PROCESSES OF CONSTITUTIONAL DECISIONMAKING

PROCESSES OF CONSTITUTIONAL DECISIONMAKING
CASES AND MATERIALS

Third Edition

Paul Brest
Dean and Richard E. Lang Professor of Law
Stanford University

Sanford Levinson
The W. St. John Garwood and W. St. John Garwood, Jr.,
Regents Chair in Law
University of Texas at Austin

LAW SCHOOL CASEBOOK SERIES

Little, Brown and Company
Boston Toronto London

Library of Congress Catalog No. 91-75793

ISBN 0-316-10787-5

Fourth Printing

Published simultaneously in Canada
by Little, Brown & Company (Canada) Limited

Printed in the United States of America

To Iris, Hilary, and Jeremy,
for the countless hours discussing
the issues in this book — P.B.

To the memory of
Professor Robert G. McCloskey (1916-1969),
a wonderful teacher,
and to the faculty of the University
of Texas Law School, wonderful colleagues — S.L.

Summary of Contents

Summary of Contents

PART ONE

Contents

PART TWO
CONSTITUTIONAL ADJUDICATION IN A NONORIGINALIST WORLD 545

Chapter 6
The Limits of History: The Constitutional Treatment of Race 581

Chapter 9

Judicial Enforcement of Nontextually Based Fundamental Rights 943

Chapter 12
The Reach of the Constitution: The State Action Dilemma 1301

Chapter 13
Constituting an American Community 1355

Chapter 14
The Allocation of Decisionmaking Authority 1459

Preface

The first edition of Processes of Constitutional Decisionmaking, published in 1975, was born out of personal frustration with teaching the introductory course in constitutional law from existing casebooks. After invariably beginning with Marbury v. Madison and several introductory sections on judicial review, those books proceeded to examine bodies of substantive doctrine, subject by subject. Questions of *how* the courts arrived at their decisions continually arose but were not systematically examined. The same was true of questions concerning the decisionmaking roles of legislatures and other nonjudicial institutions. The message of the existing casebooks, regardless of their authors' intentions to the contrary, appeared to be that the Constitution is only what the Supreme Court has said it is. When the Court had not spoken, the implication seemed to be that there was no constitutional law on the matter at all.

The conventional format seemed uncongenial to analyzing issues of methodology, process, and allocation of decisionmaking authority; yet it seemed impossible to present a coherent and undistorted view of constitutional doctrine in isolation from them. The first edition was shaped by the belief that an explicit focus on the processes of constitutional decisionmaking offered an understanding of the structure and operation, as well as of the doctrines, of American constitutional law, that the conventional organization could not offer.

The second edition, published in 1983, though reflecting those initial concerns, also responded to lessons learned while teaching from the first edition and to changes in our own thinking about constitutional law. In particular, Part One of the second edition was explicitly organized on historical-chronological lines, so that students would confront the legal consciousness of a particular period in the context of several different constitutional doctrines. We also made an effort to address constitutional law as articulated by nonjudicial institutions. With some notable additions and omissions, this third edition maintains the essential structure of the second edition.[1]

1. In response to suggestions from students and instructors using the book and our own continuing thought, we have added materials on the separation of powers (with emphasis on presidential power), aspects of the religion clauses of the First Amendment, the Second Amendment, the constitutional protection accorded private property, and constitutional aspects of the cultural pluralism that characterizes American society.

The addition of new material, including the updating of important doctrinal areas, has required the elimination of some materials contained in the second edition. We readily abandoned the chapter dealing with "the structuring of constitutional litigation" and problems such as standing, ripeness, and mootness, relegating these issues to advanced courses in civil procedure and federal jurisdiction where they are typically covered. More difficult was our decision to eliminate a substantial chapter devoted to the free speech and press aspects of the First Amendment. We do treat the issue of "subversive" speech throughout Part One, and Chapter 8 focuses on symbolic speech. Many law schools have full-scale courses on freedom of speech and of the press; this is not the casebook for such courses.

Chapter 1 introduces many of the recurring themes of the course. The chapter focuses on the constitutional issues surrounding the first two banks of the United States. The reader first approaches these issues through the conflicting views of Representative James Madison, Secretary of State Thomas Jefferson, and Secretary of the Treasury Alexander Hamilton. Chief Justice Marshall's renowned opinion comes later in the chapter, followed by contemporary critical commentary and President Andrew Jackson's message vetoing a bill to recharter the second bank. We also include substantial discussion of the Kentucky and Virginia Resolutions of 1798-1799, especially as they present the notion of the Constitution as a compact among the states (in contrast to Marshall's assertion of popular sovereignty in *McCulloch*) and the concomitant authority of the states to engage in independent constitutional review of disputed congressional legislation such as the Sedition Act of 1798. The materials thus introduce the concept of constitutional government, the allocation of decisionmaking authority between the judiciary and nonjudicial institutions, and some basic problems of constitutional interpretation, while placing the constitutional controversy in a broader social and political context.

Part One, consisting of the first five chapters, is organized historically. It examines recurring constitutional issues of federalism, property rights, racial equality, governmental (and, more particularly, presidential) authority in time of war, treatment of speech thought to be subversive, and judicial review. These are considered concurrently within each of several periods: the Marshall and Taney Courts; from the end of the Civil War to the mid-1930s; and 1937 to the 1980s.

Without sacrificing doctrinal continuity — by the end of Part One, students will know the development of the Commerce Clause from Gibbons v. Ogden (1824) to Garcia v. San Antonio Metropolitan Transit Authority (1985) — this organization illuminates relationships among seemingly discrete bodies of legal doctrine and between the constitutional system and the society in which it operates. A separate aim, pursued primarily in the first two chapters, covering the Marshall Court, is to introduce various strategies of interpreting the Constitution.

A colleague sympathetic to our historical approach has suggested that the period from 1937 to approximately 1980 should now be recognized as having a unity similar to that of the earlier periods. That is, the legal consciousness that serves to explain much of what the Supreme Court did following 1937 has, in important ways, come to its end, being replaced by the strikingly different approaches identified with Chief Justice Rehnquist, Justice Scalia, and other justices appointed by Presidents Reagan and Bush. We suspect there is much merit to this point, but its full realization must await the next edition, when the nature and extent of any changes in legal consciousness will be clearer. However, students should be aware that some of what this casebook describes as "modern" constitutional doctrine may be in the process of replacement.

Part Two is entitled Constitutional Adjudication in a Nonoriginalist World. Doctrinally it focuses on modern issues under the equal protection clause and the due process clause — the latter especially insofar as it has been viewed as the source of "fundamental rights" not explicitly mentioned in the text of the Constitution. Methodologically, Part Two is concerned with strategies of constitutional decisionmaking when the text of the Constitution and the history surrounding its adoption do not provide significant guidance for the resolution of constitutional disputes.

Part Two also contains chapters on "state action," political participation, and the Constitution in the welfare state, a chapter that brings together issues that encompass a broad range of doctrinal issues.

Chapter 13, Constituting the American Community, has already been mentioned above. It examines constitutional implications of the cultural pluralism that characterizes American society, focusing on the ways that individuals can gain or lose their citizenship, the rights of resident aliens, and the limits of toleration toward citizens with markedly different practices than those of most of their compatriots. (We examine nineteenth-century Mormons following the tenet of their faith mandating polygamy, Jehovah's Witnesses refusing to salute the American flag, Amish parents trying to maintain their community in the face of state compulsory education laws, and Native Americans smoking peyote as part of traditional religious ceremonies.)

Chapter 14, The Allocation of Constitutional Decisionmaking Authority, focuses on issues of institutional competence and authority. After examining the "political question" doctrine, we consider the Congress's decisionmaking authority under Article III and section 5 of the Fourteenth Amendment.

Not only in the last chapter but throughout, we take seriously constitutional decisionmaking by nonjudicial institutions, ranging from the Kentucky and Virginia legislatures in the late eighteenth century, to the President and Congress of the United States, to particular individuals such as senatorial candidates Abraham Lincoln and Stephen Douglas and the noted abolitionist Frederick Douglass. Nonetheless, the overwhelming bulk of the book consists of decisions of the Supreme Court of the United States. This editorial choice is supported by rationales besides adherence to the conventional emphasis (which we wish to question) on the Court as the uniquely authoritative interpreter of the Constitution: Most important federal constitutional issues eventually come before the Supreme Court, which provides, far more than is generally true of other decisionmaking institutions, elaborate written justifications for its constitutional decisions. While a well-trained lawyer should be aware that state constitutions treat many of these same issues, there are pragmatic advantages to focusing on the constitution of a single jurisdiction, especially when it presents enough issues to keep even the most industrious teachers and students occupied for a year.

The organization of any casebook is inevitably ideological — especially in a subject as fraught with ideology as constitutional law. No approach to the study of constitutional law is independent of the instructors' or casebook editors' more general intellectual and political interests. For example, we devote more space to the topic of slavery than do other casebooks. In addition to the doctrinal interest of the slave cases, this reflects our belief that students should understand the extent to which the legal ownership of one human being by another — in the United States, almost inevitably the ownership of a black by a white — pervaded American law prior to 1865 and set the stage for subsequent epic social and constitutional struggles that show no signs of abating.

The first edition of Processes of Constitutional Decisionmaking explicitly adopted the ideology of the legal process tradition identified with Albert Sacks and Henry Hart, who were especially influential teachers at the Harvard Law

School following World War II (and with whom Paul Brest studied during the early 1960s). Hart and Sacks argued that there existed apolitical decisionmaking procedures, adherence to which could provide substantively acceptable and politically legitimate decisions. Although the validity of this hypothesis remains a central concern of the book — for it is crucial matter about which every student must come to his or her own judgment — the second edition manifested our skepticism about the legitimating power of process and, indeed, about the meaning of "legitimacy" itself. Nothing that has happened since 1981, when the second edition was prepared, has lessened our skepticism. The 1980s were a time of especially vigorous and often acrimonious debates about central constitutional issues. And these debates were not confined to the pages of law reviews or the conversations of legal academics. The 1987 confirmation hearing of Robert Bork brought the critique of the post-World War II judiciary and many of its most important cases to the living rooms of American citizens. We have tried to bring to the surface these and similar issues where they can be confronted explicitly. But, of course, for every assumption that is consciously illuminated, others remain hidden in the shadows. You will get the most out of the course taught from this casebook if you take its agendas seriously even while keeping a sharp eye out for its unstated assumptions.

Acknowledgments

Paul Brest gratefully acknowledges the assistance of Matt Gonzalez, Marty Hansen, Elizabeth Leff, Lisa Yanney, and Ellen Zalman in preparing the third edition.

Sanford Levinson wishes to express his gratitude to his University of Texas Law School colleagues, including Jack Balkin, Philip Bobbitt, Doug Laycock, Scot Powe, and Jordan Steiker. Dean Mark Yudof has provided both individual and institutional support throughout the long time between the last and current editions of this casebook. Meira Levinson provided invaluable research assistance on Chapter 11. The authors are also grateful to Niva Elkin-Koren for her work on the index.

Both authors have also benefitted from the responses of a number of friends at other institutions. They include, especially, Akhil Reed Amar, Milner Ball (who pressed the claims of Native Americans to be treated as an important part of the American constitutional narrative), Walter Dellinger (who initially suggested including material from the Lincoln-Douglas debates), Paul Finkelman, Lewis LaRue, Peter Linzer, Robert Post, and Stephen Seigel.

The authors also gratefully acknowledge permission to print excerpts from the following materials:

Aleinikoff, Alexander, Theories of Loss of Citizenship, 84 Mich. L. Rev. 1471 (1986). Copyright © 1986 by the Michigan Law Review. Reprinted by permission of the author and the Michigan Law Review.

Anderson, David, The Origins of the Press Clause, 30 U.C.L.A. L. Rev. 455 (1983). Copyright © 1983 by the Regents of the University of California. All rights reserved. Reprinted by permission of the UCLA Law Review and Fred B. Rothman & Co.

Bator, Paul, The State Courts and Federal Constitutional Litigation, 22 Wm. & Mary L. Rev. 605 (1981). Copyright © 1981 by Paul M. Bator. Reprinted by permission.

Bell, Derrick, Introduction: Awakening after *Bakke*, 14 Harv. C.P.-C.L.L. Rev. 1 (1979). Copyright © 1979 by the President and Fellows of Harvard College. Reprinted by permission of the Harvard Civil Rights-Civil Liberties Law Review.

Berle, A.A., Constitutional Limitations on Corporate Activity — Protection of Personal Rights from Invasion Through Economic Power, 100 U. Pa. L. Rev. 933 (1952). Copyright © 1952 by the University of Pennsylvania Law Review. Reprinted by permission of the University of Pennsylvania Law Review and Fred B. Rothman & Co.

Bestor, Arthur, The American Civil War as a Constitutional Crisis, 69 Am. Historical Rev. 327-352 (1964). Copyright © 1964. Reprinted by permission.

Bice, Scott, Rationality Analysis in Constitutional Law, 65 Minn. L. Rev. 1. Copyright © 1980. Reprinted by permission of the author and the University of Minnesota Law Review.

Bickel, Alexander, The Least Dangerous Branch. Copyright © 1962 by Bobbs-Merrill Company, Inc. Reprinted by permission of the Bobbs-Merrill Co.

Bickel, Alexander, The Original Understanding and the Segregation Decision, 69 Harv. L. Rev. 1 (1955). Copyright © 1955 by the Harvard Law Review Association. Reprinted by permission.

Black, Charles, Impeachment: A Handbook. Copyright © 1974 by the Yale University Press. Reprinted by permission of Yale University Press.

Black, Charles, The Lawfulness of the Segregation Decisions, 69 Yale L.J. 421 (1960). Copyright © 1959. Reprinted by permission of the Yale Law Journal Company and Fred B. Rothman and Co.

Brant, Irving, Impeachment: Trials and Errors. Copyright © 1972 by Irving Brant. Reprinted by permission of Alfred A. Knopf, Inc.

Brest, Paul, Congress as a Constitutional Decisionmaker and Its Power to Counter Judicial Doctrine, 21 Ga. L. Rev. 57 (1986). Copyright © 1986. Reprinted by permission of the University of Georgia Law Review.

Brest, Paul, The Misconceived Quest for the Original Understanding, 60 B.U.L. Rev. 204, 224 (1980). Copyright © 1980. Reprinted by permission of the Boston University Law Review.

Brest, Paul, Palmer v. Thompson: An Approach to the Problem of Unconstitutional Legislative Motive, 1971 Sup. Ct. Rev. 95. Copyright © 1971 by the University of Chicago. Reprinted by permission of The University of Chicago Press.

Burt, Robert, *Miranda* and Title II: A Morganatic Marriage, 1969 Sup. Ct. Rev. 81. Copyright © 1969 by The University of Chicago. Reprinted by permission of The University of Chicago.

Colker, Ruth, Anti-Subordination Above All: Sex, Race, and Equal Protection, 61 N.Y.U.L. Rev. 1003 (1986). Copyright © 1986. Reprinted by permission of the New York University Law Review.

Corwin, Edward S., The President: Office and Powers. Copyright © 1957 by New York University. Reprinted by permission of New York University Press.

Cox, Archibald, The Role of Congress in Constitutional Determinations, 40 U. Cin. L. Rev. 199 (1971). Copyright © 1971. Reprinted by permission of the author and the University of Cincinnati Law Review.

Dahl, Robert, Decision-Making in a Democracy: The Supreme Court as National Policy-Maker, 6 J. Pub. L. 279 (1957). Copyright © 1957. Reprinted by permission of the Journal of Public Law of Emory University School of Law.

Deutsch, Jan, Neutrality, Legitimacy, and the Supreme Court, 20 Stan. L. Rev. 169 (1968). Copyright © 1968 by the Board of Trustees of the Leland Stanford Junior University. Reprinted by permission of the Stanford Law Review and Fred B. Rothman & Co.

Ely, John, Democracy and Distrust: A Theory of Judicial Review. Copyright © 1980 by the President and Fellows of Harvard College. Reprinted by permission of the Harvard University Press.

Fine, Sidney, Laissez Faire and the General Welfare State (1956). Copyright © 1956. Reprinted by permission of the University of Michigan Press.

Foner, Eric, Life and Writings of Frederick Douglass, vol. II (1953). Copyright © 1953. Reprinted by permission of International Publishers.

Gordon, Robert, Legal Thought and Legal Practice in the Age of American Enterprise, 1870-1920, in Professions and Professional Ideologies in American, 1730-1940. Copyright © 1983. Reprinted by permission of the author and the University of North Carolina Press.

Grey, Thomas, Procedural Fairness and Substantive Rights, from Due Process (Nomos XVIII) (1977). Copyright © 1977 by New York University. Reprinted by permission of New York University Press.

Gunther, Gerald, Learned Hand and the Origins of Modern First Amendment Doctrine: Some Fragments of History, 27 Stanford L. Rev. 719 (1975). Copyright © 1975 by the Board of Trustees of the Leland Stanford Junior University. Reprinted by permission of the author and Fred B. Rothman and Co.

Henkin, Louis, Shelley v. Kraemer: Notes for a Revised Opinion, 110 U. Pa. L. Rev. 473 (1962). Copyright © 1962. Reprinted by permission of the University of Pennsylvania Law Review.

Jensen, Merrill, 75 Harv. L. Rev. 456 (1961). Copyright © 1961. Reprinted by permission of the Harvard Law Review.

Jacobs, James, Race Relations and the Prison Subculture, in 1 Crime and Justice: An Annual Review of Research. Copyright © 1979 by The University of Chicago. Reprinted by permission of the University of Chicago Press.

Kelly, Alfred, The School Desegregation Case, in Quarrels That Have Shaped the Constitution (John A. Garraty, ed.). Copyright © 1964 by Harper & Row, Publishers, Inc. Reprinted by permission of the publisher.

Lawrence, Charles R., III, The Id, the Ego, and Equal Protection: Reckoning with Unconscious Racism, 39 Stan. L. Rev. 317 (1987). Copyright © 1987 by the Board of Trustees of the Leland Stanford Junior University. Reprinted by permission of the Stanford Law Review and Fred B. Rothman & Co.

Laycock, Douglas, Due Process and Separation of Powers: The Efforts to Make the Due Process Clauses Nonjusticiable, 60 Tex. L. Rev. 875 (1982). Copyright © 1982 by the Texas Law Review Association. Reprinted by permission.

Laycock, Douglas, A Survey of Religious Liberty in the United States, 47 Ohio St. L.J. 409 (1986). Copyright © 1986. Reprinted by permission of the author and the Ohio State Law Journal.

Levinson, Sanford, Suffrage and Community: Who Should Vote?, 1989 Fla. L. Rev. 545. Copyright © 1989. Reprinted by permission of the Florida Law Review.

Levy, Leonard W., Freedom of Speech and Press in Early American History: Legacy of Suppression. Copyright © 1960. Reprinted by permission.

Littleton, Christine, Reconstructing Sexual Equality, 75 Cal. L. Rev. 1279 (1986). Copyright © 1986. Reprinted by permission of the California Law Review.

McCloskey, Robert, The American Supreme Court. Copyright © 1960 by The University of Chicago. Reprinted by permission of the University of Chicago Press.

McCloskey, Robert, Economic Due Process and the Supreme Court: An Exhumation and Reburial, 1962 Sup. Ct. Rev. 34. Copyright © 1969 by The University of Chicago. Reprinted by permission of the University of Chicago Press.

McConnell, Michael, The Role of Democratic Politics in Transforming Moral Convictions into Law, 98 Yale L.J. 1501 (1989). Copyright © 1989. Reprinted by permission of the Yale Law Journal.

MacKinnon, Catherine A., Toward a Feminist Theory of the State, Chapter 12 (1989). Copyright © 1989 by Catherine A. MacKinnon. Reprinted by permission of Harvard University Press.

MacKinnon, Catherine, Whose Culture? A Case Note on Martinez v. Santa Clara Pueblo (1983), in Feminism Unmodified: Discourses on Life and Law 65-69 (1987). Copyright © 1987 by the President and Fellows of Harvard College. Reprinted by permission of Harvard University Press.

Mashaw, Jerry, The Supreme Court's Due Process Calculus, 44 U. Chi. L. Rev. 28 (1977). Copyright © 1977 by The University of Chicago. Reprinted by permission of the author and the University of Chicago Law Review.

Michelman, Frank, On Protecting the Poor Through the Fourteenth Amendment, 83 Harv. L. Rev. 7 (1969). Copyright © 1969 by the Harvard Law Review Association. Reprinted by permission.

Monaghan, Henry P., Presidential War-Making, 50 B.U.L. Rev. 19 (1970). Copyright © 1970. Reprinted by permission of the Boston University Law Review.

Monaghan, Henry, Stare Decisis and Constitutional Adjudication, 88 Colum. L. Rev. 723 (1988). Copyright © 1988 by the Directors of the Columbia Law Review Association, Inc. All rights reserved. Reprinted by permission.

Moskos, Charles, Army Women, The Atlantic, Aug. 1990, at 71-78. Copyright © 1990. Reprinted by permission of the author.

New York Times, Transcript of Frost-Nixon Interview, May 20, 1977, at A16. Copyright © 1977 by the New York Times Company. Reprinted by permission.

Olsen, Frances, Statutory Rape: A Feminist Critique of Rights Analysis, 63 Tex. L. Rev. 387 (1984). Copyright © 1984 by the Texas Law Review Review Association. Reprinted by permission.

Oral History Collection of Columbia University, Conversations with Mr. Justice Frankfurter. Copyright © 1972 by the Trustees of Columbia University. Reprinted by permission.

Powell, H. Jefferson, The Original Understanding of Original Intent, 98 Harv. L. Rev. 885 (1985). Copyright © 1985. Reprinted by permission of the Harvard Law Review.

Raphael, Alan, Discriminatory Jury Selection: Lower Court Implementation of Batson v. Kentucky, 25 Willamette L. Rev. 293 (1989). Copyright © 1989. Reprinted by permission of Willamette Law Review.

Redish, Martin, Freedom of Expression: A Critical Analysis. Copyright © 1984 by the Michie Company. Reprinted by permission of the Michie Company, Charlottesville, Va.

Regan, Donald, The Supreme Court and State Protectionism: Making Sense of the Dormant Commerce Clause, 84 Mich. L. Rev. 1091 (1986). Copyright © 1986 by the Michigan Law Review. Reprinted by permission of the Michigan Law Review.

Richards, David A.J., Free Speech and Obscenity Law: Toward a Moral Theory of the First Amendment, 123 U. Pa. L. Rev. 45 (1974). Copyright © 1974 by the University of Pennsylvania Law Review. Reprinted by permission.

Richards, David, Sexual Autonomy and the Constitutional Right to Privacy: A Case Study in Human Rights and the Unwritten Constitution, 30 Hastings L. Rev. 957, 976 (1979). Copyright © 1979. Reprinted by permission of the Hastings Law Journal.

Rosenfeld, Michel, Decoding *Richmond*: Affirmative Action and the Elusive Meaning of Constitutional Equality, 87 Mich. L. Rev. 1729 (1989). Copyright © 1989 by the Michigan Law Review. Reprinted by permission of the author and the Michigan Law Review.

Sandalow, Terrance, Comments on Powell v. McCormack, 17 U.C.L.A.L. Rev. 1 (1969). Copyright © 1969 by the Regents of the University of California. Reprinted by permission.

Schmidt, Benno, Principle and Prejudice: The Supreme Court and Race in the Progressive Era, Part 2: The Peonage Cases, 82 Colum. L. Rev. 646 (1982). Copyright © 1982 by the Directors of the Columbia Law Review Association, Inc. All rights reserved. Reprinted by permission.

Shapiro, Martin, Law and Politics in the Supreme Court. Copyright © 1964 by The Free Press, a Divison of Macmillan Publishing Co., Inc. Reprinted by permission of Macmillan Publishing Co., Inc.

Stern, Robert, That Commerce Which Concerns More States That One, 47 Harv. L. Rev. 1335 (1934). Copyright © 1934. Reprinted by permission of the Harvard Law Review.

Still, Jonathan, Political Equality and Election Systems, 91 Ethics (1981). Copyright © 1981. Reprinted by permission.

Stone, Geoffrey, Restriction of Speech Because of Its Content: The Peculiar Case of Subject-Matter Restrictions, 46 U. Chi. L. Rev. 81 (1978). Copyright © 1978. Reprinted by permission of the University of Chicago Law Review.

Sullivan, Kathleen, Sins of Discrimination: Last Term's Affirmative Action Cases, 100 Harv. L. Rev. 78 (1986). Copyright © 1986. Reprinted by permission of the Harvard Law Review.

tenBroek, Jacobus, Admissibility and Use by the United States Supreme Court of Extrinsic Aids in Constitutional Construction, 26 Calif. L. Rev. 287 (1938), 27 Calif. L. Rev. 157 (1939). Copyright © 1939. Reprinted by permission of the California Law Review.

Tribe, Laurence, American Constitutional Law (2d ed. 1988). Copyright © 1988. Reprinted by permission of Foundation Press.

Tribe, Laurence, N.Y. Times, July 3, 1989. Copyright © 1989 by the New York Times Company. Reprinted by permission.

Tussman, Joseph, & Jacobus tenBroek, The Equal Protection of the Laws, 37 Calif. L. Rev. 341, 346-353 (1949). Copyright © 1949 by the California Law Review, Inc. Reprinted by permission of the California Law Review and Fred B. Rothman & Co.

Tyack, David, Thomas James & Aaron Benavot, Law and the Shaping of Public Education, 1785-1954 (1987). Copyright © 1987. Reprinted by permission of the University of Wisconsin Press.

Wall Street Journal, The Lords of the Manor, June 1, 1984, at 18. Copyright © 1984 by Dow Jones & Co., Inc. All rights reserved. Reprinted by permission of the Wall Street Journal.

Wasserstrom, Richard, The Judicial Decision: Toward a Theory of Legal Justification. Copyright © 1961 by the Board of Trustees of the Leland Stanford Junior University. Reprinted by permission of the author and Stanford University Press.

Wasserstrom, Richard, Racism, Sexism, and Preferential Treatment, 24 U.C.L.A.L. Rev. 581 (1977). Copyright © 1977 by the Regents of the University of California. Reprinted by permission.

Wechsler, Herbert, The Political Safeguards of Federalism: The Role of the States in the Composition and Selection of the National Government, in Principles, Politics and Fundamental Law. Copyright © 1960 by the President and Fellows of Harvard College. Copyright renewed 1989 by Herbert Wechsler. Reprinted by permission of the Harvard University Press.

Wechsler, Herbert, Toward Neutral Principles of Constitutional Law, 73 Harv. L. Rev. 1 (1959). Copyright © 1959 by the Harvard Law Review Association. Reprinted by permission of the Harvard Law Review.

Wilkins, Roger, The Black Poor Are Different, N.Y. Times, Aug. 22, 1989, at A19. Copyright © 1989 by the New York Times Company. Reprinted by permission.

Williams, Wendy, The Equality Crisis: Some Reflections on Culture, Courts, and Feminism, 7 Women's Rights L. Rep. 175 (1982). Copyright © 1982. Reprinted by permission of the author.

Williams, Wendy, Equality's Riddle: Pregnancy and the Equal Treatment/Special Treatment Debate, 13 N.Y.U. Rev. L. & Soc. Change 325 (1984-1985). Copyright © 1985. Reprinted by permission of the New York University Review of Law and Social Change.

Wofford, John, The Blinding Light: The Uses of History in Constitutional Interpretation, 31 U. Chi. L. Rev. 502 (1964). Copyright © 1964 by The University of Chicago. Reprinted by permission.

Woodward, C. Vann, The Strange Career of Jim Crow (3d rev. ed.). Copyright © 1974 by Oxford University Press, Inc. Reprinted by permission.

The Constitution of the United States

We the People of the United States, in Order to form a more perfect Union, establish Justice, insure domestic Tranquility, provide for the common defence, promote the general Welfare, and secure the Blessings of Liberty to ourselves and our Posterity, do ordain and establish this Constitution for the United States of America.

ARTICLE I

Section 1. All legislative Powers herein granted shall be vested in a Congress of the United States, which shall consist of a Senate and House of Representatives.

Section 2. [1] The House of Representatives shall be composed of Members chosen every second Year by the People of the several States, and the Electors in each State shall have the Qualifications requisite for Electors of the most numerous Branch of the State Legislature.

[2] No Person shall be a Representative who shall not have attained to the Age of twenty five Years, and been seven Years a Citizen of the United States, and who shall not, when elected, be an Inhabitant of that State in which he shall be chosen.

[3] Representatives and direct Taxes shall be apportioned among the several States which may be included within this Union, according to their respective Numbers, which shall be determined by adding to the whole Number of free Persons, including those bound to Service for a Term of Years, and excluding Indians not taxed, three fifths of all other Persons.[1] The actual Enumeration shall be made within three Years after the first Meeting of the Congress of the United States, and within every subsequent Term of ten Years, in such Manner as they shall by Law direct. The Number of Representatives shall not exceed one for every thirty Thousand, but each State shall have at Least one Representative; and until such enumeration shall be made, the State of New Hampshire shall be entitled to chuse three, Massachusetts eight, Rhode Island and Providence Plantations one, Connecticut five, New York six, New Jersey four, Pennsylvania eight, Delaware one, Maryland six, Virginia ten, North Carolina five, South Carolina five, and Georgia three.

[4] When vacancies happen in the Representation from any State, the Executive Authority thereof shall issue Writs of Election to fill such Vacancies.

[5] The House of Representatives shall chuse their Speaker and other Officers; and shall have the sole Power of Impeachment.

Section 3. [1] The Senate of the United States shall be composed of two Senators from each State, chosen by the Legislature thereof,[2] for six Years; and each Senator shall have one Vote.

1. Changed by section 2 of the Fourteenth Amendment.
2. Changed by clause 1 of the Seventeenth Amendment.

[2] Immediately after they shall be assembled in Consequence of the first Election, they shall be divided as equally as may be into three Classes. The Seats of the Senators of the first Class shall be vacated at the Expiration of the second Year, of the second Class at the Expiration of the fourth Year, and of the third Class at the Expiration of the sixth Year, so that one third may be chosen every second Year; and if Vacancies happen by Resignation, or otherwise, during the Recess of the Legislature of any State, the Executive thereof may make temporary Appointments until the next Meeting of the Legislature, which shall then fill such Vacancies.[3]

[3] No Person shall be a Senator who shall not have attained to the Age of thirty Years, and been nine Years a Citizen of the United States, and who shall not, when elected, be an Inhabitant of that State for which he shall be chosen.

[4] The Vice President of the United States shall be President of the Senate, but shall have no Vote, unless they be equally divided.

[5] The Senate shall chuse their other Officers, and also a President pro tempore, in the absence of the Vice President, or when he shall exercise the Office of President of the United States.

[6] The Senate shall have the sole Power to try all Impeachments. When sitting for that Purpose, they shall be on Oath or Affirmation. When the President of the United States is tried, the Chief Justice shall preside: And no Person shall be convicted without the Concurrence of two thirds of the Members present.

[7] Judgment in Cases of Impeachment shall not extend further than to removal from Office, and disqualification to hold and enjoy any Office of honor, Trust or Profit under the United States: but the Party convicted shall nevertheless be liable and subject to Indictment, Trial, Judgment and Punishment, according to Law.

Section 4. [1] The Times, Places and Manner of holding Elections for Senators and Representatives, shall be prescribed in each State by the Legislature thereof; but the Congress may at any time by Law make or alter such Regulations, except as to the Places of chusing Senators.

[2] The Congress shall assemble at least once in every Year, and such Meeting shall be on the first Monday in December, unless they shall by Law appoint a different Day.[4]

Section 5. [1] Each House shall be the Judge of the Elections, Returns and Qualifications of its own Members, and a Majority of each shall constitute a Quorum to do Business; but a smaller Number may adjourn from day to day, and may be authorized to compel the Attendance of absent Members, in such Manner, and under such Penalties as each House may provide.

[2] Each House may determine the Rules of its Proceedings, punish its Members for disorderly Behavior, and, with the Concurrence of two thirds, expel a Member.

[3] Each House shall keep a Journal of its Proceedings, and from time to time publish the same, excepting such Parts as may in their Judgment require Secrecy; and the Yeas and Nays of the Members of either House on any question shall, at the Desire of one fifth of those Present, be entered on the Journal.

3. Changed by clause 2 of the Seventeenth Amendment.
4. Changed by section 2 of the Twentieth Amendment.

[4] Neither House, during the Session of Congress, shall, without the Consent of the other, adjourn for more than three days, nor to any other Place than that in which the two Houses shall be sitting.

Section 6. [1] The Senators and Representatives shall receive a Compensation for their Services, to be ascertained by Law, and paid out of the Treasury of the United States. They shall in all Cases, except Treason, Felony and Breach of the Peace, be privileged from Arrest during their Attendance at the Session of their respective Houses, and in going to and returning from the same; and for any Speech or Debate in either House, they shall not be questioned in any other Place.

[2] No Senator or Representative shall, during the Time for which he was elected, be appointed to any civil Office under the Authority of the United States, which shall have been created, or the Emoluments whereof shall have been encreased during such time; and no Person holding any Office under the United States, shall be a member of either House during his Continuance in Office.

Section 7. [1] All Bills for raising Revenue shall originate in the House of Representatives; but the Senate may propose or concur with Amendments as on other Bills.

[2] Every Bill which shall have passed the House of Representatives and the Senate, shall, before it become a Law, be presented to the President of the United States; If he approve he shall sign it, but if not he shall return it, with his Objections to the House in which it shall have originated, who shall enter the Objections at large on their Journal, and proceed to reconsider it. If after such Reconsideration two thirds of that House shall agree to pass the Bill, it shall be sent, together with the Objections, to the other House, by which it shall likewise be reconsidered, and if approved by two thirds of that House, it shall become a Law. But in all such Cases the Votes of both Houses shall be determined by Yeas and Nays, and the Names of the Persons voting for and against the Bill shall be entered on the Journal of each House respectively. If any Bill shall not be returned by the President within ten Days (Sundays excepted) after it shall have been presented to him, the Same shall be a Law, in like Manner as if he had signed it, unless the Congress by their Adjournment prevents its Return, in which Case it shall not be a Law.

[3] Every Order, Resolution, or Vote to Which the Concurrence of the Senate and House of Representatives may be necessary (except on a question of Adjournment) shall be presented to the President of the United States; and before the Same shall take Effect, shall be approved by him, or being disapproved by him, shall be repassed by two thirds of the Senate and House of Representatives, according to the Rules and Limitations prescribed in the Case of a Bill.

Section 8. [1] The Congress shall have Power To lay and collect Taxes, Duties, Imposts and Excises, to pay the Debts and provide for the common Defence and general Welfare of the United States; but all Duties, Imposts and Excises shall be uniform throughout the United States;

[2] To borrow money on the credit of the United States;

[3] To regulate Commerce with foreign Nations, and among the several States, and with the Indian Tribes;

[4] To establish an uniform Rule of Naturalization, and uniform Laws on the subject of Bankruptcies throughout the United States;

[5] To coin Money, regulate the Value thereof, and of foreign Coin, and fix the Standard of Weights and Measures;

[6] To provide the Punishment of counterfeiting the Securities and current Coin of the United States;

[7] To establish Post Offices and post Roads;

[8] To promote the Progress of Science and useful Arts, by securing for limited Times to Authors and Inventors the exclusive Right to their respective Writings and Discoveries;

[9] To constitute Tribunals inferior to the supreme Court;

[10] To define and punish Piracies and Felonies committed on the high Seas, and Offenses against the Laws of Nations;

[11] To declare War, grant Letters of Marque and Reprisal, and make Rules concerning Captures on Land and Water;

[12] To raise and support Armies, but no Appropriation of Money to that Use shall be for a longer Term than two Years;

[13] To provide and maintain a Navy;

[14] To make Rules for the Government and Regulation of the land and naval Forces;

[15] To provide for calling forth the Militia to execute the Laws of the Union, suppress Insurrections and repel Invasions;

[16] To provide for organizing, arming, and disciplining, the Militia, and for governing such Part of them as may be employed in the Service of the United States, reserving to the States respectively, the Appointment of the Officers, and the Authority of training the Militia according to the discipline prescribed by Congress;

[17] To exercise exclusive Legislation in all Cases whatsoever, over such District (not exceeding ten Miles square) as may, by Cessation of particular States, and the Acceptance of Congress, become the Seat of the Government of the United States, and to exercise like Authority over all Places purchased by the Consent of the Legislature of the State in which the Same shall be, for the Erection of Forts, Magazines, Arsenals, dock-Yards, and other needful Buildings; — And

[18] To make all Laws which shall be necessary and proper for carrying into Execution the foregoing Powers, and all other Powers vested by this Constitution in the Government of the United States, or in any Department or Officer thereof.

Section 9. [1] The Migration or Importation of such Persons as any of the States now existing shall think proper to admit, shall not be prohibited by the Congress prior to the Year one thousand eight hundred and eight, but a Tax or duty may be imposed on such Importation, not exceeding ten dollars for each Person.

[2] The privilege of the Writ of Habeas Corpus shall not be suspended, unless when in Cases of Rebellion or Invasion the public Safety may require it.

[3] No Bill of Attainder or ex post facto Law shall be passed.

[4] No Capitation, or other direct, Tax shall be laid, unless in Proportion to the Census or Enumeration herein before directed to be taken.[5]

[5] No Tax or Duty shall be laid on Articles exported from any State.

5. But see the Sixteenth Amendment.

[6] No Preference shall be given by any Regulation of Commerce or Revenue to the Ports of one State over those of another: nor shall Vessels bound to, or from, one State, be obliged to enter, clear, or pay Duties in another.

[7] No Money shall be drawn from the Treasury, but in Consequence of Appropriations made by Law; and a regular Statement and Account of the Receipts and Expenditures of all public Money shall be published from time to time.

[8] No Title of Nobility shall be granted by the United States: And no Person holding any Office of Profit or Trust under them, shall, without the Consent of the Congress, accept of any present, Emolument, Office, or Title, of any kind whatever, from any King, Prince, or foreign State.

Section 10. [1] No State shall enter into any Treaty, Alliance, or Confederation; grant Letters of Marque and Reprisal; coin Money; emit Bills of Credit; make any Thing but gold and silver Coin a Tender in Payment of Debts; pass any Bill of Attainder, ex post facto Law, or Law impairing the Obligation of Contracts, or grant any Title of Nobility.

[2] No State shall, without the Consent of the Congress, lay any Imposts or Duties on Imports or Exports, except what may be absolutely necessary for executing its inspection Laws: and the net Produce of all Duties and Imposts, laid by any State on Imports or Exports, shall be for the Use of the Treasury of the United States; and all such Laws shall be subject to the Revision and Controul of the Congress.

[3] No State shall, without the Consent of Congress, lay any Duty of Tonnage, keep Troops, or Ships of War in time of Peace, enter into any Agreement or Compact with another State, or with a foreign Power, or engage in War, unless actually invaded, or in such imminent Danger as will not admit of delay.

Article II

Section 1. [1] The executive Power shall be vested in a President of the United States of America. He shall hold his Office during the Term of four Years, and, together with the Vice President, chosen for the same Term, be elected, as follows:

[2] Each State shall appoint, in such Manner as the Legislature thereof may direct, a number of Electors, equal to the whole Number of Senators and Representatives to which the State may be entitled in the Congress: but no Senator or Representative, or Person holding an Office of Trust or Profit under the United States, shall be appointed an Elector.

[3] The Electors shall meet in their respective States, and vote by Ballot for two Persons, of whom one at least shall not be an Inhabitant of the same State with themselves. And they shall make a List of all the Persons voted for, and of the Number of Votes for each; which List they shall sign and certify, and transmit sealed to the Seat of the Government of the United States, directed to the President of the Senate. The President of the Senate shall, in the Presence of the Senate and House of Representatives, open all the Certificates, and the Votes shall then be counted. The Person having the greatest Number of Votes shall be the President, if such Number be a Majority of the whole Number of Electors appointed; and if there be more than one who have such Majority, and have an equal Number of Votes, then the House of Representatives shall immediately chuse by Ballot one of them for President; and if no Person have a Majority, then

from the five highest on the List the said House shall in like Manner chuse the President. But in chusing the President, the Votes shall be taken by States, the Representation from each State having one Vote; a quorum for this Purpose shall consist of a Member or Members from two thirds of the States, and a Majority of all the States shall be necessary to a Choice. In every Case, after the Choice of the President, the Person having the greatest Number of Votes of the Electors shall be the Vice President. But if there should remain two or more who have equal Votes, the Senate shall chuse from them by Ballot the Vice President.[6]

[4] The Congress may determine the Time of chusing the Electors, and the Day on which they shall give their Votes; which Day shall be the same throughout the United States.

[5] No person except a natural born Citizen, or a Citizen of the United States, at the time of the Adoption of this Constitution, shall be eligible to the Office of President; neither shall any Person be eligible to that Office who shall not have attained to the Age of thirty five Years, and been fourteen Years a Resident within the United States.

[6] In case of the removal of the President from Office, or of his Death, Resignation or Inability to discharge the Powers and Duties of the said Office, the Same shall devolve on the Vice President, and the Congress may by Law provide for the Case of Removal, Death, Resignation or Inability, both of the President and Vice President, declaring what Officer shall then act as President, and such Officer shall act accordingly, until the Disability be removed, or a President shall be elected.[7]

[7] The President shall, at stated Times, receive for his Services, a Compensation, which shall neither be increased nor diminished during the Period for which he shall have been elected, and he shall not receive within that Period any other Emolument from the United States, or any of them.

[8] Before he enter on the Execution of his Office, he shall take the following Oath or Affirmation: "I do solemnly swear (or affirm) that I will faithfully execute the Office of President of the United States, and will to the best of my Ability, preserve, protect and defend the Constitution of the United States."

Section 2. [1] The President shall be Commander in Chief of the Army and Navy of the United States, and of the Militia of the several States, when called into the actual Service of the United States; he may require the Opinion, in writing, of the principal Officer in each of the executive Departments, upon any subject relating to the Duties of their respective Offices, and he shall have Power to grant Reprieves and Pardons for Offenses against the United States, except in Cases of Impeachment.

[2] He shall have Power, by and with the Advice and Consent of the Senate, to make Treaties, provided two thirds of the Senators present concur; and he shall nominate, and by and with the Advice and Consent of the Senate, shall appoint Ambassadors, other public Ministers and Consuls, Judges of the supreme Court, and all other Officers of the United States, whose Appointments are not herein otherwise provided for, and which shall be established by Law: but the Congress may by Law vest the Appointment of such inferior Officers, as they think proper, in the President alone, in the Courts of Law, or in the Heads of Departments.

6. Superseded by the Twelfth Amendment.
7. Changed by the Twenty-fifth Amendment.

[3] The President shall have Power to fill up all Vacancies that may happen during the Recess of the Senate, by granting Commissions which shall expire at the End of their next Session.

Section 3. He shall from time to time give to the Congress Information of the State of the Union, and recommend to their Consideration such Measures as he shall judge necessary and expedient; he may, on extraordinary Occasions, convene both Houses, or either of them, and in Case of Disagreement between them, with Respect to the Time of Adjournment, he may adjourn them to such Time as he shall think proper; he shall receive Ambassadors and other public Ministers; he shall take Care that the Laws be faithfully executed, and shall Commission all the Officers of the United States.

Section 4. The President and all civil Officers of the United States, shall be removed from Office on Impeachment for, and Conviction of, Treason, Bribery, or other high Crimes and Misdemeanors.

ARTICLE III

Section 1. The judicial Power of the United States, shall be vested in one supreme Court, and in such inferior Courts as the Congress may from time to time ordain and establish. The Judges, both of the supreme and inferior Courts, shall hold their Offices during good Behaviour, and shall, at stated Times, receive for their Services, a Compensation, which shall not be diminished during their Continuance in Office.

Section 2. [1] The Judicial Power shall extend to all Cases, in Law and Equity, arising under this Constitution, the Laws of the United States, and Treaties made, or which shall be made, under their Authority; — to all Cases affecting Ambassadors, other public Ministers and Consuls; — to all Cases of admiralty and maritime Jurisdiction; — to Controversies to which the United States shall be a Party; — to Controversies between two or more States; — between a State and Citizens of another State; — between Citizens of different States; — between Citizens of the same State claiming Lands under Grants of different States, and between a State, or the Citizens thereof, and foreign States, Citizens or Subjects.

[2] In all Cases affecting Ambassadors, other public Ministers and Consuls, and those in which a State shall be a Party, the supreme Court shall have original Jurisdiction. In all the other Cases before mentioned, the supreme Court shall have appellate Jurisdiction, both as to Law and Fact, with such Exceptions, and under such Regulations as the Congress shall make.

[3] The trial of all Crimes, except in Cases of Impeachment, shall be by Jury; and such Trial shall be held in the State where the said Crimes shall have been committed; but when not committed within any State, the Trial shall be at such Place or places as the Congress may by Law have directed.

Section 3. [1] Treason against the United States, shall consist only in levying War against them, or in adhering to their Enemies, giving them Aid and Comfort. No person shall be convicted of Treason unless on the Testimony of two Witnesses to the same overt Act, or on Confession in open Court.

[2] The Congress shall have Power to declare the Punishment of Treason, but no Attainder of Treason shall work Corruption of Blood, or Forfeiture except during the Life of the Person attainted.

Article IV

Section 1. Full Faith and Credit shall be given in each State to the public Acts, and Records, and judicial Proceedings of every other State. And the Congress may by general Laws prescribe the Manner in which such Acts, Records and Proceedings shall be proved, and the Effect thereof.

Section 2. [1] The Citizens of each State shall be entitled to all Privileges and Immunities of Citizens in the several States.

[2] A Person charged to any State with Treason, Felony, or other Crime, who shall flee from Justice, and be found in another State, shall on demand of the executive Authority of the State from which he fled, be delivered up, to be removed to the State having Jurisdiction of the Crime.

[3] No Person held to Service or Labour in one State, under the Laws thereof, escaping into another, shall, in Consequence of any Law or Regulation therein, be discharged from such Service or Labour, but shall be delivered up on Claim of the Party to whom such Service or Labour may be due.[8]

Section 3. [1] New States may be admitted by the Congress into this Union; but no new State shall be formed or erected within the Jurisdiction of any other State; nor any State be formed by the Junction of two or more States, or Parts of States, without the Consent of the Legislatures of the States concerned as well as of the Congress.

[2] The Congress shall have Power to dispose of and make all needful Rules and Regulations respecting the Territory or other Property belonging to the United States; and nothing in this Constitution shall be so construed as to Prejudice any Claims of the United States, or of any particular State.

Section 4. The United States shall guarantee to every State in this Union a Republican Form of Government, and shall protect each of them against Invasion; and on Application of the Legislature, or of the Executive (when the Legislature cannot be convened) against domestic Violence.

Article V

The Congress, whenever two thirds of both Houses shall deem it necessary, shall propose Amendments to this Constitution, or, on the Application of the Legislatures of two thirds of the several States, shall call a Convention for proposing Amendments, which, in either Case, shall be valid to all Intents and Purposes, as part of this Constitution, when ratified by the Legislatures of three fourths of the several States, or by Conventions in three fourths thereof, as the one or the other Mode of Ratification may be proposed by the Congress; Provided that no Amendment which may be made prior to the Year One thousand eight hundred and eight shall in any Manner affect the first and fourth Clauses in the Ninth Section of the first Article; and that no State, without its Consent, shall be deprived of its equal Suffrage in the Senate.

8. Superseded by the Thirteenth Amendment.

ARTICLE VI

[1] All Debts contracted and Engagements entered into, before the Adoption of this Constitution, shall be a valid against the United States under this Constitution, as under the Confederation.

[2] This Constitution, and the Laws of the United States which shall be made in Pursuance thereof; and all Treaties made, or which shall be made, under the Authority of the United States, shall be the supreme Law of the Land; and the Judges in every State shall be bound thereby, any Thing in the Constitution or Laws of any State to the Contrary notwithstanding.

[3] The Senators and Representatives before mentioned, and the Members of the several State Legislatures, and all executive and judicial Officers, both of the United States and of the several States, shall be bound by Oath or Affirmation, to support this Constitution; but no religious Test shall ever be required as a Qualification to any Office or public Trust under the United States.

ARTICLE VII

The Ratification of the Conventions of nine States shall be sufficient for the Establishment of this Constitution between the States so ratifying the Same.[9]

Done in Convention by the Unanimous Consent of the States present the Seventeenth Day of September in the Year of our Lord one thousand seven hundred and Eighty seven and of the Independence of the United States of America the Twelfth.

ARTICLES IN ADDITION TO, AND AMENDMENT OF, THE CONSTITUTION OF THE UNITED STATES OF AMERICA, PROPOSED BY CONGRESS, AND RATIFIED BY THE LEGISLATURES OF THE SEVERAL STATES, PURSUANT TO THE FIFTH ARTICLE OF THE ORIGINAL CONSTITUTION[10]

AMENDMENT I [1791]

Congress shall make no law respecting an establishment of religion, or prohibiting the free exercise thereof; or abridging the freedom of speech, or of the press; or the right of the people peaceably to assemble, and to petition the Government for a redress of grievances.

AMENDMENT II [1791]

A well regulated Militia, being necessary to the security of a free State, the right of the people to keep and bear Arms, shall not be infringed.

9. The ninth state ratified the Constitution on June 21, 1788. Virginia and New York ratified later in 1788, North Carolina in 1789, and Rhode Island in 1790. George Washington was inaugurated as the first President on April 30, 1789.

10. The Twenty-first Amendment was ratified by state conventions.

AMENDMENT III [1791]

No Soldier shall, in time of peace be quartered in any house, without the consent of the Owner, nor in time of war, but in a manner to be prescribed by law.

AMENDMENT IV [1791]

The right of the people to be secure in their persons, houses, papers, and effects, against unreasonable searches and seizures, shall not be violated, and no Warrants shall issue, but upon probable cause, supported by Oath or affirmation, and particularly describing the place to be searched, and the persons or things to be seized.

AMENDMENT V [1791]

No person shall be held to answer for a capital, or otherwise infamous crime, unless on a presentment or indictment of a Grand Jury, except in cases arising in the land or naval forces, or in the Militia, when in actual service in time of War or public danger; nor shall any person be subject for the same offence to be twice put in jeopardy of life or limb; nor shall be compelled in any criminal case to be a witness against himself, nor be deprived of life, liberty, or property, without due process of law; nor shall private property be taken for public use, without just compensation.

AMENDMENT VI [1791]

In all criminal prosecutions, the accused shall enjoy the right to a speedy and public trial, by an impartial jury of the State and district wherein the crime shall have been committed, which district shall have been previously ascertained by law, and to be informed of the nature and cause of the accusation; to be confronted with the witnesses against him; to have compulsory process for obtaining witnesses in his favor, and to have the Assistance of Counsel for his defence.

AMENDMENT VII [1791]

In Suits at common law, where the value in controversy shall exceed twenty dollars, the right of trial by jury shall be preserved, and no fact tried by a jury, shall be otherwise re-examined in any Court of the United States, than according to the rules of the common law.

AMENDMENT VII [1791]

Excessive bail shall not be required, nor excessive fines imposed, nor cruel and unusual punishments inflicted.

AMENDMENT IX [1791]

The enumeration in the Constitution, of certain rights, shall not be construed to deny or disparage others retained by the people.

AMENDMENT X [1791]

The powers not delegated to the United States by the Constitution, nor prohibited by it to the States, are reserved to the States respectively, or to the people.

AMENDMENT XI [1798]

The Judicial power of the United States shall not be construed to extend to any suit in law or equity, commenced or prosecuted against one of the United States by Citizens of another State, or by Citizens or Subjects of any Foreign State.

AMENDMENT XII [1804]

The Electors shall meet in their respective states and vote by ballot for President and Vice-President, one of whom, at least, shall not be an inhabitant of the same state with themselves; they shall name in their ballots the person voted for as President, and in distinct ballots the person voted for as Vice-President, and they shall make distinct lists of all persons voted for as President, and of all persons voted for as Vice-President, and of the number of votes for each, which lists they shall sign and certify, and transmit sealed to the seat of the government of the United States, directed to the President of the Senate; — The President of the Senate shall, in the presence of the Senate and House of Representatives, open all the certificates and the votes shall then be counted; — The person having the greatest number of votes for President, shall be the President, if such number be a majority of the whole number of Electors appointed; and if no person have such majority, then from the persons having the highest numbers not exceeding three on the list of those voted for as President, the House of Representatives shall choose immediately, by ballot, the President. But in choosing the President, the votes shall be taken by states, the representation from each state having one vote; a quorum for this purpose shall consist of a member or members from two-thirds of the states, and a majority of all the states shall be necessary to a choice. And if the House of Representatives shall not choose a President whenever the right of choice shall devolve upon them, before the fourth day of March next following, then the Vice-President shall act as President, as in the case of the death or other constitutional disability of the President.[11] — The person having the greatest number of votes as Vice-President, shall be the Vice-President, if such number be a majority of the whole number of Electors appointed, and if no person have a majority, then from the two highest numbers on the list, the Senate shall choose the Vice-President; a quorum for the purpose shall consist of two-thirds of the whole number of Senators, and a majority of the whole number shall be necessary to a choice. But no person constitutionally ineligible to the office of President shall be eligible to that of Vice-President of the United States.

11. Superseded by section 3 of the Twentieth Amendment.

AMENDMENT XIII [1865]

Section 1. Neither slavery nor involuntary servitude, except as a punishment for crime whereof the party shall have been duly convicted, shall exist within the United States, or any place subject to their jurisdiction.

Section 2. Congress shall have power to enforce this article by appropriate legislation.

AMENDMENT XIV [1868]

Section 1. All persons born or naturalized in the United States, and subject to the jurisdiction thereof, are citizens of the United States and of the State wherein they reside. No State shall make or enforce any law which shall abridge the privileges or immunities of citizens of the United States; nor shall any State deprive any person of life, liberty, or property, without due process of law; nor deny to any person within its jurisdiction the equal protection of the laws.

Section 2. Representatives shall be apportioned among the several States according to their respective numbers, counting the whole number of persons in each State, excluding Indians not taxed. But when the right to vote at any election for the choice of electors for President and Vice President of the United States, Representatives in Congress, the Executive and Judicial officers of a State, or the members of the Legislature thereof, is denied to any of the male inhabitants of such State, being twenty-one years of age, and citizens of the United States, or in any way abridged, except for participation in rebellion, or other crime, the basis of representation therein shall be reduced in the proportion which the number of such male citizens shall bear to the whole number of male citizens twenty-one years of age in such State.

Section 3. No person shall be a Senator or Representative in Congress, or elector of President and Vice President, or hold any office, civil or military, under the United States, or under any State, who, having previously taken an oath, as a member of Congress, or as an officer of the United States, or as a member of any State legislature, or as an executive or judicial officer of any State, to support the Constitution of the United States, shall have engaged in insurrection or rebellion against the same, or given aid or comfort to the enemies thereof. But Congress may by a vote of two-thirds of each House, remove such disability.

Section 4. The validity of the public debt of the United States, authorized by law, including debts incurred for payment of pensions and bounties for services in suppressing insurrection or rebellion, shall not be questioned. But neither the United States nor any State shall assume or pay any debt or obligation incurred in aid of insurrection or rebellion against the United States, or any claim for the loss of emancipation of any slave; but all such debts, obligations and claims shall be held illegal and void.

Section 5. The Congress shall have power to enforce, by appropriate legislation, the provisions of this article.

AMENDMENT XV [1870]

Section 1. The right of citizens of the United States to vote shall not be denied or abridged by the United States or by any State on account of race, color, or previous condition of servitude.

Section 2. The Congress shall have power to enforce this article by appropriate legislation.

AMENDMENT XVI [1913]

The Congress shall have power to lay and collect taxes on incomes, from whatever source derived, without apportionment among the several States, and without regard to any census or enumeration.

AMENDMENT XVII [1913]

[1] The Senate of the United States shall be composed of two Senators from each State, elected by the people thereof, for six years; and each Senator shall have one vote. The electors in each State shall have the qualifications requisite for electors of the most numerous branch of the State legislatures.

[2] When vacancies happen in the representation of any State in the Senate, the executive authority of such State shall issue writs of election to fill such vacancies: *Provided,* That the legislature of any State may empower the executive thereof to make temporary appointments until the people fill the vacancies by election as the legislature may direct.

[3] This amendment shall not be so construed as to affect the election or term of any Senator chosen before it becomes valid as part of the Constitution.

AMENDMENT XVIII [1919]

Section 1. After one year from the ratification of this article the manufacture, sale, or transportation of intoxicating liquors within, the importation thereof into, or the exportation thereof from the United States and all territory subject to the jurisdiction thereof for beverage purposes is hereby prohibited.

Section 2. The Congress and the several States shall have concurrent power to enforce this article by appropriate legislation.

Section 3. This article shall be inoperative unless it shall have been ratified as an amendment to the Constitution by the legislatures of the several States, as provided in the Constitution, within seven years from the date of the submission hereof to the States by the Congress.[12]

AMENDMENT XIX [1920]

[1] The right of citizens of the United States to vote shall not be denied or abridged by the United States or by any State on account of sex.

[2] Congress shall have power to enforce this article by appropriate legislation.

AMENDMENT XX [1933]

Section 1. The terms of the President and Vice President shall end at noon on the 20th day of January, and the terms of Senators and Representatives at noon on the 3d day of January, of the years in which such terms would have ended if

12. Repealed by the Twenty-first Amendment.

this article had not been ratified; and the terms of their successors shall then begin.

Section 2. The Congress shall assemble at least once in every year, and such meeting shall begin at noon on the 3d day of January, unless they shall by law appoint a different day.

Section 3. If, at the time fixed for the beginning of the term of the President, the President elect shall have died, the Vice President elect shall become President. If a President shall not have been chosen before the time fixed for the beginning of his term, or if the President elect shall have failed to qualify, then the Vice President elect shall act as President until a President shall have qualified; and the Congress may by law provide for the case wherein neither a President elect nor a Vice President elect shall have qualified, declaring who shall then act as President, or the manner in which one who is to act shall be selected, and such person shall act accordingly until a President or Vice President shall have qualified.

Section 4. The Congress may by law provide for the case of the death of any of the persons from whom the House of Representatives may choose a President whenever the right of choice shall have devolved upon them, and for the case of the death of any of the persons from whom the Senate may choose a Vice President whenever the right of choice shall have devolved upon them.

Section 5. Sections 1 and 2 shall take effect on the 15th day of October following the ratification of this article.

Section 6. This article shall be inoperative unless it shall have been ratified as an amendment to the Constitution by the legislatures of three-fourths of the several States within seven years from the date of its submission.

Amendment XXI [1933]

Section 1. The eighteenth article of amendment to the Constitution of the United States is hereby repealed.

Section 2. The transportation or importation into any State, Territory, or possession of the United States for delivery or use therein of intoxicating liquors, in violation of the laws thereof, is hereby prohibited.

Section 3. This article shall be inoperative unless it shall have been ratified as an amendment to the Constitution by conventions in the several States, as provided in the Constitution, within seven years from the date of the submission hereof to the States by the Congress.

Amendment XXII [1951]

Section 1. No person shall be elected to the office of the President more than twice, and no person who has held the office of President, or acted as President, for more than two years of a term to which some other person was elected President shall be elected to the office of the President more than once. But this Article shall not apply to any person holding the office of President when this Article was proposed by the Congress, and shall not prevent any person who may be holding the office of President, or acting as President, during the term within which this Article becomes operative from holding the office of President or acting as President during the remainder of such term.

Section 2. This article shall be inoperative unless it shall have been ratified as an amendment to the Constitution by the legislatures of three-fourths of the several States within seven years from the date of its submission to the States by the Congress.

AMENDMENT XXIII [1961]

Section 1. The District constituting the seat of Government of the United States shall appoint in such manner as the Congress may direct:

A number of electors of President and Vice President equal to the whole number of Senators and Representatives in Congress to which the District would be entitled if it were a State, but in no event more than the least populous State; they shall be in addition to those appointed by the States, but they shall be considered, for the purposes of the election of President and Vice President, to be electors appointed by a State; and they shall meet in the District and perform such duties as provided by the twelfth article of amendment.

Section 2. The Congress shall have power to enforce this article by appropriate legislation.

AMENDMENT XXIV [1964]

Section 1. The right of citizens of the United States to vote in any primary or other election for President or Vice President, for electors for President or Vice President, or for Senator or Representative in Congress, shall not be denied or abridged by the United States or any State by reason of failure to pay any poll tax or other tax.

Section 2. The Congress shall have power to enforce this article by appropriate legislation.

AMENDMENT XXV [1967]

Section 1. In case of the removal of the President from office or of his death or resignation, the Vice President shall become President.

Section 2. Whenever there is a vacancy in the office of Vice President, the President shall nominate a Vice President who shall take office upon confirmation by a majority vote of both Houses of Congress.

Section 3. Whenever the President transmits to the President pro tempore of the Senate and the Speaker of the House of Representatives his written declaration that he is unable to discharge the powers and duties of his office, and until he transmits to them a written declaration to the contrary, such powers and duties shall be discharged by the Vice President as Acting President.

Section 4. Whenever the Vice President and a majority of either the principal officers of the executive departments or of such other body as Congress may by law provide, transmit to the President pro tempore of the Senate and the Speaker of the House of Representatives their written declaration that the President is unable to discharge the powers and duties of his office, the Vice President shall immediately assume the powers and duties of the office as Acting President.

Thereafter, when the President transmits to the President pro tempore of the Senate and the Speaker of the House of Representatives his written declaration that no inability exists, he shall resume the powers and duties of his office unless the Vice President and a majority of either the principal officers of the executive department or of such other body as Congress may by law provide, transmit within four days to the President pro tempore of the Senate and the Speaker of the House of Representatives their written declaration that the President is unable to discharge the powers and duties of his office. Thereupon Congress shall decide the issue, assembling within forty-eight hours for that purpose if not in session. If the Congress, within twenty-one days after receipt of the latter written declaration, or, if Congress is not in session, within twenty-one days after Congress is required to assemble, determines by two-thirds vote of both Houses that the President is unable to discharge the powers and duties of his office, the Vice President shall continue to discharge the same as Acting President; otherwise, the President shall resume the powers and duties of his office.

AMENDMENT XXVI [1971]

Section 1. The right of citizens of the United States, who are eighteen years of age or older, to vote shall not be denied or abridged by the United States or by any State on account of age.

Section 2. The Congress shall have power to enforce this article by appropriate legislation.

Editorial Note

Throughout this book, additions to and deletions from quoted material are indicated by brackets and ellipses except that (without notice) citations are modified and eliminated, footnotes are eliminated, and paragraphs are modified to make edited excerpts coherent. Footnote numbers in opinions and other quoted material have been changed to consecutive letters. The authors' own footnotes, including those inserted into quoted material and cases for purposes of editorial comment, are indicated by numbers, running consecutively through each chapter.

PROCESSES OF CONSTITUTIONAL DECISIONMAKING

PART ONE
FEDERALISM, PROPERTY, RACE, NATIONAL SECURITY, AND JUDICIAL REVIEW (1776-1940)

Part One examines five subjects that were the focus of constitutional controversy during the first century and a half of the United States. In the main, the chapters are organized according to the periods conventionally used by constitutional historians: John Marshall's chief-justiceship (1801-1835); that of his successor, Roger Taney (1836-1864); from the end of the Civil War through the mid-1930s (this chapter is further subdivided into the periods before and after about 1890); and from 1934 through the early 1940s.[1] Any division of events into periods is necessarily imposed, contingent, and value laden; we encourage you to be alert to, and critical of, any claims implicit in our organization.

The issues of Part One — especially those of federalism, property rights, and race — have roots in the period between the Declaration of Independence and the adoption of the Constitution of 1787. We begin with a survey of this preconstitutional period.

I. *Background to the Constitution*

In June 1776, the Continental Congress, meeting in Philadelphia, appointed committees to draft a declaration of independence and to prepare "the form of a confederation to be entered into between these colonies."[2] Within a month, the Congress approved a Declaration drafted mostly by Thomas Jefferson. The Articles of Confederation were submitted to the states the following year and were ratified by the last state, Maryland, in 1781.

Although the new nation was called The United States of America, "the Articles of Confederation were in many ways more like a treaty among a group of small nations" than a charter for a single nation.[3] Article II provided: "Each state retains its sovereignty, freedom, and independence, and every power, jurisdiction, and right, which is not by this Confederation expressly delegated to the

1. The second part of this final chapter of Part One deviates from the general organization by tracing the doctrines of federalism through to the present day.
2. Quoted in The Formation of the Union (National Archives Pub. No. 70-13) at 34.
3. Id.

United States, in Congress assembled."[4] Representation in the Congress was by states, each of which had one vote (although up to seven delegates could participate in the Congress). The delegates were subject to recall by their states, and their salaries were paid from the state treasuries. The legislative powers of the Congress were narrowly limited. It had no authority to regulate interstate or foreign commerce. It was not empowered to raise money by taxing citizens of the United States but had instead to rely on contributions from state treasuries. Although the Congress was empowered to coin money, the states retained the power to issue paper money, which some did with abandon.

The Articles did not establish a national judiciary or a real executive branch. They authorized Congress to establish such "committees and civil officers as may be necessary for managing the general affairs of the united states under their direction" and to appoint a "president" of the Congress, who could serve only a single one-year term in any three years. In 1781, Congress established departments of Foreign Affairs, War, Marine, and Treasury, each under a single secretary.

Government under the Articles proved unsatisfactory. One weakness lay in the United States' "financial incompetence, in turn ascribable to its lack of taxing power and the habitual failure of the states to meet their assessments promptly."[5] To pay the army and meet other expenses, the Continental Congress was reduced to printing paper money — money that gave rise to the phrase "not worth a continental." In the absence of congressional power to regulate commerce, the states were free to negotiate trade agreements with each other or erect trade barriers just as one nation might do with respect to others. New York took advantage of its position as a port of entry to lay duties on goods bound for New Jersey and Connecticut, which in turn taxed commerce originating in New York.

However, the problems of the new nation were not limited to the inadequacies of the federal government. The Revolutionary War had left the country in a severe depression. The United States was excluded from the British mercantile system and foreclosed from trade with the West Indies. The war, which ended only in 1783, had devastated New England's fishing industry, while "the loss of English bounties on rice and indigo had much to do with the agricultural decay of the South."[6] "Within most of the states, a continuous struggle went on between a paper-money faction, composed of small farmers, debtors, and artisans, and a hard-money faction, composed of creditors, merchants, and large planters."[7] Legislative victories by debtors, particularly in Rhode Island, stirred great concern within the creditor classes. Shay's Rebellion in 1786, the result of economic distress, confirmed fears that the new nation was on the verge of collapse.

Any government would have faced severe problems in the United States in the 1780s. "Yet to conservatives in the Confederation period the economic difficulties of the day appeared to rise in considerable part out of the weakness of the government, and the economic crisis thus contributed to the impetus for constitutional reform."[8] As early as 1783, Alexander Hamilton called for "a General

4. This and other quotations from the Articles are taken from Sources and Documents Illustrating the American Revolution 1764-1788 and the Formation of the Federal Constitution (Morison ed., 2d ed. 1965) at 178-186.

5. Alfred Kelly & Winfred Harbison, The American Constitution: Its Origin and Development 97 (5th ed. 1976).

6. Id. at 104.

7. Id. at 103.

8. Id. at 104.

Convention for the purpose of revising and amending the federal Government." The call was opposed by James Madison, who feared that such a convention would only excite "pernicious jealousies" among the states.[9] A convention was again proposed in 1786 — this time by representatives from Virginia. One hundred seventy years later, Justice Robert Jackson described the background of Virginia's call:

> When victory relieved the Colonies from the pressure for solidarity that war had exerted, a drift toward anarchy and commercial warfare between the states began. ". . . Each State would legislate according to its estimate of its own interest, the importance of its own products, and the local advantages or disadvantages of its position in a political or commercial view." This came "to threaten at once the peace and safety of the Union." Story, The Constitution. . . . The sole purpose for which Virginia initiated the movement which ultimately produced the Constitution was "to take into consideration the trade of the United States; to examine the relative situations and trade of the said States; to consider how far a uniform system in their commercial regulations may be necessary to their common interests and their permanent harmony" and for that purpose the General Assembly of Virginia in 1786 named commissioners and proposed their meeting with those from other states.[10]

At a convention held in 1786 at Annapolis, Maryland, sentiment for a more general revision of the Articles was balanced by pessimism. Madison observed that "Gentlemen both within & without Congs. wish to make this Meeting subservient to a Plenipotentiary Convention for amending the Confederation. Tho' my wishes are in favor of such an event, yet I despair so much of its accomplishment at the present crisis that I do not extend my views beyond a Commercial Reform. To speak the truth I almost despair even of this."[11]

The report of the Annapolis Convention proposed another meeting "to devise such further provisions as shall appear . . . necessary to render the constitution of the Foederal Government adequate to the exigencies of the Union."[12] And in February 1787 Congress authorized a convention "for the sole and express purpose of revising the Articles of Confederation and reporting to Congress and the several legislatures such alterations and provisions therein as shall when agreed to in Congress and confirmed by the States render the federal constitution adequate to the exigencies of Government & the preservation of the union."[13]

The Convention that met in Philadelphia in 1787 ended up drafting a new Constitution. The delegates knew they were exceeding their congressional authorization. Edmund Randoph, the Governor of Virginia, who would later become the first Attorney General of the United States, said, "There are great seasons when persons with limited powers are justified in exceeding them, and a

9. 9 Papers of James Madison 115-119 (Rutland & Rachal eds. 1975).

10. H. P. Hood & Co. v. DuMond, 336 U.S. 525 (1949). Historians differ about the extent to which the nation was actually on the brink of dissolution. Justice Jackson, like Story, was a strong nationalist, and he expresses a view widely held at least since John Fiske's influential book, The Critical Period of American History (1888). For an important revisionist history of the period see Merrill Jensen, The New Nation: A History of the United States During the Confederation, 1781-1789 (1950).

11. Madison to Jefferson, August 12, 1786, in 9 Papers, supra note 9, at 96.

12. Formation of the Union, supra note 2, at 50.

13. Id.

person would be contemptible not to risk it."[14] Alexander Hamilton remarked that "To rely on & propose any plan not adequate to these exigencies, merely because it was not clearly within our powers, would be to sacrifice the means to the end."[15] During the campaign for ratification, Madison defended the Convention's actions in The Federalist No. 40, writing that the delegates "must have borne in mind, that as the plan to be framed and proposed was to be submitted *to the people themselves* . . . its approbation [would] blot out antecedent errors and irregularities."

The Philadelphia Convention nearly deadlocked over the formula for state representation in a new and more powerful Congress. The Virginia Plan, which served as a working draft for much of the document, in effect proposed that representation in both houses be based on the number of free inhabitants in each state. This met with opposition from less populous states and from many Southern states: Although it was thought that the population of the South would grow more rapidly than the North, the South feared Northern domination of the Congress and the concomitant threat to the institution of slavery. After more than a month of passionate controversy, the Convention agreed on a compromise: The states would be represented equally in the Senate, while representation in the House would be proportionate to the sum of the "whole number of free persons" and "three-fifths of all other persons" in each state.

The Constitution's two other allusions to slavery — the "migration or importation" clause of Article I and the "fugitive from service or labor" clause of Article IV — also refer to the institution indirectly and euphemistically. However willing the authors of the Constitution were to acquiesce in slavery to create a single nation, they seemed ashamed to acknowledge its existence overtly in the founding document. Luther Martin remarked that a revolution "grounded upon the preservation of *those rights* to which God and nature had entitled *us,* not in *particular,* but in common with all the rest of *mankind* . . . , ended up by making a Constitution that was an *insult to that God* . . . who views with equal eye the poor *African slave* and his *American master.*[16]

On September 17, 1787, four months after they had convened, the members of the Philadelphia Convention signed the draft Constitution and transmitted it to Congress. Article XIII of the Articles of Confederation, the document under whose authority the Congress was operating, allowed modification of its terms only by unanimous consent of all thirteen state legislatures. Nevertheless, the Congress sent to the States the Constitution, with its Article VII, which required only the "Ratification of the Conventions [not the legislatures] of nine States" in order to negate the old Articles and validate the new Constitution — at least for the States "so ratifying the Same." Bruce Ackerman describes Articles VII's "assertion that nine state 'Conventions' could adequately ratify on behalf of the People [as] plainly an extra-legal assertion of democratic authority."[17]

14. 1 Records of the Federal Convention of 1787, at 262 (Farrand ed. 1937) (speech of June 16, 1787).

15. Id. at 283 (June 18, 1787). See also id. at 346 (George Mason).

16. Quoted in Staughton Lynd, Slavery and the Founding Fathers, in Black History 119-131 (Drimmer ed. 1968).

17. Ackerman, The Storrs Lectures: Discovering the Constitution, 93 Yale L.J. 1013, 1017 n.6 (1984).

The heated campaign over ratification produced a series of extraordinary articles by James Madison, Alexander Hamilton, and John Jay — now known as the Federalist Papers — defending the Constitution, and some brilliant articles opposing its ratification, now largely forgotten.[18] One common concern, voiced in the conventions as well as the publications, was that the Constitution contained no Bill of Rights similar to those contained in the new state constitutions written after the Revolution. In the 84th Federalist, Hamilton responded with an argument, later voiced by James Wilson at the Philadelphia Convention, based on the observation that the national government, by contrast to the states, was only one of limited, delegated powers:

> I affirm that the bills of rights . . . are not only unnecessary in the proposed constitution, but would even be dangerous. They would contain various exceptions to powers which are not granted; and on this very account, would afford a colourable pretext to claim more than were granted. For why declare that things shall not be done which there is no power to do? Why, for instance, should it be said, that the liberty of the press shall not be restrained, when no power is given by which restrictions may be imposed? I will not contend that such a provision would confer a regulating power; but it is evident that it would furnish to men disposed to usurp, a plausible pretence for claiming that power. They might urge with a semblance of reason, that the constitution ought not to be charged with the absurdity of providing against the abuse of an authority, which was not given, and that the provision against restraining the liberty of the press afforded a clear implication, that a power to prescribe proper regulations concerning it, was intended to be vested in the national government. This may serve as a specimen of the numerous hurdles which would be given to the doctrine of constructive powers, by the indulgence of an injudicious zeal for bills of rights.

The principal anti-Federalist response to this argument emphasized the limitations contained in Article I, Section 9. Why, if the powers of the national government were limited to assigned powers, was it necessary to prohibit Congress from, say, granting titles of nobility?

In any event, one of the first acts of the First Congress was to pass and submit to the states twelve amendments, ten of which were ratified in 1791. The rejected amendments concerned the numerical basis of representation in Congress and the procedure for Congressional pay raises.

II. The Issues of Part One

Part One examines the development of constitutional doctrines concerning federalism, property rights, race, national security (and freedom of expression), and judicial review during the first 150 years of the Republic.

Of these five issues, federalism is the most difficult to grasp for anyone born after the New Deal. Christopher Tiedman, a conservative nineteenth-century le-

18. See The Complete Anti-Federalist (Herbert Storing, ed. 1981), the first of whose seven volumes is an introductory essay on "What the Anti-Federalists Were For." A very good shorter collection is The Antifederalists (Kenyon ed. 1966).

gal scholar, described the problem of federalism lucidly and with the passion that animated lawyers, politicans, and judges on both sides of the issue.[19]

> [T]he local pride and prejudices of the people were not the only serious obstacles in the way of an increase of the powers of the Federal Government, which fell short of a complete extinction of the States as independent bodies politic. It was idle to advocate the absorption of the States into one composite state. The people would have rejected such a proposition with vehemence and indignation. And yet history had never produced a federal government which was not a league. The Federal Union, under the Articles of Confederation, was only a league, and neither claimed nor exercised any authority over the individual citizen. The experience of the people under these Articles of Confederation had demonstrated the futility of the attempt of the Federal Government to assume the powers of government, without the ability and right to compel the obedience of the individual to its commands; and yet the past experience of the world suggested no relief or remedy. It was reserved for an American to create an absolutely new political idea of the most transcendent importance, and which has ultimately solved the problem of combining a strong central government with an independent local government.
>
> In February, 1753, Pelatial Webster published A Dissertation on the Political Union and Constitution of the Thirteen United States of North America, which was a year later followed by another of the same tenor, by Noah Webster, in both of which was proposed "a new system of government which should act, *not on the States, but directly on individuals*, and vest in Congress full power to carry its laws into effect." When we consider for a moment the wonderfulness of two separate and in many respects independent governmental agencies exerting their powers over the same territory, and each within its own sphere commanding the obedience of the same people, there is no occasion for surprise that it required a century of experience under the new government to fully appreciate its significance and effect. The successful maintenance of the separate autonomy of the Federal and State governments for a century, through all the vicissitudes of political fortune which fell to the lot of the people of the United States, furnished an enigmatical contradiction of the prevalent notions of an indivisible sovereignty.
>
> If there be such a thing in politics as sovereignty, it is necessarily indivisible, and hence it is impossible to subject a territory and people to two separate and independent governments without one of them becoming subordinate to, and the instrument of, the other. And I am satisfied that the political leaders of the day, such as Hamilton, Madison, and Randolph, who made such strenuous efforts to establish a strong federal government, put no faith in the feasibility of a dual government of this sort. For, upon the assembling of the constitutional convention, these statesmen advocated the establishment of a supreme federal government, which would reduce the States to subordinate provinces; and they did not yield to the demands of the advocates of State rights until it was demonstrated that the convention would not adopt a centralized government. They feared, and the struggles of seventy-five years justified their fears, that the two governmental agencies could not maintain their independent autonomy. But against their will and in spite of their fears this became the fundamental principle of the American governmental agencies, about which the political forces played with more or less vehemence for three quarters of a century, until, as a declaration of the results of the mighty crisis, the Supreme Court of the United States pronounced this country to be "an indestructible Union composed of indestructible States."

19. Christopher Tiedman, The Unwritten Constitution of the United States 32-34 (1890).

The issue of property rights is easier to understand. The post-Revolutionary conflicts between creditors and debtors, merchants and farmers, wealthy and poor, have reappeared throughout our history. Courts, as well as legislatures, have always played a role in resolving these conflicts through the elaboration of common law doctrine. During the nineteenth century and well into the twentieth, propertyholders, creditors, and business enterprises that had lost in the legislatures frequently turned to the courts for constitutional redress.

The issue of race is the least difficult to describe, for it remains with us today. Slavery, never mentioned by name in the Constitution, became the central constitutional issue for the Taney Court. And during the remainder of the period studied in Part One, the Court joined with the rest of the nation to quash most hopes the Civil War Amendments — the Thirteenth, Fourteenth, and Fifteenth — held out to black citizens.

Issues of national security have implicated the first amendment protections of speech and the press as well as the allocation of powers between the President and Congress. And judicial review, our fifth concern, cuts across all the other four areas. Courts, and especially the Supreme Court of the United States, have played a central role in our constitutional history. The source and scope of judicial authority to revise the constitutional judgments of other decisionmakers, and the methods of constitutional adjudication, themselves remain significant issues of constitutional law.

Chapter 1
The Bank of the United States: A Case Study

This chapter focuses mainly on one of the first constitutional questions confronted by the new federal government: whether chartering a national bank was within the powers delegated to Congress by Article I. We move from the last decade of the eighteenth century, when the issue came before the legislative and executive branches, through the early decades of the nineteenth century, when it was faced by the Supreme Court and again by the President. Besides introducing the issue of federalism, Chapter 1 presents some themes that pervade the book, including the strategies of constitutional interpretation and the allocation of decisionmaking authority among the branches of government. The chapter concludes by examining the constitutional issues surrounding the Sedition Act of 1798.

I. *Early Background*

"There is nothing in the Constitution about banks and banking, though there might well have been, for the subject was already of both economic and political importance when the Constitution was being written."[1] In 1781, the Continental Congress had chartered the Bank of North America. Probably few members of that Congress disputed James Madison's assertion that this exceeded Congress' authority under the Articles of Confederation.[2] Rather, the bank was justified by its sheer necessity in helping finance the war for independence against Great Britain.

At the Philadelphia Convention in 1787, Madison himself proposed that Congress be authorized "to grant charters of incorporation where the interest of the U.S. might require & the legislative provisions of individual States may be incompetent."[3] Rufus King of Massachusetts objected to the proposal on the ground that the "States will be prejudiced and divided into parties by it"; King referred

1. Bray Hammond, Banks and Politics in America from the Revolution to the Civil War 103 (1957).

2. Madison initially opposed incorporation of the bank because of "the absence within the Articles of Confederation of any authority, even that of 'inferred necessity,' to create a bank to carry on the war." 3 Papers of James Madison 175 n.16 (1963). When the ordinance of incorporation came to a vote, he cast what he later termed "an acquiescing rather than an affirmative vote." See 4 id. at 19, 21 n.7, 23 (1965).

3. 2 Records of the Federal Convention of 1787 615-616 (Farrand ed. 1937) (hereinafter Farrand). No general corporation laws existed in the eighteenth and early nineteenth centuries. Corporate charters, typically giving exclusive rights to quasi-public entities, were tailor-made for the occasion. See Lawrence Friedman, A History of American Law 166-169 (1973).

specifically to the concerns of the New York and Philadelphia banking and business communities that Congress might charter a competing banking institution.[4] "Other advocates of the power held back from putting the question to a vote lest it be lost and the record be definitely against it, whereas if not acted on it could be held . . . that the power existed."[5] Gouverneur Morris of Pennsylvania dissuaded his colleague, Robert Morris, from proposing a national bank lest such a provision in the Constitution jeopardize its ratification.[6] The only related proposal brought to a vote, a motion to authorize Congress to charter corporations for the construction of canals, was defeated eight to three.[7]

II. The First Bank of the United States

In the late eighteenth and early nineteenth centuries, banks served two main functions. First, they were depositories for money. Second, they issued bank notes, on deposits or on other security, which served somewhat the same function as paper money in the absence of a national currency.[8] In December 1790, soon after ratification of the Constitution, Secretary of the Treasury Alexander Hamilton submitted a plan for a national bank to be chartered by Congress and owned jointly by private shareholders and the United States. The bank would strengthen the national government: It would aid in the collection of taxes and administration of the public finances and could provide loans to the government.[9] The Senate, half of whose 20 members had attended the Philadelphia Convention, unanimously adopted Hamilton's proposal.[10]

A. Madison's View

James Madison opened the debate in the House of Representatives by denouncing the proposed bank as beyond Congress' constitutionally delegated authority.

JAMES MADISON'S SPEECH TO THE HOUSE OF REPRESENTATIVES (1791)

2 Gales & Seaton's Debates and Proceedings of the Congress of the United States 1944-1952 (1834)

He had entertained this opinion from the date of the Constitution. His impression might, perhaps, be the stronger, because he well recollected that a power to

4. 2 Farrand, supra note 3, at 615-616.
5. Hammond, supra note 1, at 104-105.
6. Id. at 105.
7. 2 Farrand, supra note 3, at 615-616.
8. Article I, §10 prohibits states from coining money or emitting bills of credit. Article I, §8 authorizes Congress to coin money (though not in terms to issue bills of credit). Not until after the Civil War did Congress authorize the issuance of paper money.
9. Hammond, supra note 1, at 114-115.
10. R.K. Moulton, Legislative and Documentary History of the Banks of the United States 13 (1834).

grant charters of incorporation had been proposed in the general convention and rejected.

Is the power of establishing an incorporated Bank among the powers vested by the Constitution in the Legislature of the United States? This is the question to be examined. After some general remarks on the limitations of all political power, he took notice of the peculiar manner in which the Federal Government is limited. It is not a general grant, out of which particular powers are excepted; it is a grant of particular powers only, leaving the general mass in other hands. So it has been understood by its friends and its foes, and so it was to be interpreted.

As preliminaries to the right interpretation, he laid down the following rules:

An interpretation that destroys the very characteristic of the Government cannot be just.

Where the meaning is clear, the consequences, whatever they may be, are to be admitted — where doubtful, it is fairly triable by its consequences.

In controverted cases, the meaning of the parties to the instrument, if to be collected by reasonable evidence, is a proper guide.

Contemporary and concurrent expositions are a reasonable evidence of the meaning or the parties.

In admitting or rejecting a constructive authority, not only the degree of its incidentality to an express authority is to be regarded, but the degree of its importance also; since on this will depend the probability or improbability of its being left to construction.

Reviewing the Constitution with an eye to these positions, it was not possible to discover in it the power to incorporate a Bank. The only clauses under which such a power could be pretended, are either:

1. The power to lay and collect taxes to pay the debts, and provide for the common defence and general welfare: Or,
2. The power to borrow money on the credit of the United States: Or,
3. The power to pass all laws necessary and proper to carry into execution those powers.

The bill did not come within the first power. It laid no taxes to pay the debts, or provide for the general welfare. It laid no tax whatever. It was altogether foreign to the subject.

No argument could be drawn from the terms "common defence, and general welfare." The power as to these general purposes was limited to acts laying taxes for them; and the general purposes themselves were limited and explained by the particular enumeration subjoined. To understand these terms in any sense, that would justify the power in question, would give the Congress an unlimited power; would render nugatory the enumeration of particular powers; would supercede all the powers reserved to the State Governments. . . .

The cases of the Bank established by the former Congress has been cited as a precedent. This was known, he said, to have been the child of necessity. It never could be justified by the regular powers of the articles of Confederation. . . .

The second clause to be examined is that which empowers Congress to borrow money.

Is this bill to borrow money? It does not borrow a shilling. Is there any fair construction by which the bill can be deemed an exercise of the power to borrow money? The obvious meaning of the power to borrow money, is that of accepting it from, and stipulating payment to those who are able and willing to lend. . . .

The third clause is that which gives the power to pass all laws necessary and proper to execute the specified powers.

Whatever meaning this clause may have, none can be admitted, that would give an unlimited discretion to Congress.

Its meaning must, according to the natural and obvious force of the terms and the context, be limited to means necessary to the end, and incident to the nature of the specified powers.

The clause is in fact merely declaratory of what would have resulted by unavoidable implication, as the appropriate, and, as it were, technical means of executing those powers. In this sense it has been explained by the friends of the Constitution, and ratified by the State Conventions.

The essential characteristic of the Government, as composed of limited and enumerated powers, would be destroyed, if instead of direct and incidental means, any means could be used which, in the language of the preamble to the bill, "might be conceived to be conducive to the successful conducting of the finances, or might be conceived to tend to give facility to the obtaining of loans. . . ."

If, proceeded he, Congress, by virtue of the power to borrow, can create the means of lending, and, in pursuance of these means, can incorporate a Bank, they may do any thing whatever creative of like means. . . .

If, again, Congress by virtue of the power to borrow money, can create the ability to lend, they may, by virtue of the power to levy money, create the ability to pay it. The ability to pay taxes depends on the general wealth of the society, and this, on the general prosperity of agriculture, manufactures, and commerce. Congress then may give bounties and make regulations on all these objects. . . .

Mark the reasoning on which the validity of the bill depends. To borrow money is made the end, and the accumulation of capitals implied as the means. The accumulation of money is then the end, and the Bank implied as the means. The Bank is then the end, and a charter of incorporation, a monopoly, . . . &c. implied as the means.

If implications, thus remote and thus multiplied, can be linked together, a chain may be formed that will reach every object of legislation, every object within the whole compass of political economy.

The latitude of interpretation required by the bill is condemned by the rule furnished by the Constitution itself.

Congress have power "to regulate the value of money;" yet it is expressly added, not left to be implied, that counterfeiters may be punished.

They have the power "to declare war," to which armies are more incident, than incorporated banks to borrowing; yet the power "to raise and support armies" is expressly added; and to this again, the express power "to make rules and regulations for the government of armies;" a like remark is applicable to the powers as to the navy.

The regulation and calling out of militia are more appurtenant to war than the proposed Bank to borrowing; yet the former is not left to construction.

The very power to borrow money is a less remote implication from the power of war, than an incorporated monopoly Bank from the power of borrowing; yet the power is not left to implication.

It is not pretended that every insertion or omission in the Constitution is the effect of systematic attention. This is not the character of any human work, particularly the work of a body of men. The examples cited, with others that might be added, sufficiently inculcate, nevertheless, a rule of interpretation very different from that on which the bill rests. They condemn the exercise of any power, particularly a great and important power, which is not evidently and necessarily involved in an express power.

He here adverted to a distinction, which he said has not been sufficiently kept in view, between a power necessary and proper for the Government or Union, and a power necessary and proper for executing the enumerated powers.

In the latter case, the powers included in each of the enumerated powers were not expressed, but drawn from the nature of each. In the former, the powers composing the Government were expressly enumerated. This constituted the peculiar nature of the Government, no power, therefore, not enumerated could be inferred from the general nature of Government. Had the power of making treaties, for example, been omitted, however necessary it might have been, the defect could only have been lamented, or supplied by an amendment of the Constitution.

But the proposed Bank could not be called necessary to the Government; at most could be but convenient. Its uses to the Government could be supplied by keeping the taxes a little in advance; by loans from individuals; by other Banks, over which the Government would have equal command; nay greater, as it might grant or refuse to these the privilege (a free and irrevocable gift to the proposed Bank) of using their notes in the Federal Revenue.

Most of the other participants in the House debate argued for a broader notion of congressional power, along the lines later articulated by Hamilton in his memorandum to President Washington (excerpted infra). The House adopted the bill chartering the bank by a vote of 39 to 20. Of the seven Representatives who had attended the Philadelphia Convention, four voted for the measure and three against it.

Passage of the bill did not end the debate over its constitutionality. George Washington, who had been President of the Philadelphia Convention before becoming the first President under the new Constitution, asked his cabinet to prepare memoranda on the constitutional questions. Edmund Randolph, the Attorney General, thought the bill unconstitutional, as did Secretary of State Thomas Jefferson. Hamilton, as already noted, supported the measure.

B. Jefferson's Critique of the Bank

Jefferson referred to the Philadelphia Convention's rejection of the congressional power to incorporate canals: "[O]ne of the reasons for rejection urged in the debate was, that then they would have a power to erect a bank, which would render the great cities, where there were prejudices and jealousies on the subject, adverse to the reception of the Constitution." Continuing in a more general vein he wrote:[11]

> I consider the foundation of the Constitution as laid on this ground: That "all powers not delegated to the United States, by the Constitution, nor prohibited by it to the States, are reserved to the States or to the people." To take a single step beyond the boundaries thus specially drawn around the powers of Congress is to take possession of a boundless field of power, no longer susceptible of any definition.
>
> The incorporation of a bank, and the powers assumed by this bill, have not, in my opinion, been delegated to the United States, by the Constitution. . . .
>
> It has been urged that a bank will give great facility or convenience in the collection of taxes. Suppose this were true: yet the Constitution allows only the means which are *"necessary,"* not those which are merely "convenient" for effecting the enumerated powers. If such a latitude of construction be allowed to this phrase as to give any non-enumerated power, it will go to every one, for there is not one which ingenuity may not torture into a *convenience* in some instance *or other,* to *some one* of so long a list of enumerated powers. It would swallow up all the delegated powers, and reduce the whole to one power, as before observed. Therefore it was that the Constitution restrained them to the *necessary* means, that is to say, to those means without which the grant of power would be nugatory. . . .
>
> The negative of the President is the shield provided by the Constitution to protect against the invasions of the legislature: 1. the right of the Executive. 2. of the Judiciary. 3. of the States and State legislatures. The present is the case of a right remaining exclusively with the States, and consequently one of those intended by the Constitution to be placed under its protection.
>
> It must be added, however, that unless the President's mind on a view of everything which is urged for and against this bill, is tolerably clear that it is unauthorized by the Constitution; if the pro and the con hang so even as to balance his judgment, a just respect for the wisdom of the legislature would naturally decide the balance in favor of their opinion. It is chiefly for the cases where they are clearly misled by error, ambition, or interest, that the Constitution as placed a check in the negative of the President.

C. Hamilton's Defense

ALEXANDER HAMILTON, OPINION ON THE CONSTITUTIONALITY OF AN ACT TO ESTABLISH A BANK (1791)

8 Papers of Alexander Hamilton 97 (1965)

The Secretary of the Treasury having perused with attention the papers containing the opinions of the Secretary of State and Attorney General concerning the constitutionality of the bill for establishing a National Bank proceeds according to the order of the President to submit the reasons which have induced him to entertain a different opinion.

It will naturally have been anticipated that, in performing this task he would feel uncommon solicitude. Personal considerations alone arising from the reflec-

11. Opinion on the Constitutionality of the Bill for Establishing a National Bank, in 19 Papers of Thomas Jefferson 275, 279-280 (1974).

tion that the measure originated with him would be sufficient to produce it: The sense which he has manifested of the great importance of such an institution to the successful administration of the department under his particular care; and an expectation of serious ill consequences to result from a failure of the measure, do not permit him to be without anxiety on public accounts. But the chief solicitude arises from a firm persuasion, that principles of construction like those espoused by the Secretary of State and the Attorney General would be fatal to the just & indispensable authority of the United States.

In entering upon the argument it ought to be premised, that the objections of the Secretary of State and Attorney General are founded on a general denial of the authority of the United States to erect corporations. The latter indeed expressly admits, that if there be any thing in the bill which is not warranted by the constitution, it is the clause of incorporation.

Now it appears to the Secretary of the Treasury, that this *general principle* is *inherent* in the very *definition* of *Government* and *essential* to every step of the progress to be made by that of the United States; namely — that every power vested in a Government is in its nature *sovereign,* and includes by *force* of the *term,* a right to employ all the *means* requisite, and fairly *applicable* to the attainment of the *ends* of such power; and which are not precluded by restrictions & exceptions specified in the constitution; or not immoral, or not contrary to the essential ends of political society. . . .

This general & indisputable principle puts at once an end to the *abstract* question — Whether the United States have power to *erect a corporation?* that is to say, to give a *legal* or *artificial capacity* to one or more persons, distinct from the natural. For it is unquestionably incident to *sovereign power* to erect corporations, and consequently to *that* of the United States, in *relation to the objects* intrusted to the management of the government. The difference is this — where the authority of the government is general, it can create corporations in *all cases;* where it is confined to certain branches of legislation, it can create corporations only in those cases. . . .

It is not denied, that there are *implied,* as well as *express* powers, and that the former are as effectually delegated as the latter. . . .

Then it follows, that as a power of erecting a corporation may as well be *implied* as any other thing; it may as well be employed as an *instrument* or *mean* of carrying into execution any of the specified powers, as any other instrument or mean whatever. The only question must be, in this as in every other case, whether the mean to be employed, or in this instance the corporation to be erected, has a natural relation to any of the acknowledged objects or lawful ends of the government. Thus a corporation may not be erected by congress, for superintending the police of the city of Philadelphia because they are not authorized to *regulate* the *police* of that city; but one may be erected in relation to the collection of the taxes, or to the trade with foreign countries, or to the trade between the States, or with the Indian Tribes, because it is the province of the federal government to regulate those objects & because it is incident to a general *sovereign* or *legislative power* to *regulate* a thing, to employ all the means which relate to its regulation to the *best & greatest advantage.* . . .

To this mode of reasoning respecting the right of employing all the means requisite to the execution of the specified powers of the Government, it is objected that none but *necessary* & proper means are to be employed, & the Secretary of

State maintains, that no means are to be considered as *necessary,* but those without which the grant of the power would be *nugatory.* . . .

All the arguments therefore against the constitutionality of the bill derived from the accidental existence of certain State-banks: institutions which *happen* to exist to day, & for ought that concerns the government of the United States, may disappear to morrow, must not only be rejected as fallacious, but must be viewed as demonstrative, that there is a *radical* source of error in the reasoning.

It is essential to the being of the National government, that so erroneous a conception of the meaning of the word *necessary,* should be exploded.

It is certain, that neither the grammatical, nor popular sense of the term requires that construction. According to both, *necessary* often means no more than *needful, requisite, incidental, useful,* or *conducive to.* It is a common mode of expression to say, that it is *necessary* for a government or a person to do this or that thing, when nothing more is intended or understood, than that the interests of the government or person require, or will be promoted, by the doing of this or that thing. The imagination can be at no loss for exemplifications of the use of the word in this sense.

And it is the true one in which it is to be understood as used in the constitution. The whole turn of the clause containing it, indicates, that it was the intent of the convention, by that clause to give a liberal latitude to the exercise of the specified powers. . . .

[The alternative] construction would beget endless uncertainty & embarrassment. The cases must be palpable & extreme in which it could be pronounced with certainty, that a measure was absolutely necessary, or one without which the exercise of a given power would be nugatory. There are few measures of any government, which would stand so severe a test. To insist upon it, would be to make the criterion of the exercise of any implied power a *case of extreme necessity;* which is rather a rule to justify the overleaping of the bounds of constitutional authority, than to govern the ordinary exercise of it. . . .

The *degree* in which a measure is necessary, can never be a test of the *legal* right to adopt it. That must ever be a matter of opinion; and can only be a test of expediency. The *relation* between the *measure* and the *end,* between the *nature* of the *mean* employed towards the execution of a power and the object of that power, must be the criterion of constitutionality not the more or less of *necessity* or *utility.*

The practice of the government is against the rule of construction advocated by the Secretary of State. Of this the act concerning light houses, beacons, buoys & public piers, is a decisive example. This doubtless must be referred to the power of regulating trade, and is fairly relative to it. But it cannot be affirmed, that the exercise of that power, in this instance, was strictly necessary; or that the power itself would be *nugatory* without that of regulating establishments of this nature.

This restrictive interpretation of the word *necessary* is also contrary to this sound maxim of construction namely, that the powers contained in a constitution of government, especially those which concern the general administration of the affairs of a country, its finances, trade, defence &c ought to be construed liberally, in advancement of the public good. . . .

[T]he doctrine which is contended for . . . does not affirm that the National government is sovereign in all respects, but that it is sovereign to a certain extent: that is, to the extent of the objects of its specified powers.

sovereign vs supremacy?

It leaves therefore a criterion of what is constitutional, and of what is not so. This criterion is the *end* to which the measure relates as a *mean.* If the end be clearly comprehended within any of the specified powers, & if the measure have an obvious relation to that end, and is not forbidden by any particular provision of the constitution — it may safely be deemed to come within the compass of the national authority. . . .

end justifies the means

To establish [the National government's power to charter a corporation,] it remains to shew the relation of such an institution to one or more of the specified powers of the government.

Accordingly it is affirmed, that it has a relation more or less direct to the power of collecting taxes; to that of borrowing money; to that of regulating trade between the states; and to those of raising, supporting & maintaining fleets & armies. To the two former, the relation may be said to be *immediate.*

And, in the last place, it will be argued, that it is, *clearly,* within the provision which authorizes the making of all *needful* rules & *regulations* concerning the *property* of the United States, as the same has been practiced upon by the Government.

A Bank relates to the collection of taxes in two ways; *indirectly,* by increasing the quantity of circulating medium & quickening circulation, which facilitates the means of paying — *directly,* by creating a *convenient species* of *medium* in which they are to be paid.

The legislative power of borrowing money, & of making all laws necessary & proper for carrying into execution that power, seems obviously competent to the appointment of the organ through which the abilities and wills of individuals may be most efficaciously exerted, for the accommodation of the government by loans. . . .

The institution of a bank has also a natural relation to the regulation of trade between the States: in so far as it is conducive to the creation of a convenient medium of *exchange* between them, and to the keeping up a full circulation by preventing the frequent displacement of the metals in reciprocal remittances. Money is the very hinge on which commerce turns. And this does not mean merely gold & silver, many other things have served the purpose with different degrees of utility. Paper has been extensively employed. . . .

[A]s the bill under consideration contemplates the government in the light of a joint proprietor of the stock of the bank, it brings the case within the provision of the clause of the constitution which immediately respects the property of the United States.

On February 25, 1791, President Washington signed the act incorporating the Bank of the United States.[12]

12. Hammond, supra note 1, at 118.

III. The Second Bank

When the bank's 20-year charter lapsed in 1811, Congress refused to renew it. Opposition to the bank came from both Jeffersonian agrarians — though Jefferson himself now publicly supported the Bank — and from the private business and banking community. Of the 39 members of Congress who spoke on the issue of renewal, 35 addressed the constitutionality of the bank. Whether because of constitutional doubts or, more likely, because of the strength of antinational forces in Congress, renewal failed by one vote.[13]

Four years later, however, Congress established the second Bank of the United States. The intervening period had been one of some economic turmoil, partly the result of the War of 1812 and partly the result of irresponsible fiscal practices by state banks, and the federal government had been seriously inconvenienced by its need to rely on state banks to borrow money and to pay national debts.[14] The constitutionality of the bank was scarcely discussed in the debates over its rechartering. Indeed, Madison stated that the issue was settled "by repeated recognitions, under varied circumstances, of the validity of such an institution."[15]

Like its predecessor, the second bank was by no means a purely governmental agency. Private investors owned 80 percent of the stock and the government the remaining 20 percent. Of its 25 directors, 20 were elected by the shareholders, while the president appointed the other 5. The bank did act as the government's primary fiscal agent: The secretary of the treasury was required to deposit all public funds in the bank; it was required to keep, transfer, and disburse all government monies given it; and its notes were made legal tender for the payment of government debts.

The constitutional dispute over the bank was not over, however. A number of states remained intensely hostile and enacted nearly annihilative taxes on the bank.[16] It was in this context that McCulloch v. Maryland came before the Court.

IV. Judicial Examination of Congress' Authority to Create the Bank

Note on Reading and Editing Cases

The Supreme Court Justices' opinions in constitutional cases are often very long, and we have edited most of the cases in this book in order to focus the issues, to keep the book to a manageable length while covering a variety of issues, and to mitigate tedium. We have not edited *McCulloch,* however.

We suggest that you read Chief Justice Marshall's opinion through once to get a sense of its structure and arguments. Then read it again with a blue pencil (im-

13. Id. at 210-222.
14. Id. at 227-233.
15. Quoted in id. at 233.
16. Id. at 263.

aginary or real, depending on the projected resale value of this book), trying to omit as much superfluity as you can.

Our own experience as editors is that there is no better way to understand the substance and structure of a person's writing than to edit it. We also hope that you will gain some appreciation of the problems of editing an opinion — not, we hasten to add, so that you will appreciate our hard work, but so you will be skeptical about the relationship between any edited version and the original.

McCULLOCH v. MARYLAND

[The first question]

17 U.S. (4 Wheat.) 316 (1819)

Error to the Court of Appeals of the State of Maryland

[In 1818, the Maryland Assembly enacted a law imposing an annual tax of $15,000 on all banks or branches of banks in the state not chartered by the state legislature. The only bank that fit this description was the Bank of the United States, whose local cashier, J.W. McCulloch, refused to pay the tax. Maryland successfully sued McCulloch in its own courts to recover the statutory penalty for failure to comply with the statute.]

MARSHALL, C.J. . . .

[1] In the case now to be determined, the defendant, a sovereign State, denies the obligation of a law enacted by the legislature of the Union, and the plaintiff, on his part, contests the validity of an act which has been passed by the legislature of that State. The constitution of our country, in its most interesting and vital parts, is to be considered; the conflicting powers of the government of the Union and of its members, as marked in that constitution, are to be discussed; and an opinion given, which may essentially influence the great operation of the government. No tribunal can approach such a question without a deep sense of its importance, and of the awful responsibility involved in its decision. But it must be decided peacefully, or remain a source of hostile legislation, perhaps of hostility of a still more serious nature; and if it is to be so decided, by this tribunal alone can the decision be made. On the Supreme Court of the United States has the constitution of our country devolved this important duty.

[2] The first question made in the cause is, has Congress power to incorporate a bank?

[3] It has been truly said, that this can scarcely be considered as an open question, entirely unprejudiced by the former proceedings of the nation respecting it. The principle now contested was introduced at a very early period of our history, has been recognized by many successive legislatures, and has been acted upon by the judicial department, in cases of peculiar delicacy, as a law of undoubted obligation.

¶1. Marshall refers to Maryland as a "sovereign State." What does "sovereign" mean? What would be entailed in viewing Maryland as a "sovereign State"?

With respect to the last two sentences: What provisions of the Constitution "devolve" the duty to construe the Constitution? Whatever your answer to this question, does the Constitution devolve that duty on the Supreme Court (or the judiciary in general) "alone"?

[4] It will not be denied, that a bold and daring usurpation might be resisted, after an acquiescence still longer and more complete than this. But it is conceived that a doubtful question, one on which human reason may pause, and the human judgment be suspended, in the decision of which the great principles of liberty are not concerned, but the respective powers of those who are equally the representatives of the people, are to be adjusted; if not put at rest by the practice of the government, ought to receive a considerable impression from that practice. An exposition of the constitution, deliberately established by legislative acts, on the faith of which an immense property has been advanced, ought not to be lightly disregarded.

[5] The power now contested was exercised by the first Congress elected under the present constitution. The bill for incorporating the bank of the United States did not steal upon an unsuspecting legislature, and pass unobserved. Its principle was completely understood, and was opposed with equal zeal and ability. After being resisted, first in the fair and open field of debate, and afterwards in the executive cabinet, with as much persevering talent as any measure has ever experienced, and being supported by arguments which convinced minds as pure and as intelligent as this country can boast, it became a law. The original act was permitted to expire; but a short experience of the embarrassments to which the refusal to revive it exposed the government, convinced those who were most prejudiced against the measure of its necessity, and induced the passage of the present law. It would require no ordinary share of intrepidity to assert that a measure adopted under these circumstances was a bold and plain usurpation, to which the constitution gave no countenance.

[6] These observations belong to the cause; but they are not made under the impression that, were the question entirely new, the law would be found irreconcilable with the constitution.

[7] In discussing this question, the counsel for the State of Maryland have deemed it of some importance, in the construction of the constitution, to consider that instrument not as emanating from the people, but as the act of sovereign and independent States. The powers of the general government, it has been said, are delegated by the States, who alone are truly sovereign; and must be exercised in subordination to the States, who alone possess supreme dominion.

¶¶4-6. What bearing does the 1791 debate over the first Bank have on the decision in *McCulloch*? Would it make a difference if the bill had passed "unobserved" by an "unsuspecting" legislature?

What is the implication of Marshall's assertion that this case does not involve "a great principle of liberty"? Would more aggressive monitoring by the judiciary be appropriate if such a principle were involved? Is it clear that congressional power to charter banks (and thus establish mechanisms for controlling the development of the national economy) does not involve such a principle?

¶¶7-11. Why might "counsel for the State of Maryland have deemed it of some importance, in the construction of the constitution, to consider that instrument not as emanating from the people, but as the act of sovereign and independent states"? Note that eighteenth-century political theory allowed sovereignty to repose in only one entity. This, as the anti-Federalists urged during the ratification campaign, posed problems for the proposed constitution, under which two sovereignties operated simultaneously in the same jurisdiction. The Federalists responded ingeniously by denying sovereignty to both federal and state governments and placing it in "the people." See Gordon Wood, The Creation of the American Republic, 1776-1787 ch. 13 (1969).

One can perhaps best understand the placement of these paragraphs early in Marshall's opinion by reference to Professor H. Jefferson Powell's point that a "maxim of political law" during the eighteenth century was that a sovereign can be deprived of any of its powers only by its express consent narrowly construed. Should the states — or the people of the states qua states — be deemed sovereign, the implication of this maxim was that the Constitution should be given "the most strict construction that the instrument will bear" in favor of the retention of power by these sovereigns. See Powell, The Original Understanding of Original Intent, 98 Harv. L. Rev. 885, 929-931 (1985) (quoting the Virginia lawyer St. George Tucker). Placement of sovereignty in the national people would

[8] It would be difficult to sustain this proposition. The Convention which framed the constitution was indeed elected by the State legislatures. But the instrument, when it came from their hands, was a mere proposal, without obligation, or pretensions to it. It was reported to the then existing Congress of the United States, with a request that it might "be submitted to a Convention of Delegates, chosen in each State by the people thereof, under the recommendation of its Legislature, for their assent and ratification." This mode of proceeding was adopted; and by the Convention, by Congress, and by the State Legislatures, the instrument was submitted to the people. They acted upon it in the only manner in which they can act safely, effectively, and wisely, on such a subject, by assembling in Convention. It is true, they assembled in their several States — and where else should they have assembled? No political dreamer was ever wild enough to think of breaking down the lines which separate the States, and of compounding the American people into one common mass. Of consequence, when they act, they act in their States. But the measures they adopt do not, on that account, cease to be the measures of the people themselves, or become the measures of the State governments.

[9] From these Conventions the constitution derives its whole authority. The government proceeds directly from the people; is "ordained and established" in the name of the people; and is declared to be ordained, "in order to form a more perfect union, establish justice, ensure domestic tranquility, and secure the blessings of liberty to themselves and to their posterity." The assent of the States, in their sovereign capacity, is implied in calling a Convention, and thus submitting that instrument to the people. But the people were at perfect liberty to accept or reject it; and their act was final. It required not the affirmance, and could not be negatived, by the State governments. The constitution, when thus adopted, was of complete obligation, and bound the State sovereignties.

[10] It has been said, that the people had already surrendered all their powers to the State sovereignties, and had nothing more to give. But, surely, the question whether they may resume and modify the powers granted to government does not remain to be settled in this country. Much more might the legitimacy of the general government be doubted, had it been created by the States. The powers delegated to the State sovereignties were to be exercised by themselves, not by a distinct and independent sovereignty, created by themselves. To the formation

---

still presumably call for "strict construction" against derogation of their rights, but the crucial point is that popular (as opposed to state) sovereignty deprives states of any special claim to having their ostensible rights privileged over the competing claims of the national government.

Marshall appears to offer three models for who was "sovereign": (1) The people of each state, organized in some meaningful way state by state; (2) the state governments; and (3) the people of an undifferentiated whole called the United States. Marshall sets up the dispute as if it involves a choice between the second and third, and argues that because it can't be the second (why not?), then it must be the third. He keeps referring to "the people" (see especially ¶9), but the central question is *which* people? In any event, what is the role of the first model?

Consider the August 7, 1787, draft of the Constitution, which had the following preamble:

> We the people of the States of New-Hampshire, Massachusetts, Rhode-Island and Providence Plantations [and the other 13 original States] do ordain, declare and establish the following Constitution or the Government of Ourselves and our Posterity.

Does it matter that this was changed, for reasons that are wholly unclear, by the Committee on Style? What is the consequence for the "Unionist" argument of Article VII, which sets out the mode of ratification (or of Article V, which sets out the process by which the Constitution is amended)? How does Marshall respond to Maryland's invocation of Article VII? Is the response satisfactory?

of a league, such as was the confederation, the State sovereignties were certainly competent. But when, "in order to form a more perfect union," it was deemed necessary to change this alliance into an effective government, possessing great and sovereign powers, and acting directly on the people, the necessity of referring it to the people, and of deriving its powers directly from them, was felt and acknowledged by all.

[11] The government of the Union, then, (whatever may be the influence of this fact on the case,) is, emphatically, and truly, a government of the people. In form and in substance it emanates from them. Its powers are granted by them, and are to be exercised directly on them, and for their benefit.

[12] This government is acknowledged by all to be one of enumerated powers. The principle, that it can exercise only the powers granted to it, would seem too apparent to have required to be enforced by all those arguments which its enlightened friends, while it was depending before the people, found it necessary to urge. That principle is now universally admitted. But the question respecting the extent of the powers actually granted, is perpetually arising, and will probably continue to arise, as long as our system shall exist.

[13] In discussing these questions, the conflicting powers of the general and State governments must be brought into view, and the supremacy of their respective laws, when they are in opposition, must be settled.

[14] If any one proposition could command the universal assent of mankind, we might expect it would be this — that the government of the Union, though limited in its powers, is supreme within its sphere of action. This would seem to result necessarily from its nature. It is the government of all; its powers are delegated by all; it represents all, and acts for all. Though any one State may be willing to control its operations, no State is willing to allow others to control them. The nation, on those subjects on which it can act, must necessarily bind its component parts. But this question is not left to mere reason: the people have, in express terms, decided it, by saying, "this constitution, and the laws of the United States, which shall be made in pursuance thereof," "shall be the supreme law of the land," and by requiring that the members of the State legislatures, and the officers of the executive and judicial departments of the States, shall take the oath of fidelity to it.

[15] The government of the United States, then, though limited in its powers, is supreme; and its laws, when made in pursuance of the constitution, form the supreme law of the land, "any thing in the constitution or laws of any State to the contrary notwithstanding."

[16] Among the enumerated powers, we do not find that of establishing a bank or creating a corporation. But there is no phrase in the instrument which, like the

¶16. Marshall is contrasting the Tenth Amendment with Article II of the Articles of Confederation, which provided: "Each state retains its sovereignty, freedom and independence, and every power, jurisdiction, and right which is not by this confederation expressly delegated to the United States in Congress assembled."

In Marbury v. Madison, 5 U.S. (1 Cranch) 137 (1803), in Chapter 2 infra, Marshall wrote: "it cannot be presumed that any clause in the constitution is intended to be without effect: and therefore, such a construction is inadmissible, unless the words require it." Does Marshall's construction of the Tenth Amendment give it any effect? Could he properly have read "expressly" into the Tenth Amendment, and, if so, what difference should it make to the outcome of the case?

How does Marshall establish that Article I marks only the "great outlines" of congressional power, and what follows from the proposition? What is the argument based on Article I, §9? Why else might its limitations have been introduced?

articles of confederation, excludes incidental or implied powers; and which requires that every thing granted shall be expressly and minutely described. Even the 10th amendment, which was framed for the purpose of quieting the excessive jealousies which had been excited, omits the word "expressly," and declares only that the powers "not delegated to the United States, nor prohibited to the States, are reserved to the States or to the people;" thus leaving the question, whether the particular power which may become the subject of contest has been delegated to the one government, or prohibited to the other, to depend on a fair construction of the whole instrument. The men who drew and adopted this amendment had experienced the embarrassments resulting from the insertion of this word in the articles of confederation, and probably omitted it to avoid those embarrassments. A constitution, to contain an accurate detail of all the subdivisions of which its great powers will admit, and of all the means by which they may be carried into execution, would partake of the prolixity of a legal code, and could scarcely be embraced by the human mind. It would probably never be understood by the public. Its nature, therefore, requires, that only its great outlines should be marked, its important objects designated, and the minor ingredients which compose those objects be deduced from the nature of the objects themselves. That this idea was entertained by the framers of the American constitution, is not only to be inferred from the nature of the instrument, but from the language. Why else were some of the limitations, found in the ninth section of the 1st article, introduced? It is also, in some degree, warranted by their having omitted to use any restrictive term which might prevent its receiving a fair and just interpretation. In considering this question, then, we must never forget, that it is *a constitution we are expounding*.

[17] Although, among the enumerated powers of government, we do not find the word "bank" or "incorporation," we find the great powers to lay and collect taxes; to borrow money; to regulate commerce; to declare and conduct a war; and to raise and support armies and navies. The sword and the purse, all the external relations, and no inconsiderable portion of the industry of the nation, are entrusted to its government. It can never be pretended that these vast powers draw after them others of inferior importance, merely because they are inferior. Such an idea can never be advanced. But it may with great reason be contended, that a government, entrusted with such ample powers, on the due execution of which the happiness and prosperity of the nation so vitally depends, must also be entrusted with ample means for their execution. The power being given, it is the interest of the nation to facilitate its execution. It can never be their interest, and cannot be presumed to have been their intention, to clog and embarrass its execution by withholding the most appropriate means. Throughout this vast republic, from the St. Croix to the Gulf of Mexico, from the Atlantic to the Pacific, revenue is to be collected and expended, armies are to be marched and supported. The exigencies of the nation may require that the treasure raised in the north should be transported to the south, *that* raised in the east conveyed to the west, or that this order should be reversed. Is that construction of the constitution to be preferred which would render these operations difficult, hazardous, and expensive? Can we adopt that construction, (unless the words imperiously require it,) which would impute to the framers of that instrument, when granting these powers for the public good, the intention of impeding their exercise by withholding a choice of means? If, indeed, such be the mandate of the constitution, we have only to

obey; but that instrument does not profess to enumerate the means by which the powers it confers may be executed; nor does it prohibit the creation of a corporation, if the existence of such a being be essential to the beneficial exercise of those powers. It is, then, the subject of fair inquiry, how far such means may be employed.

[18] It is not denied, that the powers given to the government imply the ordinary means of execution. That, for example, of raising revenue, and applying it to national purposes, is admitted to imply the power of conveying money from place to place, as the exigencies of the nation may require, and of employing the usual means of conveyance. But it is denied that the government has its choice of means; or, that it may employ the most convenient means, if, to employ them, it be necessary to erect a corporation.

[19] On what foundation does this argument rest? On this alone: The power of creating a corporation, is one appertaining to sovereignty, and is not expressly conferred on Congress. This is true. But all legislative powers appertain to sovereignty. The original power of giving the law on any subject whatever, is a sovereign power; and if the government of the Union is restrained from creating a corporation, as a means for performing its functions, on the single reason that the creation of a corporation is an act of sovereignty; if the sufficiency of this reason be acknowledged, there would be some difficulty in sustaining the authority of Congress to pass other laws for the accomplishment of the same objects.

[20] The government which has a right to do an act, and has imposed on it the duty of performing that act, must, according to the dictates of reason, be allowed to select the means; and those who contend that it may not select any appropriate means, that one particular mode of effecting the object is excepted, take upon themselves the burden of establishing that exception.

[21] The creation of a corporation, it is said, appertains to sovereignty. This is admitted. But to what portion of sovereignty does it appertain? Does it belong to one more than to another? In America, the powers of sovereignty are divided between the government of the Union, and those of the States. They are each sovereign, with respect to the objects committed to it, and neither sovereign with respect to the objects committed to the other. We cannot comprehend that train of reasoning which would maintain, that the extent of power granted by the people is to be ascertained, not by the nature and terms of the grant, but by its date. Some State constitutions were formed *before,* some *since* that of the United States. We cannot believe that their relation to each other is in any degree dependent upon this circumstance. Their respective powers must, we think, be precisely the same as if they had been formed at the same time. Had they been formed at the same time, and had the people conferred on the general government the power contained in the constitution, and on

¶¶18-22. Counsel for Maryland conceded arguendo that "the powers given to the government imply the ordinary means of execution," but contended that chartering a corporation was extraordinary. In England, only the Crown had the power to incorporate, and in early nineteenth-century America — before the advent of general state corporation laws — charters were regarded as quite special privileges, granted by legislatures on a case-by-case basis. See Chapter 3 infra. How does Marshall meet Maryland's argument that Congress would have the authority to issue charters only if Article I explicitly granted it? Marshall's response consists in part of the assertion that those who contend that Congress may not employ a particular means in furtherance of an enumerated power have the burden of proof. Is this self-evident? Might one not draw the opposite conclusion from the nature of the federal system and the text of the Tenth Amendment?

the States the whole residuum of power, would it have been asserted that the government of the Union was not sovereign with respect to those objects which were entrusted to it, in relation to which its laws were declared to be supreme? If this could not have been asserted, we cannot well comprehend the process of reasoning which maintains, that a power appertaining to sovereignty cannot be connected with that vast portion of it which is granted to the general government, so far as it is calculated to subserve the legitimate objects of that government. The power of creating a corporation, though appertaining to sovereignty, is not, like the power of making war, or levying taxes, or of regulating commerce, a great substantive and independent power, which cannot be implied as incidental to other powers, or used as a means of executing them. It is never the end for which other powers are exercised, but a means by which other objects are accomplished. No contributions are made to charity for the sake of an incorporation, but a corporation is created to administer the charity; no seminary of learning is instituted in order to be incorporated, but the corporate character is conferred to subserve the purposes of education. No city was ever built with the sole object of being incorporated, but is incorporated as affording the best means of being well governed. The power of creating a corporation is never used for its own sake, but for the purpose of effecting something else. No sufficient reason is, therefore, perceived, why it may not pass as incidental to those powers which are expressly given, if it be a direct mode of executing them.

[22] But the constitution of the United States has not left the right of Congress to employ the necessary means, for the execution of the powers conferred on the government, to general reasoning. To its enumeration of powers is added that of making "all laws which shall be necessary and proper, for carrying into execution the foregoing powers, and all other powers vested by this constitution, in the government of the United States, or in any department thereof."

[23] The counsel for the State of Maryland have urged various arguments, to prove that this clause, though in terms a grant of power, is not so in effect; but is really restrictive of the general right, which might otherwise be implied, of selecting means for executing the enumerated powers.

[24] In support of this proposition, they have found it necessary to contend, that this clause was inserted for the purpose of conferring on Congress the power of making laws. That, without it, doubts might be entertained, whether Congress could exercise its powers in the form of legislation.

[25] But could this be the object for which it was inserted? A government is created by the people, having legislative, executive, and judicial powers. Its legislative powers are vested in a Congress, which is to consist of a Senate and House of Representatives. Each house may determine the rule of its proceedings; and it is declared that every bill which shall have passed both houses, shall, before it becomes a law, be presented to the President of the United States. The 7th section describes the course of

¶¶22-26. Marshall begins by invoking the necessary and proper clause as affirmative support for the exercise of congressional power but immediately turns to defend against Maryland's contention that the clause restricts that power. Marshall deals summarily with the argument that, but for the clause, Article I would not have vested Congress with any legislative authority, and then considers the argument that "necessary" restricts Congress to the "most direct and simple" means of implementing the enumerated powers.

proceedings, by which a bill shall become a law; and, then, the 8th section enumerates the powers of Congress. Could it be necessary to say, that a legislature should exercise legislative powers, in the shape of legislation? After allowing each house to prescribe its own course of proceeding, after describing the manner in which a bill should become a law, would it have entered into the mind of a single member of the Convention, that an express power to make laws was necessary to enable the legislature to make them? That a legislature, endowed with legislative powers, can legislate, is a proposition too self-evident to have been questioned.

[26] But the argument on which most reliance is placed, is drawn from the peculiar language of this clause. Congress is not empowered by it to make all laws, which may have relation to the powers conferred on the government, but such only as may be "*necessary and proper*" for carrying them into execution. The word "*necessary,*" is considered as controlling the whole sentence, and as limiting the right to pass laws for the execution of the granted powers, to such as are indispensable, and without which the power would be nugatory. That it excludes the choice of means, and leaves to Congress, in each case, that only which is most direct and simple.

[27] Is it true, that this is the sense in which the word "necessary" is always used? Does it always import an absolute physical necessity, so strong, that one thing, to which another may be termed necessary, cannot exist without that other? We think it does not. If reference be had to its use, in the common affairs of the world, or in approved authors, we find that it frequently imports no more than that one thing is convenient, or useful, or essential to another. To employ the means necessary to an end, is generally understood as employing any means calculated to produce the end, and not as being confined to those single means, without which the end would be entirely unattainable. Such is the character of human language, that no word conveys to the mind, in all situations, one single definite idea; and nothing is more common than to use words in a figurative sense. Almost all compositions contain words, which, taken in their rigorous sense, would convey a meaning different from that which is obviously intended. It is essential to just construction, that many words which import something excessive, should be understood in a more mitigated sense — in that sense which common usage justifies. The word "necessary" is of this description. It has not a fixed character peculiar to itself. It admits of all degrees of comparison; and is often connected with other words, which increase or diminish the impression the mind receives of the urgency it imports. A thing may be necessary, very necessary, absolutely or indispensably necessary. To no mind would the same idea be conveyed, by these several phrases. This comment on the word is well illustrated, by the passage cited at the bar, from the 10th section of the 1st article of the constitution. It is, we think, impossible to compare the sentence which prohibits a State from laying "imposts, or duties on imports or exports, except what may be *absolutely* necessary for executing its inspection laws," with that which authorizes Congress "to

¶27. Note the sources to which Marshall alludes to support his interpretation of "necessary." What other sources were available? (Had he looked at Samuel Johnson's Dictionary of the English Language (1755) he would have found the "rigorous" definition: "needful, indispensably requisite." The first American dictionary, Noah Webster's Compendious Dictionary of the English Language (1806), included "proper.")

make all laws which shall be necessary and proper for carrying into execution" the powers of the general government, without feeling a conviction that the convention understood itself to change materially the meaning of the word "necessary," by prefixing the word "absolutely." This word, then, like others, is used in various senses; and, in its construction, the subject, the context, the intention of the person using them, are all to be taken into view.

[28] Let this be done in the case under consideration. The subject is the execution of those great powers on which the welfare of a nation essentially depends. It must have been the intention of those who gave these powers, to insure, as far as human prudence could insure, their beneficial execution. This could not be done by confiding the choice of means to such narrow limits as not to leave it in the power of Congress to adopt any which might be appropriate, and which were conducive to the end. This provision is made in a constitution intended to endure for ages to come, and, consequently, to be adapted to the various *crises* of human affairs. To have prescribed the means by which government should, in all future time, execute its powers, would have been to change, entirely, the character of the instrument, and give it the properties of a legal code. It would have been an unwise attempt to provide, by immutable rules, for exigencies which, if foreseen at all, must have been seen dimly, and which can be best provided for as they occur. To have declared that the best means shall not be used, but those alone without which the power given would be nugatory, would have been to deprive the legislature of the capacity to avail itself of experience, to exercise its reason, and to accommodate its legislation to circumstances. If we apply this principle of construction to any of the powers of the government, we shall find it so pernicious in its operation that we shall be compelled to discard it. The powers vested in Congress may certainly be carried into execution, without prescribing an oath of office. The power to exact this security for the faithful performance of duty, is not given, nor is it indispensably necessary. The different departments may be established; taxes may be imposed and collected; armies and navies may be raised and maintained; and money may be borrowed, without requiring an oath of office. It might be argued, with as much plausibility as other incidental powers have been assailed, that the Convention was not unmindful of this subject. The oath which might be exacted — that of fidelity to the constitution — is prescribed, and no other can be required. Yet, he would be charged with insanity who should contend, that the legislature might not add to the oath as directed by the constitution, such other oath of office as its wisdom might suggest.

[29] So, with respect to the whole penal code of the United States: whence arises the power to punish in cases not prescribed by the constitution? All admit that the government may, legitimately, punish any violation of its laws; and yet, this is not among the enumerated powers of Congress. The right to enforce the observance of law, by punishing its infraction, might be denied with the more plausibility, because it is expressly given in some cases. Congress is empowered "to provide for the punishment of counterfeiting the securities and current coin of the United States," and "to define and punish piracies and felonies committed on the high seas, and offences against the law of nations." The several powers of

¶¶28-32. To support his "figurative" reading of the word, Marshall looks to the "subject, the context, [and] the intention of the person" using it. What is the argument of ¶28? Does it have any force independent of the counterexamples that follow in ¶¶29-30? Is the argument by counterexample persuasive?

Congress may exist, in a very imperfect state to be sure, but they may exist and be carried into execution, although no punishment should be inflicted in cases where the right to punish is not expressly given.

[30] Take, for example, the power "to establish post offices and post roads." This power is executed by the single act of making the establishment. But, from this has been inferred the power and duty of carrying the mail along the post road, from one post office to another. And, from this implied power, has again been inferred the right to punish those who steal letters from the post office, or rob the mail. It may be said, with some plausibility, that the right to carry the mail, and to punish those who rob it, is not indispensably necessary to the establishment of a post office and post road. This right is indeed essential to the beneficial exercise of the power, but not indispensably necessary to its existence. So, of the punishment of the crimes of stealing or falsifying a record or process of a Court of the United States, or of perjury in such Court. To punish these offences is certainly conducive to the due administration of justice. But courts may exist, and may decide the causes brought before them, though such crimes escape punishment.

[31] The baneful influence of this narrow construction on all the operations of the government, and the absolute impracticability of maintaining it without rendering the government incompetent to its great objects, might be illustrated by numerous examples drawn from the constitution, and from our laws. The good sense of the public has pronounced, without hesitation, that the power of punishment appertains to sovereignty, and may be exercised whenever the sovereign has a right to act, as incidental to his constitutional powers. It is a means for carrying into execution all sovereign powers, and may be used, although not indispensably necessary. It is a right incidental to the power, and conducive to its beneficial exercise.

[32] If this limited construction of the word "necessary" must be abandoned in order to punish, whence is derived the rule which would reinstate it, when the government would carry its powers into execution by means not vindictive in their nature? If the word "necessary" means "needful," "requisite," "essential," "conducive to," in order to let in the power of punishment for the infraction of law; why is it not equally comprehensive when required to authorize the use of means which facilitate the execution of the powers of government without the infliction of punishment?

[33] In ascertaining the sense in which the word "necessary" is used in this clause of the constitution, we may derive some aid from that with which it is associated. Congress shall have power "to make all laws which shall be necessary and *proper* to carry into execution" the powers of the government. If the word "necessary" was used in that strict and rigorous sense for which the counsel for the State of Maryland contend, it would be an extraordinary departure from the usual course of the human mind, as exhibited in composition, to add a word, the only possible effect of which is to qualify that strict and rigorous meaning; to present to the mind the idea of some choice of means of legislation not straitened and compressed within the narrow limits for which gentlemen contend.

¶33. Is Marshall correct that "proper" would be superfluous if "necessary" were read in its rigorous sense? Might "proper" mean "not prohibited by Article I, §9"? Doesn't Marshall's interpretation of "necessary" make "proper" superfluous — at least unless "necessary" is given a somewhat restrictive meaning?

[34] But the argument which most conclusively demonstrates the error of the construction contended for by the counsel for the State of Maryland, is founded on the intention of the Convention, as manifested in the whole clause. To waste time and argument in proving that, without it, Congress might carry its powers into execution, would be not much less idle than to hold a lighted taper to the sun. As little can it be required to prove, that in the absence of this clause, Congress would have some choice of means. That it might employ those which, in its judgment, would most advantageously effect the object to be accomplished. That any means adapted to the end, any means which tended directly to the execution of the constitutional powers of the government, were in themselves constitutional. This clause, as construed by the State of Maryland, would abridge, and almost annihilate this useful and necessary right of the legislature to select its means. That this could not be intended, is, we should think, had it not been already controverted, too apparent for controversy. We think so for the following reasons:

[35] 1st. The clause is placed among the powers of Congress, not among the limitations on those powers.

[36] 2nd. Its terms purport to enlarge, not to diminish the powers vested in the government. It purports to be an additional power, not a restriction on those already granted. No reason has been, or can be assigned for thus concealing an intention to narrow the discretion of the national legislature under words which purport to enlarge it. The framers of the constitution wished its adoption, and well knew that it would be endangered by its strength, not by its weakness. Had they been capable of using language which would convey to the eye one idea, and, after deep reflection, impress on the mind another, they would rather have disguised the grant of power, than its limitation. If, then, their intention had been, by this clause, to restrain the free use of means which might otherwise have been implied, that intention would have been inserted in another place, and would have been expressed in terms resembling these. "In carrying into execution the foregoing powers, and all others," &c. "no laws shall be passed but such as are necessary and proper." Had the intention been to make this clause restrictive, it would unquestionably have been so in form as well as in effect.

[37] The result of the most careful and attentive consideration bestowed upon this clause is, that if it does not enlarge, it cannot be construed to restrain the powers of Congress, or to impair the right of the legislature to exercise its best judgment in the selection of measures to carry into execution the constitutional powers of the government. If no other motive for its insertion can be suggested, a sufficient one is found in the desire to remove all doubts respecting the right to legislate on that vast mass of incidental powers which must be involved in the constitution, if that instrument be not a splendid bauble.

[38] We admit, as all must admit, that the powers of the government are limited, and that its limits are not to be transcended. But we think the sound con-

¶¶34-37. ¶34 seems largely introductory to the perceptive argument of ¶¶35-36 based on the location and phraseology of the clause. But doesn't it suggest an argument in Maryland's favor that Marshall ought to meet: that if Congress would have broad ancillary powers without the clause, and a document should presumptively be read so as to make no clause superfluous, then the necessary and proper clause must be designed to restrict congressional power? Is the response implicit in ¶37 satisfactory?

¶38. This is one of the most quoted paragraphs in the American constitutional corpus. Would it be fair to paraphrase it as "Congress can do whatever it wants so long as it does not contravene an ex-struction of the constitution must allow to the national legislature that discretion, with respect to the means by which the powers it confers are to be carried into execution, which will enable that body to perform the high duties assigned to it, in the manner most beneficial to the people. Let the end be legitimate, let it be within the scope of the constitution, and all means which are appropriate, which are plainly adapted to that end, which are not prohibited, but consist with the letter and spirit of the constitution, are constitutional.

[39] That a corporation must be considered as a means not less usual, not of higher dignity, not more requiring a particular specification than other means, has been sufficiently proved. If we look to the origin of corporations, to the manner in which they have been framed in that government from which we have derived most of our legal principles and ideas, or to the uses to which they have been applied, we find no reason to suppose that a constitution, omitting, and wisely omitting, to enumerate all the means for carrying into execution the great powers vested in government, ought to have specified this. Had it been intended to grant this power as one which should be distinct and independent, to be exercised in any case whatever, it would have found a place among the enumerated powers of the government. But being considered merely as a means, to be employed only for the purpose of carrying into execution the given powers, there could be no motive for particularly mentioning it.

[40] The propriety of this remark would seem to be generally acknowledged by the universal acquiescence in the construction which has been uniformly put on the 3rd section of the 4th article of the constitution. The power to "make all needful rules and regulations respecting the territory or other property belonging to the United States," is not more comprehensive, than the power "to make all laws which shall be necessary and proper for carrying into execution" the powers of the government. Yet all admit the constitutionality of a territorial government, which is a corporate body.

[41] If a corporation may be employed indiscriminately with other means to carry into execution the powers of the government, no particular reason can be assigned for excluding the use of a bank, if required for its fiscal operations. To use one, must be within the discretion of Congress, if it be an appropriate mode of executing the powers of government. That it is a convenient, a useful, and essential instrument in the prosecution of its fiscal operations, is not now a subject of controversy. All those who have been concerned in the administration of our finances, have concurred in representing its importance and necessity; and so strongly have they been felt, that statesmen of the first class, whose previous opinions against it had been confirmed by every circumstance which can fix the human judgment, have yielded those opinions to the exigencies of the nation. Under the confederation, Congress, justifying the measure by its necessity, transcended perhaps its power to obtain the advantage of a bank; and our own legislation attests the universal conviction of the utility of this measure. The time has passed away when it can be necessary to enter into any discussion in order to prove the importance of this instrument, as a means to effect the legitimate objects of the government.

---

press and specific prohibition contained in this text." How well does this culminating paragraph fit with Marshall's acknowledgement in paragraphs 15 and 16 that the national government is one of limited and enumerated powers?

[42] But, were its necessity less apparent, none can deny its being an appropriate measure; and if it is, the degree of its necessity, as has been very justly observed, is to be discussed in another place. Should Congress, in the execution of its powers, adopt measures which are prohibited by the constitution; or should Congress, under the pretext of executing its powers, pass laws for the accomplishment of objects not entrusted to the government; it would become the painful duty of this tribunal, should a case requiring such a decision come before it, to say that such an act was not the law of the land. But where the law is not prohibited, and is really calculated to effect any of the objects entrusted to the government, to undertake here to inquire into the degree of its necessity, would be to pass the line which circumscribes the judicial department, and to tread on legislative ground. This court disclaims all pretensions to such a power.

[43] After this declaration, it can scarcely be necessary to say, that the existence of State banks can have no possible influence on the question. No trace is to be found in the constitution of an intention to create a dependence of the government of the Union on those of the States, for the execution of the great powers assigned to it. Its means are adequate to its ends; and on those means alone was it expected to rely for the accomplishment of its ends. To impose on it the necessity of resorting to means which it cannot control, which another government may furnish or withhold, would render its course precarious, the result of its measures uncertain and create a dependence on other governments, which might disappoint its most important designs, and is incompatible with the language of the constitution. But were it otherwise, the choice of means implies a right to choose a national bank in preference to State banks, and Congress alone can make the election.

[44] After the most deliberate consideration, it is the unanimous and decided opinion of this Court, that the act to incorporate the Bank of the United States is a law made in pursuance of the constitution, and is a part of the supreme law of the land.

[45] The branches, proceeding from the same stock, and being conducive to the complete accomplishment of the object, are equally constitutional. It would have been unwise to locate them in the charter, and it would be unnecessarily inconvenient to employ the legislative power in making those subordinate arrangements. The great duties of the bank are prescribed; those duties require branches; and the bank itself may, we think, be safely trusted with the selection of places where those branches shall be fixed; reserving always to the government the right to require that a branch shall be located where it may be deemed necessary.

A. The Reaction to *McCulloch*

When *McCulloch* was decided in 1819, few persons of stature in the national political community genuinely disputed the constitutionality of the national bank. Yet Marshall's opinion stirred great controversy, for it went far beyond the specifics

¶42. To some extent this paragraph is designed to reassure readers that Congress does not in fact have plenary power. What *is* a "pretext"? What kinds of inquiry would be necessary in order to demonstrate its existence?

of the bank, to portray a powerful vision of the new nation. During the months following the decision a number of critical essays appeared in the Richmond Enquirer.[17]

One author, writing under the pseudonym of Amphictyon, criticized the breadth of Marshall's opinion:[18]

> Whether the power of the federal government were delegated to it, by the states in their sovereign capacity, or by the people, can make but little difference as to the extent of those powers. In either case, it is still true that the powers of that government are limited by the charter which called it into existence.

With respect to the source of the government's power, Amphictyon wrote:

> If the powers of the federal government are to be viewed as the grant of the people, without regard to the distinctive features of the states, then it would follow that if a majority of the whole sovereign population of the United States had ratified the constitution, it would immediately have been binding on the minority, although that minority should consist of every individual in one or more states. But we would know that such was not the case. Each state was an independent political society. The constitution was not binding on any state, even the smallest, without its own free and voluntary consent. . . . The respective states then in their sovereign capacity did delegate the federal government its powers, and in so doing were parties to the compact.[19]

The source of the federal government's power had been a matter of controversy at least from the time of the ratification campaigns. In the Virginia ratifying convention, Patrick Henry, a staunch opponent of the new Constitution, demanded why the Preamble to the Constitution said "*We, the people,* instead of *We the States*? States are the characteristics and the soul of a confederation. If the States be not the agents of this compact, it must be one great consolidated government of the people of all States."[20] A delegate responded that no one "but the people have a right to form government,"[21] to which Henry, referring to the fear that a "consolidated government" would ride roughshod over individual liberty, replied that "the principles of this system are extremely pernicious, impolitic, and dangerous."[22] Patrick Henry was expressing a belief, widely held in that and other times, that liberty depended on government by small political units subject to close citizen participation and control.[23] The new Constitution, by contrast, established a national government, having vastly greater powers than the Confederation and the authority over a large and expanding territory.[24]

17. See John Marshall's Defense of the Constitution (Gunther ed. 1969) (hereinafter cited as Gunther).
18. Id. at 55.
19. Id. at 56.
20. Quoted in Sources and Documents Illustrating the American Revolution, 1764-1788 and the Formation of the Federal Constitution 309 (Morison ed. 1965).
21. Id. at 315.
22. Id. at 321-322.
23. See Hannah Arendt, On Revolution (1963); Gordon Wood, Creation of the American Republic, 1776-1787 (1969).
24. In The Federalist No. 14, Madison argued that republican liberty could survive in an area as large as the United States.

Madison and Jefferson had also asserted strong claims of state sovereignty at the very end of the eighteenth century in their Virginia and Kentucky Resolutions challenging the constitutionality of the Alien and Sedition Acts of 1798.[25] Jefferson had written in the Kentucky Resolution:

> [T]he several states who formed [the Constitution], being sovereign and independent, have the unquestionable right to judge of its infraction, and . . . a nullification, by those sovereignties, of all unauthorized acts done under colour of that instrument, is the rightful remedy.[26]

Amphictyon's essays on *McCulloch* reprinted much of Madison's Virginia Resolution, which similarly asserted that the states were "duty bound to interpose" their authority in order to arrest the evil of "deliberate, palpable, and dangerous exercise of other powers not granted by the said compact."[27] Jefferson's response to *McCulloch* can be garnered from an 1820 letter describing the national judiciary as:

> . . . the subtle core of sappers and miners constantly working under ground to undermine the foundations of our confederated fabric. They are construing our Constitution from a coordination of general [i.e., national] and special [i.e., state] government to a general and supreme one alone. This will lay all things at their feet.[28]

Returning to the notion of the Virginia Resolution, Jefferson suggested that the people of two-thirds of the states could, through resolutions of nullification, overrule unconstitutional Supreme Court decisions. Only in this way could the principle be vindicated that the Constitution "is a compact of many independent powers, every single one of which claims an equal right to understand it, and to require its observance."[29]

Writing under the name of Hampden in the Richmond Enquirer, Spencer Roane, Chief Justice of the Virginia Supreme Court, also responded to *McCulloch*. Among other arguments, he invoked Johnson's Dictionary, "which is believed to be the best in the English language" to show that "necessary" was there defined as "needful" or "indispensably requisite."[30] Roane's arguments drew an admiring letter from Madison, who noted:[31]

> It could not but happen, and was foreseen at the birth of the Constitution, that difficulties and differences of opinion might occasionally arise in expounding terms and phrases necessarily used in such a charter; more especially those which divide legislation between the general and local governments; and that it might require a regular course of practice to liquidate and settle the meaning of some of them. But it was anticipated, I believe, by few, if any, of the friends of the Constitution, that a rule of

25. 1 Stat. 566, 570, 577, 696. The laws gave the president the power to imprison or deport aliens and in effect made anyone who criticized the government liable to criminal sanctions. See generally Leonard Levy, Freedom and Speech in Early American History: Legacy of Suppression (1963).

26. The Portable Jefferson 286 (Peterson ed. 1975) (hereinafter Peterson).

27. Gunther, supra note 17, at 51. These arguments were later invoked by South Carolina in its efforts to nullify federal laws and in the justification for Southern secession in 1860-1861. See The Nullification Era: A Documentary Record (Freehling ed. 1967).

28. Dumas Malone, 6 Jefferson and His Time 356 (1981) (letter to Thomas Ritchie).

29. Merrill D. Peterson, Thomas Jefferson and the New Nation 994-995 (1970).

30. Gunther, supra note 17, at 133.

31. Letter of September 2, 1819, in 3 Farrand, supra note 3, at 435.

construction would be introduced as broad and pliant as what has occurred. And those who recollect, and still more, those who shared in what passed in the State conventions, through which the people ratified the Constitution, with respect to the extent of the powers vested in Congress, cannot easily be persuaded that the avowal of such a rule would not have prevented its ratification.

B. Marshall's Methods of Constitutional Interpretation[32]

In the course of his opinion, Marshall relies on at least five sources of constitutional interpretation:

1. The text. Recall the discussion of the language of the Tenth Amendment; the implications of Article I, section 9; and the location of the necessary and proper clause. How would you characterize Marshall's approach to interpreting the constitutional text?

2. The theory and structure of the government established by the Constitution. In Structure and Relationship in Constitutional Law (1969), Professor Charles Black, Jr., argues for a strategy of constitutional interpretation based on "inference from the structures and relationships created by the constitution." He points to *McCulloch* as an example, commenting that "Marshall does not place principal reliance on the [necessary and proper] clause as a ground of decision; . . . before he reaches it he has already decided, on the basis of far more general implications, that Congress possesses the power, not expressly named, of establishing a bank and chartering corporations; . . . he addresses himself to the necessary and proper clause only in response to counsel's arguing its *restrictive* force."[33] Identify the "more general implications" underlying Marshall's argument. From what sources does Marshall construct a theory of the Constitution?

Of what relevance is it that "it is *a constitution* we are expounding"? Recall the paragraph (¶16) in which the phrase appears and in which Marshall contrasts the "great outlines" of Article I with "the prolixity of a legal code." Recall also the paragraph (¶28) in which he makes the same comparison and notes that Article I is a provision "made in a constitution intended to endure for ages to come, and, consequently to be adapted to the various crises of human affairs." What do these observations contribute to the interpretation of the necessary and proper clause? Does it follow from the nature of a federal constitution that the national legislative power should be construed expansively? To be sure, our nation would be very different had arguments like those of Maryland prevailed in Congress and the Court; perhaps we would not have survived long as one nation. But would we have been proceeding on a *misconception* of the nature of a federal constitution or simply on a *different* conception — one much less nationalist than Marshall's but more so than the Confederation or that desired by the more avid anti-Federalists? Is Marshall's conception of "*a constitution*" correct, in other words, not neces-

32. See generally Philip Bobbitt, Constitutional Fate (1982), an expanded version of Constitutional Fate, 58 Tex. L. Rev. 695 (1980), which subtly develops a six-fold morphology of constitutional arguments, classifying them as textual, historical, structural, doctrinal, prudential, and ethical.

33. Charles Black, Structure and Relationship in Constitutional Law 7, 14 (1969).

sarily as sound documentary interpretation but as (in our view) good government policy?

3. The consequences of decision: the argument reductio ad absurdum. In paragraph 17, Marshall refers to "[t]he exigencies of the nation" and rejects a "construction of the constitution that would render" the performance of government functions "difficult, hazardous, and expensive." This is an instance of the *reductio* argument frequently used in legal (and other) reasoning: "If proposition *p* is true, then consequences *c* would follow; *c* is ridiculous, therefore *p* cannot be true." With respect to Marshall's particular application of the *reductio* argument here, however, consider Madison's point in the penultimate paragraph of his speech against the first bank, supra.

4. The history surrounding the adoption of the text. Recall Marshall's discussion of the purposes of the Tenth Amendment. How do you suppose he knows the purposes of the amendment?

In arguing against the first bank, Jefferson noted that the Philadelphia Convention had rejected a proposal to authorize Congress to charter certain corporations. Marshall does not mention this history. This may not be (only) because it would not have helped his argument: Judicial references to legislative history were virtually unheard of in eighteenth-century Anglo-American jurisprudence.

5. Precedent. Although Marshall cites no judicial decisions, he nonetheless invokes as precedent the incorporation by Congress in 1791 of the First Bank to support the constitutionality of the 1816 decision to incorporate the Second Bank. And we have seen that Madison justified signing the bill establishing the Second Bank by reference to "repeated recognitions, under varied circumstances, of the validity of such an institution," even though he had denounced the validity of the 1791 incorporation. Precedential argument always presents the very existence of previous decisions as justifying the outcome in the later case. Why should precedent ever be relevant to constitutional decisionmaking, even assuming its appropriateness as a methodology in nonconstitutional areas? See Karl Llewellyn, The Bramble Bush 64-66 (1930).

Consider Justice Scalia's dissent in South Carolina v. Gathers, 490 U.S. 95 (1989), where he called for overruling Booth v. Maryland, 482 U.S. 496 (1987), a decision limiting the state's right to refer to the consequences of a murder on the victim's survivors to a sentencing jury:

> It has been argued that we should not overrule so recent a decision, lest our action "appear to be . . . occasioned by nothing more than a change in the Court's personnel," and the rules we announce no more than " 'opinions of a small group of men who temporarily occupy high office.' " I doubt that overruling *Booth* will so shake the citizenry's faith in the Court. Overrulings of precedent rarely occur without a change in the Court's personnel. The only distinctive feature here is that the overruling would follow not long after the original decision. But that is hardly unprecedented. See, e.g., Daniels v. Williams, 474 U.S. 327 (1986)(overruling Parratt v. Taylor, 451 U.S. 527 (1981)); United States v. Scott, 437 U.S. 82 (1978)(overruling United States v. Jenkins, 420 U.S. 358 (1975)); West Virginia Board of Education v.

> Barnette, 319 U.S. 624 (1943)(overruling Minersville School District Board of Education v. Gobitis, 310 U.S. 586 (1940)).
>
> Indeed, I had thought that the respect accorded prior decisions increases, rather than decreases, with their antiquity, as the society adjusts itself to their existence, and the surrounding law becomes premised upon their validity. The freshness of error not only deprives it of the respect to which long-established practice is entitled, but also counsels that the opportunity of correction be seized at once, before state and federal laws and practices have been adjusted to embody it. . . .
>
> In any case, I would think it a violation of my oath to adhere to what I consider a plainly unjustified intrusion upon the democratic process in order that the Court might save face. With some reservation concerning decisions that have become so embedded in our system of government that return is no longer possible . . . I agree with Justice Douglas: "A judge looking at a constitutional decision may have compulsions to revere past history and accept what was once written. But he remembers above all else that it is the Constitution which he swore to support and defend, not the gloss which his predecessors may have put on it." Douglas, Stare Decisis, 49 Colum. L. Rev. 735, 736 (1949). Or as the Court itself has said: "[W]hen convinced of former error, this Court has never felt constrained to follow precedent. In constitutional questions, where correction depends upon amendment and not upon legislative action this Court throughout its history has freely exercised its power to reexamine the basis of its constitutional decisions." Smith v. Allwright, 321 U.S. 649, 665 (1944).

The Court did overrule both *Booth* and *Gaithers* in Payne v. Tennessee, 111 S. Ct. — (1991). Writing for the five-member majority, Chief Justice Rehnquist stated that "[c]onsiderations in favor of *stare decisis* are at their acme in cases involving property and contract rights, where reliance interests are involved; the opposite is true in cases such as the present involving procedural and evidentiary rules." He also noted that both "*Booth* and *Gaithers* were decided by the narrowest of margins [i.e., they were both 5-4 decisions], over spirited dissents challenging the basic underpinnings of those dissents." In his dissent, Justice Marshall castigated the majority for disregarding precedent:

> Taking into account [one of the] majority's . . . criteri[a] for overruling — that a case either was decided or reaffirmed by a 5-4 margin 'over spirited dissent' — the continued vitality of literally scores of decisions must be understood to depend on nothing more than the proclivities of the individuals who *now* compromise a majority of the court. [Case citations omitted.]
>
> . . . Contrary to what the majority suggests, *stare decisis* is important not merely because individuals rely on precedent to structure their commercial activity but because fidelity to precedent is part and parcel of a conception of "the judiciary as a source of impersonal and reasoned judgments." Indeed, the function of *stare decisis* is in many respects even *more* critical in adjudication involving commercial entitlements. Because enforcement of the Bill of Rights and the Fourteenth Amendment frequently requires this Court to rein in the forces of democratic politics, the Court can legitimately lay claim to compliance with its directives only if the public understands the Court to be implementing "principles . . . founded in the law rather than in the proclivities of individuals." Thus . . . the "stron[g] presumption of validity" to which "recently decided cases" are entitled "is an essential thread in the mantle of protection that the law affords the individual. . . ."
>
> Carried to its logical conclusion, the majority's debilitated conception of *stare decisis* would destroy the Court's very capacity to resolve authoritatively the abiding con-

flicts between those with power and those without. It can hardly expect them to be treated more respectfully by the state actors whom these decisions are supposed to bind. . . . [T]he majority invites state actors to renew the very policies deemed unconstitutional in the hope that this Court may now reverse course, even if it has only recently reaffirmed the constitutional liberty in question.

Note: Uncertainties of Meaning[34]

The language of a provision in a written document is usually susceptible of more than one meaning; it can be ambiguous, vague, or figurative.

1. Ambiguity

A word or expression is ambiguous if it admits of two or more *rather different* meanings. Ambiguity is often desirable in literature; it is essential to puns. But (as distinguished from vagueness) it is usually undesirable in legal documents.

Language is pervasively ambiguous, but even a very general understanding of the purpose of a provision resolves most serious ambiguities. As an experiment, glance at some sections of the Constitution and try to understand their meanings while consciously avoiding considering their purposes. Consider, for example, Article II, §1, cl. 5: "No person except a natural born Citizen . . . shall be eligible to the Office of President. . . ." Is the meaning of "natural born citizen" inherently clear? What might the phrase mean in a revised constitution of Scotland drafted by Macbeth (had he survived)?[35] What does the phrase mean in our Constitution, and how do you know? Consider the phrase in its full context: "No person except a natural born Citizen or a Citizen of the United States, at the time of the Adoption of this Constitution, shall be eligible to the Office of President. . . ." What does this contribute to clarifying its meaning, and how? (Was George Romney, a Michigan governor who ran for the presidency in 1968 and who was the child of United States citizens and hence a citizen at his birth, but born in Chihuahua, Mexico, eligible to the office?)

34. See generally William Alston, Philosophy of Language ch. 5 (1964): William Empson, Seven Types of Ambiguity (2d ed. 1947): Willard Van Orman Quine, Word and Object ch. 4 (1960); I.A. Richards, The Philosophy of Rhetoric (1936): E. Allan Farnsworth, "Meaning" in the Law of Contracts, 76 Yale L.J. 939 (1967): Fredrich Waismann, Analytic-Synthetic V, 13 Analysis 1 (1952).

35. Recall the second apparition's assurance in Macbeth, Act IV, scene i:

> Be bloody, bold, and resolute; laugh to scorn
> The power of man, for none of woman born
> Shall harm Macbeth.

and Macbeth's ensuing confidence and his subsequent downfall (Act V, scene vii):

> *Macbeth:* Let fall thy blade on vulnerable crests;
> I bear a charmed life, which must not yield
> To one of woman born.
> *Macduff:* Despair thy charm;
> And let the Angel, whom thou still hast serv'd
> Tell thee, Macduff was from his mother's womb
> Untimely ripp'd.

2. Vagueness

Whereas ambiguous meanings tend to differ discretely, vagueness involves marginal indefiniteness in the meaning and application of words.[36]

> Thus, "middle-aged" is vague, for it is not clear whether a person aged 40 or a person aged 59 is middle-aged. Of course there are uncontroversial areas of application and nonapplication. At age 5 or 80 one is clearly not middle-aged, and at age 45 one clearly is. But on either side of the area of clear application there are indefinitely bounded areas of uncertainty. . . . [T]here is no definite answer to the question, Is a person aged 40 middle-aged? . . . Our inability [to give an answer] is not the result of lack of information about such things as blood pressure and metabolic rate. No additional information would settle the matter, except indirectly by leading us to tighten up the meaning of the word. The indeterminacy is due to an aspect of the meaning of the term rather than to the current state of our knowledge.

Not only abstract concepts but ordinary (nonproper) nouns naming physical objects and intangible things are usually vague — and incurably so. For many things are defined by the confluence of a number of attributes (a, b, c, . . . n), and one can never fully describe the combinations of attributes necessary or sufficient for proper application of the noun to particular things:[37]

> Consider the term "lemon," for example. Lemons normally have certain characteristics: a yellow color when ripe, skin of a certain thickness with a waxy texture, ovoid shape, acid taste, a size and hardness that falls within a certain range, and so on. If an object has all these properties, it is definitely a lemon. It might happen that in a particular region of the world, due to atomic fallout, lemon trees started producing fruit of a pinkish color and with a sweet taste, but having all the other characteristics of ordinary lemons. These fruits would doubtless still be lemons: pink lemons or sweet pink lemons. A thing cannot lack all, or even very many, of the typical lemon properties, and still be a lemon; but there is no one property, or group of two or three properties, which an object must have to be properly called a lemon. It must simply have some combination of the cluster or properties which lemons typically have.

Some provisions of the Constitution are quite precise: Article II, §1, cl. 5 requires that the president be at least 35 years old, not that he be at least "middle-aged." Many other provisions are quite vague: What is the "*Commerce* . . . among the several States" that Article I, §8, cl. 3 empowers Congress to regulate? And some provisions, such as the Fourth Amendment's prohibition of "*unreasonable* searches and seizures," seem designedly vague.

36. William Alston, Vagueness, in 8 Encyclopedia of Philosophy 218 (Edwards ed. 1967).

37. George Pitcher, The Philosophy of Wittgenstein 221 (1964) (borrowing an example from Michael Scriven). See also Alston, supra note 34, at 94-95 (1964), Fredrich Waismann, Verifiability, in Logic and Language — First Series (Flew ed. 1952).

3. Nonliteral usage

Article I, §8, cl. 8 empowers Congress "[t]o promote the Progress of Science and useful Arts, by securing for limited Times to Authors and Inventors the exclusive Right to their respective Writings and Discoveries." Does "writings" include anything besides letters inscribed on a surface? Does it include inscriptions by means other than hand (by printing or photo process), inscriptions of things other than letters (maps, charts, drawings), three-dimensional objects (sculptures, casseroles, automobiles), things not created by humans (driftwood), things not visually perceptible (the contents of phonograph records); ideas (the one-way toll bridge); intangible creations (theater productions, television broadcasts) and systems (computer programs, accounting systems)?[38]

The word "writings" is, to be sure, vague. But the questions posed in the previous paragraph do not involve vagueness so much as they do the literalness with which the word should be read. The Oxford English Dictionary defines the "literal" meaning of a word as its "relatively primary sense . . . as distinguished from any metaphorical or merely suggested meaning." True metaphors are rare in legal documents, but other kinds of nonliteral, or figurative, usage are very common. Interpreters are frequently called upon to determine how literally or figuratively to understand a term or, to put it another way, how narrowly or broadly to define the concept that the term represents. Does the copyright clause protect only "graphic" works, does it protect only "tangible" works, or does it protect all "expressions of intellectual creation"? It seems obvious that the proper scope of the concept represented by a term depends on the context in which, and the purpose for which, the term is used.

We recur so often to the inherent indeterminacy of language that it is important to emphasize that its indeterminacy is not unlimited; the very concept of "interpretation" implies that the interpreter is not free to stipulate the meanings of the terms he is interpreting. The reason for this is suggested by Wittgenstein's insightful analogy between language and a game. As Gilbert Ryle put it:[39]

> The significance of an expression and the powers or functions in chess of a pawn, a knight or the queen have much in common. To know what the knight can and cannot do, one must know the rules of chess, as well as be familiar with various kinds of chess situations which may arise. . . . Similarly to know what an expression means is to know how it may and may not be employed.

Just as a player who stipulates that his knight may move forward one square at a time is not playing chess, someone who stipulates that a word or expression shall mean something without regard to its accepted usage is not engaging in interpretation.

38. See generally 1 Melville Nimmer, Copyright §8 (1973).
39. Gilbert Ryle, The Theory of Meaning, in British Philosophy in the Mid-Century 255 (Mace ed. 1957).

Recall Humpty Dumpty's attempt to persuade Alice that unbirthdays are better than birthdays, and consider the mess that would result if he understood others as he expects them to understand him:[40]

> "[T]here are three hundred and sixty-four days when you might get unbirthday presents — "
>
> "Certainly," said Alice.
>
> "And only *one* for birthday presents, you know. There's glory for you!"
>
> "I don't know what you mean by 'glory,' " Alice said.
>
> Humpty Dumpty smiled contemptuously. "Of course you don't — till I tell you. I meant 'there's a nice knock-down argument for you!' "
>
> "But 'glory' doesn't mean 'a nice knock-down argument,' " Alice objected.
>
> "When *I* use a word," Humpty Dumpty said, in rather a scornful tone, "it means just what I choose it to mean — neither more nor less."
>
> "The question is," said Alice, "whether you *can* make words mean so many different things."
>
> "The question is," said Humpty Dumpty, "which is to be master — that's all."

Note: National Power over Foreign Relations

Prior to the federal Constitution, state lawmaking power was plenary, limited only by the states' own constitutions and (minimally) by prior interstate arrangements such as the Articles of Confederation. The states derive no lawmaking authority from the federal Constitution. On the contrary, the Constitution imposes various restrictions on the exercise of state power. By contrast, the national government enjoys only those powers granted it by the Constitution.

Is the national government's power over foreign affairs, which has always been treated as plenary, an exception to the last statement? Examine the relevant grants of power in Articles I and II, and consider:[41]

> Where is the power to recognize other states or governments, to maintain or break diplomatic relations, to open consulates elsewhere and permit them here, to acquire or cede territory, to give or withhold foreign aid, to proclaim a Monroe Doctrine or an Open-Door Policy, indeed to determine all the attitudes and carry out all the details in the myriads of relationships with other nations that are "the foreign policy" and "the foreign relations" of the United States? The power to make treaties is granted, but where is the power to break, denounce, or terminate them? The power to declare war is there, but where is the power to make peace, to proclaim neutrality in the wars of others, to recognize or deny rights to belligerents or insurgents? Congress can punish violations of international law but where is the power to assert rights or to carry out obligations under international law, to make new international law or to disregard or violate law? Congress can regulate foreign commerce but where is the power to make other laws relating to our foreign relations — to regulate immigration, or the status and rights of aliens, or activities of citizens at home or abroad affecting our foreign relations? These "missing" powers, and a host of others, were clearly intended for and have

40. Lewis Carroll, Through the Looking Glass ch. 6 (1865).
41. Louis Henkin, Foreign Affairs and the Constitution 16-17 (1972).

always been exercised by the federal government, but where does the Constitution say that it shall be so?

The Court has not taken the *McCulloch* route in explaining national authority over foreign affairs. Instead, it has referred to a theory proposed by Justice Sutherland in dictum in United States v. Curtiss-Wright Export Corp., 299 U.S. 304 (1936):

> [I]n respect of our internal affairs . . . , the primary purpose of the Constitution was to carve from the general mass of legislative powers *then possessed by the states* such portions as it was thought desirable to vest in the federal government, leaving those not included in the enumeration still in the states. . . . [But] since the states severally never possessed international powers, such powers could not have been carved from the mass of state powers but obviously were transmitted to the United States from some other source. During the colonial period, those powers were possessed exclusively by and were entirely under the control of the Crown. . . .
>
> Even before the Declaration [of Independence], the colonies were a unit in foreign affairs, acting through a common agency — namely the Continental Congress, composed of delegates from the thirteen colonies. . . . Rulers come and go; governments end and forms of government change; but sovereignty survives. A political society cannot endure without a supreme will somewhere. Sovereignty is never held in suspense. When, therefore, the external sovereignty of Great Britain in respect of the colonies ceased, it immediately passed to the Union. That fact was given practical application almost at once. The treaty of peace, made on September 23, 1783, was concluded between his Britannic Majesty and the "United States of America."
>
> The Union existed before the Constitution, which was ordained and established among other things to form "a more perfect Union." Prior to that event, it is clear that the Union, declared by the Articles of Confederation to be "perpetual," was the sole possessor of external sovereignty and in the Union it remained without change save in so far as the Constitution in express terms qualified its exercise. . . .
>
> It results that the investment of the federal government with the powers of external sovereignty did not depend upon the affirmative grants of the Constitution. The powers to declare and wage war, to conclude peace, to make treaties, to maintain diplomatic relations with other sovereignties, if they had never been mentioned in the Constitution, would have vested in the federal government as necessary concomitants of nationality. . . .

Justice Sutherland's history and metaphysics are open to criticism,[42] but his analysis at least suggests the spirit in which the particular grants of power to Congress and the executive have been amalgamated to create a whole greater than the sum of its parts.

42. See, e.g., Charles Lofgren, United States v. Curtiss-Wright Corporation: An Historical Reassessment, 83 Yale L.J. 1 (1973). See also the penultimate paragraph of Madison's argument against the bank, supra.

V. *The States' Power to Tax the Bank of the United States*

McCULLOCH v. MARYLAND
[The second question]

[46] It being the opinion of the Court, that the act incorporating the bank is constitutional; and that the power of establishing a branch in the State of Maryland might be properly exercised by the bank itself, we proceed to inquire —

[47] 2. Whether the State of Maryland may, without violating the constitution, tax that branch?

[48] That the power of taxation is one of vital importance; that it is retained by the States; that it is not abridged by the grant of a similar power to the government of the Union; that it is to be concurrently exercised by the two governments: are truths which have never been denied. But, such is the paramount character of the constitution, that its capacity to withdraw any subject from the action of even this power, is admitted. The States are expressly forbidden to lay any duties on imports or exports, except what may be absolutely necessary for executing their inspection laws. If the obligation of this prohibition must be conceded — if it may restrain a State from the exercise of its taxing power on imports and exports; the same paramount character would seem to restrain, as it certainly may restrain, a State from such other exercise of this power, as is in its nature incompatible with, and repugnant to, the constitutional laws of the Union. A law, absolutely repugnant to another, as entirely repeals that other as if express terms of repeal were used.

[49] On this ground the counsel for the bank place its claim to be exempted from the power of a State to tax its operations. There is no express provision for the case, but the claim has been sustained on a principle which so entirely pervades the constitution, is so intermixed with the materials which compose it, so interwoven with its web, so blended with its texture, as to be incapable of being separated from it, without rending it into shreds.

[50] This great principle is, that the constitution and the laws made in pursuance thereof are supreme; that they control the constitution and laws of the respective States, and cannot be controlled by them. From this, which may be almost termed an axiom, other propositions are deduced as corollaries, on the truth or error of which, and on their application to this case, the cause has been supposed to depend. These are, 1st. That a power to create implies a power to preserve. 2nd. That a power to destroy, if wielded by a different hand, is hostile to, and incompatible with these powers to create and to preserve. 3d. That where this repugnancy exists, that authority which is supreme must control, not yield to that over which it is supreme.

[51] These propositions, as abstract truths, would, perhaps, never be controverted. Their application to this case, however, has been denied; and, both in maintaining the affirmative and the negative, a splendor of eloquence, and strength of argument, seldom, if ever, surpassed, have been displayed.

[52] The power of Congress to create, and of course to continue, the bank, was the subject of the preceding part of this opinion; and is no longer to be considered as questionable.

[53] That the power of taxing it by the States may be exercised so as to destroy it, is too obvious to be denied. But taxation is said to be an absolute power, which acknowledges no other limits than those expressly prescribed in the constitution, and like sovereign power of every other description, is trusted to the discretion of those who use it. But the very terms of this argument admit that the sovereignty of the State, in the article of taxation itself, is subordinate to, and may be controlled by the constitution of the United States. How far it has been controlled by that instrument must be a question of construction. In making this construction, no principle not declared, can be admissible, which would defeat the legitimate operations of a supreme government. It is of the very essence of supremacy to remove all obstacles to its action within its own sphere, and so to modify every power vested in subordinate governments, as to exempt its own operations from their own influence. This effect need not be stated in terms. It is so involved in the declaration of supremacy, so necessarily implied in it, that the expression of it could not make it more certain. We must, therefore, keep it in view while construing the constitution.

[54] The argument on the part of the State of Maryland, is, not that the States may directly resist a law of Congress, but that they may exercise their acknowledged powers upon it, and that the constitution leaves them this right in the confidence that they will not abuse it.

[55] Before we proceed to examine this argument, and to subject it to the test of the constitution, we must be permitted to bestow a few considerations on the nature and extent of this original right of taxation, which is acknowledged to remain with the States. It is admitted that the power of taxing the people and their property is essential to the very existence of government, and may be legitimately exercised on the objects to which it is applicable, to the utmost extent to which the government may chuse to Carry it. The only security against the abuse of this power, is found in the structure of the government itself. In imposing a tax the legislature acts upon its constituents. This is in general a sufficient security against erroneous and oppressive taxation.

[56] The people of a State, therefore, give to their government a right of taxing themselves and their property, and as the exigencies of government cannot be limited, they prescribe no limits to the exercise of this right, resting confidently on the interest of the legislator, and on the influence of the constituents over their representative, to guard them against its abuse. But the means employed by the government of the Union have no such security, nor is the right of a State to tax them sustained by the same theory. Those means are not given by the people of a particular State, not given by the constituents of the legislature, which claim the right to tax them, but by the people of all the States. They are given by all, for the benefit of all — and upon theory, should be subjected to that government only which belongs to all.

[57] It may be objected to this definition, that the power of taxation is not confined to the people and property of a State. It may be exercised upon every object brought within its jurisdiction.

[58] This is true. But to what source do we trace this right? It is obvious, that it is an incident of sovereignty, and is co-extensive with that to which it is an incident. All subjects over which the sovereign power of a State extends, are objects of taxation; but those over which it does not extend, are, upon the soundest prin-

ciples, exempt from taxation. This proposition may almost be pronounced self-evident.

[59] The sovereignty of a State extends to every thing which exists by its own authority, or is introduced by its permission; but does it extend to those means which are employed by Congress to carry into execution powers conferred on that body by the people of the United States? We think it demonstrable that it does not. Those powers are not given by the people of a single State. They are given by the people of the United States, to a government whose laws, made in pursuance of the constitution, are declared to be supreme. Consequently, the people of a single State cannot confer a sovereignty which will extend over them.

[60] If we measure the power of taxation residing in a State, by the extent of sovereignty which the people of a single State possess, and can confer on its government, we have an intelligible standard, applicable to every case to which the power may be applied. We have a principle which leaves the power of taxing the people and property of a State unimpaired; which leaves to a State the command of all its resources, and which places beyond its reach, all those powers which are conferred by the people of the United States on the government of the Union, and all those means which are given for the purpose of carrying those powers into execution. We have a principle which is safe for the States, and safe for the Union. We are relieved, as we ought to be, from clashing sovereignty; from interfering powers; from a repugnancy between a right in one government to pull down what there is an acknowledged right in another to build up; from the incompatibility of a right in one government to destroy what there is a right in another to preserve. We are not driven to the perplexing inquiry, so unfit for the judicial department, what degree of taxation is the legitimate use, and what degree may amount to the abuse of the power. The attempt to use it on the means employed by the government of the Union, in pursuance of the constitution, it itself an abuse, because it is the usurpation of a power which the people of a single State cannot give.

[61] We find, then, on just theory, a total failure of this original right to tax the means employed by the government of the Union, for the execution of its powers. The right never existed, and the question whether it has been surrendered, cannot arise.

[62] But, waiving this theory for the present, let us resume the inquiry, whether this power can be exercised by the respective States, consistently with a fair construction of the constitution?

[63] That the power to tax involves the power to destroy; that the power to destroy may defeat and render useless the power to create; that there is a plain repugnance, in conferring on one government a power to control the constitutional measures of another, which other, with respect to those very measures, is declared to be supreme over that which exerts the control, are propositions not to be denied. But all inconsistencies are to be reconciled by the magic of the word CONFIDENCE. Taxation, it is said, does not necessarily and unavoidably destroy. To carry it to the excess of destruction would be an abuse, to presume which, would banish that confidence which is essential to all government.

[64] But is this a case of confidence? Would the people of any one State trust those of another with a power to control the most insignificant operations of their State government? We know they would not. Why, then, should we suppose that the people of any one State should be willing to trust those of another with a

power to control the operations of a government to which they have confided their most important and most valuable interests? In the legislature of the Union alone, are all represented. The legislature of the Union alone, therefore, can be trusted by the people with the power of controlling measures which concern all, in the confidence that it will not be abused. This, then, is not a case of confidence, and we must consider it as it really is.

[65] If we apply the principle for which the State of Maryland contends, to the constitution generally, we shall find it capable of changing totally the character of that instrument. We shall find it capable of arresting all the measures of the government, and of prostrating it at the foot of the States. The American people have declared their constitution, and the laws made in pursuance thereof, to be supreme; but this principle would transfer the supremacy, in fact, to the States.

[66] If the States may tax one instrument, employed by the government in the execution of its powers, they may tax any and every other instrument. They may tax the mail; they may tax the mint; they may tax patent rights; they may tax the papers of the custom-house; they may tax judicial process; they may tax all the means employed by the government, to an excess which would defeat all the ends of government. This was not intended by the American people. They did not design to make their government dependent on the States.

[67] Gentlemen say, they do not claim the right to extend State taxation to these objects. They limit their pretensions to property. But on what principle is this distinction made? Those who make it have furnished no reason for it, and the principle for which they contend denies it. They contend that the power of taxation has no other limit than is found in the 10th section of the 1st article of the constitution; that, with respect to every thing else, the power of the States is supreme, and admits of no control. If this be true, the distinction between property and other subjects to which the power of taxation is applicable, is merely arbitrary, and can never be sustained. This is not all. If the controlling power of the States be established; if their supremacy as to taxation be acknowledged; what is to restrain their exercising this control in any shape they may please to give it? Their sovereignty is not confined to taxation. That is not the only mode in which it might be displayed. The question is, in truth, a question of supremacy; and if the right of the States to tax the means employed by the general government be conceded the declaration that the constitution, and the laws made in pursuance thereof, shall be the supreme law of the land, is empty and unmeaning declamation.

[68] In the course of the argument, the Federalist has been quoted; and the opinions expressed by the authors of that work have been justly supposed to be entitled to great respect in expounding the constitution. No tribute can be paid to them which exceeds their merit; but in applying their opinions to the cases which may arise in the progress of our government, a right to judge of their correctness must be retained; and, to understand the argument, we must examine the proposition it maintains, and the objections against which it is directed. The subject of those numbers, from which passages have been cited, is the unlimited power of taxation which is vested in the general government. The objection to this unlimited power, which the argument seeks to remove, is stated with fullness and clearness. It is, "that an indefinite power of taxation in the latter (the government of the Union) might, and probably would, in time, deprive the former (the government of the States) of the means of providing for their own necessities; and

would subject them entirely to the mercy of the national legislature. As the laws of the Union are to become the supreme law of the land; as it is to have power to pass all laws that may be necessary for carrying into execution the authorities with which it is proposed to vest it; the national government might at any time abolish the taxes imposed for State objects, upon the pretence of an interference with its own. It might allege a necessity for doing this, in order to give efficacy to the national revenues; and thus all the resources of taxation might, by degrees, become the subjects of federal monopoly, to the entire exclusion and destruction of the State governments."

[69] The objections to the constitution which are noticed in these numbers, were to the undefined power of the government to tax, not to the incidental privilege of exempting its own measures from State taxation. The consequences apprehended from this undefined power were, that it would absorb all the objects of taxation, "to the exclusion and destruction of the State governments." The arguments of the Federalist are intended to prove the fallacy of these apprehensions; not to prove that the government was incapable of executing any of its powers, without exposing the means it employed to the embarrassments of State taxation. Arguments urged against these objections, and these apprehensions, are to be understood as relating to the points they mean to prove. Had the authors of those excellent essays been asked, whether they contended for that construction of the constitution, which would place within the reach of the States those measures which the government might adopt for the execution of its powers; no man, who has read their instructive pages, will hesitate to admit, that their answer must have been in the negative.

[70] It has also been insisted, that, as the power of taxation in the general and State governments is acknowledged to be concurrent, every argument which would sustain the right of the general government to tax banks chartered by the States, will equally sustain the right of the States to tax banks chartered by the general government.

[71] But the two cases are not on the same reason. The people of all the States have created the general government, and have conferred upon it the general power of taxation. The people of all the States, and the States themselves, are represented in Congress, and, by their representatives, exercise this power. When they tax the chartered institutions of the States, they tax their constituents; and these taxes must be uniform. But, when a State taxes the operations of the government of the United States, it acts upon institutions created, not by their own constituents, but by people over whom they claim no control. It acts upon the measures of a government created by others as well as themselves, for the benefit of others in common with themselves. The difference is that which always exists, and always must exist, between the action of the whole on a part, and the action of a part on the whole — between the laws of a government declared to be supreme, and those of a government which, when in opposition to those laws, is not supreme.

[72] But if the full application of this argument could be admitted, it might bring into question the right of Congress to tax the State banks, and could not prove the right of the States to tax the Bank of the United States.

[73] The Court has bestowed on this subject its most deliberate consideration. The result is a conviction that the States have no power, by taxation or otherwise, to retard, impede, burden, or in any manner control, the operations of the consti-

tutional laws enacted by Congress to carry into execution the powers vested in the general government. This is, we think, the unavoidable consequence of that supremacy which the constitution has declared.

[74] We are unanimously of opinion, that the law passed by the legislature of Maryland, imposing a tax on the Bank of the United States, is unconstitutional and void.

[75] This opinion does not deprive the States of any resources which they originally possessed. It does not extend to a tax paid by the real property of the bank, in common with the other real property within the State, nor to a tax imposed on the interest which the citizens of Maryland may hold in this institution, in common with other property of the same description throughout the State. But this is a tax on the operations of the bank, and is, consequently, a tax on the operation of an instrument employed by the government of the Union to carry its powers into execution. Such a tax must be unconstitutional.

Discussion

1. *Marshall's interpretive strategy.* Outline Marshall's argument in the second part of *McCulloch.* Which of the methods of constitutional interpretation discussed at pp. 34-35 does Marshall employ?

2. *Possible alternative holdings.* Under the principles announced in the first part of the opinion, Congress could have enacted legislation immunizing the Bank of the United States from the Maryland tax. Are you persuaded that the Constitution, by its own force, prohibits the tax? If some of the bank's functions and property, but not others, are constitutionally immune from state taxation, how can one determine which?

Recall that the Maryland tax by its terms fell only on banks not chartered by the state. Only the Bank of the United States fit that category. Could Marshall have assumed for the sake of argument that a tax on *all* banks could be upheld as applied to the national bank, but nonetheless invalidated this tax on the ground that it discriminated against the Bank of the United States? Which of Marshall's comments in *McCulloch* suggest the basis for such a holding?

3. *Questions of degree.* In the first part of the opinion Marshall writes that, if the Court concludes that the bank is "appropriate," then "the degree of its necessity is to be discussed in another place," apparently referring to Congress. If Marshall were a senator or representative, how do you suppose he would approach the question of the bank's "degree of necessity" — as a constitutional question or a political issue? Compare Hamilton's argument for the first bank, supra. (What is the difference between "constitutional" and "political" in this context?) If the "degree of necessity" remains a constitutional question even after "appropriateness" has been determined, why shouldn't the Court, as well as Congress, address it?

With respect to Marshall's "rhetorical absolute"[43] in the second part of *McCulloch,* is it true that "the power to tax is the power to destroy," or is this just a "seductive cliche"?[44] Might Marshall's absolutism have responded in part to a desire to avoid "the perplexing inquiry, so unfit for the judiciary department, what degree of taxation is the legitimate use, and what degree may amount to the abuse of power"? If so, consider the light this sheds on the "degree of necessity" discus-

43. New York v. United States, 326 U.S. 572, 576 (1946) (Frankfurter, J.).
44. Graves v. O'Keefe, 306 U.S. 466, 489 (1939) (Frankfurter, J., concurring).

sion in the first part of the opinion. If so, consider also whether a purely institutional consideration of this sort — i.e., one based on the Court's self-perceived competence rather than the meaning of the Constitution itself — justifies depriving the states of a legitimate power. (What other options were open to the Court?)

Justice Holmes, dissenting in Panhandle Oil Co. v. Knox, 277 U.S. 218, 223 (1928), observed: "In those days it was not recognized as it is today that most of the distinctions of the law are distinctions of degree. If the States had any power it was assumed that they had all power, and that the necessary alternative was to deny it altogether." (Holmes went on to write, "The power to tax is not the power to destroy while this Court sits.") Holmes implies that Marshall's "rhetorical absolute" may not have been based (merely) on the Court's institutional limitations, but on its conception of the law.

In approaching the cases in the following chapter, consider the hypothesis that "legal" analysis for Marshall consists of *categorizing* activities and other things, while "political" decisionmaking consists of weighing the costs and benefits of a proposed course of action, and that, notwithstanding the emergence of an instrumental conception of law, Marshall perceived a clear distinction between law and policymaking.

4. *Federal immunities today.* Many of the early bank's governmental functions are now performed by the Treasury itself or the Federal Reserve system. In First Agricultural Natl. Bank v. State Tax Commn., 392 U.S. 339 (1968), Justice Marshall, joined by Justices Harlan and Stewart, dissented from the Court's interpretation of a congressional enactment to immunize national banks from state sales and property taxes, and went on to state their belief that national banks can no longer claim the inherent constitutional immunity conferred by *McCulloch.* But cf. Department of Employment v. United States, 385 U.S. 355 (1966), unanimously holding that the American National Red Cross is an instrumentality of the United States, immune from a state unemployment compensation tax, and that Congress has not waived its immunity.

Over the years, the Court has also dealt with the related issue of the immunity of federal governmental activities from state *regulation.* Johnson v. Maryland, 254 U.S. 51 (1920), held that, in the absence of any federal regulation on the subject, a Post Office employee driving a government vehicle on official business was not required to possess a state driver's license. Citing *McCulloch,* Justice Holmes wrote:

> It seems to us that the immunity of instruments of the United States from state control in the performance of their duties extends to a requirement that they desist from performance until they satisfy a state officer upon examination that they are competent for a necessary part of them and pay a fee for permission to go on. Such a requirement does not merely touch the Government servants remotely by a general rule of conduct; it lays hold of them in their specific attempt to obey orders and requires qualifications in addition to those that the Government has pronounced sufficient. It is the duty of the Department to employ persons competent for their work and that duty it must be presumed has been performed.

Holmes cautioned, however, that "an employee of the United States does not secure a general immunity from state law while acting in the course of his employment" and suggested that "when the United States has not spoken, the subjection to local law would extend to general rules that might affect incidentally the mode of carrying out the employment — as, for instance, a statute or ordinance regulating the mode of turning at the corners of streets." What is the basis for this distinction?

The basic principle of federal immunity has been extended to exempt federal contractors from state licensing requirements, Leslie Miller, Inc. v. Arkansas, 352 U.S. 187 (1956); to exempt fertilizer shipped by a federal agency to farmers from a state inspection requirement, Mayo v. United States, 319 U.S. 441 (1943); to exempt milk sold to military installations from a state minimum price regulation, Paul v. United States, 371 U.S. 245 (1963); and to exempt carriers transporting goods under federal contract from state rate regulations, California Public Utilities Commission v. United States, 355 U.S. 534 (1958), and United States v. Georgia Public Service Commission, 371 U.S. 285 (1963).

VI. The Demise of the Second Bank

The national consensus that had supported the Bank of the United States in 1816 had collapsed by the time Congress passed a bill extending its charter in 1832. President Andrew Jackson's veto of the measure was accompanied by a message to the Senate addressing not only the merits but also the question of the allocation of authority to interpret the Constitution.

ANDREW JACKSON, VETO MESSAGE, JULY 10, 1832

2 Messages and Papers of the Presidents 576-589 (Richardson ed. 1897)

The bill "to modify and continue" the act entitled "An act to incorporate the subscribers to the bank of the United States" was presented to me on the 4th July instant. Having considered it with that solemn regard to the principles of the Constitution which the day was calculated to inspire, and come to the conclusion that it ought not to become a law, I herewith return it to the Senate, in which it originated, with my objections. . . .

It is maintained by the advocates of the bank that its constitutionality in all its features ought to be considered as settled by precedent and by the decision of the Supreme Court. To this conclusion I can not assent. Mere precedent is a dangerous source of authority, and should not be regarded as deciding questions of constitutional power except where the acquiescence of the people and the States can be considered as well settled. So far from this being the case on this subject, an argument against the bank might be based on precedent. One Congress, in 1791, decided in favor of a bank; another, in 1811, decided against it. One Congress, in 1815, decided against a bank; another, in 1816, decided in its favor. Prior to the present Congress, therefore, the precedents drawn from that source were equal. If we resort to the States, the expressions of legislative, judicial, and executive opinions against the bank have been probably to those in its favor as 4 to 1. There is nothing in precedent, therefore, which, if its authority were admitted, ought to weigh in favor of the act before me.

If the opinion of the Supreme Court covered the whole ground of this act, it ought not to control the coordinate authorities of this Government. The Congress, the Executive, and the Court must each for itself be guided by its own opinion of the Constitution. Each public officer who takes an oath to support the Constitution swears that he will support it as he understands it, and not as it is understood by others. It is as much the duty of the House of Representatives, of the Senate, and of the President to decide upon the constitutionality of any bill or resolution which may be presented to them for passage or approval as it is of the supreme judges when it may be brought before them for judicial decision. The opinion of the judges has no more authority over Congress than the opinion of Congress has over the judges, and on that point the President is independent of both. The authority of the Supreme Court must not, therefore, be permitted to control the Congress or the Executive when acting in their legislative capacities, but to have only such influence as the force of their reasoning may deserve.

But in the case relied upon the Supreme Court have not decided that all the features of this corporation are compatible with the Constitution. It is true that the court have said that the law incorporating the bank is a constitutional exercise of power by Congress; but taking into view the whole opinion of the court and the reasoning by which they have come to that conclusion, I understand them to have decided that inasmuch as a bank is an appropriate means for carrying into effect the enumerated powers of the General Government, therefore the law incorporating it is in accordance with that provision of the Constitution which declares that Congress shall have power "to make all laws which shall be necessary and proper for carrying those powers into execution." Having satisfied themselves that the word "necessary" in the Constitution means "needful," *"requisite," "essential," "conducive to,"* and that "a bank" is a convenient, a useful, and essential instrument in the prosecution of the Government's "fiscal operations," they conclude that to "use one must be within the discretion of Congress" and that "the act to incorporate the Bank of the United States is a law made in pursuance of the Constitution"; "but," say they, *"where the law is not prohibited and is really calculated to effect any of the objects intrusted to the Government, to undertake here to inquire into the degree of its necessity would be to pass the line which circumscribes the judicial department and to tread on legislative ground."*

The principle here affirmed is that the "degree of its necessity," involving all the details of a banking institution, is a question exclusively for legislative consideration. A bank is constitutional, but it is the province of the Legislature to determine whether this or that particular power, privilege, or exemption is "necessary and proper" to enable the bank to discharge its duties to the Government, and from their decision there is no appeal to the courts of justice. Under the decision of the Supreme Court, therefore, it is the exclusive province of Congress and the President to decide whether the particular features of this act are *necessary* and *proper* in order to enable the bank to perform conveniently and efficiently the public duties assigned to it as a fiscal agent, and therefore constitutional, or *unnecessary* and *improper,* and therefore unconstitutional.

Without commenting on the general principle affirmed by the Supreme Court, let us examine the details of this act in accordance with the rule of legislative action which they have laid down. It will be found that many of the powers and privileges conferred on it can not be supposed necessary for the purpose for which it is proposed to be created, and are not, therefore, means necessary to attain the end in view, and consequently not justified by the Constitution. . . .

This act authorizes and encourages transfers of its stock to foreigners and grants them an exemption from all State and national taxation. So far from being *"necessary and proper"* that the bank should possess this power to make it a safe and efficient agent of the Government in its fiscal operations, it is calculated to convert the Bank of the United States into a foreign bank, to impoverish our people in time of peace, to disseminate a foreign influence through every section of the Republic, and in war to endanger our independence.

The several States reserved the power at the formation of the Constitution to regulate and control titles and transfers of real property, and most, if not all, of them have laws disqualifying aliens from acquiring or holding lands within their limits. But this act, in disregard of the undoubted right of the States to prescribe such disqualifications, gives to alien stockholders in this bank an interest and title, as members of the corporation, to all the real property it may acquire within any of the States of this Union. This privilege granted to aliens is not *"necessary"* to enable the bank to perform its public duties, nor in any sense *"proper,"* because it is vitally subversive of the rights of the States. . . .

It is maintained by some that the bank is a means of executing the constitutional power "to coin money and regulate the value thereof." Congress have established a mint to coin money and passed laws to regulate the value thereof. The money so coined, with its value so regulated, and such foreign coins as Congress may adopt are the only currency known to the Constitution. But if they have other power to regulate the currency, it was conferred to be exercised by themselves, and not to be transferred to a corporation. If the bank be established for that purpose, with a charter unalterable without its consent, Congress have parted with their power for a term of years, during which the Constitution is a dead letter. It is neither necessary nor proper to transfer its legislative power to such a bank, and therefore unconstitutional.

By its silence, considered in connection with the decision of the Supreme Court in the case of McCulloch against the State of Maryland, this act takes from the States the power to tax a portion of the banking business carried on within their limits, in subversion of one of the strongest barriers which secured them against Federal encroachments. Banking, like farming, manufacturing, or any other occupation or profession, is *a business*. . . .

Upon the formation of the Constitution the States guarded their taxing power with peculiar jealousy. They surrendered it only as it regards imports and exports. In relation to every other object within their jurisdiction, whether persons, property, business, or professions, it was secured in as ample a manner as it was before possessed. . . .

There is no more appropriate subject of taxation than banks, banking, and bank stocks, and none to which the States ought more pertinaciously to cling.

It can not be *necessary* to the character of the bank as a fiscal agent of the Government that its private business should be exempted from that taxation to which all the State banks are liable, nor can I conceive it *"proper"* that the substantive and most essential powers reserved by the States shall be thus attacked and annihilated as a means of executing the powers delegated to the General Government. . . .

If our power over means is so absolute that the Supreme Court will not call in question the constitutionality of an act of Congress the subject of which "is not prohibited, and is really calculated to effect any of the objects intrusted to the Government," although, as in the case before me, it takes away powers expressly granted to Congress and rights scrupulously reserved to the States, it becomes us to proceed in our legislation with the utmost caution. Though not directly, our own powers and the rights of the States may be indirectly legislated away in the use of means to execute substantive powers. . . . We may not pass an act prohibiting the States to tax the banking business carried on within their limits, but we may, as a means of executing our powers over other objects, place that business in the hands of our agents and then declare it exempt from State taxation in their hands. Thus may our own powers and the rights of the States, which we can not directly curtail or invade, be frittered away and extinguished in the use of means employed by us to execute other powers. That a bank of the United States, competent to all the duties which may be required by the Government, might be so organized as not to infringe on our own delegated powers or the reserved rights of the States I do not entertain a doubt. Had the Executive been called upon to furnish the project of such an institution, the duty would have been cheerfully performed. In the absence of such a call it was obviously proper that he should confine himself to pointing out those prominent features in the act presented which in his opinion make it incompatible with the Constitution and sound policy. . . .

It is to be regretted that the rich and powerful too often bend the acts of government to their selfish purposes. Distinctions in society will always exist under every just government. Equality of talents, of education, or of wealth can not be produced by human institutions. In the full enjoyment of the gifts of Heaven and the fruits of superior industry, economy, and virtue, every man is equally entitled to protection by law; but when the laws undertake to add to these natural and just advantages artificial distinctions, to grant titles, gratuities, and exclusive privileges, to make the rich richer and the potent more powerful, the humble members of society — the farmers, mechanics, and laborers — who have neither the time nor the means of securing like favors to themselves, have a right to complain of the injustice of their Government. There are no necessary evils in government. Its evils exist only in its abuses. If it would confine itself to equal protection, and, as Heaven does its rains, shower its favors alike on the high and the low, the rich and the poor, it would be an unqualified blessing. In the act before me there seems to be a wide and unnecessary departure from these just principles.

Nor is our Government to be maintained or our Union preserved by invasions of the rights and powers of the several States. In thus attempting to make our General Government strong we make it weak. Its true strength consists in leaving individuals and States as much as possible to themselves — in making itself felt, not in its power, but in its beneficence; not in its control, but in its protection; not in binding the States more closely to the center, but leaving each to move unobstructed in its proper orbit.

Discussion

1. Jackson's assertion that even "[i]f the opinion of the Supreme Court covered the whole ground of this act, it ought not to control the coordinate authorities of this Government" presents a fundamental issue of the allocation of constitutional

decisionmaking authority among the branches of the national government, to which we return at length in Part Two. Jackson goes on to note that the Supreme Court in *McCulloch* had *not* "decided that all features of this corporation are compatible with the Constitution." He concludes that "it is the exclusive province of Congress and the President to decide whether the particular features of this act are *necessary* and *proper*. . . ." Is this question one of constitutional law, of politics, or both?

2. The history surrounding the adoption of the President's veto power does not shed much light on its scope.[45] Of the early history of its use, Edward Corwin writes:[46]

> . . . [T]he veto power did not escape the early talent of Americans for conjuring up constitutional limitations out of thin air. The veto was solely a self-defensive weapon of the President; it was the means furnished him for carrying out his oath to "preserve, protect and defend the Constitution" and was not validly usable for any other purpose; it did not extend to revenue bills, never having been so employed by the King of England; it did not extend to "insignificant and trivial" matters like private pension bills; it was never intended to give effect merely to presidential desires, but its use must rest on considerations of great weight, and so on and so forth. Although efforts of this sort to forge shackles for the power derived a certain specious plausibility from the rarity of the veto's use in English history, they met with failure from the first. Washington exercised the power twice, once on constitutional grounds, once on grounds of expediency. Neither Adams nor Jefferson exercised it at all. Of Madison's six vetoes four urged constitutional objections to the measure involved, two objections of policy. Summing the matter up for the first century under the Constitution, the leading authority on the subject says: "From Jackson's administration to the Civil War vetoes on grounds of expediency became more frequent, but they were still in a decided minority. Since the [Civil] War constitutional arguments in a veto message have been almost unknown." The latter statement applies moreover equally to more recent years, if exception be made for one or two vetoes by Presidents Taft and Coolidge, both of whom had a special penchant for constitutional niceties. . . .

3. Jackson's veto was not overridden, and the charter of the Bank of the United States lapsed in 1836.

Note: Congressional Spending for the "General Welfare"

Congressional authority to finance "internal improvements" was a recurring issue in the early republic. It was argued, particularly by Hamiltonians, that Congress had such power under its authority to spend for the "general welfare." However, the most significant bill mandating such an expenditure was vetoed by President James Madison:[47]

> Having considered the bill . . . entitled "An act to set apart and pledge certain funds for internal improvements," and which sets apart and pledges funds "for con-

45. Edward Corwin, The President: Office and Powers 278 (4th ed. 1957).
46. Id. at 279 (quoting Edward Mason, The Veto Power (1891)).
47. James Richardson, ed., 1 Messages and Papers of the Presidents (1897) 584-85.

structing roads and canals, and improving the navigation of water courses, in order to facilitate, promote, and give security to internal commerce among the several States, and to render more easy and less expensive the means and provisions for the common defense," I am constrained by the insuperable difficulty I feel in reconciling the bill with the Constitution of the United States to [veto it]. . . . [I]t does not appear that the power proposed to be exercised by the bill is among the enumerated powers, or that it falls by any just interpretation within the power to make laws necessary and proper for carrying into execution those or other powers vested by the Constitution in the Government of the United States.

"The power to regulate commerce among the several States" can not include such a commerce without a latitude of construction departing from the ordinary import of the terms strengthened by the known inconveniences which doubtless led to the grant of this remedial power to Congress.

To refer the power in question to the clause "to provide for the common defense and general welfare" would be contrary to the established and consistent rules of interpretation, as rendering the special and careful enumeration of powers which follow the clause nugatory and improper. Such a view of the Constitution would have the effect of giving to congress a general power of legislation instead of the defined and limited one hitherto understood to belong to them, the terms "common defense and general welfare" embracing every object and act within the purview of a legislative trust. It would have the effect of subjecting both the Constitution and laws of the several States in all cases not specifically exempted to be superseded by laws of Congress. . . . Such a view of the Constitution, finally, would have the effect of excluding the judicial authority of the United States from its participation in guarding the boundary between legislative powers of the General and State Governments, inasmuch as questions relating to the general welfare, being questions of policy and expediency, are unsusceptible of judicial cognizance and decision.

A restriction of the power "to provide for the common defense and general welfare" to cases which are to be provided for by the expenditure of money would still leave within legislative power of Congress all the great and most important measures of Government, money being the ordinary and necessary means of carrying them into execution.

If a general power to construct roads and canals, and to improve the navigation of water courses, with the train of powers incident thereto, be not possessed by Congress, the assent of the States in the mode provided in the bill can not confer the power. The only cases in which the consent and cession of particular States can extend the power of Congress are those specified and provided for in the Constitution.

I am not unaware of the great importance of roads and canals and the improved navigation of water courses, and that a power in the National Legislature to provide for them might be exercised with signal advantage to the general prosperity. But seeing that such a power is not expressly given by the Constitution, and believing that it can not be deduced from any part of it without an inadmissible latitude of construction and a reliance on insufficient precedents; believing also that the permanent success of the Constitution depends on a definite partition of powers between the General and the State Governments, and that no adequate landmarks would be left by the constructive extension of the powers of Congress as proposed in the bill, I have no option but to withhold my signature from it, and to cherishing the hope that its beneficial objects may be attained by a resort for the necessary powers to the same wisdom and virtue in the nation which established the Constitution in its actual form and providently marked out in the instrument itself a safe and practicable mode of improving it as experience might suggest.

Discussion

Madison's veto was constitutionally motivated. Apparently, he viewed internal improvements as "beneficial" and would have supported a constitutional amendment specifically authorizing them. The veto exemplifies the significance of non-judicial constitutional decisionmaking. President Monroe, his successor, also vetoed an internal improvements bill in 1822 on constitutional grounds. This, of course, was after the intervening opinion of Chief Justice Marshall in *McCulloch*. (Would Marshall have upheld the financing of "internal improvements" as within the power of Congress?)

Note: What Is a Case (and Why Read One)?

The preceding pages present a case study of the controversy surrounding the Bank of the United States. Marshall's opinion in *McCulloch* is only one of several opinions addressing the constitutionality of the bank. Madison's speech, Jefferson's and Hamilton's memoranda, and Jackson's veto message are opinions on the same issue. What, if anything, distinguishes Marshall's opinion from the others? How does *McCulloch* differ from any other thoughtful essay on the nature of the Union and of the Constitution?

We are all influenced by John Marshall and his visions of a powerful national government and Supreme Court. Most of us find it difficult to escape the feeling that the Court alone can authoritatively resolve constitutional disputes. Yet Madison, Jefferson, Jackson, and many others have disputed the broadest claims of judicial power, and the scope of the Court's authority remains unresolved today.

This book, like all other casebooks in the constitutional law, consists primarily of judicial opinions — mostly those of the United States Supreme Court. (The familiar subtitle, "cases and materials," is a giveaway.) This reflects our acknowledgment of Marshall's heritage as well as the fact that most important federal constitutional questions eventually come before the Court and are usefully focused by its opinions. As a practical matter, limitations of space and time preclude presenting other "cases" as completely as this study of the Bank of the United States, but Chapter One should indicate the costs of removing judicial opinions from the rich environment of the political and ideological contexts in which they arise.

The question remains: For what *purposes* do we read cases? One answer is: To learn constitutional doctrine. Perhaps this is done adequately by reading treatises, which was virtually the exclusive method of law school teaching in the United States until the late nineteenth century and remains the dominant method of continental legal education. Had you taken this course a century or so ago, its text would not have been a casebook, but perhaps Justice Story's Commentaries on the Constitution.

If as citizens we are Marshall's children, as law students and teachers we are Christopher Columbus Langdell's. Langdell, who became Dean of Harvard Law School in 1870, introduced the case method in order to make the law a "science" studied through what he believed to be its primary sources: the decisions of judges.[48] Langdell's notion of science seems rather parochial today — especially when taken together with his antagonism towards constitutions and statutes, which he regarded as distorting excrescences on the common law. Nonetheless, there *is* something to be said for learning doctrine from original sources rather than through the eyes of a treatise writer.

Another reason for reading cases may be to learn how to engage in constitutional analysis and interpretation and, more broadly, how to "think like a lawyer." From this perspective, the processes of justifying and criticizing opinions, rather than the doctrines they establish, are of primary importance.

One can also study cases to understand how politicians, lawyers, and judges of a particular era thought about certain issues. For example, the controversy over the Bank of the United States provides insights into the social and political history of the United States in the early nineteenth century. In reading opinions from this perspective, it is useful to remember that — whatever be the nature of constitutions — judicial opinions are not necessarily intended to endure for ages to come (or to withstand analytical dissection in the classroom). Some perceived deficiencies in judicial reasoning may make more sense if one understands the opinions as directed toward particular communities in particular political contexts.

Still more broadly, one might read opinions to learn how lawyers and judges in different periods conceived of and analyzed legal issues. This is intrinsically interesting. Moreover, the decisions of earlier times can cast light on our own legal culture by offering points of contrast and similarity. The concern here is with the Court's assumptions, structure, and style of argumentation. For these purposes, no treatise can replace the close examination of the original writers' discourse.

By way of contrast to the essentially ideological concerns mentioned in the preceding paragraphs, one may also study judicial decisions as responses to social, political, and economic forces and interest groups. The analysis of constitutional history in these terms is often coupled with the name of Charles Beard and his An Economic Interpretation of the Constitution (1913). As described by a later historian, Beard construed the Constitution "as a conservative economic document framed by an unrepresentative minority employing undemocratic means to protect personal property interests by establishing a central government responsive to their needs and able to thwart populistic majorities in the states. He viewed the Constitution as the work of personalty interests as opposed to realty interests, in short, as Beard put it, 'capital as opposed to land.' Minority business groups — manufacturers, merchants, shippers, speculators in land values, and above all, public securities holders — manipulated the call for the Convention in the hope of obtaining what Beard called 'the adoption of a revolutionary program.' "[49]

Beard's own work has been the object of considerable criticism, but "neo-Beardians" like Merrill Jensen and Jackson Turner Main continue to engage in

48. See Lawrence Friedman, A History of American Law 531-533 (1973); Robert Stevens, Two Cheers for 1870: The American Law School, in 5 Perspectives in American History 403 (1971); Marcia Speziale, Langdell's Concept of Law as Science, 5 Vt. L. Rev. 1 (1980).

49. Leonard Levy, Introduction to Essays on the Making of the Constitution xx-xxi (Levy ed. 1969). Professor Lynd similarly attributes the North's acquiescence in slavery not only to its racism but to its commitment to property rights. Staughton Lynd, Class Conflict, Slavery, and the United States Constitution (1967).

close study of the relationships between economic interests and political programs.[50] Whatever the controversy over any particular claim, few if any historians deny the importance of economic interests in shaping constitutional events. Throughout Part One, we shall examine judicial decisions in their economic context as well as others.

The learning of doctrine is thus one rationale, but only one of several, for reading cases. It is one objective, but only one of several, for this book.

VII. Freedom of Expression and States' Rights in the Late Eighteenth Century: The Sedition Act of 1798

Late eighteenth-century debates involving issues of federalism and constitutional interpretation were not confined to disputes over the legitimacy of a national bank. The Bill of Rights, though adopted with relatively little fanfare, soon became the focal point of an intense controversy regarding the scope of the first amendment guaranties of freedom of speech and press. In 1798, the Congress, narrowly divided along Federalist and Republican party lines, enacted a Sedition Act. Section 2 of the Act provided:

> That if any person shall write, print, utter or publish . . . any false, scandalous and malicious writing or writings against the government of the United States, or either house of the Congress of the United States, or the President of the United States, with intent to defame the said government, or either house of the said Congress, or the said President, or to bring them, or either of them, into contempt or disrepute; or to excite against them, or either or any of them, the hatred of the good people of the United States, or to stir up sedition within the United States, or to excite any unlawful combinations therein, for opposing or resisting any law of the United States, or any act of the President of the United States, done in pursuance of any such law, or of the powers in him vested by the constitution of the United States, or to resist, oppose, or defeat any such law or act, or to aid, encourage or abet any hostile designs of any foreign nation against the United States, their people or government, then such person, being thereof convicted before any court of the United States having jurisdiction thereof, shall be punished by a fine not exceeding two thousand dollars, and by imprisonment not exceeding two years.[51]

50. For excerpts from the continuing debate, see Levy, supra note 49; and The Reinterpretation of the American Revolution, 1763-1789 (Greene ed. 1968).

51. 1 Stat. 596 (1798)(expired 1801). Section 1 proscribes combinations or conspiracies with intent to oppose, prevent, or intimidate government laws or operations and that "counsel, advise or attempt to procure any insurrection, riot, unlawful assembly, or combination." Section 3 establishes that defendants can give the truth of the allegedly libelous material as evidence in their defense. In addition, the act gave the jury "a right to determine the law and the fact." Section 4 makes the Act law through March 3, 1801. Libel defendants and freedom of speech advocates had sought the two Section 3 reforms for many years. Under traditional seditious libel laws, courts would not allow the truth of the libel to be proved in court because a true libel was considered more dangerous than a false one. Furthermore, the jury had previously been allowed to decide only the question of whether the defendant had in fact published the libelous material. Judges decided the questions of law: whether the defendant made the remarks with malice and whether they were "of a bad tendency" to sedition.

Many perceived the Sedition Act of 1798 as a Federalist measure to silence the opposition and keep themselves in power. Indeed, federal prosecutors were vigorous in using the Act against critics of the government. As Professor Powe notes, "the Federalists identified opposition to their policies with support for France, and their name for the Republicans — the 'internal foe' — expressed their view that the Republican party was a threat to the republic."[52] The leading Republican papers were the targets of the prosecutions, and three were forced to cease publication, two permanently.[53] The passage of the Act, and its implementation, sparked fiery debates over the scope of the First Amendment and the proper realms of state and federal power.

A. The Meaning of the First Amendment

The history of the adoption of the First Amendment is sparse. Although there was a broad consensus that the Constitution should guarantee the freedoms of speech and press, few of the new nation's intellectual and political leaders discussed the content and extent of the First Amendment. Freedom of speech and press in 1789 England meant "freedom from prior restraint": Government could no longer censor political material prior to its publication. Once the material was in print, however, its author, printer, and publisher could still be punished for criminal libel. The central question is whether this limited meaning of freedom of the press also held true in the new United States, which had been heavily influenced by its English heritage yet had rebelled against what had come to be seen as tyrannical elements of the British constitutional order.[54]

1. *The Original Understanding*

Did the framers of the Bill of Rights intend the First Amendment to do more than protect speech and press from prior restraint? In Freedom of Speech and Press in Early American History: Legacy of Suppression, Leonard W. Levy argues that they did not. Levy examines legislative proceedings, criminal cases in the courts and legislatures, and writings of political and intellectual leaders in America. He concludes that the evidence shows that none of them advocated any change in the common law of libel as it existed prior to 1798.[55]

> Freedom [of speech and press in the colonial period] . . . did not include a right to criticize the legislature. . . . Legislative proceedings could not be published without

52. Lucas A. Powe, Jr., The Fourth Estate and the Constitution: Freedom of the Press in America 58 (1991).

53. Id. at 59.

54. Seditious libel was the most repressive class of libel, according to Leonard W. Levy, Freedom of Speech and Press in Early American History: Legacy of Suppression 10 (1960). Although difficult to define, "[j]udged by actual prosecutions, the crime consisted of criticizing the government: its form, constitution, officers, laws, symbols, conduct, policies, and so on. In effect, any comment about the government which could be construed to have the bad tendency of lowering it in the public's esteem or of disturbing the peace was seditious libel, subjecting the speaker or writer to criminal prosecution."

55. Id. at 68.

prior license; legislative measures were protected by parliamentary privilege from fault finders. Animadversion was regarded as subversion. Any verbal attack on government officials or policies which might be deemed an affront to the authority or honor of the legislature was subject to a power of repression from which not all the writs precious to the liberty of the subject could effect a rescue. If an exercise of parliamentary privilege was not the appropriate means of silencing an opponent, there were others of an extralegal nature. Vigilantism may be a necessary ingredient in the making of a revolution, and there may even have been occasions when its existence among the patriots was understandably provoked. But there is no denying that it did exist on a widespread scale, and it was always ugly, always a denial of due process, and always, before the outbreak of the war, directed not at an enemy but a fellow citizen whose opinions differed. There were even occasions when that citizen was a staunch patriot whose judgment in the opinion of extremists needed correction by drastic methods for the good of the cause. . . .

The evidence forces the conclusion that Chief Justice Hutchinson had accurately summarized the situation when he acidly observed that the Adamses and their supporters were "contending for an unlimited Freedom of Thought and Action, which they would confine wholly to themselves."[56] Free speech for one side only is not free speech at all, or at best is an extraordinarily narrow concept of it. That, indeed, is the whole point: during the entire colonial period, from the time of the first settlements to the Revolutionary War and the framing of the first bills of rights, America had very little experience with freedom of speech or press as a meaningful condition of life. Nor did colonial America produce or inherit a broad concept of freedom of speech or press. . . .[57]

Turning to the revolutionary period, Levy writes: "No cause was more honored by rhetorical declamation and dishonored in practice than that of freedom of expression . . . from the 1760's through the cessation of hostilities."[58] The states enacted laws punishing criticism of the revolutionary government.[59] Many post-Revolutionary state constitutions included no protection for speech or press,[60] and, of course, neither did the Constitution of 1787. In response to criticisms by the anti-Federalists, the Federalists eventually proposed a Bill of Rights. Levy comments on the process of state ratification:

State action on the proposed Bill of Rights apparently occasioned slight comment either in or out of the legislatures, except in Virginia. Nine states perfunctorily approved the Bill of Rights by mid-June of 1790. Since records of legislative debates are nonexistent, there is no way of expressly knowing what the First Amendment freedoms were understood to mean. Private correspondence, newspapers, and tracts are unilluminating. Many may have cared about protecting freedom of speech-and-press, but no one seems to have cared enough to clarify what he meant by the subject upon which he lavished praise. If definition were unnecessary because of the existence of a tacit and widespread understanding of "liberty of the press," only the received or traditional understanding could have been possible. To assume the existence of a general, latitudinarian understanding that veered substantially from the common-law definition is incredible, given the total absence of argumenta-

56. Josiah Quincy, Jr., ed., Reports of Cases Argued and Adjudged in the Superior Court of Judicature of the Province of Massachusetts Bay, Between 1761 and 1772 (Boston 1865).
57. Levy at 85-87.
58. Id. at 63.
59. Id. at 181-82.
60. Id. at 184-85.

tive analysis of the meaning of the clause on speech and press. Any novel definition expanding the scope of free expression or repudiating, even altering, the concept of seditious libel would have been the subject of public debate or comment. Not even the Anti-Federalists offered the argument that the clause on speech and press was unsatisfactory because insufficiently protective. . . .

But the history of the ratification indicates no passion on the part of anyone to grind underfoot the common law of liberty of the press. Indeed the history of the framing and ratification of the First Amendment and the other nine scarcely manifests a passion on the part of anyone connected with the process. Considering its immediate background, our precious Bill of Rights was in the main the chance result of certain Federalists' having been reluctantly forced to capitalize for their own cause the propaganda that had been originated in vain by the Anti-Federalists for ulterior purposes. Thus the party that had first opposed a Bill of Rights inadvertently wound up with the responsibility for its framing and ratification, while the party that had at first professedly wanted it discovered too late that its framing and ratification were not only embarrassing but inexpedient.[61]

Although many readers accepted Levy's view of the meaning of freedom of speech and the press in eighteenth-century America and his revisionist claim that the First Amendment was not intended to nullify the common law of criminal libel, several commentators have nevertheless chastised Levy for a crabbed reading of his evidence. For example, Merrill Jensen writes:

The impression given is that there was no freedom anywhere in America, either before or after 1763. But can we assume that the relatively few prosecutions before 1763 silenced all discussion? Did the "rude hand of the law," as Gouverneur Morris called it, touch every man who opposed governmental policies and officeholders? I doubt it. Levy goes on to assert flatly that "speech and the press were not free anywhere during the Revolution." He shows that this was correct as a matter of law but pays little attention to practice. No reader of the newspapers of the revolutionary era could accept such a statement. Of course the newspapers and people who supported Great Britain were suppressed when independence drew the line, but any nation, new or old, would do the same thing whatever its laws might be. But the debate among Americans about constitutions, governmental policies, and politicians continued with unabated fervor, and in terms that were libelous by whatever standard one applies. The prosecutions cited give one no idea of what day-to-day journalism was like. . . . Because [Levy] is concerned with seditious libel, and concentrates on the purely legal aspects, he tends to underrate the importance of practice. . . .

Another weakness of the legal approach is that it cannot explain that which is essentially political, where the law was a tool in political battles, not the guiding force. . . . [An] example is Pennsylvania during the Revolution. Levy sees no freedom of expression there because the law did not change. Yet the Pennsylvania newspapers between 1776 and 1789 contain vast amounts of some of the bitterest, most dishonest (and seditious) writing in American political history. Despite the law there was freedom of expression in fact. No governmental institution, political faction, or individual was free from attacks such as few newspapers today would dare to print.[62]

Another reviewer takes issue with the conclusion Levy draws from the inconsistency between the broad popular expression of support for the freedom of

61. Id. at 224-225, 233.
62. Merrill Jensen, 75 Harv. L. Rev. 456, 457 (1961).

speech and press and widespread public intolerance for differing views. "The serious question is whether Dean Levy is correct in saying that this broad popular spirit is meaningless because the colonists failed to demonstrate tolerance of opposing views. When our concern is with a constitutional statement of first principles, should we not be concerned with the popular ideal rather than with the gulf between principles and practice?"[63] And John Cound argues that rather than depicting a legacy of suppression, Levy's evidence actually

> shows the legacy . . . to be one of a continuing and enlarging concern for freedom. If the first amendment is a living and growing idea, as he argues, rather than a fixed statement, its growth began at least a century and a half before 1790. There were those men who, while accepting the doctrine of seditious libel (or at least not openly rejecting it) nonetheless carved out protections for free expression. . . . [I]t seems an oversimplification to say of men who had attacked prosecution after prosecution as groundless and abusive, and who by their own words courted indictment, that "they accepted in substance the Blackstone-Mansfield definition [of freedom of the press]: freedom, under law, from prior restraint," simply because they did not deny the possibility that a government can be libeled.[64]

In 1983, David Anderson, in The Origins of the Press Clause, 30 U.C.L.A.L. Rev. 455, reexamined the historical materials and vigorously attacked Levy's thesis, concluding his article as follows:

> Though scholars today may debate whether the press clause has any significance independent of the speech clause, historically there is no doubt that it did. Freedom of the press — not freedom of speech — was the primary concern of the generation that wrote the Declaration of Independence, the Constitution, and the Bill of Rights. Freedom of speech was a late addition to the pantheon of rights; freedom of the press occupied a central position from the very beginning.
>
> By the time the press clause became part of our Constitution in 1791, it had a considerable legislative history. The revolutionary state constitutions, the ratifying conventions, and the First Congress produced numerous expressions of the idea. These expressions and freedom-of-the-press literature from which they were drawn leave little doubt that press freedom was viewed as being closely related to the experiment of representative self-government. . . . The issue was born of the conflict with England, and its first expressions as a binding principle of law came in the state constitutions drafted contemporaneously with the Declaration of Independence. In these earliest expressions, the relation between freedom of the press and the idea of self-government was explicit. The press was a "bulwark of liberty," "essential to the security of freedom in a state." It had to be protected, not for its own sake, but because it provided a necessary restraint on what the patriots viewed as government's natural tendency toward tyranny and despotism.
>
> In the minds of members of the First Congress, the press clause was part of the new plan of government, no less than if it had been in the original Constitution. To the Anti-Federalists, it was an essential modification of the original Constitution; to

63. 13 Stan. L. Rev. 991, 993 (1961). In 1985, Levy published Emergence of a Free Press, an updated version of Legacy of Suppression. Although he modified some of his arguments, he continued to maintain that the framers of the first amendment cannot be shown to have intended to abolish the common law of seditious libel. For critical reviews, see Rabban, The Ahistorical Historian: Leonard Levy on Freedom of Expression in Early American History, 37 Stan. L. Rev. 795 (1985); Anderson, Levy vs. Levy, 84 Mich. L. Rev. 777 (1986).

64. John J. Cound, 36 N.Y.U.L. Rev. 253, 256 (1961).

the Federalists, it expressed what was already implicit in the Constitution. Their quarrel was only over the necessity of specifically guaranteeing freedom of the press. Neither side doubted its utility. Its value lay, as Professor Blasi says, in "checking the inherent tendency of government officials to abuse the power entrusted to them." Because it plays this role, it is, in Justice Stewart's words, "a structural provision of the Constitution."

That the press clause has a distinct history does not mean, of course, that it must be given a meaning different from the speech clause today, or even that it had a different meaning in 1791. It is possible that checking government power was also the purpose of the speech clause. My own guess, however, is that the latter was more closely related to the incipient notion of individual autonomy that underlay the religion clauses. But in either event, most modern analysis, by focusing on the speech clause, gets the matter upside down. As a means of checking government power, speech was an afterthought, if it was viewed as serving that function at all; the press was expected to be the primary source of restraint.

The legislative history of the press clause has been ignored, largely because it is inconsistent with the conclusions of Leonard Levy, whose work in first amendment history has become the conventional wisdom of our generation. Levy's view is that freedom of the press meant nothing more to the Framers than freedom from prior restraint; the first amendment was not intended to enlarge that common law meaning. . . . If Levy is right, the press could hardly have been expected to occupy any significant structural role. The press would have been at the mercy (except for prior restraints) of most of those whose abuses it was supposed to check.

Levy's thesis is not unassailable. It requires us to accept several remarkable propositions. We must believe that the press clause was directed at what was in America a non-issue — prior restraint — rather than at seditious libel, which had been the primary form of restraint on the press during the colonial period. We must believe that the press clauses that were included in nine state constitutions were intended to do nothing more than preserve the English common law. We must believe that the Framers were oblivious to, or hypocritical about, their own sedition in criticizing the government under the Articles of Confederation. We must believe that they did not understand that citizens of representative democracy must be free to criticize government until the Sedition Act taught that lesson a few years later. We must believe that Madison in 1799 misrepresented (or misunderstood) his own views of ten years earlier. . . . A thesis that requires so many suspensions of disbelief ought not be preclusive.

2. *The Kentucky and Virginia Resolutions of 1798-1799*

The Sedition Act of 1798 gave rise to the first major controversy over the scope of the First Amendment and the federal government's power to punish seditious libel. The Act was vehemently opposed by resolutions adopted by the legislatures of Kentucky and Virginia. The Kentucky Resolutions of 1798 were drafted by Thomas Jefferson, the Virginia Resolutions by James Madison.[65]

65. Both Resolutions also attacked the Alien Act of 1798, which authorized the President to order deportation of any alien he judged "dangerous to the peace and safety of the United States" or whom he had "reasonable grounds to suspect [was] concerned in any treasonable or secret machinations against the government." 1 Stat. 570 (1798) (expired 1800). See The Virginia Report 27-28, 162-167 (J.W. Randolph, ed., 1850).

Madison also wrote the Virginia Report of 1800, which elaborated and defended Virginia's position in the face of counter-resolutions by other states.[66]

The fifth of the Virginia Resolutions asserted that the Sedition Act was an

> alarming infraction[] of the Constitution, [which] exercises . . . a power not delegated by the Constitution, but on the contrary expressly and positively forbidden by one of the amendments thereto; a power which more than any other ought to produce universal alarm, because it is leveled against that right of freely examining public characters and measures, and of free communication among the people thereon, which has ever been justly deemed the only effectual guardian of every other right.

In the Virginia Report Madison writes:

> In the attempts to vindicate the "Sedition Act," it has been contended . . . [t]hat the "freedom of the press" is to be determined by the meaning of these terms in the common law . . . The freedom of the press under the common law, is, in the defences of the Sedition Act, made to consist in an exemption from all *previous* restraint on printed publications, by persons authorized to inspect or prohibit them. It appears to the committee, that this idea of the freedom of the press, can never be admitted to be the American idea of it: since a law inflicting penalties on printed publications would have a similar effect with a law authorizing a previous restraint on them. It would seem a mockery to say, that no law should be passed, preventing publications from being made, but that laws might be passed for punishing them in case they should be made.[67]

Madison also argues that the different natures of the British and American governments demonstrate why freedom of the press in America cannot be equated with the English common law restriction against prior restraint of seditious libel: In England, the people's rights need only be protected from the executive because Parliament has absolute power. In the United States, however, the people retain absolute sovereignty, and the power of *all* the branches of government is limited. Since the common law protects the press from the executive's prior restraint only, and not also from legislatively prescribed punishment, "[t]he state of the press, . . . under the common law, cannot . . . be the standard of its freedom in the United States."[68]

The Kentucky Resolutions also declared that the Sedition Act violated the First Amendment. Levy comments: "The reason for the sudden if belated emergence of a sharply articulated body of 'Jeffersonian' thought on freedom of speech and press was the threat that the government of the United States under the Adams administration might attempt to eliminate political criticism, create a one-party press in the country, and by controlling public opinion insure a Federalist victory in the elections of 1800."[69] In any event, Jefferson's and Madison's substantive reading of the freedoms of speech and press laid the foundation for all subsequent interpretations of the First Amendment. Opponents of the Sedition Act maintained that the Constitution granted the *federal* government no power over speech or the press. They did not argue that the *states* were deprived

66. Id. at 189-237.
67. Id. at 219-220.
68. Id. at 220.
69. Levy, supra note 49, at 258.

of the power to control speech. As we shall see below, the First Amendment's limitations regarding speech were not deemed applicable to the states until 1925.

B. Federalism and States' Rights

The Third Kentucky Resolution provides:

> That . . . no power over the freedom of religion, freedom of speech, or freedom of the press, being delegated to the United States by the Constitution, nor prohibited by it to the states, all lawful powers respecting the same did of right remain, and were reserved to the states, or to the people; that thus was manifested their determination to retain to themselves the right of judging how far the licentiousness of speech and of the press may be abridged without lessening their useful freedom, and how far those abuses which cannot be separated from their use, should be tolerated rather than destroyed; and . . . [a] special provision has been made by one of the amendments to the Constitution, which expressly declares, that "Congress shall make no law respecting an establishment of religion, or prohibiting the free exercise thereof, or abridging the freedom of speech, or of the press," . . . and that libels, falsehoods, and defamations, equally with heresy and false religion, are withheld from the cognizance of federal tribunals: that therefore the [Sedition Act] . . . , which does abridge the freedom of the press, is not law, but is altogether void and of no effect.

The fourth Virginia Resolution similarly provides:

> That the General Assembly doth also express its deep regret that a spirit has in sundry instances been manifested by the Federal Government, to enlarge its powers by forced constructions of the constitutional charter which defines them; and that indications have appeared of a design to expound certain general phrases . . . , so as to destroy the meaning and effect of the particular enumeration, which necessarily explains and limits the general phrases, and so as to consolidate the States by degrees into one sovereignty, the obvious tendency and inevitable result of which would be to transform the present republican system of the United States into an absolute, or at best, a mixed monarchy.

C. The Doctrine of Nullification

Who had the authority to assess the constitutionality of the Sedition Act? Would a declaration of unconstitutionality necessarily invalidate (or "nullify") its power? Both Virginia and Kentucky claimed authority to declare the Act unconstitutional. And Kentucky seemed to suggest that its declaration would deprive the statute of legal force. Thus the Kentucky legislature resolved, in its first and ninth Resolutions:

> That the several states composing the United States of America, are not united on the principle of unlimited submission to their general government; but that by compact, under the style and title of a Constitution for the United States, and of amendments thereto, they constituted a general government for special purposes, delegated to that government certain definite powers, reserving, each state to itself,

> the residuary mass of right to their own self government; and that whensoever the general government assumes undelegated powers, its acts are unauthoritative, void, and of no force: That to this compact each state acceded as a state, and is an integral party, its co-states forming as to itself, the other party: That the government created by this compact was not made the exclusive or final *judge* of the extent of the powers delegated to itself; since that would have made its discretion, and not the Constitution, the measure of its powers; but that, as in all other cases of compact among parties having no common judge, each party has an equal right to judge for itself, as well of infractions, as of the mode and measure of redress. . . .
>
> That this commonwealth does, therefore, call on its co-states for an expression of their sentiments on the acts concerning aliens, and for the punishment of certain crimes herein before specified, plainly declaring whether these acts are or are not authorized by the Federal compact. And it doubts not that . . . they will view [the general government] as seizing the rights of the states, and consolidating them in the hands of the general government with a power assumed to bind the states, (not merely in cases made federal,) but in all cases whatsoever, by laws made, not with their consent, but by others against their consent . . . ; and that the co-states, recurring to their natural right in cases not made federal, will concur in declaring these acts void and of no force, and will each unite with this commonwealth, in requesting their repeal at the next session of Congress.

The final sentence is ambiguous. Can the states themselves invalidate the Sedition Act, or can they only urge Congress to repeal it? The Kentucky Resolutions of 1799 clarified Jefferson's position in asserting that "the several states who formed [the Constitution], being sovereign and independent, have the unquestionable right to judge of its infraction and that a nullification, by those sovereignties, of all unauthorized acts done under colour of that instrument, is the rightful remedy."[70]

The Virginia Resolutions also address the issue of state nullification:

> That this Assembly doth explicitly and peremptorily declare that it views the powers of the Federal Government as resulting from the compact, to which the States are parties, as limited by the plain sense and intention of the instrument constituting that compact; as no further valid than they are authorized by the grants enumerated in that compact; and that in case of a deliberate, palpable, and dangerous exercise of other powers not granted by the said compact, the States, who are the parties thereto, have the right, and are in duty bound, to interpose for arresting the progress of the evil, and for maintaining within their respective limits, the authorities, rights, and liberties appertaining to them.

The Virginia Report elaborates:

> It appears . . . to be a plain principle, founded in common sense, illustrated by common practice, and essential to the nature of compacts, that, where resort can be had to no tribunal superior to the authority of the parties, the parties themselves must be the rightful judges, in the last resort, whether the bargain made has been pursued or violated. The Constitution of the United States was formed by the sanction of the states given by each in its sovereign capacity. It adds to the stability and dignity, as well as to the authority of the Constitution, that it rests on this legitimate and solid foundation. The states, then, being the parties to the constitutional compact, and in

70. N.E. Cunningham, Jr., ed., The Early Republic, 1789-1828, 145-146 (1968).

their sovereign capacity, it follows of necessity, that there can be no tribunal above their authority, to decide in the last resort, whether the compact made by them be violated; and, consequently, that, as the parties to it, they must themselves decide, in the last resort, such questions as may be of sufficient magnitude to require their interposition.

It does not follow, however, that because the states, as sovereign parties to their constitutional compact, must ultimately decide whether it has been violated, that such a decision ought to be interposed, either in a hasty manner, or on doubtful and inferior occasions. . . . But in the case of an intimate and constitutional union, like that of the United States, it is evident that the interposition of the parties, in their sovereign capacity, can be called for by occasions only, deeply and essentially affecting the vital principles of their political system.[71]

In the Virginia Report, Madison also responds to the objection "that the judicial authority is to be regarded as the sole expositor of the Constitution, in the last resort":

On this objection it might be observed *first,* that there may be instances of usurped power, which the forms of the Constitution would never draw within the control of the judicial department; *secondly,* that if the decisions of the judiciary be raised above the authority of the sovereign parties to the Constitution, the decision of the other departments, not carried by the forms of the Constitution before the judiciary, must be equally authoritative and final with the decisions of that department. But the proper answer to the objection is, that the resolution of the General Assembly relates to those great and extraordinary cases, in which all the forms of the Constitution may prove ineffectual against infractions dangerous to the essential rights of the parties to it. The resolution supposes that dangerous powers, not delegated, may not only be usurped and executed by the other departments, but that the judicial department also may exercise or sanction dangerous powers beyond the grant of the Constitution; and, consequently, that the ultimate right of the parties to the Constitution, to judge whether the compact has been dangerously violated, must extend to violations by one delegated authority, as well as by another; by the judiciary, as well as by the executive, or the legislature.

However true, therefore, it may be, that the judicial department, is, in all questions submitted to it by the forms of the Constitution, to decide in the last resort, this resort must necessarily be deemed the last in relation to the authorities of the other departments of the government; not in relation to the rights of the parties to the constitutional compact, from which the judicial, as well as the other departments hold their delegated trusts. On any other hypothesis, the delegation of judicial power would annul the authority delegating it; and the concurrence of this department with the others in usurped powers, might subvert for ever, and beyond the possible reach of any rightful remedy, the very Constitution which all were instituted to preserve.

The North Carolina legislature, though agreeing that the legislation was unconstitutional, refused to support the proposal that states take countermeasures against the Federal government. The Rhode Island legislature passed a resolution stating that Article III, Section 2, of the Constitution places "in the federal courts, exclusively, and in the Supreme Court of the United States, ultimately, the authority of deciding on the constitutionality of any act or law of the Congress

71. The Virginia Report at 195-96.

of the United States." It further resolved that "this legislature, in their public capacity, do not feel themselves authorized to consider and decide on the constitutionality of the Sedition and Alien laws, (so called) yet they are called upon, by the exigency of this occasion to declare that, in their private opinions, these laws are within the powers delegated to Congress, and promotive of the welfare of the United States."[72]

Rhode Island rejected not only the doctrine of nullification, but also the very idea that it had the authority to assess the Act's constitutionality. This may be the earliest suggestion of a strong notion of judicial supremacy regarding constitutional interpretation. Does rejection of the doctrine of nullification necessarily entail "exclusive" authority of assessment in the judiciary (or any other specific institution)? Contrast the view of the Rhode Island legislature with that of Andrew Jackson in his message vetoing the national bank. See also the discussion following Marbury v. Madison, infra.

Discussion

1. Return to ¶¶7-11 of McCulloch v. Maryland. Marshall, a Virginian, was clearly aware of the Kentucky and Virginia Resolutions, described by Professor H. Jefferson Powell as "among the most influential extraconstitutional, nonjudicial texts in American constitutional history" with their "vision of the United States as a league of sovereign states."[73] If you consider those paragraphs as a specific response to the Resolutions, which position do you find more persuasive?

2. The controversy that began in 1790 with Hamilton's proposal for the first national bank "demonstrated at the very outset that the Constitution had not displaced rival principles or reconciled them but had become their dialectical arena."[74] And the issues of federalism engendered by the bank controversy have continued to appear in other forms. For example, in his Inaugural Address of January 20, 1981 — without alluding to Marshall's partly contrary assertion in *McCulloch* — President Ronald Reagan remarked that "all of us need to be reminded that the Federal Government did not create the states; the states created the Federal Government"[75]

3. Does rejection of Marshall's conception of "popular sovereignty" in favor of some version of the Kentucky and Virginia Resolutions entail the legitimacy of secession, based perhaps on a notion of "breach of contract" and dissolution of the obligations to maintain membership in the political order established by the Constitution? (Might the Union, even if established by state compact, resemble marriage under the doctrines of the Roman Catholic Church, that is, indissoluble even though originating between separate persons without prior obligations to one another?) Although Madison insisted that the "Doctrines of '98" offered no support for the legitimacy of secession, many advocates of secession repeatedly cited the Resolutions to justify their position.

4. It is obvious that the "hostility" that Marshall fears in ¶1 of *McCulloch* manifested itself in 1861 with the Civil War. Consider that several of the Southern

72. The responses of Rhode Island, Massachusetts, and Vermont are reprinted in Walter Murphy, James Fleming, and Will Harris, American Constitutional Interpretation 264-265 (1986).

73. H. Jefferson Powell, The Original Understanding of Original Intent, 98 Harv. L. Rev. 885, 927 (1985).

74. Hammond, supra note 1, at 120.

75. New York Times, Jan. 21, 1981, p. 81.

States submitted the question of secession to the electorate. In Texas, for example, a referendum held on February 23, 1861, voted 46,129 to 14,697 in favor of the ordinance of secession. The electorate of some of the other states — Tennessee, North Carolina, Arkansas, and Missouri — in effect voted against secession, though three of these four then seceded. Consider the following inscription from the memorial to the Southern Confederacy in front of the Texas State Capitol:

> DIED FOR STATE RIGHTS GUARANTEED UNDER THE CONSTITUTION
>
> THE PEOPLE OF THE SOUTH, ANIMATED BY THE SPIRIT OF 1776, TO PRESERVE THEIR RIGHTS, WITHDREW FROM THE FEDERAL COMPACT IN 1861. THE NORTH RESORTED TO COERCION. THE SOUTH, AGAINST OVERWHELMING NUMBERS AND RESOURCES, FOUGHT UNTIL EXHAUSTED.

What is your response to this inscription? Consider these possibilities:

a. It expresses a clearly mistaken view of the 1787 Constitution, and the State of Texas should clearly indicate this.

b. Though it expresses an intellectually defensible view of the 1787 Constitution, that view has not prevailed, and the State of Texas should clearly indicate this.

c. The State of Texas should do absolutely nothing and leave it up to viewers to decide for themselves what they think of the inscription.

d. The State of Texas, whatever its decision about the existing inscription, should build a monument to the Union war dead, with an inscription indicating that they fought to vindicate the Constitution of 1787.

Note that none of these possibilities directly addresses the role of slavery in triggering the Civil War. We shall touch further on slavery and the onset of the war in Chapter 2. For now, consider this final possibility: The State of Texas should build a memorial to the slaves with an inscription that the war, whatever its constitutional merits (about which reasonable people may differ), was undoubtedly justified because it overthrew an iniquitous regime of chattel slavery.

Chapter 2
The Marshall Court

I. *Before Marshall; 1789-1801*[1]

The Supreme Court of the United States was not an important institution during the first decade of the new Republic. Presidents Washington and Adams had some difficulty attracting people to serve, and the rate of turnover was high. Three men were appointed chief justice during the first twelve years. John Jay resigned after six years to run for governor of New York. His successor, John Rutledge, had been appointed as an Associate in 1789 but had resigned in 1791, without ever sitting, to go to the more prestigious South Carolina Supreme Court. He was nominated to become Chief Justice of the United States Supreme Court in 1795 but failed to receive Senate confirmation. Thereafter, Oliver Ellsworth was nominated and confirmed in 1796; he served until 1800, when he resigned to accept a diplomatic post in France.

One source of discontent was the onerous duty of "riding circuit," which required each Justice to travel twice a year to sit in the federal circuit court districts. The trips were strenuous and time-consuming. In refusing President Adams' offer of reappointment as Chief Justice in 1801, Jay commented that "under a system so defective" the Court would never "obtain the energy, weight and dignity which were essential to its affording due support to the National Government, nor [would it] acquire the public confidence and respect which, as the last resort of the justice of the nation, it should possess."[2]

Without much fanfare, the Court simply assumed a power to both review the validity of state legislation that conflicted with federal treaties and statutes and to construe federal legislation in light of presumably binding constitutional requirements. Ware v. Hylton, 3 U.S. (3 Dall.) 199 (1796); Hylton v. United States, 3 U.S. (3 Dall.) 171 (1796).[3] The only decision of this period to attract much publicity — most of it negative — was Chisholm v. Georgia, 2 U.S. (2 Dall.) 419 (1793). This was a suit by two citizens of South Carolina, who were the executors of a British creditor, against the State of Georgia to recover on bonds confiscated by the state. The Supreme Court's holding that a state was liable to suit by private individuals, even though it had not waived sovereign immunity, prompted the adoption of the Eleventh Amendment: "The judicial power of the United States shall not be

1. See generally Edward Corwin, John Marshall and the Constitution (1919); Julius Goebel, Jr., 1 History of the Supreme Court of the United States, Antecedents and Beginnings to 1801 (1971); 1 Charles Warren, The Supreme Court in United States History chs. 1-3 (rev. ed. 1932).

2. Quoted in Corwin, supra note 1, at 23-24.

3. See David Currie, The Constitution in the Supreme Court: 1789-1801, 38 U. Chi. L. Rev. 819 (1981).

construed to extend to any suit in law or equity, commenced or prosecuted against one of the United States by Citizens of another State, or by Citizens or Subjects of any Foreign State."[4]

II. The Marshall Court

Between about 1796 and 1800, the Federalist Party had controlled the national government to the almost total exclusion of the Republicans, the other major party of the day. In 1800, toward the end of John Adams' term, it was evident that the Republicans would gain the presidency and control of the Congress. Federalist hopes for retaining some power lay in the judiciary. Ellsworth resigned in December 1800, and John Jay declined to serve again because of advancing age and the rigors of circuit riding. Adams then nominated his secretary of state, John Marshall, who was quickly confirmed despite doubts about the strength of his Federalist partisanship. On February 4, 1801, Marshall assumed the chief justiceship (also retaining his position as secretary of state for the month remaining of Adams' term).

References to the "________ Court," filling in the blank with the name of a Chief Justice, are sometimes simply a shorthand for periods of years and should not be taken to imply either that the Chief Justice was especially influential or that the period differed strikingly from the one that preceded or followed it. Whatever the problems of identifying a complex, multi-member court with its Chief Justice, though, it is hard to resist designating the Court of 1803-1834 as "The Marshall Court," for he was clearly the dominant figure of that period, particularly during the first two decades of his tenure, and under his leadership the Supreme Court became an important institution in the federal polity.[5]

Before Marshall, it was the practice for the justices to deliver their opinions seriatim, one after the other, in the English manner. Marshall instituted the current practice of having an "opinion of the Court" and established a tradition — not always followed in his own time and now completely dissipated — of outward unanimity.[6] Marshall himself wrote most of the Court's major constitutional opinions.

"Marshall, according to received learning, consciously furthered the political goals of the Federalist party, first by stretching the Constitution's meaning to increase national power at the expense of state power, and second, by designing constitutional doctrines that protected the upper classes' privileges against the growing democratic onslaught that in 1829 finally placed Andrew Jackson in the White House."[7] There is little doubt that the Marshall Court provided the constitutional foundations for a strong national government and created a powerful national judiciary, solicitous of property rights. But, though its decisions were

4. The amendment was drafted with the particular facts of *Chisholm*, rather than the general issue, in mind.

5. See G. Edward White, The Marshall Court and Cultural Change 1815-35 (1988).

6. See Lawrence Friedman, A History of American Law 117-118 (1973); Donald Morgan, Justice William Johnson: The First Dissenter (1954).

7. William Nelson, The Eighteenth Century Background of John Marshall's Jurisprudence, 76 Mich. L. Rev. 894 (1978).

surely motivated by these broad political ends, it would be a mistake to analyze them solely in terms of party politics. Some of the strongest pro-federalist decisions were issued — and were often unanimous — after 1811, when appointees of the Republican Presidents Jefferson and Madison constituted a majority of the Court.

III. Judicial Review of the Constitutionality of Legislation

A. Judicial Review of State Legislation

In *McCulloch,* the Marshall Court struck down Maryland's law imposing a tax on the national bank on the ground that it was inconsistent with powers delegated to and exercised by the Congress of the United States. Consider whether the *federal judiciary's* authority to examine the constitutionality of state legislation can be inferred from a combination of Articles VI and III. Here is Professor Herbert Wechsler's defense of such authority, made in response to Judge Learned Hand's claim that it is not authorized by the text of the Constitution:

H. HERBERT WECHSLER, TOWARD NEUTRAL PRINCIPLES OF CONSTITUTIONAL LAW

73 Harv. L. Rev. 1, 3-5 (1959)

... Though I have learned from past experience that disagreement with Judge Hand is usually nothing but the sheerest folly, I must make clear why I believe the power of the courts is grounded in the language of the Constitution and is not a mere interpolation. To do this you must let me quote the supremacy clause, which is mercifully short: "This Constitution, and the Laws of the United States which shall be made in Pursuance thereof; and all Treaties made, or which shall be made, under the Authority of the United States, shall be the supreme Law of the Land; and the Judges in every State shall be bound thereby, any Thing in the Constitution or Laws of any State to the Contrary notwithstanding." Judge Hand concedes that under this clause "state courts would at times have to decide whether state laws and constitutions, or even a federal statute, were in conflict with the federal constitution" but he adds that "the fact that this jurisdiction was confined to such occasions, and that it was thought necessary specifically to provide such a limited jurisdiction, looks rather against than in favor of a general jurisdiction."[8]

Are you satisfied, however, to view the supremacy clause in this way, as a grant of jurisdiction to state courts, implying a denial of the power and the duty of all others? This certainly is not its necessary meaning; it may be construed as a mandate to all of officialdom including courts, with a special and emphatic admonition that it binds the judges of the previously independent states. That the latter

8. Learned Hand, The Bill of Rights (1958).

is the proper reading seems to me persuasive when the other relevant provisions of the Constitution are brought into view.

Article III, section 1 declares that the federal judicial power "shall be vested in one supreme Court, and in such inferior Courts as the Congress may from time to time ordain and establish." This represented, as you know, one of the major compromises of the Constitutional Convention and relegated the establishment vel non of lower federal courts to the discretion of the Congress. None might have been established, with the consequence that, as in other federalisms, judicial work of first instance would all have been remitted to state courts. Article III, section 2 goes on, however, to delineate the scope of the federal judicial power, providing that it "shall extend [inter alia] to all Cases, in Law and Equity, arising under this Constitution . . ." and, further, that the Supreme Court "shall have appellate jurisdiction" in such cases "with such Exceptions, and under such Regulations as the Congress shall make." Surely this means, as section 25 of the Judiciary Act of 1789 took it to mean, that if a state court passes on a constitutional issue, as the supremacy clause provides that it should, its judgment is reviewable, subject to congressional exceptions, by the Supreme Court, in which event that Court must have no less authority and duty to accord priority to constitutional provisions than the court that it reviews. And such state cases might have encompassed every case in which a constitutional issue could possibly arise, since, as I have said, Congress need not and might not have exerted its authority to establish "inferior" federal courts. . . .

Although the Court's assertion of the power to review state legislation was not, as such, controversial, its assertion of the power to review and revise the judgments of state courts encountered some resistance. At issue was the constitutionality of section 25 of the Judicial Act of 1789, which provided for the Supreme Court review of final judgments of "the highest court . . . of a State in which a decision in the suit could be had" in three classes of cases:

> [1] . . . where is drawn in question the validity of a treaty or statute of, or an authority exercised under, the United States, and a decision is had against their validity;
>
> [2] . . . where is drawn in question the validity of a statute of, or an authority exercised under any State, on the ground of their being repugnant to the constitution, treaties or laws of the United States, and the decision is in favor of such their validity;
>
> [3] . . . where is drawn in question the construction of any clause of the constitution, or of a treaty, or statute of, or commission held under the United States, and the decision is against the title, right, privilege or exemption specially set up or claimed under it.[9]

In Martin v. Hunter's Lessee, 14 U.S. (1 Wheat.) 304 (1816), the Virginia Court of Appeals had refused to obey the Supreme Court's mandate reversing the judgment in a case involving the preemption of state laws by federal treaties. The state court had held unanimously that section 25 of the Judiciary Act of 1789, conferring federal appellate jurisdiction, was unconstitutional. The

9. The current version of §25 is 28 U.S.C. §1257.

Supreme Court again heard the case and again reversed (though to avoid another conflict, it bypassed the Virginia Court of Appeals and issued its mandate directly to the state trial court).[10] Justice Story wrote:

> [T]he constitution . . . is crowded with provisions which restrain or annul the sovereignty of the states in some of the highest branches of their prerogatives. The tenth section of the first article contains a long list of disabilities and prohibitions imposed upon the states. . . . The language of the constitution is also imperative upon the states as to the performance of many duties. It is imperative upon the state legislatures to make laws prescribing the time, places, and manner of holding elections for senators and representatives, and for electors of president and vice-president. And in these, as well as some other cases, congress have a right to revise, amend, or supercede the laws which may be passed by state legislatures. When, therefore, the states are stripped of some of the highest attributes of sovereignty, and the same are given to the United States; when the legislatures of the state are, in some respects, under the control of congress, and in every case are, under the constitution, bound by the paramount authority of the United States; it is certainly difficult to support the argument that the appellate power over the decisions of state courts is contrary to the genius of our institutions. . . .
>
> It is . . . argued, that no great public mischief can result from a construction which shall limit the appellate power of the United States to cases in their own courts . . . because state judges are bound by an oath to support the constitution of the United States, and must be presumed to be men of learning and integrity . . . [A]dmitting that the judges of the state courts are, and will be, of as much learning, integrity, and wisdom, as those of the courts of the United States, (which we very cheerfully admit,) it does not aid the argument. It is manifest that the constitution has . . . presumed (whether rightly or wrongly we do not inquire) that state attachments, state prejudices, state jealousies, and state interests, might sometimes obstruct, or control, or be supposed to obstruct or control, the regular administration of justice. . . .
>
> This is not all. A motive of another kind, perfectly compatible with the most sincere respect for state tribunals, might induce the grant of appellate power over their decisions. That motive is the importance, and even necessity of *uniformity* of decisions throughout the whole United States, upon all subjects within the purview of the constitution. Judges of equal learning and integrity, in different states, might differently interpret a statute, or a treaty of the United States, or even the constitution itself: If there were no revising authority to control these jarring and discordant judgments, and harmonize them into uniformity, the laws, the treaties, and the constitution of the United States would be different in different States, and might perhaps, never have precisely the same construction, obligation, or efficacy, in any two states. The public mischiefs that would attend such a state of things would be truly deplorable. . . .

The Court again addressed the constitutionality of section 25 in Cohens v. Virginia, 19 U.S. (6 Wheat.) 264 (1821), in which appellants, convicted of selling lottery tickets in violation of state law, claimed immunity under a congressional enactment permitting the District of Columbia to establish a lottery. Chief Justice Marshall rejected Virginia's argument that Article III did not confer appellate jurisdiction over state criminal cases:

10. 1 Charles Warren, The Supreme Court in United States History 450 (1926).

With the ample powers confided to this supreme government . . . are connected many express and important limitations on the sovereignty of the States, which are made for the same purposes. The powers of the Union, on the great subjects of war, peace, and commerce, and on many others, are in themselves limitations of the sovereignty of the States. . . . [T]he judicial power of every well-constituted government must be co-extensive with the legislative, and must be capable of deciding every judicial question which grows out of the constitution and laws. . . .

In many States the judges are dependent for office and for salary on the will of the legislature. . . . When we observe the importance which [the Constitution of the United States] attaches to the independence of judges, we are the less inclined to suppose that it can have intended to leave these constitutional questions to tribunals where this independence may not exist, in all cases where a State shall prosecute an individual who claims the protection of an act of Congress. . . .

The mischievous consequences of the construction contended for on the part of Virginia, are also entitled to great consideration. It would prostrate, it has been said, the government and its laws at the feet of every State in the Union. And would not this be its effect? What power of the government could be executed by its own means, in any State disposed to resist its execution by a course of legislation? The laws must be executed by individuals acting within the several States. If these individuals may be exposed to penalties, and if the Courts of the Union cannot correct the judgments by which these penalties may be enforced, the course of the government may be, at any time, arrested by the will of one of its members. Each member will possess a *veto* on the will of the whole. . . .

Let it be admitted, that the cases which have been put are extreme and improbable, yet there are gradations of opposition to the laws, far short of those cases, which might have a baneful influence on the affairs of the nation. Different States may entertain different opinions on the true construction of the constitutional powers of Congress. We know, that at one time, the assumption of the debts contracted by the several States, during the war of our revolution, was deemed unconstitutional by some of them. We know, too, that at other times, certain taxes, imposed by Congress have been pronounced unconstitutional. Other laws have been questioned partially, while they were supported by the great majority of the American people. We have no assurance that we shall be less divided than we have been. . . .

These collisions may take place in times of no extraordinary commotion. But a constitution is framed for ages to come, and is designed to approach immortality as nearly as human institutions can approach it. Its course cannot always be tranquil. It is exposed to storms and tempests, and its framers must be unwise statesmen indeed, if they have not provided it, as far as its nature will permit, with the means of self-preservation from the perils it may be destined to encounter. No government ought to be so defective in its organization, as not to contain within itself the means of securing the execution of its own laws against other dangers than those which occur every day. Courts of justice are the means most usually employed; and it is reasonable to expect that a government should repose on its own Courts, rather than on others.

(Upon reaching the merits, the Court held that the statute did not authorize the sale of lottery tickets beyond the city limits of Washington and affirmed the judgment of the state court.)

During the century and a half since these decisions — most recently in the wake of the *School Desegregation* cases — states have sometimes thwarted the orders and mandates of the federal judiciary.[11] But *Martin* and *Cohens* effectively settled the Supreme Court's authority to revise the judgments of state courts and, in effect, settled the federal judicial power to determine the constitutionality of state laws.

B. Judicial Review of Congressional Legislation

Oliver Wendell Holmes, Jr.:

> I do not think the United States would come to an end if we lost our power to declare an Act of Congress void. I do think the Union would be imperiled if we could not make that declaration as to the laws of the several states.[12]

Robert H. Jackson:

> [T]he power of the Supreme Court to declare acts of the *states* void under the federal Constitution presents an entirely separate issue in our history . . . [and] rests on quite different [and stronger] foundations than does the power to strike down *federal* legislation as unconstitutional.[13]

1. The Precedents for Judicial Review[14]

No provision of the Constitution explicitly authorizes the federal judiciary to review the constitutionality of acts of Congress. The extent to which those who framed and adopted the Constitution assumed or intended that the courts would exercise this power has been the subject of continuing scholarly controversy.

England provided no direct precedent for judicial review. As late as the seventeenth century, the lawmaking and law-declaring (or judicial) functions of the "High Court of Parliament" were not sharply differentiated, so that England lacked the concept of separation of powers that underlies the American institution of judicial review. Despite the settled notion that the common law embodied principles of natural or fundamental law (see pp. 105-107 infra) and despite Lord Coke's famous dictum in Bonham's Case,[15] the common law courts never assumed the authority to review acts of Parliament. England had

11. See Ch. 6 infra.
12. Oliver Wendell Holmes, Jr., Collected Legal Papers 295-296 (1920).
13. Robert H. Jackson, The Struggle for Judicial Supremacy 15 (1941).
14. See generally Judicial Review and the Supreme Court 1-12 (Levy ed. 1967); Alan Westin, Introduction and Historical Bibliography to Charles Beard, The Supreme Court and the Constitution 1-34, 133-146 (Westin ed. 1962). Compare Charles Beard, The Supreme Court and the Constitution (1912), Raoul Berger, Congress v. The Supreme Court (1969), and Henry Hart, Professor Crosskey and Judicial Review, 67 Harv. L. Rev. 1456 (1954) (book review), with Louis Boudin, Government by Judiciary (1932), Edward Corwin, Court over Constitution: A Study of Judicial Review as an Instrument of Popular Government (1938), and 2 William Crosskey, Politics and the Constitution in the History of the United States (1953).
15. 8 Co. Rep. 107a, 77 Eng. Rep. 638 (1610): "When an Act of Parliament is against common right and reason, or repugnant, or impossible to be performed, the common law will controul it, and adjudge such Act to be void. . . ." See Theodore Plucknett, Bonham's Case and Judicial Review, 40 Harv. L. Rev. 30 (1926); S.E. Thorne, Dr. Bonham's Case, 54 L.Q. Rev. 543 (1938).

no written constitution, and parliamentary supremacy was firmly established at the time of the framing of the first American constitutions. "[I]f the parliament will positively enact a thing to be done which is unreasonable," wrote Blackstone in 1765, "I know of no power in the ordinary forms of the constitution that is vested with authority to control it. . . ."[16]

Some American colonists had invoked principles of natural law to contend that the colonial courts should not enforce oppressive English legislation, and the American Revolution was justified on natural-law grounds. But if the received natural-law tradition created an atmosphere in which judicial review could flourish, that innovative American institution owed still more to John Locke's Second Treatise of Government (1690). The premise of Locke's social compact was that sovereignty did not reside in any agency of government but in "the people" themselves, who (through the American invention of written constitutions) delegated limited authority to those agencies. The legislature was the direct voice of the people, and the early republicans placed a virtually unlimited, populistic faith in the representative branch. But in the years following the Revolutionary War, as state legislatures authorized the issuance of worthless paper money, enacted sweeping debtor relief legislation, and directed oppressive measures against British loyalists, the possibility of legislative abuse — of tyranny of the majority — became increasingly apparent. One remedy was bicameralism, which the states adopted in various forms. Judicial review emerged as another remedy; if the people were sovereign, and the legislature merely their agent, then (as Hamilton later put it in The Federalist, No. 78) "where the will of the legislature declared in its statutes, stands in opposition to that of the people, declared in the constitution, the judges ought to be governed by the latter, rather than the former. They ought to regulate their decisions by the fundamental laws. . . ."[17]

By 1787, several state courts had asserted the authority to nullify legislative enactments (almost always invoking the fundamental law of the written constitution rather than unwritten natural law). Most of these tentative ventures were met with criticism, however, and some even with threats of discipline and impeachment. Thus, it cannot be said that the institution of judicial review was "established" in the states by the time of the Philadelphia convention.[18]

The "intent of the framers" is still the subject of dispute. For present purposes, it suffices to note that the general idea of judicial review was much abroad when the Constitution was framed and ratified. Whether there was a clear consensus that the federal judiciary should review the constitutionality of acts of Congress, there certainly was no consensus that it might not. The question was open, and though *Marbury* met with some criticism, it took no one by surprise.

16. Blackstone, Commentaries *91. See J.W. Gough, Fundamental Law in English Constitutional History (1955); Charles McIlwain, The High Court of Parliament and Its Supremacy (1910); Edward Corwin, The "Higher Law" Background of American Constitutional Law, 42 Harv. L. Rev. 149, 365 (1928-1929).

17. See Bernard Bailyn, The Ideological Origins of the American Revolution (1967); Carl Becker, The Declaration of Independence (1922); M.J.C. Vile, Constitutionalism and the Separation of Powers (1967); Gordon Wood, The Creation of the American Republic, 1776-1787 (1969).

18. See William Nelson, Changing Conceptions of Judicial Review: The Evolution of Constitutional Theory in the States, 1790-1860, 120 U. Pa. L. Rev. 1166 (1972).

2. *The Political Context of 1801-1803*[19]

In 1803, when *Marbury* was decided, public attention focused on the (Federalist) Court's assertion of the power — not actually exercised in the case — to restrain the conduct of the (Republican) executive. The Republicans criticized the Court both for the assertion and for examining the merits at all when it concededly lacked jurisdiction to hear the case. In the highly charged political atmosphere of the day, the fact that the Court struck down an act of Congress was a secondary issue.

In section II of this chapter, we described the events that culminated in John Marshall's appointment as Chief Justice. Two other events occurred that February that would bear on the decision in *Marbury*. First, on February 13, the Federalist Congress enacted the Circuit Court Act, which created 16 new circuit judgeships and eliminated the circuit-riding responsibilities of the justices of the Supreme Court. Although these clearly were needed reforms, the purpose and effect of the act were to cement Federalist control of the judiciary. A blatantly political provision of the Act — and no reform measure — decreased the size of the Supreme Court from six to five in order to deny the incoming Republican president the opportunity to appoint a successor to Justice Cushing, who was expected to resign shortly because of ill health. Second, and also politically motivated, was the passage two weeks later of the Organic Act of the District of Columbia, which created 42 positions for justices of the peace in the district.

Adams acted quickly to nominate party members to fill the positions under both acts, and on March 2 and 3 the Senate hastily confirmed the nominations. Jefferson was to assume the presidency on March 4, and the night of March 3 found Secretary of State John Marshall affixing the great seal of the United States to the appointees' commissions, while his brother James carted them out by the armload to deliver them. All of the commissions were signed and sealed, but in the haste and confusion of these last moments, those of several justices of the peace, including William Marbury, were left behind. Upon assuming office, Jefferson instructed James Madison, his future secretary of state, to withhold their delivery. Although Jefferson later appointed many of Adams' nominees, he did not appoint Marbury and three others, who instituted an action in the Supreme Court to compel delivery of their commissions.

In 1802, the Republican Congress repealed the Circuit Court Act (though not the Organic Act), thereby eliminating the positions of the so-called midnight judges. In order to forestall a constitutional test of the repeal and to delay the Court's decision in Marbury's case, Congress effectively abolished the 1802 terms of the Court.[20] Thus, it was not until 1803 that the Court was able to hear *Marbury*.

19. See generally Donald Dewey, Marshall Versus Jefferson: The Political Background of Marbury v. Madison (1970); 1 Warren, The Supreme Court in United States History chs. 4-5 (1926); Leonard Baker, John Marshall, A Life in the Law 394-417 (1974).

20. Section 1 of the Judiciary Act of 1789 provided that the Supreme Court "shall hold annually . . . two sessions, the one commencing the first Monday of February, and the other the first Monday of August." The Circuit Court Act of 1801 changed the two terms of court to June and December. In April 1802, immediately after abolishing the new circuit judgeships, Congress abolished the June and December terms and restored the old February, but not the old August, term. Thus the Court was adjourned from December 1801 until February 1803. (The constitutionality of the repeal act was hotly contested within and without the Congress: It was never passed on by the courts. See Felix Frankfurter & James Landis, The Business of the Supreme Court 28 n.79 (1928).)

MARBURY v. MADISON[21]

5 U.S. (1 Cranch) 137 (1803)
On Petition for Mandamus

[1] At the last term, viz. December term, 1801, William Marbury [and others] . . . moved the court for a rule to James Madison, Secretary of State of the United States, to show cause why a mandamus should not issue commanding him to cause to be delivered to them respectively their several commissions as justices of the peace in the District of Columbia. This motion was supported by affidavits of the following facts; that notice of this motion had been given to Mr. Madison; that Mr. Adams, the late president of the United States, nominated the applicants to the senate for their advice and consent to be appointed justices of the peace of the district of Columbia; that the senate advised and consented to the appointments; that commissions in due form were signed by the said president appointing them justices, &c. and that the seal of the United States was in due form affixed to the said commissions by the secretary of state; that the applicants have requested Mr. Madison to deliver them their said commissions, who has not complied with that request; and that their said commissions are withheld from them; that the applicants have made application to Mr. Madison as secretary of state of the United States at his office, for information whether the commissions were signed and sealed as aforesaid; that explicit and satisfactory information has not been given in answer to that inquiry, either by the secretary of state or any officer in the department of state; that application has been made to the secretary of the Senate for a certificate of the nomination of the applicants, and of the advice and consent of the senate, who has declined giving such a certificate; whereupon a rule was laid to show cause on the 4th day of this term. . . . Afterwards, on the 24th of February, the following opinion of the court was delivered by the Chief Justice.

[2] At the last term on the affidavits then read and filed with the clerk, a rule was granted in this case, requiring the secretary of state to show cause why a mandamus should not issue, directing him to deliver to William Marbury his commission as a justice of the peace for the county of Washington, in the district of Columbia.

[3] No cause has been shown, and the present motion is for a mandamus. The peculiar delicacy of this case, the novelty of some of its circumstances, and the real difficulty attending the points which occur in it, require a complete exposition of the principles, on which the opinion to be given by the court, is founded. . . .

[4] In the order in which the court has viewed this subject, the following questions have been considered and decided.

21. See generally William Van Alstyne, A Critical Guide to Marbury v. Madison, 1969 Duke L.J. 1.

¶¶1, 2. A writ of mandamus is an order issued by a court to a government officer or lower court commanding the performance of a ministerial (i.e., nondiscretionary) duty pertaining to the office.

¶4. In the course of the opinion, the court holds (first) that on the facts and law Marbury is entitled to the commission; (second) that a judicial remedy will not interfere improperly with the executive's constitutional discretion; and (third) that mandamus is the appropriate remedy, that respondent Madison cannot assert sovereign immunity, that §13 of the Judiciary Act of 1789 authorizes the issuance of mandamus in this case; but that §13 is unconstitutional.

This is an extraordinary way to order the issues. Courts customarily determine initially whether they have jurisdiction to decide the case and only then, if the answer is affirmative, proceed to other issues. See, e.g., Ex parte McCardle, 74 U.S. (7 Wall.) 506, 512, 514 (1869):

1st. Has the applicant a right to the commission he demands?

2dly. If he has a right, and that right has been violated, do the laws of his country afford him a remedy?

3dly. If they do afford him a remedy, is it a mandamus issuing from this court?

[5] The first object of inquiry is, 1st. Has the applicant a right to the commission he demands?

[6] His right originates in an act of congress passed in February 1801, concerning the district of Columbia . . . [which] enacts, "that there shall be appointed . . . such number of discreet persons to be justices of the peace as the president of the United States shall, from time to time think expedient, to continue in office for five years.

[7] It appears, from the affidavits, that in compliance with this law, a commission for William Marbury as a justice of peace for the county of Washington, was signed by John Adams, then president of the United States; after which the seal of the United States was affixed to it; but the commission has never reached the person for whom it was made out. . . .

[8] Some point of time must be taken, when the power of the executive over an officer, not removable at his will, must cease. That point of time must be, when the constitutional power of appointment has been exercised. And this power has been exercised, when the last act, required from the person possessing the power has been performed: this last act is the signature of the commission. . . .

[9] The commission being signed, the subsequent duty of the secretary of state is prescribed by law, and not to be guided by the will of the president. He is to affix the seal of the United States to the commission, and is to record it. This is not a proceeding which may be varied, if the judgment of the executive shall suggest one more eligible; but is a precise course accurately marked out by law, and is to be strictly pursued. . . .

> The first question necessarily is that of jurisdiction; for if the act . . . takes away the jurisdiction [of this Court], it is useless, if not improper, to enter into any discussion of other questions. . . . Without jurisdiction the court cannot proceed at all in any cause. Jurisdiction is power to declare the law, and when it ceases to exist, the only function remaining to the court is that of announcing the fact and dismissing the cause.

Professor William Van Alstyne notes that Marshall has been criticized for deciding unnecessary questions in *Marbury*: "If the Court determined that it had no jurisdiction, it would have no occasion to reach the matter of 'peculiar delicacy' [i.e., the amenability of a cabinet officer to suit]. . . . It was therefore improper for Marshall to begin as he did" (supra note 21, at 7). But Van Alstyne comes to Marshall's defense:

> Of at least equal delicacy was the question of the Court's . . . capacity to second guess the constitutionality of acts of Congress. Since the Court might avoid the necessity of confronting the constitutionality of the Judiciary Act by disposing of the case on other grounds (assuming that it were to find Marbury not entitled to his commission), it should seek to do so where possible, as here. . . . Under this view, perhaps Marshall cannot be faulted for postponing consideration of judicial review and the constitutionality of the Judiciary Act until he had first exhausted other possible bases for disposing of the case.

How valid is this defense? Granting that it is desirable to avoid unnecessary constitutional questions, Marshall did not in fact avoid any constitutional question. Is Van Alstyne suggesting that it was important that Marshall demonstrate that he *could not* avoid the constitutional question? Is Van Alstyne implying that a judicial opinion does or should describe fully and chronologically the justices' thought processes leading to a decision, rather than "justify" a decision once it is arrived at?

Note Van Alstyne's suggestion that there was "clearly an 'issue' of sorts which preceded any of those touched upon in the opinion. Specifically, it would appear that Marshall should have recused himself in view of his substantial involvement in the background of this controversy" (supra note 21, at 8). See note, Disqualification of Judges and Justices in the Federal Courts, 86 Harv. L. Rev. 736 (1973).

[10] It has also occurred as possible, and barely possible, that the transmission of the commission, and the acceptance thereof, might be deemed necessary to complete the right of the plaintiff. The transmission of the commission is a practice, directed by convenience, but not by law. It cannot, therefore, be necessary to constitute the appointment. . . . The appointment is the sole act of the president; the transmission of the commission is the sole act of the officer to whom that duty is assigned, and may be accelerated or retarded by circumstances which can have no influence on the appointment. A commission is transmitted to a person already appointed; not to a person appointed or not, as the letter inclosing the commission should happen to get into the post-office and reach him in safety, or to miscarry. . . .

[11] If the transmission of a commission be not considered as necessary to give validity to an appointment, still less is its acceptance. The appointment is the sole act of the president; the acceptance is the sole act of the officer, and is, in plain common sense, posterior to the appointment. As he may resign, so may he refuse to accept: but neither the one nor the other is capable of rendering the appointment a nonentity. . . .

[12] It is, therefore, decidedly the opinion of the court, that when a commission has been signed by the president, the appointment is made; and that the commission is complete, when the seal of the United States has been affixed to it by the secretary of state.

[13] Where an officer is removable at the will of the executive, the circumstance which completes his appointment is of no concern; because the act is at any time revocable; and the commission may be arrested, if still in the office. But when the officer is not removable at the will of the executive, the appointment is not revocable, and cannot be annulled: it has conferred legal rights which cannot be resumed. The discretion of the executive is to be exercised, until the appointment has been made. But having once made the appointment, his power over the office is terminated, in all cases where, by law, the officer is not removable by him. The right to the office is then in the person appointed, and he has the absolute unconditional power of accepting or rejecting it.

[14] Mr. Marbury, then, since his commission was signed by the President and sealed by the secretary of state, was appointed; and as the law creating the office, gave the officer a right to hold for five years, independent of the executive, the appointment was not revocable, but vested in the officer legal rights, which are protected by the laws of his country.

[15] To withhold his commission, therefore, is an act deemed by the court not warranted by law, but violative of a vested legal right.

[16] This brings us to the second inquiry; which is, 2dly. If he has a right, and that right has been violated, do the laws of his country afford him a remedy?

[17] The very essence of civil liberty certainly consists in the right of every individual to claim the protection of the laws whenever he receives an injury. One of the first duties of government is to afford that protection. . . .

[18] The government of the United States has been emphatically termed a government of laws, and not of men. It will certainly cease to deserve this high appellation, if the laws furnish no remedy for the violation of a vested legal right.

¶14. Marshall's assumption that Congress generally can prevent the president from revoking executive appointments was disapproved in Myers v. United States, 272 U.S. 52 (1926).

[19] If this obloquy is to be cast on the jurisprudence of our country, it must arise from the peculiar character of the case.

[20] It behooves us then to inquire whether there be in its composition any ingredient which shall exempt it from legal investigation, or exclude the injured party from legal redress. . . .

[Marshall then holds that Madison is not entitled to "sovereign immunity" merely because he is sued in his official capacity as secretary of state. The justiciability of executive conduct depends, rather, on its nature. Certain matters — "political questions" — are not meet for judicial determination because they are committed to the executive's discretion.]

[21] . . . But where a specific duty is assigned by law, and individual rights depend upon the performance of that duty, it seems equally clear that the individual who considers himself injured, has a right to resort to the laws of his country for a remedy. . . .

[22] The power of nominating to the senate, and the power of appointing the person nominated, are political powers, to be exercised by the President according to his own discretion. When he has made an appointment, he has exercised his whole power, and his discretion has been completely applied to the case. . . .

[23] The question, whether a right has vested or not, is in its nature, judicial, and must be tried by the judicial authority. . . .

[24] So, if [Marbury] conceives that, by virtue of his appointment, he has a legal right, either to the commission which has been made out for him, or to a copy of that commission, it is . . . a question examinable in a court. . . .

[25] It is then the opinion of the court,

1st. That by signing the commission of Mr. Marbury, the president of the United States appointed him a justice of peace, for the county of Washington, in the district of Columbia; and that the seal of the United States, affixed thereto by the secretary of state, is conclusive testimony of the verity of the signature, and of the completion of the appointment; and that the appointment conferred on him a legal right to the office for the space of five years.

[26] 2dly. That, having this legal title to the office, he has a consequent right to the commission; a refusal to deliver which, is a plain violation of that right, for which the laws of his country afford him a remedy.

[27] It remains to be inquired whether,

3dly. He is entitled to the remedy for which he applies. This depends on,

1st. The nature of the writ applied for, and,

2dly. The power of this court. . . .

[Marshall discusses the circumstances under which mandamus is appropriate at common law, to conclude:]

[28] This, then, is a plain case for a mandamus, either to deliver the commission, or a copy of it from the record; and it only remains to be inquired,

Whether it can issue from this court.

[29] The act to establish the judicial courts of the United States authorizes the supreme court "to issue writs of mandamus, in cases warranted by the principles and usages of law, to any courts appointed, or persons holding office, under the authority of the United States,"

¶¶29-30. The relevant provision is §13 of the Judiciary Act of 1789:

[30] The secretary of state, being a person holding an office under the authority of the United States, is precisely within the letter of the description; and if this court is not authorized to issue a writ of mandamus to such an officer, it must be because the law is unconstitutional, and therefore absolutely incapable of conferring the authority, and assigning the duties which its words purport to confer and assign.

[31] The constitution vests the whole judicial power of the United States in one supreme court, and such inferior courts as congress shall, from time to time, ordain and establish. This power is expressly extended to all cases arising under the laws of the United States; and consequently, in some form, may be exercised over the present case; because the right claimed is given by a law of the United States.

> [T]he Supreme Court shall have exclusive jurisdiction of all controversies of a civil nature, where a state is a party, except between a state and its citizens; and except also between a state and citizens of other states, or aliens, in which latter case it shall have original but not exclusive jurisdiction. And shall have exclusively all such jurisdiction of suits or proceedings against ambassadors, or other public ministers, or their domestics, or domestic servants, as a court of law can have or exercise consistently with the law of nations: and original, but not exclusive jurisdiction of all suits brought by ambassadors, or other public ministers, or in which a consul, or vice consul, shall be a party. And the trial of issues in fact in the Supreme Court, in all actions at law against citizens of the United States, shall be by jury. The Supreme Court shall also have appellate jurisdiction from the circuit courts and courts of the several states, in the cases herein after specially provided for; and shall have power to issue writs of prohibition to the district courts, when proceeding as courts of admiralty and maritime jurisdiction, and writs of mandamus, in cases warranted by the principles and usages of law, to any courts appointed, or persons holding office, under the authority of the United States.

Note that the first portion of §13, following Article III, §2, of the Constitution, grants the Supreme Court original jurisdiction in cases affecting, inter alia, "public ministers." Read in isolation, the term might be thought to include the secretary of state of the United States, but the context and history of Article III make quite clear that "this refers to diplomatic and consular representatives accredited to the United States by foreign powers. . . ." Ex parte Gruber, 269 U.S. 302 (1925). See also The Federalist, No. 81 (Hamilton). Why does Article III put those cases that it does within the Court's original jurisdiction?

Marshall asserts, virtually without discussion, that §13 grants the Court jurisdiction to issue a writ of mandamus in this case. Is this the most plausible interpretation of §13? Consider the location of the "mandamus" sentence in the provision and the relevant punctuation. Cf. 28 U.S.C. §1651: "Writs: The Supreme Court and all courts established by Act of Congress may issue all writs necessary or appropriate in aid of their respective jurisdictions and agreeable to the usages and principles of law." Should Marshall have been influenced by the fact that many of the same persons who drafted Article III also drafted the Judiciary Act of 1789 and by the canon (long established in England) that ambiguous statutes should be construed, where possible, in a manner consistent with fundamental law (in this case the fundamental written law of the Constitution)?

¶¶31-41. ¶¶31-41 hold §13 of the Judiciary Act of 1789 unconstitutional insofar as it authorizes the Court to issue an original writ of mandamus in a case not within its original jurisdiction. Outline Marshall's reasoning. An important step in the argument applies the sensible presumption that every clause of the Constitution (or of any written document) has meaning and effect. Marshall contends that any construction of Article III, §2, other than his own would make surplusage of parts of Article III. But is this necessarily so? If Congress cannot diminish the original jurisdiction conferred by the Constitution, does it follow, either as a matter of textual interpretation or policy, that Congress cannot *add* to it?

Note that the provision of Article III, §2, conferring original jurisdiction is not qualified (as is the provision conferring appellate jurisdiction) by the clause allowing congress to make "exceptions" and "regulations." Does this suggest a reading of Article III besides Marshall's that would give it both meaning and purpose? Professor Van Alstyne finds it ironic that Marshall's construction of Article III weakens the Court's power "in the very case celebrated because of its alleged aggrandizement of judicial power. Under Marshall's construction, Congress may not add to the Court's original jurisdiction, but it may, by simple act, *subtract* from the Court's appellate jurisdiction, such jurisdiction being subject to 'such Exceptions . . . as the Congress shall make.' It is really cases within its appellate jurisdiction, however, where nearly all of the Court's significant work is done." Van Alstyne also argues that Article III can be read to provide "that Congress may except certain cases otherwise subject only to

[32] In the distribution of this power it is declared that "the supreme court shall have original jurisdiction in all cases affecting ambassadors, other public ministers and consuls, and those in which a state shall be a party. In all other cases, the supreme court shall have appellate jurisdiction."

[33] It has been insisted, at the bar, that as the original grant of jurisdiction, to the supreme and inferior courts, is general, and the clause, assigning original jurisdiction to the supreme court, contains no negative or restrictive words; the power remains to the legislature, to assign original jurisdiction to that court in other cases than those specified in the article which has been recited; provided those cases belong to the judicial power of the United States.

[34] If it had been intended to leave it in the discretion of the legislature to apportion the judicial power between the supreme and inferior courts according to the will of that body, it would certainly have been useless to have proceeded further than to have defined the judicial power, and the tribunals in which it should be vested. The subsequent part of the section is mere surplusage, is entirely without meaning, if such is to be the construction. If congress remains at liberty to give this court appellate jurisdiction, where the constitution has declared their jurisdiction shall be original; and original jurisdiction where the constitution has declared it shall be appellate; the distribution of jurisdiction, made in the constitution, is form without substance.

[35] Affirmative words are often, in their operation, negative of other objects than those affirmed; and in this case, a negative or exclusive sense must be given to them or they have no operation at all.

[36] It cannot be presumed that any clause in the constitution is intended to be without effect; and therefore such a construction is inadmissible, unless the words require it.

[37] If the solicitude of the convention, respecting our peace with foreign powers, induced a provision that the supreme court should take original jurisdiction in cases which might be supposed to affect them; yet the clause would have proceeded no further than to provide for such cases, if no further restriction on the powers of congress had been intended. That they should have appellate jurisdiction in all other cases, with such exceptions as congress might make, is no restriction; unless the words be deemed exclusive of original jurisdiction.

[38] When an instrument organizing fundamentally a judicial system, divides it into one supreme, and so many inferior courts as the legislature may ordain and establish; then enumerates its powers, and proceeds so far to distribute them, as to define the jurisdiction of the supreme court by declaring the cases in which it shall take original jurisdiction, and that in others it shall take appellate jurisdiction; the plain import of the words seems to be, that in one class of cases its jurisdiction is original, and not appellate; in the other it is appellate, and not original. If any other construction would render the clause inoperative, that is an ad-

the Court's appellate jurisdiction [only] *by adding them to the Court's original jurisdiction*" (supra note 21, at 32-33). Is this persuasive?

Marbury's holding that the original jurisdiction of the Supreme Court cannot be enlarged remains the law. But the dictum that Congress cannot confer appellate jurisdiction in the enumerated cases within the Court's original jurisdiction has not been followed. See, e.g., Ames v. Kansas, 111 U.S. 449 (1884).

ditional reason for rejecting such other construction, and for adhering to their obvious meaning.

mandamus = appellate

[39] To enable this court then to issue a mandamus, it must be shown to be an exercise of appellate jurisdiction, or to be necessary to enable them to exercise appellate jurisdiction.

[40] It has been stated at the bar that the appellate jurisdiction may be exercised in a variety of forms, and that if it be the will of the legislature that a mandamus should be used for that purpose, that will must be obeyed. This is true, yet the jurisdiction must be appellate, not original.

[41] It is the essential criterion of appellate jurisdiction, that it revises and corrects the proceedings in a cause already instituted, and does not create that cause. Although, therefore, a mandamus may be directed to courts, yet to issue such a writ to an officer for the delivery of a paper, is in effect the same as to sustain an original action for that paper, and therefore seems not to belong to appellate, but to original jurisdiction. Neither is it necessary in such a case as this, to enable the court to exercise its appellate jurisdiction.

[42] The authority, therefore, given to the supreme court, by the act establishing the judicial courts of the United States, to issue writs of mandamus to public officers, appears not to be warranted by the constitution; and it becomes necessary to inquire whether a jurisdiction, so conferred, can be exercised.

[43] The question, whether an act, repugnant to the constitution, can become the law of the land, is a question deeply interesting to the United States; but, happily, not of an intricacy proportioned to its interest. It seems only necessary to recognize certain principles, supposed to have been long and well established, to decide it.

[44] That the people have an original right to establish, for their future government, such principles as, in their opinion, shall most conduce to their own happiness, is the basis, on which the whole American fabric has been erected. The exercise of this original right is a very great exertion; nor can it, nor ought it to be frequently repeated. The principles, therefore, so established, are deemed fundamental. And as the authority, from which they proceed, is supreme, and can seldom act, they are designed to be permanent.

¶¶44-50. What do these paragraphs establish? Although Marshall has not yet explicitly addressed the question of *judicial* review of the constitutionality of congressional enactments, doesn't this discussion strongly imply that, in the absence of a check by the judiciary, the Constitution would be "alterable when the legislature shall please to alter it" (¶47)? To analyze this argument, one must understand the ambiguities inherent in "shall please," a term that can connote at least three different things. See Ronald Dworkin, The Model of Rules, 35 U. Chi. L. Rev. 14, 32-34 (1967), on which the following relies heavily:

1. *Plenary discretion.* A decisionmaker may be able to "do as he pleases" in the sense that no standards (rules, principles, or other criteria) set by an official authority govern his decisions in a particular sphere. In this sense, the president may do as he pleases in decorating the Oval Room of the White House. We may criticize his taste, but we cannot criticize him for disregarding or misinterpreting officially set standards or misapplying them to the facts. To give another example, the president may well have plenary discretion, subject only to limited review by the Senate (see Article II, §2, cl. 2), to choose his cabinet officers and plenary discretion subject to no review to choose most other advisers. We may criticize the president for choosing fools or fanatics but not for disregarding any standards to which he is obligated to adhere.

2. *Standard-application discretion.* A decisionmaker may have discretion in interpreting and applying standards by which he is bound. Discretion of this sort exists whenever the governing standards are vague or where the decision must depend on his considering and weighing many factors. A committee charged with awarding a prize "to that student who has made the greatest contribution to the school" has discretion of this sort, as does a law school professor charged with recommending to a

Rousseau!

[45] This original and supreme will organizes the government, and assigns, to different departments, their respective powers. It may either stop here; or establish certain limits not to be transcended by those departments.

[46] The government of the United States is of the latter description. The powers of the legislature are defined, and limited; and that those limits may not be mistaken, or forgotten, the constitution is written. To what purpose are powers limited, and to what purpose is that limitation committed to writing, if these limits may, at any time, be passed by those intended to be restrained? The distinction, between a government with limited and unlimited powers, is abolished, if those limits do not confine the persons on whom they are imposed, and if acts prohibited and acts allowed, are of equal obligation. It is a proposition too plain to be contested, that the constitution controls any legislative act repugnant to it; or, that the legislature may alter the constitution by an ordinary act.

[47] Between these alternatives there is no middle ground. The constitution is either a superior, paramount law, unchangeable by ordinary means, or it is on a level with ordinary legislative acts, and like other acts, is alterable when the legislature shall please to alter it.

[48] If the former part of the alternative be true, then a legislative act contrary to the constitution is not law: if the latter part be true, then written constitutions are absurd attempts, on the part of the people, to limit a power, in its own nature illimitable.

[49] Certainly all those who have framed written constitutions contemplate them as forming the fundamental and paramount law of the nation, and consequently the theory of every such government must be, that an act of the legislature, repugnant to the constitution, is void.

---

judge the student who will make the "best law clerk." In both cases, the delegations of authority implicitly make some criteria relevant and others irrelevant, but decisionmakers may disagree whether a particular criterion is relevant and may disagree as to the weight to be given it. A decisionmaker with this kind of discretion may be criticized for misinterpreting the standards implicit in the delegation or for exercising "poor judgment" in the weighting of particular standards or in applying them to the facts. (Standard-application discretion is independent of whether the decisionmaker's decision is final and unreviewable. The prize committee may have the final say; the clerkship committee's decision is reviewable by the judge to whom it recommends.)

3. *Finality.* A decisionmaker may have the power to do "as he pleases" in the sense that his decision is final and unreviewable. The power of finality may be exercised within or without the sphere of the decisionmaker's discretion. For example: the president's choice of decor for the Oval Room is a final exercise of plenary discretion. A soccer referee's decision to award a point to one or the other team is final, even if she acts in willful disregard of the facts or the rules of the game. We may criticize her decision as erroneous — even lawless — and may bar her from refereeing future games. But there is no remedy for a particular instance of error or abuse of power (save disobedience to the rules that make her decision final). Similarly, a criminal jury's decision to acquit is final — even in the face of unequivocal evidence of guilt and in disregard of the judge's proper instructions.

Getting back to *Marbury,* in what sense can Congress "do as it pleases" if there is no judicial review of the constitutionality of its enactment? In what sense can the Court "do as it pleases" if it has the final say as to constitutionality? Consider Charles Evans Hughes' remark that "we are under a Constitution, but the Constitution is what the judges say it is." Speech Before the Elmira Chamber of Commerce, in Hughes, Addresses and Papers 133, 139 (1908). Consider Justice Story's statement in Martin v. Hunter's Lessee, 14 U.S. (1 Wheat.) 304 (1816): "It is always a doubtful course, to argue against the use or existence of a power, from the possibility of its abuse. . . . From the very nature of things, the absolute right of decision, in the last resort, must rest somewhere — wherever it may be vested it is susceptible of abuse."

[50] This theory is essentially attached to a written constitution, and is consequently to be considered, by this court, as one of the fundamental principles of our society. It is not therefore to be lost sight of in the further consideration of this subject.

[51] If an act of the legislature, repugnant to the constitution, is void, does it, notwithstanding its invalidity, bind the courts, and oblige them to give it effect? Or, in other words, though it be not law, does it constitute a rule as operative as if it was a law? This would be to overthrow in fact what was established in theory; and would seem, at first view, an absurdity too gross to be insisted on. It shall, however, receive a more attentive consideration.

[52] It is emphatically the province and duty of the judicial department to say what the law is. Those who apply the rule to particular cases, must of necessity expound and interpret that rule. If two laws conflict with each other, the courts must decide on the operation of each.

¶¶51-54. What is Marshall's argument based on the "province and duty of the judicial department"? If one concedes that the Constitution is "law" and that it is paramount to legislative enactments, does it necessarily follow that the *judiciary* has authority to decide whether a congressional enactment violates the Constitution? Is the Constitution a law, just like other laws that come within a court's purview? Consider Judge Learned Hand's response:

> It is of course true that, when a court decides whether a constitution authorizes a statute, it must first decide what each means, and that, so far, is the kind of duty that courts often exercise, just as they decide conflicts between earlier and later precedents. But if a court, having concluded that a constitution did not authorize the statute, goes on to annul it, its power to do so depends upon an authority that is not involved when only statutes or precedents are involved. For a later statute will prevail over an earlier, if they conflict, because a legislature confessedly has authority to change the law as it exists. So too when a court finds two precedents in conflict, it must follow the later one, if that be a decision of a higher court, and it is free to do so if it be one of its own, because, again, confessedly it has authority to change its mind. But when a court declares that a constitution does not authorize a statute, it reviews and reverses an earlier decision of the legislature: and however well based its authority to do so may be, it does not follow from what it does in other instances in which the same question does not arise. . . .

The Bill of Rights, 9-10 (1958).

What earlier decision of the legislature does a court review and reverse when it "declares that a constitution does not authorize a statute"? Does Congress implicitly make a constitutional decision with respect to each piece of legislation it enacts?

In appraising Marshall's argument, consider that many European and South American nations have written constitutions as well as courts that perform essentially the same functions as our courts, but that their courts often do not adjudge the substantive constitutionality of legislation. Note also that, in nonconstitutional contexts, courts are sometimes required to accept as binding legal and factual determinations by other bodies, even though the courts may believe such determinations to be erroneous. See, e.g., 9 U.S.C. §10; United Steelworkers v. Enterprise Wheel & Car Corp., 363 U.S. 593 (1960).

Compare Marshall's argument with Hamilton's in The Federalist, No. 78:

> The interpretation of the laws is the proper and peculiar province of the courts. A constitution is, in fact, and must be regarded by the judges as a fundamental law. It therefore belongs to them to ascertain its meaning, as well as the meaning of any particular act proceeding from the legislative body. If there should happen to be an irreconcilable variance between the two, that which has the superior obligation and validity ought, of course, to be preferred; or, in other words, the Constitution ought to be preferred to the statute, the intention of the people of the intention of their agents.
>
> Nor does this conclusion by any means suppose a superiority of the judicial to the legislative power. It only supposes that the power of the people is superior to both; and that where the will of the legislature, declared in its statutes, stands in opposition to that of the people, declared in the Constitution, the judges ought to be governed by the latter rather than the former. They ought to regulate their decisions by the fundamental laws, rather than by those which are not fundamental.

[53] So if a law be in opposition to the constitution; if both the law and the constitution apply to a particular case, so that the court must either decide that case conformably to the law, disregarding the constitution; or conformably to the constitution, disregarding the law; the court must determine which of these conflicting rules governs the case. This is of the very essence of judicial duty.

move on why written const. are good but could be destroyed

[54] If then the courts are to regard the constitution; and the constitution is superior to any ordinary act of the legislature, the constitution, and not such ordinary act, must govern the case to which they both apply.

[55] Those then who controvert the principle that the constitution is to be considered, in court, as a paramount law, are reduced to the necessity of maintaining that courts must lose their eyes on the constitution, and see only the law.

[56] This doctrine would subvert the very foundation of all written constitutions. It would declare that an act, which, according to the principles and theory of our government, is entirely void; is yet, in practice, completely obligatory. It would declare, that if the legislature shall do what is expressly forbidden, such act, notwithstanding the express prohibition, is in reality effectual. It would be giving to the legislature a practical and real omnipotence, with the same breath which professes to restrict their powers within narrow limits. It is prescribing limits, and declaring that those limits may be passed at pleasure.

[57] That it thus reduces to nothing what we have deemed the greatest improvement on political institutions — a written constitution — would of itself be sufficient, in America, where written constitutions have been viewed with so much reverence, for rejecting the construction. But the peculiar expressions of the constitution of the United States furnish additional arguments in favour of its rejection.

¶56. This paragraph implies an argument for judicial review reminiscent of Hamilton's in The Federalist, No. 78:

> By a limited Constitution, I understand one which contains certain specified exceptions to the legislative authority; such, for instance, as that it shall pass no bills of attainder, no ex-post-facto laws, and the like. Limitations of this kind can be preserved in practice no other way than through the medium of courts of justice, whose duty it must be to declare all acts contrary to the manifest tenor of the Constitution void. Without this, all the reservations of particular rights or privileges would amount to nothing. . . .
>
> If it be said that the legislative body are themselves the constitutional judges of their own powers, and that the construction they put upon them is conclusive upon the other departments, it may be answered, . . . [i]t is far more rational to suppose, that the courts were designed to be an intermediate body between the people and the legislature, in order, among other things, to keep the latter within the limits assigned to their authority. . . .
>
> [The] independence of judges is . . . requisite to guard the Constitution and the rights of individuals from the effects of those ill humours which the arts of designing men, or the influence of particular conjunctures, sometimes disseminate among the people themselves, and which, though they speedily give place to better information, and more deliberate reflection, have a tendency in the meantime, to occasion dangerous innovations in the government, and serious oppressions of the minor party in the community.

See also Ronald Dworkin's defense of Marshall's argument at ¶¶51-56 — that "the principle that no man should be judge in his own cause [was] so fundamental a part of the idea of legality that Marshall would have been entitled to disregard it only if the Constitution had expressly denied judicial review." Dworkin, The Jurisprudence of Richard Nixon, The New York Review of Books, May 4, 1972, at 27. In other words, the legislature may not be the final arbiter of the constitutionality of its own enactments.

¶57. Here, as in ¶¶49-50, Marshall seeks support for his argument in the fact that ours is a *written* constitution. Granting that the argument for judicial review would be more difficult to maintain if our constitution were not written, does the fact that it is written affirmatively support the argument? What purposes, other than providing guidance for the judiciary, can a written constitution serve? In

[58] The judicial power of the United States is extended to all cases arising under the constitution.

[59] Could it be the intention of those who gave this power, to say that, in using it, the constitution should not be looked into? That a case arising under the constitution should be decided without examining the instrument under which it arises?

[60] This is too extravagant to be maintained.

[61] In some cases then, the constitution must be looked into by the judges. And if they can open it at all, what part of it are they forbidden to read, or to obey?

[62] There are many other parts of the constitution which serve to illustrate this subject.

[63] It is declared that "no tax or duty shall be laid on articles exported from any state." Suppose a duty on the export of cotton, of tobacco, or of flour; and a suit instituted to recover it. Ought judgment to be rendered in such a case? Ought the judges to close their eyes on the constitution, and only see the law?

[64] The constitution declares that "no bill of attainder of ex post facto law shall be passed."

[65] If, however, such a bill should be passed and a person should be prosecuted under it; must the court condemn to death those victims whom the constitution endeavors to preserve?

[66] "No person," says the constitution, "shall be convicted of treason unless on the testimony of two witnesses to the same overt act, or on confession in open court."

---

any case, wouldn't you expect the authorization for judicial review, if there were any, to appear in the text of a written constitution?

¶¶58-61. Marshall here makes an argument based on the text of Article III, §2 — "The judicial Power shall extend to all Cases . . . arising under this Constitution. . . ." Outline the necessary steps of the argument, some of which may be only implicit in Marshall's discussion.

Note initially that Article III, §2, is in terms only a grant of jurisdiction. Some jurisdictional provisions — e.g., the Article III provisions relating to admiralty and suits between states — have been held to confer a general lawmaking power. See Hart & Wechsler 264-267, 809-821. But jurisdiction does not entail a general lawmaking or law-interpreting authority over all or any issues in the case. For example, in cases coming within the diversity jurisdiction, federal courts must adhere to (even erroneous) state court interpretations of state statutes and constitutions as well as to state judge-made law. See Erie R.R. v. Tompkins, 304 U.S. 64 (1938); Hart & Wechsler 667-755.

Nonetheless, wouldn't it be pointless to confer federal jurisdiction over "Cases arising under this Constitution" if no issues of constitutional interpretation were open to the courts? But if one concedes this much, does it follow that *all* issues of constitutional interpretation are open to federal judiciary, and in particular does it follow that issues of the constitutionality of acts of Congress are open? At least two other kinds of cases might arise under the Constitution. First, as we discussed above, pp. 71-75, the argument for federal judicial review of allegedly unconstitutional acts of *state* legislatures, judges, and officials is very strong, but without the "arising under the Constitution" clause, there would be no federal jurisdiction in many such cases. Second, it might be thought that the courts should consider claims that *federal officers* have acted unconstitutionally. The colonial experience gave the framers good cause to distrust executive officials; moreover, might not one reasonably conclude that less deference is due the actions of lower-level officers than those of Congress or of the president himself?

(The question posed in the last sentence of ¶61 is the wrong one, isn't it? It is not a matter of what *parts* of the Constitution the judges may look into, but under what circumstances they may look into it.)

¶¶62-68. You will not again encounter such easy constitutional issues as these. Does the possibility that Congress might enact blatantly unconstitutional legislation entail or imply judicial authority to hold the legislation unconstitutional? To whom is each of these provisions immediately addressed? To whom is the provision involved in *Marbury* immediately addressed?

[67] Here the language of the constitution is addressed especially to the courts. It prescribes, directly for them, a rule of evidence not to be departed from. If the legislature should change that rule, and declare one witness, or a confession *out* of court, sufficient for conviction, must the constitutional principle yield to the legislative act?

[68] From these, and many other selections which might be made, it is apparent, that the framers of the constitution contemplated that instrument, as a rule for the government of *courts*, as well as of the legislature.

[69] Why otherwise does it direct the judges to take an oath to support it? This oath certainly applies, in an especial manner, to their conduct in their official character. How immoral to impose it on them, if they were to be used as the instruments, and the knowing instruments, for violating what they swear to support!

[70] The oath of office, too, imposed by the legislature, is completely demonstrative of the legislative opinion on this subject. It is in these words, "I do solemnly swear that I will administer justice without respect to persons, and do equal right to the poor and to the rich; and that I will faithfully and impartially discharge all the duties incumbent on me as ______, according to the best of my abilities and understanding, agreeably to *the constitution,* and laws of the United States."

¶¶69-71. Does Marshall's "oath of office" argument prove too much? See Article VI, cl. 3, which requires all state and federal officials to swear or affirm to support the Constitution, and consider this excerpt from Judge Gibson's dissent in Eakin v. Raub, 12 Serg. & Rawle 330 (Pa. 1825), which involved the authority of the Pennsylvania Supreme Court to review the constitutionality of acts of the state legislature. Judge Gibson's opinion refers to and counters almost every one of Marshall's arguments in *Marbury:*

> The oath to support the constitution is not peculiar to the judges, but is taken indiscriminately by every officer of the government and is designed rather as a test of the political principles of the man, than to bind the officer in the discharge of his duty: otherwise, it were difficult to determine, what operation it is to have in the case of a recorder of deeds, for instance, who, in the execution of his office, has nothing to do with the constitution. But granting it to relate to the official conduct of the judge, as well as every other officer, and not to his political principles, still, it must be understood in reference to supporting the constitution, *only as far as that may be involved in his official duty;* and consequently, if his official duty does not comprehend an inquiry into the authority of the legislature, neither does his oath.
>
> . . . Granting that the object of the oath is to secure a support of the constitution in the discharge of official duty, its terms may be satisfied by restraining it to official duty in the exercise of the *ordinary* judicial powers. Thus, the constitution may furnish a rule of construction, where a particular interpretation of a law would conflict with some constitutional principle; and such interpretation, where it may, is always to be avoided. But the oath was more probably designed to secure the powers of each of the different branches from being usurped by any of the rest; for instance, to prevent the house of representatives from erecting itself into a court of judicature, or the supreme court from attempting to control the legislature: and in this view, the oath furnishes an argument equally plausible *against* the right of the judiciary. . . . The official oath, then, relates only to the official conduct of the officer, and does not prove that he ought to stray from the path of his ordinary business, to search for violations of duty in the business of others: nor does it, as supposed, define the powers of the officer.
>
> But do not the judges do a *positive* act in violation of the constitution, when they give effect to an unconstitutional law? Not if the law has been passed according to the forms established in the constitution. The fallacy of the question is, in supposing that the judiciary adopts the acts of the legislature as its own; whereas, the enactment of a law and the interpretation of it are not concurrent acts, and as the judiciary is not required to concur in the enactment, neither is it in the breach of the constitution which may be the consequence of the enactment; the fault is imputable to the legislature, and on it the responsibility exclusively rests.

[71] Why does a judge swear to discharge his duties agreeably to the constitution of the United States, if that constitution forms no rule for his government? If it is closed upon him, and cannot be inspected by him?

[72] If such be the real state of things, this is worse than solemn mockery. To prescribe, or to take this oath, becomes equally a crime.

[73] It is also not entirely unworthy of observation, that in declaring what shall be the *supreme* law of the land, the *constitution* itself is first mentioned; and not the laws of the United States generally, but those only which shall be made in *pursuance* of the constitution, have that rank.

[74] Thus, the particular phraseology of the constitution of the United States confirms and strengthens the principle, supposed to be essential to all written constitutions, that a law repugnant to the constitution is void; and that *courts*, as well as other departments, are bound by that instrument.

[75] The rule must be discharged.

¶¶73-74. Chief Justice Marshall makes an almost offhand reference to the supremacy clause of Article VI of the Constitution. Recall Professor Wechsler's argument based on Articles VI and III. If Wechsler is persuasive in arguing that federal judges can properly inquire into any question under the United States Constitution that state judges can inquire into, does it also imply that state judges can inquire into the constitutionality of congressional legislation? (Professor Wechsler assumes that it does, but does not explain why.)

Note the different way that Article VI treats "laws" and "treaties" and consider Van Alstyne's suggestion that "[t]he phrase 'in pursuance' might also mean merely that only those statutes adopted by Congress *after* the re-establishment and reconstitution of Congress pursuant to the Constitution itself shall be the supreme law of the land, whereas acts of the earlier Continental Congress constituted merely under the Articles of Confederation, would not necessarily be supreme and binding upon the several states" (supra note 21, at 21).

Assuming that you find the Marshall-Wechsler argument or, for that matter, any other textual argument for judicial review, persuasive, does it entail that the scope or nature of judicial review is what *Marbury* held it to be? Consider Dietze, Judicial Review in Europe, 55 Mich. L. Rev. 539, 541 (1957): "European courts have usually tested the formal constitutionality of the laws. This consists of a review of the process of enactment. If it was discovered that the procedural requirements of the constitution had not been complied with, the law in question was declared void. On the other hand, the testing of the content of a legislative act for its 'intrinsic' constitutionality was the exception rather than the rule."

¶75. Consider Robert McCloskey, The American Supreme Court 40-42 (1960):

> The decision is a masterwork of indirection, a brilliant example of Marshall's capacity to sidestep danger while seeming to court it, to advance in one direction while his opponents are looking in another. . . . The danger of a head-on clash with the Jeffersonians was averted by the denial of jurisdiction: but, at the same time, the declaration that the commission was illegally withheld scotched any impression that the Court condoned the administration's behavior. These negative maneuvers were artful achievements in their own right. But the touch of genius is evident when Marshall, not content with having rescued a bad situation, seizes the occasion to set forth the doctrine of judicial review. It is easy for us to see in retrospect that the occasion was golden. The attention of the Republicans was focused on the question of Marbury's commission, and they cared very little how the Court went about justifying a hands-off policy so long as that policy was followed. Moreover, the Court was in a delightful position, so common in its history but so confusing to its critics, of rejecting and assuming power in a single breath, for the Congress had tried here to give the judges an authority they could not constitutionally accept and the judges were high-mindedly refusing. The moment for immortal statement was at hand all right, but only a judge of Marshall's discernment could have recognised it.

Note: The First and Last Word

Marbury can read more or less imperialistically — to claim more or less power for the judicial branch. Nothing in the opinion, or in any subsequent opinion of the Supreme Court, implies that *only* the judiciary may make constitutional decisions. Nothing implies, for example, that Congress and the Executive are relieved of their responsibility to assess the constitutionality of their proposed conduct before they act — as the first Congress and Executive did with respect to the chartering of the first Bank of the United States. What was, and continues to be, an open question is whether and when the Court has the last word. Recall President Jackson's view on this when vetoing the bill to re-charter the Bank of the United States. Other Presidents, Congresses, and officials have also asserted the power to determine constitutional questions contrary to prior judicial determinations.

The question of who (if anyone) has the last word has been perennial at least since *Marbury* and will arise throughout this casebook.

C. Judicial Review in a Democratic Polity

1. The Countermajoritarian Difficulty

"The root difficulty," wrote the late Alexander Bickel, "is that judicial review is a counter-majoritarian force in our society":

> There are various ways of sliding over this ineluctable reality. Marshall did so when he spoke of enforcing, in behalf of "the people," the limits that they have ordained for the institutions of a limited government. And it has been done ever since in much the same fashion by all too many commentators. Marshall himself followed Hamilton, who in the 78th Federalist denied that judicial review implied a superiority of the judicial over the legislative power — denied, in other words, that judicial review constituted control by an unrepresentative minority of an elected majority. "It only supposes," Hamilton went on, "that the power of the people is superior to both; and that where the will of the legislature, declared in its statutes, stands in opposition to that of the people, declared in the Constitution, the judges ought to be governed by the latter rather than the former." But the word "people" so used is an abstraction . . . obscuring the reality that when the Supreme Court declares unconstitutional a legislative act or the action of an elected executive, it thwarts the will of representatives of the actual people of the here and now; it exercises control, not in behalf of the prevailing majority, but against it. That, without mystic overtones, is what actually happens. It is an altogether different kettle of fish, and it is the reason the charge can be made that judicial review is undemocratic.
>
> Most assuredly, no democracy operates by taking continuous nose counts on the broad range of daily governmental activities. Representative democracies — that is to say, all working democracies — function by electing certain men for certain periods of time, then passing judgment periodically on their conduct of public office. . . . The elected officials, however, are expected to delegate some of their tasks to men of their own appointment, who are not directly accountable at the polls. The whole operates under public scrutiny and criticism — but not at all times or in all parts. What we mean by democracy, therefore, is much more sophisticated and complex

than the making of decisions in town meeting by a show of hands. It is true also that even decisions that have been submitted to the electoral process in some fashion are not continually resubmitted, and they are certainly not continually unmade. Once run through the process, once rendered by "the people" (using the term now in its mystic sense, because the reference is to the people in the past), myriad decisions remain to govern the present and the future despite what may well be fluctuating majorities against them at any given time. A high value is put on stability, and that is also a counter-majoritarian factor. Nevertheless, although democracy does not mean constant reconsideration of decisions once made, it does mean that a representative majority has the power to accomplish a reversal. This power is of the essence, and no less so because it is often merely held in reserve.

... [N]othing in the further complexities and perplexities of the system ... can alter the essential reality that judicial review is a deviant institution in the American democracy.[22]

At the end of this section we will reconsider the premise that "judicial review is a deviant institution in the American polity." For the moment, however, assume the truth of the premise. Being deviant, the practice of judicial review then demands some special justification.

2. *Justifications for Judicial Review*

a. Supervising Inter- and Intra-governmental Relations

The federal judiciary has at times supervised two systems of governmental relations: (1) the federal system, involving relations between the national and state governments and relations among the states themselves; and (2) the internal national system, involving the allocation of powers among the legislative, executive, and judicial branches.

1. Much of Part One examines judicial supervision of the federal system, focusing on the limits of congressional and state powers under the commerce clause. The essential legitimacy of federal judicial review of state legislation has not been seriously questioned since Martin v. Hunter's Lessee. As Justices Holmes and Jackson remarked (page 75 supra), the practice was essential to the realization and maintenance of the federalist vision. On the other hand, judicial review of congressional legislation, designed to protect the states against incursions by the national government, has been controversial, and the Court has scarcely engaged in judicial review of this sort since 1937.

2. Although the allocation of powers within the national government is hedged with checks and balances among the various branches, the Court has not played a major role in policing the boundaries between its coordinate branches. Its interventions have been infrequent and problematic enough to lead one modern commentator to propose that the Court withdraw entirely from the field. Professor Jesse Choper writes:

22. Alexander Bickel, The Least Dangerous Branch 16-18 (1962).

The federal judiciary should not decide constitutional questions concerning the respective powers of Congress and the President vis-à-vis one another; rather, the ultimate constitutional issues of whether executive action (or inaction) violates the prerogatives of Congress or whether legislative action (or inaction) transgresses the realm of the President should be held to be nonjusticiable, their final resolution to be remitted to the interplay of the national political process.[23]

b. Preserving Fundamental Values

Alexander Bickel argued that the protection of fundamental values was a primary justification for judicial review. Bickel recognized that the Court's justification in *Marbury,* based on judicial competence to interpret the written text of the Constitution, did not encompass many of the Court's decisions, consider, e.g., part 2 of *McCulloch,* but went on to argue for institutional competence of a different sort:

> [M]any actions of government have two aspects: their immediate, necessarily intended, practical effects, and their perhaps unintended or unappreciated bearing on values we hold to have more general and permanent interest. It is a premise we deduce not merely from the fact of a written constitution but from the history of the race, and ultimately as a moral judgment of the good society, that government should serve not only what we conceive from time to time to be our immediate material needs but also certain enduring values. This in part is what is meant by government under law. But such values do not present themselves ready-made. They have a past always, to be sure, but they must be continually derived, enunciated, and seen in relevant application. And it remains to ask which institution of our government — if any single one in particular — should be the pronouncer and guardian of such values.
>
> Men in all walks of public life are able occasionally to perceive this second aspect of public questions. Sometimes they are also able to base their decisions on it; that is one of the things we like to call acting on principle. Often they do not do so, however, particularly when they sit in legislative assemblies. There, when the pressure for immediate results is strong enough and emotions ride high enough, men will ordinarily prefer to act on expediency rather than take the long view. Possibly legislators — everything else being equal — are as capable as other men of following the path of principle, where the path is clear or at any rate discernible. Our system, however, like all secular systems, calls for the evolution of principle in novel circumstances, rather than only for its mechanical application. Not merely respect for the rule of established principles but the creative establishment and renewal of a coherent body of principled rules — that is what our legislatures have proven themselves ill equipped to give us . . .
>
> [C]ourts have certain capacities for dealing with matters of principle that legislatures and executives do not possess: judges have, or should have, the leisure, the training, and the insulation to follow the ways of the scholar in pursuing the ends of government. This is crucial in sorting out the enduring values of a society, and it is not something that institutions can do well occasionally, while operating for the most part with a different set of gears. It calls for a habit of mind, and for undeviating

23. Jesse Choper, Judicial Review and the National Political Process 263 (1980).

institutional customs. Another advantage that courts have is that questions of principle never carry the same aspect for them as they did for the legislature or the executive. Statutes, after all, deal typically with abstract or dimly foreseen problems. The courts are concerned with the flesh and blood of an actual case. This tends to modify, perhaps to lengthen everyone's view. It also provides an extremely salutary proving ground for all abstractions; it is conducive, in a phrase of Holmes, to thinking things, not words, and thus to the evolution of principle by a process that tests as it creates.

Their insulation and the marvelous mystery of time give courts the capacity to appeal to men's better natures, to call forth their aspirations, which may have been forgotten in the moment's hue and cry. This is what Justice Stone called the opportunity for "the sober second thought." Hence it is that the courts . . . are also a great and highly effective educational institution. . . . The Justices in Dean Rostow's phrase, "are inevitably teachers in a vital national seminar." No other branch of the American government is nearly so well equipped [as the judiciary] to conduct one. And such a seminar can do a great deal to keep our society from becoming so riven that no court will be able to save it. Of course, we have never quite been that society in which the spirit of moderation is so richly in flower that no court need save it.

Thus, as Professor Henry M. Hart, Jr., has written, . . . the Court appears "predestined in the long run, not only by the thrilling tradition of Anglo-American law but also by the hard facts of its position in the structure of American institutions, to be a voice of reason, charged with the creative function of discerning afresh and of articulating and developing impersonal and durable principles. . . ." This line of thought may perhaps blunt, if it does not meet, the force of all the arguments on the other side. No doubtful consistency with democratic theory has not been established. The heat of the democratic faith is government by the consent of the governed. The further premise is not incompatible that the good society not only will want to satisfy the immediate needs of the greatest number but also will strive to support and maintain enduring general values. I have followed the view that the elected institutions are ill fitted, or not so well fitted as the courts, to perform the latter task. This rests on the assumption that the people themselves, by direct action at the ballot box, are surely incapable of sustaining a working system of general values specifically applied. But that much we assume throughout, being a representative, deliberative democracy. Matters of expediency are not generally submitted to direct referendum. Nor should matters of principle, which require even more intensive deliberation, be so submitted.[24]

c. Protecting the Integrity of Democratic Processes

In Democracy and Distrust: A Theory of Judicial Review (1980), John Hart Ely rejects the vindication of fundamental values as a justification for judicial review and offers instead what he calls a "participation-oriented, representation-reinforcing" model. His theory builds on Justice Stone's suggestion in footnote 4 of United States v. Carolene Products Co., p. 545 infra, that the judiciary should scrutinize legislation (1) that "restricts those political processes which can ordinarily be expected to bring about repeal of undesirable legislation" or (2) that is based on "prejudice against discrete and insular minorities, which tends seriously to curtail the operation of those political processes ordinarily to be relied upon to protect minorities." Ely's thesis is that, "unlike an approach geared to the judicial

24. Bickel, supra note 22, at 24-27.

imposition of 'fundamental values,' the representation reinforcing orientation . . . is not inconsistent with, but on the contrary is entirely supportive of, the American system of representative democracy. It [is devoted] to policing the mechanisms by which the system seeks to ensure that our elected representatives will actually represent." (Ely, Democracy and Distrust at 101-102.)

Paralleling Justice Stone's two categories, Ely argues that democratic "malfunction occurs when the *process* is undeserving of trust" — when "(1) the ins are choking off the channels of political changes to ensure that they will stay in and the outs will stay out, or (2) though no one is actually denied a voice or a vote, representatives beholden to an effective majority are systematically disadvantaging some minority out of simple hostility or a prejudiced refusal to recognize commonalities of interest, and thereby denying that minority the protection afforded other groups by a representative system." (Id. at 103.) Representation-reinforcing judicial review protects interests of three sorts: (1) It protects freedom of speech and freedom of the press "because they are critical to the functioning of an open and effective democratic process" (Id. at 104); (2) it protects voting rights of the sort involved in the one person/one vote cases and the poll tax case, because the franchise is "central to a right of participation in the democratic process"; and (3) through the suspect classification doctrine, it protects minorities against defects of democratic process resulting from prejudice.[25]

3. *The Countermajoritarian Difficulty Challenged*

Several contemporary political scientists have challenged the premise that judicial review presents a "countermajoritarian difficulty." In his influential article, Decision-Making in a Democracy: The Supreme Court as a National Policy-Maker,[26] Professor Robert Dahl questions the very assumption that "the Court's policy decisions can be interpreted sensibly in terms of a 'majority' versus a 'minority' ":[27]

> In this respect the Court is no different from the rest of the political leadership. Generally speaking, policy at the national level is the outcome of conflicts, bargaining, and agreement among minorities; the process is neither minority rule nor majority rule but what might better be called *minorities* rule, where one aggregation of minorities achieves policies opposed by another aggregation.

Conceding that judicial review would nonetheless pose a problem if the Court systematically thwarted congressional policy, Dahl suggests that the rate of change of the Court's personnel makes this unlikely:[28]

> Over the whole history of the Court, on the average one new justice has been appointed every twenty-two months. Thus a president can expect to appoint about two

25. Professor Ely's thesis has hardly gone unchallenged. See, e.g., Symposium on Democracy and Distrust, 77 Va. L. Rev. 631 (1991).
26. 6 J. Pub. L. 279 (1957).
27. Id. at 294.
28. Id. at 284-285.

> new justices during one term of office; and if this were not enough to tip the balance on a normally divided Court, he is almost certain to succeed in two terms. . . . The fact is, then, that the policy views dominant on the Court are never for long out of line with the policy views dominant among the lawmaking majorities of the United States. Consequently it would be most unrealistic to suppose that the Court would, for more than a few years at most, stand against any major alternatives sought by a lawmaking majority.[29]

Dahl goes on to examine instances in which the Court has struck down significant congressional legislation: In all but a few cases, either the Court reflected an actual or nascent consensus (e.g., the post-Reconstruction compromise with the South), or else its decisions were quickly reversed or overcome. The Court substantially delayed the implementation of national policy in only three areas — the income tax, child labor laws, and worker's compensation for longshoremen and harbor workers. Dahl concludes:[30]

> Except for short-lived transitional periods when the old alliance is disintegrating and the new one is struggling to take control of political institutions, the Supreme Court is inevitably part of the dominant national alliance. As an element in the political leadership of the dominant alliance, the Court of course supports the major policies of the alliance. By itself the Court is almost powerless to affect the course of national policy. . . .
>
> The Supreme Court is not, however, simply an *agent* of the alliance. It is an essential part of the political leadership and possesses some bases of power of its own, the most important of which is the unique legitimacy attributed to its interpretations of the Constitution. This legitimacy the Court jeopardizes if it flagrantly opposes the major policies of the dominant alliance; such a course of action, as we have seen, is one in which the Court will not normally be tempted to engage.
>
> It follows that within the somewhat narrow limits set by the basic policy goals of the dominant alliance, the Court *can* . . . often determine important questions of timing, effectiveness, and subordinate policy. . . .
>
> [T]he Court is least likely to be successful in blocking a determined and persistent lawmaking majority on a major policy and most likely to succeed against a "weak" majority; e.g., a dead one, a transient one, a fragile one, or one weakly united upon a policy of subordinate importance.

In Freedom of Speech: The Supreme Court amd Judicial Review (1966), Martin Shapiro builds on Dahl's observations to make a different defense of judicial review. Whether or not the Court's policies generally mirror those of the "political branches" of the national government, the political branches are far from the paradigms of democracy our civics textbooks make them out to be; by compensating for defects elsewhere in the system, the Court may actually contribute to the overall representativeness of the government. Shapiro surveys the congressional committee system, the role of seniority, the power of lobbyists, the presidential nominating conventions, the electoral college, the myriad federal agencies, and the relations among those agencies, their parallel congressional committees, and the industries subject to agency regulation, to conclude:

29. From 1952 to 1975, thirteen new justices were appointed (an average interval of 21 months). President Eisenhower appointed five justices during his two terms: Kennedy, two: Johnson, two; and Nixon four in one term.

30. Dahl, supra note 26, at 293-294, 286 (the last paragraph is taken from earlier in the article).

> Now, the lawmaker, whom the modest [i.e., those favoring judicial restraint] so reverently endow with democracy's banner, is none other than precisely this combination of bureaucracy, President, and Congress, for quite obviously, all three are major participants in the shaping of our laws. In short, the lawmaker to whom the nasty old undemocratic Supreme Court is supposed to yield so reverently because of his greater democratic virtues is the entire mass of majoritarian-anti-majoritarian, elected-appointed, special interest-general interest, responsible-irresponsible elements that make up American national politics. If we are off on a democratic quest, the dragon begins to look better and St. George worse and worse. . . . In fact there are not three branches of government but many centers of decision-making which range from more to less "democratic" and from greater to lesser power, depending on the particular issue involved. . . .

Professor Choper rejects the "sophisticated" argument that "the so-called political branches . . . are by no means as democratic as standard belief would hold and that the Court is much more subject to the popular will than conventional wisdom would grant." He asserts that, all things considered, "the Supreme Court is not as democratic as the Congress or President, and the institution of judicial review is not as majoritarian as the lawmaking process." Choper also responds to the argument that judicial review promotes democracy by protecting individual liberties.[31]

> The difficulty with this position is that it commingles substance with procedure. The Supreme Court does advance democratic values by rejecting political action that threatens individual liberty. . . . But irrespective of the *content* of its decisions, the *process* of judicial review is not democratic because the Court is not a politically responsible institution. . . . Although the Supreme Court may play a vital role in the preservation of the American democratic system, the procedure of judicial review is in conflict with a fundamental principle of democracy — majority rule under conditions of political freedom.

The persuasiveness of Choper's response may depend on what one means by "democracy." Most critics as well as advocates of activist judicial review hold to a concept of democracy that includes minority rights as well as majority rule, what Robert Bork describes as "Madisonian democracy," as distinguished from a purely majoritarian or populist concept:

> A Madisonian system is not completely democratic, if by "democratic" we mean completely majoritarian. It assumes that in wide areas of life majorities are entitled to rule for no better reason [than] that they are majorities. . . . The model also has a counter-majoritarian premise, however, for it assumes that there are some areas of life a majority should not control. There are some things a majority should not do to us no matter how democratically it decides to do them. These are areas properly left to individual freedom, and coercion by the majority in these aspects of life is tyranny. . . .
>
> Some see the model as containing an inherent, perhaps an insoluble, dilemma. Majority tyranny occurs if legislation invades the areas properly left to individual freedom. Minority tyranny occurs if the majority is prevented from ruling where its

31. Choper, supra note 23, at 58.

power is legitimate. Yet, quite obviously, neither the majority nor the minority can be trusted to define the freedom of the other.[32]

Can the dilemma be solved? If not, how can one defend a choice between judicial activism and restraint?[33]

IV. The Protection of Property Rights

FLETCHER v. PECK

10 U.S. (6 Cranch) 87 (1810)

Error to the Circuit Court for the District of Massachusetts

[This case arose out of the notorious Yazoo land-grant scandal. In 1795, a majority of the Georgia legislature had been bribed to convey some 35 million acres of state land to private companies at the bargain price of about 1½¢ per acre. In 1796 the legislature rescinded the grant, but not before large parcels had been sold to northern investors. A suit on a warranty of title presented the question whether the 1796 rescission could affect the rights of bona fide purchasers.[34]]

MARSHALL, C.J. . . .

The importance and the difficulty of the questions, presented by these pleadings, are deeply felt by the court. The lands in controversy vested absolutely in James Gunn and others, the original grantees, by the conveyance of the governor, made in pursuance of an act of assembly, to which the legislature was fully competent. Being thus in full possession of the legal estate, they, for a valuable consideration, conveyed portions of the land to those who were willing to purchase. If the original transaction was infected with fraud, these purchasers did not participate in it, and had no notice of it. They were innocent. Yet the legislature of Georgia has involved them in the fate of the first parties to the transaction, and, if the act be valid, has annihilated their rights also. The legislature of Georgia was a party to this transaction; and for a party to pronounce its own deed invalid, whatever cause may be assigned for its invalidity, must be considered as a mere act of power, which must find its vindication in a train of reasoning not often heard in courts of justice. . . .

If a suit be brought to set aside a conveyance obtained by fraud, and the fraud be clearly proved, the conveyance will be set aside, as between the parties; but the rights of third persons, who are purchasers without notice, for a valuable consideration, cannot be disregarded. . . . All titles would be insecure, and the intercourse between man and man would be very seriously obstructed, if this principle be overturned. A court of chancery, therefore, had a bill been brought to set aside the conveyance made to James Gunn and others, as being obtained by improper practices with the legislature, whatever might have been its decision as

32. Robert Bork, Neutral Principles and Some First Amendment Problems, 47 Ind. L.J. 1, 2-3 (1971).

33. See Paul Brest, The Fundamental Rights Controversy: The Essential Contradictions of Normative Constitutional Scholarship, 90 Yale L.J. 1063, 1096-1105 (1981).

34. See C. Peter Magrath, Yazoo — Law and Politics in the New Republic (1966).

respected the original grantees, would have been bound, by its own rules, and by the clearest principles of equity, to leave unmolested those who were purchasers, without notice, for a valuable consideration.

If the legislature felt itself absolved from those rules of property which are common to all the citizens of the United States, and from those principles of equity which are acknowledged in all our courts, its act is to be supported by its power alone, and the same power may divest any other individual of his lands, if it shall be the will of the legislature so to exert it.

It is not intended to speak with disrespect of the legislature of Georgia, or of its acts. Far from it. The question is a general question, and is treated as one. For although such powerful objections to a legislative grant, as are alleged against this, may not again exist, yet the principle, on which alone this rescinding act is to be supported, may be applied to every case to which it shall be the will of any legislature to apply it. The principle is this: that a legislature may, by its own act, divest the vested estate of any man whatever, for reasons which shall, by itself, be deemed sufficient. . . .

Is the power of the legislature competent to the annihilation of such title, and to a resumption of the property thus held? The principle asserted is, that one legislature is competent to repeal any act which a former legislature was competent to pass; and that one legislature cannot abridge the powers of a succeeding legislature. The correctness of this principle, so far as respects general legislation, can never be controverted. But, if an act be done under a law, a succeeding legislature cannot undo it. The past cannot be recalled by the most absolute power. Conveyances have been made, those conveyances have vested legal estates, and, if those estates may be seized by the sovereign authority, still, that they originally vested is a fact, and cannot cease to be a fact. When, then, a law is in its nature a contract, when absolute rights have vested under that contract, a repeal of the law cannot divest those rights; and the act of annulling them, if legitimate, is rendered so by a power applicable to the case of every individual in the community.

It may well be doubted, whether the nature of society and of government does not prescribe some limits to the legislative power; and if any be prescribed, where are they to be found, if the property of an individual, fairly and honestly acquired, may be seized without compensation? . . . The constitution of the United States declares that no state shall pass any bill of attainder, ex post facto law, or law impairing the obligation of contracts.

Does the case now under consideration come within this prohibitory section of the constitution? In considering this very interesting question, we immediately ask ourselves, what is a contract? Is a grant a contract? A contract is a compact between two or more parties, and is either executory or executed. An executory contract is one in which a party binds himself to do, or not to do, a particular thing; such was the law under which the conveyance was made by the governor. A contract executed is one in which the object of contracts is performed; and this, says Blackstone, differs in nothing from a grant. The contract between Georgia and the purchasers was executed by the grant. A contract executed, as well as one which is executory, contains obligations binding on the parties. A grant, in its own nature, amounts to an extinguishment of the right of the grantor, and implies a contract not to re-assert that right. A party is, therefore, always estopped by his own grant.

Since, then, in fact, a grant is a contract executed, the obligation of which still continues, and since the constitution uses the general term contract, without distinguishing between those which are executory and those which are executed, it must be construed to comprehend the latter as well as the former. . . .

If, under a fair construction of the constitution, grants are comprehended under the term contracts, is a grant from the state excluded from the operation of the provision? Is the clause to be considered as inhibiting the state from impairing the obligation of contracts between two individuals, but as excluding from that inhibition contracts made with itself? The words themselves contain no such distinction. They are general, and are applicable to contracts of every description. If contracts made with the state are to be exempted from their operation, the exception must arise from the character of the contracting party, not from the words which are employed.

Whatever respect might have been felt for the state sovereignties, it is not to be disguised, that the framers of the constitution viewed, with some apprehension, the violent acts which might grow out of the feelings of the moment; and that the people of the United States, in adopting that instrument, have manifested a determination to shield themselves and their property from the effects of those sudden and strong passions to which men are exposed. The restrictions on the legislative power of the states are obviously founded in this sentiment; and the constitution of the United States contains what may be deemed a bill of rights for the people of each state.

No state shall pass any bill of attainder, ex post facto law, or law impairing the obligation of contracts. A bill of attainder may affect the life of an individual, or may confiscate his property, or may do both. In this form, the power of the legislature over the lives and fortunes of individuals is expressly restrained. What motive, then, for implying, in words which import a general prohibition to impair the obligation of contracts, an exception in favor of the right to impair the obligation of those contracts into which the state may enter?

The state legislatures can pass no ex post facto law. An ex post facto law is one which renders an act punishable in a manner in which it was not punishable when it was committed. Such a law may inflict penalties on the person, or may inflict pecuniary penalties which swell the public treasury. The legislature is then prohibited from passing a law by which a man's estate, or any part of it, shall be seized for a crime which was not declared, by some previous law, to render him liable to that punishment. Why, then, should violence be done to the natural meaning of words for the purpose of leaving to the legislature the power of seizing, for public use, the estate of an individual, in the form of a law annulling the title by which he holds that estate? The court can perceive no sufficient grounds for making this distinction. This rescinding act would have the effect of an ex post facto law. It forfeits the estate of Fletcher for a crime not committed by himself, but by those from whom he purchased. This cannot be effected in the form of an ex post facto law, or bill of attainder; why then, is it allowable in the form of a law annulling the original grant?

The argument in favor of presuming an intention to except a case, not excepted by the words of the constitution, is susceptible of some illustration from a principle originally ingrafted in that instrument, though no longer a part of it. The constitution, as passed, gave the courts of the United States jurisdiction in suits brought against individual states. A state, then, which violated its own contract was suable in the courts of the United States for that violation. Would it have been a defence in such a suit to say, that the state had passed a law absolving itself from the contract? It is scarcely to be conceived, that such a defence could be set up. And yet, if a state is neither restrained by the general principles of our political institutions, nor by the words of the constitution, from impairing the obligation of its own contracts, such a defence would be a valid one. This feature is no longer found in the constitution; but it aids in the construction of those clauses with which it was originally associated.

It is, then, the unanimous opinion of the court, that, in this case, the estate having passed into the hands of a purchaser for a valuable consideration, without notice, the state of Georgia was restrained, either by general principles which are common to our free institutions, or by the particular provisions of the constitution of the United States, from passing a law whereby the estate of the plaintiff in the premises so purchased could be constitutionally and legally impaired and rendered null and void. . . .

JOHNSON, J.

In this case, I entertain, on two points, an opinion different from that which has been delivered by the court.

I do not hesitate to declare, that a state does not possess the power of revoking its own grants. But I do it, on a general principle, on the reason and nature of things; a principle which will impose laws even on the Deity. . . .

The right of jurisdiction is essentially connected to, or rather identified with, the national sovereignty. To part with it, is to commit a species of political suicide. In fact, a power to produce its own annihilation, is an absurdity in terms. It is a power as utterly incommunicable to a political as to a natural person. But it is not so with the interests or property of a nation. Its possessions nationally are in no wise necessary to its political existence; they are entirely accidental, and may be parted with, in every respect, similarly to those of the individuals who compose the community. When the legislature have once conveyed their interest or property in any subject to the individual, they have lost all control over it; have nothing to act upon; it has passed from them; is vested in the individual; becomes intimately blended with his existence, as essentially so as the blood that circulates through his system. The government may indeed demand of him the one or the other, not because they are not his, but because whatever is his, is his country's. . . .

I have thrown out these ideas, that I may have it distinctly understood, that my opinion on this point is not founded on the provision in the constitution of the United States, relative to laws impairing the obligation of contracts. It is much to be regretted, that words of less equivocal signification had not been adopted in that article of the constitution. There is reason to believe, from the letters of Publius, which are well known to be entitled to the highest respect, that the object of the convention was to afford a general protection to individual rights against the acts of the state legislatures. Whether the words, "acts impairing the obligation of contracts," can be construed to have the same force as must have been given to the words "obligation and *effect* of contracts," is the difficulty in my mind.

There can be no solid objection to adopting the technical definition of the word "contract," given by Blackstone. The etymology, the classical signification, and the civil law idea of the word, will all support it. But the difficulty arises on the word "obligation," which certainly imports an existing moral or physical necessity. Now, a grant or conveyance by no means necessarily implies the continuance of an obligation, beyond the moment of executing it. . . .

I enter with great hesitation upon this question, because it involves a subject of the greatest delicacy and much difficulty. The states and the United States are continually legislating on the subject of contracts, prescribing the mode of authentication, the time within which suits shall be prosecuted for them, in many cases, affecting existing contracts by the laws which they pass, and declaring them to cease or lose their effect for want of compliance, in the parties, with such statutory provisions. All these acts appear to be within the most correct limits of legislative powers, and most beneficially exercised, and certainly could not have been intended to be affected by this constitutional provision; yet where to draw the line, or how to define or limit the words, "obligation of contracts," will be found a subject of extreme difficulty.

To give it the general effect of a restriction of the state powers in favor of private rights, is certainly going very far beyond the obvious and necessary import of the words, and would operate to restrict the states in the exercise of that right which every community must exercise, of possessing itself of the property of the individual, when necessary for public uses; a right which a magnanimous and just government will never exercise without amply indemnifying the individual, and which perhaps amounts to nothing more than a power to oblige him to sell and convey, when the public necessities require it. . . .

Discussion

1. *Language and purpose.* During the depression following the Revolutionary War, many states enacted debtor relief laws, which modified contractual obligations or the procedures available to creditors for enforcing the obligations (for example, by staying proceedings to foreclose mortgages). The contract clause of Article I, section 10, was designed to preclude a recurrence of such legislation. See Home Building & Loan Association v. Blaisdell, 290 U.S. 398 (1934) (Sutherland, J., dissenting), page 343 infra.

Given this background of the clause, is Marshall's approach to the contract clause consistent with his suggestion in *McCulloch* that interpretation requires reading the language of a provision in the light of the purpose for which it was adopted? The answer may depend on the *level of generality* on which the purpose is conceived. Articulate the purpose of the contract clause narrowly enough to foreclose its application to the Georgia statute in *Fletcher*. Now articulate it broadly enough to justify Marshall's interpretation. How can one determine which is the correct level of generality on which to articulate the purpose of the provision?

2. *Judicial inquiry into legislative motivation.* The Court in *Fletcher* was also asked to invalidate the grant because of the Georgia legislature's corruption in enacting the original conveyance. Marshall responded:

> That corruption should find its way into the governments of our infant republics, and contaminate the very source of legislation, or that impure motives should contribute to the passage of a law, or the formation of a legislative contract, are circumstances most deeply to be deplored. How far a court of justice would, in any case, be competent, on proceedings instituted by the state itself, to vacate a contract thus

formed, and to annul rights acquired, under that contract, by third persons having no notice of the improper means by which it was obtained, is a question which the court would approach with much circumspection. It may well be doubted how far the validity of a law depends upon the motives of its framers, and how far the particular inducements, operating on members of the supreme sovereign power of a state, to the formation of a contract by that power, are examinable in a court of justice. If the principle be conceded, that an act of the supreme sovereign power might be declared null by a court, in consequence of the means which procured it, still would there be much difficulty in saying to what extent those means must be applied to produce this effect. Must it be direct corruption, or would interest or undue influence of any kind be sufficient? Must the vitiating cause operate on a majority, or on what number of the members? Would the act be null, whatever might be the wish of the nation, or would its obligation or nullity depend upon the public sentiment?

If the majority of the legislature be corrupted, it may well be doubted, whether it be within the province of the judiciary to control their conduct, and, if less than a majority act from impure motives, the principle by which judicial interference would be regulated, is not clearly discerned.

Whatever difficulties this subject might present, when viewed under aspects of which it may be susceptible, this court can perceive none in the particular pleadings now under consideration.

This is not a bill brought by the state of Georgia, to annul the contract, nor does it appear to the court, by this count, that the state of Georgia is dissatisfied with the sale that has been made. The case, as made out in the pleadings, is simply this. One individual who holds lands in the state of Georgia, under a deed covenanting that the title of Georgia was in the grantor, brings an action of covenant upon this deed, and assigns, as a breach, that some of the members of the legislature were induced to vote in favour of the law, which constituted the contract, by being promised an interest in it, and that therefore the act is a mere nullity.

This solemn question cannot be brought thus collaterally and incidentally before the court. It would be indecent, in the extreme, upon a private contract, between two individuals, to enter into an inquiry respecting the corruption of the sovereign power of a state. If the title be plainly deduced from a legislative act, which the legislature might constitutionally pass, if the act be clothed with all the requisite forms of a law, a court, sitting as a court of law, cannot sustain a suit brought by one individual against another founded on the allegation that the act is a nullity, in consequence of the impure motives which influenced certain members of the legislature which passed the law.

3. *Other contract clause decisions.* Marshall's expansive interpretation of the contract clause continued in Dartmouth College v. Woodward, 17 U.S. (4 Wheat.) 518 (1819), which held that New Hampshire could not unilaterally modify a private institution's charter to place it under public control. Marshall wrote:

It is more than possible that the preservation of rights of this description was not particularly in the view of the framers of the constitution, when the clause under consideration was introduced into that instrument. It is probable, that interferences of more frequent recurrence, to which the temptation was stronger, and of which the mischief was more extensive, constituted the great motive for imposing this restriction on the State legislatures. But although a particular and a rare case may not, in itself, be of sufficient magnitude to induce a rule, yet it must be governed by the rule, when established, unless some plain and strong reason for excluding it can be given. It is not enough to say, that this particular case was not in the mind of the

> Convention, when the article was framed, nor of the American people, when it was adopted. It is necessary to go further, and to say that, had this particular case been suggested, the language would have been so varied, as to exclude it, or it would have been made a special exception.

In Sturges v. Crowninshield, 17 U.S. (4 Wheat.) 122 (1819), Marshall also wrote the Court's opinion, holding that a New York bankruptcy law could not operate retroactively to discharge a debt incurred before the law was enacted.

In *Fletcher,* Marshall notes that Article I, section 10, besides prohibiting the impairment of the obligation of contracts, prohibits ex post facto laws and bills of attainder. An ex post facto law is a criminal law applied to conduct occurring before its enactment. A bill of attainder is a legislative act finding that specified individuals are guilty of a crime and punishing them for it. Bills of attainder were typically also ex post facto laws. Thus, these prohibited legislative measures share the feature that they apply retroactively to defeat settled expectations.

The distinction between retroactive and prospective interference with contractual obligations turned out to be of great significance in contract clause doctrine. Concurring in *Dartmouth College,* Justice Story observed that legislative grants might explicitly reserve to the state the power to amend the charters. And in Ogden v. Saunders, 25 U.S. (12 Wheat.) 213 (1827), the Court limited *Sturges* to the retroactive application of bankruptcy laws to preexisting contracts, holding that a statute in existence at the time the contract is made becomes "part of the contract."

In his only dissent in a constitutional case, the Chief Justice, joined by Justices Story and Duvall, argued from principles of natural law and social contract and from the language of the contract clause that government could not (in effect) dictate in advance the terms of private contracts in order to release obligors in the event of their insolvency. Marshall began by pointing to the origins of freedom of contract in natural right: "[I]ndividuals do not derive from government their right to contract, but bring that right with them into society; that obligation is not conferred upon contracts by positive law, but is intrinsic, and is conferred by the act of the parties." Society is not without any powers at all to affect the right to contract; it can control the formalities of contract formation or prohibit specific contracts as violations of public policy. Moreover, Marshall accepted the right of a state to pass laws affecting contract remedies, but he rejected the relevance of that concession by arguing that bankruptcy laws are not merely remedial, because what they do is to turn "obligatory" contracts into de facto "conditional" promises. He feared that "one of the most important features in the Constitution of the United States . . . would lie prostrate, and be construed into an inanimate, inoperative, unmeaning clause." The dissenters read the language of the clause as barring prospective as well as retrospective legislation and viewed *Ogden* as offering a method for returning to the preconstitutional era by which state legislatures felt free to pass allegedly ruinous debtor-relief legislation.

Stephen Siegel points out that a key question lurking behind the bankruptcy issue was the validity of so-called reserve clauses, whereby the legislature put into its grant of corporate charters a proviso "reserving" the right to change their terms.[35] "Until the twentieth century, property had a dual signification in Liberal thought. In one sense property denoted, as it still does, all items of wealth. In the other sense property denoted only those valuables whose acquisition was open to all individuals, typically through competition in the free market. Property, in this latter sense, stood in contrast to privilege, which signified wealth that only certain individuals could acquire, usually through designation by affirmative governmental act." Regulation of privilege was far more acceptable than regulation of ordinary property, including contract rights protected by the contract clause. It was one thing to allow reservations in charters awarded by the state because such charters were viewed as awarding a privilege to their recipients. It was quite another to allow ordinary contracts to be subject to broad reservations, and in fact no state ever enacted a general "reserve" clause governing private contracts. "[O]ver time," says Siegel, "jurists simply assumed they were unconstitutional."

4. *Appellate review and natural law.* G. Edward White, in his recent study of the Marshall Court, emphasizes the difference in treatment between appeals to the Supreme Court from state court decisions based on Section 25 of the Judiciary Act of 1789 and appeals from lower federal courts, especially those arising under diversity jurisdiction. He suggests that only in non-Section 25 cases did the Court feel free to refer to the "general law," including norms of natural law or natural justice, whereas in Section 25 appeals the Court ostensibly limited itself to constitutional issues and to a far more positivistic, textual conception of the law it was authorized to enforce. White notes that *Fletcher* "was a diversity case, meaning that the Court could draw upon general principles of federal law as well as the Constitution for its sources." Justice Washington later wrote that "no where" in *Fletcher* is it "intimated . . . that a state statute, which divests a vested right, is repugnant to the constitution of the United States." Because *Fletcher* originated in a federal court it was appropriate to refer to general norms of justice; in a Section 25 case arising from a state court, on the other hand, the Supreme Court could only invalidate the statute where it was "repugnant to the *constitution of the United States.*"[36]

On this analysis, are only those parts of *Fletcher* relying on constitutional text rather than unenumerated norms truly "constitutional"? If so, what is the source of the Court's authority to strike down a state law on non-"constitutional" "general legal" grounds?

Note: Natural Law, Vested Rights, and the Written Constitution; Sources for Judicial Review

The reliance in *Fletcher* on "general principles" of law may sound strange, especially coming from Marshall, who seven years earlier had treated judicial review (of congressional legislation) merely as the application of the positive law of the written Constitution. This note surveys the concepts of "rights" extant in the late eighteenth and early nineteenth centuries.

35. Stephen A. Siegel, Understanding the Nineteenth Century Contract Clause, The Role of the Property-Privilege Distinction and "Takings" Clause Jurisprudence, 60 So. Cal. L. Rev. 1 (1986).
36. White, The Marshall Court and Cultural Change 1815-1835 at 611, 657-59.

1. The natural law tradition.[37] Although its influence has often been exaggerated, the concept of natural or fundamental law — a universal law superior to all man-made laws — pervaded eighteenth-century American intellectual and legal thought. Three features of the English natural law tradition influenced the development of constitutionalism in America. First, the received jurisprudence was that judges did not "make" the common law. Rather, through the "artificial reason of the law," they discovered immutable legal principles, which, together with more specific applications deduced from them, constituted the corpus of the English common law.[38] Second, centuries of revisionist history had transformed the Magna Carta (1215) from a partisan political document to a declaration of the natural rights of Englishmen, and the Petition of Right (1628) and Bill of Rights (1688-1689), as well as the Declaration of Independence (1776), were usually claimed not to establish new principles but to declare preexisting ones. The third source of natural law doctrine was John Locke's Second Treatise on Civil Government (1690). Reasoning deductively from the pregovernmental "state of nature" to the "social compact" formed to improve on that state, Locke derived both the supremacy of the legislature and limitations on its exercise of powers. Of his three basic rights of individuals — "life, liberty, and estate" — the last was most fundamental: Property was an extension of the individual, and the social compact was largely designed to protect whatever distributions of wealth came about through the varying talents and efforts of the members of society.

These elements of the natural law tradition coalesced in the eighteenth-century American view that

> the written constitution [is] . . . a species of social compact, entered into by sovereign individuals in a state of nature. . . . [G]overnmental authority . . . is a trust which, save for the grant of it effected by the written constitution, were non-existent, and private rights, since they precede the constitution, gain nothing of authoritativeness from being enumerated in it, though possibly something of security. These rights are not, in other words, fundamental because they find mention in the written instrument; they find mention there because fundamental. . . . The written constitution is, in short, but a nucleus or core of a much wider region of private rights, which

37. See Bernard Bailyn, The Ideological Origins of the American Revolution (1967); Carl Becker, The Declaration of Independence ch. 2 (1922); J.W. Gough, Fundamental Law in English Constitutional History (1955); Charles Mullett, Fundamental Law and the American Revolution (1933); Gordon Wood, The Creation of the American Republic, 1776-1787 (1969); Benjamin Wright, American Interpretations of Natural Law (1931); Edward Corwin, The "Higher Law" Background of American Constitutional Law, 42 Harv. L. Rev. 149, 365 (1928-1929); Corwin, The Basic Doctrine of American-Constitutional Law, 12 Mich. L. Rev. 247 (1914).

38. The quoted phrase is Sir Edward Coke's. James I had claimed that the king was entitled to decide cases, arguing "the law was founded upon reason, and that he and others had reason, as well as the Judges." Coke replied "[T]rue it was that God had endowed his majesty with excellent science, and great endowments of nature; but his Majesty was not learned in the laws of his realm of England, and causes which concern the life, or inheritance, or goods, or fortunes of his subjects, are not to be decided by natural reason but by the artificial reason and judgment of the law, which law is an act which requires long study and experience, before that a man can attain the cognizance of it. . . ." The king "was greatly offended" at the notion that "he should be under the law, which was treason to affirm." Coke responded, quoting Bracton and invoking fundamental law: "Quod Rex non debet esse sub homine, sed sub Deo et lege" (the King ought to be under no man, but under God and the law). Prohibitions Del Roy, 12 Co. 63, 77 Eng. Rep. 1342 (1609). On the life of Coke, see Katherine Bowen, The Lion and the Throne (1957). See also Gough, supra note 37, ch. 3; David Little, Religion, Order and Law: A Study in Pre-Revolutionary England ch. 6 (1969).

> though not reduced to black and white, are as fully entitled to the protection of government as if defined in the minutest detail.[39]

The natural rights of individuals were generally understood to be those that, through judicial "discovery" and the absorption of the Magna Carta, inhered in the common law. As restated in Blackstone's Commentaries 129-139 (1765), the three "absolute rights of individuals" were: "the right of personal security [which] consists in a person's legal and uninterrupted enjoyment of his life, his limbs, his body, his health, and his reputation"; the right of "personal liberty [which] consists in the power of loco-motion, of changing situation, or moving one's person to whatsoever place one's own inclination may direct, without imprisonment or restraint, unless by due course of law"; and "the absolute right, inherent in every Englishman . . . of property: which consists in the free use, enjoyment, and disposal of all his acquisitions, without any control or diminution, save only by the laws of the land."

2. *The judicial protection of vested rights.* The substantive legal issue involved in both *Marbury* and *Fletcher* was the protection of "vested rights." The President was free to appoint or not to appoint Marbury as a justice of the peace. But once Marbury's right to the commission "vested," the Government could no more deprive him of it than a seller of real property could take it back after title had vested in the purchaser.

The doctrine of vested rights did not encompass all expectations. In his well-known nineteenth-century treatise, Constitutional Limitations, Thomas Cooley explained:

> [A] right cannot be considered a vested right, unless it is something more than such a mere expectation as may be based upon an anticipated continuance of the present general laws: it must have become a title, legal or equitable, to the present or future enjoyment of property, or to the present or future enforcement of a demand, or a legal exemption from a demand, made by another.[40]

The doctrine assumed, in other words, that the basic structure of entitlements was determined by the common law as modified by legislation — that these determined the procedures by which property interests were created and transferred. But once an interest had vested in an individual — once it *belonged* to her — it was immune from government divestment. As Chancellor James Kent wrote in his comprehensive Commentaries on American Law (1826), a statute "affecting and changing vested rights is very generally considered in this country as founded on unconstitutional principles, and consequently inoperative and void."[41]

When Kent characterized a law violating vested rights as *unconstitutional* he was not referring to the United States Constitution or even to written state constitutions, but rather to what were understood to be *general* constitutional limitations implicit in all free governments — limitations based on natural rights and the nature of the social compact.

The vested rights doctrine developed and flourished primarily in the state courts. It made its first and least equivocal Supreme Court appearance in Calder v. Bull, 3

39. Corwin, The Basic Doctrine of American Constitutional Law, supra note 37, at 247-248.
40. Thomas Cooley, 2 Constitutional Limitations 749 (Carrington ed., 8th ed. 1927).
41. Quoted in id. at 449.

U.S. (3 Dall.) 386 (1798). A Connecticut probate court had disapproved a will designating the respondents beneficiaries, thus allowing petitioners to inherit as decedent's heirs at law. The Connecticut legislature passed a resolution setting aside the decree and granting a new hearing, at which the will was approved. To petitioners' claim that the legislative act was an ex post facto law in violation of Article I, section 10, the Court responded that the clause was limited to criminal legislation. But Justice Chase, who wrote the most comprehensive of several seriatim opinions, went on to consider whether, apart from this or any other specific provision of the Constitution, a government could deprive a citizen of a vested property right:

> I cannot subscribe to the omnipotence of a state legislature, or that it is absolute and without control; although its authority should not be expressly restrained by the Constitution, or fundamental law, of the State. The people of the United States erected their Constitutions, or forms of government, to establish justice, to promote the general welfare, to secure the blessings of liberty; and to protect their persons and property from violence. The purposes for which men enter into society will determine the nature and terms of the social compact; and as they are the foundation of the legislative power, they will decide what are the proper objects of it. The nature and ends of legislative power will limit the exercise of it. This fundamental principle flows from the very nature of our free Republican governments, that no man should be compelled to do what the laws do not require, nor to refrain from acts which the laws permit. There are acts which the Federal or State Legislature cannot do, without exceeding their authority. There are certain vital principles in our free Republican governments, which will determine and overrule an apparent and flagrant abuse of legislative power; as to authorize manifest injustice by positive law; or to take away that security for personal liberty, or private property, for the protection whereof the government was established. An ACT of the Legislature (for I cannot call it a law) contrary to the great first principles of the social compact, cannot be considered a rightful exercise of legislative authority. The obligation of a law in governments established on express compact, and on republican principles, must be determined by the nature of the power on which it is founded. A few instances will suffice to explain what I mean. A law that punished a citizen for an innocent action, or, in other words, for an act, which, when done, was in violation of no existing law; a law that destroys, or impairs, the lawful private contracts of citizens; a law that makes a man a judge in his own cause; or a law that takes property from A. and gives it to B. It is against all reason and justice, for a people to intrust a Legislature with such powers; and, therefore, it cannot be presumed that they have done it. The genius, the nature, and the spirit of our State Governments, amount to a prohibition of such acts of legislation; and the general principles of law and reason forbid them. The Legislature may enjoin, permit, forbid, and punish; they may declare new crimes; and establish rules of conduct for all its citizens in future cases; they may command what is right, and prohibit what is wrong; but they cannot change innocence into guilt; or punish innocence as a crime; or violate the right of an antecedent lawful private contract; or the right of private property. To maintain that our Federal or State Legislature possesses such powers, if they had not been expressly restrained; would, in my opinion, be a political heresy, altogether inadmissible in our free republican governments.

Applying this theory to the case at bar, Justice Chase found that Connecticut's actions had not deprived the petitioners of a vested property right, since no right vested by the first decree.

Justice Iredell, in his separate opinion, challenged the basic premise of Chase's inquiry:

It is true, that some speculative jurists have held, that a legislative act against natural justice must, in itself, be void; but I cannot think that, under such a government, any Court of Justice would possess a power to declare it so. Sir William Blackstone, having put the strong case of an act of Parliament which, should authorize a man to try his own cause, explicitly adds, that even in that case, "there is no court that has power to defeat the intent of the Legislature, when couched in such evident and express words, as leave no doubt whether it was the intent of the Legislature, or no." 1 Bl. Comm. 91.

In order, therefore, to guard against so great an evil, it has been the policy of all the American States, which have, individually, framed their state constitutions since the revolution, and of the people of the United States, when they framed the Federal Constitution, to define with precision the objects of the legislative power, and to restrain its exercise within marked and settled boundaries. If any act of Congress, or of the Legislature of a State, violates those constitutional provisions, it is unquestionably void; though, I admit, that as the authority to declare it void is of a delicate and awful nature, the Court will never resort to that authority, but in a clear and urgent case. If, on the other hand, the Legislature of the Union, or the Legislature of any member of the Union, shall pass a law, within the general scope of their constitutional power, the Court cannot pronounce it to be void, merely because it is, in their judgment, contrary to the principles of natural justice. The ideas of natural justice are regulated by no fixed standard; the ablest and the purest men have differed upon the subject; and all that the Court could properly say, in such an event, would be, that the Legislature, possessed of an equal right of opinion, had passed an act which, in the opinion of the judges, was inconsistent with the abstract principles of natural justice.

3. The explicit federal constitutional protection of rights. The vested rights doctrine aside, judicial protection of individual rights depended mainly on the written provisions of state constitutions and the United States Constitution. Article I, section 10, prohibited states from passing bills of attainder, ex post facto laws, and laws impairing the obligation of contracts. Article I, section 9, applied the first two prohibitions to the federal government and limited the government's power to suspend the writ of habeas corpus. In 1791, the Constitution was supplemented by a Bill of Rights, which the Court held in Barron v. Baltimore, 32 U.S. (7 Pet.) 243 (1833), applied only to the federal government.[42]

4. The Ninth Amendment.[43] The title of Bennett Patterson's 1955 book, The Forgotten Ninth Amendment, accurately captures the status of this provision of the Bill of Rights throughout most of our constitutional history.[44] Nonetheless, if any provision of the United States Constitution seems to embody the concept of natural rights, it is the Ninth Amendment: "The enumeration in the Constitution, of certain rights, shall not be construed to deny or disparage others retained by the people." The purpose of the amendment is ambiguous, however. Was it designed to safeguard individual liberties not enumerated in the first eight

42. Does anything in the language of the amendments suggest that some of them might be applicable to the states? Compare the First and Seventh Amendments with the others.

43. See generally Leslie Dunbar, James Madison and the Ninth Amendment, 42 Va. L. Rev. 627 (1956); Alfred Kelly, Clio and the Court: An Illicit Love Affair, 1965 Sup. Ct. Rev. 119, 149-155; Randy Barnett, ed., The Rights Retained by the People: The History and Meaning of the Ninth Amendment (1989).

44. But see Chapter 8 infra.

amendments or only to protect the states against the national government's assumption of powers not delegated by Articles I, II, and III?

Much anti-Federalist opposition to the Constitution in the state conventions focused on the absence of a bill of rights. The Federalist response was that a bill of rights was unnecessary and dangerous — unnecessary because the national government, being one of delegated powers, was not authorized to infringe individual liberties; dangerous because the enumeration would imply the existence of broader powers than were delegated. A bill of rights, Alexander Hamilton wrote in The Federalist, No. 84,

> would contain various exceptions to powers which are not granted; and on this very account, would afford a colorable pretext to claim more than were granted. For why declare that things shall not be done which there is no power to do? Why, for instance, should it be said that the liberty of the press shall not be restrained, when no power is given by which restrictions may be imposed?[45] I will not contend that such a provision would confer a regulating power; but it is evident that it would furnish, to men disposed to usurp, a plausible pretense for claiming that power.

James Wilson similarly argued in the Pennsylvania ratifying convention: "If we attempt an enumeration, everything that is not enumerated is presumed to be given. The consequence is, that an imperfect enumeration would throw all implied power into the scale of the government, and the rights of the people would be rendered incomplete."[46]

James Madison, principal author of the Bill of Rights, shared the concern that it might imply broader federal powers than were granted. Additionally, he wrote to Jefferson,[47] "there is great reason to fear that a positive declaration of some of the most essential rights could not be obtained in the requisite latitude. I am sure that the rights of conscience, in particular, if submitted to public definition would be narrowed much more than they are likely ever to be by an assumed power." In presenting to the First Congress the provision that became the Ninth Amendment, Madison explained:[48]

> It has been objected also against a bill of rights, that, by enumerating particular exceptions to the grant of power, it would disparage those rights which were not placed in that enumeration; and it might follow by implication, that those rights which were not singled out, were intended to be assigned into the hands of the General Government, and were consequently insecure. This is one of the most plausible arguments I have ever heard urged against the admission of a bill of rights into this system; but, I conceive, that it may be guarded against. I have attempted it, as gentlemen may see by turning to the last clause of the fourth resolution [the Ninth Amendment]. . . .

Neither Wilson nor Madison seemed to draw a sharp line between restricting the powers of the national government and protecting individual liberties, and there is no reason to believe that those who adopted and ratified the Ninth

45. Is this a plausible argument in view of the Federalists' view of the necessary and proper clause?
46. 2 Debates in the Several State Conventions of the Adoption of the Federal Constitution 436 (Elliot ed. 1836).
47. 5 Writings of James Madison 271-272 (Hunt ed. 1904) (letter of Oct. 17, 1788).
48. 1 Annals of Cong. 439 (1789).

Amendment had a unitary view of its purpose. Furthermore, any attempt to elucidate the amendment's purposes must deal with some enigmatic data.

On the one hand, if the amendment were concerned primarily with safeguarding federalism, it would make surplusage of the Tenth Amendment, which speaks explicitly of powers "reserved to the States." On the other hand, if the amendment were concerned primarily with safeguarding individual liberties, one might expect to find similar provisions in some of the bills of rights of contemporary state constitutions. There is a further complexity here. In 1791, the Ninth Amendment was unique, but the bills of rights of many nineteenth-century state constitutions paraphrase the amendment.[49]

V. *Regulation of the Interstate Economy*

GIBBONS v. OGDEN

22 U.S. (9 Wheat.) 1 (1824)

Appeal from the Court for the Trial of Impeachments and Corrections of Errors of the State of New York

[The New York State Legislature granted Robert Livingston and Robert Fulton the exclusive right to operate steamboats in New York waters for a period of years. Livingston and Fulton assigned to Ogden the exclusive right to operate steamboats between New York City and various places in New Jersey. Ogden brought this action in New York Chancery Court to enjoin Gibbons from operating steamboats between New York and Elizabethtown, New Jersey. Gibbons responded that his boats were licensed pursuant to a 1793 Act of Congress entitled "an act for enrolling and licensing ships and vessels to be employed in the coasting trade and fisheries, and for regulating the same," and that the licenses entitled him to navigate between New York and New Jersey notwithstanding the state-granted monopoly.

The New York courts held for Ogden. The state appellate court held that the federal statute was designed solely "to establish a criterion of *national character,* with a view to enforce the laws which impose *discriminating duties* [favoring] *American* vessels [over] those of foreign countries. The term 'license' seems not be used in the sense. . . . [of] a *permit to trade,*" because "it is perfectly clear that such a vessel, coasting from one state to another, would have exactly the same right to trade, and the same right of transit, whether she had the coasting license or not. . . . Whether Congress have the power to authorize the coasting trade to be carried on, in vessels propelled by steam, so as to give a *paramount right,* in opposition to the special license given by this state, is a question not yet presented to us. No such act of Congress yet exists. . . ." The Supreme Court reversed.]

MARSHALL, C.J. . . .

As preliminary to the very able discussions of the constitution, which we have heard from the bar, and as having some influence on its construction, reference has been made to the political situation of these states, anterior to its formation. It has been said, that they were sovereign, were completely independent, and were

49. See John Ely, Democracy and Distrust 202-204 (1980).

connected with each other only by a league. This is true. But when these allied sovereigns converted their league into a government, when they converted their congress of ambassadors, deputed to deliberate on their common concerns, and to recommend measures of general utility, into a legislature, empowered to enact laws on the most interesting subjects, the whole character in which the states appear, underwent a change, the extent of which must be determined by a fair consideration of the instrument by which that change was effected.

This instrument contains an enumeration of powers expressly granted by the people to their government. It has been said, that these powers ought to be construed strictly. . . . What do gentlemen mean, by a strict construction? If they contend only against that enlarged construction, which would extend words beyond their natural and obvious import, we might question the application of the term, but should not controvert the principle. If they contend for that narrow construction which, in support of some theory not to be found in the constitution, would deny to the government those powers which the words of the grant, as usually understood, import, and which are consistent with the general views and objects of the instrument — for that narrow construction, which would cripple the government, and render it unequal to the objects for which it is declared to be instituted, and to which the powers given, as fairly understood, render it competent — then we cannot perceive the propriety of this strict construction, nor adopt it as the rule by which the constitution is to be expounded. As men, whose intentions require no concealment, generally employ the words which most directly and aptly express the ideas they intend to convey, the enlightened patriots who framed our constitution, and the people who adopted it, must be understood to have employed words in their natural sense, and to have intended what they have said. If, from the imperfection of human language, there should be serious doubts respecting the extent of any given power, it is a well-settled rule, that the objects for which it was given, especially, when those objects are expressed in the instrument itself, should have great influence in the construction. . . . We know of no rule for construing the extent of such powers, other than is given by the language of the instrument which confers them, taken in connection with the purposes for which they were conferred.

The words are, "congress shall have power to regulate commerce with foreign nations, and among the several states, and with the Indian tribes." The subject to be regulated is commerce; and our constitution being, as was aptly said at the bar, one of enumeration, and not of definition, to ascertain the extent of the power, it becomes necessary to settle the meaning of the word. The counsel for the appellee would limit it to traffic, to buying and selling, or the interchange of commodities, and do not admit that it comprehends navigation. This would restrict a general term, applicable to many objects, to one of its significations. Commerce, undoubtedly, is traffic, but it is something more — it is intercourse. It describes the commercial intercourse between nations, and parts of nations, in all its branches, and is regulated by prescribing rules for carrying on that intercourse. . . .

All America understands, and has uniformly understood, the word "commerce," to comprehend navigation. It was so understood, and must have been so understood, when the constitution was framed. The power over commerce, including navigation, was one of the primary objects for which the people of America adopted their government, and must have been contemplated in forming it. The convention must have used the word in that sense, because all have understood it in that sense; and the attempt to restrict it comes too late. . . .

The word used in the constitution, then comprehends, and has been always understood to comprehend, navigation within its meaning; and a power to regulate navigation, is as expressly granted, as if that term had been added to the word "commerce." To what commerce does this power extend? The constitution informs us, to commerce "with foreign nations, and among the several states, and with the Indian tribes." It has, we believe, been universally admitted, that these words comprehend every species of commercial intercourse between the United States and foreign nations. No sort of trade can be carried on between this country and any other, to which this power does not extend. It has been truly said, that commerce, as the word is used in the constitution, is a unit, every part of which is indicated by the term.

If this be the admitted meaning of the word, in its application to foreign nations, it must carry the same meaning throughout the sentence, and remain a unit, unless there be some plain intelligible cause which alters it. The subject to which the power is next applied, is to commerce, "among the several states." The word "among" means intermingled with. A thing which is among others, is intermingled with them. Commerce among the states, cannot stop at the external boundary line of each state, but may be introduced into the interior. It is not intended to say, that these words comprehend that commerce, which is completely internal, which is carried on between man and man in a state, or between different parts of the same state, and which does not extend to or affect other states. Such a power would be inconvenient, and is certainly unnecessary. Comprehensive as the word "among" is, it may very properly be restricted to that commerce which concerns more states than one. . . . The genius and character of the whole government seem to be, that its action is to be applied to all the external concerns of the nation, and to those internal concerns which affect the states generally; but not to those which are completely within a particular state, which do not affect other states, and with which it is not necessary to interfere, for the purpose of executing some of the general powers of the government. The completely internal commerce of a state, then may be considered as reserved for the state itself.

But in regulating commerce with foreign nations, the power of congress does not stop at the jurisdictional lines of the several states. It would be a very useless power, if it could not pass those lines. The commerce of the United States with foreign nations, is that of the whole United States; every district has a right to participate in it. The deep streams which penetrate our country in every direction, pass through the interior of almost every state in the Union, and furnish the means of exercising this right. If congress has the power to regulate it, that power must be exercised whenever the subject exists. If it exists within the states, if a foreign voyage may commence or terminate at a port within a state, then the power of congress may be exercised within a state.

This principle is, if possible, still more clear, when applied to commerce "among the several states." They either join each other, in which case they are separated by a mathematical line, or they are remote from each other, in which case other states lie between them. What is commerce "among" them; and how is it to be conducted? Can a trading expedition between two adjoining states, commence and terminate outside of each? And if the trading intercourse be between two states remote from each other, must it not commence in one, terminate in the other, and probably pass through a third? Commerce among the states must, of necessity, be commerce with the states. In the regulation of trade with the Indian tribes, the action of the law, especially, when the constitution was made, was chiefly within a state. The power of congress, then, whatever it may be, must be exercised within the territorial jurisdiction of the several states. . . .

We are now arrived at the inquiry — what is this power? It is the power to regulate; that is, to prescribe the rule by which commerce is to be governed. This power, like all others vested in congress, is complete in itself, may be exercised to its utmost extent, and acknowledges no limitations, other than are prescribed in the constitution. These are expressed in plain terms, and do not affect the questions which arise in this case, or which have been discussed at the bar. If, as has always been understood, the sovereignty of congress, though limited to specified objects, is plenary as to those objects, the power over commerce with foreign nations, and among the several states, is vested in congress as absolutely as it would be in a single government, having in its constitution the same restrictions on the exercise of the power as are found in the constitution of the United States. The wisdom and the discretion of congress, their identity with the people, and the influence which their constituents possess at elections, are, in this, as in many other instances, as that, for example, of declaring war, the sole restraints on which they have relied, to secure them from its abuse. They are the restraints on which the people must often rely solely, in all representative governments. The power of congress, then, comprehends navigation, within the limits of every state in the Union; so far as that navigation may be, in any manner, connected with "commerce with foreign nations, or among the several states, or with the Indian tribes." It may, of consequence, pass the jurisdictional line of New York, and act upon the very waters to which the prohibition now under consideration applies.

But it has been urged . . . [that] the states may severally exercise the same power, within their respective jurisdictions. In support of this argument, it is said, that they possessed it as an inseparable attribute of sovereignty, before the formation of the constitution, and still retain it, except so far as they have surrendered it by that instrument; that this principle results from the nature of the government, and is secured by the tenth amendment; that an affirmative grant of power is not exclusive, unless in its own nature it be such that the continued exercise of it by the former possessor is inconsistent with the grant, and that this is not of that description. The appellant, conceding these postulates, except the last, contends, that full power to regulate a particular subject, implies the whole power, and leaves no residuum; that a grant of the whole is incompatible with the existence of a right in another to any part of it. Both parties have appealed to the constitution, to legislative acts, and judicial decisions; and have drawn arguments from all these sources, to support and illustrate the propositions they respectively maintain.

The grant of the power to lay and collect taxes is, like the power to regulate commerce, made in general terms, and has never been understood to interfere with the exercise of the same power by the states; and hence has been drawn an argument which has been applied to the question under consideration. But the two grants are not, it is conceived, similar in their terms or their nature. Although many of the powers formerly exercised by the states, are transferred to the government of the Union, yet the state governments remain, and constitute a most important part of our system. The power of taxation is indispensable to their existence, and is a power which, in its own nature, is capable of residing in, and being exercised by, different authorities, at the same time. We are accustomed to see it placed, for different purposes, in different hands. Taxation is the simple operation of taking small portions from a perpetually accumulating mass, susceptible of almost infinite division; and a power in one to take what is necessary for certain purposes, is not, in its nature, incompatible with a power in another to take what is necessary for other purposes. Congress is authorized to lay and collect taxes, &c., to pay the debts, and provide for the common defence and general welfare of the United States. This does not interfere with the power of the states to tax for the support of their own governments; nor is the exercise of that power by the states, an exercise of any portion of the power that is granted to the United States. In imposing taxes for state purposes, they are not doing what congress is empowered to do. Congress is not empowered to tax for those purposes which are within the exclusive province of the states. When, then, each government exercises the power of taxation, neither is exercising the power of the other. But when a state proceeds to regulate commerce with foreign nations, or among the several states, it is exercising the very power that is granted to congress, and is doing the very thing which congress is authorized to do. There is no analogy, then, between the power of taxation and the power of regulating commerce.

In discussing the question, whether this power is still in the states, in the case under consideration, we may dismiss from it the inquiry, whether it is surrendered by the mere grant to congress, or is retained until congress shall exercise the power. We may dismiss that inquiry, because it has been exercised, and the regulations which congress deemed it proper to make, are now in full operation. The sole question is, can a state regulate commerce with foreign nations and among the states, while congress is regulating it?

The counsel for the respondent answer this question in the affirmative, and rely very much on the restrictions in the 10th section, as supporting their opinion. They say, very truly, that limitations of a power furnish a strong argument in favor of the existence of that power, and that the section which prohibits the states from laying duties on imports or exports, proves that this power might have been exercised, had it not been expressly forbidden; and, consequently, that any other commercial regulation, not expressly forbidden, to which the original power of the state was competent, may still be made. That this restriction shows the opinion of the convention, that a state might impose duties on exports and imports, if not expressly forbidden, will be conceded; but that it follows, as a consequence, from this concession, that a state may regulate commerce with foreign nations and among the states, cannot be admitted.

We must first determine, whether the act of laying "duties or imposts on imports or exports," is considered in the constitution, as a branch of the taxing power, or of the power to regulate commerce. We think it very clear, that it is considered as a branch of the taxing power. It is so treated in the first clause of the 8th section: "Congress shall have power to lay and collect taxes, duties, imposts and excises"; and before commerce is mentioned, the rule by which the exercise of this power must be governed, is declared. It is, that all duties, imposts and excises shall be uniform. In a separate clause of the enumeration, the power to regulate commerce is given, as being entirely distinct from the right to levy taxes and imposts, and as being a new power, not before conferred. The constitution, then, considers these powers as substantive, and distinct from each other;

and so places them in the enumeration it contains. The power of imposing duties on imports is classed with the power to levy taxes, and that seems to be its natural place. But the power to levy taxes could never be considered as abridging the right of the states on that subject; and they might, consequently, have exercised it, by levying duties on imports or exports, had the constitution contained no prohibition on this subject. This prohibition, then, is an exception from the acknowledged power of the states to levy taxes, not from the questionable power to regulate commerce.

But the inspection laws are said to be regulations of commerce, and are certainly recognised in the constitution, as being passed in the exercise of a power remaining with the states. That inspection laws may have a remote and considerable influence on commerce, will not be denied; but that a power to regulate commerce is the source from which the right to pass them is derived, cannot be admitted. The object of inspection laws, is to improve the quality of articles produced by the labor of a country; to fit them for exportation; or, it may be, for domestic use. They act upon the subject, before it becomes an article of foreign commerce, or of commerce among the states, and prepare it for that purpose. They form a portion of that immense mass of legislation, which embraces everything within the territory of a state, not surrendered to the general government; all which can be most advantageously exercised by the states themselves. Inspection laws, quarantine laws, health laws of every description, as well as laws for regulating the internal commerce of a state, and those which respect of this mass.

No direct general power over these objects is granted to congress; and, consequently, they remain subject to state legislation. If the legislative power of the Union can reach them, it must be for national purposes; it must be, where the power is expressly given for a special purpose, or is clearly incidental to some power which is expressly given. It is obvious, that the government of the Union, in the exercise of its express powers, that, for example, of regulating commerce with foreign nations and among the states, may use means that may also be employed by a state, in the exercise of its acknowledged powers; that, for example, of regulating commerce within the state. If congress license vessels to sail from one port to another, in the same state, the act is supposed to be, necessarily, incidental to the power expressly granted to congress, and implies no claim of a direct power to regulate the purely internal commerce of a state, or to act directly on its system of police. So, if a state, in passing laws on subjects acknowledged to be within its control, and with a view to those subjects, shall adopt a measure of the same character with one which congress may adopt, it does not derive its authority from the particular power which has been granted, but from some other, which remains with the state, and may be executed by the same means. All experience shows, that the same measures, or measures scarcely distinguishable from each other, may flow from distinct powers; but this does not prove that the powers themselves are identical. Although the means used in their execution may sometimes approach each other so nearly as to be confounded, there are other situations in which they are sufficiently distinct, to establish their individuality.

In our complex system, presenting the rare and difficult scheme of one general government, whose action extends over the whole, but which possesses only certain enumerated powers; and of numerous state governments, which retain and exercise all powers not delegated to the Union, contests respecting power must arise. Were it even otherwise, the measures taken by the respective governments to execute their acknowledged powers, would often be of the same description, and might, sometimes, interfere. This, however, does not prove that the one is exercising, or has a right to exercise, the powers of the other. . . .

It has been contended by the counsel for the appellant, that, as the word "to regulate" implies in its nature, full power over the thing to be regulated, it excludes, necessarily, the action of all others that would perform the same operation on the same thing. That regulation is designed for the entire result, applying to those parts which remain as they were, as well as to those which are altered. It produces a uniform whole, which is as much disturbed and deranged by changing what the regulating power designs to leave untouched, as that on which it has operated. There is great force in this argument, and the court is not satisfied that it has been refuted.

Since, however, in exercising the power of regulating their own purely internal affairs, whether of trading or police, the states may sometimes enact laws, the validity of which depends on their interfering with, and being contrary to, an act of congress passed in pursuance of the constitution, the court will enter upon the inquiry, whether the laws of New York, as expounded by the highest tribunal of that state, have, in their application to this case, come into collision with an act of congress, and deprived a citizen of a right to which that act entitles him. Should this collision exist, it will be immaterial, whether those laws were passed in virtue of a concurrent power "to regulate commerce with foreign nations and among the several states," or, in virtue of a power to regulate their domestic trade and police. In one case and the other, the acts of New York must yield to the law of congress. . . .

To the court, it seems very clear, that the whole act on the subject of the coasting trade, according to those principles which govern the construction of statutes, implies, unequivocally, an authority to licensed vessels to carry on the coasting trade. . . .

[Marshall goes on to conclude, contrary to the New York courts, that Gibbons' license under the 1793 federal statute entitled him to engage in interstate navigation and trade, notwithstanding Ogden's claims to the exclusive franchise granted by the New York legislature.]

[Justice William Johnson concurred, adopting the theory only broached by Marshall, i.e., that the power to regulate commerce was exclusively Congress'. During the colonial period, Johnson asserted, "the States had submitted, with murmurs to the commercial restrictions imposed by the parent State." Following independence, they found "themselves in the unlimited possession of those powers over their own commerce, which they had so long been deprived of, and so earnestly coveted, that selfish principle which, well controlled, is so salutary, and which, unrestricted, is so unjust and tyrannical," and consequently began passing a host of "commercial regulations, destructive to the harmony of the States, and fatal to their commercial interests abroad."]

This was the immediate cause that led to the forming of a convention.

The history of the times will, therefore, sustain the opinion, that the grant of power over commerce, if intended to be commensurate with the evils existing, and the purpose of remedying those evils, could be only commensurate with the power of the States over the subject. . . .

The "power to regulate commerce," here meant to be granted, was that power to regulate commerce which previously existed in the States. But what was that power? The States were, unquestionably, supreme; and each possessed that power over commerce, which is acknowledged to reside in every sovereign State. [The] power of a sovereign state over commerce, therefore, amounts to nothing more than a power to limit and restrain it at pleasure. And since the power to prescribe the limits to its freedom, necessarily implies the power to determine what shall remain unrestrained, it follows, that the power must be exclusive; it can reside but in one potentate; and hence, the grant of this power carries with it the whole subject, leaving nothing for the State to act upon. . . .

[With respect to the coasting license ultimately relied on by Marshall to invalidate the New York law,] I cannot overcome the conviction, that if the licensing act was repealed to-morrow, the rights of the appellant to a reversal of the decision complained of, would be as strong. . . .

But the principal objections to these opinions arise, 1st. From the unavoidable action of some of the municipal powers of the States, upon commercial subjects.

2d. From passages in the constitution, which are supposed to imply a concurrent power in the States in regulating commerce.

It is no objection to the existence of distinct, substantive powers, that, in their application, they bear upon the same subject. The same bale of goods, the same cask of provisions, or the same ship, that may be the subject of commercial regulation, may also be the vehicle of disease. And the health laws that require them to be stopped and ventilated, are no more intended as regulations on commerce, than the laws which permit their importation, are intended to inoculate the community with disease. Their different purposes mark the distinction between the powers brought into action; and while frankly exercised, they can produce no serious collision. . . . Inspection laws are of a more equivocal nature, and it is obvious that the constitution has viewed that subject with much solicitude. But so far from sustaining an inference in favour of the power of the States over commerce, I cannot but think that the guarded provisions of the 10th section, on this subject, furnish a strong argument against that inference. It was obvious, that inspection laws must combine municipal with commercial regulations; and, while the power over the subject is yielded to the States, for obvious reasons, an absolute control is given over State legislation on the subject, as far as that legislation may be exercised, so as to affect the commerce of the country. The inferences, to be correctly drawn, from this whole article, appear to me to be altogether in favour of the exclusive grants to Congress of power over commerce, and the reverse of that which the appellee contends for.

. . . [Article 1, Section 10] negatives the exercise of [the commerce] power to the States, as to the only two objects which could ever tempt them to assume the exercise of that power, to wit, the collection of a revenue from imposts and duties on imports and exports; or from a tonnage duty. As to imposts on imports or exports, such a revenue might have been aimed at directly, by express legislation, or indirectly, in the form of inspection laws; and it became necessary to guard against both. Hence, first, the consent of Congress to such imposts or duties, is made necessary; and as to inspection laws, it is limited to the minimum of expenses. Then, the money so raised shall be paid in to the treasury of the United States, or may be sued for since it is declared to be for their use. And lastly, all such laws may be modified, or repealed, by an act of Congress. It is impossible for a right to be more guarded. . . .

It would be in vain to deny the possibility of a clashing and collision between the measures of the two governments. The line cannot be drawn with sufficient distinctness between the municipal powers of the one, and the commercial powers of the other. . . . Whenever the powers of the respective governments are frankly exercised, with a distinct view to the ends of such powers, they may act upon the same object, or use the same means, and yet the powers be kept perfectly distinct. A resort to the same means, therefore, is no argument to prove the identity of their respective powers. . . .

Discussion

Like *McCulloch,* decided five years earlier, *Gibbons* is an essay on federalism, presenting Marshall's solution to the novel American problem of two sovereigns occupying the same physical space.

1. Marshall's binary view. In Marshall's view, on what theory does the Constitution permit both Congress and the states to levy taxes? Why may not both Congress and the states regulate interstate commerce?

What is Ogden's argument based on Article I, section 10, and how does Marshall respond to it? Is it possible that the laying of "duties or imposts on imports or exports" might be a branch of both the taxing power *and* the power to regulate commerce?

How does Marshall respond to Ogden's argument that state inspection (and quarantine) laws are regulations of interstate commerce? Why is it important to Marshall that they *not* be?

Consider the relationship between Marshall's analysis of these issues and his discussions of questions of "degree" in *McCulloch.*

2. The purposes of the commerce power. Consider the role that the "objects" or "purposes" of constitutional provisions play in Marshall's scheme.

Toward the beginning of the opinion, in discussing interpretation of the commerce power, Marshall refers to "the well-settled rule, that the objects for which [a power] was given . . . should have great influence in the construction." For what purposes was the commerce power given? What light is shed on these by the following description of proceedings at the Philadelphia convention?

> The Virginia delegation, led by Washington, Madison, and Randolph, feeling largely responsible for the calling of the Convention, had prepared a series of resolutions as a basis for discussion. The sixth of these resolutions, proposed by Governor Randolph four days after the Convention assembled, read in part as follows:
>
> ". . . that the National Legislature ought to be impowered to enjoy the Legislative Rights vested in Congress by the Confederation & moreover to legislate in all cases to which the separate States are incompetent, or in which the harmony of the United States may be interrupted by the exercise of individual Legislation."
>
> The broad standard thus proposed for the division of power between state and nation was criticized by some of the delegates as being too indefinite, but was approved by the Convention on May 31st by a vote of nine states in favor, none against, one divided. . . .
>
> Shortly afterwards Paterson proposed his New Jersey plan, which included in a very short enumeration of federal powers the provision that Congress could "pass Acts for the regulation of trade & commerce as well with foreign nations as with each

other." In the language of James Wilson, subsequently a Supreme Court Justice, in comparing the two plans, under the Virginia Plan "The National Legislature is to make laws in all cases at which the several states are incompetent"; under the New Jersey Plan, "In place of this cong. are to have additional power in a few cases only." The New Jersey Plan was rejected and the Virginia Plan reapproved, on June 19th, by a vote of seven states to three, one being divided.

On July 17th, when Randolph's resolution on the division of powers again came up for debate, Sherman of Connecticut, who alone had opposed the resolution originally, moved that it be amended to add the expression.

"To make laws binding on the people of the United States in all cases which may concern the common interests of the Union; but not to interfere with the Government of the individual States in any matters of internal police which respect the Gov. of such States only, and wherein the general welfare of the U. States is not concerned."

". . . [This] was defeated, and a motion by Bedford of Delaware to clarify the wording adopted by a vote of eight to two. The resolution then read as follows:

"Resolved that the national legislature ought

"1. to possess the legislative rights in Congress by the confederation; and
"2. moreover, to legislate in all cases for the general interests of the Union, and
"3. also in those to which the states are separately incompetent, or
"4. in which the harmony of the United States may be interrupted by the exercise of individual legislation."

With the other resolutions approved by the Convention, this resolution was then sent to the "Com. of detail . . . to . . . report the Constitution." This committee made its report on August 6th, ten days later. It had changed the indefinite language of Resolution VI into an enumeration of the powers of Congress closely resembling Article 1, Section 8 of the Constitution as it was finally adopted. . . .

[T]he Convention did not at any time challenge the radical change made by the committee in the form of the provision for the division of powers between state and nation. It accepted *without discussion* the enumeration of powers made by a committee which had been directed to prepare a constitution based upon the general propositions that the Federal Government was "to legislate in all cases for the general interests of the Union . . . and in those to which the states are separately incompetent." With a few changes and additions, the enumeration by the committee became the present Section 8 of Article I of the Constitution.[50]

3. The purposes of congressional regulation. In discussing the allocation of state and national powers under the clause, Marshall writes that inspection, quarantine, and health laws, "form a portion of that immense mass of legislation, which embraces everything within the territory of a state, not surrendered to the national government." He comments that "No direct general power over these objects is granted to congress; and, consequently they remain subject to state legislation. If the legislative power of the Union can reach them, it must be for national purposes. . . ."

This suggests that the scope of national power may depend, not only on the *substance* of the regulation, but also on the *purposes* for which the regulation was adopted — on the congruence between the purposes underlying the regulation and the constitutional grant of power. Recall, in this respect, Marshall's discussion of "pretext" in paragraph 42 of *McCulloch:*

50. Robert Stern, That Commerce Which Concerns More States than One, 47 Harv. L. Rev. 1335, 1338-1340 (1934).

> Should Congress, . . . under the pretext of executing its powers, pass laws for the accomplishment of objects not entrusted to the government; it would become the painful duty of this tribunal, should a case requiring such a decision come before it, to say that such an act was not the law of the land.

Think of an example of a congressional regulation of interstate commerce that might preempt a state inspection, quarantine, or health law. Think of an example of a congressional regulation of interstate commerce that is a "pretext"—i.e., that is not done to accomplish any of the objects entrusted to the national government.

Can you reconcile the "pretext" language of *McCulloch* with Marshall's statements in *Gibbons* that the "[commerce] power, like all others vested in congress, is complete in itself, may be exercised to its utmost extent, and acknowledges no limitations, other than are prescribed in the constitution," and that "the sovereignty of congress, though limited to specified objects, is plenary as to those objects, [and] the power over commerce . . . among the several states, is vested in congress as absolutely as it would be in a single government"?

4. State regulation of interstate commerce—substance and purpose. *Gibbons* holds that a valid congressional regulation of interstate commerce (the 1793 statute) preempts inconsistent state regulations. But may a state regulate interstate commerce in the absence of congressional legislation?

Counsel for Gibbons argued that the Constitution by its own terms completely deprives the states of any powers to regulate interstate commerce: "as the word 'to regulate' implies in its nature, full power over the thing to be regulated, it excludes, necessarily, the action of all others that would perform the same operation on the same thing." Marshall found "great force in this argument," but went on to decide the case on the narrower grounds of statutory preemption.

Several years later in Willson v. Black Bird Creek Marsh Co., 27 U.S. (2 Pet.) 245 (1829), the Court addressed the constitutionality of state law in the absence of a preemptive federal regulation. The state of Delaware had authorized the plaintiff company to build a dam across a navigable waterway. Defendants, the owners of a sloop licensed and enrolled under the federal act involved in *Gibbons,* broke the plaintiff company's dam. In an action for damages, defendants argued that a state law authorizing construction of the dam conflicted with the commerce clause. Chief Justice Marshall wrote:

> [T]he question is to be considered, whether the act incorporating the Black-bird Creek Marsh company is repugnant to the constitution, so far as it authorizes a dam across the creek. The plea states the creek to be navigable, in the nature of a highway, through which the tide ebbs and flows. The act of assembly by which the plaintiffs were authorized to construct their dam, shows plainly that this is one of those many creeks, passing through a deep level marsh, adjoining the Delaware, up which the tide flows for some distance. The value of the property on its banks must be enhanced by excluding the water from the marsh, and the health of the inhabitants probably improved. Measures calculated to produce these objects, provided they do not come into collision with the powers of the general government, are undoubtedly within those which are reserved to the states. But the measure authorized by this act stops a navigable creek, and must be supposed to abridge the rights of those who

have been accustomed to use it. But this abridgment, unless it comes in conflict with the constitution or a law of the United States, is an affair between the government of Delaware and its citizens, of which this court can take no cognizance.

The counsel for the plaintiffs in error insist, that it comes in conflict with the power of the United States "to regulate commerce with foreign nations, and among the several states." If congress had passed any act which bore upon the case; any act in execution of the power to regulate commerce, the object of which was to control state legislation over those small navigable creeks into which the tide flows, and which abound throughout the lower country of the middle and southern states; we should feel not much difficulty in saying, that a state law coming to conflict with such act would be void. But congress has passed no such act. The repugnancy of the law of Delaware to the constitution is placed entirely on its repugnancy to the power to regulate commerce with foreign nations and among the several states; a power which has not been so exercised as to affect the question. We do not think, that the act empowering the Black Bird Creek Marsh company to place a dam across the creek, can, under all the circumstances of the case, be considered as repugnant to the power to regulate commerce in its dormant state, or as being in conflict with any law passed on the subject.

William Wirt, counsel for the respondent company, characterized the Delaware act as a "health" measure, and described the Black Bird Creek as "one of those sluggish reptile streams, that do not run but creep, and which, wherever it passes, spreads its venom, and destroys the health of all those who inhabit its marshes." "Can it be asserted," he asked, "that a law authorizing the erection of a dam, and the formation of banks which will draw off the pestilence, and give to those who have before suffered from disease, health and vigor, is unconstitutional?"

1. How do you suppose the case would have come out if the creek had been a major interstate waterway?

2. If the proper scope of congressional exercise of the commerce power sometimes depends on the purposes for which it is exercised, the same might be true of state law affecting interstate commerce. Might the outcome have been different had Wirt characterized the law, not as a health measure, but as a regulation of navigation on the state's waterways?

Recall Marshall's attraction to the argument in *Gibbons* that the very grant of a power to one government (the United States) precludes "the action of all others that would perform the same operation on the same thing." Is *Black Bird Creek* consistent with this view?

We have not omitted any part of Marshall's analysis in the *Black Bird Creek* case. The opinion concludes, elliptically, that "under all the circumstances of the case" the law authorizing erection of the dam does not conflict with the commerce clause or with any federal statute. What do you suppose are the relevant "circumstances"? One possible circumstance is that this was a health law as distinguished from a commercial regulation. Do you suppose that this rationale would have sufficed to sustain damming up a major interstate waterway? If not, did the "circumstances" of the case include the perception that the benefits of damming the creek substantially outweighed any impediments to interstate navigation? Does anything in Marshall's opinion in *Black Bird Creek* suggest this reading, and if so, is it consistent with the jurisprudence of *McCulloch* and *Gibbons*?

Note: Language, Purpose, and Meaning[51]

1. Language and Purpose

Aristotle:

All law is universal but about some things it is not possible to make a universal statement which shall be correct. In those cases then in which it is necessary to speak universally but not possible to do so correctly, the law takes the usual case, though it is not ignorant of the possibility of error. And it is none the less correct; for the error is not in the law nor in the legislator but in the nature of the thing, since the matter of practical affairs is of this kind from the start. When the law speaks universally, then, and a case arises under it which is not covered by the universal statement, then it is right, where the legislator fails us and has erred by oversimplicity, to correct the omission — to say what the legislator himself would have put into his law, if he had known. . . . And this is the nature of the equitable, a correction of law where it is defective owing to its universality.[52]

Plowden:

A law of a certain state provides that foreigners scaling the walls of the city shall be capitally punished. But it happened that foreigners innocently passing through the city heard an outcry that enemies had suddenly attacked the city and were making inroads. The foreigners scaled the walls before the citizens, and, defending the city, they saved it. Now, therefore, what of the law? Ought they to die, as the law says? . . .

In order to form a right judgment when the letter of a statute is restrained, and when enlarged, by equity, it is a good way, when you peruse a statute, to suppose that the law-maker is present, and that you have [asked] him the question you want to know touching the equity, then you must give yourself such an answer as you may imagine he would have done, if he had been present. As for example, . . . where the strangers scale the walls, and defend the city, suppose the lawmaker to be present with you, and in your mind put this question to him, shall the strangers be put to death? Then give yourself the same answer which you imagine he, being an upright and reasonable man, would have given, and you will find that he would have said "They shall not be put to death." . . . And therefore when such cases happen which are within the letter, or out of the letter, of a statute, and yet don't directly fall within the plain and natural purport of the letter, but are in some measure to be conceived in a different idea from that in which the text seems to express, it is a good way to give questions and give answers to yourself thereupon, in the same manner as if you were actually conversing with the maker of such laws, and by this means you will easily find out what is the equity of those cases. And if the law-maker would have followed the equity, notwithstanding the words of the law . . . you may safely do the like, for while you do no more than the law-maker would have done, you do not act contrary to the law, but in conformity to it.[53]

To read a provision without regard to its context and likely purposes will yield either unresolvable indeterminacies or plain nonsense. Some judges and scholars

51. See generally Paul Brest, The Misconceived Quest for the Original Understanding, 60 B.U.L. Rev. 204 (1980); Michael Moore, the Semantics of Judging, 54 S. Cal. L. Rev. 151 (1981).

52. Aristotle, Ethics, Book V. ch. 10, fol. 1137.

53. 2 Plowden 459, 466, 467, quoted in Learned Hand, The Bill of Rights 20-22 (1958).

have asserted that "[t]he whole aim of construction, as applied to a provision of the Constitution, is to discover the meaning, to ascertain and give effect to the intent, of its framers and the people who adopted it.[54] Others maintain that an interpreter should inquire into the "purpose of the provision." For example, Justice Frankfurter wrote:[55]

> You may have observed that I have not yet used the word "intention." All these years I have avoided speaking of the "legislative intent." . . . Legislation has an aim; it seeks to obviate some mischief, to supply an inadequacy, to effect a change of policy, to formulate a plan of government. That aim, that policy is not drawn, like nitrogen, out of the air; it is evidenced in the language of the statute, as read in the light of other external manifestations of purpose. That is what the judge must seek and effectuate, and he ought not to be led off the trail by tests that have overtones of subjective design. We are not concerned with anything subjective. We do not delve into the minds of legislators or their draftsmen, or committee members.

Can the "purpose" of a provision be distinguished from the "intent" of those who drafted or adopted it? Taken *literally*, Justice Frankfurter's statement makes no sense. Things — including statutes and constitutional provisions — do not have "purposes" or "aims"; they do not "seek to obviate" mischiefs. These terms require animate subjects. *Figuratively* speaking, one might describe the "purpose of a provision" tautologously with its language: "the purpose of Article I, §8, cl. 3 is to permit Congress to regulate commerce . . . among the several States." But this seems a fruitless enterprise, and any other figurative reading of the term seems ultimately to refer to the purposes, aims, or seekings — in short the "intent" — of those who framed and adopted the provision.[56]

Nonetheless, Frankfurter's remarks are evocative of a real distinction. The (subjective) aims of those who drafted or adopted a provision can be described on different levels of generality. A rather general description would be: "Their purpose in adopting Article I, §8, cl. 3 was to permit Congress to legislate [in matters of commerce] where the States were separately incompetent." Much more specifically, one might describe the adopters' view of a particular fact situation: "They wanted to prevent the States from imposing tariffs." All other things being equal, a general or vague characterization is likely to describe the aims of more people than a precise or detailed characterization — the target is easier to hit. As one moves from the more specific to the less specific characterization of, or inquiry into, the aims of the framers, one moves from "intent" to "purpose." One can talk about the "purpose of the provision" simply because it must have been the purpose of (nearly) everyone who voted for the provision and, indeed, understood to be their purpose even by those who voted against it.[57]

54. Home Bldg. & Loan Assn. v. Blaisdell, 290 U.S. 398 (1934) (Sutherland, J., dissenting).

55. Felix Frankfurter, Some Reflections on the Reading of Statutes, 1947 Colum. L. Rev. 527, 538-539.

56. The concept of purpose incorporates an element of will. It would simply be a misuse of language to say that a thing's purpose is anything it does or can do, apart from human intention. For example, it is not a purpose of an automobile to pollute, maim, or kill, and only by using a figurative anthropomorphism is it an automobile's purpose to transport passengers.

57. On a somewhat related point, can one meaningfully talk about the purpose or intent of those who framed or adopted a provision where there is no evidence that they explicitly considered the particular application of the provision about which their views are sought? Some scholars have suggested a person has no intent whatsoever with respect to a question he did not think about. See, e.g.,

These more and less general characterizations of the framers' objectives correlate roughly with different approaches to interpretation. One who inquires into "purpose" may not look much beyond the language of the provision, for the language, when read in the context of the generally understood structure and values of a society, will usually indicate the society's reasons for adopting it. (This suggests why, without being tautologous, many speak anthropomorphically of the "purpose of the provision.") One who inquires into "intent," on the other hand, will examine closely the proceedings and debates that led to the provision's adoption.

The language and purposes of a provision enjoy a symbiotic relationship. The meaning (or application) of a provision is ascertained by examining its language and purposes. The language sets the boundaries of possible meanings and yields the initial — and often the primary — indication of its purposes. At the same time, the purposes of the provision circumscribe the range of its plausible meanings.

2. Discovering the Adopters' Purposes[58]

Four sets of proceedings bear directly on the original understanding of the constitutional provisions: the federal Constitutional Convention held in Philadelphia in 1787, the state ratification conventions, congressional proceedings in which amendments were proposed pursuant to Article V, and the state legislative proceedings in which they were ratified. Of these, the reports of the secret[59] proceedings of the Philadelphia convention are probably most often cited and are as problematic as any others. John Wofford writes:[60]

> Max Farrand, in the introduction to his compilation of all accounts of the Convention extant in 1911 [The Records of the Federal Convention of 1787], states that the official journal, apparently containing all motions and votes, was delivered to Washington, then president of the Congress of the Confederation, who in 1796 deposited the

---

John Chipman Gray, The Nature and Sources of the Law 172-173 (2d ed. 1921). The contrary view is now generally accepted. See, e.g., Lon Fuller, The Morality of Law 83-87 (1964); Gerald MacCallum, Legislative Intent, 75 Yale L.J. 754 (1966); Henry Hart & Albert Sacks, The Legal Process: Basic Problems in the Making and Application of Law 98 (tent. ed. 1958):

> What is the significance of advertance or inadvertance in the concept of "intention"? Of course, one may "intend" some specific consequences to which he did not consequently advert. If a master tells a servant to "take care of the house" during his absence, he no doubt intends that the servant will do his best to extinguish a fire in the house started by lightning, even though this contingency never actually occurred to him. But does one "intend" everything within the reach of his words which he does not consciously "exclude"? [Wittgenstein writes:] "Someone says to me: 'Show the children a game.' I teach them gaming with dice, and the other says, "I didn't mean that sort of game." Must the exclusion of the game with dice have come before his mind when he gave me the order [to make this last statement true]?"

58. See generally Jacobus tenBroek, Admissibility and Use by the United States Supreme Court of Extrinsic Aids in Constitutional Construction, 26 Calif. L. Rev. 287, 437, 664 (1938); 27 Calif. L. Rev. 157, 399 (1939).

59. See Max Farrand, The Framing of the Constitution of the United States 58-59 (1913).

60. Wofford, The Blinding Light: The Uses of History in Constitutional Interpretation, 31 U. Chi. L. Rev. 502, 504-506 (1964). See also Donald Dewey, James Madison Helps Clio Interpret the Constitution, 15 Am. J. Legal Hist. 38 (1971); James Hutson, The Creation of the Constitution: The Integrity of the Documentary Record, 65 Tex. L. Rev. 1 (1986).

papers in the Department of State. There they remained, untouched, until Congress by joint resolution in 1818 ordered them printed. Farrand reports that President Monroe requested his Secretary of State, John Quincy Adams, to take charge of the publication: "The task proved to be a difficult one. The papers were," according to Adams, "no better than the daily minutes from which the regular journal ought to have been, but never was, made out." Adams reports that at his request William Jackson, the secretary of the Convention, called upon him and "looked over the papers, but he had no recollection of them which could remove the difficulties arising from their disorderly state, nor any papers to supply the deficiency of the missing papers." With the expenditure of considerable time and labor, and with the exercise of no little ingenuity, Adams was finally able to collate the whole to his satisfaction. General Bloomfield supplied him with several important documents from the papers of David Brearley; Charles Pinckney sent him a copy of the plan he "believed" to be one he presented to the Convention; Madison furnished the means of completing the records of the last four days. . . . As thus compiled, the Journal, Acts and Proceedings of the Convention . . . Which Formed the Constitution of the United States was printed in 1819. Adams felt that he there presented a "correct and tolerably clear view of the proceedings of the convention. . . ." Farrand's own judgment, however, is more critical: "As Adams had nothing whatever to guide him in his work of compilation and editing, mistakes were inevitable, and not a few of these were important. . . . With notes so carelessly kept, as were evidently those of the secretary, the Journal cannot be relied upon absolutely. The statement of questions is probably accurate in most cases, but the determination of those questions and in particular the votes upon them should be accepted somewhat tentatively."

Material in addition to the Journal has, of course, been discovered; this enabled Farrand to speak of "mistakes" in the Journal itself. Most important are the notes which Madison made during the proceedings. Madison himself described how he made the notes, and how he then used them to reconstruct a more complete account: "I chose a seat in front of the presiding member, with the other members, on my right and left hand. In this favorable position for hearing all that passed I noted in terms legible and in abbreviations and marks intelligible to myself what was read from the Chair or spoken by the members; and losing not a moment unnecessarily between the adjournment and reassembling of the Convention I was enabled to write out my daily notes during the session or within a few finishing days after its close." Madison's notes were not published exactly as he had transcribed them after each session. For after the publication of the official — and inaccurate — Journal, Madison went over his notes and made numerous changes in them. According to Farrand, these emendations "seriously impaired the value of his notes," since many of the Journal's errors were simply duplicated.

By 1911, when Farrand published all of the known records of the Convention, the Journal and Madison's Debates had been supplemented by other (and shorter) records made contemporaneously with the Convention and by statements made later by those who had been present. We know that other records once existed, although Farrand notes that it is "not probable . . . that any such new material would modify to any great extent our conceptions of the Convention's work."

In short, we have a picture of the Philadelphia proceedings, the various parts of which are generally consistent with each other. What we do not have, and indeed will never have, is any external check upon completeness of that picture. The conceptions of what occurred at Philadelphia remain, as Farrand put it, "ours."[61]

61. The main source of proceedings at the state conventions, which also contains material relating to the Philadelphia convention, is Debates in the Several State Conventions (Elliott ed., 2d ed. 1836-1845) (five volumes). Congressional proceedings are found in the Congressional Globe, later the Congressional Record. State legislative debates are not published in most states, although an official record of actions is kept.

The Court has often discovered the "intent of the framers" in their nonofficial utterances — correspondence, papers, and publications. For example, in Reynolds v. United States, 98 U.S. 145 (1879), in holding that the free exercise clause did not immunize a Mormon from a prosecution for bigamy, the Court cited Thomas Jefferson's assertion in his letter to the Danbury Baptists that the First Amendment built "a wall of separation between church and state." Chief Justice Waite explained: "Coming as this does from an acknowledged leader of the advocates of the measure, it may be accepted almost as an authoritative declaration of the scope and effect of the amendment. . . ."[62] What implicit assumptions does Waite make?

Without doubt, the most frequently cited nonofficial source is The Federalist Papers, which the Court has typically treated as an authoritative manifestation of the intent of the framers. Consider Professor Jacobus tenBroek's comment on this practice.[63]

> There can be little doubt that if the writers of The Federalist had dedicated themselves in all sincerity to the preparation of a purely impartial account of the will of the fathers, their work would have come as near to absolute historical accuracy as human limitations would permit in the circumstances. In that case, both by reason of ability and opportunity, their situation would have been unexcelled.[a] But the doctrine that they actually revealed the collective intent of the Constitution formulators, involves the assumptions that they, in framing their articles divested themselves of their former protagonistic biases and attitudes, and that The Federalist was composed in an atmosphere of calm disinterestedness. The first of these is only conjecturally possible and the second is historically false. The Federalist was composed as an argument on one side of a bitterly controverted question. It was calculated to put the Constitution in the light which would make it most acceptable to the ratifying conventions. It did not even purport to express the intention of the framers.
>
> At bottom, the Court's theory comes down to the proposition that the authors of The Federalist, having been members of the Constitutional Convention, had a first hand opportunity to know the intention of the men there assembled. Yet that identical experience has not been regarded as similarly endowing others who were not measurably less capable. Thus, Luther Martin's commentary on the Constitution appears infrequently in the reports, and then generally with disparaging comment. Likewise, the able series of articles written over the name of "Brutus" by Judge Robert Yates has never, to my knowledge, been cited by the Supreme Court. . . . We must conclude, therefore, that the difference in the position of Madison and Hamilton, on the one hand, and Martin and Yates, on the other, lies not in any difference of opportunity to know the will of the fathers, nor yet possibly in any difference of merit. It lies rather in the not altogether incidental fact that Madison and Hamilton were on the side which turned out to be victorious, and this fact, taken together with their entire careers, has made them great in the eye of posterity — a fact which has given their words a quality of persuasion which has never attached to the utterances

62. See also McCollum v. Board of Educ., 333 U.S. 203, 211 (1948). For an excellent criticism of the Court's use of history in construing the religion clauses, see Mark de Wolfe Howe, The Garden and Wilderness (1965).

63. tenBroek, supra note 58, 27 Calif. L. Rev. 157, 162-164 (1939).

a. This statement is substantially correct but must be modified in some degree by the fact that John Jay, one of the authors of The Federalist, had not been a delegate to the Constitutional Convention. However, only five out of the eighty-five articles composing The Federalist are attributed to Jay, and these, curiously enough, are almost never cited by the Supreme Court, although this is probably due more to their subject matter than to their authorship. [Also, after the first month, Hamilton attended the convention only sporadically.]

> of Martin and Yates. It is this circumstance which explains the pre-eminent popularity of The Federalist with the United States Supreme Court as against all other contemporary partisan commentators, and not the judicially asserted fact that they possessed peculiar opportunity to inform themselves on the issue of formulative intent.[64]

Is the Court justified in giving more weight to the views of the proponents than of the opponents of the Constitution?

The Court has also cited the enactments of early Congresses as indicative of the original understanding of constitutional provisions. For example, in Myers v. United States, 272 U.S. 52 (1926), in holding that a statutory provision requiring the Senate's consent for the removal of postmasters unconstitutionally usurped executive power, Chief Justice Taft relied on the debates over, and enactment of, a 1789 law that recognized the president's plenary power to remove his secretary of foreign affairs. Taft argued that the Congress had affirmed the president's exclusive constitutional authority to remove executive appointees, and explained:

> We have devoted much space to this discussion and decision of the question of the Presidential power of removal in the First Congress, not because a Congressional conclusion on a constitutional issue is conclusive, but, first, because of our agreement with the reasons upon which it was avowedly based; second, because this was the decision of the First Congress, on a question of primary importance in the organization of the Government, made within two years after the Constitutional Convention and within a much shorter time after its ratification; and, third, because that Congress numbered among its leaders those who had been members of the Convention.

Much earlier, in Martin v. Hunter's Lessee, 14 U.S. (1 Wheat.) 304 (1816), Justice Story thus concluded his argument that the Supreme Court had appellate jurisdiction over state courts.[65]

> It is an historical fact, that at the time when the Judiciary Act was submitted to the deliberations of the first congress, composed, as it was, not only of men of great learning and ability, but of men who had acted principal part in framing, supporting, or opposing that constitution, the same exposition was explicitly declared and admitted by the friends and by the opponents of that system.

What assumptions are implicit in these uses of the actions of early Congresses? With respect to the 1789 provision relied on in *Myers*, consider Professor Charles Miller's suggestions that "one reason why the First Congress had exerted little effort on its own behalf was that George Washington was President, and no legisla-

64. The Federalist has also often been touted as a reliable gauge of opinion in the ratifying conventions, on the ground that it was widely published in the states prior to ratification and was the chief means by which the intent of the Convention was transmitted to the states. See, e.g., Legal Tender Cases, 79 U.S. (12 Wall.) 457, 585, 608 (1870). But even if the articles persuaded all who read them, "a considerable number of the conventions in the states had ratified the Constitution while a varying number of The Federalist papers were as yet unpublished. . . ." tenBroek, supra note 58, 27 Calif. L. Rev. at 171.

65. Note also that Oliver Ellsworth, who was Chief Justice of the Supreme Court from 1796 to 1800, played a major role in the framing of both Article III and the Judiciary Act of 1789. Michael Kraus, Oliver Ellsworth, in the 1 The Justices of the United States Supreme Court 273 (Friedman & Israel eds. 1969). But cf. Marbury v. Madison, page 78 supra.

tor dared question his wisdom by denying him the right to remove a member of his own cabinet," and that the outcome of Congress' action was largely the result of clever parliamentary maneuvering by James Madison, who managed to divide and conquer two factions, which, for different reasons, believed that the Senate's consent *should* be necessary for presidential removals.[66]

VI. Slavery

THE ANTELOPE

23 U.S. (10 Wheat.) 66 (1825)
Appeal from the Circuit Court of Georgia

[In 1808 Congress prohibited the importation of slaves into the United States. A series of subsequent federal enactments punished persons engaged in the slave trade, forfeited their ships, and provided that the Negroes be returned to Africa. The ship Antelope, bearing 280 Africans, most of whom had been seized by pirates from slave ships, was apprehended off the coast of Florida by a United States revenue cutter for suspected violation of the slave trade acts. The vice consuls of Spain and Portugal claimed the Africans as the property of citizens of their countries. The United States appealed from the circuit courts decision for the foreign claimants. The issue before the Court was whether the federal statutes applied to forfeit slaves owned by foreign nationals.[67]]

MARSHALL, C.J. . . .

In prosecuting this appeal, the United States assert no property in themselves. They appear in the character of guardians, or next friends, of these Africans, who are brought, without any act of their own, into the bosom of our country, insist on their right to freedom, and submit their claim to the laws of the land, and to the tribunals of the nation. The consuls of Spain and Portugal, respectively, demand these Africans as slaves, who have, in the regular cause of legitimate commerce, been acquired as property, by the subjects of their respective sovereigns, and claim their restitution under the laws of the United States.

In examining claims of this momentous importance — claims in which the sacred rights of liberty and of property come in conflict with each other — which have drawn from the bar a degree of talent and of eloquence, worthy of the questions that have been discussed, this court must not yield to feelings which might seduce it from the path of duty, and must obey the mandate of the law.

That the course of opinion on the slave-trade should be unsettled, ought to excite no surprise. The Christian and civilized nations of the world, with whom we have most intercourse, have all been engaged in it. However abhorrent this traffic may be to a mind whose original feelings are not blunted by familiarity with the practice, it has been sanctioned, in modern times, by the laws of all na-

66. Charles Miller, The Supreme Court and the Uses of History ch. 4 (1969).

67. The actual facts are considerably more complex. For a rich description of the case and its contents, see John Noonan, Jr., The Antelope: The Ordeal of the Recaptured Africans in the Administrations of James Monroe and John Quincy Adams (1977).

tions who possess distant colonies, each of whom has engaged in it as a common commercial business, which no other could rightfully interrupt. It has claimed all the sanction which could be derived from long usage and general acquiescence. That trade could not be considered as contrary to the law of nations which was authorized and protected by the laws of all commercial nations; the right to carry on which was claimed by each, and allowed by each.

The course of unexamined opinion, which was founded on this inveterate usage, received its first check in America; and, as soon as these states acquired the right of self-government, the traffic was forbidden by most of them. In the beginning of this century, several human and enlightened individuals of Great Britain devoted themselves to the cause of the Africans; and by frequent appeals to the nation, in which the enormity of this commerce was unveiled and exposed to the public eye, the general sentiment was at length roused against it, and the feelings of justice and humanity, regaining their long-lost ascendency, prevailed so far in the British parliament, as to obtain an act for its abolition. The utmost efforts of the British government, as well as of that of the United States, have since been assiduously employed in its suppression. It has been denounced by both, in terms of great severity, and those concerned in it are subjected to the heaviest penalties which law can inflict. In addition to these measures, operating on their own people, they have used all their influence to bring other nations into the same system, and to interdict this trade by the consent of all. Public sentiment has, in both countries, kept pace with the measures of government; and the opinion is extensively, if not universally, entertained, that this unnatural traffic ought to be suppressed. While its illegality is asserted by some governments, but not admitted by all; while the detestation in which it is held, is growing daily, and even those nations who tolerate it, in fact, almost disavow their own conduct, and rather connive at, than legalize, the acts of their subjects, it is not wonderful, that public feeling some at in advance of strict law, and that opposite opinions should be entertained on the precise cases in which our own laws may control and limit the practice of others. Indeed, we ought not to be surprised, if, in this novel series of cases, even courts of justice should, in some instances, have carried the principle of suppression further than a more deliberate consideration of the subject would justify. . . .

The question, whether the slave-trade is prohibited by the law of nations has been seriously propounded, and both the affirmative and negative of the proposition have been maintained with equal earnestness. That it is contrary to the law of nature, will scarcely be denied. That every man has a natural right to the fruits of his own labor, is generally admitted; and that no other person can rightfully deprive him of those fruits, and appropriate them against his will, seems to be the necessary result of this admission. But from the earliest times, war has existed, and war confers rights in which all have acquiesced. Among the most enlightened nations of antiquity, one of these was, that the victor might enslave the vanquished. This, which was the usage of all, could not be pronounced repugnant to the law of nations, which is certainly to be tried by the test of general usage. That which has received the assent of all, must be the law of all. Slavery, then, has its origin in force; but as the world has agreed, that it is a legitimate result of force, the state of things which is thus produced by general consent, cannot be pronounced unlawful.

Throughout Christendom, this harsh rule has been exploded, and war is no longer considered, as giving a right to enslave captives. But this triumph of humanity has not been universal. The parties of the modern law of nations do not propagate their principles by force, and Africa has not yet adopted them. Throughout the whole extent of that immense continent, so far as we know its history, it is still the law of nations, that prisoners are slaves. Can those who have themselves renounced this law, be permitted to participate in its effects, by purchasing the beings who are its victims? Whatever might be the answer of a moralist to this question, a jurist must search for its legal solution, in those principles of action which are sanctioned by the usages, the national acts, and the general assent, of that portion of the world of which he considers himself as a part, and to whose law the appeal is made. If we resort to this standard, as the test of international law, the question, as has already been observed, is decided in favor of the legality of the trade. Both Europe and America embarked in it; and for nearly two centuries, it was carried on, without opposition, and without censure. A jurist could not say, that a practice, thus supported, was illegal, and that those engaged in it might be punished, either personally or by deprivation of property. In this commerce thus sanctioned by universal assent, every nation had an equal right to engage. How is this right to be lost? Each may renounce it for its own people; but can this renunciation effect others?

No principle of general law is more universally acknowledged, than the perfect equality of nations. Russia and Geneva have equal rights. It results from this equality, that no one can rightfully impose a rule on another. Each legislates for itself, but its legislation can operate on itself alone. A right, then, which is vested in all, by the consent of all, can be divested only by consent; and this trade, in which all have participated, must remain lawful to those who cannot be induced to relinquish it. As no nation can prescribe a rule for others, none can make a law of nations; and this traffic remains lawful to those whose governments have not forbidden it. If it be consistent with the law of nations, it cannot in itself be piracy. It can be made so only by statute; and the obligation of the statute cannot transcend the legislative power of the state which may enact it.

If it be neither repugnant to the law of nations, nor piracy, it is almost superfluous to say, in this court, that the right of bringing in for adjudication, in time of peace, even where the vessel belongs to a nation which has prohibited the trade, cannot exist. The courts of no country execute the penal laws of another; and the courts of the American government, on the subject of visitation and search, would decide any case in which that right had been exercised by an American cruiser, on the vessel of a foreign nation, not violating our municipal laws, against the captors. It follows, that a foreign vessel engaged in the African slave-trade, captured on the high seas, in time of peace, by an American cruiser, and brought in for adjudication, would be restored. . . .

The general question being disposed of, it remains to examine the circumstances of the particular case. [The Court denied the Portuguese claims, taking judicial notice of the fact that] Americans, and others who cannot use the flag of their own nations, carry on this criminal and inhuman traffic, under the flags of other countries. . . . [The real owner of the Africans claimed by Portugal] belongs to some other nation; and feels the necessity of concealment. [Because the Court was evenly divided over the legitimacy of the Spanish claim, it affirmed the lower court's decree, though it reduced the number of Africans to be restored to the Spanish owners.]

Discussion[68]

1. Although The Antelope does not arise under the Constitution, slavery presented the most divisive constitutional issue of the first 70 years of the Republic. Even if The Antelope did not directly affect domestic slavery, Marshall was well aware that anything the Court said about the matter would be critically read, and he might also have been concerned not to antagonize the two powerful foreign nations whose nationals claimed to own the slaves.

2. In suggesting that some courts may "have carried the principle of suppression further than a deliberate consideration of the subject would justify," Marshall may have been referring to the circuit court decision in United States v. La Jeune Eugenie, 26 F. Cas. 832 (No. 15,551) (C.C. Mass. 1822), in which Justice Story condemned the slave trade as

> repugnant to the great principles of Christian duty, the dictates of natural religion, the obligations of good faith and morality, and the eternal maxims of social justice. When any trade can be truly said to have these ingredients, it is impossible that it can be consistent with any system of law that purports to rest on the authority of reason or revelation. And it is sufficient to stamp any trade as interdicted by public law, when it can be justly affirmed, that it is repugnant to the general principles of justice and humanity.

In The Antelope, Marshall also condemns slavery on moral grounds. If slavery violates principles of natural law, how could the Court order the return of any of the Negroes seized on the Antelope? One answer is that a claim of natural right — the right not to be divested of property — was being asserted on the other side. Another, not inconsistent, answer involves the distinction between natural and positive law. In 1772, in Somerset's Case, Lord Mansfield ordered discharged from service a slave who had been brought by his Virginia master to England, noting that "the state of slavery is of such a nature, that it is incapable of being introduced on any reasons . . . but only by positive law. . . . It is so odious, that nothing can be suffered to support it but positive law."[69] Marshall's decision in The Antelope is consistent with this view if, as seems likely, he regarded the unwritten but venerable "law of nations" as positive law.

3. Robert Cover writes:[70]

> In a static and simplistic model of law, the judge caught between law and morality has only four choices. He may apply the law against his conscience. He may apply conscience and be faithless to the law. He may resign. Or he may cheat: He may state that the law is not what he believes it to be; and, thus preserve an appearance (to others) of conformity of law and morality. Once we assume a more realistic model of law and of the judicial process, these four positions become only poles setting limits to a complex field of action and motive. For in a dynamic model, law is always becoming. And the judge has a legitimate role in determining what it is that the law will become.

68. See generally Robert Cover, Justice Accused: Antislavery and the Judicial Process (1975).
69. Quoted in id. at 6.
70. Id.

Based on Marshall's opinions in *McCulloch, Gibbons,* and *Fletcher,* where would you locate him on a continuum between a "static" and "dynamic" conception of law?

VII. American Indians and the American Political Community

American Indians — Native Americans — were recognized by European settlers as members of distinct tribal entities even as the settlers proceeded to displace them. The United States government frequently negotiated with Indian tribes — although history reveals "numerous accounts of threats, coercion, bribery, and outright fraud by the negotiators for the United States."[71]

Indians were not deemed citizens of the new United States. Although the 1790 federal naturalization law restricting admission to free white aliens appeared to foreclose Indian naturalization, several subsequent treaties and statutes contemplated the possibility of Indian citizenship. For example, the Cherokee treaties of 1817 and 1819 included provisions granting land to heads of families "who may wish to become citizens of the United States."[72] It was clear, though, that an Indian who chose to remain a formal member of his tribe could not become a citizen. As James Kettner writes, "the tribes themselves . . . could be considered quasi-sovereign nations, enforcing their own laws and customs and requiring the immediate allegiance of their members."[73]

Just as the tension between nation and states, exemplified by *McCulloch,* has remained a pervasive reality in American constitutional law, so the relations between Indian tribes and the other units of American government have never been fully resolved. One of the earliest judicial decisions involving these relations provoked what Charles Warren, a leading historian of the Supreme Court, termed "the most serious crisis in the history of the Court."[74] At the height of the crisis, former President John Quincy Adams exclaimed that "the Union is in the most imminent danger of dissolution."[75]

CHEROKEE NATION v. GEORGIA
30 U.S. (5 Pet. 1) (1831)

[The Cherokees had by various treaties with the United States been allotted approximately four million acres of lands within the territory of Georgia. In 1827 gold was discovered on tribal lands, and the same year the Cherokee Nation declared themselves an independent nation and adopted a constitution.[76] The Georgia legislature responded by passing "Indian laws" that, among other things,

71. Wilkinson & John M. Volkman, Judicial Review of Indian Treaty Abrogation: "As Long as Water Flows or Grass Grows upon the Earth" — How Long a Time Is That? 63 Calif. L. Rev. 601, 610 (1975).
72. James Kettner, The Development of American Citizenship, 1608-1870, 292 (1978).
73. Id. at 294.
74. Charles Warren, The Supreme Court in American History 189 (1923).
75. A. Beveridge, John Marshall 544 (1919).
76. See G. Edward White, The Marshall Court and Cultural Change 715 (1987).

annulled all of the Cherokee "laws, usages, and customs," divided their lands into separate counties under state jurisdiction, and prohibited the Cherokee legislature and courts from meeting. As an assertion of Georgia's sovereignty over the tribe, the state tried and convicted George Tassels for an 1830 homicide he committed on the reservation against another Cherokee. Tassel appealed to the United States Supreme Court, which granted a writ of error directing the state to appear. In response, Georgia's governor ordered Tassel's immediate execution.

The Cherokee Nation appealed to the federal government to support their claims against Georgia's abrogation of its treaty rights. President Jackson, who was promoting a policy of Indian removal west of the Mississippi, responded that "the President of the United States has no power to protect them against the laws of Georgia."[77] The Cherokee Nation then attempted to invoke original jurisdiction of the United States Supreme Court by describing itself as "a foreign state, not owing allegiance to the United States, nor to any state of this union. . . ."[78] On the merits, the Nation claimed that Georgia had violated the Contract Clause, since "treaties . . . are contracts of the highest character and of the most solemn obligation."

The Court rejected the Cherokee Nation's assertion that it was a foreign state and dismissed the claim for lack of jurisdiction. There was no majority opinion. Chief Justice Marshall wrote an opinion for himself and Justice McLean alone. Justices Johnson and Baldwin concurred in the result, but not the reasoning, and Justice Story joined in Justice Thompson's dissent.]

MARSHALL, C.J.

This bill is brought by the Cherokee nation, praying an injunction to restrain the state of Georgia from the execution of certain laws of that state, which, as is alleged, go directly to annihilate the Cherokees as a political society, and to seize, for the use of Georgia, the lands of the nation which have been assured to them by the United States in solemn treaties repeatedly made and still in force.

If courts were permitted to indulge their sympathies, a case better calculated to excite them can scarcely be imagined. A people once numerous, powerful, and truly independent, found by ancestors in the quiet and uncontrolled possession of an ample domain, gradually sinking beneath our superior policy, our arts and our arms, have yielded their lands by successive treaties, each of which contains a solemn guarantee of the residue, until they retain no more of their formerly extensive territory than is deemed necessary to their comfortable subsistence. To preserve this remnant, the present application is made.

Before we can look into the merits of the case, a preliminary inquiry presents itself. Has this Court jurisdiction of the cause? . . . Is the Cherokee nation a foreign state in the sense in which that term is used in the constitution?

. . . So much of the [plaintiff's] argument as was intended to prove the character of the Cherokees as a state, as a distinct political society, separated from others, capable of managing its own affairs and governing itself, has, in the opinion of a majority of the judges, been completely successful. They have been uniformly treated as a state from the settlement of our country. The numerous treaties made with them by the United States recognize them as a people capable of maintaining the relations of peace and war, of being responsible in their politi-

77. 30 U.S. (5 Pet.) 8.
78. Id. at 2.

cal character for any violation of their engagements, or for any aggression committed on the citizens of the United States by any individual of their community. Laws have been enacted in the spirit of these treaties. The acts of our government plainly recognize the Cherokee nation as a state, and the Courts are bound by those acts.

A question of much more difficulty remains. Do the Cherokees constitute a foreign state in the sense of the constitution?

The counsel have shown conclusively that they are not a state of the union, and have insisted that individually they are aliens, not owing allegiance to the United States. An aggregate of aliens composing a state must, they say, be a foreign state. Each individual being foreign, the whole must be foreign.

. . . In the general, nations not owing a common allegiance are foreign to each other. . . . But the relation of the Indians to the United States is marked by peculiar and cardinal distinctions which exist no where else. . . .

Though the Indians are acknowledged to have an unquestionable, and, heretofore, unquestioned right to the lands they occupy, until that right shall be extinguished by a voluntary cession to our government; yet it may well be doubted whether those tribes which reside within the acknowledged boundaries of the United States can, with strict accuracy, be denominated foreign nations. They may, more correctly, perhaps, be denominated domestic dependent nations. They occupy a territory to which we assert a title independent of their will. . . . Meanwhile they are in a state of pupilage. Their relation to the United States resembles that of a ward to his guardian.

They look to our government for protection; rely upon its kindness and its power; appeal to it for relief to their wants; and address the president as their great father. They and their country are considered by foreign nations, as well as by ourselves, as being so completely under the sovereignty and dominion of the United States, that any attempt to acquire their lands, or to form a political connexion with them, would be considered by all as an invasion of our territory, and an act of hostility.

These considerations go far to support the opinion, that the framers of our constitution had not the Indian tribes in view, when they opened the Courts of the union to controversies between a state or the citizens thereof, and foreign states. . . .

[T]he peculiar relations between the United States and the Indians occupying our territory are such, that we should feel much difficulty in considering them as designated by the term foreign state, were there no other part of the Constitution which might shed light on the meaning of these words. But we think that in construing them, considerable aid is furnished by that clause in the eighth section of the third article, which empowers Congress to "regulate commerce with foreign nations, and among the several states, and with the Indian tribes."

In this clause they are as clearly contradistinguished by a name appropriate to themselves, from foreign nations, as from the several states composing the union. They are designated by a distinct appellation; and as this appellation can be applied to neither of the others, neither can the appellation distinguishing either of the others be in fair construction applied to them. The objects, to which the power of regulating commerce might be directed, are divided into three distinct classes — foreign nations, the several states, and Indian tribes. When forming this article, the convention considered them as entirely distinct. We cannot assume that the distinction was lost in framing a subsequent article, unless there be something in its language to authorize the assumption. . . .

The Court has bestowed its best attention on this question, and after mature deliberation, the majority is of opinion that an Indian tribe or nation within the United States is not a foreign state in the sense of the constitution, and cannot maintain an action in the Courts of the United States.

A serious additional objection exists to the jurisdiction of the Court. Is the matter of the bill the proper subject for judicial inquiry and decision? It seeks to restrain a state from the forcible exercise of legislative power over a neighbouring people, asserting their independence; their right to which the state denies. On several of the matters alleged in the bill, for example on the laws making it criminal to exercise the usual powers of self government in their own country by the Cherokee nation, this Court cannot interpose; at least in the form in which those matters are presented.

That part of the bill which respects the land occupied by the Indians, and prays the aid of the Court to protect their possession, may be more doubtful. The mere question of right might perhaps be decided by this Court in a proper case with proper parties. But the Court is asked to do more than decide on the title. The bill requires us to control the legislature of Georgia, and to restrain the exertion of its physical force. The propriety of such an interposition by the Court may be well questioned. It savours too much of the exercise of political power to be within the proper province of the judicial department. But the opinion on the point respecting parties makes it unnecessary to decide this question.

If it be true that the Cherokee nation have rights, this is not the tribunal in which those rights are to be asserted. If it be true that wrongs have been inflicted, and that still greater are to be apprehended, this is not the tribunal which can redress the past or prevent the future.

The motion for an injunction is denied.

JOHNSON, J., concurring.

. . . With the morality of the case I have no concern; I am called upon to consider it as a legal question. . . .

I think it very clear that the constitution neither speaks of them as states or foreign states, but as just what they were, Indian tribes; an anomaly unknown to the books that treat of states, and which the law of nations would regard as nothing more than wandering hordes, held together only by ties of blood and habit, and having neither laws or government, beyond what is required in a savage state. The distinction is clearly made in that section which vests in Congress power to regulate commerce between the United States with foreign nations and the Indian tribes.

The language must be applied in one of three senses; either in that of the law of nations, or of the vernacular use, or that of the constitution. In the first, although it means any state not subject to our laws, yet it must be a state and not a hunter horde: in the vernacular, it would not be applied to a people within our limits and at our very doors: and in the constitution the two epithets are used in direct contradistinction. The latter words were unnecessary, if the first included the Indian tribes. There is no ambiguity, though taken literally; and if there were, facts and circumstances altogether remove it.

But had I been sitting alone in this cause, I should have waived the consideration of personal description altogether; and put my rejection of this notion upon the nature of the claim set up, exclusively.

I cannot entertain a doubt that it is one of a political character altogether, and wholly unfit for the cognizance of a judicial tribunal. There is no possible view of the subject, that I can perceive, in which a Court of justice can take jurisdiction of the questions made in the bill. . . .

What [do the Cherokee] allegations exhibit but a state of war, and the fact of invasion? . . . [T]he contest is distinctly a contest for empire. It is not a case of meum and tuum in the judicial but in the political sense. Not an appeal to laws but to force. A case in which a sovereign undertakes to assert his right upon his sovereign responsibility; to right himself, and not to appeal to any arbiter but the sword, for the justice of his cause. . . . In the exercise of sovereign right, the sovereign is sole arbiter of his own justice. The penalty or wrong is war and subjugation.

But there is still another ground in this case, which alone would have prevented me from assuming jurisdiction and that is the utter impossibility of doing justice, at least even handed justice, between the parties. . . .

There is still another view in which this cause of action may be considered in regard to its political nature. The United States finding themselves involved in conflicting treaties, or at least in two treaties respecting the same property, under which two parties assert conflicting claims; one of the parties, putting itself upon its sovereign right, passes laws which in effect declare the laws and treaties under which the other party claims, null and void. It proceeds to carry into effect those laws by means of physical force; and the other party appeals to the executive department for protection. Being disappointed there, the party appeals to this Court, indirectly to compel the executive to pursue a course of policy, which his sense of duty of ideas of the law may indicate should not be pursued. That is, to declare war against a state, or to use the public force to repel the force and resist the laws of a state, when his judgment tells him the evils to grow out of such a course may be incalculable.

What these people may have a right to claim of the executive power is one thing: whether we are to be the instruments to compel another branch of the government to make good the stipulations of treaties, is a very different question. Courts of justice are properly excluded from all considerations of policy, and therefore are very unfit instruments to control the action of that branch of government; which may often be compelled by the highest considerations of public policy to withhold even the exercise of a positive duty. . . .

[A dissenting opinion by Justice Baldwin is omitted.]

THOMPSON, J., joined by Story, J., dissenting.

. . . Is the Cherokee nation a competent party to sue in this Court?

. . . The terms state and nation are used in the law of nations, as well as in common parlance, as importing the same thing; and imply a body of men, united together, to procure their mutual safety and advantage by means of their union. . . . Every nation that governs itself, under what form soever, without any dependence on a foreign power, is a sovereign state. Its rights are naturally the same as those of any other state. Such are moral persons who live together in a natural society, under the law of nations. It is sufficient if it be really sovereign and independent: that is, it must govern itself by its own authority and laws. We ought, therefore, to reckon in the number of sovereigns those states that have bound themselves to another more powerful, although by an unequal alliance. The conditions of these unequal alliances may be infinitely varied; but whatever they are, provided the inferior ally reserves to itself the sovereignty or the right to govern its own body, it ought to be considered an independent state. Consequently, a weak state, that, in order to provide for its safety, places itself under the protection of a more powerful one, without stripping itself of the right of government and sovereignty, does not cease on this account to be placed among the sovereigns who acknowledge no other power. . . .

I do not understand it is denied by a majority of the Court, that the Cherokee Indians form a sovereign state according to the doctrine of the law of nations; but that, although a sovereign state, they are not considered a foreign state within the meaning of the constitution.

Whether the Cherokee Indians are to be considered a foreign state or not, is a point on which we cannot expect to discover much light from the law of nations. We must derive this knowledge chiefly from the practice of our own government, and the light in which the nation has been viewed and treated by it. . . . [The Cherokees] have never been, by conquest, reduced to the situation of subjects to any conqueror, and thereby lost their separate national existence, and the rights of self-government, and become subject to the laws of the conqueror. Whenever wars have taken place, they have been followed by regular treaties of peace, containing stipulations on each side according to existing circumstances; the Indian nation always preserving its distinct and separate national character. And notwithstanding we do not recognize the right of the Indians to transfer the absolute title of their lands to any other than ourselves [i.e., the government of the United States], the right of occupancy is still admitted to remain in them, accompanied with the right of self-government, according to their own usages and customs; and with the competency to act in a national capacity, although placed under the protection of the whites, and owing a qualified subjection so far as is requisite for public safety. But the principle is universally admitted, that this occupancy belongs to them as matter of right, and not by mere indulgence. They cannot be disturbed in the enjoyment of it, or deprived of it, without their free consent; or unless a just and necessary war should sanction their dispossession.

In this view of their situation, there is as full and complete recognition of their sovereignty, as if they were the absolute owners of the soil. The progress made in civilization by the Cherokee Indians cannot surely be considered as in any measure destroying their national or foreign character, so long as they are permitted to maintain a separate and distinct government; it is their political condition that constitutes their foreign character, and in that sense must the term foreign be understood as used in the constitution. It can have no relation to local, geographical, or territorial position. . . . It is the political relation in which one government or country stands to another, which constitutes it foreign to the other. The Cherokee territory being within the chartered limits of Georgia, does not affect the question. When Georgia is spoken of as a state, reference is had to its political character, and not to boundary. . . .

[I]f . . . a separate and distinct jurisdiction or government is the test by which to decide whether a nation be foreign or not; I am unable to perceive any sound and substantial reason why the Cherokee nation should not be so considered. It is governed by its own laws, usages and customs: it has no connexion with any other government or jurisdiction, except by way of treaties entered into with like form and ceremony as with other foreign nations. . . .

[Thompson then addresses the argument based on the language in the Commerce Clause:]

This appears to me to partake too much of a mere verbal criticism, to draw after it the important conclusion that Indian tribes are not foreign nations. . . .

Cases may arise where the trade with a particular tribe may require to be regulated, and which might not have been embraced under the general description of the term nation, or it might at least have left the case somewhat doubtful; as the clause was intended to vest in Congress the power to regulate all commercial intercourse, this phraseology was probably adopted to meet all possible cases; and the provision would have been imperfect, if the term Indian tribes had been omitted. . . . Or, it may be that the term tribe is here used as importing the same thing as that of nation, and adopted merely to avoid the repetition of the term nation. . . . No very important conclusion I think, therefore, can be drawn from the use of the term "tribe" in this clause of the constitution; intended merely for commercial regulations. . . .

Other instances occur in the constitution where different terms are used importing the same thing. Thus, in the clause giving jurisdiction to this Court, the term "foreign states" is used instead of "foreign nations," as in the clause relating to commerce. And again, in Art. I, §10, a still different phraseology is employed. "No state, without the consent of Congress, shall enter into any agreement of compact with a 'foreign power.' " But each of these terms, nation, state, power, as used in different parts of the constitution, imports the same thing, and does not admit of a different interpretation. In the treaties made with the Indians, they are sometimes designated under the name of tribe, and sometimes that of nation. . . .

The idea of the Cherokees being considered citizens is entirely inconsistent with several of our treaties with them. . . . And if not citizens, they must be aliens or foreigners, and such must be the character of each individual belonging to the nation. And it was, therefore, very aptly asked on the argument, and I think not very easily answered, how a nation composed of aliens or foreigners can be other than a foreign nation. . . .

Other departments of the government, whose right it is to decide what powers shall be recognised as sovereign and independent nations, have treated this nation as such. They have considered it competent, in its political and national capacity, to enter into contracts of the most solemn character; and if these contracts contain matter proper for judicial inquiry, why should we refuse to entertain jurisdiction of the case? . . .

[Justice Thompson concludes that it would be proper for the Court to enjoin Georgia from enforcing many of its new statutes inasmuch as they violate the treaty rights of the Cherokee Nation.]

Discussion

1. Describe Marshall's mode of analysis in *Cherokee Nation*. How does the resolution desired by the Cherokees savor more "of the exercise of political power" than the Court's striking down Maryland's tax in *McCulloch* or invalidating Georgia's attempted rescission of the Yazoo land grants in *Fletcher*? Should the

Supreme Court generally attempt to avoid accepting jurisdiction when it is foreseeable that a given decision might be met by outright defiance by those to whom it is directed? Professor White noted the widespread perception at the time that "if the Cherokees should win on the jurisdictional issue, and also on the merits, Georgia and the Jackson administration, with the tacit support of Congress, might well decline to endorse the Court's judgment, thereby isolating the Court."[79] Indeed, Georgia symbolized its view that the dispute was entirely a domestic matter by refusing even to appear before the Court to present its opposition to the Cherokee's position.

2. Describe Johnson's mode of analysis. How does it square with his concurrence in Fletcher v. Peck? Can a judge who believes that ascertainable norms of natural justice bind even the Deity, let alone states of the United States, adopt the strict separation between law and morality that is suggested in the first paragraph of opinion?

3. In Worcester v. Georgia, 31 U.S. (6 Pet.) 515 (1832), the Court, with only Justice Baldwin dissenting, held that Georgia's anti-Cherokee laws were unconstitutional. The State had sentenced Worcester to four years imprisonment for residing within Cherokee lands without procuring a license from Georgia. "The Cherokee nation," Chief Justice Marshall wrote, "is a distinct community, occupying its own territory . . . , in which the laws of Georgia can have no force. . . . The whole intercourse between the United States and this nation, is, by our constitution and laws, vested in the government of the United States." It was this decision that supposedly led to the almost certainly apocryphal remark attributed to President Jackson, "John Marshall has made his decision; now let him enforce it."[80] A recent biographer of Marshall notes that even if Jackson did not say this, it described his attitude. The Supreme Court's decision, however much it seemed to protect the Cherokees from Georgia, did nothing to protect them from the United States itself. Led by Jackson, the United States embarked on the policy that forced most Cherokees to march on the "Trail of Tears" to forced relocation in Oklahoma.

79. White, supra note 76, at 723.
80. Leonard Baker, John Marshall: A Life in Law 745 (1974).

Chapter 3
The Taney Court, 1835-1864

The first party system of Federalists and Republicans began to fade in the aftermath of the War of 1812. A second party system began to emerge after the Era of Good Feelings, a period of supposed consensus under the presidency of James Monroe. One faction, which became the Whig Party, was led by John Quincy Adams, who was elected President by a sharply divided House of Representatives in 1824. The nascent Democrats were led by Andrew Jackson and John Calhoun, who were elected President and Vice President in 1828.[1]

The Democrats dominated national politics during the period covered by this chapter, which is often labeled the age of Jacksonian democracy:

> Jacksonian democracy was a national movement in that it opposed disunion and knew no geographical limits. . . . But it was anti-national in rejecting Henry Clay's "American System" [under which Congress would have participated in developing systems of interstate transportation]. That is, the Democrats wanted roads, canals, and (in a few years) railroads to be chartered and aided by the states, but no Federal Government messing into the operations or sharing the expected profits. Jacksonians spoke for the men on the make who resented government grants of special privileges to rival entrepreneurs and who preferred laissez-faire to the positive state. . . . [T]he Jackson men identified themselves with the movement toward more equality. Yet they believed in equality only for white men; they were far less charitable toward the Indian and the Negro than their "aristocratic" foes. Jacksonian Democracy was not "leveling" in the European sense, having no desire to pull down men of wealth to a common plane; but it wanted a fair chance for every man to level up.[2]

Under the Democratic leadership, Congress did little to exploit Marshall's federalistic legacy. (Recall, also, that Jackson vetoed rechartering the Bank of the United States.) The construction of a national transportation system was left to the states and to private initiative.[3]

Roger B. Taney, a Maryland aristocrat and former Federalist, had aligned with the Democrats in the 1820s. Jackson first appointed him Attorney General and Secretary of the Treasury and then, on John Marshall's death in 1835, Chief Justice of the United States. Carl Swisher writes:

1. See generally Morton Borden, Parties and Politics in the Early Republic, 1789-1815 (1969); Shaw Livermore, Twilight of Federalism: The Disintegration of the Federalist Party, 1815-1830 (1962); Richard McCormick, The Second American Party System: Jacksonian Era (1966).

2. Samuel Eliot Morison, Henry Steele Commager & William E. Leuchtenberg, The Growth of the American Republic 419-420 (7th ed. 1980).

3. See Lawrence Friedman, A History of American Law, ch. 3 (1973); Carter Goodrich, Government Promotion of American Canals and Railroads, 1800-1890 (1960).

> Taney went to the Court with a conviction as to the sanctity of rights of physical and tangible property, and the community rights connected therewith; . . . he distrusted mercantile and banking interests that were strong enough and ruthlessly selfish enough to endanger the interests of stable property and of the community; . . . he had a deep sense of local patriotism for Maryland, which easily extended to the southern states with a similar culture; . . . although he favored voluntary and responsible loosening of the bonds of slavery, he was firmly opposed to wholesale and largely irresponsible manumission as a result of northern coercion; . . . he was committed to the position that the Negro was basically inferior to the white man and had no assured constitutional rights; and . . . although a firm believer in the Union he was also apparently in greater degree a believer in the rights of states and of what was to become the minority region of the South.[4]

Although Taney's attitudes were representative of the pre-Civil War Court, its members included judges committed to nationalism and opposed to slavery, such as the Ohioan John McLean and the New Englander Joseph Story, who had been appointed in 1811 and remained on the Court until 1845. The Taney Court therefore never enjoyed the seeming consensus of the Marshall years, and the slavery issue tore it apart as it did the entire nation.

I. The Protection of Property Rights

Economic development in the mid-nineteenth century was accompanied by a noticeable increase in the use of eminent domain by state and municipal governments and quasi-public corporations. The state courts began elaborating doctrine under state constitutional provisions governing compensation for takings of property.[5] Before the Civil War, the only federal constitutional provision directly concerned with economic rights was the contract clause. In The Contract Clause of the Constitution 62-63 (1931), Benjamin Wright comments on this period:

> It is one of the generally accepted dogmas of American constitutional history that Chief Justice Taney and his Court [1836-1864] were concerned with the protection of the public interest rather than the rights of private property. [For example, it is said that] "Jacksonian judges from agrarian states broke down the historic safeguards thrown around property rights by the letter of the Constitution and the jurisprudence of John Marshall." . . . But the decisions of the Court do not bear out the theory. . . . [T]he Taney period is not properly classified either as an era of contraction or one of expansion of the contract clause. Rather it is one of consolidation and application. With very few exceptions, the contract clause principles of John Marshall were those of Taney, and during his chief justiceship the clause was applied much more frequently and to a wide variety of subject matter.

Still, two of the most noted decisions of the Taney Court were protective of state powers. Charles River Bridge v. Warren Bridge, 36 U.S. (11 Pet.) 420

4. Carl Swisher, Mr. Chief Justice Taney, in Mr. Justice 38-39 (Dunham & Kurland eds. 1964).
5. See Harry Scheiber, The Road to *Munn:* Eminent Domain and the Concept of Public Purpose in State Courts, in Law in American History 329 (Fleming & Baily eds. 1971).

(1837), established the principle that public franchises should be narrowly construed: Since petitioner's charter to operate a toll bridge was not in terms exclusive, it would not be read to prevent the state from chartering a bridge nearby. In West River Bridge Co. v. Dix, 47 U.S. (6 How.) 507 (1848), the Court held that petitioner's franchise did not preclude the state from expropriating its bridge upon payment of compensation: All government grants are implicitly subject to the state's power of eminent domain.

CHARLES RIVER BRIDGE v. WARREN BRIDGE

36 U.S. (11 Pet.) 420 (1837)
Error to the Supreme Judicial Court of Massachusetts

[In 1650, the Massachusetts legislature granted Harvard College a franchise to run a ferry from Charlestown to Boston. In 1785, the legislature passed an act incorporating a company, The Proprietors of the Charles River Bridge, which was empowered to erect a bridge in place of the ferry route and to collect tolls for a period of 40 years. During this time, the company would pay Harvard £200 a year as "reasonable annual compensation for the annual income of the ferry, which might have been received had not the said bridge been erected." At the expiration of the charter the bridge would become property of the commonwealth. The bridge was opened in 1786, and several years later the charter was extended to 70 years.

In 1828 the Massachusetts legislature chartered another corporation to construct a bridge adjacent to the Charles River Bridge. The Warren Bridge, by the terms of its charter, was to be surrendered to the state as soon as the proprietors recouped their expenses. Subsequently, the state took over the bridge and did away with the toll, thereby entirely destroying the value of the Charles River Bridge franchise.]

TANEY, C.J. . . .

The plaintiffs in error insist, mainly, upon two grounds: 1st. That by virtue of the grant of 1650, Harvard College was entitled, in perpetuity, to the right of keeping a ferry between Charlestown and Boston; that this right was exclusive; and that the legislature had not the power to establish another ferry on the same line of travel, because it would infringe the rights of the college; and that these rights, upon the erection of the bridge in the place of the ferry, under the charter of 1785, were transferred to, and became vested in "The Proprietors of the Charles River Bridge"; and that under, and by virtue of this transfer of the ferry-right, the rights of the bridge company were as exclusive in that line of travel, as the rights of the ferry. 2d. That independently of the ferry-right, the acts of the legislature of Massachusetts, of 1785 and 1792, by their true construction, necessarily implied, that the legislature would not authorize another bridge, and especially, a free one, by the side of this, and placed in the same line of travel, whereby the franchise granted to the "Proprietors of the Charles River Bridge" should be rendered of no value; and the plaintiffs in error contend, that the grant of the ferry to the college, and of the charter to the proprietors of the bridge, are both contracts on the part of the state; and that the law authorizing the erection of the Warren bridge in 1828, impairs the obligation of one or both of these contracts.

It is very clear, that in the form in which this case comes before us (being a writ of error to a state court), the plaintiffs, in claiming under either of these rights, must place themselves on the ground of contract, and cannot support themselves upon the principle, that the law divests vested rights. It is well settled, by the decisions of this court, that a state law may be retrospective in its character, and may divest vested rights, and yet not violate the constitution of the United States, unless it also impairs the obligation of a contract. . . . [The plaintiffs] must show, that the state had entered into a contract with them, or those under whom they claim, not to establish a free bridge at the place where the Warren bridge is erected. Such, and such only, are the principles upon which the plaintiffs in error can claim relief in this case.

The nature and extent of the ferry right granted to Harvard College, in 1650, must depend upon the laws of Massachusetts. . . . [The Court concludes that the ferry right was not transferred to the plaintiffs.]

This brings us to the act of the legislature of Massachusetts, of 1785, by which the plaintiffs were incorporated . . . , and it is here, and in the law of 1792, prolonging their charter, that we must look for the extent and nature of the franchise conferred upon the plaintiffs. Much has been said in the argument of the principles of construction by which this law is to be expounded, and what undertakings, on the part of the state, may be implied. The court think there can be no serious difficulty on that head. It is the grant of certain franchises, by the public, to a private corporation, and in a matter where the public interest is concerned. The rule of construction in such cases is well settled, both in England, and by the decisions of our own tribunals. In the case of the Proprietors of the Stourbridge Canal v. Wheeley and others, 2 B. & Ad. 793, the court says, "the canal having been made under an act of parliament, the rights of the plaintiffs are derived entirely from that act. This, like many other cases, is a bargain between a company of adventurers and the public, the terms of which are expressed in the statute; and the rule of construction in all such cases, is now fully established to be this — that any ambiguity in the terms of the contract, must operate against the adventurers, and in favor of the public, and the plaintiffs can claim nothing that is not clearly given them by the act." And the doctrine thus laid down is abundantly sustained by the authorities referred to in this decision.

Borrowing, as we have done, our system of jurisprudence from the English law; and having adopted, in every other case, civil and criminal, its rules for the construction of statutes; is there anything in our local situation, or in the nature of our political institutions, which should lead us to depart from the principle, where corporations are concerned?

. . . We think not; and it would present a singular spectacle, if, while the courts in England are restraining, within the strictest limits, the spirit of monopoly, and exclusive privileges in nature of monopolies, and confining corporations to the privileges plainly given to them in their charter; the courts of this country should be found enlarging these privileges by implication; and construing a statute more unfavorably to the public, and to the rights of community, than would be done in a like case in an English court of justice.

But we are not now left to determine, for the first time, the rules by which public grants are to be construed in this country. The subject has already been considered in this court; and the rule of construction, above stated, fully established.

In the case of the United States v. Arredondo, 8 Pet. 738, the leading cases upon this subject are collected together by the learned judge who delivered the opinion of the court; and the principle recognised, that in grants by the public, nothing passes by implication.

. . . [T]he object and end of all government is to promote the happiness and prosperity of the community by which it is established; and it can never be assumed, that the government intended to diminish its power of accomplishing the end for which it was created. And in a country like ours, free, active and enterprising, continually advancing in numbers and wealth, new channels of communication are daily found necessary, both for travel and trade, and are essential to the comfort, convenience and prosperity of the people. A state ought ever to be presumed to surrender this power, because, like the taxing power, the whole community have an interest in preserving it undiminished. And when a corporation alleges, that a state has surrendered, for seventy years, its power of improvement and public accommodation, in a great and important line of travel, along which a vast number of its citizens must daily pass, the community have a right to insist, in the language of this court, above quoted, "that its abandonment ought not to be presumed, in a case, in which the deliberate purpose of the state to abandon it does not appear." The continued existence of a government would be of no great value, if, by implications and presumptions, it was disarmed of the powers necessary to accomplish the ends of its creation, and the functions it was designed to perform, transferred to the hands of privileged corporations. . . .

Adopting the rule of construction above stated as the settled one, we proceed to apply it to the charter of 1785, to the proprietors of the Charles River bridge. . . . There is no exclusive privilege given to them over the waters of Charles River, above or below their bridge; no right to erect another bridge themselves, nor to prevent other persons from erecting one, no engagement from the state, that another shall not be erected; and no undertaking not to sanction competition, nor to make improvements that may diminish the amount of its income.

. . . If a contract on that subject can be gathered from the charter, it must be by implication; and cannot be found in the words used. Can such an agreement be implied? The rule of construction before stated is an answer to the question: in charters of this description, no rights are taken from the public, or given to the corporation, beyond those which the words of the charter, by their natural and proper construction, purport to convey. . . .

Indeed, the practice and usage of almost every state in the Union, old enough to have commenced the work of internal improvement, is opposed to the doctrine contended for on the part of the plaintiffs in error. Turnpike roads have been made in succession, on the same line of travel; the later ones interfering materially with the profits of the first. These corporations have, in some instances, been utterly ruined by the introduction of newer and better modes of transportation and travelling. In some cases, railroads have rendered the turnpike roads on the same line of travel so entirely useless, that the franchise of the turnpike corporation is not worth preserving. Yet in none of these cases have the corporation supposed that their privileges were invaded, or any contract violated on the part of the state.

. . . The absence of any such controversy, when there must have been so many occasions to give rise to it, proves, that neither states, nor individuals, nor corporations, ever imagined that such a contract could be implied from such charters. . . .

And what would be the fruits of this doctrine of implied contracts, on the part of the states, and of property in a line of travel, by a corporation, if it would now be sanctioned by this court? To what results would it lead us? . . . Let it once be understood, that such charters carry with them these implied contracts, and give this unknown and undefined property in a line of travelling; and you will soon find the old turnpike corporations awakening from their sleep, and calling upon this court to put down the improvements which have taken their place. The millions of property which have been invested in railroads and canals, upon lines of travel which had been before occupied by turnpike corporations, will be put in jeopardy. We shall be thrown back to the improvements of the last century, and obliged to stand still, until the claims of the old turnpike corporations shall be satisfied; and they shall consent to permit these states to avail themselves of the lights of modern science, and to partake of the benefit of those improvements which are now adding to the wealth and prosperity, and the convenience and comfort, of every other part of the civilized world. Nor is this all. This court will find itself compelled to fix, by some arbitrary rule, the width of this new kind of property in a line of travel; for if such a right of property exists, we have no lights to guide us in marking out its extent. . . .

STORY, J., dissenting. . . .

I admit, that where the terms of a grant are to impose burdens upon the public, or to create a restraint injurious to the public interest, there is sound reason for interpreting the terms, if ambiguous, in favor of the public. But at the same time, I insist, that there is not the slightest reason for saying, even in such a case, that the grant is not to be construed favorably to the grantee, so as to secure him in the enjoyment of what is actually granted. . . .

It should also be constantly kept in mind, that in construing this charter, we are not construing a statute involving political powers and sovereignty. . . . We are construing a grant of the legislature, which though in the form of a statute, is still but a solemn contract. In such a case, the true course is, to ascertain the sense of the parties, from the terms of the instrument; and that once ascertained, to give it full effect. . . .

But with a view to induce the court to withdraw from all the common rules of reasonable and liberal interpretation in favor of grants, we have been told at the argument, that this very charter is a restriction upon the legislative power; that it is in derogation of the rights and interests of the state, and the people; that it tends to promote monopolies and exclusive privileges; and that it will interpose an insuperable barrier to the progress of improvement. Now, upon every one of these propositions, which are assumed, and not proved, I entertain a directly opposite opinion; and if I did not, I am not prepared to admit the conclusion for which they are adduced. If the legislature has made a grant, which involves any or all of these consequences, it is not for courts of justice to overturn the plain sense of the grant, because it has been improvidently or injuriously made.

But I deny the very ground-work of the argument. This charter is not (as I have already said) any restriction upon the legislative power; unless it be true, that because the legislature cannot grant again, what it has already granted, the legislative power is restricted. If so, then every grant of the public land is a restriction upon that power; a doctrine, that has never yet been established, nor (so far as I know) ever contended for. Every grant of a franchise is, so far as that grant extends, necessarily exclusive; and cannot be resumed or interfered with. All the learned judges in the state court admitted, that the franchise of Charles River bridge, whatever it be, could not be resumed or interfered with. The legislature could not recall its grant, or destroy it. It is a contract, whose obligation cannot be constitutionally impaired. In this respect, it does not differ from a grant of lands. In each case, the particular land, or the particular franchise, is withdrawn from the legislative operation. The identical land, or the identical franchise, cannot be regranted, or avoided by a new grant. But the legislative power remains unrestricted. The subject-matter only (I repeat it) has passed from the hands of the government. . . .

Then, again, as to the grant being against the interests of the people. I know not how that is established; and certainly, it is not to be assumed. It will hardly be contended, that every grant of the government is injurious to the interests of the people; or that every grant of a franchise, must necessarily be so. The erection of a bridge may be of the highest utility to the people. It may essentially promote the public convenience, and aid the public interests, and protect the public property. And if no persons can be found willing to undertake such a work, unless they receive in return the exclusive privilege of erecting it, and taking toll; surely, it cannot be said, as of course, that such a grant, under such circumstances, is, per se, against the interests of the people. Whether the grant of a franchise is, or is not, on the whole, promotive of the public interests, is a question of fact and judgment, upon which different minds may entertain different opinions. It is not to be judicially assumed to be injurious, and then the grant to be reasoned down. It is a matter exclusively confided to the sober consideration of the legislature; which is invested with full discretion, and possesses ample means to decide it. . . .

But it has been argued, and the argument has been pressed in every form which ingenuity could suggest, that if grants of this nature are to be construed liberally, as, conferring any exclusive rights on the grantees, it will interpose an effectual barrier against all general improvements of the country. For myself, I profess not to feel the cogency of this argument, either in its general application to the grant of franchises, or in its special application to the present grant. This is a subject upon which different minds may well arrive at different conclusions, both as to policy and principle. Men may, and will, complexionally differ upon topics of this sort, according to their natural and acquired habits of speculation and opinion. For my own part, I can conceive of no surer plan to arrest all public improvements, founded on private capital and enterprise, than to make the outlay of that capital uncertain and questionable, both as to security and as to productiveness. No man will hazard his capital in any enterprise, in which, if there be a loss, it must be borne exclusively by himself; and if there be success, he has not the slightest security of enjoying the rewards of that success, for a single moment. If the government means to invite its citizens to enlarge the public comforts and conveniences, to establish bridges, or turnpikes, or canals, or railroads, there must be some pledge, that the property will be safe; that the enjoyment will be coextensive with the grant; and that success will not be the signal of a general combination to overthrow its rights and to take away its profits. . . .

I have thus endeavored to answer, and I think I have successfully answered all the arguments (which indeed run into each other) adduced to justify a strict construction of the present character. I go further, and maintain, not only that it is not a case for strict construction; but that the charter, upon its very face, by its terms, and for its professed objects, demands from the court, upon undeniable principles of law, a favorable construction for the grantees. In the first place, the legislature has declared, that the erecting of the bridge will be of great public utility; and this exposition of its own motives for the grant, requires the court to give a liberal interpretation, in order to promote, and not to destroy, an enterprise of great public utility. In the next place, the grant is a contract for a valuable consideration, and a full and adequate consideration. The proprietors are to lay out a large sum of money (and in those times it was a large outlay of capital) in erecting a bridge; they are to keep it in repair, during the whole period of forty years; they are to surrender it in good repair, at the end of that period, to the state, as its own property; they are to pay, during the whole period, an annuity of £200 to Harvard College; and they are to incur other heavy expenses and burdens, for the public accommodation. In return for all these charges, they are entitled to no more than the receipt of the tolls, during the forty years, for the reimbursement of capital, interest and expenses. With all this, they are to take upon themselves the chances of success; and if the enterprise fails, the loss is exclusively their own. . . .

Now, I put it to the common sense of every man, whether if, at the moment of granting the charter, the legislature had said to the proprietors; you shall build the bridge; you shall bear the burdens; you shall be bound by the charges; and your sole reimbursement shall be from the tolls of forty years: and yet we will not even guaranty you any certainty of receiving any tolls; on the contrary; we reserve to ourselves the full power and authority to erect other bridges, toll or free bridges, according to our own free will and pleasure, contiguous to yours, and having the same termini with yours; and if you are successful, we may thus supplant you, divide, destroy your profits, and annihilate your tolls, without annihilating your burdens: if, I say, such had been the language of the legislature, is there a man living, of ordinary discretion or prudence, who would have accepted such a charter, upon such terms? I fearlessly answer, no. There would have been such a gross inadequacy of consideration, and such a total insecurity of all the right of property, under such circumstances, that the project would have dropped still-born. . . .

To sum up, then, the whole argument on this head: I maintain, that, upon the principles of common reason and legal interpretation, the present grant carries with it a necessary implication, that the legislature shall do no act to destroy or essentially to impair the franchise; that (as one of the learned judges of the state court expressed it) there is an implied agreement that the state will not grant another bridge between Boston and Charlestown, so near as to draw away the custom from the old one; and (as another learned judge expressed it) that there is an implied agreement of the state to grant the undisturbed use of the bridge and its tolls, so far as respect any acts of its own, or of any persons acting under its authority. In other words, the state of the contracts not to resume its grant, or to do any act to the prejudice or destruction of its grant. I maintain, that there is no authority or principle established in relation to the construction of crown grants, or legislative grants, which does not concede and justify this doctrine. Where the thing is given, the incidents, without which it cannot be enjoyed, are also given; ut res magis valeat quam pereat. I maintain, that a different doctrine is utterly repugnant to all the principles of the common law, applicable to all franchises of a like nature; and that we must overturn some of the best securities of the rights of property, before it can be established. I maintain, that the common law is the birthright of every citizen of Massachusetts, and that he holds the title deeds of his property, corporeal and incorporeal, under it. I maintain, that under the principles of the common law, there exists no more right in the legislature of Massachusetts, to erect the Warren bridge, to the ruin of the franchise of the Charles River bridge, than exists to transfer the latter to the former, or to authorize the former to demolish the latter. If the legislature does not mean in its grant to give any exclusive rights, let it say so, expressly, directly, and in terms admitting of no misconstruction. The grantees will then take at their peril, and must abide the results of their overweening confidence, indiscretion and zeal.

Discussion

1. Contrast Taney's and Story's views of the scope of the contract clause and the relationships between economic development and protection of private property or contractual expectations.

2. Several years before *Charles River Bridge,* in his inaugural lecture as Dane Professor of Law at Harvard,[6] Joseph Story outlined the task of the bar:

> The sacred rights of property are to be guarded at every point. I call them sacred because, if they are unprotected, all other rights become worthless or visionary. What is personal liberty if it imparts only perpetual poverty to us and all our posterity? What is the privilege of a vote, if a majority of the hour may sweep away the earning of our whole lives, to ratify the rapacity of the indolent, the cunning, or the profligate, who are borne into power upon the tide of a temporary popularity? . . .
>
> One of the glorious, and not unfrequently perilous duties of the Bar is the protection of property; and not of property only, but of personal rights, and personal character; of domestic peace, and parental authority. The lawyer is placed, as it were, upon the outpost of defence, as a public sentinel, to watch the approach of danger, and to sound the alarm when oppression is at hand.[7]

To what extent does Story's dissent seem based on views like these? To what extent is it based on an instrumental view, albeit a different one from Taney's? Morton Horwitz writes:

> The *Charles River Bridge* case represented the last great contest in America between two different models of economic development. For Justice Putnam of the Massachusetts court and for Justice Story of the Supreme Court, the essential elements for economic progress were certainty of expectation and predictability of legal consequences. . . . Justice Morton [of the Massachusetts court], on the other hand, though conceding that "exclusive rights for short periods sometimes encourage enterprise, of public usefulness," believed nevertheless that "generally their tendency is to impede the march of public improvement, and to interrupt that fair and equal competition which it has ever been the policy of our country to encourage."[8]

6. Story, while a Justice of the United States Supreme Court, held the Dane Professorship at Harvard Law School from 1829 until his death in 1845.

7. Quoted in The Legal Mind in America from Independence to the Civil War 180-181 (Miller ed. 1969) (hereinafter Miller).

8. Morton Horwitz, The Transformation of American Law, 1780-1860, 134 (1977). See also Stanley Kutler, Privilege and Creative Destruction: The Charles River Bridge Case (1978).

How do you suppose Marshall would have decided *Charles River Bridge?*

3. Although both Taney and Story claim support from the common law, the tenor of their opinions is very different — more so than can appear from our excerpts. Taney's opinion is Marshallian in its sweeping style and direct statements. Story's requires a reader to slog through 67 pages of English and American common law cases and analyses of Coke, Blackstone, and other noted legal commentators. In style as well as substance, in constitutional as well as common law judgments, Story represented the old order — an ideology criticized by Massachusetts lawyer Robert Rantoul in a Fourth of July speech delivered in 1836 in Scituate, after the state court had decided the *Charles River Bridge* case. Rantoul referred specifically to defenders of the Proprietors of the Charles River Bridge when he criticized judges who "administer Common Law as it came down from the dark ages, except what has been repealed by the Constitution and the statutes, which exception they are always careful to reduce to the narrowest possible limits. With them, wrong is right, if wrong has existed from time immemorial; precedents are every thing: the spirit of the age is nothing."[9]

4. Legislatures continued to grant special charters of the sort issued to the Proprietors of the Charles River Bridge, although, in response to decisions such as *Dartmouth College* (p. 103 supra), the charters often explicitly reserved to the state the right to modify them. During the nineteenth century, the general state law of corporations was significantly changed, however:

> In the early 19th century . . . the legislature granted charters by statute, one by one. Every charter was in theory tailor-made to the case at hand.
>
> In this colonial period, this system was not at all inappropriate. . . . But as the economy developed, entrepreneurs demanded access to the corporate form, as an efficient way to structure and finance their business ventures. If each charter had to be scrutinized, its clauses cut to order for the particular case, legislatures would have been simply unable to handle the demand. Except for projects of special importance, charters became stylized, standardized, matters of rote. They were finally replaced . . . by general incorporation laws.[10]

5. *Charles River Bridge* is, of course, a quintessential construction of a state charter awarding a privilege, and the earlier discussion of Ogden v. Saunders suggested that early nineteenth-century lawyers and judges were more hesitant to sustain state legislation affecting contracts between private parties. But although these jurists held that contract *rights* were sacrosanct, they believed that contract *remedies* could be modified even retroactively. (Recall Marshall's dissent in *Ogden.*) This distinction between rights and remedies could have provided the basis for significant state intervention in private contracts.

Ironically, it was the Jacksonian Taney who prevented this development. Bronson v. Kinzie, 42 U.S. (1 How.) 311 (1843), involved the retrospective application of a statute disallowing the judicial sale of foreclosed property where the auction bid was less than two-thirds of its market value; moreover, mortgagors were given the right to redeem their property for a year after its sale by foreclosure. With only Justice McLean dissenting, Taney emphasized the linkage between preservation of contract remedies and rights and went on to invalidate the

9. Quoted in Miller, supra note 7, at 225.
10. Friedman, supra note 3, at 166-167.

state law in the name of "maintain[ing] the integrity of contracts" in the constitutional scheme: "[I]t would but ill become this court, under any circumstances, to depart from the plain meaning of the words used, and to sanction a distinction between the right and the remedy, which would render this provision illusive and nugatory; mere words of form, affording no protection and producing no practical result." Accordingly, retrospective legislation "burdening the proceedings with new conditions and restrictions so as to make the remedy hardly worth pursuing" could not pass constitutional muster: "[A]lthough a new remedy may be deemed less convenient than the old one, and may in some degree render the recovery of debts more tardy and difficult, yet it will not follow that the law is unconstitutional. . . . [However] it would be unjust to the memory of the distinguished men who framed [the Constitution], to suppose that it was designed to protect a mere barren and abstract right, without any practical operation upon the business of life."

Professor Stephen Siegel notes that "[d]istinguishing remedial alterations that were acceptably burdensome from those that were unacceptably burdensome [not only] produced a number of difficultly reasoned precedents [but also] challenged any attempt to maintain a commitment to nondiscretionary judicial method" — for now *degree* of burdensomeness was crucial.[11]

Note: General Principles of Constitutional and Common Law

1. General Constitutional Law

Gelpcke v. Dubuque, 68 U.S. (1 Wall.) 175 (1864), was a diversity action by the holders of municipal bonds issued as part of a railroad promotion. The city defended on the ground that issuance of the bonds was beyond its authority under the Iowa Constitution. The city's interpretation of the state constitution was supported by an 1862 Iowa Supreme Court ruling, which had overruled a number of earlier decisions holding that cities must make good on such debts. In *Gelpcke,* the United States Supreme Court declined to follow the state supreme court's current interpretation. Justice Swayne noted that the Court had said a year earlier that it would follow "the latest settled [state] adjudication" construing a state statute or constitution. Leffingwell v. Warren, 67 U.S. (2 Black) 599 (1863). However, "[i]t cannot be expected that this court will follow every such oscillation, from whatever cause arising, that may possibly occur," and the earlier decisions "are sustained by reason and authority":

> The late case in Iowa, and two other cases of a kindred character in another State, also overruling earlier adjudications, stand out, as far as we are advised, in unenviable solitude and notoriety. However we may regard the late case in Iowa as affecting the future, it can have no effect on the past. "The sound and true rule is, that if the contract, when made, was valid by the laws of the State as then expounded by all departments of the government, and administered in its courts of justice, its validity and obligation cannot be impaired by any subsequent action of legislation, or decision of its courts altering the construction of the law." [Citing an Iowa decision.]

11. Siegel, Understanding the Nineteenth Century Contract Clause, The Role of the Property-Privilege Distinction and "Takings" Clause Jurisprudence, 60 So. Cal. L. Rev. 1, 8 (1986).

The same principle applies where there is a change of judicial decision as to the constitutional power of the Legislature to enact the law. To this rule, thus enlarged, we adhere. It is the law of this court. It rests upon the plainest principles of justice. To hold otherwise would be as unjust as to hold that rights acquired under a statute may be lost by its repeal.

We are not unmindful of the importance of uniformity in the decisions of this court, and those of the highest local courts, giving constructions to the laws and constitutions of their own States. It is the settled rule of this court in such cases, to follow the decisions of the state courts. But there have been heretofore, in the judicial history of this court, as doubtless there will be hereafter, many exceptional cases. We shall never immolate truth, justice, and the law, because a state tribunal has erected the altar and decreed the sacrifice.

2. The Federalization of Commercial Law: Swift v. Tyson

In view of the emerging "instrumental" conception of the common law, and the Taney Court's generally antifederalist stance, a noteworthy case is Swift v. Tyson, 41 U.S. (16 Pet.) 1 (1842). There, the Court substantially federalized the subject of commercial law by holding that federal courts should decide commercial litigation with reference to "the general principles and doctrines of commercial jurisprudence" rather than to the "decisions of local tribunals." The substantive issue in *Swift* was whether the owner of a negotiable instrument had acquired it free of the defenses available between the original parties. The action was brought in a federal court in New York, whose state decisions arguably — and against prevailing doctrine — held that, under the circumstances, the owner was not a holder in due course. In an opinion by Justice Story, the Supreme Court decided to follow the "general" commercial law, which was otherwise. The decision was based on section 34 of the Judiciary Act of 1789, also known as the Rules of Decision Act, which provided "that the laws of the several states . . . shall be regarded as the rules of decision . . . in courts of the United States." Story wrote that state judicial decisions were "at most, only evidence of what the laws are, and are not, of themselves, laws."

This invocation of the eighteenth-century notion of the common law as discovered rather than made may seem to run counter to the general change of jurisprudential climate, aspects of which were reflected in Story's contemporaneous scholarly writings on conflicts of laws.[12] But the decision to reject a peculiar state rule in favor of widely followed commercial practice, rooted in the law merchant, was entirely consistent with instrumentalist objectives. The particular holding, cutting off the debtor's defenses, facilitated negotiability (and helped creditors). Also, *Swift's* foundation of a uniform common law of negotiable instruments facilitated interstate trade generally. As Story wrote, "The law respecting negotiable instruments may be truly declared in the language of Cicero . . . to be in great measure, not the law of a single country only, but of the commercial world."

Although the state courts remained free to adjudicate disputes based on their own common law doctrines, *Swift* gave rise to an independent body of "federal common law," applied in the increasing number of commercial disputes coming

12. Horwitz, supra note 8, at 248-249.

within the federal courts' diversity jurisdiction. Grant Gilmore writes that the decision in *Swift*

> was immediately and enthusiastically accepted. No one suggested that it was an unconstitutional usurpation of power by power-crazed judges or that it was a trick played by a wily Federalist judge on his unsuspecting Jacksonian colleagues. No bumper stickers called for Justice Story's impeachment. On the contrary, the doctrine of the general commercial law was warmly welcomed and expansively construed, not only by the lower federal courts but by the state courts as well. For the next half century the Supreme Court of the United States became a great commercial law court.[13]

II. Interstate and Foreign Commerce and Personal Mobility

The Taney Court, reflecting the general political climate of the time, was protective of state autonomy. Whereas Marshall had suggested that the states might be barred from regulating interstate commerce even in the absence of congressional legislation, Taney asserted that the commerce clause by itself imposed no constraints on state regulation. Neither of these positions gained a majority, however, and the Taney era ended without resolving the scope of state and national power under the commerce clause.

A. The States' "Police Powers" as a Constraint on the National Commerce Power

New York v. Miln, one of the Taney Court's earliest commerce clause decisions, arose out of the rapidly increasing flow of immigrants from Ireland and Northern Europe into the United States. Although national policy encouraged immigration, the Atlantic seaboard states were wary of indigent immigrants. There were no national, or even state, welfare systems at the time. Rather, the poor were a local problem. *Miln* should be read with the knowledge that towns had prevented the in-migration of paupers since Colonial times.

MAYOR OF THE CITY OF NEW YORK v. MILN

36 U.S. (11 Pet.) 102 (1837)

Certificate of Division from the Circuit Court of the Southern District of New York

[An 1824 New York State law required the master of a vessel arriving in New York from another country or state to provide a detailed report on "every person brought as a passenger in the ship . . . from any country outside of the United States or from any of the United States, into the port of New York, or into any of the United States, and of all persons landed from the ship, during the voyage at any place, or put on board, or suffered to go on board any other vessel, with in-

13. Grant Gilmore, The Ages of American Law 34 (1977).

tention of proceeding to the city of New York." The law further required the master to post security for the maintenance of immigrants and their children who became wards of the city[14] and to remove any noncitizen whom the mayor deemed likely to become dependent. This was an action to recover $15,000 penalties for violation of the act.]

BARBOUR, J. . . .

It is contended by the counsel for the defendant, that the act in question is a regulation of commerce; that the power to regulate commerce is, by the constitution of the United States, granted to congress; that this power is exclusive, and that consequently, the act is a violation of the constitution of the United States.

On the part of the plaintiff, it is argued, that an affirmative grant of power previously existing in the states to congress, is not exclusive; except, 1st, where it is so expressly declared in terms, by the clause giving the power; or 2d, where a similar power is prohibited to the states; or 3d, where the power in the states would be repugnant to, and incompatible with, a similar power in congress; that this power falls within neither of these predicaments; that it is not, in terms, declared to be exclusive; that it is not prohibited to the states; and that it is not repugnant to, nor incompatible with, a similar power in congress; and that having pre-existed in the states, they, therefore, have a concurrent power in relation to the subject; and that the act in question would be valid, even if it were a regulation of commerce, it not contravening any regulation made by congress. But they deny that it is a regulation of commerce; on the contrary, they assert, that it is a mere regulation of internal police, a power over which is not granted to congress; and which, therefore, as well upon the true construction of the constitution, as by force of the tenth amendment to that instrument, is reserved to, and resides in, the several states.

We shall not enter into any examination of the question, whether the power to regulate commerce, be or be not exclusive of the states, because the opinion which we have formed renders it unnecessary: in other words, we are of opinion, that the act is not a regulation of commerce, but of police; and that being thus considered, it was passed in the exercise of a power which rightfully belonged to the states.

That the state of New York possessed power to pass this law, before the adoption of the constitution of the United States, might probably be taken as a truism, without the necessity of proof. But as it may tend to present it in a clearer point of view, we will quote a few passages from a standard writer upon public law, showing the origin and character of this power. Vattel, book 2, ch. 7, §94. "The sovereign may forbid the entrance of his territory, either to foreigners in general, or in particular cases, or to certain persons, or for certain particular purposes, according as he may think it advantageous to the state." Ibid. ch. 8, §100. "Since the lord of the territory may, whenever he thinks proper, forbid its being entered, he has, no doubt, a power to annex what conditions he pleases, to the permission to enter." The power then of New York to pass this law having undeniably existed at the formation of the constitution, the simple inquiry is, whether by that instru-

14. A 1788 New York statute explicitly enjoined that "[e]very city and town shall support and maintain their own poor." See Friedman, supra note 3, at 187-191.

ment it was taken from the states, and granted to congress; for if it were not, it yet remains with them.

If, as we think, it be a regulation, not of commerce, but police; then it is not taken from the states. To decide this let us examine its purpose, the end to be attained, and the means of its attainment. It is apparent, from the whole scope of the law, that the object of the legislature was, to prevent New York from being burdened by an influx of persons brought thither in ships, either from foreign countries, or from any other of the states; and for that purpose, a report was required of the names, places of birth, &c., of all passengers, that the necessary steps might be taken by the city authorities, to prevent them from becoming chargeable as paupers. Now, we hold, that both the end and the means here used, are within the competency of the states, since a portion of their powers were surrendered to the federal government. Let us see, what powers are left with the states. The Federalist, No 45, speaking of this subject, says, the powers reserved to the several states, all extend to all the objects, which in the ordinary course of affairs, concern the lives, liberties and properties of the people; and the internal order, improvement and prosperity of the state. And this court, in the case of Gibbons v. Ogden, . . . in speaking of the inspection laws of the states, say, they form a portion of that immense mass of legislation which embraces everything within the territory of a state, not surrendered to the general government, all which can be most advantageously exercised by the states themselves. Inspection laws, quarantine laws, health laws of every description, as well as laws for regulating the internal commerce of a state, and those which respect turnpike-roads, ferries, &c., are component parts of this mass.

Now, if the act in question be tried by reference to the delineation of power laid down in the preceding quotations, it seems to us, that we are necessarily brought to the conclusion, that it falls within its limits. There is no aspect in which it can be viewed, in which it transcends them. If we look at the place of its operation, we find it to be within the territory, and therefore, within the jurisdiction of New York. If we look at the person on whom it operates, he is found within the same territory and jurisdiction. If we look at the persons for whose benefit it was passed, they are the people of New York, for whose protection and welfare the legislature of that state are authorized and in duty bound to provide. If we turn our attention to the purpose to be attained, it is to secure that very protection, and to provide for that very welfare. If we examine the means by which these ends are proposed to be accomplished, they bear a just, natural and appropriate relation to those ends.

But we are told, that it violates the constitution of the United States, and to prove this, we have been referred to two cases in this court; the first, that of Gibbons v. Ogden, 9 Wheat. 1, and the other that of Brown v. State of Maryland, 12 Ibid. 419. . . .

Now, there is not, in this case, one of the circumstances which existed in that of Gibbons v. Ogden, which, in the opinion of the court, rendered it obnoxious to the charge of unconstitutionality. On the contrary, the prominent facts of this case are in striking contrast with those which characterized that. In that case, the theatre on which the law operated was navigable water, over which the court say that the power to regulate commerce extended; in this, it was the territory of New York, over which that state possesses an acknowledged, an undisputed jurisdiction for every purpose of internal regulation; in that, the subject-matter on which it operated, was a vessel claiming the right of navigation; a right which the court say is embraced in the power to regulate commerce; in this, the subjects on which it operates are persons whose rights and whose duties are rightfully prescribed and controlled by the laws of the respective states within whose territorial limits they are found; in that, say the court, the act of a state came into direct collision with an act of the United States; in this, no such collision exists.

Nor is there the least likeness between the facts of this case, and those of Brown v. State of Maryland. . . .[15] [In *Brown*] the court did indeed extend the power to regulate commerce, so as to protect the goods imported from a state tax, after they were landed, and were yet in bulk. . . . But how can this apply to persons? They are not the subject of commerce; and not being imported goods, cannot fall within a train of reasoning founded upon the construction of a power given to congress to regulate commerce, and the prohibition to the states from imposing a duty on imported goods. . . .

[The defendant contended that the state law conflicted with and therefore was preempted by federal statutes, enacted in 1799 and 1819, which required the masters of vessels to report on passengers and cargo transported in foreign commerce. Justice Barbour responded that the federal laws were only designed to prevent smuggling, to assure the comfort of passengers, and to "form an accurate estimate of the increase of population by emigration." In any event,] it is obvious that these laws only affect through the power over navigation, the passengers, whilst on their voyage, and until they shall have landed . . . , and can, with no propriety of language, be said to come into conflict with a law of a state, whose operation only begins when that of the laws of congress ends; whose operation is not even on the same subject. . . .

15. Brown v. Maryland (1827) held (as Chief Justice Taney later summarized it)

> that an article authorized by a law of Congress to be imported continued to be a part of the foreign commerce of the country while it remained in the hands of the importer for sale, in the original bale, package, or vessel in which it was imported; that the authority given to import necessarily carried with it the right to sell the imported article in the form and shape in which it was imported, and that no State, either by direct assessment or by requiring a license from the importer before he was permitted to sell, could impose any burden upon him or the property imported beyond what the law of Congress had itself imposed; but that when the original package was broken up for use or for retail by the importer, and also when the commodity had passed from his hands into the hands of a purchaser, it ceased to be an import, or a part of foreign commerce, and became subject to the laws of the State, and might be taxed for State purposes, and the sale regulated by the State, like any other property.

Taney, C.J., concurring in the License Cases, 46 U.S. (5 How.) 504 (1847). Taney went on to explain:

> The immense amount of foreign products used and consumed in this country are imported, landed, and offered for sale in a few commercial cities, and a very small portion of them are intended or expected to be used in the States in which they are imported. . . . And where they are in the hands of the importer . . . they may be regarded as merely in transit, on their way to the distant cities, villages, and country for which they are destined, and where they are expected to be used and consumed, and for the supply of which they were in truth imported. And a tax upon them . . . would be hardly be more justifiable in principle than a transit duty upon the merchandise when passing through a State. . . . And if a State is permitted to levy it in any form, it will put in the power of a maritime importing State to raise a revenue for the support of its own government from citizens of other States, as certainly and effectively as if the tax was laid openly and without disguise as a duty on imports. Such a power in a State would defeat one of the principal objects of forming and adopting the Constitution. And as it cannot be done directly [see Article I, §10], it could hardly be a just and sound construction of the constitution which would enable a State to accomplish precisely the same thing under another name, and in a different form.

There is, then, no collision between the law in question, and the acts of congress just commented on; and therefore, if the state law were to be considered as partaking of the nature of a commercial regulation; it would stand the test of the most rigid scrutiny, if tried by the standard laid down in the reasoning of the court, quoted from the case of Gibbons v. Ogden.

But we do not place our opinion on this ground. We choose rather to plant ourselves on what we consider impregnable positions. They are these: That a state has the same undeniable and unlimited jurisdiction over all persons and things, within its territorial limits, as any foreign nation; where that jurisdiction is not surrendered or restrained by the constitution of the United States. That, by virtue of this, it is not only the right, but the bounden and solemn duty of a state, to advance the safety, happiness and prosperity of its people, and to provide for its general welfare, by any and every act of legislation, which it may deem to be conducive to these ends; where the power over the particular subject, or the manner of its exercise is not surrendered or restrained, in the manner just stated. That all those powers which relate to merely municipal legislation, or what may, perhaps, more properly be called *internal police,* are not thus surrendered or restrained; and that, consequently, in relation to these, the authority of a state is complete, unqualified and exclusive.

We are aware, that it is at all times difficult to define any subject with proper precision and accuracy; if this be so in general, it is emphatically so, in relation to a subject so diversified and multifarious as the one which we are now considering. If we were to attempt it, we would say, that every law came within this description which concerned the welfare of the whole people of a state, or any individual within it . . . and whose operation was within the territorial limits of the state, and upon the persons and things within its jurisdiction. But we will endeavor to illustrate our meaning rather by exemplification, than by definition. No one will deny, that a state has a right to punish any individual found within its jurisdiction, who shall have committed an offence within its jurisdiction, against its criminal laws. . . . We suppose it to be equally clear, that a state has as much right to guard, by anticipation, against the commission of an offence against its laws, as to inflict punishment upon the offender, after it shall have been committed. The right to punish, or to prevent crime, does in no degree depend upon the citizenship of the party who is obnoxious to the law. The alien who shall just have set his foot upon the soil of the state, is just as subject to the operation of the law, as one who is a native citizen. . . .

Now, in relation to the section in the act immediately before us, that is obviously passed with a view to prevent her citizens from being oppressed by the support of multitudes of poor persons, who come from foreign countries, without possessing the means of supporting themselves. There can be no mode in which the power to regulate internal police could be more appropriately exercised. New York, from her particular situation, is, perhaps, more than any other city in the Union, exposed to the evil of thousands of foreign emigrants arriving there, and the consequent danger of her citizens being subjected to a heavy charge in the maintenance of those who are poor. It is the duty of the state to protect its citizens from this evil; they have endeavored to do so, by passing, amongst other things, the section of the law in question. We should, upon principle, say that it had a right to do so.

Let us compare this power with a mass of power, said by this court, in Gibbons v. Ogden, not to be surrendered to the general government. They are inspection laws, quarantine laws, health laws of every description, as well as laws for regulating the internal commerce of a state, &c. . . .

We . . . think, that if the stronger powers, under the necessity of the case, by inspection laws and quarantine laws, to delay the landing of a ship and cargo, which are the subjects of commerce and navigation, and to remove or even to destroy unsound and infectious articles, also the subject of commerce, can be rightfully exercised, then, that it must follow, as a consequence, that powers less strong, such as the one in question, which operates upon no subject either of commerce or navigation, but which operates alone within the limits and jurisdiction of New York, upon a person, at the time, not even engaged in navigation, is still more clearly embraced within the general power of the states to regulate their own internal police, and to take care that no detriment come to the commonwealth. We think it as competent and as necessary for a state to provide precautionary measures against the moral pestilence of paupers, vagabonds, and possibly convicts; as it is to guard against the physical pestilence, which may arise from unsound and infectious articles imported, or from a ship, the crew of which may be laboring under an infectious disease. . . .

THOMPSON, J. . . .

It is not necessary, in this case, to fix any limits upon the legislation of congress and of the states, on this subject; or to say how far congress may, under the power to regulate commerce, control state legislation in this respect. It is enough to say, that whatever the power of congress may be, it has not been exercised so as, in any manner, to conflict with the state law; and if the mere grant of the power to congress does not necessarily imply a prohibition of the states to exercise the power, until congress assumes to exercise it, no objection, on that ground, can arise to this law. Nor is it necessary to decide, definitively, whether the provisions of this law may be considered as at all embraced within the power to regulate commerce. Under either view of the case, the law of New York, so far at least as it is drawn in question in the present suit, is entirely unobjectionable. . . .

The case of Willson v. Blackbird Creek Marsh Company, 2 Pet. 251, is a strong case to show that a power admitted to fall within the power to regulate commerce, may be exercised by the states, until congress assumes the exercise. . . . By the same rule of construction, the law of New York, not coming in conflict with any act of congress, is not void by reason of the *dormant* power to regulate commerce; even if it should be admitted, that the subject embraced in that law fell within such power. . . .

Whether, therefore, the law of New York, so far as it is drawn in question in this case, be considered as relating purely to the police and internal government of the state, and as part of the system of poor-laws in the city of New York, and in this view belonging exclusively to the legislation of the state; or whether the subject-matter of the law be considered as belonging concurrently to the state and to congress, but never having been exercised by the latter; no constitutional objection can be made to it. . . .

STORY, J., dissenting. . . .

The questions then presented for our consideration under these circumstances are: 1st. Whether this act assumes to regulate trade and commerce between the port of New York and foreign ports? 2d. If it does, whether it is unconstitutional and void? . . .

I admit, in the most unhesitating manner, that the states have a right to pass health laws and quarantine laws, and other police laws, not contravening the laws of congress rightfully passed under their constitutional authority. I admit, that they have a right to pass poor-laws, and laws to prevent the introduction of paupers into the state, under the like qualifications. I go further, and admit, that in the exercise of their legitimate authority over any particular subject, the states may generally use the same means which are used by congress, if these means are suitable to the end. But I cannot admit, that the states have authority to enact laws, which act upon subjects beyond their territorial limits, or within those limits and which trench upon the authority of congress in its power to regulate commerce. . . .

It has been argued, that the act of New York is not a regulation of commerce, but is a mere police law upon the subject of paupers; and it has been likened to the cases of health laws, quarantine laws, ballast laws; gunpowder laws, and others of a similar nature. . . . I have already said, that I admit the power of the states to pass such laws, and to use the proper means to effectuate the objects of them; but it is with this reserve, that these means are not exclusively vested in congress. A state cannot make a regulation of commerce, to enforce its health laws, because it is a means withdrawn from its authority. It may be admitted, that it is a means adapted to the end; but it is quite a different question, whether it be a means within the competency of the state jurisdiction. . . .

But how can it be truly said, that the act of New York is not a regulation of commerce? No one can well doubt, that if the same act had been passed by congress, it would have been a regulation of commerce; and in that way, and in that only, would it be a constitutional act of congress. The right of congress to pass such an act has been expressly conceded at the argument. The act of New York purports, on its very face, to regulate the conduct of masters, and owners and passengers, in foreign trade; and in foreign ports and places [by requiring] a report of the passengers taken or landed [there]. . . . I listened with great attention to the argument, to ascertain upon what ground the act of New York was to be maintained not to be a regulation of commerce. I confess, that I was unable to ascertain any, from the reasoning of either of the learned counsel, who spoke for the plaintiff. Their whole argument on this point seemed to me to amount to this: that if it were a regulation of commerce, still it might also be deemed a regulation of police, and a part of the system of poor-laws; and therefore, justifiable as a means to attain the end. In my judgment, for the reasons already suggested, that is not a just consequence, or a legitimate deduction. If the act is a regulation of commerce, and that subject belongs exclusively to congress, it is a means cut off from the range of state sovereignty and state legislation.

And this leads me more distinctly to the consideration of the other point in question; and that is, whether, if the act of New York be a regulation of commerce, it is void and unconstitutional? If the power of congress to regulate commerce be an exclusive power; or if the subject-matter has been constitutionally regulated by congress, so as to exclude all additional or conflicting legislation by the states, then, and in either case, it is clear, that the act of New York is void and unconstitutional. Let us consider the question under these aspects.

It has been argued, that the power of congress to regulate commerce is not exclusive, but concurrent with that of the states. If this were a new question in this court, wholly untouched by doctrine or decision, I should not hesitate to go into a full examination of all the grounds upon which concurrent authority is attempted to be maintained. But in point of fact, the whole argument on this very question, as presented by the learned counsel on the present occasion, was presented by the learned counsel who argued the case of Gibbons v. Ogden, 9 Wheat. 1; and it was then deliberately examined, and deemed inadmissible by the court. Mr. Chief Justice Marshall, with his accustomed accuracy and fulness of illustration, reviewed at that time the whole grounds of the controversy; and from that time to the present, the question has been considered (so far as I know) to be at rest. The power given to congress to regulate commerce with foreign nations, and among the states, has been deemed exclusive, from the nature and objects of the power, and the necessary implications growing out of its exercise. Full power to regulate a particular subject, implies the whole power, and leaves no residuum; and a grant of the whole to one, is incompatible with a grant to another of a part. When a state proceeds to regulate commerce with foreign nations, or among the states, it is doing the very thing which congress is authorized to do. Gibbons v. Ogden, 9 Wheat. 198-199. And it has been remarked, with great cogency and accuracy, that the regulation of a subject indicates and designates the entire result; applying to those parts which remain as they were, as well as to those parts which are altered. It produces a uniform whole, which is as much disturbed and deranged by changing what the regulating power designs to leave untouched, as that upon which it has operated. Gibbons v. Ogden, 9 Wheat. 209.

This last suggestion is peculiarly important in the present case; for congress has, by the act of the 2d of March 1819, ch. 170, regulated passenger ships and vessels. Subject to the regulations therein provided, passengers may be brought into the United States from foreign ports. These regulations, being all which congress have chosen to enact, amount, upon the reasoning already stated, to a complete exercise of its power over the whole subject, as well in what is omitted as what is provided for. Unless, then, we are prepared to say, that wherever congress has legislated upon this subject, clearly within its constitutional authority, and made all such regulations, as, in its own judgment and discretion, were deemed expedient; the states may step in and supply all other regulations, which they may deem expedient, as complementary to those of congress, thus subjecting all our trade, commerce and navigation, and intercourse with foreign nations, to the double operations of distinct and independent sovereignties, it seems to me, impossible to maintain the doctrine, that the states have a concurrent jurisdiction with congress on the regulation of commerce, whether congress has or has not legislated upon the subject; a fortiori, when it has legislated.

There is another consideration, which ought not to be overlooked in discussing this subject. It is, that congress, by its legislation, has, in fact, authorized not only the transportation but the introduction of passengers into the country. The act of New York imposes restraints and burdens upon this right of transportation and introduction. It goes even further, and authorizes the removal of passengers, under certain circumstances, out of the state, and at the expense of the master and owner in whose ship they have been introduced; and this, though they are citizens of the United States, and were brought from other states. Now, if this act be constitutional to this extent, it will justify the states in regulating, controlling, and, in effect, interdicting the transportation of passengers from one state to another, in steamboats and packets. They may levy a tax upon all such passengers; they may require bonds from the master, that no such passengers shall become chargeable to the state; they may require such passengers to give bonds, that they shall not become so chargeable; they may authorize the immediate removal of such passengers back to the place from which they came. These would be most burdensome and inconvenient regulations respecting passengers, and would entirely defeat the object of congress in licensing the trade or business. And yet, if the argument which we have heard be well founded, it is a power strictly within the authority of the states, and may be exerted, at the pleasure of all or any of them, to the ruin and, perhaps, annihilation of our passenger navigation. It is no answer to the objection, to say, that the states will have too much wisdom and prudence to exercise the authority to so great an extent. Laws were actually passed, of a retaliatory nature, by the states of New York, New Jersey and Connecticut, during the steamboat controversy, which threatened the safety and security of the Union; and demonstrated the necessity, that the power to regulate commerce among the states should be exclusive in the Union, in order to prevent the most injurious restraints upon it.

In the case of Brown v. State of Maryland, 12 Wheat. 419, the state had by an act, required, that every importer of foreign goods, selling the same by wholesale, should, before he was authorized to sell the same, take out a license for which he should pay fifty dollars; and in default, the importer was subjected to a penalty. The question was, whether the state legislature could constitutionally require the importer of foreign goods to take out such a license, before he should be permitted to sell the same in the imported package? The court held, that the act was unconstitutional and void, as laying a duty on imports, and also as interfering with the power of congress to regulate commerce. On that occasion, arguments were addressed to the court on behalf of the state of Maryland, by their learned counsel, similar to those which have been addressed to us on the present occasion; and in a particular manner, the arguments, that the act did not reach the property, until after its arrival within the territorial limits of the state; that it did not obstruct the importation, but only the sale of goods, after the importation. The court said, "there is no difference, in effect, between the power to prohibit the sale of an article, and the power to prohibit its introduction into the country; the one would be a necessary consequence of the other; none would be imported, if none could be sold." "It is obvious, that the same power which imposes a light duty, can impose a heavy one, which amounts to a prohibition. Questions of power do not depend on the degree to which it may be exercised; if it may be exercised at all, it must be exercised at the will of those in whose hands it is placed." "The power claimed by the state is, in its nature, in conflict with that given to congress (to regulate commerce); and the greater or less extent to which it may be exercised, does not enter into the inquiry concerning its existence.: Any charge on the introduction and incorporation of the articles into and with the mass of property in the country, must be hostile to the power given to congress to regulate commerce; since an essential part of that regulation, and principal object of it, is to prescribe the regular means of accomplishing that introduction and incorporation."

This whole reasoning is directly applicable to the present case; if, instead of the language respecting the introduction and importation of goods, we merely substitute the words, respecting the introduction and importation of passengers, we shall instantly perceive its full purpose and effect. The result of the whole reasoning is, that whatever restrains or prevents the introduction or importation of passengers or goods into the country, authorized and allowed by congress, whether in the shape of a tax or other charge, or whether before or after their arrival in port, interferes with the exclusive right of congress to regulate commerce.

Such is a brief view of the grounds upon which my judgment is, that the act of New York is unconstitutional and void. In this opinion, I have the consolation to know, that I had the entire concurrence, upon the same grounds, of that great constitutional jurist, the late Mr. Chief Justice Marshall. Having heard the former arguments, his deliberate opinion was, that the act of New York was unconstitutional; and that the present case fell directly within the principles established in the case of Gibbons v. Ogden and Brown v. State of Maryland. . . .

Discussion

1. Justice Story grants states the right "to prevent the introduction of paupers into the state" but denies them the right to enact laws "which trench upon the authority of congress in its power to regulate commerce." How, in principle or in practice could New York exercise its right to exclude paupers without running afoul of the commerce clause?

2. Justices Thompson and Story seem to address the constitutionality of the New York law in similar terms, though of course they reach different conclusions. Justice Barbour's opinion for the Court has a different focus altogether. After concluding that the law is not preempted by any congressional statutes, he remarks that "we do not place our opinion on this ground. We choose rather to plant ourselves on what we consider impregnable positions," referring to the powers of "*internal police*" that are not surrendered by the states and with respect to which "the authority of the state is complete, unqualified, and exclusive." What is Barbour's theory? How, if at all, does his concept of the role of these state powers in the federal constitutional scheme differ from Marshall's in *Gibbons*? How does Barbour differentiate the realms of national and state authority?

3. Barbour's emphasis on the traditional authority of states to define their character by regulating immigration was articulated even more forcefully by Chief Justice Taney, dissenting in The Passenger Cases, 48 U.S. (7 How.) 283 (1849). The Court invalidated New York and Massachusetts laws that imposed a landing fee on alien passengers in order to pay for the support or medical care of foreign paupers. There was no majority opinion; the majority was divided between those justices who viewed the regulations as an unconstitutional regulation of foreign commerce and others who struck them down as taxes on imports in violation of Article I, section 10.

Taney denied the existence of any federal power at all over the immigration of persons into the states, which he viewed as a "reserved" power, impervious to limitation by federal treaty or congressional legislation. "[T]he people of the several States" retained the power to expel "from their borders any person, or class or persons, whom it might deem dangerous to its peace, or likely to produce a physical or moral evil among its citizens. . . . [T]he State has the exclusive right to determine, in its sound discretion, whether the danger does or does not exist, free from the control of the general government."

Taney's zeal on the point is motivated by slavery, as is made clear by his illustration of the danger of the majority's position:

> I cannot believe that it was ever intended to vest in Congress . . . this overwhelming power over the States [of deciding who should or should not be permitted to reside among its citizens]. For [Congress could then grant] the emancipated slaves of the West Indies . . . the absolute right to reside, hire houses, and traffic and trade throughout the Southern States, in spite of any State law to the contrary; inevitably producing the most serious discontent, and ultimately leading to the most painful consequences. . . .

4. Consider, in the light of *Miln,* the South Carolina Negro Seaman's Act of 1822. That act, among other things, provided that "any free negroes or persons of color" brought into a South Carolina port by "any vessel" coming "from any other state or foreign port" shall "be seized and confined in gaol until such vessel shall clear out and depart from this state." The vessel's captain was liable for the payment of expenses incurred by the State for the detention; refusal to pay was itself an offense punishable by a fine of not less than $1,000 and imprisonment of not less than two months. Moreover, the persons detained "shall be deemed and taken as absolute slaves, and sold . . ." by the State. The act was applied to a member of the crew of "the ship Homer, a British ship trading from Liverpool" to Charleston. Justice Johnson, sitting on circuit, described its purpose as "to prohibit ships coming into this port employing colored seamen." He went on to invalidate the act in Elkison v. Deliesseline, 8 F. Cas. 493 (1823), on the ground that it violated the Commerce Clause.

He first generalized what was at issue: "[I]f this state can prohibit Great Britain from employing her colored subjects . . . [or] her subjects of the African race, why not prohibit her from using those of Irish or Scottish nativity? . . ." After pointing out that the Act applied to domestic as well as foreign vessels, he noted that the enforcement of the Act might well encourage retaliation against South Carolina ships by the affected governments.

> [T]he commerce of this city, feeble and sickly, comparatively, as it already is, might be fatally injured. Charleston seamen, Charleston owners, Charleston vessels, might, eo nomine, be excluded from their commerce, or the United States involved in war and confusion. . . . These considerations show its utter incompatibility with the power delegated to congress to regulate commerce with foreign nations and our sister states. . . .
>
> The seaman's offense, therefore, is coming into the state in a ship or vessel; that of the captain consists in bringing him in, and not taking him out of the state, and paying all expenses. Now, according to the laws and treaties of the United States, it was both lawful for this seaman to come into this port, in this vessel, and for the captain to bring him in the capacity of a seaman; and yet these are the very acts for which the state law imposes these heavy penalties. Is there no clashing in this? It is in effect a repeal of the laws of the United States, pro tanto, converting a right into a crime.
>
> . . . [T]he right of the general government to regulate commerce with the sister states and foreign nations is a paramount and exclusive right; and this conclusion we arrive at, whether we examine it with reference to the words of the constitution, or the nature of the grant. . . . In the constitution of the United States, the most wonderful instrument ever drawn by the hand of man, there is a comprehension and

> precision that is unparalleled. . . . It is true that it contains no prohibition on the states to regulate foreign commerce. Nor was such a prohibition necessary, for the words of the grant sweep away the whole subject, and leave nothing for the states to act upon. Wherever this is the case, there is no prohibitory clause interposed in the constitution. Thus, the states are not prohibited from regulating the value of foreign coins or fixing a standard of weights and measures, for the very words imply a total, unlimited grant. . . .
>
> But to all this the plea of necessity is urged; and of the existence of that necessity we are told the state alone is to judge. Where is this to land us? Is it not asserting the right in each state to throw off the federal constitution at its will and pleasure? . . . But I deny that the state surrendered a single power necessary to its security, against this species of property. What is to prevent their being confined to their ships, if it is dangerous for them to go abroad? This power may be lawfully exercised. To land their cargoes, take in others, and depart, is all that is necessary to ordinary commerce.
>
> . . . But if the policy of this law was to keep foreign free persons from holding communion with our slaves, it certainly pursues a course altogether inconsistent with its object. . . . [T]he method of disposing of offenders by detaining them here presents the finest facilities in the world for introducing themselves lawfully into the very situation in which they would enjoy the best opportunities of pursing their designs. Now, if this plea of necessity could avail at all against the constitution and laws of the United States, certainly that law cannot be pronounced necessary which may defeat its own ends; much less when other provisions of unexceptionable legality may be resorted to, which would operate solely to the end proposed, viz., the effectual exclusion of dangerous characters.

This may help explain why Johnson wrote a concurring opinion the next year in *Gibbons* adopting the theory that Marshall was willing only to suggest — that Congress' power to regulate commerce was exclusive, even absent specific legislation.

How do you think that Justice Johnson would have voted in *Miln*? Given the result in *Miln*, how do you think the Supreme Court would have handled the South Carolina statute? Would your answer change had the majority adopted Justice Thompson's view of the concurrent power of a State? Do you think that Justice Story would agree with Justice Johnson's comments about the constitutionality of a more modest statute simply confining black seamen to their ships?

B. The *Cooley* Accommodation

Two years after the Passenger Cases, with only two dissents, the Court took an entirely new approach to analyzing state laws affecting interstate transportation.

COOLEY v. BOARD OF WARDENS

53 U.S. (12 How.) 299 (1851)

Error to the Supreme Court of Pennsylvania

[An 1803 Pennsylvania law required vessels entering and leaving the port of Philadelphia to engage a local pilot to guide them through the harbor. The penalty for noncompliance was one-half the regular fee (for the use of the Society for the Relief of Distressed and Decayed Pilots, their widows and children). This was an action by the Board of Wardens to recover the penalty from the consignee of noncomplying vessels engaged in the coastwise trade between New York and Philadelphia. The state courts held for the Board.[16]

CURTIS, J. . . .

We think this particular regulation concerning half-pilotage fees, is an appropriate part of a general system of regulations of this subject. Testing it by the practice of commercial States and countries legislating on this subject, we find it has usually been deemed necessary to make similar provisions. . . . [The laws] rest upon the propriety of securing lives and property exposed to the perils of a dangerous navigation, by taking on board a person peculiarly skilled to encounter or avoid them; upon the policy of discouraging the commanders of vessels from refusing to receive such persons on board at the proper times and places; and upon the expediency, and even intrinsic justice, of not suffering those who have incurred labor, and expense, and danger, to place themselves in a position to render important service generally necessary, to go unrewarded, because the master of a particular vessel either rashly refuses their proffered assistance, or, contrary to the general experience, does not need it. . . .

It remains to consider the objection, that it is repugnant to the third clause of the eighth section of the first article. "The Congress shall have power to regulate commerce with foreign nations and among the several States, and with the Indian tribes."

That the power to regulate commerce includes the regulation of navigation, we consider settled. And . . . the regulation of the qualifications of pilots, of the modes and times of offering and rendering their services . . . do constitute regulations of navigation, and consequently of commerce, within the just meaning of this clause of the Constitution. . . .

It is true that . . . the pilot is on board only during a part of the voyage between port of different States, or between ports of the United States and foreign countries; but if he is on board for such a purpose and during so much of the voyage as to be engaged in navigation, the power to regulate navigation extends to him while thus engaged, as clearly as it would if he were to remain on board throughout the whole passage, from port to port. For it is a power which extends to every part of the voyage, and may regulate those who conduct or assist in conducting navigation in one part of a voyage as much as in another part, or during the whole voyage.

Nor should it be lost sight of, that this subject of the regulation of pilots and pilotage has an intimate connection with, and an important relation to, the general subject of commerce with foreign nations and among the several States, over which it was one main object of the Constitution to create a national control. Con-

16. In the course of their opinions, Justices Curtis and McLean both refer to a congressional act of 1789 providing: "That all pilots in the bays, inlets, rivers, harbors, and ports of the United States shall continue to be regulated in conformity with the existing laws of the States, respectively, wherein such pilots may be, or with such laws as the States may respectively hereafter enact for the purpose, until further legislative provision shall be made by Congress." For reasons not of present concern, the Justices did not hold that the challenged Pennsylvania law was authorized by this statute; they therefore treated the state law as if Congress had not legislated on the issue. However, the majority did invoke the federal statute in support of its conclusion that the regulation of pilotage was a local matter, not a national one.

flicts between the laws of neighboring States, and discriminations favorable or adverse to commerce with particular foreign nations, might be created by State laws regulating pilotage, deeply affecting that equality of commercial rights, and that freedom from State interference, which those who formed the Constitution were so anxious to secure, and which the experience of more than half a century has taught us to value so highly. . . .

[A] majority of the court are of opinion, that a regulation of pilots is a regulation of commerce, within the grant to Congress of the commercial power, contained in the third clause of the eighth section of the first article of the Constitution. . . .

[W]e are brought directly and unavoidably to the consideration of the question, whether the grant of the commercial power to Congress, did per se deprive the States of all power to regulate pilots. This question has never been decided by this court, nor, in our judgment, has any case depending upon all the considerations which must govern this one, come before this court. The grant of commercial power to Congress does not contain any terms which expressly exclude the States from exercising an authority over its subject-matter. If they are excluded it must be because the nature of the power, thus granted to Congress, requires that a similar authority should not exist in the States. If it were conceded on the one side, that the nature of this power, like that to legislate for the District of Columbia, is absolutely and totally repugnant to the existence of similar power in the States, probably no one would deny that the grant of the power to Congress, as effectually and perfectly excludes the States from all future legislation on the subject, as if express words had been used to exclude them. And on the other hand, if it were admitted that the existence of this power in Congress, like the power of taxation, is compatible with the existence of a similar power in the States, then it would be in conformity with the contemporary exposition of the Constitution, (Federalist, No. 32), and with the judicial construction, given from time to time by this court, after the most deliberate consideration, to hold that the mere grant of such a power to Congress, did not imply a prohibition on the States to exercise the same power; that it is not the mere existence of such a power, but its exercise by Congress, which may be incompatible with the exercise of the same power by the States, and that the States may legislate in the absence of congressional regulations. Sturges v. Crowninshield, 4 Wheat. 193; Moore v. Houston, 5 Wheat. 1; Willson v. Blackbird Creek Co., 2 Pet. 251.

The diversities of opinion, therefore, which have existed on this subject, have arisen from the different views taken of the nature of this power. But when the nature of a power like this is spoken of, when it is said that the nature of the power requires that it should be exercised exclusively by Congress, it must be intended to refer to the subjects of that power, and to say they are of such a nature as to require exclusive legislation by Congress. Now the power to regulate commerce, embraces a vast field, containing not only many, but exceedingly various subjects, quite unlike in their nature; some imperatively demanding a single uniform rule, operating equally on the commerce of the United States in every port; and some, like the subject now in question, as imperatively demanding that diversity, which alone can meet the local necessities of navigation.

Either absolutely to affirm, or deny that the nature of this power requires exclusive legislation by Congress, is to lose sight of the nature of the subjects of this power, and to assert concerning all of them, what is really applicable but to a part.

Whatever subjects of this power are in their nature national, or admit only of one uniform system, or plan of regulation, may justly be said to be of such a nature as to require exclusive legislation by Congress. That this cannot be affirmed of laws for the regulation of pilots and pilotage, is plain. The act of 1789 contains a clear and authoritative declaration by the first Congress, that the nature of this subject is such, that until Congress should find it necessary to exert its power, it should be left to the legislation of the States; that it is local and not national; that it is likely to be the best provided for, not by one system, or plan of regulations, but by as many as the legislative discretion of the several States should deem applicable to the local peculiarities of the ports within their limits. . . .

The practice of the States, and of the national government, has been in conformity with this declaration, from the origin of the national government to this time; and the nature of the subject when examined, is such as to leave no doubt of the superior fitness and propriety, not to say the absolute necessity, of different systems of regulation, drawn from local knowledge and experience, and conformed to local wants. How then can we say, that by the mere grant of power to regulate commerce, the States are deprived of all the power to legislate on this subject, because from the nature of the power the legislation of Congress must be exclusive. This would be to affirm that the nature of the power is in any case, something different from the nature of the subject to which, in such case, the power extends, and that the nature of the power necessarily demands, in all cases, exclusive legislation by Congress, while the nature of one of the subjects of that power, not only does not require such exclusive legislation, but may be best provided for by many different systems enacted by the States, in conformity with the circumstances of the ports within their limits. In construing an instrument designed for the formation of a government, and in determining the extent of one of its important grants of power to legislate, we can make no such distinction between the nature of the power and the nature of the subject on which that power was intended practically to operate, nor consider the grant more extensive by affirming of the power, what is not true of its subject now in question.

It is the opinion of a majority of the court that the mere grant to Congress of the power to regulate commerce, did not deprive the States of power to regulate pilots, and that although Congress has legislated on this subject, its legislation manifests an intention . . . not to regulate this subject, but to leave its regulation to the several States. . . .

We have not adverted to the practical consequences of holding that the States possess no power to legislate for the regulation of pilots, though in our apprehension these would be of the most serious importance. For more than sixty years this subject has been acted on by the States. . . .

If the grant of commercial power in the Constitution has deprived the States of all power to legislate for the regulation of pilots, if their laws on this subject are mere usurpations upon the exclusive power of the general government, and utterly void, . . . how are the legislatures of the States to proceed in future, to watch over and amend these laws, as the progressive wants of a growing commerce will require . . . ?

We are of opinion that this State law was enacted by virtue of a power, residing in the State to legislate; that it is not in conflict with any law of Congress; that it does not interfere with any system which Congress has established by making regulations, or by intentionally leaving individuals to their own unrestricted action; that this law is therefore valid, and the judgment of the Supreme Court of Pennsylvania in each case must be affirmed.

Mr. Justice M'Lean and Mr. Justice Wayne dissented; and Mr. Justice Daniel, although he concurred in the judgment of the court, yet dissented from its reasoning.

MCLEAN, J.

It is with regret that I feel myself obliged to dissent from the opinion of a majority of my brethren in this case. . . .

As expressing my views on the question involved, I will copy a few sentences from the opinion of Chief Justice Marshall in the opinion in Gibbons v. Ogden. . . .

That a State may regulate foreign commerce, or commerce among the States, is a doctrine which has been advanced by individual judges of this court; but never before, I believe, has such a power been sanctioned by the decision of this court. In this case, the power to regulate pilots is admitted to belong to the commercial power of Congress; and yet it is held, that a State, by virtue of its inherent power, may regulate the subject, until such regulation shall be annulled by Congress. This is the principle established by this decision. Its language is guarded, in order to apply the decision only to the case before the court. But such restrictions can never operate, so as to render the principle inapplicable to other cases. And it is in this light that the decision is chiefly to be regretted. The power is recognized in the State, because the subject is more appropriate for State than Federal action; and consequently, it must be presumed the Constitution cannot have intended to inhibit State action. This is not a rule by which the Constitution is to be construed. It can receive but little support from the discussions which took place on the adoption of the Constitution, and none at all from the earlier decisions of this court.

It will be found that the principle in this case, if carried out, will deeply affect the commercial prosperity of the country. If a State has power to regulate foreign commerce, such regulation must be held valid, until Congress shall repeal or annul it. . . .

How can the unconstitutional acts of Louisiana, or of any other state which has ports on the Mississippi, or the Ohio, or on any of our other rivers, be corrected, without the action of Congress? And when Congress shall act, the state has only to change its ground, in order to enact and enforce its regulations. Louisiana now imposes a duty upon vessels for mooring in the river opposite the city of New Orleans, which is called a levee tax, and which, on some boats performing weekly trips to that city, amounts to from $3,000 to $4,000 annually. What is there to prevent the thirteen or fourteen states bordering upon the two rivers first-named, from regulating navigation on those rivers, although Congress may have regulated the same at some prior period? I speak not of the effect of this doctrine theoretically in this matter, but practically. And if the doctrine be true, how can this court say that such regulations of commerce are invalid? If this doctrine be sound, the passenger cases were erroneously decided. In those cases there was no direct conflict between the acts of the states taxing passengers and the acts of Congress.

From this race of legislation between Congress and the states, and between the states, if this principle be maintained, will arise a conflict similar to that which existed before the adoption of the Constitution. The states favorably situated, as

Louisiana, may levy a contribution upon the commerce of other states which shall be sufficient to meet the expenditures of the states. . . .

[A dissenting opinion by Justice Daniel is omitted.]

Discussion

Justice Curtis' opinion seems to break sharply with both Marshall's and Taney's view of the commerce clause. (*Cooley* is rare among commerce clause opinions of the period in not even mentioning Gibbons v. Ogden.) Viewed in retrospect, *Cooley* presaged a later, functional approach to adjudicating state regulations affecting interstate transportation. But Curtis' approach turned out to be aberrant in its own time, and the opinion was widely ignored. For example, in Paul v. Virginia, 75 U.S. (8 Wall.) 168 (1869), the Court upheld a Virginia law that imposed discriminatorily burdensome requirements on out-of-state companies selling insurance policies in the state. Under the *Cooley* doctrine, the Court would have held that the sale of insurance might be regulated by diverse states. Apparently, however, the Court in *Paul* reverted to Marshall's binary view, under which the states were entirely foreclosed from regulating interstate commerce. The Court held that the interstate sale of insurance was not interstate commerce. See also the decisions discussed in Carter v. Carter Coal Co., 298 U.S. 238 (1936), Chapter 4 infra.

Note on Congressional Consent

The *Wheeling Bridge* cases presented the first situation in which Congress attempted to authorize a state law that the Court had earlier, in the absence of congressional legislation, struck down as an invalid regulation of interstate commerce.[17] The cases arose out of competition between Pennsylvania and Virginia over where the Cumberland Road — one of the major national thoroughfares of the time — would cross the Ohio River. In 1847, the Virginia legislature chartered a corporation to build a bridge across the river in Wheeling (now in West Virginia). In Pennsylvania v. Wheeling & Belmont Bridge Co., 54 U. S. (13 How.) 518 (1852), Pennsylvania sought to enjoin construction of the bridge. By the time the case was heard, the bridge had been built. Justice McLean wrote for the Court, holding that the bridge impermissibly obstructed interstate navigation and ordering it raised to a specified height. (Chief Justice Taney dissented, relying on Willson v. Black Bird Creek Marsh Co.)

Virginia took its fight to Congress, which attached a rider to a post office appropriation bill by which the bridge was declared to be a lawful structure in its existing position and elevation and was declared to be a post road for the passage of mails. The bill was passed in the face of Pennsylvania's protest against this attempt to "reverse or render inoperative, the solemn adjudication of the Supreme Court."[18] The bridge collapsed in a storm in 1854. Invoking the judgment in the first case, plaintiffs sought to enjoin its rebuilding. In the second *Wheeling Bridge*

17. The facts surrounding the case are taken from Carl Swisher, 5 History of the Supreme Court of the United States: The Taney Period, 1836-64, 408-420 (1974).

18. Id. at 415.

case, 59 U.S. (18 How.) 421 (1855), a divided Court sustained the statute and denied the injunction. Justice Nelson wrote:

> So far . . . as this bridge created an obstruction to the free navigation of the river, in view of the previous acts of congress, they are to be regarded as modified by this subsequent legislation; and, although it still may be an obstruction in fact, it is not so in the contemplation of law. . . . The regulation of commerce includes intercourse and navigation, and, of course, the power to determinate what shall or shall not be deemed in judgment of law, an obstruction to navigation.

Justice McLean, who had written for the majority in the first case, dissented, asserting that Congress "may . . . declare that no bridge shall be built which shall be an obstruction to the use of a navigable water. And this, it would seem, is as far as the commercial power by congress can be exercised."

Since *Wheeling Bridge* it has been established that Congress can consent to state regulation of interstate commerce which otherwise would be held to run afoul of the commerce clause.[19]

For example, in Leisy v. Hardin, 135 U.S. 100 (1890), the Court relied on the "original package doctrine," p. 156 supra, to hold that Iowa could not enforce its prohibition laws by seizing sealed cases and kegs of beer shipped by an Illinois brewery into Iowa for sale there. Shortly thereafter, Congress enacted the Wilson Act, which provided that

> all intoxicating liquors . . . transported into any state . . . for use, consumption, sale, or storage therein, shall upon arrival in such state or territory be subject to the operation and effect of the laws . . . enacted in the exercise of its police powers, to the same extent and in the same manner as though such . . . liquors had been produced in such state.

In re Rahrer, 140 U.S. 545 (1891), sustained the Wilson Act, affirming a conviction for sellig imported liquor in the original package. Chief Justice Fuller wrote:

> The Constitution does not provide that interstate commerce shall be free, but, by the grant of this exclusive power to regulate it, it was left free except as Congress might impose restraint. Therefore, it has been determined that the failure of Congress to exercise this exclusive power in any case is an expression of its will that the subject shall be free from restrictions or impositions upon it by the several States.
>
> The laws of Iowa under consideration in Leisy v. Hardin . . . inhibited the receipt of an imported commodity, or its disposition before it had ceased to become an article of trade between one State and another. . . . Hence, it was held that inasmuch as interstate commerce, consisting in the transportation, purchase, sale and exchange of commodities, is national in its character and must be governed by a uniform system, so long as Congress did not pass any law to regulate it specifically, or in such way as to allow the laws of the State to operate upon it, Congress thereby indicated its will that such commerce should be free and untrammelled, and therefore that the laws of Iowa, referred to, were inoperative, in so far as they amounted to regulations of foreign or interstate commerce. . . .

19. Cf. Article I, §10, cl. 2: "No State shall, without the Consent of the Congress, lay any Imposts or Duties on Imports or Exports . . ." This clause does not apply to trade within the United States. Woodruff v. Parham, 75 U.S. (8 Wall.) 123 (1869).

> It does not admit of argument that Congress can neither delegate its own powers nor enlarge those of a State. This being so, it is urged that the act of Congress cannot be sustained as a regulation of commerce, because the Constition, in the matter of interstate commerce, operates ex proprio vigore as a restraint upon the power of Congress to so regulate it as to bring any of its subjects within the grasp of the police power of the State. . . . Thus the grant to the general government of a power designed to prevent embarrassing restrictions upon interstate commerce by any State, would be made to forbid any restraint whatever. We do not concur in this view. . . .
>
> Congress has not attempted to delegate the power to regulate commerce, or to exercise any power reserved to the States, or to grant a power not possessed by the States, or to adopt state laws. It has taken its own course and made its own regulation, applying to these subjects of interstate commerce one common rule, whose uniformity is not affected by variations in state laws in dealing with such property. . . .
>
> No reason is perceived why, if Congress chooses to provide that certain designated subjects of interstate commerce shall be governed by a rule which divests them of that character at an earlier period of time than would otherwise be the case, it is not within its competency to do so.

In Clark Distilling Co. v. Western Maryland Railway, 242 U.S. 311 (1917), the Court similarly sustained the Webb-Kenyon Act of 1913, which prohibited the very shipment of alcoholic beverages into a state where their possession or use was unlawful.

The most recent case reaffirming congressional power to legitimize state regulations that would otherwise violate the commerce clause is Northeast Bancorp, Inc. v. Board of Governors of the Federal Reserve System, 472 U.S. 159 (1985). The "Douglas Amendment" to the Bank Holding Company Act prohibits the Federal Reserve Board from approving the application of a bank located in one state to acquire a bank located in a different state in the absence of specific authorization "by the statute laws of the State in which such bank is located, by language to that effect and not merely by implication." Until 1972 the Amendment effectively precluded interstate banking, because no state passed such authorization.

Recently, however, a number of states have begun allowing acquisition by out-of-state banks, though with conditions. Massachusetts in 1982 passed a law specifically providing that an out-of-state bank holding company with its principal place of business in one of the surrounding New England states (i.e., Connecticut, Maine, New Hampshire, Rhode Island, and Vermont) can establish or acquire a Massachusetts bank or bank holding company so long as the home New England state accords reciprocal privileges to Massachusetts banks. Connecticut in 1983 passed a similar statute, and Rhode Island and Maine have also passed relevant legislation. Many other states have considered similar legislation. In the words of the Supreme Court, "One predictable effect of the regionally restrictive statutes will aparently be to allow the growth of regional multistate bank holding companies which can compete with the established giants in New York, California, Illinois, and Texas."

Citicorp, a New York bank, filed statements of opposition before the Federal Reserve Board to several proposed acquisitions by Connecticut and Massachusetts banks. Citicorp also challenged the constitutionality of the Massachusetts and Connecticut statutes under the commerce, compact, and equal protection clauses of the Constitution. The Supreme Court, through Justice Rehnquist, sustained the statutes. Regarding the commerce clause, the Court wrote:

> There can be little dispute that the dormant Commerce Clause would prohibit a group of States from establishing a system of regional banking by excluding bank holding companies from outside the region if Congress had remained completely silent on the subject. Nor can there be serious question that an individual State acting entirely on its own authority would run afoul of the dormant Commerce Clause if it sought to comprehensively regulate acquisitions of local banks by out-of-state holding companies.
>
> But that is not our case. Here the commerce power of Congress is not dormant, but has been exercised by that body when it enacted the Bank Holding Company Act and the Douglas Amendment to the Act. Congress has authority by the latter Amendment the Massachusetts and Connecticut statutes which petitioners challenge as violative of the Commerce Clause. When Congress so chooses, state actions which it plainly authorizes are invulnerable to constitutional attack under the Commerce Clause.

It is now well established that Congress' plenary power to regulate interstate commerce includes the power to permit whatever state regulation it wishes. The theory underlying this doctrine is less clear. Prudential Insurance Co. v. Benjamin, 328 U.S. 408 (1946), sustained Congress' consent to state regulation and taxation of the interstate insurance business, which the Court had earlier held beyond states' authority because of its "interstate character." Justice Rutledge noted that the Court had never invalidated a consent to state regulation of commerce:

> It is true that rationalizations have differed concerning those decisions. . . . But . . . whenever Congress' judgment has been uttered affirmatively to contradict the Court's previously expressed view that specific action taken by the states in Congress' silence was forbidden by the commerce clause, this body has accommodated its previous judgment to Congress' express approval. Some part of this readjustment may be explained in ways acceptable on any theory of the commerce clause and the relations of Congress and the courts toward its functioning. Such explanations, however, hardly go to the root of the matter. For the fact remains that, in these instances, the sustaining of Congress' overriding action has involved something beyond correction of erroneous factual judgment in deference to Congress' presumably better-informed view of the facts, and also beyond giving due deference to its conception of the scope of its powers, when it repudiates, just as when its silence is thought to support, the inference that it has forbidden state action.

"At this point," writes Professor Noel T. Dowling, "it seemed almost as if Mr. Justice Rutledge were leading to a mountain top from which he would point out the 'something beyond' which really went to the root of the matter. But after looking at this point and at that on the broad landscape of his opinion, I was still not sure that my vision had caught the 'something beyond.' "[20]

The short of it is that invalidations of state regulations under the commerce clause are less like pure "constitutional" decisions than like decisions holding state laws "preempted" by supervening congressional policy. Only the congres-

20. Noel Dowling, Interstate Commerce and State Power — Revised Version, 1947 Colum. L. Rev. 547.

sional policy is not — as otherwise it usually is — manifested in any enactment. In an earlier article, Professor Dowling proposed the following doctrine for this area.[21]

> [I]n the absence of affirmative consent a Congressional negative will be presumed in the courts against state action which in its effect upon interstate commerce constitutes an unreasonable interference with national interests, the presumption being rebuttable at the pleasure of Congress. Such a doctrine would free the states from any constitutional disability but at the same time would not give them license to take such action as they see fit irrespective of its effect upon interstate commerce. With respect to such commerce, the question whether the state may act upon it would depend upon the will of Congress expressed in such form as it may choose. State action falling short of such interference would prevail unless and until superseded or otherwise nullified by Congressional action.

C. The Privileges and Immunities of State Citizenship and Personal Mobility Among the States

The commerce clause is not the only part of the Constitution that addresses relationships among the states. The privileges and immunities clause of Article IV, section 2, provides, "The citizens of each State shall be entitled to all privileges and immunities of citizens in the several States." Furthermore, the Court has protected individuals' rights to move and resettle among the states, based on its understanding of the structure of federalism and independent of any particular constitutional provision. This section surveys these other federalistic limitations on state action as they existed in the mid-nineteenth century. Although several of the cases mentioned were decided after the Civil War, they are consistent with the attitudes and doctrines of the Taney Court.

1. *The Privileges and Immunities Clause of Article IV*

The privileges and immunities clause of Article IV is based on the fourth article of the Articles of Confederation, which provided:

> The better to secure and perpetuate mutual friendship and intercourse among the people of the different States in this Union, the free inhabitants of each of these States, paupers, vagabonds, and fugitives from justice excepted, shall be entitled to all the privileges and immunities of free citizens in the several States; and the people of each State shall have free ingress and regress to and from any other States, and shall enjoy therein all the privileges of trade and commerce, subject to the same duties, impositions, and restrictions as the inhabitants thereof respectively.

The privileges and immunities clause of Article IV does not give a citizen any rights against her *own* state. Rather, with qualifications, it entitles a citizen of state *A*, who is present in state *B*, to the same treatment by state *B* as *B* accords its own citizens. As the Court wrote in Paul v. Virginia, 75 U.S. (8 Wall.) 168 (1869),

21. Noel Dowling, Interstate Commerce and State Power, 27 Va. L. Rev. 1, 20 (1940).

It was undoubtedly the object of the clause . . . to place the citizens of each State upon the same footing with citizens of other States, so far as the advantages resulting from citizenship in those States are concerned. It relieves them from the disabilities of alienage in other States; it inhibits discriminating legislation against them by other States; it gives them the right of free ingress into other States, and egress from them; it insures to them in other States the same freedom possessed by the citizens of those States in the acquisition and enjoyment of property and in the pursuit of happiness; and it secures to them in other States the equal protection of their laws. It has justly been said that no provision in the Constitution has tended so strongly to constitute the citizens of the United States one people as this.

Indeed, without some provision of the kind removing from the citizens of each State the disabilities of alienage in the other States, and giving them equality of privilege with citizens of those States, the Republic would have constituted little more than a league of States. . . .

Does the privileges and immunities clause require that state *B* accord a citizen of state *A* *every* benefit it accords its own citizens? At least during the nineteenth century, the Court answered "no," frequently citing Justice Bushrod Washington's circuit court opinion in Corfield v. Coryell, F. Cas. No. 3,230 (D. Pa. 1823), which sustained a New Jersey statute forbidding anyone not "an actual inhabitant and resident" of the state to gather clams and oysters from the state's waters.

[T]he privileges and immunities of citizens of the several States . . . [are those] which are *fundamental;* which belong of right to the citizens of all free governments. . . . What these fundamental principles are, it would be more tedious than difficult to enumerate. They may all, however, be comprehended under the following general heads: protection by the government, with the right to acquire and possess property of every kind, and to pursue and obtain happiness and safety, subject, nevertheless, to such restraints as the government may prescribe for the general good of the whole. . . .

[However,] we cannot accede to the proposition which was insisted on by the counsel, that, under this provision of the Constitution, the citizens of the several States are permitted to participate in all *the rights* which belong exclusively to the citizens of any other particular State, merely upon the ground that they are enjoyed by those citizens; much less, that in regulating the use of the common property of the citizens of such States, the legislature is bound to extend to the citizens of all the other States the same advantages secured to their own citizens.

The court held that fish within the state's waters were the common property of all of the state's citizens, and that it would be "going quite too far to construe the grant of privileges and immunities of citizens, as amounting to a grant of a cotenancy in the common property of the States, to the citizens of all the other states."

Paul v. Virginia held that a state could forbid an out-of-state corporation from doing business in the state. The corporation was not itself a "citizen" and incorporation was a special privilege which Virginia was not required to extend to the foreign incorporators. Justice Field went on to express an instrumental concern for the state's regulatory powers over corporations, which were proliferating under the regime of general corporation laws:

At the present day corporations are multiplied to an almost indefinite extent. There is scarcely a business pursued requiring the expenditure of large capital, or the union of large numbers, that is not carried on by corporations. It is not too much to say that the wealth and business of the country are to a great extent controlled by them. And if, when composed of citizens of one State, their corporate powers and franchises could be exercised in other States without restriction, it is easy to see that, with the advantages thus possessed, the most important business of those States would soon pass into their hands. The principal business of every State would, in fact, be controlled by corporations created by other States.

If the right asserted of the foreign corporation, when composed of citizens of one State, to transact business in other States were even restricted to such business as corporations of those States were authorized to transact, it would still follow that those States would be unable to limit the number of corporations doing business therein. They could not charter a company for any purpose, however restricted, without at once opening the door to a flood of corporations from other States to engage in the same pursuits. They could not repel an intruding corporation, except on the condition of refusing incorporation for a similar purpose to their own citizens; and yet it might be of the highest public interest that the number of corporations in the State should be limited; that they should be required to give publicity to their transactions; to submit their affairs to proper examination; to be subject to forfeiture of their corporate rights in case of mismanagement, and that their officers should be held to a strict accountability for the manner in which the business of the corporations is managed, and be liable to summary removal.

2. *Interstate Mobility*

CRANDALL v. NEVADA, 73 U.S. (6 Wall.) 35 (1868): [The Court struck down a Nevada statute that imposed "a capitation tax of one dollar upon every person leaving the State by any railroad, stage coach, or other vehicle engaged or employed in the business of transporting passengers for hire" and required the carrier to collect the tax from the passengers and turn it over to the state. Crandall, the agent for a stagecoach company, was prosecuted for refusing to pay the tax.

Justice Miller described the issue as "the right of a State to levy a tax upon persons residing in the State who may wish to get out of it, and upon persons not residing in it who may have occasion to pass through it." He rejected petitioner's argument that the tax violated the prohibition of Article 1, section 10, against state "Imposts or Duties on Imports or Exports," holding that citizens travelling from one state to another were not imports or exports. With respect to the claim that the tax violated the commerce clause, he relied on Cooley v. Board of Wardens, 53 U.S. (12 How.) 299 (1851), reasoning as follows.]

MILLER, J. . . . It may be that under the power to regulate commerce among the States, Congress has authority to pass laws, the operation of which would be inconsistent with the tax imposed by the State of Nevada, but we know of no such statute now in existence. Inasmuch, therefore, as the tax does not itself institute any regulation of commerce of a national character, or which has a uniform operation over the whole country, it is not easy to maintain [that it violates the commerce clause]. . . .

[But] we do not concede that the question before us is to be determined by [these] two clauses of the Constitution. . . .

The people of these United States constitute one nation. They have a government in which all of them are deeply interested. This government has necessarily a capital established by law, where its principal operations are conducted. . . . That government has a right to call to this point any or all of its citizens to aid in its service, as members of the Congress, of the courts, of the executive departments, and to fill all its other offices; and this right cannot be made to depend upon the pleasure of a State over whose territory they must pass to reach the point where these services must be rendered. The government, also, has its offices of secondary importance in all other parts of the country. . . . In all these it demands the services of its citizens, and is entitled to bring them to those points from all quarters of the nation, and no power can exist in a State to obstruct this right that would not enable it to defeat the purposes for which the government was established. . . .

But if the government has these rights on her own account, the citizen also has correlative rights. He has the right to come to the seat of government to assert any claim he may have upon that government, or to transact any business he may have with it. To seek its protection, to share its offices, to engage in administering its functions. He has a right to free access to its sea-ports, through which all the operations of foreign trade and commerce are conducted, to the sub-treasuries, the land offices, the revenue offices, and the courts of justice in the several States, and this right is in its nature independent of the will of any State over whose soil he must pass in the exercise of it.

The views here advanced are neither novel nor unsupported by authority. The question of the taxing power of the States, as its exercise has affected the functions of the Federal government, has been repeatedly considered by this court, and the right of the States in this mode to impede or embarrass the constitutional operations of that government, or the rights which its citizens hold under it, has been uniformly denied.

The leading case of this class is that of McCulloch v. Maryland. . . . It will be observed that it was not the extent of the tax in that case which was complained of, but the right to levy any tax of that character. So in the case before us it may be said that a tax of one dollar for passing through the State of Nevada by stage coach or by railroad, cannot sensibly affect any function of the government, or deprive a citizen of any valuable right. But if the State can tax a railroad passenger one dollar, it can tax him one thousand dollars. If one State can do this, so can every other State. And thus one or more States covering the only practicable routes of travel from the east to the west, or from the north to the south, may totally prevent or seriously burden all transportation of passengers from one part of the country to the other. . . .

[T]he principles here laid down may be found more clearly stated in the dissenting opinion of the Chief Justice in [the Passenger Cases], and with more direct pertinency to the case now before us than anywhere else. After expressing his views fully in favor of the validity of the tax, which he said had exclusive reference to foreigners, so far as those cases were concerned, he proceeds to say, for the purpose of preventing misapprehension, that so far as the tax affected American citizens it could not in his opinion be maintained. He then adds: "Living as we do under a common government, charged with the great concerns of the whole Union, every citizen of the United States from the most remote States or territories, is entitled to free access, not only to the principal departments established at Washington, but also to its judicial tribunals and public offices in every

State in the Union. . . . For all the great purposes for which the Federal government was formed we are one people, with one common country. We are all citizens of the United States, and as members of the same community must have the right to pass and repass through every part of it without interruption, as freely as in our own States. And a tax imposed by a State, for entering its territories or harbors, is inconsistent with the rights which belong to citizens of other States as members of the Union, and with the objects which that Union was intended to attain. Such a power in the States could produce nothing but discord and mutual irritation, and they very clearly do not possess it."

Although these remarks are found in a dissenting opinion, they do not relate to the matter on which the dissent was founded. They accord with the inferences which we have already drawn from the Constitution itself, and from the decisions of this court in exposition of that instrument.

Those principles, as we have already stated them in this opinion, must govern the present case.

[Justice Clifford and Chief Justice Chase concurred in the judgment solely on the ground that the state law violated the commerce clause.]

Discussion

1. How do you suppose *Crandall* would have been decided by the Court that decided *Miln?* Is Justice Miller's rejection of the Commerce Clause argument consistent with the spirit of *Cooley?*

2. Note that *Crandall* is an almost unique instance — another one being the second part of *McCulloch* — of constitutional interpretation based exclusively on the theory and structure of the federal system without any recourse to the *text* of the Constitution.[22] Note also that Justice Miller makes two rather distinct "structural" arguments, which have different implications for the scope of the citizen's right of interstate mobility.

III. Slavery

Slavery first became a prominent national political issue in 1819 with the debate over the admission of Missouri as a state. After the Louisiana Purchase, slaveholders migrated to the northern portions of the territory, where they established wheat and cotton plantations. The petition for statehood, which would have established Missouri as a slave state, occasioned a heated conflict in Congress and resulted in the Missouri Compromise, which, among other things, admitted Missouri as a slave state but prohibited slavery in the territories north of latitude 36° 30′. "Angry passions quickly subsided, the sectional alignment dissolved, and politics resumed their delusive tranquility. But a veil had been lifted for the moment, re-

22. In United States v. Guest, 383 U.S. 745 (1966), Justice Stewart wrote for the Court, sustaining a federal indictment for conspiracy to interfere with the rights of black citizens to travel interstate:

> Although the Articles of Confederation provided that "the people of each State shall have free ingress and regress to and from any other State," that right finds no explicit mention in the Constitution. The reason, it has been suggested, is that a right so elementary was conceived from the beginning to be a necessary concomitant of the stronger Union the Constitution created.

vealing a bloody prospect ahead. 'This monumental question, like a fire bell in the night, awakened and filled me with terror,' wrote Jefferson. 'I considered it at once as the knell of the union.' And J.Q. Adams recorded in his diary: 'I take it for granted that the present question is a mere preamble — a title-page to a great, tragic volume.' "[23] Under the chief justiceship of Roger Taney, the Supreme Court played a significant role in the tragic drama predicted by Adams.

A. The Interstate Slave Trade

GROVES v. SLAUGHTER, 40 U.S. (15 Pet.) 449 (1841): [A provision of the Mississippi Constitution of 1832, which arguably forbade importing slaves into the state for sale there, was attacked as an impermissible restriction of interstate commerce. Mississippi was, of course, a slave state, and the provision was designed to protect its own slave trade against competition from other states. As Justice Baldwin described the provision in a concurring opinion, it "does not purport to be a regulation of police, for any defined object connected with the internal tranquility of the State, the health, or morals of the people; it is general in its terms; it is aimed at the introduction of slaves as merchandise from other States, not with the intention of excluding diseased, convicted, or insurgent slaves, or such as may be otherwise dangerous to the peace or welfare of the State. Its avowed purpose is to prevent them from being the subjects of intercourse with other States, when introduced for the purpose of sale. . . ."

Justice Thompson's opinion for the Court avoided the issue entirely by construing the state constitution to require the passage of activating legislation. Three concurring justices carried on a vigorous side debate over the issues that the majority artfully avoided.]

McLEAN, J., concurring. [For Justice McLean, an Ohioan and a Marshallian nationalist, the case presented a dilemma. If slaves were an item of commerce, Congress could, if it so chose, prohibit the interstate slave trade by ordinary legislation under the commerce power. But the Marshallian view of congressional exclusivity suggested in *Gibbons* cast doubt on the validity of any state laws regulating the slave trade; it did not distinguish between Mississippi's pro-slavery, protectionist law and Ohio's ban on the slave trade as part of its prohibition of slavery in general. McLean tried to straddle the dilemma. He denied that slaves were an item of commerce: Even "if slaves are considered in some of the States as merchandise, that cannot divest them of the leading and controlling quality of persons by which they are designated in the Constitution." He went on to argue that the states were free to deal with slavery as they wished.]

. . . The power over slavery belongs to the States respectively. It is local in its character, and in its effects; and the transfer or sale of slaves cannot be separated from this power. It is, indeed, an essential part of it.

Each state has a right to protect itself against the avarice and intrusion of the slave dealer; to guard its citizens against the inconveniences and dangers of a slave population.

The right to exercise this power by a State is higher and deeper than the Constitution. The evil involves the prosperity and may endanger the existence of a

23. Morison, Commager & Leuchtenborg, supra note 2, at 398-399.

State. Its power to guard against, or to remedy the evil, rests upon the law of self-preservation; a law vital to every community, and especially to a sovereign State. . . .

TANEY, C.J. [claimed that he addressed the issue only because McLean had raised it, and came to the same conclusion] . . . In my judgment the power over this subject is exclusively with the several States . . . and the action of the several States upon this subject, cannot be controlled by Congress, either by virtue of its power to regulate commerce, or by virtue of any other power. . . .

BALDWIN, J. [Justice Baldwin, who like McLean was a nationalist, argued that although a state could abolish slavery entirely, it could not allow slavery and prohibit the slave trade, for slaves were items of commerce and the regulation of interstate commerce lay within the exclusive domain of Congress. In elaborating this position, he made explicit some broader concerns of slavery and federalism.] . . . As each state has plenary power to legislate on this subject, its laws are the test of what is property; if they recognise slaves as the property of those who hold them, they become the subjects of commerce between the states which so recognise them, and the traffic in them may be regulated by congress, as the traffic in other articles; but no further. Being property, by the law of any state, the owners are protected from any violations of the rights of property by congress, under the fifth amendment of the constitution; these rights do not consist merely in ownership; the right of disposing of property of all kinds, is incident to it, which congress cannot touch. The mode of disposition is regulated by the state of common law; and but for the first clause in the second section of the fourth article of the constitution of the United States, a state might authorize its citizens to deal in slaves, and prohibit it to all others. But that clause secures to the citizens of all the states, "all privileges and immunities of citizens" of any other state, whereby any traffic in slaves or other property, which is lawful to the citizens or settlers of Mississippi, with each other, is equally protected when carried on between them and the citizens of Virginia. Hence, it is apparent, that no state can control this traffic, so long as it may be carried on by its own citizens, within its own limits; as part of its purely internal commerce, any state may regulate it according to its own policy; but when such regulation purports to extend to other states or their citizens, it is limited by the constitution, putting the citizens of all on the same footing as their own. It follows, likewise, that any power of congress over the subject is, as has been well expressed by one of the plaintiffs' counsel, conservative in its character, for the purpose of protecting the property of the citizens of the United States, which is a lawful subject of commerce among the states, from any state law which affects to prohibit its transmission for sale from one state to another, through a third or more states.

Thus, in Ohio, and those states to which the ordinance of 1787 applies, or in those where slaves are not property, not subjects of dealing or traffic among its own citizens, they cannot become so, when brought from other states; their condition is the same as those persons of the same color already in the state; subject in all respects to the provisions of its law, if brought there for the purposes of residence or sale. If, however, the owner of slaves in Maryland, in transporting them to Kentucky or Missouri, should pass through Pennsylvania or Ohio, no law of either state could take away or affect his right of property; nor, if passing from one slave state to another, accident or distress should compel him to touch at any place within a state, where slavery did not exist. Such transit of property, whether of slaves or bales of goods is lawful commerce among the several states, which none can prohibit or regulate, which the constitution protects, and congress may, and ought, to preserve from violation. . . .

But where no object of police is discernible in a state law or constitution, nor any rule of policy, other than that which gives to its own citizens a "privilege," which is denied to citizens of other states, it is wholly different. The direct tendency of all such laws is partial, anti-national, subversive of the harmony which should exist among the states, as well as inconsistent with the most sacred principles of the constitution. . . . For these reasons, my opinion is, that had the contract in question been invalid by the constitution of Mississippi, it would be valid by the constitution of the United States. These reasons are drawn from those principles on which alone this government must be sustained: the leading one of which is, that wherever slavery exists, by the laws of a state, slaves are property in every constitutional sense, and for every purpose, whether as subjects of taxation, as the basis of representation, as articles of commerce, or fugitives from service. To consider them as persons merely, and not property, is, in my settled opinion, the first step towards a state of things to be avoided only by a firm adherence to the fundamental principles of the state and federal governments, in relation to this species of property. If the first step taken be a mistaken one, the successive ones will be fatal to the whole system. I have taken my stand on the only position which, in my judgment, is impregnable; and feel confident in its strength, however it may be assailed in public opinion, here or elsewhere.

B. Fugitive Slaves

PRIGG v. PENNSYLVANIA

41 U.S. (16 Pet.) 536 (1842)
Error to the Supreme Court of Pennsylvania

[The Fugitive Slave Act of 1793, enacted pursuant to Article IV of the Constitution, authorized the owner to seize a fugitive slave and bring him or her before a federal judge or state magistrate, who, upon satisfactory proof "that the person so seized or arrested doth, under the laws of the state or territory from which he or she fled, owe service or labor to the person claiming him or her, it shall be the duty of such judge or magistrate to give a certificate thereof to such claimant. . . ."

Prigg, the agent of a Maryland slave owner, applied to a Pennsylvania magistrate for a certificate of removal for an escaped slave. When the certificate was refused, Prigg forcibly removed the slave from Pennsylvania and returned her to Maryland. Prigg was convicted under an 1826 Pennsylvania statute expressly designed to prevent self-help in the return of fugitive slaves.

The Supreme Court reversed the conviction and held the state law unconstitutional. Justice Story wrote for the Court; six Justices wrote separate opinions, some disagreeing sharply with aspects of the opinion. We excerpt portions of Story's opinion, Taney's opinion concurring in the result, and McLean's dissent.]

STORY, J. . . .

Few questions which have ever come before this court involve more delicate and important considerations; and few upon which the public at large may be presumed to feel a more profound and pervading interest. . . .

Before, however, we proceed to the points more immediately before us, it may be well, in order to clear the case of difficulty, to say, that in the exposition of this part of the constitution, we shall limit ourselves to those considerations which appropriately and exclusively belong to it, without laying down any rules of interpretation of a more general nature. It will, indeed, probably, be found, when we look to the character of the constitution itself, the objects which it seeks to attain, the powers which it confers, the duties which it enjoins, and the rights which it secures, as well as the known historical fact, that many of its provisions were matters of compromise of opposing interests and opinions, that no uniform rule of interpretation can be applied to it, which may not allow, even if it does not positively demand, many modifications, in its actual application to particular clauses. And, perhaps, the safest rule of interpretation, after all, will be found to be to look to the nature and objects of the particular powers, duties and rights, with all the lights and aids of contemporary history; and to give to the words of each just such operation and force, consistent with their legitimate meaning, as may fairly secure and attain the ends proposed.

There are two clauses in the constitution upon the subject of fugitives, which stand in juxtaposition with each other, and have been thought mutually to illustrate each other. They are both contained in the second section of the fourth article, and are in the following words: "A person charged in any state with treason, felony or other crime, who shall flee from justice, and be found in another state, shall, on demand of the executive authority of the state from which he fled, be delivered up, to be removed to the state having jurisdiction of the crime." "No person held to service or labor in one state, under the laws thereof, escaping into another, shall, in consequence of any law or regulation therein, be discharged from such service or labor; but shall be delivered up, on claim of the party to whom such service or labor may be due."

The last clause is that, the true interpretation whereof is directly in judgment before us. Historically, it is well known, that the object of this clause was to secure to the citizens of the slave-holding states the complete right and title of ownership in their slaves, as property, in every state in the Union into which they might escape from the state where they were held in servitude. The full recognition of this right and title was indispensable to the security of this species of property in all the slave-holding states; and, indeed, was so vital to the preservation of their domestic interests and institutions, that it cannot be doubted, that it constituted a fundamental article, without the adoption of which the Union could not have been formed. Its true design was, to guard against the doctrines and principles prevalent in the non-slave-holding states, by preventing them from intermeddling with, or obstructing, or abolishing the rights of the owners of slaves.

By the general Law of nations, no nation is bound to recognise the state of slavery, as to foreign slaves found within its territorial dominions, when it is in opposition to its own policy and institutions, in favor of the subjects of other nations where slavery is recognised. If it does it, it is as a matter of comity, and not as a matter of international right. The state of slavery is deemed to be a mere municipal regulation, founded upon and limited to the range of the territorial laws. It is manifest, from this consideration, that if the constitution had not contained this clause, every non-slave-holding state in the Union would have been at liberty to have declared free all runaway slaves coming within its limits, and to have given them entire immunity and protection against the claims of their masters; a course which would have created the most bitter animosities, and engendered perpetual strife between the different states. The clause was, therefore, of the last importance to the safety and security of the southern states, and could not have been surrendered by them, without endangering their whole property in slaves. The clause was accordingly adopted into the constitution, by the unanimous consent of the framers of it; a proof at once of its intrinsic and practical necessity.

How, then, are we to interpret the language of the clause? The true answer is, in such a manner as, consistently with the words, shall fully and completely effectuate the whole objects of it. If, by one mode of interpretation, the right must become shadowy and unsubstantial, and without any remedial power adequate to the end, and by another mode, it will attain its just end and secure its manifest purpose, it would seem, upon principles of reasoning, absolutely irresistible, that the latter ought to prevail. No court of justice can be authorized so to construe any clause of the constitution as to defeat its obvious ends, when another construction, equally accordant with the words and sense thereof, will enforce and protect them.

The clause manifestly contemplates the existence of a positive, unqualified right on the part of the owner of the slave, which no state law or regulation can in any way qualify, regulate, control or restrain. The slave is not to be discharged from service or labor, in consequence of any state law or regulation. Now, certainly, without indulging in any nicety of criticism upon words, it may fairly and reasonably be said, that any state law or state regulation, which interrupts, limits, delays or postpones the right of the owner to the immediate possession of the slave, and the immediate command of his service and labor, operates, pro tanto, a discharge of the slave therefrom. The question can never be, how much the slave is discharged from; but whether he is discharged from any, by the natural or necessary operation of state laws or state regulations. The question is not one of quantity or degree, but of withholding or controlling the incidents of a positive and absolute right.

. . . Upon this ground, we have not the slightest hesitation in holding, that under and in virtue of the constitution, the owner of a slave is clothed with entire authority, in every state in the Union, to seize and recapture his slave, whenever he can do it, without any breach of the peace or any illegal violence. In this sense, and to this extent, this clause of the constitution may properly be said to execute itself, and to require no aid from legislation, state or national.

But the clause of the constitution does not stop here; nor, indeed, consistently with its professed objects, could it do so. Many cases must arise, in which, if the remedy of the owner were confined to the mere right of seizure and recaption, he would be utterly without any adequate redress. He may not be able to lay his hands upon the slave. He may not be able to enforce his rights against persons, who either secrete or conceal, or withhold the slave. He may be restricted by local legislation, as to the mode of proofs of his ownership; as to the courts in which he shall sue, and as to the actions which he may bring; or the process he may use to compel the delivery of the slave. Nay! the local legislation may be utterly inadequate to furnish the appropriate redress . . . ; and this may be innocently as well as designedly done, since every state is perfectly competent, and has the exclusive right, to prescribe the remedies in its own judicial tribunals, to limit the time as well as the mode of redress, and to deny jurisdiction over cases, which its own policy and its own institutions either prohibit or discountenance. If, therefore, the clause of the constitution had stopped at the mere recognition of the right, without providing or contemplating any means by which it might be established and enforced, in cases where it did not execute itself, it is plain, that it would have been, in a great variety of cases, a delusive and empty annunciation. . . .

And this leads us to the consideration of the other part of the clause, which implies at once a guarantee and duty. It says, "but he (the slave) shall be delivered up, on claim of the party to whom such service or labor may be due." Now, we think it exceedingly difficult, if not impracticable, to read this language, and not to feel, that it contemplated some further remedial redress than that which might be administered at the hands of the owner himself. . . . If, indeed, the constitution guarantees the right, and if it requires the delivery upon the claim of the owner (as cannot well be doubted), the natural inference certainly is, that the national government is clothed with the appropriate authority and functions to enforce it. . . . The clause is found in the national constitution, and not in that of any state. It does not point out any state functionaries, or any state action, to carry its provisions into effect. The states cannot, therefore, be compelled to enforce them; and it might well be deemed an unconstitutional exercise of the power of interpretation, to insist, that the states are bound to provide means to carry into effect the duties of the national government, nowhere delegated or intrusted to them by the constitution. On the contrary, the natural, if not the necessary, conclusion is, that the national government, in the absence of all positive provisions to the contrary, is bound, through its own proper departments, legislative, judicial or executive, as the case may require, to carry into effect all the rights and duties imposed upon it by the constitution. . . .

Congress has taken this very view of the power and duty of the national government. As early as the year 1791, the attention of congress was drawn to it (as we shall hereafter more fully see), in consequence of some practical difficulties arising under the other clause, respecting fugitives from justice escaping into other states. The result of their deliberations was the passage of the act of the 12th of February 1793, ch. 51, which, after having, in the first and second sections, provided by the case of fugitives from justice, by a demand to be made of the delivery, through the executive authority of the state where they are found, proceeds in the third section to provide, that when a person held to labor or service in any of the United States, shall escape into any other of the states or territories the person to whom such labor or service may be due, his agent or attorney, is hereby empowered to seize or arrest such fugitive from labor and take him or her before any judge of the circuit or district courts of the United States, residing or being within the state, or before any magistrate of a county, city or town corporate, wherein such seizure or arrest shall be made; and upon proof, to the satisfaction of such judge or magistrate, either by oral evidence or affidavit, &c, that the person so seized or arrested, doth, under the laws of the state or territory from which he or she fled, owe service or labor to the person claiming him or her, it shall be the duty of such judge or magistrate, to give a certificate thereof to such claimant, his agent or attorney, which shall be sufficient warrant for removing the said fugitive from labor, to the state or territory from which he or she fled.

The fourth section provides a penalty against any person, who shall knowingly and willingly obstruct or hinder such claimant, his agent or attorney, in so seizing or arresting such fugitive from labor, or rescue such fugitive from the claimant, or his agent or attorney, when so arrested, or who shall harbor or conceal such fugitive, after notice that he is such; and it also saves to the person claiming such labor or service, his right of action for or on account of such injuries.

In a general sense, this act may be truly said to cover the whole ground of the constitution, . . . because it points out fully all the modes of attaining those objects, which congress, in their discretion, have as yet deemed expedient or proper to meet the exigencies of the constitution. If this be so, then it would seem, upon just principles of construction, that the legislation of congress, if constitutional, must supersede all state legislation upon the same subject; and by necessary implication prohibit it. For, if congress have a constitutional power to regulate a particular subject, and they do actually regulate it in a given manner, and in a certain form, it cannot be, that the state legislatures have a right to interfere, and as it were, by way of compliment to the legislation of congress, to prescribe additional regulations, and what they may deem auxiliary provisions for the same purpose. In such a case, the legislation of congress, in what it does prescribe, manifestly indicates, that it does not intend that there shall be any further legislation to act upon the subject-matter. Its silence as to what it does not do, is as expressive of what its intention is, as the direct provisions made by it. . . . [W]here congress have exercised a power over a particular subject given them by the constitution, it is not competent for state legislation to add to the provisions of congress upon that subject; for that the will of congress upon the whole subject is as clearly established by what it has not declared, as by what it has expressed.

But it has been argued, that the act of congress is unconstitutional, because it does not fall within the scope of any of the enumerated powers of legislation confided to that body; and therefore, it is void. Stripped of its artificial and technical structure, the argument comes to this, that although rights are exclusively secured by, or duties are exclusively imposed upon, the national government, yet, unless the power to enforce these rights or to execute these duties, can be found among the express powers of legislation enumerated in the constitution, they remain without any means of giving them effect by any act of congress; and they must operate solely proprio vigore, however defective may be their operation; nay, even although, in a practical sense, they may become a nullity, from the want of a proper remedy to enforce them, or to provide against their violation. If this be the true interpretation of the constitution, it must, in a great measure, fail to attain many of its avowed and positive objects, as a security of rights, and a recognition of duties. Such a limited construction of the constitution has never yet been adopted as correct, either in theory or practice. No one has ever supposed, that congress could, constitutionally, by its legislation, exercise powers, or enact laws, beyond the powers delegated to it by the constitution. But it has, on various occasions, exercised powers which were necessary and proper as means to carry into effect rights expressly given, and duties expressly enjoined thereby. The end being required, it has been deemed a just and necessary implication, that the means to accomplish it are given also; or, in other words, that the power flows as a necessary means to accomplish the end. . . .

[T]he nature of the provision and the objects to be attained by it, require that it should be controlled by one and the same will, and act uniformly by the same system of regulations throughout the Union. If, then, the states have a right, in the absence of legislation by congress, to act upon the subject, each state is at liberty to prescribe just such regulations as suit its own policy, local convenience and local feelings. The legislation of one state may not only be different from, but utterly repugnant to and incompatible with, that of another. . . .

It is scarcely conceivable, that the slave-holding states would have been satisfied with leaving to the legislation of the non-slave-holding states, a power of regulation, in the absence of that of congress, which would or might practically amount to a power to destroy the rights of the owner. If the argument, therefore, of a concurrent power in the states to act upon the subject-matter, in the absence of legislation by congress, be well founded; then, if congress had never acted at all, or if the act of congress should be repealed, without providing a substitute, there would be a resulting authority in each of the states to regulate the whole subject, at its pleasure, and to dole out its own remedial justice, or withhold it, at its pleasure, and according to its own views of policy and expediency. Surely, such a state of things never could have been intended, under such a solemn guarantee of right and duty. On the other hand, construe the right of legislation as exclusive in congress, and every evil and every danger vanishes. The right and the duty are then co-extensive and uniform in remedy and operation throughout the whole Union. The owner has the same security, and the same remedial justice, and the same exemption from state regulation and control, through however many states he may pass with his fugitive slave in his possession, in transit to his own domicile. . . .

These are some of the reasons, but by no means all, upon which we hold the power of legislation on this subject to be exclusive in congress. To guard, however, against any possible misconstruction of our views, it is proper to state, that we are by no means to be understood, in any manner whatsoever, to doubt or to interfere with the police power belonging to the states, in virtue of their general sovereignty. That police power extends over all subjects within territorial limits of the states, and has never been conceded to the United States. It is wholly distinguishable from the right and duty secured by the provision now under consideration; which is exclusively derived from and secured by the constitution of the United States, and owes its whole efficacy thereto. We entertain no doubt whatsoever, that the states, in virtue of their general police power, possess full jurisdiction to arrest and restrain runaway slaves, and remove them from their borders, and otherwise to secure themselves against their depredations and evil example, as they certainly may do in cases of idlers, vagabonds and paupers. The rights of the owners of fugitive slaves are in no just sense interfered with, or regulated, by such a course; and in many cases, the operations of this police power, although designed generally for other purposes, for protection, safety and peace of the state, may essentially promote and aid the interests of the owners. But such regulations can never be permitted to interfere with, or to obstruct, the just rights of the owner to reclaim his slave, derived from the constitution of the United States, or with the remedies prescribed by congress to aid and enforce the same.

Upon these grounds, we are of opinion, that the act of Pennsylvania upon which this indictment is founded, is unconstitutional and void. It purports to punish as a public offence against that state, the very act of seizing and removing a slave, by his master, which the constitution of the United States was designed to justify and uphold. . . .

TANEY, C.J., concurring. . . .

The opinion of the court maintains, that the power over this subject is so exclusively vested in congress, that no state, since the adoption of the constitution, can pass any law in relation to it. In other words, according to the opinion just delivered, the state authorities are prohibited from interfering, for the purpose of protecting the right of the master, and aiding him in the recovery of his property. I think, the states are not prohibited; and that, on the contrary, it is enjoined upon them as a duty, to protect and support the owner, when he is endeavoring to obtain possession of his property found within their respective territories. The language used in the constitution does not, in my judgment, justify the construction given to it by the court. It contains no words prohibiting the several states from passing laws to enforce this right. They are, in express terms, forbidden to make any regulation that shall impair it; but there the prohibition stops. And according to the settled rules of construction for all written instruments, the prohibition being confined to laws injurious to the right, the power to pass laws to support and enforce it, is necessarily implied. And the words of the article which direct that the fugitive "shall be delivered up," seem evidently designed to impose it as a duty upon the people of the several states, to pass laws to carry into execution, in good faith, the compact into which they thus solemnly entered with each other. The constitution of the United States, and every article and clause in it, is a part of the law of every state in the Union; and is the paramount law. The right of the master, therefore, to seize his fugitive slave, is the law of each state; and no state has the power to abrogate or alter it. And why may not a state protect a right of property, acknowledged by its own paramount law? Besides, the laws of the different states, in all other cases, constantly protect the citizens of other states in their rights of property, when it is found within their respective territories; and no one doubts their power to do so. And in the absence of any express prohibition, I perceive no reason for establishing, by implication, a different rule in this instance; where, by the national compact, this right of property is recognised as an existing right in every state of the Union.

. . . [I]t is manifest, from the face of the law, that an effectual remedy was intended to be given, by the act of 1793. It never designed to compel the master to encounter the hazard and expense of taking the fugitive, in all cases, to the distant residence of one of the judges of the courts of the United States; for it authorized him also, to go before any magistrate of the county, city or town corporate wherein the seizure should be made. And congress evidently supposed, that it had provided a tribunal at the place of the arrest, capable of furnishing the master with the evidence of ownership, to protect him more effectually from unlawful interruption. So far from regarding the state authorities as prohibited from interfering in cases of this description, the congress of that day must have counted upon their cordial co-operation; they legislated with express reference to state support.

MCLEAN, J., dissenting. . . .

In my judgment, there is not the least foundation in the act for the right asserted in the argument, to take the fugitive by force and remove him out of the state.

Such a proceeding can receive no sanction under the act, for it is in express violation of it. The claimant having seized the fugitive, is required by the act, to take him before a federal judge within the state, or a state magistrate within the county, city or town corporate, within which the seizure was made. Now, can there be any pretence, that after the seizure under the statute, the claimant may disregard the other express provision of it, by taking the fugitive, without claim, out of the state. But it is said, the master may seize his slave wherever he finds him, if by doing so, he does not violate the public peace; that the relation of master and slave is not affected by the laws of the state, to which the slave may have fled, and where he is found. . . .

It is admitted, that the rights of the master, so far as regards the services of the slave, are not impaired by this change; but the mode of asserting them, in my opinion, is essentially modified. In the state where the service is due, the master needs no other law than the law of force, to control the action of the slave. But can this law be applied by the master, in a state which makes the act unlawful? . . .

In a state where slavery is allowed, every colored person is presumed to be a slave; and on the same principle, in a non-slave-holding state, every person is presumed to be free, without regard to color. On this principle, the states, both slave-holding and non-slave-holding, legislate. The latter may prohibit, as Pennsylvania has done, under a certain penalty, the forcible removal of a colored person out of the state. . . .

It is very clear, that no power to seize and forcibly remove the slave, without claim, is given by the act of congress. Can it be exercised under the constitution? Congress have legislated on the constitutional power, and have directed the mode in which it shall be executed. The act, it is admitted, covers the whole ground; and that it is constitutional, there seems to be no reason to doubt. Now, under such circumstances, can the provisions of the act be disregarded, and an assumed power set up under the constitution? This is believed to be wholly inadmissible by any known rule of construction. The terms of the constitution are general, and like many other powers in that instrument, require legislation. In the language of this court, in Martin v. Hunter, 1 Wheat. 304, "the powers of the constitution are expressed in general terms, leaving to the legislature, from time to time, to adopt its own means to effectuate legitimate objects, and to mould and model the exercise of its powers, as its own wisdom and the public interests should require." This congress have done by the act of 1793. . . .

I cannot perceive how any one can doubt that the remedy given in the constitution, if, indeed, it give any remedy, without legislation, was designed to be a peaceful one; a remedy sanctioned by judicial authority; a remedy guarded by the forms of law. But the inquiry is reiterated, is not the master entitled to his property? I answer, that he is. His right is guarantied by the constitution, and the most summary means for its enforcement is found in the act of congress; and neither the state nor its citizens can obstruct the prosecution of this right. . . .

The presumption of the state that the colored person is free, may be erroneous in fact; and if so, there can be no difficulty in proving it. But may not the assertion of the master be erroneous also; and if so, how is his act of force to be remedied? The colored person is taken and forcibly conveyed beyond the jurisdiction of the state. This force, not being authorized by the act of congress nor by the constitution, may be prohibited by the state. As the act covers the whole power in the constitution, and carries out, by special enactments, its provisions, we are, in my judgment, bound by the act. We can no more, under such circumstances, administer a remedy under the constitution, in disregard of the act, than we can exercise a commercial or other power in disregard of an act of congress on the same subject. This view respects the rights of the master and the rights of the state; it neither jeopards nor retards the reclamation of the slave; it removes all state action prejudicial to the rights of the master; and recognises in the state a power to guard and protect its own jurisdiction, and the peace of its citizen.

It appears, in the case under consideration, that the state magistrate before whom the fugitive was brought refused to act. In my judgment, he was bound to perform the duty required of him by a law paramount to any act, on the same subject, in his own state. But this refusal does not justify the subsequent action of the claimant; he should have taken the fugitive before a judge of the United States, two of whom resided within the state. . . .

Discussion

1. *Prigg* held that Article IV, section 2, clause 3, was self-executing (i.e., operated of its own force without the need for implementing congressional legislation) and that it authorized a slave owner to use self-help in capturing a fugitive slave. The Court held that the 1793 act was constitutional, at least insofar as it authorized federal judges to render fugitive slaves. The Court also intimated that the statute, if not the Constitution, precluded state courts from playing any role whatever in returning fugitive slaves.[24]

Consider Story's analysis of these issues on the merits — especially in the light of McLean's and Taney's criticisms. Can the Court's approval of self-help be reconciled with the Fifth Amendment's requirement that no person shall be "deprived of life, liberty, or property, without due process of law"?

2. The introductory paragraphs of Justice Story's opinion indicate that he regarded the issues in *Prigg* as extraordinary. Story came from Boston, a stronghold of the abolitionist movement, and he often returned to sit as circuit judge. Judicial enforcement of the fugitive slave law was opposed by the abolitionist bar and, especially after *Prigg*, by extralegal methods as well.[25] As circuit judge, Story had condemned slavery and, in La Jeune Eugenie, 26 F. Cas. 832 (No. 15,551) (C.C.D. Mass. 1822), he had held, in effect, that the slave trade violated the law of nations. Marshall was likely referring to this decision when, three years later in The Antelope, Chapter 2 supra, he commented that "even courts of

24. The fugitive slave clause aside, the current doctrine is that Congress may choose to make federal jurisdiction exclusive or to grant state courts concurrent jurisdiction over any case arising under federal laws or the Constitution. The history and modern doctrine concerning the duty of state courts to entertain actions based on federal statutes is summarized in Testa v. Katt, 330 U.S. 386 (1947). Justice Black wrote:

> Enforcement of federal laws by state courts did not go unchallenged. Violent public controversies existed throughout the first part of the Nineteenth Century until the 1860's concerning the existence of the constitutional supremacy of the Federal Government. During that period there were instances in which this Court and state courts broadly questioned the power and duty of state courts to exercise their jurisdiction to enforce United States civil and penal statutes or the power of the Federal Government to require them to do so. But after the fundamental issues of federal supremacy had been resolved by war, this Court took occasion in 1876 to review the phase of the controversy concerning the relationship of state courts to the Federal Government. . . . It repudiated the assumption that federal laws can be considered by the states as though they were laws emanating from a foreign sovereign. . . . It asserted that the obligation of states to enforce these federal laws is not lessened by reason of the form in which they are cast or the remedy which they provide.

25. See Robert Cover, Justice Accused (1975).

justice . . . have carried the principle of suppression further than a more deliberate consideration of the subject would justify."

But *Prigg* involved a different issue at a different time. Story was a fervent nationalist, who feared the Union endangered by the slavery issue. His characterization of the historical significance of the fugitive slave clause seems more a reflection of contemporary concerns than those of the adopters of the Constitution.[26] Professor William Nelson cites Story's version of the original history as evidence that the opinion "rested in an instrumentalist concern for national unity."[27] However, Professor Robert Cover attributes Story's opinion in *Prigg* to a rigidly formalist, noninstrumental jurisprudence. Cover recurs to his taxonomy of the limited options available to abolitionist judges to suggest that Story's opinion was "a highly formalistic abdication of responsibility to weigh and consider policy and moral implications of constitutional law." Confronted with a perceived conflict between morality and positive law, Story "was disabled from acting as a creative control and adjustment force to settle a moral-formal conflict. Instead he retreated to formalism."[28] On the other hand, William Story, the Justice's son, asserted that his father had sought to sabotage enforcement of the fugitive slave law by "leaving the slaveholder to his constitutional remedy of self-help or to recourse to the federal judges — too few and far between to be of practical value."[29]

Note: Freedom of Speech, Federalism, and Slavery

During the 1830s abolitionists began sending material detailing the iniquity of slavery through the United States mails to leaders of public opinion in the Southern states, who would presumably be persuaded to use their power to end it.[30] In response, several slave states passed laws prohibiting the circulation of antislavery publications. Indeed, Clement Eaton states that after 1835 there was "a virtual censorship of the mails crossing the Mason and Dixon line." Although these laws necessarily touched on the powers of federal postal officials and thus raised delicate constitutional problems, they were never litigated, primarily because the federal officials involved were altogether willing to comply with the laws.

A legal test of sorts with respect to the freedom of the mails arose in 1857. Mississippi required imprisonment and fine "if any white person circulate or put forth any book, paper, magazine, or pamphlet, containing any sentiment, doctrine, advice, or innuendoes, calculated to produce a disorderly, dangerous, or rebellious disaffection among the colored population." A deputy postmaster in Yazoo City, Mississippi, refused to deliver abolitionist material mailed from Ohio, arguing that its delivery would violate the Mississippi statute. The publica-

26. Don Feherenbacher writes, "The clause was not a significant issue in the Convention. Introduced late in the proceedings by a South Carolina delegate, it aroused little debate and received unanimous approval. There is little evidence to support the assertion frequently made in later years that without the clause the Constitution would have failed." Feherenbacher, The *Dred Scott* Case 25 (1978).

27. Nelson, The Impact of the Antislavery Movement upon Styles of Judicial Reasoning in Nineteenth Century America, 87 Harv. L. Rev. 513, 539-540 (1974).

28. Robert Cover, Justice Accused 241 (1975).

29. Id.

30. See Clement Eaton, The Freedom-of-Thought Struggle in the Old South, Chapter VIII, "Censorship of the Mails" (revised ed. 1964). All of the quotations in this paragraph are taken from this chapter.

tion in question, the Cincinnati Gazette, challenged the practice, and the Postmaster General turned to Attorney General Caleb Cushing for an opinion. Cushing, though from Massachusetts, was an active member of the pro-slavery wing of the Democratic Party that had elected Franklin Pierce and was soon to send James Buchannan, of Pennsylvania, to the presidency. Cushing issued his opinion on March 2, 1857, just before he left office upon the inauguration of the new President two days later.[31]

Federal law prohibits a postmaster from "unlawfully detain[ing]" any mail. The question, therefore, is whether the Yazoo City detention was "lawful." Cushing began by noting:

> [E]ach State has, and must have, jurisdiction as regards the matter of insurrection or treason. To deny this would be to deny to the inhabitants of a State the power of self-preservation. That cannot be denied. In constitutional language, it is a right inalienable and imprescriptible. No political society can *effectively* cede away the power of self-preservation. If it should undertake to do so, in whatever explicitness of expression, such an act would be null and of no effect. Of course, it does not need to go into the inquiry, whether the law of the State of Mississippi be constitutionally maintainable as a provision of police. It is that, but it is much more. It is a law of self-conservation, in the category of those, which lie at the foundation of all possible forms of human society.
>
> [Given this assumption,] we have the main question very much simplified. It is this: Has a citizen of one of the United States plenary indisputable right to employ the functions and the officers of the Union as the means of enabling him to produce insurrection in another of the United States? Can the officers of the Union lawfully lend its functions to the citizens of one of the States for the purpose of promoting insurrection in another State?

It can surely be no surprise, given his assumption and statement of the question, that the postmaster's failure to deliver the Gazette was vindicated. Cushing notes that one of the lawyers had "intimated . . . that, to permit a deputy postmaster to detain a newspaper because of its imputed unlawfulness, would be to erect him into a censor of the press. These are but words of rhetorical exaggeration." Moreover, he noted that the federal official was not the censor; rather, he was merely honoring the legislative decision made by Mississippi.

> [I]n regard to municipal legislation, for the most part, the several United States are foreign each to the other. And the citizens of the State of Mississippi are the only competent judges of how much they may be inconvenienced by the impeded circulation among them of this or that pamphlet or newspaper. That is a question of self-government, which it belongs to them to answer for themselves, not to the citizens of Ohio to answer for them. . . . Moreover, there is here a balance of inconveniences. Insurrections are inconvenient things. It is inconvenient to the people of one State to have their houses burned by means of incendiary missiles projected from behind the secure legal shelter of the boundary line of an adjoining State. If the non-circulation of this or that foreign newspaper in a particular State be an inconvenience to somebody, it is, in the aggregate of all public interests, a much less inconvenience than the occurrence, or even the danger, of insurrection in that State.

31. 8 Opinions of Attorneys General 489.

> It may be unpleasant to some person in Ohio to find that he is not free to promote insurrection in Mississippi. Nevertheless, even at the risk of not accommodating any such perverse taste, each State of the Union has the right to protect itself against domestic violence, and to invoke to that end the friendly co-operation, or at least the neutrality, of the United States.

Cushing did concede that the actual insurrectionary nature of the publication might be a disputable question, so that persons who believed that their rights to have their mail delivered had been violated could challenge the classification in State or Federal court.

Note the complete absence of any discussion of the First Amendment. With respect to Mississippi's own law, the reason for the omission is doctrinally simple: In the 1833 decision of Barron v. Baltimore, 32 U.S. (7 Pet.) 243, Chief Justice Marshall held, for a unanimous Court, that the Bill of Rights applied only to the national government. Not until 1925 was the freedom of speech clause of the First Amendment made applicable to the States through incorporation in the Fourteenth Amendment. (See pp. 546-550 infra.) This, however, does not explain the absence of discussion of the First Amendment's application to the national government's refusal to deliver the mail. Might it be that Congress had not affirmatively required the limitation of delivery in question? That is, should the First Amendment be read as a limitation on *Congress'* powers rather than a categorical limit on the power of the national government as a whole? Given Cushing's assumptions, it is questionable whether the opinion would have been any different even had the First Amendment been considered. See Chapter 4 infra, for further discussion of the First Amendment and the "clear-and-present-danger" test.

C. Prelude to Secession

Antagonism between the North and South increased during the years following *Prigg,* and was exacerbated by the dispute over the status of slavery in California. By the so-called Compromise of 1850, California was admitted to the union as a free state, New Mexico and Utah were organized as territories with the issue of slavery being left to future legislation, the slave trade was abolished in the District of Columbia, and a more stringent fugitive slave law was adopted. The Fugitive Slave Act of 1850 provided for the appointment of federal commissioners, who were authorized to issue certificates of removal on the ex parte testimony or affidavits of slaveholders or their agents. Testimony by the alleged slave was excluded and, as if this were not sufficient to bias the outcome, the act paid the commissioner $10 for issuing the certificate but only $5 if he denied it.

The new Act was the focus of bitter controversy in the North.[32] Justice McLean, sitting as a circuit court judge in Miller v. McQuerry, 17 F. Cas. 332 (No. 9,583) (C.C.D. Ohio, 1853), rejected a challenge to its constitutionality. In Ableman v. Booth, 62 U.S. (21 How.) 506 (1859) — in what, for Taney, was a strikingly nationalist opinion — the Chief Justice wrote for the Court sustaining the Act and holding that a Wisconsin state court could not issue a writ of habeas corpus to free a federal prisoner convicted of violating it:

32. See id. ch. 11.

> [N]o State can authorize one of its judges or courts to exercise judicial power, by habeas corpus or otherwise, within the jurisdiction of another and independent Government. And although the State of Wisconsin is sovereign within its territorial limits to a certain extent, yet that sovereignty is limited and restricted by the Constitution of the United States. . . .
>
> The Constitution was not formed merely to guard the State against danger from foreign nations, but mainly to secure union and harmony at home; . . . and to accomplish this purpose, it was felt by the statesmen who framed the Constitution, and by the people who adopted it, that it was necessary that many of the rights of sovereignty which the States possessed should be ceded to the General Government; and that, in the sphere of action assigned to it, it should be supreme, and strong enough to execute its own laws by its own tribunals, without interruption from a State or from State authorities.

The holding concerning the relation between federal and state courts was entirely consistent with the principles of federalism developed in cases such as McCulloch v. Maryland; it remains the law today. The decision upholding the Fugitive Slave Act of 1850 confirmed the Court's pro-slavery position — if confirmation were needed after its catastrophic decision in the *Dred Scott* case two years earlier.

Dred Scott arose out of the other major legal problem of slavery in a federal nation — the status of *non*fugitive slaves in free states. Some Northern states had forbidden visiting slave-owners from bringing their slaves with them, and several state courts had freed slaves brought into the jurisdiction.[33] The federal constitutionality of these laws was never conclusively determined. In Strader v. Graham, 51 U.S. (10 How.) 81 (1850), however, the Supreme Court held, as a (nonconstitutional) matter of conflicts of law, that a Kentucky court, adjudicating a claim that a slave owned by a state resident was entitled to freedom by virtue of having been brought into Ohio, properly applied the Kentucky rather than Ohio law. (Under Kentucky law, the master's dominion continued.)

Dred Scott was a slave owned by a Missourian, John Emerson, who had sojourned with Emerson and his family in Illinois (a free state) and in the Missouri Territory north of the compromise line before returning to Missouri. After Emerson's death the administration of his estate was assumed by John Sanford (whose name is misspelled in the United States Reports), a citizen of New York. Dred Scott, alleging federal jurisdiction based on diversity of citizenship, brought this action, in which he claimed in effect that his earlier residence in the free state and territory liberated him from slavery. Sanford entered a plea in abatement, contesting the court's jurisdiction on the ground that a "negro of African descent" was not a citizen of Missouri or the United States. The court denied the plea but decided for Sanford on the ground that, although Scott was entitled to his freedom while in Illinois and the northern Missouri Territory, his status as a slave reattached upon his return to Missouri. Scott appealed to the Supreme Court.[34]

The Court affirmed, in an opinion by Chief Justice Taney. Six Justices wrote concurring opinions; Justices McLean and Curtis dissented. Taney decided three

33. See Paul Finkelman, An Imperfect Union: Slavery, Federalism, and Comity ch. 4 (1981); Commonwealth v. Aves, 35 Mass. (18 Pick.) 193 (1836).

34. This is an attenuated description of the background and facts of the case. See Feherenbacher, supra note 26.

issues: (1) As a matter of conflict of laws, Dred Scott's status was governed by the law of the forum state, Missouri. This reaffirmed Strader v. Graham; (2) the Missouri Compromise was unconstitutional on the grounds that (a) Article I did not authorize Congress to legislate for the territories once the settlers were able to legislate for themselves and (b) "an act of Congress which deprives a citizen . . . of his . . . property, merely because he came or brought his property into a particular Territory . . . could hardly be dignified with the name of due process of law"; and (3) the federal court lacked jurisdiction over Scott's claim because blacks were not "citizens" within the meaning of the diversity jurisdiction clause of Article III. We excerpt portions of Taney's opinion for the Court and Curtis' dissent addressing the last of these issues.

DRED SCOTT v. SANDFORD

60 U.S. (19 How.) 393 (1857)

Error from the Circuit Court of the United States for the District of Missouri

TANEY, C.J. . . .

The question is simply this: Can a negro, whose ancestors were imported into this country, and sold as slaves, become a member of the political community formed and brought into existence by the Constitution of the United States, and as such become entitled to all the rights, and privileges, and immunities, guarantied by that instrument to the citizen? One of which rights is the privilege of suing in a court of the United States in the cases specified in the Constitution.

It will be observed, that the plea applies to that class of persons only whose ancestors were negroes of the African race, and imported into this country, and sold and held as slaves. The only matter in issue before the court, therefore, is whether the descendants of such slaves, when they shall be emancipated, or who are born of parents who had become free before their birth, are citizens of a State, in the sense in which the word citizen is used in the Constitution of the United States. . . .

The words "people of the United States" and "citizens" are synonymous terms, and mean the same thing. They both describe the political body who, according to our republican institutions, form the sovereignty, and who hold the power and conduct the Government through their representatives. . . .

The question before us is, whether the class of persons described in the plea in abatement compose a portion of this people, and constituent members of this sovereignty? We think they are not. . . . [T]hey were at [the time of the adoption of the Constitution] considered as a subordinate and inferior class of beings, who had been subjugated by the dominant race, and, whether emancipated or not, yet remained subject to their authority, and had no rights or privileges but such as those who held the power and the Government might choose to grant them.

It is not the province of the court to decide upon the justice or injustice, the policy or impolicy, of these laws. The decision of that question belonged . . . to those who formed the sovereignty and framed the Constitution. The duty of the court is, to interpret the instrument they have framed, with the best lights we can obtain on the subject, and to administer it as we find it, according to its true intent and meaning when it was adopted.

In discussing this question, we must not confound the rights of citizenship which a State may confer within its own limits, and the rights of citizenship as a member of the Union. It does not by any means follow, because he has all the rights and privileges of a citizen of a State, that he must be a citizen of the United States. He may have all of the rights and privileges of the citizen of a State, and yet not be entitled to the rights and privileges of a citizen in any other State. For, previous to the adoption of the Constitution of the United States, every State had the undoubted right to confer on whomsoever it pleased the character of citizen, and to endow him with all its rights. But this character of course was confined to the boundaries of the State, and gave him no rights or privileges in other States beyond those secured to him by the laws of nations and the comity of States. Nor have the several States surrendered the power of conferring these rights and privileges by adopting the Constitution of the United States. Each State may still confer them upon an alien, or any one it thinks proper . . . ; yet he would not be a citizen in the sense in which that word is used in the Constitution of the United States, nor entitled to sue as such in one of its courts, nor to the privileges and immunities of a citizen in the other States. The rights which he would acquire would be restricted to the State which gave them. . . .

It is very clear, therefore, that no State can, by any act or law of its own . . . introduce a new member into the political community created by the Constitution of the United States. . . . [I]t cannot introduce any person, or description of persons, who were not intended to be embraced in this new political family, which the Constitution brought into existence, but were intended to be excluded from it. . . .

It becomes necessary, therefore, to determine who were citizens of the several States when the Constitution was adopted. And in order to do this, we must recur to the Governments and institutions of the thirteen colonies, when they separated from Great Britain and formed new sovereignties, and took their places in the family of independent nations. We must inquire who, at that time, were recognised as the people or citizens of a State, whose rights and liberties had been outraged by the English Government; and who declared their independence, and assumed the powers of Government to defend their rights by force of arms.

In the opinion of the court, the legislation and histories of the times, and the language used in the Declaration of Independence, show, that neither the class of persons who had been imported as slaves, nor their descendants, whether they had become free or not, were then acknowledged as a part of the people, nor intended to be included in the general words used in that memorable instrument.

It is difficult at this day to realize the state of public opinion in relation to that unfortunate race, which prevailed in the civilized and enlightened portions of the world at the time of the Declaration of Independence, and when the Constitution of the United States was framed and adopted. But the public history of every European nation displays it in a manner too plain to be mistaken.

They had for more than a century before been regarded as beings of an inferior order, and altogether unfit to associate with the white race, either in social or political relations; and so far inferior, that they had no rights which the white man was bound to respect; and that the negro might justly and lawfully be reduced to slavery for his benefit. He was bought and sold, and treated as an ordinary article of merchandise and traffic, whenever a profit could be made by it. This opinion was at that time fixed and universal in the civilized portion of the white race. It was regarded as an axiom in morals as well as in politics, which no one thought of disputing, or supposed to be open to dispute; and men in every grade and position in society daily and habitually acted upon it in their private pursuits, as well as in matters of public concern, without doubting for a moment the correctness of this opinion.

And in no nation was this opinion more firmly fixed or more uniformly acted upon than by the English Government and English people. They not only seized them on the coast of Africa, and sold them or held them in slavery for their own use; but they took them as ordinary articles of merchandise to every country where they could make a profit on them, and were far more extensively engaged in this commerce than any other nation in the world.

The opinion thus entertained and acted upon in England was naturally impressed upon the colonies they founded on this side of the Atlantic. And, accordingly, a negro of the African race was regarded by them as an article of property, and held, and bought and sold as such, in every one of the thirteen colonies which united in the Declaration of Independence, and afterwards formed the Constitution of the United States. The slaves were more or less numerous in the different colonies, as slave labor was found more or less profitable. But no one seems to have doubted the correctness of the prevailing opinion of the time.

The legislation of the different colonies furnishes positive and indisputable proof of this fact. . . . [Taney here quotes Massachusetts and Maryland statutes punishing racial intermarriage.]

[These laws] show that a perpetual and impassable barrier was intended to be erected between the white race and the one which they had reduced to slavery, and governed as subjects with absolute and despotic power, and which they then looked upon as so far below them in the scale of created beings, that intermarriages between white persons and negroes or mulattoes were regarded as unnatural and immoral, and punished as crimes, not only in the parties, but in the person who joined them in marriage. And no distinction in this respect was made between the free negro or mulatto and the slave, but this stigma, of the deepest degradation, was fixed upon the whole race.

We refer to these historical facts for the purpose of showing the fixed opinions concerning that race, upon which the statesmen of that day spoke and acted. It is necessary to do this, in order to determine whether the general terms used in the Constitution of the United States, as to the rights of man and the rights of the people, was intended to include them, or to give to them or their posterity the benefit of any of its provisions.

The language of the Declaration of Independence is equally conclusive. . . .

"We hold these truths to be self-evident: that all men are created equal; that they are endowed by their Creator with certain unalienable rights; that among them is life, liberty, and the pursuit of happiness; that to secure these rights, Governments are instituted, deriving their just powers from the consent of the governed."

The general words above quoted would seem to embrace the whole human family, and if they were used in a similar instrument at this day would be so understood. But it is too clear for dispute, that the enslaved African race were not intended to be included, and formed no part of the people who framed and adopted this declaration; for if the language, as understood in that day, would embrace them, the conduct of the distinguished men who framed the Declaration of Independence would have been utterly and flagrantly inconsistent with the principles they asserted; and instead of the sympathy of mankind, to which they so confidently appealed, they would have deserved and received universal rebuke and reprobation.

Yet the men who framed this declaration were great men — high in literary acquirement — high in their sense of honor, and incapable of asserting principles inconsistent with those on which they were acting. They perfectly understood the meaning of the language they used, and how it would be understood by others; and they knew that it would not in any part of the civilized world be supposed to embrace the negro race, which, by common consent, had been excluded from civilized Governments and the family of nations, and doomed to slavery. They spoke and acted according to the then established doctrines and principles, and in the ordinary language of the day, and no one misunderstood them. The unhappy black race were separated from the white by indelible marks, and laws long before established, and were never thought of or spoken of except as property, and when the claims of the owner or the profit of the trader were supposed to need protection.

This state of public opinion had undergone no change when the Constitution was adopted, as is equally evident from its provisions and language.

The brief preamble sets forth by whom it was formed, for what purposes, and for whose benefit and protection. It declares that it is formed by the *people* of the United States; that is to say, by those who were members of the different political communities in the several States; and its great object is declared to be to secure the blessings of liberty to themselves and their posterity. It speaks in general terms of the *people* of the United States, and of *citizens* of the several States, when it is providing for the exercise of the powers granted or the privileges secured to the citizen. It does not define what description of persons are intended to be included under these terms, or who shall be regarded as a citizen and one of the people. It uses them as terms so well understood, that no further description or definition was necessary.

But there are two clauses in the Constitution which point directly and specifically to the negro race as a separate class of persons, and show clearly that they were not regarded as a portion of the people or citizens of the Government then formed.

One of these clauses reserves to each of the thirteen States the right to import slaves until the year 1808, if it thinks proper. And the importation which it thus sanctions was unquestionably of persons of the race of which we are speaking, as the traffic in slaves in the United States had always been confined to them. And by the other provision the States pledge themselves to each other to maintain the right of property of the master, by delivering up to him any slave who may have escaped from his service, and be found within their respective territories. By the first above-mentioned clause, therefore, the right to purchase and hold this property is directly sanctioned and authorized for twenty years by the people who framed the Constitution. And by the second, they pledge themselves to maintain and uphold the right of the master in the manner specified, as long as the Government they then formed should endure. And these two provisions show, conclusively, that neither the description of persons therein referred to, nor their descendants, were embraced in any of the other provisions of the Constitution; for certainly these two clauses were not intended to confer on them or their posterity the blessings of liberty, or any of the personal rights so carefully provided for the citizen. . . .

Indeed, when we look to the condition of this race in the several States at the time, it is impossible to believe that these rights and privileges were intended to be extended to them.

It is very true, that in that portion of the Union where the labor of the negro race was found to be unsuited to the climate and unprofitable to the master, but few slaves were held at the time of the Declaration of Independence; and when the Constitution was adopted, it had entirely worn out in one of them, and measures had been taken for its gradual abolition in several others. But this change had not been produced by any change of opinion in relation to this race; but because it was discovered, from experience, that slave labor was unsuited to the climate and productions of these States: for some of the States, where it had ceased or nearly ceased to exist, were actively engaged in the slave trade, procuring cargoes on the coast of Africa, and transporting them for sale to those parts of the Union where their labor was found to be profitable, and suited to the climate and productions. And this traffic was openly carried on, and fortunes accumulated by it, without reproach from the people of the States where they resided. And it can hardly be supposed that, in the States where it was then countenanced in its worst form — that is, in the seizure and transportation — the people could have regarded those who were emancipated as entitled to equal rights with themselves.

And we may here again refer, in support of this proposition, to the plain and unequivocal language of the laws of the several States, some passed after the Declaration of Independence and before the Constitution was adopted, and some since the Government went into operation.

We need not refer, on this point, particularly to the laws of the present slaveholding States. . . . As relates to these States, it is too plain for argument, that they have never been regarded as a part of the people or citizens of the State, nor supposed to possess any political rights which the dominant race might not withold or grant at their pleasure. . . .

And if we turn to the legislation of the States where slavery had worn out, or measures taken for its speedy abolition, we shall find the same opinions and principles equally fixed and equally acted upon. . . . [A description of state laws prohibiting racial intermarriage and restricting the liberties of blacks is omitted.]

Chancellor Kent, whose accuracy and research no one will question, states in the sixth edition of his Commentaries, (published in 1848, 2 vol., 258, note b,) that in no part of the country except Maine, did the African race, in point of fact, participate equally with the whites in the exercise of civil and political rights.

The legislation of the States therefore shows, in a manner not to be mistaken, the inferior and subject condition of that race at the time the Constitution was adopted, and long afterwards, throughout the thirteen States by which that instrument was framed; and it is hardly consistent with the respect due to these States, to suppose that they regarded at that time, as fellow-citizens and members of the sovereignty, a class of beings whom they had thus stigmatized; whom, as we are bound, out of respect to the State sovereignties, to assume they had deemed it just and necessary thus to stigmatize, and upon whom they had impressed such deep and enduring marks of inferiority and degradation; or, that when they met in convention to form the Constitution, they looked upon them as a portion of their constituents, or designed to include them in the provisions so carefully inserted for the security and protection of the liberties and rights of their citizens. It cannot be supposed that they intended to secure to them rights, and privileges, and rank, in the new political body throughout the Union, which every one of them denied within the limits of its own dominion. More especially, it cannot be believed that the large slaveholding States regarded them as included in the word citizens, or would have consented to a Constitution which might compel them to receive them in that character from another State. For if they were so received, and entitled to the privileges and immunities of citizens, it would exempt them from the operation of the special laws and from the police regulations which they considered to be necessary for their own safety. It would give to persons of the negro race, who were recognised as citizens in any one State of the Union, the right to enter every other State whenever they pleased, singly or in companies, without pass or passport, and without obstruction, to sojourn there as long as they pleased, to go where they pleased at every hour of the day or night without molestation, unless they committed some violation of law for which a white man would be punished; and it would give them the full liberty of speech in public and in private upon all subjects upon which its own citizens might speak; to hold public meetings upon political affairs, and to keep and carry arms wherever they went. And all of this would be done in the face of the subject race of the same color, both free and slaves, and inevitably producing discontent and insubordination among them, and endangering the peace and safety of the State.

It is impossible, it would seem, to believe that the great men of the slave-holding States, who took so large a share in framing the Constitution of the United States, and exercised so much influence in procuring its adoption, could have been so forgetful or regardless of their own safety and the safety of those who trusted and confided in them.

Besides, this want of foresight and care would have been utterly inconsistent with the caution displayed in providing for the admission of new members into this political family. For, when they gave to the citizens of each State the privileges and immunities of citizens in the several States, they at the same time took from the several States the power of naturalization, and confined that power exclusively to the Federal Government. No State was willing to permit another State to determine who should or should not be admitted as one of its citizens, and entitled to demand equal rights and privileges with their own people, within their own territories. The right of naturalization was therefore, with one accord, surrendered by the States, and confided to the Federal Government. And this power granted to Congress to establish an uniform rule of *naturalization* is, by the well-understood meaning of the word, confined to persons born in a foreign country, under a foreign Government. It is not a power to raise to the rank of a citizen any one born in the United States, who from birth or parentage, by the laws of the country, belongs to an inferior and subordinate class. And when we find the States guarding themselves from the indiscreet or improper admission by other States of emigrants from other countries, by giving the power exclusively to Congress, we cannot fail to see that they could never have left with the States a much more important power — that is, the power of transforming into citizens a numerous class of persons, who in that character would be much more dangerous to the peace and safety of a large portion of the Union, than the few foreigners one of the States might improperly naturalize. . . .

To all this mass of proof we have still to add, that Congress has repeatedly legislated upon the same construction of the Constitution that we have given. . . . [Two laws] are particularly worthy of notice, because many of the men who assisted in framing the Constitution, and took an active part in procuring its adoption, were then in the halls of legislation, and certainly understood what they meant when they used the words "people of the United States" and "citizen" in that well-considered instrument.

The first of these acts is the naturalization law, which was passed at the second session of the first Congress, March 26, 1790, and confines the right of becoming citizens "*to aliens being free white persons.*" . . .

Another of the early laws of which we have spoken, is the first militia law, which was passed in 1792, at the first session of the second Congress. The language of this law is equally plain and significant with the one just mentioned. It directs that every "free able-bodied white male citizen" shall be enrolled in the militia. The word *white* is evidently used to exclude the African race, and the word "citizen" to exclude unnaturalized foreigners; the latter forming no part of the sovereignty, owing it no allegiance, and therefore under no obligation to defend it. The African race, however, born in the country, did owe allegiance to the Government, whether they were slave or free; but it is repudiated, and rejected from the duties and obligations of citizenship in marked language. . . .

The conduct of the Executive Department of the Government has been in perfect harmony upon this subject with this course of legislation. The question was brought officially before the late William Wirt, when he was the Attorney General of the United States, in 1821, and he decided that the words "citizens of the United States" were used in the acts of Congress in the same sense as in the Constitution; and that free persons of color were not citizens, within the meaning of the Constitution and laws; and this opinion has been confirmed by that of the late Attorney General, Caleb Cushing, in a recent case, and acted upon by the Secretary of State, who refused to grant passports to them as "citizens of the United States." . . .

No one, we presume, supposes that any change in public opinion or feeling, in relation to this unfortunate race, in the civilized nations of Europe or in this country, should induce the court to give to the words of the Constitution a more liberal construction in their favor than they were intended to bear when the instrument was framed and adopted. Such an argument would be altogether inadmissible in any tribunal called on to interpret it. If any of its provisions are deemed unjust, there is a mode prescribed in the instrument itself by which it may be amended; but while it remains unaltered, it must be construed now as it was understood at the time of its adoption. It is not only the same in words, but the same in meaning, and delegates the same powers to the Government, and reserves and secures the same rights and privileges to the citizen; and as long as it continues to exist in its present form, it speaks not only in the same words, but with the same meaning and intent with which it spoke when it came from the hands of its framers, and was voted on and adopted by the people of the United States. Any other rule of construction would abrogate the judicial character of this court, and make it the mere reflex of the popular opinion or passion of the day. This court was not created by the Constitution for such purposes. Higher and graver trusts have been confided to it, and it must not falter in the path of duty. . . .

CURTIS, J., dissenting. . . .

When . . . the Constitution speaks of citizenship of the United States, existing at the time of the adoption of the Constitution, it must necessarily refer to citizenship under the Government which existed prior to and at the time of such adoption. . . .

That Government was simply a confederacy of the several States, possessing a few defined powers over subjects of general concern, each State retaining every power, jurisdiction, and right, not expressly delegated to the United States in Congress assembled. And no power was thus delegated to the Government of the Confederation, to act on any question of citizenship, or to make any rules in respect thereto. The whole matter was left to stand upon the action of the several States, and to the natural consequence of such action, that the citizens of each State should be citizens of that Confederacy into which that State had entered, the style whereof was, "The United States of America."

To determine whether any free persons, descended from Africans held in slavery, were citizens of the United States under the Confederation, and consequently at the time of the adoption of the Constitution of the United States, it is only necessary to know whether any such persons were citizens of either of the States under the Confederation, at the time of the adoption of the Constitution.

Of this there can be not doubt. At the time of the ratification of the Articles of Confederation, all free native-born inhabitants of the States of New Hampshire, Massachusetts, New York, New Jersey, and North Carolina, though descended from African slaves, were not only citizens of those States, but such of them as had the other necessary qualifications possessed the franchise of electors, on equal terms with other citizens. . . . [A discussion of state electoral laws is omitted.]

New York, by its Constitution of 1820, required colored persons to have some qualifications as prerequisites for voting, which white persons need not possess. And New Jersey, by its present Constitution, restricts the right to vote to white male citizens. But these changes can have no other effect upon the present inquiry, except to show, that before they were made, no such restrictions existed; and colored in common with white persons, were not only citizens of those States, but entitled to the elective franchise on the same qualifications as white persons, as they now are in New Hampshire and Massachusetts. I shall not enter into an examination of the existing opinions of that period respecting the African race, nor into any discussion concerning the meaning of those who asserted, in the Declaration of Independence, that all men are created equal; that they are endowed by their Creator with certain inalienable rights; that among these are life, liberty, and the pursuit of happiness. My own opinion is, that a calm comparison of these assertions of universal abstract truths, and of their own individual opinions and acts, would not leave these men under any reproach of inconsistency; that the great truths they asserted on that solemn occasion, they were ready and anxious to make effectual, wherever a necessary regard to circumstances, which no statesman can disregard without producing more evil than good, would allow; and that it would not be just to them, nor true in itself, to allege that they intended to say that the Creator of all men had endowed the white race, exclusively, with the great natural rights which the Declaration of Independence asserts. But this is not the place to vindicate their memory. . . .

The fourth of the fundamental articles of the Confederation was as follows: "The free inhabitants of each of these States, paupers, vagabonds, and fugitives from justice, excepted, shall be entitled to all the privileges and immunities of free citizens in the several States."

The fact that free persons of color were citizens of some of the several States, and the consequence, that this fourth article of the Confederation would have the effect to confer on such persons the privileges and immunities of general citizenship, were not only known to those who framed and adopted those articles, but the evidence is decisive, that the fourth article was intended to have that effect, and that more restricted language, which would have excluded such persons, was deliberately and purposely rejected.

On the 25th of June, 1778, the Articles of Confederation being under consideration by the Congress, the delegates from South Carolina moved to amend this fourth article, by inserting after the word "free," and before the word "inhabitants," the word "white," so that the privileges and immunities of general citizenship would be secured only to white persons. Two States voted for the amendment, eight States against it, and the vote of one State was divided. The language of the article stood unchanged, and both by its terms of inclusion, "free inhabitants," and the strong implication from its terms of exclusion, "paupers, vagabonds, and fugitives from justice," who alone were excepted, it is clear, that under the Confederation, and at the time of the adoption of the Constitution, free colored persons of African descent might be, and, by reason of their citizenship in certain States, were entitled to the privileges and immunities of general citizenship of the United States.

Did the Constitution of the United States deprive them or their descendants of citizenship?

That Constitution was ordained and established by the people of the United States, through the action, in each State, of those persons who were qualified by its laws to act thereon, in behalf of themselves and all other citizens of that State. In some of the States, as we have seen, colored persons were among those qualified by law to act on this subject. . . . It would be strange, if we were to find in that instrument anything which deprived of their citizenship any part of the people of the United States who were among those by whom it was established.

I can find nothing in the Constitution which proprio vigore, deprives of their citizenship any class of persons who were citizens of the United States at the time of its adoption, or who should be native-born citizens of any State after its adoption; nor any power enabling Congress to disfranchise persons born on the soil of any State, and entitled to citizenship of such State by its Constitution and laws. And my opinion is, that, under the Constitution of the United States, every free person born on the soil of a State, who is a citizen of that State by force of its Constitution or laws, is also a citizen of the United States. . . .

The first section of the second article of the Constitution uses the language, "a natural-born citizen." It thus assumes that citizenship may be acquired by birth. . . . The Constitution has left to the States the determination what persons, born within their respective limits, shall acquire by birth citizenship of the United States; it has not left to them any power to prescribe any rule for the removal of the disabilities of alienage. This power is exclusively in Congress.

It has been . . . objected, that if free colored persons born within a particular State, and made citizens of that State by its Constitution and laws, are thereby made citizens of the United States, then, under the second section of the fourth article of the Constitution, such persons would be entitled to all the privileges and immunities of citizens in the several states; and if so, then colored persons could vote, and be eligible to not only Federal, but offices even in those States whose Constitutions and laws disqualify colored persons from voting or being elected to office.

But this position rests upon an assumption which I deem untenable. Its basis is, that no one can be deemed a citizen of the United States who is not entitled to enjoy all the privileges and franchises which are conferred on any citizen. That this is not true, under the Constitution of the United States, seems to be clear.

... So, in all the States, numerous persons, though citizens, cannot vote, or cannot hold office, either on account of their age, or sex, or that want of the necessary legal qualifications. The truth is, that citizenship, under the Constitution of the United States, is not dependent on the possession of any particular political or even of all civil rights; and any attempt so to define it must lead to error. To what citizens the elective franchise shall be confided, is a question to be determined by each State, in accordance with its own views of the necessities or expediencies of its condition. What civil rights shall be enjoyed by its citizens, and whether all shall enjoy the same, or how they may be gained or lost, are to be determined in the same way.

... [T]his clause of the Constitution does not confer on the citizens of one State, in all other States, specific and enumerated privileges and immunities. They are entitled to such as belong to citizenship, but not to such as belong to particular citizens attended by other qualifications.... It rests with the States themselves so to frame their Constitutions and laws as not to attach a particular privilege or immunity to mere naked citizenship....

It has sometimes been urged that colored persons are shown not to be citizens of the United States by the fact that the naturalization laws apply only to white persons. But whether a person born in the United States be or be not a citizen, cannot depend on laws which refer only to aliens, and do not affect the *status* of persons born in the United States. The utmost effect which can be attributed to them is, to show that Congress has not deemed it expedient generally to apply the rule to colored aliens. That they might do so, if thought fit, is clear....

I do not deem it necessary to review at length the legislation of Congress having more or less bearing on the citizenship of colored persons. It does not seem to me to have any considerable tendency to prove that it has been considered by the legislative department of the Government, that no such persons are citizens of the United States. Undoubtedly they have been debarred from the exercise of particular rights or privileges extended to white persons, but, I believe, always in terms which, by implication, admit they may be citizens. Thus the act of May 17, 1792, for the organization of the militia, directs the enrollment of "every free, able-bodied, white male citizen." An assumption that none but white persons are citizens, would be as inconsistent with the just import of this language, as that all citizens are able-bodied, or males....

Discussion

1. Taney believed that the decision in *Dred Scott* would settle the slavery issue. Instead, the decision became the nation's symbol of the irreconcilable division between North and South.

2. One doctrinal irony created by *Dred Scott* was that, while free blacks were not citizens for purposes of diversity jurisdiction, corporations were.[35]

> In 1789 [Congress] provided for federal jurisdiction in suits "between a citizen of the State where the suit is brought, and a citizen of another State." There shortly arose the question as to whether a corporation — a creature of state law — is to be deemed a "citizen" for purposes of the statute. This Court, through Chief Justice Marshall, initially responded in the negative, holding that a corporation was not a "citizen" and that it might sue and be sued under the diversity statute only if none of its shareholders was a co-citizen of any opposing party. In 1844 the Court reversed itself and ruled that a corporation was to be treated as a citizen of the State which created it. Ten years later, the Court reached the same result by a different approach. In a compromise destined to endure for over a century, the Court indulged in the fiction that, although a corporation was not itself a citizen for diversity purposes, its shareholders would conclusively be presumed citizens of the incorporating State.

3. *Dred Scott* is of limited continuing doctrinal importance. Restrictions on congressional power to bar slavery in the territories were rendered irrelevant by the Thirteenth Amendment, and the holding denying citizen status to native-born blacks was overruled by section 1 of the Fourteenth Amendment. Professor Lewis LaRue, however, notes a common thread between *Dred Scott* and modern constitutional law:[36]

> [A] key move in [Taney's] argument was the bifurcation of citizenship into two kinds of citizenship: state citizenship and national citizenship. . . . Taney did not declare that Massachusetts could not recognize free blacks as citizens of Massachusetts; he did not care about that. . . . The real issue . . . is whether Massachusetts's action would have any national relevance. . . .
>
> What many have failed to bear in mind is that this part of *Dred Scott,* the dichotomy of state and national citizenship, is still part of our law to this day. . . .

Professor LaRue discusses Sadat v. Mertes, 615 F.2d 1176 (7th Cir. 1980), a diversity torts case that cited *Dred Scott* as authority for excluding a plaintiff from federal court. Sadat was a Pennsylvania citizen who left the state in order to accept a job abroad. He had earlier been involved in an automobile accident while driving to Chicago's O'Hare airport following his job training in Wisconsin. While domiciled in Egypt he filed suit in federal court, alleging diversity from the Wisconsin defendant and his Connecticut insurance company. The Seventh Circuit rejected the case. Professor LaRue writes:

> The rationale of the *Sadat* court's opinion is as follows: The statute requires that the plaintiff and the defendant be citizens of different states; even though Sadat was a

35. United Steelworkers v. R.H. Bouligny, Inc., 382 U.S. 145 (1965). The Court has held that corporations are not "citizens" protected by the privileges and immunities clause of Article IV and the Fourteenth Amendment, Blake v. McClung, 172 U.S. 239 (1898); Paul v. Virginia, 75 U.S. (8 Wall.) 168 (1868); and not "persons" protected against self-incrimination by the Fifth Amendment, Hale v. Henkel, 201 U.S. 43 (1906). However, corporations are "persons" protected by the due process and equal protection clauses of the Fourteenth Amendment, see, e.g., Santa Clara Co. v. Southern Pacific Railroad, 118 U.S. 394 (1886), and also "people" protected by the Fourth Amendment prohibition of unreasonable searches and seizures. Silverthrone Lumber Co. v. United States, 251 U.S. 385 (1920).

36. Lewis LaRue, The Continuing Presence of *Dred Scott*, 42 Wash. & Lee L. Rev. 57, 58-59 (1985).

> citizen of the United States, he was not a citizen of any one of the several states; consequently, the requisite diversity was lacking. . . . The key step in this logic is the second step: Sadat could be a citizen of the United States without being a citizen of one of the several states. [The converse, after the Fourteenth Amendment, is a legal impossibility.] The Seventh Circuit cited *Dred Scott* for the proposition that there is a dichotomy between state and national citizenship. . . .

More than access to federal court may depend on state, rather than national, citizenship. One's right to vote for President (or for any federal office) is entirely a function of state citizenship: Only U.S. citizens who are also citizens of one of the 50 states or the District of Columbia can vote.

4. *Dred Scott* raises some interesting questions of constitutional interpretation. Assuming the accuracy of Taney's description of eighteenth-century laws regarding free Negroes, for example, how could you determine whether they *were* "citizens" as that term is used in the diversity of citizenship clause of Article III?

If you conclude that they were not citizens in 1789, does this entail that they were not citizens in 1857? Consider the controversy over the meaning of the word "state" in the diversity clause.

In Hepburn v. Ellzey, 6 U.S. (2 Cranch) 445 (1804), the Supreme Court held that the District of Columbia was not a "state" within the meaning of the provision of the Judiciary Act of 1789 that conferred federal jurisdiction in suits between citizens of different states. Chief Justice Marshall conceded that "Columbia is a distinct political society; and is, therefore, 'a State,' according to the definition of writers on general law." But he assumed that the statutory grant of diversity jurisdiction was coterminous with the Article III grant, and, examining provisions of Articles I and II, he concluded:

> [T]he word State is used in the constitution as designating a member of the Union, and excludes from the term the signification attached to it by writers on the law of nations. When the same term which has been used plainly in this limited sense in the articles respecting the legislative and executive departments, is also employed in that which respects the judicial department, it must be understood as retaining the sense originally given to it.

In 1940, Congress amended the judicial code to confer federal jurisdiction in suits between "citizens of the District of Columbia . . . and any State. . . ." In National Mutual Insurance Co. v. Tidewater Transfer Co., 337 U.S. 582 (1949), a majority of the Court reaffirmed Marshall's implicit constitutional holding.[37] In an opinion joined by Justice Reed, Justice Frankfurter wrote:

> No provisions of the Constitution, barring only those that draw on arithmetic, as in prescribing the qualifying age for a President and members of a Congress or the length of their tenure of office, are more explicit and specific than those pertaining

37. Nonetheless, the Court upheld the provision. Justices Murphy and Rutledge would have overruled *Hepburn*. Justices Black, Jackson, and Burton, through adhering to *Hepburn*, would have held that Congress' power under Article I, §8, cl. 17, to legislate for the District of Columbia empowered it to authorize citizens of the District to sue in federal court independently of the provisions of Article III — a position from which Murphy and Rutledge dissented. "And so," wrote Justice Frankfurter, "conflicting minorities in combination bring to pass a result — paradoxical as it may appear — which differing majorities of the Court find insupportable."

> to courts established under Article III. "The judicial power" which is "vested" in these tribunals and the safeguards under which their judges function are enumerated with particularity. Their tenure and compensation, the controversies which may be brought before them, and the distribution of original and appellate jurisdiction among these tribunals are defined and circumscribed, not left at large by vague and elastic phrasing. The precision which characterizes these portions of Article III is in striking contrast to the imprecision of so many other provisions of the Constitution dealing with other very vital aspects of government. This was not due to chance or ineptitude on the part of the Framers. The differences in subject-matter account for the drastic differences in treatment. Great concepts like "Commerce . . . among the several States," "due process of law," "liberty," "property" were purposely left to gather meaning from experience. For they relate to the whole domain of social and economic fact, and the statesmen who founded this Nation knew too well that only a stagnant society remains unchanged. But when the Constitution in turn gives strict definition of power or specific limitations upon it we cannot extend the definition or remove the translation. Precisely because "it is *a constitution* we are expounding," McCulloch v. Maryland, 4 Wheat. 316, 407, we ought not to take liberties with it. . . .
>
> The very subject-matter of §§1 and 2 of Article III is technical in the esteemed sense of that term. These sections do not deal with generalities expanding with experience. Provisions for the organization of courts and their jurisdiction presuppose definiteness and precision of phrasing. These requirements were heeded and met by those who were concerned with framing the Judiciary Article; Wilson and Madison and Morris and Rutledge and Sherman were lawyers of learning and astuteness. The scope of the judicial power with which the federal courts were to be entrusted was, as I have said, one of the most sharply debated and thoroughly canvassed subjects in Independence Hall. When the Framers finally decided to extend the judicial Power to controversies "between Citizens of different States," they meant to be restrictive in the use of that term. They were not unaware of the fact that outside the States there was the Northwest Territory, and that there was to be a Seat of Government. Considering their responsibility, their professional habits, and their alertness regarding the details of Article III, the precise enumeration of the heads of jurisdiction made by the Framers ought to preclude the notion that they shared the latitudinarian attitude of Alice in Wonderland toward language.[38]

Justice Rutledge, joined by Justice Murphy, disagreed. Referring to Hepburn v. Ellzey, Rutledge wrote:

> Whether or not [Marshall's] answer was adequate at the time, our Constitution today would be very different from what it is if such a narrow and literal construc-

38. Justice Frankfurter was not the first to suggest a two-clause theory. In 1924, Professor Edward S. Corwin wrote:

> [I]t will be generally found that words which refer to governing institutions, like "jury," "legislature," "election" have been given their strictly historical meaning, while words defining the subject-matter of power or of rights like "commerce," "liberty," "property," have been deliberately moulded to the views of contemporary society. Nor is the reason for this difference hard to discover. Not only are words of the former category apt to have the more definite, and so more easily ascertainable, historical denotation, but the Court may very warrantably feel that if the people wish to have their governmental institutions altered, they should go about the business in accordance with the forms laid down by the basic institution. Questions of power or of right, on the other hand, are apt to confront the Court with problems that are importunate for solution.

Corwin, Judicial Review in Action, 74 U. Pa. L. Rev. 639, 659-660 (1926).

tion of each of its terms had been transmuted into an inflexible rule of constitutional interpretation. It is to be remembered, as bearing on the very issue before us, that the Sixth Amendment's guarantee of "an impartial jury of the State . . . wherein the crime shall have been committed" extends to criminal prosecutions in the Nation's capital.[39]

Key words like "state," "citizen," and "person" do not always and invariably mean the same thing. [Marshall's] literal application disregarded any possible distinction between the purely political clauses and those affecting civil rights of citizens. . . .

What rationales do Frankfurter and Rutledge provide for their approaches to the diversity jurisdiction clause? Does the disagreement turn on their different views of the purpose of the clause or of its present-day utility? Diversity jurisdiction was designed to provide an unbiased forum for persons forced to litigate in an alien state. Rutledge asserts that the clause involves the "civil rights of citizens" and, elsewhere in his opinion, states that the case concerns the "political status and equality" of citizens of the district, and "their civil rights . . . in . . . equal access to the federal courts. . . ." In contrast, Frankfurter characterizes the clause as "technical" and, elsewhere in his opinion, asserts that "no great public interest or libertarian principle is at stake" in the continuing debate over the curtailment of diversity jurisdiction. Do these positions imply a general theory of constitutional construction? A viable one?[40]

Note: Radical Interpretation

This casebook is pervasively concerned with the methods and limits of "interpretation." William Lloyd Garrison, one of the leading white Abolitionists, held the conventional view that the Constitution sanctioned slavery and referred to the Founding Document as "A Covenant with Death and an Agreement with Hell." Frederick Douglass, the leading black Abolitionist, disputed the conventional interpretation.

39. Rutledge conceded that the leading case concerning the right to jury trial in the District, Callan v. Wilson, 127 U.S. 540 (1888), "rested in large measure on the more inclusive language of Article III, §2," which also guarantees trial by jury. Despite later statements that the Sixth Amendment guarantees jury trial in the District, the Court has not been required to consider the amendment's force independent of Article III. If the Article III guarantee did not exist, *should* the Sixth Amendment be so construed?

40. The question whether the District of Columbia is a "state or territory" has arisen in other contexts. Compare, e.g., Hurd v. Hodge, 334 U.S. 24 (1948), with District of Columbia v. Carter, 409 U.S. 418 (1973), involving 42 U.S.C. §§1982 and 1983, respectively. Section 1982 originated in the Civil Rights Act of 1866, adopted to enforce the Thirteenth Amendment, and provides: "All citizens of the United States shall have the same right, in every State and Territory, as is enjoyed by white citizens . . . [respecting] real and personal property." Section 1983 originated in the Ku Klux Klan Act of 1871, adopted to enforce the Fourteenth Amendment, and provides a civil remedy against "[e]very person who, under color of any . . . [law] of any State or Territory, subjects . . . any . . . person within the jurisdiction thereof to the deprivation of any rights . . . secured by the Constitution and laws. . . ." A unanimous Court in *Hurd* entertained "no doubt that, for the purposes of [§1982] the District of Columbia is included within the phrase 'every State and Territory.' " *Carter* unanimously held the contrary with respect to §1983, relying on the difference between the Thirteenth Amendment's general prohibition of "slavery . . . within the United States," and the Fourteenth Amendment's more limited prohibition of "State" laws that deny equal protection, etc.

FREDERICK DOUGLASS, THE CONSTITUTION OF THE UNITED STATES: IS IT PRO-SLAVERY OR ANTI-SLAVERY?

Speech delivered in Glasgow, Scotland, March 26, 1860[41]

[F]irst let me state what is not the question. It is not whether slavery existed in the United States at the time of the adoption of the Constitution; it is not whether slaveholders took part in framing the Constitution; it is not whether those slaveholders, in their hearts, intended to secure certain advantages in that instrument for slavery; it is not whether the American Government has been wielded during seventy-two years in favour of the propagation and permanence of slavery; it is not whether a pro-slavery interpretation has been put upon the Constitution by the American Courts. . . . The real and exact question . . . may be fairly stated thus: — 1st, Does the United States Constitution guarantee to any class or description of people . . . the right to enslave, or hold as property, any other class or description of people. . . ? 2nd, Is the dissolution of the union between the slave and free States required by fidelity to the slaves, or by the just demands of conscience? . . .

I . . . deny that the Constitution guarantees the right to hold property in man, and believe that the way to abolish slavery in America is to vote such men into power as will use their powers for the abolition of slavery. . . . I think we had better ascertain what the Constitution itself is. . . I will tell you. It is no vague, indefinite, floating, unsubstantial, ideal something, coloured according to any man's fancy, now a weasel, now a whale, and now nothing. On the contrary, it is a plainly written document, not in Hebrew or Greek, but in English. . . . The American Constitution is a written instrument full and complete in itself. No Court in America, no Congress, no President, can add a single word thereto, or take a single word therefrom. . . . [I]t should be borne in mind that the mere text, and only the text, and not any commentaries or creeds written by those who wished to give the text a meaning apart from its plain reading, was adopted as the Constitution of the United States. It should also be borne in mind that the intentions of those who framed the Constitution, be they good or bad, for slavery or against slavery, are to be respected so far, and so far only, as will find those intentions plainly stated in the Constitution. It would be the wildest of absurdities, and lead to endless confusion and mischiefs, if, instead of looking to the written paper itself, for its meaning, it were attempted to make us search it out, in the secret motives, and dishonest intentions, of some of the men who took part in writing it. It was what they said that was adopted by the people, not what they were ashamed or afraid to say, and really omitted to say. Bear in mind, also, and the fact is an important one, that the framers of the Constitution sat with closed doors, and that this was done purposely, that nothing but the result of their labours should be seen, and that result should be judged of by the people free from any of the bias shown in the debates. It should also be borne in mind, and the fact is still more important, that the debates in the convention that framed the Constitution, and by means of which a pro-slavery interpretation is now attempted to be forced

41. In 2 Life and Writings of Frederick Douglass 467-480 (P. Foner, ed., 1950). Douglass was the son of an unknown white man and a part-Indian slave. He spent most of his life in slavery, but was taught how to read and write. Upon his escape, he became a member of the Massachusetts Anti-Slavery Society and became a significant force in the antislavery movement, publishing a paper for slaves, and counselling President Lincoln during the Civil War.

upon that instrument, were not published till more than a quarter of a century after the presentation and the adoption of the Constitution.

These debates were purposely kept out of view, in order that the people should adopt, not the secret motives or unexpressed intentions of any body, but the simple text of the paper itself. Those debates form no part of the original agreement. I repeat, the paper itself, and only the paper itself, with its own plainly-written purposes, is the Constitution. It must stand or fall, flourish or fade, on its own individual and self-declared character and objects. Again, where would be the advantage of a written Constitution, if, instead of seeking its meaning in its words, we had to seek them in the secret intentions of individuals who may have had something to do with writing the paper. What will the people of America a hundred years hence care about the intentions of the scriveners who wrote the Constitution? These men are already gone from us, and in the course of nature were expected to go from us. They were for a generation, but the Constitution is for ages. . . . Common sense, and common justice, and sound rules of interpretation all drive us to the words of the law for the meaning of the law. The practice of the Government is dwelt upon with much fervour and eloquence as conclusive to the slaveholding character of the Constitution. . . . But good as this argument is, it is not conclusive. A wise man has said that few people have been found better than their laws, but many have been found worse. To this last rule America is no exception. Her laws are one thing, her practice is another. . . . After all, the fact that men go out of the Constitution to prove it pro-slavery, whether that going out is to the practice of the Government, or to the secret intentions of the writers of the paper, the fact that they do go out is very significant. . . . It is an admission that the thing for which they are looking is not to be found where only it ought to be found, and that is in the Constitution itself. . . .

[B]ecause upon its face [the Constitution does not support a pro-slavery interpretation, my opponent] sums up what he calls the slaveholding provisions of the Constitution[: Article I, sections 2, 8, and 9, and Article IV, section 2.] It so happens that no such words as "African slave trade," no such words as "slave representation," no such words as "fugitive slaves," no such words as "slave insurrections," are anywhere used in that instrument. [Douglass then reads to his audience the text of these four provisions.] Let us look at them just as they stand, one by one. Let us grant, for sake of the argument, that the first of these provisions, referring to the basis of representation and taxation, does refer to slaves. . . . [G]iving the provisions the very worst construction, what does it amount to? I answer — It is a downright disability laid upon the slaveholding States; one which deprives those States of two-fifths of their natural basis of representation. A black man in a free State is worth just two-fifths more than a black man in a slave State, as a basis of political power under the Constitution. Therefore, instead of encouraging slavery, the Constitution encourages freedom by giving an increase of "two-fifths" of political power to free over slave States. So much for the three-fifths clause; taking it as its worst, it still leans to freedom, not to slavery; for, be it remembered that the Constitution nowhere forbids a coloured man to vote. I come to the next, that which is said guaranteed the continuance of the African slave trade for twenty years. I will also take that for just what my opponent alleges it to have been. . . . [W]hat follows? why, this — that this part of the Constitution, so far as the slave trade is concerned, became a dead letter more than 50 years ago, and now binds no man's conscience for the continuance of any slave trade whatever. . . . But there is still more to be said about this abolition of the slave trade. Men [in 1787], both in England and in America, looked upon the slave trade as the life of slavery. The abolition of the slave trade was supposed to be the certain death of slavery. . . .

American statesmen, in providing for the abolition of the slave trade, thought they were providing for the abolition of slavery. . . . All regarded slavery as an expiring and doomed system, destined to speedily disappear from the country. . . . [T]his very provision, if made to refer to the African slave trade at all, makes the Constitution anti-slavery rather than for slavery, for it says to the slave States, the price you will have to pay for coming into the American Union is, that the slave trade, which you would carry on indefinitely out of the Union, shall be put an end to in twenty years if you come into the Union. . . . [T]he intentions of the framers of the Constitution were good, not bad. . . . I go to the "slave insurrection" clause, though, in truth, there is no such clause. . . . But I will be generous here, as well as elsewhere, and grant that it applies to slave insurrections. Let us suppose that an anti-slavery man is President of the United States (and the day that shall see this the case is not distant) and this very power of suppressing slave insurrection would put an end to slavery. The right to put down an insurrection carries with it the right to determine the means by which it shall be put down. If it should turn out that slavery is a source of insurrection, that there is no security from insurrection while slavery lasts, why, the Constitution would be best obeyed by putting an end to slavery, and an anti-slavery Congress would do that very thing. Thus, you see, the so-called slave-holding provisions of the American Constitution, which a little while ago looked so formidable, are, after all, no defence or guarantee for slavery whatever. But there is one other provision. This is called the "Fugitive Slave Provision." It is called so by those who wish to make it subserve the interest of slavery. . . . But it may be asked — if this clause does not apply to slaves, to whom does it apply?

I answer, that when adopted, it applied to a very large class of persons — namely, redemptioners — persons who had come to America from Holland, from Ireland, and other quarters of the globe . . . and had, for a consideration duly paid, become bound to "serve and labour" for the parties to whom their service and labour was due. It applies to indentured apprentices and others who had become bound for a consideration, under contract duly made, to serve and labour. To such persons this provision applies, and only to such persons. The plain reading of this provision shows that it applies, and that it can only properly and legally apply, to persons "bound to service." Its object plainly is, to secure the fulfillment of contracts for "service and labour." . . . The legal conditions of the slave puts him beyond the operation of this provision. He is not described in it. He is a simple article of property. He does not owe and cannot owe service. He cannot even make a contract. . . . The provision, then, only respects persons who owe service, and they only can owe service who can receive an equivalent and make a bargain. The slave cannot do that, and is therefore exempted from the operation of this fugitive provision. In all matters where laws are taught to be made the means of oppression, cruelty, and wickedness, I am for strict construction. I will concede nothing. It must be shown that it is so nominated in the bond. . . . The very nature of law is opposed to all such wickedness. . . . Law is not merely an arbitrary enactment with regard to justice, reason, or humanity. . . . [Douglass' adversary] laid down some rules of legal interpretation. These rules send us to the history of the law for its meaning. I have no objection to such a course in ordinary cases of doubt. But where human liberty and justice are at stake, the case falls under an entirely different class of rules. There must be something more than history — something more than tradition. The Supreme Court of the United States lays down this rule, and it meets the case exactly — "Where rights are infringed — where the fundamental principles of the law are overthrown — where the general system of the law is departed from, the legislative intention must be expressed with irresistible clearness." The same court says that the language of the law must be construed strictly in favour of justice and liberty. Again, there is another rule of law. It is — Where a law is susceptible of two meanings, the one making it accomplish an innocent purpose, and the other making it accomplish a wicked purpose, we must in all cases adopt that which makes it accomplish an innocent purpose. . . . I only ask you to look at the American Constitution in the light of [these rules of interpretation], and you will see with me that no man is guaranteed a right of property in man, under the provisions of that instrument. If there are two ideas more distinct in their character and essence than another, those ideas are "persons" and "property," "men" and "things." Now, when it is proposed to transform persons into "property" and men into beasts of burden, I demand that the law that contemplates such a purpose shall be expressed with irresistible clearness. The things must not be left to inference, but must be done in plain English. . . .

[Douglass turns to the Preamble of the Constitution, which he quotes.] It has been said that Negroes are not included within the benefits sought under this declaration. This is said by the slaveholders in America . . . but it is not said by the Constitution itself. Its language is "we the people;" not we the white people, not even we the citizens, not we the privileged class, not we the high, not we the low, but we the people; . . . , we the human inhabitants; and, if Negroes are people, they are included in the benefits for which the Constitution of America was ordained and established. . . . I undertake to say, as the conclusion of the whole matter, that the constitutionality of slavery can be made out only by disregarding the plain and common-sense reading of the Constitution itself; by discrediting and casting away as worthless the most beneficent rules of legal interpretation; by ruling the Negro outside of these beneficent rules; by claiming everything for slavery; by denying everything for freedom; by assuming that the Constitution does not mean what it says, and that it says what it does not mean; by disregarding the written Constitution, and interpreting it in the light of a secret understanding. . . . The Constitution declares that no person shall be deprived of life, liberty, or property without due process of law; it secures to every man the right of trial by jury, the privilege of the writ of habeas corpus . . . it secures to every State a republican form of government. Any one of these provisions, in the hands of abolition statesmen, and backed by a right moral sentiment, would put an end to slavery in America. The Constitution forbids the passing of a bill of attainder: that is, a law entailing upon the child the disabilities and hardships imposed upon the parent. Every slave law in America might be repealed on this very ground. . . .

I am, therefore, for drawing the bond of the Union more closely, and bringing the Slave States more completely under the power of the Free States. . . . I have much confidence in the instincts of the slaveholders. They see that the Constitution will afford slavery no protection when it shall cease to be administered by slaveholders. They see, moreover, that if there is once a will in the people of America to abolish slavery, there is no word, no syllable in the Constitution to forbid that result.

Discussion

Having now read Story, Taney, and Douglass (among others) on the status of slavery under the Constitution, whom do you find most persuasive as a constitutional interpreter? Why?

D. Judicial Supremacy and *Dred Scott:* The Lincoln-Douglas Debates

Dred Scott figured centrally in the exchanges between Abraham Lincoln and Stephen Douglas during their campaign for the United States Senate in 1858. Lincoln, in his famous "House Divided" Speech of June 16, 1858, had denounced the *Dred Scott* decision and, indeed, suggested that it was part of a conspiracy to nationalize slavery. On July 9, Douglas attacked Lincoln's views about the validity of *Dred Scott:*

> The right and the province of expounding the Constitution, and construing the law, is vested in the judiciary established by the Constitution. — As a lawyer, I feel at liberty to appear before the Court and controvert any principle of law while the question is pending before the tribunal; but when the decision is made, my private opinion, your opinion, all other opinions must yield to the majesty of that authoritative adjudication. . . . What security have you for your property, for your reputation, and for your personal rights, if the courts are not upheld, and their decisions respected when once firmly rendered by the highest tribunal known to the Constitution? . . .
>
> I am opposed to this doctrine of Mr. Lincoln, by which he proposes to take an appeal from the decision of the Supreme Court of the United States, upon this high constitutional question to a Republican caucus sitting in the country. Yes, or any other caucus or town meeting, whether it be Republican, American, or Democratic. I respect the decisions of that august tribunal; I shall always bow in deference to them.

Lincoln responded on the next day:

> I have expressed heretofore, and I now repeat, my opposition to the *Dred Scott* decision, but I should be allowed to state the nature of that opposition. . . . What is fairly implied by the term Judge Douglas has used "resistance to the decision"? I do not resist it. If I wanted to take Dred Scott from his master, I would be interfering with property. . . . But I am doing no such thing as that, but all that I am doing is refusing to obey it as a political rule. If I were in Congress, and a vote should come up on a question whether slavery should be prohibited in a new territory, in spite of that

Dred Scott decision, I would vote that it should. [Applause; "good for you"; "we hope to see it"; "that's right."]

We will try to reverse that decision. . . . Somebody has to reverse that decision, since it is made, and we mean to reverse it, and we mean to do it peaceably. . . .

Judge Douglas will have it that all hands must take this extraordinary decision, made under . . . extraordinary circumstances, and give their vote in Congress in accordance with it, yield to it and obey it in every possible sense. Circumstances alter cases. Do not gentlemen here remember the case of that same Supreme Court, some twenty-five or thirty years ago, deciding that a national bank was constitutional? . . . The bank charter ran out, and a re-charter was granted by Congress. That re-charter was laid before General Jackson. It was urged upon him, when he denied the constitutionality of the bank, that the Supreme Court had decided that it was constitutional; and that General Jackson then said that the Supreme Court had no right to lay down a rule to govern a co-ordinate branch of the government, the members of which had sworn to support the Constitution — that each member had sworn to support that Constitution as he understood it. I will venture here to say, that I have heard Judge Douglas say that he approved of General Jackson for that act. What has now become of all his tirade about "resistance to the Supreme Court?"

Douglas answered a week later, on July 17, in Springfield:

The court pronounces that law, prohibiting slavery, unconstitutional and void, and Mr. Lincoln is going to pass an act reversing that decision and making it valid. I have never heard before of an appeal being taken from the Supreme Court to the Congress of the United States to reverse its decision. . . .

Mr. Lincoln intimates that there is another mode by which he can reverse the *Dred Scott* decision. How is that? Why, he is going to appeal to the people to elect a President who will appoint judges who will reverse the *Dred Scott* decision. Well, let us see how that is going to be done. . . . [W]hy, the Republican President is to call up the candidates and catechize them, and ask them, "How will you decide this case if I appoint you judge?" [Shouts of laughter.] . . . Suppose you get a Supreme Court composed of such judges, who have been appointed by a partisan President upon their giving pledges how they would decide a case before it arise, what confidence would you have in such a court? ["None, none."] . . . It is a proposition to make that court the corrupt, unscrupulous tool of a political party. But Mr. Lincoln cannot conscientiously submit, he thinks, to the decision of a court composed of a majority of Democrats. If he cannot, how can he expect us to have confidence in a court composed of a majority of Republicans, selected for the purpose of deciding against the Democracy, and in favor of the Republicans? [Cheers.] The very proposition carries with it the demoralization and degradation destructive of the judicial department of the federal government.

Lincoln responded later that day:

I think, that in respect for judicial authority, my humble history would not suffer in a comparison with that of Judge Douglas. He would have the citizen conform his vote to that decision; the member of Congress, his; the President, his use of the veto power. He would make it a rule of political action for the people and all the departments of the government. I would not. By resisting it as a political rule, I disturb no right of property, create no disorder, excite no mobs.

Lincoln went on to read from an 1820 letter of Thomas Jefferson to a Mr. Jarvis, the author of a publication called the "Republican":

> You seem . . . to consider the judges as the ultimate arbiters of all constitutional questions — a very dangerous doctrine indeed and one which would place us under the despotism of an oligarchy. Our judges see as honest as other men, and not more so. They have, with others, the same passions for party, for power, and the privilege of their corps. . . . [T]heir power is the more dangerous as they are in office for life, and not responsible, as the other functionaries are, to the elective control. The constitution has erected no such single tribunal, knowing that to whatever hands confided, with the corruptions of time and party, its members would become despots. It has more wisely made all the departments co-equal and co-sovereign within themselves.

Discussion

Douglas accuses Lincoln of wishing to "catechize" potential nominees to the Supreme Court in regard to their views about *Dred Scott.* Consider the fact that recent Republican Party platforms call for the appointment of judges "who recognize the sanctity of human life," and Republican Presidents Reagan and Bush certainly appear to have sought out nominees who are skeptical about Roe v. Wade, the 1973 decision invalidating many states' restrictions on abortion. One presumes that the Presidents, whether by "catechizing" potential nominees or simply by making astute inquiries about them, have sought to determine the predispositions of their nominees on the issue of abortion. Is there anything improper about this?

What is the duty of the Senate, with its constitutional duty to "advise and consent" to appointments to the Court, in regard to ascertaining the views of nominees on abortion (or any other issue)? In her confirmation hearings, the first Reagan appointee, Sandra Day O'Connor, refused to answer many questions on *Roe,* saying that she could not

> tell you how I might vote on a particular issue which may come before the Court, or *endorse or criticize specific Supreme Court decisions presenting issues which may well come before the Court again.* To do so would mean I have prejudged the matter or have morally committed myself to a certain position. Such a statement by me as to how I might resolve a particular issue or what I might do in a future Court action might make it necessary to disqualify myself on the matter.[42]

Does Justice O'Connor's statement imply that it would be equally improper for a nominee to be asked (or answer) questions about the propriety of Justice Marshall's opinions in *McCulloch* and *Gibbons,* which presented an expansive reading of Congress' powers under Article I, the core issue of many contemporary cases involving the scope of national authority under purportedly limited assignment of powers.

Consider the meaning of "prejudgment." If academic appointees to the bench have published vigorous criticism of current judicial doctrines, calling for their overruling at the earliest possible time, should they be expected to answer questions about their writings? If confirmed, should they recuse themselves when those issues come up? Consider a statement by a dissenting Justice indicating hope for future

42. Quoted in Levinson, Should Supreme Court Nominees Have Opinions, The Nation, October 17, 1981, at 375 (emphasis added).

reversal by the Court of its mistaken decision. Does *that* indicate such "prejudgment" as to require recusal when the issue next comes before the Court?[43]

ARTHUR BESTOR, THE AMERICAN CIVIL WAR AS A CONSTITUTIONAL CRISIS

69 American Historical Review 327-352 (1964)[44]

The secession crisis of 1860-1861 was obviously . . . a constitutional catastrophe in the most direct sense, for it resulted in a civil war that destroyed, albeit temporarily, the fabric of the Union.

There is, however, another sense — subtler, but perhaps more significant — in which the American Civil War may be characterized as a constitutional crisis. To put the matter succinctly, the very form that the conflict finally took was determined by the preexisting form of the constitutional system. The way the opposing forces were arrayed against each other in war was a consequence of the way the Constitution had operated to array them in peace. Because the Union could be, and frequently had been, viewed as not more than a compact among sovereign states, the dissolution of the compact was a conceivable thing. . . .

Since the American system was a federal one, secession, when it finally occurred, put the secessionists into immediate possession of fully organized governments, capable of acting as no ad hoc insurrectionary regime could possibly have acted.

If slavery had been a static system, confined geographically to the areas where the institution was an inheritance from earlier days, then the demand of the slaveholding states for unrestricted, "sovereign" power to deal with it was a demand to which the majority of Americans would probably have reconciled themselves for a long time. In 1861, at any rate, even Lincoln and the Republicans were prepared to support an ironclad guarantee that the Constitution would never be amended in such a way as to interfere with the institution within the slaveholding states. An irrepealable amendment to that effect passed both houses of Congress by the necessary two-thirds vote during the week before Lincoln's inauguration. The incoming President announced that he had "no objection" to the pending amendment, and three states (two of them free) actually gave their ratifications in 1861 and 1862. . . .

[T]he proposed amendment never came close to meeting the demands of the proslavery forces. These demands, and the crisis they produced, stemmed directly from the fact that slavery was not a static and local institution; it was a prodigiously expanding one. . . . By 1860 the census revealed that more than half the slaves in the nation were held in bondage *outside* the boundaries of the thirteen states that had composed the original Union. . . .

Within the space of precisely a decade, between the beginning of 1845 and the end of 1854, four successive annexations added a million and a quarter square miles to the area under undisputed American sovereignty. Expansionism itself

43. See, e.g., the conclusion of Justice O'Connor's dissent in the *Garcia* case, p. 420 infra, where, quoting Justice Rehnquist, she indicated that the dissenters' views " 'will, I am confident, in time again command the support of a majority of this Court.' "

44. Reprinted in Lawrence Friedman and Harry Scheiber, American Law and the Constitutional Order: Historical Perspectives 219 (enlarged ed. 1988).

was explosive; its interaction with the smoldering controversy over slavery made the latter issue explosive also. . . .

[Between 1845 and 1854 there] was an actual doubling of the area of the United States within which organized civil governments existed. . . . The process of territorial organization brought into the very center of the crisis . . . the constitutional [factor]. The organization of new territories and the admission of new states were, after all, elements in a constitution-making process. Territorial expansion drastically changed the character of the dispute over slavery by entangling it with the constitutional problem of devising forms of government for the rapidly settling West. Slavery at last became, in the most direct and immediate sense, a constitutional question, and thus a question capable of disrupting the Union. It did so by assuming the form of a question about the power of Congress to legislate for the territories. . . .

A centralized national state could have employed a number of different methods of dealing with the question of slavery. Against most of these the American Constitution interposed a barrier that was both insuperable and respected. By blocking every form of frontal attack, it compelled the adoption of a strategy so indirect as to appear on the surface almost timid and equivocal. In effect, the strategy adopted was a strategy of "containment." Lincoln traced it to the founding fathers themselves. They had, he asserted, put into effect a twofold policy with respect to slavery: "restricting it from the new Territories where it had not gone, and legislating to cut off its source by the abrogation of the slave trade." Taken together these amounted to "putting the seal of legislation against its spread." The second part of their policy was still in effect, but the first, said Lincoln, had been irresponsibly set aside. To restore it was his avowed object: "I believe if we could arrest the spread [of slavery] and place it where Washington, and Jefferson, and Madison placed it, it would be in the course of ultimate extinction, and the public mind would, as for eighty years past, believe that it was in the course of ultimate extinction. The crisis would be past."

. . . [D]efenders of slavery regarded the policy of containment as so dangerous to their interests that they interpreted it as signifying "that a war must be waged against slavery until it shall cease throughout the United States." On the other hand, the opponents of slavery took an uncompromising stand in favor of this particular policy because it was the only one that the Constitution appeared to leave open. . . .

Of all the ambiguities in the written Constitution, . . . the most portentous proved in fact to be the ones that lurked in the clause dealing with territory: "The Congress shall have Power to dispose of and make all needful Rules and Regulations respecting the Territory or other Property belonging to the United States." . . . What did the Constitution mean by mingling both "Territory" and "other Property," and speaking first of the power "to dispose of" such property? Was Congress in reality given a power to govern, or merely a proprietor's right to make regulations for the orderly management of the real estate he expected eventually to sell? If it were a power to govern, did it extend to all the subjects on which a full-fledged state was authorized to legislate? Did it therefore endow Congress with powers that were not federal powers at all but municipal ones, normally reserved to the states? In particular, did it bestow upon Congress, where the territories were concerned, a police power competent to deal with domestic relations and institutions like slavery?

This chain of seemingly trivial questions . . . led inexorably to the gravest question of the day: the future of slavery in an impetuously expanding nation. . . . A single article [barring slavery] in the Ordinance of 1787 [passed under the Articles of Confederation] had eventuated in the admission of one free state after another in the old Northwest. The omission of a comparable article from other territorial enactments had cleared the way for the growth of a black belt of slavery from Alabama through Arkansas. An identical conclusion was drawn by both sides. The power to decide the question of slavery for the territories was the power to determine the future of slavery itself. . . .

[Bestor emphasizes a constitutional understanding that held firm throughout the crisis: the inability of Congress to use its Commerce Clause grant of authority to bar the interstate slave trade just as it had prohibited the international slave trade.] Careful students of constitutional history have long been at pains to point out that the broad interpretation that John Marshall gave to the commerce clause in [*Gibbons*] represented a strengthening of federal power in only one of its two possible dimensions. The decision upheld the power of Congress to sweep aside every obstruction to the free flow of interstate commerce. Not until the end of the nineteenth century, however, did the commerce power begin to be used extensively for the purpose of regulation in the modern sense, that is to say, restrictive regulation. . . . [It is a] dramatic illustration of the difference between nineteenth- and twentieth-century views of the Constitution that . . . the commerce clause was never seriously invoked in connection with the slavery dispute. The same fact illustrates another point as well: how averse to innovation in constitutional matters the antislavery forces actually were. . . .

IV. The President as Commander-in-Chief in Behalf of Preservation of the Union[45]

In his First Inaugural Speech, Lincoln emphasized his devotion to the Union and his rejection of any theory that would countenance secession.

> I hold, that in contemplation of universal law, and of the Constitution, the Union of these States is perpetual. Perpetuity is implied, if not expressed, in the fundamental law of all national governments. It is safe to assert that no government proper, ever had a provision in its organic law for its own termination. . . .[46]
>
> Again, if the United States be not a government proper, but an association of States in the nature of contract merely, can it, as a contract, be peaceably unmade, by less than all the parties who made it? One party to a contract may violate it — break it, so to speak; but does it not require all to lawfully rescind it?

45. See James G. Randall, Constitutional Problems Under Lincoln (revised edition, 1964).

46. See, however, the Constitution of the Union of Soviet Socialist Republics. Article 70 defined the USSR as "an integral, federal, multinational state formed on the principle of socialist federalism as a result of the free self-determination of nations and the voluntary association of equal Soviet Socialist Republics." Article 72 went on to state: "Each Union Republic shall retain the right freely to secede from the USSR." It is Article 72 that served as the basis of several secessionist movements within the republics of the Soviet Union before the dissolution of that country. Exclusive of one's views about communism, did the existence of Article 72 establish that the Soviet Constitution created "no government proper" insofar as it seemingly legitimated the possibility of withdrawal?

Descending from these general principles, we find the proposition that, in legal contemplation, the Union is perpetual, confirmed by the history of the Union itself. The Union is much older than the Constitution. It was formed in fact, by the Articles of Association in 1774. It was matured and continued by the Declaration of Independence in 1776. It was further matured and the faith of all the then thirteen States expressly plighted and engaged that it should be perpetual, by the Articles of Confederation in 1778. And finally, in 1787, one of the declared objects for ordaining and establishing the Constitution, was "to form a more perfect union."

But if destruction of the Union, by one, or by a part only, of the States, be lawfully possible, the Union is less perfect than before the Constitution, having lost the vital element of perpetuity.

It follows from these views that no State, upon its own mere motion, can lawfully get out of the Union, — that resolves and ordinances to that effect are legally void, and that acts of violence, within any State or States, against the authority of the United States, are insurrectionary or revolutionary, according to circumstances.

I therefore consider that, in view of the Constitution and the laws, the Union is unbroken; and, to the extent of my ability, I shall take care, as the Constitution itself expressly enjoins upon me, that the laws of the Union be faithfully executed in all the States.

A. The Authority of the President to Repel Attacks on the Union

Lincoln was inaugurated on March 4, 1861; shots were fired on Fort Sumter on April 12. Three days later, Lincoln called for a special session of Congress to meet on July 4. In the interim, he made several important decisions. Some of them, such as calling out the militia, were scarcely controversial. Others were much more so. On April 19 and 27 he issued proclamations blockading Confederate ports and authorizing the seizure of ships caught carrying goods to them. The shipowners sued, claiming that this was beyond the President's authority in the absence of a congressional declaration of war, which did not occur until July 13. The Supreme Court upheld the Proclamation in a 5 to 4 decision, with Justice Grier writing for the majority.

PRIZE CASES
67 U.S. (2 Black) 635 (1863)

Let us enquire whether, at the time this blockade was instituted, a state of war existed which would justify a resort to these means of subduing the hostile force. . . .

By the Constitution, Congress alone has the power to declare a national or foreign war. It cannot declare war against a State, or any number of States, by virtue of any clause in the Constitution. The Constitution confers on the President the whole Executive power. He is bound to take care that the laws be faithfully executed. He is Commander-in-chief of the Army and Navy of the United States, and of the militia of the several States when called into the actual service of the

United States. He has no power to initiate or declare a war either against a foreign nation or a domestic State. But by the Acts of Congress of February 28th, 1795, and 3d of March, 1807, he is authorized to call out the militia and use the military and naval forces of the United States in case of invasion by foreign nations, and to suppress insurrection against the government of a State or of the United States.

If a war be made by invasion of a foreign nation, the President is not only authorized but bound to resist force by force. He does not initiate the war, but is bound the accept the challenge without waiting for any special legislative authority. And whether the hostile party be a foreign invader, or States organized in rebellion, it is none the less a war, although the declaration of it be "*unilateral.*" . . .

The President was bound to meet [the Civil War] in the shape it presented itself, without waiting for Congress to baptize with a name; and no name given to it by him or them could change the fact. . . .

Whether the President in fulfilling his duties, as Commander-in-chief, in suppressing an insurrection, has met with such armed hostile resistance, and a civil war of such alarming proportions as will compel him to accord to them the character of belligerents, is a question to be decided *by him*, and this court must be governed by the decisions and acts of the Political Department of the government to which this power was intrusted. "He must determine what degree of force the crisis demands." The proclamation of blockade is, itself, official and conclusive evidence to the court that a state of war existed which demanded and authorized a recourse to such a measure, under the circumstances peculiar to the case.

If it were necessary to the technical existence of a war, that it should have a legislative sanction, we find it in almost every act passed at the extraordinary session of the Legislature of 1861, which was wholly employed in enacting laws to enable the Government to prosecute the war with vigor and efficiency. And finally, in 1861, we find Congress . . . passing an act "approving, legalizing, and making valid all the acts, proclamations, and orders of the President, &c., as if they had been *issued and done under the previous express authority* and direction of the Congress of the United States."

Without admitting that such an act was necessary under the circumstances, it is plain that if the President had in any manner assumed powers which it was necessary should have the authority or sanction of Congress, . . . this ratification has operated to perfectly cure the defect. . . .

NELSON, J., dissenting, joined by Taney, C.J., and Catron and Clifford, JJ.

In the case of a rebellion or resistance of a portion of the people of a country against the established government, there is no doubt, if in its progress and enlargement the government thus thought to be overthrown sees fit, it may by the competent power recognize or declare the existence of a state of civil war, which will draw after it all the consequences and rights of war between the contending parties. . . . But before this insurrection against the established Government can be dealt with on the footing of a civil war, within the meaning of the law of nations and the Constitution of the United States, and which will draw after it belligerent rights, it must be recognized or declared by the war-making power of the Government. . . .

Now, in one sense, no doubt this is war, and may be a war of the most extensive and threatening dimensions and effects, but it is a statement simply of its existence in a material sense, and has no relevancy or weight when the question is what constitutes war in a legal sense, in the sense of the law of nations, and of the Constitution of the United States. For it must be a war in this sense to attach to it all the consequences that belong to belligerent rights. . . . [T]o constitute a civil war in the sense in which we are speaking, before it can exist, in contemplation of law, it must be recognized or declared by the sovereign power of the State, and which sovereign power by our Constitution is lodged in the Congress of the United States — civil war, therefore, under our system of government, can exist only by an act of Congress, which requires the assent of two of the great departments of the Government, the Executive and Legislative.

. . . But we are asked, what would become of the peace and integrity of the Union in case of an insurrection at home or invasion from abroad if this power could not be exercised by the President in the recess of Congress and until that body could be assembled?

The framers of the Constitution fully comprehended this question, and provided for the contingency. . . . The Constitution declares that Congress shall have power "to provide for calling forth the militia to execute the laws of the Union, suppress insurrections, and repel invasions." Another clause, "that the President shall be Commander-in-chief of the Army and Navy of the United States, and of the militia of the several States when called into the actual service of the United States;" and, again, "He shall take care that the laws shall be faithfully executed." Congress passed laws on this subject in 1792 and 1795.

. . . The 2d section [of the Act of 1795] provides, that when the laws of the United States shall be opposed, or the execution obstructed in any State by combinations too powerful to be suppressed by the course of judicial proceedings, it shall be lawful for the President to call forth the militia of such State, or of any other State or States as may be necessary to suppress such combinations; and by the Act 3 March, 1807 (2 U.S. Laws, 443.) it is provided that in case of insurrection of obstruction of the laws, either in the United States or of any State or Territory, where it is lawful for the President to call forth the militia for the purpose of suppressing such insurrection, and causing the laws to be executed, it shall be lawful to employ for the same purpose such part of the land and naval forces of the United States as shall be judged necessary.

It will be seen, therefore, that ample provision has been made under the Constitution and laws against any sudden and unexpected disturbance of the public peace from insurrection at home or invasion from abroad. The whole military and naval power of the country is put under the control of the President to meet the emergency. . . .

The Acts of 1795 and 1807 did not, and could not under the Constitution, confer on the President the power of declaring war against a State of this Union, or of deciding that war existed, and upon that ground authorized the capture and confiscation of the property of every citizen of the State whenever it was found on the waters. . . . This great power over the business and property of the citizen is reserved to the legislative department by the express words of the Constitution. It cannot be delegated or surrendered to the Executive. Congress alone can determine whether war exists or should be declared; and until they have acted, no citizen of the State can be punished in his person or property, unless he has committed some offence against a law of Congress passed before the act was committed, which made it a crime, and defined the punishment. . . .

Discussion

1. What precisely is the relevance of the Act of August 6, 1861, by which the members of Congress "hereby approve and in all respects legalize and make valid" the acts done by the President "as if they had been issued and done under the previous express authority and direction of the Congress of the United States"? Can any violation of separation of powers be in effect negated if its institutional "victim" acquiesces?

2. What if Congress had passed an Act (or joint resolution) specifically repudiating the President's act? If Justice Grier's basic analysis is correct, could Congress have retroactively rendered it illegal by disaffirming it?

B. Lincoln and the Suspension of Habeas Corpus[47]

On April 27, 1861, President Lincoln issued an order to Commanding General Winfield Scott authorizing him to suspend the writ of habeas corpus (by which persons deprived of liberty can challenge the legality of their detention in a court). On May 25, military troops arrested John Merryman for participating in the destruction of railroad bridges following an antiwar riot in Baltimore.

The Constitution, in section 9 of Article I, specifically authorizes the suspension of habeas corpus "when in cases or rebellion or invasion the public safety may require it." The question is: Who can make such a determination?

1. *Chief Justice Taney on the Exclusive Authority of Congress*

Merryman was a prominent politician; his father and Chief Justice Taney had attended Dickinson College together. Merryman's lawyer filed a writ of habeas corpus before the Chief Justice. The writ was addressed to General George Cadwalader, who refused either to attend the May 27 hearing before Taney or to produce Merryman, who ignored it, refusing even to attend the May 27 hearing. Cadwalader refused to comply with a second order to be present the following day. Upon further noncompliance, Taney read a statement asserting that Merryman's detention was illegal on two grounds:

> 1. The President, under the Constitution and laws of the United States, cannot suspend the privilege of the writ of habeas corpus, nor authorize any military officer to do so.
>
> 2. A military officer has no right to arrest and detain a person, not subject to the rules and articles of war, for an offence against the laws of the United States, except in and of the judicial authority and subject to its control — and if the party is arrested by the military, it is the duty of the officer to deliver him over immediately to the civil authority, to be dealt with according to law.

Taney indicated his intention to write a fuller opinion elaborating his conclusions to "report them with these proceedings to the President of the United

47. See Carl Swisher, 5 History of the Supreme Court of the United States: The Taney Period 1836-64, Chapter 14 (1974).

States, and call upon him to perform his constitutional duty to enforce the laws. In other words, to enforce the process of this Court." He issued his opinion the following week in Ex parte Merryman, 17 F. Cas. 144 (1861):

> I understand that the President not only claims the right to suspend the writ of habeas corpus himself, at his discretion, but to delegate that discretionary power to a military officer, and to leave it to him to determine whether he will or will not obey judicial process that may be served upon him. . . . I certainly listened to [the argument] with some surprise, for I had supposed it to be one of those points of constitutional law upon which there was no difference of opinion, and that it was admitted on all hands, that the privilege of the writ could not be suspended, except by act of congress. . . . [B]elieving, as I do, that the president has exercised a power which he does not possess under the constitution, a proper respect for the high office he fills, requires me to state plainly and fully the grounds of my opinion. . . .
>
> The clause of the constitution, which authorizes the suspension of the privilege of the writ of habeas corpus, is in the 9th section of the first article. This article is devoted to the legislative department of the United States, and has not the slightest reference to the executive department. . . .
>
> It is the second article of the constitution that provides for the organization of the executive department, enumerates the powers conferred on it, and prescribes its duties. And if the high power over the liberty of the citizen now claimed, was intended to be conferred on the president, it would undoubtedly be found in plain words in this article; but here is not a word in it that can furnish the slightest ground to justify the exercise of the power.
>
> . . . The only power, therefore, which the president possesses, where the "life, liberty or property" of a private citizen is concerned, is the power and duty prescribed in the third section of the second article, which requires "that he shall take care that the laws shall be faithfully executed." He is not authorized to execute them himself, or through agents or officers, civil or military, appointed by himself, but he is to take care that they be faithfully carried into execution, as they are expounded and adjudged by the co-ordinate branch of the government to which that duty is assigned by the constitution. It is thus made his duty to come in aid of the judicial authority, if it shall be resisted by a force too strong to be overcome without the assistance of the executive arm; but in exercising this power he acts in subordination to judicial authority, assisting it to execute its process and enforce its judgments.
>
> With such provisions in the constitution, expressed in language too clear to be misunderstood by any one, I can see no ground whatever for supposing that the president, in any emergency, or in any state of things, can authorize the suspension of the privileges of the writ of habeas corpus, except in aid of the judicial power. He certainly does not faithfully execute the laws, if he takes upon himself legislative power, by suspending the writ of habeas corpus, and the judicial power also, by arresting and imprisoning a person without due process of law.
>
> Nor can any argument be drawn from the nature of sovereignty, or the necessity of government, for self-defence in times of tumult and danger. The government of the United States is one of delegated and limited power; it derives its existence and authority altogether from the constitution, and neither of its branches, executive, legislative or judicial, can exercise any of the powers of government beyond those specified and granted; for the tenth article of the amendments to the constitution, in express terms, provides that "the powers not delegated to the United States by the constitution, not prohibited by it to the states, are reserved to the states, respectively, or to the people."

. . . The right of the subject to the benefit of the writ of habeas corpus, it must be recollected, was one of the great points in controversy, during the long struggle in England between arbitrary government and free institutions, and must therefore have strongly attracted the attention of the statesmen engaged in framing a new one and, as they supposed, a freer government than the one which they had thrown off by the revolution. From the earliest history of the common law, if a person were imprisoned, no matter by what authority, he had a right to the writ of habeas corpus to bring his case before the king's bench. . . .

[Blackstone writes that] "the happiness of our constitution is, that it is not left to the executive power to determine when the danger of the state is so great as to render [suspension of habeas corpus] expedient. It is the parliament only or legislative power that, whenever it sees proper, can authorize the crown by suspending the habeas corpus for a short and limited time, to imprison suspected persons without giving any reason for so doing." If the president of the United States may suspend the writ, then the constitution of the United States has conferred upon him more regal and absolute power over the liberty of the citizen, than the people of England have thought it safe to entrust to the crown; a power which the queen of England cannot exercise at this day, and which could not have been lawfully exercised by the sovereign even in the reign of Charles the First.

Ultimately, the Administration indicted Merryman for treason by a civil grand jury. He was released on bail and never tried.

2. *The President Asserts Executive Authority*

Lincoln did not respond directly to Taney, but delivered this message to Congress on July 4:

Soon after the first call for militia, it was considered a duty to authorize the Commanding General, in proper cases, according to his discretion, to suspend the privilege of the writ of habeas corpus; or, in other words, to arrest, and detain, without resort to the ordinary processes and forms of law, such individuals as he might deem dangerous to the public safety. This authority has purposely been exercised but very sparingly. Nevertheless, the legality and propriety of what has been done under it, are questioned; and the attention of the country has been called to the proposition that one who is sworn to "take care that the laws be faithfully executed," should not himself violate them. Of course some consideration was given to the questions of power, and propriety, before this matter was acted upon. The whole of the laws which were required to be faithfully executed, were being resisted, and failing of execution, in nearly one-third of the States. Must they be allowed to finally fail of execution, even had it been perfectly clear, that by the use of the means necessary to their execution, some single law, made in such extreme tenderness of the citizen's liberty, that practically, it relieves more of the guilty, than of the innocent, should, to a very limited extent, be violated? To state the question more directly, are all the laws, but one, to go unexecuted, and the government itself go to pieces, lest that one be violated? Even in such a case, would not the official oath be broken, if the government should be overthrown, when it was believed that disregarding the single law, would tend to preserve it? But it was not believed that this question was presented. It was not believed that any law was violated. The provision of the Constitution . . . is equivalent to a provision — is a provision — that such privilege may be suspended when, in cases of rebellion, or invasion, the public safety does require it. It was decided that we have a case of rebellion, and that the public safety does require the qualified suspension of the privilege of the writ which was authorized to be made. Now it is insisted that Congress, and not the Executive, is vested with this power. But the Constitution itself, is silent as to which, or who, is to exercise the power; and as the provision was plainly made for a dangerous emergency, it cannot be believed the framers of the instrument intended, that in every case, the danger should run its course, until Congress could be called together; the very assembling of which might be prevented, as was intended in this case, by the rebellion.

Discussion

1. It is not clear whether Congress' retroactive approval, on August 6, of "all the acts, proclamations, and orders of the President . . . respecting the army and navy of the United States" included the suspension of the writ of habeas corpus. On March 3, 1863, Congress passed a habeas corpus act providing that "during the present rebellion the President of the United States, whenever, in his judgment, the public safety may require it, is authorized to suspend the privilege of the writ of habeas corpus in any case throughout the United States or any part thereof." Does this congressional authorization affect the power that President Lincoln held prior to its enactment? If so, was his original order suspending habeas corpus unconstitutional? (Some have argued that the suspension was legitimate only so long as Congress was not in session, but that Congress' failure specifically to enact a suspension when it reconvened invalidated further enforcement of the Presidential order.)

C. Lincoln: The Great Emancipator

In his First Inaugural Address, Lincoln assumed a moderate stance toward slavery. Though he vigorously opposed its extension into the territories, he stated: "I have no purpose, directly or indirectly, to interfere with the institution of slavery in the States where it exists. I believe that I have no lawful right to do so, and I have no inclination to do so." In the address, Lincoln reiterated his support of the 1860 Republican platform, which endorsed "the maintenance inviolate of the rights of the States, and especially the right of each State to order and control its own domestic institutions according to its own judgment exclusively."

Congress did not attempt to abolish slavery until it proposed the Thirteenth Amendment, which was ratified on December 6, 1865. However, on January 1, 1863, Lincoln issued the famous Emancipation Proclamation:

> I, Abraham Lincoln, President of the United States, by virtue of the power in me vested as Commander-in-Chief, of the Army and Navy of the United States in time of actual armed rebellion against authority and government of the United States, and as a fit and necessary war measure for suppressing said rebellion, do . . . order and designate as the States and parts of States wherein the people thereof respectively, are this day in rebellion against the United States, the following, to wit: Arkansas, Texas, Louisiana, (except the Parishes of St. Bernard, Plaquemines, Jefferson, St. Johns, St. Charles, St. James[,] Ascension, Assumption, Terrebonne, Lafourche, St. Mary, St. Martin, and Orleans, including the City of New Orleans)[,] Mississippi, Alabama, Florida, Georgia, South-Carolina, North-Carolina, and Virginia, (except the forty-eight counties designated as West Virginia, and also the

counties of Berkeley, Accomac, Northampton, Elizabeth-City, York, Princess Ann, and Norfolk, including the cities of Norfolk & Portsmouth[)]; and which excepted parts are, for the present, left precisely as if this proclamation were not issued.

And by virtue of the power, and for the purpose aforesaid, I do order and declare that all persons held as slaves within the designated States . . . are, and henceforward shall be free; and that the Executive government of the United States, including the military and naval authorities thereof, will recognize and maintain the freedom of said persons. . . .

And upon this act, sincerely believed to an act of justice, warranted by the Constitution, upon military necessity, I invoke the considerate judgment of mankind, and the gracious favor of Almighty God. . . .

The Emancipation Proclamation is not a general declaration of freedom. Indeed, as late as July of 1864, Lincoln reiterated that he was "unprepared . . . to declare a constitutional competency in Congress to abolish slavery in [the] States." Instead he emphasized the President's power as commander-in-chief to take actions warranted by "military necessity": "As Commander-in-Chief, I suppose I have a right to take any measure which may best subdue the enemy." Beyond this there was the President's duty to preserve the Union: "I felt that measures otherwise unconstitutional might become lawful by becoming indispensable to the preservation of the Constitution through the preservation of the nation."[48]

Note: Former Justice Curtis Dissents

The Emancipation Proclamation scarcely received universal support, even from the North. One critic, for example, was Benjamin R. Curtis, whom you earlier read vigorously dissenting from the majority's egregious views in *Dred Scott*, and who resigned from the Court shortly thereafter. In October 1862 he published a pamphlet on "executive power" that expressed strong reservations about a number of Lincoln's actions, including the Proclamation.[49]

The persons who are the subjects of this proclamation are held to service by the laws of the respective States in which they reside, enacted by State authority as clear and unquestionable, under our system of government, as any law passed by any State on any subject.

This proclamation, then, by an executive decree, proposes to repeal and annul valid State laws which regulate the domestic relations of their people. . . .

[T]his executive decree holds out this proposed repeal of State laws as a threatened penalty for the continuance of a governing majority of the people of each State, or part of a State, in rebellion against the United States. So that the President hereby assumes to himself the power to denounce it as a punishment against the entire people of a State, that the valid laws of that State which regulate the domestic condition of its inhabitants shall become null and void, at a certain future date, by reason of the criminal conduct of a governing majority of its people.

This penalty . . . is not to be inflicted on those persons who have been guilty of treason. The freedom of their slaves was already provided for by the act of Con-

48. See Randall, supra note 45, pp. 351, 358.
49. Benjamin R. Curtis, ed., 2 A Memoir of Benjamin Robbins Curtis 306-335 (1879).

gress, recited in a subsequent part of the proclamation.[50] It is not, therefore, as a punishment of guilty persons that the commander-in-chief decrees the freedom of slaves. It is upon the slaves of loyal persons, or of those who, from their tender years, or other disability, cannot be either disloyal or otherwise, that the proclamation is to operate, if at all; and it is to operate to set them free, in spite of the valid laws of their States. . . .

It has never been doubted that the power to abolish slavery within the States was not delegated to the United States by the Constitution, but was reserved to the States. If the President, as commander-in-chief of the army and navy in time of war, may, by an executive decree, exercise this power to abolish slavery in the States, because he is of opinion that he may thus "best subdue the enemy," what other power, reserved to the States or to the people, may not be exercised by the President, for the same reason that he is of opinion he may thus best subdue the enemy? . . .

Besides, all the powers of the President are executive merely. He cannot make a law. He cannot repeal one. He can only execute the laws. . . .

These conclusions concerning the powers of the President cannot be shaken by the assertion that "rebels have no rights." The assertion itself is not true, in reference either to the seceding States or their people.

It is not true of those States; for the Government of the United States has never admitted, and cannot admit, that as States, they are in rebellion. . . . [T]he Constitution is as much the supreme law of the land in Tennessee to-day, as it was before the void act of secession was attempted by a part of its people. Else the act was effectual, and the State is independent of the Government of the United States, and the war is a war of conquest and subjugation.

Nor is the assertion that "rebels have no rights" applicable to the people of those States. . . . When many millions of people are involved in civil war, humanity, and that public law which in modern times is humane, forbid their treatment as outlaws. And if public law and the Constitution and laws of the United States are now their rules of duty towards us, on what ground shall we deny that public law and the Constitution, and the laws made under it, are also our rules of duty towards them? . . .

But, if were conceded that "rebels have no rights," there would still be matter demanding the greatest consideration. For the inquiry which I have invited is not what are their rights, but what are our rights. . . .

It is among the rights of all of us that the executive power should be kept within its prescribed constitutional limits, and should not legislate, by its decrees, upon subjects of transcendent importance to the whole people.

Whether such decrees are wise or unwise, whether their subjects are citizens or not, if they are usurpations of power, our rights are both infringed and endangered. They are infringed, because the power to decide and to act is taken from the people without their consent. They are endangered, because, in a constitutional government, every usurpation of power dangerously disorders the whole framework of the State.

. . . Among all the causes of alarm which now distress the public mind, there are few more terrible . . . than the tendency to lawlessness which is manifesting itself in so many directions. No stronger evidence of this could be afforded than the open

50. Curtis is referring to the Second Confiscation Act, passed in July 1862, which, in the words of Professor Swisher, was "linked with provisions dealing with the punishment of treason" and

> applied to the property of all civil and military officers serving under the Confederacy; to the property of any person residing in the North who should assist and give aid and comfort to the rebellion; and to the property of persons 'in any state' who, being engaged in the rebellion, did not reestablish their allegiance to the United States within sixty days after a proclamation of warning by the President. Slaves were to be liberated in areas occupied by the armed forces, and the return of fugitive slaves to rebel owners was forbidden.

declaration of a respectable and widely circulated journal, that "nobody cares" whether a great public act of the President of the United States is in conformity with or is subversive of the supreme law of the land . . . ; that our public affairs have become so desperate, and our ability to retrieve them by the use of honest means is so distrusted, and our willingness to use other means so undoubted, that our great public servants may themselves break the fundamental law of the country, and become usurpers of vast powers not intrusted to them, in violation of their solemn oath of office; and "nobody cares."

Discussion

1. Could Congress have abolished slavery by ordinary legislation? Could the war powers have justified its abolition in the border states, such as Maryland, Kentucky, and Missouri, with whom the United States was not at war? Consider that the Federal Fugitive Slave Acts of 1793 and 1850 were enforced to permit the recovery by loyal slave owners in Union states until they were repealed on June 28, 1864.

2. Speaking in 1838, Lincoln declared:[51]

> Let every American, every lover of liberty, every well wisher to his posterity, swear by the blood of the Revolution, never to violate in the least particular, the laws of the country; and never to tolerate their violation by others. As the patriots of seventy-six did to the support of the Declaration of Independence, so to the support of the Constitution and Laws, let every American pledge his life, his property, and his sacred honor; — let every man remember that to violate the law, is to trample on the blood of his father, and to tear the character [charter?] of his own, and his children's liberty. Let reverence for the laws, be breathed by every American mother, to the lisping babe, that prattles on her lap — let it be taught in schools, in seminaries, and in colleges; — let it be written in Primers, spelling books, and in Almanacs; — let it be preached from the pulpit, proclaimed in legislative halls, and enforced in courts of justice. And, in short, let it become the political religion of the nation; and let the old and the young, the rich and poor, the grave and the gay, of all sexes and tongues, and colors and conditions, sacrifice unceasingly upon its altars. . . .
>
> When I so pressingly urge a strict observance of all the laws, let me not be understood that there are no bad laws, nor that grievances may not arise, for the redress of which, no legal provisions have been made. I mean to say no such thing. But I do mean to say, that, although bad laws, if they exist, should be repealed as soon as possible, still while they continue in force, for the sake of example, they should be religiously observed.

Lincoln concluded his impassioned speech by calling for "a reverence for the constitution and laws."

3. Lincoln wrote the following in an 1863 letter to Ohio Democrats upon their passage of a resolution denouncing his policy of military arrests and suspension of habeas corpus:[52]

> You ask, in substance, whether I really claim that I may override all the guarantied rights of individuals, on the plea of conserving the public safety — when I may choose to say the public safety requires it. This question, divested of the phraseology calculated to represent me as struggling for an arbitrary personal prerogative, is either simply a question who shall decide, or an affirmation that nobody shall decide,

51. Quoted in The Political Thought of Abraham Lincoln, 16-17 (Richard Current, ed., 1967).
52. Id. at 262.

what the public safety does require, in cases of Rebellion of Invasion. The constitution contemplates the question as likely to occur for decision, but it does not expressly declare who is to decide it. By necessary implication, when Rebellion or Invasion comes, the decision is to be made, from time to time; and I think the man whom, for the time, the people have, under the constitution, made the commander-in-chief, of their Army and Navy, is the man who holds the power, and bears the responsibility of making it. If he uses the power justly, the same people will probably justify him; if he abuses it, he is in their hand, to be dealt with by all the modes they have reserved to themselves in the constitution.

Compare with Lincoln's argument James Madison's defense of the Philadelphia Convention's exceeding its delegated authority by drafting a new Constitution: "the plan to be framed and proposed was to be submitted to the people themselves" and their "approbation [would] blot out antecedent errors and irregularities." (The Federalist No. 40.) May a President take constitutionally debatable action on behalf of (what he perceives to be) the public good, leaving it to citizens and the Congress to decide either that the "justice" of his actions legitimates them, or, on the other hand, that they represent a sufficient threat to the constitutional order to merit impeachment?

Did Lincoln display a "reverence" for the Constitution? Did he comply with the oath of office? Might the President's pledge to "preserve, protect and defend the Constitution of the United States" include the commission of acts that would be "unconstitutional" in normal times? Consider Thomas Jefferson's defense of the Louisiana purchase, even as he acknowledged that it exceeded the powers delegated to the President (and consider as well that two of the most sacred shrines within America's "political religion" are the Jefferson and Lincoln memorials):[53]

A strict observance of the written law is doubtless one of the high duties of a good citizen but it is not the highest. The laws of necessity, of self-preservation, of saving our country when in danger, are of higher obligation. To lose our country by a scrupulous adherence to the written law, would be to lose the law itself, with life, liberty, property and all those who are enjoying them with us; thus absurdly sacrificing the end to the means.

Consider this excerpt from a television interview of former President Richard Nixon by David Frost:[54]

Mr. Frost: So what in a sense you're saying is that there are certain situations . . . where the President can decide that it's in the best interests of the nation or something, and do something illegal.

Mr. Nixon: Well, when the President does it, that means that it is not illegal.

Mr. Frost: By definition.

Mr. Nixon: Exactly. If the President, for example, approves something, approves an action because of national security, or, in this case, because of a threat to internal peace and order, of significant magnitude, then the President's decision in that instance is one that enables those who carry it out to carry it out without violating a law. Otherwise they're in an impossible position.

53. Letter to John Colvin (September 20, 1810), in Gerald Stourzh, Alexander Hamilton and the Idea of a Republican Government 34 (1970).

54. Transcript of Frost-Nixon Interview, New York Times, May 20, 1977, at A16.

Chapter 4
1864 to 1934

This chapter covers more years than the Marshall and Taney Courts combined and includes the Chief Justiceships of Salmon Chase (1864-1873), Morrison Waite (1874-1888), Melville Fuller (1888-1910), Edward White (1910-1921), William Taft (1921-1930), and the earlier years of Charles Evans Hughes (1930-1941). During these years, the United States underwent many changes in technology, industry, economic and social structure, and legal consciousness.

I. Race Discrimination

A. History of the Adoption of the Fourteenth Amendment[1]

In 1865, shortly before the close of the Civil War, the Thirty-eighth Congress proposed the Thirteenth Amendment, which was ratified that December.[2] Although the amendment abolished slavery, the Black Codes, adopted by many southern states immediately after the war, threatened to restore freedmen to their antebellum status. The codes

> perpetuated or created many discriminations in the criminal law by applying unequal penalties to Negroes for recognized offenses and by specifying offenses for Negroes only. Laws which prohibited Negroes from keeping weapons or from selling liquor were typical of the latter. Examples of discriminatory penalties were the laws which made it a capital offense for a Negro to rape a white woman, or to assault a white woman with intent to rape. . . . In addition to the discriminations of the criminal laws, post-war black codes hedged in the Negroes with a series of restraints on their business dealings of even the simplest form. Though in many states the Negro could acquire property, Mississippi put sharp limitations on that right. But most re-

1. The following materials are based primarily on a comprehensive study by Alexander Bickel. See Bickel, The Original Understanding and the Segregation Decision, 69 Harv. L. Rev. 1 (1955). See also Charles Fairman, Reconstruction and Reunion, 1864-1888 (pt. 1), in 6 History of the Supreme Court of the United States (Freund ed. 1971).

2. The Congress that proposed the Amendment did not include representatives of the Confederate states, but by the time of ratification — December 1865 — the War was over and the defeated states all had functioning legislatures capable of exercising legal responsibilities. Thus seven of the Southern states — Virginia, Louisiana, Arkansas, South Carolina, Alabama, North Carolina, and Georgia — were among the 27 states that ratified the Amendment. That was the minimum number needed, given the presumed existence of 36 states, including the eleven states of the Confederacy.

> strictive were the provisions concerning contracts for personal service. Many statutes called for specific enforcement of labor contracts against freedmen, with provisions to facilitate capture should a freedman try to escape. Vagrancy laws made it a misdemeanor for a Negro to be without a long-term contract of employment; conviction was followed by a fine, payable by a white man who could then set the criminal to work for him until the benefactor had been completely reimbursed for his generosity.[3]

Thus, it remained for the Thirty-ninth and later Congresses to go beyond the formal abolition of slavery and to guarantee other basic rights to the freedman. The most lasting achievement of the Thirty-ninth Congress was the Fourteenth Amendment, proposed in June of 1866 and ratified two years later.[4] Any inquiry to determine what basic rights its framers sought to guarantee must begin with the Civil Rights Act of 1866.

The Civil Rights Act of 1866. A key phrase in the dispute over the scope of the Thirty-ninth Congress' concern with racial discrimination was the prohibition of discrimination in "civil rights or immunities" — the "civil rights formula" — which first appeared in the ill-fated Freedman's Bureau Bill[5] and reappeared in the Civil Rights Bill, introduced in the Senate in January 1866. Section 1 of the Civil Rights Bill provided:

> That there shall be no discrimination in civil rights or immunities among the inhabitants of any State or Territory of the United States on account of race, color, or previous condition of slavery; but the inhabitants of every race and color, without regard to any previous condition of slavery or involuntary servitude, except as a punishment for crime whereof the party shall have been duly convicted, shall have the same right to make and enforce contracts, to sue, be parties, and give evidence, to inherit, purchase, lease, sell, hold, and convey real and personal property, and to full and equal benefit of all laws and proceedings for the security of person and

3. John Frank & Robert Munro, The Original Understanding of "Equal Protection of the Laws," 1972 Wash. U.L.Q. 421, 445-446.

4. This somewhat bland sentence masks formidable constitutional problems, which Bruce Ackerman calls the "Thirteenth-Fourteenth Amendment Paradox." See Ackerman, Constitutional Politics/Constitutional Law, 99 Yale L.J. 453, 502 (1989). The paradox is derived from two sets of facts. The first (see footnote 2 above) involves the role given the governments of the Southern states. At one moment, they are considered sufficiently legitimate to count in the number needed to ratify the Thirteenth Amendment, but two weeks before the official proclamation of the ratification, Congress excluded the Representatives and Senators from these same states. This meant that the bare two-thirds majority that proposed the Fourteenth Amendment included no Southern representation. "Southern exclusion . . . was a necessary political condition for the Republicans to gain the two-thirds vote required by Article Five for the proposal of a constitutional amendment." Id. at 503. The second set of circumstances centers around the fact that the refusal of the Southern legislatures to ratify the Amendment triggered military Reconstruction. Among other aspects of Reconstruction was the requirement that states ratify the Fourteenth Amendment before they would be allowed representation in Congress. It is Ackerman's thesis that the Fourteenth Amendment, though legitimate, cannot accurately be described as an "Article V" amendment, given the circumstances surrounding its proposal and ratification.

5. The Freedman's Bureau Bill required the president to "extend military protection" in the rebellious states whenever Negroes were denied, inter alia, "civil rights or immunities belonging to white persons." The paucity of debate over the formula is probably explained by the bill's geographic limitation. It posed no danger to northern Democrats and conservative Republicans who, indeed, hoped that they could appease the Radical Republicans by acceding to the measure and avoiding a confrontation between President Johnson and the Congress. Their effort failed. Johnson vetoed the bill and the conservatives refused to override the veto.

> property, and shall be subject to like punishment, pains, and penalties, and to none other, any law, statute, ordinance, regulation, or custom to the contrary notwithstanding.

Almost without exception, supporters of the bill asserted that the only rights it secured were those specifically enumerated in section 1 and that a broader construction was not intended. For example, Lyman Trumball (Republican, Illinois), the bill's Senate sponsor, explained that section 1 would insure for blacks "the rights of citizens": "[t]he great fundamental rights set forth in this bill: the right to acquire property, the right to go and come at pleasure, the right to enforce rights in the courts, to make contracts, and to inherit and dispose of property." When James A. McDougall (Democrat, California), fearful that the phrase encompassed suffrage, pressed for a definition of "civil rights," Trumball responded by quoting the enumeration of rights in section 1 and assuring him that there was no reference to "political" rights (i.e., the right to vote).

Still, Democrats and conservative Republicans objected vigorously that the phrase "civil rights" might well be construed much more broadly than its sponsors said they intended. Willard Saulsbury (Democrat, Delaware), also fearful of black suffrage, responded to Trumball's disclaimer of "political" rights:

> The question is not what the senator means, but what is the legitimate meaning and import of the terms employed in the bill. . . . What are civil rights? What are the rights which you, I, or any citizen of this country enjoy? . . . [H]ere you use a generic term which in its most comprehensive signification includes every species of right that man can enjoy other than those the foundation of which rests exclusively in nature and in the law of nature.

And Edward Cowan, a conservative Republican from Pennsylvania, warned about segregation:

> Now, as I understand the meaning and intent of this bill, it is that there shall be no discrimination made between the inhabitants of the several States of this Union, none in any way. In Pennsylvania, for the greater convenience of the people, and for the greater convenience, I may say, of both classes of the people, in certain districts the Legislature has provided schools for colored children, has discriminated as between the two classes of children. We put the African children in this school house, . . . and educate them there as best we can. Is this amendment to the Constitution of the United States abolishing slavery[6] to break up that system which Pennsylvania has adopted for the education of her white and colored children? Are the school directors who carry out that law and who make this distinction between classes of children to be punished for a violation of this statute of the United States? To me it is monstrous.

No one responded to Cowan's point, nor indeed was the issue of segregation ever squarely faced in the debates. And despite objections that its language was too broad, the bill passed in the Senate, 33 to 12.

James F. Wilson (Iowa), a Radical Republican, presented the bill to the House of Representatives with assurances of its limited objectives:

6. Proponents of the Civil Rights Bill argued that it implemented the Thirteenth Amendment.

[Section 1] provides for the equality of citizens of the United States in the enjoyment of "civil rights and immunities." What do these terms mean? Do they mean that in all things civil, social, political, all citizens without distinction of race or color, shall be equal? By no means can they be so construed. Do they mean that all citizens shall vote in the several States? No. . . . Nor do they mean that all citizens shall sit on the juries, or that their children shall attend the same schools. These are not civil rights or immunities. Well, what is the meaning? What are civil rights? I understand civil rights to be simply the absolute rights of individuals, such as — "The right of personal security, the right of personal liberty, and the right to acquire and enjoy property." "Right itself, in civil society, is that which any man is entitled to have, or to do, or to require from others, within the limits of prescribed law." Kent's Commentaries, vol. I, p. 199. . . .

But what of the term "immunities"? . . . It merely secures to citizens of the United States equality in the exemptions of the law. A colored citizen shall not, because he is colored, be subjected to obligations, duties, pains. . . . This is the spirit and scope of the bill, and it goes not one step beyond. . . .

Laws barbaric and treatment inhuman are the rewards meted out by our white enemies to our colored friends. We should put a stop to this at once and forever.

Later he countered what he conceived as an attack on the breadth of the term "civil rights" by John Bingham of Ohio:

[Bingham] tells the House that civil rights involve all the rights that citizens have under the Government . . . , that this bill is not intended merely to enforce equality of rights, so far as they relate to citizens of the United States, but invades the States to enforce equality of rights in respect to those things which properly and rightfully depend on State regulations and laws. My friend . . . knows as every man knows, that this bill refers to those rights which belong to men as citizens of the United States and none other; and when he talks of setting aside the school laws and jury laws and franchise laws of the States by the bill . . . he steps beyond what he must know to be the rule of construction which must apply here, and as a result of which this bill can only relate to matters within the control of Congress.

The narrow scope of the bill was emphasized by other Radicals. Russell Thayer (Pennsylvania) said the bill simply declared that "all men born upon the soil of the United States shall enjoy the fundamental rights of citizenship. What rights are these? Why, sir, in order to avoid any misapprehension they are stated in the bill. The same section goes on to define with greater particularity the civil rights and immunities which are to be protected by the bill." William Windom (Minnesota) believed that the measure did not do enough because it only protected "civil" rights, not "political" rights.

Still, objections to the breadth of the language resounded in the House as they had in the Senate. Andrew Jackson Rogers (Democrat, New Jersey) declared: "As a white man is by law authorized to marry a white woman, so does this bill compel the State to grant to the negro the same right of marrying a white woman." Columbus Delano (moderate Republican, Ohio) feared that the bill would confer "upon the emancipated race the right of being jurors":

I presume that the gentleman himself will shrink from the idea of conferring upon this race now, at this particular moment, the right of being jurors, or from so wording this bill as to leave it a serious question and render it debatable hereafter in the

> courts or elsewhere. . . . [W]e once had in the State of Ohio a law excluding the black population from any participation in the public schools. . . . That law did not of course, place the black population upon an equal footing with the white, and would, therefore, under the terms of this bill be void.

The objection that the bill might grant the franchise to freedmen inspired the heaviest substantive assault. George S. Shanklin (Democrat, Kentucky) requested an amendment stating explicitly that the bill did not confer suffrage. Wilson objected to the addition because "it is in the bill now." Rogers countered: "All the rights that we enjoy, except our natural rights, are derived from Government. Therefore, there are really but two kinds of rights, natural rights and civil rights. This bill, then, would prevent a State from refusing negro suffrage under the broad acceptation of the term 'civil rights and immunities.'" And Anthony Thornton (Democrat, Illinois) insisted:

> It is said that the words "civil rights" do not include the right of suffrage, because that is a political right. . . . I do not assume . . . that [they] do . . . but with the loose and liberal mode of construction adopted in this age, who can tell what rights may not be conferred by virtue of the terms as used in this bill? Where is it to end? Who can tell how it may be defined, how it may be construed? Why not, then, if it is not intended to confer the right of suffrage upon this class, accept a proviso that no such design is entertained?

The leadership finally acceded to an amendment "[t]hat nothing in this act shall be so construed as to affect the laws of any State concerning the right of suffrage," though Wilson still maintained that the amendment "will not change my construction of the bill. I do not believe the term civil rights includes the right of suffrage."

In addition to substantive objections to the breadth of the language of the Civil Rights Bill, many congressmen doubted whether the Thirteenth Amendment, which only abolished slavery, empowered Congress to enact the measure. Michael C. Kerr (Democrat, Indiana) asked:

> Is it slavery or involuntary servitude to forbid a free negro, on account of race or color, to testify against a white man? Is it either to deny to free negroes, on the same account, the privilege of engaging in certain kinds of business . . . such as retailing spiritous liquors? Is it either to deny to children of free negroes or mulattoes on the like account, the privilege of attending the common schools of a State with the children of white men?

Andrew Jackson Rogers also asserted that the bill would prohibit public school segregation and argued that Congress was without constitutional authority to do this.

This Democratic attack might have been ignored had not similar doubts about the constitutionality of the bill been expressed by some influential Republicans, including Congressman John Bingham (Ohio), a Radical Republican and principal draftsman of both the "Bingham amendment" and the Fourteenth Amendment. Bingham construed the civil rights formula broadly:

> [T]he term civil rights includes every right that pertains to the citizen under the Constitution, laws, and Government of this country. . . . [A]re not political rights all

> embraced in the term "civil rights," and must it not of necessity be so interpreted? . . . [T]here is scarcely a State in this Union which does not, by its constitution or by its statute laws, make some discrimination on account of race or color between citizens of the United States in respect of civil rights. . . . By the Constitution of my own State neither the right of the elective franchise nor the franchise of office can be conferred . . . save upon a white citizen of the United States.

He moved to recommit the bill to committee with instructions to strike the civil rights formula and to replace the penal provision of section 2, which made it a misdemeanor to deprive anyone of a right secured by section 1, with a civil enforcement provision:

> [A]lthough the objections which I urge against the bill must, in the very nature of the case, apply, to the proposed instructions, I venture to say no candid man, no rightminded man, will deny that by amending as proposed the bill will be less oppressive, and therefore less objectionable. Doubting, as I do, the power of Congress to pass the bill, I urge the instructions with a view to take from the bill what seems to me its oppressive and I might say its unjust provisions.

In referring to "oppressive" and "unjust" provisions, Bingham may have had section 2 chiefly in mind. In the course of his lengthy and wandering speech, he objected that section 2 would "make it a penal offense for the judges of the States to obey the constitution and laws of their States. . . . I deny your power to do this. You cannot make an official act, done under color of law . . . and from a sense of public duty, a crime." But Bingham referred to "provisions" in the plural, and his motion to strike and remarks show no less a concern over the breadth of the civil rights formula.

Did Bingham object to the formula only on the ground that it was not authorized by the Thirteenth Amendment, or did he also oppose, as a matter of policy, granting the wide range of guarantees he deemed the language to comprehend? His earlier allegiance to radical antislavery ideals and the broad language he later used in drafting and defending his amendments imply that the objection was only constitutional. But the remarks quoted above also imply policy objections, and nowhere in the debates did Bingham explicitly favor the general prohibition of discrimination in "civil rights and immunities" as he favored protecting the enumerated rights, which he said "should be the law of every State, by voluntary act of every State." Moreover, Bingham made no pretense that his instructions to strike would cure the constitutional infirmity of the bill. Bingham voted against the bill even as amended, and it seems plausible that he offered the instructions in an effort to make the law conform more closely to his own racial policy, recognizing that it would be enacted despite his constitutional objection.

The bill was recommitted and the civil rights formula struck. In presenting the amended bill to the House, James Wilson stated: "Mr. Speaker, the amendment which has just been read proposes to strike out the general terms relating to civil rights. I do not think it materially changes the bill; but some gentlemen were apprehensive that the words we propose to strike out might give warrant for a latitudinarian construction not intended." Wilson also explained that the amendment made it unnecessary explicitly to exclude the franchise from the bill's coverage. The House and then the Senate passed the amended Civil Rights Act of 1866 and subsequently overrode a presidential veto.[7]

The Fourteenth Amendment. Meanwhile, the Joint Committee on Reconstruction, or Committee of Fifteen, was also addressing the problem of racial discrimination. Early in its deliberations over a possible constitutional amendment to supplement the Thirteenth, the committee rejected the civil rights formula. The committee's first product, the Bingham amendment, provided: "The Congress shall have power to make all laws which shall be necessary and proper to secure to the citizens of each State all privileges and immunities of citizens in the several States (Art. 4, Sec. 2); and to all persons in the several States equal protection in the rights of life, liberty and property (5th Amendment)." The proposal met bipartisan opposition in the House. Democrats and moderate and conservative Republicans opposed the broad delegation of power to Congress. Some Radicals were concerned that the amendment was not self-executing and left the protection of blacks to the fluctuating whims of majorities. Under this combined opposition, the amendment was tabled in the House and was never brought before the Senate.

The committee began to consider the Fourteenth Amendment after the Civil Rights Act of 1866 was on the books and the Bingham amendment had been tabled. In drafting section 1 of the Fourteenth Amendment, the committee vacillated between the civil rights formula and Bingham's language, finally reporting out the latter: "No state shall make or enforce any law which shall abridge the privileges or immunities of citizens of the United States; nor shall any state deprive any person of life, liberty or property without due process of law, nor deny to any person within its jurisdiction the equal protection of the laws."

The House and Senate debates paid little attention to the reach of section 1. Other provisions of the proposed amendment, disfranchising much of the white southern electorate, were far more controversial.[8] Apparently, most legislators identified section 1 with the Civil Rights Act, which they had only recently enacted after lengthy debate. The old Radical Republican, Thaddeus Stevens (Pennsylvania), alluded to the connection in introducing the amendment in the House:

> This amendment . . . allows Congress to correct the unjust legislation of the States, so far that the law which operates upon one man shall operate *equally* upon all. Whatever law punishes a white man for a crime shall punish the black man precisely in the same way. . . . Whatever law protects the white man shall afford "equal" protection to the black man. Whatever means of redress is afforded to one shall be afforded to all. Whatever law allows the white man to testify in court shall allow the man of color to do the same. These are great advantages over their present codes. . . . I need not enumerate these partial and oppressive laws. Unless the Constitution should restrain them those States will . . . crush to death the hated freed-

7. The text of the amended Act is as follows:

> citizens of every race and color, . . . shall have the same right, in every State and Territory in the United States, to make and enforce contracts, to sue, be parties, and give evidence, to inherit, purchase, lease, sell, hold and convey real and personal property, and to full and equal benefit of all laws and proceedings for the security of person and property, as is enjoyed by white citizens.

8. These culminated in §2 of the Fourteenth Amendment.

> men. Some answer, "Your civil rights bill secures the same things." That is partly true, but a law is repealable by a majority. And I need hardly say that the first time that the South with their Copperhead allies obtain the command of Congress it will be repealed. . . . This Amendment once adopted cannot be amended without two-thirds of Congress. That they will hardly get.

Many other Republicans asserted that section 1 merely constitutionalized the Civil Rights Act. "As I understand it," said M. Russell Thayer (Pennsylvania), "it is but incorporating in the Constitution . . . the principle of the civil rights bill . . . [so that it] shall be forever incorporated." John Broomall, also of Pennsylvania, referred to the amendment as the equivalent of the Civil Rights Act "in another shape."

Only a few congressmen insisted that the amendment guaranteed too much. Andrew Jackson Rogers' principal concern was the privileges and immunities clause:

> What are privileges and immunities? Why, sir, all the rights we have under the laws of the country are embraced under the definition of privileges and immunities. The right to vote is a privilege. The right to marry is a privilege. The right to contract is a privilege. The right to be a juror is a privilege. The right to be a judge or President of the United States is a privilege. I hold if that ever becomes a part of the fundamental law of the land it will prevent any State from refusing to allow anything to anybody embraced under this term of privileges and immunities. . . . It will result in a revolution worse than that through which we have just passed.

Whether or not Rogers' argument was made in good faith, it was not fatuous. The vague terms of the Fourteenth Amendment had been employed by the abolitionists to encompass an undefinable variety of rights and had no settled meanings. And, during the debates on section 1 of the Fourteenth Amendment, a number of its proponents made remarks inconsistent with an assumption that its broad language was strictly limited to the enumerations of the Civil Rights Act. For example, Senator Timothy Howe, a Wisconsin Radical, though not referring to segregation, suggested that the amendment might prevent racial inequality of educational expenditures:

> The right to hold land . . . the right to collect their wages by the processes of the law . . . the right to appear in the courts as suitors . . . the right to give testimony. . . . [B]ut, sir, these are not the only rights that can be denied. . . . I have taken considerable pains to look over the actual legislation [in the South]. . . . I read not long since a statute enacted by the Legislature of Florida for the education of her colored people. . . . They make provision for the education of their white children also, and everybody who has any property there is taxed for the education of the white children. Black and white are taxed alike for that purpose; but for the education of colored children a fund is raised only from colored men.

And Bingham himself, in a typically sweeping and unilluminating statement, implied that the boundaries of the amendment were amorphous.

> There . . . remains a want now, in the Constitution . . . which the proposed amendment will supply. . . . It is the power in the people . . . to protect by national law the

privileges and immunities of all the citizens of the Republic and the inborn rights of every person within its jurisdiction whenever the same shall be abridged or denied by the unconstitutional acts of any State. . . .

But, sir, it has been suggested . . . [that if the amendment] does not confer suffrage the need of it is not perceived. To all such I beg leave again to say, that many instances of State injustice and oppression have already occurred in the State legislation of this Union, of flagrant violations of the guaranteed privileges of citizens of the United States, for which the national Government furnished and could furnish by law no remedy whatever. Contrary to the express letter of your Constitution, "cruel and unusual punishments" have been inflicted under State laws . . . not only for crimes committed, but for sacred duty done. . . .

Sir, the words of the Constitution that "the citizens of each State shall be entitled to all privileges and immunities of citizens in the several States" include, among other privileges, the right to bear true allegiance to the Constitution and laws of the United States, and to be protected in life, liberty, and property.

The Fourteenth Amendment was sent to the country on June 13, 1866, and section 1 received as little attention in the ensuing election campaign and ratification proceedings as it had in Congress.

B. Early Doctrine

STRAUDER v. WEST VIRGINIA
100 U.S. 303 (1880)
Error to the Supreme Court of Appeals of the State of West Virginia

[Petitioner, a black, was convicted of murder in state court by a jury from which blacks were excluded by a statute providing: "All white male persons who are twenty-one years of age and who are citizens of this State shall be liable to serve as jurors. . . ." Before the trial, he unsuccessfully sought to remove the case to a federal court[9] and was thereafter unsuccessful in quashing in jury venire and challenging the jury panel. The state supreme court affirmed his conviction. The United States Supreme Court reversed.]

STRONG, J. . . .

[The controlling question is whether] by the Constitution and laws of the United States, every citizen of the United States has a right to a trial of an indictment against him by a jury selected and impanelled without discrimination against his race or color, because of race or color. . . .

It is to be observed that the [question] is not whether a colored man, when an indictment has been preferred against him, has a right to a grand or a petit jury composed in whole or in part of persons of his own race or color, but it is whether, in the composition or selection of jurors by whom he is to be indicted or

9. See 28 U.S.C. §1443: "Any of the following civil actions or criminal prosecutions, commenced in a State court may be removed by the defendant to the district court of the United States for the district and division embracing the place wherein it is pending: (1) Against any person who is denied or cannot enforce in the courts of such State a right under any law providing for the equal civil rights of citizens of the United States, or all persons within the jurisdiction thereof. . . ."

tried, all persons of his race or color may be excluded by law, solely because of their race or color, so that by no possibility can any colored man sit upon the jury. . . .

[The Fourteenth Amendment] is one of a series of constitutional provisions having a common purpose; namely, securing to a race recently emancipated, a race that through many generations had been held in slavery, all the civil rights that the superior race enjoy. The true spirit and meaning of the amendments, as we said in the Slaughter-House Cases (16 Wall. 36), cannot be understood without keeping in view the history of the times when they were adopted, and the general objects they plainly sought to accomplish. At the time when they were incorporated into the Constitution, it required little knowledge of human nature to anticipate that those who had long been regarded as an inferior and subject race would, when suddenly raised to the rank of citizenship, be looked upon with jealousy and positive dislike, and that State laws might be enacted or enforced to perpetuate the distinctions that had before existed. Discriminations against them had been habitual. It was well known that in some States laws making such discriminations then existed, and others might well be expected. The colored race, as a race, was abject and ignorant, and in that condition was unfitted to command the respect of those who had superior intelligence. Their training had left them mere children, and as such they needed the protection which a wise government extends to those who are unable to protect themselves. They especially needed protection against unfriendly action in the States where they were resident. It was in view of these considerations the Fourteenth Amendment was framed and adopted. It was designed to assure to the colored race the enjoyment of all the civil rights that under the law are enjoyed by white persons, and to give to that race the protection of the general government, in that enjoyment, whenever it should be denied by the States. . . .

If this is the spirit and meaning of the amendment, whether it means more or not, it is to be construed liberally, to carry out the purposes of its framers. It ordains . . . that the law in the States shall be the same for the black as for the white; that all persons, whether colored or white, shall stand equal before the laws of the States, and, in regard to the colored race, for whose protection the amendment was primarily designed, that no discrimination shall be made against them by law because of their color. . . . [The amendment guarantees] the right to exemption from unfriendly legislation against them distinctively as colored, — exemption from legal discriminations, implying inferiority in civil society, lessening the security of their enjoyment of the rights which others enjoy, and discriminations which are steps towards reducing them to the condition of a subject race.

That the West Virginia statute respecting juries — the statute that controlled the selection of the grand and petit jury in the case of the plaintiff in error — is such a discrimination ought not to be doubted. Nor would it be if the persons excluded by it were white men. If in those States where the colored people constitute a majority of the entire population a law should be enacted excluding all white men from jury service, thus denying to them the privilege of participating equally with the blacks in the administration of justice, we apprehend no one would be heard to claim that it would not be a denial to white men of the equal protection of the laws. Nor if a law should be passed excluding all naturalized

Celtic Irishmen, would there be any doubt of its inconsistency with the spirit of the amendment. The very fact that colored people are singled out and expressly denied by a statute all right to participate in the administration of the law, as jurors, because of their color, though they are citizens, and may be in other respects fully qualified, is practically a brand upon them, affixed by the law, an assertion of their inferiority, and a stimulant to that race prejudice which is an impediment to securing to individuals of the race that equal justice which the law aims to secure to all others.

The right to a trial by jury is guaranteed to every citizen of West Virginia by the Constitution of that State, and the constitution of juries is a very essential part of the protection such a mode of trial is intended to secure. The very idea of a jury is a body of men composed of the peers or equals of the person whose rights it is selected or summoned to determine; that is, of his neighbors, fellows, associates, persons having the same legal status in society as that which he holds. . . . It is well known that prejudices often exist against particular classes in the community, which sway the judgment of jurors, and which, therefore, operate in some cases to deny to persons of those classes the full enjoyment of that protection which others enjoy. . . . The framers of the constitutional amendment must have known full well the existence of such prejudice and its likelihood to continue against the manumitted slaves and their race, and that knowledge was doubtless a motive that led to the amendment. . . .

In view of these considerations, . . . how can it be maintained that compelling a colored man to submit to a trial for his life by a jury drawn from a panel from which the State has expressly excluded every man of his race, because of color alone, however well qualified in other respects, is not a denial to him of equal legal protection?

We do not say that within the limits from which it is not excluded by the amendment a State may not prescribe the qualifications of its jurors, and in so doing make discriminations. It may confine the selection to males, to freeholders, to citizens, to persons within certain ages, or to persons having educational qualifications. We do not believe the Fourteenth Amendment was ever intended to prohibit this. Looking at its history, it is clear it had no such purpose. Its aim was against discrimination because of race or color. As we have said more than once, its design was to protect an emancipated race, and to strike down all possible legal discriminations against those who belong to it . . . .[10]

Discussion

1. *The reasoning in* Strauder. How does the Court justify its conclusion that the Fourteenth Amendment prohibits the systematic exclusion of Negroes from juries? To what extent does the conclusion flow from the text of the Amendment? Is the Court's interpretation compatible with the "intentions" or "purposes" of the Amendment's framers?

2. *The harm resulting from jury exclusion.* Had Strauder been a Negro excluded from serving on a jury, his legal claim would have been straightforward: The State denied him an opportunity (serving on a jury) purely on the ground of race. This claim rests on the premise that there is no legally cognizable reason to be-

10. Justice Field and Justice Clifford dissented without opinion.

lieve that blacks are different from whites for the purposes of jury service.[11] Indeed, the majority condemns the statute for denying to blacks "the privilege of participating equally . . . in the administration of justice" and putting "a brand upon them, affixed by the law, an assertion of their inferiority." The Court has since recognized the standing of potential jurors to sue on their own behalf. See, e.g., Carter v. Jury Commission of Greene County, 396 U.S. 320 (1970).

Strauder, however, was not an excluded juror, but the defendant. Did his claim depend on the implicit argument that blacks and whites are *dissimilar* in relevant respects — that they are likely to perceive the world differently in ways that have legal consequences? If not, how was Strauder harmed by being tried by an all-white jury? Can one denounce racial classifications because they rest on irrelevant or nonexistent distinctions and simultaneously assert that outcomes would be different if the perspectives of the excluded group were recognized? Consider in this context Peters v. Kiff, 407 U.S. 493 (1972), which held that a white civil rights worker could challenge the exclusion of blacks from the grand jury that indicted him.[12]

3. Note carefully how many separate classifications were used by West Virginia in constituting its juries. Which of them do you find objectionable as a matter of political philosophy? Is this synonymous with believing that they are barred by the Fourteenth Amendment? Why or why not?

4. Justice Strong writes that, "[i]f *in those States where the colored people constitute a majority of the entire population* a law should be enacted excluding all white men from jury service," the Fourteenth Amendment would operate to strike it down. How important are the emphasized words to his analysis? Would the sentence have the same meaning if these words were eliminated?

5. Note that Justice Strong assumes, without any explicit discussion, that jury service is an issue of "civil rights" covered by the Fourteenth Amendment. Return to the debates about both the Civil Rights Act of 1866 and the Fourteenth Amendment. Is it clear that jury service would be covered by either? Consider Mark Tushnet's conclusions in The Politics of Equality in Constitutional Law, 74 Journal of American History 884 (1987):

> The lawmakers who discussed equality during Reconstruction accepted midcentury conceptions that distinguished equality with respect to civil rights, to social rights, and to political rights. The core of each conception was also well defined: The core of civil rights included the rights to sue and testify; social rights included the right to select one's associates; voting was the central political right.

Assume that *Strauder* had involved the deprivation of the ballot rather than of the right to jury service. Are you confident that Strong would have written the same opinion? Consider the material in the following Note.

11. As we shall see in Part Two, this is a standard Equal Protection argument: *A*, who is denied a benefit that *B* enjoys, claims that she is identical in all relevant respects to *B* and is therefore entitled to equal treatment.

12. Justice Marshall, joined by Justices Douglas and Stewart, would have based the holding in *Peters* in part on petitioner's standing to assert the rights of potential jurors and in part on the possible prejudice to petitioner himself: "When any large and identifiable segment of the community is excluded from jury service, the effect is to remove from the jury room qualities of human nature and varieties of human experience, the range of which is unknown and perhaps unknowable. . . ." Justice White, joined by Justices Brennan and Powell, found petitioner's standing supported by a federal statute forbidding jury exclusion based on race. Chief Justice Burger and Justices Blackmun and Rehnquist dissented.

Note: Is Voting a Political (or a Civil) Right, and Does It Matter?

Consider the following comments by Professor Kaczorowski:[13]

> [A]lthough Republicans were virtually unanimous in their support for the protection of the civil rights of blacks, they divided over the question of securing blacks' voting rights. Ultimately, suffrage was intentionally excluded from the rights that the fourteenth amendment and Civil Rights Act of 1866 were to guarantee. The exclusion of suffrage thus helped to reduce political opposition to the measures by neutralizing racist opposition within the Republican party. . . .
>
> The exclusion of suffrage from the framers' definition of civil rights was also dictated by prevailing legal opinion. Legal thinkers defined suffrage as a political privilege to be exercised by competent individuals, not as a natural right of free men. Thus principles of law buttressed political expediency.

States were not given carte blanche regarding suffrage. Indeed, perhaps the most vigorously debated part of the Amendment was its now forgotten section 2, which declared that a state's representation in the House of Representatives would be reduced should the right to vote be "denied to any of the male inhabitants of such State, being twenty-one years of age, and citizens of the United States, or in any way abridged, except for participation in rebellion, or other crime." Many of the framers argued that section 2 represented an implicit acceptance of a state's right to exclude blacks from voting, so long as it was willing to pay the price of reduced representation in Congress. Others argued that it served only as a specific penalty to be imposed on a state if it violated its presumed constitutional duty to be fair in enfranchising its citizens.[14]

It was section 2 that led Susan B. Anthony, Elizabeth Cady Stanton, and other leaders of the women's suffrage movement to oppose ratification of the Fourteenth Amendment because, as Eric Foner writes, "the second clause for the first time introduced the word 'male' into the Constitution. Alone among suffrage restrictions, those founded on sex would not reduce a state's representation."[15]

Professor Kaczorowski further notes that "the primary reason that the fourteenth amendment was criticized by Radical Republicans as too moderate or conservative was that it did not provide the same protection for voting rights that it did for civil rights." Thus the radical abolitionist Wendell Phillips denounced the Fourteenth Amendment as a "fatal and total surrender." Black enfranchisement awaited the passage two years later of the Fifteenth Amendment.[16]

Another 50 years would pass before the Nineteenth Amendment would bar denial of the suffrage on account of gender. In Minor v. Happersett, 88 U.S. 162

13. Robert Kaczorowski, Revolutionary Constitutionalism in the Era of the Civil War and Reconstruction, 61 N.Y.U.L. Rev. 863, 881-883 (1986). See also Michael Kent Curtis, No State Shall Abridge: The Fourteenth Amendment and the Bill of Rights (1986); Eric Foner, Reconstruction: America's Unfinished Revolution, 239-261 (1988).

14. Thus Representative Bingham described section 2 as "a penalty, and nothing but a penalty, inflicted on the State if its ruling class disregard and violate the guarantees of the Constitution of the political right of all the free people therein, being male citizens of the United States of full age, to participate in the choice of electors. . . ." Quoted in William W. Van Alstyne, The Fourteenth Amendment, The "Right" to Vote, and the Understanding of the Thirty-Ninth Congress, 1965 Sup. Ct. Rev. 52.

15. Eric Foner, Reconstruction: America's Unfinished Revolution 255 (1988).

16. Stanton and Anthony, incidentally, opposed ratification of the Fifteenth Amendment because of its "humiliat[ing] rejection of extending suffrage to women." Id. at 447.

(1874), the Supreme Court explicitly rejected Virginia Minor's assertion of a right to vote under the Fourteenth Amendment. Chief Justice Waite wrote for a unanimous Court:

> There is no doubt that women may be citizens. . . . [I]t did not need [the Fourteenth Amendment] to give them that position. . . .
>
> Whoever . . . was one of the people of [one of the] States when the Constitution of the United States was adopted, became ipso facto a citizen — a member of the nation created by its adoption. He was one of the persons associating together to form the nation, and was, consequently, one of its original citizens. . . .
>
> [S]ex has never been made one of the elements of citizenship in the United States. In this respect men have never had an advantage over women. The same laws precisely apply to both. The fourteenth amendment did not affect the citizenship of women any more than it did of men. In this particular, therefore, the rights of Mrs. Minor do not depend upon the amendment. . . .
>
> If the right of suffrage is one of the necessary privileges of a citizen of the United States, then the constitution and laws of Missouri confining it to men are in violation of the Constitution of the United States. . . . The direct question is, therefore, presented whether all citizens are necessarily voters.
>
> The Constitution does not define the privileges and immunities of citizens. For that definition we must look elsewhere. In this case we need not determine what they are, but only whether suffrage is necessarily one of them.
>
> It certainly is nowhere made so in express terms. . . . The amendment did not add to the privileges and immunities of a citizen. It simply furnished an additional guaranty for the protection of such as he already had. No new voters were necessarily made by it. . . .
>
> [Was] suffrage coextensive with the citizenship of the States at the time of its adoption[?] If it was, then it may with force be argued that suffrage was one of the rights which belonged to citizenship. . . .
>
> When the Federal Constitution was adopted, all the States, with the exception of Rhode Island and Connecticut [which operated under charters from the Crown], had constitutions of their own. . . . Upon an examination of those constitutions we find that in no State were all citizens permitted to vote. . . [The limitation of suffrage to males was explicit in New Hampshire, Massachusetts, New York, and South Carolina. Pennsylvania, Maryland, and North Carolina referred to "freeman" or "freemen," while New Jersey spoke of "all inhabitants" and Georgia of "citizens and inhabitants of the State." All had property qualifications for the vote.]
>
> In this condition of the law in respect to suffrage in the several States it cannot for a moment be doubted that if it had been intended to make all citizens of the United States voters, the framers of the Constitution would not have left it to implication. So important a change in the condition of citizenship as it actually existed, if intended, would have been expressly declared.
>
> But if further proof is necessary to show that no such change was intended, it can easily be found both in and out of the Constitution. [Waite quotes the "privileges and immunities" clause of Article 4, section 2.] If suffrage is necessarily a part of citizenship, then the citizens of each State must be entitled to vote in the several States precisely as their citizens are. This is more than asserting that they may change their residence and become citizens of the State and thus be voters. It goes to the extent of insisting that while retaining their original citizenship they may vote in any State. This, we think, has never been claimed. [Waite then quotes section 2 of the Fourteenth Amendment.] Why this [language], if it was not in the power of the legislature to deny the right of suffrage to some male inhabitants? And if suffrage was necessarily one of the absolute rights of citizenship, why confine the operations of

the limitation to male inhabitants? Women and children are, as we have seen, "persons." They are counted in the enumeration upon which the apportionment is to be made, but if they were necessarily voters because of their citizenship unless clearly excluded, why inflict the penalty for the exclusion of males alone? Clearly, no such form of words would have been selected to express the idea here indicated if suffrage was the absolute right of all citizens.

And still again, after the adoption of the fourteenth amendment, it was deemed necessary to adopt the fifteenth. . . . If suffrage was one of [the] privileges and immunities [protected by the fourteenth amendment], why amend the Constitution to prevent its being denied on account of race? . . .

It is true that the United States guarantees to every State a republican form of government. . . . No particular government is designated as republican. . . . All the States had governments when the Constitution was adopted. . . . In all, save perhaps New Jersey, [the right of suffrage] was only bestowed upon men and not upon all of them. Under these circumstances it is certainly now too late to contend that a government is not republican, within the meaning of this guaranty in the Constitution, because women are not made voters. . . .

[W]e have already sufficiently considered the proof found upon the inside of the Constitution. That upon the outside is equally effective. . . .

No new State has ever been admitted to the Union which has conferred the right of suffrage upon women, and this has never been considered a valid objection to her admission. On the contrary, . . . the right of suffrage was withdrawn from women as early as 1807 in the State of New Jersey. . . . Since then the governments of the insurgent States have been reorganized under a requirement that before their representatives could be admitted to seats in Congress they must have adopted new constitutions, republican in form. In no one of these constitutions was suffrage conferred upon women, and yet the States have all been restored to their original position as States in the Union.

Besides this, citizenship has not in all cases been made a condition precedent to the enjoyment of the right of suffrage. Thus, in Missouri, persons of foreign birth, who have declared their intention to become citizens of the United States, may under certain circumstances vote. The same provision is to be found in the constitutions of Alabama, Arkansas, Florida, Georgia, Indiana, Kansas, Minnesota, and Texas.

Certainly, if the courts can consider any question settled, this is one. For nearly ninety years the people have acted upon the idea that the Constitution, when it conferred citizenship, did not necessarily confer the right of suffrage. If uniform practices long continued can settle the construction of so important an instrument as the Constitution of the United States confessedly is, most certainly it has been done here.

No argument as to women's need of suffrage can be considered. We can only act upon her rights as they exist. It is not for us to look at the hardship of withholding. Our duty is at an end if we find it is within the power of a State to withhold.

Discussion

1. Compare the style of constitutional interpretation in *Minor* with Chief Justice Taney's in *Dred Scott*.

2. Would a contrary ruling necessarily have entailed the grant of suffrage to other disfranchised citizens, such as minors? (Every state had an age requirement of 21.) If so, does that imply that Mrs. Minor properly lost her suit, at least if predicated on the privileges and immunities clause? Or might the right to vote be a "presumptive" privilege, to be restricted only if the state has a very

good reason? What constitute good reasons for denying persons the right to vote?

3. Why didn't Mrs. Minor claim a violation of the equal protection clause? See p. 269 infra.

4. As you will see in Chapter 6, infra, the modern Supreme Court treats voting as embraced by the Fourteenth Amendment, and Congress has used its legislative powers under the Amendment to bar states from depriving persons over 18 years old of the right to vote in federal elections.[17] This development did not occur without dissent: Justice Harlan argued vigorously that the history of the Fourteenth Amendment foreclosed its application to voting and that any suffrage complaints arising only under that Amendment should be dismissed "for failure to state a claim of federal right."[18] Professor Van Alstyne responded to Justice Harlan's analysis as follows:

> [T]he case can safely be made that there was an original understanding that §1 of the proposed Fourteenth Amendment would not itself immediately invalidate state suffrage laws severely restricting the right to vote. With all of it, however, we cannot safely declare that there was also a clear, uniform understanding that the open-ended phrases of §1 — "privileges or immunities of citizens of the United States . . . life, liberty, or property . . . the equal protection of the laws" — would foreclose a different application in the future. . . . The question whether the original understanding was itself intended equally to bind the indefinite future becomes more lively when we note that the Thirty-ninth Congress did not adopt a second alternative: to accomplish specific, narrowly defined ends by producing an equally specific and narrowly defined amendment that, by clear language, could never be applied to suffrage. The failure to pursue that alternative, moreover, could scarcely have been inadvertent.[19]

C. Establishment of the "Separate but Equal" Doctrine

Strauder contains language that, read for all it is worth, promises full racial equality. But Justice Strong also refers to the Negroes' "abject and ignorant" condition, "unfitted to command the respect of those who had superior intelligence." Although the Court did not retreat from the specific holding in *Strauder*, some of its decisions during the ensuing several decades appear more responsive to this assumption of Negro inferiority than to the goal of racial equality. The Court was not alone in this, and its decisions of the period are illuminated by C. Vann Woodward's description of their social and political context. The year 1877 is generally regarded as the watershed. Under the so-called Compromise of 1877, southern Democrats abandoned their support for Democrat Samuel J. Tilden, who they claimed had been legally elected president, and supported the seating of Republican Rutherford B. Hayes in exchange, essentially, for the end of Reconstruction. Woodward writes:[20]

17. See Oregon v. Mitchell, 400 U.S. 112 (1970).
18. Carrington v. Rash, 380 U.S. 89, 99 (1965).
19. Van Alstyne, supra note 14, at 72-73. Professor Van Alstyne's argument is based on one earlier articulated by Alexander Bickel in regard to school segregation, supra.
20. C. Vann Woodward, The Strange Career of Jim Crow 6, 69-70 (3d rev. ed. 1974).

The phase that began in 1877 was inaugurated by the withdrawal of federal troops from the South, the abandonment of the Negro as a ward of the nation, the giving up of the attempt to guarantee the freedman his civil and political equality, and the acquiescence of the rest of the country in the South's demand that the whole problem be left to the disposition of the dominant Southern white people. What the new status of the Negro would be was not at once apparent, nor were the Southern white people themselves so united on that subject at first as has been generally assumed. The determination of the Negro's "place" took shape gradually under the influence of economic and political conflicts among divided white people — conflicts that were eventually resolved in part at the expense of the Negro. . . .

The South's adoption of extreme racism was due not so much to a conversion as it was to a relaxation of the opposition. All the elements of fear, jealousy, proscription, hatred, and fanaticism had long been present, as they are present in various degrees of intensity in any society. What enabled them to rise to dominance was not so much cleverness or ingenuity as it was a general weakening and discrediting of the numerous forces that had hitherto kept them in check. The restraining forces included not only Northern liberal opinion in the press, the courts, and the government, but also internal checks imposed by the prestige and influence of the Southern conservatives, as well as by the idealism and zeal of the Southern radicals. What happened toward the end of the century was an almost simultaneous — and sometimes not unrelated — decline in the effectiveness of restraint that had been exercised by all three forces: Northern liberalism, Southern conservatism, and Southern radicalism.

The acquiescence of Northern liberalism in the Compromise of 1877 defined the beginning, but not the ultimate extent, of the liberal retreat on the race issue. The Compromise merely left the freedman to the custody of the conservative Redeemers upon their pledge that they would protect him in his constitutional rights. But as these pledges were forgotten or violated and the South veered toward proscription and extremism, Northern opinion shifted to the right, keeping pace with the South, conceding point after point, so that at no time were the sections very far apart on race policy. The failure of the liberals to resist this trend was due in part to political factors. Since reactionary politicians and their cause were identified with the bloody-shirt issue and the demagogic exploitation of sectional animosities, the liberals naturally felt themselves strongly drawn toward the cause of sectional reconciliation. And since the Negro was the symbol of sectional strife, the liberals joined in deprecating further agitation of his cause and in defending the Southern view of race in its less extreme forms. It was quite common in the 'eighties and 'nineties to find in the Nation, Harper's Weekly, the North American Review, or the Atlantic Monthly, Northern liberals and former abolitionists mouthing the shibboleths of white supremacy regarding the Negro's innate inferiority, shiftlessness, and hopeless unfitness for full participation in the white man's civilization. Such expressions doubtless did much to add to the reconciliation of North and South, but they did so at the expense of the Negro. Just as the Negro gained his emancipation and new rights through a falling out between white men, he now stood to lose his rights through the reconciliation of white men.

PLESSY v. FERGUSON
163 U.S. 537 (1896)
In Error to the Supreme Court of Louisiana

[A Louisiana statute required railroads carrying passengers within the state to "provide equal but separate accommodations for the white and colored races" and made it a misdemeanor for a passenger to insist on "going into a coach or compartment to which by race he does not belong. . . ." In a prosecution for refusing to leave the white coach, Plessy challenged the statute.[21] The Supreme Court held that the statute did not violate the Fourteenth Amendment.]

BROWN, J. . . .

The object of the amendment was undoubtedly to enforce the absolute equality of the two races before the law, but in the nature of things it could not have been intended to abolish distinctions based upon color, or to enforce social, as distinguished from political equality, or a commingling of the two races upon terms unsatisfactory to either. Laws permitting, and even requiring, their separation in places where they are liable to be brought into contact do not necessarily imply the inferiority of either race to the other, and have been generally, if not universally, recognized as within the competency of the state legislatures in the exercise of their police power. The most common instance of this is connected with the establishment of separate schools for white and colored children, which has been held to be a valid exercise of the legislative power even by courts of States where the political rights of the colored race have been longest and most earnestly enforced. . . . [The Court here cites decisions in states including Massachusetts, New York, Ohio, and California.]

Laws forbidding the intermarriage of the two races may be said in a technical sense to interfere with the freedom of contract, and yet have been universally recognized as within the police power of the State.

The distinction between laws interfering with the political equality of the negro and those requiring the separation of the two races in schools, theatres and railway carriages has been frequently drawn by this court. Thus in Strauder v. West Virginia, 100 U.S. 303, it was held that a law of West Virginia limiting to white male persons, 21 years of age and citizens of the State, the right to sit upon juries, was a discrimination which implied a legal inferiority in civil society, which lessened the security of the right of the colored race, and was a step toward reducing them to a condition of servility. . . .

In this connection, it is also suggested by the learned counsel for the plaintiff in error that the same argument that will justity the state legislature in requiring railways to provide separate accommodations for the two races will also authorize them to require separate cars to be provided for people whose hair is of a certain color, or who are aliens, or who belong to certain nationalities, or to enact laws requiring colored people to walk upon one side of the street, and white people upon the other, or requiring white men's houses to be painted white, and colored men's black, or their vehicles or business signs to be of different colors, upon the theory that one side of the street is as good as the other, or that a house or vehicle of one color is as good as one of another color. The reply to all this is that every exercise of the police power must be reasonable, and extend only to such laws as are enacted in good faith for the promotion for the public good, and not for the annoyance or oppression of a particular class. . . .

21. Plessy maintained, among other things, that he was entitled to sit in the coach for whites by virtue of being seven-eighths Caucasian and looking white. The Court held that the issue of his proper classification was a matter of state law. For a thorough treatment of all aspects of the case, see Charles A. Lofgren, The Plessy Case: A Legal-Historical Interpretation (1987).

So far, then, as a conflict with the Fourteenth Amendment is concerned, the case reduces itself to the question whether the statute of Louisiana is a reasonable regulation, and with respect to this there must necessarily be a large discretion on the part of the legislature. In determining the question of reasonableness it is at liberty to act with reference to the established usages, customs and traditions of the people, and with a view to the promotion of their comfort, and the preservation of the public peace and good order. Gauged by this standard, we cannot say that a law which authorizes or even requires the separation of the two races in public conveyances is unreasonable, or . . . obnoxious to the Fourteenth Amendment. . . .

We consider the underlying fallacy of the plaintiff's argument to consist in the assumption that the enforced separation of the two races stamps the colored race with a badge of inferiority. If this be so, it is not by reason of anything found in the act, but solely because the colored race chooses to put that construction upon it. The argument necessarily assumes that if, as has been more than once the case, and is not unlikely to be so again, the colored race should become the dominant power in the state legislature, and should enact a law in precisely similar terms, it would thereby relegate the white race to an inferior position. We imagine that the white race, at least, would not acquiesce in this assumption. The argument also assumes that social prejudices may be overcome by legislation, and that equal rights cannot be secured to the negro except by an enforced commingling of the two races. We cannot accept this proposition. If the two races are to meet upon terms of social equality, it must be the result of natural affinities, a mutual appreciation of each other's merits and a voluntary consent of individuals. . . . Legislation is powerless to eradicate racial instincts or to abolish distinctions based upon physical differences, and the attempt to do so can only result in accentuating the difficulties of the present situation. If the civil and political rights of both races be equal one cannot be inferior to the other civilly or politically. If one race be inferior to the other socially, the Constitution of the United States cannot put them upon the same plane. . . .

HARLAN J., dissenting. . . .

It was said in argument that the statute of Louisiana does not discriminate against either race, but prescribes a rule applicable alike to white and colored citizens. But this argument does not meet the difficulty. Every one knows that the statute in question had its origin in the purpose, not so much to exclude white persons from railroad cars occupied by blacks, as to exclude colored people from coaches occupied by or assigned to white persons. Railroad corporations of Louisiana did not make discrimination among whites in the matter of accommodation for travellers. The thing to accomplish was, under the guise of giving equal accommodation for whites and blacks, to compel the latter to keep to themselves while travelling in railroad passenger coaches. No one would be so wanting in candor as to assert the contrary. The fundamental objection, therefore, to the statute is that it interferes with the personal freedom of citizens. . . . If a State can prescribe, as a rule of civil conduct, that whites and blacks shall not travel as passengers in the same railroad coach, why may it not so regulate the use of the streets of its cities and towns as to compel white citizens to keep on one side of a street and black citizens to keep on the other? Why may it not, upon like grounds, punish whites and blacks who ride together in street cars or in open vehicles on a public road or street? Why may it not require sheriffs to assign whites to one side of a court-room and blacks to the other? And why may it not also prohibit the commingling of the two races in the galleries of legislative halls or in public assemblages convened for the consideration of the political questions of the day? Further, if this statute of Louisiana is consistent with the personal liberty of citizens, why may not the State require the separation in railroad coaches of native and naturalized citizens of the United States, or of Protestants and Roman Catholics?

The answer given at the argument to these questions was that regulations of the kind they suggest would be unreasonable, and could not, therefore, stand before the law. Is it meant that the determination of questions of legislative power depends upon the inquiry whether the statute whose validity is questioned is, in the judgment of the courts, a reasonable one, taking all the circumstances into consideration? A statute may be unreasonable merely because a sound public policy forbade its enactment. But I do not understand that the courts have anything to do with the policy or expediency of legislation. . . .

The white race deems itself to be the dominant race in this country. And so it is, in prestige, in achievements, in education, in wealth and in power. So, I doubt not, it will continue to be for all time, if it remains true to its great heritage and holds fast to the principles of constitutional liberty. But in view of the Constitution, in the eye of the law, there is in this country no superior, dominant, ruling class of citizens. There is no caste here. Our Constitution is color-blind, and neither knows nor tolerates classes among citizens. In respect of civil rights, all citizens are equal before the law. The humblest is the peer of the most powerful. The law regards man as man, and takes no account of his surroundings or of his color when his civil rights as guaranteed by the supreme law of the land are involved. . . .

In my opinion, the judgment this day rendered will, in time, prove to be quite as pernicious as the decision made by this tribunal in the *Dred Scott* case. . . . The present decision, it may well be apprehended, will not only stimulate aggressions, more or less brutal and irritating, upon the admitted rights of colored citizens, but will encourage the belief that it is possible, by means of state enactments, to defeat the beneficent purposes which the people of the United States had in view when they adopted the recent amendments of the Constitution. . . . The destinies of the two races, in this country, are indissolubly linked together, and the interests of both require that the common government of all shall not permit the seeds of race hate to be planted under the sanction of law. What can more certainly arouse race hate, what more certainly create and perpetuate a feeling of distrust between these races, than state enactments, which, in fact, proceed on the ground that colored citizens are so inferior and degraded that they cannot be allowed to sit in public coaches occupied by white citizens? That, as all will admit, is the real meaning of such legislation as was enacted in Louisiana.

The sure guarantee of the peace and security of each race is the clear, distinct, unconditional recognition by our governments, National and State, of every right that inheres in civil freedom, and of the equality before the law of all citizens of the United States without regard to race. State enactments, regulating the enjoyment of civil rights, upon the basis of race, and cunningly devised to defeat legitimate results of the war, under the pretence of recognizing equality of rights, can have no other result than to render permanent peace impossible, and to keep alive a conflict of races, the continuance of which must do harm to all concerned. This question is not met by the suggestion that social equality cannot exist between the white and black races in this country. That argument, if it can be properly regarded as one, is scarcely worthy of consideration; for social equality no more exists between two races when travelling in a passenger coach or a public highway than when members of the same races sit by each other in a street car or in the jury box, or stand or sit with each other in a political assembly, or when they use in common the streets of a city or town, or when they are in the same room for the purpose of having their names placed on the registry of voters, or when they approach the ballot-box in order to exercise the high privilege of voting. . . .

The arbitrary separation of citizens, on the basis of race, while they are on a public highway, is a badge of servitude wholly inconsistent with the civil freedom and the equality before the law established by the Constitution. It cannot be justified upon any legal grounds.

If evils will result from the commingling of the two races upon public highways established for the benefit of all, they will be infinitely less than those that will surely come from state legislation regulating the enjoyment of civil rights upon the basis of race. We boast of the freedom enjoyed by our people above all other peoples. But it is difficult to reconcile that boast with a state of the law which, practically, puts the brand of servitude and degradation upon a large class of our fellow-citizens, our equals before the law. The thin disguise of "equal" accommodations for passengers in railroad coaches will not mislead any one, nor atone for the wrong this day done.

Discussion

1. Justice Brown indicates that the equal protection clause was designed to assure "political" though not "social" equality. Is he correct as to its assuring "political" equality? (Do you believe that Brown considered the Fifteenth Amendment merely redundant?) As to the distinction between social and other forms of equality, Professor Tushnet in The Politics of Equality in Constitutional Law, 74 Journal of American History 884 (1987) writes:

> Equality in political and civil rights did not mean, as a legal matter, that blacks could insist on equal treatment in the ordinary course of social life. Whites could refuse to have social contacts with blacks and could exclude blacks from their homes. More significant, the rejection of [social] equality [as a command of the Fourteenth Amendment] was widely believed to imply that segregated education was permissible, as were laws prohibiting racial intermarriage.

2. The Court implicitly contrasts "discrimination" with mere "segregation" and holds that the Constitution prohibits only the former. This view was elaborated by Professor Herbert Wechsler, a distinguished constitutional scholar, in criticizing the Court's 1954 decision in Brown v. Board of Education, Chapter 6 infra:

> For me, assuming equal facilities, the question posed by state-enforced segregation is not one of discrimination at all. Its human and its constitutional dimensions lie entirely elsewhere, in the denial by the state of freedom to associate, a denial that

impinges in the same way on any groups or races that may be involved. I think, and I hope not without foundation, that the Southern white also pays heavily for segregation, not only in the sense of guilt that he must carry but also in the benefits he is denied. In the days when I was joined with Charles H. Houston in a litigation in the Supreme Court, before the present building was constructed, he did not suffer more than I in knowing that we had to go to Union Station to lunch together during the recess. . . .

But if the freedom of association is denied by segregation, integration forces an association upon those for whom it is unpleasant or repugnant. Is this not the heart of the issue involved, a conflict in human claims of high dimension, not unlike many others that involve the highest freedoms — conflicts that Professor Sutherland has recently described. Given a situation where the state must practically choose between denying the association to those individuals who wish it or imposing it on those who would avoid it, is there a basis in neutral principles for holding that the Constitution demands that the claims for association should prevail?[22]

Do you agree with Professor Wechsler that the Constitition provides no guidance in this basic choice of values?

3. The Court states that "every exercise of the police power must be reasonable, and extend only to such laws as are enacted in good faith for the promotion for the public good, and not for the annoyance or oppression of a particular class." Presumably, if a race-based law were enacted with an improper motive or were simply a pretext for "annoyance and oppression," the Court would strike it down. Note the similarity to the "pretext" qualification in paragraph 42 of *McCulloch,* supra. Would you trust the Supreme Court to determine accurately when racial laws like those in *Plessy* meet the standard immediately above?

4. The Court asserts that nothing intrinsic to the segregation law "stamps the colored race with a badge of inferiority." Might the distinction between segregation and discrimination rest in part on the social meaning of the separation? Compare, for example, the contemporary social meaning of restrooms segregated by race and by gender. The modern Court would immediately strike down the former; the latter would certainly be upheld. (Even, one strongly suspects, had the ERA been ratified.) What accounts for the distinction?

Note that the law in *Plessy* was not an isolated enactment but part of a pervasive scheme of Jim Crow laws, in every Southern and border state, "that extended to churches and schools, to housing and jobs, to eating and drinking . . . to virtually all forms of public transportation, to sports and recreations, to hospitals, orphanages, prisons, and asylums, and ultimately to funeral homes, morgues, and cemeteries."[23] Did the Court in *Plessy* wrongly ignore the cultural meaning of state-imposed segregation? If so, what does this imply for the "process" rationale of judicial review? Consider in this context the following defense of the Court's 1954 decision in Brown v. Board of Education, Chapter 6, infra, which held "separate but equal" schooling unconstitutional.

22. Herbert Wechsler, Toward Neutral Principles of Constitutional Law, 73 Harv. L. Rev. 1, 34 (1959).

23. Woodward, supra note 20, at 8.

CHARLES BLACK, THE LAWFULNESS OF THE SEGREGATION DECISIONS

69 Yale L.J. 421, 424-427 (1960)

. . . I was raised in the south, in a Texas city where the pattern of segregation was firmly fixed. I am sure it never occurred to anyone, white or colored, to question its meaning. The fiction of "equality" is just about on a level with the fiction of "finding" in the action of trover. I think few candid southerners deny this. Northern people may be misled by the entirely sincere protestations of many southerners that segregation is "better" for the Negroes, is not intended to hurt them. But I think a little probing would demonstrate that what is meant is that it is better for the Negroes to accept a position of inferiority, at least for the indefinite future. . . .

Segregation in the South comes down in apostolic succession from slavery and the *Dred Scott* case. The South fought to keep slavery, and lost. Then it tried the Black Codes, and lost. Then it looked around for something else and found segregation. The movement for segregation was an integral part of the movement to maintain and further "white supremacy.". . . Segregation in the South grew up and is kept going because and only because the white race has wanted it that way. . . . [T]he life of a southern community [is not one] of mutual separation of whites and Negroes, but of one in-group enjoying full normal communal life and one out-group that is barred from this life and forced into an inferior life of its own. . . . When you are in Leeville and hear someone say "Leeville High," you know he has reference to the white high school; the Negro school will be called something else — Carver High, perhaps, or Lincoln High to our shame. . . .

Segregation is historically and contemporaneously associated in a functioning complex with practices which are indisputably and grossly discriminatory. I have in mind especially the long-continued and still largely effective exclusion of Negroes from voting. . . . [S]egregation is the pattern of law in communities where the extralegal patterns of discrimination against Negroes are the tightest, where Negroes are subjected to the strictest codes of "unwritten law" as to job opportunities, social intercourse, patterns of housing, going to the back door, being called by the first name, saying "Sir," and all the rest of the whole sorry business. . . .

"Separate but equal" facilities are almost never really equal. Sometimes this concerns small things — if the "white" men's room has mixing hot and cold taps, the "colored" men's room will likely have separate taps; it is always the back of the bus for the Negroes; "Lincoln Beach" will rarely if ever be as good as the regular beach. Sometimes it concerns the most vital matter — through the whole history of segregation, colored schools have been so disgracefully inferior to white schools. . . .

Attention is usually focused on these inequalities as things in themselves, correctible by detailed decrees. I am more interested in their very clear character as *evidence* of what segregation means to the people who impose it and to the people who are subjected to it. . . .

Further arguments could be piled on top of one another, for we have here to do with the most conspicuous characteristic of a whole regional culture. It is actionable defamation in the South to call a white man a Negro. A small proportion of Negro "blood" puts one in the inferior race for segregation purposes; this is the way in which one deals with a taint, such as a carcinogen in cranberries.

The various items I have mentioned differ in weight; not every one would suffice in itself to establish the character of segregation. Taken together they are of irrefragable strength. The society that has just lost the Negro as a slave, that has just lost out in an attempt to put him under quasi-servile "Codes," the society that views his blood as a contamination and his name as an insult, the society that extralegally imposes on him every humiliating mark of low caste and that until yesterday kept him in line by lynching — this society, careless of his consent, moves by law, first to exclude him from voting, and secondly to cut him off from mixing in the general public life of the community. The Court that refused to see inequality in this cutting off would be making the only kind of law that can be warranted outrageous in advance — law based on selfinduced blindness, on flagrant contradiction of known fact.

I have stated all these points shortly because they are matters of common notoriety, matters not so much for judicial notice as for the background knowledge of educated men who live in the world. A court may advise itself of them as it advises itself of the facts that we are a "religious people," that the country is more industrialized than in Jefferson's day, that children are the natural objects of fathers' bounty, that criminal sanctions are commonly thought to deter, that steel is a basic commodity in our economy, that the imputation of unchastity is harmful to a woman. Such judgments, made on such a basis, are in the foundations of all law, decisional as well as statutory; it would be the most unneutral of principles, improvised ad hoc, to require that a court faced with the present problem refuse to note a plain fact about the society of the United States — the fact that the social meaning of segregation is the putting of the Negro in a position of walled-off inferiority — or the other equally plain fact that such treatment is hurtful to human beings. Southern courts, on the basis of just such a judgment, have held that the placing of a white person in a Negro railroad car is an actionable humiliation; must a court pretend not to know that the Negro's situation there is humiliating?

Note: The Spirit of Plessy

Viewed in terms of the Compromise of 1877, *Strauder* and *Plessy* are not inconsistent with one another. Central to most political compromises is the saving of face. The law struck down in *Strauder,* by its very terms, treated Negroes unequally by excluding them from juries. The law upheld in *Plessy* was neutral in appearance, favoring neither blacks nor whites: The inequality appeared only when one looked behind the words of the statute, and this — though it hardly required much scrutiny — the Court refused to do.

Many of the Court's other decisions from about 1880 to 1930 support C. Vann Woodward's suggestion that "[t]he [C]ourt, like the liberals, was engaged in a bit of reconciliation . . . achieved at the Negro's expense."[24] Pace v. Alabama, 106 U.S. 583 (1883), upheld the prohibition of interracial marriage; Justice Field wrote for a unanimous Court that the law did not discriminate since it applied

24. Id. at 71. For detailed and extensive surveys of the law during this period, see Charles Mangum, The Legal Status of the Negro (1940); Edward Waite, The Negro in the Supreme Court, 30 Minn. L. Rev. 219 (1946).

"the same punishment to both offenders, the white and the black." *Plessy* was reaffirmed in several cases,[25] and in Gong Lum v. Rice, 275 U.S. 78 (1927), it was extended to school segregation. See also Cumming v. Richmond Co. Bd. of Educ., 175 U.S. 528 (1899); Berea College v. Kentucky, 211 U.S. 45 (1908).

The only major exception to this line of decisions is the curious case of Buchanan v. Warley, 245 U.S. 60 (1917), in which a unanimous Court held invalid under the due process clause a Louisville ordinance prohibiting black persons from residing in a block in which a majority of houses were occupied by whites, and white persons from residing in a block in which a majority of the houses were occupied by blacks. *Buchanan* was a collusive suit by a white seller to compel specific performance of a contract for the purchase of a house by a black buyer, who ostensibly defended on the ground that the ordinance made the contract illegal. Justice Day was not impressed with arguments that the ordinance prevented miscegenation and preserved property values. Although he did take seriously the argument that the ordinance "will promote the public peace by preventing race conflicts," this was held not to outweigh the seller's right to dispose of his property. *Plessy* was distinguished with the cryptic explanation that "in that case there was no attempt to deprive persons of color of transportation in the coaches of the public carrier, and the express requirements were for equal though separate accommodations." *Buchanan* probably is best explained in terms of the supposed uniqueness of real property and the then-prevailing doctrine of economic due process.[26]

It is difficult to assess the extent to which the spirit of compromise affected the Court's handling of some other areas of constitutional doctrine. Although *Strauder* had forbidden the statutory exclusion of Negroes from juries, exclusion brought about by the discriminatory action of state officials remained pervasive. The Court did intervene in some egregious instances,[27] and its failure to intervene more readily and significantly may have been due to difficulties of proof and to a tenable, though narrow, construction of jurisdictional provisions.[28] In the area of voting rights, the Court struck down several blatant statutory attempts to circumvent the requirements of the Fifteenth Amendment;[29] but the disfranchisement of southern blacks was achieved by a variety of other means, which the Court would not or could not deal with.[30]

25. E.g., Chesapeake & O. Ry. v. Kentucky, 179 U.S. 388 (1900); Chiles v. Chesapeake & O. Ry., 218 U.S. 71 (1910); McCabe v. Atchison, T. & S.F.R., 235 U.S. 151 (1914) (in which the Court held, however, that a state could not permit carriers to provide sleeping and dining facilities only for whites). See Hall v. DeCuir, 95 U.S. 485 (1877) (commerce clause); Louisville, N.O. & T. Ry. v. Mississippi, 133 U.S. 587 (1890).

26. See, however, Benno C. Schmidt, Principle and Prejudice: The Supreme Court and Race in the Progressive Era. Part 1: The Heyday of Jim Crow, 82 Colum. L. Rev. 444, 498, 523 (1982), for a more generous interpretation of the Supreme Court's motivation in *Buchanan*.

27. E.g., Neal v. Delaware, 103 U.S. 370 (1881); Carter v. Texas, 177 U.S. 442 (1900); Rogers v. Alabama, 192 U.S. 226 (1904). Cf. Yick Wo v. Hopkins, 118 U.S. 356 (1886).

28. See, e.g., Virginia v. Rives, 100 U.S. 313 (1880), holding that absent a discriminatory statute, a defendant could not remove his trial to federal court by alleging and offering to prove racial exclusion; In re Wood, 140 U.S. 278 (1891), holding that jury exclusion cannot be challenged on habeas corpus; Thomas v. Texas, 212 U.S. 278 (1909), deferring to state court's finding of no discrimination.

29. E.g., Guinn v. United States, 238 U.S. 347 (1915), striking down Oklahoma's "grandfather clause," which exempted from a literacy test all those entitled to vote in 1866 and their lineal descendants.

30. E.g., Giles v. Harris, 189 U.S. 475 (1903), holding that an action in equity could not be maintained to require supervision of voting in Montgomery County, Alabama; Giles v. Teasley, 193 U.S. 146 (1904), denying legal relief arising out of the same disfranchisement scheme.

The Court's invalidation of the Civil Rights Act of 1875 is consistent with this spirit of compromise and with its restrictive view of the scope of congressional powers.

D. Creation of the State Action Doctrine

THE CIVIL RIGHTS CASES

109 U.S. 3 (1883)

In error to, or on certificates of division in opinion between the Judges of, the Circuit Courts of the United States for the District of Kansas, District of California, Western District of Missouri, Southern District of New York, and Western District of Tennessee

[Section 1 of the Civil Rights Act of 1875 provides: "That all persons within the jurisdiction of the United States shall be entitled to the full and equal enjoyment of the accommodations, advantages, facilities, and privileges of inns, public conveyances on land or water, theatres, and other places of public amusement; subject only to the conditions and limitations established by law, and applicable alike to citizens of every race and color, regardless of any previous condition of servitude."

Section 2 makes violation of section 1 a misdemeanor and also permits an aggrieved party to recover a civil fine.

These consolidated cases, from California, Kansas, Missouri, New York, and Tennessee, arose out of the exclusion of Negroes from inns, theaters, and a railroad on account of their race.]

BRADLEY, J. . . .

[T]he primary and important question in all the cases is the constitutionality of the law . . . [the essence of which is to declare that] . . . colored citizens, whether formerly slaves or not, and citizens of other races, shall have the same accommodations and privileges in all inns, public conveyances, and places of amusement as are enjoyed by white citizens; and vice versa. . . .

Has Congress constitutional power to make such a law? Of course, no one will contend that the power to pass it was contained in the Constitution before the adoption of the last three amendments. The power is sought, first, in the Fourteenth Amendment. . . .

It is State action of a particular character that is prohibited [by the Fourteenth Amendment]. Individual invasion of individual rights is not the subject-matter of the amendment. . . . [T]he last section of the amendment invests Congress with power to enforce it by appropriate legislation. To enforce what? To enforce the prohibition. To adopt appropriate legislation for correcting the effects of such prohibited State laws and State acts, and thus to render them effectually null, void, and innocuous. . . .

And so in the present case, until some State law has been passed, or some State action through its officers or agents has been taken, adverse to the rights of citizens sought to be protected by the Fourteenth Amendment, no legislation of the United States under said amendment, nor any proceeding under such legislation, can be called into activity: for the prohibitions of the amendment are against State Laws and acts done under State authority. . . .

An inspection of the [1875 Act] shows that it makes no reference whatever to any supposed or apprehended violation of the Fourteenth Amendment on the part of the States. It is not predicated on any such view. It proceeds ex directo to declare that certain acts committed by individuals shall be deemed offenses, and shall be prosecuted and punished by proceedings in the courts of the United States. It does not profess to be corrective of any constitutional wrong committed by the States; it does not make its operation to depend upon any such wrong committed. It applies equally to cases arising in States which have the justest laws respecting the personal rights of citizens, and whose authorities are ever ready to enforce such laws, as to those which arise in States that may have violated the prohibition of the amendment. In other words, it steps into the domain of local jurisprudence, and lays down rules for the conduct of individuals in society towards each other, and imposes sanctions for the enforcement of those rules, without referring in any manner to any supposed action of the State or its authorities.

If this legislation is appropriate for enforcing the prohibitions of the amendment, it is difficult to see where it is to stop. Why may not Congress with equal show of authority enact a code of laws for the enforcement and vindication of all rights of life, liberty, and property? . . .

[C]ivil rights, such as are guaranteed by the Constitution against State aggression, cannot be impaired by the wrongful acts of individuals, unsupported by State authority in the shape of laws, customs, or judicial or executive proceedings. The wrongful act of an individual, unsupported by any such authority, is simply a private wrong, or a crime of that individual; an invasion of the rights of the injured party, it is true, whether they affect his person, his property, or his reputation; but if not sanctioned in some way by the State, or not done under State authority, his rights remain in full force, and may presumably be vindicated by resort to the laws of the State for redress. An individual cannot deprive a man of his right to vote, to hold property, to buy and sell, to sue in the courts, or to be a witness or a juror; he may, by force or fraud, interfere with the enjoyment of the right in a particular case; he may commit an assault against the person, or commit murder, or use ruffian violence at the polls, or slander the good name of a fellow citizen; but, unless protected in these wrongful acts by some shield of State law or State authority, he cannot destroy or injure the right; he will only render himself amenable to satisfaction or punishment; and amenable therefor to the laws of the State where the wrongful acts are committed. . . .

The law in question . . . is not corrective legislation; it is primary and direct; it takes immediate and absolute possession of the subject of the right of admission to inns, public conveyances, and places of amusement. It supersedes and displaces State legislation on the same subject, or only allows it permissive force. It ignores such legislation, and assumes that the matter is one that belongs to the domain of national regulation. Whether it would not have been a more effective protection of the rights of citizens to have clothed Congress with plenary power over the whole subject, is not now the question. What we have to decide is, whether such plenary power has been conferred upon Congress by the Fourteenth Amendment; and, in our judgment, it has not.

We have discussed the question presented by the law on the assumption that a right to enjoy equal accommodations and privileges in all inns, public conveyances, and places of public amusement, is one of the essential rights of the citizens which no State can abridge or interfere with. Whether it is such a right, or not, is a different question which, in the view we have taken of the validity of the law on the ground already stated, it is not necessary to examine. . . .

But the power of Congress to adopt direct and primary, as distinguished from corrective legislation, on the subject in hand, is sought, in the second place, from the Thirteenth Amendment, which abolishes slavery. This amendment declares "that neither slavery, nor involuntary servitude, except as a punishment for crime, whereof the party shall have been duly convicted, shall exist within the United States, or any place subject to their jurisdiction"; and it gives Congress power to enforce the amendment by appropriate legislation. . . . [S]uch legislation may be primary and direct in its character; for the amendment is not a mere prohibition of State laws establishing or upholding slavery, but an absolute declaration that slavery or involuntary servitude shall not exist in any part of the United States.

. . . [I]t is assumed, that the power vested in Congress to enforce the article by appropriate legislation, clothes Congress with power to pass all laws necessary and proper for abolishing all badges and incidents of slavery in the United States: and upon this assumption it is claimed, that this is sufficient authority for declaring by law that all persons shall have equal accommodations and privileges in all inns, public conveyances, and places of amusement; the argument being, that the denial of such equal accommodations and privileges is, in itself, a subjection to a species of servitude within the meaning of the amendment. Conceding the major proposition to be true, that Congress has a right to enact all necessary and proper laws for the obliteration and prevention of slavery with all its badges and incidents, is the minor proposition also true, that the denial to any person of admission to the accommodations and privileges of an inn, a public conveyance, or a theatre, does subject that person to any form of servitude, or tend to fasten upon him any badge of slavery? . . .

Can the act of a mere individual, the owner of the inn, the public conveyance or place of amusement, refusing the accommodation, be justly regarded as imposing any badge of slavery or servitude upon the applicant, or only as inflicting an ordinary civil injury, properly cognizable by the laws of the State, and presumably subject to redress by those laws until the contrary appears? . . . It would be running the slavery argument into the ground to make it apply to every act of discrimination which a person may see fit to make as to the guests he will entertain, or as to the people he will take into his coach or cab or car, or admit to his concert or theatre, or deal with in other matters of intercourse or business. Innkeepers and public carriers, by the laws of all the States, so far as we are aware, are bound, to the extent of their facilities, to furnish proper accommodation to all unobjectionable persons who in good faith apply for them. If the laws themselves make any unjust discrimination, amenable to the prohibitions of the Fourteenth Amendment, Congress has full power to afford a remedy under that amendment and in accordance with it.

When a man has emerged from slavery, and by the aid of beneficent legislation has shaken off the inseparable concomitants of that state, there must be some stage in the progress of his elevation when he takes the rank of a mere citizen, and ceases to be the special favorite of the laws, and when his rights as a citizen, or a man, are to be protected in the ordinary modes by which other men's rights are protected. There were thousands of free colored people in this country before the abolition of slavery, enjoying all the essential rights of life, liberty and property the same as white citizens; yet no one, at that time, thought that it was any invasion of his personal status as a freeman because he was not admitted to all the privileges enjoyed by white citizens, or because he was subjected to discriminations in the enjoyment of accommodations in inns, public conveyances and places of amusement. Mere discriminations on account of race or color were not regarded as badges of slavery. . . .

[T]he first and second sections of the act of Congress of March 1st, 1875, entitled "An Act to protect all citizens in their civil and legal rights," are unconstitutional and void. . . .

HARLAN, J., dissenting.

The opinion in these cases proceeds, it seems to me, upon grounds entirely too narrow and artificial. I cannot resist the conclusion that the substance and spirit of the recent amendments of the Constitution have been sacrificed by a subtle and ingenious verbal criticism. . . .

The Thirteenth Amendment, it is conceded, did something more than to prohibit slavery as an *institution,* resting upon distinctions of race, and upheld by positive law. . . . Was it the purpose of the nation simply to destroy the institution, and then remit the race, theretofore held in bondage, to the several States for such protection, in their civil rights, necessarily growing out of freedom, as those States, in their discretion, might choose to provide? Were the States against whose protest the institution was destroyed, to be left free, so far as national interference was concerned, to make or allow discriminations against that race, as such, in the enjoyment of those fundamental rights which by universal concession, inhere in a state of freedom?

That there are burdens and disabilities which constitute badges of slavery and servitude, and that the power to enforce by appropriate legislation the Thirteenth Amendment may be exerted by legislation of a direct and primary character, for the eradication, not simply of the institution, but of its badges and incidents, are propositions which ought to be deemed indisputable. They lie at the foundation of the Civil Rights Act of 1866. . . . Congress, by the act of 1866, passed in view of the Thirteenth Amendment, before the Fourteenth was adopted, undertook to remove certain burdens and disabilities, the necessary incidents of slavery, and to secure to all citizens of every race and color, and without regard to previous servitude, those fundamental rights which are the essence of civil freedom, namely, the same right to make and enforce contracts, to sue, be parties, give evidence, and to inherit, purchase, lease, sell, and convey property as is enjoyed by white citizens. . . .

I do not contend that the Thirteenth Amendment invests Congress with authority, by legislation, to define and regulate the entire body of the civil rights which citizens enjoy, or may enjoy, in the several States. But I hold that since slavery . . . was the moving or principal cause of the adoption of that amendment, and since that institution rested wholly upon the inferiority, as a race, of those held in bondage, their freedom necessarily involved immunity from, and protection against, all discrimination against them, because of their race, in respect of such civil rights as belong to freemen of other races. Congress, therefore, under its express power to enforce that amendment, by appropriate legislation, may enact laws to protect that people against the deprivation, *because of their race,* of any civil rights granted to other freemen in the same State; and such legislation may be of a direct and primary character, operating upon States, their officers and agents, and, also, upon, at least, such individuals and corporations as exercise public functions and wield power and authority under the State. . . .

It remains now to inquire what are the legal rights of colored persons in respect of the accommodations, privileges and facilities of public conveyances, inns and places of public amusement?

First, as to public conveyances on land and water. . . . In Olcott v. Supervisors, 16 Wall. 678, it was ruled that railroads are public highways, established by authority of the State for the public use; that they are none the less public highways, because controlled and owned by private corporations; that it is a part of the function of government to make and maintain highways for the convenience of the public; that no matter who is the agent, or what is the agency, the function performed is *that of the State;* that although the owners may be private companies, they may be compelled to permit the public to use these works in the manner in which they can be used; that, upon these grounds alone, have the courts sustained the investiture of railroad corporations with the State's right of eminent domain, or the right of municipal corporations, under legislative authority, to assess, levy and collect taxes to aid in the construction of railroads. . . .

Such being the relations these corporations hold to the public, it would seem that the right of a colored person to use an improved public highway, upon the terms accorded to freemen of other races, is as fundamental, in the state of freedom established in this country, as are any of the rights which my brethren concede to be so far fundamental as to be deemed the essence of civil freedom. "Personal liberty consists," says Blackstone, "in the power of locomotion, of changing situation, or removing one's person to whatever places one's own inclination may direct, without restraint, unless by due course of law." But of what value is this right of locomotion, if it may be clogged by such burdens as Congress intended by the act of 1875 to remove? They are burdens which lay at the very foundation of the institution of slavery as it once existed. . . .

Second, as to inns. The same general observations which have been made as to railroads are applicable to inns. . . . In Rex v. Ivens, 7 Carrington & Payne, 213, 32 E.C.L. 495, the court, speaking by Mr. Justice Coleridge, said:

> An indictment lies against an innkeeper who refuses to receive a guest, he having at the time room in his house; and either the price of the guest's entertainment being tendered to him, or such circumstances occurring as will dispense with that tender. This law is founded in good sense. The innkeeper is not to select his guests. He has no right to say to one, you shall come to my inn, and to another you shall not, as every one coming and conducting himself in a proper manner has a right to be received; and for this purpose innkeepers are a sort of public servants, they having in return a kind of privilege of entertaining travellers and supplying them with what they want.

. . . [A] keeper of an inn is in the exercise of a quasi-public employment. The law gives him special privileges and he is charged with certain duties and responsibilities to the public. The public nature of his employment forbids him from discriminating against any person asking admission as a guest on account of the race or color of that person.

Third. As to places of public amusement. . . . [P]laces of public amusement, within the meaning of the act of 1875, are such as are established and maintained under direct license of the law. The authority to establish and maintain them comes from the public. The colored race is a part of that public. The local government granting the license represents them as well as all other races within its jurisdiction. A license from the public to establish a place of public amusement, imports, in law, equality of right, at such places, among all the members of that public. . . .

I am of the opinion that such discrimination practised by corporations and individuals in the exercise of their public or quasi-public functions is a badge of servitude the imposition of which Congress may prevent under its power, by appropriate legislation, to enforce the Thirteenth Amendment; and consequently, without reference to its enlarged power under the Fourteenth Amendment, the act of March 1, 1875, is not, in my judgment, repugnant to the Constitution.

It remains now to consider these cases with reference to the power Congress has possessed since the adoption of the Fourteenth Amendment. Much that has been said as to the power of Congress under the Thirteenth Amendment is applicable to this branch of the discussion, and will not be repeated. . . .

The assumption that this amendment consists wholly of prohibitions upon State laws and State proceedings in hostility to its provisions, is unauthorized by its language. The first clause of the first section — "All persons born or naturalized in the United States, and subject to the jurisdiction thereof, are citizens of the United States, and of the State wherein they reside" — is of a distinctly affirmative character. . . .

The citizenship thus acquired, by [the colored] race, in virtue of an affirmative grant from the nation, may be protected, not alone by the judicial branch of the government, but by congressional legislation of a primary direct character; this, because the power of Congress is not restricted to the enforcement of prohibitions upon State laws or State action. It is, in terms distinct and positive, to enforce "the *provisions* of *this article*" of amendment; not simply those of a prohibitive character, but the provisions — *all* of the provisions — affirmative and prohibitive, of the amendment. . . .

It is, therefore, an essential inquiry what, if any, right, privilege or immunity was given, by the nation, to colored persons when they were made citizens of the State in which they reside. . . . That they became entitled, upon the adoption of the Fourteenth Amendment, "to all privileges and immunities of citizens in the several States," within the meaning of section 2 of article 4 of the Constitution, no one, I suppose, will for a moment question. What are the privileges and immunities to which, by that clause of the Constitution, they became entitled? To this it may be answered, generally, upon the authority of the adjudged cases, that they are those which are fundamental in citizenship in a free republican government, such as are "common to the citizens in the latter States under their constitutions and laws by virtue of their being citizens." . . .

But what was secured to colored citizens of the United States — as between them and their respective States — by the national grant to them of State citizenship? With what rights, privileges, or immunities did this grant invest them? There is one, if there be no other — exemption from race discrimination in respect of any civil right belonging to citizens of the white race in the same State.

That, surely, is their constitutional privilege when within the jurisdiction of other States. And such must be their constitutional right, in their own State, unless the recent amendments be splendid baubles, thrown out to delude those who deserved fair and generous treatment at the hands of the nation. Citizenship in this country necessarily imports at least equality of civil rights among citizens of every race in the same State. . . . If the grant to colored citizens of the United States of citizenship in their respective States, imports exemption from race discrimination, in their States, in respect of such civil rights as belong to citizenship, then, to hold that the amendment remits that right to the States for their protection, primarily, and stays the hands of the nation, until it is assailed by State laws or State proceedings, is to adjudge that the amendment, so far from enlarging the powers of Congress — as we have heretofore said it did — not only curtails them, but reverses the policy which the general government has pursued from its very organization. . . .

But if it were conceded that the power of Congress could not be brought into activity until the rights specified in the act of 1875 had been abridged or denied by some State law or State action, I maintain that . . . [t]here has been adverse State Action within the Fourteenth Amendment. . . .

In every material sense applicable to the practical enforcement of the Fourteenth Amendment, railroad corporations, keepers of inns, and managers of places of public amusement are agents or instrumentalities of the State, because they are charged with duties to the public, and are amenable, in respect of their duties and functions, to governmental regulation. It seems to me that . . . a denial, by these instrumentalities of the State, to the citizen, because of his race, of that equality of civil rights secured to him by law, is a denial by the State, within the meaning of the Fourteenth Amendment. If it be not, then that race is left, in respect of the civil rights in question, practically at the mercy of corporations and individuals wielding power under the States. . . .

Discussion

1. The Civil Rights Cases established three distinct propositions:

a. The Thirteenth Amendment, though it addresses private persons as well as governments, does not prohibit, or empower Congress to prohibit, most racially discriminatory practices other than involuntary servitude (which it prohibits regardless of race). This holding was substantially undercut by Jones v. Alfred H. Mayer Co., 392 U.S. 409 (1968), Chapter 10 infra.

b. The Fourteenth Amendment does not empower Congress to forbid discrimination by private persons. This holding was partly questioned by a majority of the justices participating in United States v. Guest, 383 U.S. 745 (1966), but the Court has not formally addressed the issue.

c. A fortiori from b, the Fourteenth Amendment does not of its own force prevent private discrimination, as distinguished from discrimination imposed or supported by the state. This remains the articulated doctrine today: The Fourteenth Amendment reaches "only such action as may fairly be said to be that of the States." Yet Shelley v. Kraemer, 334 U.S. 1 (1948), Chapter 10 infra, the very case in which that statement was made, is generally thought to undermine the "state action" doctrine significantly. The notion of what is "fairly" attributable to the states has expanded to an extent not readily inferred from this formulation.

2. Focusing on the Thirteenth Amendment as a possible source of congressional power forces us to confront what precisely constitute the evils of chattel slavery. If the evil lies in the system of racial oppression, can we say that slavery continued in the United States even after the abolition of the particular labor structure usually identified with that practice?

3. None of the owners of public accommodations in the Civil Rights Cases claimed an "ultimate" constitutional right to engage in the discriminatory conduct at issue. The protection extends only against federal regulation; state antidiscrimination regulation is presumptively legitimate. Contrast this with conduct protected under the First Amendment, where it is essentially irrelevant whether the claimed right is abridged at the federal, state, or local level. See also Justice Miller's concern in the Slaughter-House Cases, page 263 infra, over the implications for federalism of an expansive reading of the Privileges and Immunities Clause. Similarly, the Civil Rights Cases can be viewed as emphasizing the minimal role of the national government as a guarantor of "personal" rights and liberties. Should the Civil War Amendments be read as only minimally changing the antebellum relationship between national and state government?

4. As part of his attack on the majority's niggardly reading of Congress' power to implement the Thirteenth and Fourteenth Amendments, Justice Harlan notes the quite different approach to analyzing congressional power in Prigg v. Pennsylvania, Chapter 3 supra, which upheld the Fugitive Slave Law of 1793. Justice Harlan described *Prigg* as resting on the propositions

> That a clause of the Constitution conferring a right [in that instance the Fugitive Slave Clause of Article IV] should not be so construed as to make it shadowy, or unsubstantial, or leave the citizen without a remedial power adequate for its protection, when another construction equally accordant with the words and the sense in which they were used, would enforce and protect the right granted;
>
> That Congress is not restricted to legislation for the execution of its expressly granted powers; but, for the protection of rights guaranteed by the Constitution, may employ such means, not prohibited, as are necessary and proper; or such as are appropriate, to attain the ends proposed;
>
> That the Constitution recognized the master's right of property in his fugitive slave, and, as incidental thereto, the right of seizing and recovering him, regardless of any State law, or regulation, or local custom whatsoever; and
>
> That the right of the master to have his slave, thus escaping, delivered up on claim, being guaranteed by the Constitution, the fair implication was that the national government was clothed with appropriate authority and functions to enforce it.

Harlan appears to be arguing that, whereas the pre-War Constitution protected the rights of the slaveowner (and thus implicitly authorized Congress to pass legislation assuring the practical enforcement of his rights), the newly amended post-War Constitution, through the Thirteenth and Fourteenth Amendments, now protects the rights of Americans to be free from racial discrimination (and thus should be interpreted as authorizing Congress to pass whatever legislation it deems necessary to assure the practical enforcement of *those* rights). The majority does not suggest that the hotel owners and other purveyors of public accommodations have a right to engage in the discriminatory conduct; it appears to assume that such conduct is barred by the common law and that states will indeed enforce the right of nondiscriminatory access to public accommodations. It holds only that Congress is without the power to offer federal protection to the victims of such discrimination, thus leaving them to whatever procedures the states wish to adopt.

Pennsylvania had not formally resisted its obligations to return fugitive slaves; it merely insisted that slaveowners submit themselves to Pennsylvania procedures designed to assure that those asserted to be fugitive slaves were actually so. Yet those laws were struck down, and Congress was deemed to have power to supplant them by passing national legislation. Is it fair to describe the Court as more imaginative, in regard to its interpretation of federal power, regarding the rights of slaveowners than those of the new African-American citizens of the United States?

II. The Protection of Economic Rights

A. The Fourteenth Amendment Limited

The central purpose of the Thirteenth (1865), Fourteenth (1868), and Fifteenth (1870) Amendments — sometimes called the "Civil War" or "Reconstruction" amendments — was to help provide what Lincoln might have termed "a new birth of freedom" for the recently emancipated slaves. The central question posed to constitutional interpreters of the Fourteenth Amendment was what comprised the rights and freedoms presumably guaranteed. For example, did the Fourteenth Amendment protect the former slaves by preventing only discriminatory treatment of them (and other blacks) relative to the majority white population? Or, instead, did it guarantee to blacks (and the general population, including nonblacks) a *substantive* set of rights that were protected against governmental interference? The Court readily decided that the Amendment did not protect the political rights of access to the ballot. But this was a different question from what constituted the "civil" rights that all parties to the debate conceded, at least in the abstract, were to be protected by the new constitutional language.

Rogers Smith argues that the Thirteenth and Fourteenth Amendments must be understood in the context of the "free labor" ideology of the Republican Party, with its Lockean insistence "that although the races might not be fully equal in all respects, every human being had a natural right to pursue his trade and reap the fruits of his labor."[31] The first case testing the meaning of "free labor" as a civil right was the Slaughter-House Cases, where, writes Smith, "New Orleans butchers challenged a monopolistic slaughterhouse charter, granted by the state's North-dominated Reconstruction legislature, which forced them to work at the Crescent City Slaughter-House Company's facilities or give up their trade." In Smith's words, the butchers claimed that by depriving them of the chance to practice their trade outside of the monopoly's facilities, the law "violated the most fun-

31. Rogers Smith, "One United People": Second-Class Female Citizenship and the American Quest for Community, 1 Yale J. of L. & Humanities 229, 257 (1989). The classic scholarly treatment of this ideology is Eric Foner, Free Soil, Free Labor, Free Men (1970). See also Eric Foner, Reconstruction: America's Unfinished Revolution 1863-1877, 228-280 (1988).

damental right in liberal 'free labor' ideology, the right to labor productively, to pursue their vocation and reap the fruits of their efforts."[32] On behalf of the butchers, former Supreme Court Justice John Campbell argued that the citizenship protected by the Fourteenth Amendment "was based on the liberal commitment to securing fundamental rights against all threats, including any from the states. High among these rights, as 'property of a sacred kind,' was the 'right to labor . . . and to the product of one's faculties.' "[33]

THE SLAUGHTER-HOUSE CASES

83 U.S. (16 Wall.) 36 (1873)
Error to the Supreme Court of Louisiana

[In 1869, Louisiana enacted a statute entitled "An act to protect the health of the city of New Orleans, to locate the stock-landings and slaughter-houses, and to incorporate the Crescent City Live-Stock Landing and Slaughter-House Company." The act authorized the company to construct a large slaughterhouse, available to any butcher in the city on payment of reasonable compensation, and prohibited the maintenance of any other abattoirs. Its purpose, as described by the Court, was "to remove from the more densely populated part of the city, the noxious slaughter-houses, and large and offensive collections of animals necessarily incident to the slaughtering business of a large city, and to locate them where the convenience, health, and comfort of the people require. . . ."]

MILLER, J. . . .

It is not, and cannot be successfully controverted, that it is both the right and the duty of the legislative body — the supreme power of the State or municipality — to prescribe and determine the localities where the business of slaughtering for a great city may be conducted. To do this effectively it is indispensable that all persons who slaughter animals for food shall do it in those places *and nowhere else.*

The statute under consideration defines these localities and forbids slaughtering in any other. It does not, as has been asserted, prevent the butcher from doing his own slaughtering. On the contrary, the Slaughter-House Company is required, under a heavy penalty, to permit any person who wishes to do so, to slaughter in their houses; and they are bound to make ample provision for the convenience of all the slaughtering for the entire city. The butcher then is still permitted to slaughter, to prepare, and to sell his own meats; but he is required to slaughter at a specified place and to pay a reasonable compensation for the use of the accommodations furnished him at that place.

The wisdom of the monopoly granted by the legislature may be open to question, but it is difficult to see a justification for the assertion that the butchers are deprived of the right to labor in their occupation, or the people of their daily service in preparing food, or how this statute, with the duties and guards imposed upon the company, can be said to destroy the business of the butcher, or seriously interfere with its pursuit.

32. Smith, supra note 31, at 259.
33. Id.

The power here exercised by the legislature of Louisiana is, in its essential nature, one which has been, up to the present period in the constitutional history of this country, always conceded to belong to the States, however it may *now* be questioned in some of its details.

"Unwholesome trades, slaughter-houses, operations offensive to the senses, the deposit of powder, the application of steam power to propel cars, the building with combustible materials, and the burial of the dead, may all," says Chancellor Kent, "be interdicted by law, in the midst of dense masses of population, on the general and rational principle, that every person ought so to use his property as not to injure his neighbors; and that private interests must be made subservient to the general interests of the community." This is called the police power. . . .

This power is, and must be from its very nature, incapable of any very exact definition or limitation. Upon it depends the security of social order, the life and health of the citizen, the comfort of an existence in a thickly populated community, the enjoyment of private and social life, and the beneficial use of property. "It extends . . . to the protection of the lives, limbs, health, comfort, and quiet of all persons, and the protection of all" property within the State; . . . and persons and property are subjected to all kinds of restraints and burdens in order to secure the general comfort, health, and prosperity of the State. Of the perfect right of the legislature to do this no question ever was, or, upon acknowledged general principles, ever can be made, so far as natural persons are concerned."

The regulation of the place and manner of conducting the slaughtering of animals, and the business of butchering within a city, and the inspection of the animals to be killed for meat, and of the meat afterwards, are among the most necessary and frequent exercises of this power. It is not, therefore, needed that we should seek for a comprehensive definition, but rather look for the proper source of its exercise.

In Gibbons v. Ogden, Chief Justice Marshall, speaking of inspection laws passed by the States, says: "They form a portion of that immense mass of legislation which controls everything within the territory of a State not surrendered to the General Government — all which can be most advantageously administered by the States themselves. . . ."

The exclusive authority of State legislation over this subject is strikingly illustrated in the case of the City of New York v. Miln. . . .

It cannot be denied that the statute under consideration is aptly framed to remove from the more densely populated part of the city, the noxious slaughter-houses, and large and offensive collections of animals necessarily incident to the slaughtering business of a large city, and to locate them where the convenience, health, and comfort of the people require they shall be located. And it must be conceded that the means adopted by the act for this purpose are appropriate, are stringent, and effectual. But it is said that in creating a corporation for this purpose, and conferring upon it exclusive privileges — privileges which it is said constitute a monopoly — the legislature has exceeded its power. If this statute had imposed on the city of New Orleans precisely the same duties, accompanied by the same privileges, which it has on the corporation which it created, it is believed that no question would have been raised as to its constitutionality. In that case the effect on the butchers in pursuit of their occupation and on the public would have been the same as it is now. Why cannot the legislature confer the same powers on another corporation, created for a lawful and useful public object, that it can on the municipal corporation already existing? That wherever a legislature has the right to accomplish a certain result, and that result is best attained by means of a corporation, it has the right to create such a corporation, and to endow it with the powers necessary to effect the desired and lawful purpose, seems hardly to admit of debate. The proposition is ably discussed and affirmed in the case of McCulloch v. The State of Maryland, in relation to the power of Congress to organize the Bank of the United States to aid in the fiscal operations of the government. . . .

Unless, therefore, it can be maintained that the exclusive privilege granted by this charter to the corporation, is beyond the power of the legislature of Louisiana, there can be no just exception to the validity of the statute. And in this respect we are not able to see that these privileges are especially odious or objectionable. . . .

It may, therefore, be considered as established, that the authority of the legislature of Louisiana to pass the present statute is ample, unless some restraint in the exercise of that power be found in the constitution of that State or in the amendments to the Constitution of the United States, adopted since the date of the decisions we have already cited.

If any such restraint is supposed to exist in the constitution of the State, the Supreme Court of Louisiana having necessarily passed on that question, it would not be open to review in this court.

The plaintiffs in error accepting this issue, allege that the statute is a violation of the Constitution of the United States in these several particulars:

That it creates an involuntary servitude forbidden by the thirteenth article of amendment;

That it abridges the privileges and immunities of citizens of the United States;

That it denies to the plaintiffs the equal protection of the laws; and,

That it deprives them of their property without due process of law; contrary to the provisions of the first section of the fourteenth article of amendment.

This court is thus called upon for the first time to give construction to these articles. . . .

The most cursory glance at these articles discloses a unity of purpose, when taken in connection with the history of the times, which cannot fail to have an important bearing on any question of doubt concerning their true meaning. Nor can such doubts, when any reasonably exist, be safely and rationally solved without a reference to that history; for in it is found the occasion and the necessity for recurring again to the great source of power in this country, the people of the States, for additional guarantees of human rights; additional powers to the Federal government; additional restraints upon those of the States. Fortunately that history is fresh within the memory of us all, and its leading features, as they bear upon the matter before us, free from doubt. . . .

We repeat, then, in the light of this recapitulation of events, almost too recent to be called history, but which are familiar to us all; and on the most casual examination of the language of these amendments, no one can fail to be impressed with the one pervading purpose found in them all, lying at the foundation of each, and without which none of them would have been even suggested; we mean the freedom of the slave race, the security and firm establishment of that freedom, and the protection of the newly-made freeman and citizen from the oppressions of those who had formerly exercised unlimited dominion over him. It is true that only the fifteenth amendment, in terms, mentions the negro by speaking of his color and his slavery. But it is just as true that each of the other articles was addressed to the grievances of that race, and designed to remedy them as the fifteenth.

We do not say that no one else but the negro can share in this protection. Both the language and spirit of these articles are to have their fair and just weight in any question of construction. Undoubtedly while negro slavery alone was in the mind of the Congress which proposed the thirteenth article, it forbids any other kind of slavery, now or hereafter. If Mexican peonage or the Chinese coolie labor system shall develop slavery of the Mexican or Chinese race within our territory, this amendment may safely be trusted to make it void. And so if other rights are assailed by the States which properly and necessarily fall within the protection of these articles, that protection will apply, though the party interested may not be of African descent. But what we do say, and what we wish to be understood, is, that in any fair and just construction of any section or phrase of these amendments, it is necessary to look to the purpose which we have said was the pervading spirit of them all, the evil which they were designed to remedy, and the process of continued addition to the Constitution, until that purpose was supposed to be accomplished, as far as constitutional law can accomplish it. . . . [Justice Miller summarily dismisses appellants' claim based on the Thirteenth Amendment.]

The first section of the fourteenth article, to which our attention is more specially invited, opens with a definition of citizenship — not only citizenship of the United States, but citizenship of the States. No such definition was previously found in the Constitution, nor had any attempt been made to define it by act of Congress . . . . But it had been held by this court, in the celebrated *Dred Scott* case, only a few years before the outbreak of the civil war, that a man of African descent, whether a slave or not, was not and could not be a citizen of a State or of the United States. This decision, while it met the condemnation of some of the ablest statesmen and constitutional lawyers of the country, had never been overruled; and if it was to be accepted as a constitutional limitation of the right of citizenship, then all the negro race who had recently been made freemen, were still, not only not citizens, but were incapable of becoming so by anything short of an amendment to the Constitution.

To remove this difficulty primarily, and to establish a clear and comprehensive definition of citizenship which should declare what should constitute citizenship of the United States, and also citizenship of a State, the first clause of the first section was framed.

"All persons born or naturalized in the United States, and subject to the jurisdiction thereof, are citizens of the United States and of the State wherein they reside."

The first observation we have to make on this clause is, that it puts at rest both the questions which we stated to have been the subject of differences of opinion. It declares that persons may be citizens of the United States without regard to their citizenship of a particular State, and it overturns the *Dred Scott* decision by making *all persons* born within the United States and subject to its jurisdiction citizens of the United States. That its main purpose was to establish the citizenship of the negro can admit of no doubt. The phrase, "subject to its jurisdiction" was intended to exclude from its operation children of ministers, consuls, and citizens or subjects of foreign States born within the United States.

The next observation is more important in view of the arguments of counsel in the present case. It is, that the distinction between citizenship of the United States and citizenship of a State is clearly recognized and established. Not only may a man be a citizen of the United States without being a citizen of a State, but an important element is necessary to convert the former into the latter. He must reside within the State to make him a citizen of it, but it is only necessary that he should be born or naturalized in the United States to be a citizen of the Union.

It is quite clear, then, that there is a citizenship of the United States, and a citizenship of a State, which are distinct from each other, and which depend upon different characteristics or circumstances in the individual.

[*Privileges or immunities.*] We think this distinction and its explicit recognition in this amendment of great weight in this argument, because the next paragraph of this same section, which is the one mainly relied on by the plaintiffs in error, speaks only of privileges and immunities of citizens of the United States, and does not speak of those of citizens of the several States. The argument, however, in favor of the plaintiffs rests wholly on the assumption that the citizenship is the same, and the privileges and immunities guaranteed by the clause are the same.

The language is, "No State shall make or enforce any law which shall abridge the privileges or immunities of citizens of *the United States.*" It is a little remarkable, if this clause was intended as a protection to the citizen of a State against the legislative power of his own State, that the word citizen of the State should be left out when it is so carefully used, and used in contradistinction to citizens of the United States, in the very sentence which precedes it. It is too clear for argument that the change in phraseology was adopted understandingly and with a purpose.

Of the privileges and immunities of the citizen of the United States, and of the privileges and immunities of the citizen of the State, and what they respectively are, we will presently consider; but we wish to state here that it is only the former which are placed by this clause under the protection of the Federal Constitution, and that the latter, whatever they may be, are not intended to have any additional protection by this paragraph of the amendment.

If, then, there is a difference between the privileges and immunities belonging to a citizen of the United States as such, and those belonging to the citizen of the State as such the latter must rest for their security and protection where they have heretofore rested; for they are not embraced by this paragraph of the amendment. . . .

The first and the leading case on the [privileges and immunities clause of Article IV] is that of Corfield v. Coryell, decided by Mr. Justice Washington in the Circuit Court for the District of Pennsylvania in 1823. "The inquiry," he says, "is, what are the privileges and immunities of citizens of the several States? We feel no hesitation in confining these expressions to those privileges and immunities which are *fundamental;* which belong of right to the citizens of all free governments, and which have at all times been enjoyed by citizens of the several States which compose this Union, from the time of their becoming free, independent, and sovereign. What these fundamental principles are, it would be more tedious than difficult to enumerate. They may all, however, be comprehended under the following general heads: protection by the government, with the right to acquire and possess property of every kind, and to pursue and obtain happiness and safety, subject, nevertheless, to such restraints as the government may prescribe for the general good of the whole." . . .

In the case of Paul v. Virginia, the court, in expounding this clause of the Constitution, says that "the privileges and immunities secured to citizens of each State in the several States, by the provision in question, are those privileges and immunities which are common to the citizens in the latter States under their constitution and laws by virtue of their being citizens." . . .

Was it the purpose of the fourteenth amendment, by the simple declaration that no State should make or enforce any law which shall abridge the privileges and immunities of *citizens of the United States,* to transfer the security and protection of all the civil rights which we have mentioned, from the States to the Federal government? And where it is declared that Congress shall have the power to enforce that article, was it intended to bring within the power of Congress the entire domain of civil rights heretofore belonging exclusively to the States?

All this and more must follow, if the proposition of the plaintiffs in error be sound. For not only are these rights subject to the control of Congress whenever in its discretion any of them are supposed to be abridged by State legislation, but that body may also pass laws in advance, limiting and restricting the exercise of legislative power by the States, in their most ordinary and usual functions, as in its judgment it may think proper on all such subjects. And still further, such a construction followed by the reversal of the judgments of the Supreme Court of Louisiana in these cases, would constitute this court a perpetual censor upon all legislation of the States, on the civil rights of their own citizens, with authority to nullify such as it did not approve as consistent with those rights, as they existed at the time of the adoption of this amendment. The argument we admit is not always the most conclusive which is drawn from the consequences urged against the adoption of a particular construction of an instrument. But when, as in the case before us, these consequences are so serious, so far-reaching and pervading, so great a departure from the structure and spirit of our institutions; when the effect is to fetter and degrade the State governments by subjecting them to the control of Congress, in the exercise of powers heretofore universally conceded to them of the most ordinary and fundamental character; when in fact it radically changes the whole theory of the relations of the State and Federal governments to each other and of both these governments to the people; the argument has a force that is irresistible, in the absence of language which expresses such a purpose too clearly to admit of doubt.

We are convinced that no such results were intended by the Congress which proposed these amendments, nor by the legislatures of the States which ratified them.

But lest it should be said that no such privileges and immunities are to be found if those we have been considering are excluded, we venture to suggest some which owe their existence to the Federal government, its National character, its Constitution, or its laws.

One of these is well described in the case of Crandall v. Nevada, 73 U.S. (6 Wall.) 35 (1867). It is said to be the right of the citizen of this great country, protected by implied guarantees of its Constitution, "to come to the seat of government to assert any claim he may have upon that government, to transact any business he may have with it, to seek its protection, to share its offices, to engage in administering its functions. He has the right of free access to its seaports, through which all operations of foreign commerce are conducted, to the subtreasuries, land offices, and courts of justice in the several States." . . .

Another privilege of a citizen of the United States is to demand the care and protection of the Federal government over his life, liberty, and property when on the high seas or within the jurisdiction of a foreign government. Of this there can be no doubt, nor that the right depends upon his character as a citizen of the United States. The right to peaceably assemble and petition for redress of grievances, the privilege of the writ of habeas corpus, are rights of the citizen guaranteed by the Federal Constitution. The right to use the navigable waters of the United States, however they may penetrate the territory of the several States, all rights secured to our citizens by treaties with foreign nations, are dependent upon citizenship of the United States, and not citizenship of a State. One of these privileges is conferred by the very article under consideration. It is that a citizen of the United States can, of his own volition, become a citizen of any State of the Union by a bona fide residence therein, with the same rights as other citizens of that State. To these may be added the rights secured by the thirteenth and fifteenth articles of amendment, and by the other clause of the fourteenth, next to be considered. . . .

[*Due process.*] The argument has not been much pressed in these cases that the defendant's charter deprives the plaintiffs of their property without due process of law, or that it denies to them the equal protection of the law. The first of these paragraphs has been in the Constitution since the adoption of the fifth amendment, as a restraint upon the Federal power. It is also to be found in some form of expression in the constitutions of nearly all the States, as a restraint upon the power of the States. This law, then, has practically been the same as it now is during the existence of the government, except so far as the present amendment may place the restraining power over the States in this matter in the hands of the Federal government.

We are not without judicial interpretation, therefore, both State and National, of the meaning of this clause. And it is sufficient to say that under no construction of that provision that we have ever seen, or any that we deem admissible, can the restraint imposed by the State of Louisiana upon the exercise of their trade by the butchers of New Orleans be held to be a deprivation of property within the meaning of that provision. . . .

[*Equal protection.*] In the light of the history of these amendments, and the pervading purpose of them, . . . it is not difficult to give a meaning to [the equal protection] clause. The existence of laws in the States where the newly emancipated negroes resided, which discriminated with gross injustice and hardship against them as a class, was the evil to be remedied by this clause, and by it such laws are forbidden.

FIELD, J., dissenting. . . .

No one will deny the abstract justice which lies in the position of the plaintiffs in error; and I shall endeavor to show that the position has some support in the fundamental law of the country.

It is contended in justification for the act in question that it was adopted in the interest of the city, to promote its cleanliness and protect its health, and was the legitimate exercise of what is termed the police power of the State. That power undoubtedly extends to all regulations affecting the health, good order, morals, peace, and safety of society, and is exercised on a great variety of subjects, and in almost numberless ways. All sorts of restrictions and burdens are imposed under it, and when these are not in conflict with any constitutional prohibitions, or fundamental principles, they cannot be successfully assailed in a judicial tribunal. With this power of the State and its legitimate exercise I shall not differ from the majority of the court. But under the pretence of prescribing a police regulation the State cannot be permitted to encroach upon any of the just rights of the citizen, which the Constitution intended to secure against abridgment.

In the law in question there are only two provisions which can properly be called police regulations — the one which requires the landing and slaughtering of animals below the city of New Orleans, and the other which requires the inspection of the animals before they are slaughtered. When these requirements are complied with, the sanitary purposes of the act are accomplished. In all other particulars the act is a mere grant to a corporation created by it of special and exclusive privileges by which the health of the city is in no way promoted. It is plain that if the corporation can, without endangering the health of the public, carry on the business of landing, keeping, and slaughtering cattle within a district below the city embracing an area of over a thousand square miles, it would not endanger the public health if other persons were also permitted to carry on the same business within the same district under similar conditions as to the inspection of the animals. . . .

It is also sought to justify the act in question on the same principle that exclusive grants for ferries, bridges, and turnpikes are sanctioned. But it can find no support there. The grant, with exclusive privileges of a right thus appertaining to the government, is a very different thing from a grant, with exclusive privileges, of a right to pursue one of the ordinary trades or callings of life, which is a right appertaining solely to the individual. . . .

The act of Louisiana presents the naked case, unaccompanied by any public considerations, where a right to pursue a lawful and necessary calling, previously enjoyed by every citizen, and in connection with which a thousand persons were daily employed, is taken away and vested exclusively for twenty-five years, for an extensive district and a large population, in a single corporation. . . .

If exclusive privileges of this character can be granted to a corporation of seventeen persons, they may, in the discretion of the legislature, be equally granted to a single individual. If they may be granted for twenty-five years they may be equally granted for a century, and in perpetuity. If they may be granted for the landing and keeping of animals intended for sale or slaughter they may be equally . . . granted for any of the pursuits of human industry, even in its most simple and common forms. Indeed, upon the theory on which the exclusive privileges granted by the act in question are sustained, there is no monopoly, in the most odious form, which may not be upheld.

The question presented is, therefore, one of the gravest importance, not merely to the parties here, but to the whole country. It is nothing less than the question whether the recent amendments to the Federal Constitution protect the citizens of the United States against the deprivation of their common rights by State legislation. In my judgment the fourteenth amendment does afford such protection, and was so intended by the Congress which framed and the States which adopted it. . . .

[Under the] first clause of the fourteenth amendment . . . , [a] citizen of a State is now only a citizen of the United States residing in that State. The fundamental rights, privileges, and immunities which belong to him as a free man and a free citizen, now belong to him as a citizen of the United States, and are not dependent upon his citizenship of any State. . . .

If under the fourth article of the Constitution equality of privileges and immunities is secured between citizens of different States, under the fourteenth amendment the same equality is secured between citizens of the United States.

It will not be pretended that under the fourth article of the Constitution any State could create a monopoly in any known trade or manufacture in favor of her own citizens, or any portion of them, which would exclude an equal participation in the trade or manufacture monopolized by citizens of other States. She could not confer, for example, upon any of her citizens the sole right to manufacture shoes, or boots, or silk, or the sole right to sell those articles in the State so as to exclude non-resident citizens from engaging in a similar manufacture or sale. . . .

Now, what the clause in question does for the protection of citizens of one State against the creation of monopolies in favor of citizens of other States, the fourteenth amendment does for the protection of every citizen of the United States against the creation of any monopoly whatever. The privileges and immunities of citizens of the United States, of every one of them, is secured against abridgment in any form by any State. The fourteenth amendment places them under the guardianship of the National authority. All monopolies in any known trade or manufacture are an invasion of these privileges, for they encroach upon the liberty of citizens to acquire property and pursue happiness. . . .

That amendment was intended to give practical effect to the declaration of 1776 of inalienable rights, rights which are the gift of the Creator, which the law does not confer, but only recognizes. . . .

[The] equality of right, with exemption from all disparaging and partial enactments, in the lawful pursuits of life, throughout the whole country, is the distinguishing privilege of citizens of the United States. To them, everywhere, all pursuits, all professions, all avocations are open without other restrictions than such as are imposed equally upon all others of the same age, sex, and condition. The State may prescribe such regulations for every pursuit and calling of life as will promote the public health, secure the good order and advance the general prosperity of society, but when once prescribed, the pursuit or calling must be free to be followed by every citizen who is within the conditions designated, and will conform to the regulations. This is the fundamental idea upon which our institutions rest, and unless adhered to in the legislation of the country our government will be a republic only in name. The fourteenth amendment, in my judgment, makes it essential to the validity of the legislation of every State that this equality of right should be respected. . . .

I am authorized by the Chief Justice, Mr. Justice Swayne, and Mr. Justice Bradley, to state that they concur with me in this dissenting opinion.

BRADLEY, J., also dissenting:

I concur in the opinion which has just been read by Mr. Justice Field; but desire to add a few observations for the purpose of more fully illustrating my views on the important question decided in these cases, and the special grounds on which they rest. . . .

The people of this country brought with them to its shores the rights of Englishmen; the rights which had been wrested from English sovereigns at various periods of the nation's history. One of these fundamental rights was expressed in these words, found in Magna Carta: "No freeman shall be taken or imprisoned or be dissected of his freehold or liberties or free customs, or be outlawed or exiled, or any otherwise destroyed; nor will we pass upon him or condemn him but by lawful judgment of his peers or by the law of the land." English constitutional writers expound this article as rendering life, liberty, and property inviolable, except by due process of law. This is the very right which the plaintiffs in error claim in this case. . . . Blackstone classifies these fundamental rights under three heads, as the absolute rights of individuals, to wit: the right of personal security, the right of personal liberty, and the right of private property. . . . These are the fundamental rights which can only be taken away by due process of law, and which can only be interfered with, or the enjoyment of which can only be modified, by lawful regulations necessary or proper for the mutual good of all; and these rights, I contend, belong to the citizens of every free government.

For the preservation, exercise, and enjoyment of these rights the individual citizen, as a necessity, must be left free to adopt such calling, profession, or trade as may seem to him most conducive to that end. Without this right he cannot be a freeman. This right to choose one's calling is an essential part of that liberty which it is the object of government to protect; and a calling, when chosen, is a man's property and right. Liberty and property are not protected where these rights are arbitrarily assailed. . . .

The Constitution, it is true, as it stood prior to the recent amendments, specifies, in terms, only a few of the personal privileges and immunities of citizens, but they are very comprehensive in their character. The States were merely prohibited from passing bills of attainder, ex post facto laws, laws impairing the obligation of contracts, and perhaps one or two more. But others of the greatest consequence were enumerated, although they were only secured, in express terms, from invasion by the Federal government; such as the right of habeas corpus, the right of trial by jury, of free exercise of religious worship, the right of free speech and a free press, the right peaceably to assemble for the discussion of public measures, the right to be secure against unreasonable searches and seizures, and above all, and including almost all the rest, the right of *not being deprived of life, liberty, or property, without due process of law.* These, and still others are specified in the original Constitution, or in the early amendments of it, as among the privileges and immunities of citizens of the United States, or, what is still stronger for the force of the argument, the rights of all persons, whether citizens or not. . . .

Admitting . . . that formerly the States were not prohibited from infringing any of the fundamental privileges and immunities of citizens of the United States, except in a few specified cases, that cannot be said now, since the adoption of the fourteenth amendment. In my judgment, it was the intention of the people of this country in adopting that amendment to provide National security against violation by the States of the fundamental rights of the citizen.

. . . [A]ny law which establishes a sheer monopoly, depriving a large class of citizens of the privilege of pursuing a lawful employment, does abridge the privileges of those citizens. . . . [It also deprives them] of liberty as well as property, without due process of law. Their right of choice is a portion of their liberty; their occupation is their property. Such a law also deprives those citizens of the equal protection of the laws, contrary to the last clause of the section. . . .

It is futile to argue that none but persons of the African race are intended to be benefited by this amendment. They may have been the primary cause of the amendment, but its language is general, embracing all citizens, and I think it was purposely so expressed.

The mischief to be remedied was not merely slavery and its incidents and consequences; but that spirit of insubordination and disloyalty to the National government which had troubled the country for so many years in some of the States, and that intolerance of free speech and free discussion which often rendered life and property insecure, and led to much unequal legislation. The amendment was an attempt to give voice to the strong National yearning for that time and that condition of things, in which American citizenship should be a sure guaranty of safety, and in which every citizen of the United States might stand erect on every portion of its soil, in the full enjoyment of every right and privilege belonging to a freeman, without fear of violence or molestation. . . .

Discussion

1. General constitutional law. Before Justice Miller comes to the Reconstruction amendments, he discusses whether the Louisiana statute is within the state's police power. This may have been gratuitous, especially since the Slaughter-House Cases came before the Court on writ of error to the Louisiana Supreme Court. But, especially taken together with Justice Miller's opinion a year later in Loan Association v. Topeka, 87 U.S. (20 Wall.) 655 (1874), it indicates that the notion of a "general constitutional law" remained alive and well after the Civil War. *Loan Association* invalidated municipal bonds, issued for the benefit of a private ironworks, on the ground that their issuance lay beyond the state's taxing power:

> It must be conceded that there are such rights in every free government beyond the control of the State. A government which recognized no such rights, which held the lives, the liberty, and the property of its citizens subject at all times to the absolute disposition and unlimited control of even the most democratic depository of power, is after all but a despotism. . . .
>
> The theory of our governments, State and National, is opposed to the deposit of unlimited power anywhere. The executive, the legislative, and the judicial branches of these governments are all of limited and defined powers.
>
> There are limitations on such power which grow out of the essential nature of all free governments. Implied reservations of individual rights, without which the social compact could not exist, and which are respected by all governments entitled to the name. No court, for instance, would hesitate to declare void a statute which enacted that *A.* and *B.* who were husband and wife to each other should be so no longer, but that *A.* should thereafter be the husband of *C.*, and *B.* the wife of *D.* Or which should enact that the homestead now owned by *A.* should no longer be his, but should henceforth be the property of *B.*
>
> Of all the powers conferred upon government that of taxation is most liable to abuse. . . . The power to tax is . . . the strongest, the most pervading of all the powers of government, reaching directly or indirectly to all classes of the people. It was said by Chief Justice Marshall, in the case of McCulloch v. The State of Maryland, that the power to tax is the power to destroy. . . .
>
> To lay with one hand the power of the government on the property of the citizen, and with the other to bestow it upon favored individuals to aid private enterprises and build up private fortunes, is none the less a robbery because it is done under the

> forms of law and is called taxation. This is not legislation. It is a decree under legislative forms. . . .[34]

Several years later, in Davidson v. Louisiana, 96 U.S. 97 (1878), the Court drew a sharp jurisdictional boundary between general constitutional law and the clauses of the Fourteenth Amendment. On appeal from the Louisiana Supreme Court, the owners of real estate in New Orleans claimed that a certain property tax deprived them of property without due process of law. Justice Miller noted that the due process clause was increasingly being invoked to bring before the Supreme Court "the abstract opinions of every unsuccessful litigant in a State court of the justice of the decision against him, and of the merits of the legislation on which such a decision may be founded." Miller wrote that the city tax "may violate some provision of the State Constitution against unequal taxation; but the Federal Constitution imposes no restraints on the States in that regard. . . . It may possibly violate some of those principles of general constitutional law, of which we could take jurisdiction if we were sitting in review of a Circuit Court of the United States, as we were in Loan Association v. Topeka. . . ."

2. *"Privileges or immunities."* Justice Miller reaffirmed the Court's earlier holding that the privileges or immunities clause of Article IV, section 2, had no substantive content: The clause did not require a state to grant any particular right to any person, but only prevented a state from conferring certain benefits on its own citizens while denying them to citizens of other states. The Court acknowledged that the Fourteenth Amendment "privileges or immunities" clause, by contrast, protected certain rights of citizens against infringement even by their own state. What are these rights?

Rights arising out of a citizen's relationship with the national government. Justice Miller wrote for the Court that the Fourteenth Amendment clause protects rights "which owe their existence to the Federal government, its National character, its Constitution, or its laws." His hodgepodge of illustrations does not illuminate. Some of the examples simply incorporate the privileges or immunities clause of Article IV and other provisions of the Civil War amendments. Others, such as the right to federal protection "on the high seas or within the jurisdiction of a foreign country," seem beyond a state's ability to infringe. But certain interests that might be thought to arise out of a citizen's relationship with the national government are susceptible to infringement by the states, for example, the rights to assemble to discuss matters pertaining to the government and to petition the government

34. Only Justice Clifford dissented, writing:

> State constitutions may undoubtedly restrict the power of the legislature to pass laws, and it is plain that any law passed in violation of such a prohibition is void, but the better opinion is that where the constitution of the State contains no prohibition upon the subject, express or implied, neither the State nor Federal courts can declare a statute of the State void as unwise, unjust, or inexpedient, nor for any other cause, unless it be repugnant to the Federal Constitution. Except where the Constitution has imposed limits upon the legislative power the role of law appears to be that the power of legislation must be considered as practically absolute, whether the law operates according to natural justice or not in any particular case. . . .
>
> Courts cannot nullify an act of the State legislature on the vague ground that they think it opposed to a general latent spirit supposed to pervade or underlie the constitution, where neither the terms nor the implications of the instrument disclose any such restriction. Such a power is denied to the courts, because to concede it would be to make the courts sovereign over both the constitution and the people, and convert the government into a judicial despotism.

and the right of access to federal courts and to other federal agencies. See Hague v. CIO, 307 U.S. 496 (1939). To be sure, even without the privileges or immunities clause, Congress could enact legislation under its Article I powers to secure these rights — indeed, to secure them for noncitizens as well as citizens and against infringement by private persons as well as by states. But the privileges or immunities clause provides an explicit guarantee of the rights of citizens against state invasion that is self-executing — i.e., binding on the states and enforceable by the judiciary even in the absence of congressional implementing legislation.

Fundamental or natural rights. Justice Field asserted broadly that the clause "was intended to give practical effect to the declaration of 1776 of inalienable rights, rights which are gift of the Creator, which the law does not confer but only recognizes." And Justice Bradley asserted that among the rights of citizens are Blackstone's "three absolute rights of individuals," which encompass the "privilege of engaging in any lawful employment for a livelihood." Field and Bradley were, at the least, trying to read the privileges or immunities clause of the Fourteenth Amendment to incorporate "general constitutional principles" — though it is hardly clear that the Louisiana monopoly ran afoul of those principles.

The provisions of the Bill of Rights. Justice Bradley also suggested that the privileges and immunities of citizens of the United States include the guarantees of the first eight amendments to the Constitution. Although the Court never held that any clause of the Fourteenth Amendment fully incorporates the Bill of Rights, almost all of the provisions have been made binding on the states through "selective incorporation" into the due process clause. See the Introduction to Part Two, infra.

3. "Due process." The due process clause of the Fourteenth Amendment is identical to the due process clause of the Fifth Amendment. The Fifth Amendment clause, as its language implies, was generally understood to address the *procedures* by which individuals' rights and liabilities were adjudicated. Procedural due process is not concerned with the validity of laws that deprive people of life, liberty, or property under specified conditions, but rather with the procedures that must be followed in determining whether those conditions in fact exist. Shortly before the Civil War, in Murray v. Hoboken Land & Improvement Co., 59 U.S. (18 How.) 272 (1855), Justice Curtis thus described the origin and scope of the due process clause of the Fifth Amendment:

> The words, "due process of law," were undoubtedly intended to convey the same meaning as the words, "by the law of the land," in Magna Carta. Lord Coke, in his commentary on those words says they mean due process of law. The constitutions which had been adopted by the several States before the formation of the federal constitution, following the language of the great charter more closely, generally contained the words, "but by the judgment of his peers, or the law of the land." . . .
>
> The constitution contains no description of those processes which it was intended to allow or forbid. It does not even declare what principles are to be applied to ascertain whether it be due process. It is manifest that it was not left to the legislative power to enact any process which might be devised. The article is a restraint on the legislative as well as on the executive and judicial powers of the government, and cannot be so construed as to leave congress free to make any process "due process of law," by its mere will. To what principles, then, are we to resort to ascertain whether this process, enacted by congress, is due process? To this the answer must be two-fold. We must examine the constitution itself, to see whether this process be in con-

flict with any of its provisions. If not found to be so, we must look to those settled usages and modes of proceeding existing in the common and statute law of England, before the emigration of our ancestors, and which are shown not to have been unsuited to their civil and political condition by having been acted on by them after the settlement of this country.[35]

Plaintiffs in the Slaughter-House Cases were not attacking an adjudicatory procedure but rather the substantive appropriateness or fairness of the slaughterhouse monopoly. Recall that, in Dred Scott v. Sandford, 60 U.S. (19 How.) 393 (1857), Chapter 3 supra, Taney had similarly attacked the Missouri Compromise on the ground that it deprived slaveholders of their property and liberty without due process of law. In other words, the plaintiffs in the Slaughter-House Cases and Taney in *Dred Scott* were concerned, not with the fairness of procedures by which rights and obligations are adjudicated, but with the substantive ordering of those rights. Justice Miller's quick dismissal of the *substantive due process* claim may have reflected both the majority's acknowledgment of the historical purpose of the clause and its aversion to the *Dred Scott* decision, from which the Court was still smarting. But it may also have reflected the view that plaintiff's claim was without merit on any constitutional (large or small "c") theory. For only a year later, in Bartemeyer v. Louisiana, 85 U.S. (18 Wall.) 129 (1874), Miller commented that the application of a state prohibition law to liquor held for sale before the law's enactment would present the "very grave question . . . [w]hether this would be a statute depriving [the owner] of his property without due process of law."

4. Slaughter-House and bifurcated citizenship. Professor LaRue sees "a clear continuity, on a question of citizenship, between *Dred Scott* and the Slaughterhouse Cases." By stating that "the distinction between citizenship of the United States and citizenship of a State is clearly recognized" by the Fourteenth Amendment, Justice Miller "preserved one of the most important features" of the earlier case. He holds "that the privileges and immunities of the two types of citizenship are different, and that the United States Constitution protects only the national privileges," which are in fact of limited import.

[T]he true import of the bifurcation is that all of the important rights are left to the protection of the state governments. . . .

At this point the Slaughterhouse Cases begin to look like the deep mirror image of *Dred Scott.* Taney declared that blacks could not be citizens; . . . the fundamental purpose behind this move was to prevent blacks from claiming the privileges and immunities of citizenship. With the adoption of the fourteenth amendment, blacks become citizens, but Miller gutted the meaning of that by stripping citizenship of any important legal consequences. So long as blacks cannot be citizens, enormous importance is attached to the concept; as soon as blacks can become citizens, the concept is drained of all meaning. (It is this sort of thing that gives paranoia a good name.)[36]

35. The Court has not adhered to this static view of procedural due process and has developed an extensive doctrine concerning the procedures — e.g., notice, opportunity to be heard, opportunity to confront adverse witnesses, the impartiality of the tribunal — in various circumstances. See Chapter 9 infra.

36. Lewis LaRue, The Continuing Presence of *Dred Scott,* 42 Wash. & Lee L. Rev. 57, 60-61 (1985).

5. *The original understanding of the Fourteenth Amendment.* Compare Justice Miller's characterization of the "one pervading purpose" of the Reconstruction amendments with Justice Bradley's broader description of "the mischief to be remedied." Bradley is correct that, in reaction to threats to the institution of slavery, Confederate states had egregiously infringed civil liberties and that this had been a source of national concern.[37] Although the congressional debates over the Fourteenth Amendment reveal only vague, conflicting, and self-contradictory statements about its purpose and scope,[38] the clear focus was on racial discrimination, not on civil liberties as such. On the other hand, the language of the Fourteenth Amendment was not limited to racial concerns, and some of its phrases had been used expansively in the debates over slavery preceding the Civil War. Abolitionists indiscriminately invoked natural law, the Bill of Rights, "the inherent rights of citizens," the rights to "protection of the laws" and against the "deprivation of liberty without due process of law" to urge that slavery violated the Constitution.[39] As *Dred Scott* indicates, apologists for slavery countered in similar terms.

6. *Justice Field and Jacksonian egalitarianism.* In his message vetoing the rechartering of the Bank of the United States, Andrew Jackson cautioned that "[t]here are no necessary evils in government. Its evils exist only in its abuses. If it would confine itself to equal protection, and, as Heaven does its rains, shower its favors alike on the high and the low, the rich and the poor, it would be an unqualified blessing." Recall the distinction, relevant to the scope of the contract clause, between ordinary property, which is presumed to be the result of the "natural," prepolitical market process, and "privilege." (See p. 105 supra.) Justice Field opposed the state-mandated monopoly in the Slaughter-House Cases precisely because it represented a use of state power to establish privileges that were in direct opposition to the kind of "equal protection" sought by Jacksonian ideology. Consider Michael Les Benedict's comment:

> [O]ne must recognize that there were two related but distinct justifications for the laissez-faire principle in the later nineteenth century. The first was based directly upon classical economists' conception of the "laws" of economics. It suggested that almost any government effort to overcome or channel those laws was doomed to failure. The second was based on a concept of human liberty implicit in the principles of classical economics. It militated only against certain kinds of government interferences in the economy, not against all interference. That concept was that the power of government could not legitimately be exercised to benefit one person or group at the expense of others. It was this conviction — not the notion that all gov-

37. See, e.g., Clement Eaton, Freedom of Thought in the Old South (1940).

38. See, e.g., Charles Fairman, Reconstruction and Reunion 1864-88 (Part One), in 6 History of the Supreme Court of the United States chs. 20-21 (1971); Fairman, Does the Fourteenth Amendment Incorporate the Bill of Rights? The Original Understanding, 2 Stan. L. Rev. 5 (1949); Alexander Bickel, The Original Understanding and the Segregation Decision, 69 Harv. L. Rev. 1 (1955).

39. See Jacobus tenBroek, Equal Under Law (1965), an expanded version of his Antislavery Origins of the Fourteenth Amendment (1951); Howard Graham, The Early Antislavery Backgrounds of the Fourteenth Amendment, 1950 Wis. L. Rev. 479, 610; Graham, Our "Declaratory" Fourteenth Amendment, 7 Stan. L. Rev. 3 (1954). These articles are reprinted in Graham, Everyman's Constitution, 152, 295 (1968). On the proslavery arguments, see especially id. at 212-213, 253-254 (discussing an 1836 report of a House committee advising on the unconstitutionality of abolishing slavery in the District of Columbia).

> ernment economic activity violated "immutable" economic laws — that lay at the heart of laissez-faire constitutionalism. . . . [It] received wide support in late nineteenth-century America not because it was based on widely adhered to economic principles and certainly not because it protected entrenched economic privilege, but rather because it was congruent with a well-established and accepted principle of American liberty.[40]

Field came out of a tradition that bitterly opposed "class legislation." William Leggett, a Jacksonian writer, commented that "[p]ower and wealth are continually stealing from the many to the few." The rich and powerful are constantly seeking "to monopolize the advantages of the Government, to hedge themselves around with exclusive privileges, and elevate themselves at the expense of the great body of the people."[41] Although the great fear concerned the rich and the wellborn, Benedict notes that Jacksonians did not accept "class legislation" that benefitted the poor. Instead, the watchword was an abstract notion of "equal rights," with individuals free to make whatever use of such rights they wished within the economic marketplace.

Consider also Washington University v. Rouse, 75 U.S. (8 Wall.) 439 (1869), which concerned the validity of a Missouri charter that guaranteed the University permanent immunity from state taxation. Such tax exemptions were quite common and oft-litigated. The Supreme Court, in two 1854 decisions, Ohio Life Ins. & Trust Co. v. Debolt, 57 U.S. 416, and Piqua Branch Bank v. Knoup, 57 U.S. 369, held that an explicit grant of a tax exemption could not be rescinded without violating the contract clause. Critics argued that the legislature retained an "inalienable power" to tax in behalf of the public welfare and that one legislature could not bind its successor. Thus many jurists "began distinguishing between police power regulations promoting the public health, safety and morals from those promoting the public convenience. The former were, and the latter were not, sufficiently crucial to social welfare to justify the revocation of express charter provisions."[42] The majority in *Rouse* easily upheld the exemption. Justice Miller dissented, joined by Chief Justice Chase and Justice Field: "[N]o hindrance can be seen, in the principle adopted by the court, to rich corporations, as railroads and express companies or rich men, making contracts with the Legislatures, as they best may, and with appliances as it is known they do use, for perpetual exemption from all the burdens of supporting the government. The result of such a principle, under the growing tendency to special and partial legislation, would be, to exempt the rich from taxation, and cast all the burden of the support of government, and the payment of its debts, on those who are too poor or too honest to purchase such immunity." From a modern perspective, it may seem that Justice Field and other laissez-faire constitutionalists were too insensitive to the opportunities for abuse allowed the well-off within a market featuring dramatic inequalities of wealth, but it would oversimplify to describe them merely as apologists for existing inequalities of wealth.

40. Laissez-Faire and Liberty: A Re-Evaluation of the Meaning and Origins of Laissez-Faire Constitutionalism, 3 Law and History Review 293, 298 (1985).

41. Theodore Sedgewick, ed., Political Writings of William Leggett, i, 66-67 (1840), quoted in id. at 319.

42. Stephen A. Siegel, Understanding the Nineteenth Century Contract Clause, The Role of the Property-Privilege Distinction and "Takings" Clause Jurisprudence, 60 S. Cal. L. Rev. 1, 52 (1986).

Note: Myra Bradwell, Privileges and Immunities, and the Practice of Law

Rogers Smith writes that "the same clash between a liberal free labor interpretation of the [fourteenth amendment] and states' rights republican views" reappeared almost immediately in another case claiming a substantive right based on the privileges and immunities clause. The Illinois Supreme Court refused Myra Bradwell a license to practice law solely because she was a woman; no one doubted that she otherwise qualified. Her attorney, Republican Senator Matthew Hale Carpenter, cited the rights of the Declaration of Independence as among the "privileges and immunities" protected by the new amendment; among the specific rights protected was that of laboring in one's chosen vocation. "[I]n the pursuit of happiness," said Carpenter, "all avocations, all honors, all positions, are alike open to every one[;] in the protection of these rights all are equal before the law." As Smith notes, "[b]y resting his case on the liberal right to labor and drawing an analogy between the discrimination against women and the racial oppressions the amendment was universally acknowledged to oppose, Carpenter made a very strong argument. He also faced no opposing counsel."[43] Nonetheless, the Court rebuffed Bradwell's claim.

Justice Miller reiterated the limited scope of the privileges and immunities clause. The "right" to practice law

> in no sense depends on citizenship of the United States. It has not, as far as we know, ever been made in any State, or in any case, to depend on citizenship at all. Certainly many prominent and distinguished lawyers have been admitted to practice . . . who were not citizens of the United States or of any State. But, on whatever basis this right may be placed, so far as it can have any relation to citizenship at all, it would seem that, as to the courts of a State, it would relate to citizenship of the State, and as to Federal courts, it would relate to citizenship of the United States.
>
> . . . . [U]nless we are wholly and radically mistaken in the principles on which [the Slaughter-House Cases] are decided, the right to control and regulate the granting of licenses to practice law in the courts of a State is one of those powers which are not transferred for its protection to the Federal government, and its exercise is in no manner governed or controlled by citizenship of the United States in the party seeking such licensure.

Justice Bradley wrote a concurring opinion joined by Justices Swayne and Field, both of whom had dissented in the Slaughter-House Cases. Describing Bradwell as claiming "that it is one of the privileges and immunities of women as citizens to engage in any and every profession, occupation, or employment in civil life," he responded:

> It certainly cannot be affirmed, as an historical fact, that this has ever been established as one of the fundamental privileges and immunities of the sex. On the contrary, the civil law, as well as nature herself, has always recognized a wide difference in the respective spheres and destinies of man and woman. Man is, or should be, woman's protector and defender. The natural and proper timidity and delicacy which belongs to the female sex evidently unfits it for many of the occupations of

43. Smith, supra note 31, at 260.

civil life. The constitution of the family organization, which is founded in the divine ordinance, as well as in the nature of things, indicates the domestic sphere as that which properly belongs to the domain and functions of womanhood. The harmony, not to say identity, of interests and views which belong, or should belong, to the family institution is repugnant to the idea of a woman adopting a distinct and independent career from that of her husband. . . .

It is true that many women are unmarried and not affected by any of the duties, complications, and incapacities arising out of the married state, but these are exceptions to the general rule. The paramount destiny and mission of woman are to fulfil the noble and benign offices of wife and mother. This is the law of the Creator. And the rules of civil society must be adapted to the general constitution of things, and cannot be based upon exceptional cases.

The humane movements of modern society, which have for their object the multiplication of avenues for woman's advancement, and of occupations adapted to her condition and sex, have my heartiest concurrence. But I am not prepared to say that it is one of her fundamental rights and privileges to be admitted into every office and position, including those which require highly special qualifications and demanding special responsibilities.

Chief Justice Chase, who had been one of the leading abolitionists lawyers during the 1850s, dissented without opinion.

Discussion

As in Minor v. Hapersett, *Bradwell* did not consider the equal protection clause as a possible source of vindication of Bradwell's claims. What does this suggest about the views held by late-nineteenth-century lawyers of the clause? What, if anything, should that tell us about our own interpretation of the equal protection clause today? (We shall consider this topic again in Part Two, infra.)

B. Pressures for Intervention and the Rise of Substantive Due Process, 1874-1890[44]

Although the Court resisted making substantive use of the due process clause for the next 15 years, by 1890 it essentially embraced the theory of Justice Bradley's dissent in the Slaughter-House Cases. The history of this transformation and the period that followed can be viewed from a variety of perspectives. After briefly describing the rise of economic regulation and the corporate bar's response to it, we reproduce Lochner v. New York, which has come to be the symbol of the era of substantive due process. Following *Lochner,* we raise some further questions about the social and intellectual context in which it was decided.

The decades following the Civil War were times of widespread social protest, stemming from

the great pace of industrialization and, more particularly, from the swift concentration of economic power in the large corporation. Midwestern and Southern farm-

44. See generally Sidney Fine, Laissez Faire and the General Welfare State (1956); Richard Hofstadter, Social Darwinism in American Thought (rev. ed. 1955); Arnold Paul, Conservative Crisis and the Rule of Law (1960); Benjamin Twiss, Lawyers and the Constitution: How Laissez Faire Came to the Supreme Court (1942).

> ers, unable to control their marketing through organization and suffering from a long-term international price decline, complained bitterly of monopolistic rates by railroads, grain elevators, and banks. Factory workers and miners, crowded in slums with insecure status in a rapidly changing economy, periodically rebelled at low wages, long hours, and bad working conditions. Small businessmen, faced with the more efficient, and frequently more ruthless, competition of the large corporation, charged that the continued consolidation of capital was destroying individual opportunity. And many professional and white-collar people, uneasy over the accumulation of great wealth and the growing disparity of rich and poor, feared that the traditional fluidity of American society was fast disappearing. . . . Under the pressure of social discontent, legislators had begun to act in the 1870's and 1880's in regard to railroad and grain elevator rates, labor relations, and other matters affecting large business concerns. In turn, corporation lawyers had been pressing the courts to protect more vigilantly the rights of property against legislative regulation.[45]

After the Slaughter-House Cases, corporations could not expect aid from the privileges or immunities clause of the Fourteenth Amendment. Although Justice Miller's opinion gave even shorter shrift to the due process clause, the natural law tradition clinging to that clause and its inviting references to "property" and "liberty" led corporate lawyers to seize on it.

The state courts were the first to respond. In Matter of Jacobs, 98 N.Y. 98 (1885), the New York Court of Appeals struck down a statute prohibiting the manufacture of cigars in tenement houses. The court dismissed the ostensible public health rationale of the law to hold that it "interferes with the profitable and free use of his property by the owner or lessee of a tenement house" and "arbitrarily deprives him of his property and of some portion of his personal liberty."[46] In Godcharles v. Wigeman, 113 Pa. 431, 6 A. 354 (1886), the Pennsylvania Supreme Court held "utterly unconstitutional and void" a law requiring mining and manufacturing companies to pay wages in cash (rather than in vouchers redeemable only at the company store):

> [An attempt has been made by the legislature to do what, in this country, cannot be done; that is, prevent persons who are sui juris [i.e., persons who possess full legal rights and capacity] from making their own contracts. The Act is an infringement alike of the right of the employer and the employe; more than this, it is an insulting attempt to put the laborer under legislative tutelage, which is not only degrading to his manhood, but subversive of his rights as a citizen of the United States.
>
> He may sell labor for what he thinks best, whether money or goods, just as his employer may sell his iron or coal, and any and every law that proposes to prevent him from so doing is an infringement of his constitutional privileges, and consequently vicious and void.

Although not all state courts were so hostile to social legislation and some were avowedly sympathetic, decisions like these became increasingly common.

The early pressures for federal judicial intervention came mostly from regulated industries, and the Court first intervened in 1890, not against social legisla-

45. Paul, supra note 44, at 1-2, 5. But cf. Gabriel Kolko, Railroads and Regulation, 1877-1916 (1965).

46. In fact, New York's contribution antedates the Civil War. In Wynehamer v. New York, 12 N.Y. 378 (1856), Judge Comstock, in one of several seriatim opinions, invoked the due process clause of the New York Constitution to invalidate a law prohibiting the sale of intoxicating liquor.

tion but against railroad rate regulation. The following paragraphs trace the growth of the federal doctrine of substantive due process.

The first decision, and the "bete noire of laissez faire conservatism,"[47] was Munn v. Illinois, 94 U.S. 113 (1877), which upheld a state law limiting the rates charged by Chicago grain-storage warehouses. Writing for the Court, Chief Justice Waite began by asserting that a state had inherent authority — the "police power" — to regulate "the conduct of its citizens one towards another, and the manner in which each shall use his own property, when such regulation becomes necessary for the public good." He then noted that it was the practice in England, the colonies, and the states "to regulate ferries, common carriers, hackmen, bakers, millers, wharfingers, innkeepers, &c., and in so doing to fix a maximum of charge to be made for services rendered, accommodations furnished, and articles sold," and that the practice was followed in the District of Columbia, which was subject to the Fifth Amendment due process clause. "From this it is apparent that . . . it was not supposed that statutes regulating the use, or even the price of the use, of private property necessarily deprived an owner of his property without due process of law. Under some circumstances they may, but not under all."

This brought the Chief Justice "to inquire as to the principles upon which this power of regulation rests." For the answer, he turned to Lord Chief Justice Hale's seventeenth-century treatise, De Portibus Maris, to conclude that private property may be regulated when it is "affected with a public interest" and that property becomes "clothed with a public interest when used in a manner to make it of public consequence, and affect the community at large." The warehouses clearly fell within this description — indeed, the complainants had "a virtual monopoly" on the storage of grain bound from the Midwest to national markets.

Finally, the Court refused to hear an argument that the maximum permissible rates were "unreasonable."

> Undoubtedly, in mere private contracts, relating to matters in which the public has no interest, what is reasonable must be ascertained judicially. But this is because the legislature has no control over such a contract. . . . The controlling fact is the power to regulate at all. If that exists, the right to establish the maximum of charge, as one of the means of legislation, is implied. . . . We know that this is a power which may be abused; but that is no argument against its existence. For protection against abuses by legislatures the people must resort to the polls, not to the courts.

Justice Field, joined by Justice Strong, dissented.

The Court reaffirmed *Munn* in the Railroad Commission Cases, 116 U.S. 307 (1886), which upheld state regulation of railroad tariffs (notwithstanding a provision in the railroad's 1884 charter empowering it to set its own charges). Again Chief Justice Waite wrote that the reasonableness of rates was a legislative question. But he went on to caution:

> From what has thus been said, it is not to be inferred that this power of limitation or regulation is itself without limit. This power to regulate is not a power to destroy, and limitation is not the equivalent of confiscation. Under pretence of regulating fares and freights, the State cannot require a railroad corporation to carry persons or property without reward; neither can it do that which in law amounts to a taking

47. Paul, supra note 44, at 8.

of private property for public use without just compensation, or without due process of law.

That same year, in Santa Clara County v. Southern Pacific Railroad, 118 U.S. 394, the Court held that the word "person" in the due process clause of the Fourteenth Amendment encompassed artificial persons, i.e., corporations.[48]

Viewed in retrospect, these decisions indicate a gradual weakening of the Court's rejection of substantive due process in the Slaughter-House Cases. Waite's opinion in *Munn* implied that the Constitution might forbid state regulation of matters that were not "affected with a public interest"; the Railroad Commission Cases explicitly suggested that in extreme cases "reasonableness" might be meet for judicial inquiry; and the Court's definition of "persons" opened the way for direct challenges to regulations by corporations.

Of the justices who had participated in the Slaughter-House Cases, only Field, Bradley, and Miller remained on the Court in 1890. That year in the Minnesota Rate Cases, 134 U.S. 418, the Court struck down a statute granting a state railroad commission unreviewable authority to set rates. Justice Blatchford wrote that the reasonableness of rates "is eminently a question for judicial investigation, requiring due process of law for its determination": "If the company is deprived of the power of charging reasonable rates for the use of its property, and such deprivation takes place in the absence of investigation by judicial machinery, it is deprived of the lawful use of its property, and thus, in substance and effect, of the property itself, without due process of law." Justice Bradley, joined by Justices Gray and Lamar, dissented vigorously.

At first glance, the Minnesota Rate Cases seem to build on the tradition of procedural due process to require notice and an opportunity to be heard in the courts before rates could be imposed on the railroads. Such judicializing of administrative rate-making was itself an innovation. But the opinion implied that the judiciary's role was not simply to review the application of legislative criteria to particular cases but to determine — independent of any legislative or administrative criteria — whether the rates established were "reasonable."[49] The broad implications of the decision were not lost on the corporate bar, which rejoiced in it, nor on Justice Bradley, who remarked in dissent with no joy that it "practically overrules Munn v. Illinois."[50]

48. On the real and supposed understanding of the framers of the Fourteenth Amendment on this matter, see Graham, Everyman's Constitution, supra note 39, chs. 1-2, 10-12, which includes Graham's well-known article, The "Conspiracy Theory" of the Fourteenth Amendment, 47 Yale L.J. 371, 48 id. 171 (1938). Corporations were held not to be "citizens" under the privileges or immunities clause. See Paul v. Virginia, 75 U.S. (8 Wall.) 168 (1868); Blake v. McClung, 172 U.S. 239 (1898).

49. The basic formula was announced eight years later in Smyth v. Ames, 169 U.S. 466 (1898): rates must yield a fair return upon the present value of the company's assets. For nearly 40 years, the Court was rate-maker and accountant. In FPC v. Natural Gas Pipeline Co., 315 U.S. 575 (1942), the Court noted that "[t]he Constitution does not bind rate-making bodies to the service of any single formula," and in FPC v. Hope Natural Gas Co., 320 U.S. 591 (1944), it expressly repudiated the rule of Smyth v. Ames.

50. Bradley's dissent in *Chicago, Milwaukee & St. Paul* calls for some explanation, since the Court's decision might well be viewed as adopting the dissenting position espoused in his dissent in the Slaughter-House Cases. Bradley's earlier dissent evinces a concern for the plight of small entrepreneurs at the hands of the state-sanctioned monopoly. In a nonconstitutional decision, also written in 1873, he had rejected a railroad's attempt to disclaim common law liability, noting that the carrier and its customer do "not stand on a footing of equality." Railroad Co. v. Lockwood, 84 U.S. (17 Wall.) 357, 379 (1873). From this point of view, there was no inconsistency in upholding legislation constraining

Within a decade, the Court expanded its inquiries beyond rate regulation to review the substantive validity of legislation of almost every sort. Economic and social theories largely abandoned in the academies and legislative chambers found their last refuge in the judiciary.

Note: Incorporation of the Eminent Domain Clause

Pumpelly v. Green Bay Company, 13 Wall. 166 (1871), presented the question whether, by authorizing the erection of a dam that flooded appellant's land, Wisconsin had "taken" Pumpelly's property and therefore had a duty to compensate him. Justice Miller wrote for the Court that "though the Constitution of the United States provides that private property shall not be taken for public use without just compensation, it is well settled that this is a limitation on the power of the Federal government, and not on the States." *Pumpelly* thus reaffirmed the holding of Barron v. Baltimore, 32 U.S. (7 Pet.) 243 (1833), that the Bill of Rights did not apply to the states, and, like the Slaughter-House Cases two years later, declined to hold that the Fourteenth Amendment "incorporated" any portion of the first ten amendments.

Ironically, the first clause of the Bill of Rights in effect made applicable to state legislation was the Fifth Amendment right to just compensation for property taken by the State. In Chicago, Burlington and Quincy Railroad v. Chicago, 166 U.S. 226 (1897), the Court considered Illinois' practice of delegating essentially final authority to a jury to determine the compensation due someone whose property has been taken. In the particular case, the railroads complained that the jury's award of a dollar for seizing its right of way to build a street violated the due process and equal protection clauses of the Fourteenth Amendment.

Justice Harlan wrote for the Court, rejecting the city's claim that the United States Constitution did not apply to the case:

> It is proper now to inquire whether the due process of law enjoined by the Fourteenth Amendment requires compensation to be made or adequately secured to the owner of private property taken for public use under the authority of a State.
>
> . . . Due protection of the rights of property has been regarded as a vital principle of republican institutions. . . . The requirement that the property shall not be taken for public use without just compensation is but "an affirmance of a great doctrine established by the common law for the protection of private property. It is founded in natural equity, and is laid down by jurists as a principle of universal law. Indeed, in a free government almost all rights would become worthless if the government possessed an uncontrollable power over the private fortune of every citizen."

"the burdens and charges which those who own [public means of transportation] are authorized to impose upon the public."

Bradley argued, moreover, that the Court should accord legislation a presumption of constitutionality:

> I do not mean to say that the legislature, or . . . other legislative agency, may not so act as to deprive parties of their property without due process of law. The Constitution contemplates the possibility of such an invasion of rights. But, acting within their jurisdiction, (as in these cases they have done,) the invasion should be clear and unmistakable to bring the case within that category.

Bradley's position in this respect is similar to Justice Holmes' dissent in *Lochner*.

But if, as this court has adjudged [in Davidson v. Louisiana, supra p. 274], a legislative enactment assuming arbitrarily to take the property of one individual and give it to another individual, would not be due process of law as enjoined by the Fourteenth Amendment, it must be that the requirement of due process of law in that amendment is applicable to the direct appropriation by the State to public use and without compensation of the private property of the citizen. The legislature may prescribe a form of procedure to be observed in the taking of private property for public use, but it is not due process of law if provision be not made for compensation. . . . Due process of law as applied to judicial proceedings instituted for the taking of private property for public use means, therefore, such process as recognizes the right of the owner to be compensated if his property be wrested from him and transferred to the public. The mere form of the proceeding instituted against the owner, even if he be admitted to defend, cannot convert the process used into due process of law, if the necessary result be to deprive him of his property without compensation. . . .

"It in nowise detracts from the power of the public to take whatever may be necessary for its uses; while on the other hand, it prevents the public from loading upon one individual more than his just share of the burdens of government, and says that, when he surrenders to the public something more and different from that which is exacted from other members of the public, a full and just equivalent shall be returned to him." . . .

In our opinion, a judgment of a state court, even if it be authorized by statute, whereby private property is taken for the State or under its direction for public use, without compensation made or secured to the owner, is upon principle and authority, wanting in the due process of law required by the Fourteenth Amendment of the Constitution of the United States.

The Court went on to hold that the treatment accorded the railroads was in fact legitimate and not in violation of the Fourteenth Amendment. Justice Brewer dissented from this latter part of the Court's opinion.

C. The Heyday of Judicial Activism, 1890-1934

LOCHNER v. NEW YORK

198 U.S. 45 (1905)

Error to the County Court of Oneida County, State of New York

[In April 1895, both houses of the New York legislature unanimously passed legislation stating that "[n]o employee shall be required, permitted or suffered to work in a [bakery] more than sixty hours in any one week, or more than ten hours in any one day, unless for the purpose of making a shorter work day on the last day of the week. . . ."[51] Joseph Lochner was convicted of employing a baker in excess of 60 hours in one week.]

PECKHAM, J. . . .

The statute necessarily interferes with the right of contract between the employer and employés, concerning the number of hours in which the latter may

51. See Paul Kens, Judicial Power and Reform Politics: The Anatomy of *Lochner v. New York* 58-59 (1990). Professor Kens notes that the act was amended specifically to state "employee" rather than "person" so as to avoid any inference that a self-employed baker was precluded from working in excess of the hours indicated.

labor in the bakery of the employer. The general right to make a contract in relation to his business is part of the liberty of the individual protected by the Fourteenth Amendment of the Federal Constitution. Allgeyer v. Louisiana, 165 U.S. 578 (1897). Under that provision no State can deprive any person of life, liberty or property without due process of law. The right to purchase or to sell labor is part of the liberty protected by this amendment, unless there are circumstances which exclude the right. There are, however, certain powers, existing in the sovereignty of each State in the Union, somewhat vaguely termed police powers, the exact description and limitation of which have not been attempted by the courts. Those powers, broadly stated and without, at present, any attempt at a more specific limitation, relate to the safety, health, morals and general welfare of the public. Both property and liberty are held on such reasonable conditions as may be imposed by the governing power of the State in the exercise of those powers, and with such conditions the Fourteenth Amendment was not designed to interfere.

The State, therefore, has power to prevent the individual from making certain kinds of contracts, and in regard to them the Federal Constitution offers no protection. If the contract be one which the State, in the legitimate exercise of its police power, has the right to prohibit, it is not prevented from prohibiting it by the Fourteenth Amendment. Contracts in violation of a statute, either of the Federal or state government, or a contract to let one's property for immoral purposes, or to do any other unlawful act, could obtain no protection from the Federal Constitution, as coming under the liberty of person or of free contract. Therefore, when the State, by its legislature, in the assumed exercise of its police powers, has passed an act which seriously limits the right to labor or the right of contract in regard to their means of livelihood between persons who are sui juris (both employer and employé), it becomes of great importance to determine which shall prevail — the right of the individual to labor for such time as he may choose, or the right of the State to prevent the individual from laboring or from entering into any contract to labor beyond a certain time prescribed by the State.

This court has recognized the existence and upheld the exercise of the police powers of the States in many cases which might fairly be considered as border ones. . . . [For example, in Holden v. Hardy, 169 U.S. 336 (1898), a] provision in the act of the legislature of Utah was . . . under consideration, the act limiting the employment of workmen in all underground mines or workings . . . [and] in smelting and other institutions for the reduction or refining of ores or metals to eight hours per day. . . . The act was held to be a valid exercise of the police powers of the State. . . It was held that the kind of employment, mining, smelting, etc., and the character of the employees in such kinds of labor, were such as to make it reasonable and proper for the State to interfere to prevent the employees from being constrained by the rules laid down by the proprietors in regard to labor. . . . There is nothing in Holden v. Hardy which covers the case now before us. . . .

It must, of course, be conceded that there is a limit to the valid exercise of the police power by the State. . . . Otherwise . . . it would be enough to say that any piece of legislation was enacted to conserve the morals, the health or the safety of the people; such legislation would be valid, no matter how absolutely without foundation the claim might be. The claim of the police power would be a mere pretext — become another and delusive name for the supreme sovereignty of the State to be exercised free from constitutional restraint. This is not contended for. In every case that comes before this court, therefore, where legislation of this character is concerned and where the protection of the Federal Constitution is sought, the question necessarily arises: Is this a fair, reasonable and appropriate exercise of the police power of the State, or is it an unreasonable, unnecessary and arbitrary interference with the right of the individual to his personal liberty or to enter into those contracts in relation to labor which may seem to him appropriate or necessary for the support of himself and his family? Of course the liberty of contract relating to labor includes both parties to it. The one has as much right to purchase as the other to sell labor.

This is not a question of substituting the judgment of the court for that of the legislature. If the act be within the power of the State it is valid, although the judgment of the court might be totally opposed to the enactment of such a law. But the question would still remain: Is it within the police power of the State? and that question must be answered by the court.

The question whether this act is valid as a labor law, pure and simple, may be dismissed in a few words. There is no reasonable ground for interfering with the liberty of person or the right of free contract, by determining the hours of labor, in the occupation of a baker. There is no contention that bakers as a class are not equal in intelligence and capacity to men in other trades or manual occupations, or that they are not able to assert their rights and care for themselves without the protecting arm of the State, interfering with their independence of judgment and of action. They are in no sense wards of the State. . . . The law must be upheld, if at all, as a law pertaining to the health of the individual engaged in the occupation of a baker. It does not affect any other portion of the public than those who are engaged in that occupation. Clean and wholesome bread does not depend upon whether the baker works but ten hours per day or only sixty hours a week. . . .

The mere assertion that the subject relates though but in a remote degree to the public health does not necessarily render the enactment valid. The act must have a more direct relation, as a means to an end, and the end itself must be appropriate and legitimate, before an act can be held to be valid which interferes with the general right of an individual to be free in his person and in his power to contract in relation to his own labor. . . .

We think the limit of the police power has been reached and passed in this case. There is, in our judgment, no reasonable foundation for holding this to be necessary or appropriate as a health law. . . .

We think that there can be no fair doubt that the trade of a baker, in and of itself, is not an unhealthy one to that degree which would authorize the legislature to interfere with the right to labor, and with the right of free contract on the part of the individual, either as employer or employé. In looking through statistics regarding all trades and occupations, it may be true that the trade of a baker does not appear to be as healthy as some other trades, and is also vastly more healthy than still others. . . . It might be safely affirmed that almost all occupations more or less affect the health. There must be more than the mere fact of the possible existence of some small amount of unhealthiness to warrant legislative interference with liberty. . . . No trade, no occupation, no mode of earning one's living, could escape this all-pervading power, and the acts of the legislature in limiting the hours of labor in all employments would be valid, although such limitation might seriously cripple the ability of the laborer to support himself and his family. . . .

It is also urged, pursuing the same line of argument, that it is to the interest of the State that its population should be strong and robust, and therefore any legislation which may be said to tend to make people healthy must be valid as health laws, enacted under the police power. If this be a valid argument and a justification for this kind of legislation, it follows that the protection of the Federal Constitution from undue interference with liberty of person and freedom of contract is visionary, wherever the law is sought to be justified as a valid exercise of the police power. Scarcely any law but might find shelter under such assumptions, and conduct, properly so called, as well as contract, would come under the restrictive sway of the legislature. Not only the hours of employés, but the hours of employers, could be regulated, and doctors, lawyers, scientists, all professional men, as well as athletes and artisans, could be forbidden to fatigue their brains and bodies by prolonged hours of exercise, lest the fighting strength of the State be impaired. . . . Statutes of the nature of that under review, limiting the hours in which grown and intelligent men may labor to earn their living, are mere meddlesome interferences with the rights of the individual, and they are not saved from condemnation by the claim that they are passed in the exercise of the police power and upon the subject of the health of the individual whose rights are interfered with, unless there be some fair ground, reasonable in and of itself, to say that there is material danger to the public health or to the health of the employés, if the hours of labor are not curtailed. . . . All that [the State] could properly do has been done by it with regard to the conduct of bakeries, as provided for in the other sections of the act. . . . These several sections provide for the inspection of the premises where the bakery is carried on, with regard to furnishing proper wash-rooms and water-closets, apart from the bake-room, also with regard to providing proper drainage, plumbing and painting. . . . These various sections . . . certainly go to the full extent of providing for the cleanliness and the healthiness, so far as possible, of the quarters in which bakeries are to be conducted. . . .

It was further urged . . . that restricting the hours of labor in the case of bakers was valid because it tended to cleanliness on the part of the workers, as a man was more apt to be cleanly when not overworked, and if cleanly then his "output" was also more likely to be so. . . . In our judgment it is not possible in fact to discover the connection between the number of hours a baker may work in the bakery and the healthful quality of the bread made by the workman. The connection, if any exists, is too shadowy and thin to build any argument for the interference of the legislature. If the man works ten hours a day it is all right, but if ten and a half or eleven his health is in danger and his bread may be unhealthful, and, therefore, he shall not be permitted to do it. This, we think, is unreasonable and entirely arbitrary. When assertions such as we have adverted to become necessary in order to give, if possible, a plausible foundation for the contention that the law is a "health law," it gives rise to at least a suspicion that there was some other motive dominating the legislature than the purpose to subserve the public health or welfare. . . .

It is impossible for us to shut our eyes to the fact that many of the laws of this character, while passed under what is claimed to be the police power for the purpose of protecting the public health or welfare, are, in reality, passed from other motives. We are justified in saying so when, from the character of the law and the subject upon which it legislates, it is apparent that the public health or welfare bears but the most remote relation to the law. The purpose of a statute must be determined from the natural and legal effect of the language employed; and whether it is or is not repugnant to the Constitution of the United States must be determined from the natural effect of such statutes when put into operation, and not from their proclaimed purpose. . . . It seems to us that the real object and purpose were simply to regulate the hours of labor between the master and his employés (all being men, sui juris), in a private business, not dangerous in any degree to morals or in any real and substantial degree, to the health of the employés. Under such circumstances the freedom of master and employés to contract with each other in relation to their employment, and in defining the same, cannot be prohibited or interfered with, without violating the Federal Constitution.

Reversed.

HARLAN, J., joined by White and Day, JJ., dissenting. . . .

Granting . . . that there is a liberty of contract which cannot be violated even under the sanction of direct legislative enactment, but assuming, as according to settled law we may assume, that such liberty of contract is subject to such regulations as the State may reasonably prescribe for the common good and the well-being of society, what are the conditions under which the judiciary may declare such regulations to be in excess of legislative authority and void? Upon this point there is no room for dispute; for, the rule is universal that . . . the power of the courts to review legislative action in respect of a matter affecting the general welfare exists *only* ". . . if a statute purporting to have been enacted to protect the public health, the public morals or the public safety, has no real or substantial relation to those objects, or is, beyond all question, a plain, palpable invasion of rights secured by the fundamental law.". . . If there be doubt as to the validity of the statute, that doubt must therefore be resolved in favor of its validity, and the courts must keep their hands off, leaving the legislature to meet the responsibility for unwise legislation. If the end which the legislature seeks to accomplish be one to which its power extends, and if the means employed to that end, although not the wisest or best, are yet not plainly and palpably unauthorized by law, then the court cannot interfere. In other words, when the validity of a statute is questioned, the burden of proof, so to speak, is upon those who assert it to be unconstitutional.

Let these principles be applied to the present case. . . .

It is plain that this statute was enacted in order to protect the physical well-being of those who work in bakery and confectionery establishments. It may be that the statute had its origin, in part, in the belief that employers and employés in such establishments were not upon an equal footing, and that the necessities of the latter often compelled them to submit to such exactions as unduly taxed their strength. Be this as it may, the statute must be taken as expressing the belief of the people of New York that, as a general rule, and in the case of the average man, labor in excess of sixty hours during a week in such establishments may endanger the health of those who thus labor. . . . I find it impossible, in view of common experience, to say that there is here no real or substantial relation between the means employed by the State and the end sought to be accomplished by its legislation. . . .

Professor Hirt in his treatise on the Diseases of the Workers has said: "The labor of the bakers is among the hardest and most laborious imaginable, because it has to be performed under conditions injurious to the health of those engaged in it. It is hard, very hard work, not only because it requires a great deal of physical exertion in an overheated workshop and during unreasonably long hours, but more so because of the erratic demands of the public, compelling the baker to perform the greater part of his work at night, thus depriving him of an opportunity to enjoy the necessary rest and sleep, a fact which is highly injurious to his health." Another writer says: "The constant inhaling of flour dust causes inflammation of the lungs and of the bronchial tubes. The eyes also suffer through this dust, which is responsible for the many cases of running eyes among the bakers. The long hours of toil to which all bakers are subjected produce rheumatism, cramps and swollen legs. The intense heat in the workshops induces the workers to resort to cooling drinks, which together with their habit of exposing the greater part of their bodies to the change in the atmosphere, is another source of a number of diseases of various organs. Nearly all bakers are pale-faced and of more delicate health than the workers of other crafts, which is chiefly due to their hard work and their irregular and unnatural mode of living, whereby the power or resistance against disease is greatly diminished. The average age of a baker is below that of other workmen; they seldom live over their fiftieth year, most of them dying between the ages of forty and fifty. . . ."

We judicially know that the question of the number of hours during which a workman should continuously labor has been, for a long period, and is yet, a subject of serious consideration among civilized peoples, and by those having special knowledge of the laws of health. . . .

I do not stop to consider whether any particular view of this economic question presents the sounder theory. What the precise facts are it may be difficult to say. It is enough for the determination of this case, and it is enough for this court to know, that the question is one about which there is room for debate and for an honest difference of opinion. There are many reasons of a weighty, substantial character, based upon the experience of mankind, in support of the theory that, all things considered, more than ten hours' steady work each day, from week to week, in a bakery or confectionery establishment, may endanger the health, and shorten the lives of the workmen, thereby diminishing their physical and mental capacity to serve the State, and to provide for those dependent upon them.

If such reasons exist that ought to be the end of this case, for the State is not amenable to the judiciary, in respect of its legislative enactments, unless such enactments are plainly, palpably, beyond all questions, inconsistent with the Constitution of the United States.

HOLMES, J., dissenting.

I regret sincerely that I am unable to agree with the judgment in this case, and that I think it my duty to express my dissent.

This case is decided upon an economic theory which a large part of the country does not entertain. If it were a question whether I agreed with that theory, I should desire to study it further and long before making up my mind. But I do not conceive that to be my duty, because I strongly believe that my agreement or disagreement has nothing to do with the right of a majority to embody their opinions in law. It is settled by various decisions of this court that state constitutions and state laws may regulate life in many ways which we as legislators might think as injudicious or if you like as tyrannical as this, and which equally with this interfere with the liberty to contract. Sunday laws and usury laws are ancient examples. A more modern one is the prohibition of lotteries. The liberty of the citizen to do as he likes so long as he does not interfere with the liberty of others to do the same, which has been a shibboleth for some well-known writers, is interfered with by school laws, by the Post Office, by every state or municipal institution which takes his money for purposes thought desirable, whether he likes it or not. The Fourteenth Amendment does not enact Mr. Herbert Spencer's Social Statics. . . . [A] constitution is not intended to embody a particular economic theory, whether of paternalism and the organic relation of the citizen to the State or of laissez faire. It is made for people of fundamentally differing views, and the accident of our finding certain opinions natural and familiar or novel and even shocking ought not to conclude our judgment upon the question whether statutes embodying them conflict with the Constitution of the United States.

General propositions do not decide concrete cases. The decision will depend on a judgment or intuition more subtle than any articulate major premise. But I think that the proposition just stated, if it is accepted, will carry us far toward the end. Every opinion tends to become a law. I think that the word liberty in the Fourteenth Amendment is perverted when it is held to prevent the natural outcome of a dominant opinion, unless it can be said that a rational and fair man necessarily would admit that the statute proposed would infringe fundamental principles as they have been understood by the traditions of our people and our law. It does not need research to show that no such sweeping condemnation can be passed upon the statute before us. A reasonable man might think it a proper measure on the score of health. Men whom I certainly could not pronounce unreasonable would uphold it as a first instalment of a general regulation of the hours of work. Whether in the latter aspect it would be open to the charge of inequality I think it unnecessary to discuss.

1. The Transformation and Federalization of General Constitutional Law

Lochner (which we use as a shorthand for the jurisprudence of constitutional rights of this period) expanded the scope of federal jurisdiction by, in effect, federalizing the principles of "general constitutional law," which federal courts had previously been able to invoke only in diversity cases. This might not have been of great practical consequence were it not for an accompanying change in the content of those principles. Recall that, throughout the Marshall and Taney eras, the core of general constitutional law was the vested rights doctrine, which assumed the validity of a given legal regime for the most part, but protected individuals against the *retroactive* impairment of rights acquired under the regime. Although the jurisprudence of general constitutional law also established the legitimate bounds of the legislature's police, taxing, and eminent domain powers (recall Loan Association v. Topeka, p. 273 supra), the police power in particular was thought to be of broad scope. In contrast, *Lochner* signals a restricted view of the police power. As Duncan Kennedy has suggested, the Court during this era viewed individual autonomy and the government police power as two mutually exclusive, nonoverlapping domains. Within such a domain, each actor had absolute sovereignty — much as the Court, even during the Marshall and Taney eras, viewed the realms of state and federal powers. The Court conceived its own mission to be the policing of the boundaries between them.[52]

2. *The Meanings of "Liberty," "Property," and "Process"*

Liberty. At the beginning of the Court's opinion in *Lochner,* Justice Peckham asserts: "The general right to make a contract in relation to his business is part of the liberty of the individual protected by the Fourteenth Amendment of the Federal Constitution. Allgeyer v. Louisiana. . . . The right to purchase or to sell labor is part of the liberty protected by this amendment, unless there are circumstances which exclude the right." In Allgeyer v. Louisiana, 165 U.S. 578 (1897), Justice Peckham had written for the Court:

> The "liberty" mentioned in [the Fourteenth Amendment] means, not only the right of the citizen to be free from the mere physical restraint of his person, as by incarceration, but the term is deemed to embrace the right of the citizen to be free in the enjoyment of all his faculties; to be free to use them in all lawful ways; to live and work where he will; to earn his livelihood by any lawful calling; to pursue any livelihood or avocation, and for that purpose to enter into all contracts which may be proper, necessary and essential to his carrying out to a successful conclusion the purposes above mentioned.

The Court's adoption of this notion of "liberty" incurred considerable scholarly criticism. For example, Charles Warren wrote:[53]

> The phrase, "life, liberty or property without due process of law" came to us from the English common law; and there seems to be little question that, under the common law, the word "liberty" meant simply "liberty of the person," or, in other words, "the right to have one's person free from physical restraint." . . . There is no intimation . . . that this phrase in the Bill of Rights in . . . early State Constitutions meant anything more than it meant at common law. . . . It is unquestionable that when the First Congress adopted the Fifth Amendment and inserted the Due Process Clause, . . . they took it with the meaning it then bore.

The main object of Charles Warren's attack on the "new liberty" was Gitlow v. New York, 268 U.S. 652 (1925), in which the Court explicitly "assume[d] that freedom of speech and press — which are protected by the First Amendment from abridgement by Congress — are among the fundamental personal rights

52. Duncan Kennedy, The Rise and Fall of Classical Legal Thought, 1850-1940 (unpublished manuscript, 1975).

53. Charles Warren, The New "Liberty" Under the Fourteenth Amendment, 39 Harv. L. Rev. 431, 440 (1926). See also Charles Shattuck, The True Meaning of the Term "Liberty" in Those Clauses in the Federal and State Constitutions Which Protect "Life, Liberty, and Property," 4 Harv. L. Rev. 365 (1891).

and liberties protected by the Fourteenth Amendment from impairment by the states."[54]

Property. Even if the word "liberty" were construed narrowly, the due process clause also explicitly protects "property." In Coppage v. Kansas, 236 U.S. 1 (1915), in holding unconstitutional a statute prohibiting "yellow dog" contracts (contracts forbidding employees to join labor unions), the Court wrote: "Included in the right of personal liberty and the *right of private property* . . . is the right to make contracts. . . ." (Emphasis added.) Other substantive due process cases have similarly relied on the deprivation of property.

Of course, one might assert that the Court also construed "property" too broadly — that the term should be limited to the core common law concepts of realty and personalty.[55]

Process. Even if "liberty" and "property" may be read expansively, what about "process"? In cases like *Lochner,* what process has been inadequate — the legislative process by which the maximum hours regulation was enacted? The judicial process by which Lochner was convicted?

3. The Scope of the Police Power: Permissible and Impermissible Objectives

The Court notes at the outset that "the statute necessarily interferes with the rights of contract" but also asserts that "property and liberty are held on such reasonable conditions as may be imposed by the governing power of the state in the exercise of [its police] powers." What are the proper ends for which the police power may be exercised, and what objectives lie beyond them? Recall, in this respect, how Justice Peckham distinguished Holden v. Hardy in *Lochner.* Consider also Baltimore & Ohio R. Co. v. Interstate Commerce Commission, 221 U.S. 612 (1911), in which the Court upheld limitations on the hours of railroad employees. Justice Hughes wrote:

> The length of hours of service has a direct relation to the efficiency of the human agencies upon which protection to life and property necessarily depends. . . . In its power suitably to provide for the safety of employees and travelers, Congress was not limited to the enactment of laws relating to mechanical appliances, but it was also competent to consider, and to endeavor to reduce, the dangers incident to the strain of excessive hours of duty on the part of engineers, conductors, train dispatchers, telegraphers, and other persons embraced within the class defined by the act. And in imposing restrictions having reasonable relation to this end there is no interference with liberty of contract as guaranteed by the Constitution.

What does the *Lochner* Court find wrong with the New York statute "as a labor law, pure and simple"? Consider Professor C.G. Tiedeman's assertion that the "proper limits" of the police powers are "to compel every one to so use his own property and so conduct himself as not to injure his neighbor or infringe upon

54. See pp. 546-550 infra.

55. But see William Van Alstyne, The Demise of the Right-Privilege Distinction in Constitutional Law, 81 Harv. L. Rev. 1439 (1968); Reich, The New Property, 73 Yale L.J. 733 (1964).

his rights."[56] Consider also the following excerpt from Coppage v. Kansas, 236 U.S. 1 (1915).

> As to the interest of the employed, it is said . . . to be a matter of common knowledge that "employés, as a rule, are not financially able to be as independent in making contracts for the sale of their labor as are employers in making contracts of purchase thereof." No doubt, wherever the right of private property exists, there must and will be inequalities of fortune; and thus it naturally happens that parties negotiating about a contract are not equally unhampered by circumstances. This applies to all contracts, and not merely to that between employer and employé. Indeed a little reflection will show that wherever the right of private property and the right of free contract co-exist, each party when contracting is inevitably more or less influenced by the question whether he has much property, or little, or none; for the contract is made to the very end that each may gain something that he needs or desires more urgently than that which he proposes to give in exchange. And, since it is self-evident that, unless all things are held in common, some persons must have more property than others, it is from the nature of things impossible to uphold freedom of contract and the right of private property without at the same time recognizing as legitimate those inequalities of fortune that are the necessary result of the exercise of those rights. But the Fourteenth Amendment, in declaring that a State shall not "deprive any person of life, liberty or property without due process of law," gives to each of these an equal sanction; it recognizes "liberty" and "property" as co-existent human rights, and debars the States from any unwarranted interference with either.
>
> And since a State may not strike them down directly it is clear that it may not do so indirectly, as by declaring in effect that the public good requires the removal of those inequalities that are but the normal and inevitable result of their exercise, and then invoking the police power in order to remove the inequalities, without other object in view. The police power is broad, and not easily defined, but it cannot be given the wide scope that is here asserted for it, without in effect nullifying the constitutional guaranty.
>
> We need not refer to the numerous and familiar cases in which this court has held that the power may properly be exercised for preserving the public health, safety, morals, or general welfare, and that such police regulations may reasonably limit the enjoyment of personal liberty, including the right of making contracts. . . . An evident and controlling distinction is this: that in those cases it has been held permissible for the States to adopt regulations fairly deemed necessary to secure some object directly affecting the public welfare, even though the enjoyment of private rights of liberty and property be thereby incidentally hampered; while in that portion of the Kansas statute which is now under consideration — that is to say, aside from coercion, etc. — there is no object or purpose, expressed or implied, that is claimed to have reference to health, safety, morals, or public welfare, beyond the supposed desirability of leveling inequalities of fortune by depriving one who has property of some part of what is characterized as his "financial independence." In short, an interference with the normal exercise of personal liberty and property rights is the primary object of the statute, and not an incident to the advancement of the general welfare.

Can Muller v. Oregon, 208 U.S. 412 (1908), be distinguished from *Lochner* and *Coppage? Muller* upheld a statute limiting the workday of women in factories and laundries to ten hours. Justice Brewer wrote for the Court:

56. Christopher Tiedeman, A Treatise on the Limitations of Police Power in the United States 8 (1886).

> That woman's physical structure and the performance of maternal functions place her at a disadvantage in the struggle for subsistence is obvious. This is especially true when the burdens of motherhood are upon her. Even when they are not, by abundant testimony of the medical fraternity continuance for a long time on her feet at work, repeating this from day to day, tends to injurious effects upon the body, and as healthy mothers are essential to vigorous offspring, the physical well-being of woman becomes an object of public interest and care in order to preserve the strength and vigor of the race.
>
> Still again, history discloses the fact that woman has always been dependent upon man. He established his control at the outset by superior physical strength, and this control in various forms, with diminishing intensity, has continued to the present. As minors, though not to the same extent, she has been looked upon in the courts as needing especial care that her rights may be preserved. Education was long denied her, and while now the doors of the school room are opened and her opportunities for acquiring knowledge are great, yet even with that and the consequent increase of capacity for business affairs it is still true that in the struggle for subsistence she is not an equal competitor with her brother. Though limitations upon personal and contractual rights may be removed by legislation, there is that in her disposition and habits of life which will operate against a full assertion of those rights. She will still be where some legislation to protect her seems necessary to secure a real equality of right. Doubtless there are individual exceptions, and there are many respects in which she has an advantage over him; but looking at it from the viewpoint of the effort to maintain an independent position in life, she is not upon an equality. Differentiated by these matters from the other sex, she is properly placed in a class by herself, and legislation designed for her protection may be sustained, even when like legislation is not necessary for men and could not be sustained. It is impossible to close one's eyes to the fact that she still looks to her brother and depends upon him. Even though all restrictions on political, personal and contractual rights were taken away, and she stood, so far as statutes are concerned, upon an absolutely equal plane with him, it would still be true that she is so constituted that she will rest upon and look to him for protection; that her physical structure and a proper discharge of her maternal functions — having in view not merely her own health, but the well-being of the race — justify legislation to protect her from the greed as well as the passion of man. The limitations which this statute places upon her contractual powers, upon her right to agree with her employer as to the time she shall labor, are not imposed solely for her benefit, but also largely for the benefit of all. Many words cannot make this plainer. The two sexes differ in structure of body, in the functions to be performed by each, in the amount of physical strength, in the capacity for long-continued labor, particularly when done standing, the influence of vigorous health upon the future well-being of the race, the self-reliance which enables one to assert full rights, and in the capacity to maintain the struggle for subsistence.

How do the dissenting opinions of Justices Harlan and Holmes in *Lochner* differ with respect to whether "a labor law, pure and simple" is within the police power?

4. Burdens of Proof and Questions of Degree

Justice Peckham considers whether the New York statute can be upheld as a regulation protecting the health of bakery employees or consumers in terms of the standard: "There [must] be some fair ground, reasonable in and of itself, to say that there is a material danger to the public health, or to the health of the employee, if the hours of labor are not curtailed." How does this differ, theoretically or in application, from Justice Harlan's criterion that the law must "have a real or substantial relation" to the promotion of health? Harlan sets out a number of facts about the health of bakers, to conclude that "there is room for debate and for an honest difference of opinion" whether long hours are injurious.[57] Peckham does not explicitly deny that there may be. On what basis, then, does the Court strike down the New York statute?

One possibility is that the majority and dissent apply essentially the same standard, but with different burdens of proof or with the burden of proof on different parties.

Another possibility, not inconsistent with the first, lies in their different concepts of the nature of permissible state regulation — of the "police power." If Peckham implicitly acknowledges that the difference between *Lochner* and the decision in Holden v. Hardy sustaining maximum hours for miners (from which he dissented) is one of degree, his opinion nevertheless has an air of categorizing occupations as intrinsically hazardous or not, rather than weighing or balancing along a continuum. Harlan's seems more pragmatically and empirically oriented.

Compare also the majority's and Justice Harlan's treatment of judicial deference to state legislation in *Lochner* with their positions in *Plessy*. What accounts for the apparent reversal of positions?

5. Laissez Faire, Lawyers, and Legal Scholarship

Opponents of nineteenth-century rate and labor regulations typically argued, in the language of traditional conservatism, that the rights of property were insecure in the hands of popularly controlled state legislatures. And they also invoked the laissez faire doctrines of the eighteenth-century economist Adam Smith and the nineteenth-century social Darwinists Herbert Spencer and William Graham Sumner.

57. In Muller v. Oregon, p. 294 supra, the Court relied on an abundance of similar data, contained in a 113-page brief filed by Louis Brandeis in support of Oregon's maximum-hour legislation for women. Justice Brewer wrote for the Court, upholding the law:

> In patent cases counsel are apt to open the argument with a discussion of the state of the art. It may not be amiss, in the present case, before examining the constitutional question, to notice the course of legislation as well as expressions of opinion from other than judicial sources. In the brief filed by Mr. Louis D. Brandeis, for the defendant in error, is a very copious collection of all these matters, an epitome of which is found in the margin.
>
> The legislation and opinions referred to in the margin may not be, technically speaking, authorities, and in them is little or no discussion of the constitutional question presented to us for determination, yet they are significant of a widespread belief that woman's physical structure, and the functions she performs in consequence thereof, justify special legislation restricting or qualifying the conditions under which she should be permitted to toil. Constitutional questions, it is true, are not settled by even a consensus of present public opinion, for it is the peculiar value of a written constitution that it places in unchanging form limitations upon legislative action, and thus gives a permanence and stability to popular government which otherwise would be lacking. At the same time, when a question of fact is debated and debatable, and the extent to which a special constitutional limitation goes is affected by the truth in respect to that fact, a widespread and long continued belief concerning it is worthy of consideration. We take cognizance of all matters of general knowledge.

Briefs of this sort have come to be called "Brandeis briefs" and have been submitted in a wide variety of cases.

Smith is the father of free market theory. In modern and much oversimplified terms, individuals are motivated by self-interest, which leads to competition in the marketplace, which regulates itself so as to produce just the right quantity and quality of goods and services demanded and to allocate them in the most efficient manner.[58]Government plays a legitimate role by providing public goods (e.g., armies and police), regulating monopolies, requiring activities to internalize the external costs they generate (e.g., by preventing or providing damage remedies for "nuisances"), and subsidizing activities (e.g., education) to the extent they produce external benefits. But government-operated enterprises and government intervention in the private sector generally are inefficient and undesirable, and government redistribution of income may subvert incentive and distort the market. Since efficient operation of the market depends on the ability of individuals and firms to transact freely with each other, government constraints on private contracting are especially destructive.

The social Darwinists provided an independent justification for government nonintervention and especially for inequalities of wealth. From the process of natural selection, Herbert Spencer, an Englishman, derived the notion that only the "fittest" ought to survive. His Social Statics (1850) argued against public education, health and safety regulations (except to prevent nuisances), medical licensing, and welfare. Those "sufficiently complete to live . . . *do* live, and it is well that they should live. If they are not sufficiently complete to live, they die, and it is best that they should die." The destitute are "unfit" and "the whole effort of nature is to get rid of such, to clear the world of them, and make room for better."[59] Sumner, a professor of sociology at Yale, brought Spencer's social theory and policy to America with a vengeance:[60] "Let it be understood that we cannot go outside of this alternative: liberty, inequality, survival of the fittest; not-liberty, equality, survival of the unfittest. The former carries society forward and favors all its best members; the latter carries society downwards and favors all its worst members."

Laissez faire economics and social Darwinism were in vogue among American intellectuals in the mid-nineteenth century. But opposition to both the pure theories and their social implications began to arise among economists, sociologists, theologians, and statesmen. By the close of the nineteenth century, the notion of the purely negative state was giving way to a different view of the role of government. A modern advocate of the positive state writes:[61]

> Those who advocated a policy of laissez faire in the years after the Civil War seemingly were conforming to the best traditions of European and American liberalism. . . . Since liberalism originated essentially as a protest against an authoritarian order in religion, politics, and economics, it was at the outset a purely negative faith, one aimed at removing the artificial restrictions that blocked human progress. Thus, with respect to government and economics, it became associated with laissez faire and economic freedom. In a complex industrial society, however, if the liberal objec-

58. "Efficiency" is, today, an economic term of art. An allocation of resources among individuals is efficient (or Pareto-optimal) when no alternative distribution could make some individuals better off without making at least one worse off. Conversely, an allocation is inefficient or suboptimal when some individuals could be made better off by a different allocation without making anyone worse off.

59. Herbert Spencer, Social Statics 414-415 (1850).

60. 2 Essays of William Graham Sumner 56 (Keller & Davie eds. 1934).

61. Sidney Fine, Laissez Faire and the General Welfare State 30-32 (1956).

> tives of individual freedom and equality of opportunity are to be realized it becomes necessary to extend the sphere of social control. The result has been that liberalism, which started out as an essentially negative creed designed to do away with obstructions to individual progress, "has developed as a positive effort to better man's estate by constructive action."
>
> Those who in the industrial order that was emerging in the United States after the Civil War continued to advocate the laissez-faire brand of liberalism tended to establish economic freedom as an end in itself rather than as a means to an end, and were out of harmony with the true spirit of liberalism. They were blind to the compelling necessity for social and economic reform and refused to recognize that some positive action on the part of the state was essential to assure the effective liberty of the individual. Laissez faire in the years after 1865 was the doctrine of the conservatives.

Classical liberalism suited the needs of the corporate bar, and a reactionary spirit pervaded the two most important constitutional law texts of the period — Thomas M. Cooley's A Treatise on the Constitutional Limitations Which Rest upon the Legislative Power of the States of the American Union (1868) and Christopher G. Tiedeman's A Treatise on the Limitations of Police Power in the United States (1886).

The central thesis of both texts was that the regulatory power of the states — the so-called police power — was narrowly circumscribed by fundamental law and written constitutions. The thesis was ahistorical. In the early Republic, when most constitutions had been adopted, the bounds of government regulation had been amorphous and broad. If Locke's theory of the state implied a narrow concept of the public good, Americans (no less than others, and no less than now) picked and chose and often ignored their philosophers. In opposition to Locke, there was Hobbes' expansive notion of the salus populi — the welfare of the people — and a tradition of government regulation going back to the colonies and England. The states had long intervened in the private sector to regulate the prices of labor and commodities and to protect consumers against unhealthy products and fraudulent merchant practices.[62] But Cooley and Tiedeman, with the characteristic dogmatism of treatise writers, asserted that their views were "the law."

Tiedeman argued that the police power could be used only to enforce the maxim "sic utere tuo ut alienum non laedas" — use your own property so as not to injure another's — and to protect public health and morality. He and Cooley agreed that "class legislation" (for example, laws aiding an employee against his employer) and legislation interfering with an individual's freedom to make contracts were plainly beyond the scope of legislative power. The treatises are as dull as most legal texts, but their moving spirit is nicely captured in Tiedeman's almost hysterical introduction:

> Governmental interference is proclaimed and demanded everywhere as a sufficient panacea for every social evil which threaten the prosperity of society. Socialism, Communism, and Anarchism are rampant throughout the civilized world. The

62. See Lawrence Friedman, A History of American Law 65-71, 161-163 (1973); Oscar Handlin, Commonwealth: A Study of the Role of Government in the American Economy: Massachusetts, 1774-1861 (rev. ed. 1969); Louis Hartz, Economic Policy and Democratic Thought: Pennsylvania, 1776-1860 (1948).

> State is called on to protect the weak against the shrewdness of the stronger, to determine what wages a workman shall receive for his labor, and how many hours daily he shall labor. . . .
>
> Contemplating these extraordinary demands of the great army of discontents, and their apparent power, . . . the conservative classes stand in constant fear of the advent of an absolutism more tyrannical and more unreasoning than any before experienced by man, the absolutism of a democratic majority. . . .
>
> If the author succeeds in any measure in his attempt to awaken the public mind to a full appreciation of the power of constitutional limitations to protect private rights against the radical experimentations of social reformers, he will feel that he has been amply rewarded for his labors in the cause of social order and personal liberty.

Lochner was only one manifestation of the spirit of nineteenth-century liberalism, which extended to other spheres of constitutional doctrine and generally pervaded the legal ethos. See Robert Gordon, Legal Thought and Legal Practice in the Age of American Enterprise, 1870-1920, in Professions and Professional Ideologies in America, 1730-1940 (Stone & Geison eds. (1983)).

6. *A Survey of the Court's Work*[63]

Writing of the era of economic due process, Justice Frankfurter remarked that "Adam Smith was treated as though his generalizations had been imparted to him on Sinai and not as a thinker who addressed himself to the elimination of restrictions which had become fetters upon initiative and enterprise in his day. Basic human rights expressed by the constitutional concept of 'liberty' were equated with theories of laissez-faire. The result was that economic views of confined validity were treated by lawyers and judges as though the Framers had enshrined them in the Constitution."[64]

Between 1890 and 1934, the Supreme Court struck down some 200 statutory and administrative regulations, mostly under the due process clause of the Fourteenth Amendment. The received history tends to exaggerate the Court's perverseness, however, just as it minimizes the facts that the Court sustained at least as many regulations as it invalidated, that it declined to review many others, and that Holmes and Brandeis — the progressive heroes of the period — did not invariably dissent from substantive due process invalidations or always agree with each other.[65] The Court was considerably more restrained than some of the state supreme courts, and though it certainly never "judged social legislation on the basis of any consistent pattern of ideas which can properly bear the name of an

63. See generally William Swindler, Court and Constitution in the Twentieth Century: The Old Legality, 1889-1932 (1969); Benjamin Wright, The Growth of American Constitutional Law 153-168 (1942); The Constitution of the United States of America, Analysis and Interpretation 1602-1612, 1643-1709 (Lib. of Cong. rev. ed. 1973). For a sympathetic analysis of the economics of substantive due process, see Richard Posner, Economic Analysis of Law ch. 19 (1973); cf. Milton Friedman, Capitalism and Freedom (1962); Harold Demsetz, Minorities in the Market Place, 43 N.C.L. Rev. 271 (1965).

64. AFL v. American Sash & Door Co., 335 U.S. 538, 543 (1949) (concurring).

65. Note, however, that the practice of writing dissenting opinions was much less common than it is today. Many justices dissented only if they were strongly opposed to a decision, and, having noted their disagreement in the first decision to establish a doctrine, they often acquiesced in its subsequent applications.

economic theory,"[66] its decisions gain some coherence if one reads them in the context of the ideologies of the times.

The Court let stand most laws that appeared to protect the health, safety, or morals of the general public or to prevent consumer deception. The few exceptions usually involved extraordinarily burdensome regulations where less onerous ones would have served substantially as well. E.g., Jay Burns Baking Co. v. Bryan, 264 U.S. 504 (1924) (law requiring precisely standardized weight for bread loaves), and Weaver v. Palmer Bros. Co., 270 U.S. 402 (1926) (law forbidding use of shoddy in quilts). The Court continued to permit government regulation of rates of railroads and public utilities. But it reviewed the reasonableness of these rates and narrowed the concept of "affected with a public interest" to restrict the kinds of businesses that were subject to price regulation of any sort. Legislatures could not set maximum charges for the resale of theater tickets, Tyson & Brother v. Banton, 273 U.S. 418 (1927); for services of an employment agency, Ribnik v. McBride, 277 U.S. 350 (1928); or for the sale of gasoline, Williams v. Standard Oil Co., 278 U.S. 235 (1929). These interferences with the free market were held unwarranted by monopoly power or any other compelling factor.

In the area of labor relations, the Court distinguished *Lochner* in sustaining the limitation of women's working hours in Muller v. Oregon, 208 U.S. 412 (1908), and disregarded *Lochner* in sustaining a ten-hour maximum workday for male factory employees in Bunting v. Oregon, 243 U.S. 426 (1917). But in Adair v. United States, 208 U.S. 161 (1908), and Coppage v. Kansas, 236 U.S. 1 (1915), the Court held that yellow dog contracts could not be outlawed. And in Adkins v. Children's Hospital, 261 U.S. 525 (1923), it invalidated a District of Columbia minimum wage law for women, noting, inter alia, that the Nineteenth Amendment (1920) had reduced the civil inferiority of women almost "to the vanishing point." Justice Holmes dissented in *Adkins,* stating:

> I confess that I do not understand the principle on which the power to fix a minimum for the wages of women can be denied by those who admit the power to fix a maximum for their hours of work. . . . The bargain is equally affected whichever half you regulate. . . . It will need more than the Nineteenth Amendment to convince me that there are no differences between men and women, or that legislation cannot take those differences into account.

But the Court believed that there was a real difference between maximum hour and minimum wage laws. The former looked like regulations promoting health, a legitimate objective. Minimum wage laws, like laws prohibiting yellow dog contracts, seemed obviously designed to readjust the market in favor of one party to the contract — and this was entirely at odds with the underlying principle of laissez faire.

7. *The Demise of the Eleventh Amendment*

The Eleventh Amendment provides:

66. Lawrence Friedman, Freedom of Contract and Occupational Licensing, 1890-1910, 53 Calif. L. Rev. 487, 525 (1965).

> The judicial power of the United States shall not be construed to extend to any suit in law or equity, commenced or prosecuted against one of the United States by Citizens of another State, or by Citizens or Subjects of any Foreign State.

Although the amendment was (rather generously) interpreted to immunize an unconsenting state from suits brought even by its own citizens (Hans v. Louisiana, 134 U.S. 1 (1890)), this proved not to be a barrier to federal actions to enjoin the state from unconstitutional action. The watershed case was Ex parte Young, 209 U.S. 123 (1908), in which railroads sued the Minnesota attorney general to enjoin him from enforcing railroad tariffs, on the ground that the allegedly confiscatory rates deprived the corporations of property without due process of law. As in *Lochner,* Justice Peckham wrote for the majority, and Justice Harlan dissented. Peckham disposed of the Eleventh Amendment defense in this manner:

> The act to be enforced is alleged to be unconstitutional; and if it be so, the use of the name of the state to enforce an unconstitutional act to the injury of complainants is a proceeding without the authority of, and one which does not affect, the state in its sovereign or governmental capacity. It is simply an illegal act upon the part of a state official in attempting, by the use of the name of the state, to enforce a legislative enactment which is void because unconstitutional. If the act which the state attorney general seeks to enforce be a violation of the Federal Constitution, the officer, in proceeding under such enactment, comes into conflict with the superior authority of that Constitution, and he is in that case stripped of his official or representative character and is subjected in his person to the consequences of his individual conduct. The state has no power to impart to him any immunity from responsibility to the supreme authority of the United States. . . . If the question of unconstitutionality, with reference, at least, to the Federal Constitution, be first raised in a Federal court, that court, as we think is shown by the authorities cited hereafter, has the right to decide it, to the exclusion of all other courts. . . .
>
> To await proceedings against the company in a state court, grounded upon a disobedience of the act, and then, if necessary obtain a review in this court by writ of error to the highest state court, would place the company in peril of large loss and its agents in great risk of fines and imprisonment if it should be finally determined that the act was valid. This risk the company ought not to be required to take. Over eleven thousand millions of dollars, it is estimated, are invested in railroad property, owned by many thousands of people, who are scattered over the whole country, from ocean to ocean, and they are entitled to equal protection from the laws and from the courts, with the owners of all other kinds of property, — no more, no less. The courts having jurisdiction, Federal or state, should, at all times, be opened to them as well as to others, for the purpose of protecting their property and their legal rights.

Only Justice Harlan dissented:

> Let it be observed that the suit instituted . . . was, as to the defendant Young, one against him *as, and only because he was,* attorney general of Minnesota. No relief was sought against him individually, but only in his capacity *as* attorney general. And the manifest, indeed the avowed and admitted, object of seeking such relief, was *to tie the hands* of the *state* so that it could not in any manner or by any mode of proceeding, *in its own courts,* test the validity of the statutes and orders in question. It would therefore seem clear that within the true meaning of the 11th Amendment the suit brought in the Federal court was one, in legal effect, against the state, — as much as

if the state had been formally named on the record as a party — and therefore it was a suit to which, under the Amendment, so far as the state or its attorney general was concerned, the judicial power of the United States did not and could not extend. . . .

[T]he intangible thing called a state, however extensive its powers, can never appear or be represented or known in any court in a litigated case, except by and through its officers. . . .

This principle [of the majority], if firmly established, would work a radical change in our governmental system. It would inaugurate a new era in the American judicial system and in the relations of the national and state governments. It would enable the subordinate Federal courts to supervise and control the official action of the states as if they were "dependencies" or provinces. It would place the states of the Union in a condition of inferiority never dreamed of when the Constitution was adopted or when the 11th Amendment was made a part of the supreme law of the land.[67]

D. Freedom of Contract and the Problem of "Involuntary Servitude"

In Nothing but Freedom, historian Eric Foner notes that all societies that have ended slavery have struggled over the extent of actual freedom to be enjoyed by the newly emancipated slaves.[68] The title of his book is taken from the comment, by Confederate General Robert V. Richardson, that "[t]he emancipated slaves own nothing, because nothing but freedom has been given to them."[69] Suggestions by blacks and some of the so-called Radical Reconstructionists that the former slaves be given at least "40 acres and a mule" to embark on their new lives were rejected. For example, Horace Greeley, the editor of the New York Tribune who fancied himself an avid opponent of slavery, dismissed the agitation for confiscation of slaveholders' land and redistribution to former slaves as "either knavery or madness:" "People who want farms work for them. The only class we know that takes other people's property because they want it is largely represented in Sing Sing."

Thus, Southern blacks were relegated to the market with no resources besides their own labor, which white employers sought to control and exploit. The notorious Black Codes, enacted by many Southern states immediately after the Civil War, established new modes of discipline over the black labor force. For example, Mississippi required that every January all blacks be able to present written evidence of their employment for the next year, and also empowered all white persons to arrest any blacks who left the service of their employers.[70] The Civil Rights Act of 1966 formally invalidated the Black Codes, but the struggle over

67. Professor Owen Fiss comments that "Ex parte Young was viewed as an integral part of the judicial assault on Progressivism, and the reaction to it was aggravated by the specter of a federal judge holding the attorney general of the state in contempt. . . ." Fiss, The Civil Rights Injunction 3 (1978). Ironically, the decision was of much less importance to business interests during the *Lochner* era than it was a half-century later to civil rights and civil liberties litigants seeking to enjoin school segregation and other practices. The scope of the Eleventh Amendment in civil rights actions is examined in Edelman v. Jordan, 415 U.S. 651 (1974), and Fitapatrick v. Bitzer, 427 U.S. 445 (1976).

68. Eric Foner, Nothing but Freedom: Emancipation and Its Legacy (1983).

69. Id. at 55.

70. To put this in perspective, as late as 1875 English law enforced criminal penalties for breach of contract. Id. at 49, 51.

control of the labor force continued. Pete Daniel, the leading authority on the history of peonage, explains:

> Lacking land or capital of their own, blacks had little choice but to sign yearly contracts. . . . As military control became less strict in the South, a labor pattern emerged. Most blacks signed annual contracts. Improvident, they took advances on their expected share of the crop. When settlement time came the next fall, the laborers often discovered that their share of the crop did not cover what they owed the supply merchant or the planter. . . . [S]ome planters demanded that workers remain until they had worked out their entire debt, and when planters used indebtedness as an instrument of compulsion, the system became peonage.[71]

Foner and Daniel both indicate that peonage depended on the formal mechanism of contract, supplemented by the use of the criminal law to punish its breach. This practice finally came before the Supreme Court in 1911.

BAILEY v. ALABAMA
219 U.S. 219 (1911)
Error to the Supreme Court of Alabama

[Section 4730 of the Alabama Code made criminal the breach of a written contract for performance labor if the money for such services had been paid in advance and the breaching employee was unable to refund the advance. The statute required an "intent to injure or defraud" the employer, but "the refusal or failure of any person, who enters into [a contract for the performance of any act or service] to perform such act or service . . . or refund such money [as was advanced] . . . shall be prima facie evidence of the intent to injure his employer or landlord or defraud him." Moreover, another Alabama rule of evidence prohibited rebuttal testimony by the employee "as to his uncommunicated motives, purposes or intention."

Alonzo Bailey, who was black, had received a $15 advance on December 26, 1907, as consideration for his agreeing to work as a farmhand for one year at a salary of $12/month. (He would receive $10.75/month, given his advance.) Bailey left his job in February 1908 without repaying the advance. He was thereupon charged with violating the statute and was convicted by a jury, which found damages of $15. He was sentenced by the court to pay a $30 fine plus costs "and in default thereof to hard labor 'for twenty days in lieu of said fine and one hundred and sixteen days on account of said costs.' " The Alabama Supreme Court upheld the constitutionality of the statute under which Bailey was convicted, and appeal was taken to the United States Supreme Court.]

HUGHES, J. . . .

We at once dismiss from consideration the fact that the plaintiff in error is a black man. . . . The statute, on its face, makes no racial discrimination, and the record fails to show its existence in fact. No question of a sectional character is presented, and we may view the legislation in the same manner as if it had been

71. Pete Daniel, The Shadow of Slavery: Peonage in the South 1901-1969, 19-20 (1972). See also Daniel, The Metamorphosis of Slavery, 1865-1900, 66 J. Am. Hist. 88 (1979).

enacted in New York or in Idaho. Opportunities for coercion and oppression, in varying circumstances, exist in all parts of the Union, and the citizens of all the States are interested in the maintenance of the constitutional guarantees. . . .

[Justice Hughes emphasizes the importance of the evidentiary presumption about intent.]

The money received and repayable, nothing more being shown, constitutes a mere debt. The asserted difficulty of proving the intent to injure or defraud is thus made the occasion for dispensing with such proof . . . [Thus,] the mere breach of a contract for personal service, coupled with the mere failure to pay a debt which was to be liquidated in the course of such service, is made sufficient to warrant a conviction. . . .

[States generally have the power to prescribe their own rules of evidence, including statutes making proof of one fact prima facie evidence of another, so long as "the inference is not purely arbitrary and there is a rational relation between the two facts." However,] [t]he power to create presumptions is not a means of escape from constitutional restrictions. And the State may not in this way interfere with matters withdrawn from its authority by the Federal Constitution or subject an accused to conviction for conduct which it is powerless to proscribe.

In the present case it is urged that the statute as amended, through the operation of the presumption for which it provides, violates the Thirteenth Amendment of the Constitution of the United States and the act of Congress passed for its enforcement. . . .

The language of the Thirteenth Amendment was not new. It reproduced the historic words of the ordinance of 1787 for the government of the Northwest Territory and gave them unrestricted application within the United States and all places subject to their jurisdiction. While the immediate concern was with African slavery, the Amendment was not limited to that. It was a charter of universal civil freedom for all persons, of whatever race, color or estate, under the flag.

The words involuntary servitude have a "larger meaning than slavery." "It was very well understood that in the form of apprenticeship for long terms, as it had been practiced in the West India Islands, on the abolition of slavery by the English government, or by reducing the slaves to the condition of serfs attached to the plantation, the purpose of the article might have been evaded, if only the word slavery had been used." Slaughter House Cases, 16 Wall. p. 69. The plain intention was to abolish slavery of whatever name and form and all its badges and incidents; to render impossible any state of bondage; to make labor free, by prohibiting that control by which the personal service of one man is disposed of or coerced for another's benefit which is the essence of involuntary servitude.

While the Amendment was self-executing, so far as its terms were applicable to any existing condition, Congress was authorized to secure its complete enforcement by appropriate legislation.

The act of March 2, 1867 (Rev. Stat., §§1990, 5526, supra), was a valid exercise of this express authority. Clyatt v. United States, 197 U.S. 207. It declared that all laws of any State, by virtue of which any attempt should be made "to establish, maintain, or enforce, directly or indirectly, the voluntary or involuntary service or labor of any persons or peons, in liquidation of any debt or obligation, or otherwise," should be null and void.

Peonage is a term descriptive of a condition which has existed in Spanish America, and especially in Mexico. The essence of the thing is compulsory service in payment of a debt. A peon is one who is compelled to work for his creditor until his debt is paid. And in this explicit and comprehensive enactment, Congress was not concerned with mere names or manner of description, or with a particular place or section of the country. It was concerned with a fact, wherever it might exist; with a condition, however named and wherever it might be established, maintained or enforced.

The fact that the debtor contracted to perform the labor which is sought to be compelled does not withdraw the attempted enforcement from the condemnation of the statute. The full intent of the constitutional provision could be defeated with obvious facility if, through the guise of contracts under which advances had been made, debtors could be held to compulsory service. It is the compulsion of the service that the statute inhibits, for when that occurs the condition of servitude is created, which would be not less involuntary because of the original agreement to work out the indebtedness. The contract exposes the debtor to liability for the loss due to the breach, but not to enforced labor. . . .

The act of Congress, nullifying all state laws by which it should be attempted to enforce the "service or labor of any persons as peons, in liquidation of any debt or obligation, or, otherwise," necessarily embraces all legislation which seeks to compel the service or labor by making it a crime to refuse or fail to perform it. Such laws would furnish the readiest means of compulsion. The Thirteenth Amendment prohibits involuntary servitude except as punishment for crime. But the exception, allowing full latitude for the enforcement of penal laws, does not destroy the prohibition. It does not permit slavery or involuntary servitude to be established or maintained through the operation of the criminal law by making it a crime to refuse to submit to the one or to render service which would constitute the other. The State may impose involuntary servitude as a punishment for crime, but it may not compel one man to labor for another in payment of a debt, by punishing him as a criminal if he does not perform the service or pay the debt.

What the State may not do directly it may not do indirectly. If it cannot punish the servant as a criminal for the mere failure or refusal to serve without paying his debt, it is not permitted to accomplish the same result by creating a statutory presumption which upon proof of no other fact exposes him to conviction and punishment. Without imputing any actual motive to oppress, we must consider the natural operation of the statute here in question (Henderson v. Mayor, 92 U.S. p. 268), and it is apparent that it furnishes a convenient instrument for the coercion which the Constitution and the act of Congress forbid; an instrument of compulsion peculiarly effective as against the poor and the ignorant, its most likely victims. There is no more important concern than to safeguard the freedom of labor upon which alone can enduring prosperity be based. The provisions designed to secure it would soon become a barren form if it were possible to establish a statutory presumption of this sort and to hold over the heads of laborers the threat of punishment for crime, under the name of fraud but merely upon evidence of failure to work out their debts. The act of Congress deprives of effect all legislative measures of any State through which directly or indirectly the prohibited thing, to wit, compulsory service to secure the payment of a debt may be established or maintained; and we conclude that §4730, as amended, of the Code of Alabama, in so far as it makes the refusal or failure to perform the act or service, without refunding the money or paying for the property received, prima facie evidence of the commission of the crime which the section defines, is in conflict with the Thirteenth Amendment and the legislation authorized by that Amendment, and is therefore invalid.

In this view it is unnecessary to consider the contentions which have been made under the Fourteenth Amendment.

HOLMES, J., joined by Lurton, J., dissenting.

We all agree that this case is to be considered and decided in the same way as if it arose in Idaho or New York. Neither public document nor evidence discloses a law which by its administration is made something different from what it appears on its face, and therefore the fact that in Alabama it mainly concerns the blacks does not matter. Yick Wo v. Hopkins, 118 U.S. 356, does not apply. I shall begin then by assuming for the moment what I think is not true and shall try to show not to be true, that this statute punishes the mere refusal to labor according to contract as a crime, and shall inquire whether there would be anything contrary to the Thirteenth Amendment or the statute if it did, supposing it to have been enacted in the State of New York. I cannot believe it. The Thirteenth Amendment does not outlaw contracts for labor. That would be at least as great a misfortune for the laborers as for the man that employed him. For it certainly would affect the terms of the bargain unfavorably for the laboring man if it were understood that the employer could do nothing in case the laborer saw fit to break his word. But any legal liability for breach of a contract is a disagreeable consequence which tends to make the contractor do as he said he would. Liability to an action for damages has that tendency as well as a fine. If the mere imposition of such consequences as tend to make a man keep to his promise is the creation of peonage when the contract happens to be for labor, I do not see why the allowance of a civil action is not, as well as an indictment ending in fine. Peonage is service to a private master at which a man is kept by bodily compulsion against his will. But the creation of the ordinary legal motives for right conduct does not produce it. Breach of a legal contract without excuse is wrong conduct, even if the contract is for labor, and if a State adds to civil liability a criminal liability to fine, it simply intensifies the legal motive for doing right, it does not make the laborer a slave.

But if a fine may be imposed, imprisonment may be imposed in case of a failure to pay it. Nor does it matter if labor is added to the imprisonment. Imprisonment with hard labor is not stricken from the statute books. On the contrary, involuntary servitude as a punishment for crime is excepted from the prohibition of the Thirteenth Amendment in so many words. Also the power of the States to make breach of contract a crime is not done away with by the abolition of slavery. But if breach of contract may be made a crime at all, it may be made a crime with all the consequences usually attached to crime. There is produced a sort of illusion if a contract to labor ends in compulsory labor in a prison. But compulsory work for no private master in a jail is not peonage. If work in a jail is not condemned in itself, without regard to what the conduct is it punishes, it may be made a consequence of any conduct that the State has power to punish at all. I do not blink the fact that the liability to imprisonment may work as a motive when a fine without it would not, and that it may induce the laborer to keep on when he would like to leave. But it does not strike me as an objection to a law that it is effective. If the contract is one that ought not to be made, prohibit it. But if it is a perfectly fair and proper contract, I can see no reason why the State should not throw its weight on the side of performance. There is no relation between its doing so in the manner supposed and allowing a private master to use private force upon a laborer who wishes to leave.

But all that I have said so far goes beyond the needs of the case as I understand it. I think it a mistake to say that this statute attaches its punishment to the mere breach of a contract to labor. It does not purport to do so; what it purports to punish is fraudulently obtaining money by a false pretense of an intent to keep the written contract in consideration of which the money is advanced. (It is not necessary to cite cases to show that such an intent may be the subject of a material false representation.) But the import of the statute is supposed to be changed by the provision that a refusal to perform, coupled with a failure to return the money advanced, shall be prima facie evidence of fraudulent intent. I agree that if the statute created a conclusive presumption it might be held to make a disguised change in the substantive law. Keller v. United States, 213 U.S. 138, 150. But it only makes the conduct prima facie evidence, a very different matter. Is it not evidence that a man had a fraudulent intent if he receives an advance upon a contract over night and leaves in the morning? I should have thought that it very plainly was. Of course the statute is in general terms and applies to a departure at any time without excuse or repayment, but that does no harm except on a tacit assumption that this law is not administered as it would be in New York, and that juries will act with prejudice against the laboring man. For prima facie evidence is only evidence, and as such may be held by the jury insufficient to make out guilt. This being so, I take it that a fair jury would acquit, if the only evidence were a departure after eleven months' work, and if it received no color from some special well-known course of events. But the matter well may be left to a jury, because their experience as men of the world may teach them that in certain conditions it is so common for laborers to remain during a part of the season, receiving advances, and then to depart at the period of need in the hope of greater wages at a neighboring plantation, that when a laborer follows that course there is a fair inference of fact that he intended it from the beginning. The Alabama statute, as construed by the state court and as we must take it, merely says, as a court might say, that the prosecution may go to the jury. This means and means only that the court cannot say, from its knowledge of the ordinary course of events, that the jury could not be justified by its knowledge in drawing the inference from the facts proved. In my opinion the statute embodies little if anything more than what I should have told the jury was the law without it. The right of the State to regulate laws of evidence is admitted, and the statute does not go much beyond the common law. Commonwealth v. Rubin, 165 Massachusetts, 453.

I do not see how the result that I have reached thus far is affected by the rule laid down by the court, but not contained in the statute, that the prisoner cannot testify to his uncommunicated intentions, and therefore, it is assumed, would not be permitted to offer a naked denial of an intent to defraud. If there is an excuse for breaking the contract it will be found in external circumstances, and can be proved. So the sum of the wrong supposed to be inflicted is that the intent to go off without repaying may be put further back then it would be otherwise. But if there is a wrong it lies in leaving the evidence to the jury, a wrong that is not affected by the letting in or keeping out an item evidence on the other side. I have stated why I think it was not a wrong.

To sum up, I think that obtaining money by fraud may be made a crime as well as murder or theft; that a false representation, expressed or implied, at the time of making a contract of labor that one intends to perform it and thereby obtaining an advance, may be declared a case of fraudulently obtaining money as well as any other; that if made a crime it may be punished like any other crime, and that an unjustified departure from the promised service without repayment may be declared a sufficient case to go to the jury for their judgment; all without in any way infringing the Thirteenth Amendment or the statutes of the United States.

Several years after *Bailey*, in United States v. Reynolds, 235 U.S. 133 (1914), the Court unanimously struck down Alabama's criminal surety system. The Alabama Code authorized a person to appear as a surety for a defendant convicted of a misdemeanor and pay his fine in exchange for the defendant's entering into an employment contract to repay the surety: The defendant thus avoided imprisonment, but was subject to damages and another conviction if he broke the contract. Of course, the defendant could avoid serving time for breach of the surety contract by entering into a contract with another surety. Reynolds's first labor contract was for 10 months (compared to the 2 months he would have had to spend at hard labor in prison). The second contract bound him for 20 months (compared to less than 4 months of prison labor). As Justice Day described the cycle in his opinion for the Court, "the convict is thus kept chained to an ever-turning wheel of servitude to discharge the obligation which he has incurred to his surety." The criminal surety system was part of a larger scheme designed to provide white employers with cheap black labor:

> If there is no white man to pay him out, or if his crime is too serious to be paid out, he goes to the chain-gang — and in several states he is thus hired out to private contractors. The private employer then gets him sooner or later. Some of the largest farms in the South are operated by chain-gang labor. The demand for more convicts by white employers is exceedingly strong. . . . The natural tendency . . . is to convict as many Negroes as possible, and to punish the offences charged as severely as possible.[72]

The sureties in *Reynolds* were charged with violating a federal statute, enacted pursuant to the Thirteenth Amendment, that prohibited enforcing "the voluntary or involuntary service or labor of any persons as peons, in liquidation of any debt or obligation." Striking down the Alabama criminal surety system presented a problem for the Court. Benno Schmidt explains:

> The Court was not prepared to cast doubt on the legality of convict leasing, which was also characterized by forced servitude for private masters, often under barbarous conditions. Moreover, there could be nothing wrong with contracts whereby convicts got the money to pay fines and escape imprisonment. Finally, the state's enforcement of the obligations of such contracts by its criminal law undoubtedly increased the opportunities for convicts to make such agreements. . . . But looked at as a whole, with the distorting effects of racism in the system of law enforcement and

72. Ray Stannard Baker, Following the Color Line 98 (1964).

> the history of black forced labor given their due, the Alabama criminal-surety system stood as a major support of involuntary servitude. The Court could not know this, however, or at least it could not claim that it did. The court had no knowledge about criminal justice system in operation; it had only the indictments . . . before it.[73]

Justice Day approached the problem by noting that the convict had not been re-arrested for failing to pay the fine and costs assessed by the State — for the surety had erased that debt. Instead, he had been arrested and convicted for violating his contract with the surety. The Court concluded that forcing the convict to work to repay the debt under the constant threat of another arrest and eventual imprisonment qualified as involuntary servitude. In a brief concurring opinion, Justice Holmes wrote:

> There seems to me nothing in the Thirteenth Amendment of the Revised Statutes that prevents a State from making a breach of contract, as well a reasonable contract for labor as for other matters, a crime and punishing it as such. But impulsive people with little intelligence or foresight may be expected to lay hold of anything that affords a relief from present pain even though it will cause greater trouble by and by. The successive contracts, each for a longer term than the last, are the inevitable, and must be taken to have been the contemplated outcome of the Alabama laws. On this ground I am inclined to agree that the statutes in question disclose the attempt to maintain service that the Revised Statutes forbid.[74]

In Principle and Prejudice, Benno Schmidt places *Bailey* and the problem of involuntary servitude within the general context of contract theory:[75]

> Does the *Bailey* decision put forward a plausible constitutional theory, indicating, as both Hughes and Holmes insisted, that the racial aspect of peonage should be ignored? Or should the decision be understood as a doctrinally disguised response to the continuing legacy of forced labor for blacks in the South? Answers to these questions are elusive, but are nonetheless of first importance in appraising the Supreme Court's work during the Progressive era. If *Bailey* is credible in its professions of race-neutrality and its attempt to ground its constitutional doctrine in "the freedom of labor," it belongs where it is virtually never placed by students of constitutional history, in the camp of decisions, such as *Lochner*, *Adair*, and *Coppage*, that based rights and legislative inhibitions on the labor contract, and that made freedom of

73. Benno C. Schmidt, Jr., Principle and Prejudice: The Supreme Court and Race in the Progressive Era, Part 2: The *Peonage Cases*, 82 Colum. L. Rev. 646, 699 (1982).

74. In two other cases, the Court declined to strike down government practices challenged under the Thirteenth Amendment. The appellant in Butler v. Perry, 240 U.S. 328 (1916), was convicted under a Florida law that required males between 21 and 45 either to work for six ten-hour days on roads and bridges each year or to avoid the task by providing an able-bodied substitute or paying $3 per day to the county road and bridge fund. Writing for a unanimous Court, Justice McReynolds wrote that the Thirteenth Amendment was not designed to end the ancient tradition of requiring residents to provide labor for road upkeep: "The great purpose in view was liberty under the protection of effective government, not the destruction of the latter by depriving it of essential powers." In the Selective Draft Law Cases, 245 U.S. 366, 390 (1918), the Court upheld the Selective Draft Law of 1917: "[W]e are unable to conceive upon what theory the exaction by government from the citizen of the performance of his supreme and noble duty of contributing to the defense of the rights and honor of the nation . . . can be said to be the imposition of involuntary servitude in violation of the prohibitions of the Thirteenth Amendment."

75. Schmidt, supra note 73, at 702-703. See also President Schmidt's interesting discussion of the "contradiction between freedom and obligation that lies at the heart of the theory of freedom of contract." Should one's contract voluntarily placing oneself in the position of a slave be enforced?

contract theory the backbone of laissez-faire constitutionalism. *Bailey* is an unsettling presence among these warhorses of substantive due process, both conceptually and as a revelation of judicial attitudes. How could a Court devoted to freedom of contract find in the thirteenth amendment a freedom from strict enforcement of contract? To this day, there hovers over the freedom of contract cases the odor of class bias or, at least, benighted indifference to the cruel realities of the laborer's bargaining power in an industrial society. Yet *Bailey's* protection of workers from airtight enforcement of their labor contracts is a constitutional profession on behalf of free labor that is wholly out of sympathy with the interest of employers in having an effective legal deterrent to breach of labor contracts on farms and plantations, where constancy of labor may be critical in the planting and harvest seasons. As such, it supports the sincerity, if not the realism, of the protestations of worker-interest that mark many of the substantive due process decisions generally thought to be most damaging to the welfare of working people. On the other hand, if *Bailey* is viewed as a result-oriented response to the exploitation of black workers, it marks an instance of vigorous legal realism that sheds light both on the White Court's style of judicial statecraft and on its attitudes toward racial justice.[76]

III. Congressional Regulation of Interstate Commerce and of the National Economy

Before the Civil War, the focus of adjudication under the commerce clause was the validity of state regulation of commerce when Congress was silent. This continued to be a staple of the Court's docket throughout the nineteenth century and much of the twentieth, and we shall return to doctrines under the "dormant" commerce clause in the next chapter. Of more interest in the post-War period, however, is adjudication over the scope of *Congress'* legislative powers — an issue scarcely confronted by the Court since *McCulloch.*[77] An early case illustrates the application to federal regulation of concepts developed in the state regulation-of-commerce cases of the Marshall and Taney eras. In United States v. DeWitt, 76 U.S. (9 Wall.) 41 (1869), Chief Justice Chase wrote for a unanimous Court, holding that a congressional safety regulation prohibiting the sale of highly combustible illuminating oils lay beyond the congressional power:

> [T]he express grant of power to regulate commerce among the States has always been understood as limited by its terms; and as a virtual denial of any power to interfere with the internal trade and business of the separate States. . . . [The illuminating oil law] is a regulation of police. . . . As a police regulation, relating exclusively to the internal trade of the States, it can only have effect where the legislative authority of Congress excludes, territorially, all State legislation, as for example, in the District of Columbia. Within State limits, it can have no constitutional operation.

The law struck down in *DeWitt* was a minor and isolated congressional attempt to use the commerce power to regulate trade. Only toward the end of the nineteenth century, with the Interstate Commerce Act of 1887 and the Sherman An-

76. Id. at 705-713.
77. Marbury v. Madison and Dred Scott v. Sandford both invalidated congressional statutes, but neither involved the major Article I powers of commerce, taxing, and spending.

titrust Act of 1890, did Congress begin to intervene significantly in the burgeoning interstate economy. The Supreme Court's response was mixed and paralleled its reaction to state social and economic legislation in many respects. Almost anything connected with railroads was held to be within Congress' power.[78] For example, in Southern Railway v. United States, 22 U.S. 20 (1911), the Court upheld the Federal Safety Appliance Acts as applied to railroad cars with defective couplers moving solely within a state, noting that railroads are "highways of both interstate and intrastate commerce" and that "whatever brings delay or disaster to one [train], or results in disabling one of its operatives, is calculated to impede the progress and imperil the safety of other trains." On the same theory, the Court sustained congressional regulation of the hours of employees working on the intrastate operations of railroads that also conducted interstate operations. Baltimore & Ohio Railroad Co. v. Interstate Commerce Commission, 221 U.S. 612 (1911), p. 293 supra. And in the *Shreveport Rate* case, Houston, E. & W.T. Ry. v. United States, 234 U.S. 342 (1914), the Court held that the Interstate Commerce Commission could prohibit railroads from charging lower rates for transportation within Texas than the rates set by the ICC for identical distances between Texas and other states.

Judicial doctrine under the Sherman Act was more complex.[79] In the first decision under the Act, United States v. E.C. Knight Co., 156 U.S. 1 (1895) (the *Sugar Trust* case), the Court dismissed an action brought under the Sherman Act to set aside the American Sugar Refining Company's acquisition of four other sugar refining companies. Chief Justice Fuller wrote: "It is vital that the independence of the commercial power and of the police power . . . should always be recognized and observed, for while the one furnishes the strongest bond of the union, the other is essential to the preservation of the autonomy of the States." American already produced 65 percent of the sugar refined in the United States, and acquisition of the companies would give it 98 percent of the market. But the power to prevent a monopoly in "manufacture," as distinguished from the "commerce" that follows manufacture, belonged exclusively to the states.

Three doctrinal issues recur throughout the cases of this period. One, suggested by the *Sugar Trust* case, is whether the particular *subject* of congressional regulation is "interstate commerce" as distinguished from some local activity.

Second, are the *purposes* of a regulation consistent with the purposes for which Congress was delegated the power to regulate interstate commerce? Recall, in this respect, Marshall's "pretext" statement in *McCulloch:* "[S]hould congress, under the pretext of executing its powers, pass laws for the accomplishment of objects not intrusted to the government, it would become the painful duty of this tribunal to say that such an act was not the law of the land." By way of elaboration on Marshall's point, consider these points:

(1) General legislative authority resides in the states. (2) Lawmaking authority is delegated to the national government to achieve certain objectives. (3) There is no justification for exercising authority beyond the scope of the purposes for which it is given.

78. In Railroads and Regulation, 1877-1916 (1965), Gabriel Kolko argues that the railroads welcomed national rate regulation as a means of curbing competition.

79. See Lawrence Friedman, A History of American Law 407-408 (1973); Charles McCurdy, The *Knight* Sugar Decision of 1895 and the Modernization of American Corporation Law, 1869-1903, 53 Bus. Hist. Rev. 304 (1979).

The last statement may seem to beg the question. Consider, however, that this notion is taken for granted and applied widely outside of the area of constitutional law. Consider the consequences if government officials, private trustees, and ordinary individuals — who constantly act under authorization from others — were bound only by the substantive terms of a delegation, not by the purposes for which it was made. Consider, indeed, how often an agent's pursuit of objectives beyond those underlying the delegation is a ground for criticism and even the imposition of civil and criminal penalties. For example, a trustee who administers assets in order to injure the beneficiary or to aid a third party without regard to the beneficiary's interests may be held liable; while another trustee, whose objective conduct is no different but who acted in good faith, may not be chargeable. If the concept of ultra vires action — action outside the scope of authority — is generally concerned with purposes as well as the operative terms of the delegation, should it be different in the case of constitutional delegations of power?

The third recurring issue of the period is whether, independent of the first or second issues, a particular instance of congressional regulation of interstate commerce runs afoul of the reservation of powers to the states recognized by the Tenth Amendment. In *McCulloch,* Marshall asserted that the Tenth Amendment was a tautology. During the period considered in this section, however, the Court treated it as at least the symbol, if not the source, of what Edward Corwin called the doctrine of "dual federalism" — the view that "the coexistence of the states and their powers is itself a limitation upon national power," which restricts Congress' use of the delegated powers to purposes and results that are not reserved to the states.[80]

CHAMPION v. AMES

[The *Lottery* case]
188 U.S. 321 (1903)
Appeal from the Circuit Court of the United States from the
Northern District of Illinois

[An 1895 congressional act prohibited sending lottery tickets through the mails, or from one state to another by any means. Appellants were indicted for conspiring to transport tickets of the Pan-American Lottery Company (based in Asunción, Paraguay) from Texas to California, shipping them by railroad with Wells Fargo Express Co. They challenged the indictment on constitutional grounds.]

HARLAN, J. . . .

The appellant insists that the carrying of lottery tickets from one State to another State by an express company engaged in carrying freight and packages from State to State, although such tickets may be contained in a box or package, does not constitute, and cannot by any act of Congress be legally made to constitute, *commerce* among the States within the meaning of the clause of the Constitution. . . .

80. Edward Corwin, Congress' Power to Prohibit Commerce, 18 Cornell L.Q. 477, 482 (1933) (emphasis omitted).

The Government insists that express companies when engaged, for hire, in the business of transportation from one State to another, are instrumentalities of commerce among the States; that the carrying of lottery tickets from one State to another is commerce which Congress may regulate; and that as a means of executing the power to regulate interstate commerce Congress may make it an offence against the United States to cause lottery tickets to be carried from one State to another.

The questions presented by these opposing contentions are of great moment, and are entitled to receive, as they have received, the most careful consideration.

What is the import of the word "commerce" as used in the Constitution? It is not defined by that instrument. Undoubtedly, the carrying from one State to another by independent carriers of things or commodities that are ordinary subjects of traffic, and which have in themselves a recognized value in money, constitutes interstate commerce. . . .

It was said in argument that lottery tickets are not of any real or substantial value in themselves, and therefore are not subjects of commerce. If that were conceded to be the only legal test as to what are to be deemed subjects of the commerce that may be regulated by Congress, we cannot accept as accurate the broad statement that such tickets are of no value. Upon their face they showed that the lottery company offered a large capital prize, to be paid to the holder of the ticket winning the prize at the drawing advertised to be held at Asuncion, Paraguay. . . .

But it is said that the statute in question does not regulate the carrying of lottery tickets from State to State, but by punishing those who cause them to be so carried Congress in effect prohibits such carrying; that in respect of the carrying from one State to another of articles or things that are, in fact, or according to usage in business, the subjects of commerce, the authority given Congress was not to *prohibit,* but only to *regulate.* This view was earnestly pressed at the bar by learned counsel, and must be examined. . . .

In determining whether regulation may not under some circumstances properly take the form or have the effect of prohibition, the nature of the interstate traffic which it was sought by the act of May 2, 1895, to suppress cannot be overlooked. When enacting that statute Congress no doubt shared the views upon the subject of lotteries heretofore expressed by this court. In Phalen v. Virginia, 8 How. 163, 168, after observing that the suppression of nuisances injurious to public health or morality is among the most important duties of Government, this court said: "Experience has shown that the common forms of gambling are comparatively innocuous when placed in contrast with the widespread pestilence of lotteries. The former are confined to a few persons and places, but the latter infests the whole community; it enters every dwelling; it reaches every class; it preys upon the hard earnings of the poor; it plunders the ignorant and simple." In other cases we have adjudged that authority given by legislative enactment to carry on a lottery, although based upon a consideration in money, was not protected by the contract clause of the Constitution; this, for the reason that no State may bargain away its power to protect the public morals, nor excuse its failure to perform a public duty by saying that it had agreed, by legislative enactment, not to do so. Stone v. Mississippi, 101 U.S. 814; Douglas v. Kentucky, 168 U.S. 488.

If a State, when considering legislation for the suppression of lotteries within its own limits, may properly take into view the evils that inhere in the raising of money, in that mode, why may not Congress, invested with the power to regulate commerce among the several States, provide that such commerce shall not be polluted by the carrying of lottery tickets from one State to another? In this connection it must not be forgotten that the power of Congress to regulate commerce among the States is plenary, is complete in itself, and is subject to no limitations except such as may be found in the Constitution. What provision in that instrument can be regarded as limiting the exercise of the power granted? . . .

If it be said that the act of 1895 is inconsistent with the Tenth Amendment, reserving to the States respectively or to the people the powers not delegated to the United States, the answer is that the power to regulate commerce among the States has been expressly delegated to Congress.

Besides, Congress, by that act, does not assume to interfere with traffic or commerce in lottery tickets carried on exclusively within the limits of any State, but has in view only commerce of that kind among the several States. It has not assumed to interfere with the completely internal affairs of any State, and has only legislated in respect of a matter which concerns the people of the United States. As a State may, for the purpose of guarding the morals of its own people, forbid all sales of lottery tickets within its limits, so Congress, for the purpose of guarding the people of the United States against the "widespread pestilence of lotteries" and to protect the commerce which concerns all the States, may prohibit the carrying of lottery tickets from one State to another. In legislating upon the subject of the traffic in lottery tickets, as carried on through interstate commerce, Congress only supplemented the action of those States — perhaps all of them — which, for the protection of the public morals, prohibit the drawing of lotteries, as well as the sale or circulation of lottery tickets, within their respective limits. It said, in effect, that it would not permit the declared policy of the States, which sought to protect their people against the mischiefs of the lottery business, to be overthrown or disregarded by the agency of interstate commerce. We should hesitate long before adjudging that an evil of such appalling character, carried on through interstate commerce, cannot be met and crushed by the only power competent to that end. We say competent to that end, because Congress alone has the power to occupy, by legislation, the whole field of interstate commerce. . . .

FULLER, C.J., joined by Brewer, Shiras, and Peckham, JJ., dissenting. . . .

The power of the State to impose restraints and burdens on persons and property in conservation and promotion of the public health, good order and prosperity is a power originally and always belonging to the States, not surrendered by them to the General Government nor directly restrained by the Constitution of the United States, and essentially exclusive, and the suppression of lotteries as a harmful business falls within this power, commonly called of police. Douglas v. Kentucky, 168 U.S. 488.

It is urged, however, that because Congress is empowered to regulate commerce between the several States, it, therefore, may suppress lotteries by prohibiting the carriage of lottery matter. Congress may indeed make all laws necessary and proper for carrying the powers granted to it into execution, and doubtless an act prohibiting the carriage of lottery matter would be necessary and proper to the execution of a power to suppress lotteries; but that power belongs to the States and not to Congress. To hold that Congress has general police power would be to hold that it may accomplish objects not entrusted to the General Government, and to defeat the operation of the Tenth Amendment. . . .

But apart from the question of bona fides, this act cannot be brought within the power to regulate commerce among the several States, unless lottery tickets are articles of commerce, and, therefore, when carried across state lines, of interstate commerce; or unless the power to regulate interstate commerce includes the absolute and exclusive power to prohibit the transportation of anything or anybody from one State to another. . . .

Is the carriage of lottery tickets from one State to another commercial intercourse?

The lottery ticket purports to create contractual relations and to furnish the means of enforcing a contract right.

This is true of insurance policies, and both are contingent in their nature. Yet this court has held that the issuing of fire, marine, and life insurance policies, in one State, and sending them to another, to be there delivered to the insured on payment of premium, is not interstate commerce. Paul v. Virginia, 8 Wall. 168; Hooper v. California, 155 U.S. 648; New York Life Insurance Company v. Cravens, 178 U.S. 389.

In Paul v. Virginia [p. 173 supra], Mr. Justice Field, in delivering the unanimous opinion of the court, said: "Issuing a policy of insurance is not a transaction of commerce. The policies are simple contracts of indemnity against loss by fire, entered into between the corporations and the assured, for a consideration paid by the latter. These contracts are not articles of commerce in any proper meaning of the word. They are not subjects of trade and barter offered in the market as something having an existence and value independent of the parties to them. They are not commodities to be shipped or forwarded from one State to another, and then put up for sale. They are like other personal contracts between parties which are completed by their signature and the transfer of the consideration. Such contracts are not interstate transactions, though the parties may be domiciled in different States. The policies do not take effect — are not executed contracts — until delivered by the agent in Virginia. They are, then, local transactions, and are governed by the local law. They do not constitute a part of the commerce between the States any more than a contract for the purchase and sale of goods in Virginia by a citizen of New York whilst in Virginia would constitute a portion of such commerce." . . .

If a lottery ticket is not an article of commerce, how can it become so when placed in an envelope or box or other covering, and transported by an express company? To say that the mere carrying of an article which is not an article of commerce in and of itself nevertheless becomes such the moment it is to be transported from one State to another, is to transform a non-commercial article into a commercial one simply because it is transported. I cannot conceive that any such result can properly follow.

It would be to say that everything is an article of commerce the moment it is taken to be transported from place to place, and of interstate commerce if from State to State.

An invitation to dine, or to take a drive, or a note of introduction, all become articles of commerce under the ruling in this case, by being deposited with an express company for transportation. This in effect breaks down all the differences between that which is, and that which is not, an article of commerce, and the necessary consequence is to take from the States all jurisdiction over the subject so far as interstate communication is concerned. It is a long step in the direction of wiping out all traces of state lines, and the creation of a centralized Government. . . .

The Constitution gives no countenance to the theory that Congress is vested with the full powers of the British Parliament, and that, although subject to constitutional limitations, it is the sole judge of their extent and application; and the decisions of this court from the beginning have been to the contrary.

"To what purpose are powers limited, and to what purpose is that limitation committed to writing, if these limits may, at any time, be passed by those intended to be restrained?" asked Marshall, in Marbury v. Madison, 1 Cranch, 137, 176.

"Should Congress," said the same great magistrate in McCulloch v. Maryland, 4 Wheat. 316, 423, "under the pretext of executing its powers, pass laws for the accomplishment of objects not entrusted to the Government; it would become the painful duty of this tribunal, should a case requiring such a decision come before it, to say that such an act was not the law of the land."

Does the grant to Congress of the power to regulate interstate commerce impart the absolute power to prohibit it? . . .

The power to prohibit the transportation of diseased animals and infected goods over railroads or on steamboats is an entirely different thing [from the prohibition of lottery tickets], for they would be in themselves injurious to the transaction of interstate commerce, and, moreover, are essentially commercial in their nature. And the exclusion of diseased persons rests on different ground, for nobody would pretend that persons could be kept off the trains because they were going from one State to another to engage in the lottery business. However enticing that business may be, we do not understand these pieces of paper themselves can communicate bad principles by contact. . . .

Discussion

1. *The commerce power vs. the "police power."* How do Fuller's and Harlan's views of federal and state powers relate to the views of the Marshall and Taney periods? Would Fuller or Harlan permit a state to prohibit the importation of lottery tickets in the absence of congressional legislation?

How do the Justices' conceptions of the police power relate to their conceptions of the police power in *Lochner?* (Note that Justice Harlan, who dissented in *Lochner,* wrote for the majority in the *Lottery* case, and that Justice Peckham, who wrote for the Court in *Lochner,* was among the dissenters in the *Lottery* case.)

2. *"Pretext."* In the penultimate paragraph of his dissent, Fuller quotes Marshall's "pretext" statement in *McCulloch,* implying that the *purposes* underlying the act are not those for which the commerce power was granted. Why not? Would Fuller's position be stronger if, contrary to the Court's assertion, most states permitted the sale of lottery tickets?

3. *The subject of congressional regulation.* Justice Peckham distinguishes lottery tickets from diseased animals and infected goods, which he says Congress can prohibit from being transported interstate. Consider the possible analogue to his implicit distinction in *Lochner* between occupations that are inherently unhealthy and those that are not.

HAMMER v. DAGENHART
247 U.S. 251 (1918)
Appeal from the District Court of the United States
for the Western District of North Carolina

DAY, J. . . .

A bill was filed in the United States District Court for the Western District of North Carolina by a father in his own behalf and as next friend of his two minor sons, one under the age of fourteen years and the other between the ages of fourteen and sixteen years, employees in a cotton mill at Charlotte, North Carolina, to enjoin the enforcement of the act of Congress intended to prevent interstate commerce in the products of child labor. . . .

The District Court held the act unconstitutional and entered a decree enjoining its enforcement. This appeal brings the case here. The first section of the act is in the margin.[a]

The controlling question for decision is: Is it within the authority of Congress in regulating commerce among the States to prohibit the transportation in interstate commerce of manufactured goods, the product of a factory in which, within thirty days prior to their removal therefrom, children under the age of fourteen have been employed or permitted to work, or children between the ages of fourteen and sixteen years have been employed or permitted to work more than eight hours in any day, or more than six days in any week, or after the hour of seven o'clock P.M. or before the hour of 6 o'clock A.M.?

The power essential to the passage of this act, the Government contends, is found in the commerce clause of the Constitution which authorizes Congress to regulate commerce with foreign nations and among the States. . . .

[I]t is insisted that adjudged cases in this court establish the doctrine that the power to regulate given to Congress incidentally includes the authority to prohibit the movement of ordinary commodities and therefore that the subject is not open for discussion. The cases demonstrate the contrary. They rest upon the character of the particular subjects dealt with and the fact that the scope of governmental authority, state or national, possessed over them is such that the authority to prohibit is as to them but the exertion of the power to regulate.

The first of these cases is Champion v. Ames, 188 U.S. 321 (1903), the so-called *Lottery* case, in which it was held that Congress might pass a law having the effect to keep the channels of commerce free from use in the transportation of tickets used in the promotion of lottery schemes. In Hipolite Egg Co. v. United States, 220 U.S. 45 (1911), this court sustained the power of Congress to pass the Pure Food and Drug Act which prohibited the introduction into the States by means of interstate commerce of impure foods and drugs. In Hoke v. United

a. That no producer, manufacturer, or dealer shall ship or deliver for shipment in interstate or foreign commerce any article or commodity the product of any mine or quarry, situated in the United States, in which within thirty days prior to the time of the removal of such product therefrom children under the age of sixteen years have been employed or permitted to work, or any article or commodity the product of any mill, cannery, workshop, factory, or manufacturing establishment, situated in the United States, in which within thirty days prior to the removal of such product therefrom children under the age of fourteen years have been employed or permitted to work, or children between the ages of fourteen years and sixteen years have been employed or permitted to work more than eight hours in any day, or more than six days in any week, or after the hour of seven o'clock postmeridian, or before the hour of six o'clock antemeridian.

States, 227 U.S. 308 (1913), this court sustained the constitutionality of the so-called "White Slave Traffic Act" whereby the transportation of a woman in interstate commerce for the purpose of prostitution was forbidden. . . .

In Caminetti v. United States, 242 U.S. 470 (1917), we held that Congress might prohibit the transportation of women in interstate commerce for the purposes of debauchery and kindred purposes. In Clark Distilling Co. v. Western Maryland Ry. Co., 242 U.S. 311 (1917), the power of Congress over the transportation of intoxicating liquors was sustained. . . .

In each of these instances the use of interstate transportation was necessary to the accomplishment of harmful results. In other words, although the power over interstate transportation was to regulate, that could only be accomplished by prohibiting the use of the facilities of interstate commerce to effect the evil intended.

This element is wanting in the present case. The thing intended to be accomplished by this statute is the denial of the facilities of interstate commerce to those manufacturers in the States who employ children within the prohibited ages. The act in its effect does not regulate transportation among the States, but aims to standardize the ages at which children may be employed in mining and manufacturing within the States. The goods shipped are of themselves harmless. The act permits them to be freely shipped after thirty days from the time of their removal from the factory. When offered for shipment, and before transportation begins, the labor of their production is over, and the mere fact that they were intended for interstate commerce transportation does not make their production subject to federal control under the commerce power. . . .

It is further contended that the authority of Congress may be exerted to control interstate commerce in the shipment of child-made goods because of the effect of the circulation of such goods in other States where the evil of this class of labor has been recognized by local legislation, and the right to thus employ child labor has been more rigorously restrained than in the State of production. In other words, that the unfair competition, thus engendered, may be controlled by closing the channels of interstate commerce to manufacturers in those States where the local laws do not meet what Congress deems to be the more just standard of other States.

There is no power vested in Congress to require the States to exercise their police power so as to prevent possible unfair competition. Many causes may cooperate to give one State, by reason of local laws or conditions, an economic advantage over others. The Commerce Clause was not intended to give to Congress a general authority to equalize such conditions. In some of the States laws have been passed fixing minimum wages for women, in others the local law regulates the hours of labor of women in various employments. Business done in such States may be at an economic disadvantage when compared with States which have no such regulations; surely, this fact does not give Congress the power to deny transportation in interstate commerce to those who carry on business where the hours of labor and the rate of compensation for women have not been fixed by a standard in use in other States and approved by Congress.

The grant of power to Congress over the subject of interstate commerce was to enable it to regulate such commerce, and not to give it authority to control the States in their exercise of the police power over local trade and manufacture.

The grant of authority over a purely federal matter was not intended to destroy the local power always existing and carefully reserved to the States in the Tenth Amendment to the Constitution. . . .

The power of the States to regulate their purely internal affairs by such laws as seem wise to the local authority is inherent and has never been surrendered to the general government. To sustain this statute would not be in our judgment a recognition of the lawful exertion of congressional authority over interstate commerce, but would sanction an invasion by the federal power of the control of a matter purely local in its character, and over which no authority has been delegated to Congress in conferring the power to regulate commerce among the States. . . .

In our view the necessary effect of this act is, by means of a prohibition against the movement in interstate commerce of ordinary commercial commodities, to regulate the hours of labor of children in factories and mines within the States, a purely state authority. Thus the act in a twofold sense is repugnant to the Constitution. It not only transcends the authority delegated to Congress over commerce but also exerts a power as to a purely local matter to which the federal authority does not extend. The far reaching result of upholding the act cannot be more plainly indicated than by pointing out that if Congress can thus regulate matters entrusted to local authority by prohibition of the movement of commodities in interstate commerce, all freedom of commerce will be at an end, and the power of the States over local matters may be eliminated and thus our system of government be practically destroyed.

HOLMES, J., dissenting.

The single question in this case is whether Congress has power to prohibit the shipment [of certain goods] in interstate or foreign commerce. . . . The objection urged against the power is that the States have exclusive control over their methods of production and that Congress cannot meddle with them, and taking the proposition in the sense of direct intermeddling I agree to it and suppose that no one denies it. But if an act is within the powers specifically conferred upon Congress, it seems to me that it is not made any less constitutional because of the indirect effects that it may have, however obvious it may be that it will have those effects, and that we are not at liberty upon such grounds to hold it void.

The first step in my argument is to make plain what no one is likely to dispute — that the statute in question is within the power expressly given to Congress if considered only as to its immediate effects and that if invalid it is so only upon some collateral ground. The statute confines itself to prohibiting the carriage of certain goods in interstate or foreign commerce. Congress is given power to regulate such commerce in unqualified terms. It would not be argued today that the power to regulate does not include the power to prohibit. Regulation means the prohibition of something, and when interstate commerce is the matter to be regulated I cannot doubt that the regulation may prohibit any part of such commerce that Congress sees fit to forbid. At all events it is established by the *Lottery* case and others that have followed it that a law is not beyond the regulative power of Congress merely because it prohibits certain transportation out and out. . . . So I repeat that this statute in its immediate operation is clearly within the Congress's constitutional power.

The question then is narrowed to whether the exercise of its otherwise constitutional power by Congress can be pronounced unconstitutional because of its possible reaction upon the conduct of the States in a matter upon which I have admitted that they are free from direct control. I should have thought that matter had been disposed of so fully as to leave no room for doubt. I should have thought that the most conspicuous decisions of this Court had made it clear that the power to regulate commerce and other constitutional powers could not be cut down or qualified by the fact that it might interfere with the carrying out of the domestic policy of any State. . . .

[I]f there is any matter upon which civilized countries have agreed — far more unanimously than they have with regard to intoxicants and some other matters over which this country is now emotionally aroused — it is the evil of premature and excessive child labor. . . .

But I had thought that the propriety of the exercise of a power admitted to exist in some cases was for the consideration of Congress alone and that this Court always had disavowed the right to intrude its judgment upon questions of policy or morals. It is not for this Court to pronounce when prohibition is necessary to regulation if it ever may be necessary — to say that it is permissible as against strong drink but not as against the product of ruined lives.

The act does not meddle with anything belonging to the States. They may regulate their internal affairs and their domestic commerce as they like. But when they seek to send their products across the state line they are no longer within their rights. If there were no Constitution and no Congress their power to cross the line would depend upon their neighbors. Under the Constitution such commerce belongs not to the States but to Congress to regulate. It may carry out its views of public policy whatever indirect effect they may have upon the activities of the States. Instead of being encountered by a prohibitive tariff at her boundaries the State encounters the public policy of the United States which it is for Congress to express. The public policy of the United States is shaped with a view to the benefit of the nation as a whole. If, as has been the case within the memory of men still living, a State should take a different view of the propriety of sustaining a lottery from that which generally prevails, I cannot believe that the fact would require a different decision from that reached in Champion v. Ames. Yet in that case it would be said with quite as much force as in this that Congress was attempting to intermeddle with the State's domestic affairs. The national welfare as understood by Congress may require a different attitude within its sphere from that of some self-seeking State. It seems to me entirely constitutional for Congress to enforce its understanding by all the means at its command. . . .

Mr. Justice McKenna, Mr. Justice Brandeis and Mr. Justice Clarke concur in this opinion.

Discussion

The Child Labor Act, by its terms, operated directly upon interstate commerce. In purely formal terms, does the act differ from the prohibitions of the Federal Lottery Act, the Pure Food and Drug Act, and the White Slave Traffic Act? If not, why was it beyond the commerce power?

Were the *objectives* underlying the Child Labor Act categorically different from those underlying the other acts? In this respect, did the government overplay its hand by making the "unfair competition" argument? Recall that in the *Lottery* case the Court thought that perhaps all of the states forbade the sale of lottery tickets. The Court might have made similar assumptions about state policies concerning adulterated food and prostitution. But the very point of the "unfair competition" was that not all states prohibited child labor.[81]

If, after the *Child Labor* case, in the (judicially enforced) silence of Congress, a state had attempted to exclude goods made using child labor, this trade barrier almost surely would have been deemed an impermissible state regulation of interstate commerce. (See Chapter 5 infra.) Equally surely, in the silence of Congress, a state *could* exclude diseased cattle. What is the difference, and does it provide any further insight into the Court's restriction on *Congress'* power in the *Child Labor* case?

After the *Child Labor* case, could Congress have authorized the states to exclude goods made using child labor, under the "consent" doctrines discussed at pp. 169-173 supra?

Note: Binary Oppositions and Congressional Ability to Invoke Its Power Under the Commerce Clause

Hammer illustrates the importance of binary oppositions deemed crucial to ascertaining whether Congress had the power to act under the Commerce Clause. In addition to the distinction between inherently dangerous and harmless goods, the Court refers to another important opposition central to many cases of this period: "manufacture" versus "commerce." As the Court wrote in Kidd v. Pearson, 128 U.S. 1 (1888), "Manufacture is transformation — the fashioning of raw materials into a change of form for use. The functions of commerce are different." In United States v. E.C. Knight Co., 156 U.S. 1 (1895), the Court refused to apply the Sherman Act to a trust that manufactured 95 percent of the sugar sold in the United States. Chief Justice Fuller wrote: "Commerce succeeds to manufacture, and is not part of it. The fact that an article is manufactured for export to another State does not itself make it an article of interstate commerce." An important pre-1937 New Deal case, Carter v. Carter Coal Co., 298 U.S. 238 (1936), relied on the manufacture-commerce distinction to invalidate a provision of the Bituminous Coal Conservation Act of 1936 that required coal companies to engage in collective bargaining with their employees. Justice Sutherland defined "commerce" as "the equivalent of the phrase 'intercourse for the purpose of trade.' " "Plainly, the incidents leading up to and culminating in the mining of coal do not constitute such intercourse. The employment of men, the fixing of their wages, hours of labor and working conditions, the bargaining in respect of these things . . . — each and all constitute intercourse for the purposes of production, not trade. . . . Commerce in the coal mined is not brought into being by force of [the activities covered by the Act]. Mining brings the subject matter of commerce into existence. Commerce disposes of it."

Linked to the distinction between "manufacture" and "commerce" was that between "direct" and "indirect" effects on commerce. Justice Sutherland in *Carter* conceded that "the production of every commodity intended for interstate sale

81. For an interesting discussion of the facts, politics, and law of child labor, see Stephen Wood, Constitutional Politics in the Progressive Era (1968).

and transportation has some effect upon interstate commerce." Moreover, "[m]uch stress is put upon the evils which come from the struggle between employers and employees," including the resulting strikes, curtailment and irregularity of production and effect on prices; and it is insisted that interstate commerce is *greatly* affected thereby.

> But . . . the conclusive answer is that the evils are all local evils over which the federal government has no legislative control. . . . Working conditions are obviously local conditions. The employees are not engaged in or about commerce, but exclusively in producing a commodity. . . . Such effect as they may have upon commerce, however extensive it may be, is secondary and indirect. An increase in the greatness of the effect adds to its importance. It does not alter its character.

Sutherland suggested that "[t]he word 'direct' implies that the activity or condition invoked or blamed shall operate proximately — not mediately, remotely, or collaterally — to produce the effect. It connotes the absence of an efficient intervening agency or condition." The dichotomy was categorical rather than one of degree: "The matter of degree has no bearing upon the question here, since that question is not — What is the *extent* of the local activity or condition, or the *extent* of the effect produced upon interstate commerce? but — What is the *relation* between the activity or condition and the effect?" Sutherland did not deny that labor disputes about the conditions of coal mining might have "extensive" consequences for the availability of coal to be shipped in interstate commerce. But any such effects were "secondary and indirect. An increase in the greatness of the effect adds to its importance. It does not alter its character."

In trying to make sense of this distinction, recall discussions about causation in your torts or criminal law classes. Consider the difference involved, for example, in finding that a particular injury was "proximately caused" by the actions of the defendant and a determination that it was merely "caused in fact" by those actions.

The Court also distinguished on occasion between items in the "flow" of commerce and those not in the flow either because they had not yet entered it or because the flow had come to an end. For example, Swift & Co. v. U.S., 196 U.S. 375 (1905), upheld the application of the Sherman Act to the price-fixing practices of stockyard owners. As Justice Sutherland later described this case, "livestock was consigned and delivered to stockyards — not as a place of final destination, but, as . . . 'a throat through which the current flows.' " The pre-1937 Court refused to extend *Swift* beyond its facts. Thus, Schecter Poultry Corp. v. United States, 295 U.S. 495 (1935), struck down federal regulation of the live poultry industry in New York because "the commodity in question [i.e., chickens], although shipped from another state, had come to rest in the state of its destination, and, as the court pointed out, was no longer in a current or flow of interstate commerce."

As you will soon see, all of these categorical distinctions disappeared in the maelstrom of the post-1937 transformations of the Commerce Clause.

Note on the Taxing Power

Shortly after the decision in Hammer v. Dagenhart, Congress enacted the Child Labor Tax Law of 1919, which imposed a 10 percent tax on the net income of any manufacturer employing children below specified ages. In the *Child Labor Tax* case, Bailey v. Drexel Furniture Co., 259 U.S. 20 (1922), the Court struck it down, with only Justice Clarke dissenting. Chief Justice Taft observed that "a court must be blind not to see that the so-called tax is imposed to stop the employment of children. . . . Its prohibitory and regulatory effect and purpose are palpable." He continued:

> Grant the validity of this law, and all that Congress would need to do, hereafter, in seeking to take over to its control any one of the great number of subjects of public interest, jurisdiction of which the States have never parted with, and which are reserved to them by the Tenth Amendment, would be to enact a detailed measure of complete regulation of the subject and enforce it by a so-called tax upon departures from it. To give such magic to the word "tax" would be to break down all constitutional limitation of the powers of Congress and completely wipe out the sovereignty of the States.
>
> The difference between a tax and a penalty is sometimes difficult to define and yet the consequences of the distinction in the required method of their collection often are important. Where the sovereign enacting the law has power to impose both tax and penalty the difference between revenue production and mere regulation may be immaterial,[82] but not so when one sovereign can impose a tax only, and the power of regulation rests in another. Taxes are occasionally imposed in the discretion of the legislature on proper subjects with the primary motive of obtaining revenue from them and with the incidental motive of discouraging them by making their continuance onerous. They do not lose their character as taxes because of the incidental motive. But there comes a time in the extension of the penalizing features of the so-called tax when it loses it character as such and becomes a mere penalty with the characteristics of regulation and punishment. Such is the case in the law before us. . . .
>
> The analogy of the *Dagenhart* case is clear. The congressional power over interstate commerce is, within its proper scope, just as complete and unlimited as the congressional power to tax, and the legislative motive in its exercise is just as free from judicial suspicion and inquiry. Yet when Congress threatened to stop interstate commerce in ordinary and necessary commodities, unobjectionable as subjects of transportation, and to deny the same to the people of a State in order to coerce them into compliance with Congress's regulation of state concerns, the court said this was not in fact regulation of interstate commerce, but rather that of State concerns and was invalid. So here the so-called tax is a penalty to coerce people of a State to act as Congress wishes them to act in respect of a matter completely the business of the state government under the Federal Constitution. This case requires as did the *Dagenhart* case the application of the principle announced by Chief Justice Marshall in McCulloch v. Maryland, in [the "pretext" passage, p. 31 supra].

82. Veazie Bank v. Fenno, 75 U.S. (8 Wall.) 533 (1869), is an example. The Court sustained a 10 percent federal tax on personal and state bank notes, apparently designed to deter the use of such notes, commenting:

> Having. . . , in the exercise of undisputed constitutional powers, undertaken to provide a currency for the whole country, it cannot be questioned that Congress may, constitutionally, secure the benefit of it to the people by appropriate legislation. To this end, Congress has denied the quality of legal tender to foreign coins, and has provided by law against the imposition of counterfeit and base coin on the community. To the same end, Congress may restrain, by suitable enactments, the circulation as money of any notes not issued under its own authority. Without this power, indeed, its attempts to secure a sound and uniform currency for the country must be futile.

Hill v. Wallace, 259 U.S. 44 (1922), decided on the same day as the *Child Labor Tax* case, held invalid as a regulation of the (local) business of grain trading a tax of 20¢ per bushel on grain future contracts except those made through "boards of trade" designated by the secretary of agriculture upon their compliance with detailed regulations specified in the statute. United States v. Constantine, 296 U.S. 287 (1935), struck down a federal excise tax of $1,000 imposed on liquor dealers carrying on business in violation of state or local law; the Court held that the exaction was a penalty rather than a revenue-raising measure.

During the same period, the Court also upheld some federal taxes that appeared to regulate what it viewed as "local" matters. McCray v. United States, 195 U.S. 27 (1904), sustained a law, designed to discourage the sale of margarine that looked like butter, that taxed yellow margarine at 10¢ per pound and white margarine at only ¼¢. United States v. Doremus, 249 U.S. 86 (1919), sustained burdensome federal record-keeping requirements on sellers of narcotics, ostensibly designed to enforce a tax on the drugs. In the *Child Labor Tax* case, Chief Justice Taft distinguished these laws on the ground that, on their face, they were tax rather than regulatory measures.

Note on the Spending Power

Recall Madison's veto of an "internal improvements" measure in 1817. His constricted interpretation of congressional power did not in fact prevail, although the vetoes of Madison and Monroe and the political agendas of Jacksonian Democrats kept such measures off the political agenda for some years. When they reemerged in the aftermath of the Civil War, the Supreme Court rejected Madison's analysis. Nonetheless, the scope of a congressional "spending power," independent of the other enumerated powers, remained unclear. In the California Railroad Cases, 127 U.S. 1 (1888), which unanimously upheld the partial congressional financing of interstate railroads, Justice Bradley relied on the commerce power:

> It cannot at the present day be doubted that Congress, under the power to regulate commerce among the several States, as well as to provide for postal accommodations and military exigencies, had authority to pass these laws. The power to construct, or to authorize individuals or corporations to construct, national highways and bridges from State to State, is essential to the complete control and regulation of interstate commerce. Without authority in Congress to establish and maintain such highways and bridges, it would be without authority to regulate one of the most important adjuncts of commerce. This power in former times was exerted to a very limited extent, the Cumberland or National road being the most notable instance. Its exertion was but little called for, as commerce was then mostly conducted by water, and many of our statesman entertained doubts as to the existence of the power to establish ways of communication by land. But since, in consequence of the expansion of the country, the multiplication of its products, and the invention of railroads and locomotion by steam, land transportation has so vastly increased, a sounder consideration of the subject has prevailed and led to the conclusion that Congress has plenary power over the whole subject.

The question of Congress' power to spend federal funds in the pursuit of ends not within the enumerated powers of Article I, section 8, was addressed most importantly in United States v. Butler. While explicitly rejecting Madison's view of the spending power, the Court nonetheless invalidated the Agricultural Adjustment Act of 1933. The Act, designed to raise farm prices by reducing surplus production, authorized the secretary of agriculture to spend federal funds as consideration for the contractual agreement of farmers to reduce their productive acreage. Ironically, *Butler* confirmed the doctrinal basis for what has become a centrally important use of congressional power in the age of the modern administrative state.

UNITED STATES v. BUTLER, 297 U.S. 1 (1936): ROBERTS, J. . . . There should be no misunderstanding as to the function of this court in such a case. It is sometimes said that the court assumes a power to overrule or control the action of the people's representatives. This is a misconception. The Constitution is the supreme law of the land ordained and established by the people. All legislation must conform to the principles it lays down. When an act of Congress is appropriately challenged in the courts as not conforming to the constitutional mandate the judicial branch of the Government has only one duty, — to lay the article of the Constitution which is invoked beside the statute which is challenged and to decide whether the latter squares with the former. All the court does, or can do, is to announce its considered judgment upon the question. The only power it has, if such it may be called, is the power of judgment. This court neither approves nor condemns any legislative policy. Its delicate and difficult office is to ascertain and declare whether the legislation is in accordance with, or in contravention of, the provisions of the Constitution; and, having done that, its duty ends.

. . . Since the foundation of the Nation sharp differences of opinion have persisted as to the true interpretation of the ["general welfare" clause]. Madison asserted it amounted to no more than a reference to the other powers enumerated in the subsequent clauses of the same section; that, as the United States is a government of limited and enumerated powers, the grant of power to tax and spend for the general national welfare must be confined to the enumerated legislative fields committed to the Congress. In this view the phrase is mere tautology, for taxation and appropriation are or may be necessary incidents of the exercise of any of the enumerated legislative powers. Hamilton, on the other hand, maintained the clause confers a power separate and distinct from those later enumerated, is not restricted in meaning by the grant of them, and Congress consequently has a substantive power to tax and to appropriate, limited only by the requirement that it shall be exercised to provide for the general welfare of the United States. Each contention has had the support of those whose views are entitled to weight. This court has noticed the question, but has never found it necessary to decide which is the true construction. Mr. Justice Story, in his Commentaries, espouses the Hamiltonian position. We shall not review the writings of public men and commentators or discuss the legislative practice. Study of all these leads us to conclude that the reading advocated by Mr. Justice Story is the correct one. While, therefore, the power to tax is not unlimited, its confines are set in the clause which confers it, and not in those of §8 which bestow and define the legislative powers of the Congress. It results that the power of Congress to authorize expenditure of public moneys for public purposes is not limited by the direct grants of legislative power found in the Constitution.

But the adoption of the broader construction leaves the power to spend subject to limitations. . . . Hamilton, in his well known Report on Manufactures, states that the purpose must be "general, and not local.". . .

We are not now required to ascertain the scope of the phrase "general welfare of the United States" or to determine whether an appropriation in aid of agriculture falls within it. Wholly apart from that question, another principle embedded in our Constitution prohibits the enforcement of the Agricultural Adjustment Act. The act invades the reserved rights of the states. It is a statutory plan to regulate and control agricultural production, a matter beyond the powers delegated to the federal government. The tax, the appropriation of the funds raised, and the direction for their disbursement, are but parts of the plan. They are but means to an unconstitutional end.

From the accepted doctrine that the United States is a government of delegated powers, it follows that those not expressly granted, or reasonably to be implied from such as are conferred, are reserved to the states or to the people. To forestall any suggestion to the contrary, the Tenth Amendment was adopted. The same proposition, otherwise stated, is that powers not granted are prohibited. None to regulate agricultural production is given, and therefore legislation by Congress for that purpose is forbidden.

It is an established principle that the attainment of a prohibited end may not be accomplished under the pretext of the exertion of powers which are granted. [Quoting Marshall's "pretext" statement in *McCulloch,* p. 31 supra.] . . .

[The *Child Labor Tax* case and similar] decisions demonstrate that Congress could not, under the pretext of raising revenue, lay a tax on processors who refuse to pay a certain price for cotton, and exempt those who agree so to do, with the purpose of benefiting producers.

If the taxing power may not be used as the instrument to enforce a regulation of matters of state concern with respect to which the Congress has no authority to interfere, may it, as in the present case, be employed to raise the money necessary to purchase a compliance which the Congress is powerless to command? The Government asserts that whatever might be said against the validity of the plan if compulsory, it is constitutionally sound because the end is accomplished by voluntary cooperation. There are two sufficient answers to the contention. The regulation is not in fact voluntary. The farmer, of course, may refuse to comply, but the price of such refusal is the loss of benefits. The amount offered is intended to be sufficient to exert pressure on him to agree to the proposed regulation. The power to confer or withhold unlimited benefits is the power to coerce or destroy. If the cotton grower elects not to accept the benefits, he will receive less for his crops; those who receive payments will be able to undersell him. The result may well be financial ruin. The coercive purpose and intent of the statute is not obscured by the fact that it has not been perfectly successful. . . .

But if the plan were one for purely voluntary cooperation it would stand no better so far as federal power is concerned. At best it is a scheme for purchasing with federal funds submission to federal regulation of a subject reserved to the states. . . . The Congress cannot invade state jurisdiction to compel individual action; no more can it purchase such action. . . .

It does not help to declare that local conditions throughout the nation have created a situation of national concern; for this is but to say that whenever there is a widespread similarity of local conditions, Congress may ignore constitutional limitations upon its own powers and usurp those reserved to the states. If, in lieu of compulsory regulation of subjects within the states' reserved jurisdiction, which is prohibited, the Congress could invoke the taxing and spending power as a means to accomplish the same end, clause 1 of §8 of Article I would become the instrument for total subversion of the governmental powers reserved to the individual states. . . .

STONE, J., joined by Brandeis and Cardozo, JJ., dissenting.

The present stress of widely held and strongly expressed differences of opinion of the wisdom of the Agricultural Adjustment Act makes it important, in the interest of clear thinking and sound result, to emphasize at the outset certain propositions which should have controlling influence in determining the validity of the Act. They are:

1. The power of courts to declare a statute unconstitutional is subject to two guiding principles of decision which ought never to be absent from judicial consciousness. One is that courts are concerned only with the power to enact statutes, not with their wisdom. The other is that while unconstitutional exercise of power by the executive and legislative branches of the government is subject to judicial restraint, the only check upon our own exercise of power is our own sense of self-restraint. For the removal of unwise laws from the statute books appeal lies not to the courts but to the ballot and to the processes of democratic government.

2. The constitutional power of Congress to levy an excise tax upon the processing of agricultural products is not questioned. The present levy is held invalid, not for any want of power in Congress to lay such a tax to defray public expenditures, including those for the general welfare, but because the use to which its proceeds are put is disapproved. . . .

[Federal expenditures] would fail of their purpose and thus lose their constitutional sanction if the terms of payment were not such that by their influence on the action of the recipients the permitted end would be attained. The power of Congress to spend is inseparable from persuasion to action over which Congress has no legislative control. . . .

The spending power of Congress is in addition to the legislative power and not subordinate to it. This independent grant of the power of the purse, and its very nature, involving in its exercise the duty to insure expenditure within the granted power, presuppose freedom of selection among divers ends and aims, and the capacity to impose such conditions as will render the choice effective. It is a contradiction in terms to say that there is power to spend for the national welfare, while rejecting any power to impose conditions reasonably adapted to the attainment of the end which alone would justify the expenditure. . . .

A tortured construction of the Constitution is not to be justified by recourse to extreme examples of reckless congressional spending which might occur if courts could not prevent — expenditures which, even if they could be thought to effect any national purpose, would be possible only by action of a legislature lost to all sense of public responsibility. Such suppositions are addressed to the mind accustomed to believe that it is the business of courts to sit in judgment on the wisdom of legislative action. Courts are not the only agency of government that must be assumed to have capacity to govern. Congress and the courts both unhappily may falter or be mistaken in the performance of their constitutional duty. But interpretation of our great charter of government which proceeds on any assumption that the responsibility for the preservation of our institutions is the exclusive concern of any one of the three branches of government, or that it alone can save them from destruction is far more likely, in the long run, "to obliterate the constituent members" of "an indestructible union of indestructible states" than the frank recognition that language, even of a constitution, may mean what it says: that the power to tax and spend includes the power to relieve a nationwide economic maladjustment by conditional gifts of money.

Note on State Immunity from Federal Taxation

In dictum, Marshall asserted that the rationale of *McCulloch* did not imply a reciprocal state immunity from federal taxation. See ¶¶70-71 of *McCulloch* in Chapter 1 supra.

A half-century later, however, the Court relied on a different argument from the structure and theory of governmental institutions to hold that intergovernmental tax immunities are reciprocal. Collector v. Day, 78 U.S. (11 Wall.) 113 (1871), struck down a federal income tax as applied to the salary of a Massachusetts probate judge. Justice Nelson wrote:

> In Dobbins v. The Commissioners of Erie County, 41 U.S. (16 Pet.) 435 (1842), it was decided that it was not competent for the legislature of a State to levy a tax upon the salary or emoluments of an office of the United States. The decision was placed mainly upon the ground that the officer was a means or instrumentality employed for carrying into effect some of the legitimate powers of the government, which could not be interfered with by taxation or otherwise by the States, and that the salary or compensation for the service of the officer was inseparably connected with the office; that if the officer, as such, was exempt, the salary assigned for his support or maintenance while holding the office was also, for like reasons, equally exempt. . . .
>
> And we shall now proceed to show that, upon the same construction of [the Constitution], and for like reasons, that government is prohibited from taxing the salary of the judicial officer of a State.
>
> It is a familiar rule of construction of the Constitution of the Union, that the sovereign powers vested in the State governments by their respective constitutions, remained unaltered and unimpaired, except so far as they were granted to the government of the United States. . . . The government of the United States, therefore, can claim no powers which are not granted to it by the Constitution, and the powers actually granted must be such as are expressly given, or given by necessary implication.
>
> The general government and the States, although both exist within the same territorial limits, are separate and distinct sovereignties, acting separately and independently of each other, within their respective spheres. The former in its appropriate sphere is supreme; but the States within the limits of their powers not granted, or, in

the language of the tenth amendment, "reserved," are as independent of the general government as that government within its sphere is independent of the States. . . .

Such being the separate and independent condition of the States in our complex system, as recognized by the Constitution, . . . it would seem to follow, as a reasonable, if not a necessary consequence, that the means and instrumentalities employed for carrying on the operations of their governments, for preserving their existence, and fulfilling the high and responsible duties assigned to them in the Constitution, should be left free and unimpaired, should not be liable to be crippled, much less defeated by the taxing power of another government, which power acknowledges no limits but the will of the legislative body imposing the tax. And, more especially, those means and instrumentalities which are the creation of their sovereign and reserved rights, one of which is the establishment of the judicial department, and the appointment of officers to administer their laws. Without this power, and the exercise of it, we risk nothing in saying that no one of the States under the [republican] form of government guaranteed by the Constitution could long preserve its existence. . . .

The supremacy of the general government, therefore, so much relied on in the argument of the counsel for the plaintiff in error, in respect to the question before us, cannot be maintained. The two governments are upon an equality. . . . And if the means and instrumentalities employed by [the national] government to carry into operation the powers granted to it are, necessarily, and, for the sake of self-preservation, exempt from taxation by the States, why are not those of the States depending upon their reserved powers, for like reasons, equally exempt from Federal taxation? Their unimpaired existence in the one case is as essential as in the other. It is admitted that there is no express provision in the Constitution that prohibits the general government from taxing the means and instrumentalities of the States, nor is there any prohibiting the States from taxing the means and instrumentalities of that government. In both cases the exemption rests upon necessary implication, and is upheld by the great law of self-preservation; as any government, whose means employed in conducting its operations, if subject to the control of another and distinct government, can exist only at the mercy of that government. Of what avail are these means if another power may tax them at discretion?

Only Justice Bradley dissented, reiterating, in essence, the distinction made by Marshall in *McCulloch.* Is the Court's reasoning in Collector v. Day less persuasive than the reasoning in *McCulloch?*

Day involved a claim of "derivative" immunity, i.e., an immunity claimed by someone other than the government itself by virtue of a relationship with the government. The doctrine of derivative immunity has largely been abandoned with respect to both state and federal taxation. For example, the incomes of state and federal employees are now taxable by federal and state governments. Helvering v. Gerhardt, 304 U.S. 405 (1938) (sustaining federal income tax on salary of employees of the Port of New York Authority); Graves v. O'Keefe, 306 U.S. 466 (1939) (sustaining state income tax on salary of employees of federally owned Home Owners' Loan Corporation). The present scope of primary state immunity from federal taxation is not certain. See New York v. United States, 326 U.S. 572 (1946). The issue of state immunity from federal regulation is discussed below at pp. 406-422.

IV. *"When a Nation Is at War": World War I and the First Amendment*

The First Amendment assumed a significant place in American constitutional jurisprudence in response to governmental attempts to suppress opposition to United States participation in World War I.[83] The first cases immediately followed Congress' establishment of a military draft in 1917. Emma Goldman, Alexander Berkman, and other prominent radicals were indicted and convicted for conspiring to induce eligible people not to register for the draft. The Supreme Court readily upheld the convictions, responding to the defendants' protests that they had not in fact advised people to disobey the law by noting that this question was within the province of the jury.[84]

In June 1917, two months after American entry into the war against Germany, Congress passed an Espionage Act that, among other things, prohibited speech inciting insubordination in the military and naval forces of the United States or the refusal of service in the armed forces. The basic framework for future elaboration of the meaning of the First Amendment was established in four cases decided in 1919 — Schenck v. United States, 249 U.S. 47 (1919); Sugarman v. United States, 249 U.S. 182 (1919); Frohwerk v. United States, 249 U.S. 204 (1919); Debs v. United States, 249 U.S. 211 (1919).

Debs v. United States affirmed the conviction of Eugene V. Debs, the acknowledged leader of American socialism, who had gained over a million votes as the Socialist candidate for the presidency in 1912, for violating the Espionage Act. The conviction was based on a speech, delivered in 1918 in Canton, Ohio, expressing his deep opposition to the war. In an opinion that never refers to Debs by name or identifies him as a prominent dissident, Justice Holmes described the speech as follows:

> The main theme of the speech was socialism, its growth, and a prophecy of its ultimate success. With that we have nothing to do, but if a part or the manifest intent of the more general utterances was to encourage those present to obstruct the recruiting service and if in passages such encouragement was directly given, the immunity of the general theme may not be enough to protect the speech. The speaker began by saying that he had just returned from a visit to the workhouse in the neighborhood where three of their most loyal comrades were paying the penalty for their devotion to the working class — these being Wagenknecht, Baker and Ruthenberg, who had been convicted of aiding and abetting another in failing to register for the draft. He said that he had to be prudent and might not be able to say all that he thought, thus intimating to his hearers that they might infer that he meant more, but he did say that those persons were paying the penalty for standing erect and for seeking to pave the way to better conditions for all mankind. Later he added further eulogies and said that he was proud of them. He then expressed opposition to Prussian militarism in a way that naturally might have been thought to be intended to include the mode of proceeding in the United States.

83. See David Rabban, The First Amendment in Its Forgotten Years, 90 Yale L.J. 514 (1981). See also Mark A. Graber, Transforming Free Speech: The Ambiguous Legacy of Civil Litertarianism (1991).

84. Goldman v. United States, 245 U.S. 474 (1918). *Goldman* and companion cases are discussed in David Rabban, The Emergence of Modern First Amendment Doctrine, 50 U. Chi. L. Rev. 1205, 1244-1246 (1984).

> After considerable discourse that it is unnecessary to follow, he took up the case of Kate Richards O'Hare, convicted of obstructing the enlistment service, praised her for her loyalty to socialism and otherwise, and said that she was convicted on false testimony, under a ruling that would seem incredible to him if he had not had some experience with a Federal Court. We mention this passage simply for its connection with evidence put in at the trial. The defendant spoke of other cases, and then, after dealing with Russia, said that the master class has always declared the war and the subject class has always fought the battles — that the subject class has had nothing to gain and all to lose, including their lives; that the working class, who furnish the corpses, have never yet had a voice in declaring war and have never yet had a voice in declaring peace. "You have your lives to lose; you certainly ought to have the right to declare war if you consider a war necessary." The defendant next mentioned Rose Pastor Stokes, convicted of attempting to cause insubordination and refusal of duty in the military forces of the United States and obstructing the recruiting service. He said that she went out to render her service to the cause in this day of crises, and they sent her to the penitentiary for ten years; that she had said no more than the speaker had said that afternoon; that if she was guilty so was he, and that he would not be cowardly enough to plead his innocence; but that her message that opened the eyes of the people must be suppressed, and so, after a mock trial before a packed jury and a corporation tool on the bench, she was sent to the penitentiary for ten years.
>
> There followed personal experiences and illustrations of the growth of socialism, a glorification of minorities, and a prophecy of the success of the international socialist crusade, with the interjection that "you need to know that you are fit for something better than slavery and cannon fodder." The rest of the discourse had only the indirect though not necessarily ineffective bearing on the offences alleged that is to be found in the usual contrasts between capitalists and laboring men, sneers at the advice to cultivate war gardens, attribution to plutocrats of the high price of coal, &c., with the implication running through it all that the working men are not concerned in the war, and a final exhortation "Don't worry about the charge of treason to your masters; but be concerned about the treason that involves yourselves." The defendant addressed the jury himself, and while contending that his speech did not warrant the charges said "I have been accused of obstructing the war. I admit it. Gentlemen, I abhor war. I would oppose the war if I stood alone." The statement was not necessary to warrant the jury in finding that one purpose of the speech, whether incidental or not does not matter, was to oppose not only war in general but this war, and that the opposition was so expressed that its natural and intended effect would be to obstruct recruiting. If that was intended and if, in all the circumstances, that would be its probable effect, it would not be protected by reason of its being part of a general program and expressions of a general and conscientious belief.

Justice Holmes responded to Debs' constitutional argument by referring to Schenck v. United States, issued a week earlier, in which Holmes had written for a unanimous Court.

> It well may be that the prohibition of laws abridging the freedom of speech is not confined to previous restraints, although to prevent them may have been the main purpose. . . . We admit that in many places and in ordinary times the defendants . . . would have been within their constitutional rights. But the character of every act depends upon the circumstances in which it is done. The most stringent protection of free speech would not protect a man in falsely shouting fire in a theatre and causing a panic. . . . The question in every case is whether the words used are used in such circumstances and are of such a nature as to create a clear and present danger that

they will bring about the substantive evils that Congress has a right to prevent. It is a question of proximity and degree. When a nation is at war many things that might be said in time of peace are such a hindrance to its effort that their utterance will not be endured so long as men fight and that no Court could regard them as protected by any constitutional right. It seems to be admitted that if an actual obstruction of the recruiting service were proved, liability for words that produced that effect might be enforced. The statute of 1917 in §4 punishes conspiracies to obstruct as well as actual obstruction. If the act, . . . its tendency and the intent with which it is done are the same, we perceive no ground for saying that success alone warrants making the act a crime.

Holmes concluded that in Debs "the jury were most carefully instructed that they could not find the defendant guilty for advocacy of any of his opinions unless the words used had as their natural tendency and reasonably probable effect to obstruct the recruiting service, &c., and unless the defendant had the specific intent to do so in his mind."

The same year as *Debs*, Holmes wrote an impassioned dissent, joined by Justice Brandeis, in Abrams v. United States, 250 U.S. 616 (1919), which marks the emergence of the clear and present danger test as a constitutional standard (as distinguished from construction of the Act or definition of inchoate crimes connected with it). The Court in *Abrams* affirmed conspiracy convictions under a 1918 amendment to the act which punished urging curtailment of the production of war material "with the intent . . . to cripple or hinder the United States in the prosecution of the war." Defendants had distributed leaflets which said: "Workers in the ammunition factories, you are producing bullets, bayonets, and cannon to murder not only the Germans, but also your dearest, best, who are in Russia fighting for your freedom. . . . Workers, our reply to [America's] barbaric intervention [to destroy the Bolshevik Revolution] has to be a general strike." Justice Clarke wrote for the Court:

It will not do to say . . . that the only intent of these defendants was to prevent injury to the Russian cause. Men must be held to have intended, and to be accountable for, the effects which their acts were likely to produce. Even if their primary purpose and intent was to aid the cause of the Russian Revolution, the plan of action which they adopted necessarily involved, before it could be realized, defeat of the war program of the United States, for the obvious effect of this appeal, if it should become effective, as they hoped it might, would be to persuade persons . . . not to work in ammunition factories.

In a dissent joined by Brandeis, Holmes wrote:

[A]s against dangers peculiar to war, as against others, the principle of the right to free speech is always the same. It is only the present danger of immediate evil or an intent to bring it about that warrants Congress in setting a limit to the expression of opinion where private rights are not concerned. Congress certainly cannot forbid all effort to change the mind of the country. Now nobody can suppose that the surreptitious publishing of a silly leaflet by an unknown man, without more, would present any immediate danger that its opinions would hinder the success of the government arms or have any appreciable tendency to do so. Publishing those opinions for the very purpose of obstructing however, might indicate a great danger and at any rate would have the quality of an attempt. So I assume that the . . . leaflet if published for

> the [purpose of hindering the prosecution of the war] might be punishable. But it seems pretty clear to me that nothing less than that would bring these papers within the scope of this law. An actual intent in the sense that I have explained is necessary, to constitute an attempt, where a further act of the same individual is required to complete the substantive crime. . . . It is necessary where the success of the attempt depends upon others because if that intent is not present the actor's aim may be accomplished without bringing about the evils sought to be checked. An intent to prevent interference with the revolution in Russia might have been satisfied without any hindrance to carrying on the war in which we were engaged. I do not see how anyone can find the intent required by the statute in any of the defendants' words.

Holmes wrote an influential dissent in Gitlow v. New York, 268 U.S. 652 (1925), in which the Court, even as it upheld the conviction of Benjamin Gitlow, a communist (and former state legislator), for violating New York's criminal anarchy law, nonetheless for the first time agreed that the States were limited in their power by the First Amendment. The New York law in question prohibited, *inter alia,* publication of any material that "advocates, advises or teaches the duty, necessity or propriety of overthrowing or overturning organized government by force or violence, . . . or by any unlawful means." Justice Clarke's opinion for the Court emphasized the constitutional legitimacy of New York's determination, "through its legislative body, that utterances advocating the overthrow of organized government by force, violence and unlawful means, are so inimical to the general welfare and involve such danger of substantive evil that they may be penalized in the exercise of its police power." By contrast to *Schenck* and companion cases where the speech in question was punished only as part of the commission of a different substantive offense, i.e., obstruction of recruiting, in *Gitlow* the "legislative body ha[d] determined generally, in the constitutional exercise of its discretion, that utterances of a certain kind involve such danger of substantive evil that they be punished."

Holmes wrote in dissent:

> Mr. Justice Brandeis and I are of the opinion that this judgment should be reversed. . . . I think that the criterion sanctioned by the full Court in Schenck v. United States, 249 U.S. 47, 52, applies. "The question in every case is whether the words used are in such circumstances and are of such a nature as to create a clear and present danger that they will bring about the substantive evils that [the State] has a right to prevent." . . . If what I think the correct test is applied, it is manifest that there was no present danger of an attempt to overthrow the government by force on the part of the admittedly small minority who shared the defendant's views. It is said that this manifesto was more than a theory, that it was an incitement. Every idea is an incitement. It offers itself for belief and if believed it is acted on unless some other belief outweighs it or some failure of energy stifles the movement at its birth. The only difference between the expression of an opinion and an incitement in the narrower sense is the speaker's enthusiasm for the result. Eloquence may set fire to reason. But whatever may be thought of the redundant discourse before us it had no chance of starting a present conflagration. If in the long run the beliefs expressed in proletarian dictatorship are destined to be accepted by the dominant forces of the community, the only meaning of free speech is that they should be given their chance and have their way.
>
> If the publication of this document had been laid as an attempt to induce an uprising against government at once and not at some indefinite time in the future it

would have presented a different question. The object would have been one with which the law might deal, subject to the doubt whether there was any danger that the publication could produce any result, or in other words whether it was not futile and too remote from possible consequences. But the indictment alleges the publication and nothing more.

Discussion

Justices Holmes and Brandeis, who are major architects of the twentieth-century American theory of freedom of speech, never indicated that they had second thoughts about the convictions of Debs and others upheld in the March 1919 cases. What, then, distinguishes *Debs* from the later cases (and the speech-protective theories enunciated in them)?

1. *The status of the speaker.* In *Abrams,* Holmes derides the possibility that the country faced any danger from "the surreptitious publishing of a silly leaflet by an unknown man." Does this suggest that a jury (or a reviewing court) can properly take into account the speaker's status or the cogency of the ideas presented in deciding whether speech is punishable? Over a million Americans had demonstrated by their ballots that they did not consider Eugene Debs to be articulating "silly" ideas. Is Debs' very prominence a justification for jailing him for ten years for the crime of opposing service in the armed forces during World War I (the "War to end War")? If not, then why was Abrams to be freed, according to Justice Holmes, from the sentence visited upon Debs?

2. *Imminence of the danger presented.* How close to actuality must the threatened danger be in order to make its advocacy punishable? (It is a feature of almost all of the major freedom of speech cases that the threatened danger did not in fact occur. For example, no evidence was presented that Debs actually persuaded anyone to resist the draft or that anyone accepted Gitlow's beseeching advice to work toward overthrow of the state.) Although Holmes never elaborated the precise dimensions of "presentness" within the clear-and-present-danger test, he joined in Brandeis' opinion in Whitney v. California, 274 U.S. 652 (1925), which stated:

> There must be reasonable ground to believe that the danger apprehended is imminent. . . . Every denunciation of existing law tends in some measure to increase the probability that there will be a violation of it. . . . But even advocacy of violation, however reprehensible morally, is not a justification for denying free speech where the advocacy falls short of incitement and there is nothing to indicate that the advocacy would be immediately acted on. The wide difference between advocacy and incitement, between preparation and attempt, between assembling and conspiracy, must be borne in mind. . . .
>
> [N]o danger flowing from speech can be deemed clear and present unless the incidence of the evil apprehended is so imminent that it may befall before there is opportunity to full discussion. If there be time to expose through discussion the falsehood and fallacies, to avert the evil by the processes of education, the remedy to be applied is more speech, not enforced silence. Only an emergency can justify repression.

Could Debs possibly be convicted under this version of the clear-and-present-danger test? Does the *Whitney* opinion therefore represent a significant, albeit unackowledged, expansion of the limitations on state regulation suggested in the earlier opinions? (Brandeis' opinion was technically a concurrence upholding Ms. Whitney's conviction, but in effect it represented a full-scale attack on the majority rationale that upheld the conviction.)

3. *Seriousness of the offense*. Justice Brandeis wrote in *Whitney*: "To justify suppression of free speech there must be reasonable ground to fear that *serious evil* will result if free speech is practiced" (emphasis added). He continued:

> [E]ven imminent danger cannot justify prohibition of [speech] . . . unless the evil apprehended is relatively serious. Prohibition of free speech and assembly is a measure so stringent that it would be inappropriate as the means for averting a relatively trivial harm to society. A policy measure may be unconstitutional merely because the remedy, though effective as means of protection, is unduly harsh or oppressive. Thus, a State might, in the exercise of its police power, make any trespass upon the land of another a crime, regardless of the results or of the intent or purpose of the trespasser. It might, also, punish an attempt, a conspiracy, or an incitement to commit the trespass. But it is hardly conceivable that this Court would hold constitutional a statute which punished as a felony the mere voluntary assembly with a society formed to teach that pedestrians had the moral right to cross unenclosed, unposted, waste lands and to advocate their doing so, even if there was imminent danger that advocacy would lead to a trespass. The fact that speech is likely to result in some violence or in destruction of property is not enough to justify its suppression. There must be the probability of serious injury to the State. Among free men, the deterrents ordinarily to be applied to prevent crime are education and punishment for violations of the law, not abridgment of the rights of free speech and assembly.

Should the degree of imminence required for conviction ever vary depending on the seriousness of the offense? That is, should the state be required to tolerate the same risk of perceived catastrophe as of, say, trespass or some other distinctly noncatastrophic event? In Dennis v. United States, 241 U.S. 404 (1951), the Supreme Court, though stating that it was operating with the ambit of Holmes' "clear and present danger" test, adopted a formula proffered by Judge Learned Hand: "In each case [courts] must ask whether the gravity of the 'evil,' discounted by its improbability, justifies such invasion of free speech as is necessary to avoid the danger." As Robert McCloskey points out, "The requirement of a 'present' danger is subordinated to the requirement of a 'probable' one. Immediacy is still relevant but only insofar as it may affect probability."[85] Critics of *Dennis*, including Justices Black and Douglas, argued that this test was far too accepting of the suppression of speech. Moreover, it is wholly unclear what would ever authorize a court's setting aside a legislative assessment of gravity and likelihood: "[T]he judicial inquiry becomes by this formulation as broad and as conjectural as the legislative process itself." Indeed, the concurring opinions by Justices Jackson and Frankfurter, like Justice Clarke's opinion in *Gitlow*, "were pervaded with the idea that the judiciary was unqualified to second-guess Congress about such far-flung judgments and on issues of such magnitude."

Not at all coincidentally, *Dennis* arose during the midst of the Cold War and involved the jailing of top leaders of the Communist Party. No one seriously suggested that there was any immediate likelihood (i.e., "clear and present danger")

85. Robert McCloskey, The Modern Supreme Court 80 (1972). The quotations in this and the next paragraph are taken from pp. 80-82 of the chapter "The Vinson Court."

of overthrowing the constituted form of government (or, indeed, that the leaders were even on the brink of fomenting an attempted revolution). This seemed irrelevant, though, once the even-minimal likelihood was multiplied by the almost infinite gravity of a loss of American liberty. As McCloskey says, the *Dennis* test "simply provided a metaphorical way of explaining why the judiciary felt unable to challenge, on substantive grounds, the congressional will to scotch the Red Menace."

For many analysts, the repression of speech permitted by *Dennis* was enough to discredit the Hand formula. But should a legislature or court completely ignore the evil threatened? Should one be as formally indifferent to an estimated 40 percent chance of a racial massacre, if that is what is being advocated, as to a 40 percent probability of peaceful trespass or even disruption of rush-hour traffic? If your answer is no, then does this inevitably lead to a re-invention of some version of the Hand formula?

What do you think that Justice Brandeis means by his reference to "injury to the State"? Can the state deter injury to the property or person of "private" individuals by criminalizing the making of speeches likely to bring them about?

Justice Holmes in *Schenck* takes note of the fact that the case arose while the nation was "at war." Abrams' violation also arose during World War I, though Gitlow's took place only afterward. In any event, what precisely is the relevance of the war-time status of the country as a whole in determining the boundaries of free speech?

4. *Institutional competence.* The constitutional standards discussed above are concerned with questions of "fact." How relevant should it be that a jury made a purportedly context-specific determination that the particular speech in question presented a threat to public order, or that the New York legislature made a blanket determination in passing its criminal anarchy law that New York would be threatened by any such exercise of subversive speech?

One of the recurrent issues in First Amendment cases concerns the relative roles of legislature, jury, and reviewing court in determining the potential threat offered by speech. You have previously seen Holmes as the resolute champion of legislative rights in such cases as *Lochner, Hammer,* and *Bailey,* where he stressed that judges were not licensed to override even "tyrannical" legislation in the absence of a specific constitutional mandate to do so. Here, on the other hand, Holmes and Brandeis, another prominent defender of legislative prerogative in the "social" realm, would limit legislative power. One might, of course, distinguish regulation of wages and hours from regulation of speech simply by reference to the language of the First Amendment. Justice Hugo Black would later argue in mid-century, the "no law" language of the First Amendment entails the invalidity of *any* law criminalizing *any* speech. But Holmes offers no such textual argument. What, then, justifies less judicial deference to the legislature in free speech cases than in wages-and-hours cases? Might one have greater mistrust for the legislative capacity to make wise decisions in the former than the latter? If so, why? And what about juries? Why should not a jury's determination that a given speech constituted a clear-and-present danger be dispositive in the same way that its determination of any other legal "fact" is?

5. *Context versus formal content.* The "clear and present danger" test has been extremely influential in later development of First Amendment doctrine. Was this test, however, the only or even the best way of delimiting accountability for

violation of the Espionage Act? Would an "advocacy of unlawful action" or a still narrower "criminal solicitation" approach have been preferable? In Masses Publishing Co. v. Patten, 244 F. 535 (S.D.N.Y. 1917), Judge Learned Hand held for the plaintiffs in an action to compel the postmaster to accept their magazine in the mails, which he had refused to do on the ground that it violated the Espionage Act. The magazine vehemently criticized American participation in the war and expressed sympathy and admiration for conscientious objectors to conscription. Judge Hand conceded that it might in fact "cause" insubordination and resistance, but held that this was not sufficient to bring it within the Act:

> One may not counsel or advise others to violate the law as it stands. Words are not only the keys of persuasion, but the triggers of action, and those which have no purport but to counsel the violation of law cannot by any latitude of interpretation be a part of that public opinion which is the final source of government in a democratic state. The defendant asserts . . . that the magazine . . . counsels and advises resistance to existing law, especially to the draft. . . . To counsel or advise a man to an act is to urge upon him either that it is his interest or his duty to do it. While, of course, this may be accomplished as well by indirection as expressly, since words carry the meaning that they impart, the definition is exhaustive, I think, and I shall use it. Political agitation, by the passions it arouses or the convictions it engenders, may in fact stimulate men to the violation of law. Detestation of existing policies is easily transformed into forcible resistance of the authority which puts them in execution, and it would be folly to disregard the causal relation between the two. Yet to assimilate agitation, legitimate as such, with direct incitement to violent resistance, is to disregard the tolerance of all methods of political agitation which in normal times is a safeguard of free government. The distinction is not a scholastic subterfuge, but a hard-bought acquisition in the fight for freedom. . . . If one stops short of urging upon others that it is their duty or their interest to resist the law, it seems to me one should not be held to have attempted to cause its violation. If that be not the test, I can see no escape from the conclusion that under this section every political agitation which can be shown to be apt to create a seditious temper is illegal. I am confident that by such language Congress had no such revolutionary purpose in view.

6. Does the clear and present danger test, as compared to possible alternatives, adequately accommodate the competing interests at stake in the Espionage Act cases? Is it a judicially administrable test as applied to the Espionage Act? Consider Gerald Gunther's discussion of the *Masses* alternative.[86]

> [Hand] did not think that tightening the required chain of causation was an apt or effective method of protecting speech. To second-guess enforcement officials about probable consequences of subversive speech was to him a questionable judicial function: judges had no special competence to foresee the future. Moreover, even if predictions about the consequences of words were thought to be appropriate court business, the task would ordinarily fall not to the judge but to the jury, a body reflecting majoritarian sentiments unlikely to be conducive to the protection of dissent in wartime.
>
> Hand's solution to the problem of an appropriate and effective judicial role was to focus on the speaker's words, not in their probable consequences. Instead of ask-

86. Gerald Gunther, Learned Hand and the Origins of Modern First Amendment Doctrine: Some Fragments of History, 27 Stan. L. Rev. 719, 725, 729 (1975). See also David Rabban, The First Amendment in Its Forgotten Years, 90 Yale L.J. 514 (1981).

ing in the circumstances of each case whether the words had a tendency or even a probability of producing unlawful conduct, he sought a more "absolute and objective test" focusing on "language" — "a qualitative formula, hard, conventional, difficult to evade," as he said in his letters. What he urged was essentially an incitement test, "a test based upon the nature of the utterance itself": if the words constituted solely a counsel to law violation, they could be forbidden: all other utterances were permissible. . . .

Here was a strict, literal, perhaps even strained doctrine in the interest of speech protection. The approach had its problems. As contemporaries recognized, it could not easily deal with the indirect but purposeful incitement of Marc Anthony's oration over the body of Caesar. Although Hand recognized that advocacy could be accomplished by "indirection," he insisted on starting with the "literal meaning" of the words and never completely explained how far beyond he was willing to go.

7. *Subsequent developments.* A full elaboration of constitutional doctrine concerning "subversive" speech is beyond the scope of this casebook. However, you should be aware of the Court's most recent major statement — in Brandenburg v. Ohio. 395 v. 444 (1969), which reversed the conviction of a leader of the Ku Klux Klan for violating the Ohio Criminal Syndicalism statute by "advocat[ing] . . . the duty, necessity, or propriety of crime, sabotage, violence, or unlawful methods of terrorism as a means of accomplishing industrial or political reform" and for "voluntarily assembl[ing]" for those purposes. Speaking before a Klan rally, Brandenburg had called for "revengence" against Jews, blacks, and three branches of the national government. In a per curiam opinion, the Court unanimously struck down the Act and Brandenburg's conviction under it, in the process formally overruling *Whitney's* upholding of the California Criminal Syndicalism Act. The Court wrote:

[T]he constitutional guarantees of free speech and free press do not permit a State to forbid or proscribe advocacy of the use of force or of law violation except where such advocacy is directed to inciting or producing imminent lawless action and likely to incite or produce such action. . . . "[T]he mere abstract teaching . . . of the moral propriety or even moral necessity for a resort to force and violence, is not the same as preparing a group for violent action and steeling it to such action." A statute which fails to draw this distinction impermissibly . . . sweeps within its condemnation speech which our Constitution has immunized from governmental control. . . . Statutes affecting the right of assembly, like those touching on freedom of speech, must observe the established distinctions between mere advocacy and incitement to imminent lawless action. . . . [The Ohio] statute falls within the condemnation of the First and Fourteenth Amendments.

Professor Gunther comments:[87]

In one sense, *Brandenburg* combines the most protective ingredients of the *Masses* incitement emphasis with the most useful elements of the clear and present danger heritage. . . .

The incitement emphasis is Hand's; the reference to "imminent" reflects a limited influence of Holmes, combined with later experience; and the "likely to incite or produce such action" addition in the *Brandenburg* standard is the only reference to

87. Gunther, supra note 86, at 754-755.

the need to guess about future consequences of speech, so central to the *Schenck* approach. Under *Brandenburg,* probability of harm is no longer the central criterion for speech limitations.

The inciting language of the speaker — the Hand focus on "objective" words — is the major consideration. And punishment of the harmless inciter is prevented by the *Schenck*-derived requirement of a likelihood of dangerous consequences.

And so, via Justice Harlan and the Supreme Court majority at the end of the Warren era, the language-oriented incitement criterion, so persistently urged by Hand in *Masses* and in [his] letters, has become central to the operative law of the land. *Brandenburg* is the most speech-protective standard yet evolved by the Supreme Court.

Chapter 5
The Decline of Judicial Intervention and the Current Doctrine of Federalism

In 1934 the nation was in the midst of a disastrous economic depression. Both the national government and the states had adopted emergency measures, designed to palliate or cure. At first, the Supreme Court seemed to acquiesce in these measures — by a margin of one vote. In 1935 and 1936, however, the Court took up battle, striking down a half-dozen regulatory schemes on the ground that they were beyond congressional authority and reasserting its own authority to review the merits of state economic legislation. In 1937, the Court again acquiesced, virtually abandoning both economic due process and judicial supervision of Congress' exercise of the Article I powers.

This chapter chronicles the end of judicial intervention against state and federal economic regulation. It also completes our survey of the constitutional law of federalism — with respect both to the scope of national powers and the limits of state regulation in the silence of Congress. In Part Two we will consider contemporary equal protection doctrine and the renascence of substantive due process.

I. The Retreat from Intervention Against State Economic Regulation[1]

A. 1934

Two decisions in 1934 presaged the Court's withdrawal from intervention against state economic regulation. The first rejected a conventional substantive due process challenge to a price regulation; the second involved not due process but the contract clause.

The appellant in Nebbia v. New York, 291 U.S. 502 (1934), was a storekeeper convicted for selling milk below the minimum retail price of 9¢ a quart fixed by the New York Milk Control Board, an agency established in 1933 pursuant to the recommendation of a legislative committee. The committee attributed the critically depressed state of milk farmers to price-cutting among milk distributors

1. See generally Robert McCloskey, The American Supreme Court 161-169, 174-179 (1960); William Swindler, Court and Constitution in the Twentieth Century: The New Legality, 1932-1968 (1970).

and suggested that this destructive competition could be mitigated, inter alia, by setting minimum retail prices. In an opinion by Justice Roberts, the Court upheld the regulation. Stating that "the guaranty of due process . . . demands only that the law shall not be unreasonable, arbitrary or capricious, and that the means selected shall have a real and substantial relation to the object sought to be attained," he quoted at length from the legislative committee's report to conclude that the regulation "appears not to be unreasonable or arbitrary, or without relation to the purpose to prevent ruthless competition from destroying the wholesale price structure on which the farmer depends for his livelihood, and the community for an assured supply of milk." Justice Roberts then turned to the appellant's contentions, supported by prior decisions of the Court, that price fixing was per se unconstitutional except in "businesses affected with a public interest" and that these were limited to franchised public utilities and monopolies. Conceding that the milk industry did not fit this description, Justice Roberts noted that the industry was nonetheless subject to some sorts of regulation in the public interest, and he went on to write:

> [No] constitutional principle bars the state from correcting existing maladjustments by legislation touching prices. . . . The due process clause makes no mention of sales or of prices any more than it speaks of business or contracts or buildings or other incidents of property. . . . It is clear that there is no closed class or category of businesses affected with a public interest. . . . The phrase "affected with a public interest" can, in the nature of things, mean no more than that an industry, for adequate reason, is subject to control for the public good.

Justice McReynolds, joined by Justices Van Devanter, Sutherland, and Butler, dissented: The milk industry was not affected with a public interest. And although "[r]egulation to prevent recognized evils in [any] business has long been upheld as permissible legislative action . . . , fixation of the price at which *A*, engaged in an ordinary business, may sell, in order to enable *B*, a producer, to improve his condition, has not been regarded as within legislative power. This is not regulation, but . . . amounts to the deprivation of the fundamental right which one has to conduct his own affairs honestly and along customary lines." In any case, McReynolds argued, the judiciary had abdicated its responsibility to determine for itself whether the New York law is reasonably related to its goals: "Are federal rights subject to extinction by the reports of committees?" Independently evaluating the committee's data, Justice McReynolds concluded that the problem lay in the reduced buying power of consumers, and that since demand was insufficient even at low prices it was unreasonable to believe that "higher charges at stores to impoverished customers when the output is excessive and sale prices by producers are unrestrained, can possibly increase receipts at the farm."

The constitutional jurisprudence of *Lochner*, while not permitting government regulation of wages in the "private" relationship between employer and employee, did allow regulation (albeit judicially supervised) of certain "businesses affected with a public interest," such as railroads. If *Nebbia* took a relatively expansive view of this category, it did not constitute a sharp break with existing doctrine. The decision in the *Minnesota Mortgage Moratorium* case, however, seems more clearly incompatible with the spirit of *Lochner*.

HOME BUILDING & LOAN ASSOCIATION v. BLAISDELL

[The *Minnesota Mortgage Moratorium* case]
290 U.S. 398 (1934)
Appeal from the Supreme Court of Minnesota

[In 1933, the Minnesota legislature enacted the Mortgage Moratorium Law, an emergency measure, which expired in May 1935, granting temporary relief from mortgage foreclosures and execution sales of real estate. The particular section involved here authorized a court to extend the period during which a defaulting mortgagor might redeem his property following a foreclosure execution sale. During the period of the extension, the mortgagor was required to pay all or a reasonable part of the reasonable rental value of the property as determined by the court, including taxes, insurance, and mortgage interest. The statute did not reduce mortgage indebtedness or affect the right of a mortgagee to title in fee, or his right to obtain a deficiency judgment, if the mortgagor failed to redeem within the prescribed period.

The Blaisdells' house had been mortgaged to Home Building & Loan. Upon default, the association foreclosed and then purchased the property at the execution sale for approximately two-thirds of its market value. The Blaisdells obtained an extension of the redemption period until May 1935, during which they were required to pay the judicially ascertained fair rental value of $40 per month.

The loan company challenged the Mortgage Moratorium Law on the ground, inter alia, that it violated the contract clause, Article I, section 10, clause 1. The Minnesota Supreme Court upheld the law, and the association appealed.]

HUGHES, C.J. . . .

In determining whether the provision for this temporary and conditional relief exceeds the power of the State by reason of the clause in the Federal Constitution prohibiting impairment of the obligations of contracts, we must consider the relation of emergency to constitutional power, the historical setting of the contract clause, the development of the jurisprudence of this Court in the construction of that clause, and the principles of construction which we may consider to be established.

Emergency does not create power. Emergency does not increase granted power or remove or diminish the restrictions imposed upon power granted or reserved. The Constitution was adopted in a period of grave emergency. Its grants of power to the Federal Government and its limitations of the power of the States were determined in the light of emergency and they are not altered by emergency. . . .

The constitutional question presented in the light of an emergency is whether the power possessed embraces the particular exercise of it in response to particular conditions. . . . When the provisions of the Constitution, in grant or restriction, are specific, so particularized as not to admit of construction, no question is presented. Thus, emergency would not permit a State to have more than two Senators in the Congress, or permit the election of President by a general popular vote without regard to the number of electors to which the States are respectively entitled, or permit the States to "coin money" or to "make anything but gold and silver coin a tender in payment of debts." But where constitutional grants and limitations of power are set forth in general clauses, which afford a broad outline, the process of construction is essential to fill in the details. That is true of the contract clause. . . .

In the construction of the contract clause, the debates in the Constitutional Convention are of little aid. But the reasons which led to the adoption of that clause, and of the other prohibitions of Section 10 of Article I, are not left in doubt and have frequently been described with eloquent emphasis. The widespread distress following the revolutionary period, and the plight of debtors, had called forth in the States an ignoble array of legislative schemes for the defeat of creditors and the invasion of contractual obligations. Legislative interferences had been so numerous and extreme that the confidence essential to prosperous trade had been undermined and the utter destruction of credit was threatened. "The sober people of America" were convinced that some "thorough reform" was needed which would "inspire a general prudence and industry, and give a regular course to the business of society." The Federalist, No. 44. It was necessary to interpose the restraining power of a central authority in order to secure the foundations even of "private faith." . . .

But full recognition of the occasion and general purpose of the clause does not suffice to fix its precise scope. Nor does an examination of the details of prior legislation in the States yield criteria which can be considered controlling. To ascertain the scope of the constitutional prohibition we examine the course of judicial decisions in its application. These put it beyond question that the prohibition is not an absolute one and is not to be read with literal exactness like a mathematical formula. . . .

The obligation of a contract is "the law which binds the parties to perform their agreement." This Court has said that ". . . [n]othing can be more material to the obligation than the means of enforcement. . . . The ideas of validity and remedy are inseparable, and both are parts of the obligation, which is guaranteed by the Constitution against invasion." . . . [But it] "is competent for the States to change the form of the remedy, or to modify it otherwise, as they may see fit, provided no substantial right secured by the contract is thereby impaired. No attempt has been made to fix definitely the line between alterations of the remedy, which are to be deemed legitimate, and those which under the form of modifying the remedy, impair substantial rights. Every case must be determined upon its own circumstances" . . . [and] "[i]n all such cases the question becomes, therefore, one of reasonableness, and of that the legislature is primarily the judge." . . .

The policy of protecting contracts against impairment presupposes the maintenance of a government by virtue of which contractual relations are worth while, — a government which retains adequate authority to secure the peace and good order of society. This principle of harmonizing the constitutional prohibition with the necessary residuum of state power has had progressive recognition in the decisions of this Court. . . .

The legislature cannot "bargain away the public health or the public morals." Thus, the constitutional provision against the impairment of contracts was held not to be violated by an amendment of the state constitution which put an end to a lottery theretofore authorized by the legislature. . . . A similar rule has been applied to the control by the State of the sale of intoxicating liquors. The States retain adequate power to protect the public health against the maintenance of nuisances despite insistence upon existing contracts. Legislation to protect the public safety comes within the same category of reserved power. . . .

The argument is pressed that in the cases we have cited the obligation of contracts was affected only incidentally. This argument proceeds upon a misconception. The question is not whether the legislative action affects contracts incidentally, or directly or indirectly, but whether the legislation is addressed to a legitimate end and the measures taken are reasonable and appropriate to that end. Another argument, which comes more closely to the point, is that the state power may be addressed directly to the prevention of the enforcement of contracts only when these are of a sort which the legislature in its discretion may denounce as being in themselves hostile to public morals, or public health, safety or welfare, or where the prohibition is merely of injurious practices; that interference with the enforcement of other and valid contracts according to appropriate legal procedure, although the interference is temporary and for a public purpose, is not permissible. . . . Undoubtedly, whatever is reserved of state power must be consistent with the fair intent of the constitutional limitation of that power. . . . This principle precludes a construction which would permit the State to adopt as its policy the repudiation of debts or the destruction of contracts or the denial of means to enforce them. But it does not follow that conditions may not arise in which a temporary restraint of enforcement may be consistent with the spirit and purpose of the constitutional provision and thus be found to be within the range of the reserved power of the State to protect the vital interests of the community. . . .

Whatever doubt there may have been that the protective power of the State, its police power, may be exercised — without violating the true intent of the provision of the Federal Constitution — in directly preventing the immediate and literal enforcement of contractual obligations, by a temporary and conditional restraint, where vital public interests would otherwise suffer, was removed by our decisions relating to the enforcement of provisions of leases during a period of scarcity of housing. Marcus Brown Holding Co. v. Feldman, 256 U.S. 170 (1921); Edgar A. Levy Leasing Co. v. Siegel, 258 U.S. 242 (1922). . . . The statutes of New York, declaring that a public emergency existed, directly interfered with the enforcement of covenants for the surrender of the possession of premises on the expiration of leases. Within the City of New York and contiguous counties, the owners of dwellings, including apartment and tenement houses. . . , were wholly deprived until November 1, 1922, of all possessory remedies for the purpose of removing from their premises the tenants or occupants in possession when the laws took effect, . . . providing the tenants or occupants were ready, able and willing to pay a reasonable rent or price for their use and occupation. . . .

It is manifest from this review of our decisions that there has been a growing appreciation of public needs and of the necessity of finding ground for a rational compromise between individual rights and public welfare. The settlement and consequent contraction of the public domain, the pressure of a constantly increasing density of population, the interrelation of the activities of our people and the complexity of our economic interests, have inevitably led to an increased use of the organization of society in order to protect the very bases of individual opportunity. Where, in earlier days, it was thought that only the concerns of individuals or of classes were involved, and that those of the State itself were touched only remotely, it has later been found that the fundamental interests of the State are directly affected; and that the question is no longer merely that of one party to a contract as against another, but of the use of reasonable means to safeguard the economic structure upon which the good of all depends.

It is no answer to say that this public need was not apprehended a century ago, or to insist that what the provision of the Constitution meant to the vision of that day it must mean to the vision of our time. If by the statement that what the Constitution meant at the time of its adoption it means to-day, it is intended to say that the great clauses of the Constitution must be confined to the interpretation which the framers, with the conditions and outlook of their time, would have placed upon them, the statement carries its own refutation. It was to guard against such a narrow conception that Chief Justice Marshall uttered the memorable warning — "We must never forget that it is *a constitution* we are expounding" (McCulloch v. Maryland, 4 Wheat. 316, 407) — "a constitution intended to endure for ages to come, and consequently, to be adapted to the various *crises* of human affairs." When we are dealing with the words of the Constitution, said this Court in Missouri v. Holland, 252 U.S. 416, 433, "we must realize that they have called into life a being the development of which could not have been foreseen completely by the most gifted of its begetters. . . . The case before us must be considered in the light of our whole experience and not merely in that of what was said a hundred years ago."

When we consider the contract clause and the decisions which have expounded it in harmony with the essential reserved power of the States to protect the security of their peoples, we find no warrant for the conclusion that the clause has been warped by these decisions from its proper significance or that the founders of our Government would have interpreted the clause differently had they had occasion to assume that responsibility in the conditions of the later day. The vast body of law which has been developed was unknown to the fathers, but it is believed to have preserved the essential content and the spirit of the Constitution. With a growing recognition of public needs and the relation of individual right to public security, the court has sought to prevent the perversion of the clause through its use as an instrument to throttle the capacity of the States to protect their fundamental interests. This development is a growth from the seeds which the fathers planted. . . .

Applying the criteria established by our decisions we conclude:

1. An emergency existed in Minnesota which furnished a proper occasion for the exercise of the reserved power of the State to protect the vital interests of the community. . . . As the Supreme Court of Minnesota said, the economic emergency which threatened "the loss of homes and lands which furnish those in possession the necessary shelter and means of subsistence" was a "potent cause" for the enactment of the statute.

2. The legislation was addressed to a legitimate end, that is, the legislation was not for the mere advantage of particular individuals but for the protection of a basic interest of society.

3. In view of the nature of the contracts in question — mortgages of unquestionable validity — the relief afforded and justified by the emergency, in order not to contravene the constitutional provision, could only be of a character ap-

propriate to that emergency and could be granted only upon reasonable conditions.

4. The conditions upon which the period of redemption is extended do not appear to be unreasonable. . . . The relief afforded by the statute has regard to the interest of mortgagees as well as to the interest of mortgagors. The legislation seeks to prevent the impending ruin of both by a considerate measure of relief. . . .

5. The legislation is temporary in operation. It is limited to the exigency which called it forth. . . .

We are of the opinion that the Minnesota statute as here applied does not violate the contract clause of the Federal Constitution. Whether the legislation is wise or unwise as a matter of policy is a question with which we are not concerned. . . .

Judgment affirmed.

SUTHERLAND, J., joined by Van Devanter, McReynolds, and Butler, JJ., dissenting. . . .

The whole aim of construction, as applied to a provision of the Constitution, is to discover the meaning, to ascertain and give effect to the intent, of its framers and the people who adopted it. The necessities which gave rise to the provision, the controversies which preceded, as well as the conflicts of opinion which were settled by its adoption, are matters to be considered to enable us to arrive at a correct result. The history of the times, the state of things existing when the provision was framed and adopted, should be looked to in order to ascertain the mischief and the remedy. As nearly as possible we should place ourselves in the condition of those who framed and adopted it. . . .

An application of these principles to the question under review removes any doubt, if otherwise there would be any, that the contract impairment clause denies to the several states the power to mitigate hard consequences resulting to debtors from financial or economic exigencies by an impairment of the obligation of contracts of indebtedness. A candid consideration of the history and circumstances which led up to and accompanied the framing and adoption of this clause will demonstrate conclusively that it was framed and adopted with the specific and studied purpose of preventing legislation designed to relieve debtors *especially* in time of financial distress. . . .

Following the Revolution, and prior to the adoption of the Constitution, the American people found themselves in a greatly impoverished condition. Their commerce had been well-nigh annihilated. They were not only without luxuries, but in great degree were destitute of the ordinary comforts and necessities of life. In these circumstances they incurred indebtedness in the purchase of imported goods and otherwise, far beyond their capacity to pay. . . .

In an attempt to meet the situation recourse was had to the legislatures of the several states under the Confederation; and these bodies passed, among other acts, the following: laws providing for the emission of bills of credit and making them legal tender for the payment of debts, and providing also for such payment by the delivery of specific property at a fixed valuation; instalment laws, authorizing payment of overdue obligations at future intervals of time; stay laws and laws temporarily closing access to the courts; and laws discriminating against British creditors. . . .

In the midst of this confused, gloomy, and seriously exigent condition of affairs, the Constitutional Convention of 1787 met at Philadelphia. . . . Shortly prior to the meeting of the Convention, Madison had assailed a bill pending in the Virginia Assembly, proposing the payment of private debts in three annual instalments on the ground that "no legislative principle could vindicate such an interposition of the law in private contracts.". . .

In the plan of government especially urged by Sherman and Ellsworth there was an article proposing that the legislatures of the individual states ought not to possess a right to emit bills of credit, etc., "or in any manner to obstruct or impede the recovery of debts, whereby the interests of foreigners or the citizens of any other state may be affected." And on July 13, 1787, Congress in New York, acutely conscious of the evils engendered by state laws interfering with existing contracts, passed the Northwest Territory Ordinance, which contained the clause: "And, in the just preservation of rights and property, it is understood and declared, that no law ought ever to be made or have force in the said territory, that shall, in any manner whatever, interfere with or affect private contracts, or engagements, bona fide, and without fraud previously formed." It is not surprising, therefore, that, after the Convention had adopted the clauses, no state shall "emit bills of credit," or "make any thing but gold and silver coin a tender in payment of debts," Mr. King moved to add a "prohibition on the states to interfere in private contracts." This was opposed by Gouverneur Morris and Colonel Mason. Colonel Mason thought that this would be carrying the restraint too far; that cases would happen that could not be foreseen where some kind of interference would be essential. This was on August 28. But Mason's view did not prevail, for, on September 14 following, the first clause of Art. I, §10, was altered so as to include the provision, "No state shall . . . pass any . . . law impairing the obligation of contracts," and in that form it was adopted.

Luther Martin, in an address to the Maryland House of Delegates, declared his reasons for voting against the provision. He said that he considered there might be times of such great public calamity and distress as should render it the duty of a government in some measure to interfere by passing laws totally or partially stopping courts of justice, or authorizing the debtor to pay by instalments; that such regulations had been found necessary in most or all of the states "to prevent the wealthy creditor and the moneyed man from totally destroying the poor, though industrious debtor. Such times may again arrive." And he was apprehensive of any proposal which took from the respective states the power to give their debtor citizens "a moment's indulgence, however necessary it might be, and however desirous to grant them aid."

On the other hand, Sherman and Ellsworth defended the provision in a letter to the Governor of Connecticut. In the course of the Virginia debates, Randolph declared that the prohibition would be promotive of virtue and justice, and preventive of injustice and fraud; and he pointed out that the reputation of the people had suffered because of frequent interferences by the state legislatures with private contracts. . . .

The provision was strongly defended in The Federalist, both by Hamilton in No. 7 and Madison in No. 44. . . .

Contemporaneous history is replete with evidence of the sharp conflict of opinion with respect to the advisability of adopting the clause. . . .

If it be possible by resort to the testimony of history to put any question of constitutional intent beyond the domain of uncertainty, the foregoing leaves no reasonable ground upon which to base a denial that the clause of the Constitution now under consideration was meant to foreclose state action impairing the obligation of contracts *primarily and especially* in respect of such action aimed at giving relief to debtors *in time of emergency*. And if further proof be required to strengthen what already is inexpugnable, such proof will be found in the previous decisions of this court. . . .

The present exigency is nothing new. From the beginning of our existence as a nation, periods of depression, of industrial failure, of financial distress, of unpaid and unpayable indebtedness, have alternated with years of plenty. . . .

The defense of the Minnesota law is made upon grounds which were discountenanced by the makers of the Constitution and have many times been rejected by this court. That defense should not now succeed because it constitutes an effort to overthrow the constitutional provision by an appeal to facts and circumstances identical with those which brought it into existence. With due regard for the processes of logical thinking, it legitimately cannot be urged that conditions which produced the rule may now be invoked to destroy it. . . .

I quite agree with the opinion of the court that whether the legislation under review is wise or unwise is a matter with which we have nothing to do. Whether it is likely to work well or work ill presents a question entirely irrelevant to the issue. The only legitimate inquiry we can make is whether it is constitutional. If it is not, its virtues, if it have any, cannot save it; if it is, its faults cannot be invoked to accomplish its destruction. If the provisions of the Constitution be not upheld when they pinch as well as when they comfort, they may as well be abandoned. Being unable to reach any other conclusion than that the Minnesota statute infringes the constitutional restriction under review, I have no choice but to say so.

CARDOZO, J. [unpublished concurring opinion].

"We must never forget that it is *a constitution* we are expounding." Marshall, C.J., in McCulloch v. Maryland. . . . "A constitution [is] intended to endure for ages to come, and, consequently, to be adapted to the various *crises* of human affairs." Ibid. . . .

"The case before us must be considered in the light of our whole experience and not merely in that of what was said a hundred years ago." Holmes, J. in Missouri v. Holland. . . .

A hundred years ago when this court decided Bronson v. Kinzie . . . property might be taken without due process of law through the legislation of the states, and the courts of the nation were powerless to give redress, unless indeed they could find that a contract had been broken. Dartmouth College v. Woodward . . . ; Fletcher v. Peck. . . . The judges of those courts had not yet begun to speak of the police power except in an off hand way or in expounding the effect of the commerce clause upon local regulations. The License Cases. . . . Due process in the states was whatever the states ordained. In such circumstances there was jeopardy, or the threat of it, in encroachment, however slight, upon the obligation to adhere to the letter of a contract. Once reject that test, and no other was available, or so it might well have seemed. The states could not be kept within the limits of reason and fair dealing for such restraints were then unknown as curbs upon their power. It was either all or nothing.

The Fourteenth Amendment came, and with it a profound change in the relation between the federal government and the governments of the states. No longer were the states invested with arbitrary power. Their statutes affecting property or liberty were brought within supervision of independent courts and subjected to the rule of reason. The dilemma of "all or nothing" no longer stared us in the face.

Upon the basis of that amendment, a vast body of law unknown to the fathers has been built in treatise and decision. The economic and social changes wrought by the industrial revolution and by the growth of population have made it necessary for government at this day to do a thousand things that were beyond the experience or the thought of a century ago. With the growing recognition of this need, courts have awakened to the truth that the contract clause is perverted from its proper meaning when it throttles the capacity of the states to exert their governmental power in response to crying needs. Block v. Hirsh . . . ; Marcus Brown Co. v. Feldman . . . ; Levy Leasing Co. v. Siegel. . . . The early cases dealt with the problem as one affecting the conflicting rights and interests of individuals and classes. This was the attitude of the courts up to the Fourteenth Amendment; and the tendency to some extent persisted even later. Edwards v. Kearzey . . . ; Burnitz v. Beverly. . . . The rights and interests of the state itself were involved, as it seemed, only indirectly and remotely, if they were thought to be involved at all. We know better in these days, with the passing of the frontier and of the unpeopled spaces of the west. With these and other changes, the welfare of the social organism in any of its parts is bound up more inseparably than ever with the welfare of the whole. A gospel of laissez-faire — of individual initiative — of thrift and industry and sacrifice — may be inadequate in that great society we live in to point the way to salvation, at least for economic life. The state when it acts today by statutes like the one before us is not furthering the selfish good of individuals or classes as ends of ultimate validity. It is furthering its own good by maintaining the economic structure on which the good of all depends. Such at least is its endeavor, however much it miss the mark. The attainment of that end, so august and impersonal, will not be barred and thwarted by the obstruction of a contract set up along the way.

Looking back over the century, one perceives a process of evolution too strong to be set back. The decisions brought together by the Chief Justice [Hughes] show with impressive force how the court in its interpretation of the contract clause has been feeling its way toward a rational compromise between private rights and public welfare. From the beginning it was seen that something must be subtracted from the words of the Constitution in all their literal and stark significance. This was forcefully pointed out by Johnson, J., in Ogden v. Saunders, 12 Wheat. 213, 286. At first refuge was found in the distinction between right and remedy with all its bewildering refinements. Gradually the distinction was perceived to be inadequate. The search was for a broader base, for a division that would separate the lawful and the forbidden by lines more closely in correspondence with the necessities of government. The Fourteenth Amendment was seen to point the way. Contracts were still to be preserved. There was to be no arbitrary destruction of their binding force, nor any arbitrary impairment. There was to be no impairment, even though not arbitrary, except with the limits of fairness, of moderation, and of pressing and emergent need. But a promise exchanged between individuals was not to paralyze the state in its endeavor in times of direful crisis to keep its lifeblood flowing.

To hold this may be inconsistent with things that men said in 1787 when expounding to compatriots the newly written constitution. They did not see the changes in the relation between states and nation or in the play of social forces that lay hidden in the womb of time. It may be inconsistent with things that they believed or took for granted. Their beliefs to be significant must be adjusted to the world they knew. It is not in my judgment inconsistent with what they say today nor with what today they would believe, if they were called upon to interpret "in the light of our whole experience" the constitution that they framed for the needs of an expanding future.

With this supplemental statement I concur in all that has been written in the opinion of the court.

Discussion

Nebbia and *Blaisdell* present strikingly different issues of constitutional interpretation. The historical basis for the doctrine of substantive due process was certainly problematic. The Constitution, however, explicitly prohibits states from impairing contractual obligations; Justice Sutherland correctly observes that the framers intended to prevent the enactment of laws like the Minnesota mortgage moratorium.

Is there any theory, consistent with both the text and the "intent" of the contract clause, under which the Minnesota mortgage moratorium could have been upheld? Charles Miller argues:[2]

> Justice Sutherland's history (and that of the Court) is right as to the particular impairment the framers of the Constitution had in mind, but it is irrelevant to the basic problem recognized by the people of the time. Pursuing this reasoning it might be argued, first, that in construing the contract clause the large purpose, the smooth functioning of the economy, should be more important in later constitutional adjudication than the specific means designed to promote this end in the 1780's; and second, that the debtor legislation of the 1930's was designed to effectuate the broader aims of the clause. According to the leading historian of the contract clause, "relief legislation of the Confederation period was almost entirely the result of the existing shortage of a stable currency." One hundred and fifty years later, when the same kind of legislation was enacted in Minnesota, economic conditions were completely different. Although in form the same, the laws passed in the two eras are seen to be opposite in significance when viewed in the light of the different economic conditions. The earlier relief legislation exacerbated economic instability. The modern relief laws were designed to bring economic instability to a halt, that is, to achieve the underlying aim of the contract clause. Could the Minnesota law not be upheld on the ground of agreement with the basic intention of the framers of the Constitution?

Assuming that one ought to be faithful to the adopters' intent, does Miller express their intent at the proper *level of abstraction*?

2. Minnesota passed its law (and the Supreme Court considered it) within not only the general context of the Great Depression and its massive economic dis-

2. Charles Miller, The Supreme Court and the Uses of History 45-46 (1969).

ruptions, but also within more particular circumstances of social disorder and violence. For example, angry farmers denounced and in some instances forcibly stopped foreclosure of their farms. In Iowa, a local judge who refused to suspend foreclosure proceedings was dragged from a courtroom and had a rope put around his neck before the crowd let him go. The governor of Iowa also declared martial law in six counties and called out the National Guard in order to forestall the perceived threat of rural violence. A New York newspaper editorially noted that instead of worrying about a merely fantasized threat of a "red revolution" in the cities, Americans should become aware "that actual revolution already exists in the farm belt," provoked by the anguish of "conservatives fighting for the right to hold their homesteads."[3]

Do these facts bear on the constitutionality of Minnesota's "moratorium"? If so, why? Because people were suffering? Because judges and legal officials were threatened with violence? To what extent should the social impact of, or popular reaction to, a law influence the determination of its constitutionality? Would your views of, say, Plessy v. Ferguson change if you were persuaded that racially integrated transportation or schools would have been met with a violent response from racists?

B. 1935-1937

The Court that decided *Nebbia* and *Blaisdell* consisted of three progressives (Stone, Brandeis, and Cardozo), the reactionary "four horsemen" (Van Devanter, McReynolds, Sutherland, and Butler), and two swing members (Roberts and Chief Justice Hughes). Roberts wrote *Nebbia* and joined in *Blaisdell*, but "as the New Deal was revealed in all its terrifying dimensions to the conservatives of the nation, he became ready for persuasion. As for the Chief Justice, he was neither clearly liberal nor stubbornly conservative, but he seemed to be much concerned for the Court's own dignity and was likely sometimes to swing with a conservative majority to avoid the criticism that might follow a 5 to 4 decision. In 1935, therefore, the majority shifted, and for two busy terms the Court waged what is surely the most ambitious dragon-fight in its long and checkered history."[4]

The most significant decisions of these terms struck down recovery measures of the New Deal.[5] For present purposes, however, the most interesting decision is Morehead v. Tipaldo, 298 U.S. 587 (1936), which invalidated a New York minimum wage law for women on authority of Adkins v. Children's Hospital (1923). Justice Butler wrote for the five-man majority (including Roberts but not Hughes) that "the State is without power by any form of legislation to prohibit, change or nullify contracts between employers and adult women workers as to the amount of wages to be paid."

Morehead was decided in June 1936, toward the close of the term. Roosevelt was reelected in November, and in early February 1937, "with characteristic indirection, [he] presented Congress with a judiciary plan that purported to cope

3. See Arthur Schlesinger, The Coming of the New Deal 42-44 (1959).
4. Robert McCloskey, The American Supreme Court 164-165 (1960).
5. See, e.g., Schechter Poultry Corp. v. United States, 295 U.S. 495 (1935); Carter v. Carter Coal Co., 298 U.S. 238 (1936); United States v. Butler, 297 U.S. 1 (1936); Ch. 4 supra.

with the supposed problem of overcrowded federal court dockets. It would have enabled him to appoint a new judge to supplement any judge over seventy who failed to retire (retirement could not of course be made compulsory, for the Constitution protects judicial tenure 'during good behavior'). The significant fact was that the plan would permit the President to appoint six new Supreme Court justices, and thus to insure approval of the New Deal program. It was, as it was called, a 'court-packing plan.' . . . And it was offered by a President who had just received an overwhelming popular vote of confidence and who had not yet been denied in Congress any of his important demands. Even the five or six judges who had provoked this threat must have slept rather uneasily for a few months."[6]

The Court's dramatic shift began less than two months later in West Coast Hotel Co. v. Parrish, 300 U.S. 379 (1937), which explicitly overruled *Adkins*. Chief Justice Hughes wrote for the Court:

> [T]he violation alleged by those attacking minimum wage regulation for women is deprivation of freedom of contract. What is this freedom? The Constitution does not speak of freedom of contract. It speaks of liberty and prohibits the deprivation of liberty without due process of law. In prohibiting that deprivation the Constitution does not recognize an absolute and uncontrollable liberty. Liberty in each of its phases has its history and connotation. But the liberty safeguarded is liberty in a social organization which requires the protection of law against the evils which menace the health, safety, morals and welfare of the people. Liberty under the Constitution is thus necessarily subject to the restraints of due process, and regulation which is reasonable in relation to its subject and is adopted in the interests of the community is due process. . . . What can be closer to the public interest than the health of women and their protection from unscrupulous and overreaching employers? And if the protection of women is a legitimate end of the exercise of state power, how can it be said that the requirement of the payment of a minimum wage fairly fixed in order to meet the very necessities of existence is not an admissible means to that end? The legislature of the State was clearly entitled to consider the situation of women in employment, the fact that they are in the class receiving the least pay, and that they are the ready victims of those who would take advantage of their necessitous circumstances. The legislature was entitled to adopt measures to reduce the evils of the "sweating system," the exploiting of workers at wages so low as to be insufficient to meet the bare cost of living, thus making their very helplessness the occasion of a most injurious competition. The legislature had the right to consider that its minimum wage requirements would be an important aid in carrying out its policy of protection. The adoption of similar requirements by many States evidences a deep-seated conviction both as to the presence of the evil and as to the means adapted to check it. Legislative response to that conviction cannot be regarded as arbitrary or capricious, and that is all we have to decide. Even if the wisdom of the policy be regarded as debatable and its effects uncertain, still the legislature is entitled to its judgment.
>
> There is an additional and compelling consideration which recent economic experience has brought into a strong light. The exploitation of a class of workers who are in an unequal position with respect to bargaining power and are thus relatively defenseless against the denial of a living wage is not only detrimental to their health and well being but casts a direct burden for their support upon the community. What these workers lose in wages the taxpayers are called upon to pay. The bare cost

6. McCloskey, supra note 4, at 169. See also William Leuchtenburg, The Origins of Franklin D. Roosevelt's "Court-Packing" Plan, 1966 Sup. Ct. Rev. 347.

of living must be met. We may take judicial notice of the unparalleled demands for relief which arose during the recent period of depression and still continue to an alarming extent despite the degree of economic recovery which has been achieved. It is unnecessary to cite official statistics to establish what is of common knowledge through the length and breadth of the land. While in the instant case no factual brief has been presented, there is no reason to doubt that the State of Washington has encountered the same social problem that is present elsewhere. The community is not bound to provide what is in effect a subsidy for unconscionable employers. The community may direct its law-making power to correct the abuse which springs from their selfish disregard of the public interest. . . .

Our conclusion is that the case of Adkins v. Children's Hospital should be, and it is, overruled.

Justices Van Devanter, McReynolds, Sutherland, and Butler dissented.

West Coast Hotel was soon followed by decisions upholding New Deal legislation under the commerce and spending powers.[7] Just what brought about this sudden about-face remains somewhat obscure. The central figure is Owen Roberts, whose vote made the difference between *Morehead* and *West Coast Hotel.* Although there are indications that he cast his sustaining vote in the later case before Roosevelt presented Congress with the court-packing bill,[8] the received notion is that Roberts' fear of the bill caused him to make "the switch in time that saved nine." Whatever Roberts' motivation, Roosevelt's court-packing plan ultimately failed. (The plan had been widely criticized and very likely would have failed in any event.) But "[c]onstitutional doctrine emerged from those months of crisis profoundly altered. . . . As the Civil War had settled the basic question underlying the nation-state conflict, so the Depression and the New Deal had resolved the basic question of economic control. Significant economic issues remained to be decided, of course, even after the nation had made the basic decision against laissez-faire, but the Court by its own intransigence had disqualified itself to assist in the process by which those decisions were reached."[9]

C. The Modern Doctrine of Economic Due Process

1. The Case Law

The year after *West Coast Hotel,* in United States v. Carolene Products Co., 304 U.S. 144 (1938), the Court rejected a due process challenge to a federal enactment prohibiting the interstate shipment of "filled milk."[10] "We may assume for

7. E.g., NLRB v. Jones & Laughlin Steel Corp., 301 U.S. 1 (1937); Steward Machine Co. v. Davis, 301 U.S. 548 (1937); section II of this chapter, infra.

8. See Felix Frankfurter, Mr. Justice Roberts, 104 U. Pa. L. Rev. 311 (1955).

9. McCloskey, supra note 4, at 177-178.

10. Filled milk is skimmed milk compounded with nondairy fats. The statute included a declaration that filled milk was unhealthy and a fraud upon the public. Professor Geoffrey Miller has argued that what explains the ban in fact was the power of the dairy industry that was fearful of the economic challenge posed by the new purveyors of filled milk. See Miller, The True Story of Carolene Products, 1987 Supreme Court Review 397. He describes the "scientific case against filled milk" as "entirely bogus from the start" (p.420) and argues that the background of *Carolene Products* is best analyzed as "one discrete minority — the nation's dairy farmers and their allies — obtained legislation harmful to consumers and the public at large" (p.428) by serving to raise the price of milk.

present purposes," Justice Stone wrote, "that . . . disproof in judicial proceedings of all facts which would show or tend to show that a statute . . . had a rational basis" would invalidate the statute.

> [But] the existence of facts supporting the legislative judgment is to be presumed, for regulatory legislation affecting ordinary commercial transactions is not to be pronounced unconstitutional unless in the light of the facts made known or generally assumed it is of such a character as to preclude the assumption that it rests upon some rational basis within the knowledge and experience of the legislators. . . . [Our inquiry,] where the legislative judgment is drawn in question, must be restricted to the issue whether any state of facts either known or which could reasonably be assumed affords support for it. Here the demurrer challenges the validity of the statute on its face and it is evident from all the considerations presented to Congress, and those of which we may take judicial notice, that the question is at least debatable whether commerce in filled milk should be left unregulated, or in some measure restricted, or wholly prohibited.

Between 1937 and 1941 the Court's composition changed radically. The progressive justices were succeeded by other progressives,[11] and the old conservatives (Van Devanter, McReynolds, Butler, and Sutherland) were replaced by New Dealers.[12] It became increasingly doubtful whether economic regulations had to meet even the minimal requirements suggested by *West Coast Hotel* and *Carolene Products.*

In Olsen v. Nebraska, 313 U.S. 236 (1941), a unanimous Court overruled Ribnik v. McBride, 277 U.S. 350 (1928), to uphold a statute fixing the maximum fee that an employment agency could collect from an employee. Justice Douglas wrote:

> We are not concerned . . . with the wisdom, need, or appropriateness of the legislation. Differences of opinion on that score suggest a choice which "should be left where . . . it was left by the Constitution — to the States and to Congress." There is no necessity for the state to demonstrate before us that evils persist despite the competition which attends the bargaining in this field. In final analysis, the only constitutional prohibitions or restraints which respondents have suggested for the invalidation of this legislation are those notions of public policy embodied in earlier decisions of this Court but which, as Mr. Justice Holmes long admonished, should not be read into the Constitution. Since they do not find expression in the Constitution we cannot give them continuing vitality as standards by which the constitutionality of the economic and social programs of the states is to be determined.

The same year, in United States v. Darby, 312 U.S. 100 (1941), the Court sustained the federal Fair Labor Standards Act of 1938 against a variety of constitutional challenges. With respect to the due process objection to the act's fixing of maximum hours and minimum wages for men, Justice Stone was content to write for the Court:

11. Frankfurter replaced Cardozo (1939), who himself had replaced Holmes in 1932; Douglas replaced Brandeis (1939); Stone succeeded Hughes to the chief justiceship (1941); Jackson succeeded to Stone's seat as associate justice (1941).

12. Black replaced Van Devanter (1937); Reed replaced Sutherland (1938); Murphy replaced Butler (1940); and Byrnes replaced McReynolds (1941). Roberts, who had abandoned his conservative brethren, remained on the Court until 1945.

> Since our decision in West Coast Hotel Co. v. Parrish, it is no longer open to question that the fixing of a minimum wage is within the legislative power and that the bare fact of its exercise is not a denial of due process under the Fifth more than under the Fourteenth Amendment. Nor is it any longer open to question that it is within the legislative power to fix maximum hours. Similarly the statute is not objectionable because applied alike to both men and women.

There were no dissents. In Lincoln Federal Labor Union v. Northwestern Iron & Metal Co., 335 U.S. 525 (1949), a unanimous Court sustained a state prohibition of closed shops. Justice Black noted that the Court had rejected "the *Allgeyer-Lochner-Adair-Coppage* constitutional doctrine" and had returned "to the earlier constitutional principle that states have power to legislate against what are found to be injurious practices in their internal commercial and business affairs, so long as their laws do not run afoul of some specific federal constitutional prohibition." In Day-Brite Lighting, Inc. v. Missouri, 342 U.S. 421 (1952), the Court sustained a law allowing employees four hours' leave with full pay on election day. Justice Douglas wrote that the legislature's judgment "may be a debatable one. . . . But if our recent cases mean anything, they leave debatable issues as respects business, economic, and social affairs to legislative decision." Justice Frankfurter concurred in the result without opinion, and Justice Jackson dissented, stating that "[g]etting out the vote is not the business of employers. . . . It is either the voter's own business or the State's business." In Ferguson v. Skrupa, 372 U.S. 726 (1963), which sustained a Kansas statute prohibiting anyone except lawyers from engaging in the business of "debt adjusting,"[13] Justice Black wrote for the Court:

> [T]he Kansas Legislature was free to decide for itself that legislation was needed to deal with the business of debt adjusting. Unquestionably, there are arguments showing that the business of debt adjusting has social utility, but such arguments are properly addressed to the legislature, not to us. We refuse to sit as a "super-legislature to weigh the wisdom of legislation." . . . Whether the legislature takes for its textbook Adam Smith, Herbert Spencer, Lord Keynes, or some other is no concern of ours. The Kansas debt adjusting statute may be wise or unwise. But relief, if any be needed, lies not with us but with the body constituted to pass laws for the State of Kansas.

That there is at least a theoretical difference between the abdication or withdrawal of review espoused by Justice Black in *Lincoln Union* and Ferguson v. Skrupa and the "rational relation" standard of review is suggested by Mr. Justice Harlan's brief notation in the latter case: "Mr. Justice Harlan concurs in the judgment on the ground that this state measure bears a rational relation to a constitutionally permissible objective. See Williamson v. Lee Optical Co., 348 U.S. 483, 491." We next consider the case that Justice Harlan cited to suggest that there is a difference.

13. Debt adjusting is "the making of a contract . . . with a particular debtor whereby the debtor agrees to pay a certain amount of money periodically to the person engaged in the debt adjusting business who shall for a consideration distribute the same among certain specified creditors in accordance with a plan agreed upon."

WILLIAMSON v. LEE OPTICAL CO.

348 U.S. 483 (1955)

Appeal from the United States District Court for the Western District of Oklahoma

DOUGLAS, J. . . .

This suit was instituted in the District Court to have an Oklahoma law declared unconstitutional and to enjoin state officials from enforcing it for the reason that it allegedly violated various provisions of the Federal Constitution. The matter was heard by a District Court of three judges, as required by 28 U.S.C. §2281. That court held certain provisions of the law unconstitutional. The case is here by appeal.

The District Court held unconstitutional portions of three sections of the Act. First, it held invalid under the Due Process Clause of the Fourteenth Amendment the portions of §2 which make it unlawful for any person not a licensed optometrist or ophthalmologist to fit lenses to a face or to duplicate or replace into frames lenses or other optical appliances, except upon written prescriptive authority of an Oklahoma licensed ophthalmologist or optometrist.

An ophthalmologist is a duly licensed physician who specializes in the care of the eyes. An optometrist examines eyes for refractive error, recognizes (but does not treat) diseases of the eye, and fills prescriptions for eyeglasses. The optician is an artisan qualified to grind lenses, fill prescriptions, and fit frames.

The effect of §2 is to forbid the optician from fitting or duplicating lenses without a prescription from an ophthalmologist or optometrist. In practical effect, it means that no optician can fit old glasses into new frames or supply a lens, whether it be a new lens or one to duplicate a lost or broken lens, without a prescription. The District Court conceded that it was in the competence of the police power of a State to regulate the examination of the eyes. But it rebelled at the notion that a State could require a prescription from an optometrist or ophthalmologist "to take old lenses and place them in new frames and then fit the completed spectacles to the *face* of the eyeglass wearer." . . . The Court found that through mechanical devices and ordinary skills the optician could take a broken lens or a fragment thereof, measure its power, and reduce it to prescriptive terms. The Court held that "Although on this precise issue of duplication, the legislature in the instant regulation was dealing with a matter of public interest, the particular means chosen are neither reasonably necessary nor reasonably related to the end sought to be achieved." It was, accordingly, the opinion of the court that this provision of the law violated the Due Process Clause by arbitrarily interfering with the optician's right to do business. . . .

The Oklahoma law may exact a needless, wasteful requirement in many cases. But it is for the legislature, not the courts, to balance the advantages and disadvantages of the new requirement. It appears that in many cases the optician can easily supply the new frames or new lenses without reference to the old written prescription. It also appears that many written prescriptions contain no directive data in regard to fitting spectacles to the face. But in some cases the directions contained in the prescription are essential, if the glasses are to be fitted so as to correct the particular defects of vision or alleviate the eye condition. The legislature might have concluded that the frequency of occasions when a prescription is necessary was sufficient to justify this regulation of the fitting of eyeglasses. Likewise, when it is necessary to duplicate a lens, a written prescription may or may not be necessary. But the legislature might have concluded that one was needed often enough to require one in every case. Or the legislature may have concluded that eye examinations were so critical, not only for correction of vision but also for detection of latent ailments or diseases, that every change in frames and every duplication of a lens should be accompanied by a prescription from a medical expert. To be sure, the present law does not require a new examination of the eyes every time the frames are changed or the lenses duplicated. For if the old prescription is on file with the optician, he can go ahead and make the new fitting or duplicate the lenses. But the law need not be in every respect logically consistent with its aims to be constitutional. It is enough that there is an evil at hand for correction, and that it might be thought that the particular legislative measure was a rational way to correct it. . . .

Secondly, the District Court held that it violated the Equal Protection Clause of the Fourteenth Amendment to subject opticians to this regulatory system and to exempt, as §3 of the Act does, all sellers of ready-to-wear glasses.

Third, the District Court held unconstitutional, as violative of the Due Process Clause of the Fourteenth Amendment, that portion of §3 which makes it unlawful "to solicit the sale of . . . frames, mountings . . . or any other optical appliances.". . . [R]egulation of the advertising of eyeglass frames was said to intrude "into a mercantile field only casually related to the visual care of the public" and restrict "an activity which in no way can detrimentally affect the people."

An eyeglass frame, considered in isolation, is only a piece of merchandise. But an eyeglass frame is not used in isolation . . . ; it is used with lenses; and lenses, pertaining as they do to the human eye, enter the field of health. Therefore, the legislature might conclude that to regulate one effectively it would have to regulate the other. Or it might conclude that both the sellers of frames and the sellers of lenses were in a business where advertising should be limited or even abolished in the public interest. . . . The advertiser of frames may be using his ads to bring in customers who will buy lenses. If the advertisement of lenses is to be abolished or controlled, the advertising of frames must come under the same restraints; or so the legislature might think. We see no constitutional reason why a State may not treat all who deal with the human eye as members of a profession who should use no merchandising methods for obtaining customers.

Fourth, the District Court held unconstitutional, as violative of the Due Process Clause of the Fourteenth Amendment, the provision of §4 of the Oklahoma Act which reads as follows: "No person, firm, or corporation engaged in the business of retailing merchandise to the general public shall rent space, sublease departments, or otherwise permit any person purporting to do eye examination or visual care to occupy space in such retail store."

It seems to us that this regulation . . . is an attempt to free the profession, to as great an extent as possible, from all taints of commercialism. It certainly might be easy for an optometrist with space in a retail store to be merely a front for the retail establishment. In any case, the opportunity for that nexus may be too great for safety, if the eye doctor is allowed inside the retail store. Moreover, it may be deemed important to effective regulation that the eye doctor be restricted to geographical locations that reduce the temptations of commercialism. Geographical location may be an important consideration in a legislative program which aims to raise the treatment of the human eye to a strictly professional level. We cannot say that the regulation has no rational relation to that objective and therefore is beyond constitutional bounds. . . .

Discussion

1. *Objectives.* What does the Court suppose are the objectives of sections 2, 3, and 4 of the Oklahoma statute? How does the Court determine that they are permissible? What might the Oklahoma legislature's "real" objectives have been in enacting the law? Are these legitimate?

2. *The ends-means relationship.* What relationship does the Court require between a regulation and its supposed objectives? Who has the burden of demonstrating that the regulation does or does not promote the objectives, and what is the measure or degree of the burden?

Is the "minimum rationality" test of *Lee Optical* identical to the standards invoked by Justice Harlan's dissent in *Lochner* and Justice Roberts' majority opinion in *Nebbia?* Does the Oklahoma statute satisfy those standards? Can you imagine any plausible regulation that cannot meet the *Lee Optical* test?

3. *The constitutional basis for economic due process.* Does the Constitution impose even a minimum obligation on legislatures to assure that economic interests are not heedlessly injured? Or is the correct view that "[l]aws are not unconstitutional merely because they are shown to be useless" but only if they contravene "a constitutional criterion found elsewhere in the Constitution than in the due process clause itself"?[14]

2. *How the Court Arrived Where It Did: Two Perspectives*

ROBERT McCLOSKEY, ECONOMIC DUE PROCESS AND THE SUPREME COURT: AN EXHUMATION AND REBURIAL
1962 Sup. Ct. Rev. 34, 38-44[15]

When [the modern due process] cases were taken together with a companion series in which the Equal Protection Clause was given a similarly permissive scope, there could be little doubt as to the practical result: no claim of substantive economic rights would now be sustained by the Supreme Court. The judiciary had abdicated the field.

This was the result. But it is of some interest to note how the result had been achieved. Obviously two paths lay open. One was . . . to repudiate in explicit and unmistakable terms the very bases for the Court's jurisdiction over economic questions. Such a course was at least imaginable. The Justices might . . . have held in so many words that economic legislation was no longer subject to judicial review on the question whether it had a "rational basis." This possibility may have been in Stone's mind . . . when in *Carolene Products* he only assumed "for present purposes" that the rational basis test was still relevant. . . . Certainly Douglas came close to it in *Olsen.* A few years later, in the *Lincoln Union* case, Black came

14. Hans Linde, Without "Due Process": Unconstitutional Law in Oregon, 49 Ore. L. Rev. 125, 174 (1970).

15. The University of Chicago Press. Copyright © 1962 by the University of Chicago.

even closer when he implied that the only constitutional limits in the economic field were the specific prohibitions of the Constitution.

The other possibility was to retain the rhetoric of the rational basis standard, but to apply it so tolerantly that no law was ever likely to violate it. This was the course ultimately chosen, one more consonant with Stone's view that such issues were better dealt with "gradually and by intimation." Even Douglas seems to have accepted the rational basis concept for these rhetorical purposes.

This was perhaps the "judicial" way to bring the result about. It preserved some shreds of the idea of continuity, and that idea, myth or not, is important to the constitutional tradition. It enabled the Justices to feel their way along toward a policy whose contours were probably not yet clear in their own minds. It may have helped to maintain unanimity. . . .

So much at least can be said for the approach chosen, leaving aside for the moment the question whether the result itself was desirable. But the matter has another aspect. When policies are established "gradually and by intimation," when the question of their existence is partially obscured by preservation of the old rhetoric, there is always a chance that the destruction of those policies will not be recognized. A flat decision to discard substantive due process root-and-branch would have compelled the Justices to explain themselves, to examine the basis for their abnegation. In the actual event they have never fully done so, at least in public, and this leaves, to say the least, a large gap in the rationale that underlies the structure of modern constitutional law. . . .

Why did the Court move all the way from the inflexible negativism of the old majority to the all-out tolerance of the new? Why did it not establish a halfway house between the extremes, retaining a measure of control over economic legislation but exercising that control with discrimination and self-restraint? . . . [T]he court would [then] not strike down an arguably rational law, but it would require some showing by the State that there was a basis for believing it to be rational and would consider evidence to the contrary presented by the affected business. Laws like those involved in the *Lee Optical* case . . . might be invalidated, or at any rate more sharply queried.

Assuming then that this standard — this modest residue of the old economic supervision — was consciously and purposefully rejected, what explains the rejection? And, to make the difficulty a little more acute, what accounts for the fact that such survivors of the old Court as Stone and Roberts concurred in the choice, that the *Olsen* opinion was unanimous? A couple of "behavioral" or psychological explanations come to mind as possibilities. They are put forward diffidently, for motive is hard to ascertain with respect to only one man; when a group of nine highly sophisticated individuals is involved, the complexities become awesome.

For one thing, it may be that Stone and Roberts joined in the movement so as to preserve the rhetoric of supervision and thus some faint shadow of doctrinal continuity. Black, as his biographer says, wanted to "reject utterly and completely the doctrine . . . that the due-process clause gives to courts the power to determine the reasonableness of regulations." Considering his well-known enthusiasm for calling a spade a spade, we can well believe that Black would have liked to spell this out in an explicit abdication speech. We cannot tell how many of his brethren would have joined him then. But by the spring of 1941, there were, besides himself, four Roosevelt appointees on the Court, and further appointments were obviously pending. The veterans may have felt that the most they could hope for was the fictional survival of the rational basis test.

A second possible explanation may be more fruitful, since it relates, not only to the question why the veterans were willing to retreat so far, but also why the newer Justices seemed resolved to do so. It is that extremism had bred extremism in thinking about the role of the Supreme Court. Between 1923 and 1937, a conservative majority had, from time to time, embraced a policy of adamant resistance to economic experiment, and this obstructionist spirit had reached its zenith in the judicial reaction against the New Deal. . . . This intransigence had tended to discredit the whole concept of judicial supervision in the minds of those who felt that government must have reasonable leeway to experiment with the economic order. . . .

Factors like these may help to explain the impulse to discard the old due process doctrine, bag and baggage. Yet one would like to think that a more thoughtful process was going on somewhere below the surface, that the policy of virtual abdication was not merely a reflex against the excesses of the past but a considered and justified decision about the proper scope of judicial review. The written record to support such a supposition is not, alas, very convincing. Scattered remarks in decisions cited above, and in others, assailed the dead horse of "the *Allgeyer-Lochner-Adair-Coppage*" doctrine, i.e., the Justices argued against "social dogma" and for "increased deference to the legislative judgment" in the economic field. But they did not explain why the abuses of power in those earlier decisions justified abandonment of the power itself, nor why the deference to the legislature should be carried to the point of complete submission. The nearest thing to an explanation is perhaps to be found in Mr. Justice Frankfurter's concurrence in American Federation of Labor v. American Sash & Door Co. [335 U.S. 538, 544 (1949)], where he argued that "the judiciary is prone to misconceive the public good" and that matters of policy, depending as they do on imponderable value issues, are best left to the people and their representatives. . . .

ROBERT GORDON, LEGAL THOUGHT AND LEGAL PRACTICE IN THE AGE OF AMERICAN ENTERPRISE, 1870-1920

in Professions and Professional Ideologies in America, 1730-1940
(Stone & Geison eds. 1983)

[The classical mind-set] began to collapse in the 1890's, which produced challenges to all three of the basic aims of Liberal legal science: (1) the aim of the formal equality of juristic persons, which came to seem less attractive when such persons as U.S. Steel claimed to be endowed with the standard package of rights; (2) the aim of seeing all action within spheres of autonomy as resulting from free will, which came up against both sharper perceptions of visible coercion in the workplace and revised theories of social causation; and (3) the aim of formal realizability through the deductive process of neutral adjudication, which appeared increasingly silly and unjust in the attempt to practice it and also theoretically impossible. The very abstraction and generality that the Liberals had sought to impart to legal form now seemed its chief defect. In such forms the law was incapable of dealing with the realities of concrete social and economic problems; it concealed "real" interests under meaningless categories; and if this were not enough, it could not even approach the Liberal ideal of predictable application. Some Progressive critics (who came to include the "Legal Realists" of the 1920's and 30's) delighted not only in showing the class bias of Liberal legalisms as practiced, but in exploding its aspirations to technical coherence: The famous "principles" were exposed as empty formulae that could lead by logical manipulation, to totally contradictory results. Judging, far from being non-discretionary, involved at each logical step the necessity of social choice; but the abstraction of Liberalism shrouded in illegitimate obscurity the social bases of decision. (The first-year law school curriculum to this very day consists of an enthusiastic Oedipal slaying of our grandfathers — the authors of "formalism" in private law and "Lochnerism" in Constitutional law.)

By the "rule of law" Liberals meant the subjection of all social actors to a regime of general rules that were to specify in advance the limits of autonomous conduct and guarantee to abstain totally from regulating conduct within those limits. The Progressives, concluding that such line-drawing was impossible, also gave up on the ideal of abstention. They saw conflict between social groups as inevitable, but still manageable. When interests of social actors conflicted, each might have legitimate claims to recognition; in such a case they had to be *balanced;* questions of how far each actor could go were questions not of absolute right (having the right or not having it) but of *degree,* and so bound to vary with varying circumstances.

3. The Contract Clause, 1934-1983

The *Minnesota Mortgage Moratorium* case did not mark the end of the contract clause. During the two following years, the Court distinguished *Blaisdell* to strike down a number of state laws under the clause. Most of the decisions were unanimous. For example, W.B. Worthen Co. v. Thomas, 292 U.S. 426 (1934), held that an Arkansas law exempting the proceeds of insurance policies from garnishment could not be applied to a garnishment effected before its enactment. Chief Justice Hughes wrote for the Court that this law, unlike the Minnesota statute, contained "no limitations as to time, amount, circumstances, or need." Justice Cardozo invoked these same distinctions in W.B. Worthen Co. v. Kavanaugh, 295 U.S. 56 (1935), to strike down another Arkansas law for the relief of mortgagors. And Justice Brandeis in effect read the contract clause into the Fifth Amendment due process clause in Louisville Joint Stock Land Bank v. Radford, 295 U.S. 555 (1935), to invalidate farm mortgage moratorium provisions of the federal Frazier-Lemke Act.[16]

Since 1937, the clause has seen only sporadic litigation — partly because of the paucity of offending legislation, but at least equally because of the Court's general withdrawal from review of economic legislation. Anderson v. Brand, 303 U.S. 95 (1938), struck down an Indiana law repealing teacher tenure rights, and Wood v. Lovett, 313 U.S. 362 (1941), held that land bought at a tax sale under a statute curing irregularities that might otherwise have been raised by the owner

16. See also Treigle v. Acme Homestead Assn., 297 U.S. 189 (1936); International Steel Co. v. Surety Co., 297 U.S. 657 (1936).

was immune from a subsequent repeal of the statute when the original owner sought to recover the property from the purchaser at the sale.

In El Paso v. Simmons, 379 U.S. 497 (1965), the state of Texas had sold large amounts of land on installment contracts under which forfeiting purchasers retained a perpetual right to redeem upon payment of back interest. The state subsequently imposed a five-year statute of limitations on the right of redemption. The Court sustained the statute against a contract clause attack, holding that the state's interest in the integrity of the market, title stability, and the avoidance of litigation imbroglios outweighed the burden imposed on purchasers and their assigns. Only Justice Black dissented, arguing that the Court had "balanced away the plain guarantee" of the clause and that it had assumed that *Blaisdell* "practically read the Contract Clause out of the Constitution."

For better or worse, Justice Black's observation was generally assumed to be correct — until the late 1970s, when the Court invalidated two laws on the ground that they impaired the obligations of contracts. United States Trust Co. v. New Jersey, 431 U.S. 1 (1977), held that New York and New Jersey could not repeal a 1962 covenant that limited the ability of the jointly established Port Authority to subsidize rail transportation from revenues and reserves pledged as security for bonds issued by the Authority. The covenant had been enacted to promote the marketability of the bonds. Its repeal in 1974 was designed to promote mass transportation and thus energy conservation and environmental protection. Although the effect of the repeal on the value of the bonds was uncertain, the states had neither offered the bondholders any compensation nor replaced the covenant with an arguably comparable security provision. Under these circumstances, Justice Blackmun concluded for a majority of four, outright repeal of the covenant "totally eliminated an important security provision and this impaired the obligation of the States' contract." Justice Brennan, joined by Justices White and Marshall, dissented. (Justices Stewart and Powell did not participate.)

Allied Structural Steel v. Spannus, 438 U.S. 234 (1978), invalidated the Minnesota Private Pension Benefits Protection Act as applied retroactively to existing pension plans. Before passage of the Act in 1974, an employer could terminate a pension plan at will. Under the Act, an employer who terminated a plan or closed offices in the State was liable to a "pension funding charge" designed to supplement the existing pension funds if they were not sufficient to cover full pensions for all employees who had worked at least ten years. Justice Stewart wrote that "the first inquiry must be whether the state law has, in fact, operated as a substantial impairment of a contractual relationship. The severity of the impairment measures the height of the hurdle the state legislation must clear. Minimal alteration of contractual obligations may end the inquiry at its first stage. Severe impairment, on the other hand, will push the inquiry to a careful examination of the nature and purpose of the state legislation." Justice Stewart observed that the act "nullifies express terms of the company's contractual obligations and imposes a completely unexpected liability in potentially disabling amounts," and continued:

> This Minnesota law simply does not possess the attributes of those state laws that in the past have survived challenge under the Contract Clause of the Constitution. The law was not even purportedly enacted to deal with a broad, generalized economic or social problem. Cf. Home Building & Loan Assn. v. Blaisdell. It did not

> operate in an area already subject to state regulation at the time the company's contractual obligations were originally undertaken, but invaded an area never before subject to regulation by the State. It did not effect simply a temporary alteration of the contractual relationships of those within its coverage, but worked a severe, permanent, and immediate change in those relationships — irrevocably and retroactively. And its narrow aim was leveled, not at every Minnesota employer, not even at every Minnesota employer who left the State, but only at those who had in the past been sufficiently enlightened as voluntarily to agree to establish pension plans for their employees.

In a dissenting opinion joined by Justices White and Marshall, Justice Brennan argued that the contract clause was concerned only with legislative diminution of existing contractual obligations and not with the imposition of additional obligations on contracting parties:

> Today's conversion of the Contract Clause into a limitation on the power of States to enact laws that impose duties additional to obligations assumed under private contracts must inevitably produce results difficult to square with any rational conception of a constitutional order. Under the Court's opinion, any law that may be characterized as "superimposing" new obligations on those provided for by contract is to be regarded as creating "sudden, substantial, and unanticipated burdens" and then to be subjected to the most exacting scrutiny. . . .
>
> To permit this level of scrutiny of laws that interfere with contract-based expectations is an anomaly. There is nothing sacrosanct about expectations rooted in contract that justify according them a constitutional immunity denied other property rights.

Justice Blackmun summarized current Contract Clause doctrine in his opinion for Court in Energy Reserves Group v. Kansas Power and Light Co., 459 U.S. 400 (1983). The Kansas legislature had passed a statute subsequent to passage of the Natural Gas Policy Act of 1978 by Congress. That Act, while generally moving toward deregulation of natural gas, authorized States "to establish or enforce any maximum lawful price for the first sale of natural gas which does not exceed the applicable maximum lawful price, if any, under Title I of this Act." The Kansas statute had the effect of limiting price increases by the Energy Reserves Group that would otherwise have been allowed under a contract signed between the Group and the Kansas Power and Light Co., a public utility. The Supreme Court rejected Energy Reserves' claim that the Kansas statute violated the Contract Clause.

> The severity of the impairment is said to increase the level of scrutiny to which the legislation will be subjected. Total destruction of contractual expectations is not necessary for a finding of substantial impairment. On the other hand, state regulation that restricts a party to gains it reasonably expected from the contract does not necessarily constitute a substantial impairment. In determining the extent of the impairment, we are to consider whether the industry the complaining party has entered has been regulated in the past. . . .
>
> If the state regulation constitutes a substantial impairment, the State, in justification, must have a significant and legitimate public purpose behind the regulation, such as the remedying of a broad and general social or economic problem. Furthermore, since *Blaisdell*, the Court has indicated that the public purpose need not be

> addressed to an emergency or temporary situation. One legitimate state interest is the elimination of unforeseen windfall profits. The requirement of a legitimate public purpose guarantees that the State is exercising its police power, rather than providing a benefit to special interests.
>
> Once a legitimate public purpose has been identified, the next inquiry is whether the adjustment of "the rights and responsibilities of contracting parties [is based] upon reasonable conditions and [is] of a character appropriate to the public purpose justifying [the legislation's] adoption. Unless the State itself is a contracting party, "[a]s is customary in reviewing economic and social regulation, . . . courts properly defer to legislative judgment as to the necessity and reasonableness of a particular measure."

Applying the balancing test enunciated above, the Court unanimously held that Kansas had not "substantially" impaired ERG's contractual rights so as to trigger the Contract Clause's prohibition. Examining the particular background of the contract in question, including the "significant . . . fact that the parties are operating in a heavily regulated industry," the Court found that "ERG's reasonable expectations have not been impaired by the Kansas Act."

The Court also emphasized the "significant and legitimate state interests" justifying the statute. "The State reasonably could find that higher gas prices have caused and will cause hardship among those who use gas heat but must exist on limited fixed incomes." It also pointed to Kansas' interest in coordinating the price levels of inter- and intrastate gas. Justice Powell, joined by Chief Justice Burger and Justice Rehnquist, declined to join this part of the opinion on the grounds that the case was fully disposed of once the Court had determined that no reasonable expectations had been violated by the statute.

4. *The Takings Clause*[17]

In 1897 the Court held that the due process clause of the Fourteenth Amendment in effect incorporated and bound the states to the Fifth Amendment provision, "nor shall private property be taken for public use, without just compensation." Chicago, Burlington and Quincy Railroad v. Chicago, 166 U.S. 226 (1897). Although federal courts have played a relatively minor role in eminent domain law compared to state courts applying state constitutions, the takings clause does impose some restrictions on state regulation of property rights.

The central and vexing question of the constitutional doctrine of eminent domain is: What, short of a physical invasion and outright transfer of title, constitutes a "taking" for which compensation must be paid? Recall Pumpelly v. Green Bay Co., supra page 284: Although the Court there held that the Fourteenth Amendment did not require Wisconsin to pay compensation, it nonetheless reached the takings issue in construing the Wisconsin constitution. The Green Bay Company, after flooding Pumpelly's land, argued that his property had not been "taken" because he retained full title to it, including the freedom to sell it.

17. See generally Bruce Ackerman, Private Property and the Constitution (1977); Richard Epstein, Takings: Private Property and Eminent Domain (1985); Frank Michelman, Property, Utility and Fairness: Comments on the Ethical Foundations of "Just Compensation Law," 80 Harv. L. Rev. 1165 (1967); Carol Rose, *Mahon* Reconstructed: Why the Takings Issue Is Still a Muddle, 57 S. Cal. L. Rev. 561 (1984).

That the property was now underwater diminished its value, but, it was maintained, this alone did not establish a taking. The Court responded:

> It would be a very curious and unsatisfactory result, if in construing a provision of constitutional law, always understood to have been adopted for protection and security to the rights of the individual as against the government, and which . . . place[ed] the just principles of the common law on that subject beyond the power of ordinary legislation to change or control, . . . it shall be held that if the government refrains from the absolute conversion of real property to the uses of the public it can destroy its value entirely, can inflict irreparable and permanent injury to any extent, can, in effect, subject it to total destruction without making any compensation, because, in the narrowest sense of that word, it is not *taken* for public use. Such a construction would pervert the constitutional provision.

Pumpelly falls squarely within the established common law doctrine that states may only "take" property through the exercise of eminent domain. Few cases at the Supreme Court level, however, involve the combination of physical trespass and almost total negation of economic value as in *Pumpelly*; most involve state actions that diminish economic value but do not involve physical trespass.

1. Mahon *and the regulatory taking.* Pennsylvania Coal Co. v. Mahon, 260 U.S. 393 (1922), offers a paradigmatic example of the modern takings problem: An 1878 deed reserved to the grantor company the right to subterraneous mining, with the grantees assuming all attendant risks. The legislature subsequently enacted a statute that forbade mining causing the subsidence of any residential structure. The statute rendered the company's reservation practically valueless. The Court held that the regulation exceeded the permissible limits of the state's police powers and that compensation had to be paid. Wrote Justice Holmes:

> As applied in this case, the statute is admitted to destroy previously existing rights of property and contract. The question is whether the police power can be stretched so far.
>
> Government hardly could go on if, to some extent, values incident to property could not be diminished without paying for every such change in the general law. As long recognized, some values are enjoyed under an implied limitation, and must yield to the police power. But obviously the implied limitation must have its limits or the contract and due process clauses are gone. One fact for consideration in determining such limits is the extent of the diminution. When it reaches a certain magnitude, in most if not in all cases there must be an exercise of eminent domain and compensation to sustain the act. So the question depends upon the particular facts. The greatest weight is given to the judgment of the legislature, but it always is open to interested parties to contend that the legislature has gone beyond its constitutional power.
>
> This is the case of a single private house. . . . [The Act] is not justified as a protection of public safety. That could be provided for by notice. Indeed, the very foundation of this bill is that the defendant gave timely notice of its intent to mine under the house. On the other hand, the extent of the taking is great. It purports to abolish what is recognized in Pennsylvania as an estate in land, — a very valuable estate, — and what is declared by the court below to be a contract hitherto binding the plaintiffs. If we were called upon to deal with the plaintiffs' position alone we should

think it clear that the statute does not disclose a public interest sufficient to warrant so extensive a destruction of the defendant's constitutionally protected rights. . . .

It is our opinion that the act cannot be sustained as an exercise of the police power, so far as it affects the mining of coal under streets or cities in places where the right to mine such coal has been reserved. . . . What makes the right to mine coal valuable is that it can be exercised with profit. To make it commercially impracticable to mine certain coal has very nearly the same effect for constitutional purposes as appropriating or destroying it. This we think that we are warranted in assuming that the statute does. . . .

The rights of the public in a street purchased or laid out by eminent domain are those that it has paid for. If in any case its representatives have been so shortsighted as to acquire only surface rights, without the right of support, we see no more authority for supplying the latter without compensation than there was for taking the right of way in the first place, and refusing to pay for it because the public wanted it very much. The protection of private property in the 5th Amendment presupposes that is wanted for public use, but provides that it shall not be taken for such use without compensation. . . . When this seemingly absolute protection is found to be qualified by the police power, the natural tendency of human nature is to extend the qualification more and more until at last private property disappears. But that cannot be accomplished in this way under the Constitution of the United States.

The general rule, at least, is that while property may be regulated to a certain extent, if regulation goes too far it will be recognized as a taking. . . . As we have already said, this is a question of degree — and therefore cannot be disposed of by general propositions.

Writing for himself alone — in one of the few instances in which he and Holmes divided on a major issue — Brandeis dissented:

Every restriction upon the use of property, imposed in the exercise of the police power, deprives the owner of some right theretofore enjoyed, and is, in that sense, an abridgement by the state of rights of property without making compensation. But restrictions imposed to protect the public health, safety, or morals from dangers threatened is not a taking. The restriction here in question is merely the prohibition of a noxious use. The property so restricted remains in the possession of its owner. The state does not appropriate it or make any use of it. The state merely prevents the owner from making a use which interferes with paramount rights of the public. Whenever the use prohibited ceases to be noxious — as it may because of further change in local or social conditions, the restriction will have to be removed, and the owner will again be free to enjoy his property as heretofore.

. . . [T]he purpose of a restriction does not cease to be public because incidentally some private persons may thereby receive gratuitously valuable special benefits. Thus, owners of low buildings may obtain, through statutory restrictions upon the height of neighboring structures, benefits equivalent to an easement of light and air. . . . [T]o keep coal in place is surely an appropriate means of preventing subsidence of the surface; and ordinarily it is the only available means. Restriction upon use does not become inappropriate as a means, merely because it deprives the owner of the only use to which the property can then be profitably put. . . .

It is said . . . that the restriction upon mining cannot be justified as a protection of personal safety, since that could be provided for by notice. . . . May we say that notice would afford adequate protection of the public safety where the legislature and the highest court of the state, with greater knowledge of local conditions, have declared, in effect, that it would not? If public safety is imperiled, surely neither grant nor contract can prevail against the exercise of the police power. The rule that the state's power to take appropriate measures to guard the safety of all who may be within its jurisdiction may not be bargained away was applied to compel carriers to establish grade crossings at their own expense, despite contracts to the contrary; and, likewise, to supersede, by an employes' liability act, the provision of a charter exempting a railroad from liability for death of employees, since the civil liability was deem. Nor can existing contracts between private individuals preclude exercise of the police power. "One whose rights, such as they are, are subject to state restriction, cannot remove them from the power of the state by making a contract about them."

Assume that the 1878 price for surface rights reflected the coal company's reservation of the right to mine. Could one then characterize the Pennsylvania Act as a legislative attempt to secure a redistributive windfall to homeowners? Does your answer depend on the relevant balance of bargaining power between the coal companies and the homeowners?

2. *Legitimation of comprehensive zoning.* Zoning is the primary means by which the political community controls the use of private land, and as such it came under attack as an infringement of property rights protected by the Fourteenth Amendment. In Village of Euclid v. Ambler Realty Co., 272 U.S. 365 (1926), the Court upheld a zoning regulation in an opinion that broadly legitimized the growing practice of comprehensive zoning. The realty company challenged a comprehensive zoning ordinance passed by the Village of Euclid, Ohio, that the company alleged had reduced the value of one parcel of its real estate from $10,000 to $2,500 an acre, and reduced another from $150 to $50 a square foot. The Supreme Court upheld the law in an opinion written by one of its most conservative members, Justice Sutherland. (Three other conservatives, Justices Van Devanter, McReynolds, and Butler, dissented without filing an opinion.)

Building zone laws are of modern origin. They began in this country about twenty-five years ago. Until recent years, urban life was comparatively simple; but with the great increase and concentration of population, problems have developed, and constantly are developing, which require, and will continue to require, additional restrictions in respect of the use and occupation of private lands in urban communities. Regulations, the wisdom, necessity and validity of which, as applied to existing conditions, are so apparent that they are now uniformly sustained, a century ago, or even half a century ago, probably would have been rejected as arbitrary and oppressive. Such regulations are sustained, under the complex conditions of our day, for reasons analogous to those which justify traffic regulations, which, before the advent of automobiles and rapid transit street railways, would have been condemned as fatally arbitrary and unreasonable. And in this there is no inconsistency, for while the meaning of constitutional guaranties never varies, the scope of their application must expand or contract to meet the new and different conditions which are constantly coming within the field of their operation. In a changing world, it is impossible that it should be otherwise. But although a degree of elasticity is thus imparted, not the meaning, but the application of constitutional principles, statutes and ordinances, which, after giving due weight to the new conditions, are found clearly not to conform to the Constitution, of course, must fall.

The ordinance now under review, and all similar laws and regulations, must find their justification in some aspect of the police power, asserted for the public welfare. The line which in this field separates the legitimate from the illegitimate assumption of power is not capable of precise delimitation. It varies with circumstances and conditions. A regulatory zoning ordinance, which would be clearly valid as applied to the great cities, might be clearly invalid as applied to rural communities. . . . Thus the question whether the power to forbid the erection of a building of a particular kind or for a particular use, is to be determined, not by an abstract consideration of the building or of the thing considered apart, but by considering it in connection with the circumstances and the locality. A nuisance may be merely a right thing in the wrong place, — like a pig in the parlor instead of the barnyard. If the validity of the legislative classification for zoning purposes be fairly debatable, the legislative judgment must be allowed to control. . . .

The matter of zoning has received much attention at the hands of commissions and experts, and the results of their investigation have been set forth in comprehensive reports. These reports, which bear every evidence of painstaking consideration, concur in the view that the segregation of residential, business, and industrial buildings will make it easier to provide fire apparatus suitable for the character and intensity of the development in each section; that it will increase the safety and security or home life; greatly tend to prevent street accidents, especially to children, by reducing the traffic and resulting confusion in residential sections; decrease noise and other conditions which produce or intensify nervous disorders; preserve a more favorable environment in which to rear children, etc. With particular reference to apartment houses, it is pointed out that the development of detached house sections is greatly retarded by the coming of apartment houses, which has sometimes resulted in destroying the entire section for private house purposes; that in such sections very often the apartment house is a mere parasite, constructed in order to take advantage of the open spaces and attractive surroundings created by the residential character of the district. Moreover, the coming of one apartment house is followed by others . . . until, finally, the residential character of the neighborhood and its desirability as a place of detached residences are utterly destroyed. Under these circumstances, apartment houses, which in a different environment would be not only entirely unobjectionable but highly desirable, come very near to being nuisances.

If these reasons, thus summarized, do not demonstrate the wisdom or sound policy in all respects of those restrictions which we have indicated as pertinent to the inquiry, at least, the reasons are sufficiently cogent to preclude us from saying, as it must be said before the ordinance can be declared unconstitutional, that such provisions are clearly arbitrary and unreasonable, having no substantial relation to the public health, safety, morals, or general welfare.

Discussion

Zoning laws might be characterized as essentially redistributive, transferring value from one private property owner to another. (If everyone felt benefitted by zoning restrictions, then zoning would not be one of the most contentious subjects of local politics, which it invariably is.) Are distributive consequences relevant in determining the constitutionality of zoning restrictions? Should it matter whether "the community" as a whole, rather than a specific subset of the community, benefits from the zoning? (What *is* the community as a whole?)

Zoning laws might also serve to deter the immigration of perceived undesirables into an established community. Professor Michael Wolf notes that the laws upheld in *Euclid* involved an attempt by the local community to prevent an influx of ethnic Eastern Europeans from the nearby city of Cleveland, most of whom could only afford apartments. Consider again Justice Sutherland's reference to an apartment house as "a mere parasite," and Justice Baldwin's evocation of "vicious paupers" in *Miln*, supra Chapter 3. Should the demographic consequences of zoning laws be constitutionally relevant?[18]

3. "Forced choices" and the duty to compensate. In Miller v. Schoene, 276 U.S. 272 (1928), the Virginia state entomologist, acting under authority of the Virginia Cedar Rust Act, ordered the destruction of a large number of ornamental red cedar trees. The Act sought to protect apple orchards, an important aspect of Virginia's economy; although cedar rust does not affect the value of the cedar tree, it can infect apple trees and destroy their fruit and foliage. Cedar tree owners demanded compensation for their losses. The Court, through Justice Stone, unanimously ruled against them:

> The only practicable method of controlling the disease and protecting apple trees from its ravages is the destruction of all red cedar trees subject to the infection, located within 2 miles of apple orchards.
>
> The red cedar, aside from its ornamental use, has occasional use and value as lumber. . . . [I]ts value throughout the state is shown to be small as compared with that of the apple orchards of the state. . . .
>
> [T]he state was under the necessity of making a choice between the preservation of one class or property and that of the other, wherever both existed in dangerous proximity. It would have been none the less a choice if, instead of enacting the present statute, the state, by doing nothing, had permitted serious injury to the apple orchards within its border to go on unchecked. When forced to such a choice the state does not exceed its constitutional powers by deciding upon the destruction of one class of property in order to save another which, in the judgment of the legislature, is of greater value to the public. It will not do to say that the case is merely one of a conflict of two private interests and that the misfortune of apple growers may not be shifted to cedar owners by ordering the destruction of their property; for it is obvious that there may be, and that here there is, a preponderant public concern in the preservation of the one interest over the other. . . .
>
> [W]here, as here, the choice is unavoidable, we cannot say that its exercise, controlled by considerations of social policy which are not unreasonable, involves any denial of due process.

If you believe that the cedar tree owners deserved compensation, would you be equally sympathetic (and compensatory toward) apple tree owners had the state chosen to pass no act at all, resulting in huge losses to apple orchards? What if the state, committed to preserving the cedar trees as a means of attracting tourists, had *forbidden* the destruction of cedar trees without specific state authorization?

4. Subsequent cases. The modern Court has taken a permissive stance toward zoning and other regulatory measures. Penn Central Trans. Co. v. New York City, 438 U.S. 104 (1978), upheld a historic landmark law that imposed substantial restrictions on land use. See also PruneYard Shopping Center v. Robins, 447 U.S. 74 (1980), infra. On the other hand, the Court has treated more traditional trespassory acts as takings. Kaiser Aetna v. United States, 444 U.S. 1645 (1979), held that the Army Corps of Engineers had taken petitioner's property when it granted public access to a privately owned lagoon. And Loretto v. Teleprompter Manhattan CATV Corp., 458 U.S. 419 (1982), held that a city law that required a

18. See Chapter 6, infra, where this issue is discussed with respect to race.

landlord to permit the installation of cable television facilities on its property was "a permanent physical occupation authorized by government [and thus] a taking without regard to the public interests that it may serve."

In a number of recent decisions, however, several Justices would have supported a more active takings doctrine. Keystone Bituminous Coal Association v. DeBenedictis, 480 U.S. 470 (1987), presented a situation similar to that in *Mahon*. The Pennsylvania Bituminous Mine Subsidence and Land Conservation Act of 1966 prohibited mining that might cause subsidence damage to various structures. In accordance with the Act, the Commonwealth's Department of Environmental Resources prohibited the removal of more than 50 percent of the coal beneath protected structures so as to ensure adequate surface support. Should mining affect protected structures, operators were required, within six months, to pay for or repair the damage.

A five-Justice majority, through Justice Stevens, distinguished *Mahon* and upheld the Act based on the two-part test enunciated in Agins v. Tiburon, 447 U.S. 255 (1980): A land use regulation may constitute a taking if it "does not substantially advance legitimate state interests, . . . or denies an owner economically viable use of his land."

Describing *Mahon* as "merely . . . a balancing of the private economic interests of coal companies against the private interests of the surface owners," Justice Stevens asserted that the Act here served "important public interests" concerning "health, the environment, and the fiscal integrity of the area." Pennsylvania cannot be "estop[ped] . . . from exercising its police power to abate activity akin to a public nuisance. . . . [C]ircumstances may so change in time . . . as to clothe with such a [public] interest what at other times . . . would be a matter of purely private concern."

With respect to the second factor, "petitioners have not shown any deprivation significant enough to satisfy the heavy burden placed upon one alleging a regulatory taking." The affected coal represented no more than approximately 2 percent of the companies' resources: 27 million tons of coal were covered by the Act, out of over 1.46 billion tons available. Justice Stevens rejected the petitioners' attempt to disaggregate the affected coal into "discrete segments," writing that "where an owner possesses a full 'bundle' of property rights, the destruction of one 'strand' of the bundle is not a taking because the aggregate must be viewed in its entirety."

> Many zoning ordinances place limits on the property owner's right to make profitable use of some segments of his property. A requirement that a building occupy no more than a specified percentage of the lot on which it is located could be characterized as a taking of the vacant area. . . . Similarly, under petitioners' theory one could always argue that a set-back ordinance requiring that no structure be built within a certain distance from the property line constitutes a taking because the footage represents a distinct segment of property for takings law purposes. There is no basis for treating the less than 2% of petitioners' coal as a separate parcel of property.

Petitioners did not show that their "reasonable 'investment-backed expectations' have been materially affected by the additional duty to retain the small percentage that must be used to support the structures protected" by the Act.

The Association also argued that the Act violated the Contract Clause inasmuch as it vitiated contracts in which surface owners agreed to waive liability for subsidence damage. Although Justice Stevens conceded that the Act "operated as 'a substantial impairment of a contractual relationship,'" he stated that "it is well-settled that the prohibition against impairing the obligation of contracts is not to be read literally." He also noted that, because most of the contractual waivers had been obtained over 70 years ago "[n]o question of enforcement of such a waiver against the original covenantor is presented; rather, petitioners claim a right to enforce the waivers against subsequent owners of the surface."

> [I]t is petitioners' position that, because they contracted with some previous owners of property generations ago, they have a constitutionally protected legal right to conduct their mining operations in a way that would make a shambles of all those buildings and cemeteries. . . . [T]he Commonwealth has a strong public interest in preventing this type of harm, the environmental effect of which transcends any private agreement between contracting parties.
>
> Of course, the finding of a significant and legitimate public purpose is not, by itself, enough to justify the impairment of contractual obligations. A court must also satisfy itself that the legislature's "adjustment of 'the rights and responsibilities of contracting parties [is based] upon reasonable conditions and [is] of a character appropriate to the public purpose justifying [its] adoption.'" But, we have repeatedly held that unless the state is itself a contracting party, courts should "'properly defer to legislative judgment as to the necessity and reasonableness of a particular measure.'" . . . By requiring the coal companies either to repair the damage or to give the surface owner funds to repair the damage, the Commonwealth accomplishes both deterrence [of deleterious mining practices] and restoration of the environment to its previous condition.

Chief Justice Rehnquist dissented, joined by Justices Powell, O'Connor, and Scalia, arguing that the differences between *Mahon* and the instant cases "verge on the trivial": The statute struck down in the earlier case served a "public purpose," and the Court in *Mahon* "made clear that the mere existence of a public purpose was insufficient to release the government from the compensation requirement."

The 1966 Act could not be justified under the "nuisance exception" to the takings clause, under which the Court had upheld regulations for "discrete and narrow" purposes: "The central purposes of the Act, though including public safety, reflect a concern for preservation of buildings, economic development, and maintenance of property values to sustain the Commonwealth's tax base. We should hesitate to allow a regulation based on essentially economic concerns to be insulated from the dictates of the Fifth Amendment by labeling it nuisance regulation." Moreover, the Act extinguished "all beneficial use of petitioners' property." Responding to the majority's assimilation of the 27 million tons affected into the overall corpus of the petitioners' resources, Chief Justice Rehnquist argued that even limited physical invasions of property interests must be compensated.

> [T]here is no need for further analysis where the government by regulation extinguishes the whole bundle of rights in an identifiable segment of property, for the effect of this action on the holder of the property is indistinguishable from the effect

> of a physical taking. . . . [T]here is no question that [the 27 million tons] is an identifiable and separable property interest. Unlike many property interests, the 'bundle' of rights in this coal is sparse. " 'For practical purposes, the right to coal consists in the right to mine it.' " From the relevant perspective — that of the property owners — this interest has been destroyed every bit as much as if the government had proceeded to mine the coal for its own use. The regulation, then, does not merely inhibit one strand in the bundle, but instead destroys completely any interest in a segment of property.

The dissenters did not reach the Contract Clause issue.

Professor Richard Epstein, the most vocal academic proponent of vigorous constitutional protection of property against state regulation,[19] characterizes *De Benedictis* as "the court at its worst" in continuing "the old pattern of massive judicial resignation in the face of manifest confiscation." He notes, however, that two other 1987 cases — First English Evangelical Lutheran Church v. County of Los Angeles and Nollan v. California Coastal Commission — "hold out the possibility of a judicial revolution in the takings area, at least as it applies to local governments."[20]

In First English Evangelical Lutheran Church v. County of Los Angeles, 482 U.S. 304 (1987), the Church had operated a camp, which was destroyed in a 1977 flood. In 1979 Los Angeles County adopted an "interim" ordinance prohibiting building in the flood plain, arguably rendering the church's property practically useless. The Church sued for damages, claiming that the ordinance was a taking that required compensation.

The California courts did not determine whether the ordinance constituted a taking. Rather, they held that state law limits the victim of a "regulatory taking" to an injunction against the operation of the offending ordinance, and permits damages only for subsequent violation of the injunction, and not, as the church claimed, for damages from the date of the ordinance. A six-Justice majority, in an opinion written by Chief Justice Rehnquist (joined by Justices Brennan and Marshall, among others), held the California remedial rule unconstitutional: " 'Temporary' takings which, as here, deny a landowner all use of his property, are not different in kind from permanent takings, for which the Constitution clearly requires compensation." Therefore, "where the government's activities have already worked a taking of all use of property, no subsequent action by the government can relieve it of the duty to provide compensation for the period during which the taking was effective." Justice Stevens, joined in part by Justices Blackmun and O'Connor, dissented.

In Nollan v. California Coastal Commission, 483 U.S. 825 (1987), the state made the issuance of a building permit for petitioners' beachfront house conditional upon conveyance to the public of an easement across their property above the high-tide line. (The state owns the property up to that line.) The property was located between two public beaches, and the easement was intended to facilitate passage from one beach to the other.

The Coastal Commission argued that the new house would block public view of the ocean and contribute to the development of "a 'wall' of residential structures" preventing public realization that "a stretch of coastline exists nearby that

19. See Epstein, Takings: Private Property and the Power of Eminent Domain (1985).
20. Epstein, Private Property Makes a Comeback, The Wall Street Journal, July 23, 1987, at 26.

they have every right to visit." The California Court of Appeal upheld the Commission's claim, ruling that imposition of an access condition was permissible whenever a project contributed to a need for public access, even if the need for access was not created by the project alone and notwithstanding the indirect relation between the condition imposed and the problem sought to be remedied. The state court also pointed out that the Nollans were not deprived of all reasonable use of their property, even if its value was diminished somewhat by the easement.

In a 5-to-4 decision the Court reversed. Justice Scalia began by hypothesizing the imposition of a similar easement on an existing built-up beachfront property. He noted that such an easement would constitute a "permanent physical occupation" of the land involved, thus taking the case out of the realm of "regulatory takings."

The question remained whether the easement could be imposed as a condition for obtaining a building permit. The majority assumed that the Commission could prevent the building entirely if necessary to preserve a public interest, including the public's ability to see the ocean. It could also condition building on meeting requirements to preserve that interest, including "the requirement that the Nollans provide a viewing spot on their property for passersby with whose sighting of the ocean their new house would interfere":

> Although such a requirement, constituting a permanent grant of continuous access to the property, would have to be considered a taking if it were not attached to a development permit, the Commission's assumed power to forbid construction of the house in order to protect the public's view of the beach must surely include the power to condition construction upon some concession by the owner, even a concession of property rights, that serves the same end. . . .
>
> The evident constitutional propriety disappears, however, if the condition substituted for the prohibition utterly fails to further the end advanced as the justification for the prohibition. . . . [T]he lack of nexus between the condition and the original purpose of the building restriction converts that purpose to something other than what it was. The purpose then becomes, quite simply, the obtaining of an easement to serve some valid governmental purpose, but without payment of compensation.

Justice Brennan, joined by Justice Marshall, accused the majority of applying an "unreasonably demanding standard for determining the rationality of state regulation" and of potentially hampering "innovative efforts to preserve an increasingly fragile national resource." He also argued that the effect on the Nollans' investment-backed expectations was, at most, negligible. "Appellants can make no tenable claim that either their enjoyment of their property or its value is diminished by the public's ability merely to pass and re-pass a few feet closer to the seawall beyond which appellants' house is located." Justices Blackmun and Stevens also dissented in separate opinions.

Discussion

1. Professor Epstein suggests that *Nollan* calls into question such standard modern practices as conditioning the development of a housing subdivision on setting aside land for a public park or permitting a new high-rise apartment house only if a percentage of the space is reserved for low-income families. Are these examples doctrinally distinguishable from *Nollan*?

2. Compare *Nollan* with PruneYard Shopping Center v. Robins, 447 U.S. 74 (1980), where the Court unanimously upheld a California Supreme Court decision holding that the California Constitution protects "speech and petitioning, reasonably exercised, in shopping centers even when the centers are privately owned." The owner of the shopping center claimed that requiring that it permit Robins access to solicit signatures for a petition operated as a taking. Justice Rehnquist responded:

> It is true that one of the essential sticks in the bundle of property rights is the right to exclude others. . . . But it is well established that "not every destruction or injury to property by governmental action has been held to be a 'taking' in the constitutional sense." Rather, the determination whether a state law unlawfully infringes a landowner's property in violation of the Taking Clause requires an examination of whether the restriction on private property "forc[es] some people alone to bear public burdens which, in all fairness and justice, should be borne by the public as a whole." This examination entails inquiry into such factors as the character of the governmental action, its economic impact, and its interference with reasonable investment-backed expectations. . . .
>
> Here the requirement that appellants permit appellees to exercise state-protected rights of free expression and petition on shopping center property clearly does not amount to an unconstitutional infringement of appellants' property rights under the Taking Clause. There is nothing to suggest that preventing appellants from prohibiting this sort of activity will unreasonably impair the value or use of their property as a shopping center. . . . The decision of the California Supreme Court makes it clear that the PruneYard may restrict expressive activity by adopting time, place, and manner regulations that will minimize any interference with its commercial functions. . . . In these circumstances, the fact that [Robins] may have "physically invaded" appellants' property cannot be viewed as determinative. . . . [A]ppellants have failed to demonstrate that the "right to exclude others" is so essential to the use or economic value of their property that the state-authorized limitation of it amounted to a "taking."

The Court quoted from the opinion of the California Supreme Court, which, after noting that over 25,000 persons daily enter the property in order to shop, stated: "It bears repeated emphasis that we do not have under consideration the property or privacy rights of an individual homeowner. . . ."[21]

Note: The "Public Use" Component of Eminent Domain

The finding that a taking has occurred and compensation offered does not conclude the constitutional inquiry, for the Fifth Amendment also limits takings to "public uses." Consider in this context Hawaii Housing Authority v. Midkiff, 467 U.S. 229 (1984). As a result of Hawaii's unique history in which property had been controlled by the Hawaiian monarchy, 47 percent of the land in the state was held by only 72 private landowners; indeed, 18 landholders, with tracts in

21. Professor Epstein condemns Justice Rehnquist's opinion for "its intellectual weakness." He argues that "[t]he idea of property embraces the absolute right to exclude. . . . Nothing therefore allows the state to place conditions upon the owners' right to admit or exclude. . . . The restrictions that the state places upon the exclusive possession of land constitute a partial taking for which compensation is prima facie required." Epstein, supra note 19, at 65.

excess of 21,000 acres, owned more than 40 percent of this land. Twenty-two landholders owned 72.5 percent of the fee simple titles on Oahu, the most urbanized of Hawaii's islands. The Hawaiian legislature, finding this concentration of ownership undesirable, enacted the Land Reform Act of 1967, which transferred the fee ownership of certain residential tracts to existing lessors and paid compensation to the original owners.

In a suit brought by some property owners, the Court of Appeals struck down the Act as "a naked attempt on the part of the state of Hawaii to take the private property of *A* and transfer it to *B* solely for *B*'s private use and benefit." The Supreme Court reversed in a unanimous opinion by Justice O'Connor (Justice Marshall did not participate).

> The starting point for our analysis of the Act's constitutionality is the Court's decision in Berman v. Parker, 348 U.S. 26 (1954). In *Berman,* the Court held constitutional the District of Columbia Redevelopment Act of 1945. That Act provided both for the comprehensive use of the eminent domain power to redevelop slum areas and for the possible sale or lease of the condemned lands to private interests. In discussing whether the takings authorized by that Act were for a "public use," the Court stated:
>
> > We deal, in other words, with what traditionally has been known as the police power. An attempt to define its reach or trace its outer limits is fruitless, for each case must turn on its own facts. The definition is essentially the product of legislative determination addressed to the purpose of government, purposes neither abstractly nor historically capable of complete definition. Subject to specific constitutional limitations, when the legislature has spoken, the public interest has been declared in terms well-nigh conclusive. In such cases the legislature, not the judiciary, is the main guardian of the pubic needs to be served by social legislation, whether it be Congress legislating concerning the District of Columbia . . . or the States legislating concerning local affairs. . . . This principle admits of no exception merely because the power of eminent domain is involved.
>
> The Court explicitly recognized the breadth of the principle it was announcing, noting:
>
> > Once the object is within the authority of Congress, the right to realize it through the exercise of eminent domain is clear. For the power of eminent domain is merely the means to the end. . . . Once the object is within the authority of Congress, the means by which it will be attained is also for Congress to determine. Here one of the means chosen is the use of private enterprise for redevelopment of the area. Appellants argue that this makes the project a taking from one businessman for the benefit of another businessman. But the means of executing the project are for Congress and Congress alone to determine, once the public purpose has been established.
>
> The "public use" requirement is thus coterminous with the scope of a sovereign's police powers.
>
> There is, of course, a role for courts to play in reviewing a legislature's judgment of what constitutes a public use, even when the eminent domain power is equated with the police power. But the Court in *Berman* made clear that it is "an extremely narrow" one. The Court in *Berman* cited with approval the Court's decision in Old Dominion Co. v. United States, 269 U.S. 55, 66 (1925), which held that deference to the legislature's "public use" determination is required "until it is shown to involve

an impossibility." . . . In short, the Court has made clear that it will not substitute its judgment for a legislature's judgment as to what constitutes a public use "unless the use be palpably without reasonable foundation."

To be sure, the Court's cases have repeatedly stated that "one person's property may not be taken for the benefit of another private person without a justifying public purpose, even though compensation be paid." Thompson v. Consolidated Gas Corp., 300 U.S. 55, 80 (1937). But where the exercise of the eminent domain power is rationally related to a conceivable public purpose, the Court has never held a compensated taking to be proscribed by the Public Use Clause.

On this basis, we have no trouble concluding that the Hawaii Act is constitutional. The people of Hawaii have attempted, much as the settlers of the original 13 Colonies did, to reduce the perceived social and economic evils of a land oligopoly traceable to their monarchs. The land oligopoly has, according to the Hawaii Legislature, created artificial deterrents to the normal functioning of the State's residential land market and forced thousands of individual home-owners to lease, rather than buy, the land underneath their homes. Regulating oligopoly and the evils associated with it is a classic exercise of a State's police powers. We cannot disapprove of Hawaii's exercise of this power.

Nor can we condemn as irrational the Act's approach to correcting the land oligopoly problem. The Act presumes that when a sufficiently large number of persons declare that they are willing but unable to buy lots at fair prices the land market is malfunctioning. When such a malfunction is signaled, the Act authorizes HHA to condemn lots in the relevant tract. The Act limits the number of lots any one tenant can purchase and authorizes HHA to use public funds to ensure that the market dilution goals will be achieved. This is a comprehensive and rational approach to identifying and correcting market failure.

. . . When the legislature's purpose is legitimate and its means are not irrational, our cases make clear that empirical debates over the wisdom of takings — no less than debates over the wisdom of other kinds of socioeconomic legislation — are not to be carried out in the federal courts. Redistribution of fees simple to correct deficiencies in the market determined by the state legislature to be attributable to land oligopoly is a rational exercise of the eminent domain power. Therefore, the Hawaii statute must pass the scrutiny of the Public Use Clause.

Discussion

1. An editorial in the Wall Street Journal[22] criticized *Midkiff* as a fundamental incursion on property rights. It began with the following hypothetical:

> Suppose the U.S. Department of Housing and Urban Development decided to achieve integration once and for all. Say it proceeded to take homes at random in a white middle-class suburb through eminent domain and resell them through state housing agencies to minority applicants or, vice versa, to condemn black-occupied brownstones in the inner city and put them up for Yuppie gentrification. Most Americans, not to mention the displaced families, might feel something unconstitutional had happened. Up to this week, they would have been right.

The editorial also accuses the majority of "engineer[ing] a vast expansion of governmental powers."

22. Lords of the Manor, The Wall Street Journal, June 1, 1984, at 18.

> Even with adequate compensation, which the Constitution of course still requires, involuntary dislocation disrupts an individual's privacy, his family life, in short the sphere of existence that our system tries to protect from excessive government intrusion. A well-intentioned court has just opened this sphere to a host of unforeseeable harassments. We may all live to regret the day we heard about Hawaiian land reform.

Does this position imply that the "urban renewal" program upheld in *Berman* is equally unconstitutional? So long as compensation is paid, does the Constitution, as interpreted in *Berman* and *Midkiff*, prevent a legislature from enacting a statute declaring "that the homestead now owned by *A* should no longer be his, but should henceforth be the property of *B*"?[23] *Should* the Constitution be interpreted to do this, or to prevent the Journal's hypothetical integration program?

2. *What are "the facts," and do they matter?* Professor Powe[24] relates certain facts of the case not found in the Court's opinion: One of the parties challenging the statute was the Bishop Estate, which owned 22 percent of all private land on Oahu. It was established by Bernice Pauahi Bishop, the last lineal descendant of King Kemahameha the Great, to be "a perpetual educational trust for the support of descendants of the original Hawaiians." Its income comes from 3 percent of its landholdings; the remainder have no commercial value at present.

Hawaii's 175,000 residents with Hawaiian ancestry tend to be found toward the bottom of various statistical distributions: The median income for Hawaiians of Chinese descent is more than $21,000, with whites and Japanese-Americans sharing a median of $19,000. "For those with some Hawaiian ancestry it is $13,000, and for pure Hawaiians it's under $9300. Not surprisingly, behind these figures are others showing that Hawaiian employment is overwhelmingly blue collar — as a class fewer than half graduate from high school and less than 5 percent from college; and their life expectancy is the lowest of any group in the Islands." Thus Powe suggests that the actual social dynamic behind this case was *not* "the people" versus "feudal estates," but rather relatively well-off persons of non-Hawaiian ancestry versus the native Hawaiians who benefited from the Bishop Estate.

Although the Bishop Estate will be entitled to "just compensation" for its land, it will likely be considerably less than the amount necessary to persuade the Estate to sell its land voluntarily. Professor Powe describes *Midkiff* as "that most unusual case: it's a reverse Robin Hood," taking in effect from the poor to give to the better off. Should that fact change the result in the case?

23. In Poletown Neighborhood Council v. City of Detroit, 304 N.W.2d 455 (1981), a divided Michigan Supreme Court upheld Detroit's exercise of eminent domain to condemn a large tract of residential property to allow General Motors to construct an assembly plant that would add "jobs and taxes to the economic base of the municipality and state." Justice Ryan, in dissent, described the plan as "sweeping away a tightly-knit residential enclave of first- and second-generation Americans, for many of whom their home was their single most valuable and cherished asset and their stable ethnic neighborhood the unchanging symbol of the security and quality of their lives," and denounced the majority for accepting the legitimacy "of condemning private property for conveyance to another private party because the use of it by the new owner promises greater public 'benefit' than the old use."

24. See Reality, Not Theory, 3 Constitutional Commentary (Summer 1986).

II. Abandonment of Constraints on Congressional Regulation

Although the ultimate outcome was the same, the Court's treatment of congressional powers from 1934 to 1937 differed from its treatment of state social and economic regulation under the due process clause. The 1936 decision in Morehead v. Tipaldo, 298 U.S. 586, p. 352 supra, reasserting the unconstitutionality of minimum wage laws, was an isolated decision made against the background of *Nebbia* and *Blaisdell.* During this period, by contrast, the Court struck down the National Industrial Recovery Act of 1933, the Bituminous Coal Conservation Act of 1936, the Agricultural Adjustment Act of 1933, and the Railroad Retirement Act.[25]

A. The Commerce Power

Judicial abandonment of substantive due process was abrupt. *West Coast Hotel* flatly overruled *Adkins* (see p. 352 supra). The abandonment of judicial constraints on the exercise of congressional powers was not so clearly signaled, but it was no less complete.

NLRB v. Jones & Laughlin Steel Corp., 301 U.S. 1 (1937), the watershed case, purported to maintain continuity with the past. At issue was the National Labor Relations Act of 1935, which prohibits employers "from engaging in any unfair labor practice affecting commerce." The act defines "commerce" as "trade, traffic, commerce, transportation, or communication among the several States," and defines "affecting commerce" as "in commerce, or burdening or obstructing commerce or the free flow of commerce, or having led or tending to lead to a labor dispute burdening or obstructing commerce or the free flow of commerce." Respondent was charged with interfering with the rights of employees to organize and bargain collectively in its Aliquippa, Pennsylvania, steel manufacturing plant.

As the Court noted, the respondent corporation with its 19 subsidiaries was a "completely integrated [multistate] enterprise, owning and operating ore, coal and limestone properties, lake and river transportation facilities and terminal railroads. . . ." This made especially appealing the government's argument that the manufacturing process, though not itself commerce, was in the "stream" or "flow" of commerce. Cf. Stafford v. Wallace, 258 U.S. 495 (1922). But the Court refused to restrict its analysis to this metaphor. Rather, Chief Justice Hughes wrote:

> Burdens and obstructions may be due to injurious action springing from other sources. The fundamental principle is that the power to regulate commerce is the

25. Schechter Poultry Corp. v. United States, 295 U.S. 495 (1935) (N.R.A.); Carter v. Carter Coal Co., 298 U.S. 238 (1936) (Coal Conservation Act); United States v. Butler, 297 U.S. 1 (1936) (A.A.A.); Railroad Retirement Board v. Alton, 295 U.S. 330 (1935). Some historians have usefully divided the New Deal into an earlier period of corporatism, in which legislation such as the N.R.A. delegated regulatory power to industrial organizations, and a later period of welfarism, exemplified by the Fair Labor Standards Act and the Social Security Act. See, e.g., Paul Conklin, The New Deal (1967); Ellis Hawley, The New Deal and the Problem of Monopoly (1966). Although most of the legislation struck down by the Court was from the earlier period, the breadth of the holdings does not suggest that the Court was motivated by populist sentiments.

> power to enact "all appropriate legislation" for its "protection and advancement." . . . That power is plenary and may be exerted to protect interstate commerce "no matter what the source of the dangers which threaten it." Although activities may be intrastate in character when separately considered, if they have such a close and substantial relation to interstate commerce that their control is essential or appropriate to protect that commerce from burdens and obstructions, Congress cannot be denied the power to exercise that control. Undoubtedly, the scope of this power must be considered in light of our dual system of government and may not be extended so as to embrace effects upon interstate commerce so indirect and remote that to embrace them, in view of our complex society, would effectively obliterate the distinction between what is national and what is local and create a completely centralized government. The question is necessarily one of degree. . . .
>
> It is thus apparent that the fact that the employees here concerned were engaged in production is not determinative. The question remains as to the effect upon interstate commerce of the labor practice involved. In the *Schechter* case we found that the effect there was so remote as to be beyond the federal power. To find "immediacy or directness" there was to find it "almost everywhere," a result inconsistent with the maintenance of our federal system. . . .
>
> [T]he stoppage of [respondent's manufacturing] operations by industrial strife would have a most serious effect upon interstate commerce. In view of respondent's far-flung activities, it is idle to say that the effect would be indirect or remote. It is obvious that it would be immediate and might be catastrophic.

In NLRB v. Friedman-Harry Marks Clothing Co., 301 U.S. 58 (1937), decided on the same day as *Jones & Laughlin,* the Court upheld the NLRA as applied to a small clothing manufacturer located in Virginia, most of whose materials came from, and most of whose finished products were marketed in, other states. In a brief opinion, the court cited *Jones & Laughlin* and referred to the size, importance, and interstate character of the clothing industry and the interstate impact of a strike.

Justice McReynolds, joined by Justices Van Devanter, Sutherland, and Butler, dissented from both Labor Relations Act decisions, arguing that any "effect on interstate commerce by the discharge of the employees shown there would be indirect and remote in the highest degree."

In 1938, Congress passed a second Agricultural Adjustment Act, premised on the commerce rather than the spending power. The act included congressional findings that excess production moving in interstate commerce caused disorderly marketing, and the act imposed penalties for marketing farm commodities in excess of quotas set by the secretary of agriculture. Justice Roberts, who had written the Court's opinion in *Butler* striking down the 1933 act, wrote for the Court in Mulford v. Smith, 307 U.S. 38 (1939), sustaining the 1938 act as applied to tobacco warehousemen penalized for marketing excessive tobacco. He noted that "[t]he statute does not purport to control production" but only regulates interstate commerce, "which it reaches and affects at the throat where tobacco enters the stream of commerce, — the marketing warehouse." He stated in broad terms:

> Any rule . . . which is intended to foster, protect and conserve interstate commerce, or to prevent the flow of commerce from working harm to the people of the nation, is within the competence of Congress. Within these limits the exercise of the power,

> the grant being unlimited in its terms, may lawfully extend to the absolute prohibition of such commerce, and a fortiori to limitation of the amount of a given commodity which may be transported in such commerce.

Justices Butler and McReynolds dissented.

If it was unlikely that the old Court would have held for the government in *Mulford,* there could be no doubt that United States v. Darby, 312 U.S. 100 (1941), and Wickard v. Filburn, 317 U.S. 111 (1942), marked a new era for the commerce clause.

UNITED STATES v. DARBY
312 U.S. 100 (1941)
Appeal from the District Court of the United States for the Southern District of Georgia

[Sections 6 and 7 of the Fair Labor Standards Act of 1938 prescribe minimum wage and maximum hours for employees engaged in the production of goods related to interstate commerce as described in the opinion below. Appellee, a Georgia lumber manufacturer, was indicted for violating the act. The government appealed from the district court's judgment quashing the indictment.]

STONE, J. . . .

THE PROHIBITION OF SHIPMENT OF THE PROSCRIBED GOODS IN INTERSTATE COMMERCE

Section 15(a)(1) prohibits, and the indictment charges, the shipment in interstate commerce, of goods produced for interstate commerce by employees whose wages and hours of employment do not conform to the requirements of the Act. Since this section is not violated unless the commodity shipped has been produced under labor conditions prohibited by §6 and §7, the only question arising under the commerce clause with respect to such shipments is whether Congress has the constitutional power to prohibit them.

While manufacture is not of itself interstate commerce, the shipment of manufactured goods interstate is such commerce and the prohibition of such shipment by Congress is indubitably a regulation of the commerce. . . .

But it is said that . . . while the prohibition is nominally a regulation of the commerce its motive or purpose is regulation of wages and hours of persons engaged in manufacture, the control of which has been reserved to the states and upon which Georgia and some of the States of destination have placed no restriction; that the effect of the present statute is not to exclude the proscribed articles from interstate commerce in aid of state regulation . . . but instead, under the guise of a regulation of interstate commerce, it undertakes to regulate wages and hours within the state contrary to the policy of the state which has elected to leave them unregulated.

The power of Congress over interstate commerce "is complete in itself, may be exercised to its utmost extent, and acknowledges no limitations other than are prescribed in the Constitution." Gibbons v. Ogden. That power can neither be enlarged nor diminished by the exercise or non-exercise of state power. . . . Congress, following its own conception of public policy concerning the restrictions which may appropriately be imposed on interstate commerce, is free to exclude from the commerce articles whose use in the states for which they are destined it may conceive to be injurious to the public health, morals or welfare, even though the state has not sought to regulate their use. . . .

Such regulation is not a forbidden invasion of state power merely because either its motive or its consequence is to restrict the use of articles of commerce within the states of destination; and is not prohibited unless by other Constitutional provisions. It is no objection to the assertion of the power to regulate interstate commerce that its exercise is attended by the same incidents which attend the exercise of the police power of the states.

The motive and purpose of the present regulation are plainly to make effective the Congressional conception of public policy that interstate commerce should not be made the instrument of competition in the distribution of goods produced under substandard labor conditions, which competition is injurious to the commerce and to the states from and to which the commerce flows. The motive and purpose of a regulation of interstate commerce are matters for the legislative judgment upon the exercise of which the Constitution places no restriction and over which the courts are given no control. . . . [W]e conclude that the prohibition of the shipment interstate of goods produced under the forbidden substandard labor conditions is within the constitutional authority of Congress. . . .

Hammer v. Dagenhart has not been followed. The distinction on which the decision was rested that Congressional power to prohibit interstate commerce is limited to articles which in themselves have some harmful or deleterious property — a distinction which was novel when made and unsupported by any provision of the Constitution — has long since been abandoned. The thesis of the opinion that the motive of the prohibition or its effect to control in some measure the use or production within the states of the article thus excluded from the commerce can operate to deprive the regulation of its constitutional authority has long since ceased to have force. And finally we have declared "The authority of the federal government over interstate commerce does not differ in extent or character from that retained by the states over intrastate commerce."

The conclusion is inescapable that Hammer v. Dagenhart was a departure from the principles which prevailed in the interpretation of the commerce clause. . . . It should be and now is overruled.

Validity of the Wage and Hour Requirements

Section 15(a)(2) and §§6 and 7 require employers to conform to the wage and hour provisions with respect to all employees engaged in the production of goods for interstate commerce. As appellee's employees are not alleged to be "engaged in interstate commerce" the validity of the prohibition turns on the question whether the employment, under other than the prescribed labor standards, of employees engaged in the production of goods for interstate commerce is so related to the commerce and so affects it as to be within the reach of the power of Congress to regulate it.

. . . As the Government seeks to apply the statute in the indictment, and as the court below construed the phrase "produced for interstate commerce," it embraces at least the case where an employer engaged, as is appellee, in the manufacture and shipment of goods in filling orders of extrastate customers, manufactures his product with the intent or expectation that according to the normal course of his business all or some part of it will be selected for shipment to those customers.

... The obvious purpose of the Act was not only to prevent the interstate transportation of the proscribed product, but to stop the initial step toward transportation, production with the purpose of so transporting it. Congress was not unaware that most manufacturing businesses shipping their product in interstate commerce make it in their shops without reference to its ultimate destination and then after manufacture select some of it for shipment interstate and some intrastate according to the daily demands of their business, and that it would be practically impossible, without disrupting manufacturing businesses, to restrict the prohibited kind of production to the particular pieces of lumber, cloth, furniture or the like which later move in interstate rather than intrastate commerce....

There remains the question whether such restriction on the production of goods for commerce is a permissible exercise of the commerce power. The power of Congress over interstate commerce is not confined to the regulation of commerce among the states. It extends to those activities intrastate which so affect interstate commerce or the exercise of the power of Congress over it as to make regulation of them appropriate means to the attainment of a legitimate end, the exercise of the granted power of Congress to regulate interstate commerce....

Congress, having by the present Act adopted the policy of excluding from interstate commerce all goods produced for the commerce which do not conform to the specified labor standards, it may choose the means reasonably adapted to the attainment of the permitted end, even though they involve control of intrastate activities....

We think also that §15(a)(2), now under consideration, is sustainable independently of §15(a)(1), which prohibits shipment or transportation of the proscribed goods. As we have said the evils aimed at by the Act are the spread of substandard labor conditions through the use of the facilities of interstate commerce for competition by the goods so produced with those produced under the prescribed or better labor conditions; and the consequent dislocation of the commerce itself caused by the impairment or destruction of local businesses by competition made effective through interstate commerce. The Act is thus directed at the suppression of a method or kind of competition in interstate commerce which it has in effect condemned as "unfair." ...

The means adopted by §15(a)(2) for the protection of interstate commerce by the suppression of the production of the condemned goods for interstate commerce is so related to the commerce and so affects it as to be within the reach of the commerce power.... So far as Carter v. Carter Coal Co. is inconsistent with this conclusion, its doctrine is limited in principle by ... decisions under the Sherman Act and the National Labor Relations Act....

Our conclusion is unaffected by the Tenth Amendment which provides: "The powers not delegated to the United States by the Constitution, nor prohibited by it to the States, are reserved to the States respectively, or to the people." The amendment states but a truism that all is retained which has not been surrendered. There is nothing in the history of its adoption to suggest that it was more than declaratory of the relationship between the national and state governments as it had been established by the Constitution before the amendment or that its purpose was other than to allay fears that the new national government might seek to exercise powers not granted, and that the states might not be able to exercise fully their reserved powers. . . .

Reversed.

In Wickard v. Filburn, 317 U.S. 111 (1942), the secretary of agriculture sought to penalize a farmer for growing wheat in excess of his allotment under the Agricultural Adjustment Act of 1938. Although appellee's 239-bushel surplus was intended wholly for consumption on his farm and not for sale, it was deemed "available for marketing" within the act. The district court enjoined enforcement. In an opinion by Justice Jackson, the Supreme Court unanimously reversed.

> Whether the subject of the regulation in question was "production," "consumption," or "marketing" is . . . not material for purposes of deciding the question of federal power before us. That an activity is of local character . . . might help in determining whether in the absence of Congressional action it would be permissible for the state to exert its power on the subject matter, even though in so doing it to some degree affected interstate commerce. But even if appellee's activity be local and though it may not be regarded as commerce, it may still, whatever its nature, be reached by Congress if it exerts a substantial economic effect on interstate commerce, and this irrespective of whether such effect is what might at some earlier time have been defined as "direct" or "indirect.". . .
>
> The wheat industry has been a problem industry for some years . . . The decline in the export trade has left a large surplus in production which, in connection with an abnormally large supply of wheat and other grains in recent years, caused congestion in a number of markets. . . .
>
> The effect of consumption of home-grown wheat on interstate commerce is due to the fact that it constitutes the most variable factor in the disappearance of the wheat crop. Consumption on the farm where grown appears to vary in an amount greater than 20 percent of average production. The total amount of wheat consumed as food varies but relatively little, and use as seed is relatively constant.
>
> The maintenance by government regulation of a price for wheat undoubtedly can be accomplished as effectively by sustaining or increasing the demand as by limiting the supply. The effect of the statute before us is to restrict the amount which may be produced for market and the extent as well to which one may forestall resort to the market by producing to meet his own needs. That appellee's own contribution to the demand for wheat may be trivial by itself is not enough to remove him from the scope of federal regulation where, as here, his contribution, taken together with that of many others similarly situated, is far from trivial.
>
> It is well established by decision of this Court that the power to regulate commerce includes the power to regulate the prices at which commodities in that commerce are dealt in and practices affecting such prices. One of the primary purposes of the Act in question was to increase the market price of wheat, and to that end to limit the volume thereof that could affect the market. It can hardly be denied that a factor of such volume and variability as home-consumed wheat would have a substantial influence on price and market conditions. This may arise because being in marketable condition such wheat overhangs the market and, if induced by rising prices, tends to flow into the market and check price increases. But if we assume that it is never marketed, it supplies a need of the man who grew it which would other-

wise be reflected by purchases in the open market. Homegrown wheat in this sense competes with wheat in commerce. The stimulation of commerce is a use of the regulatory function quite as definitely as prohibitions or restrictions thereon. This record leaves us in no doubt that Congress may properly have considered that wheat consumed on the farm where grown, if wholly outside the scheme of regulation, would have a substantial effect in defeating and obstructing its purpose to stimulate trade therein at increased prices.

Discussion

1. Does *Darby* indicate that there are no implicit constitutional constraints on Congress' power to prohibit commerce or only that the Court, for institutional reasons such as its inability to inquire into Congress' motives, cannot impose any constraints? Does it suggest that there are any constraints on the boot-strapping principle employed as the first alternative justification of Section 15(a)(2)?

2. Does the principle of aggregate harm employed in *Wickard* leave anything to the requirement that an activity have a substantial effect on interstate commerce? Is the effect of any activity on interstate commerce ever de minimis if the effects of all persons engaging in the activity are aggregated? Apart from this, does *Wickard* imply a different and broader concept of interstate commerce than do the earlier decisions?

3. In 1961, Congress extended the Fair Labor Standards Act of 1938 to every employee "employed in an enterprise engaged in commerce or in the production of goods for commerce." Such an enterprise is defined as one that "has employees engaged in commerce or in the production of goods for commerce," with the effect of covering the fellow employees of employees covered by the 1938 act. In 1966, the act was further extended to the employees of hospitals, elementary and secondary schools, and institutions of higher education, including those owned and operated by states. In Maryland v. Wirtz, 392 U.S. 183 (1968), the Court upheld the act as amended. Justice Harlan wrote that the 1961 amendment could be sustained on either of two theories, one rooted in *Darby,* the other in *Jones & Laughlin.* The act prevented "unfair competition" with enterprises in other states, for "[w]hen a company does an interstate business, its competition with companies elsewhere is affected by all its significant labor costs, not merely by the wages and hours of those employees who have physical contact with the goods in question." The act also prevented labor strife that might disrupt the flow of goods in commerce. Justice Harlan deemed the second rationale especially applicable to the 1966 amendments: hospitals and schools are "major users of goods imported from other States," and strikes and work stoppages by their employees "obviously interrupt and burden this flow of goods across state lines."

Justice Douglas, joined by Justice Stewart, dissented. He did not suggest that the subjects regulated were beyond the reach of the commerce power but argued that principles of state sovereignty prohibited Congress from imposing the minimum wages and maximum hours regulations upon the *state-run* institutions that were the subject of the suit:

> States spend billions of dollars each year on programs that purchase goods from interstate commerce, hire employees whose labor strife could disrupt interstate commerce, and act on such commerce in countless subtle ways. If constitutional principles of federalism raise no limits to the commerce power where regulation of state activities are concerned, . . . then the National Government could devour the

essentials of state sovereignty, though that sovereignty is attested by the Tenth Amendment.

The Court adopted the dissenting view in National League of Cities v. Usery, infra.

B. The Taxing Power

The post-1937 taxing power cases are not different in tone or outcome from some earlier decisions, such as *McCray*. For example, Sonzinsky v. United States, 300 U.S. 506 (1937), upheld a law requiring persons dealing in certain firearms (e.g., machine guns with silencers, sawed-off shotguns and rifles) to register with the collector of internal revenue and pay a $200 annual tax. Petitioner argued that the act — another provision of which imposed a $200 tax on each transfer of such firearms — was not designed to raise revenue but to prohibit transfer of the weapons. Justice Stone responded:

> The case is not one where the statute contains regulatory provisions related to a purported tax in such a way as has enabled this Court to say in other cases that the latter is a penalty resorted to as means of enforcing the regulation. See *Child Labor Tax* cases, Hill v. Wallace. Nor is the subject of the tax described or treated as criminal by the taxing statute. Compare United States v. Constantine. Here §2 contains no regulation other than the mere registration provisions, which are obviously supportable in aid of a revenue purpose. On its face it is only a taxing measure. . . .
>
> Every tax is in some measure regulatory. To some extent it interposes an economic impediment to the activity taxed as compared with others not taxed. But a tax is not any the less a tax because it has a regulatory effect; and it has long been established that an Act of Congress which on its face purports to be an exercise of the taxing power is not any the less so because the tax is burdensome or tends to restrict or suppress the things taxed.
>
> Inquiry into the hidden motives which may move Congress to exercise a power constitutionally conferred upon it is beyond the competency of courts. They will not undertake by collateral inquiry as to the measure of the regulatory effect of a tax, to ascribe to Congress an attempt, under the guise of taxation, to exercise another power denied by the Federal Constitution.

C. The Spending Power

The major post-1937 challenge to Congress' spending power involved the unemployment compensation scheme created by the Social Security Act of 1935, upheld in Steward Machine Co. v. Davis.

STEWARD MACHINE COMPANY v. DAVIS, 301 U.S. 548 (1937): [A tax was imposed on employers, based on their employees' wages. The proceeds went into the United States Treasury (like internal revenue collections generally) and were not earmarked for any purpose; however, a credit of up to 90 percent of the federal tax was allowed to the extent the employer contributed to a state unemployment fund that met detailed requirements specified in the act and was approved by the Social Security Board. Some of the federal requirements, as the Court described them, "are designed to give assurance that the state unemployment compensation law shall be one in substance as well as name. Others are designed to give assurance that the contributions shall be protected against loss after payment to the state." Among the latter was the requirement that contributions to the state fund be turned over immediately to the Treasury, which would invest, administer, and disburse them.]

CARDOZO, J. . . . The excise is not void as involving the coercion of the States in contravention of the Tenth Amendment or of restrictions implicit in our federal form of government. . . .

[Petitioner argues] that the tax and the credit in combination are weapons of coercion, destroying or impairing the autonomy of the states. . . .

To draw the line intelligently between duress and inducement there is need to remind ourselves of facts as to the problem of unemployment that are now matters of common knowledge. . . . During the years 1929 to 1936, when the country was passing through a cyclical depression, the number of the unemployed mounted to unprecedented heights. . . . The fact developed quickly that the states were unable to give the requisite relief. The problem had become national in area and dimensions. There was need of help from the nation if the people were not to starve. It is too late today for the argument to be heard with tolerance that in a crisis so extreme the use of the moneys of the nation to relieve the unemployed and their dependents is a use for any purpose narrower than the promotion of the general welfare. . . .

Before Congress acted, unemployment compensation insurance was still, for the most part, a project and no more. Wisconsin was the pioneer. Her statute was adopted in 1931. At time bills for such insurance were introduced elsewhere, but they did not reach the stage of law. . . . But if states had been holding back before the passage of the federal law, inaction was not owing, for the most part, to the lack of sympathetic interest. Many held back through alarm lest, in laying such a toll upon their industries, they would place themselves in a position of economic disadvantage as compared with neighbors or competitors. Two consequences ensued. One was that the freedom of a state to contribute its fair share to the solution of a national problem was paralyzed by fear. The other was that in so far as there was failure by the states to contribute relief according to the measure of their capacity, a disproportionate burden, and a mountainous one, was laid upon the resources of the Government of the nation.

The Social Security Act is an attempt to find a method by which all these public agencies may work together to a common end. Every dollar of the new taxes will continue in all likelihood to be used and needed by the nation as long as states are unwilling, whether through timidity or for other motives, to do what can be done at home. At least the inference is permissible that Congress so believed, though retaining undiminished freedom to spend the money as it pleased. On the other hand fulfillment of the home duty will be lightened and encouraged by crediting the taxpayer upon his account with the Treasury of the nation to the extent that his contributions under the laws of the locality have simplified or diminished the problem of relief and the probable demand upon the resources of the fisc. Duplicated taxes, or burdens that approach them, are recognized hardships that government, state or national, may properly avoid. If Congress believed that the general welfare would better be promoted by relief through local units than by the system then in vogue, the cooperating localities ought not in all fairness to pay a second time.

Who then is coerced through the operation of this statute? Not the taxpayer. He pays in fulfillment of the mandate of the local legislature. Not the state. . . . For all that appears she is satisfied with her choice, and would be sorely disappointed if it were now to be annulled. . . . [E]very rebate from a tax when condition upon conduct is in some measure a temptation. But to hold that . . . temptation is equivalent to coercion is to plunge the law in endless difficulties. The outcome of such a doctrine is the acceptance of a philosophical determinism by which choice becomes impossible. Till now the law has been guided by a robust common sense which assumes the freedom of the will as a working hypothesis in the solution of its problems. The wisdom of the hypothesis has illustration in this case. Nothing in the case suggests the exertion of a power akin to undue influence, if we assume that such a concept can ever be applied with fitness to the relations between state and nation. . . . We cannot say that [Alabama] was acting, not of her unfettered will, but under the strain of a persuasion equivalent to undue influence, when she chose to have relief administered under laws of her own making, by agents of her own selection, instead of under federal laws, administered by federal officers, with all the ensuing evils, at least to many minds, of federal patronage and power. . . .

In ruling as we do, we leave many questions open. We do not say that a tax is valid, when imposed by act of Congress, if it is laid upon the condition that a state may escape its operation through the adoption of a statue unrelated in subject matter to activities fairly within the scope of national policy and power. No such question is before us. In the tender of this credit Congress does not intrude upon fields foreign to its function. The purpose of its intervention, as we have shown, is to safeguard its own treasury and as an incident to that protection to place the states upon a footing of equal opportunity. Drains upon its own resources are to be checked; obstructions to the freedom of the states are to be leveled. . . .

United States v. Butler is cited by petitioner as a decision to the contrary. . . . The decision was by a divided court, a minority taking the view that the objections were untenable. None of them is applicable to the situation here developed.

(a) The proceeds of the tax in controversy are not earmarked for a special group.

(b) The unemployment compensation law which is a condition of the credit has had the approval of the state and could not be a law without it.

(c) The condition is not linked to an irrevocable agreement, for the state at its pleasure may repeal its unemployment law, terminate the credit, and place itself where it was before the credit was accepted.

(d) The condition is not directed to the attainment of an unlawful end, but to an end, the relief of unemployment, for which nation and state may lawfully cooperate.

The statute does not call for a surrender by the states of powers essential to their quasi-sovereign existence. . . . A wide range of judgment is given to the several states as to the particular type of statute to be spread upon their books. . . . What they may not do, if they would earn the credit, is to depart from those standards which in the judgment of Congress are to be ranked as fundamental. . . . In determining essentials Congress must have the benefit of a fair margin of discretion. One cannot say with reason that this margin has been exceeded, or that the basic standards have been determined in any arbitrary fashion. . . .

In a companion case, Helvering v. Davis, 301 U.S. 619 (1937), with only Justices McReynolds and Butler dissenting, the Court upheld the old-age benefit provisions of the Social Security Act:

> The problem is plainly national in area and dimensions. Moreover, laws of the separate states cannot deal with it effectively. . . . State and local governments are often lacking in the resources that are necessary to finance an adequate program of security for the aged. . . . Apart from the failure of resources, states and local governments are at times reluctant to increase so heavily the burden of taxation to be borne by their residents for fear of placing themselves in a position of economic disadvantage as compared with neighbors or competitors. . . . A system of old age pensions has special dangers of its own, if put in force in one state and rejected in another. The existence of such a system is a bait to the needy and dependent elsewhere, encouraging them to migrate and seek a haven of repose. Only a power that is national can serve the interests of all.

III. The National Powers Today: Some Normative Questions

The doctrine of "dual federalism" was subject to extensive academic as well as political criticism. For example, Robert Cushman wrote:[26]

> Its general result is to deny Congress the right to exercise its granted powers for broad national purposes; and it is logically defective because the reserved powers of the states which it is alleged may not be disturbed by the exercise of the powers granted to Congress are by definition merely those powers which have not been given to Congress or denied to the states. If Congress is exercising a delegated power, then, by the very language of the tenth amendment, it cannot possibly be exercising a power reserved to the states.

And the demise of dual federalism was generally acclaimed.[27]

In a literal sense, the Tenth Amendment is, indeed, a tautology, and any argument for constitutional limitations based on it is logically defective. Marshall implied as much in *McCulloch,* Chapter 1 supra, and Justice Stone said so explicitly in *Darby,* supra. But Marshall also spoke of the "spirit" as well as the letter of the Constitution. This section inquires whether, in the exercise of its delegated powers, Congress should be constrained by any constitutional limitations implicit in the "spirit" or structure of the federal system.

26. Robert Cushman, Social and Economic Control Through Federal Taxation, 18 Minn. L. Rev. 759, 781 (1934).

27. See, e.g., Edward Corwin, The Passing of Dual Federalism, 36 Va. L. Rev. 1 (1950); Robert Stern, The Commerce Clause and the National Economy, 1933-1946, 59 Harv. L. Rev. 645, 883 (1946).

The Court's withdrawal of judicial supervision since 1937 may reflect its view that, so long as Congress is regulating matters affecting interstate commerce to any extent or is taxing or spending, it has plenary authority to pursue any objectives whatsoever. Language in commerce clause decisions like *Darby* suggests this. But the Court's withdrawal is also consistent with the position that, even though the judiciary is institutionally incapable of enforcing implicit constitutional limitations, Congress may be constrained by them. Language in some of the opinions supports this position as well.

In any case, this section does not examine judicial review as such, but rather the substance of constitutional doctrine itself. We ask you to assume the same attitude that Andrew Jackson took toward *McCulloch* when he vetoed the extension of the second bank's charter: that the Supreme Court's noninterventionist posture, far from relieving Congress and the President from the duty of considering the constitutionality of their act, makes the fulfillment of this duty all the more crucial.

A. The Scope of the Commerce, Taxing, and Spending Powers

KATZENBACH v. McCLUNG

379 U.S. 294 (1964)

Appeal from the United States District Court for the Northern District of Alabama

CLARK, J.

This case was argued with Heart of Atlanta Motel v. United States, 379 U.S. 241 (1964), decided this day, in which we upheld the constitutional validity of Title II of the Civil Rights Act of 1964 against an attack by hotels, motels, and like establishments. This complaint for injunctive relief against appellants attacks the constitutionality of the Act as applied to a restaurant. The case was heard by a three-judge United States District Court, and an injunction was issued restraining appellants from enforcing the Act against the restaurant. On direct appeal, we noted probable jurisdiction. We now reverse the judgment. . . .

2. THE FACTS

Ollie's Barbecue is a family-owned restaurant in Birmingham, Alabama, specializing in barbecued meats and homemade pies, with a seating capacity of 220 customers. It is located on a state highway 11 blocks from an interstate one and a somewhat greater distance from railroad and bus stations. The restaurant caters to a family and white-collar trade with a take-out service for Negroes. It employs 36 persons, two-thirds of whom are Negroes.

In the 12 months preceding the passage of the Act, the restaurant purchased locally approximately $150,000 worth of food, $69,683 or 46 percent of which was meat that it bought from a local supplier who had procured it from outside the State. The District Court expressly found that a substantial portion of the food served in the restaurant had moved in interstate commerce. The restaurant has refused to serve Negroes in its dining accommodations since its original opening in 1927, and since July 2, 1964, it has been operating in violation of the Act. The court below concluded that if it were required to serve Negroes it would lose a substantial amount of business.

On the merits, the District Court held that . . . [there must be] a close and substantial relation between local activities and interstate commerce which requires control of the former in the protection of the latter. The court concluded, however, that the Congress, rather than finding facts sufficient to meet this rule, had legislated a conclusive presumption that a restaurant affects interstate commerce if it serves or offers to serve interstate travelers or if a substantial portion of the food which it serves has moved in commerce. This, the court held, it could not do because there was no demonstrable connection between food purchased in interstate commerce and sold in a restaurant and the conclusion of Congress that discrimination in the restaurant would affect that commerce.

. . . [I]n *Heart of Atlanta Motel* . . . we outlined the overall purpose and operational plan of Title II and found it a valid exercise of the power to regulate interstate commerce insofar as it requires hotels and motels to serve transients without regard to their race or color.[28] In this case we consider its application to restaurants which serve food a substantial portion of which has moved in commerce.

3. The Act As Applied

Section 201(a) of Title II commands that all persons shall be entitled to the full and equal enjoyment of the goods and services of any place of public accommodation without discrimination or segregation on the ground of race, color, religion, or national origin; and §201(b) defines establishments as places of public accommodation if their operations affect commerce or segregation by them is supported by state action. Sections 201(b)(2) and (c) place any "restaurant . . . principally engaged in selling food for consumption on the premises" under the Act "if . . . it serves or offers to serve interstate travelers or a substantial portion of the food which it serves . . . has moved in commerce."

Ollie's Barbecue admits that it is covered by these provisions of the Act. The Government makes no contention that the discrimination at the restaurant was supported by the State of Alabama. There is no claim that interstate travelers frequented the restaurant. The sole question, therefore, narrows down to whether Title II, as applied to a restaurant annually receiving about $70,000 worth of food which has moved in commerce, is a valid exercise of the power of Congress.

28. Under §201(c), establishments providing lodging to transient guests are, with narrow exceptions, deemed to "affect commerce," as are restaurants that serve "interstate travelers." In *Heart of Atlanta Motel,* Justice Clark noted that the movement of persons across state lines had long been held encompassed by the commerce clause and referred to extensive testimony before congressional committees to the effect that discrimination in public accommodations seriously burdened the interstate travel of minorities. With respect to the objective of the provision, he wrote: "In framing Title II of this Act Congress was also dealing with what it considered a moral problem. But that fact does not detract from the overwhelming evidence of the disruptive effect that racial discrimination has had on commercial intercourse. It was this burden which empowered Congress to enact appropriate legislation, and given this basis for the exercise of its power, Congress was not restricted by the fact that the particular obstruction to interstate commerce with which it was dealing was also deemed a moral and social wrong." Is the impact of discrimination by local enterprises on interstate travel any less "direct" (or whatever) than the effects of the railroad safety and rate regulations sustained in *Southern Railway* and the *Shreveport Rate* case in Ch. 3 supra?

The Government has contended that Congress had ample basis upon which to find that racial discrimination at restaurants which receive from out of state a substantial portion of the food served does, in fact, impose commercial burdens of national magnitude upon interstate commerce. The appellees' major argument is directed to this premise. They urge that no such basis existed. It is to that question that we now turn.

4. THE CONGRESSIONAL HEARINGS

As we noted in *Heart of Atlanta Motel* both Houses of Congress conducted prolonged hearings on the Act. And, as we said there, while no formal findings were made, which of course are not necessary, it is well that we make mention of the testimony at these hearings the better to understand the problem before Congress and determine whether the Act is a reasonable and appropriate means toward its solution. The record is replete with testimony of the burdens placed on interstate commerce by racial discrimination in restaurants. A comparison of per capita spending by Negroes in restaurants, theaters, and like establishments indicated less spending, after discounting income differences, in areas where discrimination is widely practiced. This condition, which was especially aggravated in the South, was attributed in the testimony of the Under Secretary of Commerce to racial segregation. This diminutive spending springing from a refusal to serve Negroes and their total loss as customers has, regardless of the absence of direct evidence, a close connection to interstate commerce. The fewer customers a restaurant enjoys the less food it sells and consequently the less it buys. In addition, the Attorney General testified that this type of discrimination imposed "an artificial restriction on the market" and interfered with the flow of merchandise. In addition, there were many references to discriminatory situations causing wide unrest and having a depressant effect on general business conditions in the respective communities. . . . Likewise, it was said, that discrimination deterred professional, as well as skilled, people from moving into areas where such practices occurred and thereby caused industry to be reluctant to establish there.

We believe that this testimony afforded ample basis for the conclusion that established restaurants in such areas sold less interstate goods because of the discrimination, that interstate travel was obstructed directly by it, that business in general suffered and that many new businesses refrained from establishing there as a result of it. Hence the District Court was in error in concluding that there was no connection between discrimination and the movement of interstate commerce. The court's conclusion that such a connection is outside "common experience" flies in the face of stubborn fact.

It goes without saying that, viewed in isolation, the volume of food purchased by Ollie's Barbecue from sources supplied from out of state was insignificant when compared with the total foodstuffs moving in commerce. But, as our late Brother Jackson said for the Court in Wickard v. Filburn, 317 U.S. 111 (1942): "That appellee's own contribution to the demand for wheat may be trivial by itself is not enough to remove him from scope of federal regulation where, as here, his contribution, taken together with that of many other similarly situated, is far from trivial." . . .

5. THE POWER OF CONGRESS TO REGULATE LOCAL ACTIVITIES

. . . Much is said about a restaurant business being local but "even if appellee's activity be local and though it may not be regarded as commerce, it may still, whatever its nature, be reached by Congress if it exerts a substantial economic effect on interstate commerce. . . ." Wickard v. Filburn. The activities that are beyond the reach of Congress are "those which are completely within a particular State, which do not affect other States, and with which it is not necessary to interfere, for the purpose of executing some of the general powers of the government." Gibbons v. Ogden, 9 Wheat. 1, 195 (1824). This rule is as good today as it was when Chief Justice Marshall laid it down almost a century and a half ago. . . .

The appellees contend that Congress has arbitrarily created a conclusive presumption that all restaurants meeting the criteria set out in the Act "affect commerce." Stated another way, they object to the omission of a provision for a case-by-case determination — judicial or administrative — that racial discrimination in a particular restaurant affects commerce.

But Congress' action in framing this Act was not unprecedented. In United States v. Darby, 312 U.S. 100 (1941), this Court held constitutional the Fair Labor Standards Act of 1938. . . . The appellees in that case argued, as do the appellees here, that the Act was invalid because it included no provision for an independent inquiry regarding the effect on commerce of substandard wages in a particular business. But the Court rejected that argument, observing that: "[S]ometimes Congress itself has said that a particular activity affects the commerce, as it did in the present Act, the Safety Appliance Act and the Railway Labor Act. In passing on the validity of legislation of the class last mentioned the only function of courts is to determine whether the particular activity regulated or prohibited is within the reach of the federal power."

Here, as there, Congress has determined for itself that refusals of service to Negroes have imposed burdens both upon the interstate flow of food and upon the movement of products generally. Of course, the mere fact that Congress has said when a particular activity shall be deemed to affect commerce does not preclude further examination by this Court. But where we find that the legislators, in light of the facts and testimony before them, have a rational basis for finding a chosen regulatory scheme necessary to the protection of commerce, our investigation is at an end. The only remaining question — one answered in the affirmative by the court below — is whether the particular restaurant either serves or offers to serve interstate travelers or serves food a substantial portion of which has moved in interstate commerce. . . .

Confronted as we are with the facts laid before Congress, we must conclude that it had a rational basis for finding that racial discrimination in restaurants had a direct and adverse effect on the free flow of interstate commerce. Insofar as the sections of the Act here relevant are concerned, §§201(b)(2) and (c), Congress prohibited discrimination only in those establishments having a close tie to interstate commerce, i.e., those, like the McClungs', serving food that has come from out of the State. We think in so doing that Congress acted well within its power to protect and foster commerce in extending the coverage of Title II only to those restaurants offering to serve interstate travelers or serving food, a substantial portion of which has moved in interstate commerce.

The absence of direct evidence connecting discriminatory restaurant service with the flow of interstate food, a factor on which the appellees place much reliance, is not, given the evidence as to the effect of such practices on other aspects of commerce, a crucial matter.

The power of Congress in this field is broad and sweeping; where it keeps within its sphere and violates no express constitutional limitation it has been the rule of this Court, going back almost to the founding days of the Republic, not to interfere. The Civil Rights Act of 1964, as here applied, we find to be plainly appropriate in the resolution of what the Congress found to be a national commercial problem of the first magnitude. We find it in no violation of any express limitations of the Constitution and we therefore declare it valid. . . .

Reversed.

[Justices Black, Douglas, and Goldberg each wrote a concurring opinion. All agreed that Title II could be sustained under the commerce power. Justices Black and Goldberg implied, and Justice Douglas stated explicitly, that Congress also had power to prohibit discrimination in privately owned places of public accommodation under section 5 of the Fourteenth Amendment (cf. Chapters 10 and 12 infra).]

1. *The Substantiality of the Effect on Interstate Commerce*

(a) Recall the aggregating doctrine adopted in *Wickard:* Congress can reach an individual activity, the isolated effect of which is de minimis, if the aggregate of all such activities is not insignificant. Is this a sound doctrine, consistent with principles of federalism implicit in the Constitution?

(b) Is the aggregating doctrine sufficient to support application of Title II of the Civil Rights Act of 1964 to Ollie's Barbecue? Consider also Daniel v. Paul, 395 U.S. 298 (1969), and Perez v. United States, 402 U.S. 146 (1971).

In *Daniel,* the Court applied Title II to the Lake Nixon Club, "a 232-acre amusement area with swimming, boating, sun bathing, picknicking, miniature golf, and dancing facilities and a snack bar," located near Little Rock, Arkansas. Under section 201(c)(4), an entire establishment is covered by the act if any covered facility "is physically located within its premises." The Court found that the snack bar was covered both because it offered to serve interstate travelers and because it served food that had moved in interstate commerce. Although the club advertised only in local media, these included a magazine distributed to guests at Little Rock hotels and restaurants. Justice Brennan wrote that "it would be unrealistic to assume that none of the 100,000 patrons actually served by the Club each season was an interstate traveler." Additionally, the snack bar served "a limited fare — hotdogs and hamburgers on buns, soft drinks, and milk. The District Court took judicial notice of the fact that the 'principal ingredients going into the bread were produced and processed in other States' and that 'certain ingredients [of the soft drinks] were probably obtained from out-of-State sources.' . . . Thus, at the very least, three of the four food items sold at the snack bar contain ingredients originating outside of the State. There can be no serious doubt that a 'substantial portion of the food' served at the snack bar has moved in interstate commerce." Justice Black dissented. He objected to the Court's speculative assumptions of fact and concluded that the act could not be applied to "this country people's recreation center, lying in what may be, so far as we know, a little 'sleepy hollow' between Arkansas hills miles away from any interstate highway. This would be stretching the Commerce Clause so as to give the Federal Government complete control over every little remote country place of recreation in every nook and cranny of every precinct and county in every one of the 50 states."[29]

The petitioner in *Perez* lent money to one Miranda and exacted increasingly large payments from him under threats of injuring him and his family. All of the events took place within New York State. The Court affirmed petitioner's conviction under the Federal Consumer Credit Protection Act for engaging in "extortionate credit transactions." Justice Douglas noted that the testimony before congressional committees supported the Act's findings that "[o]rganized crime is interstate and international in character. . . . A substantial part of the income of organized crime is generated by extortionate credit transactions. . . . Extortionate credit transactions are carried on to a substantial extent in interstate and foreign commerce and through the means and instrumentalities of such commerce. Even where extortionate credit transactions are purely intrastate in character, they nevertheless directly affect interstate and foreign commerce." To petitioner's argument that there was no evidence that his conduct had any interstate ramifications, Justice Douglas responded (citing *Darby* and *McClung*):

> Petitioner is clearly *a member of the class* which engages in extortionate credit transactions as defined by Congress. . . . Where the *class of activities* is regulated and that *class* is within the reach of federal power, the courts have no power "to excise as trivial, individual instances" of the class.

Only Justice Stewart dissented:

> [U]nder the statute before us a man can be convicted without any proof of interstate movement, of the use of the facilities of interstate commerce, or of facts showing that his conduct affected interstate commerce. I think the Framers of the Constitution never intended that the National Government might define as a crime and prosecute such wholly local activity through the enactment of federal criminal laws.
>
> In order to sustain this law we would, in my view, have to be able at the least to say that Congress could rationally have concluded that loan sharking is an activity with interstate attributes that distinguish it in some substantial respect from other local crime. But it is not enough to say that loan sharking is a national problem, for all crime is a national problem. It is not enough to say that some loan sharking has interstate characteristics, for any crime may have an interstate setting. And the circumstance that loan sharking has an adverse impact on interstate business is not a distinguishing attribute, for interstate business suffers from almost all criminal activity, be it shoplifting or violence in the streets.
>
> Because I am unable to discern any rational distinction between loan sharking and other local crime, I cannot escape the conclusion that this statute was beyond the

29. Justice Black believed that application of the act to the Lake Nixon Club could have been sustained under §5 of the Fourteenth Amendment but noted that, with respect to establishments of this sort, Congress had "tied the Act and limited its protection" to the commerce power.

power of Congress to enact. The definition and prosecution of local, intrastate crime are reserved to the States under the Ninth and Tenth Amendments.

Might application of the statute in *Perez* have been upheld on the ground that in any particular case it is difficult to trace "the connection between the loanshark on the street and the organization behind him" and that "this inherent difficulty . . . necessitates regulation of *all* loansharks, in order to be certain of reaching those that *do* affect commerce through their link to organized crime"?[30] Cf. Westfall v. United States 274 U.S. 256 (1927): "when it is necessary in order to prevent an evil to make the law embrace more than the precise thing to be prevented it may do so."[31] Might application of the statute in Daniel v. Paul be sustained on the same basis?

(c) During the years immediately preceding enactment of the Civil Rights Act of 1964, many people were convicted in state courts for criminal trespass when they refused to leave places of public accommodation after discriminatorily being denied service. In Hamm v. City of Rock Hill, 379 U.S. 306 (1964), the Court construed Title II to abate all pending sit-in convictions, assuming without discussion that the commerce power authorized retroactive application of the act. In dissent, Justices Black, Harlan, Stewart, and White criticized the Court's interpretation of the act. Justices Black and Harlan also asserted that the interpretation presented constitutional difficulties, the latter noting that "the legislative record is barren of any evidence showing that giving effect to *past* state trespass convictions would result in placing any burden on *present* interstate commerce. Such evidence, at the very least, would be a prerequisite to the validity of any purported exercise of the Commerce power in this regard." Are these constitutional doubts well founded?

(d) In McDermott v. Wisconsin, 228 U.S. 115 (1913), a Wisconsin grocer had received cans of food from an Illinois wholesaler, labeled as required by federal law but mislabeled under Wisconsin law. The Court reversed his state conviction for possessing mislabeled cans, holding that the state law, which would have required the grocer to remove or obliterate the label required for interstate shipment, was preempted by the federal statute. In United States v. Sullivan, 332 U.S. 689 (1948), a Chicago drug manufacturer shipped bottles containing 1,000 sulfathiazone tablets to a wholesaler in Atlanta, Georgia. The bottles displayed warnings required by the Federal Food, Drug, and Cosmetic Act of 1938. The wholesaler sold one bottle to Sullivan, a Columbus, Georgia, retail druggist, who resold twelve of the pills in a box without the requisite warning. A divided Court construed the federal statute to apply to Sullivan's act of mislabeling and held that Congress had power "under the commerce clause to regulate the branding of articles that have completed an interstate shipment and are being held for future sales in purely local or intrastate commerce." Justice Black's opinion for the Court contained no independent analysis but relied on *McDermott.* Was application of the statute in *McDermott* supportable under the commerce clause? If so, does the result in *Sullivan* follow? In what salient way was Sullivan's conduct related to interstate commerce?

30. Note, 49 Tex. L. Rev. 568, 573 (1971).

31. See generally Robert Stern, The Commerce Clause Revisited — The Federalization of Intrastate Crime, 15 Ariz. L. Rev. 271 (1973).

2. *The Objectives of Congressional Action*

a. The Taxing Power

UNITED STATES v. KAHRIGER, 345 U.S. 22 (1953): [A divided Court upheld a federal provision requiring persons engaged in the business of accepting wagers to pay a $50 occupational tax and register with the collector of internal revenues. Appellee argued, inter alia, that the tax was only a pretext for penalizing intrastate gambling and thus infringed "the police power which is reserved to the states."]

REED, J. . . . It is conceded that a federal excise tax does not cease to be valid merely because it discourages or deters the activities taxed. Nor is the tax invalid because the revenue obtained is negligible. Appellee, however, argues that the sole purpose of the statute is to penalize only illegal gambling in the states through the guise of a tax measure. As with [other] excise taxes which we have held to be valid, the instant tax has a regulatory effect. But regardless of its regulatory effect, the wagering tax produces revenue. . . .

It is axiomatic that the power of Congress to tax is extensive and sometimes falls with crushing effect on businesses deemed unessential or inimical to the public welfare, or where, as in dealings with narcotics, the collection of the tax also is difficult. As is well known, the constitutional restraints on taxing are few. . . . The difficulty of saying when the power to lay uniform taxes is curtailed, because its use brings a result beyond the direct legislative power of Congress, has given rise to diverse decisions. In that area of abstract ideas, a final definition of the line between state and federal power has baffled judges and legislators.

While the Court has never questioned the ["pretext" statement] of Mr. Chief Justice Marshall in the *McCulloch* case the application of the rule has brought varying holdings on constitutionality. Where federal legislation has rested on other congressional powers, such as the Necessary and Proper Clause or the Commerce Clause, this Court has generally sustained the statutes, despite their effect on matters ordinarily considered state concern. When federal power to regulate is found, its exercise is a matter for Congress. Where Congress has employed the taxing clause a greater variation in the decisions has resulted. The division in this Court has been more acute. . . . It is hard to understand why the power to tax should raise more doubts because of indirect effects than other federal powers.

Penalty provisions in tax statutes added for breach of a regulation concerning activities in themselves subject only to state regulation have caused this Court to declare the enactments invalid. Unless there are provisions extraneous to any tax need, courts are without authority to limit the exercise of the taxing power. All the provisions of this excise are adapted to the collection of a valid tax.[32]

[Justice Jackson concurred, "but with such doubt that if the minority agreed upon an opinion which did not impair legitimate use of the taxing power I probably would join it." Justice Black, joined by Justice Douglas, dissented solely on the ground that the act compelled self-incrimination. Justice Frankfurter also dissented, focusing mainly on the federalistic problems presented by the statute.]

32. The court also rejected appellee's argument that the registration provision compelled him to incriminate himself in violation of the Fifth Amendment. In Marchetti v. United States, 390 U.S. 39 (1968), the Court overruled *Kahriger* and invalidated the wagering tax scheme solely on this ground.

FRANKFURTER, J., dissenting. . . . The Court's opinion manifests a natural difficulty in reaching its conclusion. Constitutional issues are likely to arise whenever Congress draws on the taxing power not to raise revenue but to regulate conduct. This is so, of course, because of the distribution of legislative power as between the Congress and the State Legislatures in the regulation of conduct.

To review in detail the decisions of this Court, beginning with Veazie Bank v. Fenno dealing with this ambivalent type of revenue enactment, would be to rehash the familiar. Two generalizations may, however, safely be drawn from this series of cases. Congress may make an oblique use of the taxing power in relation to activities with which Congress may deal directly, as for instance, commerce between the States. Thus, if the dissenting views of Mr. Justice Holmes in Hammer v. Dagenhart had been the decision of the Court, as they became in United States v. Darby the effort to deal with the problem of child labor through an assertion of the taxing power in the statute considered in *Child Labor Tax* case would by the latter case have been sustained. However, when oblique use is made of the taxing power as to matters which substantively are not within the powers delegated to Congress, the Court cannot shut its eyes to what is obviously, because designedly, an attempt to control conduct which the Constitution left to the responsibility of the States, merely because Congress wrapped the legislation in the verbal cellophane of a revenue measure.

Concededly the constitutional questions presented by such legislation are difficult. On the one hand, courts should scrupulously abstain from hobbling congressional choice of policies, particularly when the vast reach of the taxing power is concerned. On the other hand, to allow what otherwise is excluded from congressional authority to be brought within it by casting legislation in the form of a revenue measure could, as so significantly expounded in the *Child Labor Tax* case offer an easy way for the legislative imagination to control "any one of the great number of subjects of public interest, jurisdiction of which the States have never parted with. . . ." I say "significantly" because Mr. Justice Holmes and two of the Justices who had joined his dissent in Hammer v. Dagenhart, McKenna and Brandeis, JJ., agreed with the opinion in the *Child Labor Tax* case. Issues of such gravity affecting the balance of powers within our federal system are not susceptible of comprehensive statement by smooth formulas such as that a tax is none the less a tax although it discourages the activities taxed, or that a tax may be imposed although it may effect ulterior ends. . . .

[T]he context of the circumstances which brought forth this enactment . . . emphatically supports what was revealed on the floor of Congress, namely, that what was formally a means of raising revenue for the Federal Government was essentially an effort to check if not to stamp out professional gambling. . . .

Mr. Justice Douglas, while not joining in the entire opinion, agrees with the views expressed herein that this tax is an attempt by the Congress to control conduct which the Constitution has left to the responsibility of the States.

Discussion

Does Justice Reed confuse or avoid the central issue by focusing on the "indirect effects" or "indirect results" of the wagering tax law? Is Justice Frankfurter's complaint based on the results or effects of the law?

Once the issue is recast in terms of the objectives or purposes of the federal scheme, is it still so "hard to understand why the power to tax should raise more doubts . . . than other federal powers"? Are there certain objectives that Congress may not properly pursue as the sole or primary objectives of exercise of the taxing power? Is Congress also foreclosed from pursuing these as objectives ancillary to the raising of revenue?

b. The Commerce Power

Even if an activity substantially affects interstate commerce, do principles of federalism limit the objectives for which Congress may legitimately regulate the activity? Are any limitations suggested by the history of the commerce clause in the constitutional convention (see pp. 119-120 supra)? Consider the Virginia resolution from which the clause in large measure derived:

> that the National Legislature ought to be impowered to . . . legislate in all cases to which the separate States are incompetent, or in which the harmony of the United States may be interrupted by the exercise of individual Legislation.

Consider also Professor Gerald Gunther's letter of June 5, 1963, to the Department of Justice, urging that the public accommodations provisions of the administration's civil rights bill be premised on the Fourteenth Amendment rather than on the commerce clause:[33]

> The proposed end run by way of the commerce clause seems to me ill-advised in every respect. . . . I know of course that the commerce power is a temptingly broad one. But surely responsible statutory drafting should have a firmer basis than, for example, some of the loose talk in recent newspaper articles about the widely accepted, unrestricted availability of the commerce clause to achieve social ends. Some qualifications seem in order. Thus, most of the obviously "social" laws, as with lottery and prostitution legislation, have their immediate impact on the interstate movement and rest on the power to prohibit that movement. Most "social" laws are not directly aimed at intrastate affairs, are not attempts to regulate internal activities as such. Where immediate regulations of intrastate conduct have been imposed, a demonstrable economic effect on interstate commerce, business, trade has normally been required. That kind of showing has been made, for example, with regard to the control of "local" affairs in the labor relations and agricultural production fields. The commerce clause "hook" has been put to some rather strained uses in the past, I know; but the substantive content of the commerce clause would have to be drained beyond any point yet reached to justify the simplistic argument that all intrastate activity may be subjected to any kind of national regulation merely because some formal crossing of an interstate boundary once took place, without regard to the relationship between the aim of the regulation and interstate trade. The aim of the proposed anti-discrimination legislation, I take it, is quite unrelated to any concern with national commerce in any substantive sense. It would, I think, pervert the meaning and purpose of the commerce clause to invoke it as the basis for this legislation.

Does Professor Gunther's criticism apply to the "interstate travel" aspect of Title II, upheld in *Heart of Atlanta Motel,* note 28 supra, to the extent that Congress

33. Quoted in Gerald Gunther & Noel Dowling, Constitutional Law 335-336 (8th ed. 1970).

was actually concerned with removing obstacles to interstate movement? Would the criticism apply to the "interstate food" aspect of Title II, upheld in *McClung,* if Congress had actually been concerned to increase the volume of food sold or moving interstate? Is his criticism valid with respect to what obviously was the central purpose of the interstate food provision — preventing discrimination by local restaurants?

Does Professor Gunther assume too readily that there are no implicit constraints on the purposes for which Congress may regulate or prohibit the interstate movement of goods? This seems to be the Court's position in *Darby,* supra. But is it correct? Does the Virginia resolution suggest constraints?

B. The Residue of State Sovereignty

Assuming that the objectives of congressional regulation are entirely "national" and that the nexus with a delegated power is substantial, is the exercise of congressional power subject to other constraints implicit in the structure of the federal system?

1. Inherently Local Subjects

United States v. Oregon, 366 U.S. 643 (1961), was a contest between the federal government and the state over the estate of an Oregon resident who died intestate and without legal heirs in a United States Veterans Administration Hospital in Oregon. The state claimed under a general escheat statute. The United States claimed under a federal statute providing that the personal property of a veteran dying in a VA hospital under such circumstances "shall immediately vest in and become the property of the United States as trustee for the sole use and benefit of the General Post Fund" to be used for recreation in veterans' homes and hospitals. Justice Black summarily rejected Oregon's constitutional attack on the federal statute:

> Congress undoubtedly has the power — under its constitutional powers to raise armies and navies and to conduct wars — to pay pensions, and to build hospitals and homes for veterans. We think it plain that the same sources of power authorize Congress to require that the personal property left by its wards when they die in government facilities shall be devoted to the comfort and recreation of other ex-service people who must depend upon the Government for care. The fact that this law pertains to the devolution of property does not render it invalid. Although it is true that this is an area normally left to the States, it is not immune under the Tenth Amendment from laws passed by the Federal Government which are, as is the law here, necessary and proper to the exercise of a delegated power.

Justice Douglas, joined by Justice Whittaker, dissented:

> I do not see how this decedent's estate can constitutionally pass to the United States. The succession of real and personal property is traditionally a state matter under our federal system. . . . Oregon has provided how the property of one who

dies intestate and without heirs shall be distributed; and that is its constitutional right under the Tenth Amendment. . . .

[T]he Supremacy Clause is not without limits. For a federal law to have supremacy it must be made "in pursuance" of the Constitution. The Court, of course, recognizes this; and it justifies this federal law governing devolution of property under the Necessary and Proper Clause of Art. I, §8.

The power to build hospitals and homes for veterans and to pay them pensions is plainly necessary and proper to the powers to raise and support armies and navies and to conduct wars. The power to provide for the administration of the estates of veterans . . . is to me a far cry from any such power. . . .

The Tenth Amendment does not, of course, dilute any power delegated to the national government. That is one face of the truism that runs through our decisions. . . . But when the Federal Government enters a field as historically local as the administration of decedents' estates, some clear relation of the asserted power to one of the delegated powers should be shown. The need of the Government to enter upon the administration of veterans' estates — made up of funds not owing from the United States — is no crucial phase of the ability of the United States to care for ex-service men and women or to manage federal fiscal affairs.

Today's decision does not square with our conception of federalism. There is nothing more deeply imbedded in the Tenth Amendment, as I read history, than the disposition of the estates of deceased people. I do not see how a scheme for administration of decedents' estates of the kind we have here can possibly be necessary and proper to any power delegated to Congress.

Does the structure of federalism demand a stronger nexus with a delegated power where a statute deals with traditionally state matters? Is the succession of property more traditionally local than the regulation of agricultural production, labor relations, and welfare? Could Congress properly enact legislation pursuant to the commerce clause dealing with matters such as negotiable instruments, automobile tort liability, and marriage and divorce?[34]

2. *Coercion of the States Under the Spending Power*

In Steward Machine Co. v. Davis, 301 U.S. 548 (1937), petitioner argued that the Social Security Act did not merely aid or encourage the states but coerced them to establish unemployment compensation programs; petitioner further argued that the federal eligibility requirements for such programs were so detailed and pervasive as to intrude impermissibly on state sovereignty. The Court held that the Social Security Act did not coerce and did not go too far, but Justice Cardozo's opinion did not reject the possibility that the spending power was subject to such implicit limiting principles.

Federal aid to state and local governments — for welfare, education, health, and a variety of municipal functions — has increased enormously since 1937. The proper extent of federal supervision of the state use of federal monies has been a continuing subject of dispute, and there have been advocates of every position, from unrestricted bloc grants to closely regulated categorical programs. In

34. Note that certain "local" subjects, including domestic relations, have generally been excluded from federal diversity jurisdiction. Hart & Wechsler's The Federal Courts and the Federal System 1172-1192 (Bator et al. eds., 2d ed. 1973).

Oklahoma v. United States Civil Service Commission, 330 U.S. 127 (1947), the Court held that Congress could properly condition the expenditure of highway funds on a state's compliance with a provision of the Hatch Act prohibiting state officials principally employed in federally funded programs from taking "any active part" in political activities. It sustained the Civil Service Commission's order removing a state highway commissioner who was also chairman of the state Democratic party. Justice Reed wrote for the Court (over dissents without opinion by Justices Black and Rutledge):[35]

> While the United States is not concerned with, and has no power to regulate, local political activities as such of state officials, it does have power to fix the terms upon which its money allotments to states shall be disbursed. . . . The end sought by Congress through the Hatch Act is better public service by requiring those who administer funds for national needs to abstain from active political partisanship. So even though the action taken by Congress does have an effect upon certain activities within the state, it has never been thought that such effect made the federal act invalid. . . . The offer of benefits to a state by the United States dependent upon cooperation by the state with federal plans, assumedly for the general welfare, is not unusual.

In South Dakota v. Dole, 483 U.S. 203 (1987), Chief Justice Rehnquist, wrote for the Court to uphold a congressional statute that directed the Secretary of Transportation to withhold from a state a percentage of federal highway funds it would otherwise be entitled to should the state permit the purchase or public possession of alcohol by a person under 21. South Dakota, which allowed 19-year-olds to purchase beer, argued that the statute was unconstitutional under the Twenty-first Amendment, which the Court had earlier found "grants the State virtually complete control over whether to permit importation or sale of liquor and how to structure the liquor distribution system." California Retail Liquor Dealers Assn. v. Midcal Aluminum, Inc., 445 U.S. 97, 110 (1980). South Dakota asserted that it would therefore be unconstitutional for Congress to pass a national drinking-age law and that indirect control through the withholding of federal funds was also unconstitutional.

Chief Justice Rehnquist wrote that "we need not decide . . . [whether the Twenty-first Amendment] would prohibit an attempt by Congress to legislate directly a national minimum drinking age. Here, Congress has acted indirectly under its spending power to encourage uniformity in the State's drinking ages. . . . [W]e find this legislative effort within constitutional bounds even if Congress may not regulate drinking ages directly."

Citing a number of cases going back to *Butler*, the Court stated that "objectives not thought to be within Article I's 'enumerated legislative fields,' may nevertheless be attained through the use of the spending power and the conditional grant of federal funds." To be sure, Congress' power under the spending power is not unlimited: "First, the exercise of the spending power must be in pursuit of 'the general welfare,' " though Congress is entitled to considerable deference in re-

35. In a companion case, United Public Workers v. Mitchell, 330 U.S. 75 (1947), the Court sustained the Hatch Act against a First Amendment challenge. In United States Civil Service Commn. v. National Assn. of Letter Carriers, 413 U.S. 548 (1973), a divided court again rejected a First Amendment attack on the statute, and in Broadrick v. Oklahoma, 413 U.S. 601 (1973), it sustained a similar state scheme (adopted 22 years after the case discussed in the text).

gard to judgments about what constitutes such welfare. "Second, we have required that if Congress desires to condition the States' receipt of federal funds, it 'must do so unambiguously . . . , enabl[ing] the States to exercise their choice knowingly, cognizant of the consequences of their participation. Third, our cases have suggested (without significant elaboration) that conditions on federal grants might be illegitimate if they are unrelated 'to the federal interest in particular national projects or programs.' . . . Finally, we have noted that other constitutional provisions may provide an independent bar to the conditional grant of federal funds." The statute met the first three requirements:

> Congress found that the differing drinking ages in the States created particular incentives for young persons to combine their desire to drink with their ability to drive, and that this interstate problem required a national solution. The means it chose to address this dangerous situation were reasonably calculated to advance the general welfare. The conditions upon which States receive the funds, moreover, could not be more clearly stated by Congress. . . . Indeed, the condition imposed by Congress is directly related to one of the main purposes for which highway funds are expended — safe interstate travel. This goal of the interstate highway system had been frustrated by varying drinking ages among the States. A presidential commission appointed to study alcohol-related accidents and fatalities on the Nation's highways concluded that the lack of uniformity in the States' drinking ages created 'an incentive to drink and drive' because 'young persons commut[e] to border States where the drinking age is lower.' By enacting, Congress conditioned the receipt of federal funds in a way reasonably calculated to address this particular impediment to a purpose for which the funds are expended.

The fourth question was "whether the Twenty-first Amendment constitutes an 'independent constitutional bar' to the conditional grant of federal funds." Citing Oklahoma v. Civil Service Commn. and Steward Machine Co. v. Davis, the Court described "the language in our earlier opinions" as standing "for the unexceptionable proposition that the power may not be used to induce the States to engage in activities that would themselves be unconstitutional. Thus, for example, a grant of federal funds conditioned on invidiously discriminatory state action or the infliction of cruel and unusual punishment" would be unconstitutional. Here, though, the policy being pressed upon South Dakota — the raising of the minimum drinking age — would violate no one's constitutional rights. The Court also noted that South Dakota would lose only 5 percent of its allotted funds for its failure to follow federal policy. This "mild encouragement" by Congress did not approach the point "at which 'pressure turns into compulsion.' " *Davis.*

Justice O'Connor dissented, arguing that "the Court's application of the requirement that the condition imposed be reasonably related to the purpose for which the funds are expended, is cursory and unconvincing."

> The Court reasons that Congress wishes that the roads it builds may be used safely, that drunk drivers threaten highway safety, and that young people are more likely to drive while under the influence of alcohol under existing law than would be the case if there were a uniform national drinking age of 21. It hardly needs saying, however, that if the purpose is to deter drunken driving, it is far too over- and under-inclusive. It is over-inclusive because it stops teenagers from drinking even

when they are not about to drive on interstate highways. It is under-inclusive because teenagers pose only a small part of the drunken driving problem in this Nation.

Thus she found too "attenuated" the linkage between the national interest and the particular conditions imposed. To allow the statute to operate in this case in effect allowed Congress to

> regulate almost any area of a State's social, political, or economic life on the theory that use of the interstate transportation system is somehow enhanced. If, for example, the United States were to condition highway moneys upon moving the state capital, I suppose it might argue that interstate transportation is facilitated by locating local governments in places easily accessible to interstate highways — or, conversely, that highways might become overburdened if they had to carry traffic to and from the state capital. In my mind, such a relationship is hardly more attenuated than the one which the Court finds supports §158.

Justice O'Connor cited *Butler* for the distinction between spending and regulation. There Justice Roberts noted "[t]here is an obvious difference between a statute stating the conditions upon which moneys shall be expended and one effective only upon assumption of a contractual obligation to submit to a regulation which otherwise could not be enforced." According to Justice O'Connor, "the *Butler* Court saw the Agricultural Adjustment Act for what it was — an exercise of regulatory, not spending, power. The error in *Butler* was not the Court's conclusion that the Act was essentially regulatory, but rather its crabbed view of the extent of Congress' regulatory power under the Commerce Clause."

Justice Brennan also dissented, on the ground "that regulation of the minimum age of purchasers of liquor falls squarely within the ambit of those powers reserved to the States by the Twenty-first Amendment. Since States possess this constitutional power, Congress can not condition a federal grant in a manner that abridges this right."

Discussion

Consider Hans Linde's criticism of the Court's summary treatment of federalist limits on the spending power in Oklahoma v. United States Civil Service Commission:[36]

> The fiscal powers of Congress inexorably draw to Washington, D.C., the power to make decisions that shape the public sector. The effect is to restrict state and local authorities' choices of policy in spending even their own resources, for Congress may condition federal contributions on compliance with federal standards. Because federal grants go to many separate agencies at different levels of state and local government, and because costs attributable to the federally-aided programs cannot always be neatly separated from other state and local costs, probably no one can say today how much state and local tax revenue — the life-blood of local autonomy — is committed to programs the standards for which are set and controlled under federal law. Yet there must be limits on such conditions if the political values of federalism are to be preserved despite this fiscal centralization. . . .

36. Linde, Justice Douglas on Freedom in the Welfare State, 39 Wash. L. Rev. 4, 28, 30-31 (1964).

Mr. Justice Reed's easy generalizations about conditioned federal benefits prove too much. Even the liberal dissenters in 1936 had found the power to spend not beyond constitutional limitations[:] "it may not be used to coerce action left to state control."[a] If Congress chose to forbid any state officer who spends federal grants to take part in a political campaign, could Oklahoma not choose to have an elected highway commission? State officers, from governors to legislators to city councilmen and school board members, increasingly administer programs aided by federal funds; may Congress constitutionally determine which may be elected, which others politically appointed, and which must be in a nonpartisan career status? Surely a line may be perceived between such conditions and conditions that go to the substance of the federally supported project, for instance that it fit a national plan, or be soundly engineered, or meet prescribed standards of hours, wages, or nondiscrimination in employment, or be fairly and honestly administered. "Whether and where such a line is drawn could determine, as much as any tax immunity, the role of federalism as a safeguard of political democracy in a centripetal public economy."

Does Chief Justice Rehnquist's opinion in South Dakota v. Dole allay any of Justice Linde's concerns?

Consider a grant of federal highway funds contingent on the state's willingness to move its state capital to the most geographically "efficient" location. Coyle v. Smith, 221 U.S. 559 (1911), continues to be cited for the proposition that Congress cannot directly tell a state where its capital is to be. But does the Constitution prevent Congress from "encouraging" a particular location through conditional granting of funds? Can funds be conditioned on reorganizing the state government, say, by changing the attorney general from an elected to an appointed position?[37]

Does it matter what the amounts involved actually are? The *Dole* majority emphasizes that the cutback of funds was only 5 percent. Does the Constitution prohibit a 50 percent cutoff or even a 100 percent cutoff? Consider in this context Title VI of the Civil Rights Act of 1964, which provides:

> §601. No person in the United States shall, on the ground of race, color, or national origin, be excluded from participation in, be denied the benefits of, or be subjected to discrimination under any program or activity receiving Federal financial assistance.
>
> §602. Each Federal department and agency which is empowered to extend Federal financial assistance to any program or activity, by way of grant, loan, or contract . . . is authorized and directed to effectuate the provisions of section 601 . . . by issuing rules, regulations, or orders of general applicability. . . .

Title VI has resulted in considerable federal regulation of traditionally local functions, such as education, as has Title IX of the Educational Amendments of 1972. But these provisions do not necessarily present the same federalistic difficulties as those considered above. From one viewpoint, they simply transfer decisionmaking authority from the federal judiciary (acting directly under the Fourteenth Amendment to secure equal protection) to administrative agencies, which may be better equipped to assure the enforcement of civil rights with mini-

a. United States v. Butler, 297 U.S. 1, at 87 (1936).

37. See Albert Rosenthal, Conditional Spending and the Constitution, 39 Stan. L. Rev. 1103, 1138 (1987).

mal intrusion on other aspects of the state programs.[38] Assume, however, that the spending and general welfare clauses were the only available sources of congressional authority: Would the federal regulations be constitutional?

3. *State Immunity from Direct Federal Regulation*

In United States v. California, 297 U.S. 175 (1936), the Court upheld a fine against a railroad wholly owned by the state for a violation of the Federal Safety Appliance Act. Justice Stone wrote for a unanimous Court:

> [W]e think it unimportant to say whether the state conducts its railroad in its "sovereign" or in its "private" capacity. That . . . it is acting within a power reserved to the states cannot be doubted. The only question we need consider is whether the exercise of that power, in whatever capacity, must be in subordination to the power to regulate interstate commerce, which has been granted specifically to the national government. The sovereign power of the states is necessarily diminished to the extent of the grants of power to the federal government in the Constitution. . . .
>
> The analogy of the constitutional immunity of state instrumentalities from federal taxation . . . is not illuminating. That immunity is implied from the nature of our federal system and the relationship within it of state and national governments, and is equally a restriction on taxation by either of the instrumentalities of the other. . . . But there is no such limitation upon the plenary power [of Congress] to regulate commerce. . . .
>
> The federal Safety Appliance Act is remedial, to protect employees and the public from injury because of defective railway appliances, and to safeguard interstate commerce itself from obstruction and injury due to defective appliances upon locomotives and cars used on the highways of interstate commerce, even though their individual use is wholly intrastate. The danger to be apprehended is as great and commerce may be equally impeded whether the defective appliance is used on a railroad which is state-owned or privately-owned.

Since United States v. California, states have been held subject to a variety of federal labor laws enacted pursuant to the commerce power. See California v. Taylor, 353 U.S. 553 (1957) (Railway Labor Act); Parden v. Terminal Railway, 377 U.S. 184 (1964) (Federal Employers' Liability Act); Maryland v. Wirtz, 392 U.S. 183 (1968) (Fair Labor Standards Act).

In Maryland v. Wirtz, 392 U.S. 183 (1968), the Court upheld the minimum wage requirements of the Fair Labor Standards Act as applied to state hospital and school employees. Justice Douglas, joined by Justice Stewart, dissented, asserting that "the constitutional scheme of federalism imposes limits" on the commerce power in order to prevent the destruction of "state sovereignty" and that application of the law would "disrupt the fiscal policy of the States and threaten their autonomy in the regulation of health and education." In 1974, Congress extended the minimum wage and maximum hour regulations to almost all state and municipal employees. In National League of Cities v. Usery, 426 U.S. 833

38. Aspects of the remedial schemes have been controversial. Grove City College v. Bell, 465 U.S. 555 (1984), held that a covered institution did not lose federal funding for all of its programs by virtue of discrimination in a particular program. The institution-wide remedy was restored by the Civil Rights Restoration Act of 1987.

(1976), in the first decision since the 1930s to strike down a federal regulation on the ground that it exceeded Congress' Article I powers, the Court overruled Maryland v. Wirtz.

NATIONAL LEAGUE OF CITIES v. USERY

426 U.S. 833 (1976)

Appeal from the United States District Court for the District of Columbia

REHNQUIST, J.

. . . Appellants in no way challenge [our] decisions establishing the breadth of authority granted Congress under the commerce power. Their contention, on the contrary, is that when Congress seeks to regulate directly the activities of States as public employers, it transgresses an affirmative limitation on the exercise of its power akin to other commerce power affirmative limitations contained in the Constitution. Congressional enactments which may be fully within the grant of legislative authority contained in the Commerce Clause may nonetheless be invalid because found to offend against the right to trial by jury contained in the Sixth Amendment, United States v. Jackson, 390 U.S. 570 (1968), or the Due Process Clause of the Fifth Amendment, Leary v. United States, 395 U.S. 6 (1969). Appellants' essential contention is that the 1974 amendments to the Act, while undoubtedly within the scope of the Commerce Clause, encounter a similar constitutional barrier because they are to be applied directly to the States and subdivisions of States as employers.

This Court has never doubted that there are limits upon the power of Congress to override state sovereignty, even when exercising its otherwise plenary powers to tax or to regulate commerce which are conferred by Art. I of the Constitution. . . . In Fry v. United States, 421 U.S. 542 (1975), the Court recognized that an express declaration of this limitation is found in the Tenth Amendment:

> While the Tenth Amendment has been characterized as a "truism," stating merely that "all is retained which has not been surrendered," United States v. Darby, 312 U.S. 100, 124 (1941), it is not without significance. The Amendment expressly declares the constitutional policy that Congress may not exercise power in a fashion that impairs the States' integrity or their ability to function effectively in a federal system.

. . . It is one thing to recognize the authority of Congress to enact laws regulating individual businesses necessarily subject to the dual sovereignty of the government of the Nation and of the State in which they reside. It is quite another to uphold a similar exercise of congressional authority directed, not to private citizens, but to the States as States. We have repeatedly recognized that there are attributes of sovereignty attaching to every state government which may not be impaired by Congress, not because Congress may lack an affirmative grant of legislative authority to reach the matter, but because the Constitution prohibits it from exercising the authority in that manner. . . . Coyle v. Oklahoma, 221 U.S. 559 (1911) [see p. 405, supra]. . . .

One undoubted attribute of state sovereignty is the States' power to determine the wages which shall be paid to those whom they employ in order to carry out their governmental functions, what hours those persons will work, and what compensation will be provided where these employees may be called upon to work overtime. The question we must resolve here, then, is whether these determinations are " 'functions essential to separate and independent existence,' " so that Congress may not abrogate the States' otherwise plenary authority to make them. . . .

Judged solely in terms of increased costs in dollars, [the FLSA makes] a significant impact on the functioning of the governmental bodies involved. The Metropolitan Government of Nashville and Davidson County, Tenn., for example, asserted that the Act will increase its costs of providing essential police and fire protection, without any increase in service or in current salary levels, by $938,000 per year. . . . The State of California, which must devote significant portions of its budget to fire-suppression endeavors, estimated that application of the Act to employment practices will necessitate an increase in its budget of between $8 million and $16 million.

Increased costs are not, of course, the only adverse effects which compliance with the Act will visit upon state and local governments, and in turn upon the citizens who depend upon those governments. In its complaint in intervention, for example, California asserted that it could not comply with the overtime costs (approximately $750,000 per year) which the Act required to be paid to California Highway Patrol cadets during their academy training program. California reported that it had thus been forced to reduce its academy training program from 2,080 hours to only 960 hours, a compromise undoubtedly of substantial importance to those whose safety and welfare may depend upon the preparedness of the California Highway Patrol. . . .

Quite apart from the substantial costs imposed upon the States and their political subdivisions, the Act displaces state policies regarding the manner in which they will structure delivery of those governmental services which their citizens require. The Act, speaking directly to the States qua States, . . . supplants the considered policy choices of the States' elected officials and administrators as to how they wish to structure pay scales in state employment. The State might wish to employ persons with little or no training, or those who wish to work on a casual basis, or those who for some other reason do not possess minimum employment requirements, and pay them less than the federally prescribed minimum wage. It may wish to offer part-time or summer employment to teenagers at a figure less than the minimum wage, and if unable to do so may decline to offer such employment at all. But the Act would forbid such choices by the States. . . .

This dilemma presented by the minimum wage restrictions may seem not immediately different from that faced by private employers, who have long been covered by the Act and who must find ways to increase their gross income if they are to pay higher wages while maintaining current earnings. The difference, however, is that a State is not merely a factor in the "shifting economic arrangements" of the private sector of the economy, but is itself a coordinate element in the system established by the Framers for governing our Federal Union. . . .

This congressionally imposed displacement of state decisions may substantially restructure traditional ways in which the local governments have arranged their affairs. . . . The requirement imposing premium rates upon any employment in excess of what Congress has decided is appropriate for a governmental employee's workweek, for example, appears likely to have the effect of coercing the States to structure work periods in some employment areas, such as police and fire protection, in a manner substantially different from practices which have long been commonly accepted among local governments of this Nation. In addition, appellee represents that the Act will require that the premium compensation for overtime worked must be paid in cash, rather than with compensatory time off, unless such compensatory time is taken in the same pay period. This too appears likely to be highly disruptive of accepted employment practices in many governmental areas where the demand for a number of employees to perform important jobs for extended periods on short notice can be both unpredictable and critical. Another example of congressional choices displacing those of the States in the area of what are without doubt essential governmental decisions may be found in the practice of using volunteer firemen, a source of manpower crucial to many of our smaller towns' existence. Under the regulations proposed by appellee, whether individuals are indeed "volunteers" rather than "employees" subject to the minimum wage provisions of the Act are questions to be decided in the courts. . . .

Our examination of the effect of the 1974 amendments, as sought to be extended to the States and their political subdivisions, satisfies us that both the minimum wage and the maximum hour provisions will impermissibly interfere with the integral governmental functions of these bodies. . . . [The amendments will] significantly alter or displace the States' abilities to structure employer-employee relationships in such areas as fire prevention, police protection, sanitation, public health, and parks and recreation. These activities are typical of those performed by state and local governments in discharging their dual functions of administering the public law and furnishing public services. Indeed, it is functions such as these which governments are created to provide, services such as these which the States have traditionally afforded their citizens. If Congress may withdraw from the States the authority to make those fundamental employment decisions upon which their systems for performance of these functions must rest, we think there would be little left of the States' " 'separate and independent existence.' " Thus, even if appellants may have overestimated the effect which the Act will have upon their current levels and patterns of governmental activity, the dispositive factor is that Congress has attempted to exercise its Commerce Clause authority to prescribe minimum wages and maximum hours to be paid by the States in their capacities as sovereign governments. In so doing, Congress has sought to wield its power in a fashion that would impair the States' "ability to function effectively in a federal system." This exercise of congressional authority does not comport with the federal system of government embodied in the Constitution. We hold that insofar as the challenged amendments operate to directly displace the States' freedom to structure integral operations in areas of traditional governmental functions, they are not within the authority granted Congress by Art. I, §8, cl. 3.[a] . . .

Wirtz must be overruled.

a. We express no view as to whether different results might obtain if Congress seeks to affect integral operations of state governments by exercising authority granted it under other sections of the Constitution such as the spending power, Art. I, §8, cl. 1, or §5 of the Fourteenth Amendment.

BLACKMUN, J., concurring. . . .

I may misinterpret the Court's opinion, but it seems to me that it adopts a balancing approach, and does not outlaw federal power in areas such as environmental protection, where the federal interest is demonstrably greater and where state facility compliance with imposed federal standards would be essential. With this understanding on my part of the Court opinion, I join it.

BRENNAN, J., joined by White and Marshall, JJ., dissenting. . . .

My Brethren do not successfully obscure today's patent usurpation of the role reserved for the political process by their purported discovery in the Constitution of a restraint derived from sovereignty of the States on Congress' exercise of the commerce power. Mr. Chief Justice Marshall recognized that limitations "prescribed in the constitution," Gibbons v. Ogden, restrain Congress' exercise of the power. Thus laws within the commerce power may not infringe individual liberties protected by the First Amendment, the Fifth Amendment, or the Sixth Amendment. . . . But there is no restraint based on state sovereignty requiring or permitting judicial enforcement anywhere expressed in the Constitution; our decisions over the last century and a half have explicitly rejected the existence of any such restraint on the commerce power. . . .

[N]othing in the Tenth Amendment constitutes a limitation on congressional exercise of powers delegated by the Constitution to Congress. . . .

[D]evoid of meaningful content is my Brethren's argument that the 1974 amendments "displac[e] State policies." The amendments neither impose policy objectives on the States nor deny the States complete freedom to fix their own objectives. My Brethren boldly assert that the decision as to wages and hours is an "undoubted attribute of state sovereignty," and then never say why. Indeed, they disclaim any reliance on the costs of compliance with the amendments in reaching today's result. This would enable my Brethren to conclude that, however insignificant that cost, any federal regulation under the commerce power "will nonetheless significantly alter or displace the State's abilities to structure employer-employee relationships." This then would mean that, whether or not state wages are paid for the performance of an "essential" state function (whatever that may mean), the newly discovered state-sovereignty constraint could operate as a flat and absolute prohibition against congressional regulation of the wages and hours of state employees under the Commerce Clause. The portent of such a sweeping holding is so ominous for our constitutional jurisprudence as to leave one incredulous.

Certainly the paradigm of sovereign action — action qua State — is in the enactment and enforcement of state laws. Is it possible that my Brethren are signaling abandonment of the heretofore unchallenged principle that Congress "can, if it chooses, entirely displace the States to the full extent of the far-reaching Commerce Clause"? Bethlehem Steel Co. v. New York State Board, 330 U.S. 767, 780 (1947) (opinion of Frankfurter, J.). . . . [T]he ouster of state laws obviously curtails or prohibits the States' prerogatives to make policy choices respecting subjects clearly of greater significance to the "State qua State" than the minimum wage paid to state employees. The Supremacy Clause dictates this result under "the federal system of government embodied in the Constitution.". . .

reject Bethlehem?

My Brethren do more than turn aside longstanding constitutional jurisprudence that emphatically rejects today's conclusion. More alarming is the startling restructuring of our federal system, and the role they create therein for the federal judiciary. This Court is simply not at liberty to erect a mirror of its own conception of a desirable governmental structure. . . .

STEVENS, J., dissenting.

The Court holds that the Federal Government may not interfere with a sovereign State's inherent right to pay a substandard wage to the janitor at the state capitol. The principle on which the holding rests is difficult to perceive.

The Federal Government may, I believe, require the State to act impartially when it hires or fires the janitor, to withhold taxes from his paycheck, to observe safety regulations when he is performing his job, to forbid him from burning too much soft coal in the capitol furnace, from dumping untreated refuse in an adjacent waterway, from overloading a state-owned garbage truck, or from driving either the truck or the governor's limousine over 55 miles an hour. Even though these and many other activities of the capitol janitor are activities of the State qua State, I have no doubt that they are subject to federal regulation.

. . . Since I am unable to identify a limitation on that federal power that would not also invalidate federal regulation of state activities that I consider unquestionably permissible, I am persuaded that this statute is valid. . . .

New York Times reporter Linda Greenhouse once described *National League of Cities* as a kiss that turned a "constitutional frog" into a "prince" by lifting the Tenth Amendment "from decades of scorn and neglect" and reviving it "for battle in the service of states' rights." But the prince was short-lived: No subsequent decision struck down a congressional regulation of state entities, and in 1985 the Court explicitly overruled *National League of Cities.*

GARCIA v. SAN ANTONIO METROPOLITAN TRANSIT AUTHORITY

469 U.S. 528 (1985)

On Appeal from the United States District Court for the Western District of Texas

[The Department of Labor issued an opinion stating that, notwithstanding *National League of Cities*, the operations of the San Antonio Metropolitan Transit Authority (SAMTA) "are not constitutionally immune from the application of the Fair Labor Standard Act" and ordering the municipally owned transportation service to comply with federal minimum wage laws. A federal district court struck down the order, and the Secretary of Labor appealed directly to the Supreme Court. After hearing oral argument in 1983, the Court ordered reargument and requested the parties to brief "[w]hether or not the principles of the Tenth Amendment as set forth in *National League of Cities* . . . should be reconsidered."]

BLACKMUN, J.

[T]he attempt to draw the boundaries of state regulatory immunity in terms of "traditional governmental function" is not only unworkable but is inconsistent with established principles of federalism on which *National League of Cities* purported to rest. That case, accordingly, is overruled. . . .

II

. . . The controversy in the present cases has focused on the . . . *Hodel* requirement that the challenged federal statute trench on "traditional governmental functions." The District Court voiced a common concern: "Despite the abundance of adjectives, identifying which particular state functions are immune remains difficult." Just how troublesome the task has been is revealed by the results reached in other federal cases. [Justice Blackmun notes cases that had found ambulance services, municipal airports, and solid waste disposal to be "traditional governmental functions" while other cases denied this designation to the issuance of industrial development bonds, regulation of intrastate natural gas sales and air transportation, and operation of telephone systems and a mental health facility.] We find it difficult, if not impossible, to identify an organizing principle that places each of the cases in the first group on one side of a line and each of the cases in the second group on the other side. . . .

Thus far, this Court itself has made little headway in defining the scope of the governmental functions deemed protected under *National League of Cities*. . . . The only other case in which the Court has had occasion to address the problem is [Transportation Union v. Long Island Railroad Co., 455 U.S. 678 (1982), where a unanimous Court held that a state-owned commuter rail service was not a "traditional governmental function" and thus that its employees could exercise a federally protected right to strike]. We relied in large part there on "the *historical reality* that the operation of railroads is not among the functions *traditionally* performed by state and local governments," but we simultaneously disavowed "a static historical view of state functions generally immune from federal regulation." We held that the inquiry into a particular function's "traditional" nature was merely a means of determining whether the federal statute at issue unduly handicaps "basic state prerogatives," but we did not offer an explanation of what makes one state function a "basic prerogative" and another function not basic. Finally, having disclaimed a rigid reliance on the historical pedigree of state involvement in a particular area, we nonetheless found it appropriate to emphasize the extended historical record of *federal* involvement in the field of rail transportation.

Many constitutional standards involve "undoubte[d] . . . gray areas," and, despite the difficulties that this Court and other courts have encountered so far, it normally might be fair to venture the assumption that case-by-case development would lead to a workable standard for determining whether a particular governmental function should be immune from federal regulation under the Commerce Clause. A further cautionary note is sounded, however, by the Court's experience in the related field of state immunity from federal taxation. In South Carolina v. United States, 199 U.S. 437 (1905), the Court held for the first time that the state tax immunity recognized in Collector v. Day, 11 Wall. 113 (1870), extended only to the "ordinary" and "strictly governmental" instrumentalities of state government and not to instrumentalities "used by the State in the carrying on of an ordinary private business." While the Court applied the distinction outlined in *South Carolina* for the following 40 years, at no time during that period did the Court develop a consistent formulation of the kinds of governmental functions that were entitled to immunity. The Court identified the protected functions at various times as "essential," "usual," "traditional," or "strictly governmental." . . .

If these tax immunity cases had any common thread, it was in the attempt to distinguish between "governmental" and "proprietary" functions. To say that the distinction between "governmental" and "proprietary" proved to be stable, however, would be something of an overstatement. In 1911, for example, the Court declared that the provision of a municipal water supply "is no part of the essential governmental functions of a State." Flint v. Stone Tracy Co., 220 U.S. 107, 172. Twenty-six years later, without any intervening change in the applicable legal standards, the Court simply rejected its earlier position and decided that the provision of a municipal water supply *was* immune. . . . Brush v. Commissioner, 300 U.S., at 370-373. At the same time that the Court was holding a municipal water supply to be immune from federal taxes, it had held that a state-run commuter rail system was *not* immune. Helvering v. Powers, 293 U.S. 214 (1934). . . . It was this uncertainty and instability that led the Court shortly thereafter, in New York v. United States, 326 U.S. 572 (1946), unanimously to conclude that the distinction between "governmental" and "proprietary" functions was "untenable" and must be abandoned. . . .

The distinction the Court discarded as unworkable in the field of tax immunity has proved no more fruitful in the field of regulatory immunity under the Commerce Clause. Neither do any of the alternative standards that might be employed to distinguish between protected and unprotected governmental functions appear manageable. We rejected the possibility of making immunity turn on a purely historical standard of "tradition" in *Long Island*, and properly so. The most obvious defect of a historical approach to state immunity is that it prevents a court from accommodating changes in the historical functions of States, changes that have resulted in a number of once-private functions like education being assumed by the States and their subdivisions.[a] At the same time, the only apparent virtue of a rigorous historical standard, namely, its promise of a reasonably objective measure for state immunity is illusory. Reliance on history as an organizing principle results in linedrawing of the most arbitrary sort; the genesis of state governmental functions stretches over a historical continuum from before the Revolution to the present, and courts would have to decide by fiat precisely how longstanding a pattern of state involvement had to be for federal regulatory authority to be defeated.

A nonhistorical standard for selecting immune governmental functions is likely to be just as unworkable as is a historical standard. The goal of identifying "uniquely" governmental functions, for example, has been rejected by the Court in the field of government tort liability in part because the notion of a "uniquely" governmental function is unmanageable. See Indian Towing Co. v. United States, 350 U.S. 61, 64-69 (1955). . . . Another possibility would be to confine immunity to "necessary" governmental services, that is, services that would be pro-

a. Indeed, the "traditional" nature of a particular governmental function can be a matter of historical nearsightedness; today's self-evidently "traditional" function is often yesterday's suspect innovation. Thus, *National League of Cities* offered the provision of public parks and recreation as an example of a traditional governmental function. A scant 80 years earlier, however, in Shoemaker v. United States, 147 U.S. 282 (1893), the Court pointed out that city commons originally had been provided not for recreation but for grazing domestic animals "in common," and that "[i]n the memory of men now living, a proposition to take private property [by eminent domain] for a public park . . . would have been regarded as a novel exercise of legislative power." Id., at 297.

vided inadequately or not at all unless the government provided them. The set of services that fits into this category, however, may well be negligible. The fact that an unregulated market produces less of some service than a State deems desirable does not mean that the State itself must provide the service; in most if not all cases, the State can "contract out" by hiring private firms to provide the service or simply by providing subsidies to existing suppliers. It also is open to question how well equipped courts are to make this kind of determination about the workings of economic markets.

We believe, however, that there is a more fundamental problem at work here, a problem that explains why the Court was never able to provide a basis for the governmental/proprietary distinction in the intergovernmental tax immunity cases and why an attempt to draw similar distinctions with respect to federal regulatory authority under *National League of Cities* is unlikely to succeed regardless of how the distinctions are phrased. The problem is that neither the governmental/proprietary distinction nor any other that purports to separate out important governmental functions can be faithful to the role of federalism in a democratic society. The essence of our federal system is that within the realm of authority left open to them under the Constitution, the States must be equally free to engage in any activity that their citizens choose for the common weal, no matter how unorthodox or unnecessary anyone else — including the judiciary — deems state involvement to be. Any rule of state immunity that looks to the "traditional," "integral," or "necessary" nature of governmental functions inevitably invites an unelected federal judiciary to make decisions about which state policies it favors and which ones it dislikes. . . .

We therefore now reject, as unsound in principle and unworkable in practice, a rule of state immunity from federal regulation that turns on a judicial appraisal of whether a particular governmental function is "integral" or "traditional." Any such rule leads to inconsistent results at the same time that it dissevers principles of democratic self-governance, and it breeds inconsistency precisely because it is divorced from those principles. If there are to be limits on the Federal Government's power to interfere with state functions — as undoubtedly there are — we must look elsewhere to find them. We accordingly return to the underlying issue that confronted this Court in *National League of Cities* — the manner in which the Constitution insulates States from the reach of Congress' Power under the Commerce Clause.

III

. . . What has proved problematic is not the perception that the Constitution's federal structure imposes limitations on the Commerce Clause, but rather the nature and content of those limitations. One approach to defining the limits on Congress' authority to regulate the States under the Commerce Clause is to identify certain underlying elements of political sovereignty that are deemed essential to the States' "separate and independent existence." Lane County v. Oregon, 7 Wall. 71, 76 (1869) . . .

We doubt that courts ultimately can identify principled constitutional limitations on the scope of Congress' Commerce Clause powers over the States merely by relying on *a priori* definitions of state sovereignty. In part, this is because of the elusiveness of objective criteria for "fundamental" elements of state sovereignty, a problem we have witnessed in the search for "traditional governmental functions." There is, however, a more fundamental reason: the sovereignty of the States is limited by the Constitution itself. A variety of sovereign powers, for example, are withdrawn from the States by Article I, §10. Section 8 of the same Article works an equally sharp contraction of state sovereignty by authorizing Congress to exercise a wide range of legislative powers and (in conjunction with the Supremacy Clause of Article VI) to displace contrary state legislation. By providing for final review of questions of federal law in this Court, Article III curtails the sovereign power of the States' judiciaries to make authoritative determinations of law. See Martin v. Hunter's Lessee, 1 Wheat. 304 (1816). Finally, the developed application, through the Fourteenth Amendment, of the greater part of the Bill of Rights to the States limits the sovereign authority that States otherwise would possess to legislate with respect to their citizens and to conduct their own affairs. . . .

As a result, to say that the Constitution assumes the continued role of the States is to say little about the nature of that role. . . . With rare exceptions, like the guarantee, in Article IV, §3, of state territorial integrity, the Constitution does not carve out express elements of state sovereignty that Congress may not employ its delegated powers to displace. . . . In short, we have no license to employ freestanding conceptions of state sovereignty when measuring congressional authority under the Commerce Clause.

When we look for the States' "residuary and inviolable sovereignty," The Federalist No. 39, p.285 (B. Wright ed. 1961) (J. Madison), in the shape of the constitutional scheme rather than in predetermined notions of sovereign power, a different measure of state sovereignty emerges. Apart from the limitation on federal authority inherent in the delegated nature of Congress' Article I powers, the principal means chosen by the Framers to ensure the role of the States in the federal system lies in the structure of the Federal Government itself. It is no novelty to observe that the composition of the Federal Government was designed in large part to protect the States from overreaching by Congress. The Framers thus gave the States a role in the selection both of the Executive and the Legislative Branches of the Federal Government. The States were vested with indirect influence over the House of Representatives and the Presidency by their control of electoral qualifications and their role in presidential elections. U.S. Const., Art. I, §2, and Art. II, §1. They were given more direct influence in the Senate, where each State received equal representation and each Senator was to be selected by the legislature of his State. Art. I, §3. The significance attached to the States' equal representation in the Senate is underscored by the prohibition of any constitutional amendment divesting a State of equal representation without the State's consent. Art. V.

The extent to which the structure of the Federal Government itself was relied on to insulate the interests of the States is evident in the views of the Framers. James Madison explained that the Federal Government "will partake sufficiently of the spirit [of the States], to be disinclined to invade the rights of the individual States, or the prerogatives of their governments." The Federalist No. 46, p.332 (B. Wright ed. 1961). Similarly, James Wilson observed that "it was a favorite object in the Convention" to provide for the security of the States against federal encroachment and that the structure of the Federal Government itself served that end. 2 Elliot, at 438-439. . . . In short, the Framers chose to rely on a federal system in which special restraints on federal power over the States inhered principally in the workings of the National Government itself, rather than in discrete limitations on the objects of federal authority. . . .

We realize that changes in the structure of the Federal Government have taken place since 1789, not the least of which has been the substitution of popular election of Senators by the adoption of the Seventeenth Amendment in 1913, and that these changes may work to alter the influence of the States in the federal political process. Nonetheless, against this background, we are convinced that the fundamental limitation that the constitutional scheme imposes on the Commerce Clause to protect the "States as States" is one of process rather than one of result. Any substantive restraint on the exercise of Commerce Clause powers must find its justification in the procedural nature of this basic limitation, and it must be tailored to compensate for possible failings in the national political process rather than to dictate a "sacred province of state autonomy." EEOC v. Wyoming, 460 U.S., at 236.

Insofar as the present cases are concerned, then, we need go no further than to state that we perceive nothing in the overtime and minimum-wage requirements of the FLSA, as applied to SAMTA, that is destructive of state sovereignty or violative of any constitutional provision. SAMTA faces nothing more than the same minimum-wage and overtime obligations that hundreds of thousands of other employers, public as well as private, have to meet.

In these cases, the status of public mass transit simply underscores the extent to which the structural protections of the Constitution insulate the States from federally imposed burdens. When Congress first subjected state mass-transit systems to FLSA obligations in 1966, and when it expanded those obligations in 1974, it simultaneously provided extensive funding for state and local mass transit through [the Urban Mass Transportation Act of 1964 (UMTA)]. In the two decades since its enactment, UMTA has provided over $22 billion in mass transit aid to States and localities. . . . SAMTA and its immediate predecessor have received a substantial amount of UMTA funding, including over $12 million during SAMTA's first two fiscal years alone. . . . Congress' treatment of public mass transit reinforces our conviction that the national political process systematically protects States from the risk of having their functions in that area handicapped by Commerce Clause regulation.[b]

IV

This analysis makes clear that Congress' action in affording SAMTA employees the protections of the wage and hour provisions of the FLSA contravened no affirmative limit on Congress' power under the Commerce Clause. The judgment of the District Court therefore must be reversed.

Of course, we continue to recognize that the States occupy a special and specific position in our constitutional system and that the scope of Congress' authority under the Commerce Clause must reflect that position. But the principal and basic limit on the federal commerce power is that inherent in all congressional

b. Our references to UMTA are not meant to imply that regulation under the Commerce Clause must be accompanied by countervailing financial benefits under the Spending Clause. The application of the FLSA to SAMTA would be constitutional even had Congress not provided federal funding under UMTA.

action — the built-in restraints that our system provides through state participation in federal governmental action. The political process ensures that laws that unduly burden the States will not be promulgated. In the factual setting of these cases the internal safeguards of the political process have performed as intended. . . .

National League of Cities v. Usery, 426 U.S. 833 (1976), is overruled. . . .

POWELL, J., dissenting, joined by Burger, C.J., Rehnquist and O'Connor, JJ.

. . . Because I believe this decision substantially alters the federal system embodied in the Constitution, I dissent.

I

. . . The stability of judicial decision, and with it respect for the authority of this Court, are not served by the precipitous overruling of multiple precedents that we witness in this case.

Whatever effect the Court's decision may have in weakening the application of *stare decisis,* it is likely to be less important than what the Court has done to the Constitution itself. . . . Despite some genuflecting in the Court's opinion to the concept of federalism, today's decision effectively reduces the Tenth Amendment to meaningless rhetoric when Congress acts pursuant to the Commerce Clause. . . .

II

A

Much of the Court's opinion is devoted to arguing that it is difficult to define *a priori* "traditional governmental functions." *National League of Cities* neither engaged in, nor required, such a task. . . . [N]owhere does [the Court] mention that *National League of Cities* adcpted a familiar type of balancing test for determining whether Commerce Clause enactments transgress constitutional limitations imposed by the federal nature of our system of government. . . .

B

Today's opinion does not explain how the States' role in the electoral process guarantees that particular exercises of the Commerce Clause power will not infringe on residual State sovereignty.[a] Members of Congress are elected from the

a. Late in its opinion, the Court suggests that after all there may be some "affirmative limits the constitutional structure might impose on federal action affecting the States under the Commerce Clause." The Court asserts that "[i]n the factual setting of these cases the internal safeguards of the political process have performed as intended." The Court does not explain the basis for this judgment. Nor does it identify the circumstances in which the "political process" may fail and "affirmative limits" are to be imposed. Presumably, such limits are to be determined by the Judicial Branch even though it is "unelected." Today's opinion, however, has rejected the balancing standard and suggests no other standard that would enable a court to determine when there has been a malfunction of the "political process." The Court's failure to specify the "affirmative limits" on federal power, or when and how these limits are to be determined, may well be explained by the transparent fact that any such attempt would be subject to precisely the same objections on which it relies to overrule *National League of Cities.*

various States, but once in office they are members of the federal government.[b] Although the States participate in the Electoral College, this is hardly a reason to view the President as a representative of the States' interest against federal encroachment. We noted recently "the hydraulic pressure inherent within each of the separate Branches to exceed the outer limits of its power." INS v. Chadha, 462 U.S. 919 (1983). The Court offers no reason to think that this pressure will not operate when Congress seeks to invoke its powers under the Commerce Clause, notwithstanding the electoral role of the States.[c]

The Court apparently thinks that the States' success at obtaining federal funds for various projects and exemptions from the obligations of some federal statutes is indicative of the "effectiveness of the federal political process in preserving the States' interests." But such political success is not relevant to the question whether the political *processes* are the proper means of enforcing constitutional limitations. The fact that Congress generally does not transgress constitutional limits on its power to reach State activities does not make judicial review any less necessary to rectify the cases in which it does do so. The States' role in our system of government is a matter of constitutional law, not of legislative grace. . . .

More troubling than the logical infirmities in the Court's reasoning is the result of its holding, i.e., that federal political officials, invoking the Commerce Clause, are the sole judges of the limits of their own power. This result is inconsistent with the fundamental principles of our constitutional system. . . .

III

A

In our federal system, the States have a major role that cannot be preempted by the national government. As contemporaneous writings and the debates at the ratifying conventions make clear, the States' ratification of the Constitution was predicated on this understanding of federalism. Indeed, the Tenth Amendment was adopted specifically to ensure that the important role promised the States by the proponents of the Constitution was realized. [Justice Powell then reviewed the history of the 10th Amendment.] [J]udicial enforcement of the Tenth Amendment is essential to maintaining the federal system so carefully designed by the Framers and adopted in the Constitution.

b. One can hardly imagine this Court saying that because Congress is composed of individuals, individual rights guaranteed by the Bill of Rights are amply protected by the political process. Yet, the position adopted today is indistinguishable in principle. The Tenth Amendment also is an essential part of the Bill of Rights.

c. At one time in our history, the view that the structure of the federal government sufficed to protect the States might have had a somewhat more practical, although not a more logical, basis. . . . [However,] "a variety of structural and political changes in this century have combined to make Congress particularly *insensitive* to state and local values." Advisory Commn. on Intergovernmental Relations [ACIR], Regulatory Federalism: Policy, Process, Impact and Reform 50 (1984). The adoption of the Seventeenth Amendment (providing for direct election of senators), the weakening of political parties on the local level, and the rise of national media, among other things, have made Congress increasingly less representative of State and local interests, and more likely to be responsive to the demands of various national constituencies. Id., at 50-51. . . . Thus, even if one were to ignore the numerous problems with the Court's position in terms of constitutional theory, there would remain serious questions as to its factual premises.

B . . .

The Framers believed that the separate sphere of sovereignty reserved to the States would ensure that the States would serve as an effective "counterpoise" to the power of the federal government. The States would serve this essential role because they would attract and retain the loyalty of their citizens. The roots of such loyalty, the Founders thought, were found in the objects peculiar to state government. . . .

Thus, the harm to the States that results from federal overreaching under the Commerce Clause is not simply a matter of dollars and cents. Nor is it a matter of the wisdom or folly of certain policy choices. Rather, by usurping functions traditionally performed by the States, federal overreaching under the Commerce Clause undermines the constitutionally mandated balance of power between the States and the federal government, a balance designed to protect our fundamental liberties. . . .

D

. . . The Court maintains that the standard approved in *National League of Cities* "dissevers principles of democratic self government." In reaching this conclusion, the Court looks myopically only to persons elected to positions in the federal government. It disregards entirely the far more effective role of democratic self-government at the state and local levels. One must compare realistically the operation of the state and local governments with that of the federal government. Federal legislation is drafted primarily by the staffs of the congressional committees. In view of the hundreds of bills introduced at each session of Congress and the complexity of many of them, it is virtually impossible for even the most conscientious legislators to be truly familiar with many of the statutes enacted. Federal departments and agencies customarily are authorized to write regulations. Often these are more important than the text of the statutes. As is true of the original legislation, these are drafted largely by staff personnel. The administration and enforcement of federal laws and regulations necessarily are largely in the hands of staff and civil service employees. These employees may have little or no knowledge of the States and localities that will be affected by the statutes and regulations for which they are responsible. In any case, they hardly are as accessible and responsible as those who occupy analogous positions in State and local governments.

. . . [M]embers of the immense federal bureaucracy are not elected, know less about the services traditionally rendered by States and localities, and are inevitably less responsive to recipients of such services, than are state legislatures, city councils, boards of supervisors, and state and local commissions, boards, and agencies. It is at these state and local levels — not in Washington, as the Court so mistakenly thinks — that "democratic self-government" is best exemplified.

IV

The question presented in this case is whether the extension of the FLSA to the wages and hours of employees of a city-owned transit system unconstitutionally impinges on fundamental state sovereignty. The Court's sweeping holding does far more than simply answer this question in the negative. In overruling *National League of Cities,* today's opinion apparently authorizes federal control, under the auspices of the Commerce Clause, over the terms and conditions of employment of all state and local employees. . . . The Court's action reflects a serious misunderstanding, if not an outright rejection, of the history of our country and the intention of the Framers of the Constitution.

I return now to the balancing test approved in *National League of Cities* and accepted in *Hodel, Long Island R. Co.,* and FERC v. Mississippi. The Court does not find in this case that the "federal interest is demonstrably greater." 426 U.S., at 856 (Blackmun, J., concurring). No such finding could have been made, for the state interest is compelling. The financial impact on States and localities of displacing their control over wages, hours, overtime regulations, pensions, and labor relations with their employees could have serious, as well as unanticipated, effects on state and local planning, budgeting, and the levying of taxes. . . .

The Court emphasizes that municipal operation of an intra-city mass transit system is relatively new in the life of our country. It nevertheless is a classic example of the type of service traditionally provided by local government. It is *local* by definition. It is indistinguishable in principle from the traditional services of providing and maintaining streets, public lighting, traffic control, water, and sewerage systems. Services of this kind are precisely those "with which citizens are more familiarly and minutely conversant." The Federalist, No. 46, p.316. State and local officials of course must be intimately familiar with these services and sensitive to their quality as well as cost. Such officials also know that their constituents and the press respond to the adequacy, fair distribution, and cost of these services. It is this kind of state and local control and accountability that the Framers understood would insure the vitality and preservation of the federal system that the Constitution explicitly requires.

V

Although the Court's opinion purports to recognize that the States retain some sovereign power, it does not identify even a single aspect of state authority that would remain when the Commerce Clause is invoked to justify federal regulation. . . .

As I view the Court's decision today as rejecting the basic precepts of our federal system and limiting the constitutional role of judicial review, I dissent.

[A dissenting opinion by Justice O'Connor, joined by Justices Powell and Rehnquist, concluded:]

I would not shirk the duty acknowledged by *National League of Cities* and its progeny, and I share Justice Rehnquist's belief [that the earlier principle will "in time again command the support of a majority of this Court" and that the Court will] again assume its constitutional responsibility.

Discussion

1. Note that *Garcia* overruled *National League of Cities,* which in turn had overruled Maryland v. Wirtz. Note also that Justices Rehnquist and O'Connor expressed their hope that *Garcia* would be overruled at some later date. What do these developments suggest about the importance of precedent in constitutional

decisionmaking? Recall Justice Scalia's comments concerning stare decisis in Chapter 1, supra.

2. Consider the following "accountability" rationale for the result reached in *National League of Cities*: The Constitution forbids Congress from imposing costly requirements on the states unless it also provides the revenues to pay for them. What effect might such a rationale have, for example, on federal environmental protection laws? Should states have a constitutional right to burn dirty coal unless Congress underwrites the cost of using cleaner coal?

3. Consider Justice Blackmun's statement in *Garcia* that "the principle and basic limit on the federal commerce power" consists of "the built-in restraints that our system provides through state participation in federal governmental action." Is Blackmun suggesting that, apart from the delegated powers of Article I, the Constitution's procedural rules provide the sole constraints on federal legislation? If not, what additional substantive limits might the Constitution impose on federal action affecting state interests? Assuming that the process rationale of *Garcia* exhausts the constraints on federal control over the states, how convincing is Justice Powell's extension of the rationale to individual rights (used by Justice Powell to show the absurdity of the position)? In what sense do constitutional procedural rules protect the rights of individuals against federal encroachment?

4. Justice Blackmun's argument for abandoning the traditional/nontraditional governmental function distinction of *National League of Cities* rests primarily on the unpredictability of and judicial discretion necessarily involved in making these determinations. To what extent, however, is such judicial line-drawing unique to the federalism issues raised in the preceding cases?

In South Carolina v. Baker, 485 U.S. 505 (1988), South Carolina challenged the constitutionality of Section 310 (b)(1) of the Tax Equity and Fiscal Responsibility Act of 1982 (TEFRA), which eliminated the exemption from federal income tax of interest earned on nonregistered bonds issued by states and local municipalities. The exemption was maintained for registered bonds, whose ownership is recorded on a central list. Both private and public bonds were affected, because Congress determined that nonregistered "bearer bonds" lent themselves to tax avoidance and to use in illegal activities. The State claimed that the regulation of its bonds violated the Tenth Amendment.[39] As a result of TEFRA, states now issue only registered bonds, because the sale of nonregistered bonds would require the payment of substantially higher interest rates in order to overcome the loss of the tax exemption.

The Court upheld the provision. Justice Brennan, writing for the majority, treated the statute as a functional prohibition of nonregistered bonds. He found the Tenth Amendment claim foreclosed by *Garcia*, which he described as holding that the limits of Congress' authority to regulate state activities "are structural — not substantive — i.e., that States must find their protection from congressional regulation through the national political process, not through judicially defined spheres of unregulatable state activity." South Carolina claimed that §310(b)(1) was "imposed by the vote of an uninformed Congress relying on incomplete information." Justice Brennan countered that South Carolina pre-

39. South Carolina also claimed that the tax violated the doctrine of intergovernmental tax immunity. See p. 328 supra.

sented no evidence of such "extraordinary defects in the national political process" as to justify judicial intervention. "Where, as here, the national political *process* did not operate in a defective manner, the Tenth Amendment is not implicated."

Chief Justice Rehnquist and Justice Scalia, concurring in separate opinions, rejected Justice Brennan's reading of *Garcia.* Justice Scalia described that case "as explicitly disclaiming the proposition attributed to it," and quoted, with emphasis, the following sentence from *Garcia*: "These cases do not require us to identify or define what affirmative limits *the constitutional structure* might impose on federal action affecting the States under the Commerce Clause." He went on to say, "I agree only that that structure does not prohibit what the Federal Government has done here."

Chief Justice Rehnquist argued that South Carolina would lose even under *National League of Cities* because the facts showed that the provision had no practical impact on state borrowing practices since tax exemption (and thus lower interest rates) was still available for registered bonds:

> This well-supported conclusion that Section 310(b)(1) has had a *de minimis* impact on the States should end, rather than begin, the Court's constitutional inquiry. Even the more expansive conception of the Tenth Amendment espoused in *National League of Cities* recognized that only congressional action that "operate[s] to directly displace the States' freedom to structure integral operations in areas of traditional governmental functions" runs afoul of the authority granted Congress. The Special Master determined that no such displacement has occurred through the implementation of the TEFRA requirements; I see no need to go further, as the majority does, to discuss the possibility of defects in the national political process that spawned TEFRA.

Justice O'Connor dissented.

Discussion

How might one test South Carolina's assertion that TEFRA was passed by an "uninformed Congress relying on incomplete information"? Does the Constitution require Congress to be informed about matters it regulates? If so, on whom does enforcement of this duty fall? Recall Marshall's opinion in Fletcher v. Peck concerning inquiry into the possibility of illicit motivation.

C. The Political Safeguards of Federalism

In a 1960 article entitled The Political Safeguards of Federalism: The Role of the States in the Composition and Selection of the National Government,[40] Professor Herbert Wechsler argued that

> the national political process in the United States — and especially the role of the states in the composition and selection of the central government — is intrinsically well-adapted to retarding or restraining new intrusions by the center on the domain of the states. Far from a national authority that is expansionist by nature, the inher-

40. Herbert Wechsler, Principles, Politics, and Fundamental Law 49 (1960).

> ent tendency in our system is precisely the reverse, necessitating the widest support before intrusive measures of importance can receive significant consideration, reacting readily to opposition in resistance within the states.

Some of the political safeguards invoked by Professor Wechsler, such as the equal representation of states in the Senate, remain intact. Others, including the extent of state control over the federal election process, have been limited by subsequent judicial decisions, congressional legislation, and constitutional amendments requiring the apportionment of congressional districts on a "one person, one vote" basis, the elimination of poll taxes and literacy tests, limitations on durational residency requirements for voting, and the enfranchisement of citizens over 18.

Professor Wechsler's argument has recently been revived and expanded by Jesse Choper in Judicial Review and the National Political Process (1980). Professor Choper argues that "the Senate . . . was originally intended to be a national legislative guardian against usurpation of state interests," and that legislators "reflect and embody state opinions and are particularly sensitive to local concerns." He adds that "national legislators generally choose to act and vote in conformity with their perceived regional interests, even when these are in conflict with the dictates of political party allegiance" and that "presidential candidates and incumbents [are] sensitive to local public officials in order to secure their nomination or renomination and reelection."

Choper urges the Court to adopt his "federalism proposal":

> The federal judiciary should not decide constitutional questions respecting the ultimate power of the national government vis-à-vis the states; rather the constitutional issue of whether federal action is beyond the authority of the central government and thus violates "states' rights" should be treated as nonjusticiable, final resolution being relegated to the political branches — i.e., Congress and the President.

Choper asserts that "whatever the constitutional limits of national authority in this field may be, the federal political branches are fully capable of guarding against the states' being swallowed up by a central monolith."

Choper's assumptions have been questioned on a number of grounds. Lewis Kaden describes the enormous expansion of federal spending programs administered through state institutions, and comments:

> As Congress increasingly implements national policy by directing the governmental activity of the states, the people in whom sovereignty ultimately resides are left without a clear sense of the persons they may call to account — the national legislators who conceived and ordered a program, or the state officials charged with its implementation. And as the states find their resources and energies increasingly consumed in meeting obligations imposed by the national government, they confront a system of federalism more coopting than cooperative, in which the basic values of pluralism, creativity, participation, and liberty are progressively undermined.[41]

One might also question Choper's analysis if one views the main issue of federalism not as "the states" versus the "central government," but as contests among different regions of the United States for control of national power.

41. Lewis Kaden, Politics, Money, and State Sovereignty, 1979 Colum. L. Rev. 847.

IV. State Regulation of Interstate Commerce: The Current Doctrine and Its Problems

Judicial treatment of the "dormant" (or "negative") commerce clause, involving constraints on the state's authority to regulate interstate commerce even where Congress has not affirmatively exercised its power, did not parallel the decline of economic due process. This section focuses on doctrinal problems posed by contemporary judicial enforcement of the dormant commerce clause.

A. "Anti-Protectionism" and the Movement of Goods

1. The Basic Rationale for Restricting State Power

In a survey of judicial limitations on state power under the commerce clause, Professor Donald Regan states that the American political system embodies a "compromise between unlimited state autonomy and perfect national unity."[42] The former would treat states as nations entitled to set their own policies, while under the latter states would act as mere administrative units bound to enforce a single national policy. Under the compromise "states may not single out foreigners for disadvantageous treatment just because of their foreignness. But, provided they do not single out foreigners, the states need not attend positively to the foreign effects of laws they adopt nor to the distribution between locals and foreigners of the benefits and burdens of those laws." Regan views the possibility of a "protectionist purpose" as central to the continued vitality of the dormant commerce clause. A protectionist statute is one "adopted for the purpose of improving the competitive position of local (in-state) economic actors." Such a statute "seeks only a transfer of wealth from foreigners to their local competitors, which is an improper goal for a state in the context of federal union."

Under Regan's theory, the absence of a protectionist purpose insulates a state law from judicial scrutiny even if it imposes high costs on foreign producers or distributors. Moreover, a protectionist purpose alone does not suffice to invalidate legislation; the statute must also be "analogous in form to the traditional instruments of protectionism — the tariff, the quota, or the outright embargo."

2. The Case Law

In dealing with state laws that are not protectionist on their face, the Court has often weighed the state's interests in achieving its legitimate (nondiscriminatory) objectives against the burden imposed on interstate trade. In Hannibal & St. Joseph Railroad v. Husen, 95 U.S. 465 (1877), the Court struck down a Missouri statute, enacted ostensibly to prevent disease, that prohibited the importation of Texan, Mexican, or Indian cattle during nine months of the year:

42. Donald Regan, The Supreme Court and State Protectionism: Making Sense of the Dormant Commerce Clause, 84 Mich. L. Rev. 1091 (1986).

While we unhesitatingly admit that a State may pass sanitary laws, and laws for the protection of life, liberty, health, or property within its borders; while it may prevent persons and animals suffering under contagious or infectious diseases, or convicts, etc., from entering the State; while for the purpose of self-protection it may establish quarantine and reasonable inspection laws, it may not interfere with transportation into or through the State, beyond what is absolutely necessary for its self-protection. It may not, under the cover of exerting its police powers, substantially prohibit or burden either foreign or interstate commerce.

The Court held that the prohibition was overbroad in terms of the state's legitimate health interests. (See also Minnesota v. Barber, 136 U.S. 313 (1890), invalidating a statute requiring that all meat intended for human consumption be from animals inspected in the state 24 hours before slaughter.) But the Court has sustained more narrowly drawn regulations of the same sort. See, e.g., Kimmish v. Ball, 129 U.S. 217 (1889) (upholding an Iowa law prohibiting possession of cattle that had not wintered north of the southern boundaries of Missouri and Kansas); Mintz v. Baldwin, 289 U.S. 346 (1933) (upholding a New York law prohibiting the importation of cattle unless they were from herds certified free from Bang's disease).

The Court's current approach is illustrated by Dean Milk Co. v. Madison, 340 U.S. 349 (1951), in which appellant, an Illinois milk producer with plants located some distance from the city of Madison, successfully challenged an ordinance requiring that all milk sold in the city be pasteurized within a five-mile radius of downtown. Justice Clark noted that the sanitary regulation of milk was an important objective:

But this regulation . . . in practical effect excludes from distribution in Madison wholesome milk produced and pasteurized in Illinois. . . . In thus erecting an economic barrier protecting a major local industry against competition from without the State, Madison plainly discriminates against interstate commerce. This it cannot do, even in the exercise of its unquestioned power to protect the health and safety of its people, if reasonable nondiscriminatory alternatives, adequate to conserve legitimate local interests, are available. A different view, that the ordinance is valid simply because it professes to be a health measure, would mean that the Commerce Clause of itself imposes no limitation on state action other than those laid down by the Due Process Clause, save for the rare instance where a state artlessly discloses an avowed purpose to discriminate against interstate goods. Our issue then is whether the discrimination inherent in the Madison ordinance can be justified in view of the character of the local interests and the available methods of protecting them.

The Court concluded that "reasonable and adequate alternatives" were available: The city could send its own inspectors to appellant's Illinois plants and charge for the cost of the inspections, or it could adopt §11 of the Model Milk Ordinance recommended by the United States Public Health Service, pursuant to which Illinois officials would inspect the milk under uniform standards, with occasional spot checks by the Public Health Service. Wisconsin health officials had testified that the latter method was as satisfactory as the challenged ordinance.[43]

43. Elsewhere in his opinion, Justice Clark implied that the ordinance may have been discriminatory. He noted that "at the time of trial the Madison milkshed was not of 'Grade A' quality by the standards recommended by the United States Public Health Service, and no milk labeled 'Grade A'

Justice Black, joined by Justices Douglas and Minton, dissented: The ordinance did not "discriminate" against interstate commerce since it prohibited "the sale of milk in Madison by interstate and intrastate producers who prefer to pasteurize over five miles distant from the city"; the Court should not strike down a "bona fide health law . . . on the ground that some other method of safeguarding health would be as good, or better"; and the proposed options were not in fact as good, since "the fee method gives rise to prolonged litigation over the calculation and collection of the charges" and the alternative requires the city to rely on inspection standards and inspectors over which it lacks control and supervision.

In most "protectionist" cases, the complainants are out-of-state manufacturers or distributors who seek unimpeded access to the local market. Philadelphia v. New Jersey, 437 U.S. 617 (1978), involved a modern twist on this situation. A New Jersey law prohibited importing "solid or liquid waste which originated or was collected outside the territorial limits of the State." The law did not benefit the New Jersey landfill owners, who presumably benefitted from the presence of out-of-state bidders for the scarce landfill space. Rather, the law aided local cities and businesses who wanted unimpeded access to the landfills. The Court, with Justice Rehnquist and Chief Justice Burger dissenting, struck down the law. Justice Stewart explained that the state sought to achieve the "presumably legitimate goal" of conservation of landfill facilities "by the illegitimate means of isolating the State from the national economy. . . . [T]here is no basis to distinguish out-of-state waste from domestic waste. If one is inherently harmful, so is the other. Yet New Jersey has banned the former while leaving its landfill sites open to the latter." The law was "an obvious effort to saddle those outside the State with the entire burden of slowing the flow of refuse into New Jersey's remaining landfill sites. That legislative effort is clearly impermissible under the Commerce Clause of the Constitution."[44]

More complicated have been the attempts by states to regulate interstate commerce in order to protect the integrity of otherwise perfectly valid regulatory schemes. For example, in 1933 New York established a minimum price to be paid by milk dealers to producers, later upheld in *Nebbia,* supra; the law also forbade the sale in New York of milk that was purchased outside the state at less than the New York minimum price. Without such a law, milk distributors would purchase

---

was distributed in Madison," while "the milk which appellant seeks to sell in Madison . . . is labeled 'Grade A' under the Chicago ordinance."

In Mintz v. Baldwin, supra, the Court was apparently unaware of the fact that, while New York excluded foreign cattle unless their herds were certified free from Bang's disease, "the disease was widespread in the State and no steps were being taken to see that incoming cattle were being placed in clean herds." Taylor, Burtis & Waugh, Barriers to Internal Trade in Farm Products 93 (1939).

44. Ironically, New Jersey, which now exports more than half its garbage to out-of-state landfills, has recently emerged as a leading opponent of congressional legislation authorizing states to ban such imports. The fight for this legislation is being led by senators from Ohio and Indiana. See Allan Gold, New Jersey Defends Its Policy of Exporting Trash, New York Times, July 19, 1990, at A10. In 1988, Ohio received 1.5 million tons of trash from New Jersey out of a total of 2.4 million tons of imported garbage. Between 1971-1991, the number of landfills in Ohio will have declined from 360 to approximately 130. According to an official of the municipal solid waste program of the Environmental Protection Agency, persons in states like Ohio and Indiana "go through all the trouble of siting a new landfill, or working out a recycling program and they think they have done themselves a favor. Instead, they wake up one day and find they did New Jersey a favor." See William Schmidt, The Midwest Tries to Slow the Flow of Eastern Trash, New York Times, Oct. 1, 1989, at E4. Can New Jersey respond that, at least since 1976, it was forced by the Supreme Court to do other states "a favor" and if the legislation passed would be punished for having done its duty as a member of the *United* States?

cheaper milk from outside the state and thus defeat the purpose of the domestic regulation. Nonetheless, in Baldwin v. G.A.F. Seelig, Inc., 294 U.S. 511 (1935), the Supreme Court unanimously held that New York could not bar a distributor who had purchased milk in Vermont below the New York minimum price from selling it in New York. Justice Cardozo wrote:

> Such a power, if exerted will set a barrier to traffic between one state and another as effective as if customs duties, equal to the price differential, had been laid upon the thing transported. . . . Nice distinctions have been made at times between direct and indirect burdens. They are irrelevant when the avowed purpose of the obstruction, as well as its necessary tendency, is to suppress or mitigate the consequences of competition between the states. Such an obstruction is direct by the very terms of the hypothesis. We are reminded in the opinion below that a chief occasion of the commerce clause was "the mutual jealousies and aggressions of the States, taking form in customs barriers and other economic retaliation." If New York, in order to promote the economic welfare of her farmers, may guard them against competition with the cheaper prices of Vermont, the door has been opened to rivalries and reprisals that were meant to be averted by subjecting commerce between the states to the power of the nation.
>
> . . . [T]he Constitution was framed . . . upon the theory that the peoples of the several states must sink or swim together, and that in the long run prosperity and salvation are in union and not division. . . .
>
> Neither the power to tax nor the police power may be used by the state of destination with the aim and effect of establishing an economic barrier against competition with the products of another state. . . . Restrictions so contrived are an unreasonable clot on the mobility of Commerce. They set up what is the equivalent of a rampart of customs duties designed to neutralize advantages belonging to the place of origin. They are thus hostile in conception as well as burdensome in result.

Two years after *Seelig*, in Henneford v. Silas Mason Co. 300 U.S. 577 (1937), the Court upheld the state of Washington's use tax. Washington imposed a 2 percent sales tax on articles sold within the state and a "compensating tax" of 2 percent on the price of goods (plus their transportation to Washington) purchased out of the state and used in Washington; a prorated exemption was allowed for sales taxes paid in other states. As in *Seelig*, Justice Cardozo wrote for a unanimous Court:

> [One effect of the scheme] must be that retail sellers in Washington will be helped to compete upon terms of equality with retail dealers in other states who are exempt from a sales tax or any corresponding burden. Another effect . . . must be to avoid the likelihood of a drain upon the revenues of the state, buyers being no longer tempted to place their orders in other states in the effort to escape payment of the tax on local sales. . . .
>
> Equality is the theme that runs through all sections of the statute. . . . When the account is made up, the stranger from afar is subject to no greater burdens as a consequence of ownership than the dweller within the gates. . . . In each situation the burden borne by the owner is balanced by an equal burden when the sale is strictly local. . . .
>
> Baldwin v. G.A.F. Seelig, Inc. is invoked by appellees as decisive of the controversy, but the case is far apart from this one. . . . New York was attempting to project its legislation within the borders of another state by regulating the price to be paid in that state for milk acquired there. She said in effect to farmers in Vermont: your

milk cannot be sold by dealers to whom you ship it in New York unless you sell it to them in Vermont at a price determined here. What Washington is saying to sellers beyond her borders is something very different. In substance what she says is this: You may ship your goods in such amounts and at such prices as you please, but the goods when used in Washington after the transit is completed, will share an equal burden with goods that have been purchased here.

. . . [Appellees seek to stigmatize the tax] as equivalent to a protective tariff. . . . Catch words and labels, such as the words "protective tariff," are subject to the dangers that lurk in metaphors and symbols, and must be watched with circumspection. . . . A tariff, whether protective or for revenue, burdens the very act of importation, and if laid by a state upon its commerce with another is equally unlawful whether protection or revenue is the motive back of it. But a tax upon use . . . after importation is over, is not a clog on the process of importation at all.

Are *Silas Mason* and *Seelig* distinguishable in terms of national policy, or is the difference only formal? Would the Court have sustained a New York tax on milk purchased out of state for sale in New York equal to the difference between the price paid the foreign producer and New York's minimum price for domestic producers?

More recently, in Hunt v. Washington State Apple Advertising Commission, 432 U.S. 333 (1977), a unanimous Court (Justice Rehnquist not participating) invalidated a North Carolina statute that required all closed containers of apples shipped into the state to be marked with "no grade other than the applicable U.S. grade or standard," with the effect of excluding containers displaying the apple grades of the state of Washington. Chief Justice Burger wrote that North Carolina's legitimate interest in protecting its consumers against confusion and deception from the variety of state grading schemes must be accommodated with the interest of a "national 'common market.' "

In Minnesota v. Clover Leaf Creamery Co., 449 U.S. 459 (1981), Justice Brennan distinguished *Hunt* and Philadelphia v. New Jersey, in upholding a Minnesota law banning the retail sale of milk in plastic nonreturnable, nonrefillable containers, while permitting its sale in other nonreturnable, nonrefillable containers, such as paperboard cartons. He concluded that the law was not motivated by economic protectionist aims, and that its burden fell on manufacturers both within and without the state. "Even granting that the out-of-state plastics industry is burdened relatively more heavily than the Minnesota pulpwood industry, we find that this burden is not 'clearly excessive' in light of the substantial state interest in promoting conservation of energy and easing solid waste disposal problems." Justices Powell and Stevens dissented, arguing that the record did not justify the Court's assertion that the statute was motivated by legitimate concerns.

Finally, a series of cases involve State *A*'s conditioning its treatment of the products of other states on the treatment by those states of State *A*'s products. In Sporhase v. Nebraska, 458 U.S. 941 (1982), the Court considered a provision of a Nebraska law that conditioned the withdrawal of groundwater from any well within Nebraska intended for use in an adjoining state upon reciprocal treatment by that state. The appellants owned contiguous tracts of land in adjoining Nebraska and Colorado counties and used the groundwater from the Nebraska property to irrigate both the Nebraska and Colorado tracts. Colorado law forbids the exportation of its groundwater. The Nebraska Supreme Court upheld an injunction prohibiting transfer of the Nebraska water to Colorado, and the well owners appealed.

Justice Stevens wrote for the Court, striking down the Nebraska statute:

> The only purpose that appellee advances for §46-613.01 is to conserve and preserve diminishing sources of ground water. The purpose is unquestionably legitimate and highly important, and the other aspects of Nebraska's ground water regulation demonstrate that it is genuine. . . .
>
> Moreover, in the absence of a contrary view expressed by Congress, we are reluctant to condemn as unreasonable measures taken by a State to conserve and preserve for its own citizens this vital resource in times of severe shortage. Our reluctance stems from the "confluence of [several] realities." Hicklin v. Orbeck, 437 U.S. 518, 534 (1978). First, a State's power to regulate the use of water in times and places of shortage for the purpose of protecting the health of its citizens — and not simply the health of its economy — is at the core of its police power. For Commerce Clause purposes, we have long recognized a difference between economic protectionism, on the one hand, and health and safety regulation, on the other. Second, the legal expectation that under certain circumstances each State may restrict water within its borders has been fostered over the years not only by our equitable apportionment decrees, but also by the negotiation and enforcement of interstate compacts. Our law therefore has recognized the relevance of state boundaries in the allocation of scarce water resources. Third, although appellee's claim to public ownership of Nebraska ground water cannot justify a total denial of federal regulatory power, it may support a limited preference for its own citizens in the utilization of the resource. In this regard, it is relevant that appellee's claim is logically more substantial than claims to public ownership of other natural resources. Finally, given appellee's conservation efforts, the continuing availability of ground water in Nebraska is not simply happenstance; the natural resource has some indicia of a good publicly produced and owned in which a State may favor its own citizens in times of shortage. . . .
>
> Appellants, however, do challenge the requirement that "the state in which the water is to be used grants reciprocal rights to withdraw and transport ground water from that state for use in the State of Nebraska" — the reciprocity provision that troubled the Chief Justice of the Nebraska Supreme Court. Because Colorado forbids the exportation of its ground water, the reciprocity provision operates as an explicit barrier to commerce between the two States. The State therefore bears the initial burden of demonstrating a close fit between the reciprocity requirement and its asserted local purpose.
>
> The reciprocity requirement fails to clear this initial hurdle. For there is no evidence that this restriction is narrowly tailored to the conservation and preservation rationale. Even though the supply of water in a particular well may be abundant, or perhaps even excessive, and even though the most beneficial use of that water might be in another State, such water may not be shipped into a neighboring State that does not permit its water to be used in Nebraska. If it could be shown that the State as a whole suffers a water shortage, that the intrastate transportation of water from areas of abundance to areas of shortage is feasible regardless of distance, and that the importation of water from adjoining States would roughly compensate for any exportation to those States, then the conservation and preservation purpose might be credibly advanced for the reciprocity provision. A demonstrably arid state conceivably might be able to marshall evidence to establish a close means-end relationship between even a total ban on the exportation of water and a purpose to conserve and preserve water. Appellee, however, does not claim that such evidence exists. We therefore are not persuaded that the reciprocity requirement — when superim-

posed on the first three restrictions in the statute — significantly advances the State's legitimate conservation and preservation interest; it surely is not narrowly tailored to serve the purpose. The reciprocity requirement does not survive the "strictest scrutiny" reserved for facially discriminatory legislation. . . .

The reciprocity requirement of Neb. Rev. Stat. §46-613.01 violates the Commerce Clause. We leave to the state courts the question whether the invalid portion is severable.

More recently, in New Energy Co. of Indiana v. Limbach, 486 U.S. 269 (1988), the Court reviewed an Ohio law awarding a tax credit for the sale by fuel dealers of ethanol produced in Ohio or in a state that granted a similar tax advantage to Ohio-produced ethanol. An Indiana producer challenged the constitutionality of the statute. Justice Scalia wrote for a unanimous Court invalidating the law.

The Ohio provision at issue here explicitly deprives certain products of generally available beneficial tax treatment because they are made in certain other states, and thus on its face appears to violate the cardinal requirement of nondiscrimination. [Ohio] argue[s], however, that the availability of the tax credit to some out-of-state manufacturers (those in States that give tax advantages to Ohio-produced ethanol) shows that the Ohio provision, far from discriminating against interstate commerce, is likely to promote it, by encouraging other States to enact similar tax advantages that will spur the interstate sale of ethanol. We rejected a similar contention in an earlier "reciprocity" case, Great Atlantic & Pacific Tea Co. v. Cottrell, 424 U.S. 366 (1976). The regulation at issue there permitted milk from out of State to be sold in Mississippi only if the State of origin accepted Mississippi milk on a reciprocal basis. Mississippi put forward, among other arguments, the assertion that "the reciprocity requirement is in effect a free-trade provision, advancing the identical national interest that is served by the Commerce Clause." In response, we said that "Mississippi may not use the threat of economic isolation as a weapon to force sister States to enter into even a desirable reciprocity agreement." More recently, we characterized a Nebraska reciprocity requirement for the export of ground water from the State as "facially discriminatory legislation" which merited " 'strictest scrutiny.' " Sporhase v. Nebraska, 458 U.S. 941, 958 (1982).

It is true that in *Cottrell* and *Sporhase* the effect of a State's refusal to accept the offered reciprocity was total elimination of all transport of the subject product into or out of the offering State; whereas in the present case the only effect of refusal is that the out-of-state product is placed at a substantial commercial disadvantage through discriminatory tax treatment. That makes no difference for purposes of Commerce Clause analysis.

3. *On "Balancing"*

Professor Regan offers his antiprotectionist thesis not only as the best normative approach to the dormant commerce clause, but also as an accurate description of the case law. He denies that the Court has used a "balancing test" in movement-of-goods cases to invalidate nonprotectionist laws that have too costly an impact on interstate commerce.

Although a number of cases, including *Dean Milk* and *Hunt,* supra, may be ambiguous in this respect, Pike v. Bruce Church, Inc., 397 U.S. 137 (1970), which the Court frequently cites, presents a counter-example to Professor Regan's thesis. The case involved an Arizona statute requiring that all cantaloupes grown in Arizona and offered for sale be packed in Arizona before shipment for sale out of state. The statute was challenged by Bruce Church, which wished to ship uncrated cantaloupes to nearby facilities in Blythe, California, for packing and processing. The stipulated facts indicated that it would cost the company about $200,000 to build a packing facility within Arizona.

Justice Stewart, writing for a unanimous Court, noted that "statutes expressly requiring that certain kinds of processing be done in the home State before shipment to a sister State . . . have been consistently invalidated by this Court under the Commerce Clause." He then stated what has become known as the "*Pike* test" for analyzing the constitutionality of legislation under the dormant commerce clause:

> Although the criteria for determining the validity of state statutes affecting interstate commerce have been variously stated, the general rule that emerges can be phrased as follows: Where the statute regulates evenhandedly to effectuate a legitimate local public interest, and its effects on interstate commerce are only incidental, it will be upheld unless the burden imposed in such commerce is clearly excessive in relation to the putative local benefits. If a legitimate local purpose is found, then the question becomes one of degree. And the extent of the burden that will be tolerated will of course depend on the nature of the local interest involved, and on whether it could be promoted as well with a lesser impact on interstate activities. Occasionally the Court has candidly undertaken a balancing approach in resolving these issues, Southern Pacific Co. v. Arizona, 325 U.S. 761, but more frequently it has spoken in terms of "direct" and "indirect" effects and burdens.

Applying this test, Justice Stewart proceeded to invalidate the Arizona statute, finding Arizona's interest in protecting the reputation of its produce "minimal" when placed against the requirement that the packer "build and operate an unneeded $200,000 packing plant in the state."

Professor Regan argues that the same result would be reached under his own antiprotectionist analysis.[45] He notes that the "asserted purpose is protectionist," since "the state wants these cantaloupes labeled as Arizona cantaloupes because that will improve the competitive position of the Arizona cantaloupe industry." Regan views the Arizona statute as "an explicit embargo on the export of unprocessed goods," whose "inevitable tendency is to advantage Arizona packing workers."

It is by no means clear, however, that the Court has adopted the categorical analysis proposed by Regan rather than the *Pike* balancing test. Consider Maine v. Taylor, 477 U.S. 131 (1986). Taylor, a dealer in live bait fish, had attempted to import 158,000 golden shiners, a species of minnow, in spite of a Maine statute prohibiting the importation of live bait fish. The shipment was intercepted by federal authorities, who charged him with violating a federal statute making it a crime "to import . . . any fish . . . in violation of any law or regulation of any State. . . ." Taylor defended on the ground that the underlying Maine law was unconstitutional.

45. Professor Regan discusses the case at 84 Mich. L. Rev. 1209-1220, from which the quotations immediately below are taken.

Justice Blackmun, in upholding the Maine statute, emphasized the distinction "between state statutes that burden interstate transactions only incidentally, and those that affirmatively discriminate against such transactions." The first category of statutes "violate the Commerce Clause only if the burdens they impose on interstate trade are 'clearly excessive in relation to the putative local benefits,' Pike v. Bruce Church." Statutes in the second category "are subject to more demanding scrutiny." "[O]nce a state law is shown to discriminate against interstate commerce 'either on its face or in practical effect,' the burden falls on the State to demonstrate both that the statute 'serves a legitimate local purpose,' and that this purpose could not be served as well by available nondiscriminatory means."

Justice Blackmun then considered the evidence in this case:

> Maine offered three scientific experts who testified that live baitfish imported into the State posed two significant threats to Maine's unique and fragile fisheries. First, Maine's population of wild fish — including its own indigenous golden shiners — would be placed at risk by three types of parasites prevalent in out-of-state-baitfish, but not common to wild fish in Maine. Second, non-native species inadvertently included in shipments of live baitfish could disturb Maine's aquatic ecology to an unpredictable extent by competing with native fish for food or habitat, by preying on native species, or by disrupting the environment in more subtle ways. . . .
>
> Maine has a legitimate interest in guarding against imperfectly understood environmental risks, despite the possibility that they may ultimately prove to be negligible. "[T]he constitutional principles underlying the commerce clause cannot be read as requiring the State of Maine to sit idly by and wait until potentially irreversible environmental damage has occurred or until the scientific community agrees on what disease organisms are or are not dangerous before it acts to avoid such consequences."

The Court also agreed with the district court in rejecting the proffered evidence of Maine's protectionist bias. Thus the law was constitutional. Justice Stevens dissented.

The Court cited Professor Regan's analysis in CTS Corp. v. Dynamics Corp. of America, 481 U.S. 69 (1987), which upheld an Indiana law designed to limit hostile takeovers of corporations chartered in Indiana by allowing "disinterested" shareholders to limit the voting rights of those seeking to take over the corporation. As Justice Powell explained: "The practical effect of [the law] is to condition acquisition of control of a corporation on approval of a majority of the pre-existing disinterested shareholders."

The respondent argued that it primarily affected out-of-state entities because, "as a practical matter, most hostile tender offers are launched by offerors outside Indiana." However, the Court found it important that the law did not formally discriminate between in-state and out-of-state tender offers. " 'The fact that the burden of a state regulation falls on some interstate companies does not, by itself, establish a claim of discrimination against interstate commerce.' Because nothing in the Indiana Act imposes a greater burden on out-of-state offerors than it does on similarly situated Indiana offerors, we reject the contention that the Act discriminates against interstate commerce."[46]

46. The Court of Appeals below, through Judge Posner, had argued that the Act violated the Commerce Clause because of its potential to hinder tender offers and thus render less efficient the national marketplace, in whose exchanges CTS stock was freely traded. The Supreme Court empha-

B. State Regulation of Transportation

Recall Cooley v. Board of Wardens, 53 U.S. (12 How.) 299 (1851), Chapter 3 supra, which articulated a functional standard for adjudicating dormant commerce clause cases. Note that *Cooley* involved interstate transportation, as did several earlier cases, such as *Blackbird Creek Marsh,* and *Wheeling Bridge,* both of which involved hindrances to the navigability of rivers. Professor Regan concedes that "transportation" cases should be covered by a somewhat different principle than his "anti-protectionist" doctrine outlined above: "[T]he existence of an effective transportation network is essential to genuine political union just as the suppression of protectionism is essential to genuine political union."

Although the actual *Cooley* doctrine went into a long hibernation almost as soon as it was born, transportation cases continued to come regularly before the Court. Instead of analyzing state laws in the terms suggested by *Cooley* — whether the subject being regulated demanded diverse or uniform regulation, the Court distinguished between "direct" and "indirect" burdens on interstate commerce.

The attack on the direct/indirect approach was led by Justice Stone, who is largely responsible for the modernization of dormant commerce clause doctrine. In DiSanto v. Pennsylvania, 273 U.S. 34 (1927), the Court struck down a state license fee for travel agents selling steamship tickets to foreign countries, granted only on proof of good character and fitness, on the ground that "[a] state statute which by its necessary operation directly interferes with or burdens foreign commerce is a prohibited regulation and invalid, regardless of the purpose with which it was passed." Joined by Justices Brandeis and Holmes, Justice Stone dissented:[47]

> In this case the traditional test of the limit of state action by inquiring whether the interference with commerce is direct or indirect seems to be too mechanical, too uncertain in its application, and too remote from actualities to be of value. In this making use of the expressions, "direct" and "indirect interference" with commerce, we are doing little more than using labels to describe a result rather than any trustworthy formula by which it is reached.

---

sized that traditional role of the state "as overseer of corporate governance" and stated that "[t]he Constitution does not require the States to subscribe to any particular economic theory." Justice Powell wrote:

> The very commodity that is traded in the [national] securities market is one whose characteristics are defined by state law. Similarly, the very commodity that is traded in the 'market for corporate control' — the corporation — is one that owes its existence to state law. Indiana need not define these commodities as other States do; it need only provide that residents and nonresidents have equal access to them.

Justice White, joined by Justices Blackmun and Stevens, dissented, arguing that the Commerce Clause "was included in our Constitution by the Framers to prevent the very type of economic protectionism Indiana's Control Share Chapter represents." They noted that one of the articulated goals of the Chapter was to enable the shareholders of Indiana corporations more easily to prevent the takeover of corporations by persons who might move the corporate assets to other states. The means of such prevention is the refusal of voting rights, which Justice White saw likely to have the effect of "prevent[ing] individual investors, including out-of-state stockholders, from selling their stock to an out-of-state tender offeror." According to the dissenters, "the Chapter will inevitably be used to block interstate transactions in [the stock of Indiana corporations]. Because the Commerce Clause protects the 'interstate market' in such securities, and because the Control Share Chapter substantially interferes with this interstate market, the Chapter clearly conflicts with the Commerce Clause."

47. *DiSanto* was overruled in California v. Thompson, 313 U.S. 109 (1941).

> . . . [I]t seems clear that those interferences not deemed forbidden are to be sustained, not because the effect on commerce is nominally indirect, but because a consideration of all the facts and circumstances such as the nature of the regulation, its function, the character of the business involved and the actual effect on the flow of commerce, lead to the conclusion that the regulation concerns interests peculiarly local and does not infringe the national interest in maintaining the freedom of commerce across state lines.

In the 1930s and 1940s, largely under Stone's influence, the *Cooley* standard began to reemerge and to provide the foundation for contemporary doctrine concerning state regulations of interstate transportation.

SOUTH CAROLINA STATE HIGHWAY DEPT. v. BARNWELL BROTHERS, 303 U.S. 177 (1938): [A trucking company challenged a state law that excluded from South Carolina's highways trucks wider than 90 inches or weighing more than 20,000 pounds. The extensive record showed that 85 to 90 percent of trucks in interstate commerce were 96 inches wide and had a loaded gross weight greater than ten tons. Every state other than South Carolina permitted trucks 96 inches wide, and only four other states had such low weight limitations. The district court found that excessive axle weight, rather than gross weight, caused highway deterioration and that if loads were properly distributed among the axles, gross weights greater than ten tons would not damage the roads. On the other hand, it found that the width limitations did increase visibility and make it safer to pass, especially on 100 miles of the state's highways that were unusually narrow; that 60 percent of the state's highways were of substandard strength and durability; and that it was more difficult to police an axle weight than a gross weight requirement. The district court nonetheless struck down the law as an unreasonable burden on interstate commerce.

In reversing the judgment, Justice Stone articulated a two-part inquiry: "whether the state legislature . . . has acted within its province, and whether the means of regulation chosen are reasonably adapted to the end sought." With respect to the first, he noted that South Carolina's regulation was nondiscriminatory and "a safety measure and . . . a means of securing the economical use of its highways".]

STONE, J. . . . Ever since Willson v. Black Bird Creek Marsh Co. and Cooley v. Board of Port Wardens, it has been recognized that there are matters of local concern, the regulation of which unavoidably involves some regulation of interstate commerce but which, because of their local character and their number and diversity, may never be fully dealt with by Congress. Notwithstanding the commerce clause, such regulation in the absence of Congressional action has for the most part been left to the states by the decisions of this Court, subject to the other applicable constitutional restraints.

. . . Few subjects of state regulation are so peculiarly of local concern as is the use of state highways. . . . Unlike the railroads, local highways are built, owned and maintained by the state or its municipal subdivisions. The state has a primary and immediate concern in their safe and economical administration. The present regulations, or any others of like purpose, if they are to accomplish their end, must be applied alike to interstate and intrastate traffic both moving in large volume over the highways. The fact that they affect alike shippers in interstate and intrastate commerce in large numbers within as well as without the state is a safeguard against their abuse. . . .

[With respect to the second inquiry he wrote:] [C]ourts do not sit as legislatures, either state or national. They cannot act as Congress does when, after weighing all the conflicting interests, state and national, it determines when and how much the state regulatory power shall yield to the larger interests of a national commerce. And in reviewing a state highway regulation where Congress has not acted, a court is not called upon, as are state legislatures, to determine what, in its judgment, is the most suitable restriction to be applied of those that are possible, or to choose that one which in its opinion is best adapted to all the diverse interests affected. When the action of a legislature is within the scope of its power, fairly debatable questions as to its reasonableness, wisdom and propriety are not for the determination of courts, but for the legislative body on which rests the duty and responsibility of decision. . . .

Hence, in reviewing the present determination we examine the record, not to see whether the findings of the court below are supported by evidence, but to ascertain upon the whole record whether it is possible to say that the legislative choice is without rational basis. Not only does the record fail to exclude that possibility, but it shows affirmatively that there is adequate support for the legislative judgment.

Discussion

1. How would *Barnwell* have been decided under the *Cooley* uniform-local standard? Does the fact that the state owns its highways make the regulation "local" in the sense that *Cooley* uses the concept? In some other sense? (Massive federal funding of highways is a fairly recent phenomenon. But should it have made any difference if appellants had argued only for the right to use highways financed in part by federal funds, or only for the right to use highways designated "interstate"?) Is the width or weight of trucks a matter demanding national uniformity? Is the South Carolina regulation likely to conflict with requirements imposed by other states?

2. Is there a similarity between the commerce clause challenge to the South Carolina statute in *Barnwell* (1938) and the substantive due process challenge to, say, the filled-milk statute in *Carolene Products* (1938), p. 354 supra? Is there a similarity in the Court's approach to reviewing state legislation challenged under these clauses?

3. In Buck v. Kuykendall, 267 U.S. 307 (1925), appellant, who wished to transport passengers and freight by road between Seattle, Washington, and Portland, Oregon, obtained a certificate of public convenience and necessity from Oregon but was denied a like certificate by Washington on the ground that the route was already adequately served by other carriers. The Court held that a state could not require a certificate for interstate carriage, Justice Brandeis writing:

> [The state's] primary purpose is not regulation with a view to safety or to conservation of the highways, but the prohibition of competition. . . . Moreover, it determines whether the prohibition shall be applied by resort, through state officials, to a test which is peculiarly within the province of the federal action — the existence of

> adequate facilities for conducting interstate commerce. The vice of the legislation is dramatically exposed by the fact that the state of Oregon has issued its certificate which may be deemed equivalent to a legislative declaration that, despite existing facilities, public convenience and necessity required the establishment by Buck of the auto stage line between Seattle and Portland. Thus, the provision of the Washington statute is a regulation, not of the use of its own highways, but of interstate commerce. Its effect upon such commerce is not merely to burden, but to obstruct, it. Such state action is forbidden by the Commerce Clause . . .

In Bradley v. Public Utilities Commission, 289 U.S. 92 (1933), the Court sustained Ohio's denial of a certificate of public convenience and necessity to operate a motor carrier line between Cleveland and Flint, Michigan. The state commission had determined that the road "is so badly congested by established motor vehicle operations, that the addition of the applicant's proposed service would create and maintain an excessive and undue hazard to the safety and security of the traveling public, and the property upon such highway." Justice Brandeis again wrote for the Court:

> [In Buck v. Kuykendall] the promotion of safety was merely an incident of the denial. Its purpose was to prevent competition deemed undesirable. . . . In the case at bar, the purpose of the denial was to promote safety; and the test employed was congestion of the highway. The effect of the denial upon interstate commerce was merely an incident.
>
> Protection against accidents, as against crime, presents a local problem. Regulation to ensure safety is an exercise of the police power. It is primarily a state function whether the locus be private property or the public highways. . . . Safety may require that no additional vehicles be admitted to the highway. The Commerce Clause is not violated by denial of the certificate to the appellant, if upon adequate evidence denial is deemed necessary to promote the public safety. . . . The evidence [of traffic congestion] was adequate to support the finding . . .

The utility of anticompetitive regulation is a subject of continuing dispute; however, the restriction of competition on particular transportation routes is a venerable governmental practice. Nothing in Buck v. Kuykendall denigrates the notion of such regulation in general. Why, then, did the Court forbid Washington to limit the number of interstate carriers to prevent excessive competition but allow Ohio to limit the number of carriers to promote highway safety? Is the distinction responsive to the *Cooley* standard? To the somewhat different notion of "localness" adopted in *Barnwell?* Did the legislation in *Buck* pose a greater danger of discrimination against another state than that in *Bradley?*

SOUTHERN PACIFIC CO. v. ARIZONA, 325 U.S. 761 (1945): [The state sued to recover statutory penalties against appellant for violations of the Arizona Train Limit Law of 1912, which prohibited operating trains of more than 14 passenger or 70 freight cars within Arizona. The appellant argued that the statute unconstitutionally burdened interstate commerce. The state defended the law as a measure against "slack action" accidents caused by the cumulative whip-like effect of the free movement between cars. The Court invalidated the statute.]

STONE, C.J. . . . [I]n the absence of conflicting legislation by Congress, there is a residuum of power in the state to make laws governing matters of local concern which nevertheless in some measure affect interstate commerce or even to some extent, regulate it. Thus the states may regulate matters which, because of their number and diversity, may never be adequately dealt with by Congress. When the regulation of matters of local concern is local in character and effect, and its impact on the national commerce does not seriously interfere with its operation, and the consequent incentive to deal with them nationally is slight, such regulation has been generally held to be within state authority.

But ever since Gibbons v. Ogden, the states have not been deemed to have authority to impede substantially the free flow of commerce from state to state, or to regulate those phases of the national commerce which because of the need of national uniformity, demand that their regulation, if any, be prescribed by a single authority.[a] Whether or not this long-recognized distribution of power between the national and the state governments is predicated upon the implications of the commerce clause itself, . . . or upon the presumed intention of Congress, where Congress has not spoken, the result is the same.

In the application of these principles some enactments may be found to be plainly within and others plainly without state power. But between these extremes lies the infinite variety of cases, in which regulation of local matters may also operate as a regulation of commerce, in which reconciliation of the conflicting claims of state and national power is to be attained only by some appraisal and accommodation of the competing demands of the state and national interests involved. . . .

Hence the matters for ultimate determination here are the nature and extent of the burden which the state regulation of interstate trains, adopted as a safety measure, imposes on interstate commerce, and whether the relative weights of the state and national interests involved are such as to make inapplicable the rule, generally observed, that the free flow of interstate commerce and its freedom from local restraints in matters requiring uniformity of regulation are interests safeguarded by the commerce clause from state interference.

. . . [T]he facts found by the state trial court . . . show that the operation of long trains, that is trains of more than fourteen passenger and more than seventy freight cars, is standard practice over the main lines of the railroads of the United States and that, if the length of trains is to be regulated at all, national uniformity in the regulation adopted, such as only Congress can prescribe, is practically indispensable to the operation of an efficient and economical national railway system. . . .

In Arizona, approximately 93% of the freight traffic and 95% of the passenger traffic is interstate. Because of the Train Limit Law appellant is required to haul over 30% more trains in Arizona than would otherwise have been necessary. The record shows a definite relationship between operating costs and the length of trains, the increase in length resulting in a reduction of operating costs per car. The additional cost of operation of trains complying with the Train Limit Law in Arizona amounts for the two railroads traversing that state to about $1,000,000 a year. The reduction in train lengths also impedes efficient operation. . . .

a. In applying this rule the Court has often recognized that to the extent that the burden of state regulation falls on interests outside the state, it is unlikely to be alleviated by the operation of those political restraints normally exerted when interests within the state are affected.

The unchallenged findings leave no doubt that the Arizona Train Limit Law imposes a serious burden on the interstate commerce conducted by appellant. . . . Compliance with a state statute limiting train lengths requires interstate trains of a length lawful in other states to be broken up and reconstituted as they enter each state according as it may impose varying limitations upon train lengths. The alternative is for the carrier to conform to the lowest train limit restriction of any of the states through which its trains pass, whose laws thus control the carriers' operations both within and without the regulating state. . . .

If one state may regulate train lengths, so may all the others, and they need not prescribe the same maximum limitation. The practical effect of such regulation is to control train operations beyond the boundaries of the state exacting it because of the necessity of breaking up and reassembling long trains, at the nearest terminal points before entering and after leaving the regulating state. The serious impediment to the free flow of commerce by the local regulation of train lengths and the practical necessity that such regulation, if any, must be prescribed by a single body having a nation-wide authority are apparent.

The trial court found that the Arizona law had no reasonable relation to safety, and made train operation more dangerous. Examination of the evidence and the detailed findings makes it clear that this conclusion was rested on facts found which indicate that such increased danger of accident and personal injury as may result from the greater length of trains is more than offset by the increase in the number of accidents resulting from the larger number of trains when train lengths are reduced. In considering the effect of the statute as a safety measure, therefore, the . . . decisive question is whether in the circumstances the total effect of the law as a safety measure in reducing accidents and casualties is so slight or problematical as not to outweigh the national interest in keeping interstate commerce free from interferences which seriously impede it and subject it to local regulation which does not have a uniform effect on the interstate train journey which it interrupts.

We think, as the trial court found, that the Arizona Train Limit Law, viewed as a safety measure, affords at most slight and dubious advantage, if any, over unregulated train lengths, because it results in an increase in the number of trains and train operations and the consequent increase in train accidents of a character generally more severe than those due to slack action. Its undoubted effect on the commerce is the regulation, without securing uniformity, of the length of trains operated in interstate commerce, which lack is itself a primary cause of preventing the free flow of commerce by delaying it and by substantially increasing its cost and impairing its efficiency. . . .

Appellees especially rely on the full train crew cases,[48] . . . and also on South Carolina Highway Dept. v. Barnwell Bros. as supporting the state's authority to regulate the length of interstate trains. While the full train crew laws undoubtedly placed an added financial burden on the railroads in order to serve a local interest, they did not obstruct interstate transportation or seriously impede it. They had no effects outside the state beyond those of picking up and setting down the extra employees at the state boundaries; they involved no wasted use of

48. Chicago, R.I. & P.R. Co. v. Arkansas, 219 U.S. 453 (1911); St. Louis, I.M. & S.R. Co. v. Arkansas, 240 U.S. 518 (1916); Missouri Pac. R. Co. v. Norwood, 283 U.S. 249 (1931), 290 U.S. 600 (1933), sustaining laws specifying the minimum number of employees who must serve as part of a train crew. See Brotherhood of Locomotive Firemen v. Chicago, R.I. & P.R. Co., 393 U.S. 129 (1968).

facilities or serious impairment of transportation efficiency, which are among the factors of controlling weight here. In sustaining those laws the Court considered the restriction a minimal burden on the commerce. . . .

South Carolina Highway Dept. v. Barnwell Bros. was concerned with the power of the state to regulate the weight and width of motor cars passing interstate over its highways, a legislative field over which the state has a far more extensive control than over interstate railroads. . . . [W]e were at pains to point out that there are few subjects of state regulation affecting interstate commerce which are so peculiarly of local concern as is the use of the state's highways. Unlike the railroads local highways are built, owned and maintained by the state or its municipal subdivisions. The state is responsible for their safe and economical administration. Regulations affecting the safety of their use must be applied alike to intrastate and interstate traffic. The fact that they affect alike shippers in interstate and intrastate commerce in great numbers, within as well as without the state, is a safeguard against regulatory abuses. Their regulation is akin to quarantine measures, game laws, and like local regulations of rivers, harbors, piers, and docks, with respect to which the state has exceptional scope for the exercise of its regulatory power, and which, Congress not acting, have been sustained even though they materially interfere with interstate commerce.

The contrast between the present regulation and the full train crew laws in point of their effects on the commerce, and the like contrast with the highway safety regulations, in point of the nature of the subject of regulation and the state's interest in it, illustrate and emphasize the considerations which enter into a determination of the relative weights of state and national interests where state regulation affecting interstate commerce is attempted. Here examination of all the relevant factors makes it plain that the state interest is outweighed by the interest of the nation in an adequate, economical and efficient railway transportation service, which must prevail.

BLACK, J., dissenting. . . . Congress knew about the Arizona law. It is common knowledge that the Interstate Commerce Committees of the House and the Senate keep in close and intimate touch with the affairs of railroads and other national means of transportation. . . . The history of congressional consideration of this problem leaves little if any room to doubt that the choice of Congress to leave the state free in this field was a deliberate choice, which was taken with a full knowledge of the complexities of the problems and the probable need for diverse regulations in different localities. . . .

When we finally get down to the gist of what the Court today actually decides, it is this: Even though more railroad employees will be injured by "slack action" movements on long trains than on short trains, there must be no regulation of this danger in the absence of "uniform regulations." That means that no one can legislate against this danger except the Congress; and even though the Congress is perfectly content to leave the matter to the different state legislatures, this Court, on the ground of "lack of uniformity," will require it to make an express avowal of that fact before it will permit a state to guard against that admitted danger.

We are not left in doubt as to why, as against the potential peril of injuries to employees, the Court tips the scales on the side of "uniformity." For the evil it finds in a lack of uniformity is that it (1) delays interstate commerce, (2) increases its cost and (3) impairs its efficiency. All three of these boil down to the same thing, and that is that running shorter trains would increase the cost of railroad operations. . . .

This record in its entirety leaves me with no doubt whatever that many employees have been seriously injured and killed in the past, and that many more are likely to be so in the future, because of "slack movement" in trains. Everyday knowledge as well as direct evidence presented at the various hearings, substantiates the report of the Senate Committee, that the danger from slack movement is greater in long trains than in short trains. It may be that offsetting dangers are possible in the operation of short trains. The balancing of these probabilities, however, is not in my judgment a matter for judicial determination, but one which calls for legislative consideration. Representatives elected by the people to make their laws, rather than judges appointed to interpret those laws, can best determine the policies which govern the people. That at least is the basic principle on which our democratic society rests. I would affirm the judgment of the Supreme Court of Arizona.

DOUGLAS, J., dissenting. . . . I have expressed my doubts whether the courts should intervene in situations like the present and strike down state legislation on the grounds that it burdens interstate commerce. My view has been that the courts should intervene only where the state legislation discriminated against interstate commerce or was out of harmony with laws which Congress had enacted. . . .

[T]he question presented is whether the total effect of Arizona's train-limit as a safety measure is so slight as not to outweigh the national interest in keeping interstate commerce free from interferences which seriously impede or burden it. . . . If I sat as a member of the Interstate Commerce Commission or of a legislative committee to decide whether Arizona's train-limit law should be superseded by a federal regulation, the question would not be free from doubt for me. . . . Whether the question arises under the Commerce Clause or the Fourteenth Amendment, I think the legislation is entitled to a presumption of validity. . . . I am not persuaded that the evidence adduced by the railroads overcomes the presumption of validity to which this train-limit law is entitled. . . .

Note: "Representation Reinforcement" and the Dormant Commerce Clause

In both *Barnwell* and *Southern Pacific* Justice Stone is concerned with the possibility that states may insufficiently weigh the interests of out-of-staters unless there is reason to believe that the latter are "represented" by an in-state group whose interests are similar and similarly affected. In *Barnwell* the purported "fact that [the South Carolina requirements] affect alike shippers in interstate and intrastate commerce in large numbers within as well as without the state is a safeguard against their abuse." (Justice Stone mentioned no evidence to support this surmise. Can you think of any reason why it might not be true?) Stone moves from the particular to a more general theory in footnote a of *Southern Pacific*. The absence of "political restraints normally exerted when interests within the state are affected" is presented as a rationale for judicial review, which serves as a kind of "representation reinforcement"[49] of groups whose interests, though putatively entitled to be taken into account by state legislators, are likely to be ignored. This approach, linked with Stone's footnote in *Carolene Products* (1938), p. 545 infra, has been enormously influential in a wide range of doctrinal areas.

Its contemporary use in the context of the dormant commerce clause is evident in Raymond Motor Transportation, Inc. v. Rice, 434 U.S. 429 (1978), where the Court considered a Wisconsin statute prohibiting trucks longer than 55 feet or pulling more than one other vehicle, though the statute allowed a variety of exceptions that were frequently granted. Appellant motor carriers, after being denied permission to operate 65-foot double trailers on interstate highways in Wisconsin, challenged the regulation and presented uncontradicted evidence not only that the statute increased the costs of their operations but also that the double trailers were at least as safe as trucks permitted by the statute.

Writing for a unanimous Court, Justice Powell invalidated the Wisconsin law. Although he noted that "[i]n no field has deference to state regulation been greater than that of highway safety regulation" and "those who would challenge state regulations said to promote highway safety must overcome a strong presumption of validity," he was nonetheless "persuaded by the record in this case that the challenged regulations unconstitutionally burden interstate commerce." It was significant that the state allowed frequent exemptions and that it was unable to show that the prohibition increased safety.

Justice Powell, alluding to "process" considerations, noted that "[t]he Court's special deference to state highway regulations derives in part from the assumption that where such regulations do not discriminate on their face against interstate commerce, their burden usually falls on local economic interests." The shared burden insures "that a State's own political processes will serve as a check against unduly burdensome regulations." He suggested that the statutory exemptions may reflect a "compromise between forces within the State that seek to retain the State's general truck-length limit, and industries within the State that complain that the general limit is unduly burdensome. Exemptions of this kind, however, weaken the presumption in favor of the validity of the general limit" by undermining the assumptions noted in the *Southern Pacific* footnote.[50]

Kassell v. Consolidated Freightways Corp., 450 U.S. 662 (1981), involved an Iowa ban on 65-foot double-trailer trucks. There was no majority opinion. Writing for a plurality of four, Justice Powell relied heavily on trial court findings that the law substantially burdened interstate commerce without significantly promoting safety. However, both Justice Stevens and Justice Brennan, in separate

49. The phrase is from John Hart Ely, Democracy and Distrust (1980). He applies his theory to the dormant commerce clause at pp. 82-83, 90-91.

50. Justice Blackmun wrote a concurring opinion joined by Chief Justice Burger and Justices Brennan and Rehnquist which rejected the use of *Pike* made by the majority:

> In *Pike* itself the Court noted that it did not confront "state legislation in the field of safety where the property of local regulation has long been recognized." In other words, if safety justifications are not illusory, the Court will not second-guess legislative judgment about their importance in comparison with related burdens on interstate commerce. . . . Here, the Court does not engage in a balance of policies; it does not make a legislative choice. Instead, after searching the factual record developed by the parties, it concludes that the safety interests have not been shown to exist as a matter of law.

concurrences (the latter joined by Justice Marshall) noted that Iowa seemed motivated by a desire to deflect through traffic to neighboring states. Justice Brennan wrote that "this purpose, being *protectionist* in nature, is *impermissible*. . . . Iowa may not shunt off its fair share of the burden of maintaining truck routes, nor may it create increased hazards on the highways of neighboring States in order to decrease the hazards on Iowa highways." Because Iowa's decisionmakers were interested only in promoting "*Iowa's* safety and other interests at the direct expense of the safety and other interests of neighboring States," their decision "merits . . . no deference" (emphasis in original).[51]

Professor Regan argues against this "process" approach to dormant commerce clause cases on the ground that states have no general duty to take account of out-of-state interests.[52]

> [Process theory] requires review of laws no one would normally think of as requiring judicial scrutiny. If Minnesota adopts an advertising campaign to try to discourage smoking among its population, or if it forbids smoking in enough stores, offices, and places of public assembly to affect significantly the total number of cigarettes smoked, then the law should be judicially inspected to see that it does not unjustly harm tobacco growers in North Carolina. If a major city adopts a rent control ordinance, judicial review is required to protect the interests of people living elsewhere who might have moved to the city except for the increased difficulty of securing housing. If a state has a stingy workmen's compensation program that attracts employers, the courts must stand ready to consider whether representation in that state's legislature of foreign workers [whose interests are clearly in reducing the number of plant closings and shifts to the first state] might not have produced a program that was more generous.

Indeed, in New Energy Co. of Indiana v. Limbach, supra, Justice Scalia wrote:

> It has not escaped our notice that the appellant here, which is eligible to receive a cash subsidy under Indiana's program for in-state ethanol producers, is the potential beneficiary of a scheme no less discriminatory than the one that it attacks, and no less effective in conferring a commercial advantage over out-of-state competitors. . . . The Commerce Clause does not prohibit all state action designed to give its residents an advantage in the marketplace, but only action of that description *in connection with the State's regulation of interstate commerce*. Direct subsidization of domestic

51. Justice Rehnquist, joined by Chief Justice Burger and Justice Stewart, dissented. He argued that the district court was incorrect in asking whether the Iowa regulation marginally promoted safety as compared to the alternative regulations of neighboring states. Instead, the proper question was whether it promoted safety as compared to no regulation at all. "Any direct balancing of marginal safety benefits against burdens on commerce would make the burdens on commerce the sole significant factor, and make likely the odd result that similar state laws enacted for identical safety reasons might violate the Commerce Clause in one part of the country but not others," depending on the prevailing regulations of the region. He also disagreed with Brennan's suggestion that the Court should discern the legislator's actual purpose rather than accept the purpose proffered by the state's lawyer before the courts. See pp. 578-579 infra.

52. Regan, supra note 42, at 1162. Professor Regan also notes an important argument first made by James O'Fallon in The Commerce Clause: A Theoretical Comment, 61 Or. L. Review 395, 409, 413 (1982). In Regan's words: "If we regard legislation as procedure for weighing and combining pressures from constituents and generating laws which point in the direction of the resultant vector," simply requiring that some attention be paid to potential out-of-state interests would not seem to suffice. Instead, "the scheme of virtual [or reinforced] representation must respond as accurately as possible to the sheer numerical magnitude of all affected interests." Regan at 1163 n.130.

industry does not ordinarily run afoul of that prohibition; discriminatory taxation of out-of-state manufacturers does.

Although granting such a subsidy is presumably unfriendly from the perspective of non-Indiana producers, the Court did not suggest that Indiana was under any duty to take their interests into account when deciding whether or not to grant funds to the Indiana producers. Regan suggests that the rejection of the propriety of judicial oversight in such cases discredits the entire "process" approach under the commerce clause. Do you agree? Should Wisconsin citizens have any recourse against Iowa's lack of concern about their safety besides asking Congress to enact a federal law that would preempt state regulation of the transportation in question?

Note: The Special Burdens of Inconsistent Regulations

BIBB v. NAVAJO FREIGHT LINES, INC., 359 U.S. 520 (1959): [A unanimous Court struck down an Illinois requirement that all trucks using the state's highways be equipped with contoured mudguards. At least 45 other states permitted conventional straight mudflaps, which were the norm on interstate vehicles, and Arkansas required straight mudflaps. The district court found that "since it is impossible for a carrier operating in interstate commerce to determine which of its equipment will be used in a particular area, or on a particular day, or days, carriers operating into or through Illinois . . . will be required to equip all of their trailers in accordance with the [Illinois] requirements," at a cost of at least 30 dollars per truck. The Illinois requirement also hampered "interline" operations — the interchanging of trailers between an originating carrier and another carrier that serves an area not served by the former, especially important in the shipment of perishable goods and explosives. Additionally, a vehicle could not travel through both Illinois and Arkansas without changing mudguards, a several-hour operation. On the merits of the safety regulation, the court found that the contoured mudguards did not work better than conventional ones to prevent debris from being thrown behind the truck and that the contoured guards tended to cause excessive heat in the brake drum and to fall off more readily than the conventional kind. The Court affirmed the district court's holding that the Illinois regulation unconstitutionally burdened interstate commerce.]

DOUGLAS, J. . . . The power of the State to regulate the use of its highways is broad and pervasive. We have recognized the peculiarly local nature of this subject of safety. . . . The regulation of highways [is a subject] with respect to which the state has exceptional scope for the exercise of its regulatory power. . . .

These safety measures carry a strong presumption of validity when challenged in court. If there are alternative ways of solving a problem, we do not sit to determine which of them is best suited to achieve a valid state objective. . . . Unless we can conclude on the whole record that "the total effect of the law as a safety measure in reducing accidents and casualties is so slight or problematical as not to outweigh the national interest in keeping interstate commerce free from interferences which seriously impede it" (Southern Pacific Co. v. Arizona) we must uphold the statute.

. . . If we had here only a question whether the cost of adjusting an interstate operation to these new local safety regulations prescribed by Illinois unduly burdened interstate commerce, we would have to sustain the law under the authority of the *Sproles, Barnwell,* and *Maurer* cases.[53] The same result would obtain if we had to resolve the much discussed issues of safety presented in this case.

This case presents a different issue. The equipment in [those] cases could pass muster in any State. . . . We were not faced there with the question whether one State could prescribe standards for interstate carriers that would conflict with the standards of another State, making it necessary, say, for an interstate carrier to shift its cargo to differently designed vehicles once another state line was reached. We had a related problem in *Southern Pacific*. . . . More closely in point is Morgan v. Virginia, 328 U.S. 373 (1946), where a local law required a reseating of passengers on interstate busses entering Virginia in order to comply with a local segregation law. Diverse seating arrangements for people of different races imposed by several states interfered, we concluded, with "the need for national uniformity in the regulations for interstate travel.". . .

[Justice Douglas then emphasized the conflict between the Illinois and Arkansas regulations and the burden on interline operations, concluding:] This is one of those cases — few in number — where local safety measures that are nondiscriminatory place an unconstitutional burden on interstate commerce. This conclusion is especially underlined by the deleterious effect which the Illinois law will have on the "interline" operation of interstate motor carriers. The conflict between the Arkansas regulation and the Illinois regulation also suggests that this regulation of mudguards is not one of those matters "admitting of diversity of treatment according to the special requirements of local conditions." . . . A State which insists on a design out of line with the requirements of almost all the other States may sometimes place a great burden of delay and inconvenience on those interstate motor carriers entering or crossing its territory. Such a new safety device — out of line with the requirements of the other States — may be so compelling that the innovating State need not be the one to give way. But the present showing — balanced against the clear burden of commerce — is far too inconclusive to make the mudguard meet that test. We deal not with absolutes, but with questions of degree. . . .

HARLAN, J., joined by Stewart, J., concurring.

The opinion of the Court clearly demonstrates the heavy burden, in terms of cost and interference with "interlining," which the Illinois statute here involved imposes on interstate commerce. In view of the findings . . . that the contour mudflap "possesses no advantages" in terms of safety, . . . and indeed creates certain safety hazards, this heavy burden cannot be justified on the theory that the Illinois statute is a necessary, appropriate, or helpful local safety measure. Accordingly, I concur in the judgment of the Court.

53. Sproles v. Binford, 286 U.S. 374 (1932), upheld a state highway weight limitation. Maurer v. Hamilton, 309 U.S. 598 (1940), upheld a state prohibition of vehicles carrying cars above the height of the cab of the carrier vehicle.

Discussion

1. In CTS Corp. v. Dynamics Corp. of America, supra, the Court cited five cases that involved "statutes that may adversely affect interstate commerce by subjecting activities to inconsistent regulations." *Cooley, Southern Pacific,* and *Kassel* involve transportation. Edgar v. MITE Corp., 457 U.S. 624 (1982), concerned the regulation of corporate takeovers. Brown-Forman Distillers Corp. v. New York State Liquor Authority, 476 U.S. 573 (1986), invalidated a New York law requiring liquor distributors to sell to New York wholesalers at a price no higher than the lowest price the distiller charged wholesalers in any other state. The law prevented the distributor from offering lower prices in any other state for a month once the price to New York wholesalers was posted. The consequence was therefore to control liquor prices in the other states. An earlier decision suggesting that such laws were constitutional led to their proliferation and therefore "greatly multiplied the likelihood that a seller will be subjected to inconsistent obligations in different states."

Consider a manufacturer of toasters who wishes to distribute nationally. If 49 states have no regulations and one state requires toasters to meet certain safety standards, there is presumably no conflict: The manufacturer can design all toasters to conform with the regulating state's guidelines. What if two or more states adopt mutually inconsistent toaster regulations? At what point, if any, should a court invalidate such regulations? Should it invalidate *all* the state regulations, or invalidate only certain ones? Consider California's requirement of antipollution devices for its cars that are not required by any other state. Congress in fact authorized such special requirements. If Congress had not passed authorizing legislation, could General Motors win a suit to invalidate the California regulation on the basis of the cases in this subsection?

Note: A Skeptical Look at the Dormant Commerce Clause

In Tyler Pipe Industries v. Washington State Department of Revenue, 483 U.S. 232 (1987), the Court invalidated a Washington State tax on the ground that it fell more heavily on interstate than on intrastate commerce. Justice Scalia, in a dissent joined by Chief Justice Rehnquist, leveled a general attack on the notion that the judiciary has a legitimate role to play in enforcing the dormant commerce clause, at least where state legislation does not overtly select out foreign commerce for invidious treatment, and suggested that the task of monitoring the impact of state regulation on interstate commerce was more properly left to Congress. He emphasized "the lack of any clear theoretical underpinning for judicial 'enforcement' of the Commerce Clause," which he described as "a charter for Congress, not the courts, to ensure 'an area of trade free from interference by the States.'" He also rejected the argument that the Constitution assigns Congress the exclusive power to regulate commerce.

> [U]nlike the District Clause, which empowers Congress "To exercise exclusive Legislation," Art. I, §8, cl. 17, the language of the Commerce Clause gives no indication of exclusivity. Nor can one assume generally that Congress' Article I powers are exclusive; many of them plainly coexist with concurrent authority in the States. See Kewanee Oil Co. v. Bicron Corp., 416 U.S. 470, 479 (1974) (patent power); Gold-

stein v. California, 412 U.S. 546, 560 (1973) (copyright power); Houston v. Moore, 5 Wheat. 1, 25, (1820) (court martial jurisdiction over the militia); Sturges v. Crowninshield, 4 Wheat. 122, 193-196 (1819) (bankruptcy power). Furthermore, there is no correlative denial of power over commerce to the States in Art. I, §10, as there is, for example, with the power to coin money or make treaties. And both the States and Congress assumed from the date of ratification that at least some state laws regulating commerce were valid.

After noting the expansive meaning of "interstate commerce" given by post-1937 decisions of the Court, Justice Scalia considered the *Cooley* distinction between local regulation and regulation of those subjects that "are in their nature national, or admit only of one uniform system." Whatever the wisdom of such a distinction, he argued that "it is hard to see why judges rather than legislators are fit to determine what areas of commerce 'in their nature' require national regulation." He furthermore denounced the distinction as having

no conceivable basis in the text of the Commerce Clause, which treats "Commerce . . . among the several States" as a unitary subject. And attempting to limit the Clause's pre-emptive effect to state laws *intended* to regulate commerce (as opposed to those intended, for example, to promote health), while perhaps a textually possible construction of the phrase "regulate Commerce," is a most unlikely one. Distinguishing between laws with the *purpose* of regulating commerce and "police power" statutes with that *effect* is, as Taney demonstrated in the License Cases, 5 How. 504, 582-583 (1847), more interesting as a metaphysical exercise than useful as a practical technique for marking out the powers of separate sovereigns.

The least plausible theoretical justification of all is the idea that in enforcing the negative Commerce Clause the Court is not applying a constitutional command at all, but is merely interpreting the will of Congress, whose silence in certain fields of interstate commerce (but not in others) is to be taken as a prohibition of regulation. There is no conceivable reason why congressional inaction under the Commerce Clause should be deemed to have the same pre-emptive effect elsewhere accorded only congressional action. There, as elsewhere, "Congress' silence is just that — silence. . . ." Alaska Airlines, Inc. v. Brock, 480 U.S. 678 (1987).[a]

The historical record provides no grounds for reading the Commerce Clause to be other than what it says — an authorization for Congress to regulate commerce. The strongest evidence in favor of a negative Commerce Clause — that version of it which renders federal authority over interstate commerce exclusive — is Madison's comment during the Convention that "Whether the States are now restrained from laying tonnage duties depends on the extent of the power 'to regulate commerce.' These terms are vague but seem to exclude the power of the States." This comment, however, came during discussion of what became Art. I, §10, cl. 3: "No State shall, without the Consent of Congress, lay any Duty of Tonnage. . . ." The fact that it is difficult to conceive how the power to regulate commerce would *not* include the power to impose duties; and the fact that, despite this apparent coverage, the Convention went on to adopt a provision prohibiting States from levying duties on tonnage without congressional approval; suggest that Madison's assumption of

a. Unfortunately, this "legislation by inaction" theory of the negative Commerce Clause seems to be the only basis for the doctrine . . . that Congress can authorize States to enact legislation that would otherwise violate the negative Commerce Clause. See Prudential Ins. Co. v. Benjamin, 328 U.S. 408 (1946). Nothing else could explain the *Benjamin* principle that what was invalid state action can be rendered valid state action through "congressional consent." There is surely no area in which Congress can permit the States to violate the Constitution. . . .

exclusivity of the federal commerce power was ill considered and not generally shared.

... Madison does not seem to have exaggerated when he described the Commerce Clause as an addition to the powers of the national government "which few oppose and from which no apprehensions are entertained." The Federalist No. 45. I think it beyond question that many "apprehensions" would have been "entertained" if supporters of the Constitution had hinted that the Commerce Clause, despite its language, gave this Court the power it has since assumed....

[T]o the extent that we have gone beyond guarding against rank discrimination against citizens of other States — which is regulated not by the Commerce Clause but by the Privileges and Immunities Clause, Art. IV, §2, cl. 1 — the Court for over a century has engaged in an enterprise that it has been unable to justify by textual support or even coherent nontextual theory, that it was almost certainly not intended to undertake, and that it has not undertaken very well. It is astonishing that we should be expanding our beachhead in this impoverished territory, rather than being satisfied with what we have already acquired by a sort of intellectual adverse possession.

Recall the taxonomy of modes of constitutional interpretation introduced following Marshall's opinion in *McCulloch.* It is clear that Justice Scalia finds the negative commerce clause, as developed by the judiciary, to be wholly without *textual* or *historical* support. He does not, however, consider whether there might be a *structural* rationale. Professor Regan argues that a structural account emphasizing the compromise earlier mentioned between genuine state sovereignty and national uniformity is "no doubt the strongest argument for forbidding state protectionism."[54] Judge Posner has similarly suggested that the negative commerce clause corrects against the "danger that, like independent nations, states might be led by [internal] interest-group pressures to establish trade barriers" against commerce from other states. Posner describes the negative commerce clause as "one device ... for preventing states from abusing their 'market power.'"[55]

Even if one is persuaded that the structure of the Constitution generates limitations on state regulation involving interstate commerce, does it follow that the judiciary should enforce the limitation (subject to congressional override)? Perhaps it is easiest to defend the judicial role by adopting one of the two other modes of justification examined earlier, i.e., either *doctrinal* or *consequential.* Whatever its initial provenance, a series of decisions now supports the Court's power to intervene when state regulations interfere sufficiently with interstate commerce. Still, one might wonder what entitles *this* doctrine to greater respect than the economic due process doctrine swept aside in 1937. Once one accepts the practice of overruling past "mistaken" decisions, however long those decisions have been accepted, can "intellectual adverse possession" ever operate to still debate?

Can one justify the current judicial practice in terms of political exigency? In the area of dormant commerce clause doctrine, the political check of congressional overruling limits the costs of possible judicial mistakes. Nevertheless, the

54. Regan, supra note 42, at 1111.

55. Richard Posner, The Constitution as an Economic Document, 56 Geo. Wash. L. Rev. 4, 17 (1987).

underlying premise of this argument is simply that the current practice is useful. Justice Scalia would apparently reject the premise. Do you?

C. State Restrictions on Production and on the Expropriation and Exportation of Natural Resources

1. *Laws Not Discriminatory on Their Face*

The Court has generally been solicitous of state regulatory schemes that, though having extraterritorial impact, apply only to activities conducted within the state. Several years after *Seelig,* p. 427 supra, for example, the Court held in Milk Control Board v. Eisenberg Farm Products Co., 306 U.S. 346 (1939), that respondent, who purchased and processed milk in Pennsylvania for sale in New York, was not exempt from Pennsylvania's requirements that it obtain a license, file a bond for the protection of producers, and pay farmers minimum prices fixed by the Pennsylvania Milk Control Board. Justice Roberts wrote for the Court (Justices McReynolds and Butler dissenting):

> The purpose of the statute under review obviously is to reach a domestic situation in the interest of the welfare of the producers and consumers of milk in Pennsylvania. Its provisions with respect to license, bond, and regulation of prices to be paid to producers are appropriate means to the ends in view. The question is whether the prescription of prices to be paid producers in the effort to accomplish these ends constitutes a prohibited burden on interstate commerce, or an incidental burden which is permissible until superseded by Congressional enactment. . . .
>
> The Commonwealth does not essay to regulate or to restrain the shipment of the respondent's milk into New York or to regulate its sale or the price at which respondent may sell it in New York. If dealers conducting receiving stations in various localities in Pennsylvania were free to ignore the requirements of the statute on the ground that all or a part of the milk they purchase is destined to another state the uniform operation of the statute locally would be crippled and might be impracticable. Only a small fraction of the milk produced by farmers in Pennsylvania is shipped out of the Commonwealth. There is, therefore, a comparatively large field remotely affecting and wholly unrelated to interstate commerce within which the statute operates. These considerations we think justify the conclusion that the effect of the law on interstate commerce is incidental and not forbidden by the Constitution, in the absence of regulation by Congress.
>
> None of the decisions on which the court below and the respondent rely rules the instant case. . . . In Baldwin v. Seelig this court condemned an enactment aimed solely at interstate commerce attempting to affect and regulate the price to be paid for milk in a sister state, and we indicated that the attempt amounted in effect to a tariff barrier set up against milk imported into the enacting state.

More recently, in Commonwealth Edison Co. v. Montana, 453 U.S. 609 (1981), the Court upheld the appellee state's "severance tax" of up to 30 percent of the contract sales price of coal mined in the state. (Montana has approximately 25 percent of all known coal reserves in the United States and more than 50 percent of the low-sulfur coal. Approximately 90 percent of its coal is exported to other States.) Justice Marshall subjected the tax to a four-part inquiry, developed in prior decisions, to determine whether the tax "is applied to an activity with a substantial nexus with the taxing State, is fairly apportioned, does not discriminate against interstate commerce, and is fairly related to services produced by the State." The appellant power companies focused on the third and fourth aspects. To the argument that the tax discriminated against interstate commerce, Justice Marshall responded:

> [T]here is no real discrimination in this case; the tax burden is borne according to the amount of coal consumed and not according to any distinction between in-state and out-of-state consumers. Rather, appellants assume that the Commerce Clause gives residents of one State a right of access at "reasonable" prices to resources located in another State that is richly endowed with such resources, without regard to whether and on what terms residents of the resource-rich States have access to the resources. We are not convinced that the Commerce Clause, of its own force, gives the residents of one State the right to control in this fashion the terms of resource development and depletion in a sister State.

Turning to the fourth criterion, Marshall wrote that it only requires that the "measure of the tax must be reasonably related to the extent of the contact [of the taxed activity to the state], since it is the activities or presence of the taxpayer in the State that may properly be made to bear a 'just share of the tax burden.'" Marshall rejected appellants' argument that the tax must be related to costs incurred by the state from mining operations:

> [T]he appropriate level or rate of taxation is essentially a matter for legislative, and not judicial, resolution. . . . In the first place, it is doubtful whether any legal test could adequately reflect the numerous and competing economic, geographic, demographic, social, and political considerations that must inform a decision about an acceptable rate or level of state taxation. . . . But even apart from the difficulty of the judicial undertaking, . . . questions about the appropriate level of state taxes must be resolved through the political process. Under our federal system, the determination is to be made by state legislatures in the first instance and, if necessary, by Congress when particular state taxes are thought to be contrary to federal interests.

Justice Blackmun, joined by Justices Powell and Stevens, dissented, agreeing that the four-part test was appropriate, but arguing that the measure of a tax must be scrutinized when its burden falls so heavily on interstate commerce that its burden "is not likely to be alleviated by those political restraints which are normally exerted on legislation where it affects adversely interests within the state:"

> It is true that a trial in this case would require "complex factual inquiries" into whether economic conditions are such that Montana is in fact able to export the burden of its severance tax. . . . If the trial court were to determine that the tax is exported, it would then have to determine whether the tax is "fairly related." . . . If the tax is in fact a legitimate general revenue measure identical or roughly comparable to taxes imposed upon similar industries, a court's inquiry is at an end; on the other hand, if the tax singles out this particular interstate activity and charges it with a grossly disproportionate share of the general costs of government, the court must determine whether there is some reasonable basis for the

legislative judgment that the tax is necessary to compensate the State for the particular costs imposed by the activity. . . . [T]he task is likely to prove to be a formidable one; but its difficulty does not excuse our failure to undertake it. This case poses extremely grave issues that threaten both to "polarize the Nation" and to reawaken "the tendencies toward economic Balkanization" that the Commerce Clause was designed to remedy.

Justice White wrote a brief concurring opinion, emphasizing that "Congress is so far content to let the matter rest, and we are counseled by the Executive Branch through the Solicitor General not to overturn the Montana tax."

Commonwealth Edison is only one of a vast body of cases dealing with the intersection of state taxation and the commerce clause. If all interstate activities were immune from state taxation, the states would quickly go bankrupt, and it has long been established that interstate commerce must "pay its own way." On the other hand, if every state having some relationship with a particular interstate activity could tax it without limitation, many businesses might accumulate taxes exceeding 100 percent of their property, gross receipts, or net income. In its attempt to develop limiting doctrines on a case-by-case basis, the Court has created a body of doctrine as ramified and confusing as any other. There has been some congressional legislation in the area, as well as a multi-state tax compact. If you had taken this course 30 years ago, you would have spent many hours studying the state taxation of interstate commerce. Although, as *Commonwealth Edison* illustrates, these cases continue to arise,[56] we shall not deal further with them.

2. *Discrimination Favoring State Citizens and Enterprises: Intersections of the Commerce Clause and the Privileges and Immunities Clause of Article IV*

McCready v. Virginia, 94 U.S. 391 (1876), held that the privileges and immunities clause of Article IV, section 2, did not prohibit Virginia from granting its citizens the exclusive privilege of planting oysters in the state's tidal waters. Chief Justice Waite wrote:

> [E]ach State owns the beds of all tide-waters within its jurisdiction, . . . the tide-waters themselves, and the fish in them, so far as they are capable of ownership while running. For this purpose the State represents its people, and the ownership is that of the people in their united sovereignty. . . . The right which the people of the State thus acquire comes not from their citizenship alone, but from their citizenship and property combined. It is, in fact, a property right, and not a mere privilege and immunity of citizenship. . . . [T]he citizens of one State are not invested by [the privileges and immunities] clause of the Constitution with any interest in the common property of the citizens of another State.[57]

56. See also, e.g., Maryland v. Louisiana, 451 U.S. 725 (1981) (state tax on exported natural gas). For further reference, see Walter Hellerstein, Commerce Clause Restraints on State Taxation: Purposeful Economic Protectionism and Beyond, 85 Mich. L. Rev. 758 (1987); Walter Hellerstein, State Taxation and the Supreme Court, 1989 Sup. Ct. Rev. 223.

57. He went on to note that the commerce clause was not germane, since "[t]here is here no question of transportation or exchange of commodities, but only of cultivation and production. Commerce has nothing to do with land while producing, but only with the product after it has become the subject of trade."

Toomer v. Witsell, 334 U.S. 385 (1948), held that the privileges and immunities clause prohibited South Carolina from exacting a discriminatory license fee from nonresidents shrimping in its territorial waters. The state relied on *McCready,* invoking the common law notion that its citizens enjoyed common ownership of fish and wildlife within the jurisdiction. Chief Justice Vinson distinguished *McCready* in property law terms but went on to assert that "[t]he whole ownership theory . . . is now generally regarded as but a fiction expressive in legal shorthand of the importance to its people that a State have power to preserve and regulate the exploitation of an important resource." The case was decided on the principle that "one of the privileges which [the privileges and immunities] clause guarantees to citizens of State *A* is that of doing business in State *B* on terms of substantial equality with the citizens of that State." Justice Frankfurter, joined by Justice Jackson, concurred in the judgment but disagreed with the Court's application of the privileges and immunities clause:

> It is not conceivable that the framers of the Constitution meant to obliterate all special relations between a State and its citizens. . . . A State may care for its own in utilizing the bounties of nature within her borders because it has technical ownership of such bounties or, when ownership is in no one, because the State may for the common good exercise all the authority that technical ownership ordinarily confers.
>
> When the Constitution was adopted, such, no doubt, was the common understanding regarding the power of States over their fisheries. . . . The *McCready* case . . . is the symbol of one of the weightiest doctrines in our law. . . . [I]n our own day this Court formulated the amplitude of the *McCready* doctrine by referring to "the regulation or distribution of the public domain, or of the common property or resources of the people of the State, the enjoyment of which may be limited to its citizens as against both aliens and the citizens of other States."

In Geer v. Connecticut, 161 U.S. 519 (1896), and Hudson County Water Co. v. McCarter, 209 U.S. 349 (1908), the court upheld a Connecticut prohibition of the export of wild game killed within the state and a New Jersey prohibition of the export of water from its lakes and streams. Unlike the law in *Toomer,* these did not discriminate against foreign citizens as such, and the Court dealt with them under the commerce clause. The underlying theory of these decisions was essentially the same one invoked in *McCready. Geer* rested on the notions that the people of a state have a "common ownership" in wild animals and that the taker of wild game acquires only a "qualified ownership" subject to the state's power to "confine the use of such game to those who own it, the people of that State." In *Hudson County,* Justice Holmes wrote for the Court that the state as "guardian of the public welfare" had a strong interest in protecting the state's natural advantages.

Paralleling *Toomer,* later decisions have limited the scope of these commerce clause holdings. In Pennsylvania v. West Virginia, 262 U.S. 553 (1923), the Court invalidated a West Virginia requirement that all domestic needs for natural gas be satisfied before any gas could be transported outside the state. Justice Van Devanter wrote:

> Natural gas is a lawful article of commerce, and its transmission from one state to another for sale and consumption in the latter is interstate commerce. A state law, whether of the state where the gas is produced or that where it is to be sold, which by

> necessary operation prevents, obstructs or burdens such transmission is a regulation of interstate commerce — a prohibited interference. . . .
>
> [West Virginia urges] that gas is a natural product of the state and has become a necessity therein, that the supply is waning and no longer sufficient to satisfy local needs and be used abroad, and that the act is therefore a legitimate measure of conservation in the interest of the people of the state. If the situation be as stated, it affords no ground for that assumption by the state of power to regulate interstate commerce, which is what the act attempts to do. That power is lodged elsewhere. . . .
>
> Gas, when reduced to possession, is a commodity; it belongs to the owner of the land, and, when reduced to possession, is his individual property subject to sale by him.

The Court did not allude to *Geer* and *McCarter.* Justice Holmes, joined by Justice Brandeis, dissented, citing those decisions "to confirm what I think should be plain without them, that the Constitution does not prohibit a state from securing a reasonable preference for its own inhabitants in the enjoyment of its products even when the effect of its law is to keep property within its boundaries that otherwise would have passed outside." (Justices McReynolds and Brandeis also dissented, on the ground that the case was not in a posture meet for adjudication.)

Foster-Fountain Packing Co. v. Haydel, 278 U.S. 1 (1928), invalidated a Louisiana statute prohibiting the shipment of shrimp out of state until their heads and hulls had been removed, putatively so that these parts could be used as fertilizer. The Court found Pennsylvania v. West Virginia controlling, and distinguished *Geer* on the ground that Louisiana did not require that the parts removed be retained for use in the state and, indeed, that most of them were ultimately sold out of state. The decision may rest in part on the Court's belief that the purpose of the law was "not to retain the shrimp for the use of the people of Louisiana . . . , [but] to favor the canning of the meat and manufacture of bran in Louisiana by withholding raw or unshelled shrimp from [Mississippi] plants." It was on the basis of *Foster-Fountain* that Justice Frankfurter concurred in *Toomer:*

> [A] State cannot project its powers over its own resources by seeking to control the channels of commerce among the States. It is one thing to say that a food supply that may be reduced to control by a State for feeding its own people should only be locally consumed. The State has that power and the Privileges-and-Immunities clause is no restriction upon its exercise. It is a wholly different thing for the State to provide that only its citizens shall be engaged in commerce among the States, even though based on a locally available food supply. That is not the exercise of the basic right of a State to feed and maintain and give enjoyment to its own people.

BALDWIN v. MONTANA FISH AND GAME COMMISSION

436 U.S. 371 (1978)

Appeal from the United States District Court for the District of Montana

BLACKMUN, J.

This case presents issues, under the Privileges and Immunities Clause of the Constitution's Art. IV, §2, and the Equal Protection Clause of the Fourteenth Amendment, as to the constitutional validity of disparities, as between residents and nonresidents, in a State's hunting license system. . . .

II

The relevant facts are not in any real controversy and many of them are agreed. . . .

For the 1976 season, the Montana resident could purchase a license solely for elk for $9. The nonresident, in order to hunt elk, was required to purchase a combination license at a cost of $225; this entitled him to take one elk, one deer, one black bear, and game birds, and to fish with hook and line. A resident was not required to buy any combination of licenses, but if he did, the cost to him of all the privileges granted by the nonresident combination license was $30. The nonresident thus paid 7½ times as much as the resident, and if the nonresident wished to hunt only elk, he paid 25 times as much as the resident. . . .

Montana maintains significant populations of big game, including elk, deer, and antelope. Its elk population is one of the largest in the United States. Elk are prized by big-game hunters who come from near and far to pursue the animals for sport. . . . Elk are not hunted commercially in Montana. Nonresident hunters seek the animal for its trophy value; the trophy is the distinctive set of antlers. The interest of resident hunters more often may be in the meat. . . .

Elk management is expensive. In regions of the State with significant elk population, more personnel time of the Fish and Game Commission is spent on elk than on any other Species of big game. . . . The animal's preservation depends upon conservation. . . .

Privileges and immunities. Appellants strongly urge here that the Montana licensing scheme for the hunting of elk violates the Privileges and Immunities Clause of Art. IV, §2, of our Constitution. . . .

Perhaps because of the imposition of the Fourteenth Amendment upon our constitutional consciousness and the extraordinary emphasis that the Amendment received, it is not surprising that the contours of Art. IV, §2, cl. 1, are not well developed, and that the relationship, if any, between the Privileges and Immunities Clause and the "privileges or immunities" language of the Fourteenth Amendment is less than clear. We are, nevertheless, not without some pronouncements by this Court as to the Clause's significance and reach. There are at least three general comments that deserve mention:

The first is that of Mr. Justice Field, writing for a unanimous Court in Paul v. Virginia, 8 Wall., 168, 180 (1869). He emphasized nationalism, the proscription of discrimination, and the assurance of equality of all citizens within any State:

> It was undoubtedly the object of the clause in question to place the citizens of each State upon the same footing with citizens of other States, so far as the advantages resulting from citizenship in those States are concerned. It relieves them from the disabilities of alienage in other States: it inhibits discriminating legislation against them by other States; it gives them the right of free ingress into other States, and egress from them; it insures to them in other States the same freedom possessed by the citizens of those States in the acquisition and enjoyment of property and in the pursuit of happiness; and it secures to them in other States the equal protection of their laws. It has been justly said that no provision in the Constitution has tended so strongly to constitute the citizens of the United States one people as this.

The second came 70 years later when Mr. Justice Roberts, writing for himself and Mr. Justice Black in Hague v. CIO, 307 U.S. 496, 511 (1939), summed up the history of the Clause and pointed out what he felt to be the difference in analysis in the earlier cases from the analysis in later ones:

> At one time it was thought that this section recognized a group of rights which, according to the jurisprudence of the day, were classed as natural rights; and that the purpose of the section was to create rights of citizens of the United States by guaranteeing the citizens of every State the recognition of this group of rights by every other State. Such was the view of Justice Washington.
>
> While this description of the civil rights of the citizens of the States has been quoted with approval, it has come to be the settled view that Article IV, §2, does not import that a citizen of one State carries with him into another fundamental privileges and immunities which come to him necessarily by the mere fact of his citizenship in the State first mentioned, but, on the contrary, that in any State every citizen of any other State is to have the same privileges and immunities which the citizens of that State enjoy. The section, in effect, prevents a State from discriminating against citizens of other States in favor of its own.

The third and most recent general pronouncement is that authored by Mr. Justice Marshall for a nearly unanimous Court in Austin v. New Hampshire, 420 U.S. 656, 660-661 (1975), stressing the Clause's "norm of comity" and the Framers' concerns:

> The Clause thus establishes a norm of comity without specifying the particular subjects as to which citizens of one State coming within the jurisdiction of another are guaranteed equality of treatment. The origins of the Clause do reveal, however, the concerns of central import to the Framers. During the preconstitutional period, the practice of some States denying to outlanders the treatment that its citizens demanded for themselves was widespread. The fourth of the Articles of Confederation was intended to arrest this centrifugal tendency with some particularity. . . .

When the Privileges and Immunities Clause has been applied to specific cases, it has been interpreted to prevent a State from imposing unreasonable burdens on citizens of other States in their pursuit of common callings within the State; in the ownership and disposition of privately held property within the state; and in access to the courts of the State.

It has not been suggested, however, that state citizenship or residency may never be used by a State to distinguish among persons. Suffrage, for example, always has been understood to be tied to an individual's identification with a particular State. See, e.g., Dunn v. Blumstein, 405 U.S. 330 (1972). No one would suggest that the Privileges and Immunities Clause requires a State to open its polls to a person who declines to assert that the State is the only one where he claims a right to vote. The same is true as to qualification for an elective office of the State. . . . Some distinctions between residents and nonresidents merely reflect the fact that this is a Nation composed of individual States, and are permitted; other distinctions are prohibited because they hinder the formation, the purpose, or the development of a single Union of those States. Only with respect to those "privileges" and "immunities" bearing upon the vitality of the Nation as a single entity must the State treat all citizens, resident and nonresident, equally. Here we must decide into which category falls a distinction with respect to access to recreational big-game hunting.

Many of the early cases embrace the concept that the States had complete ownership over wildlife within their boundaries, and, as well, the power to preserve this bounty for their citizens alone. It was enough to say "that in regulating the use of the common property of the citizens of [a] state, the legislature is [not] bound to extend to the citizens of all the other states the same advantages as are secured to their own citizens." Corfield v. Coryell, 6 F. Cas. 546, 552 (No. 3,230) (CCED Pa. 1825). . . . [See also] McCready v. Virginia, 94 U.S. 391 (1877); Geer v. Connecticut, 161 U.S. 519 (1896). . . .

In more recent years, however, the Court has recognized that the States' interest in regulating and controlling those things they claim to "own," including wildlife, is by no means absolute. States may not compel the confinement of the benefits of their resources, even their wildlife, to their own people whenever such hoarding and confinement impedes interstate commerce. Foster-Fountain Packing Co. v. Haydel, 278 U.S. 1 (1928); Pennsylvania v. West Virginia, 262 U.S. 553 (1923); Oklahoma v. Kansas Natural Gas Co., 221 U.S. 229 (1911). Nor does a State's control over its resources preclude the proper exercise of federal power. Douglas v. Seacoast Products, Inc., 431 U.S. 265 (1977);[58] Kleppe v. New Mexico, 426 U.S. 529 (1976); Missouri v. Holland, 252 U.S. 416 (1920). And a State's interest in its wildlife and other resources must yield when, without reason, it interferes with a nonresident's right to pursue a livelihood in a State other than his own, a right that is protected by the Privileges and Immunities Clause. Toomer v. Witsell, 334 U.S. 385 (1948). See Takahashi v. Fish & Game Commn., 334 U.S. 410 (1948).

Appellants contend that the doctrine on which *Corfield, McCready,* and *Geer* all relied has no remaining vitality. We do not agree. . . .[59]

58. Douglas v. Seacoast Products, Inc., 431 U.S. 265 (1977), held that late eighteenth-century federal laws "enrolling" vessels engaged in domestic or coastwide trade preempted Virginia regulations that in effect prohibited nonresidents from catching menhaden in Chesapeake Bay and barred noncitizens from obtaining commercial fishing permits. Justice Marshall relied heavily on Chief Justice Marshall's decision in Gibbons v. Ogden, 22 U.S. (9 Wheat.) 1 (1824). Justice Marshall responded to the State's invocation of *McCready* and *Geer* that their " 'ownership' language . . . must be understood as no more than a 19th century legal fiction expressing 'the importance to its people that a State have power to preserve and regulate the exploitation of an important resource.' Under modern analysis, the question is simply whether the State has exercised its police power in conformity with the federal laws and Constitution." Noting that "reasonable and evenhanded conservation measures, so essential to the the preservation of our vital marine sources of food supply, stand unaffected by our decision," he concluded:

> Our decision is very much in keeping with sound policy considerations of federalism. The business of commercial fishing must be conducted by peripatetic entrepreneurs moving like their quarry, without regard for state boundary lines. Menhaden that spawn in the open ocean or in coastal waters of a southern State may swim into Chesapeake Bay and live there for their first summer, migrate south for the following winter, and appear off the shores of New York or Massachusetts in succeeding years. A number of coastal States have discriminatory fisheries laws, and with all natural resources becoming increasingly scarce and more valuable, more such restrictions would be a likely prospect, as both protective and retaliatory measures. Each State's fishermen eventually might be effectively limited to working in the territorial waters of their residence, or in the federally controlled fishery beyond the three-mile limit. Such proliferation of residency requirements for commercial fishermen would create precisely the sort of Balkanization of interstate commercial activity which the Constitution was intended to prevent.

59. The Court overruled Geer v. Connecticut in Hughes v. Oklahoma, 441 U.S. 322 (1979), in which it struck down an Oklahoma statute prohibiting the transport of minnows out of the state. With only Justice Rehnquist and the Chief Justice dissenting, Justice Brennan wrote for the Court:

> A State may no longer "keep the property, if the sovereign so chooses, always within its jurisdiction for every purpose." Geer v. Connecticut, 161 U.S., at 530. The fiction of state owner-

In his opinion in *Coryell,* Mr. Justice Washington, although he seemingly relied on notions of "natural rights" when he considered the reach of the Privileges and Immunities Clause, included in his list of situations, in which he believed the States would be obligated to treat each other's residents equally, only those where a nonresident sought to engage in an essential activity or exercise a basic right. He himself used the term "fundamental," in the modern as well as the "natural right" sense. Certainly Mr. Justice Field and the Court invoked the same principle in the language quoted above from Paul v. Virginia. So, too, did the Court in [other cases] . . . concerned with the pursuit of common callings, the ability to transfer property, and access to courts. . . . And comparable status of the activity involved was apparent in *Toomer,* the commercial-licensing case. With respect to such basic and essential activities, interference with which would frustrate the purposes of the formation of the Union, the States must treat residents and nonresidents without unnecessary distinctions.

Does the distinction made by Montana between residents and nonresidents in establishing access to elk hunting threaten a basic right in a way that offends the Privileges and Immunities Clause? Merely to ask the question seems to provide the answer. . . . Elk hunting by nonresidents in Montana is a recreation and a sport.

Appellants' interest in sharing this limited resource on more equal terms with Montana residents simply does not fall within the purview of the Privileges and Immunities Clause. Equality in access to Montana elk is not basic to the maintenance or well-being of the Union. Appellants do not — and cannot — contend that they are deprived of a means of a livelihood by the system or of access to any part of the State to which they may seek to travel. We do not decide the full range of activities that are sufficiently basic to the livelihood of the Nation that the States may not interfere with a nonresident's participation therein without similarly interfering with a resident's participation. Whatever rights or activities may be "fundamental" under the Privileges and Immunities Clause, we are persuaded, and hold, that elk hunting by nonresidents in Montana is not one of them.

V

Equal protection. Appellants urge, too, that distinctions drawn between residents and nonresidents are not permissible under the Equal Protection Clause of the Fourteenth Amendment when used to allocate access to recreational hunting. . . .

[There is] no irrationality in the differences the Montana Legislature has drawn in the costs of its licenses to hunt elk. The legislative choice was an eco-

---

ship may no longer be used to force those outside the State to bear the full costs of "conserving" the wild animals within its borders when equally effective nondiscriminatory conservation measures are available.

Far from choosing the least discriminatory alternative, Oklahoma has chosen to "conserve" its minnows in the way that most overtly discriminates against interstate commerce. The State places no limits on the numbers of minnows that can be taken by licensed minnow dealers; nor does it limit in any way how these minnows may be disposed of within the State. Yet it forbids the transportation of any commercially significant number of natural minnows out of the State for sale. [The statute] is certainly not a "last ditch" attempt at conservation after nondiscriminatory alternatives have proved unfeasible. It is rather a choice of the most discriminatory means even though nondiscriminatory alternatives would seem likely to fulfill the State's purported legitimate local purpose more effectively.

nomic means not unreasonably related to the preservation of a finite resource and a substantial regulatory interest of the State. It serves to limit the number of hunter days in the Montana elk country. There is, to be sure, a contrasting cost feature favorable to the resident, and, perhaps, the details and the figures might have been more precisely fixed and more closely related to basic costs to the State. But, as has been noted, appellants concede that a differential in cost between residents and nonresidents is not in itself invidious or unconstitutional. And "a statutory classification impinging upon no fundamental interest . . . need not be drawn so as to fit with precision the legitimate purposes animating it. . . . That [Montana] might have furthered its underlying purpose more artfully, more directly, or more completely, does not warrant a conclusion that the method it chose is unconstitutional." Hughes v. Alexandria Scrap Corp., 426 U.S. 794, 813 (1976).

BRENNAN, J., joined by White and Marshall, JJ., dissenting.

Far more troublesome than the Court's narrow holding — elk hunting in Montana is not a privilege or immunity entitled to protection under Art. IV, §2, cl. 1, of the Constitution — is the rationale of the holding that Montana's elk-hunting licensing scheme passes constitutional muster. The Court concludes that because elk hunting is not a "basic and essential activit[y], interference with which would frustrate the purposes of the formation of the Union," the Privileges and Immunities Clause of Art. IV, §2 — "The Citizens of each State shall be entitled to all Privileges and Immunities of Citizens in the several States" — does not prevent Montana from irrationally, wantonly, and even invidiously discriminating against nonresidents seeking to enjoy natural treasures it alone among the 50 States possesses. I cannot agree that the Privileges and Immunities Clause is so impotent a guarantee that such discrimination remains wholly beyond the purview of that provision.

I . . .

Mr. Justice Roberts' analysis of the Privileges and Immunities Clause of Art. IV, §2, in Hague v. CIO, supra, was the first noteworthy modern pronouncement on the Clause from this Court. Not only did Mr. Justice Roberts recognize that *Corfield's* view of the Privileges and Immunities Clause might, and should be, properly interred as the product of a bygone era, but he went on to emphasize the interpretation of the scope of the Clause proposed in Paul v. Virginia, supra, namely that "[t]he section, in effect, prevents a State from discriminating against citizens of other States in favor of its own." . . .

Less than a decade after *Hague,* Toomer v. Witsell, supra, embraced and applied the Roberts interpretation of the Clause. . . . After stating that the Clause "was designed to insure to a citizen of State *A* who ventures into State *B* the same privileges which the citizens of State *B* enjoy," the Court set out the standard against which a State's differential treatment of nonresidents would be evaluated.

> Like many other constitutional provisions, the privileges and immunities clause is not an absolute. It does bar discrimination against citizens of other States *where there is no substantial reason for the discrimination beyond the mere fact that they are citizens of other States*. . . .

I think the time has come to confirm explicitly that which has been implicit in our modern privileges and immunities decisions, namely that an inquiry into whether a given right is "fundamental" has no place in our analysis of whether a State's discrimination against nonresidents — who "are not represented in the [discriminating] State's legislative halls" . . . — violates the Clause. Rather, our primary concern is the State's justification for its discrimination. Drawing from the principles announced in *Toomer*, . . . a State's discrimination against nonresidents is permissible where (1) the presence or activity of nonresidents is the source or cause of the problem or effect with which the State seeks to deal, and (2) the discrimination practiced against nonresidents bears a substantial relation to the problem they present. . . .

II

It is clear that under a proper privileges and immunities analysis Montana's discriminatory treatment of nonresident big-game hunters in this case must fall. Putting aside the validity of the requirement that nonresident hunters desiring to hunt elk must purchase a combination license that resident elk hunters need not buy, there are three possible justifications for charging nonresident elk hunters an amount at least 7.5 times the fee imposed on resident big-game hunters. The first is conservation. The State did not attempt to assert this as a justification for its discriminatory licensing scheme in the District Court, and apparently does not do so here. Indeed, it is difficult to see how it could consistently with the first prong of a modern privileges and immunities analysis. First, there is nothing in the record to indicate that the influx of nonresident hunters created a special danger to Montana's elk or to any of its other wildlife species. . . . Second, if Montana's discriminatorily high big-game license fee is an outgrowth of general conservation policy to discourage elk hunting, this too fails as a basis for the licensing scheme. Montana makes no effort similarly to inhibit its own residents. As we said in Douglas v. Seacoast Products, Inc., 431 U.S. 265, 285 n.21 (1977), "[a] statute that leaves a State's residents free to destroy a natural resource while excluding aliens or nonresidents is not a conservation law at all."

The second possible justification for the fee differential Montana imposes on nonresident elk hunters — the one presented in the District Court and principally relied upon here — is a cost justification. . . . The District Court . . . [found] that "[o]n a consideration of [the] evidence . . . and with due regard to the presumption of constitutionality . . . the ratio of 7.5 to 1 cannot be justified on any basis of cost allocation." This finding is not clearly erroneous, and the Court does not intimate otherwise. . . .

The third possible justification for Montana's licensing scheme, the doctrine of McCready v. Virginia, 94 U.S. 391 (1877), is actually no justification at all, but simply an assertion that a State "owns" the wildlife within its borders in trust for its citizens and may therefore do with it what it pleases. See Geer v. Connecticut, 161 U.S. 519 (1896). The lingering death of the *McCready* doctrine as applied to a State's wildlife . . . finally became a reality in Douglas v. Seacoast Products, Inc. . . .

Note

In Hicklin v. Orbeck, 437 U.S. 518 (1978), the Court struck down, as violative of the privileges and immunities clause of Article IV, an Alaska statute requiring that Alaska residents be preferred to nonresidents for jobs connected with oil and gas pipelines. Writing for a unanimous Court, Justice Brennan assumed for the sake of argument that a state could constitutionally deal with its unemployment problem by requiring private employers to discriminate against nonresidents, if the nonresidents were the unique source of the problem. He noted that Alaska's unemployment resulted from indigenous factors such as its residents' lack of education and training, rather than from an influx of job-seekers as such. Moreover, the statutory preference extended to all Alaskans, not just the unemployed.

SUPREME COURT OF NEW HAMPSHIRE v. PIPER
470 U.S. 274 (1985)
Appeal from the First Circuit Court of Appeals

[Kathryn Piper, a resident of Lower Waterford, Vermont — about 400 yards from the New Hampshire border — applied in 1979 to take the New Hampshire bar examination. With her application, she submitted a statement of intent to become a New Hampshire resident. After passing the examination, she was informed by the New Hampshire Board of Bar Examiners that she would have to establish a home address in New Hampshire before she could be sworn in as a member of that state's bar. The New Hampshire Supreme Court rejected a request for a dispensation of the residency requirement; Ms. Piper thereupon sued in federal court, claiming a violation of the Privileges and Immunities Clause, Article IV, section 2.

The District Court ruled in her favor, finding both that the opportunity to practice law a "fundamental right" within the meaning of Baldwin v. Montana Fish and Game Commission, and that the State had denied this right without a "substantial reason." The First Circuit Court of Appeals, sitting en banc, affirmed. Upon appeal, the United States Supreme Court affirmed, with seven Justices joining Justice Powell's opinion for the Court.]

II

A

. . . Like the occupations considered in our earlier cases, the practice of law is important to the national economy. As the Court noted in *Goldfarb* [v. Virginia State Bar, 421 U.S. 773, 788], the "activities of lawyers play an important part in commercial intercourse."

The lawyer's role in the national economy is not the only reason that the opportunity to practice law should be considered a "fundamental right." We believe that the legal profession has a noncommercial role and duty that reinforce the view that the practice of law falls within the ambit of the Privileges and Immunities Clause. Out-of-state lawyers may — and often do — represent persons who raise unpopular federal claims. In some cases, representation by nonresident counsel may be the only means available for the vindication of federal rights. The lawyer who champions unpopular causes surely is as important to the "maintenance or well-being of the Union," *Baldwin,* as was the shrimp fisherman in *Toomer* or the pipeline worker in [Hicklin v. Orbeck, 437 U.S. 518 (1978)].[60]

B

The State asserts that the Privileges and Immunities Clause should be held inapplicable to the practice of law because a lawyer's activities are "bound up with the exercise of judicial power and the administration of justice." Its contention is based on the premise that the lawyer is an "officer of the court," who "exercises state power on a daily basis." The State concludes that if it cannot exclude nonresidents from the bar, its ability to function as a sovereign political body will be threatened.

Lawyers do enjoy a "broad monopoly . . . to do things other citizens may not lawfully do." In re Griffiths, 413 U.S. 717, 731 (1971).[61] We do not believe, however, that the practice of law involves an "exercise of state power" justifying New Hampshire's residency requirement. In In re Griffiths, we held that the State could not exclude an alien from the bar on the ground that a lawyer is an " 'officer of the Court who' . . . is entrusted with the 'exercise of actual government power.' " We concluded that a lawyer is not an "officer" within the ordinary meaning of that word. He " 'makes his own decisions, follows his own best judgment, collects his own fees and runs his own business.' " Moreover, we held that the state powers entrusted to lawyers do not "involve matters of state policy or acts of such unique responsibility that they should be entrusted only to citizens."

Because, under *Griffiths,* a lawyer is not an "officer" of the State in any political sense, there is no reason for New Hampshire to exclude from its bar nonresidents. We therefore conclude that the right to practice law is protected by the Privileges and Immunities Clause.

III

The conclusion that Rule 42 deprives nonresidents of a protected privilege does not end our inquiry. . . . The Clause does not preclude discrimination against nonresidents where: (i) there is a substantial reason for the difference in treatment; and (ii) the discrimination practiced against nonresidents bears a substantial relationship to the State's objective. In deciding whether the discrimination bears a close or substantial relationship to the State's objective, the Court has considered the availability of less restrictive means.

The Supreme Court of New Hampshire offers several justifications for its refusal to admit nonresidents to the bar. It asserts that nonresident members would be less likely: (i) to become, and remain, familiar with local rules and procedures;

60. See discussion of *Hicklin* at page 459 supra.

61. In In re Griffiths, appellant, a resident alien, was denied permission to take the state bar examination solely because of a U.S. citizenship requirement imposed by the state. The Court struck down the requirement as violative of the Equal Protection Clause, stating that the state "has not established that it must exclude all aliens from the practice of law in order to vindicate its undoubted interest in high professional standards."

(ii) to behave ethically; (iii) to be available for court proceedings; and (iv) to do *pro bono* and other volunteer work in the State. We find that none of these reasons meets the test of "substantiality," and that the means chosen do not bear the necessary relationship to the State's objectives.[a]

There is no evidence to support the State's claim that nonresidents might be less likely to keep abreast of local rules and procedures. Nor may we assume that a nonresident lawyer — any more than a resident — would disserve his clients by failing to familiarize himself with the rules. As a practical matter, we think that unless a lawyer has, or anticipates, a considerable practice in the New Hampshire courts, he would be unlikely to take the bar examination and pay the annual dues of $125.[b]

We also find the State's second justification to be without merit, for there is no reason to believe that a nonresident lawyer will conduct his practice in a dishonest manner. . . . Furthermore, a nonresident lawyer may be disciplined for unethical conduct. . . .

There is more merit to the State's assertion that a nonresident member of the bar at times would be unavailable for court proceedings. . . . Nevertheless, we do not believe that this type of problem justifies the exclusion of nonresident members from the state bar. One may assume that a high percentage of nonresident lawyers willing to take the state bar examination and pay the annual dues will reside in places reasonably convenient to New Hampshire. Furthermore, in those cases where the nonresident counsel will be unavailable on short notice, the State can protect its interests through less restrictive means. The trial court, by rule or as an exercise of discretion, may require any lawyer who resides at a great distance to retain a local attorney who will be available for unscheduled meetings and hearings.

The final reason advanced by the State is that nonresident members of its bar would be disinclined to do their share of *pro bono* and volunteer work. Perhaps this is true to a limited extent, particularly where the member resides in a distant location. We think it is reasonable to believe, however, that most lawyers who become members of a state bar will endeavor to perform their share of these services. . . . Furthermore, nonresident bar members, like the resident member, could be required to represent indigents and perhaps to participate in formal legal-aid work.

In summary, the State neither advances a "substantial reason" for its discrimination against nonresident applicants to the bar, nor demonstrates that

a. A former president of the American Bar Association has suggested another possible reason for the rule: "Many of the states that have erected fences against out-of-state lawyers have done so primarily to protect their own lawyers from professional competition." Smith, Time for a National Practice of Law Act, 64 A.B.A.J. 557 (1978). This reason is not substantial. The Privileges and Immunities Clause was designed primarily to prevent such economic protectionism.

b. Because it is markedly overinclusive, the residency requirement does not bear a substantial relationship to the State's objective. A less restrictive alternative would be to require mandatory attendance at periodic seminars on state practice. There already is a rule requiring all new admittees to complete a "practical skills course" within one year of their admission.

New Hampshire's "simple residency" requirement is underinclusive as well, because it permits lawyers who move away from the State to retain their membership in the bar. There is no reason to believe that a former resident would maintain a more active practice in the New Hampshire courts than would a nonresident who had never lived in the State.

the discrimination practiced bears a close relationship to its proffered objectives. . . .

[An opinion by Justice White concurring in the judgment is omitted.]

REHNQUIST, J., dissenting.

[Given that a State may require its lawmakers and judges to be residents,] it is reasonable for a State to decide that those people who have been trained to analyze law and policy are better equipped to write those state laws and adjudicate cases arising under them. The State therefore may decide that it has an interest in maximizing the number of resident lawyers, so as to increase the quality of the pool from which its lawmakers can be drawn. A residency law such as the one at issue is the obvious way to accomplish these goals. Since at any given time within a State there is only enough legal work to support a certain number of lawyers, each out-of-state lawyer who is allowed to practice necessarily takes legal work that could support an in-state lawyer, who would otherwise be available to perform various functions that a State has an interest in promoting.

Nor does the State's interest end with enlarging the pool of qualified lawmakers. A State similarly might determine that because lawyers play an important role in the formulation of State policy through their adversary representation, they should be intimately conversant with the local concerns that should inform such policies. And the State likewise might conclude that those citizens trained in the law are likely to bring their useful expertise to other important functions that benefit from such expertse and are of interest to state governments — such as trusteeships, or directorships of corporations, or school board positions, or merely the role of the interested citizen at a town meeting. . . .

It is no answer to these arguments that many lawyers simply will not perform these functions, or that out-of-state lawyers can perform them equally well, or that the State can devise less restrictive alternatives for accomplishing these goals. Conclusory second-guessing of difficult legislative decisions, such as the Court resorts to today, is not an attractive way for federal courts to engage in judicial review. . . .

Note: Subsequent Cases

The Court relied on *Piper* to strike down residency requirements in Supreme Court of Virginia v. Friedman, 487 U.S. 59 (1988), and Virgin Islands Bar Association v. Thorsten, 489 U.S. 546 (1989). Virginia allowed exemptions from the state bar exam to permanent residents who had previously been admitted to practice in another state. Chief Justice Rehnquist and Justice Scalia dissented. The Virgin Islands required one year of residence and the declaration of an intention to continue residing and practicing law in the Islands. Rehnquist also dissented in *Thorsten*, this time joined by Justices White and O'Connor: "[a]ccepting *Piper*'s view of the Privileges and Immunities Clause, I think the unique circumstances of legal practice in the Virgin Islands as compared to the mainland States could justify upholding this simple residency requirement." Thus he would remand for a full trial in which the facts purportedly justifying the Virgin Islands requirement could be developed.

REEVES, INC. v. STAKE

447 U.S. 429 (1980)

Certiorari to the Court of Appeals for the Eighth Circuit

BLACKMUN, J.

The issue in this case is whether, consistent with the Commerce Clause, U.S. Const., Art. I, §8, cl. 3, the State of South Dakota, in a time of shortage, may confine the sale of the cement it produces solely to its residents.

I

In 1919, South Dakota undertook plans to build a cement plant. The project, a product of the state's then prevailing Progressive political movement, was initiated in response to recent regional cement shortages that "interfered with and delayed both public and private enterprises," and that were "threatening the people of this state." . . .

The plant, however, located at Rapid City, soon produced more cement than South Dakotans could use. Over the years, buyers in no less than nine nearby States purchased cement from the State's plant. Between 1970 and 1977, some 40% of the plant's output went outside the State.

The plant's list of out-of-state cement buyers included petitioner Reeves, Inc. . . . From the beginning of its operations in 1958, and until 1978, Reeves purchased about 95% of its cement from the South Dakota plant.

As the 1978 construction season approached, difficulties at the plant slowed production. Meanwhile, a booming construction industry spurred demand for cement both regionally and nationally. The plant found itself unable to meet all orders. Faced with the same type of "serious cement shortage" that inspired the plant's construction, the Commission "reaffirmed its policy of supplying all South Dakota customers first and to honor all contract commitments, with the remaining volume allocated on a first come, first served basis." . . .

Reeves, which had no pre-existing long-term supply contract, was hit hard and quickly by this development. On June 30, 1978, the plant informed Reeves that it could not continue to fill Reeves' orders, and on July 5, it turned away a Reeves truck. Unable to find another supplier, Reeves was forced to cut production by 76% in mid-July.

On July 19, Reeves brought this suit against the Commission, challenging the plant's policy of preferring South Dakota buyers, and seeking injunctive relief. After conducting a hearing and receiving briefs and affidavits, the District Court found no substantial issue of material fact and permanently enjoined the Commission's practice. The court reasoned that South Dakota's "hoarding" was inimical to the national free market envisioned by the Commerce Clause.

[The Eighth Circuit reversed, relying on Hughes v. Alexandria Scrap Corp., 426 U.S. 794 (1976).]

II

A

Alexandria Scrap concerned a Maryland program designed to remove abandoned automobiles from the State's roadways and junkyards. To encourage recycling, a "bounty" was offered for every Maryland-titled junk car converted into scrap. Processors located both in and outside Maryland were eligible to collect these subsidies. . . . [However, a 1974] law imposed more exacting documentation requirements on out-of-state than in-state processors. By making it less remunerative for suppliers to transfer vehicles outside Maryland, the reform triggered a "precipitate decline in the number of bounty-eligible hulks supplied to appellee's [Virginia] plant from Maryland sources." Indeed, "[t]he practical effect was substantially the same as if Maryland had withdrawn altogether the availability of bounties on hulks delivered by unlicensed suppliers to licensed non-Maryland processors." . . .

[The Supreme Court reversed the District Court below, which held that Maryland's law violated the commerce clause.]

In the Court's view, however, *Alexandria Scrap* did not involve "the kind of action with which the Commerce Clause is concerned." Unlike prior cases voiding state laws inhibiting interstate trade, "Maryland has not sought to prohibit the flow of hulks, or to regulate the conditions under which it may occur. Instead, it has entered into the market itself to bid up their price," "as a purchaser, in effect, of a potential article of interstate commerce," and has restricted "its trade to its own citizens or businesses within the State."

Having characterized Maryland as a market participant, rather than as a market regulator, the Court found no reason to "believe the Commerce Clause was intended to require independent justification for [the State's] action." The Court couched its holding in unmistakably broad terms. "Nothing in the purposes animating the Commerce Clause prohibits a State, in the absence of congressional action, from participating in the market and exercising the right to favor its own citizens over others."

B

The basic distinction drawn in *Alexandria Scrap* between States as market participants and States as market regulators makes good sense and sound law. As that case explains, the Commerce Clause responds principally to state taxes and regulatory measures impeding free private trade in the national marketplace. . . .

There is no indication of a constitutional plan to limit the ability of the States themselves to operate freely in the free market.

III

South Dakota, as a seller of cement, unquestionably fits the "market participant" label more comfortably than a State acting to subsidize local scrap processors. Thus, the general rule of *Alexandria Scrap* plainly applies here. Petitioner argues, however, that the exemption for marketplace participation necessarily admits of exceptions. While conceding that possibility, we perceive in this case no sufficient reason to depart from the general rule.

A

In finding a Commerce Clause violation, the District Court emphasized "that the Commission . . . made an election to become part of the interstate commerce system." The gist of this reasoning, repeated by petitioner here, is that one good turn deserves another. Having long exploited the interstate market, South Dakota should not be permitted to withdraw from it when a shortage arises. This argument is not persuasive. It is somewhat self-serving to say that South Dakota has "exploited" the interstate market. An equally fair characterization is that neighboring States long have benefited from South Dakota's foresight and industry. Viewed in this light, it is not surprising that *Alexandria Scrap* rejected an argument that the 1974 Maryland legislation challenged there was invalid because cars abandoned in Maryland had been processed in neighboring States for five years. As in *Alexandria Scrap,* we must conclude that "this chronology does not distinguish the case, for Commerce Clause purposes, from one in which a State offered [cement] only to domestic [buyers] from the start."

Our rejection of petitioner's market-exploitation theory fundamentally refocuses analysis. It means that to reverse we would have to void a South Dakota "residents only" policy even if it had been enforced from the plant's very first days. Such a holding, however, would interfere significantly with a State's ability to structure relations exclusively with its own citizens. It would also threaten the future fashioning of effective and creative programs for solving local problems and distributing government largesse. A healthy regard for federalism and good government renders us reluctant to risk these results.

B

Undaunted by these considerations, petitioner advances [other] arguments for reversal:

First, petitioner protests that South Dakota's preference for its residents responds solely to the "non-governmental objectiv[e]" of protectionism. Therefore, petitioner argues, the policy is per se invalid. See Philadelphia v. New Jersey, 437 U.S. 617, 624 (1978).

We find the label "protectionism" of little help in this context. The State's refusal to sell to buyers other than South Dakotans is "protectionist" only in the sense that it limits benefits generated by a state program to those who fund the state treasury and whom the State was created to serve. Petitioner's argument apparently also would characterize as "protectionist" rules restricting to state residents the enjoyment of state educational institutions, energy generated by a state-run plant, police and fire protection, and agricultural improvement and business development programs. Such policies, while perhaps "protectionist" in a loose sense, reflect the essential and patently unobjectionable purpose of state government — to serve the citizens of the State.

Second, petitioner echoes the District Court's warning:

> If a state in this union, were allowed to hoard its commodities or resources for the use of their own residents only, a drastic situation might evolve. For example, Pennsylvania or Wyoming might keep their coal, the northwest its timber, and the mining states their minerals. The result being that embargo may be retaliated by embargo and commerce would be halted at state lines.

This argument, although rooted in the core purpose of the Commerce Clause, does not fit the present facts. Cement is not a natural resource, like coal, timber, wild game, or minerals. Cf. Hughes v. Oklahoma, 441 U.S. 322 (1979) (minnows); Philadelphia v. New Jersey, supra (landfill sites); Pennsylvania v. West Virginia, 262 U.S. 553 (1923) (natural gas); West v. Kansas Natural Gas Co., 221 U.S. 229 (1911) (same). It is the end product of a complex process whereby a costly physical plant and human labor act on raw materials. South Dakota has not sought to limit access to the State's limestone or other materials used to make cement. Nor has it restricted the ability of private firms or sister States to set up plants within its borders. Moreover, petitioner has not suggested that South Dakota possesses unique access to the materials needed to produce cement. Whatever limits might exist on a State's ability to invoke the *Alexandria Scrap* exemption to hoard resources which by happenstance are found there, those limits do not apply here. . . .

C

We conclude, then, that the arguments for invalidating South Dakota's resident-preference program are weak at best. . . .

The judgment of the United States Court of Appeals is affirmed.

POWELL, J., joined by Brennan, White, and Stevens, JJ., dissenting.

. . . I agree with the Court that the State of South Dakota may provide cement for its public needs without violating the Commerce Clause. But I cannot agree that South Dakota may withhold its cement from interstate commerce in order to benefit private citizens and businesses within the State.

I

. . . This case presents a novel constitutional question. The Commerce Clause would bar legislation imposing on private parties the type of restraint on commerce adopted by South Dakota. Conversely, a private business constitutionally could adopt a marketing policy that excluded customers who come from another State. This case falls between those polar situations. The State, through its Commission, engages in a commercial enterprise and restricts its own interstate distribution. The question is whether the Commission's policy should be treated like state regulation of private parties or like the marketing policy of a private business.

The application of the Commerce Clause to this case should turn on the nature of the governmental activity involved. If a public enterprise undertakes an "integral operatio[n] in areas of traditional governmental functions," National League of Cities v. Usery, 426 U.S. 833, 852 (1976), the Commerce Clause is not directly relevant. If, however, the State enters the private market and operates a commercial enterprise for the advantage of its private citizens, it may not evade the constitutional policy against economic Balkanization.

This distinction derives from the power of governments to supply their own needs, see Perkins v. Lukens Steel Co., 310 U.S. 113, 127 (1940); Atkin v. Kansas, 191 U.S. 207 (1903), and from the purpose of the Commerce Clause itself, which is designed to protect "the natural functioning of the interstate market." Hughes v. Alexandria Scrap Corp., supra, at 806. In procuring goods and services for the operation of government, a State may act without regard to the private marketplace and remove itself from the reach of the Commerce Clause. See American Yearbook Co. v. Askew, 339 F. Supp. 719 (M.D. Fla.), summarily aff'd, 409 U.S. 904 (1972). But when a State itself becomes a participant in the private market for other purposes, the Constitution forbids actions that would impede the flow of interstate commerce. These categories recognize no more than the "constitutional line between the State as government and the State as trader." New York v. United States, 326 U.S. 572, 579 (1946).

The Court holds that South Dakota, like a private business, should not be governed by the Commerce Clause when it enters the private market. But precisely because South Dakota is a State, it cannot be presumed to behave like an enterprise " 'engaged in an entirely private business.' " A State frequently will respond to market conditions on the basis of political rather than economic concerns. To use the Court's terms, a State may attempt to act as a "market regulator" rather than a "market participant." In that situation, it is a pretense to equate the State with a private economic actor. State action burdening interstate trade is no less state action because it is accomplished by a public agency authorized to participate in the private market.

II

The threshold issue is whether South Dakota has undertaken integral government operations in an area of traditional governmental functions, or whether it has participated in the marketplace as a private firm. If the latter characterization applies, we also must determine whether the State Commission's marketing policy burdens the flow of interstate trade. This analysis highlights the differences between the state action here and that before the Court in Hughes v. Alexandria Scrap Corp.

A

As the Court today notes, *Alexandria Scrap* determined that Maryland's bounty program constituted direct state participation in the market for automobile hulks. But the critical question — the second step in the opinion's analysis — was whether the bounty program constituted an impermissible burden on interstate commerce. Recognizing that the case did not fit neatly into conventional Commerce Clause theory. we found no burden on commerce.

The Court first observed:

> Maryland has not sought to prohibit the flow of hulks, or to regulate the conditions under which it may occur. Instead, it has entered into the market itself to bid up their price. There has been an impact upon the interstate flow of hulks only because . . . Maryland effectively has made it more lucrative for unlicensed suppliers to dispose of their hulks in Maryland. . . .

We further stated "that the novelty of this case is not its presentation of a new form of 'burden' upon commerce, but that appellee should characterize Maryland's action as a burden which the Commerce Clause was intended to make suspect." The opinion then emphasized that "no trade barrier of the type forbidden by the Commerce Clause, and involved in previous cases, impedes th[e] movement [of hulks] out of State." Rather, the hulks "remain within Maryland in response to market forces, including that exerted by money from the State." The Court concluded that the subsidies provided under the Maryland program erected no barriers to trade. Consequently, the Commerce Clause did not forbid the Maryland program.

B

Unlike the market subsidies at issue in *Alexandria Scrap,* the marketing policy of the South Dakota Cement Commission has cut off interstate trade. The State can raise such a bar when it enters the market to supply its own needs. In order to ensure an adequate supply of cement for public uses, the State can withhold from interstate commerce the cement needed for public projects. Cf. National League of Cities v. Usery, supra.

The State, however, has no parallel justification for favoring private, in-state customers over out-of-state customers. In response to political concerns that likely would be inconsequential to a private cement producer, South Dakota has shut off its cement sales to customers beyond its borders. That discrimination constitutes a direct barrier to trade "of the type forbidden by the Commerce Clause, and involved in previous cases. . . ." The effect on interstate trade is the same as if the state legislature had imposed the policy on private cement producers. The Commerce Clause prohibits this severe restraint on commerce.

Note: On the State's Spending Power

In White v. Massachusetts Council of Construction Employers, 460 U.S. 204 (1983), and United Building and Construction Trades Council of Camden County and Vicinity v. Mayor and Council of the City of Camden, 465 U.S. 208 (1984), the Court examined attempts by Boston, Massachusetts, and Camden, New Jersey, to condition the award of public construction contracts on the guarantee that bidders would hire a substantial percentage (50 percent and 40 percent, respectively) of their workers from within the city. In both cases labor unions challenged the constitutionality of the city policies.

Justice Rehnquist wrote for seven Justices in *White,* upholding the Boston mayor's order against a commerce clause challenge. He emphasized the market regulator-market participant analysis (developed in *Alexandria Scrap* and *Reeves*) and determined that the latter applied to Boston, given that it was allocating its own funds for the construction. "If the city is a market participant, then the Commerce Clause establishes no barrier to conditions such as these which the city demands for its participation." That the mayor's order affected out-of-state workers was irrelevant: "Impact on out-of-state residents figures in the equation only after it is decided that the city is regulating the market rather than participating in it. . . ."

Justice Blackmun, joined by Justice White, dissented. He took issue with the majority's use of the regulator-participant distinction and argued that the order was a de facto regulation of the private employment market subject to the restraints of the Commerce Clause:

> The simple unilateral refusals to deal the Court encountered in *Reeves* and *Alexandria Scrap* were relatively pure examples of a seller's or purchaser's simply choosing its bargaining partners, "long recognized" as the right of traders in our free enterprise system. The executive order in this case, in notable contrast, by its terms is a direct attempt to govern private economic relationships. The power to dictate to another with whom *he* may deal is viewed with suspicion and closely limited in the context of purely private economic relations. When exercised by government, such a power is the essence of regulation. . . .
>
> A requirement that firms wishing to deal with the State hire a certain percentage of their workforce from among state residents in practice may constrict the opportunities of nonresidents to work on projects with no connection whatever with the governmental entity imposing the condition. A firm that relies to any significant extent on a permanent workforce will be compelled to favor local residents for these positions. . . . The effect of such "conditions" on the ability of nonresidents to deal with affected firms would be virtually identical to the effect of a conventional market regulation requiring such practices.
>
> . . . It might be argued that because the city could have chosen to build the projects covered by the order itself and, free from dormant Commerce Clause restraint, could have hired local residents, the city may contract to have the work done by private firms on the condition that the firms hire local residents. But the Court never has suggested that the State's special sovereign interest in determining whom it will hire, and in setting the terms and conditions of public employment, extends to dictating whom private parties with which it contracts will hire, or the terms and conditions of private employment. In my view, the State's interest in managing its relations with its employees is fully safeguarded by its power to do the work itself if it so chooses. . . .
>
> Boston has at its disposal reasonable alternatives to accomplish its central goal — the alleviation of unemployment among Boston residents. It can create training programs for its unemployed residents or establish aggressive referral practices aimed at promoting employment for its residents at *all* construction projects without implicating Commerce Clause concerns. [What it cannot do is impose] discriminatory restraints on the private market.

Justice Rehnquist responded to the dissent in a footnote.

> We agree with Justice Blackmun that there are some limits on a state or local government's ability to impose restrictions that reach beyond the immediate parties with which the government transacts business. We find it unnecessary in this case to define those limits with precision, except to say that we think the Commerce Clause does not require the city to stop at the boundary of formal privity of contract. In this case, the mayor's executive order covers a discrete, identifiable class of economic ac-

tivity in which the city is a major participant. Everyone affected by the order is, in a substantial if informal sense, "working for the city." Wherever the limits of the market participation exception may lie, we conclude that the executive order in this case falls well within the scope of *Alexandria Scrap* and *Reeves*.

White involved only a Commerce Clause challenge, and the Court specifically reserved the question of the status of the program under the Privileges and Immunities Clause. The *Camden* case addressed the latter issue. The New Jersey Supreme Court had "decline[d] to apply the Privileges and Immunities Clause in the context of a municipal ordinance that has identical effects upon out-of-state citizens and New Jersey citizens not residing in the locality." Justice Rehnquist again wrote for the Court and reversed the New Jersey Supreme Court, with only Justice Blackmun dissenting:

We first address the argument, accepted by the Supreme Court of New Jersey, that the Clause does not even apply to a *municipal* ordinance such as this. Two separate contentions are advanced in support of this position: first, that the Clause only applies to laws passed by a *State* and second, that the Clause only applies to laws that discriminate on the basis of *state* citizenship.

The first argument can be quickly rejected. . . . First of all, one cannot easily distinguish municipal from state action in this case: the municipal ordinance would not have gone into effect without express approval by the State Treasurer. . . .

More fundamentally, a municipality is merely a political subdivision of the State from which its authority derives. . . . Thus, even if the ordinance had been adopted solely by Camden, and not pursuant to a state program or with state approval, the hiring preference would still have to comport with the Privileges and Immunities Clause.

The second argument merits more consideration. . . . Given the Camden ordinance, an out-of-state citizen who ventures into New Jersey will not enjoy the same privileges as the New Jersey citizen residing in Camden. It is true that New Jersey citizens not residing in Camden will be affected by the ordinance as well as out-of-state citizens. And it is true that the disadvantaged New Jersey residents have no claim under the Privileges and Immunities Clause. The Slaughter-House Cases, 16 Wall. 36, 77 (1872). But New Jersey residents at least have a chance to remedy at the polls any discrimination against them. Out-of-state citizens have no such opportunity, and they must "not be restricted to the uncertain remedies afforded by diplomatic processes and official retaliation." Toomer v. Witsell, 334 U.S. 385, 395 (1948).[a] We conclude that Camden's ordinance is not immune from constitutional

a. The dissent [rejects the application of the Privileges and Immunities Clause to municipal preferences that work against other citizens of the same state and] suggests that New Jersey citizens not residing in Camden will adequately protect the interests of out-of-state residents. . . . What the dissent fails to appreciate is that the Camden ordinance at issue in this case was adopted pursuant to a comprehensive, state-wide program applicable in all New Jersey cities. . . . [E]very New Jersey city is free to adopt a similar protectionist measure. Some have already done so. Thus, it is hard to see how New Jersey residents living outside Camden will protect the interests of out-of-state citizens.

More fundamentally, the dissent's proposed blanket exemption for all classifications that are less than state-wide would provide States with a simple means for evading the strictures of the Privileges and Immunities Clause. Suppose, for example, that California wanted to guarantee that all employees of contractors and subcontractors working on construction projects funded in whole or in part by state funds are state residents. Under the dissent's analysis, the California legislature need merely divide the State in half, providing one resident-hiring preference for Northern Californians on all such projects taking place in Northern California, and one for Southern Californians on all projects taking place in Southern California. State residents generally would benefit from the law at the expense of out-of-state residents; yet, the law would be immune from scrutiny under the Clause review at the behest of out-of-state residents merely because some in-state residents are similarly disadvantaged.

Application of the Privileges and Immunities Clause to a particular instance of discrimination against out-of-state residents entails a two-step inquiry. . . . As a threshold matter. . . , we must determine whether an out-of-state resident's interest in employment on public works contracts in another state is sufficiently "fundamental" to the promotion of interstate harmony so as to "fall within the purview of the Privileges and Immunities Clause." *Baldwin*. . . .

Certainly, the pursuit of a common calling is one of the most fundamental of those privileges protected by the Clause. . . . Public employment, however, is qualitatively different from employment in the private sector. . . . And, in *White*, we held that for purposes of the Commerce Clause everyone employed on a city public works project is, "in a substantial if informal sense, 'working for the city.' "

. . . [However,] we decline to transfer mechanically into this context an analysis fashioned to fit the Commerce Clause. . . . [T]he distinction between market participant and market regulator relied upon in *White* to dispose of the Commerce Clause challenge is not dispositive in this context. The two Clauses have different aims and set different standards for state conduct.

The Commerce Clause acts as an implied restraint upon state regulatory Power. . . . When the State acts solely as a market participant, no conflict between state *regulation* and federal regulatory authority can arise. The Privileges and Immunities Clause, on the other hand, imposes a direct restraint on state action in the interests of interstate harmony. This concern with comity cuts across the market regulator-market participant distinction that is crucial under the Commerce Clause. It is discrimination against out-of-state residents on matters of fundamental concern which triggers the Clause, not regulation affecting interstate commerce. Thus, the fact that Camden is merely setting conditions on its expenditures for goods and services in the marketplace does not preclude the possibility that those conditions violate Privileges and Immunities Clause. . . . In sum, Camden may, without fear of violating the Commerce Clause, pressure private employers engaged in public works projects funded in whole or in part by the city to hire city residents. But that same exercise of power to bias the employment decisions of private contractors and subcontractors against out-of-state residents may be called to account under the Privileges and Immunities Clause. A determination of whether a privilege is "fundamental" for purposes of that Clause does not depend on whether the employees of private contractors and subcontractors engaged in public works projects can or cannot be said to be "working for the city." The opportunity to seek employment with such private employers is "sufficiently basic to the livelihood of the Nation," *Baldwin*, as to fall within the purview of the Privileges and Immunities Clause even though the contractors and subcontractors are themselves engaged in projects funded in whole or part by the city.

The conclusion that Camden's ordinance discriminates against a protected privilege does not, of course, end the inquiry. We have stressed in prior cases that "[l]ike many other constitutional provisions, the privileges and immunities clause is not an absolute." Toomer v. Witsell, 334 U.S. 385, 396 (1948). It does not preclude discrim-

---

simply because it was not phrased in terms of *state* citizenship or residency. Such a formalistic construction would effectively write the Clause out of the Constitution.

[To this Justice Blackmun responded, in his dissent, that "[t]he fact that no State has attempted anything resembling the Court's proposed maneuver in the two centuries since the adoption of the Clause, despite the fact that none of this Court's precedents has foreclosed the option, strongly suggests that the state political processes can be trusted to prevent this kind of Balkanization. The Court cannot justify deforming the Constitution's response to real problems by invoking imaginary and urealistic ones."]

ination against citizens of other States where there is a "substantial reason" for the difference in treatment. . . . As part of any justification offered for the discriminatory law, nonresidents must somehow be shown to "constitute a peculiar source of the evil at which the statute is aimed." Id., at 398.

The city of Camden contends that its ordinance is necessary to counteract grave economic and social ills. . . . The resident hiring preference is designed, the city contends, to increase the number of employed persons living in Camden and to arrest the "middle class flight" currently plaguing the city. The city also argues that all non-Camden residents employed on city public works projects . . . "live off" Camden without "living in" Camden. Camden contends that the scope of the discrimination practiced in the ordinance, with its municipal residency requirement, is carefully tailored to alleviate this evil without unreasonably harming nonresidents, who still have access to 60% of the available positions. . . .

[W]e find it impossible to evaluate Camden's justification on the record as it now stands. No trial has ever been held in the case. No findings of fact have been made. . . . It would not be appropriate for this Court either to make factual determinations as an initial matter or to take judicial notice of Camden's decay. We, therefore, deem it wise to remand the case to the New Jersey Supreme Court.

Justice White's opinion in South-Central Timber Development v. Wunnicke, 467 U.S. 82 (1984), revealed significant uncertainty by at least half the Court regarding the market regulator-market participant distinction and the concomitant scope of contractual freedom permitted the state. Petitioner, almost all of whose business involved exporting timber to Japan, objected to having to contract with Alaska that all timber taken from state lands would be processed in-state before export. Alaska responded that Congress had authorized the state's imposition of such a requirement and that even in the absence of congressional authorization the state could impose the requirement as a contractual condition for entry onto state-owned land by private businesses.

Justice White spoke for a majority of six Justices in finding no congressional authorization. However, only three justices joined that part of his opinion that considered Alaska's constitutional defense.[62] Justice White distinguished both *Reeves* and *White,* upon which Alaska relied.

Although the Court in *Reeves* did strongly endorse the right of a State to deal with whomever it chooses when it participates in the market, it did not — and did not purport to — sanction the imposition of any terms the State might desire. For example, the Court expressly noted in *Reeves* that "Commerce Clause scrutiny may well be more rigorous when a restraint on foreign commerce is alleged"; that a natural resource "like coal, timber, wild game, or minerals," was not involved, but instead the cement was "the end product of a complex process whereby a costly physical plant and human labor act on raw materials"; and that South Dakota did not bar resale of South Dakota cement to out-of-state purchasers. In this case, all three of the elements that were not present in *Reeves* — foreign commerce, a natural resource, and restrictions on resale — are present. . . .

Contrary to the State's contention, the [*White*] doctrine is not carte blanche to impose any conditions that the State has the economic power to dictate, and does not validate any requirement merely because the State imposes it upon someone with whom it is in contractual privity.

62. Justice Powell, joined by Chief Justice Burger, would have remanded the case to the Court of Appeals for its consideration of Alaska's Commerce Clause argument. Justice Marshall did not participate in the case.

> The limit of the market-participant doctrine must be that it allows a State to impose burdens on commerce within the market in which it is a participant, but allows it to go no further. The State may not impose conditions, whether by statute, regulation, or contract, that have a substantial regulatory effect outside of that particular market [within which it is a major participant]. Unless the "market" is relatively narrowly defined, the doctrine has the potential of swallowing up the rule that States may not impose substantial burdens on interstate commerce.

Justice White found that Alaska was not a participant in the timber-processing market and therefore that its efforts to influence the operation of that market by requiring in-state processing violated the test established by Pike v. Bruce Church.[63]

Justice Rehnquist, joined by Justice O'Connor, dissented. "The contractual term at issue here no more transforms Alaska's sale of timber into 'regulation' of the processing industry than the resident-hiring preference imposed by the city of Boston in *White* constituted regulation of the construction industry." Cf. Dole v. South Dakota, pp. 402-404 supra. See also the discussion of "unconstitutional conditions" in Chapter 11 infra.

D. Federal Preemption of State Regulation

In Gibbons v. Ogden, 22 U.S. (9 Wheat.) 1 (1824), Chapter 2 supra, the first Supreme Court decision involving the commerce clause, the appellant argued that a steamboat monopoly granted by New York to the appellee was prohibited by the clause of its own force and that the monopoly conflicted with an act of Congress licensing appellant to engage in the coastal trade. In dictum, Chief Justice Marshall noted that the former argument had "great force," but he went on to hold that the congressional enactment preempted the state grant. Gibbons' two-pronged argument has become more common as Congress has increasingly legislated pursuant to the commerce and other enumerated powers. Federal preemption of state laws has not been limited to instances of explicit conflicts. Rather, the inquiry is "whether under the circumstances, . . . [the state] law stands as an obstacle to the accomplishment and execution of the full purposes and objectives of Congress."[64] As Justice Douglas wrote in Rice v. Santa Fe Elevator Corp., 331 U.S. 218 (1947):

> The question in each case is what the purpose of Congress was. . . . [This] may be evidenced in several ways. The scheme of federal regulation may be so pervasive as to make reasonable the inference that Congress left no room for the state to supplement it. Or the Act of Congress may touch a field in which the federal interest is so dominant that the federal system will be assumed to preclude enforcement of state laws on the same subject. . . . Or the state policy may produce a result inconsistent with the objective of the federal statute.

The root question in any preemption case is at least formally one of statutory interpretation — of legislative purpose. But some of the decisions indicate

63. The case was remanded to the Court of Appeals "for proceedings consistent with the opinion of this Court." Does it remain open to the Ninth Circuit to consider the Commerce Clause claim on the merits?

64. Hines v. Davidowitz, 312 U.S. 52 (1941) (holding a state law requiring alien registration preempted by national policies governing aliens).

that the Court has adopted the same weighing of interests approach in pre-emption cases that it uses to determine whether a state law unjustifiably burdens interstate commerce. In a number of situations the Court has invalidated statutes on the pre-emption ground when it appeared that the state laws sought to favor local economic interests at the expense of the interstate market. On the other hand, when the Court has been satisfied that valid local interests, such as those in safety or in the reputable operation of local business, outweigh the restrictive effect on interstate commerce, the Court has rejected the pre-emption argument and allowed state regulation to stand.[65]

Burbank v. Lockheed Air Terminal, Inc., 411 U.S. 624 (1973), is a good example of this mixed approach. A closely divided Court held that the Federal Aviation Act of 1958, as amended by the Noise Control Act of 1972, preempted a local noise abatement ordinance prohibiting jet aircraft from taking off from the Hollywood-Burbank Airport between 11:00 P.M. and 7:00 A.M. After considering the 1972 amendments and the joint role of the Federal Aviation Administration and the Environmental Protection Agency in dealing with the problem, Justice Douglas explained that "the pervasive nature of the scheme of federal regulation of aircraft noise . . . leads us to conclude that there is pre-emption" and also noted that "[i]f we were to uphold the Burbank ordinance and a significant number of municipalities followed suit, it is obvious that fractionalized control of the timing of take-offs and landings would severely limit the flexibility of the FAA in controlling air traffic flow" throughout the navigable airspace. Justice Rehnquist, joined by Justices Stewart, White, and Marshall, dissented, chiefly on the ground that the language and legislative history of the statutes indicated a congressional intent not to preempt local noise regulation of aircraft. But his opinion also sounded in the conventional language of commerce clause adjudication:

> Because noise regulation has traditionally been an area of local, not national, concern, in determining whether congressional legislation has, by implication, foreclosed remedial local enactments "we start with the assumption that the historic police powers of the States were not to be superseded by the Federal Act unless that was the clear and manifest purpose of Congress." This assumption derives from our basic constitutional division of legislative competence between the States and Congress; from "due regard for the presuppositions of our embracing federal system. . . ."

V. *The Constitution in Time of War*

A. Japanese-American Exclusion Cases

KOREMATSU v. UNITED STATES

323 U.S. 214 (1944)

Certiorari to the Circuit Court of Appeals for the Ninth Circuit

[Full American participation in World War II began on December 7, 1941, after the Japanese attack on Pearl Harbor. On February 19, 1942, President

65. Note, Pre-emption as a Preferential Ground: A New Canon of Construction, 12 Stan. L. Rev. 208, 220-221 (1959).

Roosevelt issued Executive Order No. 9066, which gave Military Commanders the discretion to "prescribe military areas . . . from which any or all persons may be excluded, and with respect to which the right of any person to enter, remain in, or leave shall be subject to whatever restrictions" the Commander might impose. Within two weeks, General DeWitt, Military Commander of the Western Defense Command, declared that the Pacific Coast states were "particularly subject to attack, to attempted invasion . . . and, in connection therewith, is subject to espionage and acts of sabotage." Military zones were established; all persons of Japanese, German, or Italian ancestry residing in Military Area No. 1, which comprised most of the Western United States, were ordered to deliver to authorities a Change of Residence Notice if they wished to move from their habitual residences.

On March 21, 1942, Congress passed a statute making it a criminal offense for anyone to "enter, remain in, leave, or commit any act in any military area or military zone . . . contrary to the restrictions applicable to any such area or zone." On May 3, General DeWitt issued Civilian Exclusion Order No. 34, which stated that, by noon on May 9, all persons of Japanese ancestry were to be removed from Military Area No. 1 to detention camps. Fred Korematsu, convicted of disobeying the Order, challenged its constitutionality.[66] By a vote of 6 to 3, the Court upheld Korematsu's conviction for violating the exclusion order.]

BLACK, J., delivered the opinion of the Court.

It should be noted, to begin with, that all legal restrictions which curtail the civil rights of a single racial group are immediately suspect. That is not to say that all such restrictions are unconstitutional. It is to say that courts must subject them to the most rigid scrutiny. Pressing public necessity may sometimes justify the existence of such restrictions; racial antagonism never can. . . .

[A previous military order] subjected all persons of Japanese ancestry in prescribed West Coast military areas to remain in their residences from 8 P.M. to 6 A.M. As is the case with the exclusion order here, that prior curfew order was designed as a "protection against espionage and against sabotage." In Hirabayashi v. United States, 320 U.S. 81, we sustained a conviction obtained for violation of the curfew order. The Hirabayashi conviction and this one thus rest on the same 1942 Congressional Act and the same basic executive and military orders, all of which orders were aimed at the twin dangers of espionage and sabotage.

The 1942 Act was attacked in the *Hirabayashi* case as an unconstitutional delegation of power; it was contended that the curfew order and other orders on which it rested were beyond the war powers of the Congress, the military authorities and of the President, as Commander in Chief of the Army; and finally that to apply the curfew order against none but citizens of Japanese ancestry amounted

66. See Peter Irons, Justice at War (1983), for a complete review of the Japanese exclusion litigation. Irons demonstrates what some might regard as obvious: The policy adopted was saturated with racism. Less obvious, though, was that the Government was aware, by the time of the argument before the Supreme Court, that General DeWitt's fear of Japanese-Americans was wholly unfounded, but failed to inform the Court of this. In 1984, a Federal District Court in San Francisco reversed Korematsu's conviction on the basis of evidence brought forth by Irons. Korematsu v. United States, 584 F. Supp. 1406 (N.D. Cal. 1984). In 1988 Congress passed a measure formally apologizing to the Japanese-American community for the measures adopted under Executive Order 9066 and awarding each detention survivor $20,000. See generally, Peter Irons, ed., Justice Delayed: The Record of the Japanese American Internment Cases (1989), which details the relitigation in the 1980s of several of the most important cases of the 1940s.

to a constitutionally prohibited discrimination solely on account of race. To these questions, we gave the serious consideration which their importance justified. We upheld the curfew order as an exercise of the power of the government to take steps necessary to prevent espionage and sabotage in an area threatened by Japanese attack.

In the light of the principles we announced in the *Hirabayashi* case, we are unable to conclude that it was beyond the war power of Congress and the Executive to exclude those of Japanese ancestry from the West Coast war area at the time they did. True, exclusion from the area in which one's home is located is a far greater deprivation than constant confinement to the home from 8 P.M. to 6 A.M. Nothing short of apprehension by the proper military authorities of the gravest imminent danger to the public safety can constitutionally justify either. . . . The military authorities, charged with the primary responsibility of defending our shores, concluded that curfew provided inadequate protection and ordered exclusion. They did so . . . in accordance with Congressional authority to the military to say who should, and who should not, remain in the threatened areas.

In this case the petitioner challenges the assumptions upon which we rested our conclusions in the *Hirabayashi* case. He also urges that by May 1942, when Order No. 34 was promulgated, all danger of Japanese invasion of the West Coast had disappeared. After careful consideration of these contentions we are compelled to reject them.

. . . Like curfew, exclusion of those of Japanese origin was deemed necessary because of the presence of an unascertained number of disloyal members of the group, most of whom we have no doubt were loyal to this country. It was because we could not reject the finding of the military authorities that it was impossible to bring about an immediate segregation of the disloyal from the loyal that we sustained the validity of the curfew order as applying to the whole group. In the instant case, temporary exclusion of the entire group was rested by the military on the same ground. The judgment that exclusion of the whole group was for the same reason a military imperative answers the contention that the exclusion was in the nature of group punishment based on antagonism to those of Japanese origin. That there were members of the group who retained loyalties to Japan has been confirmed by investigations made subsequent to the exclusion. Approximately five thousand American citizens of Japanese ancestry refused to swear unqualified allegiance to the United States and to renounce allegiance to the Japanese Emperor, and several thousand evacuees requested repatriation to Japan.

We uphold the exclusion order as of the time it was made and when the petitioner violated it. . . . Since the petitioner has not been convicted of failing to report or to remain in an assembly or relocation center, we cannot in this case determine the validity of those separate provisions of the order. It is sufficient here for us to pass upon the order which petitioner violated. . . .

It is said that we are dealing here with the case of imprisonment of a citizen in a concentration camp solely because of his ancestry, without evidence or inquiry concerning his loyalty and good disposition towards the United States. Our task would be simple, our duty clear, were this a case involving the imprisonment of a loyal citizen in a concentration camp because of racial prejudice. Regardless of the true nature of the assembly and relocation centers — and we deem it unjustifiable to call them concentration camps with all the ugly connotations that term implies — we are dealing specifically with nothing but an exclusion order. To cast this case into outlines or racial prejudice, without reference to the real military dangers which were presented, merely confuses the issue. Korematsu was not excluded from the Military Area because of hostility to him or his race. He *was* excluded because we are at war with the Japanese Empire, because the properly constituted military authorities feared an invasion of our West Coast and felt constrained to take proper security measures, because they decided that the military urgency of the situation demanded that all citizens of Japanese ancestry be segregated from the West Coast temporarily, and finally, because Congress, reposing its confidence in this time of war in our military leaders — as inevitably it must — determined that they should have the power to do just this. There was evidence of disloyalty on the part of some, the military authorities considered that the need for action was great, and time was short. We cannot — by availing ourselves of the calm perspective of hindsight — now say that at that time these actions were unjustified.

FRANKFURTER, J., concurring.

The provisions of the Constitution which confer on the Congress and the President powers to enable this country to wage war are as much part of the Constitution as provisions looking to a nation at peace. . . . [T]he war power of the Government is "the power to wage war successfully." Therefore, the validity of action under the war power must be judged wholly in the context of war. That action is not to be stigmatized as lawless because like action in times of peace would be lawless. To talk about a military order that expresses an allowable judgment of war needs by those entrusted with the duty of conducting war as "an unconstitutional order" is to suffuse a part of the Constitution with an atmosphere of unconstitutionality. The respective spheres of action of military authorities and of judges are of course very different. But within their sphere, military authorities are no more outside the bounds of obedience to the Constitution than are judges within theirs. . . . To recognize that military orders are "reasonably expedient military precautions" in time of war and yet to deny them constitutional legitimacy makes of the Constitution an instrument of dialectic subtleties not reasonably to be attributed to the hard-headed Framers, of whom a majority had actual participation in war. If a military order such as that under review does not transcend the means appropriate for conducting war, such action by the military is as constitutional as would be any authorized action by the Interstate Commerce Commission within the limits of the constitutional power to regulate commerce. And being an exercise of the war power explicitly granted by the Constitution for safeguarding the power to enforce such a valid military order by making its violation an offense triable in the civil courts. To find that the Constitution does not forbid the military measures now complained of does not carry with it approval of that which Congress and the Executive did. That is their business, not ours.

ROBERTS, J., dissenting.

[This] is the case of convicting a citizen as a punishment for not submitting to imprisonment in a concentration camp, based on his ancestry, and solely because of his ancestry, without evidence or inquiry concerning his loyalty and good disposition towards the United States. . . . I need hardly labor the conclusion that Constitutional rights have been violated. . . .

MURPHY, J., dissenting.

This exclusion of "all persons of Japanese ancestry, both alien and non-alien," from the Pacific Coast area on a plea of military necessity in the absence of martial law ought not to be approved. Such exclusion goes over "the very brink of constitutional power" and falls into the ugly abyss of racism.

JACKSON, J., dissenting.

Korematsu was born on our soil, of parents born in Japan. The Constitution makes him a citizen of the United States by nativity and a citizen of California by residence. No claim is made that he is not loyal to this country. There is no suggestion that apart from the matter involved here he is not law-abiding and well disposed. Korematsu, however, has been convicted of an act not commonly a crime. It consists merely of being present in the state whereof he is a citizen, near the place where he was born, and where all his life he has lived.

Even more unusual is the series of military orders which made this conduct a crime. They forbid such a one to remain, and they also forbid him to leave. They were so drawn that the only way Korematsu could avoid violation was to give himself up to the military authority. This meant submission to custody, examination, and transportation out of the territory, to be followed by indeterminate confinement in detention camps.

A citizen's presence in the locality, however, was made a crime only if his parents were of Japanese birth. . . . Now, if any fundamental assumption underlies our system, it is that guilt is personal and not inheritable. . . . [H]ere is an attempt to make an otherwise innocent act a crime merely because this prisoner is the son of parents as to whom he had no choice, and belongs to a race from which there is no way to resign. If Congress in peace-time legislation should enact such a criminal law, I should suppose this Court would refuse to enforce it.

But the "law" which this prisoner is convicted of disregarding is not found in an act of Congress, but in a military order. . . . And it is said that if the military commander had reasonable military grounds for promulgating the orders, they are constitutional and become law, and the Court is required to enforce them. There are several reasons why I cannot subscribe to this doctrine.

It would be impracticable and dangerous idealism to expect or insist that each specific military command in an area of probable operations will conform to conventional tests of constitutionality. . . . The armed forces must protect a society, not merely its Constitution. . . . No court can require . . . a commander in such circumstances to act as a reasonable man; he may be unreasonably cautious and exacting. . . .

But if we cannot confine military expedients by the Constitution, neither would I distort the Constitution to approve all that the military may deem expedient. That is what the Court appears to be doing, whether consciously or not. I cannot say, from any evidence before me, that the orders of General DeWitt were not reasonably expedient military precautions, nor could I say that they were. But even if they were permissible military procedures, I deny that it follows that they are constitutional. If, as the Court holds, it does follow, then we may as well say that any military order will be constitutional and have done with it.

The limitation under which courts always will labor in examining the necessity for a military order are illustrated by this case. How does the Court know that these orders have a reasonable basis in necessity? No evidence whatever on that subject has been taken by this or any other court. There is sharp controversy as to the credibility of the DeWitt report. So the Court, having no real evidence before it, has no choice but to accept General DeWitt's own unsworn, self-serving statement, untested by any cross-examination, that what he did was reasonable. And thus it will always be when courts try to look into the reasonableness of a military order.

In the very nature of things, military decisions are not susceptible of intelligent judicial appraisal. They do not pretend to rest on evidence, but are made on information that often would not be admissible and on assumptions that could not proved. Information in support of an order could not be disclosed to courts without danger that it would reach the enemy. Neither can courts act on communications made in confidence. Hence courts can never have any real alternative to accepting the mere declaration of the authority that issued the order that it was reasonably necessary from a military viewpoint.

Much is said of the danger to liberty from the Army program for deporting and detaining these citizens of Japanese extraction. But a judicial construction of the due process clause that will sustain this order is a far more subtle blow to liberty than the promulgation of the order itself. A military order, however unconstitutional, is not apt to last longer than the military emergency. . . . But once a judicial opinion rationalizes such an order to show that it conforms to the Constitution, or rather rationalizes the Constitution to show that the Constitution sanctions such an order, the Court for all time has validated the principle of racial discrimination in criminal procedure and of transplanting American citizens. The principle then lies about like a loaded weapon ready for the hand of any authority that can bring forward a plausible claim of an urgent need. . . . [T]he passing incident becomes the doctrine of the Constitution. There it has a generative power of its own, and all that it creates will be in its own image. Nothing better illustrates this danger than does the Court's opinion in this case.

It argues that we are bound to uphold the conviction of Korematsu because we upheld one in *Hirabayashi,* where we sustained these orders in so far as they applied a curfew requirement to a citizen of Japanese ancestry. I think we should learn something from that experience.

In that case we were urged to consider only the curfew feature. . . . We yielded, and the Chief Justice guarded the opinion as carefully as language will do. . . . However, in spite of our limiting words we did validate a discrimination on the basis of ancestry for mild and temporary deprivation of liberty. Now the principle of racial discrimination is pushed from temporary deprivations to indeterminate ones. . . . How far the principle of this case would be extended before plausible reasons would play out, I do not know.

I should hold that a civil court cannot be made to enforce an order which violates constitutional limitations even if it is a reasonable exercise of military authority. The courts can exercise only the judicial power, can apply only law, and must abide by the Constitution, or they cease to be civil courts and become instruments of military policy.

. . . I would not lead people to rely on this Court for a review that seems to me wholly delusive. . . . The chief restraint upon those who command the physical forces of the country, in the future as in the past, must be their responsibility to the political judgments of their contemporaries and to the moral judgments of history.

My duties as a justice as I see them do not require me to make a military judgment as to whether General DeWitt's evacuation and detention program was a reasonable military necessity. I do not suggest that the courts should have attempted to interfere with the Army in carrying out its task. But I do not think they may be asked to execute a military order that has no place in law under the Constitution. I would reverse the judgment and discharge the prisoner.

Discussion

Critics of *Korematsu* often emphasize its blatant racism. As Justice Jackson wrote, "Had Korematsu been one of four — the others being, say, a German alien enemy, an Italian alien enemy, and a citizen of American-born ancestors, convicted of treason but out on parole — only Korematsu's presence would have violated the order." If it is racism alone that stirs your opposition, does this suggest that the evil would have been cured had Executive Order 9066 been applied to *all* of the ethnic groups whose loyalties might have been subject to suspicion during World War II? That is, would Korematsu still have had good (constitutional) cause to complain had the United States been as eager to round up and detain German- and Italian-Americans as it was Japanese-Americans? If so, on what ground?

B. The Steel Seizure Case

Less than five years after the cessation of World War II, the United States became involved in the conflict between South Korea (supported by the United Nations) and North Korea. Following President Truman's decision to cross the 38th parallel and move toward the northern border of North Korea, the People's Republic of China entered the fray. (The war thereafter bogged down, to be finally ended in 1953 with an armistice that maintained the division of Korea into two countries, one allied with the West, the other with the Communist bloc.)

In April 1952, following months of efforts at mediation between the United Steelworkers of America and the management of the country's major steel producers, the Union announced its intention to begin a nationwide strike on April 9. President Truman ordered the Secretary of the Treasury, John Sawyer, to seize the steel mills and to operate them in the name of the United States. He claimed that uninterrupted production of steel was vital to the successful prosecution of the Korean War. Truman notified Congress of his action; Congress took no action. The affected companies immediately filed suit claiming that the seizure violated the Constitution.

At the trial before the District Court, Assistant Attorney General Baldridge, representing the United States, made the following claims about the power of the President:[67]

The Court: So you contend the Executive has unlimited power in time of an emergency?

Mr. Baldridge: He has the power to take such action as is necessary to meet the emergency.

The Court: If the emergency is great, it is unlimited, is it?

Mr. Baldridge: I suppose if you carry it to its logical conclusion, that is true. But I do want to point out that there are two limitations on the Executive power. One is the ballot box and the other is impeachment. . . .

The Court: Let me put a case to you. . . . Supposing the President should declare that the public interest required the seizure of your home and directed an agent to seize it and to dispossess you: Do you think or do you contend that the court could not restrain that act because the President had declared an emergency and because he had directed an agent to carry out his will?

Mr. Baldridge: I would rather, Your Honor, not answer a case in that extremity. We are dealing here with a situation involving a grave national emergency . . . that requires the exercise of rather unusual powers in these particular circumstances. I do not believe any President would exercise such unusual power unless, in his opinion, there was a grave and an extreme national emergency existing. . . .

The Court: [I]s it not . . . your view that the powers of the Government are limited by and enumerated in the Constitution of the United States?

Mr. Baldridge: That is true, Your Honor, with respect to legislative powers.

The Court: But it is not true, you say, as to the Executive?

Mr. Baldridge: No. Section 1, of Article II of the Constitution . . . reposes all of the executive power in the Chief Executive. . . . In so far as the Executive is concerned, all executive power is vested in the President. In so far as legislative powers are concerned, the Congress has only those powers that are specifically delegated to it, plus the implied power to carry out the powers specifically enumerated.

The Court: So, when the sovereign people adopted the Constitution, it enumerated the powers set up in the Constitution but limited the powers of the Congress and limited the powers of the judiciary, but it did not limit the powers of the Executive. Is that what you say?

Mr. Baldridge: That is the way we read Article II of the Constitution. . . . It is our position that the President is accountable only to the country, and that the decisions of the President are conclusive. . . . [H]aving a broad grant of power[,] the executive, particularly in times of national emergency, can meet whatever situation endangers the national safety of the country. . . . I want to say that we had an emergency situation here. Somebody had to deal with it. The legislative [route, i.e., asking Congress for specific authority to seize the mills] was too slow. As of April 8th, midnight, the Taft-Hartley [route] was too slow. In either event, there would have been an indefinite stoppage of steel production. Are we to say, then, that there is no power in Government any place to meet as serious a situation as this, when it confronts the security of this nation? . . . I just say that as of midnight on April 8th this seizure procedure appeared to be the only effective way to avoid a strike and to avoid a cessation for an indefinite period of production of steel necessary to national security and national defense.

67. See Maeva Marcus, Truman and the Steel Seizure Case: The Limits of Presidential Power (1977), for an historical overview of the case.

District Judge Pine ("the Court" in this colloquy) enjoined the seizure. The Court of Appeals for the District of Columbia stayed the order, and the Supreme Court immediately granted certiorari. Justice Black wrote for six justices (two of whom had been appointed by President Truman) affirming issuance of the injunction.

YOUNGSTOWN SHEET & TUBE CO. v. SAWYER

343 U.S. 579 (1952)

Certiorari to the United States Court of Appeals for the District of Columbia Circuit

BLACK, J., delivered the opinion of the Court.

II

The President's power, if any, to issue the order must stem either from an act of Congress or from the Constitution itself. There is no statute that expressly authorizes the President to take possession of property as he did here. Nor is there any act of Congress to which our attention has been directed from which such a power can fairly be implied. Indeed, we do not understand the Government to rely on statutory authorization for this seizure. . . .

Moreover, the use of the seizure technique to solve labor disputes in order to prevent work stoppages was not only unauthorized by any congressional enactment; prior to this controversy, Congress had refused to adopt that method of settling labor disputes. . . .

It is clear that if the President had authority to issue the order he did, it must be found in some provision of the Constitution. And it is not claimed that express constitutional language grants this power to the President. The contention is that presidential power should be implied from the aggregate of his powers under the Constitution. Particular reliance is placed on provisions in Article II which say that "The executive Power shall be vested in a President . . ."; that "he shall take Care that the Laws be faithfully executed"; and that he "shall be Commander in Chief of the Army and Navy of the United States."

The order cannot properly be sustained as an exercise of the President's military power as Commander in Chief of the Armed Forces. The Government attempts to do so by citing a number of cases upholding broad powers in military commanders engaged in day-to-day fighting in a theater of war. Such cases need not concern us here. Even though "theater of war" be an expanding concept, we cannot with faithfulness to our constitutional system hold that the Commander in Chief of the Armed Forces has the ultimate power as such to take possession of private property in order to keep labor disputes from stopping production. That is a job for the Nation's lawmakers, not for its military authorities.

Nor can the seizure order be sustained because of the several constitutional provisions that grant executive power to the President. In the framework of our Constitution, the President's power to see that the laws are faithfully executed refutes the idea that he is to be a lawmaker. The Constitution limits his functions in the lawmaking process to the recommending of laws he thinks wise and the vetoing of laws he thinks bad. And the Constitution is neither silent nor equivocal about who shall make laws which the President is to execute. . . .

FRANKFURTER, J., concurring.

... A proposal that the President be given powers to seize plants to avert a shutdown where the "health or safety" of the Nation was endangered was thoroughly canvassed by Congress [in 1947] and rejected. No room for doubt remains that the proponents as well as the opponents of the bill which became the Labor Management Relations Act of 1947 ["Taft-Hartley"] clearly understood that as a result of that legislation the only recourse for preventing a shutdown in any basic industry, after failure of mediation, was Congress. Authorization for seizure as an available remedy for potential dangers was unequivocally put aside. . . . Congress chose not to lodge this power in the President. It chose not to make available in advance a remedy to which both industry and labor were fiercely hostile. . . .

It cannot be contended that the President would have had power to issue this order had Congress explicitly negated such authority in formal legislation. Congress has expressed its will to withhold this power from the President as though it had said so in so many words. The authoritatively expressed purpose of Congress to disallow such power to the President and to require him, when in his mind the occasion arose for such a seizure, to put the matter to Congress and ask for specific authority from it, could not be more decisive if it had been written into . . . the Labor Management Relations Act of 1947. . . .

The utmost that the Korean conflict may imply is that it may have been desirable to have given the President further authority, a freer hand in these matters. Absence of authority in the President to deal with a crisis does not imply want of power in the Government. Conversely the fact that power exists in the Government does not vest it in the President. The need for new legislation does not enact it. Nor does it repeal or amend existing law. . . .

Apart from his vast share of responsibility for the conduct of our foreign relations, the embracing function of the President is that "he shall take Care that the Laws be faithfully executed. . . ." Art. II, §3. . . . The powers of the President are not as particularized as are those of Congress. But unenumerated powers do not mean undefined powers. The separation of powers built into our Constitution gives essential content to undefined provisions in the frame of our government.

To be sure, the content of the three authorities of government is not to be derived from an abstract analysis. The areas are partly interacting, not wholly disjointed. The Constitution is a framework for government. Therefore the way the framework has consistently operated fairly establishes that it has operated according to its true nature. Deeply embedded traditional ways of conducting government cannot supplant the Constitution of legislation, but they give meaning to the words of the text or supply them. It is an inadmissibly narrow conception of American constitutional law to confine it to the words of the Constitution and to disregard the gloss which life has written upon them. In short, a systematic, unbroken, executive practice, long pursued to the knowledge of the Congress and never before questioned, engaged in by Presidents who have also sworn to uphold the Constitution, making as it were such exercise of power part of the structure of our government, may be treated as a gloss on "executive Power" vested in the President by §1 of Art. II.

Such was the case of United States v. Midwest Oil Co., 236 U.S. 459. The contrast between the circumstances of that case and this one helps to draw a clear line between authority not explicitly conferred yet authorized to be exercised by the

President and the denial of such authority. In both instances it was the concern of Congress under express constitutional grant to make rules and regulations for the problems with which the President dealt. In the one case he was dealing with the protection of property belonging to the United States; in the other with the enforcement of the Commerce Clause and with raising and supporting armies and maintaining the Navy. In the *Midwest Oil* case, lands which Congress had opened for entry were, over a period of 80 years and in 252 instances, and by Presidents learned and unlearned in the law, temporarily withdrawn from entry so as to enable Congress to deal with such withdrawals. No remotely comparable practice can be vouched for executive seizure of property at a time when this country was not at war, in the only constitutional way in which it can be at war. It would pursue the irrelevant to reopen the controversy over the constitutionality of some acts of Lincoln during the Civil War. Suffice it to say that he seized railroads in territory where armed hostilities had already interrupted the movement of troops to the beleaguered Capital, and his order was ratified by Congress.

The only other instances of seizures are those during the periods of the first and second World Wars. . . . In this case, reliance on the powers that flow from declared war has been commendably disclaimed by the Solicitor General. . . . [T]he list of executive assertions of the power of seizure in circumstances comparable to the present reduces to three in the six-month period from June to December of 1941. . . . Without passing on their validity, as we are not called upon to do, it suffices to say that these three isolated instances do not add up, either in number, scope, duration or contemporaneous legal justification, to the kind of executive construction of the Constitution revealed in the *Midwest Oil* case. Nor do they come to us sanctioned by long-continued acquiescence of Congress giving decisive weight to a construction by the Executive of its powers. . . .

DOUGLAS, J., concurring.

There can be no doubt that the emergency which caused the President to seize these steel plants was one that bore heavily on the country. But the emergency did not create power; it merely marked an occasion when power should be exercised. And the fact that it was necessary that measures be taken to keep steel in production does not mean that the President, rather than the Congress, had the constitutional authority to act. The Congress, as well as the President, is trustee of the national welfare. The President can act more quickly than the Congress. The President with the armed services at his disposal can move with force as well as with speed. All executive power — from the reign of ancient kings to the rule of modern dictators — has the outward appearance of efficiency.

Legislative power, by contrast, is slower to exercise. There must be delay while the ponderous machinery of committees, hearings, and debates is put into motion. That takes time; and while the Congress slowly moves into action, the emergency may take its toll in wages, consumer goods, war production, the standard of living of the people, and perhaps even lives. Legislative action may indeed often be cumbersome, time-consuming, and apparently inefficient. But as Mr. Justice Brandeis stated in his dissent in Myers v. United States, 272 U.S. 52, 293:

> The doctrine of the separation of powers was adopted by the Convention of 1787 not to promote efficiency but to preclude the exercise of arbitrary power. The purpose was not to avoid friction, but, by means of the inevitable friction incident to the

distribution of the governmental powers among three departments, to save the people from autocracy.

We therefore cannot decide this case by determining which branch of government can deal most expeditiously with the present crisis. The answer must depend on the allocation of powers under the Constitution. . . .

The legislative nature of the action taken by the President seems to me to be clear. When the United States takes over an industrial plant to settle a labor controversy, it is condemning property. . . . But though the seizure is only for a week or a month, the condemnation is complete and the United States must pay compensation for the temporary possession. . . .

I have no doubt but that condemnation of a plant, factory, or industry in order to promote industrial peace would be constitutional. But there is a duty to pay for all property taken by the Government. The command of the Fifth Amendment is that no "private property be taken for public use, without just compensation." That constitutional requirement has an important bearing on the present case.

The President has no power to raise revenues. That power is in the Congress by Article I, Section 8 of the Constitution. The President might seize and the Congress by subsequent action might ratify the seizure. But until and unless Congress acted, no condemnation would be lawful. The branch of government that has the power to pay compensation for a seizure is the only one able to authorize a seizure or make lawful one that the President had effected. That seems to me to be the necessary result of the condemnation provision in the Fifth Amendment. It squares with the theory of checks and balances expounded by Mr. Justice Black in the opinion of the Court in which I Join.

JACKSON, J., concurring in the judgment and opinion of the court.

That comprehensive and undefined presidential powers hold both practical advantages and grave dangers for the country will impress anyone who has served as legal adviser to a President in time of transition and public anxiety. [Justice Jackson had, before being named to the Supreme Court, served as Solicitor General and Attorney General under President Roosevelt.] While an interval of detached reflection may temper teachings of that experience, they probably are a more realistic influence on my views than the conventional materials of judicial decision which seem unduly to accentuate doctrine and legal fiction. But as we approach the question of presidential power, we half overcome mental hazards by recognizing them. The opinions of judges, no less than executives and publicists, often suffer the infirmity of confusing the issue of a power's validity with the cause it is invoked to promote, of confounding the permanent executive office with its temporary occupant. The tendency is strong to emphasize transient results upon policies — such as wages or stabilization — and lose sight of enduring consequences upon the balanced power structure of our Republic.

A judge, like an executive adviser, may be surprised at the poverty of really useful and unambiguous authority applicable to concrete problems of executive power as they actually present themselves. Just what our forefathers did envision, or would have envisioned had they foreseen modern conditions, must be divined from materials almost as enigmatic as the dreams Joseph was called upon to interpret for Pharaoh. A century and a half of partisan debate and scholarly speculation yields no net result but only supplies more or less apt quotations from respected sources on each side of any question. They largely cancel each other. And court decisions are indecisive because of the judicial practice of dealing with the largest questions in the most narrow way.

The actual art of governing under our Constitution does not and cannot conform to judicial definitions of the power of any of its branches based on isolated clauses or even single Articles torn from context. While the Constitution diffuses power the better to secure liberty, it also contemplates that practice will integrate the dispersed powers into a workable government. It enjoins upon its branches separateness but interdependence, autonomy but reciprocity.

Presidential powers are not fixed but fluctuate, depending upon their disjunction or conjunction with those of Congress. We may well begin by a somewhat over-simplified grouping of practical situations in which a President may doubt, or others may challenge, his powers, and by distinguishing roughly the legal consequences of this factor of relativity.

1. When the President acts pursuant to an express or implied authorization of Congress, his authority is at its maximum, for it includes all that he possesses in his own right plus all that Congress can delegate. In these circumstances, and in these only, may he be said (for what it may be worth), to personify the federal sovereignty. If his act is held unconstitutional under these circumstances, it usually means that the Federal Government as an undivided whole lacks power. A seizure executed by the President pursuant to an Act of Congress would be supported by the strongest of presumptions and the widest latitude of judicial interpretation, and the burden of persuasion would rest heavily upon any who might attack it.

2. When the President acts in absence of either a congressional grant or denial of authority, he can only rely upon his own independent powers, but there is a zone of twilight in which he and Congress may have concurrent authority, or in which its distribution is uncertain. Therefore, congressional inertia, indifference or quiescence may sometimes, at least as a practical matter, enable, if not invite, measures on independent presidential responsibility. In this area, any actual test of power is likely to depend on the imperatives of events and contemporary imponderables rather than on abstract theories of law.

3. When the President takes measures incompatible with the expressed or implied will of Congress, his power is at its lowest ebb, for then he can rely only upon his own constitutional powers minus any constitutional powers of Congress over the matter. Courts can sustain exclusive Presidential control in such a case only by disabling the Congress from acting upon the subject. Presidential claim to a power at once so conclusive and preclusive must be scrutinized with caution, for what is at stake is the equilibrium established by our constitutional system.

Into which of these classifications does this executive seizure of the steel industry fit? It is eliminated from the first by admission, for it is conceded that no congressional authorization exists for this seizure. . . . Can it then be defended under flexible tests available to the second category? It seems clearly eliminated from that class because Congress has not left seizure of private property an open field but has covered it by three statutory policies inconsistent with this seizure. . . . In choosing a different and inconsistent way of his own, the President cannot claim that it is necessitated or invited by failure of Congress to legislate upon the occasions, grounds and methods for seizure of industrial properties.

This leaves the current seizure to be justified only by the severe tests under the third grouping, where it can be supported only by any remainder of executive power after subtraction of such powers as Congress may have over the subject. In short, we can sustain the President only by holding that seizure of such strike-bound industries is within his domain and beyond control by Congress. Thus, this Court's first review of such seizures occurs under circumstances which leave Presidential power most vulnerable to attack and in the least favorable of possible constitutional postures.

I did not suppose, and I am not persuaded, that history leaves it open to question, at least in the courts, that the executive branch, like the Federal Government as a whole, possesses only delegated powers. The purpose of the Constitution was not only to grant power, but to keep it from getting out of hand. However, because the President does not enjoy unmentioned powers does not mean that the mentioned ones should be narrowed by a niggardly construction. Some clauses could be made almost unworkable, as well as immutable, by refusal to indulge some latitude of interpretation for changing times. I have heretofore, and do now, give to the enumerated powers the scope and elasticity afforded by what seem to be reasonable practical implications instead of the rigidity dictated by a doctrinaire textualism.

The Solicitor General seeks the power of seizure in three clauses of the Executive Article, the first reading, "The executive Power shall be vested in a President of the United States of America." Lest I be thought to exaggerate, I quote the interpretation which his brief puts upon it: "In our view, this clause constitutes a grant of all the executive powers of which the Government is capable." If that be true, it is difficult to see why the forefathers bothered to add several specific items, including some trifling ones.

The example of such unlimited executive power that must have most impressed the forefathers was the prerogative exercised by George III, and the description of its evils in the Declaration of Independence leads me to doubt that they were creating their new Executive in his image. Continental European examples were no more appealing. And if we seek instruction from our own times, we can match it only from the executive powers in those governments we disparagingly describe as totalitarian. I cannot accept the view that this clause is a grant in bulk of all conceivable executive power but regard it as an allocation to the presidential office of the generic powers thereafter stated.

The clause on which the Government next relies is that "The President shall be Commander in Chief of the Army and Navy of the United States. . . ." These cryptic words have given rise to some of the most persistent controversies in our constitutional history. Of course, they imply something more than an empty title. But just what authority goes with the name has plagued Presidential advisers who would not waive or narrow it by nonassertion yet cannot say where it begins or ends. It undoubtedly puts the Nation's armed forces under Presidential command. Hence, this loose appellation is sometimes advanced as support for any Presidential action, internal or external, involving use of force, the idea being that it vests power to do anything, anywhere, that can be done with an army or navy.

That seems to be the logic of an argument tendered at our bar — that the President having, on his own responsibility, sent American troops abroad derives from that act "affirmative power" to seize the means of producing a supply of steel for them. . . . Thus, it is said he has invested himself with "war powers."

I cannot foresee all that it might entail if the Court should indorse this argument. Nothing in our Constitution is plainer than that declaration of a war is entrusted only to Congress. Of course, a state of war may in fact exist without a formal declaration. But no doctrine that the Court could promulgate would seem to me more sinister and alarming than that a President whose conduct of foreign affairs is so largely uncontrolled, and often even is unknown, can vastly enlarge his mastery over the internal affairs of the country by his own commitment of the Nation's armed forces to some foreign venture.

I do not, however, find it necessary or appropriate to consider the legal status of the Korean enterprise to discountenance argument based on it.

Assuming that we are in a war de facto, whether it is or is not a war de jure, does that empower the Commander-in-Chief to seize industries he thinks necessary to supply our army? The Constitution expressly places in Congress power 'to raise and support Armies' and 'to provide and maintain a Navy.' This certainly lays upon Congress primary responsibility for supplying the armed forces. Congress alone controls the raising of revenues and their appropriation and may determine in what manner and by what means they shall be spent for military and naval procurement. I suppose no one would doubt that Congress can take over war supply as a Government enterprise. On the other hand, if Congress sees fit to rely on free private enterprise collectively bargaining with free labor for support and maintenance of our armed forces can the Executive because of lawful disagreements incidental to that process, seize the facility for operation upon Government-imposed terms? There are indications that the Constitution did not contemplate that the title Commander-in-Chief of the Army and Navy will constitute him also Commander-in-Chief of the country, its industries and its inhabitants. He has no monopoly of 'war powers,' whatever they are. While Congress cannot deprive the President of the command of the army and navy, only Congress can provide him an army or navy to command. It is also empowered to make rules for the 'Government and Regulation of land and naval forces,' by which it may to some unknown extent impinge upon even command functions.

That military powers of the Commander-in-Chief were not to supersede representative government of internal affairs seems obvious from the Constitution and from elementary American history. Time out of mind, and even now in many parts of the world, a military commander can seize private housing to shelter his troops. Not so, however, in the United States, for the Third Amendment says, "No Soldier shall, in time of peace be quartered in any house, without the consent of the Owner, nor in time of war, but in a manner to be prescribed by law." Thus, even in war time, his seizure of needed military housing must be authorized by Congress. It also was expressly left to Congress to 'provide for calling forth the Militia to execute the Laws of the Union, suppress Insurrections and repel Invasions. . . ." Such a limitation on the command power, written at a time when the militia rather than a standing army was contemplated as the military weapon of the Republic, underscores the Constitution's policy that Congress, not the Executive, should control utilization of the war power as an instrument of domestic policy. Congress, fulfilling that function, has authorized the President to use the army to enforce certain civil rights. On the other hand, Congress has forbidden him to use the army for the purpose of executing general laws except when expressly authorized by the Constitution or by Act of Congress.

While broad claims under this rubric often have been made, advice to the President in specific matters usually has carried overtones that powers, even under this head, are measured by the command functions usual to the topmost officer of the army and navy. Even then, heed has been taken of any efforts to negative his authority.

We should not use this occasion to circumscribe, much less to contract, the lawful role of the President as Commander-in-Chief. I should indulge the widest latitude of interpretation to sustain his exclusive function to command the instruments of national force, at least when turned against the outside world for the security of our society. But, when it is turned inward, not because of rebellion but because of a lawful economic struggle between industry and labor, it should have no such indulgence. His command power is not such an absolute as might be implied from that office in a militaristic system but is subject to limitations consistent with a constitutional Republic whose law and policy-making branch is a representative Congress. The purpose of lodging dual titles in one man was to insure that the civilian would control the military, not to enable the military to subordinate the presidential office. No penance would ever expiate the sin against free government of holding that a President can escape control of executive powers by law through assuming his military role. What the power of command may include I do not try to envision, but I think it is not a military prerogative, without support of law, to seize persons or property because they are important or even essential for the military and naval establishment.

The third clause in which the Solicitor General finds seizure powers is that "he shall take Care that the Laws be faithfully executed. . . ." That authority must be matched against words of the Fifth Amendment that "No person shall be . . . deprived of life, liberty, or property, without due process of law. . . ." One gives a governmental authority that reaches so far as there is law, the other gives a private right that authority shall go no farther. These signify about all there is of the principle that ours is a government of laws, not of men, and that we submit ourselves to rulers only if under rules.

The Solicitor General lastly grounds support of the seizure upon nebulous, inherent powers never expressly granted but said to have accrued to the office from the customs and claims of preceding administrations. The plea is for a resulting power to deal with a crisis or an emergency according to the necessities of the case, the unarticulated assumption being that necessity knows no law.

Loose and irresponsible use of adjectives colors all non-legal and much legal discussion of presidential powers. "Inherent" powers, "implied" powers, "incidental" powers, "plenary" powers, "war" powers and "emergency" powers are used, often interchangeably and without fixed or ascertainable meanings.

The vagueness and generality of the clauses that set forth presidential powers afford a plausible basis for pressures within and without an administration for presidential action beyond that supported by those whose responsibility it is to defend his actions in court. The claim of inherent and unrestricted presidential powers has long been a persuasive dialectical weapon in political controversy. While it is not surprising that counsel should grasp support from such unadjudicated claims of power, a judge cannot accept self-serving press statements of the attorney for one of the interested parties as authority in answering a constitutional question, even if the advocate was himself. [Justice Jackson here is referring to the Government's citation of his own opinion, written while Attorney General, upholding broad executive power in behalf of President Roosevelt.] But prudence has counseled that actual reliance on such nebulous claims stop short of provoking a judicial test.

The Solicitor General, acknowledging that Congress has never authorized the seizure here, says practice of prior Presidents has authorized it. . . . [Justice Jackson analyzes the key instance, concluding that it] yield[s] to distinctions so decisive that it cannot be regarded as even a precedent, much less an authority for the present seizure.

The appeal, however, that we declare the existence of inherent powers *ex necessitate* to meet an emergency asks us to do what many think would be wise, although it is something the forefathers omitted. They knew what emergencies were, knew the pressures they engender for authoritative action, knew, too, how they afford a ready pretext for usurpation. We may also suspect that they suspected that emergency powers would tend to kindle emergencies. Aside from suspension of the privilege of the writ of habeas corpus in time of rebellion or invasion, when the public safety may require it, they made no express provision for exercise of extraordinary authority because of a crisis. I do not think we rightfully may so amend their work, and, if we could, I am not convinced it would be wise to do so, although many modern nations have forthrightly recognized that war and economic crises may upset the normal balance between liberty and authority. Their experience with emergency powers may not be irrelevant to the argument here that we should say that the Executive, of his own volition, can invest himself with undefined emergency powers.

[After briefly discussing France and Germany, Justice Jackson notes that] Great Britain also has fought both World Wars under a sort of temporary dictatorship created by legislation. As Parliament is not bound by written constitutional limitations, it established a crisis government simply by delegation to its Ministers of a larger measure than usual of its own unlimited power, which is exercised under its supervision by Ministers whom it may dismiss. This has been called the "highwater mark in the voluntary surrender of liberty," but, as Churchill put it, "Parliament stands custodian of these surrendered liberties, and its most sacred duty will be to restore them in their fullness when victory has crowned our exertions and our perseverance." Thus, parliamentary control made emergency powers compatible with freedom.

This contemporary foreign experience may be inconclusive as to the wisdom of lodging emergency powers somewhere in a modern government. But it suggests that emergency powers are consistent with free government only when their control is lodged elsewhere than in the Executive who exercises them. That is the safeguard that would be nullified by our adoption of the 'inherent powers' formula. Nothing in my experience convinces me that such risks are warranted by any real necessity, although such powers would, of course, be an executive convenience.

In the practical working of our Government we already have evolved a technique within the framework of the Constitution by which normal executive powers may be considerably expanded to meet an emergency. Congress may and has granted extraordinary authorities which lie dormant in normal times but may be called into play by the Executive in war or upon proclamation of a national emergency. In 1939, upon congressional request, the Attorney General listed ninety-nine such separate statutory grants by Congress of emergency or war-time executive powers. They were invoked from time to time as need appeared. Under this procedure we retain Government by law — special, temporary law, perhaps, but law nonetheless. The public may know the extent and limitations of the powers that can be asserted, and persons affected may be informed from the statute of their rights and duties.

In view of the ease, expedition and safety with which Congress can grant and has granted large emergency powers, certainly ample to embrace this crisis, I am quite unimpressed with the argument that we should affirm possession of them without statute. Such power either has no beginning or it has no end. If it exists, it need submit to no legal restraint. I am not alarmed that it would plunge us straightway into dictatorship, but it is at least a step in that wrong direction.

As to whether there is imperative necessity for such powers, it is relevant to note the gap that exists between the President's paper powers and his real powers. The Constitution does not disclose the measure of the actual controls wielded by the modern presidential office. That instrument must be understood as an Eighteenth-Century sketch of a government hoped for, not as a blueprint of the Government that is. Vast accretions of federal power, eroded from that reserved by the States, have magnified the scope of presidential activity. Subtle shifts take place in the centers of real power that do not show on the face of the Constitution.

Executive power has the advantage of concentration in a single head in whose choice the whole Nation has a part, making him the focus of public hopes and expectations. In drama, magnitude and finality his decisions so far overshadow any others that almost alone he fills the public eye and ear. No other personality in public life can begin to compete with him in access to the public mind through modern methods of communications. By his prestige as head of state and his influence upon public opinion he exerts a leverage upon those who are supposed to check and balance his power which often cancels their effectiveness.

Moreover, rise of the party system has made a significant extraconstitutional supplement to real executive power. No appraisal of his necessities is realistic which overlooks that he heads a political system as well as a legal system. Party loyalties and interests, sometimes more binding than law, extend his effective control into branches of government other than his own and he often may win, as a political leader, what he cannot command under the Constitution. . . . I cannot be brought to believe that this country will suffer if the Court refuses further to aggrandize the presidential office, already so potent and so relatively immune from judicial review, at the expense of Congress.

But I have no illusion that any decision by this Court can keep power in the hands of Congress if it is not wise and timely in meeting its problems. A crisis that challenges the President equally, or perhaps primarily, challenges Congress. If not good law, there was worldly wisdom in the maxim attributed to Napoleon that "The tools belong to the man who can use them." We may say that power to legislate for emergencies belongs in the hands of Congress, but only Congress itself can prevent power from slipping through its fingers.

The essence of our free Government is "leave to live by no man's leave, underneath the law" — to be governed by those impersonal forces which we call law. Our Government is fashioned to fulfill this concept so far as humanly possible.

The Executive, except for recommendation and veto, has no legislative power. The executive action we have here originates in the individual will of the President and represents an exercise of authority without law. No one, perhaps not even the President, knows the limits of the power he may seek to exert in this instance and the parties affected cannot learn the limit of their rights. We do not know today what powers over labor or property would be claimed to flow from Government possession if we should legalize it, what rights to compensation would be claimed or recognized, or on what contingency it would end. With all its defects, delays and inconveniences, men have discovered no technique for long preserving free government except that the Executive be under the law, and that the law be made by parliamentary deliberations. Such institutions may be destined to pass away. But it is the duty of the Court to be last, not first, to give them up.

[A concurring opinion by Justice Burton is omitted.]

VINSON, C.J., joined by Reed and Minton, JJ., dissenting. . . .

I

In passing upon the question of Presidential powers in this case, we must first consider the context in which those powers were exercised.

Those who suggest that this is a case involving extraordinary powers should be mindful that these are extraordinary times. A world not yet recovered from the devastation of World War II has been forced to face the threat of another and more terrifying global conflict. . . . For almost two full years, our armed forces have been fighting in Korea, suffering casualties of over 108,000 men. . . . Defendant's brief informs us that the Soviet Union maintains the largest air force in the world and maintains ground forces much larger than those presently available to the United States and the countries joined with us in mutual security arrangements. Constant international tensions are cited to demonstrate how precarious is the peace. . . . Congress also directed the President to build up our own defenses. Congress, recognizing the "grim fact . . . that the United States is now engaged in a struggle for survival" and that "it is imperative that we now take those necessary steps to make our strength equal to the peril of the hour," granted authority to draft men into the armed forces. As a result, we now have over 3,500,000 men in our armed forces. . . .

Even before Korea, steel production at levels above theoretical 100% capacity was not capable of supplying civilian needs alone. Since Korea, the tremendous military demand for steel has far exceeded the increases in productive capacity. [A congressional committee] emphasized that the shortage of steel, even with the mills operating at full capacity, coupled with increased civilian purchasing power, presented grave danger of disastrous inflation. [Elsewhere in the opinion, Chief Justice Vinson quotes an affidavit filed by the Secretary of Defense indicating that "a work stoppage in the steel industry will result immediately in serious curtailment of production of essential weapons and munitions of all kinds." Other affidavits "disclose an enormous demand for steel in such vital defense programs as the expansion of facilities in atomic energy, petroleum, power, transportation and industrial production, including steel production. Those charged with administering allocations and priorities swore to the vital part steel production plays in our economy. The affidavits emphasize the critical need for steel in our defense program, the absence of appreciable inventories of steel, and the drastic results of any interruption in steel production.]

The President has the duty to execute the . . . legislative programs [dealing with national security and the economy]. Their successful execution depends upon continued production of steel and stabilized prices for steel. Accordingly, when the collective bargaining agreements between the Nation's steel producers and their employees, represented by the United Steel Workers, were due to expire on December 31, 1951, and a strike shutting down the entire basic steel industry was threatened, the President acted to avert a complete shutdown of steel production. On December 22, 1951, he certified the dispute to the Wage Stabilization Board, requesting that the Board investigate the dispute and promptly report its recommendation as to fair and equitable terms of settlement. The Union complied with the President's request and delayed its threatened strike while the dispute was before the Board. . . . [T]he full Wage Stabilization Board submitted its report and recommendations to the President on March 20, 1952. The Board's report was acceptable to the Union but was rejected by plaintiffs. The Union gave notice of its intention to strike as of 12:01 A.M., April 9, 1952, but bargaining between the parties continued with hope of settlement until the evening of April 8, 1952. After bargaining had failed to avert the threatened shutdown of steel production, the President [seized the mills and immediately notified Congress of his action]. . . .

Twelve days passed without action by Congress. On April 21, 1952, the President sent a letter to the President of the Senate in which he again described the purpose and need for his action and again stated his position that "The Congress can, if it wishes, reject the course of action I have followed in this matter." Congress has not so acted to this date. . . .

One is not here called upon even to consider the possibility of executive seizure of a farm, a corner grocery store or even a single industrial plant. Such considerations arise only when one ignores the central fact of this case — that the Nation's entire basic steel production would have shut down completely if there had been no Government seizure. Even ignoring for the moment whatever confidential information the President may possess as "the Nation's organ for foreign affairs," Chicago & Southern Air Lines v. Waterman S.S. Corp., 333 U.S. 103, 111 (1948), the uncontroverted affidavits in this record amply support the finding that "a work stoppage would immediately jeopardize and imperil our national defense."

Plaintiffs do not remotely suggest any basis for rejecting the President's finding that any stoppage of steel production would immediately place the Nation in peril. . . .

Accordingly, if the President has any power under the Constitution to meet a critical situation in the absence of express statutory authorization, there is no basis whatever for criticizing the exercise of such power in this case.

II

. . . Admitting that the Government could seize the mills, plaintiffs claim that the implied power of eminent domain can be exercised only under an Act of Congress; under no circumstances, they say, can that power be exercised by the President unless he can point to an express provision in enabling legislation. . . .

Consideration of this view of executive impotence calls for further examination of the nature of the separation of powers under our tripartite system of Government. . . .

The whole of the "executive Power" is vested in the President. . . . Only by instilling initiative and vigor in all of the three departments of Government, declared Madison, could tyranny in any form be avoided. Hamilton added:

> Energy in the Executive is a leading character in the definition of good government. It is essential to the protection of the community against foreign attack; it is not less essential to the steady administration of the laws; to the protection of property against those irregular and highhanded combinations which sometimes interrupt the ordinary course of justice; to the security of liberty against the enterprises and assaults of ambition, of faction, and of anarchy.

It is thus apparent that the Presidency was deliberately fashioned as an office of power and independence. Of course, the Framers created no autocrat capable of arrogating any power unto himself at any time. But neither did they create an automaton impotent to exercise the powers of Government at a time when the survival of the Republic itself may be at stake. . . . [W]e are not called upon today to expand the Constitution to meet a new situation. For, in this case, we need only look to history and time-honored principles of constitutional law — principles that have been applied consistently by all branches of the Government throughout our history. It is those who assert the invalidity of the Executive Order who seek to amend the Constitution in this case.

III

A review of executive action demonstrates that our Presidents have on many occasions exhibited the leadership contemplated by the Framers when they made the President Commander in Chief, and imposed upon him the trust to "take Care that the Laws be faithfully executed." With or without explicit statutory authorization, Presidents have at such times dealt with national emergencies by acting promptly and resolutely to enforce legislative programs, at least to save those programs until Congress could act. Congress and the courts have responded to such executive initiative with consistent approval. [The next fourteen pages of the opinion are devoted to detailing such instances.]

IV

Focusing now on the situation confronting the President on the night of April 8, 1952, we cannot but conclude that the President was performing his duty under the Constitution to "take Care that the Laws be faithfully executed." . . .

Much of the argument in this case has been directed at straw men. We do not now have before us the case of a President acting solely on the basis of his own notions of the public welfare. Nor is there any question of unlimited executive power in this case. The President himself closed the door to any such claim when he sent his Message to Congress stating his purpose to abide by any action of Congress, whether approving or disapproving his seizure action. Here, the President immediately made sure that Congress was fully informed of the temporary action he had taken only to preserve the legislative programs from destruction until Congress could act.

The absence of a specific statute authorizing seizure of the steel mills as a mode of executing the laws — both the military procurement program and the anti-inflation program — has not until today been thought to prevent the President from executing the laws. . . .

There is no statute prohibiting seizure as a method of enforcing legislative programs. . . .

Whatever the extent of Presidential power on more tranquil occasions, and whatever the right of the President to execute legislative programs as he sees fit without reporting the mode of execution to Congress, the single Presidential purpose disclosed on this record is to faithfully execute the laws by acting in an emergency to maintain the status quo, thereby preventing collapse of the legislative programs until Congress could act. The President's action served the same purposes as a judicial stay entered to maintain the status quo in order to preserve the jurisdiction of a court. . . . Consequently, there is no evidence whatever of any Presidential purpose to defy Congress or act in any way inconsistent with the legislative will.

In United States v. Midwest Oil Co., this Court approved executive action where, as here, the President acted to preserve an important matter until Congress could act — even though his action in that case was contrary to an express statute. In this case, there is no statute prohibiting the action taken by the President in a matter not merely important but threatening the very safety of the Nation. Executive inaction in such a situation, courting national disaster, is foreign to the concept of energy and initiative in the Executive as created by the Founding Fathers. . . . There is no cause to fear Executive tyranny so long as the laws of Congress are being faithfully executed.

Certainly there is no basis for fear of dictatorship when the Executive acts, as he did in this case, only to save the situation until Congress could act.

V

Plaintiffs place their primary emphasis on the Labor Management Relations Act of 1947, hereinafter referred to as the Taft-Hartley Act, but do not contend that Act contains any provision prohibiting seizure. . . .

VI. . .

The broad executive power granted by Article II to an officer on duty 365 days a year cannot, it is said, be invoked to avert disaster. Instead, the President must confine himself to sending a message to Congress recommending action. Under this messenger-boy concept of the Office, the President cannot even act to preserve legislative programs from destruction so that Congress will have something left to act upon. There is no judicial finding that the executive action was unwarranted because there was in fact no basis for the President's finding of the existence of an emergency for, under this view, the gravity of the emergency and the immediacy of the threatened disaster are considered irrelevant as a matter of law. . . .

Presidents have been in the past, and any man worthy of the Office should be in the future, free to take at least interim action necessary to execute legislative programs essential to survival of the Nation. . . .

There is no question that the possession was other than temporary in character and subject to congressional direction — either approving, disapproving or regulating the manner in which the mills were to be administered and returned to the owners. The President immediately informed Congress of his action and clearly stated his intention to abide by the legislative will. No basis for claims of arbitrary action, unlimited powers or dictatorial usurpation of congressional power appears from the facts of this case. On the contrary, judicial, legislative and executive precedents throughout our history demonstrate that in this case the President acted in full conformity with his duties under the Constitution.

Discussion

1. Are the description and importance of the "facts" consistent throughout the various opinions? To what extent does the result turn on the unique context of the case?

2. Professor Philip Bobbitt has characterized Justice Black's method of constitutional interpretation as paradigmatically "textual," based on the notion that the Constitution's commands can be derived directly from the plain meaning of the text.[68] Bobbitt contrasts this to a "prudential argument," which he defines as "constitutional argument actuated by the political and economic circumstances surrounding the decision. Thus, prudentialists generally hold that in times of national emergency even the plainest of constitutional limitations can be ignored" if it is the public interest to do so.[69] Is Chief Justice Vinson's dissent a "prudentialist" opinion?

3. Note the rather divergent rationales offered by Justices Black and Frankfurter. Which seems most responsive to the concerns of the dissenters?

4. Both Justice Frankfurter and Justice Jackson indicate a reluctance to define the Korean "enterprise" as a "war" despite the engagement of American troops. Assume that Congress had formally declared war on Korea. Would the seizure then have been constitutionally proper?

5. Consider Justice Jackson's assertion, early in his opinion, that

> A judge, like an executive adviser, may be surprised at the poverty of really useful and unambiguous authority applicable to concrete problems of executive power as they actually present themselves. Just what our forefathers did envision, or would have envisioned had they foreseen modern conditions, must be divined from materials almost as enigmatic as the dreams Joseph was called upon to interpret for Pharaoh. A century and a half of partisan debate and scholarly speculation yields no net result but only supplies more or less apt quotations from respected sources on each

68. Philip Bobbitt, Constitutional Fate 25 (1982).
69. Id. at 61.

side of any question. They largely cancel each other. And court decisions are indecisive because of the judicial practice of dealing with the largest questions in the most narrow way.

Are these observations unique to the issue of presidential power, or might they apply more generally to other themes that you have encountered thus far in this book?

Note: Presidential Power to Commit Troops Without a Congressional Declaration of War

Congress has not formally declared war on an enemy since 1941. Yet the United States has been involved in recurrent military hostilities since the end of World War II, including the Korean, Vietnamese, and Iraqi conflicts. Although in none of these did Congress opt to invoke its Article I power "to declare war," it authorized expenditures for the military activities, and it adopted the 1964 Gulf of Tonkin Resolution authorizing the President to engage in retaliation for alleged attacks on American military forces in Vietnam, which served as the legal underpinning for the subsequent buildup of American forces. In addition, there have been numerous "minor" military actions, in areas of the world ranging from Lebanon to the Dominican Republic and Grenada. There has been recurrent debate about the constitutional legitimacy of these military actions.

Consider Henry P. Monaghan's analysis:[70]

> If one examines the text of the constitution, he is at once struck by the differences between the powers conferred upon congress by article I and those given to the president by article II. The great powers that one identifies with the national government are conferred upon congress. . . . By contrast, the textual powers conferred upon the president are both few and of uncertain dimension. Some are plainly of a trivial character. The few more open-ended clauses upon which "strong" presidents have based their authority are [the Executive Power, the Commander in Chief, and the "Take Care" Clauses]. But, textually, none of these powers need be read as a significantly independent, substantive power. . . . The president's power as commander in chief, so heavily relied upon by modern presidents, could be read only as constituting the president, in Hamilton's phrase, "the first general and admiral of the confederacy," and not as an independent authority for making decisions that, in turn, require use of the armed forces to back them up[, and] the "take care" clause could be taken as simply declaratory of a presidential obligation to enforce existing congressional policy. Not surprisingly, therefore, the presidency was not originally viewed as a great office. The dominant mood was that of legislative prerogative.
>
> But the measure of presidential power cannot be gleaned simply from the words of Article II alone, nor from references by eighteenth century statesmen as to the appropriate distribution of legislative and executive power. . . . [T]here has been a vast accretion of power in the presidency [relative to that of Congress], particularly in this century. . . . "Presidential government" has, therefore, emerged as the dominant aspect of modern American political life. . . .

70. Henry P. Monaghan, Presidential War-Making, 50 B.U.L. Rev. 19 (1970).

By and large the broad expansion of presidential power has occurred as a result of large, open-ended legislative grants from congress itself. . . . However, . . . "strong" presidents have always asserted the power to act in the absence of statute where there was an emergency. . . . It seems to me indefensible to assert that even on internal matters the president must invariably point to a statute to justify his conduct. Should an emergency arise, the president must and will act so as to protect the nation's interest as he conceives it. To require the existence of a statute would leave an enormous gap in the nation's power to meet an emergency, a doctrine not likely to commend itself to men of affairs. And I would add that the existence of an emergency is largely a political not a judicial question. If the president abuses that power, the only recourse is subsequent congressional action and, ultimately, the displeasure of the electorate.

As it does with respect to internal matters, the constitutional text assigns broad powers to congress in the area of foreign affairs. . . . The president is also expressly vested with some powers bearing on foreign relations. . . . More importantly, from the beginning the Hamiltonian contention that the president possessed broad "inherent" powers in representing the nation in our foreign relations gained considerable currency. Thus Marshall could refer to the president as "the sole organ of the nation in its external relations, and its sole representative with foreign nations." By 1935 the supreme court, undoubtedly influenced by the long and steady growth of presidential activity, characterized the presidential prerogative to conduct foreign affairs as "delicate, plenary and exclusive."[a]

Not surprisingly, therefore, most writers recognize that the respective ambits of congressional and executive powers in controlling the direction of American policy cannot be resolved simply by an appeal to the constitutional text. That document "is remarkably inexact concerning the distribution of responsibilities . . . for the making of foreign policy"; it seems to permit the exercise of considerable power over this subject matter in both branches.[b]

Writing in 1957, Professor Corwin accurately summarized the situation: "[C]onsidered only for its affirmative grants of power capable of affecting the issue, [the constitution] is an invitation to struggle for the privilege of directing American foreign policy. . . ."

Accordingly, even if one were inclined to accept [the] view that presidential action within the United States must be grounded in a statute, there is no basis for applying such a rigid concept of separation of powers past our shorelines.

The general view for which I have been contending is that analysis of the doctrine of separation of powers should focus more on a recognition that often what is being separated are institutions and not necessarily "powers." To some degree these institutions have unique powers; one would not expect the president to promulgate an income tax code merely because in his judgment congress should have done so. But there are gray areas where joint power exists — where both branches have tremendous and overlapping power and where any "conflict" must be resolved on the political, not the legal, level. This seems to me indisputably true in the area of foreign affairs. And the consequences of this view are of course evident: the existence of the congressional power over the subject of foreign affairs will not support a nar-

a. United States v. Curtiss-Wright Export Corp. 299 U.S. 304, 320 (1936).

b. Professor Black argues, however, that the textual powers of the president to conduct foreign affairs are in fact minimal. Accordingly, he is of the opinion that the constitutional text presupposed congressional supremacy in the area of foreign affairs corresponding to a similar supremacy in internal affairs. C. Black, Perspectives in Constitutional Law 57-59 (1963). . . . I tend to agree with this view. Historical necessity has, however, expanded the content of such terms as "executive power" and "commander in chief" and it has given sanction to the Hamiltonian view of "inherent" powers — i.e. to powers not in the constitutional text.

row definition of presidential power. Absent congressional action, the president has (to use a conclusory term) "inherent" constitutional power in the conduct of our foreign affairs. . . .

The occasions on which presidents have refused to take military action abroad because of a lack of prior congressional authorization are few in number and increasingly rare. From the beginning of our constitutional history, presidents have both deployed the armed forces abroad and committed them to actual hostilities without explicit congressional authorization. In excess of one hundred and twenty instances of such action exist. . . . Thus, argues the state department, "practice and precedent have confirmed the constitutional authority of the president to commit the armed forces to battle without a declaration of war."

The strength of the "practice and precedent" has, however, not gone unchallenged. Most writers who seek constitutionally based restrictions on the president's war-making power argue that the precedents are not compelling. Indeed, it has been suggested that there is only one prior illustration of presidential commitment of armed forces to war without congressional authorization, namely, Korea. The other instances cited, it is argued, were simply presidential responses to reprisals, or "relatively minor and short-lived occurrences [that] do not establish precedent for the massive and long-lasting [Vietnam] war. . .": "minor" and "short-lived" from whose point of view? . . . To dismiss American interventions in Latin America as "minor" amounts to recognition of presidential power to wage war against weak opponents for limited purposes. . . .

Whatever the intention of the framers, the military machine has become simply an instrument for the achievement of foreign policy goals, which, in turn, have become a central responsibility of the presidency. Congress has seldom objected on legal grounds, and so the only limitation upon presidential power has been that imposed by political considerations. That is the teaching of our history.

Discussion

1. *The original understanding.* Professor Monaghan repeatedly refers to possible "original" understandings of the allocation of power with respect to the commitment of armed forces. There is considerable controversy over what this original understanding may have been. Professor Lofgren, in an extensive analysis, concluded that the framers intended to grant only very limited independent presidential power to commit troops.[71] Consider in this context Thomas Jefferson's actions taken in response to North African pirates. Without congressional authorization, he sent the American fleet to the Mediterranean, where it battled the Tripolitan fleet. On December 8, 1801, he sent a message to Congress in which he said:

> Tripoli, the least considerable of the Barbary States, had come forward with demands unfounded either in right or in compact, and had permitted itself to denounce war on our failure to comply before a given day. The style of the demand admitted but one answer. I sent a small squadron of frigates into the Mediterranean . . . with orders to protect our commerce against the threatened attack. . . . Our commerce in the Mediterranean was blockaded, and that of the Atlantic in peril. . . . One of the Tripolitan cruisers having fallen in with, and engaged the small schooner Enterprise, . . . was captured, after a heavy slaughter of her men. . . . Unauthorized by the constitution, without the sanction of Congress, to go beyond the line of defence,

71. Charles Lofgren, War-Making Under the Constitution: The Original Understanding, 81 Yale L.J. 672 (1972).

the vessel being disabled from committing further hostilities, was liberated with its crew. The legislature will doubtless consider whether, by authorizing measures of offence, also, they will place our force on an equal footing with that of its adversaries. I communicate all material information on this subject, that in the exercise of the important function confided by the constitution to the legislature exclusively, their judgment may form itself on a knowledge and consideration of every circumstance of weight.

Even assuming that Jefferson acted in accordance with the original understanding of the President's powers, how much weight does it deserve? Professor Monaghan states that whether presidential invocation of power " 'defeats' the framers' intention is . . . a profitless speculation. We do not and cannot know, what, specifically, they would have thought about a world so different from their own. Nor would we really care." Monaghan cites Justice Holmes' opinion in Missouri v. Holland, 252 U.S. 416, 433 (1920):

[W]hen we are dealing with words that also are a constituent act, like the Constitution of the United States, we must realize that the framers have called into life a being the development of which could not have been foreseen completely by the most gifted of its begetters. It was enough for them to realize or to hope that they had created an organism; it has taken a century and has cost their successors much sweat and blood to prove that they created a nation. The case before us must be considered in the light of our whole experience and not merely in that of what was said a hundred years ago.

2. *The legitimacy of specific congressional limitation.* There has been substantial debate over the propriety of congressional legislation limiting the President's independent power to commit troops. Justice Clark, concurring in the Steel Seizure Case, wrote:

One of this Court's first pronouncements upon the powers of the President under the Constitution was made by Chief Justice John Marshall some one hundred and fifty years ago. In Little v. Barreme, 2 Cranch 170 (1804) he used this characteristically clear language in discussing the power of the President to instruct the seizure of the 'Flying-Fish,' a vessel bound from a French port: "It is by no means clear that the President of the United States whose high duty it is to 'take care that the laws be faithfully executed,' and who is commander in chief of the armies and navies of the United States, might not, without any special authority for that purpose, in the then existing state of things, have empowered the officers commanding the armed vessels of the United States, to seize and send into port for adjudication, American vessels which were forfeited by being engaged in this illicit commerce. But when it is observed that (an act of Congress) gives a special authority to seize on the high seas, and limits that authority to the seizure of vessels bound or sailing to a French port, the legislature seem to have prescribed that the manner in which this law shall be carried into execution, was to exclude a seizure of any vessel not bound to a French port." Accordingly, a unanimous Court held that the President's instructions had been issued without authority and that they could not "legalize an act which without those instructions would have been a plain trespass." I know of no subsequent holding of this Court to the contrary.

The limits of presidential power are obscure. . . . Some of our Presidents, such as Lincoln, "felt that measures otherwise unconstitutional might become lawful by becoming indispensable to the preservation of the Constitution through the preservation of the nation." Others, such as Theodore Roosevelt, thought the President to be capable, as a "steward" of the people, of exerting all power save that which is specifically prohibited by the Constitution or the Congress. In my view — taught me not only by the decision of Chief Justice Marshall in Little v. Barreme, but also by a score of other pronouncements of distinguished members of this bench — the Constitution does grant to the President extensive authority in times of grave and imperative national emergency. In fact, to my thinking, such a grant may well be necessary to the very existence of the Constitution itself. . . . In describing this authority I care not whether one calls it "residual," "inherent," "moral," "implied," "aggregate," "emergency," or otherwise. I am of the conviction that those who have had the gratifying experience of being the President's lawyer [Justice Clark had served as Attorney General under President Truman] have used one or more of these adjectives only with the utmost of sincerity and the highest of purpose.

I conclude that where Congress has laid down specific procedures to deal with the type of crisis confronting the President, he must follow those procedures in meeting the crisis; but that in the absence of such action by Congress, the President's independent power to act depends upon the gravity of the situation confronting the nation. I cannot sustain the seizure in question because here, as in Little v. Barreme, Congress had prescribed methods to be followed by the President in meeting the emergency at hand.

3. *The relevance of* Curtiss-Wright. Professor Monaghan describes United States v. Curtiss-Wright, 299 U.S. 304 (1935), as accepting the doctrine of "inherent" presidential power over foreign affairs. Compare Justice Jackson's analysis of *Curtiss-Wright* in his opinion in the Steel Seizure Case:

United States v. Curtiss-Wright Export Corp. involved, not the question of the President's power to act without congressional authority, but the question of his right to act under and in accord with an Act of Congress. The constitutionality of the Act under which the President had proceeded was assailed on the ground that it delegated legislative powers to the President. Much of the Court's opinion is dictum, but the ratio decidendi is contained in the following language:

"When the President is to be authorized by legislation to act in respect of a matter intended to affect a situation in foreign territory, the legislator properly bears in mind the important consideration that the form of the President's action — or, indeed, whether he shall act at all — may well depend, among other things, upon the nature of the confidential information which he has or may thereafter receive, or upon the effect which his action may have upon our foreign relations. This consideration, in connection with what we have already said on the subject, discloses the unwisdom of requiring Congress in this field of governmental power to lay down narrowly definite standards by which the President is to be governed. As this court said in Mackenzie v. Hare, 239 U.S. 299, 311, 'As a government, the United States is invested with all the attributes of sovereignty. As it has the character of nationality it has the powers of nationality, especially those which concern its relations and intercourse with other countries. *We should hesitate long before limiting or embarrassing such powers.*' (Italics supplied.)"

That case does not solve the present controversy. It recognized internal and external affairs as being in separate categories, and held that the strict limitation upon congressional delegations of power to the President over internal affairs does not apply with respect to delegations of power in external affairs. It was intimated that the President might act in external affairs without congressional authority, but not that he might act contrary to an Act of Congress.

4. In the aftermath of the Vietnam War, Congress passed, over President Nixon's veto, the War Powers Resolution of 1973.[72] Its central purpose was to increase Congress' role in decisionmaking regarding the commitment of American troops. It requires the President to submit a report to Congress within 48 hours of the introduction of American troops, in the absence of a declaration of war,

> (1) into hostilities or into situations where imminent involvement in hostilities is clearly indicated by the circumstances;
> (2) into the territory, airspace or waters of a foreign nation, while equipped for combat, except for deployments which relate solely to supply, replacement, repair, or training of such forces; or
> (3) in numbers which substantially enlarge United States Armed Forces equipped for combat already located in a foreign country.

Submission of such a report triggers a 60-day decisionmaking period. At the end of that period, "the President shall terminate any use of United States Armed forces" reported on "unless the Congress (1) has declared war or has enacted a specific authorization for such use of United States Armed Forces, (2) has extended by law such sixty-day period, or (3) is physically unable to meet as a result of an armed attack upon the United States." This 60-day period can also be extended by 30 additional days should the President notify Congress "that unavoidable military necessity respecting the safety of United States Armed Forces requires the continued use of such armed forces in the course of bringing about a prompt removal of such forces." However, in the absence of a declaration of war or specific congressional authorization, "such forces shall be removed by the President if the Congress so directs by concurrent resolution."

The War Powers Act has been the topic of major constitutional debate, in large measure because of the specific process chosen for invocation of congressional power. Thus, presidential authority to commit troops seemingly expires unless Congress affirmatively authorizes the commitment, and the President is given no opportunity to veto the concurrent resolution directly. Every President since Nixon has argued that this aspect of the Act is unconstitutional. Congress has not yet attempted to use the War Powers Act to limit presidential action. Dramatic examples of the practical irrelevance of the Act involved President Reagan's and Bush's commitments of American military forces to the Persian Gulf. Congressional majorities self-consciously avoided invoking of the Act, over the heated protest of several legislators.

Imagine that Congress, over the President's objections, passed a law directing the removal of American troops from a particular theater of involvement. Would the statute be constitutional?

5. Consider the *institutional* role of the Supreme Court in adjudicating conflicts between the Congress and the President over military policy. Professor Monaghan regards "the precise relationship between the executive and the legislative branches [as] a matter for the political process." He therefore "see[s] no role for the courts to play. A contention that the president of the United States

72. See Louis Fisher, Constitutional Conflicts Between Congress and the President 307-318 (1985); Ely, Suppose Congress Wanted a War Powers Act that Worked, 88 Colum. L. Rev. 1379 (1988).

must defend his decision to commit troops to combat before a federal district judge in Boston, Milwaukee or Seattle strikes me as wholly untenable."

Does a judicial injunction against the commitment of troops seem less tenable than other areas involving judicial invalidation of political acts?

6. *Subsequent case.* In Dames & Moore v. Regan, 453 U.S. 654 (1981), the Court considered the constitutionality of executive orders under which President Carter, in an agreement with Iran for the release of over 400 American hostages, "nullified attachments and liens on Iranian assets in the United States, directed that these assets be transferred to Iran, and suspended claims against Iran that may be presented to an International Claims Tribunal." Following his inauguration, President Reagan "ratified" the orders.

Dames & Moore had sued the government of Iran, an Iranian agency, and several Iranian banks for services performed under a contract. A federal district court attached the property of several defendants in order to secure any judgment that might be entered against them. The Court subsequently found in favor of Dames & Moore, which then attempted to execute the judgment by having the attached property sold. Prior to sale, however, the district court stayed execution of its judgment and "ordered that all prejudgment attachments obtained against the Iranian defendants be vacated and that further proceedings against the bank defendants be stayed in light of the Executive Orders." Dames & Moore complained that the orders were unconstitutional. The Supreme Court granted a writ of certiorari.

Justice Rehnquist, writing for a unanimous Court on the point at issue, emphasized that "we attempt to lay down no general 'guidelines' covering other situations not involved here, and attempt to confine the opinion only to the very questions necessary to decision of the case." The Court noted that "the President's action in nullifying the attachments and ordering the transfer of the assets was taken pursuant to specific congressional authorization." As to "the President's authority to suspend claims pending in American courts," there was no such statutory authorization, though statutory provisions are nonetheless "highly relevant in the looser sense of indicating congressional acceptance of a broad scope for executive action in circumstances such as those presented in this case." Justice Rehnquist also noted "a history of congressional acquiescence in conduct of the sort engaged in by the President" and went on to pronounce as "[c]rucial to our decision today . . . the conclusion that Congress has implicitly approved the practice of claim settlement by executive agreement."

Professor Mark Tushnet maintains that *Dames & Moore* approves "an exercise of presidential authority indistinguishable in its essentials from that disapproved in the *Steel Seizure Case,*" for there the Court "could have found equally 'persuasive' authority if it had chosen to uphold the President's actions."[73] *Dames & Moore* differs from its predecessor, Tushnet argues, in that it arose at a moment of "greater enthusiasm for the imperial presidency." The Court "could not possibly have gotten away with invalidating the Iranian Hostage Accords, while the Court in 1952, facing a politically weakened President who had — horror of horrors — trampled on the prerogatives of property, could get away with what it did."

73. Mark Tushnet, The Burger Court: The Counter-Revolution that Wasn't, 132 U. Pa. L. Rev. 1257 (1984). See also Symposium: Dames & Moore v. Regan, 29 U.C.L.A.L. Rev. 977 (1981).

C. The Pentagon Papers Case

NEW YORK TIMES v. UNITED STATES
403 U.S. 713 (1971)
Certiorari to the United States Court of Appeals for the Second Circuit

[On June 13, 1971, the New York Times began publishing a series of articles concerning the involvement of the Kennedy and Johnson Administrations in the origins of the Vietnam War. These articles were based on internal documents of the Department of Defense, prepared for a classified history of the War. The documents had been procured by Daniel Ellsberg, who had helped prepare the history but then grew disillusioned with the War, and who viewed their release as a means of encouraging protest against continued American involvement. On June 15, the Nixon Administration sought an injunction against further publication of the "Pentagon Papers," as they came to be called, on the ground that it threatened vital national interests.

A district judge refused to grant the injunction. On appeal, the Second Circuit reversed and enjoined further publication. When the Washington Post began publishing similar stories, the Administration sought injunctive relief in the District of Columbia. It was denied, and the United States immediately appealed. Oral argument was held on June 26, and the Court issued its *per curiam* opinion four days later:][74]

[T]he United States seeks to enjoin the New York Times and the Washington Post from publishing the contents of a classified study entitled "History of U.S. Decision-Making Process on Viet Nam Policy." "Any system of prior restraints of expression comes to this Court bearing a heavy presumption against its constitutional validity." Bantam Books, Inc. v. Sullivan, 372 U.S. 58, 70 (1963). The Government "thus carries a heavy burden of showing justification for the imposition of such a restraint." [The court below] held that the Government had not met that burden. We agree.

[Each Justice wrote an opinion explaining his position.]

BLACK, J., joined by Douglas, J., concurring:

[T]he Government's case against the Washington Post should have been dismissed and the injunction against the New York Times should have been vacated without oral argument when the cases were first presented to this Court. I believe that every moment's continuance of the injunctions against these newspapers amounts to a flagrant, indefensible, and continuing violation of the First Amendment. . . . In my view it is unfortunate that some of my Brethren are apparently willing to hold that the publication of news may sometimes be enjoined. Such a holding would make a shambles of the First Amendment.

. . . [T]he federal courts are asked to hold that the First Amendment does not mean what it says, but rather means that the Government can halt the publication of current news of vital importance to the people of this country.

In seeking injunctions against these newspapers and in its presentation to the Court, the Executive Branch seems to have forgotten the essential purpose and history of the First Amendment. . . . The Bill of Rights changed the original Con-

74. See Sanford Ungar, The Papers and the Papers (1972).

stitution into a new charter under which no branch of government could abridge the people's freedoms of press, speech, religion, and assembly. Yet the Solicitor General argues and some members of the Court appear to agree that the general powers of the Government adopted in the original Constitution should be interpreted to limit and restrict the specific and emphatic guarantees of the Bill of Rights adopted later. I can imagine no greater perversion of history. Madison and the other Framers of the First Amendment, able men that they were, wrote in language they earnestly believed could never be misunderstood: "Congress shall make no law . . . abridging the freedom . . . of the press . . ." Both the history and language of the First Amendment support the view that the press must be left free to publish news, whatever the source, without censorship, injunctions, or prior restraints.

In the First Amendment the Founding Fathers gave the free press the protection it must have to fulfill its essential role in our democracy. The press was to serve the governed, not the governors. The Government's power to censor the press was abolished so that the press would remain forever free to censure the Government. The press was protected so that it could bare the secrets of government and inform the people. Only a free and unrestrained press can effectively expose deception in government. And paramount among the responsibilities of a free press is the duty to prevent any part of the government from deceiving the people and sending them off to distant lands to die of foreign fevers and foreign shot and shell. In my view, far from deserving condemnation for their courageous reporting, the New York Times, the Washington Post, and other newspapers should be commended for serving the purpose that the Founding Fathers saw so clearly. In revealing the workings of government that led to the Vietnam war, the newspapers nobly did precisely that which the Founders hoped and trusted they would do.

. . . [T]he Government argues in its brief that in spite of the First Amendment, "[t]he authority of the Executive Department to protect the nation against publication of information whose disclosure would endanger the national security stems from two interrelated sources: the constitutional power of the President over the conduct of foreign affairs and his authority as Commander-in-Chief."

In other words, we are asked to hold that despite the First Amendment's emphatic command, the Executive Branch, the Congress, and the Judiciary can make laws enjoining publication of current news and abridging freedom of the press in the name of "national security." The Government does not even attempt to rely on any act of Congress. Instead it makes the bold and dangerously far-reaching contention that the courts should take it upon themselves to "make" a law abridging freedom of the press in the name of equity, presidential power and national security, even when the representatives of the people in Congress have adhered to the command of the First Amendment and refused to make such a law. To find that the President has "inherent power" to halt the publication of news by resort to the courts would wipe out the First Amendment and destroy the fundamental liberty and security of the very people the Government hopes to make "secure." No one can read the history of the adoption of the First Amendment without being convinced beyond any doubt that it was injunctions like those sought here that Madison and his collaborators intended to outlaw in this Nation for all time. . . .

DOUGLAS, J., joined by Black, J., concurring.

[The language of the First Amendment] leaves, in my view, no room for governmental restraint on the press.

There is, moreover, no statute barring the publication by the press of the material which the Times and the Post seek to use. . . . So any power that the Government possesses must come from its "inherent power."

The power to wage war is "the power to wage war successfully." See Hirabayashi v. United States. But the war power stems from a declaration of war. The Constitution by Art. I, §8, gives Congress, not the President, power "[t]o declare War." Nowhere are presidential wars authorized. We need not decide therefore what leveling effect the war power of Congress might have.

These disclosures may have a serious impact. But that is no basis for sanctioning a previous restraint on the press. As stated by Chief Justice Hughes in Near v. Minnesota, 283 U.S. 697,

> While reckless assaults upon public men, and efforts to bring obloquy upon those who are endeavoring faithfully to discharge official duties, exert a baleful influence and deserve the severest condemnation in public opinion, it cannot be said that this abuse is greater, and it is believed to be less, than that which characterized the period in which our institutions took shape. Meanwhile, the administration of government has become more complex, the opportunities for malfeasance and corruption have multiplied, crime has grown to most serious proportions, and the danger of its protection by unfaithful officials and of the impairment of the fundamental security of life and property by criminal alliances and official neglect, emphasizes the primary need of a vigilant and courageous press, especially in great cities. The fact that the liberty of the press may be abused by miscreant purveyors of scandal does not make any the less necessary the immunity of the press from previous restraint in dealing with official misconduct.

. . . The Government says that it has inherent powers to go into court and obtain an injunction to protect the national interest, which in this case is alleged to be national security. Near v. Minnesota repudiated that expansive doctrine in no uncertain terms.

The dominant purpose of the First Amendment was to prohibit the widespread practice of governmental suppression of embarrassing information. . . . Secrecy in government is fundamentally anti-democratic, perpetuating bureaucratic errors. Open debate and discussion of public issues are vital to our national health. On public questions there should be "uninhibited, robust, and wide-open" debate.

BRENNAN, J., concurring.

I . . .

So far as I can determine, never before has the United States sought to enjoin a newspaper from publishing information in its possession. . . .

II . . .

[T]he First Amendment tolerates absolutely no prior judicial restraints of the press predicated upon surmise or conjecture that untoward consequences may result. Our cases, it is true, have indicated that there is a single, extremely narrow class of cases in which the First Amendment's ban on prior judicial restraint may be overridden. Our cases have thus far indicated that such cases may arise only when the Nation "is at war," Schenck v. United States, 249 U.S. 47, 52 (1919), during which times "[n]o one would question but that a government might prevent actual obstruction to its recruiting service or the publication of the sailing dates of transports or the number and location of troops." *Near*. Even if the present world situation were assumed to be tantamount to a time of war, or if the power of presently available armaments would justify even in peacetime the suppression of information that would set in motion a nuclear holocaust, in neither of these actions has the Government presented or even alleged that publication of items from or based upon the material at issue would cause the happening of an event of that nature. "[T]he chief purpose of [the First Amendment's] guaranty [is] to prevent previous restraints upon publication." Thus, only governmental allegation and proof that publication must inevitably, directly, and immediately cause the occurrence of an event kindred to imperiling the safety of a transport already at sea can support even the issuance of an interim restraining order. In no event may mere conclusions be sufficient: for if the Executive Branch seeks judicial aid in preventing publication, it must inevitably submit the basis upon which that aid is sought to scrutiny by the judiciary. And therefore, every restraint issued in this case, whatever its form, has violated the First Amendment — and not less so because that restraint was justified as necessary to afford the courts an opportunity to examine the claim more thoroughly. Unless and until the Government has clearly made out its case, the First Amendment commands that no injunction may issue.

STEWART, J., joined by White, J., concurring.

In the governmental structure created by our Constitution, the Executive is endowed with enormous power in the two related areas of national defense and international relations. This power, largely unchecked by the Legislative and Judicial branches, has been pressed to the very hilt since the advent of the nuclear missile age. . . .

In the absence of the governmental checks and balances present in other areas of our national life, the only effective restraint upon executive policy and power in the areas of national defense and international affairs may lie in an enlightened citizenry — in an informed and critical public opinion which alone can here protect the values of democratic government. For this reason, it is perhaps here that a press that is alert, aware, and free most vitally serves the basic purpose of the First Amendment. For without an informed and free press there cannot be an enlightened people.

Yet it is elementary that the successful conduct of international diplomacy and the maintenance of an effective national defense require both confidentiality and secrecy. Other nations can hardly deal with this Nation in an atmosphere of mutual trust unless they can be assured that their confidences will be kept. And within our own executive departments, the development of considered and intelligent international policies would be impossible if those charged with their formulation could not communicate with each other freely, frankly, and in confidence. In the area of basic national defense the frequent need for absolute secrecy is, of course, self-evident.

I think there can be but one answer to this dilemma, if dilemma it be. The responsibility must be where the power is. If the Constitution gives the Executive a large degree of unshared power in the conduct of foreign affairs and the maintenance of our national defense, then under the Constitution the Executive must have the largely unshared duty to determine and preserve the degree of internal security necessary to exercise that power successfully. . . . [I]t is clear to me that it is the constitutional duty of the Executive — as a matter of sovereign prerogative and not as a matter of law as the courts know law — through the promulgation and enforcement of executive regulations, to protect the confidentiality necessary to carry out its responsibilities in the fields of international relations and national defense.

This is not to say that Congress and the courts have no role to play. Undoubtedly Congress has the power to enact specific and appropriate criminal laws to protect government property and preserve government secrets. Congress has passed such laws, and several of them are of very colorable relevance to the apparent circumstances of these cases. And if a criminal prosecution is instituted, it will be the responsibility of the courts to decide the applicability of the criminal law under which the charge is brought. Moreover, if Congress should pass a specific law authorizing civil proceedings in this field, the courts would likewise have the duty to decide the constitutionality of such a law as well as its applicability to the facts proved.

But in the cases before us we are asked neither to construe specific regulations nor to apply specific laws. We are asked, instead, to perform a function that the Constitution gave to the Executive, not the Judiciary. We are asked, quite simply, to prevent the publication by two newspapers of material that the Executive Branch insists should not, in the national interest, be published. I am convinced that the Executive is correct with respect to some of the documents involved. But I cannot say that disclosure of any of them will surely result in direct, immediate, and irreparable damage to our Nation or its people. That being so, there can under the First Amendment be but one judicial resolution of the issues before us. I join the judgments of the Court.

WHITE, J., joined by Stewart, J., concurring.

I concur in today's judgments, but only because of the concededly extraordinary protection against prior restraints enjoyed by the press under our constitutional system. . . .

The Government's position is simply stated: The responsibility of the Executive for the conduct of the foreign affairs and for the security of the Nation is so basic that the President is entitled to an injunction against publication of a newspaper story whenever he can convince a court that the information to be revealed threatens "grave and irreparable" injury to the public interest; and the injunction should issue whether or not the material to be published is classified, whether or not publication would be lawful under relevant criminal statutes enacted by Congress, and regardless of the circumstances by which the newspaper came into possession of the information.

At least in the absence of legislation by Congress, based on its own investigations and findings, I am quite unable to agree that the inherent powers of the Executive and the courts reach so far as to authorize remedies having such sweeping potential for inhibiting publications by the press. Much of the difficulty inheres in the "grave and irreparable danger" standard suggested by the United States. If the United States were to have judgment under such a standard in these cases, our decision would be of little guidance to other courts in other cases, for the material at issue here would not be available from the Court's opinion or from public records, nor would it be published by the press. Indeed, even today where we hold that the United States has not met its burden, the material remains sealed in court records and it is properly not discussed in today's opinion. . . . To sustain the Government in these cases would start the courts down a long and hazardous road that I am not willing to travel, at least without congressional guidance and direction. . . .

[T]erminating the ban on publication of the relatively few sensitive documents the Government now seeks to suppress does not mean that the law either requires or invites newspapers or others to publish them or that they will be immune from criminal action if they do. Prior restraints require an unusually heavy justification under the First Amendment; but failure by the Government to justify prior restraints does not measure its constitutional entitlement to a conviction for criminal publication. That the Government mistakenly chose to proceed by injunction does not mean that it could not successfully proceed in another way.

. . . The Criminal Code contains numerous provisions potentially relevant to these cases. [One section] makes it a crime to publish certain photographs or drawings of military installations. [Another], also in precise language, proscribes knowing and willful publication of any classified information concerning the cryptographic systems or communication intelligence activities of the United States as well as any information obtained from communication intelligence operations. If any of the material here at issue is of this nature, the newspapers are presumably now on full notice of the position of the United States and must face the consequences if they publish. I would have no difficulty in sustaining convictions under these sections on facts that would not justify the intervention of equity and the imposition of a prior restraint. . . .

It is thus clear that Congress has addressed itself to the problems of protecting the security of the country and the national defense from unauthorized disclosure of potentially damaging information. It has not, however, authorized the injunctive remedy against threatened publication. It has apparently been satisfied to rely on criminal sanctions and their deterrent effect on the responsible as well as the irresponsible press. I am not, of course, saying that either of these newspapers has yet committed a crime or that either would commit a crime if it published all the material now in its possession. That matter must await resolution in the context of a criminal proceeding if one is instituted by the United States. In that event, the issue of guilt or innocence would be determined by procedures and standards quite different from those that have purported to govern these injunctive proceedings.

MARSHALL, J., concurring.

. . . The issue is whether this Court or the Congress has the power to make law. In these cases there is no problem concerning the President's power to classify information as "secret" or "top secret." Congress has specifically recognized Presidential authority . . . to classify documents and information. Nor is there any issue here regarding the President's power as Chief Executive and Commander in Chief to protect national security by disciplining employees who disclose information and by taking precautions to prevent leaks.

The problem here is whether in these particular cases the Executive Branch has authority to invoke the equity jurisdiction of the courts to protect what it believes to be the national interest. The Government argues that in addition to the inherent power of any government to protect itself, the President's power to conduct foreign affairs and his position as Commander in Chief give him authority to impose censorship on the press to protect his ability to deal effectively with foreign nations and to conduct the military affairs of the country. Of course, it is beyond cavil that the President has broad powers by virtue of his primary responsibility for the conduct of our foreign affairs and his position as Commander in Chief. And in some situations it may be that under whatever inherent powers the Government may have, as well as the implicit authority derived from the President's mandate to conduct foreign affairs and to act as Commander in Chief, there is a basis for the invocation of the equity jurisdiction of this Court as an aid to prevent the publication of material damaging to "national security," however that term may be defined.

It would, however, be utterly inconsistent with the concept of separation of powers for this Court to use its power of contempt to prevent behavior that Congress has specifically declined to prohibit. There would be a similar damage to the basic concept of these co-equal branches of Government if when the Executive Branch has adequate authority granted by Congress to protect "national security" it can choose instead to invoke the contempt power of a court to enjoin the threatened conduct. The Constitution provides that Congress shall make laws, the President execute laws, and courts interpret laws. *Youngstown Sheet & Tube Co.* It did not provide for government by injunction in which the courts and the Executive Branch can "make law" without regard to the action of Congress. It may be more convenient for the Executive Branch if it need only convince a judge to prohibit conduct rather than ask the Congress to pass a law, and it may be more convenient to enforce a contempt order than to seek a criminal conviction in a jury trial. Moreover, it may be considered politically wise to get a court to share the responsibility for arresting those who the Executive Branch has probable cause to believe are violating the law. But convenience and political considerations of the moment do not justify a basic departure from the principles of our system of government. . . .

On at least two occasions Congress has refused to enact legislation that would have made the conduct engaged in here unlawful and given the President the power that he seeks in this case. . . . It is not for this Court to fling itself into every breach perceived by some Government official nor is it for this Court to take on itself the burden of enacting law, especially a law that Congress has refused to pass.

HARLAN, J., joined by Burger, C.J., and Blackmun, J., dissenting.

. . . With all respect, I consider that the Court has been almost irresponsibly feverish in dealing with these cases. . . .

Forced as I am to reach the merits of these cases, I dissent from the opinion and judgments of the Court. Within the severe limitations imposed by the time constraints under which I have been required to operate, I can only state my reasons in telescoped form. . . .

It is plain to me that the scope of the judicial function in passing upon the activities of the Executive Branch of the Government in the field of foreign affairs is very narrowly restricted. This view is, I think, dictated by the concept of separation of powers upon which our constitutional system rests.

In a speech on the floor of the House of Representatives, Chief Justice John Marshall, then a member of that body, stated: "The President is the sole organ of the nation in its external relations, and its sole representative with foreign nations."

From that time, shortly after the founding of the Nation, to this, there has been no substantial challenge to this description of the scope of executive power. See United States v. Curtiss-Wright Export Corp., 299 U.S. 304, 319-321 (1936), collecting authorities.

From this constitutional primacy in the field of foreign affairs, it seems to me that certain conclusions necessarily follow. Some of these were stated concisely by President Washington, declining the request of the House of Representatives for the papers leading up to the negotiation of the Jay Treaty: "The nature of foreign negotiations requires caution, and their success must often depend on secrecy; and even when brought to a conclusion a full disclosure of all the measures, demands, or eventual concessions which may have been proposed or contemplated would be extremely impolitic; for this might have a pernicious influence on future negotiations, or produce immediate inconveniences, perhaps danger and mischief, in relation to other powers."

The power to evaluate the "pernicious influence" of premature disclosure is not, however, lodged in the Executive alone. I agree that, in performance of its duty to protect the values of the First Amendment against political pressures, the judiciary must review the initial Executive determination to the point of satisfying itself that the subject matter of the dispute does lie within the proper compass of the President's foreign relations power. Constitutional considerations forbid "a complete abandonment of judicial control." Moreover the judiciary may properly insist that the determination that disclosure of the subject matter would irreparably impair the national security be made by the head of the Executive Department concerned — here the Secretary of State or the Secretary of Defense — after actual personal consideration by that officer. This safeguard is required in the analogous area of executive claims of privilege for secrets of state.

But in my judgment the judiciary may not properly go beyond these two inquiries and redetermine for itself the probable impact of disclosure on the national security. . . .

Even if there is some room for the judiciary to override the executive determination, it is plain that the scope of review must be exceedingly narrow. I can see no indication in the opinions of either the District Court or the Court of Appeals in the Post litigation that the conclusions of the Executive were given even the deference owing to an administrative agency, much less that owing to a co-equal branch of the Government operating within the field of its constitutional prerogative. . . .

Pending further hearings in each case conducted under the appropriate ground rules, I would continue the restraints on publication. I cannot believe that the doctrine prohibiting prior restraints reaches to the point of preventing courts from maintaining the status quo long enough to act responsibly in matters of such national importance as those involved here.

BLACKMUN, J., dissenting.

. . . The First Amendment, after all, is only one part of an entire Constitution. Article II of the great document vests in the Executive Branch primary power over the conduct of foreign affairs and places in that branch the responsibility for the Nation's safety. Each provision of the Constitution is important, and I cannot subscribe to a doctrine of unlimited absolutism for the First Amendment at the cost of downgrading other provisions. . . . What is needed here is a weighing, upon properly developed standards, of the broad right of the press to print and of the very narrow right of the Government to prevent. Such standards are not yet developed. The parties here are in disagreement as to what those standards should be. But even the newspapers concede that there are situations where restraint is in order and is constitutional. Mr. Justice Holmes gave us a suggestion [in *Schenck*].

[A dissenting opinion by Chief Justice Burger is omitted.]

Discussion

On prior restraints. Twentieth-century interpretations of the First Amendment often emphasize the particular dangers of prior restraints on speech, and historians agree that the amendment was at the very least intended to prohibit the English practice of requiring licenses prior to publication. The evils of prior restraint are exemplified in Near v. Minnesota, cited by several of the Justices as the foundation of the modern doctrine.

Minnesota sought to shut down Near's newspaper based on the "scandalous" nature of past publications. Although the state did not allege that he was about to publish a specific article that would cause harm, it argued that the content of previous issues justified prohibiting any future publication by Near. The Supreme Court, by a 5-to-4 vote, rejected the argument.[75]

How does *New York Times* differ from *Near*? Assuming that the publication of the Pentagon Papers could be punished after the fact, why should the First Amendment prohibit an injunction against publication when it would tolerate punishment after publication?[76]

People who wish to engage in conduct that they believe to be constitutionally protected, but that may fall within the prohibition of a criminal statute, often seek declaratory and injunctive relief before engaging in the conduct. Does an injunction sought by the government to define in advance the specific expression that will be unprotected, afford the same advantages — especially when the criminal

75. See Fred Friendly, Minnesota Rag (1981). See also Symposium, Near v. Minnesota, 50th Anniversary, 66 Minn. L. Rev. 1 (1981).

76. See Martin Redish, The Proper Role of the Prior Restraint Doctrine in First Amendment Theory, in Freedom of Expression: A Critical Analysis 127-172 (1984), and Vince Blasi, Toward a Theory of Prior Restraint: The Central Linkage, 66 Minn. L. Rev. 11 (1981), for two radically different answers to this question.

statute is bound to be somewhat vague? Might the possibility of criminal punishment conceivably "chill" more speech than a narrowly drawn injunction prohibiting the publication of very specific material?

Consider some aspects of injunctions that are not protective of free speech:

a. In many circumstances a person who violates an injunction may not contest its validity in defense to a charge of contempt. See Walker v. Birmingham, 388 U.S. 307 (1967).

b. Although a severe penalty may not be imposed without a jury trial, Bloom v. Illinois, 391 U.S. 194 (1968), a judge may impose a fine or even a jail sentence for contempt.

c. The relative inexpensiveness of seeking an injunction, as compared to a full-scale criminal trial after publication, may result in greater use of the injunctive remedy. Note in this context that no newspaper editor was ever prosecuted for publishing the Pentagon Papers.

d. It is extremely difficult to predict *ex ante* the consequences of publication before the material is actually published. One might predict, however, that governmental officials will almost never *under*estimate the potential harms of publication and may often overestimate them.

Suppose, though, that these aspects of injunctions were absent — that the scope of an injunction could be challenged in a collateral contempt proceeding, that trial by jury was required for a conviction, that there were no economic differences between prior restraint and subsequent punishment, and that the harmful consequences of expression could be predicted accurately. Also, suppose that the legislature had specifically authorized seeking injunctions prohibiting publication under carefully limited circumstances. Would you still differentiate between prior restraint and subsequent punishment?

Consider the Intelligence Identities Protection Act of 1982, which prohibits the disclosure of the names of American intelligence agents. Assume (contrary to fact) that Congress had specifically authorized the Attorney General to seek an injunction preventing the publication of such names. A newspaper is about to publish the names of intelligence agents. What are the prospects for an injunction against the publication of the specific names? What are the prospects for postpublication conviction for violation of the Act?

VI. The Process of Decisionmaking in the Contemporary Administrative State

A. The Rise of the Administrative Agency and the Delegation of Discretionary Power

This chapter has traced, among other things, the development of the "administrative state," characterized by the ever-increasing role of administrative agencies in the modern scheme of government. The origins of the administrative state reach back over 100 years to the Interstate Commerce Commission, established under the Interstate Commerce Act of 1887, which "undoubtedly ranks as the most important legislative enactment of the latter nineteenth century, for it introduced a new organ of government unforeseen by the Framers — the administrative agency. . . . Although it would be two decades before Congress created another administrative agency [the Food and Drug Administration], the ICC became the model; its operations provided the initial building blocks of the entirely new subject of administrative law, with its own unique rules and procedures."[77]

The five commissioners of the ICC were appointed by the President and confirmed by the Senate. They differed from other executive appointees in two important respects. First, they held office for a fixed term (often extending beyond the administration of the appointing President). Second, whereas presidents may dismiss most high level officials by requesting their resignations, members of the independent administrative agencies can be removed only through congressional impeachment or upon demonstration of "cause" by the executive. There have, in fact, been no such removals in the history of the major federal agencies.

The ICC, which was charged primarily with the regulation of interstate shipment of goods by rail, heard complaints, examined records, and issued cease-and-desist orders against offending railroads. (Later, other modes of interstate shipment, such as trucking, also came under its jurisdiction.) Although the ICC did not set rates directly, it effectively fixed maximum rates by prohibiting "unreasonable" tolls.

Administrative agencies do not readily fit within the traditional framework of the separated powers of government. The ICC, for example, was required to administer the Interstate Commerce Act, an executive function. However, it mimicked the legislature by issuing general regulations having the force of law. Finally, by holding hearings, taking evidence, and ultimately adjudicating quite specific conflicts, it acted like a court. The judiciary's first reaction to this anomaly was one of hostility: The Court initially limited the ICC's power. Congress responded with legislation increasing the agency's power, to which the Court eventually acquiesced in Interstate Commerce Commission v. Illinois Central Railroad Co., 206 U.S. 452 (1910).

Two major achievements of Woodrow Wilson's first term (1913-1917) were the creation of the Federal Trade Commission, charged with enforcing antitrust laws, and the Federal Reserve Board. The next decade saw the establishment of the Federal Radio Commission, transformed into the Federal Communications Commission in 1934. President Roosevelt's New Deal, particularly the period from 1933 to 1937, created numerous "alphabet" agencies, including the SEC (Securities and Exchange Commission) and NLRB (National Labor Relations Board).

Many administrative statutes mandate that agencies regulate in "the public interest" but provide relatively little guidance as to what the public interest might be. On essentially this ground, a number of New Deal agencies were initially challenged as unconstitutional delegations of legislative power. However, the Court only twice invalidated a congressional statute on this ground. See Panama Refining Co. v. Ryan, 293 U.S. 388 (1935), and A.L.A. Schecter Poultry Corp. v. U.S., 295 U.S. 495 (1935). The nondelegation doctrine is widely regarded as another casualty of the post-1937 developments traced in this chapter, and it has not

77. Melvin Urofsky, A March of Liberty: A Constitutional History of the United States 523 (1988).

played a significant role in contemporary constitutional jurisprudence.[78] As Justice Scalia recently observed:[79]

> [W]hile the doctrine of unconstitutional delegation is unquestionably a fundamental element of our constitutional system, it is not an element readily enforceable by the courts. Once it is conceded, as it must be, that no statute can be entirely precise, and that some judgments, even some judgments involving policy considerations, must be left to the officers executing the law and to the judges applying it, the debate over unconstitutional delegation becomes a debate not over a point of principle but over a question of degree. As Chief Justice Taft expressed the point for the Court in the landmark case of J.W. Hampton, Jr. & Co. v. U.S., 276 U.S. 394, 406 (1928), the limits of delegation "must be fixed according to common sense and the inherent necessities of the governmental co-ordination."

Hampton required that Congress "lay down by legislative act an intelligible principle to which the person or body authorized to [exercise the delegated authority] is directed to conform." In practice this has not served as a significant constraint on legislative delegations of authority. Justice Blackmun described the modern Court's attitude when he wrote that in "[a]pplying this 'intelligible principle' test to congressional delegations, our jurisprudence has been driven by a practical understanding that in our increasingly complex society, replete with ever changing and more technical problems, Congress simply cannot do its job absent an ability to delegate power under broad general directives."[80]

78. Mistretta v. United States, 488 U.S. 361 (1989) (Scalia, J., dissenting).

79. Id.

80. See, however, Justice Rehnquist's concurrence in Industrial Union Dept., AFL-CIO v. American Petroleum, 448 U.S. 607 (1980), and dissent (joined by Chief Justice Burger) in American Textile Manufacturers Institute v. Donovan, 452 U.S. 490 (1981). Both cases involved §6(b)(5) of the Occupational Safety and Health Act of 1970, which requires the Secretary of Labor

> in promulgating standards dealing with toxic materials or harmful physical agents under this subsection [to] set the standard which most adequately assures, *to the extent feasible,* on the basis of the best available evidence, that no employee will suffer material impairment of health or functional capacity even if such employee has regular exposure to the hazard dealt with by such standard for the period of his working life. (Emphasis added.)

Did the statute forbid, permit, or even mandate the Secretary to engage in "cost-benefit" analysis balancing the increased safety of a standard against its cost? According to Justice Rehnquist,

> [Congress] unconstitutionally delegated to the Executive Branch the authority to make the "hard policy choices" properly the task of the legislature. . . . The "feasibility standard" is no standard at all. . . . The words "to the extent feasible" were used to mask a fundamental policy disagreement in Congress. I have no doubt that if Congress had been required to choose whether to mandate, permit, or prohibit the Secretary from engaging in a cost-benefit analysis, there would have been no bill for the President to sign. . . .
>
> I do not mean to suggest that Congress, in enacting a statute, must resolve all ambiguities or must "fill in all of the blanks." . . . [L]egislation is the art of compromise, and . . . an important, controversial bill is seldom enacted by Congress in the form in which it is first introduced. It is not unusual for the various factions supporting or opposing a proposal to accept some departure from the language they would prefer and to adopt substitute language agreeable to all. But that sort of compromise is a far cry from this case, where Congress simply abdicated its responsibility for the making of a fundamental and most difficult policy choice — whether and to what extent "the statistical possibility of future deaths should . . . be disregarded in light of the economic costs of preventing those deaths." That is a "quintessential legislative" choice and must be made by the elected representatives of the people, not by nonelected officials in the Executive Branch.

452 U.S. 543-547.

B. The Legislative Veto

The broad delegation of power to administrative agencies gave rise to political controversies over particular administrative decisions. In response, Congress developed ways in which it might control undesired exercises of administrative authority. One method which is constitutionally unproblematic is for Congress to pass legislation overruling specific agency policy. A second method, which first appeared in 1918, was the "legislative veto," by which administrative regulations promulgated under a statute could be overturned without the passage of new legislation. As described by Professor Donald Elliott: "To create a 'legislative veto,' Congress simply reserves power to overrule an official's subsequent actions as part of a statute that delegates broad, discretionary powers to an administrative agency or executive branch official. Most of the legislative veto statutes prescribe that this power can be exercised by passing a resolution of disapproval in one house of Congress."[81]

Since 1918 Congress has included legislative veto provisions in over 200 statutes — covering every area of national policy from the economy to foreign affairs to governmental reorganization. The Supreme Court first addressed the legitimacy of the legislative veto in 1983.

IMMIGRATION AND NATURALIZATION SERVICE v. CHADHA

462 U.S. 919 (1983)

On Appeal from the United States Court of Appeals for the Ninth Circuit

[The Immigration and Nationality Act §244(c)(2), 8 U.S.C. §1254(c)(2), authorizes either House of Congress, by resolution, to invalidate decisions of the Executive Branch allowing aliens otherwise subject to deportation to remain in the United States. The Immigration and Naturalization Service sought to deport Jagdish Chadha, an East Indian born in Kenya holding a British passport, for remaining in the United States beyond the expiration of his nonimmigrant student visa. An immigration judge ordered that Chadha's deportation be suspended, finding that he met the requirements of §244(a)(1): He had resided continuously in the United States for more than seven years, he was of good moral character, and he would suffer "extreme hardship" if deported. The Attorney General adopted the recommendation and conveyed it to Congress, as required by statute.

On December 12, 1975, Representative Eilberg introduced a resolution opposing the recommendation. On December 16, the House Judiciary Committee submitted the resolution to the entire House for a vote. The resolution had not been printed and was not available to other Members of the House prior to or at the time it was voted on. The House consideration of the resolution was based on Representative Eilberg's statement from the floor that "[i]t was the feeling of the committee, after reviewing 340 cases, that the aliens contained in the resolution [Chadha and five others] did not meet these statutory requirements, particularly as it relates to hardship; and it is the opinion of the committee that their deporta-

81. E. Donald Elliot, Why Our Separation of Powers Jurisprudence Is So Abysmal, 57 Geo. Wash. L. Rev., 506, 513 (1989).

tion should not be suspended." The resolution was passed without debate or recorded vote.

The immigration judge thereupon ordered Chadha deported. Chadha appealed, claiming that the statute's legislative veto provision was unconstitutional. The INS agreed; the Court of Appeals therefore invited both the Senate and the House of Representatives to participate as amici curiae. The Court of Appeals struck down the provision, finding that the legislative veto violated the constitutional doctrine of separation of powers. The Supreme Court granted certiorari in two cases brought by the House and the Senate.]

BURGER, C.J.

III

A

. . . We turn now to the question whether action of one House of Congress under §244(c)(2) violates strictures of the Constitution. We begin, of course, with the presumption that the challenged statute is valid. . . .

Our inquiry is sharpened rather than blunted by the fact that Congressional veto provisions are appearing with increasing frequency in statutes which delegate authority to executive and independent agencies:

> Since 1932, when the first veto provision was enacted into law, 295 congressional veto-type procedures have been inserted in 196 different statutes as follows: from 1932 to 1939, five statutes were affected; from 1940-49, nineteen statutes; between 1950-59, thirty-four statutes; and from 1960-69, forty-nine. From the year 1970 through 1975, at least one hundred sixty-three such provisions were included in eighty-nine laws. [Abourezk, The Congressional Veto: A Contemporary Response to Executive Encroachment on Legislative Prerogatives, 52 Ind. L. Rev. 323, 324, (1977).]

Justice White undertakes to make a case for the proposition that the one House veto is a useful "political invention," and we need not challenge that assertion. We can even concede this utilitarian argument although the long range political wisdom of this "invention" is arguable. . . . But policy arguments supporting even useful "political inventions" are subject to the demands of the Constitution which defines powers and, with respect to this subject, sets out just how those powers are to be exercised.

Explicit and unambiguous provisions of the Constitution prescribe and define the respective functions of the Congress and of the Executive in the legislative process. Since the precise terms of those familiar provisions are critical to the resolution of this case, we set them out verbatim. Art. I provides:

> All legislative Powers herein granted shall be vested in a Congress of the United States, which shall consist of a Senate *and* a House of Representatives. [Art. I, §1. (Emphasis added).]
>
> Every Bill which shall have passed the House of Representatives *and* the Senate, *shall* before it become a Law, be presented to the President of the United States; . . . [Art. I, §7, cl. 2. (Emphasis added).]

> *Every* Order, Resolution, or Vote to which the Concurrence of the Senate and House of Representatives may be necessary (except on a question of Adjournment) *shall be* presented to the President of the United States; and before the Same shall take Effect, *shall be* approved by him, or being disapproved by him, *shall be* repassed by two thirds of the Senate and House of Representatives, according to the Rules and Limitations prescribed in the Case of a Bill. [Art. I, §7, cl.3. (Emphasis added).]

These provisions of Art. I are integral parts of the constitutional design for the separation of powers. We have recently noted that "[t]he principle of separation of powers was not simply an abstract generalization in the minds of the Framers: it was woven into the documents that they drafted in Philadelphia in the summer of 1787." Buckley v. Valeo, supra 424 U.S., at 124. . . . [T]he purposes underlying the Presentment Clauses, Art I, §7, cls. 2, 3, and the bicameral requirements of Art. I, §1 and §7, cl. 2, guide our resolution of the important question presented in this case. The very structure of the articles delegating and separating powers under Arts. I, II, and III exemplify the concept of separation of powers and we now turn to Art. I.

B. THE PRESENTMENT CLAUSES

The records of the Constitutional Convention reveal that the requirement that all legislation be presented to the President before becoming law was uniformly accepted by the Framers. Presentment to the President and the Presidential veto were considered so imperative that the draftsmen took special pains to assure that these requirements could not be circumvented. During the final debate on Art. I. §7, cl.2, James Madison expressed concern that it might easily be evaded by the simple expedient of calling a proposed law a "resolution" or "vote" rather than a "bill." As a consequence, Art. I, §7, cl.3, ante, at 2781, was added.

The decision to provide the President with a limited and qualified power to nullify proposed legislation by veto was based on the profound conviction of the Framers that the powers conferred on Congress were the powers to be most carefully circumscribed. It is beyond doubt that lawmaking was a power to be shared by both Houses and the President. In The Federalist No. 73 (H. Lodge ed. 1888), Hamilton focused on the President's role in making laws:

> If even no propensity had ever discovered itself in the legislative body to invade the rights of the Executive, the rules of just reasoning and theoretic propriety would of themselves teach us that the one ought not to be left to the mercy of the other, but ought to possess a constitutional and effectual power of self-defense. [Id., at 457-458.]

See also The Federalist No. 51. . . .

The President's role in the lawmaking process also reflects the Framers' careful efforts to check whatever propensity a particular Congress might have to enact oppressive, improvident, or ill-considered measures. The President's veto role in the legislative process was described later during public debate on ratification:

> It establishes a salutary check upon the legislative body, calculated to guard the community against the effects of faction, precipitancy, or of any impulse unfriendly to the public good which may happen to influence a majority of that body. . . . The primary inducement to conferring the power in question upon the Executive is to enable him to defend himself; the secondary one is to increase the chances in favor of the community against the passing of bad laws through haste, inadvertence, or design. [The Federalist No. 73, supra, at 458 (A. Hamilton).]

The Court also has observed that the Presentment Clauses serve the important purpose of assuring that a "national" perspective is grafted on the legislative process:

> The President is a representative of the people just as the members of the Senate and of the House are, and it may be, at some times, on some subjects, that the President elected by all the people is rather more representative of them all than are the members of either body of legislature whose constituencies are local and not country-wide. . . ." [Myers v. United States]

C. BICAMERALISM

The bicameral requirement of Art. I, §§1, 7 was of scarcely less concern to the Framers than was the Presidential veto and indeed the two concepts are interdependent. By providing that no law could take effect without the concurrence of the prescribed majority of the Members of both Houses, the Framers reemphasized their belief, already remarked upon in connection with the Presentment Clauses, that legislation should not be enacted unless it has been carefully and fully considered by the Nation's elected officials. In the Constitutional Convention debates on the need for a bicameral legislature, James Wilson, later to become a Justice of this Court, commented:

> Despotism comes on mankind in different shapes. Sometimes in an Executive, sometimes in a military, one. Is there danger of a Legislative despotism? Theory & practice both proclaim it. If the Legislative authority be not restrained, there can be neither liberty nor stability; and it can only be restrained by dividing it within itself, into distinct and independent branches. In a single house there is no check, but the inadequate one, of the virtue & good sense of those who compose it. [1. M. Farrand, supra, at 254.]

Hamilton argued that a Congress comprised of a single House was antithetical to the very purposes of the Constitution. Were the Nation to adopt a Constitution providing for only one legislative organ, he warned:

> we shall finally accumulate, in a single body, all the most important prerogatives of sovereignty, and thus entail upon our posterity one of the most execrable forms of government that human infatuation ever contrived. Thus we should create in reality that very tyranny which the adversaries of the new Constitution either are, or affect to be, solicitous to avert. [The Federalist No. 22, supra, at 135.]

However familiar, it is useful to recall that apart from their fear that special interests could be favored at the expense of public needs, the Framers were also concerned, although not of one mind, over the apprehensions of the smaller states. Those states feared a commonality of interest among the larger states would work to their disadvantage; representatives of the larger states, on the other hand, were skeptical of a legislature that could pass laws favoring a minority of the people. It need hardly be repeated here that the Great Compromise, under which one House was viewed as representing the people and the other the states, allayed the fears of both the large and small states.

We see therefore that the Framers were acutely conscious that the bicameral requirement and the Presentment Clauses would serve essential constitutional functions. . . . It emerges clearly that the prescription for legislative action in Art. I, §§1, 7 represents the Framers' decision that the legislative power of the Federal government be exercised in accord with a single, finely wrought and exhaustively considered, procedure.

IV

The Constitution sought to divide the delegated powers of the new federal government into three defined categories, legislative, executive and judicial, to assure, as nearly as possible, that each Branch of government would confine itself to its assigned responsibility. The hydraulic pressure inherent within each of the separate Branches to exceed the outer limits of its power, even to accomplish desirable objectives, must be resisted.

Although not "hermetically" sealed from one another, the powers delegated to the three Branches are functionally identifiable. When any Branch acts, it is presumptively exercising the power the Constitution has delegated to it. When the Executive acts, it presumptively acts in an executive or administrative capacity as defined in Art. II. And when, as here, one House of Congress purports to act, it is presumptively acting within its assigned sphere.

Beginning with this presumption, we must nevertheless establish that the challenged action under §244(c)(2) is of the kind to which the procedural requirements of Art. I, §7 apply. Not every action taken by the either House is subject to the bicameralism and presentment requirements of Art. I. Whether actions taken by either House are, in law and fact, an exercise of legislative power depends not on their form but upon "whether they contain matter which is properly to be regarded as legislative in its character and effect." S. Rep. No. 1335, 54th Cong., 2d Sess., 8 (1897).

Examination of the action taken here by one House pursuant to §244(c)(2) reveals that it was essentially legislative in purpose and effect. In purporting to exercise power defined in Art. I, §8, cl. 4 to "establish a uniform Rule of Naturalization," the House took action that had the purpose and effect of altering the legal rights, duties and relations of persons, including the Attorney General, Executive Branch officials and Chadha, all outside the legislative branch. Section 244(c)(2) purports to authorize one House of Congress to require the Attorney General to deport an individual alien whose deportation otherwise would be cancelled under §244. The one-House veto operated in this case to overrule the Attorney General and mandate Chadha's deportation; absent the House action, Chadha would remain in the United States. Congress has *acted* and its action has altered Chadha's status.

The legislative character of the one-House veto in this case is confirmed by the character of the Congressional action it supplants. Neither the House of Representatives nor the Senate contends that, absent the veto provision in §244(c)(2), either of them or both of them acting together, could effectively require the Attorney General to deport an alien once the Attorney General, in the exercise of legislatively delegated authority, had determined the alien should remain in the United States. Without the challenged provision in §244(c)(2), this could have been achieved, if at all, only by legislation requiring deportation. Similarly, a veto by one House of Congress under §244(c)(2) cannot be justified as an attempt at amending the standards set out in §244(a)(1), or as a repeal of §244 as applied to Chadha. Amendment and repeal of statutes, no less than enactment, must conform with Art. I.[a]

The nature of the decision implemented by the one-House veto in this case further manifests its legislative character. After long experience with the clumsy, time consuming private bill procedure, Congress made a deliberate choice to delegate to the Executive Branch, and specifically to the Attorney General, the authority to allow deportable aliens to remain in this country in certain specified circumstances. It is not disputed that this choice to delegate authority is precisely the kind of decision that can be implemented only in accordance with the procedures set out in Art. I. Disagreement with the Attorney General's decision on Chadha's deportation — that is, Congress' decision to deport Chadha — no less than Congress' original choice to delegate to the Attorney General the authority to make that decision, involves determinations of policy that Congress can implement in only one way; bicameral passage followed by presentment to the President. Congress must abide by its delegation of authority until that delegation is legislatively altered or revoked.

Finally, we see that when the Framers intended to authorize either House of Congress to act alone and outside of its prescribed bicameral legislative role, they narrowly and precisely defined the procedure for such action. There are but four provisions in the Constitution, explicit and unambiguous, by which one House may act alone with the unreviewable force of law, not subject to the President's veto:

a. Congress protests that affirming the Court of Appeals in this case will sanction "lawmaking by the Attorney General. . . . Why is the Attorney General exempt from submitting his proposed changes in the law to the full bicameral process?" Brief of the United States House of Representatives 40. To be sure, some administrative agency action — rule making, for example — may resemble "lawmaking." . . . This Court has referred to agency activity as being "quasi-legislative" in character. Humphrey's Executor v. United States, 295 U.S. 602, 628 (1935). Clearly, however, "[i]n the framework of our Constitution, the President's power to see that the laws are faithfully executed refutes the idea that he is to be lawmaker." *Youngstown.* When the Attorney General performs his duties pursuant to §244, he does not exercise "legislative" power. The bicameral process is not necessary as a check on the Executive's administration of the laws because his administrative activity cannot reach beyond the limits of the statute that created it. . . . The courts, when a case or controversy arises, can always "ascertain whether the will of Congress has been obeyed," Yakus v. United States, 321 U.S. 414, 425 (1944), and can enforce adherence to statutory standards. It is clear, therefore, that the Attorney General acts in his presumptively Art. II capacity when he administers the Immigration and Nationality Act. Executive action under legislatively delegated authority that might resemble "legislative" action in some respects is not subject to the approval of both Houses of Congress and the President for the reason that the Constitution does not so require. That kind of Executive action is always subject to check by the terms of the legislation that authorized it; and if that authority is exceeded it is open to judicial review as well as the power of Congress to modify or revoke the authority entirely.

(a) The House of Representatives alone was given the power to initiate impeachments. Art. I, §2, cl.6;
(b) The Senate alone was given the power to conduct trials following impeachment on charges initiated by the House and to convict following trial. Art. I. §3, cl.5;
(c) The Senate alone was given final unreviewable power to approve or to disapprove presidential appointments. Art. II, §2, cl.2;
(d) The Senate alone was given unreviewable power to ratify treaties negotiated by the President. Art. II, §2, cl.2.

Clearly, when the Draftsmen sought to confer special powers on one House independent of the other House, or of the President, they did so in explicit, unambiguous terms.[b] These carefully defined exceptions from presentment and bicameralism underscore the difference between the legislative functions of Congress and other unilateral but important and binding one-House acts provided for in the Constitution. These exceptions are narrow, explicit, and separately justified; none of them authorize the action challenged here. On the contrary, they provide further support for the conclusion that Congressional authority is not to be implied and for the conclusion that the veto provided for in §244(c)(2) is not authorized by the constitutional design of the powers of the Legislative Branch.

Since it is clear that the action by the House under §244(c)(2) was not within any of the express constitutional exceptions authorizing one House to act alone, and equally clear that it was an exercise of legislative power, that action was subject to the standards prescribed in Article I. . . .[c]

b. An exception from the Presentment Clauses was ratified in Hollingsworth v. Virginia, 3 Dall. 378 (1798). There the Court held presidential approval was unnecessary for a proposed constitutional amendment which had passed both Houses of Congress by the requisite two-thirds majority.

One might also include another "exception" to the rule that Congressional action having the force of law be subject to the bicameral requirement and the Presentment Clauses. Each House has the power to act alone in determining specified internal matters. . . .

Although the bicameral check was not provided for in any of these provisions for independent Congressional action, precautionary alternative checks are evident. For example, Art. II., §2 requires that two-thirds of the Senators present concur in the Senate's consent to a treaty, rather than the simple majority required for the passage of legislation. See the Federalist No. 64 (J. Jay); The Federalist No. 66 (A. Hamilton); The Federalist No. 75 (A. Hamilton). Similarly, the Framers adopted an alternative protection, in the stead of Presidential veto and bicameralism, by requiring the concurrence of two-thirds of the Senators present for a conviction of impeachment. Art. I, §3. We also note that the Court's holding in *Hollingsworth*, supra, that a resolution proposing an amendment to the Constitution need not be presented to the President, is subject to two alternative protections. First, a constitutional amendment must command the votes of two-thirds of each House. Second, three-fourths of the states must ratify any amendment.

c. Justice White suggests that the Attorney General's action under §244(c)(1) suspending deportation is equivalent to a *proposal* for legislation and that because Congressional approval is indicated "by failure to veto, the one-House veto satisfies the requirement of bicameral approval." However, as the Court of Appeals noted, that approach "would analogize the effect of the one house disapproval to the failure of one house to vote affirmatively on a private bill." Even if it were clear that Congress entertained such an arcane theory . . . this would amount to nothing less than an amending of Art. I. The legislative steps outlined in Art. I. are not empty formalities; they were designed to assure that both Houses of Congress and the President participated in the exercise of lawmaking authority. This does not mean that legislation must always be preceded by debate; on the contrary, we have said that it is not necessary for a legislative body to "articulate its reasons for enacting a statute." United States Railroad Retirement Board v. Fritz. But the steps required by Art. I. §§1, 7 make certain that there is an opportunity for deliberation and debate.

The veto authorized by §244(c)(2) doubtless has been in many respects a convenient shortcut; the "sharing" with the Executive by Congress of its authority over aliens in this manner is, on its face, an appealing compromise. In purely practical terms, it is obviously easier for action to be taken by one House without submission to the President; but it is crystal clear from the records of the Convention, contemporaneous writings and debates, that the Framers ranked other values higher than efficiency. The records of the Convention and debates in the States preceding ratification underscore the common desire to define and limit the exercise of the newly created federal powers affecting the states and the people. There is unmistakable expression of a determination that legislation by the national Congress be a step-by-step, deliberate and deliberative process.

The choices we discern as having been made in the Constitutional Convention impose burdens on governmental processes that often seem clumsy, inefficient, even unworkable, but those hard choices were consciously made by men who had lived under a form of government that permitted arbitrary governmental acts to go unchecked. There is no support in the Constitution or decisions of this Court for the proposition that the cumbersomeness and delays often encountered in complying with explicit constitutional standards may be avoided, either by the Congress or by the President. See Youngstown Sheet & Tube Co. v. Sawyer, 343 U.S. 579 (1952). With all the obvious flaws of delay, untidiness, and potential for abuse, we have not yet found a better way to preserve freedom than by making the exercise of power subject to the carefully crafted restraints spelled out in the Constitution.

V

We hold that the Congressional veto provision in §244(c)(2) is severable from the Act and that it is unconstitutional. Accordingly, the judgment of the Court of Appeals is

Affirmed.

POWELL, J., concurring in the judgment.

The Court's decision, based on the Presentment Clauses, Art. I, §7, cl. 2 and 3, apparently will invalidate every use of the legislative veto. The breadth of this holding gives one pause. Congress has included the veto in literally hundreds of statutes, dating back to the 1930s. Congress clearly views this procedure as essential to controlling the delegation of power to administrative agencies. One reasonably may disagree with Congress' assessment of the veto's utility, but the respect due its judgment as a coordinate branch of Government cautions that our holding should be no more extensive than necessary to decide these cases. In my view, the case may be decided on a narrower ground. When Congress finds that a particular person does not satisfy the statutory criteria for permanent residence in this country it has assumed a judicial function in violation of the principle of separation of powers. Accordingly, I concur in the judgment.

To allow Congress to evade the strictures of the Constitution and in effect enact Executive proposals into law by mere silence cannot be squared with Art. I.

I

A

The Framers perceived that "[t]he accumulation of all powers legislative, executive and judiciary in the same hands, whether of one, a few or many, and whether hereditary, self appointed, or elective, may justly be pronounced the very definition of tyranny." The Federalist No. 47, p.324 (J. Cooke ed. 1961) (J. Madison). Theirs was not a baseless fear.

One abuse that was prevalent during the Confederation was the exercise of judicial power by the state legislatures. The Framers were well acquainted with the danger of subjecting the determination of the rights of one person to the "tyranny of shifting majorities." Jefferson observed that members of the General Assembly in his native Virginia had not been prevented from assuming judicial power, and " '[t]hey have accordingly *in many* instances *decided rights* which should have been left to *judiciary controversy*.' " The Federalist No. 48, p.336 (J. Cooke ed. 1961) (emphasis in original) (quoting T. Jefferson, Notes on the State of Virginia 196 (London edition 1787)). The same concern also was evident in the reports of the Council of the Censors, a body that was charged with determining whether the Pennsylvania Legislature had complied with the state constitution. The Council found that during this period "[t]he constitutional trial by jury had been violated; and powers assumed, which had not been delegated by the Constitution. . . . [C]ases belonging to the judiciary department, frequently [had been] drawn within legislative cognizance and determination." Id., at 336-337.

It was to prevent the recurrence of such abuses that the Framers vested the executive, legislative, and judicial powers in separate branches. Their concern that a legislature should not be able unilaterally to impose a substantial deprivation on one person was expressed not only in this general allocation of power, but also in more specific provisions, such as the Bill of Attainder Clause, Art. I, §9, cl. 3. . . . This Clause, and the separation of powers doctrine generally, reflect the Framers' concern that trial by a legislature lacks the safeguards necessary to prevent the abuse of power.

B

The Constitution does not establish three branches with precisely defined boundaries. Rather, as Justice Jackson wrote, "[w]hile the Constitution diffuses power the better to secure liberty, it also contemplates that practice will integrate the dispersed powers into a workable government. It enjoins upon its branches separateness but interdependence, autonomy but reciprocity." Youngstown Sheet & Tube Co. v. Sawyer, 343 U.S. 579, 635 (1952) (concurring opinion). The Court thus has been mindful that the boundaries between each branch should be fixed "according to common sense and the inherent necessities of the governmental co-ordination." J.W. Hampton, Jr. & Co. v. United States, 276 U.S. 394, 406 (1928). But where one branch has impaired or sought to assume a power central to another branch, the Court has not hesitated to enforce the doctrine.

Functionally, the doctrine may be violated in two ways. One branch may interfere impermissibly with the other's performance of its constitutionally assigned function. Alternatively, the doctrine may be violated when one branch assumes a function that more properly is entrusted to another. This case presents the latter situation.

II

... On its face, the House's action appears clearly adjudicatory. The House did not enact a general rule; rather it made its own determination that six specific persons did not comply with certain statutory criteria. It thus undertook the type of decision that traditionally had been left to other branches. Even if the House did not make a de novo determination, but simply reviewed the Immigration and Naturalization Service's findings, it still assumed a function ordinarily entrusted to the federal courts. See 5 U.S.C. §704 (providing generally for judicial review of final agency action). Where, as here, Congress has exercised a power "that cannot possibly be regarded as merely in aid of the legislative function of Congress," Buckley v. Valeo, 424 U.S., at 138, the decisions of this Court have held that Congress impermissibly assumed a function that the Constitution entrusted to another branch.

The impropriety of the House's assumption of this function is confirmed by the fact that its action raises the very danger the Framers sought to avoid — the exercise of unchecked power. In deciding whether Chadha deserves to be deported, Congress is not subject to any internal constraints that prevent it from arbitrarily depriving him of the right to remain in this country. Unlike the judiciary or an administrative agency, Congress is not bound by established substantive rules. Nor is it subject to the procedural safeguards, such as the right to counsel and a hearing before an impartial tribunal, that are present when a court or an agency adjudicates individual rights. The only effective constraint on Congress' power is political, but Congress is most accountable politically when it prescribes rules of general applicability. When it decides rights of specific persons, those rights are subject to "the tyranny of a shifting majority."

Chief Justice Marshall observed: "It is the peculiar province of the legislature to prescribe general rules for the government of society; the application of those rules would seem to be the duty of other departments." Fletcher v. Peck, 6 Cranch 87, 136 (1810). In my view, when Congress undertook to apply its rules to Chadha, it exceeded the scope of its constitutionally prescribed authority. I would not reach the broader question whether legislative vetoes are invalid under the Presentment Clauses.

WHITE, J., dissenting.

Today the Court not only invalidates §244(c)(2) of the Immigration and Nationality Act, but also sounds the death knell for nearly 200 other statutory provisions in which Congress has reserved a "legislative veto." For this reason, the Court's decision is of surpassing importance. And it is for this reason that the Court would have been well-advised to decide the case, if possible, on the narrower grounds of separation of powers, leaving for full consideration the constitutionality of other congressional review statutes operating on such varied matters as war powers and agency rulemaking, some of which concern the independent regulatory agencies.

The prominence of the legislative veto mechanism in our contemporary political system and its importance to Congress can hardly be overstated. It has become a central means by which Congress secures the accountability of executive and independent agencies. Without the legislative veto, Congress is faced with a Hobson's choice: either to refrain from delegating the necessary authority, leaving itself with a hopeless task of writing laws with the requisite specificity to cover endless special circumstances across the entire policy landscape, or in the alternative, to abdicate its lawmaking function to the executive branch and independent agencies. . . .

I

The legislative veto developed initially in response to the problems of reorganizing the sprawling government structure created in response to the Depression. The Reorganization Acts established the chief model for the legislative veto. . . .

Shortly after adoption of the Reorganization Act of 1939, Congress and the President applied the legislative veto procedure to resolve the delegation problem for national security and foreign affairs. World War II occasioned the need to transfer greater authority to the President in these areas. The legislative veto offered the means by which Congress could confer additional authority while preserving its own constitutional role. . . .

Over the quarter century following World War II, Presidents continued to accept legislative vetoes by one or both Houses as constitutional, while regularly denouncing provisions by which Congressional committees reviewed Executive activity. . .

During the 1970's the legislative veto was important in resolving a series of major constitutional disputes between the President and Congress over claims of the President to broad impoundment, war, and national emergency powers. The key provision of the War Powers Resolution, 50 U.S.C. §1544(c), authorizes the termination by concurrent resolution of the use of armed forces in hostilities. A similar measure resolved the problem posed by Presidential claims of inherent power to impound appropriations. Congressional Budget and Impoundment Control Act of 1974, 31 U.S.C. §1403. In conference, a compromise was achieved under which permanent impoundments, termed "rescissions," would require approval through enactment of legislation. In contrast, temporary impoundments, or "deferrals," would become effective unless disapproved by one House. This compromise provided the President with flexibility, while preserving ultimate Congressional control over the budget. . . .

In the energy field, the legislative veto served to balance broad delegations in legislation emerging from the energy crisis of the 1970's. In the educational field, it was found that fragmented and narrow grant programs "inevitably lead to Executive-Legislative confrontations" because they inaptly limited the Commissioner of Education's authority. The response was to grant the Commissioner of Education rulemaking authority, subject to a legislative veto. In the trade regulation area, the veto preserved Congressional authority over the Federal Trade Commission's broad mandate to make rules to prevent businesses from engaging in "unfair or deceptive acts or practices in commerce."

Even this brief review suffices to demonstrate that the legislative veto is more than "efficient, convenient, and useful." It is an important if not indispensable political invention that allows the President and Congress to resolve major constitutional and policy differences, assures the accountability of independent regulatory agencies, and preserves Congress' control over lawmaking. Perhaps there are other means of accommodation and accountability, but the increasing reliance of Congress upon the legislative veto suggests that the alternatives to which Congress must now turn are not entirely satisfactory.

The history of the legislative veto also makes clear that it has not been a sword with which Congress has struck out to aggrandize itself at the expense of the other branches — the concerns of Madison and Hamilton. Rather, the veto has been a means of defense, a reservation of ultimate authority necessary if Congress is to fulfill its designated role under Article I as the nation's lawmaker. While the President has often objected to particular legislative vetoes, generally those left in the hands of congressional committees, the Executive has more often agreed to legislative review as the price for a broad delegation of authority. To be sure, the President may have preferred unrestricted power, but that could be precisely why Congress thought it essential to retain a check on the exercise of delegated authority.

II

For all these reasons, the apparent sweep of the Court's decision today is regrettable. The Court's Article I analysis appears to invalidate all legislative vetoes irrespective of form or subject. Because the legislative veto is commonly found as a check upon rulemaking by administrative agencies and upon broad-based policy decisions of the Executive Branch, it is particularly unfortunate that the Court reaches its decision in a case involving the exercise of a veto over deportation decisions regarding particular individuals. Courts should always be wary of striking statutes as unconstitutional; to strike an entire class of statutes based on consideration of a somewhat atypical and more-readily indictable exemplar of the class is irresponsible. . .

If the legislative veto were as plainly unconstitutional as the Court strives to suggest, its broad ruling today would be more comprehensible. But, the constitutionality of the legislative veto is anything but clearcut. The issue divides scholars, courts, attorneys general, and the two other branches of the National Government. . . .

The Constitution does not directly authorize or prohibit the legislative veto. Thus, our task should be to determine whether the legislative veto is consistent with the purpose of Art. I and the principles of Separation of Powers which are reflected in that Article and throughout the Constitution. . . . [T]he wisdom of the Framers was to anticipate that the nation would grow and new problems of governance would require different solutions. Accordingly, our Federal Government was intentionally chartered with the flexibility to respond to contemporary needs without losing sight of fundamental democratic principles. In my view, neither Article I of the Constitution nor the doctrine of separation of powers is violated by this mechanism by which our elected representatives preserve their voice in the governance of the nation.

III . . .

[T]he Court maintains that the provisions of §244(c)(2) are inconsistent with the requirement of bicameral approval, implicit in Art. I, §1, and the requirement that all bills and resolutions that require the concurrence of both Houses be presented to the President, Art. I, §7, cl. 2 and 3.

I do not dispute the Court's truismatic exposition of these clauses. . . . [T]he Third Part of the Court's opinion is entirely unexceptionable.

It does not, however, answer the constitutional question before us. The power to exercise a legislative veto is not the power to write new law without bicameral approval or presidential consideration. The veto must be authorized by statute and may only negative what an Executive department or independent agency has proposed. On its face, the legislative veto no more allows one House of Congress to make law than does the presidential veto confer such power upon the President. Accordingly, the Court properly recognizes that it "must establish that the challenged action under §244(c)(2) is of the kind to which the procedural requirements of Art. I, §7 apply" and admits that "not every action taken by either House is subject to the bicameralism and presentation requirements of Art. I."

A

The terms of the Presentment Clauses suggest only that bills and their equivalent are subject to the requirements of bicameral passage and presentment to the President. . . .

James Madison observed that if the President's veto was confined to bills, it could be evaded by calling a proposed law a "resolution" or "vote" rather than a "bill." Accordingly, he proposed that "or resolve" should be added after "bill" in what is now clause 2 of §7. 2 M. Farrand, The Records of the Federal Convention of 1787, 301-302. After a short discussion on the subject, amendment was rejected. On the following day, however, Randolph renewed the proposal in the substantial form as it now appears, and the motion passed. The chosen language, Madison's comment, and the brevity of the Convention's consideration, all suggest a modest role was intended for the Clause and no broad restraint on Congressional authority was contemplated. See Stewart, Constitutionality of the Legislative Veto, 13 Harv. J. Legisl. 593, 609-611 (1976). This reading is consistent with the historical background of the Presentment Clause itself which reveals only that the Framers were concerned with limiting the methods for enacting new legislation. The Framers were aware of the experience in Pennsylvania where the legislature had evaded the requirements attached to the passing of legislation by the use of "resolves," and the criticisms directed at this practice by the Council of Censors. There is no record that the Convention contemplated, let alone intended, that these Article I requirements would someday be invoked to restrain the scope of Congressional authority pursuant to duly-enacted law.[a]

a. Although the legislative veto was not a feature of Congressional enactments until the twentieth century, the practices of the first Congresses demonstrate that the constraints of Article I were not envisioned as a constitutional straightjacket. The First Congress, for example, began the practice of arming its committees with broad investigatory powers without the passage of legislation. See A. Josephy, On the Hill: A History of the American Congress 81-83 (1975). More directly pertinent is the First Congress' treatment of the Northwest Territories Ordinance of 1787. The ordinance, ini-

When the Convention did turn its attention to the scope of Congress' law-making power, the Framers were expansive. The Necessary and Proper Clause, Art. I, §8, cl. 18, vests Congress with the power "to take all laws which shall be necessary and proper for carrying into Execution the foregoing Powers [the enumerated powers of §8], and all other Powers vested by this Constitution in the government of the United States, or in any Department or Officer thereof." It is long-settled that Congress may "exercise its best judgment in the selection of measures to carry into execution the constitutional powers of the government," and "avail itself of experience, to exercise its reason, and to accommodate its legislation to circumstances." McCulloch v. Maryland, 4 Wheat. 316, 415-416, 420 (1819).

B

The Court heeded this counsel in approving the modern administrative state. The Court's holding today that all legislative-type action must be enacted through the lawmaking process ignores that legislative authority is routinely delegated to the Executive branch, to the independent regulatory agencies, and to private individuals and groups. . . .

This Court's decisions sanctioning such delegations make clear that Article I does not require all action with the effect of legislation to be passed as a law.

Theoretically, agencies and officials were asked only to "fill up the details," and the rule was that "Congress cannot delegate any part of its legislative power except under a limitation of a prescribed standard." United States v. Chicago, Milwaukee R. Co. Chief Justice Taft elaborated the standard in J.W. Hampton & Co. v. United States, 276 U.S. 394, 409 (1928): "If Congress shall lay down by legislative act an intelligible principle to which the person or body authorized to fix such rates is directed to conform, such legislative action is not a forbidden delegation of legislative power." In practice, however, restrictions on the scope of the power that could be delegated diminished and all but disappeared. In only two instances did the Court find an unconstitutional delegation. Panama Refining Co. v. Ryan, 293 U.S. 388 (1935); Schechter Poultry Corp. v. United States,

---

tially drafted under the Articles of Confederation on July 13, 1787, was the document which governed the territory of the United States northwest of the Ohio River. The ordinance authorized the territories to adopt laws, subject to disapproval in Congress. "The governor and judges, or a majority of them, shall adopt and publish in the district, such laws of the original states, criminal and civil, as may be necessary and best suited to the circumstances of the district, *and report them to Congress,* from time to time; which laws shall be in force in the district until the organization of the general assembly therein, *unless disapproved by Congress;* but afterwards the legislature shall have authority to alter them as they shall think fit." (emphasis added)

After the Constitution was enacted, the ordinance was reenacted to conform to the requirements of the Constitution. Act of Aug. 7, 1789, ch. VIII, §1, 1 Stat. 50-51. Certain provisions, such as one relating to appointment of officials by Congress, were changed because of constitutional concerns, but the language allowing disapproval by Congress was retained. Subsequent provisions for territorial laws contained similar language. See e.g., 48 U.S.C. §1478 (1970). . . .

The histories of the territories, the correspondence of the era, and the Congressional reports contain no indication that . . . resolutions disapproving of territorial laws were to be presented to the President or that the authorization for such a "congressional veto" in the Act of August 7, 1789 was of doubtful constitutionality.

The practice of the First Congress are not so clear as to be dispositive of the constitutional question now before us. But it is surely significant that this body, largely composed of the same men who authored Article I and secured ratification of the Constitution, did not view the Constitution as forbidding a precursor of the modern day legislative veto.

295 U.S. 495 (1935). In other cases, the "intelligible principle" through which agencies have attained enormous control over the economic affairs of the country was held to include such formulations as "just and reasonable," Tagg Bros. & Moorhead v. United States, 280 U.S. 420 (1930), "public interest," New York Central Securities Corp. v. United States, 287 U.S. 12 (1932), "public convenience, interest, or necessity," Federal Radio Comm. v. Nelson Bros. Bond & Mortgage Co., 289 U.S. 266, 285 (1933), and "unfair methods of competition." FTC v. Gratz, 253 U.S. 421 (1920).

The wisdom and the constitutionality of these broad delegations are matters that still have not been put to rest. But for present purposes, these cases establish that by virtue of congressional delegation, legislative power can be exercised by independent agencies and Executive departments without the passage of new legislation. For some time, the sheer amount of law — the substantive rules that regulate private conduct and direct the operation of government — made by the agencies has far outnumbered the lawmaking engaged in by Congress through the traditional process. There is no question but that agency rulemaking is lawmaking in any functional or realistic sense of the term. . . .[b] These regulations bind courts and officers of the federal government, may preempt state law, and grant rights to and impose obligations on the public. In sum, they have the force of law.

If Congress may delegate lawmaking power to independent and executive agencies, it is most difficult to understand Article I as forbidding Congress from also reserving a check on legislative power for itself. Absent the veto, the agencies receiving delegations of legislative or quasi-legislative power may issue regulations having the force of law without bicameral approval and without the President's signature. It is thus not apparent why the reservation of a veto over the exercise of that legislative power must be subject to a more exacting test. In both cases, it is enough that the initial statutory authorizations comply with the Article I requirements.

Nor are there strict limits on the agents that may receive such delegations of legislative authority so that it might be said that the legislature can delegate authority to others but not to itself. While most authority to issue rules and regulations is given to the executive branch and the independent regulatory agencies, statutory delegations to private persons have also passed this Court's scrutiny. In Currin v. Wallace, 306 U.S. 1 (1939), the statute provided that restrictions upon the production or marketing of agricultural commodities was to become effective only upon the favorable vote by a prescribed majority of the affected farmers. United States v. Rock Royal Co-operative, 307 U.S. 533, 577 (1939), upheld an act which gave producers of specified commodities the right to veto marketing orders issued by the Secretary of Agriculture. Assuming *Currin* and *Rock Royal Co-operative* remain sound law, the Court's decision today suggests that Congress

b. "Legislative, or substantive, regulations are 'issued by an agency pursuant to statutory authority and . . . implement the statute, as for example, the proxy rules issue by the Securities and Exchange Commission . . . Such rules have the force and effect of law.' U.S. Dept. of Justice, Attorney General's Manual on the Administrative Procedures Act 30 n.3 (1947)." Batterton v Francis, 432 U.S. 416, 425 n.9 (1977).

Substantive agency regulations are clearly exercises of lawmaking authority; agency interpretations of their statutes are only arguably so. But as Henry Monaghan has observed, "Judicial deference to agency 'interpretation' of law is simply one way of recognizing a delegation of lawmaking authority to an agency." H. Monaghan, *Marbury* and the Administrative State, 83 Colum. L. Rev. 1, 26 (1983).

may place a "veto" power over suspensions of deportation in private hands or in the hands of an independent agency, but is forbidden from reserving such authority for itself. Perhaps this odd result could be justified on other constitutional grounds, such as the separation of powers, but certainly it cannot be defended as consistent with the Court's view of the Article I presentment and bicameralism commands.[c] . .

The Court suggests . . . that the Attorney General acts in an Article II capacity because "[t]he courts when a case or controversy arises, can always 'ascertain whether the will of Congress has been obeyed,' Yakus v. United States, and can enforce adherence to statutory standards." This assumption is simply wrong, as the Court itself points out: "We are aware of no decision . . . where a federal court has reviewed a decision of the Attorney General suspending deportation of an alien pursuant to the standards set out in §244(a)(1). This is not surprising, given that no party to such action has either the motivation or the right to appeal from it." It is perhaps on the erroneous premise that judicial review may check abuses of the §244 power that the Court also submits that "The bicameral process is not necessary as a check on the Executive's administration of the laws because his administrative activity cannot reach beyond the limits of the statue that created it — a statute duly enacted pursuant to Art. I, §§1,7." On the other hand, the Court's reasoning does persuasively explain why a resolution of disapproval under §244(c)(2) need not again be subject to the bicameral process. Because it serves only to check the Attorney General's exercise of the suspension authority granted by §244, the disapproval resolution — unlike the Attorney General's action — "cannot reach beyond the limits of the statute that created it — a statute duly enacted pursuant to Article I."

More fundamentally, even if the Court correctly characterizes the Attorney General's authority under §244 as an Article II Executive power, the Court concedes that certain administrative agency action, such as rulemaking, "may resemble lawmaking" and recognizes that "[t]his Court has referred to agency activity as being 'quasi-legislative' in character." Such rules and adjudications by the agencies meet the Court's own definition of legislative action for they "alter the legal rights, duties, and relations of persons . . . outside the legislative branch," and involve "determinations of policy." Under the Court's analysis, the Executive Branch and the independent agencies may make rules with the effect of law while Congress, in whom the Framers confided the legislative power, Art. I, §1, may not exercise a veto which precludes such rules from having operative force. If the effective functioning of a complex modern government requires the delegation of vast authority which, by virtue of its breadth, is legislative or "quasi-legislative" in character, I cannot accept that Article I — which is, after all, the source of the

c. As the Court acknowledges, the "provisions of Art. I are integral parts of the constitutional design for the separation of powers." But these separation of power concerns are that legislative power be exercised by Congress, executive power by the President, and judicial power by the Courts. A scheme which allows delegation of legislative power to the President and the departments under his control, but forbids a check on its exercise by Congress itself obviously denigrates the separation of power concerns underlying Article I. To be sure, the doctrine of separation of powers is also concerned with checking each branch's exercise of its characteristic authority. Section 244(c)(2) is fully consistent with the need for checks upon Congressional authority, and the legislative veto mechanism, more generally is an important check upon Executive authority.

non-delegation doctrine — should forbid Congress from qualifying that grant with a legislative veto.[d]

C

The Court also takes no account of perhaps the most relevant consideration: However resolutions of disapproval under §244(c)(2) are formally characterized, in reality, a departure from the status quo occurs only upon the concurrence of opinion among the House, Senate, and President. Reservations of legislative authority to be exercised by Congress should be upheld if the exercise of such reserved authority is consistent with the distribution of and limits upon legislative power that Article I provides.

1

As its history reveals, §244(c)(2) withstands this analysis. Until 1917, Congress had never established laws concerning the deportation of aliens. The Immigration Act of 1924 enlarged the categories of aliens subject to mandatory deportation, and substantially increased the likelihood of hardships to individuals by abolishing in most cases the previous time limitation of three years within which deportation proceedings had to be commenced. Thousands of persons, who either had entered the country in more lenient times or had been smuggled in as children, or had overstayed their permits, faced the prospect of deportation. . . . Congress provided relief in certain cases through the passage of private bills.

In 1933, when deportations reached their zenith, the Secretary of Labor temporarily suspended numerous deportations on grounds of hardship and proposed legislation to allow certain deportable aliens to remain in the country. The Labor Department bill was opposed, however, as "grant[ing] too much discretionary authority," 78 Cong. Rec. 11790 (remarks of Rep. Dirksen), and it failed decisively.

d. The Court's other reasons for holding the legislative veto subject to the presentment and bicameral passage requirements require but brief discussion. First, the Court posits that the resolution of disapproval should be considered equivalent to new legislation because absent the veto authority of §244(c)(2) neither House could, short of legislation, effectively require the Attorney General to deport an alien once the Attorney General has determined that the alien should remain in the United States. The statement is neither accurate nor meaningful. The Attorney General's power under the Act is only to "suspend" the order of deportation: the "suspension" does not cancel the deportation or adjust the alien's status to that of a permanent resident alien. Cancellation of deportation and adjustment of status must await favorable action by Congress. More important, the question is whether §244(c)(2) as written is constitutional and no law is amended or repealed by the resolution of disapproval which is, of course, expressly authorized by that section.

The Court also argues that "the legislative character of the challenged action of one House is confirmed by the fact that when the Framers intended to authorize either House of Congress to act alone and outside of its prescribed bicameral legislative role, they narrowly and precisely defined the procedure for such action." Leaving aside again the above-refuted premise that all action with a legislative character requires passage in a law, the short answer is that all of these carefully defined exceptions to the presentment and bicameralism strictures do not involve action of the Congress pursuant to a duly-enacted statute. Indeed, for the most part these powers — those of impeachment, review of appointments, and treaty ratification — are not legislative powers at all. The fact that it was essential for the Constitution to stipulate that Congress has the power to impeach and try the President hardly demonstrates a limit upon Congress' authority to reserve itself a legislative veto, through statutes over subjects within its lawmaking authority.

The following year, the administration proposed bills to authorize an inter-Departmental committee to grant permanent residence to deportable aliens who had lived in the United States for 10 years or who had close relatives here. These bills were also attacked as an "abandonment of congressional control over the deportation of undesirable aliens," and were not enacted. A similar fate awaited a bill introduced in the 75th Congress that would have authorized the Secretary to grant permanent residence to up to 8,000 deportable aliens. The measure passed the House, but did not come to a vote in the Senate.

The succeeding Congress again attempted to find a legislative solution to the deportation problem. . . . The compromise solution, the immediate predecessor to §244(c), allowed the Attorney General to suspend the deportation of qualified aliens. Their deportation would be canceled and permanent residence granted if the House and Senate did not adopt a concurrent resolution of disapproval. The Executive Branch played a major role in fashioning this compromise, and President Roosevelt approved the legislation, which became the Alien Registration Act of 1940, P.L. No. 670, 54 Stat. 670.

In 1947, the Department of Justice requested legislation authorizing the Attorney General to cancel deportations without congressional review. The purpose of the proposal was to "save time and energy of everyone concerned. . . ." . . . Congress not only rejected the Department's request for final authority but amended the Immigration Act to require that cancellation of deportation be approved by a concurrent resolution of the Congress. President Truman signed the bill without objection.

Practice over the ensuing several years convinced Congress that the requirement of affirmative approval was "not workable . . . and would, in time, interfere with the legislative work of the House." In preparing the comprehensive Immigration and Nationality Act of 1952, the Senate Judiciary Committee recommended that for certain classes of aliens the adjustment of status be subject to the disapproval of either House; but deportation of an alien "who is of the criminal, subversive, or immoral classes or who overstays his period of admission," would be cancelled only upon a concurrent resolution disapproving the deportation. Legislation reflecting this change was passed by both Houses, and enacted into law as part of the Immigration and Nationality Act of 1952 over President Truman's veto, which was not predicated on the presence of a legislative veto. In subsequent years, the Congress refused further requests that the Attorney General be given final authority to grant discretionary relief for specified categories of aliens, and §244 remained intact to the present.

Section 244(A)(1) authorizes the Attorney General, in his discretion, to suspend the deportation of certain aliens who are otherwise deportable and, upon Congress' approval, to adjust their status to that of aliens lawfully admitted for permanent residence. In order to be eligible for this relief, an alien must have been physically present in the United States for a continuous period of not less than seven years, must prove he is of good moral character, and must prove that he or his immediate family would suffer "extreme hardship" if he is deported. Judicial review of a denial of relief may be sought. Thus, the suspension proceeding "has two phases: a determination whether the statutory conditions have been met, which generally involves a question of law, and a determination whether relief shall be granted, which [ultimately] . . . is confided to the sound discretion of the Attorney General [and his delegates]." 2 C. Gordon & H. Rosenfield, Immigration Law and Procedure §7.9a(5) at 7-134.

There is also a third phase to the process. Under §244(c)(1) the Attorney General must report all such suspensions, with a detailed statement of facts and reasons, to the Congress. Either House may then act, in that session or the next, to block the suspension of deportation by passing a resolution of disapproval. Upon Congressional approval of the suspension — by its silence — the alien's permanent status is adjusted to that of a lawful resident alien.

The history of the Immigration Act makes clear that §244(c)(2) did not alter the division of actual authority between Congress and the Executive. At all times, whether through private bills, or through affirmative concurrent resolutions, or through the present one-House veto, a permanent change in a deportable alien's status could be accomplished only with the agreement of the Attorney General, the House, and the Senate.

2

The central concern of the presentation and bicameralism requirements of Article I is that when a departure from the legal status quo is undertaken, it is done with the approval of the President and both Houses of Congress — or, in the event of a presidential veto, a two-thirds majority in both Houses. This interest is fully satisfied by the operation of §244(c)(2). The President's approval is found in the Attorney General's action in recommending to Congress that the deportation order for a given alien be suspended. The House and the Senate indicate their approval of the Executive's action by not passing a resolution of disapproval within the statutory period. Thus, a change in the legal status quo — the deportability of the alien — is consummated only with the approval of each of the three relevant actors. The disagreement of any one of the three maintains the alien's pre-existing status: the Executive may choose not to recommend suspension; the House and Senate may each veto the recommendation. The effect on the rights and obligations of the affected individuals and upon the legislative system is precisely the same as if a private bill were introduced but failed to receive the necessary approval. "The President and the two Houses enjoy exactly the same say in what the law is to be as would have been true for each without the presence of the one-House veto, and nothing in the law is changed absent the concurrence of the President and a majority in each House." Atkins v. United States, 556 F.2d 1028, 1064 (Ct. Claims, 1977). . . .

Thus understood, §244(c)(2) fully effectuates the purposes of the bicameralism and presentation requirements. I now briefly consider possible objections to the analysis.

First, it may be asserted that Chadha's status before legislative disapproval is one of nondeportation and that the exercise of the veto, unlike the failure of a private bill, works a change in the status quo. This position plainly ignores the statutory language. At no place in §244 has Congress delegated to the Attorney General any final power to determine which aliens shall be allowed to remain in the United States. Congress has retained the ultimate power to pass on such changes in deportable status. By its own terms, §244(a) states that whatever power the Attorney General has been delegated to suspend deportation and adjust status is to be exercisable only "as hereinafter prescribed in this section." Subsection (c) is part of that section. A grant of "suspension" does not cancel the alien's deportation or adjust the alien's status to that of a permanent resident alien. A suspension order is merely a "deferment of deportation," which can mature into a cancellation of deportation and adjustment of status only upon the approval of Congress — by way of silence — under §244(c)(2). . . . Until that ratification occurs, the executive's action is simply a recommendation that Congress finalize the suspension — in itself, it works no legal change.

Second, it may be said that this approach leads to the incongruity that the two-House veto is more suspect than its one-House brother. Although the idea may be initially counter-intuitive, on close analysis, it is not at all unusual that the one-House veto is of more certain constitutionality than the two-House version. If the Attorney General's action is a proposal for legislation, then the disapproval of but a single House is all that is required to prevent its passage. Because approval is indicated by the failure to veto, the one-House veto satisfies the requirement of bicameral approval. The two-House version may present a different question. The concept that "neither branch of Congress, when acting separately, can lawfully exercise more power than is conferred by the Constitution on the whole body." Kilbourn v. Thompson, 103 U.S. 168, 182 (1881) is fully observed.

Third, it may be objected that Congress cannot indicate its approval of legislative change by inaction. In the Court of Appeals' view, inaction by Congress "could equally imply endorsement, acquiescence, passivity, indecision or indifference," and the Court appears to echo this concern. This objection appears more properly directed at the wisdom of the legislative veto than its constitutionality. The Constitution does not and cannot guarantee that legislators will carefully scrutinize legislation and deliberate before acting. In a democracy it is the electorate that holds the legislators accountable for the wisdom of their choices. It is hard to maintain that a private bill receives any greater individualized scrutiny than a resolution of disapproval under §244(c)(2). Certainly the legislative veto is no more susceptible to this attack than the Court's increasingly common practice of according weight to the failure of Congress to disturb an Executive or independent agency's action. Earlier this Term, the Court found it important that Congress failed to act on bills proposed to overturn the Internal Revenue Service's interpretation of the requirements for tax-exempt status under §501(c)(3) of the tax code. Bob Jones University v. United States, 103 S. Ct. 2017 (1983). If Congress may be said to have ratified the Internal Revenue Service's interpretation without passing new legislation, Congress may also be said to approve a suspension of deportation by the Attorney General when it fails to exercise its veto authority. The requirements of Article I are not compromised by the Congressional scheme.

IV

The Court of Appeals struck §244(c)(2) as violative of the constitutional principle of separation of powers. It is true that the purpose of separating the authority of government is to prevent unnecessary and dangerous concentration of power in one branch. For that reason, the Framers saw fit to divide and balance the powers of government so that each branch would be checked by the others. Virtually every part of our constitutional system bears the mark of this judgment.

But the history of the separation of powers doctrine is also a history of accommodation and practicality.

Our decisions reflect this judgment. As already noted, the Court, recognizing that modern government must address a formidable agenda of complex policy issues, countenanced the delegation of extensive legislative authority to executive and independent agencies. The separation of powers doctrine has heretofore led to the invalidation of government action only when the challenged action violated some express provision in the Constitution. . . . Because we must have a workable efficient government, this is as it should be.

This is the teaching of Nixon v. Administrator of Gen. Servs., 433 U.S. 425 (1977), which, in rejecting a separation of powers objection to a law requiring that the Administrator take custody of certain presidential papers, set forth a framework for evaluating such claims:

> [I]n determining whether the Act disrupts the proper balance between the coordinate branches, the proper inquiry focuses on the extent to which it prevents the Executive Branch from accomplishing its constitutionally assigned functions. Only where the potential for disruption is present must we then determine whether that impact is justified by an overriding need to promote objectives within the constitutional authority of Congress. [433 U.S., at 443.]

Section 244(c)(2) survives this test. The legislative veto provision does not "prevent the Executive Branch from accomplishing its constitutionally assigned functions." First, it is clear that the Executive Branch has no "constitutionally assigned" function of suspending the deportation of aliens. "'Over no conceivable subject is the legislative power of Congress more complete than it is over' the admission of aliens." Kleindienst v. Mandel, 408 U.S. 753, 766 (1972), quoting Oceanic Steam Navigation Co. v. Stranahan, 214 U.S. 320, 339 (1909). Nor can it be said that the inherent function of the Executive Branch in executing the law is involved. The Steel Seizure Case resolved that the Article II mandate for the President to execute the law is a directive to enforce that law which Congress has written. "The duty of the President to see that the laws be executed is a duty that does not go beyond the laws or require him to achieve more than Congress sees fit to leave within his power." Myers v. United States, 272 U.S., at 177 (Holmes, J., dissenting); 272 U.S., at 247 (Brandeis, J., dissenting). Here, §244 grants the executive only a qualified suspension authority and it is only that authority which the President is constitutionally authorized to execute.

Moreover, the Court believes that the legislative veto we consider today is best characterized as an exercise of legislative or quasi-legislative authority. Under this characterization, the practice does not, even on the surface, constitute an infringement of executive or judicial prerogative. The Attorney General's suspension of deportation is equivalent to a proposal for legislation. The nature of the Attorney General's role as recommendatory is not altered because §244 provides for congressional action through disapproval rather than by ratification. In comparison to private bills, which must be initiated in the Congress and which allow a Presidential veto to be overriden by a two-thirds majority in both Houses of Congress, §244 augments rather than reduces the executive branch's authority. So understood, congressional review does not undermine, as the Court of Appeals thought, the "weight and dignity" that attends the decisions of the Executive Branch.

Nor does §244 infringe on the judicial power, as Justice Powell would hold. Section 244 makes clear that Congress has reserved its own judgment as part of the statutory process. Congressional action does not substitute for judicial review of the Attorney General's decisions. The Act provides for judicial review of the refusal of the Attorney General to suspend a deportation and to transmit a recommendation to Congress. But the courts have not been given the authority to review whether an alien should be given permanent status; review is limited to whether the Attorney General has properly applied the statutory standards for essentially denying the alien a recommendation that his deportable status be changed by the Congress. Moreover, there is no constitutional obligation to provide any judicial review whatever for a failure to suspend deportation. "The power of Congress, therefore, to expel, like the power to exclude aliens, or any specified class of aliens, from the country, may be exercised entirely through executive officers; or Congress may call in the aid of the judiciary to ascertain any contested facts on which an alien's right to be in the country has been made by Congress to depend." Fon Yue Ting v. United States, 149 U.S. 698, 713-714 (1893).

I do not suggest that all legislative vetoes are necessarily consistent with separation of powers principles. A legislative check on an inherently executive function, for example that of initiating prosecutions, poses an entirely different question. But the legislative veto device here — as in many other settings — is far from an instance of legislative tyranny over the Executive. It is a necessary check on the unavoidably expanding power of the agencies, both executive and independent, as they engage in exercising authority delegated by Congress.

V

I regret that I am in disagreement with my colleagues on the fundamental questions that this case presents. But even more I regret the destructive scope of the Court's holding. It reflects a profoundly different conception of the Constitution than that held by the Courts which sanctioned the modern administrative state. Today's decision strikes down in one fell swoop provisions in more laws enacted by Congress than the Court has cumulatively invalidated in its history. I fear it will now be more difficult "to insure that the fundamental policy decisions in our society will be made not by an appointed official but by the body immediately responsible to the people," Arizona v. California, 373 U.S. 546, 626 (1963) (Harlan, J. dissenting). I must dissent.

Discussion

1. The War Powers Act of 1972 authorizes the President to commit armed forces in potentially risky situations, but requires prompt notification of Congress of such action. Congress may, through joint resolution, subsequently require the withdrawal of troops. Does the joint resolution provision survive *Chadha*?

2. Compare Chief Justice Burger's reasoning with that of Justice White's dissent. Critics of the majority opinion find it overly formalistic, similar to the discredited "conceptualism" of the *Lochner* era, with its indifference to

developing social and political needs. Critics of Justice White's dissent, on the other hand, might accuse it of substituting policy for legal analysis. Do you find either critique persuasive? Does Justice Powell offer an acceptable alternative to both?

3. Soon after the Court's ruling in *Chadha,* the New York Times published the following Letter to the Editor from Barry Karl, Professor of History at the University of Chicago:

> The debate over the legislative veto and the Supreme Court's recent decision concerning it can easily be confused by a misunderstanding of the history of its origins.
>
> The legislative veto appeared initially in the Overman Act of 1918, prepared largely by President Woodrow Wilson and designed to give him greater authority to reorganize the agencies created to cope with the World War I emergency. Its reappearance in legislation for Hoover in 1932 was again in response to an emergency, the deepening Depression. Both instances were based on Congress's concern with efficiency and economy and both Presidents' interest in managing emergency agencies more effectively.
>
> The provision for a legislative veto in the Executive Reorganization Act of 1939 was designed to give the President greater authority in such reorganizations while allowing Congress authority to overrule them within 60 days. It was a simple and very specific device intended to balance the increase in the President's authority to manage the Presidency with a Congressional power to reject, but to reject specific proposals within a specific period of time.
>
> Unfortunately, that way of presenting the history obscures another side of the story, which was part of an entirely different debate.
>
> Ever since 1914, jurists had been commenting somewhat ruefully on the growth of administrative power in American government. They were referring specifically to the independent commissions and the Federal agencies created by Progressive-era reforms. They saw in the new rule-making powers a possible drift toward the bureaucratic systems of Europe . . . managed by courts and lawyers rather than by responsible legislators and knowledgeable executives.
>
> Through the 1920's, writers like Felix Frankfurter and A.A. Berle Jr. expressed an uncertainty about the effects of such a transformation on American government, but no doubts about the direction. The onset of the Great Depression and the coming of the New Deal proved them right.
>
> The battle has always been over delegation of growing administrative powers required by a Federal Government increasingly involved in the detailed management of national life. Unwilling to give expanded managerial authority to the President and aware of the difficulties a legislative body faced in attempting to exercise control, Congress continued the process of allowing what it could not prevent.
>
> The authority of administrative agencies grew apace, as did court systems for dealing with the disputes that arose over the decisions and a Washington legal profession skilled at mediating those disputes. Successive Presidents were destined to look for ways to control what they politely called "administrative management" but more angrily labeled "the bureaucrats."
>
> Unfortunately, however, history played some dirty tricks on them. Vietnam and Watergate loomed as public symbols of their problems with executive power. Monstrous millstones, they dragged everything else down with them. The split between Presidential power and effective management was so badly obscured that even the proximity of two recent Supreme Court decisions, the one on the legislative veto, the

other on passive restraints for automobile passengers,[82] appears to have gone unnoticed.

The first seems to say that Congress can no longer claim control over executive actions of which it might disapprove. The second seems to say that the President cannot claim control over actions of administrative agencies if he wants to change them. Both decisions, taken together, would then suggest that administrative agencies can still be independent of both the [executive] and the legislative branches of government.

What the Court has done, in fact, is to affirm the authority of the courts as the only body capable of mediating the relation between the executive and the legislative branches. . . . I have great difficulty seeing the outcome as one intended by the framers of the Constitution of 1787.

BOWSHER v. SYNAR, 478 U.S. 714 (1986): [The Court applied *Chadha* to the 1985 Gramm-Rudman-Hollings Act, which set maximum federal budget deficit amounts for fiscal years 1986 through 1991. The Act requires across-the-board spending cuts whenever the year's projected deficit exceeds a targeted amount. Half of the cuts must come from defense, and the remainder from nondefense programs, with the exception of certain priority programs.

The Act establishes complicated administrative procedures: Each year the Office of Management of Budget (OMB) and the Congressional Budget Office (CBO) estimate the prospective deficit. If the deficit exceeds the permitted amount, the offices independently calculate the necessary reductions. They next report jointly to the Comptroller General (CG), who in turn reviews these reports and communicates his conclusions to the President, who must then issue a "sequestration" order mandating the reductions specified by the CG. Congress has a limited period within which to pass legislation obviating the need for the reductions; if Congress fails to act, the order automatically becomes effective.

The CG is appointed by the President with consent of the Senate. Although a CG is not subject to presidential removal, Congress may dismiss a CG by joint resolution. (The CG can also be removed by impeachment.) In signing the Act, President Reagan issued a statement questioning the Act's constitutionality insofar as an official not removable by the President could exercise de facto executive authority.

In a suit challenging the delegation of authority, the District Court held the Act unconstitutional. The Supreme Court affirmed. Chief Justice Burger, writing for the majority, stated:]

The Constitution does not contemplate an active role for Congress in the supervision of officers charged with the execution of the laws it enacts. . . . A direct congressional role in the removal of officers . . . is inconsistent with separation of powers. . . .

This was made clear in debate in the First Congress in 1789 [concerning a statute that authorized the President to remove the Secretary of Foreign Affairs

82. In Motor Vehicle Mfrs. Assn. v. State Farm Mut., 463 U.S. 29 (1983), the Court held that the National Highway Traffic Safety Administration, in revoking a rule requiring passive restraints (automatic seatbelts or airbags) in new automobiles, had violated the "arbitrary and capricious" standard of administrative action in failing to provide an adequate explanation for rescinding the requirement. The decision to revoke the rule came at the urging of Andrew Lewis, Secretary of Transportation in the Reagan Administration, and overturned the decision of his predecessor in the Carter Administration.

without Senate consent]. James Madison urged rejection of a congressional role in the removal of Executive Branch officers, other than by impeachment, saying in debate:

> Perhaps there was no argument urged with more success, or more plausibly grounded against the Constitution, under which we are now deliberating, than that founded on the mingling of the Executive and Legislative branches of the Government in one body. It has been objected that the Senate have too much of the Executive power even, by having a control over the President in the appointment to office. Now, shall we extend this connexion between the Legislative and Executive departments, which will strengthen the objection, and diminish the responsibility we have in the head of the Executive? 1 Annals of Cong. 380.

Madison's position ultimately prevailed, and a congressional role in the removal process was rejected. . . .

This Court first directly addressed this issue in *Myers,* [which involved] a statute providing that certain postmasters could be removed only "by and with the advice and consent of the Senate."

The Court invalidated the statute, saying that Congress could not "draw to itself, or to either branch of it, the power to remove or the right to participate in the exercise of that power. . . ." *Humphrey's Executor* involved congressional limitation of presidential removal power. Humphrey had been a commissioner of the Federal Trade Commission; commissioners can be removed "by the President," but only for "inefficiency, neglect of duty, or malfeasance in office." That is, political disagreement with the decisions of the Commissioner do not warrant removal, unlike, for example, any ordinary Cabinet officer. The Court upheld this limitation, stating, through Justice Sutherland, that "illimitable power of removal is not possessed by the President" with respect to members of the Federal Trade Commission and, presumably, all so-called independent agencies. The case was distinguished from *Myers* on the ground that Congress was not attempting to reserve a role for itself in regard to the termination of Humphrey's appointment. . . .

In light of these precedents, we conclude that Congress cannot reserve for itself the power of removal of an officer charged with the execution of the laws except by impeachment. To permit the execution of the laws to be vested in an officer answerable only to Congress would, in practical terms, reserve in Congress control over the execution of the laws. . . .

Our decision in *Chadha* supports this conclusion. . . . To permit an officer controlled by Congress to execute the laws would be, in essence, to permit a congressional veto. Congress could simply remove, or threaten to remove, an officer for executing the laws in any fashion found to be unsatisfactory to Congress. This kind of congressional control over the execution of the laws, *Chadha* makes clear, is constitutionally impermissible. . . .

With these principles in mind, we turn to consideration of whether the Comptroller General is controlled by Congress.

Appellants urge that the Comptroller General performs his duties independently and is not subservient to Congress. . . . [T]his contention does not bear close scrutiny.

The critical factor lies in the provisions of the statute defining the Comptroller General's office relating to removability. [Congress can by joint resolution remove the CG for] "(i) permanent disability; (ii) inefficiency; (iii) neglect of duty; (iv) malfeasance; or (v) a felony or conduct involving moral turpitude."[a] This provision was included, as one Congressman explained in urging passage of the Act, because Congress "felt that [the Comptroller General] should be brought under the sole control of Congress, so that Congress . . . could remove him without the long, tedious process of a trial by impeachment." . . .

Justice White contends that "[t]he statute does not permit anyone to remove the Comptroller at will; removal is permitted only for specified cause, with the existence of cause to be determined by Congress following a hearing. Any removal under the statute would presumably be subject to post-termination judicial review to ensure that a hearing had in fact been held and the finding of cause for removal was not arbitrary." That observation by the dissenter rests on at least two arguable premises: (a) that the enumeration of certain specified causes of removal excludes the possibility of removal for other causes, cf. Shurtleff v. United States, 189 U.S. 311, 315-316 (1903); and (b) that any removal would be subject to judicial review, a position that appellants were unwilling to endorse.

Glossing over these difficulties, the dissent's assessment of the statute fails to recognize the breadth of the grounds for removal. . . . [The terms of the statute] are very broad and, as interpreted by Congress, could sustain removal of a Comptroller General for any number of actual or perceived transgressions of the legislative will. The Constitutional Convention chose to permit impeachment of executive officers only for "Treason, Bribery, or other high Crimes and Misdemeanors." It rejected language that would have permitted impeachment for "maladministration," with Madison arguing that "[s]o vague a term will be equivalent to a tenure during pleasure of the Senate.". . .

Justice White, however, assures us that "[r]ealistic consideration" of the "practical result of the removal provision" reveals that the Comptroller General is unlikely to be removed by Congress. The separated powers of our Government cannot be permitted to turn on judicial assessment of whether an officer exercising executive power is on good terms with Congress. The Framers recognized that, in the long term, structural protections against abuse of power were critical to preserving liberty. In constitutional terms, the removal powers over the Comptroller General's office dictate that he will be subservient to Congress. . . .

[W]e see no escape from the conclusion that, because Congress has retained removal authority over the Comptroller General, he may not be entrusted with executive powers. The remaining question is whether the Comptroller General has been assigned such powers. . . .

The primary responsibility of the Comptroller General under the instant Act is the preparation of a "report." This report must contain detailed estimates of projected federal revenues and expenditures. The report must also specify the reductions, if any, necessary to reduce the deficit to the target for the appropriate fiscal year. . . .

a. Although the President could veto such a joint resolution, the veto could be overridden by a two-thirds vote of both Houses of Congress. Thus, the Comptroller General could be removed in the face of Presidential opposition. . . . [W]e therefore read the removal provision as authorizing removal by Congress alone.

In preparing the report, the Comptroller is to have "due regard" for the estimates and reductions set forth in a joint report submitted to him by the Director of CBO and the Director of OMB, the President's fiscal and budgetary advisor. However, the Act plainly contemplates that the Comptroller General will exercise his independent judgment and evaluation with respect to those estimates. . . . [W]e view these functions as plainly entailing execution of the law in constitutional terms. . . .

We conclude the District Court correctly held that the powers vested in the Comptroller General . . . violate the command of the Constitution that the Congress play no direct role in the execution of the laws. . . .

[Justice Stevens, joined by Justice Marshall, concurred only in the judgment. He rejected the majority's emphasis on the removal power:]

[T]he Comptroller General must be characterized as an agent of Congress because of his longstanding statutory responsibilities; that the powers assigned to him under the Gramm-Rudman Act require him to make policy that will bind the Nation; and that, when Congress, or a component or an agent of Congress, seeks to make policy that will bind the Nation, it must follow the procedures mandated by Article I of the Constitution — through passage by both Houses and presentment to the President.

[Justice White dissented, decrying the majority's "distressingly formalistic view of separation of powers as a bar to the attainment of governmental objectives through the means chosen by the Congress and the President in the legislative process established by the Constitution. . . . I cannot accept . . . that the exercise of authority by an officer removable for cause by a joint resolution of Congress is analogous to the impermissible execution of the law by Congress itself, nor would I hold that the congressional role in the removal process renders the Comptroller an 'agent' of the Congress, incapable of receiving 'executive' power."

Justice White also strongly criticized the majority's reliance on *Chadha*:]

[T]he Court overlooks or deliberately ignores the decisive difference between the congressional removal provision and the legislative veto struck down in *Chadha:* under the Budget and Accounting Act, Congress may remove the Comptroller only through a joint resolution which by definition must be passed by both Houses and signed by the President [or passed by a two-thirds majority overriding a presidential veto]. In other words, a removal of the Comptroller under the statute *satisfies the requirements of bicameralism and presentment laid down in Chadha.* The majority's citation of *Chadha* for the proposition that Congress may only control the acts of officers of the United States "by passing new legislation" in no sense casts doubt on the legitimacy of the removal provision, for that provision allows Congress to effect removal only through action that constitutes legislation as defined in *Chadha.*

[Justice Blackmun also dissented, arguing that even if Congress' control over the CG is unconstitutional, the proper remedy, given the clear import of the Gramm-Rudman-Hollings Act, is to save it by invalidating congressional removal of the Comptroller rather than invalidating the Act "in order to preserve a cumbersome, 65-year-old removal power that has never been exercised and appears to have been all but forgotten until this litigation."]

Discussion

Note that the Court did not address the issue proffered by President Reagan — the unconstitutionality of executive action carried out by officials not removable by the President. Does *Bowsher*, in conjunction with *Chadha,* give any indication how the Court might resolve this issue in the future? See Morrison v. Olson, 108 S. Ct. 2597 (1988), where the Court upheld the constitutionality of so-called independent prosecutors appointed to consider allegations of executive misconduct and removable only "for cause." However, Justice Scalia filed a heated dissent, and Justice Thomas, prior to his nomination to the Supreme Court, had indicated that he thought that *Morrison* was deeply flawed, and he praised Justice Scalia's dissent. It is, therefore, altogether possible that the constitutionality of the independent agencies will continue to be an issue on the Court's docket.

PART TWO
CONSTITUTIONAL ADJUDICATION IN A NONORIGINALIST WORLD

Part Two has two concurrent aims: (1) to examine the methods of adjudication when neither the text nor the original understanding of the Constitution provides much guidance for the resolution of particular issues; and (2) to study a variety of contemporary doctrines under the equal protection and due process clauses.

We use the term "originalist" to refer to constitutional decisionmaking that accords binding authority to the text of the Constitution or the intentions of its adopters and is significantly guided by one or both of these sources. The title of Part Two is not meant to suggest that the decisions examined in Part One were mostly originalist. On the contrary, we think that some of the most durable and venerated decisions we have examined — as well as some that happily did not endure — have rather weak originalist credentials. To the extent that Part One examined the methods of interpretation, however, it focused on interpretation of text and original history. Here, we focus on methods of adjudication that involve the interpretation of nonoriginalist sources — for example, precedent, tradition, and social values.

Part Two examines decisions concerned with discrimination based on race and sex and with individual liberties and entitlements not explicitly mentioned in the Constitution.

I. The Carolene Products *Footnote*

It is useful to place the contemporary decisions in historical perspective. The Court's retreat from intervention after 1937 was accompanied by a significant shift of power from the states to the national government. In the years following World War II, the Court regained institutional confidence, and its interventions followed the centralizing spirit of the times: The Court again began to nationalize individual rights, though it focused on a different cluster of rights than those favored during the *Lochner* era.

Hints of the new activism came as early as 1938 in an aside in United States v. Carolene Products Co., 304 U.S. 144 (1938), Chapter 5 supra, an otherwise inconsequential decision upholding a regulatory statute against a substantive due process attack. In the text of the opinion, Justice Stone emphasized the "presumption of constitutionality" to be accorded statutes of this sort. But in the now-famous footnote 4 of the decision, he remarked:

> There may be narrower scope for operation of the presumption of constitutionality when legislation appears on its face to be within a specific prohibition of the Constitution, such as those of the first ten amendments, which are deemed equally specific when held to be embraced within the Fourteenth. See Stromberg v. California, 283 U.S. 359, 369-370; Lovell v. Griffin, 303 U.S. 444, 452.
>
> It is unnecessary to consider now whether legislation which restricts those political processes which can ordinarily be expected to bring about repeal of undesirable legislation, is to be subjected to more exacting judicial scrutiny under the general prohibitions of the Fourteenth Amendment than are most other types of legislation. On restrictions upon the right to vote, see Nixon v. Herndon, 273 U.S. 536; Nixon v. Condon, 286 U.S. 73; on restraints upon the dissemination of information, see Near v. Minnesota ex rel. Olson, 283 U.S. 697, 713-714, 718-720, 722; Grosjean v. American Press Co., 297 U.S. 233; Lovell v. Griffin, supra; on interferences with political organizations, see Stromberg v. California, supra, 369; Fiske v. Kansas, 274 U.S. 380; Whitney v. California, 274 U.S. 357, 373-378; Herndon v. Lowry, 301 U.S. 242; and see Holmes, J., in Gitlow v. New York, 268 U.S. 652, 673; as to prohibition of peaceable assembly, see De Jonge v. Oregon, 299 U.S. 353, 365.
>
> Nor need we enquire whether similar considerations enter into the review of statutes directed at particular religions, Pierce v. Society of Sisters, 268 U.S. 510, or national, Meyer v. Nebraska, 262 U.S. 390; Bartels v. Iowa, 262 U.S. 404; Farrington v. Tokushige, 273 U.S. 484, or racial minorities, Nixon v. Herndon, supra; Nixon v. Condon, supra; whether prejudice against discrete and insular minorities may be a special condition, which tends seriously to curtail the operation of those political processes ordinarily to be relied upon to protect minorities, and which may call for a correspondingly more searching judicial inquiry. Compare McCulloch v. Maryland, 4 Wheat. 316, 428; South Carolina v. Barnwell Bros., 303 U.S. 177, 184, n.2, and cases cited.

Part Two is concerned, among other things, with the second and third paragraphs of footnote 4. Although a detailed interpretation of much of the first paragraph now lies within the domain of criminal procedure, the book would be incomplete without some mention of the history behind the nationalization of the Bill of Rights.

II. "Incorporation" of the Bill of Rights into the Fourteenth Amendment

Recall that in Barron v. Baltimore, 32 U.S. (7 Pet.) 243 (1833), the Marshall Court held that the Bill of Rights applied only to the national government and that 40 years later in the Slaughter-House Cases, 82 U.S. (16 Wall.) 36 (1873), the Court rejected the notion that the Fourteenth Amendment incorporated the Bill of Rights. At the very end of the nineteenth century, however, in Chicago, B. & Q.R. Co. v. Chicago, 166 U.S. 226 (1897), the Court held that the just compensation clause of the Fifth Amendment applied to the states. Twenty-eight years later the Court noted that portions of the First Amendment were binding on the states. Justice Sanford wrote in Gitlow v. New York, 268 U.S. 652 (1925):

> For present purposes we may and do assume that the freedom of speech and of the press — which are protected by the First Amendment from abridgment by Congress — are among the fundamental personal rights and "liberties" protected by the due process clause of the Fourteenth Amendment from impairment by the States.

The free exercise and establishment of religion clauses were incorporated, respectively, in Cantwell v. Connecticut, 310 U.S. 296 (1940), and Everson v. Board of Education, 330 U.S. 1 (1947).

The most heated controversies involved those parts of the Bill of Rights dealing with criminal procedure, particularly the Fourth, Fifth, and Sixth Amendments. Until the 1960s, the ex post facto and bill of attainder clauses of Article I, section 10, and the due process clause of the Fourteenth Amendment were the only federal constraints on the states' administration of criminal justice. The first two were rarely invoked, and the due process clause came into play only when the Court was faced with egregious instances of injustice. In 1947, in Adamson v. California, 332 U.S. 46, Justices Frankfurter and Black engaged in the classic debate over incorporation, each relying on his own conception of the original understanding of the Fourteenth Amendment. By a five-to-four decision, the Court rejected Black's argument that the entire Bill of Rights was meant to apply to the states and determined instead to inquire on a case-by-case basis whether particular procedures "offend those canons of decency and fairness which express the notions of justice of English-speaking peoples even toward those charged with the most heinous offenses." Malinski v. New York, 324 U.S. 401 (1945) (Frankfurter, J.).

If Frankfurter won the battle, Black eventually won the war, for the Court has made almost all of the provisions of the Bill of Rights binding on the states through the process of "selective incorporation."[1]

The Court's current approach to incorporation is described in Justice White's opinion for the Court in Duncan v. Louisiana, 391 U.S. 145 (1968), which made the Sixth Amendment right to jury trial binding on the states:

> The Fourteenth Amendment denies the States the power to "deprive any person of life, liberty, or property, without due process of law." In resolving conflicting claims concerning the meaning of this spacious language, the Court has looked increasingly to the Bill of Rights for guidance; many of the rights guaranteed by the first eight Amendments to the Constitution have been held to be protected against state action by the Due Process Clause of the Fourteenth Amendment. That clause now protects the right to compensation for property taken by the State;[a] the rights of speech, press, and religion covered by the First Amendment;[b] the Fourth Amendment rights to be free from unreasonable searches and seizures and to have ex-

1. The only provisions of the first eight amendments that have escaped incorporation are the Second and Third Amendments, the Fifth Amendment's requirement of grand jury indictment, and the Seventh Amendment. The Second Amendment is discussed below. There has been virtually no litigation involving the Third Amendment. But see United States v. Valenzuela, 95 F. Supp. 363 (S.D. Cal. 1951) (Housing and Rent Act of 1947 unsuccessfully attacked as "an incubator and hatchery of swarms of bureaucrats to be quartered as storm troopers on the people").

a. Chicago, B. & Q.R. Co. v. Chicago, 166 U.S. 226 (1897).

b. See, e.g., Fiske v. Kansas, 274 U.S. 380 (1927).

cluded from criminal trials any evidence illegally seized;[c] the right guaranteed by the Fifth Amendment to be free of compelled self-incrimination;[d] and the Sixth Amendment rights to counsel,[e] to a speedy[f] and public[g] trial, to confrontation of opposing witnesses,[h] and to compulsory process for obtaining witnesses.[i]

The test for determining whether a right extended by the Fifth and Sixth Amendments with respect to federal criminal proceedings is also protected against state action by the Fourteenth Amendment has been phrased in a variety of ways in the opinions of this Court. The question has been asked whether a right is among those " 'fundamental principles of liberty and justice which lie at the base of all our civil and political institutions,' " Powell v. Alabama, 287 U.S. 45, 67 (1932); whether it is "basic in our system of jurisprudence," In re Oliver, 333 U.S. 257, 273 (1948); and whether it is "a fundamental right, essential to a fair trial," Gideon v. Wainwright, 372 U.S. 335, 343-344 (1963); Malloy v. Hogan, 378 U.S. 1, 6 (1964); Pointer v. Texas, 380 U.S. 400, 403 (1965). The claim before us is that the right to trial by jury guaranteed by the Sixth Amendment meets these tests. The position of Louisiana, on the other hand, is that the Constitution imposes upon the States no duty to give a jury trial in any criminal case, regardless of the seriousness of the crime or the size of the punishment which may be imposed. Because we believe that trial by jury in criminal cases is fundamental to the American scheme of justice, we hold that the Fourteenth Amendment guarantees a right of jury trial in all criminal cases which — were they to be tried in a federal court — would come within the Sixth Amendment's guarantee.[j] Since we consider the appeal before us to be such a case, we hold

c. See Mapp v. Ohio, 367 U.S. 643 (1961).
d. Malloy v. Hogan, 378 U.S. 1 (1964).
e. Gideon v. Wainwright, 372 U.S. 335 (1963).
f. Mopfer v. North Carolina, 386 U.S. 213 (1967).
g. In re Oliver, 333 U.S. 257 (1948).
h. Pointer v. Texas, 380 U.S. 400 (1965).
i. Washington v. Texas, 388 U.S. 14 (1967).

j. In one sense recent cases applying provisions of the first eight Amendments to the States represent a new approach to the "incorporation" debate. Earlier the Court can be seen as having asked, when inquiring into whether some particular procedural safeguard was required of a State, if a civilized system could be imagined that would not accord the particular protection. For example, Palko v. Connecticut, 302 U.S. 319, 325 (1937), stated: "The right to trial by jury and the immunity from prosecution except as the result of an indictment may have value and importance. Even so, they are not of the very essence of a scheme of ordered liberty. . . . Few would be so narrow or provincial as to maintain that a fair and enlightened system of justice would be impossible without them." The recent cases, on the other hand, have proceeded upon the valid assumption that state criminal processes are not imaginary and theoretical schemes but actual systems bearing virtually every characteristic of the common-law system that has been developing contemporaneously in England and in this country. The question thus is whether given this kind of system a particular procedure is fundamental — whether, that is, a procedure is necessary to an Anglo-American regime of ordered liberty. It is this sort of inquiry that can justify the conclusions that state courts must exclude evidence seized in violation of the Fourth Amendment, Mapp v. Ohio, 367 U.S. 643 (1961); that state prosecutors may not comment on a defendant's failure to testify, Griffin v. California, 380 U.S. 609 (1965); and that criminal punishment may not be imposed for the status of narcotics addiction, Robinson v. California, 370 U.S. 660 (1962). Of immediate relevance for this case are the Court's holdings that the States must comply with certain provisions of the Sixth Amendment, specifically that the States may not refuse a speedy trial, confrontation of witnesses, and the assistance, at state expense if necessary, of counsel. Of each of these determinations that a constitutional provision originally written to bind the Federal Government should bind the States as well it might be said that the limitation in question is not necessarily fundamental to fairness in every criminal system that might be imagined but is fundamental in the context of the criminal processes maintained by the American States.

When the inquiry is approached in this way the question whether the States can impose criminal punishment without granting a jury trial appears quite different from the way it appeared in the older cases opining that States might abolish jury trial. See, e.g., Maxwell v. Dow, 176 U.S. 581 (1900). A criminal process which was fair and equitable but used no juries is easy to imagine. It would make use of alternative guarantees and protections which would serve the purposes that the jury serves in the English and American systems. Yet no American State has undertaken to construct such a system.

that the Constitution was violated when appellant's demand for jury trial was refused.

Justice Black, joined by Justice Douglas, concurred. He was "happy to support this selective process through which our Court has . . . held most of the specific Bill of Rights' protections applicable to the States to the same extent they are applicable to the Federal Government." But he reiterated his contention, first made in Adamson v. California, supra, that the Fourteenth Amendment makes the entire Bill of Rights binding on the states. Justice Fortas concurred, noting that, although the due process clause requires jury trials in state criminal cases,

> [it does not] automatically import all of the ancillary rules which have been or may hereafter be developed incidental to the right to jury trial in the federal courts. I see no reason whatever, for example, to assume that our decision today should require us to impose federal requirements such as unanimous verdicts or a jury of 12 upon the States. We may well conclude that these and other features of federal jury practice are by no means fundamental — that they are not essential to due process of law — and that they are not obligatory on the States.

Justice Harlan, joined by Justice Stewart, dissented. But he agreed with Justice Fortas' analysis and attacked the "illogic" of selectively incorporating an entire clause "jot-for-jot and case-for-case":

> If the problem is to discover and articulate the rules of fundamental fairness in criminal proceedings, there is no reason to assume that the whole body of rules developed in this Court constituting Sixth Amendment jury trial must be regarded as a unit. The requirement of trial by jury in federal criminal cases has given rise to numerous subsidiary questions respecting the exact scope and content of the right. It surely cannot be that every answer the Court has given, or will give, to such a question is attributable to the Founders; or even that every rule announced carries equal conviction of this Court; still less can it be that every such subprinciple is equally fundamental to ordered liberty.[2]

Instead, every American State, including Louisiana, uses the jury extensively, and imposes very serious punishments only after a trial at which the defendant has a right to a jury's verdict. In every State, including Louisiana, the structure and style of the criminal process — the supporting framework and the subsidiary procedures — are of the sort that naturally complement jury trial, and have developed in connection with and in reliance upon jury trial.

2. Two years later, in Williams v. Florida, 399 U.S. 78 (1970), a divided Court held that the Sixth Amendment permits trial by a jury composed of six persons. Justice Harlan concurred in the result. He reiterated his views in *Duncan* and argued that the Court was now "diluting constitutional protections within the federal system itself" in order to "allow the States more elbow room in ordering their own criminal systems":

> The internal logic of the selective incorporation doctrine cannot be respected if the Court is both committed to interpreting faithfully the meaning of the federal Bill of Rights and recognizing the governmental diversity that exists in this country. The "backlash" in *Williams* exposes the malaise, for there the Court dilutes a federal guarantee in order to reconcile the logic of "incorporation," the "jot-for-jot and case-for-case" application of the federal right to the States, with the reality of federalism. Can one doubt that had Congress tried to undermine the common-law right to trial by jury before *Duncan* came on the books the history today recited would have barred such action? Can we expect repeat performances when this Court is called upon to give definition and meaning to other federal guarantees that have been "incorporated"?

In Apodaca v. Oregon, 406 U.S. 404 (1972), a sharply divided Court upheld a state conviction by a nonunanimous jury verdict. Jurtice White, who had written for the Court in *Duncan* and *Williams*,

After several decades of quiescence, the question of the original history of the Fourteenth Amendment with respect to incorporation of the Bill of Rights was raised again by Attorney General Edwin Meese III in a 1985 speech to the American Bar Association on the "jurisprudence of original intention":[3]

> Since [1925] a good portion of constitutional adjudication has been aimed at extending the scope of the doctrine of incorporation. But the most that can be done is to expand the scope; nothing can be done to expand the shaky foundation upon which the doctrine rests. And nowhere has the principle of federalism been dealt so politically violent and constitutionally suspect a blow as by the theory of incorporation.

Notwithstanding the Attorney General's views, the Solicitor General did not attempt to persuade the Supreme Court to abandon the doctrine of selective incorporation.

Note: An Incorporation Conundrum: The Second Amendment[4]

Among the few amendments that have not been incorporated is the second: "A well regulated Militia, being necessary to the security of a free State, the right of the people to keep and bear Arms, shall not be infringed." Unlike the Seventh Amendment — also not incorporated and not a source of much controversy — the Second Amendment not only raises significant dilemmas for anyone who purports to take constitutional interpretation seriously, but is also a subject of important political contention: The National Rifle Association, which has almost 3 million members, predicates its opposition to almost all gun-control measures on the Second Amendment.

What constraints does the amendment impose on the *national* government? The only Supreme Court opinion that discusses the issue at any length is United States v. Miller, 307 U.S. 174 (1939). The defendant was charged with violating the National Firearms Act of 1934 by moving a sawed-off shotgun in interstate commerce. Among other things, he had not registered the firearm as required by the Act. The court below had dismissed the charge, accepting Miller's argument

---

now wrote for a plurality, including Chief Justice Burger and Justices Blackmun and Rehnquist, that the Sixth Amendment does not require jury unanimity. Justices Douglas, Brennan, Stewart, and Marshall dissented, arguing that the Sixth Amendment does require unanimity for conviction. Justice Powell cast the deciding vote to uphold the Oregon provision, but he disavowed the plurality's "major premise . . . that the concept of jury trial, as applicable to the States under the Fourteenth Amendment, must be identical in every respect to the concept required in federal courts by the Sixth Amendment." For Powell, the question was "whether unanimity is . . . so fundamental to the essentials of jury trial" as to bring it "within the mandate of due process," and he believed that unanimity was not fundamental. Thus, in *Apodaca,* eight justices thought that the Sixth Amendment applied with full force to the states; five justices thought that the Sixth Amendment required unanimous jury verdicts. Yet because Justice Powell, who adhered to the latter position, did not adhere to the former, the Court held that a unanimous verdict was not required in the states. Powell succeeded to a position that has had strong and respected adherents, including Cardozo, Frankfurter, and Harlan. However, it is not clear that any member of the present Court (1991) holds this view.

3. In The Great Debate, Interpreting Our Written Constitution (Federalist Society, 1986).

4. See, for an elaboration of the arguments suggested in this Note, Levinson, The Embarrassing Second Amendment, 99 Yale L.J. 637 (1989).

that the Act violated the Second Amendment. The Supreme Court reversed unanimously. Justice McReynolds emphasized that there was no evidence showing that a sawed-off shotgun "at this time has some reasonable relationship to the preservation or efficiency of a well regulated militia. . . . Certainly it is not within judicial notice that this weapon is any part of the ordinary military equipment or that its use could contribute to the common defense." (Does this argument contain a negative predicate suggesting that Miller might have had a more tenable argument had he been keeping or bearing a bazooka, a machine gun, or an assault rifle?)

Justice McReynolds went on to explain that the Amendment was intended "to assure the continuation and render possible the effectiveness" of the militia. He contrasted the militia with troops of a standing army, which the Constitution indeed forbids the states to keep without the explicit consent of Congress: "The sentiment of the time strongly disfavored standing armies; the common view was that adequate defense of country and laws could be secured through the Militia — civilians primarily, soldiers on occasion." And McReynolds noted that "the debates in the Convention, the history and legislation of Colonies and States, and the writings of approved commentators" all "[s]how plainly enough that the Militia comprised all males physically capable of acting in concert for the common defense."

Whatever its scope, can the Second Amendment's limitation on the national government be logically extended to *state* governments? Professor Laurence Tribe answers "no," writing that the history of the Amendment "indicate[s] that the central concern of [its] framers was to prevent such federal interference with the state militia as would permit the establishment of a standing national army and the consequent destruction of local autonomy."[5] Although he acknowledges that "the debates surrounding congressional approval of the second amendment do contain references to individual self-protection as well as states' rights," he argues that the preamble to the amendment and the qualifying phrase "well regulated" make "any invocation of the amendment as a restriction on state or local gun control measures extremely problematic."

Some historians have argued that the Amendment guarantees individuals the right "to possess arms for their own personal defense."[6] It would not be surprising if this were so, in view of the fact that the development of a professionalized police force in American cities did not occur until the mid-nineteenth century. One might accept this "self-defense" notion but believe that the development of professional public police forces has made superfluous — and even dangerous — the assignment to private individuals of what today is viewed as the quintessential "public" activity of controlling wrongdoers through force of arms.

More fundamentally, some historians maintain that the Second Amendment protects a *communitarian*, rather than an individual interest.[7] If so, there remain interesting problems in defining the relationship between the community and the state apparatus. Return once again to the preamble's reference to the importance of a well-regulated militia. As Justice McReynolds suggested in *Miller*, there

5. Tribe, American Constitutional Law 299 n.6 (2d ed. 1988).

6. See Robert Shalhope, Ideological Origins of the Second Amendment, 69 J. Amer. Hist. 599 (1982).

7. See, e.g., Lawrence D. Cress, An Armed Community: The Origins and Meaning of the Right to Bear Arms, 71 J. Amer. Hist. 22 (1984).

is strong evidence in the historical literature that "militia" refers to all of the people, or at least all of those treated as full citizens of the community. For example, when George Mason, one of the Virginians who refused to sign the Constitution because of its lack of a Bill of Rights, asked "Who are the Militia?" he answered, "They consist now of the whole people." Similiarly, the Federal Farmer, another important anti-Federalist opponent of the Constitution, referred to a "militia, when properly formed, [as] in fact the people themselves."[8]

This notion of a "universal militia" is linked to the particular political theory of "republicanism," which many American historians have thought to be an important foundation of the theory of American constitutionalism. An important English republican theorist was James Harrington, who (it has been said) made "the most significant contribution to English libertarian attitudes toward arms, the individual, and society."[9] For Harrington, preservation of republican liberty requires independence, which rests primarily on possession of adequate property to make individuals free from coercion by employers or landlords. But ownership of land is not sufficient. "[T]hese independent yeomen, armed and embodied in a militia, are also a popular government's best protection against its enemies, whether they be aggressive foreign monarchs or scheming demagogues within the nation itself."[10]

Central to eighteenth-century American political thought was the concern about political corruption and consequent governmental tyranny. For example, James Madison speaks in the 46th Federalist of "the advantage of being armed, which the Americans possess over the people of almost every other nation." This "advantage" was not merely the defense of American borders, but the protection of political liberty against domestic threats. It is therefore no surprise that the anti-Federalist Federal Farmer wrote that "to preserve liberty, it is essential that the whole body of the people always possess arms, and be taught alike, especially the young, how to use them."[11] Similarly, in his influential Commentaries on the Constitution, Joseph Story emphasized the importance of the Second Amendment and described the militia as "the natural defence of a free country" not only "against sudden foreign invasions" and "domestic insurrections," but also against "domestic usurpations of power by rulers." "The right of the people to keep and bear arms has justly been considered as the palladium of the liberties of a republic; since it offers a strong moral check against the usurpation and arbitrary power of rulers; and will generally, even if these are successful in the first instance, enable the people to resist and triumph over them."[12]

The strongest version of the republican argument would hold the right to keep and bear arms to be a "privilege and immunity of United States citizenship." Ironically, the principal judicial source supporting this argument is Chief Justice Taney's opinion in *Dred Scott*, supra Chapter 4. Taney argued that, because it was inconceivable that the framers would have given African Americans the right to possess arms, they did not envision them as citizens.

8. Both of these quotations come from Don Kates, Handgun Prohibition and the Original Meaning of the Second Amendment, 82 Mich. L. Rev. 204, 216 n.51 (1983).

9. Shalhope, supra note 5, at 602.

10. Edmund Morgan, Inventing the People 156 (1988).

11. Letters from the Federal Farmer to the Republican 124 (W. Bennett ed. 1978).

12. 3 Commentaries §1890 (1833), excerpted in Philip Kurland and Ralph Lerner, eds., 5 The Founders Constitution 214 (1987).

Citizens of the states, trained in the use of arms, could provide potential protection against a tyrannical national government. Indeed, several governors threatened to call out state militias at the time of the 1800 deliberations over the recent election if the Federalists took advantage of pre-Twelfth Amendment procedures to elect Aaron Burr rather than their hated enemy Thomas Jefferson, who was the popular choice.[13]

Consider, then, the possibility — supported by implications from the Second, Ninth, and Tenth Amendments — that the vertical structure of the American polity has not two, but three components: the national government, the states, and the citizenry itself insofar as it stands ready to defend republican liberty against the depredations of the other two structures.

One might note, in this regard, James Madison's extraordinarily influential critique, especially in the 14th Federalist paper, of what had theretofore been the traditional emphasis on the desirability of small states as preservers of republican liberty. He transformed this debate by arguing that the states would be *less* likely to preserve liberty because they could so easily fall under the sway of a local dominant faction, whereas an extended republic would guard against this danger. Although the Bill of Rights rights implies that it is "retained by the people" against both levels of government, its provisions are only applied to the national government.

As mentioned above, the process of selective application of provisions of the Bill of Rights to the states through the Fourteenth Amendment began with the just compensation clause. Chicago, B. & Q.R. Co. v. Chicago, 166 U.S. 226 (1897). Twenty years earlier, in United States v. Cruikshank, 92 U.S. 542 (1875), Chief Justice Waite rejected the argument that the right to keep and bear arms was one of the "privileges or immunities of United States citizenship" protected by the Fourteenth Amendment, writing that "it is not a right granted by the Constitution. . . . The Second Amendment declares that it shall not be infringed, but this . . . means no more than that it shall not be infringed by Congress. This is one of the amendments that has no other effect than to restrict the powers of the National government." The Court cited this passage in Presser v. Illinois, 116 U.S. 252 (1886), in upholding the punishment of Herman Presser for violating an Illinois statute making unlawful "any body of men whatever, other than the regular organized volunteer militia of this state, and the troops of the United States, [associating] themselves together as a military company or organization, or to drill or parade with arms in any city, or town, of this state."[14]

13. Jefferson and Burr had received the same number of votes in the electoral college because the original Constitution, Art. I, §1, cl. 3, required each elector, without differentiating between candidates for the presidency and vice-presidency, to vote for two "persons." The one with the most votes, assuming it was at least a majority of the total, became President, the runner-up the Vice President. The framers assumed, among other things, the absence of a party system, but by 1800 there were in fact two parties that ran president and vice-presidential candidates as a ticket. What happened, therefore, is that all of the Republican electors voted for Jefferson and Burr, which by definition meant that they received an equal number of votes, thereby sending the election to the House of Representatives for choice between them. Republicans were fearful that Federalists might take advantage of this constitutional glitch to vote for Burr and thus deprive Jefferson of the office to which he had clearly been elected by the populace. It was in order to prevent future such episodes that the Twelfth Amendment, requiring separate votes for President and Vice President, was adopted.

14. For the background of the Illinois statute see Paul Avrich, The Haymarket Tragedy 45 (1984):

Since *Chicago, B. & Q.R. Co.* was not decided until after *Cruikshank* and *Presser*, it is not evident whether the earlier cases focused on the nonincorporation of the Second Amendment in particular rather than rejecting incorporation of the Bill of Rights in general. Of course, if you agree with Tribe that the Second Amendment is simply a federalist protection of state rights, then there is nothing to incorporate. But if you read the amendment as a substantive limitation on the ability of the national government to regulate the private possession of arms, based on either the "individualist" or "neo-republican" theories sketched above, then is there any reason not to follow the "incorporationist" logic applied to other amendments and limit the state's power to regulate and prohibit such possession?

III. "Rationality" Analysis

While the *Carolene Products* footnote held out the promise that the Court would carefully scrutinize certain types of legislation, the actual holding of the case stands for the proposition that much, indeed most, legislation will scarcely be scrutinized. That decision sustained a dubious statute designed in order to protect the dairy industry against so-called filled milk.[15] The holding is typical of the Court's approach to most legislation that does not implicate the concerns mentioned in the famous footnote. When most such legislation is challenged under the due process or equal protection clauses, the Court applies only a "minimum rationality" review (recall Williamson v. Lee Optical Co., p.357 supra).

A paradigmatic case capturing the post-1937 view of "ordinary" equal protection analysis is Railway Express Agency v. New York, 336 U.S. 106 (1949), which involved a New York City regulation providing that "[n]o person shall operate . . . in or upon any street an advertising vehicle; provided that nothing herein contained shall prevent the putting of business notices upon business delivery vehicles, so long as such vehicles are engaged in the usual business or regular work of the owner and are not used merely or mainly for advertising." The ostensible purpose of this ordinance was to increase traffic safety by limiting potential distractions to drivers. What this meant, practically speaking, was that the Railway Express Agency, which owned hundreds of delivery vans, could not rent space on the side of its delivery vans to businesses wishing to advertise their products. R.E.A. was convicted for violating the ordinance after carrying advertisements

---

> As early as 1875, a small group of Chicago socialists, most of them German immigrants, had formed an armed club to protect the workers against police and military assaults, as well as against physical intimidation at the polls. . . .
>
> In the eyes of its supporters, . . . the need for such a group was amply demonstrated by the behavior of the police and [state-controlled] militia during the [Great Strike of 1877], a national protest by labor triggered by a 10 percent cut in wages by the Baltimore and Ohio Railroad, which included the breaking up of workers' meetings, the arrest of socialist leaders, [and] the use of club, pistol, and bayonet against strikers and their supporters. . . . Workers . . . were resolved never again to be shot and beaten without resistance. Nor would they stand idly by while their meeting places were invaded or their wives and children assaulted. They were determined, as [Albert Parsons, a leader of the anarchist movement in Chicago,] expressed it, to defend both "their persons and their rights."

See also L.H. LaRue, Constitutional Law and Constitutional History, 36 Buffalo L. Rev. 373, 386-390 (1988).

15. See page 354 supra, text and footnote 10.

for cigarettes, a radio station, and a circus. However, the New York Times Company, which also owned hundreds of delivery trucks, could freely advertise The New York Times on the sides of *its* trucks. Without dissent,[16] the Court upheld the ordinance against R.E.A.'s equal protection challenge.

Writing for the Court, Justice Douglas noted R.E.A.'s contention

> that unequal treatment on the basis of such a distinction is not justified by the aim and purpose of the regulation. It is said, for example, that one of appellant's trucks carrying the advertisement of a commercial house would not cause any greater distraction of pedestrians and vehicle drivers than if the commercial house carried the same advertisement on its own truck. . . . It is therefore contended that the classification which the regulation makes has no relation to the traffic problem since a violation turns not on what kind of advertisements are carried on trucks but on whose trucks they are carried.

Justice Douglas, however, described this analysis as "superficial," for he declared that "local authorities may well have concluded that those who advertise their own wares on their trucks do not present the same traffic problem in view of the nature or extent of the advertising which they use. It would take a degree of omniscience which we lack to say that such is not the case." On that assumption, then, the Court "cannot say that the judgment is not an allowable one." The classification at issue relates "to the purpose for which it is made and does not contain the kind of discrimination against which the Equal Protection Clause affords protection."

Dallas v. Stanglin, 490 U.S. 19 (1989), is typical of contemporary cases applying the minimum rationality standard. A Dallas, Texas, ordinance limited admission to certain dance halls to youths between the ages of 14 and 18. Stanglin operated, within the same building, both the Twilight Skating Rink, open to persons of all ages, and (separated from the rink only by plastic pylons) a dance hall, open only to the designated teenagers. The ordinance prohibited Stanglin from opening the dance hall to everyone, and he sued, claiming, inter alia, that it violated the equal protection clause of the Fourteenth Amendment. The Court rejected the claim. Chief Justice Rehnquist wrote the majority opinion,[17] which was joined by, among others, Justices Scalia, Brennan, and Marshall, who presumably occupied opposite ends of the Court's ideological spectrum. They all agreed that Dallas' ordinance easily passed constitutional muster.[18]

The Court quoted the testimony of a Dallas planner, who described "older kids" as being likely to have more "access [to] drugs and alcohol," with "more mature sexual attitudes, more liberal sexual attitudes in general. . . . And we're concerned about mixing up these [older] individuals with youngsters that have not fully matured." Similarly, the Court noted the testimony of a police officer that the age restriction was designed to discourage juvenile crime.

16. Though Justice Rutledge acquiesced in the Court's opinion, "dubitante on the question of equal protection of the laws."

17. There was no dissent, although Justice Stevens, joined by Justice Blackmun, concurred without reaching the equal protection analysis, as the issue was "neither reviewed by the Texas Court of Appeals nor briefed before us."

18. One measure of the perceived ease of the case is that, after hearing argument on March 1, 1989, the Court handed down its opinion only one month later, on April 3.

Respondent claims that this restriction "has no real connection with the City's stated interests and objectives." Except for saloons and teenage dance halls, respondent argues, teenagers and adults in Dallas may associate with each other, including at the skating area of the Twilight Skating Rink. Respondent also states, as did the court below, that the city can achieve its objectives through increased supervision, education, and prosecution of those who corrupt minors.

We think respondent's arguments misapprehend the nature of rational-basis scrutiny, which is the most relaxed and tolerant form of judicial scrutiny under the Equal Protection Clause. In Dandridge v. Williams, 397 U.S. 471 (1970), . . . the Court said,

> [A] State does not violate the Equal Protection Clause merely because the classifications made by its laws are imperfect. If the classification has some "reasonable basis," it does not offend the Constitution simply because the classification "is not made with mathematical nicety or because in practice it results in some inequality." Lindsley v. Natural Carbonic Gas Co., 220 U.S. 61, 78 (1911). "The problems of government are practical ones and may justify, if they do not require, rough accommodations — illogical, it may be, and unscientific." Metropolis Theatre Co. v. City of Chicago, 228 U.S. 61, 69-70 (1913). . . .

We think that similar considerations support the age considerations at issue here. As we said in New Orleans v. Duke, 427 U.S. 297, 303-304 (1976), "in the local economic sphere, it is only the invidious discrimination, the wholly arbitrary act, which cannot stand consistently with the Fourteenth Amendment." The city could reasonably conclude . . . the teenagers might be susceptible to corrupting influence if permitted, unaccompanied by their parents, to frequent a dance hall with older persons. See 7 E. McQuillin, Law of Municipal Corporations §24.210 (3d ed. 1981) ("Public dance halls have been regarded as being in that category of businesses and vocations having potential evil consequences"). The city could properly conclude that limiting dance-hall contacts between juveniles and adults would make less likely illicit or undesirable juvenile involvement with alcohol, illegal drugs, and promiscuous sex. It is true that the city allows teenagers and adults to roller-skate together, but skating involves less physical contact than dancing. The differences between the two may not be striking, but differentiation need not be striking in order to survive rational-basis scrutiny.

A. The Problem of Classification and Generalization

It should be obvious that the Fourteenth Amendment does not prohibit "discrimination" as such, at least if "discrimination" simply means "distinctions among individuals or classes of individuals." The major business of any legislative body is deciding who among its citizens or their activities should receive certain benefits or bear certain burdens. Indeed, can you think of *any* laws that apply universally to all persons, things, or activities, that is, that do not classify at all?

Thus, the essential evil to which the equal protection clause is responsive is not classification as such, but rather defects in *generalization* attendant to any scheme of classification. A classic discussion of the problem of generalization is found in Joseph Tussman and Jacobus tenBroek, The Equal Protection of the Laws, 37 Calif. L. Rev. 341, 346-353 (1949):

> The purpose of a law may be either the elimination of a public "mischief" or the achievement of some positive public good. To simplify the discussion we shall refer

to the purpose of a law in terms of the elimination of mischief, since the same argument holds in either case. We shall speak of the defining character or characteristics of the legislative classification as the trait. We can thus speak of the relation of the classification to the purpose of the law as the relation of the Trait to the Mischief.

A problem arises at all because the classification in a law usually does not have as its defining Trait the possession of or involvement with the Mischief at which the law aims. For example, let us suppose that a legislature proposes to combat hereditary criminality — an admitted mischief — and that the sterilization of transmitters of hereditary criminality is a permissible means to that end. Now if the legislature were to pass a law declaring that for the purpose of eliminating hereditary criminality, all individuals who are tainted with inheritable criminal tendencies are to be sterilized, and if it provided for proper administrative identification of transmitters of hereditary criminality, our problem would largely disappear. The class, being defined directly in terms of the Mischief, automatically includes all who are similarly situated with respect to the purpose of the law.

This procedure requires, however, delegation of considerable discretion to administrators to determine which individuals to sterilize. Legislators, reluctant to confer such discretion, tend to classify by Traits which limit the range of administrative freedom. Suppose then, that they pass a law providing for the sterilization of all persons convicted of three felonies. The "reasonableness" of this classification depends upon the relation between the class of three-time felons and the class of hereditary criminals.[19]

In other words, we are really dealing with the relation of two classes to each other. The first class consists of all individuals possessing the defining Trait; the second class consist of all individuals possessing, or rather, tainted by, the Mischief at which the law aims. The former is the legislative classification; the latter is the class of those similarly situated with respect to the purpose of the law. We shall refer to these two classes as *T* and *M* respectively.

Now, since the reasonableness of any class *T* depends entirely upon its relation to a class *M*, it is obvious that it is impossible to pass judgment on the reasonableness of a classification without taking into consideration, or identifying, the purpose of the law. . . .

There are five possible relationships between the class defined by the Trait and the class defined by the Mischief. These relationships can be indicated by the following diagrams:

(1)

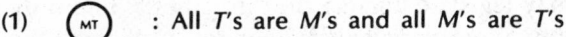

: All *T*'s are *M*'s and all *M*'s are *T*'s

(2)

: No *T*'s are *M*'s

(3)

: All *T*'s are *M*'s but some *M*'s are not *T*'s

(4)

: All *M*'s are *T*'s but some *T*'s are not *M*'s

(5)

: Some *T*'s are *M*'s; some *T*'s are not *M*'s; and some *M*'s are not *T*'s

One of these five relationships holds in fact in any case of legislative classification, and we will consider each from the point of view of its "reasonableness."

The first two situations represent respectively the ideal limits of reasonableness and unreasonableness. In the first case, the classification in the law coincides completely with the class of those similarly situated with respect to the purpose of the

19. The example is taken from Skinner v. Oklahoma, 316 U.S. 535 (1942).

law. It is perfectly reasonable. In the second case, no member of the class defined in the law is tainted with the mischief at which the law aims. The classification is, therefore, perfectly unreasonable. These two situations need not detain us.

Classification of the third type may be called "under-inclusive." All who are included in the class are tainted with the mischief, but there are others also tainted whom the classification does not include. Since the classification does not include all who are similarly situated with respect to the purpose of the law, there is a prima facie violation of the equal protection requirement of reasonable classification. . . .

The fourth type of classification imposes a burden upon a wider range of individuals than are included in the class of those tainted with the mischief at which the law aims. It can thus be called "over-inclusive." Herod, ordering the death of all male children born on a particular day because one of them would some day bring about his downfall, employed such a classification. It is exemplified by the quarantine and the dragnet. The wartime treatment of American citizens of Japanese ancestry is a striking recent instance of the imposition of burdens upon a large class of individuals because some of them were believed to be disloyal. . . .

The final situation to be considered is one in which the previously discussed factors of under-inclusiveness and over-inclusiveness are both present. While it may seem paradoxical to assert that a classification can be at once over-inclusive and under-inclusive, many classifications do, in fact, fall into this category, that is, they can be challenged separately on both grounds.

For example, in the *Hirabayashi*[a] case, the classification of "American citizens of Japanese ancestry" for the purpose of meeting the dangers of sabotage can be challenged both on the grounds that it is under-inclusive, since others — American citizens of German or Italian ancestry — are equally under the strain of divided loyalties, and that it is over-inclusive, since it is not supposed that all American citizens of Japanese ancestry are disloyal. . . .

Discussion

Note the following general features of equality-based argument:

1. "Pure" equality suits never challenge the end presumptively sought by the challenged legislation; they challenge *only* the classifications used to distinguish who comes within a given statute from those left outside its domain. Thus the Tussman-tenBroek formal analysis of trait/mischief relationships assumes, without discussion, that the state may legislate against the "mischief." The only inquiry is whether the classifications chosen are legitimate in terms of some theory of rational "fit" with their (possible) purposes.

Challenging the legitimacy of the end involves an entirely different kind of argument from an egalitarian one. The argument must either be rights based or claim *ultra vires* conduct by the legislature or other decisionmaker. That is, you can claim either that no agency of government can limit your particular right (e.g., your right to engage in speech critical of the government) or that, even if *some* agency could, the particular agency that attempted to cannot because it has not been assigned the power to do so under the relevant constitutional or statutory scheme.

2. A "pure" concern with equality requires only that *A* and *B* be treated alike if they are "similarly situated." But if they are *not* similarly situated, it is permissible to treat them differently. The one thing that equal protection cannot plausibly

a. Hirabayashi v. United States, 320 U.S. 81 (1943).

mean is that government must give everyone the "same thing" (e.g., amount of goods, services, scrutiny by the FBI, punishment, etc.).

3. The formal nature of an equality argument is revealed in the inevitable ambiguity regarding the *remedy* for a violation of the equality norm (whatever that turns out to be). Imagine that *A* sues, claiming the right to be treated similarly to *B*, who under some legislative scheme gets *X* units of some good while *A* gets none. Assume that *A* wins; that is, the court rules that *A* does indeed have a right to similar treatment. Is the remedy that *A* gets what *B* gets (*X* units) or that *B* gets what *A* gets (no units)? The equality condition is *always* satisfied by either result.

Imagine, for example, that a man challenges a state law that provides that only women can get alimony and that the court invalidates the classification. Is the proper remedy to treat men like women (i.e., everybody can get alimony) or women like men (i.e., no one can get alimony, at least until the legislature passes a new law saying that everybody can)? One can easily enough imagine two different male plaintiffs: *X*, who is rich, wants a declaration that no one can get alimony; *Y*, a poor man married to a rich woman, wants a declaration that everyone can get alimony. Should the relief depend on what the plaintiff wants? What if *X*'s and *Y*'s suits are decided by the Supreme Court on the same day? What, if anything, should guide a court in deciding what the relief is?

Sometimes the remedy appears "obvious" because we have a strong sense of the existence of a background "right" pushing in a particular direction. Thus, contemporary First Amendment doctrine increasingly uses a basically egalitarian notion that the state cannot regulate speech on the basis of its content. That is, all points of view must be treated equally. Imagine that a state university prohibits the distribution of leaflets criticizing United States foreign policy. That prohibition would clearly be content based and would be unconstitutional. The obvious remedy is to allow the distribution of the prohibited leaflet because of the First Amendment's presumption in favor of free speech. Imagine another state university that prohibits the distribution of *all* leaflets on campus. If no one can pass out a leaflet, then everyone is treated equally. If the state may not do this, it is *only* because of some notion of a *right* to freedom of speech protected against state interference. See Chapter 8 infra.

B. Anatomy of the Rational Classification Standard

Suppose that one were to take seriously the notion that legislative classifications violated the equal protection clause if (but only if) they were absolutely irrational. Under what circumstances would this standard be violated?

1. *The Basic Criteria of Rational Classification*

There has been almost no systematic analysis of the criteria that determine the bounds of reasonable classification. The following is proposed as a starting point. For a classification to meet the requirements of one or more of these criteria is a *sufficient,* but not a necessary, condition for upholding it under the rational relation standard.

Let *X* and *Y* be two individuals or things similarly situated in all respects except as described below. The purpose and effect of the regulation are to reduce or eliminate a "mischief." It is not irrational to impose the regulation on *X* but not on *Y* if:

1. Application of the regulation to *X* reduces the total amount of mischief more than would its application to *Y*; or
2. *X* causes a greater amount of mischief than *Y* causes; or
3. *Y*'s cost of complying with the regulation is greater than *X*'s; or
4. exempting *Y* from the burden of the regulation will serve an ancillary objective; or
5. a. *X* possesses trait *T*, and
   b. on the average, persons or objects possessing *T* are situated with respect to persons not possessing *T* as *X* (in 1 through 4) is situated with respect to *Y*; and
   c. employing *T* as a classifying trait is more efficient than employing a narrower, more individualized trait.

Some of these criteria are usefully illustrated by reference to Professor John Ely's "deadstop brake" example:[20]

> [T]he political branches [are] granted discretion by courts to honor their own value preferences in deciding which goal to promote at the expense of which other goal. If, for example, a new and unusually effective truck brake, the deadstop brake, were developed, courts would not interfere with a legislative judgment concerning the extent to which one of the acceptable goals of traffic regulation, safety and owner economy,[a] should be promoted at the expense of the other. The legislature could permissibly opt for maximum safety by requiring all trucks to install the brake, or for minimum owner cost by not requiring its installation at all. Courts *would* require, however, that any legislative choice be rationally relatable to the effectuation of *one* of the acceptable goals.
>
> Assume the legislature passes the following law: "*All trucks whose weight exceeds five tons must install the deadstop brake.*" If the state can make out a plausible case . . . that the heavier a truck is, the harder it is to stop with an ordinary brake (or the more damage it will cause if it is not stopped), the distinction drawn by this law, between heavier and lighter trucks, would be upheld as rationally relatable to the goal of promoting traffic safety. Of course safety would be maximally promoted by requiring all trucks to install the brake, but the distinction here drawn is sustainable because, in light of the proof, "Requiring deadstop brakes on heavy trucks promotes safety *to a greater extent* than requiring them on light trucks" can be labeled rational. Or assume that the legislature decrees: "*All trucks manufactured henceforth must install the deadstop brake.*"
>
> If the state can make out a plausible case that installation costs are higher for an already existing truck than they are for one not yet produced, the distinction drawn by this law, between existing and future trucks, would be upheld as rationally relat-

20. John Ely, Legislative and Administrative Motivation in Constitutional Law, 79 Yale L.J. 1205, 1237-1239 (1970).

a. . . . Of course the Court might well recognize other acceptable goals; the example is deliberately oversimplified for illustrative purposes.

able to the goal of reducing owner cost. That goal would be maximally promoted by not requiring the brake at all, but the choice made is sustainable because "Excusing an existing truck from the requirement reduced the cost to the owner *to a greater extent* than excusing a future truck" can also be labeled rational.

Assume, however, that the legislature enacts a law which provides "*Blue trucks must install the deadstop brake,*" or, more likely politically, "*All trucks save those carrying seafood must install the deadstop brake.*" Both of these laws would fall, because neither of the distinctions drawn is rationally relatable to the promotion either of safety or of owner economy. Specifically, the following claims (barring proof which would surprise me greatly) must be labeled irrational.

Requiring deadstop brakes on blue trucks (or trucks not carrying seafood) promotes safety to a greater extent than requiring them on others.

Excusing non-blue trucks (or trucks carrying seafood) reduces the cost to the owner to a greater extent than excusing others.

Criteria 1 and 2. Criteria *1* and *2* are both met by a regulation requiring the installation of deadstop brakes on all trucks weighing more than five tons, assuming that any heavier truck is more difficult to stop than a lighter truck. (Under the same criteria, it would also be rational to draw the line at 4 or 6 tons.) Criterion *1* is satisfied because installation of the brake on a truck weighing more than five tons (*X*) reduced the total mischief (i.e., the total cost of accidents) more than its installation on a truck weighing less than five tons (*Y*). Criterion *2* is met because a truck weighing more than five tons (*X*) causes more mischief (i.e., is less likely to stop in time to avert an accident) than a truck weighing less (*Y*).

Criteria *1* and *2* are often coextensive, but one can conceive of cases in which they would not be. Consider, for example, the decision to require the installation of exhaust emission control devices on vehicles. Suppose that vehicle *Q* produces 1,000 units of pollutants, and vehicle *R* produces 500 units; but for technical reasons, installation of the control device will reduce *Q*'s output by only 200 units, while the same device will reduce *R*'s output by 400 units. Requiring *R* but not *Q* to install the device would satisfy criterion *1*: the choice would be premised on efficency — attaining the greatest reduction in pollution per dollar. Requiring *Q* but not *R* to install the device would satisfy criterion *2*: the choice here would be premised on the arguable fairness of imposing the costs of the regulation on those who impose the greatest pollution costs on society.[21]

Criterion 3. Criterion *3* is met by a regulation that requires only trucks manufactured henceforth to install the deadstop brake. The mischief caused by trucks manufactured before and after the effective date is identical, but the cost of a retrofit on an existing truck is greater than the factory installation cost.

Criterion 4. Criterion *4* would be met by a regulation that prohibits all trucks weighing more than five tons from using certain highways (this itself meets criterion *1*, cf. South Carolina Highway Department v. Barnwell Brothers, 303 U.S. 177 (1938), page 434 supra) but exempts fire engines and other emergency vehicles in order to protect endangered persons and property. Affording such protection is obviously not the primary objective of the regulation. It is, rather, the objective of the exception to the regulation, or, if one likes, an ancillary objective of the provision taken as a whole.

21. Cf. Richard Epstein, A Theory of Strict Liability, 2 J. Legal Studies 151 (1973); George Fletcher, Fairness and Utility in Tort Theory, 85 Harv. L. Rev. 537 (1972).

Does the equal protection clause limit the ancillary objectives that may be pursued in a given regulatory context? Consider Smith v. Cahoon, 283 U.S. 553 (1931). This was an equal protection challenge to a Florida statute that required commercial carriers to post liability bonds to indemnify persons injured through the carriers' negligence. Exempted from the requirement were carriers engaged exclusively in transporting farm, fish, and seafood products. A unanimous Court held the legislation invalid; Chief Justice Hughes wrote:

> [T]he constitutional guaranty of equal protection of the laws is interposed against discriminations that are entirely arbitrary. In determining what is within the range of discretion and what is arbitrary, regard must be had to the particular subject of the State's action. In the present instance, the regulation as to the giving of a bond or insurance policy to protect the public generally, in order to be sustained, must be deemed to relate to the public safety. This is a matter of grave concern as the highways become increasingly crowded with motor vehicles, and we entertain no doubt of the power of the State to insist upon suitable protection for the public against injuries through the operations on its highways of carriers for hire, whether they are common carriers or private carriers. But in establishing such a regulation, there does not appear to be the slightest justification for making a distinction between those who carry for hire farm products, or milk or butter, or fish or oysters, and those who carry for hire bread or sugar, or tea or coffee, or groceries in general, or other useful commodities. So far as the statute was designed to safeguard the public with respect to the use of the highways, we think that the discrimination it makes between the private carriers which are relieved of the necessity of obtaining certificates and giving security, and a carrier such as the appellant, was wholly arbitrary and constituted a violation of the appellant's constitutional right.

The Court in Smith v. Cahoon completely ignored a plausible objective of the Florida regulation. "Obviously the exemption did not stem from a legislative belief that the exempted drivers were any more careful than the drivers covered by the statute; it was obviously motivated by a desire to foster the production of farm and seafood products. Although this is a goal which can properly be served by classifications made in other statutory settings, and it plainly was the goal the legislators had in mind, the Court refused to refer to it in order to uphold the classification." As Professor Ely continues, *Cahoon* implicitly rejects the view that "government officials should be privileged to pursue in any context any goal they may acceptably pursue in any other context. This view would imply, for example, that because farming can constitutionally be encouraged by subsidies, it can also be encouraged by limiting driver's licenses to farmers or free public education to their children."[22] Ely explains:

> In cases like *Cahoon* — which subsequent developments make clear is not simply a derelict surviving from the "overactive" early 1930's[a] — the Court apparently is ap-

22. Ely, supra note 20, at 1225-1226.

a. In Railway Express Agency, Inc. v. New York, 336 U.S. 106 (1949), . . . the Court declined to rest its decision on the theory that since owner operation can obviously be encouraged in other ways, it can be encouraged in this way. . . . Instead, it chose the vastly more tortured route of attempting, not altogether successfully, to postulate a rational relation between the challenged distinction and something it was willing to credit as an acceptable goal, increased traffic safety. . . . [Cf. Jackson, J., concurring.] See Daniel v. Family Sec. Life Ins. Co., 336 U.S. 220 (1949), and Williamson v. Lee Optical Co., 348 U.S. 483 (1955), for other examples of the Court's having to strain to find a distinction

plying a sort of "consensus" theory, asking not what motivation underlay the specific distinction in question, but rather what such laws are generally concerned with, what most legislators intend to accomplish by most such laws considered in their entirety. Where a law has generally to do with traffic safety, the Court is saying, classifications must — regardless of the motivation underlying the specific classification in issue — be justifiable in terms of traffic safety. (Economy to the owner surely would count as an acceptable goal as well. If the installation of a safety device on one sort of vehicle is significantly more costly than its installation on another sort of vehicle, its installation could be required on the one but not the other.)[b] A subsidy program or a tax code may constitute an appropriate vehicle for legislative promotion of whatever activity is deemed to advance the general welfare, but a motor vehicle code does not.

Why, however, may the Florida legislature not protect what it deems an important industry by exempting it from a possibly onerous bond requirement? Neither the Court nor Professor Ely has suggested an answer, and it is not apparent that there is a good one. Two possible justifications appear, but neither seems entirely satisfactory. First, to permit exemptions from a regulatory burden to be justified as an indirect subsidy or protection of the exempted industry or activity is to allow in by the back door the very sort of political expediency that the equal protection clause seemingly protects against. The contextual limitation tends to force subsidies into the open where they are subject to public scrutiny. But *should* the equal protection clause serve this prophylactic function? Second, a cash subsidy or tax break generally is financed, more or less, by the public at large. The subsidy forbidden in *Cahoon* would have been paid for by the accidentally selected few persons injured by unbonded and impecunious seafood carriers. But is this allocation of resources plainly irrational or unfair?

Criterion 5. Criteria *1* through *4* concern the treatment of *individual* persons or things. But actual legislation deals with *classes* of persons and things, and, without criterion *5*, no legislation could be sustained under the rational classification requirement. It is this principle that defines permissible bounds of under- and over-inclusion. Suppose that the all-trucks-over-five-tons regulation is challenged by the owner of a seven-ton truck. He concedes that the regulation is reasonable with respect to most trucks but not as applied to *his* truck, which, because of special design, stops as well without the deadstop brake as do the trucks weighing less than five tons, which are not subject to the regulation.

The government's response would refer to the practical necessity of legislative classifications based on valid generalizations that may nonetheless not hold true for each member of a class. The government would point out that the challenged regulation, though overinclusive (and probably underinclusive as well) is less costly to administer and less subject to maladministration than one whose application depended on individualized determinations of stopping ability.

The court would sustain the regulation on this basis. For to refuse to allow departures from congruence to be justified in terms of efficiency, or (in other words) to require governments to hear and determine every claim that a particu-

---

rationally defensible because of its unwillingness to credit as acceptable the goal the legislature plainly had intended to serve in making the challenged distinction, even though that goal could properly have been served by distinctions in other statutory settings.

b. If, moreover, carriers of farm and seafood products could have been shown to be financially more secure, and therefore better able to pay in case of accident, the *Cahoon* distinction presumably would have been upheld. Cf. Morey v. Doud, 354 U.S. 457 (1957).

lar individual does not cause the mischief (or a suitable quantity of it) that the regulation seeks to prevent, would increase the costs of governmental regulation so as to price most regulation out of existence. Consider almost any regulations you can think of, and the point becomes clear.[23]

Note that criterion 5 focuses on the *average* mischief caused by persons or objects possessing *T*. A regulation is not necessarily rational merely because the *aggregate* mischief caused by the class defined by *T* is greater than that caused by those not possessing the trait. Otherwise, assuming that there are more blue trucks in operation than trucks of other colors, it would be permissible to require only blue trucks to install the deadstop brake.

Discussion

Analyze, in terms of the foregoing criteria, the ordinances challenged in *Stanglin* and *Railway Express*.

2. *The "Step-at-a-Time" Justification*

The criteria set out above may state sufficient conditions for upholding classifications as rational. But are they exhaustive? Do they state the only circumstances under which a classification should be upheld? The existence of an additional validating principle is asserted in a number of the Court's equal protection decisions. In Railway Express Agency v. New York City, supra, the Court recognized that New York City had not chosen, in its campaign against "distracting" advertisements, to eliminate "the vivid displays on Times Square." The Court stated, though, that "the fact that New York City sees fit to eliminate from traffic [one] kind of distraction but does not touch what may be even greater ones in a different category . . . is immaterial. *It is no requirement of equal protection that all evils of the same genus be eradicated or none at all.*" [Emphasis added.]

In McDonald v. Board of Election, 394 U.S. 802 (1969), the Court rejected the argument of qualified Cook County voters, incarcerated in the Cook County jail awaiting trial, that Illinois could not constitutionally deny them absentee ballots when ballots were provided to four other classes: persons absent from their county of residence for any reason, the physically incapacitated, those whose observance of a religious holiday precludes attendance at the polls, and poll watchers in precincts other than their own. Writing for a unanimous Court, Chief Justice Warren suggested that the distinction might "reflect a legislative determination that without the protection of the voting booth, local officials might be too tempted to try to influence the local vote of in-county inmates." But this was not the Court's primary rationale. Rather, the Chief Justice emphasized that over a period of 50 years the state had extended the availability of absentee ballots to one class at a time:

> [A] legislature traditionally has been allowed to take reform "one step at a time, addressing itself to the phase of the problem which seems most acute to the legislative

23. This is not to say that it may not *also* be rational for governments to allow individualized exemptions form general regulatory criteria. Regulations sometimes explicitly permit waivers or exemptions on a showing that the individual does not cause the mischief that the regulation seeks to prevent.

mind," Williamson v. Lee Optical of Oklahoma, Inc., 348 U.S. 483, 489 (1955); and a legislature need not run the risk of losing an entire remedial scheme simply because it failed, through inadvertence or otherwise, to cover every evil that might conceivably have been attacked. . . . Illinois could, of course, make voting easier for all concerned by extending absentee voting privileges to those in appellants' class. Its failure to do so, however, hardly seems arbitrary, particularly in view of the many other classes of Illinois citizens not covered by the absentee provisions, for whom voting may be extremely difficult, if not practically impossible.[a]

We are satisfied then that appellants' challenge to the allegedly unconstitutional incompleteness of Illinois' absentee voting provisions cannot be sustained. Ironically, it is Illinois' willingness to go further than many States in extending the absentee voting privileges so as to include even those attending to election duties that has provided appellants with a basis for arguing that the provisions operate in an invidiously discriminatory fashion to deny them a more convenient method of exercising the franchise. Indeed, appellants' challenge seems to disclose not an arbitrary scheme or plan but, rather, the very opposite — a consistent and laudable state policy of adding, over a 50-year period, groups to the absentee coverage as their existence comes to the attention of the legislature. That Illinois has not gone still further, as perhaps it might, should not render void its remedial legislation, which need not, as we have stated before, "strike at all evils at the same time."

There seem to be two related bases for the step-at-a-time justification. One is that the legislature cannot feasibly consider most issues of policy systematically and completely. An issue often comes before the legislature triggered by a particular event and, hence, is framed in limited terms — e.g., a veteran's organization lobbies for absentee ballots for soldiers. Limited time and resources may prevent the legislature from going much beyond the particular issue presented to it, and the equal protection clause therefore permits the legislature to deal with problems in a piecemeal fashion. Second, even when the legislature could feasibly consider the problem in a broader perspective, it may wish to intervene cautiously and experimentally.

If the step-at-a-time justification is sometimes proper and independent of the other validating criteria, surely not every instance of noncongruence can be thus justified. What, then, determines when the justification can be successfully invoked? Can one do better than to rely on an intuitive notion of what can reasonably be expected of an "imperfect" legislative process?[24]

a. A number of identifiable groups are not yet entitled to vote absentee under Illinois legislation: those serving on juries within the county of their residence, mothers with children who cannot afford a baby sitter, persons attending ill relations within their own counties, servicemen stationed in their own counties, doctors who are often called on to do emergency work, and businessmen called away from their precincts on business. On the other hand, any person in the above groups, including an unsentenced prisoner, presumably can get an absentee ballot if he is outside his resident county, ill, or observing a religious holiday.

24. *Note on political necessity as a possible justification for noncongruence.* How should one respond to a proffered justification for underinclusiveness — say, the exemption of self-advertisers from a general prohibition on advertising on vehicles — that "this is all we can do within the limits set by certain political considerations, such as the necessity of winning re-election or appeasing powerful pressure groups"? Tussman and tenBroek concede that "it is impossible altogether to ignore the pressure situation in which legislatures operate." The Equal Protection of the Laws, 37 Calif. L. Rev. 341, 350 (1949). However, they agree with Justice Jackson in *Railway Express Agency*, supra, that the function of the equal protection clause is to impose external constraints on political decisions and that the demand for equal protection makes no sense if any classification can be justified by a showing of political necessity. Should a legislature be precluded from enacting a desirable reform measure if it can only

3. *Objectives: The Level of Generality*

The objectives of a provision can be characterized on different levels of generality. Consider, for example, the objectives of a regulation requiring the installation of exhaust emission devices on cars: (1) to reduce automobile exhaust emissions, (2) to reduce air pollution, (3) to protect health and the environment, or (4) to promote the general welfare. If car owners complain that the regulation denies them equal protection, which of these is the court to posit as the objective of the regulation in terms of which it must be justified, and how does the court know with what nonregulated activity to compare the regulation of cars? To describe the objective in terms of level (1) achieves perfect congruence between the mischief and the classifying trait. But any regulation can be validated in terms of a tautological objective — a regulation limited to blue cars has the objective of reducing emissions from blue cars — and such self-validation is obviously inconsistent with any criterion of rationality.[25] If, on the other hand, one chooses the broadest characterization, (4), the task of adjudication is seemingly endless. One must compare the regulation of cars with every conceivable unregulated or less regulated activity — the sale of alcohol, the use of guns, allowing potholes to go unrepaired — until one finds, or is certain that one cannot find, an activity that it is irrational not to regulate while regulating automobile exhaust emissions. Of course, as one moves to higher levels of generality, the likelihood of finding rational grounds for distinction increases. But where to stop? How does one know that cars are to be compared with trucks and buses, and perhaps with airplanes and factories, but not with cigars, jack-hammers, and pornography?

Courts and commentators assume without discussion that a particular level of generality — somewhere between (1) and (4) — is appropriate; they assume, with respect to the things to be compared, that some activities "fall within the natural perimeter" of others. Walz v. Tax Commission, 397 U.S. 664 (1970) (separate opinion of Harlan, J.) (establishment of religion case). A particular society at a particular time probably has widely shared intuitions about the location of the "natural perimeter" of a regulated activity, within which nonregulated activities must be rationally distinguished. It is doubtful, however, that one can formulate objective criteria to determine these bounds.

4. *"Discretionary Choices"*

The rationality standards assume that the issue before the court can (in principle) be reduced to an empirical inquiry into the relationship between a law and its objectives. Application of the standards is, therefore, futile where the assertion that a law promotes a particular objective is not subject to verification or falsification. Even if one avoids the pitfall of characterizing the objectives in tautological terms, this danger may lurk in what Professor John Ely has termed "discretionary choices."

---

gain the necessary votes by exempting a group that cannot be rationally distinguished from those covered?

25. See Note, Legislative Purpose, Rationality, and Equal Protection, 82 Yale L.J. 123, 128-132 (1972).

Ely identifies two major categories of discretionary choices. The first encompasses the regulation, inter alia, of aesthetics and morality:[26]

> Courts *can* evaluate the "rationality" of the relation between various choices and the goal of promoting physical health . . . : a distinction between rubbers and sneakers as acceptable rainy day footwear is rationally related to that goal, a distinction between black and blue rubbers is irrational with respect to it. However, the relation between various choices and [another] goal, the promotion of good taste, cannot be thus labeled rational or irrational. The statements "Outlawing sneakers promotes good taste to a greater extent than outlawing loafers," and, for that matter, "Outlawing loafers promotes good taste to a greater extent than outlawing sneakers," can be labeled neither rational nor irrational by courts. They are judgments of taste — like saying that spinach is tastier than broccoli; or that Raphael's Madonnas are more beautiful than Leonardo's. Unlike claims of increased safety or economy, their "validity" depends on no reasoned elaboration of the choice's actual or projected results. Of course people can argue about loafers and sneakers, or Raphael and Leonardo. But courts sensibly appreciate that they could "review" judgments like the two hypothesized only by substituting their own aesthetic judgment for that of the political branches — a kind of revisory authority which would negate the assumed grant of authority to the political branches to promote good taste.

The second category of discretionary choices involves what Ely terms the "umbrella goal," promotion of the general welfare:

> The usual demand that choices be rationally related to the effectuation of some acceptable goal would be similarly inapposite were the Court to define the acceptable goals of the area of choice in question not as some set of goals of varying precision but rather as one goal, the promotion of the "general welfare." "Encouraging industrial growth promotes the general welfare to a greater extent than encouraging the arts," and "Protecting private property promotes the general welfare to a greater extent than protecting physical security," are claims which courts can label neither rational nor irrational. Of course we can disagree and argue about them, but after the smoke clears, the choice still reduces to a value preference.[a] . . .
>
> [The rationality standards might seem applicable] to legislative decisions to encourage a particular occupation or activity by the creation of taxing or spending discrepancies and decisions to punish one crime more severely than another (or to make one act rather than another a crime in the first place). Of course such choices will ultimately take their direction from the decision maker's definition of the general welfare. But what appear, on one level at any rate, to be "rational" defenses can be mounted in support of such choices. Thus giving a tax break to oilmen but not to artists can be justified in terms of the promotion of industry. "Encouraging oil production promotes industry to a greater extent than encouraging artists" appears to be rational in the same sense as "Requiring brakes on heavy trucks promotes safety to a greater extent than requiring them on light trucks." Of course the choice of oilmen over artists involves a choice of the goal of promoting industry over the goal of promoting the arts, but there is nothing in the ordinary demand for a rational choice/goal relation which limits the discretion of the political branches to choose one goal over another when they conflict. The requirement is simply that the choice

26. Ely, supra note 20, at 1239-1240, 1246-1247.

a. Deciding which goal to promote at the expense of which other goal always involves a value preference. What is special about these "discretionary goal" situations is that the relation between the choice under attack and such a goal can be evaluated only in terms of a value judgment. . . .

be rationally relatable to *some* acceptable goal. And is it not clear that this choice is thus relatable — the goal being the promotion of industry? By a similar process, a decision to punish burglary more harshly than battery could be defended in terms of its promotion of the goal of protecting property.

But of course *any* politically imaginable decision to encourage one occupation or activity more than another, or to punish one act more harshly than another, is defensible in just such terms — a realization that should raise questions about the aptness of our model of review. A decision to aid artists rather than oilmen is defensible in terms of promoting the arts; punishing battery more harshly than burglary is defensible in terms of the safeguarding of physical security. And so is any such choice thus defensible, because courts are prepared to credit as acceptable any goal the political branches view as contributing to the general welfare. Thus each choice will import its own goal, each goal will count as acceptable, and the requirement of a "rational" choice-goal relation will be satisfied by the very making of the choice.

If the areas of "discretionary choice" could be delineated and isolated, they would simply constitute domains within which the rationality standards are inapplicable. To the extent that these areas cannot be contained, however, they pose a serious threat to the overall viability of the rationality standards. This danger materializes when regulations that cannot be justified in terms of "regulatory" objectives, such as health and safety, can be "justified" on aesthetic or "general welfare" grounds:[27]

So long as even one acceptable goal in a given context is thus "discretionary," even if others are not, an across-the-board demand that all choices be "rationally" related to the effectuation of some acceptable goal is impossible, and the [rationality standards] of review cannot be imposed. . . .

As the class of acceptable goals limiting an area of choice expands from a comparative few to a substantial number, the requirement that every choice be rationally connected to the effectuation of an acceptable goal obviously becomes less of a restriction. But the demand remains intelligible — evaluation can take place — so long as the class of acceptable goals remains finite (and the goals remain relatively precise). *When, however — because the courts stand ready to credit as acceptable any goal the political branches regard as conducive to the general welfare — the class of acceptable (sub)goals is infinitely expandable at the discretion of the political branches, a requirement of a rational choice/goal relation for every choice is no demand at all.* An infinitely expandable "set" of acceptable subgoals, one to fit every choice the political branches will make, is more realistically and economically viewed as one umbrella goal, the promotion of the general welfare. . . . [T]he relation between such a goal and various choices is not amenable to evaluation in terms of rationality.

Consider how easily the laws challenged in *Railway Express Agency* and Williamson v. Lee Optical Co., 348 U.S. 483 (1955), could have been upheld on the grounds that they promoted particular industries — newspapers and optometrists, respectively — favored by the regulations. (Could *Stanglin* have been defended on such a basis?) Note Judge Hans Linde's comment on *Williamson*: "If Oklahoma had said that it gave independent optometrists a monopoly on fitting eyeglass frames in order to assure their financial ability to render their other professional services at prices people could afford, there should be no need to

27. Ely, supra note 20, at 1240, 1247-1248.

demonstrate any health risks from having frames fitted by opticians or in drug stores."[28]

C. The Rationale for Rationality Review

SCOTT BICE, RATIONALITY ANALYSIS IN CONSTITUTIONAL LAW
65 Minn. L. Rev. 1 (1980)

Several scholars have recently commented on . . . two competing models used to describe legislative bodies.[a] One view — "idealistic, somewhat communal, and perhaps sentimental" — is that legislators struggle in good faith to identify and achieve social good.[b] Under this view, legislation is a means of achieving what a majority of the legislature has identified as desirable "social objectives." As Professor Michelman describes the "social good" model, the legislature is the "forum for identifying [objectives], and acting toward those ends. The process is one of mutual search through joint deliberation. . . . [M]oral insight, sociological understanding, and goodwill are all legislative virtues."[c] . . .

An opposing view of the legislative process that is realistic and individualistic, assumes that the legislature is simply a "market-like arena" in which individuals and special interest groups trade with each other through representatives to further their own private ends.[d] There is no "public interest," no identifiable "social good"; there are only bargains struck between those helped by legislation and those who are harmed. Under this "public choice" model of the legislative process, . . . it makes no sense . . . to speak of "evaluating the rationality" of legislative action. All collective action by the legislature is, by definition, arational: the legislature simply does what it does — means and ends are merged.

As *descriptions*, both the social good and the public choice models — like all fairly simple theories — provide only rough approximations of an incredibly

28. Hans Linde, Without "Due Process": Unconstitutional Law in Oregon, 49 Or. L. Rev. 125, 177 n.154 (1970).

a. See, e.g., Michelman, Political Markets and Community Self-Determination: Competing Judicial Models of Local Government Legitimacy, 53 Ind. L.J. 145, 148-157 (1978).

b. Id. at 149. Michelman posits that this model depends on a belief in public values and ends for human action, a view associated with Kant and Rousseau. See A. Levine, The Politics of Autonomy: A Kantian Reading of Rousseau's Social Contract 56 (1976).

c. Michelman, supra note [a], at 149. The ultimate social good can be conceived of in at least three ways: as a utilitarian concept in which the legislature aims to increase the net individual utility; as a more limited, though still utilitarian, concept in which the legislature aims to increase net utility so that the "gainers" benefit enough that they would be willing to compensate the "losers"; and as a non-utilitarian "moral" concept in which the legislature transfers wealth from losers to gainers because it is "just" or "fair." See Michelman, Norms and Normativity in the Economic Theory of Law, 62 Minn. L. Rev. 1015, 1024-1027 (1978); Posner, Utilitarianism, Economics, and Legal Theory, 8 J. Legal Stud. 103, 104-11 (1979). For present purposes, we need not decide which of these or other conceptions of the ultimate public good is the most valid. Whichever theory is adopted, the important fact about the social good model is that is views most legislation as an *instrumental* attempt to achieve *discrete* social goods that are compatible with some ultimate normative conception of good. . . .

d. This model is rooted in skepticism about the reality or even the possibility of public values. It posits that the only intelligible conception of the "public" good is the maximum feasible satisfaction of *individual* preferences. See R. Posner, Economic Analysis of Law 10-12 (2d ed. 1977). Thus, assuming that the legislature operates as a proper market, legislation is, by definition, an accurate expression of that maximum satisfaction.

complex and probably "unmodelable" reality. One might still ask, however, which model gives the "more useful" picture of the legislative process. The answer depends on the reason one needs a model. If a political scientist is seeking the model that will best explain why certain legislation was enacted, the public choice model is probably most appropriate. On the other hand, if one is choosing a model that will best interpret legislative commands in ambiguous cases, the social good model seems more useful.

As *normative* prescriptions for legislative action, the models present very different visions of representative government. The social good model posits legislators as statesmen who, although informed by public opinion, strive to do what is "right," and submit their conception of the social good to periodic review by the electorate. By contrast, the public choice model views legislators as conduits who respond to relevant exertions of power, much like traders in a market. The choice between these two opposing visions is a central question of the theory of representation and an important issue of political morality.

. . . [C]ourts have adopted the social good model in interpreting statutes and determining whether legislation is directed toward illegitimate ends. Adoption of the social good model in these contexts allows courts to employ rationality to *interpret* legislative behavior. Using the social good model for this interpretive purpose does not, however, require legislatures to adhere precisely to it. Rather, the model serves only as a basis for giving meaning to legislative actions. Legislatures are perfectly free to follow the public choice model in their deliberations, although they will doubtlessly "dress up" their enactments to give the proper signals for later judicial interpretation.

[A court might also adopt] . . . the social good model as a predicate for *evaluative* rationality analysis. Once again, it is not necessary that legislators actually behave in the manner the social good model postulates, but the effect of invalidating legislation on the basis of the rationality requirement is a strong normative exhortation by the judiciary that legislators should act in accordance with the model. . . .

Because evaluative rationality in law is premised on the social good model of legislation, an ultimate judgment about the legitimacy of the rational basis test depends on whether constitutional theory requires fidelity to the social good model. Although the content of constitutional theory may differ, there are three different contexts in which the issue can arise: federal constitutional norms for federal legislation, state constitutional norms for state legislation, and federal constitutional norms for state legislation.

In his extensive and illuminating discussion of the rational basis test, Justice Linde argues forcefully that legislatures should *not* be required to act in a rational manner. According to Linde, to legislate rationally the legislature must identify goals, obtain information about the extent to which those goals are not presently realized, and select the means that will advance them:

> Rational lawmaking, if we take the formula seriously, would oblige this collective body to reach and to articulate some agreement on a desired goal. It would oblige legislators to inform themselves in some fashion about the existing conditions on which the proposed law would operate, and about the likelihood that the proposal would in fact further the intended purpose. In order to weigh the anticipated

> benefits for some against the burdens the law would impose on others, legislators must inform themselves also about those burdens.

Linde observes that such a rational decisionmaking process is certainly not descriptive of a vast amount of legislation. More important, he urges, legislatures should not be required to act in this fashion because, first, such a process imposes enormous time demands and, second, "nonrational" decision-making is simply an acceptable way of accommodating conflicting political pressures — a legitimate function of legislatures. Linde in effect reasons that legislatures should not be required to act rationally in accord with the social good model because of the cumbersomeness of rational decision-making and the acceptability of nonrational decision-making.

In response, it should first be noted that Linde seems to overstate the requirements of rational decision-making that the social good model would impose on legislatures. He appears to say that the model requires that *each legislator* act rationally and that individual actions be aggregated systematically into a group decision. The requirements of the social good model can be stated far more modestly, however. The model requires only that an observer be able to characterize the final legislative output in plausible means-ends terms when rational action is necessary. This allows wide variation in the methods that legislators can follow.

Second, the social good model does not entirely preclude nonrational action. For example, it allows some expressive or "discretionary" actions, actions that cannot be meaningfully characterized in means-ends terms. . . .

This is simply to say, however, that fidelity to the social good model is feasible. The question then becomes whether the model is desirable. In other words, what is the affirmative argument supporting the assertion that legislatures should conform to the social good model? Here issues of "first principles" are confronted: which view of collective legislative action — "market arena" or "search for the public good" — does the relevant constitution adopt? The answer may differ from one constitution to another, but most American governments at least *aspire* to the social good model, treating it as the ideal to be achieved. For example, politicians typically justify legislation by showing how the enactments serve some conception of the public interest; they rarely defend their actions on the ground that the legislation is simply an accommodation of competing private wants. Of course, legislators sometimes admit to political compromise, but the compromise is usually cited as justification for failing to pursue the public interest to the full extent, rather than as the sole justification for the legislation. Even when legislation benefits a narrow group or a single corporation, politicians stress the public benefits of the enactment. A legislator who sought to justify such legislation simply in terms of a desire to accommodate private ends would probably be widely condemned as "caving in" to powerful "special interests."

Some might argue, however, that while political rhetoric may retain the trappings of loyalty to the social good model, recent developments in American government demonstrate the superficiality of this professed allegiance. The realities of single-issue interest groups, powerful lobbyists and large sum political contributions lead to legislative behavior that is more in accord with the public choice model. At the very least, these developments demonstrate an ambivalence about the desirability of the social good model. . . .

Yet even assuming that the social good model is accepted, the question remains as to whether *judicial* invalidation of nonrational legislation serves any useful function. Since invalidation does not prevent the legislature from reenacting the same statutory provision with a citation of additional goals, critics have questioned the utility of evaluative rationality analysis. Although the legislature may have the power to reenact the same law, it probably will not do so when the additional goals needed to revise the legislation are politically controversial. Hence, the required acknowledgment of the new goals may, for practical purposes, preclude reenactment of the law. Even if the legislation is reenacted in substantially the same form, reenactment can be beneficial. The invalidation of legislation by the courts forces the legislature to reconsider the justification for the law. This process of reassessment, even if it generates a substantially similar law, can be democratically beneficial in providing those *currently* burdened by the legislation with an opportunity to participate in a decision that affects them. Thus, if one concludes that relevant constitutional norms support adherence to the social good model, courts invested with the power of judicial review seem justified in applying evaluative rationality analysis.

Discussion

1. *Why should legislation be subject to general rationality review?* Assume that it is desirable, as a matter of policy, that legislation be able to meet the minimal rationality standards of the due process and equal protection clauses. For the sake of argument, put aside doubts as to whether the text or original understanding of these clauses justifies judicial intervention. The question remains: What *functions* are served by judicial review of legislation to assure its rationality?

One possibility is that legislators may simply have *overlooked* a complex legislative scheme's effect on some group. Had they been aware of the effect, they would have avoided it, but inertia makes it unlikely that the group can now get the legislature's ear, whereas a court is structured to hear individualized claims. (Similarly, social or economic facts may have changed so as to make irrational what was an entirely reasonable regulation at the time of enactment.) Is this plausible? Which, if any, of the due process or equal protection minimum rationality decisions does it explain?

Another possibility is that the legislators knew what they were doing and responded to a particular interest group either by exempting it from a general regulation or by legislating against its competitors. To use the equal protection clause to limit such legislation clearly requires endorsement of a certain conception of "proper" legislative activities or procedures.

2. *Why should the standard of review be so low?* If courts are to review the reasonableness of classifications at all, what justifies review under so weak a criterion as "minimum rationality," rather than requiring, say, that the law or classification "have a real and substantial relation to the object sought to be attained"? Nebbia v. New York, 291 U.S. 502 (1934) (due process). Why, to use a common expression, does the legislation come with so strong a "presumption of constitutionality"?

The heavy presumption of constitutionality has been justified on two grounds, one having to do with the putative superior fact-finding competence of legislatures, the other with the "deference" that the courts should accord to other decisionmaking bodies. In Oregon v. Mitchell, 400 U.S. 112 (1970), for example, Justices Brennan, White, and Marshall wrote that the presumption is responsive to the fact that

> the nature of the judicial process makes it an inappropriate forum for the determination of complex factual questions of the kind so often involved in constitutional adjudication. Courts, therefore, will overturn a legislative determination of a factual question only if the legislature's finding is so clearly wrong that it may be characterized as "arbitrary," "irrational," or "unreasonable."

Justice Harlan explicitly disagreed, asserting that "[j]udicial deference is based, not on relative factfinding competence, but on due regard for the decision of the body constitutionally appointed to decide."

Legislatures, and executive and administrative decisionmakers as well, have available a variety of means for gathering and evaluating empirical data relevant to proposed regulations. Legislative committees with expert staff, legislative reference services, and special commissions sometimes perform these tasks superbly.[29] But because of cost, time, lack of interest, and lack of disinterest, these methods are often misused or not used at all.[30] The courts also have means (not always used or used properly) for assisting the judge: the parties may conduct experiments or surveys and may present expert testimony; the court may appoint its own experts, or appoint a special master to determine complex empirical issues. In one respect, the court may be in an advantageous position: even a conscientious legislature cannot investigate every empirical question underlying every aspect of the application of a regulation that might arise in the future; but the regulation typically comes before the court after it has gone into effect and with the factual issues more narrowly focused.

Whether or not a legislature possesses any inherently superior fact-finding competence, efficiency in the utilization of institutional resources — avoiding duplication of the task — may favor some sort of a presumption supporting its findings. But this does not entail an almost insurmountable presumption.

Discussions of "deference . . . based on . . . due regard for the decision of the body constitutionally appointed to decide" seldom go beyond asserting that the judiciary must show respect for and give comity to legislative acts.[31] But there is a functional justification for such deference: Only a strong presumption of constitutionality can insure that the court does not upset legislative judgments on questions of policy and values.

The reason for this lies in the fact that most governmental decisions are based on empirical assumptions, the probable validity of which is considerably less than certainty; and an important aspect of the decisionmaking process is the legislature's assessment of what probabilities justify particular governmental actions. *It may be perfectly rational for the legislature to make a decision based on facts that it recognizes are likely* not *to exist.* For example, it is not irrational to prohibit the sale of a drug or food additive that *may* cause cancer even if the link is only tenuously es-

29. See ABA Department of Legislation, Fact Finding for Legislation, 49 ABAJ 791 (1963).

30. See, e.g., Julius Cohen & Reginald Robson, The Lawyer and the Legislative Process, 33 Neb. L. Rev. 523 (1954).

31. See, e.g., the most venerable discussion of the presumption of constitutionality, Thayer, The Origin and Scope of the American Doctrine of Constitutional Law, 7 Harv. L. Rev. 129 (1893).

tablished. The decision whether to ban the chemical will turn on a variety of factors, such as what the probable danger seems to be, what substitute products exist, and how efficient and expensive they are. (Compare, for example, the federal government's decision to prohibit the use of cyclamates in food products while not prohibiting the use of oral contraceptives.) Judgments of this sort, which often subsume judgments involving the distribution of benefits and costs, are highly value-laden. By employing any standard of proof less than "beyond a reasonable doubt," the court would be substituting its judgment on these (essentially nonempirical) questions for that of the legislature. (For example, if the complainant's burden were only a "preponderance of the evidence," the ban on cyclamates and other possibly carcinogenic chemicals might be invalid.) The high presumption of constitutionality leaves such judgments in the hands of the "political" branches.

D. Rationality Plus

GERALD GUNTHER, IN SEARCH OF EVOLVING DOCTRINE ON A CHANGING COURT: A MODEL FOR A NEWER EQUAL PROTECTION

86 Harv. L. Rev. 1, 20-21, 44-48 (1972)

The model . . . would have the Court take seriously a constitutional requirement that has never been formally abandoned: that legislative means must substantially further legislative ends. . . . Putting consistent new bite into the old equal protection would mean that the Court would be less willing to supply justifying rationales by exercising its imagination. It would have the Court assess the means in terms of legislative purposes that have substantial basis in actuality, not merely in conjecture. Moreover, it would have the Justices gauge the reasonableness of questionable means on the basis of materials that are offered to the court, rather than resorting to rationalizations created by perfunctory judicial hypothesizing. . . .

Modest interventionism would certainly differ from the "all-out tolerance" of the old equal protection and from the attitude of the hands off due process era. It would place a greater burden on the state to come forth with explanations about the contributions of its means to its ends. But that demand would reinforce, not conflict with, one of the most pervasively articulated themes in the thinking about the Court's modern role: safeguarding the structure of the political process has been acknowledged as a major judicial obligation since the 1930's. . . . Means scrutiny . . . can improve the quality of the political process — without second-guessing the substantive validity of its results — by encouraging a fuller airing in the political arena of the grounds for legislative action. Examination of means in light of asserted state purposes would directly promote public consideration of the benefits assertedly sought by the proposed legislation; indirectly, it would stimulate fuller political examination, in relation to those benefits, of the costs that would be incurred if the proposed means were adopted.

A common defense of extreme judicial abdication is that the state has considered the contending considerations. Too often the only assurance that the state has thought about the issues is the judicial presumption that it has. Means scrutiny would provide greater safeguards that the presumed process corresponds to reality — and would thereby give greater content to the underlying premise for deferring to the state's resolution of the competing issues. . . .

There is no inherent lack of judicial capacity to demand more of the state than the Court required in Williamson v. Lee Optical Co., [348 U.S. 483 (1955), Chapter 5 supra], for example. The statute under attack in that case barred opticians from placing old lenses in new frames without written authority from those with greater professional training. The opticians claimed that prescriptions were typically unnecessary for that largely mechanical task. It was enough for Justice Douglas that the legislature "might have concluded" that prescriptions were necessary with sufficient frequency to require the regulation. A demand that some evidence to justify the restriction be brought forward, or at least some evidence that the state had thought about the rationale that satisfied the Court, would have helped safeguard against the exploitative potential of the statute.

The model concededly would provide only limited assurance that competing considerations had been aired. First of all, a legislature could comply with the model without specifying the *costs* of the means adopted in relation to the ends achieved. But in any public debate encouraged by requiring the legislature to explain the benefits sought, the costs would be likely to emerge. Second, and more serious, the model would not have the Court inquire into the motivations of legislatures. But under the model, a legislature wanting simply to give optometrists a guild advantage over opticians, could do so in only two ways: first, by articulating the guild purpose; second, by stating plausible health reasons as a credible facade. Under the first route, the acceptability of the legislative objective would be exposed at once to critical public debate. And even under the second route, in addition to the indirect encouragement of debate on costs, the public scrutiny of the proposed legislation would ultimately pierce any *fragile* facade obscuring real objectives. Either route seems a healthier one for the political process than the Court's approach in *Lee Optical*. There, legislative silence was sufficient to legitimate possible arbitrariness; the Court supplied the "conceivable" rationale. Making the state address itself to supporting arguments in the first instance would serve the function Justice Jackson advocated in *Railway Express* for means-focused equal protection: not a total denial of legislative power, but a narrow, intermediate safeguard against arbitrariness. . . .

The model sketched here has the vices, if also the virtues, of a model: it is relatively simple to describe, but the description may obscure difficulties in its application. . . .

The identification of state purposes illustrates the complex problems likely to be encountered in the task of elaborating techniques capable of disciplined and consistent application. The model asks that the Court assess the rationality of the means in terms of the *state's* purposes, rather than hypothesizing conceivable justifications on its own initiative. But identifying the purposes against which the means are to be measured is not a simple undertaking. What are the relevant data regarding purpose? The model would not call for a delving into actual legislative motivation. The obstacles to judicial inquiry into motivation are as formidable here as elsewhere. Nor, at the other extreme, would the only judicially cognizable purpose be one explicitly set forth in a statutory preamble or the legislative history. A state court's or attorney general office's description of purpose should be acceptable. If the Court were to require an articulation of purpose from an authoritative state source, rather than hypothesizing one on its own, there would at least be indirect pressure on the legislature to state its own reasons for selecting particular means and classifications. And that pressure would further the political process aims of the moderate intervention model.

The call for testing the rationality of means on the basis of state-articulated purposes raises other complications as well. A legislature may legitimately have a multiplicity of purposes, especially in carving exceptions from the scope of a general statute. Court inquiry should not be limited to a primary purpose; subsidiary purposes may also support the rationality of a means. The model would call on the Court to be receptive to all purposes, few or many, articulated by the state. . . . . Although this approach obviously will encourage imagination in the defenders of legislation to articulate a range of legitimating purposes, that need not imply that the model encourages futile judicial gestures. Articulation of legitimating purposes would avoid judicial invalidation, to be sure. But it would do so at the cost of greater explicitness as to the reasons justifying the legislative means; and it would encourage the airing and critique of those reasons in the state's political process.

Nor are the difficulties ended once the articulated purposes are identified. The model requires that there be an affirmative relation between means and ends — or, in more traditional equal protection terms, that there be a genuine difference in terms of the state's objective between the group within the classification and those without. To a large extent, that is an empirical inquiry. The model would have the Court assess the justification for the classification largely in terms of information presented by the defenders of the law rather than hypothesizing data of its own. But such an inquiry would be neither mechanical nor value-free. Requiring compulsively neat logical correlations between classification and objective would ignore legitimate demands for legislative flexibility. The inquiry, like others entrusted to the Court, would involve questions of degree, turning on sensitivity to legislative realities and not on purely abstract considerations of fairness. Still, the value judgments involved in that inquiry would be of drastically narrower dimension than efforts to identify new fundamental interests and to proscribe varieties of legislative objectives. Indeed, perhaps the greatest difficulty in applying the model will be to delineate the boundary between the narrow value judgments required in evaluating means and the broad ones implicit in choosing among ends — in short, to avoid a disguised examination of legislative ends, such as *Baird's* excessively intense concentration on actual state objectives. The line between means and ends will be drawn primarily in such terms of breadth of value judgments; it will present the most difficult questions of degree.

The model is, in sum, not a simple formula capable of automatic, problem-free application. It is a suggestion of a direction for modest interventionism with substantial promise of feasibility as well as substantial attractiveness for the changing Court. The challenge of developing disciplined techniques for the evolving means does not seem to be an insurmountable one. . . .

Discussion

1. What are Professor Gunther's proposals for limiting the objectives in terms of which a law may be justified and for more meaningful evaluation of the

means/ends relationship? Are they likely, directly or indirectly, to exert pressure on the legislature to give greater consideration to its ends and means?

2. Professor Gunther refers to Justice Jackson's concurrence in Railway Express Agency v. New York City, supra, where he wrote that

> there is no more effective practical guaranty against arbitrary and unreasonable government than to require that the principles of law which officials would impose upon a minority must be imposed generally. Conversely, nothing opens the door to arbitrary action so effectively as to allow those officials to pick and choose only a few to whom they will apply legislation and thus to escape the political retribution that might be visited upon them if larger numbers were affected.

After noting the "interests . . . of the great metropolitan newspapers" that might well have contributed to the exemption for advertising one's own businesses, Jackson noted as well that "[t]here is not even a pretense here that the traffic hazard created by the advertising which is forbidden is in any manner or degree more hazardous than that which is permitted."

Still, he upheld the ordinance:

> The question in my mind comes to this. Where individuals contribute to an evil or danger in the same way and to the same degree, may those who do so for hire be prohibited, while those who do so for their own commercial ends but not for hire be allowed to continue? I think the answer has to be that the hireling may be put in a class by himself and be dealt with differently than those who act on their own. But this is not merely because such a discrimination will enable the lawmaker to diminish the evil. That might be done by many classifications, which I should think wholly unattainable. It is rather because there is a real difference between doing in self-interest and doing for hire.

What, if anything, does the actuality of the Jackson opinion suggest about the practical meaning of Professor Gunther's invocation of it as a possible move toward strengthening the Court's review of legislation challenged under the equal protection clause?

3. Why shouldn't "the only judicially cognizable purpose be one explicitly set forth in a statutory preamble or the legislative history"? Note, though, that legislative declarations of purpose are typically vague and conclusory. They seldom explain any details of, or exclusions from, a regulation — upon which equal protection challenges focus. Consider the "declaration of policy" that preceded the Oklahoma optical appliance regulations upheld in *Williamson:*

> It is the public policy of the State of Oklahoma that the citizens of Oklahoma shall receive the best possible visual care, through the efforts of well trained and qualified physicians . . . and optometrists . . . and that no unqualified person shall be permitted to visually correct for compensation the eyes of another.

The objectives were further stated — as they frequently are — in the title of the act: "An Act relating to visual care; . . . prohibiting dishonest and dangerous practices in the sale of optical goods and devices."

With respect to judicial use of legislative history, note that many states do not regularly publish the reports of legislative committees and debates within the legislatures. Moreover, the objectives stated in committee reports and by proponents of a measure typically are not more informative than those stated in the preambles to statutes.

4. Professor Gunther asserts that "a state court's or attorney general office's description of purpose should be acceptable" and suggests that it would at least impose "indirect pressure on the legislature to state its own reasons for selecting particular means and classifications." Why wouldn't counsel proffer *all* plausible legitimate objectives that might sustain a challenged law, even if no one suggested them in a committee report or in the legislature? Should lawyers be limited to purposes actually stated? (Does this mean, then, that states *must* begin publishing legislative records in order to provide evidence of the purposes underlying its handiwork?) Consider the debate between Justice Brennan and then-Justice Rehnquist in Kassel v. Consolidated Freightways Corp., 450 U.S. 662 (1981), in which the Court invalidated Iowa's prohibition of 65-foot double-trailer trucks as a burden on interstate commerce. In his concurring opinion, Justice Brennan examined the legislative history and concluded that the regulation was motivated by protectionist purposes. He continued in a more general vein:

> . . . My brother Rehnquist claims that the "argument" that a Court should defer to the actual purposes of the lawmakers rather than to the post hoc justifications of counsel "has been consistently rejected by the Court in other contexts." Apparently, he has overlooked such cases as Allied Stores of Ohio, Inc. v. Bowers, 358 U.S. 522 (1959), where we described the rationale for our earlier decision in Wheeling Steel Corp. v. Glander, 337 U.S. 562 (1949):
>
> > The statutes, on their face admittedly discriminatory against nonresidents, themselves declared their purpose. . . . Having themselves specifically declared their purpose, the Ohio statute left no room to conceive of any other purpose for their existence. And the declared purpose having been found arbitrarily discriminatory against nonresidents, the Court could hardly escape the conclusion. . . .
>
> And in Weinberger v. Wiesenfeld, 420 U.S. 636, 648, n.16 (1975), we said:
>
> > This Court need not . . . accept at face value assertions of legislative purposes, when an examination of the legislative scheme and its history demonstrates that the asserted purpose could not have been a goal of the legislation.
>
> And in Massachusetts Board of Retirement v. Murgia, 427 U.S. 307, 314 (1976), we stated that a classification challenged as being discriminatory will be upheld only if it "rationally furthers the purpose identified by the State."
>
> The extent to which we may rely upon post hoc justifications of counsel depends on the circumstances surrounding passage of the legislation. Where there is no evidence bearing on the actual purpose for a legislative classification, our analysis necessarily focuses on the suggestions of counsel. Even then, "marginally more demanding scrutiny" is appropriate to "test the plausibility of the tendered purpose." Schweiker v. Wilson, 450 U.S. 221, 245 (1981) (Powell, J., dissenting). But where the lawmakers' purposes in enacting a statute are explicitly set forth, or are clearly discernible from the legislative history, this Court should not take — and, with the possible exception of United States Railroad Retirement Board v. Fritz, 449 U.S. 166 (1980), see id. at 187-193 (Brennan, J., dissenting), has not taken — the extraordinary step of disregarding the actual purpose in favor of some "imaginary basis or purpose." The principle of separation of powers requires, after all, that we defer to the elected lawmakers' judgment as to the appropriate means to accomplish an end, not that we defer to the arguments of lawyers.

> If, as here, the only purpose ever articulated by the State's lawmakers for maintaining a regulation is illegitimate, I consider it contrary to precedent as well as to sound principles of constitutional adjudication for the courts to base their analysis on purposes never conceived by the lawmakers.

Justice Rehnquist, who dissented, specifically rejected Brennan's argument, claiming as well that it "has been consistently rejected by the Court in other contexts . . ." He specified some of the problems ostensibly attached to such a position.

> To name just a few, it assumes that individual legislators are motivated by one discernible "actual" purpose, and ignores the fact that different legislators may vote for a single piece of legislation for widely different reasons. How, for example, would a court adhering to the views expressed in the concurring opinion approach a statute, the legislative history of which indicated that 10 votes were based on safety considerations, 10 votes were based on protectionism, and the statute passed by a vote of 40-20? What would the *actual* purpose of the *legislature* have been in that case? This Court has wisely "never insisted that a legislative body articulate its reasons for enacting a statute." [United States Railroad Retirement Board v.] Fritz.

5. Would the range of objectives in terms of which a law could be justified be usefully and properly narrowed if the reviewing court limited those objectives to the ones that *plausibly*, rather than conceivably, were the legislature's objectives.

6. With respect to the ends/means relationship, what kinds of data, and in what form, would Professor Gunther have government counsel present to the court? How strongly or persuasively must the relationship be established? Is this aspect of the Gunther model consistent with its goal of avoiding judicial intrusion into matters of legislative judgment?

Chapter 6
The Limits of History: The Constitutional Treatment of Race

This chapter focuses on the meaning of the equal protection clause of the Fourteenth Amendment: "No state shall . . . deny to any person within its jurisdiction the equal protection of the laws" in the context of classification by race. We begin by using the occasion of the *School Desegregation* case to examine in greater detail the original understanding of the equal protection clause and its current implications. The rest of the chapter considers contemporary issues of racial discrimination, both to study constitutional decisionmaking that is not significantly constrained by the text and original understanding and to address substantive constitutional issues that are important in their own right.

I. The Original Understanding

A. Background to the School Desegregation Case

Recall that in footnote 4 of *Carolene Products*, p. 546 supra, Justice Stone suggested that the Court might intervene to protect "discrete and insular minorities." In the years following World War II, the Court began to make good on its promise.

ALFRED KELLY, THE SCHOOL DESEGREGATION CASE
in Quarrels That Have Shaped the Constitution
243, 247-249, 253 (Garraty ed. 1964)

[T]he World War II crisis worked . . . substantial acceleration in the growth of the Negro's national political power and influence. First, it created an unprecedentedly large demand for Negro labor in the great cities of the North. This not only produced a new wave of migration from the South which increased the voting power of the Northern urban community; it also forced the Negro into jobs, pay ratings, union memberships, and the like never open to him before. . . .

Second, the equalitarian ideology of American war propaganda, which presented the United States as a champion of democracy engaged in a death struggle with the German racists, created in the minds and hearts of most white persons a new and intense awareness of the shocking contrast between the country's too comfortable image of itself and the cold realities of American racial segregation. Both pragmatic propaganda interests and the new idealism demanded certain steps for the Negro's further integration, both in society and in the war effort.

Some of this crisis-imposed, wartime integration took place on an official level: in a series of executive orders, the Roosevelt administration expanded the employment of Negroes in the federal bureaucracy, wrote "no discrimination" clauses into war contracts, established in 1941 a Fair Employment Practices Commission, and even took a few hesitant steps toward racial integration in the armed forces. Meantime, in 1939, Attorney General Frank Murphy, already something of a radical idealist on the integration and Negro civil rights questions, had established a Civil Rights Division in the Department of Justice, which in turn undertook what was to prove to be a generation-long legal quest for new federal guarantees against lynching and new safeguards for Negro voting rights. Congress, also, bestirred itself. The Soldiers Vote Act of 1942 abolished the poll tax as a prerequisite for voting by members of the armed services, while the so-called La Follette Civil Liberties Committee began its own investigation into the lynching problem.

It was inevitable that the Negro's new nationalized political power, his enhanced economic position, and the vast improvement in ideological climate in the country presently would spill over into the courts, to produce a new series of decisions reflecting the altered position of the Negro in America. The dynamics of this process are hardly very mysterious. Several of the Roosevelt appointees to the Court after 1937 were practical politicians whom the exigencies of the New Deal had made intensely aware of the "political power shift" implicit in the Negro's new party role. Hugo Black, Robert Jackson, Frank Murphy, and Wiley Rutledge all fell into this category. Or, like Felix Frankfurter and William O. Douglas, the new appointees were legal academicians who reflected the equalitarian idealism of the liberal university communities of the North. . . .

It needs only to be added here that the succession of justices appointed to the Court after the war — Fred M. Vinson, Harold Burton, Sherman Minton, and Tom Clark — while they tended generally to be more conservative than New Deal era justices, nonetheless had been trained in the hard practical school of politics and shared to the full an awareness of the altered position of the Negro in American society. Earl Warren, the mild-mannered middle-of-the-road Republican who came to the chief justiceship in 1953, epitomized as no one else could have this new politico-judicial understanding. The Negro's altered role was no mere matter of New Deal radical idealism. It was a point of view which had been thoroughly absorbed by the working politicians of both parties.

It is hardly open to question, then, that this flow of Democratic and Republican appointees to the High Court after 1937 would in no great length of time have produced something of a constitutional revolution in the Negro's status. But this process, inevitable as it may well have been, was vastly accelerated by the legal assault on segregation first launched in the late 1930's by a powerful and dedicated Negro interest group, the National Association for the Advancement of Colored People. The desegregation campaign commenced about 1935 by the NAACP got under way very slowly, but it continued without interruption and with growing success for the next generation. It was a campaign which would make the NAACP the "cutting edge" of all the complex social and political forces that were at work to produce a desegregated America.

[The NAACP's postwar school desegregation began with] . . . a series of suits to force the admission of Negroes to Southern graduate professional schools, above all state university law schools. Several major considerations led NAACP officials to adopt this scheme. First, most Southern states did not even attempt to maintain a facade of equality in professional educational facilities for Negroes, so that their classic "separate but equal" defense, the Association hoped, would prove to be inapplicable. Second, NAACP lawyers believed that if the Southern states countered this strategy by trying to provide genuinely equal facilities for Negroes in graduate education, the effort would prove to be both awesomely expensive and impossible of actual achievement. . . .

The NAACP lawyers were also deliberately exploiting a peculiarity of Southern racial sentiment. The South . . . regarded racial mixing in graduate and professional education as far less invidious than in primary and secondary schools or even in collegiate education. As a consequence, they hoped, Southern officials might be expected to resist graduate school integration with less emotional conviction than would be the case for lower-level schools. As [Thurgood] Marshall, with characteristic humor, later put the matter: "Those racial supremacy boys somehow think that little kids of six or seven are going to get funny ideas about sex and marriage just from going to school together, but for some equally funny reason youngsters in law school aren't supposed to feel that way. We didn't get it but we decided that if that was what the South believed, then the best thing for the moment was to go along."

The NAACP's strategy was successful.[1] Missouri ex rel. Gaines v. Canada, 305 U.S. 337 (1938), held that Missouri did not provide equal protection by paying the tuition for black students at out-of-state law schools while denying them admission to the state school. Chief Justice Hughes wrote that petitioner was entitled to "facilities [within the state] substantially equal to those which the State there afforded for persons of the white race" and that in the absence of such facilities he must be admitted to the one state school. Justice McReynolds, joined by Justice Butler, dissented, arguing that the state had made a "fair effort" to solve a difficult problem and that its solution was "far from [an] unmistakable disregard of [petitioner's] rights." A unanimous Court reaffirmed *Gaines* ten years later in Sipuel v. University of Oklahoma Board of Regents, 332 U.S. 631 (1948). (Justices McReynolds and Butler had resigned in the interim and been replaced by Justices Rutledge and Murphy.) The Court held that petitioner had a constitutional right to an equal education and could not be denied entrance to a state law school solely because of her race. However, on remand, a trial court gave the state the option of establishing a separate black law school, and the Supreme Court, in Fisher v. Hurst, 333 U.S. 147 (1948), refused to order the state to desegregate its law school.

Two years later, however, in Sweatt v. Painter, 339 U.S. 629 (1950), the Court held that a hastily established law school for black law students did not and probably could not provide an education equal to that offered by the University of Texas Law School. Chief Justice Vinson wrote for the Court:

1. See Mark Tushnet, The NAACP's Legal Strategy Against Segregated Education, 1925-1950 (1987).

In terms of number of the faculty, variety of courses and opportunity for specialization, size of the student body, scope of the library, availability of law review and similar activities, the University of Texas Law School is superior. What is more important, the University of Texas Law School possesses to a far greater degree those qualities which are incapable of objective measurement but which make for greatness in a law school. Such qualities, to name but a few, include reputation of the faculty, experience of the administration, position and influence of the alumni, standing in the community, traditions and prestige. . . .

The law school, the proving ground for legal learning and practice, cannot be effective in isolation from the individuals and institutions with which the law interacts. . . . The law school to which Texas is willing to admit petitioner excludes from its student body members of the racial groups which number 85% of the population of the State and include most of the lawyers, witnesses, jurors, judges and other officials with whom petitioner will inevitably be dealing when he becomes a member of the Texas Bar.

McLaurin v. Oklahoma State Regents, 339 U.S. 637 (1950), decided the same day as *Sweatt,* held that petitioner, having been admitted to the state university to pursue a graduate program not offered at the state's school for blacks, could not be required to sit in separate sections of the classroom, library, and cafeteria. Chief Justice Vinson again wrote for a unanimous Court, stating that the "restrictions impair and inhibit [petitioner's] ability to study, to engage in discussions and exchange views with other students, and, in general, to learn his profession." To the argument that petitioner might still be set apart by his fellow students, Vinson responded:

[T]here is a vast difference — a Constitutional difference — between restrictions imposed by the state which prohibit the intellectual commingling of students, and the refusal of individuals to commingle where the state presents no such bar. . . . The removal of the state restrictions will not necessarily abate individual and group predilections, prejudices and choices. But at the very least, the state will not be depriving appellant of the opportunity to secure acceptance by his fellow students on his own merits.

In 1952, the NAACP presented the Court with the issue of segregation in elementary and secondary public schools. Brown v. Board of Education, 347 U.S. 483 (1954), and its four companion cases were first argued during the 1952 term of the Supreme Court. Toward the close of the term, on June 8, 1953, the Court set the cases for reargument and requested counsel "[i]n their briefs and on oral argument . . . to discuss particularly the following questions . . .":

1. What evidence is there that the Congress which submitted and the State legislatures and conventions which ratified the Fourteenth Amendment contemplated or did not contemplate, understood or did not understand, that it would abolish segregation in the public schools?

2. If neither the Congress in submitting nor the States in ratifying the Fourteenth Amendment understood that compliance with it would require the immediate abolition of segregation in public schools, was it nevertheless the understanding of the framers of the Amendment

(a) that future Congresses might, in the exercise of their power under section 5 of the Amendment, abolish such segregation, or

(b) that it would be within the judicial power, in light of future conditions, to construe the Amendment as abolishing segregation of its own force?

3. On the assumption that the answers to questions 2(a) and (b) do not dispose of the issue, is it within the judicial power, in construing the Amendment, to abolish segregation in public schools?

The parties in *Brown* responded to the Court's questions on the original understanding with lengthy historical briefs.[2] See Chapter 4 for a summary of the historical evidence.

B. The School Desegregation Case

BROWN v. BOARD OF EDUCATION

347 U.S. 483 (1954)
Appeal from the United States District Court
for the District of Kansas[a]

WARREN, C.J.

These cases come to us from the States of Kansas, South Carolina, Virginia, and Delaware. They are premised on different facts and different local conditions, but a common legal question justifies their consideration together in this consolidated opinion.

In each of the cases, minors of the Negro race, through their legal representatives, seek the aid of the courts in obtaining admission to the public schools of their community on a nonsegregated basis. In each instance, they had been denied admission to schools attended by white children under laws requiring or permitting segregation according to race. This segregation was alleged to deprive the plaintiffs of the equal protection of the laws under the Fourteenth Amendment. In each of the cases other than the Delaware case, a three-judge federal district court denied relief to the plaintiffs on the so-called "separate but equal" doctrine announced by this Court in Plessy v. Ferguson, 163 U.S. 537. Under the doctrine, equality of treatment is accorded when the races are provided substantially equal facilities, even though these facilities be separate. In the Delaware case, the Supreme Court of Delaware adhered to that doctrine, but ordered that the plaintiffs be admitted to the white schools because of their superiority to the Negro schools.

The plaintiffs contend that segregated public schools are not "equal" and cannot be made "equal," and that hence they are deprived of the equal protection of the laws. Because of the obvious importance of the question presented, the Court took jurisdiction. Argument was heard in the 1952 Term, and reargument was heard this Term on certain questions propounded by the Court.

2. The petitioners in *Brown* commissioned various historians, including Howard J. Graham, Alfred H. Kelly, C. Vann Woodward, John Hope Franklin, and Horace Bond, to prepare monographs for their use. See generally Kelly, supra page 581.

a. Together with Briggs v. Elliott, on appeal from the United States District Court for the Eastern District of South Carolina; Davis v. County School Board of Prince Edward County, Virginia; on appeal from the United States District Court for the Eastern District of Virginia; and Gebhart v. Belton, on certiorari to the Supreme Court of Delaware.

Reargument was largely devoted to the circumstances surrounding the adoption of the Fourteenth Amendment in 1868. It covered exhaustively consideration of the Amendment in Congress, ratification by the states, then existing practices in racial segregation, and the views of proponents and opponents of the Amendment. This discussion and our own investigation convince us that, although these sources cast some light, it is not enough to resolve the problem with which we are faced. At best, they are inconclusive. The most avid proponents of the post-War Amendments undoubtedly intended them to remove all legal distinctions among "all persons born or naturalized in the United States." Their opponents, just as certainly, were antagonistic to both the letter and the spirit of the Amendments and wished them to have the most limited effect. What others in Congress and the state legislatures had in mind cannot be determined with any degree of certainty.

An additional reason for the inconclusive nature of the Amendment's history, with respect to segregated schools, is the status of public education at that time.[b] In the South, the movement toward free common schools, supported by general taxation, had not yet taken hold. Education of white children was largely in the hands of private groups. Education of Negroes was almost nonexistent, and practically all of the race were illiterate. In fact, any education of Negroes was forbidden by law in some states. Today, in contrast, many Negroes have achieved outstanding success in the arts and sciences as well as in the business and professional world. It is true that public school education at the time of the Amendment had advanced further in the North, but the effect of the Amendment on Northern States was generally ignored in the congressional debates. Even in the North, the conditions of public education did not approximate those existing today. The curriculum was usually rudimentary; ungraded schools were common in rural areas; the school term was but three months a year in many states; and compulsory school attendance was virtually unknown. As a consequence, it is not surprising that there should be so little in the history of the Fourteenth Amendment relating to its intended effect on public education.

In the first cases in this Court construing the Fourteenth Amendment, decided shortly after its adoption, the Court interpreted it as proscribing all state-imposed discriminations against the Negro race.[c] The doctrine of "separate but equal" did not make its appearance in this Court until 1896 in the case of Plessy v. Ferguson, supra, involving not education but transportation.[d] American courts have since labored with the doctrine for over half a century. In this Court, there

b. . . . Although the demand for free public schools followed substantially the same pattern in both the North and the South, the development in the South did not begin to gain momentum until about 1850, some twenty years after that in the North. . . . In the country as a whole, but particularly in the South, the War virtually stopped all progress in public education. The low status of Negro education in all sections of the country, both before and immediately after the War, is described in Beale, A History of Freedom of Teaching in American Schools (1941). . . . Compulsory school attendance laws were not generally adopted until after the ratification of the Fourteenth Amendment, and it was not until 1918 that such laws were in force in all the states. . . .

c. Slaughter-House Cases, 16 Wall. 36, 67-72 (1873); Strauder v. West Virginia, 100 U.S. 303, 307-308 (1880). . . .

d. The doctrine apparently originated in Roberts v. City of Boston, 59 Mass. 198, 206 (1850), upholding school segregation against attack as being violative of a state constitutional guarantee of equality. Segregation in Boston public schools was eliminated in 1855. Mass. Acts 1855, c. 256. But elsewhere in the North segregation in public education has persisted in some communities until recent years. It is apparent that such segregation has long been a nationwide problem, not merely one of sectional concern.

have been six cases involving the "separate but equal" doctrine in the field of public education. In Cumming v. County Board of Education, 175 U.S. 528, and Gong Lum v. Rice, 275 U.S. 78, the validity of the doctrine itself was not challenged.[e] In more recent cases, all on the graduate school level, inequality was found in that specific benefits enjoyed by white students were denied to Negro students of the same educational qualifications. Missouri ex rel. Gaines v. Canada, 305 U.S. 337; Sipuel v. Oklahoma, 332 U.S. 631; Sweatt v. Painter, 339 U.S. 629; McLaurin v. Oklahoma State Regents, 339 U.S. 637. In none of these cases was it necessary to re-examine the doctrine to grant relief to the Negro plaintiff. And in Sweatt v. Painter, supra, the Court expressly reserved decision on the question whether Plessy v. Ferguson should be held inapplicable to public education.

In the instant cases, that question is directly presented. Here, unlike Sweatt v. Painter, there are findings below that the Negro and white schools involved have been equalized, or are being equalized, with respect to buildings, curricula, qualifications and salaries of teachers, and other "tangible" factors. Our decision, therefore, cannot turn on merely a comparison of these tangible factors in the Negro and white schools involved in each of the cases. We must look instead to the effect of segregation itself on public education.

In approaching this problem, we cannot turn the clock back to 1868 when the Amendment was adopted, or even to 1896 when Plessy v. Ferguson was written. We must consider public education in the light of its full development and its present place in American life throughout the Nation. Only in this way can it be determined if segregation in public schools deprives these plaintiffs of the equal protection of the laws.

Today, education is perhaps the most important function of state and local governments. Compulsory school attendance laws and the great expenditures for education both demonstrate our recognition of the importance of education to our democratic society. It is required in the performance of our most basic public responsibilities, even service in the armed forces. It is the very foundation of good citizenship. Today it is a principal instrument in awakening the child to cultural values, in preparing him for later professional training, and in helping him to adjust normally to his environment. In these days, it is doubtful that any child may reasonably be expected to succeed in life if he is denied the opportunity of an education. Such an opportunity, where the state has undertaken to provide it, is a right which must be made available to all on equal terms.

We come then to the question presented: Does segregation of children in public schools solely on the basis of race, even though the physical facilities and other "tangible" factors may be equal, deprive the children of the minority group of equal educational opportunities? We believe that it does.

In Sweatt v. Painter, supra, in finding that a segregated law school for Negroes could not provide them equal educational opportunities, this Court relied in large part on "those qualities which are incapable of objective measurement but which make for greatness in a law school." In McLaurin v. Oklahoma State Re-

e. In the *Cumming* case, Negro taxpayers sought an injunction requiring the defendant school board to discontinue the operation of a high school for white children until the board resumed operation of a high school for Negro children. Similarly, in the *Gong Lum* case, the plaintiff, a child of Chinese descent contended only that state authorities had misapplied the doctrine by classifying him with Negro children and requiring him to attend a Negro school.

gents, supra, the Court, in requiring that a Negro admitted to a white graduate school be treated like all other students, again resorted to intangible considerations: ". . . his ability to study, to engage in discussions and exchange views with other students, and, in general, to learn his profession." Such considerations apply with added force to children in grade and high schools. To separate them from others of similar age and qualifications solely because of their race generates a feeling of inferiority as to their status in the community that may affect their hearts and minds in a way unlikely ever to be undone. The effect of this separation on their educational opportunities was well stated by a finding in the Kansas case by a court which nevertheless felt compelled to rule against the Negro plaintiffs:

> Segregation of white and colored children in public schools has a detrimental effect upon the colored children. The impact is greater when it has the sanction of the law; for the policy of separating the races is usually interpreted as denoting the inferiority of the negro group. A sense of inferiority affects the motivation of a child to learn. Segregation with the sanction of law, therefore, has a tendency to [retard] the educational and mental development of negro children and to deprive them of some of the benefits they would receive in a racial[ly] integrated school system.[f]

Whatever may have been the extent of psychological knowledge at the time of Plessy v. Ferguson, this finding is amply supported by modern authority.[g] Any language in Plessy v. Ferguson contrary to this finding is rejected.

We conclude that in the field of public education the doctrine of "separate but equal" has no place. Separate educational facilities are inherently unequal. Therefore, we hold that the plaintiffs and others similarly situated for whom the actions have been brought are, by reason of the segregation complained of, deprived of the equal protection of the laws guaranteed by the Fourteenth Amendment. This disposition makes unnecessary any discussion whether such segregation also violates the Due Process Clause of the Fourteenth Amendment.

Because these are class actions, because of the wide applicability of this decision, and because of the great variety of local conditions, the formulation of decrees in these cases presents problems of considerable complexity. On reargument, the consideration of appropriate relief was necessarily subordinated to the primary question — the constitutionality of segregation in public education. We have now announced that such segregation is a denial of the equal protection of the laws. In order that we may have the full assistance of the parties in formulating decrees, the cases will be restored to the docket, and the parties are requested to present further argument on Questions 4 and 5 previously pro-

f. A similar finding was made in the Delaware case: "I conclude from the testimony that in our Delaware society, State-imposed segregation in education itself results in the Negro children, as a class, receiving educational opportunities which are substantially inferior to those available to white children otherwise similarly situated."

g. [The Court's note 11.] K.B. Clark, Effect of Prejudice and Discrimination on Personality Development (Midcentury White House Conference on Children and Youth, 1950); Witmer and Kotinsky, Personality in the Making (1952), c. VI; Deutscher and Chein, The Psychological Effects of Enforced Segregation: A Survey of Social Science Opinion, 26 J. Psychol. 259 (1948): Chein, What Are the Psychological Effects of Segregation Under Conditions of Equal Facilities?, 3 Int. J. Opinion and Attitude Res. 299 (1949); Brameld, Educational Costs, in Discrimination and National Welfare (MacIver, ed., 1949), 44-48; Frazier, The Negro in the United States (1949), 674-681. And see generally Myrdal, An American Dilemma (1944).

pounded by the Court for the reargument this Term.[h] The Attorney General of the United States is again invited to participate. The Attorneys General of the states requiring or permitting segregation in public education will also be permitted to appear as amici curiae upon request to do so by September 15, 1954, and submission of briefs by October 1, 1954.

It is so ordered.

C. The Current Meaning of the Original Understanding

Our reproduction of *Brown* does not omit any portion of the Court's discussion of the history bearing on the adoption of the Fourteenth Amendment. Is the Court's holding consistent with the original history?

1. *Whose Intent?*

Chief Justice Warren writes: "What others in Congress [besides those who spoke in the debates] and the state legislatures had in mind cannot be determined with any degree of certainty." The Fourteenth Amendment was initially rejected by several Southern states, which were then required to ratify the Amendment as a condition for sending representatives and senators to Congress. Thus, the tangled history of the Amendment, connected as it was with the political turmoil of Reconstruction and the unorthodox process of its addition to the Constitution makes it especially difficult to determine what lay in the minds of its supporters. Even had the history been less complex, however, problems of ascertaining the intent of a multimember body would remain. Consider Justice Peckham's opinion for the Court in United States v. Trans-Missouri Freight Association, 166 U.S. 290 (1897), an early decision construing the Sherman Act:

> All that can be determined from the debates and [committee] reports is that various members had various views, and we are left to determine the meaning of this act, as we determine the meaning of other acts, from the language used therein.
>
> There is, too, a general acquiescence in the doctrine that debates in Congress are not appropriate sources of information from which to discover the meaning of the language of a statute passed by that body.

h. "4. Assuming it is decided that segregation in public schools violates the Fourteenth Amendment

"(a) would a decree necessarily follow providing that, within the limits set by normal geographic school districting, Negro children should forthwith be admitted to schools of their choice, or

"(b) may this Court, in the exercise of its equity powers, permit an effective gradual adjustment to be brought about from existing segregated systems to a system not based on color distinctions?

"5. On the assumption on which questions 4 (a) and (b) are based, and assuming further that this Court will exercise its equity powers to the end described in question 4 (b),

"(a) should this Court formulate detailed decrees in these cases;

"(b) if so, what specific issues should the decrees reach;

"(c) should this Court appoint a special master to hear evidence with a view to recommending specific terms for such decrees;

"(d) should this Court remand to the courts of first instance with directions to frame decrees in these cases, and if so what general directions should the decrees of this Court include and what procedures should the courts of first instance follow in arriving at the specific terms of more detailed decrees?"

> The reason is that it is impossible to determine with certainty what construction was put upor an act by the members of a legislative body that passed it by resorting to the speeches of individual members thereof. Those who did not speak may not have agreed with those who did; and those who spoke might differ from each other; the result being that the only proper way to construe a legislative act is from the language used in the act, and, upon occasion, by a resort to the history of the times when it was passed.

Is the problem any more tractable in the interpretation of constitutional provisions?

Even if the Philadelphia convention or Congress (in the case of amendments) had an ascertainable corporate intent, what about the state conventions (or legislatures) whose ratification of constitutional provisions was essential? Consider John Wofford, The Blinding Light: The Uses of History in Constitutional Interpretation.[3]

> [I]f we are really searching for the states of mind of those responsible for the presence in the Constitution of a particular provision, it is hard to understand why we should be particularly concerned only with those who drafted the provision or supported it actively. Responsibility is more widely distributed; in order to become part of the Constitution, the provision had to be accepted by the Philadelphia Convention or by the Congress, and then ratified by the states acting either through legislatures or through special conventions.
>
> In this sense, interpreting the Constitution is profoundly different from interpreting documents which result from the deliberations of fewer persons. A will purports to be the expressed intent of one person; a contract the expressed intent of two or more; and a statute the expressed intent of one or two deliberative bodies. The Constitution, however, purports to be the expressed intent of a widely dispersed and numerically large sovereign electorate: "We the People of the United States . . . do ordain and establish this Constitution." However mythical the notion of the People as Sovereign may be, it is not at all unrealistic to state that a large number of people were responsible for the Constitution as it emerged and as it was later, from time to time, amended.
>
> Yet to admit the relevance of such a large number of states of mind is to set forth a task virtually impossible to fulfill. Joseph Story long ago pointed out that the varying interpretations of the Constitution presented in the state conventions make the debates in those conventions at best uncertain and inconclusive criteria. The delegates to the ratifying conventions were advocates, using every possible argument for either the support or rejection of the proposed Constitution. To what extent is the mental acceptance or rejection of such arguments relevant? Indeed, to what extent can such acceptance or rejection on the part of those who voted in all of the state ratifying conventions ever be discovered?

Referring specifically to the original understanding of the Fourteenth Amendment, however, Alexander Bickel wrote:[4]

> [T]he debates of the Congress which submitted, and the journals and documents of the legislatures which ratified, the amendment provide the most direct and unim-

3. 31 U. Chi. L. Rev. 502, 508-509 (1964).

4. Alexander Bickel, The Original Understanding and the Segregation Decision, 69 Harv. L. Rev. 1 (1955).

peachable indication of original purpose and understanding — to the extent, of course, that any such indication is to be found. Of these two sets of materials the congressional debates are in this case the richer, and they rank, in any event, first in importance. It may perhaps be said that whatever they establish constitutes a rebuttable presumption. For it is not unrealistic, in the main, to assume notice of Congressional purpose in the state legislatures. A showing of ratification on the basis of an understanding different from that revealed by congressional materials must carry the burden of proof. And, of course, the ratifying states are a chorus of voices; a discordant one among them proves little.

2. *What Was Their Intent?*

In Government by Judiciary (1977), Raoul Berger argues that "[t]he key to an understanding of the Fourteenth Amendment is that the North was shot through with Negrophobia, [and] that the Republicans, except for a minority of extremists, were swayed by the racism that gripped their constituents rather than by abolitionist ideology." (Id. at 10.) After examining the debates in the Thirty-ninth Congress, he concludes that the adopters of the Fourteenth Amendment merely intended to ensure the constitutionality of the Civil Rights Act of 1866 and that *Brown* and almost all other Supreme Court decisions under the Fourteenth Amendment are incorrect.

Much of the scholarly response to Berger's thesis has been critical of his reading of history, historiographic methods, and assumptions about the processes of constitutional interpretation. For example, Aviam Soifer takes Berger to task for focusing narrowly on the official proceedings in Congress, arguing that one cannot understand the debates without placing them in the context of "major changes in political thought and legal theory during and after the Civil War — including ideas about federalism and natural law — and the congressional reaction to President Johnson's veto of the Civil Rights Act, which drove many moderate Republicans into the waiting arms of the Radical wing of the dominant Republican party."[5] In Democracy and Distrust, John Ely comments on Berger's "key" to understanding the amendment:

> Perhaps the most insisted upon implication of this "key" is found in Berger's repeated assertion that given their racism the Fourteenth Amendment's framers could not conceivably have intended to draft a provision capable one day of supporting the inference that blacks were entitled to vote. Curiously lacking is any attempt whatever to account for the fact that the Fifteenth Amendment, explicitly granting blacks the vote, was proposed and ratified *only two years later*. . . . Obviously there was racism in the Thirty-Ninth Congress — though recognizing racism in one's constituents and being racist oneself are not equivalent. The recognition that there was racism in society doubtless was one reason the framers chose open-ended language capable of developing over time. In any event the claim that race prejudice is the "key" to interpreting the Fourteenth Amendment is one that borders on perversity:

5. Soifer, Book Review, 54 N.Y.U.L. Rev. 651, 656-659 (1979). For other book reviews see Clark, 56 Tex. L. Rev. 947 (1978); Murphy, 87 Yale L.J. 1762 (1978); Nathanson, 56 Tex. L. Rev. 579 (1978). See generally Symposium, 6 Hastings Const. L.Q. 403-635 (1979).

it is roughly akin to a claim that censorship is the key to understanding the First Amendment.[6]

ALEXANDER BICKEL, THE ORIGINAL UNDERSTANDING AND THE SEGREGATION DECISION

69 Harv. L. Rev. 1, 59-63 (1955)

If the fourteenth amendment were a statute, a court might very well hold, on the basis of what has been said so far, that it was foreclosed from applying it to segregation in public schools. The evidence of congressional purpose is as clear as such evidence is likely to be, and no language barrier stands in the way of construing the section in conformity with it. But we are dealing with a constitutional amendment, not a statute. The tradition of a broadly worded organic law not frequently or lightly amended was well-established by 1866, and, despite the somewhat revolutionary fervor with which the Radicals were pressing their changes, it cannot be assumed that they or anyone else expected or wished the future role of the Constitution in the scheme of American government to differ from the past. Should not the search for congressional purpose, therefore, properly be twofold? One inquiry should be directed at the congressional understanding of the immediate effect of the enactment on conditions then present. Another should aim to discover what if any thought was given to the long-range effect, under future circumstances, of provisions necessarily intended for permanence.

That the Court saw the need for two such inquiries with respect to the original understanding on segregation is clearly indicated by the questions it propounded at the 1952 Term. The Court asked first whether Congress and the state legislatures contemplated that the fourteenth amendment would abolish segregation in public schools. It next asked whether, assuming that the immediate abolition of segregation was not contemplated, the framers nevertheless understood that Congress acting under section 5, or the Court in the exercise of the judicial function would, in light of future conditions, have power to abolish segregation.

With this double aspect of the inquiry in mind, certain other features of the legislative history — not inconsistent with the conclusion earlier stated, but complementary to it — became significant. Thus, section 1 of the fourteenth amendment, on its face, deals not only with racial discrimination, but also with discrimination whether or not based on color. This cannot have been accidental, since the alternative considered by the Joint Committee, the civil rights formula, did apply only to racial discrimination. Everyone's immediate preoccupation in the 39th Congress — insofar as it did not go to partisan questions — was, of course, with hardships being visited on the colored race. Yet the fact that the proposed constitutional amendment was couched in more general terms could not have escaped those who voted for it. And this feature of it could not have been deemed to be included in the standard identification of section 1 with the Civil Rights Act. Again, when it rejected the civil rights formula in reporting out the abortive Bingham amendment, the Joint Committee elected to submit an equal protection clause limited to the rights of life, liberty, and property, supplemented by a necessary and proper clause. Now the choice was in favor of a due process

6. John Ely, Democracy and Distrust: A Theory of Judicial Review 201 n.70 (1980).

clause limited the way the equal protection clause had been in the earlier draft, but of an equal protection clause not so limited: equal protection "of the laws." Presumably the lesson taught by the defeat of the Bingham amendment had been learned. Congress was not to have unlimited discretion, and it was not to have the leeway represented by "necessary and proper" power. One would have to assume a lack of familiarity with the English language to conclude that a further difference between the Bingham amendment and the new proposal was not also perceived, namely, the difference between equal protection in the rights of life, liberty, and property, a phrase which so aptly evoked the evils uppermost in men's minds at the time, and equal protection of the laws, a clause which is plainly capable of being applied to all subjects of state legislation. Could the comparison have failed to leave the implication that the new phrase, while it did not necessarily, and certainly not expressly, carry greater coverage than the old, was nevertheless roomier, more receptive to "latitudinarian" construction? . . .

Finally, it is noteworthy that the shorthand argument characterizing the fourteenth amendment as the constitutional embodiment of the Civil Rights Act was often accompanied on the Republican side by generalities about the self-evident demands of justice and the natural rights of man. This was true both in Congress and in the course of the election which followed. To all this should be added the fact that while the Joint Committee's rejection of the civil rights formula is quite manifest, there is implicit also in its choice of language a rejection — presumably as inappropriate in a constitutional provision — of such a specific and exclusive enumeration of rights as appeared in section 1 of the Civil Rights Act.

These bits and pieces of additional evidence do not contradict and could not in any event override the direct proof showing the specific evils at which the great body of congressional opinion thought it was striking. But perhaps they provide sufficient basis for the formulation of an additional hypothesis. It remains true that an explicit provision going further than the Civil Rights Act could not have been carried in the 39th Congress; also that a plenary grant of legislative power such as the Bingham amendment would not have mustered the necessary majority. But may it not be that the Moderates and the Radicals reached a compromise permitting them to go to the country with language which they could, where necessary, defend against damaging alarms raised by the opposition, but which at the same time was sufficiently elastic to permit reasonable future advances? This is thoroughly consistent with rejection of the civil rights formula and its implications. That formula could not serve the purpose of such a compromise. It had been under heavy attack at this session, and among those who had expressed fears concerning its reach were Republicans who would have to go forth and stand on the platform of the fourteenth amendment. Bingham, of course, was one of these men, and he could not be required to go on the hustings and risk being made to eat his own words. If the party was to unite behind a compromise which consisted neither of an exclusive listing of a limited series of rights, nor of a formulation dangerously vulnerable to attacks pandering to the prejudices of the people, new language had to be found. Bingham himself supplied it. It had both sweep and the appearance of a careful enumeration of rights, and it had a ring to echo in the national memory of libertarian beginnings. To put it another way, the Moderates . . . consolidated the victory they had achieved in the Civil Rights Act debate. They could go forth and honestly defend themselves against charges that on the day after ratification Negroes were going to become white men's "social equals," marry their daughters, vote in their elections, sit on their juries, and attend schools with their children. The Radicals . . . obtained what early in the session had seemed a very uncertain price indeed: a firm alliance, under Radical leadership, with the Moderates in the struggle against the President, and thus a good, clear chance at increasing and prolonging their political power. In the future, the Radicals could, in one way or another, put through such further civil rights provisions as they thought the country would take, without being subject to the sort of effective constitutional objections which haunted them when they were forced to operate under the thirteenth amendment. . . .

Whatever other support this hypothesis may have, it has behind it the very authoritative voice of [the distinguished Radical Republican] Thaddeus Stevens, who held it, and twice gave notice of it in speaking on the fourteenth amendment. It was Stevens who dutifully defined section 1 . . . in . . . narrow terms . . . ; it fell short of his wishes. And it was Stevens, his hopes fulfilled, who [upon the enactment of the Fourteenth Amendment] powerfully and candidly emphasized the political opportunities which the amendment gained for the Radicals, and who looked to the future for better things "in further legislation, in enabling acts or other provisions." . . . It need hardly be added that in view of Stevens' remarks, and in view also of the nature of the other evidence which supports it, this hypothesis cannot be disparaged as putting forth an undisclosed, conspiratorial purpose such as has been imputed to Bingham and others with regard to protection of corporations. Indeed, no specific purpose going beyond the coverage of the Civil Rights Act is suggested; rather an awareness on the part of these framers that it was *a constitution* they were writing, which led to a choice of language capable of growth.

It is such a reading as this of the original understanding, in response to the second of the questions propounded by the Court, that the Chief Justice must have had in mind when he termed the materials "inconclusive." For up to this point they tell a clear story and are anything but inconclusive. From this point on the word is apt, since the interpretation of the evidence just set out comes only to this, that the question of giving greater protection than was extended by the Civil Rights Act was deferred, was left open, to be decided another day under a constitutional provision with more scope than the unserviceable thirteenth amendment.

3. *The Manifold Nature of "Intent"*

In The Misconceived Quest for the Original Understanding, 60 B.U.L. Rev. 204 (1980), Paul Brest examines the complexities of "intentionalist" interpretation.[7] The article first defines the concepts of "interpretive intent" and "the intended specificity of a provision."

Interpretive intent refers to "the canons by which the adopters intended their provisions to be interpreted." The article asserts:

7. For a useful discussion of the complexities of the conceptions of "intention," see Ronald Dworkin, The Forum of Principle, 56 N.Y.U.L. Rev. 447 (1981).

> The practice of statutory interpretation from the 18th through at least the mid-19th century suggests that the adopters assumed — if they assumed anything at all — a mode of interpretation that was more textualist than intentionalist. The plain meaning rule was frequently invoked: judicial recourse to legislative debate was virtually unknown and generally considered improper. Even after references to extrinsic sources became common, courts and commentators frequently asserted that the plain meaning of the text was the surest guide to the intent of the adopters.

The intended specificity of a provision is a matter of how much discretion the adopters intended to delegate to those charged with applying a provision:

> Consider, for example, the possible intentions of the adopters of the cruel and unusual punishment clause of the eighth amendment. They might have intended that the language serve only as a shorthand for the Stuart tortures which were their exemplary applications of the clause. Somewhat more broadly, they might have intended the clause to be understood to incorporate the principle of ejusdem generis — to include their exemplary applications and other punishments that they found or would have found equally repugnant.
>
> What of instances where the adopters' substantive intent was indeterminate — where even if they had adverted to a proposed application they would not have been certain how the clause should apply? Here it is plausible that — if they *had* a determinate interpretive intent — they intended to delegate to future decision makers the authority to apply the clause in light of the general principles underlying it. To use Ronald Dworkin's terms, the adopters would have intended future interpreters to develop their own "conceptions" of cruel and unusual punishment within the framework of the adopters' general "concept" of such punishments.
>
> What of a case where the adopters viewed a certain punishment as not cruel and unusual? This is not the same as saying that the adopters "intended not to prohibit the punishment." For even if they expected their laws to be interpreted by intentionalist canons, the adopters may have intended that their own views not always govern. Like parents who attempt to instill values in their child by both articulating and applying a moral principle, they may have accepted, or even invited, the eventuality that the principle would be applied in ways that diverge from their own views. The adopters may have understood that, even as to instances to which they believe the clause ought or ought not to apply, further thought by themselves or others committed to its underlying principle might lead them to change their minds. Not believing in their own omniscience or infallibility, they delegated the decision to those charged with interpreting the provision.[8] If such a motivation is plausible with respect to applications of the clause in the adopters' contemporary society, it is even more likely with respect to its application by future interpreters, whose un-

8. Cf. Garrison Keillor, Laying on Our Backs Looking up at the Stars, Newsweek, July 4, 1988, at 33.

> And we are hopeful about the progress of liberty and believe that the idea of equal rights that Americans have struggled with for two hundred years will be more perfectly realized and understood by our children and grandchildren.
>
> You will grow up less weighted down by fears and shame and all the rocks we carried in our pockets. You being easier about who you are will be less troubled by people who are different from you, whose names are strange, who are another color, who speak another language, pray to a different God or don't pray at all, whose feelings and opinions seem odd and even wrong, who put pickles on their hot dogs instead of onions and mustard; you will take them in stride as people.

derstanding of the clause will be affected by changing knowledge, technology, and forms of society.

The article then describes the interpreter-historian's task:

> The interpreter's task as historian can be divided into three stages or categories. First, she must immerse herself in the world of the adopters to try to understand constitutional concepts and values from their perspective. Second, at least the intentionalist must ascertain the adopters' interpretive intent and the intended scope of the provision in question. Third, she must often "translate" the adopters' concepts and intentions into our time and apply them to situations that the adopters did not foresee.
>
> The first stage is common to originalists of all persuasions. Although the textualist's aim is to understand and apply the language of a constitutional provision, she must locate the text in the linguistic and social contexts in which it was adopted. Similarly, the originalist "structuralist" interpreter must situate the institutions in their original contexts. The intentionalist . . . [must try] to discover a consensus of the adopters as manifested in the text of the provision itself, the history surrounding its adoption, and the ideologies and practices of the time.
>
> The essential difficulty posed by the distance that separates the modern interpreter from the objects of her interpretation has been succinctly stated by Quentin Skinner in addressing the analogous problem facing historians of political theory: "[I]t will never in fact be possible simply to study what any given classic writer has *said* . . . without bringing to bear some of one's own expectations about what he must have been saying. . . . [T]hese models and preconceptions in terms of which we unavoidably organize and adjust our perceptions and thoughts will themselves tend to act as determinants of what we think or perceive. We must classify in order to understand, and we can only classify the unfamiliar in terms of the familiar. The perpetual danger, in our attempts to enlarge our historical understanding, is thus that our expectations about what someone must be saying or doing will themselves determine that we understand the agent to be doing something which he would not — or even could not — himself have accepted as an account of what he *was* doing."
>
> The intentionalist interpreter must next ascertain the adopters' interpretive intent and the intended breadth of their provisions. That is, she must determine what the adopters intended future interpreters to make of their substantive views. Even if she can learn how the adopters intended contemporary interpreters to construe the Constitution, she cannot assume they intended the same canons to apply one or two hundred years later. Perhaps they wanted to bind the future as closely as possible to their own notions. Perhaps they intended a particular provision to be interpreted with increasing breadth as time went on. Or — more likely than not — the adopters may have had no intentions at all concerning these matters.
>
> For purposes of analytic clarity I have distinguished between (1) the adopters' interpretive intent and the intended scope of a provision and (2) their substantive intent concerning the application of the provision. If interpretive intent and intended scope can be ascertained at all, they may instruct the interpreter to adopt different canons of interpretation than she would prefer. Under these circumstances, the intentionalist interpreter may wish to ignore these intentions and limit her inquiry to the adopters' substantive intentions. Leaving aside the normative difficulty of such selective infidelity, this is a problematic strategy: To be a coherent theory of interpretation, intentionalism must distinguish between the adopters' personal *views* about an issue and their *intentions* concerning its constitutional resolution. And it is only by reference to their interpretive intent and the intended scope of a provision that this distinction can be drawn.

The interpreter's final task is to translate the adopters' intentions into the present in order to apply them to the question at issue. Consider, for example, whether the cruel and unusual punishment clause of the eighth amendment prohibits the imposition of the death penalty today. The adopters of the clause apparently never doubted that the death penalty was constitutional. But was death the same event for inhabitants of the American colonies in the late 18th century as it is two centuries later? Death was not only a much more routine and public phenomenon then, but the fear of death was more effectively contained within a system of religious belief. Twentieth-century Americans have a more secular cast of mind and seem less willing to accept this dreadful, forbidden, solitary, and shameful event. The interpreter must therefore determine whether we view the death penalty with the same attitude — whether of disgust or ambivalence — that the adopters viewed their core examples of cruel and unusual punishment.

Intentionalist interpretation frequently requires translations of this sort. For example, to determine whether the commerce clause applies to transactions taking place wholly within the boundaries of one state, or whether the first amendment protects the mass media, the interpreter must abstract the adopters' concepts of federalism and freedom of expression in order to find their analogue in our contemporary society with its different technology, economy, and systems of communication. The alternative would be to limit the application of constitutional provisions to the particular events and transactions with which the adopters were familiar. Even if such an approach were coherent, however, it would produce results that even a strict intentionalist could likely reject: Congress could not regulate any item of commerce or any mode of transportation that did not exist in 1789; the first amendment would not protect any means of communication not then known.

However difficult the earlier stages of her work, the interpreter was only trying to understand the past. The act of translation required here is different in kind, for it involves the counterfactual and imaginary act of projecting the adopters' concepts and attitudes into a future they probably could not have envisioned. When the interpreter engages in this sort of projection, she is in a fantasy world more of her own than of the adopters' making.

In The Original Understanding of Original Intent, 98 Harv. L. Rev. 885 (1985), Professor H. Jefferson Powell argues that the 1787 framers of the Constitution almost certainly did not view the Constitution as embodying their specific "intentions." Although judicial decisions of the time sometimes referred to "intent," this had little or nothing to do with "the subjective purposes of the author." Rather: "The late eighteenth century common lawyer conceived an instrument's 'intent' — and therefore its meaning — not as what the drafters meant by their words but rather as what judges, employing the 'artificial reason and judgment of law,' understood 'the reasonable and legal meaning' of those words to be." Similarly, courts when interpreting statutes made no use of legislative history. "English judges professed themselves bound to honor the true import of the 'express words' of Parliament. The 'intent of the act' and the 'intent of the legislature' were interchangeable terms; neither term implied that the interpreter looked at any evidence concerning that 'intent' other than the words of the text and the common law background of the statute."

Powell goes on specifically to discuss "James Madison's Theory of Constitutional Interpretation":

Madison's interpretive theory rested primarily on the distinction he drew between the public meaning or intent of a state paper, a law, or a constitution, and the personal opinions of the individuals who had written or adopted it. The distinction was implicit in the common law's treatment of the concept of "intent," but Madison made it explicit and thereby illuminated its implications and underlying rationale. . . . Responding to President Andrew Jackson's citation of a veto message Madison had sent Congress in 1817, Madison wrote [Martin Van Buren in 1830] that Jackson's use of his message had misconceived his personal views. But Madison conceded that Jackson might have correctly interpreted the public meaning of the message: "I am aware that the document must speak for itself, and that that intention cannot be substituted for [the intention derived through] the established rules of interpretation."

. . . With respect to the Constitution, Madison described his knowledge of the views actually held by the delegates to the Philadelphia and Virginia conventions as a possible source of "bias" in his constitutional interpretations. . . . "As a guide in expounding and applying the provisions of the Constitution, the debates and incidental decisions of the Convention can have no authoritative character."

Madison employed the distinction between public meaning and private intent to differentiate the relative value of the various sources of information to which constitutional interpreters might turn for evidence on "the intention of the States." The text itself, of course, was the primary source from which that intention was to be gathered, but Madison's awareness of the imperfect nature of human communication led him to concede that the text's import would frequently be unclear. Madison thought it proper to engage in structural inference in the classic contractual mode of the Virginia and Kentucky Resolutions, and to consult the direct expressions of state intention available in the resolutions of the ratifying conventions. He regarded the debates in those conventions to be of real yet limited value for the interpreter: evidentiary problems with the surviving records and Madison's insistence on distinguishing the binding public intention of the state from the private opinions of any individuals, or group of individuals, including those gathered at a state convention, led him to conclude that the state debates could bear no more than indirect and corroborative witness to the meaning of the Constitution. Madison allowed that the contemporaneous expositions of the document by its supporters were of some value, but he cautioned that such statements were to be regarded strictly as private opinions, useful chiefly in shedding light upon the meaning of words and phrases that the fluidity of language might gradually change over time. Last and least in value were the records of the Philadelphia convention. . . .

The dichotomy between public meaning and private intent also informed Madison's view of constitutional precedent. He consistently thought that "*usus,*" the exposition of the Constitution provided by actual governmental practice and judicial precedents, could "settle its meaning and the intention of its authors." Here, too, he was building on a traditional foundation: the common law had regarded usage as valid evidence of the meaning of ancient instruments, and had regarded judicial determinations of that meaning even more highly. Applying this view of interpretation to the Constitution, Madison felt himself compelled to change his position on the controversial issue of Congress's constitutional power to incorporate a national bank. In the first Congress, Representative Madison opposed on constitutional grounds the bill establishing the First Bank of the United States; as President, Madison twenty years later signed into law the act creating the Second Bank. "But even here the inconsistency," Madison assured a correspondent, "is apparent only, not real." His own "abstract opinion of the text" remained unchanged: the words of the Constitution did not authorize Congress to establish the bank. Nevertheless, he recognized that Congress, the President, the Supreme Court, and (most important, by failing to use their amending power) the American people had for two decades accepted the existence and made use of the services of the First Bank, and he viewed this wide-spread acceptance as "a construction put on the Constitution by the nation, which, having made it, had the supreme right to declare its meaning." He had signed the Second Bank bill, Madison declared, in accordance with his "early and unchanged opinion" that such a construction by usage and precedent should override the intellectual scruples of the individual. . . . In Madison's eyes, precedents — at least those derived from "authoritative, deliberate, and continued decisions" — served to "fix the interpretation of a law." Furthermore, Madison claimed, this view represented not just his opinion, but the general expectation — the "interpretive intention" — that prevailed at the time of the Constitution's framing and ratification: "It could not but happen, and was foreseen at the birth of the Constitution, that difficulties and differences of opinion might occasionally arise in expounding terms and phrases necessarily used in such charter . . . and that it might require a regular course of practice to liquidate and settle the meaning of some of them."

. . . To the end of his life, Madison warned his fellow citizens against expansive innovations in constitutional interpretation, "new principles and new constructions, that may remove the landmarks of power." But however strongly he might have fought constitutional error when it first appeared, for Madison there could be no return to the unadorned text from interpretations that had received the approbation of the people. The Constitution is a public document, and its interpretation, for Madison, was in the end a public process.

Discussion

Can you make a plausible argument that an interpreter should focus only on the adopters' "substantive intent" and not feel bound by their "interpretive intent" (to the extent it can be ascertained)? How readily can an author's substantive and interpetive intent be separated?

Perhaps the best known contemporary proponent of "the jurisprudence of original intent" is former Judge Robert H. Bork, who has written that "[t]he interpretation of the Constitution according to the original understanding . . . is the only method that can preserve the Constitution, the separation of powers, and the liberties of the people."[9] During the hearings following his (ultimately unsuccessful) nomination to the Supreme Court by President Ronald Reagan Pennsylvania Senator Arlen Specter asked Judge Bork about his support for *Brown,* in view of its apparent deviation from the original understanding of the framers of the Fourteenth Amendment. Bork responded:[10]

> [P]assing [some] historical evidence, which I think casts some doubt on the flat assumption that the 14th Amendment really meant separate but equal, let me say this. [The framers] wrote a clause that does not say anything about separation. They wrote a clause that says "equal protection of the laws."
>
> I think it may well be true . . . that they had an assumption . . . that equality could be achieved with separation. Over the years it became clear that that assumption would not be borne out in reality ever. Separation would never produce equality.
>
> I think when the background assumption proved false, it was entirely proper for the court to say "we will carry out the rule they wrote" and if they would have been a

9. Bork, The Tempting of America: The Political Seduction of the Law 159 (1989).

10. Nomination of Robert H. Bork to be Associate Justice of the Supreme Court of the United States, Hearings Before the Committee on the Judiciary, United States Senate, Part I, 284-286 (1987).

little surprised that it worked out this way, that is too bad. That is the rule they wrote and they assumed something that is not true.

And in that way I do not think any damage is done — you can even look at it more severely. You could say suppose they had written a clause that said "we want equality and that can be achieved by separation and we want that too."

By 1954 it was perfectly apparent that you could not have both equality and separation. Now the court has to violate one aspect or the other of that clause, as I have framed it hypothetically. It seems to me that the way the actual amendment was written, it was natural to choose the equality segment, and the court did so. I think it was proper constitutional law, and I think we are all better off for it.

Note that Judge Bork's hypothetical amendment subordinates the goal of maintaining separation to that of equality, so that if they come into conflict, the former should give way. Suppose, however, that the hypothetical amendment read, "We want equality, but not if it requires mixing the races in schools or other such places." Is one or the other hypothetical version more plausible as an historical reconstruction? Does our presumed preference for Bork's version rest on anything more than the more attractive contemporary outcomes that it allows?

4. *Some Other Examples of Fourteenth Amendment Decisions Having Problematic Originalist Roots*

a. The Original Understanding of the Fifth Amendment

Whatever your conclusions about *Brown,* is Bolling v. Sharpe, 347 U.S. 497 (1954), consistent with originalism of any sort? In *Bolling,* which was decided on the same day as *Brown,* the Court held that the due process clause of the Fifth Amendment prohibited racial segregation in the District of Columbia schools. Chief Justice Warren wrote for the Court:

The Fifth Amendment, which is applicable in the District of Columbia, does not contain an equal protection clause as does the Fourteenth Amendment which applies only to the states. But the concepts of equal protection and due process, both stemming from our American ideal of fairness, are not mutually exclusive. The "equal protection of the laws" is a more explicit safeguard of prohibited unfairness than "due process of law," and, therefore, we do not imply that the two are always interchangeable phrases. But, as this Court has recognized, discrimination may be so unjustifiable as to be violative of due process. . . .

Although the Court has not assumed to define "liberty" with any great precision, that term is not confined to mere freedom from bodily restraint. Liberty under law extends to the full range of conduct which the individual is free to pursue, and it cannot be restricted except for a proper governmental objective. Segregation in public education is not reasonably related to any proper governmental objective, and thus it imposes on Negro children of the District of Columbia a burden that constitutes an arbitrary deprivation of their liberty in violation of the Due Process Clause.

In view of our decision that the Constitution prohibits the states from maintaining racially segregated public schools, it would be unthinkable that the same Constitution would impose a lesser duty on the Federal Government. We hold that racial segregation in the public schools of the District of Columbia is a denial of the due process of law guaranteed by the Fifth Amendment to the Constitution.

In 1789, the due process clause of the Fifth Amendment concerned only the fairness of adjudicatory procedures (e.g., notice, the opportunity for a hearing). Compare Chapter 9, infra. In this light, consider the following exerpt from the Senate confirmation hearings of Judge Bork.[11]

Senator Specter: [H]ow can you justify Bolling v. Sharpe applying the due process clause to stopping segregation?

Judge Bork: I do not know that anybody ever has. I think that has been a case that has left people puzzled, and I have been told that some Justices on the Supreme Court felt very queasy afterwards about Bolling v. Sharpe. . . . I think that constitutionally that is a troublesome case.

Now it has been suggested that if the Supreme Court had struck down segregation in all of the States under the equal protection clause, Congress most certainly would have stopped segregation in the District of Columbia. And it would have been a national scandal if they had not.

Bolling v. Sharpe seems to have been propelled by a feeling that if we are going to do this to all of the States, we cannot let the federal government do it. I understand that feeling. . . . [But] if they apply the due process clause that way, . . . [y]ou are off and running with substantive due process which I have long thought is a pernicious constitutional idea. . . .

Senator Specter: Final question: Do you accept Bolling v. Sharpe or not?

Judge Bork: I have not thought of a rationale for it. . . .

Senator Specter: You say you have or have not?

Judge Bork: Have not. . . . [I]f you say it is due process and we will do whatever is fair or good under due process, the court's powers are unlimited. That is the problem I have with that substantive due process.

Consider also Professor Hans Linde's rejoinder to *Bolling:*[12]

[T]here is nothing difficult or even surprising in the thought that the "same Constitution," in the equal protection clause of 1868, might impose upon the states congressionally enforceable standards of equal treatment beyond that imposed upon the federal government by the Fifth Amendment in 1791 — at least nothing unthinkable if the premises for this thought are to be found in the text, the history, or the political structure of the Constitution. What defied thought in *Bolling* was the suggestion that a mere doctrinal distinction between the Fifth and Fourteenth Amendments could confine the scope of a revolution in the constitutional law of race relations. . . . But the unthinkable often bears thought.

11. Id. at 286-287.
12. Hans Linde, Judges, Critics, and the Realist Tradition, 82 Yale L.J. 227, 233-234 (1972). Professor Linde goes on to suggest that Congress would have prohibited segregation in the District of Columbia within a few years.

b. The Fourteenth Amendment and Voting Rights

Since the 1964 *Reapportionment Cases*, p. 1073 infra, the Court has held that the equal protection clause prohibits discrimination in matters affecting the franchise. In the first reapportionment decision, Reynolds v. Sims, 377 U.S. 533 (1964), Justice Harlan argued in dissent that this contradicted the original understanding of the Fourteenth Amendment. He noted that many proponents of the Amendment expressly stated that section 1 did not interfere with states' regulation of the franchise, that section 2 provides the Amendment's sole remedy for a state's denial of suffrage, and that it required the Fifteenth Amendment to prohibit abridging the right to vote "on account of race, color, or previous condition of servitude" and the Nineteenth Amendment to add sex to the prohibited classifications. Although the original understanding of the Amendment is arguably more complex, there is considerable scholarly support for Justice Harlan's reading of the history.[13] Imagine a Constitution that does not include the Fifteenth and Nineteenth Amendments but *does* include the Thirteenth and Fourteenth. Even if you agree with Justice Harlan's reading of the original history of the Fourteenth Amendment, does this necessarily prevent Congress or the courts from prohibiting racial or gender discrimination in the franchise under sections 1 and 5 of the Fourteenth Amendment?

5. *Against Originalism?*

In Lions Under the Throne 3 (1947), Charles Curtis asserts that "[t]he intention of the framers of the Constitution, even assuming we could discover what it was, when it is not adequately expressed in the Constitution, that is to say, what they meant when they did not say it, surely has no binding force on us." On what theories might you argue for fidelity to the text of the Constitution but not to the intentions of its adopters?

In the article excerpted above (at 224), Brest argues normatively that, while an interpreter should take *account* of the text and original understanding of the Constitution, she is not *bound* by either:

> What authority does the written Constitution have in our system of constitutional government? This is not an empty question. The English experience demonstrates that a constitutional democracy — a government of limited powers ultimately responsible to its citizens — need not be premised on a written document. And although article VI declares that the Constitution is the "supreme law of the land," a document cannot achieve the status of law, let alone supreme law, merely by its own assertion.
>
> According to the political theory most deeply rooted in the American tradition, the authority of the Constitution derives from the consent of its adopters. Even if the adopters freely consented to the Constitution, however, this is not an adequate basis for continuing fidelity to the founding document, for their consent cannot

13. See Minor v. Happersatt and accompanying discussion, page 241 supra.

bind succeeding generations. We did not adopt the Constitution, and those who did are dead and gone.

Given the questionable authority of the American Constitution — indeed, of any (quasi) revolutionary constitution at the moment of its inception — it is only through a history of continuing assent or acquiescence that the document could become law. Our constitutional tradition, however, has not focused on the document alone, but on the decisions and practices of courts and other institutions. And this tradition has included major elements of nonoriginalism. The doctrines described in the conclusion to Part One[14] are as well-settled parts of the constitutional landscape as most originalist-based doctrines. They are among the principal subjects that occupy professionals who "do" constitutional law — lawyers, judges, law professors and law students — and are considered part of constitutional law by the media and by the lay public. A description of the American legal system that omitted them or treated them as aberrational would be extraordinarily inaccurate. To make the point affirmatively, the practice of supplementing and derogating from the text and original understanding is itself part of our constitutional tradition.

The fact of this tradition undermines the exclusivity of the written document. It does not, however, establish the legitimacy of nonoriginalism. Acquiescence is not the same as "consent," which must be informed and knowingly and freely given. Those conditions have not in fact been met, and perhaps can never be met in a large industrial society.

Actual consent is not, then, a practicable measure of the legitimacy of any system of government, and a fortiori not of a particular practice or institution. Owen Fiss has suggested that it is not even an appropriate measure of institutional legitimacy: "Consent goes to the system, not the particular institution; it operates on the whole rather than on each part. The legitimacy of particular institutions, such as courts, depends not on the consent — implied or otherwise — of the people, but rather on their *competence,* on the special contribution they make to the quality of our social life. Legitimacy depends on the capacity of the institution to perform a function within the political system and its willingness to respect the limitations on that function." Whether or not the practices of constitutional decisionmaking should ideally be validated by consent as well as competence, I think we must accept Professor Fiss' observation faute de mieux.

To whatever extent this argument is plausible, it raises the obvious question: If an interpreter is not bound by the text of the Constitution or the intentions of its adopters, then what *does* bind her? This question was presented by a number of the cases in Part One and is a central and explicit issue throughout Part Two, which will examine various approaches to nonoriginalist adjudication. For the moment, consider Professor Henry Monaghan's suggestion that stare decisis may play an essential role.

14. Part One concludes that "an originalist, whether of textualist or intentionalist persuasion, would have difficulties justifying (1) the incorporation of the principles of equal protection into the fifth amendment, (2) the incorporation of provisions of the Bill of Rights into the fourteenth amendment, (3) the more general notion of substantive due process, including the minimal rational relationship standard, and (4) the practice of judicial review of congressional legislation established by Marbury v. Madison. Although these doctrines strain or go beyond the text of the Constitution, . . . one cannot say with certainty that they are not authorized by the original understanding. However, the legitimacy of their origins cannot be established with much certainty."

HENRY MONAGHAN, STARE DECISIS AND CONSTITUTIONAL ADJUDICATION

88 Colum. L. Rev. 723, 728-729, 744-753, 757-758 (1988)

. . . [D]ifficulties with originalism emerge once the existing constitutional order is actually examined. The Supreme Court's repeated invocations of the Framers' understanding notwithstanding, a significant portion of our constitutional order cannot reasonably be reconciled with original understanding. For example, it is now increasingly acknowledged "that those who wrote and ratified the Fourteenth Amendment believed that it would permit racial segregation in public schools." Consequently, unless they are willing to see it overruled, Brown v. Board of Education presents deep difficulties for those who insist upon original understanding as the only legitimate canon for constitutional adjudication. . . .

In addition to *Brown,* it seems evident that the abortion cases, the reapportionment cases, and the sex discrimination cases are also inconsistent with any constrained conception of the original understanding.

Nor is that the end of the difficulties. Even on the assumption, itself controversial, that the fourteenth amendment was intended to make the Bill of Rights applicable to the states, much of the actual judicial development of the Bill of Rights has taken very little from original understanding. . . .

[S]tare decisis plays a very large role in constitutional law. Many constitutional issues are so far settled that they are simply off the agenda. For example, it seems clear that under the 1789 Constitution only metal could constitute legal tender. In fact, until driven to do so by the exigencies of the Civil War, the national government never attempted to impart that quality to paper. When the government did take this step the result was a series of post-Civil War decisions, collectively known as the *Legal Tender Cases.* While they "have [now] disappeared below the surface of American constitutional law . . . [m]easured by the intensity of the public debate at the time, [these cases raised] one of the leading constitutional controversies in American history." Following this painful conflict and one of the most widely criticized overrulings of precedent, use of paper money as legal tender was sustained. Over one hundred years later, in our age of checks, credit cards and electronic banking, the issue is off the agenda: no Supreme Court would now reexamine the merits, no matter how closely wedded it was to original intent theory and no matter how certain it was of its predecessor's error.

. . . [M]any of the fundamental transformations in our governmental structure legitimated by the Supreme Court in this century are unquestionably above challenge. Is it conceivable that the Court would outlaw the administrative state? Certainly administrative legislation, in some substantial form, is a permanent feature of our constitutional order. And while the Court may or may not honor *Garcia* in the future, it cannot be doubted that as a constitutional matter the federal government's regulatory power is more aptly described as limitless than limited. The constitutional law, if not the political dimensions of the New Deal, is here to stay.

The operation of stare decisis in these contexts is agenda limiting in nature. The Court could not fairly look at these issues *res nova.* Regardless of whether the Court thought these issues rightly decided, consciously or unconsciously any challenge would be screened out *in limine*. History counts. The only significant question is how. . . .

At this juncture the pertinent question is whether stare decisis should have any substantial role in cases where the issues remain contested. . . .

Suppose that the Court were composed of a solid majority who believe that *Roe* was incorrectly decided. What *should* happen? Whether *Roe* should be overruled is a question not reducible to whether *Roe* was decided correctly. One can imagine the Court drawing precisely such a distinction and refusing to overrule *Roe*. Of course, to make this distinction one needs a general theory of constitutional interpretation that includes some account of precedent. . . .

Precedent is, of course, part of our understanding of what law is. But that acknowledgement does not resolve the question why it plays such an important role. Generally, judicial adherence to precedent is defended by pointing to the important values in decisionmaking that are promoted thereby: consistency, coherence, fairness, equality, predictability and efficiency. Perhaps, as is sometimes suggested, these values are largely obtainable without any formal doctrine of stare decisis. Be that as it may, I believe that any meaningful role for stare decisis in constitutional adjudication must draw on more powerful considerations, weighty enough to predominate even when the consitutional issues involved are of the first order. For us, those considerations are bottomed upon the concept of legitimation. . . .

At its most general level, stare decisis operates to promote system-wide stability and continuity by ensuring the survival of governmental norms that have achieved unsurpassed importance in American society. Such norms include the freedom from racial discrimination by the government, the general reach of the commerce clause, and even the legality of paper money. Expectations, tangible and symbolic, have developed around the critical decisions; the massive destabilization following a successful attack on any of these would threaten the functioning of the federal government, if not the viability of the constitutional order itself. . . .

Stability and continuity, however, are not the only important constitutional values, and sometimes even these values cannot be achieved without change. Thus, even this argument cannot establish the absolute priority of precedent over text. But constitutional law is in the end a matter of government, and the Court is a part of that Government. Although *Brown* will forever remind us that the Supreme Court can occasionally act as a catalyst in generating profound social change, the Court also plays an important role in our government by conserving and perpetuating shared values. In that respect, the very existence of a body of precedent is a conservative, stabilizing force. . . .

There is, however, a second, and perhaps more universal justification for the application of stare decisis to contested matters, one that also arises from a rationale concerned with stability and continuity. Namely, the Court must strive to demonstrate — at least to elites — the continuing legitimacy of judicial review. A general judicial adherence to constitutional precedent supports a consensus about the rule of law, specifically the belief that all organs of government, including the Court, are bound by the law. At first blush it may seem perverse to defend the idea that the Court maintains its subservience to the fundamental law by upholding decisions that depart from that law. But this difficulty is not insurmountable. What the Constitution requires is often a matter for debate, and once having been adequately canvassed and resolved by the Court, an issue might presumptively remain at rest. Even when the prior judicial resolution seems plainly wrong to a majority of the present Court, adherence to precedent can contribute to the important notion that the law is impersonal in character, that the Court believes itself to be following a "law which binds [it] as well as the litigants." In listing the weighty considerations supporting adherence to precedent, Justice Harlan included "the necessity of maintaining public faith in the judiciary as a source of impersonal and reasoned judgments."

. . . [S]tare decisis must require more of a court than simply exploring the precedents as possible models for current decisionmaking. In some sense, the second must feel *bound* by the precedent. . . .

In the American common law, stare decisis states a conditional obligation: precedent binds absent a showing of substantial countervailing considerations. This formulation is not vacuous, or rather, it need not be. Nearly one-half century ago, Dean Pound wrote:

> Just how binding is "binding authority" in our common law technique? A single decision has never been regarded as absolutely binding at all events. But, on the other hand, it had become established that nothing less than an overriding conviction that a precept fixed by a prior decision was contrary to the principles of the law so that it had an ill effect upon the process of determining new questions by analogical reasoning and was, as Blackstone puts it, "flatly" unjust in its results, could justify judicial rejection of it.

A similar formulation seems appropriate for constitutional adjudication. Even an "overriding conviction" of prior error is not enough; the precedent must have some palpable adverse consequences beyond its existence. . . .

[Recall the debate between Justices Scalia and Marshall, pp. 35-37 supra.]

Note: Reflections on the Opinion in **Brown**

Few opinions of the Supreme Court have been more controversial than Chief Justice Warren's in Brown v. Board of Education. Any decision dealing with so sensitive an issue was bound to be controversial, but both the reasoning and style of *Brown* were criticized even by commentators who supported the outcome. For example, the day after the decision, May 18, 1954, James Reston wrote in the New York Times that the Court had rejected "history, philosophy, and custom" in basing its decision in "the primacy of the general welfare. . . . Relying more on the social scientists than on legal precedents — a procedure often in controversy in the past — the Court insisted on equality of the mind and heart rather than on equal school facilities. . . . The Court's opinion read more like an expert paper on sociology than a Supreme Court opinion."[15]

Warren's desire had been to write an opinion that was "short, readable by the lay public, nonrhetorical, unemotional and, above all, non-accusatory."[16] When

15. Quoted in Richard Kluger, Simple Justice 711 (1975), a detailed and excellent study of the background of *Brown*. See also Edmund Kahn, Jurisprudence, 30 N.Y.U.L. Rev. 150 (1955) (criticizing reliance on problematic social science evidence).

16. Kluger, supra note 15, at 711.

Justice Jackson asked his law clerk, Barrett Prettyman, what he thought of the draft opinion circulated by the Chief Justice, Prettyman commented:

> I wished that it had more law in it but I didn't find anything glaringly unacceptable in it. The genius of the Warren opinion was that it was so simple and unobtrusive. He had come from political life and had a keen sense of what you could say in this opinion without getting everybody's back up. His opinion took the sting off the decision, it wasn't accusatory, and it didn't pretend that the Fourteenth Amendment was more helpful than the history suggested — he didn't equivocate on that point.[17]

However well you think the opinion succeeded in its goals, the fact is that Earl Warren *had* goals — "extralegal" ones, if you like — for it. Besides those already mentioned, he strongly desired that the Court speak with one voice on this controversial question: Achieving unanimity, even among Justices who were committed to the outcome, was no small accomplishment.[18] Moreover, it was only in the last week before the decision was handed down that the Chief Justice persuaded Justice Reed not to file a dissenting opinion:

> After the Chief Justice had left, Reed asked [his law clerk, George] Mickum, who had been raised in a community with segregated schools, how he felt about the Justice's going along with the rest of the Court. Mickum, a man not notably more convinced of the natural equality of the Negro than Reed himself was, suggested that the demands of conscience seemed to require his going beyond the knowable facts in the case and asking himself, as Warren had, what was best for America. "I think he was really troubled by the possible consequences of his position," Mickum adds. "Because he was a Southerner, even a lone dissent by him would give a lot of people a lot of grist for making trouble. For the good of the country, he put aside his own basis for dissent." The only condition he extracted from Warren for going along, Mickum believes, was a pledge that the Court implementation decree would allow segregation to be dismantled gradually instead of being wrenched apart.[19]

It is difficult to achieve even an "opinion of the Court," let alone a unanimous opinion, without compromises of language and, sometimes, the scope of the holding as well. Consider, for example, Justice Frankfurter's recollection of Justice Holmes' opinion for the Court in the *Pipe Line Cases*, 234 U.S. 548 (1914), which sustained a congressional act declaring interstate pipe lines to be common carriers and requiring the major oil producers who owned them to carry the oil of minor competitors:[20]

> The *Pipeline* case was an important case, but not complicated on its facts, and it didn't require a vast amount of what we call legal research, certainly not for Holmes. One thing is incontestable, and that is that it took all this time to get the case out not because Holmes took a lot of time to write the opinion. Considering the nature of the legislation and the make-up of the Court, one can be sure that there were differences within the Court. The ground that seems to you and to me obvious on which to sustain the constitutionality of the statute, namely, that under the Commerce Clause

17. Id. at 697.
18. See id. at 582-699.
19. Id. at 698.
20. Conversations with Mr. Justice Frankfurter 292-296 (Oral History Collection of Columbia University 1956). See also Frankfurter Reminisces 344-346 (Phillips ed. 1960).

> Congress has power to deal with the more or less economic monopoly as much as it has in dealing with a legal monopoly such as a franchise implies, that ground which, I have no doubt, would commend itself to Holmes in the light of his past opinions and might commend itself to one or two other people on the Court, might be a little frightening to others on the Court to whom "liberty of contract" and the distinction between private carrier and common carrier is almost as deep and immutable as the differences between the sexes. Therefore, the problem was to get out an opinion that is not disturbing for the future, which sustains this legislation, and gives little further encouragement to the underlying economic impulse behind the legislation which some of the boys certainly feared. . . .
>
> When I came into possession of . . . the opinion as originally circulated in the *Pipeline* case and the opinion that finally became the opinion of the Court, the documents revealed that Holmes did go on this essentially economic justification for Congressional interference, but the boys wouldn't stand for it. In all the years Holmes was on the Court, from 1902 to 1932, in no other case did he write and re-write and circulate and re-circulate with a view to getting an agreement on the part of the Court, and the thing that now appears is an eviscerated document, a castration really, not an evisceration, a castration of his original opinion. And in his own annotation on his copy of the opinion . . . Holmes wrote in his own handwriting, "This is a wholly unsatisfactory opinion," and then stated why it was unsatisfactory. . . . The vital fact is that the statute was sustained. When you have to have at least five people to agree on something, they can't have that comprehensive completeness of candor which is open to a single man, giving his own reasons untrammeled by what anybody else may do or not do if he put that out. . . .[21]

From the cases read so far, you have noticed that the Court has often issued judgments without being unanimous. When and why might the Justices subordinate individual differences and strive to speak with (more or less) one voice? *Brown* suggests one occasion — when the Justices believe that the decision is likely to meet with resistance and therefore wish to invoke the impersonal authority of "the Court." (The decision in United States v. Nixon, 418 U.S. 683 (1974), requiring President Nixon to turn over certain tapes to the Watergate special prosecutor was also unanimous.)[22]

Justice Reed's comments suggest that the judges who silently concur, as well as opinion-writers themselves, must sometimes choose between the desire to express personal views and the benefits of an institutional view. The justices' propensity to write separate concurring and dissenting opinions has varied at different times. Leaving aside the early Court's practice of issuing seriatim opinions, the number of separate opinions may now be at an all-time high. In Furman v. Georgia, 408 U.S. 238 (1972), which struck down various schemes for impos-

21. At this point, the interviewer (Harlan Phillips), who had interviewed John W. Davis several years earlier, recounted the following story to Justice Frankfurter:

> You may be interested in a story I got from John W. Davis on the *Pipeline* case, the first case he argued as Solicitor General. As he put it, he jumped into the stream as it flowed by, and he waited all year for the opinion. After it came down, he had occasion to visit Justice Holmes, and he made some comment to the effect that he was glad the government won, but that he was not entirely happy with the opinion. Mr. Davis reported that Holmes said, "Well, that's the trouble. I write out my opinions, and I send them around to my brethren. One of them picks out a plum here, and the other picks out a plum there, and they send it back to me with nothing but a shapeless mass of dough to father!"

22. See Scott Armstrong and Robert Woodward, The Brethren 285-347 (1979), for a description of the Court's internal bargaining to achieve unanimity in this case.

ing the death penalty, there were nine separate opinions and no opinion for the Court. There were eight separate opinions in the *Pentagon Papers* case, New York Times Co. v. United States, 403 U.S. 713 (1971), p.530 supra. The differences among the opinions in such cases often seem matters more of nuance than of disagreement over fundamental legal principles. "The variety," Archibald Cox suggests, "must be attributed partly to unwillingness to yield personal preferences and partly to the desire to influence the future."[23] As a consequence, the Court fails "to achieve the consensus necessary to maintain an ever-growing yet continuous body of law." That is to say, one cannot tell what the Court held.

The preceding discussion raises a more fundamental question. Opinion writing has always been the general practice in Anglo-American courts,[24] but why *should* courts write opinions to support the judgments they render? Besides the criticism directed at Chief Justice Warren's opinion in *Brown,* the Court was criticized for a series of per curiam decisions — summary decisions not accompanied by any opinion — immediately following *Brown*. Herbert Wechsler wrote:[25]

> Here . . . the Court has written on the merits of the constitutional issue posed by state segregation only once. . . . The original opinion, you recall, was firmly focused on state segregation in the public schools, its reasoning accorded import to the nature of the educational process, and its conclusion was that separate educational facilities are "inherently unequal."
>
> What shall we think then of the Court's extension of the ruling to other public facilities, such as public transportation, parks, golf courses, bath houses, and beaches, which no one is obliged to use — all by per curiam decisions? That these situations present a weaker case against state segregation is not, of course, what I am saying. I am saying that the question whether it is stronger, weaker, or of equal weight appears to me to call for principled decision. I do not know, and I submit you cannot know, whether the per curiam affirmance in the *Dawson* case, involving public bath houses and beaches, embraced the broad opinion of the circuit court that all state-enforced racial segregation is invalid or approved only its immediate result and, if the latter, on what ground. Is this "process of law," to borrow the words Professor Brown has used so pointedly in writing of such unexplained decisions upon matters far more technical — the process that alone affords the Court its title and its duty to adjudicate a claim that state action is repugnant to the Constitution?

23. Archibald Cox, Freedom of Expression in the Burger Court, 94 Harv. L. Rev. 1, 25 (1980). But see Frank Easterbrook, Ways of Criticizing the Court, 95 Harv. L. Rev. 802 (1982).

24. See Report of the Committee of Managers on the Causes of the Duration of Mr. Hastings Trial, 4 Speeches of Edmund Burke 200-201 (1816): "Your committee do not find any positive law which binds the judges of the courts in Westminister-Hall publicly to give a reasoned opinion from the bench, in support of their judgments upon matters that are stated before them. But the course has prevailed from the oldest times. It hath been so general and so uniform, that it must be considered the law of the land." Cf. Goldberg v. Kelly, 397 U.S. 254 (1970), holding that due process requires an administrative official to support his decision with reasons. The constitutions or statutes of several states require written opinions. See, e.g., Cal. Const., art. VI, §2: "all decisions of the [Supreme Court] . . . shall be given in writing, and the ground of the decision shall be stated." See Max Radin, The Requirement of Written Opinions, 18 Calif. L. Rev. 486 (1930). For a comparative perspective, see Jean Louis Goutal, The Dynamics of Justification: A Comparative Study of Reasons in Civil Judgments (1974) (unpublished thesis in Stanford Law School Library). But see David Currie, The Constitution in the Supreme Court: 1789-1801, 48 U. Chi. L. Rev. 819 (1981) (U.S. Supreme Court seldom wrote opinions in the eighteenth century). Even today, federal district courts and courts of appeals do not publish all of their opinions.

25. Herbert Wechsler, Toward Neutral Principles of Constitutional Law, 73 Harv. L. Rev. 1, 22-23 (1959). See also Albert Sacks, Foreword to the Supreme Court, 1953 Term, 68 Harv. L. Rev. 96 (1954).

Richard Wasserstrom explains the reasons for judicial opinion-writing in this way:[26]

> [I]f the legal system ought to be free from the biases, partialities, and like peculiarities of the judges who render decisions, [the procedures for deciding cases] must have at least three characteristics. First, under such procedures there should be certain independent criteria by which the one who makes a decision can evaluate the conclusion reached or the course of action decided upon. This requirement ensures, among other things, that the proponent of any plan of behavior must first persuade himself on "external" grounds of the desirability of his proposal. The second, and perhaps a more significant, requirement is that the justification for any proposal should be submitted to and should be able to withstand public examination. For the prerequisite of publicity provides what has consistently proved to be the most effective means by which the enthusiasms of the advocate and the visions of the would-be seer can be measured against the less personal and more sober and disinterested wisdom of the community. To require that the grounds of a decision be made public is to insist that an avenue of independent verification and criticism be kept open. The third requirement, which is closely related to the first two, stipulates that *all* the grounds or reasons for the decision be both revealed and evaluated. It insists that the processes of argumentation, justification, and enlightened persuasion not be prematurely cut short. It demands that the process of justification continue until the "ultimate" premise upon which any decision stands and from which it draws its claim for acceptability is fully revealed. For it is only after this point has been reached that it is legitimate — if it is ever legitimate — to conclude that grounds for intelligent discussion no longer in fact exist. To urge that these requirements be present is to insist that men be *rational* — in the best sense of the word — so that the conclusions they have reached may be as accurate as possible, and the conduct undertaken as beneficial as possible.
>
> The central role that rational inquiry and justification should play in the law has been nicely indicated in an essay by John Dewey, entitled Logical Method and Law. "Courts not only reach decisions; they expound them, and the exposition must state justifying reasons. . . . Exposition implies that a definitive solution is reached, that the situation is now determinate with respect to its legal implication. Its purpose is to set forth grounds for the decision reached so that it will not appear as an arbitrary dictum, and so that it will indicate a rule for dealing with similar cases in the future. It is highly probable that the need of justifying to others conclusions reached and decisions made has been the chief cause of the origin and development of logical operations in the precise sense; of abstraction, generalization, regard for consistency of implications. It is quite conceivable that if no one had ever had to account to others for his decisions, logical operations would never have developed, but men would use exclusively methods of inarticulate intuition and impression, feeling; so that only after considerable experience in accounting for their decisions to others who demanded a reason, or exculpation, and were not satisfied till they got it, did men begin to give an account to themselves of the process of reaching a conclusion in a justified way. However this may be, it is certain that in judicial decisions the only alternative to arbitrary dicta, accepted by the parties to a controversy only because of the authority or prestige of the judge, is a rational statement which formulates grounds and exposes connecting or logical links."

As Wasserstrom suggests, the practice of publishing opinions serves other interests besides "testing" the validity of decisions. Suppose that the Court usually

26. Richard Wasserstrom, The Judicial Decision 92-97 (1961).

stated the facts of the case and announced its judgments ("affirmed," "reversed," etc.) without opinion. Consider the difficulties that citizens, legislatures, officials, courts, and the Supreme Court itself at a later time would have determining the scope and implications of particular decisions. And consider the effect such a practice would have on the ability of lawyers and academic commentators to make informed criticisms of the Court's work.[27]

D. Three Decades of School Desegregation

1. Brown *and Its Immediate Aftermath*

The Court's opinion in Brown v. Board of Education concluded by setting the cases for reargument on the question of appropriate relief. In *Brown II*, 349 U.S. 294 (1955), Chief Justice Warren again wrote for a unanimous Court:

> Full implementation of [the principle announced in *Brown*] may require solution of varied local school problems. School authorities have the primary responsibility for elucidating, assessing, and solving these problems; courts will have to consider whether the action of school authorities constitutes good faith implementation of the governing constitutional principles. Because of their proximity to local conditions and the possible need for further hearings, the courts which originally heard these cases can best perform this judicial appraisal. Accordingly, we believe it appropriate to remand the cases to those courts.
>
> In fashioning and effectuating the decrees, the courts will be guided by equitable principles. Traditionally, equity has been characterized by a practical flexibility in shaping its remedies and by a facility for adjusting and reconciling public and private needs. These cases call for the exercise of these traditional attributes of equity power. At stake is the personal interest of the plaintiffs in admission to public schools as soon as practicable on a nondiscriminatory basis. To effectuate this interest may call for elimination of a variety of obstacles in making the transition to school systems operated in accordance with the constitutional principles set forth in our

27. Any recent volume of the United States Reports will show that the Court often cites and sometimes responds to critical law review articles. In Erie R.R. v. Tompkins, 304 U.S. 64 (1938), the Court relied heavily on Charles Warren's New Light on the History of the Federal Judiciary Act of 1789, 37 Harv. L. Rev. 49 (1923), in overruling Swift v. Tyson, 41 U.S. (16 Pet.) 1 (1842). See also Clyde Jacobs, Law Writers and the Courts (1954), studying the influence of the academy on the course of economic due process. See Charles Evans Hughes, Foreword, 50 Yale L.J. 737 (1941):

> I well remember that thirty years ago Mr. Justice Holmes would refer somewhat scornfully to the "notes" in law school reviews which ventured, not always with modesty, to criticise pronouncements of the Supreme Court. I recall that at one time he admonished counsel who had the temerity to refer to them in argument that they were merely the "work of boys." He thought the limit had been reached when what he had said in his judicial opinions was approved by the students as being "a correct statement of the law." But through the intensive discipline of the law schools and the selection of review editors from the best students, there has been a growing regard for these "notes" as helpful analyses of decisions, while the articles contributed to the reviews by eminent legal experts have given lawyers and judges the benefit of wide research and exploration, not infrequently blazing new trails in preference to old but less desirable paths. It is not too much to say that, in confronting any serious problem, a wide-awake and careful judge will at once look to see if the subject has been discussed, or the authorities collated and analyzed, in a good law periodical. If some members of this "fourth estate" of the law, conscious of their prestige and influence, may seem at times to assume an attitude approaching arrogance, they are at once subject to counter-attack and a balance of sound criticism is attained, with advantage to all concerned. . .

May 17, 1954, decision. Courts of equity may properly take into account the public interest in the elimination of such obstacles in a systematic and effective manner. But it should go without saying that the vitality of these constitutional principles cannot be allowed to yield simply because of disagreement with them.

While giving weight to these public and private considerations, the courts will require that the defendants make a prompt and reasonable start toward full compliance with our May 17, 1954, ruling. Once such a start has been made, the courts may find that additional time is necessary to carry out the ruling in an effective manner. The burden rests upon the defendants to establish that such time is necessary in the public interest and is consistent with good faith compliance at the earliest practicable date. To that end, the courts may consider problems related to administration, arising from the physical condition of the school plant, the school transportation system, personnel, revision of school districts and attendance areas into compact units to achieve a system of determining admission to the public schools on a nonracial basis, and revision of local laws and regulations which may be necessary in solving the foregoing problems. They will also consider the adequacy of any plans the defendants may propose to meet these problems and to effectuate a transition to a racially nondiscriminatory school system. During this period of transition, the courts will retain jurisdiction of these cases.

The . . . cases are remanded to the District Courts to take such proceedings and enter such orders and decrees consistent with this opinion as are necessary and proper to admit to public schools on a racially nondiscriminatory basis with all deliberate speed the parties to these cases.

Desegregation in the thousand districts affected by *Brown* followed no single pattern but varied with the attitudes and behavior of school officials, their white constituents, and federal district and appellate judges. The Supreme Court allowed controversies to develop and occasionally to resolve themselves in the inferior federal courts until the late 1960s, when it finally intervened to establish a national policy.

a. Massive Resistance

The District of Columbia and some school districts in the border states began to desegregate their schools almost immediately. The South responded to *Brown* with a barrage of measures designed to preserve and entrench segregation. State legislatures adopted resolutions of "nullification" and "interposition," which declared that the Court's decisions were without effect.[28] They enacted statutes mandating school segregation; ordering state and local officials to take all measures within their authority to preserve segregation; terminating state funds for racially mixed schools; placing the public schools directly under the authority of the governor or state board of education with plenary power to close them; providing tuition grants to enable pupils to attend private schools; and repealing compulsory attendance laws.[29]

28. See Note, Interposition vs. Judicial Power — A Study of Ultimate Authority in Constitutional Questions, 1 Race Rel. L. Rep. 465 (1956); Robert McKay; "With All Deliberate Speed" — A Study of School Desegregation, 31 N.Y.U.L. Rev. 911, 1017-39 (1956).

29. See McKay, supra note 28, at 1039-1049; McKay, "With All Deliberate Speed": Legislative Reaction and Judicial Development 1956-57, 43 Va. L. Rev. 1205, 1216-28 (1957). Only Mississippi has not yet reinstated compulsory public education.

Most of these schemes were struck down by lower federal courts.[30] The Supreme Court's two major interventions were Cooper v. Aaron, 358 U.S. 1 (1958), which required Little Rock, Arkansas, to proceed with school desegregation in the face of state-inspired opposition, violence, and disorder; and Griffin v. Prince Edward County School Board, 377 U.S. 218 (1964), which ordered a county school system reopened after it had been closed for five years to avoid desegregation.[31]

b. Pupil Placement

Massive resistance was followed by adoption of "pupil placement" acts in the late 1950s and early 1960s. The Alabama act, which served as the model for many southern states, directed districts to assign pupils to schools in accordance with a variety of nonracial factors, including the availability of school plants, staff, and transportation; the suitability of school curricula to the pupil's academic preparation and abilities; his morals, conduct, health, personal standards, and home environment; the psychological effect on the pupil; the effect of his admission on prevailing academic standards; and the possibility of friction, disorder, and ill will within the school and the community.[32] Pupils were initially assigned as a matter of course to the school maintained for their race.

> The particular genius of the assignment statutes derives from the provisions designed to individualize consideration of requests for transfers. Local school boards are . . . prohibited by most of the acts from authorizing the transfer of any individual or group without separate consideration of each application and a finding that each transfer would be consistent with the criteria declared to embody the educational policy of the state. In short, the statutes, functioning as intended, make mass integration almost impossible, place the burden of altering the status quo upon individual Negro pupils and their parents, establish a procedure that is difficult and time-consuming to complete, and prescribe standards so varied and vague that it is extremely difficult to establish that any individual denial is attributable to racial considerations.[33]

In 1958 the Supreme Court summarily affirmed the decision of a three-judge district court holding that the Alabama plan was not unconstitutional on its face.[34] The major issue became whether black schoolchildren could maintain

30. See, e.g., Poindexter v. Louisiana Financial Assistance Comm., 275 F. Supp. 833 (E.D. La. 1967), aff'd, 389 U.S. 571 (1968); id., 296 F. Supp. 686 (E.D. La.), aff'd. sub nom. Louisiana Educ. Commn. for Needy Children v. Poindexter, 393 U.S. 17 (1968); Lee v. Macon County Bd. of Educ., 267 F. Supp. 458 (M.D. Ala.), aff'd sub nom. Wallace v. United States, 389 U.S. 215 (1967).

31. The Court also thwarted the attempts of several states to harass or oust the NAACP and others seeking to implement *Brown*. See NAACP v. Alabama, 357 U.S. 449 (1958); NAACP v. Button, 371 U.S. 415 (1963). For a more recent example of massive resistance, in the context of housing segregation, see Spallone v. United States, 110 S. Ct. 625 (1990). Cf. Missouri v. Jenkins, 110 S. Ct. 1651 (1990) (federal court can require a school district to levy taxes to fund school desegregation plan).

32. Ala. Code tit. 52, §§61(1) to (12) (1958). See generally Note, The Federal Courts and Integration of Southern Schools: Troubled Status of the Pupil Placement Acts, 1962 Colum. L. Rev. 1448; United States Commission on Civil Rights, Education 22-31 (1961).

33. Note, supra note 32, at 1452-1453.

34. Shuttlesworth v. Birmingham Bd. of Educ., 358 U.S. 101., aff'g 162 F. Supp. 372 (N.D. Ala. 1958).

class actions seeking school desegregation notwithstanding the statutes, or whether each child who wished to transfer to a white school would first have to exhaust administrative remedies before the school board before he could seek judicial relief. By the mid-1960s, it was established that pupil placement schemes could not bar class judicial relief.[35]

2. *Desegregation in the 1960s*

During the 1960s, the lower courts approved two types of desegregation plans — assignment on the basis of residence and "freedom of choice."

Southern districts had traditionally assigned pupils to the schools nearest their homes, employing dual, overlapping attendance zones for the black and white schools. It would have been relatively simple to consolidate the dual zones into unitary ones. Because of the contiguity of black and white neighborhoods in many southern communities, this would often have produced substantial desegregation, relegating white pupils to the formerly black schools, which, apart from their social status were inferior in every traditional measure of school quality.[36] For these reasons, unitary zoning was not common, and where adopted it was implemented on a grade-a-year basis and with a provision that pupils could transfer from any school in which their race was in the minority to one in which they would be in the majority. In Goss v. Knoxville Board of Education, 373 U.S. 683 (1963), the Supreme Court unanimously held these minority-to-majority transfer provisions unconstitutional on the ground that they were "based solely on racial factors which . . . inevitably lead toward segregation of the students by race." Assignment by residence lost what little appeal it had for most districts.

The second and by far the more popular school desegregation scheme was freedom of choice, under which each child could opt to attend either a formerly white or black school. As ultimately perfected, the plan required each pupil (or his parent) to exercise a choice each year, thus precluding automatic assignment to the school formerly maintained for his race in the absence of a choice. The district was required to furnish transportation to the nearest school of the pupil's "opposite" race. No choice could be denied for any reason other than overcrowding, in which event preference was based solely on geographic proximity. Faculty and staff, and all facilities, activities, and programs were to be desegregated, and the districts were required to bring inferior black schools up to the level of the white schools or else close them.[37]

By the late 1960s freedom of choice was prevalent. It seldom yielded much desegregation. The United States Commission on Civil Rights explained.[38]

35. See Note, supra note 32. The courts held that the initial assignment on the basis of race was unconstitutional.

36. Even some liberal commentators seemed to assume that whites should not be sent to such schools (see Alexander Bickel, The Decade of School Desegregation, 1964 Colum. L. Rev. 193, 212), apparently without questioning why only black pupils should bear this burden.

37. See, e.g., the "model decree" in United States v. Jefferson County Bd. of Educ., 380 F.2d 385 (5th Cir. 1967), aff'g en banc 372 F.2d 836 (5th Cir. 1966).

38. U.S. Commission on Civil Rights, Survey of School Desegregation in the Southern and Border States, 1965-66, at 51-52 (1966). See also the commission's report, Southern School Desegregation, 1966-67, at 88 (1967).

Freedom of choice plans . . . have not disestablished the dual and racially segregated school systems involved, for the following reasons:

a. Negro and white schools have tended to retain their racial identity;
b. White students rarely elect to attend Negro schools;
c. Some Negro students are reluctant to sever normal school ties, made stronger by the racial identification of their schools;
d. Many Negro children and parents in Southern States, having lived for decades in positions of subservience, are reluctant to assert their rights;
e. Negro children and parents in Southern States frequently will not choose a formerly all-white school because they fear retaliation and hostility from the white community;
f. In some school districts in the South, school officials have failed to prevent or punish harassment by white children of Negro children who have elected to attend white schools;
g. In some areas in the South where Negroes have elected to attend formerly all-white schools, the Negro community has been subjected to retaliatory violence, evictions, loss of jobs, and other forms of intimidation.

Ten years after *Brown*, less than 1 percent of black children in the Deep South attended schools with whites. Not only were the court-approved desegregation plans inadequate, but school districts did not desegregate voluntarily, so that each one had to be sued in a separate action.[39] Almost all school litigation in the South was conducted by the NAACP Legal Defense and Educational Fund, Inc., a private organization whose small central staff, aided by handfuls of local cooperating attorneys, obviously could not take on each of the thousand-odd districts.[40] Delay was on the defendants' side. Many judges were hostile to *Brown* and to the plaintiffs and attorneys seeking to implement it; many other judges were subjected to strong pressures from the communities in which they lived.[41] Moreover, school desegregation cases, unlike most other litigation, never ended. The courts retained jurisdiction of each case, and their dockets were crowded with motions to modify or supplement orders as factual circumstances and the law changed.[42]

39. This was a result of the highly decentralized nature of most southern states' school systems. In 1967, however, as a result of Governor Wallace's actions to prevent desegregation of certain Alabama school districts, the court did enter a statewide decree. Lee v. Macon County Bd. of Educ., supra note 30.

40. The Legal Defense Fund began as the legal arm of the NAACP, but in 1939 it became an independent organization.

41. Southern Justice 165-227 (Friedman ed. 1965); J.W. Peltason, Fifty-Eight Lonely Men (1961); United States Commission on Civil Rights, Federal Enforcement of School Desegregation 48-54 (1969); Note, Judicial Performance in the Fifth Circuit, 73 Yale L.J. 90 (1963).

42. Some notion of the magnitude is suggested by the reported appellate decisions in Singleton v. Jackson Municipal Separate School Dist. The case begins as Evers v. Jackson Municipal Separate School Dist., 328 F.2d 408 (5th Cir. 1964) (exhaustion of administrative remedies under pupil placement scheme not required), and it continues in 348 F.2d 729 (1965) (ordering freedom of choice plans for four grades); 355 F.2d 865 (1966) (modifying plan); 357 F.2d 653 (1966) (holidng that, notwithstanding the district court's evidentiary findings of Negro inferiority and harmfulness of desegregation, it was bound to order desegregation); 404 F.2d 353 (1968) (reversing district court's approval of deviations from model freedom-of-choice plan); 419 F.2d 1211 (1969) (requiring full desegregation by September 1970), rev'd, 396 U.S. 290 (Jan. 14, 1970) (requiring full desegregation immediately); 425 F.2d 1211 (Jan. 21, 1970) (requiring full desegregation by Feb. 1, 1970); 426 F.2d 1364 (May 1970) (disapproving district court's plan as inadequate); 430 F.2d 368 (July 1970) (modifying previous mandate in some details); 432 F.2d 927 (Aug. 1970) (disapproving revised district court plan). In addition, the district court issued at least 15 to 20 unreported orders of one or another sort over the life of this case, which reached a state of repose in June 1971, with the district court's approval of a plan agreed upon by all parties. But cf. Singleton v. Jackson Municipal Separate School Dist., 332 F. Supp. 984 (S.D. Miss. 1971) (enjoining state officials from withholding state funds to dis-

In Watson v. City of Memphis, 373 U.S. 526 (1963), the Supreme Court began to indicate its impatience. In rejecting the city's request for delay in desegregating recreational facilities, the Court added in dictum:

> Given the extended time which has elapsed [since *Brown*,] it is far from clear that the mandate of the second *Brown* decision requiring that desegregation proceed with "all deliberate speed" would today be fully satisfied by types of plans or programs for desegregation of public educational facilities which eight years ago might have been deemed sufficient. *Brown* never contemplated that the concept of "deliberate speed" would countenance indefinite delay in elimination of racial barriers in schools.

A year later, in ordering the Prince Edward County schools to be reopened, Justice Black wrote that "[t]here has been entirely too much deliberation and not enough speed" and that at least for this recalcitrant district "[t]he time for mere 'deliberate speed' has run out. . . ."[43]

In 1964 Congress enacted the first comprehensive civil rights act since Reconstruction. Titles IV and IX of the Civil Rights Act of 1964 authorized the attorney general to initiate and intervene in school desegregation suits.[44] More important, Title VI prohibited discrimination in programs receiving federal financial assistance and required each department responsible for federally funded programs to issue regulations to achieve this end. Congress appropriated $2.4 billion under the Elementary and Secondary Education Act of 1965, much of it for school districts having "educationally disadvantaged" children. The Department of Health, Education and Welfare issued regulations and guidelines requiring most recipient districts to adopt freedom-of-choice plans.[45]

1963 had seen some increase in the pace of school desegregation, probably due to the neutralization of pupil placement schemes, and Title VI of the Civil Rights Act of 1964 accelerated the process. Nonetheless, in 1968, more than three-quarters of all Negro children in the South still attended the "formerly" black schools — which remained all-black — and the formerly white schools were still clearly identifiable as white, though some of them were now sprinkled with handfuls of black children who had the courage and stamina to choose them. As difficult as it was to supervise and enforce court orders and the HEW guidelines, the core problem lay in the substance of the orders and guidelines themselves — in their acceptance of freedom of choice.

---

trict). See also Owen Fiss, Injunctions 417-421 (1972), listing 77 docket entries between 1964 and 1969 in United States v. Montgomery County Bd. of Educ., 395 U.S. 225 (1969).

43. Griffin v. Prince Edward County School Bd., 377 U.S. 218 (1964).

44. Prior to the adoption of Title IX, the government had sometimes effectively intervened as "amicus curiae," playing a much more active role than amici traditionally do.

45. 45 C.F.R. §80.1 et seq. (1968) (1964 regulations); 45 C.F.R. §181.1 (1968) (1966 guidelines). The HEW guidelines influenced judge-made remedial doctrine, and in some circuits they were simply adopted by the courts; but there were also conflicts between HEW and the courts. See generally James Dunn, Title VI, the Guidelines and School Desegregation in the South, 53 Va. L. Rev. 42 (1967); Note, The Courts, HEW, and Southern School Desegregation, 77 Yale L.J. 321 (1967); United States v. Jefferson County Bd. of Educ., 372 F.2d 836 (1966), aff'd en banc, 380 F.2d 385 (5th Cir. 1967). See also Adams v. Richardson, 356 F. Supp. 92 (D.D.C. 1973) (finding that HEW had inadequately enforced Title VI and ordering it to commence enforcement proceedings against noncomplying districts).

3. *The Demise of Freedom of Choice and of Southern Rural Segregation*

The adequacy of freedom of choice was as much an issue of substantive doctrine as of remedy. The Legal Defense Fund continually urged that the constitutional objective was the elimination of racially identifiable schools and that, measured in these terms, freedom-of-choice plans were unconstitutional. The school districts responded that, absent improper coercion, a well-designed freedom-of-choice plan succeeded by definition: The Constitution required no more than that black and white children have the option to attend schools with children of the other race.[46]

As early as 1966, HEW and the Court of Appeals for the Fifth Circuit had accepted the former view in principle.[47] Two years later, freedom of choice remained virtually the sole means of desegregation within the circuit, however, and some other courts had not even accepted the principle. In Green v. New Kent County School Board, the Supreme Court finally intervened.

GREEN v. NEW KENT COUNTY SCHOOL BOARD, 391 U.S. 430 (1968): [The Court held that a small school district, which was not residentially segregated and which had only two schools, could not employ a freedom-of-choice plan when its effect was to perpetuate the long-standing tradition of segregation. The decision was unanimous.]

BRENNAN, J. . . . The pattern of separate "white" and "Negro" schools in the New Kent County school system established under compulsion of state laws is precisely the pattern of segregation to which *Brown I* and *Brown II* were particularly addressed, and which *Brown I* declared unconstitutionally denied Negro school children equal protection of the laws. Racial identification of the system's schools was complete, extending not just to the composition of student bodies at the two schools but to every facet of school operations — faculty, staff, transportation, extracurricular activities and facilities. In short, the State, acting through the local school board and school officials, organized and operated a dual system, part "white" and part "Negro."

It was such dual systems that 14 years ago *Brown I* held unconstitutional and a year later *Brown II* held must be abolished; school boards operating such school systems were *required* by *Brown II* "to effectuate a transition to a racially nondiscriminatory school system." It is of course true that for the time immediately after *Brown II* the concern was with making an initial break in a long-established pattern of excluding Negro children from schools attended by white children. The principal focus was on obtaining for those Negro children courageous enough to break with tradition a place in the "white" schools. Under *Brown II* that immediate goal was only the first step, however. The transition to a unitary, nonracial system of public education was and is the ultimate end to be brought about. . . .

46. Support for this position was typically sought in the offhand remark of the district court in Briggs v. Elliott, 132 F. Supp. 776, 777 (E.D.S.C. 1955), one of the cases consolidated with *Brown*, that [t]he Constitution . . . does not require integration. It merely forbids [segregation]."

47. See United States v. Jefferson County Bd. of Educ., supra note 45. See especially 372 F.2d at 846 n.5, which discusses and rejects the "Briggs dictum" (note 46 supra).

In the context of the state-imposed segregated pattern of long standing, the fact that in 1965 the Board opened the doors of the former "white" school to Negro children and of the "Negro" school to white children merely begins, not ends, our inquiry whether the Board has taken steps adequate to abolish its dual, segregated system. *Brown II* was a call for the dismantling of well-entrenched dual systems tempered by an awareness that complex and multifaceted problems would arise which would require time and flexibility for a successful resolution. School boards such as the respondent then operating state-compelled dual systems were nevertheless clearly charged with the affirmative duty to take whatever steps might be necessary to convert to a unitary system in which racial discrimination would be eliminated root and branch. . . .[a]

In determining whether respondent School Board met that command by adopting its "freedom-of-choice" plan, it is relevant that this first step did not come until some 11 years after *Brown I* was decided and 10 years after *Brown II* directed the making of a "prompt and reasonable start." This deliberate perpetuation of the unconstitutional dual system can only have compounded the harm of such a system. . . . The burden on a school board today is to come forward with a plan that promises realistically to work, and promises realistically to work *now*. . . .

We do not hold that "freedom of choice" can have no place in such a plan. We do not hold that a "freedom-of-choice" plan might of itself be unconstitutional, although that argument has been urged upon us. Rather, all we decide today is that in desegregating a dual system a plan utilizing "freedom of choice" is not an end in itself. As Judge Sobeloff has put it,

> "Freedom of choice" is not a sacred talisman; it is only a means to a constitutionally required end — the abolition of the system of segregation and its effects. If the means prove effective, it is acceptable, but if it fails to undo segregation, other means must be used to achieve this end. The school officials have the continuing duty to take whatever action may be necessary to create a "unitary, non-racial system."

The New Kent School Board's "freedom-of-choice" plan cannot be accepted as a sufficient step to "effectuate a transition" to a unitary system. In three years of operation not a single white child has chosen to attend Watkins school and . . . 85% of the Negro children in the system still attend the all-Negro Watkins school. . . . The Board must be required to formulate a new plan and in light of other courses which appear open to the Board, such as zoning,[b] fashion steps

a. "We bear in mind that the court has not merely the power but the duty to render a decree which will so far as possible eliminate the discriminatory effects of the past as well as bar like discrimination in the future." Louisiana v. United States, 380 U.S. 145, 154.

b. "In view of the situation found in New Kent County, where there is no residential segregation, the elimination of the dual school system and the establishment of a 'unitary, non-racial system' could be readily achieved with a minimum of administrative difficulty by means of geographic zoning — simply by assigning students living in the eastern half of the county to the New Kent School and those living in the western half of the county to the Watkins School. Although a geographical formula is not universally appropriate, it is evident that here the Board, by separately busing Negro children across the entire county to the 'Negro' school, and the white children to the 'white' school, is deliberately maintaining a segregated system which would vanish with non-racial geographic zoning. The conditions in this county present a classical case for this expedient." Petitioners have also suggested that the Board could consolidate the two schools, one site (e.g., Watkins) serving grades 1-7 and the other (e.g., New Kent) serving grades 8-12, this being the grade division respondent makes between elementary and secondary levels. Petitioners contend this would result in a more efficient system by

which promise realistically to convert promptly to a system without a "white" school and a "Negro" school, but just schools. . . .

After some initial delay in the implementation of *Green*,[48] most Southern districts replaced freedom of choice with geographic zoning. In many rural areas and smaller cities where large-scale residential segregation is not pervasive, this has eliminated interschool segregation. But it has not eliminated all forms of racial discrimination. Some school boards have desegregated by closing adequate Negro schools and busing only black students.[49] Many other districts have replicated aspects of the dual school system within a "desegregated" school, through ability grouping or tracking; segregation of classrooms, buses, and other facilities; discrimination in the hiring and assignment of personnel; and discrimination in disciplinary treatment, athletics, and other student activities.[50]

The implementation of *Green* resulted in some "white flight" from districts with high percentages of black students to other areas or to private schools.[51] The Court alluded to the issue of white flight in Monroe v. Board of Commissioners, 391 U.S. 450 (1968), which invalidated a "free transfer" provision ancillary to a geographic zoning plan. Although the scheme was not limited to minority-to-majority transfers, it permitted a " 'considerable number' of white or Negro students . . . to return, at the implicit invitation of the Board [from desegregated schools] to the comfortable security of the old, established discriminatory pattern." The Court responded to the school district's argument that "without the transfer option . . . white students will flee the school system altogether," by quoting *Brown II*: "the vitality of these constitutional principles cannot be allowed to yield simply because of disagreement with them."

4. *Constitutional Limitations on Government Aid to Private Segregated Schools*

NORWOOD v. HARRISON, 413 U.S. 455 (1973): [The Court held unanimously[52] that Mississippi could not lend textbooks to students attending private

---

eliminating costly duplication in this relatively small district while at the same time achieving immediate dismantling of the dual system.

These are two suggestions the District Court should take into account upon remand, along with any other proposed alternatives and in light of considerations respecting other aspects of the school system such as the matter of faculty and staff desegregation remanded to the court by the Court of Appeals.

48. See Alexander v. Holmes County Bd. of Educ., 396 U.S. 19 (1969); Carter v. West Feliciana Parish School Bd., 396 U.S. 226, 290 (1969); Northcross v. Board of Educ., 397 U.S. 232 (1970); Note, The Supreme Court, 1969 Term, 84 Harv. L. Rev. 1, 32 (1970).

49. See Note, Inequality in Desegregation: Black School Closings, 39 U. Chi. L. Rev. 658 (1972); American Friends Service Committee, The Status of School Desegregation in the South 1970.

50. See American Friends Service Committee, supra note 49.

51. See Richard Fields, The Status of Private Segregated Academies in Eleven Southern States (NAACP Legal Defense & Educational Fund, Sept. 1972); Norwood v. Harrison, 413 U.S. 455 (1973).

52. Justices Douglas and Brennan concurred in the result.

segregated schools pursuant to a long-standing program of providing free textbooks to all public and private school students.]

BURGER, C.J. . . . This Court has consistently affirmed decisions enjoining state tuition grants to students attending racially discriminatory private schools. A textbook lending program is not legally distinguishable from the forms of state assistance foreclosed by the prior cases. Free textbooks, like tuition grants directed to private school students, are a form of financial assistance inuring to the benefit of the private schools themselves. An inescapable educational cost for students in both public and private schools is the expense of providing all necessary learning materials. When, as here, that necessary expense is borne by the State, the economic consequence is to give aid to the enterprise; if the school engages in discriminatory practices the State by tangible aid in the form of textbooks thereby gives support to such discrimination. Racial discrimination in state-operated schools is barred by the Constitution and "[i]t is also axiomatic that a state may not induce, encourage or promote private persons to accomplish what it is constitutionally forbidden to accomplish." Lee v. Macon County Board of Education, 267 F. Supp. 458, 475-476 (M.D. Ala. 1967).

We do not suggest that a State violates its constitutional duty merely because it has provided *any* form of state service that benefits private schools said to be racially discriminatory. Textbooks are a basic educational tool and, like tuition grants, they are provided only in connection with schools; they are to be distinguished from generalized services government might provide to schools in common with others. Moreover, the textbooks provided to private school students by the State in this case are a form of assistance readily available from sources entirely independent of the State — unlike, for example, "such necessities of life as electricity, water, and police and fire protection." Moose Lodge No. 107 v. Irvis, 407 U.S. 163, 173 (1972). The State has neither an absolute nor operating monopoly on the procurement of school textbooks; anyone can purchase them on the open market.

The District Court laid great stress on the absence of showing by appellants that "any child enrolled in private school, if deprived of free textbooks, would withdraw from private school and subsequently enroll in the public schools." We can accept this factual assertion; we cannot and do not know, on this record at least, whether state textbook assistance is the determinative factor in the enrollment of any students in any of the private schools in Mississippi. We do not agree with the District Court in its analysis of the legal consequences of this uncertainty, for the Constitution does not permit the State to aid discrimination even when there is no precise causal relationship between state financial aid to a private school and the continued well-being of that school. A State may not grant the type of tangible financial aid here involved if that aid has a significant tendency to facilitate, reinforce, and support private discrimination. "[D]ecisions on the constitutionality of state involvement in private discrimination do not turn on whether the state aid adds up to 51 percent or adds up to only 49 percent of the support of the segregated institution." Poindexter v. Louisiana Financial Assistance Commn., 275 F. Supp. 833, 854 (E.D. La. 1967).

The recurring theme of appellees' argument is a sympathetic one — that the State's textbook loan program is extended to students who attend racially segregated private schools only because the State sincerely wishes to foster quality education for all Mississippi children, and, to that end, has taken steps to insure that no sub-group of school children will be deprived of an important educational tool merely because their parents have chosen to enroll them in segregated private schools. We need not assume that the State's textbook aid to private schools has been motivated by other than a sincere interest in the educational welfare of all Mississippi children. But good intentions as to one valid objective do not serve to negate the State's involvement in violation of a constitutional duty. "The existence of a permissible purpose cannot sustain an action that has an impermissible effect." Wright v. Council of City of Emporia, 407 U.S. 451, 462 (1972). The Equal Protection Clause would be a sterile promise if state involvement in possible private activity could be shielded altogether from constitutional scrutiny simply because its ultimate end was not discrimination but some higher goal.

The District Court offered as further support for its holding the finding that Mississippi's public schools "were fully established as unitary schools throughout the state no later than 1970-71 [and] continue to attract 90% of the state's educable children." We note, however, that overall statewide attendance figures do not fully and accurately reflect the impact of private schools in particular school districts.[a] In any event, the constitutional infirmity of the Mississippi textbook program is that it significantly aids the organization and continuation of a separate system of private schools which, under the District Court holding, may discriminate if they so desire. A State's constitutional obligation requires it to steer clear, not only of operating the old dual system of racially segregated schools, but also of giving significant aid to institutions that practice racial or other invidious discrimination. That the State's public schools are not fully unitary, as the District Court found, is irrelevant.

Appellees and the District Court also placed great reliance on our decisions in Everson v. Board of Education, 330 U.S. 1 (1947), and Board of Education v. Allen, 392 U.S. 236 (1968). In *Everson,* we held that the Establishment Clause of the First Amendment did not prohibit New Jersey from "spending tax-raised funds to pay the bus fares of parochial school pupils as a part of a general program under which it pays the fares of pupils attending public and other schools." *Allen,* following *Everson,* sustained a New York law requiring school textbooks to be lent free of charge to all students, including those in attendance at parochial schools, in specified grades.

Neither *Allen* nor *Everson* is dispositive of the issue before us in this case. Religious schools "pursue two goals, religious instruction and secular education." Board of Education v. Allen. And, where carefully limited so as to avoid the prohibitions of the "effect" and "entanglement" tests,[53] States may assist church-

a. In Tunica County, for example, where appellants reside, in response to . . . Alexander v. Holmes County Board of Education, 396 U.S. 19 (1969), all white children were withdrawn from public schools and placed in a private academy housed in local church facilities and staffed by the principal and 17 high school teachers of the county system, who resigned in mid-year to accept jobs at the new academy. See United States v. Tunica County School district, 323 F. Supp. 1019 (N.D. Miss. 1970), aff'd, 440 F.2d 377 (CA5 1971). As of the time of the filing of this lawsuit, the successor Tunica Institute of Learning enrolled 495 students, all white, and would not attest to an open enrollment policy. Similar histories of Holmes County, Canton Municipal Separate School District, Jackson Municipal Separate School District, Amite County, Indianola Municipal Separate School District, and Grenada Municipal Separate School District are recited, without challenge by appellees, in Brief for Appellants.

53. "Every analysis in [the establishment of religion] area must begin with consideration of the cumulative criteria developed by the Court over many years. Three such tests may be gleaned from our cases. First, the statute must have a secular legislative purpose: second, its principal or primary

related schools in performing their secular functions, not only because the States have a substantial interest in the quality of education being provided by private schools, but more importantly because assistance properly confined to the secular functions of sectarian schools does not substantially promote the readily identifiable religious mission of those schools and it does not interfere with the free exercise rights of others.

Like a sectarian school, a private school — even one that discriminates — fulfills an important educational function; however, the difference is that in the context of this case the legitimate educational function cannot be isolated from discriminatory practices — if such in fact exist. Under Brown v. Board of Education, 347 U.S. 483 (1954), discriminatory treatment exerts a pervasive influence on the entire educational process. The private school that closes its doors to defined groups of students on the basis of constitutionally suspect criteria manifests, by its own actions, that its educational processes are based on private belief that segregation is desirable in education. There is no reason to discriminate against students for reasons wholly unrelated to individual merit unless the artificial barriers are considered an essential part of the educational message to be communicated to the students who are admitted. Such private bias is not barred by the Constitution, nor does it invoke any sanction of laws, but neither can it call on the Constitution for material aid from the State.

Our decisions under the Establishment Clause reflect the "internal tension in the First Amendment between the Establishment Clause and the Free Exercise Clause," Tilton v. Richardson, 403 U.S. 672, 677 (1971). This does not mean, as we have already suggested, that a State is constitutionally obligated to provide even "neutral" services to sectarian schools. But the transcendent value of free religious exercise in our constitutional scheme leaves room for "play in the joints" to the extent of cautiously delineated secular governmental assistance to religious schools, despite the fact that such assistance touches on the conflicting values of the Establishment Clause by indirectly benefiting the religious schools and their sponsors.

In contrast, although the Constitution does not proscribe private bias, it places no value on discrimination as it does on the values inherent in the Free Exercise Clause. Invidious private discrimination may be characterized as a form of exercising freedom of association protected by the First Amendment, but it has never been accorded affirmative constitutional protections. . . .

Discussion

In McGlotten v. Connally, 338 F. Supp. 448 (D.D.C. 1972), the court held that the secretary of the treasury could not allow charitable deductions for gifts to fraternal orders that excluded nonwhites and could not grant federal income tax exemptions to such organizations. The court recognized that every tax deduction "provides a benefit to the class who may take advantage of it" and conceded that this alone would not impermissibly involve the government in the private discrimination. But "[t]he rationale for allowing the deduction of charitable contributions has historically been that by doing so, the Government relieves itself of the burden of meeting public needs. . . ." This, together with "the degree of con-

---

effect must be one that neither advances nor inhibits religion: finally, the statute must not foster 'an excessive government entanglement with religion.' " Lemon v. Kurtzman, 403 U.S. 602 (1971).

trol the Government has retained as to the purposes and organizations which may benefit, and the aura of government approval inherent in an exempt ruling by the Internal Revenue Service, all serve to distinguish the benefits at issue from the general run of deductions" and make the Government "sufficiently entwined with private parties to call forth a duty to ensure compliance with the Fifth Amendment. . . ." For similar reasons, the Court held that the exemption of the passive investment income of fraternal orders amounted to government "approval of the organizations and hence their discriminatory practice, and [aid to] that discrimination by the provision of federal tax benefits." But the Court upheld the exemption of membership dues from the taxable income of a discriminatory nonprofit club. This did "not operate to provide a grant of federal funds through the tax system" but simply reflected a congressional determination that "where individuals have banded together to provide recreational facilities on a mutual basis, it would be conceptually erroneous to impose a tax on the organization as a separate entity." All clubs "organized and operated exclusively for pleasure, recreation and other nonprofitable purposes" were entitled to this treatment; the exemption did not carry any implicit government approval; and "Congress does not violate the Constitution by *failing to tax* private discrimination where there is no other act of Government involvement."[54]

Does the fact that a state is obligated to eradicate all vestiges of its past de jure segregation mean that it may be forbidden to aid a private discriminatory activity, while a state that has not engaged in de jure segregation may grant the same aid? Norwood v. Harrison implied that the loan of textbooks to pupils attending segregated private schools is unconstitutional, independent of the state's obligation to desegregate the public schools. Contrast Gilmore v. City of Montgomery, 417 U.S. 556 (1974). Here the Court held that the district court properly enjoined the city from permitting the exclusive use of its recreational facilities (e.g., basketball and tennis courts, football and baseball fields) by private segregated schools, where "exclusive use" meant temporary but complete control of an entire facility.[55] The Court remanded for further evidence on whether the schools' use of facilities such as zoos and museums in common with others constituted unlawful state action. And it held that the record did not support an injunction against the use of facilities by private segregated organizations and groups other than schools.

With respect to exclusive use by private segregated schools, Justice Blackmun relied heavily on the city's history of circumventing a court order to desegregate its recreational facilities and on the effect of the city's policy upon desegregation of the Montgomery County school system:

> Certainly, the city officials were . . . responsible for seeing that no actions on their part would significantly impede the progress of school desegregation in the city. . . . Here the city's actions significantly enhanced the attractiveness of segregated private schools, formed in reaction against the federal court school order, by enabling

54. For a discussion of the decision, see Boris Bittker & Kenneth Kaufman, Taxes and Civil Rights: "Constitutionalizing" the Internal Revenue Code, 82 Yale L.J. 51 (1972).

55. Justice Blackmun wrote: "We understand the term 'exclusive use' not to include the situation where only part of a facility may be allocated to or used by a group, even though that allocation or use results in the pro tanto exclusion of others. For example, the use of two of a total of 10 tennis courts by a private school group would not constitute an exclusive use: the use of all 10 courts would."

> them to offer complete athletic programs. The city's provision of stadiums and recreational fields resulted in capital savings for those schools and enabled them to divert their own funds to other educational programs. It also provided the opportunity for the schools to operate concessions that generated revenues. . . . [T]his assistance significantly tended to undermine the federal court order mandating the establishment and maintenance of a unitary school system in Montgomery.

However, the record was not clear whether nonexclusive use of recreational facilities would have the same effect and whether "a particular use constitutes a vestige of the type of state-sponsored racial segregation in public recreational facilities that was prohibited in the parks [desegregation] decree . . . ."

5. The Amelioration of Southern Metropolitan Segregation

In the larger Southern cities, the assignment of pupils by residential zones often produced patterns of school segregation superficially indistiguishable from those common in Northern cities. The Court first addressed this problem in 1971 in the context of a district encompassing the city of Charlotte, North Carolina, and surrounding Mecklenburg County.

SWANN v. CHARLOTTE-MECKLENBURG BOARD OF EDUCATION, 402 U.S. 1 (1971): [About 24,000 (29 percent) of the pupils in the Charlotte-Mecklenburg schools were black. The system had operated under a court-approved plan since 1965, and by the 1968-1969 school year, about half of the black pupils attended formerly white schools; the other half remained in virtually all-black schools. On petitioners' motion for further relief following *Green*, the district court ordered the school board to come forward with an effective desegregation plan. The court found the proposed plan unacceptable, appointed its own expert, and adopted its own plan, which would have assured that no elementary school had fewer than 9 percent or more than 38 percent black students. The plan incorporated a scheme of noncontiguous zoning, grouping several outlying white schools with one black inner city school. Black students in the first four grades were bused to the outlying schools, and white fifth- and sixth-graders were bused to the city schools. The Court of Appeals for the Fourth Circuit vacated this aspect of the plan, fearing that "the pairing and grouping of elementary schools would place an unreasonable burden on the board and the system's pupils."

The Supreme Court unanimously reversed. The main burden of Chief Justice Burger's opinion was that district courts may exercise very broad equitable discretion in formulating remedial desegregation plans. More specifically, the Court addressed itself to four major questions:]

> (1) to what extent racial balance or racial quotas may be used as an implement in a remedial order to correct a previously segregated system;
> (2) whether every all-Negro and all-white school must be eliminated as an indispensable part of a remedial process of desegregation;

(3) what the limits are, if any, on the rearrangement of school districts and attendance zones, as a remedial measure; and
(4) what the limits are, if any, on the use of transportation facilities to correct state-enforced racial school segregation.

(1) *Racial Balances or Racial Quotas*. . . . [The District Court directed]

> that efforts should be made to reach a 71-29 ratio in the various schools so that there will be no basis for contending that one school is racially different from the others . . . , [t]hat no school [should] be operated with an all-black or predominantly black student body, [and] [t]hat pupils of all grades [should] be assigned in such a way that as nearly as practicable the various schools at various grade levels have about the same proportion of black and white students.

The District Judge went on to acknowledge that variation "from that norm may be unavoidable." This contains intimations that the "norm" is a fixed mathematical racial balance reflecting the pupil constituency of the system. If we were to read the holding of the District Court to require, as a matter of substantive constitutional right, any particular degree of racial balance or mixing, that approach would be disapproved and we would be obliged to reverse. The constitutional command to desegregate schools does not mean that every school in every community must always reflect the racial composition of the school system as a whole. . . .

As we said in *Green* [however,] a school authority's remedial plan or a district court's remedial decree is to be judged by its effectiveness. Awareness of the racial composition of the whole school system is likely to be a useful starting point in shaping a remedy to correct past constitutional violations. In sum, the very limited use made of mathematical ratios was within the equitable remedial discretion of the District Court.[56]

(2) *One-race Schools*. The record in this case reveals the familiar phenomenon that in metropolitan areas minority groups are often found concentrated in one part of the city. In some circumstances certain schools may remain all or largely of one race until new schools can be provided or neighborhood patterns change. . . .

In light of the above, it should be clear that the existence of some small number of one-race, or virtually one-race, schools within a district is not in and of itself the mark of a system that still practices segregation by law. The district judge or school authorities should make every effort to achieve the greatest possible degree of actual desegregation and will thus necessarily be concerned with the elimination of one-race schools. . . . The court should scrutinize such schools, and the burden upon the school authorities will be to satisfy the court that their

56. See also United States v. Montgomery County Bd. of Educ., 395 U.S. 225 (1969). District Judge Frank Johnson, after finding that the respondent board had not made adequate progress under a general order to desegregate faculty, required that the board move, according to an annual schedule, "toward a goal under which 'in each school the ratio of white to Negro faculty members is substantially the same as it is throughout the system.' " The court of appeals, characterizing the goal as requiring "fixed mathematical" ratios, eliminated it. The Supreme Court unanimously reversed. Justice Black wrote for the Court that the district court's order "might possibly be more troublesome if we read [it] as being absolutely rigid and inflexible," but that it could not properly be so read.

racial composition is not the result of present or past discriminatory action on their part. . . . Provision for optional transfer to those in the majority racial group of a particular school to other schools where they will be in the minority is an indispensible remedy for those students willing to transfer to other schools in order to lessen the impact on them of the state-imposed stigma of segregation. In order to be effective, such a transfer arrangement must grant the transferring student free transportation and space must be made available in the school to which he desires to move. . . .

(3) *Remedial Altering of Attendance Zones.* . . . Absent a constitutional violation there would be no basis for judicially ordering assignment of students on a racial basis. All things being equal, with no history of discrimination, it might well be desirable to assign pupils to schools nearest their homes. But all things are not equal in a system that has been deliberately constructed and maintained to enforce racial segregation. . . .

No fixed or even substantially fixed guidelines can be established as to how far a court can go, but it must be recognized that there are limits. The objective is to dismantle the dual school system. "Racially neutral" assignment plans proposed by school authorities to a district court may be inadequate; such plans may fail to counteract the continuing effects of past school segregation resulting from discriminatory location of school sites or distortion of school size in order to achieve or maintain an artificial racial separation. . . .[57]

We hold that the pairings and groupings of noncontiguous school zones is a permissible tool and such action is to be considered in light of the objectives sought. . . .

(4) *Transportation of Students.* . . . Bus transportation has been an integral part of the public education system for years, and was perhaps the single most important factor in the transition from the one-room schoolhouse to the consolidated

57. Earlier in the opinion, the Chief Justice had written:

> The construction of new schools and the closing of old ones are two of the most important functions of local school authorities and also two of the most complex. They must decide questions of location and capacity in light of population growth, finances, land values, site availability, through an almost endless list of factors to be considered. The result of this will be a decision which, when combined with one technique or another of student assignment, will determine the racial composition of the student body in each school in the system. Over the long run, the consequence of the choices will be far reaching. People gravitate toward school facilities, just as schools are located in response to the needs of people. The location of schools may thus influence the patterns of residential development of the metropolitan area and have important impact on composition of inner-city neighborhoods.
>
> In the past, choices in this respect have been used as a potent weapon for creating or maintaining a state-segregated school system. In addition to the classic pattern of building schools specifically intended for Negro or white students, school authorities have sometimes, since *Brown*, closed schools which appeared likely to become racially mixed through changes in neighborhood residential patterns. This was sometimes accompanied by building new schools in the areas of white suburban expansion farthest from Negro population centers in order to maintain the separation of the races with a minimum departure from the formal principles of "neighborhood zoning." Such a policy does more than simply influence the short-run composition of the student body of a new school. It may well promote segregated residential patterns which, when combined with "neighborhood zoning," further lock the school system into the mold of separation of the races. . . .
>
> In ascertaining the existence of legally imposed school segregation, the existence of a pattern of school construction and abandonment is thus a factor of great weight. In devising remedies where legally imposed segregation has been established, it is the responsibility of local authorities and district courts to see to it that future school construction and abandonment are not used and do not serve to perpetuate or re-establish the dual system.

school. Eighteen million of the Nation's public school children, approximately 39%, were transported to their schools by bus in 1969-1970 in all parts of the country.

The decree provided that the buses used to implement the plan would operate on direct routes. Students would be picked up at schools near their homes and transported to the schools they were to attend. The trips for elementary school pupils average about seven miles and the District Court found that they would take "not over 35 minutes at the most." This system compares favorably with the transportation plan previously operated in Charlotte under which each day 23,600 students on all grade levels were transported an average of 15 miles one way for an average trip requiring over an hour. In these circumstances, we find no basis for holding that the local school authorities may not be required to employ bus transportation as one tool of school desegregation. Desegregation plans cannot be limited to the walk-in school.

An objection to transportation of students may have validity when the time or distance of travel is so great as to either risk the health of the children or significantly impinge on the educational process. . . . The reconciliation of competing values in a desegregation case is, of course, a difficult task with many sensitive facets but fundamentally no more so than remedial measures courts of equity have traditionally employed. . . .

At some point, these school authorities and others like them should have achieved full compliance with this Court's decision in *Brown*. The system would then be "unitary" in the sense required by our decision in *Green*. . . .

It does not follow that the communities served by such systems will remain demographically stable, for in a growing, mobile society, few will do so. Neither school authorities nor district courts are constitutionally required to make year-by-year adjustments of the racial composition of student bodies once the affirmative duty to desegregate has been accomplished and racial discrimination through official action is eliminated from the system. This does not mean that federal courts are without power to deal with future problems; but in the absence of a showing that either the school authorities or some other agency of the State has deliberately attempted to fix or alter demographic patterns to affect the racial composition of the schools, further intervention by a district court should not be necessary.

Note

Pasadena City Board of Education v. Spangler, 427 U.S. 424 (1976), invoked the closing paragraphs of *Swann* to hold that after four years under a court-ordered plan requiring cross-district busing to assure that no school had more than 50 percent minority students, the school board need not continue to reassign students on the basis of race to compensate for demographic changes. Justice Marshall, joined by Justice Brennan, dissented, arguing that the Court should have deferred to the District Court's finding that "the Pasadena Plan has not had the cooperation from the Board that permits a realistic measure of its educational success or failure" and that the Board had not yet fulfilled its affirmative duty to desegregate.

In Board of Education of Oklahoma City v. Dowell, 111 S. Ct. 630 (1991), the district court dissolved a ten-year-old desegregation decree against the school district. The court found that the original plan was no longer workable, that the district had complied with the court's orders in good faith, and that district's Student Reassignment Plan, which would return a number of previously desegregated schools to one-race schools for the asserted purpose of alleviating busing burdens on black pupils was not designed with discriminatory intent. The court of appeals reversed, holding that the injunction should remain in effect unless the school district could show "grievous wrong evolved by new and unforeseen conditions." The Court reversed, Chief Justice Rehnquist writing:

> From the very first, federal supervision of local school systems was intended as a temporary measure to remedy past discrimination. . . . The legal justification for displacement of local authority in a school desegregation case by an injunctive decree is a violation of the Constitution by local authorities. Dissolving a desegregation decree after the local authorities have operated in compliance with it for a reasonable period of time properly recognizes that "necessary concern for the important values of local control of public schools dictates that a federal court's regulatory control of such systems does not extend beyond the time required to remedy the effects of past intentional discrimination." . . . In considering whether the vestiges of *de jure* segregation have been eliminated as far as practicable, the District Court should look not only at student assignments, but to "every facet of school operation — faculty, staff, transportation, extra-curricular activities, and facilities."

Justice Marshall, joined by Justices Blackmun and Stevens, dissented:

> I believe a desegregation decree cannot be lifted so long as conditions likely to inflict the stigmatic injury condemned in *Brown I* persist and there remain feasible methods of eliminating such conditions. . . . [T]he record here shows . . . that feasible steps could have been taken to avoid one-race schools. . . . Consistent with the mandate of *Brown I* our cases have imposed on school districts an unconditional duty to eliminate *any* condition that perpetuates the message of racial inferiority inherent in the policy of state-sponsored segregation. The racial identifiability of a district's schools is such a condition. . . . In a district with a history of state-sponsored school segregation, racial separation, in my view, *remains* inherently unequal.

6. *Varieties of Northern School Segregation*

KEYES v. SCHOOL DISTRICT NO. 1, DENVER, COLORADO

413 U.S. 189 (1973)

Certiorari to the United States Court of Appeals for the Tenth Circuit

[The Denver school system, with a composition of 66 percent Anglo, 20 percent Hispanic, and 14 percent black, was highly segregated.[58] Unlike Southern school systems, however, the Denver school system had never been segregated by the mandate of any state law. Plaintiffs claimed that the schools nonetheless were de jure segregated as the result of the school board's race-conscious manipulation

58. The Court here treated schools with a "combined predominance of Negroes and Hispanos" as "segregated," based on the observation that both groups had suffered economic and cultural deprivation and discrimination.

of attendance zones and selection of school sites. The district court found that the board had engaged in such practices in an outlying community, Park Hill, but found no evidence of discrimination with respect to the segregated inner-city schools. The district court nonetheless ordered district-wide desegregation in order to assure the inner-city students "equal educational opportunity." The Tenth Circuit Court of Appeals reversed the portion of the decree requiring desegregation of the inner-city schools. The Supreme Court reversed.]

BRENNAN, J. . . .

II

. . . [T]he District Court found that "[b]etween 1960 and 1969 the Board's policies with respect to these northeast Denver schools show an undeviating purpose to isolate Negro students" in segregated schools "while preserving the Anglo character of [other] schools." This finding did not relate to an insubstantial or trivial fragment of the school system. . . . In addition, there was uncontroverted evidence that teachers and staff had for years been assigned on the basis of a minority teacher to a minority school throughout the school system.

This is not a case . . . where a statutory dual system has ever existed. Nevertheless, where plaintiffs prove that the school authorities have carried out a systematic program of segregation affecting a substantial portion of the students, schools, teachers, and facilities within the school system, it is only common sense to conclude that there exists a predicate for a finding of the existence of a dual school system. Several considerations support this conclusion. First, it is obvious that a practice of concentrating Negros in certain schools by structuring attendance zones or designating "feeder" schools of the basis of race has the reciprocal effect of keeping other nearby schools predominantly white. Similarly, the practice of building a school . . . to a certain size and in a certain location, "with conscious knowledge that it would be a segregated school," has a substantial reciprocal effect on the racial composition of other nearby schools. So also, the use of mobile classrooms, the drafting of student transfer policies, the transportation of students, and the assignment of faculty and staff, on racially identifiable bases, have the clear effect of earmarking schools according to their racial composition, and this, in turn, together with the elements of student assignment and school construction, may have a profound reciprocal effect on the racial composition of residential neighborhoods within a metropolitan area, thereby causing further racial concentration within the schools. . . .

III

The District Court proceeded on the premise that the finding as to the Park Hill schools was irrelevant to the consideration of the rest of the district, and began its examination of the core city schools by requiring that petitioners prove all of the essential elements of de jure segregation — that is, stated simply, a current condition of segregation resulting from intentional state action directed specifically to the core city schools. . . .

[P]etitioners presented evidence tending to show that the Board, through its actions over a period of years, intentionally created and maintained the segregated character of the core city schools. Respondents countered this evidence by arguing that the segregation in these schools is the result of a racially neutral "neighborhood school policy" and that the acts of which petitioners complain are explicable within the bounds of that policy. . . .

[There is a] well-stated evidentiary principle that "the prior doing of other similar acts, whether clearly a part of a scheme or not, is useful as reducing the possibility that the act in question was done with innocent intent." 2 J. Wigmore, Evidence 200 (3d ed. 1940). . . . [I]n the special context of school desegregation cases, we hold that a finding of intentionally segregative school board actions in a meaningful portion of a school system, as in this case, creates a presumption that other segregated schooling within the system is not adventitious. It establishes, in other words, a prima facie case of unlawful segregative design on the part of school authorities, and shifts to those authorities the burden of proving that other segregated schools within the system are not also the result of intentionally segregative actions. This is true even if it is determined that different areas of the school district should be viewed independently of each other because, even in that situation, there is high probability that where school authorities have effectuated an intentionally segregative policy in a meaningful portion of the school system, similar impermissible considerations have motivated their actions in other areas of the system. We emphasize that the differentiating factor between de jure segregation and so-called de facto segregation to which we referred in *Swann* is *purpose* or *intent* to segregate. Where school authorities have been found to have practiced purposeful segregation . . . in a meaningful or significant segment of a school system, as in the case, . . . it is both fair and reasonable to require that the school authorities bear the burden of showing that their actions as to other segregated schools within the system were not also motivated by segregative intent. . . .

In discharging that burden, it is not enough, of course, that the school authorities rely upon some allegedly logical, racially neutral explanation for their actions. Their burden is to adduce proof sufficient to support a finding that segregative intent was not among the factors that motivated their actions. . . . [Otherwise] it can rebut the prima facie case only by showing that its past segregative acts did not create or contribute to the current segregated condition of the core city schools.

IV

In summary, the District Court on remand, first, will afford respondent School Board the opportunity to prove its contention that the Park Hill area is a separate, identifiable and unrelated section of the school district that should be treated as isolated from the rest of the district. If respondent School Board fails to prove that contention, the District Court, second, will determine whether respondent School Board's conduct over almost a decade after 1960 in carrying out a policy of deliberate racial segregation in the Park Hill schools constitutes the entire school system as a dual school system. If the District Court determines that the Denver school system is a dual school system, respondent School Board has the affirmative duty to desegregate the entire system "root and branch." Green v. County School Board, 391 U.S. at 438. If the District Court determines, however, that the Denver school system is not a dual school system by reason of the Board's actions in Park Hill, the court, third, will afford respondent School Board the opportunity to rebut petitioners' prima facie case of intentional segregation in the core city schools raised by the finding of intentional segregation in the Park Hill schools. There, the Board's burden is to show that its policies and practices with respect to school-site location, school size, school renovations and additions, student-attendance zones, student assignment and transfer options, mobile classroom units, transportation of students, assignment of faculty and staff, etc., considered together and premised on the Board's so-called "neighborhood school" concept, either were not taken in effectuation of a policy to create or maintain segregation in the core city schools, or, if unsuccessful in that effort, were not factors in causing the existing condition of segregation in these schools. Considerations of "fairness" and "policy" demand no less in light of the Board's intentionally segregative actions. If respondent Board fails to rebut petitioners' prima facie case, the District Court must, as in the case of Park Hill, decree all-out desegregation of the core city schools.[59]

REHNQUIST, J., dissenting. . . .

[I]n a school district the size of Denver's, it is quite conceivable that the School Board might have engaged in the racial gerrymandering of the attendance boundary between two particular schools in order to keep one largely Negro and Hispano, and the other largely Anglo, as the District Court found to have been the fact in this case. Such action would have deprived affected minority students who were the victims of such gerrymandering of their consititutional right to equal protection of the laws. But if the school board had been evenhanded in its drawing of the attendance lines for other schools in the district, minority students required to attend other schools within the district would have suffered no such deprivation. . . .

Underlying the Court's entire opinion is its apparent thesis that a district judge is at least permitted to find that if a single attendance zone between two individual schools in the large metropolitan district is found by him to have been "gerrymandered," the school district is guilty of operating a "dual" school system, and is apparently a candidate for what is in practice a federal receivership. Not only the language of the Court in the opinion, but its reliance on the case of Green v. County School Board, 391 U.S. 430, 437-438 (1968), indicates that such would be the case. It would therefore presumably be open to the District Court to require, inter alia, that pupils be transported great distances throughout the district to and from schools whose attendance zones have not been gerrymandered. . . .

The drastic extension of *Brown* which *Green* represented was barely, if at all, explicated in the latter opinion. To require that a genuinely "dual" system be disestablished, in the sense that the assignment of a child to a particular school is not made to depend on his race, is one thing. To require that school boards affirmatively undertake to achieve racial mixing in schools were such mixing is not achieved in sufficient degree by neutrally drawn boundary lines is quite obviously something else.

The court's own language in *Green* makes it unmistakably clear that this significant extension of *Brown's* prohibition against discrimination, and the conversion of that prohibition into an affirmative duty to integrate, was made in the context of a school system which had for a number of years rigidly excluded Negroes from attending the same schools as were attended by whites. Whatever may be

59. Justice White did not participate in the case. Chief Justice Burger concurred in the result. Justice Douglas wrote a brief concurring opinion.

the soundness of that decision in the context of a genuinely "dual" school system, where segregation of the races had once been mandated by law, I can see no constitutional justification for it in a situation such as that which the record shows to have obtained in Denver.

POWELL, J., concurring in part and dissenting in part. . . .

I

In my view we should abandon a distinction which long since has outlived its time, and formulate constitutional principles of national rather than merely regional application. When Brown v. Board of Education, 347 U.S. 483 (1954) (*Brown*), was decided, the distinction between de jure and de facto segregation was consistent with the limited constitutional rationale of that case. The situation confronting the Court, largely confined to the southern States, was officially imposed racial segregation in the schools extending back for many years and usually embodied in constitutional and statutory provisions. . . .

But the doctrine of *Brown I*, as amplified by *Brown II*, 349 U.S. 294 (1955), did not retain its original meaning. In a series of decisions extending from 1954 to 1971 the concept of state neutrality was transformed into the present constitutional doctrine requiring affirmative state action to desegregate school systems. The keystone case was *Green*.

In *Swann*, . . . the Court refrained from even considering whether the evolution of constitutional doctrine from *Brown* to *Green/Swann* undercut whatever logic once supported the de facto/de jure distinction. In imposing on metropolitan southern school districts an affirmative duty, entailing large-scale transportation of pupils, to eliminate segregation in the schools, the Court required these districts to alleviate conditions which in large part did *not* result from historic, state-imposed de jure segregation. Rather, the familiar root cause of segregated schools in *all* the biracial metropolitan areas of our country is essentially the same: one of segregated residential and migratory patterns the impact of which on the racial composition of the schools was often perpetuated and rarely ameliorated by action of public school authorities. This is a national, not a southern, phenomenon. And it is largely unrelated to whether a particular State had or did not have segregative school laws.

II

. . . I concur in the Court's position that the public school authorities are the responsible agency of the State, and that if the affirmative-duty doctrine is sound constitutional law for Charlotte, it is equally so for Denver. I would not, however, perpetuate the de jure/de facto distinction nor would I heave to petitioners the initial tortuous effort of identifying "segregative acts" and deducing "segregative intent." I would hold, quite simply, that where segregated public schools exist within a school district to a substantial degree, there is a prima facie case that the duly constituted public authorities (I will usually refer to them collectively as the "school board") are sufficiently responsible[a] to warrant imposing upon them a

a. A prima facie case of constitutional violation exists when segregation is found to a substantial degree in the schools of a particular district. It is recognized, of course, that this term is relative and

nationally applicable burden to demonstrate they nevertheless are operating a genuinely integrated school system.

A

The principal reason for abandonment of the de jure/de facto distinction is that, in view of the evolution of the holding in *Brown I* into the affirmative-duty doctrine, the distinction no longer can be justified on a principled basis. In decreeing remedial requirements for the Charlotte-Mecklenburg school district, *Swann* dealt with a metropolitan, urbanized area in which the basic causes of segregation were generally similar to those in all sections of the country, and also largely irrelevant to the existence of historic, state-imposed segregation at the time of the *Brown* decision. Further, the extension of the affirmative-duty concept to include compulsory student transportation went well beyond the mere remedying of that portion of school segregation for which former state segregation laws were ever responsible. Moreover, as the Court's opinion today abundantly demonstrates, the facts deemed necessary to establish de jure discrimination present problems of subjective intent which the courts cannot fairly resolve.

At the outset, one must try to identify the constitutional right which is being enforced. I would define it as the right, derived from the Equal Protection Clause, to expect that once the State has assumed responsibility for education, local school boards will operate *integrated school systems* within their respective districts. This means that school authorities, consistent with the generally accepted educational goal of attaining quality education for all pupils, must make and implement their customary decisions with a view toward enhancing integrated school opportunities.

The term "integrated school system" presupposes, of course, a total absence of any laws, regulations, or policies supportive of the type of "legalized" segregation condemned in *Brown.* A system would be integrated in accord with constitutional standards if the responsible authorities had taken appropriate steps to (i) integrate faculties and administration; (ii) scrupulously assure equality of facilities, instruction, and curriculum opportunities throughout the district; (iii) utilize their authority to draw attendance zones to promote integration; and (iv) locate new schools, close old ones, and determine the size and grade categories with this same objective in mind. Where school authorities decide to undertake the transportation of students, this also must be with integrative opportunities in mind.

The foregoing prescription is not intended to be either definitive or all-inclusive, but rather an indication of the contour characteristics of an *integrated school system* in which all citizens and pupils may justifiably be confident that racial discrimination is neither practiced nor tolerated. An integrated school system does not mean — and indeed could not mean in view of the residential patterns of most of our major metropolitan areas — that *every school* must in fact be an integrated unit. A school which happens to be all or predominantly white or all or

provides no precise standards. But circumstances, demographic and otherwise, vary from district to district and hard-and-fast rules should not be formulated. The existence of a substantial percentage of schools populated by students from one race only or predominantly so populated, should trigger the inquiry.

predominantly black is not a "segregated" school in an unconstitutional sense if the system itself is a genuinely integrated one. . . .

Public schools are creatures of the State, and whether the segregation is state-created or state-assisted or merely state-perpetuated should be irrelevant to constitutional principle. The school board exercises pervasive and continuing responsibility over the long-range planning as well as the daily operations of the public school system. It sets policies on attendance zones, faculty employment and assignments, school construction, closings and consolidations, and myriad other matters. School board decisions obviously are not the sole cause of segregated school conditions. But if, after such detailed and complete public supervision, substantial school segregation still persists, the presumption is strong that the school board, by its acts or omissions, is in some part responsible. Where state action and supervision are so pervasive and where, after years of such action, segregated schools continue to exist within the district to a substantial degree, this Court is justified in finding a prima facie case of a constitutional violation. The burden then must fall on the school board to demonstrate it is operating an "integrated school system."

It makes little sense to find prima facie violations and the consequent affirmative duty to desegregate solely in those States with state-imposed segregation at the time of the *Brown* decision. The history of state-imposed segregation is more widespread in our country than the de jure/de facto distinction has traditionally cared to recognize.[b] . . .

B

There is thus no reason as a matter of constitutional principle to adhere to the de jure/de facto distinction in school desegregation cases. In addition, there are reasons of policy and prudent judicial administration which point strongly toward the adoption of a uniform national rule. . . .

The litigation will focus as a consequence of the Court's decision on whether segregation has resulted in any "meaningful or significant" portion of a school system from a school board's "segregative intent." The intractable problems involved in litigating this issue are obvious to any lawyer. . . .

This Court has recognized repeatedly that it is "extremely difficult for a court to ascertain the motivation, or collection of different motivations, that lie behind a legislative enactment," Palmer v. Thompson, 403 U.S. 217, 224 (1971); McGinnis v. Royster, 410 U.S. 263, 276-277 (1973); United States v. O'Brien, 391 U.S. 367, 381 (1968). Whatever difficulties exist with regard to a single statute will be compounded in a judicial review of years of administration of a large and complex school system. Every act of a school board and school administration, and indeed every failure to act where affirmative action is indicated, must now be subject to scrutiny. The most routine decisions with respect to the operation of schools, made almost daily, can affect in varying degrees the extent to which schools are initially segregated, remain in that condition, are desegregated, or — for the long term future — are likely to be one or the other. These decisions in-

b. Indeed, if one goes back far enough, it is probable that all racial segregation, wherever occurring and whether or not confined to the schools, has at some time been supported or maintained by government action. . . .

clude action or nonaction with respect to school building construction and location; the timing of building new schools and their size; the closing and consolidation of schools; the drawing or gerrymandering of student attendance zones; the extent to which a neighborhood policy is enforced; the recruitment, promotion and assignment of faculty and supervisory personnel; policies with respect to transfers from one school to another; whether, and to what extent, special schools will be provided, where they will be located, and who will qualify to attend them; the determination of curriculum, including whether there will be "tracks" that lead primarily to college or to vocational training, and the routing of students into these tracks; and even decisions as to social, recreational, and athletic policies. . . .

[Justice Powell then discussed the appropriate remedies for segregation, emphasizing the importance of neighborhood schools and the disruptiveness of extensive transportation.]

Where school authorities have defaulted in their duty to operate an integrated school system, district courts must insure that affirmative desegregative steps ensue. Many of these can be taken effectively without damaging state and parental interests in having children attend schools within a reasonable vicinity of home. Where desegregative steps are possible within the framework of a system of "neighborhood education," school authorities must pursue them. For example, boundaries of neighborhood attendance zones should be drawn to integrate, to the extent practicable, the school's student body. Construction of new schools should be of such a size and at such a location as to encourage the likelihood of integration. Faculty integration should be attained throughout the school system. An optional majority-to-minority transfer program, with the State providing free transportation to desiring students, is also a helpful adjunct to a desegregated school system. It hardly need be repeated that allocation of resources within the school district must be made with scrupulous fairness among all schools. . . .

[T]here would be no prohibition on court-ordered student transportation in furtherance of desegregation. But it would require that the legitimate community interests in neighborhood school systems be accorded far greater respect. In the balancing of interests so appropriate to a fair and just equitable decree, transportation orders should be applied with special caution to any proposal as disruptive of family life and interests — and ultimately of education itself — as extensive transportation of elementary-age children solely for desegregation purposes. . . .

Note: After Keyes

In Dayton Board of Education v. Brinkman, 433 U.S. 406 (1977), the Court held that the District Court's findings of fact did not justify a systemwide desegregation remedy. The District Court had found a "cumulative violation" based on racial imbalance in schools throughout the system, the use of optional high school attendance zones that permitted white students to avoid attending three predominantly black schools, and the school board's rescission of earlier resolutions acknowledging responsibility for and calling for the remedy of racial imbalance. Justice Rehnquist wrote that racial imbalance did not violate the Equal

Protection Clause absent proof of segregative intent; that even if the high school optional attendance zones were designed with segregative intent, this did not justify a remedy extending to other schools; and that the rescission of school board resolutions was not unconstitutional unless the board was constitutionally obligated to take the action that it rescinded. Justice Rehnquist concluded:

> The duty of both the District Court and of the Court of Appeals in a case such as this, where mandatory segregation by law of the races in the schools has long since ceased, is to first determine whether there was an action in the conduct of the business of the school board which was intended to, and did in fact, discriminate against minority pupils, teachers or staff. Washington v. Davis. . . . If such violations are found, the District Court in the first instance, subject to review by the Court of Appeals, must determine how much incremental segregative effect these violations had on the racial distribution of the Dayton school population as presently constituted, when that distribution is compared to what it would have been in the absence of such constitutional violations. The remedy must be designed to redress that difference, and only if there has been a systemwide impact may there be a systemwide remedy. *Keyes*.

Because of the confused state of the record, the Court remanded to the District Court for further proceedings.

Justice Stevens concurred, noting that "the relevant finding of intent in a case of this kind necessarily depends primarily on objective evidence concerning the effect of the Board's action, rather than the subjective motivation of one or more members of the Board." Justice Brennan concurred in the judgment. He agreed that the findings were not of themselves sufficient to support a systemwide remedy "when considered solely as unconstitutional *actions*," but noted that

> they clearly are very significant as indicia of *intent* on the part of the school board. As we emphasized in *Keyes*, "Plainly, a finding of intentional segregation as to a portion of a school system is not devoid of probative value with respect to other parts of the same school system." Once segregative intent is found, the District Court may more readily conclude that not only blatant, but also subtle actions — and in some circumstances even inaction — justify a finding of unconstitutional segregation that must be redressed by a [systemwide] remedial busing order.

(Justice Marshall did not participate.)

On remand the district court denied relief, finding no evidence that the district was segregated as a result of purposeful segregation. The court of appeals reversed, holding that the district was unconstitutionally segregated at the time of *Brown*, and that the Board had not only failed in its affirmative duty to disestablish its dual school system but had engaged in some intentional segregative practices in the interim, all of which justified a systemwide desegregation remedy.

The Court affirmed in Dayton Board of Education v. Brinkman, 443 U.S. 526 (1979), and in the companion case of Columbus Board of Education v. Penick, 443 U.S. 449 (1979), it upheld a systemwide desegregation order against another Northern school district.

DAYTON BOARD OF EDUCATION v. BRINKMAN, 443 U.S. 526 (1979): WHITE, J. . . . Given intentionally segregated schools in 1954, . . . the Court of Appeals was quite right in holding that the Board was thereafter under a continuing duty to eradicate the effects of that system, and that the system-wide nature of the violation furnished prima facie proof that current segregation in the Dayton schools was caused at least in part by prior intentionally segregative official acts. Thus, judgment for the plaintiffs was authorized and required absent sufficient countervailing evidence by the defendant school officials. At the time of trial, Dunbar High School and the three black elementary schools, or the schools that succeeded them, remained black schools; and most of the schools in Dayton were virtually one-race schools, as were 80% of the classrooms. " '*Every* school which was 90 percent or more black in 1951-52 *or* 1963-64 *or* 1971-72 and which is still in use today remains 90 percent or more black. Of the 25 white schools in 1972-73, *all* opened 90 percent or more white and, if open, were 90 percent or more white in 1971-72, 1963-64 and 1951-52.' " Against this background, the Court of Appeals held "[that] [t]he evidence of record demonstrates convincingly that defendants have failed to eliminate the continuing systemwide effects of their prior discrimination and have intentionally maintained a segregated school system down to the time the complaint was filed in the present case." At the very least, defendants had failed to come forward with evidence to deny "that the current racial composition of the school population reflects the systemwide impact" of the Board's prior discriminatory conduct.

Part of the affirmative duty imposed by our cases, is the obligation not to take any action that would impede the process of disestablishing the dual system and its effects. The Dayton Board, however, had engaged in many post-*Brown* actions that had the effect of increasing or perpetuating segregation. The District Court ignored this compounding of the original constitutional breach on the ground that there was no direct evidence of continued discriminatory purpose. But the measure of the post-*Brown* conduct of a school board under an unsatisfied duty to liquidate a dual system is the effectiveness, not the purpose, of the actions in decreasing or increasing the segregation caused by the dual system. As was clearly established in *Keyes* and *Swann*, the Board had to do more than abandon its prior discriminatory purpose. The Board has had an affirmative responsibility to see that pupil assignment policies and school construction and abandonment practices "are not used and do not serve to perpetuate or reestablish the dual school system," and the Board has a " 'heavy burden' " of showing that actions that increased or continued the effects of the dual system serve important and legitimate ends.

The Board has never seriously contended that it fulfilled its affirmative duty or the heavy burden of explaining its failure to do so. Though the Board was often put on notice of the effects of its acts or omissions, the District Court found that "with one [counterproductive] exception . . . no attempt was made to alter the racial characteristics of any of the schools." The Court of Appeals held that far from performing its constitutional duty, the Board had engaged in "post-1954 actions which actually have exacerbated the racial separation existing at the time of *Brown I*." The court reversed as clearly erroneous the District Court's finding that intentional faculty segregation had ended in 1951; the Court of Appeals found that it had effectively continued into the 1970's. This was a systemwide practice and strong evidence that the Board was continuing its efforts to segregate students. Dunbar High School remained as a black high school until 1962, when a new Dunbar High School opened with a virtually all-black faculty and student body. The old Dunbar was converted into an elementary school to which children from two black grade schools were assigned. Furthermore, the Court of Appeals held that since 1954 the Board had used some "optional attendance zones for racially discriminatory purposes in clear violation of the Equal Protection Clause." The District Court's finding to the contrary was clearly erroneous. At the very least, the use of such zones amounted to a perpetuation of the existing dual school system. Likewise, the Board failed in its duty and perpetuated racial separation in the schools by its pattern of school construction and site selection, recited by the District Court, that resulted in 22 of the 24 new schools built between 1950 and the filing of the complaint opening 90% black or white. The same pattern appeared with respect to additions of classroom space made to existing schools. Seventy-eight of a total of 86 additions were made to schools that were 90% of one race. We see no reason to disturb these factual determinations, which conclusively show the breach of duty found by the Court of Appeals. . . .

Finally, petitioners contend that the District Court correctly interpreted our earlier decision in this litigation as requiring respondents to prove with respect to each individual act of discrimination precisely what effect it has had on current patterns of segregation. This argument results from a misunderstanding of *Dayton,* where the violation that had then been established included at most a few high schools. We have found no reason to fault the Court of Appeals' findings after our remand that a sufficient case of current, systemwide effect had been established. In reliance on its decision in *Columbus,* the Court of Appeals held that:

> First, the dual school system extant at the time of *Brown I* embraced "a systemwide program of segregation affecting a substantial portion of the schools, teachers, and facilities" of the Dayton schools, and, thus, clearly had systemwide impact. . . . Secondly, the post-1954 failure of defendants to desegregate the school system in contravention of their affirmative constitutional duty obviously had systemwide impact. . . . The impact of defendants' practices with respect to the assignment of faculty and students, use of optional attendance zones, school construction and site selection, and grade structure and reorganization clearly was systemwide in that actions perpetuated and increased public school segregation in Dayton.

As we note in *Columbus* today, this is not a misuse of *Keyes,* "where we held that purposeful discrimination in a substantial part of a school system furnishes a sufficient basis for an inferential finding of a systemwide discriminatory intent unless otherwise rebutted, and that given the purpose to operate a dual school system one could infer a connection between such a purpose and racial separation in other parts of the school system." The Court of Appeals was also quite justified in utilizing the Board's total failure to fulfill its affirmative duty — and indeed its conduct resulting in increased segregation — to trace the current, systemwide segregation back to the purposefully dual system of the 1950's and to the subsequent acts of intentional discrimination.

[Justice Rehnquist, joined by Justice Powell, dissented in both *Columbus* and *Dayton.* The essence of his lengthy opinion in the former case is captured by the remark in the latter that "the Court's cascade of presumptions . . . sweeps away the distinction between de facto and de jure segregation." (Justice Powell also wrote separately in dissent.) Justice Stewart, joined by Chief Justice Burger, argued that because of the subtlety of the factual issues in school desegregation cases such as these, "appellate courts should accept even more readily the factual findings of courts of first instance." He thus dissented in *Dayton,* but concurred in the result in *Columbus,* where the trial court had found the school district unconstitutionally segregated.]

7. *Interdistrict School Segregation and Remedies*

MILLIKEN v. BRADLEY, 418 U.S. 717 (1974): [The district court, having found de jure segregation within the city of Detroit, entered a decree that included 53 surrounding suburban districts. Although the city was predominantly black and the suburbs white, there was no substantial evidence of race-dependent action (such as manipulating boundaries) designed to segregate the city's blacks from the suburbs' whites. On this basis, and emphasizing the importance of local control over public schools, the Supreme Court reversed.]

BURGER, C.J. . . . The controlling principle consistently expounded in our holdings is that the scope of the remedy is determined by the nature and extent of the constitutional violation. Before the boundaries of separate and autonomous school districts may be set aside by consolidating the separate units for remedial purposes or by imposing a cross-district remedy, it must first be shown . . . that racially discriminatory acts of the state or local school districts, or of a single school district have been a substantial cause of inter-district segregation. Thus an inter-district remedy might be in order where the racially discriminatory acts of one or more school districts caused racial segregation in an adjacent district, or where district lines have been deliberately drawn on the basis of race. In such circumstances an inter-district remedy would be appropriate to eliminate the inter-district segregation directly caused by the constitutional violation. Conversely, without an inter-district violation and inter-district effect, there is no constitutional wrong calling for an inter-district remedy.

. . . To approve the remedy ordered by the court would impose on the outlying districts, not shown to have committed any constitutional violation, a wholly impermissible remedy based on a standard not hinted at in *Brown I* and *II* or any holding of this Court.[60]

WHITE, J., joined by Douglas, Brennan, and Marshall, JJ., dissenting. . . .

I am . . . mystified how the Court can ignore the legal reality that the constitutional violations, even if occurring locally, were committed by governmental entities for which the State is responsible and that it is the State that must respond to the command of the Fourteenth Amendment. An interdistrict remedy for the infringements that occurred in this case is well within the confines and powers of

60. Chief Justice Burger distinguished the Court's earlier decisions in Wright v. Emporia, 407 U.S. 451 (1972), and United States v. Scotland Neck Bd. of Educ., 407 U.S. 484 (1972), where the Court forbade carving new (largely white) school districts from exerting de jure segregated districts in the process of dismantling dual school systems. Although the evident purpose of the secessions was to create segregated enclaves, the Court in the 1972 decisions relied solely on the effects and characterized the lower courts' inquiry into purpose as fruitless and irrelevant.

the State, which is the governmental entity ultimately responsible for desegregating its schools. . . .

The result reached by the Court certainly cannot be supported by the theory that the configuration of local governmental units is immune from alteration when necessary to redress constitutional violations. . . . [T]he Court has elsewhere required the public bodies of a State to restructure the State's political subdivisions to remedy infringements of the constitutional rights of certain members of its populace, notably in the reapportionment cases. In Reynolds v. Sims, 377 U.S. 533 (1964), for example, which held that equal protection of the laws demands that the seats in both houses of a bicameral state legislature be apportioned on a population basis, thus necessitating wholesale revision of Alabama's voting districts, the Court remarked: "Political subdivisions of States — counties, cities, or whatever — never were and never have been considered as sovereign entities. Rather, they have been traditionally regarded as subordinate governmental instrumentalities created by the State to assist in the carrying out of state governmental functions." And even more pointedly, the Court declared in Gomillion v. Lightfoot, 364 U.S. 339, 344-345 (1960), that "[l]egislative control of municipalities, no less than other state power, lies within the scope of relevant limitations imposed by the United States Constitution."

MARSHALL, J., dissenting. . . . [Justice Marshall emphasized the state's control over public education and suggested how the state's action might have contributed to the disparity between the racial makeup of Detroit and of its surrounding suburbs.] . . . The State's creation, through de jure acts of segregation, of a growing core of all-Negro schools inevitably acted as a magnet to attract Negroes to the areas served by such schools and to deter them from settling either in other areas of the city or in the suburbs. By the same token, the growing core of all-Negro schools inevitably helped drive whites to other areas of the city or to the suburbs. . . . The rippling effects on residential patterns caused by purposeful acts of segregation do not automatically subside at the school district border. With rare exceptions, these effects naturally spread through all the residential neighborhoods within a metropolitan area.

The State must also bear part of the blame for the white flight to the suburbs which would be forthcoming from a Detroit-only decree and would render such a remedy ineffective. Having created a system where whites and Negroes were intentionally kept apart so that they could not become accustomed to learning together, the State is responsible for the fact that many whites will react to the dismantling of that segregated system by attempting to flee to the suburbs. Allowing that flight to the suburbs to succeed, the Court today allows the State to profit from its own wrong and to perpetuate for years to come the separation of the races it achieved in the past by purposeful state action.

Discussion

1. The Court nominally adheres to two principles: (a) that the Fourteenth Amendment prohibits de jure but not de facto segregation, and (b) that "the scope of the remedy is determined by the nature and extent of the constitutional violation." Milliken v. Bradley, supra. Which, if any, of the post-*Brown* decisions go beyond these principles?

2. What arguments can you make supporting or rejecting the distinction between de jure and de facto school segregation? Does the original understanding of the Fourteenth Amendment support or disfavor the distinction?

3. *Should* the scope of a remedy be determined by the nature and extent of the violation? Dissenting in *Milliken,* Justice Marshall wrote:

> The majority asserts . . . that involvement of outlying districts would do violence to the accepted principle that "the nature of the violation determines the scope of the remedy." Not only is the majority's attempt to find in this single phrase the answer to the complex and difficult questions presented in this case hopelessly simplistic, but more importantly, the Court reads these words in a manner which perverts their obvious meaning. The nature of a violation determines the scope of the remedy simply because the function of any remedy is to cure the violation to which it is addressed. In school segregation cases, as in other equitable causes, a remedy which effectively cures the violation is what is required. No more is necessary, but we can tolerate no less. To read this principle as barring a District Court from imposing the only effective remedy for past segregation and remitting the court to a patently ineffective alternative is, in my view, to turn a simple commonsense rule into a cruel and meaningless paradox. Ironically, by ruling out an inter-district remedy, the only relief which promises to cure segregation in the Detroit public schools, the majority flouts the very principle on which it purports to rely.

4. In Swann v. Charlotte-Mecklenburg Board of Education, 431 F.2d 128 (4th Cir. 1970), the Court of Appeals noted:

> The district judge pointed out that black residences are concentrated in the northwest quadrant of Charlotte as a result of both public and private action. North Carolina courts, in common with many courts elsewhere, enforced racially restrictive covenants on real property until Shelley v. Kraemer, 334 U.S. 1 (1945), prohibited this discriminatory practice. Presently the city zoning ordinances differentiate between black and white residential areas. . . . The district judge also found that urban renewal projects, supported by heavy federal financing and the active participation of local government, contributed to the city's racially segregated housing patterns. The school board, for its part, located schools in black residential areas and fixed the size of the schools to accommodate the needs of immediate neighborhoods. Predominantly black schools were the inevitable result. The interplay of these policies on both residential and educational segregation previously has been recognized by this and other courts. The fact that similar forces operate in cities throughout the nation under the mask of de facto segregation provides no justification for allowing us to ignore the part that government plays in creating segregated neighborhood schools.

In the Supreme Court, Chief Justice Burger wrote that "[w]e do not reach in this case the question whether a showing that school segregation is a consequence of other types of state action, without any discriminatory action by a school desegregation decree." If the Court did reach the question, how should it be resolved?

5. The Court in *Milliken* emphasized the importance of community control over public schools, which would be endangered by the structure and dynamics of an interdistrict decree. Some black leaders and organizations have argued against school desegregation and for black community-controlled schools. If a large proportion of a black community so desired, would it be constitutionally

permissible (a) to allow segregation to continue in a formerly de jure segregated system, (b) to fail to remedy de facto segregation in order to maintain segregated black schools? To what extent are the factors that disfavor racial classifications present in these situations? Does the constitutionality of "voluntary" segregation depend upon its objectives?

II. The Antidiscrimination Principle and the "Suspect Classification" Standard

The opinion in *Brown* emphasized the particular harms caused by segregation in the classroom. The per curiam decisions that quickly followed, extending the holding to prohibit state-mandated segregation in *all* spheres, provided no clue about how the principles of *Brown* applied, say, to segregated restrooms. The Jim Crow system was so obviously evil that the Court had no need to articulate the parameters of the antidiscrimination principle implicit in these holdings. As we shall see, however, the problems of remedying school segregation and the issues surrounding affirmative action required, and still require, a return to first principles. We therefore take leave of the original history of the Fourteenth Amendment to inquire into the seemingly obvious questions of when and why it is improper for the government to use race as a criterion for classifying people.

A. The Antidiscrimination Principle

PAUL BREST, FOREWORD: IN DEFENSE OF THE ANTIDISCRIMINATION PRINCIPLE

90 Harv. L. Rev. 1, 6-11 (1976)

By the "antidiscrimination principle" I mean the general principle disfavoring classifications and other decisions and practices that depend on the race (or ethnic origin) of the parties affected.[a] The antidiscrimination principle guards against certain defects in the *process* by which race-dependent decisions are made and also against certain harmful *results* of race-dependent decisions. Restricting the principle to a unitary purpose vitiates its moral force and requires the use of sophisticated reasoning to explain applications that seem self-evident.

1. Defects of Process

The antidiscrimination principle is designed to prevent both irrational and unfair infliction of injury.

Race-dependent decisions are irrational insofar as they reflect the assumption that members of one race are less worthy than other people. Not all such decisions are necessarily irrational, however. For example, if black laborers tend to be

a. For the moment, I leave open whether the antidiscrimination principle disfavors so-called "benign" race-dependent practices — practices designed to benefit, and that seem in fact to benefit, the member of traditionally disadvantaged minorities.

absent from work more often than their white counterparts — for whatever reason — it is not irrational for an employer to prefer white applicants for the job. If Americans of Japanese ancestry were more prone to disloyalty than Caucasians during World War II, it was not irrational for the United States government to take special precautions against sabotage and espionage by them. Regulations and decisions based on statistical generalizations are commonplace in all developed societies and essential to their functioning. And it is often rational for decisionmakers to rely on weak and even dubious generalizations. Consider, for example, a fire department's or airline's policy against employing overweight personnel, based on the rather slight probability that they will suffer a heart attack while on duty.

In short, the mere fact that most blacks are industrious and most Japanese-Americans loyal does not make the employer's or the Government's decision irrational. Indeed, if all race-dependent decisions were irrational, there would be no need for an antidiscrimination principle, for it would suffice to apply the widely held moral, constitutional, and practical principle that forbids treating persons irrationally. The antidiscrimination principle fills a special need because — as even a glance at history indicates — race-dependent decisions that are rational and purport to be based solely on legitimate considerations are likely in fact to rest on assumptions of the differential worth of racial groups or on the related phenomenon of racially selective sympathy and indifference.

Mr. Justice Black focused on the first of these dangers in Korematsu v. United States, the case in which the Government sought to justify its policy of interning Japanese-Americans, and in which the Court first enunciated the modern "suspect classification" doctrine. He wrote for the majority:

> [A]ll legal restrictions which curtail the civil rights of a single racial group are immediately suspect. . . . [C]ourts must subject them to the most rigid scrutiny. Pressing public necessity may sometimes justify the existence of such restrictions; racial antagonism never can.

Mr. Justice Black chose the word "suspect" advisedly. For, although a court often cannot ascertain the true motives underlying a decision, our history and traditions provide strong reasons to suspect that racial classifications ultimately rest on assumptions of the differential worth of racial groups. These racial value judgments appear in forms besides "racial antagonism" — for example in paternalistic assumptions of racial inferiority.

By the phenomenon of racially selective sympathy and indifference I mean the unconscious failure to extend to a minority the same recognition of humanity, and hence the same sympathy and care, given as a matter of course to one's own group.

Although racially selective sympathy and indifference (hereafter, just indifference) is an inevitable consequence of attributing intrinsic value to membership in a racial group, it may also result from a desire to enhance our own power and esteem by enhancing the power and esteem of members of groups to which we belong. And it may also result — often unconsciously — from our tendency to sympathize most readily with those who seem most like ourselves. Whatever its cause, decisions that reflect this phenomenon, like those reflecting overt racial hostility, are unfair; for by hypothesis, they are decisions disadvantaging minority persons that would not be made under the identical circumstances if they disadvantaged members of the dominant group. The unequal treatment could be justified only if one group were in fact more worthy than the other. This justification failing, such treatment violates the cardinal rule of fairness — the Golden Rule.

2. Harmful Results

A second and independent rationale for the antidiscrimination principle is the prevention of the harms which may result from race-dependent decisions. Often, the most obvious harm is the denial of the opportunity to secure a desired benefit — a job, a night's lodging at a motel, a vote. But this does not completely describe the consequences of race-dependent decisionmaking. Decisions based on assumptions of intrinsic worth and selective indifference inflict psychological injury by stigmatizing their victims as inferior. Moreover, because acts of discrimination tend to occur in pervasive patterns, their victims suffer especially frustrating, cumulative and debilitating injuries.

The prevention of stigmatic harm played a major role in Strauder v. West Virginia, the first race discrimination case to reach the Supreme Court after the Civil War. On alternative grounds, the Court struck down a state law excluding blacks from juries. Although the first ground was the black defendant's right to a jury composed of a cross-section of the community, the second involved the rights of the members of the black community themselves. Mr. Justice Strong reasoned that the fourteenth amendment protects Negroes "from legal discriminations, implying their inferiority in civil society," and held that the West Virginia statute was "practically a brand upon them . . . , an assertion of their inferiority." Dissenting in Plessy v. Ferguson, Mr. Justice Harlan likewise observed that the segregation of railway passengers was a "badge of servitude" because it proceeded "on the ground that colored citizens are . . . inferior and degraded."

Similarly, the essence of Brown v. Board of Education lay in Chief Justice Warren's observation that the segregation of black public school pupils "generates a feeling of inferiority as to their status in the community that may affect their hearts and minds in a way unlikely ever to be undone." As Charles L. Black noted, the Court could not properly have ignored "a plain fact about the society of the United States — the fact that the social meaning of segregation is the putting of the Negro in a position of walled-off inferiority — or the other equally plain fact that such treatment is hurtful to human beings."

Recognition of the stigmatic injury inflicted by discrimination explains applications of the antidiscrimination principle where the material harm seems slight or problematic. For example, it fully explains the harmfulness of de jure school segregation without the need to invoke controversial social science evidence concerning the effects of segregation on achievement, interracial attitudes, and the like, and thus explains the Supreme Court's casual extension of *Brown* to prohibit the segregation of public beaches, parks, golf courses and buses. It also explains how present practices that are racially neutral may nonetheless perpetuate the harms of past de jure segregation.

Racial generalizations usually inflict psychic injury whether or not they are in fact premised on assumptions of differential moral worth. Although all of us recognize that institutional decisions must depend on generalizations based on objective characteristics of persons and things rather than on individualized judgments, we nonetheless tend to feel unfairly treated when disadvantaged by a generalization that is not true as applied to us. Generalizations based on immutable personal traits such as race or sex are especially frustrating because we can do nothing to escape their operation. These generalizations are still more pernicious, for they are often premised on the supposed correlation between the inherited characteristic and the undesirable voluntary behavior of those who possess the characteristic — for example, blacks are less industrious, trustworthy or clean than whites. Because the behavior is voluntary, and hence the proper object of moral condemnation, individuals as to whom the generalization is inaccurate may justifiably feel that the decisionmaker has passed moral judgment on them.

The psychological injury inflicted by generalizations based on race is compounded by the frustrating and cumulative nature of their material injuries. Racial generalizations are pervasive and have traditionally operated in the same direction — to the disadvantage of members of the minority group. A person who is denied one opportunity because he or she is short or overweight will find other opportunities, for in our society height and weight do not often serve as the bases for generalizations determining who will receive benefits. By contrast, at least until very recently, a black was not denied *an* opportunity because of his or her race, but denied virtually *all* desirable opportunities. As door after door is shut in one's face, the individual acts of discrimination combine into a systematic and grossly inequitable frustration of opportunity.

The cumulative disadvantage caused by the use of race as a proxy even for legitimate characteristics provides an independent ground for disfavoring nonbenign race-dependent decisions regardless of the integrity of the process by which they were made. To the unprejudiced employer who would prefer white applicants to blacks solely for reasons of efficiency, the antidiscrimination principle says in effect: "If you were the only one to do this, we would permit you to make efficient generalizations based on race. But so many other firms might employ similar generalizations that black individuals would suffer great cumulative harms. And, in the absence of an overriding justification, this cannot be permitted."

In Democracy and Distrust (1980), John Ely emphasizes the defects of legislative process that the antidiscrimination principle may remedy. He puts forward alternative justifications for the treatment of racial classifications as "suspect." One ground for suspicion (id. at 153) is "first degree prejudice":

> If the doctrine of suspect classifications is a roundabout way of uncovering official attempts to inflict inequality for its own sake — to treat a group worse not in the service of some overriding social goal but largely for the sake of simply disadvantaging its members — it would seem to follow that one set of classifications we should treat as suspicious are those that disadvantage groups we know to be the object of widespread vilification, groups we know others (specifically those who control the legislative process) might wish to injure.

The alternative ground for suspicion is "second degree prejudice." Although legislation inevitably involves overgeneralization, we should be suspicious of "a generalization whose incidence of counterexample is significantly higher than the legislative authority appears to have thought it was" (id.):

> [T]o disadvantage — in the perceived service of some overriding social goal — a thousand persons that a more individualized (but more costly) test or procedure would exclude, under the impression that only five hundred fit that description, is to deny the five hundred to whose existence you are oblivious their right to equal concern and respect, by valuing their welfare at zero.

"The rub comes in how the Court should go about identifying" prejudice in the second degree. Building on the observation that "prejudice is a lens that distorts reality," Professor Ely continues (id. at 158-159):

> In deciding how much presumptive credit to extend a given generalization in our everyday lives, we would want to know where it came from — who came up with it and whether it is one that serves their interests. This commonsense insight . . . seems relevant to the constitutional inquiry as well. The choice between classifying on the basis of a comparative generalization and attempting to come up with a more discriminating formula always involves balancing the increase in fairness that greater individualization will produce against the added costs it will entail. Where the generalization involved is one that serves the interests of the decision-makers, however, certain dangers that are inherent in any balancing process are significantly intensified. Where it tangibly enhances their fortunes, the dangers may be most obvious. . . . But even where no tangible gain can be identified, there are psychic rewards in self-flattering generalizations. . . . "The easiest idea to sell anyone is that he is better than someone else," and it is a rare person who isn't delighted to hear and prone to accept comparative characterizations of ethnic or other groups that suggest the relative superiority of those groups to which he belongs. . . .
>
> Thus generalizations to the effect, say, that whites in general are smarter or more industrious than blacks, men more stable emotionally than women, or native-born Americans more patriotic than Americans born elsewhere, are likely to go down pretty easily . . . with groups whose demography is that of the typical American legislature. . . . By seizing upon the positive myths about groups to which they belong and the negative myths about those to which they don't, or for that matter the realities respecting some or most members of the two classes, legislators, like the rest of us, are likely to assume too readily that not many of "them" will be unfairly deprived, nor many of "us" unfairly benefited, by a classification of this type.

Do the theories of "process" and "result" defects fully capture your aversion to discriminatory laws and practices? Consider two radically opposed views of the equal protection clause — a "color-blind" and an "anti-subordination" conception.

> Some people say: "Well, the fourteenth amendment mandates that government be color-blind (period)." This is not a theory, however; it is an assertion in need of a theory or justification. What might that be?
>
> The Court has never addressed the question systematically, but some opinions suggest that it is unfair to burden anyone because of characteristics that are beyond his or her control. In *Bakke* [p.710 infra], Justices Brennan et al. referred to "our

deep belief that legal burdens should bear some relationship to individual responsibility or wrongdoing." . . .

I doubt that the original history of the equal protection clause provides much support for this position. Rather, its source lies in our culture, traditions, and psychology — a psychology that tells us that it is frustrating and painful, even if we are not stigmatized or the objects of prejudice, to be classified and disadvantaged based on characteristics beyond our control. Yet there are many areas besides race and sex and the traditional suspect-type classifications where this happens to us all the time and we are willing to accept it. To develop this theory, one must at least distinguish the circumstances where being disadvantaged because of an immutable characteristic is constitutionally permissible and those where it should be disfavored or forbidden.[61]

RUTH COLKER, ANTI-SUBORDINATION ABOVE ALL: SEX, RACE, AND EQUAL PROTECTION

61 N.Y.U.L. Rev. 1003, 1005-1014 (1986)

. . . Under the anti-differentiation perspective, it is inappropriate to treat individuals differently on the basis of a particular normative view about race or sex. It is an individual rights perspective in two respects. First, it focuses on the motivation of the individual institution that has allegedly discriminated, without attention to the larger societal context in which the institution operates. Second, the anti-differentiation perspective focuses on the specific effect of the alleged discrimination on discrete individuals, rather than on groups. Race- and sex-specific policies or actions are invalid under this perspective because they reflect invidious motivation and result in dissimilar treatment for similarly situated individuals. It is equally invidious for white men to be treated differently from black women as for black women to be treated differently from white men under this perspective, because both situations violate the preeminent norm of equal treatment. Anti-differentiation advocates therefore argue for "color-blindness" or "sex-blindness" in the development and analysis of legislative and institutional policies, and frequently criticize affirmative action as violating that principle.

In this Article, I argue that courts should analyze equal protection cases from an anti-subordination perspective. Under the anti-subordination perspective, it is inappropriate for certain groups in society to have subordinated status because of their lack of power in society as a whole. This approach seeks to eliminate the power disparities between men and women, and between whites and non-whites, through the development of laws and policies that directly redress those disparities. From an anti-subordination perspective, both facially differentiating and facially neutral policies are invidious only if they perpetuate racial or sexual hierarchy.

In contrast to the anti-differentiation approach, the anti-subordination perspective is a group-based perspective, in two ways. First, it focuses on society's role in creating subordination. Second, it focuses on the way in which this subordination affects, or has affected groups of people. It is more invidious for women

61. Paul Brest, Affirmative Action and the Constitution: Three Theories, 72 Iowa L. Rev. 281 (1987). The author is, in fact, deeply skeptical about the possibility of a satisfactory justification for a color-blind standard.

or blacks to be treated worse than white men than for men or whites to be treated worse than black women under this perspective, because of the differing histories and contexts of subordination faced by these groups. Anti-subordination proponents therefore advocate the use of race- or sex-specific policies, such as affirmative action, when those policies redress the subordination of racial minorities or women.

The courts have struggled with the choice between the anti-differentiation and anti-subordination perspectives. The most obvious sources of this tension have been the affirmative action cases, where the courts have grappled with the issue of whether the princple of anti-differentiation should be compromised by accommodation of race- or sex-specific policies that are instituted to overcome a prior history of subordination of racial minorities or women. . . .

Although much of the scholarship on equal protection doctrine assumes that the anti-differentiation principle is justifiably the dominant perspective, . . . the anti-subordination principle better explains both much of the law and the aversion we feel to race and sex discrimination.

. . . [T]he anti-subordination perspective is consistent with the history of the equal protection clause and reflects a living aspiration that will help us move towards a world of equality. Historically, the equal protection principle developed to remedy a history of subordination against a particular group in society, blacks. Aspirationally, it reminds us that no group should remain subordinated in our society and that we should therefore take seriously the claims of women and of other discrete minorities that they have been subjected to pervasive discrimination in our society.

The anti-differentiation principle, in contrast, does a disservice to this history and fundamental aspiration by asserting that discrimination against whites is as problematic as discrimination against blacks. We have not decided, as a nation, that all distinctions are invidious. We permit distinctions on the basis of intelligence or ability. We only prohibit distinctions that we have good reasons to believe are biased or irrational, and it is group-based experiences that primarily inform us as to which kinds of distinctions are biased or irrational. Thus, the anti-subordination principle, by recognizing and drawing on the historical subordination of blacks and women, offers a substantive explanation for why certain distinctions are subjected to closer scrutiny. . . .

Discussion

1. What is the relationship between the "process" and "result" aspects of the antidiscrimination principle as described by Brest and Ely, and the antidifferentiation and antisubordination principles described by Colker?

2. Assume that Colker's antisubordination principle is in fact the best approach to the Fourteenth Amendment. Whom would you trust to make the kinds of empirical judgments required by the principle? In particular, would you expect members of the judiciary to be especially skilled and/or trustworthy in making these judgments? Recall Plessy v. Ferguson, p.245 supra, and the promise that the Court would not tolerate measures designed for the "annoyance or oppression of a particular race." Are there "neutral" tests to determine what counts as an "annoyance" or "oppression" or what is invidiously "subordinating" as opposed to "reasonable"? Does one need some special training in social interpreta-

tion — e.g., training in interpretive sociology or anthropology — in order to make such judgments, and do law schools offer such training?

B. Operational Criteria for Implementing the Antidiscrimination Principle

The preceding discussions caution against the use of racial classifications, but do not determine under what circumstances, if any, racial classifications may be employed. There are at least three possibilities: (1) The dangers inherent in using race are so great that, as a prophylactic measure, government must never use it as a decisionmaking criterion — that is, racial classifications are per se impermissible; (2) the dangers are such that any use of race is justified only if it is necessary to the promotion of extraordinarily important government interests; (3) in each case, the decisionmaker should inquire to what extent the regulation gives rise to the dangers inherent in the use of race and then weigh these dangers against the governmental interest promoted. Consider the approaches that were and should have been taken in resolving the following issues.

1. The Imposition of Unequal Burdens Based on Race

Recall Korematsu v. United States, p.474 supra, in which the Court upheld a conviction of a Japanese-American for refusing to obey Executive Order 9066 excluding all Japanese-Americans from the West Coast states during World War II. Justice Black, writing for the Court, stated the criterion under which the exclusion order was tested:

> [A]ll legal restrictions which curtail the civil rights of a single racial group are immediately suspect. That is not to say that all such restrictions are unconstitutional. It is to say that courts must subject them to the most rigid scrutiny. Pressing public necessity may sometimes justify the existence of such restrictions; racial antagonism never can.

Although the Court recognized that excluding Korematsu and many thousands of other Japanese-Americans from their homes constituted an extreme deprivation, it nonetheless found it a reasonable exercise of political-military judgment. The Court pointed to the probability that *some* Japanese-Americans were disloyal as legitimating the general exclusion given that the specific "number and strength [of the disloyal] could not be precisely and quickly ascertained. We cannot say that the war-making branches of the Government did not have ground for believing that in a critical hour such persons could not readily be isolated and separately dealt with."

It is doubtful that Justice Black disagreed with the dissenting justices that the classification was both underinclusive (in leaving German- and Italian-Americans untouched) and overinclusive (in excluding *all* Japanese-Americans and not simply those against whom evidence of disloyalty existed). Still, according to the majority, the classification was reasonable, with "reasonableness" inextricably related to the magnitude of the interest asserted by the United States government.

Discussion

1. In a 1960 lecture criticizing the Court's willingness to balance First Amendment rights against countervailing governmental interests, Justice Black asserted:[62]

> The great danger of the judiciary balancing process is that in times of emergency and stress it gives Government the power to do what it thinks necessary to protect itself, regardless of the rights of individuals. If the need is great, the right of Government can always be said to outweigh the rights of the individual. If "balancing" is accepted as the test, it would be hard for any conscientious judge to hold otherwise in times of dire need. And laws adopted in times of dire need are often very hasty and oppressive laws. . . . Misuse of government power, particularly in times of stress, has brought suffering to humanity in all ages about which we have authentic history.

Is the Court's criterion in *Korematsu* — the "suspect classification" standard — the proper one in the circumstances, or should the Court have held that racially discriminatory burdens are unconstitutional per se whatever the countervailing interests? Assuming that the Court's criterion is proper, did the Court apply it correctly? What more information, if any, is necessary to answer this? Is Justice Murphy's analysis tenable?

2. *Korematsu* was the last Supreme Court decision to uphold an overt racial discrimination. The Court's only subsequent intimation that (nonremedial) discrimination or segregation might be permitted came in Lee v. Washington, 390 U.S. 333 (1968). There, the Court summarily affirmed an order directing desegregation of the Alabama prison system, noting, however, that nothing in the order precluded "allowance for the necessities of prison security and discipline." In a one-paragraph concurrence, Justices Black, Harlan, and Stewart made explicit "something that is left to be gathered only by implication from the Court's opinion. This is that prison authorities have the right, acting in good faith and in particularized circumstances, to take into account racial tensions in maintaining security, discipline, and good order in prisons and jails."

Would racial segregation in prisons be a permissible response to conditions of the sort described in the following material by James Jacobs?[63]

> The inmate leaders, except one, were black, even though almost 50 percent of the inmates were white. The white prisoners were unable to organize. Consequently, they were highly vulnerable to exploitation.
>
> "The exploitation matrix typically consists of four groups, and the form of exploitation found in each is fairly clear cut. At the top normally is a black leader called a 'heavy.' He is followed closely by three or four black lieutenants. The third group,

62. Hugo Black, The Bill of Rights, 35 N.Y.U.L. Rev. 865, 878-879 (1960).

63. James Jacobs, Race Relations and the Prison Subculture, in 1 Crime and Justice: An Annual Review of Research (Morris & Toury eds. 1979). Jacobs adds:

> Aside from Italian cliques clothed in the Mafia mystique, white cliques are too weak to offer individuals any protection in the predatory prisoner subculture. Only in California does it appear that white prisoners have been able to achieve a strong enough organization to protect themselves. It is significant that such organization has been achieved by groups which already had some sense of group consciousness ("okies" and "bikers"), and only then by an extreme emphasis upon white racism. Neo-Nazi prisoner movements have also appeared in Illinois, especially at Menard, and may in the long run be the basis on which white prisoners achieve solidarity.

a mixture of eight to sixteen black and white youths, do the bidding of those at the top. This group is divided into a top half of mostly blacks, known as 'alright guys,' with the bottom half comprised mostly of whites, designated as 'chumps.' One or two white scapegoats make up the fourth group in each cottage. These scapegoats become the sexual victims of the first three groups." . . .

Numbers will not fully explain the hegemony of black and other minority prisoners, even when the dominant group is also a majority. The key to black dominance is their greater solidarity and ability to intimidate whites. As the distinct minority in the larger society, blacks have long experienced racial discrimination. They have necessarily defined themselves in terms of their racial identity and have linked their opportunities in the larger society to the fate of their race. Whites, especially outside the south, have had almost no experience in grouping together on the basis of being white. Ethnicity has been a more important basis for social interaction, although even ethnicity has been a weaker basis of collective action for whites than race for blacks. "Whiteness" simply possesses no ideological or cultural significance in American society, except for racist fringe groups. Consequently, whites face imprisonment alone or in small cliques based on outside friendships, neighborhood, or ethnic background.

Note: Custody, Adoption, and Race

In Palmore v. Sidoti, 466 U.S. 429 (1984), the Supreme Court unanimously invalidated "a judgment of a state court divesting a natural mother of the custody of her infant child because of her remarriage to a person of a different race." When Linda and Anthony Sidoti, both white, divorced in May 1980, the Florida court awarded custody of their three-year-old daughter to the mother. In September 1981, Anthony petitioned for a modification of that judgment on the ground, among others, that Linda was living with an African-American man (whom she had married by the time of the hearing). Although the court specifically found that Linda remained a fit parent and that her husband was "respectable," it awarded custody to Anthony. The court apparently took into account a counselor's conclusion that Linda "has chosen for herself and for her child, a life-style unacceptable to her father *and to society* . . ." (emphasis supplied by the Supreme Court). The Florida court added:

> [D]espite the strides that have been made in bettering relations between the races in this country, it is inevitable that Melanie will, if allowed to remain in her present situation and attain[ ] school age and thus [become] more vulnerable to peer pressures, suffer from the social stigmatization that is sure to come.

Chief Justice Burger observed that "it is clear that the outcome would have been different had petitioner married a Caucasian male of similar respectability," and that "the action of the Florida court must be tested by "the most exacting scrutiny."

> [The best interest of the child is] indisputably a substantial governmental interest for purposes of the Equal Protection Clause.
>
> It would ignore reality to suggest that racial and ethnic prejudices do not exist. . . . There is a risk that a child living with a step-parent of a different race may be

subject to a variety of pressures and stresses not present if the child were living with parents of the same racial or ethnic origin.

The question, however, is whether the reality of private biases and the possible injury they might inflict are permissible considerations for removal of an infant child from the custody of its natural mother. We have little difficulty concluding that they are not. The Constitution cannot control such prejudices but neither can it tolerate them. Private biases may be outside the reach of the law, but the law cannot, directly or indirectly, give them effect. . . .

This is by no means the first time that acknowledged racial prejudice has been invoked to justify racial classifications. In Buchannan v. Warley, 245 U.S. 60 (1917), for example, this Court invalidated a Kentucky law forbidding Negroes from buying homes in white neighborhoods. "It is urged that this proposed segregation will promote the public peace by preventing race conflicts. Desirable as this is, and important as is the preservation of the public peace, this aim cannot be accomplished by laws or ordinances which deny rights created or protected by the Federal Constitution." Whatever problems racially-mixed households may pose for children in 1984 can no more support a denial of constitutional rights than could the stresses that residential integration was thought to entail in 1917. The effects of racial prejudice, however real, cannot justify a racial classification removing an infant child from the custody of its natural mother found to be an appropriate person to have such custody.

Many adoption agencies seek to "match" children to their prospective adoptive parents on the basis of religion (almost always based on the biological mother), race and ethnic background (e.g., Italian, Polish, "Mediterranean"), and physical appearance (height, hair and eye color). Is a conscious attempt to achieve a racial "match" constitutional? Professor James S. Bowen[64] strongly endorses racial matching: "A Black child must be raised as a Black child," and "[g]iven a situation of equipoise between two possible adoptive families, race may be a determinative factor in deciding the placement of a Black child in contemporary American society." Indeed, he proposes the adoption of an "Afro-American Child Welfare Act," specifically modelled after the Indian Child Welfare Act of 1978, that would codify such racial factors. One section of the proposed Act would have Congress declare "that it is the policy of this Nation to protect the best interests of Afro-American children and to promote the stability and security of Afro-American children and to promote the stability and security of Afro-American people and families by the establishment of minimum federal standards for the placement of such children in foster or adoptive homes which will reflect the unique values of Afro-American culture." Professor Bowen argues that "[r]ather than use race as a mechanism for erecting or maintaining group domination or hierarchy, the utility of race [under his plan] is as a means to facilitate redress of past racial injustice." (How does a racial preference for adoption rectify "past racial injustice"?)

Would Professor Bowen's Act survive *Sidoti*? Professor Elizabeth Bartholet writes in Where Do Black Children Belong? The Politics of Race Matching in Adoption, 139 U. Pa. L. Rev. 1163 (1991), that "[c]urrent racial matching policies are in conflict with the basic law of the land on race discrimination." Although she notes that "[a]lmost no one advocates the elimination of any preference whatsoever for inrace placement," she insists that many current

64. James S. Bowen, Cultural Convergences and Divergences: The Nexus Between Putative Afro-American Family Values and the Best Interests of the Child, 26 J. Fam. L. 487 (1987-88).

race-matching policies are harmful to children insofar as they significantly hinder transracial adoptions even where in-race placement is not an option. She concludes that "[e]stablishment of a regime in which there is no official preference [even presumably as a tiebreaker] for same-race placement seems the wise course and the direction in which we should move." Even Professor Bowen would require "equipoise between two possible adoptive families" before invoking racial preference as a tiebreaker. Can *Sidoti* be distinguished on the basis that the judge in that case was indeed "us[ing] race as a mechanism for . . . maintaining group domination"? But if race can be used as a tiebreaker (i.e., it receives one point), why can't it receive two or even ten points and overcome other significant attributes of the nonsimilar-race family? If you oppose this emphasis on race, then why not simply flip a coin even in those presumably rare cases of genuine "equipoise"?

2. *"Equal" Treatment of Whites and Blacks*

In McLaughlin v. Florida, 379 U.S. 184 (1964), the Court invalidated a statute that punished interracial cohabitation more severely than cohabitation by persons of the same race. In Loving v. Virginia, 388 U.S. 1 (1967), the Court struck down Virginia's antimiscegenation law. Both decisions were unanimous. The Court rejected the "equal application" theory espoused in Pace v. Alabama, 106 U.S. 583 (1883). Although the statutes applied equally to both parties, they drew "racial classifications" and, as Justice White wrote for the Court in *McLaughlin:*

> [W]e deal here with a classification based upon the race of the participants, which must be viewed in light of the historical fact that the central purpose of the Fourteenth Amendment was to eliminate racial discrimination emanating from official sources in the States. This strong policy renders racial classifications "constitutionally suspect," and subject to the "most rigid scrutiny," and "in most circumstances irrelevant" to any constitutionally acceptable legislative purposes. . . .
>
> There is involved here an exercise of the state police power which trenches upon the constitutionally protected freedom from invidious official discrimination based on race. Such a law, even though enacted pursuant to a valid state interest, bears a heavy burden of justification . . . and will be upheld only if it is necessary, and not merely rationally related, to the accomplishment of a permissible state policy.

In *Loving,* the Court rejected as impermissible the objectives invoked by the state court to uphold the statute — the preservation of "racial pride," "the racial integrity of its citizens," and the prevention of "corruption of blood" and "a mongrel breed of citizens." The state's assertion that "the scientific evidence [of the harms resulting from intermarriage] is substantially in doubt" was taken as an admission that the state had failed to meet its burden of showing a "legitimate overriding purpose."

Justice Stewart, joined by Justice Douglas, concurred in *McLaughlin* but wished to disassociate himself from the implication "that a criminal law of the kind here involved might be constitutionally valid if a State could show 'some overriding statutory purpose' ": "This is an implication in which I cannot join, because I cannot conceive of a valid legislative purpose under our Constitution for a state law which makes the color of a person's skin the test of whether his conduct is a criminal offense. . . . Discrimination of that kind is invidious per se." Justice Stewart reiterated this point in *Loving*. (Is his position consistent with his concurrence in Washington v. Lee, the prison desegregation case?)

3. Gathering and Disseminating Racial Information

In Anderson v. Martin, 375 U.S. 399 (1964), the Court unanimously invalidated a Louisiana statute requiring that the ballots in all elections designate the race of the candidates. The Court rejected the state's argument that the requirement was nondiscriminatory since the labeling provision applied equally to black and white candidates. Justice Clark wrote:

> [B]y directing the citizen's attention to the single consideration of race or color, the State indicates that a candidate's race or color is an important — perhaps paramount — consideration in the citizen's choice, which may decisively influence the citizens to cast his ballot along racial lines. . . . The vice lies . . . in the placing of the power of the State behind a racial classification that induces racial prejudice at the polls.

The same year, in Tancil v. Wools, 379 U.S. 19 (1964), the Court summarily affirmed the judgment of a three-judge district court invalidating Virginia laws that required officials to keep voting and property-owner records on a racially segregated basis, but sustaining a law that required that every divorce decree recite the race of the spouses.

Were these cases decided correctly — in view of the policies underlying the "suspect" classification criterion?

4. The Nature of the "Suspect Classification" Test

Korematsu focused on the importance of the ends served by the Japanese removal laws and placed somewhat less emphasis on the closeness of the "fit" between ends and means, i.e., on the degree of congruence between the regulation and its objective and on whether the objective could be achieved by less drastic means. In *McLaughlin,* by contrast, the Court's test focused on means: a racial classification "will be upheld only if it is necessary, and not merely rationally related, to the accomplishment of a permissible state policy." Did the Court purposely say "permissible" rather than "important," and, if so, was it correct?

A student commentator asserts that *McLaughlin* is properly indifferent to the importance of ends:[65]

> [T]he goal served by the classification need be only permissible, not compelling. Thus, if the classification is perfect or justifiably imperfect, the reviewing court should not proceed to inquire into how compelling the asserted state interest is. [I]f the Court's concern in suspect classification cases is with purity of process rather than with a specific substantive interest (as in the case when a deprivation of First

65. Note, Mental Illness: A Suspect Classification?, 83 Yale L.J. 1237, 1257 (1974).

Amendment or other "fundamental" rights is at issue), it seems inappropriate for the Court to test for a compelling state interest.

Is "purity of process" the only concern? Even if it is, does the commentator's conclusion follow? How should a court treat a school principal's decision, based solely on aesthetics, to have black and white students sit "on opposite sides of the stage at the graduation ceremony?"

John Ely, whose rationale for the antidiscrimination principle also centers on the decisionmaking process, argues that a court should invalidate a suspect law unless "the state come[s] up with a goal of substantial weight and (2) show[s] that the classification fits that goal with virtual perfection," explaining that these "fit" and "weight" requirements are not penalties for being suspect but "ways of extending the initial inquiry, of determining whether the initial suspicions aroused by the classification are well founded or rather on fuller exploration can be allayed." (Democracy and Distrust 147 (1980).)

C. Alternative Forms of Race-Dependent Decisions

The most overt race-dependent decision is a statute that in terms classifies people by race. Like the jury-exclusion law struck down in *Strauder,* such a law might impose different burdens or confer different benefits on one race than on another. Or, like the segregation, cohabitation, and marriage laws struck down in *Brown, Loving,* and *McLaughlin,* it may apply with formal equality to persons of both races but nonetheless run afoul of the antidiscrimination principle.

Race-dependent decisions are not always embodied in statutes nor always overt, however. For example, an employer may deny someone a job because of her race while explaining the decision on entirely other grounds.

Do different kinds of race-dependent decisions have different legal consequences? In answering this question, it is important to keep two questions conceptually separate. (1) What obligations does the antidiscrimination principle impose on the *initial decisionmaker,* e.g., an employer, an official, a legislator? (2) Under what circumstances will a *reviewing court* inquire whether that decisionmaker's decision was race-dependent? The rest of this section deals with the first question. The second is taken up in Section D.

1. *Discriminatory Administration*

Laws that do not classify on the basis of race may nonetheless be administered in a race-dependent manner. For example, in Yick Wo v. Hopkins, 118 U.S. 356 (1886), the San Francisco Board of Supervisors, which had authority to issue permits to operate laundries in wooden buildings, had granted permits to none of 200 Chinese applicants and to all but one of about 80 Caucasian applicants. The Court reversed petitioners' convictions for operating laundries without permits, Justice Matthews writing:

> [T]he facts shown establish an administration directed so exclusively against a particular class of persons as to warrant and require the conclusion, that, whatever may have been the intent of the ordinances as adopted, they are applied by the public authorities charged with their administration, and thus representing the State itself, with a mind so unequal and oppressive as to amount to a practical denial by the State of that equal protection of the laws which is secured to the petitioners, as to all other persons, by the broad and benign provisions of the Fourteenth Amendment to the Constitution of the United States. Though the law itself be fair on its face and impartial in appearance, yet if it is applied and administered by public authority with an evil eye and an unequal hand, so as practically to make unjust and illegal discriminations between persons in similar circumstances, material to their rights, the denial of equal justice is still within the prohibition of the Constitution. . . .
>
> The present cases, as shown by the facts disclosed in the record, are within this class. It appears that both petitioners have complied with every requisite, deemed by the law or by the public officers charged with its administration, necessary for the protection of neighboring property from fire, or as a precaution against injury to the public health. No reason whatever, except the will of the supervisors, is assigned why they should not be permitted to carry on, in the accustomed manner, their harmless and useful occupation, on which they depend for a livelihood. And while this consent of the supervisors is withheld from them and from two hundred others who have also petitioned, all of whom happen to be Chinese subjects, eighty others, not Chinese subjects, are permitted to carry on the same business under similar conditions. The fact of this discrimination is admitted. No reason for it is shown, and the conclusion cannot be resisted, that no reason for it exists except hostility to the race and nationality to which the petitioners belong, and which in the eye of the law is not justified.

Courts have frequently relied on statistical evidence of this sort to find unlawful patterns of racial discrimination in jury selection, employment, voter registration, and pupil and teacher assignment.

Does the San Francisco Board of Supervisors' unpublished rule differ, in a constitutionally relevant way, from an ordinance explicitly prohibiting Chinese from operating laundries in wooden buildings?

2. *The Race-Dependent Decision to Adopt a Nonracially Specific Regulation or Law*

Laws, regulations, and policies that do not classify on the basis of race and are administered without regard to race may nonetheless be adopted for race-dependent reasons. For example, in Ho Ah Kow v. Nunan, 12 F. Cas. 252 (No. 6546) (C.C.D. Cal. 1879), a San Francisco ordinance required that every male imprisoned in the county jail have his hair "cut or clipped to an uniform length of one inch from the scalp thereof." Plaintiff, a Chinese national, defaulted on a fine imposed for a housing code violation and was imprisoned and shorn. On demurrer, the Circuit Court for the District of California sustained his action against the sheriff for damages. Justice Field wrote:

The complaint avers that it is the custom of Chinamen to shave the hair from the front of the head and to wear the remainder of it braided into a queue; that the deprivation of the queue is regarded by them as a mark of disgrace, and is attended, according to their religious faith, with misfortune and suffering after death; that the defendant knew of this custom and religious faith of the Chinese, and knew also that the plaintiff venerated the custom and held the faith; yet, in disregard of his rights, inflicted the injury complained of. . . .

The cutting off the hair of every male person within an inch of his scalp, on his arrival at the jail, was not intended and cannot be maintained as a measure of discipline or as a sanitary regulation. The act by itself has no tendency to promote discipline, and can only be a measure of health in exceptional cases. Had the ordinance contemplated a mere sanitary regulation it would have been limited to such cases and made applicable to females as well as to males, and to persons awaiting trial as well as to persons under conviction. . . . It is special legislation on the part of the supervisors against a class of persons who, under the constitution and laws of the United States, are entitled to the equal protection of the laws. The ordinance was intended only for the Chinese in San Francisco. This was avowed by the supervisors on its passage, and was so understood by every one. The ordinance is known in the community as the "Queue Ordinance," being so designated from its purpose to reach the queues of the Chinese, and it is not enforced against any other persons. The reason advanced for its adoption, and now urged for its continuance, is, that only the dread of the loss of his queue will induce a Chinaman to pay his fine. . . .

The class character of this legislation is none the less manifest because of the general terms in which it is expressed. . . .

During the various periods of English history, legislation, general in its character, has often been enacted with the avowed purpose of imposing special burdens and restrictions upon Catholics; but that legislation has since been regarded as not less odious and obnoxious to animadversion than if the persons at whom it was aimed had been particularly designated. But in our country hostile and discriminating legislation by a state against persons of any class, sect, creed or nation, in whatever form it may be expressed, is forbidden by the fourteenth amendment of the constitution.

In Gomillion v. Lightfoot, 364 U.S. 339 (1960), the Alabama legislature changed the boundaries of the city of Tuskegee from a square to what Justice Frankfurter described as "an uncouth twenty-eight-sided figure"; the effect was to remove all but a handful of black voters, but not a single white voter, from the city limits. The Court struck down the law, finding these facts "tantamount for all practical purposes to a mathematical demonstration that the legislature is solely concerned with segregating white and colored voters by fencing Negro citizens out of town."

In Griffin v. Prince Edward County School Board, 377 U.S. 218 (1964), the school board closed down the school system after a court had ordered that it be desegregated. The Supreme Court ordered it reopened, stating:

[T]he record in the present case could not be clearer that Prince Edward's public schools were closed and private schools operated in their place with state and county assistance, for one reason and one reason only: to ensure . . . that white and colored children in Prince Edward County would not, under any circumstances, go to the same school. Whatever nonracial grounds might support a State's allowing a county to abandon public schools, the object must be a constitutional one, and grounds of race and opposition to desegregation do not qualify as constitutional.

3. *Transferred de Jure Discrimination*

A practice that does not itself take race into account may disproportionately disadvantage a racial minority as a result of *causally related* de jure discrimination. Suppose, for example, that the residential segregation in our hypothetical school district was the result of unconstitutional discrimination. Although the Court has not addressed this precise issue,[66] it dealt with an analogous one in a statutory context in Gaston County v. United States, 395 U.S. 235 (1969). The Voting Rights Act of 1965 prohibits a state or local government from using a test "for the purpose or with the effect of denying or abridging the right to vote on account of race or color." The issue in *Gaston County* was whether the act permitted the county to use a voting literacy test that disproportionately disfranchised blacks. The Court accepted the county's claim that it administered the tests in a fair and impartial manner, but noted that blacks who are now eligible to vote had been educated in the country's segregated and inferior schools. Justice Harlan wrote:

> It is only reasonable to infer that among the black children compelled to endure a segregated and inferior education, fewer will achieve any given degree of literacy than will their better-educated white contemporaries. And . . . it was certainly proper to infer that Gaston County's inferior Negro schools provide many of its Negro residents with a subliterate education, and gave many others little inducement to enter or remain in school. . . . From this record, we cannot escape the sad truth that throughout the years Gaston County systematically deprived its black citizens of the education opportunities it granted to its white citizens. "Impartial" administration of the literacy test today would serve only to perpetuate these inequalities in a different form.

There is no standard term for describing the voting registrar's action in *Gaston County*. Perhaps "transferred de jure discrimination" is as good as any.

In the preceding sections the causal connection between a race-dependent decision and its effects was typically direct and obvious. This section examines a variety of situations in which the causal connection is attenuated; it also considers the constitutionality of racially disproportionate impact which cannot be causally traced to any (particular) race-dependent decisions at all.

Note on Terminology

Covert race-dependent decisions are frequently referred to as "racially motivated" decisions and sometimes as "unconstitutionally motivated" (since race-dependent decisions usually end up being unconstitutional). The word "motivation" gives rise to a potential ambiguity in this context and probably in most others as well. One might use it to mean either "race-dependent" decisions,

66. In Swann v. Charlotte-Mecklenburg Bd. of Educ., page 624 supra, the district court found that the local, state, and federal governments were responsible for residential segregation, which, combined with a proximity assignment plan, resulted in school segregation. The Supreme Court affirmed a judgment requiring school desegregation on other grounds, noting that "[w]e do not reach in this case the question whether a showing that school segregation [that] is a consequence of other types of state action, without any discriminatory action by the school authorities, is a constitutional violation requiring remedial action by a school desegregation decree."

or race-dependent decisions that are based on "prejudice" or "hostility" (as distinguished from those that are rationally based). In this book we use it simply to mean "race-dependent" decisions — so that a decisionmaker's taking account of race for any purposes whatever is a race-"motivated" decision.

D. Judicial Review of Covert Race-Dependent Decisions: The Inquiry into Motivation

VILLAGE OF ARLINGTON HEIGHTS v. METROPOLITAN HOUSING DEVELOPMENT CORP.

429 U.S. 252 (1977)

Certiorari to the United States Court of Appeals for the Seventh Circuit

POWELL, J., delivered the opinion of the Court.

In 1971 respondent Metropolitan Housing Development Corporation (MHDC) applied to petitioner, the Village of Arlington Heights, Ill., for the rezoning of a 15-acre parcel from single-family to multiple-family classification. Using federal financial assistance, MHDC planned to build 190 clustered townhouse units for low- and moderate-income tenants. The Village denied the rezoning request. . . . [MHDC] alleged that the denial was racially discriminatory and that it violated, inter alia, the Fourteenth Amendment and the Fair Housing Act of 1968, 82 Stat. 81, 42 U.S.C. §3601 et seq. . . . The Court of Appeals for the Seventh Circuit . . . [found] that the "ultimate effect" of the denial was racially discriminatory, and that the refusal to rezone therefore violated the Fourteenth Amendment. We . . . reverse.

I . . .

. . . [In 1970] MHDC and [a private seller] entered into a 99-year lease and an accompanying agreement of sale covering a 15-acre site. . . . MHDC engaged an architect and proceeded with the project, to be known as Lincoln Green. . . .

The planned development did not conform to the Village's zoning ordinance and could not be built unless Arlington Heights rezoned the parcel to . . . its multiple-family housing classification. Accordingly, MHDC filed with the Village Plan Commission a petition for rezoning, accompanied by supporting materials describing the development and specifying that it would be subsidized under §236. The materials made clear that one requirement under §236 is an affirmative marketing plan designed to assure that a subsidized development is racially integrated. MHDC also submitted studies demonstrating the need for housing of this type and analyzing the probable impact of the development. . . .

During the spring of 1971, the Plan Commission considered the proposal at a series of three public meetings, which drew large crowds. Although many of those attending were quite vocal and demonstrative in opposition to Lincoln Green, a number of individuals and representatives of community groups spoke in support of rezoning. Some of the comments, both from opponents and supporters, addressed what was referred to as the "social issue," the desirability or undesirability of introducing at this location in Arlington Heights low- and moderate-income housing, housing that would probably be racially integrated. Many of the opponents, however, focused on the zoning aspects of the petition, stressing two arguments. First, the area always had been zoned single-family, and the neighboring citizens had built or purchased there in reliance on that classification. Rezoning threatened to cause a measurable drop in property value for neighboring sites. Second, the Village's apartment policy, adopted by the Village Board in 1962 and amended in 1970, called for [multiple-family] zoning primarily to serve as a buffer between single-family development and land uses thought incompatible, such as commercial or manufacturing districts. Lincoln Green did not meet this requirement, as it adjoined no commercial or manufacturing district.

At the close of the third meeting, the Plan Commission adopted a motion to recommend to the Village's Board of Trustees that it deny the request. . . . After a public hearing, the Board denied the rezoning by a 6-1 vote.

The following June MHDC and three Negro individuals filed this lawsuit against the Village, seeking declaratory and injunctive relief. . . . [T]he District Court held that the petitioners were not motivated by racial discrimination or intent to discriminate against low-income groups when they denied rezoning, but rather by a desire "to protect property values and the integrity of the Village's zoning plan."

A divided Court of Appeals reversed. It first approved the District Court's finding that the defendants were motivated by a concern for the integrity of the zoning plan, rather than by racial discrimination. Deciding whether their refusal to rezone would have discriminatory effects was more complex. The court observed that the refusal would have a disproportionate impact on blacks. Based upon family income, blacks constituted 40% of those Chicago area residents who were eligible to become tenants of Lincoln Green, although they composed a far lower percentage of total area population. The court reasoned, however, that under our decision in James v. Valtierra, 402 U.S. 137 (1971), such a disparity in racial impact alone does not call for strict scrutiny of a municipality's decision that prevents the construction of the low-cost housing.

There was another level to the court's analysis of allegedly discriminatory results. . . . [T]he Court of Appeals ruled that the denial of rezoning must be examined in light of its "historical context and ultimate effect." Northwest Cook County was enjoying rapid growth in employment opportunities and population, but it continued to exhibit a high degree of residential segregation. The court held that Arlington Heights could not simply ignore this problem. Indeed, it found that the Village had been "exploiting" the situation by allowing itself to become a nearly all white community. The Village had no other current plans for building low- and moderate-income housing, and no other [appropriately zoned] parcels in the Village were available to MHDC at an economically feasible price.

Against this background, the Court of Appeals ruled that the denial of the Lincoln Green proposal had racially discriminatory effects and could be tolerated only if it served compelling interests. Neither the buffer policy nor the desire to protect property values met this exacting standard. The court therefore concluded that the denial violated the Equal Protection Clause of the Fourteenth Amendment. . . .

III

Our decision last Term in Washington v. Davis, 426 U.S. 229 (1976),[67] made it clear that official action will not be held unconstitutional solely because it results in a racially disproportionate impact. "Disproportionate impact is not irrelevant, but it is not the sole touchstone of an invidious racial discrimination." Proof of racially discriminatory intent or purpose is required to show a violation of the Equal Protection Clause. Although some contrary indications may be drawn from some of our cases,[a] the holding in Davis reaffirmed a principle well established in a variety of contexts.

Davis does not require a plaintiff to prove that the challenged action rested solely on racially discriminatory purposes. Rarely can it be said that a legislature or administrative body operating under a broad mandate made a decision motivated solely by a single concern, or even that a particular purpose was the "dominant" or "primary" one.[b] In fact, it is because legislators and administrators are properly concerned with balancing numerous competing considerations that courts refrain from reviewing the merits of their decisions, absent a showing of arbitrariness or irrationality. But racial discrimination is not just another competing consideration. When there is a proof that a discriminatory purpose has been a motivating factor in the decision, this judicial deference is no longer justified.

Determining whether invidious discriminatory purpose was a motivating factor demands a sensitive inquiry into such circumstantial and direct evidence of intent as may be available. The impact of the official action whether it "bears more heavily on one race than another" may provide an important starting point. Sometimes a clear pattern, unexplainable on grounds other than race, emerges from the effect of the state action even when the governing legislation appears neutral on its face. Yick Wo v. Hopkins, 118 U.S. 356 (1886); Guinn v. United States, 238 U.S. 347 (1915); Lane v. Wilson, 307 U.S. 268 (1939); Gomillion v. Lightfoot, 364 U.S. 339 (1960). The evidentiary inquiry is then relatively easy.[c] But such cases are rare. Absent a pattern as stark as that in *Gomillion* or *Yick Wo*, impact alone is not determinative,[d] and the Court must look to other evidence.

The historical background of the decision is one evidentiary source, particularly if it reveals a series of official actions taken for invidious purposes. See Lane v. Wilson, supra; Griffin v. School Board, 377 U.S. 218 (1964). The specific sequence of events leading up the challenged decision also may shed some light on the decisionmaker's purposes. For example, if the property involved here always had been zoned [multiple family] but suddenly was changed to [single family]

67. In Washington v. Davis, page 689 infra, the Court emphasized that segregation did not violate the equal protection clause absent a "*purpose* or *intent* to segregate."

a. Palmer v. Thompson, 403 U.S. 217, 225 (1971).

b. In McGinnis v. Royster, 410 U.S. 263 (1973), in a somewhat different context, we observed: "The search for legislative purpose is often elusive enough without a requirement that primacy be ascertained. Legislation is frequently multipurposed: the removal of even a 'subordinate' purpose may shift altogether the consensus of legislative judgment supporting the statute."

c. Several of our jury-selection cases fall into this category. Because of the nature of the jury-selection task, however, we have permitted a finding of constitutional violation even when the statistical pattern does not approach the extremes of *Yick Wo* or *Gomillion*.

d. This is not to say that a consistent pattern of official racial discrimination is a necessary predicate to a violation of the Equal Protection Clause. A single invidiously discriminatory governmental act in the exercise of the zoning power as elsewhere would not necessarily be immunized by the absence of such discrimination in the making of other comparable decisions. See City of Richmond v. United States, 422 U.S. 358 (1975).

when the town learned of MHDC's plans to erect integrated housing,[e] we would have a far different case. Departures from the normal procedural sequence also might afford evidence that improper purposes are playing a role. Substantive departures too may be relevant, particularly if the factors usually considered important by the decisionmaker strongly favor a decision contrary to the one reached.[f]

The legislative or administrative history may be highly relevant, especially where there are contemporary statements by members of the decisionmaking body, minutes of its meetings, or reports. In some extraordinary instances the members might be called to the stand at trial to testify concerning the purpose of the official action, although even then such testimony frequently will be barred by privilege.[g]

The foregoing summary identifies, without purporting to be exhaustive, subjects of proper inquiry in determining whether racially discriminatory intent existed. With these in mind, we now address the case before us.

IV

. . . [B]oth courts below understood that at least part of their function was to examine the purpose underlying the decision. In making its findings on this issue, the District Court noted that some of the opponents of Lincoln Green who spoke at the various hearings might have been motivated by opposition to minority groups. The court held, however, that the evidence "does not warrant the conclusion that this motivated the defendants." On appeal the Court of Appeals focused primarily on respondents' claim that the Village's buffer policy had not been consistently applied and was being invoked with a strictness here that could only demonstrate some other underlying motive. The court concluded that the buffer policy, though not always applied with perfect consistency, had on several occasions formed the basis for the Board's decision to deny other rezoning proposals. "The evidence does not necessitate a finding that Arlington Heights administered this policy in a discriminatory manner." The Court of Appeals therefore approved the District Court's findings concerning the Village's purposes in denying rezoning to MHDC. We also have reviewed the evidence. The impact of the Village's decision does arguably bear more heavily on racial minori-

e. See e.g., Progress Development Corp. v. Mitchell, 286 F.2d 222 (C.A.7 1961) (park board allegedly condemned plaintiffs' land for a park upon learning that the homes plaintiffs were erecting there would be sold under a marketing plan designed to assure integration); Kennedy Park Homes Assn. v. City of Lackawanna, 436 F.2d 108 (C.A.2 1970), cert. denied, 401 U.S. 1010 (1971) (town declared moratorium on new subdivisions and rezoned area for parkland shortly after learning of plaintiffs' plans to build low income housing). To the extent that the decision in *Kennedy Park Homes* rested solely on a finding of discriminatory impact, we have indicated our disagreement. Washington v. Davis.

f. See Dailey v. City of Lawton, 425 F.2d 1037 (C.A.10 1970). The plaintiffs in Dailey planned to build low-income housing on the site of a former school that they had purchased. The city refused to rezone the land from PF, its public facilities classification, to R-4, high-density residential. All the surrounding area was zoned R-4, and both the present and the former planning director for the city testified that there was no reason "from a zoning standpoint" why the land should not be classified R-4. Based on this and other evidence, the Court of Appeals ruled that "the record sustains the (District Court's) holding of racial motivation and of arbitrary and unreasonable action."

g. This Court has recognized, ever since Fletcher v. Peck, 6 Cranch 87 (1810), that judicial inquiries into legislative or executive motivation represent a substantial intrusion into the workings of other branches of government. Placing a decisionmaker on the stand is therefore "usually to be avoided." . . .

ties. Minorities constitute 18% of the Chicago area population, and 40% of the income groups said to be eligible for Lincoln Green. But there is little about the sequence of events leading up to the decision that would spark suspicion. The area around the Victorian property has been zoned [single family] since 1959, the year when Arlington Heights first adopted a zoning map. Single-family homes surround the 80-acre site, and the Village is undeniably committed to single-family homes as its dominant residential land use. The rezoning request progressed according to the usual procedures. The Plan Commission even scheduled two additional hearings, at least in part to accommodate MHDC and permit it to supplement its presentation with answers to questions generated at the first hearing.

The statements by the Plan Commission and Village Board members, as reflected in the official minutes, focused almost exclusively on the zoning aspects of the MHDC petition, and the zoning factors on which they relied are not novel criteria in the Village's rezoning decisions. There is no reason to doubt that there has been reliance by some neighboring property owners on the maintenance of single-family zoning in the vicinity. The Village originally adopted its buffer policy long before MHDC entered the picture and has applied the policy too consistently for us to infer discriminatory purpose from its application in this case. Finally, MHDC called one member of the Village Board to the stand at trial. Nothing in her testimony supports an inference of invidious purpose.

In sum, the evidence does not warrant overturning the concurrent findings of both courts below. Respondents simply failed to carry their burden of proving that discriminatory purpose was a motivating factor in the Village's decision.[h] This conclusion ends the constitutional inquiry. The Court of Appeals' further finding that the Village's decision carried a discriminatory "ultimate effect" is without independent constitutional significance.

V

Respondents' complaint also alleged that the refusal to rezone violated the Fair Housing Act of 1968, 42 U.S.C. §3601 et seq. They continue to urge here that a zoning decision made by a public body may, and that petitioners' action did, violate §3604 or §3617. The Court of Appeals, however, proceeding in a somewhat unorthodox fashion, did not decide the statutory question. We remand the case for further consideration of respondents' statutory claims.

Mr. Justice Stevens took no part in the consideration or decision of this case.

MARSHALL, J., joined by Brennan, J., concurring in part and dissenting in part.

h. Proof that the decision by the Village was motivated in part by a racially discriminatory purpose would not necessarily have required invalidation of the challenged decision. Such proof would, however, have shifted to the Village the burden of establishing that the same decision would have resulted even had the impermissible purpose not been considered. If this were established, the complaining party in a case of this kind no longer fairly could attribute the injury complained of to improper consideration of a discriminatory purpose. In such circumstances, there would be no justification for judicial interference with the challenged decision. But in this case respondents failed to make the required threshold showing. See Mt. Healthy City School Dist. Bd. of Education v. Doyle, 429 U.S. 274 (1977).

I concur in Parts I-III of the Court's opinion. However, I believe the proper result would be to remand this entire case to the Court of Appeals for further proceedings. . . .

WHITE, J., dissenting.

. . . I would vacate the judgment of the Court of Appeals and remand the case for consideration of the statutory issue and, if necessary, for consideration of the constitutional issue in light of Washington v. Davis.

BATSON v. KENTUCKY, 476 U.S. 79 (1986): [Peremptory challenges, by which a party to litigation can strike prospective jurors without having to give reasons, have been part of the Anglo-American system of jury trial since the earliest recorded period. In criminal cases involving black defendants, it is a common practice for prosecutors to exercise peremptory challenges to remove all blacks from the petit jury.[68]

In Swain v. Alabama, 380 U.S. 202 (1965), the Court had unanimously reaffirmed Strauder v. West Virginia (page 237 supra), in holding that a "State's purposeful or deliberate denial to Negroes on account of race of participation as jurors in the administration of justice violates the Equal Protection Clause." However, the Court went on, over the dissent of three Justices, to require the person challenging the prosecutor's use of peremptory challenges in a particular case to demonstrate that exclusion of blacks from juries was part of a systematic policy of purposeful discrimination. The exclusionary result in a particular case, including Swain's, was insufficient proof of systematic "perversion" of the long-established practice of peremptory challenges.

The Court overruled this limiting condition in Batson v. Kentucky, in which the prosecutor had peremptorily removed all four blacks on the venire from the petit jury of a black man charged with burglary and receipt of stolen goods, who was convicted by the all-white jury.

Justice Powell wrote for the Court that lower courts had understood *Swain* to place "a crippling burden of proof" on defendants, so that "prosecutors' peremptory challenges [became] largely immune from constitutional scrutiny." This was "inconsistent with standards that have been developed since *Swain* for asserting a prima facie case under the Equal Protection Clause":]

The showing necessary to establish a prima facie case of purposeful discrimination in selection may be discerned in this Court's decisions. E.g., Castaneda v. Partida, 430 U.S. 482, 494-495 (1977); Alexander v. Louisiana, 405 U.S. 625, 631-632. The defendant initially must show that he is a member of a racial group capable of being singled out for differential treatment. In combination with that evidence a defendant may then make a prima facie case by proving that in the particular jurisdiction members of his race have not been summoned for jury service over an extended period of time. Proof of systematic exclusion from the

68. Some prosecutors also strike blacks from the juries in cases involving white defendants, apparently because prosecutors view blacks as generally less likely to credit police testimony. A study of 100 felony trials that took place in Dallas County, Texas, in 1983-1984 showed that prosecutors used their peremptory challenges to eliminate 405 out of 467 eligible black jurors. An otherwise qualified black member of the jury venire had a one-in-ten chance of becoming a member of the petit jury, compared to a 50 percent chance for a white.

venire raises an inference of purposeful discrimination because the "result bespeaks discrimination."

Since the ultimate issue is whether the State has discriminated in selecting the defendant's venire, however, the defendant may establish a prima facie case "in other ways than by evidence of long-continued unexplained absence" of members of his race "from many panels." In cases involving the venire, this Court has found a prima facie case on proof that members of the defendant's race were substantially underrepresented on the venire from which his jury was drawn, and that the venire was selected under a practice providing "the opportunity for discrimination." This combination of factors raises the necessary inference of purposeful discrimination because the Court has declined to attribute to chance the absence of black citizens on a particular jury array where the selection mechanism is subject to abuse. When circumstances suggest the need, the trial court must undertake a "factual inquiry" that "takes into account all possible explanatory factors" in the particular case.

Thus, since the decision in *Swain*, this Court has recognized that a defendant may make a prima facie showing of purposeful racial discrimination in selection of the venire by relying solely on the factors concerning its selection *in his case*. These decisions are in accordance with the proposition, articulated in *Arlington Heights*, that "a consistent pattern of official racial discrimination" is not "a necessary predicate to a violation of the Equal Protection Clause. A single invidiously discriminatory governmental" act is not "immunized by the absence of such discrimination in the making of other comparable decisions." . . .

These principles support our conclusion that a defendant may establish a prima facie case of purposeful discrimination in selection of the petit jury solely on evidence concerning the prosecutor's exercise of peremptory challenges at the defendant's trial. To establish such a case, the defendant must first establish membership in a cognizable racial group and that the prosecutor has exercised peremptory challenges to remove from the venire members of the defendant's race. Second, the defendant is entitled to rely on the fact, as to which there can be no dispute, that peremptory challenges constitute a jury selection practice that permits "those to discriminate who are of a mind to discriminate." Finally, the defendant must show that these facts and any other relevant circumstances raise an inference that the prosecutor used that practice to exclude the veniremen from the petit jury on account of their race. This combination of factors in the empanelling of the petit jury . . . raises the necessary inference of purposeful discrimination. . . .

Once the defendant makes a prima facie showing, the burden shifts to the State to come forward with a neutral explanation for challenging black jurors. Though this requirement imposes a limitation in some cases on the full peremptory character of the historic challenge, we emphasize that the prosecutor's explanation need not rise to the level justifying exercise of a challenge for cause. But the prosecutor may not rebut the defendant's prima facie case of discrimination by stating merely that he challenged jurors of the defendant's race on the assumption — or his intuitive judgment — that they would be partial to the defendant because of their shared race. . . . Nor may the prosecutor rebut the defendant's case merely by denying that he had a discriminatory motive or "affirming his good faith in individual selections." . . . The prosecutor therefore must articulate a neutral explanation related to the particular case to be tried.

[Justices White, Marshall, Stevens (joined by Brennan), and O'Connor each wrote concurring opinions. Justice Marshall wrote that the "end [of] of racial discrimination that peremptories inject into the jury-selection process . . . can be accomplished only by eliminating peremptory challenges entirely," and he would apply such a ban to defense attorneys as well as prosecutors. In the absence of such a complete ban, "trial courts face the difficult burden of assessing prosecutors' motives. Any prosecutor can easily assert facially neutral reasons for striking a juror, and trial courts are ill-equipped to second-guess those reasons." Justice Marshall went on to argue that "outright prevarication by prosecutors" is not the only danger of the *Batson* approach. "A prosecutor's own conscious or unconscious racism may lead him easily to the conclusion that a prospective black juror is 'sullen,' or 'distant,' a characterization that would not have come to his mind if a white juror had acted identically. A judge's own conscious or unconscious racism may lead him to accept such an explanation as well supported."[69]

Chief Justice Burger, joined by Justice Rehnquist, dissented. He quoted at length from United States v. Leslie, 783 F.2d 541 (1986) (en banc). The Fifth Circuit, upholding the prosecutor's use of peremptory challenges, distinguished peremptory challenges from exclusion from the jury venire, on the basis that the latter "implies that the government (usually the legislative or judicial branch) . . . has made the general determination that those excluded are unfit to try *any* case." A peremptory challenge, on the other hand, "represents the discrete decision, made by one of two or more opposed *litigants* in the trial phase of our adversary system of justice, that the challenged" juror is likely to be "more unfavorable to that litigant in that *particular case* than others on the same venire. . . . To suggest that a particular race is unfit to judge in any case is racially insulting. To suggest that each race may have its own special concerns, or even may tend to favor its own, is not." The Chief Justice continued:]

[P]eremptory challenges are often lodged, of necessity, for reasons "normally thought irrelevant to legal proceedings or official action, namely, the race, religion, nationality, occupation or affiliations of people summoned for jury duty." Moreover, in making peremptory challenges, both the prosecutor and defense attorney necessarily act on limited information or hunch. . . . As a result, unadulterated equal protection analysis is simply inapplicable to peremptory challenges exercised in any particular case. A clause that requires a minimum "rationality" in government actions has no application to " 'an arbitrary and capricious right.' " . . .

[Moreover,] if conventional equal protection principles apply, then presumably defendants could object to exclusions on the basis of not only race, but also sex; religious or political affiliation; mental capacity; number of children; living arrangements; and employment in a particular industry, or profession. [Case citations omitted.]

In short, it is quite possible that every peremptory challenge could be objected to on the basis that, because it excluded a venireman who had some characteristic

69. Justice Marshall cited a case from California, where the State constitution had been interpreted as imposing a rule similar to that articulated in *Batson*. There a prosecutor sought to rebut an inference of prejudice by offering among his reasons for striking potential jurors that they " 'never cracked a smile' and, therefore did not possess the sensitivity to realistically look at the issues and decide the facts in this case" and that a juror "had a son about the same age as defendant." People v. Hall, 35 Cal. 3d 161, 672 P.2d 854, 856 (1983).

not shared by the remaining members of the venire, it constituted a "classification" subject to equal protection scrutiny. . . .

Peremptory challenges have long been viewed as a means to achieve an impartial jury that will be sympathetic toward neither an accused nor witnesses for the State on the basis of some shared factor of race, religion, occupation, or other characteristic. Nearly a century ago the Court stated that the peremptory challenge is "essential to the fairness of trial by jury." Lewis v. U.S. 370, 376 (1892). Under conventional equal protection principles, a state interest of this magnitude and ancient lineage might well overcome an equal protection objection to the application of peremptory challenges. However, the Court is silent on the strength of the state's interest. . . .

To rebut a prima facie case, the Court requires a "neutral explanation" for the challenge, but is at pains to "emphasize" that the "explanation need not rise to the level justifying exercise of a challenge for cause." I am at a loss to discern the governing principles here. . . . Apparently the Court envisions permissible challenges short of a challenge for cause that are just a little bit arbitrary — but not too much. While our trial judges are "experienced in supervising *voir dire,*" they have no experience in administering rules like this.

[Justice Rehnquist also wrote a separate dissent, joined by Chief Justice Burger:]

I cannot subscribe to the Court's unprecedented use of the Equal Protection Clause to restrict the historic scope of the peremptory challenge. . . . In my view, there is simply nothing "unequal" about the State using its peremptory challenges to strike blacks from the jury in cases involving black defendants, so long as such challenges are also used to exclude whites in cases involving white defendants, Hispanics in cases involving Hispanic defendants, Asians in cases involving Asian defendants, and so on. This case-specific use of peremptory challenges by the State does not single out blacks, or members of any other race for that matter, for discriminatory treatment.[a] Such use of peremptories is at best based upon seat-of-the-pants instincts, which are undoubtedly crudely stereotypical and may in many cases be hopelessly mistaken. But as long as they are applied across the board to jurors of all races and nationalities, I do not see — and the Court most certainly has not explained — how their use violates the Equal Protection Clause.

Note: Subsequent Cases

Although *Batson* emphasizes the racial identity of the defendant with the excluded potential jurors, the Court dropped this requirement in Holland v. Illinois, 493 U.S. 474 (1990), which was decided under the Sixth Amendment, and in Powers v. Ohio, 499 U.S. — (1991), where the equal protection clause was held to allow any criminal defendant, regardless of race, to protest a prosecutor's race-based exclusion of persons from the petit jury. (Recall the discussion following *Strauder* above.)

a. I note that the Court does not rely on the argument that, because there are fewer "minorities" in a given population than there are "majorities," the equal use of peremptory challenges against members of "majority" racial groups has an equal impact. The flaws in this argument are demonstrated in Judge Garwood's thoughtful opinion for the en banc Fifth Circuit in U.S. v. Leslie.

In Edmonson v. Leesville Concrete Co., 111 S. Ct. 2077 (1991), the Court, sharply divided 6-3, further extended *Batson* to apply to private civil litigation. The central issue was the presence, vel non, of "state action," and the case is considered at some length in Chapter 12. Given *Edmonson*, may a defense attorney in a criminal case strike African-Americans from a jury trying white police officers accused of wrongfully killing an African-American (as happened several years ago in Florida)?

Note: Interpreting "Neutral" Explanations

Batson and its progeny require that a prosecutor must, in certain circumstances, provide a racially neutral explanation for the use of peremptory challenges to strike racial minorities from a jury. At this point, the inquiry shifts to what counts as a racially "neutral" explanation. In Hernandez v. New York, 111 S. Ct. 1859 (1991), a prosecutor in a criminal case had exercised peremptory challenges to exclude bilingual jurors, who, he said, would not necessarily rely on the official interpreter for English translation of testimony given by Spanish-speaking witnesses. The two jurors in question were Latino, and Hernandez argued that the prosecutor's rationale was not race neutral.

Although the court was fragmented, all of the justices agreed that *Batson* (as modified by *Price*) would apply to Latinos or Hispanics. However, six justices rejected Hernandez's claim that the exclusion was accurately described as racial. On behalf of a four-justice plurality that included Chief Justice Rehnquist and Justices White and Souter, Justice Kennedy wrote that "[a] neutral explanation . . . means an explanation based on something other than the race of the juror."

> [The prosecutor] did not rely on language ability without more, but explained that the specific responses and the demeanor of the two individuals during *voir dire* caused him to doubt their ability to defer to the official translation of Spanish-language testimony. . . .
>
> The prosecutor's articulated basis for these challenges divided potential jurors into two classes: those whose conduct during *voir dire* would persuade him they might have difficulty in accepting the translator's rendition of Spanish language testimony and those potential jurors who gave no such reason for doubt. Each category would include both Latinos and non-Latinos. While the prosecutor's criterion might well result in the disproportionate removal of prospective Latino jurors, that disproportionate impact does not turn the prosecutor's actions into a *per se* violation of the Equal Protection Clause. . . .
>
> Unless a government actor adopted a criterion with the intent of causing the impact asserted, that impact itself does not violate the principle of race-neutrality.

The plurality went on to assess the trial court's finding below that the prosecutor's rationale was not a mere pretext for constitutionally prohibited exclusion of Latinos from the jury. The plurality noted the potential for widespread exclusion of Latinos, given "common knowledge in the locality that a significant percentage of the Latino population speaks fluent Spanish, and that many consider it their preferred language, the one chosen for personal communication, the one selected for speaking with the most precision and power, the one used to define the self." Moreover, Justice Kennedy noted that no attempts were made to suggest an alternative to dismissal, such as allowing "Spanish-speaking jurors . . . to advise the judge in a discreet way of any concerns with the translation during the course of trial." The plurality held, however, that the determination of a prosecutor's motivation was a question of fact, and that the trial judge's conclusion was therefore entitled in deference.

> [W]e decline to overturn the state trial court's finding on the issue of discriminatory intent unless convinced that its determination was clearly erroneous. . . .
>
> We discern no clear error in the state trial court's determination that the prosecutor did not discriminate on the basis of the ethnicity of Latino jurors. We have said that "[w]here there are two permissible views of the evidence, the factfinder's choice between them cannot be clearly erroneous." . . . Apart from the prosecutor's demeanor, which of course we have no opportunity to review, the court could have relied on the fact that the prosecutor defended his use of peremptory challenges without being asked to do so by the judge, that he did know which jurors were Latinos, and that the ethnicity of the victims and prosecution witnesses tended to undercut any motive to exclude Latinos from the jury. Any of these factors could be taken as evidence of the prosecutor's sincerity. The trial court, moreover, could rely on the fact that only three challenged jurors can with confidence be identified as Latinos, and that the prosecutor had a verifiable and legitimate explanation for two of those challenges. Given these factors, that the prosecutor also excluded one or two Latino venirepersons on the basis of a subjective criterion having a disproportionate impact on Latinos does not leave us with a "definite and firm conviction that a mistake has been committed."
>
> . . . Our decision today does not imply that exclusion of bilinguals from jury service is wise, or even that it is constitutional in all cases. . . . We would face a quite different case if the prosecutor had justified his peremptory challenges with the explanation that he did not want Spanish-speaking jurors. It may well be, for certain ethnic groups and in some communities, that proficiency in a particular language, like skin color, should be treated as a surrogate for race under an equal protection analysis. . . . And, as we make clear, a policy of striking all who speak a given language, without regard to the particular circumstances of the trial or the individual responses of the jurors, may be found by the trial judge to be a pretext for racial discrimination. But that case is not before us.

Justice O'Connor, joined by Justice Scalia, concurred only in the judgment, stating that "the plurality opinion goes farther than it needs to in assessing the constitutionality of the prosecutor's asserted justification for his peremptory strikes."

Justice Stevens, joined by Justice Marshall, dissented:[70]

> Even assuming the prosecutor's explanation in rebuttal was advanced in good faith, the justification was insufficient to dispel the existing inference of racial animus.
>
> The prosecutor's explanation was insufficient for three reasons. First, the justification would inevitably result in a disproportionate disqualification of Spanish-speaking venirepersons. An explanation that is "race-neutral" on its face is nonetheless unacceptable if it is merely a proxy for a discriminatory practice. Second, the prosecutor's concern could easily have been accommodated by less drastic means. As is the practice in many jurisdictions, the jury could have been instructed that the official translation alone is evidence; bilingual jurors could

70. Justice Blackmun dissented without opinion, stating that he substantially agreed with the part of Justice Stevens' opinion quoted below.

have been instructed to bring to the attention of the judge any disagreements they might have with the translation so that any disputes could be resolved by the court. Third, if the prosecutor's concern was valid and substantiated by the record, it would have supported a challenge for cause. The fact that the prosecutor did not make any such challenge should disqualify him from advancing the concern as a justification for a peremptory challenge.

Each of these reasons considered alone might not render insufficient the prosecutor's facially neutral explanation. In combination, however, they persuade me that his explanation should have been rejected as a matter of law.

Discussion

Consider the "neutrality" of the following justifications presented by prosecutors following *Batson*:[71]

1. In a case where the prosecutor used nine of his ten peremptories to remove African-Americans from the (ultimately all-white) jury trying an African-American defendant for burglary, the reasons for exclusion included that one juror "was close to defendant's age, unmarried, moved very recently, and was very attentive to defendant's counsel during his *voir dire*," while another was "unmarried, had no children, had been at current job for only six weeks, had insufficient community ties, and put name in wrong place on jury form." See Johnson v. State, 740 S.W.2d 868 (Tex. Ct. App. 1987).

2. A dismissed African-American was cited as being a member of the Church of Christ, described by the prosecutor as "a little bit away from the mainstream," while another was struck for being a Jehovah's Witness (a "fringe religious group") and unmarried and having no children. See Chambers v. State, 724 S.W.2d 440 (Tex. Ct. App. 1987).

These last examples, of course, raise independent questions about the constitutional propriety of basing challenges even on certain nonracial attributes, such as religion. Consider a prosecutor who strikes males, but not females, from a jury hearing a rape case.

Palmer v. Thompson, 403 U.S. 217 (1971), involved an equal protection challenge to a decision by the city council of Jackson, Mississippi to close the city's public swimming pools following a federal court order to desegregate them in 1962. The District Court found that the closing was justified to preserve peace and order and because the pools could not be operated economically on an integrated basis and held that the city's action did not deny black citizens equal protection of the laws. The Supreme Court affirmed. Although Washington v. Davis, *Arlington Heights* and *Batson* effectively overruled *Palmer*'s broadest implications, the opinion usefully discusses some of the problems inherent in judicial review of legislative motivation.[72] Justice Black, writing for the Court, stated:

71. See, generally, Alan Raphael, Discriminatory Jury Selection: Lower Court Implementation of Batson v. Kentucky, 25 Williamette L. Rev. 293 (1989), from which the following examples are taken.

72. Several years later, in Washington v. Davis, 426 U.S. 229 (1976), infra, Justice White wrote: "To the extent that *Palmer* suggests a generally applicable proposition that legislative purpose is irrelevant in constitutional adjudication, our prior cases . . . are to the contrary." Shortly after *Palmer*, in Lemon v. Kurtzman, 403 U.S. 602 (1971), a unanimous Court reaffirmed that legislation subsidizing church-related schools requires close judicial scrutiny of the statute's purpose.

Petitioners have . . . argued that respondents' action violates the Equal Protection Clause because the decision to close the pools was motivated by a desire to avoid integration of the races. But no case in this Court has held that a legislative act may violate equal protection solely because of the motivations of the men who voted for it. . . .

[I]t is extremely difficult for a court to ascertain the motivation, or collection of different motivations, that lie behind a legislative enactment. Here, for example, petitioners have argued that the Jackson pools were closed because of ideological opposition to racial integration in swimming pools. Some evidence in the record appears to support this argument. On the other hand the courts below found that the pools were closed because the city council felt they could not be operated safely and economically on an integrated basis. There is substantial evidence in the record to support this conclusion. It is difficult or impossible for any court to determine the "sole" or "dominant" motivation behind the choices of a group of legislators. Furthermore, there is an element of futility in a judicial attempt to invalidate a law because of the bad motives of its supporters. If the law is struck down for this reason, rather than because of its facial content or effect, it would presumably be valid as soon as the legislature or relevant governing body repassed it for different reasons. . . .

Petitioners have argued strenuously that a city's possible motivations to ensure safety and save money cannot validate an otherwise impermissible state action. This proposition is, of course, true. Citizens may not be compelled to forgo their constitutional rights because officials fear public hostility or desire to save money. But the issue here is whether black citizens in Jackson *are* being denied their constitutional rights when the city has closed the public pools to black and white alike. Nothing in the history or the language of the Fourteenth Amendment nor in any of our prior cases persuades us that the closing of the Jackson swimming pools to all its citizens constitutes a denial of "the equal protection of the laws."

Justice White, joined by Justices Brennan and Marshall, dissented:

Jackson, Mississippi, closed its swimming pools when a district judge struck down [in Clark v. Thompson] the city's tradition of segregation in municipal services and made clear his expectation that public facilities would be integrated. The circumstances surrounding this action and the absence of other credible reasons for the closings leave little doubt that shutting down the pools was nothing more or less than a most effective expression of official policy that Negroes and whites must not be permitted to mingle together when using the services provided by the city. . . .

On May 24, 1962, nine days after the District Court's decision in Clark v. Thompson, the Jackson Daily News quoted Mayor Thompson as saying: " 'We will do all right this year at the swimming pools . . . but if these agitators keep up their pressure, we would have five colored swimming pools because we are not going to have any intermingling.' ". . .

Mayor Thompson filed an affidavit [in the present action] which stated: "Realizing that the personal safety of all of the citizens of the City and the maintenance of law and order would prohibit the operation of swimming pools on an integrated basis, and realizing that the said pools could not be operated economically on an integrated basis, the City made the decision subsequent to the Clark case to close all pools owned and operated by the City to members of both races." . . .

There . . . can be no disagreement that the desegregation ruling in Clark v. Thompson was the event that precipitated the city's decision to cease furnishing public swimming facilities to its citizens. . . . The official's sworn affidavits, accepted by the courts below, stated that loss of revenue and danger to the citizens would ob-

> viously result from operating the pools on an integrated basis. Desegregation, and desegregation alone, was the catalyst that would produce these undesirable consequences. . . .
>
> The conclusion of city officials that integrated pools would not be "economical" was no more than "personal speculation." . . . The prediction that the pools could not be operated safely if they were desegregated was nothing more than a "vague disquietude." . . . [T]here is no factual evidence that city law enforcement authorities would be unable to cope with any disturbances that might arise. . . . Officials may take effective action to control violence or to prevent it when it is reasonably imminent. But the anticipation of violence in this case rested only on unsupported assertion, to which the *permanent* closing of swimming pools was a wholly unjustified response.

Concurring opinions by Chief Justice Burger and Justice Blackmun and dissenting opinions by Justices Douglas and Marshall have been omitted.

Discussion[73]

1. How does Justice Black's opinion in *Palmer* square with the notion that, under the antidiscrimination principle, a finding that a decision was *race dependent* triggers strict scrutiny, at which point the government is required to meet the compelling-interest standard? Did the Court assume that petitioners had to prove not only that the decision was race *dependent* but that it was motivated by racial *prejudice*?

2. In view of the underlying reasons for deeming certain motivations unconstitutional, should a law be overturned only if the decisionmaker's sole or dominant purpose was illicit, or should it be sufficient that illicit motivation played a nontrivial role in the decisionmaking process so that it might have affected the outcome? In a footnote to the Court's opinion in *Arlington*, Justice Powell writes:

> Proof that the decision by the Village was motivated in part by a racially discriminatory purpose would not necessarily have required invalidation of the challenged decision. Such proof would, however, have shifted to the Village the burden of establishing that the same decision would have resulted even had the impermissible purpose not been considered. If this were established, the complaining party in a case of this kind no longer fairly could attribute the injury complained of to improper consideration of a discriminatory purpose. In such circumstances, there would be no justification for judicial interference with the challenged decision.

In Hunter v. Underwood, 471 U.S. 222 (1985), the Court cited *Arlington* in striking down a provision of the Alabama Constitution that disenfranchised persons convicted of certain enumerated felonies and misdemeanors, including "any . . . crime involving moral turpitude." Appellees, one of whom was black and the other white, were disenfranchised after being convicted of presenting worthless checks. The lower court found that, although the provision was neutral on its face, it had a racially discriminatory impact on blacks. Justice Rehnquist, writing for a unanimous Court, stated that the proper inquiry was whether the provision

73. See generally Paul Brest, Palmer v. Thompson: An Approach to the Problem of Unconstitutional Legislative Motive, 1971 Sup. Ct. Rev. 95; Theodore Eisenberg, Disproportionate Impact and Illicit Motive: Theories of Constitutional Adjudication, 52 N.Y.U.L. Rev. 36 (1977); John Ely, Legislative and Administrative Motivation in Constitutional Law, 79 Yale L.J. 1205 (1970); Michael Perry, The Disproportionate Impact Theory of Racial Discrimination, 125 U. Pa. L. Rev. 540 (1977); Symposium, Legislative Motivation, 15 San Diego L. Rev. 925 (1978).

was adopted with a discriminatory purpose and that "[o]nce racial discrimination is shown to have been a 'substantial' or 'motivating' factor behind enactment of the law, the burden shifts to the law's defenders to demonstrate that the law would have been enacted without this factor." After reviewing the circumstances of its adoption in 1901, the Court found that racial animus "was a motivating factor for the provision, and that [it] would not have been adopted . . . in the absence of the racially discriminatory motivation." In response to evidence that the provision was also motivated by a desire to disenfranchise poor whites, the Court held that "an additional purpose to discriminate against poor whites would not render nugatory the purpose to discriminate against all blacks, and it is beyond peradventure that the latter was a 'but-for' motivation for the enactment of [the provision]." The Court concluded: "Without deciding whether [the provision] would be valid if enacted today without any impermissible motivation, we simply observe that its original enactment was motivated by a desire to discriminate against blacks on account of race and the section continues to this day to have that effect. As such, it violates equal protection under *Arlington Heights*."

3. Can a legislature be held to have pursued the objectives stated in the statute? In Truax v. Raich, 239 U.S. 33 (1915), the Court struck down an Arizona law restricting the private employment of aliens and entitled: "An act to protect the citizens of the United States in their employment against non-citizens of the United States." Chief Justice Hughes rejected the state's argument that "the act proceeds upon the assumption that 'the employment of aliens unless restrained was a peril to the public welfare,' " noting that the act made discrimination against aliens "an end in itself." In Hawkins v. North Carolina State Board of Education, Civ. No. 2067 (W.D.N.C. 31 March 1966), 11 Race Rel. L. Rep. 745, the court invalidated an act permitting school closings, tuition grants, and exemptions from compulsory education, noting that the law contained its own declaration of unlawful purpose, viz: "Our people need to be assured that no child will be forced to attend school with children of another race in order to get an education." And in Parr v. Municipal Court, 3 Cal. 3d 861, 479 P.2d 353 (1971), the court found an unconstitutional "discriminatory purpose" in the official declaration that accompanied an ordinance prohibiting lying and sitting on lawns — viz: "The City Council of Carmel-by-the-Sea has observed an undesirable influx of undesirable and unsanitary visitors to the City, sometimes known as 'hippies,' and finds that unless proper regulations are adopted immediately the use and enjoyment of public property will be jeopardized."

Typically, illicit motivation can be established, if at all, only by circumstantial evidence. With what assurance can one characterize the decisionmakers' motivations in *Yick Wo*, *Gomillion*, and *Griffin*?[74] Was Justice Frankfurter justified in United States v. Kahriger, 345 U.S. 22 (1953) (dissenting opinion), in concluding

74. "The juxtaposition of a decision with some prior event or sequence of events often bears on the inference of illicit motivation. The following chronological sequence, for example, is typical of a variety of cases: the decisionmaker enforces a discriminatory . . . rule: a court enjoins this practice: the decisionmaker then adopts a constitutionally 'innocent' rule that effectively maintains the status quo ante. For example, state voting officials are enjoined from refusing to register black applicants and the state then adopts difficult but apparently neutral registration requirements: or, school districts are ordered to cease assigning students by race and the state then enacts a tuition grant law, or abandons a public school system, or engages in other practices that tend to maintain segregation," Brest, supra note 73, at 122-123. The University of Chicago Press.

from the "detailed scheme of administration [of the wagering tax laws] beyond the [government's] obvious fiscal needs" that "what was formally a means of raising revenue for the Federal Government was essentially an effort to check if not to stamp out professional gambling"?

4. What does Justice Black mean in *Palmer* by the "futility" of invalidating a law because of improper motives? That the law may be reenacted for proper reasons? That it may be reenacted for (better concealed) illicit reasons? Consider the proposal that[75]

> [the court should] presume that the decisionmaker continues to entertain the motives that led to the original decision (and to its invalidation). In operational terms, the court should enjoin an administrative decisionmaker from making the same decision again unless he comes forward with persuasive evidence that this time it will be made only for legitimate reasons. Sometimes a material change of circumstances, or the passage of time accompanied by a change of community attitudes, will be persuasive of the decisionmaker's good faith. In other circumstances the decisionmaker may be required to demonstrate that the proposed decision is in fact desirable on the merits and that no practicable alternative is less burdensome to the class at whom the original decision was adversely aimed. . . . If the court invalidates a legislative enactment, it should similarly scrutinize reenactment of the identical or a similar law if it is challenged in a properly maintained action.

5. It has been asserted that "a finding of impure motive sufficient to void an act of a legislature impugns [its] essential integrity"[76] and that judicial review of legislative motivation manifests disrespect for the "the station" of the legislature.[77] Consider the following confession and avoidance:[78]

> This argument has some force. To declare a law unconstitutional on its merits is to hold that the decisionmaker made an error. But a finding of illicit motivation often is tantamount to an accusation that the decisionmaker violated his constitutional oath of office. Especially where the decisionmaker claims to have pursued only legitimate objectives, a judicial determination of illicit motivation carries an element of insult; it is an attack on the decisionmaker's honesty. These concerns apply to lower-echelon officials as well as to legislators and high executive officials. Our constitutional traditions, however, accord greater respect to the integrity of the higher agencies.
>
> Nevertheless, legislators sometimes do act out of illicit motivations. And against the argument for nonintervention one must set the interests favoring judicial invalidation of an illicitly motivated legislative act — the injury and insult felt by those at whom it is aimed; the harm to the integrity of a system of government that pretends officially not to know what everyone knows is true. The critical commentators themselves have conceded the propriety of invalidation when the case is clear, and the courts have so acted. Herein lies the proper reconciliation of these competing interests: the courts should not refuse to inquire into the motivation of any governmental body, but they should not invalidate a decision on the ground that it was designed to serve illicit objectives unless that fact has been established by clear and convincing evidence.

75. Id. at 126-127.
76. Note, Developments in the Law — Equal Protection, 82 Harv. L. Rev. 1065, 1093 (1969).
77. Alexander Bickel, The Least Dangerous Branch 214 (1962).
78. Brest, supra note 73, at 129-130.

6. On the record in *Palmer,* could the Court have concluded that Jackson closed its swimming pools (a) simply to avoid integration, (b) to avert interracial violence and the loss of revenues that might result if the pools were operated on an integrated basis? If the former motivation is plainly unconstitutional, is the latter? Should the latter at least be treated as "suspect" and thus demand (as Justice White would demand) a stronger demonstration than respondents made that the predicted dangers would occur?

Note: Other Debates Concerning Motive Inquiry

In Rogers v. Lodge, 458 U.S. 613 (1982), a district court found that although a Georgia county's at-large voting system was "racially neutral when adopted, [it] is being *maintained* for invidious purposes," and ordered the establishment of single-member electoral districts. The Supreme Court affirmed. Justice Powell, joined by Justice Rehnquist, dissented, arguing that the complainants had not proved discriminatory intent. Justice Stevens also dissented with a wide-ranging discussion of the problems of assessing and remedying the motivation of political acts. Justice Stevens first observed that the county's demographics could change so that blacks would have more representation under the at-large scheme invalidated by the district court than under a single-member district system. He argued that "constitutional adjudication that is premised on a case-by-case appraisal of the subjective intent of local decisionmakers cannot possibly satisfy the requirement of impartial administration of the law that is embodied in the Equal Protection Clause of the Fourteenth Amendment."

> In the future, it is not inconceivable that the white officials who are likely to remain in power under the District Court's plan will desire to perpetuate that system and to continue to control a majority of seats on the county commission. Under this Court's standard, if some of those officials harbor such an intent or an "invidious" reason, the District Court's plan will itself become unconstitutional. It is not clear whether the invidious intent would have to be shared by all three white commissioners, by merely a majority of two, or by simply one if he were influential. It is not clear whether the issue would be affected by the intent of the two black commissioners, who might fear that a return to an at-large system would undermine the certainty of two black seats. Of course, if the subjective intent of these officials were such as to mandate a change to a governmental structure that would permit black voters to elect an all-black commission — and if black voters did so — those black officials could not harbor an intent to maintain the system to keep whites from returning to power. . . .
>
> The costs and the doubts associated with litigating questions of motive, which are often significant in routine trials, will be especially so in cases involving the "motives" of legislative bodies. . . . Assuming that it is the intentions of the "state actors" that is critical, how will their mental processes be discovered? Must a specific proposal for change be defeated? What if different motives are held by different legislators or, indeed, by a single official? Is a selfish desire to stay in office sufficient to justify a failure to change a governmental system? . . .
>
> Certainly governmental action should not be influenced by irrelevant considerations. I am not convinced, however, that the Constitution affords a right — and this is the *only* right the Court finds applicable in this case — to have every official decision made without the influence of considerations that are in some way "discrimina-

tory." Is the failure of a state legislature to ratify the Equal Rights Amendment invalid if a federal judge concludes that a majority of the legislators harbored stereotypical views of the proper role of women in society? Is the establishment of a memorial for Jews slaughtered in World War II unconstitutional if civil leaders believe that their cause is more meritorious than that of victimized Palestinian refugees? Is the failure to adopt a state holiday for Martin Luther King, Jr. invalid if it is proved that state legislators believed that he does not deserve to be commemorated? Is the refusal to provide Medicaid funding for abortions unconstitutional if officials intend to discriminate against women who would abort a fetus?

A rule that would invalidate all governmental action motivated by racial, ethnic or political considerations is too broad. Moreover, in my opinion the Court is incorrect in assuming that the intent of elected officials is invidious when they are motivated by a desire to retain control of the local political machinery. For such an intent is surely characteristic of politicians throughout the country. In implementing that sort of purpose, dominant majorities have used a wide variety of techniques to limit the political strength of aggressive minorities. In this case the minority is defined by racial characteristics, but minority groups seeking an effective political voice can, of course, be identified in many other ways. The Hasidic Jews in Kings County, New York, the Puerto Ricans in Chicago, the Spanish-speaking citizens in Dallas, the Bohemians in Cedar Rapids, the Federalists in Massachusetts, the Democrats in Indiana, and the Republicans in California have all been disadvantaged by deliberate political maneuvers by the dominant majority. As I have stated, a device that serves no purpose other than to exclude minority groups from effective political participation is unlawful under objective standards. But if a political majority's intent to maintain control of a legitimate local government is sufficient to invalidate any electoral device that makes it more difficult for a minority group to elect candidates — regardless of the nature of the interest that gives the minority group cohesion — the Court is not just entering a "political thicket"; it is entering a vast wonderland of judicial review of political activity.

Justice Scalia, dissenting in Edwards v. Aguillard, 482 U.S. 578 (1987), categorically attacked the cogency of motive analysis. The case concerned the constitutionality of a Louisiana statute requiring that "creation science" be taught in classes where evolution is presented as a possible explanation for the origin of life. The Supreme Court struck down the statute under a doctrine that invalidated a law if its purpose was "to endorse or disapprove of religion." Justice Scalia suggests that:

> Our cases interpreting and applying the purpose test have made such a maze of the Establishment Clause that even the most conscientious government officials can only guess what motives will be held unconstitutional. . . .
>
> But the difficulty is knowing how or where to find it. For while it is possible to discern the objective "purpose" of a statute (i.e., the public good at which its provisions appear to be directed), or even the formal motivation for a statute where that is explicitly set forth (as it was [in the preamble] to no avail, here) discerning the subjective motivation of those enacting the statute is, to be honest, almost always an impossible task. The number of possible motivations, to begin with, is not binary, or indeed even finite. In the present case, for example, a particular legislator need not have voted for the Act either because he wanted to foster religion or because he wanted to improve education. He may have thought the bill would provide jobs for his district, or may have wanted to make amends with a faction

of his party he had alienated on another vote, or he may have been a close friend of the bill's sponsor, or he may have been repaying a favor he owed the Majority Leader, or he may have hoped the Governor would appreciate his vote and make a fundraising appearance for him, or he may have been seeking favorable publicity, or he may have been reluctant to hurt the feelings of a loyal staff member who worked on the bill, or he may have been settling an old score with a legislator who opposed the bill, or he may have been mad at his wife who opposed the bill, or he may have been intoxicated and utterly *un*motivated when the vote was called, or he may have accidentally voted "yes" instead of "no," or, of course, he may have had (and very likely did have) a combination of some of the above reasons and many other motivations. To look for *the sole purpose* of even a single legislator is probably to look for something that does not exist.

Putting that problem aside, however, where ought we to look for the individual legislator's purpose? We cannot of course assume that every member present (if, as is unlikely, we know who or even how many they were) agreed with the motivation expressed in a particular legislator's pre-enactment floor or committee statement. Quite obviously, "[w]hat motivates one legislator to make a speech about a statute is not necessarily what motivates scores of others to enact it." United States v. O'Brien, 391 U.S. 367, 384 (1968). Can we assume, then, that they all agree with the motivation expressed in the staff-prepared committee reports they might have read — even though we are unwilling to assume that they agreed with the motivation expressed in the very statute that they voted for? Should we consider post-enactment floor statements? Or post-enactment testimony from legislators, obtained expressly for the lawsuit? Should we consider media reports on the realities of the legislative bargaining? All of these sources, of course are eminently manipulable. Legislative histories can be contrived and sanitized, favorable media coverage orchestrated, and post-enactment recollections conveniently distorted. Perhaps most valuable of all would be more objective indications — for example, evidence regarding the individual legislators' religious affiliations. And if that, why not evidence regarding the fervor or tepidity of their beliefs?

Having achieved, through these simple means, an assessment of what individual legislators intended, we must still confront the question (yet to be adressed in any of our cases) how *many* of them must have the invalidating intent. If a state senate approves a bill by vote of 36 to 35, and only one of the 26 intended solely to advance religion [or exhibit racial prejudice], is the law unconstitutional? What if 13 of the 26 had that intent? What if 3 of the 26 had the impermissible intent, but 3 of the 25 voting against the bill were motivatied by religious hostility or were simply attempting to "balance" the votes of their impermissibly motivated colleagues? Or is it possible that the intent of the bill's sponsor is alone enough to invalidate it — on a theory, perhaps that even though everyone else's intent was pure, what they produced was the fruit of a forbidden tree?

Because there are no good answers to these questions, this court has recognized . . . that determining the subjective intent of legislators is a perilous enterprise. It is perilous, I might note, not just for the judges who will very likely reach the wrong result, but also for the legislators who find that they must assess the validity of proposed legislation — and risk the condemnation of having voted for an unconstitutional measure — not on the basis of what the legislation contains, nor even on the basis of what they themselves intend, but on the basis of what *others* have in mind.

Given the many hazards in assuming the subjective intent of governmental decisionmakers, the [duty to ascertain purpose] is defensible, I think, only if the text of the Establishment Clause demands it. That is surely not the case.

Discussion

Do you agree with Justice Scalia's general argument? Can the Fourteenth Amendment be applied without demanding inquiries into purpose?

McCLESKEY v. KEMP

481 U.S. 279 (1987)
Certiorari to the 11th Circuit

POWELL, J. delivered the opinion of the Court.

This case presents the question whether a complex statistical study that indicates a risk that racial considerations enter into capital sentencing determinations proves that petitioner McCleskey's capital sentence is unconstitutional under the . . . Fourteenth Amendment.

I

[Warren McCleskey, an African-American, was convicted of killing a white police officer while committing an armed robbery. The jury that convicted him also held a separate penalty hearing following conviction. Georgia law allows the imposition of the death penalty only if the jury finds beyond reasonable doubt that the murder was accompanied by "aggravating circumstances." Two such circumstances, both found by McCleskey's jury, are the commission of the murder during the course of an armed robbery and the victim's being a peace officer engaged in the performance of his duties. The jury sentenced McCleskey to death.

McCleskey challenged the sentence on the ground that the Georgia capital sentencing process was administered in a racially discriminatory manner. His principal evidence was a complex statistical study performed by three researchers, the chief of whom was David Baldus of the University of Iowa.]

The Baldus study is actually two sophisticated statistical studies that examine over 2,000 murder cases that occurred in Georgia during the 1970s. The raw numbers collected by Professor Baldus indicate that defendants charged with killing white persons received the death penalty in 11% of the cases, but defendants charged with killing blacks received the death penalty in only 1% of the cases. The raw numbers also indicate a reverse racial disparity according to the race of the defendant: 4% of the black defendants received the death penalty, as opposed to 7% of the white defendants.

Baldus also divided the cases according to the combination of the race of the defendant and the race of the victim. He found that the death penalty was assessed in:

[1] 22% of the cases involving black defendants and white victims;
[2] 8% of the cases involving white defendants and white victims;
[3] 1% of the cases involving black defendants and black victims; and
[4] 3% of the cases involving white defendants and black victims.

Similarly, Baldus found that prosecutors sought the death penalty in

[1] 70% of the cases involving black defendants and white victims;

[2] 32% of the cases involving white defendants and white victims;
[3] 15% of the cases involving black defendants and black victims;
[4] and 19% of the cases involving white defendants and black victims.

Baldus subjected his data to an extensive analysis, taking account of 230 variables that could have explained the disparities on nonracial grounds. One of his models concludes that, even after taking account of 39 nonracial variables, defendants charged with killing white victims were 4.3 times as likely to receive a death sentence as defendants charged with killing blacks. According to this model, black defendants were 1.1 times as likely to receive a death sentence as other defendants. Thus, the Baldus study indicates that black defendants, such as McCleskey, who kill white victims have the greatest likelihood of receiving the death penalty.[a] . . .

II

McCleskey's first claim is that the Georgia capital punishment statute violates the Equal Protection Clause of the Fourteenth Amendment.[b] . . . As a black defendant who killed a white victim, McCleskey claims that the Baldus study demonstrates that he was discriminated against because of his race and because of the race of his victim. . . . We agree with the Court of Appeals, and every other court that has considered such a challenge, that this claim must fail.

A

. . . [T]o prevail under the Equal Protection Clause, McCleskey must prove that the decisionmakers in his case acted with discriminatory purpose. He offers no evidence specific to his own case that would support an inference that racial considerations played a part in his sentence. Instead, he relies wholly on the Baldus study. . . .

The Court has accepted statistics as proof of intent to discriminate in certain limited contexts. First, this Court has accepted statistical disparities as proof of an equal protection violation in the selection of the jury venire in a particular district. . . . Second, this Court has accepted statistics in the form of multiple regression analysis to prove statutory violations under Title VII.

But the nature of the capital sentencing decision, and the relationship of the statistics to that decision, are fundamentally different from the corresponding elements in the venire-selection or Title VII cases. Most importantly, each particular decision to impose the death penalty is made by a petit jury selected from a properly constituted venire. Each jury is unique in its composition, and the Constitution requires that its decision rest on consideration of innumerable factors that vary ac-

a. Baldus' 230-variable model divided cases into eight different ranges, according to the estimated aggravation level of the offense. Baldus argued in his testimony to the District Court that the effects of racial bias were most striking in the mid-range cases. "[W]hen the cases become tremendously aggravated so that everybody would agree that if we're going to have a death sentence, these are the cases that should get it, the race effects go away. It's only in the mid-range of cases where the decision makers have a real choice as to what to do. If there's room for the exercise of discretion, then the [racial] factors begin to play a role." Under this model, Baldus found that 14.4% of the black-victim mid-range cases received the death penalty, and 34.4% of the white-victim cases received the death penalty. According to Baldus, the facts of McCleskey's case placed it within the mid-range.

b. . . . [W]e assume the study is valid statistically. . . .

cording to the characteristics of the individual defendant and the facts of the particular capital offense. Thus, the application of an inference drawn from the general statistics to a specific decision in a trial and sentencing simply is not comparable to the application of an inference drawn from general statistics to a specific venire-selection or Title VII case. In those cases, the statistics relate to fewer entities, and fewer variables are relevant to the challenged decisions.[c]

Another important difference between the cases in which we have accepted statistics as proof of discriminatory intent and this case is that, in the venire-selection and Title VII contexts, the decisionmaker has an opportunity to explain the statistical disparity. Here, the State has no practical opportunity to rebut the Baldus study. "[C]ontrolling considerations of . . . public policy" dictate that jurors "cannot be called . . . to testify to the motives and influences that led to their verdict." Similarly, the policy considerations behind a prosecutor's traditionally "wide discretion" suggest the impropriety of our requiring prosecutors to defend their decisions to seek death penalties, "often years after they were made." Moreover, absent far stronger proof, it is unnecessary to seek such a rebuttal, because a legitimate and unchallenged explanation for the decision is apparent from the record: McCleskey committed an act for which the United States Constitution and Georgia laws permit imposition of the death penalty.

Finally, McCleskey's statistical proffer must be viewed in the context of his challenge. McCleskey challenges decisions at the heart of the State's criminal justice system. . . . Implementation of [the criminal law] necessarily requires discretionary judgments. Because discretion is essential to the criminal justice process, we would demand exceptionally clear proof before we would infer that the discretion has been abused. . . . Accordingly, we hold that the Baldus study is clearly insufficient to support an inference that any of the decisionmakers in McCleskey's case acted with discriminatory purpose.

B

McCleskey also suggests that the Baldus study proves that the State as a whole has acted with a discriminatory purpose. He appears to argue that the State has violated the Equal Protection Clause by adopting the capital punishment statute and allowing it to remain in force despite its allegedly discriminatory application. But " '[d]iscriminatory purpose' . . . implies more than intent as volition or intent as awareness of consequences. It implies that the decisionmaker, in this case a state legislature, selected or reaffirmed a particular course of action at least in part 'because of,' not merely 'in spite of,' its adverse effects upon an identifiable group." For this claim to prevail, McCleskey would have to prove that the Georgia Legislature enacted or maintained the death penalty statute because of an anticipated racially discriminatory effect. [There is no evidence supporting such a proposition.]

c. In venire-selection cases, the factors that may be considered are limited, usually by state statute. . . . While employment decisions may involve a number of relevant variables, these variables are to a great extent uniform for all employees because they must all have a reasonable relationship to the employee's qualifications to perform the particular job at issue. . . . In contrast, a capital sentencing jury may consider any factor relevant to the defendant's background, character, and the offense. There is no common standard by which to evaluate all defendants who have or have not received the death penalty.

Nor has McCleskey demonstrated that the legislature maintains the capital punishment statute because of the racially disproportionate impact suggested by the Baldus study. . . . Accordingly, we reject McCleskey's equal protection claims. . . .

IV

B

. . . [McCleskey] further contends that the Georgia capital punishment system is arbitrary and capricious in application, and therefore his sentence is excessive, because racial considerations may influence capital sentencing decisions in Georgia. We now address this claim.

To evaluate McCleskey's challenge, we must examine exactly what the Baldus study may show. Even Professor Baldus does not contend that his statistics prove that race enters into any capital sentencing decisions or that race was a factor in McCleskey's particular case. Statistics at most may show only a likelihood that a particular factor entered into some decisions. There is, of course, some risk of racial prejudice influencing a jury's decision in a criminal case. . . . The question "is at what point that risk becomes constitutionally unacceptable." McCleskey asks us to accept the likelihood allegedly shown by the Baldus study as the constitutional measure of an unacceptable risk of racial prejudice influencing capital sentencing decisions. This we decline to do. . . .

The capital sentencing decision requires the individual jurors to focus their collective judgment on the unique characteristics of a particular criminal defendant. . . .

McCleskey's argument that the Constitution condemns the discretion allowed decisionmakers in the Georgia capital sentencing system is antithetical to the fundamental role of discretion in our criminal justice system. . . . [A] capital-punishment system that did not allow for discretionary acts of leniency "would be totally alien to our notions of criminal justice."

C

At most, the Baldus study indicates a discrepancy that appears to correlate with race. Apparent disparities in sentencing are an inevitable part of our criminal justice system. . . . Where the discretion that is fundamental to our criminal process is involved, we decline to assume that what is unexplained is invidious. In light of the safeguards designed to minimize racial bias in the process, the fundamental value of jury trial in our criminal justice system, and the benefits that discretion provides to criminal defendants, we hold that the Baldus study does not demonstrate a constitutionally significant risk of racial bias affecting the Georgia capital-sentencing process.

V

. . . . [I]f we accepted McCleskey's claim that racial bias has impermissibly tainted the capital sentencing decision, we could soon be faced with similar claims as to other types of penalty.[d] Moreover, the claim that his sentence rests on the irrelevant factor of race easily could be extended to apply to claims based on unexplained discrepancies that correlate to membership in other minority groups, and even to gender. . . . Also, there is no logical reason that such a claim need be limited to racial or sexual bias. If arbitrary and capricious punishment is the touchstone under the Eighth Amendment, such a claim could — at least in theory — be based upon any arbitrary variable, such as the defendant's facial characteristics, or the physical attractiveness of the defendant or the victim, that some statistical study indicates may be influential in jury decisionmaking. As these examples illustrate, there is no limiting principle to the type of challenge brought by McCleskey. The Constitution does not require that a State eliminate any demonstrable disparity that correlates with a potentially irrelevant factor in order to operate a criminal justice system that includes capital punishment. As we have stated specifically in the context of capital punishment, the Constitution does not "plac[e] totally unrealistic conditions on its use."

[Justice Brennan, joined by Justices Marshall, Blackmun, and Stevens, dissented, focusing primarily on doctrinal aspects of the Eighth Amendment. Parts of his opinion were relevant to the Equal Protection claim as well:]

II

At some point in this case, Warren McCleskey doubtless asked his lawyer whether a jury was likely to sentence him to die. A candid reply to this question would have been disturbing. First, counsel would have to tell McCleskey that few of the details of the crime or of McCleskey's past criminal conduct were more important than the fact that his victim was white. . . . The story could be told in a variety of ways, but McCleskey could not fail to grasp its essential narrative line: there was a significant chance that race would play a prominent role in determining if he lived or died. . . .

The statistical evidence in this case . . . relentlessly documents the risk that McCleskey's sentence was influenced by racial considerations. This evidence shows that there is a better than even chance in Georgia that race will influence the decision to impose the death penalty: a majority of defendants in white-victim crimes would not have been sentenced to die if their victims had been black. . . .

C

Evaluation of McCleskey's evidence cannot rest solely on the numbers themselves. We must also ask whether the conclusion suggested by those numbers is consonant with our understanding of history and human experience. Georgia's legacy of a race-conscious criminal justice system, as well as this Court's own recognition of the persistent danger that racial attitudes may affect criminal proceedings, indicate that McCleskey's claim is not a fanciful product of mere statistical artifact. . . .

d. Studies already exist that allegedly demonstrate a racial disparity in the length of prison sentences.

The ongoing influence of history is acknowledged, as the majority observes, by our " 'unceasing efforts' to eradicate racial prejudice from our criminal justice system." These efforts, however, signify not the elimination of the problem but its persistence. Our cases reflect a realization of the myriad of opportunities for racial considerations to influence criminal proceedings: in the exercise of peremptory challenges; in the selection of the grand jury; in the selection of the petit jury; in the exercise of prosecutorial discretion; in the conduct of argument; and in the conscious or unconscious bias of jurors. . . .

V

. . . Warren McCleskey's evidence confronts us with the subtle and persistent influence of the past. His message is a disturbing one to a society that has formally repudiated racism, and a frustrating one to a Nation accustomed to regarding its destiny as the product of its own will. Nonetheless, we ignore him at our peril, for we remain imprisoned by the past as long as we deny its influence in the present.

BLACKMUN, J., joined by Marshall, Stevens, and Brennan, JJ., dissenting.

I

A

. . . The Court states that it will not infer a discriminatory purpose on the part of the state legislature because "there were legitimate reasons for the Georgia Legislature to adopt and maintain capital punishment."

. . . The Court on numerous occasions during the past century has recognized that an otherwise legitimate basis for a conviction does not outweigh an equal protection violation. In cases where racial discrimination in the administration of the criminal justice system is established, it has held that setting aside the conviction is the appropriate remedy. . . .

B

. . . The Court correctly points out: "In its broadest form, McCleskey's claim of discrimination extends to every actor in the Georgia capital sentencing process, from the prosecutor who sought the death penalty and the jury that imposed the sentence, to the State itself that enacted the capital punishment statute and allows it to remain in effect despite its allegedly discriminatory application." Having recognized the complexity of McCleskey's claim, however, the Court proceeds to ignore a significant element of that claim. . . . [That element is the role of the prosecutor,] the quintessential state actor in a criminal proceeding. . . . I concentrate on the decisions within the prosecutor's office through which the State decided to seek the death penalty and, in particular, the point at which the State proceeded to the penalty phase after conviction. This is the step at which the evidence of the effect of the racial factors was especially strong, but is ignored by the Court.

II

A

A criminal defendant alleging an equal protection violation must prove the existence of purposeful discrimination. He may establish a prima facie case of purposeful discrimination "by showing that the totality of the relevant facts gives rise to an inference of discriminatory purpose." Once the defendant establishes a prima facie case, the burden shifts to the prosecution to rebut that case. . . .

McCleskey must meet a three-factor standard. First, he must establish that he is a member of a group "that is a recognizable, distinct class, singled out for different treatment." Second, he must make a showing of a substantial degree of differential treatment. Third, he must establish that the allegedly discriminatory procedure is susceptible to abuse or is not racially neutral.

B

There can be no dispute that McCleskey has made the requisite showing under the first prong of the standard. The Baldus study demonstrates that black persons are a distinct group that are singled out for different treatment in the Georgia capital-sentencing system. . . .

With respect to the second prong, McCleskey must prove that there is a substantial likelihood that his death sentence is due to racial factors. The Court of Appeals assumed the validity of the Baldus study and found that it "showed that systemic and substantial disparities existed in the penalties imposed on homicide defendants in Georgia based on the race of homicide victim, that the disparities existed at a less substantial rate in death sentencing based on race of defendants, and that the factors of race of the victim and defendant were at work in Fulton County." The question remaining therefore is at what point does that disparity become constitutionally unacceptable. . . .

McCleskey demonstrated the degree to which his death sentence was affected by racial factors by introducing multiple-regression analyses that explain how much of the statistical distribution of the cases analyzed is attributable to the racial factors. McCleskey established that because he was charged with killing a white person he was 4.3 times as likely to be sentenced to death as he would have been had he been charged with killing a black person. McCleskey also demonstrated that it was more likely than not that the fact that the victim he was charged with killing was white determined that he received a sentence of death — 20 out of every 34 defendants in McCleskey's mid-range category would not have been sentenced to be executed if their victims had been black. The most persuasive evidence of the constitutionally significant effect of racial factors in the Georgia capital-sentencing system is McCleskey's proof that the race of the victim is more important in explaining the imposition of a death sentence than is the factor whether the defendant was a prime mover in the homicide.[e] Similarly, the race-

e. A defendent's chances of receiving a death sentence increase by a factor of 4.3 if the victim is white, but only by 2.3 if the defendant was the prime mover behind the homicide.

of-victim factor is nearly as crucial as the statutory aggravating circumstance whether the defendant had a prior record of a conviction for a capital crime.[f]

The Court has noted elsewhere that Georgia could not attach "the 'aggravating' label to factors that are constitutionally impermissible or totally irrelevant to the sentencing process, such as for example the race, religion, or political affiliation of the defendant." What we have held to be unconstitutional if included in the language of the statute, surely cannot be constitutional because it is a de facto characteristic of the system.

McCleskey produced evidence concerning the role of racial factors at the various steps in the decisionmaking process, focusing on the prosecutor's decision as to which cases merit the death sentence. McCleskey established that the race of the victim is an especially significant factor at the point where the defendant has been convicted of murder and the prosecutor must choose whether to proceed to the penalty phase of the trial and create the possibility that a death sentence may be imposed or to accept the imposition of a sentence of life imprisonment. McCleskey demonstrated this effect at both the statewide level and in Fulton County where he was tried and sentenced. The statewide statistics indicated that black defendant/white victim cases advanced to the penalty trial at nearly five times the rate of the black defendant/black victim cases (70% vs. 15%), and over three times the rate of white defendant/black victim cases (70% vs. 19%). . . .

As to the final element of the prima facie case, McCleskey showed that the process by which the State decided to seek a death penalty in his case and to pursue that sentence throughout the prosecution was susceptible to abuse. . . .

[A]t every stage of a prosecution, the Assistant District Attorney exercised much discretion. . . .

In addition to this showing that the challenged system was susceptible to abuse, McCleskey presented evidence of the history of prior discrimination in the Georgia system. . . . This historical background of the state action challenged "is one evidentiary source" in this equal protection case. . . .

[McCleskey's] showing is of sufficient magnitude that, absent evidence to the contrary, one must conclude that racial factors entered into the decisionmaking process that yielded McCleskey's death sentence. . . . [The state] must demonstrate that legitimate racially neutral criteria and procedures yielded this racially skewed result. . . .

III

The Court's explanations for its failure to apply this well-established equal protection analysis to this case are not persuasive. . . .

I disagree with the Court's assertion that there are fewer variables relevant to the decisions of jury commissioners or prosecutors in their selection of jurors, or to the decisions of employers in their selection, promotion, or discharge of employees. Such decisions involve a multitude of factors, some rational, some irrational. Second, I disagree with the comment that the venire-selection and employment decisions are "made by fewer entities." Certainly in the employment context, personnel decisions are often the product of several levels of decisionmaking within the busi-

f. A prior record of a conviction for murder, armed robbery, rape, or kidnaping with bodily injury increases the chances of a defendant's receiving a death sentence by a factor of 4.9. . . .

ness or government structure. The Court's statement that the decision to impose death is made by the petit jury also disregards the fact that the prosecutor screens the cases throughout the pretrial proceedings and decides to seek the death penalty and to pursue a capital case to the penalty phase where a death sentence can be imposed. McCleskey's claim in this regard lends itself to analysis under the framework we apply in assessing challenges to other prosecutorial actions. . . .

IV

A

One of the final concerns discussed by the Court may be the most disturbing aspect of its opinion. Granting relief to McCleskey in this case, it is said, could lead to further constitutional challenges. That, of course, is no reason to deny McCleskey his rights under the Equal Protection Clause. If a grant of relief to him were to lead to a closer examination of the effects of racial considerations throughout the criminal-justice system, the system, and hence society, might benefit. . . .

[A dissenting opinion by Justice Stevens, joined by Justice Blackmun, is omitted.]

Recall, p. 559 supra, that even successful equal protection challenges always lend themselves to at least two formally adequate remedies. Assuming that *A* at the outset is treated better than *B*, the remedy could be either to give *B* what *A* now gets or to reduce *A*'s benefits to the level of *B*'s. What should the remedy have been if McCleskey's claim of unequal treatment had been upheld? However you might treat the case of the particular complainant, Warren McCleskey (who was ultimately executed by Georgia in 1991), what more general changes in Georgia's death penalty process might have emerged from a victory by McCleskey?

The lawyers pressing McCleskey's claim were associated with the NAACP Legal Defense Fund, which is strongly opposed to capital punishment. They would surely have sought an overall reduction in the use of the death penalty. But consider the following comment by Randall Kennedy:[79]

> My critique of McCleskey v. Kemp does not proceed from abolitionist premises. Rather, it seeks to delineate a response to race-of-the-victim disparities that vindicate the claims of racial justice — with or without capital punishment. I am more concerned with the plight of black communities whose welfare is slighted by criminal justice systems that respond more forcefully to the killing of whites than the killing of blacks than I am concerned with the plight of murderers, black or white. McCleskey understandably portrayed the case in a defendant-oriented fashion. I portray the case, by contrast, in a community-oriented fashion. I conceptualize *McCleskey* as an instance of racial inequality in the provision of public goods. Whereas other cases have involved the racially unequal provision of street lights, sidewalks and sewers, *McCleskey* involves racial inequality in the provision of a peculiar sort of public good — capital sentencing.

79. McCleskey v. Kemp: Race, Capital Punishment, and the Supreme Court, 101 Harv. L. Rev. 1388, 1394 (1988).

III. Alternatives to Race-Dependency as a Trigger for Equal Protection Scrutiny

A. A Definitional Introduction: De Jure and de Facto

People can be described in terms of an unlimited number of characteristics and traits: race, gender, income, residence, weight, ownership of dogs. In the population at large, these traits may correlate with each other positively, negatively, or not at all. For example, weight correlates positively with height, negatively with being female, and (probably) randomly with owning a dog. To the extent that a correlation exists between any one trait (*T1*) and another (*T2*), a law classifying according to *T1* will by definition have a nonrandom, or disproportionate, impact with respect to *T2*. That is, a *T1*-dependent decision (or a "de jure" classification according to *T1*) will have a "de facto" impact with respect to *T2*.

For example, consider a school district's regulation, adopted solely to assure safe and efficient transportation, requiring that children be assigned to the schools closest to their homes. The regulation classifies (de jure) on the basis of residence. Suppose that the district is residentially segregated — through no unconstitutional action on anyone's part. The regulation still classifies according to residence, but it now has a disproportionate impact on race; the schools will be de facto segregated.

The school segregation is de facto even if the school board *knows* that the proximity assignment plan will result in segregated schools. If, however, the school board adopts the plan with the *motive* or *purpose* of bringing about segregation, the result is accurately characterized as de jure segregation, for the board is (perhaps covertly) using race as a decisionmaking factor.[80]

The distinction between race-dependent decisions or de jure discrimination on the one hand and de facto discrimination or disproportionate impact on the other is a conventional one and provides a common terminology for discussing constitutional doctrines involving race. This section asks the question, among others, whether the distinction may not manifest a socially oversimplified and morally and constitutionally problematic world view.

B. Disproportionate Racial Impact

Griggs v. Duke Power Co., 401 U.S. 424 (1971), construed Title VII of the Civil Rights Act of 1964 to prohibit an employer from requiring high school diplomas of job applicants and subjecting them to a general intelligence test, where the effect was to disadvantage black applicants and where the criteria had not been demonstrated to predict job performance. Chief Justice Burger wrote for a unanimous Court:

80. A common error is to characterize foreseeable segregation as "intentional" and hence de jure by invoking the saw that "actors intend the foreseeable or foreseen consequences of their conduct." This not only obliterates the conceptual distinction between de jure and de facto but carries a misleading emotive charge. It does not reflect ordinary usage to say that whenever an actor foresees that her conduct will work to someone's detriment, the actor "intends to injure" him.

> What is required by Congress is the removal of artificial, arbitrary, and unnecessary barriers to employment where the barriers operate invidiously to discriminate on the basis of racial or other impermissible classification. . . . The Act proscribes not only overt discrimination but also practices that are fair in form, but discriminatory in operation. The touchstone is business necessity. If an employment practice which operates to exclude Negroes cannot be shown to be related to job performance, the practice is prohibited.
>
> On the record before us, neither the high school completion requirement nor the general intelligence test is shown to bear a demonstrable relationship to successful performance of the jobs for which it was used. Both were adopted, as the Court of Appeals noted, without meaningful study of their relationship to job-performance ability. . . . The evidence . . . shows that employees who have not completed high school or taken the tests have continued to perform satisfactorily and make progress in departments for which the high school and test criteria are now used. The promotion record of present employees who would not be able to meet the new criteria thus suggests the possibility that the requirements may not be needed for the limited purpose of preserving the avowed policy of advancement within the Company. . . .
>
> The Court of Appeals held that the Company had adopted the diploma and test requirements without any "intention to discriminate against Negro employees." We do not suggest that either the District Court or the Court of Appeals erred in examining the employer's intent; but good intent or absence of discriminatory intent does not redeem employment procedures or testing mechanisms that operate as "built-in headwinds" for minority groups and are unrelated to measuring job capability. . . . Congress directed the thrust of the Act to the consequences of employment practices, not simply the motivation. More than that, Congress has placed on the employer the burden of showing that any given requirement must have manifest relationship to the employment in question.

The effective impact of *Griggs* was qualified by Wards Cove Packing Co. v. Atonio, 490 U.S. 642 (1989). Nonwhite cannery workers at petitioner's salmon cannery claimed illegal discrimination in hiring practices based on the disparate-impact strand of Title VII. The Court of Appeals found that the disparity between the percentage of nonwhites in unskilled cannery jobs, on the one hand, and skilled and unskilled noncannery jobs on the other, was sufficient to make out a prima facie case of disparate impact. The Supreme Court reversed. Justice White, writing for a 5-to-4 majority, first held that although the comparison "between the racial composition of the qualified persons in the labor market and the persons holding at-issue jobs . . . generally forms the proper basis for the initial inquiry in a disparate impact case . . . , with respect to the skilled noncannery jobs at issue here, the cannery work force in no way reflected 'the pool of *qualified* job applicants' or the '*qualified* population in the labor force.' " As to the unskilled noncannery positions, Justice White wrote: "As long as there are no barriers or practices deterring qualified nonwhites from applying for noncannery positions, if the percentage of selected applicants who are nonwhite is not significantly less than the percentage of qualified applicants who are nonwhite, the employer's selection mechanism probably does not operate with a disparate impact on minorities." Justice White further held that, to establish a prima facie case, respondents "have to demonstrate that the disparity they complain of is the result of one or more of the employment practices that they are attacking here, specifically showing that each challenged practice has a significantly disparate impact on employment opportunities for whites and nonwhites." After the employee establishes a prima facie case, "the employer carries the burden of producing evidence of a business justification for his employment practice. The burden of persuasion, however, remains with the disparate-impact plaintiff."

Justice Stevens, in a dissent joined by Justices Brennan, Marshall, and Blackmun, took issue with the Court's handling of the burden of proof requirements, and argued that "while the employer's burden in a disparate treatment case is simply one of coming forward with evidence of legitimate business purpose, its burden in a disparate impact case is proof of an affirmative defense of business necessity." Justice Stevens also wrote that the Court's requirement that discriminatory practices be identified with particularity "tip[ped] the scales in favor of employers."

Justice Blackmun, joined by Justices Brennan and Marshall, also dissented. Arguing that the decision "essentially immunizes" certain discriminatory employment practices from attack under Title VII, he wrote: "One wonders whether the majority still believes that race discrimination — or, more accurately, race discrimination against nonwhites — is a problem in our society, or even remembers that it ever was."[81]

Griggs was decided solely on the basis of Title VII of the Civil Rights Act of 1964. In Washington v. Davis, the Court declined to read the disparate impact standard into the Fourteenth Amendment.

WASHINGTON v. DAVIS
426 U.S. 229 (1976)
Certiorari to the United States Court of Appeals for the District of Columbia

[Respondents were blacks whose applications to become police officers in the District of Columbia had been rejected because they had failed a written personnel test ("Test 21," developed and widely used by the Civil Service Commission). They sued to invalidate the test on the ground that it was racially discriminatory in violation of the Fifth Amendment. (At the time respondents filed suit, Title VII of the Civil Rights Act of 1964 did not cover municipal employees.) The Court of Appeals invalidated the test solely on the ground that it disproportionately excluded minorities and that petitioners had not proved that it related to job performance. In effect, the Court of Appeals incorporated into the Fifth and (by implication) the Fourteenth Amendments the Supreme Court's interpretation of Title VII in *Griggs*. The Supreme Court reversed.]

WHITE, J. . . .

Because the Court of Appeals erroneously applied the legal standards applicable to Title VII cases in resolving the constitutional issue before it, we reverse its judgment in respondents' favor. . . .

As the Court of Appeals understood Title VII, employees or applicants proceeding under it need not concern themselves with the employer's possibly discriminatory purpose but instead may focus solely on the racially differential impact of the challenged hiring or promotion practices. This is not the constitutional rule. We have never held that the constitutional standard for adjudicating claims of invidious racial discrimination is identical to the standards applicable under Title VII, and we decline to do so today.

81. In response to *Wards Cove*, the Civil Rights Act of 1991 requires an employer to "demonstrate that the challenged practice is job-related for the position in question and consistent with business necessity." Complainants must still specify the particular practices alleged to have a disparate impact.

The central purpose of the Equal Protection Clause of the Fourteenth Amendment is the prevention of official conduct discriminating on the basis of race. It is also true that the Due Process Clause of the Fifth Amendment contains an equal protection component prohibiting the United States from invidiously discriminating between individuals or groups. But our cases have not embraced the proposition that a law or other official act, without regard to whether it reflects a racially discriminatory purpose, is unconstitutional *solely* because it has a racially disproportionate impact.

Almost 100 years ago, Strauder v. West Virginia, 100 U.S. 303 (1880), established that the exclusion of Negroes from grand and petit juries in criminal proceedings violated the Equal Protection Clause, but the fact that a particular jury or a series of juries does not statistically reflect the racial composition of the community does not in itself make out an invidious discrimination forbidden by the Clause. "A purpose to discriminate must be present which may be proven by systematic exclusion of eligible jurymen of the proscribed race or by unequal application of the law to such an extent as to show intentional discrimination." Akins v. Texas, 325 U.S. 398, 403-404 (1945). A defendant in a criminal case is entitled "to require that the State not deliberately and systematically deny to members of his race the right to participate as jurors in the administration of justice." Alexander v. Louisiana, 405 U.S. 625, 628-629 (1972).

The rule is the same in other contexts. Wright v. Rockefeller, 376 U.S. 52 (1964), upheld a New York congressional apportionment statute against claims that district lines had been racially gerrymandered. The challenged districts were made up predominantly of whites or of minority races, and their boundaries were irregularly drawn. The challengers did not prevail because they failed to prove that the New York Legislature "was either motivated by racial considerations or in fact drew the districts on racial lines"; the plaintiffs had not shown that the statute "was the product of a state contrivance to segregate on the basis of race or place of origin."...

The school desegregation cases have also adhered to the basic equal protection principle that the invidious quality of a law claimed to be racially discriminatory must ultimately be traced to a racially discriminatory purpose. That there are both predominantly black and predominantly white schools in a community is not alone violative of the Equal Protection Clause. The essential element of de jure segregation is "a current condition of segregation resulting from intentional state action." Keyes v. School Dist. No. 1, 413 U.S. 189, 205 (1973). "The differentiating factor between de jure segregation and so-called de facto segregation ... is *purpose* or *intent* to segregate." Id. The Court has also recently rejected allegations of racial discrimination based solely on the statistically disproportionate racial impact of various provisions of the Social Security Act because "[t]he acceptance of appellants' constitutional theory would render suspect each difference in treatment among the grant classes, however lacking in racial motivation and however otherwise rational the treatment might be." Jefferson v. Hackney, 406 U.S. 535, 548 (1972)....

This is not to say that the necessary discriminatory racial purpose must be express or appear on the face of the statute, or that a law's disproportionate impact is irrelevant in cases involving Constitution-based claims of racial discrimination.

A statute, otherwise neutral on its face, must not be applied so as invidiously to discriminate on the basis of race. Yick Wo v. Hopkins, 118 U.S. 356 (1886). It is also clear from the cases dealing with racial discrimination in the selection of juries that the systematic exclusion of Negroes is itself such an "unequal application of the law . . . as to show intentional discrimination." Akins v. Texas. A prima facie case of discriminatory purpose may be proved as well by the absence of Negroes on a particular jury combined with the failure of the jury commissioners to be informed of eligible Negro jurors in a community or with racially non-neutral selection procedures. With a prima facie case made out, "the burden of proof shifts to the State to rebut the presumption of unconstitutional action by showing that permissible racially neutral selection criteria and procedures have produced the monochromatic result."

Necessarily, an invidious discriminatory purpose may often be inferred from the totality of the relevant facts, including the fact, if it is true, that the law bears more heavily on one race than another. It is also not infrequently true that the discriminatory impact — in the jury cases for example, the total or seriously disproportionate exclusion of Negroes from jury venires — may for all practical purposes demonstrate unconstitutionality because in various circumstances the discrimination is very difficult to explain on nonracial grounds. Nevertheless, we have not held that a law, neutral on its face and serving ends otherwise within the power of government to pursue, is invalid under the Equal Protection Clause simply because it may affect a greater proportion of one race than of another. Disproportionate impact is not irrelevant, but it is not the sole touchstone of an invidious racial discrimination forbidden by the Constitution. Standing alone, it does not trigger the rule, McLaughlin v. Florida, 379 U.S. 184 (1964), that racial classifications are to be subjected to the strictest scrutiny and are justifiable only by the weightiest of considerations.

There are some indications to the contrary in our cases. In Palmer v. Thompson, 403 U.S. 217 (1971), the city of Jackson, Miss., following a court decree to this effect, desegregated all of its public facilities save five swimming pools which had been operated by the city and which, following the decree, were closed by ordinance pursuant to a determination by the city council that closure was necessary to preserve peace and order and that integrated pools could not be economically operated. Accepting the finding that the pools were closed to avoid violence and economic loss, this Court rejected the argument that the abandonment of this service was inconsistent with the outstanding desegregation decree and that the otherwise seemingly permissible ends served by the ordinance could be impeached by demonstrating that racially invidious motivations had prompted the city council's action. The holding was that the city was not overtly or covertly operating segregated pools and was extending identical treatment to both whites and Negroes. The opinion warned against grounding decision on legislative purpose or motivation, thereby lending support for the proposition that the operative effect of the law rather than its purpose is the paramount factor. But the holding of the case was that the legitimate purposes of the ordinance — to preserve peace and avoid deficits — were not open to impeachment by evidence that the councilmen were actually motivated by racial considerations. Whatever dicta the opinion may contain, the decision did not involve, much less invalidate, a statute or ordinance having neutral purposes but disproportionate racial consequences.[a]

Wright v. Council of City of Emporia, 407 U.S. 451 (1972), also indicates that in proper circumstances, the racial impact of a law, rather than its discriminatory purpose, is the critical factor. That case involved the division of a school district. The issue was whether the division was consistent with an outstanding order of a federal court to desegregate the dual school system found to have existed in the area. The constitutional predicate for the District Court's invalidation of the divided district was "the enforcement until 1969 of racial segregation in a public school system of which Emporia had always been a part." There was thus no need to find "an independent constitutional violation." Ibid. Citing Palmer v. Thompson, we agreed with the District Court that the division of the district had the effect of interfering with the federal decree and should be set aside.

That neither *Palmer* nor *Wright* was understood to have changed the prevailing rule is apparent from Keyes v. School Dist. No. 1, supra, where the principal issue in litigation was whether and to what extent there had been purposeful discrimination resulting in a partially or wholly segregated school system. . . .

Both before and after Palmer v. Thompson, however, various Courts of Appeals have held in several contexts, including public employment, that the substantially disproportionate racial impact of a statute or official practice standing alone and without regard to discriminatory purpose, suffices to prove racial discrimination violating the Equal Protection Clause absent some justification going substantially beyond what would be necessary to validate most other legislative classifications. The cases impressively demonstrate that there is another side to the issue; but, with all due respect, to the extent that those cases rested on or expressed the view that proof of discriminatory racial purpose is unnecessary in making out an equal protection violation, we are in disagreement.

As an initial matter, we have difficulty understanding how a law establishing a racially neutral qualification for employment is nevertheless racially discriminatory and denies "any person . . . equal protection of the laws" simply because a greater proportion of Negroes fail to qualify than members of other racial or ethnic groups. Had respondents, along with all others who had failed Test 21, whether white or black, brought an action claiming that the test denied each of them equal protection of the laws as compared with those who had passed with high enough scores to qualify them as police recruits, it is most unlikely that their challenge would have been sustained. Test 21, which is administered generally to prospective Government employees, concededly seeks to ascertain whether those who take it have acquired a particular level of verbal skill; and it is untenable that the Constitution prevents the Government from seeking modestly to upgrade the communicative abilities of its employees rather than to be satisfied with some lower level of competence, particularly where the job requires special ability to communicate orally and in writing. Respondents, as Negroes, could no more successfully claim that the test denied them equal protection than could white applicants who also failed. The conclusion would not be different in the face of proof that more Negroes than whites had been disqualified by Test 21. That other Ne-

a. To the extent that *Palmer* suggests a generally applicable proposition that legislative purpose is irrelevant in constitutional adjudication, our prior cases — as indicated in the text — are to the contrary. . . .

groes also failed to score well would, alone, not demonstrate that respondents individually were being denied equal protection of the laws by the application of an otherwise valid qualifying test being administered to prospective police recruits.

Nor on the facts of the case before us would the disproportionate impact of Test 21 warrant the conclusion that it is a purposeful device to discriminate against Negroes and hence an infringement of the constitutional rights of respondents as well as other black applicants. . . .

Under Title VII, Congress provided that when hiring and promotion practices disqualifying substantially disproportionate numbers of blacks are challenged, discriminatory purpose need not be proved, and that it is an insufficient response to demonstrate some rational basis for the challenged practices. It is necessary, in addition, that they be "validated" in terms of job performance in any one of several ways, perhaps by ascertaining the minimum skill, ability or potential necessary for the position at issue and determining whether the qualifying tests are appropriate for the selection of qualified applicants for the job in question. However this process proceeds, it involves a more probing judicial review of, and less deference to, the seemingly reasonable acts of administrators and executives than is appropriate under the Constitution where special racial impact, without discriminatory purpose, is claimed. We are not disposed to adopt this more rigorous standard for the purposes of applying the Fifth and the Fourteenth Amendments in cases such as this.

A rule that a statute designed to serve neutral ends is nevertheless invalid, absent compelling justification, if in practice it benefits or burdens one race more than another would be far-reaching and would raise serious questions about, and perhaps invalidate, a whole range of tax, welfare, public service, regulatory, and licensing statutes that may be more burdensome to the poor and to the average black than to more affluent whites.[b]

Given that rule, such consequences would perhaps be likely to follow. However, in our view, extension of the rule beyond those areas where it is already applicable by reason of statute, such as in the field of public employment, should await legislative prescription. . . .

STEVENS, J., concurring.

While I agree with the Court's disposition of this case, I add these comments on the constitutional issue. . . .

The requirement of purposeful discrimination is a common thread running through the cases summarized [by the Court]. . . . Frequently the most probative evidence of intent will be objective evidence of what actually happened rather than evidence describing the subjective state of mind of the actor. For normally the actor is presumed to have intended the natural consequences of his deeds. This is particularly true in the case of governmental action which is frequently the product of compromise of collective decisionmaking, and of mixed motiva-

b. Goodman, De Facto School Segregation: A Constitutional and Empirical Analysis, 60 Calif. L. Rev. 275, 300 (1972), suggests that disproportionate-impact analysis might invalidate "tests and qualifications for voting, draft deferment, public employment, jury service, and other government-conferred benefits and opportunities . . . ; [s]ales taxes, bail schedules, utility rates, bridge tolls, license fees, and other state-imposed charges." It has also been argued that minimum age and usury laws as well as professional licensing requirements would require major modifications in light of the unequal-impact rule. Silverman, Equal Protection, Economic Legislation, and Racial Discrimination, 25 Vand. L. Rev. 1183 (1972). See also Demsetz, Minorities in the Market Place, 43 N.C.L. Rev. 271 (1965).

tion. It is unrealistic, on the one hand, to require the victim of alleged discrimination to uncover the actual subjective intent of the decisionmaker or, conversely, to invalidate otherwise legitimate action simply because an improper motive affected the deliberation of a participant in the decisional process. A law conscripting clerics should not be invalidated because an atheist voted for it.

My point in making this observation is to suggest that the line between discriminatory purpose and discriminatory impact is not nearly as bright, and perhaps not quite as critical, as the reader of the Court's opinion might assume. I agree, of course, that a constitutional issue does not arise every time some disproportionate impact is shown. On the other hand, when the disproportion is as dramatic as in Gomillion v. Lightfoot, 364 U.S. 339, or Yick Wo v. Hopkins, 1 18 U.S. 356, it really does not matter whether the standard is phrased in terms of purpose or effect. Therefore, although I accept the statement of the general rule in the Court's opinion, I am not yet prepared to indicate how that standard should be applied in the many cases which have formulated the governing standard in different language. . . .

There are two reasons why I am convinced that the challenge to Test 21 is insufficient. First, the test serves the neutral and legitimate purpose of requiring all applicants to meet a uniform minimum standard of literacy. Reading ability is manifestly relevant to the police function, there is no evidence that the required passing grade was set at an arbitrarily high level, and there is sufficient disparity among high schools and high school graduates to justify the use of a separate uniform test. Second, the same test is used throughout the federal service. The applicants for employment in the District of Columbia Police Department represent such a small fraction of the total number of persons who have taken the test that their experience is of minimal probative value in assessing the neutrality of the test itself. That evidence, without more, is not sufficient to overcome the presumption that a test which is this widely used by the Federal Government is in fact neutral in its effect as well as its "purpose" as that term is used in constitutional adjudication. . . .

[Justices Brennan and Marshall dissented on grounds unrelated to the constitutional issue of racially disproportionate impact.]

Discussion[82]

1. Griggs *versus* Davis. The legislative history of Title VII provides scant support for holding that disproportionate impact, as such, supports an employment discrimination claim. This makes all the more interesting the question why the Court held that disproportionate impact stated a claim in *Griggs* and not in *Davis*. One possibility lies in the fact that the statute is limited in scope to employment, while the Fourteenth Amendment covers discrimination of every possible sort. The Court may have believed that *Griggs* was good employment policy yet thought that a constitutionally compelled disproportionate impact principle was undesirable, unpredictable, or uncontainable. Could the Court have plausibly limited a Fourteenth Amendment disproportionate-impact principle to particular subject areas of discrimination?

The facts of the two cases may also have played a role. Someone reading the record in *Griggs* and similar cases brought at the time could easily conclude that

82. See generally Eisenberg, supra note 73, and Perry, supra note 73.

the defendants were engaging in intentional discrimination — albeit discrimination that was often difficult and expensive to prove. The jobs that plaintiffs were denied had traditionally been held only by whites. By contrast, the chief of the Washington, D.C., Police Department was black and the department had many black officers. (If this is a plausible explanation for the different outcomes, is it a persuasive justification?)

2. *The parade of horribles.* Justice White concludes his opinion for the Court in *Davis* by mentioning some far-reaching consequences of adopting a disproportionate impact rule. You have probably encountered "parade of horribles" arguments before and perhaps have made them yourself. What are the implicit premises of this kind of argument? Are they inconsistent with John Ely's comment that "the observation that a constitutional doctrine will have far reaching implications cannot count as a refutation; whatever else we may or may not know about the adoption of the Fourteenth Amendment, it plainly was intended to make a difference." (Ely, Legislative and Administrative Motivation in Constitutional Law, 79 Yale L.J. 1205, 1256 (1970).)

3. *Washington v. Davis and the antidiscrimination principle.* Does the antidiscrimination principle support or weigh against the outcome of *Davis?* Consider first two arguments drawing on the *process* rationale for the antidiscrimination principle.

a. Justice White notes that a racially disproportionate impact may be evidence that a decision or pattern of decisionmaking was race-dependent. Recall Yick Wo v. Hopkins and Gomillion v. Lightfoot. Would this rationale have justified a different holding in *Davis?*

b. Would a different holding have been justified by a finding that the disproportionate black failure rate on Test 21 was the result of past de jure discrimination against blacks? In a book review in 35 Stan. L. Rev. 831 (1983), Professor Charles R. Lawrence III writes:

> [T]he discriminatory impact of the test on blacks could easily be traced to the history of racial discrimination in the city's school system. In Bolling v. Sharpe, 347 U.S. 497 (1954), a companion case to *Brown*, the Supreme Court held the District of Columbia's statutorily segregated school system unconstitutional. In Hobson v. Hansen, 269 F. Supp. 401 (D.D.C. 1967), aff'd sub nom. Smuck v. Hobson, 408 F.2d 175 (D.C. Cir. 1969), the court found that the D.C. school district had perpetuated segregated classrooms through the tracking of students. Thus, police training applicants in *Davis*, which arose only five years after *Hansen*, most likely spent the greater part of their public school careers in unconstitutionally segregated schools.

If it would be appropriate for Congress, legislating under section 5 of the Fourteenth Amendment, to prohibit certain tests on this rationale, are there any reasons for the Court not to do so? Does the decision turn on facts, or require determinations of policy, that seem more appropriate for legislative than judicial resolution?

Now consider a theory drawing on the *result* rationale of the antidiscrimination principles. Might the disproportionate disadvantage or exclusion of minorities sometimes give rise to individual and social costs produced solely because of the race of the people affected — costs that would not arise from the identical practices if their impact were random with respect to race? Recall Justice Powell's separate opinion in Keyes v. Denver School District (p. 628 supra), and consider the possible harms caused by school segregation. As a justification for the *Griggs* rule (or for a policy of racially preferential employment) consider the hypothesis that the disproportionately low socioeconomic status of certain minority groups inflicts race-specific harms on their members; that improvement in the status and income of some members of an impoverished minority community produces external benefits, increasing the wealth, status, and power of the community as a whole; that the very presence of minorities in traditionally white occupations, associations, and unions may undermine stereotypes that perpetuate prejudice and provide minorities with the leverage to prevent discrimination against others of their group; that successful minority individuals may provide role models for youths who would not otherwise aspire to certain occupations; and that even minorities regularly employed in lower level occupations may serve as role models for learning industrial discipline and bring needed stability to their communities. Assuming that this provides a basis for legislative policymaking, would it justify constitutionalizing the *Griggs* rule? More generally, can one justify a constitutional principle that requires remedy of race-specific harms but not other equally severe injuries — a principle, for example, under which a school district must spend $X to prevent $Y amount of harm by integrating the schools, but need not spend the same amount of money to prevent the same amount of harm to mentally or physically handicapped children or to white children from impoverished environments?

Do you find any merit in this result-focused rationale? If not, is it because you think that some defect of process is a necessary ingredient to a violation of the antidiscrimination principle? Assuming the rationale has merit, might it be more appropriate that Congress, rather than the Court, implement this rationale in a case such as *Davis?*

4. *The remedies for racially disproportionate employment practices.* The remedy imposed by *Griggs* and *Gaston County* was to suspend the employment and voting tests for *all* applicants, whatever their race. Would the more appropriate remedy have been to suspend the tests only for members of the disproportionately disadvantaged minority group? If such selective suspension would be "reverse discrimination" and might itself invoke the antidiscrimination principle, isn't it also "reverse discrimination" for suspension of the tests (for everyone) to be *triggered* only by disproportionate impact on minorities?

C. The Cultural Meaning of Racially Disproportionate Practices

CHARLES R. LAWRENCE III, THE ID, THE EGO, AND EQUAL PROTECTION: RECKONING WITH UNCONSCIOUS RACISM

39 Stan. L. Rev. 317, 319-326, 357-358 (1987)

. . . Critics of Washington v. Davis advance two principal arguments. The first is that a motive-centered doctrine of racial discrimination places a very heavy, and often impossible, burden of persuasion on the wrong side of the dispute. . . .

The second objection . . . is more fundamental. It argues that the injury of racial inequality exists irrespective of the decisionmakers' motives. Does the black child in a segregated school experience less stigma and humiliation because the local school board did not consciously set out to harm her? Are blacks less prisoners of the ghetto because the decision that excludes them from an all-white neighborhood was made with property values and not race in mind? Those who make this second objection reason that the "facts of racial inequality are the real problem." They urge that racially disproportionate harm should trigger heightened judicial scrutiny without consideration of motive.

Supporters of the intent requirement are equally adamant in asserting the doctrine's propriety. They echo the four main arguments that the Court itself set forth in *Davis:* (1) A standard that would subject all governmental action with a racially disproportionate impact to strict judicial scrutiny would cost too much; such a standard, the Court argues, would substantially limit legitimate legislative decisionmaking and would endanger the validity of a "whole range of [existing] tax, welfare, public service, regulatory and licensing statutes"; (2) a disproportionate impact standard would make innocent people bear the costs of remedying a harm in which they played no part; (3) an impact test would be inconsistent with equal protection values, because the judicial decisionmaker would have to explicitly consider race; and (4) it would be inappropriate for the judiciary to choose to remedy the racially disproportionate impact of otherwise neutral governmental actions at the expense of other legitimate social interests.

My own sympathies lie with the critics of the doctrine of discriminatory purpose. . . . But I do not intend to simply add another chapter to the intent/impact debate. Rather, I wish to suggest another way to think about racial discrimination, a way that more accurately describes both its origins and the nature of the injury it inflicts.

Much of one's inability to know racial discrimination when one sees it results from a failure to recognize that racism is both a crime and a disease. This failure is compounded by a reluctance to admit that the illness of racism infects almost everyone. Acknowledging and understanding the malignancy are prerequisites to the discovery of an appropriate cure. But the diagnosis is difficult, because our own contamination with the very illness for which a cure is sought impairs our comprehension of the disorder.

. . . Traditional notions of intent do not reflect the fact that decisions about racial matters are influenced in large part by factors that can be characterized as neither intentional — in the sense that certain outcomes are self-consciously sought — nor unintentional — in the sense that the outcomes are random, fortuitous, and uninfluenced by the decisionmaker's beliefs, desires, and wishes.

Americans share a common historical and cultural heritage in which racism has played and still plays a dominant role. Because of this shared experience, we also inevitably share many ideas, attitudes, and beliefs that attach significance to an individual's race and induce negative feelings and opinions about nonwhites. To the extent that this cultural belief system has influenced all of us, we are all racists. At the same time, most of us are unaware of our racism. We do not recognize the ways in which our cultural experience has influenced our beliefs about race or the occasions on which those beliefs affect our actions. In other words, a large part of the behavior that produces racial discrimination is influenced by unconscious racial motivation.

There are two explanations for the unconscious nature of our racially discriminatory beliefs and ideas. First, Freudian theory states that the human mind defends itself against the discomfort of guilt by denying or refusing to recognize those ideas, wishes, and beliefs that conflict with what the individual has learned is good or right. While our historical experience has made racism an integral part of our culture, our society has more recently embraced an ideal that rejects racism as immoral. When an individual experiences conflict between racist ideas and the societal ethic that condemns those ideas, the mind excludes his racism from consciousness.

Second, the theory of cognitive psychology states that the culture — including, for example, the media and an individual's parents, peers, and authority figures — transmits certain beliefs and preferences. Because these beliefs are so much a part of the culture, they are not experienced as explicit lessons. Instead, they seem part of the individual's rational ordering of her perceptions of the world. The individual is unaware, for example, that the ubiquitous presence of a culture stereotype has influenced her perception that blacks are lazy or unintelligent. Because racism is so deeply ingrained in our culture, it is likely to be transmitted by understandings: Even if a child is not told that blacks are inferior, he learns that lesson by observing the behavior of others. These tacit understandings, because they have never been articulated, are less likely to be experienced at a conscious level.

In short, requiring proof of conscious or intentional motivation as a prerequisite to constitutional recognition that a decision is race-dependent ignores much of what we understand about how the human mind works. It also disregards both the irrationality of racism and the profound effect that the history of American race relations has had on the individual and collective unconscious.

It may often be appropriate for the legal system to disregard the influence of the unconscious on individual or collective behavior. But where the goal is the eradication of invidious racial discrimination, the law must recognize racism's primary source. The equal protection clause requires the elimination of governmental decisions that take race into account without good and important reasons. Therefore, equal protection doctrine must find a way to come to grips with unconscious racism.

In pursuit of that goal, this article proposes a new test to trigger judicial recognition of race-based behavior. It posits a connection between unconscious racism and the existence of cultural symbols that have racial meaning. It suggests that the "cultural meaning" of an allegedly racially discriminatory act is the best available analogue for, and evidence of, a collective unconscious that we cannot observe directly. This test would thus evaluate governmental conduct to determine whether it conveys a symbolic message to which the culture attaches racial significance. A finding that the culture thinks of an allegedly discriminatory governmental action in racial terms would also constitute a finding regarding the beliefs and motivations of the governmental actors: The actors are themselves part of the culture and presumably could not have acted without being influenced by racial considerations, even if they are unaware of their racist beliefs. Therefore, the court would apply strict scrutiny.

Thus, an action such as the construction of a wall between white and black communities in Memphis[a] would have a cultural meaning growing out of a long history of whites' need to separate themselves from blacks as a symbol of their superiority. Individual members of the city council might well have been unaware that their continuing need to maintain their superiority over blacks,[b] or their failure to empathize with how construction of the wall would make blacks feel, influenced their decision. But if one were to ask even the most self-deluded among them what the residents of Memphis would take the existence of the wall to mean, the obvious answer would be difficult to avoid. If one told the story leading to the wall's construction while omitting one vital fact — the race of those whose vehicular traffic the barrier excluded — and then asked Memphis citizens to describe the residents of the community claiming injury, few, if any, would not guess that they were black.

The current racial meanings of governmental actions are strong evidence that the process defects of group vilification and misapprehension of costs and benefits have occurred whether or not the decisionmakers were conscious that race played a part in their decisionmaking. Moreover, actions that have racial meaning within the culture are also those actions that carry a stigma for which we should have special concern. This is not the stigma that occurs only because of a coincidental congruence between race and poverty. The association of a symbol with race is a residuum of overtly racist practices in the past: The wall conjures up racial inferiority, not the inferiority of the poor or the undesirability of vehicular traffic. And stigma that has racial meaning burdens all blacks and adds to the pervasive, cumulative, and mutually reinforcing system of racial discrimination.

This proposal is relatively modest. It does not abandon the judicial search for unconstitutional motives, nor does it argue that all governmental action with discriminatory impact should be strictly scrutinized. Instead, it urges a more complete understanding of the nature of human motivation. While it is grounded in the Court's present focus on individual responsibility, it seeks to understand individual responsibility in light of modern insights into human personality and collective behavior. In addition, this proposal responds directly to the concern that abandoning the Washington v. Davis doctrine will invalidate a broad range of legitimate, race-neutral governmental actions. By identifying those cases where race unconsciously influences governmental action, this new test leaves untouched nonrace-dependent decisions that disproportionately burden blacks

a. City of Memphis v. Greene, 451 U.S. 100 (1981).

b. Several scholars have criticized Memphis as a poor application of the intent test: The closing was effected by the erection of a barrier at the point of separation between the black and white neighborhoods. It was a unique step, not part of a uniform city planning effort, taken at the request of white property owners who expressed concern about excess traffic and danger to children. One person soliciting signatures for a petition in favor of the street closing had referred to the traffic as "undesirable traffic."

The Court refused to probe beneath the surface of the residents' expressed purposes, asserting that, because the plaintiffs had sued the mayor and city council, it is the latter's motivation that must be ascertained. The Court similarly refused to hold that the history of resistance to desegregation in Memphis, the fact that the white neighborhood in question developed as a result of pre-World War II segregation, and evidence of present racial animus required the district court to find that the city council's action was racially motivated, since there was no showing that "the residents of Hein Park would have welcomed the heavy flow of transient traffic through their neighborhood if the drivers had been predominantly white." Weinzweig, "Discriminatory Impact and Intent Under the Equal Protection Clause: The Supreme Court and the Mind-Body Problem," 1 Law and Inequality 277 (1983).

only because they are over-represented or underrepresented among the decision's targets or beneficiaries.

This effort to inform the discriminatory intent requirement with the learning of twentieth century psychology is important for at least three reasons. First, the present doctrine, by requiring proof that the defendant was aware of his animus against blacks, severely limits the number of individual cases in which the courts will acknowledge and remedy racial discrimination.

Second, the existing intent requirement's assignment of individualized fault or responsibility for the existence of racial discrimination distorts our perceptions about the causes of discrimination and leads us to think about racism in a way that advances the disease rather than combating it. By insisting that a blameworthy perpetrator be found before the existence of racial discrimination can be acknowledged, the Court creates an imaginary world where discrimination does not exist unless it was consciously intended. And by acting as if this imaginary world was real and insisting that we participate in this fantasy, the Court and the law it promulgates subtly shape our perceptions of society. The decision to deny relief no longer finds its basis only in raw political power or economic self-interest; it is now justifiable on moral grounds. If there is no discrimination, there is no need for a remedy; if blacks are being treated fairly yet remain at the bottom of the socioeconomic ladder, only their own inferiority can explain their subordinate position.

Finally, the intent doctrine's focus on the narrowest and most unrealistic understanding of individual fault has also engendered much of the resistance to and resentment of affirmative action programs and other race-conscious remedies for past and continuing discrimination. If there can be no discrimination without an identifiable criminal, then "innocent" individuals will resent the burden of remedying an injury for which the law says they are not responsible. Understanding the cultural source of our racism obviates the need for fault, as traditionally conceived, without denying our collective responsibility for racism's eradication. We cannot be individually blamed for unconsciously harboring attitudes that are inescapable in a culture permeated with racism. And without the necessity for blame, our resistance to accepting the need and responsibility for remedy will be lessened.

D. Disproportionate Impact, Racial Classification, or What?

HUNTER v. ERICKSON
393 U.S. 385 (1969)
Appeal from the Supreme Court of Ohio

[Most ordinances adopted by the City Council of Akron, Ohio, become effective thirty days after passage, subject to repeal by referendum initiated by 10 percent of the voters. Section 137 of the Akron City Charter provided for a special procedure for ordinances regulating the sale and leasing of real property "on the basis of race, color, religion, national origin or ancestry": They became effective only if approved by a majority of the electors voting at a general or special election. The Court held that section 137 violated the equal protection clause.]

WHITE, J. . . .

[Section 137 makes] an explicitly racial classification treating racial housing matters differently from other racial and housing matters . . .

Only laws to end housing discrimination based on "race, color, religion, national origin or ancestry" must run §137's gauntlet. It is true that the section draws no distinctions among racial and religious groups. Negroes and whites, Jews and Catholics are all subject to the same requirements if there is housing discrimination against them which they wish to end. But §137 nevertheless disadvantages those who would benefit from laws barring racial, religious, or ancestral discriminations as against those who would bar other discriminations or who would otherwise regulate the real estate market in their favor. The automatic referendum system does not reach housing discrimination on sexual or political grounds, or against those with children or dogs, nor does it affect tenants seeking more heat or better maintenance from landlords, nor those seeking rent control, urban renewal, public housing, or new building codes.

Moreover, although the law on its face treats Negro and white, Jew and gentile in an identical manner, the reality is that the law's impact falls on the minority. The majority needs no protection against discrimination and if it did, a referendum might be bothersome but no more than that. Like the law requiring specification of candidates' race on the ballot, Anderson v. Martin, 375 U.S 399 (1964), §137 places special burdens on racial minorities within the governmental process. This is no more permissible than denying them the vote, on an equal basis with others. . . .

Because the core of the Fourteenth Amendment is the prevention of meaningful and unjustified official distinctions based on race, racial classifications are "constitutionally suspect," and subject to the "most rigid scrutiny." They "bear a far heavier burden of justification" than other classifications.

We are unimpressed with any of Akron's justifications for its discrimination. Characterizing it simply as a public decision to move slowly in the delicate area of race relations emphasizes the impact and burden of §137, but does not justify it. The amendment was unnecessary either to implement a decision to go slowly, or to allow the people of Akron to participate in that decision. . . . Even though Akron might have proceeded by majority vote at town meeting on all its municipal legislation, it has instead chosen a more complex system. Having done so, the State may no more disadvantage any particular group by making it more difficult to enact legislation in its behalf than it may dilute any person's vote or give any group a smaller representation than another of comparable size.

We hold that §137 discriminates against minorities, and constitutes a real, substantial, and invidious denial of the equal protection of the laws.

HARLAN, J., joined by Stewart, J., concurring. . . .

Most laws which define the structure of political institutions . . . are designed with the aim of providing a just framework within which the diverse political groups in our society may fairly compete and are not enacted with the purpose of assisting one particular group in its struggle with its political opponents. Consider, for example, Akron's procedure which requires that almost any ordinance be submitted to a general referendum if 10% of the electorate signs an appropriate petition. This rule obviously does not have the purpose of protecting one particular group to the detriment of all others. It will sometimes operate in favor of one faction; sometimes in favor of another. Akron has adopted the referendum system because its citizens believe that whenever an action of the City Council raises the emotional opposition of *any* significant group in the community, the people should have a right to decide the matter directly. Statutes of this type, which are grounded upon general democratic principle, do not violate the Equal Protection Clause simply because they occasionally operate to disadvantage Negro political interests. If a governmental institution is to be fair, one group cannot always be expected to win. If the Council's fair housing legislation were defeated at a referendum, Negroes would undoubtedly lose an important political battle, but they would not thereby be denied equal protection. . . .

In the case before us, however, the city of Akron has not attempted to allocate governmental power on the basis of any general principle. Here we have a provision that has the clear purpose of making it more difficult for certain racial and religious minorities to achieve legislation that is in their interest. Since the charter amendment is discriminatory on its face, Akron must "bear a far heavier burden of justification" than is required in the normal case. McLaughlin v. Florida, 379 U.S. 184, 194 (1964). And Akron has failed to sustain this burden. The city's principal argument in support of the charter amendment relies on the undisputed fact that fair housing legislation may often be expected to raise the passions of the community to their highest pitch. It was not necessary, however, to pass this amendment in order to assure that particularly sensitive issues will ultimately be decided by the general electorate. Akron has already provided a procedure, which is grounded in neutral principle, that requires a general referendum on this issue if 10% of the voters insist. If the prospect of fair housing legislation really arouses passionate opposition, the voters will have the final say. Consequently, the charter amendment will have its real impact only when fair housing does *not* arouse extraordinary controversy. This being the case, I can perceive no legitimate state interest which in any degree vindicates the action taken by the City here.

As I read the Court's opinion to be entirely consistent with the basic principles which I believe control this case, I join in it.

[A dissenting opinion by Justice Black is omitted.]

Discussion

Does section 137 classify on the basis of race? If not, should it be treated as suspect? Suppose that section 137 applied to ordinances dealing with a number of controversial subjects besides civil rights. Would the treatment of laws regulating discrimination in the sale and leasing of property still constitute a "racial classification" in *Hunter's* sense? Formulate a general principle that justifies *Hunter* and that is otherwise consistent with relevant existing judicial doctrine.

WASHINGTON v. SEATTLE SCHOOL DISTRICT NO. 1

458 U.S. 457 (1982)

On Writ of Certiorari to the United States Court of Appeals for the Ninth Circuit

[In 1978, 66 percent of the voters of the State of Washington approved Initiative 350, which provided that "no school board . . . shall directly or indirectly require any student to attend a school other than the school which is geographically nearest or next nearest the student's place of residence. . . ." Several school districts that had noncomplying desegregation plans challenged Initiative 350 under the equal protection clause.]

BLACKMUN, J. . . .

We are presented here with an extraordinary question: whether an elected local school board may use the Fourteenth Amendment to *defend* its program of busing for integration from attack by the State. . . .

II

. . . [T]he Fourteenth Amendment . . . reaches "a political structure that treats all individuals as equals," Mobile v. Bolden, 446 U.S. 55, 84 (1980) (Stevens, J., concurring in the judgment), yet more subtly distorts governmental processes in such a way as to place special burdens on the ability of minority groups to achieve beneficial legislation.

This principle received its clearest expression in Hunter v. Erickson, a case that involved attempts to overturn antidiscrimination legislation in Akron, Ohio. . . .

Lee v. Nyquist, 318 F. Supp. 710 (W.D.N.Y. 1970) (three-judge court), offers an application of the *Hunter* doctrine in a setting strikingly similar to the one now before us. That case involved the New York education system, which made use of both elected and appointed school boards and which conferred extensive authority on state education officials. In an effort to eliminate de facto segregation in New York's schools, those officials had directed the city of Buffalo — a municipality with an appointed school board — to implement an integration plan. While these developments were proceeding, however, the New York Legislature enacted a statute barring state education officials and appointed — though not elected — school boards from "assign[ing] or compell[ing] [students] to attend any school on account of race . . . or for the purpose of achieving [racial] equality in attendance . . . at any school."

Applying *Hunter,* the three-judge District Court invalidated the statute, noting that under the provision "[t]he Commissioner [of Education] and local appointed officials are prohibited from acting in [student assignment] matters only where racial criteria are involved." In the court's view, the statute therefore "place[d] *burdens* on the implementation of educational policies designed to deal with race on the local level" by "treating educational matters involving racial criteria differently from other educational matters and making it more difficult to deal with racial imbalance in the public schools." (emphasis in original). This drew an impermissible distinction "between the treatment of problems involving racial matters and that afforded other problems in the same area." This Court affirmed the District Court's judgment without opinion. 402 U.S. 935 (1971).

These cases yield a simple but central principle. As Justice Harlan noted while concurring in the Court's opinion in *Hunter,* laws structuring political institutions or allocating political power according to "neutral principles" — such as the executive veto, or the typically burdensome requirements for amending state constitutions — are not subject to equal protection attack, though they may "make it more difficult for minorities to achieve favorable legislation." Because such laws make it more difficult for *every* group in the community to enact comparable laws, they "provid[e] a just framework within which the diverse political groups in our society may fairly compete." Thus, the political majority may generally restructure the political process to place obstacles in the path of everyone seeking to secure the benefits of governmental action. But a different analysis is required when the State allocates governmental power non-neutrally, by explicitly using *racial* nature of a decision to determine the decisionmaking process. State action of this kind, the Court said, "places *special* burdens on racial minorities within the governmental process," (emphasis added), thereby "making it *more* difficult for certain racial and religious minorities [than for other members of the community] to achieve legislation that is in their interest." (emphasis added) (Harlan, J., concurring). Such a structuring of the political process, the Court said, was "no more permissible than [is] denying [members of a racial minority] the vote, on an equal basis with others."

III

We believe that the Court of Appeals properly focused on *Hunter* and *Lee,* for we find the principle of those cases dispositive of the issue here. . . .

A

Noting that Initiative 350 nowhere mentions "race" or "integration," appellants suggest that the legislation has no racial overtones; they maintain that *Hunter* is inapposite because the initiative simply permits busing for certain enumerated purposes while neutrally forbidding it for all other reasons. We find it difficult to believe that appellants' analysis is seriously advanced, however, for despite its facial neutrality there is little doubt that the initiative was effectively drawn for racial purposes. . . . Proponents of the initiative candidly "represented that there would be no loss of school district flexibility other than in busing for desegregation purposes." . . . Initiative 350 in fact allows school districts to bus their students "for most, if not all," of the non-integrative purposes required by their educational policies.

Even accepting the view that Initiative 350 was enacted for such a purpose, the United States — which has changed its position during the course of this litigation, and now supports the State — maintains that busing for integration, unlike the fair housing ordinance involved in *Hunter,* is not a peculiarly "racial" issue at all. Again, we are not persuaded. It undoubtedly is true, as the United States suggests, that the proponents of mandatory integration cannot be classified by race: Negroes and whites may be counted among both the supporters and the opponents of Initiative 350. And it should be equally clear that white as well as Negro children benefit from exposure to "ethnic and racial diversity in the classroom." Columbus Board of Education v. Penick, 443 U.S. 449, 486 (1979) (Powell, J., dissenting). See Milliken v. Bradley, 418 U.S. 717, 783 (1974) (Marshall, J., dissenting). But neither of these factors serves to distinguish *Hunter,* for we may fairly assume that members of the racial majority both favored and benefited from Akron's fair housing ordinance. For present purposes, it is enough that minorities may consider busing for integration to be "legislation that is in their interest." Hunter v. Erickson, 393 U.S., at 395 (Harlan, J., concurring). Given the racial focus of Initiative 350, this suffices to trigger application of the *Hunter* doctrine.

B

We are also satisfied that the practical effect of Initiative 350 is to work a reallocation of power of the kind condemned in *Hunter.* The initiative removes the authority to address a racial problem — and only a racial problem — from the existing decisionmaking body, in such a way as to burden minority interests. Those favoring the elimination of de facto school segregation now must seek relief from the state legislature, or from the statewide electorate. Yet authority over all other student assignment decisions, as well as over most other areas of educational policy, remains vested in the local school board. . . . As in *Hunter,* then, the community's political mechanisms are modified to place effective decisionmaking authority over a racial issue at a different level of government. . . .

The state appellants and the United States, in response to this line of analysis, argue that Initiative 350 has not worked *any* reallocation of power. They note that the State necessarily retains plenary authority over Washington's system of education, and therefore they suggest that the initiative amounts to nothing more than an unexceptional example of a State's intervention in its own school system. In effect, they maintain that the State functions as a "super school board," which typically involves itself in all areas of educational policy. And, the argument continues, if the State is the body that usually makes decisions in this area, Initiative 350 worked a simple change in policy rather than a forbidden reallocation of power. Cf. Crawford v. Los Angeles Board of Education, 458 U.S. 527 (1982).

[In *Crawford,* decided the same day, the Court, with only Justice Marshall dissenting, upheld a California proposition, passed by referendum, that barred state courts from using busing as a remedy for school segregation that was illegal under state, but not federal, law. (The California Constitution had been interpreted to prohibit de facto segregation.)]

. . . But . . . [t]he issue here, after all, is not whether Washington has the authority to intervene in the affairs of local school boards; it is, rather, whether the State has exercised that authority in a manner consistent with the Equal Protection Clause. . . . Before adoption of the initiative, the power to determine what programs would most appropriately fill a school district's educational needs — including programs involving student assignment and desegregation — was firmly committed to the local board's discretion. . . . After passage of Initiative 350, authority over all but one of those areas remained in the hands of the local board. By placing power over desegregative busing at the state level, then, Initiative 350 plainly "differentiates between the treatment of problems involving racial matters and that afforded other problems in the same area." Lee v. Nyquist.

C

To be sure, "the simple repeal or modification of desegregation or anti-discrimination laws, without more, never has been viewed as embodying a presumptively invalid racial classification." Crawford v. Los Angeles Board of Education. As Justice Harlan noted in *Hunter,* the voters of the polity may express their displeasure through an established legislative or referendum procedure when particular legislation "arouses passionate opposition." (concurring opinion). Had Akron's fair housing ordinance been defeated at a referendum, for example,

"Negroes would undoubtedly [have lost] an important political battle, but they would not thereby [have been] denied equal protection."

Initiative 350, however, works something more than the "mere repeal" of a desegregation law by the political entity that created it. It burdens all future attempts to integrate Washington schools in districts throughout the State, by lodging decisiomaking authority over the question at a new and remote level of government. . . .

IV

In the end, appellants are reduced to suggesting that *Hunter* has been effectively overruled by more recent decisions of this Court. As they read it, *Hunter* applied a simple "disparate impact" analysis: it invalidated a facially neutral ordinance because of the law's adverse effects upon racial minorities. Appellants therefore contend that *Hunter* was swept away, along with the disparate impact approach to equal protection, in Washington v. Davis, 426 U.S. 229 (1976). . . .

Appellants unquestionably are correct when they suggest that "purposeful discrimination is 'the condition that offends the Constitution,'" for the "central purpose of the Equal Protection Clause . . . is the prevention of official conduct discriminating on the basis of race." Washington v. Davis. Thus, when facially neutral legislation is subjected to equal protection attack, an inquiry into intent is necessary, to determine whether the legislation in some sense was designed to accord disparate treatment on the basis of racial considerations. Appellants' suggestion that this analysis somehow conflicts with *Hunter,* however, misapprehends the basis of the *Hunter* doctrine. We have not insisted on a particularized inquiry into motivation in all equal protection cases: "A racial classification, regardless of purported motivation, is presumptively invalid and can be upheld only upon an extraordinary justification." And legislation of the kind challenged in *Hunter* similarly falls into an inherently suspect category.

There is one immediate and crucial difference between *Hunter* and the cases cited by appellants. While decisions such as Washington v. Davis . . . considered classifications facially unrelated to race, the charter amendment at issue in *Hunter* dealt in explicitly racial terms with legislation designed to benefit minorities "as minorities," not legislation intended to benefit some larger group of underprivileged citizens among whom minorities were disproportionately represented. This does not mean, of course, that every attempt to address a racial issue gives rise to an impermissible racial classification. But when the political process or the decisionmaking mechanism used to *address* racially conscious legislation — and only such legislation — is singled out for peculiar and disadvantageous treatment, the governmental action plainly "rests on 'distinctions based on race.'" And when the State's allocation of power places unusual burdens on the ability of racial groups to enact legislation specifically designed to overcome the "special condition" of prejudice, the governmental action seriously "curtail[s] the operation of those political processes ordinarily to be relied upon to protect minorities." United States v. Carolene Products Co., 304 U.S. 144, 152-153, n.4 (1938). In a most direct sense, this implicates the judiciary's special role in safeguarding the interests of those groups that are "relegated to such a position of political powerlessness as to command extraordinary protection from the majoritarian political process." San Antonio School Dist. v. Rodriguez, 411 U.S. 1, 28 (1973). . . .

POWELL, J., with whom Burger, C.J., and Rehnquist and O'Connor, JJ., join, dissenting.

. . . In the absence of a constitutional violation, no decision of this Court compels a school district to adopt or maintain a mandatory busing program for racial integration. Accordingly, the Court does not hold that the adoption of a neighborhood school policy by *local* school districts would be unconstitutional. Rather, it holds that the adoption of such a policy at the *State* level — rather than at the local level — violates the Equal Protection Clause of the Fourteenth Amendment. . . .

II

. . . The Constitution does not dictate to the States a particular division of authority between legislature and judiciary or between state and local governing bodies. It does not define institutions of local government.

Thus, a State may choose to run its schools from the state legislature or through local school boards just as it may choose to address the matter of race relations at the State or local level. There is no constitutional requirement that the State establish or maintain local institutions of government or that it delegate particular powers to these bodies. The only relevant constitutional limitation on a State's freedom to order its political institutions is that it may not do so in a fashion designed to "[place] *special* burdens on racial minorities within the governmental process." Hunter v. Erickson (emphasis added). . . .

III

. . . In this case, by Initiative 350, the State has adopted a policy of racial neutrality in student assignments. The policy in no way interferes with the power of State or Federal Courts to remedy constitutional violations. And if such a policy had been adopted by any of the school districts in this litigation there could have been no question that the policy was constitutional.

The issue here arises only because the Seattle School District — in the absence of a then established State policy — chose to adopt race specific school assignments with extensive busing. It is not questioned that the District itself, at any time thereafter, could have changed its mind and canceled its integration program without violating the Federal Constitution. Yet this Court holds that neither the legislature or the people of the State of Washington could alter what the District had decided.

The Court argues that the people of Washington by Initiative 350 created a racial classification, and yet must agree that identical action by the Seattle School District itself would have created no such classification. This is not an easy argument to answer because it seems to make no sense. School boards are the creation of supreme State authority, whether in a State Constitution or by legislative enactment. Until today's decision no one would have questioned the authority of a State to abolish school boards altogether, or to require that they conform to any lawful State policy. And in the State of Washington, a neighborhood school policy would have been lawful.

Under today's decision this heretofore undoubtedly supreme authority of a State's electorate is to be curtailed whenever a school board — or indeed any other state board or local instrumentality — adopts a race specific program that arguably benefits racial minorities. Once such a program is adopted, *only* the local or subordinate entity that approved it will have authority to change it. The Court offers no authority or relevant explanation for this extraordinary subordination of the ultimate sovereign power of a State to act with respect to racial matters by subordinate bodies. It is a strange notion — alien to our system — that local governmental bodies can forever preempt the ability of a State — the sovereign power — to address a matter of compelling concern to the State. The Constitution of the United States does not require such a bizarre result.

. . . Initiative 350 [does not] authorize or approve segregation in any form or degree. It is neutral on its face, and racially neutral as public policy. Children of all races benefit from neighborhood schooling, just as children of all races benefit from exposure to "ethnic and racial diversity in the classroom."

Finally, Initiative 350 places no "special burdens on racial minorities within the governmental process," Hunter v. Erickson, such that interference with the State's distribution of authority is justified. Initiative 350 is simply a reflection of the State's political process at work. It does not alter that process in any respect. It does not require, for example, that all matters dealing with race or with integration in the schools — must henceforth be submitted to a referendum of the people. Cf. Hunter v. Erickson. The State has done no more than precisely what the Court has said that it should do: It has "resolved through the political process" the "desirability and efficacy of [mandatory] school desegregation" where there has been no unlawful segregation.

The political process in Washington, as in other States, permits persons who are dissatisfied at a local level to appeal to the State legislature or the people of the State for redress. It permits the people of a State to preempt local policies; and to formulate new programs and regulations. Such a process is inherent in the continued sovereignty of the States. This is our system. Any time a State chooses to address a major issue some persons or groups may be disadvantaged. In a democratic system there are winners and losers. But there is no inherent unfairness in this and certainly no Constitutional violation.

IV

. . . In *Hunter* the people of Akron passed a charter amendment that "not only suspended the operation of the existing ordinance forbidding housing discrimination, but also required the approval of the electors before any future [anti-discrimination] ordinance could take effect." Although the charter amendment was facially neutral, the Court found that it could be said to embody a racial classification: "[T]he reality is that the law's impact falls on the minority. The majority needs no protection against discrimination." By making it more difficult to pass legislation in favor of racial minorities, the amendment placed "special burdens on racial minorities within the governmental process."

Nothing in *Hunter* supports the Court's extraordinary invasion into the State's distribution of authority. Even could it be assumed that Initiative 350 imposed a burden on racial minorities, it simply does not place unique political obstacles in the way of racial minorities. In this case, unlike in *Hunter*, the political system has *not* been redrawn or altered. The authority of the State over the public school system, acting through Initiative or the legislature, is plenary. Thus, the State's political system is not altered when it adopts for the first time a policy, concededly within the area of its authority, for the regulation of local school districts. And certainly racial minorities are not uniquely or comparatively burdened by the State's adoption of a policy that would be lawful if adopted by any School District in the State.

Hunter, therefore, is simply irrelevant. It is the *Court* that by its decision today disrupts the normal course of State government.

IV. "Preferential" Treatment for Racial Minorities

A. The Basic Issues: University of California v. Bakke

The "suspect classification" doctrine, treating racial classification as presumptively unconstitutional, was developed in response to discrimination against the members of minority groups that were the objects of hostility and prejudice. In Strauder v. West Virginia, 100 U.S. 303 (1880), Justice Strong suggested, "If . . . a law should be enacted excluding all white men from jury service, . . . we apprehend that no one would be heard to claim that it would not be a denial of the equal protection of the laws. Nor if a law should be passed excluding all naturalized Celtic Irishmen, would there be any doubt of its inconsistency with the spirit of the amendment." But until several decades after *Brown* the Court had no occasion to consider the permissibility of race-dependent decisions designed to benefit rather than disadvantage the members of such minorities.

The Court first addressed these issues in United States v. Montgomery County Board of Education, 395 U.S. 225 (1969), and Swann v. Charlotte-Mecklenburg Board of Education, 402 U.S. 1 (1971), where it cautiously approved of the race-conscious assignment of teachers and pupils to remedy deeply entrenched patterns of state-mandated segregation. Whatever political and constitutional problems these remedies engendered, they were not generally perceived as selectively burdening the members of one race, but rather as imposing burdens and granting benefits to minorities and nonminorities alike.

In University of California Regents v. Bakke, 438 U.S. 265 (1978), the Court for the first time[83] confronted the constitutionality of "preferential treatment" (or "affirmative action" or "reverse discrimination" — each phrase has its own emotional and political connotations) that appeared to benefit minorities at the expense of nonminorities.[84]

83. In DeFunis v. Odegaard, 416 U.S. 312 (1974), petitioner, who had been denied admission to the University of Washington Law School, challenged the school's preferential admissions program, claiming a violation of equal protection. The Court, however, failed to reach the merits due to mootness (the petitioner, who had been ordered admitted by a lower court, was nearing graduation).

84. Many of the cases in this section present issues under civil rights statutes (for example, Titles VI and VII of the Civil Rights Act of 1964) as well as under the Constitution. In the eyes of most of the Justices, the statutory and constitutional demands largely coincide; but for at least some of the Jus-

REGENTS OF THE UNIVERSITY OF CALIFORNIA v. BAKKE
438 U.S. 265 (1978)
Certiorari to the Supreme Court of California

POWELL, J.

This case presents a challenge to the special admissions program of the petitioner, the Medical School of the University of California at Davis, which is designed to assure the admission of a specified number of students from certain minority groups. . . . The Supreme Court of California . . . [found] the special admissions program unlawful . . . enjoin[ed] petitioner from considering the race of any applicant. . . . [and ordered Bakke's] admission.

For the reasons stated in the following opinion, I believe that so much of the judgment of the California court as holds petitioner's special admissions program unlawful and directs that respondent be admitted to the Medical School must be affirmed. For the reasons expressed in a separate opinion, my Brothers The Chief Justice, Mr. Justice Stewart, Mr. Justice Rehnquist, and Mr. Justice Stevens concur in this judgment.

I also conclude for the reasons stated in the following opinion that the portion of the court's judgment enjoining petitioner from according any consideration to race in its admissions process must be reversed. For reasons expressed in separate opinions, my Brothers Mr. Justice Brennan, Mr. Justice White, Mr. Justice Marshall, and Mr. Justice Blackmun concur in this judgment.

Affirmed in part and reversed in part.

I[a]

[Justice Powell began with a comparison of Davis' special and regular admissions programs. Under the regular procedure, an admissions committee rated applicants on the basis of the candidate's overall grade point average, scores on the Medical College Admissions Test (MCAT), letters of recommendation, extracurricular activities, other biographical data, and interview evaluations. Candidates whose undergraduate grade point averages fell below 2.5 on a scale of 4.0 were summarily rejected. A separate committee, a majority of whose members were minorities, reviewed special admissions. In 1973, "special admissions" students were those who identified themselves as "economically and/or educationally disadvantaged"; in 1974, only students who were members of a "minority group," made up of "Blacks," "Chicanos," "Asians," and "American Indians," were considered. For special admissions applicants, the 2.5 grade point average cutoff did not apply. Special admissions candidates were not rated against general applicants, but could be rejected for failure to meet certain requirements. Applicants continued to be considered and accepted until the prescribed number of 16 special admissions students had been admitted.[85]

tices, with respect to certain issues, they may diverge. The underlying issues of justice and public policy are, in any event, identical, and we suggest that you read the cases with a defeasible presumption that the doctrines are congruent.

a. Mr. Justice Brennan, Mr. Justice White, Mr. Justice Marshall, and Mr. Justice Blackmun join Parts I and V-C of this opinion. Mr. Justice White also joins Part III-A of this opinion.

85. From 1971 to 1974, 63 minority students (21 black, 30 Mexican-American, and 12 Asians) were admitted through the special admissions program, and 44 minority students (1 black, 6 Mexican-Americans, and 33 Asians) were admitted through the regular admissions program. Justice Pow-

Bakke, a white male whose application was considered under the general admissions program, was denied admission in 1973 and 1974. In both years, applicants were admitted under the special program with "significantly lower" scores than Bakke. After the second rejection, Bakke sued the University. The trial court held that the special admissions program violated the Federal and state constitutions, as well as Title VI, but refused to order Bakke's admission, holding that he had failed to prove that he would have been admitted but for the special program. Both Bakke and the University appealed. Justice Powell went on to describe the California Supreme Court decision:]

[T]he Supreme Court . . . agreed that the goals of integrating the medical profession and increasing the number of physicians willing to serve members of minority groups were compelling state interests, [but] concluded that the special admissions program was not the least intrusive means of achieving those goals. . . . [T]he California court held that the Equal Protection Clause of the Fourteenth Amendment required that "no applicant may be rejected because of his race, in favor of another who is less qualified, as measured by the standards applied without regard to race."

Turning to Bakke's appeal, the court ruled that since Bakke had established that the University had discriminated against him on the basis of his race, the burden of proof shifted to the University to demonstrate that he would not have been admitted even in the absence of the special admissions program. . . . In its petition for rehearing below, however, the University conceded its inability to carry that burden. The California court thereupon amended its opinion to direct that the trial court enter judgment ordering Bakke's admission to the Medical School. . . .

II

. . . At the outset we face the question whether a right of action for private parties exists under Title VI. . . . We assume, only for the purposes of this case, that respondent has a right of action under Title VI. . . .

The language of §601, 78 Stat. 252, like that of the Equal Protection Clause, is majestic in its sweep:

> No person in the United States shall, on the ground of race, color, or national origin, be excluded from participation in, be denied the benefits of, or be subjected to discrimination under any program or activity receiving Federal financial assistance.

[After reviewing the legislative history of Title VI, Justice Powell concluded:] In view of the clear legislative intent, Title VI must be held to proscribe only those racial classifications that would violate the Equal Protection Clause or the Fifth Amendment.

---

ell notes, "[a]lthough disadvantaged whites applied to the special program in large numbers, none received an offer of admission through that process. Indeed, in 1974, at least, the special committee explicitly considered only 'disadvantaged' special applicants who were members of one of the designated minority groups."

III

A

[Justice Powell then turned to the constitutional claims:] The parties . . . disagree as to the level of judicial scrutiny to be applied to the special admissions program. Petitioner argues that the court below erred in applying strict scrutiny, as this inexact term has been applied in our cases. That level of review, petitioner asserts, should be reserved for classifications that disadvantage "discrete and insular minorities." Respondent, on the other hand, contends that the California court correctly rejected the notion that the degree of judicial scrutiny accorded a particular racial or ethnic classification hinges upon membership in a discrete and insular minority. . . .

En route to this crucial battle over the scope of judicial review, the parties fight a sharp preliminary action over the proper characterization of the special admissions program. Petitioner prefers to view it as establishing a "goal" of minority representation in the Medical School. Respondent, echoing the courts below, labels it a racial quota.

This semantic distinction is beside the point: The special admissions program is undeniably a classification based on race and ethnic background. To the extent that there existed a pool of at least minimally qualified minority applicants to fill the 16 special admissions seats, white applicants could compete only for 84 seats in the entering class, rather than the 100 open to minority applicants. Whether this limitation is described as a quota or a goal, it is a line drawn on the basis of race and ethnic status.

The guarantees of the Fourteenth Amendment extend to all persons. . . . It is settled beyond question that the "rights created by the first section of the Fourteenth Amendment are, by its terms, guaranteed to the individual. The rights established are personal rights." The guarantee of equal protection cannot mean one thing when applied to one individual and something else when applied to a person of another color. If both are not accorded the same protection, then it is not equal.

Nevertheless, petitioner argues that the court below erred in applying strict scrutiny to the special admissions program because white males, such as respondent, are not a "discrete and insular minority" requiring extraordinary protection from the majoritarian political process. This rationale, however, has never been invoked in our decisions as a prerequisite to subjecting racial or ethnic distinctions to strict scrutiny. Nor has this Court held that discreteness and insularity constitute necessary preconditions to a holding that a particular classification is invidious. These characteristics may be relevant in deciding whether or not to add new types of classifications to the list of "suspect" categories or whether a particular classification survives close examination. Racial and ethnic classifications, however, are subject to stringent examination without regard to these additional characteristics. . . .

B

This perception of racial and ethnic distinctions is rooted in our Nation's constitutional and demographic history. The Court's initial view of the Fourteenth

Amendment was that its "one pervading purpose" was "the freedom of the slave race, the security and firm establishment of that freedom, and the protection of the newly-made freeman and citizen from the oppressions of those who had formerly exercised dominion over him." Slaughter-House Cases, 16 Wall. 36, 71 (1873). . . . [But] [i]t was only as the era of substantive due process came to a close, that the Equal Protection Clause began to attain a genuine measure of vitality.

By that time it was no longer possible to peg the guarantees of the Fourteenth Amendment to the struggle for equality of one racial minority. During the dormancy of the Equal Protection Clause, the United States had become a Nation of minorities. Each had to struggle — and to some extent struggles still — to overcome the prejudices not of a monolithic majority, but of a "majority" composed of various minority groups of whom it was said — perhaps unfairly in many cases — that a shared characteristic was a willingness to disadvantage other groups. As the Nation filled with the stock of many lands, the reach of the Clause was gradually extended to all ethnic groups seeking protection from official discrimination. . . .

Although many of the Framers of the Fourteenth Amendment conceived of its primary function as bridging the vast distance between members of the Negro race and the white "majority," Slaughter-House Cases, supra, the Amendment itself was framed in universal terms, without reference to color, ethnic origin, or condition of prior servitude. . . . Indeed, it is not unlikely that among the Framers were many who would have applauded a reading of the Equal Protection Clause that states a principle of universal application and is responsive to the racial, ethnic, and cultural diversity of the Nation.

Over the past 30 years, this Court has embarked upon the crucial mission of interpreting the Equal Protection Clause with the view of assuring to all persons "the protection of equal laws," *Yick Wo*, supra, in a Nation confronting a legacy of slavery and racial discrimination. Because the landmark decisions in this area arose in response to the continued exclusion of Negroes from the mainstream of American society, they could be characterized as involving discrimination by the "majority" white race against the Negro minority. But they need not be read as depending upon that characterization for their results. It suffices to say that "[o]ver the years, this Court has consistently repudiated '[d]istinctions between citizens solely because of their ancestry' as being 'odious to a free people whose institutions are founded upon the doctrine of equality.'" Loving v. Virginia (1967).

Petitioner urges us to adopt for the first time a more restrictive view of the Equal Protection Clause and hold that discrimination against members of the white "majority" cannot be suspect if its purpose can be characterized as "benign." The clock of our liberties, however, cannot be turned back to 1868. It is far too late to argue that the guarantee of equal protection to *all* persons permits the recognition of special wards entitled to a degree of protection greater than that accorded others. "The Fourteenth Amendment is not directed solely against discrimination due to a 'two-class theory' — that is, based upon differences between 'white' and Negro."

Once the artificial line of a "two-class theory" of the Fourteenth Amendment is put aside, the difficulties entailed in varying the level of judicial review according to a perceived "preferred" status of a particular racial or ethnic minority are intractable. The concepts of "majority" and "minority" necessarily reflect temporary arrangements and political judgments. As observed above, the white "majority" itself is composed of various minority groups, most of which can lay claim to a history of prior discrimination at the hands of the State and private individuals. Not all of these groups can receive preferential treatment and corresponding judicial tolerance of distinctions drawn in terms of race and nationality, for then the only "majority" left would be a new minority of white Anglo-Saxon Protestants. There is no principled basis for deciding which groups would merit "heightened judicial solicitude" and which would not. Courts would be asked to evaluate the extent of the prejudice and consequent harm suffered by various minority groups. Those whose societal injury is thought to exceed some arbitrary level of tolerability then would be entitled to preferential classifications at the expense of individuals belonging to other groups. Those classifications would be free from exacting judicial scrutiny. As these preferences began to have their desired effect, and the consequences of past discrimination were undone, new judicial rankings would be necessary. The kind of variable sociological and political analysis necessary to produce such rankings simply does not lie within the judicial competence — even if they otherwise were politically feasible and socially desirable.

Moreover, there are serious problems of justice connected with the idea of preference itself. First, it may not always be clear that a so-called preference is in fact benign. Courts may be asked to validate burdens imposed upon individual members of particular groups in order to advance the group's general interest. Nothing in the Constitution supports the notion that individuals may be asked to suffer otherwise impermissible burdens in order to enhance the societal standing of their ethnic groups. Second, preferential programs may only reinforce common stereotypes holding that certain groups are unable to achieve success without special protection based on a factor having no relationship to individual worth. Third, there is a measure of inequity in forcing innocent persons in respondent's position to bear the burdens of redressing grievances not of their making.

By hitching the meaning of the Equal Protection Clause to these transitory considerations, we would be holding, as a constitutional principle, that judicial scrutiny of classifications touching on racial and ethnic background may vary with the ebb and flow of political forces. Disparate constitutional tolerance of such classifications well may serve to exacerbate racial and ethnic antagonisms rather than alleviate them. Also, the mutability of a constitutional principle, based upon shifting political and social judgments, undermines the chances for consistent application of the Constitution from one generation to the next, a critical feature of its coherent interpretation. In expounding the Constitution, the Court's role is to discern "principles sufficiently absolute to give them roots throughout the community and continuity over significant periods of time, and to lift them above the level of the pragmatic political judgments of a particular time and place." A. Cox, The Role of the Supreme Court in American Government 114 (1976).

If it is the individual who is entitled to judicial protection against classifications based upon his racial or ethnic background because such distinctions impinge upon personal rights, rather than the individual only because of his membership in a particular group, then constitutional standards may be applied consistently. Political judgments regarding the necessity for the particular classification may be weighed in the constitutional balance, Korematsu v. United States, 323 U.S. 214 (1944), but the standard of justification will remain constant. This is as it should be, since those political judgments are the product of rough compromise struck by contending groups within the democratic process. When they touch upon an individual's race or ethnic background, he is entitled to a judicial determination that the burden he is asked to bear on that basis is precisely tailored to serve a compelling governmental interest. . . .

C

Petitioner contends that on several occasions this Court has approved preferential classifications without applying the most exacting scrutiny. Most of the cases upon which petitioner relies are drawn from three areas: school desegregation, employment discrimination, and sex discrimination. Each of the cases cited presented a situation materially different from the facts of this case.

The school desegregation cases are inapposite. Each involved remedies for clearly determined constitutional violations. Racial classifications thus were designed as remedies for the vindication of constitutional entitlement.[b] Moreover, the scope of the remedies was not permitted to exceed the extent of the violations. Here, there was no judicial determination of constitutional violation as a predicate for the formulation of a remedial classification.

The employment discrimination cases also do not advance petitioner's cause. For example, in Franks v. Bowman Transportation Co., 424 U.S. 747 (1976), we approved a retroactive award of seniority to a class of Negro truckdrivers who had been the victims of discrimination — not just by society at large, but by the respondent in that case. . . . But we have never approved preferential classifications in the absence of proved constitutional or statutory violations.

Nor is petitioner's view as to the applicable standard supported by the fact that gender-based classifications are not subjected to this level of scrutiny. . . . [T]he Court has never viewed such classification as inherently suspect or as comparable to racial or ethnic classifications for the purpose of equal protection analysis. . . .

In this case . . . there has been no determination by the legislature or a responsible administrative agency that the University engaged in a discriminatory practice requiring remedial efforts. Moreover, the operation of petitioner's special admissions program is quite different from the remedial measures approved in those cases. It prefers the designated minority groups at the expense of other individuals who are totally foreclosed from competition for the 16 special admissions seats in every Medical School class. . . .

IV

We have held that in "order to justify the use of a suspect classification, a State must show that its purpose or interest is both constitutionally permissible and substantial, and that its use of the classification is 'necessary . . . to the accomplish-

b. . . . Respondent's position is wholly dissimilar to that of a pupil bused from his neighborhood school to a comparable school in another neighborhood in compliance with a desegregation decree. Petitioner did not arrange for respondent to attend a different medical school in order to desegregate Davis Medical School: instead, it denied him admission and may have deprived him altogether of a medical education.

ment' of its purpose or the safeguarding of its interest." . . . The special admissions program purports to serve the purposes of: (i) "reducing the historic deficit of traditionally disfavored minorities in medical schools and in the medical profession"; (ii) countering the effects of societal discrimination; (iii) increasing the number of physicians who will practice in communities currently underserved; and (iv) obtaining the educational benefits that flow from an ethnically diverse student body. It is necessary to decide which, if any, of these purposes is substantial enough to support the use of a suspect classification.

A

If petitioner's purpose is to assure within its student body some specified percentage of a particular group merely because of its race or ethnic origin, such a preferential purpose must be rejected not as insubstantial but as facially invalid. Preferring members of any one group for no reason other than race or ethnic origin is discrimination for its own sake. This the Constitution forbids.

B

The State certainly has a legitimate and substantial interest in ameliorating, or eliminating where feasible, the disabling effects of identified discrimination. . . . We have never approved a classification that aids persons perceived as members of relatively victimized groups at the expense of other innocent individuals in the absence of judicial, legislative, or administrative findings of constitutional or statutory violations. After such findings have been made, the governmental interest in preferring members of the injured groups at the expense of others is substantial, since the legal rights of the victims must be vindicated. In such a case, the extent of the injury and the consequent remedy will have been judicially, legislatively, or administratively defined. Also, the remedial action usually remains subject to continuing oversight to assure that it will work the least harm possible to other innocent persons competing for the benefit. . . .

Petitioner does not purport to have made, and is in no position to make, such findings. Its broad mission is education, not the formulation of any legislative policy or the adjudication of particular claims of illegality. For reasons similar to those stated in Part III of this opinion, isolated segments of our vast governmental structures are not competent to make those decisions, at least in the absence of legislative mandates and legislatively determined criteria.[c] Before relying upon these sorts of findings in establishing a racial classification, a governmental body must have the authority and capability to establish, in the record, that the classification is responsive to identified discrimination. . . .

C

Petitioner simply has not carried its burden of demonstrating that it must prefer members of particular ethnic groups over all other individuals in order to

c. For example, the University is unable to explain its selection of only the four favored groups — Negroes, Mexican-Americans, American Indians, and Asians — for preferential treatment. The inclusion of the last group is especially curious in light of the substantial numbers of Asians admitted through the regular admissions process.

promote better health-care delivery to deprived citizens. Indeed, petitioner has not shown that its preferential classification is likely to have any significant effect on the problem.

D

The fourth goal asserted by petitioner is the attainment of a diverse student body. This clearly is a constitutionally permissible goal for an institution of higher education. Academic freedom, though not a specifically enumerated constitutional right, long has been viewed as a special concern of the First Amendment. The freedom of a university to make its own judgments as to education includes the selection of its student body. . . .

Thus, in arguing that its universities must be accorded the right to select those students who will contribute the most to the "robust exchange of ideas," petitioner invokes a countervailing constitutional interest, that of the First Amendment. In this light, petitioner must be viewed as seeking to achieve a goal that is of paramount importance in the fulfillment of its mission. . . .

Physicians serve a heterogeneous population. An otherwise qualified medical student with a particular background — whether it be ethnic, geographic, culturally advantaged or disadvantaged — may bring to a professional school of medicine experiences, outlooks, and ideas that enrich the training of its student body and better equip its graduates to render with understanding their vital service to humanity.

. . . As the interest of diversity is compelling in the context of a university's admissions program, the question remains whether the program's racial classification is necessary to promote this interest.

V

A

. . . The diversity that furthers a compelling state interest encompasses a far broader array of qualifications and characteristics of which racial or ethnic origin is but a single though important element. Petitioner's special admissions program, focused *solely* on ethnic diversity, would hinder rather than further attainment of genuine diversity. . . .

The experience of other university admissions programs, which take race into account in achieving the educational diversity valued by the First Amendment, demonstrates that the assignment of a fixed number of places to a minority group is not a necessary means toward that end. An illuminating example is found in the Harvard College program:

> In recent years Harvard College has expanded the concept of diversity to include students from disadvantaged economic, racial and ethnic groups. Harvard College now recruits not only Californians or Louisianans but also blacks and Chicanos and other minority students. . . .
>
> In practice, this new definition of diversity has meant that race has been a factor in some admission decisions. When the Committee on Admissions reviews the large middle group of applicants who are "admissible" and deemed capable of doing good

> work in their courses, the race of an applicant may tip the balance in his favor just as geographic origin or a life spent on a farm may tip the balance in other candidates' cases. . . .
>
> In Harvard college admissions the Committee has not set target-quotas for the number of blacks, or of musicians, football players, physicists or Californians to be admitted in a given year. . . .[86] But that awareness [of the necessity of including more than a token number of black students] does not mean that the Committee sets a minimum number of blacks or of people from west of the Mississippi who are to be admitted. It means only that in choosing among thousands of applicants who are not only "admissible" academically but have other strong qualities, the Committee, with a number of criteria in mind, pays some attention to distribution among many types and categories of students.

In such an admissions program, race or ethnic background may be deemed a "plus" in a particular applicant's file, yet it does not insulate the individual from comparison with all other candidates for the available seats. The file of a particular black applicant may be examined for his potential contribution to diversity without the factor of race being decisive when compared, for example, with that of an applicant identified as an Italian-American if the latter is thought to exhibit qualities more likely to promote beneficial educational pluralism. . . . In short, an admissions program operated in this way is flexible enough to consider all pertinent elements of diversity in light of the particular qualifications of each applicant, and to place them on the same footing for consideration, although not necessarily according them the same weight. Indeed, the weight attributed to a particular quality may vary from year to year depending upon the "mix" both of the student body and the applicants for the incoming class.

This kind of program treats each applicant as an individual in the admissions process. The applicant who loses out on the last available seat to another candidate receiving a "plus" on the basis of ethnic background will not have been foreclosed from all consideration for that seat simply because he was not the right color or had the wrong surname. It would mean only that his combined qualifications, which may have included similar nonobjective factors, dd not outweigh those of the other applicant. His qualifications would have been weighed fairly and competitively, and he would have no basis to complain of unequal treatment under the Fourteenth Amendment.

86. The elision is Justice Powell's. The omitted text (which is set out in the appendix to Justice Powell's opinion) reads:

> At the same time the Committee is aware that if Harvard College is to provide a truly heterogeneous environment that reflects the rich diversity of the United States, it cannot be provided without some attention to numbers. It would not make sense, for example, to have 10 or 20 students out of 1,100 whose homes are west of the Mississippi. Comparably, 10 or 20 black students could not begin to bring to their classmates and to each other the variety of points of view, backgrounds and experiences of blacks in the United States. Their small numbers might also create a sense of isolation among the black students themselves and thus make it more difficult for them to develop and achieve their potential. Consequently, when making its decisions, the Committee on Admissions is aware that there is some relationship between numbers and achieving the benefits to be derived from a diverse student body, and between numbers and providing a reasonable environment for those students admitted.

It has been suggested that an admissions program which considers race only as one factor is simply a subtle and more sophisticated — but no less effective — means of according racial preference than the Davis program. A facial intent to discriminate, however, is evident in petitioner's preference program and not denied in this case. No such facial infirmity exists in an admissions program where race or ethnic background is simply one element — to be weighed fairly against other elements — in the selection process. . . .

B

In summary, it is evident that the Davis special admissions program involves the use of an explicit racial classification never before countenanced by this Court. It tells applicants who are not Negro, Asian, or Chicano that they are totally excluded from a specific percentage of the seats in an entering class. No matter how strong their qualifications, quantitative and extracurricular, including their own potential for contribution to educational diversity, they are never afforded the chance to compete with applicants from the preferred groups for the special admissions seats. At the same time, the preferred applicants have the opportunity to compete for every seat in the class.

The fatal flaw in petitioner's preferential program is its disregard of individual rights as guaranteed by the Fourteenth Amendment. . . .

C

In enjoining petitioner from ever considering the race of any applicant, however, the courts below failed to recognize that the State has a substantial interest that legitimately may be served by a properly devised admissions program involving the competitive consideration of race and ethnic origin. For this reason, so much of the California court's judgment as enjoins petitioner from any consideration of the race of any applicant must be reversed.

VI

With respect to respondent's entitlement to an injunction directing his admission to the Medical School, petitioner has conceded that it could not carry its burden of proving that, but for the existence of its unlawful special admissions program, respondent still would not have been admitted. Hence, respondent is entitled to the injunction, and that portion of the judgment must be affirmed.

BRENNAN, WHITE, MARSHALL, and BLACKMUN, JJ., concurring in the judgment in part and dissenting in part. . . .

We agree with Mr. Justice Powell that, as applied to the case before us, Title VI goes no further in prohibiting the use of race than the Equal Protection Clause of the Fourteenth Amendment itself. . . . Since we conclude that the affirmative admissions program at the Davis Medical School is constitutional, we would reverse the judgment below in all respects. Mr. Justice Powell agrees that some uses of race in university admissions are permissible and, therefore, he joins with us to make five votes reversing the judgment below insofar as it prohibits the University from establishing race-conscious programs in the future....

II

The threshold question we must decide is whether Title VI of the Civil Rights Act of 1964 bars recipients of federal funds from giving preferential consideration to disadvantaged members of racial minorities as part of a program designed to enable such individuals to surmount the obstacles imposed by racial discrimination. We join Parts I and V-C of our Brother Powell's opinion and three of us agree with his conclusion in Part II that this case does not require us to resolve the question whether there is a private right of action under Title VI.

In our view, Title VI prohibits only those uses of racial criteria that would violate the Fourteenth Amendment if employed by a State or its agencies; it does not bar the preferential treatment of racial minorities as a means of remedying past societal discrimination to the extent that such action is consistent with the Fourteenth Amendment....

III

A . . .

Our cases have always implied that an "overriding statutory purpose," McLaughlin v. Florida, 379 U.S. 184, 192 (1964), could be found that would justify racial classifications....

We conclude, therefore, that racial classifications are not per se invalid under the Fourteenth Amendment. Accordingly, we turn to the problem of articulating what our role should be in reviewing state action that expressly classifies by race.

B

... [Justice Brennan first considered the applicability of "strict scrutiny" analysis to the University's special admissions program:] We have held that a government practice or statute which restricts "fundamental rights" or which contains "suspects classifications" is to be subjected to "strict scrutiny" and can be justified only if it furthers a compelling government purpose and, even then, only if no less restrictive alternative is available. But no fundamental right is involved here. Nor do whites as a class have any of the "traditional indicia of suspectness: the class is not saddled with such disabilities, or subjected to such a history of purposeful unequal treatment, or relegated to such a position of political powerlessness as to command extraordinary protection from the majoritarian political process." ...

On the other hand, the fact that this case does not fit neatly into our prior analytic framework for race cases does not mean that it should be analyzed by applying the very loose rational-basis standard of review that is the very least that is always applied in equal protection cases. " '[T]he mere recitation of a benign, compensatory purpose is not an automatic shield which protects against any inquiry into the actual purposes underlying a statutory scheme.' " Califano v. Webster, 430 U.S. 313, 317 (1977), quoting Weinberger v. Wiesenfeld, 420 U.S. 636,

648 (1975). Instead, a number of considerations — developed in gender-discrimination cases but which carry even more force when applied to racial classifications — lead us to conclude that racial classifications designed to further remedial purposes " 'must serve important governmental objectives and must be substantially related to achievement of those objectives.' "[a]

First, race, like "gender-based classifications too often [has] been inexcusably utilized to stereotype and stigmatize politically powerless segments of society." While a carefully tailored statute designed to remedy past discrimination could avoid these vices, we nonetheless have recognized that the line between honest and thoughtful appraisal of the effects of past discrimination and paternalistic stereotyping is not so clear and that a statute based on the latter is patently capable of stigmatizing all women with a badge of inferiority. State programs designed ostensibly to ameliorate the effects of past racial discrimination obviously create the same hazard of stigma, since they may promote racial separatism and reinforce the views of those who believe that members of racial minorities are inherently incapable of succeeding on their own.

Second, race, like gender and illegitimacy, is an immutable characteristic which its possessors are powerless to escape or set aside. While a classification is not per se invalid because it divides classes on the basis of an immutable characteristic, it is nevertheless true that such divisions are contrary to our deep belief that "legal burdens should bear some relationship to individual responsibility or wrongdoing," and that advancement sanctioned, sponsored, or approved by the State should ideally be based on individual merit or achievement, or at the least on factors within the control of an individual.

Because this principle is so deeply rooted it might be supposed that it would be considered in the legislative process and weighed against the benefits of programs preferring individuals because of their race. But this is not necessarily so: The "natural consequence of our governing processes [may well be] that the most 'discrete and insular' of whites . . . will be called upon to bear the immediate, direct costs of benign discrimination." Moreover, it is clear from our cases that there are limits beyond which majorities may not go when they classify on the basis of immutable characteristics. Thus, even if the concern for individualism is weighed by the political process, that weighing cannot waive the personal rights of individuals under the Fourteenth Amendment.

In sum, because of the significant risk that racial classifications established for ostensibly benign purposes can be misused, causing effects not unlike those created by invidious classifications, it is inappropriate to inquire only whether there

a. We disagree with our Brother Powell's suggestion that the presence of "rival groups which can claim that they, too, are entitled to preferential treatment" distinguishes the gender cases or is relevant to the question of scope of judicial review of race classifications. We are not asked to determine whether groups other than those favored by the Davis program should similarly be favored. All we are asked to do is to pronounce the constitutionality of what Davis has done.

But, were we asked to decide whether any given rival group — German-Americans for example — must constitutionally be accorded preferential treatment, we do have a "principled basis," for deciding this question, one that is well established in our cases: The Davis program expressly sets out four classes which receive preferred status. The program clearly distinguishes whites, but one cannot reason from this a conclusion that German-Americans, as a national group, are singled out for invidious treatment. And even if the Davis Program had a differential impact on German-Americans, they would have no constitutional claim unles they could prove that Davis intended invidiously to discriminate against German-Americans. . . . Thus, claims of rival groups, although they may create thorny political problems, create relatively simple problems for the courts.

is any conceivable basis that might sustain such a classification. Instead, to justify such a classification an important and articulated purpose for its use must be shown. In addition, any statute must be stricken that stigmatizes any group or that singles out those least well represented in the political process to bear the brunt of a benign program. Thus, our review under the Fourteenth Amendment should be strict — not " 'strict' in theory and fatal in fact," because it is stigma that causes fatality — but strict and searching nonetheless.

IV

Davis' articulated purpose of remedying the effects of past societal discrimination is, under our cases, sufficiently important to justify the use of race-conscious admissions programs where there is a sound basis for concluding that minority underrepresentation is substantial and chronic, and that the handicap of past discrimination is impeding access of minorities to the Medical School.

A

At least since Green v. County School Board, 391 U.S. 430 (1968), it has been clear that a public body which has itself been adjudged to have engaged in racial discrimination cannot bring itself into compliance with the Equal Protection Clause simply by ending its unlawful acts and adopting a neutral stance. Three years later, Swann v. Charlotte-Mecklenburg Board of Education, 402 U.S. 1 (1971), . . . [held] that school boards, even in the absence of a judicial finding of past discrimination, could voluntarily adopt plans which assigned students with the end of creating racial pluralism by establishing fixed ratios of black and white students in each school.

. . . Congress can and has outlawed actions which have a disproportionately adverse and unjustified impact upon members of racial minorities and has required or authorized race-conscious action to put individuals disadvantaged by such impact in the position they otherwise might have enjoyed. See Franks v. Bowman Transportation Co., 424 U.S. 747 (1976); Teamsters v. United States, 431 U.S. 324 (1977). Such relief does not require as a predicate proof that recipients of preferential advancement have been individually discriminated against; it is enough that each recipient is within a general class of persons likely to have been the victims of discrimination. Nor is it an objection to such relief that preference for minorities will upset the settled expectations of nonminorities. . . .

These cases cannot be distinguished simply by the presence of judicial findings of discrimination, for race-conscious remedies have been approved where such findings have not been made. Indeed, the requirement of a judicial determination of a constitutional or statutory violation as a predicate for race-conscious remedial actions would be self-defeating. Such a requirement would severely undermine efforts to achieve voluntary compliance with the requirements of law. And, our society and jurisprudence have always stressed the value of voluntary efforts to further the objectives of the law. Judicial intervention is a last resort to achieve cessation of illegal conduct or the remedying of its effects rather than a prerequisite to action.

Thus, our cases under Title VII of the Civil Rights Act have held that, in order to achieve minority participation in previously segregated areas of public life,

Congress may require or authorize preferential treatment for those likely disadvantaged by societal racial discrimination. Such legislation has been sustained even without a requirement of findings of intentional racial discrimination by those required or authorized to accord preferential treatment, or a case-by-case determination that those to be benefited suffered from racial discrimination. These decisions compel the conclusion that States also may adopt race-conscious programs designed to overcome substantial, chronic minority underrepresentation where there is reason to believe that the evil addressed is a product of past racial discrimination.[b]

B

Properly construed, therefore, our prior cases unequivocally show that a state government may adopt race-conscious programs if the purpose of such programs is to remove the disparate racial impact its actions might otherwise have and if there is reason to believe that the disparate impact is itself the product of past discrimination, whether its own or that of society at large. There is no question that Davis' program is valid under this test.

Certainly, on the basis of the undisputed factual submissions before this Court, Davis had a sound basis for believing that the problem of underrepresentation of minorities was substantial and chronic and that the problem was attributable to handicaps imposed on minority applicants by past and present racial discrimination. Until at least 1973, the practice of medicine in this country was in fact, if not in law, largely the prerogative of whites. In 1950, for example, while Negroes constituted 10% of the total population, Negro physicians constituted only 2.2% of the total number of physicians. The overwhelming majority of these, moreover, were educated in two predominantly Negro medical schools, Howard and Meharry. By 1970, the gap between the proportion of Negroes in medicine and their proportion in the population had widened: The number of Negroes employed in medicine remained frozen at 2.2% while the Negro population had increased to 11.1%. The number of Negro admittees to predominantly white medical schools, moreover, had declined in absolute numbers during the years 1955 to 1964.

Moreover, Davis had very good reason to believe that the national pattern of underrepresentation of minorities in medicine would be perpetuated if it retained a single admissions standard. For example, the entering classes in 1968 and 1969, the years in which such a standard was used, included only 1 Chicano

b. We do not understand Mr. Justice Powell to disagree that providing a remedy for past racial prejudice can constitute a compelling purpose sufficient to meet strict scrutiny. Yet, because petitioner is a corporation administering a university, he would not allow it to exercise such power in the absence of "judicial, legislative, or administrative findings of constitutional or statutory violations." . . .

Generally, the manner in which a State chooses to delegate govermental functions is for it to decide. California, by constitutional provision, has chosen to place authority over the operation of the University of California in the Board of Regents. Control over the University is to be found not in the legislature, but rather in the Regents who have been vested with full legislative (including policymaking), administrative, and adjudicative powers by the citizens of California. This is certainly a permissible choice, see *Sweezy*, supra, and we, unlike our Brother Powell, find nothing in the Equal Protection Clause that requires us to depart from established principle by limiting the scope of power the Regents may exercise more narrowly than the powers that may constitutionally be wielded by the Assembly. . . .

and 2 Negroes out of the 50 admittees for each year. Nor is there any relief from this pattern of underrepresentation in the statistics for the regular admissions program in later years.

Davis clearly could conclude that the serious and persistent underrepresentation of minorities in medicine depicted by these statistics is the result of handicaps under which minority applicants labor as a consequence of a background of deliberate, purposeful discrimination against minorities in education and in society generally, as well as in the medical profession. From the inception of our national life, Negroes have been subjected to unique legal disabilities impairing access to equal educational opportunity. . . .

C

The second prong of our test — whether the Davis program stigmatizes any discrete group or individual and whether race is reasonably used in light of the program's objectives — is clearly satisfied by the Davis program.

It is not even claimed that Davis' program in any way operates to stigmatize or single out any discrete and insular, or even any identifiable, nonminority group. Nor will harm comparable to that imposed upon racial minorities by exclusion or separation on grounds of race be the likely result of the program. It does not, for example, establish an exclusive preserve for minority students apart from and exclusive of whites. Rather, its purpose is to overcome the effects of segregation by bringing the races together. . . .

Nor was Bakke in any sense stamped as inferior by the Medical School's rejection of him. . . . Unlike discrimination against racial minorities, the use of racial preferences for remedial purposes does not inflict a pervasive injury upon individual whites in the sense that wherever they go or whatever they do there is a significant likelihood that they will be treated as second-class citizens because of their color. . . .

In addition, there is simply no evidence that the Davis program discriminates intentionally or unintentionally against any minority group which it purports to benefit. The program does not establish a quota in the invidious sense of a ceiling on the number of minority applicants to be admitted. Nor can the program reasonably be regarded as stigmatizing the program's beneficiaries or their race as inferior. The Davis program does not simply advance less qualified applicants; rather, it compensates applicants, who it is uncontested are fully qualified to study medicine, for educational disadvantages which it was reasonable to conclude were a product of state-fostered discrimination. . . .

D

We disagree with the lower courts' conclusion that the Davis program's use of race was unreasonable in light of its objectives. First, as petitioner argues, there are no practical means by which it could achieve its ends in the foreseeable future without the use of race-conscious measures. With respect to any factor (such as poverty or family educational background) that may be used as a substitute for race as an indicator of past discrimination, whites greatly outnumber racial minorities simply because whites make up a far larger percentage of the total population and therefore far outnumber minorities in absolute terms at every socioeconomic level. . . .

Second, the Davis admissions program does not simply equate minority status with disadvantage. Rather, Davis considers on an individual basis each applicant's personal history to determine whether he or she has likely been disadvantaged by racial discrimination. The record makes clear that only minority applicants likely to have been isolated from the mainstream of American life are considered in the special program; other minority applicants are eligible only through the regular admissions program. . . .

E

Finally, Davis' special admissions program cannot be said to violate the Constitution simply because it has set aside a predetermined number of places for qualified minority applicants rather than using minority status as a positive factor to be considered in evaluating the applications of disadvantaged minority applicants. For purposes of constitutional adjudication, there is no difference between the two approaches. In any admissions program which accords special consideration to disadvantaged racial minorities, a determination of the degree of preference to be given is unavoidable, and any given preference that results in the exclusion of a white candidate is no more or less constitutionally acceptable than a program such as that at Davis. Furthermore, the extent of the preference inevitably depends on how many minority applicants the particular school is seeking to admit in any particular year so long as the number of qualified minority applicants exceeds that number. There is no sensible, and certainly no constitutional, distinction between, for example, adding a set number of points to the admissions rating of disadvantaged minority applicants as an expression of the preference with the expectation that this will result in the admission of an approximately determined number of qualified minority applicants and setting a fixed number of places for such applicants as was done here.

. . . That the Harvard approach does not . . . make public the extent of the preference and the precise workings of the system while the Davis program employs a specific, openly stated number, does not condemn the latter plan for purposes of Fourteenth Amendment adjudication. It may be that the Harvard plan is more acceptable to the public than is the Davis "quota." If it is, any State, including California, is free to adopt it in preference to a less acceptable alternative, just as it is generally free, as far as the Constitution is concerned, to abjure granting any racial preferences in its admissions program. But there is no basis for preferring a particular preference program simply because in achieving the same goals that the Davis Medical School is pursuing, it proceeds in a manner that is not immediately apparent to the public.

V

Accordingly, we would reverse the judgment of the Supreme Court of California holding the Medical School's special admissions program unconstitutional and directing respondent's admission, as well as that portion of the judgment enjoining the Medical School from according any consideration to race in the admissions process. . . .

STEVENS, J., joined by Burger, C.J., and Stewart and Rehnquist, JJ., concurring in the judgment in part and dissenting in part. . . .

The University, through its special admissions policy, excluded Bakke from participation in its program of medical education because of his race. The University also acknowledges that it was, and still is, receiving federal financial assistance. The plain language of [Title VI of the Civil Rights Act of 1964] therefore requires affirmance of the judgment below. A different result cannot be justified unless that language misstates the actual intent of the Congress that enacted the statute or the statute is not enforceable in a private action. Neither conclusion is warranted.

[The Justices' discussion of the legislative history is omitted.]

Discussion

1. Justice Stevens, joined by Chief Justice Burger and Justices Stewart and Rehnquist, did not address the constitutional question; he concluded only that Davis' quota system violated Title VI of the Civil Rights Act of 1964. Justice Brennan, joined by Justices White, Marshall, and Blackmun, concluded that the admissions program did not violate either the equal protection clause of the Fourteenth Amendment or Title VI (which he believed "prohibits only those uses of racial criteria that would violate the Fourteenth Amendment"). Justice Powell held the swing vote. He agreed with Justice Brennan's equation of Title VI with the equal protection clause but concluded that Davis' fixed quota system was unconstitutional and therefore unlawful. What did the *Court* hold?[87]

2. How do the language, purposes, and history surrounding the adoption of the Fourteenth Amendment bear on the issue in *Bakke?*

3. How do the *process* and *result* rationales for the antidiscrimination principle bear on *Bakke?* John Ely, whose view of the equal protection clause is heavily, if not exclusively, process oriented, writes:

> There is no danger that the coalition that makes up the white majority in our society is going to deny to whites generally their right to equal concern and respect. Whites are not going to discriminate against all whites for reasons of racial prejudice, and neither will they be tempted to underestimate the needs and deserts of whites relative to those, say, of blacks or to overestimate the costs of devising a more finely tuned classification system that would extend to certain whites the advantages that they are extending to blacks. The function of the Equal Protection Clause . . . is largely to protect against substantive outrages by requiring that those who would harm others must at the same time harm themselves — or at least widespread elements of their constituency on which they depend for reelection. The argument does not work the other way around, however: similar reasoning supports no insistence that our representatives cannot hurt themselves, or the majority on whose support they depend, without at the same time hurting others as well. Whether or not it is more blessed to give than to receive, it is surely less suspicious.[88]

4. Professor Ely focuses on the injuries to those who are dispreferred under a preferential admissions program. The "white majority," as Ely would doubtless

87. See Vincent Blasi, *Bakke* as Precedent: Does Mr. Justice Powell Have a Theory?, 67 Calif. L. Rev. 21 (1979).

88. John Ely, Democracy and Distrust 170-171 (1980). See also John Ely, The Constitutionality of Reverse Discrimination, 41 U. Chi. L. Rev. 723 (1974).

agree, is not monolithic, but is composed of the members of a variety of ethnic, religious, and cultural groups. How does this fact bear on the application of a process-based theory to *Bakke?* Can you imagine circumstances in which an affirmative action program would reflect prejudice against, or racially selective indifference to, certain minorities among the dispreferred white majority and hence violate the antidiscrimination principle with respect to them?[89] Does the Davis program fit this description?

5. Consider Casteneda v. Partida, 430 U.S. 482 (1977), for whatever light it sheds on the issues raised above. In *Casteneda,* the defendant in a criminal prosecution claimed that Mexican-Americans were systematically excluded from the county's juries. The district court held that a prima facie statistical case of discriminatory exclusion of Mexican-Americans from juries was rebutted by the fact that Mexican-Americans constituted a "governing majority" of the county. In an opinion by Justice Blackmun, the Supreme Court reversed:

> [T]he District Court's "governing majority" theory . . . did not dispel the presumption of purposeful discrimination in the circumstances of this case. Because of the many facets of human motivation, it would be unwise to presume as a matter of law that human beings of one definable group will not discriminate against other members of their group. . . . The problem is a complex one, about which widely differing views can be held, and, as such, it would be somewhat precipitous to take judicial notice of one view over another on the basis of a record as barren as this.[a]
>
> Furthermore, the relevance of a governing majority of elected officials to the grand jury selection process is questionable. The fact that certain elected officials are Mexican-American demonstrates nothing about the motivations and methods of the grand jury commissioners who select persons for grand jury lists. The only arguably relevant fact in this record on the issue is that three of the five jury commissioners in respondent's case were Mexican-American. Knowing only this, we would be forced to rely on the reasoning that we have rejected — that human beings would not discriminate against their own kind — in order to find that the presumption of purposeful discrimination was rebutted. Without the benefit of this simple behavioral presumption, discriminatory intent can be rebutted only with evidence in the record about the way in which the commissioners operated and their reasons for doing so. It was the State's burden to supply such evidence, once respondent established his prima facie case. The State's failure in this regard leaves unchallenged respondent's proof of purposeful discrimination.
>
> Finally, even if a "governing majority" theory has general applicability in cases of this kind, the inadequacy of the record in this case does not permit such an ap-

89 See United Jewish Organizations v. Carey, 430 U.S. 144 (1977), involving a State's deliberate use of racial criteria in redrawing district lines to maintain black voting strength in voluntary compliance with the Federal Voting Rights Act of 1965. The redistricting splintered the voting power of a community made up of about 30,000 Hasidic Jews. A divided Court found the plan valid under the Fourteenth and Fifteenth Amendments. Justice White, in a plurality opinion joined by Justices Stevens and Rehnquist, argued that, even apart from the Voting Rights Act, "as long as whites . . . as a group, were provided with fair representation, we cannot conclude that there was a cognizable discrimination against whites." Justice Stewart, joined by Justice Powell, concurred in the judgment, arguing that the circumstances "foreclose[d] any finding that the [New York Legislature] acted with the invidious purpose of discriminating against white voters."

a. This is not a case where a majority is practicing benevolent discrimination in favor of a traditionally disfavored minority, although that situation illustrates that motivations not immediately obvious might enter into discrimination against "one's own kind."

proach. Among the evidentiary deficiencies are the lack of any indication of how long the Mexican-Americans have enjoyed "governing majority" status, the absence of information about the relative power inherent in the elective offices held by Mexican-Americans, and the uncertain relevance of the general political power to the specific issue in this case.

In a dissenting opinion joined by Chief Justice Burger and Justice Rehnquist, Justice Powell responded:

In this case, the following critical facts are beyond dispute: the judge who appointed the jury commissioners and later presided over respondent's trial was Mexican-American: three of the five jury commissioners were Mexican-American: 10 of the 20 members of the grand jury array were Mexican-American: five of the 12 grand jurors who returned the indictment, including the foreman, were Mexican-American, and seven of the 12 petit jurors who returned the verdict of guilt were Mexican-American. In the year in which respondent was indicted, 52.5% of the persons on the grand jury list were Mexican-American. In addition, a majority of the elected officials in Hidalgo County were Mexican-American, as were a majority of the judges. That these positions of power and influence were so held is not surprising in a community where 80% of the population is Mexican-American. As was emphasized by District Judge Garza, the able Mexican-American jurist who presided over the habeas proceedings in the District Court, this case *is* unique. Every other jury discrimination case reaching this Court has involved a situation where the governing majority, and the resulting power over the jury selection process, was held by a white electorate and white officials.[a]

. . . In these circumstances, where Mexican-Americans control both the selection of jurors and the political process, rational inferences from the most basic facts in a democratic society render improbable respondent's claim of an intent to discriminate against him and other Mexican-Americans. As Judge Garza observed, "If people in charge can choose whom they want, it is unlikely they will discriminate against themselves."

See also City of Richmond v. J.A. Croson Co., p.758 infra.

6. Dissenting in Fullilove v. Klutznick, 448 U.S. 448 (1980), Justice Stevens wrote:

If the National Government is to make a serious effort to define racial classes by criteria that can be administered objectively, it must study precedents such as the

a. I do not suggest, of course, that the mere fact that Mexican-Americans constitute a majority in Hidalgo County is dispositive. There are many communities in which, by virtue of historical or other reasons, a majority of the population may not be able at a particular time to control or significantly influence political decisions or the way the system operates. But no one can contend seriously that Hidalgo County is such a community. The classic situation in which a "minority group" may suffer discrimination in a community is where it is "relegated to . . . a position of political powerlessness." San Antonio School District v. Rodriguez, 41 1 U.S. 1, 28 (1973). Here the Mexican-Americans are not politically "powerless": they *are* the majoritarian political element of the community, with demonstrated capability to elect and protect their own.

Nor do I suggest that persons in positions of power can never be shown to have discriminated against other members of the same ethnic or racial group. I would hold only that respondent's statistical evidence, without more, is insufficient to prove a claim of discrimination in this case.

> First Regulation to the Reichs Citizenship Law of November 14, 1935. . . : "1. A Jew is anyone who descended from at least three grandparents who were racially full Jews. . . . 2. A Jew is also one who descended from two full Jewish parents, if. . . ."

Stevens might just as readily have looked to American laws defining "Negro."[90] Until 1910, Virginia's school segregation law drew the line at one-fourth black; that year the fraction was changed to one-sixteenth; and in 1930 it was amended again to provide that any amount of "Negro blood" made one black. Arizona's and Montana's antimiscegenation laws similarly prohibited a white from marrying a person with any trace of Negro blood, while Nebraska and North Dakota drew the line at one-eighth Negro.

William Van Alstyne suggests that by permitting racial preferences, the Court will confront a variety of second-order issues: "Among the more obvious issues, as additional groups, people, agencies, and parties are inevitably drawn in, are these: *which* races, *how much* to each race, *by what test* is each of us to be assigned "our" race?"[91]

7. Justice Brennan wrote that a state *may* adopt a race-conscious program where there is "reason to believe" that substantial minority underrepresentation is due to past discrimination, but indicates that such a program *must* be adopted only where the state "intended invidiously to discriminate" against a minority. Suppose the University, noticing a dearth of Italian-American graduates from its medical program, set aside 16 places for Italian-American applicants on the belief that the discrepancy was due to past discrimination. Would such a plan, on Brennan's theory, be constitutional? Would it survive an equal protection challenge brought by blacks, Mexican-Americans, Native Americans, and Asians charging invidious discrimination in that the plan excluded them from consideration for 16 slots?

8. Is Davis' program constitutionally problematic because of its effect on members of the *preferred* minority groups? If so, is it because of process- or result-oriented concerns? Is there a difference, in these terms, between preferentially admitting minorities and preferentially grading or graduating them?

9. If none of these rationales for the antidiscrimination principle seems clearly applicable to a program like Davis', but you nonetheless intuitively find it troublesome, can you articulate an alternative rationale of constitutional magnitude? Consider the "color-blind" conception discussed in part III A, supra.

10. If preferential treatment of minorities should give rise to a cause of action under the equal protection clause, what is the appropriate standard for assessing a program such as Davis'? The suspect classification test? Something less demanding? An ad hoc accommodation of the interests and potential harms involved? What standard did the various Justices in *Bakke* purport to apply, and with what justification? Did they in fact use the standards they articulated?

11. Assuming that a preferential admissions program demands some substantial justification, how persuasive do you find the following justifications in general, as well as in the unique context of Davis' program?

90. See Charles Mangum, The Legal Status of the Negro 1-17 (1940).

91. William Van Alstyne, Rites of Passage: Race, The Supreme Court, and the Constitution, 46 U. Chi. L. Rev. 775 (1979).

a. *Preventive.* A school might prefer minorities in the proportion that they would be admitted if race were *not* taken into account — to assure that the admissions officers do not engage in de jure discrimination.

b. *Compensatory.* The principle that if *A* injures *B*, *A* must compensate *B* is deeply rooted in our morality and laws. The law has recognized extensions of the rights and obligation beyond the protagonists to their estates, which can sue and be sued. Certainly, governments and white-dominated organizations and individuals have inflicted massive injuries on blacks through the institution of slavery and the following century of discrimination. Other racial and ethnic minorities have suffered discrimination to varying degrees.

To the extent a preferential admissions program has compensatory aims, consider (i) how closely the programs benefit the actual victims of discrimination, (ii) who pays the cost of compensation and the cost-payers' responsibility for the wrongdoing or relationship to the wrongdoers, and (iii) how far back into the past the moral obligations of compensatory justice extend.

c. *Distributive.* A distributive rationale for preferential admissions might hold that it is prima facie unjust for any racial or ethnic group in a society to be appreciably less well off than other groups and that this injustice does not depend on how the distributional disparity came about (which distinguishes the distributive from the compensatory rationale). Since good education leads to good jobs, and good jobs provide income and status, redistributing education (and jobs) promotes a more equal sharing of social benefits and burdens.

Why should the fact that a larger portion of blacks than whites are poor entitle a particular black applicant who is poor to more than an equally poor white applicant? If you believe that government should redistribute wealth from the rich to the poor, does it follow that government should redistribute to minorities who, as a group, are poor? Is admission to medical school an appropriate way of redistributing wealth?

A preferential admissions program may also be designed to have indirect redistributive effects. For example, a professional school might believe that its minority graduates are more likely than nonminorities to work in inadequately served minority communities — and more likely to do so effectively because of factors such as language, trust, and familiarity with cultural norms. The school might also believe that minority graduates who choose a middle-class practice indirectly benefit less-advantaged minorities by exercising power on their behalf and by serving as role models for minority youths. If these beliefs were substantiated, what sort of preferential program would they justify? Does the Fourteenth Amendment require that they be substantiated?

d. *Educational.* One might believe that the education of all students at a law or medical school is enriched and improved by the diversity of viewpoints provided by students from a variety of ethnic and cultural backgrounds.

12. Are some of the objectives of preferential admissions programs more appropriately pursued by a state legislature than, say, the Regents of the University of California? The Fourteenth Amendment treats the "state" as an entity and is generally indifferent to the state's allocation of authority among agencies and subdivisions. If, in his separate opinion in *Bakke*, Justice Powell was suggesting that the allocation of state powers presents a federal constitutional issue, he was proposing a radically new constitutional doctrine. Consider two, not mutually inconsistent, readings of his opinion. (a) As a matter of *state* law, the Regents are

limited to pursuing educational objectives and will not be heard to justify their preferential admissions program on grounds that lie beyond their delegated authority. (b) Even if the California constitution or legislature authorized the Regents to consider broader social goals, a federal court should give less *deference* to the judgment of such an agency than it would give to the state legislature itself, because the legislature is more representative, has a broader perspective on general issues of social justice, and is the state's highest policy-making institution.

13. Professor Derrick Bell faults both the the Court and the University for failing to take cognizance of "the upper class bias of standards based on grades and test scores":

> Studiously ignored were the many special preferences which colleges and professional schools offer . . . to those fortunate enough to be born into upper income homes where quality schools and upper social class environment increase the likelihood of top grades and test scores.[a] Most beneficiaries of these longstanding preferences are, of course, both upper class and white. While not based directly on race, these socioeconomic preferences do disadvantage minorities and, for that reason, arguably are constitutionally suspect. Yet schools have not been required to prove that these socioeconomic preferences serve a compelling state interest. By assuming the validity of general admissions programs which indirectly disadvantage racial minorities, and by attacking minority admissions programs which involve direct racial quotas, the advocates of "merit" have managed to transfer the burden of justification from the preferences that favor the white elite to the preferences forged by minorities in order partially to correct the bias which results from the socioeconomic preferences.

The University's failure to recognize the discriminatory bias inherent in traditional meritocratic evaluations, argues Bell, was itself a manifestation of racial discrimination:

> Given the choice of acknowledging that their admissions practices disadvantaged racial minorities in that they did not accurately predict minority applicants' performance in medical school, or casting doubt on the intellectual abilities of minority students by implying that the tests were valid but that minorities simply had trouble with them because of some vague, undefined disadvantage, the Regents chose the latter. In doing so, they committed the kind of group defamation that white liberals, as far back as the abolitionists, have felt free to impose on blacks as a condition of their support. . . . In what was potentially the most important civil rights case since Brown v. Board of Education, racial disadvantage, like a birth defect, was treated as an unfortunate accident of nature for which charity was appropriate, not as a massive, historic, and intentional racial crime for which virtually all institutions are responsible and for which a compensatory remedy is essential.[92]

a. Even college-bound students from low and moderate income families perform poorly on standardized tests of academic ability and achievement, compared to students from upper income homes. For example, a survey of 674,320 students who were given the Scholastic Aptitude Test (SAT) in 1974-75 showed that the average mean family income of students with the lowest test scores, 200 to 249 points, was $9,583, while the average family income of students with scores in the highest range, 750 to 800 points, was $27,999. Between these two extremes, test scores increase in almost direct proportion to increase in family income.

92. Derrick A. Bell, Jr., Introduction: Awakening After *Bakke*, 14 Harv. C.R.-C.L.L. Rev. 1 (1979).

Issues Concerning Race-Conscious Affirmative Action Programs

Starting with *Bakke*, all members of the Court have agreed that purportedly "benign" programs that classify on the basis of race deserve some measure of heightened judicial scrutiny. Justice Powell in *Bakke* maintained that *all* racial classifications, including those for benign purposes, warrant strict judicial scrutiny to ensure that the burdens imposed are "precisely tailored to serve a compelling governmental interest." In his partial concurrence, Justice Brennan, joined by Justices Marshall, Blackmun, and White, argued that preferential programs resting on racial classifications require only an intermediate level of scrutiny, such that they "serve important governmental objectives and . . . [are] substantially related to the achievement of those objectives." In the years since *Bakke*, a plurality has fairly consistently articulated a strict (or quite strict) standard of scrutiny in reviewing constitutional challenges to affirmative action plans, with a unified trio of justices (Brennan, Marshall, and Blackmun) unfailingly advocating intermediate scrutiny as the proper standard of review.[93]

In the cases that follow, observe how each Justice applies the standard of scrutiny articulated to the facts of the case. How consistently or predictably are these standards applied? Is the Court's level of scrutiny as demanding as in the area of nonbenign racial classifications, or is it somewhat more flexible? How strict is the intermediate standard of review advanced by Brennan et al? After reading the cases, consider what type of preferential program might fail this lower level of scrutiny.

The affirmative action programs considered in the following cases arguably serve various goals and allocate burdens and benefits through different means. They were also adopted through different routes, including voluntary adoption by the employer, consent decrees, and judicial imposition. The following paragraphs present some concepts and issues designed to help guide your reading of the cases.

1. Goals

A. Relief for actual victims of past discrimination. All members of the Court agree that, at the very minimum, an employer who has engaged in prior illegal discriminatory conduct against particular individuals may or must provide "make-whole" relief to those victims. Certain Justices have indicated that an affirmative action program may not legitimately go beyond this goal and that mere membership in the disadvantaged class is insufficient to warrant preferential treatment.[94] If relief is reserved only for those who were actual victims of prior discrimination, should this even be characterized as a race-dependent remedy?

93. In Sheet Metal Workers v. EEOC (1986, p.735 below) and United States v. Paradise (1987, p.750 below), Justice Brennan wrote the opinion for the Court upholding an affirmative action plan against constitutional attack, but on both occasions avoided resolving the issue of the proper level of review, stating that the plans survived even strict scrutiny.

94. See, e.g., Firefighters v. Stotts, 467 U.S. 561 (1984), where Justice White, writing for the majority, stated in dicta that, to be entitled to the relief in question, "each individual must prove that the discriminatory practice had an impact on him." This position is echoed in Justice Scalia's concurrence in City of Richmond v. Croson (1989), p.769 infra.

B. Remedy for the lingering effects of past discrimination. The Court has proven itself most willing to uphold race-conscious preferential programs benefitting nonvictims where low minority participation is found to be a result of past discrimination against members of the minority group. In reading the cases that follow, consider: What types of evidence will support the necessary determination of past discrimination? How "direct" must such discrimination be to justify the program? How specific to the employer must a finding of past discrimination be? Are judicial findings given greater deference than admissions by the employer involved?

C. Nonremedial goals. In *Bakke*, Justice Powell embraced certain nonremedial goals as compelling justifications for race-based preferential programs. Nevertheless, since *Bakke*, the Court has been at least skeptical of nonremedial rationales.[95] As you read the following cases, consider the nonremedial justifications proffered by the supporters of affirmative action plans. Are they persuasive? Does the Court's preference for looking backward to redress past "specific sins of racism" rather than forward to promote a "racially integrated future" make sense?[96]

2. Means

A. Burden on "innocent" nonminorities. In reviewing preferential programs, the Court has shown considerable sensitivity to the burdens imposed upon dispreferred nonminority individuals who are not themselves directly responsible for the prior discrimination against the preferred minority group. The affirmative action decisions since *Bakke* reveal a particular unwillingness to frustrate settled expectations of nonminority members. Thus, while the Court has upheld hiring and promotion or admissions plans benefitting minorities, it has consistently struck down affirmative action plans mandating disproportionate layoffs of nonminority employees.

B. Quotas versus factors. Recall Justice Powell's opinion in *Bakke*, rejecting the University's specific numerical target for minority admissions but embracing its consideration of race as a "factor" to be considered in the admissions process. This distinction between "rigid" numerical quotas and more "flexible" and temporary goals has permeated subsequent affirmative action debate on the Court. In reading the cases that follow, consider how the preference for flexible goals relates to the Court's reluctance to place undue burdens on nonminorities. Does it make a difference to the dispreferred nonminority that a flexible rather than a rigid goal was used? Is there something in the nature of rigid quotas themselves that make them insufficiently narrowly tailored? Also, in determining the tightness of a plan's "fit" with the articulated goal, what types of numerical or statistical comparisons does the Court find relevant?

95. See, e.g., Wygant v. Jackson Board of Educ., 476 U.S. 267 (1986), p.738 infra.
96. The quotes are from Sullivan, Sins of Discrimination: Last Term's Affirmative Action Cases, 100 Harv. L. Rev. 78 (1986).

3. Who Adopted or Imposed the Program?

Does it matter whether a race-conscious affirmative action program was adopted voluntarily or by a consent decree or imposed by a court upon a resisting employer? Consider George Rutherglen's and Daniel Ortiz's argument that "voluntary preferences should receive more lenient treatment under both Title VII and the Constitution . . . [because] both sources of law embody fundamental principles of government that favor voluntary resolution of disputes over government coercion and litigation."[97]

4. Equal Protection v. Statutory Claims

Recall the different Justices' views in *Bakke* about the relationship between the equal protection clause and Title VI. The relationship between constitutional and statutory antidiscrimination provisions has also arisen in the employment cases considered below. In United Steelworkers v. Weber, infra, the Court stated that Title VII did not "incorporate and particularize the commands of the Fifth and Fourteenth Amendments," thus suggesting that the standards of review under statutory and equal protection claims might differ. In Johnson v. Transportation Agency, 480 U.S. 616 (1987), involving an affirmative action program benefitting women, five Justices agreed that preferential programs under Title VII require only showing of a "manifest imbalance"[98] between the percentage of minorities employed and the percentage of minorities in the population, rather than the stricter equal protection standard of a "firm" basis in the evidence. The remaining four justices argued that Title VII and the Constitution impose identical evidentiary requirements on employers seeking to justify affirmative action plans.[99] In reading the opinions that follow, try to uncover whether the source of the antidiscrimination law has ever been dispositive to the outcome of a case. Note that in 1972, public employers were added to the definition of "employer" in Title VII. If a public employer's affirmative action plan is challenged under both Title VII and the Constitution, which standard should the Court apply?[100]

B. The Employment Context

1. *Hiring and Promotion Goals*

The year after *Bakke*, in United Steelworkers v. Weber, 443 U.S. 193 (1979), a divided Court upheld a private employer's affirmative action plan under Title

97. Rutherglen & Ortiz, Affirmative Action Under the Constitution and Title VII: From Confusion to Convergence, 35 U.C.L.A.L. Rev. 467 (1988).

98. The language is from *Weber*.

99. Justice O'Connor wrote that under both Title VII and the Constitution, an employer would have a "firm" evidentiary basis if it could "point to a statistical disparity sufficient to support a prima facie claim under Title VII by the employee beneficiaries of the affirmative action plan." A prima facie claim under Title VII looks to the disparity between the percentage of minorities employed and the percentage of qualified minorities in the relevant labor pool. See Wards Cove Packing v. Atonio, 490 U.S. 642 (1989).

100. See Rutherglen and Ortiz, Affirmative Action Under the Constitution and Title VII: From Confusion to Convergence, 35 U.C.L.A.L. Rev. 467 (1988).

VII of the Civil Rights Act of 1964, without addressing any constitutional issues. A white employee challenged a plan — collectively bargained by the petitioner union and the Kaiser Aluminum Corp. — that reserved 50 percent of the openings in an in-plant craft training program for blacks until the percentage of black craft workers in a plant was commensurate with the percentage of blacks in the local labor force. Justice Brennan emphasized the "narrowness of our inquiry. Since the Kaiser-USWA plan does not involve state action, this case does not present an alleged violation of the Equal Protection Clause.[101] . . . [And since the plan] was adopted voluntarily, we are not concerned with what Title VII requires or with what a court might order to remedy a past proven violation of the Act. The only question before us is the narrow statutory issue of whether Title VII *forbids* private employers and unions from voluntarily agreeing upon bona fide affirmative action plans that accord racial preferences." After a lengthy discussion of the language and legislative history of the statute, Justice Brennan concluded:

> The purposes of the plan mirror those of the statute. Both were designed to break down patterns of racial segregation and hierarchy. Both were structured to "open employment opportunities for Negroes in occupations which have been traditionally closed to them." At the same time the plan does not unnecessarily trammel the interests of the white employees. The plan does not require the discharge of white workers and their replacement with new black hires. Nor does the plan create an absolute bar to the advancement of white employees; half of those trained in the program will be white. Moreover, the plan is a temporary measure; it is not intended to maintain racial balance, but simply to eliminate a manifest racial imbalance.

Justice Rehnquist, joined by Chief Justice Burger, dissented, arguing that the legislative history and language of Title VII "irrefutably demonstrates that Congress meant precisely what it said . . . — that *no* racial discrimination in employment is permissible under Title VII, not even preferential treatment of minorities to correct racial imbalance." Rehnquist concluded that in passing Title VII, "Congress outlawed *all* racial discrimination, recognizing that no discrimination based on race is benign, that no action disadvantaging a person because of his color is affirmative." Justices Powell and Stevens did not participate.

In Sheet Metal Workers v. EEOC, 478 U.S. 421 (1986), the Court upheld an affirmative action program imposed upon a union found to have engaged in illegal discrimination under Title VII. The program established a 29 percent minority membership goal based on the percentage of minorities in the relevant labor pool, to be achieved within six years. In 1982 and 1983 the union was found in contempt for failing to fulfill the court order; the District Court subsequently amended the plan and extended the deadline for compliance to 1987.

Justice Brennan, joined by Justices Marshall, Blackmun, and Stevens, first adressed the statutory claim, and concluded that §706(g)[102] does not preclude the

101. Justice Brennan stated that Title VII, in contrast to Title VI which the majority in *Bakke* held to be coextensive with the Equal Protection Clause, "was enacted pursuant to the commerce power to regulate purely private decisionmaking and was not intended to incorporate and particularize the commands of the Fifth and Fourteenth Amendments."

102. Section 706(g) provides:

> If the court finds that the respondent has intentionally engaged in or is intentionally engaging in an unlawful employment practice, . . . the court may enjoin the respondent from engaging in such unlawful employment practice, and order such affirmative action as may be appropriate, which may include, but is not limited to, reinstatement or hiring of employees, with or

use of racial preferences to remedy Title VII violations. Although "race-conscious affirmative measures [should] not be invoked simply to create a racially balanced work force," "[w]here an employer or union has engaged in particularly longstanding or egregious discrimination, . . . requiring recalcitrant employers or unions to hire and to admit qualified minorities roughly in proportion to the number of qualified minorities in the work force may be the only effective way to ensure the full enjoyment of the rights protected by Title VII." Justice Brennan held that Title VII did not forbid remedial relief for individuals who were not actual proven victims of past discrimination, finding such relief "appropriate where an employer or a labor union has engaged in persistent or egregious discrimination, or where necessary to dissipate the lingering effects of pervasive discrimination." Justice Brennan also found the measures sufficiently temporary and narrowly tailored to fulfill the State's purposes without "unnecessarily trammel[ling] the interests of white employees." Turning to the equal protection claim, the plurality maintained that, although the Court had failed to agree on the proper standard of review, the plan "pass[ed] even the most rigorous test — it is narrowly tailored to further the Government's compelling interest in remedying past discrimination."

Justice Powell agreed that the union's "egregious" violations of Title VII established a compelling state purpose justifying remedial action, and upheld the measures imposed, writing that "[t]he flexible application of the goal requirement in this case demonstrates that it is not a means to achieve racial balance."

Justice O'Connor would have invalidated the plan solely on the statutory claim, holding that the membership goal established a "rigid racial quota" and as such could not be imposed by a court consistent with the terms of Title VII. Justice White conceded that race-conscious preferential plans adopted under Title VII may at times benefit nonvictims of discrimination, but, like Justice O'Connor, found the strict racial quota prohibited.

Justice Rehnquist, joined by Chief Justice Burger, held that Title VII only permitted relief to actual victims of unlawful discrimination.

On the same day as *Sheet Metal Workers*, the Court also held in Firefighters v. Cleveland, 478 U.S. 501 (1986), that §706(g) of Title VII permitted a consent decree benefitting nonvictims of defendant's discrimination. In 1980, a group of black and Hispanic firefighters filed suit against the city of Cleveland, charging racial discrimination in violation of the Constitution. The city, having previously been found guilty of discrimination in similar lawsuits, submitted a consent decree which was subsequently approved by a district court. The local firefighters union then brought this action, claiming that the decree violated Title VII. Justice Brennan first emphasized that "Congress intended voluntary compliance to be the preferred means of achieving the objectives of Title VII." Citing *Weber*, he stated that voluntary compliance "may include reasonable race-conscious relief that benefits individuals who were not actual victims of

---

without back pay, . . . or any other equitable relief as the court deems appropriate. . . . No order of the court shall require the admission or reinstatement of an individual as a member of a union, or the hiring, reinstatement, or promotion of an individual as an employee, or the payment to him of any back pay, if such individual was refused employment or advancement or was suspended or discharged for any reason other than discrimination on account of race, color, religion, sex, or national origin in violation of . . . this title.

discrimination." Identifying the "voluntary nature of a consent decree [as] its most fundamental characteristic," Justice Brennan found that §706(g) limited only the power of federal courts, and did not in any way "restrict the ability of employers or unions to enter into voluntary agreements providing for race-conscious remedial action." He further maintained that a "court is not barred from entering a consent decree merely because it might lack authority under §706(g) to do so after trial."

Justice O'Connor, concurring, emphasized the narrowness of the Court's holding, adding in dicta that "nonminority employees . . . remain free to challenge the race-conscious measures contemplated by a proposed consent decree as violative of their rights under [other provisions of Title VII] or the Fourteenth Amendment."[103]

Justice White dissented, arguing that because the city had never made the requisite finding of its own prior discriminatory practices, the decree was unjustified. He also found the consent decree/trial distinction inapposite, stating "[t]here is no statutory authority for concluding that if an employer desires to discriminate against a white applicant or employee on racial grounds he may do so without violating Title VII but may not be ordered to do so if he objects."

Justice Rehnquist, joined by Chief Justice Burger, also dissented, maintaining that §706(g) applied to the facts of the case, and that the legitimate scope of a consent decree was limited to what a court could impose. He found it "simply incredible that the Court today virtually reads [§706(g)] out of existence."

103. In Martin v. Wilks, 490 U.S. 755 (1989), the Court held that nonminority employees not privy to a consent decree could nonetheless challenge it. An employee's failure to intervene in the initial proceedings did not bar subsequent challenge to the decree under the Federal Rules of Civil Procedure: "Joinder as a party, rather than knowledge of a lawsuit and an opportunity to intervene, is the method by which potential parties are subjected to the jurisdiction of the court and bound by a judgement or decree." Responding to the claim that identification and joinder of all possible future dispreferred employees placed an undue burden on civil rights litigation, Chief Justice Rehnquist wrote:

> The difficulties petitioners foresee . . . are undoubtedly present, but they arise from the nature of the relief sought and not because of any choice between mandatory intervention and joinder. . . . [P]laintiffs who seek the aid of the courts to alter existing employment policies, or the employer who might be subject to conflicting decrees, are best able to bear the burden of designating those who would be adversely affected if plaintiffs prevail. . . . Petitioners' alternative does not eliminate the need for, or difficulty of, identifying persons who, because of their interests, should be included in a lawsuit. It merely shifts that responsibility to less able shoulders.

Justice Stevens, joined by Justices Brennan, Marshall, and Blackmun, dissented, arguing that the majority confused a consent decree's practical impact with being legally bound by its terms: "The fact that one of the effects of a decree is to curtail the job opportunities of nonparties does not mean that the nonparties have been deprived of legal rights or that they have standing to appeal from that decree without becoming parties." Justice Stevens feared that the majority's holding would "destroy the integrity of litigated judgements, would lead to an abundance of vexatious litigation, and would subvert the interest in comity between courts." He added: "Just as white employees in the past were innocent beneficiaries of illegal discriminatory practices, so is it inevitable that some of the same white employees will be innocent victims who must share some of the burdens resulting from the redress of the past wrongs."

The Civil Rights Act of 1991 prohibits challenges to dissent decrees by individuals who had a reasonable opportunity to object to the decree or whose interests were adequately represented by another party.

2. *Protecting Recently Hired Minorities Against Layoffs*

WYGANT v. JACKSON BOARD OF EDUCATION
476 U.S. 267 (1986)
On Certiorari to the Sixth Circuit Court of Appeals

[In 1972, against a background of several years of racial tension in Jackson, Michigan, the Jackson Board of Education and the local teachers' union, the Jackson Education Association, agreed to the following contract provision (Article XII) involving layoffs:

> In the event that it becomes necessary to reduce the number of teachers through layoff from employment by the Board, teachers with the most seniority in the district shall be retained, except that at no time will there be a greater percentage of minority personnel laid off than the current percentage of minority personnel employed at the time of the layoff.

"Minorities" were defined as "those employees who are Black, American Indian, Oriental, or of Spanish descendancy." The Board also had an affirmative action hiring program, though only the layoff provision was challenged in this case.

In the 1976-1977 and 1981-1982 school years, job layoffs were instituted under the contract, and nonminority teachers were laid off while minority teachers with less seniority were retained. Several of the displaced nonminority teachers sued, claiming that the provision violated, inter alia, the Fourteenth Amendment. A fragmented Supreme Court upheld their claim.]

POWELL, J., announced the judgment of the Court and delivered an opinion in which Chief Justice Burger and Justice Rehnquist joined, and in all but Part IV of which Justice O'Connor joined.

II

. . . We must decide whether the layoff provision is supported by a compelling state purpose and whether the means chosen to accomplish that purpose are narrowly tailored.

III

A

The Court of Appeals, relying on the reasoning and language of the District Court's opinion, held that the Board's interest in providing minority role models for its minority students, as an attempt to alleviate the effects of societal discrimination, was sufficiently important to justify the racial classification embodied in the layoff provision. The court discerned a need for more minority faculty role models by finding that the percentage of minority teachers was less than the percentage of minority students.

This Court never has held that societal discrimination alone is sufficient to justify a racial classification. Rather, the Court has insisted upon some showing of prior discrimination by the governmental unit involved before allowing limited use of racial classifications in order to remedy such discrimination. . . .

[T]he role model theory employed by the District Court has no logical stopping point [and] allows the Board to engage in discriminatory hiring and layoff practices long past the point required by any legitimate remedial purpose. . . . Moreover, because the role model theory does not necessarily bear a relationship to the harm caused by prior discriminatory hiring practices, it actually could be used to escape the obligation to remedy such practices by justifying the small percentage of black teachers by reference to the small percentage of black students. Carried to its logical extreme, the idea that black students are better off with black teachers could lead to the very system the Court rejected in *Brown*. . . .

B

Respondents also now argue that their purpose in adopting the layoff provision was to remedy prior discrimination against minorities by the Jackson School District in hiring teachers. Public schools, like other public employers, operate under two interrelated constitutional duties. They are under a clear command from this court . . . to eliminate every vestige of racial segregation and discrimination in the schools. Pursuant to that goal, race-conscious remedial action may be necessary. On the other hand, public employers, including public schools, also must act in accordance with a "core purpose of the Fourteenth Amendment," which is to "do away with all governmentally imposed distinctions based on race." Palmore v. Sidoti, 466 U.S., at 432. These related constitutional duties are not always harmonious; reconciling them requires public employers to act with extraordinary care. In particular, a public employer like the Board must ensure that, before it embarks on an affirmative action program, it has convincing evidence that remedial action is warranted. That is, it must have sufficient evidence to justify the conclusion that there has been prior discrimination.

Evidentiary support for the conclusion that remedial action is warranted becomes crucial when the remedial program is challenged in court by nonminority employees. . . . In such a case, the trial court must make a factual determination that the employer had a strong basis in evidence for its conclusion that remedial action was necessary. The ultimate burden remains with the employees to demonstrate the unconstitutionality of an affirmative action program. But unless such a determination is made, an appellate court reviewing a challenge to remedial action by nonminority employees cannot determine whether the race-based action is justified as a remedy for prior discrimination.

Despite the fact that Article XII has spawned years of litigation and three separate lawsuits, no such determination ever had been made. [The Board had initially denied the existence of prior discrimination in its hiring practices. The current Board] now contends that, given another opportunity, it could establish the existence of prior discrimination. . . .[a] [W]e need not consider the question

a. Justice Marshall. . . . engages in an unprecedented reliance on nonrecord documents that respondent has "lodged" with this Court. This selective citation to factual materials not considered by the District Court or the Court of Appeals below is unusual enough by itself. My disagreement with Justice Marshall, however, is more fundamental. . . . It is disagreement as to what constitutes a "legitimate factual predicate." If the necessary factual predicate is prior discrimination — that is, that race-based state action is taken to remedy prior discrimination by the governmental unit involved — then since we conclude below that the layoff provision was not a legally appropriate means of achieving even a compelling purpose.

IV

The Court of Appeals examined the means chosen to accomplish the Board's race-conscious purpose under a test of "reasonableness." That standard has no support in the decisions of this Court. . . . [O]ur decisions always have employed a more stringent standard — however articulated — to test the validity of the means chosen by a state to accomplish its race-conscious purposes. Under strict scrutiny the means chosen to accomplish the State's asserted purpose must be specifically and narrowly framed to accomplish that purpose.

We have recognized, however, that in order to remedy the effects of prior discrimination, it may be necessary to take race into account. As part of this Nation's dedication to eradicating racial discrimination, innocent persons may be called upon to bear some of the burden of the remedy. . . .[b]

We have previously expressed concern over the burden that a preferential layoffs scheme imposes on innocent parties. Firefighters v. Stotts[104]. . . . In cases involving valid hiring goals, the burden to be borne by innocent individuals is diffused to a considerable extent among society generally. Though hiring goals may burden some innocent individuals, they simply do not impose the same kind of injury that layoffs impose. Denial of a future employment opportunity is not as intrusive as loss of an existing job.

---

the very nature of appellate review requires that a factfinder determine whether the employer was justified in instituting a remedial plan. Nor can the respondent unilaterally insulate itself from this key constitutional question by conceding that it has discriminated in the past, now that it is in its interest to make such a concession. Contrary to the dissent's assertion, the requirement of such a determination by the trial court is not some arbitrary barrier set up by today's opinion. Rather, it is a necessary result of the requirement that state-based state action be remedial.

b. Of course, when a state implements a race-based plan that requires such a sharing of the burden, it cannot justify the discriminatory effect on some individuals because other individuals had approved the plan. Any "waiver" of the right not to be dealt with by the government on the basis of one's race must be made by those affected. Yet Justice Marshall repeatedly contends that the fact that Article XII was approved by a majority vote of the Union somehow validates this plan. He sees this case not in terms of individual constitutional rights, but as an allocation of burdens "between two racial groups." Thus, Article XII becomes a political compromise that "avoided placing the entire burden of layoffs on either the white teachers as a group or the minority teachers as a group." But the petitioners before us are not "the white teachers as a group." They are Wendy Wygant and other individuals who claim that they are fired from their jobs because of their race. That claim cannot be waived by petitioner's more senior colleagues. In view of the way union seniority works, it is not surprising that while a straight freeze on minority layoff was overwhelmingly rejected, a "compromise" eventually was reached that placed the entire burden of the compromise on the most junior union members. The more senior union members simply had nothing to lose from such a compromise. . . . The Constitution does not allocate constitutional rights to be distributed like bloc grants within discrete racial groups, and until it does, petitioners' more senior union colleagues cannot vote away petitioners' rights. . . .

104. Firefighters v. Stotts, 467 U.S. 561 (1984), held that Title VII did not authorize a court, in modifying a consent decree, to order an affirmative action layoff provision that disrupted an existing state seniority system. Justice White, writing for the majority, held that because "Title VII protects bona fide seniority systems," it "precludes a district court from displacing a nonminority employee with seniority under the contractually established seniority system absent either a finding that the seniority system was adopted with discriminatory intent or a determination that such a remedy was necessary to make whole a proven victim of discrimination." In dicta, Justice White identified the policy behind Title VII as "provid[ing] make-whole relief only to those who have been actual victims of illegal discrimination." Justice O'Connor filed a concurring opinion, while Justice Stevens joined only in the judgment. Justice Blackmun, joined by Justices Brennan and Marshall, dissented.

Many of our cases involve union seniority plans with employees who are typically heavily dependent on wages for their day-to-day living. Even a temporary layoff may have adverse financial as well as psychological effects. A worker may have invested many productive years in one job and one city with the expectation of earning the stability and security of seniority. "At that point, the rights and expectations surrounding seniority make up what is probably the most valuable capital asset that the worker 'owns,' worth even more than the current equity in his home." Fallon & Weiler, Conflicting Models of Racial Justice, 1984 S. Ct. Rev. 1, 58. Layoffs disrupt these settled expectations in a way that general hiring goals do not. . . .

We therefore hold that, as a means of accomplishing purposes that otherwise may be legitimate, the Board's layoff plan is not sufficiently narrowly tailored. Other, less intrusive means of accomplishing similar purposes — such as the adoption of hiring goals — are available. For these reasons, the Board's selection of layoffs as the means to accomplish even a valid purpose cannot satisfy the demands of the Equal Protection Clause.[c]

IV

We accordingly reverse the judgment of the Court of Appeals for the Sixth Circuit.

O'CONNOR, J., concurring in part and concurring in the judgment. . . .

The Court is in agreement that, whatever the formulation employed, remedying past or present racial discrimination by a state actor is a sufficiently weighty state interest to warrant the remedial use of a carefully constructed affirmative action program. This remedial purpose need not be accompanied by contemporaneous findings of actual discrimination to be accepted as legitimate as long as the public actor has a firm basis for believing that remedial action is required. Additionally, although its precise contours are uncertain, a state interest in the promotion of racial diversity has been found sufficiently "compelling," at least in the context of higher education, to support the use of racial considerations in futhering that interest. And certainly nothing the Court has said here today necessarily forecloses the possibility that the Court will find other governmental interests which have been relied upon in the lower courts but which have not been passed on here to be sufficiently "important" or "compelling" to sustain the use of affirmative action policies. . . .

In the final analysis, the diverse formulations and the number of separate writings put forth by various members of the Court in these difficult cases do not necessarily reflect an intractable fragmentation in opinion with respect to certain core principles. Ultimately, the Court is at least in accord in believing that a public employer, consistent with the Constitution, may undertake an affirmative action program which is designed to further a legitimate remedial purpose and which

c. The Board's definition of minority to include blacks, orientals, American Indians, and persons of Spanish descent further illustrates the undifferentiated nature of the plan. There is no explanation of why the Board chose to favor these particular minorities or how in fact members of some of the categories can be identified. Moreover, respondents have never suggested — much less formally found — that they have engaged in prior, purposeful discriminination against members of each of these minority groups.

implements that purpose by means that do not impose disproportionate harm on the interests, or unnecessarily trammel the rights, of innocent individuals directly and adversely affected by a plan's racial preference. . . .

I agree with the Court that a governmental agency's interest in remedying "societal" discrimination, that is, discrimination not traceable to its own actions, cannot be deemed sufficiently compelling to pass constitutional muster under strict scrutiny. I also concur in the Court's assessment that use by the courts below of a "role model" theory to justify the conclusion that this plan had a legitimate remedial purpose was in error. . . .

The imposition of a requirement that public employers make findings that they have engaged in illegal discrimination before they engage in affirmative action programs would severely undermine public employers' incentive to meet voluntarily their civil rights obligations. This result would clearly be at odds with this Court's and Congress' consistent emphasis on "the value of voluntary efforts to further the objectives of the law." *Bakke*. The value of voluntary compliance is doubly important when it is a public employer that acts, both because of the example its voluntary assumption of responsibility sets and because the remediation of governmental discrimination is of unique importance. Imposing a contemporaneous findings requirement would produce the anomalous result that what private employers may do to correct apparent violations of Title VII, Steelworkers v. Weber, public employers are constitutionally forbidden to do to correct their statutory and constitutional transgressions. . . .

Of course, . . . in order to provide some measure of protection to the interests of its nonminority employees and the employer itself in the event that its affirmative action plan is challenged, the public employer must have a firm basis for determining that affirmative action is warranted. Public employers are not without reliable benchmarks in making this determination. For example, demonstrable evidence of a disparity between the percentage of qualified blacks on a school's teaching staff and the percentage of qualified minorities in the relevant labor pool sufficient to support a prima facie Title VII pattern or practice claim by minority teachers would lend a compelling basis for a competent authority such as the School Board to conclude that implementation of a voluntary affirmative action plan is appropriate to remedy apparent prior employment discrimination. . . .

In sum, I do not think that the layoff provision was constitutionally infirm simply because the School Board, the Commission, or a court had not made particularized findings of discrimination at the time the provision was agreed upon. But when the plan was challenged, the District Court and the Court of Appeals did not make the proper inquiry into the legitimacy of the Board's asserted remedial purposes; instead, they relied upon governmental purposes that we have deemed insufficient to withstand strict scrutiny, and therefore failed to isolate a sufficiently important governmental purpose that could support the challenged provision.

There is, however, no need to inquire whether the provision actually had a legitimate remedial purpose based on the record, such as it is, because the judgment is vulnerable on yet another ground: the courts below applied a "reasonableness" test . . . that is plainly incorrect under any of the standards articulated by this Court. Nor is it necessary, in my view, to resolve the troubling questions of whether any layoff provision could survive strict scrutiny or whether this particular layoff provision could, when considered without reference to the hiring goal it was intended to further, pass the onerous "narrowly tailored" requirement. Petitioners have met their burden of establishing that this layoff provision is not "narrowly tailored" to achieve its asserted remedial purpose by demonstrating that the provision is keyed to a hiring goal that itself has no relation to the remedying of employment discrimination.

Although the constitutionality of the hiring goal as such is not before us, it is impossible to evaluate the necessity of the layoff provision as a remedy for the apparent prior employment discrimination absent reference to that goal. In this case, the hiring goal that the layoff provision was designed to safeguard was tied to the percentage of minority students in the school district, not to the percentage of qualified minority teachers within the relevant labor pool. The disparity between the percentage of minorities on the teaching staff and the percentage of minorities in the student body is not probative of employment discrimination; it is only when it is established that availability of minorities in the relevant labor pool substantially exceeded those hired that one may draw an inference of deliberate discrimination in employment. Because the layoff provision here acts to maintain levels of minority hiring that have no relation to remedying employment discrimination, it cannot be adjudged "narrowly tailored" to effectuate its asserted remedial purpose.

WHITE, J., concurring in the judgment.

... Whatever the legitimacy of hiring goals or quotas may be, the discharge of white teachers to make room for blacks, none of whom has been shown to be a victim of any racial discrimination, is quite a different matter. I cannot believe that in order to integrate a work force, it would be permissible to discharge whites and hire blacks until the latter comprised a suitable percentage of the work force.... The layoff policy in the case — laying off whites who would otherwise be retained in order to keep blacks on the job — has the same effect and is equally violative of the Equal Protection Clause. I agree with the plurality that this official policy is unconstitutional and hence concur in the judgment.

MARSHALL, J., with whom Brennan and Blackmun, JJ., join, dissenting.

... [T]he District Court should have the opportunity to develop a factual record adequate to resolve the serious issue raised by the case....

I, too, believe that layoffs are unfair. But unfairness ought not be confused with constitutional injury. Paying no heed to the true circumstances of petitioners' plight, the plurality would nullify years of negotiation and compromise designed to solve serious educational problems in the public schools of Jackson, Michigan. Because I believe that a public employer, with the full agreement of its employees, should be permitted to preserve the benefits of a legitimate and constitutional affirmative-action hiring plan even while reducing its work force, I dissent....

II

... The sole question posed by this case is whether the Constitution prohibits a union and a local school board from developing a collective-bargaining agreement that apportions layoffs between two racially determined groups as a means of preserving the effects of an affirmative hiring policy, the constitutionality of which is unchallenged.

III

[Justice Marshall reviewed the different standards of review that have been adopted by various members of the Court in a number of opinions.] In this case, it should not matter which test the Court applies. What is most important, under any approach to the constitutional analysis, is that a reviewing court genuinely consider the circumstances of the provision at issue. The history and application of Article XII, assuming verification upon a proper record, demonstrate that this provision would pass constitutional muster, no matter which standard the Court should adopt.

IV

The principal state purpose supporting Article XII is the need to preserve the levels of faculty integration achieved through the affirmative hiring policy adopted in the early 1970's. Justification for the hiring policy itself is found in the turbulent history of the effort to integrate the Jackson Public Schools — not even mentioned in the majority opinion — which attests to the bona fides of the Board's current employment practices. . . .

Instead of subjecting an already volatile school system to the further disruption of formal accusations and trials, it appears that the Board set about achieving the goals articulated in the [1969 settlement of a claim of discrimininination filed by the Jackson NAACP against the Board of Education before the Michigan Civil Rights Commission]. . . .

An explicit Board admission or judicial determination of culpability, which the petitioners and even the Solicitor General urge us to hold was required before the Board could undertake a race-conscious remedial plan, would only have exposed the Board in this case to futher litigation and liability. . . . It would have contributed nothing to the advancement of the community's urgent objective of integrating its schools. . . .

Moreover, under the apparent circumstances of this case, we need not rely on any general awareness of "societal discrimination" to conclude that the Board's purpose is of sufficient importance to justify its limited remedial efforts. There are allegations that the imperative to integrate the public schools was urgent. Racially motivated violence had erupted at the schools, interfering with all educational objectives. . . .

Were I satisfied with the record before us, I would hold that the state purpose of preserving the integrity of a valid hiring policy — which in turn sought to achieve diversity and stability for the benefit of all students — was sufficient, in this case, to satisfy the demands of the Constitution.

V

The second part of any constitutional assessment of the disputed plan requires us to examine the means chosen to achieve the state purpose. . . .

A

Testimony of both Union and school officials illustrates that the Board's obligation to integrate its faculty could not have been fulfilled meaningfully as long as layoffs continued to eliminate the last hired. . . . The testimony suggests that the lack of some layoff protection would have crippled the efforts to recruit minority applicants. Adjustment of the layoff hierarchy under these circumstances was a necessary corollary of an affirmative action hiring policy.

B

Under Justice Powell's approach, the community of Jackson, having painfully watched the hard-won benefits of its integration efforts vanish as a result of massive layoffs, would be informed today, simply, that preferential layoff protection is never permissible because hiring policies serve the same purpose at a lesser cost. As a matter of logic as well as fact, a hiring policy achieves no purpose at all if it is eviscerated by layoff. . . .

Any per se prohibition against layoff protection . . . must rest upon a premise that the tradition of basing layoff decisions on seniority is so fundamental that its modification can never be permitted. Our cases belie that premise. . . .

[Reviewing a number of prior decisions involving layoffs, Justice Marshall concluded:] These cases establish that protection from layoff is not altogether unavailable as a tool for achieving legitimate societal goals. . . .

C

. . . [N]either petitioners nor any Justice of this Court has suggested an alternative to Article XII that would have attained the stated goal in any narrower or more equitable a fashion. Nor can I conceive of one.

VI

It is no accident that this least burdensome of all conceivable options is the very provision that the parties adopted. For Article XII was forged in the crucible of clashing interests. All of the economic powers of the predominantly white teachers' union were brought to bear against those of the elected Board, and the process yielded consensus. . . .

The best evidence that Article XII is a narrow means to serve important interests is that representatives of all affected persons, starting from diametrically opposed perspectives, have agreed to it — not once, but six times since 1972.

VII

. . . I believe the conclusion is inescapable that Article XII meets, and indeed surpasses, any standard for ensuring that race-conscious programs are necessary to achieve remedial purposes. When an elected school board and a teachers' union collectively bargain a layoff provision designed to preserve the effects of a valid minority recruitment plan by apportioning layoffs between two racial groups, as a result of a settlement achieved under the auspices of a supervisory state agency charged with protecting the civil rights of all citizens, that provision should not be upset by this Court on constitutional grounds. . . .

STEVENS, J., dissenting.

In my opinion, it is not necessary to find that the Board of Education has been guilty of racial discrimination in the past to support the conclusion that it has a legitimate interest in employing more black teachers in the future. Rather than analyzing a case of this kind by asking whether minority teachers have some sort of special entitlement to jobs as a remedy for sins that were committed in the past, I believe that we should first ask whether the Board's action advances the public interest in educating children for the future. If so, I believe we should consider whether that public interest, and the manner in which it is pursued, justifies any adverse effects on the disadvantaged group.

I

. . . In the context of public education, it is quite obvious that a school board may reasonably conclude that an integrated faculty will be able to provide benefits to the student body that could not be provided by an all white, or nearly all white, faculty. For one of the most important lessons that the American public schools teach is that the diverse ethnic, cultural, and national backgrounds that have been brought together in our famous "melting pot" do not identify essential differences among the human beings that inhabit our land. It is one thing for a white child to be taught by a white teacher that color, like beauty, is only "skin deep"; it is far more convincing to experience that truth on a day to day basis during the routine, ongoing learning process. . . .

Thus, there was a rational and unquestionably legitimate basis for the Board's decision to enter into the collective-bargaining agreement that petitioners have challenged, even though the agreement required special efforts to recruit and retain minority teachers.

II

. . . There is . . . a critical difference between a decision to exclude a member of a minority race because of his or her skin color and a decision to include more members of the minority in a school faculty for that reason.

The exclusionary decision rests on the false premise that differences in race, or in the color of a person's skin, reflect real differences that are relevant to a person's right to share in the blessings of a free society. . . . [T]hat premise is "utterly irrational," and repugnant to the principles of a free and democratic society. Nevertheless, the fact that persons of different races do, indeed, have differently colored skin, may give rise to a belief that there is some significant difference between such persons. The inclusion of minority teachers in the educational process inevitably tends to dispel that illusion whereas their exclusion could only tend to foster it. The inclusionary decision is consistent with the principle that all men are created equal; the exclusionary decision is at war with that principle. One decision accords with the Equal Protection Clause of the Fourteenth Amendment; the other does not. Thus, consideration of whether the consciousness of race is exclusionary or inclusionary plainly distinguishes the Board's valid purpose in this case from a race-conscious decision that would reinforce assumptions of inequality.

III

Even if there is a valid purpose to the race consciousness, however, the question that remains is whether that public purpose transcends the harm to the white teachers who are disadvantaged by the special preference the Board has given to its most recently hired minority teachers. In my view, there are two important inquiries in assessing the harm to the disadvantaged teacher. The first is an assessment of the procedures that were used to adopt, and implement, the race-conscious action. The second is an evaluation of the nature of the harm itself.

In this case, there can be no question about either the fairness of the procedures used to adopt the race-conscious provision, or the propriety of its breadth. As Justice Marshall has demonstrated, the procedures for adopting this provision were scrupulously fair. The Union that represents the petitioners negotiated the provision and agreed to it; the agreement was put to a vote of the membership, and overwhelmingly approved. . . . Similarly, the provision is specifically designed to achieve its objective — retaining the minority teachers that have been specially recruited to give the Jackson schools, after a period of racial unrest, an integrated faculty. Thus, in striking contrast to the procedural inadequacy and unjustified breadth of the race-based classification in *Fullilove,* the race-conscious layoff policy here was adopted with full participation of the disadvantaged individuals and with a narrowly circumscribed berth for the policy's operation.

Finally, we must consider the harm to the petitioners. . . . [P]etitioners have been laid off for a combination of two reasons: The economic conditions that have led Jackson to lay off some teachers, and the special contractual protections intended to preserve the newly integrated character of the faculty in the Jackson schools. Thus, the same harm might occur if a number of gifted young teachers had been given special contractual protection because their specialties were in short supply and if the Jackson Board of Education faced a fiscal need for layoffs. A Board decision to grant immediate tenure to a group of experts in computer technology, an athletic coach, and a language teacher, for example, might reduce the pool of teachers eligible for layoffs during a depression and therefore have precisely the same impact as the racial preference at issue here. In either case, the harm would be generated by the combination of economic conditions and the special contractual protection given a different group of teachers — a protection that, as discussed above, was justified by a valid and extremely strong public interest.[a]

a. The fact that the issue arises in a layoff context, rather than a hiring context, has no bearing on the equal protection question. For if the Board's interest in employing more minority teachers is sufficient to justify providing them with an extra incentive to accept jobs in Jackson, Michigan, it is also sufficient to justify their retention when the number of available jobs is reduced. Justice Powell's suggestion that there is a distinction of constitutional significance under the Equal Protection Clause between a racial preference at the time of hiring and an identical preference at the time of discharge is thus wholly unpersuasive. He seems to assume that a teacher who has been working for a few years suffers a greater harm when he is laid off than the harm suffered by an unemployed teacher who is refused a job for which he is qualified. In either event, the adverse decision forecloses "only one of several opportunities" that may be available to the disappointed teacher. Moreover, the distinction is artificial, for the layoff provision at issue in this case was included as part of the terms of the hiring of minority and other teachers under the collective-bargaining agreement.

Discussion

1. Justice Powell states that hiring and promotion goals "simply do not impose the same kinds of injury that layoffs impose," largely due to the effects of layoffs on the "settled expectations" of employees. What role do people's subjective expectations play in constitutional analysis under the equal protection clause? Might promotion goals also upset expectations?

2. Justice Powell objects to the "role model" theory on two grounds. First, the theory "allows the Board to engage in discriminatory hiring and layoff practices long past the point required by any legitimate remedial purpose." Does the role model theory purport to serve remedial goals? Is Justice Powell's treatment of nonremedial goals in *Wygant* consistent with his views in *Bakke*? Second, "the idea that black students are better off with black teachers could lead to the very system the Court rejected in *Brown*." Consider, however, Justice Steven's distinction between the inclusion and exclusion of minorities on the basis of race.

3. Justice Powell states that affirmative action is justified only where there is a "strong basis" in the evidence for concluding that remedial action is necessary. Imagine that you are on a school board and are considering implementing an affirmative action plan. What types of evidence would you present to support the plan?

4. Justice O'Connor writes that, in evaluating the "fit" of a remedial plan, one must compare the percentage of minorities employed with the percentage of qualified minorities in the relevant labor pool. Why? Might the absence of minorities in the pool of qualified teachers itself be the result of past discrimination against minorities elsewhere in society? Does this rationale prove too much? May (or should) the School Board take into account other societal discrimination in formulating the scope of its plan?

5. With respect to the "societal discrimination" rationale, consider Professor Roger Wilkins' argument that the urban black poor occupy a unique historical and social position in American life and may therefore require race-based programs specially tailored to their needs:

> No matter how much more politically palatable general programs might be, the black poor need programs designed specifically for them because some of the black poor are different. . . . [T]he racially inflicted economic, cultural, and psychological damage [the black poor] suffer is unique and hideously destructive and requires specially tailored remedies.
>
> The inner city poor are poor because they have been scarred more deeply by the legacy of slavery than the rest of us. Racism has always hurt some blacks more than others. At the time of the Revolution, some blacks were free, literate and living in Boston; others were little better than beasts of burden and sexual chattel in South Carolina.
>
> Some blacks came North before Emancipation and others were slammed back into semislavery during and especially after Reconstruction. Some of their descendants remained illiterate peasants in the South in the sixth and even seventh decades of this century. They were driven off the land by the mechanization of agriculture.
>
> When they got to the major cities, millions of the unskilled jobs that the underclasses from Europe and earlier black emigres from the South had used as ladders to the middle class were disappearing. Some survived this transition while others became disoriented and redundant in the cities' hard and dirty backwaters. . . .

> Economically superfluous people engulfed by societal opprobrium, environmental ugliness and cultural desolation experience the same sense of futurelessness that people under wartime bombardment do. They live under constant stress. Many do not play by the rules generated by people for whom society works. . . .
>
> Children born into this chaos are victims at birth and on their way to becoming societal burdens or menaces at 15. If these children are to be saved, we must find ways to nurse health back into families in the inner cities, where family disintegration is ripping black culture apart, putting an enormous segment of the black future at risk.[105]

6. Professor Kathleen Sullivan has argued that, in the area of race-based preferences, the Court operates almost exclusively under a retrospective, "sin"-based paradigm that circumscribes the justifications for both the goals of, and the burdens imposed by, affirmative action. With respect to goals, the Court demands evidence of a guilty perpetrator and "has approved affirmative action only as precise penance for the specific sins of racism a government, union, or employer has committed in the past." The guilt perspective similarly infects the Court's treatment of burdens; although the "innocence" of dispreferred individuals has not led to a complete rejection of preferential programs, it has resulted in a "utilitarian balancing of hardships to determine how the 'punishment' imposed by affirmative action will be distributed." Sullivan suggests an alternative to the sin paradigm focusing more directly on prospective justifications:

> Public and private employers might choose to implement affirmative action for many reasons other than to purge their own past sins of discrimination. The Jackson school board, for example, said it had done so in part to improve the quality of education in Jackson — whether by improving black students' performance or by dispelling for black and white students alike any idea that white supremacy governs our social institutions. Other employers might advance different forward-looking reasons for affirmative action: improving their services to black constituencies, averting racial tension over the allocation of jobs in a community, or increasing the diversity of a work force, to name but a few examples. Or they might adopt affirmative action simply to eliminate from their operations all de facto embodiment of a system of racial caste. All of these reasons aspire to a racially integrated future, but none reduces to "racial balancing for its own sake."
>
> If such aspirations for the future rather than past sin were the basis for affirmative action, would white claims of "innocence" count for less? They should, for it is easier to show that displacing "innocent" whites is narrowly tailored to goals that turn on integrating institutions now than it is to show that doing so is narrowly tailored to purging past sins of discrimination that the displaced whites did not themselves "commit.". . .
>
> In the absence of any . . . strong basis to claim that race can never be a factor in politics or private bargaining, voluntary affirmative action is as defensible as the architecture of a better future as it is as a remedy for sins of discrimination past. And by turning to such forward-looking justification, the Court might more effectively quiet protests about windfalls to nonvictims and injustice to innocents than it has by treating affirmative action as penance for past sins.[106]

105. Wilkins, The Black Poor Are Different, New York Times, Aug. 22, 1989, at A19.

106. Kathleen Sullivan, Sins of Discrimination: Last Term's Affirmative Action Cases, 100 Harv. L. Rev. 78 (1986).

Do you agree with Sullivan's assessment that the burdens imposed on nonminorities are more justifiable when based on a prospective as opposed to a retrospective purpose?

UNITED STATES v. PARADISE, 480 U.S. 149 (1987): [This case arose out of protracted litigation over racial discrimination by the Alabama Department of Public Safety. In 1972, the Department was found to have systematically excluded blacks from employment. In 1983, following a determination that the Department had failed to develop racially nondiscriminatory promotion procedures, the District Court, in Justice Brennan's words, imposed a minimum 50 percent promotional quota in the upper ranks, but only if there were qualified black candidates, if the rank were less than 25 percent black, and if the Department had not developed and implemented a promotion plan without adverse impact for the relevant rank. The court highlighted the temporary nature and flexible design of the relief ordered, stating that it was "specifically tailored" to eliminate the lingering effects of past discrimination, to remedy effects of past discrimination, to remedy the delayed compliance with the consent decrees and to ensure prompt implementation of lawful procedures. The Court of Appeals affirmed, and the United States filed a petition for certiorari challenging the constitutionality of the order.[107] The Court upheld the order in a 5-4 decision, with no opinion gaining the assent of a majority of the Justices.

Justice Brennan wrote for a plurality that included Justices Marshall, Blackmun, and Powell. He emphasized that "the Department's prior employment practices and conduct during this lawsuit bear directly on the constitutionality of any race-conscious remedy imposed upon it."]

... It is now well established that government bodies, including courts, may constitutionally employ racial classifications essential to remedy unlawful treatment of racial or ethnic groups subject to discrimination. ... But although this Court has consistently held that some elevated level of scrutiny is required when a racial or ethnic distinction is made for remedial purposes, it has yet to reach consensus on the appropriate constitutional analysis. We need not do so in this case, however, because we conclude that the relief ordered survives even strict scrutiny analysis. ...

The government unquestionably has a compelling interest in remedying past and present discrimination by a state actor. ... [T]he pervasive, systematic, and obstinate discriminatory conduct of the Department created a profound need and a firm justification for the race-conscious relief ordered by the District Court.

[Petitioners] maintain that the Department was found guilty only of discrimination in hiring, and not in its promotional practices. They argue that no remedial relief is justified in the promotion context because the intentional discrimination was without effect in the upper ranks, and because the Department's promotional procedure was not discriminatory. There is no merit in either premise.

107. Although the United States originally challenged the Department's practices, under the Reagan Administration the United States joined the Department in seeking reversal of the District Court promotion procedure.

Discrimination at the entry-level necessarily precluded blacks from competing for promotions, and resulted in a departmental hierarchy dominated exclusively by nonminorities. . . . It is too late for the Department to attempt to segregate the results achieved by its hiring practices and those achieved by its promotional practices. . . .

Finally, . . . the District Court's enforcement order is "supported not only by the governmental interest in eradicating [the Department's] discriminatory practices, it is also supported by the societal interest in compliance with the judgments of federal courts." The relief at issue was imposed upon a defendant with a consistent history of resistance to the District Court's order, and only after the Department failed to live up to its court-approved commitments.

III

While conceding that the District Court's order serves a compelling interest, the Government insists that it was not narrowly tailored to accomplish its purposes. . . .

In determining whether race-conscious remedies are appropriate, we look to several factors, including the necessity for the relief and the efficacy of alternative remedies, the flexibility and duration of the relief, including the availability of waiver provisions; the relationship of the numerical goals to the relevant labor market; and the impact of the relief on the rights of third parties. When considered in light of these factors, it was amply established, and we find that the one-for-one promotion requirement was narrowly tailored to serve its several purposes, both as applied to the initial set of promotions to the rank of corporal and as a continuing contingent order with respect to the upper ranks.

B

. . . Most significantly, the one-for-one requirement is ephemeral; the term of its application is contingent upon the Department's own conduct. The requirement endures only until the Department comes up with a procedure that does not have a discriminatory impact on blacks — something the Department was enjoined to do in 1972 and expressly promised to do by 1980. . . .

C

. . . [Although] the Government concedes that a one-to-three requirement would have been lawful, [it challenged the one-for-one requirement adopted by the District Court because it is substantially higher than the percentage of blacks in the relevant labor market (approximately 25%)]. This argument ignores that the 50% figure is not itself the goal; rather it represents the speed at which the goal of 25% will be achieved. . . .

The figure selected to compensate for past discrimination and delay necessarily involved a delicate calibration of the rights and interests of the plaintiff class, the Department, and the white troopers. . . . This Court should not second-guess the lower court's carefully considered choice of the figure necessary to achieve its many purposes, especially when that figure is hedged about with specific qualifying measures designed to prevent any unfair impact that might arise from rigid application.

D

The one-for-one requirement did not impose an unacceptable burden on innocent third parties. As stated above, the temporary and extremely limited nature of the requirement substantially limits any potential burden on white applicants for promotion. It was used only once at the rank of corporal and may not be utilized at all in the upper ranks. Nor has the court imposed an "absolute bar" to white advancement. In the one instance in which the quota was employed, 50% of those elevated were white.

The one-for-one requirement does not require the layoff and discharge of white employees and therefore does not impose burdens of the sort that concerned the plurality in *Wygant*. . . . Because the one-for-one requirement is so limited in scope and duration, it only postpones the promotion of qualified whites. Consequently, like a hiring goal, it "impose[s] a diffuse burden, . . . foreclosing only one of several opportunities." . . . Finally, the basic limitation, that black troopers promoted must be qualified, remains. . . .

E

. . . [W]e conclude that the District Judge properly balanced the individual and collective interests at stake, including the interests of the white troopers eligible for promotion, in shaping this remedy. . . .

[Concurring opinions by Justices Powell and Stevens are omitted.]

O'CONNOR, J., joined by Chief Justice Rehnquist and Justice Scalia, dissenting.

. . . The Court today purports to apply strict scrutiny, and concludes that the order in this case was narrowly tailored for its remedial purpose. Because the Court adopts a standardless view of "narrowly tailored" far less stringent than that required by strict scrutiny, I dissent. . . .

The order at issue in this case clearly had one purpose — and one purpose only — to compel the Department to develop a promotion procedure that would not have an adverse impact on blacks. Although the Court and the courts below suggest that the order also had the purpose of "eradicat[ing] the ill effects of the Department's delay in producing" such a promotion procedure, the District Court's subsequent implementation of the order makes clear that the order cannot be defended on the basis of such a purpose.

. . . The one-for-one promotion quota used in this case far exceeded the percentage of blacks in the trooper force, and there is no evidence in the record that such an extreme quota was necessary to eradicate the effects of the Department's delay. . . . The Court attempts to defend this one-for-one promotion quota as merely affecting the speed by which the Department attains the goal of 25% black representation in the upper ranks. Such a justification, however, necessarily eviscerates any notion of "narrowly tailored" because it has no stopping point; even a 100% quota could be defended on the ground that it merely "determined how quickly the Department progressed toward" some ultimate goal. If strict scrutiny is to have any meaning, therefore, a promotion goal must have a closer relationship to the percentage of blacks eligible for promotions. . . .

[Justice O'Connor also criticized the District Court for failing to consider alternatives to the plan adopted: "[T]he least that strict scrutiny requires is that the District Court expressly evaluate the available alternative remedies," such as appointment of a trustee to develop a new promotion procedure or the leveling of stiff fines and other penalties for contempt of court in failing to develop the required procedures.]

[Justice White, who "agree[d] with much of what Justice O'Connor [had] written," found that the District Court had exceeded its equitable powers in devising the remedy.]

Discussion

1. The majority in *Paradise* justified the District Court's order partly based on the Department's intransigence and "the societal interest in compliance with the judgments of federal courts." Since the brunt of any affirmative action program in the workplace falls on dispreferred employees, can this rationale justify an otherwise overly burdensome preferential program? What other alternatives were available to the Court?

2. Justice Brennan stated that the one-for-one hiring plan in *Paradise* represents the speed at which the Department was to reach the goal of 25 percent minority representation. Could the judge have ordered a 100 percent black hiring plan? Would the Department's intransigence have justified a layoff provision similar to that invalidated in *Wygant*?

C. National and State Powers over Affirmative Action: Preferences for Minority-Owned Businesses

This section consists of three decisions: Fullilove v. Klutznick, 448 U.S. 448 (1980), City of Richmond v. J.A. Croson Co., 488 U.S. 469 (1989), and Metro Broadcasting, Inc. v. FCC, 110 S. Ct. 2997 (1990). *Fullilove* upheld a federal statute requiring that a certain percentage of public contracts be set aside for minority contractors. *Croson* struck down a similar provision adopted by the Richmond, Virginia, City Council. In *Metro Broadcasting*, one of Justice Brennan's last majority opinions before retiring from the Court, he distinguished *Croson* on the ground that Congress had broader powers over affirmative action than state and local governments. This section examines the rationale for that distinction and considers more generally the constitutional issues raised by the preferential provisions.

FULLILOVE v. KLUTZNICK, 448 U.S. 448 (1980): [The Court upheld the "minority business enterprise" (MBE) provision of the Public Works Employment Act of 1977, which requires that 10 percent of federal funds granted for local public works projects must be used to procure services or supplies from businesses owned by minority group members. The provision was responsive to the concern, evinced in its legislative history, that difficulties confronting minority contractors —

such as lack of working capital, inability to meet bonding requirements, and unfamiliarity with bidding opportunities and procedures — were often the results of past discrimination. As administered, the MBE program contemplates the award of contracts to MBE's even if they are not the lowest bidders where the bids are inflated as a result of past discrimination. The regulations allow waiver of the 10 percent requirement on a showing that it cannot reasonably be met.

The complainants were associations of contractors and subcontractors who alleged economic injury from enforcement of the MBE provision and challenged it under the Fifth and Fourteenth Amendments.

There was no majority opinion; Chief Justice Burger announced the judgment of the Court sustaining the statute in an opinion joined by Justices White and Powell.]

BURGER, C.J. . . . [T]he objectives of the MBE program are within the power of Congress under §5 "to enforce by appropriate legislation," the equal protection guarantees of the Fourteenth Amendment.

. . . Although the Act recites no preambulary "findings" on the subject, we are satisfied that Congress had abundant historical basis from which it could conclude that traditional procurement practices, when applied to minority businesses, could perpetuate the effects of prior discrimination. Accordingly, Congress reasonably determined that the prospective elimination of these barriers to minority firm access to public contracting opportunities generated by the 1977 Act was appropriate to ensure that those businesses were not denied equal opportunity to participate in federal grants to state and local governments, which is one aspect of the equal protection of the laws. Insofar as the MBE program pertains to the actions of state and local grantees, Congress could have achieved its objectives by use of its power under §5 of the Fourteenth Amendment. . . .

[Turning to "the question whether, as a *means* to accomplish these plainly constitutional objectives, Congress may use racial and ethnic criteria," the Chief Justice emphasized the limited and remedial nature of the MBE provision. He cited the Court's school desegregation cases to reject the contention that in the remedial context the Congress must act in a "wholly 'color-blind' fashion." Without articulating the standard of judicial review being applied, he characterized the injury to the complainant as "relatively light" and wrote that "[w]hen effectuating a limited and properly tailored remedy to cure the effects of prior discrimination such a 'sharing of the burden' by innocent parties is not impermissible." The Chief Justice noted that "[t]his opinion does not adopt . . . the formulas of analysis articulated in such cases as University of California Regents v. Bakke. However, our analysis demonstrates that the MBE provision would survive judicial scrutiny under either 'test' articulated in the several *Bakke* opinions."

Justice Powell concurred. He said that he "would place greater emphasis than the Chief Justice on the need to articulate judicial standards of review in conventional terms" and went on to apply the analysis set out in his opinion in *Bakke*. The three basic questions were "(i) whether Congress is competent to make findings of unlawful discrimination; (ii) if so, whether sufficient findings have been made to establish that unlawful discrimination has affected adversely minority business enterprises, and (iii) whether the 10 percent set-aside is a permissible means for redressing identifiable past discrimination." Congress' competence was "beyond question," and the legislative history "demonstrates that Congress reasonably concluded that private and governmental discrimination had contributed to the negligible percentage of public contracts awarded minority contractors." Since the government interest in redressing this discrimination was "compelling," this left only the question of whether the means were "necessary." Justice Powell believed that in enforcing the Civil War amendments, Congress had "the authority to select reasonable remedies. . . . Courts must be sensitive to the possibility that less intrusive means might serve the compelling state interest equally as well. . . . Congress' choice of remedy should be upheld, however, if the means selected are equitable and reasonably necessary to the redress of identifiable discrimination." Justice Powell also discussed the problem posed by the sparse legislative history of the MBE provision:]

The petitioners contend that the legislative history of §103(f)(2) reflects no congressional finding of statutory or constitutional violations. Crucial to that contention is the assertion that a reviewing court may not look beyond the legislative history of the PWEA itself for evidence that Congress believed it was combating invidious discrimination. But petitioners' theory would erect an artificial barrier to full understanding of the legislative process.

Congress is not an adjudicatory body called upon to resolve specific disputes between competing adversaries. Its constitutional role is to be representative rather than impartial, to make policy rather than to apply settled principles of law. The petitioners' contention that this Court should treat the debates on §103(f)(2) as the complete "record" of congressional decisionmaking underlying that statute is essentially a plea that we treat Congress as if it were a lower federal court. But Congress is not expected to act as though it were duty bound to find facts and make conclusions of law. The creation of national rules for the governance of our society simply does not entail the same concept of recordmaking that is appropriate to a judicial or administrative proceeding. Congress has no responsibility to confine its vision to the facts and evidence adduced by particular parties. Instead, its special attribute as a legislative body lies in its broader mission to investigate and consider all facts and opinions that may be relevant to the resolution of an issue. One appropriate source is the information and expertise that Congress acquires in the consideration and enactment of earlier legislation. After Congress has legislated repeatedly in an area of national concern, its Members gain experience that may reduce the need for fresh hearings or prolonged debate when Congress again considers action in that area.

Acceptance of petitioners' argument would force Congress to make specific factual findings with respect to each legislative action. Such a requirement would mark an unprecedented imposition of adjudicatory procedures upon a coordinate branch of Government. Neither the Constitution nor our democratic tradition warrants such a constraint on the legislative process. I therefore conclude that we are not confined in this case to an examination of the legislative history of §103(f)(2) alone. Rather, we properly may examine the total contemporary record of congressional action dealing with the problems of racial discrimination against minority business enterprises.

[Justice Marshall, joined by Justices Brennan and Blackmun, concurred in the judgment on the basis of their separate opinion (with Justice White) in *Bakke*.] In our view . . . the proper inquiry is whether racial classifications designed to further remedial purposes serve important governmental objectives and are substantially related to achievement of those objectives. . . . Judged under this standard, the 10 percent minority set-aside provision at issue in this case is plainly constitutional. Indeed, the question is not even a close one.

[Justice Stewart, joined by Justice Rehnquist, dissented on the ground that the government may never act to the detriment of a person solely because of that person's race, whether or not the person is a member of a racial minority. Congress has no greater authority than a court to impose detriments on the basis of race, and "a judicial decree that imposes burdens on the basis of race can be upheld only where its sole purpose is to eradicate the actual effects of illegal race discrimination." Justice Stewart thought that the MBE provision went beyond this because it sought "racial balance as a goal in and of itself" and "may have been enacted to compensate for the effects of social, educational, and economic 'disadvantage.' "]

STEVENS, J., dissenting. . . . I am not convinced that the Clause contains an absolute prohibition against any statutory classification based on race. I am nonetheless persuaded that it does impose a special obligation to scrutinize any governmental decisionmaking process that draws nationwide distinctions between citizens on the basis of their race and incidentally also discriminates against noncitizens in the preferred racial classes. For just as procedural safeguards are necessary to guarantee impartial decisionmaking in the judicial process, so can they play a vital part in preserving the impartial character of the legislative process.[a]

In both its substantive and procedural aspects this Act is markedly different from the normal product of the legislative decisionmaking process. The very fact that Congress for the first time in the Nation's history has created a broad legislative classification for entitlement to benefits based solely on racial characteristics identifies a dramatic difference between this Act and the thousands of statutes that preceded it. This dramatic point of departure is not even mentioned in the statement of purpose of the Act or in the Reports of either the House or the Senate Committee that processed the legislation, and was not the subject of any testimony or inquiry in any legislative hearing on the bill that was enacted. It is true that there was a brief discussion on the floor of the House as well as in the Senate on two different days, but only a handful of legislators spoke and there was virtually no debate. This kind of perfunctory consideration of an unprecedented policy decision of profound constitutional importance to the Nation is comparable to the accidental malfunction of the legislative process that led to what I regarded as a totally unjustified discrimination in Delaware Tribal Business Committee v. Weeks, 430 U.S., at 97.

Although it is traditional for judges to accord the same presumption of regularity to the legislative process no matter how obvious it may be that a busy Con-

a. See Linde, Due Process of Lawmaking, 55 Neb. L. Rev. 197, 255 (1976):

> For the last few years have reawakened our appreciation of the primacy of process over product in a free society, the knowledge that no ends can be better than the means of their achievement. "The highest morality is almost always the morality of process," Professor Bickel wrote about Watergate a few months before his untimely death. If the republic is remembered in the distant history of law, it is likely to be for its enduring adherence to legitimate institutions and processes, not for its perfection of unique principles of justice and certainly not for the rationality of its laws. This recognition now may well take our attention beyond the processes of adjudication and of executive government to a new concern with the due process of lawmaking.

gress has acted precipitately, I see no reason why the character of their procedures may not be considered relevant to the decision whether the legislative product has caused a deprivation of liberty or property without due process of law.[b] Whenever Congress creates a classification that would be subject to strict scrutiny under the Equal Protection Clause of the Fourteenth Amendment if it had been fashioned by a state legislature, it seems to me that judicial review should include a consideration of the procedural character of the decisionmaking process.[c] A holding that the classification was not adequately preceded by a consideration of less drastic alternatives or adequately explained by a statement of legislative purpose would be far less intrusive than a final determination that the substance of the decision is not "narrowly tailored to the achievement of that goal." If the general language of the Due Process Clause of the Fifth Amendment authorizes this Court to review Acts of Congress under the standards of the Equal Protection Clause of the Fourteenth Amendment — a clause that cannot be found in the Fifth Amendment — there can be no separation-of-powers objection to a more tentative holding of unconstitutionality based on a failure to follow procedures that guarantee the kind of deliberation that a fundamental constitutional issue of this kind obviously merits.[d]

. . . I would hold this statute unconstitutional on a narrower ground. It cannot fairly be characterized as a "narrowly tailored" racial classification because it simply raises too many serious questions that Congress failed to answer or even to address in a responsible way.[e] The risk that habitual attitudes toward classes of persons, rather than analysis of the relevant characteristics of the class, will serve as a basis for a legislative classification is present when benefits are distributed as well as when burdens are imposed. In the past, traditional attitudes too often provided the only explanation for discrimination against

b. "It is not a new thought that 'to guarantee the democratic legitimacy of political decisions by establishing essential rules for the political process' is the central function of judicial review, as Dean Rostow and Professor Strong, among others, have argued." Linde, supra, 55 Neb. L. Rev., at 251.

c. See Sandalow, Judicial Protection of Minorities, 75 Mich. L. Rev. 1162, 1188 (1977):

> [I]f governmental action trenches upon values that may reasonably be regarded as fundamental, that action should be the product of a deliberate and broadly based political judgment. The stronger the argument that governmental action does encroach upon such values, the greater the need to assure that it is the product of a process that is entitled to speak for the society. Legislation that has failed to engage the attention of Congress, like the decisions of subordinate governmental institutions, does not meet that test, for it is likely to be the product of partial political pressures that are not broadly reflective of the society as a whole.

d. The conclusion to the Chief Justice's opinion states: "Any preference based on racial or ethnic criteria must necessarily receive a *most searching* examination to make sure that it does not conflict with constitutional guarantees." I agree with this statement but it seems to me that due process requires that the "most searching examination" be conducted in the first instance by Congress rather than by a federal court.

e. For example, why were these six racial classifications, and no others, included in the preferred class? Why are aliens excluded from the preference although they are not otherwise ineligible for public contracts? What percentage of Oriental blood or what degree of Spanish-speaking skill is required for membership in the preferred class? How does the legacy of slavery and the history of discrimination against the descendants of its victims support a preference for Spanish-speaking citizens who may be directly competing with black citizens in some overpopulated communities? Why is a preference given only to owners of business enterprises and why is that preference unaccompanied by any requirement concerning the employment of disadvantaged persons? Is the preference limited to a subclass of persons who can prove that they are subject to a special disability caused by part discrimination, as the Court's opinion indicates? Or is every member of the racial class entitled to a preference as the statutory language seems plainly to indicate? Are businesses formed just to take advantage of the preference eligible?

women, aliens, illegitimates, and black citizens. Today there is a danger that awareness of past injustice will lead to automatic acceptance of new classifications that are not in fact justified by attributes characteristic of the class as a whole.

When Congress creates a special preference, or a special disability, for a class of persons, it should identify the characteristic that justifies the special treatment. When the classification is defined in racial terms, I believe that such particular identification is imperative.

In this case, only two conceivable bases for differentiating the preferred classes from society as a whole have occurred to me: (1) that they were the victims of unfair treatment in the past and (2) that they are less able to compete in the future. Although the first of these factors would justify an appropriate remedy for past wrongs, for reasons that I have already stated, this statute is not such a remedial measure. The second factor is simply not true.

Discussion

1. *The standard of (substantive) review.* What standards of review did the Justices purport to apply in *Fullilove?* What standards did they actually apply?

2. *The argument for procedural review.* Recall that in the first case in this book, McCulloch v. Maryland, the Court referred approvingly to the process by which the First Congress enacted the law incorporating the Bank of the United States. The petitioners in *Fullilove* argued that the MBE provision was vulnerable because the legislative process was inadequate. While both Chief Justice Burger and Justice Powell reject the petitioners' argument, Justice Stevens adopts it. What are Justice Stevens' objections to the congressional process in this case? What kind of process would Justice Stevens find necessary to sustain the provision? What would be the benefits and costs, to Congress and the judiciary, of requiring such process?[108]

CITY OF RICHMOND v. J.A. CROSON CO.

488 U.S. 469 (1989)

Appeal from the U.S. Court of Appeals for the Fourth Circuit

[Justice O'Connor announced the judgment of the Court and delivered the opinion of the Court with respect to Parts I, III-B, and IV, an opinion with respect to Part II, in which Chief Justice Rehnquist and Justice White joined, and an opinion with respect to Parts III-A and V, in which Justice Kennedy also joined.]

108. See also Textile Workers Union v. Lincoln Mills, 353 U.S. 448 (1957), where the Court upheld a federal statute (§301 of the Taft-Hartley Act) involving complex constitutional issues of federal jurisdiction which obviously had received inadequate attention by Congress. In a dissenting opinion, Justice Frankfurter noted in passing: "In the wise distribution of governmental powers, this Court cannot do what a President sometimes does in returning a bill to Congress. We cannot return this provision to Congress and respectfully request that body to face the responsibility placed upon it by the Constitution. . . ." Compare Alexander Bickel & Harry Wellington, Legislative Purpose and the Judicial Function: The *Lincoln Mills* Case, 71 Harv. L. Rev. 1 (1957), which argues that the Court can properly perform a "remanding function" and that it has in fact done so in the guise, inter alia, of avowedly construing statutes to avoid serious constitutional problems.

I

On April 11, 1983, the Richmond City Council adopted the Minority Business Utilization Plan . . . [which] required prime contractors to whom the city awarded construction contracts to subcontract at least 30% of the dollar amount of the contract to one or more Minority Business Enterprises (MBEs). The 30% set-aside did not apply to city contracts awarded to minority-owned prime contractors.

The Plan defined an MBE as "[a] business at least fifty-one (51) percent of which is owned and controlled . . . by minority group members." "Minority group members" were defined as "[c]itizens of the United States who are Blacks, Spanish-speaking, Orientals, Indians, Eskimos, or Aleuts." There was no geographic limit to the Plan; an otherwise qualified MBE from anywhere in the United States could avail itself of the 30% set-aside. The Plan declared that it was "remedial" in nature, and enacted "for the purpose of promoting wider participation by minority business enterprises in the construction of public projects." The Plan expired on June 30, 1988, and was in effect for approximately five years.

[A provision, formulated by a city administrative agency, permitted waiver of the requirement only where it could be shown that "sufficient, relevant, qualified [MBEs] . . . are unavailable or unwilling to participate in the contract to enable meeting the 30% MBE goal." Although there was no direct administrative appeal from a denial of waiver, once a contract had been awarded to another firm, a bidder denied a contract for failure to fulfill the MBE requirements had a "general right of protest."]

The Plan was adopted by the Richmond City Council after a public hearing. Seven members of the public spoke to the merits of the ordinance: five were in opposition, two in favor. Proponents of the set-aside provision relied on a study which indicated that, while the general population of Richmond was 50% black, only .67% of the city's prime construction contracts had been awarded to minority businesses in the 5-year period from 1978 to 1983. It was also established that a variety of contractors' associations, whose representatives appeared in opposition to the ordinance, had virtually no minority businesses within their membership. . . .

There was no direct evidence of race discrimination on the part of the city in letting contracts or any evidence that the city's prime contractors had discriminated against minority-owned subcontractors.

Opponents of the ordinance questioned both its wisdom and its legality. . . . Representatives of various contractors' associations questioned whether there were enough MBEs in the Richmond area to satisfy the 30% set-aside requirement. [One representative] noted that only 4.7% of all construction firms in the United States were minority owned and that 41% of these were located in California, New York, Illinois, Florida, and Hawaii. He predicted that the ordinance would thus lead to a windfall for the few minority firms in Richmond. . . . Some of the representatives of the local contractors organizations indicated that they did not discriminate on the basis of race and were in fact actively seeking out minority members. . . . [T]he ordinance was enacted by a vote of six to two. . . .

[The ordinance was challenged by a contractor whose request for a waiver of the MBE requirement had been denied. The first time the case reached the Supreme Court, it remanded for further consideration in light of Wygant v.

Jackson Board of Education. On remand, a divided panel of the Court of Appeals struck down the Richmond set-aside program.]

II

The parties and their supporting amici fight an initial battle over the scope of the city's power to adopt legislation designed to address the effects of past discrimination. Relying on our decision in *Wygant,* appellee argues that the city must limit any race-based remedial efforts to eradicating the effects of its own prior discrimination. This is essentially the position taken by the Court of Appeals below. Appellant argues that our decision in *Fullilove* is controlling, and that as a result the city of Richmond enjoys sweeping legislative power to define and attack the effects of prior discrimination in its local construction industry. We find that neither of these two rather stark alternatives can withstand analysis. . . .

[In the principal opinion in *Fullilove,* Chief Justice Burger] stressed two factors in upholding the MBE set-aside. First was the unique remedial powers of Congress under §5 of the Fourteenth Amendment:

> . . . It is fundamental that in no organ of government, state or federal, does there repose a more comprehensive remedial power than in the Congress, expressly charged by the Constitution with competence and authority to enforce equal protection guarantees.

. . . [Chief Justice Burger also] focused on the evidence before Congress that a nationwide history of past discrimination had reduced minority participation in federal construction grants. . . . The Chief Justice concluded that "Congress had abundant historical basis from which it could conclude that traditional procurement practices, when applied to minority businesses, could perpetuate the effects of prior discrimination."

The second factor emphasized by the principal opinion in *Fullilove* was the flexible nature of the 10% set-aside. . . .

[In his concurring opinion, Justice Powell] made it clear that other governmental entities might have to show more than Congress before undertaking race-conscious measures: "The degree of specificity required in the findings of discrimination and the breadth of discretion in the choice of remedies may vary with the nature and authority of the governmental body."

Appellant and its supporting amici rely heavily on *Fullilove* for the proposition that a city council, like Congress, need not make specific findings of discrimination to engage in race-conscious relief. . . .

What appellant ignores is that Congress, unlike any State or political subdivision, has a specific constitutional mandate to enforce the dictates of the Fourteenth Amendment. The power to "enforce" may at times also include the power to define situations which Congress determines threaten principles of equality and to adopt prophylatic rules to deal with those situations. See Katzenbach v. Morgan. The Civil War Amendments themselves worked a dramatic change in the balance between congressional and state power over matters of race. . . .

That Congress may identify and redress the effects of society-wide discrimination does not mean that, a fortiori, the State and their political subdivisions are free to decide that such remedies are appropriate. Section 1 of the Fourteenth

Amendment is an explicit constraint on state power, and the States must undertake any remedial efforts in accordance with that provision. To hold otherwise would be to cede control over the content of the Equal Protection Clause to the 50 state legislatures and their myriad political subdivisions. The mere recitation of a benign or compensatory purpose for the use of a racial classification would essentially entitle the States to exercise the full power of Congress under §5 of the Fourteenth Amendment and insulate any racial classification from judicial scrutiny under §1. We believe that such a result would be contrary to the intentions of the Framers of the Fourteenth Amendment, who desired to place clear limits on the State's use of race as a criterion for legislative action, and to have the federal courts enforce those limitations. . . .

It would seem equally clear, however, that a state or local subdivision (if delegated the authority from the State) has the authority to eradicate the effects of private discrimination within its own legislative jurisdiction. . . . Our decision in *Wygant* is not to the contrary. . . . It was in the context of addressing the school board's power to adopt a race-based layoff program affecting its own work force that the *Wygant* plurality indicated that the Equal Protection Clause required "some showing of prior discrimination by the governmental unit involved." As a matter of state law, the city of Richmond has legislative authority over its procurement policies, and can use its spending powers to remedy private discrimination, if it identifies that discrimination with the particularity required by the Fourteenth Amendment. . . .

Thus, if the city could show that it had essentially become a "passive participant" in a system of racial exclusion practiced by elements of the local construction industry, we think it clear that the city could take affirmative steps to dismantle such a system. It is beyond dispute that any public entity, state or federal, has a compelling interest in assuring that public dollars, drawn from the tax contributions of all citizens, do not serve to finance the evil of private prejudice.

III

A

. . . As this Court has noted in the past, the "rights created by the first section of the Fourteenth Amendment are, by its terms, guaranteed to the individual. The rights established are personal rights." The Richmond Plan denies certain citizens the opportunity to compete for a fixed percentage of public contracts based solely upon their race. To whatever racial group these citizens belong, their "personal rights" to be treated with equal dignity and respect are implicated by a rigid rule erecting race as the sole criterion in an aspect of public decisionmaking.

Absent searching judicial inquiry into the justification for such race-based measures, there is simply no way of determining what classifications are "benign" or "remedial" and what classifications are in fact motivated by illegitimate notions of racial inferiority or simple racial politics. . . .

Classifications based on race carry a danger of stigmatic harm. Unless they are strictly reserved for remedial settings, they may in fact promote notions of racial inferiority and lead to a politics of racial hostility. We thus reaffirm the view expressed by the plurality in *Wygant* that the standard of review under the Equal

Protection Clause is not dependent on the race of those burdened or benefited by a particular classification.

Our continued adherence to the standard of review employed in *Wygant,* does not, as Justice Marshall's dissent suggests, indicate that we view "racial discrimination as largely a phenomenon of the past" or that "government bodies need no longer preoccupy themselves with rectifying racial injustice." . . . Rather, our interpretation of §1 stems from our agreement with the view expressed by Justice Powell in *Bakke,* that "[t]he guarantee of equal protection cannot mean one thing when applied to one individual and something else when applied to a person of another color."

Under the standard proposed by Justice Marshall's dissent, "[r]ace-conscious classifications designed to further remedial goals," are forthwith subject to a relaxed standard of review. How the dissent arrives at the legal conclusion that a racial classification is "designed to further remedial goals," without first engaging in an examination of the factual basis for its enactment and the nexus between its scope and that factual basis we are not told. However, once the "remedial" conclusion is reached, the dissent's standard is singularly deferential, and bears little resemblance to the close examination of legislative purpose we have engaged in when reviewing classifications based either on race or gender.

Even were we to accept a reading of the guarantee of equal protection under which the level of scrutiny varies according to the ability of different groups to defend their interests in the representative process, heightened scrutiny would still be appropriate in the circumstances of this case. One of the central arguments for applying a less exacting standard to "benign" racial classifications is that such measures essentially involve a choice made by dominant racial groups to disadvantage themselves. If one aspect of the judiciary's role under the Equal Protection Clause is to protect "discrete and insular minorities" from majoritarian prejudice or indifference, some maintain that these concerns are not implicated when the "white majority" places burdens upon itself. See J. Ely, Democracy and Distrust 170 (1980).

In this case, blacks comprise approximately 50% of the population of the city of Richmond. Five of the nine seats on the City Council are held by blacks. The concern that a political majority will more easily act to the disadvantage of a minority based on unwarranted assumptions or incomplete facts would seem to militate for, not against, the application of heightened judicial scrutiny in this case. See Ely, The Constitutionality of Reverse Racial Discrimination, 41 U. Chi. L. Rev. 723, 739, n.58 (1974) ("Of course it works both ways: a law that favors Blacks over Whites would be suspect if it were enacted by a predominantly Black legislature"). . . .

B

We think it clear that the factual predicate offered in support of the Richmond Plan suffers from the same two defects identified as fatal in *Wygant.* . . . Like the "role model" theory employed in *Wygant,* a generalized assertion that there has been past discrimination in an entire industry provides no guidance for a legislative body to determine the precise scope of the injury it seeks to remedy. It "has no logical stopping point." *Wygant.* "Relief" for such an ill-defined wrong could extend until the percentage of public contracts awarded to MBEs in Richmond mirrored the percentage of minorities in the population as a whole.

Appellant argues that it is attempting to remedy various forms of past discrimination that are alleged to be responsible for the small number of minority businesses in the local contracting industry. Among these the city cites the exclusion of blacks from skilled construction trade unions and training programs. This past discrimination has prevented them "from following the traditional path from laborer to entrepreneur." The city also lists a host of nonracial factors which would seem to face a member of any racial group attempting to establish a new business enterprise, such as deficiencies in working capital, inability to meet bonding requirements, unfamiliarity with bidding procedures, and disability caused by an inadequate track record.

While there is no doubt that the sorry history of both private and public discrimination in this country has contributed to a lack of opportunities for black entrepreneurs, this observation, standing alone, cannot justify a rigid racial quota in the awarding of public contracts in Richmond, Virginia. Like the claim that discrimination in primary and secondary schooling justifies a rigid racial preference in medical school admissions, an amorphous claim that there has been past discrimination in a particular industry cannot justify the use of an unyielding racial quota. . . .

Defining these sorts of injuries as "identified discrimination" would give local governments license to create a patchwork of racial preferences based on statistical generalizations about any particular field of endeavor.

These defects are readily apparent in this case. The 30% quota cannot in any realistic sense be tied to any injury suffered by anyone. The District Court relied upon five predicate "facts" in reaching its conclusion that there was an adequate basis for the 30% quota: (1) the ordinance declares itself to be remedial; (2) several proponents of the measure stated their views that there had been past discrimination in the construction industry; (3) minority businesses received .67% of prime contracts from the city while minorities constituted 50% of the city's population; (4) there were very few minority contractors in local and state contractors' associations; and (5) in 1977, Congress made a determination that the effects of past discrimination had stifled minority participation in the construction industry nationally.

None of these "findings," singly or together, provide the city of Richmond with a "strong basis in evidence for its conclusion that remedial action was necessary." There is nothing approaching a prima facie case of a constitutional or statutory violation by anyone in the Richmond construction industry.

The District Court accorded great weight to the fact that the city council designated the Plan as "remedial." But the mere recitation of a "benign" or legitimate purpose for a racial classification, is entitled to little or no weight. . . .

The District Court also relied on the highly conclusionary statement of a proponent of the Plan that there was racial discrimination in the construction industry "in this area, and the State, and around the nation." It also noted that the city manager had related his view that racial discrimination still plagued the construction industry in his home city of Pittsburg. These statements are of little probative value in establishing identified discrimination in the Richmond construction industry. The factfinding process of legislative bodies is generally entitled to a presumption of regulatory and deferential review by the judiciary. But when a legislative body chooses to employ a suspect classification, it cannot rest upon a generalized assertion as to the classification's relevance to its goals. . . .

Reliance on the disparity between the number of prime contracts awarded to minority firms and the minority population of the city of Richmond is similarly misplaced. . . .

In the employment context, we have recognized that for certain entry level positions or positions requiring minimal training, statistical comparisons of the racial composition of an employer's workforce to the racial composition of the relevant population may be probative of a pattern of discrimination. But where special qualifications are necessary, the relevant statistical pool for purposes of demonstrating discriminatory exclusion must be the number of minorities qualified to undertake the particular task.

In this case, the city does not even know how many MBEs in the relevant market are qualified to undertake prime or subcontracting work in public construction projects. Nor does the city know what percentage of total city construction dollars minority firms now receive as subcontractors on prime contracts let by the city.

To a large extent, the set-aside of subcontracting dollars seems to rest on the unsupported assumption that white prime contractors simply will not hire minority firms.[a] . . . Without any information on minority participation in subcontracting, it is quite simply impossible to evaluate overall minority representation in the city's construction expenditures.

The city and the District Court also relied on evidence that MBE membership in local contractors' associations was extremely low. Again, standing alone this evidence is not probative of any discrimination in the local construction industry. There are numerous explanations for this dearth of minority participation, including past societal discrimination in education and economic opportunities as well as both black and white career and entrepreneurial choices. . . . The mere fact that black membership in these trade organizations is low, standing alone, cannot establish a prima facie case of discrimination.

For low minority membership in these associations to be relevant, the city would have to link it to the number of local MBEs eligible for membership. If the statistical disparity between eligible MBEs and MBE membership were great enough, an inference of discriminatory exclusion could arise. In such a case, the city would have a compelling interest in preventing its tax dollars from assisting these organizations in maintaining a racially segregated construction market.

Finally, the city and the District Court relied on Congress' finding in connection with the set-aside approved in *Fullilove* that there had been nationwide discrimination in the construction industry. The probative value of these findings for demonstrating the existence of discrimination in Richmond is extremely limited. By its inclusion of a waiver procedure in the national program addressed in

a. Since 1975 the city of Richmond has had an ordinance on the books prohibiting both discrimination in the award of public contracts and employment discrimination by public contracts. The city points to no evidence that its prime contracts have been violating the ordinance in either their employment or subcontracting practices. The complete silence of the record concerning enforcement of the city's own anti-discrimination ordinance flies in the face of the dissent's vision of a "tight-knit industry" which has prevented blacks from obtaining the experience necessary to participate in construction contracting.

Fullilove, Congress explicitly recognized that the scope of the problem would vary from market area to market area.

Moreover, as noted above, Congress was exercising its powers under §5 of the Fourteenth Amendment. . . . While the States and their subdivisions may take remedial action when they possess evidence that their own spending practices are exacerbating a pattern of prior discrimination, they must identify that discrimination, public or private, with some specificity before they may use race-conscious relief. . . . If all a state or local government need do is find a congressional report on the subject to enact a set-aside program, the constraints of the Equal Protection Clause will, in effect, have been rendered a nullity.

. . . The "evidence" relied upon by the dissent, the history of school desegregation in Richmond and numerous congressional reports, does little to define the scope of any injury to minority contractors in Richmond or the necessary remedy. The facts relied upon by the dissent could justify a preference of any size or duration. . . .

In sum, none of the evidence presented by the city points to any identified discrimination in the Richmond construction industry. We, therefore, hold that the city has failed to demonstrate a compelling interest in apportioning public contracting opportunities on the basis of race. . . .

The foregoing analysis applies only to the inclusion of blacks within the Richmond set-aside program. There is absolutely no evidence of past discrimination against Spanish-speaking, Oriental, Indian, Eskimo, or Aleut persons in any aspect of the Richmond construction industry. . . . The random inclusion of racial groups that, as a practical matter, may never have suffered from discrimination in the construction industry in Richmond, suggests that perhaps the city's purpose was not in fact to remedy past discrimination. . . .

IV

As noted by the court below, it is almost impossible to assess whether the Richmond Plan is narrowly tailored to remedy prior discrimination since it is not linked to identified discrimination in any way. We limit ourselves to two observations in this regard.

First, there does not appear to have been any consideration of the use of race-neutral means to increase minority business participation in city contracting. Many of the barriers to minority participation in the construction industry relied upon by the city to justify a racial classification appear to be race neutral. If MBEs disproportionately lack capital or cannot meet bonding requirements, a race-neutral program of city financing for small firms would, a fortiori, lead to greater minority participation. The principal opinion in *Fullilove* found that Congress had carefully examined and rejected race-neutral alternatives before enacting the MBE set-aside. There is no evidence in this record that the Richmond City Council has considered any alternatives to a race-based quota.

Second, the 30% quota cannot be said to be narrowly tailored to any goal, except perhaps outright racial balancing. It rests upon the "completely unrealistic" assumption that minorities will choose a particular trade in lockstep proportion to their representation in the local population. . . .

As noted above, the congressional scheme upheld in *Fullilove* allowed for a waiver of the set-aside provision where an MBE's higher price was not attributable to the effects of past discrimination. Based upon proper findings, such programs are less problematic from an equal protection standpoint because they treat all candidates individually, rather than making the color of an applicant's skin the sole relevant consideration. Unlike the program upheld in *Fullilove*, the Richmond Plan's waiver system focuses solely on the availability of MBEs; there is no inquiry into whether or not the particular MBE seeking a racial preference has suffered from the effects of past discrimination by the city or prime contractors.

Given the existence of an individualized procedure, the city's only interest in maintaining a quota system rather than investigating the need for remedial action in particular cases would seem to be simple administrative convenience. But the interest in avoiding the bureaucratic effort necessary to tailor remedial relief to those who truly have suffered the effects of prior discrimination cannot justify a rigid line drawn on the basis of a suspect classification. Under Richmond's scheme, a successful black, Hispanic, or Oriental entrepreneur from anywhere in the country enjoys an absolute preference over other citizens based solely on their race. We think it obvious that such a program is not narrowly tailored to remedy the effects of prior discrimination.

V

Nothing we say today precludes a state or local entity from taking action to rectify the effects of identified discrimination within its jurisdiction. If the city of Richmond had evidence before it that nonminority contractors were systematically excluding minority businesses from subcontracting opportunities it could take action to end the discriminatory exclusion. Where there is a significant statistical disparity between the number of qualified minority contractors willing and able to perform a particular service and the number of such contractors actually engaged by the locality or the locality's prime contractors, an inference of discriminatory exclusion could arise. Under such circumstances, the city could act to dismantle the closed business system by taking appropriate measures against those who discriminate on the basis of race or other illegitimate criteria. In the extreme case, some form of narrowly tailored racial preference might be necessary to break down patterns of deliberate exclusion.

Nor is local government powerless to deal with individual instances of racially motivated refusals to employ minority contractors. Where such discrimination occurs, a city would be justified in penalizing the discriminator and providing appropriate relief to the victim of such discrimination. Moreover, evidence of a pattern of individual discriminatory acts can, if supported by appropriate statistical proof, lend support to a local government's determination that broader remedial relief is justified.

Even in the absence of evidence of discrimination, the city has at its disposal a whole array of race-neutral devices to increase the accessibility of city contracting opportunities to small entrepreneurs of all races. Simplification of bidding procedures, relaxation of bonding requirements, and training and financial aid for disadvantaged entrepreneurs of all races would open the public contracting market to all those who have suffered the effects of past societal discrimination or neglect. . . . Business as usual should not mean business pursuant to the unthinking exclusion of certain members of our society from its rewards.

In the case at hand, . . . it is simply impossible to say that the city has demonstrated "a strong basis in evidence for its conclusion that remedial action was necessary." *Wygant.*

Proper findings in this regard are necessary to define both the scope of the injury and the extent of the remedy necessary to cure its effects. Such findings also serve to assure all citizens that the deviation from the norm of equal treatment of all racial and ethnic groups is a temporary matter, a measure taken in the service of the goal of equality itself. Absent such findings, there is a danger that a racial classification is merely the product of unthinking stereotypes or a form of racial politics. . . . Because the city of Richmond has failed to identify the need for remedial action in the awarding of its public construction contracts, its treatment of its citizens on a racial basis violates the dictates of the Equal Protection Clause. Accordingly, the judgment of the Court of Appeals for the Fourth Circuit is Affirmed.

STEVENS, J., concurring in part and concurring in the judgment.

A central purpose of the Fourteenth Amendment is to further the national goal of equal opportunity for all our citizens. In order to achieve that goal we must learn from our past mistakes, but I believe the Constitution requires us to evaluate our policy decisions — including those that govern the relationships among different racial and ethnic groups — primarily by studying their probable impact on the future. I therefore do not agree with the premise that seems to underlie today's decision. . . that governmental decision that rests on a racial classification is never permissible except as a remedy for a past wrong.[a] I do, however, agree with the Court's explanation of why the Richmond ordinance cannot be justified as a remedy for past discrimination, and therefore join Parts I, III-B, and IV of its opinion. I write separately to emphasize three aspects of the case that are of special importance to me.

First, the city makes no claim that the public interest in the efficient performance of its construction contracts will be served by granting a preference to minority-business enterprises. This case is therefore completely unlike *Wygant*, in which I thought it quite obvious that the School Board had reasonably concluded that an integrated faculty could provide educational benefits to the entire student body that could not be provided by an all-white, or nearly all-white faculty. . . .

Second, this litigation involves an attempt by a legislative body, rather than a court, to fashion a remedy for a past wrong. Legislatures are primarily policy-making bodies that promulgate rules to govern future conduct. . . . It is the judicial system, rather than the legislative process, that is best equipped to identify

a. In my view the Court's approach to this case gives unwarranted deference to race-based legislative action that purports to serve a purely remedial goal, and overlooks the potential value of race-based determinations that may serve other valid purposes. With regard to the former point . . . I am not prepared to assume that even a more narrowly tailored set-aside program supported by stronger findings would be constitutionally justified. Unless the legislature can identify both the particular victims and the particular perpetrators of past discrimination, which is precisely what a court does when it makes findings of fact and conclusions of law, a remedial justification for race-based legislation will almost certainly sweep too broadly. With regard to the latter point: I think it unfortunate that the Court in neither *Wygant* nor this case seems prepared to acknowledge that some race-based policy decisions may serve a legitimate public purpose. I agree, of course, that race is so seldom relevant to legislative decisions on how best to foster the public good that legitimate justifications for race-based legislation will usually not be available. But unlike the Court, I would not totally discount the legitimacy of race-based decisions that may produce tangible and fully justified future benefits.

past wrongdoers and to fashion remedies that will create the conditions that presumably would have existed had no wrong been committed.

Third, instead of engaging in a debate over the proper standard of review to apply in affirmative-action litigation, I believe it is more constructive to try to identify the characteristics of the advantaged and disadvantaged classes that may justify their disparate treatment. In this case that approach convinces me that, instead of carefully identifying the characteristics of the two classes of contractors that are respectively favored and disfavored by its ordinance, the Richmond City Council has merely engaged in the type of stereotypical analysis that is a hallmark of violations of the Equal Protection Clause. Whether we look at the class of persons benefited by the ordinance or at the disadvantaged class, the same conclusion emerges.

The justification for the ordinance is the fact that in the past white contractors — and presumably other white citizens in Richmond — have discriminated against black contractors. The class of persons benefited by the ordinance is not, however, limited to victims of such discrimination — it encompasses persons who have never been in business in Richmond as well as minority contractors who may have been guilty of discriminating against members of other minority groups. Indeed, for all the record shows, all of the minority-business enterprises that have benefited from the ordinance may be firms that have prospered notwithstanding the discriminatory conduct that may have harmed other minority firms years ago. Ironically, minority firms that have survived in the competitive struggle, rather than those that have perished, are most likely to benefit from an ordinance of this kind.

The ordinance is equally vulnerable because of its failure to identify the characteristics of the disadvantaged class of white contractors that justify the disparate treatment. . . . Thus, the composition of the disadvantaged class of white contractors presumably includes some who have been guilty of unlawful discrimination, some who practiced discrimination before it was forbidden by law, and some who have never discriminated against anyone on the basis of race. Imposing a common burden on such a disparate class merely because each member of the class is of the same race stems from reliance on a stereotype rather than fact or reason.

There is a special irony in the stereotypical thinking that prompts legislation of this kind. Although it stigmatizes the disadvantaged class with the unproven charge of past racial discrimination, it actually imposes a greater stigma on its supposed beneficiaries. . . .

Accordingly, I concur in parts I, III-B, and IV of the Court's opinion, and in the judgment.

KENNEDY, J., concurring in part and concurring in the judgment.

I join all but Part II of Justice O'Connor's opinion and give this further explanation. . . .

The process by which a law that is an equal protection violation when enacted by a State becomes transformed to an equal protection guarantee when enacted by Congress poses a difficult proposition for me; but as it is not before us, any reconsideration of that issue must await some further case. For purposes of the ordinance challenged here, it suffices to say that the State has the power to eradicate racial discrimination and its effects in both the public and private sectors, and the absolute duty to do so where those wrongs were caused intentionally by the State itself. The Fourteenth Amendment ought not to be interpreted to reduce a State's authority in this regard, unless, of course, there is a conflict with federal law or a state remedy is itself a violation of equal protection. The latter is the case presented here.

The moral imperative of racial neutrality is the driving force of the Equal Protection Clause. Justice Scalia's opinion underscores this position, quite properly, in my view. The rule suggested in his opinion, which would strike down all preferences which are not necessary remedies to victims of unlawful discrimination, would eliminate the necessity for courts to pass upon each racial preference that is enacted. . . .

Nevertheless, given that a rule of automatic invalidity for racial preferences in almost every case would be a significant break with our precedents that require a case-by-case test, I am not convinced we need adopt it at this point. On the assumption that it will vindicate the principle of race neutrality found in the Equal Protection Clause, I accept the less absolute rule contained in Justice O'Connor's opinion, a rule based on the proposition that any racial preference must face the most rigorous scrutiny by the courts. My reasons for doing so are as follows. First, I am confident that, in application, the strict scrutiny standard will operate in a manner generally consistent with the imperative of race neutrality, because it forbids the use even of narrowly drawn racial classifications except as a last resort. Second, the rule against race-conscious remedies is already less than an absolute one, for that relief may be the only adequate remedy after a judicial determination that a State or its instrumentality has violated the Equal Protection Clause. I note, in this connection, that evidence which would support a judicial finding of intentional discrimination may suffice also to justify remedial legislative action, for it diminishes the constitutional responsibilities of the political branches to say they must wait to act until ordered to do so by a court. Third, the strict scrutiny rule is consistent with our precedents, as Justice O'Connor's opinion demonstrates.

The ordinance before us falls far short of the standard we adopt. [The ordinance is] open to the fair charge that is not a remedy but is itself a preference which will cause the same corrosive animosities that the Constitution forbids in the whole sphere of government and that our national policy condemns in the rest of society as well. . . .

SCALIA, J., concurring in the judgment.

I agree with much of the Court's opinion, and, in particular, with its conclusion that strict scrutiny must be applied to all governmental classification by race, whether or not its asserted purpose is "remedial" or "benign." I do not agree, however, with the Court's dicta suggesting that, despite the Fourteenth Amendment, state and local governments may in some circumstances discriminate on the basis of race in order (in a broad sense) "to ameliorate the effects of past discrimination." The benign purpose of compensating for social disadvantages, whether they have been acquired by reason of prior discrimination or otherwise, can no more be pursued by the illegitimate means of racial discrimination than can other assertedly benign purposes we have repeatedly rejected. The difficulty of overcoming the effects of past discrimination is as nothing compared with the difficulty of eradicating from our society the source of those effects, which is the tendency — fatal to a nation such as ours — to classify and judge men and women on the basis of their country of origin or the color of their skin. A solution to the first problem that aggravates the second is no solution at all. . . .

We have in some contexts approved the use of racial classifications by the Federal Government to remedy the effects of past discrimination. I do not believe that we must or should extend those holdings to the States. . . .

A sound distinction between federal and state (or local) action based on race rests not only upon the substance of the Civil War Amendments, but upon social reality and governmental theory. . . . The struggle for racial justice has historically been a struggle by the national society against oppression in the individual States. And the struggle retains that character in modern times. . . . What the record shows, in other words, is that racial discrimination against any group finds a more ready expression at the state and local than at the federal level. To the children of the Founding Fathers, this should come as no surprise. An acute awareness of the heightened danger of oppression from political factions in small, rather than large, political units dates to the very beginning of our national history. . . .

Richmond [enacted] a set-aside clearly and directly beneficial to the dominant political group, which happens also to be the dominant racial group. The same thing has no doubt happened before in other cities (though the racial basis of the preference has rarely been made textually explicit) — and blacks have often been on the receiving end of the injustice. Where injustice is the game, however, turnabout is not fair play.

In my view there is only one circumstance in which the States may act by race to "undo the effects of past discrimination": where that is necessary to eliminate their own maintenance of a system of unlawful racial classification. . . .

A State can, of course, act "to undo the effects of past discrimination" in many permissible ways that do not involve classification by race. . . . And, of course, a State may "undo the effects of past discrimination" in the sense of giving the identified victim of state discrimination that which it wrongfully denied him. . . . That is worlds apart from the system here, in which those to be disadvantaged are identified solely by race.

I agree with the Court's dictum that a fundamental distinction must be drawn between the effects of "societal" discrimination and the effects of "identified" discrimination, and that the situation would be different if Richmond's plan were "tailored" to identify those particular bidders who "suffered from the effects of past discrimination by the city or prime contractors." In my view, however, the reason that would make a difference is not, as the Court states, that it would justify race-conscious action, but rather that it would enable race-neutral remediation. . . . In other words, far from justifying racial classification, identification of actual victims of discrimination makes it less supportable than ever, because more obviously unneeded. . . .

It is plainly true that in our society blacks have suffered discrimination immeasurably greater than any directed at other racial groups. But those who believe that racial preferences can help to "even the score" display, and reinforce, a manner of thinking by race that was the source of the injustice and that will, if it endures within our society, be the source of more injustice still. . . . Racial preferences appear to "even the score" (in some small degree) only if one embraces the proposition that our society is appropriately viewed as divided into races, making it right that an injustice rendered in the past to a black man should be compensated for by discriminating against a white. Nothing is worth that embrace. Since blacks have been disproportionately disadvantaged by racial discrimination, any race-neutral remedial program aimed at the disadvantaged as such will have a disproportionately beneficial impact on blacks. Only such a program, and not one that operates on the basis of race, is in accord with the letter and the spirit of our Constitution.

Since I believe that the appellee here had a constitutional right to have its bid succeed or fail under a decisionmaking process uninfected with racial bias, I concur in the judgment of the Court.

MARSHALL, BLACKMUN, and BRENNAN, JJ., dissenting.

It is a welcome symbol of racial progress when the former capital of the Confederacy acts forthrightly to confront the effects of racial discrimination in its midst. In my view, nothing in the Constitution can be construed to prevent Richmond, Virginia, from allocating a portion of its contracting dollars for businesses owned or controlled by members of minority groups. . . .

A majority of this Court holds today, however, that the Equal Protection Clause of the Fourteenth Amendment blocks Richmond's initiative. The essence of the majority's position is that Richmond has failed to catalogue adequate findings to prove that past discrimination has impeded minorities from joining or participating fully in Richmond's construction contracting industry. I find deep irony in second-guessing Richmond's judgment on this point. As much as any municipality in the United States, Richmond knows what racial discrimination is; a century of decisions by this and other federal courts has richly documented the city's disgraceful history of public and private racial discrimination. In any event, the Richmond City Council has supported its determination that minorities have been wrongly excluded from local construction contracting. Its proof includes statistics showing that minority-owned businesses have received virtually no city contracting dollars and rarely if ever belonged to area trade associations; testimony by municipal officials that discrimination has been widespread in the local construction industry; and the same exhaustive and widely publicized federal studies relied on in *Fullilove*, studies which showed that pervasive discrimination in the Nation's tight-knit construction industry had operated to exclude minorities from public contracting. These are precisely the types of statistical and testimonial evidence which, until today, this Court had credited in cases approving of race-conscious measures designed to remedy past discrimination.

More fundamentally, today's decision marks a deliberate and giant step backward in this Court's affirmative action jurisprudence. Cynical of one municipality's attempt to redress the effects of past racial discrimination in a particular industry, the majority launches a grapeshot attack on race-conscious remedies in general. The majority's unnecessary pronouncements will inevitably discourage or prevent governmental entities, particularly States and localities, from acting to rectify the scourge of past discrimination. This is the harsh reality of the majority's decision, but it is not the Constitution's command.

I

As an initial matter . . . the majority downplays the fact that the City Council had before it a rich trove of evidence that discrimination in the Nation's construction industry had seriously impaired the competitive position of businesses owned or controlled by members of minority groups. . . . The majority's refusal to recognize that Richmond has proven itself no exception to the dismaying pattern of national exclusion which Congress so painstakingly identified infects its entire analysis of this case. . . .

The congressional program upheld in *Fullilove* was based upon an array of congressional and agency studies which documented the powerful influence of racially exclusionary practices in the business world. A 1975 report by the House Committee on Small Business concluded:

> The effects of past inequities stemming from racial prejudice have not remained in the past. The Congress has recognized the reality that past discriminatory practices have, to some degree, adversely affected our present economic system.
>
> "While minority persons comprise about 16 percent of the Nation's population, of the 13 million businesses in the United States, only 382,000, or approximately 3.0 percent, are owned by minority individuals. The most recent data from the Department of Commerce also indicates that the gross receipts of all businesses in this country totals about $2,540.8 billion, and of this amount only $16.6 billion, or about 0.65 percent was realized by minority business concerns. . . .
>
> Currently, we more often encounter a business system which is racially neutral on its face, but because of past overt social and economic discrimination is presently operating, in effect, to perpetuate these past inequities. Minorities, until recently, have not participated to any measurable extent, in our total business system generally, or in the construction industry in particular."

Congress further found that minorities seeking initial public contracting assignments often faced immense entry barriers which did not confront experienced nonminority contractors. . . .

Thus, as of 1977, there was "abundant evidence" in the public domain "that minority businesses ha[d] been denied effective participation in public contracting opportunities by procurement practices that perpetuated the effects of prior discrimination." Significantly, this evidence demonstrated that discrimination had prevented existing or nascent minority-owned businesses from obtaining not only federal contracting assignments, but state and local ones as well.[a]

The members of the Richmond City Council were well aware of these exhaustive congressional findings, a point the majority, tellingly, elides. The transcript of the session at which the Council enacted the local set-aside initiative contains numerous references to the 6-year-old congressional set-aside program, to the evidence of nationwide discrimination barriers described above, and to the *Fullilove* decision itself.

The City Council's members also heard . . . testimony from city official as to the exclusionary history of the local construction industry. As the District Court

a. Numerous congressional studies undertaken after 1977 and issued before the Richmond City Council convened in April 1983 found that the exclusion of minorities had continued virtually unabated — and that, because of this legacy of discrimination, minority businesses across the nation had still failed, as of 1983, to gain a real toehold in the business world. . . .

noted, not a single person who testified before the City Council denied that discrimination in Richmond's construction industry had been widespread. So long as one views Richmond's local evidence of discrimination against the backdrop of systematic nationwide racial discrimination which Congress had so painstakingly identified in this very industry, this case is readily resolved.

II

. . . My view has long been that race-conscious classifications designed to further remedial goals "must serve important governmental objectives and must be substantially related to achievement of those objectives" in order to withstand constitutional scrutiny. Analyzed in terms of this two-prong standard, Richmond's set-aside, like the federal program on which it was modeled, is "plainly constitutional."

A

1

Turning first to the governmental interest inquiry, Richmond has two powerful interests in setting aside a portion of public contracting funds for minority-owned enterprises. The first is the city's interest in eradicating the effects of past racial discrimination. It is far too late in the day to doubt that remedying such discrimination is a compelling, let alone an important, interest. . . .

Richmond has a second compelling interest in setting aside, where possible, a portion of its contracting dollars. That interest is the prospective one of preventing the city's own spending decisions from reinforcing and perpetuating the exclusionary effects of past discrimination. . . .

The majority is wrong to trivialize the continuing impact of government acceptance or use of private institutions or structures once wrought by discrimination. When government channels all its contracting funds to a white-dominated community of established contractors whose racial homogeneity is the product of private discrimination, it does more than place its imprimatur on the practices which forged and which continue to define that community. It also provides a measurable boost to those economic entities that have thrived within it, while denying important economic benefits to those entities which, but for prior discrimination, might well be better qualified to receive valuable government contracts. In my view, the interest in ensuring that the government does not reflect and reinforce prior private discrimination in dispensing public contracts is every bit as strong as the interest in eliminating private discrimination — an interest which this Court has repeatedly deemed compelling. . . . Cities like Richmond may not be constitutionally required to adopt set-aside plans. But there can be no doubt that when Richmond acted affirmatively to stem the perpetuation of patterns of discrimination through its own decisionmaking, it served an interest of the highest order.

2

The remaining question with respect to the "governmental interest" prong of equal protection analysis is whether Richmond has proffered satisfactory proof of past racial discrimination to support its twin interests in remediation and in governmental nonperpetuation. Although the Members of this Court have differed on the appropriate standard of review for race-conscious remedial measures, we have always regarded this factual inquiry as a practical one. Thus, the Court has eschewed rigid tests which require the provision of particular species of evidence, statistical or otherwise. At the same time we have required that government adduce evidence that, taken as a whole, is sufficient to support its claimed interest and to dispel the natural concern that it acted out of mere "paternalistic stereotyping, not on a careful consideration of modern social conditions." . . . Our unwillingness to go beyond . . . generalized standards to require specific types of proof in all circumstances reflects, in my view, an understanding that discrimination takes a myriad of "ingenious and pervasive forms." The varied body of evidence on which Richmond relied provides a "strong," "firm," and "unquestionably legitimate" basis upon which the City Council could determine that the effects of past racial discrimination warranted a remedial and prophylactic governmental response. . . . Richmond acted against a backdrop of congressional and Executive Branch studies which demonstrated with such force the nationwide pervasiveness of prior discrimination that Congress presumed that " 'present economic inequities' " in construction contracting resulted from " 'past discriminatory systems.' " The city's local evidence confirmed that Richmond's construction industry did not deviate from this pernicious national pattern. The fact that just .67% of public construction expenditures over the previous five years had gone to minority-owned prime contractors, despite the city's racially mixed population, strongly suggest that construction contracting in the area was rife with "present economic inequities." To the extent this enormous disparity did not itself demonstrate that discrimination had occurred, the descriptive testimony of Richmond's elected and appointed leaders drew the necessary link between the pitifully small presence of minorities in construction contracting and past exclusionary practices. That no one who testified challenged this depiction of widespread racial discrimination in area construction contracting lent significant weight to these accounts. The fact that area trade associations had virtually no minority members dramatized the extent of present inequities and suggested the lasting power of past discriminatory systems. In sum, to suggest that the facts on which Richmond has relied do not provide a sound basis for its finding of past racial discrimination simply blinks credibility. . . .

[T]he majority's criticisms of individual items of Richmond's evidence rest on flimsy foundations. The majority states, for example, that reliance on the disparity between the share of city contracts awarded to minority firms (.67%) and the minority population of Richmond (approximately 50%) is "misplaced." It is true that, when the factual predicate needed to be proved is one of present discrimination, we have generally credited statistical contrasts between the racial composition of a work force and the general population as proving discrimination only where this contrast revealed "gross statistical disparities." But this principle does not impugn Richmond's statistical contrast, for two reasons. First, considering how minuscule the share of Richmond public construction contracting dollars received by minority-owned businesses is, it is hardly unreasonable to conclude that this case involves a "gross statistical disparit[y]." . . .

Second, and more fundamentally, where the issue is not present discrimination but rather whether past discrimination has resulted in the continuing exclusion of minorities from an historically tight-knit industry, a contrast between population and work force is entirely appropriate to help gauge the degree of the exclusion. . . . This contrast is especially illuminating in cases like this, where a main avenue of introduction into the work force — here, membership in the trade associations whose members presumably train apprentices and help them procure subcontracting assignments — is itself grossly dominated by nonminorities. The majority's assertion that the city "does not even know how many MBE's in the relevant market are qualified" is thus entirely beside the point. If Richmond indeed has a monochromatic contracting community — a conclusion reached by the District Court — this most likely reflects the lingering power of past exclusionary practices. Certainly this is the explanation Congress has found persuasive at the national level. The city's requirement that prime public contractors set aside 30% of their subcontracting assignments for minority-owned enterprises, subject to the ordinance's provision for waivers where minority-owned enterprises are unavailable or unwilling to participate, is designed precisely to ease minority contractors into the industry.

The majority's perfunctory dismissal of the testimony of Richmond's appointed and elected leaders is also deeply disturbing. . . . [B]y disregarding the testimony of local leaders and the judgment of local government, the majority does violence to the very principles of comity within our federal system which this Court has long championed. Local officials, by virtue of their proximity to, and their expertise with, local affairs, are exceptionally well-qualified to make determinations of public good "within their respective spheres of authority." The majority, however, leaves any traces of comity behind in its headlong rush to strike down Richmond's race-conscious measure.

Had the majority paused for a moment on the facts of the Richmond experience, it would have discovered that the city's leadership is deeply familiar with what racial discrimination is. The members of the Richmond City Council have spent long years witnessing multifarious acts of discrimination, including, but not limited to, the deliberate diminution of black residents' voting rights, resistance to school desegregation, and publicly sanctioned housing discrimination. Numerous decisions of federal courts chronicle this disgraceful recent history. . . .

When the legislatures and leaders of cities with histories of pervasive discrimination testify that past discrimination has infected one of their industries, armchair cynicism like that exercised by the majority has no place. . . . Disbelief is particularly inappropriate here in light of the fact that appellee Croson, which had the burden of proving unconstitutionality at trial, has at no point come forward with any direct evidence that the City Council's motives were anything other than sincere.

Finally, I vehemently disagree with the majority's dismissal of the congressional and Executive Branch findings noted in *Fullilove* as having "extremely limited" probative value in this case. . . . The majority, inexplicably, would forbid Richmond to "share" in this information, and permit only Congress to take note of these ample findings. In thus requiring that Richmond's local evidence be severed from the context in which it was prepared, the majority would require cities seeking to eradicate the effects of past discrimination within their borders to reinvent the evidentiary wheel and engage in unnecessarily duplicative, costly, and time-consuming factfinding.

No principle of federalism or of federal power, however, forbids a state or local government from drawing upon a nationally relevant historical record prepared by the Federal Government. Of course, Richmond could have built an even more compendious record of past discrimination, one including additional stark statistics and additional individual accounts of past discrimination. But nothing in the Fourteenth Amendment imposes such onerous documentary obligations upon States and localities once the reality of past discrimination is apparent.

B

In my judgment, Richmond's set-aside plan also comports with the second prong of the equal protection inquiry, for it is substantially related to the interests it seeks to serve in remedying past discrimination and in ensuring that municipal contract procurement does not perpetuate that discrimination. The most striking aspect of the city's ordinance is the similarity it bears to the "appropriately limited" federal set-aside provision upheld in *Fullilove*. Like the federal provision, Richmond's is limited to five years in duration and was not renewed when it came up for reconsideration in 1988. Like the federal provision, Richmond's contains a waiver provision freeing from its subcontracting requirements those nonminority firms that demonstrate that they cannot comply with its provisions. Like the federal provision, Richmond's has a minimal impact on innocent third parties. While the measure affects 30% of public contracting dollars, that translates to only 3% of overall Richmond area contracting.

Finally, like the federal provision, Richmond's does not interfere with any vested right of a contractor to a particular contract; instead it operates entirely prospectively. . . .

The majority takes issue . . . with two aspects of Richmond's tailoring: the city's refusal to explore the use of race-neutral measures to increase minority business participation in contracting and the selection of a 30% set-aside figure. The majority's first criticism is flawed in two respects. First, the majority overlooks the fact that since 1975, Richmond has barred both discrimination by the city in awarding public contracts and discrimination by public contractors. The virtual absence of minority businesses from the city's contracting rolls, indicated by the fact that such businesses have received less than 1% of public contracting dollars, strongly suggests that this ban has not succeeded in redressing the impact of past discrimination or in preventing city contract procurement from reinforcing racial homogeneity. Second, the majority's suggestion that Richmond should have first undertaken such race-neutral measures as a program of city financing for small firms ignores the fact that such measures, while theoretically appealing, have been discredited by Congress as ineffectual in eradicating the effects of past discrimination in this very industry. . . .[b]

As for Richmond's 30% target, the majority states that this figure "cannot be said to be narrowly tailored to any goal, except perhaps outright racial bal-

b. The majority also faults Richmond's ordinance for including within its definition of "minority group members" not only black citizens, but also citizens who are "Spanish-speaking, Oriental, Indian, Eskimo, or Aleut persons." This is, of course, precisely the same definition Congress adopted in its set-aside legislation. Even accepting the majority's view that Richmond's ordinance is overbroad because it includes groups, such as Eskimos or Aleuts, about whom no evidence of local discrimination has been proffered, it does not necessarily follow that the balance of Richmond's ordinance should be invalidated.

ancing." The majority ignores two important facts. First, the set-aside measure affects only 3% of overall city contracting; thus, any imprecision in tailoring has far less impact than the majority suggests. But more important, the majority ignores the fact that Richmond's 30% figure was patterned directly on the *Fullilove* precedent. Congress' 10% figure fell "roughly halfway between the present percentage of minority contractors and the percentage of minority group members in the Nation." The Richmond City Council's 30% figure similarly falls roughly halfway between the present percentage of Richmond-based minority contractors (almost zero) and the percentage of minorities in Richmond (50%). In faulting Richmond for not presenting a different explanation for its choice of a set-aside figure, the majority honors *Fullilove* only in the breach.

III

I would ordinarily end my analysis at this point and conclude that Richmond's ordinance satisfies both the governmental interest and substantial relationship prongs of our Equal Protection Clause analysis. However, I am compelled to add more, for the majority has gone beyond the facts of this case to announce a set of principles which unnecessarily restrict the power of governmental entities to take race-conscious measures to redress the effects of prior discrimination.

A

Today, for the first time, a majority of this Court has adopted strict scrutiny as its standard of Equal Protection Clause review of race-conscious remedial measures. This is an unwelcome development. A profound difference separates governmental actions that themselves are racist, and governmental actions that seek to remedy the effects of prior racism or to prevent neutral governmental activity from perpetuating the effects of such racism.

Racial classifications "drawn on the presumption that one race is inferior to another or because they put the weight of government behind racial hatred and separatism" warrant the strictest judicial scrutiny because of the very irrelevance of these rationales. By contrast, racial classifications drawn for the purpose of remedying the effects of discrimination that itself was race-based have a highly pertinent basis: the tragic and indelible fact that discrimination against blacks and other racial minorities in this Nation has pervaded our Nation's history and continues to scar our society. . . .

In concluding that remedial classifications warrant no different standard of review under the Constitution than the most brute and repugnant forms of state-sponsored racism, a majority of this Court signals that it regards racial discrimination as largely a phenomenon of the past, and that government bodies need no longer preoccupy themselves with rectifying racial injustice. I, however, do not believe this Nation is anywhere close to eradicating racial discrimination or its vestiges. In constitutionalizing its wishful thinking, the majority today does a grave disservice not only to those victims of past and present racial discrimination in this Nation whom government has sought to assist, but also to this Court's long tradition of approaching issues of race with the utmost sensitivity.

B

I am also troubled by the majority's assertion that, even if it did not believe generally in strict scrutiny of race-based remedial measures, "the circumstances of this case" require this Court to look upon the Richmond City Council's measure with the strictest scrutiny. The sole such circumstance which the majority cites, however, is the fact that blacks in Richmond are a "dominant racial grou[p]" in the city. In support of this characterization of dominance, the majority observes that "blacks comprise approximately 50% of the population of the city of Richmond" and that "[f]ive of the nine seats on the City Council are held by blacks."

While I agree that the numerical and political supremacy of a given racial group is a factor bearing upon the level of scrutiny to be applied, this Court has never held that numerical inferiority, standing alone, makes a racial group "suspect" and thus entitled to strict scrutiny review. Rather, we have identified other "traditional indicia of suspectness": whether a group has been "saddled with such disabilities, or subjected to such a history of purposeful unequal treatment, or relegated to such a position of political powerlessness as to command extraordinary protection from the majoritarian political process."

It cannot seriously be suggested that nonminorities in Richmond have any "history of purposeful unequal treatment." Nor is there any indication that they have any of the disabilities that have characteristically afflicted those groups this Court has deemed suspect. Indeed, the numerical and political dominance of nonminorities within the State of Virginia and the Nation as a whole provide an enormous political check against the "simple racial politics" at the municipal level which the majority fears. If the majority really believes that groups like Richmond's nonminorities, which comprise approximately half the population but which are outnumbered even marginally in political fora, are deserving of suspect class status for these reasons alone, this Court's decisions denying suspect status to women and to persons with below-average incomes stand on extremely shaky ground.

In my view, the "circumstances of this case," underscore the importance of not subjecting to a strict scrutiny straitjacket the increasing number of cities which have recently come under minority leadership and are eager to rectify, or at least prevent the perpetuation of, past racial discrimination. . . . This history of "purposefully unequal treatment" forced upon minorities, not imposed by them, should raise an inference that minorities in Richmond had much to remedy — and that the 1983 set-aside was undertaken with sincere remedial goals in mind, not "simple racial politics.". . . .

The majority's view that remedial measures undertaken by municipalities with black leadership must face a stiffer test of Equal Protection Clause scrutiny than remedial measures undertaken by municipalities with white leadership implies a lack of political maturity on the part of this Nation's elected minority officials that is totally unwarranted. Such insulting judgments have no place in constitutional jurisprudence.

C

Today's decision, finally, is particularly noteworthy for the daunting standard it imposes upon States and localities contemplating the use of race-conscious measures to eradicate the present effects of prior discrimination and prevent its perpetuation. The majority restricts the use of such measures to situations in which a State or locality can put forth "a prima facie case of a constitutional or statutory violation." . . .

Nothing in the Constitution or in the prior decisions of this Court supports limiting state authority to confront the effects of past discrimination to those situations in which a prima facie case of a constitutional or statutory violation can be made out. By its very terms, the majority's standard effectively cedes control of a large component of the content of that constitutional provision to Congress and to state legislatures. If an antecedent Virginia or Richmond law had defined as unlawful the award to nonminorities of an overwhelming share of a city's contracting dollars, for example, Richmond's subsequent set-aside initiative would then satisfy the majority's standard. But without such a law, the initiative might not withstand constitutional scrutiny. The meaning of "equal protection of the laws" thus turns on the happenstance of whether a State or local body has previously defined illegal discrimination. . . .

[Similarly, i]f Congress tomorrow dramatically expanded Title VII . . . or alternatively, if it repealed that legislation altogether — the meaning of equal protection would change precipitously along with it. Whatever the Framers of the Fourteenth Amendment had in mind in 1868, it certainly was not that the content of their Amendment would turn on the amendments to or the evolving interpretations of a federal statute passed nearly a century later.[c]

To the degree that this parsimonious standard is grounded on a view that either §1 or §5 of the Fourteenth Amendment substantially disempowered States and localities from remedying past racial discrimination, the majority is seriously mistaken. With respect, first, to §5, our precedents have never suggested that this provision — or, for that matter, its companion federal-empowerment provisions in the Thirteenth and Fifteenth Amendments — was meant to pre-empt or limit state police power to undertake race-conscious remedial measures. . . .

As for §1, it is too late in the day to assert seriously that the Equal Protection Clause prohibits States — or for that matter, the Federal Government, to whom the equal protection guarantee has largely been applied, from enacting race-conscious remedies. Our cases in the areas of school desegregation, voting rights, and affirmative action have demonstrated time and again that race is constitutionally germane, precisely because race remains dismayingly relevant in American life.

In adopting its prima facie standard for States and localities, the majority closes its eyes to this constitutional history and social reality. . . .

The fact is that Congress' concern in passing the Reconstruction Amendments, and particularly their congressional authorization provisions, was that

c. Although the majority purports to "adher[e] to the standard of review employed in *Wygant*," the "prima facie case" standard it adopts marks an implicit rejection of the more generally framed "strong basis in evidence" test endorsed by the *Wygant* plurality, and the similar "firm basis" test endorsed by Justice O'Connor in her separate concurrence in that case. Under those tests, proving a prima facie violation of Title VII would appear to have been but one means of adducing sufficient proof to satisfy Equal Protection Clause analysis. . . .

States would not adequately respond to racial violence or discrimination against newly freed slaves. To interpret any aspect of these Amendments as proscribing state remedial responses to these very problems turns the Amendments on their heads. . . .

In short, there is simply no credible evidence that the Framers of the Fourteenth Amendment sought "to transfer the security and protection of all the civil rights . . . from the States to the Federal government." The three Reconstruction Amendments undeniably "worked a dramatic change in the balance between congressional and state power." . . . But nothing in the Amendments themselves, or in our long history of interpreting or applying those momentous charters, suggests that States, exercising their police power, are in any way constitutionally inhibited from working alongside the Federal Government in the fight against discrimination and its effects.

IV

The majority today sounds a full-scale retreat from the Court's longstanding solicitude to race-conscious remedial efforts "directed toward deliverance of the century-old promise of equality of economic opportunity." The new and restrictive tests it applies scuttle one city's effort to surmount its discriminatory past, and imperil those of dozens more localities. I, however, profoundly disagree with the cramped vision of the Equal Protection Clause which the majority offers today and with its application of that vision to Richmond, Virginia's, laudable set-aside plan. The battle against pernicious racial discrimination or its effects is nowhere near won. I must dissent.

[Justice Blackmun wrote a brief dissent supporting Justice Marshall's opinion.]

Discussion

1. The majority in *Croson* distinguishes *Fullilove* by asserting (among other things) that Congress has unique remedial powers under §5 of the Fourteenth Amendment that the states don't share. Is the underlying rationale for the distinction (as Justice Scalia suggests) that state and local political units are more susceptible to factional control than Congress, and consequently that "racial discrimination against any group finds a more ready expression at the state and local than at the federal level"? Or is redressing general, nonparticularized discrimination simply beyond state or local legislative competence?

2. Professor Michel Rosenfeld has written:

> In contrast to their disagreements concerning the applicable constitutional standard and how that standard may be met, the Justices in *Croson* do agree on the principle facts. Yet, paradoxically, the bitter split between the Court's majority and the dissenters ultimately revolves more around the proper interpretation of commonly accepted facts than around disputes concerning constitutional doctrine. Indeed, acceptance of the same principal facts leads to diametrically opposed conclusions concerning the meaning and existence of compensable discrimination, the causal links between such discrimination and a compensable injury or disadvantage, and suitable remedies to redress the injury or eliminate the disadvantage. Moreover,

> these opposite conclusions are traceable to reliance on contrasting modes of interpretation. The first of these — to which I will refer as the atomistic mode of interpretation — is a more discrete mechanical mode of interpretation, relying on the disconnection of facts from the context in which they are embedded, and on the recombination of such disconnected facts into mechanistic causal chains made up of direct and linear links. The second mode of interpretation — which I will refer to as the ecological mode of interpretation — is more holistic and systemic in nature, approaching social facts and events in terms of the interaction between individuals, groups, and their social, political, and historical environment. Moreover, under an ecological mode of interpretation, causal relationships need not be direct or linear. Instead, they may be indirect and multifaceted as they are shaped by the historical sequence of adaptations and disruptions that characterize the interactions between human actors and their intersubjective environment.[109]

Rosenfeld asserts that the majority in *Croson* applies an atomistic mode of interpretation and thus "imposes a very stringent standard for the establishment of the proper nexus between discrimination and resulting injury. [This approach] requires that the links between discrimination and its effects be tightly and directly drawn, and appears to go to great lengths to present a series of events, which would ordinarily be viewed as being related, as though they were utterly disconnected."

What types of facts might Justice O'Connor have found sufficient to justify the Richmond plan? An admission of racial discrimination by certain members of the construction industry? A prior judicial finding of illegal discrimination by the local contractors' organization?

3. Drew S. Days III, who represented the United States before the Supreme Court in *Fullilove*, argued in a 1987 article that courts should seek to compel "principled decisionmaking" by public and private actors adopting race-conscious remedies:

> Government agencies establishing set-asides should be held to a higher standard than at present, although they should not have to satisfy the procedural and evidentiary requirements demanded of courts or administrative tribunals engaged in resolving specific discrimination claims. State and local agencies creating set-asides should, for example, be able to rely in part upon federal legislative or agency findings and judicial determinations regarding nationwide discrimination against minority business enterprises as predicates for considering the propriety of set-asides in their respective jurisdictions. But it is essential that state and local agencies also establish the presence of discrimination in their own bailiwicks, based either upon their own fact-finding processes or upon determinations made by other competent institutions, such as courts and administrative agencies.[110]

Do you agree with Justice O'Connor that Richmond had engaged in insufficient fact-finding of its own?

4. Soon after *Richmond* was announced, a number of constitutional scholars and law school deans jointly published a statement concerning the impact of the Court's ruling on the future of affirmative action:

109. Michel Rosenfeld, Decoding *Richmond*: Affirmative Action and the Elusive Meaning of Constitutional Equality, 87 Mich. L. Rev. 1729 (1989).

110. Drew S. Days, Fullilove, 96 Yale L.J. 453 (1987).

> In light of the Supreme Court's January 1989 decision in City of Richmond v. Croson, some have recently argued that race-conscious remedies by local and state governments should be regarded as conflicting with the Constitution. As long-time students of constitutional law, we regard this assessment as wrong. The Supreme Court has insisted that affirmative action programs be carefully designed — not dismantled. A call for fairness and flexibility in affirmative action programs should never be equated with a call for retrenchment and retreat. It would defy not only the Supreme Court's decisions but the fundamental purposes of the Equal Protection Clause to conclude that the Constitution forbids all such inclusive remedial measures, or requires that such measures be treated in exactly the same way as the invidious discrimination of the nation's past.
>
> Therefore, while it would be irresponsible for local governments to avoid whatever steps are necessary to adjust their minority contract programs to the Supreme Court's ruling in the Croson decision, it would be equally irresponsible for others to claim that this opinion casts doubt on the overall constitutionality of properly constructed race-conscious remedies.[111]

The statement prompted Professor Charles Fried, who was Solicitor General of the United States from June 1985 until January 1989, to respond:

> Appearing originally as a *cri de coeur* and moral exhortation on the part of those disappointed by the Court's decision in City of Richmond v. Croson, the constitutional scholars' statement was an entirely familiar example of attempted "spin control" and as such required no response. Offered recently in the pages of this major law review it draws the comment that as a statement of the law it is at best curious and at worst misleading. . . . It is misleading in so far as it suggests that no proposition of significance was enunciated, and that those propositions which were enunciated somehow embrace rather than severely limit the availability of racial quotas and preferences. . . .
>
> *Croson* is . . . a welcome clarification and coming together by this Court under its new leadership of some themes that have been troubling the Court for more than a decade. I am glad that the Court has made clear that a governmental unit may act to remedy not only its own past discrimination but that of identified others in its jurisdiction. But of surpassing importance is the unequivocal affirmation that the Equal Protection Clause protects all equally, and that all invocations of the power of government in racial terms must overcome the highest burdens of scrutiny, even those designated as benign.[112]

Which interpretation seems more compelling? Might both statements be engaging in their own version of "spin control"?

5. Consider this provision adopted by the Texas legislature in 1989:

> Sec. 70.08 Undergraduate Admissions. (a) The board of regents of The University of Texas System may provide for the admission and enrollment of not more than 2,000 entering freshman students at The University of Texas at Dallas. . . .
>
> (d) It is the intent of the legislature that minority students be full participants in the educational opportunities created by the admission of lower-division undergraduates to The University of Texas at Dallas primarily in programs leading to degrees in natural sciences, mathematics, and engineering. Therefore, until the

111. Lawrence Tribe, et al., Constitutional Scholars' Statement on Affirmative Action After City of Richmond v. Croson, 99 Yale L.J. 1711 (1989).

112. Charles Fried, Response, 99 Yale L.J. 155 (1989).

minority student populations at The University of Texas at Dallas are fully representative of the state's minority populations, the board shall cause to be set aside for each academic year from among the enrollments targeted by the academic plan for that academic year a number of enrollments equal to not less than five percent of the targeted number, and those enrollments are to be reserved exclusively for admission of minority students.

Is this provision consistent with *Bakke*? With *Croson*? Suppose the statute is constitutional on its face. Must it be applied to include as preferred minority students (a) a Jewish immigrant from the Soviet Union, and (b) a person with a white mother and an African-American father?[113]

Suppose that you are general counsel for the University of Texas, and you conclude that the Texas statute is unconstitutional under current Supreme Court decisions. What are your obligations? Should you wait for, or encourage, a Texas equivalent of Allan Bakke to sue? If suit is brought, should you defend the law or suggest that the Texas legislature hire independent counsel to defend it?

METRO BROADCASTING, INC. v. FEDERAL COMMUNICATIONS COMMISSION

110 S. Ct. 2997 (1990)

Certiorari to the United States Court of Appeals for the District of Columbia Circuit

BRENNAN, J.

The issue in these cases, consolidated for decision today, is whether certain minority preference policies of the Federal Communications Commission violate the equal protection component of the Fifth Amendment. The policies in question are (1) a program awarding an enhancement for minority ownership in comparative proceedings for new licenses, and (2) the minority "distress sale" program, which permits a limited category of existing radio and television broadcast stations to be transferred only to minority-controlled firms. We hold that these policies do not violate equal protection principles.

I

A

The policies before us today can best be understood by reference to the history of federal efforts to promote minority participation in the broadcasting industry.[a] In the Communications Act of 1934, as amended, Congress assigned to the Federal Communications Commission (FCC or Commission) exclusive authority

113. See Felicity Barringer, Mixed-Race Generation Emerges but Is Not Sure Where It Fits, New York Times, September 24, 1989, at 14, noting that "about one million Americans of mixed parentage have been born here in the last 20 years. In 1987, the latest year for which records are available, at least 100,000 such children were born, as against 30,000 born in 1968. Children of mixed parentage now represent about 3 percent of all births in the United States. . . . Of the 100,000 mixed-race children born in 1987, almost 40% came from black-white couples; 36% from Asian-white couples; and about 18% from Indian-white couples. The remainder were born of Asian-black or black-Indian unions."

a. The FCC has defined the term "minority" to include "those of Black, Hispanic Surnamed, American Eskimo, Aleut, American Indian and Asiatic American extraction."

to grant licenses, based on "public convenience, interest, or necessity," to persons wishing to construct and operate radio and television broadcast stations in the United States. Although for the past two decades minorities have constituted at least one-fifth of the United States population, during this time relatively few members of minority groups have held broadcast licenses. . . . [I]n 1978, minorities owned less than 1 percent of the Nation's radio and television stations; and in 1986, they owned just 2.1 percent of the more than 11,000 radio and television stations in the United States. Moreover, these statistics fail to reflect the fact that, as late entrants who often have been able to obtain only the less valuable stations, many minority broadcasters serve geographically limited markets with relatively small audiences. The Commission has recognized that the viewing and listening public suffers when minorities are underrepresented among owners of television and radio stations:

> Acute underrepresentation of minorities among the owners of broadcast properties is troublesome because it is the licensee who is ultimately responsible for identifying and serving the needs and interests of his or her audience. Unless minorities are encouraged to enter the mainstream of the commercial broadcasting business, a substantial portion of our citizenry will remain underserved and the larger, non-minority audience will be deprived of the views of minorities.

The Commission has therefore worked to encourage minority participation in the broadcast industry. The FCC began by formulating rules to prohibit licensees from discriminating against minorities in employment. Initially, the FCC did not consider minority status as a factor in licensing decisions, maintaining as a matter of Commission policy that no preference to minority ownership was warranted where the record in a particular case did not give assurances that the owner's race likely would affect the content of the station's broadcast service to the public. . . .

[After a conference on minority ownership policies in 1977,] the FCC concluded:

> [W]e are compelled to observe that the views of racial minorities continue to be inadequately represented in the broadcast media. This situation is detrimental not only to the minority audience but to all of the viewing and listening public. Adequate representation of minority viewpoints in programming serves not only the needs and interests of the minority community but also enriches and educates the non-minority audience. It enhances the diversified programming which is a key objective not only of the Communications Act of 1934 but also of the First Amendment.

Describing its actions as only "first steps," the FCC outlined two elements of a minority ownership policy. First, the Commission pledged to consider minority ownership . . . in a comparative hearing as a "plus" to be weighed together with all other relevant factors. The "plus" is awarded only to the extent that a minority owner actively participates in the day-to-day management of the station.

Second, the FCC outlined a plan to increase minority opportunities to receive reassigned and transferred licenses through the so-called "distress sale" policy. As a general rule, a licensee whose qualifications to hold a broadcast license come into question may not assign or transfer that license until the FCC has resolved its doubts in a noncomparative hearing. The distress sale policy is an exception to that practice, allowing a broadcaster whose license has been designated for a revocation hearing, or whose renewal application has been designated for hearing, to assign the license to an FCC-approved minority enterprise. The assignee must meet the FCC's basic qualifications, and the minority ownership must exceed 50 percent or be controlling. . . .

B

1

Metro Broadcasting, Inc. (Metro) challenges the Commission's policy awarding preferences to minority owners in comparative licensing proceedings. [A competitor of Metro, Rainbow, was awarded the license in part because of its having received] a substantial enhancement on the ground that it was 90 percent Hispanic-owned, whereas Metro had only one minority partner who owned 19.8 percent of the enterprise. The [FCC] Review Board found that Rainbow's minority credit outweighed Metro's local residence and civic participation advantage. The Commission denied review of the Board's decision largely without discussion, stating merely that it "agree(d) with the Board's resolution of this case."

2

The dispute in [the second case] emerged from a series of attempts by Faith Center, Inc., the licensee of a Hartford, Connecticut television station, to execute a minority distress sale.

In December 1983, respondent Shurberg Broadcasting of Hartford, Inc. (Shurberg) applied to the Commission for a permit to build a television station in Hartford. The application was mutually exclusive with Faith Center's renewal application, then still pending. In June 1984, Faith Center again sought the FCC's approval for a distress sale, requesting permission to sell the station to Astroline Communications Company, Limited Partnership (Astroline), a minority applicant. Shurberg opposed the sale to Astroline on a number of grounds, including that the FCC's distress sale program violated Shurberg's right to equal protection. Shurberg therefore urged the Commission to deny the distress sale request and to schedule a comparative hearing to examine the application Shurberg had tendered alongside Faith Center's renewal request. In December 1984, the FCC approved Faith Center's petition for permission to assign its broadcast license to Astroline pursuant to the distress sale policy. The FCC rejected Shurberg's equal protection challenge to the policy as "without merit."

II

It is of overriding significance in these cases that the FCC's minority ownership programs have been specifically approved — indeed, mandated — by Congress. We explained [in *Fullilove*] that deference was appropriate in light of Congress' institutional competence as the national legislature, as well as Congress' powers under the Commerce Clause, the Spending Clause, and the Civil War Amendments.[b] A majority of the Court in *Fullilove* did not apply strict scrutiny to the

b. Justice O'Connor's suggestion that the deference to Congress described in *Fullilove* rested entirely on Congress' powers under §5 of the Fourteenth Amendment is simply incorrect. The Chief Justice expressly noted that in enacting the provision at issue, "Congress employed an amalgam of its specifically delegated powers." 448 U.S., at 473.

race-based classification at issue. Three Members inquired "whether the objectives of th[e] legislation are within the power of Congress" and "whether the limited use of racial and ethnic criteria is a constitutionally permissible means for achieving the congressional objectives." Three other Members would have upheld benign racial classifications that "serve important governmental objectives and are substantially related to achievement of those objectives." We apply that standard today. We hold that benign race-conscious measures mandated by Congress[c] — even if those measures are not "remedial" in the sense of being designed to compensate victims of past governmental or societal discrimination — are constitutionally permissible to the extent that they serve important governmental objectives within the power of Congress and are substantially related to achievement of those objectives.

Our decision last Term in Richmond v. J.A. Croson Co., concerning a minority set-aside program adopted by a municipality, does not prescribe the level of scrutiny to be applied to a benign racial classification employed by Congress. . . . In fact, much of the language and reasoning in *Croson* reaffirmed the lesson of *Fullilove* that race-conscious classifications adopted by Congress to address racial and ethnic discrimination are subject to a different standard than such classifications prescribed by state and local governments. . . .

We hold that the FCC minority ownership policies pass muster under the test we announce today. First, we find that they serve the important governmental objective of broadcast diversity. Second, we conclude that they are substantially related to the achievement of that objective.

A

Congress found that "the effects of past inequities stemming from racial and ethnic discrimination have resulted in a severe underrepresentation of minorities in the media of mass communication." Congress and the Commission do not justify the minority ownership policies strictly as remedies for victims of this discrimination, however. Rather, Congress and the FCC have selected the minority ownership policies primarily to promote programming diversity, and they urge that such diversity is an important governmental objective that can serve as a constitutional basis for the preference policies. We agree.

We have long recognized that "(b)ecause of the scarcity of (electromagnetic) frequencies, the Government is permitted to put restraints on licensees in favor of others whose views should be expressed on this unique medium." Red Lion Broadcasting Co. v. FCC, 395 U.S. 367, 390 (1969). The Government's role in distributing the limited number of broadcast licenses is not merely that of a "traffic officer"; rather, it is axiomatic that broadcasting may be regulated in light of the rights of the viewing and listening audience and that "the widest possible dissemination of information from diverse and antagonistic sources is essential to

c. We fail to understand how Justice Kennedy can pretend that examples of "benign" race-conscious measures include South African apartheid, the "separate-but-equal" law at issue in Plessy v. Ferguson, and the internment of American citizens of Japanese ancestry upheld in Korematsu v. United States, 323 U.S. 214 (1944). We are confident that an "examination of the legislative scheme and its history," will separate benign measures from other types of racial classifications. Of course, "the mere recitation of a benign, compensatory purpose is not an automatic shield which protects against any inquiry into the actual purposes underlying a statutory scheme."

the welfare of the public." Safeguarding the public's right to receive a diversity of views and information over the airwaves is therefore an integral component of the FCC's mission.

Against this background, we conclude that the interest in enhancing broadcast diversity is, at the very least, an important governmental objective and is therefore a sufficient basis for the Commission's minority ownership policies. Just as a "diverse student body" contributing to a " 'robust exchange of ideas' " is a "constitutionally permissible goal" on which a race-conscious university admissions program may be predicated, University of California Regents v. Bakke, 438 U.S. 265, 311-313 (1978) (opinion of Powell, J.), the diversity of views and information on the airwaves serves important First Amendment values. The benefits of such diversity are not limited to the members of minority groups who gain access to the broadcasting industry by virtue of the ownership policies; rather, the benefits redound to all members of the viewing and listening audience. As Congress found, "the American public will benefit by having access to a wider diversity of information sources."

B

We also find that the minority ownership policies are substantially related to the achievement of the Government's interest. One component of this inquiry concerns the relationship between expanded minority ownership and greater broadcast diversity; both the FCC and Congress have determined that such a relationship exists. Although we do not " 'defer' to the judgment of the Congress and the Commission on a constitutional question," and would not "hesitate to invoke the Constitution should we determine that the Commission has not fulfilled its task with appropriate sensitivity" to equal protection principles, we must pay close attention to the expertise of the Commission and the factfinding of Congress when analyzing the nexus between minority ownership and programming diversity. With respect to this "complex" empirical question, we are required to give "great weight to the decisions of Congress and the experience of the Commission."

1

The FCC has determined that increased minority participation in broadcasting promotes programming diversity. The FCC's conclusion that there is an empirical nexus between minority ownership and broadcasting diversity is a product of its expertise, and we accord its judgment deference.

Furthermore, the FCC's reasoning with respect to the minority ownership policies is consistent with longstanding practice under the Communications Act. From its inception, public regulation of broadcasting has been premised on the assumption that diversification of ownership will broaden the range of programming available to the broadcast audience. The Commission has never relied on the market alone to ensure that the needs of the audience are met. Indeed, one of the FCC's elementary regulatory assumptions is that broadcast content is not purely market-driven; if it were, there would be little need for consideration in licensing decisions of such factors as integration of ownership and management, local residence, and civic participation. . . .

2

Congress also has made clear its view that the minority ownership policies advance the goal of diverse programming. In recent years, Congress has specifically required the Commission, through appropriations legislation, to maintain the minority ownership policies without alteration.

Congress has twice extended the prohibition on the use of appropriated funds to modify or repeal minority ownership policies and has continued to focus upon the issue.

As revealed by the historical evolution of current federal policy, both Congress and the Commission have concluded that the minority ownership programs are critical means of promoting broadcast diversity. We must give great weight to their joint determination.

C

The judgment that there is a link between expanded minority ownership and broadcast diversity does not rest on impermissible stereotyping. Congressional policy does not assume that in every case minority ownership and management will lead to more minority-oriented programming or to the expression of a discrete "minority viewpoint" on the airwaves. Neither does it pretend that all programming that appeals to minority audiences can be labeled "minority programming" or that programming that might be described as "minority" does not appeal to nonminorities. Rather, both Congress and the FCC maintain simply that expanded minority ownership of broadcast outlets will, in the aggregate, result in greater broadcast diversity. A broadcasting industry with representative minority participation will produce more variation and diversity than will one whose ownership is drawn from a single racially and ethnically homogeneous group. The predictive judgment about the overall result of minority entry into broadcasting is not a rigid assumption about how minority owners will behave in every case but rather is akin to Justice Powell's conclusion in *Bakke* that greater admission of minorities would contribute, on average, "to the 'robust exchange of ideas.'" To be sure, there is no ironclad guarantee that each minority owner will contribute to diversity. But neither was there an assurance in *Bakke* that minority students would interact with nonminority students or that the particular minority students admitted would have typical or distinct "minority" viewpoints.

Although all station owners are guided to some extent by market demand in their programming decisions, Congress and the Commission have determined that there may be important differences between the broadcasting practices of minority owners and those of their nonminority counterparts. This judgment — and the conclusion that there is a nexus between minority ownership and broadcasting diversity — is corroborated by a host of empirical evidence.[d] Evidence

d. For example, the Congressional Research Service (CRS) analyzed data from some 8,720 FCC-licensed radio and TV stations and found a strong correlation between minority ownership and diversity of programming. While only 20 percent of stations with no Afro-American ownership responded that they attempted to direct programming at Afro-American audiences, 65 percent of stations with Afro-American ownership reported that they did so. Only 10 percent of stations without Hispanic ownership stated that they targeted programming at Hispanic audiences, while 59 percent of stations with Hispanic owners said they did. The CRS concluded: "(A)n argument can be made that FCC policies that enhanced minority . . . station ownership may have resulted in more minority and

suggests that an owner's minority status influences the selection of topics for news coverage and the presentation of editorial viewpoint, especially on matters of particular concern to minorities. "[M]inority ownership does appear to have specific impact on the presentation of minority images in local news," inasmuch as minority-owned stations tend to devote more news time to topics of minority interest and to avoid racial and ethnic stereotypes in portraying minorities. In addition, studies show that a minority owner is more likely to employ minorities in managerial and other important roles where they can have an impact on station policies.[e] While we are under no illusion that members of a particular minority group share some cohesive, collective viewpoint, we believe it a legitimate inference for Congress and the Commission to draw that as more minorities gain ownership and policymaking roles in the media, varying perspectives will be more fairly represented on the airwaves. The policies are thus a product of " 'analysis' " rather than a " 'stereotyped reaction' " based on " '[h]abit.' " *Fullilove*, 448 U.S., at 534, n.4 (Stevens, J., dissenting).

Our cases demonstrate that the reasoning employed by the Commission and Congress is permissible. We have recognized, for example, that the fair cross-section requirement of the Sixth Amendment forbids the exclusion of groups on the basis of such characteristics as race and gender from a jury venire because "[w]ithout that requirement, the State could draw up jury lists in such manner as to produce a pool of prospective jurors disproportionately ill disposed towards one or all classes of defendants, and thus more likely to yield petit juries with similar disposition." It is a small step from this logic to the conclusion that including minorities in the electromagnetic spectrum will be more likely to produce a "fair cross section" of diverse content.

D

We find that the minority ownership policies are in other relevant respects substantially related to the goal of promoting broadcast diversity. First, the Commission adopted and Congress endorsed minority ownership preferences only after long study and painstaking consideration of all available alternatives. For many years, the FCC attempted to encourage diversity of programming content without consideration of the race of station owners.[f] . . .

---

other audience targeted programming. To the degree that increasing minority programming across audience markets is considered adding to programming diversity, then, based on the FCC survey data, an argument can be made that the FCC preference policies contributed, in turn, to programming diversity.". . .

e. Afro-American-owned radio stations, for example, have hired Afro-Americans in top management and other important job categories at far higher rates than have white-owned stations, even those with Afro-American-oriented formats. The same has been true of Hispanic hiring at Hispanic-owned stations, compared to Anglo-owned stations with Spanish-language formats. As of September 1986, half of the 14 Afro-American or Hispanic general managers at TV stations in the United States worked at minority-owned or controlled stations.

In 1981, 13 of the 15 Spanish-language radio stations in the United States owned by Hispanics also had a majority of Hispanics in management positions, while only a third of Anglo-owned Spanish-language stations had a majority of Hispanic managers, and 42 percent of the Anglo-owned Spanish-language stations had no Hispanic managers at all.

f. The Commission has eschewed direct federal control over discrete programming decisions by radio and television stations. In order to ensure diversity by means of administrative decree, the Commission would have been required to familiarize itself with the needs of every community and to monitor the broadcast content of every station. Such a scheme likely would have presented

[T]he Commission established minority ownership preferences only after long experience demonstrated that race-neutral means could not produce adequate broadcasting diversity. . . . In endorsing the minority ownership preferences, Congress agreed with the Commission's assessment that race-neutral alternatives had failed to achieve the necessary programming diversity. . . .

Although it has underscored emphatically its support for the minority ownership policies, Congress has manifested that support through a series of appropriations acts of finite duration, thereby ensuring future reevaluations of the need for the minority ownership program as the number of minority broadcasters increases. In addition, Congress has continued to hold hearings on the subject of minority ownership. Furthermore, there is provision for administrative and judicial review of all Commission decisions, which guarantees both that the minority ownership policies are applied correctly in individual cases, and that there will be frequent opportunities to revisit the merits of those policies. Congress and the Commission have adopted a policy of minority ownership not as an end in itself, but rather as a means of achieving greater programming diversity. Such a goal carries its own natural limit, for there will be no need for further minority preferences once sufficient diversity has been achieved.

Finally, we do not believe that the minority ownership policies at issue impose impermissible burdens on nonminorities. Although the nonminority challengers in these cases concede that they have not suffered the loss of an already-awarded broadcast license, they claim that they have been handicapped in their ability to obtain one in the first instance. But just as we have determined that "[a]s part of this Nation's dedication to eradicating racial discrimination, innocent persons may be called upon to bear some of the burden of the remedy," *Wygant,* 476 U.S., at 280-281 (opinion of Powell, J.), we similarly find that a congressionally mandated benign race-conscious program that is substantially related to the achievement of an important governmental interest is consistent with equal protection principles so long as it does not impose undue burdens on nonminorities.

In the context of broadcasting licenses, the burden on nonminorities is slight. The FCC's responsibility is to grant licenses in the "public interest, convenience, or necessity," and the limited number of frequencies on the electromagnetic spectrum means that "[n]o one has a First Amendment right to a license." Applicants have no settled expectation that their applications will be granted without consideration of public interest factors such as minority ownership. Award of a preference in a comparative hearing or transfer of a station in a distress sale thus contravenes "no legitimate firmly rooted expectation[s]" of competing applicants.

Respondent Shurberg insists that because the minority distress sale policy operates to exclude nonminority firms completely from consideration in the transfer of certain stations, it is a greater burden than the comparative hearing preference for minorities, which is simply a "plus" factor considered together with other characteristics of the applicants. We disagree that the distress sale pol-

insurmountable practical difficulties, in light of the thousands of broadcast outlets in the United States and the myriad local variations in audience tastes and interests. Even were such an ambitious policy of central planning feasible, it would have raised "serious First Amendment issues" if it denied a broadcaster the ability to "carry a particular program or to publish his own views," if it risked "government censorship of a particular program," or if it led to "the official government view dominating public broadcasting." The Commission, with the approval of this Court, has therefore "avoid[ed] unnecessary restrictions on licensee discretion" and has interpreted the Communications Act as "seek[ing] to preserve journalistic discretion while promoting the interests of the listening public.". . .

icy imposes an undue burden on nonminorities. By its terms, the policy may be invoked at the Commission's discretion only with respect to a small fraction of broadcast licenses — those designated for revocation or renewal hearings to examine basic qualification issues — and only when the licensee chooses to sell out at a distress price rather than to go through with the hearing. The distress sale policy is not a quota or fixed quantity set-aside. . . . In practice, distress sales have represented a tiny fraction — less than four tenths of one percent — of all broadcast sales since 1979. Nonminority firms are free to compete for the vast remainder of license opportunities available in a market that contains over 11,000 broadcast properties. The burden on nonminority firms is at least as "relatively light" as that created by the program at issue in *Fullilove*, which set aside for minorities 10 percent of federal funds granted for local public works projects.

III

The Commission's minority ownership policies bear the imprimatur of longstanding congressional support and direction and are substantially related to the achievement of the important governmental objective of broadcast diversity.

[A concurring opinion by Justice Stevens is omitted.]

KENNEDY, J., with whom Justice Scalia joins, dissenting.

. . . [In Plessy v. Ferguson, the] Court concluded that the "race-conscious measures" it reviewed were reasonable because they served the governmental interest of increasing the riding pleasure of railroad passengers. . . . Today the Court grants Congress latitude to employ "benign race-conscious measures . . . [that] are not . . . designed to compensate victims of past governmental or societal discrimination," but that "serve important governmental objectives . . . and are substantially related to achievement of those objectives." The interest the Court accepts to uphold the Commission's race-conscious measures is "broadcast diversity." Furthering that interest, we are told, is worth the cost of discriminating among citizens on the basis of race because it will increase the listening pleasure of media audiences. In upholding this preference, the majority exhumes *Plessy's* deferential approach to racial classifications. The Court abandons even the broad societal remedial justification for racial preferences . . . and now will allow the use of racial classifications by Congress untied to any goal of addressing the effects of past race discrimination. All that need be shown under the new approach . . . is that the future effect of discriminating among citizens on the basis of race will advance some "important" governmental interest.

Once the Government takes the step, which itself should be forbidden, of enacting into law the stereotypical assumption that the race of owners is linked to broadcast content, it follows a path that becomes ever more tortuous. It must decide which races to favor. While the Court repeatedly refers to the preferences as favoring "minorities," and purports to evaluate the burdens imposed on "nonminorities," it must be emphasized that the discriminatory policies upheld today operate to exclude the many racial and ethnic minorities that have not made the Commission's list. The enumeration of the races to be protected is borrowed from a remedial statute, but since the remedial rationale must be disavowed in order to sustain the policy, the race classifications bear scant relation to the asserted governmental interest. The Court's reasoning provides little justification for welcoming the return of racial classifications to our Nation's laws.[a] I cannot agree with the Court that the Constitution permits the Government to discriminate among its citizens on the basis of race in order to serve interests so trivial as "broadcast diversity." In abandoning strict scrutiny to endorse this interest the Court turns back the clock on the level of scrutiny applicable to federal race-conscious measures. Strict scrutiny is the surest test the Court has yet devised for holding true to the constitutional command of racial equality. The majority cannot achieve its goal of upholding the quotas here under the rigor of this standard, and so must devise an intermediate test.

The Court insists that the programs under review are "benign." Justice Stevens agrees. "[T]he reason for the classification — the recognized interest in broadcast diversity — is clearly identified and does not imply any judgment concerning the abilities of owners of different races or the merits of different kinds of programming. Neither the favored nor the disfavored class is stigmatized in any way."[b] A fundamental error of the *Plessy* Court was its similar confidence in its ability to identify "benign" discrimination.

Although the majority is "confident" that it can determine when racial discrimination is benign, it offers no explanation as to how it will do so. Policies of racial separation and preference are almost always justified as benign, even when it is clear to any sensible observer that they are not. The following statement, for example, would fit well among those offered to uphold the Commission's racial preference policy: "The policy is not based on any concept of superiority or inferiority, but merely on the fact that people differ, particularly in their group associations, loyalties, cultures, outlook, modes of life and standards of development." See South Africa and the Rule of Law 37 (1968) (official publication of the South African Government). The history of governmental reliance on race demonstrates that racial policies defended as benign often are not seen that way by the individuals affected by them. Although the majority disclaims it, the FCC policy seems based on the demeaning notion that members of the defined racial groups ascribe to certain "minority views" that must be different from those of other citizens. Special preferences also can foster the view that members of the favored groups are inherently less able to compete on their own. And, rightly or wrongly, special preference programs often are perceived as targets for exploitation by opportunists who seek to take advantage of monetary rewards without advancing the stated policy of minority inclusion.[c]

a. The Court fails to address the difficulties, both practical and constitutional, with the task of defining members of racial groups that its decision will require. The Commission, for example, has found it necessary to trace an applicant's family history to 1492 to conclude that the applicant was "Hispanic" for purposes of a minority tax certificate policy. See Storer Broadcasting Co., 87 F.C.C. 2d 190 (1981). I agree that "the very attempt to define with precision a beneficiary's qualifying racial characteristics is repugnant to our constitutional ideals." Fullilove v. Klutznick, 448 U.S. 448, 534, n.5 (1980) (Stevens, J., dissenting). "If the National Government is to make a serious effort to define racial classes by criteria that can be administered objectively, it must study precedents such as the First Regulation to the Reichs Citsizenship Law of November 14, 1935, translated in 4 Nazi Conspiracy and Aggression, Document No. 1417-PS, pp. 8-9 (1946)." Id., at 534, n.5. Other examples are available. See Population Registration Act No. 30 of 1950, Statutes of the Republic of South Africa 71 (1985).

b. Justice Stevens' assertion . . . is curious. If this policy which explicitly arrives at the ultimate goal of altering programming content, does not "imply any judgement concerning . . . different kinds of programming" then it is difficult to see how the FCC's policy serves any governmental interest, let alone substantially furthers one.

c. The record in one of these two cases indicates that Astroline Communications Company, the beneficiary of the distress sale policy in this case has a total capitalization of approximately

The perceptions of the excluded class must also be weighed, with attention to the cardinal rule that our Constitution protects each citizen as an individual, not as a member of a group. There is the danger that the "stereotypical thinking" that prompts policies such as the FCC rules here "stigmatizes the disadvantaged class with the unproven charge of past racial discrimination." Whether or not such programs can be described as "remedial," the message conveyed is that it is acceptable to harm a member of the group excluded from the benefit or privilege. If this is to be considered acceptable under the Constitution, there are various possible explanations. One is that the group disadvantaged by the preference should feel no stigma at all, because racial preferences address not the evil of intentional discrimination but the continuing unconscious use of stereotypes that disadvantage minority groups. But this is not a proposition that the many citizens, who to their knowledge "have never discriminated against anyone on the basis of race," will find easy to accept.

Another explanation might be that the stigma imposed upon the excluded class should be overlooked, either because past wrongs are so grievous that the disfavored class must bear collective blame, or because individual harms are simply irrelevant in the face of efforts to compensate for racial inequalities. But these are not premises that the Court even appears willing to address in its analysis. Until the Court is candid about the existence of stigma imposed by racial preferences on both affected classes, candid about the "animosity and discontent" they create, and open about defending a theory that explains why the cost of this stigma is worth bearing and why it can consist with the Constitution, no basis can be shown for today's casual abandonment of strict scrutiny.

Perhaps the Court can succeed in its assumed role of case-by-case arbiter of when it is desirable and benign for the Government to disfavor some citizens and favor others based on the color of their skin. Perhaps the tolerance and decency to which our people aspire will let the disfavored rise above hostility and the favored escape condescension. But history suggests much peril in this enterprise, and so the Constitution forbids us to undertake it. I regret that after a century of judicial opinions we interpret the Constitution to do no more than move us from "separate but equal" to "unequal but benign."

O'CONNOR, J., with whom The Chief Justice and Justices Scalia, and Kennedy join, dissenting.

At the heart of the Constitution's guarantee of equal protection lies the simple command that the Government must treat citizens "as individuals, not 'as simply components of a racial, religious, sexual or national class.' " Social scientists may debate how peoples' thoughts and behavior reflect their background, but the Constitution provides that the Government may not allocate benefits and burdens among individuals based on the the assumption that race or ethnicity determines how they act or think. To uphold the challenged programs, the Court departs from these fundamental principles and from our traditional requirement that racial classifications are permissible only if necessary and narrowly tailored to achieve a compelling interest. This departure marks a renewed toleration of racial classifications and a repudiation of our recent affirmation that the Constitution's equal protection guarantees extend equally to all citizens. The

$24,000,000. Its sole minority principle was a Hispanic-American who held 21% of Astroline's overall equity and 71% of its voting equity. His total cash contribution was $210.

Court's application of a lessened equal protection standard to congressional actions finds no support in our cases or in the Constitution. I respectfully dissent.

I

This Court's precedents in no way justify the Court's marked departure from our traditional treatment of race classifications and its conclusion that different equal protection principles apply to these federal actions.

In both the challenged policies, the FCC provides benefits to some members of our society and denies benefits to others based on race or ethnicity. Except in the narrowest of circumstances, the Constitution bars such racial classifications as a denial to particular individuals, of any race or ethnicity, of "the equal protection of the laws." The dangers of such classifications are clear. They endorse race-based reasoning and the conception of a Nation divided into racial blocs, thus contributing to an escalation of racial hostility and conflict. Such policies may embody stereotypes that treat individuals as the product of their race, evaluating their thoughts and efforts — their very worth as citizens — according to a criterion barred to the Government by history and the Constitution. Racial classifications, whether providing benefits to or burdening particular racial or ethnic groups, may stigmatize those groups singled out for different treatment and may create considerable tension with the Nation's widely shared commitment to evaluating individuals upon their individual merit.

In Bolling v. Sharpe, . . . the Court held that equal protection principles embedded in the Fifth Amendment's Due Process Clause prohibited the Federal Government from maintaining racially segregated schools in the District of Columbia: "[I]t would be unthinkable that the same Constitution would impose a lesser duty on the Federal Government." Consistent with this view, the Court has repeatedly indicated that "the reach of the equal protection guarantee of the Fifth Amendment is coextensive with that of the Fourteenth."

Nor does the congressional role in prolonging the FCC's policies justify any lower level of scrutiny. As with all instances of judicial review of federal legislation, the Court does not lightly set aside the considered judgment of a coordinate branch. Nonetheless, the respect due a coordinate branch yields neither less vigilance in defense of equal protection principles nor any corresponding diminution of the standard of review. The Court has not varied its standard of review when entertaining other equal protection challenges to congressional measures.

Congress has considerable latitude, presenting special concerns for judicial review, when it exercises its "unique remedial powers under §5 of the Fourteenth Amendment," see *Croson* (opinion of O'Connor, J.), but this case does not implicate those powers. Section 5 empowers Congress to act respecting the States, and of course this case concerns only the administration of federal programs by federal officials. Reflecting the Fourteenth Amendment's "dramatic change in the balance between congressional and state power over matters of race," that section provides to Congress a particular, structural role in the oversight of certain of the States' actions.

The Court asserts that *Fullilove* supports its novel application of intermediate scrutiny to "benign" race conscious measures adopted by Congress. Three reasons defeat this claim. First, . . . [a]lthough the various opinions in *Fullilove* referred to several sources of congressional authority, the opinions make clear that it was §5 that led the Court to apply a different form of review to the challenged program. Last Term, *Croson* resolved any doubt that might remain regarding this point. We distinguished *Fullilove*, in which we upheld a similar set-aside enacted by Congress, on the ground that in *Fullilove* "Congress was exercising its powers under §5 of the Fourteenth Amendment." *Croson* indicated that the decision in *Fullilove* turned on "the unique remedial powers of Congress under §5," and that the latitude afforded Congress in identifying and redressing past discrimination rested on §5's "specific constitutional mandate to enforce the dictates of the Fourteenth Amendment."

Second, *Fullilove* applies at most only to congressional measures that seek to remedy identified past discrimination. The Court upheld the challenged measures in *Fullilove* only because Congress had identified discrimination that had particularly affected the construction industry and had carefully constructed corresponding remedial measures. *Fullilove* indicated that careful review was essential to ensure that Congress acted solely for remedial rather than other, illegitimate purposes. The FCC and Congress are clearly not acting for any remedial purpose, and the Court today expressly extends its standard to racial classifications that are not remedial in any sense.

Finally, even if *Fullilove* applied outside a remedial exercise of Congress' §5 power, it would not support today's adoption of the intermediate standard of review proffered by Justice Marshall but rejected in *Fullilove*. Although the Court correctly observes that a majority did not apply strict scrutiny, six Members of the Court rejected intermediate scrutiny in favor of some more stringent form of review.

The Court's reliance on "benign racial classifications" is particularly disturbing. "'Benign' racial classification" is a contradiction in terms. Governmental distinctions among citizens based on race or ethnicity, even in the rare circumstances permitted by our cases, exact costs and carry with them substantial dangers. To the person denied an opportunity or right based on race, the classification is hardly benign. The right to equal protection of the laws is a personal right, securing to each individual an immunity from treatment predicated simply on membership in a particular racial or ethnic group. The Court's emphasis on "benign racial classifications" suggests confidence in its ability to distinguish good from harmful governmental uses of racial criteria. History should teach greater humility. Untethered to narrowly confined remedial notions, "benign" carries with it no independent meaning, but reflects only acceptance of the current generation's conclusion that a politically acceptable burden, imposed on particular citizens on the basis of race, is reasonable.

This dispute regarding the appropriate standard of review may strike some as a lawyers' quibble over words, but it is not. The standard of review establishes whether and when the Court and Constitution allow the Government to employ racial classifications. A lower standard signals that the Government may resort to racial distinctions more readily. The Court's departure from our cases is disturbing enough, but more disturbing still is the renewed toleration of racial classifications that its new standard of review embodies.

II

Our history reveals that the most blatant forms of discrimination have been visited upon some members of the racial and ethnic groups identified in the challenged programs. Many have lacked the opportunity to share in the Nation's wealth and to participate in its commercial enterprises. It is undisputed that minority participation in the broadcasting industry falls markedly below the demographic representation of those groups, and this shortfall may be traced in part to the discrimination and the patterns of exclusion that have widely affected our society. As a Nation we aspire to create a society untouched by that history of exclusion, and to ensure that equality defines all citizens' daily experience and opportunities as well as the protection afforded to them under law.

For these reasons, and despite the harms that may attend the Government's use of racial classifications, we have repeatedly recognized that the Government possesses a compelling interest in remedying the effects of identified race discrimination. We subject even racial classifications claimed to be remedial to strict scrutiny, however, to ensure that the Government in fact employs any race-conscious measures to further this remedial interest and employs them only when, and no more broadly than, the interest demands.

Yet it is equally clear that the policies challenged in these cases were not designed as remedial measures and are in no sense narrowly tailored to remedy identified discrimination. The FCC appropriately concedes that its policies embodied no remedial purpose and has disclaimed the possibility that discrimination infected the allocation of licenses. The congressional action at most simply endorsed a policy designed to further the interest in achieving diverse programming. . . . The Court evaluates the policies only as measures designed to increase programming diversity. I agree that the racial classifications cannot be upheld as remedial measures.

III

Under the appropriate standard, strict scrutiny, only a compelling interest may support the Government's use of racial classifications. Modern equal protection doctrine has recognized only one such interest: remedying the effects of racial discrimination. The interest in increasing the diversity of broadcast viewpoints is clearly not a compelling interest. It is simply too amorphous, too insubstantial, and too unrelated to any legitimate basis for employing racial classifications. The Court does not claim otherwise. Rather, it employs its novel standard and claims that this asserted interest need only be, and is, "important." This conclusion twice compounds the Court's initial error of reducing its level of scrutiny of a racial classification. First, it too casually extends the justifications that might support racial classifications, beyond that of remedying past discrimination. . . .

Second, it has initiated this departure by endorsing an insubstantial interest, one that is certainly insufficiently weighty to justify tolerance of the Government's distinctions among citizens based on race and ethnicity. . . . An interest capable of justifying race-conscious measures must be sufficiently specific and verifiable, such that it supports only limited and carefully defined uses of racial classifications. In *Croson*, we held that an interest in remedying societal discrimination cannot be considered compelling. We determined that a "generalized assertion" of past discrimination "has no logical stopping point" and would support unconstrained uses of race classifications. In *Wygant*, we rejected the asserted interest in "providing minority role models for [a public school system's] minority students, as an attempt to alleviate the effects of societal discrimination," because "[s]ocietal discrimination, without more, is too amorphous a basis for imposing a racially classified remedy" and would allow "remedies that are ageless in their reach into the past, and timeless in their ability to affect the future." Both cases condemned those interests because they would allow distribution of goods essentially according to the demographic representation of particular racial and ethnic groups.

The asserted interest in this case suffers from the same defects. The interest is certainly amorphous: the FCC and the majority of this Court understandably do not suggest how one would define or measure a particular viewpoint that might be associated with race, or even how one would assess the diversity of broadcast viewpoints. . . .

The asserted interest would justify discrimination against members of any group found to contribute to an insufficiently diverse broadcasting spectrum, including those groups currently favored. In *Wygant*, we rejected as insufficiently weighty the interest in achieving role models in public schools, in part because that rationale could as readily be used to limit the hiring of teachers who belonged to particular minority groups. The FCC's claimed interest could similarly justify limitations on minority members' participation in broadcasting. It would be unwise to depend upon the Court's restriction of its holding to "benign" measures to forestall this result. Divorced from any remedial purpose and otherwise undefined, "benign" means only what shifting fashions and changing politics deem acceptable. Members of any racial or ethnic group, whether now preferred under the FCC's policies or not, may find themselves politically out of fashion and subject to disadvantageous but "benign" discrimination.

Under the majority's holding, the FCC may also advance its asserted interest in viewpoint diversity by identifying what constitutes a "Black viewpoint," an "Asian viewpoint," an "Arab viewpoint," and so on; determining which viewpoints are underrepresented; and then using that determination to mandate particular programming or to deny licenses to those deemed by virtue of their race or ethnicity less likely to present the favored views. Indeed, the FCC has, if taken at its word, essentially pursued this course, albeit without making express its reasons for choosing to favor particular groups or for concluding that the broadcasting spectrum is insufficiently diverse.

We should not accept as adequate for equal protection purposes an interest unrelated to race, yet capable of supporting measures so difficult to distinguish from proscribed discrimination. The remedial interest may support race classifications because that interest is necessarily related to past racial discrimination; yet the interest in diversity of viewpoints provides no legitimate, much less important, reason to employ race classifications apart from generalizations impermissibly equating race with thoughts and behavior. And it will prove impossible to distinguish naked preferences for members of particular races from preferences for members of particular races because they possess certain valued views: no matter what its purpose, the Government will be able to claim that it has favored certain persons for their ability, stemming from race, to contribute distinctive views or perspectives.

Even considered as other than a justification for using race classifications, the asserted interest in viewpoint diversity falls short of being weighty enough. The Court has recognized an interest in obtaining diverse broadcasting viewpoints as a legitimate basis for the FCC, acting pursuant to its "public interest" statutory mandate, to adopt limited measures to increase the number of competing licensees and to encourage licensees to present varied views on issues of public concern. We have also concluded that these measures do not run afoul of the First Amendment's usual prohibition of Government regulation of the marketplace of ideas, in part because First Amendment concerns support limited but inevitable Government regulation of the peculiarly constrained broadcasting spectrum. But the conclusion that measures adopted to further the interest in diversity of broadcasting viewpoints are neither beyond the FCC's statutory authority nor contrary to the First Amendment hardly establishes the interest as important for equal protection purposes.

The FCC's extension of the asserted interest in diversity of views in this case presents, at the very least, an unsettled First Amendment issue. The FCC has concluded that the American broadcasting public receives the incorrect mix of ideas and claims to have adopted the challenged policies to supplement programming content with a particular set of views. Although we have approved limited measures designed to increase information and views generally, the Court has never upheld a broadcasting measure designed to amplify a distinct set of views or the views of a particular class of speakers. Indeed, the Court has suggested that the First Amendment prohibits allocating licenses to further such ends. Even if an interest is determined to be legitimate in one context, it does not suddenly become important enough to justify distinctions based on race.

IV

Our traditional equal protection doctrine requires, in addition to a compelling state interest, that the Government's chosen means be necessary to accomplish and narrowly tailored to further the asserted interest. This element of strict scrutiny is designed to "ensur[e] that the means chosen 'fit' [the] compelling goal so closely that there is little or no possibility that the motive for the classification was illegitimate racial prejudice or stereotype." The chosen means, resting as they do on stereotyping and so indirectly furthering the asserted end, could not plausibly be deemed narrowly tailored. The Court instead finds the racial classifications to be "substantially related" to achieving the Government's interest, a far less rigorous fit requirement. The FCC's policies fail even this requirement.

1

The FCC claims to advance its asserted interest in diverse viewpoints by singling out race and ethnicity as peculiarly linked to distinct views that require enhancement. The FCC's choice to employ a racial criterion embodies the related notions that a particular and distinct viewpoint inheres in certain racial groups, and that a particular applicant, by virtue of race or ethnicity alone, is more valued than other applicants because "likely to provide [that] distinct perspective." The policies impermissibly value individuals because they presume that persons think in a manner associated with their race.

The FCC assumes a particularly strong correlation of race and behavior. The FCC justifies its conclusion that insufficiently diverse viewpoints are broadcast by reference to the percentage of minority owned stations. This assumption is correct only to the extent that minority owned stations provide the desired additional views, and that stations owned by individuals not favored by the preferences cannot, or at least do not, broadcast underrepresented programming. Additionally, the FCC's focus on ownership to improve programming assumes that preferences linked to race are so strong that they will dictate the owner's behavior in operating the station, overcoming the owner's personal inclinations and regard for the market.

The majority addresses this point by arguing that the equation of race with distinct views and behavior is not "impermissible" in this particular case. Apart from placing undue faith in the Government and courts' ability to distinguish "good" from "bad" stereotypes, this reasoning repudiates essential equal protection principles that prohibit racial generalizations. The Court embraces the FCC's reasoning that an applicant's race will likely indicate that the applicant possesses a distinct perspective, but notes that the correlation of race to behavior is "not a rigid assumption about how minority owners will behave in every case." The corollary to this notion is plain: individuals of unfavored racial and ethnic backgrounds are unlikely to possess the unique experiences and background that contribute to viewpoint diversity. Both the reasoning and its corollary reveal but disregard what is objectionable about a stereotype: the racial generalization inevitably does not apply to certain individuals, and those persons may legitimately claim that they have been judged according to their race rather than upon a relevant criterion. Similarly disturbing is the majority's reasoning that different treatment on the basis of race is permissible because efficacious "in the aggregate." In Wiesenfeld [v. Weinberger], we rejected similar reasoning: "Obviously, the notion that men are more likely than women to be the primary supporters of their spouses and children is not entirely without empirical support. But such a gender-based generalization cannot suffice to justify the denigration of the efforts of women who do work and whose earnings contribute significantly to their families' support." Similarly in this case, even if the Court's equation of race and programming viewpoint has some empirical basis, equal protection principles prohibit the Government from relying upon that basis to employ racial classifications.

2

Moreover, the FCC's selective focus on viewpoints associated with race illustrates a particular tailoring difficulty. The asserted interest is in advancing the Nation's different "social, political, esthetic, moral, and other ideas and experiences," yet of all the varied traditions and ideas shared among our citizens, the FCC has sought to amplify only those particular views it identifies through the classifications most suspect under equal protection doctrine. Even if distinct views could be associated with particular ethnic and racial groups, focusing on this particular aspect of the Nation's views calls into question the Government's genuine commitment to its asserted interest.

Our equal protection doctrine governing intermediate review indicates that the Government may not use race and ethnicity as "a 'proxy for other, more germane bases of classification.' " The FCC has used race as a proxy for whatever views it believes to be underrepresented in the broadcasting spectrum. This reflexive or unthinking use of a suspect classification is the hallmark of an unconstitutional policy. The ill fit of means to end is manifest. The policy is overinclusive: many members of a particular racial or ethnic group will have no interest in advancing the views the FCC believes to be underrepresented, or will find them utterly foreign. The policy is underinclusive: it awards no preference to disfavored individuals who may be particularly well versed in and committed to presenting those views. The FCC has failed to implement a case-by-case determination, and that failure is particularly unjustified when individualized hearings already occur, as in the comparative licensing process. Even in the remedial context, we have required that the Government adopt means to ensure that the award of a particular preference advances the asserted interest.

Moreover, the FCC's programs cannot survive even intermediate scrutiny because race-neutral and untried means of directly accomplishing the governmental interest are readily available. The FCC could directly advance its interest by requiring licensees to provide programming that the FCC believes would add to diversity. The FCC and the Court suggest that First Amendment interests in some manner should exempt the FCC from employing this direct, race-neutral means to achieve its asserted interest. They essentially argue that we may bend our equal protection principles to avoid more readily apparent harm to our First Amendment values. But the FCC cannot have it both ways: either the First Amendment bars the FCC from seeking to accomplish indirectly what it may not accomplish directly; or the FCC may pursue the goal, but must do so in a manner that comports with equal protection principles. And if the FCC can direct programming in any fashion, it must employ that direct means before resorting to indirect race-conscious means.

Other race-neutral means also exist, and all are at least as direct as the FCC's racial classifications. The FCC could evaluate applicants upon their ability to provide and commitment to offer whatever programming the FCC believes would reflect underrepresented viewpoints. Additionally, if the FCC believes that certain persons by virtue of their unique experiences will contribute as owners to more diverse broadcasting, the FCC could simply favor applicants whose particular background indicates that they will add to the diversity of programming, rather than rely solely upon suspect classifications. . . .

The FCC has never attempted to assess what alternatives to racial classifications might prove effective. [T]he FCC has never determined that it has any need to resort to racial classifications to achieve its asserted interest, and it has employed race-conscious means before adopting readily available race-neutral, alternative means.

The FCC seeks to avoid the tailoring difficulties by focusing on minority ownership rather than the asserted interest in diversity of broadcast viewpoints. The Constitution clearly prohibits allocating valuable goods such as broadcast licenses simply on the basis of race. Yet the FCC refers to the lack of minority ownership of stations to support the existence of a lack of diversity of viewpoints, and has fitted its programs to increase ownership. This repeated focus on ownership supports the inference that the FCC seeks to allocate licenses based on race, an impermissible end, rather than to increase diversity of viewpoints, the asserted interest. And this justification that links the use of race preferences to minority ownership rather than to diversity of viewpoints ensures that the FCC's programs, like that at issue in *Croson,* "cannot be said to be narrowly tailored to any goal, except perhaps outright racial balancing." *Croson,* 488 U.S., at 507.

3

Even apart from these tailoring defects in the FCC's policies, one particular flaw underscores the Government's ill fit of means to end. The FCC's policies assume and rely upon the existence of a tightly bound "nexus" between the owners' race and the resulting programming. . . .

Three difficulties suggest that the nexus between owners' race and programming is considerably less than substantial. First, the market shapes programming to a tremendous extent. Members of minority groups who own licenses might be thought, like other owners, to seek to broadcast programs that will attract and retain audiences, rather than programs that reflect the owner's tastes and preferences. Second, station owners have only limited control over the content of programming. The distress sale presents a particularly acute difficulty of this sort. Unlike the comparative licensing program, the distress sale policy provides preferences to minority owners who neither intend nor desire to manage the station in any respect. Whatever distinct programming may attend the race of an owner actively involved in managing the station, an absentee owner would have far less effect on programming.

Third, the FCC had absolutely no factual basis for the nexus when it adopted the policies and has since established none to support its existence. . . . In the mid-1980s, the FCC, prompted by this Court's decisions indicating that a factual predicate must be established to support use of race classifications, unanimously sought to examine whether, and to what extent, any nexus existed between an owner's race and programming. As the Chairman of the FCC explained to Congress:

> To the extent that heightened scrutiny requires certain factual predicates, we discovered notwithstanding our statements in the past regarding the assumed nexus between minority or female ownership and program diversity, a factual predicate has never been established.

Through the appropriations measures, Congress barred the FCC's attempt to initiate that examination. Even apart from the limited nature of the Court's claims, little can be discerned from the congressional action. First, the Court's survey does not purport to establish that the FCC or Congress has identified any particular deficiency in the viewpoints contained in the broadcast spectrum. Second, no degree of congressional endorsement may transform the equation of race with behavior and thoughts into a permissible basis of governmental action. . . . Third, we should hesitate before accepting as definitive any declaration regarding even the existence of a nexus. The two legislative reports that claim some nexus to exist refer to sources that provide no support for the proposition. Congress through appropriations measures sought to foreclose examination of an issue that the FCC believed to be entirely unresolved. Especially where Congress rejects the considered judgment of the executive officials possessing particular expertise regarding the matter in issue, courts are hardly bound to accept the congressional declaration. Additionally, the FCC created the challenged policies. Congress has, through the appropriations process, frozen those policies in place by preventing the FCC from reexamining or altering them. That congressional action does not amount to an endorsement of the reasoning and empirical claims originally asserted and then abandoned by the FCC, and does not reflect the same considered judgment embodied in measures crafted through the legislative process and subject to the hearings and deliberation accompanying substantive legislation.

4

Finally, the Government cannot employ race classifications that unduly burden individuals who are not members of the favored racial and ethnic groups. The challenged policies fail this independent requirement, as well as the other constitutional requirements. The comparative licensing and distress sale programs provide the eventual licensee with an exceptionally valuable property and with a rare and unique opportunity to serve the local community. The distress sale imposes a particularly significant burden. The FCC has at base created a specialized market reserved exclusively for minority controlled applicants. There is no more rigid quota than a 100% set-aside. This fact is not altered by the observation that the FCC and seller have some discretion over whether stations may be sold through the distress program. For the would-be purchaser or person who seeks to compete for the station, that opportunity depends entirely upon race or ethnicity. The Court's argument that the distress sale allocates only a small percentage of all license sales also misses the mark. This argument readily supports complete preferences and avoids scrutiny of particular programs: it is no response to a person denied admission at one school, or discharged from one job, solely on the basis of race, that other schools or employers do not discriminate.

The comparative licensing program, too, imposes a significant burden. The Court's emphasis on the multifactor process should not be confused with the claim that the preference is in some sense a minor one. It is not. The basic nonrace criteria are not difficult to meet, and, given the sums at stake, applicants have every incentive to structure their ownership arrangement to prevail in the comparative process. Applicants cannot alter their race, of course, and race is clearly the dispositive factor in a substantial percentage of comparative proceedings. Petitioner Metro asserts that race is overwhelmingly the dispositive factor. In reply, the FCC admits that it has not assessed the operation of its own program and the Court notes only that "minority ownership does not guarantee that an applicant will prevail." . . .

In sum, the Government has not met its burden even under the Court's test that approves of racial classifications that are substantially related to an important governmental objective. Of course, the programs even more clearly fail the strict scrutiny that should be applied. The Court has determined, in essence, that Congress and all federal agencies are exempted, to some ill-defined but significant degree, from the Constitution's equal protection requirements. This break with our precedents greatly undermines equal protection guarantees, and permits distinctions among citizens based on race and ethnicity which the Constitution clearly forbids. I respectfully dissent.

Discussion

With the resignation of Justices Brennan and Marshall, it is unclear whether the distinction drawn in *Metro Broadcasting* between the powers of the FCC (and of Congress) and those of the States, as delineated in *Croson,* will survive. In any event, are you persuaded that Congress has greater power to require racial preferences than do States? Recall that the Fourteenth Amendment does not apply to the national government. Does acceptance of Bolling v. Sharpe necessarily imply that the limitations placed on the United States by the due process clause of the Fifth Amendment are identical to those placed on the States by the Fourteenth Amendment?

Chapter 7
Classifications Based on Sex

The previous chapter explored the heightened scrutiny accorded to classifications based on race. Given the history of the Fourteenth Amendment, this presents perhaps the most straightforward and uncontroversial application of the equal protection clause as a constraint on government. The Court has also, however, interpreted the clause to disfavor classifications based on some traits besides race, and commentators have urged that still other traits be included within the special protection of the clause. This chapter focuses on classifications based on sex and, more generally, on the methodology for deciding what classifications besides race should demand an extraordinary justification (i.e., more than minimum rationality) and how heavy a justification should be required.

I. Evolution of the "Intermediate Standard"

Throughout most of its history, the Supreme Court was reluctant to support the demands of women to become full participants in American society. As we saw in Chapter 4, the Court found no constitutional impediments to the Illinois law that rejected Myra Bradwell's right to practice law solely because she was female. The Illinois Supreme Court had upheld the state prohibition in an oral opinion noting that, as a married woman, Bradwell "would be bound neither by her express contracts nor by those implied contracts which it is the policy of the law to create between attorney and client."[1] In affirming Bradwell v. Illinois, 83 U.S. (16 Wall.) 130 (1873), the Supreme Court pointed to the "natural and proper timidity and delicacy which belongs to the female sex [and] evidently unfits it for many of the occupations of civil life." Justice Bradley's concurrence has become notorious:

> [T]he civil law, as well as nature herself, has always recognized a wide difference in the respective spheres and destinies of man and woman. . . . The constitution of the family organization, which is founded in the divine ordinance, as well as in the nature of things, indicates the domestic sphere as that which properly belongs to the domain and functions of womanhood. . . . The paramount destiny and mission of woman are to fulfill the noble and benign offices of wife and mother. This is the law of the Creator.

1. At common law married women lacked the legal capacity to contract or convey property. Women were also not considered criminally responsible for actions done at the instruction of their husbands.

Two years later, in Minor v. Happersett, 88 U.S. (21 Wall.) 162 (1875), p.241 supra, the Court upheld a Missouri law that limited voting rights to men. Although the Court acknowledged that women were citizens of the United States, it held without dissent that the right to vote was not a privilege or immunity of United States citizenship. Presumably because of the decisions in the *Slaughter-House* and *Bradwell* cases, the Court did not even consider that the equal protection clause might constrain this gender classification.

Women scarcely acquiesed: The movement for women's suffrage was one of the major political movements of the late nineteenth and early twentieth centuries.[2] The women's suffrage movement achieved its ultimate success in 1920 by bringing about passage of the Nineteenth Amendment, which removed from the states the right to limit suffrage on grounds of sex.

The first major case concerning women after the Amendment was Adkins v. Children's Hospital, 261 U.S. 525 (1923). The dispute involved a District of Columbia law requiring that women (but not men) receive a minimum wage. After noting the restraint on freedom of contract and the purported lack of evidence supporting differential treatment of women and men, the Court invalidated the law as a violation of the due process clause of the Fifth Amendment. Justice Sutherland, writing for the court, stated:

> [T]he ancient inequality of the sexes, otherwise than physical . . . has continued "with diminishing intensity." In view of the great — not to say revolutionary — changes which have taken place since [Muller v. Oregon], in the contractual, political and civil status of women, culminating in the Nineteenth Amendment, it is not unreasonable to say that these differences have not come almost, if not quite, to the vanishing point. In this aspect of the matter, while the physical differences must be recognized in appropriate cases, and legislation fixing hours or conditions of work may properly take them into account, we cannot accept the doctrine that women of mature age, *sui juris,* require or may be subjected to restrictions upon their liberty of contract which could not lawfully be imposed in the case of men under similar circumstances.[3]

Whatever promise *Adkins* held for the equal treatment of women in the employment context[4] was essentially repudiated in Goesaert v. Cleary, 335 U.S. 464 (1948), which applied the minimum rationality standard to sustain a Michigan statute forbidding a woman to work as a bartender unless she was the "wife or daughter of the male owner" of the establishment. Justice Frankfurter began the majority opinion by stating that it was "beyond question" that Michigan could draw "a sharp line between the sexes" and "forbid all women from working behind a bar." (He did not, however, address whether Michigan could prevent women from joining the Bar.) Noting that Michigan

2. The women's movement, of course, preceded the late nineteenth century, see Ellen DuBois, Feminism and Suffrage: The Emergence of an Independent Women's Movement in America, 1848-1869 (1978). You may recall from Chapter 4 that several prominent early feminists opposed the Fourteenth Amendment on the grounds that section 2 legitimized the denial of voting rights to women by penalizing states only for denying certain "males" the vote.

3. Cf. Muller v. Oregon, 208 U.S. 412 (1908), Chapter 4, supra. *Adkins* was overruled in West Coast Hotel Co. v. Parish 300 U.S. 379 (1937). In 1941 the Court upheld federal maximum hours and minimum wage requirements for both men and women.

4. See Kirp and Yudof, Gender Justice (1987), for a strong argument that *Adkins,* if followed later, could have been a liberating decision for women.

did allow some women to tend bar, Frankfurter wrote that "while Michigan may deny to all women opportunities for tending bar, Michigan cannot play favorites among women without rhyme or reason." Sufficient rhyme and reason was found in Michigan's presumed assumption that "the oversight assured through ownership of a bar by a barmaid's husband or father minimizes hazards that may confront a barmaid without such protecting oversight. This Court is certainly not in a position to gainsay such belief by the Michigan legislature."[5]

The 1960s, which would become a decade of extraordinary change in American life, began with the Court's acceptance, in Hoyt v. Florida, 368 U.S. 57 (1961), of a law that put women on jury lists only at their request: A "woman is still regarded as the center of home and family life."[6]

Presumably as a result of heightened social consciousness, associated with the 1960s, the legal treatment of gender classifications began to change. The watershed decision was Reed v. Reed, 404 U.S. 71 (1971). Although *Reed* purported to apply only the minimal rationality standard, the Court struck down an Idaho law that required, as between a man and woman equally qualified to be administrator of an estate, that the man be chosen. The question of whether *Reed* was truly a "minimal rationality" case and the appropriate standard of review regarding gender classifications became the focus of analysis in the subsequent case of Frontiero v. Richardson.

FRONTIERO v. RICHARDSON
411 U.S. 677 (1973)
On Appeal from the United States District Court
for the Middle District of Alabama

BRENNAN, J., joined by Douglas, White, and Marshall, JJ.

The question before us concerns the right of a female member of the uniformed services to claim her spouse as a "dependent" for the purposes of obtaining increased quarters allowances and medical and dental benefits under 37 U.S.C. §§401, 403, and 10 U.S.C. §§1072, 1076, on an equal footing with male members. Under these statutes, a serviceman may claim his wife as a "dependent" without regard to whether she is in fact dependent upon him for any part of her support. A servicewoman, on the other hand, may not claim her husband as a "dependent" under these programs unless he is in fact dependent upon her for over one-half of his support. Thus, the question for decision is whether this difference in treatment constitutes an unconstitutional discrimination against servicewomen in violation of the Due Process Clause of the Fifth Amendment. . . .

5. Justice Rutledge dissented, joined by Justices Douglas and Murphy, pointing out the lack of congruence between the law and its purported objectives: "A male owner, although he himself is always absent from the bar, may employ his wife and daughter as barmaids. A female owner may neither work as a barmaid herself nor employ her daughter in that position, even if a man is always present in the establishment to keep order."

6. *Hoyt* was overruled by Taylor v. Louisiana, 419 U.S. 522 (1975), which held that a criminal defendant was deprived of his Sixth Amendment right to a jury composed of a cross-section of the community by a practice of automatically exempting women from jury duty unless they had filed a declaration of their desire to serve. See also Duren v. Missouri, 439 U.S. 357 (1979).

I

In an effort to attract career personnel through reenlistment, Congress established a scheme for the provision of fringe benefits to members of the uniformed services on a competitive basis with business and industry. Thus, a member of the uniformed services with dependents is entitled to an increased "basic allowance for quarters" and a member's dependents are provided comprehensive medical and dental care.

Appellant Sharron Frontiero, a lieutenant in the United States Air Force, sought increased quarters allowances, and housing and medical benefits for her husband, appellant Joseph Frontiero, on the ground that he was her "dependent." Although such benefits would automatically have been granted with respect to the wife of a male member of the uniformed services, appellant's application was denied because she failed to demonstrate that her husband was dependent on her for more than one-half of his support. Appellants then commenced this suit, contending that, by making this distinction, the statutes unreasonably discriminate on the basis of sex in violation of the Due Process Clause of the Fifth Amendment.[a] In essence, appellants asserted that the discriminatory impact of the statutes is twofold: first, as a procedural matter, a female member is required to demonstrate her spouse's dependency, while no such burden is imposed upon male members; and second, as a substantive matter, a male member who does not provide more than one-half of his wife's support receives benefits, while a similarly situated female member is denied such benefits. Appellants therefore sought a permanent injunction against the continued enforcement of these statutes and an order directing the appellees to provide Lieutenant Frontiero with the same housing and medical benefits that a similarly situated male member would receive.

Although the legislative history of these statutes sheds virtually no light on the purposes underlying the differential treatment accorded male and female members, a majority of the three-judge District Court surmised that Congress might reasonably have concluded that, since the husband in our society is generally the "bread-winner" in the family — and the wife typically the "dependent" partner — "it would be more economical to require married female members claiming husbands to prove actual dependency than to extend the presumption of dependency to such members." Indeed, given the fact that approximately 99% of all members of the uniformed services are male, the District Court speculated that such differential treatment might conceivably lead to a "considerable saving of administrative expense and manpower."

II

At the outset, appellants contend that classifications based upon sex, like classifications based upon race, alienage, and national origin, are inherently suspect and must therefore be subjected to close judicial scrutiny. We agree and, indeed, find

a. "[W]hile the Fifth Amendment contains no equal protection clause, it does forbid discrimination that is 'so unjustifiable as to be violative of due process.'" Schneider v. Rusk, 377 U.S. 163, 168 (1964).

at least implicit support for such an approach in our unanimous decision only last Term in Reed v. Reed, 404 U.S. 71 (1971).

In *Reed,* the Court considered the constitutionality of an Idaho statute providing that, when two individuals are otherwise equally entitled to appointment as administrator of an estate, the male applicant must be preferred to the female. Appellant, the mother of the deceased, and appellee, the father, filed competing petitions for appointment as administrator of their son's estate. Since the parties, as parents of the deceased, were members of the same entitlement class, the statutory preference was invoked and the father's petition was therefore granted. Appellant claimed that this statute, by giving a mandatory preference to males over females without regard to their individual qualifications, violated the Equal Protection Clause of the Fourteenth Amendment.

The Court noted that the Idaho statute "provides that different treatment be accorded to the applicants on the basis of their sex; it thus establishes a classification subject to scrutiny under the Equal Protection Clause." Under "traditional" equal protection analysis, a legislative classification must be sustained unless it is "patently arbitrary" and bears no rational relationship to a legitimate governmental interest.

In an effort to meet this standard, appellee contended that the statutory scheme was a reasonable measure designed to reduce the workload on probate courts by eliminating one class of contests. Moreover, the appellee argued that the mandatory preference for male applicants was in itself reasonable since "men [are] as a rule more conversant with business affairs than . . . women." Indeed, appellee maintained that "it is a matter of common knowledge, that women still are not engaged in politics, the professions, business or industry to the extent that men are." And the Idaho Supreme Court, in upholding the constitutionality of this statute, suggested that the Idaho Legislature might reasonably have "concluded that in general men are better qualified to act as an administrator than are women."

Despite these contentions, however, the Court held the statutory preference for male applicants unconstitutional. In reaching this result, the Court implicitly rejected appellee's apparently rational explanation of the statutory scheme, and concluded that, by ignoring the individual qualifications of particular applicants, the challenged statute provided "dissimilar treatment for men and women who are . . . similarly situated."

The Court therefore held that, even though the State's interest in achieving administrative efficiency "is not without some legitimacy," "[t]o give a mandatory preference, to members of either sex over members of the other, merely to accomplish the elimination of hearings on the merits, is to make the very kind of arbitrary legislative choice forbidden by the [Constitution]. . . ." This departure from "traditional" rational-basis analysis with respect to sex-based classifications is clearly justified.

There can be no doubt that our Nation has had a long and unfortunate history of sex discrimination.[b] Traditionally, such discrimination was rationalized by an attitude of "romantic paternalism" which, in practical effect, put women, not on a

b. Indeed, the position of women in this country at its inception is reflected in the view expressed by Thomas Jefferson that women should be neither seen nor heard in society's decisionmaking councils.

pedestal, but in a cage. Indeed, this paternalistic attitude became so firmly rooted in our national consciousness that, 100 years ago, a distinguished Member of this Court was able to proclaim:

> Man is, or should be, woman's protector and defender. The natural and proper timidity and delicacy which belongs to the female sex evidently unfits it for many of the occupations of civil life. The constitution of the family organization, which is founded in the divine ordinance, as well as in the nature of things, indicates the domestic sphere as that which properly belongs to the domain and functions of womanhood. The harmony, not to say identity, of interests and views which belong, or should belong, to the family institution is repugnant to the idea of a woman adopting a distinct and independent career from that of her husband. . . .
>
> The paramount destiny and mission of woman are to fulfill the noble and benign offices of wife and mother. This is the law of the Creator. Bradwell v. [Illinois, 83 U.S. (16 Wall.)] 130, 141 (1573) (Bradley, J., concurring).

As a result of notions such as these, our statute books gradually became laden with gross, stereotyped distinctions between the sexes and, indeed, throughout much of the 19th century the position of women in our society was, in many respects, comparable to that of blacks under the pre-Civil War slave codes. Neither slaves nor women could hold office, serve on juries, or bring suit in their own names, and married women traditionally were denied the legal capacity to hold or convey property or to serve as legal guardians of their own children. And although blacks were guaranteed the right to vote in 1870, women were denied even that right — which is itself "preservative of other basic civil and political rights" — until adoption of the Nineteenth Amendment half a century later.

It is true, of course, that the position of women in America has improved markedly in recent decades. Nevertheless, it can hardly be doubted that, in part because of the high visibility of the sex characteristic, women still face pervasive although at times more subtle, discrimination in our educational institutions, in the job market and, perhaps most conspicuously, in the political arena.[c]

Moreover, since sex, like race and national origin, is an immutable characteristic determined solely by the accident of birth, the imposition of special disabilities upon the members of a particular sex because of their sex would seem to violate "the basic concept of our system that legal burdens should bear some relationship to individual responsibility. . . ." And what differentiates sex from such non-suspect statuses as intelligence or physical disability, and aligns it with the recognized suspect criteria, is that the sex characteristic frequently bears no relation to ability to perform or contribute to society. As a result, statutory distinctions between the sexes often have the effect of invidiously relegating the entire class of females to inferior legal status without regard to the actual capabilities of its individual members.

We might also note that, over the past decade, Congress has itself manifested an increasing sensitivity to sex-based classifications. In Tit. VII of the Civil Rights

c. It is true, of course, that when viewed in the abstract, women do not constitute a small and powerless minority. Nevertheless, in part because of past discrimination, women are vastly underrepresented in this Nation's decisionmaking councils. There has never been a female President, nor a female member of this Court. Not a single woman presently sits in the United States Senate, and only 14 women hold seats in the House of Representatives. And, as appellants point out, this underrepresentation is present throughout all levels of our State and Federal Government.

Act of 1964, for example, Congress expressly declared that no employer, labor union, or other organization subject to the provisions of the Act shall discriminate against any individual on the basis of "race, color, religion, *sex,* or national origin." Similarly, the Equal Pay Act of 1963 provides that no employer covered by the Act "shall discriminate . . . between employees on the basis of *sex,*" and §1 of the Equal Rights Amendment, passed by Congress on March 22, 1972, and submitted to the legislatures of the States for ratification, declares that "[e]quality of rights under the law shall not be denied or abridged by the United States or by any State on account of sex." Thus, Congress itself has concluded that classifications based upon sex are inherently invidious, and this conclusion of a coequal branch of Government is not without significance to the question presently under consideration.

With these considerations in mind, we can only conclude that classifications based upon sex, like classifications based upon race, alienage, or national origin, are inherently suspect, and must therefore be subjected to strict judicial scrutiny. Applying the analysis mandated by that stricter standard of review, it is clear that the statutory scheme now before us is constitutionally invalid.

III

The sole basis of the classification established in the challenged statutes is the sex of the individuals involved. . . . [T]he statutes operate so as to deny benefits to a female member, such as appellant Sharron Frontiero, who provides less than one-half of her spouse's support, while at the same time granting such benefits to a male member who likewise provides less than one-half of his spouse's support. Thus, to this extent at least, it may fairly be said that these statutes command "dissimilar treatment for men and women who are . . . similarly situated." Reed v. Reed.

Moreover, the Government concedes that the differential treatment accorded men and women under these statutes serves no purpose other than mere "administrative convenience." In essence, the Government maintains that, as an empirical matter, wives in our society frequently are dependent upon their husbands, while husbands rarely are dependent upon their wives. Thus, the Government argues that Congress might reasonably have concluded that it would be both cheaper and easier simply conclusively to presume that wives of male members are financially dependent upon their husbands, while burdening female members with the task of establishing dependency in fact.[d]

The Government offers no concrete evidence, however, tending to support its view that such differential treatment in fact saves the Government any money. In order to satisfy the demands of strict judicial scrutiny, the Government must demonstrate, for example, that it is actually cheaper to grant increased benefits with respect to *all* male members, than it is to determine which male members are in fact entitled to such benefits and to grant increased benefits only to those members whose wives actually meet the dependency requirement. Here, however, there is substantial evidence that, if put to the test, many of the wives of

d. It should be noted that these statutes are not in any sense designed to rectify the effects of past discrimination against women. On the contrary, these statutes seize upon a group — women who have historically suffered discrimination in employment, and rely on the effects of this past discrimination as a justification for heaping on additional economic disadvantages.

male members would fail to qualify for benefits. And in light of the fact that the dependency determination with respect to the husbands of female members is presently made solely on the basis of affidavits, rather than through the more costly hearing process, the Government's explanation of the statutory scheme is, to say the least, questionable.

In any case, our prior decisions make clear that, although efficacious administration of governmental programs is not without some importance, "the Constitution recognizes higher values than speed and efficiency." And when we enter the realm of "strict judicial scrutiny," there can be no doubt that "administrative convenience" is not a shibboleth, the mere recitation of which dictates constitutionality. On the contrary, any statutory scheme which draws a sharp line between the sexes, *solely* for the purpose of achieving administrative convenience, necessarily commands "dissimilar treatment for men and women who are . . . similarly situated," and therefore involves the "very kind of arbitrary legislative choice forbidden by the [Constitution]. . . ." We therefore conclude that, by according differential treatment to male and female members of the uniformed services for the sole purpose of achieving administrative convenience, the challenged statutes violate the Due Process Clause of the Fifth Amendment insofar as they require a female member to prove the dependency of her husband.[e]

Reversed.

Mr. Justice Stewart concurs in the judgment, agreeing that the statutes before us work an invidious discrimination in violation of the Constitution. Reed v. Reed, 404 U.S. 71.

POWELL, J., joined by Burger, C.J., and Blackmun, J., concurring.

I agree that the challenged statutes constitute an unconstitutional discrimination against servicewomen in violation of the Due Process Clause of the Fifth Amendment, but I cannot join the opinion of Mr. Justice Brennan, which would hold that all classifications based upon sex, "like classifications based upon race, alienage, and national origin," are "inherently suspect and must therefore be subjected to close judicial scrutiny." It is unnecessary for the Court in this case to characterize sex as a suspect classification, with all of the far-reaching implications of such a holding. Reed v. Reed, 404 U.S. 71 (1971), which abundantly supports our decision today, did not add sex to the narrowly limited group of classifications which are inherently suspect. In my view, we can and should decide this case on the authority of *Reed* and reserve for the future any expansion of its rationale. There is another, and I find compelling, reason for deferring a general categorizing of sex classifications invoking the strictest test of judicial scrutiny. The Equal Rights Amendment, which if adopted will resolve the substance of this precise question, has been approved by the Congress and submitted for ratification by the States. If this Amendment is duly adopted, it will represent the will of the people accomplished in the manner prescribed by the Constitution. By acting prematurely and unnecessarily, as I view it, the Court has assumed a decisional responsibility at the very time when state legislatures, functioning within the traditional democratic process, are debating the proposed Amendment. It

e. As noted earlier, the basic purpose of these statutes was to provide fringe benefits to members of the uniformed services in order to establish a compensation pattern which would attract career personnel through reenlistment. Our conclusion in no wise invalidates the statutory schemes except insofar as they require a female member to prove the dependency of her spouse.

seems to me that this reaching out to pre-empt by judicial action a major political decision which is currently in process of resolution does not reflect appropriate respect for duly prescribed legislative processes.

There are times when this Court, under our system, cannot avoid a constitutional decision on issues which normally should be resolved by the elected representatives of the people. But democratic institutions are weakened, and confidence in the restraint of the Court is impaired, when we appear unnecessarily to decide sensitive issues of broad social and political importance at the very time they are under consideration within the prescribed constitutional processes.

REHNQUIST, J., dissents for the reasons stated by Judge Rives in his opinion for the District Court, Frontiero v. Laird, 341 F. Supp. 201 (1972).

Discussion

Between 1971, when *Reed* was decided, and 1976, the Court did not settle on a standard for reviewing gender-based classifications. This was partly because of the fact that several of the intervening cases involved statutes that arguably *benefited* women, and the Court was uncertain about how to deal with "reverse" discrimination even in the more familiar area of race. In Craig v. Boren, 429 U.S. 190 (1976), a majority of the Justices finally agreed upon an *"intermediate"* standard of review — presumably intermediate between the rational classification and the full-blown suspect classification standards. A classification based on gender *"must serve important governmental objectives and must be substantially related to achievement of those objectives."*

Hovering over this entire chapter, in some ways, is the Equal Rights Amendment and the implications to be drawn first from its proposal by Congress and secondly from its ultimate inability to be ratified by the required 38 states in order to become part of the Constitution. See section VII infra. Consider the use that Justices Brennan and Powell made of the fact that it had been proposed by Congress and submitted to the states for ratification. What precisely is the point of the Amendment and the use of the Article V amending process if Justice Brennan's interpretation of the existing, nonamended constitution, is correct? Might it be that, whereas Justice Brennan would allow at least *some* gender classifications, i.e., those that pass strict scrutiny, the proposed amendment would require an absolutely "gender-blind" Constitution that would tolerate *no* use of gender as a classification? Is this plausible, either as a legal or a political matter?

II. Why Should Gender Classifications Be Accorded Any Special Scrutiny?

Why should gender classifications be subject to *any* special standard of review at all? This question is not merely of historical interest. Some of the doctrines in this area are not firmly settled, and the demise of a proposed equal rights amendment in 1982 indicates a lack of contemporary agreement about how sex discrimination should be treated. The same considerations that underlie one's attempt to answer the question may, moreover, provide a foundation for determining whether classifications based on other traits should be deemed suspect. To place the theoretical inquiry in a concrete economic and social context, we first survey some examples of traditional gender classifications in the area of employment.

A. Introduction: A Survey of Gender-Dependent Employment Practices

The laws upheld in *Bradwell* and *Goesaert* are extreme examples of so-called protective laws restricting women's occupational opportunities. Legislatures also enacted minimum wage and maximum hours regulations for women. These laws were aimed at terrible work conditions — which legislatures tried to ameliorate for men as well — and were also designed to protect American laborers against competition from immigrants willing to work longer hours at lower wages.[7] Whatever the motives of those who supported the laws, it was only the *Lochner* Court's sexism that sustained any of them. (Compare Justice Brewer's opinion in Muller v. Oregon, 208 U.S. 412 (1908), Chapter 4 supra, with the language in *Bradwell.*)

Today, legislation regulating the terms and conditions of employment without regard to sex is pervasive and accepted as constitutional. When the Civil Rights Act of 1964 was enacted, however, sexually discriminatory protective legislation was also pervasive. An early regulation, promulgated by the Equal Employment Opportunity Commission to implement Title VII of the Act, provided:[8]

> (1) Many States have enacted laws or promulgated administrative regulations with respect to the employment of females. Among these laws are those which prohibit or limit the employment of females, e.g., the employment of females in certain occupations, in jobs requiring the lifting or carrying of weights exceeding certain prescribed limits, during certain hours of the night, or for more than a specified number of hours per day or per week.
>
> (2) The Commission believes that such laws and regulations, although originally promulgated for the purpose of protecting females, have ceased to be relevant to our technology or to the expanding role of the female worker in our economy. The Commission has found that such laws and regulations do not take into account the capacities, preferences, and abilities of individual females and tend to discriminate rather than protect. Accordingly the Commission has concluded that such laws and regulations conflict with Title VII of the Civil Rights Act of 1964. . . .

Before the enforcement of Title VII of the Civil Rights Act of 1964 and the Equal Pay Act, 29 U.S.C. §206(d), employers commonly excluded women from various positions and paid women less than men for performing identical jobs. To whatever extent de jure discrimination of this sort persists, its illegality is not

7. See Elisabeth Landes, The Effect of State Maximum-Hours Laws on the Employment of Women in 1920, 88 J. Pol. Econ. 476 (1980).

8. 29 C.F.R. §1604. 1(b) (1970). Section 703 of the Civil Rights Act, 42 U.S.C. §2000e-2, provides: "It shall be an unlawful employment practice for an employer . . . to fail or refuse to hire or to discharge any individual, or otherwise to discriminate against any individual with respect to his compensation, terms, conditions, or privileges of employment because of such individual's race, color, religion, sex, or national origin." As originally introduced in Congress, Title VII did not include sex, which was added by Southern opponents of the bill in an attempt to defeat it.

in doubt. There has, however, been litigation over section 703(e), the "BFOQ" exception to Title VII's general prohibition of sex discrimination:

> Notwithstanding any other provision of this title, it shall not be an unlawful employment practice to an employer to hire and employ employees . . . on the basis of . . . religion, sex, or national origin in those certain instances where religion, sex, or national origin is a bona fide occupational qualification [BFOQ] reasonably necessary to the normal operation of that particular business or enterprise.

In Phillips v. Martin Marietta Corp., 400 U.S. 542 (1971), the Court reversed the lower courts' summary approval of respondent's policy of not employing women with preschool children, while employing similarly situated men:

> The existence of . . . conflicting family obligations, if demonstrably more relevant to job performance for a woman than for a man, could arguably be a basis for distinction under section 703(e) of the Act. But that is a matter of evidence. . . . [W]e remand for fuller development of the record.

Justice Marshall concurred, but argued that no conceivable record could justify the discrimination. He understood the bfoq exception to apply "only to job situations that require specific physical characteristics necessarily possessed by only one sex."

In Dothard v. Rawlinson, 433 U.S. 321 (1977), the Court sustained the Alabama Board of Corrections' Administrative Regulation 204, which assigned guards to maximum security facilities based on gender, with the effect of excluding women from 75 percent of the available "correctional counsellor" positions in the Alabama prison system. Justice Stewart wrote:

> In [the prisons'] environment of violence and disorganization, it would be an oversimplification to characterize Regulation 204 as an exercise in "romantic paternalism." In the usual case, the argument that a particular job is too dangerous for women may appropriately be met by the rejoinder that it is the purpose of Title VII to allow the individual woman to make that choice for herself. More is at stake in this case, however. . . . The essence of a correctional counsellor's job is to maintain prison security. A woman's relative ability to maintain order in a male, maximum-security, unclassified penitentiary of the type Alabama now runs could be directly reduced by her womanhood. There is a basis in fact for expecting that sex offenders who have criminally assaulted women in the past would be moved to do so again if access to women were established within the prison. There would also be a real risk that other inmates, deprived of a normal heterosexual environment, would assault women guards because they were women. In a prison system where violence is the order of the day, where inmate access to guards is facilitated by dormitory living arrangements, where every institution is understaffed, and where a substantial portion of the inmate population is composed of sex offenders mixed at random with other prisoners, there are few visible deterrents to inmate assaults on women custodians.

Justice Marshall, joined by Justice Brennan, dissented:

> [T]he fundamental justification for the decision is that women as guards will generate sexual assaults. With all respect, this rationale perpetuates one of the most insidious of the old myths about women — that women, wittingly or not, are se-

ductive sexual objects. The effect of the decision . . . is to punish women because their very presence might provoke sexual assaults. It is women who are made to pay the price in lost job opportunities for the threat of depraved conduct by prison inmates. . . .

The Court points to no evidence in the record to support the asserted "likelihood that inmates would assault a woman because she was a woman." Perhaps the Court relies upon common sense, or "innate recognition." Brief for Appellants. But the danger in this emotionally laden context is that common sense will be used to mask the " 'romantic paternalism' " and persisting discriminatory attitudes that the Court properly eschews.[9]

Discussion

1. Is it a "myth" to believe that women at least "unwittingly . . . are seductive sexual objects"? Is it not a central point of feminism that men all too often view women in precisely such a fashion? Is not the question, then, the extent to which Alabama in effect can take this fact into account in determining who can become a prison guard?

2. Justice Marshall assumes that the rationale for Alabama's policy is merely "paternalistic," i.e., to protect female guards from sexual assault by men. But what if Alabama instead argued that it is trying to prevent increased disruption, instability, and possible violence attached to the entry of women into the maximum-security prisons for males. Would that change Justice Marshall's views on the constitutional issue?

3. Assume that the duties of prison guards include the observation of prisoners while taking showers. Is it legitimate to limit this duty to members of the same sex as the prisoners? If you would not accept any such limitation with respect to race, what accounts for the different reaction?

B. Text and History

How do the text and history of the equal protection clause bear on the constitutionality of discrimination on the basis of sex as compared to race? Consider the different levels of abstraction on which one can describe the *purposes* of the clause or the *principles* attributed to it. Articulate and defend the lowest-order (i.e., narrowest) principle that one would have to attribute to the equal protection clause in order to encompass gender as well as race discrimination.

Recall Brennan in *Frontiero*: "[T]hroughout much of the 19th century the position of women in our society was, in many respects, comparable to that of blacks under the pre-Civil War slave codes." Is the historical discrimination of women similar to that of racial or ethnic minorities?

9. Justice Marshall also noted that, in an unrelated case, a court had held that the prison conditions invoked by the majority to justify Regulation 204 violated the cruel and unusual punishment clause of the Eighth Amendment. Referring to the language of the bfoq exception to Title VII, he argued that "no governmental 'business' may operate 'normally' in violation of the Constitution." See also Catharine MacKinnon, Toward a Feminist Theory of the State 226 (1989): "Excluding women is always an option if sex equality feels in tension with the pursuit itself. . . . For example, women have been excluded from contact jobs in male-only prisons in the name of 'their very womanhood' because they might get raped, the Court taking the view of the reasonable rapist in women's employment opportunities. The conditions that create women's rapability are not seen as susceptible to legal change, nor is predicating women's employment on their inevitability seen as discriminatory."

C. Reasoning from Race

The first instinct of many judges, commentators, and students in addressing the constitutionality of sex discrimination is to treat race discrimination as a point of comparison and to inquire to what extent gender classifications share the characteristics that call race classifications into disfavor. There are two overlapping strategies: (a) to recall the rationales for treating racial classifications as suspect and ask whether they apply to gender classifications; (b) to identify the features of race that make it seem special and ask whether gender shares these features.

With respect to (a), recall the process, result, and color-blind rationales for the antidiscrimination principle. With respect to (b), consider the following description of the features of racial classifications within a system of discrimination of the sort that existed in parts of the United States until several decades ago. Racial classifications are based on a congenital and unalterable, morally neutral trait (e.g., whiteness of skin). The trait is infused with moral value so that those who possess the trait deem themselves superior to those who do not, and the latter are stigmatized. The trait is possessed by a majority of the society, or a majority of those holding power in the society. The trait correlates poorly with legitimate policymaking criteria but is nonetheless pervasively used as a basis for differential treatment in such a manner that those who possess the desirable trait obtain more benefits than those who do not.

D. Views from the Academy

RICHARD WASSERSTROM, RACISM, SEXISM, AND PREFERENTIAL TREATMENT[10]

24 U.C.L.A.L. Rev. 581, 587-592 (1977)

It is even clearer in the case of sex than in the case of race that one's sexual identity is a centrally important, crucially relevant category within our culture. I think, in fact, that it is more important and more fundamental than one's race. It is evident that there are substantially different role expectations and role assignments to persons in accordance with their sexual physiology, and that the positions of the two sexes in the culture are distinct. We do have a patriarchal society in which it matters enormously whether one is a male or a female. By almost all important measures it is more advantageous to be a male rather than a female. . . .

As is true for race, it is also a significant social fact that to be a female is to be an entity or creature viewed as different from the standard, fully developed person who is male as well as white. But to be female, as opposed to being black, is not to be conceived of as simply a creature of less worth. That is one important thing that differentiates sexism from racism: The ideology of sex, as opposed to the ideology of race, is a good deal more complex and confusing. Women are both put on a pedestal and deemed not fully developed persons. They are idealized;

10. The ideas in this piece are treated in greater detail and in somewhat different form in two essays: Racism and Sexism, and Preferential Treatment, both contained in Wasserstrom, Philosophy and Social Issues: Five Studies (1980).

their approval and admiration is sought; and they are at the same time regarded as less competent than men and less able to live fully developed, fully human lives — for that is what men do. At best, they are viewed and treated as having properties and attributes that are valuable and admirable for humans of this type. For example, they may be viewed as especially empathetic, intuitive, loving, and nurturing. At best, these qualities are viewed as good properties for women to have, and, provided they are properly muted, are sometimes valued within the more well-rounded male. Because the sexual ideology is complex, confusing, and variable, it does not unambiguously proclaim the lesser value attached to being female rather than being male, nor does it unambiguously correspond to the existing social realities. For these, among other reasons, sexism could plausibly be regarded as a deeper phenomenon than racism. It is more deeply embedded in the culture, and thus less visible. Being harder to detect, it is harder to eradicate. Moreover, it is less unequivocally regarded as unjust and unjustifiable. That is to say, there is less agreement within the dominant ideology that sexism even implies an unjustifiable practice or attitude. Hence, many persons announce, without regret or embarrassment, that they are sexists or male chauvinists; very few announce openly that they are racists. For all of these reasons sexism may be a more insidious evil than racism, but there is little merit in trying to decide between two seriously objectionable practices which one is worse. . . .

Viewed from the perspective of social reality it should be clear, too, that racism and sexism should not be thought of as phenomena that consist simply in taking a person's race or sex into account, or even simply in taking a person's race or sex into account in an arbitrary way. Instead, racism and sexism consist in taking race and sex into account in a certain way, in the context of a specific set of institutional arrangements and a specific ideology which together create and maintain a *system* of unjust institutions and unwarranted beliefs and attitudes. That system is and has been one in which political, economic, and social power and advantage are concentrated in the hands of those who are white and male.

Discussion

Wasserstrom believes that sexism "is more deeply embedded in the culture, and thus less visible" than racism. Must we conclude that classifications based on gender should receive more heightened scrutiny than classifications based on race?

JOHN ELY, DEMOCRACY AND DISTRUST
164-170 (1980)

The case of women is timely and complicated. Instances of first-degree prejudice are obviously rare, but just as obviously exaggerated stereotyping — typically to the effect that women are unsuited to the work of the world and therefore belong at home — has long been rampant throughout the male population and consequently in our almost exclusively male legislatures in particular. It may all be in apparent good humor, even perceived as protective, but it has cost women dearly. Absent a strong demonstration of mitigating factors, therefore, we would have to treat gender-based classifications that act to the disadvantage of women as suspicious. If the stereotyping has been clear, however, so has the noninsularity of the group affected. The degree of contact between men and women could hardly be greater, and neither, of course, are women "in the closet" as homosexuals historically have been. Finally, lest you think I missed it, women have about half the votes, apparently more. As if it weren't enough that they're not discrete and insular, they're not even a minority!

Despite that seeming avalanche of rebuttal, there remains something that seems right in the claim that women have been operating at an unfair disadvantage in the political process, though it's tricky pinning down just what gives rise to that intuition. . . . [I]f women have "chosen" not to avail themselves of their opportunities, either by voting or by personally influencing those men with whom they come in contact, to correct the exaggerated stereotype that many men hold and on the basis of which they have often legislated . . . [it can] plausibly be argued . . . that many women have *accepted* the overdrawn stereotype and thus have seen nothing to "correct." . . . That could, of course, imply that it wasn't so exaggerated a stereotype after all, but it could mean something else too, that our society, including the women in it, has been so pervasively dominated by men that women quite understandably have accepted men's stereotypes, of women as well as on other subjects.

The general idea is one that in some contexts has merit. A sufficiently pervasive prejudice can block its own correction not simply by keeping its victims "in the closet" but also by convincing even them of its correctness. In Castaneda v. Partida, decided in 1977, the Court held that a prima facie case of intentional discrimination against Mexican-Americans in the selection of grand jurors was not constitutionally affected by the fact that Mexican-Americans enjoyed "governing majority" status in the county involved. Concurring, Justice Marshall gave the reason why: "Social scientists agree that members of minority groups frequently respond to discrimination and prejudice by attempting to disassociate themselves from the group, even to the point of adopting the majority's negative attitudes towards the minority." . . .

To apply all this to the situation of women in America in 1980, however, is to strain a metaphor past the breaking point. . . .

The very stereotypes that gave rise to laws "protecting" women by barring them from various activities are under daily and publicized attack, and are the subject of equally spirited defense. . . . Given such open discussion of the traditional stereotypes, the claim that the numerical majority is being "dominated," that women are in effect "slaves" who have no realistic choice but to assimilate the stereotypes, is one it has become impossible to maintain except at the most inflated rhetorical level. . . .

[T]he date of passage seems unquestionably relevant to what our analysis has suggested is a more promising approach to the question of suspiciousness — one geared to the existence of official or unofficial blocks on the opportunities of those the law disadvantages to counter by argument or example the overdrawn stereotypes we might, from the demography of the decision-making body, otherwise suspect were operative. . . .

[Suppose that the Court struck down a gender classification enacted in an earlier era, and that a contemporary legislature] reconsidered and repassed the same or a similar law. The fact that due process of lawmaking was denied in 1908 or even in 1939 needn't imply that it was in 1982 as well and consequently the new law should be upheld as constitutional. In fact I may be wrong in supposing that because women now are in a position to protect themselves they will, that we are thus unlikely to see in the future the sort of official gender discrimination that has marked our past. But if women don't protect themselves from sex discrimination in the future, it won't be because they can't. It will rather be because for one reason or another — substantive disagreement or most likely the assignment of a low priority to the issue — they don't choose to. Many of us may condemn such a choice as benighted on the merits, but that is not a constitutional argument.

Discussion

1. Professor Ely adopts a purely process-oriented rationale for the antidiscrimination principle. Does this rationale entail his conclusion that a gender classification adopted in the 1990s should not be subject to judicial scrutiny?

2. In a reference to Castaneda v. Parida, Ely cites Marshall, who says "minority groups . . . disassociate themselves from the group, even to the point of adopting the majority's negative attitudes towards the minority." Could this explain why women "don't choose to" use their votes to force change? And if such a choice is unconscious or indicative of the dominant male hegemony, why does Ely say that it "is not a constitutional argument"?

3. Responding to the concluding lines of the excerpt just quoted, Paul Brest wrote:

> Until I read these sentences I never fully grasped what the Court meant when it said in Shelley v. Kraemer that the rights established by the Fourteenth Amendment are "*personal* rights." I do now. Imagine, if you will, explaining to a woman who is excluded by protective legislation from a "man's job" for which she is qualified, "Well you had a choice to vote down this legislation but you didn't choose to." *Who* didn't choose to? Suppose that *she* did what she could to vote it down, but other women embrace the stereotype it embodies.[11]

SYLVIA LAW, RETHINKING SEX AND THE CONSTITUTION

132 U. Pa. L. Rev. 955, 965 (1984)

There are . . . important points of difference between sex- and race-based discrimination. There is no reason to believe that black and white people are inherently different in any way that should ever be allowed to matter in the law. Men and women, by contrast, are different in significant sex-specific physical ways. Most differences between men and women are like differences between blacks and whites: statistical generalizations, which are more or less true in the aggregate but untrue in relation to particular individuals. Accurate statistical differences between men and women that are false in individual cases include weight, height, longevity, mathematical aptitude, aggression, capacity for nurturance, and physical strength. There are, however, other categorical differences between men and women that are not simply statistical generalizations, but rather sex-based physical differences relating to reproductive capacity. By categorical sex-based differences, what is meant, and *all that is meant*, is that most women and no men possess the capacity to reproduce the species.

11. Paul Brest, The Substance of Process, 42 Ohio St. L.J. 131 (1981).

III. The Rejection of "Archaic and Overbroad Generalizations"[12]

A. Discrimination Against Women

In Weinberger v. Wiesenfeld, 420 U.S. 636 (1975), the Court invalidated the "mother's insurance benefit" provision of the Social Security Act, 42 U.S.C. §402(g), which provided benefits to widows (but not widowers) having minor children in their care. Justice Brennan noted that the scheme denigrated "the efforts of women who do work and whose earnings contribute significantly to their families' support." He found the scheme even more pernicious than that invalidated in Frontiero v. Richardson, because the presumption of dependency was irrebuttable and because the deceased wife "not only failed to receive for her family the same protection which a similarly situated male worker would have received, but she also was deprived of a portion of her own earnings in order to contribute to the fund out of which benefits would be paid to others. Since the Constitution forbids the gender-based differentiation premised upon assumptions of dependency made in the statutes before us in *Frontiero,* the Constitution also forbids the gender-based differentiation that results in the efforts of women workers required to pay social security taxes producing less protection for their families than is produced by the efforts of men."

The government had argued that the classification was "reasonably designed to compensate women beneficiaries as a group for the economic difficulties which still confront women who seek to support themselves and their families." Justice Brennan responded:

> [T]he mere recitation of a benign, compensatory purpose is not an automatic shield which protects against any inquiry into the actual purposes underlying a statutory scheme. Here it is apparent both from the statutory scheme itself and from the legislative history of §402(g) that Congress' purpose in providing benefits to widows with young children was not to provide an income to women who were, because of economic discrimination, unable to provide for themselves. Rather §402(g), linked as it is directly to responsibility for minor children, was intended to permit women to elect not to work and to devote themselves to the care of children. . . .
>
> Given the purpose of enabling the surviving parent to remain at home to care for a child, the gender-based distinction of §402(g) is entirely irrational. The classification discriminates against surviving children solely on the basis of the sex of the surviving parent. . . . It is no less important for a child to be cared for by its sole surviving parent when that parent is male rather than female. . . . [T]o the extent that Congress legislated on the presumption that women as a group would choose to forego work to care for children while men would not, the statutory structure, independent of the gender-based classification, would deny or reduce benefits to those men who conform to the presumed norm and are not hampered by their child-care responsibilities. Benefits under §402(g) decrease with increased earnings.

Justice Powell, joined by the Chief Justice, wrote a brief opinion concurring "in the judgment and generally in the opinion of the Court." Justice Rehnquist wrote a brief opinion concurring in the result. Justice Douglas did not participate.

12. Schlesinger v. Ballard, 419 U.S. 498, 508 (1975).

In Stanton v. Stanton, 421 U.S. 7 (1975), the Court invalidated a Utah statute which provided that the period of minority for males extended to age 21 and for females to age 18. The defendant had discontinued support payments ordered by the divorce decree for his daughter when she reached 18. Justice Blackmun delivered the opinion of the Court in an 8 to 1 decision, with only Justice Rehnquist dissenting.

It may be true, as the Utah court observed and as is argued here, that it is the man's primary responsibility to provide a home and that it is salutary for him to have education and training before he assumes that responsibility; that girls tend to mature earlier than boys; and that females tend to marry earlier than males. . . .

Notwithstanding the "old notions" to which the Utah court referred, we perceive nothing rational in the distinction drawn by §15-2-1 which, when related to the divorce decree, results in the appellee's liability for support for Sherri only to age 18 but for Rick to age 21. This imposes "criteria wholly unrelated to the objective of that statute." A child, male or female, is still a child. No longer is the female destined solely for the home and the rearing of the family, and only the male for the marketplace and the world of ideas. . . . Women's activities and responsibilities are increasing and expanding. Coeducation is a fact, not a rarity. The presence of women in business, in the professions, in government and, indeed, in all walks of life where education is a desirable, if not always a necessary, antecedent is apparent and a proper subject of judicial notice. If specified age of minority is required for the boy in order to assure him parental support while he attains his education and training, so, too, is it for the girl. . . . [I]f the female is not to be supported so long as the male, she hardly can be expected to attend school as long as he does, and bringing her education to an end earlier coincides with the role-typing society has long imposed.

Califano v. Goldfarb, 430 U.S. 199 (1977), struck down a provision of the Social Security Act under which a widow was entitled to survivors' benefits based on her deceased husband's coverage regardless of dependency, but only a widower who received at least half of his support from his deceased wife was entitled to benefits. Justice Brennan wrote for a plurality including Justices White, Marshall, and Powell. Invoking Weinberger v. Wiesenfeld, he asserted that the law must be analyzed, not as a discrimination in favor of surviving widows, but as a discrimination against covered wage-earning females, who received less protection for their spouses. After reviewing the legislative history, Justice Brennan concluded that

the differential treatment of nondependent widows and widowers results not . . . from a deliberate congressional intention to remedy the arguably greater needs of the former, but rather from an intention to aid the dependent spouses of deceased wage earners, coupled with a presumption that wives are usually dependent. This presents precisely the situation faced in *Frontiero* and *Wiesenfeld*. The only conceivable justification for writing the presumption of wives' dependency into the statute is the assumption, not verified by the Government . . . but based simply on "archaic and overbroad" generalizations, that it would save the Government time, money, and effort simply to pay benefits to all widows, rather than to require proof of dependency of both sexes. . . . [S]uch assumptions do not suffice to justify a gender-based discrimination in the distribution of employment related benefits.

Justice Stevens concurred in the judgment. He believed that "the relevant discrimination . . . is against surviving male spouses, rather than against deceased female wage earners" and that it was not invidious. A review of the legislative history persuaded him that

> this discrimination against a group of males is merely the accidental by-product of a traditional way of thinking about females . . . , [and] that a rule which effects an unequal distribution of economic benefits solely on the basis of sex is sufficiently questionable that "due process requires that there be a legitimate basis for presuming that the rule was actually intended to serve [the] interest" put forward by the Government as its justification. In my judgment, something more than accident is necessary to justify the disparate treatment of persons who have as strong a claim to equal treatment as do similarly situated surviving spouses.

Justice Rehnquist, joined by Chief Justice Burger and Justices Stewart and Blackmun, dissented. He argued that the Court should give great deference to social insurance legislation for two reasons: "the statutory scheme will typically have been expanded by amendment over a period of years so that it is virtually impossible to say that a particular amendment fits with mathematical nicety into a carefully conceived overall plan for payment of benefits"; and "considerations of 'administrative convenience' . . . bear a . . . vital relation to the overall legislative plan because of congressional concern for certainty in determination of entitlement and promptness in payment of benefits." Here the distinction was responsive to the fact that widows are much more likely to be without adequate means of support than widowers. Even if a provision that discriminated against women should receive heightened judicial scrutiny, this was not such a provision. Because "the contributions of the deceased spouse cannot be regarded as creating any sort of contractual entitlement on the part of either the deceased wife or the surviving husband," the only constitutionally relevant distinction was between widowers and widows. But because the statute worked to the advantage of widows, "it in no way perpetuates or exacerbates the economic disadvantage that has led the Court to conclude that gender-based discrimination must meet a different test than other types of classifications."[13]

In Califano v. Westcott, 443 U.S. 76 (1979), the Court invalidated a provision of the Social Security Act granting AFDC payments to families whose dependent children had been deprived of parental support due to the unemployment of the father but not of the mother. The Court found that the law discriminated against mothers who were the primary economic source of income for their families. Justice Blackmun, joined by Justices Brennan, White, Marshall, and Stevens, concluded that the classification

13. In Heckler v. Mathews, 465 U.S. 728 (1984), a unanimous Court upheld certain amendments passed by Congress in 1977 following the decision in *Goldfarb*, in which Congress repealed the dependency requirements for husbands and widows that had been invalidated in that decision. Writing for a unanimous Court, Justice Brennan noted that "Congress' purpose in adopting the exception bears no relationship to the concerns that animated the original enactment of those criteria . . . , which were premised on an assumption that females would normally be dependent on the earnings of their spouses but males would not." Here, however, the purpose was protecting the "expectations of persons, both men and women, who had planned their retirements on pre-January 1977 law . . . , not to reassert the sexist assumption rejected in *Goldfarb*. . . . The protection of reasonable reliance interests is not only a legitimate governmental objective: it provides 'an exceedingly persuasive justification' for the statute at issue here."

is not substantially related to the attainment of any important and valid statutory goals. It is, rather, part of the "baggage of sexual stereotypes," that presumes the father has the "primary responsibility to provide a home and its essentials," while the mother is the "center of home and family life." Legislation that rests on such presumptions, without more, cannot survive scrutiny under the Due Process Clause of the Fifth Amendment.

Justice Powell filed an opinion concurring in part and dissenting in part, in which Chief Justice Burger, and Justices Stewart and Rehnquist, joined.

In Wengler v. Druggists Mut. Ins. Co., 446 U.S. 142 (1980), the Court struck down a Missouri law under which widows of men who died in work-related accidents were automatically entitled to death benefits, while widowers of women who died in such accidents had to prove that they were incapacitated or actually dependent on the wife's earnings. Writing for a majority of seven, Justice White found *Weinberger, Frontiero,* and *Goldfarb* controlling, and found that the statute discriminated against both men and women.

In Kirchberg v. Feenstra, 450 U.S. 455 (1981), the Court invalidated a Louisiana statute granting a husband, as "head and master" of the family, the unilateral right to dispose of property jointly owned with his wife without her consent. In a unanimous decision, Justice Marshall noted that although the statute allowed a wife to take affirmative steps to prohibit her husband from disposing of joint property by making a "declaration by authentic act," "the 'absence of an insurmountable barrier' will not redeem an otherwise unconstitutionally discriminatory law."

B. Discrimination Against Men

The constitutional scrutiny of classifications that disadvantage males might be justified in at least two ways. (1) It might reflect a substantive rather than a process-oriented view of the equal protection clause — perhaps reflecting the notion that (most) burdens imposed on people because of an immutable characteristic such as gender are harmful and unjustified. (2) It might reflect a process-oriented concern with the *non*material injuries inflicted on women by the pattern of such classifications.

In Craig v. Boren, 429 U.S. 190 (1976) — where the Court first announced the "substantially related to important purposes" standard for reviewing gender classifications — Justice Brennan wrote for the majority invalidating an Oklahoma law that prohibited the sale of 3.2 percent beer to males under the age of 21 and females under the age of 18. The State argued that the classification reflected gender-based correlations with drunken driving. Brennan responded that the gender correlations (e.g., 1.8 percent of males and .2 percent of females between 18-20 were arrested for driving under the influence of alcohol) were too tenuous to meet the standard. While Justice Brennan did not specifically discuss why a classification disfavoring males should be subject to special judicial scrutiny, he did note that although the statute disadvantaged men, it also perpetuated "archaic and overbroad" generalizations concerning teenage males and females. "In light of the weak congruence between gender and the characteristic or trait that gender purported to represent, it was necessary that the legislatures choose either to realign their substantive laws in a gender-neutral fashion, or to adopt procedures for identifying those instances where the sex-centered generalizations actually comported to fact." He also questioned the validity of the statistics, suggesting that

> [t]he very social stereotypes that find reflection in age-differential laws . . . are likely substantially to distort the accuracy of these comparative statistics. Hence "reckless" young men who drink and drive are transformed into arrest statistics, whereas their female counterparts are chivalrously escorted home.

Chief Justice Burger and Justice Rehnquist argued in dissent that, at least where a classification does not discriminate against females, it should suffice that it has a rational basis.

Orr. v. Orr, 440 U.S. 268 (1979), invalidated an Alabama statute requiring husbands but not wives to pay alimony upon divorce. Justice Brennan wrote that the statute could not be upheld "even if sex were a reliable proxy need, and even if the institution of marriage did discriminate against women. . . . Under the statute, individualized hearings at which the parties' relative financial circumstances are considered *already* occur . . . [and] individualized hearings can determine which women were in fact discriminated against vis à vis their husbands, as well as which family unit defied the stereotype and left the husband dependent on the wife. . . ."

Chief Justice Burger, and Justices Powell and Rehnquist, dissented on the ground that, in its posture before the Court, the case did not present an actual case or controversy.

In Caban v. Mohammed, 441 U.S. 380 (1979), the Court invalidated a New York law permitting unwed mothers but not unwed fathers to block the adoption of their child by withholding consent. Justice Powell delivered the opinion of the Court, in which Justices Brennan, White, Marshall, and Blackmun, joined. He noted that

> maternal and paternal roles are not invariably different in importance. Even if unwed mothers as a class were closer than unwed fathers to their newborn infants, this generalization concerning parent-child relations would become less acceptable as a basis for legislative distinctions as the age of the child increased. The present case demonstrates that an unwed father may have a relationship with his children fully comparable to that of the mother. . . .
>
> The effect of New York's classification is to discriminate against unwed fathers even when their identity is known and they have manifested a significant paternal interest in the child. The facts of this case illustrate the harshness of classifying unwed fathers as being invariably less qualified and entitled than mothers to exercise a concerned judgment as to the fate of their children. Section 111 both excludes some loving fathers from full participation in the decision whether their children will be adopted and, at the same time, enables some alienated mothers arbitrarily to cut off the paternal rights of fathers.

Chief Justice Burger and Justices Stevens, Rehnquist, and Stewart dissented.

MISSISSIPPI UNIVERSITY FOR WOMEN v. HOGAN
458 U.S. 718 (1982)
On Writ of Certiorari to the United States Court of Appeals for the Fifth Circuit

[The Mississippi University for Women is a state school, located in Columbia, Mississippi. Since its establishment in 1884, its enrollment has been limited to women. (During much of its history, of course, enrollment was limited to white women.) In 1971 MUW opened a School of Nursing, to which Joe Hogan, a resident of Columbia, applied in 1979. Although he was offered the opportunity to audit certain nursing courses without receiving credit, he was denied admission because he is male. The District Court upheld the denial of admission; the Fifth Circuit reversed.]

O'CONNOR, J., delivered the opinion of the Court.

This case presents the narrow issue of whether a state statute that excludes males from enrolling in a state-supported professional nursing school violates the Equal Protection Clause of the Fourteenth Amendment. . . .

II

. . . [T]he party seeking to uphold a statute that classifies individuals on the basis of their gender must carry the burden of showing an "exceedingly persuasive justification" for the classification. The burden is met only by showing at least that the classification serves "important governmental objectives and that the discriminatory means employed" are "substantially related to the achievement of those objectives."

Although the test for determining the validity of a gender-based classification is straightforward, it must be applied free of fixed notions concerning the roles and abilities of males and females. Care must be taken in ascertaining whether the statutory objective itself reflects archaic and stereotypic notions. Thus, if the statutory objective is to exclude or "protect" members of one gender because they are presumed to suffer from an inherent handicap or to be innately inferior, the objective itself is illegitimate.

III

A

The State's primary justification for maintaining the single-sex admissions policy of MUW's School of Nursing is that it compensates for discrimination against women and, therefore, constitutes educational affirmative action. As applied to the School of Nursing, we find the State's argument unpersuasive.

In limited circumstances, a gender-based classification favoring one sex can be justified if it intentionally and directly assists members of the sex that is disproportionately burdened. However, we consistently have emphasized that "the mere recitation of a benign, compensatory purpose is not an automatic shield which protects against any inquiry into the actual purposes underlying a statutory scheme." Weinberger v. Wiesenfeld. . . .

It is readily apparent that a State can evoke a compensatory purpose to justify an otherwise discriminatory classification only if members of the gender benefited by the classification actually suffer a disadvantage related to the classification. . . . Mississippi has made no showing that women lacked opportunities to obtain training in the field of nursing or to attain positions of leadership in that field when the MUW School of Nursing opened its door or that women currently are deprived of such opportunities. In fact, in 1970, the year before the School of Nursing's first class enrolled, women earned 94 percent of the nursing baccalaureate degrees conferred in Mississsippi and 98.6 percent of the degrees earned nationwide. . . . As one would expect, the labor force reflects the same predominance of women in nursing. When MUW's School of Nursing began operation, nearly 98 percent of all employed registered nurses were female.

Rather than compensate for discriminatory barriers faced by women, MUW's policy of excluding males from admission to the School of Nursing tends to perpetuate the stereotyped view of nursing as an exclusively woman's job. By assuring that Mississippi allots more openings in its state-supported nursing schools to women than it does to men, MUW's admissions policy lends credibility to the old view that women, not men, should become nurses, and makes the assumption that nursing is a field for women a self-fulfilling prophecy. See Stanton v. Stanton, 421 U.S. 7 (1975). Thus, we conclude that, although the State recited a "benign, compensatory purpose," it failed to establish that the alleged objective is the actual purpose underlying the discriminatory classification.

The policy is invalid also because it fails the second part of the equal protection test, for the State has made no showing that the gender-based classification is substantially and directly related to its proposed compensatory objective. To the contrary, MUW's policy of permitting men to attend classes as auditors fatally undermines its claim that women, at least those in the School of Nursing, are adversely affected by the presence of men. . . .

POWELL, J., with whom Rehnquist, J., joins, dissenting.

The Court's opinion bows deeply to conformity. Left without honor — indeed, held unconstitutional — is an element of diversity that has characterized much of American education and enriched much of American life. The Court in effect holds today that no State now may provide even a single institution of higher learning open only to women students. . . .

It is undisputed that women enjoy complete equality of opportunity in Mississippi's public system of higher education. Of the State's eight universities and 16 junior colleges, all except MUW are coeducational. At least two other Mississippi universities would have provided respondent with the nursing curriculum that he wishes to pursue. . . .

Nor is respondent significantly disadvantaged by MUW's all-female tradition. His constitutional complaint is based upon a single asserted harm: that he must *travel* to attend the state-supported nursing schools that concededly are available to him. The Court characterizes this injury as one of "inconvenience."

I

Coeducation, historically, is a novel educational theory. From grade school through high school, college, and graduate and professional training, much of the nation's population during much of our history has been educated in sexually segregated classrooms.

The sexual segregation of students has been a reflection of, rather than an imposition upon, the preference of those subject to the policy. It cannot be disputed, for example, that the highly qualified women attending the leading women's colleges could have earned admission to virtually any college of their choice. Women attending such colleges have chosen to be there, usually expressing a preference for the special benefits of the single-sex institutions. Similar decisions were made by the colleges that elected to remain open to women only.

The arguable benefits of single-sex colleges also continue to be recognized by students of higher education. A 10-year empirical study by the Cooperative Institutional Research Program of the American Council of Education and the University of California, Los Angeles also has affirmed the distinctive benefits of single-sex colleges and universities. As summarized in A. Astin, Four Critical Years 232 (1977), the data established that

> [b]oth [male and female] single-sex colleges facilitate student involvement in several areas: academic, interaction with faculty, and verbal aggressiveness. . . . Men's and women's colleges also have a positive effect on intellectual self-esteem. Students at single-sex colleges are more satisfied than students at coeducational colleges with virtually all aspects of college life. . . . The only area where students are less satisfied is social life. . . .

II

The issue in this case is whether a State transgresses the Constitution when — within the context of a public system that offers a diverse range of campuses, curricula, and educational alternatives — it seeks to accommodate the legitimate personal preferences of those desiring the advantages of an all-women's college. In my view, the Court errs seriously by assuming — without argument or discussion — that the equal protection standard generally applicable to sex discrimination is appropriate here. That standard was designed to free women from "archaic and overbroad generalizations. . . ." In no previous case have we applied it to invalidate state efforts to *expand* women's choices. Nor are there prior sex discrimination decisions by this Court in which a male plaintiff, as in this case, had the choice of an equal benefit.

The cases cited by the Court therefore do not control the issue now before us. . . .

By applying heightened equal protection analysis to this case,[a] the Court frustrates the liberating spirit of the Equal Protection Clause. . . .

a. Even the Court does not argue that the appropriate standard here is "strict scrutiny" — a standard that none of our "sex discrimination" cases ever has adopted. Sexual segregation in education differs from the tradition, by the decision in Plessy v. Ferguson, 163 U.S. 537 (1896), of "separate but equal" racial segregation. It was characteristic of racial segregation that segregated facilities were offered, not as alternatives to increase the choices available to blacks, but as the sole alternative. MUW stands in sharp contrast. Of Mississippi's eight public universities and 16 public junior colleges, only MUW considers sex as a criterion for admission. Women consequently are free to select a coeducational education environment for themselves if they so desire; their attendance of MUW is not a matter of coercion.

Discussion

1. Would "separate but equal" male only and female only schools satisfy the majority in MUW?

2. Is convenience/location of the school important? What if MUW were located across from a co-ed nursing school?

3. Justice O'Connor's opinion presents itself as a narrow consideration of the particular facts before the Court. Indeed, she notes in a footnote that the Court was "not faced with the question of whether States can provide 'separate but equal' undergraduate institutions for males and females. Cf. Vorchheimer v. School District of Philadelphia, 532 F.2d 880 (C.A. 3 1975), *aff'd by an equally divided court,* 430 U.S. 703 (1977)." Although the Fifth Circuit below had questioned the validity of all sex segregated education within MUW, the Court refrained from addressing this issue. "[B]ecause we review judgments, not statements in opinions, Black v. Cutter Laboratories, 351 U.S. 292 (1956), we decline to address the question of whether MUW's admissions policy, as applied to males seeking admission to schools other than the School of Nursing, violates the Fourteenth Amendment."

Vorchheimer upheld the denial of admission to an all-male selective-admission public high school. Chief Justice Burger, dissenting in *Hogan*, emphasized the narrowness of the majority's holding and suggested "that a State might well be justified in maintaining, for example, the option of an all-women's business school or liberal arts program." Justice Blackmun, in a separate dissent, also noted the purported narrowness of the Court's holding, but he expressed skepticism about preventing its "spillover" into the wider issue of sex segregated education. Justice Powell could "see no principled way — in light of the Court's rationale — to reach a different result with respect to other MUW schools and departments." Can *Vorchheimer* be reconciled with *Hogan*?

4. To what extent can Mississippi's fate in *Hogan* be attributed to inept lawyering? Justice O'Connor riddles the states' claim that some sort of affirmative action is needed to encourage female Mississippians to become nurses. What if the state had argued instead that it was trying to provide maximum freedom of choice to its citizenry, including women who continued to want to attain the purported benefits of attending a single-sex school of nursing. Justice Powell quoted in his opinion comments by the President of Wellesley College and by the Mount Holyoke College Trustees Committee on Coeducation justifying the decisions of those two institutions to remain exclusively women's colleges. Thus Wellesley President Barbara Newell stated in 1973 that "[t]he research we have clearly demonstrates that women's colleges produce a disproportionate number of women leaders and women in responsible positions in society." Wellesley and Mount Holyoke are both private colleges and, for that very reason, quite expensive to attend. Is Mississippi forbidden to provide for its nonwealthy women what they could buy through the market were they wealthy and willing to leave the state, i.e., the opportunity to attend a women's college? Assuming it may do so constitutionally, should Massachusetts prohibit gender discrimination in admissions to private institutions just as it now prohibits racial discrimination?

IV. Sameness and Difference

The Court generally justifies disparate treatment according to gender based on findings that men and women *are* different in some significant way. However, a determination of "real differences" may be problematic, if only because one's notions of what counts as a relevant difference may be based on accepted stereotypes and long practiced custom. In the cases that follow, has the Court found real differences or is it perpetuating stereotypes?

A. Classification on What Basis?

In Geduldig v. Aiello, 417 U.S. 484 (1974), the Court applied only a rational classification standard to uphold California's exclusion of disabilities incident to normal pregnancies from its disability insurance scheme established for the employees of private employers. Justice Stewart explained:

> [T]his case is thus a far cry from cases like Reed v. Reed and Frontiero v. Richardson, involving discrimination based upon gender as such. The California insurance program does not exclude anyone from benefit eligibility because of gender but merely removes one physical condition — pregnancy — from the list of compensable disabilities. While it is true that only women can become pregnant, it does not follow that every legislative classification concerning pregnancy is a sex-based classification like those considered in *Reed* and *Frontiero*. Normal pregnancy is an objectively identifiable physical condition with unique characteristics. Absent a showing that distinctions involving pregnancy are mere pretexts designed to effect an invidious discrimination against the members of one sex or the other, lawmakers are constitutionally free to include or exclude pregnancy from the coverage of legislation such as this on any reasonable basis, just as with respect to any other physical condition.
>
> The lack of identity between the excluded disability and gender as such under this insurance program becomes clear upon the most cursory analysis. The program divides potential recipients into two groups — pregnant women and nonpregnant persons. While the first group is exclusively female, the second includes members of both sexes. The fiscal and actuarial benefits of the program thus accrue to members of both sexes.

Justice Brennan, joined by Justices Douglas and Marshall, dissented:

> [B]y singling out for less favorable treatment a gender-linked disability peculiar to women, the State has created a double standard for disability compensation: a limitation is imposed upon the disabilities for which women workers may recover, while men receive full compensation for all disabilities suffered, including those that affect only or primarily their sex, such as prostatectomies, circumcision, hemophilia and gout. In effect, one set of rules is applied to females and another to males. Such dissimilar treatment of men and women, on the basis of physical characteristics inextricably linked to one sex, inevitably constitutes sex discrimination.
>
> The same conclusion has been reached by the Equal Employment Opportunity Commission, the federal agency charged with enforcement of Title VII of the Civil Rights Act of 1964, as amended by the Equal Employment Opportunity Act of 1972, which prohibits employment discrimination on the basis of sex. In guidelines issued

pursuant to Title VII and designed to prohibit the disparate treatment of pregnancy disabilities in the employment context, the EEOC has declared that: "Disabilities caused or contributed to by pregnancy, miscarriage, abortion, childbirth and recovery therefrom are, for all job-related purposes, temporary disabilities and should be treated as such under any health or temporary disability insurance or sick leave plan available in connection with employment. Written and unwritten employment policies and practices involving matters such as the commencement and duration of leave, the availability of extensions, the accrual of seniority and other benefits and privileges, reinstatement, and payment under any health or temporary disability insurance or sick leave plan, formal or informal, shall be applied to disability due to pregnancy or childbirth on the same terms and conditions as they are applied to other temporary disabilities."

Discussion

Does the law in *Geduldig* classify on the basis of gender? Assume that it does not and analyze it in terms of the rationales for treating gender classifications as suspect. (By what standard should a court review a classification based on having recessive sickle-cell anemia or Tay-Sachs genes, which are carried almost exclusively by Blacks and Jews respectively?)

General Electric Co. v. Gilbert, 429 U.S. 125 (1976), relied on *Geduldig* to sustain against a Title VII challenge a corporate disability plan that excluded pregnancy-related disabilities. Justices Brennan, Marshall, and Stevens dissented.

Nashville Gas Co. v. Satty, 434 U.S. 136 (1977), held that Title VII prohibited an employer who requires a pregnant employee to take a leave of absence from depriving her of accumulated job seniority upon her return. Justice Rehnquist wrote that, by comparison to the disability plan in *Gilbert,* "petitioner has not merely refused to extend to women a benefit that men cannot and do not receive, but has imposed on women a substantial burden that men need not suffer." The district court had also invalidated the employer's policy of not awarding sick-leave pay to pregnant employees. The Supreme Court held that, absent proof that the exclusion was a pretext "designed to effect an invidious discrimination," this did not violate Title VII.

B. "Special (Favorable) Treatment" for Pregnancy

In 1978 Congress amended Title VII to prohibit discrimination "on the basis of pregnancy, childbirth, or related medical conditions." Public Law 95-555. Referring to Title VII's prohibition of discrimination "because of sex" or "on the basis of sex," the Pregnancy Discrimination Act of 1978 (PDA) provided that these terms "include, but are not limited to, because of or on the basis of pregnancy, childbirth, or related medical conditions; and women affected by pregnancy, childbirth, or related medical conditions shall be treated the same for all employment-related purposes, including receipt of benefits under fringe benefit programs, as other persons not so affected but similar in their ability or inability to work. . . ."[14]

14. In Newport News Shipbuilding and Dry Dock v. EEOC, 462 U.S. 669 (1983), the Court held that an employer's insurance program providing less extensive pregnancy benefits for spouses of

Some state legislation goes further than the federal PDA to require employers to provide special treatment for pregnancy and childbirth. For example, the California Fair Employment and Housing Act makes it unlawful "[f]or any employer to refuse to allow a female employee affected by pregnancy, childbirth, or related medical conditions . . . to take a leave on account of pregnancy for a reasonable period of time; provided such period shall not exceed four months." In California Federal Savings and Loan Association v. Guerra, 479 U.S. 272 (1987), the Supreme Court held that the California law was not preempted by the federal PDA. (The employer did not argue that the California law violated the Fourteenth Amendment, and the Court did not consider this issue.) Justice Marshall wrote:

> Congress intended the PDA to be "a floor beneath which pregnancy disability benefits may not drop — not a ceiling above which they may not rise."
>
> The context in which Congress considered the issue of pregnancy discrimination supports this view of the PDA. Congress had before it extensive evidence of discrimination *against* pregnancy, particularly in disability and health insurance programs like those challenged in *Gilbert* and Nashville Gas Co. v. Satty. The Reports, debates, and hearings make abundantly clear that Congress intended the PDA to provide relief for working women and to end discrimination against pregnant workers. . . . [T]he legislative history is devoid of any discussion of preferential treatment of pregnancy, beyond acknowledgments of the existence of state statutes providing for such preferential treatment. . . .
>
> Title VII, as amended by the PDA, and California's pregnancy disability leave statute share a common goal. The purpose of Title VII is "to achieve equality of employment opportunities and remove barriers that have operated in the past to favor an identifiable group of . . . employees over other employees." Rather than limiting existing Title VII principles and objectives, the PDA extends them to cover pregnancy. As Senator Williams, a sponsor of this Act, stated: "The entire thrust . . . behind this legislation is to guarantee women the basic right to participate fully and equally in the workforce, without denying them the fundamental right to full participation in family life."
>
> [The California statute] also promotes equal employment opportunity. By requiring employers to reinstate women after a reasonable pregnancy disability leave, [it] insures that they will not lose their jobs on account of pregnancy disability. California's approach is consistent with the dissenting opinion of Justice Brennan in General Electric Co. v. Gilbert, which Congress adopted in enacting the PDA. . . . Justice Brennan stated:
>
> > [D]iscrimination is a social phenomenon encased in a social context and, therefore, unavoidably takes its meaning from the desired end products of the relevant legislative enactment, end products that may demand due consideration of the uniqueness of the "disadvantaged" individuals. A realistic understanding of the conditions found in to-

---

male employees than for female employees discriminated against male employees in violation of Title VII. Justice Stevens, writing for the majority, held that the PDA not only overturned the specific result reached in *Gilbert*, but also rejected its reasoning that differential treatment of pregnancy is not gender-based discrimination. He stated that the PDA "makes clear that it is discriminatory to treat pregnancy-related conditions less favorably than other medical conditions. Thus petitioner's plan unlawfully gives married male employees a benefit package for their dependents that is less inclusive than the dependency coverage provided to married female employees." Justice Rehnquist, in a dissent joined by Justice Powell, concluded that the PDA only overturned *Gilbert* to the extent that it related to female employees, and that *Gilbert* was still controlling precedent for pregnancy coverage involving dependents.

day's labor environment warrants taking pregnancy into account in fashioning disability policies."

By "taking pregnancy into account," California's pregnancy disability-leave statute allows women, as well as men, to have families without losing their jobs. . . . The statute is narrowly drawn to cover only the period of actual physical disability. . . . Accordingly, unlike the protective labor legislation prevalent earlier in this century, [it] does not reflect archaic or stereotypical notions about pregnancy and the abilities of pregnant workers. A statute based on such stereotypical assumptions would, of course, be inconsistent with Title VII's goal of equal employment opportunity.

Justice White, joined by Chief Justice Rehnquist and Justice Powell, dissented.[15]

Note: Putative Parenthood

In Parham v. Hughes, 441 U.S. 347 (1979), the Court upheld a Georgia statute prohibiting an unwed father but not an unwed mother from suing for a child's wrongful death unless the father had previously legitimated the child. The Court found that avoiding the problems involving proof of paternity that are most common in cases dealing with fathers, especially after the death of the child in question, was an important state objective. Justice Stewart, joined by Chief Justice Burger and Justices Rehnquist and Stevens, argued that

> [t]he appellant, as the natural father, was responsible for conceiving an illegitimate child and had the opportunity to legitimate the child but failed to do so. Legitimation would have removed the stigma of bastardy and allowed the child to inherit from the father in the same manner as if born in wedlock. . . . Unlike the illegitimate child for whom the status of illegitimacy is involuntary and immutable, the appellant here was responsible for fostering an illegitimate child and for failing to change its status. It is thus neither illogical nor unjust for society to express its "condemnation of irresponsible liaisons beyond the bounds of marriage" by not conferring upon a biological father the statutory right to sue for the wrongful death of his illegitimate child. . . .
>
> [I]t is clear that the Georgia statute does not invidiously discriminate against the appellant simply because he is of the male sex. The fact is that mothers and fathers of illegitimate children are not similarly situated. Under Georgia law, only a father can by voluntary unilateral action make an illegitimate child legitimate. Unlike the mother of an illegitimate child whose identity will rarely be in doubt, the identity of the father will frequently be unknown.
>
> . . . [The] state interest in avoiding fraudulent claims of paternity in order to maintain a fair and orderly system of decedent's property disposition is also present in the context of actions for wrongful death. If paternity has not been established before the commencement of a wrongful-death action, a defendant may be faced with the possibility of multiple lawsuits by individuals all claiming to be the father of the deceased child. Such uncertainty would make it difficult if not impossible for a defendant to settle a wrongful death action in many cases, since there would always

15. Wimberly v. Labor & Indus. Relations Commn. of Mo., 479 U.S. 511 (1987), held that the PDA did not *require* employers to make special accommodations for pregnancy leave. The Court unanimously upheld the denial of unemployment benefits to a woman who had been on pregnancy leave pursuant to the employer's policy that she would be rehired only if a position was available when she was ready to return to work.

exist the risk of a subsequent suit by another person claiming to be the father. The State of Georgia has chosen to deal with this problem by allowing only fathers who have established paternity by legitimating their children to sue for wrongful death, and we cannot say that this solution is an irrational one.

Justice Powell concurred in the judgment.

Justice White dissented, joined by Justices Brennan, Marshall, and Blackmun. He stated that

> Appellant is the father, rather than the mother, of a deceased illegitimate child. It is conceded that for this reason alone he may not bring an action for the wrongful death of his child. Yet four Members of the Court conclude that appellant is not discriminated against "simply" because of his sex . . . because Georgia provides a means by which fathers can legitimate their children. The dispositive point is that only a father may avail himself of this process. Therefore, we are told, "[t]he fact is that mothers and fathers of illegitimate children are not similarly situated." . . . That only fathers *may* resort to the legitimizing process cannot dissolve the sex discrimination in *requiring* them to.

C. "Special (Unfavorable) Treatment" Based on Pregnancy and Fertility

Cleveland Board of Education v. LaFleur, 414 U.S. 632 (1974), invalidated a regulation that required a pregnant schoolteacher to take maternity leave five months before the expected birth of her child. Emphasizing the important interests in "freedom of personal choice in matters of marriage and family choice," Justice Stewart found the regulation unconstitutional because it contains "an irrebuttable presumption of physical incompetency and that presumption applies even when the medical evidence as to an individual woman's physical status might be wholly to the contrary."

UAW v. Johnson Controls, Inc., 111 S. Ct. 1196 (1991), held that the respondent battery manufacturer was not entitled to summary judgment in a Title VII action challenging its "fetal protection policy." The policy, designed to prevent unborn children and their mothers from suffering the adverse effects of lead exposure in respondent's battery manufacturing plant, prohibited women with childbearing capacity from holding positions that exposed them to high levels of lead. Justice Blackmun wrote for the Court holding that respondent's policy was facially discriminatory, and that the manufacturer had not established sex as a bona fide occupational qualification (BFOQ).

In sustaining the fetal protection policy, the Court of Appeals for the Seventh Circuit had applied a "business necessity" test, a three-step inquiry that considers "whether there is a substantial health risk to the fetus; whether transmission of the hazard to the fetus occurs only through women; and whether there is a less discriminatory alternative equally capable of preventing the health hazard to the fetus." The Supreme Court held that while the business necessity defense was relevant to policies that had a disparate impact, it had no application to a policy that treated employees differently based on their sex:

> . . . Johnson Controls' policy classifies on the basis of gender and childbearing capacity, rather than fertility alone. . . . Johnson Controls' policy is facially discriminatory because it requires only a female employee to produce proof that she is not capable of reproducing.
>
> Our conclusion is bolstered by the Pregnancy Discrimination Act of 1978 (PDA) . . . in which Congress explicitly provided that, for purposes of Title VII, discrimination "on the basis of sex" includes discrimination "because of or on the basis of pregnancy, childbirth, or related medical conditions." . . .
>
> The enforcement policy of the Equal Employment Opportunity Commission accords with this conclusion. On January 24, 1990, the EEOC issued a Policy Guidance in the light of the Seventh Circuit's decision in the present case. . . . The document noted: "For the plaintiff to bear the burden of proof [as done here] in a case in which there is direct evidence of a facially discriminatory policy is wholly inconsistent with settled Title VII law."

Title VII does permit an employer to discriminate where an employee's sex is a bona fide occupational qualification for the job. However, Justice Blackmun noted:

> The wording of the BFOQ defense contains several terms of restriction that indicate that the exception reaches only special situations. The statute thus limits the situations in which discrimination is permissible to "certain instances" where sex discrimination is "reasonably necessary" to the "normal operation" of the "particular" business. Each one of these terms — certain, normal, particular — prevents the use of general subjective standards and favors an objective, verifiable requirement. But the most telling term is "occupational"; this indicates that these objective, verifiable requirements must concern job-related skills and aptitudes. . . .
>
> We conclude that the language of both the BFOQ provision and the PDA which amended it, as well as the legislative history and the case law, prohibit an employer from discriminating against a woman because of her capacity to become pregnant unless her reproductive potential prevents her from performing the duties of her job. We reiterate our holdings in . . . *Dothard* that an employer must direct its concerns about a woman's ability to perform her job safely and efficiently to those aspects of the woman's job-related activities that fall within the "essence" of the particular business.
>
> We have no difficulty concluding that Johnson Controls cannot establish a BFOQ. Fertile women, as far as appears in the record, participate in the manufacture of batteries as efficiently as anyone else. . . .
>
> Nor can concerns about the welfare of the next generation be considered a part of the "essence" of Johnson Controls' business. . . . It is no more appropriate for the courts than it is for individual employers to decide whether a woman's reproductive role is more important to herself and her family than her economic role. Congress has left this choice to the woman as hers to make.

Finally, dismissing possible tort liability as a justification for Johnson Control's policy, Justice Blackmun noted: "If, under general tort principles, Title VII bans sex-specific fetal-protection policies, the employer fully informs the woman of the risk, and the employer has not acted negligently, the basis for holding an employer liable seems remote at best."

In a separate opinion, Justice White argued that the Court erred in holding "that the BFOQ defense is so narrow that it could never justify a sex-specific fetal protection policy." Although the BFOQ standard "is a difficult standard to satisfy, nothing in the statute's language indicates that it could *never* support a sex-specific fetal protection policy." One possible justification would be "to avoid substantial tort liability." Justice White deemed the Court's "speculative" dismissal of this possibility "small comfort to employers."

Justice White also argued that "[p]rior decisions construing the BFOQ defense confirm that the defense is broad enough to include considerations of cost and safety of the sort that could form the basis for an employer's adoption of a fetal protection policy." Reading *Dothard* differently from the majority, he thought the case made clear "that avoidance of sustantial safety risks to third parties is *inherently* part of both an employee's ability to perform a job and an employer's 'normal operation' of its business."

Justice Scalia also wrote a separate opinion:

> First, I think it irrelevant that there was "evidence in the record about the debilitating effect of lead exposure on the male reproductive system. . . . Even without such evidence, treating women differently "on the basis of pregnancy" constitutes discrimination "on the basis of sex," because Congress has unequivocally said so. . . .
>
> Second, [it is entirely irrelevant] . . . that "Johnson Controls has shown no factual basis for believing that all or substantially all women would be unable to perform safely the duties of the job involved. . . . As Judge Easterbrook put it in his dissent below, "Title VII gives parents the power to make occupational decisions affecting their families." . . .
>
> Third, . . . all that need be said [about the liability issue] in the present case is that Johnson has not demonstrated a substantial risk of tort liability — which is alone enough to defeat a tort-based assertion of the BFOQ exception.
>
> Last, the Court goes far afield, it seems to me, in suggesting that increased cost alone cannot support a BFOQ defense. . . . [N]othing in our prior cases suggests this, and in my view it is wrong. I think, for example, that a shipping company may refuse to hire pregnant women as crew members on long voyages because the on-board facilities for foreseeable emergencies, though quite feasible, would be inordinately expensive.

D. The Feminist Legal Debate[16]

WENDY WILLIAMS, EQUALITY'S RIDDLE: PREGNANCY AND THE EQUAL TREATMENT/SPECIAL TREATMENT DEBATE[17]

13 N.Y.U. Rev. L. & Soc. Change 325, 325-327, 329-331, 352-356, 362-364 (1984-1985)

. . . The [equal treatment] approach has been, in the words of the 1978 Pregnancy Discrimination Act (PDA), to require that "women affected by pregnancy, childbirth or related medical conditions . . . be treated the same for all employment related purposes . . . as other persons not affected but similar in their ability or inability to work."

16. See also C. Gilligan, In a Different Voice (1982), and E. Wolgast, Equality and the Rights of Women (1980).

17. Williams was counsel for the plaintiff in Geduldig v. Aiello, and counsel for NOW and several other organizations that appeared as amici in California Fed. Sav. & Loan Assn. v. Guerra to urge that the Court strike down the California law.

Today, commentators have raised questions about the wisdom and propriety of this . . . approach to pregnancy rules and laws. In Professor Ann Scales's version of the critique, she states her basic assumption as follows:

> The only differences between the sexes which apparently cannot be ignored are in utero pregnancy, and breastfeeding, the one function in the childrearing process which only women can perform. In observing that these are the capabilities which really differentiate women from men, it is crucial that we overcome any aversion to describing these functions as "unique." Uniqueness is a "trap" only in terms of an analysis, such as that generated in Geduldig v. Aiello, which assumes that maleness is the norm. "Unique" does not mean uniquely handicapped.

. . . Thus, at least superficially, the dispute centers on whether pregnancy should be viewed as comparable to other physical conditions or as unique and special. On a deeper level, the dispute is about whether pregnancy "naturally" makes women unequal and thus requires special legislative accommodation to it in order to equalize the sexes, or whether pregnancy can or should be visualized as one human experience which in many contexts, most notably the workplace, creates needs and problems similar to those arising from causes other than pregnancy, and which can be handled adequately on the same basis as are other physical conditions of employees. On the deepest level, the debate may reflect a demand by special treatment advocates that the law recognize and honor a separate identity which women themselves consider special and important and, on the equal treatment side, a commitment to a vision of the human condition which seeks to cover commonality rather than difference.

The critics believe that the "equal treatment model" precludes recognition of pregnancy's uniqueness, and thus creates for women a Procrustean bed — pregnancy will be treated as if it were comparable to male conditions when it is not, thus forcing pregnant women into a workplace structure designed for men. Such a result, they believe, denies women's special experience and does not adequately respond to the realities of women's lives.

[For] proponents of the equal treatment model, . . . the objective is to readjust the general rules for dealing with illness and disability to ensure that the rules can fairly account for the whole range of workplace disabilities that confront employed people. Pregnancy creates not "special" needs, but rather exemplifies typical basic needs.

The first proposition essential to [the equal treatment] analysis is that sex-based generalizations are generally impermissible. . . . The basis for this proposition is a belief that a dual system of rights inevitably produces gender hierarchy and, more fundamentally, treats women and men as statistical abstractions rather than as persons with individual capacities, inclinations and aspirations — at enormous cost to women and not insubstantial cost to men.

The second essential proposition is that laws and rules which do not overtly classify on the basis of sex, but which have a disproportionately negative effect upon one sex, warrant, under appropriate circumstances, placing a burden of justification upon the party defending the law or rule in court. In the view of its proponents, the proposition is an essential companion to the first proposition and is necessary for the ultimate equality of the sexes. Society has been tailored to predefined sex roles not only through overt gender classification, but also through laws and rules neutral on their face but inspired by the same assumptions, stereotypes and ideologies as sex-based classifications.

The goal of the feminist legal movement that began in the early seventies is not and never was the integration of women into a male world any more than it has been to build a separate but better place for women. . . . The second proposition (perpetrators of rules with a disparate effect must justify them) provides a doctrinal tool with which to begin to squeeze the male tilt out of a purportedly neutral legal structure and thus substitute genuine for merely formal gender neutrality. . . . That principle was recognized [in the PDA]. . . .

The "equal treatment" model separates pregnancy and childrearing and insists that each be independently analyzed. The separation has important implications. When the childrearing function is considered separately from pregnancy, it becomes apparent that parents of either sex might undertake that responsibility. To grant childrearing leave to mothers only would be, under this analysis, to discriminate against fathers. Employers who provide leaves for childrearing must therefore substitute "parental" for "maternal" leaves. This separation of early childrearing from pregnancy thus serves the objective of prohibiting workplace rules that discourage families for opting for an egalitarian or nontraditional assignment of parental roles and from ordering their lives in a way that best meets their economic and personal needs. Further, it explicitly rejects stereotypes about motherhood and fatherhood, undermining the view that holds the mother naturally and inevitably responsible, and the father exempt from responsibility, for the nurturing of young children. Finally, it may reduce the vulnerability of working single mothers by making childrearing obligations something that the employer must expect that any parent, male or female, may experience.

The separation of childbearing and childrearing also promotes reanalysis of pregnancy in the workplace context. . . . [Pregnancy] is susceptible to a functional analysis which compares the way it affects the pregnant worker to how other physical conditions affect other workers. Under a functional analysis, it becomes possible to argue that pregnancy, when not disabling, should not be a basis for termination or forced leave any more than any other nondisabling condition should be, and that when pregnancy does become disabling, the benefits appropriate for other workers should be extended to pregnant workers as well. . . .

Scales fails to see that her [special treatment] vision — a vision of the inclusion and proper accounting for pregnancy in the public sphere — is best served by the equal treatment approach. It is precisely that vision that gave birth to the equal treatment model in the first place. The model was proposed in the context of an exclusionary workplace, and it was urged to promote the "normalization" of pregnancy. In the litigation context, the model was the basis for insisting on the incorporation of pregnancy into existing benefit schemes. . . . It sought to overcome the definition of the prototypical worker as male and to promote an integrated — and androgynous — prototype.

Nonetheless, if the equal treatment approach were limited to the integration of pregnancy into the pattern of existing provisions for job security and economic benefits, Ann Scales would have good reason to protest that the [special treatment] vision cannot fully be implemented through that approach. An existing system of protections and benefits, she might point out, is structured to respond to the needs and characteristics of the typical male worker. Even if such protections and benefits are extended to women workers (and this might be especially true for those who become pregnant), they will not necessarily deliver equivalent advantages to women. Schemes set up on a male model are likely to be misconfigured from a woman's perspective. To grasp this point one need only envision what workplace rules would look like if the entire workforce were composed of women of childbearing years. The present scheme of things is thus unlikely to account for the needs and characteristics of men.

But the "equal treatment" feminists do not contend only that women who are pregnant must be treated the same as other workers in analogous situations. They also assert that apparently neutral rules that have a disproportionate effect on women, whether because of pregnancy or some other class-based characteristic, may violate Title VII.

CHRISTINE LITTLETON, RECONSTRUCTING SEXUAL EQUALITY[18]

75 Cal. L. Rev. 1279, 1284-1285, 1302, 1306-1308, 1312-1313, 1325-1326 (1986)

My proposal is easy to state, somewhat harder to fill with content, and even harder to implement. It is simply this: *The difference between human beings, whether perceived or real, and whether biologically or socially based, should not be permitted to make a difference in the lived-out equality of those persons.* I call this the model of "equality as acceptance." . . .

The Court's equality analysis could deal with overbroad generalizations, questions of closeness of fit, and even with temporary affirmative action, but a generalization that was accurate, and permanently so, was beyond the pale. The first strand of the feminist critique of equality addresses this failing, asserting that *equality analysis defines as beyond its scope precisely those issues that women find crucial to their concrete experience as women.*

Legal equality analysis "runs out" when it encounters "real" difference, and only becomes available if and when the difference is analogized to some experience men can have too. Legislative overruling of *Gilbert* by the Pregnancy Discrimination Act [PDA] was thus accomplished by making pregnancy look similar to something men experienced as well — disability. Given the way employment is structured, pregnancy renders a woman unable to work for a few days to a few months, just like illness and injury do for men. However, what makes pregnancy a *dis*ability rather than, say, an additional ability, is the structure of work, not reproduction. Normal pregnancy may make a woman unable to "work" for days, weeks or months, but it also makes her able to reproduce. From whose viewpoint is the work that she cannot do "work," and the work that she is doing *not* work? Certainly not from hers.

Thus, the second strand of the feminist critique of equality states: *Difference, which is created by the relationship of women to particular and contingent social structures, is taken as natural (that is, unchangeable and inherent), and it is located solely in the woman herself.* It is not impossible to imagine a definition of "work" that includes the "labor" of childbirth; nor is it impossible to imagine a workplace setting in which pregnancy would not be disabling.

18. Littleton was counsel for the Coalition for Reproductive Equality in the Workplace, which urged that the California law be upheld in *CalFed.*

Analogizing pregnancy to disability has created new difficulties for a legal system trying to apply an assimilationist model of equality. In California Federal Savings & Loan Association v. Guerra, an employer challenged a mandatory pregnancy leave statute, arguing that the law could be regarded as equal treatment, rather than a special bonus for women, only where men already have a right to disability leave for other reasons. Underlying the employer's argument was the assumption that the workplace is itself a gender-neutral institution that must treat all workers evenhandedly. Evenhanded treatment requires treating each worker the same as her coworkers, which means extending leave to all workers regardless of cause or denying leave to all. This reasoning falls prey to the second strand of the critique by assuming that if women have other needs for disability leave, it is because *they* are different.

It also gives rise to a third objection: that an institution structured so that women are inevitably disadvantaged by its facially neutral policies is itself phallocentric. Thus, *the third strand of the critique challenges the assumed gender-neutrality of social institutions, as well as the notion that practices must distinguish themselves from "business as usual" in order to be seen as unequal.* . . .

To summarize, from a feminist viewpoint, current equality analysis is phallocentrically biased in three respects: (1) it is inapplicable once it encounters "real" difference; (2) it locates difference in women, rather than in relationships; and (3) it fails to question the assumptions that social institutions are gender-neutral, and that women and men are therefore similarly related to those institutions. What these three strands of this critique share is their focus on "difference." A reconstructed equality analysis — one that seeks to eliminate, or at least reduce, the phallocentrism of the current model — must at some point deal with each strand of the critique. Thus, from a theoretical standpoint, symmetrical equality models, with their insistence that difference be ignored, eradicated or dissolved, are not responsive to the feminist critique of equality. . . .

The mathematical fallacy — that equal must mean similar — is one problem with the current concept of equality. Nevertheless, this would not be so severe a problem for women . . . were it not for the phallocentric fallacy that consistently leads courts (and even legal reformers) to choose the (biological or social) mode as the norm and to locate difference in the female. . . .

Consider the woman who recently lunched in the restaurant of the Beverly Rodeo Hotel. When she began breast feeding her infant the manager asked her to leave the dining room. What routes are open to her? Imagine the following dialogue:

Woman: Equality!

Restaurant: Yes, let's have equality. We don't allow men to bare their breasts in the dining room, so we can't let you do it either. (Assumption of symmetry.)

Woman: Wait a minute. There's a difference between those two situations.

Restaurant: Yes, there's a difference. Women's breasts are far more disruptive than men's breasts. Keep yours covered. (Location of difference in the woman.)

Woman: No, I have different needs and this social institution should take account of them.

Restaurant: Fine, go over there behind that screen. You can rejoin the others when you're finished. ("Accommodation" of difference leaves institution itself as rejecting the woman.)

The model of equality as acceptance responds to the first strand of the feminist critique of equality by insisting that equality can in fact be applied *across* difference. It is not, however, a "leveling" proposal. Rather, equality as acceptance calls for equalization across only those differences that the culture has encoded as gendered complements. . . .

Under the model of equality as acceptance, equality analysis does not end at the discovery of a "real" difference. Rather, it attempts to assess the "cultural meaning" of that difference, and to determine how to achieve equality despite it. This formulation responds to the second strand of the feminist critique by locating difference in the relationship between women and men rather than in women alone, as accommodation arguably does. . . .

[Some] equality theorists [assert] that male institutions should take account of women's differences by accommodating those differences. . . .

The problem with accommodation . . . is that it implicitly accepts the prevailing norm as generally legitimate, even as it urges that "special circumstances" make the norm inappropriate for the particular individual or class seeking accommodation. In addition, it falls prey to the feminist critique of equality by labeling women as deviant from the norm, thus locating the difference in women. Assimilated women are particularly vulnerable to this misperception, and are all too often persuaded to drop valid demands for inclusion on their own terms by the response that they are asking for "an exception."

The distinction between accommodation and acceptance may be illustrated by a rather commonplace example. I remember a feminist lawyer walking up to a podium to deliver a speech. The podium was high enough that she could not reach the microphone. While arrangements were being modified, she pointedly noted, "Built for a man!" Accommodation is a step platform brought for her to stand on. Acceptance is a podium whose height is adjustable.

. . . Under disparate impact doctrine . . . a woman can establish discrimination by demonstrating that women as a class are more severely affected than men by a facially neutral employment practice, such as a height requirement. The employer can, however, justify the discriminatory impact by demonstrating that the practice is "job related" or necessary to the employer's business. Moreover, the relevance of the practice is tested solely by reference to the way the job is already structured. Thus, even disparate impact analysis — as currently practiced — does not allow for challenges to male bias in the structure of businesses, occupations, or jobs.

Equality as acceptance would support challenges to government and employer policies and practices that use male norms even when such norms are considered job-related, necessary to the business, or "substantially related to an important governmental interest." Unlike the more radical version of the model of androgyny referred to above, however, acceptance would not necessarily require the *elimination* of such norms. Acceptance could instead be achieved by inventing complementary structures containing female norms. For example, assume an employer successfully defends its 5′9″ minimum height requirement as necessary to the job of sorting widgets as they pass on a conveyor belt. Equality as acceptance could be achieved by restructuring the job itself — in this case, by changing the height of the conveyor belt or by adding a second belt. Alternatively, the employer could defend the requirement by demonstrating that equal job opportunities exist in the plant for applicants shorter than 5′9″. Acceptance would thus permit de facto sex segregation in the workplace, but *only* if the predominantly male and predominantly female jobs have equal pay, status, and opportunity for promotion into decisionmaking positions.

CATHARINE A. MACKINNON, TOWARD A FEMINIST THEORY OF THE STATE

Chapter 12, On Sex Equality on Difference and Dominance (1989)

Sex discrimination law, with mainstream moral theory, sees equality and gender as issues of sameness and difference. According to this approach, which has dominated politics, law, and social perception, equality is an equivalence not a distinction, and gender is a distinction not an equivalence. The legal mandate of equal treatment — both a systemic norm and a specific legal doctrine — becomes a matter of treating likes alike and unlikes unlike, while the sexes are socially defined as such by their mutual unlikeness. That is, gender is socially constructed as difference epistemologically, and sex discrimination law bounds gender equality by difference doctrinally. Socially, one tells a woman from a man by their difference from each other, but a woman is legally recognized to be discriminated against on the basis of sex only when she can first be said to be the same as a man. A built-in tension thus exists between this concept of equality, which presupposes sameness, and this concept of sex, which presupposes difference. Difference defines the state's approach to sex equality epistemologically and doctrinally. Sex equality becomes a contradiction in terms, something of an oxymoron. The deepest issues of sex inequality, in which the sexes are most constructed as socially different, are either excluded at the threshold or precluded from coverage once in. In this way, difference is inscribed on society as the meaning of gender and written into law as the limit on sex discrimination. . . .

In this mainstream epistemologically liberal approach, the sexes are by nature biologically different, therefore socially properly differentiated for some purposes. . . . As one scholar has put it, "any prohibition against sexual classifications must be flexible enough to accommodate two legitimate sources of distinctions on the basis of sex: biological differences between the sexes and the prevailing heterosexual ethic of American society." . . . Laws or practices that express or reflect sex "stereotypes," understood as inaccurate overgeneralized attitudes often termed "archaic" or "outmoded," are at the core of this definition of discrimination. Mistaken illusions about real differences are actionable, but any distinction that can be accurately traced to biology or heterosexuality is not a discrimination but a difference.[a]

a. Doctrinally speaking, two alternative paths to sex equality for women exist within the mainstream approach to sex discrimination, paths that follow the lines of the sameness/difference tension. The leading one is: be the same as men. This path is termed "gender neutrality" doctrinally and the single standard philosophically. It is testimony to how substance becomes form in law that this rule is considered formal equality. . . . To women who want equality yet find themselves "different," the doctrine provides an alternative route: be different from men. This equal recognition of difference is termed the special benefit rule or special protection rule legally, the double standard philosophically. [These sentences actually appear elsewhere in MacKinnon's chapter. — Ed.]

From women's point of view [i.e., under the dominance analysis], gender is more an inequality of power than a differentiation that is accurate or inaccurate. To women, sex is a social status based on who is permitted to do what to whom; only derivatively is it a difference. For example, one woman reflected on her gender: "I wish I had been born a doormat, or a man." Being a doormat is definitely different from being a man. Differences between the sexes do descriptively exist. But the fact that these are a woman's realistic options, and that they are so limiting, calls into question the perspective that considers this distinction a "difference."

From this perspective, considering gender a matter of sameness and difference covers up the reality of gender as a system of social hierarchy, as an inequality. The differences attributed to sex become lines that inequality draws, not any kind of basis for it. Social and political inequality begins indifferent to sameness and difference. Differences are inequality's post hoc excuse, its conclusory artifact, its outcome presented as its origin, its sentimentalization, its damage that is pointed to as the justification for doing the damage after the damage has been done, the distinctions that perception is socially organized to notice because inequality gives them consequences for social power. . . . [A] discourse and a law of gender that center on difference serve as ideology to neutralize, rationalize, and cover disparities of power, even as they appear to criticize or problematize them. Difference is the velvet glove on the iron fist of domination. The problem then is not that differences are not valued; the problem is that they are defined by power. This is as true when difference is affirmed as when it is denied, when its substance is applauded or disparaged, when women are punished or protected in its name.

. . . If differentiation were the problem, gender neutrality would make sense as an approach to it. Since hierarchy is the problem, it is not only inadequate, it is perverse. In questioning the principledness of neutral principles, this analysis suggests that current law to rectify sex inequality is premised upon, and promotes, its continued existence.

. . . To the extent that the sexuality of one sex is a social stigma, target, and provocation to violation, while the sexuality of the other is socially a source of pleasure, adventure, power (indeed, the social definition of potency), and a focus for deification, entertainment, nurturance, and derepression, the sexuality of each is equally different, equally heterosexual or not, but not equally socially powerful.[b]

b. A rule or practice is discriminatory, in the [dominance] approach, if it participates in the systemic social deprivation of one sex because of sex. The only question for litigation is whether the policy or practice in question integrally contributes to the maintenance of an underclass or a deprived position because of gender status. The disadvantage which constitutes the injury of discrimination is not the failure to be treated "without regard to" one's sex; that is the injury of arbitrary differentiation. The unfairness lies in being deprived because of being a woman or a man, a deprivation given meaning in the social context of the dominance or preference of one sex over the other. The social problem addressed is not the failure to ignore woman's essential sameness with man, but the recognition of womanhood to women's comparative disadvantage. In this approach, few reasons, not even biological ones, can justify the institutionalized disadvantage of women. Comparability of sex characteristics is not required because policies are proscribed which transform women's sex-based differences from men into social and economic deprivations. All that is required are comparatively unequal results. . . . [From Catharine A. MacKinnon, Sexual Harassment of Working Women, 102, 117-118, 126-127 (1979). — Ed.]

V. *Other Problems of Classifications Based on Sex*

A. Statutory Rape

MICHAEL M. v. SUPERIOR COURT OF SONOMA COUNTY
450 U.S. 464 (1981)
Certiorari to the Supreme Court of California

REHNQUIST, J., announced the judgment of the Court and delivered an opinion, in which the Chief Justice, Justice Stewart, and Justice Powell joined.

The question presented in this case is whether California's "statutory rape" law, §261.5 of the Cal. Penal Code Ann. violates the Equal Protection Clause of the Fourteenth Amendment. Section 261.5 defines unlawful sexual intercourse as "an act of sexual intercourse accomplished with a female not the wife of the perpetrator, where the female is under the age of 18 years." The statute thus makes men alone criminally liable for the act of sexual intercourse.

In July 1978, a complaint was filed in the Municipal Court of Sonoma County, Cal., alleging that petitioner, then a 17½-year-old male, had unlawful sexual intercourse with a female under the age of 18, in violation of §261.5. The evidence, adduced at a preliminary hearing showed that at approximately midnight on June 3, 1978, petitioner and two friends approached Sharon, a 16½-year-old female, and her sister as they waited at a bus stop. Petitioner and Sharon, who had already been drinking, moved away from the others and began to kiss. After being struck in the face for rebuffing petitioner's initial advances, Sharon submitted to sexual intercourse with petitioner. Prior to trial, petitioner sought to set aside the information on both state and federal constitutional grounds, asserting that §261.5 unlawfully discriminated on the basis of gender. The trial court and the California Court of Appeal denied petitioner's request for relief and petitioner sought review in the Supreme Court of California.

The Supreme Court [of California] held that "section 261.5 discriminates on the basis of sex because only females may be victims, and only males may violate the section." [It] then subjected the classification to "strict scrutiny," stating that it must be justified by a compelling state interest. It found that the classification was "supported not by mere social convention but by the immutable physiological fact that it is the female exclusively who can become pregnant." Canvassing "the tragic human costs of illegitimate teenage pregnancies," including the large number of teenage abortions, the increased medical risk associated with teenage pregnancies, and the social consequences of teenage childbearing, the court concluded that the State has a compelling interest in preventing such pregnancies. Because males alone can "physiologically cause the result which the law properly seeks to avoid," the court further held that the gender classification was readily justified as a means of identifying offender and victim. For the reasons stated below, we affirm the judgment of the California Supreme Court.

... Unlike the California Supreme Court, we have not held that gender-based classifications are "inherently suspect" and thus we do not apply so-called "strict scrutiny" to those classifications. See Stanton v. Stanton, 421 U.S. 7 (1975). Our cases have held, however, that the traditional minimum rationality test takes on a somewhat "sharper focus" when gender-based classifications are challenged. See

Craig v. Boren, 429 U.S. 190, 210 n.* (1976) (Powell, J., concurring). In Reed v. Reed, 404 U.S. 71 (1971), for example, the Court stated that a gender-based classification will be upheld if it bears a "fair and substantial relationship" to legitimate state ends, while in Craig v. Boren, the Court restated the test to require the classification to bear a "substantial relationship" to "important governmental objectives."

Underlying these decisions is the principle that a legislature may not "make overbroad generalizations based on sex which are entirely unrelated to any differences between men and women or which demean the ability or social status of the affected class." Parham v. Hughes, 441 U.S. 347, 354 (1979) (plurality opinion of Stewart, J.). But because the Equal Protection Clause does not "demand that a statute necessarily apply equally to all persons" or require " 'things which are different in fact . . . to be treated in law as though they were the same,' " Rinaldi v. Yeager, 384 U.S. 305 (1966), this Court has consistently upheld statutes where the gender classification is not invidious, but rather realistically reflects the fact that the sexes are not similarly situated in certain circumstances. Parham v. Hughes, supra; Califano v. Webster, 430 U.S. 313 (1977); Schlesinger v. Ballard, 419 U.S. 498 (1975); Kahn v. Shevin, 416 U.S. 351 (1974). As the Court has stated, a legislature may "provide for the special problems of women." Weinberger v. Wiesenfeld, 420 U.S. 636 (1975).

Applying those principles to this case, the fact that the California Legislature criminalized the act of illicit sexual intercourse with a minor female is a sure indication of its intent or purpose to discourage that conduct. Precisely why the legislature desired that result is of course somewhat less clear. This Court has long recognized that "[i]nquiries into congressional motives or purposes are a hazardous matter," and the search for the "actual" or "primary" purpose of a statute is likely to be elusive. Here, for example, the individual legislators may have voted for the statute for a variety of reasons. Some legislators may have been concerned about preventing teenage pregnancies, others about protecting young females from physical injury or from the loss of "chastity," and still others about promoting various religious and moral attitudes towards premarital sex.

The justification for the statute offered by the State, and accepted by the Supreme Court of California, is that the legislature sought to prevent illegitimate teenage pregnancies. That finding, of course, is entitled to great deference. And although our cases establish that the State's asserted reason for the enactment of a statute may be rejected, if it "could not have been a goal of the legislation," Weinberger v. Wiesenfeld, supra, this is not such a case.

We are satisfied not only that the prevention of illegitimate pregnancy is at least one of the "purposes" of the statute, but also that the State has a strong interest in preventing such pregnancy. At the risk of stating the obvious, teenage pregnancies, which have increased dramatically over the last two decades, have significant social, medical, and economic consequences for both the mother and her child, and the State. Of particular concern to the State is that approximately half of all teenage pregnancies end in abortion. And of those children who are born, their illegitimacy makes them likely candidates to become wards of the State.[a]

a. The policy and intent of the California Legislature evinced in other legislation buttresses our view that the prevention of teenage pregnancy is a purpose of the statute. The preamble to the Preg-

We need not be medical doctors to discern that young men and young women are not similarly situated with respect to the problems and the risks of sexual intercourse. Only women may become pregnant, and they suffer disproportionately the profound physical, emotional and psychological consequences of sexual activity. The statute at issue here protects women from sexual intercourse at an age when those consequences are particularly severe.[b]

The question thus boils down to whether a State may attack the problem of sexual intercourse and teenage pregnancy directly by prohibiting a male from having sexual intercourse with a minor female. We hold that such a statute is sufficiently related to the State's objectives to pass constitutional muster.

Because virtually all of the significant harmful and inescapably identifiable consequences of teenage pregnancy fall on the young female, a legislature acts well within its authority when it elects to punish only the participant who, by nature, suffers few of the consequences of his conduct. It is hardly unreasonable for a legislature acting to protect minor females to exclude them from punishment. Moreover, the risk of pregnancy itself constitutes a substantial deterrence to young females. No similar natural sanctions deter males. A criminal sanction imposed solely on males thus serves to roughly "equalize" the deterrents on the sexes.

We are unable to accept petitioner's contention that the statute is impermissibly underinclusive and must, in order to pass judicial scrutiny, be *broadened* so as to hold the female as criminally liable as the male. It is argued that this statute is not *necessary* to deter teenage pregnancy because a gender-neutral statute, where both male and female would be subject to prosecution, would serve that goal equally well. The relevant inquiry, however, is not whether the statute is drawn as precisely as it might have been, but whether the line chosen by the California Legislature is within constitutional limitations. Kahn v. Shevin.

In any event, we cannot say that a gender-neutral statute would be as effective as the statute California has chosen to enact. The State persuasively contends that a gender-neutral statute would frustrate its interest in effective enforcement. Its view is that a female is surely less likely to report violations of the statute if she herself would be subject to criminal prosecution.[c] In an area already fraught with

---

nancy Freedom of Choice Act, for example, states: "The legislature finds that pregnancy among unmarried persons under 21 years of age constitutes an increasing social problem in the State of California."

Subsequent to the decision below, the California Legislature considered and rejected proposals to render §261.5 gender neutral, thereby ratifying the judgment of the California Supreme Court. That is enough to answer petitioner's contention that the statute was the " 'accidental by-product of a traditional way of thinking about females.' " Califano v. Webster. Certainly this decision of the California Legislature is as good a source as is this Court in deciding what is "current" and what is "outmoded" in the perception of women.

b. Although petitioner concedes that the State has a "compelling" interest in preventing teenage pregnancy, he contends that the "true" purpose of §261.5 is to protect the virtue and chastity of young women. As such, the statute is unjustifiable because it rests on archaic stereotypes. What we have said above is enough to dispose of that contention. The question for us — and the only question under the Federal Constitution — is whether the legislation violates the Equal Protection Clause of the Fourteenth Amendment, not whether its supporters may have endorsed it for reasons no longer generally accepted. Even if the preservation of female chastity were one of the motives of the statute, and even if that motive be impermissible, petitioner's argument must fail because "[i]t is a familiar practice of constitutional law that this court will not strike down an otherwise constitutional statute on the basis of an alleged illicit legislative motive."

c. Petitioner contends that a gender-neutral statute would not hinder prosecutions because the prosecutor could take into account the relative burdens on females and males and generally only prosecutorial difficulties, we decline to hold that the Equal Protection Clause requires a legislature to enact a statute so broad that it may well be incapable of enforcement.[d]

We similarly reject petitioner's argument that §261.5 is impermissibly overbroad because it makes unlawful sexual intercourse with prepubescent females, who are, by definition, incapable of becoming pregnant. Quite apart from the fact that the statute could well be justified on the grounds that very young females are particularly susceptible to physical injury from sexual intercourse, it is ludicrous to suggest that the Constitution requires the California Legislature to limit the scope of its rape statute to older teenagers and exclude young girls.

There remains only petitioner's contention that the statute is unconstitutional as it is applied to him because he, like Sharon, was under 18 at the time of sexual intercourse. Petitioner argues that the statute is flawed because it presumes that as between two persons under 18, the male is the culpable aggressor. We find petitioner's contentions unpersuasive. Contrary to his assertions, the statute does not rest on the assumption that males are generally the aggressors. It is instead an attempt by a legislature to prevent illegitimate teenage pregnancy by providing an additional deterrent for men. The age of the man is irrelevant since young men are as capable as older men of inflicting the harm sought to be prevented.

In upholding the California statute we also recognize that this is not a case where a statute is being challenged on the grounds that it "invidiously discriminates" against females. To the contrary, the statute places a burden on males which is not shared by females. But we find nothing to suggest that men, because of past discrimination or peculiar disadvantages, are in need of the special solicitude of the courts. Nor is this a case where the gender classification is made "solely for . . . administrative convenience," as in Frontiero v. Richardson, or rests on "the baggage of sexual stereotypes" as in Orr v. Orr. As we have held, the statute instead reasonably reflects the fact that the consequences of sexual intercourse and pregnancy fall more heavily on the female than on the male. Accordingly, the judgment of the California Supreme Court is affirmed.

STEWART, J., concurring. . . .

A

At the outset, it should be noted that the statutory discrimination, when viewed as part of the wider scheme of California law, is not as clearcut as might at first appear. Females are not freed from criminal liability in California for engaging in sexual activity that may be harmful. It is unlawful, for example, for any person, of either sex, to molest, annoy, or contribute to the delinquency of anyone under

---

prosecute males. But to concede this is to concede all. If the prosecutor, in exercising discretion, will virtually always prosecute just the man and not the woman, we do not see why it is impermissible for the legislature to enact a statute to the same effect.

d. The question whether a statute is *substantially* related to its asserted goals is at best an opaque one. . . . Where . . . differing speculations as to the effect of a statute are plausible, we think it appropriate to defer to the decision of the California Supreme Court, "armed as it was with the knowledge of the facts and circumstances concerning the passage and potential impact of [the statute], and familiar with the milieu in which that provision would operate." Reitman v. Mulkey, 387 U.S. 369 (1967).

18 years of age. All persons are prohibited from committing "any lewd or lascivious act," including consensual intercourse, with a child under 14. And members of both sexes may be convicted for engaging in deviant sexual acts with anyone under 18. Finally, females may be brought within the proscription of §261.5 itself, since a female may be charged with aiding and abetting its violation.

Section 261.5 is thus but one part of a broad statutory scheme that protects all minors from the problems and risks attendant upon adolescent sexual activity. To be sure, §261.5 creates an additional measure of punishment for males who engage in sexual intercourse with females between the ages of 14 and 17. The question then is whether the Constitution prohibits a state legislature from imposing this additional sanction on a gender-specific basis.

B

The Constitution is violated when government, state or federal, invidiously classifies similarly situated people on the basis of the immutable characteristics with which they were born. Thus, detrimental racial classifications by government always violate the Constitution, for the simple reason that, so far as the Constitution is concerned, people of different races are always similarly situated. By contrast, while detrimental gender classifications by government often violate the Constitution, they do not always do so, for the reason that there are differences between males and females that the Constitution necessarily recognizes. In this case we deal with the most basic of these differences: females can become pregnant as the result of sexual intercourse; males cannot.

As was recognized in Parham v. Hughes "a State is not free to make overbroad generalizations based on sex which are entirely unrelated to any differences between men and women or which demean the ability or social status of the affected class." Gender-based classifications may not be based upon administrative convenience, or upon archaic assumptions about the proper roles of the sexes. But we have recognized that in certain narrow circumstances men and women are not similarly situated; in these circumstances a gender classification based on clear differences between the sexes is not invidious, and a legislative classification realistically based upon those differences is not unconstitutional. "[G]ender-based classifications are not invariably invalid. When men and women are not in fact similarly situated in the area covered by the legislation in question, the Equal Protection Clause is not violated." Caban v. Mohammed, 441 U.S. 380 (dissenting opinion).

Applying these principles to the classification enacted by the California Legislature, it is readily apparent that §261.5 does not violate the Equal Protection Clause. Young women and men are not similarly situated with respect to the problems and risk associated with intercourse and pregnancy, and the statute is realistically related to the legitimate state purpose of reducing those problems and risks.

C

As the California Supreme Court's catalog shows, the pregnant unmarried female confronts problems more numerous and more severe than any faced by her male partner. She alone endures the medical risks of pregnancy or abortion.[a] She suffers disproportionately the social, educational, and emotional consequences of pregnancy. Recognizing this disproportion, California has attempted to protect teenage females by prohibiting males from participating in the act necessary for conception.

The fact that males and females are not similarly situated with respect to the risks of sexual intercourse applies with the same force to males under 18 as it does to older males. The risk of pregnancy is a significant deterrent for unwed young females that is not shared by unmarried males, regardless of their age. Experienced observation confirms the commonsense notion that adolescent males disregard the possibility of pregnancy far more than do adolescent females. And to the extent that §261.5 may punish males for intercourse with prepubescent females, that punishment is justifiable because of the substantial physical risks for prepubescent females that are not shared by their male counterparts.

D

The petitioner argues that the California Legislature could have drafted the statute differently, so that its purpose would be accomplished more precisely. "But the issue, of course, is not whether the statute could have been drafted more wisely, but whether the lines chosen by the . . . [l]egislature are within constitutional limitations." Kahn v. Shevin. That other States may have decided to attack the same problems more broadly, with gender-neutral statutes, does not mean that every State is constitutionally compelled to do so.[b]

E

In short, the Equal Protection Clause does not mean that the physiological differences between men and women must be disregarded. While those differences must never be permitted to become a pretext for invidious discrimination, no such discrimination is presented by this case. The Constitution surely does not require a State to pretend that demonstrable differences between men and women do not really exist.

BLACKMUN, J., concurring in the judgment.

It is gratifying that the plurality recognizes that "[a]t the risk of stating the obvious, teenage pregnancies . . . have increased dramatically over the last two decades" and "have significant social, medical, and economic consequences for both the mother and her child, and the State." . . .

a. There is also empirical evidence that sexual abuse of young females is a more serious problem than sexual abuse of young males. For example, a review of five studies found that 88% of sexually abused minors were female. Jaffe, Dynneson, & ten Bensel, Sexual Abuse of Children, 129 Am. J. of Diseases of Children 689, 690 (1975).

b. The fact is that a gender-neutral statute would not necessarily lead to a closer fit with the aim of reducing the problems associated with teenage pregnancy. If both parties were equally liable to prosecution, a female would be far less likely to complain; the very complaint would be self-incriminating. Accordingly, it is possible that a gender-neutral statute would result in fewer prosecutions than the one before us. In any event, a state legislature is free to address itself to what it believes to be the most serious aspect of a broader problem. "[T]he Equal Protection Clause does not require that a State must choose between attacking every aspect of a problem or not attacking the problem at all." Dandridge v. Williams, 397 U.S. 471.

I . . . cannot vote to strike down the California statutory rape law, for I think it is a sufficiently reasoned and constitutional effort to control the problem at its inception. For me, there is an important difference between this state action and a State's adamant and rigid refusal to face, or even to recognize, the "significant . . . consequences" — to the woman — of a forced or unwanted conception. . . .

BRENNAN, J., with whom Justices White and Marshall join, dissenting.

I

It is disturbing to find the Court so splintered on a case that presents such a straightforward issue: Whether the admittedly gender-based classification in §261.5 bears a sufficient relationship to the State's asserted goal of preventing teenage pregnancies to survive the "mid-level" constitutional scrutiny mandated by Craig v. Boren, 429 U.S. 190 (1976). Applying the analytical framework provided by our precedents, I am convinced that there is only one proper resolution of this issue: the classification must be declared unconstitutional. I fear that the plurality opinion and Justices Stewart and Blackmun reach the opposite result by placing too much emphasis on the desirability of achieving the State's asserted statutory goal — prevention of teenage pregnancy — and not enough emphasis on the fundamental question of whether the sex-based discrimination in the California statute is *substantially* related to the achievement of that goal.[a]

II

. . . The burden is on the government to prove both the importance of its asserted objective and the substantial relationship between the classification and that objective. And the State cannot meet that burden without showing that a gender-neutral statute would be a less effective means of achieving that goal.

The State of California vigorously asserts that the "important governmental objective" to be served by §261.5 is the prevention of teenage pregnancy. It claims that its statute furthers this goal by deterring sexual activity by males — the class of persons it considers more responsible for causing those pregnancies. But even assuming that prevention of teenage pregnancy is an important governmental objective and that it is in fact an objective of §261.5, California still has the burden of proving that there are fewer teenage pregnancies under its gender-based statutory rape law than there would be if the law were gender neutral. To meet this burden, the State must show that because its statutory rape law punishes only males, and not females, it more effectively deters minor females from having sexual intercourse.

The plurality assumes that a gender-neutral statute would be less effective than §261.5 in deterring sexual activity because a gender-neutral statute would

a. None of the three opinions upholding the California statute fairly applies the equal protection analysis this Court has so carefully developed since Craig v. Boren, 429 U.S. 190 (1976). . . . They overlook the fact that the State has not met is burden of proving that the gender discrimination in §261.5 is *substantially* related to the achievement of the State's asserted statutory goal. My Brethren seem not to recognize that California has the burden of proving that a gender-neutral statutory rape law would be less effective than §261.5 in deterring sexual activity leading to teenage pregnancy. Because they fail to analyze the issue in these terms, I believe they reach an unsupportable result.

create significant enforcement problems. The plurality thus accepts the State's assertion that "a female is surely less likely to report violations of the statute if she herself would be subject to criminal prosecution. . . ." However, a State's bare assertion that its gender-based statutory classification substantially furthers an important governmental interest is not enough to meet its burden of proof under Craig v. Boren. Rather, the State must produce evidence. The State has not produced such evidence in this case. Moreover, there are at least two serious flaws in the State's assertion that law enforcement problems created by a gender-neutral statutory rape law would make such a statute less effective than a gender-based statute in deterring sexual activity. First, the experience of other jurisdictions, and California itself, belies the plurality's conclusion that a gender-neutral statutory rape law "may well be incapable of enforcement." There are now at least 37 States that have enacted gender-neutral statutory rape laws. Although most of these laws protect young persons (of either sex) from the sexual exploitation of older individuals, the laws of Arizona, Florida, and Illinois permit prosecution of both minor females and minor males for engaging in mutual sexual conduct. California has introduced no evidence that those States have been handicapped by the enforcement problems the plurality finds so persuasive. Surely, if those States could provide such evidence, we might expect that California would have introduced it. . . .

The second flaw in the State's assertion is that even assuming that a gender-neutral statute would be more difficult to enforce, the State has still not shown that those enforcement problems would make such a statute less effective than a gender-based statute in deterring minor females from engaging in sexual intercourse. Common sense, however, suggests that a gender-neutral statutory rape law is potentially a *greater* deterrent of sexual activity than a gender-based law, for the simple reason that a gender-neutral law subjects both men and women to criminal sanctions and thus arguably has a deterrent effect on twice as many potential violators. Even if fewer persons were prosecuted under the gender-neutral law, as the State suggests, it would still be true that twice as many persons would be *subject* to arrest. The State's failure to prove that a gender-neutral law would be a less effective deterrent than a gender-based law, like the State's failure to prove that a gender-neutral law would be difficult to enforce, should have led this Court to invalidate §261.5.

III

Until very recently, no California court or commentator had suggested that the purpose of California's statutory rape law was to protect young women from the risk of pregnancy. Indeed, the historical development of §261.5 demonstrates that the law was initially enacted on the premise that young women, in contrast to young men, were to be deemed legally incapable of consenting to an act of sexual intercourse. Because their chastity was considered particularly precious, those young women were felt to be uniquely in need of the State's protection. In contrast, young men were assumed to be capable of making such decisions for themselves; the law therefore did not offer them any special protection.

It is perhaps because the gender classification in California's statutory rape law was initially designed to further these outmoded sexual stereotypes, rather than to reduce the incidence of teenage pregnancies, that the State has been unable to demonstrate a substantial relationship between the classification and its newly asserted goal. But whatever the reason, the State has not shown that Cal. Penal Code §261.5 is any more effective than a gender-neutral law would be in deterring minor females from engaging in sexual intercourse. It has therefore not met its burden of proving that the statutory classification is substantially related to the achievement of its asserted goal. I would hold that §261.5 violates the Equal Protection Clause of the Fourteenth Amendment, and I would reverse the judgment of the California Supreme Court.

STEVENS, J., dissenting.

. . . I think the plurality is quite correct in making the assumption that the joint act that this law seeks to prohibit creates a greater risk of harm for the female than for the male. But the plurality surely cannot believe that the risk of pregnancy confronted by the female — any more than the risk of venereal disease confronted by males as well as females — has provided an effective deterrent to voluntary female participation in the risk-creating conduct. Yet the plurality's decision seems to rest on the assumption that the California Legislature acted on the basis of that rather fanciful notion.

In my judgment, the fact that a class of persons is especially vulnerable to a risk that a statute is designed to avoid is a reason for making the statute applicable to that class. The argument that a special need for protection provides a rational explanation for an exemption is one I simply do not comprehend.[a]

In this case, the fact that a female confronts a greater risk of harm than a male is a reason for applying the prohibition to her — not a reason for granting her a license to use her own judgment on whether or not to assume the risk. Surely, if we examine the problem from the point of view of society's interest in preventing the risk-creating conduct from occurring at all, it is irrational to exempt 50% of the potential violators. And, if we view the government's interest as that of a parens patriae seeking to protect its subjects from harming themselves, the discrimination is actually perverse. Would a rational parent making rules for the conduct of twin children of opposite sex simultaneously forbid the son and authorize the daughter to engage in conduct that is especially harmful to the daughter? That is the effect of this statutory classification.

If pregnancy or some other special harm is suffered by one of the two participants in the prohibited act, that special harm no doubt would constitute a legitimate mitigating factor in deciding what, if any, punishment might be appropriate in a given case. But from the standpoint of fashioning a general preventive rule — or, indeed, in determining appropriate punishment when neither party in fact has suffered any special harm — I regard a total exemption for the members of the more endangered class as utterly irrational.

In my opinion, the only acceptable justification for a general rule requiring disparate treatment of the two participants in a joint act must be a legislative

a. A hypothetical racial classification will illustrate my point. Assume that skin pigmentation provides some measure of protection against cancer caused by exposure to certain chemicals in the atmosphere and, therefore, that white employees confront a greater risk than black employees in certain industrial settings. Would it be rational to require black employees to wear protective clothing but to exempt whites from that requirement? It seems to me that the greater risk of harm to white workers would be a reason for including them in the requirement — not for granting them an exemption.

judgment that one is more guilty than the other. The risk-creating conduct that this statute is designed to prevent requires the participation of two persons — one male and one female. In many situations it is probably true that one is the aggressor and the other is either an unwilling, or at least a less willing, participant in the joint act. If a statute authorized punishment of only one participant and required the prosecutor to prove that participant had been the aggressor, I assume that the discrimination would be valid. Although the question is less clear, I also assume, for the purpose of deciding this case, that it would be permissible to punish only the male participant, if one element of the offense were proof that he had been the aggressor, or at least in some respects the more responsible participant in the joint act. The statute at issue in this case, however, requires no such proof. The question raised by this statute is whether the State, consistently with the Federal Constitution, may always punish the male and never the female when they are equally responsible or when the female is the more responsible of the two.

It would seem to me that an impartial lawmaker could give only one answer to that question. The fact that the California Legislature has decided to apply its prohibition only to the male may reflect a legislative judgment that in the typical case the male is actually the more guilty party. Any such judgment must, in turn, assume that the decision to engage in the risk-creating conduct is always — or at least typically — a male decision. If that assumption is valid, the statutory classification should also be valid. But what is the support for the assumption? It is not contained in the record of this case or in any legislative history or scholarly study that has been called to our attention. I think it is supported to some extent by traditional attitudes toward male-female relationships. But the possibility that such a habitual attitude may reflect nothing more than an irrational prejudice makes it an insufficient justification for discriminatory treatment that is otherwise blatantly unfair. For, as I read this statute, it requires that one, and only one, of two equally guilty wrongdoers be stigmatized by a criminal conviction.

I cannot accept the State's argument that the constitutionality of the discriminatory rule can be saved by an assumption that prosecutors will commonly invoke this statute only in cases that actually involve a forcible rape, but one that cannot be established by proof beyond a reasonable doubt.[b] That assumption implies that a State has a legitimate interest in convicting a defendant on evidence that is constitutionally insufficient. Of course, the State may create a lesser-included offense that would authorize punishment of the more guilty party, but surely the interest in obtaining convictions on inadequate proof cannot justify a statute that punishes one who is equally or less guilty than his partner.[c]

Nor do I find at all persuasive the suggestion that this discrimination is adequately justified by the desire to encourage females to inform against their male

b. According to the State of California: "The statute is commonly employed in situations involving force, prostitution, pornography or coercion due to status relationships, and the state's interest in these situations is apparent." The State's interest in these situations is indeed apparent and certainly sufficient to justify statutory prohibition of forcible rape, prostitution, pornography, and nonforcible, but nonetheless coerced, sexual intercourse. However, it is not at all apparent to me how this state interest can justify a statute not specifically directed to any of these offenses.

c. Both Justice Rehnquist and Justice Blackmun apparently attach significance to the testimony at the preliminary hearing indicating that the petitioner struck his partner. In light of the fact that the petitioner would be equally guilty of the crime charged in the complaint whether or not that testimony is true, it obviously has no bearing on the legal question presented by this case.

partners. Even if the concept of a wholesale informant's exemption were an acceptable enforcement device, what is the justification for defining the exempt class entirely by reference to sex rather than by reference to a more neutral criterion such as relative innocence? Indeed, if the exempt class is to be composed entirely of members of one sex, what is there to support the view that the statutory purpose will be better served by granting the informing license to females rather than to males? If a discarded male partner informs on a promiscuous female, a timely threat of prosecution might well prevent the precise harm the statute is intended to minimize.

Finally, even if my logic is faulty and there actually is some speculative basis for treating equally guilty males and females differently, I still believe that any such speculative justification would be outweighed by the paramount interest in evenhanded enforcement of the law. A rule that authorizes punishment of only one of two equally guilty wrongdoers violates the essence of the constitutional requirement that the sovereign must govern impartially.

FRANCES OLSEN, STATUTORY RAPE: A FEMINIST CRITIQUE OF RIGHTS ANALYSIS

63 Tex. L. Rev. 387, 401-402, 412, 418-420, 426 (1984)

Statutory rape laws . . . pose a classic political dilemma for feminists. On one hand, they protect females; like laws against rape, incest, child molestation, and child marriage, statutory rape laws are a statement of social disapproval of certain forms of exploitation. To some extent they reduce abuse and victimization. On the other hand, statutory rape laws restrict the sexual activity of young women and reinforce the double standard of sexual morality. The laws both protect and undermine women's rights. . . .

Feminists charge that statutes such as [California's] are harmful to women on both a practical and an ideological level. First, as an effort to control the sexual activities of young women, statutory rape laws are an unwarranted governmental intrusion into their lives and an oppressive restriction upon their freedom of action. An unmarried woman under eighteen cannot legally have intercourse in California. Whether the prohibition is enforced by prosecuting her partner or by prosecuting her as an aider and abettor, the statute interferes with the sexual freedom of the underage female. In the language of rights analysis, statutory rape laws violate the female's right to privacy and her right to be as free sexually as her male counterpart.

Feminists' second common objection to statutory rape laws is ideological. Gender-based statutory rape laws reinforce the sexual stereotype of men as aggressors and women as passive victims. . . . For males, sex is an accomplishment; they gain something through intercourse. For women, sex entails giving something up. Further, for the myth of male sexual accomplishment to exist, some females must give in. The double standard divides females into two classes — virgins and whores, "good girls" whose chastity should be protected and "bad girls" who may be exploited with impunity. . . . [G]ender-based statutory rape laws violate the right of all women to be treated equally to men. . . .

A commitment to establish and protect rights for women provides us with little guidance in deciding whether to support any particular statutory rape law or to oppose all statutory rape laws. Even if we artificially simplify our task by focusing only upon the rights of women, we cannot determine how to protect these rights. Rights analysis does not help us as an analytic tool because it is indeterminate. Every effort to protect young women against private oppression by individual men risks subjecting women to state oppression, and every effort to protect them against state oppression undermines their power to resist individual oppression.

Further, any acknowledgment of the actual difference between the present situation of males and females stigmatizes females and perpetuates discrimination. But if we ignore power differences and pretend that women and men are similarly situated, we perpetuate discrimination by disempowering ourselves from instituting effective change. The strategy of protecting rights runs afoul of the conflict between rights as freedom of action and rights as security; the strategy of promoting equality runs afoul of the conflict between formal equality of opportunity and substantive equality of outcome. . . .

Brennan considered the act invalid only because it punished males and did not punish females. Michael's argument, endorsed by the dissenters, was not that the female should be as free to engage in sex as the male, but that she is equally culpable and should be punished equally. . . .

In fact, the statute discriminates in two different ways: it outlaws sexual intercourse by minor females, but not by minor males, and it protects minor females from exploitative intercourse with anyone, but does not protect minor males from exploitative intercourse with females who are above the age of consent. The dissenters ignored the first discrimination altogether and appeared confused about the second. Under a gender-neutral law forbidding intercourse with an underage person, Michael and Sharon might be considered equally culpable; each of them engaged in sexual intercourse with an underage partner. Sharon would be culpable because her partner was underage, not because she was. The dissenting opinions, however, assumed that Sharon was culpable for engaging in a "joint act" of intercourse that risked a teenage pregnancy. Justice Stevens referred to the California statute as "exempt[ing] 50% of the potential violators," and Justice Brennan argued that under a gender-neutral law "twice as many persons would be subject to arrest." This implies that the dissenters' "gender-neutral" approach would criminalize the same instances of intercourse as the California law. In other words, underage men's intercourse would remain legal; underage women's intercourse would remain illegal, but both the underage woman and her partner could be prosecuted as principals. "Neutrality" would be achieved by placing blame and criminal liability on the woman, not by treating young men as equally in need of state protection or as equally vulnerable to sexual objectification by the state.

It appears that the dissenters would uphold a statute that prosecuted both partners for having sexual intercourse when the woman was under eighteen. Presumably, they would consider such a law a legitimate state regulation to reduce the number of young women who become pregnant. But this revision would be the worst alternative for women, because it would increase the coercive elements of the California law and diminish any protective aspects it now might have. A woman would find it more difficult to use statutory rape laws as a shield against male aggression, even aggression by men who are above the age of consent. Because the woman would have to admit that she had violated the law in order to prosecute the male, he would take less seriously her threat to invoke the law. Nor would the amendment suggested by the dissenters reduce the problem of destructive and demeaning stereotypes. To be treated as a guilty culprit in need of protection against oneself as well as against males is no great improvement over being treated as a victim.

Even though the dissenting opinions would eliminate a sexist law, they are misogynic and regressive. The overt misogyny is bad enough; even worse are the assumptions that underlie the opinions — assumptions that are considered too basic to need explicit statement. The dissents imply, for example, that subordination of women is largely a problem of the past and that sex discrimination is an aberrant event, rather than a pervasive aspect of our society. They suggest that discrimination can strike anyone, male or female, and that here its victim was Michael. They treat the social and economic circumstances that make "teenage pregnancy" a greater problem when the female, not the male, is the teenager as immutable truths or as natural, inevitable facts of life. The dissenters assume that the problem of sex discrimination can be solved with tools and resources readily at our disposal, that sexual intercourse in our society is an equal and joint act, and that no major or fundamental changes in our present sexual arrangements are necessary. All of these assumptions are unjustified and apologetic. . . .

Michael M.'s liberal-legalist approach has a related but more serious political consequence: it co-opts feminists into acquiescing to a mystification of sexual intercourse. The plurality opinion characterizes Sharon and Michael as engaging in the same conduct. In this way, they treat sexual intercourse as though it were an equal interaction, which it is not in our society. In fact, men and women rarely receive equal benefits from sexual intercourse. The pretense of equality disempowers women from taking collective action to improve the conditions of their lives.

B. Women and the Military

In Rostker v. Goldberg, 453 U.S. 57 (1981), the Court upheld the constitutionality of the Military Selective Service Act, which exempted women from registration for the draft. Writing for the majority, Justice Rehnquist noted that the Court traditionally accords Congress great deference in cases arising in "the context of Congress' authority over national defense and military affairs." The Court found the exemption of women to be closely related to Congress' purpose in preparing a draft "*of combat troops*." Since women were ineligible for combat,[19] Congress concluded there was no reason to require their registration for the draft. "The Constitution requires that Congress treat similarly situated persons similarly, not that it engage in gestures of superficial equality."

The majority referred to Congress' thorough floor debate and committee action concerning the place of women in the Armed Services to suggest that ". . .

19. "The restrictions on the participation of women in combat in the Navy and Air Force are statutory. Under 10 U.S.C. §6015 'women may not be assigned to duty on vessels or in aircraft that are engaged in combat missions,' and under 10 U.S.C. §8549 female members of the Air Force 'may not be assigned to duty in aircraft engaged in combat missions.' The Army and Marine Corps preclude the use of women in combat as a matter of established policy."

the decision to exempt women from registration was not the 'accidental by-product of a traditional way of thinking about women.' Califano v. Webster. . . . The issue was considered at great length, and Congress clearly expressed its purpose and intent." The majority quoted from the Senate Report:

> The principle that women should not intentionally and routinely engage in combat is fundamental, and enjoys wide support among our people. It is universally supported by military leaders who have testified before the Committee. . . . Current law and policy exclude women from being assigned to combat in our military forces, and the Committee reaffirms this policy. . . . Men and women, because of the combat restrictions on women, are simply not similarly situated for purposes of a draft or registration for a draft.

The Court also addressed the issue that women might serve in noncombat positions "freeing men to go to the front." There was testimony that "in the event of a draft of 650,000 the military could absorb some 80,000 female inductees" in noncombat positions. The Court reasoned that this did not necessarily compel the registration of both men and women. Justice Rehnquist granted considerable deference to Congress:

> In the first place, assuming that a small number of women could be drafted for noncombat roles, Congress simply did not consider it worth the added burdens of including women in draft and registration plans. . . .
>
> Congress also concluded that whatever the need for women for noncombat roles during mobilization, whether 80,000 or less, it could be met by volunteers. . . .
>
> Most significantly, Congress determined that . . . [m]ilitary flexibility requires that a commander be able to move units or ships quickly. Units or ships not located at the front or not previously scheduled for the front nevertheless must be able to move into action if necessary. In peace and war, significant rotation of personnel is necessary. We should not divide the military into two groups — one in permanent combat and one in permanent support. Large numbers of non-combat positions must be available to which combat troops can return for duty before being redeployed.

Justice White, joined by Justice Brennan, dissented, stating that there was "some sense" to the notion that administrative burdens might be involved in registering all women for only some noncombat positions, but he insisted that "on the record before us, the number of women who could be used in the military without sacrificing combat-readiness is not at all small or insubstantial, and administrative convenience has not been sufficient justification for the kind of outright gender-based discrimination involved in registering and conscripting men but no women at all."

Justice Marshall also dissented, joined by Justice Brennan, writing "there simply is no basis for concluding in this case that excluding women from registration is substantially related to the achievement of a concededly important governmental interest in maintaining an effective defense." He argued that the majority had focused upon the wrong issue:

> The relevant inquiry under the Craig v. Boren test is not whether a *gender-neutral* classification would substantially advance important governmental interests.

> Rather, the question is whether the gender-based classification is itself substantially related to the achievement of the asserted governmental interest. Thus, the Government's task in this case is to demonstrate that excluding women from registration substantially furthers the goal of preparing for a draft of combat troops. Or to put it another way, the Government must show that registering women would substantially impede its efforts to prepare for such a draft. Under our precedents, the Government cannot meet this burden without showing that a gender-neutral statute would be a less effective means of attaining this end.

Justice Marshall rejected the argument that there was "*no military need* to draft women," and he cited Defense Department estimates that in the event of a draft, "there will not be enough women volunteers to fill the positions for which women would be eligible. . . ." He maintained that "since the purpose of registration is to protect against unanticipated shortages of volunteers, it is difficult to see how excluding women from registration can be justified by conjectures about the expected number of female volunteers." While he accepted the importance of "military flexibility" posited by the majority, he denied that this warranted the exclusion of women from registration and the draft. Marshall argued that there was nothing in the Senate Report to suggest that "staffing even a limited number of noncombat positions with women would impede military flexibility."

Discussion

1. Consider this summary of the brief filed by the National Organization of Women in *Rostker*: "[T]he exclusion of women from the draft injures their self-perception, reinforces the stereotypes of women as weak and men as aggressive, and helps perpetuate the conditions under which many women are unable to defend themselves against rape and domestic violence and men are led to believe that it is normal to assault women."[20]

2. Consider Wendy Williams, The Equality Crisis: Some Reflections on Culture, Courts, and Feminism, 7 Women's Rights Law Reporter 175, 182-185 (1982), in Herma Kay, Sex-Based Discrimination 115 (3d ed. 1988):

> Suppose you could step outside our culture, rise above its minutiae, and look at its great contours. Having done so, speculate for a moment about where society might draw the line and refuse to proceed further with gender equality. What does our culture identify as quintessentially masculine? Where is the locus of traditional masculine pride and self-identity? What can we identify in men's cultural experience that most divides it from women's cultural experience? Surely, one rather indisputable answer to that question is "war": physical combat and its modern equivalents.
>
> Not surprisingly, the Court in *Rostker* didn't come right out and say, "We've reached our cultural limits." . . . When Congress considered whether women should be drafted, it was much more forthright about its reasons and those reasons support my thesis. . . . To translate, Congress was worried that (1) sexually mixed units would not be able to function — perhaps because of sex in the foxhole; (2) if women were assigned combat, the nation might be reluctant to go to war, presumably because the specter of women fighting would deter a protective and chivalrous popu-

20. Mimi Kelber, Combat in the Erroneous Zone, The Nation, July 25-August 1, 1981, at 73. NOW also argued that the law materially disadvantaged women: "Because the military is the largest vocational trainer of men in the United States . . . women are unfairly disadvantaged. They are not given the same opportunity to serve but are penalized for not serving when they compete with veterans for jobs or promotions or when they apply for mortgages." Id.

lace; and (3) the idea that mom could go into battle and dad keep the home fires burning is simply beyond the cultural pale. In short, current notions of acceptable limits on sex-role behavior would be surpassed by putting women into combat.

3. In December 1989, the 18,000 troops involved in the American incursion into Panama included 800 women, of whom 150, including helicopter pilots were in the immediate vicinity of enemy fire. (Indeed two women were awarded Air Medals for their participation.)[21] A significant number of women were involved in the war with Iraq in 1991. Writing before that conflict, Professor Charles Moskos asked:

> [W]ill allowing qualified women to enter . . . combat . . . finally mean the resolution of [the] nettlesome issue [of] women's role in the military?
>
> Unfortunately, no. The issue is not simply "opening up" combat positions to military women. The core question — the one avoided in public debate, but the one that the women soldiers I spoke with in Panama were all too aware of — is this: Should every woman soldier be made to confront exactly the same combat liabilities as every man? All male soldiers can, if need arises, be assigned to the combat arms, whatever their normal postings. True equality would mean that women soldiers would incur the same liability. To allow women but not men the option of entering or not entering the combat arms would — rightly or wrongly — cause immense resentment among male soldiers; in a single stroke it would diminish the status and respect that female soldiers have achieved. To allow both sexes to choose whether or not to go into combat would be the end of an effective military force. Honesty requires that supporters of lifting the ban on women in combat state openly that they want to put all female soldiers at the same combat risk as all male soldiers — or that they don't.
>
> A trial program of women in combat roles which shows that women can hold their own in battle may put one argument to rest. But it will signal the start of another.

4. Imagine that you are the legislative assistant to a conscientious legislator who wants your advice about what the Constitution requires (or permits) regarding the assignment of women to positions in the military. What advice would you give her?

PERSONNEL ADMINISTRATOR OF MASSACHUSETTS v. FEENEY

442 U.S. 256 (1979)

Appeal from the United States District Court for the District of Massachusetts

[During her 12-year tenure as a state employee, the appellee, who is not a veteran, had passed a number of open competitive civil service examinations for better jobs, but because of Massachusetts' veterans' preference statute, she was ranked in each instance below male veterans who had achieved lower test scores than the appellee. Under the statute, all veterans who qualify for state civil service positions must be considered for appointment ahead of any qualifying nonveterans. The statutory preference, which is available to "any person, male or female,

21. See Charles Moskos, Army Women, The Atlantic, August 1990, at 71-78, from whom the information and quotations in this paragraph are taken.

including a nurse," who was honorably discharged from the United States Armed Forces after at least 90 days of active service, at least one day of which was during "wartime," operates overwhelmingly to the advantage of males. Appellee brought on action in Federal District Court, alleging that the absolute-preference formula established in the Massachusetts statute inevitably operates to exclude women from consideration for the best state civil service jobs and thus discriminates against women in violation of the equal protection clause of the Fourteenth Amendment. A three-judge court declared the statute unconstitutional and enjoined its operation, finding that while the goals of the preference were legitimate and the statute had not been enacted for the purpose of discriminating against women, the exclusionary impact upon women was so severe as to require the state to further its goals through a more limited form of preference.]

STEWART, J. . . .

Notwithstanding the apparent attempts by Massachusetts to include as many military women as possible within the scope of the preference, the statute today benefits an overwhelmingly male class. This is attributable in some measure to the variety of federal statutes, regulations, and policies that have restricted the number of women who could enlist in the United States Armed Forces, and largely to the simple fact that women have never been subjected to a military draft.

When this litigation was commenced, then, over 98% of the veterans in Massachusetts were male; only 1.8% were female. And over one-quarter of the Massachusetts population were veterans. During the decade between 1963 and 1973 when the appellee was actively participating in the State's merit selection system, 47,005 new permanent appointments were made in the classified official service. Forty-three percent of those hired were women, and 57% were men. Of the women appointed, 1.8% were veterans, while 54% of the men had veteran status. A large unspecified percentage of the female appointees were serving in lower paying positions for which males traditionally had not applied.

At the outset of this litigation appellants conceded that for "many of the permanent positions for which males and females have competed" the veterans' preference has "resulted in a substantially greater proportion of female eligibles than male eligibles" not being certified for consideration. The impact of the veterans' preference law upon the public employment opportunities of women has thus been severe. This impact lies at the heart of the appellee's federal constitutional claim.

II

The sole question for decision on this appeal is whether Massachusetts, in granting an absolute lifetime preference to veterans, has discriminated against women in violation of the Equal Protection Clause of the Fourteenth Amendment.

A

The equal protection guarantee of the Fourteenth Amendment does not take from the States all power of classification. . . .

Certain classifications, however, in themselves supply a reason to infer antipathy. Race is the paradigm. A racial classification, regardless of purported motivation, is presumptively invalid and can be upheld only upon an extraordinary justification. This rule applies as well to a classification that is ostensibly neutral but is an obvious pretext for racial discrimination. But, as was made clear in Washington v. Davis, 426 U.S. 229, and Arlington Heights v. Metropolitan Housing Dev. Corp., 429 U.S. 252, even if a neutral law has a disproportionately adverse effect upon a racial minority, it is unconstitutional under the Equal Protection Clause only if that impact can be traced to a discriminatory purpose.

Classifications based on gender, not unlike those based upon race, have traditionally been the touchstone for pervasive and often subtle discrimination. This Court's recent cases teach that such classifications must bear a close and substantial relationship to important governmental objectives, and are in many settings unconstitutional. . . . [A]ny state law overtly or covertly designed to prefer males over females in public employment would require an exceedingly persuasive justification to withstand a constitutional challenge under the Equal Protection Clause of the Fourteenth Amendment.

B

The cases of Washington v. Davis and Arlington Heights v. Metropolitan Housing Dev. Corp. recognize that when a neutral law has a disparate impact upon a group that has historically been the victim of discrimination, an unconstitutional purpose may still be at work. But those cases signaled no departure from the settled rule that the Fourteenth Amendment guarantees equal laws, not equal results. . . .

When a statute gender-neutral on its face is challenged on the ground that its effects upon women are disproportionately adverse, a twofold inquiry is thus appropriate. The first question is whether the statutory classification is indeed neutral in the sense that it is not gender based. If the classification itself, covert or overt, is not based upon gender, the second question is whether the adverse effect reflects invidious gender-based discrimination. In this second inquiry, impact provides an "important starting point," but purposeful discrimination is "the condition that offends the Constitution." . . .

III

A

The question whether ch. 31, §23, establishes a classification that is overtly or covertly based upon gender must first be considered. The appellee has conceded that ch. 31, §23, is neutral on its face. She has also acknowledged that state hiring preferences for veterans are not per se invalid, for she has limited her challenge to the absolute lifetime preference that Massachusetts provides to veterans. The District Court made two central findings that are relevant here: first, that ch. 31, §23, serves legitimate and worthy purposes; second, that the absolute preference was not established for the purpose of discriminating against women. The appellee has thus acknowledged and the District Court has thus found that the distinction between veterans and nonveterans drawn by ch. 31, §23, is not a pretext for gender discrimination. The appellee's concession and the District Court's finding are clearly correct.

If the impact of this statute could not be plausibly explained on a neutral ground, impact itself would signal that the real classification made by the law was in fact not neutral. But there can be but one answer to the question whether this veteran preference excludes significant numbers of women from preferred state jobs because they are women or because they are nonveterans. Apart from the fact that the definition of "veterans" in the statute has always been neutral as to gender and that Massachusetts has consistently defined veteran status in a way that has been inclusive of women who have served in the military, this is not a law that can plausibly be explained only as a gender-based classification. Indeed, it is not a law that can rationally be explained on that ground. . . . Too many men are [adversely] affected by ch. 31, §23, to permit the inference that the statute is but a pretext for preferring men over women. . . .

B

The dispositive question, then, is whether the appellee has shown that a gender-based discriminatory purpose has, at least in some measure, shaped the Massachusetts veterans' preference legislation. As did the District Court, she points to two basic factors which in her view distinguish ch. 31, §23, from the neutral rules at issue in the Washington v. Davis and *Arlington Heights* cases. The first is the nature of the preference, which is said to be demonstrably gender-biased in the sense that it favors a status reserved under federal military policy primarily to men. The second concerns the impact of the absolute lifetime preference upon the employment opportunities of women, an impact claimed to be too inevitable to have been unintended. The appellee contends that these factors, coupled with the fact that the preference itself has little if any relevance to actual job performance, more than suffice to prove the discriminatory intent required to establish a constitutional violation.

1

The contention that this veterans' preference is "inherently nonneutral" or "gender-biased" presumes that the State, by favoring veterans, intentionally incorporated into its public employment policies the panoply of sex-based and assertedly discriminatory federal laws that have prevented all but a handful of women from becoming veterans. There are two serious difficulties with this argument. First, it is wholly at odds with the District Court's central finding that Massachusetts has not offered a preference to veterans for the purpose of discriminating against women. Second, it cannot be reconciled with the assumption made by both the appellee and the District Court that a more limited hiring preference for veterans could be sustained. Taken together, these difficulties are fatal.

To the extent that the status of veteran is one that few women have been enabled to achieve, every hiring preference for veterans, however modest or extreme, is inherently gender-biased. If Massachusetts by offering such a preference can be said intentionally to have incorporated into its state employment policies the historical gender-based federal military personnel practices, the degree of the preference would or should make no constitutional difference. Invidious discrimination does not become less so because the discrimination accomplished is of a lesser magnitude. Discriminatory intent is simply not amenable to calibration. It either is a factor that has influenced the legislative choice or it is not. The District Court's conclusion that the absolute veterans' preference was not originally enacted or subsequently reaffirmed for the purpose of giving an advantage to males as such necessarily compels the conclusion that the State intended nothing more than to prefer "veterans." Given this finding, simple logic suggests that an intent to exclude women from significant public jobs was not at work in this law. To reason that it was, by describing the preference as "inherently nonneutral" or "gender-biased," is merely to restate the fact of impact, not to answer the question of intent.

To be sure, this case is unusual in that it involves a law that by design is not neutral. The law overtly prefers veterans as such. As opposed to the written test at issue in *Davis*, it does not purport to define a job-related characteristic. To the contrary, it confers upon a specifically described group — perceived to be particularly deserving — a competitive headstart. But the District Court found, and the appellee has not disputed, that this legislative choice was legitimate. The basic distinction between veterans and nonveterans, having been found not gender-based, and the goals of the preference having been found worthy, ch. 31 must be analyzed as is any other neutral law that casts a greater burden upon women as a group than upon men as a group. The enlistment policies of the Armed Services may well have discriminated on the basis of sex. See Frontiero v. Richardson, 411 U.S. 677; cf. Schlesinger v. Ballard, 419 U.S. 498. But the history of discrimination against women in the military is not on trial in this case.

2

The appellee's ultimate argument rests upon the presumption, common to the criminal and civil law, that a person intends the natural and foreseeable consequences of his voluntary actions. . . .

The decision to grant a preference to veterans was of course "intentional." So, necessarily, did an adverse impact upon nonveterans follow from that decision. And it cannot seriously be argued that the Legislature of Massachusetts could have been unaware that most veterans are men. It would thus be disingenuous to say that the adverse consequences of this legislation for women were unintended, in the sense that they were not volitional or in the sense that they were not foreseeable.

"Discriminatory purpose," however, implies more than intent as volition or intent as awareness of consequences. It implies that the decisionmaker, in this case a state legislature, selected or reaffirmed a particular course of action at least in part "because of," not merely "in spite of," its adverse effects upon an identifiable group. Yet nothing in the record demonstrates that this preference for veterans was originally devised or subsequently re-enacted because it would accomplish the collateral goal of keeping women in a stereotypic and predefined place in the Massachusetts Civil Service.

To the contrary, the statutory history shows that the benefit of the preference was consistently offered to "any person" who was a veteran. That benefit has been extended to women under a very broad statutory definition of the term veteran. . . . When the totality of legislative actions establishing and extending the Massachusetts veterans' preference are considered, the law remains what it purports to be: a preference for veterans of either sex over nonveterans of either sex, not for men over women.

STEVENS, J., joined by White, J., concurring.

While I concur in the Court's opinion, I confess that I am not at all sure that there is any difference between the two questions posed. If a classification is not overtly based on gender, I am inclined to believe the question whether it is covertly gender-based is the same as the question whether its adverse effects reflect invidious gender-based discrimination. However the question is phrased, for me the answer is largely provided by the fact that the number of males disadvantaged by Massachusetts' veterans' preference (1,867,000) is sufficiently large — and sufficiently close to the number of disadvantaged females (2,954,000) — to refute the claim that the rule was intended to benefit males as a class over females as a class.

MARSHALL, J., joined by Brennan, J., dissenting.

Although acknowledging that in some circumstances, discriminatory intent may be inferred from the inevitable or foreseeable impact of a statute, the Court concludes that no such intent has been established here. I cannot agree. In my judgment, Massachusetts' choice of an absolute veterans' preference system evinces purposeful gender-based discrimination. And because the statutory scheme bears no substantial relationship to a legitimate governmental objective, it cannot withstand scrutiny under the Equal Protection Clause.

I

The District Court found that the "prime objective" of the Massachusetts veterans' preference statute, Mass. Gen. Laws Ann., ch. 31, §23, was to benefit individuals with prior military service. . . .

That a legislature seeks to advantage one group does not, as a matter of logic or of common sense, exclude the possibility that it also intends to disadvantage another. Individuals in general and lawmakers in particular frequently act for a variety of reasons. . . . [T]he critical constitutional inquiry is not whether an illicit consideration was the primary or but-for cause of a decision, but rather whether it had an appreciable role in shaping a given legislative enactment. Where there is "proof that a discriminatory purpose has been *a* motivating factor in the decision, . . . judicial deference is no longer justified." Arlington Heights v. Metropolitan Housing Dev. Corp.

Moreover, since reliable evidence of subjective intentions is seldom obtainable, resort to inference based on objective factors is generally unavoidable. To discern the purposes underlying facially neutral policies, this Court has therefore considered the degree, inevitability, and foreseeability of any disproportionate impact as well as the alternatives reasonably available.

In the instant case, the impact of the Massachusetts statute on women is undisputed. . . . Because less than 2% of the women in Massachusetts are veterans, the absolute preference formula has rendered desirable state civil service employment an almost exclusively male prerogative.

As the District Court recognized, this consequence follows foreseeably, indeed inexorably, from the long history of policies severely limiting women's participation in the military. Although neutral in form, the statute is anything but neutral in application. . . . Where the foreseeable impact of a facially neutral policy is so disproportionate, the burden should rest on the State to establish that sex-based considerations played no part in the choice of the particular legislative scheme.

Clearly, that burden was not sustained here. The legislative history of the statute reflects the Commonwealth's patent appreciation of the impact the preference system would have on women, and an equally evident desire to mitigate that impact only with respect to certain traditionally female occupations. Until 1971, the statute and implementing civil service regulations exempted from operation of the preference any job requisitions "especially calling for women." In practice, this exemption, coupled with the absolute preference for veterans, has created a gender-based civil service hierarchy, with women occupying low-grade clerical secretarial jobs and men holding more responsible and remunerative positions.

Thus, for over 70 years, the Commonwealth has maintained, as an integral part of its veterans' preference system, an exemption relegating female civil service applicants to occupations traditionally filled by women. Such a statutory scheme both reflects and perpetuates precisely the kind of archaic assumptions about women's roles which we have previously held invalid. Particularly when viewed against the range of less discriminatory alternatives available to assist veterans,[a] Massachusetts' choice of a formula that so severely restricts public employment opportunities for women cannot reasonably be thought gender-neutral. . . .

II

To survive challenge under the Equal Protection Clause, statutes reflecting gender-based discrimination must be substantially related to the achievement of important governmental objectives. Appellants here advance three interests in support of the absolute preference system: (1) assisting veterans in their readjustment to civilian life; (2) encouraging military enlistment; and (3) rewarding those who have served their country. . . .

With respect to the first interest, facilitating veterans' transition to civilian status, the statute is plainly overinclusive. By conferring a permanent preference, the legislation allows veterans to invoke their advantage repeatedly, without regard to their date of discharge. . . .

Nor is the Commonwealth's second asserted interest, encouraging military service, a plausible justification for this legislative scheme. In its original and subsequent re-enactments, the statute extended benefits retroactively to veterans who had served during a prior specified period. . . . Moreover, even if such influence could be presumed, the statute is still grossly overinclusive in that it bestows benefits on men drafted as well as those who volunteered.

Finally, the Commonwealth's third interest, rewarding veterans, does not "adequately justify the salient features" of this preference system. Where a particular statutory scheme visits substantial hardship on a class long subject to discrimination, the legislation cannot be sustained unless " 'carefully tuned to alternative

a. Only four States afford a preference comparable in scope to that of Massachusetts. Other States and the Federal Government grant point or tie-breaking preferences that do not foreclose opportunities for women.

considerations.' " Here, there are a wide variety of less discriminatory means by which Massachusetts could effect its compensatory purposes. For example, a point preference system, such as that maintained by many States and the Federal Government, or an absolute preference for a limited duration, would reward veterans without excluding all qualified women from upper level civil service positions. Apart from public employment, the Commonwealth can, and does, afford assistance to veterans in various ways, including tax abatements, educational subsidies, and special programs for needy veterans. Unlike these and similar benefits, the costs of which are distributed across the taxpaying public generally, the Massachusetts statute exacts a substantial price from a discrete group of individuals who have long been subject to employment discrimination, and who, "because of circumstances totally beyond their control, have [had] little if any chance of becoming members of the preferred class."

Discussion

Under the majority's analysis, could a state constitutionally limit a veterans' preference to "all members of the armed forces who served in combat positions?" Given that women are statutorily excluded from combat, the provision would presumably limit the preference exclusively to males. Assuming that the legal analysis remained the same, what type of factual finding might compel the Court to strike down such a provision?

C. The Use of Gender-Specific Actuarial Tables

CITY OF LOS ANGELES v. MANHART, 435 U.S. 702 (1978): [The Court held that Title VII prohibited petitioner-employer from requiring female employees to make larger contributions than male employees to its pension fund. The Department's plan was responsive to the fact that its female employees live longer on the average than males and that the cost of a pension for a female retiree was therefore greater.]

STEVENS, J.

. . . The question . . . is whether the existence or nonexistence of "discrimination" is to be determined by comparison of class characteristics or individual characteristics. . . .

The statute makes it unlawful "to discriminate against any *individual* with respect to his compensation, terms, conditions, or privileges of employment, because of such *individual's* race, color, religion, sex, or national origin." . . . Even a true generalization about the class is an insufficient reason for disqualifying an individual to whom the generalization does not apply.

That proposition is of critical importance in this case because there is no assurance that any individual woman working for the Department will actually fit the generalization on which the Department's policy is based. Many of those individuals will not live as long as the average man. While they were working, those individuals received smaller paychecks because of their sex, but they will receive no compensating advantage when they retire.

It is true, of course, that while contributions are being collected from the employees, the Department cannot know which individuals will predecease the average woman. Therefore, unless women as a class are assessed an extra charge, they will be subsidized, to some extent, by the class of male employees. It follows, according to the Department, that fairness to its class of male employees justifies the extra assessment against all of its female employees. . . .

Even if the statutory language were less clear, the basic policy of the statute requires that we focus on fairness to individuals rather than fairness to classes. Practices that classify employees in terms of religion, race, or sex tend to preserve traditional assumptions about groups rather than thoughtful scrutiny of individuals. The generalization involved in this case illustrates the point. Separate mortality tables are easily interpreted as reflecting innate differences between the sexes; but a significant part of the longevity differential may be explained by the social fact that men are heavier smokers than women. . . .

Although we conclude that the Department's practice violated Title VII, we do not suggest that the statute was intended to revolutionize the insurance and pension industries. All that is at issue today is a requirement that men and women make unequal contributions to an employer-operated pension fund. Nothing in our holding implies that it would be unlawful for an employer to set aside equal retirement contributions for each employee and let each retiree purchase the largest benefit which his or her accumulated contributions could command in the open market. Nor does it call into question the insurance industry practice of considering the composition of an employer's work force in determining the probable cost of a retirement or death benefit plan. Finally, we recognize that in a case of this kind it may be necessary to take special care in fashioning appropriate relief. . . .

[Chief Justice Burger and Justice Rehnquist dissented on this issue.]

Discussion

1. How should *Manhart* have been decided under the Fourteenth Amendment?

2. Suppose that a government institution offers its employees both ordinary life insurance and an annuity program. All employees opting for the same coverage pay in the same amount. Based on the lower life expectancy of men than women, however, men's life insurance policies pay out less than women's, and women receive lower annuities than men. Does this scheme violate the equal protection clause? Cf. Equal Employment Opportunity Commission v. Colby College, 589 F.2d 1139 (1st Cir. 1978). Could the same government institution offer differential rates to blacks and whites based on actuarial differences in the life expectancies of the two groups?

3. Justice Stevens writes in *Manhart* that "[e]ven a true generalization about the class is an insufficient reason for disqualifying an individual to whom the generalization does not apply." Professor George Benston argues that actuarial tables do not impose group generalizations on unique individuals, but rather represent life expectancies, and that "longer life *expectancy* . . . is a characteristic shared by every individual woman." For Benston, the Court's view that certain women receive less than men under sexually segregated tables is therefore misplaced:

> To understand insurance, one must realize that the purchaser of a policy is not buying the amount that will be remitted should the unwanted event occur, but the *promise* that *if* the event occurs, the designated amount will be paid. Thus . . . after a life

> annuity contract has been executed, an annuitant who lives for thirty years and an annuitant who dies the next day have both received the same product for their money.[22]

On the basis of this analysis, Benston concludes that, because unisex actuarial tables undercompensate all men and overcompensate all women, their use violates Title VII:

> [A]ssuming for now that, all other things being equal, women are expected to live longer than men, granting the same periodic life pension to a male and a female employee of the same age who do the same work gives lower present compensation to the male than to the female. If the same amount of life insurance coverage were given to these employees, the male would receive a greater fringe benefit than the female. Because these differences in pay are determined solely by the gender of the employees, I conclude that this practice violates the Equal Pay Act and . . . Title VII.[23]

4. Professor Lea Brilmayer et al. have argued that, even if women's life expectancy can be proven to be inherently greater than men's (which they question), this leaves unresolved whether the use of sexually segregated actuarial tables is legitimate:

> [The] expectancy argument begs the question in a fundamental way. The ultimate issue is precisely whether mortality data may be classified by sex for the purpose of paying annuities — that is, whether sex may be used to predict longevity. . . . It is circular to use the expectancies generated by a predictor to justify using that predictor.[24]

The underlying issue, they argue, turns on a tension between the disparate treatment and disparate impact strands of Title VII. After reviewing the legislative history surrounding Title VII, the authors conclude that the disproportionate impact on men resulting from the use of unisex actuarial tables cannot justify the disparate treatment of women that sexually segregated tables necessarily entail: "When the ban on disparate treatment conflicts with the partial ban on disparate impact, the former must control."

Affirmative action plans often permit overt race- or sex-conscious treatment based on findings of disparate impact from which discrimination is inferred. Is this reconcilable with the conclusion above that disparate treatment cannot be justified under Title VII simply to ameliorate disparate impact?

ARIZONA GOVERNING COMMITTEE FOR TAX DEFERRED ANNUITY AND DEFERRED COMPENSATION PLANS v. NORRIS, 463 U.S. 1073 (1983): [The Court invoked *Manhart* to invalidate an Arizona statute offering state employees a right to purchase annuities from a restricted list of insurance

22. George J. Benston, The Economics of Gender Discrimination in Employee Fringe Benefits: *Manhart* Revisited, 49 U. Chi. L. Rev. 489 (1982).
23. Id.
24. Lea Brilmayer, Richard W. Hekeler, Douglas Laycock, and Teresa A. Sullivan, Sex Discrimination in Employer-Sponsored Insurance Plans: A Legal and Demographic Analysis, 47 U. Chi. L. Rev. 505 (1980).

companies, all of whom paid women a smaller sum per month than men for an equal payment. There were two "majority opinions" in the case, in effect, one concerning the statute, the other involving the remedy.

As to liability, Justice Marshall wrote for himself and Justices Brennan, White, Stevens, and O'Connor. He first considered whether Arizona could have administered such an annuity program itself without the participation of any insurance companies from the private market. "We have no hesitation in holding . . . that the classification of employees on the basis of sex is no more permissible at the pay-out stage of a retirement plan than at the pay-in stage. . . . *Manhart* squarely rejected the notion that, because women as a class live longer than men, an employer may adopt a retirement plan that treats every individual woman less favorably than every individual man."]

BRENNAN, J.

III

Since petitioners plainly would have violated Title VII if they had run the entire deferred compensation plan themselves, the only remaining question as to liability is whether their conduct is beyond the reach of the statute because it is the companies chosen by petitioners to participate that calculate and pay the retirement benefits.

Title VII "primarily govern[s] relations between employees and their employer, not between employees and third parties." *Manhart*. Recognizing this limitation on the reach of the statute, we noted in *Manhart* that

> Nothing in our holding implies that it would be unlawful for an employer to set aside equal retirement contributions for each employee and let each retiree purchase the largest benefits which his or her accumulated contributions could command in the open market.

Relying on this caveat, petitioners contend that they have not violated Title VII because the life annuities offered by the companies participating in the Arizona plan reflect what is available in the open market. Petitioners cite a statement in the stipulation of facts entered into in the District Court that "[a]ll tables presently in use provide a larger sum to a male than to a female of equal age, account value and any guaranteed payment period."

It is no defense that all annuities immediately available in the open market may have been based on sex-segregated actuarial tables. In context it is reasonably clear that the stipulation on which petitioners rely means only that all the tables used by the companies taking part in the Arizona plan are based on sex, but our conclusion does not depend upon whether petitioner's construction of the stipulation is accepted or rejected. It is irrelevant whether any other insurers offered annuities on a sex-neutral basis, since the State did not simply set aside retirement contributions and let employees purchase annuities on the open market. On the contrary, the State provided the opportunity to obtain an annuity as part of its own deferred compensation plan. It invited insurance companies to submit bids outlining the terms on which they would supply retirement benefits and selected the companies that were permitted to participate in the plan. Once the State selected these companies, it entered into contracts with them governing the terms on which benefits were to be provided to employees. Employees enrolling in the plan could obtain retirement benefits only from one of those companies, and no employee could be contacted by a company except as permitted by the State.

Under these circumstances there can be no serious question that petitioners are legally responsible for the discriminatory terms on which annuities are offered by the companies chosen to participate in the plan. Having created a plan whereby employees can obtain the advantages of using deferred compensation to purchase an annuity only if they invest in one of the companies specifically selected by the State, the State cannot disclaim responsibility for the discriminatory features of the insurers' options. Since employers are ultimately responsible for the "compensation, terms, conditions, [and] privileges of employment" provided to employees, an employer that adopts a fringe-benefit scheme that discriminates among its employees on the basis of race, religion, sex, or national origin violates Title VII regardless of whether third parties are also involved in the discrimination. In this case the State of Arizona was itself a party to contracts concerning the annuities to be offered by the insurance companies, and it is well established that both parties to a discriminatory contract are liable for any discriminatory provisions the contract contains, regardless of which party initially suggested inclusion of the discriminatory provisions. It would be inconsistent with the broad remedial purposes of Title VII to hold that an employer who adopts a discriminatory fringe benefit plan can avoid liability on the ground that he could not find a third party willing to treat his employees on a nondiscriminatory basis. An employer who confronts such a situation must either supply the fringe benefit himself, without the assistance of any third party, or not provide it at all.

[Justice Powell dissented on the issue of liability, joined by Chief Justice Burger and Justices Blackmun and Rehnquist:]

I

The State of Arizona provides its employees with a voluntary pension plan that allows them to defer receipt of a portion of their compensation until retirement. If an employee chooses to participate, an amount designated by the employee is withheld from each paycheck and invested by the State on the employee's behalf. When an employee retires, he or she may receive the amount that has accrued in one of three ways. The employee may withdraw the total amount accrued, arrange for periodic payments of a fixed sum for a fixed time, or used the accrued amount to purchase a life annuity.

There is no contention that the State's plan discriminates between men and women when an employee contributes to the fund. The plan is voluntary and each employee may contribute as much as he or she chooses. Nor does anyone contend that either of the first two methods or repaying the accrued amount at retirement is discriminatory. Thus, if Arizona had adopted the same contribution plan but provided only the first two repayment options, there would be no dispute that its plan complied with Title VII. . . . The first two options, however, have disadvantages. If an employee chooses to take a lump-sum payment, the tax liability will be substantial. The second option ameliorates the tax problem by spreading the receipt of the accrued amount over a fixed period of time. This option, however, does not guard against the possibility that the finite number of payments selected by the employee will fail to provide income for the remainder of his or her life.

The third option — the purchase of a life annuity — resolves both of these problems. It reduces an employee's tax liability by spreading the payments out over time, and it guarantees that the employee will receive a stream of payments for life. State law prevents Arizona from accepting the financial uncertainty of funding life annuities. But to achieve tax benefits under federal law, the life annuity must be purchased from a company designated by the retirement plan. Accordingly, Arizona contracts with private insurance companies to make life annuities available to its employees. The companies that underwrite the life annuities, as do the vast majority of private insurance companies in the United States, use sex-based mortality tables. Thus, the only effect of Arizona's third option is to allow its employees to purchase at a tax saving the same annuities they otherwise would purchase on the open market.

The Court holds that Arizona's voluntary plan violates Title VII. In the majority's view, Title VII requires an employer to follow one of three courses. An employer must provide unisex annuities, contract with insurance companies to provide such annuities, or provide no annuities to its employees. The first option is largely illusory. Most employers do not have either the financial resources or administrative ability to underwrite annuities. Or, as in this case, state law may prevent an employer from providing annuities. If unisex annuities are available, an employer may contract with private insurance companies to provide them. It is stipulated, however, that the insurance companies with which Arizona contracts do not provide unisex annuities, nor do insurance companies generally underwrite them. The insurance industry either is prevented by state law from doing so[a] or it views unisex mortality tables as actuarially unsound. An employer, of course, may choose the third option. It simply may decline to offer its employees the right to purchase annuities at a substantial tax saving. It is difficult to see the virtue in such a compelled choice.

II

As indicated above, the consequences of the Court's holdings are unlikely to be beneficial. If the cost to employers offering unisex annuities is prohibitive, or if insurance carriers choose not to write such annuities, employees will be denied the opportunity to purchase life annuities — concededly the most advantageous pension plan — at lower cost. If, alternatively, insurance carriers and employers choose to offer these annuities, the heavy cost burden of equalizing benefits probably will be passed on to current employees. There is no evidence that Con-

a. See Cal. Ins. Code Ann. §790.03(f) (West) (1983) (requiring differentials based on the sex of the individual insured); Spirit v. Teachers Insurance and Annuity Assn., 691 F.2d 1054, 1066 (C.A.2 1982) (noting that the State of New York has disapproved certain uses of unisex rates).

This is precisely what has happened in this case. Faced with the liability resulting from the Court of Appeal's judgment, the State of Arizona discontinued making life annuities available to its employees. Any employee who now wishes to have the security provided by a life annuity must withdraw his or her accrued retirement savings from the state pension plan, pay federal income tax on the amount withdrawn, and then use the remainder to purchase an annuity on the open market — which most likely will be sex-based. The adverse effect of today's holding apparently will fall primarily on the State's employees.

gress intended Title VII to work such a change. Nor does *Manhart* support such a sweeping reading of this statute. That case expressly recognized the limited reach of its holding — a limitation grounded in the legislative history of Title VII and the inapplicability of Title VII's policies to the insurance industry.

A

We were careful in *Manhart* to make clear that the question before us was narrow. We stated: "All that is at issue today is a requirement that men and women make unequal contributions to an *employer-operated* pension fund." And our holding was limited expressly to the precise issue before us. We stated that "[a]lthough we concluded that the Department's practice violated Title VII, we do not suggest that the statute was intended to revolutionize the insurance and pension industries."

[With the addition of Justice O'Connor's vote, however, Justice Powell gained a majority for his conclusion that the decision should be prospective only. Annuity plans purchased prior to August 1, 1983, *can* pay out different amounts to men and women based on the longevity tables used at the time of purchase. Justices Marshall, Brennan, White, and Stevens would have remanded for further consideration by the courts below as to the proper remedy, including possibly retroactivity at least to the time of *Manhart*.[25]]

Discussion

Note footnote b of Justice Powell's opinion. Assuming that he accurately summarizes the state laws of California and New York, are they constitutional under the Fourteenth Amendment? Would your answer change if one of the laws in question mandated that sex be taken into account in regard to life insurance contracts (which would mean that women would pay less than men for a policy of a given amount) but that annuity contracts be sex neutral?

VI. *Affirmative Action*

In Kahn v. Shevin, 416 U.S. 351 (1974), a widower challenged a Florida statute granting widows, but not widowers, an annual tax exemption of $500. A divided Court upheld the law. Justice Douglas noted the pervasive effects of economic discrimination against women and held that the law was not irrational:

> While the widower can usually continue in the occupation which preceded his spouse's death, in many cases the widow will find herself suddenly forced into a job market with which she is unfamiliar, and in which, because of her former economic dependency, she will have fewer skills to offer. . . . We deal here with state tax law

25. See Florida v. Long, 487 U.S. 223 (1988), striking down an award of retroactive relief granted to employees by a District Court, where the employer continued to offer optional retirement plans using sex-based actuarial tables after *Manhart*, but discontinued the option with the Court's holding in *Norris*. Justice Kennedy, writing for the majority, concluded that, given the narrowness of the holding in *Manhart*, the case did not place "Florida on notice that optional pension plans offering sex-based benefits violated Title VII."

> reasonably designed to further the state policy of cushioning the financial impact of spousal loss upon the sex for which that loss imposes a disproportionately heavy burden.

Justice Brennan dissented, in an opinion joined by Justice Marshall. He agreed with Justice Douglas' analysis, and further wrote that

> the purpose and effect of the suspect classification is ameliorative; the statute neither stigmatizes nor denigrates widowers not also benefitted by the legislation. Moreover, inclusion of needy widowers within the class of beneficiaries would not further the State's overriding interest in remedying the economic effects of past discrimination for needy victims of that discrimination.

However, Justice Brennan went on to argue that sex was a suspect trait and that sex classifications were therefore subject to strict scrutiny. Under this standard,

> the State has not borne its burden of proving that its compelling interest could not be achieved by a more precisely tailored statute or by the use of feasible less drastic means. [The statute is] plainly overinclusive, for the $500 property tax exemption may be obtained by a financially independent heiress as well as by an unemployed widow with dependent children.

Justice White also dissented on the ground that the law did not pass strict scrutiny, noting that "there are many widowers who are needy and who are in more desperate financial straits and have less access to the job market than many widows."

In Schlesinger v. Ballard, 419 U.S. 496 (1975), the Court addressed a Navy practice under which a male officer who twice fails to be selected for promotion is subject to mandatory discharge regardless of how long he has been in active service, while a female officer is subject to mandatory discharge only after 13 years of active service without promotion. The Court upheld the classification against a challenge by a male officer discharged after nine years' service. Justice Stewart wrote:

> In contrast [to *Reed* and *Frontiero*], the different treatment of men and women naval officers . . . reflects, not archaic and overbroad generalizations, but, instead, the demonstrable fact that male and female line officers in the Navy are *not* similarly situated with respect to opportunities for professional service. The appellee has not challenged the current restrictions on women officers' participation in combat and in most sea duty. . . . [I]n competing for promotion, female lieutenants will not generally have compiled records of seagoing service comparable to those of male lieutenants. In enacting and retaining [the scheme], Congress may thus quite rationally have believed that women line officers had less opportunity for promotion than did their male counterparts, and that a longer period of tenure for women officers would, therefore, be consistent with the goal to provide women officers with "fair and equitable career advancement programs." Cf. Kahn v. Shevin. . . .
>
> In both *Reed* and *Frontiero* the reason asserted to justify the challenged gender-based classifications was administrative convenience, and that alone. Here, on the contrary, the operation of the statutes in question results in a flow of promotions commensurate with the Navy's current needs and serves to motivate qualified com-

> missioned officers to so conduct themselves that they may realistically look forward to higher levels of command.

Justice Brennan dissented in an opinion joined by Justices Douglas and Marshall and agreed in "for the most part" by Justice White. He argued that the scheme should be reviewed under a "compelling interest" standard; that the legislative history demonstrated that Congress' purpose in retaining the scheme was not compensatory; and that the scheme did not in fact compensate, since men and women do not compete directly with each other for promotions. Furthermore, he found "quite troublesome the notion that a gender-based difference in treatment can be justified by another, broader, gender-based difference in treatment imposed directly and currently by the Navy itself. While it is true that the restrictions upon women officers' opportunities for professional service are not here directly under attack, . . . the Court ought at least to consider whether they *may* be valid before sustaining a provision it conceives to be based upon them."

Califano v. Webster, 430 U.S. 313 (1977) (per curiam), invoked *Kahn* and *Ballard* and distinguished *Goldfarb* and *Wiesenfeld* to uphold a social security provision that provided higher monthly old-age benefits for retired female wage earners than for males. Benefits are based on a wage earner's average monthly wage during the benefit computation years, but recipients can omit a certain number of low earning years in computing the average. Until 1972, women could exclude three more years than similarly situated male wage earners. The Court noted that "allowing women, who as such have been unfairly hindered from earning as much as men, to eliminate additional low-earning years from the calculation of their retirement benefits works directly to remedy some part of the effect of past discrimination." The provision therefore met the standard announced in Craig v. Boren, that "classifications by gender must serve important government objectives and must be substantially related to the achievement of those objectives."

Chief Justice Burger, joined by Justices Stewart, Blackmun, and Rehnquist, concurred in the judgment for the reasons stated by Justice Rehnquist's dissent in *Goldfarb*.

In Johnson v. Transportation Agency, 480 U.S. 616 (1987), a male employee who was passed over for promotion in favor of a female employee brought a Title VII suit against the county transportation agency. Without reaching any constitutional issues, Justice Brennan held that the agency did not violate Title VII by taking sex into account and promoting the female employee, despite recommendations by three Agency supervisors conducting the final interviews that the male be hired, since the decision was made

> pursuant to an Agency plan that directed that sex or race be taken into account for the purpose of remedying underrepresentation. The Agency Plan acknowledged the "limited opportunities that have existed in the past" . . . for women to find employment in certain job classifications "where women have not been traditionally employed in significant numbers." . . . The plan sought to remedy these imbalances through "hiring, training and promotion of . . . women throughout the Agency in all major job classifications where they are underrepresented." . . . The plan stressed that such goals "should not be construed as 'quotas' that must

be met," but as reasonable aspirations in correcting the imbalance in the Agency's work force.[26]

Chief Justice Rehnquist and Justices White and Scalia dissented. Justice Scalia argued that the decision "completes the process of converting [Title VII] from a guarantee that race or sex will *not* be the basis for employment determinations, to a guarantee that it often *will*. Ever so subtly . . . we effectively replace the goal of a discrimination-free society with the quite incompatible goal of proportionate representation by race and sex in the workplace."

Discussion

1. *Kahn* and *Ballard* were decided at a time when the Court had not agreed on a standard of judicial review even for nonpreferential sex discrimination and had not agreed on a standard of review for preferential treatment based on race. Might Justice Brennan's dissents have been part of a strategy to gain acceptance for the strict scrutiny of all gender classifications? In view of his position in subsequent affirmative action cases, what standard do you suppose he would apply if the cases came up today? How would you decide them?

2. There are at least three variables in these cases: (1) the *assumptions* and *purposes* underlying the classifications; (2) the *material* benefits and burdens of the gender classifications; and (3) *nonmaterial* consequences of the classifications, such as stereotyping or stigma. Do these variables change depending on whether men or women are the burdened group? Should they? Can you formulate and justify a principle that reconciles these decisions, as well as *Frontiero*, in terms of these and/or any other factors?

3. If the Supreme Court continues to follow its newly announced rule of strict scrutiny for racially based affirmative action, *Crosen*, Chapter 6 supra, but only intermediate scrutiny for gender classifications, does this mean that gender-based affirmative action programs will survive even as their race-based analogues are struck down?

VII. The Equal Rights Amendment

Between 1923 and 1972, resolutions proposing an equal rights amendment were introduced in every term of Congress. In 1972, Congress proposed the following amendment for ratification by state legislatures:

> Section 1. Equality of rights under the law shall not be denied or abridged by the United States or by any State on account of sex.

26. Although neither the District Court nor the Court of Appeals had found prior discrimination, Justice Brennan argued that the burden of proof remained with employees challenging the validity of the plan. "Once a plaintiff establishes a prima facie case that race or sex has been taken into account in an employer's employment decision, the burden shifts to the employer to articulate a nondiscriminatory rationale for its decision. The existence of an affirmative action plan provides such a rationale. If such a plan is . . . the basis for the employer's decision, the burden shifts to the plaintiff to prove that the employer's justification is pretextual. . . . [R]eliance on an affirmative action plan is [not] to be treated as an affirmative defense requiring the employer to carry the burden of proving the validity of the plan. The burden of proving its invalidity remains on the plaintiff."

Section 2. The Congress shall have the power to enforce, by appropriate legislation, the provisions of this article.

At the time of its submission, the ERA appeared relatively uncontroversial. The House of Representatives voted 354-23 in favor of the amendment; the Senate, in turn, overwhelmingly endorsed it by a vote of 84-8 on March 22, 1972.[27] Hawaii unanimously approved the amendment that very day, 25 minutes after learning of the Senate's vote. Delaware, Nebraska, and New Hampshire followed suit the next day, with Idaho and Iowa joining these states on March 24. By early 1973, 30 of the 38 states needed to ratify had endorsed the amendment, most of them unanimously or by lopsided votes. Thereafter, however, a vigorous anti-ERA movement, sparked in part by the Court's decision in *Roe* in 1973, successfully blocked approval in most of the remaining states, so that by 1977 only 35 states had endorsed the amendment. Although Congress had initially proposed a seven-year time limit for ratification, in 1979, after a heated debate with constitutional overtones,[28] Congress extended the limit to 1982. Despite the extension, the ERA failed to garner approval in any more states. (Indeed, several states attempted to rescind their prior ratifications.) The proposed amendment expired on June 30, 1982.[29]

One of the principal controversies surrounding the ERA focused on its potential legal consequences. The amendment would clearly have imposed a standard higher than "rational basis" for gender classifications, but just what the standard would have been and what practices would have been unconstitutional remained unclear. Jane Mansbridge points out that many opponents of the ERA charged that it would require the elimination of the combat exemption for women in the armed services, while proponents took conflicting positions on this.[30] Opponents also argued that the amendment would prohibit gender-segregated bathrooms, a proposition that supporters almost unanimously denied.[31]

Proponents did not argue so much that the amendment's text was unambiguous, as that Congress could control its interpretation by specifying its intentions about the ERA's reach in its deliberations. Thus an ERA advocate testified that

> the Senate and the House of Representatives control the meaning. . . . You are the legislators. . . . If the amendment is adopted, it is what the proponents say it means and what the majority reports or any reports supporting the adoption of the amendment in either House say. And if they are clear about what the amendment means, that will be controlling.[32]

27. See Jane J. Mansbridge, Why We Lost the ERA 12-13 (1986).

28. See Ruth Bader Ginsburg, Ratification of the Equal Rights Amendment: A Question of Time, 57 Tex. L. Rev. 919 (1979); Grover Rees III, Throwing Away the Key: The Unconstitutionality of the Equal Rights Amendment Extension, 58 Tex. L. Rev. 875 (1980).

29. The following states failed to ratify the ERA: Alabama, Arizona, Arkansas, Florida, Georgia, Illinois, Louisiana, Mississippi, Missouri, Nevada, North Carolina, Oklahoma, Utah, and Virginia.

30. Mansbridge, supra note 27, at 67. "[W]hile most pro-ERA pamphlets suggested that the ERA would not require Congress to send women into combat, the pamphlets never explained *why* this might be so in legal terms." Id. at 83.

31. See id. at 112-115, on argument that gender-segregated bathrooms protected "privacy" interests. Given, however, that such a rationale would be unacceptable in the case of racially segregated bathrooms, is it self-evident why "privacy" interests would permit sex-segregated bathrooms?

32. Testimony of Ann Freedman, quoted in Mansbridge, supra note 27, at 127.

1. In view of what you have learned about the interpretive history of the Fourteenth Amendment (not to mention other clauses of the Constitution), how much reliance would you place in these assurances about the ability of the Congress to "control the meaning" of the ERA? Had the amendment been ratified, how should the Court have applied it to a challenge of the Navy's ban on women serving on aircraft carriers?

2. The Canadian Constitution Act of 1982 contains a Charter of Rights and Freedoms, including the following:

> *Equality Rights*
>
> 15. (1) Every individual is equal before and under the law and has the right to the equal protection and equal benefit of the law without discrimination and, in particular, without discrimination based on race, national or ethnic origin, colour, religion, sex, age or mental or physical disability.
>
> (2) Subsection (1) does not preclude any law, program or activity that has as its object the amelioration of conditions of disadvantaged individuals or groups including those that are disadvantaged because of race, national or ethnic origin, colour, religion, sex, age or mental or physical disability.
>
> 28. Notwithstanding anything in this Charter, the rights and freedoms referred to in it are guaranteed equally to male and female persons.

Would you favor the replacement of the equal protection clause in the Fourteenth Amendment and the proposed Equal Rights Amendment by the first clause in Section 15 of the Canadian Charter? Would you favor its replacement by both clauses one and two? Why or why not?

Imagine that you are a law clerk to a justice of the Canadian Supreme Court; can you provide him any cases from the corpus of American constitutional law that give particularly useful insights into the meaning of these two sections of the Charter?

VIII. Other Suspect Bases of Classification

The Court has treated classifications based on ethnic origin[33] identically to race and has required more than a rational justification for classifications based on alienage[34] and legitimacy.[35] There are numerous other bases of classification that, it might be argued, should be treated as "suspect," including age,[36] height, intelligence,[37] appearance, and sexual orientation. See *High Tech Gays*, p.1028 infra.

33. See, e.g., Korematsu v. United States, 323 U.S. 214 (1944); Hirabayashi v. United States, 320 U.S. 81 (1943) (distinctions "between citizens solely because of their ancestry are by their very nature odious"); Hernandez v. Texas, 347 U.S. 475 (1954).

34. See, e.g., Graham v. Richardson, 403 U.S. 305 (1971); Sugarman v. Dougall, 413 U.S. 634 (1973); In re Griffiths, 413 U.S. 717 (1973); Examining Bd. v. Flores de Otero, 426 U.S. 572 (1976); Nyquist v. Mauclet, 432 U.S. 1 (1977). But see Foley v. Connelie, 435 U.S. 291 (1978); Ambach v. Norwich, 441 U.S. 68 (1979).

35. See, e.g., Levy v. Louisiana, 301 U.S. 68 (1968); Glona v. American Guar. & Liab. Co., 391 U.S. 73 (1968); Weber v. Aetna Cas. & Sur. Co., 406 U.S. 164 (1972); Trimble v. Gordon, 430 U.S. 762 (1977). Cf. Labine v. Vincent, 401 U.S. 532 (1971); Mathews v. Lucas, 427 U.S. 495 (1976).

36. But see Massachusetts Bd. of Retirement v. Murgia, 427 U.S. 307 (1976); Vance v. Bradley, 440 U.S. 93 (1979).

37. See Note, Equal Protection and Intelligence Classifications, 26 Stan. L. Rev. 647 (1974).

After our analysis of race and sex, do you have a theory of the equal protection clause that helps determine which, if any, of these other classifications should receive special scrutiny?

CITY OF CLEBURNE, TEXAS v. CLEBURNE LIVING CENTER

473 U.S. 432 (1985)

On Certiorari to the United States Court of Appeals for the Fifth Circuit

[In July 1980, a four-bedroom house in Cleburne, Texas, was purchased for lease to the Cleburne Living Centers, Inc. (CLC), to serve as a group home for 13 mentally retarded men and women who would live there under the supervision of CLC staff members. CLC intended to comply with all applicable state and federal regulations. The city determined that a special use permit, required for the construction of "[h]ospitals for the insane or feeble-minded, or alcoholic[s] or drug addicts, or penal or correctional institutions," was required as well, on the basis of its classification of the home as a "hospital for the feeble-minded." CLC applied for a permit, which the city council denied by a vote of three to one. CLC then filed suit in the Federal District Court, which found that "[i]f the potential residents of the . . . home were not mentally retarded, but the home was the same in all other respects, its use would be permitted under the city's zoning ordinance." It further found that the city council's decision "was motivated primarily by the fact that the residents of the home would be persons who are mentally retarded." Nevertheless, the court held the ordinance and its application constitutional under the standard of minimal rationality, for it was rationally related to the city's legitimate interests in "the legal responsibility of CLC and its residents, . . . the safety and fears of residents in the adjoining neighborhood," and the number of people to be housed in the facility.

The Court of Appeals for the Fifth Circuit reversed, holding that mental retardation was a quasi-suspect classification triggering an intermediate-level standard of review, which the city could not pass. The city appealed.]

WHITE, J., delivered the opinion of the Court.

. . . When social or economic legislation is at issue, the Equal Protection Clause allows the states wide latitude, and the Constitution presumes that even improvident decisions will eventually be rectified by the democratic processes.

The general rule gives way, however, when a statute classifies by race, alienage or national origin. These factors are so seldom relevant to the achievement of any legitimate state interest that laws grounded in such considerations are deemed to reflect prejudice and antipathy — a view that those in the burdened class are not as worthy or deserving as others. For these reasons and because such discrimination is unlikely to be soon rectified by legislative means, these laws are subjected to strict scrutiny and will be sustained only if they are suitably tailored to serve a compelling state interest. . . .

Legislative classifications based on gender also call for a heightened standard of review. . . . Rather than resting on meaningful considerations, statutes distributing benefits and burdens between the sexes in different ways very likely reflect outmoded notions of the relative capabilities of men and women. A gender classification fails unless it is substantially related to a sufficiently important governmental interest. Because illegitimacy is beyond the individual's control and bears "no relation to the individual's ability to participate in and contribute to society," Mathews v. Lucas, 427 U.S. 495, 505 (1976), official discriminations resting on that characteristic are also subject to somewhat heightened review. Those restrictions "will survive equal protection scrutiny to the extent they are substantially related to a legitimate state interest." Mills v. Habluetzel, 456 U.S. 91, 99 (1982).

We have declined, however, to extend heightened review to differential treatment based on age:

> While the treatment of the aged in this Nation has not been wholly free of discrimination, such persons, unlike, say, those who have been discriminated against on the basis of race or national origin, have not experienced a "history of purposeful unequal treatment" or been subjected to unique disabilities on the basis of stereotyped characteristics not truly indicative of their abilities. Massachusetts Board of Retirement v. Murgia, 427 U.S. 307, 313 (1976).

The lesson of *Murgia* is that where individuals in the group affected by a law have distinguishing characteristics relevant to interests the state has the authority to implement, the courts have been very reluctant, as they should be in our federal system and with our respect for the separation of powers, to closely scrutinize legislative choices as to whether, how and to what extent those interests should be pursued. In such cases, the Equal Protection Clause requires only a rational means to serve a legitimate end.

III

Against this background, we conclude for several reasons that the Court of Appeals erred in holding mental retardation a quasi-suspect classification calling for a more exacting standard of judicial review than is normally accorded economic and social legislation. First, it is undeniable, and it is not argued otherwise here, that those who are mentally retarded have a reduced ability to cope with and function in the everyday world. Nor are they all cut from the same pattern: as the testimony in this record indicates, they range from those whose disability is not immediately evident to those who must be constantly cared for. They are thus different, immutably so, in relevant respects, and the states' interest in dealing with and providing for them is plainly a legitimate one. How this large and diversified group is to be treated under the law is a difficult and often a technical matter, very much a task for legislators guided by qualified professionals and not by the perhaps ill-informed opinions of the judiciary. . . .

Second, the distinctive legislative response, both national and state, to the plight of those who are mentally retarded demonstrates not only that they have unique problems, but also that the lawmakers have been addressing their difficulties in a manner that belies a continuing antipathy or prejudice and a corresponding need for more intrusive oversight by the judiciary. [The Court then reviewed some recent protective legislation passed by both the federal and Texas governments.]

. . . It may be . . . that legislation designed to benefit, rather than disadvantage, the retarded would generally withstand examination under a test of heightened scrutiny. The relevant inquiry, however, is whether heightened scrutiny is constitutionally mandated in the first instance. Even assuming that many of these laws could be shown to be substantially related to an important governmental purpose, merely requiring the legislature to justify its efforts in these terms may lead it to refrain from acting at all. Much recent legislation intended to benefit the retarded also assumes the need for measures that might be perceived to disadvantage them. The [federal] Education of the Handicapped Act, for example, requires an "appropriate" education, not one that is equal in all respects to the education of non-retarded children. . . . Especially given the wide variation in the abilities and needs of the retarded themselves, governmental bodies must have a certain amount of flexibility and freedom from judicial oversight in shaping and limiting their remedial efforts.

Third, the legislative response, which could hardly have occurred and survived without public support, negates any claim that the mentally retarded are politically powerless in the sense that they have no ability to attract the attention of the lawmakers. Any minority can be said to be powerless to assert direct control over the legislature, but if that were a criterion for higher level scrutiny by the courts, much economic and social legislation would now be suspect.

Fourth, if the large and amorphous class of the mentally retarded were deemed quasi-suspect, . . . it would be difficult to find a principled way to distinguish a variety of other groups who have perhaps immutable disabilities setting them off from others, who cannot themselves mandate the desired legislative responses, and who can claim some degree of prejudice from at least part of the public at large. One need mention in this respect only the aging, the disabled, the mentally ill, and the infirm. We are reluctant to set out on that course, and we decline to do so. . . .

IV

We turn to the issue of the validity of the zoning ordinance insofar as it requires a special use permit for homes for the mentally retarded. We inquire first whether requiring a special use permit for the Featherston [Avenue] home in the circumstances here deprives respondents of the equal protection of the laws. If it does, there will be no occasion to decide whether the special use permit provision is facially invalid where the mentally retarded are involved. . . .

The constitutional issue is clearly posed. The city does not require a special use permit in an R-3 zone for apartment houses, multiple dwellings, boarding and lodging houses, fraternity or sorority houses, dormitories, apartment hotels, hospitals, sanitariums, nursing homes for convalescents or the aged (other than for the insane or feeble-minded or alcoholics or drug addicts), private clubs or fraternal orders, and other specified uses. It does, however, insist on a special permit for the Featherston home, and it does so, as the District Court found, because it would be a facility for the mentally retarded. May the city require the permit for this facility when other care and multiple dwelling facilities are freely permitted?

. . . Because in our view the record does not reveal any rational basis for believing that the Featherston home would pose any special threat to the city's legitimate interests, we affirm the judgment below insofar as it holds the ordinance invalid as applied in this case.

The District Court found that the City Council's insistence on the permit rested on several factors. First, the Council was concerned with the negative attitude of the majority of property owners located within 200 feet of the Featherston facility, as well as with the fears of elderly residents of the neighborhood. But mere negative attitudes, or fear, unsubstantiated by factors which are properly cognizable in a zoning proceeding, are not permissible bases for treating a home for the mentally retarded differently from apartment houses, multiple dwellings, and the like. . . . "Private biases may be outside the reach of the law, but the law cannot, directly or indirectly, give them effect." Palmore v. Sidoti.

Second, the Council had two objections to the location of the facility. It was concerned that the facility was across the street from a junior high school, and it feared that the students might harass the occupants of the Featherston home. But the school itself is attended by about 30 mentally retarded students, and denying a permit based on such vague, undifferentiated fears is again permitting some portion of the community to validate what would otherwise be an equal protection violation. The other objection to the home's location was that it was located on a "five hundred year flood plain." This concern with the possibility of a flood, however, can hardly be based on a distinction between the Featherston home and, for example, nursing homes, homes for convalescents or the aged, or sanitariums or hospitals, any of which could be located on the Featherston site without obtaining a special use permit. The same may be said of another concern of the Council — doubts about the legal responsibility for actions which the mentally retarded might take. . . .

Fourth, the Council was concerned with the size of the home and the number of people that would occupy it. . . . [But] there would be no restrictions on the number of people who could occupy this home as a boarding house, nursing home, family dwelling, fraternity house, or dormitory. . . . In the words of the Court of Appeals, "The City never justifies its apparent view that other people can live under such 'crowded' conditions when mentally retarded persons cannot."

In the courts below the city also urged that the ordinance is aimed at avoiding concentration of population and at lessening congestion of the streets. These concerns obviously fail to explain why apartment houses, fraternity and sorority houses, hospitals and the like, may freely locate in the area without a permit. So, too, the expressed worry about fire hazards, the serenity of the neighborhood, and the avoidance of danger to other residents fail rationally to justify singling out a home such as 201 Featherston for the special use permit. . . .

The short of it is that requiring the permit in this case appears to us to rest on an irrational prejudice against the mentally retarded, including those who would occupy the Featherston facility and who would live under the closely supervised and highly regulated conditions expressly provided for by state and federal law.

The judgment of the Court of Appeals is affirmed insofar as it invalidates the zoning ordinance as applied to the Featherston home. . . .

[A concurring opinion by Justice Stevens, joined by Chief Justice Burger, is omitted.]

MARSHALL, J., joined by Brennan and Blackmun, JJ., concurring in the judgment in part and dissenting in part.

. . . Cleburne's ordinance is invalidated only after being subjected to precisely the sort of probing inquiry associated with heightened scrutiny. . . . [H]owever labeled, the rational basis test invoked today is most assuredly not the rational basis test of *Williamson*. . . .

The Court, for example, concludes that legitimate concerns for fire hazards or the serenity of the neighborhood do not justify singling out respondents to bear the burdens of these concerns, for analogous permitted uses appear to pose similar threats. Yet under the traditional and most minimal version of the rational basis test, "reform may take one step at a time, addressing itself to the phase of the problem which seems most acute to the legislative mind." Williamson v. Lee Optical Co. The "record" is said not to support the ordinance's classifications, but under the traditional standard we do not sift through the record to determine whether policy decisions are squarely supported by a firm factual foundation. Finally, the Court further finds it "difficult to believe" that the retarded present different or special hazards than other groups. In normal circumstances, the burden is not on the legislature to convince the Court that the lines it has drawn are sensible. . . .

The refusal to acknowledge that something more than minimum rationality review is at work here is, in my view, unfortunate in at least two respects. The suggestion that the traditional rational basis test allows this sort of searching inquiry creates precedent for this Court and lower courts to subject economic and commercial classifications to similar and searching "ordinary" rational basis review — a small and regrettable step back toward the days of Lochner v. New York. Moreover, by failing to articulate the factors that justify today's "second order" rational basis review, the Court provides no principled foundation for determining when more searching inquiry is to be invoked.

II

I have long believed the level of scrutiny employed in equal protection cases should vary with "the constitutional and societal importance of the interest adversely affected and the recognized invidiousness of the basis upon which the particular classification is drawn." San Antonio Independent School District v. Rodriguez, 411 U.S. 1, 99 (1973) (dissenting). When a zoning ordinance works to exclude the retarded from all residential districts in a community, these two considerations require that the ordinance be convincingly justified as substantially furthering legitimate and important purposes.

First, the interest of the retarded in establishing group homes is substantial. . . . Excluding group homes deprives the retarded of much of what makes for human freedom and fulfillment — the ability to form bonds and take part in the life of a community.

Second, the mentally retarded have been subject to a "lengthy and tragic history," *Bakke*, of segregation and discrimination that can only be called grotesque. [In the early twentieth century, a] regime of state-mandated segregation and degradation . . . emerged that in its virulence and bigotry rivaled, and indeed paralleled, the worst excesses of Jim Crow. Massive custodial institutions were built to warehouse the retarded for life; the aim was to halt reproduction of the retarded and "nearly extinguish their race." Retarded children were categorically excluded from public schools, based on the false stereotype that all were ineducable and on the purported need to protect nonretarded children from them. State laws deemed the retarded "unfit for citizenship."

Segregation was accompanied by eugenic marriage and sterilization laws that extinguished for the retarded one of the "basic civil rights of man" — the right to marry and procreate. Marriages of the retarded were made, and in some states continue to be, not only voidable but also often a criminal offense. The purpose of such limitations, which frequently applied only to women of child bearing age, was unabashedly eugenic: to prevent the retarded from propagating. To assure this end, 29 states enacted compulsory eugenic sterilization laws between 1907 and 1931.

Prejudice, once let loose, is not easily cabined. As of 1979, most states still categorically disqualified "idiots" from voting, without regard to individual capacity and with discretion to exclude left in the hands of low-level election officials. Not until Congress enacted the Education of the Handicapped Act were the "door[s] of public education" opened wide to handicapped children. But most important, lengthy and continuing isolation of the retarded has perpetuated the ignorance, irrational fears, and stereotyping that long have plagued them.

In light of the importance of the interest at stake and the history of discrimination the retarded have suffered, the Equal Protection Clause requires us to do more than review the distinctions drawn by Cleburne's zoning ordinance as if they appeared in a taxing statute or in economic or commercial legislation. . . .

III

In its effort to show that Cleburne's ordinance can be struck down under no "more exacting standard . . . than is normally accorded economic and social legislation," the Court offers several justifications as to why the retarded do not warrant heightened judicial solicitude. These justifications, however, find no support in our heightened scrutiny precedents and cannot withstand logical analysis.

The Court downplays the lengthy "history of purposeful unequal treatment" of the retarded by pointing to recent legislative action that is said to "beli[e] a continuing antipathy or prejudice." Building on this point, the Court similarly concludes that the retarded are not "politically powerless" and deserve no greater judicial protection than "any minority" that wins some political battles and loses others. The import of these conclusions, it seems, is that the only discrimination courts may remedy is the discrimination they alone are perspicacious enough to see. Once society begins to recognize certain practices as discriminatory, in part because previously stigmatized groups have mobilized politically to lift this stigma, the Court would refrain from approaching such practices with the added skepticism of heightened scrutiny.

Courts, however, do not sit or act in a social vacuum. Moral philosophers may debate whether certain inequalities are absolute wrongs, but history makes clear that constitutional principles of equality, like constitutional principles of liberty, property and due process, evolve over time; what once was a "natural" and "self-evident" ordering later comes to be seen as an artificial and invidious constraint on human potential and freedom. Compare Plessy v. Ferguson, 163 U.S. 537 (1896), and Bradwell v. Illinois, 16 Wall. 130, 141 (1873) (Bradley, J., concurring) with Brown v. Board of Education, 347 U.S. 483 (1954) and Reed v. Reed, 404 U.S. 71 (1971). Shifting cultural, political, and social patterns at times come to make past practices appear inconsistent with fundamental principles upon which

American society rests, an inconsistency legally cognizable under the Equal Protection Clause. It is natural that evolving standards of equality come to be embodied in legislation. When that occurs, courts should look to the fact of such change as a source of guidance on evolving principles of equality. In [*Frontiero*], the Court reached this very conclusion when it extended heightened scrutiny to gender classifications and drew on parallel legislative developments to support that extension. . . .

Moreover, even when judicial action has catalyzed legislative change, that change certainly does not eviscerate the underlying constitutional principle. The Court, for example, has never suggested that race-based classifications became any less suspect once extensive legislation had been enacted on the subject.

For the retarded, just as for Negroes and women, much has changed in recent years, but much remains the same; out-dated statutes are still on the books, and irrational fears or ignorance, traceable to the prolonged social cultural isolation of the retarded, continue to stymie recognition of the dignity and individuality of retarded people. Heightened judicial scrutiny of action appearing to impose unnecessary barriers to the retarded is required in light of increasing recognition that such barriers are inconsistent with evolving principles of equality embedded in the Fourteenth Amendment.

The Court also offers a more general view of heightened scrutiny, a view focused primarily on when heightened scrutiny does not apply as opposed to when it does apply. Two principles appear central to the Court's theory. First, heightened scrutiny is said to be inapplicable where individuals in a group have distinguishing characteristics that legislatures properly may take into account in some circumstances. Heightened scrutiny is also purportedly inappropriate when many legislative classifications affecting the group are likely to be valid. . . .

If the Court's first principle were sound, heightened scrutiny would have to await a day when people could be cut from a cookie mold. Women are hardly alike in all their characteristics, but heightened scrutiny applies to them, because legislatures can rarely use gender itself as a proxy for these other characteristics. Permissible distinctions between persons must bear a reasonable relationship to their relevant characteristics, and gender per se is almost never relevant. Similarly, that some retarded people have reduced capacities in some areas does not justify using retardation as a proxy for reduced capacity in areas where relevant individual variations in capacity do exist.

The Court's second assertion — that the standard of review must be fixed with reference to the number of classifications to which a characteristic would validly be relevant — is similarly flawed. Certainly the assertion is not a logical one; that a characteristic may be relevant under some or even many circumstances does not suggest any reason to presume it relevant under other circumstances where there is reason to suspect it is not. A sign that says "men only" looks very different on a bathroom door than a courthouse door.

Our heightened scrutiny precedents belie the claim that a characteristic must virtually always be irrelevant to warrant heightened scrutiny. . . . While *Frontiero* stated that gender "frequently" and "often" bears no relation to legitimate legislative aims, it did not deem gender an impermissible basis of state action in all circumstances. Indeed, the Court has upheld some gender-based classifications. Rokster v. Goldberg, 453 U.S. 57 (1981); Michael M. v. Superior Court, 450 U.S. 464 (1981). Heightened but not strict scrutiny is considered appropriate in areas such as gender, illegitimacy, or alienage because the Court views the trait as relevant under some circumstances but not others. . . .

Potentially discriminatory classifications exist only where some constitutional basis can be found for presuming that equal rights are required. Discrimination, in the Fourteenth Amendment sense, connotes a substantive constitutional judgment that two individuals or groups are entitled to be treated equally with respect to some thing. With regard to economic and commercial matters, no basis for such a conclusion exists. . . . As a matter of substantive policy, therefore, government is free to move in any direction, or to change directions, in the economic and commercial sphere. . . .

But the Fourteenth Amendment does prohibit other results under virtually all circumstances, such as castes created by law along racial or ethnic lines, and significantly constrains the range of permissible government choices where gender or illegitimacy, for example, are concerned. Where such constraints, derived from the Fourteenth Amendment, are present, and where history teaches they have systemically been ignored, a "more searching judicial inquiry" is required. United States v. Carolene Products Co.

That more searching inquiry, be it called heightened scrutiny or "second order" rational basis review, is a method of approaching certain classifications skeptically, with judgment suspended until the facts are in and the evidence considered. The government must establish that the classification is substantially related to important and legitimate objectives, see e.g., Craig v. Boren, 429 U.S. 190 (1976), so that valid and sufficiently weighty policies actually justify the departure from equality. Heightened scrutiny does not allow courts to second guess reasoned legislative or professional judgments tailored to the unique needs of a group like the retarded, but it does seek to assure that the hostility or thoughtlessness with which there is reason to be concerned has not carried the day. . . .

As the history of discrimination against the retarded and its continuing legacy amply attest, the mentally retarded have been, and in some areas may still be, the targets of action the Equal Protection Clause condemns. With respect to a liberty so valued as the right to establish a home in the community, and so likely to be denied on the basis of irrational fears and outright hostility, heightened scrutiny is surely appropriate.

IV

In light of the scrutiny that should be applied here, Cleburne's ordinance sweeps too broadly to dispel the suspicion that it rests on a bare desire to treat the retarded as outsiders, pariahs who do not belong in the community. The Court, while disclaiming that special scrutiny is necessary or warranted, reaches the same conclusion. Rather than striking the ordinance down, however, the Court invalidates it merely as applied to respondents. I must dissent from the novel proposition that "the preferred course of adjudication" is to leave standing a legislative act resting on "irrational prejudice," thereby forcing individuals in the group discriminated against to continue to run the act's gauntlet.

. . . As a consequence, the Court's as applied remedy relegates future retarded applicants to the standardless discretion of low-level officials who have already shown an all too willing readiness to be captured by the "vague, undifferentiated fears" of ignorant or frightened residents.

Invalidating on its face the ordinance's special treatment of the "feeble-minded," in contrast, would place the responsibility for tailoring and updating Cleburne's unconstitutional ordinance where it belongs: with the legislative arm of the City of Cleburne. . . .

To my knowledge, the Court has never before treated an equal protection challenge to a statute on an as applied basis. When statutes rest on impermissibly overbroad generalizations, our cases have invalidated the presumption on its face. We do not instead leave to the courts the task of redrafting the statute through an ongoing and cumbersome process of "as applied' constitutional rulings. In Cleveland Board of Education v. LaFleur, 414 U.S. 632 (1974), for example, we invalidated inter alia a maternity leave policy that required pregnant school teachers to take unpaid leave beginning five months before their expected due date. . . . Assuming the policy might validly be applied to some teachers, particularly in the last few weeks of their pregnancy, we nonetheless invalidated it in toto, rather than simply as applied to the particular plaintiff. The Court required school boards to employ "alternative administrative means" to achieve their legitimate health and safety goal, or the legislature to enact a more carefully tailored statute.

Similarly, Caban v. Mohammed, 441 U.S. 380 (1979), invalidated a law that required parental consent to adoption from unwed mothers but not from unwed fathers. This distinction was defended on the ground, inter alia, that unwed fathers were often more difficult to locate, particularly during a child's infancy. We suggested the legislature might make proof of abandonment easier or proof of paternity harder, but we required the legislature to draft a new statute tailored more precisely to the problem of locating unwed fathers. The statute was not left on the books by invalidating it only as applied to unwed fathers who actually proved they could be located. When a presumption is unconstitutionally overbroad, the preferred course of adjudication is to strike it down.

Discussion

1. The special permit requirement in *Cleburne* applied not only to hospitals for the "feeble-minded," but also to penal and correctional institutions. Assume that CLC decided to house juvenile offenders convicted of drug dealing and that the city again required a special permit, offering the same justifications for the requirement that it offered in this case. Would the requirement pass the "rational basis" scrutiny articulated here? *Should* the cases be treated differently?

2. Professor Martha Minow has argued that the majority and dissenting opinions in *Cleburne* rest on distinct visions of the status of "difference" under the equal protection clause:

> [B]eneath the debates [in *Cleburne*] over the proper fit between ends and means of legislative action and the proper level of scrutiny for reviewing legislative classifications lies a sharp division about the meaning of difference. On one side is the perhaps contentiously labeled "abnormal persons" view, a conception of real differences used to treat certain people as legally different. On the other side is the perhaps ambiguously designated "social relations" view, which emphasizes how differences acquire significance through social attributions, rather than the other way around; how we each have relationships even with those we think are different; and how "we" are as different from those we call different as they are different from us.

> The "abnormal persons" view makes differential treatment seem natural, unavoidable, and unproblematic; the social relations view makes differential treatment a problem of social choice and meaning, a problem for which all onlookers are responsible.[38]

Where classifications of race, ethnicity, or gender are involved, the Court justifies heightened scrutiny largely on the view that such classifications *as a factual matter* are seldom relevant to legitimate state ends, and therefore are presumed to rest on prejudice and bigotry. Under Minow's analysis, is the problem with the "abnormal persons" view that as a factual matter it misperceives the nature of the difference, or rather that it unfairly ignores the perspective and feelings of the affected class?

IX. *Accommodation as a Norm: The Americans with Disabilities Act of 1990*

In the summer of 1990, President Bush proudly signed the Americans with Disabilities Act, describing it as the most important step in civil rights since the Civil Rights Act of 1964. Section 102 provides:

> (a) General Rule. No covered entity shall discriminate against a qualified individual with a disability because of the disability of such individual in regard to . . . terms, conditions, and privileges of employment.
>
> (b) Construction. As used in subsection (a), the term "discriminate" includes —
>
> (5)(A) not making reasonable accommodations to the known physical or mental limitations of an otherwise qualified individual with a disability who is an applicant or employee, unless such covered entity can demonstrate that the accommodation would impose an undue hardship on the operation of the business of such covered entity.

Section 101 provides:

> (9) The term "reasonable accommodation" may include:
>
> (A) making existing facilities used by employees readily accessible to and useable by individuals with disabilities; and
>
> (B) job restructuring, part-time or modified work schedules, reassignment to a vacant position, acquisition or modification of equipment or devices, appropriate adjustment or modifications of examinations, training materials or policies, the provision of qualified readers or interpreters, and other similar accommodations for individuals with disabilities.
>
> (10) The term "undue hardship" means an action requiring significant difficulty or expense, when considered in the light of factors [including the nature and cost of the accommodation and the overall financial resources of the covered entity and the facility involved.]

38. Martha Minow, When Difference Has Its Home: Group Homes for the Mentally Retarded, Equal Protection and Legal Treatment of Difference, 22 Harv. C.R.-C.L.L. Rev. 111, 139-140 (1987).

Discussion

Consider the proposition that the "reasonable accommodation" provision of the Americans with Disabilities Act of 1990 is, literally speaking, radically different from the antidiscrimination principle under the equal protection clause, the Civil Rights Act of 1964, and other federal civil rights statutes. Might the closest analog to the Americans with Disabilities Act be the provision of the California Fair Employment and Housing Act upheld in the *CalFed* case, supra. You will recall, however, that the litigants in that case did not raise the Fourteenth Amendment issue. What if they had? Consider, finally, that the requirement of "reasonable accommodation" may respond to the phenomenon of selective sympathy and indifference discussed earlier in this book.

Chapter 8
Selected Issues Involving Freedom of Expression

In earlier chapters we examined tensions between regulations designed to protect national security and the constitutional values of freedom of expression and the press. This chapter deals with one other part of the vast terrain of doctrine under the clause of the First Amendment that provides: "Congress shall make no law . . . abridging the freedom of speech." We place the chapter here in order to consider a right that is (more or less) explicitly protected by the Constitution before examining "fundamental rights" doctrines whose relationship to the constitutional text is problematic. Students studying those doctrines often wonder how they compare to adjudication under relatively explicit constitutional provisions — and the free speech clause of the First Amendment is about as explicit as they come. The relative specificity of the clause gives rise to a question you might keep in mind throughout the chapter: How much guidance does the Court get from the text and original history of the First Amendment, and what are the Court's other sources of guidance?

The chapter develops other themes as well. One concerns the different ways in which a law may affect a constitutional right. For example, a regulation may affect expression more or less directly; it may be "aimed" at the expression or it may be concerned with something else but nonetheless have a nontrivial impact on expression. How, if at all, should First Amendment doctrine distinguish among these situations? The appropriateness of judicial inquiry into the legislative motives underlying a regulation is closely related to this issue. A second theme, also closely related, concerns the forms that a constitutional standard may take: The Court sometimes balances the competing interests of the government and speaker on a case-by-case basis; at other times it applies relatively categorical rules. What are the advantages and disadvantages of these approaches, and when are they appropriate?

I. *Rationales for the Protection of Freedom of Expression*

In a separate opinion in Whitney v. California, 274 U.S. 357 (1927), Justice Brandeis eloquently explained "why a State is, ordinarily, denied the power to prohibit dissemination of social, economic, and political doctrine which a vast majority of its citizens believes to be false and fraught with evil consequences":

> Those who won our independence believed that the final end of the State was to make men free to develop their faculties; and that in its government the deliberative

forces should prevail over the arbitrary. They valued liberty both as an end and as a means. They believed liberty to be the secret of happiness and courage to be the secret of liberty. They believed that freedom to think as you will and to speak as you think are means indispensable to the discovery and spread of political truth; that without free speech and assembly discussion would be futile; that with them, discussion affords ordinarily adequate protection against the dissemination of noxious doctrine; that the greatest menace to freedom is an inert people; that public discussion is a political duty; and that this should be a fundamental principle of the American government. They recognized the risks to which all human institutions are subject. But they knew that order cannot be secured merely through fear of punishment for its infraction; that it is hazardous to discourage thought, hope and imagination; that fear breeds repression; that hate menaces stable government; that the path of safety lies in the opportunity to discuss freely supposed grievances and proposed remedies; and that the fitting remedy for evil counsels is good ones. Believing in the power of reason as applied through public discussion, they eschewed silence coerced by law — the argument of force in its worst form. Recognizing the occasional tyrannies of governing majorities, they amended the Constitution so that free speech and assembly should be guaranteed.

A. Protecting Representative Government

Justice Brandeis' statement implicitly focuses on political speech and assumes a political system of self-government. Within such a system, freedom of expression not only promotes each individual's self-interest in persuading others to her views, but protects the essential integrity of government and its processes. As Justice Black wrote for the Court in Mills v. Alabama, 384 U.S. 214 (1966):

> Whatever differences may exist about interpretations of the First Amendment, there is practically universal agreement that a major purpose of that Amendment was to protect the free discussion of governmental affairs. This of course includes discussions of candidates, structures and forms of government, the manner in which government is operated or should be operated, and all such matters relating to political processes. Thus the press serves and was designed to serve as a powerful antidote to any abuses of power by governmental officials and as a constitutionally chosen means for keeping officials elected by the people responsible to all of the people whom they were selected to serve.

The view that freedom of expression about political matters is essential both to assure effective representation and to check the abuses of those in power has not been seriously disputed. Rather, the controversies surrounding these rationales have focused on such matters as whether they protect the advocacy of forceful overthrow of government or of the establishment of a nonrepresentative government.

Justice Brandeis also proffers the ancillary rationale that freedom of expression promotes stability, either by assuring peaceful change or simply by serving as a psychological safety valve. This rationale depends on the value one accords stability and on a variety of empirical assumptions. Does the stability rationale provide a firm foundation on which to ground freedom of expression?

A final problem for those who emphasize the link between protected expression and maintenance of representative democracy is what protection to accord nonpolitical expression. What, for example, is the status of obscenity and pornography?

B. Advancing Knowledge and Promoting Truth

Justice Brandeis asserted that "freedom to think as you will and to speak as you think are means indispensable to the discovery and spread of political truth." Similarly, dissenting in Abrams v. United States, 250 U.S. 616 (1919), Justice Holmes wrote:

> Persecution for the expression of opinions seems to me perfectly logical. If you have no doubt of your premises or your power and want a certain result with all your heart you naturally express your wishes in law and sweep away all opposition. . . . But when men have realized that time has upset many fighting faiths, they may come to believe even more than they believe the very foundations of their own conduct that the ultimate good desired is better reached by free trade in ideas — that the best test of truth is the power of the thought to get itself accepted in the competition of the market, and that truth is the only ground upon which their wishes safely can be carried out. . . .

This view has venerable antecedents. In Areopagitica — A Speech for the Liberty of Unlicensed Printing (1644), John Milton argued: "And though all the winds of doctrine were let loose to play upon the earth, so Truth be in the field, we do injuriously, by licensing and prohibiting, to misdoubt her strength. Let her and Falsehood grapple; who ever knew Truth put to the worst, in a free and open encounter?" And John Stuart Mill argued in On Liberty (1859):

> We have . . . recognized the necessity to the mental well-being of mankind (on which all their other well-being depends) of freedom of opinion, and freedom of the expression of opinion, on four distinct grounds. . . .
>
> First, if any opinion is compelled to silence, that opinion may, for aught we can certainly know, be true. To deny this is to assume our own infallibility.
>
> Secondly, though the silenced opinion be an error, it may, and very commonly does, contain a portion of truth; and since the general or prevailing opinion on any subject is rarely or never the whole truth, it is only by the collision of adverse opinions that the remainder of the truth has any chance of being supplied.
>
> Thirdly, even if the received opinion be not only true, but the whole truth: unless it is suffered to be, and actually is, vigorously and earnestly contested, it will, by most of those who receive it, be held in the manner of a prejudice, with little comprehension or feeling of its rational grounds. And not only this, but, fourthly, the meaning of the doctrine itself will be in danger of being lost, or enfeebled, and deprived of its vital effect on the character and conduct; the dogma becoming a mere formal profession, inefficacious for good, but cumbering the ground, and preventing the growth of any real and heartfelt conviction, from reason or personal experience. . . .

The "free marketplace of ideas" argument is analogous to the more general argument for a "free market economy."[1] Indeed, one Chicago economist has argued that it is inconsistent for "liberals" to urge government intervention in one

1. See, e.g., Milton Friedman & Jane Friedman, Free to Choose (1980).

market and not the other.[2] Insofar as intervention in the economy is predicated on either the adverse consequences of an unrestricted market or on "market failure," might problems in the unregulated intellectual marketplace also justify intervention?

Alexander Meiklejohn, while arguing that the "representative government" justification extends to virtually all expression, was "[not] able to share the . . . faith that in a fair fight between truth and error truth is sure to win. And if one had that faith, it would be hard to reconcile it with the sheer stupidity of the policies of this nation — and of other nations — now driving humanity to the very edge of final destruction."[3]

If the "free marketplace" rationale holds under some conditions, is it relevant to our present-day society? Jerome Barron argues:[4]

> Our constitutional theory is in the grip of a romantic conception of free expression, a belief that the "marketplace of ideas" is freely accessible. But if ever there were a self-operating marketplace of ideas, it has long ceased to exist. . . .
>
> There is inequality in the power to communicate ideas just as there is inequality in economic bargaining power; to recognize the latter and deny the former is quixotic. The "marketplace of ideas" view has rested on the assumption that protecting the right of expression is equivalent to providing for it. But changes in the communications industry have destroyed the equilibrium in that marketplace. While it may have been still possible in 1925 to believe with Justice Holmes that every idea is "acted on unless some other belief outweighs it or some failure of energy stifles the movement at its birth," it is impossible to believe that now. Yet the Holmesian theory is not abandoned, even though the advent of radio and television has made even more evident that philosophy's unreality. A realistic view of the first amendment requires recognition that a right of expression is somewhat thin if it can be exercised only at the sufferance of the managers of mass communications.

Herbert Marcuse argues that "[u]nder the rule of monopolistic media — themselves the mere instruments of economic and political power — a mentality is created from which right and wrong, true and false are predefined whenever they affect the vital interests of society."[5]

If some ideas are intrinsically false and ought not be communicated, who should have the authority to censor them? What are the operational implications of the view that our society does not in fact enjoy a free marketplace of ideas? Marcuse argues that the remedy is a "liberating tolerance" — "intolerance against movements from the Right and tolerance of movements from the Left."[6] Less radically, Professor Barron argues that citizens are constitutionally entitled to direct access to the media.

2. See, e.g., Ronald Coase, The Market for Goods and the Market for Ideas, 64 Am. Econ. Rev.: Papers and Proceedings 384 (1974).

3. Alexander Meiklejohn, The First Amendment is an Absolute, 1961 Sup. Ct. Rev. 245, 263.

4. Jerome Barron, Access to the Press — A New First Amendment Right, 80 Harv. L. Rev. 1641, 1647-1648 (1967).

5. Herbert Marcuse, Repressive Tolerance, in Robert Wolff et al., A Critique of Pure Tolerance 95 (1965).

6. Id. at 109.

C. Protecting Individual Autonomy

Justice Brandeis' assertion that "[t]hose who won our independence believed that the final end of the State was to make men free to develop their faculties," and that they "valued liberty . . . as an end" implies a rationale for freedom of expression much broader than either of the above. A number of later commentators have also stressed the independent value of individual liberty or autonomy. For example, David A.J. Richards writes:[7]

> [P]eople are not to be constrained to communicate or not to communicate, to believe or not to believe, to associate or not to associate. The value placed on this cluster of ideas derives from the notion of self-respect that comes from a mature person's full and untrammeled exercise of capacities central to human rationality. Thus, the significance of free expression rests on the central human capacity to create and express symbolic systems, such as speech, writing, pictures, and music, intended to communicate in determinate, complex and subtle ways. Freedom of expression permits and encourages the exercise of these capacities: it supports a mature individual's sovereign autonomy in deciding how to communicate with others; it disfavors restrictions on communication imposed for the sake of the distorting rigidities of the orthodox and the established. In so doing, it nurtures and sustains the self-respect of the mature person.
>
> Further, freedom of expression protects the interest of the mature individual, with developed capacities of rational choice, in deciding whether to be an audience to a communication and in weighing the communication according to his own rational vision of life. This idea was expressed by Kant by the moving thought that each rational being is a sovereign legislator in the realm of ends. It is a contempt of human rationality for any other putative sovereign, democratic or otherwise, to decide to what communications mature people can be exposed.
>
> The value of free expression, in this view, rests on its deep relation to self-respect arising from autonomous self-determination without which the life of the spirit is meager and slavish.

C. Edwin Baker notes that the expressive function does not depend on whether the communication is persuasive to others:[8]

> To engage voluntarily in a speech act is to engage in self-definition or expression. A Vietnam war protestor may explain that when she chants "Stop This War Now" at a demonstration, she does so without any expectation that her speech will affect the continuance of the war or even that it will communicate anything to people in power; rather, she participates and chants in order to *define* herself publicly in opposition to the war. The war protestor provide a dramatic illustration of the importance of this self-expressive use of speech, independent of any effective communication to others, for self-fulfillment or self-realization.

The autonomy rationale for the protection of expression has broad appeal. (To what extent does it underlie the other rationales?) Does it prove too much, however? That is, can it be restricted to the protection of speech, while not pro-

7. David Richards, Free Speech and Obscenity Law: Toward a Moral Theory of the First Amendment, 123 U. Pa. L. Rev. 45, 62 (1974).

8. See Baker, Scope of the First Amendment Freedom of Speech, 25 U.C.L.A.L. Rev. 964, 994 (1978). See also Frederick Schaver, Freedom of Speech: A Philosophical Enquiry (1982).

tecting other conduct important to individuals' self-respect?[9] Consider Robert McCloskey's comment that

> [I]t is sometimes argued that laws limiting freedom of expression impinge on the human personality more grievously than do laws curbing mere economic liberty, and that the Court is therefore justified in protecting the former more zealously than the latter. The individual has, qua individual, "the right to be let alone." The right to free choice in the intellectual and spiritual realm is particularly precious to him. A major difficulty with this formulation is that there is the smell of the lamp about it: it may reflect the tastes of the judges and dons who advance it, rather than the real preferences of the commonality of mortals. Judges and professors are talkers both by profession and avocation. It is not surprising that they would view freedom of expression as primary to the free play of their personalities. But most men would probably feel that an economic right, such as freedom of occupation, was at least as vital to them as the right to speak their minds.[10]

The autonomy rationale is noninstrumentalist, but is its application therefore independent of any empirical assumptions? In justifying punishing speech that creates a "clear and present danger" of causing substantive harm, Justice Holmes gave a classic example of a nonautonomous audience when he wrote: "The most stringent protection of free speech would not protect a man in falsely shouting fire in a theatre and causing a panic."[11] Might there be analogous situations even in the realm of social and political discourse? Consider also how Marcuse's and Barron's criticisms of the "free marketplace of ideas" bear on the autonomy rationale.

II. *The Ambit of the First Amendment*

Justice Brandeis metaphorically attributed his assertions in *Whitney* to "those who won our independence." But what *did* they, or those who adopted and ratified the First Amendment, believe? And what should their beliefs matter to present-day decisionmaking under the Amendment?

Does the text of the First Amendment imply that it adopts or excludes any of the values underlying freedom of expression? (Consider the central clause in the context of the entire amendment and the nine other amendments that constitute the Bill of Rights.) Note that the First Amendment provides, "Congress shall make no law . . ." Does the amendment also constrain conduct by the executive and judicial branches?

The Constitution assumes, creates, and protects representative institutions. Charles Black has therefore argued that political speech and association would be

9. See, e.g., David Richards, Unnatural Acts and the Constitutional Right to Privacy: A Moral Theory, 45 Fordham L. Rev. 1281 (1977). See also Frederick Schauer, Freedom of Speech: A Philosophical Enquiry (1982).

10. Robert McCloskey, Economic Due Process and the Supreme Court: An Exhumation and Reburial, 1962 Sup. Ct. Rev. 34, 44-46. Similarly, Professor Baker argues that "[g]enerally, any individually chosen, meaningful conduct, whether public or private, expressed and further defines the actor's nature and contributes to the actor's self-realization." Supra note 8 at 994.

11. Schenck v. United States, 249 U.S. 47 (1919).

protected even in the absence of the piece of text known as the First Amendment.[12] Does the structure or theory underlying the Constitution provide any support for nonpolitical expression?

The history behind the adoption of the First Amendment is sparse and vague. (See Chapter 1, section VII.) Doubtless the framers' focus was on political speech, which had been suppressed in a variety of ways in England and the Colonies. But proponents of freedom of speech often emphasized its broader importance to individual autonomy and the search for truth. For example, in A Treatise Concerning Political Enquiry, and the Liberty of the Press (1800), Tunis Wortman argued that "[t]here is no natural right more perfect or more absolute, than that of investigating every subject which concerns us"; only through "entirely unshackeled" intellectual investigation can errors be corrected. "We are entitled to pursue every justifiable method of increasing our perceptions and invigorating our faculties. We are equally entitled to communicate our information to others."[13]

Suppose that those who adopted the First Amendment intended that government nonetheless be permitted to punish sedition, blasphemy, obscenity, and defamation. Of what relevance should this be to the interpretation of the amendment today? Roth v. United States, 354 U.S. 476 (1957), held that "obscenity is not within the area of constitutionally protected speech or press," resting in part on the original history of the First Amendment:

> The guaranties of freedom of expression in effect in 10 of the 14 States which by 1792 had ratified the Constitution, gave no absolute protection for every utterance. Thirteen of the 14 States provided for the prosecution of libel, and all of those States made either blasphemy or profanity, or both, statutory crimes. As early as 1712, Massachusetts made it criminal to publish "any filthy, obscene, or profane song, pamphlet, libel or mock sermon" in imitation or mimicking of religious services. Thus, profanity and obscenity were related offenses.
>
> In light of this history, it is apparent that the unconditional phrasing of the First Amendment was not intended to protect every utterance. This phrasing did not prevent this Court from concluding that libelous utterances are not within the area of constitutionally protected speech. At the time of the adoption of the First Amendment, obscenity law was not as fully developed as libel law, but there is sufficiently contemporaneous evidence to show that obscenity, too, was outside the protection intended for speech and press.

Consider Professor Harry Kalven's criticism that "the Court's use of history was so casual as to be alarming in terms of what other propositions might be proved by the same technique. Is it clear, for example, that blasphemy can constitutionally be made a crime today? And what would the Court say to an argument along the same lines appealing to the Sedition Act of 1798 as justification for the truly liberty-defeating crime of seditious libel?"[14]

12. Charles Black, Structure and Relationship in Constitutional Law (1969). Recall Chief Justice Marshall's comment in *McCulloch*, Ch. 1 supra: "There is no express provision for the case, but the claim has been sustained on a principle which so entirely pervades the constitution, is so intermixed with the materials that compose it, so interwoven with its web, so blended with its texture, as to be incapable of being separated from it, without rending it into shreds."

13. Quoted in Leonard Levy, Freedom of Speech and Press in Early American History 284-285 (1963).

14. Harry Kalven, The Metaphysics of the Law of Obscenity, 1960 Sup. Ct. Rev. 1, 9.

III. The Problem of Flag Desecration

Prior to the *Flag Desecration Case,* Texas v. Johnson, infra, the Court had dealt with the government regulation of conduct involving flags and other symbols on several occasions.

Stromberg v. California, 283 U.S. 359 (1931), struck down the provision of a state statute punishing "[a]ny person who displays a red flag, banner or badge . . . as a sign, symbol or emblem of opposition to organized government," thus reversing the appellant's conviction for raising a Soviet flag at the children's camp she operated. Without discussing the language of the First Amendment, Chief Justice Hughes wrote:

> It has been determined that the conception of liberty under the due process clause of the Fourteenth Amendment embraces the right of free speech. . . . The state court recognized . . . that the clause "might be construed to include the peaceful and orderly opposition to a government. . . ." The maintenance of the opportunity for free political discussion to the end that government may be responsive to the will of the people and that changes may be obtained by lawful means, an opportunity essential to the security of the Republic, is a fundamental principle of our constitutional system.

West Virginia Board of Education v. Barnette, 319 U.S. 624 (1943), p.1407 infra, held that the First Amendment's guarantee of freedom of speech, as applied to the states through the Fourteenth Amendment, entitled Jehovah's Witnesses to exemption from a requirement that public school students begin the day by saluting the American flag.[15] Justice Jackson wrote:

> There is no doubt that, in connection with the pledges, the flag salute is a form of utterance. Symbolism is a primitive but effective way of communicating ideas. The use of an emblem or flag to symbolize some system, idea, institution, or personality, is a short cut from mind to mind. . . . A person gets from a symbol the meaning he puts into it, and what is one man's comfort and inspiration is another's jest and scorn. . . . We think the action of the local authorities in compelling the flag salute and pledge transcends constitutional limitations on their power and invades the sphere of intellect and spirit which it is the purpose of the First Amendment to our Constitution reserve from all official control.

In Tinker v. Des Moines School District, 393 U.S. 503 (1969), the Court relied on *Stromberg* and *Barnette* to hold that public school pupils were constitutionally entitled to wear black armbands to protest United States involvement in Vietnam, at least where the protest engendered no disruption of the school's operation. Justice Fortas wrote:

> [T]he wearing of an armband for the purpose of expressing certain views is the type of symbolic act that is within the Free Speech Clause of the First Amendment. . . .

15. The Jehovah's Witnesses believe that saluting the flag comes within the commandment in Exodus 20:4-5: "Thou shalt not make unto thee any graven image, or any likeness of any thing that is in heaven above, or that is in the earth beneath, or that is in the water under the earth; Thou shalt not bow down thyself to them, nor serve them . . ."

> The problem posed by the present case does not relate to regulation of the length of skirts or the type of clothing, to hair style, or deportment. It does not concern aggressive, disruptive action or even group demonstrations. Our problem involves direct, primary First Amendment rights akin to "pure speech."

In Street v. New York, 394 U.S. 576 (1969), the defendant burned a flag in the street, shouting "We don't need no damned flag" and, "[i]f they let that happen to [James] Meredith [who was shot during a civil rights demonstration] we don't need an American flag." The Court reversed his conviction for flag desecration because the record indicated that he might have been convicted solely on the basis of his words.

Spence v. Washington, 418 U.S. 405 (1974), reversed the "improper use" conviction of a student who taped a peace symbol to an American flag and draped it from his window. The Court concluded that the student's conduct was protected under the First Amendment, observing that "no interest the State may have in preserving the physical integrity of a privately owned flag was significantly impaired on these facts."

In Smith v. Goguen, 415 U.S. 566 (1974), the appellee, who wore a small flag on the seat of his trousers, was convicted under a Massachusetts flag-misuse statute that subjected to criminal liability anyone who "publicly . . . treats contemptuously the flag of the United States." The Court held that the statutory language was unconstitutionally broad and vague.

TEXAS v. JOHNSON

491 U.S. 397 (1989)

On Writ of Certiorari to the Supreme Court of Criminal Appeals of Texas

BRENNAN, J., delivered the opinion of the Court.

After publicly burning an American flag as a means of political protest, Gregory Lee Johnson was convicted of desecrating a flag in violation of Texas law. This case presents the question whether his conviction is consistent with the First Amendment. We hold that it is not.

I

While the Republican National Convention was taking place in Dallas in 1984, respondent Johnson participated in a political demonstration dubbed the "Republican War Chest Tour." As explained in literature distributed by the demonstrators and in speeches made by them, the purpose of this event was to protest the policies of the Reagan administration and of certain Dallas-based corporations. The demonstrators marched through the Dallas streets, chanting political slogans and stopping at several corporate locations to stage "die-ins" intended to dramatize the consequences of nuclear war. On several occasions they spray-painted the walls of buildings and overturned potted plants, but Johnson himself took no part in such activities. He did, however, accept an American flag handed to him by a fellow protestor who had taken it from a flag pole outside one of the targeted buildings.[a]

The demonstration ended in front of Dallas City Hall, where Johnson unfurled the American flag, doused it with kerosene, and set it on fire. While the flag burned, the protestors chanted, "America, the red, white, and blue, we spit on you." After the demonstrators dispersed, a witness to the flag-burning collected the flag's remains and buried them in his backyard. No one was physically injured or threatened with injury, though several witnesses testified that they had been seriously offended by the flag-burning.

Of the approximately 100 demonstrators, Johnson alone was charged with a crime. The only criminal offense with which he was charged was the desecration of a venerated object in violation of Tex. Penal Code Ann. §42.09(a)(3) (1989).[b] After a trial, he was convicted, sentenced to one year in prison, and fined $2,000. The Court of Appeals for the Fifth District of Texas at Dallas affirmed Johnson's conviction, but the Texas Court of Criminal Appeals reversed, holding that the State could not, consistent with the First Amendment, punish Johnson for burning the flag in these circumstances. . . .

II

Johnson was convicted of flag desecration for burning the flag rather than for uttering insulting words. This fact somewhat complicates our consideration of his conviction under the First Amendment. We must first determine whether Johnson's burning of the flag constituted expressive conduct, permitting him to invoke the First Amendment in challenging his conviction. See, e.g., Spence v. Washington, 418 U.S. 405 (1974). If his conduct was expressive, we next decide whether the State's regulation is related to the suppression of free expression. See, e.g., United States v. O'Brien, 391 U.S. 367 (1968). If the State's regulation is not related to expression, then the less stringent standard we announced in United States v. O'Brien for regulations of noncommunicative conduct controls.[16] If it is, then we are outside of O'Brien's test, and we must

a. There was no evidence that Johnson himself stole the flag he burned, nor did the prosecution or the arguments urged in support of it depend on the theory that the flag was stolen. Thus, our analysis does not rely on the way in which the flag was acquired, and nothing in our opinion should be taken to suggest that one is free to steal a flag so long as one later uses it to communicate an idea. We also emphasize that Johnson was prosecuted only for flag desecration — not for trespass, disorderly conduct, or arson. [Moved from later in the opinion. — Ed.]

b. Tex. Penal Code Ann. §42.09 (1989) provides in full: "§42.09. Desecration of Venerated Object

"(a) A person commits an offense if he intentionally or knowingly desecrates:

"(1) a public monument;

"(2) a place of worship or burial; or

"(3) a state or national flag.

"(b) For purposes of this section, 'desecrate' means deface, damage, or otherwise physically mistreat in a way that the actor knows will seriously offend one or more persons likely to observe or discover his action.

"(c) An offense under this section is a Class A misdemeanor."

16. In *O'Brien*, the Court wrote: "a government regulation is sufficiently justified if it is within the constitutional power of the Government; if it furthers an important or substantial governmental interest; if the governmental interest is unrelated to the suppression of free expression; and if the incidental restriction on alleged First Amendment freedoms is no greater than is essential to the furtherance of that interest."

ask whether this interest justifies Johnson's conviction under a more demanding standard. . . .[c]

The First Amendment literally forbids the abridgement only of "speech," but we have long recognized that its protection does not end at the spoken or written word. While we have rejected "the view that an apparently limitless variety of conduct can be labeled 'speech' whenever the person engaging in the conduct intends thereby to express an idea," we have acknowledged that conduct may be "sufficiently imbued with elements of communication to fall within the scope of the First and Fourteenth Amendments."

In deciding whether particular conduct possesses sufficient communicative elements to bring the First Amendment into play, we have asked whether "[a]n intent to convey a particularized message was present, and [whether] the likelihood was great that the message would be understood by those who viewed it." Hence, we have recognized the expressive nature of students' wearing of black armbands to protest American military involvement in Vietnam, Tinker v. Des Moines Independent Community School Dist., 393 U.S. 503 (1969); of a sit-in by blacks in a "whites only" area to protest segregation, Brown v. Louisiana, 383 U.S. 131 (1966); of the wearing of American military uniforms in a dramatic presentation criticizing American involvement in Vietnam, Schacht v. United States, 398 U.S. 58 (1970); and of picketing about a wide variety of causes, see, e.g., Food Employees v. Logan Valley Plaza, Inc., 391 U.S. 308 (1968); United States v. Grace, 461 U.S. 171 (1983).

Especially pertinent to this case are our decisions recognizing the communicative nature of conduct relating to flags. Attaching a peace sign to the flag, *Spence*; saluting the flag, *Barnette*; and displaying a red flag, Stromberg v. California, 283 U.S. 359 (1931), we have held, all may find shelter under the First Amendment. That we have had little difficulty identifying an expressive element in conduct relating to flags should not be surprising. The very purpose of a national flag is to serve as a symbol of our country; it is, one might say, "the one visible manifestation of two hundred years of nationhood." Thus, we have observed: "[T]he flag salute is a form of utterance. Symbolism is a primitive but effective way of communicating ideas. The use of an emblem or flag to symbolize some system, idea, institution, or personality, is a short cut from mind to mind. Causes and nations, political parties, lodges and ecclesiastical groups seek to knit the loyalty of their followings to a flag or banner, a color or design." *Barnette*. Pregnant with expressive content, the flag as readily signifies this Nation as does the combination of letters found in "America."

We have not automatically concluded, however, that any action taken with respect to our flag is expressive. Instead, in characterizing such action for First

c. . . . Section 42.09 regulates only physical conduct with respect to the flag, not the written or spoken word, and although one violates the statute only if one "knows" that one's physical treatment of the flag "will seriously offend one or more persons likely to observe or discover his action," this fact does not necessarily mean that the statute applies only to expressive conduct protected by the First Amendment. A tired person might, for example, drag a flag through the mud, knowing that this conduct is likely to offend others, and yet have no thought of expressing any idea; neither the language nor the Texas courts' interpretations of the statute precludes the possibility that such a person would be prosecuted for flag desecration. Because the prosecution of a person who had not engaged in expressive conduct would pose a different case, and because we are capable of disposing of this case on narrower grounds, we address only Johnson's claim that §42.09 as applied to political expression like his violates the First Amendment.

Amendment purposes, we have considered the context in which it occurred. In *Spence*, for example, we emphasized that Spence's taping of a peace sign to his flag was "roughly simultaneous with and concededly triggered by the Cambodian incursion and the Kent State tragedy." The State of Washington had conceded, in fact, that Spence's conduct was a form of communication, and we stated that "the State's concession is inevitable on this record."

The State of Texas conceded for purposes of its oral argument in this case that Johnson's conduct was expressive conduct, and this concession seems to us as prudent as was Washington's in *Spence*. Johnson burned an American flag as part — indeed, as the culmination — of a political demonstration that coincided with the convening of the Republican Party and its renomination of Ronald Reagan for President. The expressive, overtly political nature of this conduct was both intentional and overwhelmingly apparent. . . . In these circumstances, Johnson's burning of the flag was conduct "sufficiently imbued with elements of communication" to implicate the First Amendment.

III

The Government generally has a freer hand in restricting expressive conduct than it has in restricting the written or spoken word. It may not, however, proscribe particular conduct because it has expressive elements. "[W]hat might be termed the more generalized guarantee of freedom of expression makes the communicative nature of conduct an inadequate basis for singling out that conduct for proscription. A law directed at the communicative nature of conduct must, like a law directed at speech itself, be justified by the substantial showing of need that the First Amendment requires." It is, in short, not simply the verbal or nonverbal nature of the expression, but the governmental interest at stake, that helps to determine whether a restriction on that expression is valid.

Thus, although we have recognized that where " 'speech' and 'nonspeech' elements are combined in the same course of conduct, a sufficiently important governmental interest in regulating the nonspeech element can justify incidental limitations on First Amendment freedoms," we have limited the applicability of *O'Brien's* relatively lenient standard to those cases in which "the governmental interest is unrelated to the suppression of free expression." In stating, moreover, that *O'Brien's* test "in the last analysis is little, if any, different from the standard applied to time, place, or manner restrictions," we have highlighted the requirement that the governmental interest in question be unconnected to expression in order to come under *O'Brien's* less demanding rule.

In order to decide whether *O'Brien's* test applies here, therefore, we must decide whether Texas has asserted an interest in support of Johnson's conviction that is unrelated to the suppression of expression. If we find that an interest asserted by the State is simply not implicated on the facts before us, we need not ask whether *O'Brien's* test applies. The State offers two separate interests to justify this conviction: preventing breaches of the peace, and preserving the flag as a symbol of nationhood and national unity. We hold that the first interest is not implicated on this record and that the second is related to the suppression of expression.

A

Texas claims that its interest in preventing breaches of the peace justifies Johnson's conviction for flag desecration. However, no disturbance of the peace actually occurred or threatened to occur because of Johnson's burning of the flag. Although the State stresses the disruptive behavior of the protestors during their march toward City Hall, it admits that "no actual breach of the peace occurred at the time of the flagburning or in response to the flagburning." The State's emphasis on the protestors' disorderly actions prior to arriving at City Hall is not only somewhat surprising given that no charges were brought on the basis of this conduct, but it also fails to show that a disturbance of the peace was a likely reaction to Johnson's conduct. The only evidence offered by the State at trial to show the reaction to Johnson's actions was the testimony of several persons who had been seriously offended by the flag-burning.

The State's position, therefore, amounts to a claim that an audience that takes serious offense at particular expression is necessarily likely to disturb the peace and that the expression may be prohibited on this basis.[d] Our precedents do not countenance such a presumption. On the contrary, they recognize that a principal "function of free speech under our system of government is to invite dispute. It may indeed best serve its high purpose when it induces a condition of unrest, creates dissatisfaction with conditions as they are, or even stirs people to anger." Terminiello v. Chicago, 337 U.S. 1, 4 (1949). It would be odd indeed to conclude both that "if it is the speaker's opinion that gives offense, that consequence is a reason for according it constitutional protection," and that the Government may ban the expression of certain disagreeable ideas on the unsupported presumption that their very disagreeableness will provoke violence.

Thus, we have not permitted the Government to assume that every expression of a provocative idea will incite a riot, but have instead required careful consideration of the actual circumstances surrounding such expression, asking whether the expression "is directed to inciting or producing imminent lawless action and is likely to incite or produce such action." Brandenburg v. Ohio, 395 U.S. 444 (1969) (reviewing circumstances surrounding rally and speeches by Ku Klux Klan). To accept Texas' arguments that it need only demonstrate "the potential for a breach of the peace," and that every flag-burning necessarily possesses that potential, would be to eviscerate our holding in *Brandenburg*. This we decline to do.

Nor does Johnson's expressive conduct fall within that small class of "fighting words" that are "likely to provoke the average person to retaliation, and thereby cause a breach of the peace." Chaplinsky v. New Hampshire, 315 U.S. 568 (1942). No reasonable onlooker would have regarded Johnson's generalized expression of dissatisfaction with the policies of the Federal Government as a direct personal insult or an invitation to exchange fisticuffs.

We thus conclude that the State's interest in maintaining order is not implicated on these facts. The State need not worry that our holding will disable it from preserving the peace. We do not suggest that the First Amendment forbids a State to prevent "imminent lawless action." *Brandenburg*. And, in fact, Texas already has a statute specifically prohibiting breaches of the peace, Tex. Penal

d. There is, of course a tension between this argument and the State's claim that one need not actually cause serious offense in order to violate §42.09.

Code Ann. §42.01 (1989), which tends to confirm that Texas need not punish this flag desecration in order to keep the peace.

B

The State also asserts an interest in preserving the flag as a symbol of nationhood and national unity. In *Spence*, we acknowledged that the Government's interest in preserving the flag's special symbolic value "is directly related to expression in the context of activity" such as affixing a peace symbol to a flag. We are equally persuaded that this interest is related to expression in the case of Johnson's burning of the flag. The State, apparently, is concerned that such conduct will lead people to believe either that the flag does not stand for nationhood and national unity, but instead reflects other, less positive concepts, or that the concepts reflected in the flag do not in fact exist, that is, we do not enjoy unity as a Nation. These concerns blossom only when a person's treatment of the flag communicates some message, and thus are related "to the suppression of free expression" within the meaning of *O'Brien*. We are thus outside of *O'Brien's* test altogether.

IV

It remains to consider whether the State's interest in preserving the flag as a symbol of nationhood and national unity justifies Johnson's conviction.

As in *Spence*, "[w]e are confronted with a case of prosecution for the expression of an idea through activity," and "[a]ccordingly, we must examine with particular care the interests advanced by [petitioner] to support its prosecution." Johnson was not, we add, prosecuted for the expression of just any idea; he was prosecuted for his expression of dissatisfaction with the policies of this country, expression situated at the core of our First Amendment values.

Moreover, Johnson was prosecuted because he knew that his politically charged expression would cause "serious offense." If he had burned the flag as a means of disposing of it because it was dirty or torn, he would not have been convicted of flag desecration under this Texas law: federal law designates burning as the preferred means of disposing of a flag "when it is in such condition that it is no longer a fitting emblem for display," 36 U.S.C. §176(k), and Texas has no quarrel with this means of disposal. The Texas law is thus not aimed at protecting the physical integrity of the flag in all circumstances, but is designed instead to protect it only against impairments that would cause serious offense to others. . . .

Whether Johnson's treatment of the flag violated Texas law thus depended on the likely communicative impact of his expressive conduct. . . . Johnson's political expression was restricted because of the content of the message he conveyed. We must therefore subject the State's asserted interest in preserving the special symbolic character of the flag to "the most exacting scrutiny."

Texas argues that its interest in preserving the flag as a symbol of nationhood and national unity survives this close analysis. Quoting extensively from the writings of this Court chronicling the flag's historic and symbolic role in our society, the State emphasizes the "special place" reserved for the flag in our Nation. The State's argument is not that it has an interest simply in maintaining the flag as a symbol of something, no matter what it symbolizes; indeed, if that were the

State's position, it would be difficult to see how that interest is endangered by highly symbolic conduct such as Johnson's. Rather, the State's claim is that it has an interest in preserving the flag as a symbol of nationhood and national unity, a symbol with a determinate range of meanings. According to Texas, if one physically treats the flag in a way that would tend to cast doubt on either the idea that nationhood and national unity are the flag's referents or that national unity actually exists, the message conveyed thereby is a harmful one and therefore may be prohibited.[e]

If there is a bedrock principle underlying the First Amendment, it is that the Government may not prohibit the expression of an idea simply because society finds the idea itself offensive or disagreeable.

We have not recognized an exception to this principle even where our flag has been involved. In Street v. New York, 394 U.S. 576 (1969), we held that a State may not criminally punish a person for uttering words critical of the flag. Rejecting the argument that the conviction could be sustained on the ground that Street had "failed to show the respect for our national symbol which may properly be demanded of every citizen," we concluded that "the constitutionally guaranteed 'freedom to be intellectually . . . diverse or even contrary,' and the 'right to differ as to things that touch the heart of the existing order,' encompass the freedom to express publicly one's opinion about our flag, including those opinions which are defiant or contemptuous." Nor may the Government, we have held, compel conduct that would evince respect for the flag. "To sustain the compulsory flag salute we are required to say that a Bill of Rights which guards the individual's right to speak his own mind, left it open to public authorities to compel him to utter what is not on his mind."

. . . In *Spence*, we held that the same interest asserted by Texas here was insufficient to support a criminal conviction under a flag-misuse statute for the taping of a peace sign to an American flag. "Given the protected character of [Spence's] expression and in light of the fact that no interest that State may have in preserving the physical integrity of a privately owned flag was significantly impaired on these facts," we held, "the conviction must be invalidated." To convict a person who had sewn a flag onto seat of his pants for "contemptuous" treatment of the flag would be "[t]o convict not to protect the physical integrity or to protect against acts interfering with the proper use of the flag, but to punish for communicating ideas unacceptable to the controlling majority in the legislature."

In short, nothing in our precedents suggests that a State may foster its own view of the flag by prohibiting expressive conduct relating to it.[f] To bring its argument outside our precedents, Texas attempts to convince us that even if its interest in preserving the flag's symbolic role does not allow it to prohibit words or

e. Our decision in Halter v. Nebraska, 205 U.S. 34 (1907), addressing the validity of a state law prohibiting certain commercial uses of the flag, is not to the contrary. That case was decided "nearly 20 years before the Court concluded that the First Amendment applies to the States by virtue of the Fourteenth Amendment." More important, as we continually emphasized in *Halter* itself, that case involved purely commercial rather than political speech. . . .

f. Texas claims that "Texas is not endorsing, protecting, avowing or prohibiting any particular philosophy." If Texas means to suggest that its asserted interest does not prefer Democrats over Socialists, or Republicans over Democrats, for example, then it is beside the point, for Johnson does not rely on such an argument. He argues instead that the State's desire to maintain the flag as a symbol of nationhood and national unity assumes that is only one proper view of the flag. Thus, if Texas means to argue that its interest does not prefer any viewpoint over another, it is mistaken; surely one's attitude towards the flag and its referents is a viewpoint.

some expressive conduct critical of the flag, it does permit it to forbid the outright destruction of the flag. The State's argument cannot depend here on the distinction between written or spoken words and nonverbal conduct. That distinction, we have shown, is of no moment where the nonverbal conduct is expressive, as it is here, and where the regulation of that conduct is related to expression, as it is here. In addition, both *Barnette* and *Spence* involved expressive conduct, not only verbal communication, and both found that conduct protected.

Texas' focus on the precise nature of Johnson's expression, moreover, misses the point of our prior decisions: their enduring lesson, that the Government may not prohibit expression simply because it disagrees with its message, is not dependent on the particular mode in which one chooses to express an idea.[g] If we were to hold that a State may forbid flag-burning wherever it is likely to endanger the flag's symbolic role, but allow it wherever burning a flag promotes that role — as where, for example, a person ceremoniously burns a dirty flag — we would be saying that when it comes to impairing the flag's physical integrity, the flag itself may be used as a symbol — as a substitute for the written or spoken word or a "short cut from mind to mind" — only in one direction. We would be permitting a State to "prescribe what shall be orthodox" by saying that one may burn the flag to convey one's attitude toward it and its referents only if one does not endanger the flag's representation of nationhood and national unity.

We never before have held that the Government may ensure that a symbol be used to express only one view of that symbol or its referents. Indeed, in Schacht v. United States, we invalidated a federal statute permitting an actor portraying a member of one of our armed forces to " 'wear the uniform of that armed force if the portrayal does not intend to discredit that armed force.' " This proviso, we held, "which leaves Americans free to praise the war in Vietnam but can send persons like Schacht to prison for opposing it, cannot survive in a country which has the First Amendment."

We perceive no basis on which to hold that the principle underlying our decision in *Schacht* does not apply to this case. To conclude that the Government may permit designated symbols to be used to communicate only a limited set of messages would be to enter territory having no discernible or defensible boundaries. Could the Government, on this theory, prohibit the burning of state flags? Of copies of the Presidential seal? Of the Constitution? In evaluating these choices under the First Amendment, how would we decide which symbols were sufficiently special to warrant this unique status? To do so, we would be forced to consult our own political preferences, and impose them on the citizenry, in the very way that the First Amendment forbids us to do.

There is, moreover, no indication — either in the text of the Constitution or in our cases interpreting it — that a separate juridical category exists for the American flag alone. Indeed, we would not be surprised to learn that the persons who framed our Constitution and wrote the Amendment that we now construe were not known for their reverence for the Union Jack. The First Amendment does

g. The dissent appears to believe that Johnson's conduct may be prohibited and, indeed, criminally sanctioned, because "his act . . . conveyed nothing that could not have been conveyed and was not conveyed just as forcefully in a dozen different ways." Not only does this assertion sit uneasily next to the dissent's quite correct reminder that the flag occupies a unique position in our society — which demonstrates that messages conveyed without use of the flag are not "just as forcefu[l]" as those conveyed with it — but it also ignores the fact that, in *Spence* we "rejected summarily" this very claim.

not guarantee that other concepts virtually sacred to our Nation as a whole — such as the principle that discrimination on the basis of race is odious and destructive — will go unquestioned in the marketplace of ideas. See Brandenburg v. Ohio, 395 U.S. 444 (1969). We decline, therefore, to create for the flag an exception to the joust of principles protected by the First Amendment.

It is not the State's ends, but its means, to which we object. It cannot be gainsaid that there is a special place reserved for the flag in this Nation, and thus we do not doubt that the Government has a legitimate interest in making efforts to "preserv[e] the national flag as an unalloyed symbol of our country." We reject the suggestion, urged at oral argument by counsel for Johnson, that the Government lacks "any state interest whatsoever" in regulating the manner in which the flag may be displayed. Congress has, for example, enacted precatory regulations describing the proper treatment of the flag, see 36 U.S.C. §§173-177, and we cast no doubt on the legitimacy of its interest in making such recommendations. To say that the Government has an interest in encouraging proper treatment of the flag, however, is not to say that it may criminally punish a person for burning a flag as a means of political protest. "National unity as an end which officials may foster by persuasion and example is not in question. The problem is whether under our Constitution compulsion as here employed is a permissible means for its achievement." *Barnette.*

We are fortified in today's conclusion by our conviction that forbidding criminal punishment for conduct such as Johnson's will not endanger the special role played by our flag or the feelings it inspires. To paraphrase Justice Holmes, we submit that nobody can suppose that this one gesture of an unknown man will change our Nation's attitude towards its flag. See Abrams v. United States, 250 U.S. 616 (1919) (Holmes, J., dissenting). Indeed, Texas' argument that the burning of an American flag "is an act having a high likelihood to cause a breach of the peace," and its statute's implicit assumption that physical mistreatment of the flag will lead to "serious offense," tend to confirm that the flag's special role is not in danger; if it were, no one would riot or take offense because a flag had been burned.

We are tempted to say, in fact, that the flag's deservedly cherished place in our community will be strengthened, not weakened, by our holding today. Our decision is a reaffirmation of the principles of freedom and inclusiveness that the flag best reflects, and of the conviction that our toleration of criticism such as Johnson's is a sign and source of our strength. Indeed, one of the proudest images of our flag, the one immortalized in our own national anthem, is of the bombardment it survived at Fort McHenry. It is the Nation's resilience, not its rigidity, that Texas sees reflected in the flag — and it is that resilience that we reassert today.

The way to preserve the flag's special role is not to punish those who feel differently about these matters. It is to persuade them that they are wrong. . . . And, precisely because it is our flag that is involved, one's response to the flag-burner may exploit the uniquely persuasive power of the flag itself. We can imagine no more appropriate response to burning a flag than waving one's own, no better way to counter a flag-burner's message than by saluting the flag that burns, no surer means of preserving the dignity even of the flag that burned than by — as one witness here did — according its remains a respectful burial. We do not consecrate the flag by punishing its desecration, for in doing so we dilute the freedom that this cherished emblem represents.

V

. . . The judgment of the Texas Court of Criminal Appeals is therefore Affirmed.

KENNEDY, J., concurring.

I write not to qualify the words Justice Brennan chooses so well, for he says with power all that is necessary to explain our ruling. I join his opinion without reservation, but with a keen sense that this case, like others before us from time to time, exacts its personal toll. This prompts me to add to our pages these few remarks.

The case before us illustrates better than most that the judicial power is often difficult in its exercise. We cannot here ask another branch to share responsibility, as when the argument is made that a statute is flawed or incomplete. For we are presented with a clear and simple statute to be judged against a pure command of the Constitution. The outcome can be laid at no door but ours.

The hard fact is that sometimes we must make decisions we do not like. We make them because they are right, right in the sense that the law and the Constitution, as we see them, compel the result. And so great is our commitment to the process that, except in the rare case, we do not pause to express distaste for the result, perhaps for fear of undermining a valued principle that dictates the decision. This is one of those rare cases.

Our colleagues in dissent advance powerful arguments why respondent may be convicted for his expression, reminding us that among those who will be dismayed by our holding will be some who have had the singular honor of carrying the flag in battle. And I agree that the flag holds one lonely place of honor in an age when absolutes are distrusted and simple truths are burdened by unneeded apologetics.

With all respect to those views, I do not believe the Constitution gives us the right to rule as the dissenting members of the Court urge, however painful this judgment is to announce. Though symbols often are what we ourselves make of them, the flag is constant in expressing beliefs Americans share, beliefs in law and peace and that freedom which sustains the human spirit. The case here today forces recognition of the costs to which those beliefs commit us. It is poignant but fundamental that the flag protects those who hold it in contempt.

For all the record shows, this respondent was not a philosopher and perhaps did not even possess the ability to comprehend how repellent his statements must be to the Republic itself. But whether or not he could appreciate the enormity of the offense he gave, the fact remains that his acts were speech, in both the technical and the fundamental meaning of the Constitution. So I agree with the Court that he must go free.

REHNQUIST, Chief Justice, with whom White, J., and O'Connor, J., join, dissenting.

In holding this Texas statute unconstitutional, the Court ignores Justice Holmes' familiar aphorism that "a page of history is worth a volume of logic." For more than 200 years, the American flag has occupied a unique position as the symbol of our Nation, a uniqueness that justifies a governmental prohibition against flag burning in the way respondent Johnson did here. . . .

[The Chief Justice surveys poetry, songs, and symbolic acts demonstrating reverence for the flag during the Revolutionary War (Ralph Waldo Emerson's "Concord Hymn"), the War of 1812 (Francis Scott Key's "The Star Spangled Banner"), the Civil War (John Greenleaf Whittier's "Barbara Frietchie"), World War II (the Marines' placing of the flag at Iwo Jima), and the Korean War (raising the flag at Inchon).]

The flag symbolizes the Nation in peace as well as in war. It signifies our national presence on battleships, airplanes, military installations, and public buildings from the United States Capitol to the thousands of county courthouses and city halls throughout the country. Two flags are prominently placed in our courtroom. Countless flags are placed by the graves of loved ones each year on what was first called Decoration Day, and is now called Memorial Day. . . .

No other American symbol has been as universally honored as the flag. . . . The American flag, then, throughout more than 200 years of our history, has come to be the visible symbol embodying our Nation. It does not represent the views of any particular political party, and it does not represent any particular political philosophy. The flag is not simply another "idea" or "point of view" competing for recognition in the marketplace of ideas. Millions and millions of Americans regard it with an almost mystical reverence regardless of what sort of social, political, or philosophical beliefs they may have. I cannot agree that the First Amendment invalidates the Act of Congress, and the laws of 48 of the 50 States, which make criminal the public burning of the flag.

More than 80 years ago in Halter v. Nebraska, 205 U.S. 34 (1907), this Court upheld the constitutionality of a Nebraska statute that forbade the use of representations of the American flag for advertising purposes upon articles of merchandise. The Court there said: "For the flag every true American has not simply an appreciation but a deep affection. . . . Hence, it has often occurred that insults to a flag have been the cause of war, and indignities put upon it, in the presence of those who revere it, have often been resented and sometimes punished on the spot."

Only two Terms ago, in San Francisco Arts & Athletics, Inc. v. United States Olympic Committee, 483 U.S. 522 (1987), the Court held that Congress could grant exclusive use of the word "Olympic" to the United States Olympic Committee. The Court thought that this "restrictio[n] on expressive speech properly [was] characterized as incidental to the primary congressional purpose of encouraging and rewarding the USOC's activities." As the Court stated, "when a word [or symbol] acquires value 'as the result of organization and the expenditure of labor, skill, and money' by an entity, that entity constitutionally may obtain a limited property right in the word [or symbol]." Surely Congress or the States may recognize a similar interest in the flag.

But the Court insists that the Texas statute prohibiting the public burning of the American flag infringes on respondent Johnson's freedom of expression. Such freedom, of course, is not absolute. See Schenck v. United States, 249 U.S. 47 (1919). In Chaplinsky v. New Hampshire, 315 U.S. 568 (1942), a unanimous Court said: "Allowing the broadest scope to the language and purpose of the Fourteenth Amendment, it is well understood that the right of free speech is not absolute at all times and under all circumstances. There are certain well-defined and narrowly limited classes of speech, the prevention and punishment of which have never been thought to raise any Constitutional problem. These include the lewd and obscene, the profane, the libelous, and the insulting or 'fighting' words — those which by their very utterance inflict injury or tend to incite an immediate breach of the peace. It has been well observed that such utterances are no essential part of any exposition of ideas, and are of such slight social value as a step to truth that any benefit that may be derived from them is clearly outweighed by the social interest in order and morality." The Court upheld Chaplinsky's conviction under a state statute that made it unlawful to "address any offensive, derisive or annoying word to any person who is lawfully in any street or other public place." Chaplinsky had told a local Marshal, "You are a God damned racketeer" and a "damned Fascist and the whole government of Rochester are Fascists or agents of Fascists."

Here it may equally well be said that the public burning of the American flag by Johnson was no essential part of any exposition of ideas, and at the same time it had a tendency to incite a breach of the peace. Johnson was free to make any verbal denunciation of the flag that he wished; indeed, he was free to burn the flag in private. He could publicly burn other symbols of the Government or effigies of political leaders. [I]t was only when he proceeded to burn publicly an American flag stolen from its rightful owner that he violated the Texas statute.

The Court could not, and did not, say that Chaplinsky's utterances were not expressive phrases — they clearly and succinctly conveyed an extremely low opinion of the addressee. The same may be said of Johnson's public burning of the flag in this case; it obviously did convey Johnson's bitter dislike of his country. But his act, like Chaplinsky's provocative words, conveyed nothing that could not have been conveyed and was not conveyed just as forcefully in a dozen different ways. As with "fighting words," so with flag burning, for purposes of the First Amendment: It is "no essential part of any exposition of ideas, and [is] of such slight social value as a step to truth that any benefit that may be derived from [it] is clearly outweighed" by the public interest in avoiding a probable breach of the peace. The highest courts of several States have upheld state statutes prohibiting the public burning of the flag on the grounds that it is so inherently inflammatory that it may cause a breach of public order.

The result of the Texas statute is obviously to deny one in Johnson's frame of mind one of many means of "symbolic speech." Far from being a case of "one picture being worth a thousand words," flag burning is the equivalent of an inarticulate grunt or roar that, it seems fair to say, is most likely to be indulged in not to express any particular idea, but to antagonize others. Only five years ago we said in Los Angeles City Council v. Taxpayers for Vincent, 466 U.S. 789 (1984), that "the First Amendment does not guarantee the right to employ every conceivable method of communication at all times and in all places." The Texas statute deprived Johnson of only one rather inarticulate symbolic form of protest — a form of protest that was profoundly offensive to many — and left him with a full panoply of other symbols and every conceivable form of verbal expression to express his deep disapproval of national policy. Thus, in no way can it be said that Texas is punishing him because his hearers — or any other group of people — were profoundly opposed to the message that he sought to convey. Such opposition is no proper basis for restricting speech or expression under the First Amendment. It was Johnson's use of this particular symbol, and not the idea that he sought to convey by it or by his many other expressions, for which he was punished. . . .

The uniquely deep awe and respect for our flag felt by virtually all of us are bundled off [by the Court] under the rubric of "designated symbols" that the First Amendment prohibits the government from "establishing." But the government has not "established" this feeling; 200 years of history have done that. The government is simply recognizing as a fact the profound regard for the American flag created by that history when it enacts statutes prohibiting the disrespectful public burning of the flag.

... Surely one of the high purposes of a democratic society is to legislate against conduct that is regarded as evil and profoundly offensive to the majority of people — whether it be murder, embezzlement, pollution, or flag burning. Our Constitution wisely places limits on powers of legislative majorities to act, but the declaration of such limits by this Court "is, at all times, a question of much delicacy, which ought seldom, if ever, to be decided in the affirmative, in a doubtful case." Fletcher v. Peck, 6 Cranch 87 (1810) (Marshall, C.J.). Uncritical extension of constitutional protection to the burning of the flag risks the frustration of the very purpose for which organized governments are instituted. The Court decides that the American flag is just another symbol, about which not only must opinions pro and con be tolerated, but for which the most minimal public respect may not be enjoined. The government may conscript men into the Armed Forces where they must fight and perhaps die for the flag, but the government may not prohibit the public burning of the banner under which they fight. I would uphold the Texas statute as applied in this case.

STEVENS, J., dissenting.

As the Court analyzes this case, it presents the question whether the State of Texas, or indeed the Federal Government, has the power to prohibit the public desecration of the American flag. The question is unique. In my judgment rules that apply to a host of other symbols, such as state flags, armbands, or various privately promoted emblems of political or commercial identity, are not necessarily controlling. Even if flag burning could be considered just another species of symbolic speech under the logical application of the rules that the Court has developed in its interpretation of the First Amendment in other contexts, this case has an intangible dimension that makes those rules inapplicable.

A country's flag is a symbol of more than "nationhood and national unity." It also signifies the ideas that characterize the society that has chosen that emblem as well as the special history that has animated the growth and power of those ideas. The fleurs-de-lis and the tricolor both symbolized "nationhood and national unity," but they had vastly different meanings. The message conveyed by some flags — the swastika, for example — may survive long after it has outlived its usefulness as a symbol of regimented unity in a particular nation.

So it is with the American flag. It is more than a proud symbol of the courage, the determination, and the gifts of nature that transformed 13 fledgling Colonies into a world power. It is a symbol of freedom, of equal opportunity, of religious tolerance, and of goodwill for other peoples who share our aspirations. The symbol carries its message to dissidents both at home and abroad who may have no interest at all in our national unity or survival.

The value of the flag as a symbol cannot be measured. Even so, I have no doubt that the interest in preserving that value for the future is both significant and legitimate. Conceivably that value will be enhanced by the Court's conclusion that our national commitment to free expression is so strong that even the United States as ultimate guarantor of that freedom is without power to prohibit the desecration of its unique symbol. But I am unpersuaded. The creation of a federal right to post bulletin boards and graffiti on the Washington Monument might enlarge the market for free expression, but at a cost I would not pay. Similarly, in my considered judgment, sanctioning the public desecration of the flag will tarnish its value — both for those who cherish the ideas for which it waves and for those who desire to don the robes of martyrdom by burning it. That tarnish is not justified by the trivial burden on free expression occasioned by requiring that an available, alternative mode of expression — including uttering words critical of the flag — be employed.

It is appropriate to emphasize certain propositions that are not implicated by this case. The statutory prohibition of flag desecration does not "prescribe what shall be orthodox in politics, nationalism, religion, or other matters of opinion or force citizens to confess by word or act their faith therein." West Virginia Board of Education v. Barnette, 319 U.S. 624 (1943). The statute does not compel any conduct or any profession of respect for any idea or any symbol.

Nor does the statute violate "the government's paramount obligation of neutrality in its regulation of protected communication." Young v. American Mini Theatres, Inc., 427 U.S. 50 (1976) (plurality opinion). The content of respondent's message has no relevance whatsoever to the case. The concept of "desecration" does not turn on the substance of the message the actor intends to convey, but rather on whether those who view the act will take serious offense. Accordingly, one intending to convey a message of respect for the flag by burning it in a public square might nonetheless be guilty of desecration if he knows that others — perhaps simply because they misperceive the intended message — will be seriously offended. Indeed, even if the actor knows that all possible witnesses will understand that he intends to send a message of respect, he might still be guilty of desecration if he knows that this understanding does not lessen the offense taken by some of those witnesses. Thus, this is not a case in which the fact that "it is the speaker's opinion that gives offense" provides a special "reason for according it constitutional protection," FCC v. Pacifica Foundation, 438 U.S. 726 (1978) (plurality opinion). The case has nothing to do with "disagreeable ideas." It involves disagreeable conduct that, in my opinion, diminishes the value of an important national asset.

The Court is therefore quite wrong in blandly asserting that respondent "was prosecuted for his expression of dissatisfaction with the policies of this country, expression situated at the core of our First Amendment values." Respondent was prosecuted because of the method he chose to express his dissatisfaction with those policies. Had he chosen to spray paint — or perhaps convey with a motion picture projector — his message of dissatisfaction on the facade of the Lincoln Memorial, there would be no question about the power of the Government to prohibit his means of expression. The prohibition would be supported by the legitimate interest in preserving the quality of an important national asset. Though the asset at stake in this case is intangible, given its unique value, the same interest supports a prohibition on the desecration of the American flag.[a]

a. The Court suggests that a prohibition against flag desecration is not content-neutral because this form of symbolic speech is only used by persons who are critical of the flag or the ideas it repre-

The ideas of liberty and equality have been an irresistible force in motivating leaders like Patrick Henry, Susan B. Anthony, and Abraham Lincoln, schoolteachers like Nathan Hale and Booker T. Washington, the Phillippine Scouts who fought at Bataan, and the soldiers who scaled the bluff at Omaha Beach. If those ideas are worth fighting for — and our history demonstrates that they are — it cannot be true that the flag that uniquely symbolizes their power is not itself worthy of protection from unnecessary desecration.

I respectfully dissent.

Discussion

1. *"Speech" and Symbolic Expression.* Can "speech" be read literally? Is all speech protected by the First Amendment — including perjury and encouraging fraudulent transactions? Is all expression that is not, literally, "speech" — *not* protected, including writing, singing, dancing, drawing, photographing, picketing, passing out handbills, displaying posters, waving flags, dumping (one's own) tea, and burning (one's own) flags? To what extent do the majority and dissenting Justices disagree about the meaning of the word "speech" in the First Amendment? If they agree that speech encompasses at least some forms of expression that are not literally "speech," how do they determine which forms are protected? Which of the interests underlying free expression might be compromised if the government could punish Johnson for his conduct?

2. *The Actor's Purposes.* Did Johnson's actions have a communicative purpose? (Do the majority and dissenting Justices differ on this issue?) Could Johnson have invoked the First Amendment's protection even if he lacked a communicative purpose? Suppose, for example, that someone uses an American flag as kindling to start a fire, not to protest anything, but simply because it is close at hand?

3. *The State's Purposes.* In Street v. New York, 394 U.S. 576 (1969), Justice Fortas dissented from the reversal of appellant's conviction under a flag desecration statute for burning his flag:

> If a state statute provided that it is a misdemeanor to burn one's shirt or trousers or shoes on the public thoroughfare, it could hardly be asserted that the citizen's constitutional right is violated. If the arsonist asserted that he was burning his shirt or trousers or shoes as a protest against the Government's fiscal policies, for example, it is hardly possible that his claim to First Amendment shelter would prevail against the State's claim of a right to avert danger to the public and to avoid obstruction to traffic as a result of the fire. This is because action, even if clearly for serious protest purposes, is not entitled to the pervasive protection that is given to speech alone. It may be subjected to reasonable regulation that appropriately takes into account the competing interests involved.

---

sents. In making this suggestion the Court does not pause to consider the far-reaching consequences of its introduction of disparate impact analysis into our First Amendment jurisprudence. It seems obvious that a prohibition against the desecration of a gravesite is content-neutral even if it denies some protesters the right to make a symbolic statement by extinguishing the flame in Arlington Cemetery where John F. Kennedy is buried while permitting others to salute the flame by bowing their heads. Few would doubt that a protestor who extinguishes the flame has desecrated the gravesite, regardless of whether he prefaces that act with a speech explaining that his purpose is to express deep admiration or unmitigated scorn for the late President. Likewise, few would claim that the protester who bows his head has desecrated the gravesite, even if he made clear that his purpose is to show disrespect. In such a case, as in a flag burning case, the prohibition against desecration has absolutely nothing to do with the content of the message that the symbolic speech is intended to convey.

> . . . If, as I submit, it is permissible to prohibit the burning of personal property on the public sidewalk, there is no basis for applying a different rule to flag burning. And the fact that the law is violated for purposes of protest does not immunize the violator.

Justice Fortas implies that there is no constitutionally relevant distinction between a statute that specifically punishes burning a flag in public and a statute that generally punishes setting fires to anything in a public place. Consider whether the statutes might have rather different purposes and perhaps, therefore, different constitutional implications. See Laurence Tribe, American Constitutional Law 580-588 (1978); John Ely, Flag Desecration: A Case Study in the Roles of Categorizing and Balancing in First Amendment Analysis, 88 Harv. L. Rev. 1482 (1975).

What are Texas's interests in punishing Johnson's conduct? Are they related to the communicative content of his conduct? (Do the majority and dissenting Justices differ on this issue?)

4. *Standards of Constitutional Scrutiny.* What standard of constitutional scrutiny did the Court apply? What standard did the dissenting Justices apply? How does the Court's standard compare to the standard for unlawful advocacy articulated in Brandenburg v. Ohio, supra page 338?

Consider four permutations of the factors involved in a case like Texas v. Johnson:

	State Law IS NOT Concerned with Communicative Content	**State Law IS Concerned with Communicative Content**
Actor INTENDS to Communicate		
Actor Does NOT Intend to Communicate		

Do some of these permutations implicate the first amendment interests more than others, and, if so, should they receive greater constitutional scrutiny? Which permutation fits the facts of Texas v. Johnson? (Do the majority and dissenting Justices differ on this issue?)

5. *The Offensiveness and Emotive Content of the Communication.* Johnson's method of communicating his dissatisfaction with the Reagan administration was emotionally charged and likely to give offense. Consider, in this respect, Cohen v. California, 403 U.S. 15 (1971), where appellant was convicted for "maliciously and willfully disturb[ing] the peace and quiet of any neighborhood or person . . . by . . . offensive conduct," for wearing a jacket bearing the words "Fuck the Draft" in a corridor of the Los Angeles Courthouse. The state court held that "offensive conduct" means "behavior which has a tendency to provoke others to acts of violence or to in turn disturb the peace." Justice Harlan wrote for the Court:

[The issue] is whether California can excise, as "offensive conduct," one particular scurrilous epithet from the public discourse, either upon the theory of the court below that its use is inherently likely to cause violent reaction or upon a more general assertion that the States, acting as guardians of public morality, may properly remove this offensive word from the public vocabulary.

The rationale of the California court is plainly untenable. At most it reflects an "undifferentiated fear or apprehension of disturbance [which] is not enough to overcome the right to freedom of expression." We have been shown no evidence that substantial numbers of citizens are standing ready to strike out physically at whoever may assault their sensibilities with execrations like that uttered by Cohen. . . .

Admittedly, it is not so obvious that the First and Fourteenth Amendments must be taken to disable the States from punishing public utterance of this unseemly expletive in order to maintain what they regard as a suitable level of discourse within the body politic. We think, however, that examination and reflection will reveal the shortcomings of a contrary viewpoint.

. . . The constitutional right of free expression is powerful medicine in a society as diverse and populous as ours. It is designed and intended to remove governmental restraints from the arena of public discussion, putting the decision as to what views shall be voiced largely into the hands of each of us, in the hope that use of such freedom will ultimately produce a more capable citizenry and more perfect polity and in the belief that no other approach would comport with the premise of individual dignity and choice upon which our political system rests.

To many, the immediate consequence of this freedom may often appear to be only verbal tumult, discord, and even offensive utterance. These are, however, within established limits, in truth necessary side effects of the broader enduring values which the process of open debate permits us to achieve. That the air may at times seem filled with verbal cacophony is, in this sense not a sign of weakness but of strength. We cannot lose sight of the fact that, in what otherwise might seem a trifling and annoying instance of individual distasteful abuse of a privilege, these fundamental societal values are truly implicated. . . .

Against this perception of the constitutional policies involved, we discern certain more particularized considerations that peculiarly call for reversal of this conviction. First, the principle contended for by the State seems inherently boundless. How is one to distinguish this from any other offensive word? Surely the State has no right to cleanse public debate to the point where it is grammatically palatable to the most squeamish among us. Yet no readily ascertainable general principle exists for stopping short of that result were we to affirm the judgment below. For, while the particular four-letter word being litigated here is perhaps more distasteful than most others of its genre, it is nevertheless often true that one man's vulgarity is another's lyric. Indeed, we think it is largely because governmental officials cannot make principled distinctions in this area that the Constitution leaves matters of taste and style so largely to the individual.

Additionally, we cannot overlook the fact, because it is well illustrated by the episode involved here, that much linguistic expression serves a dual communicative function: it conveys not only ideas capable of relatively precise, detached explication, but otherwise inexpressible emotions as well. In fact, words are often chosen as much for their emotive as their cognitive force. We cannot sanction the view that the Constitution, while solicitous of the cognitive content of individual speech, has little or no regard for that emotive function which, practically speaking, may often be the more important element of the overall message sought to be communicated. Indeed, as Mr. Justice Frankfurter has said, "[o]ne of the prerogatives of American citizenship is the right to criticize public men and measures — and that means not only informed and responsible criticism but the freedom to speak foolishly and without moderation."

Finally, and in the same vein, we cannot indulge the facile assumption that one can forbid particular words without also running a substantial risk of suppressing ideas in the process. Indeed, governments might soon seize upon the censorship of particular words as a convenient guise for banning the expression of unpopular views. We have been able, as noted above, to discern little social benefit that might result from running the risk of opening the door to such grave results. . . .

Justice Blackmun dissented, in a short opinion joined by Chief Justice Burger and Justice Black, remarking that "Cohen's absurd and immature antic, in my view, was mainly conduct and very little speech."

In recent years, "offensive speech" directed against racial and other minorities has received special attention on university campuses and in scholarly literature. This important subject and the related questions concerning the regulation of pornography are taken up in courses focusing on the First Amendment and are beyond the scope of this book. For an introduction to the literature, see Charles Lawrence, If He Hollers Let Him Go: Regulating Racist Speech on Campus, 1990 Duke L.J. 431; Mari Matsuda, Public Response to Racist Speech: Considering the Victim's Story, 87 Mich. L. Rev. 2320 (1989); Nadine Strossen, Regulating Racist Speech on Campus: A Modest Proposal, 1990 Duke L.J. 484.

6. *The Flag Protection Act of 1989*. Following *Johnson*, Professor Laurence Tribe suggested in an op-ed article in The New York Times (July 3, 1989):

Properly understood, the Court's decision upheld no right to desecrate the flag, even in political protest, but merely required that Government protection of the flag be separated from Government suppression of detested views. . . .

Thus, if a flag desecration law were written and enforced without regard to the presence or absence of any message, government could defend the values embodied in the flag without addressing the values expressed by its destruction. I believe the Court would uphold such a law.

When government undertakes to protect a special place or symbol, it need not focus on whatever message might be expressed by someone who defaces the object of such protection. The same protective impulse that animates laws against the desecration of a gravesite may properly animate laws against the desecration of a flag that might cover a casket. When government legislates to protect special places or symbols, the Constitution does not require it to ignore emotions, whether of grief or patriotism.

What is vital from a First Amendment perspective is that, when we single out particular symbolic objects for special protection, we avoid singling out those occasions on which such objects are destroyed publicly or in a manner that expresses contempt.

Thus, I believe that the existing Federal statute outlawing flag desecration — which punishes "whoever knowingly casts contempt upon any flag of the United States by publicly defacing it" — could be rendered constitutional easily.

But it is not enough to delete the reference to "contempt," as the Senate did last month. To pass muster under the First Amendment, the statute must extend to anyone who intentionally defaces the flag, in public or in private. Only this step would remove the law's gratuitous reference to the speech element.

Encouraged by the liberal Professor Tribe's analysis, as well as political prudence, many congressional Democrats joined with their Republican colleagues to support what became the Flag Protection Act of 1989, which punished anyone who "knowingly mutilates, defaces, physically defiles, burns, maintains on the floor or ground, or tramples upon" a United States flag, unless it is related to the disposal of a "worn or soiled" flag. The Act also allowed for expedited review by the Supreme Court should it be challenged, as it immediately was.

In United States v. Eichman, 110 S. Ct. 2404 (1990), the Court held the Act unconstitutional as applied to appellees, who were prosecuted under the Act for burning flags while protesting Government policies, including the Act's passage. Justice Brennan wrote for the Court:

> The Government concedes in this case, as it must, that appellees' flag-burning constituted expressive conduct, but invites us to reconsider our rejection in *Johnson* of the claim that flag-burning as a mode of expression, like obscenity or "fighting words," does not enjoy the full protection of the First Amendment. This we decline to do. The only remaining question is whether the Flag Protection Act is sufficiently distinct from the Texas statute that it may constitutionally be applied to proscribe appellees' expressive conduct.
>
> The Government contends that the Flag Protection Act is constitutional because, unlike the statute addressed in *Johnson*, the Act does not target expressive conduct on the basis of the content of its message. The Government asserts an interest in "protect[ing] the physical integrity of the flag under all circumstances" in order to safeguard the flag's identity " 'as the unique and unalloyed symbol of the Nation.' " The Act proscribes conduct (other than disposal) that damages or mistreats a flag, without regard to the actor's motive, his intended message, or the likely effects of his conduct on onlookers. . . .
>
> Although the Flag Protection Act contains no explicit content-based limitation on the scope of prohibited conduct, it is nevertheless clear that the Government's asserted interest is "related 'to the suppression of free expression,' " and concerned with the content of such expression. The Government's interest in protecting the "physical integrity" of a privately owned flag rests upon a perceived need to preserve the flag's status as a symbol of our Nation and certain national ideals. But the mere destruction or disfigurement of a particular physical manifestation of the symbol, without more, does not diminish or otherwise affect the symbol itself in any way. For example, the secret destruction of a flag in one's own basement would not threaten the flag's recognized meaning. Rather, the Government's desire to preserve the flag as a symbol for certain national ideals is implicated "only when a person's treatment of the flag communicates [a] message" to others that is inconsistent with those ideals.
>
> We concede that the Government has a legitimate interest in preserving the flag's function as an "incident of sovereignty," though we need not address today the extent to which this interest may justify any laws regulating conduct that would thwart this core function, as might a commercial or like appropriation of the image of the United States flag. Amicus does not, and cannot, explain how a statute that penalizes anyone who knowingly burns, mutilates, or defiles any American flag is designed to advance this asserted interest in maintaining the association between the flag and the Nation. Burning a flag does not threaten to interfere with this association in any way; indeed, the flag-burner's message depends in part on the viewer's ability to make this very association.
>
> Moreover, the precise language of the Act's prohibitions confirms Congress' interest in the communicative impact of flag destruction. The Act criminalizes the

conduct of anyone who "knowingly mutilates, defaces, physically defiles, burns, maintains on the floor or ground, or tramples upon any flag." 18 U.S.C.A. §700(a)(1) (Supp. 1990). Each of the specified terms — with the possible exception of "burns" — unmistakably connotes disrespectful treatment of the flag and suggests a focus on those acts likely to damage the flag's symbolic value. And the explicit exemption in §700(a)(2) for disposal of "worn or soiled" flags protects certain acts traditionally associated with patriotic respect for the flag.[a]

Justice Stevens dissented, joined by Chief Justice Rehnquist and Justices White and O'Connor:

Burning a flag is not, of course, equivalent to burning a public building. Assuming that the protester is burning his own flag, it causes no physical harm to other persons or to their property. The impact is purely symbolic, and it is apparent that some thoughtful persons believe that impact, far from depreciating the value of the symbol, will actually enhance its meaning. I most respectfully disagree. Indeed, what makes this case particularly difficult for me is what I regard as the damage to the symbol that has already occurred as a result of this Court's decision to place its stamp of approval on the act of flag burning. A formerly dramatic expression of protest is now rather commonplace. In today's marketplace of ideas, the public burning of a Vietnam draft card is probably less provocative than lighting a cigarette. Tomorrow flag burning may produce a similar reaction. There is surely a direct relationship between the communicative value of the act of flag burning and the symbolic value of the object being burned.

The symbolic value of the American flag is not the same today as it was yesterday. Events during the last three decades have altered the country's image in the eyes of numerous Americans, and some now have difficulty understanding the message that the flag conveyed to their parents and grandparents — whether born abroad and naturalized or native born. Moreover, the integrity of the symbol has been compromised by those leaders who seem to advocate compulsory worship of the flag even by individuals whom it offends, or who seem to manipulate the symbol of national purpose into a pretext for partisan disputes about meaner ends. And . . . the residual value of the symbol after this Court's decision in Texas v. Johnson is surely not the same as it was a year ago.

Given all these considerations, plus the fact that the Court today is really doing nothing more than reconfirming what it has already decided, it might be appropriate to defer to the judgment of the majority and merely apply the doctrine of stare decisis to the case at hand. That action, however, would not honestly reflect my considered judgment concerning the relative importance of the conflicting interests that are at stake. I remain persuaded that the considerations identified in my opinion in Texas v. Johnson are of controlling importance in this case as well.

a. The Act also does not prohibit flying a flag in a storm or other conduct that threatens the physical integrity of the flag, albeit in an indirect manner unlikely to communicate disrespect.

. . . Although Congress cast the Flag Protection Act in somewhat broader terms than the Texas statute at issue in *Johnson*, the Act still suffers from the same fundamental flaw: it suppresses expression out of concern for its likely communicative impact. Despite the Act's wider scope, its restriction on expression cannot be " 'justified without reference to the content of the regulated speech.' " The Act therefore must be subjected to "the most exacting scrutiny," and for the reasons stated in *Johnson*, supra, the Government's interest cannot justify its infringement on First Amendment rights. We decline the Government's invitation to reassess this conclusion in light of Congress' recent recognition of a purported "national consensus" favoring a prohibition on flag-burning. Even assuming such a consensus exists, any suggestion that the Government's interest in suppressing speech becomes more weighty as popular opposition to that speech grows is foreign to the First Amendment.

Note: The Response to Eichman

Following the Court's decision, President Bush, as he had done the previous year after *Johnson*, called for a constitutional amendment that would permit punishing flag burning. He proposed an amendment, which was endorsed by many members of Congress: "The Congress and the States shall have power to prohibit the physical desecration of the flag of the United States." (The proposed amendment died after failing to receive the constitutionally required two-thirds support of the House of Representatives.)

The Senate Judiciary Committee held a day of hearings on the proposed amendment. Among those who supported the amendment was Robert H. Bork, formerly a professor of law at Yale, Solicitor General of the United States, member of the United States Court of Appeals for the District of Columbia, and President Reagan's unsuccessful nominee for membership on the Supreme Court:[17]

> It is said that we should not tamper with the Constitution. But the fact is that the amendment would not alter but rather would restore the First Amendment to the Constitution. It is wholly unrealistic to suppose that every decision of the Supreme Court, no matter how wrong, represents the real Constitution. Texas v. Johnson and United States v. Eichman are decisions that probably no other Supreme Court in our history would have reached. . . . Indeed, Hugo Black, who described himself as a First Amendment absolutist, stated, "It passes my belief that anything in the Federal Constitution bars a State from making the deliberate burning of the American flag an offense." . . . The constitutional amendment before you would "tamper" not with the historic Constitution but with novel and incorrect decisions that a switch in just one vote would have caused to go the other way. . . . No other object even remotely resembles the flag as the symbol of our identity as a nation. . . . The American people have demonstrated in hundreds of ways and through consistent conduct over many years that the flag of the United States is a symbol different from all others.
>
> It is not true that we have never amended the Constitution to overturn a Supreme Court decision. We have done that from the beginning. The Eleventh Amendment, ratified in 1798, was ratified in order to overturn the Supreme Court's decision in Chisholm v. Georgia, 2 Dall. 419 (1793), by taking away from federal judges the power to hear suits against any State by citizens of another State or by citizens of any foreign state.
>
> It is not even true that we have never amended the Constitution to remove a freedom the Supreme Court had found in the Bill of Rights. In Dred Scott v. Sanford, 19 How. 393 (1857), the Supreme Court found in the Fifth Amendment an individual freedom or right, good against the United States, to own slaves. That judicial misreading of the Constitution, by a much larger majority than in the flag burning cases, was corrected by the Thirteenth Amendment which outlawed slavery and involuntary servitude. We should not talk today as if amending the Constitution to correct a wrong Supreme Court ruling is unheard of. There is very good historical precedent for that.
>
> There has been criticism of politicians who are using flag desecration as a political issue. That criticism seems to me wide of the mark. Of course flag burning is a political issue. Politicians and elected representatives are supposed to respond to the sentiments and beliefs of the American people. But flag burning is a political issue for

17. Measures to Protect the American Flag, Hearing before the Committee on the Judiciary, United States Senate, June 21, 1990, Serial No. J-101-77, pp. 145-151.

more profound reasons than that. The flag is the one indispensible symbol we possess of our existence as a political community.

. . . The people who oppose putting this flag desecration amendment out for debate over its ratification seem to think that the Supreme Court may change the Constitution by one vote but that the American people by a vote of three-quarters of the States must not be allowed to restore the Constitution.

The only question before you is whether the American people are entitled to have one symbol of their nationhood that they may protect from defilement and outrage. My answer is yes. The answer of others is no. I urge you to propose the amendment and let the American people decide that question for themselves.

Among the critics of the proposed amendment was Professor Cass Sunstein of the University of Chicago, who focused first on the unwisdom of any amendment at all and secondly on the particular problems attached to the proposed amendment:[18]

[I]t would be a mistake to amend the Constitution and the bill of rights to ban the desecration of the flag.

a. First: This is not the sort of matter that belongs in a Constitution at all. . . .

Constitutional amendments are acceptable and indeed desirable under two principal conditions . . . :

1. If there is a serious structural problem or omission in the document, especially from the standpoint of democracy itself, an amendment is the right course. This principle accounts for a large number of amendments and the original bill of rights. . . .

2. New moral or ethical understandings sometimes call for constitutional changes — at least if those new understandings are widely shared, and especially if those understandings involve an effort to include or protect groups excluded by previous constitutional arrangements. This principle accounts for the 13th, 14th, and 15th amendments[, among others]. . . .

In these two situations, resort to the ordinary political process is insufficient. The problem that the amendment addresses is also a very large one, calling for large-scale institutional reform. Finally, constitutional change is unlikely, in these situations, to have harmful effects on the stability of the system or on the independence of the judiciary.

It should be obvious that a constitutional amendment protecting the flag falls in neither category. . . . (The prohibition amendment might be the closest analogy. It too did not belong in the Constitution, and of course it was ultimately repealed.) . . .

b. Second: Perhaps I have described the category of desirable amendments too narrowly. Perhaps there are occasions on which the Constitution should be amended to overturn a Supreme Court decision that the majority of the citizenry condemns. . . . But even if this is so, there are several reasons why the Constitution ought not to be amended here.

Many reasonable people believe that the Supreme Court erred in one or both of its rulings on the subject of flag-burning. . . . But even those who object to the Supreme Court's decisions in this area should acknowledge that those decisions are the furthest thing from incomprehensible or out of step with prevailing free speech law. . . . One of the central tenets of first amendment law, and a commitment for which Americans have much to be grateful, is that the Constitution protects what Justice Holmes described as freedom "for the thought we hate." It is far easier to live

18. Id. at 82-93.

with this proposition as a slogan or an abstraction than it is to accept it when we are confronted, concretely, with speech that seems genuinely despicable or offensive. . . . [I]f flag-burning is to be prohibited, it will not be easy to draw the line between that activity and other sorts of expression that are also thought by many or most citizens to be harmful or offensive. In a pluralistic society, tolerance and open-mindedness are the watchwords of freedom. . . . The American commitment to freedom of speech has flourished in part precisely because there are so few exceptions. To each person seeking an exception, it has been possible to say, "Neither for you nor for anyone else do we make special provisos. Everyone benefits, overall, if the censorship of every form of political speech is placed off the political agenda." When we deny an exception to concentration camp survivors who live in Skokie[, Illinois, the site of an extremely controversial proposed march by American Nazis during the 1970s], to those who might be victimized by the Klan, to refugees from Communist and other totalitarian regimes — this is the sort of answer that the first amendment demands. The denial of an exemption is essentially mechanical. At least until now, it has involved no judgment that the particular speech to which people are objecting is less obnoxious than other forms. An amendment protecting the flag would dilute this answer and render it cynical. It would legitimate efforts to amend the Constitution or to seek exceptions in multiple other settings. . . .

Although I believe that a proposed amendment should be rejected, I do not believe that standing by itself, a decision to recommend and ultimately to ratify an amendment on this subject would by itself threaten constitutional liberty in the United States in a serious way. . . . If it is . . . thought necessary to protect the flag, through a constitutional change, we should ensure that the risks to constitutional liberty will be minimal. The central goals here should be twofold. First, we should minimize the occasions for prosecution and the kinds of expressive activity that can be criminalized. Second, we should maximize the neutrality of any legal protection accorded to the flag. On both of these fronts, there is considerable room for creativity. I will content myself with two brief observations.

First, the power to enact legislation to protect the national flag should be granted only to Congress, and not the states. The flag is a symbol of the nation, not of the states. If anyone is to be empowered to prevent its destruction, it should be the nation. . . .

Second, any constitutional amendment should treat the flag not as a religious symbol, and not as a vehicle for suppressing political protest, but instead as something in which the United States has a kind of property interest. If this is the basic understanding, then it would not matter whether the flag is destroyed through political protest or otherwise. The initial step here should be to eliminate the word "desecration." There are two major problems with that word. The first is that it intermingles the flag with the divine — an intermingling that is in serious tension with the existing constitutional structure, in particular with the religion clauses. Under our system, the state is not identified with a religion. . . .

The second problem with the word is that it conspicuously calls for criminalization of protest activity — of criticism of the government — rather than protecting the flag in a more neutral manner. A better method would be to allow Congress to protect the "physical integrity" of the flag. Of course any subsequent statute would have to be carefully drawn so as not to sweep up an excessive amount of conduct. A "physical integrity" statute might make it a criminal offense to destroy the flag inadvertently, or to tear up or dispose of the multiple entities, including newspapers and coffee cups, on which the flag is reproduced. To draw up a more neutral amendment would therefore raise a serious risk of overinclusiveness; but any amendment should attempt, to the extent possible, to avoid partisanship.

If the amendment had passed, and Congress had repassed the legislation invalidated in *Eichman*, would it legitimate punishment in the following situations?[19]

Someone makes good pictures of U.S. flags, one- or two-sided, on paper or cloth — by color photography, color photocopy, or computer with ink-jet printer — and then publicly tramples and burns the pictures.

An iconoclast uses small cloth pictures of the flag as handkerchiefs and distributes large ones as blankets to New York's homeless.

A protester projects a picture of a flag onto a white wall and then hurls mud or paint onto the image.

A protester wall-mounts a large flag behind cellophane, then paints or smears obscenities on the transparent covering.

A computer-animation programmer creates a realistic video of what seems to be a flag burning to charred shreds.

An artist uses a thousand tiny flags as minute elements in an obscene picture.

IV. Viewpoint Neutral Regulations That Affect Speech

A regulation that regulates the time, place, or manner of speech, without regard to the viewpoint being expressed, may nonetheless implicate First Amendment values. Consider the different approaches that the Court has taken to such regulations.

SCHNEIDER v. STATE

308 U.S. 147 (1939)

Certiorari to the Court of Errors and Appeals of New Jersey

[The court reviewed the constitutionality of three ordinances which prohibited the distribution of leaflets and handbills in public places.]

ROBERTS, J. . . .

The freedom of speech and of the press secured by the First Amendment against abridgment by the United States is similarly secured to all persons by the Fourteenth against abridgment by a state.

Although a municipality may enact regulations in the interest of the public safety, health, welfare or convenience, these may not abridge the individual liberties secured by the Constitution to those who wish to speak, write, print or circulate information or opinion.

Municipal authorities, as trustees for the public, have the duty to keep their communities' streets open and available for movement of people and property, the primary purpose to which the streets are dedicated. So long as legislation to this end does not abridge the constitutional liberty of one rightfully upon the street to impart information through speech or the distribution of literature, it may lawfully regulate the conduct of those using the streets. For example, a person could not exercise this liberty by taking his stand in the mid-

19. Ken Knowlton and Barbara Bean Knowlton, Scenarios and Questions for Anti-Flag-Desecration Lawmakers, reprinted as When Is a Flag Desecrated? Harpers, December 1989, at 19.

dle of a crowded street, contrary to traffic regulations, and maintain his position to the stoppage of all traffic; a group of distributors could not insist upon a constitutional right to form a cordon across the street and to allow no pedestrian to pass who did not accept a tendered leaflet; nor does the guarantee of freedom of speech or of the press deprive a municipality of power to enact regulations against throwing literature broadcast in the streets. Prohibition of such conduct would not abridge the constitutional liberty since such activity bears no necessary relationship to the freedom to speak, write, print or distribute information or opinion.

This court has characterized the freedom of speech and that of the press as fundamental personal rights and liberties. The phrase is not an empty one and was not lightly used. It reflects the belief of the framers of the Constitution that exercise of the rights lies at the foundation of free government by free men. It stresses, as do many opinions of this court, the importance of preventing the restriction of enjoyment of these liberties.

In every case, therefore, where legislative abridgment of the rights is asserted, the courts should be astute to examine the effect of the challenged legislation. Mere legislative preferences or beliefs respecting matters of public convenience may well support regulation directed at other personal activities, but be insufficient to justify such as diminishes the exercise of rights so vital to the maintenance of democratic institutions. And so, as cases arise, the delicate and difficult task falls upon the courts to weigh the circumstances and to appraise the substantiality of the reasons advanced in support of the regulation of the free enjoyment of the rights.

In Lovell v. City of Griffin, 303 U.S. 444 (1938), this court held void an ordinance which forbade the distribution by hand or otherwise of literature of any kind without written permission from the city manager. The opinion pointed out that the ordinance was not limited to obscene and immoral literature or that which advocated unlawful conduct, placed no limit on the privilege of distribution in the interest of public order, was not aimed to prevent molestation of inhabitants or misuse or littering of streets, and was without limitation as to time or place of distribution. The court said that, whatever the motive, the ordinance was bad because it imposed penalties for the distribution of pamphlets, which had become historical weapons in the defense of liberty, by subjecting such distribution to license and censorship; and that the ordinance was void on its face, because it abridged the freedom of the press. . . .

The Los Angeles, the Milwaukee, and the Worcester ordinances under review do not purport to license distribution but all of them absolutely prohibit it in the streets and, one of them, in other public places as well.

The motive of the legislation . . . is held by the courts below to be the prevention of littering of the streets and, although the alleged offenders were not charged with themselves scattering paper in the streets, their convictions were sustained upon the theory that distribution by them encouraged or resulted in such littering. We are of opinion that the purpose to keep the streets clean and of good appearance is insufficient to justify an ordinance which prohibits a person rightfully on a public street from handing literature to one willing to receive it. Any burden imposed upon the city authorities in cleaning and caring for the streets as an indirect consequence of such distribution results from the constitutional protection of the freedom of speech and press. This constitutional protection does not deprive a city of all power to prevent street littering. There are obvious methods of preventing littering. Amongst these is the punishment of those who actually throw papers on the streets. . . .

It is suggested that the Los Angeles and Worcester ordinances are valid because their operation is limited to streets and alleys and leaves persons free to distribute printed matter in other public places. But, as we have said, the streets are natural and proper places for the dissemination of information and opinion; and one is not to have the exercise of his liberty of expression in appropriate places abridged on the plea that it may be exercised in some other place. . . .

Discussion

1. The Court summarized the modern doctrine concerning regulations of the time, place, and manner of speech in Grayned v. City of Rockford, 408 U.S. 104 (1972), which affirmed the petitioner's conviction under a local ordinance providing that "no person, while on public . . . grounds adjacent to any building in which a school or any class thereof is in session, shall willfully make or assist in the making of any noise or diversion which disturbs or tends to disturb the peace or good order of such school session." With only Justice Douglas dissenting, Justice Marshall wrote:

> Clearly, government has no power to restrict [expressive activity in public streets] because of its message. Our cases make equally clear, however, that reasonable "time, place and manner" regulations may be necessary to further significant governmental interests, and are permitted. For example, two parades cannot march on the same street simultaneously, and government may allow only one. A demonstration or parade on a large street during rush hour might put an intolerable burden on the essential flow of traffic, and for that reason could be prohibited. . . . Subject to such reasonable regulation, however, peaceful demonstrations in public places are protected by the First Amendment. . . .
>
> The nature of a place, "the pattern of its normal activities, dictate the kinds of regulations of time, place, and manner that are reasonable." Although a silent vigil may not unduly interfere with a public library, Brown v. Louisiana, 383 U.S. 131 (1966), making a speech in the reading room almost certainly would. The same speech should be perfectly appropriate in a park. The crucial question is whether the manner of expression is basically incompatible with the normal activity of a particular place at a particular time. Our cases make clear that in assessing the reasonableness of a regulation, we must weigh heavily the fact that communication is involved; the regulation must be narrowly tailored to further the State's legitimate interest. . . .
>
> In light of these general principles, we do not think that Rockford's ordinance is an unconstitutional regulation of activity around a school. . . . [Although] we think it clear that the public sidewalk adjacent to school grounds may not be declared off limits for expressive activity by members of the public . . . [,] expressive activity may be prohibited if it "materially disrupts classwork or involves substantial disorder or invasion of the rights of others." . .
>
> Rockford's anti-noise ordinance . . . is narrowly tailored to further Rockford's compelling interest in having an undisrupted school session conducive to the students' learning, and does not unnecessarily interfere with First Amendment rights. . . .
>
> In Cox v. Louisiana, 379 U.S. 559 (1965), this Court indicated that, because of the special nature of the place, persons could be constitutionally prohibited from picketing "in or near" a courthouse "with the intent of interfering with, obstructing, or

impeding the administration of justice." Likewise, in Cameron v. Johnson, 390 U.S. 611 (1968), we upheld a statute prohibiting picketing "in such a manner as to obstruct or unreasonably interfere with free ingress or egress to and from any . . . county . . . courthouses." As in those two cases, Rockford's modest restriction in some peaceful picketing represents a considered and specific legislative judgment that some kinds of expressive activity should be restricted at a particular time and place, here in order to protect the schools. Such a reasonable regulation is not inconsistent with the First and Fourteenth Amendments. The anti-noise ordinance is not invalid on its face.

2. City Council of Los Angeles v. Taypayers for Vincent, 446 U.S. 789 (1984), is one of many contemporary examples of judicial consideration of the constitutionality of nonviewpoint-based regulations of the "time, place, and manner" of expression. The Court upheld a section of the Los Angeles Municipal Code that prohibits posting signs on public property, including, among other things, street lampposts, hydrants, and telephone poles, as applied to a political poster supporting a candidate for election to the Los Angeles City Council. The Court accepted the candidate's argument that the only interest at stake was "esthetic," but rejected the argument "that the City's interest in eliminating visual blight is not sufficiently weighty to justify an abridgement of speech." Noting that "the state may sometimes curtail speech when necessary to advance a significant and legitimate state interest" Justice Stevens invoked United States v. O'Brien, 391 U.S. (1968), for "the appropriate framework for reviewing a viewpoint neutral regulation of this kind":

> [A] government regulation is sufficiently justified if it is within the constitutional power of the Government; if it furthers an important or substantial govermental interest; if the governmental interest is unrelated to the suppression of free expression; and if the incidental restriction on alleged First Amendment freedoms is no greater than is essential to the furtherance of that interest.

Justice Stevens concluded: "The problem addressed by this ordinance — the visual assault on the citizens of Los Angeles presented by an accumulation of signs posted on public property — constitutes a significant substantive evil within the City's power to prohibit."

3. *The Standard for Viewpoint Neutral Regulations of Expression.* In recent years, the Court has often assessed time, place, and manner regulations in terms of the *O'Brien* standard, quoted by Justice Stevens in *Vincent.* It is evident, isn't it, that this is a less demanding standard than that used in Texas v. Johnson. Even Justice Black, who consistently argued that the First Amendment absolutely prohibited government from regulating the content of expression, agreed that regulations of the time, place, and manner of expression called for a "balancing" of competing interests.

What are the rationales for the distinction between content-based and content-neutral regulations of speech?

a. In Restrictions of Speech Because of Its Content: The Peculiar Case of Subject-Matter Restrictions." 46 U. Chi. L. Rev. 81, Dean Geoffrey Stone writes:

> 1. *Marketplace of Ideas.* There appear to be two primary reasons for the Court's strikingly speech-protective approach to content-based restrictions. First, because such

restrictions accord differential treatment to speech because of its content, they necessarily distort the ordinary working of the "marketplace of ideas" in a content-differentiated manner. Such restrictions thus leave the public with only an incomplete — and perhaps inaccurate — perception of their social and political universe. As a consequence, they tend seriously to undermine two of the principal purposes of free speech: they distort the search for truth and they distort the process, so essential to the effective operation of a self-governing society, by which the citizen makes for himself critical decisions on matters of public policy.

. . . Content-neutral restrictions may also limit the public's access to potentially relevant information and ideas. But . . . there is arguably a prima facie case that such restrictions do not have a similarly distorting effect and do not as seriously inhibit the search for truth or the process of self-government. This is not to say, however, that content-neutral restrictions can never have a content-differential impact. . . . But to meet this concern by testing all content-neutral restrictions under the same stringent standards of review employed to test content-based restrictions seems more drastic a step than first amendment requires. . . .

Content neutral restrictions may . . . distort the marketplace of ideas in a content-differential manner when, although neutral on their face, they have de facto "unequal effects on various types of messages." For example, a law prohibiting all leafletting . . . may in fact have a disproportionately harsh impact upon those who, for reasons of finances or ideology, do not have ready access to more conventional means of communication. . . . The Court has attempted to handle this problem[20] . . . [by] taking this factor into account in the balancing process only when the particular content-neutral restriction at issue is likely to have substantial and relatively clear-cut content-differential effects. . . .

2. *Government Impartiality*. The second possible explanation of the Court's strikingly speech-protective approach to content-based restrictions derives from the precept that it is per se impermissible for government to restrict speech because it disapproves of the message conveyed. . . . What, though, does this have to do with

20. Consider Justice Black's defense of the public forum, dissenting in Kovacs v. Cooper, 336 U.S. 77 (1949). The Court held that a town could exclude from its thoroughfares vehicles emitting amplified speech or music — at least when the sound was "loud and raucous." Joined by Justices Douglas and Rutledge, Justice Black wrote:

> Laws which hamper the free use of some instruments of communication thereby favor competing channels. Thus, unless constitutionally prohibited, laws like this Trenton ordinance can give an overpowering influence to views of owners of legally favored instruments of communication. This favoritism, it seems to me, is the inevitable result of today's decision. . . .
>
> There are many people who have ideas that they wish to disseminate but who do not have enough money to own or control publishing plants, newspapers, radios, moving picture studios, or chains of show places. Yet everybody knows the vast reaches of these powerful channels of communication which from the very nature of our economic system must be under the control and guidance of comparatively few people. On the other hand, public speaking is done by many men of divergent minds with no centralized control over the ideas they entertain so as to limit the causes they espouse. It is no reflection on the value of preserving freedom for dissemination of the ideas of publishers of newspapers, magazines, and other literature, to believe that transmission of ideas through public speaking is also essential to the sound thinking of a fully informed citizenry. . . . For the press, the radio, and the moving picture owners have their favorites, and it assumes the impossible to suppose that these agencies will at all times be equally fair as between the candidates and officials they favor and those whom they vigorously oppose. And it is an obvious fact that public speaking today without sound amplifiers is a wholly inadequate way to reach the people on a large scale. Consequently, to tip the scales against transmission of ideas through public speaking, as the Court does today, is to . . . [prefer] those who can obtain the support of newspapers, etc., or those who have money enough to buy advertising from newspapers, radios, or moving pictures. . . . [T]he right to freedom of expression should be protected from absolute censorship for persons without, as for persons with, wealth and power. At least, such is the theory of our society.

the Court's special treatment of content-based restrictions? Although such restrictions may in some instance derive, at least in part, from government hostility to the views suppressed, in others that factor may not have played a role at all. . . .

To avoid the necessity of such an inquiry in every case, one might . . . erect a presumption that content-based restrictions, because of their very nature, are tainted by at least the likelihood of improper motivation. . . . [T]here may be some cases in which we can be reasonably certain that the content-based restriction would have been enacted even in the absence of any improper motivation. . . . This might be so, for example, when the interest served by the restriction is truly compelling and when there is no other way to protect this interest than by use of the content-based restriction. This mode of analysis, of course, resembles, in important respects, the stringent standards of review used by the Court to test content-based restrictions.

b. In his book, Freedom of Expression: A Critical Analysis (1984), Professor Martin Redish of Northwestern University Law School writes:

The most puzzling aspect of the distinction between content-based and content-neutral restrictions is that either restriction reduces the sum total of information or opinion disseminated. That governmental regulation impedes all forms of speech, rather than only selected viewpoints or subjects, does not alter the fact that the regulation impairs the free flow of expression. . . . Whatever rationale one adopts for the constitutional protection of speech the goals behind that rationale are undermined by *any* limitation on expression, content-based or not. . . .

Content-neutral restrictions like the prohibition of the distribution of all leaflets on street corners or the requirement of disclosure of authorship on all handbills may reduce the level and quality of contributions to the free exchange of ideas as significantly as any content-based regulation. Even if we accept the often compelling criticisms leveled at the "marketplace" model of expression and adopt instead the so-called "liberty" model, premised on the preeminent value of individual self-fulfillment, we still need not accept the content distinction. Here, too, content-neutral restrictions may significantly undermine the value of free expression by imposing limitations on the opportunity for individual expression. That the expression is regulated for reasons other than its content makes it no less an interference with expression. . . .

Professor Stone's first point — that content-based restrictions leave the public with a more incomplete and inaccurate perception of social reality than do content-neutral restrictions — is neither intuitively nor empirically supportable. . . . More importantly, even if content-neutral restrictions equally affected all competing points of view, such restrictions may undermine the functioning of the marketplace by keeping the public equally ignorant of *all* positions on issues, rather than merely of one viewpoint. . . .

Professor Stone's second point — the impropriety of governmental regulation because of government disagreement with speech — is no more convincing. . . . It is true that the philosophy of the first amendment rejects government regulation of expression based on disagreement with the expression's content. But . . . that philosophy is equally undermined whenever expression is limited without a valid and compelling justification.

Of course, in some cases the government may be able to provide a compelling justification for content-neutral regulation, while in many cases the government will be unable to justify content-based regulation since mere disagreement with content is not a sufficient justification. Thus, advocates of the content distinction may be correct in the narrow sense that, in terms of individual cases, content-based regulations will and should be overturned in more instances than content-neutral restrictions. However, this difference results not because the threat to first amendment values is

> any greater in one than in the other or because the level of judicial scrutiny given to one is more demanding, but because the asserted justification is more likely to meet a strict level of scrutiny in the former than in the latter.

c. Clark v. Community for Creative Non-Violence, 468 U.S. 288 (1984), held that the National Park Service could prohibit demonstrators from sleeping in tents erected in Lafayette Park and the Mall in Washington, D.C. to protest the treatment of the homeless. Justice White assumed, for purposes of the case, that "overnight sleeping in connection with the demonstration is expressive conduct protected to some extent by the First Amendment," but went on to hold that the Park Service rule was a reasonable restriction concerning the time, place, or manner of speech.

Justice Marshall wrote in dissent:

> The Court has dramatically lowered its scrutiny of governmental regulations once it has determined that such regulations are content-neutral. The result has been the creation of a two-tiered approach to First Amendment cases: while regulations that turn on the content of the expression are subject to a strict form of judicial review, regulations that are aimed at matters other than expression receive only a minimal level of scrutiny. The minimal scrutiny prong of this two-tiered approach has led to an unfortunate diminution of First Amendment protection. By narrowly limiting its concern to whether a given regulation creates a content-based distinction, the Court has seemingly overlooked the fact that content-neutral restrictions are also capable of unnecessarily restricting protected expressive activity. . . . The Court . . . , has transformed the ban against content-distinctions from a floor that offers all persons at least equal liberty under the First Amendment into a ceiling that restricts persons to the protection of First Amendment equality — but nothing more.
>
> [There is reason to believe] that judicial administration of the First Amendment, in conjunction with a social order marked by large disparities in wealth and other sources of power, tends systematically to discriminate against efforts by the relatively disadvantaged to convey their political ideas. In the past, this Court has taken such considerations into account in adjudicating the First Amendment rights of those among us who are financially deprived. See, e.g., Martin v. City of Struthers, 319 U.S. 141 (1943) (striking down ban on door-to-door distribution of circulars in part because this mode of distribution is "essential to the poorly financed causes of little people"); Marsh v. Alabama, 326 U.S. 501 (1946) (state cannot impose criminal sanction on person for distributing literature on sidewalk of town owned by private corporation). . . .
>
> [In addition, the Court sometimes engages in] a mistaken assumption regarding the motives and behavior of government officials who create and administer content-neutral regulations. The Court's salutary skepticism of governmental decision-making in First Amendment matters suddenly dissipates once it determines that a restriction is not content-based. The Court evidently assumes that the balance struck by officials is deserving of deference so long as it does not appear to be tainted by content discrimination. What the Court fails to recognize is that public officials have strong incentives to overregulate even in the absence of an intent to censor particular views. This incentive stems from the fact that of the two groups whose interests officials must accommodate — on the one hand, the interests of the general public and on the other, the interests of those who seek to use a particular forum for First Amendment activity — the political power of the former is likely to be far greater than that of the latter.

INDIANA v. GLEN THEATRE, INC.

111 S. Ct. 2456 (1991)

On Writ of Certiorari to the United States Court of Appeals for the Seventh Circuit

REHNQUIST, C.J., announced the judgment of the Court and delivered an opinion in which Justice O'Connor and Justice Kennedy joined.

Respondents are two establishments in South Bend, Indiana, that wish to provide totally nude dancing as entertainment, and individual dancers who are employed at these establishments. They claim that the First Amendment's guarantee of freedom of expression prevents the State of Indiana from enforcing its public indecency law to prevent this form of dancing. We reject their claim.

. . . The Kitty Kat Lounge, Inc. (Kitty Kat) is located in the city of South Bend. It sells alcoholic beverages and presents "go-go dancing." Its proprietor desires to present "totally nude dancing," but an applicable Indiana statute regulating public nudity requires that the dancers wear "pasties" and a "G-string" when they dance. The dancers are not paid an hourly wage, but work on commission. They receive a 100 percent commission on the first $60 in drink sales during their performances. Darlene Miller, one of the respondents in the action, had worked at the Kitty Kat for about two years at the time this action was brought. Miller wishes to dance nude because she believes she would make more money doing so. . . .

Respondent Glen Theatre, Inc., . . . [provides] so-called adult entertainment through written and printed materials, movie showings, and live entertainment at an enclosed "bookstore." The live entertainment at the "bookstore" consists of nude and seminude performances and showings of the female body through glass panels. Customers sit in a booth and insert coins into a timing mechanism that permits them to observe the live nude and seminude dancers for a period of time.

. . . [N]ude dancing of the kind sought to be performed here is expressive conduct within the outer perimeters of the First Amendment, though we view it as only marginally so. This, of course, does not end our inquiry. We must determine the level of protection to be afforded to the expressive conduct at issue, and must determine whether the Indiana statute is an impermissible infringement of that protected activity.

Indiana, of course, has not banned nude dancing as such, but has proscribed public nudity across the board. The Supreme Court of Indiana has construed the Indiana statute to preclude nudity in what are essentially places of public accommodation. . . . The petitioner contends . . . that Indiana's restriction on nude dancing is a valid "time, place or manner" restriction under cases such as Clark v. Community for Creative Non-Violence, 468 U.S. 288 (1984).

The "time, place, or manner" test was developed for evaluating restrictions on expression taking place on public property which had been dedicated as a "public forum." . . . In *Clark* we observed that this test has been interpreted to embody much the same standards as those set forth in United States v. O'Brien, 391 U.S. 367 (1968), and we turn, therefore, to the rule enunciated in *O'Brien*.

O'Brien burned his draft card on the steps of the South Boston courthouse in the presence of a sizable crowd, and was convicted of violating a statute that prohibited the knowing destruction or mutilation of such a card. He claimed that his conviction was contrary to the First Amendment because his act was "symbolic speech" — expressive conduct. The court rejected his contention that symbolic speech is entitled to full First Amendment protection, saying:

> Even on the assumption that the alleged communicative element in O'Brien's conduct is sufficient to bring into play the First Amendment, it does not necessarily follow that the destruction of a registration certificate is constitutionally protected activity. This Court has held that when 'speech' and 'nonspeech' elements are combined in the same course of conduct, a sufficiently important governmental interest in regulating the nonspeech element can justify incidental limitations on First Amendment freedoms. To characterize the quality of the governmental interest which must appear, the Court has employed a variety of descriptive terms: compelling; substantial; subordinating; paramount; cogent; strong. Whatever imprecision inheres in these terms, we think it clear that a government regulation is sufficiently justified if it is within the constitutional power of the Government; if it furthers an important or substantial governmental interest; if the governmental interest is unrelated to the suppression of free expression; and if the incidental restriction on alleged First Amendment freedoms is no greater than is essential to the furtherance of that interest.

Applying the four-part *O'Brien* test enunciated above, we find that Indiana's public indecency statute is justified despite its incidental limitations on some expressive activity. The public indecency statute is clearly within the constitutional power of the State and furthers substantial governmental interests. It is impossible to discern, other than from the text of the statute, exactly what governmental interest the Indiana legislators had in mind when they enacted this statute, for Indiana does not record legislative history, and the state's highest court has not shed additional light on the statute's purpose. Nonetheless, the statute's purpose of protecting societal order and morality is clear from its text and history. . . . Public indecency statutes such as the one before us reflect moral disapproval of people appearing in the nude among strangers in public places. . . .

This and other public indecency statutes were designed to protect morals and public order. The traditional police power of the States is defined as the authority to provide for the public health, safety, and morals, and we have upheld such a basis for legislation. . . . Thus, the public indecency statute furthers a substantial government interest in protecting order and morality.

This interest is unrelated to the suppression of free expression. . . . It can be argued, of course, that almost limitless types of conduct — including appearing in the nude in public — are "expressive," and in one sense of the word this is true. People who go about in the nude in public may be expressing something about themselves by so doing. But the court rejected this expansive notion of "expressive conduct" in *O'Brien,* saying: "We cannot accept the view that an apparently limitless variety of conduct can be labelled 'speech' whenever the person engaging in the conduct intends thereby to express an idea." . . .

Respondents contend that even though prohibiting nudity in public generally may not be related to suppressing expression, prohibiting the performance of nude dancing is related to expression because the state seeks to prevent its erotic message. Therefore, they reason that the application of the Indiana statute to the nude dancing in this case violates the First Amendment, because it fails the third part of the *O'Brien* test, viz: the governmental interest must be unrelated to the suppression of free expression.

But we do not think that when Indiana applies its statute to the nude dancing in these nightclubs it is proscribing nudity because of the erotic message conveyed by the dancers. Presumably numerous other erotic performances are presented at these establishments and similar clubs without any interference from the state, so long as the performers wear a scant amount of clothing. Likewise, the requirement that the dancers don pasties and a G-string does not deprive the dance of whatever erotic message it conveys: it simply makes the message slightly less graphic. The perceived evil that Indiana seeks to address is not erotic dancing, but public nudity. The appearance of people of all shapes, sizes and ages in the nude at a beach, for example, would convey little if any erotic message, yet the state still seeks to prevent it. Public nudity is the evil the state seeks to prevent, whether or not it is combined with expressive activity. . . .

The fourth part of the *O'Brien* test requires that the incidental restriction on First Amendment freedom be no greater than is essential to the furtherance of the governmental interest.

As indicated in the discussion above, the governmental interest served by the text of the prohibition is societal disapproval of nudity in public places and among strangers. The statutory prohibition is not a means to some greater end, but an end in itself. It is without cavil that the public indecency statute is "narrowly tailored;" Indiana's requirement that the dancers wear at least pasties and a G-strong is modest, and the bare minimum necessary to achieve the state's purpose.

SCALIA, J., concurring in the judgment.

I agree that the judgment of the Court of Appeals must be reversed. In my view, however, the challenged regulation must be upheld, not because it survives some lower level of First-Amendment scrutiny, but because, as a general law regulating conduct and not specifically directed at expression, it is not subject to First-Amendment scrutiny at all. . . .

I

. . . On its face, this law is not directed at expression in particular. As Judge Easterbrook put it in his dissent below: "Indiana does not regulate dancing. It regulates public nudity. . . . Almost the entire domain of Indiana's statute is unrelated to expression, unless we view nude beaches and topless hot dog vendors as speech." The intent to convey a "message of eroticism" (or any other message) is not a necessary element of the statutory offense of public indecency; . . . Public indecency — including public nudity — has long been an offense at common law. . . .

II

Since the Indiana regulation is a general law not specifically targeted at expressive conduct, its application to such conduct does not in my view implicate the First Amendment.

The First Amendment explicitly protects "the freedom of speech [and] of the press" — oral and written speech — not "expressive conduct." When any law restricts speech, even for a purpose that has nothing to do with the suppression of communication (for instance, to reduce noise, to regulate election campaigns, or to prevent littering, we insist that it meet the high, First-Amendment standard of justification. But virtually every law restricts conduct, and virtually any prohibited conduct can be performed for an expressive purpose — if only expressive of the fact that the actor disagrees with the prohibition. It cannot reasonably be demanded, therefore, that every restriction of expression incidentally produced by a general law regulating conduct pass normal First-Amendment scrutiny, or even — as some of our cases have suggested, see e.g., United States v. O'Brien, 391 U.S. 367 (1968) — that it be justified by an "important or substantial" government interest. Nor do our holdings require such justification: we have never invalidated the application of a general law simply because the conduct that it reached was being engaged in for expressive purposes and the government could not demonstrate a sufficiently important state interest.

This is not to say that the First Amendment affords no protection to expressive conduct. Where the government prohibits conduct precisely because of its communicative attributes, we hold the regulation unconstitutional. . . . Where that has not been the case, however — where suppression of communicative use of the conduct was merely the incidental effect of forbidding the conduct for other reasons — we have allowed the regulation to stand. . . .

All our holdings (though admittedly not some of our discussion) support the conclusion that "the only First Amendment analysis applicable to laws that do not directly or indirectly impede speech is the threshold inquiry of whether the purpose of the law is to suppress communication. If not, that is the end of the matter so far as First Amendment guarantees are concerned; if so, the court then proceeds to determine whether there is substantial justification for the proscription." Community for Creative Non-Violence v. Watt, 703 F.2d 586, 622-623 (1983) (en banc) (Scalia, J., dissenting), rev'd Clark v. Community for Creative Non-Violence, 468 U.S. 288 (1984). Such a regime ensures that the government does not act to suppress communication, without requiring that all conduct-restricting regulation (which means in effect all regulation) survive an enhanced level of scrutiny.

We have explicitly adopted such a regime in another First Amendment context: that of Free Exercise. In Employment Division, Oregon Dept of Human Resources v. Smith, 494 U.S. (1990), [infra, Chapter 13,] we held that general laws not specifically targeted at religious practices did not require heightened First Amendment scrutiny even though they diminished some people's ability to practice their religion. . . . There is even greater reason to apply this approach to the regulation of expressive conduct. Relatively few can plausibly assert that their illegal conduct is being engaged in for religious reasons; but almost anyone can violate almost any law as a means of expression. In the one case, as in the other, if the law is not directed against the protected value (religion or expression) the law must be obeyed.

III

. . . The plurality purports to apply to this general law, insofar as it regulates this allegedly expressive conduct, an intermediate level of First Amendment scrutiny: the government interest in the regulation must be " 'important or substantial.' " As I have indicated, I do not believe such a heightened standard exists. I think we should avoid wherever possible, moreover, a method of analysis that requires judicial assessment of the "importance" of government interests — and especially of government interests in various aspects of morality. . . .

SOUTER, J., concurring in the judgment.

Not all dancing is entitled to First Amendment protection as expressive activity. This Court has previously categorized ballroom dancing as beyond the Amendment's protection, and dancing as aerobic exercise would likewise be outside the First Amendment's concern. But dancing as a performance directed to an actual or hypothetical audience gives expression at least to generalized emotion or feeling, and where the dancer is nude or nearly so the feeling expressed, in the absence of some contrary clue, is eroticism, carrying an endorsement of erotic experience. Such is the expressive content of the dances described in the record.

Although such performance dancing is inherently expressive, nudity per se is not. It is a condition, not an activity, and the voluntary assumption of that condition, without more, apparently expresses nothing beyond the view that the condition is somehow appropriate to the circumstances. . . . But when nudity is combined with expressive activity, its stimulative and attractive value certainly can enhance the force of expression, and a dancer's acts in going from clothed to nude, as in a strip-tease, are integrated into the dance and its expressive function. Thus I agree with the plurality and the dissent that an interest in freely engaging in the nude dancing at issue here is subject to a degree of First Amendment protection.

I also agree with the plurality that the appropriate analysis to determine the actual protection required by the First Amendment is the four-part enquiry described in United States v. O'Brien, for judging the limits of appropriate state action burdening expressive acts as distinct from pure speech or representation. I nonetheless write separately to rest my concurrence in the judgment, not on the possible sufficiency of society's moral views to justify the limitations at issue, but on the State's substantial interest in combating the secondary effects of adult entertainment establishments of the sort typified by respondents' establishments. . . . [W]e may legitimately consider petitioners' assertion that the statute is applied to nude dancing because such dancing "encourages prostitution, increases sexual assaults, and attracts other criminal activity."

This asserted justification for the statute may not be ignored merely because it is unclear to what extent this purpose motivated the Indiana Legislature in enacting the statute. Our appropriate focus is not an empirical enquiry into the actual intent of the enacting legislature, but rather the existence or not of a current governmental interest in the service of which the challenged application of the statute may be constitutional. . . . In my view, the interest asserted by petitioners in preventing prostitution, sexual assault, and other criminal activity, . . . is sufficient under *O'Brien* to justify the State's enforcement of the statute against the type of adult entertainment at issue here. . . .

At the outset, it is clear that the prevention of such evils falls within the constitutional power of the State, which satisfies the first *O'Brien* criterion. The second *O'Brien* prong asks whether the regulation "furthers an important or substantial governmental interest." The asserted state interest is plainly a substantial one; the only question is whether prohibiting nude dancing of the sort at issue here "furthers" that interest. I believe that our cases have addressed this question sufficiently to establish that it does.

In Renton v. Playtime Theatres, Inc., 475 U.S. 41 (1986), we upheld a city's zoning ordinance designed to prevent the occurrence of harmful secondary effects, including the crime associated with adult entertainment. . . . Of particular importance to the present enquiry, we held that the city of Renton was not compelled to justify its restrictions by studies specifically relating to the problems that would be caused by adult theaters in that city. Rather, "Renton was entitled to rely on the experiences of Seattle and other cities," which demonstrated the harmful secondary effects correlated with the presence "of even one [adult] theater in a given neighborhood."

. . . In light of *Renton's* recognition that legislation seeking to combat the secondary effects of adult entertainment need not await localized proof of those effects, the State of Indiana could reasonably conclude that forbidding nude entertainment of the type offered at the Kitty Kat Lounge and the Glen Theatre's "bookstore" furthers its interest in preventing prostitution, sexual assault, and associated crimes. [We have recognized] that "society's interest in protecting this type of expression is of a wholly different, and lesser, magnitude than the interest in untrammeled political debate," . . . The statute as applied to nudity of the sort at issue here therefore satisfies the second prong of *O'Brien*.

The third *O'Brien* condition is that the governmental interest be "unrelated to the suppression of free expression," and, on its face, the governmental interest in combating prostitution and other criminal activity is not at all inherently related to expression. . . .

Because the State's interest in banning nude dancing results from a simple correlation of such dancing with other evils, rather than from a relationship between the other evils and the expressive component of the dancing, the interest is unrelated to the suppression of free expression.

The fourth *O'Brien* condition, that the restriction be no greater than essential to further the governmental interest, requires little discussion. Pasties and a G-string moderate the expression to some degree, to be sure, but only to a degree. Dropping the final stitch is prohibited, but the limitation is minor when measured against the dancer's remaining capacity and opportunity to express the erotic message. . . .

Accordingly, I find *O'Brien* satisfied and concur in the judgment.

WHITE, J., with whom Justice Marshall, Justice Blackmun, and Justice Stevens join, dissenting. . . .

Having arrived at the conclusion that nude dancing performed as entertainment enjoys First Amendment protection, the Court states that it must "determine the level of protection to be afforded to the expressive conduct at issue, and must determine whether the Indiana statute is an impermissible infringement of that protected activity." . . .

The Court's analysis is erroneous in several respects. Both the Court and Justice Scalia in his concurring opinion overlook a fundamental and critical aspect of our cases upholding the States' exercise of their police powers. None of the cases they rely upon . . . involved anything less than truly general proscriptions on individual conduct. In *O'Brien,* for example, individuals were prohibited from destroying their draft cards at any time and in any place, even in completely private places such as the home. . . . By contrast, in this case Indiana does not suggest that its statute applies to, or could be applied to, nudity wherever it occurs, including the home. We do not understand the Court or Justice Scalia to be suggesting that Indiana could constitutionally enact such an intrusive prohibition. . . .

We are told by the Attorney General of Indiana that the Indiana Supreme Court held that the statute at issue here cannot and does not prohibit nudity as a part of some larger form of expression meriting protection when the communication of ideas is involved. Petitioners also state that the evils sought to be avoided by applying the statute in this case would not obtain in the case of theatrical productions, such as Salome or Hair. . . .

Thus, the Indiana statute is not a general prohibition of the type we have upheld in prior cases. As a result, the Court's and Justice Scalia's simple references to the State's general interest in promoting societal order and morality is not sufficient justification for a statute which concededly reaches a significant amount of protected expressive activity. Instead, in applying the *O'Brien* test, we are obligated to carefully examine the reasons the State has chosen to regulate this expressive conduct in a less than general statute. In other words, when the State enacts a law which draws a line between expressive conduct which is regulated and nonexpressive conduct of the same type which is not regulated, *O'Brien* places the burden on the State to justify the distinctions it has made. Closer inquiry as to the purpose of the statute is surely appropriate.

Legislators do not just randomly select certain conduct for proscription; they have reasons for doing so and those reasons illuminate the purpose of the law that is passed. Indeed, a law may have multiple purposes. The purpose of forbidding people from appearing nude in parks, beaches, hot dog stands, and like public places is to protect others from offense. But that could not possibly be the purpose of preventing nude dancing in theaters and barrooms since the viewers are exclusively consenting adults who pay money to see these dances. The purpose of the proscription in these contexts is to protect the viewers from what the State believes is the harmful message that nude dancing communicates. This is why Clark v. Community for Creative Non-Violence, 468 U.S. 288 (1984), is of no help to the State: "In *Clark* . . . the damage to the parks was the same whether the sleepers were camping out for fun, were in fact homeless, or wished by sleeping in the park to make a symbolic statement on behalf of the homeless." (Posner, J., concurring). That cannot be said in this case: the perceived damage to the public interest caused by appearing nude on the streets or in the parks, as I have said, is not what the State seeks to avoid in preventing nude dancing in theaters and taverns. There the perceived harm is the communicative aspect of the erotic dance. As the State now tells us, and as Justice Souter agrees, the State's goal in applying what it describes as its "content neutral" statute to the nude dancing in this case is "deterrence of prostitution, sexual assaults, criminal activity, degradation of women, and other activities which break down family structure." The attainment of these goals, however, depends on preventing an expressive activity.

The Court nevertheless holds that the third requirement of the *O'Brien* test, that the governmental interest be unrelated to the suppression of free expression, is satisfied because in applying the statute to nude dancing, the State is not "proscribing nudity because of the erotic message conveyed by the dancers." The

Court suggests that this is so because the State does not ban dancing that sends an erotic message; it is only nude erotic dancing that is forbidden. The perceived evil is not erotic dancing but public nudity, which may be prohibited despite any incidental impact on expressive activity. This analysis is transparently erroneous.

In arriving at its conclusion, the Court concedes that nude dancing conveys an erotic message and concedes that the message would be muted if the dancers wore pasties and G-strings. Indeed, the emotional or erotic impact of the dance is intensified by the nudity of the performers. . . . The nudity is itself an expressive component of the dance, not merely incidental "conduct." . . .

This being the case, it cannot be that the statutory prohibition is unrelated to expressive conduct. Since the State permits the dancers to perform if they wear pasties and G-strings but forbids nude dancing, it is precisely because of the distinctive, expressive content of the nude dancing performances at issue in this case that the State seeks to apply the statutory prohibition. It is only because nude dancing performances may generate emotions and feelings of eroticism and sensuality among the spectators that the State seeks to regulate such expressive activity, apparently on the assumption that creating or emphasizing such thoughts and ideas in the minds of the spectators may lead to increased prostitution and the degradation of women. But generating thoughts, ideas, and emotions is the essence of communication. The nudity element of nude dancing performances cannot be neatly pigeonholed as mere "conduct" independent of any expressive component of the dance.

That fact dictates the level of First Amendment protection to be accorded the performances at issue here. . . . Content based restrictions "will be upheld only if narrowly drawn to accomplish a compelling governmental interest." . . .

That the performances in the Kitty Kat Lounge may not be high art, to say the least, and may not appeal to the Court, is hardly an excuse for distorting and ignoring settled doctrine. The Court's assessment of the artistic merits of nude dancing performances should not be the determining factor in deciding this case. In the words of Justice Harlan, "it is largely because governmental officials cannot make principled decisions in this area that the Constitution leaves matters of taste and style so largely to the individual." Cohen v. California, 403 U.S. 15, 25 (1971). "While the entertainment afforded by a nude ballet at Lincoln Center to those who can pay the price may differ vastly in content (as viewed by judges) or in quality (as viewed by critics), it may not differ in substance from the dance viewed by the person who . . . wants some 'entertainment' with his beer or shot of rye." Salem Inn, Inc. v. Frank, 501 F.2d. (CA2 1974), aff'd in part, Doran v. Salem Inn, Inc., 422 U.S. 922 (1975).

The Court and Justice Souter do not go beyond saying that the state interests asserted here are important and substantial. But even if there were compelling interests, the Indiana statute is not narrowly drawn. If the State is genuinely concerned with prostitution and associated evils, . . . it can adopt restrictions that do not interfere with the expressiveness of nonobscene nude dancing performances. For instance, the State could perhaps require that, while performing, nude performers remain at all times a certain minimum distance from spectators. . . . Likewise, the State clearly has the authority to criminalize prostitution and obscene behavior. Banning an entire category of expressive activity, however, generally does not satisfy the narrow tailoring requirement of strict First Amendment scrutiny. . . .

Discussion

On what basis, if any, would the prohibition of a nude dance in Salome be distinguished, as a constitutional matter, from the prohibition of nude dancing in the Kitty Kat Lounge?

V. *Legislative Motivation and the Allocation of Constitutional Decisionmaking Responsibility*

The Universal Military Training and Service Act of 1948 provides:[21]

> Any person . . . who knowingly violates or evades any of the provisions of this title or rules and regulations promulgated pursuant thereto relating to the issuance, transfer, or possession of [any selective service certificate], shall, upon conviction, be fined not to exceed $10,000 or be imprisoned for not more than five years, or both.

Regulations promulgated under the act require each registrant to "have in his personal possession at all times" his registration certificate and notice of classification.[22] In summer of 1965, when burning draft cards had become a widely recognized symbol of protest against the war in Vietnam, Congressman Mendel L. Rivers of South Carolina introduced H.R. 10306, which amended section 12(b) also to punish any person who "knowingly destroys [or] knowingly mutilates" any selective service certificate. Strom Thurmond introduced a parallel measure in the Senate.[23] The bills were promptly referred to and reported by the respective armed services committees and were quickly enacted as an amendment to Section 12(b)(3) of the Universal Military Training and Service Act.

This section first considers the constitutional problems presented by H.R. 10306 from the viewpoint of a member of the House Committee on Armed Services. Then it examines how Congress in fact resolved these problems. Finally, it studies United States v. O'Brien, 391 U.S. 367 (1968), in which the Supreme Court upheld the 1965 amendment.

A. The Conscientious Legislator

You are counsel to the House Committee on Armed Services. A member of the committee is troubled about the constitutionality of the proposed statute and seeks your advice.

Based on the analysis in this chapter, how should you advise the committee member who wishes to know whether, consistent with her oath to uphold the Constitution, she can conscientiously vote for the draft-card destruction bill? Does the language of the bill make its purposes unequivocally clear? If not, suppose that you asked her what *her* purposes were in supporting the bill and she responded (1) solely to facilitate the mechanics of the selective service system, (2)

21. Section 12(b) (6), 50 U.S.C. app. §462(b)(6) (1968).
22. 32 C.F.R. §§1617.1 (1962), 1623.5 (1962).
23. 111 Cong. Rec. 19746, 20433-20434 (1965).

solely to suppress an effective means of antiwar protest (and that, at least for her, the first rationale was a makeweight), or (3) for a combination of the two reasons. Would your constitutional analysis differ depending on her answer?[24]

B. Congress Acts

H.R. 10306 was promptly referred to the Committee on Armed Services, which, without taking evidence, favorably reported it the following Monday. The report explained:[25]

> The House Committee on Armed Services is fully aware of, and shares in, the deep concern expressed throughout the Nation over the increasing incidences in which individuals and large groups of individuals openly defy and encourage others to defy the authority of their Government by destroying or mutilating their draft cards.
>
> While the present provisions of the Criminal Code with respect to the destruction of Government property may appear broad enough to cover all acts having to do with the mistreatment of draft cards in the possession of individuals, the committee feels that in the present critical situation of the country, the acts of destroying or mutilating these cards are offenses which pose such a grave threat to the security of the Nation that no question whatsoever should be left as to the intention of the Congress that such wanton and irresponsible acts should be punished.

On August 10, the House passed the bill 393 to 1.[26] The only speakers were Mendel Rivers, the amendment's sponsor, and William G. Bray of Indiana. Congressman Rivers explained that the bill "is a straightforward clear answer to those who would make a mockery of our efforts in South Vietnam by engaging in the mass destruction of draft cards. . . . This is the least we can do for our men in South Vietnam fighting to preserve freedom, while a vocal minority in this country thumb their noses at their own Government."[27]

Congressman Bray stated:[28]

> The need of this legislation is clear. Beatniks and so-called "campus-cults" have been publicly burning their draft cards to demonstrate their contempt for the United States and our resistance to Communist takeovers. . . .
>
> These so-called "student" mobs at home and abroad make demands and threats; they hurl rocks and ink bottles at American buildings; they publicly mutilate or burn their draft cards; they even desecrate the American flag. Chanting and screaming vile epithets, these mobs, of so-called "students" and Communist "stooges" attempt to create fear and destroy self-confidence in our country and its citizens and to downgrade the United States in the eyes of the world. . . .

24. See Paul Brest, The Conscientious Legislator's Guide to Constitutional Interpretation, 27 Stan. L. Rev. 585, 589-591 (1975).

25. H.R. Rep. No. 747, 89th Cong., 1st Sess. (1965).

26. The one dissenter, Congressman Henry P. Smith of New York, later explained that though he sympathized with the aims of the bill, the punishment "is far too excessive for this type of misdemeanor." N.Y. Times, Aug. 11, 1965, at 14, in Dean Alfange, Free Speech and Symbolic Conduct: The Draft-Card Burning Case, 1968 Sup. Ct. Rev. 1, 6, n.21.

27. 111 Cong. Rec. 19871 (1965).

28. Id. at 19871-19872.

> This proposed legislation to make it illegal to knowingly destroy or mutilate a draft card is only one step in bringing some legal control over those who would destroy American freedom. . . .
>
> The growing disrespect for our law and institutions in America holds a real threat to our country and to our freedom. Just 5 short years ago no one would have believed that disrespect for our country could have grown to the proportions that it has today. . . .
>
> If these "revolutionaries" are permitted to deface and destroy their draft cards, our entire Selective Service System is dealt a serious blow.

On August 12, the Senate Committee on Armed Services favorably reported the parallel measure:[29]

> The committee has taken notice of the defiant destruction and mutilation of draft cards by dissident persons who disapprove of national policy. If allowed to continue unchecked this contumacious conduct represents a potential threat to the exercise of the power to raise and support armies.

The Senate passed the bill on August 13. Only its sponsor, Senator Thurmond of South Carolina, spoke:[30]

> Recent incidents of mass destruction of draft cards constitute open defiance of the war-making powers of the Government and have demonstrated an urgent need for this legislation. . . .
>
> The President has acknowledged that our country is engaged in a war. Attempts to interfere with the Universal Military Training Act or service in the Armed Forces constitute treason in time of war. Such conduct as public burnings of draft cards and public pleas for persons to refuse to register for their draft should not and must not be tolerated by a society whose sons, brothers, and husbands are giving their lives in defense of freedom and countrymen against Communist aggression.

President Johnson approved the bill on August 31, 1965.

C. The Court Reviews

UNITED STATES v. O'BRIEN

391 U.S. 367 (1968)

On Petition for Writ of Certiorari to the United States Court of Appeals for the First Circuit

WARREN, C.J.

On the morning of March 31, 1966, David Paul O'Brien and three companions burned their Selective Service registration certificates on the steps of the South Boston Courthouse. . . .

For this act, O'Brien was indicted, tried, convicted, and sentenced in the United States District Court for the District of Massachusetts. He did not contest the fact that he had burned the certificate. He stated in argument to the jury that

29. S. Rep. No. 589, 89th Cong., 1st Sess. (1965).
30. 111 Cong. Rec. 20433.

he burned the certificate publicly to influence others to adopt his antiwar beliefs, as he put it, "so that other people would reevaluate their positions with Selective Service, with the armed forces, and reevaluate their place in the culture of today, to hopefully consider my position."

The indictment upon which he was tried charged that he "willfully and knowingly did mutilate, destroy, and change by burning . . . [his] Registration Certificate (Selective Service System Form No. 2); in violation of Title 50, App., United States Code, Section 462(b)." . . . In the District Court, O'Brien argued that the 1965 Amendment prohibiting the knowing destruction or mutilation of certificates was unconstitutional because it was enacted to abridge free speech, and because it served no legitimate legislative purpose. The District Court rejected these arguments, holding that the statute on its face did not abridge First Amendment rights, that the court was not competent to inquire into the motives of Congress in enacting the 1965 Amendment, and that the Amendment was a reasonable exercise of the power of Congress to raise armies.

On appeal, the Court of Appeals for the First Circuit held the 1965 Amendment unconstitutional as a law abridging freedom of speech. . . . The Court of Appeals . . . was of the opinion that conduct punishable under the 1965 Amendment was already punishable under the nonpossession regulation, and consequently that the Amendment served no valid purpose; further, that in light of the prior regulation, the Amendment must have been "directed at public as distinguished from private destruction." On this basis, the court concluded that the 1965 Amendment ran afoul of the First Amendment by singling out persons engaged in protests for special treatment. The court ruled, however, that O'Brien's conviction should be affirmed under the statutory provision, 50 U.S.C. App. §462(b)(6), which in its view made violation of the nonpossession regulation a crime, because it regarded such violation to be a lesser included offense of the crime defined by the 1965 Amendment.

The Government petitioned for certiorari, arguing that the Court of Appeals erred in holding the statute unconstitutional, and that its decision conflicted with decisions by the Courts of Appeals for the Second and Eighth Circuits upholding the 1965 Amendment against identical constitutional challenges. O'Brien cross-petitioned for certiorari, arguing that the Court of Appeals erred in sustaining his conviction on the basis of a crime of which he was neither charged nor tried. We granted the Government's petition to resolve the conflict in the circuits, and we also granted O'Brien's cross-petition. We hold that the 1965 Amendment is constitutional both as enacted and as applied. We therefore vacate the judgment of the Court of Appeals and reinstate the judgment and sentence of the District Court without reaching the issue raised by O'Brien. . . .

I

. . . We note at the outset that the 1965 Amendment plainly does not abridge free speech on its face, and we do not understand O'Brien to argue otherwise. Amended §12(b)(3) on its face deals with conduct having no connection with speech. It prohibits the knowing destruction of certificates issued by the Selective Service System, and there is nothing necessarily expressive about such conduct. The Amendment does not distinguish between public and private destruction, and it does not punish only destruction engaged in for the purpose of expressing views. Compare Stromberg v. California, 283 U.S. 359 (1931). A law prohibiting destruction of Selective Service certificates no more abridges free speech on its face than a motor vehicle law prohibiting the destruction of drivers' licenses, or a tax law prohibiting the destruction of books and records.

O'Brien nonetheless argues that the 1965 Amendment is unconstitutional in its application to him, and is unconstitutional as enacted because what he calls the "purpose" of Congress was "to suppress freedom of speech." We consider these arguments separately.

II

O'Brien first argues that the 1965 Amendment is unconstitutional as applied to him because his act of burning his registration certificate was protected "symbolic speech" within the First Amendment. His argument is that the freedom of expression which the First Amendment guarantees includes all modes of "communication of ideas by conduct," and that his conduct is within this definition because he did it in "demonstration against the war and against the draft."

We cannot accept the view that an apparently limitless variety of conduct can be labeled "speech" whenever the person engaging in the conduct intends thereby to express an idea. However, even on the assumption that the alleged communicative element in O'Brien's conduct is sufficient to bring into play the First Amendment, it does not necessarily follow that the destruction of a registration certificate is constitutionally protected activity. This Court has held that when "speech" and "nonspeech" elements are combined in the same course of conduct, a sufficiently important governmental interest in regulating the nonspeech element can justify incidental limitations on First Amendment freedoms. To characterize the quality of the governmental interest which must appear, the Court has employed a variety of descriptive terms: compelling; substantial; subordinating; paramount; cogent; strong. Whatever imprecision inheres in these terms, we think it clear that a government regulation is sufficiently justified if it is within the constitutional power of the Government; if it furthers an important or substantial governmental interest; if the governmental interest is unrelated to the suppression of free expression; and if the incidental restriction on alleged First Amendment freedoms is no greater than is essential to the furtherance of that interest. We find that the 1965 Amendment to §12(b)(3) of the Universal Military Training and Service Act meets all of these requirements, and consequently that O'Brien can be constitutionally convicted for violating it.

The constitutional power of Congress to raise and support armies and to make all laws necessary and proper to that end is broad and sweeping. The power of Congress to classify and conscript manpower for military service is "beyond question." Pursuant to this power, Congress may establish a system of registration for individuals liable for training and service, and may require such individuals within reason to cooperate in the registration system. . . . And legislation to insure the continuing availability of issued certificates serves a legitimate and substantial purpose in the system's administration. . . .

1. . . . [T]he availability of the certificates . . . relieves the Selective Service System of the administrative burden it would otherwise have in verifying the registration and classification of all suspected delinquents. Further, since both certificates are in the nature of "receipts" . . . , it is in the interest of the just and

efficient administration of the system that they be continually available, in the event, for example, of a mix-up in the registrant's file. Additionally, in a time of national crisis, reasonable availability to each registrant of the two small cards assures a rapid and uncomplicated means for determining his fitness for immediate induction, no matter how distant in our mobile society he may be from his local board.

2. The information supplied on the certificates facilitates communication between registrants and local boards, simplifying the system and benefiting all concerned. To begin with, each certificate bears the address of the registrant's local board . . . [and] the registrant's Selective Service number. . . .

3. Both certificates carry continual reminders that the registrant must notify his local board of any change of address, and other specified changes in his status. . . .

4. The regulatory scheme involving Selective Service certificates includes clearly valid prohibitions against the alteration, forgery, or similar deceptive misuse of certificates. The destruction or mutilation of certificates obviously increases the difficulty of detecting and tracing abuses such as these. Further, a mutilated certificate might itself be used for deceptive purposes.

The many functions performed by Selective Service certificates establish beyond doubt that Congress has a legitimate and substantial interest in preventing their wanton and unrestrained destruction and assuring their continuing availability by punishing people who knowingly and willfully destroy or mutilate them. And we are unpersuaded that the pre-existence of the nonpossession regulations in any way negates this interest.

In the absence of a question as to multiple punishment, it has never been suggested that there is anything improper in Congress' providing alternative statutory avenues of prosecution to assure the effective protection of one and the same interest. Here, the pre-existing avenue of prosecution was not even statutory. Regulations may be modified or revoked from time to time by administrative discretion. Certainly, the Congress may change or supplement a regulation.

Equally important, a comparison of the regulations with the 1965 Amendment indicates that they protect overlapping but not identical governmental interests, and that they reach somewhat different classes of wrong-doers. . . . [For example, the] knowing destruction or mutilation of someone else's certificates would . . . violate the statute but not the nonpossession regulations. . . .

We perceive no alternative means that would more precisely and narrowly assure the continuing availability of issued Selective Service certificates than a law which prohibits their willful mutilation or destruction. . . . When O'Brien deliberately rendered unavailable his registration certificate, he willfully frustrated this governmental interest. For this noncommunicative impact of his conduct, and for nothing else, he was convicted.

The case at bar is therefore unlike one where the alleged governmental interest in regulating conduct arises in some measure because the communication allegedly integral to the conduct is itself thought to be harmful. . . .

III

O'Brien finally argues that the 1965 Amendment is unconstitutional as enacted because what he calls the "purpose" of Congress was "to suppress freedom of speech." We reject this argument because under settled principles the purpose of Congress, as O'Brien uses that term, is not a basis for declaring this legislation unconstitutional.

It is a familiar principle of constitutional law that this Court will not strike down an otherwise constitutional statute on the basis of an alleged illicit legislative motive. As the Court long ago stated: "The decisions of this court from the beginning lend no support whatever to the assumption that the judiciary may restrain the exercise of lawful power on the assumption that a wrongful purpose or motive has caused the power to be exerted." McCray v. United States, 195 U.S. 27, 56 (1904). . . .

Inquiries into congressional motives or purposes are a hazardous matter. When the issue is simply the interpretation of legislation, the Court will look to statements by legislators for guidance as to the purpose of the legislature, because the benefit to sound decision-making in this circumstance is thought sufficient to risk the possibility of misreading Congress' purpose. It is entirely a different matter when we are asked to void a statute that is, under well-settled criteria, constitutional on its face, on the basis of what fewer than a handful of Congressmen said about it. What motivates one legislator to make a speech about a statute is not necessarily what motivates scores of others to enact it, and the stakes are sufficiently high for us to eschew guesswork. We decline to void essentially on the ground that it is unwise legislation which Congress had the undoubted power to enact and which could be reenacted in its exact form if the same or another legislator made a "wiser" speech about it. . . .

We think it not amiss, in passing, to comment upon O'Brien's legislative purpose argument. . . . We note that if we were to examine legislative purpose in the instant case, we would be obliged to consider not only these statements [of Senator Thurmond and Congressmen Rivers and Bray] but also the more authoritative reports of the Senate and House Armed Services Committees. . . . While both reports make clear a concern with the "defiant" destruction of so-called "draft cards" and with "open" encouragement to others to destroy their cards, both reports also indicate that this concern stemmed from an apprehension that unrestrained destruction of cards would disrupt the smooth functioning of the Selective Service System.

IV

Since the 1965 Amendment to §12(b)(3) of the Universal Military Training and Service Act is constitutional as enacted and as applied, the Court of Appeals should have affirmed the judgment of conviction entered by the District Court. Accordingly, we vacate the judgment of the Court of Appeals, and reinstate the judgment and sentence of the District Court. This disposition makes unnecessary consideration of O'Brien's claim that the Court of Appeals erred in affirming his conviction on the basis of the nonpossession regulation.

It is so ordered.

Mr. Justice Marshall took no part in the consideration or decision of these cases.

HARLAN, J., concurring. . . .

I wish to make explicit my understanding that [the Court] does not foreclose consideration of First Amendment claims in those rare instances when an "incidental" restriction upon expression, imposed by a regulation which furthers an "important or substantial" governmental interest and satisfies the Court's other criteria, in practice has the effect of entirely preventing a "speaker" from reaching a significant audience with whom he could not otherwise lawfully communicate. This is not such a case, since O'Brien manifestly could have conveyed his message in many ways other than by burning his draft card.[31]

Discussion

1. Recall the Court's standard in *O'Brien*:

> [A] government regulation is sufficiently justified if it is within the constitutional power of the Government; if it furthers an important or substantial governmental interest; if the governmental interest is unrelated to the suppression of free expression; and if the incidental restriction on alleged First Amendment freedoms is no greater than is essential to the furtherance of that interest.

What does Justice Harlan's concurrence add to the Court's standard?

2. How did the Court conclude that the 1965 amendment furthered an "important or substantial government" interest? Did the Court have reason to believe that Congress had reached that conclusion? If not, why did the Court assume that it did?

3. Did the Court have reason to believe that Congress' purpose (i.e., the purpose of a majority of those who voted for the 1965 amendment) was or was not to suppress speech? If not, why did the Court assume that it was not?

4. Recall Chief Justice Marshall's statements in McCulloch v. Maryland, Chapter 1 supra:

> Let the end be legitimate, let it be within the scope of the constitution, and all means which are appropriate, which are plainly adapted to that end, which are not prohibited but consist with the spirit of the constitution, are constitutional. . . .
>
> Should Congress under the pretext of executing its powers, pass laws for the accomplishment of objects not entrusted to the government; it would become the painful duty of this tribunal, should a case requiring such a decision come before it, to say that such an act was not the law of the land.

How would a Marshallian judge approach the statute reviewed in *O'Brien?*

5. Suppose that you wish to burn your draft card to protest United States military involvement abroad. Citizens, as such, are not required to take an oath to "support, protect, and defend the Constitution of the United States." (Why not?) Suppose that you nonetheless feel bound by this oath. Does *O'Brien* finally determine that your protest is not protected under the Constitution?

31. Justice Douglas dissented on grounds unrelated to the First Amendment issues.

Chapter 9
Judicial Enforcement of Nontextually Based Fundamental Rights

In earlier portions of the book we paid close attention to the text and history of certain constitutional provisions for guidance in the process of judicial decision-making. To some extent this process resembles the methodology of statutory interpretation. We began approaching the equal protection clause in a similar way, but then turned rather quickly to issues that could not be resolved by reference to originalist sources. Instead, we examined "doctrines" or "principles" of equal protection that, though not necessarily inconsistent with the original understanding, were certainly not determined by it.

This chapter completes the journey away from originalism. We study a group of modern decisions — decisions from the second era of substantive due process — in which the Court has protected rights variously described in terms of privacy, procreational choice, sexual autonomy, lifestyle choices, family integrity, and intimate association.

Those who support judicial intervention usually acknowledge that these rights cannot be justified by simple reference to the text or specific historical purposes underlying given constitutional provisions. They argue, however, that these rights are discoverable through the methods of philosophy and adjudication or in the understandings of conventional morality. Critics frequently deny that such fundamental rights and conventional values exist; they deny, in any event, that judges are capable of identifing them with the precision necessary to resolve constitutional disputes, and they also deny that courts have the political authority to bind the polity to their conclusions. This debate is the central concern of this chapter.

I. Antecedents of Fundamental Rights Adjudication

The modern doctrine of fundamental rights adjudication is heir to three traditions. On the most general level, it continues a tradition of judicial protection of rights that goes back to the doctrines of "general constitutional law" examined in Part One. Second, it is an outgrowth of the resurgence of judicial protection of individual rights that followed World War II, which we have seen manifested in the expansion of the equal protection doctrine chronicled in Chapters 6 and 7 and in the incorporation of the Bill of Rights into the Fourteenth Amendment described in the Introduction to Part Two.

Third, notwithstanding the Court's protestations to the contrary, modern doctrine owes much to the *Lochner* era. (Recall that even Justice Holmes, dissenting in *Lochner,* conceded that the judiciary could legitimately invalidate "the natural outcome of a dominant opinion" when "a rational and fair man necessarily would admit that the statute proposed would infringe fundamental principles as they have been understood by the traditions of our people and our law.") During the heyday of economic due process, the Court intervened on several occasions to protect interests that had a significant noneconomic component. The language in two of the leading cases of the period, Meyer v. Nebraska, 262 U.S. 390 (1923), and Pierce v. Society of Sisters, 268 U.S. 510 (1925), suggests that the Court did not consider "economic" and "personal" interests discrete areas of concern.

The petitioner in *Meyer* was an instructor in a parochial school, convicted under a state law prohibiting the teaching of a foreign language to any child not yet in the eighth grade. (The law reflected the animosity against German-Americans during World War I.) Over the dissents of Justices Holmes and Sutherland, the Court struck down the law, viewing it as an incursion on Meyer's right "to teach and the right of parents to engage him so to instruct their children." Justice McReynolds, writing for the Court, described the concept of substantive due process:

> While this Court has not attempted to define with exactness the liberty thus guaranteed, the term has received much consideration and some of the included things have been definitely stated. Without doubt, it denotes not merely freedom from bodily restraint but also the right of the individual to contract, to engage in any of the common occupations of life, to acquire useful knowledge, to marry, establish a home and bring up children, to worship God according to the dictates of his own conscience, and generally to enjoy those privileges long recognized by common law as essential to the orderly pursuit of happiness by free men. The established doctrine is that this liberty may not be interfered with, under the guise of protecting the public interest, by legislative action which is arbitrary or without reasonable relation to some purpose within the competency of the State to effect. Determination by the legislature of what constitutes proper exercise of the police power is not final or conclusive but is subject to supervision by the courts . . .

Pierce v. Society of Sisters and the consolidated case of Pierce v. Hill Military Academy were suits brought by parochial and private schools challenging an Oregon statute that required children to attend public schools. Justice McReynolds wrote for a unanimous Court, invalidating the statute:

> The inevitable practical result of enforcing the Act under consideration would be destruction of appellees' primary schools, and perhaps all other private primary schools for normal children within the State of Oregon. These parties are engaged in a kind of undertaking not inherently harmful, but long regarded as useful and meritorious. Certainly there is nothing in the present records to indicate that they have failed to discharge their obligations to patrons, students or the State. And there are no peculiar circumstances or present emergencies which demand extraordinary measures relative to primary education.
>
> Under the doctrine of Meyer v. Nebraska, we think it entirely plain that the Act of 1922 unreasonably interferes with the liberty of parents and guardians to direct the upbringing and education of children under their control. As often heretofore pointed out, rights guaranteed by the Constitution may not be abridged by legislation which has no reasonable relation to some purpose within the competency of the

State. The fundamental theory of liberty upon which all governments in this Union repose excludes any general power of the State to standardize its children by forcing them to accept instruction from public teachers only. The child is not the mere creature of the State; those who nurture him and direct his destiny have the right, coupled with the high duty, to recognize and prepare him for additional obligations.

Appellees are corporations and therefore, it is said, they cannot claim for themselves the liberty which the Fourteenth Amendment guarantees. Accepted in the proper sense, this is true. But they have business and property for which they claim protection. These are threatened with destruction through the unwarranted compulsion which appellants are exercising over present and prospective patrons of their schools. And this court has gone very far to protect against loss threatened by such action. . . .

Generally it is entirely true, as urged by counsel, that no person in any business has such an interest in possible customers as to enable him to restrain exercise of proper power of the State upon the ground that he will be deprived of patronage. But the injunctions here sought are not against the exercise of any *proper* power. Plaintiffs asked protection against arbitrary, unreasonable and unlawful interference with their patrons and the consequent destruction of their business and property. Their interest is clear and immediate, within the rule approved in . . . cases where injunctions have issued to protect business enterprises against interference with the freedom of patrons or customers.

Although the Court abandoned economic due process in 1937, it was far more equivocal about the protection of noneconomic rights not specifically enumerated in the Bill of Rights. In Olsen v. Nebraska, 313 U.S. 236 (1941), an economic due process case considered in Chapter 5, Justice Douglas wrote, for a unanimous Court, that "[w]e are not concerned . . . with the wisdom, need, or appropriateness of the legislation. . . . In final analysis, the only constitutional prohibitions or restraints which respondents have suggested for the invalidation of this legislation are those notions of public policy embodied in earlier decisions of this Court but which, as Mr. Justice Holmes long admonished, should not be read into the Constitution."

One year later, however, Justice Douglas also wrote for the Court in Skinner v. Oklahoma, 316 U.S. 535 (1942), invalidating Oklahoma's Habitual Criminal Sterilization Act as a violation of the Equal Protection Clause. The Act required sterilization of a criminal offender upon a third conviction of a felony "involving moral turpitude." Several felonies, including embezzlement, were specifically exempted from serving as predicate offenses triggering the sterilization penalty. Skinner had been convicted over the course of a decade of three qualifying felonies — one chicken theft and two armed robberies — and was sentenced to sterilization. Justice Douglas wrote for the Court: "if we had here only a question as to the State's classification of crimes, such as embezzlement or larceny, no substantial federal question would be raised." Instead:

We are dealing here with legislation which involves one of the basic civil rights of man. Marriage and procreation are fundamental to the very existence and survival of the race. The power to sterilize, if exercised, may have subtle, far-reaching and devastating effects. In evil or reckless hands it can cause races or types which are inimical to the dominant group to wither and disappear. There is no redemption for the individual whom the law touches. Any experiment which the State conducts is to his irreparable injury. He is forever deprived of a basic liberty. . . . [S]trict scrutiny of the classification which a State makes in a sterilization law is essential, lest unwittingly, or otherwise, invidious discriminations are made against groups or types of individuals in violation of the constitutional guaranty of just and equal laws. . . . When the law lays an unequal hand on those who have committed intrinsically the same quality of offense and sterilizes one and not the other, it has made as invidious a discrimination as if it had selected a particular race or nationality for oppressive treatment.

Justice Douglas went on to contrast the crime of grand larceny (a felony covered by the statute) with the exempted crime of embezzlement to demonstrate that in many instances the distinctions were based on technical questions of property law. He concluded that there was no basis for believing that the "inheritability of criminal traits follows the neat legal distinctions which the law has marked between those two legal offenses."

Chief Justice Stone concurred in the result on the ground that the due process clause entitled petitioner to a hearing on the heritability of his criminal tendencies before he could be subjected to "so harsh a measure."[1] Justice Jackson agreed with both Douglas and Stone, adding that "[t]here are limits to the extent to which a legislatively represented majority may conduct biological experiments at the expense of the dignity and personality and natural powers of a minority — even those who have been guilty of what the majority defines as crimes."

During the 1950s, the Court also invoked the due process clause to impose substantive limitations on the criteria for the admission of lawyers to state bars.[2] And in Aptheker v. Secretary of State, 378 U.S. 500 (1964), the Court invalidated a law that effectively denied passports to all members of the Communist Party, holding that it "sweeps unnecessarily broadly and thereby invade[s] the area of protected freedoms," specifically the "right to travel abroad," which the Court held was a "personal liberty" implicit in the Fifth Amendment.

What is sometimes called the second era of substantive due process came into full flower in 1965 with Griswold v. Connecticut.

II. Methods of Fundamental Rights Adjudication

A. The Birth of the Second Era of Substantive Due Process

GRISWOLD v. CONNECTICUT
381 U.S. 479 (1965)
Appeal from the Supreme Court of Errors of Connecticut

DOUGLAS, J.

1. Cf. Buck v. Bell, 274 U.S. 200 (1927), in which the state provided for the sterilization of institutionalized mentally defective persons after a hearing at which, apparently, the issue of heritability could be contested. Petitioner challenged not the procedure but the substantive provision itself. Noting that she was feebleminded, the mother of an illegitimate feebleminded child, and the daughter of a feebleminded woman confined to the same state institution, Justice Holmes summarily dismissed the due process challenge with the comment that "three generations of imbeciles are enough." To the equal protection claim that the sterilization law applied only to persons confined in state institutions and not to the multitudes outside, Holmes responded that "it is the usual last resort of constitutional arguments to point out shortcomings of this sort."

2. See Schware v. Board of Bar Examiners, 353 U.S. 232 (1957). See also Konigsberg v. State Bar, 353 U.S. 252 (1957). Cf. Wieman v. Updegraff, 344 U.S. 183 (1952).

Appellant Griswold is Executive Director of the Planned Parenthood League of Connecticut. Appellant Buxton is a licensed physician and a professor at the Yale Medical School who served as Medical Director for the League at its Center in New Haven — a center open and operating from November 1 to November 10, 1961, when appellants were arrested.

They gave information, instruction, and medical advice to *married persons* as to the means of preventing conception. They examined the wife and prescribed the best contraceptive device or material for her use. Fees were usually charged, although some couples were serviced free.

The statutes whose constitutionality is involved in this appeal are §§53-32 and 54-196 of the General Statutes of Connecticut (1958 rev.). The former provides: "Any person who uses any drug, medicinal article or instrument for the purpose of preventing conception shall be fined not less than fifty dollars or imprisoned not less than sixty days nor more than one year or be both fined and imprisoned."

Section 54-196 provides: "Any person who assists, abets, counsels, causes, hires or commands another to commit any offense may be prosecuted and punished as if he were the principal offender."

The appellants were found guilty as accessories and fined $100 each, against the claim that the accessory statute as so applied violated the Fourteenth Amendment. The Appellate Division of the Circuit Court affirmed. The Supreme Court of Errors affirmed that judgment. We noted probable jurisdiction.

[The Court held that appellants had standing to raise the constitutional rights of the married people with whom they had a professional relationship. See Chapter 13 infra.]

Coming to the merits, we are met with a wide range of questions that implicate the Due Process Clause of the Fourteenth Amendment. Overtones of some arguments suggest that Lochner v. New York should be our guide. But we decline that invitation as we did in West Coast Hotel v. Parrish [and] Williamson v. Lee Optical Co. We do not sit as a super-legislature to determine the wisdom, need, and propriety of laws that touch economic problems, business affairs, or social conditions. This law, however, operates directly on an intimate relation of husband and wife and their physician's role in one aspect of that relation.

The association of people is not mentioned in the Constitution nor in the Bill of Rights. The right to educate a child in a school of the parents' choice — whether public or private or parochial — is also not mentioned. Nor is the right to study any particular subject or any foreign language. Yet the First Amendment has been construed to include certain of those rights.

By Pierce v. Society of Sisters the right to educate one's children as one chooses is made applicable to the States by the force of the First and Fourteenth Amendments. By Meyer v. Nebraska the same dignity is given the right to study the German language in a private school. In other words, the State may not consistently with the spirit of the First Amendment, contract the spectrum of available knowledge. The right of freedom of speech and press includes not only the right to utter or to print, but the right to distribute, the right to receive, the right to read and freedom of inquiry, freedom of thought, and freedom to teach — indeed the freedom of the entire university community. Without those peripheral rights the specific rights would be less secure. And so we reaffirm the principle of the *Pierce* and the *Meyer* cases.

In NAACP v. Alabama, 357 U.S. 449 (1958), we protected the "freedom to associate and privacy in one's associations," noting that freedom of association was a peripheral First Amendment right. Disclosure of membership lists of a constitutionally valid association, we held, was invalid, "as entailing the likelihood of a substantial restraint upon the exercise by petitioner's members of their right to freedom of association." In other words, the First Amendment has a penumbra where privacy is protected from governmental intrusion. In like context, we have protected forms of "association" that are not political in the customary sense but pertain to the social, legal, and economic benefit of the members. NAACP v. Button 371 U.S. 415 (1963).[3] In Schware v. Board of Bar Examiners, 353 U.S. 232 (1957), we held it not permissible to bar a lawyer from practice, because he had once been a member of the Communist Party. . . .

Those cases involved more than the "right of assembly" — a right that extends to all irrespective of their race or ideology. The right of "association," like the right of belief is more than the right to attend a meeting; it includes the right to express one's attitudes or philosophies by membership in a group or by affiliation with it or by other lawful means. Association in that context is a form of expression of opinion; and while it is not expressly included in the First Amendment its existence is necessary in making the express guarantees fully meaningful.

The foregoing cases suggest that specific guarantees in the Bill of Rights have penumbras, formed by emanations from those guarantees that help give them life and substance. See Poe v. Ullman, 367 U.S. 497, 516-522 (1961) (dissenting opinion). Various guarantees create zones of privacy. The right of association contained in the penumbra of the First Amendment is one, as we have seen. The Third Amendment in its prohibition against the quartering of soldiers "in any house" in time of peace without the consent of the owner is another facet of that privacy. The Fourth Amendment explicitly affirms the "right of the people to be secure in their persons, houses, papers, and effects, against unreasonable searches and seizures." The Fifth Amendment in its Self-Incrimination Clause enables the citizen to create a zone of privacy which government may not force him to surrender to his detriment. The Ninth Amendment provides: "The enumeration in the Constitution, of certain rights, shall not be construed to deny or disparage others retained by the people."

The Fourth and Fifth Amendments were described in Boyd v. United States, 116 U.S. 616 (1886), as protection against all governmental invasions "of the sanctity of a man's home and the privacies of life." We recently referred in Mapp v. Ohio, 367 U.S. 643 (1961), to the Fourth Amendment as creating a "right to privacy, no less important than any other right carefully and particularly reserved to the people.". . .

The present case, then, concerns a relationship lying within the zone of privacy created by several fundamental constitutional guarantees. And it concerns a law which, in forbidding the *use* of contraceptives rather than regulating their manufacture or sale, seeks to achieve its goals by means having a maximum destructive impact upon that relationship. Such a law cannot stand in light of the familiar principle, so often applied by this Court, that a "governmental purpose to control or prevent activities constitutionally subject to state regulation may not be achieved by means which sweep unnecessarily broadly and thereby invade the

3. NAACP v. Button held that Virginia's prohibition of the solicitation of legal or professional business could not be employed to prevent the legal activities of the NAACP and NAACP Legal Defense and Educational Fund.

area of protected freedoms." NAACP v. Alabama. Would we allow the police to search the sacred precincts of marital bedrooms for telltale signs of the use of contraceptives? The very idea is repulsive to the notions of privacy surrounding the marriage relationship.

We deal with a right of privacy older than the Bill of Rights — older than our political parties, older than our school system. Marriage is a coming together for better or for worse, hopefully enduring, and intimate to the degree of being sacred. It is an association that promotes a way of life, not causes; a harmony in living, not political faiths; a bilateral loyalty, not commercial or social projects. Yet it is an association for as noble a purpose as any involved in our prior decisions.

Reversed.

GOLDBERG, J., joined by Warren, C.J., and Brennan, J., concurring.

I agree with the Court that Connecticut's birth-control law unconstitutionally intrudes upon the right of marital privacy, and I join in its opinion and judgment. Although I have not accepted the view that "due process" as used in the Fourteenth Amendment incorporates all of the first eight Amendments, I do agree that the concept of liberty protects those personal rights that are fundamental, and is not confined to the specific terms of the Bill of Rights. My conclusion that the concept of liberty is not so restricted and that it embraces the right of marital privacy though that right is not mentioned explicitly in the Constitution is supported . . . by the language and history of the Ninth Amendment. . . .

The Ninth Amendment . . . was proffered to quiet expressed fears that a bill of specifically enumerated rights could not be sufficiently broad to cover all essential rights and that the specific mention of certain rights would be interpreted as a denial that others were protected. . . . [T]he Framers did not intend that the first eight amendments be construed to exhaust the basic and fundamental rights which the Constitution guaranteed to the people.

. . . To hold that a right so basic and fundamental and so deep-rooted in our society as the right of privacy in marriage may be infringed because that right is not guaranteed in so many words by the first eight amendments to the Constitution is to ignore the Ninth Amendment and to give it no effect whatsoever. . . .

I do not mean to imply that the Ninth Amendment is applied against the States by the Fourteenth. Nor do I mean to state that the Ninth Amendment constitutes an independent source of rights protected from infringement by either the States or the Federal Government. Rather the Ninth Amendment simply lends strong support to the view that the "liberty" protected by the Fifth and Fourteenth Amendments from infringement by the Federal Government or the States is not restricted to rights specifically mentioned in the first eight amendments. . . .

In determining which rights are fundamental, judges are not left at large to decide cases in light of their personal and private notions. Rather, they must look to the "traditions and [collective] conscience of our people" to determine whether a principle is "so rooted [there] . . . as to be ranked as fundamental." The inquiry is whether a right involved "is of such a character that it cannot be denied without violating those 'fundamental principles of liberty and justice which lie at the base of all our civil and political institutions.' "

The entire fabric of the Constitution and the purposes that clearly underlie its specific guarantees demonstrate that the rights to marital privacy and to marry and raise a family are of similar order and magnitude as the fundamental rights specifically protected.

Although the Constitution does not speak in so many words of the right of privacy in marriage, I cannot believe that it offers these fundamental rights no protection. The fact that no particular provision of the Constitution explicitly forbids the State from disrupting the traditional relation of the family — a relation as old and as fundamental as our entire civilization — surely does not show that the Government was meant to have the power to do so. . . .

The logic of the dissents would sanction federal or state legislation that seems to me even more plainly unconstitutional than the statute before us. Surely the Government, absent a showing of a compelling subordinating state interest, could not decree that all husbands and wives must be sterilized after two children have been born to them. Yet by their reasoning such an invasion of marital privacy would not be subject to constitutional challenge because, while it might be "silly," no provision of the Constitution specifically prevents the Government from curtailing the marital right to bear children and raise a family. . . .

In a long series of cases this Court has held that where fundamental personal liberties are involved, they may not be abridged by the States simply on a showing that a regulatory statute has some rational relationship to the effectuation of a proper state purpose. "Where there is a significant encroachment upon personal liberty, the State may prevail only upon showing a subordinating interest which is compelling," Bates v. Little Rock, 361 U.S. 516 (1960). The law must be shown "necessary, and not merely rationally related, to the accomplishment of a permissible state policy." McLaughlin v. Florida, 379 U.S. 184 (1964).

Although the Connecticut birth-control law obviously encroaches upon a fundamental personal liberty, the State does not show that the law serves any "subordinating [state] interest which is compelling" or that it is "necessary . . . to the accomplishment of a permissible state policy." The State, at most, argues that there is some rational relation between this statute and what is admittedly a legitimate subject of state concern — the discouraging of extra-marital relations. It says that preventing the use of birth-control devices by married persons helps prevent the indulgence by some in such extra-marital relations. The rationality of this justification is dubious, particularly in light of the admitted widespread availability to all persons in the State of Connecticut, unmarried as well as married, of birth-control devices for the prevention of disease, as distinguished from the prevention of conception. But, in any event, it is clear that the state interest in safeguarding marital fidelity can be served by a more discriminately tailored statute, which does not, like the present one, sweep unnecessarily broadly, reaching far beyond the evil sought to be dealt with and intruding upon the privacy of all married couples. . . . The State of Connecticut does have statutes, the constitutionality of which is beyond doubt, which prohibit adultery and fornication. These statutes demonstrate that means for achieving the same basic purpose of protecting marital fidelity are available to Connecticut without the need to "invade the area of protected freedoms." . . .

In sum, I believe that the right of privacy in the marital relation is fundamental and basic — a personal right "retained by the people" within the meaning of the Ninth Amendment. Connecticut cannot constitutionally abridge this fundamental right, which is protected by the Fourteenth Amendment from infringement by the States. I agree with the Court that petitioners' convictions must therefore be reversed. . . .

[Justice Harlan concurred in the judgment in *Griswold,* stating that "the proper constitutional inquiry in this case is whether this Connecticut statute infringes the Due Process Clause of the Fourteenth Amendment because the enactment violates basic values 'implicit in the concept of ordered liberty.' . . . For reasons stated at length in my dissenting opinion in Poe v. Ullman, 367 U.S. 497 (1961), I believe that it does." *Poe* was an earlier challenge to the Connecticut anticontraception law, in which the Court dismissed the complainants' appeal on procedural grounds. In one of four dissenting opinions in *Poe,* Justice Harlan expressed his views on the merits:]

HARLAN, J., dissenting [in Poe v. Ullman]. . . .

Were due process merely a procedural safeguard it would fail to reach those situations where the deprivation of life, liberty or property was accomplished by legislation which by operating in the future could, given even the fairest possible procedure in application to individuals, nevertheless destroy the enjoyment of all three. Thus the guaranties of due process . . . have in this country "become bulwarks also against arbitrary legislation."

However it is not the particular enumeration of rights in the first eight Amendments which spells out the reach of Fourteenth Amendment due process, but rather, as was suggested in another context long before the adoption of that Amendment, those concepts which are considered to embrace those rights "which are . . . *fundamental;* which belong . . . to the citizens of all free governments," Corfield v. Coryell, 4 Wash. C.C. 371, 380, for "the purposes [of securing] which men enter into society," Calder v. Bull, 3 Dall. 386, 388. . . .

Due process has not been reduced to any formula; its content cannot be determined by reference to any code. The best that can be said is that through the course of this Court's decisions it has represented the balance which our Nation, built upon postulates of respect for the liberty of the individual, has struck between that liberty and the demands of organized society. If the supplying of content to this Constitutional concept has of necessity been a rational process, it certainly has not been one where judges have felt free to roam where unguided speculation might take them. The balance of which I speak is the balance struck by this country, having regard to what history teaches are the traditions from which it developed as well as the traditions from which it broke. That tradition is a living thing. . . .

It is this outlook which has led the Court continuingly to perceive distinctions in the imperative character of Constitutional provisions, since that character must be discerned from a particular provision's larger context. And inasmuch as this context is one not of words, but of history and purposes, the full scope of the liberty guaranteed by the Due Process Clause cannot be found in or limited by the precise terms of the specific guarantees elsewhere provided in the Constitution. This "liberty" is not a series of isolated points pricked out in terms of the taking of property; the freedom of speech, press, and religion; the right to keep and bear arms; the freedom from unreasonable searches and seizures; and so on. It is a rational continuum which, broadly speaking, includes a freedom from all substantial arbitrary impositions and purposeless restraints, see Allgeyer v. Louisiana, 165 U.S. 578; Holden v. Hardy, 169 U.S. 366; Nebbia v. New York, 291

U.S. 502; Skinner v. Oklahoma, 316 U.S. 535, 544 (concurring opinion); Schware v. Board of Bar Examiners, 353 U.S. 232, and which also recognizes, what a reasonable and sensitive judgment must, that certain interests require particularly careful scrutiny of the state needs asserted to justify their abridgment. . . .

Precisely what is involved here is this: the state is asserting the right to enforce its moral judgments by intruding upon the most intimate details of the marital relation with the full power of the criminal law. Potentially, this could allow the deployment of all the incidental machinery of the criminal law, arrests, searches and seizures; inevitably, it must mean at the very least the lodging of criminal charges, a public trial, and testimony as to the corpus delicti. Nor could any imaginable elaboration of presumptions, testimonial privileges, or other safeguards, alleviate the necessity for testimony as to the mode and manner of the married couples' sexual relations, or at least the opportunity for the accused to make denial of the charges. In sum, the statute allows the State to enquire into, prove and punish married people for the private use of their marital intimacy.

. . . This enactment involves what, by common understanding throughout the English-speaking world, must be granted to be a most fundamental aspect of "liberty," the privacy of the home in its most basic sense, and it is this which requires that the statute be subjected to "strict scrutiny."

That aspect of liberty which embraces the concept of the privacy of the home receives explicit Constitutional protection at two places only. These are the Third Amendment, relating to the quartering of soldiers, and the Fourth Amendment, prohibiting unreasonable searches and seizures. While these Amendments reach only the Federal Government, this Court has held in the strongest terms . . . that the concept of "privacy" embodied in the Fourth Amendment is part of the "ordered liberty" assured against state action by the Fourteenth Amendment.

It is clear, of course, that this Connecticut statute does not invade the privacy of the home in the usual sense, since the invasion involved here may, and doubtless usually would, be accomplished without any physical intrusion whatever into the home. What the statute undertakes to do, however, is to create a crime which is grossly offensive to this privacy, while the Constitution refers only to methods of ferreting out substantive wrongs, and the procedure it requires presupposes that substantive offenses may be committed and sought out in the privacy of the home. But such an analysis forecloses any claim to Constitutional protection against this form of deprivation of privacy, only if due process in this respect is limited to what is explicitly provided in the Constitution, divorced from the rational purposes, historical roots, and subsequent developments of the relevant provisions. . . .

It would surely be an extreme instance of sacrificing substance to form were it to be held that the Constitutional principle of privacy against arbitrary official intrusion comprehends only physical invasions by the police. . . . [I]f the physical curtilage of the home is protected, it is surely as a result of solicitude to protect the privacies of the life within. Certainly the safeguarding of the home does not follow merely from the sanctity of property rights. The home derives its pre-eminence as the seat of family life. . . .

Of [the] whole "private realm of family life" it is difficult to imagine what is more private or more intimate than a husband and wife's marital relations. . . . [T]he intimacy of husband and wife is necessarily an essential and accepted feature of the institution of marriage, an institution which the State not only must allow, but which always and in every age it has fostered and protected. It is one thing when the State exerts its power either to forbid extramarital sexuality altogether, or to say who may marry, but it is quite another when, having acknowledged a marriage and the intimacies inherent in it, undertakes to regulate by means of the criminal law the details of that intimacy. . . .

Since, as it appears to me, the statute marks an abridgment of important fundamental liberties protected by the Fourteenth Amendment, it will not do to urge in justification of that abridgment simply that the statute is rationally related to the effectuation of a proper state purpose. A closer scrutiny and stronger justification than that are required. . . . To me the very circumstance that Connecticut has not chosen to press the enforcement of this statute against individual users, while it nevertheless persists in asserting its right to do so at any time — in effect a right to hold this statute as an imminent threat to the privacy of the households of the State — conduces to the inference either that it does not consider the policy of the statute a very important one, or that it does not regard the means it has chosen for its effectuation as appropriate or necessary.

But conclusive, in my view, is the utter novelty of this enactment. Although the Federal Government and many States have at one time or other had on their books statutes forbidding or regulating the distribution of contraceptives, none, so far as I can find, has made the *use* of contraceptives a crime. . . .

WHITE, J., concurring [in *Griswold*].

In my view this Connecticut law as applied to married couples deprives them of "liberty" without due process of law, as that concept is used in the Fourteenth Amendment. I therefore concur in the judgment of the Court reversing these convictions under Connecticut's aiding and abetting statute. . . .

[T]his is not the first time this Court has had occasion to articulate that the liberty entitled to protection under the Fourteenth Amendment includes the right "to marry, establish a home and bring up children," Meyer v. Nebraska, and "the liberty . . . to direct the upbringing and education of children," Pierce v. Society of Sisters, and that these are among "the basic civil rights of man," Skinner v. Oklahoma. . . . These decisions affirm that there is a "realm of family life which the state cannot enter" without substantial justification. Prince v. Massachusetts, 321 U.S. 158 (1944). Surely the right invoked in this case, to be free of regulation of the intimacies of the marriage relationship, "come[s] to this Court with a momentum for respect lacking when appeal is made to liberties which derive merely from shifting economic arrangements.". . .

An examination of the justification offered, however, cannot be avoided by saying that the Connecticut anti-use statute invades a protected area of privacy and association or that it demeans the marriage relationship. The nature of the right invaded is pertinent, to be sure, for statutes regulating sensitive areas of liberty do, under the cases of this Court, require "strict scrutiny," Skinner v. Oklahoma, and "must be viewed in the light of less drastic means for achieving the same basic purpose." "Where there is a significant encroachment upon personal liberty, the State may prevail only upon showing a subordinating interest which is compelling." But such statutes, if reasonably necessary for the effectuation of a legitimate and substantial state interest, and not arbitrary or capricious in application, are not invalid under the Due Process Clause.

As I read the opinions of the Connecticut courts and the argument of Connecticut in this Court, the State claims but one justification for its anti-use statute. . . . [T]he statute is said to serve the State's policy against all forms of promiscuous or illicit sexual relationships, be they premarital or extramarital, concededly a permissible and legitimate legislative goal.

Without taking issue with the premise that the fear of conception operates as a deterrent to such relationships in addition to the criminal proscriptions Connecticut has against such conduct, I wholly fail to see how the ban on the use of contraceptives by married couples in any way reinforces the State's ban on illicit sexual relationships. Connecticut does not bar the importation or possession of contraceptive devices; they are not considered contraband material under state law, and their availability in that State is not seriously disputed. The only way Connecticut seeks to limit or control the availability of such devices is through its general aiding and abetting statute whose operation in this context has been quite obviously ineffective and whose most serious use has been against birth-control clinics rendering advice to married, rather than unmarried, persons. . . . Moreover, it would appear that the sale of contraceptives to prevent disease is plainly legal under Connecticut law.

In these circumstances one is rather hard pressed to explain how the ban on use by married persons in any way prevents use of such devices by persons engaging in illicit sexual relations and thereby contributes to the State's policy against such relationships. . . . At most the broad ban is of marginal utility to the declared objective. A statute limiting its prohibition on use to persons engaging in the prohibited relationship would serve the end posited by Connecticut in the same way, and with the same effectiveness, or ineffectiveness, as the broad anti-use statute under attack in this case. I find nothing in this record justifying the sweeping scope of this statute, with its telling effect on the freedoms of married persons, and therefore conclude that it deprives such persons of liberty without due process of law.

BLACK, J., joined by Stewart, J., dissenting. . . .

In order that there may be no room at all to doubt why I vote as I do, I feel constrained to add that the law is every bit as offensive to me as it is to my Brethren of the majority. . . . There is no single one of the graphic and eloquent strictures and criticisms fired at the policy of this Connecticut law either by the Court's opinion or by those of my concurring Brethren to which I cannot subscribe — except their conclusion that the evil qualities they see in the law make it unconstitutional. . . .

The Court talks about a constitutional "right of privacy" as though there is some constitutional provision or provisions forbidding any law ever to be passed which might abridge the "privacy" of individuals. But there is not. There are, of course, guarantees in certain specific constitutional provisions which are designed in part to protect privacy at certain times and places with respect to certain activities. Such, for example, is the Fourth Amendment's guarantee against "unreasonable searches and seizures." But I think it belittles that Amendment to talk about it as though it protects nothing but "privacy." . . .

One of the most effective ways of diluting or expanding a constitutionally guaranteed right is to substitute for the crucial word or words of a constitutional guarantee another word or words, more or less flexible and more or less restricted in meaning. . . . "Privacy" is a broad, abstract and ambiguous concept which can easily be shrunken in meaning but which can also, on the other hand, easily be interpreted as a constitutional ban against many things other than searches and seizures. . . . For these reasons I get nowhere in this case by talk about a constitutional "right of privacy" as an emanation from one or more constitutional provisions. I like my privacy as well as the next one, but I am nevertheless compelled to admit that government has a right to invade it unless prohibited by some specific constitutional provision. . . .

I discuss the due process and Ninth Amendment arguments together because on analysis they turn out to be the same thing — merely using different words to claim for this Court and the federal judiciary power to invalidate any legislative act which the judges find irrational, unreasonable or offensive. . . .

Of the cases on which my Brothers White and Goldberg rely so heavily, undoubtedly the reasoning of two of them supports their result here — as would that of a number of others which they do not bother to name, e.g., Lochner v. New York, Coppage v. Kansas, and Adkins v. Children's Hospital. The two they do cite and quote from, Meyer v. Nebraska, and Pierce v. Society of Sisters, were both decided in opinions by Mr. Justice McReynolds which elaborated the same natural law due process philosophy found in Lochner v. New York, one of the cases on which he relied in *Meyer,* along with such other long-discredited decisions as, e.g., Adkins v. Children's Hospital. . . . Without expressing an opinion as to whether either of those cases reached a correct result in light of our later decisions applying the First Amendment to the States through the Fourteenth, I merely point out that the reasoning stated in *Meyer* and *Pierce* was the same natural law due process philosophy which many later opinions repudiated, and which I cannot accept. . . .

My Brother Goldberg has adopted the recent discovery that the Ninth Amendment as well as the Due Process Clause can be used by this Court as authority to strike down all state legislation which this Court thinks violates "fundamental principles of liberty and justice," or is contrary to the "traditions and [collective] conscience of our people." He also states, without proof satisfactory to me, that in making decisions on this basis judges will not consider "their personal and private notions." One may ask how they can avoid considering them. Our Court certainly has no machinery with which to take a Gallup Poll. And the scientific miracles of this age have not yet produced a gadget which the Court can use to determine what traditions are rooted in the "[collective] conscience of our people." Moreover, one would certainly have to look far beyond the language of the Ninth Amendment to find that the Framers vested in this Court any such awesome veto powers over lawmaking, either by the States or by the Congress. . . . That Amendment was passed not to broaden the powers of this Court or any other department of "the General Government," but, as every student of history knows, to assure the people that the Constitution in all its provisions was intended to limit the Federal Government to the powers granted expressly or by necessary implication. . . .

The Due Process Clause with an "arbitrary and capricious" or "shocking to the conscience" formula was liberally used by this Court to strike down economic legislation in the early decades of this century, threatening, many people thought, the tranquility and stability of the Nation. That formula, based on subjective considerations of "natural justice," is no less dangerous when used to enforce this Court's view about personal rights than those about economic rights. . . .

STEWART, J., joined by Black, J., dissenting.

Since 1879 Connecticut has had on its books a law which forbids the use of contraceptives by anyone. I think this is an uncommonly silly law. . . . But we are not asked in this case to say whether we think this law is unwise, or even asinine. We are asked to hold that it violates the United States Constitution. And that I cannot do. . . .

As to the First, Third, Fourth, and Fifth Amendments, I can find nothing in any of them to invalidate this Connecticut law, even assuming that all those Amendments are fully applicable against the States. It has not even been argued that this is a law "respecting an establishment of religion, or prohibiting the free exercise thereof." And surely, unless the solemn process of constitutional adjudication is to descend to the level of a play on words, there is not involved here any abridgment of "the freedom of speech, or of the press; or the right of the people peaceably to assemble, and to petition the Government for a redress of grievances." No soldier has been quartered in any house. There has been no search, and no seizure. Nobody has been compelled to be a witness against himself.

The Court also quotes the Ninth Amendment, and my Brother Goldberg's concurring opinion relies heavily upon it. But to say that the Ninth Amendment has anything to do with this case is to turn somersaults with history. . . .

What provision of the Constitution, then, does make this state law invalid? The Court says it is the right of privacy "created by several fundamental constitutional guarantees." With all deference, I can find no such general right of privacy in the Bill of Rights, in any other part of the Constitution, or in any case ever before decided by this Court.

At the oral argument in this case we were told that the Connecticut law does not "conform to current community standards." But it is not the function of this Court to decide cases on the basis of community standards. We are here to decide cases "agreeably to the Constitution and laws of the United States." . . .

Discussion

1. Why does Justice Douglas appeal to the text instead of adopting Justice Harlan's nontextualist approach? Does Justice Douglas's analysis of the passages he cites provide sufficient "penumbral" support for his opinion? Under the Fourth Amendment, for example, the State may invade an individual's privacy when it presents to a judge a very good reason ("probable cause") and receives a warrant authorizing the invasion. Would the police, in Douglas's view, be foreclosed from searching the "sacred precincts of marital bedrooms" for evidence of ordinary crimes, like bank robberies? Note also that the Fifth Amendment has been construed (over Justice Douglas's dissent) to allow the state to compel a person to testify so long as she is granted "immunity" from having her testimony used against her.

2. Does Justice Douglas's analysis in *Griswold* imply, by analogy, that vested property rights and liberty of contract are protected by the penumbras of the contract clause and the Fifth Amendment? That is, does *Griswold* provide an independent foundation for the decisions of the *Lochner* era?

3. Identify all of the *sources,* besides the "penumbras" of the Bill of Rights, from which the Court and concurring Justices establish the liberty interest of a married couple in choosing whether to use contraceptives. Identify all of the *methods* of decisionmaking explicitly or implicitly invoked by the Court and concurring Justices. How similar and different are these sources and methods from those you encountered in adjudication under the equal protection clause? How do they compare with those of common law adjudication that you have encountered in other courses such as torts and contracts?

4. What is the nature of the interest in "privacy" protected by *Griswold?* The locational interest in one's home? The interest in freedom to choose when and to whom to disclose personal information? The interest in the integrity of the marital relationship (or of *any* intimate relationship)? The interest in autonomy, that is, in freedom from governmental control? Which of these interests are implicit in the various opinions?

5. How does Justice White's argument in *Griswold* differ from those of his concurring colleagues? How might Justice White respond if the law's stated purpose was to increase the Connecticut birth rate, an important State interest given that Connecticut's representation in Congress (and thus its ability to protect its interests at the national level) depends on the size of its population?

6. Why isn't the legislature the best institution to determine "what traditions are rooted in the '[collective] conscience of our people' "? How might Justice Harlan respond to this question? Although Justice Harlan rejects "unguided speculation" by judges, how might he recognize "guided speculation"?

7. *Subsequent decisions regarding marriage and contraception.* Several of the *Griswold* opinions emphasize the unique importance of the marital relationship. Later cases both applied *Griswold* outside the marital setting and broadened the protection surrounding the marital relationship.

In Eisenstadt v. Baird, 405 U.S. 438 (1972), the Court invoked the equal protection rational relation standard to overturn appellee's conviction for distributing contraceptive foam to individuals, both married and unmarried, at a public meeting at Boston University. After quoting the lower court's opinion that prohibiting access to contraceptive devices might violate an individual's fundamental rights, the Court stated:

> We need not and do not, however, decide that important question in this case because, whatever the rights of the individual to access to contraceptives may be, the rights must be the same for the unmarried and the married alike.
>
> If under *Griswold* the distribution of contraceptives to married persons cannot be prohibited, a ban on distribution to unmarried persons would be equally impermissible. It is true that in *Griswold* the right of privacy in question inhered in the marital relationship. Yet the marital couple is not an independent entity with a mind and heart of its own, but an association of two individuals each with a separate intellectual and emotional makeup. If the right of privacy means anything, it is the right of the *individual,* married or single, to be free from unwarranted governmental intrusion into matters so fundamentally affecting a person as the decision whether to bear or beget a child.

Five years later, in Carey v. Population Services International, 431 U.S. 648 (1977), the Court struck down a New York law prohibiting the sale of contraceptives to minors under 16, together with an ancillary provision (most likely designed to assure enforcement of the age regulation) forbidding anyone other than a licensed pharmacist to sell even nonprescription contraceptives to persons of any age. With respect to the latter provision, Justice Brennan wrote for the Court that "*Griswold* may no longer be read as holding only that a State may not prohibit a married couple's use of contraceptives." Instead, "the teaching of *Griswold* is that the Constitution protects individual decisions in matters of childbearing from unjustified intrusion by the State. Restrictions on the distribution of contraceptives clearly burden the freedom to make such decisions." New York's limitation on the distribution of nonprescription contraceptives "clearly imposes a significant burden on the right of the individuals to use contraceptives if they choose to do so. . . ." Chief Justice Burger and Justice Rehnquist dissented.

Zablocki v. Redhail, 434 U.S. 374 (1978), struck down a Wisconsin statute conditioning marriage by a resident obligated to support a minor not in his custody upon a showing that support had been provided and that any covered children were not nor were likely to become public charges. Justice Marshall, citing various opinions in which the Court had found the right to marry to be fundamental, concluded that the equal protection clause requires "critical examination of the state interests advanced" in support of a classification based on the exercise of that right. He rejected the state's asserted interest in counselling persons with child-support obligations before they incurred further obligations, noting that the statute neither required counselling nor automatically permitted marriage after counselling was completed. He also rejected Wisconsin's presentation of the law as a rational means of enforcing support obligations, noting that the state had other means for enforcing such obligations and that the statute was poorly suited to this goal. Justice Stewart, concurring in the judgment, would have invalidated the law under the due process rather than the equal protection clause. Justice Powell, also concurring in the judgment, accepted the need for heightened scrutiny (a "fair and substantial relationship") under the due process and equal protection clauses because the intrusion on the marriage decision was "contrary to deeply rooted traditions" and because it excluded indigents from a process in which the state exercised a monopoly.[4] Justice Rehnquist wrote a lone dissent.

III. Theories of Fundamental Rights Adjudication: A Basic Outline[5]

Griswold and its progeny inspired a large outpouring of scholarly literature regarding the assignment of substantive meaning to the due process clause or, its functional equivalent, the determination that certain "fundamental interests" require strict scrutiny under the equal protection clause. We consider seriatim a number of approaches to the debate.

4. See also Boddie v. Connecticut, 401 U.S. 371 (1971), p.1142 infra.

5. Much of this section is based on Paul Brest, The Fundamental Rights Controversy: The Essential Contradictions of Normative Constitutional Law Scholarship, 90 Yale L.J. 1063 (1981).

A. Conventional Morality

One view holds that the Court's task in cases such as *Griswold* is to ascertain and enforce society's conventional morality. The adjective is crucial, for this approach in no way implies the existence of trans-social norms of "natural law" or "natural justice." Philip Bobbitt has coined the term "ethical argument" to refer to

> constitutional argument whose force relies on a characterization of American institutions and the role within them of the American people. . . . [E]thical arguments are not *moral* arguments. Ethical constitutional arguments do not claim that a particular solution is right or wrong in any sense larger than that the solution comports with the sort of people we are and the means we have chosen to solve political and customary constitutional problems.[6]

On this view, even if individuals have no intrinsic natural rights, they are entitled to treatment consistent with whatever moral principles their society holds. The rationale for judicial intervention is that although legislation generally reflects conventional morality, the legislative process is subject to certain defects. Thus Harry Wellington writes:

> [T]he environment in which legislators function makes difficult a bias-free perspective. It is often hard for law-makers to resist pressure from their constituents who react to particular events . . . with a passion that conflicts with common morality. . . . Nor is it an easy matter for legislators to find conventional morality when there are well-organized interest groups insisting on moral positions of their own.[7]

Michael Perry agrees with Wellington and emphasizes that the relevant question for a court is "not whether the conduct is disapproved by conventional morality, but whether conventional morality supports state enforcement of its disapproval through criminal and civil sanctions." For example, "the issue is not whether conventional morality disfavors sodomy, but only whether it supports treating sodomy as an issue implicating the *public* morals, by criminalizing consensual sodomous conduct by adults in private."[8] Professor Wellington might be read to suggest that judicial review provides a "sober second look" at laws passed in the heat of legislative passion. In this context, consider Sanford Levinson's thesis concerning judicial explication of the inchoate rights protected by the Ninth Amendment.[9] Although conceding that "the judiciary [may not be the] better interpreter of 'our' political tradition than a legislature," he submits that judges might nevertheless "confront [legislators] with the implications of their decisions and . . . ask if they are really willing to accept the consequences." On this view, courts would inquire whether there is "good reason to believe that the legislator or any other primary decision-maker in fact considered the implications of the given piece of legislation for values that do indeed seem central to 'our' tradition

6. Philip Bobbitt, Constitutional Fate 94-95 (1982).

7. Harry Wellington, Common Law Rules and Constitutional Double Standards: Some Notes on Adjudication, 83 Yale L.J. 221, 248-249 (1973).

8. Michael Perry, Substantive Due Process Revisited: Reflections on (and Beyond) Recent Cases, 71 Nw. U.L. Rev. 417, 477 (1977).

9. Sanford Levinson, Constitutional Rhetoric and the Ninth Amendment, 64 Chi.-Kent L. Rev. 131, 156-158 (1988).

. . . [and if so,] did the consideration happen recently enough in the past that we can recognize the legislators" as truly sharing our own social world? Levinson notes that, in striking down legislation, the Court would effectively remand it to the legislature for further, presumably more thoughtful, consideration.

How might a judge identify society's conventional morality? Wellington writes that judges must "become sensitive to it, experience widely, read extensively, and ruminate, reflect, and analyze situations that seem to call moral obligations into play."[10] Other commentators have supplemented intuitive methods for ascertaining conventional morality by drawing on the methods of the social sciences, including public opinion polls. Although the Court has not made much explicit use of these methods in fundamental rights cases, some Justices invoked social science data in addressing the question of whether the death penalty was inconsistent with contemporary standards of decency. See Furman v. Georgia, 408 U.S. 238 (1972).

One of the more recent debates on the proper methodology for discerning fundamental norms arose in Stanford v. Kentucky, 492 U.S. 397 (1989). The doctrinal issue was whether the execution of 16- and 17-year-olds violated the Eighth Amendment prohibition of cruel and unusual punishment. Petitioners invoked Trop v. Dulles, 356 U.S. 86 (1958), which construed the Eighth Amendment to embody the "evolving standards of decency that mark the progress of a maturing society." Justice Scalia, writing for the Court, explained that:

> [T]his court has "not confined the prohibition embodied in the Eighth Amendment to 'barbarous' methods that were generally outlawed in the 18th century," but instead has interpreted the Amendment "in a flexible and dynamic manner." In determining what standards have "evolved," however, we have looked not to our own conceptions of decency, but to those of modern American society as a whole.[a] . . .
>
> "[F]irst" among the " 'objective indicia that reflect the public attitude toward a given sanction' " are statutes passed by society's elected representatives. . . . It is not the burden of [a state] to establish a national consensus approving what their citizens have voted to do; rather, it is the "heavy burden" of petitioners to establish a national consensus *against* it. As far as the primary and most reliable indication of consensus is concerned — the pattern of enacted laws — petitioners have failed to carry that burden. . . .
>
> [Petitioners] argue, however, that even if the laws themselves do not establish a settled consensus, the application of the laws does. That contemporary society views capital punishment of 16- and 17-year-old offenders as inappropriate is demonstrated, they say, by the reluctance of juries to impose, and prosecutors to seek, such sentences. Petitioners are quite correct that a far smaller number of offenders under 18 than over 18 have been sentenced to death in this country. . . . These statistics, however, carry little significance. Given the undisputed fact that a far smaller percentage of capital crimes is committed by persons under 18 than over 18, the discrepancy is much less than might seem. Granted, however, that a substantial discrepancy exists, that does not establish the requisite proposition that the death sentence for offenders under 18 is categorically unacceptable to prosecutors and ju-

10. Wellington, supra note 7, at 246.

a. We emphasize that it is *American* conceptions of decency that are dispositive, rejecting the contention of petitioners and their various *amici* ([and] accepted by the dissent) that the sentencing practices of other countries are relevant. [Practices of other nations] cannot serve to establish the first Eighth Amendment prerequisite, that the practice is accepted among our people.

ries. To the contrary, it is not only possible but overwhelmingly probable that the very considerations which induce petitioners and their supporters to believe that death should *never* be imposed on offenders under 18 cause prosecutors and juries to believe that it should *rarely* be imposed. . . .

Having failed to establish a consensus against capital punishment for 16- and 17-year-old offenders through state and federal statutes and the behavior of prosecutors and juries, petitioners seek to demonstrate it through other indicia, including public opinion polls, the views of interest groups and the positions adopted by various professional associations. We decline the invitation to rest constitutional law upon such uncertain foundations. A revised national consensus so broad, so clear and so enduring as to justify a permanent prohibition upon all units of democratic government must appear in the operative acts (laws and the application of laws) that the people have approved.[11]

Justice Brennan, joined by Justices Marshall, Blackmun, and Stevens, dissented. He agreed that the meaning of the Eighth Amendment "is informed . . . by an examination of contemporary attitudes toward the punishment, as evidenced in the actions of legislatures and of juries," but took issue with the Court's reading of the evidence.[12] His disagreement with Justice Scalia's analysis was more fundamental, however:

Justice Scalia forthrightly states in his separate opinion that Eighth Amendment analysis is at an end once legislation and jury verdicts relating to the punishment in question are analyzed as indicators of contemporary values. . . . [His] approach would largely return the task of defining the contours of Eighth Amendment protection to political majorities. . . . The promise of the Bill of Rights goes unfulfilled when we leave "[c]onstitutional doctrine [to] be formulated by the acts of those institutions which the Constitution is supposed to limit," as is the case under Justice Scalia's positivist approach to the definition of citizens' rights. This Court abandons its proven and proper role in our constitutional system when it hands back to the very majorities the Framers distrusted the power to define the precise scope of protection afforded by the Bill of Rights, rather than bringing its own judgment to bear on that question, after complete analysis.

B. Rights-Based Theories

A rights-based theory of fundamental rights adjudication seeks to ground the practice in rights that enjoy at least some independence from conventional moral views. For example, Professor Laurence Tribe of Harvard writes:

References to history, tradition, evolving community standards, and civilized consensus can provide suggestive parallels and occasional insights, but it is illusion to suppose that they can yield answers, much less absolve judges of responsibility for developing and defending a theory of what rights are "preferred" or "fundamental." . . .

11. Justice O'Connor did not join in the final paragraph of the opinion.

12. Justice Brennan also argued that the views of experts in the relevant fields and of other governments "merit our attention as indicators whether a punishment is acceptable in a civilized society."

> For we are talking, necessarily, about rights of individuals or groups *against* the larger community, and against the majority. . . . Subject to all of the perils of antimajoritarian judgment, courts — and all who take seriously their constitutional oaths — must ultimately define and defend rights against government in terms independent of consensus or majority will.[13]

Another rights theorist, David A.J. Richards, poses the question: "What is the constitutionally permissible content of the legal enforcement of morals?"[14] His answer invokes a liberal theory of human rights traced from Milton, Locke, Rousseau, and Kant, to Ronald Dworkin and John Rawls.

Richards asserts that underlying any concept of human rights are "two crucial assumptions: first, that persons have the capacity to be autonomous in living their life; second, that persons are entitled, as persons, to equal concern and respect in exercising their capacities for living autonomously.[15] . . . Under the constitutional order, certain human rights are elevated into legally enforceable rights, so that if a law infringes on these moral rights, the law is not valid."[16]

> This principle explains and justifies the sense in which the constitutional right to privacy is a *right*. The constitutional concept expresses an underlying moral principle resting on the enhancement of sexual autonomy, the self-determination of the role of sexuality in one's life which protects values foundational to the concept of human rights, equal concern and respect for autonomy. Accordingly, in the absence of countervailing moral argument, laws which determine how one will have sex and with what consequences are constitutionally invalid.[17]

Our "constitutional morality" incorporates these principles and, by contrast to conventional morality, is subject to the metaethical constraints of moral reasoning. It follows that

> not everything invoked by democratic majorities as justified by "public morality" is, in fact, morally justified. From the moral point of view, we must always assess such claims by whether they can be sustained by the underlying structure of moral reasoning. . . . In this regard, constitutional morality is at one with the moral point of view. The values of equal concern and respect for personal autonomy, that we have unearthed as the foundations of American constitutionalism, are the same values that recent moral theory . . . has identified as the fundamental values of the moral point of view.[18]

C. Justifications for Government Regulation

Of the various justifications for laws and regulations that arguably interfere with individual rights, two seem most prominent: the state's interests in promoting morality and the stability of the family.

13. Laurence Tribe, American Constitutional Law 1311 (2d ed. 1988).
14. David Richards, Sexual Autonomy and the Constitutional Right to Privacy: A Case Study in Human Rights and the Unwritten Constitution, 30 Hastings L.J. 957, 976 (1979).
15. Id. at 964.
16. Id. at 958.
17. Id. at 1006.
18. Id. at 977.

In Poe v. Ullman, 367 U.S. 497 (1961), Justice Harlan, while dissenting from the Court's refusal to strike down Connecticut's anticontraception law, conceded the state's authority to protect the moral welfare of its citizenry:

> [S]ociety is not limited in its objects only to the physical well-being of the community, but has traditionally concerned itself with the moral soundness of its people as well. Indeed to attempt a line between public behavior and that which is purely consensual or solitary would be to withdraw from community concern a range of subjects with which every society in civilized times has found it necessary to deal. The laws regarding marriage, which provided both when the sexual powers may be used and the legal and societal context in which children are born and brought up, as well as laws forbidding adultery, fornication, and homosexual practices which express the negative of the proposition, confining sexuality to lawful marriage, form a pattern so deeply pressed into the substance of our social life that any constitutional doctrine in this area must build upon that basis.

Although few proponents of fundamental rights adjudication have argued that the Constitution incorporates John Stuart Mill's On Liberty (1859), most have disfavored the promotion-of-decency rationale. Richards, while conceding that there is "no constitutional objection to prohibiting clearly immoral acts that threaten the existence of society," argues that enforcing mere conventional morality "is incompatible with the moral theory of human rights implicit in the constitutional order."[19] J. Harvey Wilkinson and G. Edward White, who argue for the constitutional protection of "lifestyle" choices, assert:

> The privilege of living in a free and open society entails . . . some obligation to tolerate ideals and moral choices with which one disagrees. . . . Moreover, to uphold legal proscriptions on grounds of abstract morality would permit the state to ferret out and ultimately to try and punish offenders upon the assertion, not that the given behavior was socially harmful, but that it was revolting and unnatural. Such a rule of law would invite the majority to act upon its least noble and most prejudiced impulses.[20]

The interest in protecting the traditional family has found somewhat more favor among academic commentators. For example, Tribe writes:

> [T]he stereotypical "family unit" that is so much a part of our constitutional rhetoric is becoming decreasingly central to our constitutional reality. Such exercises of familial rights and responsibilities as remain prove to be *individual* powers to resist governmental determination of who shall be born, with whom one shall live, and what values shall be transmitted.
>
> This shift might well represent an irresistible corollary of changes in the structure of American family life and social and cultural existence. Whatever its cause, the issue it raises most sharply is the recurring puzzle of liberal individualism: Once the State, whether acting through its courts or otherwise, has "liberated" the child — and the adult — from the shackles of such intermediate groups as family, what is to

19. Id. at 991, 992.

20. J. Harvey Wilkinson & G. Edward White, Constitutional Protection for Personal Lifestyles, 62 Cornell L. Rev. 563, 618 (1977).

> defend the individual against the combined tyranny of the state and her own alienation?[21]

Wilkinson and White believe that "state interests of significant strength support a prohibition of homosexuality."[22] Of these, the most significant is protecting the family by preventing homosexuality from becoming a viable alternative to heterosexual intimacy:

> Family life has been a central unifying experience throughout American society. Preserving the strength of this basic, organic unit is a central and legitimate end of the police power. The state ought to be concerned that if allegiance to traditional family arrangements declines, society as a whole may suffer. . . .
>
> Mr. Wilkinson would uphold the state's interest in the preservation of the traditional family; Mr. White would desire stronger empirical proof that the state interest is truly put in jeopardy by homosexual practices among consenting adults. Both authors acknowledge the intuitive elements in their judgments.[23]

D. Criticisms of Fundamental Rights Adjudication

Most of the criticisms of fundamental rights adjudication have focused on the problematic nature of the sources and methods available to the judiciary. The most comprehensive critique of the practice appears in John Ely's book, Democracy and Distrust: A Theory of Judicial Review (1980). Professor Ely believes that fundamental rights adjudication may be authorized by the text and history of the Constitution:

> [T]he most plausible interpretation of the Privileges or Immunities Clause is, as it must be, the one suggested by its language — that it was a delegation to future constitutional decision-makers to protect certain rights that the document neither lists, at least not exhaustively, nor even in any specific way gives directions for finding. . . . [T]he Ninth Amendment was intended to signal the existence of federal constitutional rights beyond those specifically enumerated in the Constitution. . . . [Id. at 38.]

But this is "[not] a question on which history can have the last word," for the absence of textual or historical *guidance* is crucial:

> If a principled approach to judicial enforcement of the Constitution's open-ended provisions cannot be developed, one that is not hopelessly inconsistent with our nation's commitment to representative democracy, responsible commentators must consider seriously the possibility that courts simply should stay away from them. [Id. at 41.]

21. Laurence Tribe, American Constitutional Law 987-988 (1978).
22. Wilkinson & White, supra note 20, at 593.
23. Id. at 595-596.

1. *The Critique of Consensus or Conventional Morality*

Professor Ely denies that American society shares a conventional morality:

> There is a growing literature that argues that in fact there is no consensus to be discovered (and to the extent that one may seem to exist, that is likely to reflect only the domination of some groups by others). . . . "[D]ispute concerning the legitimate role of race in governmental decision-making, whether for purposes of segregation or affirmative action, or the legitimacy of the state's allowing the cessation of the possibility of life, by abortion or euthanasia, . . . present differences of the greatest magnitude regarding conceptions of justice." [Id. at 63-64, quoting Sanford Levinson.]

Moreover, even if a conventional morality exists, it is "not reliably discoverable, at least not by courts":

> "The more concrete the allusions to this allegedly timeless moral agreement, the less convincing they become. Therefore, to make their case the proponents of objective value must restrict themselves to a few abstract ideals whose vagueness allows almost any interpretation." . . . [B]y viewing society's values through one's own spectacles . . . one can convince oneself that some invocable consensus supports almost any position a civilized person might want to see supported. [Id. at 64-67, quoting Roberto Unger.]

Ely makes a similar point about the indeterminacy and manipulability of tradition, which "can be invoked in support of almost any cause." He cites the competing American traditions regarding both malign and benign racial discrimination and quotes Garry Wills' pithy remark that "Running men out of town on a rail is at least as much an American tradition as declaring unalienable rights." (Id. at 60.)

2. *The Critique of Rights Theories*

Ely's critique of rights theories begins with two historical points. He disputes the claim, made by some proponents, that fundamental rights adjudication is heir to a natural law tradition virtually unbroken since the eighteenth century, and he illustrates how natural law "has been summoned in support of all manner of causes in this country — some worthy, others nefarious — and often on both sides of the same issue." (Id. at 50.) Ely's main argument is a metaethical one, however: Natural law does not exist — at least not in a form useful for resolving constitutional disputes.

> [T]he only propositions with a prayer of passing themselves off as "natural law" are those so uselessly vague that no one will notice — something along the "No one should needlessly inflict suffering" line. "[A]ll the many attempts to build a moral and political doctrine upon the conception of a universal human nature have failed. Either the allegedly universal ends are too few and abstract to give content to the idea of the good, or they are too numerous and concrete to be truly universal. One has to choose between triviality and implausibility." . . . [O]ur society does not,

> rightly does not, accept the notion of a discoverable and objectively valid set of moral principles. [Id. at 51-52, quoting Roberto Unger.]

If few contemporary fundamental rights theorists invoke "natural law" in quite these terms, some have suggested that "judges seek values in . . . the writings of good contemporary moral philosophers." (Id. at 58.) Ely responds:

> Some moral philosophers think utilitarianism is the answer; others feel just as strongly it is not. Some regard enforced economic redistribution as a moral imperative; others find it morally censurable. What may be the two most renowned recent works of moral and political philosophy, John Rawls's A Theory of Justice and Robert Nozick's Anarchy, State and Utopia, reach very different conclusions. There simply does not exist *a* method of philosophy. [Id.]

Ely sardonically proposes a Supreme Court opinion that reads, "We like Rawls, you like Nozick. We win 6-3." (Id.)

Although he denies the existence of absolute ethical truths, Ely believes that "[w]e *can* reason about moral issues . . . [by proceeding] from ethical principles or conclusions it is felt the reader is likely already to accept to other conclusions or principles he or she might not previously have perceived as related in the way the writer suggests." (Id. at 54.) But he disputes the claim that "moral judgments are sounder if made dispassionately, and that because of their comparative insulation judges are more likely so to make them." (Id. at 57.) Moreover, he argues that judicial reasoning results in a "systematic bias . . . in favor of the values of the upper-middle, professional class," which constitutes the "reasoning class." (Id. at 59.) "Thus, the list of values the Court and the commentators tended to enshrine as fundamental . . . [include] expression, association, education, academic freedom, the privacy of the home, personal autonomy . . ." (Id. at 59.)

In any event, how well equipped are judges to engage in moral reasoning? Michael McConnell writes:[24]

> [J]udicial decisionmaking contains very little serious deliberation on moral issues. In the abortion decision, for example, the Court majority thought it "need not resolve" the moral-legal status of the unborn child (thereby deciding it by default), while the dissenters devoted their entire opinion to issues of standing to sue and the power of the states. Of course, standing and state power are important legal issues, but surely the overriding moral-political question was how the political community goes about determining to whom it will extend the protection of the law. . . . The Court's treatment of other prominent moral-constitutional questions . . . has not been much better. The Court's analysis is typically long on manipulation of precedent and low on intelligible principle.
>
> Nor, I believe, has there been much more moral deliberation behind the curtains. The Justices are far too busy to spend much time thinking about the cases, and their conferences are largely perfunctory. Certainly they have no time to do the kind of outside reading they would need to become able to contribute to moral-political deliberation in a serious way. In contrast to the months, even years, that are devoted to major legislative deliberation, the Justices devote one hour to oral argument and somewhat less than that to discussion at conference. Amazingly, they do not even

24. Michael McConnell, The Role of Democratic Politics in Transforming Moral Convictions into Law, 98 Yale L.J. 1501, 1536-1538 (1989).

> wait to see what the dissenting opinion has to say before joining the majority. The appearance of debate and deliberation created by the opinions is largely a sham.
>
> Third, not only do Supreme Court opinions contain little serious moral reflection, but they serve as an excuse for dispensing with moral reflection at other levels of government. Supporters of a right to abortion do not have to engage in a serious discussion of their position in the state legislatures; . . . all they need to do is cite Roe v. Wade. . . .
>
> Fourth, it is difficult to avoid the conclusion that a preference for judicial rule contains a large element of class bias. Judges, as well as most of the lawyers who appear before them and the academics who comment on their work, are members of the upper-middle-class. They come from a highly educated sector of society. This class typically has a particular predisposition toward moral issues. By contrast, legislators have to listen to, and accommodate, the opinions of a broader segment of society. The one clear effect of nonoriginalism is to give upper middle class opinions a disproportionate role in public decisionmaking. Some may contend that upper middle class values are objectively the best; I suspect this is the real reason why nonoriginalism is so popular among academics. But these arguments are rarely made in public.

Recall Professor Levinson's thesis that "fundamental values" adjudication is most appropriate where there is evidence of legislative thoughtlessness. Does Professor McConnell provide sufficient reason to reject even that role for the Court?

3. *The Levels-of-Abstraction Problem*

Professor Tribe, a proponent of fundamental values adjudication, believes that private consensual homosexual conduct should be protected because sexual expression is central to the development of a person's identity. Commenting on Bowers v. Hardwick, infra, in which the Court denied constitutional protection for homosexual sodomy, Tribe concedes that there exist "instances where homosexuality has been disapproved in western history,"[25] but argues that

> in asking whether an alleged right forms a part of a traditional liberty, it is crucial to define the liberty at a high enough level of generality to permit unconventional variants to claim protection along with mainstream versions of protected conduct. The proper question, as the dissent in *Hardwick* recognized, is not whether oral sex as such has long enjoyed a special place in the pantheon of constitutional rights, but whether private, consensual, adult sexual acts partake of traditionally revered liberties of intimate association and individual autonomy.[26]

Ely criticized this type of reasoning as the "understandable temptation to vary the relevant tradition's level of abstraction to make it come out right."[27] Similarly, Professor Robert Bork criticizes *Griswold* on the ground that the Court's choice of the level on which to define the protected liberty was necessarily arbitrary. He notes that the Court surely did not adopt the very broad principle that "govern-

25. Tribe, supra note 13, at 1427.
26. Id. at 1428.
27. John Ely, Democracy and Distrust 61 (1980).

ment may not interfere with any acts done in private."[28] On the other hand, for the Court to define the principle very narrowly — "government may not prohibit the use of contraceptives by married couples" — presents problems of "neutral definition":

> Why does the principle extend only to married couples? Why, out of all forms of sexual behavior, only to the use of contraceptives? Why, out of all forms of behavior, only to sex? . . .
>
> To put the matter another way, if a neutral judge must demonstrate why principle *X* applies to cases *A* and *B* but not to case *C* . . . , he must, by the same token, also explain why the principle is defined as *X* rather than as *X minus,* which would cover *A* but not cases *B* and *C,* or as *X plus,* which would cover all cases, *A, B,* and *C.*[29]

The levels-of-abstraction problem in interpreting the due process clause was specifically addressed by Justices Scalia and Brennan in the case of Michael H. v. Gerald D., infra. In reading that case, consider whether Tribe or Bork offers a credible response to each Justice's concerns.

4. *Lochnering*[30]

For critics and proponents alike, Lochner v. New York symbolizes the negative side of fundamental rights adjudication. Tribe argues that the Court's mistake was not the mode of adjudication as such but the particular values it chose. If *Lochner* was wrong,

> the reason can *only* be that in twentieth century America, minimum wage laws, as a substantive matter, are *not* intrusions upon human freedom in any meaningful sense, but are instead entirely reasonable and just ways of attempting to combat economic subjugation and human domination. . . . What was wrong was simply that, as a picture of freedom in industrial society, the one painted by the Justices badly distorted the character and needs of the human condition and the reality of the economic situation. . . . [But] there is no escape from the difficult task of painting a better — a morally and economically truer — picture.[31]

For John Ely, however, *Lochner* illustrates the Court's intrinsic perceptual limitations:

> It may be . . . that the "right to an abortion," or noneconomic rights in general, accord more closely with "this generation's idealization of America": than the "rights" asserted in . . . *Lochner*. . . . But that attitude, of course, is *precisely* the point of the *Lochner* philosophy, which would grant unusual protection to those "rights" that somehow *seem* most pressing, regardless of whether the Constitution suggests any special solicitude for them.[32]

28. Robert Bork, Neutral Principles and Some First Amendment Problems, 47 Ind. L.J. 1, 7 (1971).
29. Id.
30. The term is John Ely's in The Wages of Crying Wolf: A Comment on Roe v. Wade, 82 Yale L.J. 920 (1973).
31. Tribe, supra note 13, at 585, 586 n.37.
32. Ely, supra note 27, at 939.

IV. The Family and Other Living Arrangements

In Village of Belle Terre v. Boraas, 416 U.S. 1 (1974), six unrelated college students challenged a local ordinance restricting land use to one-family dwellings, with "family" defined so as to exclude more than two unrelated people living together. Writing for the Court, Justice Douglas sustained the ordinance, noting that it involved no "fundamental" or "privacy" rights and that the state could use its zoning authority to safeguard "family values." Only Justice Marshall dissented on the merits.

Moore v. City of East Cleveland, 431 U.S. 494 (1977), distinguished *Belle Terre* to invalidate an ordinance that limited occupancy of a dwelling unit to members of a single family, where "family" was defined in terms of a nuclear rather than an extended family. Appellant, who lived in her home with her son and two grandsons — her son's son and his nephew — was convicted for failing to remove the nephew as an "illegal occupant." Justice Powell, writing for a plurality including Justices Brennan, Marshall, and Blackmun, contrasted *Belle Terre's* impact on unrelated individuals with East Cleveland's "slicing deeply into the family itself": "[W]hen the government intrudes on choices concerning family living arrangements, this Court must examine carefully the importance of the governmental interests advanced and the extent to which they are served by the challenged regulation." Justice Powell held that the Court's earlier decisions "establish that the Constitution protects the sanctity of the family precisely because the institution of the family is deeply rooted in this Nation's history and tradition," a protection that reaches even to extended families composed of "uncles, aunts, cousins, and especially grandparents sharing a household along with parents and children." He added that "the choice of relatives in this degree of kinship to live together may not lightly be denied by the State. . . . [T]he Constitution prevents East Cleveland from standardizing its children — and its adults — by forcing all to live in certain narrowly defined family patterns." He concluded that the city's proffered interests in preventing overcrowding, minimizing traffic and parking congestion, and avoiding burdening the school system, were marginally served by the ordinance, but were outweighed by the appellant's constitutional interests.

Justice Stevens concurred, viewing it as "a taking of property without due process and without just compensation," which cut "deeply into a fundamental right normally associated with the ownership of real property — that of an owner to decide who may reside on her property."

Justice Stewart, joined by Justice Rehnquist, dissented:

> When the Court has found that the Fourteenth Amendment placed a substantive limitation on a State's power to regulate, it has been in those rare cases in which the personal interests at issue have been deemed "implicit in the concept of ordered liberty." The interest that the appellant may have in permanently sharing a single kitchen and a suite of contiguous rooms with some of her relatives simply does not rise to that level. To equate this interest with the fundamental decisions to marry and to bear and raise children is to extend the limited substantive contours of the Due Process Clause beyond recognition.

Justice White dissented in an opinion that questioned the validity of the notion of substantive due process and argued that judicial intervention "under the general rubric of the right to privacy" should be narrowly circumscribed. (Chief Justice Burger dissented on procedural grounds.)

MICHAEL H. v. GERALD D.

491 U.S. 110 (1989)
On Appeal from the California Court of Appeals

SCALIA, J., announced the judgment of the Court and delivered an opinion in which the Chief Justice joined, and in all but note [f] of which Justice O'Connor and Justice Kennedy joined.

[Carole D., while married to Gerald D., had an affair with Michael H. In September 1980, she gave birth to Victoria. Gerald was listed as father on the birth certificate and always treated Victoria as his daughter. However, a blood test indicated with near certainty (98%) that Michael was Victoria's father. Carole and Michael intermittently lived together, and he presented Victoria as his daughter. In turn, Victoria apparently referred to him as "Daddy."

After Carole and Victoria permanently returned to Gerald, Michael's attempts to visit Victoria were rebuffed. He therefore filed a filiation action[33] in a California court to establish his paternity and right to visitation. Victoria, represented by a guardian ad litem, cross-complained that she had a right to maintain a relationship with both "fathers."

A court-ordered psychological exam recommended that Michael be allowed continued contact as long as Carole retained sole custody of Victoria. At this point, Gerald intervened and moved for summary judgment on the ground that there were no triable issues of fact as to Victoria's paternity. He invoked Cal. Evid. Code §621, which provides that "the issue of a wife cohabiting with her husband, . . . is conclusively presumed to be a child of the marriage," unless within two years of the birth, paternity has been established in another man.

The Superior Court rejected Michael and Victoria's constitutional challenges to §621, denied their motions for continued visitation. On appeal, Michael and Victoria raised a due process challenge to the statute, but the California Court of Appeals affirmed the lower court judgment and upheld the statute.]

II

The California statute that is the subject of this litigation is, in substance, more than a century old. . . .

III . . .

Michael was seeking to be declared the father of Victoria. The immediate benefit he evidently sought to obtain from that status was visitation rights. . . . But if Michael were successful in being declared the father, other rights would follow — most importantly, the right to be considered as the parent who should have custody, a status which "embrace(s) the sum of parental rights with respect to the

33. A filiation action is a special proceeding, criminal in form, but in the nature of a civil action to enforce a civil obligation or duty specifically involving a decision regarding paternity.

rearing of a child." All parental rights, including visitation, were automatically denied by denying Michael status as the father. . . . The [California courts] held that California law denies visitation, against the wishes of the mother, to a putative father who has been prevented by §621 from establishing his paternity.

Michael raises two related challenges to the constitutionality of §621. First, he asserts that requirements of procedural due process prevent the State from terminating his liberty interest in his relationship with his child without affording him an opportunity to demonstrate his paternity in an evidentiary hearing. We believe this claim derives from a fundamental misconception of the nature of the California statute. While §621 is phrased in terms of a presumption, that rule of evidence is the implementation of a substantive rule of law. California declares it to be, except in limited circumstances, irrelevant for paternity purposes whether a child conceived during and born into an existing marriage was begotten by someone other than the husband and had a prior relationship with him. As the Court of Appeal phrased it: " 'The conclusive presumption is actually a substantive rule of law based upon a determination by the Legislature as a matter of overriding social policy, that given a certain relationship between the husband and wife, the husband is to be held responsible for the child, and that the integrity of the family unit should not be impugned.' "

Of course the conclusive presumption not only expresses the State's substantive policy but also furthers it, excluding inquiries into the child's paternity that would be destructive of family integrity and privacy.[a]

. . . A conclusive presumption does, of course, foreclose the person against whom it is invoked from demonstrating, in a particularized proceeding, that applying the presumption to him will in fact not further the lawful governmental policy the presumption is designed to effectuate. But the same can be said of any legal rule that establishes general classifications, whether framed in terms of a presumption or not. In this respect there is no difference between a rule which says that the marital husband shall be irrebuttably presumed to be the father, and a rule which says that the adulterous natural father shall not be recognized as the legal father. Both rules deny someone in Michael's situation a hearing on whether, in the particular circumstances of his case, California's policies would best be served by giving him parental rights. . . . We therefore reject Michael's procedural due process challenge and proceed to his substantive claim.

Michael contends as a matter of substantive due process that because he has established a parental relationship with Victoria, protection of Gerald's and Carole's marital union is an insufficient state interest to support termination of that relationship. This argument is, of course, predicated on the assertion that Michael has a constitutionally protected liberty interest in his relationship with Victoria.

It is an established part of our constitutional jurisprudence that the term "liberty" in the Due Process Clause extends beyond freedom from physical restraint. Without that core textual meaning as a limitation, defining the scope of the Due Process Clause "has at times been a treacherous field for this Court," giving "rea-

a. In those circumstances in which California allows a natural father to rebut the presumption of legitimacy of a child born to a married woman, e.g., where the husband is impotent or sterile, or where the husband and wife have not been cohabiting, it is more likely that the husband already knows the child is not his, and thus less likely that the paternity hearing will disrupt an otherwise harmonious and apparently exclusive marital relationship.

son for concern lest the only limits to . . . judicial intervention become the predilections of those who happen at the time to be Members of this Court."

In an attempt to limit and guide interpretation of the Clause, we have insisted not merely that the interest denominated as a "liberty" be "fundamental" (a concept that, in isolation, is hard to objectify), but also that it be an interest traditionally protected by our society.[b] As we have put it, the Due Process Clause affords only those protections "so rooted in the traditions and conscience of our people as to be ranked as fundamental." Snyder v. Massachusetts, 291 U.S. 97 (1934) (Cardozo, J.). Our cases reflect "continual insistence upon respect for the teachings of history [and] solid recognition of the basic values that underlie our society. . . ." *Griswold.*

This insistence that the asserted liberty interest be rooted in history and tradition is evident, as elsewhere, in our cases according constitutional protection to certain parental rights. Michael reads the landmark case of Stanley v. Illinois, 405 U.S. 645 (1972), and the subsequent cases of Quilloin v. Walcott, 434 U.S. 246 (1978), Caban v. Mohammed, 441 U.S. 380 (1979), and Lehr v. Robertson, 463 U.S. 248 (1983), as establishing that a liberty interest is created by biological fatherhood plus an established parental relationship — factors that exist in the present case as well. We think that distorts the rationale of those cases. As we view them, they rest not upon such isolated factors but upon the historic respect — indeed, sanctity would not be too strong a term — traditionally accorded to the relationships that develop within the unitary family.[c] In *Stanley,* for example, we forbade the destruction of such a family when, upon the death of the mother, the state had sought to remove children from the custody of a father who had lived with and supported them and their mother for 18 years. . . .

Thus, the legal issue in the present case reduces to whether the relationship between persons in the situation of Michael and Victoria has been treated as a protected family unit under the historic practices of our society, or whether on any other basis it has been accorded special protection. We think it impossible to find that it has. In fact, quite to the contrary, our traditions have protected the marital family (Gerald, Carole, and the child they acknowledge to be theirs) against the sort of claim Michael asserts.[d]

b. We do not understand what Justice Brennan has in mind by an interest "that society traditionally has thought important . . . without protecting it." The protection need not take the form of an explicit constitutional provision or statutory guarantee, but it must at least exclude . . . a societal tradition of enacting laws denying the interest. Nor do we understand why our practice of limiting the Due Process Clause to traditionally protected interests turns the clause "into a redundancy." Its purpose is to prevent future generations from lightly casting aside important traditional values — not to enable this Court to invent new ones.

c. Justice Brennan asserts that only "a pinched conception of 'the family' " would exclude Michael, Carole and Victoria from protection. We disagree. The family unit accorded traditional respect in our society, which we have referred to as the "unitary family," is typified, of course, by the marital family, but also includes the household of unmarried parents and their children. Perhaps the concept can be expanded even beyond this, but it will bear no resemblance to traditionally respected relationships — and will thus cease to have any constitutional significance — if it is stretched so far as to include the relationship established between a married woman, her lover and their child, during a three-month sojourn in St. Thomas, or during a subsequent 8-month period when, if he happened to be in Los Angeles, he stayed with her and the child.

d. Justice Brennan insists that in determining whether a liberty interest exists we must look at Michael's relationship with Victoria in isolation, without reference to the circumstance that Victoria's mother was married to someone else when the child was conceived, and that that woman and her husband wish to raise the child as their own. We cannot imagine what compels this strange procedure of looking at the act which is assertedly the subject of a liberty interest in isolation from its effect upon

The presumption of legitimacy was a fundamental principle of the common law. Traditionally, that presumption could be rebutted only by proof that a husband was incapable of procreation or had had no access to his wife during the relevant period. . . . And, under the common law both in England and here, "neither husband nor wife [could] be a witness to prove access or nonaccess." The primary policy rationale underlying the common law's severe restrictions on rebuttal of the presumption appears to have been an aversion to declaring children illegitimate, thereby depriving them of rights of inheritance and succession, and likely making them wards of the state. A secondary policy concern was the interest in promoting the "peace and tranquility of States and families," a goal that is obviously impaired by facilitating suits against husband and wife asserting that their children are illegitimate. . . .

We have found nothing in the older sources, nor in the older cases, addressing specifically the power of the natural father to assert parental rights over a child born into a woman's existing marriage with another man. Since it is Michael's burden to establish that such a power (at least where the natural father has established a relationship with the child) is so deeply embedded within our traditions as to be a fundamental right, the lack of evidence alone might defeat his case. But the evidence shows that even in modern times — when . . . the rigid protection of the marital family has in other respects been relaxed — the ability of a person in Michael's position to claim paternity has not been generally acknowledged. . . .

Moreover, even if it were clear that one in Michael's position generally possesses, and has generally always possessed, standing to challenge the marital child's legitimacy, that would still not establish Michael's case. As noted earlier, what is at issue here is not entitlement to a state pronouncement that Victoria was begotten by Michael. It is no conceivable denial of constitutional right for a State to decline to declare facts unless some legal consequence hinges upon the requested declaration. What Michael asserts here is a right to have himself declared the natural father and thereby to obtain parental prerogatives.[e] What he must establish, therefore, is not that our society has traditionally allowed a natural father in his circumstances to establish paternity, but that it has traditionally accorded such a father parental rights, or at least has not traditionally denied them. Even if the law in all States had always been that the entire world could challenge the marital presumption and obtain a declaration as to who was the natural father, that would not advance Michael's claim. Thus, it is ultimately irrelevant, even for purposes of determining current social attitudes towards the alleged substantive right Michael asserts, that the present law in a number of States appears to allow the natural father — including the natural father who has not established a relationship with the child — the theoretical power to rebut the marital presumption. What counts is whether the States in fact award substantive parental rights to the

---

other people. . . The logic of Justice Brennan's position leads to the conclusion that if Michael had begotten Victoria by rape, that fact would in no way affect his possession of a liberty interest in his relationship with her.

e. According to Justice Brennan, Michael does not claim — and in order to prevail here need not claim — a substantive right to maintain a parental relationship with Victoria, but merely the right to "a hearing on the issue" of his paternity. "Michael's challenge . . . does not depend," we are told, "on his ability ultimately to obtain visitation rights." To be sure it does not depend upon his ability ultimately to obtain those rights, but it surely depends upon his asserting a claim to those rights, which is precisely what Justice Brennan denies. We cannot grasp the concept of a "right to a hearing" on the part of a person who claims no substantive entitlement that the hearing will assertedly vindicate.

natural father of a child conceived within and born into an extant marital union that wishes to embrace the child. We are not aware of a single case, old or new, that has done so. This is not the stuff of which fundamental rights qualifying as liberty interests are made.[f]

In Lehr v. Robertson, a case involving a natural father's attempt to block his child's adoption by the unwed mother's new husband, we observed that "[t]he significance of the biological connection is that it offers the natural father an opportunity that no other male possesses to develop a relationship with his offspring," and we assumed that the Constitution might require some protection of that opportunity. Where, however, the child is born into an extant marital family, the natural father's unique opportunity conflicts with the similarly unique opportunity of the husband of the marriage; and it is not unconstitutional for the State to give categorical preference to the latter. . . . In accord with our traditions, a limit is also imposed by the circumstance that the mother is, at the time of the child's conception and birth, married to and cohabitating with another man, both

f. Justice Brennan criticizes our methodology in using historical traditions specifically relating to the rights of an adulterous natural father, rather than inquiring more generally "whether parenthood is an interest that historically has received our attention and protection." There seems to us no basis for the contention that this methodology is "nove[l]." For example, in Bowers v. Hardwick we noted that at the time the Fourteenth Amendment was ratified all but 5 of the 37 States had criminal sodomy laws, that all 50 of the States had such laws prior to 1961, and that 24 States and the District of Columbia continued to have them; and we concluded from that record, regarding that very specific aspect of sexual conduct, that "to claim that a right to engage in such conduct is 'deeply rooted in this Nation's history and tradition' or 'implicit in the concept of ordered liberty' is, at best, facetious." In *Roe* we spent about a fifth of our opinion negating the proposition that there was a longstanding tradition of laws proscribing abortion. We do not understand why, having rejected our focus upon the societal tradition regarding the natural father's rights vis-à-vis a child whose mother is married to another man, Justice Brennan would choose to focus instead upon "parenthood." Why should the relevant category not be even more general — perhaps "family relationships"; or "personal relationships"; or even "emotional attachments in general"?

Though the dissent has no basis for the level of generality it would select, we do: We refer to the most specific level at which a relevant tradition protecting, or denying protection to, the asserted right can be identified. If, for example, there were no societal tradition, either way, regarding the rights of the natural father of a child adulterously conceived, we would have to consult, and (if possible) reason from, the traditions regarding natural fathers in general. But there is such a more specific tradition, and it unqualifiedly denies protection to such a parent.

One would think that Justice Brennan would appreciate the value of consulting the most specific tradition available, since he acknowledges that "[e]ven if we can agree . . . that 'family' and 'parenthood' are part of the good life, it is absurd to assume that we can agree on the content of those terms and destructive to pretend that we do." Because such general traditions provide such imprecise guidance, they permit judges to dictate rather than discern the society's views. The need, if arbitrary decision-making is to be avoided, to adopt the most specific tradition as the point of reference — or at least to announce, as Justice Brennan declines to do, some other criterion for selecting among the innumerable relevant traditions that could be consulted — is well enough exemplified by the fact that in the present case Justice Brennan's opinion and Justice O'Connor's opinion, which disapproves this footnote, both appeal to tradition, but on the basis of the tradition they select reach opposite results. Although assuredly having the virtue (if it be that) of leaving judges free to decide as they think best when the unanticipated occurs, a rule of law that binds neither by text nor by any particular, identifiable tradition, is no rule of law at all.

Finally, we may note that this analysis is not inconsistent with the result in cases such as Griswold v. Connecticut or Eisenstadt v. Baird. None of those cases acknowledged a longstanding and still extant societal tradition withholding the very right pronounced to be the subject of a liberty interest and then rejected it. Justice Brennan must do so here. In this case, the existence of such a tradition, continuing to the present day, refutes any possible contention that the alleged right is "so rooted in the traditions and conscience of our people as to be ranked as fundamental," Snyder v. Massachusetts, or "implicit in the concept of ordered liberty," Palko v. Connecticut.

of whom wish to raise the child as the offspring of their union.[g] It is a question of legislative policy and not constitutional law whether California will allow the presumed parenthood of a couple desiring to retain a child conceived within and born into their marriage to be rebutted.

We do not accept Justice Brennan's criticism that this result "squashes" the liberty that consists of "the freedom not to conform." It seems to us that reflects the erroneous view that there is only one side to this controversy — that one disposition can expand a "liberty" of sorts without contracting an equivalent "liberty" on the other side. Such a happy choice is rarely available. Here, to provide protection to an adulterous natural father is to deny protection to a marital father, and vice versa. If Michael has a "freedom not to conform" (whatever that means), Gerald must equivalently have a "freedom to conform." One of them will pay a price for asserting that "freedom" — Michael by being unable to act as father of the child he has adulterously begotten, or Gerald by being unable to preserve the integrity of the traditional family unit he and Victoria have established. Our disposition does not choose between these two "freedoms," but leaves that to the people of California. . . .

IV

We have never had occasion to decide whether a child has a liberty interest, symmetrical with that of her parent, in maintaining her filial relationship. We need not do so here because, even assuming that such a right exists, Victoria's claim must fail. Victoria's due process challenge is, if anything, weaker than Michael's. Her basic claim is not that California has erred in preventing her from establishing that Michael, not Gerald, should stand as her legal father. Rather, she claims a due process right to maintain filial relationships with both Michael and Gerald. This assertion merits little discussion, for, whatever the merits of the guardian ad litem's belief that such an arrangement can be of great psychological benefit to a child, the claim that a State must recognize multiple fatherhood has no support in the history or traditions of this country. Moreover, even if we were to construe Victoria's argument as forwarding the lesser proposition that, whatever her status vis-à-vis Gerald, she has a liberty interest in maintaining a filial relationship with her natural father, Michael, we find that, at best, her claim is the obverse of Michael's and fails for the same reasons.

[A discussion of Victoria's equal protection claim is omitted.]

O'CONNOR, J., joined by Kennedy, J., concurring in part.

I concur in all but footnote [f] of Justice Scalia's opinion. This footnote sketches a mode of historical analysis to be used when identifying liberty interests protected by the Due Process Clause of the Fourteenth Amendment that may be somewhat inconsistent with our past decisions in this area. On occasion the Court has characterized relevant traditions protecting asserted rights at levels of generality that might not be "the most specific level" available. I would not foreclose the unanticipated by the prior imposition of a single mode of historical analysis.

g. Justice Brennan chides us for thus limiting our holding to situations in which, as here, the husband and wife wish to raise her child jointly. . . . We limit our pronouncement to the relevant facts of this case because it is at least possible that our traditions lead to a different conclusion with regard to adulterous fathering of a child whom the marital parents do not wish to raise as their own. . . .

STEVENS, J., concurring in the judgment.

. . . I think cases like Stanley v. Illinois and Caban v. Mohammed demonstrate that enduring "family" relationships may develop in unconventional settings. I therefore would not foreclose the possibility that a constitutionally protected relationship between a natural father and his child might exist in a case like this. Indeed, I am willing to assume for the purpose of deciding this case that Michael's relationship with Victoria is strong enough to give him a constitutional right to try to convince a trial judge that Victoria's best interest would be served by granting him visitation rights. I am satisfied, however, that the California statute, as applied in this case, gave him that opportunity. . . .

I therefore concur in the Court's judgment of affirmance.

BRENNAN, J., with whom Marshall and Blackmun, JJ., join, dissenting.

. . . [I]t is fruitful to begin by emphasizing the common ground shared by a majority of this Court. Five Members of the Court refuse to foreclose "the possibility that a natural father might ever have a constitutionally protected interest in his relationship with a child whose mother was married to and cohabiting with another man at the time of the child's conception and birth." Five Justices agree that the flaw inhering in a conclusive presumption that terminates a constitutionally protected interest without any hearing whatsoever is a procedural one. Four Members of the Court agree that Michael H. has a liberty interest in his relationship with Victoria, and one assumes for purposes of this case that he does.

In contrast, only two Members of the Court fully endorse Justice Scalia's view of the proper method of analyzing questions arising under the Due Process Clause. Nevertheless, because the plurality opinion's exclusively historical analysis portends a significant and unfortunate departure from our prior cases and from sound constitutional decisionmaking, I devote a substantial portion of my discussion to it.

I

Once we recognized that the "liberty" protected by the Due Process Clause of the Fourteenth Amendment encompasses more than freedom from bodily restraint, today's plurality opinion emphasizes, the concept was cut loose from one natural limitation on its meaning. This innovation paved the way, so the plurality hints, for judges to substitute their own preferences for those of elected officials. Dissatisfied with this supposedly unbridled and uncertain state of affairs, the plurality casts about for another limitation on the concept of liberty.

It finds this limitation in "tradition." Apparently oblivious to the fact that this concept can be as malleable and as elusive as "liberty" itself, the plurality pretends that tradition places a discernible border around the Constitution. The pretense is seductive; it would be comforting to believe that a search for "tradition" involves nothing more idiosyncratic or complicated than poring through dusty volumes on American history. Yet, as Justice White observed in his dissent in Moore v. East Cleveland, 431 U.S. 494, 549 (1977): "What the deeply rooted traditions of the country are is arguable." Indeed, wherever I would begin to look for an interest "deeply rooted in the country's traditions," one thing is certain: I would not stop (as does the plurality) at Bracton, or Blackstone, or Kent, or even the American Law Reports in conducting my search. Because reasonable people can disagree about the content of particular traditions, and because they can disagree even about which traditions are relevant to the definition of "liberty," the plurality has not found the objective boundary that it seeks.

Even if we could agree, moreover, on the content and significance of particular traditions, we still would be forced to identify the point at which a tradition becomes firm enough to be relevant to our definition of liberty and the moment at which it becomes too obsolete to be relevant any longer. The plurality supplies no objective means by which we might make these determinations. Indeed, as soon as the plurality sees signs that the tradition upon which it bases its decision (the laws denying putative fathers like Michael standing to assert paternity) is crumbling, it shifts ground and says that the case has nothing to do with that tradition, after all. "What is at issue here," the plurality asserts after canvassing the law on paternity suits, "is not entitlement to a state pronouncement that Victoria was begotten by Michael." But that is precisely what is at issue here, and the plurality's last-minute denial of this fact dramatically illustrates the subjectivity of its own analysis.

It is ironic that an approach so utterly dependent on tradition is so indifferent to our precedents. Citing barely a handful of this Court's numerous decisions defining the scope of the liberty protected by the Due Process Clause to support its reliance on tradition, the plurality acts as though English legal treatises and the American Law Reports always have provided the sole source for our constitutional principles. They have not. Just as common-law notions no longer define the "property" that the Constitution protects, see Goldberg v. Kelly, 397 U.S. 254 (1970), neither do they circumscribe the "liberty" that it guarantees. . . .

It is not that tradition has been irrelevant to our prior decisions. Throughout our decisionmaking in this important area runs the theme that certain interests and practices — freedom from physical restraint, marriage, childbearing, childrearing, and others — form the core of our definition of "liberty." Our solicitude for these interests is partly the result of the fact that the Due Process Clause would seem an empty promise if it did not protect them, and partly the result of the historical and traditional importance of these interests in our society. In deciding cases arising under the Due Process Clause, therefore, we have considered whether the concrete limitation under consideration impermissibly impinges upon one of these more generalized interests.

Today's plurality, however, does not ask whether parenthood is an interest that historically has received our attention and protection; the answer to that question is too clear for dispute. Instead, the plurality asks whether the specific variety of parenthood under consideration — a natural father's relationship with a child whose mother is married to another man — has enjoyed such protection.

If we had looked to tradition with such specificity in past cases, many a decision would have reached a different result. Surely the use of contraceptives by unmarried couples, Eisenstadt v. Baird, or even by married couples, Griswold v. Connecticut; the freedom from corporal punishment in schools, Ingraham v. Wright, 430 U.S. 651 (1977); the freedom from an arbitrary transfer from a prison to a psychiatric institution, Vitek v. Jones, 445 U.S. 480 (1980); and even the right to raise one's natural but illegitimate children, Stanley v. Illinois, were not "interest[s] traditionally protected by our society," at the time of their consideration by this Court. If we had asked, therefore, in *Eisenstadt, Griswold, Ingraham, Vitek,* or *Stanley* itself whether the specific interest under consideration had been traditionally protected, the answer would have been a resounding "no." That we did not ask this question in those cases highlights the novelty of the interpretive method that the plurality opinion employs today.

The plurality's interpretive method is more than novel; it is misguided. It ignores the good reasons for limiting the role of "tradition" in interpreting the Constitution's deliberately capacious language. In the plurality's constitutional universe, we may not take notice of the fact that the original reasons for the conclusive presumption of paternity are out of place in a world in which blood tests can prove virtually beyond a shadow of a doubt who sired a particular child and in which the fact of illegitimacy no longer plays the burdensome and stigmatizing role it once did. Nor, in the plurality's world, may we deny "tradition" its full scope by pointing out that the rationale for the conventional rule has changed over the years; . . . instead, our task is simply to identify a rule denying the asserted interest and not to ask whether the basis for that rule — which is the true reflection of the values undergirding it — has changed too often or too recently to call the rule embodying that rationale a "tradition." Moreover, by describing the decisive question as whether Michael and Victoria's interest is one that has been "traditionally *protected by* our society," rather than one that society traditionally has thought important (with or without protecting it), and by suggesting that our sole function is to "*discern* the society's views," the plurality acts as if the only purpose of the Due Process Clause is to confirm the importance of interests already protected by a majority of the States. Transforming the protection afforded by the Due Process Clause into a redundancy mocks those who, with care and purpose, wrote the Fourteenth Amendment.

In construing the Fourteenth Amendment to offer shelter only to those interests specifically protected by historical practice, moreover, the plurality ignores the kind of society in which our Constitution exists. We are not an assimilative, homogeneous society, but a facilitative, pluralistic one, in which we must be willing to abide someone else's unfamiliar or even repellant practice because the same tolerant impulse protects our own idiosyncrasies. Even if we can agree, therefore, that "family" and "parenthood" are part of the good life, it is absurd to assume that we can agree on the content of those terms and destructive to pretend that we do. In a community such as ours, "liberty" must include the freedom not to conform. The plurality today squashes this freedom by requiring specific approval from history before protecting anything in the name of liberty.

The document that the plurality construes today is unfamiliar to me. It is not the living charter that I have taken to be our Constitution; it is instead a stagnant, archaic, hidebound document steeped in the prejudices and superstitions of a time long past. This Constitution does not recognize that times change, does not see that sometimes a practice or rule outlives its foundations. I cannot accept an interpretive method that does such violence to the charter that I am bound by oath to uphold.

II

The plurality's reworking of our interpretive approach is all the more troubling because it is unnecessary. This is not a case in which we face a "new" kind of interest, one that requires us to consider for the first time whether the Constitution protects it. On the contrary, we confront an interest — that of a parent and child in their relationship with each other — that was among the first that this Court acknowledged in its cases defining the "liberty" protected by the Constitution, and I think I am safe in saying that no one doubts the wisdom or validity of those decisions. Where the interest under consideration is a parent-child relationship, we need not ask, over and over again, whether that interest is one that society traditionally protects.

Thus, to describe the issue in this case as whether the relationship existing between Michael and Victoria "has been treated as a protected family unit under the historic practices of our society, or whether on any other basis it has been accorded special protection," is to reinvent the wheel. The better approach — indeed, the one commanded by our prior cases and by common sense — is to ask whether the specific parent-child relationship under consideration is close enough to the interests that we already have protected to be deemed an aspect of "liberty" as well. . . .

On four prior occasions, we have considered whether unwed fathers have a constitutionally protected interest in their relationships with their children. See Stanley v. Illinois; Quilloin v. Walcott; Caban v. Mohammed; and Lehr v. Robertson. Though different in factual and legal circumstances, these cases have produced a unifying theme: although an unwed father's biological link to his child does not, in and of itself, guarantee him a constitutional stake in his relationship with that child, such a link combined with a substantial parent-child relationship will do so. . . .[a]

The evidence is undisputed that Michael, Victoria, and Carole did live together as a family; that is, they shared the same household, Victoria called Michael "Daddy," Michael contributed to Victoria's support, and he is eager to continue his relationship with her. Yet they are not, in the plurality's view, a "unitary family," whereas Gerald, Carole, and Victoria do compose such a family. The only difference between these two sets of relationships, however, is the fact of marriage. . . . However, the very premise of *Stanley* and the cases following it is that marriage is not decisive in answering the question whether the Constitution protects the parental relationship under consideration. . . .

[The plurality's] pinched conception of "the family," crucial as it is in rejecting Michael and Victoria's claim of a liberty interest, is jarring in light of our many cases preventing the States from denying important interests or statuses to those whose situations do not fit the government's narrow view of the family. From Loving v. Virginia to . . . Moore v. East Cleveland, we have declined to respect a State's notion, as manifested in its allocation of privileges and burdens, of what the family should be. . . .

The plurality's focus on the "unitary family" is misdirected for another reason. It conflates the question whether a liberty interest exists with the question what procedures may be used to terminate or curtail it. It is no coincidence that we never before have looked at the relationship that the unwed father seeks to disrupt, rather than the one he seeks to preserve, in determining whether he has a liberty interest in his relationship with his child. To do otherwise is to allow the State's interest in terminating the relationship to play a role in defining the "lib-

a. The plurality's claim that "the logic of (my) position leads to the conclusion that if Michael had begotten Victoria by rape, that fact would in no way affect his possession of a liberty interest in his relationship with her," ignores my observation that a mere biological connection is insufficient to establish a liberty interest on the part of an unwed father.

erty" that is protected by the Constitution. According to our established framework under the Due Process Clause, however, we first ask whether the person claiming constitutional protection has an interest that the Constitution recognizes; if we find that she does, we next consider the State's interest in limiting the extent of the procedures that will attend the deprivation of that interest. By stressing the need to preserve the "unitary family" and by focusing not just on the relationship between Michael and Victoria but on their "situation" as well, today's plurality opinion takes both of these steps at once.

The plurality's premature consideration of California's interests is evident from its careful limitation of its holding to those cases in which "the mother is, at the time of the child's conception and birth, married to and cohabitating with another man, *both of whom wish to raise the child as the offspring of their union.*" (emphasis added). . . . The highlighted language suggests that if Carole or Gerald alone wished to raise Victoria, or if both were dead and the State wished to raise her, Michael and Victoria might be found to have a liberty interest in their relationship with each other.

But that would be to say that whether Michael and Victoria have a liberty interest varies with the State's interest in recognizing that interest, for it is the State's interest in protecting the marital family — and not Michael and Victoria's interest in their relationship with each other — that varies with the status of Carole and Gerald's relationship. It is a bad day for due process when the State's interest in terminating a parent-child relationship is reason to conclude that that relationship is not part of the "liberty" protected by the Fourteenth Amendment.

The plurality has wedged itself between a rock and a hard place. If it limits its holding to those situations in which a wife and husband wish to raise the child together, then it necessarily takes the State's interest into account in defining "liberty"; yet if it extends that approach to circumstances in which the marital union already has been dissolved, then it may no longer rely on the State's asserted interest in protecting the "unitary family" in denying that Michael and Victoria have been deprived of liberty. . . .

III

Because the plurality decides that Michael and Victoria have no liberty interest in their relationship with each other, it need consider neither the effect of §621 on their relationship nor the State's interest in bringing about that effect. It is obvious, however, that the effect of §621 is to terminate the relationship between Michael and Victoria before affording any hearing whatsoever on the issue whether Michael is Victoria's father. This refusal to hold a hearing is properly analyzed under our procedural due process cases, which instruct us to consider the State's interest in curtailing the procedures accompanying the termination of a constitutionally protected interest. [Justice Brennan's discussion of this point is omitted.] . . .

IV

The atmosphere surrounding today's decision is one of make-believe. Beginning with the suggestion that the situation confronting us here does not repeat itself every day in every corner of the country, moving on to the claim that it is tradition alone that supplies the details of the liberty that the Constitution protects, and passing finally to the notion that the Court always has recognized a cramped vision of "the family," today's decision lets stand California's pronouncement that Michael — whom blood tests show to a 98 percent probability to be Victoria's father — is not Victoria's father. When and if the Court awakes to reality, it will find a world very different from the one it expects.

WHITE, J., with whom Brennan, J., joins, dissenting.

. . . [T]he fact that Michael H. is the biological father of Victoria is to me highly relevant to whether he has rights, as a father or otherwise, with respect to the child. Because I believe that Michael H. has a liberty interest that cannot be denied without due process of the law, I must dissent.

I

Like Justices Brennan, Marshall, Blackmun and Stevens, I do not agree with the plurality opinion's conclusion that a natural father can never "have a constitutionally protected interest in his relationship with a child whose mother was married to and cohabiting with another man at the time of the child's conception and birth." . . . The basic principle enunciated in the Court's unwed father cases is that an unwed father who has demonstrated a sufficient commitment to his paternity by way of personal, financial, or custodial responsibilities has a protected liberty interest in a relationship with his child. . . .

In the case now before us, Michael H. is not a father unwilling to assume his responsibilities as a parent. To the contrary, he is a father who has asserted his interests in raising and providing for his child since the very time of the child's birth. . . . The facts in this case satisfy the *Lehr* criteria, which focused on the relationship between father and child, not on the relationship between father and mother. Under *Lehr* a "mere biological relationship" is not enough, but in light of Carole's vicissitudes, what more could Michael H. have done? It is clear enough that Michael H. more than meets the mark in establishing the constitutionally protected liberty interest. . . .

II

[Justice White's discussion of the process due Michael H. at the hearing is omitted.]

As the Court has said: "The significance of the biological connection is that it offers the natural father an opportunity that no other male possesses to develop a relationship with his offspring. If he grasps that opportunity and accepts some measure of responsibility for the child's future, he may enjoy the blessings of the parent-child relationship and make uniquely valuable contributions to the child's development." It is as if this passage was addressed to Michael H. Yet the plurality today recants. Michael H. eagerly grasped the opportunity to have a relationship with his daughter (he lived with her; he declared her to be his child; he provided financial support for her) and still, with today's opinion, his opportunity has vanished. He has been rendered a stranger to his child. . . .

Discussion

Do you agree with Justice Scalia that the fundamental right in question is that of an "[adulterous] natural father to assert parental rights over a child born into a woman's existing marriage with another man"? Or is it the right of "a parent to be heard before being deprived of any contact with his or her child" by the other parent. Is there a "neutral" or "principled" method of describing the right in question or determining the proper level of generality in construing previously recognized fundamental rights? If you agree with Justice Scalia's approach, what claim might someone like Michael H. have brought that deserved protection as a fundamental right? If you agree with Justice Brennan's approach, what sort of facts would lead you to consider a claim based on fundamental rights? For example, would you grant a hearing to a rapist father? Does Justice Brennan adequately answer Justice Scalia's charge that the rapist *would* be able to assert a "fundamental right" if Brennan's analysis were accepted?

V. *The Abortion Dilemma*

A. Roe v. Wade

ROE v. WADE
410 U.S. 113 (1973)
Appeal from the United States District Court for the Northern District of Texas

[An unmarried pregnant woman and others brought this class action challenging the constitutionality of the Texas criminal abortion laws, which prohibit procuring or attempting an abortion except for the purpose of saving the mother's life. A three-judge district court granted declaratory relief, holding that the statutes infringed plaintiff's rights protected by the Ninth Amendment, but denied injunctive relief. Plaintiff and defendant, the Texas attorney general, both appealed. The Supreme Court affirmed, holding that the statutes are unconstitutional and that a declaratory judgment to that effect sufficed.]

BLACKMUN, J.

This Texas federal appeal and its Georgia companion, Doe v. Bolton, present constitutional challenges to state criminal abortion legislation. The Texas statutes under attack here are typical of those that have been in effect in many States for approximately a century. The Georgia statutes, in contrast, have a modern cast and are a legislative product that, to an extent at least, obviously reflects the influences of recent attitudinal change, of advancing medical knowledge and techniques, and of new thinking about an old issue.

We forthwith acknowledge our awareness of the sensitive and emotional nature of the abortion controversy, of the vigorous opposing views, even among physicians, and of the deep and seemingly absolute convictions that the subject inspires. One's philosophy, one's experiences, one's exposure to the raw edges of human existence, one's religious training, one's attitudes toward life and family and their values, and the moral standards one establishes and seeks to observe, are all likely to influence and to color one's thinking and conclusions about abortion.

In addition, population growth, pollution, poverty, and racial overtones tend to complicate and not to simplify the problem.

Our task, of course, is to resolve the issue by constitutional measurement, free of emotion and of predilection. We seek earnestly to do this, and, because we do, we have inquired into, and in this opinion place some emphasis upon, medical and medical-legal history and what that history reveals about man's attitudes toward the abortion procedure over the centuries. We bear in mind, too, Mr. Justice Holmes' admonition in his now-vindicated dissent in Lochner v. New York, 198 U.S. 45, 76 (1905): "[The Constitution] is made for people of fundamentally differing views, and the accident of our finding certain opinions natural and familiar or novel and even shocking ought not to conclude our judgment upon the question whether statutes embodying them conflict with the Constitution of the United States."

I

The Texas statutes that concern us here . . . make it a crime to "procure an abortion," . . . or to attempt one, except with respect to "an abortion procured or attempted by medical advice for the purpose of saving the life of the mother." Similar statutes are in existence in a majority of the States.

V

The principal thrust of appellant's attack on the Texas statutes is that they improperly invade a right, said to be possessed by the pregnant woman, to choose to terminate her pregnancy. Appellant would discover this right in the concept of personal "liberty" embodied in the Fourteenth Amendment's Due Process Clause; or in personal, marital, familial, and sexual privacy said to be protected by the Bill of Rights or its penumbras, see Griswold v. Connecticut, or among those rights reserved to the people by the Ninth Amendment, Griswold v. Connecticut (Goldberg, J., concurring). Before addressing this claim, we feel it desirable briefly to survey, in several aspects, the history of abortion, for such insight as that history may afford us, and then to examine the state purposes and interests behind the criminal abortion laws.

VI

[Justice Blackmun divides his 18-page survey of abortion laws and practices into eight categories: (1) ancient attitudes; (2) the Hippocratic oath, (3) the common law, (4) the English statutory law, (5) the American law, (6) the position of the American Medical Association, (7) the position of the American Public Health Association, and (8) the position of the American Bar Association.

The Hippocratic oath, which, among other things, prohibited giving "to a woman an abortive remedy," was not widely accepted in ancient Greece and Rome, where abortions were common, but with the emergence of Christianity "[t]he Oath 'became the nucleus of all medical ethics.'. . ."

"It is undisputed that at the common law, abortion performed *before* 'quickening' — the first recognizable movement of the fetus in utero, appearing usually from the 16th to the 18th week of pregnancy — was not an indictable offense." Coke and Blackstone wrote that abortion after quickening was a crime, and this view was uncritically adopted by American courts. But "[whether] abortion of a *quick* fetus was a felony at common law, or even a lesser crime" now appears "doubtful."

Abortion was made a statutory crime in England in 1803. The first statute distinguished between abortion before and after quickening, with lighter penalities for the former; but later statutes dropped the distinction. The English Abortion Act of 1967 permits abortions when, inter alia, "the continuance of the pregnancy would involve risks to the . . . physical or mental health of the pregnant woman or any existing children of her family," taking account of her "actual or reasonably foreseen environment."

Justice Blackmun then turns to historical and present views of abortion in the United States:]

. . . In this country, the law in effect in all but a few States until mid-19th century was the pre-existing English common law . . . In 1828, New York enacted legislation that, in two respects, was to serve as a model for early anti-abortion statutes. First, while barring destruction of an unquickened fetus as well as a quick fetus, it made the former only a misdemeanor, but the latter second-degree manslaughter. Second, it incorporated a concept of therapeutic abortion by providing that an abortion was excused if it "shall have been necessary to preserve the life of such mother, or shall have been advised by two physicians to be necessary for such purpose." By 1840, when Texas had received the common law, only eight American States had statutes dealing with abortion. It was not until after the War Between the States that legislation began generally to replace the common law. Most of these initial statutes dealt severely with abortion after quickening but were lenient with it before quickening. . . .

Gradually, in the middle and late 19th century the quickening distinction disappeared from the statutory law of most States and the degree of the offense and the penalties were increased. By the end of the 1950's, a large majority of the jurisdictions banned abortion, however and whenever performed, unless done to save or preserve the life of the mother. . . . In the past several years, however, a trend toward liberalization of abortion statutes has resulted in adoption, by about one-third of the States, of less stringent laws, most of them patterned after the ALI Model Penal Code, §230.3.[34]

It is thus apparent that at common law, at the time of the adoption of our Constitution, and throughout the major portion of the 19th century, abortion was viewed with less disfavor than under most American statutes currently in effect. Phrasing it another way, a woman enjoyed a substantially broader right to termi-

34. Section 230.3 reads:

(1) *Unjustifed Abortion.* A person who purposely and unjustifiably terminates the pregnancy of another otherwise than by a live birth commits a felony of the third degree or, where the pregnancy has continued beyond the twenty-sixth week, a felony of the second degree.

(2) *Justifiable Abortion.* A licensed physician is justified in terminating a pregnancy if he believes there is substantial risk that continuance of the pregnancy would gravely impair the physical or mental health of the mother or that the child would be born with grave physical or mental defect, or that the pregnancy resulted from rape, incest, or other felonious intercourse. All illicit intercourse with a girl below the age of 16 shall be deemed felonious for purposes of this subsection.

nate a pregnancy than she does in most States today. At least with respect to the early stage of pregnancy, and very possibly without such a limitation, the opportunity to make this choice was present in this country well into the 19th century. Even later, the law continued for some time to treat less punitively an abortion procured in early pregnancy. . . .

[Finally, Justice Blackmun discusses the views of the American Medical Association, the American Public Health Association, and the American Bar Association: "The anti-abortion mood prevalent in this country in the late 19th century was shared by the medical profession. Indeed, the attitude of the profession may have played a significant role in the enactment of stringent criminal abortion legislation during the period." By 1970, however, an AMA committee noted that the profession was polarized and that there had been a remarkable shift of views "felt to be influenced 'by the rapid changes in state law and by the judicial decisions which tend to make abortion more freely available.' . . ." The AMA House of Delegates adopted statements emphasizing " 'the best interests of the patient,' 'sound clinical judgment,' and 'informed patient consent,' in contrast to 'mere acquiescence to the patient's demand.' " In 1970 the Executive Board of the APHA adopted standards providing, inter alia, that "rapid and simple abortion referral must be readily available through state and local public health departments, medical societies, or other nonprofit organizations." And in 1972 the ABA House of Delegates approved the quite liberal Uniform Abortion Act.]

VII

Three reasons have been advanced to explain historically the enactment of criminal abortion laws in the 19th century and to justify their continued existence.

It has been argued occasionally that these laws were the product of a Victorian social concern to discourage illicit sexual conduct. Texas, however, does not advance this justification in the present case, and it appears that no court or commentator has taken the argument seriously. . . .

A second reason is concerned with abortion as a medical procedure. When most criminal abortion laws were first enacted, the procedure was a hazardous one for the woman. . . . Thus, it has been argued that a State's real concern in enacting a criminal abortion law was to protect the pregnant woman, that is, to restrain her from submitting to a procedure that placed her life in serious jeopardy.

Modern medical techniques have altered this situation. Appellants and various amici refer to medical data indicating that abortion in early pregnancy, that is, prior to the end of the first trimester, although not without its risk, is now relatively safe. Mortality rates for women undergoing early abortions, where the procedure is legal, appear to be as low as or lower than the rates for normal childbirth. Consequently, any interest of the State in protecting the woman from an inherently hazardous procedure, except when it would be equally dangerous for her to forgo it, has largely disappeared. Of course, important state interests in the area of health and medical standards do remain. The State has a legitimate interest in seeing to it that abortion, like any other medical procedure, is performed under circumstances that insure maximum safety for the patient. This interest obviously extends at least to the performing physician and his staff, to the facilities involved, to the availability of after-care, and to adequate provision for any complication or emergency that might arise. The prevalence of high mortality rates at illegal "abortion mills" strengthens, rather than weakens, the State's interest in regulating the conditions under which abortions are performed. Moreover, the risk to the woman increases as her pregnancy continues. Thus, the State retains a definite interest in protecting the woman's own health and safety when an abortion is proposed at a late stage of pregnancy.

The third reason is the State's interest — some phrase it in terms of duty — in protecting prenatal life. Some of the argument for this justification rests on the theory that a new human life is present from the moment of conception. The State's interest and general obligation to protect life then extends, it is argued, to prenatal life. Only when the life of the pregnant mother herself is at stake, balanced against the life she carries within her, should the interest of the embryo or fetus not prevail. Logically, of course, a legitimate state interest in this area need not stand or fall on acceptance or the belief that life begins at conception or at some other point prior to live birth. In assessing the State's interest, recognition may be given to the less rigid claim that as long as at least *potential* life is involved, the State may assert interests beyond the protection of the pregnant woman alone. . . .

It is with these interests, and the weight to be attached to them, that this case is concerned.

VIII

The Constitution does not explicitly mention any right of privacy. In a [long] line of decisions, however, . . . the Court has recognized that a right of personal privacy, or a guarantee of certain areas or zones of privacy, does exist under the Constitution. In varying contexts, the Court or individual Justices have, indeed, found at least the roots of that right in the First Amendment; in the penumbras of the Bill of Rights; in the Ninth Amendment; or in the concept of liberty guaranteed by the first section of the Fourteenth Amendment. These decisions make it clear that only personal rights that can be deemed "fundamental" or "implicit in the concept of ordered liberty," Palko v. Connecticut, are included in this guarantee of personal privacy. They also make it clear that the right has some extension to activities relating to marriage, Loving v. Virginia; procreation, Skinner v. Oklahoma; contraception, Eisenstadt v. Baird; family relationships, Prince v. Massachusetts; and child rearing and education, Pierce v. Society of Sisters, Meyer v. Nebraska.

This right of privacy, whether it be founded in the Fourteenth Amendment's concept of personal liberty and restrictions upon state action, as we feel it is, or, as the District Court determined, in the Ninth Amendment's reservation of rights to the people, is broad enough to encompass a woman's decision whether or not to terminate her pregnancy. The detriment that the State would impose upon the pregnant woman by denying this choice altogether is apparent. Specific and direct harm medically diagnosable even in early pregnancy may be involved. Maternity, or additional offspring, may force upon the woman a distressful life and future. Psychological harm may be imminent. Mental and physical health may be taxed by child care. There is also the distress, for all concerned, associated with the unwanted child; and there is the problem of bringing a child into a family already unable, psychologically and otherwise, to care for it. In other cases, as in this one, the additional difficulties and continuing stigma of unwed motherhood may be involved. All these are factors the woman and her responsible physician necessarily will consider in consultation.

On the basis of elements such as these, appellant and some amici argue that the woman's right is absolute and that she is entitled to terminate her pregnancy at whatever time, in whatever way, and for whatever reason she alone chooses. With this we do not agree. Appellant's arguments that Texas either has no valid interest at all in regulating the abortion decision, or no interest strong enough to support any limitation upon the woman's sole determination, is unpersuasive. The Court's decisions recognizing a right of privacy also acknowledge that some state regulation in areas protected by that right is appropriate. As noted above, a State may properly assert important interests in safeguarding health, in maintaining medical standards, and in protecting potential life. At some point in pregnancy, these respective interests become sufficiently compelling to sustain regulation of the factors that govern the abortion decision. The privacy right involved, therefore, cannot be said to be absolute. . . .

We, therefore, conclude that the right of personal privacy includes the abortion decision, but that this right is not unqualified and must be considered against important state interests in regulation. . . .

Where certain "fundamental rights" are involved, the Court has held that regulation limiting these rights may be justified only by a "compelling state interest," . . . and that legislative enactments must be narrowly drawn to express only the legitimate state interests at stake. . . .

IX

The District Court held that the appellee failed to meet his burden of demonstrating that the Texas statute's infringement upon Roe's rights was necessary to support a compelling state interest, and that, although the appellee presented "several compelling justifications for state presence in the area of abortions," the statutes outstripped these justifications and swept "far beyond any areas of compelling state interest." Appellant and appellee both contest that holding. . . .

A

The appellee and certain amici argue that the fetus is a "person" within the language and meaning of the Fourteenth Amendment. In support of this, they outline at length and in detail the well-known facts of fetal development. If this suggestion of personhood is established, the appellant's case, of course, collapses, for the fetus' right to life is then guaranteed specifically by the Amendment. . . . [However, no case] holds that a fetus is a person within the meaning of the Fourteenth Amendment.

The Constitution does not define "person" in so many words. Section 1 of the Fourteenth Amendment contains three references to "person." The first, in defining "citizens," speaks of "persons born or naturalized in the United States." The word also appears both in the Due Process Clause and in the Equal Protection Clause. "Person" is used in other places in the Constitution. . . . But in nearly all these instances, the use of the word is such that it has application only postnatally. None indicates, with any assurance, that it has any possible prenatal application.[a]

All this, together with our observation, supra, that throughout the major portion of the 19th century prevailing legal abortion practices were far freer than they are today, persuades us that the word "person," as used in the Fourteenth Amendment, does not include the unborn. . . .

This conclusion, however, does not of itself fully answer the contentions raised by Texas, and we pass on to other considerations.

The pregnant woman cannot be isolated in her privacy. She carries an embryo and, later, a fetus, if one accepts the medical definitions of the developing young in the human uterus. The situation therefore is inherently different from marital intimacy, or bedroom possession of obscene material, or marriage, or procreation, or education, with which *Eisenstadt, Griswold, Stanley, Loving, Skinner, Pierce,* and *Meyer* were respectively concerned. As we have intimated above, it is reasonable and appropriate for a State to decide that at some point in time another interest, that of health of the mother or that of potential human life, becomes significantly involved. The woman's privacy is no longer sole and any right of privacy she possesses must be measured accordingly.

Texas urges that, apart from the Fourteenth Amendment, life begins at conception and is present throughout pregnancy, and that, therefore, the State has a compelling interest in protecting that life from and after conception. We need not resolve the difficult question of when life begins. When those trained in the respective disciplines of medicine, philosophy, and theology are unable to arrive at any consensus, the judiciary, at this point in the development of man's knowledge, is not in a position to speculate as to the answer.

It should be sufficient to note briefly the wide divergence of thinking on this most sensitive and difficult question. There has always been strong support for the view that life does not begin until live birth. This was the belief of the Stoics. It appears to be the predominant, though not the unanimous, attitude of the Jewish faith. It may be taken to represent also the position of a large segment of the Protestant community, insofar as that can be ascertained; organized groups that have taken a formal position on the abortion issue have generally regarded abortion as a matter for the conscience of the individual and her family. As we have noted, the common law found greater significance in quickening. Physicians and their scientific colleagues have regarded that event with less interest and have tended to focus either upon conception, upon live birth, or upon the interim point at which the fetus becomes "viable," that is, potentially able to live outside the mother's womb, albeit with artificial aid. Viability is usually placed at about seven months (28 weeks) but may occur earlier, even at 24 weeks. The Aristotelian theory of "mediate animation," that held sway throughout the Middle Ages and the Renaissance in Europe, continued to be official Roman Catholic dogma until the 19th century, despite opposition to this "ensoulment" theory from those in the Church who would recognize the existence of life from the moment of con-

a. When Texas urges that a fetus is entitled to Fourteenth Amendment protection as a person, it faces a dilemma. Neither in Texas nor in any other State are all abortions prohibited. Despite broad proscription, an exception always exists. The exception . . . for an abortion procured or attempted by medical advice for the purpose of saving the life of the mother, is typical. But if the fetus is a person who is not to be deprived of life without due process of law, and if the mother's condition is the sole determinant, does not the Texas exception appear to be out of line with the Amendment's command?

ception. The latter is now, of course, the official belief of the Catholic Church. As one of the briefs amicus discloses, this is a view strongly held by many non-Catholics as well, and by many physicians. Substantial problems for precise definition of this view are posed, however, by new embryological data that purport to indicate that conception is a "process" over time; rather than an event, and by new medical techniques such as menstrual extraction, the "morning-after" pill, implantation of embryos, artificial insemination, and even artificial wombs.

In areas other than criminal abortion, the law has been reluctant to endorse any theory that life, as we recognize it, begins before live birth or to accord legal rights to the unborn except in narrowly defined situations and except when the rights are contingent upon live birth. For example, the traditional rule of tort law denied recovery for prenatal injuries even though the child was born alive. That rule has been changed in almost every jurisdiction. In most States, recovery is said to be permitted only if the fetus was viable, or at least quick, when the injuries were sustained, though few courts have squarely so held. In a recent development, generally opposed by the commentators, some States permit the parents of a stillborn child to maintain an action for wrongful death because of prenatal injuries. Such an action, however, would appear to be one to vindicate the parents' interest and is thus consistent with the view that the fetus, at most, represents only the potentiality of life. Similarly, unborn children have been recognized as acquiring rights or interests by way of inheritance or other devolution of property, and have been represented by guardians ad litem. Perfection of the interests involved, again, has generally been contingent upon live birth. In short, the unborn have never been recognized in the law as persons in the whole sense.

X

In view of all this, we do not agree that, by adopting one theory of life, Texas may override the rights of the pregnant woman that are at stake. We repeat, however, that the State does have an important and legitimate interest in preserving and protecting the health of the pregnant woman, whether she be a resident of the State or a nonresident who seeks medical consultation and treatment there, and that it has still *another* important and legitimate interest in protecting the potentiality of human life. These interests are separate, and distinct. Each grows in substantiality as the woman approaches term and, at a point during pregnancy, each becomes "compelling."

With respect to the State's important and legitimate interest in the health of the mother, the "compelling" point, in the light of present medical knowledge, is at approximately the end of the first trimester. This is so because of the now established medical fact . . . that until the end of the first trimester mortality in abortion may be less than mortality in normal childbirth. It follows that, from and after this point, a State may regulate the abortion procedure to the extent that the regulation reasonably relates to the preservation and protection of maternal health. Examples of permissible state regulation in this area are requirements as to the qualifications of the person who is to perform the abortion; as to the licensure of that person; as to the facility in which the procedure is to be performed, that is, whether it must be a hospital or may be a clinic or some other place of less-than-hospital status; as to the licensing of the facility; and the like.

This means, on the other hand, that, for the period of pregnancy prior to this "compelling" point, the attending physician, in consultation with his patient, is free to determine, without regulation by the State, that, in his medical judgment, the patient's pregnancy should be terminated. If that decision is reached, the judgment may be effectuated by an abortion free of interference by the State.

With respect to the State's important and legitimate interest in potential life, the "compelling" point is at viability. This is so because the fetus then presumably has the capability of meaningful life outside the mother's womb. State regulation protective of fetal life after viability thus has both logical and biological justifications. If the State is interested in protecting fetal life after viability, it may go so far as to proscribe abortion during that period, except when it is necessary to preserve the life or health of the mother.

Measured against these standards, . . . the Texas Penal Code, in restricting legal abortions to those "procured or attempted by medical advice for the purpose of saving the life of the mother," sweeps too broadly. The statute makes no distinction between abortions performed early in pregnancy and those performed later, and it limits to a single reason, "saving" the mother's life, the legal justification for the procedure. The statute, therefore, cannot survive the constitutional attack made upon it here. . . .

XI

To summarize and to repeat:

1. A state criminal abortion statute of the current Texas type, that excepts from criminality only a *lifesaving* procedure on behalf of the mother, without regard to pregnancy stage and without recognition of the other interests involved, is violative of the Due Process Clause of the Fourteenth Amendment.

(a) For the stage prior to approximately the end of the first trimester, the abortion decision and its effectuation must be left to the medical judgment of the pregnant woman's attending physician.

(b) For the stage subsequent to approximately the end of the first trimester, the State, in promoting its interest in the health of the mother, may, if it chooses, regulate the abortion procedure in ways that are reasonably related to maternal health.

(c) For the stage subsequent to viability, the State in promoting its interest in the potentiality of human life may, if it chooses, regulate, and even proscribe, abortion except where it is necessary, in appropriate medical judgment, for the preservation of the life or health of the mother.

2. The State may define the term "physician". . . to mean only a physician currently licensed by the State, and may proscribe any abortion by a person who is not a physician as so defined.

In Doe v. Bolton, . . . procedural requirements contained in one of the modern abortion statutes are considered. That opinion and this one, of course, are to be read together.[b]

b. Neither in this opinion nor in Doe v. Bolton do we discuss the father's rights, if any exist in the constitutional context, in the abortion decision. No paternal right has been asserted in either of the cases, and the Texas and the Georgia statutes on their face take no cognizance of the father. We are aware that some statutes recognize the father under certain circumstances. North Carolina, for example, requires written permission for the abortion from the husband when the woman is a married

This holding, we feel, is consistent with the relative weights of the respective interests involved, with the lessons and examples of medical and legal history, with the lenity of the common law, and with the demands of the profound problems of the present day. The decision leaves the State free to place increasing restrictions on abortion as the period of pregnancy lengthens, so long as those restrictions are tailored to the recognized state interests. The decision vindicated the right of the physician to administer medical treatment according to his professional judgment up to the points where important state interests provide compelling justifications for intervention. Up to those points, the abortion decision in all its aspects is inherently, and primarily, a medical decision, and basic responsibility for it must rest with the physician. If an individual practitioner abuses the privilege of exercising proper medical judgment, the usual remedies, judicial and intra-professional, are available.

[A concurring opinion by Chief Justice Burger is omitted.]

[In the companion case of Doe v. Bolton, 410 U.S. 179 (1973), the Court invalidated various procedural provisions of the Georgia abortion statute. It held that the requirement that abortions, but not other surgery, only be performed in hospitals accredited by the Joint Commission on Accreditation of Hospitals "simply is not 'based on differences that are reasonably related to the purposes of the Act in which it is found.' " The requirement that abortions be performed only in "a licensed hospital, rather than [in] . . . some other appropriately licensed institution" is invalid with respect to abortions performed in the first trimester, since the state "has not presented persuasive data to show that only hospitals meet its acknowledged interest in insuring the quality of the operation and the full protection of the patient." A requirement that abortions be approved by a hospital committee "is unduly restrictive of the patient's rights and needs that, at this point, have already been medically delineated and substantiated by her personal physician." For similar reasons the state could not require that two other physicians concur in the attending doctor's judgment that an abortion is appropriate, The Court also invalidated a provision to limit abortions to residents of the State.]

DOUGLAS, J., concurring. . . .

While I join the opinion of the Court, I add a few words.

I

The Ninth Amendment obviously does not create federally enforceable rights. It merely says, "The enumeration in the Constitution, of certain rights, shall not be construed to deny or disparage others retained by the people." But a catalogue of these rights includes customary, traditional, and time-honored rights, amenities, privileges, and immunities that come within the sweep of "the Blessings of Liberty" mentioned in the preamble to the Constitution. Many of them, in my view, come within the meaning of the term "liberty" as used in the Fourteenth Amendment.

---

minor, that is, when she is less than 18 years of age: if the woman is an unmarried minor, written permission from the parents is required. We need not now decide whether provisions of this kind are constitutional.

First is the autonomous control over the development and expression of one's intellect, interests, tastes, and personality.

These are rights protected by the First Amendment and, in my view, they are absolute, permitting of no exceptions. . . .

Second is freedom of choice in the basic decisions of one's life respecting marriage, divorce, procreation, contraception, and the education and upbringing of children.

These rights, unlike those protected by the First Amendment, are subject to some control by the police power. . . . These rights are "fundamental" and we have held that in order to support legislative action the statute must be narrowly and precisely drawn and that a "compelling state interest" must be shown in support of the limitation. . . .

Third is the freedom to care for one's health and person, freedom from bodily restraint or compulsion, freedom to walk, stroll, or loaf.

These rights, though fundamental, are likewise subject to regulation on a showing of "compelling state interest." . . .

The Georgia[35] statute is at war with the clear message . . . that a woman is free to make the basic decision whether to bear an unwanted child. Elaborate argument is hardly necessary to demonstrate that childbirth may deprive a woman of her preferred lifestyle and force upon her a radically different and undesired future. For example, rejected applicants under the Georgia statute are required to endure the discomforts of pregnancy; to incur the pain, higher mortality rate, and after effects of childbirth; to abandon educational plans; to sustain loss of income; to forgo the satisfactions of careers; to tax further mental and physical health in providing child care; and, in some cases, to bear the lifelong stigma of unwed motherhood, a badge which may haunt, if not deter, later legitimate family relationships.

II

The present statute has struck the balance between the woman's and the State's interests wholly in favor of the latter. I am not prepared to hold that a State may equate, as Georgia has done, all phases of maturation preceding birth. We held in *Griswold* that the States may not preclude spouses from attempting to avoid the joinder of sperm and egg. If this is true, it is difficult to perceive any overriding public necessity which might attach precisely at the moment of conception. . . .

In summary, the enactment is overbroad. It is not closely correlated to the aim of preserving prenatal life. In fact, it permits its destruction in several cases, including pregnancies resulting from sex acts in which unmarried females are below the statutory age of consent. At the same time, however, the measure broadly proscribes aborting other pregnancies which may cause severe mental disorders. Additionally, the statute is overbroad because it equates the value of embryonic life immediately after conception with the worth of life immediately before birth.

STEWART, J., concurring.

In 1963, this Court, in Ferguson v. Skrupa, 372 U.S. 726, purported to sound the death knell for the doctrine of substantive due process. . . . As Mr. Justice

35. Justice Douglas' concurrence is addressed largely to Georgia's relatively liberal abortion statute, much of which was invalidated in Doe v. Bolton. His remarks apply a fortiori to the Texas statute.

Black's opinion for the Court in *Skrupa* put it: "We have returned to the original constitutional proposition that courts do not substitute their social and economic beliefs for the judgment of legislative bodies, who are elected to pass laws."

Barely two years later, in Griswold v. Connecticut, the Court held a Connecticut birth control law unconstitutional. In view of what had been so recently said in *Skrupa,* the Court's opinion in *Griswold* understandably did its best to avoid reliance on the Due Process Clause of the Fourteenth Amendment as the ground for decision. Yet, the Connecticut law did not violate any provision of the Bill of Rights, nor any other specific provision of the Constitution. So it was clear to me then, and it is equally clear to me now, that the *Griswold* decision can be rationally understood only as a holding that the Connecticut statute substantively invaded the "liberty" that is protected by the Due Process Clause of the Fourteenth Amendment. As so understood, *Griswold* stands as one in a long line of pre-*Skrupa* cases decided under the doctrine of substantive due process, and I now accept it as such.

"In a Constitution for a free people, there can be no doubt that the meaning of 'liberty' must be broad indeed." The Constitution nowhere mentions a specific right of personal choice in matters of marriage and family life, but the "liberty" protected by the Due Process Clause of the Fourteenth Amendment covers more than those freedoms explicitly named in the Bill of Rights. . . .

Several decisions of this Court make clear that freedom of personal choice in matters of marriage and family life is one of the liberties protected by the Due Process Clause of the Fourteenth Amendment. As recently as last Term, in Eisenstadt v. Baird, we recognized "the right of the *individual,* married or single, to be free from unwarranted governmental intrusion into matters so fundamentally affecting a person as the decision whether to bear or beget a child." That right necessarily includes the right of a woman to decide whether or not to terminate her pregnancy. "Certainly the interests of a woman in giving of her physical and emotional self during pregnancy and the interests that will be affected throughout her life by the birth and raising of a child are of a far greater degree of significance and personal intimacy than the right to send a child to private school protected in Pierce v. Society of Sisters, or the right to teach a foreign language protected in Meyer v. Nebraska."

Clearly, therefore, the Court today is correct in holding that the right asserted by Jane Roe is embraced within the personal liberty protected by the Due Process Clause of the Fourteenth Amendment.

It is evident that the Texas abortion statute infringes that right directly. Indeed, it is difficult to imagine a more complete abridgment of a constitutional freedom than that worked by the inflexible criminal statute now in force in Texas. The question then becomes whether the state interests advanced to justify this abridgment can survive the "particularly careful scrutiny" that the Fourteenth Amendment here requires.

The asserted state interests are protection of the health and safety of the pregnant woman, and protection of the potential future human life within her. These are legitimate objectives, amply sufficient to permit a State to regulate abortions as it does other surgical procedures, and perhaps sufficient to permit a State to regulate abortions more stringently or even to prohibit them in the late stages of pregnancy. But such legislation is not before us, and I think the Court today has thoroughly demonstrated that these state interests cannot constitutionally support the broad abridgment of personal liberty worked by the existing Texas law. Accordingly, I join the Court's opinion holding that that law is invalid under the Due Process Clause of the Fourteenth Amendment.

REHNQUIST, J., dissenting. . . .

I have difficulty in concluding, as the Court does, that the right of "privacy" is involved in this case. Texas by the statute here challenged, bars the performance of a medical abortion by a licensed physician on a plaintiff such as Roe. A transaction resulting in an operation such as this is not "private" in the ordinary usage of that word. Nor is the "privacy" that the Court finds here even a distant relative of the freedom from searches and seizures protected by the Fourth Amendment to the Constitution, which the Court has referred to as embodying a right to privacy.

If the Court means by the term "privacy" no more than that the claim of a person to be free from unwanted state regulation of consensual transactions may be a form of "liberty" protected by the Fourteenth Amendment, there is no doubt that similar claims have been upheld in our earlier decision on the basis of that liberty. I agree with the statement of Mr. Justice Stewart in his concurring opinion that the "liberty," against deprivation of which without due process the Fourteenth Amendment protects, embraces more than the rights found in the Bill of Rights. But that liberty is not guaranteed absolutely against deprivation, only against deprivation without due process of law. The test traditionally applied in the area of social and economic legislation is whether or not a law such as that challenged has a rational relation to a valid state objective. Williamson v. Lee Optical Co., 348 U.S. 483, 491 (1955). The Due Process Clause of the Fourteenth Amendment undoubtedly does place a limit, albeit a broad one, on legislative power to enact laws such as this. If the Texas statute were to prohibit an abortion even where the mother's life is in jeopardy, I have little doubt that such a statute would lack a rational relation to a valid state objective under the test stated in *Williamson,* supra. But the Court's sweeping invalidation of any restrictions on abortion during the first trimester is impossible to justify under that standard, and the conscious weighing of competing factors that the Court's opinion apparently substitutes for the established test is far more appropriate to a legislative judgment than to a judicial one. . . .

While the Court's opinion quotes from the dissent of Mr. Justice Holmes in Lochner v. New York, the result it reaches is more closely attuned to the majority opinion of Mr. Justice Peckham in that case. As in *Lochner* and similar cases applying substantive due process standards to economic and social welfare legislation, the adoption of the compelling state interest standard will inevitably require this Court to examine the legislative policies and pass on the wisdom of these policies in the very process of deciding whether a particular state interest put forward may or may not be "compelling." The decision here to break pregnancy into three distinct terms and to outline the permissible restrictions the State may impose in each one, for example, partakes more of judicial legislation than it does of a determination of the intent of the drafters of the Fourteenth Amendment.

The fact that a majority of the States reflecting, after all, the majority sentiment in those States, have had restrictions on abortions for at least a century is a strong indication, it seems to me, that the asserted right to an abortion is not "so rooted in the traditions and conscience of our people as to be ranked as fundamental." Even today, when society's views on abortion are changing, the very existence of the debate is evidence that the "right" to an abortion is not so universally accepted as the appellants would have us believe.

To reach its result the Court necessarily has had to find within the scope of the Fourteenth Amendment a right that was apparently completely unknown to the drafters of the Amendment. . . . By the time of the adoption of the Fourteenth Amendment in 1868, there were at least 36 laws enacted by state or territorial legislatures limiting abortion. While many States have amended or updated their laws, 21 of the laws on the books in 1868 remain in effect today. . . .

There apparently was no question concerning the validity of [the Texas] or of any of the other state statutes when the Fourteenth Amendment was adopted. The only conclusion possible from this history is that the drafters did not intend to have the Fourteenth Amendment withdraw from the States the power to legislate with respect to this matter. . . .

WHITE, J., joined by Rehnquist, J., dissenting.

At the heart of the controversy in these cases are those recurring pregnancies that pose no danger whatsoever to the life or health of the mother but are, nevertheless, unwanted for any one or more of a variety of reasons — convenience, family planning, economics, dislike of children, the embarrassment of illegitimacy, etc. The common claim before us is that for any one of such reasons, or for no reason at all, and without asserting or claiming any threat to life or health, any woman is entitled to an abortion at her request if she is able to find a medical advisor willing to undertake the procedure.

The Court for the most part sustains this position: During the period prior to the time the fetus becomes viable, the Constitution of the United States values the convenience, whim, or caprice of the putative mother more than the life or potential life of the fetus; the Constitution, therefore, guarantees the right to an abortion as against any state law or policy seeking to protect the fetus from an abortion not prompted by more compelling reasons of the mother.

With all due respect, I dissent. I find nothing in the language or history of the Constitution to support the Court's judgment. The Court simply fashions and announces a new constitutional right for pregnant mothers and, with scarcely any reason or authority for its action, invests that right with sufficient substance to override most existing state abortion statutes. The upshot is that the people and the legislatures of the 50 States are constitutionally disentitled to weigh the relative importance of the continued existence and development of the fetus, on the one hand, against a spectrum of possible impacts on the mother, on the other hand. As an exercise of raw judicial power, the Court perhaps has authority to do what it does today; but in my view its judgment is an improvident and extravagant exercise of the power of judicial review that the Constitution extends to this Court.

The Court apparently values the convenience of the pregnant mother more than the continued existence and development of the life or potential life that she carries. Whether or not I might agree with that marshaling of values, I can in no event join the Court's judgment because I find no constitutional warrant for imposing such an order of priorities on the people and legislatures of the States. In a sensitive area such as this, involving as it does issues over which reasonable men may easily and heatedly differ, I cannot accept the Court's exercise of its clear power of choice by interposing a constitutional barrier to state efforts to protect human life and by investing mothers and doctors with the constitutionally protected right to exterminate it. This issue, for the most part, should be left with the people and to the political processes the people have devised to govern their affairs. . . .

Discussion[36]

Parts VII-IX of Justice Blackmun's opinion for the Court contain the core of its reasoning: A woman has a (prima facie) right to abort her pregnancy, which can only be defeated by a compelling state interest. During the first two trimesters, the state's interest is limited to protecting the woman's health: During the first, the state can require that a physician approve and perform the abortion; during the second, it may require other health-related measures. During the third trimester, an interest in the "potentiality of human life" emerges and justifies restricting the decision to abort. (What is the operational significance of part VI — the lengthy survey of past and present laws and attitudes regarding abortion? How might different historical evidence have affected the reasoning or the outcome of the decision?)

1. The woman's interest. How does the Court establish that the due process right to privacy includes, prima facie, the right to an abortion? What is the nature of the privacy interest involved? Did Roe v. Wade establish a general right to control one's own body? (For example, are regulations affecting all medical and surgical procedures now subject to the "compelling interest" standard?) If something more of constitutional significance is involved, what is it, and what is its relation to the right of "privacy"?

2. The interest of the fetus. Is Justice Blackmun persuasive that "person" as used in the Fourteenth Amendment does not include the unborn? Could a fetus be a "person" for some legal purposes but not others? Assuming that his conclusion is correct, what follows from it? What would follow if the fetus were a "person"?[37]

What is the fundamental philosophical issue facing the Court in this portion of the opinion — and how is it characterized by Justice Blackmun? By the dissenters? Why needn't the Court "resolve the difficult question of when life begins"? What, exactly, is the nature of the state's "important and legitimate interest in protecting the potentiality of human life"? Would it be accurate to say that the basic question is whether and when the fetus is a being with a claim to life, i.e., a "person" for moral purposes? Unless one adopts the position that this claim attaches upon conception, is there any tenable basis for choosing a time, in terms of physical development or events, when this claim attaches (or when the state's interest becomes "compelling")? Consider Professor Laurence Tribe's suggestion that the asserted right to abort a viable fetus is "not only a right to *remove* an unwanted fetus from one's body, but also an entirely separate right *to ensure its*

36. See generally John Ely, The Wages of Crying Wolf, 82 Yale L.J. 920 (1973); Philip Heymann & Douglas Barzelay, The Forest and the Trees, 53 B.U.L. Rev. 765 (1973); Laurence Tribe, Toward a Model of Roles in the Due Process of Life and Law, 87 Harv. L. Rev. 1 (1973).

37. For an argument that the fetus has due process rights not to be aborted, see David Louisell, Abortion, The Practice of Medicine and the Due Process of Law, 16 U.C.L.A.L. Rev. 233 (1969). But see Donald Regan, Rewriting *Roe v. Wade*, 77 Mich. L. Rev. 1569 (1979), arguing that, even if the fetus is considered a person, general common law principles of good samaratinism would justify abortion in many contexts.

death," i.e., a right to commit infanticide.[38] Consider whether the Court might have adopted Professor Michael Tooley's position that an "organism possesses a serious right to life only if it possesses the concept of a self as a continuing subject of experiences and other mental states, and believes that it is itself such a continuing entity."[39]

3. The accommodation of the interests. In view of the fact that much of the opinion preceding part X demonstrates the lack of a consensus regarding the medico-ethical issues of abortion, should the first sentence of part X have read as follows?

> In view of all this, we cannot conclude that the Constitution adopts one particular theory of life. Therefore we cannot conclude that the Ninth or Fourteenth Amendment prevents a state from determining that the unborn child's right to life attaches at any point after conception, or that the Constitution precludes a state from making whatever accommodation of the competing interests of the mother and her unborn child it believes appropriate.

Is the Court's point that once a prima facie right to privacy is established, something more than a lack of consensus with respect to the competing interests is required to defeat it? To the extent that the mother's constitutional right to privacy is ultimately grounded in moral consensus, isn't that right qualified or weakened by a lack of consensus about whether it may ethically be exercised to abort a fetus?

4. An alternative to accommodation? Professor Laurence Tribe has suggested that Roe v. Wade might better have been decided in terms of a " 'personal question' doctrine — a doctrine embodying the concept that some types of choices ought to be remanded, on principle, to private decisionmakers unchecked by substantive governmental control":[40]

> The Court was not, after all, choosing simply between the alternatives of abortion and continued pregnancy. *It was instead choosing among alternative allocations of decisionmaking authority,* for the issue it faced was whether the woman and her doctor, rather than an agency of government, should have the authority to make the abortion decision at various stages of pregnancy. The appellant's argument in *Roe* was not that the Court should decide "for abortion," but rather that the Court should transfer the role of decisionmaker from the government to the woman herself. Despite what the Court's opinion seemed to say, the result it reached was not the simple "substitution of one non-rational judgment for another concerning the relative importance of a mother's opportunity to live the life she has planned and a fetus's opportunity to live at all," but was instead a decision about *who should make judgments of that sort.*

Does the role allocation model provide a different and useful way of analyzing Roe v. Wade? Consider *Lochner, Griswold,* and the other cases in this section in terms of the role allocation model.

38. Tribe, supra note 36, at 27.

39. Abortion and Infanticide, 2 Phil. & Pub. Affairs 37, 44 (1972). Cf. Sydney Shoemaker, Self-Knowledge and Self-Identity (1963). Tooley's position eliminates the moral dilemma of abortion and implies that infanticide may raise no serious moral issues. For discussions of the philosophical issues involving abortion, see, e.g., Daniel Callahan, Abortion: Law, Choice and Morality (1970); Judith Thompson, A Defense of Abortion, 1 Phil. & Pub. Affairs 47 (1971).

40. Tribe, supra note 36, at 32.

5. *Feminist responses to the right established in* Roe. A number of scholars have suggested that the abortion dilemma is fundamentally an issue of sexual equality and therefore might more appropriately be analyzed under equal protection doctrine.[41] By casting the issue in essentially gender-neutral terms, the Court, in this view, suppresses the extent to which abortion regulations disadvantage women in society. Professor Sylvia Law writes:

> The rhetoric of privacy, as opposed to equality, blunts our ability to focus on the fact that it is *women* who are oppressed when abortion is denied. A privacy right that demands that "the abortion decision . . . be left to the medical judgment of the pregnant woman's physician," gives doctors undue power by falsely casting the abortion decision as primarily a medical question. The rhetoric of privacy also reinforces a public/private dichotomy that is at the heart of the structures that perpetuate the powerlessness of women.[42]

Under an equal protection rationale, at what point would the rights of the mother give way to the State's interest in the fetus?[43]

B. Decisions After *Roe*

Roe has proved one of the most controversial and bitterly contested Supreme Court decisions of this century. Although a number of subsequent decisions affirmed and expanded *Roe's* holding, its authority has more recently been called into question. Justice White and Chief Justice Rehnquist have adhered to their views expressed in dissent from the 1973 decision. Four of the Justices who constituted part of the *Roe* majority — Stewart, Powell, Brennan, and Marshall — have been replaced by Justices O'Connor, Kennedy, Souter, and Thomas, respectively. Whatever their ultimate stance on the formal overruling of *Roe*, none of these justices has displayed the commitment to the case characteristic of their predecessors (or of Justice Blackmun, the lone remaining member of the 1973 majority). Justice Scalia, who joined the Court upon Chief Justice Burger's resignation in 1984, is perhaps the most insistent on overruling *Roe*.

41. See, e.g., Kenneth Karst, Foreword: Equal Citizenship Under the Fourteenth Amendment, 91 Harv. L. Rev. 1 (1977). Professor Tribe has also recognized the equality implications of *Roe*: "To give society — especially a male-dominated society — the power to sentence women to childbearing against their will is to delegate to some a sweeping and unaccountable authority over the lives of others. Any such allocation of power operates to the serious detriment of women as a class . . . [and] burden[s] the participation of women as equals in society." Tribe, American Constitutional Law 1354 (2d ed. 1988). See also Guido Calabresi, The Supreme Court, 1990 Term, Foreword: Antidiscrimination and Constitutional Accountability (What the Bork-Brennan Debate Ignores), 105 Harv. L. Rev. 80, 103-108 (1991).

42. Sylvia A. Law, Rethinking Sex and the Constitution, 132 U. Pa. L. Rev. 955, 1020 (1984) (quoting Roe v. Wade).

43. See also Jed Rubenfeld, The Right of Privacy, 102 Harv. L. Rev. 737, 782 (1989):

> [U]nderlying the idea that a woman is *defining her identity* by determining not to have a child is the very premise of those institutionalized sexual roles through which the subordination of women has for so long been maintained. Only if it were "natural" for a woman to want to bear children — and unnatural if she did not — would it make sense to insist that the decision not to have a child at one given moment was centrally definitive of a womans' identity. . . . The claim that an abortion is a fundamental act of self-definition is nothing other than a corollary to the insistence that motherhood, or at least the desire to be a mother, is the fundamental, inescapable, natural backdrop of womanhood against which every woman is defined.

In Webster v. Reproductive Health Services, 492 U.S. 490 (1989), a fragmented Court upheld a number of restrictions on abortion without (save for Justice Scalia) firmly addressing the continued vitality of *Roe*. See also Hodgson v. Minnesota, 110 S. Ct. 2926 (1990), and Ohio v. Akron Center for Reproductive Health, 110 S. Ct. 2972 (1990). In 1991, both Pennsylvania and Louisiana passed antiabortion laws that were clearly designed to test the limits of *Roe*. As this is being written, certiorari is being sought from the Supreme Court by both sides in regards to the Pennsylvania statute. By the time you read this, the Supreme Court may well have clarified its views on the extent to which abortion continues to be protected by the Constitution.

Because current abortion doctrine is so unstable, the discussion below is designed primarily to address the fundamental issues underlying *Roe*. The pre-*Webster* abortion decisions are also useful to the extent that they expose some of the trickier doctrinal complexities raised by *Roe's* tripartite scheme.[44]

In Planned Parenthood of Central Missouri v. Danforth, 428 U.S. 52 (1976), the Court scrutinized a variety of provisions in a 1974 Missouri statute concerning abortions. Justice Blackmun wrote the Court's opinion.

Viability. Section 5 of the Missouri statute prohibits an abortion not necessary to preserve the life or health of the mother "unless the attending physician certifies with reasonable certainty that the fetus is not viable." Section 2(2) defines "viability" as "that stage of fetal development when the life of the unborn child may be continued indefinitely outside the womb by natural or artificial life-supportive systems." The Court held that this definition was consistent with *Roe*, noting that "it is not the proper function of the legislature or the courts to place viability, which is essentially a medical concept, at a specific point in the gestation period." Section 2(2) reflects the fact that "[t]he time when viability is achieved may vary with each pregnancy, and the determination of whether a particular fetus is viable is, and must be, a matter for the judgment of the responsible attending physician." Justice Stewart, joined by Justice Powell, joined in the Court's opinion on this issue, noting that the statute only requires "physicians performing abortions to *certify* that the fetus to be aborted is not viable" and imposes no punishment for an erroneous determination.

Duty to preserve the life of the fetus. Section 6(1) of the statute provides:

> No person who performs or induces an abortion shall fail to exercise that degree of professional skill, care and diligence to preserve the life and health of the fetus which such person would be required to exercise in order to preserve the life and health of any fetus intended to be born and not aborted.

A physician who fails to exercise this standard of care is guilty of manslaughter and liable for damages if death results. The Court held that the provision "impermissibly requires the physician to preserve the health and life of the fetus, whatever the stage of pregnancy" and "does not specify that such care need be taken

44. The discussion that follows is not intended as a comprehensive survey of post-*Roe* litigation. In particular, we do not treat two important issues. One concerns the constitutionality of state and federal legislation excluding abortions from government programs subsidizing medical care. The other involves parental consultation and consent for minors' abortions. The first is addressed in Chapter 11. We leave the second for courses such as family or juvenile law, where they can be considered in the context of other policies concerning the legal status of minors.

only after the stage of viability has been reached." Justice White, joined by Chief Justice Burger and Justice Rehnquist, dissented on this issue. He believed that the statute could reasonably be read "to operate only in the gray area after the fetus *might* be viable but while the physician is still able to certify 'with reasonable medical certainty that the fetus is not viable.' . . . Since the State has a compelling interest, sufficient to outweigh the mother's desire to kill the fetus when the 'fetus . . . has the capability of meaningful life outside the mother's womb,' *Roe,* the statute is constitutional."

Saline amniocentesis. The Court struck down section 9 of the statute, prohibiting the use of saline amniocentesis as a method of abortion after the twelfth week of pregnancy, holding that the provision failed as a reasonable regulation for the protection of maternal health. Justice Blackmun noted that the saline method is the most commonly used method of abortion after the first trimester; that it is as safe as or safer than childbirth and most alternative means of abortion; and that the safer prostaglandin technique was not generally available in Missouri when the section was enacted and the State had not proved that it was available at the time of trial. Justice Stevens concurred, noting that, on the record, section 9 "was almost tantamount to a prohibition of any abortion in the State after the first twelve weeks of pregnancy." Justice White, joined by Chief Justice Burger and Justice Rehnquist, dissented, arguing that the record did not show that the prostaglandin method was unavailable in Missouri and indeed suggested the opposite.

Spousal consent. Section 3(3) requires the prior written consent of the spouse of a woman seeking an abortion during the first 12 weeks of pregnancy, unless the abortion is necessary to preserve the mother's life. The Court concluded that, "since the State cannot regulate or proscribe abortion during the first stage, . . . the State cannot delegate authority to any particular person, even the spouse, to prevent abortion during that same period." Justice Blackmun recognized "the deep and proper concern and interest that a devoted and protective husband has in his wife's pregnancy and in the growth and development of the fetus she is carrying," and thought that "ideally, the decision to terminate a pregnancy should be one concurred in by both the wife and her husband." But he thought it unlikely that the marital relationship would be enhanced by giving the husband a veto power exercisable for any reason whatsoever or for no reason at all" and concluded that "[i]nasmuch as it is the woman who physically bears the child and who is the more directly and immediately affected by the pregnancy, as between the two, the balance weighs in her favor." Justice Stewart, joined by Justice Powell, concurred, though noting that the Court's decisions recognizing "a man's right to father children and enjoy the association of his offspring" made this "a rather more difficult problem than the Court acknowledges." Dissenting on this issue, Justice White, joined by Chief Justice Burger and Justice Rehnquist, wrote:

> A father's interest in having a child — perhaps his only child — may be unmatched by any other interest in his life. . . . In describing the nature of a mother's interest in terminating a pregnancy, the Court in Roe v. Wade mentioned only the post-birth burdens of rearing a child, and rejected a rule based on her interest in controlling her own body during pregnancy. Missouri has a law which prevents a woman from putting a child up for adoption over her husband's objection. This law represents a judgment by the State that the mother's interest in avoiding the burdens of child

rearing do not outweigh or snuff out the father's interest in participating in bringing up his own child. That law is plainly valid, but no more so than §3(3) of the Act now before us, resting as it does on precisely the same judgment.

Recordkeeping. Sections 10 and 11 of the statute require all health facilities and physicians to keep certain records on each abortion for the purpose, among others, of "adding to the sum of medical knowledge through the compilation of relevant maternal health and life data." The information "shall be confidential and shall be used only for statistical purposes"; the records are subject to inspection by local, state, and national public health officers; the health facility must keep the records for seven years. Justice Blackmun noted that "[a]s for the first stage [of pregnancy] one may argue forcefully, as appellants do, that the State should not be able to impose any recordkeeping requirements that significantly differ from those imposed with respect to other, and comparable, medical and surgical procedures." But he concluded that "§§10 and 11, while perhaps approaching impermissible limits, are not constitutionally offensive in themselves."

In a number of cases following *Danforth,* the Court continued to protect the right to abortion from state attempts at regulation.

CITY OF AKRON v. AKRON CENTER FOR REPRODUCTIVE HEALTH

462 U.S. 416 (1983)

On Writ of Certiorari to the United States Court of Appeals for the Sixth Circuit

[In 1978 Akron, Ohio, passed an ordinance regulating abortion, which included the following provisions:

1. §1870.03, requiring that all abortions performed after the first trimester of pregnancy be performed in a hospital;
2. §1870.05, requiring parental notification and consent for abortions to be performed on minors;
3. §1870.06, requiring the attending physician to make certain specified statements to the patient about the fetus prior to performing an abortion such as "the unborn child is a human life from the moment of conception" including a detailed anatomical and physiological description of the unborn child at the gestational point at which the abortion is performed and that it may be viable;
4. §1870.07, requiring a 24-hour waiting period after the signing of a consent form for an abortion, before the abortion can be performed; and
5. §1870.70, requiring that fetal remains be "disposed of in a humane and sanitary manner."]

POWELL, J.

III . . .

A

. . . We reaffirm today that a State's interest in health regulation becomes compelling at approximately the end of the first trimester. The existence of a compelling state interest in health, however, is only the beginning of the inquiry. The State's regulation may be upheld only if it is reasonably designed to further that state interest. . . . [I]f it appears that during a substantial portion of the second trimester the State's regulation "depart[s] from accepted medical practice," the regulation may not be upheld simply because it may be reasonable for the remaining portion of the trimester. Rather, the State is obligated to make a reasonable effort to limit the effect of its regulations to the period in the trimester during which its health interest will be furthered.

B

There can be no doubt that §1870.03's second-trimester hospitalization requirement places a significant obstacle in the path of women seeking an abortion. A primary burden created by the requirement is additional cost to the woman. The Court of Appeals noted that there was testimony that a second-trimester abortion costs more than twice as much in a hospital as in a clinic. See 651 F.2d, at 1209 (in-hospital abortion costs $850-$900, wheress a dilatation-and-evacuation (D & E) abortion performed in a clinic costs $350-$400). Moreover, the court indicated that second-trimester abortions were rarely performed in Akron hospitals. Ibid. (only nine second-trimester abortions performed in Akron hospitals in the year before the trial). Thus, a second-trimester hospitalization requirement may force women to travel to find available facilities, resulting in both financial expense and additional health risk. It therefore is apparent that a second-trimester hospitalization requirement may significantly limit a woman's ability to obtain an abortion.

Akron does not contend that §1870.03 imposes only an insignificant burden on women's access to abortion, but rather defends it as a reasonable health regulation. This position had strong support at the time of Roe v. Wade. . . . Since then, however, the safety of second-trimester abortions has increased dramatically. The principal reason is that the D & E procedure is now widely and successfully used for second-trimester abortions. The Court of Appeals found that there was "an abundance of evidence that D & E is the safest method of performing post-first trimester abortions today." . . .

For our purposes, an even more significant factor is that experience indicates that D & E may be performed safely on an outpatient basis in appropriate nonhospital facilities. . . .

These developments, and the professional commentary supporting them, constitute impressive evidence that — at least during the early weeks of the second-trimester — D & E abortions may be performed as safely in an outpatient clinic as in a full-service hospital. We conclude, therefore, that "present medical knowledge" convincingly undercuts Akron's justification for requiring that *all* second-trimester abortions be performed in a hospital.

[Part IV, dealing with the parental notification and consent requirements, is omitted.]

V

The Akron ordinance provides that no abortion shall be performed except "with the informed written consent of the pregnant woman, . . . given freely and without coercion." §1870.06(A). Furthermore, "in order to insure that the consent for an abortion is truly informed consent," the woman must be "orally informed by her attending physician" of the status of her pregnancy, the development of her fetus, the date of possible viability, the physical and emotional complications that may result from an abortion, and the availability of agencies to provide her with assistance and information with respect to birth control, adoption, and childbirth. §1870.06(B). In addition, the attending physician must inform her "of the particular risks associated with her own pregnancy and the abortion technique to be employed . . . [and] other information which in his own medical judgment is relevant to her decision as to whether to have an abortion or carry her pregnancy to term." §1870.06(C).

A . . .

The validity of an informed consent requirement . . . rests on the State's interest in protecting the health of the pregnant woman. . . . This does not mean, however, that a State has unreviewable authority to decide what information a woman must be given before she chooses to have an abortion. It remains primarily the responsibility of the physician to ensure that appropriate information is conveyed to his patient, depending on her particular circumstances. *Danforth's* recognition of the State's interest in ensuring that this information be given will not justify abortion regulations designed to influence the woman's informed choice between abortion or childbirth.

B

Viewing the city's regulations in this light, we believe that §1870.06(B) attempts to extend the State's interest in ensuring "informed consent" beyond permissible limits. First, it is fair to say that much of the information required is designed not to inform the woman's consent but rather to persuade her to withhold it altogether. . . .

An additional, and equally decisive, objection to §1870.06(B) is its intrusion upon the discretion of the pregnant woman's physician. This provision specifies a litany of information that the physician must recite to each woman regardless of whether in his judgment the information is relevant to her personal decision. . . . Akron has gone far beyond merely describing the general subject matter relevant to informed consent. By insisting upon recitation of a lengthy and inflexible list of information, Akron unreasonably has placed "obstacles in the path of the doctor upon whom [the woman is] entitled to rely for advice in connection with her decision."

C

Section 1870.06(C) presents a different question. Under this provision, the "attending physician" must inform the woman

> of the particular risks associated with her own pregnancy and the abortion technique to be employed including providing her with at least a general description of the medical instructions to be followed subsequent to the abortion in order to insure her safe recovery, and shall in addition provide her with such other information which in his own medical judgment is relevant to her decision as to whether to have an abortion or carry her pregnancy to term.

The information required clearly is related to maternal health and to the State's legitimate purpose in requiring informed consent. . . . [I]n contrast to subsection (B), §1870.06(C) merely describes in general terms the information to be disclosed. It properly leaves the precise nature and amount of this disclosure to the physician's discretion and "medical judgment."

The Court of Appeals also held, however, that §1870.06(C) was invalid because it required that the disclosure be made by the "attending physician." . . .

[I]n *Roe* and subsequent cases we have . . . left no doubt that, to ensure the safety of the abortion procedure, the States may mandate that only physicians perform abortions.

We are not convinced, however, that there is as vital a state need for insisting that the physician performing the abortion, or for that matter any physician, personally counsel the patient in the absence of a request. The State's interest is in ensuring that the woman's consent is informed and unpressured; the critical factor is whether she obtains the necessary information and counseling from a qualified person, not the identity of the person from whom she obtains it. . . .

VI

The Akron ordinance prohibits a physician from performing an abortion until 24 hours after the pregnant woman signs a consent form. §1870.07.

We find that Akron has failed to demonstrate that any legitimate state interest is furthered by an arbitrary and inflexible waiting period. . . . In accordance with the ethical standards of the profession, a physician will advise the patient to defer the abortion when he thinks this will be beneficial to her. But if a woman, after appropriate counseling, is prepared to give her written informed consent and proceed with the abortion, a State may not demand that she delay the effectuation of that decision.

VII

[The Court held that §1870.70 was impermissibly vague as a definition of conduct subject to criminal prosecution, and therefore violated the Due Process Clause.]

O'CONNOR, J., joined by Rehnquist and White, JJ., dissenting. . . .

I

The trimester or "three-stage" approach adopted by the Court in *Roe,* and, in a modified form, employed by the Court to analyze the state regulations in these cases, cannot be supported as a legitimate or useful framework for accommodating the woman's right and the State's interests. The decision of the Court today graphically illustrates why the trimester approach is a completely unworkable method of accommodating the conflicting personal rights and compelling state interests that are involved in the abortion context.

As the Court indicates today, the State's compelling interest in maternal health changes as medical technology changes, and any health regulation must not "depart from accepted medical practice." In applying this standard, the Court holds that "the safety of second-trimester abortions has increased dramatically" since 1973, when *Roe* was decided. Although a regulation such as one requiring that all second-trimester abortions be performed in hospitals "had strong support" in 1973 "as reasonable health regulation," ibid., this regulation can no longer stand because, according to the Court's diligent research into medical and scientific literature, the dilation and evacuation procedure (D&E), used in 1973 only for first-trimester abortions, "is now widely and successfully used for second trimester abortions." . . .

It is not difficult to see that despite the Court's purported adherence to the trimester approach adopted in *Roe,* the lines drawn in that decision have now been "blurred" because of what the Court accepts as technological advancement in the safety of abortion procedure. The State may no longer rely on a "bright line" that separates permissible from impermissible regulation, and it is no longer free to consider the second trimester as a unit and weigh the risks posed by all abortion procedures throughout that trimester. Rather, the State must continuously and conscientiously study contemporary medical and scientific literature in order to determine whether the effect of a particular regulation is to "depart from accepted medical practice" insofar as particular procedures and particular periods within the trimester are concerned. Assuming that legislative bodies are able to engage in this exacting task, it is difficult to believe that our Constitution *requires* that they do it as a prelude to protecting the health of their citizens. It is even more difficult to believe that this Court, without the resources available to those bodies entrusted with making legislative choices, believes itself competent to make these inquiries and to revise these standards every time the American College of Obstetricians and Gynecologists (ACOG) or similar group revises its views about what is and what is not appropriate medical procedure in this area. . . .

Just as improvements in medical technology inevitably will move *forward* the point at which the State may regulate for reasons of maternal health, different technological improvements will move *backward* the point of viability at which the State may proscribe abortions except when necessary to preserve the life and health of the mother. . . .

[R]ecent studies have demonstrated increasingly earlier fetal viability. It is certainly reasonable to believe that fetal viability in the first trimester of pregnancy may be possible in the not too distant future. . . .

The *Roe* framework, then, is clearly on a collision course with itself. As the medical risks of various abortion procedures decrease, the point at which the

State may regulate for reasons of maternal health is moved further forward to actual childbirth. As medical science becomes better able to provide for the separate existence of the fetus, the point of viability is moved further back toward conception. Moreover, it is clear that the trimester approach violates the fundamental aspiration of judicial decision making through the application of neutral principles "sufficiently absolute to give them roots throughout the community and continuity over significant periods of time. . . ." A. Cox, The Role of the Supreme Court in American Government 114 (1976).

Even assuming that there is a fundamental right to terminate pregnancy in some situations, there is no justification in law or logic for the trimester framework adopted in *Roe* and employed by the Court today on the basis of stare decisis. For the reasons stated above, that framework is clearly an unworkable means of balancing the fundamental right and the compelling state interests that are indisputably implicated.

II

The Court in *Roe* correctly realized that the State has important interest "in the areas of health and medical standards" and that "[t]he State has a legitimate interest in seeing to it that abortion, like any other medical procedure, is performed under circumstances that insure maximum safety for the patient." The Court also recognized that the State has "*another* important and legitimate interest in protecting the potentiality of human life." I agree completely that the State has these interests, but in my view, the point at which these interests become compelling does not depend on the trimester of pregnancy. Rather, these interests are present *throughout* pregnancy.

The fallacy inherent in the *Roe* framework is apparent: just because the State has a compelling interest in ensuring maternal safety once an abortion may be more dangerous than childbirth, it simply does not follow that the State has *no* interest before that point that justifies state regulation to ensure that first-trimester abortions are performed as safely as possible.

The State interest in potential human life is likewise extant throughout pregnancy. In *Roe,* the Court held that although the State had an important and legitimate interest in protecting potential life, that interest could not become compelling until the point at which the fetus was viable. The difficulty with this analysis is clear: *potential* life is no less potential in the first weeks of pregnancy than it is at viability or afterward. At any stage of pregnancy, there is the *potential* for human life. Although the Court refused to "resolve the difficult question of when life begins," the Court chose the point of viability — when the fetus is *capable* of life independent of its mother — to permit the complete proscription of abortion. The choice of viability as the point at which the State interest in *potential* life becomes compelling is no less arbitrary than choosing any point before viability or any point afterward. Accordingly, I believe that the State's interest in protecting potential human life exists throughout the pregnancy.

III

Although the State possesses compelling interests in the protection of potential human life and in maternal health throughout pregnancy, not every regulation that the State imposes must be measured against the State's compelling interests and examined with strict scrutiny. . . . "*Roe* did not declare an unqualified 'constitutional right to an abortion.' . . . Rather, the right protects the woman from unduly burdensome interference with her freedom to decide whether to terminate her pregnancy." *Maher,* 432 U.S., at 473-474. The Court and its individual Justices have repeatedly utilized the "unduly burdensome" standard in abortion cases. . . .

The "unduly burdensome" standard is particularly appropriate in the abortion context because of the *nature* and *scope* of the right that is involved. . . . Rather, the *Roe* right is intended to protect against state action "drastically limiting the availability and safety of the desired service," against the imposition of an "absolute obstacle" on the abortion decision, *Danforth,* or against "official interference" and "coercive restraint" imposed on the abortion decision. That a state regulation may "inhibit" abortions to some degree does not require that we find that the regulation is invalid.

The abortion cases demonstrate that an "undue burden" has been found for the most part in situations involving absolute obstacles or severe limitations on the abortion decision. . . .

In determining whether the State imposes an "undue burden," we must keep in mind that when we are concerned with extremely sensitive issues, such as the one involved here, "the appropriate forum for their resolution in a democracy is the legislature." . . .

IV

[Justice O'Connor found that the first four Akron provisions did not place an "undue burden" on the abortion decision. She further found that the fifth provision, concerning the "humane disposal" of fetuses, required only that "fetuses will not be 'dump[ed] . . . on garbage piles,' " quoting from the brief submitted by Akron.]

Discussion

1. *Roe* holds that the State's interest in a mother's health first becomes compelling in the second trimester, because first trimester abortions are generally safer than second trimester abortions. The Court in *Akron* found that the D & E method permitted safe abortions well into the second trimester, however. As Justice O'Connor pointed out, why should the second trimester continue to serve as a benchmark for determining when the State's interest in maternal health becomes compelling?

2. The Court strikes down Akron's "informed consent" provision both because it invades the woman's protected right to privacy and because it "intru[des] upon the discretion of the pregnant woman's physician." Does this imply that the physician has a separate protected right? If so, is this right unique to the abortion context, or might it embrace all physician-patient relationships? If, on the other hand, the physician's right is simply an extension of the woman's protected right, would the Constitution protect a woman's right to have an abortion over her physician's objection?

3. In response to Justice O'Connor's critique of the unstable nature of the boundaries in *Roe's* tripartite scheme, Professor Tribe has offered a defense of viability as a proper constitutional concern:

> [A]s technology enhances the ability to relieve the pregnant woman of the burden of her pregnancy and transfer nurture of the fetus to other hands, the state's power to protect fetal life expands — *as it should.* A viability rule . . . allows society to optimize the protection of women *and* their unborn children by choosing how much to invest in the technologies pushing viability toward conception.[45]

4. In Thornburgh v. American College of Obstetricians and Gynecologists, 476 U.S. 747 (1986), the Court struck down a number of abortion regulations, including: (1) a requirement that a physician inform the patient of possible detrimental physical and psychological effects of abortion, medical assistance benefits for carrying the child to term, the father's liability for child support, and a list of agencies offering alternatives to abortion; (2) a requirement that literature be available describing the anatomical and physiological characteristics of the fetus at two-week gestational increments; (3) detailed reporting requirements; and (4) special postviability requirements, including the presence of a second physician. Justice Blackmun, writing for the Court, found that the "informed consent" requirements were "an outright attempt to wedge the Commonwealth's message discouraging abortion into the privacy of the . . . dialogue between the woman and her physician." He further found that the reporting requirements "raise the specter of public exposure and harrassment of women who choose to exercise their personal, intensely private right, with their physician, to end a pregnancy," and concluded that "States are not free, under the guise of protecting maternal health or potential life, to intimidate women into continuing pregnancies." Justice Blackmun concluded with a reaffirmation of *Roe* and its progeny:

> Constitutional rights do not always have easily ascertainable boundaries, and controversy over the meaning of our Nation's most majestic guarantees frequently has been turbulent. As judges, however, we are sworn to uphold the law even when its content gives rise to bitter dispute. We recognized at the very beginning of our opinion in *Roe* that abortion raises moral and spiritual questions over which honorable persons can disagree sincerely and profoundly. But those disagreements did not then and do not now relieve us of our duty to apply the Constitution faithfully.
>
> Our cases long have recognized that the Constitution embodies a promise that a certain private sphere of individual liberty will be kept largely beyond the reach of government. That promise extends to women as well as to men. Few decisions are more personal and intimate, more properly private, or more basic to individual dignity and autonomy, than a woman's decision — with the guidance of her physician and within the limits specified in *Roe* — whether to end her pregnancy. A woman's right to make that choice freely is fundamental. Any other result, in our view, would protect inadequately a central part of the sphere of liberty that our law guarantees equally to all.

Chief Justice Burger, dissenting, would have upheld the regulations as falling well within the permissible limits articulated in *Roe*. He stated that "every Mem-

45. Tribe, American Constitutional Law 1357-1358 (2d ed. 1988). See also Tribe, Abortion: A Clash of Absolutes (1990).

ber of the *Roe* Court rejected the idea of abortion on demand. The Court's opinion today, however, plainly undermines that important principle, and I regretfully conclude that some of the concerns of the dissenting Justices in *Roe,* as well as the concerns I expressed in my separate opinion, have now been realized. . . . If *Danforth* and today's holding really mean what they seem to say, I agree we should reexamine *Roe.*"

In a lengthy dissent, Justice White, joined by Justice Rehnquist, again attacked the notion that the abortion decision was fundamental. He favored a much more deferential standard:

> I can certainly agree with the proposition — which I deem indisputable — that a woman's ability to choose an abortion is a species of "liberty" that is subject to the general protections of the Due Process Clause. I cannot agree, however, that this liberty is so "fundamental" that restrictions upon it call into play anything other than the most minimal scrutiny.

Justice White also argued that *stare decisis* provided an insufficient basis for adhering to the right established in *Roe*:

> [D]ecisions that find in the Constitution principles or values that cannot fairly be read into that document usurp the people's authority, for such decisions represent choices that the people have never made and that they cannot disavow through corrective legislation. For this reason, it is essential that this Court maintain the power to restore authority to its proper possessors by correcting constitutional decisions that, on reconsideration, are found to be mistaken.

Justice O'Connor, in a dissent joined by Justice Rehnquist, reiterated her position from *Akron.*

Three years after *Thornburgh,* the Court seriously called into question the continued authority of its prior abortion decisions.

WEBSTER v. REPRODUCTIVE HEALTH SERVICES

492 U.S. 490 (1989)

Appeal from the United States Court of Appeals for the Eighth Circuit

REHNQUIST, C.J., for the Court with respect to Parts I, II-A, II-B, and II-C, and, with respect to Parts II-D and III, joined only by Justices White and Kennedy.

II

Decision of this case requires us to address four sections of a 1986 Missouri Act: (a) the preamble[, containing "findings" by the state legislature that "[t]he life of each human being begins at conception," and that "unborn children have protectable interests in life, health, and well-being."]; (b) the prohibition on the use of public facilities or employees to perform abortions; (c) the prohibition on public funding of abortion counseling; and (d) the requirement that physicians conduct viability tests prior to performing abortions. We address these seriatim.

A

The State contends that the preamble itself is precatory and imposes no substantive restrictions on abortions, and that appellees therefore do not have standing to challenge it. Appellees, on the other hand, insist that the preamble is an operative part of the Act intended to guide the interpretation of other provisions of the Act.

In our view, [*Akron* held] only that a State could not "justify" an abortion regulation otherwise invalid under Roe v. Wade on the ground that it embodied the State's view about when life begins. Certainly the preamble does not by its terms regulate abortion or any other aspect of appellees' medical practice. The Court has emphasized that Roe v. Wade "implies no limitation on the authority of a State to make a value judgment favoring childbirth over abortion." Maher v. Roe. The preamble can be read simply to express that sort of value judgment.

We think the extent to which the preamble's language might be used to interpret other state statutes or regulations is something that only the courts of Missouri can definitively decide.... We therefore need not pass on the constitutionality of the Act's preamble.

B

[The Court next concluded that the prohibition on the use of public facilities for abortions was permissible under Maher v. Roe and Harris v. McRae. For a discussion of these cases, see Chapter 11, below.]

C

[The Court accepted the State's claim that §188.205's prohibition on public funding of abortions "is not directed at the conduct of any physician or health care provider, private, or public, [but] is directed solely at those persons responsible for expending public funds." Because appellees contended that they were not "adversely" affected under the State's interpretation of §188.205, and therefore that there was no longer a case or controversy on this question, "the controversy over §188.205 is now moot."]

D . . .

The viability-testing provision of the Missouri Act is concerned with promoting the State's interest in potential human life rather than in maternal health. Section 188.029 creates what is essentially a presumption of viability at 20 weeks, which the physician must rebut with tests indicating that the fetus is not viable prior to performing an abortion. It also directs the physician's determination as to viability by specifying consideration, if feasible, of gestational age, fetal weight, and lung capacity. The District Court found that "the medical evidence is uncontradicted that a 20-week fetus is not viable," and that "23½ to 24 weeks gestation is the earliest point in pregnancy where a reasonable possibility of viability exists." But it also found that there may be a 4-week error in estimating gestational age, which supports testing at 20 weeks....

We think that the doubt cast upon the Missouri statute . . . is not so much a flaw in the statute as it is a reflection of the fact that the rigid trimester analysis of the course of a pregnancy enunciated in *Roe* has resulted in subsequent cases like *Colautti* and *Akron* making constitutional law in this area a virtual Procrustean bed. . . .

In the first place, the rigid *Roe* framework is hardly consistent with the notion of a Constitution cast in general terms, as ours is, and usually speaking in general principles, as ours does. The key elements of the *Roe* framework — trimesters and viability — are not found in the text of the Constitution or in any place else one would expect to find a constitutional principle. Since the bounds of the inquiry are essentially indeterminate, the result has been a web of legal rules that have become increasingly intricate, resembling a code of regulations rather than a body of constitutional doctrine.

In the second place, we do not see why the State's interest in protecting potential human life should come into existence only at the point of viability, and that there should therefore be a rigid line allowing state regulation after viability but prohibiting it before viability. . . . The tests that §188.029 requires the physician to perform are designed to determine viability. The State here has chosen viability as the point at which its interest in potential human life must be safeguarded. It is true that the tests in question increase the expense of abortion, and regulate the discretion of the physician in determining the viability of the fetus. Since the tests will undoubtedly show in many cases that the fetus is not viable, the tests will have been performed for what were in fact second-trimester abortions. But we are satisfied that the requirement of these tests permissibly furthers the State's interest in protecting potential human life, and we therefore believe §188.029 to be constitutional.

The dissent takes us to task for our failure to join in a "great issues" debate as to whether the Constitution includes an "unenumerated" general right to privacy as recognized in cases such as *Griswold* and *Roe*. But *Griswold*, unlike *Roe*, did not purport to adopt a whole framework, complete with detailed rules and distinctions, to govern the cases in which the asserted liberty interest would apply. . . . The experience of the Court in applying Roe v. Wade in later cases suggests to us that there is wisdom in not unnecessarily attempting to elaborate the abstract differences between a "fundamental right" to abortion, as the Court described it in *Akron*, a "limited fundamental constitutional right," which Justice Blackmun's dissent today treats *Roe* as having established, or a liberty interest protected by the Due Process Clause, which we believe it to be. The Missouri testing requirement here is reasonably designed to ensure that abortions are not performed where the fetus is viable — an end which all concede is legitimate — and that is sufficient to sustain its constitutionality.

The dissent also accuses us, inter alia, of cowardice and illegitimacy in dealing with "the most politically divisive domestic legal issue of our time." There is no doubt that our holding today will allow some governmental regulation of abortion that would have been prohibited under the language of cases such as Colautti v. Franklin and *Akron.* But the goal of constitutional adjudication is surely not to remove inexorably "politically divisive" issues from the ambit of the legislative process, whereby the people through their elected representatives deal with matters of concern to them. The goal of constitutional adjudication is to hold true the balance between that which the Constitution puts beyond the reach of the democratic process and that which it does not. We think we have done that today. . . .

III

Both appellants and the United States as Amicus Curiae have urged that we overrule our decision in Roe v. Wade. . . . This case . . . affords us no occasion to revisit the holding of *Roe*, which was that the Texas statute unconstitutionally infringed the right to an abortion derived from the Due Process Clause, and we leave it undisturbed. To the extent indicated in our opinion, we would modify and narrow Roe and succeeding cases. Because none of the challenged provisions of the Missouri Act properly before us conflict with the Constitution, the judgment of the Court of Appeals is reversed.

O'CONNOR, J., concurring in part and concurring in the judgment.
I concur in Parts I, II-A, II-B, and II-C of the Court's opinion. . . .

II

In its interpretation of Missouri's "determination of viability" provision, the plurality has proceeded in a manner unnecessary to deciding the question at hand. . . .

Unlike the plurality, I do not understand these viability testing requirements to conflict with any of the Court's past decisions concerning state regulation of abortion. Therefore, there is no necessity to accept the State's invitation to reexamine the constitutional validity of *Roe*. Where there is no need to decide a constitutional question, it is a venerable principle of this Court's adjudicatory processes not to do so. . . .

I do not think . . . [that] §188.029, as interpreted by the Court, imposes a degree of state regulation on the medical determination of viability that in any way conflicts with prior decisions of this Court. . . .

It is clear to me that requiring the performance of examinations and tests useful to determining whether a fetus is viable, when viability is possible, and when it would not be medically imprudent to do so, does not impose an undue burden on a woman's abortion decision. On this ground alone I would reject the suggestion that §188.029 as interpreted is unconstitutional. More to the point, however, just as I see no conflict between §188.029 and *Colautti* or any decision of this Court concerning a State's ability to give effect to its interest in potential life, I see no conflict between §188.029 and the Court's opinion in *Akron*. The second-trimester hospitalization requirement struck down in *Akron* imposed, in the majority's view, "a heavy, and unnecessary, burden," more than doubling the cost of "women's access to a relatively inexpensive, otherwise accessible, and safe abortion procedure." By contrast, the cost of examinations and tests that could usefully and prudently be performed when a woman is 20-24 weeks pregnant to determine whether the fetus is viable would only marginally, if at all, increase the cost of abortion. . . .

I would reverse. . . .

SCALIA, J., concurring in part and concurring in the judgment.

I join Parts I, II-A, II-B, and II-C of the opinion of The Chief Justice. As to Part II-D, I share Justice Blackmun's view that it effectively would overrule Roe v. Wade. I think that should be done, but would do it more explicitly. . . .

The outcome of today's case will doubtless be heralded as a triumph of judicial statesmanship. It is not that, unless it is statesmanlike needlessly to prolong this Court's self-awarded sovereignty over a field where it has little proper business since the answers to most of the cruel questions posed are political and not juridicial — a sovereignty which therefore quite properly, but to the great damage of the Court, makes it the object of the sort of organized public pressure that political institutions in a democracy ought to receive.

Justice O'Connor's assertion that a " 'fundamental rule of judicial restraint' " requires us to avoid reconsidering *Roe*, cannot be taken seriously. By finessing *Roe* we do not, as she suggests, adhere to the strict and venerable rule that we should avoid " 'decid[ing] questions of a constitutional nature.' " We have not disposed of this case on some statutory or procedural ground, but have decided, and could not avoid deciding, whether the Missouri statute meets the requirements of the United States Constitution. The only choice available is whether, in deciding that constitutional question, we should use Roe v. Wade as the benchmark, or something else. What is involved, therefore, is not the rule of avoiding constitutional issues where possible, but the quite separate principle that we will not " 'formulate a rule of constitutional law broader than is required by the precise facts to which it is to be applied.' " The latter is a sound general principle, but one often departed from when good reason exists. . . .

The real question . . . is whether there are valid reasons to go beyond the most stingy possible holding today. It seems to me there are not only valid but compelling ones. Ordinarily, speaking no more broadly than is absolutely required avoids throwing settled law into confusion; doing so today preserves a chaos that is evident to anyone who can read and count. Alone sufficient to justify a broad holding is the fact that our retaining control, through *Roe*, of what I believe to be, and many of our citizens recognize to be, a political issue, continuously distorts the public perception of the role of this Court. We can now look forward to at least another Term with carts full of mail from the public, and streets full of demonstrators, urging us — their unelected and life-tenured judges who have been awarded those extraordinary, undemocratic characteristics precisely in order that we might follow the law despite the popular will — to follow the popular will. Indeed, I expect we can look forward to even more of that than before, given our indecisive decision today. . . .

It was an arguable question today whether §188.029 of the Missouri law contravened this Court's understanding of Roe v. Wade, and I would have examined *Roe* rather than examining the contravention. Given the Court's newly contracted abstemiousness, what will it take, one must wonder, to permit us to reach the fundamental question? The result of our vote today is that we will not reconsider that prior opinion, even if most of the Justices think it is wrong, unless we have before us a statute that in fact contradicts it — and even then (under our newly discovered "no-broader-than-necessary" requirement) only minor problematical aspects of *Roe* will be reconsidered, unless one expects State legislatures to adopt provisions whose compliance with *Roe* cannot even be argued with a straight face. It thus appears that the mansion of constitutionalized abortion-law, constructed overnight in Roe v. Wade, must be disassembled door-jamb by door-jamb, and never entirely brought down, no matter how wrong it may be. . . .

Of the four courses we might have chosen today — to reaffirm *Roe*, to overrule it explicitly, to overrule it sub silentio, or to avoid the question — the last is the least responsible. On the question of the constitutionality of §188.029, I concur in the judgment of the Court and strongly dissent from the manner in which it has been reached.

BLACKMUN, J., with whom Brennan and Marshall, JJ., join, concurring in part and dissenting in part.

Today, Roe v. Wade and the fundamental constitutional right of women to decide whether to terminate a pregnancy, survive but are not secure. Although the Court extricates itself from this case without making a single, even incremental, change in the law of abortion, the plurality and Justice Scalia would overrule *Roe* (the first silently, the other explicitly) and would return to the States virtually unfettered authority to control the quintessentially intimate, personal, and life-directing decision whether to carry a fetus to term. Although today, no less than yesterday, the Constitution and the decisions of this Court prohibit a State from enacting laws that inhibit women from the meaningful exercise of that right, a plurality of this Court implicitly invites every state legislature to enact more and more restrictive abortion regulations in order to provoke more and more test cases, in the hope that sometime down the line the Court will return the law of procreative freedom to the severe limitations that generally prevailed in this country before January 22, 1973. Never in my memory has a plurality announced a judgment of this Court that so foments disregard for the law and for our standing decisions. . . .

I

A . . .

As properly construed, the viability-testing provision does not pass constitutional muster under even a rational-basis standard. . . . By mandating tests to determine fetal weight and lung maturity for every fetus thought to be more than 20 weeks gestational age, the statute requires physicians to undertake procedures, such as amniocentesis, that, in the situation presented, have no medical justification, impose significant additional health risks on both the pregnant woman and the fetus, and bear no rational relation to the State's interest in protecting fetal life. As written, §188.029 is an arbitrary imposition of discomfort, risk, and expense, furthering no discernible interest except to make the procurement of an abortion as arduous and difficult as possible. Thus, were it not for the plurality's tortured effort to avoid the plain import of §188.029, it could have struck down the testing provision as patently irrational irrespective of the *Roe* framework. . . .

If, as the plurality appears to hold, the testing provision simply requires a physician to use appropriate and medically sound tests to determine whether the fetus is actually viable when the estimated gestational age is greater than 20 weeks (and therefore within what the District Court found to be the margin of error for viability), then I see little or no conflict with *Roe*. Nothing in *Roe,* or any of its progeny, holds that a State may not effectuate its compelling interest in the potential life of a viable fetus by seeking to ensure that no viable fetus is mistakenly aborted because of the inherent lack of precision in estimates of gestational age. . . . In short, the testing provision, as construed by the plurality is consistent with the Roe framework and could be upheld effortlessly under current doctrine. . . .

B

1 . . .

With respect to the *Roe* framework, the general constitutional principle, indeed the fundamental constitutional right, for which it was developed is the right to privacy, a species of "liberty" protected by the Due Process Clause, which under our past decisions safeguards the right of women to exercise some control over their own role in procreation. . . . It is this general principle, the " 'moral fact that a person belongs to himself and not others nor to society as a whole,' " that is found in the Constitution. The trimester framework simply defines and limits that right to privacy in the abortion context to accommodate, not destroy, a State's legitimate interest in protecting the health of pregnant women and in preserving potential human life. Fashioning such accommodations between individual rights and the legitimate interests of government, establishing benchmarks and standards with which to evaluate the competing claims of individuals and government, lies at the very heart of constitutional adjudication. To the extent that the trimester framework is useful in this enterprise, it is not only consistent with constitutional interpretation, but necessary to the wise and just exercise of this Court's paramount authority to define the scope of constitutional rights. . . .

2

That numerous constitutional doctrines result in narrow differentiations between similar circumstances does not mean that this Court has abandoned adjudication in favor of regulation. Rather, these careful distinctions reflect the process of constitutional adjudication itself, which is often highly fact-specific, requiring such determinations as whether state laws are "unduly burdensome" or "reasonable" or bear a "rational" or "necessary" relation to asserted state interests. . . . If, in delicate and complicated areas of constitutional law, our legal judgments "have become increasingly intricate," it is not, as the plurality contends, because we have overstepped our judicial role. Quite the opposite: the rules are intricate because we have remained conscientious in our duty to do justice carefully, especially when fundamental rights rise or fall with our decisions. . . .

C

Having contrived an opportunity to reconsider the *Roe* framework, and then having discarded that framework, the plurality finds the testing provision unobjectionable because it "permissibly furthers the State's interest in protecting potential human life." This newly minted standard is circular and totally meaningless. Whether a challenged abortion regulation "permissibly furthers" a legitimate state interest is the *question* that courts must answer in abortion cases, not the standard for courts to apply. In keeping with the rest of its opinion, the plurality makes no attempt to explain or to justify its new standard, either in the abstract or as applied in this case. Nor could it. The "permissibly furthers" standard has no independent meaning, and consists of nothing other than what a majority of this Court may believe at any given moment in any given case. The plurality's novel test appears to be nothing more than a dressed-up version of rational-basis review, this Court's most lenient level of scrutiny. One thing is clear, however: were the plurality's "permissibly furthers" standard adopted by the Court, for all practical purposes, *Roe* would be overruled.

The "permissibly furthers" standard completely disregards the irreducible minimum of *Roe*: the Court's recognition that a woman has a limited fundamental constitutional right to decide whether to terminate a pregnancy. That right receives no meaningful recognition in the plurality's written opinion. Since, in the plurality's view, the State's interest in potential life is compelling as of the moment of conception, and is therefore served only if abortion is abolished, every hindrance to a woman's ability to obtain an abortion must be "permissible." . . .

D

Thus, "not with a bang, but a whimper," the plurality discards a landmark case of the last generation, and casts into darkness the hopes and visions of every woman in this country who had come to believe that the Constitution guaranteed her the right to exercise some control over her unique ability to bear children. The plurality does so either oblivious or insensitive to the fact that millions of women, and their families, have ordered their lives around the right to reproductive choice, and that this right has become vital to the full participation of women in the economic and political walks of American life. The plurality would clear the way once again for government to force upon women the physical labor and specific and direct medical and psychological harms that may accompany carrying a fetus to term. The plurality would clear the way again for the State to conscript a woman's body and to force upon her a "distressful life and future."

The result, as we know from experience, would be that every year hundreds of thousands of women, in desperation, would defy the law, and place their health and safety in the unclean and unsympathetic hands of back-alley abortionists, or they would attempt to perform abortions upon themselves, with disastrous results. Every year, many women, especially poor and minority women, would die or suffer debilitating physical trauma, all in the name of enforced morality or religious dictates or lack of compassion, as it may be. . . .

II

For today, at least, the law of abortion stands undisturbed. For today, the women of this Nation still retain the liberty to control their destinies. But the signs are evident and very ominous, and a chill wind blows.

I dissent.

[A separate opinion by Justice Stevens, concurring in part and dissenting in part, is omitted.]

Note: Subsequent Cases

In Hodgson v. Minnesota, 110 S. Ct. 2926 (1990), and Ohio v. Akron Center for Reproductive Health, 110 S. Ct. 2972 (1990), the Court upheld parental-notification requirements for a minor to gain access to an abortion. Under the challenged state laws, parents could not veto the abortion decision, but were entitled to notification by their daughter about her pregnancy and possible abortion. Ohio requires that only one parent be notified; Minnesota required that the child seek out both of her parents, even if they had never been married, were divorced, or were otherwise not living with one another or the child. Ohio allowed a minor to "bypass" the notification requirement by persuading a court that there was good cause. The Minnesota statute indicated that a bypass provision would automatically become part of the scheme if a court ruled that it was constitutionally required.

As usual, the Court was fragmented. Justice Scalia wrote, "concurring in the judgment in part and dissenting in part," in *Hodgson*:

> As I understand the various opinions today: . . . Justice [O'Connor] holds that two parent-notification is unconstitutional (at least in the present circumstances) without judicial bypass, but constitutional with bypass; . . . [Justices Kennedy, White, Scalia, and Chief Justice Rehnquist] would hold that two-parent notification is constitutional with or without bypass; . . . Justices [Stevens, Brennan, Marshall, and Blackmun] would hold that two-parent notification is unconstitutional with or without bypass, though the four apply two different standards; . . . Justices [White, O'Connor, Scalia, Stevens, Kennedy, and Chief Justice Rehnquist] hold that one-parent notification with bypass is constitutional, though for two different sets of reasons; and . . . Justices [Brennan, Marshall, and Blackmun] would hold one-parent notification with bypass is unconstitutional.

In her concurring opinion, Justice O'Connor agreed with the Court's statement that "[a] woman's decision to beget or to bear a child is a component of her liberty that is protected by the Due Process Clause of the Fourteenth Amendment to the Constitution." She also noted that, after *Roe*, minors could be treated differently from adults. She then restated her previously expressed view that "[i]f the particular regulation does not 'unduly burde[n]' the fundamental right, . . . then our evaluation of that regulation is limited to our determination that the regulation rationally relates to a legitimate state purpose." Applying this standard, she concluded that the Minnesota statute imposed an undue burden, by requiring, for example, a minor to notify even an abusive parent of her pregnancy.

Justice O'Connor's opinion necessarily assumes that *Roe* remains good constitutional doctrine. Much of the speculation about the eventual fate of *Roe* has focused on her willingness, or not, to countenance its overruling.

VI. Sexuality and Sexual Orientation

BOWERS v. HARDWICK
478 U.S. 186 (1986)
Certiorari to the United States Court of Appeals for the Eleventh Circuit

[On the morning of August 3, 1982, Officer K.R. Torick entered Michael Hardwick's house in Atlanta, Georgia, to serve him with an arrest warrant on a charge of failing to appear in court for drinking in public. "Torick later claimed in his official report that when he arrived to serve the arrest warrant, one of Michael's housemates answered the door and admitted the officer. 'The roommate told me [he] didn't know if Hardwick was home but said I could come in to look for him. While walking down the hallway inside the house, I saw a bedroom door partially open.' Torick entered the bedroom and promptly arrested Michael and his male companion for violating the Georgia sodomy statute."[46] Following a preliminary hearing, the District Attorney decided not to press the sodomy charge. Hardwick then filed suit in federal court challenging the constitutionality of Georgia's criminalization of consensual sodomy. After a district judge dismissed the suit, a divided panel of the Eleventh Circuit held in Hardwick's favor. Justice White, writing for the Court, reversed:]

This case does not require a judgment on whether laws against sodomy between consenting adults in general, or between homosexuals in particular, are wise or desirable. It raises no question about the right or propriety of state legislative decisions to repeal their laws that criminalize homosexual sodomy, or of state court decisions invalidating those laws on state constitutional grounds. The issue presented is whether the Federal Constitution confers a fundamental right upon homosexuals to engage in sodomy and hence invalidates the laws of the many States that still make such conduct illegal and have done so for a very long time. The case also calls for some judgment about the limits of the Court's role in carrying out its constitutional mandate.

We first register our disagreement with the Court of Appeals and with respondent that the Court's prior cases have construed the Constitution to confer a right of privacy that extends to homosexual sodomy and for all intents and purposes have decided this case. The reach of this line of cases was sketched in Carey v. Population Services International. Pierce v. Society of Sisters and Meyer v. Nebraska were described as dealing with child rearing and education; Prince v. Massachusetts, 321 U.S. 158 (1944), with family relationships; Skinner v. Oklahoma ex rel. Williamson, with procreation; Loving v. Virginia, 388 U.S. 1 (1967), with marriage; Griswold v. Connecticut and Eisenstadt v. Baird, with contraception; and Roe v. Wade, 410 U.S. 113 (1973), with abortion. The latter three cases were interpreted as construing the Due Process Clause of the Fourteenth Amendment to confer a fundamental individual right to decide whether or not to beget or bear a child. . . .

46. Peter Irons, The Courage of Their Convictions 381 (1989). The statutory provision at issue, Ga. Code Ann. §16-6-2 (1984) reads as follows:

> (a) A person commits the offense of sodomy when he performs or submits to any sexual act involving the sex organs of one person and the mouth or anus of another. . . .
> (b) A person convicted of the offense of sodomy shall be punished by imprisonment for not less than one nor more than 20 years. . . .

[W]e think it evident that none of the rights announced in those cases bears any resemblance to the claimed constitutional right of homosexuals to engage in acts of sodomy that is asserted in this case. No connection between family, marriage, or procreation on the one hand and homosexual activity on the other has been demonstrated. . . . Moreover, any claim that these cases nevertheless stand for the proposition that any kind of private sexual conduct between consenting adults is constitutionally insulated from state proscription is unsupportable. . . .

Precedent aside, however, respondent would have us announce . . . a fundamental right to engage in homosexual sodomy. This we are quite unwilling to do. It is true that despite the language of the Due Process Clauses of the Fifth and Fourteenth Amendments, which appears to focus only on the processes by which life, liberty, or property is taken, the cases are legion in which those Clauses have been interpreted to have substantive content. . . . Among such cases are those recognizing rights that have little or no textual support in the constitutional language. . . .

Striving to assure itself and the public that announcing rights not readily identifiable in the Constitution's text involves much more than the imposition of the Justices' own choice of values on the States and the Federal Government, the Court has sought to identify the nature of the rights qualifying for heightened judicial protection. In Palko v. Connecticut, 302 U.S. 319, 325, 326 (1937), it was said that this category includes those fundamental liberties that are "implicit in the concept of ordered liberty," such that "neither liberty nor justice would exist if [they] were sacrificed." A different description of fundamental liberties appeared in Moore v. East Cleveland, 431 U.S. 494, 503 (1977) (opinion of Powell, J.), where they are characterized as those liberties that are "deeply rooted in this Nation's history and tradition."

It is obvious to us that neither of these formulations would extend a fundamental right to homosexuals to engage in acts of consensual sodomy. Proscriptions against that conduct have ancient roots. See generally, Survey on the Constitutional Right to Privacy in the Context of Homosexual Activity, 40 U. Miami L. Rev. 521, 525 (1986). Sodomy was a criminal offense at common law and was forbidden by the laws of the original thirteen States when they ratified the Bill of Rights. In 1868, when the Fourteenth Amendment was ratified, all but 5 of the 37 States in the Union had criminal sodomy laws. In fact, until 1961, all 50 States outlawed sodomy, and today, 24 States and the District of Columbia continue to provide criminal penalties for sodomy performed in private and between consenting adults. Against this background, to claim that a right to engage in such conduct is "deeply rooted in this Nation's history and tradition" or "implicit in the concept of ordered liberty" is, at best, facetious.

Nor are we inclined to take a more expansive view of our authority to discover new fundamental rights imbedded in the Due Process Clause. The Court is most vulnerable and comes nearest to illegitimacy when it deals with judge-made constitutional law having little or no cognizable roots in the language or design of the Constitution. . . . There should be, therefore, great resistance to expand the substantive reach of those Clauses, particularly if it requires redefining the category of rights deemed to be fundamental. Otherwise, the Judiciary necessarily takes to itself further authority to govern the country without express constitutional authority. The claimed right pressed on us today falls far short of overcoming this resistance.

Respondent, however, asserts that the result should be different where the homosexual conduct occurs in the privacy of the home. He relies on Stanley v. Georgia, 394 U.S. 557, 565 (1969), where the Court held that the First Amendment prevents conviction for possessing and reading obscene material in the privacy of his home: "If the First Amendment means anything, it means that a State has no business telling a man, sitting alone in his house, what books he may read or what films he may watch." *Stanley* did protect conduct that would not have been protected outside the home, and it partially prevented the enforcement of state obscenity laws; but the decision was firmly grounded in the First Amendment. The right pressed upon us here has no similar support in the text of the Constitution, and it does not qualify for recognition under the prevailing principles for construing the Fourteenth Amendment. Its limits are also difficult to discern. Plainly enough, otherwise illegal conduct is not always immunized whenever it occurs in the home. Victimless crimes, such as the possession and use of illegal drugs do not escape the law where they are committed at home. *Stanley* itself recognized that its holding offered no protection for the possession in the home of drugs, firearms, or stolen goods. And if respondent's submission is limited to the voluntary sexual conduct between consenting adults, it would be difficult, except by fiat, to limit the claimed right to homosexual conduct while leaving exposed to prosecution adultery, incest, and other sexual crimes even though they are committed in the home. We are unwilling to start down that road.

Even if the conduct at issue here is not a fundamental right, respondent asserts that there must be a rational basis for the law and that there is none in this case other than the presumed belief of a majority of the electorate in Georgia that homosexual sodomy is immoral and unacceptable. This is said to be an inadequate rationale to support the law. The law, however, is constantly based on notions of morality, and if all laws representing essentially moral choices are to be invalidated under the Due Process Clause, the courts will be very busy indeed. Even respondent makes no such claim, but insists that majority sentiments about the morality of homosexuality should be declared inadequate. We do not agree, and are unpersuaded that the sodomy laws of some 25 States should be invalidated on this basis.

BURGER, C.J., concurring.

. . . [P]roscriptions against sodomy have very "ancient roots." Decisions of individuals relating to homosexual conduct have been subject to state intervention throughout the history of Western Civilization. Condemnation of those practices is firmly rooted in Judaeo-Christian moral and ethical standards. Homosexual sodomy was a capital crime under Roman law. . . .

Blackstone described "the infamous crime against nature" as an offense of "deeper malignity" than rape, an heinous act "the very mention of which is a disgrace to human nature," and "a crime not fit to be named." The common law of England, including its prohibition of sodomy, became the received law of Georgia and the other Colonies. In 1816 the Georgia Legislature passed the statute at issue here, and that statute has been continuously in force in one form or another since that time. To hold that the act of homosexual sodomy is somehow protected as a fundamental right would be to cast aside millennia of moral teaching.

This is essentially not a question of personal "preferences" but rather of the legislative authority of the State. I find nothing in the Constitution depriving a State of the power to enact the statute challenged here.

POWELL, J., concurring.

I join the opinion of the Court. I agree with the Court that there is no fundamental right — i.e., no substantive right under the Due Process Clause — such as that claimed by respondent. . . . This is not to suggest, however, that respondent may not be protected by the Eighth Amendment of the Constitution. The Georgia statute at issue in this case . . . authorizes a court to imprison a person for up to 20 years for a single private, consensual act of sodomy. In my view, a prison sentence for such conduct — certainly a sentence of long duration — would create a serious Eighth Amendment issue. . . .

In this case, however, respondent has not been tried, much less convicted and sentenced. Moreover, respondent has not raised the Eighth Amendment issue below. For these reasons this constitutional argument is not before us.

BLACKMUN, J., joined by Brennan, Marshall, and Stevens, JJ., dissenting.

This case is no more about "a fundamental right to engage in homosexual sodomy," as the Court purports to declare, than Stanley v. Georgia was about a fundamental right to watch obscene movies, or Katz v. United States, 389 U.S. 347 (1967) [holding a warrantless wiretap of a public telephone prohibited by the Fourth Amendment], was about a fundamental right to place interstate bets from a telephone booth. Rather, this case is about "the most comprehensive of rights and the right most valued by civilized men," namely, "the right to be let alone." Olmstead v. United States, 277 U.S. 438, 478 (1928) (Brandeis, J., dissenting). The statute at issue denies individuals the right to decide for themselves whether to engage in particular forms of private, consensual sexual activity. The Court concludes that [the statute] is valid essentially because "the laws of . . . many States . . . still make such conduct illegal and have done so for a very long time." But the fact that the moral judgments expressed by statutes like [this one] may be "natural and familiar . . . ought not to conclude our judgment upon the question whether statutes embodying them conflict with the Constitution of the United States." Roe v. Wade, 410 U.S. 113, 117 (1973), quoting Lochner v. New York, 198 U.S. 45, 76 (1905) (Holmes, J., dissenting). Like Justice Holmes, I believe that "[i]t is revolting to have no better reason for a rule of law than that so it was laid down in the time of Henry IV. It is still more revolting if the grounds upon which it was laid down have vanished long since, and the rule simply persists from blind imitation of the past." Holmes, The Path of the Law, 10 Harv. L. Rev. 457, 469 (1897). I believe we must analyze respondent's claim in the light of the values that underlie the constitutional right to privacy. . . .

I . . .

A fair reading of the statute and of the complaint clearly reveals that the majority has distorted the question this case presents.

First, the Court's almost obsessive focus on homosexual activity is particularly hard to justify in light of the broad language Georgia has used. Unlike the Court, the Georgia Legislature has not proceeded on the assumption that homosexuals are so different from other citizens that their lives may be controlled in a way that would not be tolerated if it limited the choices of those other citizens. Rather, Georgia has provided that "(a) person commits the offense of sodomy when he performs or submits to any sexual act involving the sex organs of one person and the mouth or anus of another." Ga. Code Ann. §16-6-2(a). The sex or status of the persons who engage in the act is irrelevant as a matter of state law. In fact, to the extent I can discern a legislative purpose for Georgia's 1968 enactment of §16-6-2, that purpose seems to have been to broaden the coverage of the law to reach heterosexual as well as homosexual activity.[a] I therefore see no basis for the Court's decision to treat this case as an "as applied" challenge to §16-6-2 or for Georgia's attempt, both in its brief and at oral argument, to defend §16-6-2 solely on the grounds that it prohibits homosexual activity. . . . [Hardwick's] claim that §16-6-2 involves an unconstitutional intrusion into his privacy and his right of intimate association does not depend in any way on his sexual orientation. . . .

In construing the right to privacy, the Court has proceeded along two somewhat distinct, albeit complementary, lines. First, it has recognized a privacy interest with reference to certain decisions that are properly for the individual to make. Second, it has recognized a privacy interest with reference to certain places without regard for the particular activities in which the individuals who occupy them are engaged. The case before us implicates both the decisional and the spatial aspects of the right to privacy.

A

The Court concludes today that none of our prior cases dealing with various decisions that individuals are entitled to make free of governmental interference "bears any resemblance to the claimed constitutional right of homosexuals to engage in acts of sodomy that is asserted in this case." While it is true that these cases may be characterized by their connection to protection of the family, the Court's conclusion that they extend no further than this boundary ignores the warning in Moore v. East Cleveland, 431 U.S. 494, 501 (1977) (plurality opinion), against "clos[ing] our eyes to the basic reasons why certain rights associated with the family have been accorded shelter under the Fourteenth Amendment's Due Process Clause." We protect those rights not because they contribute, in some direct and material way, to the general public welfare, but because they form so central a part of an individual's life. . . . And so we protect the decision whether to marry precisely because marriage "is an association that promotes a way of life, not causes; a harmony in living, not political faiths; a bilateral loyalty, not commercial or social projects." Griswold v. Connecticut, 381 U.S., at 486. We protect the decision whether to have a child because parenthood alters so dramatically an individual's self-definition, not because of demographic considerations or the Bible's command to be fruitful and multiply. And we protect the family because it contributes so powerfully to the happiness of individuals, not because of a prefer-

a. Until 1968, Georgia defined sodomy as "the carnal knowledge and connection against the order of nature, by man with man, or in the same unnatural manner with woman." Ga. Crim. Code s 26-5901 (1933). [After two Georgia Supreme Court decisions refusing to apply the statute, respectively, to lesbian activity and to heterosexual cunnilingus,] Georgia passed the act-specific statute currently in force "perhaps in response to the restrictive court decisions. . . ." Note, The Crimes Against Nature, 16 J. Pub. L. 159, 167, n.47 (1967).

ence for stereotypical households. The Court recognized in Roberts v. United States Jaycees, 468 U.S. 609, 619 (1984), that the "ability independently to define one's identity that is central to any concept of liberty" cannot truly be exercised in a vacuum; we all depend on the "emotional enrichment of close ties with others."

Only the most willful blindness could obscure the fact that sexual intimacy is "a sensitive, key relationship of human existence, central to family life, community welfare, and the development of human personality." The fact that individuals define themselves in a significant way through their intimate sexual relationships with others suggests, in a Nation as diverse as ours, that there may be many "right" ways of conducting those relationships, and that much of the richness of a relationship will come from the freedom an individual has to choose the form and nature of these intensely personal bonds. . . . The Court claims that its decision today merely refuses to recognize a fundamental right to engage in homosexual sodomy; what the Court really has refused to recognize is the fundamental interest all individuals have in controlling the nature of their intimate associations with others.

B

The behavior for which Hardwick faces prosecution occurred in his own home, a place to which the Fourth Amendment attaches special significance. The Court's treatment of this aspect of the case is symptomatic of its overall refusal to consider the broad principles that have informed our treatment of privacy in specific cases. Just as the right to privacy is more than the mere aggregation of a number of entitlements to engage in specific behavior, so too, protecting the physical integrity of the home is more than merely a means of protecting specific activities that often take place there. . . . The Court's interpretation of the pivotal case of Stanley v. Georgia, 394 U.S. 557 (1969), is entirely unconvincing. Stanley held that Georgia's undoubted power to punish the public distribution of constitutionally unprotected, obscene material did not permit the State to punish the private possession of such material. According to the majority here, *Stanley* relied entirely on the First Amendment, and thus, it is claimed, sheds no light on cases not involving printed materials. But that is not what *Stanley* said. Rather, the *Stanley* Court anchored its holding in the Fourth Amendment's special protection for the individual in his home. . . . "He is asserting the right to read or observe what he pleases — the right to satisfy his intellectual and emotional needs in the privacy of his own home." . . .

"The right of the people to be secure in their . . . houses," expressly guaranteed by the Fourth Amendment, is perhaps the most "textual" of the various constitutional provisions that inform our understanding of the right to privacy, and thus I cannot agree with the Court's statement that "[t]he right pressed upon us here has no . . . support in the text of the Constitution." Indeed, the right of an individual to conduct intimate relationships in the intimacy of his or her own home seems to me to be the heart of the Constitution's protection of privacy.

III

The Court's failure to comprehend the magnitude of the liberty interests at stake in this case leads it to slight the question whether petitioner, on behalf of the

State, has justified Georgia's infringement on these interests. I believe that neither of the two general justifications for §16-6-2 that petitioner has advanced warrants dismissing respondent's challenge for failure to state a claim.

First, petitioner asserts that the acts made criminal by the statute may have serious adverse consequences for "the general public health and welfare," such as spreading communicable diseases or fostering other criminal activity. Inasmuch as this case was dismissed by the District Court on the pleadings, it is not surprising that . . . [n]othing in the record before the Court provides any justification for finding the activity forbidden by §16-6-2 to be physically dangerous, either to the persons engaged in it or to others.

The core of petitioner's defense of §16-6-2, however, is that respondent and others who engage in the conduct prohibited by §16-6-2 interfere with Georgia's exercise of the " 'right of the Nation and of the States to maintain a decent society' " Paris Adult Theater I v. Slaton, 413 U.S. 49 (1973). . . . I cannot agree that either the length of time a majority has held its convictions or the passions with which it defends them can withdraw legislation from this Court's scrutiny. See, e.g., Loving v. Virginia, 388 U.S. 1 (1967) [invalidating state anti-miscegenation law].[b] It is precisely because the issue raised by this case touches the heart of what makes individuals what they are that we should be especially sensitive to the rights of those whose choices upset the majority.

The assertion that "traditional Judaeo-Christian values proscribe" the conduct involved cannot provide an adequate justification for §16-6-2. . . . The legitimacy of secular legislation depends instead on whether the State can advance some justification for its law beyond its conformity to religious doctrine. Thus, far from buttressing his case, [Bowers's] invocation of Leviticus, Romans, St. Thomas Aquinas, and sodomy's heretical status during the Middle Ages undermines his suggestion that §16-6-2 represents a legitimate use of secular coercive power. A State can no more punish private behavior because of religious intolerance than it can punish such behavior because of racial animus. . . .

Nor can §16-6-2 be justified as a "morally neutral" exercise of Georgia's power to "protect the public environment." Certainly, some private behavior can affect the fabric of society as a whole. . . . [But petitioner] and the Court fail to see the difference between laws that protect public sensibilities and those that enforce private morality. Statutes banning public sexual activity are entirely consistent with protecting the individual's liberty interest in decisions concerning sexual relations: the same recognition that those decisions are intensely private which justifies protecting them from governmental interference can justify protecting individuals from unwilling exposure to the sexual activities of others. But the mere fact that intimate behavior may be punished when it takes place in public cannot dictate how States can regulate intimate behavior that occurs in intimate places.

b. The parallel between *Loving* and this case is almost uncanny. There, too, the State relied on a religious justification for its law. There, too, defenders of the challenged statute relied heavily on the fact that when the Fourteenth Amendment was ratified, most of the States had similar prohibitions. There, too, at the time the case came before the Court, many of the States still had criminal statutes concerning the conduct at issue. Yet the Court held, not only that the invidious racism of Virginia's law violated the Equal Protection Clause, but also that the law deprived the Lovings of due process by denying them the "freedom of choice to marry" that had "long been recognized as one of the vital personal rights essential to the orderly pursuit of happiness by free men."

This case involves no real interference with the rights of others, for the mere knowledge that other individuals do not adhere to one's value system cannot be a legally cognizable interest, let alone an interest that can justify invading the houses, hearts, and minds of citizens who choose to live their lives differently. . . .

STEVENS, J., joined by Brennan and Marshall, JJ., dissenting.

. . . Because the Georgia statute expresses the traditional view that sodomy is an immoral kind of conduct regardless of the identity of the persons who engage in it, I believe that a proper analysis of its constitutionality requires consideration of two questions: First, may a State totally prohibit the described conduct by means of a neutral law applying without exception to all persons subject to its jurisdiction? If not, may the State save the statute by announcing that it will only enforce the law against homosexuals? The two questions merit separate discussion.

I

Our prior cases make two propositions abundantly clear. First, the fact that the governing majority in a State has traditionally viewed a particular practice as immoral is not a sufficient reason for upholding a law prohibiting the practice; neither history nor tradition could save a law prohibiting miscegenation from constitutional attack. Second, individual decisions by married persons, concerning the intimacies of their physical relationship, even when not intended to produce offspring, are a form of "liberty" protected by the Due Process Clause of the Fourteenth Amendment. Moreover, this protection extends to intimate choices by unmarried as well as married persons.

In consideration of claims of this kind, the Court has emphasized the individual interest in privacy, but its decisions have actually been animated by an even more fundamental concern. As I wrote some years ago:

> These cases do not deal with the individual's interest in protection from unwarranted public attention, comment, or exploitation. They deal, rather, with the individual's right to make certain unusually important decisions that will affect his own, or his family's, destiny. The Court has referred to such decisions as implicating "basic values," as being "fundamental," and as being dignified by history and tradition. The character of the Court's language in these cases brings to mind the origins of the American heritage of freedom — the abiding interest in individual liberty that makes certain state intrusions on the citizen's right to decide how he will live his own life intolerable. Guided by history, our tradition of respect for the dignity of individual choice in matters of conscience and the restraints implicit in the federal system, federal judges have accepted the responsibility for recognition and protection of these rights in appropriate cases. Fitzgerald v. Porter Memorial Hospital, 523 F.2d 716, 719-20 (7th Cir. 1975).

Society has every right to encourage its individual members to follow particular traditions in expressing affection for one another and in gratifying their personal desires. It, of course, may prohibit an individual from imposing his will on another to satisfy his own selfish interests. It also may prevent an individual from interfering with, or violating, a legally sanctioned and protected relationship, such as marriage. And it may explain the relative advantages and disadvantages of different forms of intimate expression. But when individual married couples are isolated from observation by others, the way in which they voluntarily choose to conduct their intimate relations is a matter for them — not the State — to decide. The essential "liberty" that animated the development of the law in cases like *Griswold, Eisenstadt,* and *Carey* surely embraces the right to engage in nonreproductive, sexual conduct that others may consider offensive or immoral.

. . . [O]ur prior cases thus establish that a State may not prohibit sodomy within "the sacred precincts of marital bedrooms," *Griswold,* or, indeed, between unmarried heterosexual adults. *Eisenstadt.* In all events, it is perfectly clear that the State of Georgia may not totally prohibit the conduct proscribed by §16-6-2 of the Georgia Criminal Code.

II

If the Georgia statute cannot be enforced as it is written — if the conduct it seeks to prohibit is a protected form of liberty for the vast majority of Georgia's citizens — the State must assume the burden of justifying a selective application of its law. Either the persons to whom Georgia seeks to apply its statute do not have the same interest in "liberty" that others have, or there must be a reason why the State may be permitted to apply a generally applicable law to certain persons that it does not apply to others.

The first possibility is plainly unacceptable. Although the meaning of the principle that "all men are created equal" is not always clear, it surely must mean that every free citizen has the same interest in "liberty" that the members of the majority share. From the standpoint of the individual, the homosexual and the heterosexual have the same interest in deciding how he will live his own life, and, more narrowly, how he will conduct himself in his personal and voluntary associations with his companions. State intrusion into the private conduct of either is equally burdensome.

The second possibility is similarly unacceptable. A policy of selective application must be supported by a neutral and legitimate interest — something more substantial than a habitual dislike for, or ignorance about, the disfavored group. Neither the State nor the Court has identified any such interest in this case. The Court has posited as a justification for the Georgia statute "the presumed belief of a majority of the electorate in Georgia that homosexual sodomy is immoral and unacceptable." But the Georgia electorate has expressed no such belief — instead, its representatives enacted a law that presumably reflects the belief that all sodomy is immoral and unacceptable. . . . [T]he Georgia statute does not single out homosexuals as a separate class meriting special disfavored treatment.

. . . Georgia's prohibition on private, consensual sodomy has not been enforced for decades. The record of nonenforcement, in this case and in the last several decades, belies the Attorney General's representations about the importance of the State's selective application of its generally applicable law. . . .

III

The Court orders the dismissal of respondent's complaint even though the State's statute prohibits all sodomy; even though that prohibition is concededly unconstitutional with respect to heterosexuals; and even though the State's post hoc explanations for selective application are belied by the State's own actions. . . .

I respectfully dissent.

Discussion

1. A lesbian student in one of the editors' classes imagined that her experience in sitting through a class discussion of *Hardwick* was similar to that of a hypothetical Negro student sitting through a discussion of *Dred Scott* in, say, 1858. *Do* gays and lesbians have any substantive rights that heterosexuals are constitutionally bound to respect?

2. Both the majority and the dissenters in *Hardwick* recognize a constitutional right to privacy. The debate concerns the proper scope of that right.

If Georgia may constitutionally prohibit homosexual sodomy, may it also ban heterosexual sodomy, including fellatio and cunnilingus? Attorney General Bowers, in his oral argument before the Court, conceded that the application of Georgia's antisodomy law to married couples would be unconstitutional because of the "right of marital privacy as identified by the Court in *Griswold*." What about its application to unmarried heterosexual couples? (Does *Eisenstadt* bear on this?)

Does Justice Blackmun adequately address the state's putative power to prohibit adultery and incest? His dissent includes the following footnote:

> Although I do not think it necessary to decide today issues that are not even remotely before us, it does seem to me that a court could find simple, analytically sound distinctions between certain private, consensual sexual conduct, on the one hand, and adultery and incest (the only two vaguely specific "sexual crimes" to which the majority points), on the other. For example, marriage, in addition to its spiritual aspects, is a civil contract that entitles the contracting parties to a variety of governmentally provided benefits. A State might define the contractual commitment necessary to become eligible for these benefits to include a commitment of fidelity and then punish individuals for breaching that contract. Moreover, a State might conclude that adultery is likely to injure third persons, in particular, spouses and children of persons who engage in extramarital affairs. With respect to incest, a court might well agree with respondent that the nature of familial relationships renders true consent to incestuous activity sufficiently problematical that a blanket prohibition of such activity is warranted.

3. "The voluminous scholarly reaction to the decision has been almost universally negative."[47] Out of the 32 articles surveyed by Professor Earl Maltz, 29 are critical, many of them "in unusually harsh terms, asserting that the Court based its judgment on blind prejudice rather than acceptable legal principles." Professor Maltz argues that the decision is unexceptionable in terms of the principles of constitutional interpretation adopted after 1937, which counselled significant deference to legislative judgments. He views the commentators' hostility to *Bowers* more as evidence of the support in recent years by the "left center" of an "activist" Court willing to give it important victories unattainable in the legislative forum than as the truly disinterested analysis of scholars committed to "acceptable legal principles" regardless of their political consequences. One's view of Maltz's critique obviously depends on one's belief in the existence of "acceptable

47. See Earl Maltz, The Court, the Academy, and the Constitution: A Comment on *Bowers v. Hardwick* and Its Critics, 1989 B.Y.U.L. Rev. 59, 60.

legal principles" and in the ability of scholars and judges to recognize and apply them. That, of course, is a major topic of this casebook.

Note: Due Process and Equal Protection — Sodomy and Homosexuality

HIGH TECH GAYS v. DEFENSE INDUSTRIAL SECURITY CLEARANCE OFFICE

895 F.2d 563 (9th Cir. 1990),
rehearing en banc denied, 909 F.2d 372 (9th Cir. 1990)

BRUNETTI, Circuit Judge.

The plaintiffs-appellees challenge whether the Department of Defense's (DoD) policy of subjecting all homosexual applicants for Secret and Top Secret clearances to expanded investigations and mandatory adjudications, and whether the alleged DoD policy and practice of refusing to grant security clearances to known or suspected gay applicants, violates the equal protection component of the Fifth Amendment's Due Process Clause. . . .

In analyzing the equal protection challenge, the district court concluded that " 'gay people are a quasi-suspect class' entitled to heightened scrutiny," and that the DoD security clearance regulations "must withstand strict scrutiny because they impinge upon the right of lesbians and gay men to engage in any homosexual activity, not merely sodomy, and thus impinge upon their exercise of a fundamental right." The district court rejected the reasons proffered by the DoD to justify its policies and found the absence of even a "rational basis for defendants' subjecting all gay applicants to expanded investigations and mandatory adjudications while not doing the same for all straight applicants." . . . We reverse. . . .

It is well established that there are three standards we may apply in reviewing the plaintiffs' equal protection challenge to the DoD Security Clearance Regulations: strict scrutiny, heightened scrutiny, and rational basis review. The plaintiffs assert that homosexuality should be added to the list of suspect or quasi-suspect classifications requiring strict or heightened scrutiny. We disagree and hold that the district court erred in applying heightened scrutiny to the regulations at issue and that the proper standard is rational basis review. . . .

The Supreme Court has ruled that homosexual activity is not a fundamental right protected by substantive due process and that the proper standard of review under the Fifth Amendment is rational basis review. . . . If for federal analysis we must reach equal protection of the Fourteenth Amendment by the Due Process Clause of the Fifth Amendment, and if there is no fundamental right to engage in homosexual sodomy under the Due Process Clause of the Fifth Amendment, it would be incongruous to expand the reach of equal protection to find a fundamental right of homosexual conduct under the equal protection component of the Due Process Clause of the Fifth Amendment.

Other circuits are in accord and have held that although the Court in *Hardwick* analyzed the constitutionality of the sodomy statute on a due process rather than equal protection basis, by the *Hardwick* majority holding that the Constitution confers no fundamental right upon homosexuals to engage in sodomy, and because homosexual conduct can thus be criminalized, homosexuals cannot constitute a suspect or quasi-suspect class entitled to greater than rational basis review for equal protection purposes.... It is apparent that while the Supreme Court has identified that legislative classifications based on race, alienage, or national origin are subject to strict scrutiny and that classifications based upon gender or illegitimacy call for a heightened standard, the Court has never held homosexuality to a heightened standard of review.

To be a "suspect" or "quasi-suspect" class, homosexuals must 1) have suffered a history of discrimination; 2) exhibit obvious, immutable, or distinguishing characteristics that define them as a discrete group; and 3) show that they are a minority or politically powerless, or alternatively show that the statutory classification at issue burdens a fundamental right....

While we do agree that homosexuals have suffered a history of discrimination, we do not believe that they meet the other criteria. Homosexuality is not an immutable characteristic; it is behavioral and hence is fundamentally different from traits such as race, gender, or alienage, which define already existing suspect and quasi-suspect classes. The behavior or conduct of such already recognized classes is irrelevant to their identification. Id.

Moreover, legislatures have addressed and continue to address the discrimination suffered by homosexuals on account of their sexual orientation through the passage of anti-discrimination legislation. Thus, homosexuals are not without political power; they have the ability to and do "attract the attention of the lawmakers," as evidenced by such legislation.

Our review compels us to agree with the other circuits that have ruled on this issue and to hold that homosexuals do not constitute a suspect or quasi-suspect class entitled to greater than rational basis scrutiny under the equal protection component of the Due Process Clause of the Fifth Amendment.

CANBY, Circuit Judge, joined by Norris, Circuit Judge, dissenting from denial of rehearing en banc [909 F.2d 372].

The class of "homosexuals" clearly qualifies as a suspect category, triggering strict judicial scrutiny of any governmental discrimination against them. The applicable criteria are properly described but improperly applied by the panel: "To be a 'suspect' or 'quasi-suspect' class, homosexuals must (1) have suffered a history of discrimination; (2) exhibit obvious, immutable, or distinguishing characteristics that define them as a discrete group; and (3) show that they are a minority or politically powerless. . . ."

The panel agrees that the first criterion is met; homosexuals have suffered a history of discrimination. Id. This point should not be put quickly out of mind, however, for this history of discrimination makes it far more likely that differential treatment is simply a resort to old prejudices. As the district court said, "[l]esbians and gays have been the object of some of the deepest prejudice and hatred in American society." That fact tends to make discrimination against them all too easy. We should be careful not to endorse that tendency.

With regard to the second criterion, the panel's opinion states: "Homosexuality is not an immutable characteristic; it is behavioral and hence is fundamentally different from traits such as race, gender, or alienage, which define already existing suspect and quasi-suspect classes." There are several problems with this conclusion. In the first place, the criterion quoted earlier by the panel required that the class, to be suspect, "exhibit obvious, immutable, *or* distinguishing characteristics that define them as a discrete group." Id. (emphasis added). The Supreme Court has more than once recited the characteristics of a suspect class without mentioning immutability. See, e.g., City of Cleburne v. Cleburne Living Center, 473 U.S. 432, 440-41 (1985); Massachusetts Bd. of Retirement v. Murgia, 427 U.S. 307, 313 (1976); *San Antonio School Dist.*, 411 U.S. 1, 28 (1973). Aliens, for example, constitute a suspect category, but the condition is not immutable. See Graham v. Richardson, 403 U.S. 365, 371-2 (1971). The real question is whether discrimination on the basis of the class's distinguishing characteristic amounts to an unfair branding or resort to prejudice, not necessarily whether the characteristic is immutable.

Immutability, of course, does make discrimination more clearly unfair. There is every reason to regard homosexuality as an immutable characteristic for equal protection purposes. It is not enough to say that the category is "behavioral." One can make "behavioral" classes out of persons who go to church on Saturday, persons who speak Spanish, or persons who walk with crutches. The question is, what causes the behavior? Does it arise from the kind of a characteristic that belongs peculiarly to a group that the equal protection clause should specially protect?

Homosexuals are physically attracted to members of their own sex. That is the source of the behavior that we notice about them. Did they choose to be attracted by members of their own sex, rather than by members of the opposite sex? The answer, by the overwhelming weight of respectable authority, is "no." Sexual identity is established at a very early age; it is not a matter of conscious or controllable choice. Can homosexuals change their orientation? Again, from everything we now know, the answer is "no." At least they cannot change it without immense difficulty. As Judge Norris has asked, what would it take to get any one of us to change his or her sexual orientation? See Watkins v. U.S. Army, 875 F.2d 699, 726 (9th Cir. 1989) (en banc) (concurring opinion).

For practical and constitutional purposes, then, homosexuality is an immutable characteristic, and the panel's opinion offers nothing to the contrary except its bare conclusion. When the government discriminates against homosexuals, it is discriminating against persons because of what they are, through no choice of their own, and what they are unable to change. Preventing such unfair discrimination is what the equal protection clause is all about.

The panel's opinion also concludes that homosexuals are not politically powerless. Its support for this proposition is that one state broadly bars employment discrimination against homosexuals, two other states more narrowly bar discrimination against homosexuals, and a few cities bar some types of discrimination. Id. That showing is clearly insufficient to deprive homosexuals of the status of a suspect classification. Compare the situation with that of blacks, who clearly constitute a suspect category for equal protection purposes. Blacks are protected by three federal constitutional amendments, major federal Civil Rights Acts of 1866, 1870, 1871, 1875 (ill-fated though it was), 1957, 1960, 1964, 1965, and 1968, as well as by antidiscrimination laws in 48 of the states. By that comparison, and by absolute standards as well, homosexuals are politically powerless. They are so because of their numbers, which most estimates put at around 10 per cent of the population, and by the fact that many of them keep their status secret to avoid discrimination. That secrecy inhibits organization of homosexuals as a pressure group. Certainly homosexuals as a class wield less political power than blacks, a suspect classification, or women, a quasi-suspect one. One can easily find examples of major political parties' openly tailoring their positions to appeal to black voters, and to female voters. One cannot find comparable examples of appeals to homosexual voters; homosexuals are regarded by the national parties as political pariahs.

Homosexuals, then, are exactly the kind of class that should trigger strict scrutiny when the government discriminates against them. The panel's opinion, by ruling that such discrimination may be justified merely by a rational basis, creates the opportunity for immense abuse.

The panel's opinion seems to suggest that even if homosexuals otherwise qualify as a suspect class, they are precluded from being so because of Bowers v. Hardwick. The suggestion is completely unfounded. In *Hardwick,* the Supreme Court held that the application of state sodomy laws to homosexuals did not violate any fundamental right of privacy protected by the due process clause. The *Hardwick* opinion pointed out, however, that no equal protection claim had been presented, and *Hardwick* is clearly not controlling on the suspect class issue.

The panel's opinion also appears to suggest that *Hardwick's* conclusion that homosexuals have no fundamental right to engage in sodomy somehow by itself precludes a heightened level of equal protection scrutiny. But there are two alternative routes to higher levels of scrutiny under the equal protection clause; a higher level of scrutiny is employed if (1) the classification impinges on a fundamental right, or (2) the classification itself is suspect or quasi-suspect. See, e.g., San Antonio Indep. School Dist. v. Rodriguez. The panel's opinion seems to collapse the two separate routes into one. . . .

The panel's opinion draws an additional point from *Hardwick,* however. It states: "because homosexual conduct can . . . be criminalized, homosexuals cannot constitute a suspect or quasi-suspect class entitled to greater than rational basis review." There are at least three problems with this proposition; the first two are important enough but the third is fundamental to the whole subject.

At the simplest level, it is no refutation of a claim of governmental discrimination that the government has the right to criminalize the activity in question. As one of the amici points out, a city would trigger the highest level of scrutiny if it jailed all blacks convicted of speeding, while it only fined whites similarly convicted. The classification is suspect even though the city is free to criminalize speeding.

It is not a proper answer to this observation to say: "yes, but *Hardwick* authorizes a state to select homosexual sodomy for prosecution." *Hardwick* establishes no such proposition. *Hardwick* involved the application of a state statute that prohibited sodomy, not homosexual sodomy. Hardwick, a homosexual who had been charged with violating the statute, brought an action contending that application of the statute violated his fundamental rights. As the Supreme Court stated, "The issue presented is whether the Federal Constitution confers a fundamental right upon homosexuals to engage in sodomy and hence invalidates the laws of the many States that still make such conduct illegal and have done so for a very long time." The Court then held that there was no such fundamental right. It also rejected the argument that homosexuals possessed a fundamental right to engage in sodomy so long as it was practiced in the privacy of a home. "[I]t would be difficult, except by fiat, to limit the claimed right to homosexual conduct while leaving exposed to prosecution adultery, incest, and other sexual crimes even though they are committed in the home."

All *Hardwick* established was that a homosexual had no fundamental right to violate the sodomy laws — laws that presumably apply (as they are written) to others not protected by some marital right. . . .

Even if *Hardwick* is read more expansively, however, it goes no farther than to hold that sodomy committed by homosexuals may be made a crime. But the most that can be said for that fact is that it authorizes a form of discrimination (criminal punishment) for the act that is made a crime. But when the act is used to define a class for the purpose of imposing disabilities not designed as punishment for the commission of the criminally-proscribed act, then there is no logical reason to preclude the examination of the class to see whether it exhibits the characteristics of a suspect category. Particularly is this so when, in half of the states, the act of sodomy has not in fact been made criminal and there is no crime to punish. When the government defines a class, the nature of the class should be examined.

The final difficulty with the panel's proposition drawn from *Hardwick* is crucial. It assumes that the class of homosexuals is entirely defined by conduct that may be criminalized. The panel's error here is fundamental. In the first place, it is not proper to assume generally that "homosexual conduct . . . can be criminalized." There are many varieties of conduct that might be characterized as homosexual, from hand-holding to sodomy. *Hardwick* establishes only that the latter may be criminalized. Yet the Department of Defense invokes its expanded security clearance procedures when there is information indicating "deviant behavior," which it defines to include "homosexuality." If there is "homosexual activity" within the past 15 years, the expanded security procedure is followed. Nothing in the record suggests that the Department is confining its view of homosexual conduct to sodomy.

Perhaps the panel would regard this discussion as quibbling, however, and would say that sodomy is very commonly the behavior that triggers an expanded investigation. That fact, if true, still does not justify the Department's discrimination against homosexuals. It is an error of massive proportions to define the entire class of homosexuals by sodomy. I will be the first to admit that homosexuals, in sexually expressing their affection for persons of their own sex, frequently engage in sodomy, as do heterosexuals sexually expressing their affection for persons of the opposite sex. Homosexuals and heterosexuals also engage in other affective conduct, criminalized nowhere. But homosexuality, like heterosexuality, is a status. As an amicus points out, one is a homosexual or a heterosexual while playing bridge just as much as while engaging in sexual activity. And the Department of Defense is discriminating against homosexuals for what they are, not what they do. The Department is not trying to send anyone to jail for sodomy. It is not asserting that acts of sodomy endanger national security. It is making the unsupported assumption that homosexuals are more likely to betray their country than other classes of persons, and it is discriminating against them because of that assumption. That is the key to this case.

VII. The Persistence of Fundamental Rights

CRUZAN v. DIRECTOR, MISSOURI DEPARTMENT OF HEALTH

110 S. Ct. 2841 (1990)
On Writ of Certiorari to the Supreme Court of Missouri

[Following severe injuries sustained during an automobile accident and unsuccessful efforts at rehabilitation, Nancy Cruzan was placed in a Missouri state hospital "in what is commonly referred to as a persistent vegetative state: generally, a condition in which a person exhibits motor reflexes but evinces no indications of significant cognitive function." She was kept alive as the result of use of artificial hydration and feeding equipment, paid for by the State of Missouri. Nancy's parents "sought a court order directing the withdrawal of their daughter's artificial feeding and hydration equipment after it became apparent that she had virtually no chance of recovering her cognitive faculties." Although the trial court granted the request, the Missouri Supreme Court reversed, holding that no one can decide that life-sustaining medical support should be withdrawn from a person "in the absence of the formalities required under Missouri's Living Will statutes or the clear and convincing, inherently reliable evidence" that the person would have desired the withdrawal. Nancy's parents appealed, claiming that Missouri's refusal to allow the withdrawal violated her constitutional right "to withdraw life-sustaining treatment from her under these circumstances."]

REHNQUIST, C.J., delivered the opinion of the Court.

[I. IS THERE A FUNDAMENTAL RIGHT TO REFUSE LIFE-SUSTAINING MEDICAL TREATMENT?[48]]

. . . This is the first case in which we have been squarely presented with the issue of whether the United States Constitution grants what is in common parlance referred to as a "right to die." State courts have available to them for decision a number of sources — state constitutions, statutes, and common law — which are not available to us. In this Court, the question is simply and starkly whether the United States Constitution prohibits Missouri from choosing the rule of decision which it did. We follow the judicious counsel of our decision in Twin City Bank v. Nebeker, 167 U.S. 196, 202 (1897), where we said that in deciding "a question of such magnitude and importance . . . it is the [better] part of wisdom not to attempt, by any general statement, to cover every possible phase of the subject."

At common law, even the touching of one person by another without consent and without legal justification was a battery. . . . This notion of bodily integrity has been embodied in the requirement that informed consent is generally required for medical treatment. Justice Cardozo, while on the Court of Appeals of New York, aptly described this doctrine: "Every human being of adult years and sound mind has a right to determine what shall be done with his own body; and a surgeon who performs an operation without his patient's consent commits an assault, for which he is liable in damages." The informed consent doctrine has become firmly entrenched in American tort law.

48. Some portions of the opinion have been reorganized by the editors in the interests of clarity.

The logical corollary of the doctrine of informed consent is that the patient generally possesses the right not to consent, that is, to refuse treatment. Until about 15 years ago and the seminal decision in In re Quinlan, 70 N.J. 10, 355 A.2d 647 (1976), the number of right-to-refuse-treatment decisions were relatively few. Most of the earlier cases involved patients who refused medical treatment forbidden by their religious beliefs, thus implicating First Amendment rights as well as common law rights of self-determination. More recently, however, with the advance of medical technology capable of sustaining life well past the point where natural forces would have brought certain death in earlier times, cases involving the right to refuse life-sustaining treatment have burgeoned.

The Fourteenth Amendment provides that no State shall "deprive any person of life, liberty, or property, without due process of law." The principle that a competent person has a constitutionally protected liberty interest in refusing unwanted medical treatment may be inferred from our prior decisions. In Jacobson v. Massachusetts, 197 U.S. 11 (1905), for instance, the Court balanced an individual's liberty interest in declining an unwanted smallpox vaccine against the State's interest in preventing disease. Decisions prior to the incorporation of the Fourth Amendment into the Fourteenth Amendment analyzed searches and seizures involving the body under the Due Process Clause and were thought to implicate substantial liberty interests. See, e.g., Breithaupt v. Abram, 352 U.S. 432 (1957) ("As against the right of an individual that his person be held inviolable . . . must be set the interests of society . . .").

Just this Term, in the course of holding that a State's procedures for administering antipsychotic medication to prisoners were sufficient to satisfy due process concerns, we recognized that prisoners possess "a significant liberty interest in avoiding the unwanted administration of antipsychotic drugs under the Due Process Clause of the Fourteenth Amendment." Washington v. Harper, 110 S. Ct. 1028 (1990). Still other cases support the recognition of a general liberty interest in refusing medical treatment.

. . . [F]or purposes of this case, we assume that the United States Constitution would grant a competent person a constitutionally protected right to refuse lifesaving hydration and nutrition.

[II. Does an Incompetent Patient Enjoy the Same Right to Refuse Lifesaving Hydration and Nutrition?]

Petitioners go on to assert that an incompetent person should possess the same right [to refuse lifesaving treatment] as is possessed by a competent person. . . .

The difficulty with petitioners' claim is that in a sense it begs the question: an incompetent person is not able to make an informed and voluntary choice to exercise a hypothetical right to refuse treatment or any other right. Such a "right" must be exercised for her, if at all, by some sort of surrogate. Here, Missouri has in effect recognized that under certain circumstances a surrogate may act for the patient in electing to have hydration and nutrition withdrawn in such a way as to cause death, but it has established a procedural safeguard to assure that the action of the surrogate conforms as best it may to the wishes expressed by the patient while competent. Missouri requires that evidence of the incompetent's wishes as to the withdrawal of treatment be proved by clear and convincing evidence. The question, then, is whether the United States Constitution forbids the establishment of this procedural requirement by the State. We hold that it does not.

. . . [D]etermining that a person has a "liberty interest" under the Due Process Clause does not end the inquiry; "whether respondent's constitutional rights have been violated must be determined by balancing his liberty interests against the relevant state interests."

Whether or not Missouri's clear and convincing evidence requirement comports with the United States Constitution depends in part on what interests the State may properly seek to protect in this situation. Missouri relies on its interest in the protection and preservation of human life, and there can be no gainsaying this interest. As a general matter, the States — indeed, all civilized nations — demonstrate their commitment to life by treating homicide as serious crime. Moreover, the majority of States in this country have laws imposing criminal penalties on one who assists another to commit suicide. We do not think a State is required to remain neutral in the face of an informed and voluntary decision by a physically-able adult to starve to death.

But in the context presented here, a State has more particular interests at stake. The choice between life and death is a deeply personal decision of obvious and overwhelming finality. We believe Missouri may legitimately seek to safeguard the personal element of this choice through the imposition of heightened evidentiary requirements. . . . Not all incompetent patients will have loved ones available to serve as surrogate decisionmakers. And even where family members are present, "[t]here will, of course, be some unfortunate situations in which family members will not act to protect a patient." A State is entitled to guard against potential abuses in such situations. Similarly, a State is entitled to consider that a judicial proceeding to make a determination regarding an incompetent's wishes may very well not be an adversarial one, with the added guarantee of accurate factfinding that the adversary process brings with it. Finally, we think a State may properly decline to make judgments about the "quality" of life that a particular individual may enjoy, and simply assert an unqualified interest in the preservation of human life to be weighed against the constitutionally protected interests of the individual.

In our view, Missouri has permissibly sought to advance these interests through the adoption of a "clear and convincing" standard of proof to govern such proceedings. . . .

No doubt is engendered by anything in this record but that Nancy Cruzan's mother and father are loving and caring parents. If the State were required by the United States Constitution to repose a right of "substituted judgment" with anyone, the Cruzans would surely qualify. But we do not think the Due Process Clause requires the State to repose judgment on these matters with anyone but the patient herself. . . . All of the reasons previously discussed for allowing Missouri to require clear and convincing evidence of the patient's wishes lead us to conclude that the State may choose to defer only to those wishes, rather than confide the decision to close family members.

The judgment of the Supreme Court of Missouri is [a]ffirmed.

O'CONNOR, J., concurring.

I agree that a protected liberty interest in refusing unwanted medical treatment may be inferred from our prior decisions and that the refusal of artificially delivered food and water is encompassed within that liberty interest. I write separately to clarify why I believe this to be so.

As the Court notes, the liberty interest in refusing medical treatment flows from decisions involving the State's invasions into the body. Because our notions of liberty are inextricably entwined with our idea of physical freedom and self-determination, the Court has often deemed state incursions into the body repugnant to the interests protected by the Due Process Clause. The State's imposition of medical treatment on an unwilling competent adult necessarily involves some form of restraint and intrusion. A seriously ill or dying patient whose wishes are not honored may feel a captive of the machinery required for life-sustaining measures or other medical interventions. Such forced treatment may burden that individual's liberty interests as much as any state coercion.

The State's artificial provision of nutrition and hydration implicates identical concerns. Artificial feeding cannot readily be distinguished from other forms of medical treatment. Whether or not the techniques used to pass food and water into the patient's alimentary tract are termed "medical treatment," it is clear they all involve some degree of intrusion and restraint. Feeding a patient by means of a nasogastric tube requires a physician to pass a long flexible tube through the patient's nose, throat and esophagus and into the stomach. Because of the discomfort such a tube causes, "[m]any patients need to be restrained forcibly and their hands put into large mittens to prevent them from removing the tube." A gastrostomy tube (as was used to provide food and water to Nancy Cruzan) or jejunostomy tube must be surgically implanted into the stomach or small intestine. Requiring a competent adult to endure such procedures against her will burdens the patient's liberty, dignity, and freedom to determine the course of her own treatment. Accordingly, the liberty guaranteed by the Due Process Clause must protect, if it protects anything, an individual's deeply personal decision to reject medical treatment, including the artificial delivery of food and water.

Today's decision, holding only that the Constitution permits a State to require clear and convincing evidence of Nancy Cruzan's desire to have artificial hydration and nutrition withdrawn, does not preclude a future determination that the Constitution requires the States to implement the decisions of a patient's duly appointed surrogate. Nor does it prevent States from developing other approaches for protecting an incompetent individual's liberty interest in refusing medical treatment. As is evident from the Court's survey of state court decisions, no national consensus has yet emerged on the best solution for this difficult and sensitive problem. Today we decide only that one State's practice does not violate the Constitution; the more challenging task of crafting appropriate procedures for safeguarding incompetents' liberty interests is entrusted to the "laboratory" of the States in the first instance. . . .

SCALIA, J., concurring.

. . . While I agree with the Court's analysis today, and therefore join in its opinion, I would have preferred that we announce, clearly and promptly, that the federal courts have no business in this field; that American law has always accorded the State the power to prevent, by force if necessary, suicide — including suicide by refusing to take appropriate measures necessary to preserve one's life; that the point at which life becomes "worthless," and the point at which the means necessary to preserve it become "extraordinary" or "inappropriate," are neither set forth in the Constitution nor known to the nine Justices of this Court any better than they are known to nine people picked at random from the Kansas City telephone directory; and hence, that even when it is demonstrated by clear and convincing evidence that a patient no longer wishes certain measures to be taken to preserve her life, it is up to the citizens of Missouri to decide, through their elected representatives, whether that wish will be honored. It is quite impossible (because the Constitution says nothing about the matter) that those citizens will decide upon a line less lawful than the one we would choose; and it is unlikely (because we know no more about "life-and-death" than they do) that they will decide upon a line less reasonable.

The text of the Due Process Clause does not protect individuals against deprivations of liberty *simpliciter*. It protects them against deprivations of liberty "without due process of law." To determine that such a deprivation would not occur if Nancy Cruzan were forced to take nourishment against her will, it is unnecessary to reopen the historically recurrent debate over whether "due process" includes substantive restrictions. It is at least true that no "substantive due process" claim can be maintained unless the claimant demonstrates that the State has deprived him of a right historically and traditionally protected against State interference. That cannot possibly be established here.

At common law in England, a suicide — defined as one who "deliberately puts an end to his own existence, or commits any unlawful malicious act, the consequence of which is his own death," 4 W. Blackstone, Commentaries *189 — was criminally liable. Although the States abolished the penalties imposed by the common law (i.e., forfeiture and ignominious burial), they did so to spare the innocent family, and not to legitimize the act. Case law at the time of the Fourteenth Amendment generally held that assisting suicide was a criminal offense. . . . The Field Penal Code, adopted by the Dakota Territory in 1877, proscribed attempted suicide and assisted suicide. And most States that did not explicitly prohibit assisted suicide in 1868 recognized, when the issue arose in the 50 years following the Fourteenth Amendment's ratification, that assisted and (in some cases) attempted suicide were unlawful. Thus, "there is no significant support for the claim that a right to suicide is so rooted in our tradition that it may be deemed 'fundamental' or 'implicit in the concept of ordered liberty.' " Marzen, O'Dowd, Crone, & Balch, Suicide: A Constitutional Right?, 24 Duquesne L. Rev. 1, 100 (1985).

Petitioners rely on three distinctions to separate Nancy Cruzan's case from ordinary suicide: (1) that she is permanently incapacited and in pain; (2) that she would bring on her death not by any affirmative act but by merely declining treatment that provides nourishment; and (3) that preventing her from effectuating her presumed wish to die requires violation of her bodily integrity. None of these suffices. Suicide was not excused even when committed "to avoid those ills which (persons) had not the fortitude to endure." 4 Blackstone, supra, at — . "The life of those to whom life has become a burden — of those who are hopelessly diseased or fatally wounded — nay, even the lives of criminals condemned to death, are under the protection of the law, equally as the lives of those who are in the full tide of life's enjoyment, and anxious to continue to live." Blackburn v. State, 23 Ohio St. 146, 163 (1873). . . . Nor would the imminence of the patient's death have affected liability. "The lives of all are equally under the protection of the law, and under that protection to their last moment. . . . [Assisted suicide] is declared by the law to be murder, irrespective of the wishes or the condition of the party to whom the poison is administered. . . ." *Blackburn,* supra, at 163; see also Commonwealth v. Bowen, 13 Mass. 356, 360 (1816).

The second asserted distinction — suggested by the recent cases canvassed by the Court concerning the right to refuse treatment — relies on the dichotomy between action and inaction. Suicide, it is said, consists of an affirmative act to end one's life; refusing treatment is not an affirmative act "causing" death, but merely a passive acceptance of the natural process of dying. I readily acknowledge that the distinction between action and inaction has some bearing upon the legislative judgment of what ought to be prevented as suicide — though even there it would seem to me unreasonable to draw the line precisely between action and inaction, rather than between various forms of inaction. It would not make much sense to say that one may not kill oneself by walking into the sea, but may sit on the beach until submerged by the incoming tide; or that one may not intentionally lock oneself into a cold storage locker, but may refrain from coming indoors when the temperature drops below freezing. Even as a legislative matter, in other words, the intelligent line does not fall between action and inaction but between those forms of inaction that consist of abstaining from "ordinary" care and those that consist of abstaining from "excessive" or "heroic" measures. Unlike action vs. inaction, that is not a line to be discerned by logic or legal analysis, and we should not pretend that it is.

But to return to the principal point for present purposes: the irrelevance of the action-inaction distinction. Starving oneself to death is no different from putting a gun to one's temple as far as the common-law definition of suicide is concerned; the cause of death in both cases is the suicide's conscious decision to "pu[t] an end to his own existence." 4 Blackstone, supra, at —. Of course the common law rejected the action-inaction distinction in other contexts involving the taking of human life as well. In the prosecution of a parent for the starvation death of her infant, it was no defense that the infant's death was "caused" by no action of the parent but by the natural process of starvation, or by the infant's natural inability to provide for itself. A physician, moreover, could be criminally liable for failure to provide care that could have extended the patient's life, even if death was immediately caused by the underlying disease that the physician failed to treat. Barrow v. State, 17 Okl. Cr. 340, 188 P. 351 (1920); People v. Phillips, 64 Cal. 2d 574, 414 P.2d 353 (1966).

It is not surprising, therefore, that the early cases considering the claimed right to refuse medical treatment dismissed as specious the nice distinction between "passively submitting to death and actively seeking it. The distinction may be merely verbal, as it would be if an adult sought death by starvation instead of a drug. If the State may interrupt one mode of self-destruction, it may with equal authority interfere with the other." John F. Kennedy Memorial Hosp. v. Heston, 58 N.J. 576, 581-582, 279 A.2d 670, 672-673 (1971). The third asserted basis of distinction — that frustrating Nancy Cruzan's wish to die in the present case requires interference with her bodily integrity — is likewise inadequate, because such interference is impermissible only if one begs the question whether her refusal to undergo the treatment on her own is suicide. It has always been lawful not only for the State, but even for private citizens, to interfere with bodily integrity to prevent a felony. That general rule has of course been applied to suicide. At common law, even a private person's use of force to prevent suicide was privileged. It is not even reasonable, much less required by the Constitution, to maintain that although the State has the right to prevent a person from slashing his wrists it does not have the power to apply physical force to prevent him from doing so, nor the power, should he succeed, to apply, coercively if necessary, medical measures to stop the flow of blood. The state-run hospital, I am certain, is not liable under 42 U.S.C. §1983 for violation of constitutional rights, nor the private hospital liable under general tort law, if, in a State where suicide is unlawful, it pumps out the stomach of a person who has intentionally taken an overdose of barbiturates, despite that person's wishes to the contrary.

The dissents of Justices Brennan and Stevens make a plausible case for our intervention here only by embracing — the latter explicitly and the former by implication — a political principle that the States are free to adopt, but that is demonstrably not imposed by the Constitution. "The State," says Justice Brennan, "has no legitimate general interest in someone's life, completely abstracted from the interest of the person living that life, that could outweigh the person's choice *to avoid medical treatment*." (emphasis added) The italicized phrase sounds moderate enough, and is all that is needed to cover the present case — but the proposition cannot *logically* be so limited. One who accepts it must also accept, I think, that the State has no such legitimate interest that could outweigh "the person's choice *to put an end to her life*." Similarly, if one agrees with Justice Brennan that "the State's general interest in life must accede to Nancy Cruzan's particularized and intense interest in self-determination *in her choice of medical treatment*," (emphasis added), he must also believe that the State must accede to her "particularized and intense interest in self-determination *in her choice whether to continue living or to die*." For insofar as balancing the relative interests of the State and the individual is concerned, there is nothing distinctive about accepting death through the refusal of "medical treatment," as opposed to accepting it through the refusal of food, or through the failure to shut off the engine and get out of the car after parking in one's garage after work. Suppose that Nancy Cruzan were in precisely the condition she is in today, except that she could be fed and digest food and water without artificial assistance. How is the State's "interest" in keeping her alive thereby increased, or her interest in deciding whether she wants to continue living reduced? It seems to me, in other words, that Justice Brennan's position ultimately rests upon the proposition that it is none of the State's business if a person wants to commit suicide. Justice Stevens is explicit on the point: "Choices about death touch the core of liberty. . . . [N]ot much may be said with confidence about death unless it is said from faith, and that alone is reason enough to protect the freedom to conform choices about death to individual conscience." This is a view that some societies have held, and that our States are free to adopt if they wish. But it is not a view imposed by our constitutional traditions, in which the power of the State to prohibit suicide is unquestionable.

What I have said above is not meant to suggest that I would think it desirable, if we were sure that Nancy Cruzan wanted to die, to keep her alive by the means at issue here. I assert only that the Constitution has nothing to say about the subject. To raise up a constitutional right here we would have to create out of nothing (for it exists neither in text nor tradition) some constitutional principle whereby, although the State may insist that an individual come in out of the cold and eat food, it may not insist that he take medicine; and although it may pump his stomach empty of poison he has ingested, it may not fill his stomach with food he has failed to ingest. Are there, then, no reasonable and humane limits that ought not to be exceeded in requiring an individual to preserve his own life? There obviously are, but they are not set forth in the Due Process Clause. What assures us that those limits will not be exceeded is the same constitutional guarantee that is the source of most of our protection — what protects us, for example, from being assessed a tax of 100% of our income above the subsistence level, from being forbidden to drive cars, or from being required to send our children to school for 10 hours a day, none of which horribles is categorically prohibited by the Constitution. Our salvation is the Equal Protection Clause, which requires the democratic majority to accept for themselves and their loved ones what they impose on you and me. This Court need not, and has no authority to, inject itself into every field of human activity where irrationality and oppression may theoretically occur, and if it tries to do so it will destroy itself.

BRENNAN, J., with whom Marshall and Blackmun JJ., join, dissenting.

. . . Today the Court, while tentatively accepting that there is some degree of constitutionally protected liberty interest in avoiding unwanted medical treatment, including life-sustaining medical treatment such as artificial nutrition and hydration, affirms the decision of the Missouri Supreme Court. The majority opinion, as I read it, would affirm that decision on the ground that a State may require "clear and convincing" evidence of Nancy Cruzan's prior decision to forgo life-sustaining treatment under circumstances such as hers in order to ensure that her actual wishes are honored. Because I believe that Nancy Cruzan has a fundamental right to be free of unwanted artificial nutrition and hydration, which right is not outweighed by any interests of the State, and because I find that the improperly biased procedural obstacles imposed by the Missouri Supreme Court impermissibly burden that right, I respectfully dissent. . . .

I

A

. . . The question before this Court is a relatively narrow one: whether the Due Process Clause allows Missouri to require a now-incompetent patient in an irreversible persistent vegetative state to remain on life-support absent rigorously clear and convincing evidence that avoiding the treatment represents the patient's prior, express choice. If a fundamental right is at issue, Missouri's rule of decision must be scrutinized under the standards this Court has always applied in such circumstances. As we said in Zablocki v. Redhail, 434 U.S. 374, 388 (1978), if a requirement imposed by a State "significantly interferes with the exercise of a fundamental right, it cannot be upheld unless it is supported by sufficiently important state interests and is closely tailored to effectuate only those interests." . . . An evidentiary rule, just as a substantive prohibition, must meet these standards if it significantly burdens a fundamental liberty interest. . . .

III

This is not to say that the State has no legitimate interests to assert here. As the majority recognizes, Missouri has a *parens patriae* interest in providing Nancy Cruzan, now incompetent, with as accurate as possible a determination of how she would exercise her rights under these circumstances. Second, if and when it is determined that Nancy Cruzan would want to continue treatment, the State may legitimately assert an interest in providing that treatment. But until Nancy's wishes have been determined, the only state interest that may be asserted is an interest in safe-guarding the accuracy of that determination.

Accuracy, therefore, must be our touchstone. Missouri may constitutionally impose only those procedural requirements that serve to enhance the accuracy of a determination of Nancy Cruzan's wishes or are at least consistent with an accurate determination. The Missouri "safeguard" that the Court upholds today does not meet that standard. The determination needed in this context is whether the incompetent person would choose to live in a persistent vegetative state on life-support or to avoid this medical treatment. Missouri's rule of decision imposes a markedly asymmetrical evidentiary burden. Only evidence of specific statements of treatment choice made by the patient when competent is admissible to support a finding that the patient, now in a persistent vegetative state, would wish to avoid further medical treatment. Moreover, this evidence must be clear and convincing. No proof is required to support a finding that the incompetent person would wish to continue treatment.

A

The majority offers several justifications for Missouri's heightened evidentiary standard. First, the majority explains that the State may constitutionally adopt this rule to govern determinations of an incompetent's wishes in order to advance the State's substantive interests, including its unqualified interest in the preservation of human life. Missouri's evidentiary standard, however, cannot rest on the State's own interest in a particular substantive result. To be sure, courts have long erected clear and convincing evidence standards to place the greater risk of erroneous decisions on those bringing disfavored claims. In such cases, however, the choice to discourage certain claims was a legitimate, constitutional policy choice. In contrast, Missouri has no such power to disfavor a choice by Nancy Cruzan to avoid medical treatment, because Missouri has no legitimate interest in providing Nancy with treatment until it is established that this represents her choice. Just as a State may not override Nancy's choice directly, it may not do so indirectly through the imposition of a procedural rule. Second, the majority offers two explanations for why Missouri's clear and convincing evidence standard is a means of enhancing accuracy, but neither is persuasive. The majority initially argues that a clear and convincing evidence standard is necessary to compensate for the possibility that such proceedings will lack the "guarantee of accurate factfinding that the adversary process brings with it." . . .

[T]he proceeding to determine Nancy Cruzan's wishes was neither ex parte nor secret. In a hearing to determine the treatment preferences of an incompetent person, a court is not limited to adjusting burdens of proof as its only means of protecting against a possible imbalance. Indeed, any concern that those who come forward will present a one-sided view would be better addressed by appointing a guardian ad litem, who could use the State's powers of discovery to gather and present evidence regarding the patient's wishes. A guardian ad litem's task is to uncover any conflicts of interest and ensure that each party likely to have relevant evidence is consulted and brought forward — for example, other members of the family, friends, clergy, and doctors. Missouri's heightened evidentiary standard attempts to achieve balance by discounting evidence; the guardian ad litem technique achieves balance by probing for additional evidence. Where, as here, the family members, friends, doctors and guardian ad litem agree, it is not because the process has failed. . . . It is because there is no genuine dispute as to Nancy's preference.

The majority next argues that where, as here, important individual rights are at stake, a clear and convincing evidence standard has long been held to be an appropriate means of enhancing accuracy, citing decisions concerning what process an individual is due before he can be deprived of a liberty interest. In those cases, however, this Court imposed a clear and convincing standard as a constitutional minimum on the basis of its evaluation that one side's interests clearly outweighed the second side's interests and therefore the second side should bear the risk of error. See Santosky v. Kramer, 455 U.S. 745, 753, 766-767 (1982) (requiring a clear and convincing evidence standard for termination of parental rights because the parent's interest is fundamental but the State has no legitimate interest in termination unless the parent is unfit, and finding that the State's interest in finding the best home for the child does not arise until the parent has been found unfit); Addington v. Texas, 441 U.S. 418, 426-427 (1979) (requiring clear and convincing evidence in an involuntary commitment hearing because the interest of the individual far outweighs that of a State, which has no legitimate interest in confining individuals who are not mentally ill and do not pose a danger to themselves or others). Moreover, we have always recognized that shifting the risk of error reduces the likelihood of errors in one direction at the cost of increasing the likelihood of errors in the other. In the cases cited by the majority, the imbalance imposed by a heightened evidentiary standard was not only acceptable but required because the standard was deployed to protect an individual's exercise of a fundamental right. . . . In contrast, the Missouri court imposed a clear and convincing standard as an obstacle to the exercise of a fundamental right.

The majority claims that the allocation of the risk of error is justified because it is more important not to terminate life-support for someone who would wish it continued than to honor the wishes of someone who would not. An erroneous decision to terminate life-support is irrevocable, says the majority, while an erroneous decision not to terminate "results in a maintenance of the status quo." But, from the point of view of the patient, an erroneous decision in either direction is irrevocable. An erroneous decision to terminate artificial nutrition and hydration, to be sure, will lead to failure of that last remnant of physiological life, the brain stem, and result in complete brain death. An erroneous decision not to terminate life-support, however, robs a patient of the very qualities protected by the right to avoid unwanted medical treatment. His own degraded existence is perpetuated; his family's suffering is protracted; the memory he leaves behind becomes more and more distorted. . . .

C

I do not suggest that States must sit by helplessly if the choices of incompetent patients are in danger of being ignored. Even if the Court had ruled that Missouri's rule of decision is unconstitutional, as I believe it should have, States would nevertheless remain free to fashion procedural protections to safeguard the interests of incompetents under these circumstances. The Constitution provides merely a framework here: protections must be genuinely aimed at ensuring decisions commensurate with the will of the patient, and must be reliable as instruments to that end. Of the many States which have instituted such protections, Missouri is virtually the only one to have fashioned a rule that lessens the likelihood of accurate determinations. In contrast, nothing in the Constitution prevents States from reviewing the advisability of a family decision, by requiring a court proceeding or by appointing an impartial guardian ad litem. . . .

D

Finally, I cannot agree with the majority that where it is not possible to determine what choice an incompetent patient would make, a State's role as *parens patriae* permits the State automatically to make that choice itself. Under fair rules of evidence, it is improbable that a court could not determine what the patient's choice would be. Under the rule of decision adopted by Missouri and upheld today by this Court, such occasions might be numerous. But in neither case does it follow that it is constitutionally acceptable for the State invariably to assume the role of deciding for the patient. A State's legitimate interest in safeguarding a patient's choice cannot be furthered by simply appropriating it.

The majority justifies its position by arguing that, while close family members may have a strong feeling about the question, "there is no automatic assurance that the view of close family members will necessarily be the same as the patient's would have been had she been confronted with the prospect of her situation while competent." I cannot quarrel with this observation. But it leads only to another question: Is there any reason to suppose that a State is more likely to make the choice that the patient would have made than someone who knew the patient intimately? . . .

A State's inability to discern an incompetent patient's choice still need not mean that a State is rendered powerless to protect that choice. But I would find that the Due Process Clause prohibits a State from doing more than that. A State may ensure that the person who makes the decision on the patient's behalf is the one whom the patient himself would have selected to make that choice for him. And a State may exclude from consideration anyone having improper motives. But a State generally must either repose the choice with the person whom the patient himself would most likely have chosen as proxy or leave the decision to the patient's family.

IV

As many as 10,000 patients are being maintained in persistent vegetative states in the United States, and the number is expected to increase significantly in the near future. . . . The 80% of Americans who die in hospitals are "likely to meet their end . . . 'in a sedated or comatose state; betubed nasally, abdominally and intravenously; and far more like manipulated objects than like moral subjects.' " A fifth of all adults surviving to age 80 will suffer a progressive dementing disorder prior to death.

. . . The new medical technology can reclaim those who would have been irretrievably lost a few decades ago and restore them to active lives. For Nancy Cruzan, it failed, and for others with wasting incurable disease it may be doomed to failure. In these unfortunate situations, the bodies and preferences and memories of the victims do not escheat to the State; nor does our Constitution permit the State or any other government to commandeer them. . . .

STEVENS, J., dissenting. . . .

I

This case is the first in which we consider whether, and how, the Constitution protects the liberty of seriously ill patients to be free from life-sustaining medical treatment. So put, the question is both general and profound. We need not, however, resolve the question in the abstract. Our responsibility as judges both enables and compels us to treat the problem as it is illuminated by the facts of the controversy before us. . . .

II

. . . An innocent person's constitutional right to be free from unwanted medical treatment is . . . categorically limited [by the court] to those patients who had the foresight to make an unambiguous statement of their wishes while competent. The Court's decision affords no protection to children, to young people who are victims of unexpected accidents or illnesses, or to the countless thousands of elderly persons who either fail to decide, or fail to explain, how they want to be treated if they should experience a similar fate. Because Nancy Beth Cruzan did not have the foresight to preserve her constitutional right in a living will, or some comparable "clear and convincing" alternative, her right is gone forever and her fate is in the hands of the state legislature instead of in those of her family, her independent neutral guardian ad litem, and an impartial judge — all of whom agree on the course of action that is in her best interests. The Court's willingness to find a waiver of this constitutional right reveals a distressing misunderstanding of the importance of individual liberty.

III

It is perhaps predictable that courts might undervalue the liberty at stake here. Because death is so profoundly personal, public reflection upon it is unusual. As this sad case shows, however, such reflection must become more common if we are to deal responsibly with the modern circumstances of death. . . .

Ultimate questions that might once have been dealt with in intimacy by a family and its physician have now become the concern of institutions. When the institution is a state hospital, as it is in this case, the government itself becomes involved. Dying nonetheless remains a part of "the life which characteristically has its place in the home," Poe v. Ullman, 367 U.S. 497, 551 (1961) (Harlan, J., dissenting). The "integrity of that life is something so fundamental that it has been found to draw to its protection the principles of more than one explicitly granted Constitutional right," id., at 551-552, and our decisions have demarcated a "private realm of family life which the state cannot enter." Prince v. Massachusetts, 321 U.S. 158, 166-167 (1944). . . . [T]his Court has long recognized that the liberty to make the decisions and choices constitutive of private life is so fundamental to our "concept of ordered liberty," Palko v. Connecticut, 302 U.S. 319, 325 (1937), that those choices must occasionally be afforded more direct protection.

Respect for these choices has guided our recognition of rights pertaining to bodily integrity. The constitutional decisions identifying those rights, like the common-law tradition upon which they built, are mindful that the "makers of our Constitution . . . recognized the significance of man's spiritual nature." Olmstead v. United States, 277 U.S. 438, 478 (1928) (Brandeis, J., dissenting). It may truly be said that "our notions of liberty are inextricably entwined with our idea of physical freedom and self determination." Thus we have construed the Due Process Clause to preclude physically invasive recoveries of evidence not only because such procedures are "brutal" but also because they are "offensive to human dignity." Rochin v. California, 342 U.S. 165, 174 (1952). We have interpreted the Constitution to interpose barriers to a State's efforts to sterilize some criminals not only because the proposed punishment would do "irreparable injury" to bodily integrity, but because "[m]arriage and procreation" concern "the basic civil rights of man." Skinner v. Oklahoma ex rel. Williamson, 316 U.S. 535, 541 (1942). . . . [J]ust as the constitutional protection for the "physical curtilage of the home . . . is surely . . . a result of solicitude to protect the privacies of the life within," Poe v. Ullman, 367 U.S., at 551 (Harlan, J., dissenting), so too the constitutional protection for the human body is surely inseparable from concern for the mind and spirit that dwell therein.

It is against this background of decisional law, and the constitutional tradition which it illuminates, that the right to be free from unwanted life-sustaining medical treatment must be understood. That right presupposes no abandonment of the desire for life. Nor is it reducible to a protection against batteries undertaken in the name of treatment, or to a guarantee against the infliction of bodily discomfort. Choices about death touch the core of liberty. Our duty, and the concomitant freedom, to come to terms with the conditions of our own mortality are undoubtedly "so rooted in the traditions and conscience of our people as to be ranked as fundamental," and indeed are essential incidents of the unalienable rights to life and liberty endowed us by our Creator.

The more precise constitutional significance of death is difficult to describe; not much may be said with confidence about death unless it is said from faith, and that alone is reason enough to protect the freedom to conform choices about death to individual conscience. We may also, however, justly assume that death is not life's simple opposite, or its necessary terminus, but rather its completion. Our ethical tradition has long regarded an appreciation of mortality as essential to understanding life's significance. It may, in fact, be impossible to live for anything without being prepared to die for something. Certainly there was no disdain for life in Nathan Hale's most famous declaration or in Patrick Henry's; their words instead bespeak a passion for life that forever preserves their own lives in the memories of their countrymen. From such "honored dead we take increased devotion to that cause for which they gave the last full measure of devotion."

These considerations cast into stark relief the injustice, and unconstitutionality, of Missouri's treatment of Nancy Beth Cruzan. Nancy Cruzan's death, when it comes, cannot be an historic act of heroism; it will inevitably be the consequence of her tragic accident. But Nancy Cruzan's interest in life, no less than that of any other person, includes an interest in how she will be thought of after her death by those whose opinions mattered to her. There can be no doubt that her life made her dear to her family, and to others. How she dies will affect how that life is remembered. The trial court's order authorizing Nancy's parents to cease their daughter's treatment would have permitted the family that cares for Nancy to bring to a close her tragedy and her death. Missouri's objection to that order subordinates Nancy's body, her family, and the lasting significance of her life to the State's own interests. The decision we review thereby interferes with constitutional interests of the highest order.

To be constitutionally permissible, Missouri's intrusion upon these fundamental liberties must, at a minimum, bear a reasonable relationship to a legitimate state end. Missouri asserts that its policy is related to a state interest in the protection of life. In my view, however, it is an effort to define life, rather than to protect it, that is the heart of Missouri's policy. Missouri insists, without regard to Nancy Cruzan's own interests, upon equating her life with the biological persistence of her bodily functions. Nancy Cruzan, it must be remembered, is not now simply incompetent. She is in a persistent vegetative state, and has been so for seven years. The trial court found, and no party contested, that Nancy has no possibility of recovery and no consciousness.

It seems to me that the Court errs insofar as it characterizes this case as involving "judgments about the 'quality' of life that a particular individual may enjoy." Nancy Cruzan is obviously "alive" in a physiological sense. But for patients like Nancy Cruzan, who have no consciousness and no chance of recovery, there is a serious question as to whether the mere persistence of their bodies is "life" as that word is commonly understood, or as it is used in both the Constitution and the Declaration of Independence. The State's unflagging determination to perpetuate Nancy Cruzan's physical existence is comprehensible only as an effort to define life's meaning, not as an attempt to preserve its sanctity.

This much should be clear from the oddity of Missouri's definition alone. Life, particularly human life, is not commonly thought of as a merely physiological condition or function. Its sanctity is often thought to derive from the impossibility of any such reduction. When people speak of life, they often mean to describe the experiences that comprise a person's history, as when it is said that somebody "led a good life." They may also mean to refer to the practical manifestation of the human spirit, a meaning captured by the familiar observation that somebody "added life" to an assembly. If there is a shared thread among the various opinions on this subject, it may be that life is an activity which is at once the matrix for and an integration of a person's interests. In any event, absent some theological abstraction, the idea of life is not conceived separately from the idea of a living person. Yet, it is by precisely such a separation that Missouri asserts an interest in Nancy Cruzan's life in opposition to Nancy Cruzan's own interests. The resulting definition is uncommon indeed.

The laws punishing homicide, upon which the Court relies, do not support a contrary inference. Obviously, such laws protect both the life and interests of those who would otherwise be victims. Even laws against suicide pre-suppose that those inclined to take their own lives have some interest in living, and, indeed, that the depressed people whose lives are preserved may later be thankful for the State's intervention. Likewise, decisions that address the "quality of life" of incompetent, but conscious, patients rest upon the recognition that these patients have some interest in continuing their lives, even if that interest pales in some eyes when measured against interests in dignity or comfort. Not so here. Contrary to the Court's suggestion, Missouri's protection of life in a form abstracted from the living is not commonplace; it is aberrant.

Nor does Missouri's treatment of Nancy Cruzan find precedent in the various state law cases surveyed by the majority. Despite the Court's assertion that state courts have demonstrated "both similarity and diversity in their approach" to the issue before us, none of the decisions surveyed by the Court interposed an absolute bar to the termination of treatment for a patient in a persistent vegetative state. . . .

In short, there is no reasonable ground for believing that Nancy Beth Cruzan has any personal interest in the perpetuation of what the State has decided is her life. As I have already suggested, it would be possible to hypothesize such an interest on the basis of theological or philosophical conjecture. But even to posit such a basis for the State's action is to condemn it. It is not within the province of secular government to circumscribe the liberties of the people by regulations designed wholly for the purpose of establishing a sectarian definition of life.

My disagreement with the Court is thus unrelated to its endorsement of the clear and convincing standard of proof for cases of this kind. Indeed, I agree that the controlling facts must be established with unmistakable clarity. The critical question, however, is not how to prove the controlling facts but rather what proven facts should be controlling. In my view, the constitutional answer is clear: the best interests of the individual, especially when buttressed by the interests of all related third parties, must prevail over any general state policy that simply ignores those interests. Indeed, the only apparent secular basis for the State's interest in life is the policy's persuasive impact upon people other than Nancy and her family. Yet, "[a]lthough the State may properly perform a teaching function," and although that teaching may foster respect for the sanctity of life, the State may not pursue its project by infringing constitutionally protected interests for "symbolic effect." The failure of Missouri's policy to heed the interests of a dying individual with respect to matters so private is ample evidence of the policy's illegitimacy.

Only because Missouri has arrogated to itself the power to define life, and only because the Court permits this usurpation, are Nancy Cruzan's life and liberty put into disquieting conflict. If Nancy Cruzan's life were defined by reference to her own interests, so that her life expired when her biological existence ceased serving any of her own interests, then her constitutionally protected interest in freedom from unwanted treatment would not come into conflict with her constitutionally protected interest in life. Conversely, if there were any evidence that Nancy Cruzan herself defined life to encompass every form of biological persistence by a human being, so that the continuation of treatment would serve Nancy's own liberty, then once again there would be no conflict between life and liberty. The opposition of life and liberty in this case are thus not the result of Nancy Cruzan's tragic accident, but are instead the artificial consequence of Missouri's effort, and this Court's willingness, to abstract Nancy Cruzan's life from Nancy Cruzan's person.

IV

Both this Court's majority and the state court's majority express great deference to the policy choice made by the state legislature. That deference is, in my view, based upon a severe error in the Court's constitutional logic. The Court believes that the liberty interest claimed here on behalf of Nancy Cruzan is peculiarly problematic because "an incompetent person is not able to make an informed and voluntary choice to exercise a hypothetical right to refuse treatment or any other right." The impossibility of such an exercise affords the State, according to the Court, some discretion to interpose "a procedural requirement" that effectively compels the continuation of Nancy Cruzan's treatment.

There is, however, nothing "hypothetical" about Nancy Cruzan's constitutionally protected interest in freedom from unwanted treatment, and the difficulties involved in ascertaining what her interests are do not in any way justify the State's decision to oppose her interests with its own. As this case comes to us, the crucial question — and the question addressed by the Court — is not what Nancy Cruzan's interests are, but whether the State must give effect to them. There is certainly nothing novel about the practice of permitting a next friend to assert constitutional rights on behalf of an incompetent patient who is unable to do so. Thus, if Nancy Cruzan's incapacity to "exercise" her rights is to alter the balance between her interests and the State's, there must be some further explanation of how it does so. The Court offers two possibilities, neither of them satisfactory.

The first possibility is that the State's policy favoring life is by its nature less intrusive upon the patient's interest than any alternative. The Court suggests that Missouri's policy "results in a maintenance of the status quo," and is subject to reversal, while a decision to terminate treatment "is not susceptible of correction" because death is irreversible. Yet, this explanation begs the question, for it assumes either that the State's policy is consistent with Nancy Cruzan's own interests, or that no damage is done by ignoring her interests. The first assumption is without basis in the record of this case, and would obviate any need for the State to rely, as it does, upon its own interests rather than upon the patient's. The second assumption is unconscionable. Insofar as Nancy Cruzan has an interest in being remembered for how she lived rather than how she died, the damage done to those memories by the prolongation of her death is irreversible. Insofar as Nancy Cruzan has an interest in the cessation of any pain, the continuation of her pain is irreversible. Insofar as Nancy Cruzan has an interest in a closure to her life consistent with her own beliefs rather than those of the Missouri legislature, the State's imposition of its contrary view is irreversible. To deny the importance of these consequences is in effect to deny that Nancy Cruzan has interests at all, and thereby to deny her personhood in the name of preserving the sanctity of her life.

The second possibility is that the State must be allowed to define the interests of incompetent patients with respect to life-sustaining treatment because there is no procedure capable of determining what those interests are in any particular case. The Court points out various possible "abuses" and inaccuracies that may affect procedures authorizing the termination of treatment. The Court correctly notes that in some cases there may be a conflict between the interests of an incompetent patient and the interests of members of her family. A State's procedures must guard against the risk that the survivors' interests are not mistaken for the patient's. Yet, the appointment of the neutral guardian ad litem, coupled with the searching inquiry conducted by the trial judge and the imposition of the clear and convincing standard of proof, all effectively avoided that risk in this case. Why such procedural safeguards should not be adequate to avoid a similar risk in other cases is a question the Court simply ignores.

Indeed, to argue that the mere possibility of error in any case suffices to allow the State's interests to override the particular interests of incompetent individuals in every case, or to argue that the interests of such individuals are unknowable and therefore may be subordinated to the State's concerns, is once again to deny Nancy Cruzan's personhood. The meaning of respect for her personhood, and for that of others who are gravely ill and incapacitated, is, admittedly, not easily defined: choices about life and death are profound ones, not susceptible of resolution by recourse to medical or legal rules. It may be that the best we can do is to ensure that these choices are made by those who will care enough about the patient to investigate her interests with particularity and caution. The Court seems to recognize as much when it cautions against formulating any general or inflexible rule to govern all the cases that might arise in this area of the law. The Court's deference to the legislature is, however, itself an inflexible rule, one that the Court is willing to apply in this case even though the Court's principal grounds for deferring to Missouri's legislature are hypothetical circumstances not relevant to Nancy Cruzan's interests.

On either explanation, then, the Court's deference seems ultimately to derive from the premise that chronically incompetent persons have no constitutionally cognizable interests at all, and so are not persons within the meaning of the Constitution. Deference of this sort is patently unconstitutional. It is also dangerous in ways that may not be immediately apparent. Today the State of Missouri has announced its intent to spend several hundred thousand dollars in preserving the life of Nancy Beth Cruzan in order to vindicate its general policy favoring the preservation of human life. Tomorrow, another State equally eager to champion an interest in the "quality of life" might favor a policy designed to ensure quick and comfortable deaths by denying treatment to categories of marginally hopeless cases. If the State in fact has an interest in defining life, and if the State's policy with respect to the termination of life-sustaining treatment commands deference from the judiciary, it is unclear how any resulting conflict between the best interests of the individual and the general policy of the State would be resolved. I believe the Constitution requires that the individual's vital interest in liberty should prevail over the general policy in that case, just as in this.

That a contrary result is readily imaginable under the majority's theory makes manifest that this Court cannot defer to any State policy that drives a theoretical wedge between a person's life, on the one hand, and that person's liberty or happiness, on the other. The consequence of such a theory is to deny the personhood of those whose lives are defined by the State's interests rather than their own. This consequence may be acceptable in theology or in speculative philosophy, but it is radically inconsistent with the foundation of all legitimate government. Our

Constitution presupposes a respect for the personhood of every individual, and nowhere is strict adherence to that principle more essential than in the Judicial Branch.

V

. . . Each of us has an interest in the kind of memories that will survive after death. . . . Lives do not exist in abstraction from persons, and to pretend otherwise is not to honor but to desecrate the State's responsibility for protecting life. A State that seeks to demonstrate its commitment to life may do so by aiding those who are actively struggling for life and health. In this endeavor, unfortunately, no State can lack for opportunities: there can be no need to make an example of tragic cases like that of Nancy Cruzan.

I respectfully dissent.

Discussion

1. Robert Bork has written, "No [current member of the Supreme Court] renounces the power to override democratic majorities when the Constitution is silent." As the phrasing might indicate, Judge Bork vigorously opposes *any* reliance on "fundamental rights" by judges. Thus for him, the famous dissent by Justice Holmes in *Lochner*, supra Chapter 4, was "spoiled" by Holmes's "accept[ance of] substantive due process" in his acknowledgment that the courts could invalidate a law upon the finding "that a rational and fair man necessarily would admit that the statute proposed would infringe fundamental principles as they have been understood by the traditions of our people and our law."[49] Turning to the present Court, Judge Bork states:

> It may be that Scalia and Rehnquist are trying to come as close as they can get [to renouncing judicial authority to enforce fundamental albeit unwritten rights] by insisting on using the most specific tradition available. But even that assumes an illegitimate power, and the limitation will prove no restriction at all when there is only a general, unfocused tradition to be found. Seven Justices, in varying degrees, reject even that slight restriction on their powers. Nothing resembling an adequate justification has ever been, is now, or ever will be offered for this taking by judges of a power that is not theirs.

How does Judge Bork's description of the Justices comport with their positions in *Cruzan*?

2. Is Justice Scalia correct in stating that no principled distinction can be offered between upholding Nancy Cruzan's right to reject treatment and her "right to commit suicide"? Consider his example of a state-run hospital sued for violation of constitutional rights "if, in a State where suicide is unlawful, it pumps out the stomach of a person who has intentionally taken an overdose of barbiturates, despite that person's wishes to the contrary." Would your answer depend on your assessment of the "rationality" of the person's desire for death? Assume that the person had written an extensive note explaining her decision to die on the basis of having been informed that she has Alzheimer's disease? Now imagine a differ-

49. Robert Bork, The Tempting of America: The Political Seduction of the Law 240, 245 (1989).

ent person, a 30-year-old male, who offers an unhappy love affair and the decision by his beloved to break off relations as the rationale for "ending it all." Would you *ever* honor the choice of a 15-year-old to die?

3. Does Justice Scalia's conundrum apply with equal force to all of the other opinions? Most of the opinions rely on individual autonomy, but is Justice Stevens's approach less dependent on that concept than the other justices?

4. Justice O'Connor's relatively brief concurring opinion focuses primarily on the presence of a protected liberty interest in cases such as Cruzan's. She also addresses a problem not directly in front of the Court, though likely to arise at some point in the future: The designation by a competent person of a "surrogate" to make a decision as to when the termination of life-support is appropriate.

> I also write separately to emphasize that the Court does not today decide the issue whether a State must also give effect to the decisions of a surrogate decisionmaker. In my view, such a duty may well be constitutionally required to protect the patient's liberty interest in refusing medical treatment. Few individuals provide explicit oral or written instructions regarding their intent to refuse medical treatment should they become incompetent. States which decline to consider any evidence other than such instructions may frequently fail to honor a patient's intent. Such failures might be avoided if the State considered an equally probative source of evidence: the patient's appointment of a proxy to make health care decisions on her behalf. Delegating the authority to make medical decisions to a family member or friend is becoming a common method of planning for the future. Several States have recognized the practical wisdom of such a procedure by enacting durable power of attorney statutes that specifically authorize an individual to appoint a surrogate to make medical treatment decisions. Some state courts have suggested that an agent appointed pursuant to a general durable power of attorney statute would also be empowered to make health care decisions on behalf of the patient. Other States allow an individual to designate a proxy to carry out the intent of a living will. These procedures for surrogate decisionmaking, which appear to be rapidly gaining in acceptance, may be a valuable additional safeguard of the patient's interest in directing his medical care. Moreover, as patients are likely to select a family member as a surrogate, giving effect to a proxy's decisions may also protect the "freedom of personal choice in matters of . . . family life."

Chapter 10
Representation Within a Republican Polity

Article IV of the Constitution speaks of a republican form of government. Although the specific meaning of the term is uncertain, most analysts would agree that a "republican" form of government is one that allows popular discussion of important issues and gives citizens an opportunity through electing public officials to influence governmental decisions on those issues. The Constitution of 1787 was silent about suffrage and thus left to the States the power to decide who could participate. At the time the Constitution was adopted, "universal suffrage" typically referred to white males who owned real property. Most property qualifications were limited or eliminated by the 1820s, though racial and gender restrictions remained.[1]

The first "federalization" of the suffrage came with the passage of the Fourteenth and Fifteenth Amendments. As noted earlier, in Chapter 4, section 2 of the Fourteenth Amendment reduced the Congressional representatives of those states that "denied [the vote] to any of the male inhabitants of such State, being twenty-one years of age, and citizens of the United States," except for "participation in rebellion, or other crime." The Fifteenth Amendment went further by formally barring states from denying the right to vote of any citizen "on account of race, color, or previous condition of servitude."

In Minor v. Hapersett, 88 U.S. 162 (1874), page 241 supra, the Supreme Court rejected Virginia Minor's argument that the privileges and immunities clause of the Fourteenth Amendment gave her a right to participate in Missouri's elections. Indeed, the Court noted that except for the Fifteenth Amendment, the Constitution did not constrain a state's decisions with respect to suffrage. The Nineteenth Amendment, adopted in 1920, prohibited denying the vote "on account of sex."

I. Participation in the Electoral Process

No political system has ever literally practiced "universal" suffrage, even among its citizens. For example, it is doubtful that any countries have ever allowed young children to vote and, at least within the United States, convicted felons are commonly denied the franchise. Thus, being a citizen does not automatically entitle one to vote. Nonetheless, the Court has interpreted the equal protection clause of the Fourteenth Amendment to limit beyond race or sex the power of states to exclude citizens from the electorate.

1. See Merrill D. Peterson, ed., Democracy, Liberty, and Property: The State Constitutional Conventions of the 1820's (1966: Anthology of Massachusetts, Virginia, New York debates); Chilton Williamson, American Suffrage from Property to Democracy: 1760-1860 (1960).

A. Paying for the Suffrage

HARPER v. VIRGINIA BOARD OF ELECTIONS
383 U.S. 663 (1966)
Appeal from the United States District Court for the Eastern District of Virginia

[Virginia levied a $1.50 annual poll tax on all persons over 21, enforced by disfranchising those who did not pay. The tax proceeds financed the public school systems and other local government functions. Petitioners sued to declare the tax unconstitutional. A three-judge district court dismissed the complaint on the authority of Breedlove v. Suttles, 302 U.S. 277 (1937), in which the Court had sustained a state poll tax against equal protection challenge. On appeal, the Supreme Court reversed.]

DOUGLAS, J. . . .

We conclude that a State violates the Equal Protection Clause of the Fourteenth Amendment whenever it makes the affluence of the voter or payment of any fee an electoral standard. Voter qualifications have no relation to wealth nor to paying or not paying this or any other tax. Our cases demonstrate that the Equal Protection Clause of the Fourteenth Amendment restrains the States from fixing voter qualifications which invidiously discriminate. . . .

Long ago in Yick Wo v. Hopkins, 118 U.S. 356 (1886), the Court referred to "the political franchise of voting" as a "fundamental political right, because preservative of all rights." Recently in Reynolds v. Sims, 377 U.S. 533 (1964), we said, "Undoubtedly, the right of suffrage is a fundamental matter in a free and democratic society. Especially since the right to exercise the franchise in a free and unimpaired manner is preservative of other basic civil and political rights, any alleged infringement of the right of citizens to vote must be carefully and meticulously scrutinized." There we were considering charges that voters in one part of the State had greater representation per person in the State Legislature than voters in another part of the State. We concluded:

> A citizen, a qualified voter, is no more nor no less so because he lives in the city or on the farm. This is the clear and strong command of our Constitution's Equal Protection Clause. This is an essential part of the concept of a government of laws and not men. This is at the heart of Lincoln's vision of "government of the people, by the people, [and] for the people." The Equal Protection Clause demands no less than substantially equal state legislative representation for all citizens, of all places as well as of all races.

We say the same whether the citizen, otherwise qualified to vote, has $1.50 in his pocket or nothing at all, pays the fee or fails to pay it. The principle that denies the State the right to dilute a citizen's vote on account of his economic status or other such factors by analogy bars a system which excludes those unable to pay a fee to vote or who fail to pay.

It is argued that a State may exact fees from citizens for many different kinds of licenses; that if it can demand from all an equal fee for a driver's license, it can demand from all an equal poll tax for voting. But we must remember that the interest of the State, when it comes to voting, is limited to the power to fix qualifications. Wealth, like race, creed, or color, is not germane to one's ability to participate intelligently in the electoral process. Lines drawn on the basis of wealth or property, like those of race (Korematsu v. United States, 323 U.S. 214, 216), are traditionally disfavored. See Edwards v. California, 314 U.S. 160, 184-185 (Jackson, J., concurring); Griffin v. Illinois, 351 U.S. 12 (1956); Douglas v. California, 372 U.S. 353 (1963). To introduce wealth or payment of a fee as a measure of a voter's qualifications is to introduce a capricious or irrelevant factor. The degree of the discrimination is irrelevant. In this context–that is, as a condition of obtaining a ballot–the requirement of fee paying causes an "invidious" discrimination (Skinner v. Oklahoma, 316 U.S. 535, 541) that runs afoul of the Equal Protection Clause. Levy "by the poll" . . . is an old familiar form of taxation; and we say nothing to impair its validity so long as it is not made a condition to the exercise of the franchise. Breedlove v. Suttles sanctioned its use as "a prerequisite of voting." To that extent the *Breedlove* case is overruled.

BLACK, J., dissenting. . . .

The equal protection cases carefully analyzed boil down to the principle that distinctions drawn and even discriminations imposed by state laws do not violate the Equal Protection Clause so long as these distinctions and discriminations are not "irrational," "irrelevant," "unreasonable," "arbitrary," or "invidious.". . . State poll tax legislation can "reasonably," "rationally" and without an "invidious" or evil purpose to injure anyone be found to rest on a number of state policies including (1) the State's desire to collect its revenue, and (2) its belief that voters who pay a poll tax will be interested in furthering the State's welfare when they vote. Certainly it is rational to believe that people may be more likely to pay taxes if payment is a prerequisite to voting. And if history can be a factor in determining the "rationality" ofdiscrimination in a state law . . . , then whatever may be our personal opinion, history is on the side of "rationality" of the State's poll tax policy. Property qualifications existed in the Colonies and were continued by many States after the Constitution was adopted. Although I join the Court in disliking the policy of the poll tax, this is not in my judgment a justifiable reason for holding this poll tax law unconstitutional. Such a holding on my part would, in my judgment, be an exercise of power which the Constitution does not confer upon me.

. . . Another reason for my dissent from the Court's judgment and opinion is that it seems to be using the old "natural-law-due-process formula" to justify striking down state laws as violations of the Equal Protection Clause. I have heretofore had many occasions to express my strong belief that there is no constitutional support whatever for this Court to use the Due Process Clause as though it provided a blank check to alter the meaning of the Constitution as written so as to add to it substantive constitutional changes which a majority of the Court at any given time believes are needed to meet present-day problems. Nor is there in my opinion any more constitutional support for this Court to use the Equal Protection Clause, as it has today, to write into the Constitution its notions of what it thinks is good governmental policy. . . .

The Court denies that it is using the "natural-law-due-process formula." It says that its invalidation of the Virginia law "is founded not on what we think governmental policy should be, but on what the Equal Protection Clause requires." I find no statement in the Court's opinion, however, which advances even a plausible argument as to why the alleged discriminations which might possibly be effected by Virginia's poll tax law are "irrational," "unreasonable," "arbitrary," or "invidious" or have no relevance to a legitimate policy which the State wishes to adopt. . . . I can only conclude that the primary, controlling, predominant, if not the exclusive reason for declaring the Virginia law unconstitutional is the Court's deep-seated hostility and antagonism, which I share, to making payment of a tax a prerequisite to voting.

The Court's justification for consulting its own notions rather than following the original meaning of the Constitution, as I would, apparently is based on the belief of the majority of the Court that for this Court to be bound by the original meaning of the Constitution is an intolerable and debilitating evil; that our Constitution should not be "shackled to the political theory of a particular era," and that to save the country from the original Constitution the Court must have constant power to renew it and keep it abreast of this Court's more enlightened theories of what is best for our society.[a]

HARLAN, J., joined by Stewart, J., dissenting. . . .

I do not propose to retread ground covered in my dissents in Reynolds v. Sims, 377 U.S. 533, 589, and Carrington v. Rash, 380 U.S. 89, 97, and will proceed on the premise that the Equal Protection Clause of the Fourteenth Amendment now reaches both state apportionment (*Reynolds*) and voter-qualification (*Carrington*) cases.[2] . . .

The Equal Protection Clause prevents States from arbitrarily treating people differently under their laws. . . . The test involved by this Court for determining whether an asserted justifying classification exists is whether such a classification can be deemed to be founded on some rational and otherwise constitutionally permissible state policy. . . .

Is there a rational basis for Virginia's poll tax as a voting qualification? I think the answer to that question is undoubtedly "yes."

Property qualifications and poll taxes have been a traditional part of our political structure. In the Colonies the franchise was generally a restricted one. Over the years these and other restrictions were gradually lifted, primarily because

a. In Brown v. Board of Education, the Court today purports to find precedent for using the Equal Protection Clause to keep the Constitution up to date. I did not vote to hold segregation in public schools unconstitutional on any such theory. I thought when *Brown* was written, and I think now, that Mr. Justice Harlan was correct in 1896 when he dissented from Plessy v. Ferguson, which held that it was not a discrimination prohibited by the Equal Protection Clause for state law to segregate white and colored people in public facilities, there railroad cars.

2. In *Reynolds*, which held that the equal protection clause of the Fourteenth Amendment required state adherence to a one-person/one-vote apportionment standard in legislative elections, Justice Harlan argued at length in dissent that the history of the adoption of the amendment, as well as §2 of the amendment's text, made clear that the amendment did not apply to the franchise. As he reiterated in Oregon v. Mitchell, 400 U.S. 112 (1970), "[T]he history of the Fourteenth Amendment with respect to suffuage qualifications is remarkably free of the problems which bedevil most attempts to find a reliable guide to present decision in the pages of the past. Instead there is virtually unanimous agreement, clearly and repeatedly expressed, that §1 of the Amendment did not reach discriminatory voter qualifications."

Recall the history of the adoption of the Fourteenth Amendment, pp. 229-237 supra. Whatever this suggests with respect to Negro suffrage, does it entail the same result with respect to the issues in *Reynolds* and *Harper*? See William Van Alstyne, The Fourteenth Amendment, the "Right" to Vote, and the Understanding of the Thirty-ninth Congress, 1965 Sup. Ct. Rev. 33; Charles Miller, The Supreme Court and the Uses of History 135-138 (1969).

popular theories of political representation had changed. Often restrictions were lifted only after wide public debate. The issue of woman suffrage, for example, raised questions of family relationships, of participation in public affairs, of the very nature of the type of society in which Americans wished to live; eventually a consensus was reached, which culminated in the Nineteenth Amendment no more than 45 years ago.

Similarly with property qualifications, it is only by fiat that it can be said, especially in the context of American history, that there can be no rational debate as to their advisability. Most of the early Colonies had them; many of the States have had them during much of their histories; and, whether one agrees or not, arguments have been and still can be made in favor of them. For example, it is certainly a rational argument that payment of some minimal poll tax promotes civic responsibility, weeding out those who do not care enough about public affairs to pay $1.50 or thereabouts a year for the exercise of the franchise. It is also arguable, indeed it was probably accepted as sound political theory by a large percentage of Americans through most of our history, that people with some property have a deeper stake in community affairs, and are consequently more responsible, more educated, more knowledgeable, more worthy of confidence, than those without means, and that the community and Nation would be better managed if the franchise were restricted to such citizens. Nondiscriminatory and fairly applied literacy tests, upheld by this Court in Lassiter v. Northampton Election Board, 360 U.S. 45, find justification on very similar grounds.

These viewpoints, to be sure, ring hollow on most contemporary ears. Their lack of acceptance today is evidenced by the fact that nearly all of the States, left to their own devices, have eliminated property or poll-tax qualifications; by the cognate fact that Congress and three-quarters of the States quickly ratified the Twenty-Fourth Amendment. . . .

Property and poll-tax qualifications, very simply, are not in accord with current egalitarian notions of how a modern democracy should be organized. It is of course entirely fitting that legislatures should modify the law to reflect such changes in popular attitudes. However, it is all wrong, in my view, for the Court to adopt the political doctrines popularly accepted at a particular moment of our history and to declare all others to be irrational and invidious, barring them from the range of choice by reasonably minded people acting through the political process. It was not too long ago that Mr. Justice Holmes felt impelled to remind the Court that the Due Process Clause of the Fourteenth Amendment does not enact the laissez-faire theory of society, Lochner v. New York. The times have changed, and perhaps it is appropriate to observe that neither does the Equal Protection Clause of that Amendment rigidly impose upon America an ideology of unrestrained egalitarianism.

I would affirm the decision of the District Court.

Discussion

1. *Wealth as a suspect basis of classification.* Assuming that the poll tax classified on the basis of wealth, to what extent does wealth share the characteristics that make race a suspect basis of classification? In Edwards v. California, 314 U.S. 160 (1941), Justice Jackson concurred in invalidating a law prohibiting bringing a nonresident indigent into the state, on the ground that "a man's mere property status, without more, cannot be used by a state to test, qualify, or limit his rights as

a citizen of the United States. 'Indigence' in itself . . . is a neutral fact — constitutionally an irrelevance, like race, creed, or color."

2. *The basis of classification.* Assuming that "wealth" should be treated as suspect, does the poll tax *classify* on the basis of wealth, or does it classify on some other basis but have a different impact on persons of differing wealth? Would it be tenable in an economy that relied on a pricing system — i.e., any modern economy — to hold that every law that classifies as the Virginia law does is suspect and demands an extraordinary justification?

3. *Rational classification?* The dissenting opinions in *Harper* suggest that the Virginia poll tax served several governmental interests: collecting revenues, promoting a responsible vote, and limiting the franchise to those with some minimal stake in the community. Can the tax be sustained, under a rational classification standard, in terms of one or more of those objectives?

4. *The justification for demanding an extraordinary justification.* If mere differential impact on persons of differing wealth is not sufficient to trigger the demand for an extraordinary justification, what additional factor is present in *Harper*? The Court concedes at the outset that there is no constitutional "right" to vote in state elections. What is it about the "interest" in voting that justifies demanding an extraordinary justification of the fee requirement in *Harper*? In what constitutional sources does the Court find guidance for deeming participation in the electoral process a "fundamental interest"?

5. *The nature of the relief granted.* Note that the decision in *Harper* invalidates the poll tax for *all* Virginians, rich and poor alike. Why can't the state impose a poll tax on the citizenry in general, save for those who submit an affidavit that they cannot afford the tax?

6. *The relevance of the Twenty-Fourth Amendment.* Justice Harlan notes that the Twenty-Fourth Amendment, which prohibited a state from imposing poll taxes as a condition for voting in elections for *federal* offices, had been adopted only two years before the Court's decision in *Harper*. If it required a constitutional amendment to prohibit poll taxes for federal elections, how plausible is the majority's reading of the Fourteenth Amendment to prohibit poll taxes in state elections? If, on the other hand, you are persuaded by Justice Douglas' opinion, was the Twenty-Fourth Amendment wholly unnecessary?

7. *Filing fees.* States and localities commonly extract filing fees from political candidates for state and local offices. In Bullock v. Carter, 405 U.S. 134 (1972), would-be candidates for state and local offices challenged a Texas requirement that they pay substantial filing fees in order to run in the primary elections. The fees, based on the "importance, emolument, and term of office," were large, in some cases amounting to 15 percent or more of the salary attached to the office.

The Court unanimously struck down the Texas scheme. Chief Justice Burger began by asking "[t]he threshold question . . . whether the filing-fee system should be sustained if it can be shown to have some rational basis, or whether it must withstand a more rigid standard of review." He noted the likely link between poor voters and candidates unable to pay the filing fees and concluded, "Because the Texas filing-fee scheme has a real and appreciable impact on the exercise of the franchise, and because this impact is related to the resources of the voters supporting a particular candidate, we conclude, as in *Harper,* that the laws must be 'closely scrutinized' and found reasonably necessary to the accomplishment of legitimate state objectives in order to pass constitutional muster."

Turning to the state's asserted interests, the Chief Justice suggested that, as a device to weed out frivolous candidates, the fee requirement might not even meet the demands of minimum rationality: "There may well be some rational relationship between a candidate's willingness to pay a filing fee and the seriousness with which he takes his candidacy, but the candidates in this case affirmatively alleged that they were *unable,* not simply *unwilling,* to pay the assessed fees and there was no contradictory evidence."[3] And though the scheme was rationally related to relieving "the State treasury of the cost of conducting the primary elections," it did not meet the "showing of necessity" demanded by the stricter standard of review. The Court was also unimpressed by the state's argument that a candidate could bypass the primary and appear on the general election ballot without paying a fee: "Apart from the fact that the primary election may be more crucial than the general election in certain parts of Texas, we can hardly accept as reasonable an alternative that requires candidates and voters to abandon their party affiliations." Without "cast[ing] doubt on the validity of reasonable candidate filing fees," the Court concluded that "Texas has [impermissibly] erected a system which utilizes the criterion of ability to pay as a condition to being on the ballot, thus [impermissibly] excluding some candidates otherwise qualified and denying an undetermined number of voters the opportunity to vote for candidates of their choice." In Lubin v. Panish, 415 U.S. 709 (1974), the Court relied on *Bullock* to invalidate California's somewhat more modest filing fees.

Although the Court relied on *Harper* for the proposition that strict scrutiny must be applied to the filing fees, it explicitly refused to "cast doubt on the validity of reasonable candidate filing fees." Why are states free to charge "reasonable candidate filing fees," but not a "reasonable poll tax"?

8. *Of poll taxes, filing fees, and postage stamps.* A basic attribute of any republican system of government is the citizenry's ability to participate in decisionmaking about vital issues of the day. At least today it seems unthinkable that the poor should be excluded from voting because they cannot pay a poll tax or be precluded from running for office because they cannot afford a filing fee.

Does republican governance require more than the right to participate in relatively infrequent elections? Consider, for example, someone who wishes to convey her view to the president or a member of Congress about the proper reaction to an unexpected event that was not even discussed in prior election campaigns. A common way to convey such views is to send letters to these officials — and this requires purchasing stamps with which to mail them. Should *Harper* stand for the proposition that at least the indigent (and perhaps all of us?) have a constitutional right to send letters to public officials at no cost? (Note that the First Amendment specifically protects the right to petition government for redress of grievances.) (See Chapter 11.)

B. Other Limitations on the Ballot

Harper stressed that the Virginia poll tax "discriminated" on the basis of wealth. The Court's strict scrutiny of laws affecting the franchise antedated *Harper,* however, and was not limited to classifications affecting wealth. Reynolds v. Sims, 377 U.S. 533 (1964), infra, the leading reapportionment decision, held that the equal

3. Is the Chief Justice correct in suggesting that the law could not be rationally justified in terms of this purpose?

protection clause required apportionment of state legislatures on a one-person/one-vote basis. And Carrington v. Rash, 380 U.S. 89 (1965), struck down a Texas constitutional provision that prohibited any member of the armed forces who moved to the state during the course of military duty from voting in any state election. The state proffered two justifications for the law. First, it prevented a military " 'takeover' of the civilian community resulting from concentrated voting by large numbers of military personnel" who might be influenced by a base commander "to vote in conformity with his predilections" and who might oppose local expenditures because they had no stake in the future of the area. Justice Stewart responded that a state could not deprive bona fide residents of the franchise "because of a fear of [their] political views." Second, the state argued that the provision assured that voters were in fact bona fide residents rather than mere transients. The Court agreed that this was a legitimate objective but held that it must be pursued through less restrictive means. "We deal here with matters close to the core of our constitutional system. . . . States may not casually deprive a class of individuals of the vote because of some remote administrative benefit. . . . By forbidding a soldier ever to controvert the presumption of nonresidence, the Texas Constitution imposes an invidious discrimination in violation of the Fourteenth Amendment."[4] Only Justice Harlan dissented, reasserting his view that the Fourteenth Amendment did not comprehend deprivations of the franchise and arguing alternatively that it sufficed that the Texas provision classified on a rational basis.

In Kramer v. Union Free School District No. 15, the Court synthesized *Reynolds, Carrington,* and *Harper,* to articulate a general criterion for measuring the constitutionality of laws depriving persons of the franchise.

KRAMER v. UNION FREE SCHOOL DISTRICT NO. 15

395 U.S. 621 (1969)

Appeal from the United States District Court for the Eastern District of New York

WARREN, C.J.

In this case we are called on to determine whether §2012 of the New York Education Law is constitutional. The legislation provides that in certain New York school districts residents who are otherwise eligible to vote in state and federal elections may vote in the school district election only if they . . . [are] either (1) . . . the owner or lessee of taxable real property located in the district, (2) . . . the spouse of one who owns or leases qualifying property, or (3) . . . the parent or guardian of a child enrolled for a specified time during the preceding year in a local district school. . . .

In determining whether or not [this] law violates the Equal Protection Clause, . . . we must give the statute a close and exacting examination. . . . Any

4. Compare Charles Black's analysis in Structure and Relationship in Constitutional Law 10-11 (1969): "Carrington, I should rather have said, was a federal soldier, recruited by the national government to perform a crucial national function. Conceding that in every other way he qualified to vote, Texas said that, solely upon the showing that he was in the performance of that function, he was not to vote. It makes little difference whether you call that a penalization of membership in the national Army. It is, in neutral terminology, the imposition, by a state, of a distinctive disadvantage based solely on membership in the Army. My thought would be that it ought to be held that no state may annex any disadvantage simply and solely to the performance of a federal duty."

unjustified discrimination in determining who may participate in political affairs or in the selection of public officials undermines the legitimacy of representative government.

. . . [S]tatutes granting the franchise to residents on a selective basis always pose the danger of denying some citizens any effective voice in the governmental affairs which substantially affect their lives. Therefore, if a challenged state statute grants the right to vote to some bona fide residents of requisite age and citizenship and denies the franchise to others, the Court must determine whether the exclusions are necessary to promote a compelling state interest.

And, for these reasons, the deference usually given to the judgment of legislators does not extend to decisions concerning which resident citizens may participate in the election of legislators and other public officials. Those decisions must be carefully scrutinized by the Court to determine whether each resident citizen has, as far as is possible, an equal voice in the selections. Accordingly, when we are reviewing statutes which deny some residents the right to vote, the general presumption of constitutionality afforded state statutes and the traditional approval given state classifications if the Court can conceive of a "rational basis" for the distinctions made are not applicable. See Harper v. Virginia Bd. of Elections. The presumption of constitutionality and the approval given "rational" classifications in other types of enactments are based on an assumption that the institutions of state government are structured so as to represent fairly all the people. However, when the challenge to the statute is in effect a challenge of this basic assumption, the assumption can no longer serve as the basis for presuming constitutionality. And, the assumption is no less under attack because the legislature which decides who may participate at the various levels of political choice is fairly elected. Legislation which delegates decision making to bodies elected by only a portion of those eligible to vote for the legislature can cause unfair representation. Such legislation can exclude a minority of voters from any voice in the decisions just as effectively as if the decisions were made by legislators the minority had no voice in selecting.

The need for exacting judicial scrutiny of statutes distributing the franchise is undiminished simply because, under a different statutory scheme, the offices subject to election might have been filled through appointment. . . .

Besides appellant and others who similarly live in their parents' homes,[5] the statute also disenfranchises the following persons (unless they are parents or guardians of children enrolled in the district public school): senior citizens and others living with children or relatives; clergy, military personnel, and others who live on tax-exempt property; boarders and lodgers; parents who neither own nor lease qualifying property and whose children are too young to attend school; parents who neither own nor lease qualifying property and whose children attend private schools. . . . All members of the community have an interest in the quality and structure of public education, appellant says, and he urges that "the decisions taken by local boards . . . may have grave consequences to the entire population." Appellant also argues that the level of property taxation affects him, even though he does not own property, as property tax levels affect the price of goods and services in the community.

5. "Appellant is a 31-year-old college-educated stockbroker who lives in his parents' home. . . . He is a citizen of the United States and has voted in federal and state elections since 1959."

We turn therefore to question whether the exclusion is necessary to promote a compelling state interest. First, appellees argue that the State has a legitimate interest in limiting the franchise in school district elections to "members of the community of interest" — those "primarily interested in such elections." Second, appellees urge that the State may reasonably and permissibly conclude that "property taxpayers" (including lessees of taxable property who share the tax burden through rent payments) and parents of the children enrolled in the district's schools are those "primarily interested" in school affairs.

We do not understand appellees to argue that the State is attempting to limit the franchise to those "subjectively concerned" about school matters. Rather, they appear to argue that the State's legitimate interest is in restricting a voice in school matters to those "directly affected" by such decisions. The State apparently reasons that since the schools are financed in part by local property taxes, persons whose out-of-pocket expenses are "directly" affected by property tax changes should be allowed to vote. Similarly, parents of children in school are thought to have a "direct" stake in school affairs and are given a vote.

Appellees argue that it is necessary to limit the franchise to those "primarily interested" in school affairs because "the ever increasing complexity of the many interacting phases of the school system and structure make it extremely difficult for the electorate fully to understand the whys and wherefores of the detailed operations of the school system." Appellees say that many communications of school boards and school administrations are sent home to the parents through the district pupils and are "not broadcast to the general public"; thus, nonparents will be less informed than parents. Further, appellees argue, those who are assessed for local property taxes (either directly or indirectly through rent) will have enough of an interest "through the burden on their pocketbooks, to acquire such information as they may need." . . .

Whether classifications allegedly limiting the franchise to those resident citizens "primarily interested" deny those excluded equal protection of the laws depends, inter alia, on whether all those excluded are in fact substantially less interested or affected than those the statute includes. In other words, the classifications must be tailored so that the exclusion of appellant and members of his class is necessary to achieve the articulated state goal.[a] Section 2012 does not meet the exacting standard of precision we require of statutes which selectively distribute the franchise. The classifications in §2012 permit inclusion of many persons who have, at best, a remote and indirect interest in school affairs and, on the other hand, exclude others who have a distinct and direct interest in the school meeting decisions.[b]

Nor do appellees offer any justification for the exclusion of seemingly interested and informed residents — other than to argue that the §2012 classifications include those "whom the State could understandably deem to be the most intimately interested in actions taken by the school board.". . . The requirements of

a. Of course, if the exclusions are necessary to promote the articulated state interest, we must then determine whether the interest promoted by limiting the franchise constitutes a compelling state interest. We do not reach that issue in this case.

b. For example, appellant resides with his parents in the school district, pays state and federal taxes and is interested in and affected by school board decisions; however, he has no vote. On the other hand, an uninterested unemployed young man who pays no state or federal taxes, but who rents an apartment in the district, can participate in the election.

§2012 are not sufficiently tailored to limiting the franchise to those "primarily interested" in school affairs to justify the denial of the franchise to appellant and members of his class. . . .

STEWART, J., joined by Black and Harlan, JJ., dissenting. . . .

[T]he appellant explicitly concedes, as he must, the validity of voting requirements relating to residence, literacy, and age. Yet he argues — and the Court accepts the argument — that the voting qualifications involved here somehow have a different constitutional status. I am unable to see the distinction.

Clearly a State may reasonably assume that its residents have a greater stake in the outcome of elections held within its boundaries than do other persons. Likewise, it is entirely rational for a state legislature to suppose that residents, being generally better informed regarding state affairs than are nonresidents, will be more likely than nonresidents to vote responsibly. And the same may be said of legislative assumptions regarding the electoral competence of adults and literate persons on the one hand, and of minors and illiterates on the other. It is clear, of course, that lines thus drawn cannot infallibly perform their intended legislative function. Just as "[i]lliterate people may be intelligent voters," nonresidents or minors might also in some instances be interested, informed, and intelligent participants in the electoral process. Persons who commute across a state line to work may well have a great stake in the affairs of the State in which they are employed; some college students under 21 may be both better informed and more passionately interested in political affairs than many adults. But such discrepancies are the inevitable concomitant of the line drawing that is essential to law making. So long as the classification is rationally related to a permissible legislative end, therefore — as are residence, literacy, and age requirements imposed with respect to voting — there is no denial of equal protection.

Thus judged, the statutory classification involved here seems to me clearly to be valid. New York has made the judgment that local educational policy is best left to those persons who have certain direct and definable interests in that policy: those who are either immediately involved as parents of school children or who, as owners or lessees of taxable property, are burdened with the local cost of funding school district operations. True, persons outside those classes may be genuinely interested in the conduct of a school district's business — just as commuters from New Jersey may be genuinely interested in the outcome of a New York City election. But . . . I see no way to justify the conclusion that the legislative classification involved here is not rationally related to a legitimate legislative purpose.

With good reason, the Court does not really argue the contrary. Instead, it strikes down New York's statute by asserting that the traditional equal protection standard is inapt in this case, and that a considerably stricter standard — under which classifications relating to "the franchise" are to be subjected to "exacting judicial scrutiny" — should be applied. But the asserted justification for applying such a standard cannot withstand analysis. . . .

The voting qualifications at issue have been promulgated, not by Union Free School District No. 15, but by the New York State Legislature, and the appellant is of course fully able to participate in the election of representatives in that body. There is simply no claim whatever here that the state government is not "structured so as to represent fairly all the people," including the appellant. . . . The appellant is eligible to vote in all state, local and federal elections in which general governmental policy is determined. He is fully able, therefore, to participate not only in the processes by which the requirements for school district voting may be changed, but also in those by which the levels of state and federal financial assistance to the District are determined. He clearly is not locked into any self-perpetuating status of exclusion from the electoral process.

. . . The appellant's status is merely that of a citizen who says he is interested in the affairs of his local public schools. If the Constitution requires that he must be given a decision-making role in the governance of those affairs, then it seems to me that any individual who seeks such a role must be given it. For as I have suggested, there is no persuasive reason for distinguishing constitutionally between the voter qualifications New York has required for its Union Free School District elections and qualifications based on factors such as age, residence, or literacy.

C. Subsequent Developments

1. Taxation and Representation

Cipriano v. City of Houma, 395 U.S. 701 (1969), decided on the same day as *Kramer,* struck down a Louisiana law permitting only property-owning taxpayers to vote in elections for municipal utilities where the bonds were to be paid solely from operation of the utilities and did not in any way burden real property. Justice Black, joined by Justice Stewart, concurred in the judgment on the ground that the classification was " 'wholly irrelevant to achievement' of the State's objective." Justice Harlan also concurred in the result, "adhering to his views" that the Fourteenth Amendment does not touch the franchise, "but considering himself bound by the Court's decisions" to the contrary.

City of Phoenix v. Kolodziejski, 399 U.S. 204 (1969), invalidated a similar state law. Here the municipal improvements were financed through general obligation bonds; a substantial portion of the indebtedness was to be paid from property taxes; and the bonds in effect constituted a lien on real property, secured by the city's taxing power. Justice White wrote for the Court that "[t]he differences between the interests of property owners and the interests of non-property owners are not sufficiently substantial to justify excluding the latter from the franchise." Nonproperty owners have a substantial interest in whether the city provides the services and facilities financed by the bonds; other local taxes besides property taxes are used to service the bonds (in Phoenix, over half of the bond obligation was met through nonproperty taxes); and a significant portion of property taxes is passed on to the tenants of property owners. Justice Stewart, joined by Chief Justice Burger and Justice Harlan, dissented, arguing that the state could rationally conclude that bonds should not be issued "without the approval of a majority of those upon whom the weight of repaying those bonds will legally fall."

In Salyer Land Co. v. Tulare Lake Basin Water Storage District, 410 U.S. 719 (1973), the Court held that *Kramer, Cipriano,* and *Kolodziejski* did not preclude California from limiting participation in a water district election to persons and corporations owning land in the district or from apportioning votes according to the assessed valuation of the land. Justice Rehnquist noted that the district's primary purpose was to provide for the acquisition, storage, and distribution of water for farming and that all costs of district projects were assessed against the land in proportion to the benefits received. He concluded that "the popular election requirements enunciated by *Reynolds* and succeeding cases are inapplicable" and went on to decide that it was not irrational to deny the franchise to nonlandowning residents, including long-term lessees — even though they might indirectly bear district costs and were affected by the district's flood control policies — and that it was permissible to apportion votes according to assessments. Justice Douglas, joined by Justices Brennan and Marshall, dissented.

Ball v. James, 451 U.S. 355 (1981), upheld the "one acre/one vote" electoral scheme of the Salt River Project Agricultural Improvement and Power District, the primary supplier of electric power to much of Phoenix and its environs. Registered voters within the district who did not meet the district's voting property requirements sued to invalidate them, alleging that the district enjoys the governmental powers to condemn land, to sell tax-exempt bonds, and to levy taxes on real property, and that, because the district sells electricity to virtually half the population of Arizona and can exercise significant influence on flood control and environmental management, its policies affect residents of the district regardless of property ownership.

The Court found *Salyer* controlling. Justice Stewart wrote that the district "cannot enact any laws governing the conduct of citizens, nor does it administer such normal functions of government as the maintenance of streets, the operation of schools, or sanitation, health, and welfare services." Nor did the district exercise control over the distribution and use of water, which, as in *Salyer,* was delivered according to land ownership. With respect to the size of the district's power operations, Justice Stewart noted that the relationship between nonvoting residents and the district was "essentially that between consumers and a business enterprise from which they buy." In sum, the district's functions are "of the narrow, special sort which justifies a departure from the popular election requirements of the *Reynolds* case."

In a footnote, Justice Stewart implicitly called *Kramer* into question by noting that the complainants "are qualified voters in Arizona and so remain equal participants in the election of state legislators who created and have the power to change the District." In a concurring opinion, Justice Powell explicitly questioned *Kramer.*

Justice White dissented, joined by Justices Brennan, Marshall, and Blackmun, criticizing the majority's assertion that "the provision of electricity and water is essentially private enterprise and not sufficiently governmental": "The purpose and authority of the Salt River District are of extreme *public* importance. The District affects the daily lives of thousands of citizens who because of the present voting scheme and powers vested in the District by the State are unable to participate in any meaningful way in the conduct of the District's operations." With respect to the continued viability of *Kramer,* Justice White wrote:

> It is suggested . . . that since the nonvoters living in the district may, of course, vote in the state legislature elections, their interests are sufficiently represented since the state legislature maintains ultimate control over the operation and authority of the District. . . . In most situations involving a state agency, or even a city, the state legislature and ultimately the people could exercise control since any municipal corpora-

tion is a creature of the State. The Fourteenth Amendment requires a far more direct sense of democratic participation in elective schemes which is not satisfied by the indirect and imprecise voter control suggested by the Court and by Justice Powell.

Discussion

In writing of the importance of a "direct sense of democratic participation in elective schemes," is Justice White suggesting that the Constitution *requires* that public officials be elected rather than appointed? The number and type of public officials elected and appointed varies significantly from state to state. New Jersey, for example, essentially mimics the Federal Government in electing only the Governor, who then appoints other members of the executive branch. New Jersey appoints its judges via nomination by the governor and confirmation by the state senate. In Texas, on the other hand, almost all public officials, including judges, are elected, and there is significant debate about the wisdom of election versus appointment as a method of selecting officials such as the Commissioner of Agriculture, members of the Board of Education, and members of the judiciary.

Suppose that the Texas legislature decides that the current scheme of electing the Commissioner of Agriculture is undesirable because the state's overwhelmingly urban electorate does not sufficiently understand the needs of the agricultural sector. However, the legislature wishes to maintain the elected status of the office. It therefore decides upon the following scheme: Only those Texans who live in "agricultural counties" (defined in terms of the local economic base) can vote for the Commissioner. Would this be unconstitutional? *Kramer,* of course, suggests an affirmative answer. Assume that a court so rules and that the legislature responds by making it an appointive office (and requiring further that the Commissioner be "an experienced farmer or rancher"). Would *that* violate the equal protection clause? If not, then why should the Constitution require egalitarian participation in electoral schemes if there need not be elections at all?

2. *Duration of Residency*

Dunn v. Blumstein, 405 U.S. 330 (1972), while explicitly recognizing the states' power to limit the franchise to bona fide residents, held that the equal protection clause limited state authority to impose durational residence requirements. Tennessee conditioned eligibility to vote on one year's residency in the state and three months' in the county. It proffered two purposes: to "insure purity of [the] ballot box" by protecting against "fraud through colonization and inability to identify persons offering to vote"; and to assure a "knowledgeable voter," one who has "become a member of the community and . . . has a common interest in all matters pertaining to its government and is, therefore, more likely to exercise his right more intelligently." Justice Marshall began by setting the Court's legal framework for decision:

> To decide whether a law violates the Equal Protection Clause, we look, in essence, to three things: the character of the classification in question; the individual interests affected by the classification; and the governmental interests asserted in support of

> the classification. In considering laws challenged under the Equal Protection Clause, this Court has evolved more than one test, depending upon the interest affected or the classification involved. First, then, we must determine what standard of review is appropriate. In the present case, whether we look to the benefit withheld by the classification (the opportunity to vote) or the basis for the classification (recent interstate travel) we conclude that the state must show a substantial and compelling reason for imposing durational residence requirements.
>
> ... [Such requirements are unconstitutional] unless the State can demonstrate that such laws are "*necessary* to promote a *compelling* governmental interest." Shapiro v. Thompson (first emphasis added); Kramer v. Union Free School District. Thus phrased, the constitutional question may sound like a mathematical formula. But legal "tests" do not have the precision of mathematical formulas. The key words emphasize a matter of degree: that a heavy burden of justification is on the State, and that the statute will be closely scrutinized in light of its asserted purposes.
>
> It is not sufficient for the State to show that durational residence requirements further a very substantial state interest. In pursuing that important interest, the State cannot choose means which unnecessarily burden or restrict constitutionally protected activity. Statutes affecting constitutional rights must be drawn with "precision," NAACP v. Button, 371 U.S. 415, 438 (1963); United States v. Robel, 389 U.S. 258, 265 (1967), and must be "tailored" to serve their legitimate objectives. Shapiro v. Thompson. And if there are other, reasonable ways to achieve those goals with a lesser burden on constitutionally protected activity, a State may not choose the way of greater interference. If it acts at all, it must choose "less drastic means." Shelton v. Tucker, 364 U.S. 479, 488 (1960).

With respect to the first justification for the durational requirements, the Court agreed that the state had a legitimate interest in preventing nonresidents from temporarily invading the jurisdiction and falsely swearing their residence in order to vote. In view of the state's primary reliance on the oath to prevent fraud and the ease of checking various indicia of residence, however, the Court believed that 30 days provides the state with "an ample period of time ... to complete whatever administrative tasks are necessary to prevent fraud."[6] To the extent that the state's interest in ensuring "knowledgeable voters" meant ensuring voters having "local" viewpoints, it is constitutionally impermissible under *Carrington,* supra. And in view of modern communication and the self-selection of those who bother to register and vote, the state's interest in an informed electorate cannot justify such lengthy durational residence requirements.

Chief Justice Burger dissented, arguing that "[s]ome lines must be drawn. To challenge such lines by the 'compelling state interest' standard is to condemn them all. So far as I am aware, no state law has ever satisfied this seemingly insurmountable standard, and I doubt that one ever will, for it demands nothing less than perfection."

6. Justice Marshall found support for this number in the Voting Rights Act of 1970, which limits durational requirements for presidential elections to 30 days, and in the fact that Tennessee closes its registration books only 30 days before an election. In Marston v. Lewis, 410 U.S. 679 (1973), and Burns v. Fortson, 410 U.S. 686 (1973), the Court approved 50-day requirements for Arizona and Georgia in view of the states' demonstrations of special needs. Justice Marshall, joined by Justices Douglas and Brennan, dissented from the two per curiam decisions.

3. *Jail Inmates and Convicted Felons*

O'Brien v. Skinner, 414 U.S. 524 (1974), held that New York must provide absentee registration and voting for persons in jail awaiting trial or convicted of misdemeanors when it provided absentee procedures for a variety of others unable to vote in person. Chief Justice Burger rejected the argument made in dissent by Justices Blackmun and Rehnquist that "New York's present statutory structure [for absentee voting] has developed by successive remedial amendments, each designed to correct a then-apparent gap. . . . And 'a legislature traditionally has been allowed to take reform one step at a time, addressing itself to the phase of the problem which seems most acute to the legislative mind.' . . . McDonald v. Board of Election Commissioners, 394 U.S. 802 (1969)." The Court distinguished *McDonald,* in which it rejected the argument of qualified Cook County voters who were incarcerated in the the county jail awaiting trial that they were entitled to absentee ballots. The Court based the distinction on the fact that the record there, unlike the present one, did not indicate that persons in jail were absolutely disabled from voting.

Richardson v. Ramirez, 418 U.S. 24 (1974), held that the equal protection clause does not prohibit a state from disfranchising convicted felons who had completed their sentences and paroles. Justice Rehnquist relied largely on the facts that many state constitutions in effect when the Fourteenth Amendment was adopted disfranchised convicted felons and that section 2 of the Fourteenth Amendment reduced the basis of representation in the House to the extent a state denied the vote to adult male citizens, "except for participation in rebellion, or other crime." He concluded that "the exclusion of felons from the vote has an affirmative sanction . . . which was not present in the case of the other restrictions on the franchise" invalidated in *Harper* and its progeny. Justice Marshall, joined by Justice Brennan, dissented.[7] He argued that section 2 is a provision of limited purpose and effect and ought not constrain the broad language of section 1 and that the permanent disfranchisement of convicted felons served no compelling state interests.

4. *Party Affiliation*

Rosario v. Rockefeller, 410 U.S. 752 (1973), upheld New York's delayed enrollment law, which required voters to enroll in the party of their choice at least 30 days before a general election in order to be eligible to vote in the next party primary, thus preventing a change in party affiliation for approximately eleven months. However, in Kusper v. Pontikes, 414 U.S. 51 (1973), the Court struck down an Illinois law prohibiting persons from voting in a primary election if they had voted in the primary of any other party within the preceding 23 months. Justice Stewart recognized the state's interest in preventing party "raiding" but held that it must be attained by less drastic means. Justices Blackmun and Rehnquist dissented.

7. Justice Douglas dissented on technical grounds.

5. *Literacy*

In Lassiter v. Northampton County Board of Elections, 360, U.S. 45 (1959), Justice Douglas wrote for a unanimous Court upholding a literacy test as a prerequisite for voting:

> Literacy and intelligence are obviously not synonymous. Illiterate people may be intelligent voters. Yet in our society where newspapers, periodicals, books, and other printed matter canvass and debate campaign issues, a State might include that only those who are literate should exercise the franchise. . . . We do not sit in judgment on the wisdom of that policy.

Justice Douglas appeared to be applying only a minimal-rationality test. Would a literacy test survive Justice Douglas's own standard in *Harper* or the Court's in *Kramer*?

The issue has been resolved for the present, since Congress in the exercise of its powers under section 5 of the Fourteenth Amendment, see Oregon v. Mitchell, 400 U.S. 112 (1970), p.1502 infra, has prohibited the use of any literary test as a voting condition.

6. *Age*

What kinds of justifications support limiting the vote to persons over a certain age? Until 1965 the Constitution said nothing about age and voting. Most states recognized 21 as the age of majority, though at least one (Kentucky) allowed 18-year-olds to vote, in part through acceptance of the slogan "if you're old enough to fight (i.e., be drafted), you're old enough to vote." (Would it have been constitutional to restrict the voters under 21 to those persons who had been drafted or enlisted in the armed forces?) In 1965, however, Congress invoked its powers under section 5 of the Fourteenth Amendment to enact a Voting Rights Act that, among other things, required states to lower their voting ages to 18. In Oregon v. Mitchell, 400 U.S. 112 (1970), p.1502 infra, four Justices believed that this aspect of the Act was constitutional and four believed that it unconstitutionally usurped the states' power to set the basic conditions of suffrage. Justice Black held that, while Congress lacked the power to invalidate state laws concerning elections for *state* offices, it did have the power to regulate elections for *federal* officials.

Although this debate was rendered moot by the ratification of the Twenty-sixth Amendment in 1971, which sets 18 as the voting age in all elections, it nonetheless remains in the background of any age limitations on voting. Consider, for example, Justice Brennan's assertion that "there is serious question whether a statute [denying the franchise] . . . to persons between the ages of 18 and 21 could withstand present scrutiny under the Equal Protection Clause." Justice Stewart responded that imposing a "compelling interest" test upon the states in regard to age qualifications "is really to deny a State any choice at all, because no State could demonstrate a 'compelling interest' in drawing the line with respect to age at one point rather than another." Consider, in this context, a post-Twenty-sixth Amendment case filed by a 17-year-old vitally interested in issues of the day.

What justifies the state in excluding her from participating in the election? Does your answer meet a "compelling interest" requirement? Should it have to?

Note: "Interest," "Community," and the Right to Vote

In explaining why Mr. Kramer has a constitutional right to vote in the Union Free School District elections, the Court emphasizes his "interest in the quality and structure of public education." How should we interpret this reliance on "interest"?[8]

> Over the past decade, one of the richest debates in American political theory has been that between "liberals" and "communitarians." Although no canonical definitions of these terms exist, certain snapshots of thought portray what are (thought to be) the different parts of the intellectual landscape. Although classical liberalism might well be identified with a specific theory of a limited state, in the contemporary debate "liberalism" is identified more often, especially by its critics, as a theory of the self and its relationship with the polity. Thus Michael Sandel, a leading communitarian political theorist, has criticized liberals for advancing the notion of an autonomous, acontextual self.[9] He emphasizes instead the various "encumbrances" of social context that not only "limit" the self but, much more importantly, serve to "constitute" a genuine self. These "encumbrances" include ways of looking at the world imparted to persons through both formal socialization processes and the everyday living of life in particular social worlds.
>
> . . . Most liberals would argue that the self develops *outside* of the political order — in families, churches, the workplace, etc. The crucial point is that the preferences held by these selves develop externally to the polity. Each self, or collective group of selves, enters the political realm in order to achieve the maximum realization of these "prepolitical" preferences. In the words of . . . Frank Michelman, for such liberals "good politics can only be a market-like medium through which variously interested and motivated individuals and groups seek to maximize their own particular preferences."[10] Self-styled "republicans," on the other hand, emphasize not only the notion of the "encumbered" self, but also the view of politics as transformative. The very conception of one's self — and of one's preferences — is shaped by participation in the political realm and the realization that the polity is far more than a mere arena for bargaining. . . . Within the theory of classical republicanism that is being revived . . . , "[p]olitical participants were to subordinate their private interests to the public good through political participation in an ongoing process of collective self-determination."[11] Active participation in contemplating and discussing the public good with one's fellow citizens is, according to Professor Michelman's reading of republicanism, "considered a positive human good because the self is understood as partially constituted by, or as coming to itself through, such engagement." This conception of politics and ultimately of the self sharply contrasts with the "pluralist" perspective "in which the primary interests of individuals appear as pre-political, and politics, accordingly, as a secondary instrumental medium for protecting or advancing those 'exogenous' interests."

8. The following excerpt is from Levinson, Suffrage and Community: Who Should Vote?, 1989 Fla. L. Rev. 545. See Gerald L. Neuman, We Are the People, 13 Mich. L. Rev. 259 (1992).
9. See Michael Sandel, Liberalism and the Limits of Justice (1982).
10. Michelman, Law's Republic, 97 Yale L.J. 1493, 1508 (1988).
11. Sunstein, Beyond the Republican Revival, 97 Yale L.J. 1539, 1547-1548 (1988).

> The eminent political scientist Robert Dahl noted [in 1970] that deciding who can participate in the political process is "a curiously neglected and yet absolutely crucial problem" for any polity, for if democracy means "in some sense 'rule by the people,' we need to clarify" who is entitled to participate in ruling through casting the ballot. . . .[12]
>
> I want to contrast two basic models of allocating the ballot. These models can be linked to the current debate between "liberals" (or "pluralists') and "communitarians" (or "neo-republicans"). One model, drawn from the liberal side of the spectrum, focuses on the presumed *interest* of the person and on the duty of the polity to allow persons to enunciate their interests through the ballot. Dahl refers to this model as the "Principle of Affected Interests": "everyone who is affected by the decisions of a government should have the right to participate in the government." Thus the liberal model assumes that all persons (or at least all citizens) who live within a jurisdiction ought to be able to vote because the legislative decisions of the jurisdiction affect them.
>
> The emphasis on the interest of voters contributes to the traditional liberal skepticism about "competence-based" limitations on the ballot, such as literacy or mental competence. After all, voters need not be particularly bright or well-read to perceive their own interests. . . . Someone who views elections as the forum for reflection on "common interest," however, might be more respectful of attempts to guarantee the competence and the proper character of voters — i.e., the intellectual capacity for reflection on the common good and the character disposition to subordinate merely "personal" interest to the common good. . . .
>
> Examining the contemporary allocation of the ballot from th[e] interest-based perspective, we immediately encounter certain problems. . . . [O]ne discovers that that allocation is grossly *under*inclusive. The current practice of allocating voting rights by geographic residence and citizenship, for example, means that many people who, by any criterion, are "interested" in the legislative outcomes are not allowed to vote. Why, for example, should New Jersey residents who work in New York not be allowed to vote in New York city and state elections. . . . How do we explain, as a matter of political theory, the fact that "[N]onresidents . . . are disenfranchised, and they are supposed to be so." As Lea Brilmayer aptly puts it, such denial of the suffrage works to separate "the shaping of the laws . . . from the sharing of its consequences."[13]

Questioning the denial of any vote at all for legal residents of state *A* who work or are otherwise closely associated with state *B* is not identical with arguing that the person in question should get a vote that is fully equal with the vote of residents of state *B*. Perhaps they should get only half-votes in state *B*. The modern interpretation of the equal protection clause encourages the view that those who may vote at all get an equal vote relative to all others entitled to vote. But we should distinguish between the two different issues of a basic entitlement to vote and the weight of the vote to which one is entitled. Under these circumstances, at least, one person/one vote may not be desirable.

One might defend excluding the nonresident simply by pointing out that those deprived of the vote are not citizens of the relevant jurisdiction, be it a city, state, or the nation as a whole. Thus Douglas Laycock has written that

12. See Robert Dahl, After the Revolution (1970).

13. Brilmayer, Shaping and Sharing in Democratic Theory: Towards a Political Philosophy of Interstate Equality, 15 Fla. St. U.L. Rev. 389, 390 (1987).

"[t]he restriction of voting . . . to the residents of each state is essential to the states' existence as separate polities." "The logic of the constitutional structure is that at any given time, each of us is a member of *one and only one* state polity"?[14] Laycock's argument is not "logical"; the constitutional concept of "stateness" need not include as a predicate the proposition that a person can be a citizen of only one state or that the ballot must be restricted only to physical residents of a given [locality]. Dual nationals, persons with completely valid legal citizenship in more than one national polity, exist in legal fact. . . . Similarly, dual citizenship *within* the United States could exist. Individuals could be citizens of more than one state, with concomitant voting rights in all of the states in which one has established the prerequisite for citizenship (e.g., residence or property ownership or holding a permanent job, etc.). One almost certainly should get only *one* vote for federal offices. [No one] should be able to vote for presidential electors or members of Congress in [two states]. Multiple votes for federal offices *would* violate important principles of equal citizenship. . . .

The discussion above assumed the relevance of citizenship in allocating the voting franchise. We thus enter the realm of the second basic theory undergirding allocation of the ballot — communal membership. Citizenship can be conceived of as the legal recognition of community membership. Limiting the franchise to citizens may be a way of saying that only genuine members of the political community can vote. Even *resident* aliens cannot vote, whatever their "interest," because they are presumed not to be genuine members of the political community. This presumption is not logically necessary. Quite a few nineteenth century state constitutions included guarantees of the right to vote for aliens who had indicated their intention to become citizens of the United States; such noncitizens voted in some states as late as 1928. Today, all states require that one must have the citizenship in hand.

For the resident alien, even the combination of permanent residence and overwhelming interest is not enough to warrant the ballot. . . .

Citizenship, however, is a purely formal category. A citizen of a given community need not actually reside in it in order to vote. . . . Why do we so automatically . . . link citizenship and the suffrage? The answer may require that we ask about the meaning of citizenship. . . . Does, or should, citizenship involve participation in a common way of life or commitment to common values? Such commonality as exists presumably affects the conception of individual "interest" held by particular individuals. It is not that citizens are without interests; rather, the classical republicanism argument is that strong communal membership in some sense tames the unfettered interest of the asocial self and joins it to a notion of common interest and common good. One defines oneself as a member of the community and, concomitantly, one's self-interest as that of the collectivity.

. . . [W]e might ask why something so important as the vote is based on citizenship, even within a communalist perspective.

I argued above that a conception of citizenship as simply a surrogate for shared interests is a fatally underinclusive category because the universe of people whose interests are vitally affected by any given election is far larger than the universe of those who are allowed to participate in the choosing of public officials (who will in turn set the public agenda). If we view citizenship as a surrogate for shared values, then it may be grossly overinclusive: the set of people sharing the (proper) values may be far smaller than the set of people designated as citizens. (Non-citizens also may share what are thought to be the requisite values.) This emphasis on shared attachment to core principles itself raises a host of questions.

14. Laycock, Equality and the Citizens of Sister States, 15 Fla. St. U.L. Rev. 431, 434 (1987) (emphasis added).

> The central question is whether as a polity we ought to require certain value commitments of those who would vote. I suspect that most traditional liberals tend to be horrified by any such suggestion insofar as they tend to see an election as the arena to which persons bring their own values and interests. (How, therefore, can a liberal justify the limitation of the franchise to citizens, whether of city, state, or nation?) On the other hand, communitarians should find it more palatable to restrict participation rights to those who are genuine members, but it is hard to see why they would be satisfied with a purely formal test of legal citizenship instead of a more complete examination of the putative member's actual commitments.[15]

Besides Professor Michelman, another proponent of "neo-republicanism" is Professor Cass Sunstein, who notes that within republican theory, citizens and representatives, "in their capacity as political actors . . . are not supposed to ask only what is in their private interest, but also what will best serve the community in general — understood as a response to the best general theory of social welfare." To the extent that we might be dubious about the likelihood of citizens "naturally" asking Sunstein's question or acting upon its answer, would we then support the State's taking various measures to develop the proper republican sensibility, whether by vigorous public education or by scrutinizing individual voters to determine whether they have the requisite understanding of (and the character to comply with) their responsibilities as unselfish members of the whole community? Imagine, for example, a "voter's oath" similar to an oath taken by all public officials to support, protect, and defend basic constitutional values, even at the cost of personal sacrifice. If you are opposed to that, is it because you cannot believe it would be efficacious, or because you think it would be wrong for the state to demand such assurances before allowing citizens to vote?[16]

II. Reapportionment and "One Person/One Vote"

A. The Decision for Justiciability

Constitutional litigation has gone beyond access to the ballot box to focus on the way that states aggregate voters in election districts. The Court was initially inhospitable to such concerns. Colegrove v. Green, 328 U.S. 549 (1946), rejected the claim that the legislative districts drawn by the Illinois legislature were unconstitutional insofar as individual legislators represented districts with significantly different populations. The Court indicated that this was a nonjusticiable "political question," inappropriate for the judiciary to address at all.

Two decades later, however, the Court agreed to review claims of "malapportionment" in the Tennessee legislature. Although the Tennessee Constitution, as implemented by a 1901 statute, had initially apportioned the state legislators essentially by population, with each legislator representing the same number of constituents, subsequent demographic developments in the state led to quite un-

15. Levinson, supra note 8.

16. Chapter 13, infra, further examines some of the constitutional problems that arise when one confronts various notions of "community" and attempts to rationalize in some manner the conflicting claims of the plurality of American cultures with the desire for some kind of national unity.

equally apportioned districts: About 40 percent of the voters elected two-thirds of the State's senators and representatives. After the legislature had repeatedly rejected appeals by the increasing urban electorate to reapportion itself, voters sued to invalidate the existing apportionment on the ground that their votes were "diluted" in violation of the equal protection clause. The district court dismissed the action, citing *Green*.

BAKER v. CARR
369 U.S. 186 (1962)

BRENNAN, J. . . .

Of course the mere fact that the suit seeks protection of a political right does not mean it presents a political question. Such an objection "is little more than a play upon words." Nixon v. Herndon, 273 U.S. 536, 540. Rather, it is argued that apportionment cases, whatever the actual wording of the complaint, can involve no federal constitutional right except one resting on the guaranty of a republican form of government,[a] and that complaints based on that clause have been held to present political questions which are nonjusticiable. . . .

It is apparent that several formulations which vary slightly according to the settings in which the questions arise may describe a political question, although each has one or more elements which identify it as essentially a function of the separation of powers. Prominent on the surface of any case held to involve a political question is found a textually demonstrable constitutional commitment of the issue to a coordinate political department; or a lack of judicially discoverable and manageable standards for resolving it; or the impossibility of deciding without an initial policy determination of a kind clearly for nonjudicial discretion; or the impossibility of a court's undertaking independent resolution without expressing lack of the respect due coordinate branches of government; or an unusual need for unquestioning adherence to a political decision already made; or the potentiality of embarrassment from multifarious pronouncements by various departments on one question.

Unless one of these formulations is inextricable from the case at bar, there should be no dismissal for nonjusticiability on the ground of a political question's presence. . . . But it is argued that this case shares the characteristics of . . . cases concerning the Constitution's guaranty, in Art. IV, §4, of a republican form of government. A conclusion as to whether the case at bar does present a political question cannot be confidently reached until we have considered those cases with special care. We shall discover that Guaranty Clause claims involve those elements which define a "political question," and for that reason and no other, they are nonjusticiable. In particular, we shall discover that the nonjusticiability of such claims has nothing to do with their touching upon matters of state governmental organization.

. . . Luther v. Borden, 7 How. 1, though in form simply an action for damages for trespass was, as Daniel Webster said in opening the argument for the defense,

a. "The United States shall guarantee to every State in this Union a Republican Form of Government, and shall protect each of them against Invasion: and on Application of the Legislature, or of the Executive (when the Legislature cannot be convened) against domestic Violence." U.S. Const., Art. IV, §4.

"an unusual case." The defendants, admitting an otherwise tortious breaking and entering, sought to justify their action on the ground that they were agents of the established lawful government of Rhode Island, which State was then under martial law to defend itself from active insurrection; that the plaintiff was engaged in that insurrection; and that they entered under orders to arrest the plaintiff. The case arose "out of the unfortunate political differences which agitated the people of Rhode Island in 1841 and 1842," and which had resulted in a situation wherein two groups laid competing claims to recognition as the lawful government. The plaintiff's rights to recover depended upon which of the two groups was entitled to such recognition; but the lower court's refusal to receive evidence or hear argument on that issue, its charge to the jury that the earlier established or "charter" government was lawful, and the verdict for the defendants, were affirmed upon appeal to this Court.

Chief Justice Taney's opinion for the Court reasoned as follows: (1) If a court were to hold the defendants' acts unjustified because the charter government had no legal existence during the period in question, it would follow that all of that government's actions — laws enacted, taxes collected, salaries paid, accounts settled, sentences passed — were of no effect; and that "the officers who carried their decisions into operation [were] answerable as trespassers, if not in some cases as criminals." There was, of course, no room for application of any doctrine of de facto status to uphold prior acts of an officer not authorized de jure, for such would have defeated the plaintiff's very action. A decision for the plaintiff would inevitably have produced some significant measure of chaos, a consequence to be avoided if it could be done without abnegation of the judicial duty to uphold the Constitution.

(2) No state court had recognized as a judicial responsibility settlement of the issue of the locus of state governmental authority. Indeed, the courts of Rhode Island had in several cases held that "it rested with the political power to decide whether the charter government had been displaced or not," and that that department had acknowledged no change.

(3) Since "[t]he question relates, altogether, to the constitution and laws of [the] . . . State," the courts of the United States had to follow the state courts' decisions unless there was a federal constitutional ground for overturning them.

(4) No provision of the Constitution could be or had been invoked for this purpose except Art. IV, §4, the Guaranty Clause. Having already noted the absence of standards whereby the choice between governments could be made by a court acting independently, Chief Justice Taney now found further textual and practical reasons for concluding that, if any department of the United States was empowered by the Guaranty Clause to resolve the issue, it was not the judiciary:

> Under this article of the Constitution it rests with Congress to decide what government is the established one in a State. For as the United States guarantee to each State a republican government, Congress must necessarily decide what government is established in the State before it can determine whether it is republican or not. And when the senators and representatives of a State are admitted into the councils of the Union, the authority of the government under which they are appointed, as well as its republican character, is recognized by the proper constitutional authority. And its decision is binding on every other department of the government, and could not be questioned in a judicial tribunal. It is true that the contest in this case did not

last long enough to bring the matter to this issue; and . . . Congress was not called upon to decide the controversy. Yet the right to decide is placed there, and not in the courts.

Clearly, several factors were thought by the Court in *Luther* to make the question there "political": the commitment to the other branches of the decision as to which is the lawful state government; the unambiguous action by the President, in recognizing the charter government as the lawful authority; the need for finality in the executive's decision; and the lack of criteria by which a court could determine which form of government was republican. . . .

We come, finally, to the ultimate inquiry whether our precedents as to what constitutes a nonjusticiable "political question" bring the case before us under the umbrella of that doctrine. A natural beginning is to note whether any of the common characteristics which we have been able to identify and label descriptively are present. We find none: The question here is the consistency of state action with the Federal Constitution. We have no question decided, or to be decided, by a political branch of government coequal with this Court. Nor do we risk embarrassment of our government abroad, or grave disturbance at home if we take issue with Tennessee as to the constitutionality of her action here challenged. Nor need the appellants, in order to succeed in this action, ask the Court to enter upon policy determinations for which judicially manageable standards are lacking. Judicial standards under the Equal Protection Clause are well developed and familiar, and it has been open to courts since the enactment of the Fourteenth Amendment to determine, if on the particular facts they must, that a discrimination reflects no policy, but simply arbitrary and capricious action. . . .

We conclude then that the nonjusticiability of claims resting on the Guaranty Clause which arises from their embodiment of questions that were thought "political," can have no bearing upon the justiciability of the equal protection claim presented in this case. Finally, we emphasize that it is the involvement in Guaranty Clause claims of the elements thought to define "political questions," and no other feature, which could render them nonjusticiable. Specifically, we have said that such claims are not held nonjusticiable because they touch matters of state governmental organization. . . . [O]nly last Term, in Gomillion v. Lightfoot, 364 U.S. 339 [1961], we applied the Fifteenth Amendment to strike down a redrafting of municipal boundaries which effected a discriminatory impairment of voting rights. . . .

We conclude that the complaint's allegations of a denial of equal protection present a justiciable constitutional cause of action upon which appellants are entitled to a trial and a decision. The right asserted is within the reach of judicial protection under the Fourteenth Amendment.

DOUGLAS, J., concurring. . . .

Universal equality is not the test; there is room for weighting [of votes]. "The prohibition of the Equal Protection Clause goes no further than the invidious discrimination."

CLARK, J., concurring. . . .

[T]he apportionment picture in Tennessee is a topsy-turvical of gigantic proportions . . . , a crazy quilt without rational basis. . . . [T]here is no requirement that any plan have mathematical exactness in its application. Only where, as here, the total picture reveals incommensurables of both magnitude and frequency can it be said that there is present an invidious discrimination. . . .

[With respect to the appropriateness of judicial intervention, a]lthough I find the Tennessee apportionment statute offends the Equal Protection Clause, I would not consider intervention by this Court into so delicate a field if there were any other relief available to the people of Tennessee. But the majority of the people of Tennessee have no "practical opportunities for exerting their political weight at the polls" to correct the existing "invidious discrimination." Tennessee has no initiative and referendum. I have searched diligently for other "practical opportunities" present under the law. . . . [T]he legislative policy has riveted the present seats in the Assembly to their respective constituencies, and by the votes of their incumbents a reapportionment of any kind is prevented. The people have been rebuffed at the hands of the Assembly; they have tried the constitutional convention route, but since the call must originate in the Assembly it, too, has been fruitless. They have tried Tennessee courts with the same result, and Governors have fought the tide only to flounder. It is said that there is recourse in Congress and perhaps that may be, but from a practical standpoint this is without substance. To date Congress has never undertaken such a task in any State. We therefore must conclude that the people of Tennessee are stymied and without judicial intervention will be saddled with the present discrimination in the affairs of their state government.

[Justice Stewart also concurred, emphasizing that the Court had only decided that the action was justiciable and had held nothing with respect to the merits.]

FRANKFURTER, J., joined by Harlan, J., dissenting [argued that the equal protection clause provided no more standards than did the guarantee clause.] . . .

The present case involves all of the elements that have made the Guarantee Clause cases non-justiciable. It is, in effect, a Guarantee Clause claim masquerading under a different label. But it cannot make the case more fit for judicial action that appellants invoke the Fourteenth Amendment rather than Art. IV, §4, where, in fact, the gist of their complaint is the same — unless it can be found that the Fourteenth Amendment speaks with greater particularity to their situation. . . . Art. IV, §4, is not committed by express constitutional terms to Congress. It is the nature of the controversies arising under it, nothing else, which has made it judicially unenforceable. . . .

What, then, is this question of legislative apportionment? Appellants invoke the right to vote and to have their votes counted. But they are permitted to vote and their votes are counted. They go to the polls, they cast their ballots, they send their representatives to the state councils. Their complaint is simply that the representatives are not sufficiently numerous or powerful — in short, that Tennessee has adopted a basis of representation with which they are dissatisfied. Talk of "debasement" or "dilution" is circular talk. One cannot speak of "debasement" or "dilution" of the value of a vote until there is first defined a standard of reference as to what a vote should be worth. What is actually asked of the Court in this case is to choose among competing bases of representation — ultimately, really, among competing theories of political philosophy — in order to establish an appropriate frame of government for the State of Tennessee and thereby for all the States of the Union. . . .

Certainly, "equal protection" is no more secure a foundation for judicial judgment of the permissibility of varying forms of representative government than is "Republican Form." Indeed since "equal protection of the laws" can only mean an equality of persons standing in the same relation to whatever governmental action is challenged, the determination whether treatment is equal presupposes a determination concerning the nature of the relationship. This, with respect to apportionment, means an inquiry into the theoretic base of representation in an acceptably republican state. . . .

The notion that representation proportioned to the geographic spread of population is so universally accepted as a necessary element of equality between man and man that it must be taken to be the standard of a political equality preserved by the Fourteenth Amendment — that it is, in appellants' words "the basic principle of representative government" — is, to put it bluntly, not true. However desirable and however desired by some among the great political thinkers and framers of our government, it has never been generally practiced, today or in the past. It was not the English system, it was not the colonial system, it was not the system chosen for the national government by the Constitution, it was not the system exclusively or even predominantly practiced by the States at the time of adoption of the Fourteenth Amendment, it is not predominantly practiced by the States today. Unless judges, the judges of this Court, are to make their private views of political wisdom the measure of the Constitution — views which in all honesty cannot but give the appearance, if not reflect the reality, of involvement with the business of partisan politics so inescapably a part of apportionment controversies — the Fourteenth Amendment . . . provides no guide for judicial oversight of the representation problem. . . .

Manifestly, the Equal Protection Clause supplies no clearer guide for judicial examination of apportionment methods than would the Guarantee Clause itself. Apportionment, by its character, is a subject of extraordinary complexity, involving — even after the fundamental theoretical issues concerning what is to be represented in a representative legislature have been fought out or compromised — considerations of geography, demography, electoral convenience, economic and social cohesions or divergencies among particular local groups, communications, the practical effects of political institutions like the lobby and the city machine, ancient traditions and ties of settled usage, respect for proven incumbents of long experience and senior status, mathematical mechanics, censuses compiling relevant data, and a host of others. Legislative responses throughout the country to the reapportionment demands of the 1960 Census have glaringly confirmed that these are not factors that lend themselves to evaluations of a nature that are the staple of judicial determinations or for which judges are equipped to adjudicate by legal training or experience or native wit. And this is the more so true because in every strand of this complicated, intricate web of values meet the contending forces of partisan politics. The practical significance of apportionment is that the next election results may differ because of it. Apportionment battles are overwhelmingly party or intra-party contests. It will add a virulent source of friction and tension in federal-state relations to embroil the federal judiciary in them. . . .

[T]here is not under our Constitution a judicial remedy for every political mischief, for every undesirable exercise of legislative power. The Framers carefully and with deliberate forethought refused so to enthrone the judiciary. In this situation, as in others of like nature, appeal for relief does not belong here. Appeal must be to an informed, civically militant electorate. In a democratic society like ours, relief must come through an aroused popular conscience that sears the conscience of the people's representatives. In any event there is nothing judicially more unseemly nor more self-defeating than for this Court to make in terrorem pronouncements, to indulge in merely empty rhetoric, sounding a word of promise to the ear, sure to be disappointing to the hope. . . .

[Justice Harlan, joined by Justice Frankfurter, wrote a dissenting opinion to the effect that the plaintiffs' complaint should have been dismissed under Federal Rule 12(b)(6) for failure to state a claim.]

B. Constitutional Standards of Apportionment

REYNOLDS v. SIMS, 337 U.S. 533 (1964): [In *Sims* and five companion cases, together known as the *Reapportionment* cases, the Court addressed the merits of various states' apportionment schemes.] WARREN, C.J. . . . A predominant consideration in determining whether a State's legislative apportionment scheme constitutes an invidious discrimination violative of rights asserted under the Equal Protection Clause is that the rights allegedly impaired are individual and personal in nature. . . . [T]he judicial focus must be concentrated upon ascertaining whether there has been any discrimination against certain of the State's citizens which constitutes an impermissible impairment of their constitutionally protected right to vote. . . . Undoubtedly, the right of suffrage is a fundamental matter in a free and democratic society. Especially since the right to exercise the franchise in a free and unimpaired manner is preservative of other basic civil and political rights, any alleged infringement of the right of citizens to vote must be carefully and meticulously scrutinized. . . .

Legislators represent people, not trees or acres. Legislators are elected by voters, not farms or cities or economic interests. . . . It could hardly be gainsaid that a constitutional claim had been asserted by an allegation that certain otherwise qualified voters had been entirely prohibited from voting for members of their state legislature. And, if a State should provide that the votes of citizens in one part of the State should be given two times, or five times, or 10 times the weight of votes of citizens in another part of the State, it could hardly be contended that the right to vote of those residing in the disfavored areas had not been effectively diluted. . . . Of course, the effect of state legislative districting schemes which give the same number of representatives to unequal numbers of constituents is identical. . . . Weighting the votes of citizens differently, by any method or means, merely because of where they happen to reside, hardly seems justifiable. . . .

State legislatures are, historically, the fountainhead of representative government in this country. . . . But representative government is in essence self-government through the medium of elected representatives of the people, and each and every citizen has an inalienable right to full and effective participation in the political processes of his State's legislative bodies. . . . Full and effective participation by all citizens in state government requires, therefore, that each citizen have an equally effective voice in the election of members of his state legislature. Modern and viable state government needs, and the Constitution demands, no less.

Logically, in a society ostensibly grounded on representative government, it would seem reasonable that a majority of the people of a State could elect a majority of that State's legislators. To conclude differently, and to sanction minority control of state legislative bodies, would appear to deny majority rights in a way that far surpasses any possible denial of minority rights that might otherwise be thought to result. . . . And the concept of equal protection has been traditionally viewed as requiring the uniform treatment of persons standing in the same relation to the government action questioned or challenged. With respect to the allocation of legislative representation, all voters, as citizens of a State, stand in the same relation regardless of where they live. Any suggested criteria for the differentiation of citizens are insufficient to justify any discrimination, as to the weight of their votes, unless relevant to the permissible purposes of legislative apportionment. Since the achieving of fair and effective representation for all citizens is concededly the basic aim of legislative apportionment, we conclude that the Equal Protection Clause guarantees the opportunity for equal participation by all voters in the election of state legislators. . . . Our constitutional system amply provides for the protection of minorities by means other than giving them majority control of state legislatures. . . .

We are told that the matter of apportioning representation in a state legislature is a complex and many-faceted one. We are advised that States can rationally consider factors other than population in apportioning legislative representation. We are admonished not to restrict the power of the States to impose differing views as to political philosophy on their citizens. We are cautioned about the dangers of entering into political thickets and mathematical quagmires. Our answer is this: a denial of constitutionally protected rights demands judicial protection; our oath and our office require no less of us. . . . To the extent that a citizen's right to vote is debased, he is that much less a citizen. The fact that an individual lives here or there is not a legitimate reason for overweighting or diluting the efficacy of his vote. . . . Population is, of necessity, the starting point for consideration and the controlling criterion for judgment in legislative apportionment controversies.

We hold that, as a basic constitutional standard, the Equal Protection Clause requires that the seats in both houses of a bicameral state legislature must be apportioned on a population basis. Simply stated, an individual's right to vote for state legislators is unconstitutionally impaired when its weight is in a substantial fashion diluted when compared with votes of citizens living in other parts of the State. . . .

Much has been written since our decision in Baker v. Carr about the applicability of the so-called federal analogy to state legislative apportionment arrangements. . . . We agree with the District Court, and find the federal analogy inapposite and irrelevant to state legislative districting schemes. . . .

The system of representation in the two Houses of the Federal Congress is one ingrained in our Constitution, as part of the law of the land. It is one conceived out of compromise and concession indispensable to the establishment of our federal republic. Arising from unique historical circumstances, it is based on the consideration that in establishing our type of federalism a group of formerly independent States bound themselves together under one national government. . . . [A]t the time of the inception of the system of representation in the Federal Congress, a compromise between the larger and smaller States on this matter averted a deadlock in the Constitutional Convention which had threatened to abort the birth of our Nation. . . .

Political subdivisions of States — counties, cities, or whatever — never were and never have been considered as sovereign entities. Rather, they have been traditionally regarded as subordinate governmental instrumentalities created by the State to assist in the carrying out of state governmental functions. . . . The relationship of the States to the Federal Government could hardly be less analogous.

HARLAN, J., dissenting [in all six cases, argued that the Fourteenth Amendment was not intended to apply to voting rights of any sort.] . . . In one or another of today's opinions, the Court declares it unconstitutional for a State to give effective consideration to any of the following in establishing legislative districts:

(1) history;
(2) "economic or other sorts of group interest";
(3) area;
(4) geographical considerations;
(5) a desire "to insure effective representation for sparsely settled areas";
(6) "availability of access of citizens to their representatives";
(7) theories of bicameralism (except those approved by the Court);
(8) occupation;
(9) "an attempt to balance urban and rural power."
(10) the preference of a majority of voters in the State.

So far as presently appears, the *only* factor which a State may consider, apart from numbers, is political subdivisions. But even "a clearly rational state policy" recognizing this factor is unconstitutional if "population is submerged as the controlling consideration. . . ."

I know of no principle of logic or practical or theoretical politics, still less any constitutional principle, which establishes all or any of these exclusions. Certain it is that the Court's opinion does not establish them. So far as the Court says anything at all on this score, it says only that "legislators represent people, not trees or acres,". . . that "citizens, not history or economic interest, cast votes,". . . that "people, not land or trees or pastures, vote." . . . All this may be conceded. But it is surely equally obvious, and, in the context of elections, more meaningful to note that people are not ciphers and that legislators can represent their electors only by speaking for their interests — economic, social, political — many of which do reflect the place where the electors live. The Court does not establish, or indeed even attempt to make a case for the proposition that conflicting interest within a State can only be adjusted by disregarding them when voters are grouped for purposes of representation. . . .

STEWART, J. . . . [T]he Equal Protection Clause demands but two basic attributes of any plan of state legislative apportionment. First, it demands that, in the light of the State's own characteristics and needs, the plan must be a rational one. Secondly, it demands that the plan must be such as not to permit the systematic frustration of the will of the majority of the electorate of the State. . . .

[Justice Stewart would have upheld New York State's apportionment scheme, under which a legislator from New York City represented many more constituents than one from upstate New York, on the theory that] New York City, with its seven million people and a budget larger than that of the State, has by virtue of its concentration of population, homogeneity of interest, and political cohesiveness, acquired an institutional power and political influence of its own hardly measurable simply by counting the number of its representatives in the legislature.

[He would have upheld the Colorado scheme on the grounds that it properly accommodated the interests of the state's four distinct regions and that it had been adopted in a state-wide constitutional referendum.

Justice Clark applied a requirement of "rationality" to concur in the judgments of some of the cases and dissent from others.]

Discussion

1. *The premise of political equality.* The premise of the *Reapportionment* cases — captured in the slogan, "one person, one vote, one value" — is that all citizens are entitled to equal voting power. Is this principle inherent in the history, theory, or structure of the American polity? Is it reflected in the Constitution? See generally Auerbach, The Reapportionment Cases, 1962 Sup. Ct. Rev. 1.

2. *Political equality versus equal apportionment.* Is the goal of individual equality necessarily served by a requirement of equal apportionment? Professor Martin Shapiro writes:[17]

> The degree of any citizen's political effectiveness is . . . determined by the degrees of organization and skill of the groups to which he belongs, the number of groups to which he belongs, and the powers of the agencies of government to which those groups have access. . . . In general, the urban and industrial sectors of society spawn groups and group action. Members of these sectors find themselves amid unions, corporations, city councils, chambers of commerce, ethnic and racial minority associations, and a wide range of government agencies especially attuned to their problems. . . .
>
> [T]he electoral process is not the only political process. Indeed, a major share of our politics consists of negotiations, both public and private, among various interest groups and segments of government. In this sphere of negotiation, political equality is difficult to attain. In fact, it is extremely difficult to assess what degrees of inequality actually exist. . . .
>
> The new decisions fundamentally ignore all that we have learned about the group nature of politics. By adopting the most simplistic view of the political process, and particularly of the process of representation, the Court equates the electoral and the political processes and thinks to assure each citizen "equal protection of the laws" in the political sphere by giving each citizen a vote equal to every other's. . . . A vision of the political process as no more than the electoral process and of each citizen as exercising his whole political power in the individual act of voting cannot properly serve even the most populistic philosophy. For in the complex politics of group bargaining and shifting temporary majorities that we actually have in the United States, inequalities in voting strength may contribute in the over-all equality of all participants in the political process as a whole. Blanket and blind enforcement of electoral equality will only decrease the political inequalities in some states at the cost of increasing them in others. The result of the Court's new rulings

17. Martin Shapiro, Law and Politics in the Supreme Court 229-239, 249 (1964).

in terms of real political equality will be largely random. In the end they may achieve somewhat greater over-all equality but only because the sum of new equalities will exceed the sum of new inequalities.

3. Recall the hypothetical offered above, regarding the election of the Texas Commissioner of Agriculture. In that situation, people either had the right to vote or they did not. Assume now that the Texas legislature both agrees that all Texans should in fact choose the Commissioner and wishes to control at least somewhat the consequences of the fact that the majority of Texans live in urban areas. It therefore assigns two votes to the roughly 20 percent of the electorate who live in agricultural counties and one vote to everyone else. Again, one must assume that *Reynolds* would invalidate this even as it would allow the legislature to remove the office from the electorate entirely. Thus the question is, once again, why read the Constitution as requiring this result?

C. The Political Question Revisited

Justice Stewart's and Professor Shapiro's view of the political process leads them to suggest a more discriminating judicial standard than equal districting. Shapiro writes:[18]

> [After Baker v. Carr] the Court as political theorist might have become Court as political scientist, analyzing the actual operation of the political forces around it. For once the democratic theorist recognizes that electoral equality is not equivalent to political equality or freedom but is simply a means that sometimes contributes to and sometimes conflicts with these ends, he must decide when, where, and how much electoral equality should be added to or subtracted from the political system in which he operates, in order to make it more democratic. Given the complexity of contemporary American politics, such assessments are always difficult, but one thing is fairly certain. Whatever the assessments, they are likely to suggest delicate adjustments rather than sledgehammer blows. It seems highly unlikely that either a continuation of the present crazy quilt of malapportionment or introduction of total and immediate equalization of votes will yield a democratically ideal result. The *Baker* decision allowed the Supreme Court to make its own case-by-case assessment of the political balance in any given state and to fit its remedies to the situations it found. When it is recalled that the processes of group politics may give to members of certain groups far greater political influence than to others and that the relative strength of various groups is markedly affected by the geographic distributions of population, resources, industries, and so forth — distributions that vary markedly from state to state — whoever attempts to achieve greater equality must be prepared to make differing adjustments in differing areas.
>
> If the Supreme Court were to be successful as democratic political theorist, it would have had to take on the chores of the political scientist, that is, the analysis of existential political relationships. . . . What the Court would have been called upon to do would have been to make rough estimates of the over-all effects of apportionment arrangements on the general complexion of politics in certain states. It would be easy enough for any political scientist to go on ad horrendum and ad nauseam about the difficulty of this sort of thing — about how little we know about state and

18. Id. at 245-247.

> local government and politics in general and about the impact of electoral arrangements on politics in particular. Nevertheless, commonsense judgments about such political questions are made constantly by voters, legislators, and administrators, indeed by all political actors. Precisely because we do not have sufficient data or methods of gathering data to render "technically correct" solutions to most political problems, we must either settle for prudent, common-sense action or for total inaction. . . .

Justice Stewart's application of the "systematic frustration of the majority" standard to the Colorado and New York apportionment schemes seems to be in the same spirit. Is the Stewart-Shapiro approach viable? Consider Professor Jan Deutsch's response:[19]

> What both Stewart and Shapiro would require the Court to do in apportionment cases is to examine the realities of the distribution of political power within the State — the existence of voting blocs, the degree of party control over voters and officials, the position of the mass media, and the extent of financial backing available to the various factions, to mention only a few of the crucial inquiries. In dissenting from the invalidation of New York's apportionment, for example, Stewart quotes Elihu Root's remarks to the New York constitutional convention of 1894, justifying the giving of fewer seats to New York City than a "one man, one vote" rule would require. . . .
>
> Whether or not it is correct to assume that the representatives of a large city are under pressure to represent only a single, homogenous interest, the quotation makes crystal clear that the formula espoused by Stewart and Shapiro would indeed require the Court to canvass the actual workings of the floor leadership in the legislative branches, the mechanisms of party control not only over voters and the city government but also over elected representatives — in short, the details of the petty corruption and networks of personal influence that all too often constitute crucial sources of power in municipal politics. Given the Court's institutional arrangements, however, it could investigate these matters only by requiring lower courts to build records on these issues. Is this a demand we can reasonably make of our courts? Even assuming that the evidence was available and would be forthcoming, is it likely that our society could accept, as a steady diet, the spectacle of the judiciary solemnly ruling on the accuracy of a political boss's testimony concerning the sources of his power over voters and the degree of control that he exercised over elected officials?

What Deutsch suggests, in other words, is that the Stewart-Shapiro approach would make legislative apportionment a political question and that the Court was faced with a choice between the total abstention advocated by Justice Frankfurter in Baker v. Carr and the equal apportionment standard of Reynolds v. Sims.[20]

19. Deutsch, Neutrality, Legitimacy, and the Supreme Court, 20 Stan. L. Rev. 169, 246-247 (1968).

20. But cf. Shapiro, supra note 17, at 249-250:

> In the light of the extreme inequalities in current state districting practices, it is undoubtedly true that the immediate effects of the new decisions will probably be to decrease many grave political inequalities. . . . [However,] the decisions must . . . be assessed on the basis not only of the immediate electoral inequities that they eliminate but also of the permanent inequities they will create, particularly in states like Michigan and California, where one geographically concentrated set of interest groups may form the permanent majority and another the permanent minority. If it had been necessary to choose between the present inequities and the long-range ones to be anticipated from the "one man, one vote" standard, one might have chosen one of two bases: preferring to clean up present inequalities, while leaving future ones to take care of

D. Subsequent Developments

1. *The Extension of* Reynolds *to Local Government Agencies*

Avery v. Midland County, 390 U.S. 474 (1968), applied the equal districting requirement to the four precincts that elected a Texas county's "Commissioners Court" — the county governing body that exercised broad functions, including running jails, hospitals, and airports, providing welfare services, building roads and bridges, setting the county's budget and tax rates, and issuing bonds. The county argued that the agency performed "administrative" rather than "legislative" functions, but Justice White could "see little difference, in terms of the application of the Equal Protection Clause . . . between the exercise of state power through legislatures and its exercise by elected officials in the cities, towns, and counties." Thus, "the Constitution permits no substantial variation from equal population in drawing districts for units of local government having general governmental powers over the entire geographic area served by the body." Justices Harlan, Fortas, and Stewart each dissented in a separate opinion.

Hadley v. Junior College District, 397 U.S. 50 (1970), extended *Avery* to a junior college district formed by eight school districts, holding that it was impermissible to give a district having 60 percent of the population the power to elect only 50 percent of the junior college district's trustees. Justice Black found that the district's powers to run the schools, levy taxes, and issue bonds were "general enough and [had] sufficient impact throughout the district" to require equal apportionment, but he went on to suggest that there were no "judicially manageable standards" for distinguishing among the "purposes" or relative significance of elections or between the elections of legislative and administrative officers:

> We therefore hold today that as a general rule, whenever a state or local government decides to select persons by popular election to perform governmental functions, the Equal Protection Clause of the Fourteenth Amendment requires that each qualified voter must be given an equal opportunity to participate in that election, and when members of an elected body are chosen from separate districts, each district must be established on a basis that will insure, as far as is practicable, that equal numbers of voters can vote for proportionally equal numbers of officials. It is of course possible that there might be some case in which a State elects certain functionaries whose duties are so far removed from normal governmental activities and so disproportionately affect different groups that a popular election in compliance with *Reynolds* . . . might not be required, but certainly we see nothing in the present case that indicates that the activities of these trustees fit in that category.

In Board of Estimate of the City of New York v. Morris, 489 U.S. 688 (1989), a unanimous Court (though Justice Blackmun joined only in the judgment) invalidated New York City's Board of Estimate, an important component of the City's government that consisted of three members elected citywide and the elected presidents of the City's five boroughs, which have widely disparate populations. The suit was brought by residents of Brooklyn, the most populous of the bor-

---

themselves, or preferring the current fluid inequalities to the future rigid ones that the new standard is likely to create. The whole point, however, is that such a cruel choice was not really necessary.

oughs, who pointed to a 132 percent deviation between its population and that of Staten Island, the smallest of the boroughs. The City defended on the ground that the Board of Estimate was not subject to *Reynolds* "because in its view the board is a nonelective, nonlegislative body." Justice White wrote:

> As an initial matter, we reject the city's suggestion that because the Board of Estimate is a unique body wielding non-legislative powers, board membership elections are not subject to review under the prevailing reapportionment doctrine. . . .
>
> That the members of New York City's Board of Estimate trigger this constitutional safeguard is certain. All eight officials become members as a matter of law upon their various elections. The Mayor, the comptroller, and the president of the City Council, who comprise the board's citywide number, are elected by votes of the entire city electorate. Each of these three cast two votes, except the Mayor has no vote on the acceptance of modification of his budget proposal. Similarly, when residents of the city's five boroughs . . . elect their respective borough presidents, the elections decide each borough's representatives on the board. These five members each have single votes on all board matters.
>
> New York law assigns to the board a significant range of functions common to municipal governments . . . , [including participation in the budget process].
>
> This considerable authority to formulate the city's budget, which last fiscal year surpassed twenty-five billion dollars, as well as the board's land use, franchise, and contracting powers over the city's seven million inhabitants, situate the Board comfortably within the category of governmental bodies whose "powers are general enough and have sufficient impact throughout the district" to require that elections to the body comply with Equal Protection strictures.
>
> The city also erroneously implies that the Board's composition survives constitutional challenge because the citywide members cast a 6-5 majority. . . . The at-large members, however, . . . often do not vote together, and when they do not, the outcome is determined by the vote of the borough presidents, each having one vote. Two citywide members, with the help of the presidents of the two least populous boroughs, the Bronx and Staten Island, will prevail over a disagreeing coalition of the third citywide member and the presidents of [Manhattan, Brooklyn, and Queens,] that contain a large majority of the city's population. Furthermore, because the Mayor has no vote on budget issues, the citywide members alone cannot control board budgetary decisions.

2. *The Extent of Permissible Deviation from Equal Apportionment*

The Court in *Board of Estimate* noted that the Board's apportionment deviated 78 percent from equal apportionment. Justice White wrote that "no case of ours has ever indicated that a deviation of some 78% would ever be justified. At the very least, the local government seeking to support such a difference between electoral districts would bear a very difficult burden." He went on to hold that New York's proferred justifications did not overcome the burden.

As Justice White's comment implies, the Court has not always required "absolute equality." It has applied a stricter standard to congressional districting than to the districting of state governmental units.

In Kirkpatrick v. Preisler, 394 U.S. 526 (1969), a divided Court held that Wesberry v. Sanders, 376 U.S. 1 (1964), "requires that the State make a good-faith effort to achieve precise mathematical equality" in apportioning congressional districts. Thus any variation from absolute equality should be de minimis. States could not defend inequality on the grounds that it avoided fragmenting political subdivisions (even if, as was argued, this would deter partisan gerrymandering). This standard was reaffirmed in White v. Weiser, 412 U.S. 383 (1973), with Chief Justice Burger and Justices Powell and Rehnquist acquiescing in the result "unless and until the Court decides to reconsider" *Kirkpatrick*.

A sharply divided 5-4 Court adhered to the *Kirkpatrick-Weiser* doctrine in Karcher v. Daggett, 462 U.S. 725 (1983). In reapportioning New Jersey's congressional districts, the state legislature adopted a plan that deviated from pure equality by an average of 0.1384 percent, about 725 people; the largest district deviated from the smallest by 3,674 people, or 0.698 percent. Justice Brennan wrote for the Court, invalidating this plan on the ground that the "legislature had before it other plans with appreciably smaller population deviations between the largest and smallest districts." Therefore, the "state must bear the burden of proving that each significant variance between districts was necessary to achieve some legitimate goal," and this, the majority held, New Jersey could not do.

States have considerably wider latitude with respect to the districting of state governmental districts. Thus, Mahan v. Howell, 410 U.S. 315 (1973), approved the Virginia legislature's redistricting plan, which produced an average percentage variance of 3.89 percent from equal apportionment and a maximum variance of 16.4 percent. Justice Rehnquist distinguished *Kirkpatrick* and reaffirmed the statements in *Reynolds* that "[s]o long as the divergences from a strict population standard are based on legitimate considerations incident to the effectuation of a rational state policy, some deviations from the equal population principle are constitutionally permissible with respect to the apportionment of seats in either or both of the two houses of a bicameral state legislature." One rational policy was "that of insuring some voice to political subdivisions, as political subdivisions." He emphasized the power of the Virginia General Assembly to enact special legislation dealing with political subdivisions. Later, in Gaffney v. Cummings, 412 U.S. 735 (1973), and White v. Regester, 412 U.S. 755 (1973), the Court held that Connecticut and Texas, respectively, did not even need to justify reapportionment plans that produced average deviations of about 2 percent and maximum variations of 8 percent and 9.9 percent, respectively. The majority in *Gaffney* described such deviations as "minor" and "insufficient to make out a prima facie case of invidious discrimination under the Fourteenth Amendment so as to require justification by the State." Justices Brennan, Douglas, and Marshall dissented in all of these cases.

Note: The Problem of the "Denominator" When Measuring the Value of a Vote

What is the unit of representation against which we measure "equality"? The numerator is one, as in one vote. What is the "denominator" that allows you, in District *A*, to measure the weight of your own vote against that of mine, in District *B*? Consider the following candidates for possible denominators:

1. all persons residing within the area, as counted by the most recent census;

2. all persons legally residing within the area;
3. all citizens residing within the area;
4. all citizens who are potentially qualified to vote;
5. all actually registered voters;
6. all actual voters.

The first category obviously produces the largest denominators; the last, the smallest. Consider Burns v. Richardson, 384 U.S. 73 (1966), in which the Court upheld Hawaii's reapportionment scheme based on the number of registered voters in a district rather than on its general population. The State argued that use of the latter denominator would assign to certain districts, particularly the island of Oahu, a significant number of armed forces personnel and other transients, which would in turn lead to Oahu's gross overrepresentation relative to, say, the island of Hawaii.

There are some obvious problems in using only registered voters as the denominator, even if we put to one side evidence that voter registration correlates with class or race.[21] Even the most affluent children cannot register to vote, nor can the most socially integrated resident alien. Yet they have interests that might better be reflected if one of the first three, maximally inclusive, standards was adopted. Consider for example, two districts chosen under the fourth standard: District *A* consists entirely of a planned retirement community with 20,000 senior citizens; district *B*, on the other hand, is composed of 20,000 adult voters and 20,000 children. Should one of the children be entitled to complain? (Could one of the voters possibly complain in his own name, given that each of the 40,000 voters has precisely the same amount of voting power?)

But it should be equally obvious that problems arise regardless of which standard is adopted. If you use what appears to be the most common standard, pure population, filtered perhaps only by requiring *legal* residency, then the 20,000 actual voters in district *B* will get the same degree of voting power as, say, *two* of the planned retirement communities with 40,000 voting senior citizens. Does the Constitution give a clue as to the proper denominator to be used?

Judge Kozinski usefully discusses this problem in Garza v. County of Los Angeles, 918 F.2d 763, 781-788 (9th Cir. 1990) (Kozinski, J., concurring and dissenting). He agreed with his colleagues that Los Angeles had drawn its supervisorial district lines to intentionally dilute Hispanic voting strength, but went on to argue that district lines had to be drawn on the basis of numbers of *citizens* rather than *total population*. Along the way he distinguished between the "principle of equal representation" and "the principle of electoral equality," and he read the Supreme Court's decisions as opting for the latter: "If the ultimate objective were to serve the representative principle, that is to equalize populations, *Burns* would be inexplicable, as it approved deviations from strict population equality that were wildly in excess of what a strict application of that principle would permit." He interpreted *Burns* to stand foursquare for "the principle of electoral equality; the Court approved the departure from strict population figures because raw population did not provide an accurate measure of whether the voting strength of each citizen was equal." Judge Kozinski conceded

21. Frances Fox Piven and Richard A. Cloward, Why Americans Don't Vote 4, 88-95, 108-112 (1988).

that some of the cases were murky and that he "would not be suprised to see [the Supreme Court] limit or abandon the principle of electoral equality in favor of a principle of representational equality." If you were a clerk for a Supreme Court justice who asked your advice as to the principle favored by the Constitution, how would you answer?

The problems of measuring equality are more difficult even than suggested above. Jonathan Still argues that "political equality is not a single concept, but a group of distinct (though related) criteria."[22] It is easy enough to think of paradigm instances of inequality — for example, "a situation in which some people are completely excluded from voting" or where some individuals receive five votes and others receive only one. (England, for example, used to give graduates of Oxford and Cambridge an additional vote.) What, however, is the paradigm of "equality"? Still begins his analysis by offering the following criterion of equality:

> 1. Universal Equal Suffrage: Everyone is allowed to vote, and everyone gets the same number of votes. . . .
>
> This criterion would appear to be an extremely simple one. But in practice even it can become complicated. For universal suffrage has never been truly universal, and no one has ever seriously suggested that it ought to be. Children are always excluded, though the age cutoff used has varied. Aliens are often excluded, as are insane people and convicted felons. . . .

Does this condition provide genuine equality? Still asks us to consider a city of 100,000 voters about to elect a mayor. The voting scheme divides the city into five geographical "units," each of which will get one "unit vote" based on the majority of votes within the unit. The candidate with the majority of unit votes will become mayor. Four of the units have 250 voters each; the fifth has 99,000. Would any egalitarian be satisfied with such a system? The presumed negative answer leads Still to offer a second criterion:

> 2. Equal Share: Each voter has the same "share in the election," defined as what that voter voted on divided by the number of voters who voted on it.
>
> . . . Universal Equal Suffrage and Equal Shares have one characteristic in common. Neither, in any way, relates the votes that are cast to the outcome of the election. This property seems peculiar in a criterion for determining the presence or absence of political equality. If all votes are to "count the same" or be "equally weighted" or "equally effective," one would think that would mean that, in some sense, all votes have the same impact on the outcome of the election.

Universal Equal Suffrage and Equal Shares are not adequate, however, as Still's next example demonstrates: a city of 100,000 voters divided into two districts, one containing 60,000 voters, the other 40,000. The winner of the first unit gets 6 unit votes; the winner of the second gets 4 unit votes. The candidate who gets a majority of the total ten unit votes wins overall election. Although the first two criteria are completely satisfied, it is obvious that the voters in the smaller district have no real say in who gets elected. Rectifying this problem leads to Still's third criterion:

22. Political Equality and Election Systems, 91 Ethics 375 (1981).

3. Equal Probabilities: Each voter has the same statistical probability of casting a vote which decides the election (under certain assumptions).

. . . The "certain" assumptions . . . are those constituting the statistical model on which the Banzhaf index is based.[23] The Banzhaf index assumes, in essence, that the election is between two alternatives (for or against a policy proposal, or between two candidates for a single office, or two political parties seeking control of a legislative body), and that each voter favors one of these alternatives (there are no abstentions). Further, it is assumed that all possible voting combinations (specifications of which voters support which of the alternatives) are equally likely to occur; this is equivalent to assuming that each voter is equally likely to favor either alternative.

A person's vote is decisive if the change in that vote would have changed the election result. . . . [T]he probability that a particular person's vote will be decisive is simply the number of voting combinations in which the vote is decisive divided by the total number of possible voting combinations. This probability is the Banzhaf index of voting power for that voter. . . . In essence, the Equal Probabilities criterion requires that all voters have the same chance, or the same number of opportunities, of having their vote determine the election result, under the assumptions described earlier.

At-large elections will always satisfy the first three criteria. But most elections in the United States take place in electoral districts. If the size of the districts differs, the Equal Probabilities criterion will be violated. But the problems run yet deeper. Imagine, for example, a five-member city council empowered to pass local ordinances upon majority vote; each member is elected from separate districts composed of 20,000 voters, thus satisfying Universal Equal Suffrage, Equal Shares, and Equal Probabilities. However, the city contains two groups of 36,000 voters each, each of which mobilizes to capture control of the council. The 36,000 members of group *A* are spread in clumps of 12,000 in three of the districts, while the members of group *B* are distributed throughout the five districts, with 7,000 voters in each of four districts and 8,000 voters in the remaining district. Group *A* will always dominate the council; Group *B* may well be unable to elect even a single council member if the two districts lacking any *A*'s nonetheless contain a sufficiently organized Group *C* who will refuse to vote for any *B*'s. Would an egalitarian be satisfied with this system?

Still suggests that the problem here is that the composition of the council depends entirely on the physical location of the specific voters. Had the voters in Group *B* been distributed differently throughout the districts, their power would have shifted accordingly. This problem would be eliminated through adoption of Still's fourth criterion:

23. The Banzhaf index is a particular method for measuring voting "power" developed by Professor John Banzhaf III. See Weighted Voting Doesn't Work: A Mathematical Analysis, 19 Rutgers L. Rev. 317 (1965); Multi-Member Electoral Districts — Do They Violate the "One Man, One Vote" Principle, 75 Yale L.J. 1309 (1966); One Man, 3,312 Votes: A Mathematical Analysis of the Electoral College, 13 Vill. L. Rev. 304 (1968). In *Board of Estimate,* the Court specifically declined to accept the Banzhaf index. Justice White noted that the Court had, in Whitcomb v. Chavis, 403 U.S. 124 (1971),

> observed that the Banzhaf methodology "remains a theoretical one" and is unrealistic in not taking into account "any political or other factors which might affect the actual voting power of the residents, which might include party affiliation, race, previous voting characteristics or other factors which go into the entire political voting situation."
>
> The personal right to vote is a value in itself, and a citizen is, without more and without mathematically calculating the power to determine the outcome of an election, shortchanged if he may vote for only one representative when citizens in a neighboring district, of equal population, vote for two.

4. Anonymity: The result of the election is the same under all possible distributions of the voters among the positions in the structure of the election system.

. . . Voters may trade places with each other in any possible manner, and the election result will not change. . . . Anonymity guarantees that each individual's vote counts the same as everyone else's in the sense that it makes no difference whether that person casts the vote or someone else casts it. . . . What counts is the votes that are cast, not who casts them (or where they are cast from).

Is Anonymity sufficient for political equality? Consider a referendum on, say, a proposed bond issue. In the election, 60 percent of the voters vote for the bond issue, and 40 percent vote against. [However, t]he bond issue is defeated because a two-thirds vote is necessary for passage. The system satisfies Anonymity; no matter how voters might trade places, the result will still be 60 percent in favor, which is short of two-thirds. Yet it could be argued that the votes of the bond issue opponents have weighed more heavily than the votes of the supporters, since the views of 40 percent have prevailed over the views of 60 percent. Similarly, it can be argued that any super-majority requirement will result in the same sort of inequality. This line of argument leads to the following criterion.

5. Majority Rule: An alternative favored by a majority of the voters will be chosen by the election system.

Note that this criterion does not attempt to deal with all situations. Specifically, it does not say what should happen if there are three or more alternatives, none of which commands a majority. The Majority Rule criterion requires only that the election system be such that, if there is one alternative which has majority support, then that alternative will be chosen. . . .

Anonymity requires that the weight of a vote not depend on who casts it or where it is cast from; but the weight is allowed to depend on the alternative for which it is cast. Majority Rule prohibits this latter form of "weighting" as well as the other types.

Does a system satisfying the first five criteria achieve equality when a ten-member city council is elected at large? Consider a 100,000-voter city divided into two groups. 60,000 votes are cast for the candidates of Party *A*, 40,000 for those of Party *B*, thus electing ten *A*'s. One way of describing this is that the *A*'s receive one seat on the city council for every 6,000 of its votes; the 40,000 *B*'s, of course, are left with no seats at all. Thus this leads Still to present his final criterion of political equality:

6. Proportional Group Representation: Each group of voters receives the same proportion of the seats in the legislative body as the number of voters in the group is of the total electorate. . . .

Proportional Group Representation bears a certain resemblance to Equal Shares. The difference is that [PGR] treats voters as having a share only in legislators they supported, whereas Equal Shares will often treat voters as having a share in legislators they opposed and with whose policy views they may strongly disagree.

Of course, proportional representation is possible only in elections for a multimember body. If there is only one winner, as in choosing a governor, majority rule is the closest one can come to proportionality. With respect to multimember bodies, such as city councils or legislatures, the obvious question is "how far along this spectrum one must go in order to reach 'meaningful' political equality." Still believes that "one would have to reach at least Anonymity. . . . [A] violation of

Anonymity means that there can be two groups of exactly the same size, and one group can get what it wants while the other group cannot. In this situation, it is difficult to see how it can be said that each person's vote counts the same as everyone else's."

Note that the preceding discussion assumes the basic framework of "one person/one vote." But the United States Senate (like the United Nations), for example, is organized on the principle of what might be termed "one entity/one vote." Does the Senate necessarily violate the theory of equality propounded by the Fourteenth Amendment and survive only because the Fourteenth Amendment has not been read to apply to national institutions themselves?

Still goes on to offer some "applications" of his criteria:

> Existing (and alternative) political institutions differ substantially in how far along the spectrum they go toward political equality. This fact will be illustrated below by several applications of these criteria to actual political institutions and changes which have been proposed or made in them.
>
> The first illustration is . . . Gray v. Sanders[, 372 U.S. 368 (1963), involving] the Georgia county unit system for selecting the Democratic nominee for Governor. . . . Each county was assigned a certain number of unit votes, all of which were awarded to the candidate carrying that county in the primary election. The winner was the candidate receiving a majority of the unit votes; a runoff between the top two was held if no candidate received a majority the first time around. Each voter had one vote in the election, and [the Court assumed that] there were no significant exclusions, so Universal Equal Suffrage was satisfied. The more populous counties had more unit votes than the smaller counties, but not nearly in proportion to population (or number of voters), so Equal Shares was not satisfied. . . . [I]t can be shown that Equal Probabilities was likewise not satisfied. Nor was Anonymity satisfied — even in a two-candidate race, a minority of the voters could elect their candidate if they were advantageously distributed with small majorities in counties having a majority of the unit votes. . . . For the same reason, Majority Rule was not satisfied. (Proportional Group Representation is inapplicable, since this was the election of a single official.)
>
> The Supreme Court declared the county unit system unconstitutional because it resulted in the unequal weighting of votes. . . . Unfortunately, the Court did not say [what criterion would have to be satisfied in order to have all votes equally weighted. What the Court did say was,] "The conception of political equality . . . can mean only one thing — one person, one vote." Taken literally, this would mean that the Court considered political equality to be synonymous with Universal Equal Suffrage. But that could not be, for the county unit system satisfied Universal Equal Suffrage, a fact that the Court acknowledged.
>
> . . . [T]he Court added a footnote at the end of its opinion[:] ". . . the [unconstitutional] weighting of votes would continue, even if unit votes were allocated strictly in proportion to population. Thus if a candidate won 6,000 of 10,000 votes in a particular county, he would get the entire unit vote, the 4,000 other votes for a different candidate being worth nothing and being counted only for the purpose of being discarded." This makes it clear that the Court did not consider Equal Shares to be sufficient for political equality, since the "reformed" county unit system it was discussing would have satisfied Equal Shares.
>
> . . . [T]he Court's rejection of any form of county unit system left Georgia with little choice but to adopt the obvious alternative — a popular vote primary election with the winner being determined by the most votes received (as is traditional in the South, provision was made for a runoff between the top vote getters if no candidate

received a majority in the initial election). It is easy to see that this system satisfies Universal Equal Suffrage, Equal Shares, and Equal Probabilities. Anonymity is also satisfied, since the result depends entirely on the number of votes each candidate receives and not on their distribution. A candidate supported by a majority of the voters will always win, so Majority Rule is satisfied. . . . By its decision in Gray v. Sanders, the Supreme Court accomplished a significant extension of political equality. [The 1964 reapportionment cases involved state legislative elections with the following general pattern:] State legislators were elected from districts (some single member, some multimember) by plurality vote. Universal Equal Suffrage was satisfied, as each voter had one vote for each legislator to be elected. Equal Shares was not satisfied, because the ratio of legislators to population varied among the districts. Equal Probabilities was also not satisfied. A group of voters constituting a majority in one district could elect a legislator, while an equal number of voters scattered among several districts could not, so Anonymity was not satisfied. A minority of the voters could win control of the legislature if they were distributed in a way giving them majorities in districts electing a majority of the legislators, so Majority Rule was not satisfied. And the fact that a minority of the voters could win a majority of the seats is also sufficient to show that Proportional Group Representation was not satisfied.

The Supreme Court held that this scheme was unconstitutional. . . . As in *Gray*, the Court did not say clearly exactly what criterion would have to be satisfied to attain political equality. But the Court did not spell out what election system would have to replace the one it was invalidating.

The change ordered by the Court was that the districts be redrawn so that the population per legislator would be the same in all districts. Of course, this system satisfies Universal Equal Suffrage and Equal Shares. Since the district sizes could still differ, Equal Probabilities is not satisfied. As before, a group of voters amounting to a majority in one district could elect a legislator, while an equal number scattered among the districts could not, so Anonymity is not satisfied. Similarly a minority of the voters which is advantageously distributed among the districts could elect a majority of the legislators, so Majority Rule is not satisfied. This possibility suffices to show that Proportional Group Representation is also not satisfied.

. . . [I]n *Gray*, the result of the Court's decision was that all of the criteria were satisfied, whereas in the reapportionment cases, the Court moved the situation only one additional step along the spectrum. And the one criterion which the Court added, Equal Shares, was precisely the one criterion which the Court had explicitly said in Gray v. Sanders would not be sufficient for political equality! . . . [I]n the reapportionment cases, the Court accomplished virtually nothing [in terms of moving states along the six-criteria spectrum developed by in this article].

Note: On the Notion of "Fair and Effective Representation" — Herein of Gerrymandering

In Reynolds v. Sims, Chief Justice Warren spoke of "fair and effective representation for all citizens [as] concededly the basic aim of legislative apportionment." There is wide agreement that fair representation requires more than mere access to a (single) ballot and that the vote is in fact counted.

Some of the opposition to ratification of the original 1787 Constitution was predicated on perceived deficiencies in the fairness of representation in the scheme adopted by the Framers. Several opponents took particular umbrage at the small number of "representatives" to be elected to the new national Congress and the consequences for the "fairness" of the ensuing representation. For example, "The Impartial Examiner" argued that "representation should be *complete*, that is, it should be such as to comprehend every species of interest within the society." Within a diverse and complex social order, it was vital that "[a]ll orders of men, who have any permanent interest in the government, as far as practicable, . . . be represented."

One of the most important critics of the Constitution, "The Federal Farmer," emphasized that the "essential parts of a free and good government are a full and equal representation of the people in the legislature." The aim of "fair representation" can be attained only if "every order of men in the community, according to the common course of elections, can have a share in it — in order to allow professional men, merchants, traders, farmers, mechanics, etc. to bring a just proportion of their best informed men respectively into the legislature."

The Federal Farmer disdained arguments that rested on the formal right of the citizen to vote for (relatively) few legislators. "It is deceiving a people to tell them they are electors, and can chuse their legislators, if they cannot, in the nature of things, chuse men from among themselves, and genuinely like themselves." The Federal Farmer was thus dubious of arguments that the fact that a representative had to compete for votes guaranteed meaningful representation of those who did not vote for the winner. Indeed, how much do *you* consider yourself to be represented by mayors, representatives and senators in the state and national legislatures, governors, and presidents of the United States when those offices are held by members of a political party other than the one that you identify with?

There is an unmistakable overtone of the notion of proportional representation in the analysis of the Federal Farmer, and it should not be surprising that Still and others argue that *Gray* and *Reynolds* "logically require . . . what the Court has not even intimated that it is ready to provide: [proportional representation] or at large election of every representative body at every level." Proportional representation, says Professor Dixon, "may be the only way of making good on 'one man-one vote' if that is interpreted, 'one man, one vote, each vote to be as *effective* a vote as possible.' "[24]

1. Race and Representation

WHITCOMB v. CHAVIS, 403 U.S. 124 (1971): [In drawing district lines for elections to the state legislature, the Indiana legislature placed Marion County in a single district with multiple members who are elected at large by all the voters in the county. Marion County was not unique: Eight of the state's 31 senatorial districts and 25 of its 39 house districts were also multimember, but Marion County, which includes Indianapolis, was by far the largest multimember district, electing 8 senators (from a total of 50) and 15 representatives (from a total of 100).

A group of Marion County residents sued to invalidate the districting scheme, alleging that it invidiously diluted the votes of Negroes and poor people living within certain Marion County census tracts, particularly the Indianapolis "ghetto": "With single-member districting . . . the ghetto area would elect three

24. Robert Dixon, Democratic Representation: Reapportionment in Law and Politics 535 (1968) (emphasis in original).

members of the house and one senator, whereas under the present districting voters in the area 'have almost no political force or control over legislators because the effect of their vote is cancelled out by other contrary interest groups' in Marion County."

The district court held for the plaintiffs, finding that senators and representatives tended to come from the better-off areas of Marion County. Almost 50 percent of the County's senators and about one-third of its representatives resided in a white "relatively wealthy suburban area" with approximately 14 percent of the County's population. By contrast, only approximately 5 percent of the senators and 6 percent of the representatives came from the ghetto area, which had almost 18 percent of the population. The court held that the voting strength of an identifiable racial group living in the ghetto area of Indianapolis "has been minimized by Marion County's multi-member senate and house district because of the strong control exercised by political parties over the selection of candidates, the inability of the Negro voters to assure themselves the opportunity to vote for prospective legislators of their choice and the absence of any particular legislators who were accountable for their legislative record to Negro voters." Upon the state's failure to redistrict voluntarily, the court imposed its own scheme, which created single-member districts throughout the state in order to protect "the legally cognizable racial minority group against dilution of its voting strength."

Indiana successfully sought a stay against implementation of the order, and the 1970 elections were held under the old scheme. Thereafter, in 1971, the legislature adopted new districting that provided for single-member house and senate districts throughout the state, including Marion County. The Supreme Court, after first holding that the case was not moot, went on to consider the issue presented by the district court's decision. Justice White wrote for the majority:]

The question of the constitutional validity of multi-member districts has been pressed in this Court since the first of the modern reapportionment cases. These questions have focused not on population-based apportionment but on the quality of representation afforded by the multi-member district as compared with single-member districts. In Lucas v. Colorado General Assembly, 377 U.S. 713 (1964), decided with Reynolds v. Sims, we noted certain undesirable features of the multi-member district but expressly withheld any intimation "that apportionment schemes which provide for the at-large election of a number of legislators from a county, or any political subdivision, are constitutionally defective." Subsequently, when the validity of the multi-member district, as such, was squarely presented, we held that such a district is not *per se* illegal under the Equal Protection Clause. But we have deemed the validity of multi-member district systems justiciable, recognizing also that they may be subject to challenge where the circumstances of a particular case may "operate to minimize or cancel out the voting strength of racial or political elements of the voting population." Fortson v. Dorsey, 379 U.S. 433, 439 (1965). Such a tendency, we have said, is enhanced when the district is large and elects a substantial proportion of the seats in either house of a bicameral legislature, if it is multi-member for both houses of the legislature or if it lacks provision for at-large candidates running from particular geographical subdistricts, as in *Fortson*. But we have insisted that the challenger carry the burden of proving that multi-member districts unconstitutionally operate to dilute or cancel the voting strength of racial or political elements. We have not yet sustained such an attack. . . .

Plaintiffs level two quite distinct challenges to the Marion County district. The first charge is that any multi-member district bestows on its voters several unconstitutional advantages over voters in single-member districts or smaller multi-member districts. The other allegation is that the Marion County district, on the record of this case, illegally minimizes and cancels out the voting power of a cognizable racial minority in Marion County. The District Court sustained the latter claim and considered the former sufficiently persuasive to be a substantial factor in prescribing uniform, single-member districts as the basic scheme of the court's own plan.

[The Court accepted the plausibility of the plaintiffs' mathematical argument that an individual's vote in a multi-member district is weightier than a vote in a single-member district because of having more chances to determine election outcomes, but went on to describe the argument as "a theoretical one" that avoids " 'tak[ing] into account any political or other factors which might affect the actual voting power of the residents, which might include party affiliation, race, previous voting characteristics or any other factors which go into the entire political voting situation.' " The Court also deemed too theoretical and lacking in empirical support an analogous argument that, because multimember legislators from a single district tend to vote as a bloc, such districts have more effective representation in the legislature than do districts with single representatives (or smaller multimember districts). Thus the Court adhered to its prior view that multimember districts do not, *per se*, violate the Equal Protection Clause. Justice White then turned to the argument concerning the invidious racial consequences of the Indiana scheme.]

[T]here is no suggestion here that Marion County's multi-member district, or similar districts throughout the State, were conceived or operated as purposeful devices to further racial or economic discrimination. As plaintiffs concede, "there was no basis for asserting that the legislative districts in Indiana were designed to dilute the vote of minorities.". . .

Nor does the fact that the number of ghetto residents who were legislators was not in proportion to ghetto population satisfactorily prove invidious discrimination absent evidence and findings that ghetto residents had less opportunity than did other Marion County residents to participate in the political processes and to elect legislators of their choice. We have discovered nothing in the record or in the court's findings indicating that poor Negroes were not allowed to register or vote, to choose the political party they desired to support, to participate in its affairs or to be equally represented on those occasions when legislative candidates were chosen. Nor did the evidence purport to show or the court find that inhabitants of the ghetto were regularly excluded from the slates of both major parties, thus denying them the chance of occupying legislative seats. It appears reasonably clear that the Republican Party won four of the five elections from 1960 to 1968, that Center Township ghetto voted heavily Democratic and that ghetto votes were critical to Democratic Party success. Although we cannot be sure of the facts since the court ignored the question, it seems unlikely that the Democratic Party could afford to overlook the ghetto in slating its candidates. . . . Nor is there any indication that the party failed to slate candidates satisfactory to the ghetto in other years. . . . [I]t seems reasonable to infer that had the Democrats won all of the elections or even most of them, the ghetto would have had no justifiable complaints about representation. . . . If this is the proper view of this case, the failure of the ghetto to have legislative seats in proportion to its population emerges more as a function of losing elections than of built-in bias against poor Negroes.

The voting power of ghetto residents may have been "cancelled out" as the District Court held, but this seems a mere euphemism for political defeat at the polls.

. . . [T]ypical American legislative elections are district-oriented, head-on races between candidates of two or more parties. As our system has it, one candidate wins, the others lose. Arguably the losing candidates' supporters are without representation since the men they voted for have been defeated. . . . But we have not yet deemed it a denial of equal protection to deny legislative seats to losing candidates, even in those so-called "safe" districts where the same party wins year after year.

Plainly, the District Court saw nothing unlawful about the impact of typical single-member district elections. The court's own plan created districts giving both Republicans and Democrats several predictably safe general assembly seats, with political, racial or economic minorities in those districts being "unrepresented" year after year. But similar consequences flowing from Marion County multi-member district elections were viewed differently. Conceding that all Marion County voters could fairly be said to be represented by the entire delegation, just as is each voter in a single-member district by the winning candidate, the District Court thought the ghetto voters' claim to the partial allegiance of eight senators and 15 representatives was not equivalent to the undivided allegiance of one senator and two representatives. As the trial court saw it, ghetto voters could not be adequately and equally represented unless some of Marion County's general assembly seats were reserved for ghetto residents serving the interests of the ghetto majority. But are poor Negroes of the ghetto any more underrepresented than poor ghetto whites who also voted Democratic and lost, or any more discriminated against than other interest groups or voters in Marion County with allegiance to the Democratic Party, or, conversely, any less represented than Republican areas or voters in years of Republican defeat? We think not. The mere fact that one interest group or another concerned with the outcome of Marion County elections has found itself outvoted and without legislative seats of its own provides no basis for invoking constitutional remedies where, as here, there is no indication that this segment of the population is being denied access to the political system. There is another gap in the trial court's reasoning. As noted by the court, the interest of ghetto residents in certain issues did not measurably differ from that of other voters. Presumably in these respects Marion County's assemblymen were satisfactorily representative of the ghetto. As to other matters, ghetto residents had unique interests not necessarily shared by others in the community and on these issues the ghetto residents were invidiously underrepresented absent their own legislative voice to further their own policy views.

Part of the difficulty with this conclusion is that the findings failed to support it. Plaintiffs' evidence purported to show disregard for the ghetto's distinctive interests; defendants claimed quite the contrary. We see nothing in the findings of the District Court indicating recurring poor performance by Marion County's delegation with respect to Center Township ghetto, nothing to show what the ghetto's interests were in particular legislative situations and nothing to indicate that the outcome would have been any different if the 23 assemblymen had been chosen from single-member districts. Moreover, even assuming bloc voting by the delegation contrary to the wishes of the ghetto majority, it would not follow that the Fourteenth Amendment had been violated unless it is invidiously discriminatory for a county to elect its delegation by majority vote based on party or candidate platforms and so to some extent predetermine legislative votes on particular issues. Such tendencies are inherent in government by elected representatives; and surely elections in single-member districts visit precisely the same consequences on the supporters of losing candidates whose views are rejected at the polls. . . .

The District Court's holding, although on the facts of this case limited to guaranteeing one racial group representation, is not easily contained. It is expressive of the more general proposition that any group with distinctive interests must be represented in legislative halls if it is numerous enough to command at least one seat and represents a majority living in an area sufficiently compact to constitute a single-member district. This approach would make it difficult to reject claims of Democrats, Republicans, or members of any political organization in Marion County who live in what would be safe districts in a single-member district system but who in one year or another, or year after year, are submerged in a one-sided multi-member district vote. There are also union oriented workers, the university community, religious or ethnic groups occupying identifiable areas of our heterogeneous cities and urban areas. Indeed, it would be difficult for a great many, if not most, multi-member districts to survive analysis under the District Court's view unless combined with some voting arrangement such as proportional representation or cumulative voting aimed at providing representation for minority parties or interests. At the very least, affirmance of the District Court would spawn endless litigation concerning the multi-member district systems now widely employed in this country.

We are not insensitive to the objections long voiced to multi-member district plans. Although not as prevalent as they were in our early history, they have been with us since colonial times and were much in evidence both before and after the adoption of the Fourteenth Amendment. . . . In our view . . . , experience and insight have not yet demonstrated that multi-member districts are inherently invidious and violative of the Fourteenth Amendment. Surely the findings of the District Court do not demonstrate it. Moreover, if the problems of multi-member districts are unbearable or even unconstitutional it is not at all clear that the remedy is a single-member district system with its lines carefully drawn to ensure representation to sizable racial, ethnic, economic, or religious groups and with its own capacity for overrepresenting and underrepresenting parties and interests and even for permitting a minority of the voters to control the legislature and government of a State. The short of it is that we are unprepared to hold that district-based elections decided by plurality vote are unconstitutional in either single- or multi-member districts simply because the supporters of losing candidates have no legislative seats assigned to them. As presently advised we hold that the District Court misconceived the Equal Protection Clause in applying it to invalidate the Marion County multi-member districts.[25]

Justice White's opinion should be read in the context of such cases as Palmer v. Thompson (handed down a week later) and Washington v. Davis, p.689 supra, which concern the relevance of intention and disproportionate impact in determining the reach of the Fourteenth Amendment. In White v. Regester, 412 U.S. 755

25. Concurring opinions by Justices Stewart and Harlan are omitted, as is a dissenting opinion by Justice Douglas, joined by Justices Brennan and Marshall.

(1973), the Court invalidated multimember districts in Texas counties including Dallas and San Antonio. Justice White wrote that "multimember districts are not *per se* unconstitutional," but went on to hold that there was sufficient evidence to support the district court's finding that the Black and Mexican-American plaintiffs in the case had not had an equal opportunity "to participate in the political processes and to elect legislators of their choice." The court below had paid careful attention to *Whitcomb* and "did not hold that every racial or political group has a constitutional right to be represented in the state legislature." Instead, it concluded, "from its own special vantage point," that multimember districts invidiously excluded the plaintiffs "from effective participation in political life, specifically in the election of representatives to the Texas House of Representatives."

However, seven years later in City of Mobile v. Bolden, 446 U.S. 55 (1980), the Court reversed a Court of Appeals decision striking down Mobile's system of at-large elections for its city council. The plurality opinion, written by Justice Stewart and joined by Chief Justice Burger and Justices Powell and Rehnquist, emphasized that the Fourteenth and Fifteenth Amendments prevent only *intentional* discrimination and that there was no evidence of discriminatory intent in the adoption of the commission system in 1911. Justice Stevens concurred in the judgment, while Justices White, Brennan, and Marshall all wrote dissenting opinions.[26]

The practical import of *Bolden* has been vitiated by a 1982 amendment to the Voting Rights Act of 1965, which generally prohibits the abridgment of the right to vote on racial grounds. The amendment establishes a violation of the Act whenever:

> based on the totality of circumstances, it is shown that the political processes leading to nomination or election in the State or political subdivision are not equally open to participation by members of a class of citizens protected by [the act] in that its members have less opportunity than other members of the electorate to participate in the political process and to elect representatives of their choice. The extent to which members of a protected class have been elected to office in the State or political subdivision is one circumstance which may be considered. *Provided*, that nothing in this section establishes a right to have members of a protected class elected in numbers equal to their proportion in the population.[27]

The report of the Senate Judiciary Committee described *Bolden* as a break with precedent that "substantially increased the burden on plaintiffs in voting discrimination cases by requiring proof of discriminatory purpose." Concluding that this places "an unacceptably difficult burden on plaintiffs," the Committee described

26. The *Bolden* decision led to renewed litigation concerning the intentions of the 1911 Mobile decisionmakers. Plaintiffs' attorneys presented a newly discovered letter to an editor written in 1909 by State Senator Frederick Bromberg, of Mobile, explaining the background of Alabama's post-Reconstruction election laws and commenting on measures then being considered by the Mobile citizenry for adoption: "We have always, as you know, falsely pretended that our main purpose was to exclude the ignorant vote when, in fact, we were trying to exclude not the ignorant vote, but the Negro vote. . . . At present, the masses of the colored people are indifferent to the right to vote and still more indifferent to the right to hold office. By adopting remedial measures now we shall cause no discontent, because of the present apathy of our colored citizens. This is fully recognized by all statesmen." A Voting Rights Letter for Congress, New York Times, April 27, 1982, at 28.

27. One issue raised by passage of the amendment, whether Congress can in effect interpret the demands of the Fourteenth or Fifteenth Amendment differently from the Supreme Court, is treated at length of Chapter 14, infra.

the purpose of the 1982 amendment as negating the requirement that discriminatory purpose be proved in order to establish a violation of the Voting Rights Act.

2. On the General Problem of Gerrymandering

Gerrymandering is an old American practice, in which an incumbent political party designs legislative districts to maximize the number of seats it can win in a general election.[28] Imagine, for example, a community of 303 persons, with 150 Democrats and 153 Republicans. All of the Democrats live north of the river that divides the community, all of the Republicans south. The community elects three members to the state legislature. Consider the four districting schemes on page 1101. The first is a single, multimember district, which would presumably elect three Republicans. The other three are single-district schemes.

Is any of these four possibilities fundamentally unfair? Is this the same as asking if any of them violates the Fourteenth Amendment? Would you answer differently if, instead of Democrats and Republicans, the relevant categories were whites and African-Americans? Would you want to know what motivated the drawing of the latter districts, e.g., a validated perception that whites generally voted Republican and African-Americans Democratic?

DAVIS v. BANDEMER

478 U.S. 109 (1986)

On Appeal from the United States District Court for the Southern District of Indiana

[In 1981 the Republican party controlled the Indiana governorship and both houses of the Indiana legislature, which consists of 100 members of the House of Representatives and 50 Senators. When the legislature turned to redrawing state legislative boundary lines pursuant to the 1980 census, its operative principle was to maximize the number of Republican seats: As one Republican House member said, "The name of the game is to keep us in power." Accordingly, Republicans alone composed the legislative conference committee that drew the new lines, and the districting map that the committee used was the product of a computerized study funded by the Republican State Committee.

The plan, as finally adopted, included single-, double-, and triple-member districts. Neither county nor city lines were consistently followed; House districts often crossed the lines of the larger Senate districts.

The 1982 election was held under the new districting plan; all of the House seats and half of the Senate seats were involved. Statewide, Democrats received 51.9 percent of the vote, but only 43 were elected to the House. For the Senate, Democrats received 53.1 percent of the vote statewide and won 52 percent (13 out of 25) of the contests. In Marion and Allen Counties, both of which had been divided into multimember House districts, Democrats attained 46.6 percent of the vote, but gained only 3 of the 21 House seats to be filled.[29]

28. The term is derived from the 1812 Massachusetts election, where the Federalists, while winning a majority of the votes, gained only 37 percent of the seats in the legislature, due to the skills of the Massachusetts Democrats led by Elbridge Gerry, the governor.

29. In 1984 Democrats earned approximately 44 percent of the statewide vote, but gained only 39 of the House seats. The two counties featuring multimember districts again proved Republican gold

PLAN 1

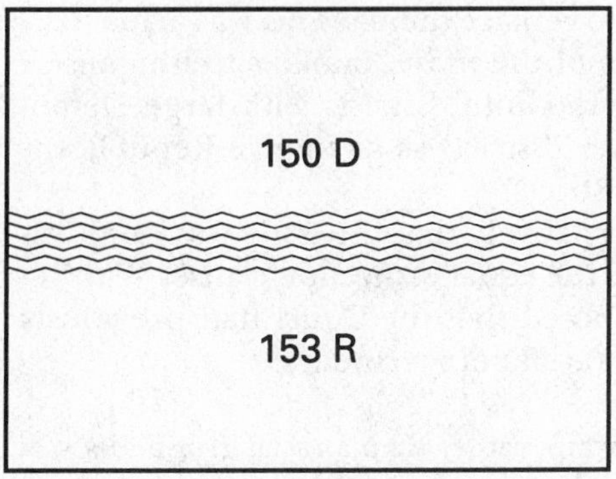

Multimember single district.
Presumed outcome: 3 Republicans.

PLAN 2

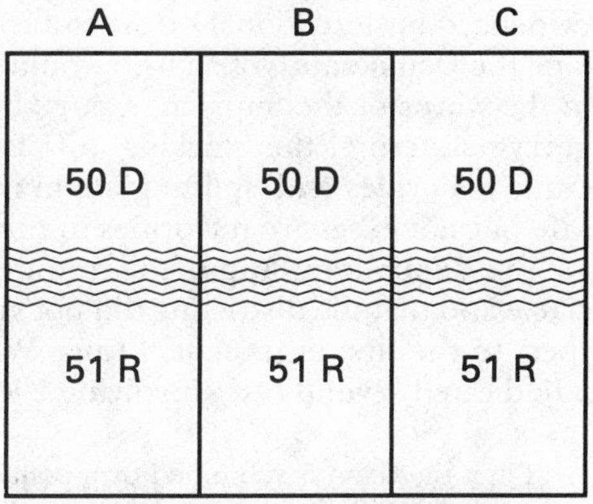

Three single-member districts.
Presumed outcome: 3 Republicans.

PLAN 3

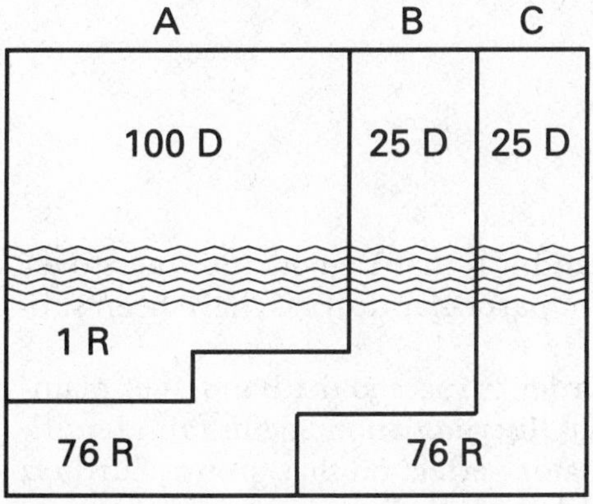

Three single-member districts.
Presumed outcome: 2 Republicans, 1 Democrat.

PLAN 4

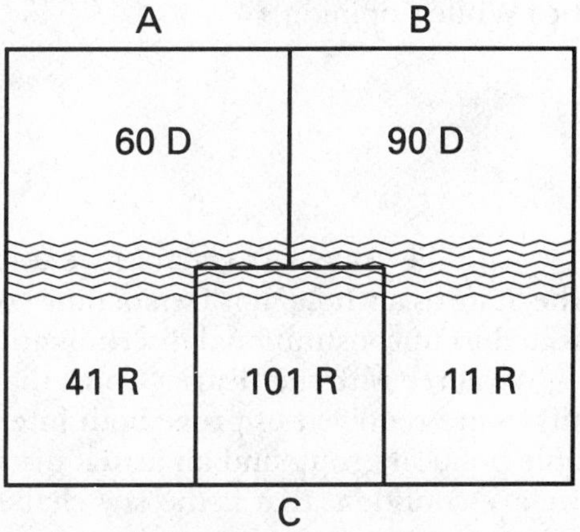

Three single-member districts.
Presumed outcome: 2 Democrats, 1 Republican.

Indiana Democrats sued to invalidate the plan, charging that they had been denied equal protection of the laws by virtue of the partisan gerrymander. In December 1984, a three-judge district court invalidated the reapportionment. Noting, *inter alia,* the irregular shape of some of the districts, the mixture of single- and multimember districts, and the failure of the boundary lines to adhere consistently to established political divisions, the court concluded that the plan evidenced an intentional effort to favor Republican incumbents and disadvantage the Democratic voters who would like to replace them. "This was achieved," in the words of the Supreme Court, by one of the most "familiar techniques of gerrymandering, the 'stacking' [of] Democrats into districts with large Democratic majorities and 'splitting' them in other districts so as to give Republicans safe but not excessive majorities in those districts."

The Republicans appealed, arguing alternatively that the issue was nonjusticiable and that the districting did not violate the equal protection clause. With respect to the first argument, Justice White noted that the Court had previously adjudicated several cases involving alleged racial gerrymanders:

> [T]hat the claim is submitted by a political group, rather than a racial group, does not distinguish it in terms of justiciability. That the characteristics of the complaining group are not immutable or that the group has not been subject to the same historical stigma may be relevant to the manner in which the case is adjudicated, but these differences do not justify a refusal to entertain such a case.

There was no consensus on the substantive constitutional issue, however. Only Justices Brennan, Marshall, and Blackmun joined in the remaining parts of Justice White's opinion:]

III

A

. . . [T]he appellee's claim as we understand it is that Democratic voters over the State as a whole, not Democratic voters in particular districts, have been subjected to unconstitutional discrimination. . . .

We agree with the District Court that in order to succeed the Bandemer plaintiffs were required to prove both intentional discrimination against an identifiable political group and an actual discriminatory effect on that group. Further, we are confident that if the law challenged here had discriminatory effects on Democrats, this record would support a finding that the discrimination was intentional. . . .

Indeed, . . . we think it most likely that whenever a legislature redistricts, those responsible for the legislation will know the likely political composition of the new districts and will have a prediction as to whether a particular district is a safe one for a Democratic or Republican candidate or a competitive district that either candidate might win. . . . As long as redistricting is done by a legislature, it should

---

mines. Republicans gained 18 of the 21 seats with approximately 62 percent of the vote. In the Senate election, where the 25 contests were the first under the new plan, the sagacity of the Republican linedrawers was again shown: Although Democratic candidates received 42.3 percent of the vote, they gained only 28% (7) of the seats.

not be very difficult to prove that the likely political consequences of the reapportionment were intended.

B

We do not accept, however, the District Court's legal and factual bases for concluding that the 1981 Act visited a sufficiently adverse effect on the appellees' constitutionally protected rights to make out a violation of the Equal Protection Clause. The District Court held that because any apportionment scheme that purposely prevents proportional representation is unconstitutional, Democratic voters need only show that their proportionate voting influence has been adversely affected. Our cases, however, clearly foreclose any claim that the Constitution requires proportional representation or that legislature in reapportioning must draw district lines to come as near as possible to allocating seats to the contending parties in proportion to what their anticipated statewide vote will be. Whitcomb v. Chavis; White v. Regester.

The typical election for legislative seats in the United States is conducted in described geographical districts, with the candidate receiving the most votes in each district winning the seat allocated to that district. If all or most of the districts are competitive — defined by the District Court in this case as districts in which the anticipated split in the party vote is within the range of 45% to 55% — even a narrow statewide preference for either party would produce an overwhelming majority for the winning party in the state legislature. This consequence, however, is inherent in winner-take-all, district-based elections. . . . [W]e cannot hold that such a reapportionment law would violate the Equal Protection Clause because the voters in the losing party do not have representation in the proportion to the statewide vote received by their party candidates. . . .

To draw district lines to maximize the representation of each major party would require creating as many safe seats for each party as the demographic and predicted political characteristics of the State would permit. This in turn would leave the minority in each safe district without a representative of its choice. We upheld the "political fairness" approach in Gaffney v. Cummings, 412 U.S. 735 (1973), despite its tendency to deny safe district minorities any realistic chance to elect their own representatives. But *Gaffney* in no way suggested that the Constitution requires the approach that Connecticut had adopted in that case.

In cases involving individual multi-member districts, we have a required a substantially greater showing of adverse effects than a mere lack of proportional representation to support a finding of unconstitutional vote dilution. Only where there is evidence that excluded groups have "less opportunity to participate in the political processes and to elect candidates of their choice" have we refused to approve the use of multi-member districts. In these cases, we have also noted the lack of responsiveness by those elected to the concerns of the relevant groups.

These holdings rest on a conviction that the mere fact that a particular apportionment scheme makes it more difficult for a particular group in a particular district to elect the representatives of its choice does not render that scheme constitutionally infirm. This conviction, in turn, stems from a perception that the power to influence the political process is not limited to winning elections. An individual or a group of individuals who votes for a losing candidate is usually deemed to be adequately represented by the winning candidate and to have as much opportunity to influence that candidate as other voters in the district. We cannot presume such a situation, without actual proof to the contrary, that the candidate elected will entirely ignore the interests of those voters. This is true even in a safe district where the losing group loses election after election. . . .

As with individual districts, where unconstitutional vote dilution is alleged in the form of statewide political gerrymandering, the mere lack of proportional representation will not be sufficient to prove unconstitutional discrimination. . . . Rather, unconstitutional discrimination occurs only when the electoral system is arranged in a manner that will consistently degrade a voter's or a group of voters' influence on the political process as a whole. . . . [A]n equal protection violation may be found only where the electoral system substantially disadvantages certain voters in their opportunity to influence the political process effectively.

. . . [S]uch a finding of unconstitutionality must be supported by evidence of continued frustration of the will of a majority of the voters or effective denial to a minority of voters of a fair chance to influence the political process. . . .

C

The District Court's findings do not satisfy this threshold condition to stating and proving a cause of action. . . .

Relying on a single election to prove unconstitutional discrimination is unsatisfactory. . . .

[The conclusion is the same with respect to multimember districts, which] appear indistinguishable from safe Republican and safe Democratic single-member districts. . . .

[I]n determining the constitutionality of multi-member districts challenged as racial gerrymanders, we have rejected the view that "any group with distinctive interests must be represented in legislative halls if it is numerous enough to command at least one seat and represents a minority living in an area sufficiently compact to constitute a single-member district." *Whitcomb,* 403 U.S., at 156. Rather, we have required that there be proof that the complaining minority "had less opportunity . . . to participate in the political processes and to elect legislators of their choice." In *Whitcomb,* we went on to observe that there was no proof that blacks were not allowed to register or vote, to choose the political party they desired to support, to participate in its affairs or to be equally represented on those occasions when candidates were chosen, or to be included among the candidates slated by the Democratic Party. Against this background, we concluded that the failure of the minority "to have legislative seats in proportion to its population emerges more as a function of losing elections than of built-in bias against poor Negroes. The voting power of ghetto residents may have been 'cancelled out' as the District Court held, but this seems a mere euphemism for political defeat at the polls.". . .

D

[Justice Powell, joined by Justice Stevens, agreed that the case was justiciable, but disagreed with the plurality (who were joined by the three Justices — Chief Justice Burger and Justices O'Connor and Rehnquist — who rejected justiciability) that no violation of the Equal Protection Clause was shown.]

In response to our approach, Justice Powell suggests an alternative method for evaluating equal protection claims of political gerrymandering. In his view, courts would look at a number of factors in considering these claims: the nature of the legislative procedures by which the challenged redistricting was accomplished and the intent behind the redistricting; the shapes of the districts and their conformity with political subdivision boundaries; and "evidence concerning population disparities and statistics tending to show vote dilution."

. . . [T]he crux of Justice Powell's analysis seems to be that — at least in some cases — the intentional drawing of district boundaries for partisan ends and for no other reason violates the Equal Protection Clause in and of itself. We disagree, however, with this conception of a constitutional violation. Specifically, even if a state legislature redistricts with the specific intention of disadvantaging one political party's election prospects, we do not believe that there has been an unconstitutional discrimination against members of that party unless the redistricting does in fact disadvantage it at the polls.

Moreover, as we discussed above, a mere lack of proportionate results in one election cannot suffice in this regard. . . .

Justice Powell's view would allow a constitutional violation to be found where the only proven effect on a political party's electoral power was disproportionate results in one (or possibly two) elections. This view, however, contains no explanation of why a lack of proportionate election results should suffice in those political gerrymandering cases while it does not in the cases involving racial gerrymandering. In fact, Justice Powell's opinion is silent as to the relevance of the substantive standard developed in the multi-member district cases to these political gerrymandering cases. . . .

In sum, we decline to adopt the approach enunciated by Justice Powell. In our view, that approach departs from our past cases and invites judicial interference in legislative districting whenever a political party suffers at the polls. We recognize that our own view may be difficult of application. Determining when an electoral system has been "arranged in a manner that will consistently degrade a voter's or a group of voters' influence on the political process as a whole," is of necessity a difficult inquiry. Nevertheless, we believe that it recognizes the delicacy of intruding on this most political of legislative functions and is at the same time consistent with our prior cases regarding individual multi-member districts, which have formulated a parallel standard.

[Justice O'Connor wrote an opinion, joined by Chief Justice Burger and Justice Rehnquist, that] would hold that the partisan gerrymandering claims of major political parties raise a nonjusticiable political question that the judiciary should leave to the legislative branch as the Framers of the Constitution unquestionably intended. . . .

The step taken today is a momentous one, which if followed in the future can only lead to political instability and judicial malaise. If members of the major political parties are protected by the Equal Protection Clause from dilution of their voting strength, then members of every identifiable group that possesses distinctive interests and tends to vote on the basis of those interests should be able to bring similar claims. Federal courts will have no alternative but to attempt to recreate the complex process of legislative apportionment in the context of adversary litigation in order to reconcile the competing claims of political, religious, ethnic, racial, occupational, and socioeconomic groups. Even if there were some way of limiting such claims to organized political parties, the fact remains that the losing party or the losing group of legislators in every reapportionment will now be invited to fight the battle anew in federal court. . . . There is simply no clear stopping point to prevent the gradual evolution of a requirement of roughly proportional representation for every cohesive political group. . . .

Baker v. Carr does not require that we hold that the right asserted in this case is similarly within the intendment of the Equal Protection Clause and determinable under the standards developed to enforce that Clause. The right asserted in *Baker* was an individual right to vote whose weight was not arbitrarily subjected to "debasement," 369 U.S., at 194. The rights asserted in this case are *group* rights to an equal share of political power and representation, and the "arbitrary and capricious" standard discussed in *Baker* cannot serve as a basis for recognizing such rights. . . .

Nor do this Court's racial gerrymandering cases require the recognition of any such group right outside the context of racial discrimination. As Justice Frankfurter observed:

> The cases involving Negro disfranchisement are no exception to the principle of avoiding federal judicial intervention into matters of state government in absence of an explicit and clear constitutional imperative. For here the controlling command of Supreme Law is plain and unequivocal. An end of discrimination against the Negro was the compelling motive of the Civil War Amendments. The Fifteenth expresses this in terms, and it is no less true of the Equal Protection Clause of the Fourteenth. *Baker,* 369 U.S., at 385-286 (Frankfurter, J., dissenting).

In my view, where a racial minority group is characterized by "the traditional indicia of suspectedness" and is vulnerable to exclusion from the political process, individual voters who belong to that group enjoy some measure of protection against dilution of their group voting strength by means of racial gerrymandering. As a matter of past history and present reality, there is a direct and immediate relationship between the racial minority's group voting strength in a particular community and the individual rights of its members to vote and to participate in the political process. . . . Even so, the individual's right is infringed only if the racial minority group can prove that it has "essentially been shut out of the political process."

Clearly, members of the Democratic and Republican parties cannot claim that they are a discrete and insular group vulnerable to exclusion from the political process by some dominant group: these political parties *are* the dominant groups, and the Court has offered no reason to believe that they are incapable of fending for themselves through the political process. . . .

[Justice O'Connor criticizes the plurality's discussion of *Gaffney*, which had upheld a bipartisan gerrymander because it was intended to "provide a rough sort of proportional representation."] As the plurality acknowledges, the scheme upheld in *Gaffney* tended to "deny safe district minorities any realistic chance to elect their own representatives." If this bipartisan arrangement between two groups of self-interested legislators is constitutionally permissible, as I believe and as the Court held in *Gaffney*, then — in terms of the rights of individuals — it should be equally permissible for a legislative majority to employ the same means to pursue its own interests over the opposition of the other party.

. . . The Court has in effect decided that it is constitutionally acceptable for both parties to "waste" the votes of individuals through a bipartisan gerrymander, so long as the *parties* themselves are not deprived of their group voting strength to an extent that will exceed the plurality's threshold requirement. This choice confers greater rights on powerful political groups than on individuals; that cannot be the meaning of the Equal Protection Clause.

II

The standard the plurality proposes exemplifies the intractable difficulties in deriving a judicially manageable standard from the Equal Protection Clause for adjudicating political gerrymandering claims. . . . In my view, this standard will over time either prove unmanageable and arbitrary or else evolve towards some loose form of proportionality. Either outcome would be calamitous for the federal courts, for the States, and for our two-party system. . . .

Of course, in one sense, a requirement of proportional representation, whether loose or absolute, is judicially manageable. . . . The flaw in such a pronouncement, however, would be the use of the Equal Protection Clause as the vehicle for making a fundamental policy choice that is contrary to the intent of its Framers and to the traditions of this republic.

. . . [T]he plurality opinion ultimately rests on a political preference for proportionality — not an outright claim that proportional results are required, but a conviction that the greater the departure from proportionality, the more suspect an apportionment plan becomes. This preference for proportionality is in serious tension with essential features of state legislative elections. Districting itself represents a middle ground between winner-take-all elections and proportional representation for political parties. . . .

The plurality's theory is also internally inconsistent. The plurality recognizes that, given a normal dispersion of party strength and winner-take-all district-based elections, it is likely that even a narrow statewide preference for one party will give that party a disproportionately large majority in the legislature. The plurality is prepared to tolerate this effect, because not to do so would spell the end of district-based elections, or require reverse gerrymandering to ensure greater proportionality for the minority party. But this means that the plurality would extend greater protection to a party that can command a majority of the statewide vote than to a party that cannot: the explanation, once again, is that the plurality has made a political judgment — in this instance, that district-based elections must be taken as a given. . . .

Racial gerrymandering should remain justiciable, for the harms it engenders run counter to the central thrust of the Fourteenth Amendment. But no such justification can be given for judicial intervention on behalf of mainstream political parties, and the risks such intervention poses to our political institutions are unacceptable.

[Much of Justice Powell's dissenting opinion has already been summarized in Justice White's plurality opinion. Additional excerpts follow:]

The Equal Protection Clause guarantees citizens that their state will govern them impartially. In the context of redistricting, that guarantee is of critical importance because the franchise provides most citizens their only voice in the legislative process. Since the contours of a voting district powerfully may affect citizens' ability to exercise influence through their vote, district lines should be determined in accordance with neutral and legitimate criteria. When deciding where those lines will fall, the state should treat its voters as standing in the same position, regardless of their political beliefs or party affiliation.

. . . The Court's decision in Reynolds v. Sims illustrates two concepts that are vitally important in evaluating an equal protection challenge to redistricting. First, the Court recognized that equal protection encompasses a guarantee of equal *representation*, requiring a State to seek to achieve through redistricting "fair and effective representation for all citizens." The concept of "representation" necessarily applies to groups: groups of voters elect representatives, individual voters do not. . . . Thus, the fact that individual voters in heavily populated districts are free to cast their ballot has no bearing on a claim of malapportionment.

Second, . . . the Court plainly recognized that redistricting should be based on a number of neutral criteria, of which districts of equal population was only one. . . . For example, the Court observed that districts should be compact and cover contiguous territory, precisely because the alternative, "[i]ndiscriminate districting," would be "an open invitation to partisan gerrymandering." Similarly, a State properly could choose to give "independent representation" to established political subdivisions. Adherence to community boundaries, the Court reasoned, would both "deter the possibilities of gerrymandering," and allow communities to have a voice in the legislature that directly controls their local interests.

Discussion

1. Does it follow from Justice O'Connor's remarks that no constitutional issue would be raised if the Indiana Republicans adopted a state-wide single district, with each voter having the opportunity to vote for up to 100 candidates for the Indiana House of Representatives?

2. How would you respond to Justice O'Connor's point that those who favor judicial intervention in the instant case would have to be willing to strike down the system of single-member district legislative elections, given the possibility (and in some instances the actuality) that slender majorities in a number of (otherwise fairly apportioned) districts will result in significant "underrepresentation" for defeated minorities? Is it enough to say that this result was not "intended," even though its possibility was easily foreseen?

3. Indiana, like most states, has a two-party system. It is certainly easy enough to imagine, though, a party structure like the one currently found in Germany, where the Free Democrats, though distinctly smaller than the Christian Democrats or the Socialist Party, nonetheless are important political actors. (There is also an even smaller Green Party.) Indeed, American history is full of "third parties"; one of our present major parties, the Republican Party, began as an insurgent movement in the 1850s and successfully displaced the Whig Party from the national political scene. In modern times New York has had as many as four parties plausibly contending for votes.

Consider a New York reapportionment plan designed and adopted by Democrats and Republicans working together that assured that the particular districts likely to elect members of the deviant parties were divided among their neighbors so that the two-party system was preserved. Would *that* apportionment be constitutionally permissible, considering the Court's treatment of the Indiana scheme? Do minority parties have only such representation rights as the majority parties choose to respect?

Note: On the Constitutionality of the Electoral College

Consider the electoral college in light of the plurality's and Justice Powell's opinions: Every state except Maine assigns its electoral votes (the sum of the number of seats in the House of Representatives plus two votes for their Senators) to the winner of the statewide poll. Thus 100 percent of California's 50+ votes go to electors favoring the winning Presidential candidate, regardless of his or her plurality. In 1984, Ronald Reagan's 60 percent of the nationwide vote translated into over 95 percent of the electoral college. As Jonathan Still notes,

> The Electoral College operates as a unit voting system for the election of the President. Universal Equal Suffrage is satisfied, as each voter has one vote in the election. Equal Shares is not satisfied, because the electoral vote of each state includes two votes for its two senators, regardless of population. It has been shown that Equal Probabilities is not satisfied. The number of votes needed to win depends on how those votes are distributed among the states, so Anonymity is not satisfied. And the minority candidate could be elected in a two-way race, so Majority Rule is not satisfied.[30]

Like the Senate, the electoral college is presumably constitutionally entrenched. Is this true of the winner-take-all feature? Presumably, states follow the winner-take-all method in order to maximize their power within the college. (For example, Senator Bentsen was chosen as the Democratic vice-presidential candidate in 1988 in the hope that he would help carry Texas for the Democrats. Were Texas' votes assigned proportionally rather than winner-take-all, someone else might well have been chosen.) In essence, all voters in a state are presumed to share an interest in maximizing the state's power. Might one question the basis for this claim of a unified state interest? Is one's "Californian-ness" or "Texan-ness" a deeper part of one's identity than one's self-conception as a Democrat or Republican, liberal or conservative?

Is the winner-take-all method justified by a *Gaffney*-like answer that, after all, the two major parties have in effect agreed to roll the electoral dice in their states? What about third-party candidates? Do they have no say in the matter?

What about a third candidate who is a member of a racial minority? The 1982 amendments to the Voting Rights Act prohibit "political processes leading to nomination or election in the State" that are "not equally open to participation by members of a class of citizens protected by [the Act] in that its members have less opportunity than other members of the electorate to participate in the political processes and to elect representatives of their choice." These amendments have been interpreted to require setting aside multimember legislative districts that result in significantly less black representation than would result from smaller single-member districts. One may doubt that Congress was focusing the electoral college when drafting this section. But is there a principled distinction between voting for a member of the state legislature and voting for a member of the electoral college?

30. Jonathan Still, supra note 22.

Chapter 11
The Constitution in the Modern Welfare State

The demise of *Lochner* and the Court's retreat from the active review of most economic regulation reflected its acquiescence to the emerging welfare state — a state not constitutionally limited to maintaining order and facilitating voluntary private transactions, but one that could legitimately intervene to adjust perceived inequities in the distribution of private power and wealth. This intervention almost invariably involved the redistribution of social resources, ranging from legal rights, such as the right not to work more than a certain number of hours, to direct transfers of income, such as welfare benefits.[1] As Neil Gilbert explains:[2]

> Capitalism encourages competition and risk-taking behavior. Although success in the economic marketplace is often well rewarded, misfortune and failure can lead to harsh consequences. There are few market mechanisms to mitigate the consequences of accident, illness, age, and vicissitudes of industrial society. And these mechanisms, such as private insurance, provide the most protection to those who are relatively well off and least in need of it. The welfare state operates through a social market that provides a sort of communal safety net for the casualties of a market economy. Ideally, as a system for distributing benefits in society, the market economy responds to individual initiative, ability, productivity, and the desire for profit. In contrast, the social market of the welfare state responds to need, dependency, and charitable impulses.

Regulation, occupational licensing, and subsidies for developing industries had existed since at least the eighteenth century, and at no point did American government adopt a posture of pure laissez-faire.[3] Still, the magnitude of state

1. Asa Briggs, in The Welfare State in Historical Perspective, defines the welfare state as

> a state in which organized power is deliberately used (through politics and administration) in an effort to modify the play of market forces in at least three directions — first, by guaranteeing individuals and families a minimum income irrespective of the market value of their property; second, by narrowing the extent of insecurity by enabling individuals and families to meet certain "social contingencies" (for example, sickness, old age, and unemployment) which lead otherwise to individual and family crises; and third, by ensuring that all citizens without distinction of status or class are offered the best standards available in relation to a certain agreed range of social services.

Quoted in Evelyn Z. Brodkin & Dennis Young, Making Sense of Privatization: What Can We Learn from Economic and Policy Analysis?, in Sheila B. Kamerman & Alfred J. Kahn, eds., Privatization and the Welfare State 140 (1989).

One question that will repeatedly arise in the course of this chapter is the extent to which the United States, either as a constitutional or an empirical matter, meets Briggs's definition of a welfare state.

2. Neil Gilbert, Capitalism and the Welfare State 4-5 (1983). See also Amy Gutmann, ed., Democracy and the Welfare State (1988).

3. See, e.g., Oscar and Mary Handlin, Commonwealth: A Study of the Role of Government in the American Economy: Massachusetts, 1774-1861 (1947); Louis Hartz, Economic Policy and Demo-

intervention in the lives of individuals and enterprises increased enormously during the New Deal and in the decades that followed.

These changes in the extent of government activity were accompanied by shifts in certain fundamental constitutional concepts. We have already seen some of the shifts in the meanings of "property" and "liberty" under the due process clause.

This chapter examines the Constitution in the modern welfare state. We begin by asking the deceptively simple question of whether the welfare state is a constitutional *requirement* or merely an option open to legislatures. We then turn to limitations imposed by the Constitution on lawmakers who, having decided to inaugurate some version of a welfare state, nonetheless wish to limit its reach or impose certain requirements on the recipients of governmental largesse.

I. Does the Constitution Guarantee Affirmative Rights?

DESHANEY v. WINNEBAGO COUNTY DEPARTMENT OF SOCIAL SERVICES

489 U.S. 189 (1989)

On Certiorari to the Court of Appeals for the Seventh Circuit

[Joshua DeShaney, born in 1979, had been placed in the custody of his father, Randy, following the divorce of Joshua's parents. In January 1982, the Winnebago (Wisconsin) County Department of Social Services (DSS) was notified by Joshua's stepmother, who at the time sought a divorce from Randy, that Randy had abused Joshua. The DSS interviewed Randy, who denied the accusations. In January 1983, Joshua was admitted to a hospital; his multiple bruises and abrasions led the examining physician to notify the DSS of potential child abuse. At the insistence of the DSS, a Wisconsin juvenile court placed Joshua in the temporary custody of the hospital. A "Child Protection Team" then considered Joshua's situation and decided that there was insufficient evidence of abuse to justify retaining custody over Joshua. It did, however, recommend, among other things, that Randy receive counseling. A month later Joshua was again taken to a hospital emergency room with "suspicious" injuries, but the DSS caseworker decided that there was no cause for further action. Over the next six months the caseworker made monthly visits to the DeShaney home, during which "she observed a number of suspicious injuries on Joshua's head." She noticed as well that Joshua had not been enrolled in school, as had been recommended by the DSS, nor had Randy's girlfriend moved out, as had also been recommended. "The caseworker dutifully recorded . . . her continuing suspicion that someone in the DeShaney household was physically abusing Joshua, but she did nothing more." In November 1983, Joshua was treated yet again for injuries believed to be the result of child abuse. "On the caseworker's next two visits to the DeShaney home, she was told that Joshua was too ill to see her. Still DDS took no action."

---

cratic Thought: Pennsylvania, 1776-1860 (1948); James Neal Primm, Economy Policy in the Development of a Western State: Missouri, 1820-1860 (1954); Leonard Levy, The Law of the Commonwealth and Chief Justice Shaw (1957); Harry N. Scheiber, Property Law, Expropriation, and Resource Allocation by Government, 33 J. Econ. Hist. 232 (1973).

Five months later, in March 1984, "Randy DeShaney beat . . . Joshua so severely that he fell into a life-threatening coma." He "did not die, but he suffered brain damage so severe that he is expected to spend the rest of his life confined to an institution for the profoundly retarded." Randy was subsequently tried and convicted of child abuse.

Joshua, through his mother, claimed that the DSS had deprived him of his fourteenth amendment rights to liberty by its failure to protect him "against a risk of violence at his father's hands of which they knew or should have known."]

REHNQUIST, C.J.

. . . The claim is one invoking the substantive rather than procedural component of the Due Process Clause; petitioners do not claim that the State denied Joshua protection without according him appropriate procedural safeguards, but that it was categorically obligated to protect him in these circumstances.

But nothing in the language of the Due Process Clause itself requires the State to protect the life, liberty, and property of its citizens against invasion by private actors. The Clause is phrased as a limitation on the State's power to act, not as a guarantee of certain minimal levels of safety and security. . . . Its purpose was to protect the people from the State, not to ensure that the State protected them from each other. The Framers were content to leave the extent of governmental obligation in the latter area to the democratic political processes.

Consistent with these principles, our cases have recognized that the Due Process Clauses generally confer no affirmative right to governmental aid, even where such aid may be necessary to secure life, liberty, or property interests of which the government itself may not deprive the individual. See, e.g., Harris v. McRae, 448 U.S. 297 [page 1242 infra] (no obligation to fund abortions or other medical services) (discussing Due Process Clause of Fifth Amendment); Lindsey v. Normet, 405 U.S. 56, 74 (1972) (no obligation to provide adequate housing) (discussing Due Process Clause of Fourteenth Amendment); see also Youngsberg v. Romeo, 457 U.S. 307, 317 (1982) ("As a general matter, a State is under no constitutional duty to provide substantive services for those within its border"). As we said in Harris v. McRae, "[a]lthough the liberty protected by the Due Process Clause affords protection against unwarranted *government* interference, . . . it does not confer an entitlement to such [governmental aid] as may be necessary to realize all the advantages of that freedom." If the Due Process Clause does not require the State to provide its citizens with particular protective services, it follows that the State cannot be held liable under the Clause for injuries that could have been averted had it chosen to provide them.[a] As a general matter, then, we conclude that a State's failure to protect an individual against private violence simply does not constitute a violation of the Due Process Clause.

[The Court also rejected the argument that the State had in effect created a "special relationship" with Joshua through such services as the DSS did in fact provide. It distinguished earlier cases that had found the State obligated to provide certain services to incarcerated prisoners or involuntarily committed mental patients on the ground that] they stand only for the proposition that when the State takes a person into its custody and holds him there against his will, the Constitution imposes upon it a corresponding duty to assume some responsibility for

a. The State may not, of course, selectively deny its protective services to certain disfavored minorities without violating the Equal Protection Clause. But no such argument has been made here.

his safety and general well-being. The rationale for this principle is simple enough: when the State by the affirmative exercise of its power so restrains an individual's liberty that it renders him unable to care for himself, and at the same time fails to provide for his basic human needs — e.g., food, clothing, shelter, medical care, and reasonable safety — it transgresses the substantive limits on state action set by the Eighth Amendment and the Due Process Clause. See Estelle v. Gamble, 429 U.S. 97 (1976); Youngberg v. Romeo, 457 U.S. 307 (1982). The affirmative duty to protect arises not from the State's knowledge of the individual's predicament or from its expressions of intent to help him, but from the limitation which it has imposed on his freedom to act on his own behalf. In the substantive due process analysis, it is the State's affirmative act of restraining the individual's freedom to act on his own behalf — through incarceration, institutionalization, or other similar restraint of personal liberty — which is the "deprivation of liberty" triggering the protections of the Due Process Clause, not its failure to act to protect his liberty interests against harms inflicted by other means.

The *Estelle-Youngberg* analysis simply has no applicability in the present case. Petitioners concede that the harms Joshua suffered did not occur while he was in the State's custody, but while he was in the custody of his natural father, who was in no sense a state actor. While the State may have been aware of the dangers that Joshua faced in the free world, it played no part in their creation, nor did it do anything to render him any more vulnerable to them. That the State once took temporary custody of Joshua does not alter the analysis, for when it returned him to his father's custody, it placed him in no worse position than that in which he would have been had it not acted at all; the State does not become the permanent guarantor of an individual's safety by having once offered him shelter. Under these circumstances, the State had no constitutional duty to protect Joshua. . . .

BRENNAN, J., joined by Marshall and Blackmun, JJ., dissenting.

. . . It may well be . . . that the Due Process Clause as construed by our prior cases creates no general right to basic government services. That, however, is not the question presented here. . . .

The Court's baseline is the absence of positive rights in the Constitution and a concomitant suspicion of any claim that seems to depend on such rights. From this perspective, the DeShaneys' claim is first and foremost about inaction (the failure, here, of respondents to take steps to protect Joshua), and only tangentially about action (the establishment of a state program specifically designed to help children like Joshua). And from this perspective, holding these Wisconsin officials liable — where the only difference between this case and one involving a general claim to protective services is Wisconsin's establishment and operation of a program to protect children — would seem to punish an effort that we should seek to promote.

I would begin from the opposite direction. I would focus first on the action that Wisconsin *has* taken with respect to Joshua and children like him, rather than on the action that the State failed to take. Such a method is not new to this Court. Both *Estelle* and *Youngberg* began by emphasizing that the States had confined J.W. Gamble to prison and Nicholas Romeo to a psychiatric hospital. This initial action rendered these people helpless to help themselves or to seek help from persons unconnected to the government. Cases from the lower courts also recognize that a State's actions can be decisive in assessing the constitutional significance of subsequent inaction. . . .

Because of the Court's initial fixation on the general principle that the Constitution does not establish positive rights, it is unable to appreciate our recognition in *Estelle* and *Youngberg* that this principle does not hold true in all circumstances. . . . In addition, the Court's exclusive attention to State-imposed restraints of "the individual's freedom to act on his own behalf" suggests that it was the State that rendered Romeo unable to care for himself, whereas in fact — with an I.Q. of between 8 and 10, and the mental capacity of an 18-month-old child — he had been quite incapable of taking care of himself long before the State stepped into his life. Thus, the fact of hospitalization was critical in *Youngberg* not because it rendered Romeo helpless to help himself, but because it separated him from other sources of aid that, we held, the State was obligated to replace. Unlike the Court, therefore, I am unable to see in *Youngberg* a neat and decisive divide between action and inaction.

. . . Thus, I would read *Youngberg* and *Estelle* to stand for the much more generous proposition that, if a State cuts off private sources of aid and then refuses aid itself, it cannot wash its hands of the harm that results from its inaction. . . .

[After discussing the complex structure established by Wisconsin in regard to child abuse, Justice Brennan wrote:] In these circumstances, a private person, or even a person working in a government agency other than DSS, would doubtless feel that her job was done as soon as she had reported her suspicions of child abuse to DSS. Through its child-welfare program, in other words, the State of Wisconsin has relieved ordinary citizens and governmental bodies other than the Department of any sense of obligation to do anything more than report their suspicions of child abuse to DSS. If DSS ignores or dismisses these suspicions, no one will step in to fill the gap. . . . Conceivably, then, children like Joshua are made worse off by the existence of this program when the persons and entities charged with carrying it out fail to do their jobs.

It simply belies reality, therefore, to contend that the State "stood by and did nothing" with respect to Joshua. Through its child-protection program, the State actively intervened in Joshua's life and, by virtue of this intervention, acquired ever more certain knowledge that Joshua was in grave danger. . . .

My disagreement with the Court arises from its failure to see that inaction can be every bit as abusive of power as action, that oppression can result when a State undertakes a vital duty and then ignores it. Today's opinion construes the Due Process Clause to permit a State to displace private sources of protection and then, at the critical moment, to shrug its shoulders and turn away from the harm that it has promised to try to prevent. Because I cannot agree that our Constitution is indifferent to such indifference, I respectfully dissent.

BLACKMUN, J., dissenting:

. . . Like the antebellum judges who denied relief to fugitive slaves, the Court today claims that its decision, however harsh, is compelled by existing legal doctrine. On the contrary, the question presented by this case is an open one, and our Fourteenth Amendment precedents may be read more broadly or narrowly depending upon how one chooses to read them. Faced with the choice, I would adopt a "sympathetic" reading, one that comports with dictates of fundamental justice and recognizes that compassion need not be exiled from the province of judging. . . .

Discussion

1. Chief Justice Rehnquist's analysis can be paraphrased as follows: The Constitution prohibits the state from depriving individuals, without due process of law, of whatever preexisting rights to life, liberty, or property they might have; but it does not require the State to *provide* anyone with resources, save for such "special circumstances" as where it confines individuals in a way that prevents them from being responsible for their own welfare.

2. United States Census figures indicate that in 1986, 22.1 percent of all children under the age of five were living in conditions of poverty.[4] In 1985 more than 2 million children lived in families with incomes less than one-half the poverty level, an increase of almost 800,000 since 1979.[5] These children face an increased risk of suffering from ills ranging from malnutrition to learning disabilities. How is the situation of these 2 million children, who might claim that their lives are blighted by a lack of social services beyond what the state is willing to provide, different from Joshua's situation?

3. Justice Brennan suggests that the state agency's intervention in situations like Joshua's may obviate others' concern for his welfare that would otherwise exist. Does this entail a constitutional requirement that once a State offers *any* services to a person, it must provide some minimal threshold that is at least as high as the putative level of support that private contributors might have been expected to give in the absence of any state action?

4. *The Constitution and "minimum needs."* Consider the following provisions from the Universal Declaration of Human Rights, adopted by the General Assembly of the United Nations on December 10, 1948:[6]

> *Article 23*
>
> 1. Everyone has the right to work, to free choice of employment, [and] to just and favourable conditions of work. . . .
>
> 3. Everyone who works has the right to just and favourable remuneration ensuring for himself and his family an existence worthy of human dignity, and supplemented, if necessary, by other means of social protection. . . .
>
> *Article 25*
>
> 1. Everyone has the right to a standard of living adequate for the health and well-being of himself and of his family, including food, clothing, housing and medical care and necessary social services, and the right to security in the event of unemployment, sickness, disability, widowhood, old age or other lack of livelihood in circumstances beyond his control.
>
> 2. Motherhood and childhood are entitled to special care and assistance. All children, whether born in or out of wedlock, shall enjoy the same social protection.

4. U.S. Bureau of the Census, Current Population Reports, Series P-60, No. 157, Money Income and Poverty Status of Families and Persons in the United States 1986 (Advance Data from the March 1987 Current Population Survey), Table 18, p.30.

5. Id., No. 158, Characteristics of the Population Below the Poverty Level: 1985, table 4, pp. 21-22; corresponding volume for 1979, table prepared by Children's Defense Fund.

6. See Human Rights: A Compilation of International Instruments 1-3 (1983).

Article 26

Everyone has the right to education. . . .

On whom might these provisions impose obligations? If they were a part of our Constitution, would they compel a ruling in Joshua's favor?

Of course, the United States Constitution does not contain these provisions. Might any of its other provisions create such rights?

Professor Frank Michelman has presented the most systematic and comprehensive argument that the Constitution guarantees some level of "minimum protection" against the effects of poverty.[7] Professor Michelman starts from the premise that a pricing system is both constitutional and desirable: "We usually regard it as both the fairest and most efficient arrangement to require each consumer to pay the full market price of what he consumes, limiting his consumption to what his income permits." However, he notes that cases such as Harper v. Virginia Board of Elections, p.1054 supra, held that a state may not charge a user fee for access to certain rights or privileges (in that case, access to the ballot). Placing this and other cases to be discussed below within the context of the ideas of political philosopher John Rawls, Michelman argues that even within a market economy that tolerates a measure of income and resource inequality, persons are both morally and constitutionally entitled to "minimum protection against economic hazard":

> As applied to economic hazards, a claim to "minimum protection" would mean that persons are entitled to have certain wants satisfied — certain existing needs filled — by government, free of any direct charge over and above the obligation to pay general taxes. . . .
>
> [It might be argued] that justice is satisfied as long as the prevailing social and economic institutions afford every one a fair opportunity to derive an income sufficient over time to provide for whatever needs are considered "basic." [But] the argument of minimum protection as applied to specific needs and occasions . . . depend[s] on the proposition that justice requires *more* than a fair opportunity to realize an income which can cover these needs or insure against them — requires . . . absolute assurance that they will be met when and as felt, free of any remote[a] contingencies pertaining to effort, thrift or foresight.
>
> We might take our clue from Professor Rawls' idea of "justice as fairness." Rawls grants that social institutions and practices may be just, even though they produce unequal incomes and accumulations. Yet for an unequal system to be just, it must be the case that a rational person, hypothetically ignorant of what particular place in society awaits him, would find the inequalities acceptable. . . .
>
> The identity of "just wants" would then be determined according to a judgment arrived at through the following process of reasoning. Assume that a man has no idea what his social and economic station in a predominantly competitive society is to be and that he fully recognizes the role of income incentives and free markets in maximizing social productivity. Will he nevertheless wish to have each person insured against the risk that certain needs will remain unfulfilled as and when they

7. See On Protecting the Poor Through the Fourteenth Amendment, 83 Harv. L. Rev. 7 (1969). For a response, see Ralph Winter, Poverty, Economic Equality, and the Equal Protection Clause, 1972 Sup. Ct. Rev. 41.

a. "Remote" is intended to save the possibility that a person might deliberately and effectively waive his claims by informed and proximate choice. Such choice could, conceivably, assume a variety of forms — monastic vows, perhaps, or deliberate waste of publicly provided food or shelter.

accrue — and what specific risks of that sort, if any, will he say should be insured against?[b] Might he, for example, say that insofar as the society provides for "democratic" political participation through such means as voting and standing for office, access to these activities should never be blocked by economic vicissitude? Or that persons must at all times be assured of effective access to some impartial and remedially competent forum for the peaceful settlement of bona fide legal disputes? Or that everyone at all times must be assured of facilities for a modicum of privacy, intimacy, confidentiality, self-expression? Or that each child must be guaranteed the means of developing his competence, self-knowledge, and tastes for living? . . .

If the relevant insight concerning payment requirements must be given a doctrinal form of statement, the appropriate construction would seem to be something like: "It is no justification for deprivation of a fundamental right (i.e., involuntary nonfulfillment of a just want) that the deprivation results from a general practice of requiring persons to pay for what they get." Such a construction focuses the inquiry on the crucial variable — the nature and quality of the deprivation — and thereby avoids the distractions, false stirring of hopes, and tunneling of vision which results from a rhetorical emphasis on acts of "discrimination" that consist of nothing more than charging a price.

Michelman indicated that the notion of "minimum protection" is more readily assimilated to the due process clause than to the equal protection clause, for it focuses not on relative but on absolute deprivation: " 'Minimum protection' radar scans, not for inequalities, but for instances in which persons have important needs or interests which they are prevented from satisfying because of traits or predicaments not adopted by free and proximate choice." But there are reasons why a court might choose to clothe a minimum protection decision "in the verbiage of inequality and discrimination." The language of the due process clause requires that the state act to deprive a person of property, something not textually mandated by the equal protection clause. Moreover, an equal protection standard provides some guidance as to how much protection must be furnished by looking to the benefits enjoyed by others in society. Finally,

it must be noted that while the idea of "just wants" or "severe deprivations" expresses an ethical precept distinct from that of "equality," detecting a failure to provide the required minimum may nonetheless depend in part upon the detection of inequalities; and elimination or reduction of inequality may be entailed in rectifying such a failure, insofar as the just minimum is understood to be a function (in part) of the existing maximum. Such an understanding could grow out of a residue of indis-

b. Here we may briefly note some possible reasons for insisting on such assurances, over and above insistence on a system of economic rewards and transfers which would tend generally to assure each household head of an income adequate to his household's important needs. Assurances may be desired against the risk that one — or the family head upon whom one is dependent — will not measure up to generally reasonable minimum standards of active participation in the economy, or against the risk that a generally fair system of judging the quality of one's participation, or the extenuating force of one's disabilities, will in a particular case miscarry. More generally, assurance may be desired against the chance that the sincerest attempts to devise and maintain a generally fair system of rewards and transfers will nevertheless leave some persons on some occasions desperately unprovisioned. Most generally, flat assurances concerning just wants may upon reflection seem a desirable way of simplifying (and thus cheapening) the continuing task of adjustment of the reward/transfer system, either because this method obviates any need to place a dollar value from time to time on the whole catalogue of just wants (a composite we may call the just minimum) or because it assures society that transferred purchasing power will not be dissipated on other wants, leaving just wants unfulfilled and, accordingly, an unsatisfied claim still outstanding. The latter point, I suspect, will eventually turn out to be the key to the argument. It provides a reason why persons in a just system would agree to receive their guaranteed minimum in kind rather than in cash.

> soluble interpenetration of the felt evils of relative deprivation and poignant hardship. Thus if the extent of society's obligation to tax itself for support of the needy depends in part upon its overall level of affluence, widening inequalities become increasingly suggestive of failure to furnish the just minimum. Or again, insofar as the components of the required (or "a decent") minimum are affected by what others have — by prevailing tastes and expectations, or by emulation — then extremity of inequality is suggestive. Standing on quite different ground is the relevance of what others have when the want in question is deemed specially significant — as education, for example, might be — because of its importance for success in competitive activities.

5. *Minimum needs rejected.* The year following Professor Michelman's article, Dandridge v. Williams, 397 U.S. 471 (1970), upheld a provision of Maryland's Aid to Families with Dependent Children that limited the monthly grant to any one family to $250, regardless of its size or computed need. As a result, individual members of a large family received less per capita than the members of smaller families, and less per capita than the state itself recognized as the minimum required for subsistence. Justice Stewart, writing for the majority, found that Maryland's program passed muster under the minimum rationality standard of the equal protection clause. "To be sure," he conceded, cases decided under that standard "have in the main involved state regulation of business or industry. The administration of public welfare assistance, by contrast, involves the most basic economic needs of impoverished human beings. We recognize the dramatically real factual differences between [those] cases and this one, but we can find no basis for applying a different constitutional standard. . . ."

In dissent, Justice Marshall, joined by Justice Brennan, objected that the Court should not apply the "rational basis test," normally reserved for business regulation, in a case involving "the literally vital interests of a powerless minority — poor families without breadwinners."

Similarly, in Lindsey v. Normet, 405 U.S. 56 (1972), the Court rejected the claim that the "need for decent shelter" rose to the level of a fundamental interest that would call for heightened scrutiny of a summary "forcible entry and wrongful detainer" procedure for the eviction of tenants after alleged nonpayment of rent. Justice White, writing for the Court, stated:

> We do not denigrate the importance of decent, safe, and sanitary housing. But the Constitution does not provide judicial remedies for every social and economic ill. We are unable to perceive in that document any constitutional guarantee of access to dwellings of a particular quality. . . . Absent constitutional mandate, the assurance of adequate housing and the definition of landlord-tenant relationships are legislative, not judicial, functions.

To the extent that there are exceptions to the cases sketched above, they arise in the context of indigents faced with defending themselves against criminal charges or seeking divorces. These cases are examined later in this chapter.

Note: Slavery, Childhood, and Joshua DeShaney

All of the questions above assume that *DeShaney* and the questions it raises are best discussed in terms of the Fourteenth Amendment. However, Professors

Akhil Reed Amar and Daniel Widawsky, in A Thirteenth Amendment Response to *DeShaney*, 105 Harv. L. Rev. — (1992), have suggested that *DeShaney* should have been argued as a Thirteenth Amendment case and, as such, decided in DeShaney's favor. "Indisputably, the amendment was designed to end slavery in America — of children as well as adults." Amar and Widawsky point out that no one doubted that "[a] mulatto slave child sired by a white slaveowner" was freed by the amendment. "Nor did the amendment protect only those slaves with some biological roots in America, for it abolished the enslavement of all persons, whatever their race or national origin." As the Court wrote in the Slaughter-House Cases, "while negro slavery alone was in the mind of the Congress which proposed the thirteenth article, it forbids any other kind of slavery, now or hereafter." Thus, the Court indicated that "Mexican peonage" or "the Chinese coolie labor system" would be made equally "void" under the amendment. "Finally," they write, "the amendment guaranteed personal freedom in all respects, not only freedom from forced labor for the master's economic enrichment: The amendment speaks to the enslavement of a person, whether the ultimate motive for such domination is greed or sadism or power lust." Thus, they conclude, the amendment "extends its affirmative protection to a slave even if (1) the slave is a child, (2) the slave child is the offspring of the master, (3) the slave child has no African roots, and (4) the slave child is not used to maximize the master's financial profit. One such slave child was Joshua DeShaney."

One question posed by Amar's and Widawsky's analysis, of course, is precisely what constitutes "involuntary servitude." The answer, they suggest, is the "unconstrained power" of one person over another, so that one cannot meaningfully find "consent" to be present in any given relationship. For the state to fail to intervene in a situation where a parent is known to be abusing a child is, they argue, to place the child in a condition of just such "involuntary servitude" relative to the parent.

One virtue of a Thirteenth Amendment analysis, according to Amar and Widawsky, is that it answers the slippery-slope fears expressed by the majority about the possibility of crime victims suing the government for inadequate police protection or of persons mired in poverty claiming that the state must supply adequate social services to rectify the situation. "Under the Thirteenth Amendment, a State has an obligation *only* in cases of slavery or involuntary servitude rather than in every case of interpersonal violence" (emphasis added).

Putting to one side the probability of the current Supreme Court's accepting this analysis, do *you* find it preferable to the Fourteenth Amendment claim alleged by DeShaney? More particularly, if you are persuaded by the majority's Fourteenth Amendment analysis would you change your mind upon being presented with Amar's and Widawsky's argument?

II. Constitutional Limitations in the Administration of a Welfare State

Regardless of whether a welfare state is constitutionally required, it is beyond doubt that our nation has witnessed the development of at least a modified welfare state in the twentieth century, as both state and national governments increasingly provide certain goods and services to members of society who are unable to purchase them on the private market. The "welfare state" is distinct from the "regulatory state" whose emergence was traced in Chapter 5. The regulatory state, characterized by statutory regulation of wages and hours, labor-management relations, the securities market, and the like, emerged in response to skepticism about the fairness of the unimpeded operations of the market. The government thus sought to redistribute power by conferring specific legal rights upon more vulnerable groups to counter the private power of those who would prevail in the absence of regulation. Much of twentieth-century constitutional law, immediately following 1937, involved the validation of the regulatory state within the constraints of established constitutional doctrine.

Most of the New Deal legislation, however, required astonishingly little increase in the direct expenditures of state funds. Though the social goal may have been redistribution of income, legislators chose to effectuate this goal by simply rearranging the legal relations between private actors. The state, for example, did not itself finance higher wages or increased benefits for union members, but rather imposed the burden on private employers. The principal governmental expenditures of many of these statutory schemes were the quite modest costs of administration and enforcement. However important to the modern regulatory state the National Labor Relations Board or Securities and Exchange Commission may be, they do not make extraordinary demands on the federal budget.

A welfare state, in contrast to a regulatory state, plays a more active role in the redistribution of resources. Beyond merely shifting the boundaries of private legal relations, the welfare state directly allocates resources to a discrete group of individuals. Examples are legion, ranging from grants to college students to food stamps to subsidies to the blind. Laws of these kinds lead to significant increases in governmental budgets.

Although the origins of this transformation can be found in the New Deal and such programs as Social Security, the number of programs and level of expenditures increased dramatically in the 1960s. Between 1964 and 1966 alone Congress passed the Economic Opportunity Act, the Demonstration Cities and Metropolitan Development Act, the Older Americans Act, the Food Stamp Act, and established the basic medical coverage programs of Medicare and Medicaid.[8] These initiatives, identified with President Lyndon Johnson's "Great Society," were substantially consolidated and in some instances expanded by the succeeding administration of President Richard Nixon. Even the comparatively minimalist welfare program of the Reagan Administration only slowed down, rather than reversed, the developments of the 1960s and '70s.

Governmental expenditure figures provide vivid confirmation of the changing political reality. Between 1927 and 1932, when the consequences of the Great Depression ravaged the nation, "public welfare" expenditures at all levels of government increased from only $161 million to $445 million. By 1936 they had climbed to nearly $1 billion. In 1960, the total expenditures were approximately $4.5 billion. By 1970 they reached approximately $17.5 billion.[9]

8. See Gilbert, supra note 2, at vii.

9. See Series Y 533-566, Federal, State, and Local Government Expenditures, by Function: 1902 to 1970, Historical Statistics of the United States, Colonial Times to 1970, Part 2, p.1120 (1975).

At the national level, only in 1962 did the federal budget first cross the $100 billion barrier. The previous high had been in 1945, the last year of World War II, when the budget was $95 billion. By 1975 the total outlays were $326 billion, and by 1978 they reached $450 billion.[10] Inflation, of course, makes the interpretation of these numbers somewhat difficult. Consider, then, that in constant 1972 prices, the nondefense budget went from $32.1 billion in 1960 to $60.9 billion in 1969 to $125 billion in 1978.[11]

More illuminating are functional budgets. Thus federal spending on elementary and secondary education went from $417 million in 1961 to $3.5 billion in 1972 and $6.5 billion in 1979. Health care services climbed from approximately $157 million in 1961 to $4.9 billion in 1966 (shortly after the passage of the Medicare legislation in 1965), to $15 billion in 1971 and $48.5 billion in 1979. Public assistance payments rose from $2.4 billion in 1961 to $5.1 billion in 1970, and $28.3 billion in 1979.[12]

Although some of this increased federal spending substitutes for expenditures previously made by states, state expenditures have also increased significantly over the past several decades.[13]

The rise of the welfare state has brought to center stage a number of important constitutional dilemmas, to which we now turn. The first set of materials concern problems that arise in the direct administration of the benefits associated with the modern welfare state.

III. The Procedural Due Process Protection of Entitlements and Other Nontraditional Property and Liberty Interests: The Basic Doctrine

The Constitution provides that a person may not be deprived of "liberty" or "property" without due process of law, or, put another way, that government may not punish you or take your property until after a hearing at which it has been determined that, as a matter of fact and law, the deprivation is authorized by an applicable statute or regulation.

What implications does this requirement have for constitutional doctrine in the welfare state? In a seminal 1964 article, Charles Reich argued that the subsi-

10. See The United States Budget in Brief, Fiscal Year 1980 (Washington: GPO, 1980), Table 8, Budget receipts and outlays, 1789-1982, p.85.

11. Id., Table 4, Composition of Budget Outlays in Current and Constant (Fiscal Year 1972) Prices: 1958-1982.

12. US Budget in Brief, FY 1972, Budget Outlays by Subfunction, 1961-1972, p.64; US Budget in Brief, Budget Outlays by Function and Subfunction: 1970-82, p.77. Some of the specific yearly figures do not agree in the two tables, but the differences are not of sufficient magnitude to affect the central point. In 1988, Medicare expenditures alone were $78.9 billion, and almost $32 billion was spent on "[e]ducation, training, employment, and social services." See Budget of the United States Government, Fiscal Year 1990 10-10 (Table 3. Outlays by Function, 1988-94).

13. See, e.g., Series Y 736-782, State Government Expenditure, by Character and Object, by Function, and State Government Debt: 1902 to 1970, Historical Statistics . . . , Part 2, pp. 1130-1131 (1975). "Public welfare" spending went from $2.221 billion in 1960 to $8.203 billion in 1970. Similar spending by local governments also shows significant increase, going from $2.183 billion in 1960 to $6.477 billion in 1970. See id., Series Y 817-848. Local Government Expenditure, by Function: 1902 to 1970.

dies and licenses characteristic of the welfare state constituted "the new property" and deserved some of the constitutional protections granted to traditional property. Reich wrote that "[r]egulation of [traditional] property has been limited, not because society had no interest in property, but because it was in the interest of society that property be free."[14] Private property, according to Reich, provided the individual some space for a private life away from, and sometimes in opposition to, the desires of the state. Those dependent on the "new property," he argued, require constitutional protection lest their dependence on governmental largesse leave them at the mercy of the state.

GOLDBERG v. KELLY

397 U.S. 254 (1970)

Appeal from the United States District Court for the Southern District of New York

BRENNAN, J.

The question for decision is whether a State that terminates public assistance payments to a particular recipient without affording him the opportunity for an evidentiary hearing prior to termination denies the recipient procedural due process in violation of the Due Process Clause of the Fourteenth Amendment.

This action was brought in the District Court for the Southern District of New York by residents of New York City receiving financial aid under the federally assisted program of Aid to Families with Dependent Children (AFDC) or under New York State's general Home Relief program. Their complaint alleged that the New York State and New York City officials administering these programs terminated, or were about to terminate, such aid without prior notice and hearing, thereby denying them due process of law. At the time the suits were filed there was no requirement of prior notice or hearing of any kind before termination of financial aid. . . .

I

The constitutional issue to be decided, therefore, is the narrow one whether the Due Process Clause requires that the recipient be afforded an evidentiary hearing *before* the termination of benefits. . . .

Appellant does not contend that procedural due process is not applicable to the termination of welfare benefits. Such benefits are a matter of statutory entitlement for persons qualified to receive them.[a] Their termination involves state

14. Charles A. Reich, The New Property, 73 Yale L.J. 733, 779 (1964).

a. It may be realistic today to regard welfare entitlements as more like "property" than a "gratuity." Much of the existing wealth in this country takes the form of rights that do not fall within traditional common-law concepts of property. It has been aptly noted that

> [s]ociety today is built around entitlement. The automobile dealer has his franchise, the doctor and lawyer their professional licenses, the worker his union membership, contract, and pension rights, the executive his contract and stock options; all are devices to aid security and independence. Many of the most important of these entitlements now flow from government: subsidies to farmers and businessmen, routes for airlines and channels for television stations; long term contracts for defense, space, and education; social security pensions for individuals. Such sources of security, whether private or public, are no longer regarded as luxuries or gratuities: to the recipients they are essentials, fully deserved, and in no sense a form of charity. It

action that adjudicates important rights. The constitutional challenge cannot be answered by an argument that public assistance benefits are "a 'privilege' and not a 'right.'" Shapiro v. Thompson, 394 U.S. 618 (1969). Relevant constitutional restraints apply as much to the withdrawal of public assistance benefits as to disqualification for unemployment compensation, Sherbert v. Verner, 374 U.S. 398 (1963); or to denial of a tax exemption, Speiser v. Randall, 357 U.S. 513 (1958); or to discharge from public employment, Slochower v. Board of Higher Education, 350 U.S. 551 (1956).[b] The extent to which procedural due process must be afforded the recipient is influenced by the extent to which he may be "condemned to suffer grievous loss," Joint Anti-Fascist Refugee Committee v. McGrath, 341 U.S. 123, 168 (1951) (Frankfurter, J., concurring), and depends upon whether the recipient's interest in avoiding that loss outweighs the governmental interest in summary adjudication. Accordingly, as we said in Cafeteria & Restaurant Workers Union v. McElroy, 367 U.S. 886, 895 (1961), "consideration of what procedures due process may require under any given set of circumstances must begin with a determination of the precise nature of the government function involved as well as of the private interest that has been affected by governmental action." See also Hannah v. Larche, 363 U.S. 420, 440, 442 (1960).

It is true, of course, that some governmental benefits may be administratively terminated without affording the recipient a pre-termination evidentiary hearing.[c] But we agree with the District Court that when welfare is discontinued, only a pre-termination evidentiary hearing provides the recipient with procedural due process. For qualified recipients, welfare provides the means to obtain essential food, clothing, housing, and medical care. Thus the crucial factor in this context — a factor not present in the case of the blacklisted government contractor, the discharged government employee, the taxpayer denied a tax exemption, or virtually anyone else whose governmental entitlements are ended — is that termination of aid pending resolution of a controversy over eligibility may deprive an *eligible* recipient of the very means by which to live while he waits. Since he lacks independent resources, his situation becomes immediately desperate. His need to concentrate upon finding the means for daily subsistence, in turn, ad-

---

> is only the poor whose entitlements, although recognized by public policy, have not been effectively enforced.

Reich, Individual Rights and Social Welfare: The Emerging Legal Issues, 74 Yale L.J. 1245, 1255 (1965). See also Reich, The New Property, 73 Yale L.J. 733 (1964).

b. See also Goldsmith v. United States Board of Tax Appeals, 270 U.S. 117 (1926) (right of a certified public accountant to practice before the Board of Tax Appeals); Hornsby v. Allen, 326 F.2d 605 (5th Cir. 1964) (right to obtain a retail liquor store license); Dixon v. Alabama State Board of Education, 294 F.2d 150 (5th Cir. 1961) (right to attend a public college).

c. One Court of Appeals has stated: "In a wide variety of situations, it has long been recognized that where harm to the public is threatened, and the private interest infringed is reasonably deemed to be of less importance, an official body can take summary action pending a later hearing." R.A. Holman & Co. v. SEC, 112 U.S. App. D.C. 43, 47, 299 F.2d 127, 131 (1962) (suspension of exemption from stock registration requirement). See also, for example, Ewing v. Mytinger & Casselberry, Inc., 339 U.S. 594 (1950) (seizure of mislabeled vitamin product); North American Cold Storage Co. v. Chicago, 211 U.S. 306 (1908) (seizure of food not fit for human use); Yakus v. United States, 321 U.S. 414 (1944) (adoption of wartime price regulations); Gonzalez v. Freeman, 118 U.S. App. D.C. 180, 334 F.2d 570 (1964) (disqualification of a contractor to do business with the Government). In Cafeteria & Restaurant Workers Union v. McElroy, supra, summary dismissal of a public employee was upheld because "[i]n [its] proprietary military capacity, the Federal Government . . . has traditionally exercised unfettered control," and because the case involved the Government's "dispatch of its own internal affairs."

versely affects his ability to seek redress from the welfare bureaucracy. . . . The same governmental interests that counsel the provision of welfare, counsel as well its uninterrupted provision to those eligible to receive it; pre-termination evidentiary hearings are indispensable to that end.

Appellant does not challenge the force of these considerations but argues that they are outweighed by countervailing governmental interests in conserving fiscal and administrative resources. These interests, the argument goes, justify the delay of any evidentiary hearing until after discontinuance of the grants. Summary adjudication protects the public fisc by stopping payments promptly upon discovery of reason to believe that a recipient is no longer eligible. Since most terminations are accepted without challenge, summary adjudication also conserves both the fisc and administrative time and energy by reducing the number of evidentiary hearings actually held.

We agree with the District Court, however, that these governmental interests are not overriding in the welfare context. The requirement of a prior hearing doubtless involves some greater expense, and the benefits paid to ineligible recipients pending decision at the hearing probably cannot be recouped, since these recipients are likely to be judgment-proof. But the State is not without weapons to minimize these increased costs. Much of the drain on fiscal and administrative resources can be reduced by developing procedures for prompt pre-termination hearings and by skillful use of personnel and facilities. . . .

II

We also agree with the District Court, however, that the pre-termination hearing need not take the form of a judicial or quasi-judicial trial. We bear in mind that the statutory "fair hearing" will provide the recipient with a full administrative review. Accordingly, the pre-termination hearing has one function only: to produce an initial determination of the validity of the welfare department's grounds for discontinuance of payments in order to protect a recipient against an erroneous termination of his benefits. Thus, a complete record and a comprehensive opinion, which would serve primarily to facilitate judicial review and to guide future decisions, need not be provided at the pre-termination stage. We recognize, too, that both welfare authorities and recipients have an interest in relatively speedy resolution of questions of eligibility, that they are used to dealing with one another informally, and that some welfare departments have very burdensome caseloads. These considerations justify the limitation of the pre-termination hearing to minimum procedural safeguards, adapted to the particular characteristics of welfare recipients, and to the limited nature of the controversies to be resolved. We wish to add that we, no less than the dissenters, recognize the importance of not imposing upon the States or the Federal Government in this developing field of law any procedural requirements beyond those demanded by rudimentary due process.

"The fundamental requisite of due process of law is the opportunity to be heard." Grannis v. Ordean, 234 U.S. 385 (1914). The hearing must be "at a meaningful time and in a meaningful manner." Armstrong v. Manzo, 380 U.S. 545 (1965). In the present context these principles require that a recipient have timely and adequate notice detailing the reasons for a proposed termination, and an effective opportunity to defend by confronting any adverse witnesses and by presenting his own arguments and evidence orally. These rights are important in cases such as those before us, where recipients have challenged proposed terminations as resting on incorrect or misleading factual premises or on misapplication of rules or policies to the facts of particular cases. . . .

The opportunity to be heard must be tailored to the capacities and circumstances of those who are to be heard. It is not enough that a welfare recipient may present his position to the decision maker in writing or secondhand through his caseworker. Written submissions are an unrealistic option for most recipients, who lack the educational attainment necessary to write effectively and who cannot obtain professional assistance. Moreover, written submissions do not afford the flexibility of oral presentations; they do not permit the recipient to mold his argument to the issues the decision maker appears to regard as important. Particularly where credibility and veracity are at issue, as they must be in many termination proceedings, written submissions are a wholly unsatisfactory basis for decision. The second-hand presentation to the decisionmaker by the caseworker has its own deficiencies; since the caseworker usually gathers the facts upon which the charge of ineligibility rests, the presentation of the recipient's side of the controversy cannot safely be left to him. Therefore a recipient must be allowed to state his position orally. . . .

In almost every setting where important decisions turn on questions of fact, due process requires an opportunity to confront and cross-examine adverse witnesses. What we said in Greene v. McElroy, 360 U.S. 474 (1959), is particularly pertinent here:

> Certain principles have remained relatively immutable in our jurisprudence. One of these is that where governmental action seriously injures an individual, and the reasonableness of the action depends on fact findings, the evidence used to prove the Government's case must be disclosed to the individual so that he has an opportunity to show that it is untrue. While this is important in the case of documentary evidence, it is even more important where the evidence consists of the testimony of individuals whose memory might be faulty or who, in fact, might be perjurers or persons motivated by malice, vindictiveness, intolerance, prejudice, or jealousy . . .

Welfare recipients must therefore be given an opportunity to confront and cross-examine the witnesses relied on by the department.

"The right to be heard would be, in many cases, of little avail if it did not comprehend the right to be heard by counsel." Powell v. Alabama, 287 U.S. 45, 68-69 (1932). We do not say that counsel must be provided at the pre-termination hearing, but only that the recipient must be allowed to retain an attorney if he so desires. Counsel can help delineate the issues, present the factual contentions in an orderly manner, conduct cross-examination, and generally safeguard the interests of the recipient. We do not anticipate that this assistance will unduly prolong or otherwise encumber the hearing. . . .

Finally, the decisionmaker's conclusion as to a recipient's eligibility must rest solely on the legal rules and evidence adduced at the hearing. Ohio Bell Tel. Co. v. PUC, 301 U.S. 292 (1937); United States v. Abilene & S.R. Co., 265 U.S. 274, 288-289 (1924). To demonstrate compliance with this elementary requirement, the decision maker should state the reasons for his determination and indicate the evidence he relied on, cf. Wichita R. & Light Co. v. PUC, 260 U.S. 48, 57-59

(1922), though his statement need not amount to a full opinion or even formal findings of fact and conclusions of law. And, of course, an impartial decision maker is essential. Cf. In re Murchison, 349 U.S. 133 (1955); Wong Yang Sung v. McGrath, 339 U.S. 33, 45-46 (1950). We agree with the District Court that prior involvement in some aspects of a case will not necessarily bar a welfare official from acting as a decision maker. He should not, however, have participated in making the determination under review.

BLACK, J., dissenting. . . .

The more than a million names on the relief rolls in New York, and the more than nine million names on the rolls of all the 50 States were not put there at random. The names are there because state welfare officials believed that those people were eligible for assistance. Probably in the officials' haste to make out the lists many names were put there erroneously in order to alleviate immediate suffering, and undoubtedly some people are drawing relief who are not entitled under the law to do so. Doubtless some draw relief checks from time to time who know they are not eligible, either because they are not actually in need or for some other reason. Many of those who thus draw undeserved gratuities are without sufficient property to enable the government to collect back from them any money they wrongfully receive. But the Court today holds that it would violate the Due Process Clause of the Fourteenth Amendment to stop paying those people weekly or monthly allowances unless the government first affords them a full "evidentiary hearing" even though welfare officials are persuaded that the recipients are not rightfully entitled to receive a penny under the law. In other words, although some recipients might be on the lists for payment wholly because of deliberate fraud on their part, the Court holds that the government is helpless and must continue, until after an evidentiary hearing, to pay money that it does not owe, never has owed, and never could owe. I do not believe there is any provision in our Constitution that should thus paralyze the government's efforts to protect itself against making payments to people who are not entitled to them.

. . . The Court, however, relies upon the Fourteenth Amendment and in effect says that failure of the government to pay a promised charitable instalment to an individual deprives that individual of *his own property,* in violation of the Due Process Clause of the Fourteenth Amendment. It somewhat strains credulity to say that the government's promise of charity to an individual is property belonging to that individual when the government denies that the individual is honestly entitled to receive such a payment. . . . Once the verbiage is pared away it is obvious that this Court today adopts the views of the District Court "that to cut off a welfare recipient in the face of . . . 'brutal need' without a prior hearing of some sort is unconscionable," and therefore, says the Court, unconstitutional. The majority reaches this result by a process of weighing "the recipient's interest in avoiding" the termination of welfare benefits against "the governmental interest in summary adjudication." Today's balancing act requires a "pre-termination evidentiary hearing," yet there is nothing that indicates what tomorrow's balance will be. Although the majority attempts to bolster its decision with limited quotations from prior cases, it is obvious that today's result does not depend on the language of the Constitution itself or the principles of other decisions, but solely on the collective judgment of the majority as to what would be a fair and humane procedure in this case.

This decision is thus only another variant of the view often expressed by some members of this Court that the Due Process Clause forbids any conduct that a majority of the Court believes "unfair," "indecent," or "shocking to their consciences." See, e.g., Rochin v. California, 342 U.S. 165, 172 (1952). Neither these words nor any like them appear anywhere in the Due Process Clause. If they did, they would leave the majority of Justices free to hold any conduct unconstitutional that they should conclude on their own to be unfair or shocking to them.[a] Had the drafters of the Due Process Clause meant to leave judges such ambulatory power to declare laws unconstitutional, the chief value of a written constitution, as the Founders saw it, would have been lost. In fact, if that view of due process is correct, the Due Process Clause could easily swallow up all other parts of the Constitution. And truly the Constitution would always be "what the judges say it is" at a given moment, not what the Founders wrote into the document.[b] A written constitution, designed to guarantee protection against governmental abuses, including those of judges, must have written standards that mean something definite and have an explicit content. I regret very much to be compelled to say that the Court today makes a drastic and dangerous departure from a Constitution written to control and limit the government and the judges and moves toward a constitution designed to be no more and no less than what the judges of a particular social and economic philosophy declare on the one hand to be fair or on the other hand to be shocking and unconscionable.

The procedure required today as a matter of constitutional law finds no precedent in our legal system. Reduced to its simplest terms, the problem in this case is similar to that frequently encountered when two parties have an ongoing legal relationship that requires one party to make periodic payments to the other. Often the situation arises where the party "owing" the money stops paying it and justifies his conduct by arguing that the recipient is not legally entitled to payment. The recipient can, of course, disagree and go to court to compel payment. But I know of no situation in our legal system in which the person alleged to owe money to another is required by law to continue making payments to a judgment-proof claimant without the benefit of any security or bond to insure that these payments can be recovered if he wins his legal argument. Yet today's decision in no way obligates the welfare recipient to pay back any benefits wrongfully received during the pretermination evidentiary hearings or post any bond, and in all "fairness" it could not do so. These recipients are by definition too poor to post a bond or to repay the benefits that, as the majority assumes, must be spent as received to insure survival.

The Court apparently feels that this decision will benefit the poor and needy. In my judgment the eventual result will be just the opposite. While today's deci-

a. I am aware that some feel that the process employed in reaching today's decision is not dependent on the individual views of the Justices involved, but is a mere objective search for the "collective conscience of mankind," but in my view that description is only a euphemism for an individual's judgment. Judges are as human as anyone and as likely as others to see the world through their own eyes and find the "collective conscience" remarkably similar to their own. Cf. Griswold v. Connecticut, 381 U.S. 479, 518-519 (1965) (Black, J., dissenting); Sniadach v. Family Finance Corp., 395 U.S. 337, 350-351 (1969) (Black, J., dissenting).

b. To realize how uncertain a standard of "fundamental fairness" would be, one has only to reflect for a moment on the possible disagreement if the "fairness" of the procedure in this case were propounded to the head of the National Welfare Rights Organization, the president of the national Chamber of Commerce, and the chairman of the John Birch Society.

sion requires only an administrative, evidentiary hearing, the inevitable logic of the approach taken will lead to constitutionally imposed, time-consuming delays of a full adversary process of administrative and review. . . . [T]he inevitable result of such a constitutionally imposed burden will be that the government will not put a claimant on the rolls initially until it has made an exhaustive investigation to determine his eligibility. While this Court will perhaps have insured that no needy person will be taken off the rolls without a full "due process" proceeding, it will also have insured that many will never get on the rolls, or at least that they will remain destitute during the lengthy proceedings followed to determine initial eligibility.

For the foregoing reasons I dissent from the Court's holding. The operation of a welfare state is a new experiment for our Nation. For this reason, among others, I feel that new experiments in carrying out a welfare program should not be frozen into our constitutional structure. They should be left, as are other legislative determinations, to the Congress and the legislatures that the people elect to make our laws.[15]

Note: Hearing Attending the Termination of Disability Benefits

In Mathews v. Eldridge, 424 U.S. 319 (1976), the Court distinguished *Goldberg,* holding that a recipient of disability benefits under the Social Security Act was not entitled to a hearing prior to termination. The Act requires a state agency to make a continuing assessment, based on information from the recipient and his sources of medical treatment, that he remains medically disabled from engaging in substantial gainful activity. Before the agency makes a final determination, the recipient is entitled to review his file and to submit additional evidence and respond to the proposed determination of noneligibility. A final determination of noneligibility is reviewed, and typically accepted, by the Social Security Agency Bureau of Disability Insurance, which notifies the recipient of the reasons for termination and of his right to de novo reconsideration by the state agency; benefits are terminated two months after the month in which medical recovery is found to have occurred. If the recipient seeks reconsideration by the state agency and the determination is adverse and accepted by the SSA, the recipient is entitled to an evidentiary hearing before an SSA administrative law judge.

Justice Powell articulated the factors to be balanced in determining the administrative procedures required by the due process clause. The Court must consider "first, the private interest that will be affected by the official action; second, the risk of an erroneous deprivation of such interest through the procedures used and the probable value, if any, of additional or substitute procedural safeguards; and finally, the Government's interest, including the function involved and the fiscal and administrative burdens that the addition or substitute procedural requisites would entail."

Turning to the facts of *Eldridge,* Justice Powell wrote: "In view of the torpidity of this administrative review process [which typically takes more than a year], and the typically modest resources of the family unit of the physically disabled

15. Dissenting opinions by Chief Justice Burger and Justice Stewart are omitted.

worker, the hardship imposed on the erroneously terminated disability recipient may be significant. Still, the disabled worker's need is likely to be less than that of a welfare recipient. In addition to the possibility of access to private resources, other forms of government assistance will become available where the termination of disability benefits places a worker or his family below the subsistence level." Moreover, the medical assessment requisite to termination "is a more sharply focused and easily documented decision than the typical determination of welfare entitlement." Fairness was further assured by the recipient's access to his file and opportunity to respond and produce additional evidence.

Justices Brennan and Marshall dissented.

A. What Procedural Safeguards Are Due?

Governments make individualized determinations adverse to citizens in a broad variety of situations. Schoolteachers grade examinations and punish students by making them stay after class or by suspending them; agencies grant or refuse licenses to drive, practice dentistry, operate bars, and construct buildings; wardens grant or deny prisoners "good time" and put them in solitary confinement; parole boards grant, deny, and revoke parole. Each situation may present the questions of *what* procedural safeguards are due and, more fundamentally, whether *any* process is due at all.

JERRY MASHAW, THE SUPREME COURT'S DUE PROCESS CALCULUS — THREE FACTORS IN SEARCH OF A THEORY

44 U. Chi. L. Rev. 28, 28-30, 46-59 (1976)

In the Court's latest attempt to formulate [a] due process calculus, Mathews v. Eldridge, Justice Powell's majority opinion articulates a set of criteria with a comprehensiveness that suggests a preliminary integration of the Court's recent efforts. In the majority's words, from which there is no dissent, the Court must consider:

> first, the private interest that will be affected by the official action; second, the risk of an erroneous deprivation of such interest through the procedures used, and the probable value, if any, of additional or substitute procedural safeguards; and finally, the Government's interest, including the function involved and the fiscal and administrative burdens that the additional or substitute procedural requisites would entail.

The thesis of this article is that the *Eldridge* approach is unsatisfactory both as employed in that case and as a general formulation of due process review of administrative procedures. The failing of *Eldridge* is its focus on questions of technique rather than on questions of value. That focus, it is argued, generates an inquiry that is incomplete because unresponsive to the full range of concerns embodied in the due process clause. . . .

The Supreme Court's analysis in *Eldridge* is not informed by systematic attention to any theory of the values underlying due process review. The approach is implicitly utilitarian but incomplete, and the Court overlooks alternative theories that might have yielded fruitful inquiry. My purpose is, first, to articulate the limits of the Court's utilitarian approach, both in *Eldridge* and as a general schema for evaluating administrative procedures, and second, to indicate the strengths and weaknesses of three alternative theories — individual dignity, equality, and tradition. These theories, at the level of abstraction here presented, require little critical justification: they are widely held, respond to strong currents in the philosophic literature concerning law, politics, and ethics, and are supported either implicitly or explicitly by the Supreme Court's due process jurisprudence.[a]

A. Utilitarianism

Utility theory suggests that the purpose of decisional procedures — like that of social action generally — is to maximize social welfare. Indeed, the three-factor analysis enunciated in *Eldridge* appears to be a type of utilitarian, social welfare function. That function first takes into account the social value at stake in a legitimate private claim; it discounts that value by the probability that it will be preserved through the available administrative procedures, and it then subtracts from that discounted value the social cost of introducing additional procedures. When combined with the institutional posture of judicial self-restraint, utility theory can be said to yield the following plausible decision-rule: "Void procedures for lack of due process only when alternative procedures would so substantially increase social welfare that their rejection seems irrational."

a. In early due process cases the Supreme Court concentrated on tradition. The oft-cited statement in Davidson v. New Orleans, 96 U.S. 97, 104 (1877), that the Court's approach to due process problems should be "by the gradual process of judicial inclusion and exclusion," epitomizes the conservative, precedent-oriented, historical approach. As governmental functions increased, however, the Court was faced with due process problems that had no compelling historical analogies. If the Court was not to be a continual stumbling block to "progress," a more flexible approach was needed. Indeed, the history of due process in the Supreme Court might be characterized as a continuous search for a theory of due process review that combines the legitimacy of the evolutionary theory with a flexibility that permits adaptation to contemporary circumstances. Dignitary or natural right, utilitarian, and egalitarian theories have all been incorporated to this end.

Dignitary ideas, although used occasionally in a supportive role both before 1900 and in some contemporary cases, were employed most frequently as the primary mode of analysis from about 1933 through the early 1950s. The proliferation of new government functions associated with the New Deal legislation and, later, with emergency war measures, stimulated a judicial reaction that was captured in the Court's emphasis on individual rights and dignitary values. The reactive natural rights style, predicated upon the Justices' perception of the "fair" solution in each case, had an ad hoc quality that soon became disturbing. The apparent inconsistency of the Supreme Court's due process jurisprudence led Sanford Kadish in a seminal article to describe the Supreme Court's decisions as in "chaotic array." Kadish, Methodology and Criteria in Due Process Adjudication — A Survey and Criticism, 66 Yale L.J. 319 (1957).

In the late 1950s and early 1960s various utilitarian formulations began to supply a structure for analysis. In Cafeteria & Restaurant Workers Local 473 v. McElroy, 367 U.S. 886, 895 (1961), for example, the Court, per Mr. Justice Stewart, stated that two factors must be considered in due process cases: "the precise nature of the government function involved . . . [and] of the private interest that has been affected by government action." The statement of the utilitarian approach culminates in the *Eldridge* opinion's three-factor calculus.

Equality as a due process value has received considerable attention in criminal (or quasi-criminal) cases, but little outside that area. Perhaps the best example of the explicit use of equality concerns with respect to an administrative function is found in Ashbacker Radio Corp. v. FCC, 326 U.S. 327, 330 (1945). There the Court, per Mr. Justice Douglas, stated that the right to a hearing "becomes an empty thing" unless all parties affected by the process have an equal opportunity to be heard.

The utilitarian calculus is not, however, without difficulties. The *Eldridge* Court conceives of the values of procedure too narrowly: it views the sole purpose of procedural protections as enhancing accuracy, and thus limits its calculus to the benefits or costs that flow from correct or incorrect decisions. No attention is paid to "process values" that might inhere in oral proceedings or to the demoralization costs that may result from the grant-withdrawal-grant-withdrawal sequence to which claimants like Eldridge are subjected. Perhaps more important, as the Court seeks to make sense of a calculus in which accuracy is the sole goal of procedure, it tends erroneously to characterize disability hearings as concerned almost exclusively with medical impairment and thus concludes that such hearings involve only medical evidence, whose reliability would be little enhanced by oral procedure. As applied by the *Eldridge* Court the utilitarian calculus tends, as cost-benefit analyses typically do, to "dwarf soft variables" and to ignore complexities and ambiguities.

The problem with a utilitarian calculus is not merely that the Court may define the relevant costs and benefits too narrowly. However broadly conceived, the calculus asks unanswerable questions. For example, what is the social value, and the social cost, of continuing disability payments until after an oral hearing for persons initially determined to be ineligible? Answers to those questions require a technique for measuring the social value and social cost of government income transfers, but no such technique exists. Even if such formidable tasks of social accounting could be accomplished, the effectiveness of oral hearings in forestalling the losses that result from erroneous terminations would remain uncertain. In the face of these pervasive indeterminacies the *Eldridge* Court was forced to retreat to a presumption of constitutionality.

Finally, it is not clear that the utilitarian balancing analysis asks the constitutionally relevant questions. The due process clause is one of those Bill of Rights protections meant to insure individual liberty in the face of contrary collective action. Therefore, a collective legislative or administrative decision about procedure, one arguably reflecting the intensity of the contending social values and representing an optimum position from the contemporary social perspective, cannot answer the constitutional question of whether due process has been accorded. A balancing analysis that would have the Court merely redetermine the question of social utility is similarly inadequate. There is no reason to believe that the Court has superior competence or legitimacy as a utilitarian balancer except as it performs its peculiar institutional role of insuring that libertarian values are considered in the calculus of decision. . . .

B. Individual Dignity

The increasingly secular, scientific, and collectivist character of the modern American state reinforces our propensity to define fairness in the formal, and apparently neutral language of social utility. Assertions of "natural" or "inalienable" rights seem, by contrast, somewhat embarrassing. Their ancestry, and therefore their moral force, are increasingly uncertain. Moreover, their role in the history of the due process clause makes us apprehensive about their eventual reach. It takes no peculiar acuity to see that the tension in procedural due process cases is the same as that in the now discredited substantive due process jurisprudence — a tension between the efficacy of the state and the individual's right to freedom from coercion or socially imposed disadvantage.

Yet the popular moral presupposition of individual dignity, and its political counterpart, self-determination, persist. State coercion must be legitimized, not only by acceptable substantive policies, but also by political processes that respond to a democratic morality's demand for participation in decisions affecting individual and group interests. At the level of individual administrative decisions this demand appears in both the layman's and the lawyer's language as the right to a "hearing" or "to be heard," normally meaning orally and in person. To accord an individual less when his property or status is at stake requires justification, not only because he might contribute to accurate determinations, but also because a lack of personal participation causes alienation and a loss of that dignity and self-respect that society properly deems independently valuable.

The obvious difficulty with a dignitary theory of procedural due process lies in defining operational limits on the procedural claims it fosters. In its purest form the theory would suggest that decisions affecting individual interests should be made only through procedures acceptable to the person affected. This purely subjective standard of procedural due process cannot be adopted: an individual's claim to a "nonalienating" procedure is not ranked ahead of all other social values. . . .

Notwithstanding its difficulties, the dignitary theory of due process might have contributed significantly to the *Eldridge* analysis. . . . While the disability decision in *Eldridge* may be narrowly characterized as a decision about the receipt of money payments, it may also be considered from various qualitative perspectives which seem pertinent in view of the general structure of the American income-support system.

That system suggests that a disability decision is a judgment of considerable social significance, and one that the claimant should rightly perceive as having a substantial moral content. The major cash income-support programs determine eligibility, not only on the basis of simple insufficiency of income, but also, or exclusively, on the basis of a series of excuses for partial or total nonparticipation in the work force: agedness, childhood, family responsibility, injury, disability. A grant under any of these programs is an official, if sometimes grudging, stamp of approval of the claimant's status as a partially disabled worker or nonworker. It proclaims, in effect, that those who obtain it have encountered one of the politically legitimate hazards to self-sufficiency in a market economy. The recipients, therefore, are entitled to society's support. Conversely, the denial of an income-maintenance claim implies that the claim is socially illegitimate, and the claimant, however impecunious, is not excused from normal work force status.

These moral and status dimensions of the disability decision indicate that there is more at stake in disability claims than temporary loss of income.[b] They also tend to put the disability decision in a framework that leads away from the superficial conclusion that disability decisions are a routine matter of evaluating medical evidence. Decisions with substantial "moral worth" connotations are generally expected to be highly individualized and attentive to subjective evidence.

b. The *Eldridge* Court, in distinguishing *Goldberg* largely on the ground that terminated welfare recipients were more desperate financially than terminated disability recipients, thus ignored a very substantial similarity. . . . The potential for feelings of demoralization, rejection, or simple righteous indignation seems essentially the same in both types of cases.

The adjudication of such issues on the basis of documents submitted largely by third parties and by adjudicators who have never confronted the claimant seems inappropriate. Instead, a court approaching an analysis of the disability claims process from the dignitary perspective might emphasize those aspects of disability decisions that focus on a particular claimant's vocational characteristics, his unique response to his medical condition, and the ultimate predictive judgment of whether the claimant should be able to work. . . .

C. Equality

. . . Notions of equality can . . . significantly inform the evaluation of any administrative process. One question we might ask is whether an investigative procedure is designed in a fashion that systematically excludes or undervalues evidence that would tend to support the position of a particular class of parties. If so, those parties might have a plausible claim that the procedure treated them unequally. Similarly, in a large-scale inquisitorial process involving many adjudicators, the question that should be posed is whether like cases receive like attention and like evidentiary development so that the influence of such arbitrary factors as location are minimized. In order to take such equality issues into account, we need only to broaden our due process horizons to include elements of procedural fairness beyond those traditionally associated with adversary proceedings. These two inquiries might have been pursued fruitfully in *Eldridge*. First, is the state agency system of decision making, which is based on documents, particularly disadvantageous for certain classes of claimants? There is some tentative evidence that it is. Cases such as *Eldridge* involving muscular or skeletal disorders, neurological problems, and multiple impairments, including psychological overlays, are widely believed to be both particularly difficult, due to the subjectivity of the evidence, and particularly prone to be reversed after oral hearing.

Second, does the inquisitorial process at the state agency level tend to treat like cases alike? If the GAO's study is indicative, the answer is decidedly no. According to that study, many, perhaps half, of the decisions are made on the basis of records that other adjudicators consider so inadequate that a decision could not be rendered. The relevance of such state agency variance to Eldridge's claim is twofold: first, it suggests that state agency determinations are unreliable and that further development at the hearing stage might substantially enhance their reliability; alternatively, it may suggest that the hierarchical or bureaucratic model of decision making, with overhead control for consistency, does not accurately describe the Social Security disability system. And if consistency is not feasible under this system, perhaps the more compelling standard for evaluating the system is the dignitary value of individualized judgment, which . . . implies claimant participation.

D. Tradition or Evolution

Judicial reasoning, including reasoning about procedural due process, is frequently and self-consciously based on custom or precedent. In part, reliance on tradition or "authority" is a court's institutional defense against illegitimacy in a political democracy. But tradition serves other values, not the least of which are predictability and economy of effort. More importantly, the inherently conservative technique of analogy to custom and precedent seems essential to the evolutionary development and the preservation of the legal system. Traditional procedures are legitimate not only because they represent a set of continuous expectations, but because the body politic has survived their use.

The use of tradition as a guide to fundamental fairness is vulnerable, of course, to objection. Since social and economic forces are dynamic, the processes and structures that proved functional in one period will not necessarily serve effectively in the next. Indeed, evolutionary development may as often end in the extinction of a species as in adaptation and survival. For this reason alone tradition can serve only as a partial guide to judgment.

Furthermore, it may be argued that reasoning by analogy from traditional procedures does not actually provide a perspective on the values served by due process. Rather, it is a decisional technique that requires a specification of the purposes of procedural rules merely in order that the decision maker may choose from among a range of authorities or customs the particular authority or custom most analogous to the procedures being evaluated.

This objection to tradition as a theory of justification is weighty, but not devastating. What is asserted by an organic or evolutionary theory is that *the purposes of legal rules cannot be fully known.* Put more cogently, while procedural rules, like other legal rules, should presumably contribute to the maintenance of an effective social order, we cannot expect to know precisely how they do so and what the long-term effects of changes or revisions might be. Our constitutional stance should therefore be preservative and incremental, building carefully, by analogy, upon traditional modes of operation. So viewed, the justification "we have always done it that way" is not so much a retreat from reasoned and purposive decision making as a profound acknowledgment of the limits of instrumental rationality.

Viewed from a traditionalist's perspective, the Supreme Court's opinion in *Eldridge* may be said to rely on the traditional proposition that property interests may be divested temporarily without hearing, provided a subsequent opportunity for contest is afforded. Goldberg v. Kelly is deemed an exceptional case, from which *Eldridge* is distinguished. . . .

Conclusion

The preceding discussion has emphasized the way that explicit attention to a range of values underlying due process of law might have led the *Eldridge* Court down analytic paths different from those that appear in Justice Powell's opinion. The discussion has largely ignored, however, arguments that would justify the result that the Court reached in terms of the alternative value theories here advanced. Those arguments are now set forth.

First, focus on the dignitary aspects of the disability decision can hardly compel the conclusion that an oral hearing is a constitutional necessity prior to the termination of benefits when a full hearing is available later. Knowledge that an oral hearing will be available at some point should certainly lessen disaffection and alienation. . . .

Second, arguments premised on equality do not necessarily carry the day for the proponent of prior hearings. . . . On balance, . . . the program that Congress enacted contains criteria that suggest a desire for both consistency and individualization. No adjudicatory process can avoid tradeoffs between the pursuit of one or the other of these goals. Thus a procedural structure incorporating (1) decisions by a single state agency based on a documentary record and subject to hierarchical quality review, followed by (2) appeal to de novo oral proceedings before independent administrative law judges, is hardly an irrational approach to the necessary compromise between consistency and individualization.

Explicit and systematic attention to the values served by a demand for due process nevertheless remains highly informative in *Eldridge* and in general. The use of analogy to traditional procedures might have helped rationalize and systematize a concern for the "desperation" of claimants that seems as impoverished in *Eldridge* as it seems profligate in *Goldberg;* and the absence in *Eldridge* of traditionalist, dignitary, or egalitarian considerations regarding the disability adjudication process permitted the Court to overlook questions of both fact and value — questions that, on reflection, seem important. The structure provided by the Court's three factors is an inadequate guide for analysis because its neutrality leaves it empty of suggestive value perspectives.

B. Lawyers and Due Process of Law

Closely connected to the right to a hearing is the right of legal representation at that hearing. Although the Sixth Amendment prohibits the state from depriving a criminal defendant of the right to be represented by a lawyer, there is no such analogue for civil suits or administrative hearings. Consider, in this regard, Walters v. National Association of Radiation Survivors, 473 U.S. 305 (1985), which upheld a congressional statute prohibiting veterans seeking benefits for service-related death or disabilities from paying an attorney more than $10. The Court held that the fee limitation did not violate the due process clause. Emphasizing the nonadversarial nature of the informal, ex parte proceedings that are involved in obtaining benefits, Justice Rehnquist wrote that legal representation was unnecessary in such a situation. In a dissent joined by Justices Brennan and Marshall, Justice Stevens argued that the right to counsel was virtually absolute.

1. The Right to Representation Under the Sixth Amendment

The Supreme Court has never found a right to appointed counsel in civil cases; however, the Sixth Amendment states that "[i]n all criminal prosecutions, the accused shall enjoy the right . . . to have the Assistance of Counsel for his defence." Although for many years this was interpreted to mean only that the state could not deprive a criminal defendant of the right to representation by retained counsel, in the 1930s the Court began holding that under certain circumstances, especially where there was a possibility of capital punishment, a criminal defendant who lacked the resources to retain a lawyer had the right to state-financed representation. See, e.g., Powell v. Alabama, 287 U.S. 45 (1932).

In Gideon v. Wainwright, 372 U.S. 335 (1963), a unanimous Court held that the Sixth Amendment required that counsel be provided to all felony defendants at trial. This was extended, by Argersinger v. Hamlin, 407 U.S. 25 (1972), to any offense "whether classified as petty, misdemeanor, or felony" that in fact results in a sentence of imprisonment.[16] For an excellent description of the litigation and facts leading up to it, see Anthony Lewis, Gideon's Trumpet (1964).

In Ross v. Moffit, 417 U.S. 600 (1974), the Court declined to expand the Sixth Amendment to require the appointment of counsel for indigents seeking discretionary review in the Supreme Court. And in Murray v. Giarratano, 492 U.S. 1 (1989), the Court ruled against inmates of Virginia's death row who claimed a right to appointed counsel to challenge their convictions in collateral proceedings. Chief Justice Rehnquist, writing for a plurality including Justices White, O'Connor, and Scalia, found the case controlled by Pennsylvania v. Finley, 481 U.S. 551 (1987), which held that the Sixth Amendment does not require states to provide counsel in postconviction proceedings generally. In a concurring opinion, Justice O'Connor emphasized that "[a] postconviction proceeding is not part of the criminal process itself, but is instead a civil action designed to overturn a presumptively valid criminal judgment."

Justice Stevens, in a dissent joined by Justices Brennan, Marshall, and Blackmun, argued that "even if it is permissible to leave an ordinary prisoner to his own resources in collateral proceedings, it is fundamentally unfair to require an indigent death row inmate to initiate collateral relief without counsel's guiding hand." He noted the presence of "significant evidence that in capital cases what is ordinarily considered direct review does not sufficiently safeguard against miscarriages of justice" to warrant the traditional presumption of finality. Thus, whereas "[f]ederal habeas courts granted relief in only 0.25% to 7% of noncapital cases in recent years, in striking contrast, the success rate in capital cases ranged from 60% to 70%. Such a high incidence of uncorrected error [at the ordinary appellate stage] demonstrates that the meaningful appellate review necessary in a capital case extends beyond the direct appellate process":

> Although in some circumstances governmental interests may justify infringements on Fourteenth Amendment rights, cf. Mathews v. Eldridge, Virginia has failed to assert any interest that outweighs respondents' right to legal assistance. The State already appoints counsel to death row inmates who succeed in filing postconviction petitions asserting at least one nonfrivolous claim; therefore, the additional cost of providing its 32 death row inmates competent counsel to prepare such petitions should be minimal. . . .
>
> Of the 37 States authorizing capital punishment, at least 18 automatically provide their indigent death row inmates counsel to help them initiate state collateral proceedings. Thirteen of the 37 States have created governmentally funded resource centers to assist counsel in litigating capital cases. Virginia is among as few as five States that fall into neither group and have no system for appointing counsel for condemned prisoners before a postconviction petition is filed.

16. A number of later decisions elaborated the circumstances under which indigent convicted criminals would be entitled to free transcripts. See, e.g., Land v. Brown, 372 U.S. 477 (1963) (indigent must be afforded free transcript of a postconviction hearing where filing of the transcript in the reviewing court was necessary to confer appellate jurisdiction); Long v. District Court, 385 U.S. 192 (1966) (free transcript required on appeal from denial of postconviction relief even if its filing is not jurisdictional); Roberts v. LaVallee, 389 U.S. 40 (1967) (entitlement to transcript of testimony of a major witness for the state at the preliminary hearing in order to aid prisoner in applying for postconviction relief).

2. *The Relevance of the Due Process and Equal Protection Clauses*

Griffin v. Illinois, 351 U.S. 12 (1956), held that a state must provide a trial transcript or its equivalent to an indigent criminal defendant appealing his conviction based on trial errors, notwithstanding the state's general practice of conditioning appeals on appellants' furnishing transcripts at their own expense. Justice Black, writing for a plurality that included Chief Justice Warren and Justices Douglas and Clark, emphasized the mixture of equal protection and due process doctrinal concerns presented by the case:

> [Our] constitutional guaranties of due process and equal protection both call for procedures in criminal trials which allow no invidious discriminations between persons and different groups of persons. Both equal protection and due process emphasize the central aim of our entire judicial system — all people charged with crime must, so far as the law is concerned, "stand on an equality before the bar of justice in every American court." . . .
>
> In criminal trials a State can no more discriminate on account of poverty than on account of religion, race, or color. Plainly the ability to pay costs in advance bears no rational relationship to a defendant's guilt or innocence and could not be used as an excuse to deprive a defendant of a fair trial. . . .
>
> There is no meaningful distinction between a rule which would deny the poor the right to defend themselves in a trial court and one which effectively denies the poor an adequate appellate review accorded to all who have money enough to pay the costs in advance. It is true that a State is not required by the Federal Constitution to provide appellate courts or a right to appellate review at all. . . . But that is not to say that a State that does grant appellate review can do so in a way that discriminates against some convicted defendants on account of their poverty. Appellate review has now become an integral part of the Illinois trial system for finally adjudicating the guilt or innocence of a defendant. Consequently at all stages of the proceedings the Due Process and Equal Protection Clauses protect persons like petitioners from invidious discriminations. . . .
>
> All of the States now provide some method of appeal from criminal convictions, recognizing the importance of appellate review to a correct adjudication of guilt or innocence. Statistics show that a substantial proportion of criminal convictions are reversed by state appellate courts. Thus to deny adequate review to the poor means that many of them may lose their life, liberty or property because of unjust convictions which appellate courts would set aside. Many States have recognized this and provided aid for convicted defendants who have a right to appeal and need a transcript but are unable to pay for it. A few have not. Such a denial is a misfit in a country dedicated to affording equal justice to all and special privileges to none in the administration of its criminal law. There can be no equal justice where the kind of trial a man gets depends on the amount of money he has. Destitute defendants must be afforded as adequate appellate review as defendants who have money enough to buy transcripts.

Justice Frankfurter wrote a brief opinion concurring in the result. Justices Reed, Burton, Minton, and Harlan dissented. With respect to the petitioner's equal protection claim, Justice Harlan argued that "[a]ll that Illinois has done is to fail to alleviate the consequences of differences in economic circumstances that exist wholly apart from any state action. . . . [T]he real issue in this case is not whether Illinois *has* discriminated but whether it has a duty *to* discriminate." With respect to the due process claim, Justice Harlan argued that the state's practice was not arbitrary and did not deprive petitioner of a right "implicit in the concept of ordered liberty."

On the same day as it decided *Gideon,* a divided Court in Douglas v. California, 372 U.S. 353 (1963), invalidated California's procedure regulating the appointment of counsel for indigent defendants appealing criminal convictions. Under state procedure, the appellate court first made "an independent investigation of the record" in order to "determine whether it would be of advantage to the defendant or helpful to the appellate court to have counsel appointed." Appellants who retained private counsel were not required to submit to this prior scrutiny. In petitioner's case, the appellate court had concluded, based on the record, that "no good whatever could be served by appointment of counsel." Justice Douglas wrote that this violated the equal protection clause by drawing "an unconstitutional line . . . between rich and poor." Without addressing the question whether due process requires having appellate review at all, the Court held that where a state *does* provide appellate review it may not impose this special burden on indigent appellants.

> [T]he discrimination is not between "possibly good and obviously bad cases," but between cases where the rich man can require the court to listen to argument of counsel before deciding on the merits, but a poor man cannot. There is lacking that equality demanded by the Fourteenth Amendment where the rich man, who appeals as of right, enjoys the benefit of counsel's examination into the record, research of the law, and marshalling of arguments on his behalf, while the indigent, already burdened by a preliminary determination that his case is without merit, is forced to shift for himself. The indigent, where the record is unclear or the errors are hidden, has only the right to a meaningless ritual, while the rich man has a meaningful appeal.[17]

Discussion

Justice Harlan, dissenting in *Douglas,* insisted on distinguishing between due process and equal protection analysis. He suggested that if the holding were justified on equal protection grounds, rather than a conception of minimal requirements under the due process clause, then "the requirement of counsel on appeal is the right to the most skilled advocate who is theoretically at the call of the defendant of means."[18]

Assuming that wealth is a suspect basis of classification, do the laws in *Griffin* and *Douglas* classify on the basis of wealth? On whatever bases the statutes classify, their effect or impact certainly is different on persons of different wealth: Their effect is to grant effective access to the appellate system for those with funds to purchase goods (transcripts) or services (lawyers), while effectively limiting access to those without such funds. Still, the Court has not held that the Con-

17. See his concurring opinion in Williams v. Illinois, 399 U.S. 235 (1970), which invalidated an Illinois statute that required convicts unable to pay their fines or court costs to "work off" their obligations by remaining in jail at an imputed rate of $5 per day, even if this would result in incarceration for a term longer than the maximum statutory term. "If equal protection implications of the Court's opinion were to be fully realized," Justice Harlan wrote, "it would require that the consequences of punishment be comparable for all individuals," which he presumably assumed would be, if not fanciful, then at least not constitutionally required.

18. The concurring opinion of Chief Justice Burger and the dissenting opinion of Justice Douglas are omitted.

stitution prohibits a state from charging user fees for many of the services it provides, whenever the consequence is to deprive access to indigents. Consider, for example, civic theaters and municipal transportation systems. Thus, something other than an abstract commitment to equality animates the decisions in *Griffin* and *Douglas*. What is it? Consider in this context the cases in the following section.

Note: Other Rights of Indigent Criminal Defendants

In Fuller v. Oregon, 417 U.S. 40 (1974), the Court held that a state may recoup legal expenses paid on behalf of a convicted defendant to the extent that he becomes able to repay and that it may condition a solvent defendant's probation on repayment. Against Fuller's argument that "a defendant's knowledge that he may remain under an obligation to repay the expenses incurred in providing him legal representation might impel him to decline the services of an appointed attorney and thus 'chill' his constitutional right to counsel," Justice Stewart responded:

> We live in a society where the distribution of legal assistance, like the distribution of all goods and services, is generally regulated by the dynamics of private enterprise. A defendant in a criminal case who is just above the line separating the indigent from the nonindigent must borrow money, sell off his meager assets, or call upon his family or friends in order to hire a lawyer. We cannot say that the Constitution requires that those only slightly poorer must remain forever immune from any obligation to shoulder the expenses of their legal defense, even when they are able to pay without hardship.
>
> This case is fundamentally different from our decisions . . . which have invalidated state and federal laws that placed a penalty on the exercise of a constitutional right. Unlike the statutes found invalid in those cases, where the provisions "had no other purpose or effect than to chill the assertion of constitutional rights by penalizing those who choose to exercise them," Oregon's recoupment statute merely provides that a convicted person who later becomes able to pay for his counsel may be required to do so.

The Court also rejected petitioner's claim that the Oregon statute unconstitutionally discriminated (1) between defendants who are convicted and those who are not convicted or whose convictions are reversed, and (2) between indigent criminal defendants furnished legal assistance by the state and other debtors, including defendants who retain private counsel. Justice Marshall, joined by Justice Brennan, explicitly reserved judgment on the issue of "chilling effect" but dissented based on the state's different treatment of indigent criminal defendants and other judgment debtors.[19]

19. James v. Strange, 407 U.S. 128 (1972), struck down a Kansas statute providing for the recoupment of all state expenditures for indigent defendants and depriving them of almost all of the usual exemptions and restrictions (e.g., limitations on wage garnishment, exemptions of personal clothing and food) afforded civil judgment debtors. The Court held that the equal protection clause required "more even treatment of indigent criminal defendants with other classes of indigents for self-sufficiency and self-respect." Rinaldi v. Yeager, 384 U.S. 305 (1966), struck down a New Jersey statute that required unsuccessful appellants confined to prisons to repay the state for the costs of transcripts, but

Almost a decade later, in Ake v. Oklahoma, 470 U.S. 68 (1985), the Court held that, in certain circumstances, a state must provide an indigent defendant with access to psychiatric assistance to make out a defense of insanity. In this case, the defendant Ake was sentenced to death for first degree murder due to aggravating circumstances after his request for psychiatric evaluation at the state's expense was denied. Justice Marshall wrote for the majority:

> We recognized long ago that mere access to the courthouse doors does not by itself assure a proper functioning of the adversary process, and that a criminal trial is fundamentally unfair if the State proceeds against an indigent defendant without making certain that he has access to the raw materials integral to the building of an effective defense. . . .
>
> In this case, we must decide whether, and under what conditions, the participation of a psychiatrist is important enough to preparation of a defense to require the State to provide an indigent defendant with access to competent psychiatric assistance in preparing the defense. Three factors are relevant to this determination. The first is the private interest that will be affected by the action of the State. The second is the governmental interest that will be affected if the safeguard is to be provided. The third is the probable value of the additional or substitute procedural safeguards that are sought, and the risk of an erroneous deprivation of the affected interest if those safeguards are not provided. . . .
>
> The private interest in the accuracy of a criminal proceeding that places an individual's life or liberty at risk is almost uniquely compelling. . . .
>
> [Second, t]he State's interest in prevailing at trial — unlike that of a private litigant — is necessarily tempered by its interest in the fair and accurate adjudication of criminal cases. Thus, also unlike a private litigant, a State may not legitimately assert an interest in maintenance of a strategic advantage over the defense, if the result of that advantage is to cast a pall on the accuracy of the verdict obtained. We therefore conclude that the governmental interest in denying Ake the assistance of a psychiatrist is not substantial, in light of the compelling interest of both that State and the individual in accurate dispositions. . . .
>
> [Finally,] when the State has made the defendant's mental condition relevant to his criminal culpability and to the punishment he might suffer, the assistance of a psychiatrist may well be crucial to the defendant's ability to marshal his defense. . . . By organizing a defendant's mental history, examination results and behavior, and other information, interpreting it in light of their expertise, and then laying out their investigative and analytic process to the jury, the psychiatrists for each party enable the jury to make its most accurate determination of the truth on the issue before them. . . .
>
> The foregoing leads inexorably to the conclusion that, without the assistance of a psychiatrist to conduct a professional examination on issues relevant to the defense, to help determine whether the insanity defense is viable, to present testimony, and to assist in preparing the cross-examination of a State's psychiatric witnesses, the risk of an inaccurate resolution of sanity issues is extremely high. . . .
>
> A defendant's mental condition is not necessarily at issue in every criminal proceeding, however. . . . When the defendant is able to make an *ex parte* threshold showing to the trial court that his sanity is likely to be a significant factor in his defense, the need for assistance of a psychiatrist is readily apparent. . . . In such a circumstance, where the potential accuracy of the jury's determination is so

---

did not exact repayment from defendants receiving suspended sentences, placed on probation, or penalized only by a fine.

dramatically enhanced, and where the interests of the individual and the State in an accurate proceeding are substantial, the State's interest in its fisc must yield.

The majority concluded that the denial of psychiatric assistance to Ake violated his due process rights to a fair trial. Chief Justice Burger concurred in the judgment. Justice Rehnquist dissented.

C. Access to the Judicial Process in Civil Cases

BODDIE v. CONNECTICUT
401 U.S. 371 (1971)
Appeal from the United States District Court for the District of Connecticut

[Persons commencing divorce proceedings in Connecticut must pay a filing fee of $45 and an average of $15 for service of process. Appellants were indigent divorce complainants who had unsuccessfully sought waiver of these costs.]

HARLAN, J. . . .

I

. . . It is to courts, or other quasijudicial official bodies, that we ultimately look for the implementation of a regularized, orderly process of dispute settlement. Within this framework, those who wrote our original Constitution, in the Fifth Amendment, and later those who drafted the Fourteenth Amendment, recognized the centrality of the concept of due process in the operation of this system. Without this guarantee that one may not be deprived of his rights, neither liberty nor property, without due process of law, the State's monopoly over techniques for binding conflict resolution could hardly be said to be acceptable under our scheme of things. Only by providing that the social enforcement mechanism must function strictly within these bounds can we hope to maintain an ordered society that is also just. It is upon this premise that this Court has through years of adjudication put flesh upon the due process principle.

Such litigation has, however, typically involved rights of defendants — not, as here, persons seeking access to the judicial process in the first instance. This is because our society has been so structured that resort to the courts is not usually the only available, legitimate means of resolving private disputes. Indeed, private structuring of individual relationships and repair of their breach is largely encouraged in American life, subject only to the caveat that the formal judicial process, if resorted to, is paramount. Thus, this Court has seldom been asked to view access to the courts as an element of due process. The legitimacy of the State's monopoly over techniques of final dispute settlement, even where some are denied access to its use, stands unimpaired where recognized, effective alternatives for the adjustment of differences remain. But the successful invocation of this governmental power by plaintiffs has often created serious problems for defendants' rights. For at that point, the judicial proceeding becomes the only effective means of resolving the dispute at hand and denial of a defendant's full access to that process raises grave problems for its legitimacy.

Recognition of this theoretical framework illuminates the precise issue presented in this case. As this Court on more than one occasion has recognized, marriage involves interests of basic importance in our society. See, e.g., Loving v. Virginia, 388 U.S. 1 (1967); Skinner v. Oklahoma, 316 U.S. 535 (1942); Meyer v. Nebraska, 262 U.S. 390 (1923). It is not surprising, then, that the States have seen fit to oversee many aspects of that institution. Without a prior judicial imprimatur, individuals may freely enter into and rescind commercial contracts, for example, but we are unaware of any jurisdiction where private citizens may covenant for or dissolve marriages without state approval. Even where all substantive requirements are concededly met, we know of no instance where two consenting adults may divorce and mutually liberate themselves from the constraints of legal obligations that go with marriage, and more fundamentally the prohibition against remarriage, without invoking the State's judicial machinery.

II

. . . Prior cases establish, first, that due process requires, at a minimum, that absent a countervailing state interest of overriding significance, persons forced to settle their claims of right and duty through the judicial process must be given a meaningful opportunity to be heard. . . . Although "[m]any controversies have raged about the cryptic and abstract words of the Due Process Clause," as Mr. Justice Jackson wrote for the Court in Mullane v. Central Hanover Tr. Co., 339 U.S. 306 (1950), "there can be no doubt that at a minimum they require that deprivation of life, liberty or property by adjudication be preceded by notice and opportunity for hearing appropriate to the nature of the case." . . .

III

. . . [T]he State's refusal to admit these appellants to its courts, the sole means in Connecticut for obtaining a divorce, must be regarded as the equivalent of denying them an opportunity to be heard upon their claimed right to a dissolution of their marriages, and, in the absence of a sufficient countervailing justification for the State's action, a denial of due process.

The arguments for this kind of fee and cost requirement are that the State's interest in the prevention of frivolous litigation is substantial, its use of court fees and process costs to allocate scarce resources is rational, and its balance between the defendant's right to notice and the plaintiff's right to access is reasonable.

In our opinion, none of these considerations is sufficient to override the interest of these plaintiff-appellants in having access to the only avenue open for dissolving their allegedly untenable marriages. . . .

Reversed.

DOUGLAS, J., concurring in the result.

I believe this case should be decided upon the principles developed in the line of cases marked by Griffin v. Illinois. . . .

The Due Process Clause on which the Court relies has proven very elastic in the hands of judges. . . .

The reach of the Equal Protection Clause is not definable with mathematical precision. But in spite of doubts by some, as it has been construed, rather definite guidelines have been developed. . . . Here the invidious discrimination is based on one of the guidelines: *poverty*. An invidious discrimination based on poverty is adequate for this case. . . .

BRENNAN, J., concurring in part. . . .

I cannot join the Court's opinion insofar as today's holding is made to depend upon the factor that only the State can grant a divorce and that an indigent would be locked into a marriage if unable to pay the fees required to obtain a divorce. A State has an ultimate monopoly of all judicial process and attendant enforcement machinery. As a practical matter, if disputes cannot be successfully settled between the parties, the court system is usually "the only forum effectively empowered to settle their disputes. . . ." I see no constitutional distinction between appellants' attempt to enforce this state statutory right and an attempt to vindicate any other right arising under federal or state law. . . .

The question that the Court treats exclusively as one of due process inevitably implicates considerations of both due process and equal protection. . . . The rationale of *Griffin* covers the present case. Courts are the central dispute-settling institutions in our society. They are bound to do equal justice under law, to rich and poor alike. They fail to perform their function in accordance with the Equal Protection Clause if they shut their doors to indigent plaintiffs altogether. Where money determines not merely "the kind of trial a man gets," Griffin v. Illinois, but whether he gets into court at all, the great principle of equal protection becomes a mockery. A State may not make its judicial processes available to some but deny them to others simply because they cannot pay a fee. Cf. Harper v. Virginia Board of Elections. In my view, Connecticut's fee requirement, as applied to an indigent, is a denial of equal protection.

[Justice Black dissented, arguing that *Griffin* and its progeny were limited to criminal cases. In civil cases, "the government is not usually involved as a party, and there is no deprivation of life, liberty, or property as punishment for crime. Our Federal Constitution, therefore, does not place such private disputes on the same high level as it places criminal trials and punishment."]

UNITED STATES v. KRAS, 409 U.S. 434 (1973): [Appellee, an indigent petitioner in bankruptcy, sought waiver of the usual fees, amounting to $50, which cover a portion of the referee's, trustee's, and clerk's costs. The district court held that the fee provisions, as applied to appellee, violated the Fifth Amendment. The government appealed.]

BLACKMUN, J. . . .

A. The appellants in *Boddie,* on the one hand, and Robert Kras, on the other, stand in materially different postures. The denial of access to the judicial forum in *Boddie* touched directly, as has been noted, on the marital relationship and on the associational interests that surround the establishment and dissolution of that relationship. On many occasions, we have recognized the fundamental importance of these interests under our Constitution. . . . Kras' alleged interest in the elimination of his debt burden, and in obtaining his desired new start in life, although important and so recognized by the enactment of the Bankruptcy Act, does not rise to the same constitutional level. See Dandridge v. Williams, 397 U.S.

471 (1970); Richardson v. Belcher, 404 U.S. 78 (1971). If Kras is not discharged in bankruptcy, his position will not be materially altered in any constitutional sense. Gaining or not gaining a discharge will effect no change with respect to basic necessities. We see no fundamental interest that is gained or lost depending on the availability of a discharge in bankruptcy. . . .

C. Nor is the government's control over the establishment, enforcement, or dissolution of debts nearly so exclusive as Connecticut's control over the marriage relationship in *Boddie.* In contrast with divorce, bankruptcy is not the only method available to a debtor for the adjustment of his legal relationship with his creditors. . . . However unrealistic the remedy may be in a particular situation, a debtor, in theory, and often in actuality, may adjust his debts by negotiated agreement with his creditors. . . .

D. We are also of the opinion that the filing fee requirement does not deny Kras the equal protection of the laws. Bankruptcy is hardly akin to free speech or marriage or to those other rights, so many of which are imbedded in the First Amendment, that the Court has come to regard as fundamental and that demand the lofty requirement of a compelling governmental interest before they may be significantly regulated. See Shapiro v. Thompson, 394 U.S. 618 (1969). Neither does it touch upon what has been said to be the suspect criteria of race, nationality, or alienage. . . .

E. There is no constitutional right to obtain a discharge of one's debts in bankruptcy. . . .

F. The rational basis for the fee requirement is readily apparent. . . .

G. If the $50 filing fees are paid in installments over six months as General Order No. 35(4) permits on a proper showing, the required average weekly payment is $1.92. If the payment period is extended for the additional three months as the Order permits, the average weekly payment is lowered to $1.28. This is a sum less than the payments Kras makes on his couch of negligible value in storage, and less than the price of a movie and little more than the cost of a pack or two of cigarettes. . . .

Reversed.

STEWART, J., joined by Douglas, Brennan, and Marshall, JJ., dissenting. . . . The violation of due process seems to me [as] clear in the present case [as in *Boddie*]. It is undisputed that Kras is making a good-faith attempt to obtain a discharge in bankruptcy, and that he is in fact indigent. As was true in *Boddie,* the "welfare income . . . barely suffices to meet the costs of the daily essentials of life and includes no allotment that could be budgeted for the expense to gain access to the courts. . . ."

Similarly, the debtor, like the married plaintiffs in *Boddie,* originally entered into his contract freely and voluntarily. But it is the government nevertheless that continues to enforce that obligation, and under our "legal system" that debt is effective only because the judicial machinery is there to collect it. The bankrupt is bankrupt precisely for the reason that the State stands ready to exact all of his debts through garnishment, attachment, and the panoply of other creditor remedies. The appellee can be pursued and harassed by his creditors since they hold his legally enforceable debts.

And in the unique situation of the indigent bankrupt, the government provides the only effective means of his ever being free of these government-imposed obligations. As in *Boddie,* there are no "recognized, effective alternatives." While the creditors of a bankrupt with assets might well desire to reach a compromise settlement, that possibility is foreclosed to the truly indigent bankrupt. With no funds and not even a sufficient prospect of income to be able to promise the payment of a $50 fee in weekly installments of $1.28, the assetless bankrupt has absolutely nothing to offer his creditors. And his creditors have nothing to gain by allowing him to escape or reduce his debts; their only hope is that eventually he might make enough income for them to attach. Unless the government provides him access to the bankruptcy court, Kras will remain in the totally hopeless situation he now finds himself. The government has thus truly preempted the only means for the indigent bankrupt to get out from under a lifetime burden of debt. . . .

The Court today holds that Congress may say that some of the poor are too poor even to go bankrupt. I cannot agree.

MARSHALL, J., dissenting. . . .

It may be easy for some people to think that weekly savings of less than $2 are no burden. But no one who has had close contact with poor people can fail to understand how close to the margin of survival many of them are. A sudden illness, for example, may destroy whatever savings they may have accumulated, and by eliminating a sense of security may destroy the incentive to save in the future. A pack or two of cigarettes may be, for them, not a routine purchase but a luxury indulged in only rarely. The desperately poor almost never go to see a movie, which the majority seems to believe is an almost weekly activity. They have more important things to do with what little money they have — like attempting to provide some comforts for a gravely ill child, as Kras must do.

It is perfectly proper for judges to disagree about what the Constitution requires. But it is disgraceful for an interpretation of the Constitution to be premised upon unfounded assumptions about how people live. . . .

The majority says that "the denial of access to the judicial forum in *Boddie* touched directly . . . on the marital relationship." It sees "no fundamental interest that is gained or lost depending on the availability of a discharge in bankruptcy." . . .

I view the case as involving the right of access to the courts, the opportunity to be heard when one claims a legal right, and not just the right to a discharge in bankruptcy. When a person raises a claim of right or entitlement under the laws, the only forum in our legal system empowered to determine that claim is a court. . . .

The legal system is of course not so pervasive as to preclude private resolution of disputes. But private settlements do not determine the validity of claims of right. Such questions can be authoritatively resolved only in courts. It is in that sense, I believe, that we should consider the emphasis in *Boddie* on the exclusiveness of the judicial forum — and give Kras his day in court.[a]

a. These evidentiary hearings, of course, must meet the minimal requirements of due process. Goldberg v. Kelly. Appellants have alleged that the hearings were deficient in several ways, . . . but neither the record nor the opinion of the Oregon court provides support for these contentions.

Discussion

1. Of what liberty or property were appellants in *Boddie* and the appellee in *Kras* deprived?

2. As of 1991 the filing fee is $120, and it appears that, more than ever, "[m]any Americans are too poor to go bankrupt." See Jason de Parle, Poor Find Going Broke Too Costly, New York Times, Dec. 11, 1991, at 24. Even if filing fees were waived, of course, the problem of finding and paying for a lawyer would remain. If you disagree with *Kras,* would you argue as well that the Constitution requires state-subsidized lawyers for persons who cannot otherwise navigate the shoals of filing for bankruptcy?

Note: Subsequent Decisions

Ortwein v. Schwab, 410 U.S. 656 (1973), summarily upheld Oregon's $25 appellate court filing fee as applied to appeals by indigents from administrative decisions reducing welfare payments:

> In *Kras,* we observed that one's interest in a bankruptcy discharge "does not rise to the same constitutional level" as one's inability to dissolve his marriage except through the courts. In this case, appellants seek increased welfare payments. This interest, like that of *Kras,* has far less constitutional significance than the interest of the *Boddie* appellants. Each of the present appellants has received an agency hearing at which it was determined that the minimum level of payments authorized by law was being provided. As in *Kras,* we see "no fundamental interest that is gained or lost depending on the availability" of the relief sought by appellants. . . .
>
> In *Kras,* the Court also stressed the existence of alternatives, not conditioned on the payment of the fees, to the judicial remedy. The Court has held that procedural due process requires that a welfare recipient be given a pretermination evidentiary hearing. Goldberg v. Kelly, 397 U.S. 254 (1970). These appellants have had hearings.[a] The hearings provide a procedure, not conditioned on payment of any fee, through which appellants have been able to seek redress. This Court has long recognized that, even in criminal cases, due process does not require a State to provide an appellate system. Under the facts of this case, appellants were not denied due process.
>
> Appellants urge that the filing fee violates the Equal Protection Clause by unconstitutionally discriminating against the poor. As in *Kras,* this litigation, which deals with welfare payments, "is in the area of economics and social welfare." No suspect classification, such as race, nationality, or alienage, is present. See Graham v. Richardson, 403 U.S. 365, 372 (1971). The applicable standard is that of rational justification. Kras v. United States.
>
> The purpose of the filing fee, as with the bankruptcy fees in *Kras,* is apparent. The Oregon court system incurs operating costs, and the fee produces some small revenue to assist in offsetting those expenses. . . . Appellants do not contend that the fee is disproportionate or that it is not an effective means to accomplish the State's goal. The requirement of rationality is met. . . .

Justices Douglas, Stewart, Brennan, and Marshall dissented.

a. These evidentiary hearings, of course, must meet the minimal requirements of due process. Goldberg v. Kelly. Appellants have alleged that the hearings were deficient in several ways, . . . but neither the record nor the opinion of the Oregon court provides support for these contentions.

In Little v. Streater, 452 U.S. 1 (1981), a unanimous Court held unconstitutional, as applied to an indigent defendant in a paternity suit, a Connecticut statute requiring the party requesting blood grouping tests to bear their costs. Chief Justice Burger invoked Mathews v. Eldridge (p.1129 supra) and *Boddie*.

On the same day, in Lassiter v. Department of Social Services, 452 U.S. 18 (1981), Justice Stewart examined the particular circumstances of a child neglect proceeding to conclude that neither "fundamental fairness" nor the *Mathews* formula (p.1129 supra) required the state to provide free counsel to an indigent mother whose child was removed from her custody.

D. Constitutional Constraints on the Government as Employer

The modern state has witnessed an explosion in the number of government employees. In 1816, the federal government had fewer than 5,000 civilian employees; in 1881, the number first exceeded 100,000. In 1940, there were 1 million federal civilian employees, and by 1970 the number had reached nearly 3 million.[20] Similar increases occurred at the state and local levels, with the result that by 1975 approximately 15 million persons, accounting for 15 percent of the nation's workforce, were employed at various levels of government.[21]

This section considers some of the constitutional problems that the Court has confronted with respect to the public workforce.

1. *Due Process and the Termination of Government Employment*

American common law in the 1800s gave employers the right to fire employees "at will,"[22] so that the only constraints on employers were those within the employment contract. To what extent does the due process clause place limits upon the ability of the government to control the employment relationship?

BOARD OF REGENTS v. ROTH, 408 U.S. 564 (1972): [Respondent was hired to teach at a state university for a term of one year. Informed without explanation that his contract would not be renewed, Roth sued to require the university to state its reasons for nonrenewal and to afford him a hearing. The Court held that Roth had not been deprived of "property."]

STEWART, J. . . . The District Court decided that procedural due process guarantees apply in this case by assessing and balancing the weights of the particular

20. Historical Statistics of the United States, Colonial Times to 1970, Part 2, pp. 1102-03: Series Y 308-317. Paid Civilian Employment of the Federal Government: 1816 to 1970. It has remained roughly at that level since. Thus the number of federal civilian employees in 1989 was approximately 3.13 million. See United States Bureau of the Census, Statistical Abstract of the United States 1991, Table 531. An additional 1.7 million Americans were members of the United States armed forces in 1988. Id., Table 545.

21. Statistical Abstract of the United States 1976, Tables 406 and 452. The number had increased to over 17.5 million by 1988. See United States Bureau of the Census, Statistical Abstract of the United States 1991, Table 497. The total labor force was approximately 115 million. Id., Table 631.

22. There has, however, been significant limitation on this right in recent years. See Clyde Summers, Individual Protection Against Unjust Dismissal, 62 Va. L. Rev. 481 (1976); William L. Mauk, Wrongful Discharge: The Erosion of 100 Years of Employer Privilege, 21 Idaho L. Rev. 201 (1985).

interests involved. It concluded that the respondent's interest in re-employment at Wisconsin State University-Oshkosh outweighed the University's interest in denying him re-employment summarily. Undeniably, the respondent's re-employment prospects were of major concern to him — concern that we surely cannot say was insignificant. And a weighing process has long been a part of any determination of the *form* of hearing required in particular situations by procedural due process. But, to determine whether due process requirements apply in the first place, we must look not to the "weight" but to the *nature* of the interest at stake. We must look to see if the interest is within the Fourteenth Amendment's protection of liberty and property.

. . . [T]he Court has fully and finally rejected the wooden distinction between "rights" and "privileges" that once seemed to govern the applicability of procedural due process rights. The Court has also made clear that the property interests protected by procedural due process extend well beyond actual ownership of real estate, chattels, or money. . . .

Yet, while the Court has eschewed rigid or formalistic limitations on the protection of procedural due process, it has at the same time observed certain boundaries. For the words "liberty" and "property" in the Due Process Clause of the Fourteenth Amendment must be given some meaning. . . .

Certain attributes of "property" interests protected by procedural due process emerge from [our] decisions. To have a property interest in a benefit, a person clearly must have more than an abstract need or desire for it. He must have more than a unilateral expectation of it. He must, instead, have a legitimate claim of entitlement to it. It is a purpose of the ancient institution of property to protect those claims upon which people rely in their daily lives, reliance that must not be arbitrarily undermined. It is a purpose of the constitutional right to a hearing to provide an opportunity for a person to vindicate those claims.

Property interests, of course, are not created by the Constitution. Rather, they are created and their dimensions are defined by existing rules or understandings that stem from an independent source such as state law — rules or understandings that secure certain benefits and that support claims of entitlement to those benefits. Thus, the welfare recipients in Goldberg v. Kelly had a claim of entitlement to welfare payments that was grounded in the statute defining eligibility for them. The recipients had not yet shown that they were, in fact, within the statutory terms of eligibility. But we held that they had a right to a hearing at which they might attempt to do so.

Just as the welfare recipients' "property" interest in welfare payments was created and defined by statutory terms, so the respondent's "property" interest in employment at Wisconsin State University-Oshkosh was created and defined by the terms of his appointment. Those terms secured his interest in employment up to June 30, 1969. But the important fact in this case is that they specifically provided that the respondent's employment was to terminate on June 30. They did not provide for contract renewal absent "sufficient cause." Indeed, they made no provision for renewal whatsoever.

Thus, the terms of the respondent's appointment secured absolutely no interest in re-employment for the next year. They supported absolutely no possible claim of entitlement to re-employment. Nor, significantly, was there any state statute or University rule or policy that secured his interest in re-employment or that created any legitimate claim to it. In these circumstances, the respondent surely had an abstract concern in being rehired, but he did not have a *property* interest sufficient to require the University authorities to give him a hearing when they declined to renew his contract of employment.

MARSHALL, J., dissenting. . . .[23] In my view, every citizen who applies for a government job is entitled to it unless the government can establish some reason for denying the employment. This is the "property" right that I believe is protected by the Fourteenth Amendment and that cannot be denied "without due process of law." And it is also liberty — liberty to work — which is the "very essence of the personal freedom and opportunity" secured by the Fourteenth Amendment.

This Court has often had occasion to note that the denial of public employment is a serious blow to any citizen. . . . Thus, when an application for public employment is denied or the contract of a government employee is not renewed, the government must say why, for it is only when the reasons underlying government action are known that citizens feel secure and protected against arbitrary government action.

Employment is one of the greatest, if not the greatest, benefits that governments offer in modern-day life. When something as valuable as the opportunity to work is at stake, the government may not reward some citizens and not others without demonstrating that its actions are fair and equitable. And it is procedural due process that is our fundamental guarantee of fairness, our protection against arbitrary, capricious, and unreasonable government action.

Roth should be read together with Perry v. Sindermann, 408 U.S. 593 (1972), decided on the same day. In his tenth year of employment at a state college under a succession of one-year contracts, Sindermann was notified that his contract would not be renewed. Unlike Roth, Sindermann alleged that his college "had a de facto tenure program, and that he had tenure under that program."[24] The Court, per Justice Stewart, held that he was entitled to prove his claim that the college had fostered the understanding that persons in his position would enjoy continued employment absent "sufficient cause":

> A written contract with an explicit tenure provision clearly is evidence of a formal understanding that supports a teacher's claim of entitlement to continued employment unless sufficient "cause" is shown. Yet absence of such an explicit contractual provision may not always foreclose the possibility that a teacher has a "property" interest in re-employment. For example, the law of contracts in most, if not all, jurisdictions long has employed a process by which agreements, though not formalized in writing, may be "implied." 3 A. Corbin on Contracts §§561-572A (1960). Explicit contractual provisions may be supplemented by other agreements implied from "the promisor's words and conduct in the light of the surrounding circumstances."

23. Justices Douglas and Brennan also wrote dissenting opinions.
24. For example, the college's faculty guide provided:

> Teacher Tenure: Odessa College has no tenure system. The administration of the College wishes the faculty member to feel that he has permanent tenure as long as his teaching services are satisfactory and as long as he displays a cooperative attitude toward his co-workers and his superiors, and as long as he is happy in his work.

Id., at §562. And, "[t]he meaning of [the promisor's] words and acts is found by relating them to the usage of the past." Ibid.

A teacher, like the respondent, who has held his position for a number of years, might be able to show from the circumstances of this service — and from other relevant facts — that he has a legitimate claim of entitlement to job tenure. Just as this Court has found there to be a "common law of a particular industry or of a particular plant" that may supplement a collective-bargaining agreement, Steelworkers v. Warrior & Gulf Co., 363 U.S. 574, 579, so there may be an unwritten "common law" in a particular university that certain employees shall have the equivalent of tenure. This is particularly likely in a college or university, like Odessa Junior College, that has no explicit tenure system even for senior members of its faculty, but that nonetheless may have created such a system in practice.

Discussion

Justice Stewart seems to distinguish *Roth* from *Sindermann* on the basis of the different expectations of continued service that Roth (who had been employed for only one year) and Sindermann (employed for ten years) might reasonably have held, especially given the common practice at colleges and universities of granting tenure after several years of employment. Justice Stewart noted that "the District Court has not found that there is anything approaching a 'common law' of re-employment . . . so strong as to require University officials to give [Roth] a statement of reasons and a hearing on their decision not to rehire him."

What if Roth had been on the faculty for ten years, rehired each year seemingly as a matter of course? Conversely, could Sindermann's college prospectively abolish its "common law" tenure system by publicly rescinding any statements or rules that imply an expectancy of continued service, even if it does not change its behavior? After *Roth,* could a state circumvent Goldberg v. Kelly by announcing that welfare recipients have no continuing right to receive payments and that henceforth a recipient's eligibility may be determined de novo each month? If not, is it because what counts is not what the state says but what is does? (Then how do you distinguish *Roth*?)

These questions were sharply debated in Arnett v. Kennedy, 416 U.S. 134 (1974), where the Court rejected the claim of a nonprobationary employee of the Office of Economic Opportunity, discharged for cause, that the statutory hearing procedures were constitutionally inadequate. There was no majority opinion. Justice Rehnquist, joined by Chief Justice Burger and Justice Stewart, found it conclusive that the hearing procedures were part of the same statutory scheme that created the interest in employment:

> The employee's statutorily defined right is not a guarantee against removal without cause in the abstract, but such a guarantee as enfored by the procedures which Congress has designed for the determination of cause. . . . [W]here the grant of a substantive right is inextricably intertwined with the limitations on the procedures which are to be employed in determining that right, a litigant in the position of appellee must take the bitter with the sweet.
>
> To conclude otherwise would require us to hold that although Congress chose to enact what was essentially a legislative compromise, and with unmistakable clarity granted governmental employees security against being dismissed without "cause," but refused to accord them a full adversary hearing for the determination of "cause," it was constitutionally disabled from making such a choice. . . . Neither the

> language of the Due Process Clause of the Fifth Amendment nor our cases construing it require any such hobbling restrictions on legislative authority in this area.

The other six Justices, though dividing on the adequacy of OEO's hearing procedures, rejected Justice Rehnquist's analysis and agreed that the due process clause imposed external constraints on such procedures.

Two years later, in Bishop v. Wood, 426 U.S. 341 (1976), a majority of the Court appeared to move closer to Justice Rehnquist's position in *Arnett.* After three years on the Marion, North Carolina, police force, an officer was dismissed without a hearing on various grounds. North Carolina law grants a public employee an enforceable expectation of continued public employment only if the employer grants some form of guarantee. The District Court interpreted the relevant Marion ordinance as not granting such right and concluded that the officer "held this position at the will and pleasure of the city." Writing for the Court, Justice Stevens adopted the District Court's interpretation of state law and concluded that since Bishop had no property interest in his job the due process clause imposed no constraints on the city's termination procedure.

In Cleveland Board of Education v. Loudermill, 470 U.S. 532 (1985), however, the Court seemed to retrace its steps. James Loudermill had been dismissed from his job by the Cleveland Board of Education. Although as a "classified civil servant" he could be dismissed only for cause and was entitled to post-termination administrative review, he claimed that the absence of a *pre*termination hearing violated his due process rights. A similar claim had been asserted in a companion case against the Parma (Ohio) Board of Education. The Court, through Justice White, held in favor of both claimants:

> Respondents' federal constitutional claim depends on their having had a property right in continued employment. If they did, the State could not deprive them of this property without due process.
>
> Property rights are not created by the Constitution, "they are created and their dimensions are defined by existing rules or understandings that stem from an independent source such as state law." Board of Regents v. Roth. The Ohio statute plainly creates such an interest. . . . Indeed, this question does not seem to have been disputed below.
>
> The Parma Board argues, however, that the property right is defined by, and conditioned on, the legislature's choice of procedures for its deprivation. The Board stresses that in addition to specifying the grounds for termination, the statute sets out procedures by which termination may take place. The procedures were adhered to in these cases. According to petitioner, "[t]o require additional procedures would in effect expand the scope of the property interest itself."
>
> This argument, which was accepted by the District Court, has its genesis in the plurality opinion in Arnett v. Kennedy, 416 U.S. 134 (1974). . . . This view garnered three votes in *Arnett,* but was specifically rejected by the other six Justices. Since then, this theory has at times seemed to gather some additional support. More recently, however, the Court has clearly rejected it. In Vitek v. Jones, 445 U.S. 480, 491 (1980), we pointed out that "minimum [procedural] requirements [are] a matter of federal law, they are not diminished by the fact that the State may have specified its own procedures that it may deem adequate for determining the preconditions to adverse official action." This conclusion was reiterated in Logan v. Zimmerman Brush Co., 455 U.S. 422, 432 (1982). . . .

In light of these holdings, it is settled that the "bitter with the sweet" approach misconceives the constitutional guarantee. If a clearer holding is needed, we provide it today. The point is straight-forward: the Due Process Clause provides that certain substantive rights — life, liberty, and property, cannot be deprived except pursuant to constitutionally adequate procedures. The categories of substance and process are distinct. Were the rule otherwise, the Clause would be reduced to a mere tautology. "Property" cannot be defined by the procedures provided for its deprivation any more than can life or liberty. The right to due process "is conferred, not by legislative grace, but by constitutional guarantee. While the legislature may elect not to confer a property interest in [public] employment, it may not constitutionally authorize the deprivation of such an interest, once conferred, without appropriate procedural safeguards." Arnett v. Kennedy, 416 U.S., at 167 (Powell, J., concurring in part and concurring in result in part).

In short, once it is determined that the Due Process Clause applied, "the question remains what process is due." Monisey v. Brewer, 408 U.S. 471, 481 (1972). The answer to that question is not to be found in the Ohio statute.

The need for some form of pretermination hearing . . . is evident from a balancing of the competing interests at stake. These are the private interests in retaining employment, the governmental interest in the expeditious removal of unsatisfactory employees and the avoidance of administrative burdens, and the risk of an erroneous termination. See Mathews v. Eldridge, 424 U.S. 319, 335 (1976). . . .

[A]ffording the employee an opportunity to respond prior to termination would impose neither a significant administrative burden nor intolerable delays. Furthermore, the employer shares the employee's interest in avoiding disruption and erroneous decisions; and until the matter is settled, the employer would continue to receive the benefit of the employee's labors. It is preferable to keep a qualified employee on than to train a new one. A governmental employer also has an interest in keeping citizens usefully employed rather than taking the possibly erroneous and counter-productive step of forcing its employees onto the welfare rolls. Finally, in those situations where the employer perceives a significant hazard in keeping the employee on the job, it can avoid the problem by suspending with pay.

The foregoing considerations indicate that the pretermination "hearing," though necessary, need not be elaborate. . . . In general, "something less" than a full evidentiary hearing is sufficient prior to adverse administrative action. Under state law, respondents were later entitled to a full administrative hearing and judicial review. The only question is what steps were required before the termination took effect. . . .

The essential requirements of due process, and all that respondents seek or the Court of Appeals required, are notice and an opportunity to respond. The opportunity to present reasons, either in person or in writing, why proposed action should not be taken is a fundamental due process requirement. The tenured public employee is entitled to oral or written notice of the charges against him, an explanation of the employer's evidence, and an opportunity to present his side of the story. To require more than this prior to termination would intrude to an unwarranted extent on the government's interest in quickly removing an unsatisfactory employee.

Justice Marshall concurred in part and concurred in the judgment; Justice Brennan concurred in part and dissented with respect to a matter not discussed above. Justice Rehnquist dissented.

Note: Views from the Academy

THOMAS GREY, PROCEDURAL FAIRNESS AND SUBSTANTIVE RIGHTS
18 Nomos (Due Process) 182, 190-202 (1977)

. . . In my view, there is a paradox here. The Constitution is indifferent to the very intense and yet fragile interests of applicants for government jobs or for clemency. . . . The Constitution is even indifferent to the question whether the benefits in question are available at all. But if the benefits are made available, and the conditions for bestowing them are defined by rules, the Constitution closely constrains the discretion of the rule-making authorities to design the procedures under which individual claims for the benefits in question are granted or rejected. . . .

It is tempting to resolve the paradox legalistically; to argue that the Constitution requires fair procedure, but not clemency or job security or welfare. . . .

The truth is that nothing in the language or historical background of the constitutional due process clauses requires or even strongly suggests such [a position]. The constitutional text forbids deprivation of "life, liberty or property without due process of law." Historically, the rights of life, liberty, and property were regarded as natural (and constitutional) rights which the legislatures could neither create nor destroy. The characterization of legislatively created benefits like job tenure or welfare payments as property — much less life or liberty — would not have occurred to the framers of our due process clause.

Traditionally, benefits such as these — benefits which governments can grant or withdraw in their discretion — have been described as "privileges" rather than rights, and as such outside the protection of the due process clauses. Where there was legislative discretion to create and define the substantive terms of a benefit program, there was equal legislative discretion to give structure to the procedures under which that program was administered. With respect to such discretionary programs, the process established by the authority with the discretion to define the program was the only process which was "due."

Modern courts have rejected this traditional position and the "right-privilege distinction" that underlies it. But their rejection cannot be based on the language or the historical meaning of the due process clauses. It must be justified by arguments from contemporary moral ideals implicit in the general concept of procedural fairness. And those arguments must confront the paradox presented by constitutional indifference to the substantive content and indeed to the very existence of benefit programs, combined with deep constitutional concern for the procedures through which those programs are administered once established.

As a first approach to the paradox, one might argue that it is not the content but the source of the programs which gives special force to the requirement that they be accurately enforced. Statutes such as those creating job security or establishing a welfare program may not themselves be required by justice or morality, but they have been passed by a democratically elected legislature, and as such represent the popular will. On this view, which stems from notions of the separation of powers, due process constraints are designed to prevent the circumvention of the legislative will by bureaucrats or executive officials through the kind of careless or intentional misapplication of statutes which can be caused or permitted by excessively informal procedures.

This attempt to justify review for procedural fairness as a device to protect legislators from bureaucrats cannot withstand analysis. Any procedure invalidated on grounds of due process has itself been either mandated directly by the legislature itself, or created by executive officials under express or implied legislative authority. Procedures lacking such legislatively granted authority are unlawful without reference to constitutional due process; they are invalid because they violate statutory law. Due process — if it is to be the vital notion it has been in our constitutional law — must be a restraint on legislative as well as on executive procedural design. . . .

A second approach [to the paradox] would treat the special concern for procedural fairness as based on the morality of contractual obligation. Where substantive norms — whatever their source or status — govern a dispute, they generate in the parties to the dispute the legitimate expectation that these norms will be accurately applied. . . . [T]he Constitution may not require governments to grant job tenure to their employees or welfare payments to their needy citizens, but statutes establishing such programs create expectations which if frustrated trigger a universal sense of injustice. . . .

[But] the promissory theory does not adequately resolve the paradox of due process. If we think of a benefit program established by law as a promise or set of promises establishing rights in the beneficiaries, why should we look only to the substantive provision of the law defining the program as terms of the promise? The program establishes not only substantive entitlements, but also procedures for determining in individual cases whether the substantive terms are met. Government employees may not be fired except for cause — as determined by the following procedure. People meeting certain conditions are entitled to welfare — as determined by the following procedure. . . .

A benefit program might be thought to generate the expectation that its substantive terms will be enforced with a "normal" or "reasonable" degree of accuracy in application. The standard of normality would be determined by reference to the sorts of procedural safeguards commonly provided for already existing programs of a similar type. The moral force of that standard is again promissory — when a new statutory right is established, its beneficiaries can fairly expect that it will be enforced with the degree of accuracy and formality of procedure with which they have been accustomed in their similar previous dealings with the state. They cannot fairly be expected to look to "the fine print" — that is, the statute's own specifications of procedure — and to modify their general procedural expectations accordingly.

The difficulty with this suggestion appears when one probes more deeply into the factors that must be considered in making the judgment what is a "normal" level of procedural formality for the administration of a given statutory benefit. . . .

In general, the promissory theory of procedural fairness is, like the separation of powers theory, inadequate to resolve the paradox of due process. Upon analysis, it turns out that judgments of the appropriate level or procedure required in the administration of a benefit program must vary according to judicial evaluation of the force of the substantive case for providing the benefit in the first place.

It thus remains a puzzle why special constitutional norms of justice should be applied to the procedures under which such benefits are provided, but the substance and even the existence of the benefit programs themselves are left to the discretion of the legislative authority.

In my view, the paradox of procedural fairness as I have stated it is not resolvable. A decision to treat a legislatively created benefit program as subject to the constitutional-moral constraints of due process, while regarding the substance or existence of the program as a matter of legislative grace, would be simply an unjustifiable anomaly. . . .

Using the example of welfare benefits, let me explain what I mean by this perhaps somewhat startling assertion. If I am correct in my thesis, the application of norms of procedural fairness to welfare decisions means that the courts regard claims to welfare benefits as claims of substantive right with a basis beyond the welfare statutes themselves. The overriding of legislative judgment as to the proper procedure for administering welfare programs means that the courts regard the *substance* of the welfare programs as no longer entirely a matter of legislative discretion, subject to legislative alteration at will and indeed to legislative withdrawal.

Surely this conclusion is contradicted by the emphatically proclaimed judicial position that the substance of welfare programs is not subject to probing judicial review, and by the general understanding that there is no judicially enforceable "constitutional right to welfare." Surely if a legislature repealed its welfare program altogether, the courts would not require it to reenact the program and enjoin it to raise tax moneys to support it. Surely, the objection continues, when the courts speak of an "entitlement" to welfare as the ground for judicial scrutiny of the procedures used in the program, they refer only to the fact that the legislature has chosen to structure the substance of existing welfare programs through reasonably definite rules governing eligibility and benefits provided. . . .

[I]t must be conceded that welfare is not a full-fledged, judicially enforceable, constitutional right. A legislature balked in its attempt to get free of procedural restrictions imposed on its welfare program would retain the power to reduce the cost of that program by cutting benefits across the board, reducing the number of recipients, or even eliminating the welfare program altogether. The courts would not closely scrutinize the steps taken and the lines drawn in such a substantive cost-cutting program — at least such is present constitutional doctrine.

The reasons for the courts' reluctance to intervene with the substance of welfare programs in this way lie, I believe, in the courts' present judgment of the proper limitations on their institutional competence and authority. Even if they considered that some guarantee of minimum material support for those unable to support themselves was a fundamental individual right — a right properly deserving of constitutional status — they might quite properly think it was a right beyond their power to enforce against infringement by direct legislative withdrawal of funds. At least — in the extreme case of total legislative withdrawal from public assistance — enforcement of the right to welfare would require the judiciary to order the disbursement of large sums of public money, to draft a complex scheme of social legislation, and to force the collection or diversion of massive tax revenues. None of these tasks are within our traditional conception of the judicial role, and that institutional consideration would probably prevent straightforward judicial protection of the right to welfare.

On the other hand, judicial enforcement of the requirements of the rule of law and of procedural fairness in the structure and the administration of welfare programs are quite reasonably within traditional conception of the judicial role. . . .

Let me try to summarize the general conception of procedural fairness suggested and tentatively sketched in this essay. Procedural fairness involves a special moral concern for the correct and accurate decision of disputes which affect substantive rights. Its norms impinge from the outside on decision-making institutions, and require of those institutions more concern for the substantive rights which would be threatened or infringed by erroneous decisions than the institutions (or officials) would otherwise be inclined to show, given the natural balance those institutions are likely to strike between the competing claims of accurate decision, cost, and institutional self-interest.

It makes sense to impose special procedural controls from outside the authoritative decision-making institution — whether through the moral check of conscience, or the external institutional check of judicial review — only when the substantive right placed at hazard has its source outside the decision-making institution itself. Thus "entitlements" created only by the decision-making institution's own rules should not be protected by external restraints of procedural fairness. These, in the old terminology of the law, are "mere privileges." The kinds of substantive rights which properly trigger due process restraints are categorical moral rights or, in the legal context, rights with a hierarchical status above the rules of the decision-making institution. In the usual case — where the decision-making institution's authority derives from the legislature — the only substantive rights having this status are constitutional rights. Some constitutional substantive rights may be judicially enforced largely or only through procedural due process constraints, because institutional constraints on judicial power prevent their more direct enforcement. . . .

DOUGLAS LAYCOCK, DUE PROCESS AND SEPARATION OF POWERS: THE EFFORTS TO MAKE THE DUE PROCESS CLAUSES NONJUSTICIABLE

60 Tex. L. Rev. 875, 879-882 (1982)

The syntax of the due process clauses indicates that "life, liberty, or property" is being taken; if so, then and only then do we determine what due process is required before the taking. We must decide what the two phrases mean to make these determinations, but even without knowing what they mean, the structure of the sentence tells us that two separate concepts are being discussed. Any theory that collapses one into the other — that allows "due process" to be defined in the course of defining "life, liberty, or property" — reduces the clauses to tautologies.

The most obvious initial hypothesis for distinguishing the two phrases is to say that "life, liberty, or property" refers to substance, and that "due process" refers to procedure. . . .

Permitting legislatures to define rights to life, liberty, or property in explicitly procedural terms leads to results that most lawyers would find erroneous and most speakers would find absurd. With respect to liberty and property, these absurdities have been hidden by confusion and disagreement over the larger question whether legislatures can define rights to liberty and property at all. It is therefore helpful to start with the right to life.

Consider two possible murder laws for the District of Columbia: (1) "Any person who murders another shall suffer death," and (2) "Any person found by a preponderance of the evidence to have murdered another shall suffer death." Under the first statute, the due process clause would require the government to prove murder beyond a reasonable doubt. What about the second statute? . . . Rehnquist should say that a defendant's "statutorily defined right is not a guarantee against [death unless he murders] in the abstract, but such a guarantee as enforced by the procedures which Congress has designated for the determination of [whether he murdered]." Thus, a preponderance of the evidence — or merely probable cause, if Congress really got tough on crime — could constitutionally support a judgment of death. And it could do so because, although the defendant would be quite dead, he would not have been deprived of "life" in the special sense in which the term is apparently used in Rehnquistian due process clauses.

Perhaps not even Rehnquist would so vote, but he would be hard pressed to distinguish his reasoning in *Arnett.* It is true that life is more important than a government job, but that difference goes to how much process is due if the due process clause applies. His *Arnett* opinion says the clause does not apply, because no life, liberty, or property has been taken.

Nor is it sufficent to say that the right to life is inherent, or derived from natural law, but that the right to property — and certainly the right to a government job — is defined by legislation. A capital punishment statute defines the scope of the right to life, just as a civil service statute defines the scope of the right to a government job. It is true that the capital punishment statute is wholly negative, specifying when life will be taken away, while the civil service statute specifies when the job will be awarded in the first place as well as when it will be taken away. This distinction may be relevant to many questions, but it is not relevant to whether the thing taken is life or property. . . . Every individual enters life subject to legislative specification of the conditions that will cause him to forfeit it. If my entitlement to a job can be defined procedurally, so can my entitlement to life. . . .

[T]he lack of consensus about the boundaries of liberty and property should not mislead us into thinking that the boundaries might be described in procedural terms.

2. *Politics and the Governmental Workforce*

The question of whether political beliefs and activities can legitimately be used as a qualification for or bar from employment or licensure arises in two different contexts. The first involves the regulation of putatively subversive views or activities. See Chapter 4. The second involves patronage systems of hiring and firing — by which affiliation in the "right" party is a necessary criterion for employment.

a. "Subversive" Politics, Employment, and Licensure

In addition to the millions of Americans directly employed by the government, additional millions are employed in industries, especially those related to defense, that contract with the government to provide goods and services.[25] To what extent can the United States, either through setting contractual conditions or through legislative and executive regulation, place political conditions on eligibility for employment?

UNITED STATES v. ROBEL

389 U.S. 258 (1967)

Appeal from the United States District Court for the Western District of Washington

WARREN, C.J.

This appeal draws into question the constitutionality of §5(a)(1)(D) of the Subversive Activities Control Act of 1950,[a] which provides that, when a Communist-action organization is under a final order to register, it shall be unlawful for any member of the organization "to engage in any employment in any defense facility." In Communist Party v. Subversive Activities Control Board, 367 U.S. 1 (1961), this Court sustained an order of the SACB requiring the Communist Party of the United States to register as a Communist-action organization under the Act. The Board's order became final on October 20, 1961. At that time appellee, a member of the Communist Party, was employed as a machinist at the Seattle, Washington, shipyard of Todd Shipyards Corporation. On August 20, 1962, the Secretary of Defense, acting under authority delegated by §5(b) of the Act, designated that shipyard a "defense facility." Appellee's continued employment at the shipyard after that date subjected him to prosecution under §5(a)(1)(D), and on May 21, 1963, an indictment was filed charging him with a violation of that section. . . .

[T]he operative fact upon which the job disability depends is the exercise of an individual's rights of association, which is protected by the provisions of the First Amendment. . . .

The Government seeks to defend the statute on the ground that it was passed pursuant to Congress' war power. . . . More specifically in this case, the Government asserts that §5(a)(1)(D) is an expression "of the growing concern shown by the executive and legislative branches of government over the risks of internal subversion in plants on which the national defense depend[s]." Yet, this concept of "national defense" cannot be deemed an end in itself, justifying any exercise of legislative power designed to promote such a goal. Implicit in the term "national defense" is the notion of defending those values and ideals which set this Nation apart. For almost

25. One reporter has estimated that 3.3 million persons were employed in defense-related industries as of 1989. See Frederick M. Biddle, As Thoughts Turn to Conversion, Boston Globe, Nov. 19, 1989, at 101. An additional 4.7 million persons — 1.7 million in the armed forces and 3 million civilians — were employed directly by the United States in 1988 in "defense-related agencies." United States Bureau of the Census, Statistical Abstract of the United States 1991, Table 545. All of these numbers have almost certainly declined with the end of the Cold War.

a. The Act was passed over the veto of President Truman. In his veto message, President Truman told Congress, "The Department of Justice, the Department of Defense, the Central Intelligence Agency, and the Department of State have all advised me that the bill would seriously damage the security and the intelligence operations for which they are responsible. They have strongly expressed the hope that the bill would not become law." H.R. Doc. No. 708, 81st Cong., 2d Sess., 1 (1950).

President Truman also observed that "the language of the bill is so broad and vague that it might well result in penalizing the legitimate activities of people who are not Communists at all, but loyal citizens."

two centuries, our country has taken singular pride in the democratic ideals enshrined in its Constitution, and the most cherished of those ideals have found expression in the First Amendment. It would indeed be ironic if, in the name of national defense, we would sanction the subversion of one of those liberties — the freedom of association — which makes the defense of the Nation worthwhile.

When Congress' exercise of one of its enumerated powers clashes with those individual liberties protected by the Bill of Rights, it is our "delicate and difficult task" to determine whether the resulting restriction on freedom can be tolerated. The Government emphasizes that the purpose of §5(a)(1)(D) is to reduce the threat of sabotage and espionage in the Nation's defense plants. The Government's interest in such a prophylactic measure is not insubstantial. But it cannot be doubted that the means chosen to implement that governmental purpose in this instance cut deeply into the right of association. Section 5(a)(1)(D) put appellee to the choice of surrendering his organizational affiliation, regardless of whether his membership threatened the security of defense facility, or giving up his job. . . . The statute quite literally establishes guilt by association alone, without any need to establish that an individual's association poses the threat feared by the Government in proscribing it. The inhibiting effect on the exercise of First Amendment rights is clear.

It has become axiomatic that "[p]recision of regulation must be the touchstone in an area so closely touching our most precious freedoms." Such precision is notably lacking in §5(a)(1)(D). That statute casts its net across a broad range of associational activities, indiscriminately trapping membership which can be constitutionally punished and membership which cannot be so proscribed. It is made irrelevant to the statute's operation that an individual may be a passive or inactive member of a designated organization, that he may be unaware of the organization's unlawful aims, or that he may disagree with those unlawful aims. It is also made irrelevant that an individual who is subject to the penalties of §5(a)(1)(D) may occupy a nonsensitive position in a defense facility. Thus, §5(a)(1)(D) contains the fatal defect of overbreadth because it seeks to bar employment both for association which may be proscribed and for association which may not be proscribed consistently with First Amendment rights. See . . . Aptheker v. Secretary of State, 378 U.S. 500 (1964).[26] This the Constitution will not tolerate.

We are not unmindful of the congressional concern over the danger of sabotage and espionage in national defense industries, and nothing we hold today should be read to deny Congress the power under narrowly drawn legislation to keep from sensitive positions in defense facilities those who would use their positions to disrupt the Nation's production facilities. We have recognized that, while the Constitution protects against invasions of individual rights, it does not withdraw from the Government the power to safeguard its vital interests. . . . Spies and saboteurs do exist, and Congress can, of course, prescribe criminal penalties for those who engage in espionage and sabotage. The Government can deny access to its secrets to those who would use such information to harm the Nation. And Congress can declare sensitive positions in national defense industries off

26. *Aptheker* involved the Fifth Amendment right to travel and held that mere Party membership, without knowledge of the Party's unlawful aims and specific intent to further them, could not constitutionally justify denying a member a passport.

limits to those who would use such positions to disrupt the production of defense materials. The Government has told us that Congress, in passing §5(a)(1)(D), made a considered judgment that one possible alternative to that statute — an industrial security screening program — would be inadequate and ineffective to protect against sabotage in defense facilities. It is not our function to examine the validity of that congressional judgment. Neither is it our function to determine whether an industrial security screening program exhausts the possible alternatives to the statute under review. We are concerned solely with determining whether the statute before us has exceeded the bounds imposed by the Constitution when First Amendment rights are at stake. The task of writing legislation which will stay within those bounds has been committed to Congress. Our decision today simply recognizes that, when legitimate legislative concerns are expressed in a statute which imposes a substantial burden on protected First Amendment activities, Congress must achieve its goal by means which have a "less drastic" impact on the continued vitality of First Amendment freedoms.[b] The Constitution and the basic position of First Amendment rights in our democratic fabric demand nothing less.[27]

BRENNAN, J., concurring in the result. . . .

Aptheker v. Secretary of State, 378 U.S. 500 (1964), held §6 of the [Subversive Activities Control] Act overbroad in that it deprived Party members of the right to travel without regard to whether they were active members of the Party or intended to further the Party's unlawful objectives, and therefore invalidly abridged, on the basis of political associations, the members' constitutionally protected right to travel. Section 5(a)(1)(D) also treats as irrelevant whether or not the members are active, or know the Party's unlawful purposes, or intend to pursue those purposes. . . .

It is true, however, as the Government points out, that Congress often regulates indiscriminately, through preventive or prophylactic measures, and that such regulation has been upheld even where fundamental freedoms are potentially affected. Each regulation must be examined in terms of its potential impact upon fundamental rights, the importance of the end sought and the necessity for the means adopted. The Government argues that §5(a)(1)(D) may be distinguished from §6 on the basis of these factors. Section 5(a)(1)(D) limits employment only in "any defense facility," while §6 deprived every Party member of the right to apply for or to hold a passport. If §5(a)(1)(D) were in fact narrowly applied, the restrictions it would place upon employment are not as great as those placed upon the right to travel by §6. The problems presented by the employ-

b. It has been suggested that this case should be decided by "balancing" the governmental interests expressed in §5(a)(1)(D) against the First Amendment rights asserted by the appellee. This we decline to do. We recognize that both interests are substantial, but we deem it inappropriate for this Court to label one as being more important or more substantial than the other. Our inquiry is more circumscribed. Faced with a clear conflict between a federal statute enacted in the interests of national security and an individual's exercise of his First Amendment rights, we have confined our analysis to whether Congress has adopted a constitutional means in achieving its concededly legitimate legislative goal. In making this determination we have found it necessary to measure the validity of the means adopted by Congress against both the goal it has sought to achieve and the specific prohibitions of the First Amendment. But we have in no way "balanced" those respective interests. We have ruled only that the Constitution requires that the conflict between congressional power and individual rights be accommodated by legislation drawn more narrowly to avoid the conflict. . . .

27. Justice Marshall took no part in the decision of the case.

ment of Party members at defense facilities, moreover, may well involve greater hazards to national security than those created by allowing Party members to travel abroad. We may assume, too, that Congress may have been justified in its conclusion that alternatives to §5(a)(1)(D) were inadequate. For these reasons, I am not persuaded to the Court's view that overbreadth is fatal to this statute, as I agreed it was in other contexts; see e.g., Keyishian v. Board of Regents, 385 U.S. 589.

[Justice Brennan went on to conclude that Congress had not properly delegated to the Secretary of Defense the authority to designate "defense facilities."]

WHITE, J., joined by Harlan, J., dissenting. . . .

The relevant cases uniformly reveal the necessity for accommodating the right of association and the public interest. . . .

Nor does the Court mandate a different course in this case. Apparently "active" members of the Communist Party who have demonstrated their commitment to the illegal aims of the Party may be barred from defense facilities. This exclusion would have the same deterrent effect upon associational rights as the statute before us, but the governmental interest in security would override that effect. Also, the Court would seem to permit barring appellee, although not an "active" member of the Party, from employment in "sensitive" positions in the defense establishment. Here, too, the interest in anticipating and preventing espionage or sabotage would outweigh the deterrent impact of job disqualification. If I read the Court correctly, associating with the Communist Party may at times be deterred by barring members from employment and nonmembership may at times be imposed as a condition of engaging in defense work. In the case before us the Court simply disagrees with the Congress and the Defense Department, ruling that Robel does not present a sufficient danger to the national security to require him to choose between membership in the Communist Party and his employment in a defense facility. Having less confidence than the majority in the prescience of this remote body when dealing with threats to the security of the country, I much prefer the judgment of Congress and the Executive Branch that the interest of appellee in remaining a member of the Communist Party, knowing that it has been adjudicated a Communist-action organization, is less substantial than the public interest in excluding him from employment in critical defense industries.

The national interest asserted by the Congress is real and substantial. . . . Given the characteristics of the Party, its foreign domination, its primary goal of government overthrow, the discipline which it exercises over its members, and its propensity for espionage and sabotage, the exclusion of members of the Party who know the Party is a Communist-action organization from certain defense plants is well within the powers of Congress.

Congress should be entitled to take suitable precautionary measures. Some Party members may be no threat at all, but many of them undoubtedly are, and it is exceedingly difficult to identify those in advance of the very events which Congress seeks to avoid. If Party members such as Robel may be barred from "sensitive positions," it is because they are a potential threat to security. For the same reason they should be excludable from employment in defense plants which Congress and the Secretary of Defense consider of critical importance to the security of the country.

The statute does not prohibit membership in the Communist Party. Nor are appellee and other Communists excluded from all employment in the United States, or even from all defense plants. The touchstones for exclusion are the requirements of national security, and the facilities designated under this standard amount to only about one percent of all the industrial establishments in the United States.

It is this impact on associational rights, although specific and minimal, which the Court finds impermissible. But as the statute's dampening effect on associational rights is to be weighed against the asserted and obvious government interest in keeping members of Communist-action groups from defense facilities, it would seem important to identify what interest Robel has in joining and remaining a member of a group whose primary goals he may not share. We are unenlightened, however, by the opinion of the Court or by the record in this case, as to the purposes which Robel and others like him may have in associating with the Party. The legal aims and programs of the Party are not identified or appraised nor are Robel's activities as a member of the Party. The Court is left with a vague and formless concept of associational rights and its own notions of what constitutes an unreasonable risk to defense facilities.

The Court says that mere membership in an association with knowledge that the association pursues unlawful aims cannot be the basis for criminal prosecution, Scales v. United States, 367 U.S. 203 (1961), or for denial of a passport, Aptheker v. Secretary of State, 378 U.S. 500 (1964). But denying the opportunity to be employed in some defense plants is a much smaller deterrent to the exercise of associational rights than denial of a passport or a criminal penalty attached solely to membership, and the Government's interest in keeping potential spies and saboteurs from defense plants is much greater than its interest in keeping disloyal Americans from traveling abroad or in committing all Party members to prison. The "delicate and difficult" judgment to which the Court refers should thus result in a different conclusion from that reached in the *Scales* and *Aptheker* cases.

Discussion

1. Near the beginning of the opinion, Chief Justice Warren asserts that "[w]hen Congress' exercise of one of its enumerated powers clashes with those individual liberties protected by the Bill of Rights, it is our 'delicate and difficult task' to determine whether the resulting restriction on freedom can be tolerated." In the concluding footnote he asserts that "we have in no way 'balanced' " the competing interests. How could the Court have reached a decision without some balancing? Does the Chief Justice perhaps mean only that the Court has not engaged in a *situational* consideration of the interests at bar, e.g., whether appellee's position in the shipyard was so sensitive as to justify excluding him from it? To what extent does the decision turn on the Court's belief that the government could achieve its legitimate goals through less drastic means? Can the Court consistently rely on the possibility of less drastic means without considering whether viable alternatives in fact exist?

2. Compare *Robel* with Keyishian v. Board of Regents, 385 U.S. 589 (1967), which struck down New York civil service and education laws that required state employees in general, and teachers in particular, to certify, as a condition for employment, that they were not members of the Communist Party. Justice Brennan wrote:

In Elfbrandt v. Russell, 384 U.S. 11, we said, "Those who join an organization but do not share its unlawful purposes and who do not participate in its unlawful activities surely pose no threat, either as citizens or as public employees." We there struck down a statutorily required oath binding the state employee not to become a member of the Communist Party with knowledge of its unlawful purpose, on threat of discharge and perjury prosecution if the oath were violated. We found that "[a]ny lingering doubts that proscription of mere knowing membership, without any showing of 'specific intent,' would run afoul of the Constitution was set at rest by our decision in *Aptheker*."...

"A law which applies to membership without the 'specific intent' to further the illegal aims of the organization infringes unnecessarily on protected freedoms. It rests on the doctrine of 'guilt by association' which has no place here." *Elfbrandt.* Thus mere Party membership, even with knowledge of the Party's unlawful goals, cannot suffice to justify criminal punishment, see Scales v. United States, 367 U.S. 203; Noto v. United States, 367 U.S. 290; Yates v. United States, 354 U.S. 298; nor may it warrant a finding of moral unfitness justifying disbarment.

These limitations clearly apply to [the civil service provision] which blankets all state employees, regardless of the "sensitivity" of their positions. But even the [education] provision, applicable primarily to activities of teachers, who have captive audiences of young minds, are subject to these limitations in favor of freedom of expression and association: the stifling effect on the academic mind from curtailing freedom of association in such manner is manifest, and has been documented in recent studies. *Elfbrandt* and *Aptheker* state the governing standard: legislation which sanctions membership unaccompanied by specific intent to further the unlawful goals of the organization or which is not active membership, violates constitutional limitations.[28]

Although *Keyishian* was decided only a year earlier, *Robel* neither cites it nor speaks in as broad language. Does *Robel* reflect second thoughts about the wholesale incorporation of the *Scales* criteria for punishment for membership into the broader area of civil disabilities? Does it nonetheless implicitly establish the *Scales* criteria as a presumption?

3. Consider whether *Robel* — and especially the Court's refusal to consider the less drastic regulatory alternatives that might be available — may implicitly reflect a mode of *procedural* rather than substantive review. That is, the Court may have concluded that Congress had not focused on the possibility of achieving its legitimate goals through less intrusive means, and in effect "remanded" the matter to Congress for its reconsideration. Consider the political climate in which the Subversive Activities Control Act of 1950 was enacted, the Court's footnote a, and the extent to which First Amendment doctrine had evolved during the intervening 27 years.

b. The Scope of Permissible Inquiry into Beliefs and Membership

Inextricably connected with the issue of membership in a political organization is the state's putative power to compel information relating to one's beliefs and membership in organizations. Three 1971 cases, concerned with attempts by

28. Justice Clark dissented, joined by Justices Harlan, Stewart, and White.

various states to deny applicants admission to the bar, illustrate the problems as well as the sharp division within the Court in regard to purported solutions.

Baird v. State Bar of Arizona, 401 U.S. 1, held that petitioner could not be denied admission to the bar for refusing to answer whether she had ever been a member of the Communist Party or any organization advocating overthrow of the United States government by force or violence. The state bar argued that it was entitled to an answer on the premise that a) it was legitimate to deny admission to the bar to anyone "who truly and sincerely believes in the overthrow of the United States Government by force and violence" and b) an affirmative answer to the question would provide a clue that further investigation of the applicant is necessary to ascertain her actual beliefs. "The Committee again emphasizes that a mere answer of 'yes' would not lead to an automatic rejection of the application," but would lead instead only "to an investigation and interrogation as to whether or not the applicant presently entertains the view that a violent overthrow of the United States Government is something to be sought after."

Justices Douglas, Brennan, and Marshall joined Justice Black's opinion ordering Ms. Baird's admission. That opinion took note of the confusion spawned by the Court's previous decisions in the area and stated that the best solution was to return to the "45 words that make up the First Amendment," which indicate, according to Black, that, "[W]hatever justification may be offered, a State may not inquire about a man's views or associations solely for the purpose of withholding a right or benefit because of what he believes." Justice Stewart, who provided the necessary fifth vote compelling Ms. Baird's admission, focused instead on the state bar's admission that it would exclude an applicant solely on the grounds of sincere belief of forbidden ideas. Citing *Scales,* he emphasized the need for both knowing membership and a "specific intent to further the organization's illegal goals."

The principal dissent, written by Justice Blackmun and joined by Chief Justice Burger and Justices Harlan and White, accepted the premise that more than "mere belief" would have to be shown to deny admission, but argued that the question was legitimate as part of the permitted inquiry into the actual content of one's views and organizational memberships. "Assurance that applicant Baird at least professes to refrain from forceful and violent overthrow of the Government of which, upon admission, she will become a true and working part . . . is a subject of legitimate inquiry."

Justices Harlan and White also wrote separate dissents. "I do maintain," said Justice Harlan, "that there is no constitutional barrier to denying admission to those who seek entry to the profession for the very purpose of doing away with the orderly processes of law, and that temperate inquiry into the character of their beliefs in this regard, which is all that is shown here, is a relevant and permissible course to that end." Justice White, in turn, emphasized the propriety of the state asking "perfectly relevant questions designed to ascertain whether an applicant considers it the proper role of the lawyer, as practitioner, to advise and advocate violence as a means for settling disputes or achieving social or political ends."

An identically divided Court ordered Ohio to admit to its bar Martin Stolar, who had previously been admitted to the New York bar. In re Stolar, 401 U.S. 23 (1971). Stolar had given Ohio all the information he had made available to New York a year earlier, including a listing of all current associational affiliations and a negative reply to a question about membership in any group seeking to effect changes in the American form of government. He did, however, refuse to answer Ohio's request for a list of organizations "of which you have been a member since registering as a law student," "of which you are or have been a member," and of organizations to which he belonged that advocated the overthrow of the United States government by force.

The first two questions were disallowed by reference to Shelton v. Tucker, 364 U.S. 479 (1960), which had struck down an Arkansas statute requiring teachers to disclose all organizations to which they had belonged within the preceding five years. The Court in *Shelton* concluded that the broad disclosure requirement violated a teacher's freedom of association by placing "pressure upon a teacher to avoid any ties which might displease those who control his professional destiny. . . ." The *Stolar* plurality thought that the Ohio questions were perceived as placing similar pressure on "[l]aw students who know they must survive this screening process before practicing their profession" and were thus unconstitutional. The third question was disallowed for substantially the same reasons given in *Baird*. Again, Justice Stewart concurred only in the judgment, and the remaining Justices dissented.

The final case decided that day was Law Students Research Council v. Wadmond, 401 U.S. 154, where Justice Stewart joined the *Baird-Stolar* dissenters and wrote an opinion for the Court upholding the screening system employed by the New York bar. The system was challenged by prospective members, none of whom had actually been refused admission. Their principal contention was that the system "by its very existence works a 'chilling effect' " on the rights of freedom of association. The Court found that the bar's criteria encompassed no more than "dishonorable conduct relevant to the legal profession." The Court also dealt with Rule 9406 and questions designed to implement its requirements that the applicant "believe in the form of government of the United States and [be] loyal to such government." Although the rule on its face might raise serious questions, Justice Stewart concluded that, as construed by the bar, it only ascertained that "an applicant is not one who 'swears to an oath [to support the Constitution] pro forma while declaring or manifesting his disagreement with or indifference to the oath.' " The Court then turned to the New York bar's implementing questions:

> 26. (a) Have you ever organized or helped to organize or become a member of any organization or group of persons which, during the period of your membership or association, you knew was advocating or teaching that the government of the United States or any state or any political subdivision thereof should be overthrown or overturned by force, violence or any unlawful means? If your answer is in the affirmative, state the facts below.
>
> (b) If your answer to (a) is in the affirmative, did you, during the period of such membership or association, have the specific intent to further the aims of such organization or group of persons to overthrow or overturn the government of the United States or any state or any political subdivision thereof by force, violence or any unlawful means?

Justice Stewart easily distinguished Question 26 from the questions he had agreed were invalid in *Baird* and *Stolar:*

Question 26 is precisely tailored to conform to the relevant decisions of this Court. Our cases establish that inquiry into associations of the kind referred to is permissible under the limitations carefully observed here. We have held that knowing membership in an organization advocating the overthrow of the Government by force or violence, on the part of one sharing the specific intent to further the organization's illegal goals, may be made criminally punishable. Scales v. United States, 367 U.S. 203. It is also well settled that Bar examiners ask about Communist affiliations as a preliminary to further inquiry into the nature of the association and may exclude an applicant for refusal to answer. Konigsberg v. State Bar, 366 U.S. 36 (1961). Surely a State is constitutionally entitled to make such an inquiry of an applicant for admission to a profession dedicated to the peaceful and reasoned settlement of disputes between men, and between a man and his government. The very Constitution that the appellants invoke stands as a living embodiment of that ideal. . . .

3. Political Patronage and the First Amendment

To what degree may government take nonsubversive political beliefs and activities into account in deciding whom to hire and fire? The First Amendment imposes significant limits on the government's power to treat individuals differently based on their political views. It would be bizarre, however, if Presidents could not consider party affiliation in deciding whom to appoint to their Cabinet or if they could not dismiss a Cabinet member who has expressed opposition to a policy supported by the chief executive.

In Elrod v. Burns, 427 U.S. 347 (1976), the Court considered for the first time the constitutionality of conditioning governmental employment on membership in, or loyalty to, the political party holding power. Although the Court rejected the Chicago patronage practice, no opinion commanded a majority. Four years later, Justice Stevens wrote for the Court in a decision extending *Elrod.*

BRANTI v. FINKEL

445 U.S. 507 (1980)

Certiorari to the United States Court of Appeals for the Second Circuit

STEVENS, J.

The question presented is whether the First and Fourteenth Amendments to the Constitution protect an assistant public defender who is satisfactorily performing his job from discharge solely because of his political beliefs. . . .

The critical facts can be summarized briefly. The Rockland County Public Defender is appointed by the County Legislature for a term of six years. He in turn appoints nine assistants who serve at his pleasure. The two respondents have served as assistants since their respective appointments in March 1971 and September 1975; they are both Republicans.

Petitioner Branti's predecessor, a Republican, was appointed in 1972 by a Republican-dominated County Legislature. By 1977, control of the legislature had shifted to the Democrats and petitioner, also a Democrat, was appointed to replace the incumbent when his term expired. As soon as petitioner was formally appointed on January 3, 1978, he began executing termination notices for six of the nine assistants then in office. Respondents were among those who were to be terminated. With one possible exception, the nine who were to be appointed or retained were all Democrats and were all selected by Democratic legislators or Democratic town chairmen on a basis that had been determined by the Democratic caucus. . . .

I

In Elrod v. Burns the Court held that the newly elected Democratic Sheriff of Cook County, Ill., had violated the constitutional rights of certain non-civil service employees by discharging them "because they did not support and were not members of the Democratic Party and had failed to obtain the sponsorship of one of its leaders." 427 U.S., at 351. That holding was supported by two separate opinions.

Writing for the plurality, Mr. Justice Brennan identified two separate but interrelated reasons supporting the conclusion that the discharges were prohibited by the First and Fourteenth Amendments. First, he analyzed the impact of a political patronage system on freedom of belief and association. Noting that in order to retain their jobs, the sheriff's employees were required to pledge their allegiance to the Democratic party, work for or contribute to the party's candidates, or obtain a Democratic sponsor, he concluded that the inevitable tendency of such a system was to coerce employees into compromising their true beliefs. That conclusion, in his opinion, brought the practice within the rule of cases like Board of Education v. Barnette, 319 U.S. 624, condemning the use of governmental power to prescribe what the citizenry must accept as orthodox opinion.

Second, apart from the potential impact of patronage dismissals on the formation and expression of opinion, Mr. Justice Brennan also stated that the practice had the effect of imposing an unconstitutional condition on the receipt of a public benefit and therefore came within the rule of cases like Perry v. Sindermann, 408 U.S. 593. In support of the holding in *Perry* that even an employee with no contractual right to retain his job cannot be dismissed for engaging in constitutionally protected speech, the Court had stated:

> For at least a quarter-century, this Court has made clear that even though a person has no "right" to a valuable governmental benefit and even though the government may deny him the benefit for any number of reasons, there are some reasons upon which the government may not rely. It may not deny a benefit to a person on a basis that infringes his constitutionally protected interests — especially, his interest in freedom of speech. For if the government could deny a benefit to a person because of his constitutionally protected speech or associations, his exercise of those freedoms would in effect be penalized and inhibited. This would allow the government to "produce a result which [it] could not command directly." Speiser v. Randall, 357 U.S. 513, 526. Such interference with constitutional rights is impermissible.
>
> Thus, the respondent's lack of a contractual or tenure "right" to reemployment for the 1969-1970 academic year is immaterial to his free speech claim. Indeed, twice before, this Court as specifically held that the nonrenewal of a nontenured public school teacher's one-year contract may not be predicated on his exercise of First and Fourteenth Amendment rights. Shelton v. Tucker, supra; Keyishian v. Board of Regents, supra. We reaffirm those holdings here. . . .

If the First Amendment protects a public employee from discharge based on what he has said, it must also protect him from discharge based on what he believes. Under this line of analysis, unless the Government can demonstrate "an overriding interest," 427 U.S., at 368, "of vital importance," id., at 362, requiring that a person's private beliefs conform to those of the hiring authority, his beliefs cannot be the sole basis for depriving him of continued public employment.

Mr. Justice Stewart's concurring opinion avoided comment on the first branch of Mr. Justice Brennan's analysis, but expressly relied on the same passage from Perry v. Sindermann that is quoted above.

Petitioner argues that Elrod v. Burns should be read to prohibit only dismissals resulting from an employee's failure to capitulate to political coercion. Thus, he argues that, so long as an employee is not asked to change his political affiliation or to contribute to or work for the party's candidates, he may be dismissed with impunity — even though he would not have been dismissed if he had had the proper political sponsorship and even though the sole reason for dismissing him was to replace him with a person who did have such sponsorship. Such an interpretation would surely emasculate the principles set forth in *Elrod.* While it would perhaps eliminate the more blatant forms of coercion described in *Elrod,* it would not eliminate the coercion of belief that necessarily flows from the knowledge that one must have a sponsor in the dominant party in order to retain one's job. More importantly, petitioner's interpretation would require the Court to repudiate entirely the conclusion of both Mr. Justice Brennan and Mr. Justice Stewart that the First Amendment prohibits the dismissal of a public employee solely because of his private political beliefs.

In sum, there is no requirement that dismissed employees prove that they, or other employees, have been coerced into changing, either actually or ostensibly, their political allegiance. To prevail in this type of an action, it was sufficient, as *Elrod* holds, for respondents to prove that they were discharged "solely for the reason that they were not affiliated with or sponsored by the Democratic Party." Id., at 350.

II

Both opinions in *Elrod* recognize that party affiliation may be an acceptable requirement for some types of government employment. Thus, if an employee's private political beliefs would interfere with the discharge of his public duties, his First Amendment rights may be required to yield to the State's vital interest in maintaining governmental effectiveness and efficiency. 427 U.S., at 366. In *Elrod,* it was clear that the duties of the employees — the chief deputy of the process division of the sheriff's office, a process server and another employee in that office, and a bailiff and security guard at the Juvenile Court of Cook County — were not of that character, for they were as Mr. Justice Stewart stated, "nonpolicymaking, nonconfidential" employees. Id., at 375.

As Mr. Justice Brennan noted in *Elrod,* it is not always easy to determine whether a position is one in which political affiliation is a legitimate factor to be considered. 427 U.S., at 367. Under some circumstances, a position may be appropriately considered political even though it is neither confidential nor policymaking in character. As one obvious example, if a State's election laws require that precincts be supervised by two election judges of different parties, a Republican judge could be legitimately discharged solely for changing his party registration. That conclusion would not depend on any finding that the job involved participation in policy decisions or access to confidential information. Rather, it would simply rest on the fact that party membership was essential to the discharge of the employee's governmental responsibilities.

It is equally clear that party affiliation is not necessarily relevant to every policymaking or confidential position. The coach of a state university's football team formulates policy, but no one could seriously claim that Republicans make better coaches than Democrats, or vice versa, no matter which party is in control of the state government. On the other hand, it is equally clear that the governor of a state may appropriately believe that the official duties of various assistants who help him write speeches, explain his views to the press, or communicate with the legislature cannot be performed effectively unless those persons share his political beliefs and party commitments. In sum, the ultimate inquiry is not whether the label "policymaker" or "confidential" fits a particular position; rather, the question is whether the hiring authority can demonstrate that party affiliation is an appropriate requirement for the effective performance of the public office involved.

Having thus framed the issue, it is manifest that the continued employment of an assistant public defender cannot properly be conditioned upon his allegiance to the political party in control of the county government. The primary, if not the only, responsibility of an assistant public defender is to represent individual citizens in controversy with the State.[a] As we recently observed in commenting on the duties of counsel appointed to represent indigent defendants in federal criminal proceedings:

> . . . [T]he primary office performed by appointed counsel parallels the office of privately retained counsel. Although it is true that appointed counsel serves pursuant to statutory authorization and in furtherance of the federal interest in insuring effective representation of criminal defendants, his duty is not to the public at large, except in that general way. His principal responsibility is to serve the undivided interests of his client. Indeed, an indispensable element of the effective performance of his responsibilities is the ability to act independently of the government and to oppose it in adversary litigation. Ferri v. Ackerman, 444 U.S. 193, 204 (1979).

Thus, whatever policymaking occurs in the public defender's office must relate to the needs of individual clients and not to any partisan political interests. Similarly, although an assistant is bound to obtain access to confidential information arising out of various attorney-client relationships, that information has no bearing whatsoever on partisan political concerns. Under these circumstances, it would undermine, rather than promote, the effective performance of an assistant public defender's office to make his tenure dependent on his allegiance to the dominant political party.

a. This is in contrast to the broader public responsibilities of an official such as a prosecutor. We express no opinion as to whether the deputy of such an official could be dismissed on grounds of political party affiliation or loyalty. Cf. Newcomb v. Brennan, 558 F.2d 825 (CA7 1977), cert. denied, 434 U.S. 968 (dismissal of deputy city attorney).

Accordingly, the entry of an injunction against termination of respondents' employment on purely political grounds was appropriate and the judgment of the Court of Appeals is Affirmed.

STEWART, J., dissenting.

I joined the judgment of the Court in Elrod v. Burns, 427 U.S. 347, because it is my view that, under the First and Fourteenth Amendments, "a nonpolicymaking, nonconfidential government employee can [not] be discharged . . . from a job that he is satisfactorily performing upon the sole ground of his political beliefs." Id., at 375. That judgment in my opinion does not control the present case for the simple reason that the respondents here clearly are not "nonconfidential" employees.

. . . [T]he employees in the *Elrod* case were three process servers and a juvenile court bailiff and security guard. The respondents in the present case are lawyers, and the employment positions involved are those of assistants in the office of the Rockland County Public Defender. The analogy to a firm of lawyers in the private sector is a close one, and I can think of few occupational relationships more instinct with the necessity of mutual confidence and trust than that kind of professional association.

I believe that the petitioner, upon his appointment as Public Defender, was not constitutionally compelled to enter such a close professional and necessarily confidential association with the respondents if he did not wish to do so.[a]

POWELL, J., joined by Rehnquist, J., (and by Stewart, J., as to Part I), dissenting.

The Court today continues the evisceration of patronage practices begun in Elrod v. Burns, 427 U.S. 347 (1976). With scarcely a glance at almost 200 years of American political tradition, the Court further limits the relevance of political affiliation to the selection and retention of public employees. Many public positions previously filled on the basis of membership in national political parties now must be staffed in accordance with a constitutionalized civil service standard that will affect the employment practices of federal, state, and local governments. Governmental hiring practices long thought to be a matter of legislative and executive discretion now will be subjected to judicial oversight. Today's decision is an exercise of judicial lawmaking that, as the Chief Justice wrote in his *Elrod* dissent, "represents a significant intrusion into the area of legislative and policy concerns." 427 U.S., at 375. I dissent.

I

The Court contends that its holding is compelled by the First Amendment. In reaching this conclusion, the Court largely ignores the substantial governmental interests served by patronage. Patronage is a long-accepted practice that never has been eliminated totally by civil service laws and regulations. The flaw in the Court's opinion lies not only in its application of First Amendment principles, see parts II-IV infra, but also in its promulgation of a new, and substantially ex-

a. Contrary to repeated statements in the Court's opinion, the present case does not involve "private political beliefs," but public affiliation with a political party.

panded, standard for determining which governmental employees may be retained or dismissed on the basis of political affiliation.

In Elrod v. Burns, three Members of the Court joined a plurality opinion concluding that nonpolicymaking employees could not be dismissed on the basis of political affiliation. 427 U.S., at 367 (opinion of Brennan, J., with whom White, J., and Marshall, J., joined). Two Members of the Court joined a concurring opinion stating that nonpolicymaking, nonconfidential employees could not be so dismissed. 427 U.S., at 375 (Stewart, J., concurring, with whom Blackmun, J., joined). Notwithstanding its purported reliance upon the holding of *Elrod,* the Court today ignores the limitations inherent in both views. The Court rejects the limited role for patronage recognized in the plurality opinion by holding that not all policymakers may be dismissed because of political affiliation. And the Court refuses to allow confidential employees to be dismissed for partisan reasons. The broad, new standard is articulated as follows: "[T]he ultimate inquiry is not whether the label 'policymaker' or 'confidential' fits a particular position; rather, the question is whether the hiring authority can demonstrate that party affiliation is an appropriate requirement for the effective performance of the public office involved."

The Court gives three examples to illustrate the standard. Election judges and certain executive assistants may be chosen on the basis of political affiliation; college football coaches may not.[a] And the Court decides in this case that party affiliation is not an appropriate requirement for selection of the attorneys in a public defender's office because "whatever policymaking occurs in the public defender's office must relate to the needs of individual clients and not to any partisan political interests."

The standard articulated by the Court is framed in vague and sweeping language certain to create vast uncertainty. Elected and appointed officials at all levels who now receive guidance from civil service laws, no longer will know when political affiliation is an appropriate consideration in filling a position. Legislative bodies will not be certain whether they have the final authority to make the delicate line-drawing decisions embodied in the civil service laws. Prudent individuals requested to accept a public appointment must consider whether their predecessors will threaten to oust them through legal action.

One example at the national level illustrates the nature and magnitude of the problem created by today's holding. The President customarily has considered political affiliation in removing and appointing United States Attorneys. Given the critical role that these key law enforcement officials play in the administration of the Department of Justice, both Democratic and Republican Attorneys General have concluded, not surprisingly, that they must have the confidence and support of the United States Attorneys. And political affiliation has been used as one indicator of loyalty.

a. The rationale for the Court's conclusion that election judges may be partisan appointments is not readily apparent. The Court states that "if a State's election laws require that precincts be supervised by two election judges of different parties, a Republican judge could be legitimately discharged solely for changing his party registration." If the mere presence of a state law mandating political affiliation as a requirement for public employment were sufficient, then the legislature of Rockland County could reverse the result of this case merely by passing a law mandating that political affiliation be considered when a Public Defender chooses his assistants. Moreover, it is not apparent that a State could demonstrate, under the standard approved today, that only a political partisan is qualified to be an impartial election judge.

Yet, it would be difficult to say, under the Court's standard, that "partisan" concerns properly are relevant to the performance of the duties of a United States Attorney. This Court has noted that "[t]he office of public prosecutor is one which must be administered with courage and independence." Imbler v. Pachtman, 424 U.S. 409, 423 (1976) quoting Pearson v. Reed, 6 Cal. App. 2d 277, 287, 44 P.2d 592, 597 (1935). Nevertheless, I believe that the President must have the right to consider political affiliation when he selects top ranking Department of Justice officials. The President and his Attorney General, not this Court, are charged with the responsibility for enforcing the laws and administering the Department of Justice. The Court's vague, overbroad decision may cast serious doubt on the propriety of dismissing United States Attorneys, as well as thousands of other policymaking employees at all levels of government, because of their membership in a national political party.

A constitutional standard that is both uncertain in its application and impervious to legislative change will not control selection and removal of key governmental personnel. Federal judges will now be the final arbiters as to who federal, state, and local governments may employ. In my view, the Court is not justified in removing decisions so essential to responsible and efficient governance from the discretion of legislative and executive officials.

II

The Court errs not only in its selection of a standard, but more fundamentally in its conclusion that the First Amendment prohibits the use of membership in a national political party as a criterion for the dismissal of public employees. In reaching this conclusion, the Court makes new law from inapplicable precedents. The Court suggests that its decision is mandated by the principle that governmental action may not "prescribe what shall be orthodox in politics, nationalism, religion, or other matters of opinion. . . ." Board of Education v. Barnette, 319 U.S. 624, 642 (1943). The Court also relies upon the decisions in Perry v. Sindermann, 408 U.S. 593 (1972), and Keyishian v. Board of Regents, 385 U.S. 589 (1967). But the propriety of patronage was neither questioned nor addressed in those cases.

Both *Keyishian* and *Perry* involved faculty members who were dismissed from state educational institutions because of their political views. In *Keyishian,* the Court reviewed a state statute that permitted dismissals of faculty members from state institutions for "treasonable or seditious" utterances or acts. The Court noted that academic freedom is "a special concern of the First Amendment, which does not tolerate laws that cast a pall of orthodoxy over the classroom." 385 U.S., at 603. Because of the ambiguity in the statutory language, the Court held that the law was unconstitutionally vague. The Court also held that membership in the Communist Party could not automatically disqualify a person from holding a faculty position in a state university. Id., at 606. In *Perry,* the Court held that the Board of Regents of a state university system could not discharge a professor in retaliation for his exercise of free speech. 408 U.S., at 598. In neither case did the State suggest that the governmental positions traditionally had been regarded as patronage positions. Thus, the Court correctly held that no substantial state interest justified the infringement of free speech. This case presents a question quite different from that in *Keyishian* and *Perry.*

The constitutionality of appointing or dismissing public employees on the basis of political affiliation depends upon the governmental interests served by patronage. No constitutional violation exists if patronage practices further sufficiently important interests to justify tangential burdening of First Amendment rights. See Buckley v. Valeo, 424 U.S. 1, 25 (1976). This inquiry cannot be resolved by reference to First Amendment cases in which patronage was neither involved nor discussed. Nor can the question in this case be answered in a principled manner without identifying and weighing the governmental interest served by patronage.

III

Patronage appointments help build stable political parties by offering rewards to persons who assume the tasks necessary to the continued functioning of political organizations. "As all parties are concerned with power they naturally operate by placing members and supporters into positions of power. Thus there is nothing derogatory in saying that a primary function of parties is patronage." J. Jupp, Political Parties 25-26 (1968). The benefits of patronage to a political organization do not derive merely from filling policymaking positions on the basis of political affiliation. Many, if not most, of the jobs filled by patronage at the local level may not involve policymaking functions. The use of patronage to fill such positions builds party loyalty and avoids "splintered parties and unrestrained factionalism [that might] do significant damage to the fabric of government." Storer v. Brown, 415 U.S. 724, 736 (1974).

Until today, I would have believed that the importance of political parties was self-evident. Political parties, dependent in many ways upon patronage serve a variety of substantial governmental interests. A party organization allows political candidates to muster donations of time and money necessary to capture the attention of the electorate. Particularly in a time of growing reliance upon expensive television advertisements, a candidate who is neither independently wealthy nor capable of attracting substantial contributions must rely upon party workers to bring his message to the voters. In contests for less visible offices, a candidate may have no efficient method of appealing to the voters unless he enlists the efforts of persons who seek reward through the patronage system. Insofar as the Court's decision today limits the ability of candidates to present their views to the electorate, our democratic process surely is weakened.

Strong political parties also aid effective governance after election campaigns end. Elected officials depend upon appointees who hold similar views to carry out their policies and administer their programs. Patronage — the right to select key personnel and to reward the party "faithful" — serves the public interest by facilitating the implementation of policies endorsed by the electorate. The Court's opinion casts a shadow over this time-honored element of our system. It appears to recognize that the implementation of policy is a legitimate goal of the patronage system and that some, but not all, policymaking employees may be replaced on the basis of their political affiliation. But the Court does not recognize that the implementation of policy often depends upon the cooperation of public employees who do not hold policymaking posts. As one commentator has written, "[w]hat the Court forgets is that, if government is to work, policy implementation is just as important as policymaking. No matter how wise the chief, he has to have the right Indians to transform his ideas into action, to get the job done." The growth of the civil service system already has limited the ability of elected politicians to effect political change. Public employees immune to public pressure "can resist changes in policy without suffering either the loss of their jobs or a cut in their salary." Such effects are proper when they follow from legislative or executive decisions to withhold some jobs from the patronage system. But the Court tips the balance between patronage and nonpatronage positions, and, in my view, imposes unnecessary constraints upon the ability of responsible officials to govern effectively and to carry out new policies.

. . . The Court ignores the substantial governmental interests served by reasonable patronage. In my view, its decision will seriously hamper the functioning of stable political parties.

IV

The facts of this case also demonstrate that the Court's decision well may impair the right of local voters to structure their government. Consideration of the form of local government in Rockland County, New York, demonstrates the antidemocratic effect of the Court's decision.

The voters of the County elect a legislative body. Among the responsibilities that the voters give to the legislature is the selection of a County Public Defender. In 1972, when the county voters elected a Republican majority in the legislature, a Republican was selected as Public Defender. The Public Defender retained one respondent and appointed the other as assistant public defender. Not surprisingly, both respondents are Republicans. In 1976, the voters elected a majority of Democrats to the legislature. The Democratic majority, in turn, selected a Democratic Public Defender who replaced both respondents with assistant public defenders approved by the Democratic legislators.

The voters of Rockland County are free to elect their Public Defender and assistant public defenders instead of delegating their selection to elected and appointed officials.[b] Certainly the Court's holding today would not preclude the voters, the ultimate "hiring authority," from choosing both Public Defenders and their assistants by party membership. The voters' choice of public officials on the basis of political affiliation is not yet viewed as an inhibition of speech; it is democracy. Nor may any incumbent contend seriously that the voters' decision not to re-elect him because of his political views is an impermissible infringement upon his right of free speech or affiliation. In other words, the operation of democratic government depends upon the selection of elected officials on precisely the basis rejected by the Court today.

Although the voters of Rockland County could have elected both the Public Defender and his assistants, they have given their legislators a representative proxy to appoint the Public Defender. And they have delegated to the Public Defender the power to choose his assistants. Presumably the voters have adopted this course in order to facilitate more effective representative government. Of course, the voters could have instituted a civil service system that would preclude the selection of either the Public Defender or his assistants on the basis of political

b. In Florida, for example, the local Public Defender is elected. See Fla. Const. Art. 5 §18; Fla. Stat. Ann. §27.50 (1974).

affiliation. But the continuation of the present system reflects the electorate's decision to select certain public employees on the basis of political affiliation.

The Court's decision today thus limits the ability of the voters of a county to structure their democratic government in the way that they please. Now those voters must elect both the Public Defender and his assistants if they are to fill governmental positions on a partisan basis. Because voters certainly may elect governmental officials on the basis of party ties, it is difficult to perceive a constitutional reason for prohibiting them from delegating that same authority to legislators and appointed officials.

V

The benefits of political patronage and the freedom of voters to structure their representative government are substantial governmental interests that justify the selection of the assistant public defenders of Rockland County on the basis of political affiliation. The decision to place certain governmental positions within a civil service system is a sensitive political judgment that should be left to the voters and to elected representatives of the people. But the Court's constitutional holding today displaces political responsibility with judicial fiat. In my view, the First Amendment does not incorporate a national civil service system. I would reverse the judgment of the Court of Appeals.

Note: Subsequent Case

Branti was extended in Rutan v. Republican Party of Illinois, 110 S. Ct. 2729 (1990). In 1980, the (Republican) governor of Illinois had ordered a freeze of all state jobs subject to his control. Gubernatorial approval was necessary to fill any vacant job, whether filled by a new hire, promotion, transfer, or recall after layoffs. Such approval was contingent on an applicant's having voted in Republican party primaries, otherwise providing support to the Republican Party and its candidates for office, or receiving the support of Republican Party officials. The plaintiffs included a rehabilitation counselor, a prison guard, and a state garage worker, all of whom claimed that they had been denied employment or promotions because of their non-Republican affiliations or lack of support by Republician Party officials. A divided Court, through Justice Brennan, held that the principles announced in the earlier cases extended to "promotion, transfer, recall or hiring decisions involving public employment positions for which party affiliation is not an appropriate requirement."

Justice Scalia, joined by Chief Justice Rehnquist and Justice Kennedy and in part by Justice O'Connor, wrote a vigorous dissent. He began by observing that

> if there is any category of jobs for whose performance party affiliation is not an appropriate requirement, it is the job of being a judge, where partisanship is not only unneeded, but positively undesirable. It is, however, rare that a federal administration of one party will appoint a judge from another party. . . . Thus, the new principle that the Court today announces will be enforced by a corps of judges (the Members of this Court included) who overwhelmingly owe their office to its violation. Something must be wrong here, and I suggest it is the Court.

The burden of Justice Scalia's opinion was that *Elrod* and *Branti* were themselves wrongly decided and should be overruled:

> If *Elrod* and *Branti* are not to be reconsidered in light of their demonstrably unsatisfactory consequences, I would go no further than to allow a cause of action when the employee has lost his position, that is, his formal title and salary. That narrow ground alone is enough to resolve the constitutional claims in the present case . . . [s]ince none of the plaintiffs has alleged loss of his position because of affiliation.

E. Political Expression and the Civil Servant

The United States and each of the 50 state governments attempt to restrict the political activity of civil servants. The regulations are variously designed to maintain a neutral public corps independent of partisan political affiliation, to protect civil servants against pressures by their superiors, and to prevent insubordination.

1. *Partisan Activity by Civil Servants*

Although public employees are permitted to vote and to engage in a modicum of political activity, their active public participation in the affairs of political parties is commonly prohibited. Under federal law, for example, employees cannot run in partisan elections, serve as officials of political parties, solicit contributions for a party, take an active role in the management of political campaigns, or circulate a partisan nominating petition.[29]

The constitutionality of such limitations was addressed in two decisions, United States Civil Service Commission v. National Association of Letter Carriers, 413 U.S. 548 (1973), and Broadrick v. Oklahoma, 413 U.S. 601 (1973), which reaffirmed an earlier decision, United Public Workers v. Mitchell, 330 U.S. 75 (1947), and upheld the limitations against First Amendment challenge. Justice White wrote in *Letter Carriers:*

> The restrictions . . . imposed on federal employees are not aimed at particular parties, groups, or points of view, but apply equally to all partisan activities of the type described. . . . Nor do they seek to control political opinions or beliefs, or to interfere with or influence anyone's vote at the polls. . . .
>
> It seems fundamental in the first place that employees in the Executive Branch of the Government, or those working for any of its agencies, should administer the law . . . without bias or favoritism for or against any political party or group or the members thereof. A major thesis of the Hatch Act is that to serve this great end of Government — the impartial execution of the laws — it is essential that federal employees, for example, not take formal positions in political parties, not undertake to play substantial roles in partisan political campaigns, and not run for office on partisan political tickets. . . . [I]t is not only important that the Government and its employees in fact avoid practicing political justice, but it is also critical that they ap-

29. See generally David Rosenbloom, Federal Service and the Constitution: The Development of the Public Employment Relationship (1971).

pear to the public to be avoiding it, if confidence in the system of representative Government is not to be eroded to a disastrous extent.

Another major concern of the restriction against partisan activities by federal employees was perhaps the immediate occasion for enactment of the Hatch Act in 1939. That was the conviction . . . that substantial barriers should be raised against the party in power — or the party out of power, for that matter — using the thousands or hundreds of thousands of federal employees, paid for at public expense, to man its political structure and political campaigns.

A related concern, and this remains as important as any other, was to further serve the goal that employment and advancement in the Government service not depend on political performance, and at the same time to make sure that Government employees would be free from pressure and from express or tacit invitation to vote in a certain way or perform political chores in order to curry favor with their superiors rather than to act out their own beliefs. . . .

Neither the right to associate nor the right to participate in political activities is absolute in any event. Nor are the management, financing, and conduct of political campaigns wholly free from governmental regulation. We agree with the basic holding of *Mitchell* that plainly identifiable acts of political management and political campaigning on the part of federal employees may constitutionally be prohibited.

2. *Control over "Nonpartisan" Speech by Government Employees*

BROWN v. GLINES
444 U.S. 348 (1980)
Certiorari to the United States Court of Appeals for the Ninth Circuit

POWELL, J.

This case involves challenges to United States Air Force regulations that require members of the service to obtain approval from their commanders before circulating petitions on Air Force bases. The first question is whether the regulations violate the First Amendment. . . .

I

The commander can deny permission only if he determines that distribution of the material would result in "a clear danger to the loyalty, discipline, or morale of members of the Air Force, or material interference with the accomplishment of a military mission. . . ."

Albert Glines was a captain in the Air Force Reserves. While on active duty at the Travis Air Force Base in California, he drafted petitions to several Members of Congress and to the Secretary of Defense complaining about the Air Force's grooming standards. Aware that he needed command approval in order to solicit signatures within a base, Glines at first circulated the petitions outside his base. During a routine training flight through the Anderson Air Force Base in Guam, however, Glines gave the petitions to an Air Force sergeant without seeking approval from the base commander. The sergeant gathered eight signatures before military authorities halted the unauthorized distribution. Glines' commander promptly removed him from active duty, determined that he had failed to meet the professional standards expected of an officer, and reassigned him to the standby reserves. Glines then brought suit in the United States District Court for the Northern District of California claiming that the Air Force regulations requiring prior approval for the circulation of petitions violated the First Amendment and 10 U.S.C. §1034. The court granted Glines' motion for summary judgment and declared the regulations facially invalid. 401 F. Supp. 127 (1975)....

II

In Greer v. Spock, 424 U.S. 828, 840 (1976), Mr. Justice Stewart wrote for the Court that "nothing in the Constitution . . . disables a military commander from acting to avert what he perceives to be a clear danger to the loyalty, discipline, or morale of troops on the base under his command." In that case, civilians who wished to distribute political literature on a military base challenged an Army regulation substantially identical to the Air Force regulations now at issue. See id., at 831, and n.2. The civilians claimed that the Army regulation was an unconstitutional prior restraint on speech, invalid on its face. We disagreed. We recognized that a base commander may prevent the circulation of material that he determines to be a clear threat to the readiness of his troops. See id., at 837-839. We therefore sustained the Army regulation. Id., at 840. For the same reasons, we now uphold the Air Force regulations.

These regulations, like the Army regulation in *Spock,* protect a substantial government interest unrelated to the suppression of free expression. See Procunier v. Martinez, 416 U.S. 396, 413 (1974). The military is, "by necessity, a specialized society separate from civilian society." Parker v. Levy, 417 U.S. 733, 743 (1974). Military personnel must be ready to perform their duty whenever the occasion arises. Ibid. To ensure that they always are capable of performing their mission promptly and reliably, the military services "must insist upon a respect for duty and a discipline without counterpart in civilian life." Schlesinger v. Councilman, 420 U.S. 738, 757 (1975); see Department of the Air Force v. Rose, 425 U.S. 352, 367-368 (1976).

" 'Speech that is protected in the civil population may . . . undermine the effectiveness of response to command.' " Parker v. Levy, supra, at 759, quoting United States v. Priest, 21 U.S.C.M.A. 564, 570, 45 C.M.R. 338, 344 (1972). Thus, while members of the military services are entitled to the protections of the First Amendment, "the different character of the military community and the military mission requires a different application of those protections." Parker v. Levy, supra, at 758. The rights of military men must yield somewhat " 'to meet certain overriding demands of discipline and duty. . . .' " Id., at 744, quoting Burns v. Wilson, 346 U.S. 137, 140 (1953) (plurality opinion). Speech likely to interfere with these vital prerequisites for military effectiveness therefore can be excluded from a military base....

Like the Army regulation that we upheld in *Spock*, the Air Force regulations restrict speech no more than is reasonably necessary to protect the substantial governmental interest. See Procunier v. Martinez, supra. Both the Army and the Air Force regulations implement the policy set forth in Department of Defense (DOD) Directive 1325.6 (1969). That directive advises commanders to preserve servicemen's "right to expression . . . to the maximum extent possible, consistent with good order and discipline and the national security." Id., II. Thus, the regulations in both services prevent commanders from interfering with the circulation of any materials other than those posing a clear danger to military loyalty, discipline, or morale. . . . Indeed, the Air Force regulations specifically prevent commanders from halting the distribution of materials that merely criticize the government or its policies. . . . The Air Force regulations also require any commander who prevents the circulation of materials within his base to notify his superiors of that decision. . . . *Spock* held that such limited restrictions on speech within a military base do not violate the First Amendment. 425 U.S., at 840; id., at 848 (Powell, J., concurring).

Spock also established that a regulation requiring members of the military services to secure command approval before circulating written materials within a military base is not invalid on its face. Id., at 840.[a] Without the opportunity to review materials before they are dispersed throughout his base, a military commander could not avert possible disruptions among his troops. Since a commander is charged with maintaining morale, discipline, and readiness, he must have authority over the distribution of materials that could affect adversely these essential attributes of an effective military force. "[T]he accuracy and effect of a superior's command depends critically upon the specific and customary reliability of [his] subordinates, just as the instinctive obedience of subordinates depends upon the unquestioned specific and customary reliability of the superior." Department of the Air Force v. Rose, 425 U.S., at 368. Because the right to command and the duty to obey ordinarily must go unquestioned, this Court long ago recognized that the military must possess substantial discretion over its internal discipline. . . . In *Spock,* we found no facial constitutional infirmity in regulations that allow a commander to determine before distribution whether particular materials pose a clear danger to the good order of his troops.[b] The Air Force regulations at issue here are identical in purpose and effect to the regulation that we upheld in *Spock.* We therefore conclude that they do not violate the First Amendment.

BRENNAN, J., dissenting. . . .

I believe that the military regulations at issue are prohibited by the First Amendment; accordingly, I would hold them to be unconstitutional, and affirm the judgments of the two Courts of Appeals.

Two sets of military regulations are challenged. Respondents in *Huff* (No. 78-599) attack Navy and Marine Corps regulations that require prior approval by

a. Glines would distinguish *Spock* on the ground that the plaintiffs in that case were civilians who had no specific right to enter a military base. The distinction is unpersuasive. Our decision in *Spock* rejected a facial challenge to a regulation that required "any person," civilian or military, to obtain prior permission for the distribution of literature within a base. Id., at 831. Unauthorized distributions of literature by military personnel are just as likely to undermine discipline and morale as similar distributions by civilians. Furthermore, the military has greater authority over a serviceman than over a civilian. See Parker v. Levy, 417 U.S. 733, 749-751 (1974). Even when not confronted with the special requirements of the military, we have held that a governmental employer may subject its employees to such special restrictions on free expression as are reasonably necessary to promote effective government. See Civil Service Commn. v. Letter Carriers, 413 U.S. 548, 565 (1973); Cole v. Richardson, 405 U.S. 676, 684 (1972); cf. Kelley v. Johnson, 425 U.S. 238, 245-248 (1976).

b. Commanders sometimes may apply these regulations "irrationally, invidiously, or arbitrarily," thus giving rise to legitimate claims under the First Amendment. Greer v. Spock, 424 U.S., at 840. . . . But Glines, who — like the civilians in *Spock* — never requested permission to circulate his materials, has not and cannot raise such a claim. Greer v. Spock, supra, at 840; id, at 849 (Powell, J., concurring).

commanding officers before the origination, distribution or circulation of petitions or other written material on ships, aircraft, military installations and "anywhere within a foreign country." FMFO 5370.3. Respondent in *Glines* (No. 78-1006) challenges parallel Air Force regulations that require command approval before the distribution or posting of nonofficial printed material and for the circulation of petitions for signature. AFR 30-1(9), 35-15(3)(a). Both the Navy and Marine and the Air Force regulations authorize withholding of approval if the commander determines that distribution would pose a "clear danger" to loyalty, discipline or morale of servicemen or if the distribution would "[m]aterially interfere" with military duties. The Air Force regulation explicitly declares, however, that "[d]istribution or posting may not be prohibited *solely* on the ground that the material is critical of Government policies or officials." (Emphasis added.)

I

Respondents contend that the regulations impermissibly interfere with First Amendment rights to communicate and petition. That contention finds solid support in First Amendment doctrine as explicated in a variety of settings by decisions of this Court. These regulations plainly establish an essentially discretionary regime of censorship that arbitrarily deprives respondents of precious communicative rights.

The circulation of petitions is indisputably protected First Amendment activity. Petitioning involves a bundle of related First Amendment rights [and] is especially suited for the exercise of all of these rights: it serves as a vehicle of communication; as a classic means of individual affiliation, with ideas or opinions; and as a peaceful yet effective method of amplifying the views of the individual signers. Indeed, the petition is a traditionally favored method of political expression and participation. . . . Thus, petitioning of officials has been expressly held to be a right secured by the First Amendment. Bridges v. California, 314 U.S. 252, 277 (1941).

This First Amendment shield for petitioning is impermissibly breached in at least three ways by the regulations before us.

First. By mandating that proposed petitions be subjected to Command approval, the regulations impose a prior restraint. . . .

Second. The command approval procedure implementing these regulations is seriously flawed. Time and again, the Court has underscored the principle that restraints upon communication must be hedged about by procedures that guarantee against infringement of protected expression and that eliminate the play of discretion that epitomizes arbitrary censorship. . . .

Third. The regulations demonstrably do not serve the military interests offered as their compelling justification, and for that reason alone violate the First Amendment. . . . The most important purpose that can be posited for them is prevention of incitement to military disorder. But if the danger of incitement necessitates prior clearance of servicemen's messages, it would be logical for the military to mandate preclearance of all messages, whether circulated by petition or disseminated orally. Since oral discussion is not subjected to preliminary censorship, doubt must be raised as to the urgency and the efficacy of such censorship when communication is by petition. In other words, inasmuch as the content of an oral communication may be identical to the content of a petition, there is no reason to single out petitions for a content preclearance requirement.

The only rational basis for disparate treatment of petitioning and oral communication would be the presence of some danger *peculiar* to *the process of petitioning.* But petitioning differs from simple oral expression only in that it involves an element of physical conduct. Insofar as that physical element of the petitioning process poses a greater threat of disruption than does simple verbal expression, recourse to content-neutral regulation of the time, place, and manner of circulation is surely an appropriate and sufficient alternative to suppression. By ordering prior official review of the content of petitions, these regulations are an excessive response to any distinctive problems of petitioning. Even the most important governmental purpose cannot justify a regulation that unduly burdens First Amendment liberties. See Shelton v. Tucker, 364 U.S. 479, 488-490 (1960).

II

All that the Court offers to palliate these fatal constitutional infirmities is a series of platitudes about the special nature and overwhelming importance of military necessity.[a]

Military (or national) security is a weighty interest, not least of all because national survival is an indispensable condition of national liberties. See United States v. Robel, 389 U.S. 258, 264 (1967). But the concept of military necessity is seductively broad, and has a dangerous plasticity. Because they invariably have the visage of overriding importance, there is always a temptation to invoke security "necessities" to justify an encroachment upon civil liberties. For that reason, the military security argument must be approached with a healthy skepticism: its very gravity counsels that courts be cautious when military necessity is invoked by the Government to justify a trespass on First Amendment rights. . . .

To be sure, generals and admirals, not federal judges, are expert about military needs. But it is equally true that judges, not military officers, possess the competence and authority to interpret and apply the First Amendment. . . .

A properly detached — rather than unduly acquiescent — approach to the military necessity argument here would doubtless have led the Court to a different result. The military's omission to regulate the content of oral communication suggests the pointlessness of controlling the identical message when embodied in a petition. It is further troubling that these regulations apply to all military bases, not merely to those that operate under combat or near-combat conditions. The "front line" and the rear echelon may be difficult to identify in the conditions of modern warfare, but there is a difference between an encampment that faces im-

a. The Court, ante, at n. [a] also suggests that curtailment of First Amendment freedoms might be warranted inasmuch as service personnel are government employees, citing Civil Service Commn. v. Letter Carriers, 413 U.S. 548 (1973). That doctrine is inapposite. The predicate for upholding liberty restrictions as a condition of public employment must, at least in part, be the voluntariness of the decision to accept government employment. At various times, however, this country has inducted citizens into military service as a matter of compulsion. Moreover, unlike other employees, servicemen may not freely resign their posts should they decide to unburden themselves of restraints upon their freedom of expression.

It is also noteworthy that the statutory scheme considered in *Letter Carriers* permitted employees to "[s]ign a political petition as an individual," *Letter Carriers,* supra, at 577, n.21, and evidently further allowed the full panoply of petitioning rights with respect to petitions addressed to the Federal Government, id., at 572-574, 587-588 (appendix).

minent conflict and a military installation that provides staging, support, or training services. It is simply impossible to credit the contention that national security is significantly promoted by the control of petitioning throughout *all* installations.

Finally, and fundamentally, the Court has been deluded into unquestioning acceptance of the very flawed assumption that discipline and morale are enhanced by restricting peaceful communication of various viewpoints. Properly regulated as to time, place, and manner, petitioning provides a useful outlet for airing complaints and opinions that are held as strongly by citizens in uniform as by the rest of society. The forced absence of peaceful expression only creates the illusion of good order; underlying dissension remains to flow into the more dangerous channels of incitement and disobedience. In that sense, military efficiency is only disserved when First Amendment rights are devalued.

III

The court egregiously errs in holding that Greer v. Spock, 424 U.S. 828 (1976), compels the validation of these regulations. I dissented in *Greer*, and continue to disagree with the decision in that case. But, in any event, *Greer* is not dispositive here; indeed, if it governs at all in these cases, *Greer* is authority that the regulations are constitutionally indefensible.

Greer arose because of the rejection by military authorities of Dr. Benjamin Spock's request to hold a presidential campaign meeting and distribute campaign literature at Fort Dix. Although the case involved a number of Army regulations restricting various expressive activities — including regulations parallel to those before us now — the actual issue in *Greer* was the exclusion of a politically partisan campaign effort. And there were three critical elements in *Greer* that prompted the Court to sustain that exclusion:

First, the Court relied upon the proposition that civilians lack expressive rights on military reservations from which they can be excluded. Significantly, the previous decision in Flower v. United States, 407 U.S. 197 (1972) (per curiam), was distinguished on the ground that leafletting in *Flower* had taken place on a portion of Fort Sam Houston that had been effectively dedicated to public use.

Second, the Court noted that servicemen stationed at Fort Dix had easy access to off-base public fora where they could be exposed to communications by Dr. Spock and others. By the same token, although not discussed in *Greer,* these off-base fora provided Dr. Spock with ample opportunity for expressive activity. Thus, from the standpoint of speaker and listeners, the Fort Dix regulations only effected a partial cutoff of communicative rights because other equivalent avenues of interchange remained open.

Finally, *Greer* repeatedly emphasized the lack of *any* claim that the Fort Dix regulations had been applied in biased fashion. It explicitly noted the complete absence of any question of "irrationa[l], invidiou[s], or arbitrar[y]" application of the Army regulations. 424 U.S., at 840. Accordingly, the Court did not confront the problem of official discrimination among political viewpoints. Indeed, *Greer* placed weight upon a perceived "American constitutional tradition" that the military be institutionally free of political entanglement, and that it avoid "the appearance of acting as a handmaiden for partisan political causes or candidates." (Id., at 839.)

These three predicates to *Greer* are wholly absent in the setting in which we review the regulations before us. On their face, and as applied in these cases, the regulations restrict the expressive activities of individuals who are mandatorily, not permissively, present on military reservations. For soldiers and sailors, as opposed to civilians, military installations *must be* the place for "free . . . communication of thoughts," Greer v. Spock, supra, at 838. Further, when service personnel are stationed abroad or at sea, the base or warship is very likely the *only* place for free communication of thoughts. Thus, in contrast to *Greer*, the regulations here permit complete foreclosure of a distinctive mode of expression by servicemen, who lack the civilian's option to depart the sphere of military authority.

These cases also differ from *Greer* because they exemplify pervasive official partiality in the regulation of messages. The orders refusing command approval of respondents' petitioning or leafletting flowed from the obviously biased official judgment that the content was "erroneous and misleading commentary," or that it "impugn[ed] by innuendo the motives and conduct" of the President. Far from being evenhanded regulation, this sort of command judgment is quintessentially political; in suppressing communication that "impugns" Presidential conduct "by innuendo," military authorities entangle themselves in national politics. Since these cases involve discriminatory regulation of communication, *Greer's* assumption of military neutrality — and, consequently, *Greer's* result — cannot govern here. Actually, the "tradition of a politically neutral military," *Greer*, supra, at 839, strongly counsels invalidation of these regulations, which demonstrably encourage commanding officers to exercise personal political judgment in deciding whether to permit petitioning.

Today's decisions, then, clash, rather than comport, with the underlying premises of Greer v. Spock. The Court unnecessarily trammels important First Amendment rights by uncritically accepting the dubious proposition that military security requires — or is furthered by — the discretionary suppression of a classic form of peaceful group expression. Servicemen and women deserve better than this. I respectfully dissent.

[Justices Stewart, Brennan, and Stevens also dissented on statutory grounds. Justice Marshall did not participate.]

Pickering v. Board of Education, 391 U.S. 563 (1968) involved an Illinois school board's attempt to dismiss a teacher under a statute allowing dismissal where the "interests of the schools" so require. Pickering had written a letter to a local newspaper criticizing actions of the school board and the district superintendent of schools. Illinois state courts had agreed that such criticism was detrimental to the school system and upheld the dismissal. The Supreme Court, with only Justice White dissenting on a marginal point, reversed.

The Court conceded "that the State has interests as an employer in regulating the speech of its employees that differ significantly from those it possesses in connection with regulation of the citizenry in general. The problem in any case is to arrive at a balance between the interests of the teacher, as a citizen, in commenting upon matters of public concern and the interest of the State, as an employer, in promoting the efficiency of the public services it performs through its employees." One way to promote efficiency, of course, is to maintain high internal cohesion, and the board argued that tolerating public opposition to its policies would negatively affect staff morale.

The Court responded by analyzing the specific content of the letter. It noted, for example, that "[t]he statements are in no way directed towards any person with whom appellant would normally be in contact in the course of his daily work as a teacher. Thus no question of maintaining either discipline by immediate superiors or harmony among coworkers is presented here." The Court described Pickering's letter as a comment on a matter of general public concern — the school's budget — rather than an attack on colleagues. Indeed, the Court went on to note that teachers may have special knowledge about educational controversies and that the public is entitled to benefit from such knowledge. "Accordingly, it is essential that they be able to speak out freely on such questions without fear of retaliatory dismissal."

In addition, the Court held that dismissal could not be based on the fact that Pickering's letter had contained some factual errors. The Court found that they were not made so carelessly or about "matters so closely related to the day-to-day operations of the schools that any harmful impact on the public would be difficult to counter because of the teacher's presumed greater access to the real facts."

In Givhan v. Western Line Consolidated School District, 439 U.S. 410 (1979), the Supreme Court unanimously held that First Amendment rights attached even to speech directed at a school principal by a teacher in the principal's office. Thus speech need not be "public" in order to be protected by the First Amendment.

In Connick v. Myers, 461 U.S. 138 (1983), the Court, in a 5-4 decision, upheld the firing of an Assistant District Attorney following her circulation to her colleagues of a questionnaire discussing, inter alia, office morale and the level of confidence regarding certain officials in the office. She also asked, "Do you ever feel pressured to work in political campaigns on behalf of office supported candidates?" At the time of circulating the questionnaire, Ms. Myers and the District Attorney were embroiled in a dispute concerning a change in responsibilities; she did not wish to accept a transfer into a different division of the office. District Attorney Connick fired Ms. Myers immediately upon learning of the questionnaire; in justification he cited her refusal to accept the transfer and her act of insubordination in distributing the questionnaire.

A district judge found Myers' dismissal invalid under *Pickering* and *Givhan* and ordered reinstatement plus back pay. The Court of Appeals for the Fifth Circuit affirmed in a one-sentence opinion. The Supreme Court reversed. Justice White stressed *Pickering's* roots in the desire to protect the rights of public employees to participate in public affairs and discussions of "matters of public concern." *Givhan*, although "private" insofar as the forum was a principal's office, nonetheless was within *Pickering* because "it is clear that her statements concerning the school district's allegedly racially discriminatory policies involved a matter of public concern." In contrast, according to Justice White, Myers' speech ultimately involved only workplace and personnel matters.

> When employee expression cannot be fairly considered as relating to any matter of political, social, or other concern to the community, government officials should enjoy wide latitude in managing their offices, without intrusive oversight by the judiciary in the name of the First Amendment. . . . We hold only that when a public

employee speaks not as a citizen upon matters of public concern, but instead as an employee upon matters only of personal interest, absent the most unusual circumstances, a federal court is not the appropriate forum in which to review the wisdom of a personnel decision taken by a public agency allegedly in reaction to the employee's behavior.

Justice White took note of the question involving pressure to work in political campaigns, and he admitted that this did raise a matter of public concern. Nevertheless, he concluded, after examining the entire context of the dispute, that it fell within the ambit of an ordinary personnel dispute, and the District Attorney was therefore allowed to act on his fear that Ms. Myers was "undermining office relations."

Justice Brennan dissented in an opinion joined by Justices Marshall, Blackmun, and Stevens. "I would hold that Myers' questionnaire addressed matters of public concern because it discussed subjects that could reasonably be expected to be of interest to persons seeking to develop informed opinions about the manner in which the Orleans Parish District Attorney, an elected offical charged with managing a vital governmental agency, discharges his responsibilities." Justice Brennan also criticized the majority for accepting Connick's assertions about the potentially disruptive effects of Myers' action rather than requiring some showing of actual disruption.

> Such extreme deference to the employer's judgment is not appropriate when public employees voice critical views concerning the operations of the agency for which they work. Although an employer's determination that an employee's statements have undermined essential working relationships must be carefully weighed in the *Pickering* balance, we must bear in mind that "the threat of dismissal from public employment is . . . a potent means of inhibiting speech." *Pickering*, at 574. . . . If the employer's judgment is to be controlling, public employees will not speak out when what they have to say is critical of their supervisors. In order to protect public employee's First Amendment right to voice critical views on issues of public importance, the courts must make their own appraisal of the effects of the speech in question.

IV. Unconstitutional Conditions

A. Prelude: A Taxonomy of Constitutionally Cognizable Rights or Interests

We have already encountered a variety of "rights" or "interests" that can affect the outcome of a constitutional dispute. Because this chapter introduces yet another one a catalog may be helpful.

1. Substantive Constitutional Rights

The archetypal constitutional "rights" are those explicit in the text of the Constitution — e.g., the rights to free exercise of religion and freedom of speech. Other substantive rights — e.g., the right to interstate mobility — may be inferred from the structure of the Constitution. Still others — e.g., the right of "privacy" — are derived from traditional and contemporary social values. These rights against government interference are not "absolute" insofar as they are subject to accommodation with competing government interests. They are absolute, however, in that they afford substantive protection to individuals without regard to the evenhandedness or procedural fairness of the interference. The First Amendment prohibits the government from censoring newspapers for political content, even if it censors all newspapers equally and even if it affords a full hearing to an editor who complains that the censor has erred.

2. *The Right to Rational Treatment*

In the "minimum rationality" modes, the due process and equal protection clauses require that every law and every classification made by a law serve *some* legitimate purpose to *some* extent. This standard would invalidate a regulation that provided, say, that only left-handed people can visit the zoo, even though no one has a substantive constitutional right that a city build or maintain a zoo.

3. *The Right to Procedural Due Process*

As we saw above, the due process clause guarantees notice, an opportunity to be heard, and other procedural safeguards, before a person can be deprived of life, liberty, or property based on an individualized determination about the person — though there are disputed issues about what constitutes liberty or property and what procedural safeguards are due. The due process clause probably requires the city to accord a hearing to an individual excluded from the zoo on the ground that she harasses the animals — a hearing on the question whether she *in fact* does harass the animals.

4. *The Right Not to Be Disfavored Because of Prejudice, etc.*

The "etc." reflects the difficulty of describing and articulating, with precision and without controversion, the equal protection standard dealing with "suspect" and kindred classifications. It is clear, however, that the equal protection clause prohibits the zoo from excluding or segregating African-Americans or women.

5. *The Right Not to Be Differentially Treated with Respect to Constitutional Rights and Important Interests*

In the concluding section of Chapter 10 we saw that the Court has scrutinized under the equal protection clause classifications affecting the franchise because of the fundamental interest attached to participation in the electoral process in a democratic polity. The Court has carefully refrained from declaring that the

Constitution guarantees a "right" to vote, per se. Rather the doctrine has the *conditional* form of other equal protection guaranties: You do not (necessarily) have a right that this official position exist at all, or that it be an elective rather than appointive office; but if it is elective you have the right to have your vote counted equally (*Reapportionment* cases), or not to be disfranchised because you cannot afford to pay a poll tax (*Harper*), or not to be excluded from the election because you are not deemed sufficiently "interested" in it (*Kramer*).

6. The Right Not to Be Required to Waive the Exercise of a Constitutional Right in Order to Receive a Privilege or Benefit — "Unconstitutional Conditions"

The archetypal constitutional violations consist of government conduct (searches and seizures, deprivations of property without hearings) forbidden by the Constitution and government prohibition of individual conduct (advocating radical changes in the structure of American government, using contraceptives) protected by the Constitution. People may, of course, voluntarily waive their constitutional rights simply by deciding not to exercise them. For example, even though the First Amendment protects individuals rights to engage in obnoxious speech, most people do not engage in such speech (most of the time); similarly, the right to travel interstate lies dormant, practically speaking, for those Americans who prefer to stay in their home states.

One can also waive rights consciously or formally. For example, although the Constitution guarantees a jury trial to anyone charged with the commission of a crime, an overwhelming number of convictions in the United States take place through the submission of guilty pleas, in which defendants choose to forgo their constitutional rights, usually in return for a "plea bargain" with the state. Even those defendants who choose to exercise their right to a jury trial may then waive their Fifth Amendment right to remain silent and take the stand in their own defense.

Are there *any* truly "inalienable rights," i.e. rights not subject to waiver? Many political theorists reject the "freedom" to sell oneself into slavery, on the ground that one cannot waive one's right to enjoy at least some degree of personal autonomy. (It should be obvious, though, that all employment contracts involve significant limitations on one's precontractual autonomy.)

As suggested above, rights are often consciously waived to gain something: In exchange for a guilty plea, the criminal defendant receives probation rather than a jail sentence. To what extent can government induce consent to an otherwise unconstitutional action by granting benefits — e.g. employment, housing, education, and welfare — only on the condition that the recipients waive their constitutional rights?

Most equal protection and procedural due process rights above would be meaningless if they were subject to induced waiver of this sort. A state could avoid the racial desegregation decisions simply by making waiver of the right not to be segregated a part of the contract of admission to public schools, zoos, and rest rooms. Indeed the requirement of termination hearings for welfare recipients or government employees could be avoided by merely requiring waiver of due process rights as a condition of receiving welfare benefits or as part of the employment contract.

Courts on occasion have asserted that the induced waiver of substantive constitutional rights presents no difficulties at all. For example, Justice Holmes, writing for the Supreme Judicial Court of Massachusetts in McAuliffe v. Mayor of New Bedford, 155 Mass. 216, 29 N.E. 517 (1892), dismissed the petition of a policeman who was fired for violating a departmental regulation against political activities with the quip: "The petitioner may have a constitutional right to talk politics, but he has no constitutional right to be a policeman. . . . [H]e takes the employment on the terms which are offered him." Much more recently Justice Blackmun wrote for the Court in Wyman v. James, 400 U.S. 309 (1971), that a state did not violate the Fourth Amendment by conditioning Aid for Dependent Children benefits on the recipient family's acquiescence to occasional "home visits" by a welfare caseworker: "[T]he visitation in itself is not forced or compelled, and . . . the beneficiary's denial of permission is not a criminal act. If consent to the visitation is withheld, no visitation takes place. The aid then never begins or merely ceases, as the case may be." Consider also South Dakota v. Dole, p.402 supra, involving the legitimacy of the Federal Government's inducing South Dakota to waive its right to set its drinking age lower than the federally "suggested" 21 by making the grant of federal highway funds contingent on the State's adoption of the congressionally desired age.

The argument against this view was forcefully stated in Frost & Frost Trucking Co. v. Railroad Commission, 271 U.S. 583 (1926). In this case, California attempted to condition the right of a trucking company to use the public roads on its agreement to follow certain limitations on charges to its customers. Justice Sutherland wrote:

> It would be a palpable incongruity to strike down an act of state legislation which, by words of express divestment, seeks to strip the citizen of rights guaranteed by the federal Constitution, but to uphold an act by which the same result is accomplished under the guise of a surrender of a right in exchange for a valuable privilege which the state threatens otherwise to withhold. . . . If the state may compel the surrender of one constitutional right as a condition of its favor, it may, in a like manner, compel a surrender of all. It is inconceivable that guarantees embedded in the Constitution of the United States may thus be manipulated out of existence.

Of course, the particular right that Justice Sutherland was protecting from coerced waiver was based on the since-discredited doctrine of economic due process. However, the concern about unconstitutional conditions is not limited to any particular substantive constitutional doctrine. Consider, for example, Justice Douglas's dissent in *Wyman,* where he condemned the willingness of the majority to acquiesce in the "invasion of the privacy of Barbara James" by viewing the state's demand for her waiver of privacy as a constitutionally tolerable predicate for the benefits given her by the state: "[T]he central question is whether the government by force of its largesse has the power to 'buy up' rights guaranteed by the Constitution. But for the assertion of her constitutional right [protected by the Fourth Amendment], Barbara James in this case would have received the welfare benefit."

Justice Douglas cited a number of cases forbidding the requirement of waivers in order to receive government benefits. For example, "[w]hile second-class mail rates may be granted or withheld by the Government, we would not allow them to be granted 'on condition that certain economic or political ideas not be disseminated.' Hannegan v. Esquire, Inc., 327 U.S. 146 (1946)." Similarly, the Court has held that a state cannot require its employees to sign broad loyalty oaths and disclaimers of membership in subversive organizations, Elfbrandt v. Russell, 384 U.S. 11 (1966); Keyishian v. Board of Regents, 385 U.S. 589 (1967), and that the state cannot condition public employment on waiver of the privilege against self-incrimination with respect to alleged misconduct connected with the activities. Lefkowitz v. Turley, 414 U.S. 70 (1973); Gardner v. Broderick, 392 U.S. 273 (1968). Based on the cases considered above and those that follow, can you devise a comprehensive theory explaining when the doctrine of unconstitutional conditions should apply and when, on the contrary, it is perfectly tolerable for the government to " 'buy up' rights guaranteed by the Constitution"?[30]

B. Can Congress Condition Tax Deductibility on Forgoing the Constitutional Right to Lobby?

REGAN v. TAXATION WITH REPRESENTATION OF WASHINGTON

461 U.S. 540 (1983)

Appeal from the United States Court of Appeals for the District of Columbia Circuit

REHNQUIST, J.

Appellee Taxation With Representation of Washington (TWR) is a nonprofit corporation organized to promote what it conceives to be the "public interest" in the area of federal taxation. It proposes to advocate its point of view before Congress, the Executive Branch, and the Judiciary. This case began when TWR applied for tax-exempt status under §501(c)(3) of the Internal Revenue Code. The Internal Revenue Service denied the application because it appeared that a substantial part of TWR's activities would consist of attempting to influence legislation, which is not permitted by §501(c)(3). . . .

TWR was formed to take over the operations of two other nonprofit corporations. One . . . was organized to promote TWR's goals by publishing a journal and engaging in litigation; it had tax-exempt status under §501(c)(3). The other . . . attempted to promote the same goals by influencing legislation; it had tax-exempt status under §501(c)(4). Neither predecessor organization was required to pay federal income taxes. For purposes of our analysis, there are two principal differences between §501(c)(3) organizations and §501(c)(4) organizations. Taxpayers who contribute to [the former] are permitted . . . to deduct the amount of their contributions on their federal income tax returns, while contributions to [the latter] are not deductible. . . .

In these cases, TWR is attacking the prohibition against substantial lobbying in §501(c)(3) because it wants to use tax-deductible contributions to support sub-

30. For further discussion of these complex problems, see Richard Epstein, The Supreme Court, 1987 Term, Foreword: Unconstitutional Conditions, State Power, and the Limits of Consent, 102 Harv. L. Rev. 4 (1988); Seth Kreimer, Allocational Sanctions: The Problem of Negative Rights in a Positive State, 132 U. Pa. L. Rev. 1293 (1984); Kathleen Sullivan, Unconstitutional Conditions, 102 Harv. L. Rev. 1413 (1989).

stantial lobbying activities. To evaluate TWR's claims, it is necessary to understand the effect of the tax-exemption system enacted by Congress.

Both tax exemptions and tax deductibility are a form of subsidy that is administered through the tax system. A tax exemption has much the same effect as a cash grant to the organization of the amount of tax it would have to pay on its income. Deductible contributions are similar to cash grants of the amount of a portion of the individual's contributions. The system Congress has enacted provides this kind of subsidy to nonprofit civic welfare organizations that do not engage in substantial lobbying. In short, Congress chose not to subsidize lobbying as extensively as it chose to subsidize other activities. . . .

TWR contends that Congress' decision not to subsidize its lobbying . . . imposes an "unconstitutional condition" on the receipt of tax-deductible contributions. [TWR relied on Speiser v. Randall, 357 U.S. 513 (1958), in which] California established a rule requiring anyone who sought to take advantage of a property tax exemption to sign a declaration stating that he did not advocate the forcible overthrow of the Government of the United States. This Court stated that "[t]o deny an exemption to claimants who engage in certain forms of speech is in effect to penalize them for such speech [and thus violates the First Amendment]."

TWR is certainly correct when it states that we have held that the government may not deny a benefit to a person because he exercises a constitutional right. See Perry v. Sindermann, [supra]. But TWR is just as certainly incorrect when it claims that this case fits the *Speiser-Perry* model. The Code does not deny TWR the right to receive tax deductible contributions to support its non-lobbying activity, nor does it deny TWR any independent benefit on account of its intention to lobby. Congress has merely refused to pay for the lobbying out of public moneys. This Court has never held that Congress must grant a benefit such as TWR claims here to a person who wishes to exercise a constitutional right.

This aspect of these cases is controlled by Cammarano v. United States, 358 U.S. 498 (1959), in which we upheld a Treasury Regulation that denied business expense deductions for lobbying activities. . . .

TWR also contends that the equal protection component of the Fifth Amendment renders the prohibition against substantial lobbying invalid. [The Internal Revenue Code] permits taxpayers to deduct contributions to veterans' organizations[, which are permitted by the Code] to lobby as much as they want in furtherance of their exempt purposes. TWR argues that because Congress has chosen to subsidize the substantial lobbying activities of veterans' organizations, it must also subsidize the lobbying of §501(c)(3) organizations. . . .

Legislatures have especially broad latitude in creating classifications and distinctions in tax statutes. . . .

The case would be different if Congress were to discriminate invidiously in its subsidies in such a way as to " 'ai[m] at the suppression of dangerous ideas.' " *Speiser,* 357 U.S. at 519. But the veterans' organizations . . . are entitled to receive tax-deductible contributions regardless of the content of any speech they may use, including lobbying. We find no indication that the statute was intended to suppress any ideas or any demonstration that it has had that effect. . . .

Congressional selection of particular entities or persons for entitlement to this sort of largesse "is obviously a matter of policy and discretion not open to judicial review unless in circumstances which here we are not able to find." . . .

We have held in several contexts that a legislature's decision not to subsidize the exercise of a fundamental right does not infringe the right, and thus is not subject to strict scrutiny. . . .

TWR contends that §501(c)(3) organizations could better advance their charitable purposes if they were permitted to engage in substantial lobbying. This may well be true. But Congress — not TWR or this Court — has the authority to determine whether the advantage the public would receive from additional lobbying by charities is worth the money the public would pay to subsidize that lobbying, and other disadvantages that might accompany that lobbying. . . . It is not irrational for Congress to decide that tax-exempt charities such as TWR should not further benefit at the expense of taxpayers at large by obtaining a further subsidy for lobbying.

It is also not irrational for Congress to decide that, even though it will not subsidize substantial lobbying by charities generally, it will subsidize lobbying by veterans' organizations. . . . Our country has a longstanding policy of compensating veterans for their past contributions by providing them with numerous advantages. This policy has "always been deemed to be legitimate." Personnel Administrator of Mass. v. Feeney, 442 U.S. 256, 279, n.25 (1979).

The issue in these cases is not whether TWR must be permitted to lobby, but whether Congress is required to provide it with public money with which to lobby. For the reasons stated above, we hold that it is not.

[Justice Blackmun, joined by Justices Brennan and Marshall, concurred in the opinion, but wrote separately to emphasize TWR's ability to return to its old organizational structure and thus gain the advantage of §501(c)(3) for its nonlobbying component. "A §501(c)(3) organization's right to speak is not infringed, because it is free to make known its views on legislation through its §501(c)(4) affiliate without losing tax benefits for its nonlobbying activities." Without this possibility, Justice Blackmun would regard the prohibition imposed on §501(c)(3) organizations as raising a significant constitutional question.]

C. Can Congress Impose Restrictions on What Can Be Said by Radio Stations Accepting Federal Subsidies?

FCC v. LEAGUE OF WOMEN VOTERS OF CALIFORNIA

468 U.S. 364 (1984)

On Appeal from the District Court of the Central District of California

[The Public Broadcasting Act of 1967 establishing the Corporation for Public Broadcasting included a section that, as amended in 1981, forbids any "noncommercial educational broadcasting station which receives a grant from the Corporation" to "engage in editorializing." 47 U.S.C. §399. The Pacifica Foundation, the principal appellee, operates several noncommercial educational stations in five major metropolitan areas and receives federal grants from the Corporation.

The Foundation challenged §399 in 1979 as a limitation on its first amendment rights and sought a declaratory judgment that it was unconstitutional.[a]

The District Court granted summary judgment in favor of Pacifica, finding that the ban on editorializing violated the First Amendment. The United States appealed directly to the Supreme Court, which, through Justice Brennan, affirmed. "Were a similar ban on editorializing applied to newspapers and magazines, we would not hesitate to strike it down as violative of the First Amendment." However, the case involved the electronic media, where, because of the scarcity of the spectrum, the Court has "never gone so far as to demand that . . . regulations serve 'compelling' governmental interests." As a result, "the broadcasting industry plainly operates under restraints not imposed upon other media." Such restraints are legitimate, though, only if the Court is "satisfied that the restriction is narrowly tailored to further a substantial governmental interest, such as ensuring adequate and balanced coverage of public issues."]

BRENNAN, J.

III

. . . Before assessing the government's proffered justifications for the statute, however, two central features of the ban against editorializing must be examined, since they help to illuminate the importance of the First Amendment interests at stake in this case.

A

First, the restriction imposed by §399 is specifically directed at a form of speech — namely, the expression of editorial opinion — that lies at the heart of First Amendment protection. . . . Indeed, the pivotal importance of editorializing as a means of satisfying the public's interest in receiving a wide variety of ideas and views through the medium of broadcasting has long been recognized by the FCC; the Commission has for the past 35 years actively encouraged commercial broadcast licensees to include editorials on public affairs in their programming. . . .

Second, the scope of §399's ban is defined solely on the basis of the content of the suppressed speech. . . . Section 399 . . . singles out noncommercial broadcasters and denies them the right to address their chosen audience on matters of public importance. Thus, in enacting §399 Congress appears to have sought . . . to limit discussion of controversial topics and thus to shape the agenda for public

a. The Department of Justice informed both Houses of the Congress that it had decided not to defend the constitutionality of the statute. Attorney General Civiletti stated that the "Department of Justice is, of course, fully mindful of its duty to support the laws enacted by Congress. Here, however, the Department has determined, after careful study and deliberation, that reasonable arguments cannot be advanced to defend the challenged statute." The suit was dismissed on the grounds that there was no justiciable controversy because the Government had decided not to enforce the statute.

Pacifica appealed; while the appeal was pending in the Ninth Circuit, the Justice Department, under the leadership of a new Attorney General appointed by Ronald Reagan, announced that it would defend the statute, and the case was remanded to the District Court. Moreover, Congress amended §399 by adding a section prohibiting all noncommercial stations from making political endorsements, regardless of whether they received federal funds. The plaintiffs, however, ultimately chose to challenge only the ban on editorializing and dropped an attack on the prohibition of political endorsements.

debate. . . . [W]e must be particularly wary in assessing §399 to determine whether it reflects an impermissible attempt "to allow the government [to] control . . . the search for political truth."

B

In seeking to defend the prohibition on editorializing imposed by §399, the Government urges that the statute was aimed at preventing two principal threats to the overall success of the Public Broadcasting Act of 1967. According to the argument, the ban was necessary, first, to protect noncommercial educational broadcasting stations from being coerced, as result of federal financing, into becoming vehicles for governmental propagandizing or the objects of governmental influence; and second, to keep these stations from becoming convenient targets for capture by private interest groups wishing to express their own partisan viewpoints. By seeking to safeguard the public's right to a balanced presentation of public issues through the prevention of either governmental or private bias, these objectives are, of course, broadly consistent with the goals identified in our earlier broadcast regulation cases[, where the Court had upheld the power of the Federal Communications Commission to impose certain "fairness" standards on electronic media]. But, in sharp contrast to the restrictions upheld in [those cases,] which left room for editorial discretion and simply required broadcast edition to grant others access to the microphone, §399 directly prohibits the broadcaster from speaking out on public issues even in a balanced and fair manner. The Government insists, however, that the hazards posed in the "special" circumstances of noncommercial educational broadcasting are so great that §399 is an indispensable means of preserving the public's First Amendment interests. We disagree.

1

. . . [A]n examination of both the overall legislative scheme established by the 1967 Act and the character of public broadcasting demonstrates that the interest asserted by the Government is not substantially advanced by §399. First, to the extent that federal financial support creates a risk that stations will lose their independence through the bewitching power of governmental largesse, the elaborate structure established by the Public Broadcasting Act already operates to insulate local stations from governmental interference. . . .

Even if these statutory protections were thought insufficient to the task, however, suppressing the particular category of speech restricted by §399 is simply not likely, given the character of the public broadcasting system, to reduce substantially the risk that the Federal Government will seek to influence or put pressure on local station. . . . [W]hat is far more likely than local station editorials to pose the kinds of dangers hypothesized by the Government are the wide variety of programs addressing controversial issues produced, often with substantial CPB funding, for national distribution to local stations. Such programs truly have the potential to reach a large audience and, because of the critical commentary they contain, to have the kind of genuine national impact that might trigger a congressional response or kindle governmental resentment. The ban imposed by §399, however, is plainly not directed at the potentially controversial content of such programs; it is, instead, leveled solely at the expression of editorial opinion by local station management, a form of expression that is far more likely to be aimed at a smaller local audience, to have less national impact, and to be confined to local issues. . . .

Furthermore, the manifest imprecision of the ban imposed by §399 reveals that its proscription is not sufficiently tailored to the harm it seeks to prevent to justify its substantial interference with broadcasters' speech. Section 399 includes within its grip a potentially infinite variety of speech, most of which would not be related in any way to governmental affairs, political candidacies or elections. Indeed, the breadth of editorial commentary is as wide as human imagination permits. But the Government never explains how, say, an editorial by local station management urging improvements in a town's parks or museums will so infuriate Congress or other Federal officials that the future of public broadcasting will be imperiled unless such editorials are suppressed. Nor is it explained how the suppression of editorials alone serves to reduce the risk of governmental retaliation and interference when it is clear that station management is fully able to broadcast controversial views so long as such views are not labeled as its own.

The Government appears to recognize these flaws in §399, because it focuses instead on the suggestion that the source of governmental influence may well be state and local governments, many of which have established public broadcasting commissions that own and operate local noncommercial educational stations. . . . The Government's argument, however, proves too much. First, §399's ban applies to the many private noncommercial community organizations that own and operate stations that are not in any way controlled by state or local government. Second, the legislative history of the Public Broadcasting Act clearly indicates that Congress was concerned with "assur[ing] complete freedom from any *Federal Government influence*." Consistently with the concern, Congress refused to create any federally owned stations and it expressly forbid the CPB to own or operate any television or radio stations. By contrast, although Congress was clearly aware in 1967 that many noncommercial educational stations were owned by state and local governments, it did not hesitate to extend Federal assistance to such stations, it imposed no special requirements to restrict state or local control over these stations, and, indeed, it ensured through the structure of the Act that these stations would be as insulated from Federal interference as the wholly private stations.

Finally, although the Government certainly has a substantial interest in ensuring that the audiences of noncommercial stations will not be led to think that the broadcaster's editorials reflect the official view of the government, this interest can be fully satisfied by less restrictive means that are readily available[, including the requirement that stations] broadcast a disclaimer every time they editorialize which would state that the editorial represents only the view of the station's management and does not in any way represent the views of the Federal Government or any of the station's other sources of funding. . . .

2

Assuming that the Government's second asserted interest in preventing noncommercial stations from becoming a "privileged outlet for the political and ideological opinions of station owners and management" is legitimate, the substantiality of this asserted interest is dubious. . . .

In short, §399 does not prevent the use of noncommercial stations for the presentation of partisan views on controversial matters; instead, it merely bars a station from specifically communicating such views on its own behalf or on behalf of its management. If the vigorous expression of controversial opinions is, as the Government assures us, affirmatively encouraged by the Act, and if local licensees are permitted under the Act to exercise editorial control over the selection of programs, controversial or otherwise, that are aired on their stations, then §399 accomplishes only one thing — the suppression of editorial speech by station management. It does virtually nothing, however, to reduce the risk that public stations will serve solely as outlets for expression of narrow partisan views. . . .

Finally, the public's interest in preventing public broadcasting stations from becoming forums for lopsided presentations of narrow partisan positions is already secured by a variety of other regulatory means that intrude far less drastically upon the "journalistic freedom" of noncommercial broadcasters. The requirements of the FCC's fairness doctrine, for instance, which apply to commercial and noncommercial stations alike, ensure that such editorializing would maintain a reasonably balanced and fair presentation of controversial issues. . . . Rather than requiring noncommercial broadcasters who express editorial opinions on controversial subjects to permit *more speech* on such subjects to ensure that the public's First Amendment interest in receiving a balanced account of the issue is met, §399 simply silences all editorial speech by such broadcasters. Since the breadth of §399 extends so far beyond what is necessary to accomplish the goals identified by the Government, it fails to satisfy the First Amendment standards that we have applied in this area. . . .

IV

[The Government also tried] to justify §399 on basis of Congress' Spending Power. Relying upon our recent decision in Regan v. Taxation with Representation, the Government argues that by prohibiting noncommercial educational stations that receive CPB grants from editorializing, Congress has, in the proper exercise of its Spending Power, simply determined that it "will not subsidize public broadcasting station editorials." In *Taxation with Representation,* the Court found that Congress could, in the exercise of its Spending Power, reasonably refuse to subsidize the lobbying activities of tax-exempt charitable organizations by prohibiting such organizations from using tax-deductible contributions to support their lobbying efforts. In so holding, however, we explained that such organizations remained free "to receive tax-deductible contributions to support non-lobbying activit[ies]." Thus, a charitable organization could create [under the Internal Revenue Code] an affiliate to conduct its non-lobbying activities using tax-deductible contributions, and, at the same time, establish . . . a separate affiliate to pursue its lobbying efforts without such contributions. . . .

In this case, however . . . , a noncommercial educational station that receives only 1 percent of its overall income from CPB grants is barred absolutely from all editorializing. . . . The station has no way of limiting the use of its Federal funds to all non-editorializing activities, and, more importantly, it is barred from using even wholly private funds to finance its editorial activity. . . .

V

In conclusion, we emphasize that our disposition of this case rests upon a narrow proposition. We do not hold that the Congress or the FCC are without power to regulate the content, timing, or character of speech by noncommercial educational broadcasting stations. Rather, we hold only that the specific interests sought to be advanced by §399's ban on editorializing are either not sufficiently substantial or are not served in a sufficiently limited manner to justify the substantial abridgement of important journalistic freedoms which the First Amendment jealously protects. Accordingly, the judgment of the District Court is affirmed.

REHNQUIST, J., joined by Chief Justice Burger and Justice White, dissenting. . . . Pacifica, well aware of §399's condition on its receipt of public money, nonetheless accepted the public money and now seeks to avoid the conditions which Congress legitimately has attached to receipt of that funding. . . .

The Court's . . . discussion of why §399, repeatedly reexamined and retained by Congress, violates the First Amendment is to me utterly unpersuasive. Congress has rationally determined that the bulk of the taxpayers whose monies provide the funds for grants by the CPB would prefer not to see the management of local educational stations promulgate its own private views on the air at taxpayers' expense. Accordingly Congress simply has decided not to subsidize stations which engage in that activity. . . .

This is not to say that the government may attach *any* condition to its largess; it is only to say that when the government is simply exercising its power to allocate its own public funds, we need only find that the condition imposed has a rational relationship to Congress' purpose in providing the subsidy and that it is not primarily "aimed at the suppression of dangerous ideas." In this case Congress' prohibition is directly related to its purpose in providing subsidies for public broadcasting, and it is plainly rational for Congress to have determined that taxpayer monies should not be used to subsidize management's views or to pay for management's exercise of partisan politics. Indeed, it is entirely rational for Congress to have wished to avoid the appearance of government sponsorship of a particular view or a particular political candidate. Futhermore, Congress' prohibition is strictly neutral. In no sense can it be said that Congress has prohibited only editorial views of one particular ideological bent. Nor has it prevented public stations from airing programs, documentaries, interviews, etc. dealing with controversial subjects, so long as management itself does not expressly endorse a particular viewpoint. And Congress has not prevented station management from communicating its own views on those subjects through any medium other than subsidized public broadcasting.

For the foregoing reasons I find this case entirely different from the so-called "unconstitutional condition" cases, wherein the Court has stated that the government "may not deny a benefit to a person on a basis that infringes his constitutionally protected interests — especially his interest in freedom of speech." Perry v. Sinderman, 408 U.S. 593, 597 (1972). In those cases the suppressed speech was not content-neutral in the same sense as here, and in those cases, there is at best only a strained argument that the legislative purpose of the condition imposed was to avoid *subsidizing* the prohibited speech. . . .

WHITE, J.

Believing that the editorializing and candidate endorsement proscription stand or fall together and being confident that Congress may condition use of its funds on abstaining from political endorsements, I join Justice Rehnquist's dissenting opinion.

STEVENS, J., dissenting.

. . . As Justice White correctly notes, the statutory prohibitions against editorializing and candidate endorsements rest on the same foundation. In my opinion that foundation is far stronger than merely a "rational basis" and it is not weakened by the fact that it is buttressed by other provisions that are also designed to avoid the insidious evils of government propaganda favoring particular points of view. The quality of the interest in maintaining government neutrality in the free market of ideas — of avoiding subtle forms of censorship and propaganda — outweigh the impact on expression that results from this statute. Indeed, by simply terminating or reducing funding, Congress could curtail much more expression with no risk whatsoever of a constitutional transgression. . . .

Neither the fact that the statute regulates only one kind of speech, nor the fact that editorial opinion has traditionally been an important kind of speech, is sufficient to identify the character or the significance of the statute's impact on speech. Three additional points are relevant. First, the statute does not prohibit Pacifica from expressing its opinion through any avenue except the radio stations for which it receives federal financial support. It eliminates the radio stations for which it receives federal financial support. It eliminates the subsidized channel of communication as a forum for Pacifica itself, and thereby deprives Pacifica of an advantage it would otherwise have over other speakers, but it does not exclude Pacifica from the marketplace for ideas. Second, the statute does not curtail the expression of opinion by individual commentators who participate in Pacifica's programs. The only comment that is prohibited is a statement that Pacifica agrees with the opinions that others may express on its programs. Third, and of greatest significance for me, the statutory restriction is completely neutral in its operation — it prohibits all editorials without any distinction being drawn concerning the subject matter or the point of view that might be expressed.

II

The statute does not violate the fundamental principle that the citizen's right to speak may not be conditioned upon the sovereign's agreement with what the speaker intends to say. On the contrary, the statute was enacted in order to protect that very principle — to avoid the risk that some speakers will be rewarded or penalized for saying things that appeal to — or are offensive to — the sovereign. The interests the statute is designed to protect are interests that underlie the First Amendment itself. . . .

The Court does not question the validity of the basic interests served by §399. Instead, it suggests that the statute does not substantially serve those interests because the Public Broadcasting Act operates in many other respects to insulate local stations from governmental interference. In my view, that is an indication of nothing more than the strength of the governmental interest involved here — Congress enacted many safeguards because the evil to be avoided was so grave.

Organs of official propaganda are antithetical to this nation's heritage and Congress understandably acted with great caution in this area. . . . No safeguard is foolproof; and the fact that funds are dispensed according to largely "objective" criteria certainly is no guarantee. Individuals must always make judgments in allocating funds, and pressure can be exerted in subtle ways as well as through outright fund cutoffs. . . .

The magnitude of the present danger that the statute is designed to avoid is admittedly a matter about which reasonable judges may disagree.[a] Moreover, I would agree that the risk would be greater if other statutory safeguards were removed. It remains true, however, that Congress has the power to prevent the use of public funds to subsidize the expression of partisan points of view, or to suppress the propagation of dissenting opinions. No matter how great or how small the immediate risk may be, there surely is more than a theoretical possibility that future grantees might be influenced by the ever present tie of the political purse strings, even if those strings are never actually pulled. "One who knows that he may dissent knows also he somehow consents when he does not dissent." Arendt, The Crisis of the Republic 88 (1972), quoting De Tocqueville, Democracy in America. . . .

D. Can the State Prohibit Disclosing Information About Abortion as a Condition of Accepting Governmental Funding?

RUST v. SULLIVAN

111 S. Ct. 1759 (1991)

On Writ of Certiorari to the United States Court of Appeals for the Second Circuit

REHNQUIST, C.J.

These cases concern a facial challenge to Department of Health and Human Services (HHS) regulations which limit the ability of Title X fund recipients to engage in abortion related activities. . . .

I

A

In 1970, Congress enacted Title X of the Public Health Service Act (Act), which provides federal funding for family planning services. The Act authorizes the Secretary to "make grants to and enter into contracts with public or nonprofit private entities to assist in the establishment and operation of voluntary family planning projects which shall offer a broad range of acceptable and effective

a. The majority argues that the Government's concededly substantial interest in ensuring that audiences of educational stations will not perceive the station to be a government propaganda organ can be fully satisfied by requiring such stations to broadcast a disclaimer each time they editorialize stating that the editorial "does not in any way represent the views of the Federal Government. . . ." This solution would be laughable were it not so Orwellian: the answer to the fact that there is a real danger that the editorials are really government propaganda is for the government to require the station to tell the audience that it is not propaganda at all.

family planning methods and services." Grants and contracts under Title X must "be made in accordance with such regulations as the Secretary may promulgate." [A section] of the Act, however, provides that "[n]one of the funds appropriated under this subchapter shall be used in programs where abortion is a method of family planning." . . .

In 1988, the Secretary promulgated new regulations designed to provide " 'clear and operational guidance' to grantees about how to preserve the distinction between Title X programs and abortion as a method of family planning." 53 Fed. Reg. 2923-2924 (1988). The regulations clarify, through the definition of the term "family planning," that Congress intended Title X funds "to be used only to support *preventive* family planning services" (emphasis added). Accordingly, Title X services are limited to "preconceptual counseling, education, and general reproductive health care," and expressly exclude "pregnancy care (including obstetric or prenatal care)." . . .

The regulations attach three principal conditions on the grant of federal funds for Title X projects. First, the regulations specify that a "Title X project may not provide counseling concerning the use of abortion as a method of family planning or provide referral for abortion as a method of family planning." Because Title X is limited to preconceptional services, the program does not furnish services related to childbirth. Only in the context of a referral out of the Title X program is a pregnant woman given transitional information. Title X projects must refer every pregnant client "for appropriate prenatal and/or social services by furnishing a list of available providers that promote the welfare of the mother and the unborn child." The list may not be used indirectly to encourage or promote abortion, "such as by weighing the list of referrals in favor of health care providers which perform abortions, by including on the list of referral providers health care providers whose principal business is the provision of abortions, by excluding available providers who do not provide abortions, or by 'steering' clients to providers who offer abortion as a method of family planning." The Title X project is expressly prohibited from referring a pregnant woman to an abortion provider, even upon specific request. One permissible response to such an inquiry is that "the project does not consider abortion an appropriate method of family planning and therefore does not counsel or refer for abortion." §59.8(b)(5).

Second, the regulations broadly prohibit a Title X project from engaging in activities that "encourage, promote or advocate abortion as a method of family planning." Forbidden activities include lobbying for legislation that would increase the availability of abortion as a method of family planning, developing or disseminating materials advocating abortion as a method of family planning, providing speakers to promote abortion as a method of family planning, using legal action to make abortion available in any way as a method of family planning, and paying dues to any group that advocates abortion as a method of family planning as a substantial part of its activities.

Third, the regulations require that Title X projects be organized so that they are "physically and financially separate" from prohibited abortion activities. To be deemed physically and financially separate, "a Title X project must have an objective integrity and independence from prohibited activities. Mere bookkeeping separation of Title X funds from other monies is not sufficient." . . .

B

Petitioners are Title X grantees and doctors who supervise Title X funds suing on behalf of themselves and their patients. Respondent is the Secretary of the Department of Health and Human Services. . . . Petitioners challenged the regulations on the grounds that they were not authorized by Title X and that they violate the First and Fifth Amendment rights of Title X clients and the First Amendment rights of Title X health providers. . . .

II

. . . We turn first to petitioners' contention that the regulations exceed the Secretary's authority under Title X and are arbitrary and capricious. [The Court rejects this argument and finds the regulations to be authorized by the congressional statute.]

III

Petitioners contend that the regulations violate the First Amendment by impermissibly discriminating based on viewpoint because they prohibit "all discussion about abortion as a lawful option — including counseling, referral, and the provision of neutral and accurate information about ending a pregnancy — while compelling the clinic or counselor to provide information that promotes continuing a pregnancy to term." They assert that the regulations violate the "free speech rights of private health care organizations that receive Title X funds, of their staff, and of their patients" by impermissibly imposing "viewpoint-discriminatory conditions on government subsidies" and thus penaliz[e] speech funded with non-Title X monies." . . . Relying on Regan v. Taxation With Representation of Wash., and Arkansas Writers Project, Inc. v. Ragland, 481 U.S. 221, 234 (1987), petitioners also assert that while the Government may place certain conditions on the receipt of federal subsidies, it may not "discriminate invidiously in its subsidies in such a way as to 'ai[m] at the suppression of dangerous ideas.' "

There is no question but that the statutory prohibition . . . is constitutional. . . . The Government can, without violating the Constitution, selectively fund a program to encourage certain activities it believes to be in the public interest, without at the same time funding an alternate program which seeks to deal with the problem in another way. . . .

The challenged regulations implement the statutory prohibition by prohibiting counseling, referral, and the provision of information regarding abortion as a method of family planning. They are designed to ensure that the limits of the federal program are observed. The Title X program is designed not for prenatal care, but to encourage family planning. A doctor who wished to offer prenatal care to a project patient who became pregnant could properly be prohibited from doing so because such service is outside the scope of the federally funded program. The regulations prohibiting abortion counseling and referral are of the same ilk; "no funds appropriated for the project may be used in programs where abortion is a method of family planning," and a doctor employed by the project may be prohibited in the course of his project duties from counseling abortion or referring for abortion. This is not a case of the Government "suppressing a dangerous idea," but of a prohibition on a project grantee or its employees from engaging in activities outside of its scope.

To hold that the Government unconstitutionally discriminates on the basis of viewpoint when it chooses to fund a program dedicated to advance certain permissible goals, because the program in advancing those goals necessarily discourages alternate goals, would render numerous government programs constitutionally suspect. When Congress established a National Endowment for Democracy to encourage other countries to adopt democratic principles, it was not constitutionally required to fund a program to encourage competing lines of political philosophy such as Communism and Fascism. Petitioners' assertions ultimately boil down to the position that if the government chooses to subsidize one protected right, it must subsidize analogous counterpart rights. But the Court has soundly rejected that proposition. . . .

Petitioners rely heavily on their claim that the regulations would not, in the circumstance of a medical emergency, permit a Title X project to refer a woman whose pregnancy places her life in imminent peril to a provider of abortions or abortion-related services. This case, of course, involves only a facial challenge to the regulations, and we do not have before us any application by the Secretary to a specific fact situation. On their face, we do not read the regulations to bar abortion referral or counseling in such circumstances. Abortion counseling as a "method of family planning" is prohibited, and it does not seem that a medically necessitated abortion in such circumstances would be the equivalent of its use as a "method of family planning." . . . Moreover, the regulations themselves contemplate that a Title X project would be permitted to engage in otherwise prohibited abortion-related activity in such circumstances. . . . Section 59.8(a)(2) provides a specific exemption for emergency care and requires Title X recipients "to refer the client immediately to an appropriate provider of emergency medical services." 42 CFR 59.8(a)(2) (1989). Section 59.5(b)(1) also requires Title X projects to provide "necessary referral to other medical facilities when medically indicated."

Petitioners also contend that the restrictions on the subsidization of abortion-related speech contained in the regulations are impermissible because they condition the receipt of a benefit, in this case Title X funding, on the relinquishment of a constitutional right, the right to engage in abortion advocacy and counseling. . . . Relying on Perry v. Sindermann, 408 U.S. 593, 597 (1972), and FCC v. League of Women Voters of Cal. 468 U.S. 364 (1984), petitioners argue that "even though the government may deny [a] . . . benefit for any number of reasons, there are some reasons upon which the government may not rely. It may not deny a benefit to a person on a basis that infringes his constitutionally protected interests — especially, his interest in freedom of speech."

Petitioners' reliance on these cases is unavailing, however, because here the government is not denying a benefit to anyone, but is instead simply insisting that public funds be spent for the purposes for which they were authorized. The Secretary's regulations do not force the Title X grantee to give up abortion-related speech; they merely require that the grantee keep such activities separate and distinct from Title X activities. Title X expressly distinguishes between a Title X grantee and a Title X project. The grantee, which normally is a health care organization, may receive funds from a variety of sources for a variety of purposes. The grantee receives Title X funds, however, for the specific and limited purpose of establishing and operating a Title X project. The regulations govern the scope of the Title X project's activities, and leave the grantee unfettered in its other activities. The Title X grantee can continue to perform abortions, provide abortion-related services, and engage in abortion advocacy; it simply is required to conduct those activities through programs that are separate and independent from the project that receives Title X funds.

In contrast, our "unconstitutional conditions" cases involve situations in which the government has placed a condition on the recipient of the subsidy rather than on a particular program or service, thus effectively prohibiting the recipient from engaging in the protected conduct outside the scope of the federally funded program. In FCC v. League of Women Voters of Cal., we invalidated a federal law providing that noncommercial television and radio stations that receive federal grants may not "engage in editorializing." Under that law, a recipient of federal funds was "barred absolutely from all editorializing" because it "is not able to segregate its activities according to the source of its funding" and thus "has no way of limiting the use of its federal funds to all noneditorializing activities." The effect of the law was that "a noncommercial educational station that receives only 1% of its overall income from [federal] grants is barred absolutely from all editorializing" and "barred from using even wholly private funds to finance its editorial activity." . . .

Similarly, in *Regan* we held that Congress could, in the exercise of its spending power, reasonably refuse to subsidize the lobbying activities of tax-exempt charitable organizations by prohibiting such organizations from using tax-deductible contributions to support their lobbying efforts. In so holding, we explained that such organizations remained free "to receive deductible contributions to support . . . nonlobbying activit[ies]." . . .

By requiring that the Title X grantee engage in abortion-related activity separately from activity receiving federal funding, Congress has . . . not denied it the right to engage in abortion-related activities. Congress has merely refused to fund such activities out of the public fisc, and the Secretary has simply required a certain degree of separation from the Title X project in order to ensure the integrity of the federally funded program.

The same principles apply to petitioners' claim that the regulations abridge the free speech rights of the grantee's staff. Individuals who are voluntarily employed for a Title X project must perform their duties in accordance with the regulation's restrictions on abortion counseling and referral. The employees remain free, however, to pursue abortion-related activities when they are not acting under the auspices of the Title X project. . . . The employees' freedom of expression is limited during the time that they actually work for the project; but this limitation is a consequence of their decision to accept employment in a project, the scope of which is permissibly restricted by the funding authority.

This is not to suggest that funding by the Government, even when coupled with the freedom of the fund recipients to speak outside the scope of the Government-funded project, is invariably sufficient to justify government control over the content of expression. For example, this Court has recognized that the existence of a Government "subsidy," in the form of Government-owned property, does not justify the restriction of speech in areas that have "been traditionally open to the public for expressive activity," or have been "expressly dedicated to speech activity." Similarly, we have recognized that the university is a traditional sphere of free expression so fundamental to the functioning of our society that the Government's ability to control speech within that sphere by means of conditions attached to the expenditure of Government funds is restricted by the vagueness and overbreadth doctrines of the First Amendment.

It could be argued by analogy that traditional relationships such as that between doctor and patient should enjoy protection under the First Amendment from government regulation, even when subsidized by the Government. We need not resolve that question here, however, because the Title X program regulations do not signficantly impinge upon the doctor-patient relationship. Nothing in them requires a doctor to represent as his own any opinion that he does not in fact hold. Nor is the doctor-patient relationship established by the Title X program sufficiently all-encompassing so as to justify an expectation on the part of the patient of comprehensive medical advice. The program does not provide postconception medical care, and therefore a doctor's silence with regard to abortion cannot reasonably be thought to mislead a client into thinking that the doctor does not consider abortion an appropriate option for her. The doctor is always free to make clear that advice regarding abortion is simply beyond the scope of the program. In these circumstances, the general rule that the Government may choose not to subsidize speech applies with full force.

IV

We turn now to petitioners' argument that the regulations violate a woman's Fifth Amendment right to choose whether to terminate her pregnancy. . . .

The difficulty that a woman encounters when a Title X project does not provide abortion counseling or referral leaves her in no different position than she would have been if the government had not enacted Title X. . . .

Petitioners also argue that by impermissibly infringing on the doctor/patient relationship and depriving a Title X client of information concerning abortion as a method of family planning, the regulations violate a woman's Fifth Amendment right to medical self-determination and to make informed medical decisions free of government-imposed harm. . . .

In [earlier cases,] we invalidated a city ordinance requiring all physicians to make specified statements to the patient prior to performing an abortion in order to ensure that the woman's consent was "truly informed." Similarly, . . . we struck down a state statute mandating that a list of agencies offering alternatives to abortion and a description of fetal development be provided to every woman considering terminating her pregnancy through an abortion. Critical to our decisions . . . was the fact that the laws in both cases required all doctors within their respective jurisdictions to provide all pregnant patients contemplating an abortion a litany of information, regardless of whether the patient sought the information or whether the doctor thought the information necessary to the patient's decision. Under the Secretary's regulations, however, a doctor's ability to provide, and a woman's right to receive, information concerning abortion and abortion-related services outside the context of the Title X project remains unfettered. It would undoubtedly be easier for a woman seeking an abortion if she could receive information about abortion from a Title X project, but the Constitution does not require that the Government distort the scope of its mandated program in order to provide that information.

Petitioners contend, however, that most Title X clients are effectively precluded by indigency and poverty from seeing a health care provider who will provide abortion-related services. But once again, even these Title X clients are in no worse position than if Congress had never enacted Title X. "The financial constraints that restrict an indigent woman's ability to enjoy the full range of constitutionally protected freedom of choice are the product not of governmental restrictions on access to abortion, but rather of her indigency."

The Secretary's regulations are a permissible construction of Title X and do not violate either the First or Fifth Amendments to the Constitution.

BLACKMUN, J., with whom Justice Marshall joins, with whom Justice Stevens joins as to Parts II and III, and with whom Justice O'Connor joins as to Part I, dissenting.

[T]he Court, for the first time, upholds viewpoint-based suppression of speech solely because it is imposed on those dependent upon the Government for economic support. Under essentially the same rationale, the majority upholds direct regulation of dialogue between a pregnant woman and her physician when that regulation has both the purpose and the effect of manipulating her decision as to the continuance of her pregnancy. I conclude that the Secretary's regulation of referral, advocacy, and counseling activities exceeds his statutory authority, and, also, that the Regulations violate the First and Fifth Amendments of our Constitution. . . .

I

The majority does not dispute that "[f]ederal statutes are to be so construed as to avoid serious doubt of their constitutionality." Machinists v. Street, 367 U.S. 740, 749 (1961). . . . [I]n its zeal to address the constitutional issues, the majority sidesteps this established canon of construction with the feeble excuse that the challenged Regulations "do not raise the sort of 'grave and doubtful constitutional questions,' . . . that would lead us to assume Congress did not intend to authorize their issuance."

This facile response to the intractable problem the Court addresses today is disingenuous at best. Whether or not one believes that these Regulations are valid, it avoids reality to contend that they do not give rise to serious constitutional questions. . . . [T]he question squarely presented by the Regulations — the extent to which the Government may attach an otherwise unconstitutional condition to the receipt of a public benefit — implicates a troubled area of our jurisprudence in which a court ought not entangle itself unnecessarily. See, e.g., Epstein, Unconstitutional Conditions, State Power, and the Limits of Consent, 102 Harv. L. Rev. 4, 6 (1988) (describing this problem as "the basic structural issue that for over a hundred years has bedeviled courts and commentators alike. . . ."); Sullivan, Unconstitutional Conditions, 102 Harv. L. Rev. 1413, 1415-1416 (1989) (observing that this Court's unconstitutional conditions cases "seem a minefield to be traversed gingerly"). . . .

Section 1008 of the Public Health Service Act provides simply: "None of the funds appropriated under this title shall be used in programs where abortion is a method of family planning." The majority concedes that this language "does not speak directly to the issues of counseling, referral, advocacy, or program integrity," and that "the legislative history is ambiguous" in this respect. Consequently, the language of §1008 easily sustains a constitutionally trouble-free interpretation.

Thus, this is not a situation in which "the intention of Congress is revealed too distinctly to permit us to ignore it because of mere misgivings as to power." Indeed, it would appear that our duty to avoid passing unnecessarily upon important constitutional questions is strongest where, as here, the language of the statute is decidedly ambiguous. It is both logical and eminently prudent to assume that when Congress intends to press the limits of constitutionality in its enactments, it will express that intent in explicit and unambiguous terms.

Because I conclude that a plainly constitutional construction of §1008 "is not only 'fairly possible' but entirely reasonable," I would reverse the judgment of the Court of Appeals on this ground without deciding the constitutionality of the Secretary's Regulations.

II

I also strongly disagree with the majority's disposition of petitioners' constitutional claims. . . .

A

. . . It cannot seriously be disputed that the counseling and referral provisions at issue in the present cases constitute content-based regulation of speech. Title X grantees may provide counseling and referral regarding any of a wide range of family planning and other topics, save abortion. . . .

The Regulations are also clearly viewpoint-based. While suppressing speech favorable to abortion with one hand, the Secretary compels anti-abortion speech with the other. For example, the Department of Health and Human Services' own description of the Regulations makes plain that "Title X projects are required to facilitate access to prenatal care and social services, including adoption services, that might be needed by the pregnant client to promote her well-being and that of her child, while making it abundantly clear that the project is not permitted to promote abortion by facilitating access to abortion through the referral process."

Moreover, the Regulations command that a project refer for prenatal care each woman diagnosed as pregnant, irrespective of the woman's expressed desire to continue or terminate her pregnancy. If a client asks directly about abortion, a Title X physician or counselor is required to say, in essence, that the project does not consider abortion to be an appropriate method of family planning. §59.8(b)(4). Both requirements are antithetical to the First Amendment.

The Regulations pertaining to "advocacy" are even more explicitly viewpoint-based. These provide: "A Title X project may not *encourage, promote or advocate* abortion as a method of family planning." [Emphasis added by Justice Blackmun.] . . . The Regulations do not, however, proscribe or even regulate anti-abortion advocacy. These are clearly restrictions aimed at the suppression of "dangerous ideas."

Remarkably, the majority concludes that "the Government has not discriminated on the basis of viewpoint; it has merely chosen to fund one activity to the exclusion of another." But the majority's claim that the Regulations merely limit a Title X project's speech to preventive or preconceptional services rings hollow in light of the broad range of non-preventive services that the Regulations authorize Title X projects to provide.[a] By refusing to fund those family-planning projects that advocate abortion because they advocate abortion, the Government plainly has targeted a particular viewpoint. . . .

[I]n addition to their impermissible focus upon the viewpoint of regulated speech, the provisions intrude upon a wide range of communicative conduct, including the very words spoken to a woman by her physician. By manipulating the content of the doctor/patient dialogue, the Regulations upheld today force each of the petitioners "to be an instrument for fostering public adherence to an ideological point of view [he or she] finds unacceptable." This type of intrusive, ideologically based regulation of speech . . . cannot be justified simply because it is a condition upon the receipt of a governmentl benefit.[b]

B

The Court concludes that the challenged Regulations do not violate the First Amendment rights of Title X staff members because any limitation of the employees' freedom of expression is simply a consequence of their decision to accept employment at a federally funded project. But it has never been sufficient to justify an otherwise unconstitutional condition upon public employment that the employee may escape the condition by relinquishing his or her job. . . .

The majority attempts to circumvent this principle by emphasizing that Title X physicians and counselors "remain free . . . to pursue abortion-related activities when they are not acting under the auspices of the Title X project." . . . Under the majority's reasoning, the First Amendment could be read to tolerate any governmental restriction upon an employee's speech so long as that restriction is limited to the funded workplace. This is a dangerous proposition. . . .

In the cases at bar, the speaker's interest in the communication is both clear and vital. In addressing the family planning needs of their clients, the physicians and counselors who staff Title X projects seek to provide them with the full range of information and options regarding their health and reproductive freedom. Indeed, the legitimate expectations of the patient and the ethical responsibilities of the medical profession demand no less. . . . The Government's articulated in-

a. In addition to requiring referral for prenatal care and adoption services, the Regulations permit general health services such as physical examinations, screening for breast cancer, treatment of gynecological problems, and treatment for sexually transmitted diseases. 53 Fed. Reg. 2927 (1988). None of the latter are strictly preventative, preconceptional services.

b. The majority attempts to obscure the breadth of its decision through its curious contention that "the Title X program regulations do not significantly impinge upon the doctor-patient relationship." That the doctor-patient relationship is substantially burdened by a rule prohibiting the dissemination by the physician of pertinent medical information is beyond serious dispute. This burden is undiminished by the fact that the relationship at issue here is not an "all-encompassing" one. A woman seeking the services of a Title X clinic has every reason to expect, as do we all, that her physician will not withhold relevant information regarding the very purpose of her visit. To suggest otherwise is to engage in uninformed fantasy. Further, to hold that the doctor-patient relationship is somehow incomplete where a patient lacks the resources to seek comprehensive healthcare from a single provider is to ignore the situation of a vast number of Americans. As Justice Marshall has noted in a different context: "It is perfectly proper for judges to disagree about what the Constitution requires. But it is disgraceful for an interpretation of the Constitution to be premised upon unfounded assumptions about how people live." United States v. Kras, 409 U.S. 434, 460 (1973) (dissenting opinion.)

terest in distorting the doctor/patient dialogue — ensuring that federal funds are not spent for a purpose outside the scope of the program — falls far short of that necessary to justify the suppression of truthful information and professional medical opinion regarding constitutionally protected conduct. Moreover, the offending Regulation is not narrowly tailored to serve this interest. For example, the governmental interest at stake could be served by imposing rigorous bookkeeping standards to ensure financial separation or adopting content-neutral rules for the balanced dissemination of family-planning and health information. By failing to balance or even to consider the free speech interests claimed by Title X physicians against the Government's asserted interest in suppressing the speech, the Court falters in its duty to implement the protection that the First Amendment clearly provides for this important message.

C

Finally, it is of no small significance that the speech the Secretary would suppress is truthful information regarding constitutionally protected conduct of vital importance to the listener. One can imagine no legitimate governmental interest that might be served by suppressing such information. Concededly, the abortion debate is among the most divisive and contentious issues that our Nation has faced in recent years. "But freedom to differ is not limited to things that do not matter much. That would be a mere shadow of freedom. The test of its substance is the right to differ as to things that touch the heart of the existing order." West Virginia Board of Education v. Barnette, 319 U.S. 624, 642 (1943).

III

By far the most disturbing aspect of today's ruling is the effect it will have on the Fifth Amendment rights of the women who, supposedly, are beneficiaries of Title X programs. The majority rejects petitioners' Fifth Amendment claims summarily. It relies primarily upon the decisions in Harris v. McRae, 448 U.S. 297 (1980), and Webster v. Reproductive Health Services, 492 U.S. 490 (1989). . . . [E]ven if one accepts as valid the Court's theorizing in those cases, the majority's reasoning in the present cases is flawed. Until today, the Court has allowed to stand only those restrictions upon reproductive freedom that, while limiting the availability of abortion, have left intact a woman's ability to decide without coercion whether she will continue her pregnancy to term. . . . Today's decision abandons that principle, and with disastrous results.

Contrary to the majority's characterization, this is not a case in which individuals seek government aid in exercising their fundamental rights. The Fifth Amendment right asserted by petitioners is the right of a pregnant woman to be free from affirmative governmental interference in her decision. Roe v. Wade, 410 U.S. 113 (1973), and its progeny are not so much about a medical procedure as they are about a woman's fundamental right to self-determination. Those cases serve to vindicate the idea that "liberty," if it means anything, must entail freedom from governmental domination in making the most intimate and personal of decisions. By suppressing medically pertinent information and injecting a restrictive ideological message unrelated to considerations of maternal health the Government places formidable obstacles in the path of Title X clients' freedom of choice and thereby violates their Fifth Amendment rights.

It is crystal-clear that the aim of the challenged provisions . . . is not simply to ensure that federal funds are not used to perform abortions, but to "reduce the incidence of abortion." 42 CFR §59.2 (1990) (in definition of "family planning"). As recounted above, the Regulations require Title X physicians and counselors to provide information pertaining only to childbirth, to refer a pregnant woman for prenatal care irrespective of her medical situation, and, upon direct inquiry, to respond that abortion is not an "appropriate method" of family planning.

The undeniable message conveyed by this forced speech, and the one that the Title X client will draw from it, is that abortion nearly always is an improper medical option. Although her physician's words, in fact, are strictly controlled by the Government and wholly unrelated to her particular medical situation, the Title X client will reasonably construe them as professional advice to forgo her right to obtain an abortion. As would most rational patients, many of these women will follow that perceived advice and carry their pregnancy to term, despite their needs to the contrary and despite the safety of the abortion procedure for the vast majority of them. Others, delayed by the Regulations' mandatory prenatal referral, will be prevented from acquiring abortions during the period in which the process is medically sound and constitutionally protected.

In view of the inevitable effect of the Regulations, the majority's conclusion that "[t]he difficulty tht a woman encounters when a Title X project does not provide abortion counseling or referral leaves her in no different position than she would have been if the government had not enacted Title X," is insensitive and contrary to common human experience. Both the purpose and result of the challenged Regulations is to deny women the ability voluntarily to decide their procreative destiny. For these women, the Government will have obliterated the freedom to choose as surely as if it had banned abortions outright. The denial of this freedom is not a consequence of poverty but of the Government's ill-intentioned distortion of information it has chosen to provide. The substantial obstacles to bodily self-determination that the Regulations impose are doubly offensive because they are effected by manipulating the very words spoken by physicians and counselors to their patients. In our society, the doctor/patient dialogue embodies a unique relationship of trust. The specialized nature of medical science and the emotional distress often attendant to health-related decisions requires that patients place their complete confidence, and often their very lives, in the hands of medical professionals. One seeks a physician's aid not only for medication or diagnosis, but also for guidance, professional judgment, and vital emotional support. Accordingly, each of us attaches profound importance and authority to the words of advice spoken by the physician. . . .

The majority [argue] that the . . . Regulations now before the Court pertain [only] to the narrow class of healthcare professionals employed at Title X projects. But the rights protected by the Constitution are personal rights. And for the individual woman, the deprivation of liberty by the Government is no less substantial because it affects few rather than many. It cannot be that an otherwise unconstitutional infringement of choice is made lawful because it touches only some of the Nation's pregnant women and not all of them. . . .[31]

Discussion

After *Rust*, could a state condition the provision of funds to public defenders or court-appointed criminal defense lawyers on their agreement not to inform their clients that the Fifth Amendment gives them the right to refuse to talk to the police or testify at trial? If the answer is no, that is because after Gideon v. Wainwright the state is constitutionally compelled to provide indigents with effective assistance of counsel, which includes providing such basic information as the client's right not to incriminate himself. The lawyer's right (indeed, duty) to provide such information is based on the Fifth or Sixth Amendments, rather than the First Amendment. Suppose the state requires state-subsidized criminal defense lawyers to tell clients, after informing them of their Fifth Amendment rights, that "refusing to tell the authorities what you know about the crime is considered an antisocial act by most right-thinking people". Would you differentiate between lawyers employed full-time by the state (e.g., public defenders) and the court-appointed private-market lawyer?

Lawyers funded by the Legal Services Corporation (LSC) are prohibited from bringing cases involving, among other things, "abortion rights, draft resistance and school desegration." See Englade, The LSC Under Siege, ABA Journal 66, 68 (Dec. 1, 1987). Do these limitations present constitutional problems? Is it permissible to allow an LSC lawyer to litigate a school desegregation case only as long "as busing is not sought as a remedy"? Could LSC lawyers be prevented from telling their clients about the availability of punitive damage remedies in regard to certain actions (and be prevented from pleading for such damages should suits be brought)?

Note the majority's reference to the special circumstances of universities. What constitutional theory underlies more protection for college professors than for doctors or lawyers?

V. The Protection of Welfare Rights under the Equal Protection Clause

As we saw earlier in this chapter, the Constitution has not been interpreted to *require* the contemporary welfare state — at least not in gross. Rather, Government provision or subsidy of food, shelter, medical care, and the like is the result of political or policy decisions by Congress and state legislatures.

Nonetheless, the state does not have unlimited discretion to selectively allocate those services it chooses to offer. We have already seen this in the equal protection doctrines concerned with suspect classifications and the interest in voting. The remainder of this chapter examines other situations in which the Constitution arguably constrains the state's ability to offer benefits on certain conditions, even though it need not offer them at all.

31. Dissenting opinions by Justices O'Connor and Stevens, which focus on the issue of statutory interpretation, are omitted.

A. Burdens on Interstate Mobility

We last encountered the constitutional protection of interstate mobility in Crandall v. Nevada, 73 U.S. (6 Wall.) 35 (1868), Chapter 3 supra, in which the Court, reasoning from the structure of the federal union, invalidated a $1 Nevada departure tax. The only significant decision between *Crandall* and Shapiro v. Thompson was Edwards v. California, 314 U.S. 160 (1941), in which the Court unanimously struck down a California law that forbade bringing indigents into the state. The Court, in an opinion by Justice Byrnes, relied on the commerce clause, asserting that the subject was one demanding uniformity under the *Cooley* standard. Justice Byrnes responded to the state's citation of the dictum in Miln v. New York, Chapter 3 supra: "Whatever may have been the notion then prevailing, we do not think that it will now be seriously contended that because a person is without employment and without funds he constitutes a 'moral pestilence.' " Justice Douglas, joined by Justices Black and Murphy, concurred on the ground that "the right to move freely from State to State is an incident of *national* citizenship protected by the privileges or immunities clause of the Fourteenth Amendment against state interference." Justice Jackson also based his concurrence on the privileges and immunities clause, but while Douglas did not reach the commerce clause issue, Jackson explicitly rejected the Court's reasoning: "the migrations of a human being, of whom it is charged that he possesses nothing that can be sold and has no wherewithal to buy, do not fit easily into my notions as to what is commerce. To hold that the measure of his rights is the commerce clause is likely to result eventually either in distorting the commercial law or in denaturing human rights."

SHAPIRO v. THOMPSON[32]

394 U.S. 618 (1969)

Appeal from the United States District Court for the District of Connecticut

BRENNAN, J. . . .

Each [of these cases] is an appeal from a decision of a three-judge District Court holding unconstitutional a State or District of Columbia statutory provision which denies welfare assistance to residents of the State or District who have not resided within their jurisdictions for at least one year immediately preceding their applications for such assistance. We affirm the judgments of the District Courts in the three cases. . . .

II

There is no dispute that the effect of the waiting-period requirement in each case is to create two classes of needy resident families indistinguishable from each other except that one is composed of residents who have resided a year or more, and the second of residents who have resided less than a year, in the jurisdiction.

32. Together with Washington v. Legrant, on appeal from the United States District Court for the District of Columbia, and Reynolds v. Smith, on appeal from the United States District Court for the Eastern District of Pennsylvania.

On the basis of this sole difference the first class is granted and the second class is denied welfare aid upon which may depend the ability of the families to obtain the very means to subsist — food, shelter, and other necessities of life. . . . On reargument, appellees' central contention is that the statutory prohibition of benefits to residents of less than a year creates a classification which constitutes an invidious discrimination denying them equal protection of the laws. We agree. The interests which appellants assert are promoted by the classification either may not constitutionally be promoted by government or are not compelling governmental interests.

III

Primarily, appellants justify the waiting-period requirement as a protective device to preserve the fiscal integrity of state public assistance programs. It is asserted that people who require welfare assistance during their first year of residence in a State are likely to become continuing burdens on state welfare programs. Therefore, the argument runs, if such people can be deterred from entering the jurisdiction by denying them welfare benefits during the first year, state programs to assist long-time residents will not be impaired by a substantial influx of indigent newcomers. . . .

We do not doubt that the one-year waiting-period device is well suited to discourage the influx of poor families in need of assistance. An indigent who desires to migrate, resettle, find a new job, and start a new life will doubtless hesitate if he knows that he must risk making the move without the possibility of falling back on state welfare assistance during his first year of residence, when his need may be most acute. But the purpose of inhibiting migration by needy persons into the State is constitutionally impermissible.

This Court long ago recognized that the nature of our Federal Union and our constitutional concepts of personal liberty unite to require that all citizens be free to travel throughout the length and breadth of our land uninhibited by statutes, rules, or regulations which unreasonably burden or restrict this movement. That proposition was early stated by Chief Justice Taney in the Passenger Cases, 7 How. 283, 492 (1849). . . .

We have no occasion to ascribe the source of this right to travel interstate to a particular constitutional provision.[a] It suffices that, as Mr. Justice Stewart said for the Court in United States v. Guest, 383 U.S. 745, 757-758 (1966): "The constitutional right to travel from one State to another . . . occupies a position fundamental to the concept of our Federal Union. It is a right that has been firmly established and repeatedly recognized. . . ."

a. In Corfield v. Coryell, 6 F. Cas. 546, 552 (No. 3230) (C.C.E.D. Pa. 1825), Paul v. Virginia, 8 Wall. 168, 180 (1869), and Ward v. Maryland, 12 Wall. 418, 430 (1871), the right to travel interstate was grounded upon the Privileges and Immunities Clauses of Art. IV, §2. See also Slaughter-House Cases, 16 Wall. 36, 79 (1873); Twining v. New Jersey, 211 U.S. 78, 97 (1908). In Edwards v. California, 314 U.S. 160, 181, 183-185 (1941) (Douglas and Jackson, JJ., concurring), and Twining v. New Jersey, supra, reliance was placed on the Privileges and Immunities Clause of the Fourteenth Amendment. See also Crandall v. Nevada, 6 Wall. 35 (1868). In Edwards v. California, supra, and the Passenger Cases, 7 How. 283 (1849), a Commerce Clause approach was employed.

See also Kent v. Dulles, 357 U.S. 116, 125 (1958); Aptheker v. Secretary of State, 378 U.S. 500, 505-506 (1964); Zemel v. Rusk, 381 U.S. 1, 14 (1965), where the freedom of Americans to travel outside the country was grounded upon the Due Process Clause of the Fifth Amendment.

Thus, the purpose of deterring the in-migration of indigents cannot serve as justification for the classification created by the one-year waiting period, since that purpose is constitutionally impermissible. If a law has "no other purpose . . . than to chill the assertion of constitutional rights by penalizing those who choose to exercise them, then it [is] patently unconstitutional."

Alternatively, appellants argue that even if it is impermissible for a State to attempt to deter the entry of all indigents, the challenged classification may be justified as a permissible state attempt to discourage those indigents who would enter the State solely to obtain larger benefits. We observe first that none of the statutes before us is tailored to serve that objective. . . .

More fundamentally, a State may no more try to fence out those indigents who seek higher welfare benefits than it may try to fence out indigents generally. Implicit in any such distinction is the notion that indigents who enter a State with the hope of securing higher welfare benefits are somehow less deserving than indigents who do not take this consideration into account. But we do not perceive why a mother who is seeking to make a new life for herself and her children should be regarded as less deserving because she considers, among other factors, the level of a State's public assistance. Surely such a mother is no less deserving than a mother who moves into a particular State in order to take advantage of its better educational facilities.

Appellants argue further that the challenged classification may be sustained as an attempt to distinguish between new and old residents on the basis of the contribution they have made to the community through the payment of taxes. . . . Appellants' reasoning would logically permit the State to bar new residents from schools, parks, and libraries or deprive them of police and fire protection. Indeed it would permit the State to apportion all benefits and services according to the past tax contributions of its citizens. The Equal Protection Clause prohibits such an apportionment of state services.[b]

We recognize that a State has a valid interest in preserving the fiscal integrity of its programs. It may legitimately attempt to limit its expenditures, whether for public assistance, public education, or any other program. But a State may not accomplish such a purpose by invidious distinctions between classes of its citizens. It could not, for example, reduce expenditures for education by barring indigent children from its schools. Similarly, in the cases before us, appellants must do more than show that denying welfare benefits to new residents saves money. The saving of welfare costs cannot justify an otherwise invidious classification.

In sum, neither deterrence of indigents from migrating to the State nor limitation of welfare benefits to those regarded as contributing to the State is a constitutionally permissible state objective.

IV

Appellants next advance as justification certain administrative and related governmental objectives allegedly served by the waiting-period requirement. They argue that the requirement (1) facilitates the planning of the welfare budget; (2) provides an objective test of residency; (3) minimizes the opportunity for recipi-

b. We are not dealing here with state insurance programs which may legitimately tie the amount of benefits to the individual's contributions.

ents fraudulently to receive payments from more than one jurisdiction; and (4) encourages early entry of new residents into the labor force.

At the outset, we reject appellants' argument that a mere showing of a rational relationship between the waiting period and these four admittedly permissible state objectives will suffice to justify the classification. The waiting-period provision denies welfare benefits to otherwise eligible applicants solely because they have recently moved into the jurisdiction. But in moving from State to State or to the District of Columbia appellees were exercising a constitutional right, and any classification which serves to penalize the exercise of that right, unless shown to be necessary to promote a *compelling* governmental interest, is unconstitutional.

[The Court concludes that the states did not in fact use the residency requirement to further (1) or (2) above; that the states could accomplish (3) by less drastic means; and that (4) does not justify treating old and new residents differently.]

We conclude therefore that appellants in these cases do not use and have no need to use the one-year requirement for the governmental purposes suggested. Thus, even under traditional equal protection tests a classification of welfare applicants according to whether they have lived in the State for one year would seem irrational and unconstitutional. But, of course, the traditional criteria do not apply in these cases. Since the classification here touches on the fundamental right of interstate movement, its constitutionality must be judged by the stricter standard of whether it promotes a *compelling* state interest. Under this standard, the waiting-period requirement clearly violates the Equal Protection Clause.

V

[The Court considers and rejects appellants' argument that Congress expressly approved the one-year waiting period and concludes that "even if we were to assume, arguendo, that Congress did approve the imposition of a one-year waiting period, . . . the provision . . . would be unconstitutional. Congress may not authorize the states to violate the Equal Protection Clause."[33]]

STEWART, J., concurring.

In joining the opinion of the Court, I add a word in response to the dissent of my Brother Harlan, who, I think, has quite misapprehended what the Court's opinion says.

The Court today does *not* "pick out particular human activities, characterize them as 'fundamental,' and give them added protection. . . ." To the contrary, the Court simply recognizes, as it must, an established constitutional right, and gives to that right no less protection than the Constitution itself demands. "The constitutional right to travel from one State to another . . . has been firmly established and repeatedly recognized.". . .

It follows, as the Court says, that "the purpose of deterring the in-migration of indigents cannot serve as justification for the classification created by the one-year waiting period, since that purpose is constitutionally impermissible." And it further follows, as the Court says, that any *other* purposes offered in support of a law that so clearly impinges upon the constitutional right of interstate travel must

33. The scope of congressional authority to determine what are and are not violations of the equal protection clause is taken up in Chapter 12.

be shown to reflect a *compelling* governmental interest. . . . As Mr. Justice Harlan wrote for the Court more than a decade ago, "[T]o justify the deterrent effect . . . on the free exercise . . . of their constitutionally protected right . . . a '. . . subordinating interest of the State must be compelling.' " NAACP v. Alabama, 357 U.S. 449 (1958). . . .

WARREN, C.J., joined by Black, J., dissenting. . . .

Congress has imposed a residence requirement in the District of Columbia and authorized the States to impose similar requirements. The issue before us must therefore be framed in terms of whether Congress may create minimal residence requirements, not whether the States, acting alone, may do so. See Prudential Insurance Co. v. Benjamin, 328 U.S. 408 (1946); In re Rahrer, 140 U.S. 545 (1891). Appellees insist that a congressionally mandated residence requirement would violate their right to travel. The import of their contention is that Congress, even under its "plenary" power to control interstate commerce, is constitutionally prohibited from imposing residence requirements. I reach a contrary conclusion for I am convinced that the extent of the burden on interstate travel when compared with the justification for its imposition requires the Court to uphold this exertion of federal power.

Congress, pursuant to its commerce power, has enacted a variety of restrictions upon interstate travel. It has taxed air and rail fares and the gasoline needed to power cars and trucks which move interstate. Many of the federal safety regulations of common carriers which cross state lines burden the right to travel. And Congress has prohibited by criminal statute interstate travel for certain purposes. E.g., 18 U.S.C. §1952. Although these restrictions operate as a limitation upon free interstate movement of persons, their constitutionality appears well settled. . . .

The Court's right-to-travel cases lend little support to the view that congressional action is invalid merely because it burdens the right to travel. Most of our cases fall into two categories: those in which *state*-imposed restrictions were involved, see, e.g., Edwards v. California, 314 U.S. 160 (1941); Crandall v. Nevada, 6 Wall. 35 (1868), and those concerning congressional decisions to remove impediments to interstate movement, see, e.g., United States v. Guest, 383 U.S. 745 (1966). Since the focus of our inquiry must be whether Congress would exceed permissible bounds by imposing residence requirements, neither group of cases offers controlling principles.

In only three cases have we been confronted with an assertion that Congress has impermissibly burdened the right to travel.[34] Kent v. Dulles, 357 U.S. 116 (1958), did invalidate a burden on the right to travel; however, the restriction was voided on the nonconstitutional basis that Congress did not intend to give the Secretary of State power to create the restriction at issue. Zemel v. Rusk, 381 U.S. 1 (1965), on the other hand, sustained a flat prohibition of travel to certain designated areas and rejected an attack that Congress could not constitutionally impose this restriction. Aptheker v. Secretary of State, 378 U.S. 500 (1964), is the only case in which this Court invalidated on a constitutional basis a congressio-

34. These decisions all involved the travel of Americans *abroad,* but in *Kent* the Court stated in dictum that "the right to travel is part of the 'liberty' of which the citizens cannot be deprived without due process of law under the Fifth Amendment. . . . Freedom of movement across frontiers, in either direction, and inside frontiers as well, was part of our heritage."

nally imposed restriction. *Aptheker* also involved a flat prohibition but in combination with a claim that the congressional restriction compelled a potential traveler to choose between his right to travel and his First Amendment right of freedom of association. It was this Hobson's choice, we later explained, which forms the rationale of *Aptheker*. *Aptheker* thus contains two characteristics distinguishing it from the appeals now before the Court: a combined infringement of two constitutionally protected rights and a flat prohibition upon travel. Residence requirements do not create a flat prohibition, for potential welfare recipients may move from State to State and establish residence wherever they please. Nor is any claim made by appellees that residence requirements compel them to choose between the right to travel and another constitutional right.

Zemel v. Rusk, the most recent of the three cases, provides a framework for analysis. The core inquiry is "the extent of the governmental restriction imposed" and the "extent of the necessity for the restriction." As already noted, travel itself is not prohibited. Any burden inheres solely in the fact that a potential welfare recipient might take into consideration the loss of welfare benefits for a limited period of time if he changes his residence. Not only is this burden of uncertain degree, but appellees themselves assert there is evidence that few welfare recipients have in fact been deterred by residence requirements. . . .

The insubstantiality of the restriction imposed by residence requirements must then be evaluated in light of the possible congressional reasons for such requirements. One fact which does emerge with clarity from the legislative history is Congress' belief that a program of cooperative federalism combining federal aid with enhanced state participation would result in an increase in the scope of welfare programs and level of benefits. Given the apprehensions of many States that an increase in benefits without minimal residence requirements would result in an inability to provide an adequate welfare system, Congress deliberately adopted the intermediate course of a cooperative program. Such a program, Congress believed, would encourage the States to assume greater welfare responsibilities and would give the States the necessary financial support for such an undertaking. Our cases require only that Congress have a rational basis for finding that a chosen regulatory scheme is necessary to the furtherance of interstate commerce. Certainly, a congressional finding that residence requirements allowed each State to concentrate its resources upon new and increased programs of rehabilitation ultimately resulting in an enhanced flow of commerce as the economic condition of welfare recipients progressively improved is rational and would justify imposition of residence requirements under the Commerce Clause. And Congress could have also determined that residence requirements fostered personal mobility. An individual no longer dependent upon welfare would be presented with an unfettered range of choices so that a decision to migrate could be made without regard to considerations of possible economic dislocation. . . .

HARLAN, J., dissenting.

The Court today . . . [expands] the comparatively new constitutional doctrine that some state statutes will be deemed to deny equal protection of the laws unless justified by a "compelling" governmental interest, and . . . [holds] that the Fifth Amendment's Due Process Clause imposes a similar limitation on federal enactments. Having decided that the "compelling interest" principle is applicable, the Court then finds that the governmental interests here asserted are either wholly impermissible or are not "compelling." For reasons which follow, I disagree both with the Court's result and with its reasoning.

I

... [T]he welfare residence requirements are alleged to be unconstitutional on two grounds: *first,* because they impose an undue burden upon the constitutional right of welfare applicants to travel interstate; *second,* because they deny to persons who have recently moved interstate and would otherwise be eligible for welfare assistance the equal protection of the laws assured by the Fourteenth Amendment (in the state cases) or the analogous protection afforded by the Fifth Amendment (in the District of Columbia case). Since the Court basically relies upon the equal protection ground, I shall discuss it first.

II

In upholding the equal protection argument, the Court has applied an equal protection doctrine of relatively recent vintage: the rule that statutory classifications which either are based upon certain "suspect" criteria or affect "fundamental rights" will be held to deny equal protection unless justified by a "compelling" governmental interest.

The "compelling interest" doctrine, which today is articulated more explicitly than ever before, constitutes an increasingly significant exception to the long-established rule that a statute does not deny equal protection if it is rationally related to a legitimate governmental objective. The "compelling interest" doctrine has two branches. The branch which requires that classifications based upon "suspect" criteria be supported by a compelling interest apparently had its genesis in cases involving racial classifications, which have, at least since Korematsu v. United States, 323 U.S. 214, 216 (1944), been regarded as inherently "suspect."... Today the list [of suspect classifications] apparently has been further enlarged to include classifications based upon recent interstate movement, and perhaps those based upon the exercise of *any* constitutional right....

I think that this branch of the "compelling interest" doctrine is sound when applied to racial classifications, for historically the Equal Protection Clause was largely a product of the desire to eradicate legal distinctions founded upon race. However, I believe that the more recent extensions have been unwise.... And when, as in ... the present case, a classification is based upon the exercise of rights guaranteed against state infringement by the Federal Constitution, then there is no need for any resort to the Equal Protection Clause; in such instances, this Court may properly and straightforwardly invalidate any undue burden upon those rights under the Fourteenth Amendment's Due Process Clause.

The second branch of the "compelling interest" principle is even more troublesome. For it has been held that a statutory classification is subject to the "compelling interest" test if the result of the classification may be to affect a "fundamental right," regardless of the basis of the classification....[a] [The notion] has

a. Analysis is complicated when the statutory classification is grounded upon the exercise of a "fundamental" right. For then the statute may come within the first branch of the "compelling interest" doctrine because exercise of the right is deemed a "suspect" criterion and also within the second because the statute is considered to affect the right by deterring its exercise.... The present case is

reappeared today in the Court's cryptic suggestion that the "compelling interest" test is applicable merely because the result of the classification may be to deny the appellees "food, shelter, and other necessities of life," as well as in the Court's statement that "[s]ince the classification here touches on the fundamental right of interstate movement, its constitutionality must be judged by the stricter standard of whether it promotes a *compelling* state interest."

I think this branch of the "compelling interest" doctrine particularly unfortunate and unnecessary. . . . When the right affected is one assured by the Federal Constitution, any infringement can be dealt with under the Due Process Clause. But when a statute affects only matters not mentioned in the Federal Constitution and is not arbitrary or irrational, I must reiterate that I know of nothing which entitles this Court to pick out particular human activities, characterize them as "fundamental," and give them added protection under an unusually stringent equal protection test. . . .

III

The next issue, which I think requires fuller analysis than that deemed necessary by the Court under its equal protection rationale, is whether a one-year welfare residence requirement amounts to an undue burden upon the right of interstate travel. Four considerations are relevant: First, what is the constitutional source and nature of the right to travel which is relied upon? Second, what is the extent of the interference with that right? Third, what governmental interests are served by welfare residence requirements? Fourth, how should the balance of the competing considerations be struck? . . .

[1. Justice Harlan discusses the first question to conclude:] the right to travel interstate is a "fundamental" right which, for present purposes, should be regarded as having its source in the Due Process Clause of the Fifth Amendment.

[2.] . . . The number or proportion of persons who are actually deterred from changing residence by the existence of [the one-year waiting period] is unknown. If one accepts evidence put forward by the appellees, to the effect that there would be only a minuscule increase in the number of welfare applicants were existing residence requirements to be done away with, it follows that the requirements do not deter an appreciable number of persons from moving interstate.

[3.] Against this indirect impact on the right to travel must be set the interests of the States, and of Congress with respect to the District of Columbia, in imposing residence conditions. There appear to be four such interests. First, it is evident that a primary concern . . . was to deny welfare benefits to persons who moved into the jurisdiction primarily in order to collect those benefits. This seems to me an entirely legitimate objective. A legislature is certainly not obliged to furnish welfare assistance to every inhabitant of the jurisdiction, and it is entirely rational to deny benefits to those who enter primarily in order to receive them, since this will make more funds available for those whom the legislature deems more worthy of subsidy.

[an] instance, insofar as welfare residence statutes both deter interstate movement and distinguish among welfare applicants on the basis of such movement. Consequently, I have not attempted to specify the branch of the doctrine upon which these decisions rest.

A second possible purpose of residence requirements is the prevention of fraud. A residence requirement provides an objective and workable means of determining that an applicant intends to remain indefinitely within the jurisdiction. . . . Third, the requirement of a fixed period of residence may help in predicting the budgetary amount which will be needed for public assistance in the future. While none of the appellant jurisdictions appears to keep data sufficient to permit the making of detailed budgetary predictions in consequence of the requirement, it is probable that in the event of a very large increase or decrease in the number of indigent newcomers the waiting period would give the legislature time to make needed adjustments in the welfare laws. Obviously, this is a proper objective. Fourth, the residence requirements conceivably may have been predicated upon a legislative desire to restrict welfare payments financed in part by state tax funds to persons who have recently made some contribution to the State's economy, through having been employed, having paid taxes, or having spent money in the State. This too would appear to be a legitimate purpose.

[4.] The next question is the decisive one: whether the governmental interests served by residence requirements outweigh the burden imposed upon the right to travel. In my view, a number of considerations militate in favor of constitutionality. First, as just shown, four separate, legitimate governmental interests are furthered by residence requirements. Second, the impact of the requirements upon the freedom of individuals to travel interstate is indirect and, according to evidence put forward by the appellees themselves, insubstantial. Third, these are not cases in which a State or States, acting alone, have attempted to interfere with the right of citizens to travel, but one in which the States have acted within the terms of a limited authorization by the National Government, and in which Congress itself has laid down a like rule for the District of Columbia. Fourth, the legislatures which enacted these statutes have been fully exposed to the arguments of the appellees as to why these residence requirements are unwise, and have rejected them. This is not, therefore, an instance in which legislatures have acted without mature deliberation.

Fifth, and of longer-range importance, the field of welfare assistance is one in which there is a widely recognized need for fresh solutions and consequently for experimentation. Invalidation of welfare residence requirements have the unfortunate consequence of discouraging the Federal and State Governments from establishing unusually generous welfare programs in particular areas on an experimental basis, because of fears that the program would cause an influx of persons seeking higher welfare payments. Sixth and finally, a strong presumption of constitutionality attaches to statutes of the types now before us. . . .

Taking all of these competing considerations into account, I believe that the balance definitely favors constitutionality. In reaching that conclusion, I do not minimize the importance of the right to travel interstate. However, the impact of residence conditions upon that right is indirect and apparently quite insubstantial. On the other hand, the governmental purposes served by the requirements are legitimate and real, and the residence requirements are clearly suited to their accomplishment. . . .

1. *The Equal Protection Mode*

It is not difficult to explain in historical terms why the Court relied on the equal protection clause in *Shapiro*. Justice Brennan and several other members of the Warren Court had been seeking to create a new equal protection jurisprudence in which the clause would protect a variety of "fundamental interests" that did not have the status of constitutional "rights." Although some sort of freedom of interstate mobility had long been recognized as a constitutional right, its sources and scope were obscure. Moreover, reliance on the equal protection clause gave Justice Brennan the opportunity to make what Justice Harlan called the "cryptic suggestion that the 'compelling interest' test is applicable merely because the result of the classification may be to deny the appellees food, shelter, and other necessities of life" — a suggestion that appeared less cryptically in a dissenting opinion only a year later.[35]

Given the Court's view that freedom of interstate mobility is an independent constitutional right, why, as an *analytic* matter, did the Court not rely directly on that right rather than, in effect, incorporating it into the equal protection clause?

Recall that the fundamental defect of the laws invalidated in cases such as Dean Milk v. Madison and Pennsylvania v. West Virginia (page 451 supra) was that they preferred one class of persons (residents of the regulating state) to another class (residents of other states). Not all laws that disadvantage residents of other states are invalid: Their constitutionality depends in part on their purpose and necessity. For example, in Mintz v. Baldwin (page 425 supra), the Court upheld New York's exclusion of cattle from herds not certified free from Bang's disease in view of the state's strong interest in curbing the spread of infection to clean herds. However, the theoretic strength of a state's justification for disadvantaging other states may be undercut by its domestic practices. New York's interest in curbing Bang's disease seems less compelling in light of the information (apparently not presented to the Court) that the state was doing virtually nothing to prevent its spread among domestic herds. More generally, Professor Robert Reinstein suggests:[36]

> [A] state can hardly demonstrate a compelling interest in regulating the conduct of Group *A* on the basis of a governmental objective that is equally applicable to an identical Group *B* which goes unregulated. If the governmental objective must be compelling in light of the effect on Group *A*'s constitutional rights, then a strong showing should be required that Group *B* is not situated similarly with Group *A* with respect to the asserted objective. . . .
>
> Stringent equal protection standards are thus necessarily intertwined in a Bill of Rights analysis of the state's justification. It is for this reason that equal protection cannot be read out of the *Shapiro* case. The maximum impact on the right to travel would have been caused by a state setting a permanent level of benefits much lower than in other states; indeed, the deterrent on the right to travel would be greatest if a state abolished its welfare program. But the state's justification for doing either would be overriding, and a court would probably not view a case challenging this action as a right to travel case at all. Even though the residence test affected the exer-

35. Dandridge v. Williams, 397 U.S. 471 (1970).

36. Reinstein, The Welfare Cases: Fundamental Rights, the Poor, and the Burden of Proof in Constitutional Litigation, 44 Temp. L.Q. 1, 39 (1970).

> cise of the right to travel to a lesser extent, the discriminatory features enhanced the constitutional challenge. . . . The four objectives asserted by the state — facilitating planning, objectively determining residence, guarding against fraudulent claims, and encouraging employment — are no doubt important in the abstract but were belied in this case by the state's failure to seek to obtain them in the much larger class of welfare recipients, and was the one factor that Justice Harlan overlooked in his balance. It is one thing to say that abolition of welfare can be justified even though it deters the freedom to travel; it is quite something else to say that newcomers to the state should be singled out for the non-enjoyment of welfare benefits.

The Court might have adopted this equal protection "mode" of analysis without reference to the equal protection clause, as it did in the commerce clause cases referred to above; however, it chose to use a provision that focuses directly on the treatment of different classes of persons.

Note the Court's similar approach in Police Department of Chicago v. Mosley, 408 U.S. 92 (1972). Respondent was picketing a high school, to protest its alleged discriminatory policies, in violation of a city ordinance prohibiting picketing near a school in session except "any school involved in a labor dispute. . . ." He sued successfully to declare the law unconstitutional. On appeal, the Supreme Court affirmed, Justice Marshall writing:

> Because Chicago treats some picketing differently from others, we analyze this ordinance in terms of the Equal Protection Clause of the Fourteenth Amendment. Of course, the equal protection claim in this case is closely intertwined with First Amendment interests. . . . [U]nder the Equal Protection Clause, not to mention the First Amendment itself, government may not grant the use of a forum to people whose views it finds acceptable, but deny use to those wishing to express less favored or more controversial views. And it may not select which issues are worth discussing or debating in public facilities. There is an "equality of status in the field of ideas," and government must afford all points of view an equal opportunity to be heard. Once a forum is opened up to assembly or speaking by some groups, government may not prohibit others from assembling or speaking on the basis of what they intend to say. Selective exclusions from a public forum may not be based on content alone, and may not be justified by reference to content alone.

Justice Marshall concluded that the ordinance in effect regulated the content of expression. He rejected the city's justification that "as a class, nonlabor picketing is more prone to produce violence than labor picketing," holding that "[t]he Equal Protection Clause requires that statutes affecting First Amendment interests be narrowly tailored to their legitimate objectives."

2. *For What Purposes May a State Abridge Freedom of Interstate Mobility?*

Recall that, consistent with the commerce clause, states may inspect and fence out infectious cattle. Might a state also inspect and fence out persons suffering from an infectious disease where unrestricted immigration would subvert a domestic disease-control program?

Could a state refuse to accept an individual it deems a "moral pestilence"? Imagine, for example, a murderer who had been paroled by state *A*. Could the state condition parole on his remaining within the state, close to supervisors? State *A* might be quite eager, though, to have the murderer move to some other jurisdiction. Could state *B* refuse him admission, or at least require that the murderer persuade state *B*'s parole board that he no longer presents any danger? Is the decision of state *A*'s parole board that he no longer endangers the public dispositive for all other states?

In *Shapiro,* Justice Brennan suggests that if persons enjoy a constitutional right of interstate mobility, it follows logically that the *purpose* of deterring the immigration of indigents is constitutionally impermissible. Do you agree? May the state nonetheless discourage people from entering the state solely to obtain larger welfare benefits?

3. The Nature and Extent of Permissible Incidental Abridgements

To what extent and under what circumstances may a state burden interstate mobility in effectuating a legitimate objective, no part of which is to deter mobility? This issue was raised by the "administrative" justifications proffered in *Shapiro* and has been presented in several subsequent cases.

In Evansville-Vanderburgh Airport Authority v. Delta Airlines, 405 U.S. 707 (1972), the Court sustained a $1 tax imposed by the airport authority on each enplaning commercial airline passenger, the proceeds to be used to defray the costs of airport facilities. Writing for the Court, Justice Brennan alluded to the statement in *Crandall* that "if the State can tax a railroad passenger one dollar, it can tax him one thousand dollars," but noted that here the travelers were only "asked to bear a fair share of the costs of providing public facilities that further travel":

> [A] charge designed only to make the user of state-provided facilities pay a reasonable fee to help defray the costs of their construction and maintenance may constitutionally be imposed on interstate and domestic users alike. The principle that burdens on the right to travel are constitutional only if shown to be necessary to promote a compelling state interest has no application in this context. . . . The facility provided at public expense aids rather than hinders the right to travel. A permissible charge to help defray the cost of the facility is therefore not a burden in the constitutional sense.

Only Justice Douglas dissented, stating that the decision in effect overruled *Crandall.*

In Dunn v. Blumstein, 405 U.S. 330 (1972), the court held that Tennessee's one-year residence requirement for voting in state elections violated the equal protection clause. (The state argued that the requirement protected against double registration and other forms of fraud and also assured that voters would be knowledgeable of state and community affairs.) The Court subjected the requirement to strict equal protection scrutiny both because it affected the franchise and because it "penalized" the right of interstate mobility. On the latter issue, Justice Marshall wrote:

In Tennessee's view, the compelling state interest test is appropriate only where there is "some evidence to indicate a deterrence of or infringement on the right to travel. . . ." Thus, Tennessee seeks to avoid the clear command of *Shapiro* by arguing that durational residence requirements for voting neither seek to nor actually do deter such travel. . . .

This view represents a fundamental misunderstanding of the law. . . . *Shapiro* did not rest upon a finding that denial of welfare actually deterred travel. Nor have other "right to travel" cases in this Court always relied on the presence of actual deterrence. In *Shapiro* we explicitly stated that the compelling-state-interest test would be triggered by "any classification which serves to *penalize* the exercise of that right [to travel]. . . ." (emphasis added). While noting the frank legislative purpose to deter migration by the poor, and speculating that "[a]n indigent who desires to migrate . . . will doubtless hesitate if he knows that he must risk" the loss of benefits, the majority found no need to dispute the "evidence that few welfare recipients have in fact been deterred [from moving] by residence requirements." (Warren, C.J., dissenting). . . . Indeed, none of the litigants had themselves been deterred. Only last Term, it was specifically noted that because a durational residence requirement for voting "operates to *penalize* those persons, and only those persons, who have exercised their constitutional right of interstate migration . . . , [it] may withstand constitutional scrutiny only upon a clear showing that the burden imposed is necessary to protect a compelling and substantial governmental interest." Oregon v. Mitchell, 400 U.S., at 238 (separate opinion of Brennan, White, and Marshall, JJ.) (emphasis added). . . .

Durational residence laws impermissibly condition and penalize the right to travel by imposing their prohibitions on only those persons who have recently exercised that right. In the present case, such laws force a person who wishes to travel and change residences to choose between travel and the basic right to vote. Absent a compelling state interest, a State may not burden the right to travel in this way.

In Memorial Hospital v. Maricopa County, 415 U.S. 250 (1974), the majority and dissenting opinions further addressed the concept of "penalizing" the right to interstate mobility. The Court held that an Arizona statute requiring one year's residence in a county as a condition for an indigent's receiving nonemergency medical care at the county's expense violated the equal protection clause. Justice Marshall first noted that it was irrelevant that the statute dealt in terms with the duration of county, rather than state, residence: "Even if we were to draw a constitutional distinction between interstate and intrastate travel, a question we do not now consider; . . . [a]ppellant Evaro has been effectively penalized for his interstate migration. . . ." He went on to address the question of penalization:

Although any durational residency requirement imposes a potential cost on migration, the Court, in *Shapiro,* cautioned that some "waiting period[s] . . . may not be penalties." In Dunn v. Blumstein the Court found that the denial of the franchise, "a fundamental political right," was a penalty requiring application of the compelling-state-interest test. In *Shapiro,* the Court found denial of the basic "necessities of life" to be a penalty. Nonetheless, the Court has declined to strike down state statutes requiring one year of residence as a condition to lower tuition at state institutions of higher education.

Whatever the ultimate parameters of the *Shapiro* penalty analysis, it is at least clear that medical care is as much "a basic necessity of life" to an indigent as welfare assistance. And, governmental privileges or benefits necessary to basic sustenance have often been viewed as being of greater constitutional significance than less essential forms of governmental entitlements. It would be odd, indeed, to find that the State of Arizona was required to afford Evaro welfare assistance to keep him from the discomfort of inadequate housing or the pangs of hunger but could deny him the medical care necessary to relieve him from the wheezing and gasping for breath that attend his illness.

The Court held that the state's proffered justifications for the law were not "compelling." Justice Douglas concurred in a separate opinion; Chief Justice Burger and Justice Blackmun concurred in the result. In dissent, Justice Rehnquist wrote:

Since the Court concedes that "some 'waiting period[s] . . . may not be penalties,' " one would expect to learn from the opinion how to distinguish a waiting period which is a penalty from one which is not. Any expense imposed on citizens crossing state lines but not imposed on those staying put could theoretically be deemed a penalty on travel; the toll exacted from persons crossing from Delaware to New Jersey by the Delaware Memorial Bridge is a "penalty" on interstate travel in the most literal sense of all. But such charges, as well as other fees for use of transportation facilities such as taxes on airport users, have been upheld by this Court against attacks based upon the right to travel. It seems to me that the line to be derived from our prior cases is that some financial impositions on interstate travelers have such indirect or inconsequential impact on travel that they simply do not constitute the type of direct purposeful barriers struck down in *Edwards* and *Shapiro.* Where the impact is that remote, a State can reasonably require that the citizen bear some proportion of the State's cost in its facilities. I would think that this standard is not only supported by this Court's decisions, but would be eminently sensible and workable. But the Court not only rejects this approach, but leaves us entirely without guidance as to the proper stand to be applied.

The Court instead resorts to ipse dixit, declaring rather than demonstrating that the right to nonemergency medical care is within the class of rights protected by *Shapiro* and *Dunn.* . . .

However clear this conclusion may be to the majority, it is certainly not clear to me. The solicitude which the Court has shown in cases involving the right to vote, and the virtual denial of entry inherent in denial of welfare benefits . . . ought not be so casually extended to the alleged deprivation here. Rather the Court should examine, as it has done in the past, whether the challenged requirement erects a real and purposeful barrier to movement, or the threat of such a barrier, or whether the effects on travel, viewed realistically, are merely incidental and remote. . . . [T]he barrier here is hardly a counterpart to the barriers condemned in earlier cases. That being so, the Court should observe its traditional respect for the State's allocation of its limited financial resources rather than unjustifiedly imposing its own preferences.

In Sosna v. Iowa, 419 U.S. 393 (1975), the Court upheld Iowa's requirement that a party reside in the state for one year before bringing a divorce action against a nonresident. Justice Rehnquist wrote:

Appellant was not irretrievably foreclosed from obtaining some part of what she sought, as was the case with the welfare recipients in *Shapiro,* the voters in *Dunn,* or the indigent patient in *Maricopa County.* She would eventually qualify for the same sort of adjudication which she demanded virtually upon her arrival in the State. . . .

A decree of divorce is not a matter in which the only interested parties are the State as a sort of "grantor," and a plaintiff such as appellant in the role of "grantee." Both spouses are obviously interested in the proceedings, since it will affect their marital status and very likely their property rights. Where a married couple has minor children, a decree of divorce would usually include provisions for their custody and support. With consequences of such moment riding on a divorce decree issued by its courts, Iowa may insist that one seeking to initiate such a proceeding have the modicum of attachment to the State required here.

Such a requirement additionally furthers the State's parallel interests in both avoiding officious intermeddling in matters in which another State has a paramount interest, and in minimizing the susceptibility of its own divorce decrees to collateral attack. A State such as Iowa may quite reasonably decide that it does not wish to become a divorce mill for unhappy spouses who have lived there as short a time as appellant had when she commenced her action in the state court after having long resided elsewhere. . . . Perhaps even more importantly, Iowa's interests extend beyond its borders and include the recognition of its divorce decrees by other States under the Full Faith and Credit Clause of the Constitution, Art. IV. §1. For that purpose, this Court has often stated that "judicial power to grant a divorce — jurisdiction, strictly speaking — is founded on domicil." Where a divorce decree is entered after a finding of domicile in ex parte proceedings, this Court has held that the finding of domicile is not binding upon another State and may be disregarded in the face of "cogent evidence" to the contrary. For that reason, the State asked to enter such a decree is entitled to insist that the putative divorce plaintiff satisfy something more than the bare minimum of constitutional requirements before a divorce may be granted. The State's decision to exact a one-year residency requirement as a matter of policy is therefore buttressed by a quite permissible inference that this requirement not only effectuates state substantive policy but likewise provides a greater safeguard against successful collateral attack than would a requirement of bona fide residence alone.

Justice Marshall, joined by Justice Brennan, dissented, criticizing the Court's failure to inquire "whether the right to obtain a divorce is of sufficient importance that its denial to recent interstate immigrants constitutes a penalty on interstate travel" and its refusal to apply a "compelling interest" test. He believed that the state's only legitimate interests lay in "protecting itself against invasion by those seeking quick divorces in a forum with relatively lax divorce laws, and . . . in avoiding collateral attacks on its decree in other States." Justice Marshall concluded that these "would adequately be protected by a simple requirement of domicile — physical presence plus intent to remain — which would remove the rigid one-year barrier while permitting the State to restrict the availability of its divorce process to citizens who are genuinely its own." Justice White dissented on technical grounds.

4. *Can the State Give More Welfare to Long-Time Residents Than to Newcomers?*

Shapiro holds that a state may not use a durational residency requirement to deny welfare benefits to new residents. But may the state award benefits on a sliding scale based on duration, where the newcomer receives something, but long-timers receive even more?

ZOBEL v. WILLIAMS, 457 U.S. 55 (1982): [The Alaska legislature passed a bill distributing some of the vast income from the development of North Slope oil directly to Alaska citizens. The amount received was a function of length of residence. "Dividend units" would be apportioned at the rate of one unit per year of residence since 1959, the first year of statehood. Each unit was worth $50 in 1979, although the State estimated that it would be worth four times as much by 1985.

The Court, by an 8 to 1 vote, declared the Alaska scheme unconstitutional. Chief Justice Burger, writing for the majority, found the statute in violation of the equal protection clause, unable to pass even a test of minimal rationality.

The State put forth three purposes for its program: "(a) creation of a financial incentive for individuals to establish and maintain residence in Alaska; (b) encouragement of prudent management of the Permanent Fund; and (c) apportionment of benefits in recognition of undefined 'contributions of various kinds, both tangible and intangible, which residents have made during their years of residency.' " The majority could see no rational relation between any of these purposes and the difference in entitlement based on past residency.

The incentive rationale might be plausible with respect to duration of residency *following* the passage of the bill; then Alaska citizens would know that the longer they stayed, the more income they would receive from the oil monies. (The Court thus "need not consider whether the State could enact the dividend program prospectively only.") But rewarding persons for their already completed residence cannot act as an incentive to do what they have already done. Nor was there a relationship between the program and prudent management of the Permanent Fund established to manage the income. Indeed, the Alaska Supreme Court itself had found these two objectives insupportable to justify the legislation. Chief Justice Burger went on:

> The last of the State's objectives — to reward citizens for past contributions — alone was relied upon by the Alaska Supreme Court to support the retrospective application of the law to 1959. However, that objective is not a legitimate state purpose. A similar "past contributions" argument was made and rejected in Shapiro v. Thompson. . . .
>
> If the States can make the amount of a cash dividend depend on the length of residence, what would preclude varying university tuition on a sliding scale based on years of residence — or even limiting access to finite public facilities, eligibility for student loans, for civil service jobs, or for government contracts by length of domicile? Could States impose different taxes based on length of residence? Alaska's reasoning could open the door to state apportionment of other rights, benefits and services according to length of residency. It would permit the states to divide citizens into expanding numbers of permanent classes. Such a result would be clearly impermissible.

Chief Justice Burger rejected two non-equal protection forms of analysis: First, "the right to travel, when applied to residency requirements, protects new residents of a state from being disadvantaged because of their migration or from otherwise being treated differently from longer-term residents. In reality, right to travel analysis refers to little more than a particular application of equal protection analysis." Second, the privileges and immunities clause of Article IV was inapplicable. "That Clause 'was designed to insure a citizen of

State *A* who ventures into State *B* the same privileges which the citizens of State *B* enjoy.' Toomer v. Witsell, 334 U.S. 385, 395, (1948)." Here, however, the challenged discrimination was that between acknowledged citizens of the same State.

Justice Brennan, although joining in the opinion, wrote a separate concurrence, joined by Justices Marshall, Blackmun, and Powell. That opinion emphasized "what has come to be called the 'right to travel'. . . , or, more precisely, the federal interest in free interstate migration." The "threat to free interstate migration" presented by the Alaska law "provides an independent rationale for holding that law unconstitutional."

Justice Brennan noted that "frequent attempts to assign the right to travel some textual source in the Constitution seem to me to have proven both inconclusive and unnecessary." Possible sources include the privileges and immunities clause of Article IV and of the Fourteenth Amendment, as well as the commerce clause. He continued:

> In any event, in the light of the unquestioned historic recognition of the principle of free interstate migration, and of its role in the development of the Nation, we need not feel impelled to "ascribe the source of this right to travel interstate to a particular constitutional provision." Shapiro v. Thompson. . . . I find its unmistakable essence in that document that transformed a loose confederation of States into one Nation. A scheme of the sort adopted by Alaska is inconsistent with the Federal structure even in its prospective operation.
>
> [To be sure, "a State may make residence within its boundaries more attractive by offering direct benefits to its citizens in the form of public services, lower taxes than any other States offer, or direct distribution of its munificence." Such rivalry] inheres in the very idea of maintaining the States as independent sovereigns within a larger framework. . . . But a State cannot *compound* its offer of direct benefits in the inventive manner exemplified by the Alaska distribution scheme: For if each State were free to reward its citizens incrementally for their years of residence, so that a citizen leaving one State would thereby forfeit his accrued seniority, only to have to begin building such seniority again in his new State of residence, then the mobility so essential to the economic progress of our Nation, and so commonly accepted as a fundamental aspect of our social order would not long survive.

Turning to the equal protection clause, Justice Brennan stated that it "does not provide for, and does not allow for degrees of citizenship based on length of residence. . . . [E]quality of citizenship is of the essence in our republic." This comment was immediately qualified, however, by the recognition that "the Constitution does not bar the States from making reasoned distinctions between citizens," and there are circumstances where duration of residence might pass constitutional muster.

> To be sure, allegiance and attachment may be rationally measured by length of residence . . . and [these] may bear some rational relationship to a very limited number of legitimate state purposes. Cf. Chimento v. Stark, 353 F. Supp. 1211 (D.N.H.), *affirmed*, 414 U.S. 802 (1973) (seven year citizenship requirement to run for governor); U.S. Const., art I, §2, cl. 2, §3, art II, §1, cl. 4. But those instances in which length of residence could provide a legitimate basis for distinguishing one citizen from another are rare.

Justice O'Connor concurred only in the judgment. She rejected the majority's equal protection analysis, stating that the Fourteenth Amendment does not render illegitimate the objective of rewarding citizens for past contributions. "[A] generalized desire to reward citizens for past endurance, particularly in a State where years of hardship only recently have produced prosperity, is not innately improper." Yet the differentiation in treatment between shorter- and longer-term citizens "conflicts with the constitutional purpose of maintaining a Union rather than a mere 'league of States.' See Paul v. Virginia, 8 Wall. 168, 180 (1869). The Court's task, therefore, should be (1) to articulate this constitutional principle, explaining its textual sources, and (2) to test the strength of Alaska's objective against the constitutional imperative." Justice O'Connor's analysis emphasized the Privileges and Immunities Clause of Article IV.]

I

Our opinions teach that Article IV's Privileges and Immunities Clause "was designed to insure to a citizen of State *A* who ventures into State *B* the same privileges which the citizens of State *B* enjoy." Toomer v. Witsell, 334 U.S. 385, 395 (1948). The Clause protects a nonresident who enters a State to work, Hicklin v. Orbeck, 437 U.S. 518 (1978), to hunt commercial game, *Toomer*, supra, or to procure medical services, Doe v. Bolton, 410 U.S. 179 (1973). A fortiori, the Privileges and Immunities Clause should protect the "citizen of State *A* who ventures into State *B*" to settle there and establish a home.

In this case, Alaska forces nonresidents settling in the State to accept a status inferior to that of old-timers.

It could be argued that Alaska's scheme does not trigger the Privileges and Immunities Clause because it discriminates among classes of residents, rather than between residents and nonresidents. This argument, however, misinterprets the force of Alaska's distribution system. Alaska's scheme classifies citizens on the basis of their former residential status, imposing a relative burden on those who have migrated to the State after 1959. Residents who arrived in Alaska after that date have a less valuable citizenship right than do the old-timers who preceded them. Citizens who arrive in the State tomorrow will receive an even smaller claim on Alaska's resources. The fact that this discrimination unfolds after the nonresident establishes residency does not insulate Alaska's scheme from scrutiny under the Privileges and Immunities Clause. Each group of citizens who migrated to Alaska in the past, or chooses to move there in the future, lives in the State on less favorable terms than those who already arrived earlier. The circumstance that some of the disfavored citizens already live in Alaska does not negate the fact that "the citizen of State *A* who ventures into [Alaska] to establish a home labors under a continuous disability."

If the Privileges and Immunities Clause applied to Alaska's distribution system, then our prior opinions describe the proper standard of review. In Baldwin v. Fish & Game Commission, 436 U.S. 371 (1978), we held that States must treat residents and nonresidents "without unnecessary distinctions" when the nonresident seeks to "engage in an essential activity or exercise a basic right." On the other hand, if the nonresident engages in conduct that is not "fundamental" because it does not "bea[r] upon the vitality of the Nation as a single entity," the Privileges and Immunities Clause affords no protection.

Once the Court ascertains that discrimination burdens an "essential activity," it will test the constitutionality of the discrimination under a two-part test. First, there must be "something to indicate that non-citizens constitute a peculiar source of the evil at which the statute is aimed." Hicklin v. Orbeck, 437 U.S. 518, 525-526 (1978) (quoting Toomer v. Witsell, 334 U.S. 385, 398 (1948)). Second, the Court must find a "substantial relationship" between the evil and the discrimination practiced against the noncitizens. Id., at 527.

Certainly the right infringed in this case is "fundamental." Alaska's statute burdens those nonresidents who choose to settle in the State. It is difficult to imagine a right more essential to the Nation as a whole than the right to establish residence in a new State. . . .

Alaska has not shown that its new residents are the "peculiar source" of any evil addressed by its disbursement scheme. The State does not argue that recent arrivals constitute a particular source of its population turnover problem. Indeed, the State urges that it has a special interest in persuading young adults, who have grown to maturity in the State, to remain there. Brief for Appellees 35, n.24. Nor is there any evidence that new residents, rather than old, will foolishly deplete the State's mineral and financial resources. Finally, although Alaska argues that its scheme compensates residents for their prior tangible and intangible contributions to the State, nonresidents are hardly a peculiar source of the "evil" of partaking in current largesse without having made prior contributions. A multitude of native Alaskans — including children and paupers — may have failed to contribute to the State in the past. Yet the State does not dock paupers for their prior failures to contribute, and it awards every person over the age of 18 dividends equal to the number of years that person has lived in the State.

Even if new residents were the peculiar source of these evils, Alaska has not chosen a cure that bears a "substantial relationship" to the malady. As the dissenting judges below observed, Alaska's scheme gives the largest dividends to residents who have lived longest in the State. The dividends awarded to new residents may be too small to encourage them to stay in Alaska. The size of these dividends appears to give new residents only a weak interest in prudent management of the State's resources. As a reward for prior contributions, finally, Alaska's scheme is quite ill-suited. While the phrase "substantial relationship" does not require mathematical precision, it demands at least some recognition of the fact that persons who have migrated to Alaska may have contributed significantly more to the State, both before and after their arrival, than have some natives.

For these reasons, I conclude that Alaska's disbursement scheme violates Article IV's Privileges and Immunities Clause. I thus reach the same destination as the Court, but along a course that more precisely identifies the evils of the challenged statute.

II

The analysis outlined above might apply to many cases in which a litigant asserts a right to travel or migrate interstate.[a] To historians, this would come as no sur-

a. Any durational residency requirement, for example, treats nonresidents who have exercised their right to settle in a State differently from longer-term residents. This is not to say, however, that

prise. Article IV's Privileges and Immunities Clause has enjoyed a long association with the rights to travel and migrate interstate.

The Clause derives from Article IV of the Articles of Confederation. The latter expressly recognized a right of "free ingress and regress to and from any other State," in addition to guaranteeing "the free inhabitants of each of these states . . . the privileges and immunities of free citizens in the several states." While the Framers of our Constitution omitted the reference to "free ingress and regress," they retained the general guaranty of "privileges and immunities." Charles Pickney, who drafted the current version of Article IV, told the Convention that this Article was "formed exactly upon the principles of the 4th article of the present Confederation." 3 M. Farrand, Records of the Federal Convention 112 (1934). Commentators, therefore, have assumed that the Framers omitted the express guaranty merely because it was redundant, not because they wished to excise the right from the Constitution.

Early opinions by the Justices of this Court also traced a right to travel or migrate interstate to Article IV's Privileges and Immunities Clause. . . .

History, therefore, supports assessment of Alaska's scheme, as well as other infringements of the right to travel, under the Privileges and Immunities Clause. This Clause may not address every conceivable type of discrimination that the Court previously has denominated a burden on interstate travel. I believe, however, that application of the Privileges and Immunities Clause to controversies involving the "right to travel" would at least begin the task of reuniting this elusive right with the constitutional principles it embodies. Because I believe that Alaska's distribution scheme violates the Privileges and Immunities Clause of Article IV, I concur in the Court's judgment insofar as it reverses the judgment of the Alaska Supreme Court.

REHNQUIST, J., dissenting.

Alaska's dividend distribution scheme represents one State's effort to apportion unique economic benefits among its citizens. Although the wealth received from the oil deposits of Prudhoe Bay may be quite unlike the economic resources enjoyed by most States, Alaska's distribution of that wealth is in substance no different from any other State's allocation of economic benefits. The distribution scheme being in the nature of economic regulation, I am at a loss to see the rationality behind the court's invalidation of it as a denial of equal protection. . . .

Despite the highly deferential approach which we invariably have taken toward state economic regulations, the Court today finds the retroactive aspect of the Alaska distribution scheme violative of the Fourteenth Amendment. The Court concludes that the State's first two jusitifications are not rationally related to the retroactive portion of the distribution scheme, and that the third justification — the reward of citizens for their past contributions — is not a legitimate

---

all such requirements would fail scrutiny under the Privileges and Immunities Clause. The durational residency requirement upheld in Sosna v. Iowa, 419 U.S. 393 (1975) (one year to obtain divorce), for example, would have survived under the analysis outlined above. In *Sosna* the State showed that nonresidents were a peculiar source of the evil addressed by its durational residency requirement. Those persons could misrepresent their attachment to Iowa and obtain divorces that would be susceptible to collateral attack in other States. Iowa adopted a reasonable response to this problem by requiring nonresidents to demonstrate their bona fide residency for one year before obtaining a divorce. I am confident that the analysis developed in Hicklin v. Orbeck, supra, will adequately identify other legitimate durational residency requirements.

state objective. But the illegitimacy of a State's recognizing the past contributions of its citizens has been established by the Court only in certain cases considering an infringment of the right to travel, and the majority itself rightly declines to apply the strict scrutiny analysis of those right-to-travel cases. The distribution scheme at issue in this case impedes no person's right to travel to and settle in Alaska; if anything, the prospect of receiving annual cash dividends would encourage immigration to Alaska. The State's third justification cannot, therefore, be dismissed simply by quoting language about its legitimacy from right-to-travel cases which have no relevance to the question before us.

So understood, this case clearly passes equal protection muster. There can be no doubt that the state legislature acted rationally when it concluded that dividends retroactive to the year of statehood would "recognize the 'contributions of various kinds, both tangible and intangible,' which residents have made during their years of state residency." Williams v. Zobel, 619 P.2d 448, 458 (Alas. 1980). Nor can there be any doubt that Alaska, perhaps more than any other State in the Union, has good reason for recognizing such contributions. Because the distribution scheme is thus rationally based, I dissent from its invalidation under the guise of equal protection analysis.[a] In striking down the Alaskan scheme, the Court seems momentarily to have forgotten "the principle that the Fourteenth Amendment gives the federal courts no power to impose upon the States their view of what constitutes wise economic or social policy." Dandridge v. Williams, 397 U.S. 471 486 (1970).

Discussion

In his article Equal Treatment for Newcomers: The Core Meaning of National and State Citizenship, 1 Constitutional Commentary 9 (1984), Professor Cohen suggests that the conceptual "disarray" generated by *Shapiro* and successor cases, including *Zobel*, can be alleviated if one adopts, in place of "right to travel" analysis, a constitutional principle of "equal state citizenship." "Under the fourteenth amendment, any United States citizen becomes a full-fledged member of the state community immediately upon establishing residence there." That principle, in turn, "demands that newcomers be treated as full members of the state community. . . . [D]urational residency requirements for state benefits and services are permissible only to the extent they respond to a reasonable concern for proof of domiciliary intent."

Consider, in terms of Professor Cohen's "equal citizenship" principle, Hooper and Hooper v. Bernalillo County Assessor, 472 U.S. 612 (1985). The New Mexico State Legislature passed a statute granting a $2,000 property tax exemption to any honorably discharged veteran of the Vietnam War who had been a resident of the state before May 8, 1976. Alvin Hooper, a Vietnam veteran who es-

a. I also disagree with the suggestion of Justice O'Connor that the Alaska distribution scheme contravenes the Privileges and Immunities Clause of Art. IV of the Constitution. That Clause assures that *nonresidents* of a State shall enjoy the same privileges and immunities as residents enjoy: "It was designed to insure to a citizen of State *A* who ventures into State *B* the same privileges which the citizens of State *B* enjoy." Toomer v. Witsell, 334 U.S. 385, 395 (1948). We long ago held that the Clause has no application to a citizen of the State whose laws are complained of. "The constitutional provision there alluded to did not create those rights, which it called privileges and immunities of citizens of the States. It threw around them in that clause no security for the citizen of the State in which they were claimed or exercised. Nor did it profess to control the power of the State governments over the rights of its own citizens." *The Slaughterhouse Cases*, 16 Wall. 36, 77 (1872).

tablished New Mexico residency in August 1981, applied to the Bernalillo County tax assessor for the $2,000 veteran's exemption but was turned down because he had not been a resident by the statutory date. Hooper and his wife challenged the denial as a violation of their rights both to equal protection and to migrate to New Mexico. After losing before the New Mexico Court of Appeals, they appealed to the United States Supreme Court, which reversed in an opinion written by Chief Justice Burger.

The majority opinion focused on one of the justifications offered by New Mexico for the distinction: "assisting 'veterans who, as [New Mexico] citizens, were dependent on [the State] during a time of upheaval in their lives.' This rationale assumes that the State accepted a special responsibility toward those veterans who 'picked up or laid down the burdens of war' as state residents."

Agreeing that New Mexico can choose to aid veterans as against nonveterans, the majority nonetheless held that the distinction drawn between the veterans was unconstitutional:

> Those who serve in the military during wartime inevitably have their lives disrupted; but it is difficult to grasp how New Mexico residents serving in the military suffered more than residents of other States who served, so that the latter would not deserve the benefits a State bestows for national military service. Moreover, the legislature provided this economic boon years after the dislocation occurred. Established state residents, by this time, presumably had become resettled in the community and the modest tax exemption hardly bears directly on the transition to civilian life long after the war's end. Finally, the benefit of the tax exemption continues for the recipient's life. The annual exemption, which will benefit this limited group of resident veterans long after the wartime disruption dissipated, is a continuing bounty for a [sic] one group of residents rather than simply an attempt to ease the veteran's return to civilian life.
>
> Even assuming that the State may legitimately grant benefits on the basis of a coincidence between military service and past residence, the New Mexico statute's distinction between resident veterans is not rationally related to the State's asserted legislative goal. The Statute is not written to require any connection between the veteran's prior residence and military service. Indeed, the veteran who resided in New Mexico as an infant long ago would immediately qualify for the exemption upon settling in the State at any time in the future regardless of where he resided before, during or after military service. . . .
>
> Stripped of its asserted justifications, the New Mexico statute suffers from the same constitutional flaw as the Alaska statute in *Zobel*. . . . The State may not favor established residents over new residents based on the view that the State may take care of "its own," if such is defined by prior residence. . . .
>
> We decline appellants' request to rule on the severability of the unconstitutional aspect of the New Mexico veteran's tax-exemption statute. If the fixed-date residence requirement, §7-37-5(C)(d), were excised from the statute, the exemption would be available to all current resident veterans who served the requisite 90 days during the Vietnam War and received honorable discharges. It is for the New Mexico courts to decide, as a matter of state law, whether the state legislature would have enacted the statute without the invalid portion.

Justice Brennan, who joined the majority opinion, wrote a one-paragraph concurrence reiterating his commitment to his views expressed in *Zobel*.

Justice Stevens, joined by Justices Rehnquist and O'Connor, dissented:

Vietnam veterans are, of course, a distinct minority of the population of New Mexico. . . .

In this case, New Mexico's legislation reflects, not only an expression of gratitude, but also an attempt to ameliorate the hardship Vietnam veterans experienced upon seeking to integrate or reintegrate themselves into New Mexican society. . . . New Mexico's modest monetary benefit can be reasonably understood as both a tangible and symbolic "welcome home" to veterans returning to New Mexico from the Far East as well as to those deciding to establish their domiciles in the state for the first time. The legislation simply reflects and recognizes the State's felt obligation to facilitate the difficult transition of veterans from the battlefields of Asia to civilian life in New Mexico.

Of course, the Legislature might have crafted a more elaborate set of eligibility criteria, but since exclusion from the favored class merely places the ineligible veteran in the same class as the majority of the citizenry, there is no constitutional objection to the use of a simple, easily administered standard. The statutory requirement of residence before May 8, 1976 is not a perfect proxy for identifying those Vietnam veterans seeking admission or readmission into New Mexican society, but "rational distinctions may be made with substantially less than mathematical exactitude." New Orleans v. Dukes, 427 U.S. 297, 303 (1976). . . .

In my opinion, the validity of the State's classification is not undermined by the fact that it takes the form of a modest annual tax exemption instead of a cash payment or gold medal. It is true that the continuing character of the exemption differentiates the eligible veteran from the rest of the citizenry over an extended period of time, but I fail to see how that fact bears on the rationality of the classification. If New Mexico had awarded gold medallions to all of its resident veterans on May 1, 1976, I believe it would be absurd for a veteran arriving in the State in 1981 to claim that he or she had a constitutional right either to a comparable medal or to have all the other medal recipients return them to the State.

In like manner, New Mexico by this legislation has provided, in effect, a modest annuity for veterans who own real property. Again, it is surely rational for the State to provide this form of assistance rather than a lump-sum cash bonus. . . .

New Mexico's statute is not at all like the Alaska dividend program struck down in *Zobel*. . . . Every recent arrival was treated less favorably than those who had arrived earlier. The vast majority of dividend recipients were thus treated more favorably than the newly arrived minority. In this case, in contrast, the alleged victim of the discrimination is being treated exactly like the vast majority of New Mexico's residents. In *Zobel*, the program had no rational justification other than a purpose to allocate a cash surplus among the majority on the basis of the duration of the veteran's residence in the State. In this case, the duration of the veteran's residence is irrelevant and the distribution to the members of the favored class is supported by a legitimate state interest. There is a world of difference between a decision to provide benefits to some, but not all, veterans and a decision to divide the entire population into a multitude of classes differentiated only by length of residence. The State's refusal to provide appellant with a veteran's benefit has not branded him with any badge of inferiority. He has not been treated as a "second class citizen" in any sense. Rather, he has merely received precisely the same treatment as the vast majority of the residents of New Mexico.

As an example of a case which asks the correct question under his equal-citizenship analysis, Professor Cohen offers Martinez v. Bynum, 461 U.S. 321 (1983), where the Court upheld the constitutionality of a Texas law denying tuition-free admission to the public schools by a minor living apart from a "parent, guardian, or other person having lawful control of him under an order of a court" if the minor's presence in the school district is "for the primary purpose of attending the public free schools." Roberto Morales, a United States citizen by birth, left his parents' home in Reynosa, Mexico, in order to reside with his sister, Oralia Martinez, in McAllen, Texas. Finding that the move was motivated primarily by the desire to attend the local schools, the McAllen Independent School District denied Morales tuition-free admission. A class action suit was filed challenging the Texas statute on its face. Both the District and Fifth Circuit courts upheld the statute against facial attack, and the Supreme Court, in an 8 to 1 vote, affirmed, with only Justice Marshall dissenting.

Still, despite Professor Cohen's analysis, the question of defining "equality" remains. Although Dunn v. Blumstein prohibited Tennessee from imposing a durational residency requirement for the franchise, Justice Brennan readily acknowledges New Hampshire's power to prohibit newcomers from running for governor until they have lived in the state for seven years. One can vote immediately, but the newcomer must wait before running for governor. Is this not a sliding scale of eligibility for participation in state politics?

Attorney General of New York v. Soto-Lopez, 476 U.S. 898 (1986), struck down a state statute that conditioned eligibility for veterans' benefits on their state residence at the time of their induction into the military. Justice Brennan, writing for a plurality of four Justices, cited "the same guiding principle" of *Zobel* and *Hooper*: "[T]he right to migrate protects residents of a State from being disadvantaged, or from being treated differently, simply because of the timing of their migration, from other similarly situated residents." At this point, he mentioned in a footnote "that not all waiting periods are impermissible." Citing Sosna v. Iowa, 419 U.S. 393 (1975), which had upheld a one-year residency requirement for those seeking a divorce in Iowa's courts, he wrote: "Weighing the fact that appellant's access to the desired state procedures was only temporarily delayed, against the State's important interest, we concluded that her right to migrate was not violated. . . . We have also sustained domicile requirements, which incorporated 1-year waiting periods, for resident tuition at state universities. Starns v. Malkerson, 401 U.S. 985 (1971); Sturgis v. Washington, 414 U.S. 1057 (1973)."

Chief Justice Burger and Justice White concurred, finding the veterans residency requirement irrational under the equal protection clause of the Fourteenth Amendment.

Justice O'Connor, joined by Justices Rehnquist and Stevens, dissented.

> [S]omething more than a negligible or minimal impact on the right to travel is required before strict scrutiny is applied. I believe that . . . the limited preference granted under the . . . New York law can[not] realistically be held to infringe or penalize the right to travel. [Moreover, t]his case presents one of those instances in which the recognition of state citizens' past sacrifices constitutes a valid state interest that does not infringe any constitutionally protected interest, including the fundamental right to settle in another State which is protected by the Privileges and Immunities Clause of Art. IV, §2.

Justice Stevens also wrote a separate dissent.

5. Congressional Consent

Federal law punishes interstate travel under certain circumstances. See 18 U.S.C. §1073 (flight to avoid prosecution or giving testimony), 18 U.S.C. §1952 (travel in aid of racketeering), 18 U.S.C. §1201 (transportation of kidnapping victim), 18 U.S.C. §2101 (travel to incite riot), 18 U.S.C. §2421 (transportation for prosecution). The Court has not suggested that they are constitutionally problematic.

Recall that the majority in Edwards v. California, supra page 1211, relied on the commerce clause to invalidate California's attempt to bar the entry of indigents during the Great Depression. In view of Congress' general power to impede or authorize the states to impede interstate commerce, could Congress prohibit indigents from crossing state lines or authorize the states to deny them admission? Your answer may depend on the source of the right to travel — whether it is derived from the relationship of the states to one another, or is based on a citizen's relationship to the federal government, or is a fundamental personal right of the individual.

Perhaps the Court decided to base *Shapiro* on the equal protection clause in order to insulate the holding against a congressional "overruling." (We will consider Congress' power to disagree with judicial interpretations of the Fourteenth Amendment in Chapter 14; but it is fair to assume that while Congress has almost plenary discretion to implement the commerce clause, its authority to interpret the equal protection clause is more limited.) If heightened equal protection scrutiny in *Shapiro* is based on the unequal treatment of persons because they exercised a constitutional "right," isn't the source of that right relevant to the question whether Congress can in effect overrule the decision?

B. Selective Nonsupport of Constitutionally Protected Choices

1. The Abortion Funding Cases

MAHER v. ROE

432 U.S. 464 (1977)

Appeal from the United States District Court for the District of Connecticut

POWELL, J. . . .

I

A regulation of the Connecticut Welfare Department limits state Medicaid benefits for first trimester abortions to those that are "medically necessary," a term defined to include psychiatric necessity. Connecticut enforces this limitation through a system of prior authorization from its Department of Social Services. In order to obtain authorization for a first trimester abortion, the hospital or clinic where the abortion is to be performed must submit, other things, a certificate from the patient's attending physician stating that the abortion is medically necessary.

This attack on the validity of the Connecticut regulation was brought against appellant Maher, the Commissioner of Social Services, by appellees Poe and Roe, two indigent women who were unable to obtain a physician's certificate of medical necessity.[a] [A three-judge district court held the statute unconstitutional.]

II

The Constitution imposes no obligation on the States to pay the pregnancy-related medical expenses of indigent women, or indeed to pay any of the medical expenses of indigents. But when a State decides to alleviate some of the hardships of poverty by providing medical care, the manner in which it dispenses benefits is subject to constitutional limitations. Appellees' claim is that Connecticut must accord equal treatment to both abortion and childbirth, and may not evidence a policy preference by funding only the medical expenses incident to childbirth. This challenge to the classifications established by the Connecticut regulation presents a question arising under the Equal Protection Clause of the Fourteenth Amendment. The basic framework of analysis of such a claim is well settled: "We must decide, first, whether [state legislation] operates to the disadvantage of some suspect class or impinges upon a fundamental right explicitly or implicitly protected by the Constitution, thereby requiring strict judicial scrutiny. . . . If not, the [legislative] scheme must still be examined to determine whether it rationally furthers some legitimate, articulated state purpose and therefore does not constitute an invidious discrimination. . . ." San Antonio School Dist. v. Rodriguez, 411 U.S. 1, 17 (1973). Applying this analysis here, we think the District Court erred in holding that the Connecticut regulation violated the Equal Protection Clause of the Fourteenth Amendment.

A

This case involves no discrimination against a suspect class. An indigent woman desiring an abortion does not come within the limited category of disadvantaged classes so recognized by our cases. Nor does the fact that the impact of the regulation falls upon those who cannot pay lead to a different conclusion. In a sense, every denial of welfare to an indigent creates a wealth classification as compared to nonindigents who are able to pay for the desired goods or services. But this Court has never held that financial need alone identifies a suspect class for purposes of equal protection analysis. See *Rodriguez,* supra, at 29; Dandridge v. Williams, 397 U.S. 471 (1970).[b] Accordingly, the central question in this case is whether the regulation "impinges upon a fundamental right explicitly or implic-

a. At the time this action was filed, Mary Poe, a 16-year-old high school junior, had already obtained an abortion at a Connecticut hospital. Apparently because of Poe's inability to obtain a certificate of medical necessity, the hospital was denied reimbursement by the Department of Social Services. As a result, Poe was being pressed to pay the hospital bill of $244. Susan Roe, an unwed mother of three children, was unable to obtain an abortion because of her physician's refusal to certify that the procedure was medically necessary. . . .

b. In cases such as Griffin v. Illinois, 351 U.S. 12 (1956) and Douglas v. California, 372 U.S. 353 (1963), the Court held that the Equal Protection Clause requires States that allow appellate review of criminal convictions to provide indigent defendants with trial transcripts and appellate counsel. These cases are grounded in the criminal justice system, a governmental monopoly in which participation is compelled. Our subsequent decisions have made it clear that the principles underlying *Griffin* and *Douglas* do not extend to legislative classifications generally.

itly protected by the Constitution." The District Court read our decisions in Roe v. Wade, 410 U.S. 113 (1973), and the subsequent cases applying it, as establishing a fundamental right to abortion and therefore concluded that nothing less than a compelling state interest would justify Connecticut's different treatment of abortion and childbirth. We think the District Court misconceived the nature and scope of the fundamental right recognized in *Roe*.

B

... The Texas law in *Roe* was a stark example of impermissible interference with the pregnant woman's decision to terminate her pregnancy. In subsequent cases, we have invalidated other types of restrictions, different in form but similar in effect, on the woman's freedom of choice. [See, e.g.,] Planned Parenthood of Central Missouri v. Danforth, 428 U.S. 52, 70-71, n.11 (1976). ...

Roe did not declare an unqualified "constitutional right to an abortion," as the District Court seemed to think. Rather, the right protects the woman from unduly burdensome interference with her freedom to decide whether to terminate her pregnancy. It implies no limitation on the authority of a State to make a value judgment favoring childbirth over abortion, and to implement that judgment by the allocation of public funds.

The Connecticut regulation before us is different in kind from the laws invalidated in our previous abortion decisions. The Connecticut regulation places no obstacles — absolute or otherwise — in the pregnant woman's path to an abortion. An indigent woman who desires an abortion suffers no disadvantage as a consequence of Connecticut's decision to fund childbirth; she continues as before to be dependent on private sources for the service she desires. The State may have made childbirth a more attractive alternative, thereby influencing the woman's decision, but it has imposed no restriction on access to abortions that was not already there. The indigency that may make it difficult — and in some cases, perhaps, impossible — for some women to have abortions is neither created nor in any way affected by the Connecticut regulation. We conclude that the Connecticut regulation does not impinge upon the fundamental right recognized in *Roe*.[c]

c. Appellees rely on Shapiro v. Thompson, 394 U.S. 618 (1969), and Memorial Hospital v. Maricopa County, 415 U.S. 250 (1974). In those cases durational residence requirements for the receipt of public benefits were found to be unconstitutional because they "penalized" the exercise of the constitutional right to travel interstate.

Appellees' reliance on the penalty analysis of *Shapiro* and *Maricopa County* is misplaced. In our view there is only a semantic difference between appellees' assertion that the Connecticut law unduly interferes with a woman's right to terminate her pregnancy and their assertion that it penalizes the exercise of that right. Penalties are most familiar to the criminal law, where criminal sanctions are imposed as a consequence of proscribed conduct. *Shapiro* and *Maricopa County* recognized that denial of welfare to one who had recently exercised the right to travel across state lines was sufficiently analogous to a criminal fine to justify strict judicial scrutiny.

If Connecticut denied general welfare benefits to all women who had obtained abortions and who were otherwise entitled to the benefits, we would have a close analogy to the facts in *Shapiro*, and strict scrutiny might be appropriate under either the penalty analysis or the analysis we have applied in our previous abortion decisions. But the claim here is that the State "penalizes" the woman's decision to have an abortion by refusing to pay for it. *Shapiro* and *Maricopa County* did not hold that States would penalize the right to travel interstate by refusing to pay the bus fares of the indigent travelers. We find no support in the right-to-travel cases for the view that Connecticut must show a compelling interest for its decision not to fund elective abortions.

C

Our conclusion signals no retreat from *Roe* or the cases applying it. There is a basic difference between direct state interference with a protected activity and state encouragement of an alternative activity consonant with legislative policy. Constitutional concerns are greatest when the State attempts to impose its will by force of law; the State's power to encourage actions deemed to be in the public interest is necessarily far broader.

This distinction is implicit in two cases cited in *Roe* in support of the pregnant woman's right under the Fourteenth Amendment. Meyer v. Nebraska, 262 U.S. 390 (1923), involved a Nebraska law making it criminal to teach foreign languages to children who had not passed the eighth grade. Nebraska's imposition of a criminal sanction on the providers of desired services makes *Meyer* closely analogous to *Roe*. In sustaining the constitutional challenge brought by a teacher convicted under the law, the Court held that the teacher's "right thus to teach and the right of parents to engage him so to instruct their children" were "within the liberty of the Amendment." 262 U.S., at 400. In Pierce v. Society of Sisters, 268 U.S. 510 (1925), the Court relied on *Meyer* to invalidate an Oregon criminal law requiring the parent or guardian of a child to send him to a public school, thus precluding the choice of a private school. Reasoning that the Fourteenth Amendment's concept of liberty "excludes any general power of the State to standardize its children by forcing them to accept instruction from public teachers only," the Court held that the law "unreasonably interfere[d] with the liberty of parents and guardians to direct the upbringing and education of children under their control."

Both cases invalidated substantial restrictions on constitutionally protected liberty interests: in *Meyer,* the parent's right to have his child taught a particular foreign language; in *Pierce,* the parent's right to choose private rather than public school education. But neither case denied to a State the policy choice of encouraging the preferred course of action. Indeed, in *Meyer* the Court was careful to state that the power of the State "to prescribe a curriculum" that included English and excluded German in its free public schools "is not questioned." 262 U.S., at 402. Similarly, *Pierce* casts no shadow over a State's power to favor public education by funding it — a policy choice pursued in some States for more than a century. See Brown v. Board of Education, 347 U.S. 483, 489 n.4 (1954). Indeed, in Norwood v. Harrison, 413 U.S. 455, 462 (1973), we explicitly rejected the argument that *Pierce* established a "right of private or parochial schools to share with public schools in state largesse," noting that "[i]t is one thing to say that a State may not prohibit the maintenance of private schools and quite another to say that such schools must, as a matter of equal protection, receive state aid." Yet, were we to accept appellees' argument, an indigent parent could challenge the state policy of favoring public rather than private schools, or of preferring instruction in English rather than German, on grounds identical in principle to those advanced here. We think it abundantly clear that a State is not required to show a compelling interest for its policy choice to favor normal childbirth any more than a State must so justify its election to fund public but not private education.[d]

d. In his dissenting opinion, Mr. Justice Brennan rejects the distinction between direct state interference with a protected activity and state encouragement of an alternative activity and argues that our previous abortion decisions are inconsistent with today's decision. But as stated above, all of those

D

The question remains whether Connecticut's regulation can be sustained under the less demanding test of rationality that applies in the absence of a suspect classification or the impingement of a fundamental right. This test requires that the distinction drawn between childbirth and nontherapeutic abortion by the regulation be "rationally related" to a "constitutionally permissible" purpose. We hold that the Connecticut funding scheme satisfies this standard.

Roe itself explicitly acknowledged the State's strong interest in protecting the potential life of the fetus. That interest exists throughout the pregnancy, "grow[ing] in substantiality as the woman approaches term." Because the pregnant woman carries a potential human being, she "cannot be isolated in her privacy. . . . [Her] privacy is no longer sole and any right of privacy she possesses must be measured accordingly." The State unquestionably has a "strong and legitimate interest in encouraging normal childbirth," an interest honored over the centuries.[e] Nor can there be any question that the Connecticut regulation rationally furthers that interest. The medical costs associated with childbirth are substantial, and have increased significantly in recent years. As recognized by the District Court in this case, such costs are significantly greater than those normally associated with elective abortions during the first trimester. The subsidizing of costs incident to childbirth is a rational means of encouraging childbirth. . . .

BRENNAN, J., joined by Marshall and Blackmun, JJ., dissenting. . . .

The stark reality for too many, not just "some," indigent pregnant women is that indigency makes access to competent licensed physicians not merely "difficult" but "impossible." As a practical matter, many indigent women will feel they have no choice but to carry their pregnancies to term because the State will pay for the associated medical services, even though they would have chosen to have abortions if the State had also provided funds for that procedure, or indeed if the State had provided funds for neither procedure. This disparity in funding by the State clearly operates to coerce indigent pregnant women to bear children they would not otherwise choose to have, and just as clearly, this coercion can only operate upon the poor, who are uniquely the victims of this form of financial pressure. . . .

None can take seriously the Court's assurance that its "conclusion signals no retreat from *Roe* or the cases applying it.". . . Indeed, it cannot be gainsaid that today's decision seriously erodes the principles that *Roe* and *Doe* announced to guide the determination of what constitutes an unconstitutional infringement of the fundamental right of pregnant women to be free to decide whether to have an abortion.

---

decisions involved laws that placed substantial state-created obstacles in the pregnant woman's path to an abortion. . . . [Justice Brennan relies on] Singleton v. Wulff, 428 U.S. 106 (1976). Yet, as Mr. Justice Blackmun was careful to note at the beginning of his opinion in *Singleton*, that case presented "issues [of standing] not going to the merits of this dispute." Significantly, Mr. Justice Brennan makes no effort to distinguish or explain the much more analogous authority of Norwood v. Harrison, 413 U.S. 455 (1973).

e. In addition to the direct interest in protecting the fetus, a State may have legitimate demographic concerns about its rate of population growth. Such concerns are basic to the future of the State and in some circumstances could constitute a substantial reason for departure from a position of neutrality between abortion and childbirth.

The Court's premise is that only an equal protection claim is presented here. Claims of interference with enjoyment of fundamental rights have, however, occupied a rather protean position in our constitutional jurisprudence. Whether or not the Court's analysis may reasonably proceed under the Equal Protection Clause, the Court plainly errs in ignoring, as it does, the unanswerable argument of appellees, and the holding of the District Court, that the regulation unconstitutionally impinges upon their claim of privacy derived from the Due Process Clause.

Roe v. Wade and cases following it hold that an area of privacy invulnerable to the State's intrusion surrounds the decision of a pregnant woman whether or not to carry her pregnancy to term. The Connecticut scheme clearly impinges upon that area of privacy by bringing financial pressures on indigent women that force them to bear children they would not otherwise have. That is an obvious impairment of the fundamental right established by Roe v. Wade. Yet the Court concludes that "the Connecticut regulation does not impinge upon [that] fundamental right." This conclusion is based on a perceived distinction, on the one hand, between the imposition of criminal penalties for the procurement of an abortion present in Roe v. Wade and Doe v. Bolton and the absolute prohibition present in Planned Parenthood of Central Missouri v. Danforth, 428 U.S. 52 (1976), and, on the other, the assertedly lesser inhibition imposed by the Connecticut scheme. . . .

We . . . rejected this approach in other abortion cases. Doe v. Bolton, the companion to Roe v. Wade, in addition to striking down the Georgia criminal prohibition against elective abortions, struck down the procedural requirements of certification of hospitals, of approval by a hospital committee, and of concurrence in the abortion decision by two doctors other than the woman's own doctor. None of these requirements operated as an absolute bar to elective abortions in the manner of the criminal prohibitions present in the other aspect of the case or in *Roe,* but this was not sufficient to save them from unconstitutionality. In *Planned Parenthood,* supra, we struck down a requirement for spousal consent to an elective abortion which the Court characterizes today simply as an "absolute obstacle" to a woman's obtaining an abortion. But the obstacle was "absolute" only in the limited sense that a woman who was unable to persuade her spouse to agree to an elective abortion was prevented from obtaining one. Any woman whose husband agreed, or could be persuaded to agree, was free to obtain an abortion, and the State never imposed directly any prohibition of its own. This requirement was qualitatively different from the criminal statutes that the Court today says are comparable, but we nevertheless found it unconstitutional. . . .

Finally, cases involving other fundamental rights also make clear that the Court's concept of what constitutes an impermissible infringement upon the fundamental right of a pregnant woman to choose to have an abortion makes new law. We have repeatedly found that infringements of fundamental rights are not limited to outright denials of those rights. First Amendment decisions have consistently held in a wide variety of contexts that the compelling-state-interest test is applicable not only to outright denials but also to restraints that make exercise of those rights more difficult. See, e.g., Sherbert v. Verner, 374 U.S. 398 (1963) (free exercise of religion); NAACP v. Button, 371 U.S. 415 (1963) (freedom of expression and association); Linmark Associates v. Township of Willingboro, 431 U.S. 85 (1977) (freedom of expression). The compelling-state-interest test has been applied in voting cases, even where only relatively small infringements upon voting power, such as dilution of voting strength caused by malapportionment, have been involved. See, e.g., Reynolds v. Sims, 377 U.S. 533, 562, 566 (1964); Chapman v. Meier, 420 U.S. 1 (1975); Connor v. Finch, 431 U.S. 407 (1977). Similarly, cases involving the right to travel have consistently held that statutes penalizing the fundamental right to travel must pass muster under the compelling-state-interest test, irrespective of whether the statutes actually deter travel. Memorial Hospital v. Maricopa County, 415 U.S. 250, 257-258 (1974); Dunn v. Blumstein, 405 U.S. 330, 339-341 (1972); Shapiro v. Thompson, 394 U.S. 618 (1969). And indigents asserting a fundamental right of access to the courts have been excused payment of entry costs without being required first to show that their indigency was an absolute bar to access. Griffin v. Illinois, 351 U.S. 12 (1956); Douglas v. California, 372 U.S. 353 (1963); Boddie v. Connecticut, 401 U.S. 371 (1971).

Until today, I had not thought the nature of the fundamental right established in *Roe* was open to question, let alone susceptible of the interpretation advanced by the Court. The fact that the Connecticut scheme may not operate as an absolute bar preventing all indigent women from having abortions is not critical. What is critical is that the State has inhibited their fundamental right to make that choice free from state interference.

Nor does the manner in which Connecticut has burdened the right freely to choose to have an abortion save its Medicaid program. The Connecticut scheme cannot be distinguished from other grants and withholdings of financial benefits that we have held unconstitutionally burdened a fundamental right. Sherbert v. Verner, supra, struck down a South Carolina statute that denied unemployment compensation to a woman who for religious reasons could not work on Saturday, but that would have provided such compensation if her unemployment had stemmed from a number of other nonreligious causes. Even though there was no proof of indigency in that case, *Sherbert* held that "the pressure upon her to forgo [her religious] practice [was] unmistakable," and therefore held that the effect was the same as a fine imposed for Saturday worship. Here, though the burden is upon the right to privacy derived from the Due Process Clause and not upon freedom of religion under the Free Exercise Clause of the First Amendment, the governing principle is the same, for Connecticut grants and withholds financial benefits in a manner that discourages significantly the exercise of a fundamental constitutional right. Indeed, the case for application of the principle actually is stronger than in *Verner* since appellees are all indigents and therefore even more vulnerable to the financial pressures imposed by the Connecticut regulation. . . .

Although appellant does not argue it as justification, the Court concludes that the State's interest "in protecting the potential life of the fetus" suffices.[a] Since only the first trimester of pregnancy is involved in this case, that justification is totally foreclosed if the Court is not overruling the holding of Roe v. Wade that "[w]ith respect to the State's important and legitimate interest in potential life, the 'compelling' point is at viability," occurring at about the end of the second tri-

a. The Court also suggests that a "State may have legitimate demographic concerns about its rate of population growth" which might justify a choice to favor live births over abortions. While it is conceivable that under some circumstances this might be an appropriate factor to be considered as part of a State's "compelling" interest, no one contends that this is the case here, or indeed that Connecticut has any demographic concerns at all about the rate of its population growth.

mester. The appellant also argues a further justification not relied upon by the Court, namely, that the State needs "to control the amount of its limited public funds which will be allocated to its public welfare budget." The District Court correctly held, however, that the asserted interest was "wholly chimerical" because the "state's assertion that it saves money when it declines to pay the cost of a welfare mother's abortion is simply contrary to undisputed facts."

HARRIS v. McRAE, 448 U.S. 297 (1980): [The Court relied on Maher v. Roe to sustain the Hyde Amendment to the Medicaid program established in Title XIX of the Social Security Act. The Medicaid program provides federal financial assistance to states that assist indigents in meeting certain medical costs (including costs incurred in connection with pregnancy). The Hyde Amendment prohibits the use of federal funds "to perform abortions except where the life of the mother would be endangered if the fetus were carried to term; or except for such medical procedures necessary for the victims of rape or incest . . . ," thereby forbidding the funding of abortions necessary to the mother's health in situations where her life is not threatened.]

STEWART, J. . . . The Hyde Amendment, like the Connecticut welfare regulation at issue in *Maher,* places no government obstacle in the path of a woman who chooses to terminate her pregnancy, but rather, by means of unequal subsidization of abortion and other medical services, encourages alternative activity deemed in the public interest. The present case does differ factually from *Maher* insofar as that case involved a failure to fund nontherapeutic abortions, whereas the Hyde Amendment withholds funding of certain medically necessary abortions. Accordingly, the appellees argue that because the Hyde Amendment affects a significant interest not present or asserted in *Maher* — the interest of a woman in protecting her health during pregnancy — and because that interest lies at the core of the personal constitutional freedom recognized in *Wade,* the present case is constitutionally different from *Maher.* It is the appellees' view that to the extent that the Hyde Amendment withholds funding for certain medically necessary abortions, it clearly impinges on the constitutional principle recognized in *Wade.*

It is evident that a woman's interest in protecting her health was an important theme in *Wade.* In concluding that the freedom of a woman to decide whether to terminate her pregnancy falls within the personal liberty protected by the Due Process Clause, the Court in *Wade* emphasized the fact that the woman's decision carries with it significant personal health implications — both physical and psychological. In fact, although the Court in *Wade* recognized that the state interest in protecting potential life becomes sufficiently compelling in the period after fetal viability to justify an absolute criminal prohibition of nontherapeutic abortions, the Court held that even after fetal viability a State may not prohibit abortions "necessary to preserve the life or health of the mother." Because even the compelling interest of the State in protecting potential life after fetal viability was held to be insufficient to outweigh a woman's decision to protect her life or health, it could be argued that the freedom of a woman to decide whether to terminate her pregnancy for health reasons does in fact lie at the core of the constitutional liberty identified in *Wade.*

But, regardless of whether the freedom of a woman to choose to terminate her pregnancy for health reasons lies at the core or the periphery of the due process liberty recognized in *Wade,* it simply does not follow that a woman's freedom of choice carries with it a constitutional entitlement to the financial resources to avail herself of the full range of protected choices. The reason why was explained in *Maher:* although government may not place obstacles in the path of a woman's exercise of her freedom of choice, it need not remove those not of its own creation. Indigency falls in the latter category. The financial constraints that restrict an indigent woman's ability to enjoy the full range of constitutionally protected freedom of choice are the product not of governmental restrictions on access to abortions, but rather of her indigency. Although Congress has opted to subsidize medically necessary services generally, but not certain medically necessary abortions, the fact remains that the Hyde Amendment leaves an indigent woman with at least the same range of choice in deciding whether to obtain a medically necessary abortion as she would have had if Congress had chosen to subsidize no health care costs at all. We are thus not persuaded that the Hyde Amendment impinges on the constitutionally protected freedom of choice recognized in *Wade.*

Although the liberty protected by the Due Process Clause affords protection against unwarranted government interference with freedom of choice in the context of certain personal decisions, it does not confer an entitlement to such funds as may be necessary to realize all the advantages of that freedom. To hold otherwise would mark a drastic change in our understanding of the Constitution. It cannot be that because government may not prohibit the use of contraceptives, Griswold v. Connecticut, 381 U.S. 479, or prevent parents from sending their child to a private school, Pierce v. Society of Sisters, 268 U.S. 510, government, therefore, has an affirmative constitutional obligation to ensure that all persons have the financial resources to obtain contraceptives or send their children to private schools. To translate the limitation on governmental power implicit in the Due Process Clause into an affirmative funding obligation would require Congress to subsidize the medically necessary abortion of an indigent woman even if Congress had not enacted a Medicaid program to subsidize other medically necessary services. Nothing in the Due Process Clause supports such an extraordinary result. Whether freedom of choice that is constitutionally protected warrants federal subsidization is a question for Congress to answer, not a matter of constitutional entitlement. Accordingly, we conclude that the Hyde Amendment does not impinge on the due process liberty recognized in *Wade.*

[The Court went on to add that the Hyde Amendment did not violate the establishment clause of the First Amendment.

Justice White wrote a short concurring opinion, asserting that the case was not distinguishable from *Maher.*

Justice Brennan, joined by Justices Marshall and Blackmun, dissented for essentially the reasons given in his dissent in *Maher.* He wrote that the "fundamental flaw in the Court's due process analysis . . . is its failure to acknowledge that the discriminatory distribution of the benefits of governmental largesse can discourage the exercise of fundamental liberties just as effectively as can an outright denial of those rights through criminal and regulatory sanctions."]

MARSHALL, J., dissenting [also relied on his dissent in *Maher,* and went on to argue that this case was distinguishable.]

. . . The result in *Maher* turned on the fact that the legislation there under consideration discouraged only nontherapeutic, or medically unnecessary, abortions. In the Court's view, denial of Medicaid funding for nontherapeutic abortions was not a denial of equal protection because Medicaid funds were available only for medically necessary procedures. Thus the plaintiffs were seeking benefits which were not available to others similarly situated. . . . [Respondents in this case] are protesting their exclusion from a benefit that is available to all others similarly situated. This, it need hardly be said, is a crucial difference for equal protection purposes.

STEVENS, J., dissenting [made the same point as Marshall. Additionally, he noted that Roe v. Wade held that even after fetal viability, a state could not prohibit an abortion to preserve the "health of the mother."]

. . . If a woman has a constitutional right to place a higher value on avoiding either serious harm to her own health or perhaps an abnormal childbirth than on protecting potential life, the exercise of that right cannot provide the basis for the denial of a benefit to which she would otherwise be entitled. . . . The Court focuses exclusively on the "legitimate interest in protecting the potential life of the fetus." It concludes that since the Hyde amendments further that interest, the exclusion they create is rational and therefore constitutional. But it is misleading to speak of the Government's legitimate interest in the fetus without reference to the context in which that interest was held to be legitimate. For Roe v. Wade squarely held that the States may not protect that interest when a conflict with the interest in a pregnant woman's health exists.

Discussion

1. Even if one disagrees with the Court's decision in Roe v. Wade, any doctrinal analysis of *Maher* makes sense only if one assumes — as the Court professed to assume — that *Roe* remains the law.

2. Should Roe v. Wade be read to prohibit Connecticut from adopting any and all measures to discourage women from having abortions? For example, can the state engage in publicity and educational campaigns promoting birth over abortion? How does this differ (constitutionally) from prohibiting abortions?

3. Should Roe v. Wade be read to invalidate a statute (antedating the legalization of abortion) providing that "all medical procedures that require introducing a surgical instrument into the human body shall be performed in licensed facilities" and setting the annual license fee at $1,000? Suppose the statute set an annual fee of $1,000 for any facility in which abortions were performed and a fee of $100 for any other facility. Cf. Doe v. Bolton, page 991 supra. What constitutional difference, if any, is there between these two hypothetical statutes?

4. Justice Blackmun described the right protected in Roe v. Wade in terms of the pregnant woman's *choice* between childbirth and abortion — her right to make a "decision whether or not to terminate her pregnancy." Would this right be interfered with in the following situations?

a. If Connecticut did not provide *any* medical assistance to indigent people?

b. If (leaving aside claims of gender discrimination) Connecticut provided medical assistance to the poor for many purposes but excluded both childbirth and abortion?

c. If the preamble to the Connecticut statute in *Maher* provided: "Whereas it is the public policy of the State to discourage abortions . . ."? How does this hypothetical statute differ constitutionally from the practices described in parts a and b of this question and from the statutes in question 3?

5. Assume that Missouri, as part of its efforts to maintain families in times of stress, offers free marriage counseling services to any couple with children that is contemplating divorce. It does not, however, offer "divorce counseling," in which efforts are made to minimize the well-documented stress attached to the process of divorce. Even if one assumes that the right to dissolve a marriage is constitutionally protected, see Boddie v. Connecticut, p.1142 supra, would there be anything unconstitutional about Missouri's policy and its decision to place public funds behind one vision of life, maintaining intact families, rather than another, aiding unhappy individuals in dissolving their marriages? Cf. *Michael H.* p.970 supra.

2. *Abortions and Public Hospital Facilities*

Maher and *Harris* deal with direct state payment either to a woman or her doctor to subsidize an abortion. The Court has relied on these decisions in dealing with policies prohibiting abortions in public hospitals even when the woman seeks no other state aid and is willing to pay the full cost of the hospital services. Thus, in Poelker v. Doe, 432 U.S. 519 (1977), the Court sustained St. Louis' policy of refusing to permit abortions in public hospitals unless there was a threat of great physiological injury or death. "For the reasons stated in *Maher,* the Constitution does not forbid a State or city, pursuant to democratic processes, from expressing a preference for normal childbirth." On the same day, Beal v. Doe, 432 U.S. 438 (1977), held that the Social Security Act does not require states to fund nontherapeutic abortions as a condition of participation in the federal Medicaid program.

The Court returned to the issue in Webster v. Reproductive Health Services, page 1009 supra, where Missouri law made it "unlawful for any public facility to be used for the purpose of performing or assisting an abortion not necessary to save the life of the mother." Chief Justice Rehnquist wrote:

> Missouri's refusal to allow . . . abortions in public hospitals leaves a pregnant woman with the same choices as if the State had chosen not to operate any public hospitals at all. The challenged provisions only restrict a woman's ability to obtain an abortion to the extent that she chooses to use a physician affiliated with a public hospital. The circumstance is more easily remedied, and thus considerably less burdensome, than indigency. . . . Having held that the State's refusal to fund abortions does not violate Roe v. Wade, it strains logic to reach a contrary result for the use of public facilities and employees. If the State may "make a value judgment favoring childbirth over abortion and . . . implement that judgment by the allocation of public funds," *Maher,* surely it may do so through the allocation of other public resources, such as hospitals and medical staff.
>
> The Court of Appeals sought to distinguish our cases on the additional ground that "[t]he evidence here showed that all of the public facility's costs in providing abortion services are recouped when the patient pays." Absent any expenditure of public funds, the court thought that Missouri was "expressing" more than "its pref-

erence for childbirth over abortions," but rather was creating an "obstacle to exercise of the right to choose an abortion [that could not] stand absent a compelling state interest." We disagree.

. . . Nothing in the Constitution requires States to enter or remain in the business of performing abortions. Nor, as appellees suggest, do private physicians and their patients have some kind of constitutional right of access to public facilities for the performance of abortions. Indeed, if the State does recoup all of its costs in performing abortions, and no state subsidy, direct or indirect, is available, it is difficult to see how any procreational choice is burdened by the State's ban on the use of its facilities or employees for performing abortions.

Maher, Poelker, and *McRae* all support the view that the State need not commit any resources to facilitating abortions, even if it can turn a profit by doing so.

Justice O'Connor, though concurring in this part of Chief Justice Rehnquist's opinion, noted that Missouri broadly defined a "public facility" as "any public institution, public facility, public equipment, or any physical asset owned, leased, or controlled by this state or any agency or political subdivisions thereof." She thought that "there may be conceivable applications of the ban on the use of public facilities that would be unconstitutional. . . . [For example,] the State could try to enforce the ban against private hospitals using public water and sewage lines, or against private hospitals leasing state-owned equipment or state land." Justice O'Connor believed that the issues need not be decided in *Webster*. In his dissent Justice Blackmun similarly emphasized the "sweeping scope" of Missouri's definition of "public facilities," and would have struck down the Missouri law on its face.[37]

Discussion

1. At the end of the penultimate paragraph quoted above from *Webster*, Chief Justice Rehnquist drops the following footnote: "A different analysis might apply if a particular State had socialized medicine and all of its hospitals and physicians were publicly funded. This case might also be different if the State barred doctors who performed abortions in private facilities from the use of public facilities for any purpose." Doesn't the hypothetical in the second sentence present quite different issues from those in *Poelker* and *Webster*? With respect to the first sentence, why would the state become obligated to provide a service if it legally monopolizes an enterprise, but not if the enterprise is left to the market? Suppose that state monopolization occurs not by force of law — i.e., competitors are prohibited — but as a consequence of market conditions — e.g., the malpractice insurance rate for abortions is prohibitively high? Suppose that all of the private hospitals in a state are operated by the Roman Catholic Church, which has a strong policy against performing abortions, even when the life of the mother is at stake?

37. Justice Blackmun noted that "in 1985, 97 percent of all Missouri hospital abortions at 16 weeks or later were performed" at the Truman Medical Center in Kansas City, "a private hospital, staffed by private doctors, and administered by a private corporation[, but] located on ground leased from a political subdivision of the State" and therefore possibly "public" under the Missouri statute.

Note: Further Reflections on the State's Control over Public Property

Recall the analysis in Reeves v. Stake, page 463 supra, that emphasized South Dakota's freedom as a "market participant" to operate its cement plant with at least some of the same freedom of a private operator with respect to the ability to choose its preferred customers. One might analyze the abortion-and-public-hospital cases by reference to the prerogatives of ownership. But nothing concerning constitutional limits on state action is simple.

In Commonwealth v. Davis, 162 Mass. 510 (1895), aff'd, 167 U.S. 53 (1897), Justice Holmes, then on the Supreme Judicial Court of Massachusetts, sustained a preacher's conviction for making a public address on the Boston Common without first securing a permit from the mayor. Holmes held that the state had the same control over "its" property that private owners have over theirs: "For the legislature absolutely or conditionally to forbid speaking in a highway or public part is no more of an infringement of the rights of a member of the public than for the owner of a private house to forbid it in his house." In affirming the decision for a unanimous Supreme Court, Justice Edward White rejected the notion of a citizen's right "to use public property in defiance of the constitution and laws of the State. . . . The right to absolutely exclude all right to use, necessarily includes the authority to determine under what circumstances such use may be availed of, as the greater power contains the lesser."

Forty-two years later, however, Justice Roberts sent the Court in a decidedly different direction, when he wrote, for a plurality in Hague v. CIO, 307 U.S. 495 (1939):

> Wherever the title of streets and parks may rest, they have immemorially been held in trust for the use of the public and, time out of mind, have been used for purposes of assembly, communicating thoughts between citizens, and discussing public questions. Such use of the streets and public places has, from ancient times, been a part of the privileges, immunities, rights and liberties of citizens.

Hague held that access to such public property could be subject to reasonable regulation, "but it must not, in the guise of regulation, be abridged or denied." In Chapter 8 we examined some of the subsequent doctrine delineating the scope of reasonable *content-neutral* regulations, see Schneider v. State, 308 U.S. 147 (1939), and Grayned v. City of Rockford, 408 U.S. 104 (1972). The case law may be broadly summarized as standing for the following propositions: 1) The state holds public property in trust for the public at large, and any limitation of access to it must be shown to serve the public interest. The state cannot exercise the (relatively) plenary discretion of a private owner to control access to it. 2) The state can, in effect, be forced to subsidize some of the costs of free expression. For example, the state in *Schneider* could not prohibit handbilling even if the activity resulted in increased costs in picking up the litter. Similarly, local governments must incur expenses to provide police protection for groups using the public streets or parks for political expression.[38] Nor is it imaginable that the U.S. Postal

38. After *DeShaney*, could the state simply refuse to provide special protection even where violence might be anticipated? Could the state, in any event, require demonstrators to post bonds adequate to cover any costs beyond those "normally budgeted" (whatever this might mean) for police services? See, e.g., Colin v. Smith, 447 F. Supp. 676 (1978), 578 F.2d. 1197 (7th Cir. 1978), which involved the

Service could offer its services, including those that are subsidized by taxpayers, only to publications that do not challenge government policy or promote disrespect for the flag. Postal workers must deliver mail they find offensive and even seditious.

Return now to the cases involving abortions in public hospitals. Recall that *Webster* said that "the State need not commit any resources to facilitating abortions, even if it can turn a profit by doing so. . . . Nothing in the Constitution requires States to enter or remain in the business of performing abortions. Nor, as appellees suggest, do private physicians and their patients have some kind of constitutional right of access to public facilities for the performance of abortions." Can you square this assertion with the free-speech cases discussed above? As long as Roe v. Wade remains the law, isn't a woman's constitutional right to choose to have an abortion as "fundamental" as that of freedom of speech? (If not, what procedure or criteria do you use for ranking constitutional rights?) If, after *Schneider*, the state cannot prohibit handbilling on public sidewalks just because one could distribute handbills in other public or private places, why can Missouri prohibit abortions in public hospitals just because they remain available in private hospitals? The first amendment cases indicate that access to public property may be limited where the intended use would be inappropriate. In view of the uses to which the property has been dedicated, can one plausibly assert that a hospital is not an appropriate place in which to perform an abortion? What governmental interest other than animosity regarding the exercise of the woman's constitutionally protected right to an abortion can justify the Missouri ordinance, which applies even if the woman is willing to pay the full costs incurred by the state?

C. The Status of Education in the Modern Welfare State

Recall that the Supreme Court in Brown v. Board of Education said:

> Today, education is the very foundation of good citizenship . . . , a principal instrument in awakening the child to cultural values, in preparing him for later professional training, and in helping him to adjust normally to his environment. In these days, it is doubtful that any child may reasonably be expected to succeed in life if he is denied the opportunity of an education. Such an opportunity, where the state has undertaken to provide it, is a right which must be made available to all on equal terms.

---

attempted prohibition by Skokie, Illinois, of a planned march by Nazis. The town required among other things, that the demonstrators obtain $3,000,000 in public liability insurance and $50,000 in property damage insurance. The Court of Appeals struck down the insurance requirement as applied, saying that "we do not need to determine now that no insurance requirement could be imposed in any circumstances, which would be a close question."

In retrospect, of course *Brown* rested not on the special status of education but on the criterion (i.e, race) on which the state classified children attending its public schools. Is education nonetheless so important or special an interest as to call for heightened scrutiny of nonracial laws that allocate educational benefits differentially? Is it so important, indeed, that the Constitution should require the state to provide at least a minimal level of education to everyone within its jurisdiction?

1. *"Equal Provision" of Public Education*

SAN ANTONIO INDEPENDENT SCHOOL DISTRICT v. RODRIGUEZ

411 U.S. 1 (1973)

Appeal from the United States District Court for the Western District of Texas

[Texas public school systems are financed through a combination of local property taxes and state funds. The state-funded "foundation program" tends to equalize disparities among district tax bases, but district expenditures nevertheless depend heavily on local property wealth. For example, in the 1967-1968 school year, the Edgewood Independent School District in San Antonio had an assessed property value per pupil of $5,960. By taxing itself at a rate of 1 percent and after paying its required share into the state program, it was able to raise $26 per pupil. State subventions brought its per pupil expenditure to $356. The Alamo Heights Independent School District, also located in San Antonio, had a tax base of $49,000 per pupil, and raised $333 locally by taxing itself at only .85 percent. State subventions brought its per-pupil expenditure to $594.

Appellees, the parents of children attending the Edgewood schools, brought this suit to invalidate the state school financing scheme on the ground that it violated the equal protection clause of the Fourteenth Amendment. On the state's appeal from the district court's judgment for appellees, the Supreme Court reversed.]

POWELL, J. . . .

I

. . . We must decide, first, whether the Texas system of financing public education operates to the disadvantage of some suspect class or impinges upon a fundamental right explicitly or implicitly protected by the Constitution, thereby requiring strict judicial scrutiny. If so, the judgment of the District Court should be affirmed. If not, the Texas scheme must still be examined to determine whether it rationally furthers some legitimate, articulated state purpose and therefore does not constitute an invidious discrimination in violation of the Equal Protection Clause of the Fourteenth Amendment.

II

. . . In concluding that strict judicial scrutiny was required [the District Court] relied on decisions dealing with the rights of indigents to equal treatment in the criminal trial and appellate processes, and on cases disapproving wealth restrictions on the right to vote. Those cases, the District Court concluded, established wealth as a suspect classification. Finding that the local property tax system discriminated on the basis of wealth, it regarded those precedents as controlling. It then reasoned, based on decisions of this Court affirming the undeniable importance of education, that there is a fundamental right to education and that, absent some compelling state justification, the Texas system could not stand.

We are unable to agree that this case, which in significant aspects is sui generis, may be so neatly fitted into the conventional mosaic of constitutional analysis under the Equal Protection Clause. Indeed, for the several reasons that follow, we find neither the suspect-classification nor the fundamental-interest analysis persuasive.

A

The wealth discrimination discovered by the District Court in this case, and by several other courts that have recently struck down school-financing laws in other States, is quite unlike any of the forms of wealth discrimination heretofore reviewed by this Court. . . .

The Texas system of school financing might be regarded as discriminating (1) against "poor" persons whose incomes fall below some identifiable level of poverty or who might be characterized as functionally "indigent," or (2) against those who are relatively poorer than others, or (3) against all those who, irrespective of their personal incomes, happen to reside in relatively poorer school districts. Our task must be to ascertain whether, in fact, the Texas system has been shown to discriminate on any of these possible bases and, if so, whether the resulting classification may be regarded as suspect.

The precedents of this Court provide the proper starting point. The individuals, or groups of individuals, who constituted the class discriminated against in our prior cases shared two distinguishing characteristics: because of their impecunity they were completely unable to pay for some desired benefit, and as a consequence, they sustained an absolute deprivation of a meaningful opportunity to enjoy that benefit. . . .

Only appellees' first possible basis for describing the class disadvantaged by the Texas school-financing system — discrimination against a class of definably "poor" persons — might arguably meet the criteria established in these prior cases. Even a cursory examination, however, demonstrates that neither of the two distinguishing characteristics of wealth classifications can be found here. First, in support of their charge that the system discriminates against the "poor," appellees have made no effort to demonstrate that it operates to the peculiar disadvantage of any class fairly definable as indigent, or as composed of persons whose incomes are beneath any designated poverty level. Indeed, there is reason to believe that the poorest families are not necessarily clustered in the poorest property districts. A recent and exhaustive study of school districts in Connecticut concluded . . . that the poor were clustered around commercial and industrial areas — those same areas that provide the most attractive sources of property tax income for school districts. Whether a similar pattern would be discovered in Texas is not known, but there is no basis on the record in this case for assuming that the poorest people — defined by reference to any level of absolute impecunity — are concentrated in the poorest districts.

Second, neither appellees nor the District Court addressed the fact that . . . lack of personal resources has not occasioned an absolute deprivation of the desired benefit. The argument here is not that the children in districts having relatively low assessable property values are receiving no public education; rather, it is that they are receiving a poorer quality education than that available to children in districts having more assessable wealth. Apart from the unsettled and disputed question whether the quality of education may be determined by the amount of money expended for it,[a] a sufficient answer to appellees' argument is that, at least where wealth is involved, the Equal Protection Clause does not require absolute equality or precisely equal advantages. . . .

For these two reasons — the absence of any evidence that the financing system discriminates against any definable category of "poor" people or that it results in the absolute deprivation of education — the disadvantaged class is not susceptible of identification in traditional terms.[b]

As suggested above, appellees and the District Court may have embraced a second or third approach, the second of which might be characterized as a theory of relative or comparative discrimination based on family income. Appellees sought to prove that a direct correlation exists between the wealth of families within each district and the expenditures therein for education. That is, along a continuum, the poorer the family the lower the dollar amount of education received by the family's children. . . .

If, in fact, [this correlation] could be sustained, . . . [a]ppellees' comparative-discrimination theory would still face serious unanswered questions, including whether a bare positive correlation or some higher degree of correlation is necessary to provide a basis for concluding that the financing system is designed to operate to the peculiar disadvantage of the comparatively poor, and whether a class of this size and diversity could ever claim the special protection accorded "suspect" classes. These questions need not be addressed in this case, however, since appellees' proof fails to support their allegations or the District Court's conclusions. . . .

This brings us, then, to the third way in which the classification scheme might be defined — *district* wealth discrimination. Since the only correlation indicated by the evidence is between district property wealth and expenditures, it may be argued that discrimination might be found without regard to the individual income characteristics of district residents. Assuming a perfect correlation between district property wealth and expenditures from top to bottom, the disadvantaged class might be viewed as encompassing every child in every district except the dis-

a. Each of appellees' possible theories of wealth discrimination is founded on the assumption that the quality of education varies directly with the amount of funds expended on it and that, therefore, the difference in quality between two schools can be determined simplistically by looking at the difference in per-pupil expenditures. This is a matter of considerable dispute among educators and commentators. . . .

b. An educational financing system might be hypothesized, however, in which the analogy to the wealth discrimination cases would be considerably closer. If elementary and secondary education were made available by the State only to those able to pay a tuition assessed against each pupil, there would be a clearly defined class of "poor" people — definable in terms of their inability to pay the prescribed sum — who would be absolutely precluded from receiving an education. That case would present a far more compelling set of circumstances for judicial assistance than the case before us today. . . .

trict that has the most assessable wealth and spends the most on education. Alternatively, . . . the class might be defined more restrictively to include children in districts with assessable property which falls below the statewide average, or median, or below some other artifically defined level.

However described, it is clear that appellees' suit asks this Court to extend its most exacting scrutiny to review a system that allegedly discriminates against a large, diverse, and amorphous class, unified only by the common factor of residence in districts that happen to have less taxable wealth than other districts. The system of alleged discrimination and the class it defines have none of the traditional indicia of suspectness: the class is not saddled with such disabilities, or subjected to such a history of purposeful unequal treatment, or relegated to such a position of political powerlessness as to command extraordinary protection from the majoritarian political process.

We thus conclude that the Texas system does not operate to the peculiar disadvantage of any suspect class. But in recognition of the fact that this Court has never heretofore held that wealth discrimination alone provides an adequate basis for invoking strict scrutiny, appellees have not relied solely on this contention. They also assert that the State's system impermissibly interferes with the exercise of a "fundamental" right and that accordingly the prior decisions of this Court require the application of the strict standard of judicial review. . . .

B

In Brown v. Board of Education, 347 U.S. 483 (1954), a unanimous Court recognized that "education is perhaps the most important function of state and local governments." . . .

Nothing this Court holds today in anyway detracts from our historic dedication to public education. We are in complete agreement with the conclusion of the three-judge panel below that "the grave significance of education both to the individual and to our society" cannot be doubted. But the importance of a service performed by the State does not determine whether it must be regarded as fundamental for purposes of examination under the Equal Protection Clause. . . .

The lesson of [Lindsey v. Normet, 405 U.S. 56 (1972); Dandridge v. Williams, 397 U.S. 471 (1970); Jefferson v. Hackney, 406 U.S. 535 (1972); and Richardson v. Belcher, 404 U.S. 78 (1971)] in addressing the question now before the Court is plain. It is not the province of this Court to create substantive constitutional rights in the name of guaranteeing equal protection of the laws. Thus, the key to discovering whether education is "fundamental" is not to be found in comparisons of the relative societal significance of education as opposed to subsistence or housing. Nor is it to be found by weighing whether education is as important as the right to travel. Rather, the answer lies in assessing whether there is a right to education explicitly or implicitly guaranteed by the Constitution. Eisenstadt v. Baird, 405 U.S. 438 (1972); Dunn v. Blumstein, 405 U.S. 330 (1972);[c] Police

c. Dunn fully canvasses this Court's voting rights cases and explains that "this Court has made clear that a citizen has a *constitutionally protected right* to participate in elections on an equal basis with other citizens in the jurisdiction." Id., at 336 (emphasis supplied). The constitutional underpinnings of the right to equal treatment in the voting process can no longer be doubted even though, as the Court noted in Harper v. Virginia Bd. of Elections, . . . "the right to vote in state elections is nowhere expressly mentioned." . . .

Dept. of Chicago v. Mosley, 408 U.S. 92 (1972);[d] Skinner v. Oklahoma, 316 U.S. 535 (1942).[e]

Education, of course, is not among the rights afforded explicit protection under our Federal Constitution. Nor do we find any basis for saying it is implicitly so protected. As we have said, the undisputed importance of education will not alone cause this Court to depart from the usual standard for reviewing a State's social and economic legislation. It is appellees' contention, however, that education is distinguishable from other services and benefits provided by the State because it bears a peculiarly close relationship to other rights and liberties accorded protection under the Constitution. Specifically, they insist that education is itself a fundamental personal right because it is essential to the effective exercise of First Amendment freedoms and to intelligent utilization of the right to vote. In asserting a nexus between speech and education, appellees urge that the right to speak is meaningless unless the speaker is capable of articulating his thoughts intelligently and persuasively. The "marketplace of ideas" is an empty forum for those lacking basic communicative tools. . . . A similar line of reasoning is pursued with respect to the right to vote.[f] Exercise of the franchise, it is contended, cannot be divorced from the educational foundation of the voter.

We need not dispute any of these propositions. The Court has long afforded zealous protection against unjustifiable governmental interference with the individual's rights to speak and to vote. Yet we have never presumed to possess either the ability or the authority to guarantee to the citizenry the most *effective* speech or the most *informed* electoral choice. . . .

Whatever merit appellees' argument might have if a State's financing system occasioned an absolute denial of educational opportunities to any of its children, that argument provides no basis for finding an interference with fundamental rights where only relative differences in spending levels are involved and where — as is true in the present case — no charge fairly could be made that the system fails to provide each child with an opportunity to acquire the basic minimal skills necessary for the enjoyment of the rights of speech and of full participation in the political process.

Furthermore, the logical limitations on appellees' nexus theory are difficult to perceive. How, for instance, is education to be distinguished from the significant personal interests in the basics of decent food and shelter? Empirical examination might well buttress an assumption that the ill-fed, ill-clothed, and ill-housed are among the most ineffective participants in the political process, and that they derive the least enjoyment from the benefits of the First Amendment. If so, ap-

d. In *Mosley*, the Court struck down a Chicago antipicketing ordinance that exempted labor picketing from its prohibitions. The ordinance was held invalid under the Equal Protection Clause after subjecting it to careful scrutiny and finding that the ordinance was not narrowly drawn. The stricter standard of review was appropriately applied since the ordinance was one "affecting First Amendment interests." . . .

e. Skinner applied the standard of close scrutiny to a state law permitting forced sterilization of "habitual criminals." Implicit in the Court's opinion is the recognition that the right of procreation is among the rights of personal privacy protected under the Constitution. See Roe v. Wade, 410 U.S. 113, 152 (1973).

f. Since the right to vote, per se, is not a constitutionally protected right, we assume that appellees' references to that right are simply shorthand references to the protected right, implicit in our constitutional system, to participate in state elections on an equal basis with other qualified voters whenever the State has adopted an elective process for determining who will represent any segment of the State's population. See n. [c] supra.

pellees' thesis would cast serious doubt on the authority of Dandridge v. Williams and Lindsey v. Normet.

. . . In one further respect we find this a particularly inappropriate case in which to subject state action to strict judicial scrutiny. The present case, in another basic sense, is significantly different from any of the cases in which the Court has applied strict scrutiny to state or federal legislation touching upon constitutionally protected rights. Each of our prior cases involved legislation which "deprived," "infringed," or "interfered" with the free exercise of some such fundamental personal right or liberty. See Skinner v. Oklahoma; Shapiro v. Thompson; Dunn v. Blumstein. Every step leading to the establishment of the system Texas utilizes today — including the decisions permitting localities to tax and expend locally, and creating and continuously expanding state aid — was implemented in an effort to *extend* public education and to improve its quality. Of course, every reform that benefits some more than others may be criticized for what it fails to accomplish. But we think it plain that, in substance, the thrust of the Texas system is affirmative and reformatory and, therefore, should be scrutinized under judicial principles sensitive to the nature of the State's efforts and to the rights reserved to the States under the Constitution.

C . . .

We need not rest our decision, however, solely on the inappropriateness of a strict-scrutiny test. A century of Supreme Court adjudication under the Equal Protection Clause affirmatively supports the application of the traditional standard of review, which requires only that the State's system be shown to bear some rational relationship to legitimate state purposes. . . .

While assuring a basic education for every child in the State, [the Texas system of school finance] permits and encourages a large measure of participation in and control of each district's schools at the local level. In an era that has witnessed a consistent trend toward centralization of the functions of government, local sharing of responsibility for public education has survived. . . . In part, local control means . . . the freedom to devote more money to the education of one's children. Equally important, however, is the opportunity it offers for participation in the decisionmaking process that determines how those local tax dollars will be spent. Each locality is free to tailor local programs to local needs. Pluralism also affords some opportunity for experimentation, innovation, and a healthy competition for educational excellence. . . .

Appellees suggest that local control could be preserved and promoted under other financing systems that resulted in more equality in educational expenditures. While it is no doubt true that reliance on local property taxation for school revenues provides less freedom of choice with respect to expenditures for some districts than for others, the existence of "some inequality" in the manner in which the State's rationale is achieved is not alone a sufficient basis for striking down the entire system. . . . Nor must the financing system fail because, as appellees suggest, other methods of satisfying the State's interest, which occasion "less drastic" disparities in expenditures, might be conceived. Only where state action impinges on the exercise of fundamental constitutional rights or liberties must it be found to have chosen the last restrictive alternative. It is also well to remember that even those districts that have reduced ability to make free decisions with respect to how much they spend on education still retain under the present system a large measure of authority as to how available funds will be allocated. They further enjoy the power to make numerous other decisions with respect to the operation of the schools. The people of Texas may be justified in believing that other systems of school financing, which place more of the financial responsibility in the hands of the State, will result in a comparable lessening of desired local autonomy. That is, they may believe that along with increased control of the purse strings at the state level will go increased control over local policies.

Appellees further urge that the Texas system is unconstitutionally arbitrary because it allows the availability of local taxable resources to turn on "happenstance." They see no justification for a system that allows, as they contend, the quality of education to fluctuate on the basis of the fortuitous positioning of the boundary lines of political subdivisions and the location of valuable commercial and industrial property. But any scheme of local taxation — indeed the very existence of identifiable local governmental units — requires the establishment of jurisdictional boundaries that are inevitably arbitrary. It is equally inevitable that some localities are going to be blessed with more taxable assets than others.[g] Nor is local wealth a static quantity. Changes in the level of taxable wealth within any district may result from any number of events, some of which local residents can and do influence. For instance, commercial and industrial enterprises may be encouraged to locate within a district by various actions — public and private.

Moreover, if local taxation for local expenditures were an unconstitutional method of providing for education then it might be an equally impermissible means of providing other necessary services customarily financed largely from local property taxes, including local police and fire protection, public health and hospitals, and public utility facilities of various kinds. . . .

In sum, to the extent that the Texas system of school financing results in unequal expenditures between children who happen to reside in different districts, we cannot say that such disparities are the product of a system that is so irrational as to be invidiously discriminatory. . . .

[A concurring opinion by Justice Stewart is omitted.]

WHITE, J., joined by Douglas and Brennan, JJ., dissenting. . . .

I cannot disagree with the proposition that local control and local decision-making play an important part in our democratic system of government. Much may be left to local option, and this case would be quite different if it were true that the Texas system, while insuring minimum educational expenditures in every district through state funding, extended a meaningful option to all local districts to increase their per-pupil expenditures and so to improve their children's education to the extent that increased funding would achieve that goal. The system would then arguably provide a rational and sensible method of achieving the stated aim of preserving an area for local initiative and decision.

The difficulty with the Texas system, however, is that it provides a meaningful option to Alamo Heights and like school districts but almost none to Edgewood and those other districts with a low per-pupil real estate tax base. In these latter

g. This Court has never doubted the propriety of maintaining political subdivisions within the States and has never found in the Equal Protection Clause any per se rule of "territorial uniformity." . . .

districts, no matter how desirous parents are of supporting their schools with greater revenues, it is impossible to do so through the use of the real estate property tax. In these districts, the Texas system utterly fails to extend a realistic choice to parents because the property tax, which is the only revenue-raising mechanism extended to school districts, is practically and legally unavailable. That this is the situation may be readily demonstrated. . . .

The Equal Protection Clause permits discriminations between classes but requires that the classification bear some rational relationship to a permissible object sought to be attained by the statute. It is not enough that the Texas system before us seeks to achieve the valid, rational purpose of maximizing local initiative; the means chosen by the State must also be rationally related to the end sought to be achieved. . . .

Neither Texas nor the majority heeds this rule. If the State aims at maximizing local initiative and local choice, by permitting school districts to resort to the real property tax if they choose to do so, it utterly fails in achieving its purpose in districts with property tax bases so low that there is little if any opportunity for interested parents, rich or poor, to augment school district revenues. Requiring the State to establish only that unequal treatment is in furtherance of a permissible goal, without also requiring the State to show that the means chosen to effectuate that goal are rationally related to its achievement, makes equal protection analysis no more than an empty gesture. In my view, the parents and children in Edgewood, and in like districts, suffer from an invidious discrimination violative of the Equal Protection Clause.

This does not, of course, mean that local control may not be a legitimate goal of a school financing system. Nor does it mean that the State must guarantee each district an equal per-pupil revenue from the state school-financing system. . . . On the contrary, it would merely mean that the State must fashion a financing scheme which provides a rational basis for the maximization of local control. . . .

MARSHALL, J., joined by Douglas, J., dissenting. . . .

I

The Court acknowledges that "substantial interdistrict disparities in school expenditures" exist in Texas, and that these disparities are "largely attributable to differences in the amounts of money collected through local property taxation." But instead of closely examining the seriousness of these disparities and the invidiousness of the Texas financing scheme, the Court undertakes an elaborate exploration of the efforts Texas has purportedly made to close the gaps between its districts in terms of levels of district wealth and resulting educational funding. Yet, however praiseworthy Texas' equalizing efforts, the issue in this case is not whether Texas is doing its best to ameliorate the worst features of a discriminatory scheme but, rather, whether the scheme itself is in fact unconstitutionally discriminatory in the face of the Fourteenth Amendment's guarantee of equal protection of the laws. . . .

Certainly the Court has recognized that to demand precise equality of treatment is normally unrealistic, and thus minor differences inherent in any practical context usually will not make out a substantial equal protection claim. But . . . we are hardly presented here with some de minimis claim of discrimination resulting from the play necessary in any functioning system; to the contrary, it is clear that the Foundation Program utterly fails to ameliorate the seriously discriminatory effects of the local property tax.

Alternatively, . . . the majority may believe that the Equal Protection Clause cannot be offended by substantially unequal state treatment of persons who are similarly situated so long as the State provides everyone with some unspecified amount of education which evidently is "enough." The basis for such a novel view is far from clear. . . . [T]his Court has never suggested that because some "adequate" level of benefits is provided to all, discrimination in the provision of services is therefore constitutionally excusable. The Equal Protection Clause is not addressed to the minimal sufficiency but rather to the unjustifiable inequalities of state action. . . .

Despite the evident discriminatory effect of the Texas financing scheme, both the appellants and the majority raise substantial questions concerning the precise character of the disadvantaged class in this case.

I believe it is sufficient that the overarching form of discrimination in this case is between the schoolchildren of Texas on the basis of the taxable property wealth of the districts in which they happen to live. . . . In their complaint appellees asserted that the Constitution does not permit local district wealth to be determinative of educational opportunity. This is simply another way of saying, as the District Court concluded, that consistent with the guarantee of equal protection of the laws, "the quality of public education may not be a function of wealth, other than the wealth of the state as a whole." Under such a principle, the children of a district are excessively advantaged if that district has more taxable property per pupil than the average amount of taxable property per pupil considering the State as a whole. By contrast, the children of a district are disadvantaged if that district has less taxable property per pupil than the state average. The majority attempts to disparage such a definition of the disadvantaged class as the product of an "artificially defined level" of district wealth. But such is clearly not the case, for this is the definition unmistakably dictated by the constitutional principle for which appellees have argued throughout the course of this litigation. And I do not believe that a clearer definition of either the disadvantaged class of Texas schoolchildren or the allegedly unconstitutional discrimination suffered by the members of that class under the present Texas financing scheme could be asked for, much less needed. Whether this discrimination, against the schoolchildren of property-poor districts, inherent in the Texas financing scheme, is violative of the Equal Protection Clause is the question to which we must now turn.

II

To avoid having the Texas financing scheme struck down because of the interdistrict variations in taxable property wealth, the District Court determined that . . . the discrimination inherent in the scheme had to be shown necessary to promote a "compelling state interest" in order to withstand constitutional scrutiny. The basis for this determination was twofold: first, the financing scheme divides citizens on a wealth basis, a classification which the District Court viewed as highly suspect; and second, the discriminatory scheme directly affects what it considered to be a "fundamental interest," namely, education. . . .

The majority today concludes, however, that the Texas scheme is not subject to such a strict standard of review under the Equal Protection Clause. Instead, in its view, the Texas scheme must be tested by nothing more than that lenient standard of rationality which we have traditionally applied to discriminatory state action in the context of economic and commercial matters. . . .

A . . .

The Court apparently seeks to establish today that equal protection cases fall into one of two neat categories which dictate the appropriate standard of review — strict scrutiny or mere rationality. But this Court's decisions in the field of equal protection defy such easy categorization. A principled reading of what this Court has done reveals that it has applied a spectrum of standards in reviewing discrimination allegedly violative of the Equal Protection Clause. This spectrum clearly comprehends variations in the degree of care with which the Court will scrutinize particular classifications, depending, I believe, on the constitutional and societal importance of the interest adversely affected and the recognized invidiousness of the basis upon which the particular classification is drawn. . . .

I therefore cannot accept the majority's labored efforts to demonstrate that fundamental interests, which call for strict scrutiny of the challenged classification, encompass only established rights which we are somehow bound to recognize from the text of the Constitution itself. To be sure, some interests which the Court has deemed to be fundamental for purposes of equal protection analysis are themselves constitutionally protected rights. . . . See Police Dept. of Chicago v. Mosley . . . ; Shapiro v. Thompson. . . . But it will not do to suggest that the "answer" to whether an interest is fundamental for purposes of equal protection analysis is *always* determined by whether that interest "is a right . . . explicitly or implicitly guaranteed by the Constitution."[a] . . .

I would like to know where the Constitution guarantees the right to procreate, Skinner v. Oklahoma, or the right to vote in state elections, e.g., Reynolds v. Sims, or the right to an appeal from a criminal conviction, e.g., Griffin v. Illinois. These are instances in which, due to the importance of the interests at stake, the Court has displayed a strong concern with the existence of discriminatory state treatment. But the Court has never said or indicated that these are interests which independently enjoy full-blown constitutional protection.

Thus, in Buck v. Bell, 247 U.S. 200 (1927), the Court refused to recognize a substantive constitutional guarantee of the right to procreate. Nevertheless, in Skinner v. Oklahoma, . . . the Court, without impugning the continuing validity of Buck v. Bell, held that "strict scrutiny" of state discrimination affecting procreation "is essential," for "[m]arriage and procreation are fundamental to the very existence and survival of the race." . . .

Similarly, . . . "this Court has made clear that a citizen has a *constitutionally protected right* to participate in elections *on an equal basis with other citizens in the jurisdiction.*" Dunn v. Blumstein (emphasis added). The final source of such protection

a. Indeed, the Court's theory would render the established concept of fundamental interests in the context of equal protection analysis superfluous, for the substantive constitutional right itself requires that this Court strictly scrutinize any asserted state interest for restricting or denying access to any particular guaranteed right. . . .

from inequality in the provision of the state franchise is, of course, the Equal Protection Clause. Yet it is clear that whatever degree of importance has been attached to the state electoral process when unequally distributed, the right to vote in state elections has itself never been accorded the stature of an independent constitutional guarantee.[b] . . .

Finally, it is likewise "true that a State is not required by the Federal Constitution to provide appellate courts or a right to appellate review at all." Griffin v. Illinois. Nevertheless, discrimination adversely affecting access to an appellate process which a State has chosen to provide has been considered to require close judicial scrutiny. See, e.g., Griffin v. Illinois; Douglas v. California.[c]

The majority is, of course, correct when it suggests that the process of determining which interests are fundamental is a difficult one. But I do not think the problem is insurmountable. And I certainly do not accept the view that the process need necessarily degenerate into an unprincipled, subjective "picking-and-choosing" between various interests or that it must involve this Court in creating "substantive constitutional rights in the name of guaranteeing equal protection of the laws." Although not all fundamental interests are constitutionally guaranteed, the determination of which interests are fundamental should be firmly rooted in the text of the Constitution. The task in every case should be to determine the extent to which constitutionally guaranteed rights are dependent on interests not mentioned in the Constitution. As the nexus between the specific constitutional guarantee and the nonconstitutional interest draws closer, the nonconstitutional interest becomes more fundamental and the degree of judicial scrutiny applied when the interest is infringed on a discriminatory basis must be adjusted accordingly. Thus, it cannot be denied that interests such as procreation, the exercise of the state franchise, and access to criminal appellate processes are not fully guaranteed to the citizen by our Constitution. But these interests have nonetheless been afforded special judicial consideration in the face of discrimination because they are, to some extent, interrelated with constitutional guarantees. Procreation is now understood to be important because of its interaction with the established constitutional right of privacy. The exercise of the state franchise is closely tied to basic civil and political rights inherent in the First Amendment. And access to criminal appellate processes enhances the integrity of the range of rights implicit in the Fourteenth Amendment guarantee of due process of law. Only if we closely protect the related interests from state discrimination do we ultimately ensure the integrity of the constitutional guarantee itself. This is the real lesson that must be taken from our previous decisions involving interests deemed to be fundamental. . . .

b. It is interesting that in its effort to reconcile the state voting rights cases with its theory of fundamentality the majority can muster nothing more than the contention that "[t]he constitutional underpinnings of the *right to equal treatment in the voting process* can no longer be doubted. . . ." (emphasis added). If, by this, the Court intends to recognize a substantive constitutional "right to equal treatment in the voting process" independent of the Equal Protection Clause, the source of such a right is certainly a mystery to me.

c. It is true that *Griffin* and *Douglas* also involved discrimination against indigents, that is, wealth discrimination. But, as the majority points out, the Court has never deemed wealth discrimination alone to be sufficient to require strict judicial scrutiny; rather, such review of wealth classifications has been applied only where the discrimination affects an important individual interest, see, e.g., Harper v. Virginia Bd. of Elections. Thus, I believe *Griffin* and *Douglas* can only be understood as premised on a recognition of the fundamental importance of the criminal appellate process.

B

It is true that this Court has never deemed the provision of free public education to be required by the Constitution. . . . Nevertheless, the fundamental importance of education is amply indicated by the prior decisions of this Court, by the unique status accorded public education by our society, and by the close relationship between education and some of our most basic constitutional values. . . . In large measure, the explanation for the special importance attached to education must rest . . . on the facts that "some degree of education is necessary to prepare citizens to participate effectively and intelligently in our open political system . . . ," and that "education prepares individuals to be self-reliant and self-sufficient participants in society." Both facets of this observation are suggestive of the substantial relationship which education bears to guarantees of our Constitution.

Education directly affects the ability of a child to exercise his First Amendment interests, both as a source and as a receiver of information and ideas, whatever interests he may pursue in life. . . . Education may instill the interest and provide the tools necessary for political discourse and debate. . . . But of most immediate and direct concern must be the demonstrated effect of education on the exercise of the franchise by the electorate. . . . Data from the Presidential Election of 1968 clearly demonstrates a direct relationship between participation in the electoral process and level of educational attainment; and, as this Court recognized in Gaston County v. United States, 395 U.S. 284, 296 (1969), the quality of education offered may influence a child's decision to "enter or remain in school." It is this very sort of intimate relationship between a particular personal interest and specific constitutional guarantees that has heretofore caused the Court to attach special significance, for purposes of equal protection analysis, to individual interests such as procreation and the exercise of the state franchise.[d]

While ultimately disputing little of this, the majority seeks refuge in the fact that the Court has "never presumed to possess either the ability or the authority to guarantee to the citizenry the most *effective* speech or the most *informed* electoral choice." . . . This serves only to blur what is in fact at stake. With due respect, the issue is neither provision of the most *effective* speech nor of the most *informed* vote. Appellees do not now seek the best education Texas might provide. They do seek, however, an end to state discrimination resulting from the unequal distribution of taxable district property wealth that directly impairs the ability of some districts to provide the same educational opportunity that other districts

d. I believe that the close nexus between education and our established constitutional values with respect to freedom of speech and participation in the political process makes this a different case from our prior decisions concerning discrimination affecting public welfare, see, e.g., Dandridge v. Williams, housing, see, e.g., Lindsey v. Normet. There can be no question that, as the majority suggests, constitutional rights may be less meaningful for someone without enough to eat or without decent housing. But the crucial difference lies in the closeness of the relationship. Whatever the severity of the impact of insufficient food or inadequate housing on a person's life, they have never been considered to bear the same direct and immediate relationship to constitutional concerns for free speech and for our political processes as education has long been recognized to bear. Perhaps, the best evidence of this fact is the unique status which has been accorded public education as the single public service nearly unanimously guaranteed in the constitutions of our State. . . . Education, in terms of constitutional values, is much more analogous, in my judgment, to the right to vote in state elections than to public welfare or public housing. Indeed, it is not without significance that we have long recognized education as an essential step in providing the disadvantaged with the tools necessary to achieve economic self-sufficiency.

can provide with the same or even substantially less tax effort. The issue is, in other words, one of discrimination that affects the quality of the education which Texas has chosen to provide its children; and, the precise question here is what importance should attach to education for purposes of equal protection analysis of that discrimination. . . .

C

The District Court found that in discriminating between Texas schoolchildren on the basis of the amount of taxable property wealth located in the district in which they live, the Texas financing scheme created a form of wealth discrimination. . . . The majority, however, considers any wealth classification in this case to lack certain essential characteristics which it contends are common to the instances of wealth discrimination that this Court has heretofore recognized. We are told that in every prior case involving a wealth classification, the members of the disadvantaged class have "shared" two distinguishing characteristics: because of their impecunity they were completely unable to pay for some desired benefit, and as a consequence, they sustained an absolute deprivation of a meaningful opportunity to enjoy that benefit." . . . I cannot agree. . . .

Under the first part of the theory announced by the majority, the disadvantaged class in *Harper,* in terms of a wealth analysis, should have consisted only of those too poor to afford the $1.50 necessary to vote. But the *Harper* Court did not see it that way. In its view, the Equal Protection Clause "bars a system which excludes [from the franchise] those unable to pay a fee to vote or who *fail to pay.*" (Emphasis added.) So far as the Court was concerned, the "degree of the discrimination [was] irrelevant." Thus, the Court struck down the poll tax in toto; it did not order merely that those too poor to pay the tax be exempted; complete impecunity clearly was not determinative of the limits of the disadvantaged class, nor was it essential to make an equal protection claim. . . .

[In Griffin v. Illinois and Douglas v. California] the right of appeal itself was not absolutely denied to those too poor to pay; but because of the cost of a transcript and of counsel, the appeal was a substantially less meaningful right for the poor than for the rich.[e] It was on these terms that the Court found a denial of equal protection, and those terms clearly encompassed degrees of discrimination on the basis of wealth which do not amount to outright denial of the affected right or interest.

This is not to say that the form of wealth classification in this case does not differ significantly from those recognized in the previous decisions of this Court. Our prior cases have dealt essentially with discrimination on the basis of personal wealth. Here, by contrast, the children of the disadvantaged Texas school districts are being discriminated against not necessarily because of their personal wealth or the wealth of their families, but because of the taxable property wealth of the residents of the district in which they happen to live. The appropriate

e. This does not mean that the Court has demanded precise equality in the treatment of the indigent and the person of means in the criminal process. We have never suggested, for instance, that the Equal Protection Clause requires the best lawyer money can buy for the indigent. We are hardly equipped with the objective standards which such a judgment would require. But we have pursued the goal of substantial equality of treatment in the face of clear disparities in the nature of the appellate process afforded rich versus poor. . . .

question, then, is whether the same degree of judicial solicitude and scrutiny that has previously been afforded wealth classifications is warranted here.

As the Court points out, no previous decision has deemed the presence of just a wealth classification to be sufficient basis to call forth rigorous judicial scrutiny of allegedly discriminatory state action. . . . That wealth classifications alone have not necessarily been considered to bear the same high degree of suspectness as have classifications based on, for instance, race or alienage may be explainable on a number of grounds. The "poor" may not be seen as politically powerless as certain discrete and insular minority groups. Personal poverty may entail much the same social stigma as historically attached to certain racial or ethnic groups. But personal poverty is not a permanent disability; its shackles may be escaped. Perhaps most importantly, though, personal wealth may not necessarily share the general irrelevance as a basis for legislative action that race or nationality is recognized to have. While the "poor" have frequently been a legally disadvantaged group, it cannot be ignored that social legislation must frequently take cognizance of the economic status of our citizens. Thus, we have generally gauged the invidiousness of wealth classifications with an awareness of the importance of the interests being affected and the relevance of personal wealth to those interests. See Harper v. Virginia Bd. of Elections, supra.

When evaluated with these considerations in mind, it seems to me that discrimination on the basis of group wealth in this case likewise calls for careful judicial scrutiny. First, it must be recognized that while local district wealth may serve other interests, it bears no relationship whatsoever to the interest of Texas school children in the educational opportunity afforded them by the State of Texas. Given the importance of that interest, we must be particularly sensitive to the invidious characteristics of any form of discrimination that is not clearly intended to serve it, as opposed to some other distinct state interest. Discrimination on the the basis of group wealth may not, to be sure, reflect the social stigma frequently attached to personal poverty. Nevertheless, insofar as group wealth discrimination involves wealth over which the disadvantaged individual has no significant control,[f] it represents in fact a more serious basis of discrimination than does personal wealth. For such discrimination is no reflection of the individual's characteristics or his abilities. And thus — particularly in the context of a disadvantaged class composed of children — we have previously treated discrimination on a basis which the individual cannot control as constitutionally disfavored. Cf. Weber v. Aetna Casualty & Surety Co., 406 U.S. 164 (1972); Levy v. Louisiana, 391 U.S. 68 (1968). . . .

Nor can we ignore the extent to which, in contrast to our prior decisions, the Stat is responsible for the wealth discrimination in this instance. *Griffin, Douglas, Williams, Tate,* and our other prior cases have dealt with discrimination on the basis of indigency which was attributable to the operation of the private sector. But we have no such simple de facto wealth discrimination here. The means for financing public education in Texas are selected and specified by the State. It is the State that has created local school districts, and tied educational funding to the local property tax and thereby to local district wealth. At the same time, govern-

f. True, a family may move to escape a property-poor school district, assuming it has the means to do so. But such a view would itself raise a serious constitutional question concerning an impermissible burdening of the right to travel, or, more precisely, the concomitant right to remain where one is. Cf. Shapiro v. Thompson.

mentally imposed land use controls have undoubtedly encouraged and rigidified natural trends in the allocation of particular areas for residential or commercial use, and thus determined each district's amount of taxable property wealth. In short, this case, in contrast to the Court's previous wealth discrimination decision, can only be seen as "unusual in the extent to which governmental action *is* the cause of the wealth classifications."

In the final analysis, then, the invidious characteristics of the group wealth classification present in this case merely serve to emphasize the need for careful judicial scrutiny of the State's justifications for the resulting interdistrict discrimination in the educational opportunity afforded to the schoolchildren of Texas.

D

The nature of our inquiry into the justifications for state discrimination is essentially the same in all equal protection cases: We must consider the substantiality of the state interests sought to be served, and we must scrutinize the reasonableness of the means by which the State has sought to advance its interests. Differences in the application of this test are, in my view, a function of the constitutional importance of the interests at stake and the invidiousness of the particular classification. In terms of the asserted state interests, the Court has indicated that it will require, for instance, a "compelling" or a "substantial" or "important" state interest to justify discrimination affecting individual interests of constitutional significance. Whatever the differences, if any, in these descriptions of the character of the state interest necessary to sustain such discrimination, basic to each is, I believe, a concern with the legitimacy and the reality of the asserted state interests. Thus, when interests of constitutional importance are at stake, the Court does not stand ready to credit the State's classification with any conceivable legitimate purpose, but demands a clear showing that there are legitimate state interests which the classification was in fact intended to serve. Beyond the question of the adequacy of the State's purpose for the classification, the Court traditionally has become increasingly sensitive to the means by which a State chooses to act as its action affects more directly interests of constitutional significance. Thus, by now, "less restrictive alternatives" analysis is firmly established in equal protection jurisprudence. It seems to me that the range of choice we are willing to accord the State in selecting the means by which it will act, and the care with which we scrutinize the effectiveness of the means which the State selects, also must reflect the constitutional importance of the interest affected and the invidiousness of the particular classification. Here both the nature of the interest and the classification dictate close judicial scutiny of the purposes which Texas seeks to serve with its present educational financing scheme and of the means it has selected to serve that purpose.

The only justification offered by appellants to sustain the discrimination in educational opportunity caused by the Texas financing scheme is local educational control. . . .

At the outset, I do not question that local control of public education, as an abstract matter, constitutes a very substantial state interest. . . . Consequently, true state dedication to local control would present, I think, a substantial justification to weigh against simply interdistrict variations in the treatment of a State's school children. But I need not now decide how I might ultimately strike the balance were we confronted with a situation where the State's sincere concern for local control inevitably produced educational inequality. For on this record, it is apparent that the State's purported concern with local control is offered primarily as an excuse rather than as a justification for interdistrict inequality.

In Texas, statewide laws regulate in fact the most minute details of local public education. . . . [But] even if we accept Texas' general dedication to local control in educational matters, it is difficult to find any evidence of such dedication with respect to fiscal matters. . . . If Texas had a system truly dedicated to local fiscal control, one would expect the quality of the educational opportunity provided in each district to vary with the decision of the voters in that district as to the level of sacrifice they wish to make for public education. In fact, the Texas scheme produces precisely the opposite result. Local school districts cannot choose to have the best education in the State by imposing the highest tax rate. Instead, the quality of the educational opportunity offered by any particular district is largely determined by the amount of taxable property located in the district — a factor over which local voters can exercise no control. . . .

In my judgment, any substantial degree of scrutiny of the operation of the Texas financing scheme reveals that the State has selected means wholly inappropriate to secure its purported interest in assuring its school districts local fiscal control.[g] At the same time, appellees have pointed out a variety of alternative financing schemes which may serve the State's purported interest in local control as well as, if not better than, the present scheme without the current impairment of the educational opportunity of vast numbers of Texas schoolchildren. I see no need, however, to explore the practical or constitutional merits of those suggested alternatives at this time for, whatever their positive or negative features, experience with the present financing scheme impugns any suggestion that it constitutes a serious effort to provide local fiscal control. . . .[h]

g. My Brother White, in concluding that the Texas financing scheme runs afoul of the Equal Protection Clause, likewise finds on analysis that the means chosen by Texas — local property taxation dependent upon local taxable wealth — is completely unsuited in its present form to the achievement of the asserted goal of providing local fiscal control. Although my Brother White purports to reach this result by application of that lenient standard of mere rationality traditionally applied in the context of commercial interests, it seems to me that the care with which he scrutinizes the practical effectiveness of the present local property tax as a device for affording local fiscal control reflects the application of a more stringent standard of review, a standard which at the least is influenced by the constitutional significance of the process of public education.

h. . . . [E]ven centralized financing would not deprive local school districts of what has been considered to be the essence of local educational control. . . . Central financing would leave in local hands the entire gamut of local educational policymaking — teachers, curriculum, school sites, the whole process of allocating resources among alternative educational objectives.

[Local fiscal control could be achieved under] the theory of district power equalization put forth by Professors Coons, Clune and Sugarman in their seminal work, Private Wealth and Public Education 201-242 (1970). Such a scheme would truly reflect a dedication to local fiscal control. Under their system, each school district would receive a fixed amount of revenue per pupil for any particular level of tax effort regardless of the level of local property tax base. Appellants criticize this scheme on the rather extraordinary ground that it would encourage poorer districts to overtax themselves in order to obtain substantial revenues for education. But under the present discriminatory scheme, it is the poor districts that are already taxing themselves at the highest rates, yet are receiving the lowest returns.

District wealth reapportionment is yet another alternative which would accomplish directly essentially what district power equalization would seek to do artificially. Appellants claim that the calculations concerning state property required by such a scheme would be impossible as a practical matter. Yet Texas is already making far more complex annual calculations — involving not only local property values but also local income and other economic factors — in conjunction with the Local Fund Assignment portion of the Minimum Foundation School Program. . . .

[A dissenting opinion by Justice Brennan is omitted.]

Discussion

1. Comparative constitutional kinship. Rank the following interests in terms of the firmness of their grounding in the text, structure, and original history of the Constitution: interstate mobility (protected in *Crandall,* page 175 supra, and *Shapiro,* page 1211 supra), privacy (protected in *Griswold* and Roe v. Wade, Chapter 9, supra), the franchise (protected in *Harper* and *Kramer,* Chapter 10, supra), subsistence (denied protection in Dandridge v. Williams 397 U.S. 471 (1970) and Lindsey v. Normet, 405 U.S. 56 (1972)), and education (denied protection in *Rodriguez,* page 1249 supra). Is Justice Powell persuasive that the Court has not picked and chosen among possible interests both in the creation of constitutional "rights" (e.g., privacy) and "fundamental interests" (e.g., political participation)? How persuasive is Justice Marshall's argument that education deserves special constitutional treatment because of its relationships with speech and the franchise? Assuming that some regulations concerning education do affect these interests, cf. Pierce v. Society of Sisters and Meyer v. Nebraska, supra, does the Texas school finance scheme affect them in a significant or in a constitutionally germane manner?

2. The methodologies of due process and equal protection. Is there a real difference between the methodologies of substantive due process — whether of the *Lochner* or Roe v. Wade variety — and "substantive equal protection"?[39] Justice Harlan believed that the new equal protection was less principled than his modest version of substantive due process. Justice Douglas argued the opposite.[40] Justice Rehnquist takes the position that the two decisionmaking processes have the same defect:[41]

> The relationship of the . . . "fundamental personal right" analysis to the constitutional guarantee of equal protection of the law is approximately the same as that of "freedom of contract" to the constitutional guarantee that no person shall be deprived of life, liberty, or property without due process of law. It is an invitation for judicial exegesis over and above the commands of the Constitution, in which values that cannot possibly have their source in that instrument are invoked to either validate or condemn the countless laws enacted by the various States.

3. The nature of the interests protected. Is there a difference between the kinds of interests that the Court has held to be constitutional "rights" independent of the equal protection clause and the interests that the Court has refused to deem "fundamental" under the equal protection clause? Is there a difference between the kinds of protection the Court has been asked to accord those interests? Recall the distinction between the "negative" state of classical liberalism and the "positive"

[Another] possibility would be to remove commercial, industrial, and mineral property from local tax rolls, to tax this property on a statewide basis, and to return the resulting revenues to the local districts in a fashion that would compensate for remaining variations in the local tax bases.

None of these particular alternatives are necessarily constitutionally compelled: rather, they indicate the breadth of choice which would remain to the State if the present interdistrict disparities were eliminated.

39. See Kenneth Karst & Harold Horowitz, Reitman v. Mulkey: A Telophase of Substantive Equal Protection, 1967 Sup. Ct. Rev. 39.

40. See Boddie v. Connecticut, 401 U.S. 371 (1971) (concurring opinion), p.1143 supra.

41. Weber v. Aetna Cas. & Sur. Co., 406 U.S. 164 (1972) (dissenting opinion).

welfare state. What are the likely implications of a decision that interests such as food, shelter, and education are independent constitutional rights?

4. The incorporation of independent constitutional "rights" into the equal protection clause. Once something has been determined to be an independent constitutional "right," whether through textual, historical, structural, or substantive due process methodology, should classifications affecting its enjoyment be subject to demanding scrutiny under the equal protection clause? Review the discussion of Shapiro v. Thompson, 394 U.S. 618 (1969) (right to interstate mobility), and Police Department of Chicago v. Mosley, 408 U.S. 92 (1972) (freedom of speech and assembly).

5. The standard of judicial review and the substantive requirements of the equal protection clause. In *Dandridge* and *Rodriguez,* Justice Marshall criticizes the Court for its binary or "two-tier"[42] approach to equal protection adjudication, under which a classification is subjected either to minimal or to very demanding scrutiny. He proposes, instead, a variable standard determined by the nature of the classifying trait and the interests affected. What are the rationales for the Court's and Justice Marshall's approaches?

In a portion of *Rodriguez* not quoted above, Justice Powell asserts: "[I]f the degree of judicial scrutiny of state legislation fluctuated depending on the majority's view of the importance of the interest affected, we would have gone 'far toward making this Court a super-legislature.' We would, indeed, then be assuming a legislative role and one for which the Court lacks both authority and competence." Do *Dandridge* and *Rodriguez* reflect the Court's *substantive* position that the equal protection clause demands nothing more than "minimum rationality" in the allocation of welfare and educational benefits or only an institutional reluctance to second-guess the legislature's application of a more demanding standard? What rationales support the two positions? If the legislature is bound to apply a more stringent standard in the first instance, what should that standard be? If Justice Marshall's criterion seems too amorphous to guide decisionmaking by a nonrepresentative judiciary, it might nonetheless speak to a legislator. It suggests that as the interests affected become more important and the classifications more invidious, the parochialism, self-interest, logrolling, and the like that pervade the political process must yield to generally shared principles of fair treatment. A conscientious legislator might take this view even if there were no equal protection clause. But the clause at least stands as a reminder of the government's commitment to fairness and provides some counterforce to callousness and expediency.

6. A "due process" minimum? Does footnote b of Justice Powell's opinion suggest that the state can neither withdraw entirely from the educational marketplace nor bar children from public schools because of their or their families' inability to pay?[43]

42. See Gerald Gunther, In Search of Evolving Doctrine on a Changing Court: A Model For a Newer Equal Protection, 86 Harv. L. Rev. 1 (1972).

43. By "public schools" we are referring to elementary and secondary schools. It is clear that public universities exclude qualified students because of their inability to pay the costs of their education, and this is not, at least currently, thought to present a constitutional problem.

2. *Is There a Right to Some Minimal Provision of Educational Resources?*

PLYLER v. DOE
457 U.S. 202 (1982)
On appeal from the United States Court of Appeals for the Fifth Circuit

[In 1975, the Texas legislature revised its education laws 1) to withhold from local school districts any state funds to pay for the education of children not "legally admitted" into the United States; and 2) to authorize local school districts to deny enrollment to such children. A class action was filed challenging the Texas legislation.]

BRENNAN, J. . . .

II

The Fourteenth Amendment provides that "No State shall . . . deprive any person of life, liberty or property, without due process of law; nor deny to *any person within its jurisdiction* the equal protection of the laws." [Emphasis added.] Appellants argue at the outset that undocumented aliens, because of their immigration status, are not "persons within the jurisdiction" of the State of Texas, and that they therefore have no right to the equal protection of Texas law. We reject this argument. Whatever his status under the immigration laws, an alien is surely a "person" in any ordinary sense of that term. Aliens, even aliens whose presence in this country is unlawful, have long been recognized as "persons" guaranteed due process of law by the Fifth and Fourteenth Amendments. Shaughnessy v. Mezei, 345 U.S. 206, 212 (1953); Wong Wing v. United States, 163 U.S. 228, 238 (1986); held that the Fifth Amendment protects aliens whose presence in this country is unlawful from invidious discrimination by the Federal Government. Mathews v. Diaz, 426 U.S. 67, 77 (1976). . . .

There is simply no support for appellants' suggestion that "due process" is somehow of greater stature than "equal protection" and therefore available to a larger class of persons. To the contrary, each aspect of the Fourteenth Amendment reflects an elementary limitation on state power. To permit a State to employ the phrase "within its jurisdiction" in order to identify subclasses of persons whom it would define as beyond its jurisdiction, thereby relieving itself of the obligation to assure that its laws are designed and applied equally to those persons, would undermine the principal purpose for which the Equal Protection Clause was incorporated in the Fourteenth Amendment. The Equal Protection Clause was intended to work nothing less than the abolition of all caste and invidious class based legislation. That objective is fundamentally at odds with the power the State asserts here to classify persons subject to its laws as nonetheless excepted from its protection.

Although the congressional debate concerning §1 of the Fourteenth Amendment was limited, that debate clearly confirms the understanding that the phrase "within its jurisdiction" was intended in a broad sense to offer the guarantee of equal protection to all within a State's boundaries, and to all upon whom the State would impose the obligations of its laws. Indeed, it appears from those debates that Congress, by using the phrase "person within its jurisdiction," sought expressly to ensure that the equal protection of the laws was provided to the alien population. Representative Bingham reported to the House the draft resolution of the Joint Committee of Fifteen on Reconstruction (H.R. 63) that was to become the Fourteenth Amendment. Cong. Globe, 39th Cong., 1st Sess., 1033 (1866). Two days later, Bingham posed the following question in support of the resolution: "Is it not essential to the unity of the Government and the unity of the people that all persons, whether citizens or strangers, within this land, shall have equal protection in every State in this Union in the rights of life and liberty and property?" Id., at 1090.

Senator Howard, also a member of the Joint Committee of Fifteen, and the floor manager of the Amendment in the Senate, was no less explicit about the broad objectives of the Amendment, and the intention to make its provisions applicable to all who "may happen to be" within the jurisdiction of a State:

> The last two clauses of the first section of the amendment disable a State from depriving not merely a citizen of the United States, but *any person, whoever he may be,* of life, liberty, or property without due process of law, or from denying to him the equal protection of the laws of the State. This abolishes all class legislation in the States, and does away with the injustice of subjecting one caste of persons to a code not applicable to another. . . . It will, if adopted by the States, forever disable every one of them from passing laws trenching upon those fundamental rights and privileges which pertain to citizens of the United States, *and to all persons who may happen to be within their jurisdiction.*

Cong. Globe, 39th Cong. 1st Sess. 2766 (1866) (emphasis added).

Use of the phrase "within its jurisdiction" thus does not detract from, but rather confirms the understanding that the protection of the Fourteenth Amendment extends to anyone, citizen or stranger, who is subject to the laws of a State, and reaches into every corner of a State's territory. That a person's initial entry into a State or into the United States, was unlawful, and that he may for that reason be expelled, cannot negate the simple fact of his presence within the State's territorial perimeter. Given such presence, he is subject to the full range of obligations imposed by the State's civil and criminal laws. And until he leaves the jurisdiction — either voluntarily, or involuntarily in accordance with the Constitution and the laws of the United States — he is entitled to the equal protection of the laws that a State may choose to establish. . . .

III

. . . We turn to a consideration of the standard appropriate for the evaluation of §21.031.

A

Sheer incapability or lax enforcement of the laws barring entry into this country, coupled with the failure to establish an effective bar to the employment of undocumented aliens, has resulted in the creation of a substantial "shadow population" of illegal migrants — numbering in the millions — within our borders.

This situation raises the specter of a permanent caste of undocumented resident aliens, encouraged by some to remain here as a source of cheap labor, but nevertheless denied the benefits that our society makes available to citizens and lawful residents. The existence of such an underclass presents most difficult problems for a Nation that prides itself on adherence to the principles of equality under law.

The children who are plaintiffs in these cases are special members of this underclass. Persuasive arguments support the view that a State may withhold its beneficence from those whose very presence within the United States is the product of their own unlawful conduct. These arguments do not apply with the same force to classifications imposing disabilities on the minor children of such illegal entrants. At the least, those who elect to enter our territory by stealth and in violation of our law should be prepared to bear the consequences, including, but not limited to, deportation. But the children of those illegal entrants are not comparably situated. Their "parents have the ability to conform their conduct to societal norms," and presumably the ability to remove themselves from the State's jurisdiction; but the children who are plaintiffs in these cases "can affect neither their parents' conduct nor their own status." Trimble v. Gordon, 430 U.S. 762, 770 (1977). Even if the State found it expedient to control the conduct of adults by acting against their children, legislation directing the onus of a parent's misconduct against his children does not comport with fundamental conceptions of justice. . . .

Public education is not a "right" granted to individuals by the Constitution. *San Antonio School District.* But neither is it merely some governmental "benefit" indistinguishable from other forms of social welfare legislation. Both the importance of education in maintaining our basic institutions, and the lasting impact of its deprivation on the life of the child, mark the distinction. The "American people have always regarded education and the acquisition of knowledge as matters of supreme importance." Meyer v. Nebraska, 262 U.S. 390, 400 (1923). We have recognized "the public school as a most vital civic institution for the preservation of a democratic system of government." Abington School District v. Schempp, 374 U.S. 203, 230 (1963) (Brennan, J., concurring), and as the primary vehicle for transmitting "the values on which our society rests." Ambach v. Norwick, 441 U.S. 68, 76 (1979). As noted early in our history, "some degree of education is necessary to prepare citizens to participate effectively and intelligently in our open political system if we are to preserve freedom and independence." Wisconsin v. Yoder, 406 U.S. 205, 221 (1972). And the historic "perceptions of the public schools as inculcating fundamental values necessary to the maintenance of a democratic political system have been confirmed by the observations of social scientists." Ambach v. Norwick, supra, at 77. In addition, education provides the basic tools by which individuals might lead economically productive lives to the benefit of us all. In sum, education has a fundamental role in maintaining the fabric of our society. We cannot ignore the significant social costs borne by our Nation when select groups are denied the means to absorb the values and skills upon which our social order rests.

In addition to the pivotal role of education in sustaining our political and cultural heritage, denial of education to some isolated group of children poses an affront to one of the goals of the Equal Protection Clause: the abolition of governmental barriers presenting unreasonable obstacles to advancement on the basis of individual merit. Paradoxically, by depriving the children of any disfavored group of an education, we foreclose the means by which that group might raise the level of esteem in which it is held by the majority. But more directly, "education prepares individuals to be self-reliant and self-sufficient participants in society." Wisconsin v. Yoder, supra, at 221. Illiteracy is an enduring disability. The inability to read and write will handicap the individual deprived of a basic education each and every day of his life. The inestimable toll of that deprivation on the social, economic, intellectual and psychological well-being of the individual, and the obstacle it poses to individual achievement, makes it most difficult to reconcile the cost or the principle of a status-based denial of basic education with the framework of equality embodied in the Equal Protection Clause. . . .

B

These well-settled principles allow us to determine the proper level of deference to be afforded §21.031. Undocumented aliens cannot be treated as a suspect class because their presence in this country in violation of federal law is not a "constitutional irrelevancy." Nor is education a fundamental right; a State need not justify by compelling necessity every variation in the manner in which education is provided to its population. See San Antonio School Dist. v. Rodriguez. But more is involved in this case than the abstract question whether §21.031 discriminates against a suspect class, or whether education is a fundamental right. Section 21.031 imposes a lifetime hardship on a discrete class of children not accountable for their disabling status. The stigma of illiteracy will mark them for the rest of their lives. By denying these children a basic education, we deny them the ability to live within the structure of our civic institutions, and foreclose any realistic possibility that they will contribute in even the smallest way to the progress of our Nation. In determining the rationality of §21.031, we may appropriately take into account its costs to the Nation and to the innocent children who are its victims. In light of these countervailing costs, the discrimination contained in §21.031 can hardly be considered rational unless it furthers some substantial goal of the State.

IV

Appellants argue that the classification at issue furthers interests in the "preservation of the state's limited resources for the education of its lawful residents." Of course, a concern for the preservation of resources standing alone can hardly justify the classification used in allocating those resources. The State must do more than justify its classification with a concise expression of an intention to discriminate. Apart from the asserted state prerogative to act against undocumented children solely on the basis of their undocumented status — an asserted prerogative that carries only minimal force in the circumstances of this case — we discern three colorable state interests that might support §21.031.

First, appellants appear to suggest that the State may seek to protect the State from an influx of illegal immigrants. While a State might have an interest in mitigating the potentially harsh economic effects of sudden shifts in population, §21.031 hardly offers an effective method of dealing with an urgent demographic or economic problem. There is no evidence in the record suggesting that illegal entrants impose any significant burden on the State's economy. To the contrary, the available evidence suggests that illegal aliens under utilize public services, while contributing their labor to the local economy and tax money to the State fisc. The dominant incentive for illegal entry into the State of Texas is the availability of employment; few if any illegal immigrants come to this country, or presumably to the State of Texas, in order to avail themselves of a free education. Thus, even making the doubtful assumption that the net impact of illegal aliens on the economy of the State is negative, we think it clear that "[c]harging tuition to undocumented children constitutes a ludicrously ineffectual attempt to stem the tide of illegal immigration," at least when compared with the alternative of prohibiting the employment of illegal aliens.

Second, while it is apparent that a state may "not . . . reduce expenditures for education by barring [some arbitrarily chosen class of] children from its schools," Shapiro v. Thompson, 394 U.S. 618, 633 (1969), appellants suggest that undocumented children are appropriately singled out for exclusion because of the special burdens they impose on the State's ability to provide high quality public education in the State. As the District Court noted, the State failed to offer any "credible supporting evidence that a proportionately small diminution of the funds spent on each child [which might result from devoting some State funds to the education of the excluded group] will have a grave impact on the quality of education." And, after reviewing the State's school financing mechanism, the District Court concluded that barring undocumented children from local schools would not necessarily improve the quality of education provided in these schools. Of course, even if improvement in the quality of education were a likely result of barring some *number* of children from the schools of the State, the State must support its selection of *this* group as the appropriate target for exclusion. In terms of educational cost and need, however, undocumented children are "basically indistinguishable" from legally resident alien children.

Finally, appellants suggest that undocumented children are appropriately singled out because their unlawful presence within the United States renders them less likely than other children to remain within the boundaries of the State, and to put their education to productive social or political use within the State. Even assuming that such an interest is legitimate, it is an interest that is most difficult to quantify. The State has no assurance that any child, citizen or not, will employ the education provided by the State within the confines of the State's borders. In any event, the record is clear that many of the undocumented children disabled by this classification will remain in this country indefinitely, and that some will become lawful residents or citizens of the United States. It is difficult to understand precisely what the State hopes to achieve by promoting the creation and perpetuation of a subclass of illiterates within our boundaries, surely adding to the problems and costs of unemployment, welfare, and crime. It is thus clear that whatever savings might be achieved by denying these children an education, they are wholly insubstantial in light of the costs involved to these children, the State, and the Nation.

V

If the state is to deny a discrete group of innocent children the free public education that it offers to other children residing within its borders, that denial must be justified by a showing that it furthers some substantial state interest. No such showing was made here. Accordingly, the judgment of the Court of Appeals in each of these cases is

Affirmed.

[Concurring opinions by Justices Blackmun and Powell have been omitted.]

BURGER, C.J., with whom White, Rehnquist, and O'Connor, JJ., join dissenting.

The dispositive issue in these cases, simply put, is whether, for purposes of allocating its finite resources, a State has a legitimate reason to differentiate between persons who are lawfully within the State and those who are unlawfully there. The distinction the State of Texas has drawn — based not only upon its own legitimate interests but on classifications established by the federal government in its immigration laws and policies — is not unconstitutional.

A

The Court acknowledges that except in those cases when state classifications disadvantage a "suspect class" or impinge upon a "fundamental right," the Equal Protection Clause permits a State "substantial latitude" in distinguishing between different groups of persons. Moreover, the Court expressly — and correctly — rejects any suggestion that illegal aliens are a suspect class, or that education is a fundamental right. Yet by patching together bits and pieces of what might be termed quasi-suspect-class and quasi-fundamental-rights analysis, the Court spins out a theory custom-tailored to the facts of these cases. In the end, we are told little more than that the level of scrutiny employed to strike down the Texas law applies only when illegal alien children are deprived of a public education. If ever a court was guilty of an unabashedly result-oriented approach, this case is a prime example.

1

The Court first suggests that these illegal alien children, although not a suspect class, are entitled to special solicitude under the Equal Protection Clause because they lack "control" over or "responsibility" for their unlawful entry into this country. Similarly, the Court appears to take the position that §21.031 is presumptively "irrational" because it has the effect of imposing "penalties" on "innocent" children. However, the Equal Protection Clause does not preclude legislators from classifying among persons on the basis of factors and characteristics over which individuals may be said to lack "control." Indeed, in some circumstances persons generally, and children in particular, may have little control over or responsibility for such things as their ill-health, need for public assistance, or place of residence. Yet a state legislature is not barred from considering, for example, relevant differences between the mentally-healthy and the mentally-ill, or between the residents of different counties, simply because these may be factors unrelated to individual choice or to any "wrongdoing." The Equal Protection Clause protects against arbitrary and irrational classifications, and against invidious discrimination stemming from prejudice and hostility; it is not an all-encompassing "equalizer" designed to eradicate every distinction for which persons are not "responsible."

The Court does not presume to suggest that appellees' purported lack of culpability for their illegal status prevents them from being deported or otherwise "penalized" under federal law. Yet would deportation be any less a "penalty" than denial of privileges provided to legal residents? Illegality of presence in the United States does not — and need not — depend on some amorphous concept of "guilt" or "innocence" concerning an alien's entry. Similarly, a State's use of federal immigration status as a basis for legislative classification is not necessarily rendered suspect for its failure to take such factors into account.

The Court's analogy to cases involving discrimination against illegitimate children is grossly misleading. The State has not thrust any disabilities upon appellees due to their "status of birth." Cf. Weber v. Aetna Casualty & Surety Co., 406 U.S. 164, 176 (1972). Rather, appellees' status is predicated upon the circumstances of their concededly illegal presence in this country, and is a direct result of Congress' obviously valid exercise of its "broad constitutional powers" in the field of immigration and naturalization. U.S. Const., Art. I, §8, cl. 4; see Takahashi v. Fish & Game Commission, 334 U.S. 410, 419 (1948). This Court has recognized that in allocating governmental benefits to a given class of aliens, one "may take into account the character of the relationship between the alien and this country." Mathews v. Diaz, 426 U.S. 67, 80 (1976). When that "relationship" is a federally-prohibited one, there can, of course, be no presumption that a State has a constitutional duty to include illegal aliens among the recipients of its governmental benefits.

2

The second strand of the Court's analysis rests on the premise that, although public education is not a constitutionally-guaranteed right, "neither is it merely some governmental 'benefit' indistinguishable from other forms of social welfare legislation." Whatever meaning or relevance this opaque observation might have in some or other context, it simply has no bearing on the issues at hand. Indeed, it is never made clear what the Court's opinion means on this score.

The importance of education is beyond dispute. Yet we have held repeatedly that the importance of a governmental service does not elevate it to the status of a "fundamental right" for purposes of equal protection analysis. In *San Antonio School District,* supra, Justice Powell, speaking for the Court, expressly rejected the proposition that state laws dealing with public education are subject to special scrutiny under the Equal Protection Clause. Moreover, the Court points to no meaningful way to distinguish between education and other governmental benefits in this context. Is the Court suggesting that education is more "fundamental" than food, shelter, or medical care? . . .

B

Once it is conceded — as the Court does — that illegal aliens are not a suspect class, and that education is not a fundamental right, our inquiry should focus on and be limited to whether the legislative classification at issue bears a rational relationship to a legitimate state purpose.

The State contends primarily that §21.031 serves to prevent undue depletion of its limited revenues available for education, and to preserve the fiscal integrity of the State's school financing system against an ever-increasing flood of illegal aliens — aliens over whose entry or continued presence it has no control. Of course such fiscal concerns alone could not justify discrimination against a group of persons. Yet I assume no member of this Court would argue that prudent conservation of finite state revenues is per se an illegitimate goal. Indeed, the numerous classifications this Court has sustained in social welfare legislation were invariably related to the limited amount of revenues available to spend on any given program or set of programs. See, e.g., Jefferson v. Hackney, 406 U.S. 535, 549-551 (1972); Dandridge v. Williams, 397 U.S. 471, 487 (1970). The significant question here is whether the requirement of tuition from illegal aliens who attend the public schools — as well as from residents of other States, for example — is a rational and reasonable means of furthering the State's legitimate fiscal ends.

Without laboring what will undoubtedly seem obvious to many, it simply is not "irrational" for a State to conclude that it does not have the same responsibility to provide benefits for persons whose very presence in the State and this country is illegal as it does to provide for persons lawfully present. By definition, illegal aliens have no right whatever to be here, and the State may reasonably, and constitutionally, elect not to provide them with governmental services at the expense of those who are lawfully in the State. In DeCanas v. Bica, 424 U.S. 351, 357 (1976), we held that a State may protect its "fiscal interests and lawfully resident labor force from the deleterious effects on its economy resulting from the employment of illegal aliens." And only recently this Court made clear that a State has a legitimate interest in protecting and preserving the quality of its schools and "the right of its own *bona fide residents* to attend such institutions on a preferential tuition basis." Vlandis v. Kline, 412 U.W. 441, 452-453 (1973) (emphasis added). See also Elkins v. Moreno, 435 U.S. 647, 663-668 (1978). The Court has failed to offer even a plausible explanation why illegality of residence in this country is not a factor that may legitimately bear upon the bona fides of state residence and entitlement to the benefits of lawful residence.

Discussion

Is a community barred from limiting the access of illegal immigrants to the emergency rooms of its public hospitals, or is the rationale of *Plyler* limited to "education"? On what theory might education be selected out for such special constitutional solicitude? Could the state respond to *Plyler* by shutting down all of its public schools?

The Court treats *Plyler* as an equal protection case, as did an earlier Court in Truax v. Raich, p.673, which struck down an Arizona law prohibiting the employment of lawful resident aliens. Might these be better understood as federal preemption cases, that is, assigning to the national government the exclusive responsibility for controlling immigration to the United States and removing from the states any power over the subject?[44] Congress has plenary authority to decide

44. See generally two student notes, The Equal Treatment of Aliens: Preemption or Equal Protection?, 31 Stan. L. Rev. 1069 (1979), and State Burdens on Resident Aliens: A New Preemption Analysis, 89 Yale L.J. 940 (1980). See also Toll v. Moreno, 458 U.S. 1 (1982), discussed in Gerald Gunther, Constitutional Law: Cases and Materials 675-676 (11th ed. 1985).

who enters the United States and, arguably, to decide on the conditions of entry. Congress has not only defined illegal aliens, but by that definition Congress has declared illegal aliens unwelcome and by recent legislation prohibited employers from hiring them. Does this violate the Fifth Amendment's implicit equal protection guarantee? If not, could Congress authorize the states to deny public services (including education) to illegal aliens? See pp. 1392-1405.

KADRMAS v. DICKINSON PUBLIC SCHOOLS, 487 U.S. 450 (1988): [As authorized by a 1979 North Dakota statute, the Dickinson Public Schools charged a fee to children using their bus service. The fee, which covered approximately 11 percent of the cost of providing the service, was $97/year for one child and $150/year for two children. About 13 percent of the district's students rode the buses. State law required certain other school districts (large ones "reorganized" through the consolidation of thinly populated, territorially smaller, districts) to provide free transportation.

Sarita Kadrmas lived approximately 16 miles from her school; her family is at or near the poverty level. In 1985, the Kadrmas family indicated that it could no longer afford the busing fee, and the public school bus stopped taking her to school; the family arranged for private transportation at a cost that proved to be greater than the school bus fee. This arrangement continued until the spring of 1987, when the Kadrmas family signed a contract for bus service from the District.

The Kadrmas family filed suit, claiming that the busing charge violated the equal protection clause. In a 5-4 decision, the Supreme Court denied the claim.]

O'CONNOR, J.

Appellants contend that Dickinson's user fee for bus service unconstitutionally deprives those who cannot afford to pay it of "minimum access to education." Sarita Kadrmas, however, continued to attend school during the time that she was denied access to the school bus. Appellants must therefore mean to argue that the busing fee unconstitutionally places a greater obstacle to education in the path of the poor than it does in the path of wealthier families. Alternatively, appellants may mean to suggest that the Equal Protection Clause affirmatively requires government to provide free transportation to school, at least for some class of students that would include Sarita Kadrmas. Under either interpretation of appellants' position, we are evidently being urged to apply a form of strict or "heightened" scrutiny to the North Dakota statute. Doing so would require us to extend the requirements of the Equal Protection Clause beyond the limits recognized in our cases, a step we decline to take.

[Plaintiffs relied principally on *Plyler*. Justice O'Connor quoted both Justices Powell and Chief Justice Burger in emphasizing *Plyler's* "unique circumstances" and its "unique confluence of theories and rationales." She thus rejected its applicability here:]

Unlike the children in [*Plyler*], Sarita Kadrmas has not been penalized by the government for illegal conduct by her parents. On the contrary, Sarita was denied access to the school bus only because her parents would not agree to pay the same user fee charged to all other families that took advantage of this service. Nor do we see any reason to suppose that this user fee will "promot[e] the creation and perpetuation of a sub-class of illiterates within our boundaries, surely adding to the problems and costs of unemployment, welfare, and crime." . . .

North Dakota does not maintain a legal or practical monopoly on the means of transporting children to school. . . . It is plain that the busing fee in this case more closely resembles the fees that were upheld in *Kras* and *Ortwein* than it resembles the fees that were invalidated in [*Griffin* and *Boddie*]. . . .

Applying the [rationality test,] we think it is quite clear that a State's decision to allow local school boards the option of charging patrons a user fee for bus service is constitutionally permissible. . . . No one denies that encouraging local school districts to provide school bus service is a legitimate state purpose or that such encouragement would be undermined by a rule requiring that general revenues be used to subsidize an optional service that will benefit a minority of the district's families. It is manifestly rational for the State to refrain from undermining its legitimate objective with such a rule.

[Plaintiffs also challenged as irrational the distinction between the "reorganized" districts that were required to provide free transportation and districts like Dickinson. Justice O'Connor responded by quoting the explanation of the North Dakota court that the purpose of the difference "is to encourage school district reorganization with a concomitant tax base expansion and an enhanced and more effective school system. The legislation provides incentive for the people to approve school district reorganization by alleviating parental concerns regarding the costs of student transportation in the reorganized district."

Justice Marshall, joined by Justice Brennan, dissented, asserting that "[a]s in *Plyler*, the State in this case has acted to burden the educational opportunities of a disadvantaged group of children who need an education to become full participants in society." Justice Stevens, joined by Justice Blackmun, also dissented.]

Discussion

The majority in *Kadrmas* insists that *Plyler* is still good law, even though its application is confined to a unique set of circumstances and blend of arguments. What meaning does *Plyler* have after *Kadrmas*? Given changes in the membership of the Supreme Court since 1988, would you advise a state legislature that it was still bound by *Plyler*?

3. *Public Funding of Religious Schools*

The preceding cases concerned constitutional limits on the funding of public schools. Here we consider the limits imposed by the Establishment Clause of the First Amendment on government funding of "private" schools.[45]

45. This section is nowhere close to a full survey of the immensely complicated, indeed many would say garbled and incoherent, law of the establishment clause, or even of the particular application of that clause to the problem of state aid to religious schools. Rather, our purpose is to introduce the problem and provide a basic literacy that students can draw on in further courses on the First Amendment or on religion and the Constitution. We defer until Chapter 12 a full discussion of what allows us to refer to state-funded schools as "private."

COMMITTEE FOR PUBLIC EDUCATION & LIBERTY v. NYQUIST

413 U.S. 756 (1973)

Appeal from the United States District Court for the Southern District of New York

[In 1972, New York established three financial aid programs for nonpublic elementary and secondary schools. Under the first, the state would give direct money grants to "qualifying" schools to be used for the "maintenance and repair of . . . school facilities and equipment to ensure the health, welfare and safety of enrolled pupils." "Qualifying" schools were those that "serv[ed] a high concentration of pupils from low-income families. . . ." This section of the legislation is prefaced by an assertion that the State "has a primary responsiblity to ensure the health, welfare and safety of children attending . . . nonpublic schools" and a finding that the "fiscal crisis in nonpublic education . . . has caused a diminution of proper maintenance and repair programs, threatening the health, welfare and safety of nonpublic school children" in low-income urban areas.

The other two aspects of the legislation consist of tuition grants and a tax benefit program. Parents having annual taxable income under $5,000 could receive limited reimbursement ($50 and $100 for each child attending elementary and high school respectively) for tuition payments to private schools. The legislature had found that the ability to choose among alternative educational programs "is diminished or even denied to children of lower-income families, whose parents, of all groups, have the least options in determining where their children are to be educated." Furthermore, the legislature found that any "precipitious decline in the number of nonpublic school pupils would cause a massive increase in public school enrollment and costs," which would "aggravate an already serious fiscal crisis in public education" and would "seriously jeopardize quality education for all children."

Finally, parents who cannot qualify for tuition reimbursement are provided some state tax relief by allowing them to deduct part of the money expended in private school tuition from their gross income. Taxpayers with less than $9,000 gross income can deduct $1,000 for each of up to three dependents. The deduction diminishes as one goes up the income scale — for example, a taxpayer with $15,000 gross income can deduct only $400 per dependent — and is eliminated at the $25,000 level.

Plaintiff-petitioners challenged the legislation on the ground that religious schools were included among "qualifying" schools. Approximately 20 percent of the New York school population attended nonpublic schools, of which 85 percent were church affiliated, most of these being Roman Catholic, with some Jewish, Lutheran, Episcopal, and Seventh Day Adventist schools as well. The Supreme Court declared all three programs unconstitutional.]

POWELL, J. . . .

II

The history of the Establishment Clause has been recounted frequently and need not be repeated here. See Everson v. Board of Education, 330 U.S. 1 (1947); McCollum v. Board of Education, 333 U.S. 203, 212 (1948) (separate opinion of Frankfurter, J.); McGowan v. Maryland, 366 U.S. 420 (1961); Engel v. Vitale, 370 U.S. 421 (1962). It is enough to note that it is now firmly established that a law may be one "respecting an establishment of religion" even though its consequence is not to promote a "state religion," Lemon v. Kurtzman, 403 U.S. 602, 612 (1971), and even though it does not aid one religion more than another but merely benefits all religions alike. It is equally well established, however, that not every law that confers an "indirect," "remote," or "incidental" benefit upon religious institutions is, for that reason alone, constitutionally invalid. What our cases require is careful examination of any law challenged on establishment grounds with a view to ascertaining whether it furthers any of the evils against which that Clause protects. Primary among those evils have been "sponsorship, financial support, and active involvement of the sovereign in religious activity." Walz v. Tax Commissioner, 397 U.S. 664, 668 (1970) [upholding tax exemptions granted to religious institutions].

. . . [A] now well-defined three-part test . . . has emerged from our decisions. . . . [T]o pass muster under the Establishment Clause the law in question, first, must reflect a clearly secular legislative purpose, second, must have a primary effect that neither advances nor inhibits religions, and third, must avoid excessive government entanglement with religion.

In applying these criteria to the three distinct forms of aid involved in this case, we need touch only briefly on the requirement of a "secular legislative purpose." . . . [E]ach measure is adequately supported by legitimate, nonsectarian state interests. We do not question the propriety, and fully secular content, of New York's interest in preserving a healthy and safe educational environment for all of its schoolchildren. And we do not doubt . . . the validity of the State's interests in promoting pluralism and diversity among its public and nonpublic schools. Nor do we hesitate to acknowledge the reality of its concern for an already overburdened public school system that might suffer in the event that a significant percentage of children presently attending nonpublic schools should abandon those schools in favor of the public schools. . . .

A

The "maintenance and repair" provisions . . . authorize direct payments to nonpublic schools, virtually all of which are Roman Catholic schools in low-income areas. The grants, totaling $30 or $40 per pupil depending on the age of the institution, are given largely without restriction on usage. . . . No attempt is made to restrict payments to those expenditures related to the upkeep of facilities used exclusively for secular purposes, nor do we think it possible within the context of these religion-oriented institutions to impose such restrictions. Nothing in the statute, for instance, bars a qualifying school from paying out of state funds the salaries of employees who maintain the school chapel, or the cost of renovating classrooms in which religion is taught, or the cost of heating and lighting those same facilities. Absent appropriate restrictions on expenditures for these and similar purposes, it simply cannot be denied that this section has a primary effect that advances religion in that it subsidizes directly the religious activities of sectarian elementary and secondary schools.

The state officials nevertheless argue that these expenditures for "maintenance and repair" are similar to other financial expenditures approved by this Court. Primarily they rely on Everson v. Board of Education, supra; Board of Education v. Allen, 392 U.S. 236 (1968); and Tilton v. Richardson, 403 U.S. 672 (1971). In each of those cases it is true that the Court approved a form of financial assistance which conferred undeniable benefits upon private, sectarian schools. But a close examination of those cases illuminates their distinguishing characteristics. In *Everson,* the Court, in a five-to-four decision, approved a program of reimbursements to parents of public as well as parochial schoolchildren for bus fares paid in connection with transportation to and from school, a program which the Court characterized as approaching the "verge" of impermissible state aid. In *Allen,* decided some 20 years later, the Court upheld a New York law authorizing the provision of *secular* textbooks for all children in grades seven through 12 attending public and nonpublic schools. Finally, in *Tilton,* the Court upheld federal grants of funds for the construction of facilities to be used for clearly *secular* purposes by public and nonpublic institutions of higher learning.

. . . *Tilton* draws the line most clearly. While a bare majority was there persuaded . . . that carefully limited construction grants to colleges and universities could be sustained, the Court was unanimous in its rejection of one clause of the federal statute in question. Under that clause, the Government was entitled to recover a portion of its grant to a sectarian institution in the event that the constructed facility was used to advance religion by, for instance, converting the building to a chapel or otherwise allowing it to be "used to promote religious interests." But because the statute provided that the condition would expire at the end of 20 years, the facilities would thereafter be available for use by the institution for any sectarian purpose. [The Court struck down the expiration provision.] If tax-raised funds may not be granted to institutions of higher learning where the possibility exists that those funds will be used to construct a facility utilized for sectarian activities 20 years hence, *a fortiori* they may not be distributed to elementary and secondary sectarian schools for the maintenance and repair of facilities without any limitations on their use. If the State may not erect buildings in which religious activities are to take place, it may not maintain such buildings or renovate them when they fall into disrepair. . . .

New York's maintenance and repair provisions violate the Establishment Clause because their effect, inevitably, is to subsidize and advance the religious mission of sectarian schools. We have no occasion, therefore, to consider the further question whether those provisions as presently written would also fail to survive scrutiny under the administrative entanglement aspect of the three-part test because assuring the secular use of all funds requires too intrusive and continuing a relationship between Church and State.

B

New York's tuition reimbursement program also fails the "effect" test, for much the same reasons that govern its maintenance and repair grants. . . .

There can be no question that these grants could not, consistently with the Establishment Clause, be given directly to sectarian schools. . . . The controlling question here, then, is whether the fact that the grants are delivered to parents rather than schools is of such significance as to compel a contrary result. The State and intervenor-appellees rely on *Everson* and *Allen* for their claim that grants to parents, unlike grants to institutions, respect the "wall of separation" required by the Constitution. It is true that in those cases the Court upheld laws that provided benefits to children attending religious schools and to their parents. . . . But . . . the fact that aid is disbursed to parents rather than to the schools is only one among many factors to be considered.

In *Everson*, the Court found the bus fare program analogous to the provision of services such as police and fire protection, sewage disposal, highways, and sidewalks for parochial schools. Such services, provided in common to all citizens, are "so separate and so indisputably marked off from the religious function" that they may fairly be viewed as reflections of a neutral posture toward religious institutions. *Allen* is founded upon a similar principle. The Court there repeatedly emphasized that upon the record in that case there was no indication that textbooks would be provided for anything other than purely secular courses. . . .[a]

The tuition grants here are subject to no such restrictions. There has been no endeavor "to guarantee the separation between secular and religious educational functions and to ensure that State financial aid supports only the former." Indeed, it is precisely the function of New York's law to provide assistance to private schools, the great majority of which are sectarian. By reimbursing parents for a portion of their tuition bill, the State seeks to relieve their financial burdens sufficiently to assure that they continue to have the option to send their children to religion-oriented schools. And while the other purposes for that aid — to perpetuate a pluralistic educational environment and to protect the fiscal integrity of overburdened public schools — are certainly unexceptionable, the effect of the aid is unmistakably to provide desired financial support for nonpublic, sectarian institutions.[b]

. . . [W]e will address briefly the subsidiary arguments made by the state officials and intervenors in [defense of the tuition grant program].

First, it has been suggested that it is of controlling significance that New York's program calls for *reimbursement* for tuition already paid rather than for direct contributions which are merely routed through the parents to the schools, in advance of or in lieu of payment by the parents. The parent is not a mere conduit,

a. *Allen* and *Everson* differ from the present litigation in a second important respect. In both cases the class of beneficiaries included *all* schoolchildren, those in public as well as those in private schools. . . . We do not agree with the suggestion in the dissent of [Chief Justice Burger] that tuition grants are an analogous endeavor to provide comparable benefits to all parents of schoolchildren whether enrolled in public or nonpublic schools. The grants to parents of private school children are given in addition to the right that they have to send their children to public schools "totally at state expense." And in any event, the argument proves too much, for it would also provide a basis for approving through tuition grants the *complete subsidization* of all religious schools on the ground that such action is necessary if the State is fully to equalize the position of parents who elect such schools — a result wholly at variance with the Establishment Clause.

Because of the manner in which we have resolved the tuition grant issue, we need not decide whether the significantly religious character of the statute's beneficiaries might differentiate the present cases from a case involving some form of public assistance (e.g., scholarships) made available generally without regard to the sectarian-nonsectarian, or public-nonpublic nature of the institution benefited. Thus, our decision today does not compel, as appellees have contended, the conclusion that the educational assistance provisions of the "G.I. Bill" impermissibly advance religion in violation of the Establishment Clause.

b. Appellees, focusing on the term "principal or primary effect" which this Court has utilized in expressing the second prong of the three-part test have argued that the Court must decide in these cases whether the "primary" effect of New York's tuition grant program is to subsidize religion or to promote these legitimate secular objectives. . . . We do not think that such metaphysical judgments are either possible or necessary. Our cases simply do not support the notion that a law found to have a "primary" effect to promote some legitimate end under the State's police power is immune from further examination to ascertain whether it also has the direct and immediate effect of advancing religions. . . .

[S]ecular objectives, no matter how desirable and irrespective of whether judges might possess sufficiently sensitive calipers to ascertain whether the secular effects outweigh the sectarian benefits, cannot serve . . . to justify . . . a direct and substantial advancement of religion.

we are told, but is absolutely free to spend the money he receives in any manner he chooses. . . .

[However,] if the grants are offered as an incentive to parents to send their children to sectarian schools by making unrestricted cash payments to them, the Establishment Clause is violated whether or not the actual dollars given eventually find their way into the sectarian institutions. Whether the grant is labeled a reimbursement, a reward, or a subsidy, its substantive impact is still the same. . . .

Second, [it is argued] that it is significant here that the tuition reimbursement grants pay only a portion or the tuition bill, and an even smaller portion of the religious school's total expenses. The New York statute limits reimbursement to 50% of any parent's actual outlay. Additionally, intervenor estimates that only 30% of the total cost of nonpublic education is covered by tuition payments, with the remaining coming from "voluntary contribution, endowments and the like." On the basis of these two statistics, appellees reason that the "maximum tuition reimbursement by the State is thus only 15% of educational costs in the nonpublic schools." And, since the compulsory education laws of the State, by necessity require significantly more than 15% of school time to be devoted to teaching secular courses," the New York statute provides "a statistical guarantee of neutrality." . . . Our cases, however, have long since foreclosed the notion that mere statistical assurances will suffice to sail between the Scylla and Charybdis of "effect" and "entanglement."

Finally, the State argues that its program of tuition grants should survive scrutiny because it is designed to promote the free exercise of religion. The State notes that only "low-income parents" are aided by this law, and without state assistance their right to have their children educated in a religious environment "is diminished or even denied." It is true, of course, that this Court has long recognized and maintained the right to choose nonpublic over public education. Pierce v. Society of Sisters, 268 U.S. 510 (1925). It is also true that a state law interfering with a parent's right to have his child educated in a sectarian school would run afoul of the Free Exercise Clause. But this Court repeatedly has recognized that tension inevitably exists between the Free Exercise and the Establishment Clauses and that it may often not be possible to promote the former without offending the latter. As a result of this tension, our cases require the State to maintain an attitude of "neutrality," neither "advancing" nor "inhibiting" religion. In its attempt to enhance the opportunities of the poor to choose between public and nonpublic education, the State has taken a step which can only be regarded as one "advancing" religion. However great our sympathy for the burdens experienced by those who must pay public school taxes at the same time that they support other schools because of the constraints of "conscience and discipline," and notwithstanding the "high social importance" of the State's purposes, neither may justify an eroding of the limitations of the Establishment Clause now firmly emplanted.

C

[The final provisions of the New York legislation] establish a system for providing income tax benefits to parents of children attending New York's nonpublic schools. . . .

In practical terms there would appear to be little difference, for purposes of determining whether such aid has the effect of advancing religion, between the tax benefit allowed here and the tuition grant [invalidated in the previous section of the opinion]. . . .

[A]ppellees place their strongest reliance on Walz v. Tax Commission, in which New York's property tax exemption for religious organizations was upheld. We think that *Walz* provides no support for appellees' position. Indeed, its rationale plainly compels the conclusion that New York's tax package violates the Establishment Clause.

Tax exemptions for church property enjoyed an apparently universal approval in this country both before and after the adoption of the First Amendment. . . . We know of no historical precedent for New York's recently promulgated tax relief program. Indeed, it seems clear that tax benefits for parents whose children attend parochial schools are a recent innovation, occasioned by the growing financial plight of nonpublic institutions. . . .

But historical acceptance without more would not alone have sufficed, as "no one acquires a vested or protected right in violation of the Constitution by long use." It was the reason underlying that long history of tolerance of tax exemptions for religion that proved controlling. A proper respect for both the Free Exercise and the Establishment Clauses compels the State to pursue a course of "neutrality" toward religion. . . . Special tax benefits . . . cannot be squared with the principle of neutrality established by the decisions of this Court. To the contrary, insofar as such benefits render assistance to parents who send their children to sectarian schools, their purpose and inevitable effect are to aid and advance those religious institutions.

Apart from its historical foundations, *Walz* is a product of the same dilemma and inherent tension found in most government-aid-to-religion controversies. To be sure, the exemption of church property from taxation conferred a benefit, albeit a direct and incidental one. Yet that "aid" was a product not of any purpose to support or to subsidize, but of a fiscal relationship designed to minimize involvement and entanglement between Church and State. "The exemption," the Court emphasized, "tends to complement and reinforce the desired separation insulating each from the other." Furthermore, "[e]limination of the exemption would tend to expand the involvement of government by giving rise to tax valuation of church property, tax liens, tax foreclosures, and the direct confrontations and conflicts that follow in the train of those legal processes." The granting of the tax benefits under the New York statute, unlike the extension of an exemption, would tend to increase rather than limit the involvement beween Church and State.

One further difference between tax exemptions for church property and tax benefits for parents should be noted. The exemption challenged in *Walz* was not restricted to a class composed exclusively or even predominantly of religious institutions. Instead, the exemption covered all property devoted to religious, educational, or charitable purposes. As the parties here must concede, tax reductions authorized by this law flow primarily to the parents of children attending sectarian, nonpublic schools. Without intimating whether this factor might have controlling significance in another context in some future case, it should be apparent that in terms of the potential divisiveness of any legislative measure the narrowness of the benefited class would be an important factor. . . .

III

Because we have found that the challenged sections have the impermissible effect of advancing religion, we need not consider whether such aid would result in entanglement of the State with religion in the sense of "[a] comprehensive, discriminating, and continuing state surveillance." Lemon v. Kurtzman, 403 U.S., at 619. But the importance of the competing societal interests implicated here prompts us to make the further observation that, apart from any specific entanglement of the State in particular religious programs, assistance of the sort here involved carries grave potential for entanglement in the broader sense of continuing political strife over aid to religion. . . .

One factor of recurring significance . . . is the potentially divisive political effect of an aid program. . . .

In this situation, where the underlying issue is the deeply emotional one of Church-State relationships, the potential for seriously divisive political consequences needs no elaboration. And while the prospect of such divisiveness may not alone warrant the invalidation of state laws that otherwise survive the careful scrutiny required by the decisions of this Court, it is certainly a "warning signal" not to be ignored.

Our examination of New York's aid provisions, in light of all relevant considerations, compels the judgment that each, as written, has a "primary effect that advances religion" and offends the constitutional prohibition against laws "respecting an establishment of religion." . . .

BURGER, C.J., joined in part by Justice White and joined by Justice Rehnquist, concurring in part and dissenting in part.

[The Chief Justice agreed that the "maintenance and repair" provision was unconstitutional "because it is a direct aid to religion," but he would have upheld the other two aspects of the program under precedents such as *Everson, Allen,* and *Walz.*]

It is admittedly difficult to articulate the reasons why a State should be permitted to reimburse parents of private school children — partially at least — to take into account the State's enormous savings in not having to provide schools for those children, when a State is not allowed to pay the same benefit directly to sectarian schools on a per-pupil basis. . . . The answer, I believe, lies in the experienced judgment of various members of this Court over the years that the balance between the policies of free exercise and establishment of religion tips in favor of the former when the legislation moves away from direct aid to religious institutions and takes on the character of general aid to individual families. This judgment reflects the caution with which we scrutinize any effort to give official support to religion and the tolerance with which we treat general welfare legislation. . . .

The tuition grant and tax relief programs now before us are, in my view, indistinguishable in principle, purpose, and effect from the statutes in *Everson* and *Allen*. . . . [T]he States have merely attempted to equalize the costs incurred by parents in obtaining an education for their children. The only discernible difference between the programs in *Everson* and *Allen* and these cases is in the method of the distribution of benefits: here the particular benefits . . . are given only to parents of private school children, while in *Everson* and *Allen* the statutory benefits were made available to parents of both public and private school children. But to regard that difference as constitutionally meaningful is to exalt form over substance. . . . [New York's statute] is no more than simple equity to grant partial relief to parents who support the public schools they do not use. . . .

However sincere our collective protestations of the debt owed by the public generally to the parochial school systems, the wholesome diversity they engender will not survive on expressions of good will.

[Justice White joined this opinion only as it related to the tuition grant and tax relief statute.]

REHNQUIST, C.J., and Justice White concur, dissenting in part.

[Justice Rehnquist dissented from the invalidation of the tuition reimbursement and tax benefit provisions:]

Here the effect of the tax benefit is trebly attenuated as compared with the outright exemption considered in *Walz*. There the result was a complete forgiveness of taxes, while here the result is merely a reduction in taxes. There the ultimate benefit was available to an actual house of worship, while here even the ultimate benefit redounds only to a religiously sponsored school. There the churches themselves received the direct reduction in the tax bill, while here it is only the parents of the children who are sent to religiously sponsored schools who receive the direct benefit. . . .

[Justice Rehnquist also emphasized the similarity of New York's plan to those upheld in *Everson* and *Allen* and justified them as similar exercises in "benevolent neutrality."]

The reimbursement and tax benefit plans today struck down, no less than the plans in *Everson* and *Allen*, are consistent with the principle of neutrality. New York has recognized that parents who are sending their children to nonpublic schools are rendering the State a service by decreasing the costs of public education and by physically relieving an already overburdened public school system. Such parents are nonetheless compelled to support public school services unused by them and to pay for their own children's education. Rather than offering "an incentive to parents to send their children to sectarian schools," as the majority suggests, New York is effectuating the secular purpose of the equalization of the cost of educating New York children that are borne by parents who send their children to nonpublic schools. As in *Everson* and *Allen*, the impact, if any, on religious education from the aid granted is significantly diminished by the fact that the benefits go to the parents rather than to the institutions. . . .

WHITE, J., joined in part by the Chief Justice and Justice Rehnquist, dissenting.

[Justice White would have upheld the New York statute in its entirety.]

About 10% of the Nation's children, approximately 5.2 million students, . . . are not being educated in public schools at public expense. [Elsewhere in his opinion, Justice White notes that of these 5.2 million, approximately 4.4 million (83 percent of the total) are enrolled in Roman Catholic schools. As of 1986, of a total of approximately 45.5 million children enrolled in elementary or secondary schools, approximately 5.6 million were enrolled in nonpublic schools.[46] In 1986 the reported enrollment of students in Catholic schools was approximately 2.43 million.[47]] Under state law these children have a right to a free public education and it would not appear unreasonable if the State, relieved of the expense of educating a child in the public school, contributed to the expense of his education elsewhere. The parents of such children pay taxes, including school taxes. They could receive in return a free education in the public schools. They prefer to send their children, as they have the right to do, to nonpublic schools that furnish the satisfactory equivalent of a public school education but also offer subjects or other assumed advantages not available in public schools. Constitutional considerations aside, it would be understandable if a State gave such parents a call on the public treasury up to the amount it would have cost the State to educate the child in public school, or, to put it another way, up to the amount the parents save the State by not sending their children to public school.

In light of the Free Exercise Clause of the First Amendment, this would seem particularly the case where the parent desires his child to attend a school that offers not only secular subjects but religious training as well. A State should put no unnecessary obstacles in the way of religious training for the young. . . .

[Justice White also notes a declining enrollment in nonpublic schools as of 1973, in part because of severe financial pressures.] Whatever the reasons, there has been, and there probably will continue to be, a movement to the public schools, with the prospect of substantial increases in public school budgets that are already under intense attack and with the States and cities that are primarily involved already facing severe financial crises. It is this prospect that has prompted some of these States to attempt, by a variety of devices, to save, or slow the demise of, the nonpublic school system, an educational resource that could deliver quality education at a cost to the public substantially below the per-pupil cost of the public schools.

There are, then, the most profound reasons . . . for this Court to proceed with the utmost care in deciding these cases. It should not, absent a clear mandate in the Constitution, invalidate these [statutes] and thereby not only scuttle state efforts to hold off serious financial problems in their public schools but also make it more difficult, if not impossible, for parents to follow the dictates of their conscience and seek a religious as well as secular education for their children.

. . . No one contends that he can discern from the sparse language of the Establishment Clause that a State is forbidden to aid religion in any manner whatsoever or, if it does not mean that, what kind of or how much aid is permissible. And one cannot seriously believe that the history of the First Amendment furnishes unequivocal answers to many of the fundamental issues of church-state relations. In the end, the courts have fashioned answers to these questions as best they can, the language of the Constitution and its history having left them a wide range of choice among many alternatives. But decision has been unavoidable; and, in choosing, the courts necessarily have carved out what they deemed to be the most desirable national policy governing various aspects of church-state relationships.

46. See Statistical Abstract of the United States 1989, p.128 (No. 207. Elementary and Secondary Schools — Enrollment and Teachers, by Type of Control, 1960 to 1987, and Projections, 1990 and 1995).

47. Id. at 142 (No. 234. Catholic Elementary and Secondary Schools: 1960 to 1987).

. . . I . . . have little difficulty in accepting the New York maintenance grant, which does not and could not, by its terms, approach the actual repair and maintenance cost incurred in connection with the secular education services performed for the State in parochial schools. . . .

At the very least I would not strike down these statutes on their face. The Court's opinion emphasizes a particular kind of parochial school, one restricted to students of particular religious beliefs and conditioning attendance on religious study. Concededly, there are many parochial schools that do not impose such restrictions. Where they do not, it is even more difficult for me to understand why the primary effect of these statutes is to advance religion. . . .

DOUGLAS LAYCOCK, A SURVEY OF RELIGIOUS LIBERTY IN THE UNITED STATES, 47 Ohio St. L.J. 409, 443-449 (1986): Government aid to religious schools has been on the Supreme Court's docket almost continuously since 1968. The Court has been unwilling either to ban all such aid or to permit all such aid. Instead, it has groped for a compromise formulation that would permit some aid but not too much. At least six inconsistent theories have been endorsed by one or more justices. . . . The result has been a series of inconsistent and almost inexplicable decisions.

1. The Possible Theories

The no-aid theory. One plausible view is the no-aid theory: that any state money paid to a religious school or its students expands the school's budget and thereby aids religion. Even if the state's money is used to buy math books, that frees some of the school's money to spend on religion, or it enables the school to lower tuition and make it easier for children to attend a religious school. . . .

The purchase-of-services theory. A second plausible view is the purchase-of-services theory: that state money paid to a religious school is simply a purchase of educational services. The state is obligated [by its constitution] to provide a free education for all its children; it can do so directly or through independent contractors. As long as the state does not pay more than the costs of the secular education provided, it is simply paying for services rendered and not subsidizing religion. . . .

The equal-treatment theory. A third plausible view is the equal-treatment theory. In its strong form, it holds that the government is obligated to pay for the secular aspects of education in religious schools; in its weak form, it holds that government is free to make such payments if it wishes.

Children have a constitutional right to attend religious schools. If they do not exercise that right and attend public schools, the state will be required to spend substantial sums on their education. If they do exercise their constitutional right, they forfeit the state subsidy of their education. This can plausibly be viewed as a penalty on the exercise of their constitutional right. . . .

The equal-treatment theory relies on the principle that government cannot discriminate against religion, which is as basic as the principle that the government cannot support religion. . . .

The child-benefit theory. A fourth plausible view of the school aid issue is the child-benefit theory: that the state can provide educational benefits directly to children or their parents, even if the benefits are used at or in connection with a religious school. But the state cannot provide the same aid directly to the school. . . .

Proponents of the no-aid theory note that aid to a school and aid to the students in that school are economically equivalent: either makes it less expensive for students to attend the school. But others have found it symbolically important that the aid goes to the child rather than to the school. Directly the aid to the child may be seen as a symbolic affirmation of the purchase-of-services or equal-treatment theory, emphasizing that these programs provide education as well as religion. . . .

The tracing theory. A fifth view of the school aid issue has attracted the Court, but it is only superficially plausible. Under the tracing theory the Court tries to divide all the activities of a religious school into components that are wholly secular and components that are, or might be, affected by religion. Then it tries to trace each dollar of government money to see what the school spent it on. The Court approves aid if, and only if, the money can be traced to a wholly secular expenditure. . . . [T]his approach cannot be applied consistently. The task of dividing school activities into secular and religious components is conceptually impossible; the whole purpose of such schools is to integrate secular and religious education. . . .

The little-bit theory. The Court occasionally alludes to a sixth theory, which may explain more of the Court's results than the theories it relies on more often. This is the theory that a little bit of aid to religious schools is permissible, but it must be structured in a way that keeps it from becoming too much. . . .

2. The Court's Results

It is hardly a surprise that this mix of theories has not produced coherent results. The variety of theories and the attempt to distinguish the indistinguishables in the tracing theory have produced distinctions that do not commend themselves to common sense.

Thus, bus transportation to and from school is permitted, *Everson,* supra, but bus transportation on field trips is forbidden[, Wolman v. Walter, 433 U.S. 229 (1977)]. Why? Because the teacher might discuss religion on the field trip. Thus, under the tracing theory, the bus ride to school is wholly secular, but the field trip might not be.

The state can loan secular textbooks to students in religious schools [*Allen,*] but it cannot loan maps, projectors, or other instructional materials [*Wolman*]. The child-benefit theory might have reconciled these holdings, because each child needs his own textbook but only the school needs maps and projectors. But that is not what the Court said. Rather, it decided the first textbook cases on a combination of child-benefit and tracing theories; then it decided the instructional materials case on the theory that any aid to the school helps religion. The Court noted that its approach to books was inconsistent with its approach to other instructional materials, but it declined to reconcile the cases. Even more strange in the very opinion [*Wolman*] in which it adopted the no-aid theory for instructional materials, it used the tracing theory to allow state-administered tests in religious schools.

The Court also used the tracing theory to hold that guidance counseling, remedial instruction, and other therapeutic services are permissible if provided by public school teachers *away* from the religious school campus [*Wolman*] but not if provided by public school teachers *on* the religious school campus[, Aguilar v. Felton, 473 U.S. 402 (1985); Grand Rapids School District v. Ball, 473 U.S. (1985)]. Why? Because the public school teachers might be influenced by the religious environment and inadvertently discuss religion with their students; that danger is insubstantial away from the religious school. However, diagnostic services are permissible even on the religious school campus because the diagnostician will not spend enough time with any one student to develop a relationship. Without a relationship he is unlikely to talk religion [*Wolman*]. . . .

The tracing theory also produced paradoxical results with respect to teacher salaries and testing expenses. The state cannot pay fifteen percent of the salary of teachers who teach secular subjects in religious schools[, *Lemon*]. It cannot pay religious schools for the cost of conducting state-mandated testing if the religious school teachers design and grade the test [Levitt v. Committee for Public Educ. and Religious Liberty, 413 U.S. 472 (1973)]. In neither case could the money be traced to wholly secular uses, because the teachers might include religious material in their classes or on the exams, even in secular subjects. But the state is permitted to administer required tests to religious school students and grade the tests itself[, *Wolman*]. State designed and administered tests present no danger of religious content; they are wholly secular.

Does it follow that the state can pay the school to administer objective secular tests designed by the state? The Court said yes [Committee for Public Education & Religious Liberty v. Regan, 444 U.S. 646 (1980)]. There was no risk of testing religious content, and paying the school to administer the tests was no more a subsidy than having the state administer the tests directly. Either approach relieved the school of the expenses. On the same rationale, the state could require religious schools to take attendance and pay for the expense of doing so. In each case the expense consisted of part of the teachers' time; the state paid as much as 5.4% of faculty payroll under this program. So, it turns out that, with enough red tape, the state can pay part of the salaries of teachers after all. The state need only identify wholly secular job components and the time required to perform them, and pay the school for that time. This carried the tracing theory to its fictional extreme. And this decision came after the Court rejected the tracing theory with respect to instructional materials.

In 1983, Mueller v. Allen[, 463 U.S. 388 (1983),] held that state income tax *deductions* for the expenses of sending children to religious schools are permissible. But ten years earlier, Committee for Public Education and Religious Liberty v. Nyquist[, 413 U.S. 756 (1973),] held that state income tax *credits* for the expenses of sending children to religious schools are forbidden. What is the difference? The Court said that the tax credits in *Nyquist* were dovetailed with a scholarship program for low income students, making it clear that the tax credits were themselves a thinly disguised scholarship. In addition, the credit applied to private school tuition only. The tax deduction in *Mueller* also applied to transportation and supply expenses, which could be claimed by parents of public school children, and to tuition payments by the handful of children attending public schools outside their own district.

Those were real differences, but they were not very significant. Again, a theory shift was more important. *Nyquist* was written on the tracing theory, or perhaps on the no-aid theory. Scholarships and tax credits were invalid under either theory because once the students paid the money to the school it went into general revenues and could not be traced. But in *Mueller* the Court emphasized the child-benefit theory and the equal-treatment theory. The Court thought it important that the tax savings went to parents instead of religious schools, and that parents decided independently whether to send their children to public or private schools. The state was not required to discriminate against religion by denying a deduction available to parents of public school children. It was irrelevant that ninety-six perent of the deductions were in fact claimed by parents of children in Catholic and Lutheran schools. This was a break with earlier cases in which the Court had thought it significant that most private schools were religious[, Meek v. Pittenger, 421 U.S. 349 (1975)]. . . .

Whatever the Court said, a comparison of tax deductions and tax credits suggests consistent application of the little-bit theory. There is no structural limit on a tax credit; a state could allow a credit for 100% of private school tuition. But a deduction can never be worth more than the private school's tuition multiplied by the state's marginal tax rate; and most state income tax rates are quite low. . . .

These tax deduction and tax credit cases also highlight an inconsistency in public perception of the issues, and probably in judicial perception as well. Tax deductions for tuition paid to religious schools are widely perceived as a form of aid that at least raise serious questions under the establishment clause. Yet tax deductions for gifts to the same schools, or to churches themselves for purely religious purposes, are widely perceived as raising no problem. It is hard to believe that both perceptions can be correct. The breadth of the charitable deduction offers weak ground for distinction, because a tuition tax deduction is always a small part of a state's efforts to finance, encourage, and subsidize education. The long-standing familiarity of the charitable contribution deduction, and the novelty of tuition deductions, explain but do not justify the differences in constitutional perception.

Many commentators thought that *Mueller's* approval of tuition tax deductions indicated a substantial shift in direction. . . . But in 1985, in Grand Rapids v. Ball and Aguilar v. Felton the Court returned to the tracing theory to strike down supplemental courses in religious schools. The political context highlights the majority's [including "liberals" like Justices Brennan and Marshall] aversion to substantial aid: *Aguilar* struck down federally funded remedial instruction for impoverished children. The Court again thought it significant that most private schools receiving the aid were religious schools. . . .

Discussion

Recall that Justice Brennan wrote a vigorous dissent in the abortion funding case, Harris v. McRae, supra. How can Justice Brennan comfortably accept Justice Powell's reading of neutrality (and noncoercion) in *Nyquist*? Consider Professor Michael McConnell's "revised" version of Justice Brennan's dissent in *Harris*. McConnell illustrates the putative contradictions in Justice Brennan's different treatment of the issues by changing the issue in *Harris* from abortion funding to the funding of a religious-based education equal to the education given by the state to citizens who conform to the state's desire to educate children in public schools:[48]

48. Michael W. McConnell, The Selective Funding Problem: Abortions and Religious Schools, 104 Harv. L. Rev. 989, 990 (1991).

> A poor woman [with school-age children] confronts two alternatives: she may elect either to [send them to secular schools] or to [send them to religious schools]. In the abstract, of course, the choice is hers alone, and the Court rightly observes that [*Lemon*] "places no governmental obstacle in the path of a woman who chooses to [send her children to religious school]." But the reality of the situation is that [the Supreme Court in its decisions] has effectively removed this choice from the indigent woman's hands. By funding all of the expenses associated with [secular education] and none of the expenses incurred in [religious education,] the Government literally makes an offer that the indigent woman cannot afford to refuse. It matters not that in this instance the Government has used the carrot rather than the stick. What is critical is the realization that as a practical matter, many poverty-stricken women will choose to [send their children to secular schools] simply because the Government provides funds for [this,] even though these same women would have chose [religious schools] if the Government had also paid for that option, or indeed if the Government had stayed out of the picture altogether and had defrayed the costs of neither.

Consider also the implications of Justice Brennan's dissent in *DeShaney,* in which he emphasized the consequences of state decisions for private decisionmaking. Does not the burden of state taxation to fund public education make it difficult even for non-indigent families to afford private secular and parochial education? Is this constitutionally relevant?

D. A Concluding Problem: Food Stamps and the Constitution

The federal food stamp program provides an in-kind income supplement for the poor as well as a subsidy for the farmers producing the food. By 1988 the annual outlay for food stamps was $12.3 billion.[49] The program has been the source of some constitutional litigation. In Department of Agriculture v. Moreno, 413 U.S. 528 (1973), the Court considered a 1971 amendment to the Food Stamp Act that excluded from participation in the food stamp program any member of a household whose members are not all related to each other. Although there is good reason to believe that Congress was attempting to prevent "hippie communes" from receiving any stamps, the plaintiffs in the case were not hippies. For example, one was a person with an acute hearing deficiency who, in order to live near a special school for the deaf, was sharing an apartment with someone on public assistance. Because they were not related, they became ineligible for the food stamps they would have received had they lived separately. Justice Brennan wrote for the Court invalidating the exclusion on the ground that it did not serve any valid legislative purpose and thus created an "irrational classification in violation of the equal protection component of the Due Process Clause of the Fifth Amendment." Justice Douglas concurred on the ground that the regulation unconstitutionally interfered with rights of association. Justice Rehnquist, joined by Chief Justice Burger, dissented, arguing that the regulation was rationally related to assuring that a household exists for some purpose other than collecting federal food stamps.

49. Budget of the United States Government, Fiscal Year 1990, 9-40.

LYNG v. INTERNATIONAL UNION, UNITED AUTO WORKERS

485 U.S. 360 (1988)

Appeal from the United States Court of Appeals for the District of Columbia Circuit

[In 1984, Congress amended the Food Stamp Act to provide that no household shall become eligible to receive food stamps while any one of its members is on strike. If the household was already receiving food stamps, its allotment would not be increased by virtue of the striker's unemployment. A congressional committee report estimated that this measure would save a total of about $165 million in fiscal years 1982, 1983, and 1984. As the Court observed, "It would be difficult to deny that this statute works at least some discrimination against strikers and their households. For the duration of the strike, those households cannot increase their allotment of food stamps even though the loss of income occasioned by the strike may well be enough to qualify them for food stamps or to increase their allotment if the fact of the strike itself were ignored."

The court below had declared the amendment unconstitutional on three different grounds. Two were based on the First Amendment: The amended act interfered with strikers' rights to associate with their families and unions as well as to express themselves freely about union matters by striking. The third was predicated on the "equal protection component of the Due Process Clause of the Fifth Amendment."]

WHITE, J.

A

The challenge to the statute based on the associational rights asserted by appellees is foreclosed by . . . Lyng v. Castillo, 477 U.S. 635 (1986). There we considered a constitutional challenge to the definition of "household" in the Food Stamp Act, which treats parents, siblings, and children who live together, but not more distant relatives or unrelated persons who do so, as a single household for purposes of defining eligibility for food stamps. Although the challenge in that case was brought solely on equal protection grounds, and not under the First Amendment, the Court was obliged to decide whether the statutory classification should be reviewed under a stricter standard than mere rational-basis review because it " 'directly and substantially' interfere[s] with family living arrangements and thereby burden[s] a fundamental right." The Court held that it did not, explaining that the definition of "household" does not "order or prevent any group of persons from dining together. Indeed, in the overwhelming majority of cases it probably has no effect at all. It is exceedingly unlikely that close relatives would choose to live apart simply to increase their allotment of food stamps, for the costs of separate housing would almost certainly exceed the incremental value of the additional stamps."

The same rationale applies in this case. . . .

The statute also does not infringe the associational rights of appellee individuals and their unions. . . . It does not "order" appellees not to associate together for the purpose of conducting a strike, or for any other purpose, and it does not "prevent" them from associating together or burden their ability to do so in any significant manner. . . .

Any impact on associational rights in this case results from the Government's refusal to extend food stamp benefits to those on strike, who are now without their wage income. Denying such benefits makes it harder for strikers to maintain themselves and their families during the strike and exerts pressure on them to abandon their union. Strikers and their union would be much better off if food stamps were available, but the strikers' right of association does not require the Government to furnish funds to maximize the exercise of that right. . . . Exercising the right to strike inevitably risks economic hardship, but we are not inclined to hold that the right of association requires the Government to minimize that result by qualifying the striker for food stamps. . . .

B

For the same reasons, we cannot agree that [the Amendment] abridges appellees' right to express themselves about union matters free of coercion by the Government. . . . It merely declines to extend additional food stamp assistance to striking individuals merely because the decision to strike inevitably leads to a decline in their income. And this Court has explicitly stated that even where the Constitution prohibits coercive governmental interference with specific individual rights, it " 'does not confer an entitlement to such funds as may be necessary to realize all the advantages of that freedom.' " Regan v. Taxation with Representation of Washington, 461 U.S. 540, 550 (1983), quoting Harris v. McRae, 448 U.S. 297, 318 (1980).

III

Because the statute challenged here has no substantial impact on any fundamental interest and does not "affect with particularity any protected class," we confine our consideration to whether the statutory classification "is rationally related to a legitimate governmental interest." Department of Agriculture v. Moreno, 413 U.S. 528, 533 (1973). . . .

The Government submits that this statute serves three objectives. Most obvious . . . is to cut federal expenditures. Second, the limited funds available were to be used where the need was likely to be greatest, an approach which Congress thought did not justify food stamps for strikers. Third was the concern that the food stamp program was being used to provide one-sided support for labor strikes; the Senate Report indicated that the amendment was intended to remove the basis for that perception and criticism.

We have little trouble in concluding that [the amendment] is rationally related to the legitimate governmental objective of avoiding undue favoritism to one side or the other in private labor disputes. . . .

Congress was in a difficult position when it sought to address the problems it had identified. Because a striking individual faces an immediate and often total drop in income during a strike, a single controversy pitting an employer against its employees can lead to a large number of claims for food stamps for as long as the controversy endures. It is the disbursement of food stamps in response to such a controversy that constitutes the sources of the concern, and of the dangers to the program, that Congress believed it was important to remedy. We are not free in this instance to reject Congress' views about "what constitutes wise economic or social policy." Dandridge v. Williams, 397 U.S. 471, 486 (1970).

It is true that in terms of the scope and extent of their ineligibility for food stamps, [the amendment] is harder on strikers than on "voluntary quitters."[a] But the concern about neutrality in labor disputes does not arise with respect to those who, for one reason or another, simply quit their jobs. As we have stated in a related context, even if the statute "provides only 'rough justice,' its treatment . . . is far from irrational." Ohio Bureau of Employment Services v. Hodory, 431 U.S. 471 491 (1977).[50]

. . . [W]e are not authorized to ignore Congress' considered efforts to avoid favoritism in labor disputes, which are evidenced also by the two significant provisos contained in the statute. The first proviso preserves eligibility for the program of any household that was eligible to receive stamps "immediately prior to such strike." The second proviso makes clear that the statutory ineligibility for food stamps does not apply "to any household that does not contain a member of strike, if any of its members refuses to accept employment at a plant or site because of a strike or lockout." In light of all this, the statute is rationally related to the stated objective of maintaining neutrality in private labor disputes.

In view of the foregoing, we need not determine whether either of the other two proffered justifications for [the amendment] would alone suffice. . . .

Appellees contend and the District Court held that the legislative classification is irrational because of the "critical" fact that it "impermissibly strikes at the striker through his family." This, however, is nothing more than a description of how the food stamp program operates as a general matter. . . . Whenever an individual takes any action that hampers his or her ability to meet the program's eligibility requirements, such as quitting a job or failing to comply with the work-registration requirements, the entire household suffers accordingly. . . . That aspect of the program does not violate the Constitution. . . .

MARSHALL, J., joined by Justices Brennan and Blackmun, dissenting:

. . . After canvassing the many absurdities that afflict the striker amendment, I conclude that it fails to pass constitutional muster under even the most deferential scrutiny. . . .

I

. . . The Court fails to note [that the rational basis] standard of review, although deferential, " 'is not a toothless one.' " Mathews v. De Castro, 429 U.S. 181, 185 (1976), quoting Mathews v. Lucas, 427 U.S. 495, 510 (1976). . . .

A

The Secretary's argument that the striker amendment will save money proves far too much. According to the Secretary's reasoning, the exclusion of any un-

a. For example, one who voluntarily quits a job is disqualified for food stamps for 90 days. Thereafter, he is eligible as long as he registers for work and cannot find a job. The striker, unless he quits his job, is disqualified for as long as he is on strike.

50. An Ohio statute denied unemployment compensation benefits to workers thrown out of work because of a labor dispute, so long as they weren't "locked out" by employers. Hodory, a nonstriking employee of a parent company that shut down after a subsidiary went on strike, was denied unemployment compensation because of this statute. The Supreme Court upheld the denial, holding that it did not violate the equal protection clause.

popular group from a public benefit program would survive rational basis scrutiny, because exclusion always would result in a decrease in governmental expenditures. . . . [T]his Court expressly has noted that "a concern for the preservation of resources standing alone can hardly justify the classification used in allocating those resources." Plyler v. Doe, 457 U.S. 202, 227. We have insisted that such classifications *themselves* be rational rather than arbitrary. . . .

B

Perhaps recognizing this necessity, the Secretary defends the singling out of strikers and their households as rationally related to the goal of channeling resources to those persons most " 'genuinely in need.' " As a threshold matter, however, households denied food stamps because of the presence of a strike are as "needy" in terms of financial resources as households that qualify for food stamps: the former are denied food stamps *despite* the fact that they meet the financial eligibility requirements [of federal law], even after strike-fund payments are counted as household income. This point has particular poignancy for the infants and children of a striking worker. Their need for nourishment is in no logical way diminished by the striker's action. The denial to these children of what is often the only buffer between them and malnourishment and disease cannot be justified as a targeting of the most needy: they *are* the most needy. The record below bears witness to this point in a heartbreaking fashion.

The Secretary argues, however, that the striker amendment is related to need at least in the sense of willingness to work, if not in the strict sense of financial eligibility. Because the Food Stamp Act generally excludes persons unwilling to work — and their households — the Secretary argues that it is consistent to exclude strikers and their households as well, on the ground that strikers remain "unwilling to work," at least at the struck business, for the duration of the strike. In the Secretary's eyes, a striker is akin to an unemployed worker who day after day refuses to accept available work. One flaw in this argument is its false factual premise. It is simply not true, as the Secretary argues, that a striker always has a job that "remains available to him." Many strikes result in the complete cessation of a business's operations, so that the decision of an individual striker to return to work would be unavailing. Moreover, many of the businesses that continue to operate during a strike hire permanent replacements for the striking workers. In this situation as well, a striker no longer has the option of returning to work. In fact, the record in this case reveals that a number of appellees were denied food stamps even though they had been permanently replaced by their employers.

But even if it were true that strikers always can return to their jobs, the Secretary's "willingness to work" rationale falls apart in light of the glaring disparity between the treatment of strikers and the treatment of those who are unwilling to work for other reasons. People who voluntarily quit their jobs are not disqualified from receiving food stamps if, after notice and hearing, they can demonstrate that they quit with "good cause." Moreover, even if the state agency determines that the quit was without good cause, the voluntary quitter is disqualified only for a period of 90 days, and the quitter's household is disqualified only if the quitter was the "head of household." In contrast, a striker is given no opportunity to demonstate that the strike was for "good cause," even though strikers frequently allege that unfair labor practices by their employer precipitated the strike. In addition, strikers and their entire households, no matter how minimal the striker's contribution to the household's income may have been, are disqualified for the duration of the strike, even if the striker is permanently replaced or business operations temporarily cease.

In a similar vein, the striker amendment expressly distinguishes between strikers and non-strikers in conditioning eligibility for food stamps on willingness to accept struck work. Unemployed workers may refuse to accept otherwise appropriate employment at a business involved in a strike or a lockout and still remain eligible to receive food stamps — as long as they are not themselves on strike. Only strikers, though they may be as "willing to work" in every salient respect, must give up their eligibility for food stamps if they refuse to cross a picket line. The Secretary's "willingness to work" argument provides no justification for this especially harsh treatment of strikers and their households.

C

Unable to explain completely the striker amendment by the "willingness to work" rationale, the Secretary relies most heavily on yet a third rationale: the promotion of governmental neutrality in labor disputes. Indeed, the Court relies solely on this explanation in rejecting appellees' Equal Protection challenge to the amendment. . . .

[T]he "neutrality" argument . . . is both deceptive and deeply flawed. Even on the most superficial level, the striker amendment does not treat the parties to a labor dispute evenhandedly: forepersons and other management employees who may become temporarily unemployed when a business ceases to operate during a strike remain eligible for food stamps. Management's burden during the course of the dispute is thus lessened by the receipt of public funds, whereas labor must struggle unaided. This disparity cannot be justified by the argument that the strike is labor's "fault," because strikes are often a direct response to illegal practices by management, such as failure to abide by the terms of a collective bargaining agreement or refusal to bargain in good faith.

On a deeper level, the "neutrality" argument reflects a profoundly inaccurate view of the relationship of the modern federal government to the various parties to a labor dispute. Both individuals and businesses are connected to the government by a complex web of supports and incentives. On the one hand, individuals may be eligible to receive a wide variety of health, education, and welfare-related benefits. On the other hand, businesses may be eligible to receive a myriad of tax subsidies through deductions, depreciation, and credits or direct subsidies in the form of government loans through the Small Business Administration (SBA). Businesses also may receive lucrative government contracts and invoke the protections of the Bankruptcy Act against their creditors. None of these governmental subsidies to businesses is made contingent on the businesses' abstention from labor disputes, even if a labor dispute is the direct cause of the claim to a subsidy. For example, a small business in need of financial support because of labor troubles may seek a loan from the SBA. And a business that claims a net operating loss as a result of a strike or a lockout presumably may carry the loss back three years and forward five years in order to maximize its tax advantage. In addition, it appears that businesses may be eligible for special tax credits for hiring replacement workers during a strike under the targeted Jobs Tax Credit program. When viewed against the network of governmental support of both labor and management, the withdrawal of the single support of food stamps — a support critical to the continued life and health of an individual worker and his or her family — cannot be seen as a "neutral" act. Altering the backdrop of governmental support in this one-sided and devastating way amounts to a penalty on strikers, not neutrality.

D

The successive failure of each of the Secretary's purported rationales for the striker amendment . . . suggests that the enactment at issue here rests on public animus toward strikers. This conclusion draws substantial support from the legislative history of the precursors of the 1981 amendment. Beginning in 1968, four years after the enactment of the Food Stamp Act, Congress considered at regular intervals proposals similar or identical to the striker amendment eventually passed in 1981. Such proposals were considered and rejected in 1968, 1970, 1971, 1972, 1973, 1974, and 1977. Each time a proposal was discussed on the floor of the House, representatives decried the "anti-union" and "anti-strike" animus that motivated it. In 1977, the House Committee on Agriculture reviewed the history of such proposals and rejected the most recent one, explaining its decision as follows:

> The real purpose of the amendment . . . was not to restore some government neutrality allegedly lost because strikers are eligible for food stamps but, on the contrary, to use a denial of food stamps as a pressure on the worker — or more accurately on his family — to help break a strike. . . .
>
> The amendment was an effort to increase the power of the management over workers, using food as a weapon in collective bargaining.

I am mindful that the views expressed on the floor of the House and in the 1977 Committee Report were from those opposed to the striker amendment. But the evidence of animus is not limited to statements by the amendment's opponents. Rather, supporters of the striker amendment likened strikers to "hippies" and "commune residents" — groups whose exclusion from the food stamp program this Court struck down fifteen years ago in Department of Agriculture v. Moreno, 413 U.S. 528, (1973). . . . Our warning in *Moreno* that "a bare congressional desire to harm a politically unpopular group cannot constitute a legitimate governmental interest," would seem directly applicable to the instant case. . . .

Note: On "Neutrality"

Both the majority and the dissenters in *Lyng*, *Nyquist*, and other cases throughout this chapter seem to share the assumptions that neutrality is a meaningful term of analysis and that neutrality goes far toward upholding a policy challenged under the establishment or equal protection clause. Which way does neutrality cut in *Lyng*, however? Is allowing strikers to receive food stamps partisan on their behalf, or does the disallowance throw the power of the state against strikers in a nonneutral manner by removing their eligibility for social welfare benefits that would otherwise be available?

These questions raise two more fundamental issues. First, do we have a jurisprudential or political theory that identifies a given constellation of social arrangements as "neutral"? And even if so, to what extent does the Constitution require those who control the apparatus of state power to constrain their partisanship when passing legislation or otherwise engaging in the business of governance?

Professor Sunstein suggests that we tend to identify as neutral those social practices that have sufficient longevity to be perceived as normal within the society.[51] Thus, throughout much of the nineteenth century, the ostensible norms of the common law were perceived to establish a baseline of vested rights in property holders that were protected against innovative legislation that redistributed the existing arrangements of legal rights. During the *Lochner* era, these arrangements were often treated as property or liberty interests protected by the Constitution. But, of course, a central tenet of modern political analysis is that any given status quo represents little, if anything, more than the congealed social power of dominant social groups at a particular time. That is, there is nothing neutral about any existing assignment of legal rights or entitlements, for all are attempts to privilege one sector of society or another.

Professor Sunstein aptly describes *Lochner* as "for more than a half-century, the most important" single case in terms of defining the central questions of contemporary constitutional theory. The questions raised in that case haunt the discussion in *Lyng*, despite the surprising shifts in the political complexion of the proponents of the various positions.

Justice Peckham did not question the existence of a state's police power; instead, he suggested that the law limiting bakers' hours had been "passed from other motives" than "protecting the public health and welfare." Peckham viewed the legislation as an attempt by the state to redistribute power from employers to employees. According to Sunstein, "the Court's concern was that maximum hour legislation was partisan rather than neutral — selfish rather than public-regarding. It was neutrality that the Due Process clause commanded, and neutrality was served only by the general or 'public purposes' comprehended by the police power." The absence of such purposes made the legislation subject to invalidation "as impermissibly partisan — what might now be called special-interest legislation."

Justice Harlan, though dissenting, did not reject Peckham's basic analysis so much as challenge the assertion that the law was not a valid means to the end of protecting public health. There is no reason to believe that Harlan would have accepted the legislative purpose of redistributing bargaining power from employers to employees. Both Peckham and Harlan, according to Sunstein, accept the basic premise that efforts to redistribute resources were constitutionally questionable and outside the permitted range of the police power. "[R]egulatory power was largely limited to the redress of harms recognized at common law," such as causing injury to one's health. "This limitation of the category of permis-

51. See Cass Sunstein, Lochner's Legacy, 87 Colum. L. Rev. 873 (1987), a masterful synthesis of a critical tradition going back at least to some of the legal realists of the 1920s. All of the quotations below from Sunstein are taken from this article.

sible ends had important implications, excluding a wide range of measures enacted by majorities."

Justice Holmes' famous dissent is written from an entirely different point of view. Sunstein writes that it "is a rejection of neutrality altogether. It comes close to modern interest-group pluralism, which treats the political process as an unprincipled struggle among self-interested groups for social resources. Under this view, *Lochner's* means-end scrutiny, examining whether there is a 'public' and hence neutral justification for the statute is difficult to understand." Sunstein describes Holmes' vision of a political process "as a kind of civil war, in which the powerful succeed."

Indeed, Holmes had earlier written in The Common Law that "[t]he first requirement of a sound body of law is, that it should correspond with the actual feelings and demands of the community, whether right or wrong."[52] Similarly, in introducing Montesquieu's Spirit of the Laws, Holmes asked his readers, "What proximate text of excellence can be found except correspondence to the actual equilibrium of force in the community — that is, conformity to the wishes of the dominant power?"[53] All of this underlies Holmes' injunction in *Lochner* that the Constitution should not be read to prevent "the natural outcome of a dominant opinion."

Standard wisdom has it that *Lochner* has long since been consigned to the doctrinal ash-heap left by the post-1937 Supreme Court. It has been the recipient of judicial scorn from all sides of the political spectrum, and almost all contemporary writers on the Constitution agree that it was wrongly decided.[54] But Professor Sunstein suggests that in important ways "*Lochner* has hardly been overruled." To understand his point one must ask what precisely was wrong with the decision. Was it the crabbed application of the standards required of the state to justify its activity under the police power? Or, on the other hand, was it the implication that a court might legitimately strike down legislation that it did not believe was in the public interest or was motivated by the illegitimate purpose of redistributing power or wealth from the haves to the have nots?

Return to *Lyng* once more and assume that Justice Marshall is correct that the amendment is rooted in antiunion animus. So what? After all, proponents might well have justified the amendment by reference to some notion of the general public interest that is disserved by unions' having "too much" power. But imagine a group of remarkably forthright proponents of the amendment who openly reject the meaningfulness of a discourse conducted in the language of "neutrality," "public interest," "partisanship," and the like. Instead, in the spirit of Holmes, they describe labor and management as two contending groups in the never-ending struggle that is pluralist politics. They indicate that they prefer management, and they have the votes to write that preference into law. Assuming that the burdened group has not been accorded the status of a "suspect class" in equal protection analysis, what constitutional problem does this present?

Finally, consider Professor Pope's remark that "[d]uring the 1950's the Supreme Court all but withdrew constitutional protection from labor picketing and stood by while a host of lower courts resolved the 'momentous question' of

52. The Common Law 36 (Howe ed., 1963).

53. Collected Legal Papers 258 (1920).

54. There are, however, exceptions, of whom the most prominent is Professor Richard Epstein of the University of Chicago. See Takings: Private Property and the Law of Eminent Domain 5 (1985).

the constitutional right to strike by summarily denying its existence."[55] What constitutional theory supports a right to strike? One of President Reagan's first actions as President was to fire several thousand members of the airline traffic controllers union for violating federal law by striking. If a legislature may prohibit public employees from striking, then what is the problem with a law prohibiting strikes in the private sector?

Do labor strikes have a sufficient impact on the national economy to justify regulation or even an outright ban? If the right to strike is *not* constitutionally protected, a legislature could presumably criminalize strikes and authorize the imprisonment of strikers. So why can't Congress choose the lesser sanction of depriving strikers (and their families) of food stamps? If there *is* a constitutionally protected right to strike, what is its source? Would the right extend to public as well as private employees, at least in the absence of a countervailing government interest?

55. James Gray Pope, Labor and the Constitution: From Abolition to Deindustrialization, 65 Tex. L. Rev. 1071 (1987). Professor Pope advocates the recognition of a constitutional right to strike, as did Archibald Cox, Strikes, Picketing and the Constitution, 4 Vand. L. Rev. 574 (1951).

Chapter 12
The Reach of the Constitution: The State Action Dilemma

I. Introduction

The distinction between government and the individual is fundamental to American constitutional theory — and to the ways most Americans ordinarily think about political matters. Almost without exception (but see the Thirteenth Amendment), the provisions of the Constitution are addressed to governmental entities and officials.[1] The central focus of the constitutional provisions concerned with individual rights and liberties is to protect against governmental infringement of the rights of the individual. A moment's reflection reveals differences between the restricted latitude of the government to deal with the citizenry and the broad liberties enjoyed by citizens in their dealings with each other. For example, the First Amendment precludes the state from expressing any views at all on certain matters, such as the truth of particular religious doctrines, and state officials may not pick and choose who may speak in public parks based on the acceptability of the speakers' views. By the same token, the First Amendment protects the right of individuals to be passionately committed to particular viewpoints and to use all resources at their disposal to promote them. It would be bizarre to expect a citizen to be as indifferent to deeply contentious public issues as we sometimes require the state to be. Reinforcing this distinction, the language used to grasp this aspect of our experienced social lives usually includes a contrast between the "private" and the "public" realm, with the Constitution ostensibly regulating only the latter and, indeed, carving out "private" realms (religious belief, contraception, and the like) for protection from government regulation. (Henceforth, we omit the quotation marks, but the clarity and even the meaningfulness of these concepts are central questions of this chapter.)

Despite the emphasis on the division, the boundaries separating the public and private sectors have never been neat or static. As government has increasingly involved itself in what was formerly the private sector, either through regulation (Chapter 5) or the assumption of direct social welfare responsibilities (Chapter 11), traditional lines have often been obscured, if not indeed obliterated. Recall, for example, the discussion in Chapter 11 about what conditions the state can place on persons or institutions that accept public funds. One central topic of the present chapter is the extent to which recipients of public funds and other privileges become subject to certain of the constraints that the Constitution imposes

1. See Larry Alexander and Paul Horton, Whom Does the Constitution Command: A Conceptual Analysis with Practical Implications (1988).

on the state. For example, does a hospital's acceptance of public funds, without more, entail that it comes under the antidiscrimination injunctions of the Fourteenth Amendment? A federal appeals court answered yes, and the Supreme Court saw no reason to review the decision.[2] However, complications immediately arise: Does the fact that a nursing home receives most of its funding from Medicaid reimbursement require that it must accord its patients due process as required of government by the Fourteenth Amendment? The Supreme Court answered in the negative.[3]

The previous paragraph addressed the implications of state involvement, through funding, in the affairs of a private entity. And we shall also address another aspect of the state action dilemma: What if the decisions of private entities take on a certain level of public import? How indeed do we recognize the difference between the public state and private entities? Sociologists, for example, often define the state as that social entity that has a legal monopoly over the means of violence or other power of profound social concern. But what if an institution denominated private in fact exercises some measure of significant power in society? Does it thereby take on sufficient attributes of the state to bring it under constitutional constraint? To what extent is it significant that the legislature could, if it wished, exercise the state's regulatory power to limit or even prohibit the conduct of private entities? Is state nonregulation sufficient to trigger an attribution of "state action"? Some analysts would describe this as a public decision to allocate decisionmaking authority to private parties and that in some circumstances (but which?) their actions take on the character of state law for purposes of the Fourteenth Amendment.

This chapter explores the reach of the Constitution — the circumstances in which an arguably private actor is defined as sufficiently "public" to become subject to constitutional constraints. You should, incidentally, be aware of the possibility that a putatively private entity might itself on occasion claim constitutional rights against governmental regulation even as it is being held in other situations to constitute the government against which *other* private entities and individuals may claim constitutional rights.

The controversy over the reach of the Constitution has centered on the Fourteenth Amendment, and especially the equal protection clause: "No State shall . . . deny to any person within its jurisdiction the equal protection of the laws." In the Civil Rights Cases, 109 U.S. 3 (1883), Chapter 4 supra, which struck down the Civil Rights Act of 1875 on the ground that the Fourteenth Amendment did not empower Congress to prohibit racial discrimination by innkeepers, railroads, and places of public amusement, Justice Bradley wrote, "It is State action of a particular character that is prohibited. Individual invasion of individual rights is not the subject-matter of the amendment. . . . [The amendment does not come into operation] until some State law has been passed, or some State action through its officers or agents has been taken. . . ."

This interpretation of the amendment was not inevitable. In dissent, Justice Harlan argued that the businesses covered by the Act were "agents" or "instrumentalities" of the state, performing "quasi-public functions." Moreover, the

2. See Simkins v. Moses H. Cone Memorial Hospital, 323 F.2d 959 (4th Cir.), cert. denied, 376 U.S. 938 (1964).

3. See Blum v. Yaretsky, 457 U.S. 991 (1982), discussed infra.

amendment might have been read to treat a state's failure to prevent discrimination by private entities as a denial of equal protection. Indeed, other parts of Bradley's opinion suggest this interpretation. But ambiguities that inhered in the Civil Rights Cases about the conceptualization of state action were resolved over time in favor of requiring some kind of active encouragement of the conduct in question. Passive acquiescence in the defendant's exercise of presumptively discretionary choices would not count as "state action."

The Civil Rights Cases involved the constitutionality of congressional implementing legislation under section 5 of the Fourteenth Amendment. Most of the subsequent cases have involved the amendment in its *self-executing* mode; that is, they have involved claims under section 1 of the amendment, independent of any implementing congressional statute, that a party has been denied equal protection or deprived of liberty or property without due process of law.

Concluding a survey of judicial decisions and scholarly commentary on the state action issue, Professor Charles Black wrote:

> Taking it as a whole, what we see exhibited is a "doctrine" without shape or line. The doctrine-in-chief is a slogan from 1883. The sub-doctrines are nothing but discordant suggestions. The whole thing has the flavor of a torchless search for a way out of a damp echoing cave. . . . The commentary confirms the inference we would draw from the decisions. The field is a conceptual disaster area; most constructive suggestions come down, one way or another, to the suggestion that attention shift from the inquiry after "state action" to some other inquiry altogether.[4]

There are several explanations for this situation. First, the doctrines of state action are not entirely independent of the substantive social issues at stake. The bulk of the decisions involve racial discrimination, and the modern Court has assumed a special responsibility for eradicating at least its most blatant forms. The Court pursued this mission largely without legislative assistance until the mid-1960s, when Congress enacted the Civil Rights Act of 1964, the Voting Rights Act of 1965, and the Fair Housing Act of 1968. If the Court's post-World War II expansion of the scope of the Fourteenth Amendment is explicable in terms of this mission, the more restrictive decisions of more recent times can be understood partly as deference to congressional determinations of the reach of national antidiscrimination policy. State action decisions in nonracial areas may reflect the Court's sympathy, or lack of sympathy, with the substantive constitutional interests asserted.

Second, the state action doctrine may respond to at least three interests or concerns, which may be more or less present in particular cases.

1. *Federalism.* The doctrine may serve to protect the autonomous sphere of state power against the incursion of national power, whether exercised by Congress or the judiciary.

2. *Individual autonomy.* The doctrine may serve to protect the sphere of individual autonomy against the incursion of government power. Justice Douglas, who consistently sought to expand the reach of the Fourteenth Amendment, nonetheless acknowledged the interest in protecting the right of individuals and groups to discriminate: "The associational rights which our system honors permit

4. Charles Black, "State Action," Equal Protection and California's Proposition 14, 81 Harv. L. Rev. 69, 95 (1967).

all white, all black, all brown, and all yellow clubs to be formed. . . . Government may not tell a man or woman who his or her associates must be. The individual can be as selective as he desires." Moose Lodge No. 107 v. Irvis, 407 U.S. 163 (1972) (dissenting opinion), infra.

3. *Separation of powers.* As applied to the self-executing aspects of the amendment, the doctrine may serve to protect the domains of legislative policymaking from incursions by the judiciary.

The characterization of action as "state" or "private" is at most a highly intuitive hermeneutic enterprise that attempts to capture generally held social and political norms of the time. At worst, it is a way of masking the fact that the distinction makes no sense in our legal culture — and of manipulating the outcomes of decisions in order to achieve covert substantive goals. The main agenda of this chapter is to understand how the interpretive enterprise might work and to see whether the worst is true.

II. The Interweaving of State and Society

BURTON v. WILMINGTON PARKING AUTHORITY

365 U.S. 715 (1961)

Appeal from the Supreme Court of Delaware

CLARK, J.

In this action for declaratory and injunctive relief it is admitted that the Eagle Coffee Shoppe, Inc., a restaurant located within an off-street automobile parking building in Wilmington, Delaware, has refused to serve appellant food or drink solely because he is a Negro. The parking building is owned and operated by the Wilmington Parking Authority, an agency of the State of Delaware, and the restaurant is the Authority's lessee. Appellant claims that such refusal abridges his rights under the Equal Protection Clause of the Fourteenth Amendment to the United States Constitution. The Supreme Court of Delaware has held that Eagle was acting in "a purely private capacity" under its lease; that its action was not that of the Authority and was not, therefore, state action within the contemplation of the prohibitions contained in that Amendment. . . .

The Authority . . . is "a public body corporate and politic, exercising public powers of the State as an agency thereof." Its statutory purpose is to provide adequate parking facilities for the convenience of the public. . . . To this end the Authority is granted wide powers including that of constructing or acquiring by lease, purchase or condemnation, lands and facilities, and that of leasing "portions of any of its garage buildings or structures for commercial use by the lessee, where, in the opinion of the Authority, such leasing is necessary and feasible for the financing and operation of such facilities.". . . Any and all property owned or used by the Authority is likewise exempt from state taxation. . . .

Before it began actual construction of the facility, the Authority was advised by its retained experts that the anticipated revenue from the parking of cars and proceeds from sale of its bonds would not be sufficient to finance the construction costs of the facility. Moreover, the bonds were not expected to be marketable if payable solely out of parking revenues. To secure additional capital . . . the Authority decided it was necessary to enter long-term leases with responsible tenants for commercial use of some of the space available in the projected "garage building." The public was invited to bid for these leases.

In April 1957 such a private lease, for 20 years and renewable for another 10 years, was made with Eagle Coffee Shoppe, Inc., for use as a "restaurant, dining room, banquet hall, cocktail lounge and bar and for no other use and purpose." The multi-level space of the building which was let to Eagle, although "within the exterior walls of the structure, has no marked public entrance leading from the parking portion of the facility into the restaurant proper. . . ." Upon completion of the building, the Authority located at appropriate places thereon official signs indicating the public character of the building, and flew from mastheads on the roof both the state and national flags. . . .

The Civil Rights Cases "embedded in our constitutional law" the principle "that the action inhibited by the first section [equal protection clause] of the Fourteenth Amendment is only such action as may fairly be said to be that of the States. That Amendment erects no shield against merely private conduct, however discriminatory or wrongful." Chief Justice Vinson in Shelley v. Kraemer, 334 U.S. 1, 13 (1948). It was language in the opinion in the Civil Rights Cases, that phrased the broad test of state responsibility under the Fourteenth Amendment, predicting its consequence upon "State action of every kind . . . which denies . . . the equal protection of the laws." And only two Terms ago, some 75 years later, the same concept of state responsibility was interpreted as necessarily following upon "state participation through any arrangement, management, funds or property." Cooper v. Aaron, 358 U.S. 1, 4 (1958). It is clear, as it always has been since the Civil Rights Cases, that "Individual invasion of individual rights is not the subject-matter of the amendment," and that private conduct abridging individual rights does no violence to the Equal Protection Clause unless to some significant extent the State in any of its manifestations has been found to have become involved in it. Because the virtue of the right to equal protection of the laws could lie only in the breadth of its application, its constitutional assurance was reserved in terms whose imprecision was necessary if the right were to be enjoyed in the variety of individual-state relationships which the Amendment was designed to embrace. For the same reason, to fashion and apply a precise formula for recognition of state responsibility under the Equal Protection Clause is an "impossible task" which "This Court has never attempted." Only by sifting facts and weighing circumstances can the nonobvious involvement of the State in private conduct be attributed its true significance.

. . . [T]he opinion of the Supreme Court as well as that of the Chancellor presents the facts in sufficient detail for us to determine the degree of state participation in Eagle's refusal to serve petitioner. In this connection the Delaware Supreme Court seems to have placed controlling emphasis on its conclusion, as to the accuracy of which there is doubt, that only some 15% of the total cost of the facility was "advanced" from public funds; that the cost of the entire facility was allocated three-fifths to the space for commercial leasing and two-fifths to parking space; that anticipated revenue from parking was only some 30.5% of the total income, the balance of which was expected to be earned by the leasing; that the Authority had no original intent to place a restaurant in the building, it being only a happenstance resulting from the bidding; that Eagle expended considerable moneys on furnishings; that the restaurant's main and marked public entrance is on Ninth Street without any public entrance direct from the parking area; and that "the only connection Eagle has with the public facility . . . is the furnishing of the sum of $28,700 annually in the form of rent which is used by the Authority to defray a portion of the operating expense of an otherwise unprofitable enterprise." While these factual considerations are indeed validly accountable aspects of the enterprise upon which the State has embarked, we cannot say that they lead inescapably to the conclusion that state action is not present. Their persuasiveness is diminished when evaluated in the context of other factors which must be acknowledged.

The land and building were publicly owned. As an entity, the building was dedicated to "public uses" in performance of the Authority's "essential governmental functions." The costs of land acquisition, construction, and maintenance are defrayed entirely from donations by the City of Wilmington, from loans and revenue bonds and from the proceeds of rentals and parking services out of which the loans and bonds were payable. Assuming that the distinction would be significant, the commercially leased areas were not surplus state property, but constituted a physically and financially integral and, indeed, indispensable part of the State's plan to operate its project as a self-sustaining unit. Upkeep and maintenance of the building, including necessary repairs, were responsibilities of the Authority and were payable out of public funds. It cannot be doubted that the peculiar relationship of the restaurant to the parking facility in which it is located confers on each an incidental variety of mutual benefits. Guests of the restaurant are afforded a convenient place to park their automobiles, even if they cannot enter the restaurant directly from the parking area. Similarly, its convenience for diners may well provide additional demand for the Authority's parking facilities. Should any improvements effected in the leasehold by Eagle become part of the realty, there is no possibility of increased taxes being passed on to it since the fee is held by a tax-exempt government agency. Neither can it be ignored, especially in view of Eagle's affirmative allegation that for it to serve Negroes would injure its business, that profits earned by discrimination not only contribute to, but also are indispensable elements in, the financial success of a governmental agency.

Addition of all these activities, obligations and responsibilities of the Authority, the benefits mutually conferred, together with the obvious fact that the restaurant is operated as an integral part of a public building devoted to a public parking service, indicates that degree of state participation and involvement in discriminatory action which it was the design of the Fourteenth Amendment to condemn. . . . As the Chancellor pointed out, in its lease with Eagle the Authority could have affirmatively required Eagle to discharge the responsibilities under the Fourteenth Amendment imposed upon the private enterprise as a consequence of state participation. But no State may effectively abdicate its responsibilities by either ignoring them or by merely failing to discharge them whatever the motive may be. It is of no consolation to an individual denied the equal protection of the laws that it was done in good faith. . . . By its inaction, the Authority, and through it the State, has not only made itself a party to the refusal of service, but has elected to place its power, property and prestige behind the admitted discrimination. The State has so far insinuated itself into a position of interdependence with Eagle that it must be recognized as a joint participant in the challenged activity, which, on that account, cannot be considered to have been so "purely private" as to fall without the scope of the Fourteenth Amendment.

Because readily applicable formulae may not be fashioned, the conclusions drawn from the facts and circumstances of this record are by no means declared as universal truths on the basis of which every state leasing agreement is to be tested. Owing to the very "largeness" of government, a multitude of relationships might appear to some to fall within the Amendment's embrace, but that, it must be remembered, can be determined only in the framework of the peculiar facts or circumstances present. Therefore respondents' prophecy of nigh universal application of a constitutional precept so peculiarly dependent for its invocation upon appropriate facts fails to take into account "Differences in circumstances [which] beget appropriate differences in law." Specifically defining the limits of our inquiry, what we hold today is that when a State leases public property in the manner and for the purpose shown to have been the case here, the proscriptions of the Fourteenth Amendment must be complied with by the lessee as certainly as though they were binding covenants written into the agreement itself.

The judgment of the Supreme Court of Delaware is reversed and the cause remanded for further proceedings consistent with this opinion.[5]

A. Post-*Burton* Developments

1. *Subsidization and Tax Relief*

Recall Norwood v. Harrison, 413 U.S. 455 (1973), and McGlotten v. Kennedy, 338 F. Supp. 448 (D.D.C. 1972), Chapter 6 supra.

2. *The Leasing and Sale of Property*

In Derrington v. Plummer, 240 F.2d 922 (5th Cir. 1956), Harris County, Texas, had furnished the basement of its newly constructed courthouse as a cafeteria and leased it to a private operator in an arms-length transaction. The lessee was required "to operate a first class cafeteria," "to keep this cafeteria open at all such times as the Court House is open," and to give a 10 percent discount to county employees. The lease was silent as to the racial practices of the lessee, who excluded Negroes from the cafeteria. The court held that plaintiffs were entitled to an injunction against renewal of the lease. Although "a county may in good faith lawfully sell and dispose of its surplus property" and may "lease for private purposes property not used or needed for county purposes," the property here

5. Justice Stewart concurred on a different ground: "In upholding Eagle's right to deny service to the appellant solely because of his race, the Supreme Court of Delaware relied upon a statute of that State which permits the proprietor of a restaurant to refuse to serve 'persons whose reception or entertainment by him would be offensive to the major part of his customers. . . .' There is no suggestion in the record that the appellant as an individual was such a person. The highest court of Delaware has thus construed this legislative enactment as authorizing discriminatory classification based exclusively on color." Cf. Reitman v. Mulkey, 387 U.S. 369 (1967). Justices Frankfurter and Harlan, the latter joined by Justice Whittaker, dissented, arguing that the state supreme court's construction of the statute was unclear and that the case should be remanded or certified to the court for clarification.

was not surplus, and "the express purpose of the lease was to furnish cafeteria service for the benefit of persons having occasion to be in the County Courthouse." The court concluded that the county was rendering service "through the instrumentality" of the lessee and that "in rendering such service the lessee stands in the place of the County."

In Tonkins v. City of Greensboro, 276 F.2d 890 (4th Cir. 1960), the court held that the bona fide outright sale of a public swimming pool to private parties did not unconstitutionally involve the state in discrimination of its new owners. In Hampton v. City of Jacksonville, 304 F.2d 320 (5th Cir. 1962), the city had sold a golf course to private parties, subject to the condition that the property revert to the city if the purchaser used it for anything else. The court of appeals held that Negro plaintiffs were entitled to use the golf course. It distinguished the outright sale in *Tonkins* and held that the conditional sale here was effectively identical to the leasing arrangement in *Derrington*. The city, which had long operated municipal golf courses, was now "permitting the private individual to perform this part of the City's function."

Could the cafeteria in *Derrington* have refused to employ blacks? Could it have refused to employ persons because of their religion or political beliefs?

3. *Government Licensing and Regulation*

In one of the sit-in cases, Garner v. Louisiana, 368 U.S. 157 (1961), Justice Douglas suggested in a concurring opinion that the municipal licensing and regulation of a restaurant were sufficient to make it a "public facility" bound by the equal protection clause; but the Court disposed of the case on narrower grounds without discussing the question. In Moose Lodge No. 107 v. Irvis, 407 U.S. 163 (1972), the Court considered this issue with respect to a "private" fraternal club.

Irvis, a guest of a member of the lodge, was refused service in its dining room and bar solely because he was black. He sued, successfully, in a federal district court to have the lodge's liquor license revoked. The court found two features of Pennsylvania's licensing scheme especially significant. First, each municipality in the state was allowed only one retail license for every 1,500 inhabitants; Moose Lodge was located in Harrisburg, whose quota had been filled for many years. Second, a licensee was subject to a variety of regulations, including a requirement that a private club "adhere to all the provisions of its constitution and by-laws"; and the Moose Lodge's constitution excluded nonwhites as members and guests.

The Supreme Court held for the lodge. Justice Rehnquist emphasized that "Moose Lodge is a private social club in a private building." He mentioned the license quota only in passing and pointed out (apparently correctly) that the state regulation requiring a licensee to enforce its own rules was designed solely to prevent the subterfuge of "a place of public accommodation masquerading as a private club."[6]

6. Nonetheless, the Court held that enforcement of this regulation should be enjoined: Although it is "neutral in its terms, the result of its application in a case where the constitution and bylaws of a club require racial discrimination would be to invoke the sanctions of the State to enforce a concededly discriminatory private rule."

Justice Douglas, joined by Justice Marshall, dissented.[7] He started from the premises that private clubs enjoy constitutional rights of privacy and association; that, all other things being equal, the Moose Lodge could be as selective as it desired in admitting members and guests; and that "the fact that a private club gets some kind of permit from the State or municipality does not make it ipso facto a public enterprise or undertaking, any more than the grant to a housekeeper of a permit to operate an incinerator puts the householder in the public domain." But, Justice Douglas asserted, Pennsylvania was far more substantially involved in the Moose Lodge's discrimination, for a state regulation in effect required the lodge to enforce its racially restrictive provisions and, more important, the state issued only a limited number of licenses:

> This state-enforced scarcity of licenses restricts the ability of blacks to obtain liquor, for liquor is commercially available *only* at private clubs for a significant portion of each week. Access by blacks to places that serve liquor is further limited by the fact that the state quota is filled. A group desiring to form a nondiscriminatory club which would serve blacks must purchase a license held by an existing club, which can exact a monopoly price for the transfer. The availability of such a license is speculative at best, however, for, as Moose Lodge itself concedes, without a liquor license a fraternal organization would be hard pressed to survive.

In Columbia Broadcasting System v. Democratic National Committee, 412 U.S. 94 (1973), the Court avoided deciding whether a television broadcaster's policy of refusing to accept paid editorial advertisements constituted governmental action, holding that it did not, in any case, contravene the First Amendment. Chief Justice Burger, joined by Justices Stewart and Rehnquist, would have held that broadcasters are not bound by the First Amendment under the present regulatory scheme, which purposely accords licensees a broad sphere of journalistic discretion:

> Were we to read the First Amendment to spell out governmental action in the circumstances presented here, few licensee decisions on the content of broadcasts or the processes of editorial evaluation would escape constitutional scrutiny. In this sensitive area so sweeping a concept of governmental action would go far in practical effect to undermine nearly a half century of unmistakable congressional purpose to maintain — no matter how difficult the task — essentially private broadcast journalism held only broadly accountable to public interest standards. . . .
>
> More profoundly, it would be anomalous for us to hold, in the name of promoting the constitutional guarantees of free expression, that the day-to-day editorial decisions of broadcast licensees are subject to the kind of restraints urged by respondents. To do so in the name of the First Amendment would be a contradiction. Journalistic discretion would in many ways be lost to the rigid limitations that the First Amendment imposes on government . . .

Justice Brennan, joined by Justice Marshall, argued in response that "the public nature of the airwaves, the governmentally created preferred status of the broadcast licensees, the pervasive regulation of broadcast programming, and the Commission's specific approval of the challenged broadcaster policy combine in this

7. Justice Brennan also wrote a dissenting opinion, which Justice Marshall joined.

case to bring the promulgation and enforcement of that policy within the orbit of constitutional imperatives."

JACKSON v. METROPOLITAN EDISON CO., 419 U.S. 345 (1974): [The Court held that state licensing and regulation of a privately owned public utility did not impose procedural due process requirements on the corporation's termination of petitioner's electric service for nonpayment.]

REHNQUIST, J. . . . Here the action complained of was taken by a utility company which is privately owned and operated, but which in many particulars of its business is subject to extensive state regulation. The mere fact that a business is subject to state regulation does not by itself convert its action into that of the State for purposes of the Fourteenth Amendment. Nor does the fact that the regulation is extensive and detailed, as in the case of most public utilities, do so. It may well be that acts of a heavily regulated utility with at least something of a governmentally protected monopoly will more readily be found to be "state" acts than will the acts of an entity lacking these characteristics. But the inquiry must be whether there is a sufficiently close nexus between the State and the challenged action of the regulated entity so that the action of the latter may be fairly treated as that of the State itself. . . .

Petitioner first argues that "state action" is present because of the monopoly status allegedly conferred upon Metropolitan by the State of Pennsylvania. As a factual matter, it may well be doubted that the State ever granted or guaranteed Metropolitan a monopoly.[a] But assuming that it had, this fact is not determinative in considering whether Metropolitan's termination of service to petitioner was "state action" for purposes of the Fourteenth Amendment. In Public Utilities Commn. v. Pollak, 343 U.S. 451 (1952), where the Court dealt with the activities of the District of Columbia Transit Company, a congressionally established monopoly, we expressly disclaimed reliance on the monopoly status of the transit authority. Similarly, although certain monopoly aspects were presented in Moose Lodge No. 107 v. Irvis, 407 U.S. 163 (1972), we found that the lodge's action was not subject to the provisions of the Fourteenth Amendment. In each of those cases, there was insufficient relationship between the challenged actions of the entities involved and their monopoly status. There is no indication of any greater connection here. . . .

We also reject the notion that Metropolitan's termination is state action because the State "has specifically authorized and approved" the termination practice. In the instant case, Metropolitan filed with the Public Utilities Commission a general tariff — a provision of which states Metropolitan's right to terminate service for non-payment. . . .

As a threshold matter, it is less than clear under state law that Metropolitan was even required to file this provision as part of its tariff or that the Commission would have had the power to disapprove it. The District Court observed that the sole connection of the Commission with this regulation was Metropolitan's simple

a. . . . There is nothing in either Metropolitan's certificate or in the statutes under which it was issued indicating that the State has granted or guaranteed to Metropolitan monopoly status. . . . As petitioner admits, such public utility companies are natural monopolies created by the economic forces of high threshold capital requirements and virtually unlimited economy of scale. Regulation was superimposed on such natural monopolies as a substitute for competition and not to eliminate it. . . .

notice filing with the Commission and the lack of any Commission action to prohibit it.

The case most heavily relied on by petitioner is Public Utilities Commn. v. Pollak. There the Court dealt with the contention that Capital Transit's installation of a piped music system on its buses violated the First Amendment rights of the bus riders. It is not entirely clear whether the Court alternatively held that Capital Transit's action was action of the "state" for First Amendment purposes, or whether it merely assumed arguendo that it was and went on to resolve the First Amendment question adversely to the bus riders. In either event, the nature of the state involvement there was quite different than it is here. The District of Columbia Public Utilities Commission, on its own motion, commenced an investigation of the effects of the piped music, and after a full hearing concluded not only that Capital Transit's practices were "not inconsistent with public convenience, comfort, and safety," but that the practice "in fact through the creation of better will among passengers, . . . tends to improve the conditions under which the public rides." Here, on the other hand, there was no such imprimatur placed on the practice of Metropolitan about which petitioner complains. The nature of governmental regulation of private utilities is such that a utility may frequently be required by the state regulatory scheme to obtain approval for practices a business regulated in less detail would be free to institute without any approval from a regulatory body. Approval by a state utility commission of such a request from a regulated utility, where the Commission has not put its own weight on the side of the proposed practice by ordering it, does not transmute a practice initiated by the utility and approved by the Commission into "state action.". . .

We also find absent in the instant case the symbiotic relationship presented in Burton v. Wilmington Parking Authority, 365 U.S. 715 (1961). . . .

We conclude that the State of Pennsylvania is not sufficiently connected with respondent's action in terminating petitioner's service so as to make respondent's conduct in so doing attributable to the State for purposes of the Fourteenth Amendment. We therefore have no occasion to decide whether petitioner's claim to continued service was "property" for purposes of that Amendment, or whether "due process of law" would require a State taking similar action to accord petitioner the procedural rights for which she contends. . . .

[Justices Douglas and Marshall each wrote a dissenting opinion on the merits.[8] The former argued that "[i]t is not enough to examine seriatim each of the factors upon which a claimant relies and to dismiss each individually as being insufficient to support a finding of state action. It is the aggregate that is controlling."]

MARSHALL, J., dissenting. . . . Our state action cases have repeatedly relied on several factors clearly presented by this case: a state-sanctioned monopoly; an extensive pattern of cooperation between the "private" entity and the state; and a service uniquely public in nature. Today the Court takes a major step in repudiating this line of authority and adopts a stance that is bound to lead to mischief when applied to problems beyond the narrow sphere of due process objections to utility terminations.

When the State confers a monopoly on a group or organization, this Court has held that the organization assumes many of the obligations of the State. . . . The

8. Justice Brennan also dissented on technical grounds.

majority . . . [implies] that since the State's purpose in regulating a natural monopoly is not to aid the company but to prevent its charging monopoly prices, the State's involvement is somehow less significant for state action purposes. . . . The difficulty inherent in this kind of economic analysis counsels against excusing natural monopolies from the reach of state action principles. To invite inquiry into whether a particular state-sanctioned monopoly might have survived without the State's express approval grounds the analysis in hopeless speculation. Worse, this approach ignores important implications of the State's policy of utilizing private monopolies to provide electric service. Encompassed within this policy is the State's determination not to permit governmental competition with the selected private company, but to cooperate with and regulate the company in a multitude of ways to ensure that the company's service will be the functional equivalent of service provided by the State.

The pattern of cooperation between Metropolitan Edison and the State has led to significant state involvement in virtually every phase of the company's business. The majority, however, accepts the relevance of the State's regulatory scheme only to the extent that it demonstrates state support for the challenged termination procedure. Moreover, after concluding that the State in this case had not approved the company's termination procedures, the majority suggests that even state authorization and approval would not be sufficient: the State would apparently have to *order* the termination practice in question to satisfy the majority's state action test.

I disagree with the majority's position on three separate grounds. First, the suggestion that the State would have to "put its own weight on the side of the proposed practice by ordering it" seems to me to mark a sharp departure from our previous state action cases. . . . [W]e have consistently indicated that state authorization and approval of "private" conduct would support a finding of state action.

Second, I question the wisdom of giving such short shrift to the extensive interaction between the company and the State, and focusing solely on the extent of state support for the particular activity under challenge. In cases where the State's only significant involvement is through financial support or limited regulation of the private entity, it may be well to inquire whether the State's involvement suggests state approval of the objectionable conduct. But where the State has so thoroughly insinuated itself into the operations of the enterprise, it should not be fatal if the State has not affirmatively sanctioned the particular practice in question.

Finally, it seems to me in any event that the State *has* given its approval to Metropolitan Edison's termination procedures. The state utility commission approved a tariff provision under which the company reserved the right to discontinue its service on reasonable notice for nonpayment of bills. . . .

The majority's conclusion that there is no state action in this case is likely guided in part by its reluctance to impose on a utility company burdens that might ultimately hurt consumers more than they would help them. Elaborate hearings prior to termination might be quite expensive, and for a responsible company there might be relatively few cases in which such hearings would do any good. The solution to this problem, however, it is to require only abbreviated pretermination procedures for all utility companies, not to free the "private" companies to behave however they see fit. . . .

What is perhaps most troubling about the Court's opinion is that it would appear to apply to a broad range of claimed constitutional violations by the company. The Court has not adopted the notion . . . that different standards should apply to state action analysis when different constitutional claims are presented. Thus, the majority's analysis would seemingly apply as well to a company that refused to extend service to Negroes, welfare recipients, or any other group that the company preferred, for its own reasons, not to serve. . . .

Discussion

1. The relevance of regulation. Does the extent of regulation of a private activity bear on its amenability to the Fourteenth Amendment? Are the nature and purposes of the regulatory scheme germane? Does the fact that a state regulates the sellers of food and other commodities and services to prevent fraud and protect health and safety imply that a regulated enterprise should be treated as "public" for purposes of the Fourteenth Amendment — at least to the extent of prohibiting discrimination among customers? Does the state have a legitimate interest in affording consumer protection even in situations or transactions one might deem "private"?

If it can be shown that certain types of regulatory schemes, by removing competitive market pressures, make it more likely that a business enterprise will indulge discriminatory tastes than in the absence of regulation,[9] should this render the private discrimination impermissible under the Fourteenth Amendment?

2. The relevance of licensing. Consider three categories of licensing schemes: (1) those used for raising revenues (e.g., hunting and fishing licenses); (2) those used for certifying qualification (e.g., driver's or doctor's licenses); and (3) those that grant an exclusive or partly exclusive right to enjoy a scarce resource — for example, the liquor license in *Moose Lodge* or the permit to operate a television station in *CBS*.[10] Do any provide a sound basis for linking private discriminatory conduct with the state?

3. The relevance of a corporate charter. Consider A.A. Berle's suggestion that individuals be accorded constitutional protections "in their dealings with private units wielding great economic power":[11]

> [T]he corporation, itself a creation of the state, [should be] as subject to constitutional limitations which limit action as is the state itself. . . . On logical analysis, a corporation, being a creature of the state, which owned, let us say, a dominant department or chain store system, could not offer its facilities to white men and refuse them to Negroes; could not, through whim or dislike, refuse to serve a family or a customer which it disliked; could not give undue favors to a group it wished to foster at the expense of the rest of its public. This would be true despite the fact that, as owner, it could theoretically do what it pleased with its own property. And this legal restraint would apply not only to rules embodied in the corporation's constitu-

9. See Ralph Winter, Improving the Economic Status of Negroes Through Laws Against Discrimination, 34 U. Chi. L. Rev. 817 (1967); Harold Demsetz, Minorities in the Market Place, 43 N.C.L. Rev. 271 (1965).

10. Cf. labor relations statutes that confer special advantages on the union chosen by a majority of the relevant class of employees. See Steele v. Louisville & N.R. Co., 323 U.S. 192 (1944); Wellingon, The Constitution, the Labor Union, and Governmental Action, 70 Yale L.J. 345 (1961).

11. A.A. Berle, Constitutional Limitations on Corporate Activity — Protection of Personal Rights from Invasion Through Economic Power, 100 U. Pa. L. Rev. 933, 942-943 (1952).

tion and by-laws, but also to its regulations, practices and day-to-day dealings. The Bill of Rights and the Fourteenth and Fifteenth Amendments would thus have direct application to and also throughout any corporation whose position gave it power. The preconditions of application are two: the undeniable fact that the corporation was created by the state and the existence of sufficient economic power concentrated in this vehicle to invade the constitutional right of an individual to a material degree.

This [would be] new as a rule of law, but it is typically American in tradition. Instead of a social attack on an enterprise as an enterprise, with nationalization or socialization as the aim, this is the application of a set of general rules to the organisms and individuals who govern them, with a view to achieving a freer order of individual life. Under this theory certain human values are protected by the American Constitution; any fraction of the governmental system, economic as well as legal, is prohibited from invading or violating them. The principle is logical because, as has been seen, the modern state has set up, and come to rely on, the corporate system to carry out functions for which in modern life by community demand the government is held ultimately responsible. It is unlimited because it follows corporate power whenever that power actually exists. It resolves the conflict between the property notion that an owner can do what he likes with his own and the governmental concept that a public agency is obliged to serve all alike within strict constitutional limitations, evenhandedly, up to the limit of its capacity. Instead of nationalizing the enterprise, this doctrine "constitutionalizes" the operation.

Note: The Relevance of an Exclusive Government License

In San Francisco Arts & Athletics, Inc. v. United States Olympic Committee, 483 U.S. 522 (1987), the Court dealt with the effects of a federal statute that prohibits anyone from using the words "Olympic" or "Olympiad" "for the purpose of trade, to induce the sale of any goods or services, or to promote any theatrical exhibition, athletic performance, or competition" without first obtaining permission from the United States Olympic Committee (USOC). The plaintiffs argued that the USOC had unconstitutionally discriminated in denying them permission to sponsor a "Gay Olympic Games," pointing out that USOC had allowed "Special Olympics" for handicapped persons and "Junior Olympics" and "Explorer Olympics" for youth.

"The fundamental inquiry is whether the USOC is a governmental actor to whom the prohibitions of the Constitution apply," and the Court held that it was not. The plaintiffs claimed that attributes of the USOC constituted state action, specifically referring to the fact that Congress had granted the USOC a corporate charter and provided some direct grants to the Committee, as well as giving it control over the key words named above. Justice Powell wrote:

The fact that Congress granted it a corporate charter does not render the USOC a government agent. All corporations act under charters granted by a government, usually by a State. They do not thereby lose their essentially private character. Even extensive regulation by the government does not transform the actions of the regulated entity into those of the government. See Jackson v. Metropolitan Edison Co. Nor is the fact that Congress has granted the USOC exclusive use of the word "Olympic" dispositive. All enforceable rights in trademarks are created by some governmental act. . . . The actions of the trademark owners nevertheless remain private. Moreover, the intent on the part of Congress to help the USOC obtain funding does not change the analysis. The Government may subsidize private entities without assuming constitutional responsibility for their actions.

... The USOC's choice of how to enforce its exclusive right to use the word "Olympic" simply is not a governmental decision. There is no evidence that the Federal Government coerced or encouraged the USOC in the exercise of its right. At most, the Federal Government, by failing to supervise the USOC's use of its rights, can be said to exercise "[m]ere approval of or acquiescence in the intiatives" of the USOC. This is not enough to make the USOC's actions those of the Government....

Justice Brennan, joined by Justice Marshall, dissented. He placed the origins of the congressional action in "dissatisfaction" about the performance of American athletes at the Olympic games, which led Congress to grant the USOC unprecedented administrative authority over all private American athletic organizations:

The legislative history reveals, contrary to the Court's assumption, that no actor in the private sector had ever performed this function, and indeed never could perform it absent enabling legislation.... [I]n the Amateur Sports Act, Congress granted the USOC the authority and ability to govern national amateur athletics related to international competition.... Its actions ... ought to be subject to constitutional limits.

Justice Brennan went on to argue that the "nexus" between the Committee and the United States brought the case within the ambit of *Burton*.

First, as in *Burton*, the relationship here confers a variety of mutual benefits.... [T]he Act gave the USOC authority and responsibilities that no private organization in this country had ever held. The Act also conferred substantial financial resources on the USOC..., and afford[ed] it unprecedented power to control the use of the word "Olympic" and related emblems to raise additional funds....

Second, in the eye of the public, both national and international, the connection between the decisions of the United States Government and those of the USOC is profound. The President of the United States has served as the Honorary President of the USOC. The national flag flies both literally and figuratively over the central product of the USOC, the United States Olympic Team....

Even more importantly, there is a close financial and legislative link between the USOC's alleged discriminatory exercise of its word-use authority and the financial success of both the USOC and the Government. It would certainly be "irony amounting to grave injustice" if, to finance the team that is to represent our political system, the USOC were free to employ government-created economic leverage to prohibit political speech.... The purpose of this grant of unique discretion was to enhance the fundraising ability of the USOC....

Indeed, the required nexus between the challenged action and the Government appears even closer here than in *Burton*. While in *Burton* the restaurant was able to pursue a policy of discrimination because the State had failed to impose upon it a policy of nondiscrimination, the USOC could pursue its alleged policy of selective enforcement only because Congress *affirmatively* granted it power that it would not otherwise have to control the use of the word "Olympic." I conclude, then, that the close nexus between the Government and the challenged action compels a finding of government action.

Justice O'Connor, joined by Justice Blackmun, indicated substantial agreement with Justice Brennan's "nexus" argument.

4. *The Receipt of Public Funds to Reimburse Private Persons for Their Services*

The social welfare responsibilities assumed by the contemporary state often include the payment or reimbursement for services provided to individuals. Under what circumstances does the receipt of such funds bind a putatively private entity to constitutional constraints? In Rendell-Baker v. Kohn, 457 U.S. 830 (1982), teachers employed by a private school claimed that its director violated the due process clause when he dismissed them without a hearing. Ninety percent of the school's funds came from the state's payment of tuition for students referred to the school by local school boards or from other state and federal agencies. Similarly, in Blum v. Yaretsky, 457 U.S. 991 (1982), a patient in a New York nursing home funded under Medicaid complained about the procedures by which he was determined to require a lower level of medical services than he desired. The Supreme Court refused to find state action in either case.

In *Rendell-Baker*, Chief Justice Burger, for a six-Justice majority,[12] rejected the argument that the level of dependence on state funds subjected the school to the First and Fourteenth Amendments. "The school, like the nursing homes [in *Blum,*] is not fundamentally different from many private corporations whose business depends primarily on contracts to build roads, bridges, dams, ships, or submarines for the government. Acts of such private contractors do not become acts of their government by reason of their significant or even total engagement in performing public contracts." The Court went on to cite Polk County v. Dodson, 454 U.S. 312 (1981), which had declined to hold that a state public defender's activities vis-à-vis her client implicated the state. Justice Marshall, joined by Justice Brennan, dissented.

The Justices' line-up was identical in *Blum;* they focused here on the private decisionmakers' independence from state coercion: "[O]ur precedents indicate that a State normally can be held responsible for a private decision only when it has exercised coercive power or has provided such significant encouragement, either overt or covert, that the choice must in law be deemed to be that of the State." Although New York did require physicians to classify patients based on a computed "score" of their need for services, the physicians retained the ultimate judgment to authorize nursing home care even if the patient had a "low score": "These decisions ultimately turn on medical judgments made by private parties according to professional standards that are not established by the State."

Discussion

To what extent does the claimed substantive violation drive the finding of state action? Imagine that there were no state or federal civil rights laws and that both the school in *Rendell-Baker* and the nursing home in *Blum*, as well as the other entities found to be private in the cases examined in this section, had adopted ra-

12. Justice White concurred only in the judgment.

cially discriminatory policies in allocating their respective services. How do you think the Supreme Court would decide these cases?

5. *Does State Membership in an Organization Make the Organization "the State"?*

NATIONAL COLLEGIATE ATHLETIC ASSOCIATION v. TARKANIAN, 488 U.S. 179 (1988): [The National Collegiate Athletic Association (NCAA), an unincorporated association, consists of approximately 960 members, including almost all American public and private universities and four-year colleges with major athletic programs. Members of the Association agree to abide by the rules — or "legislation" — adopted by it. Alleged rule violations are investigated by a Committee on Infractions, which can impose penalties. The Committee can require a member (under the threat of further penalties) to impose discipline on a named employee.

Jerry Tarkanian became head basketball coach at the University of Nevada, Las Vegas, (UNLV) in 1973. By 1977, Tarkanian succeeded in taking his team to the Final Four of the NCAA basketball tournament. Later that year, however, the NCAA determined that UNLV and Tarkanian personally had violated a number of its rules, and it placed UNLV on probation for two years, conditioned on its suspension of Tarkanian. Although the University expressed both continuing doubt that Tarkanian had in fact violated the rules and concern about the fairness of the procedures used in the investigation, it nonetheless suspended him in order to escape heavier penalties. The suspension entailed both a demotion and a significant pay cut for Tarkanian, who then sued in Nevada state court, claiming that the NCAA had deprived him of due process guaranteed by the Fourteenth Amendment. The Nevada courts agreed, and the NCAA appealed to the United State Supreme Court. Justice Stevens wrote for a five-justice majority in reversing the Nevada Supreme Court:]

In this case Tarkanian argues that the NCAA was a state actor because it misused power that it possessed by virtue of state law. He claims specifically that UNLV delegated its own functions to the NCAA, clothing the Association with authority both to adopt rules governing UNLV's athletic programs and to enforce those rules on behalf of UNLV. Similarly, the Nevada Supreme Court held that UNLV had delegated its authority over personnel decisions to the NCAA. Therefore, the court reasoned, the two entities acted jointly to deprive Tarkanian of liberty and property interests, making the NCAA as well as UNLV a state actor.

These contentions fundamentally misconstrue the facts of this case. In a typical case raising a state action issue, a private party has taken the decisive step that caused the harm to the plaintiff, and the question is whether the State was sufficiently involved to treat that decisive conduct as state action. . . .

This case uniquely mirrors the traditional state action case. Here the final act challenged by Tarkanian — his suspension — was committed by UNLV. A state university without question is a state actor. When it decides to impose a serious disciplinary sanction upon one of its tenured employees, it must comply with the terms of the Due Process Clause of the Fourteenth Amendment. . . .

The mirror image presented in this case requires us to step through an analytical looking glass to resolve it. Clearly UNLV's conduct was influenced by the rules and recommendations of the NCAA, the private party. But it was UNLV, the state entity, that actually suspended Tarkanian. Thus the question is not whether UNLV participated to a critical extent in the NCAA's activities, but whether UNLV's actions in compliance with the NCAA rules and recommendations turned the NCAA's conduct into state action.

... [Although UNLV, as a member of the NCAA had some impact on the NCAA's policy determinations,] ... the NCAA's several hundred other public and private member institutions each similarly affected those policies. Those institutions, the vast majority of which were located in States other than Nevada, did not act under color of Nevada law. It necessarily follows that the source of the legislation adopted by the NCAA is not Nevada but the collective membership, speaking through an organization that is independent of any particular State.[a]

State action nonetheless might lie if UNLV, by embracing the NCAA's rules, transformed them into state rules and NCAA into a state actor. UNLV engaged in state action when it adopted the NCAA's rules to govern its own behavior, but that would be true even if UNLV had taken no part in the promulgation of those rules. . . . Neither UNLV's decision to adopt the NCAA's standards nor its minor role in their formulation is a sufficient reason for concluding that the NCAA was acting under color of Nevada law when it promulgated standards governing athletic recruitment, eligibility, and academic performance.

Tarkanian further asserts that the NCAA's investigation, enforcement proceedings, and consequent recommendations constituted state action because they resulted from a delegation of power by UNLV. . . . It is, of course, true that a state may delegate authority to a private party and thereby make that party a state actor. Thus, we recently held that a private physician who had contracted with a state prison to attend to the inmates' medical needs was a state actor. West v. Atkins, 108 S. Ct. 2250 (1988). But UNLV delegated no power to the NCAA to take specific action against any University employee. The commitment by UNLV to adhere to NCAA enforcement procedures was enforceable only by sanctions that the NCAA might impose on UNLV itself.

Indeed, the notion that UNLV's promise to cooperate in the NCAA enforcement proceedings was tantamount to a partnership agreement or the transfer of certain University powers to the NCAA is belied by the history of this case. It is quite obvious that UNLV used its best efforts to retain its winning coach — a goal diametrically opposed to the NCAA's interest in ascertaining the truth of its investigators' reports. During the several years that the NCAA investigated the alleged violations, the NCAA and UNLV acted much more like adversaries than like partners engaged in a dispassionate search for the truth. . . . Just as a state-compensated public defender acts in a private capacity when she represents a private client in a conflict against the State, Polk County v. Dodson, 454 U.S. 312, 320 (1981), the NCAA is properly viewed as a private actor at odds with the State when it represents the interests of its entire membership in an investigation of one public university.

a. The situation would, of course, be different if the membership consisted entirely of institutions located within the same State, many of them public institutions created by the same sovereign. [Cases omitted.] The dissent apparently agrees that the NCAA was not acting under color of state law in its relationships with private universities, which constitute the bulk of its membership.

The NCAA enjoyed no governmental powers to facilitate its investigation. It had no power to subpoena witnesses, to impose contempt sanctions, or to assert sovereign authority over any individual. Its greatest authority was to threaten sanctions against UNLV. . . . Even the University's vice president acknowledged that the [NCAA] Report gave the University options other than suspension: UNLV could have retained Tarkanian and risked additional sanctions, perhaps even expulsion from the NCAA, or it could have withdrawn voluntarily from the Association.

Finally, Tarkanian argues that the power of the NCAA is so great that the UNLV had no practical alternative to compliance with its demands. We are not at all sure this is true, but even if we assume that a private monopolist can impose its will on a state agency by a threatened refusal to deal with it, it does not follow that such a private party is therefore acting under color of state law.

[Justice White dissented, joined by Justices Brennan, Marshall, and O'Connor:]

All agree that UNLV, a public university, is a state actor, and that the suspension of Jerry Tarkanian, a public employee, was state action. The question here is whether the NCAA acted jointly with UNLV in suspending Tarkanian and thereby also became a state actor. I would hold that it did.

. . . First, Tarkanian was suspended for violations of NCAA rules, which UNLV embraced in its agreement with the NCAA. . . . Second, the NCAA and UNLV also agreed that the NCAA would conduct the hearings concerning violations of its rules. . . . As a result of this agreement, the NCAA conducted the very hearings the Nevada Supreme Court held to have violated Tarkanian's rights to procedural due process.

Third, the NCAA and UNLV agreed that the findings of fact made by the NCAA at the hearings it conducted would be binding on UNLV. By becoming a member of the NCAA, UNLV did more than merely "promise to cooperate in the NCAA enforcement proceedings." It agreed . . . to accept the NCAA's "findings of fact as in some way superior to [its] own." By the terms of UNLV's membership in the NCAA, the NCAA's findings were final and not subject to review by any other body, and it was for that reason that UNLV suspended Tarkanian, despite concluding that many of those findings were wrong. . . . On these facts, the NCAA was "jointly engaged with [UNLV] officials in the challenged action," and therefore was a state actor.

. . . [T]he majority relies extensively on the fact that the NCAA and UNLV were adversaries throughout the proceedings before the NCAA. . . . But this opportunity for opposition, provided for by the terms of the membership agreement between UNLV and the NCAA, does not undercut the agreement itself. . . .

Had UNLV refused to suspend Tarkanian, and the NCAA responded by imposing sanctions against UNLV, it would be hard indeed to find any state action that harmed Tarkanian. But that is not this case. Here, UNLV did suspend Tarkanian, and it did so because it embraced the NCAA rules governing conduct of its athletic program and adopted the results of the hearings conducted by the NCAA concerning Tarkanian, as it had agreed that it would. Under these facts, I would find that the NCAA acted jointly with UNLV and therefore is a state actor.

B. The Special Problem of Judicial Enforcement of Private Agreements

SHELLEY v. KRAEMER, 334 U.S. 1 (1948): [Prior to 1948, tracts of residential property in white neighborhoods were often subject to covenants, running with the land, prohibiting the sale of the property to racial minorities. Shelley v. Kraemer was a suit to enjoin Negroes from taking possession of a lot sold to them in breach of a racially restrictive covenant. The Court noted that the private contract as such was beyond the reach of the Fourteenth Amendment but held that a state court could not constitutionally enforce it by injunction.]

VINSON, C.J. . . . That the action of state courts and judicial officers in their official capacities is to be regarded as action of the State within the meaning of the Fourteenth Amendment, is a proposition which has long been established by decisions of this Court. That principle was given expression in the earliest cases involving the construction of the terms of the Fourteenth Amendment. Thus, in Virginia v. Rives, 100 U.S. 313, 318 (1880), this Court stated: "It is doubtless true that a State may act through different agencies, — either by its legislative, its executive, or its judicial authorities; and the prohibitions of the amendment extend to all action of the State denying equal protection of the laws, whether it be action by one of these agencies or by another.". . .

[T]he examples of state judicial action which have been held by this Court to violate the Amendment's commands are not restricted to situations in which the judicial proceedings were found in some manner to be procedurally unfair. It has been recognized that the action of state courts in enforcing a substantive common-law rule formulated by those courts, may result in the denial of rights guaranteed by the Fourteenth Amendment. . . . Thus, in American Federation of Labor v. Swing, 312 U.S. 321 (1941), enforcement by state courts of the common-law policy of the State, which resulted in the restraining of peaceful picketing, was held to be state action of the sort prohibited by the Amendment's guaranties of freedom of discussion. In Cantwell v. Connecticut, 310 U.S. 296 (1940), a conviction in a state court of the common-law crime of breach of the peace was, under the circumstances of the case, found to be a violation of the Amendment's commands relating to freedom of religion. In Bridges v. California, 314 U.S. 252 (1941), enforcement of the state's common-law rule relating to contempts by publication was held to be state action inconsistent with the prohibitions of the Fourteenth Amendment.

The short of the matter is that from the time of the adoption of the Fourteenth Amendment until the present, it has been the consistent ruling of this Court that the action of the States to which the Amendment has reference includes action of state courts and state judicial officials. . . .

Against this background of judicial construction, extending over a period of some three-quarters of a century, we are called upon to consider whether enforcement by state courts of the restrictive agreements in these cases may be deemed to be the acts of those States; and, if so, whether that action has denied these petitioners the equal protection of the laws which the Amendment was intended to insure.

We have no doubt that there has been state action in these cases in the full and complete sense of the phrase. The undisputed facts disclose that petitioners were willing purchasers of properties upon which they desired to establish homes. The owners of the properties were willing sellers; and contracts of sale were accordingly consummated. It is clear that but for the active intervention of the state courts, supported by the full panoply of state power, petitioners would have been free to occupy the properties in question without restraint.

These are . . . cases in which the States have made available to such individuals the full coercive power of government to deny to petitioners, on the grounds of race or color, the enjoyment of property rights in premises which petitioners are willing and financially able to acquire and which the grantors are willing to sell. The difference between judicial enforcement and nonenforcement of the restrictive covenants is the difference to petitioners between being denied rights of property available to other members of the community and being accorded full enjoyment of those rights on an equal footing.

. . . [The Fourteenth Amendment is not] ineffective simply because the particular pattern of discrimination, which the State has enforced, was defined initially by the terms of a private agreement. State action, as that phrase is understood for the purposes of the Fourteenth Amendment, refers to exertions of state power in all forms. And when the effect of that action is to deny rights subject to the protection of the Fourteenth Amendment, it is the obligation of this Court to enforce the constitutional commands.

We hold that in granting judicial enforcement of the restrictive agreements in these cases, the States have denied petitioners the equal protection of the laws and that, therefore, the action of the state courts cannot stand. We have noted that freedom from discrimination by the States in the enjoyment of property rights was among the basic objectives sought to be effectuated by the framers of the Fourteenth Amendment. That such discrimination has occurred in these cases is clear. Because of the race or color of these petitioners they have been denied rights of ownership or occupancy enjoyed as a matter of course by other citizens of different race or color.

Respondents urge . . . that since the state courts stand ready to enforce restrictive covenants excluding white persons from the ownership or occupancy of property covered by such agreements, enforcement of covenants excluding colored persons may not be deemed a denial of equal protection of the laws to the colored persons who are thereby affected. This contention does not bear scrutiny. The parties have directed our attention to no case in which a court, state or federal, has been called upon to enforce a covenant excluding members of the white majority from ownership or occupancy of real property on grounds of race or color. But there are more fundamental considerations. The rights created by the first section of the Fourteenth Amendment are, by its terms, guaranteed to the individual. The rights established are personal rights. It is, therefore, no answer to these petitioners to say that the courts may also be induced to deny white persons rights of ownership and occupancy on grounds of race or color. Equal protection of the laws is not achieved through indiscriminate imposition of inequalities.

In Barrows v. Jackson, 346 U.S. 249 (1953), the Court, over Chief Justice Vinson's dissent, extended *Shelley* to hold that a seller could not be held liable for damages for his breach of a racially restrictive covenant. Justice Minton noted that to permit such a suit would induce potential sellers not to sell to Negroes or to sell to them at higher prices.

The issue of state action through judicial enforcement arose again in the early 1960s in a series of criminal trespass prosecutions of Negroes who had refused to leave segregated lunch counters and restaurants. Through a variety of imaginative holdings, the Court reversed the convictions in every case without deciding whether the prosecutions constituted unlawful state action.[13] But concurring and dissenting justices discussed the question. In Lombard v. Louisiana, 373 U.S. 267 (1963), Justice Douglas would have held, inter alia, that the state judiciary cannot constitutionally "put criminal sanctions behind racial discrimination in public places": "If this were an intrusion of a man's home or yard or farm or garden, the property owner could seek and obtain the aid of the State against the intruder"; a restaurant, however, has "no aura of constitutionally protected privacy about it." Justice Harlan, dissenting, characterized the sit-in cases as involving "a clash of competing constitutional claims of a high order: liberty and equality" and would have assigned considerably more weight than Justice Douglas to the restaurant owner's "[f]reedom to . . . use and dispose of his property as he sees fit." In Bell v. Maryland, 378 U.S. 226 (1964), Justice Douglas reiterated his view, arguing that "the preferences involved in Shelley v. Kraemer . . . were far more personal than the motivation of the corporate managers in the present case" and that "[w]e should put these restaurant cases in line with *Shelley*." Justice Black, joined by Justices Harlan and White, argued that *Shelley* was premised on a consensual relationship between the seller and buyer and that the state court's injunction in *Shelley* had infringed the owner's rights of "free use, enjoyment, and disposal" of his property.[14] "But equally, when one party is unwilling, as when the property owner chooses . . . *not* to admit" someone to his property, he is entitled to the law's protection. Justice Black also suggested that to deny the restaurant owner the state's assistance would leave him to self-help and "betray our whole plan for a tranquil and orderly society."

In Evans v. Abney, 396 U.S. 435 (1970), following a decision that the city of Macon, Georgia, could not maintain a segregated park as required by Senator Bacon's devise granting it to the city,[15] the Georgia Supreme Court held that the grant had failed, that the doctrine of cy pres could not properly be applied to eliminate the racial restriction,[16] and that the trust property reverted to the senator's heirs. The Supreme Court upheld the decision, Justice Black writing:

> The situation presented in this case is . . . easily distinguishable from that presented in Shelley v. Kraemer, where we held unconstitutional state judicial action which had affirmatively enforced a private scheme of discrimination against Negroes. Here the effect of the Georgia decision eliminated all discrimination against Ne-

13. See Thomas Lewis, The Sit-In Cases: Great Expectations, 1963 Sup. Ct. Rev. 101; Monrad Paulsen, The Sit-In Cases of 1964: "But Answer Came There None," 1964 Sup. Ct. Rev. 137. See also note 16 infra.

14. Quoting Buchanan v. Warley, 245 U.S. 60 (1917). Earlier in the opinion, Justice Black suggested that the interlocking convenants in *Shelley* amounted to the kind of racial zoning ordinance invalidated in *Buchanan*.

15. See Evans v. Newton, 382 U.S. 296 (1966), infra.

16. The relevant Georgia statute provides that "when a valid charitable bequest is incapable for some reason of execution in the exact manner provided by the testator, . . . a court of equity will carry it into effect in such a way as will as nearly as possible effectuate his intention." The Georgia court found that the racial requirement was an inseparable part of the senator's intent.

groes in the park by eliminating the park itself, and the termination of the park was a loss shared equally by the white and Negro citizens of Macon since both races would have enjoyed a constitutional right of equal access to the park's facilities had it continued.

Justices Douglas and Brennan dissented in separate opinions, the latter arguing, inter alia, that *Shelley* controlled:[17]

> Nothing in the record suggests that after our decisions in Evans v. Newton, . . . the City of Macon retracted its previous willingness to manage Baconsfield on a nonsegregated basis, or that the white beneficiaries of Senator Bacon's generosity were unwilling to share it with Negroes. . . . Thus, so far as the record shows, that is a case of a state court's enforcement of a racial restriction to prevent willing parties from dealing with one another. [This] . . . constitutes state action denying equal protection.[18]

Discussion

1. Distinguish *Shelley* from the precedents relied on by Chief Justice Vinson — decisions holding that "the action of state courts in enforcing a substantive common-law rule formulated by those courts, may result in the denial of rights guaranteed by the Fourteenth Amendment."

2. Should judicial enforcement be treated as an "ordinary" benefit, like police and fire protection or as a special subsidy?

If the Moose Lodge is not entitled to a federal "tax subsidy," may it invoke the state's judicial processes to evict an African-American trespasser who, but for his race, would be admitted as a member? If the lodge is granted a tax subsidy, may the state court evict the trespasser? May the state court *refuse* to evict? Is there any basis for distinguishing among judicial enforcement through injunctive relief, damages, and criminal prosecution?

3. If the state may not use its criminal processes to convict someone engaging in a sit-in for criminal trespass, may it use its law enforcement officials to remove him? If not, is the "trespasser" entitled to an injunction against the proprietor's use of self-help (i.e., force) or to damages if the proprietor injures him in the attempt to remove him?

4. Consider Professor Louis Henkin's "notes for a revised opinion" in *Shelley:*[19]

> If the competing claims of liberty and the possibility that they may sometimes prevail are recognized, Shelley v. Kraemer must be given a . . . limited reading, and new qualifications must be made to discussions of state responsibility for discrimination. *Shelley,* we would say, holds that generally a state may not enforce discrimination which it could not itself require or perpetrate. Such enforcement

17. Justice Brennan found other bases for unconstitutional state involvement, including statutory authorization for discriminatory trusts at the time of the devise, the city's acceptance of a trust with a racially discriminatory reversion clause, and the city's longtime operation of the park as a public facility. Justice Marshall did not participate in the case.

18. See also Gordon v. Gordon, 332 Mass. 197, 124 N.E.2d 228 (1955), which gave effect to a provision of a will that "[i]f any of my . . . children shall marry a person not born in the Hebrew faith then I hereby revoke the gift . . . and the provision . . . herein made to or for such child." The Supreme Judicial Court of Massachusetts asserted without discussion that *Shelley* and related cases "seem to us to involve quite different considerations from the right to dispose of property by will." The United States Supreme Court denied certiorari, 349 U.S. 947 (1955).

19. Louis Henkin, Shelley v. Kraemer: Notes for a Revised Opinion, 110 U. Pa. L. Rev. 473 (1962).

is state action, makes the state responsible for a denial of equal protection. But there are circumstances where the discriminator can invoke a protected liberty which is not constitutionally inferior to the claim of equal protection. There the Constitution requires or permits the state to favor the right to discriminate over the victim's claim to equal protection; the state, then, is not in violation of the fourteenth amendment when it legislates or affords a remedy in support of the discrimination. . . . The special cases, we suggest, are . . . those few where the state supports that basic liberty, privacy, autonomy, which outweighs even the equal protection of the laws. . . .

In the end, whether the freedom to discriminate may surpass the claim to equality and how "neutral" the forces of law may be in that conflict can only be decided in the light of a complex of considerations of varying import and relevance. The balance may be struck differently at different times, reflecting differences in prevailing philosophy and the continuing movement from laissez-faire government toward welfare and meliorism. The changes in prevailing philosophy themselves may sum up the judgment of judges as to how the conscience of our society weighs the competing needs and claims of liberty and equality in time and context.

Note: On State Repeal of Antidiscrimination Prohibitions and the "Encouragement" of Private Discrimination

The defendants in the cases read thus far almost invariably claim that they are private actors exercising autonomy traditionally protected by the law. That is, they claim that the state has had a "hands off" position with respect to the conduct in question. The plaintiffs assert that there is sufficient state involvement that the state may not be indifferent to the consequences of private discriminatory conduct.

Suppose that the state has not always been formally indifferent, but instead, having banned private conduct at one point shifts its policy to one of formal indifference. This question was raised in Reitman v. Mulkey, 387 U.S. 369 (1967), in which the Court considered the constitutionality of an amendment to the California Constitution that protected "the right of any person who is willing or desires to sell, lease or rent any part or all of his real property, to decline to sell, lease or rent such property to such person or persons as he, in his absolute discretion, chooses." The passage of the amendment by popular referendum in 1964 was widely understood to be aimed at California statutes prohibiting racial discrimination in the sale or rental of most private dwellings; it was understood to establish a constitutional right (though obviously not a duty) to discriminate.

A majority of the Supreme Court agreed with the California Supreme Court that the amendment violated the Fourteenth Amendment. The violation did not consist in the mere "repeal of an existing law prohibiting racial discriminations in housing." Rather, according to Justice White:

> Private discriminations in housing were now not only free from [the previous legislation] but they also enjoyed a far different status than was true before the passage

> of those statutes. The right to discriminate, including the right to discriminate on racial grounds, was now embodied in the State's basic charter, immune from legislative, executive, or judicial regulation at any level of the state government. Those practicing racial discriminations need no longer rely solely on their personal choice. They could now invoke express constitutional authority, free from censure or interference of any kind from official sources. . . .
>
> [The amendment] was intended to authorize, and does authorize, racial discrimination in the housing market. The right to discriminate is now one of the basic policies of the State. The California Supreme Court believes that the [amendment] will significantly encourage and involve the State in private discriminations. We have been presented with no persuasive considerations indicating that these judgments should be overturned.

The opinion drew a strong dissent from Justice Harlan, joined by Justices Black, Clark, and Stewart, which emphasized California's "neutrality" toward sellers or renters of housing: "All that has happened is that California has effected a pro tanto repeal of its prior statutes forbidding private discrimination. This runs no more afoul of the Fourteenth Amendment than would have California's failure to pass any such antidiscrimination statutes in the first instance." That the provision was constitutionally entrenched was, from the dissenters' perspective, irrelevant.

There are a number of possible descriptions of the holding in *Reitman,* among which are the following:

1. The state has an *affirmative duty* to prevent private discrimination (under some circumstances);
2. a state may not *authorize* private discrimination (how is this different from 1?);
3. a state may not *encourage* or otherwise give succor to private discrimination (how is this different from 1 and 2, at least on the facts of *Reitman*?);
4. once a state has prohibited private discrimination, it may not backtrack;
5. a state may not disable its agencies and subdivisions from prohibiting racial discrimination in the private sector (who is "the state"?);
6. state provisions that have the effect of disadvantaging a racial minority demand an extraordinary justification, and "freedom of contract" is an insufficient justification.

Which, if any, of these rationales offers the best justification for the holding in *Reitman*? To what extent do the rationales accurately describe contemporary constitutional doctrine? For example, compare *Reitman* with the Court's later cases, canvassed in Chapter 6, that require demonstration of an "intent" to discriminate, rather than merely a detrimental impact on the interests of a racial minority, as a predicate condition for Fourteenth Amendment.

Reitman was a 5-4 decision that included a vigorous dissent. Recall the discussions of precedent in Chapters 1 and 6, supra. Should the present majority, if unpersuaded by the Justice White's opinion, hesitate to overrule it?

III. The "Private" Performance of "Public Functions"

A. The Company Town Case

MARSH v. ALABAMA
326 U.S. 501 (1946)
Appeal from the Court of Appeals of Alabama

BLACK, J.

In this case we are asked to decide whether a State, consistently with the First and Fourteenth Amendments, can impose criminal punishment on a person who undertakes to distribute religious literature on the premises of a company-owned town contrary to the wishes of the town's management. The town, a suburb of Mobile, Alabama, known as Chickasaw, is owned by the Gulf Shipbuilding Corporation. Except for that it has all the characteristics of any other American town. The property consists of residential buildings, streets, a system of sewers, a sewage disposal plant and a "business block" on which business places are situated. A deputy of the Mobile County Sheriff, paid by the company, serves as the town's policeman. Merchants and service establishments have rented the stores and business places on the business block and the United States uses one of the places as a post office from which six carriers deliver mail to the people of Chickasaw and the adjacent area. The town and the surrounding neighborhood, which can not be distinguished from the Gulf property by anyone not familiar with the property lines, are thickly settled, and according to all indications the residents use the business block as their regular shopping center. To do so, they now, as they have for many years, make use of a company-owned paved street and sidewalk located alongside the store fronts in order to enter and leave the stores and the post office. Intersecting company-owned roads at each end of the business block lead into a four-lane public highway which runs parallel to the business block at a distance of thirty feet. There is nothing to stop highway traffic from coming onto the business block and upon arrival a traveler may make free use of the facilities available there. In short the town and its shopping district are accessible to and freely used by the public in general and there is nothing to distinguish them from any other town and shopping center except the fact that the title to the property belongs to a private corporation.

Appellant, a Jehovah's Witness, came onto the sidewalk we have just described, stood near the post office and undertook to distribute religious literature. In the stores the corporation had posted a notice which read as follows: "This Is Private Property, and Without Written Permission, No Street, or House Vendor, Agent or Solicitation of Any Kind Will Be Permitted." Appellant was warned that she could not distribute the literature without a permit and told that no permit would be issued to her. She protested that the company rule could not be constitutionally applied so as to prohibit her from distributing religious writings. When she was asked to leave the sidewalk and Chickasaw she declined. The deputy sheriff arrested her and she was charged in the state court with violating Title 14, §426 of the 1940 Alabama Code which makes it a crime to enter or remain on the premises of another after having been warned not to do so. Appellant contended that to construe the state statute as applicable to her activities would abridge her right to freedom of press and religion contrary to the First and Fourteenth Amendments to the Constitution. This contention was rejected [by the state courts]. . . .

Had the title to Chickasaw belonged not to a private but to a municipal corporation and had appellant been arrested for violating a municipal ordinance rather than a ruling by those appointed by the corporation to manage a company town it would have been clear that appellant's conviction must be reversed. . . . Our question then narrows down to this: Can those people who live in or come to Chickasaw be denied freedom of press and religion simply because a single company has legal title to all the town? For it is the State's contention that the mere fact that all the property interest in the town are held by a single company is enough to give that company power, enforceable by a state statute, to abridge these freedoms.

We do not agree that the corporation's property interests settle the question.[a] The state urges in effect that the corporation's right to control the inhabitants of Chickasaw is coextensive with the right of a homeowner to regulate the conduct of his guests. We cannot accept that contention. Ownership does not always mean absolute dominion. The more an owner, for his advantage, opens up his property for use by the public in general, the more do his rights become circumscribed by the statutory and constitutional rights of those who use it. Thus, the owners of privately held bridges, ferries, turnpikes and railroads may not operate them as freely as a farmer does his farm. Since these facilities are built and operated primarily to benefit the public and since their operation is essentially a public function, it is subject to state regulation. . . .

Whether a corporation or a municipality owns or possesses the town the public in either case has an identical interest in the functioning of the community in such manner that the channels of communication remain free. As we have heretofore stated, the town of Chickasaw does not function differently from any other town. The "business block" serves as the community shopping center and is freely accessible and open to the people in the area and those passing through. The managers appointed by the corporation cannot curtail the liberty of press and religion of these people consistently with the purposes of the Constitutional guarantees, and a state statute, as the one here involved, which enforces such action by criminally punishing those who attempt to distribute religious literature clearly violates the First and Fourteenth Amendments to the Constitution.

Many people in the United States live in company-owned towns.[b] These people, just as residents of municipalities, are free citizens of their State and country. Just as all other citizens they must make decisions which affect the welfare of community and nation. To act as good citizens they must be informed. In order to enable them to be properly informed their information must be uncensored. There is no more reason for depriving these people of the liberties guaranteed by

a. We do not question the state court's determination of the issue of "dedication." That determination means that the corporation could, if it so desired, entirely close the sidewalk and the town to the public and is decisive of all questions of state law which depend on the owner's being estopped to reclaim possession of, and the public's holding the title to, or having received an irrevocable easement in, the premises. . . . But determination of the issue of "dedication" does not decide the question under the Federal Constitution here involved.

b. In the bituminous coal industry alone, approximately one-half of the miners in the United States lived in company-owned houses in the period from 1922-23. The percentage varied from 9 per cent in Illinois and Indiana and 64 per cent in Kentucky, to almost 80 per cent in West Virginia. . . .

the First and Fourteenth Amendments than there is for curtailing these freedoms with respect to any other citizen.

When we balance the Constitutional rights of owners of property against those of the people to enjoy freedom of press and religion, as we must here, we remain mindful of the fact that the latter occupy a preferred position. As we have stated before, the right to exercise the liberties safeguarded by the First Amendment "lies at the foundation of free government by free men" and we must in all cases "weigh the circumstances and . . . appraise the . . . reasons . . . in support of the regulation . . . of the rights." In our view the circumstance that the property rights to the premises where the deprivation of liberty, here involved, took place, were held by others than the public, is not sufficient to justify the State's permitting a corporation to govern a community of citizens so as to restrict their fundamental liberties and the enforcement of such restraint by the application of a state statute. Insofar as the State has attempted to impose criminal punishment on appellant for undertaking to distribute religious literature in a company town, its action cannot stand. The case is reversed and the cause remanded for further proceedings not inconsistent with this opinion.

Reversed and remanded.

FRANKFURTER, J., concurring. . . .

I am unable to find legal significance in the fact that a town in which the Constitutional freedoms of religion and speech are invoked happens to be company-owned. . . . Constitutional privileges having such a reach ought not to depend upon a State court's notion of the extent of "dedication" of private property to public purposes. Local determinations of such technical matters govern controversies affecting property. But when decisions by State courts involving local matters are so interwoven with the decision of the question of Constitutional rights that one necessarily involves the other, State determination of local questions cannot control the Federal Constitutional right.

A company-owned town gives rise to a net-work of property relations. As to these, the judicial organ of a State has the final say. But a company-owned town is a town. In its community aspects it does not differ from other towns. These community aspects are decisive in adjusting the relations now before us, and more particularly in adjudicating the clash of freedoms which the Bill of Rights was designed to resolve — the freedom of the community to regulate its life and the freedom of the individual to exercise his religion and to disseminate his ideas. Title to property as defined by State law controls property relations; it cannot control issues of civil liberties which arise precisely because a company town is a town as well as a congeries of property relations. And similarly the technical distinctions on which a finding of "trespass" so often depends are too tenuous to control decision regarding the scope of the vital liberties guaranteed by the Constitution.

REED, J., joined by Stone, C.J., and Burton, J., dissenting. . . .

What the present decision establishes as a principle is that one may remain on private property against the will of the owner and contrary to the law of the state so long as the only objection to his presence is that he is exercising an asserted right to spread there his religious views. . . .

Both Federal and Alabama law permit, so far as we are aware, company towns. By that we mean an area occupied by numerous houses, connected by passways, fenced or not, as the owners may choose. These communities may be essential to furnish proper and convenient living conditions for employees on isolated operations in lumbering, mining, production of high explosives and large-scale farming. The restrictions imposed by the owners upon the occupants are sometimes galling to the employees and may appear unreasonable to outsiders. Unless they fall under the prohibition of some legal rule, however, they are a matter for adjustment between owner and licensee, or by appropriate legislation. . . .

Our Constitution guarantees to every man the right to express his views in an orderly fashion. An essential element of "orderly" is that the man shall also have a right to use the place he chooses for his exposition. The rights of the owner, which the Constitution protects as well as the right of free speech, are not outweighed by the interests of the trespasser, even though he trespasses in behalf of religion or free speech. We cannot say that Jehovah's Witnesses can claim the privilege of a license, which has never been granted, to hold their meetings in other private places, merely because the owner has admitted the public to them for other limited purposes. Even though we have reached the point where this Court is required to force private owners to open their property for the practice there of religious activities or propaganda distasteful to the owner; because of the public interest in freedom of speech and religion, there is no need for the application of such a doctrine here. Appellant, as we have said, was free to engage in such practices on the public highways, without becoming a trespasser on the company's property.

B. *Marsh*'s Progeny and Cousins

1. *The Shopping Center Cases*

In Amalgamated Food Employees Union v. Logan Valley Plaza, 391 U.S. 308 (1968), the Court extended *Marsh* to hold that the petitioner labor union could not constitutionally be enjoined from picketing a supermarket situated entirely within a privately owned shopping center. Justice Marshall wrote that the shopping center was the "functional equivalent . . . of a normal municipal business district . . . open to the public to the same extent as the commercial center of a normal town" and found that the union could not effectively reach its intended audience by picketing and canvassing outside the shopping center. To respondents' assertion of an "absolute right . . . to prohibit any use of their property by others without their consent," Justice Marshall responded:

> [U]nlike a situation involving a person's home, no meaningful claim to protection of a right of privacy can be advanced by respondents here. Nor on the facts of the case can any significant claim to protection of the normal business operation of the property be raised. Naked title is essentially all that is at issue.
>
> The economic development of the United States in the last 20 years reinforces our opinion of the correctness of the approach taken in *Marsh.* The large-scale movement of this country's population from the cities to the suburbs has been accompanied by the advent of the suburban shopping center, typically a cluster of in-

dividual retail units on a single large privately owned tract. It has been estimated that by the end of 1966 there were between 10,000 and 11,000 shopping centers in the United States and Canada, accounting for approximately 37% of the total retail sales in those two countries.

These figures illustrate the substantial consequences for workers seeking to challenge substandard working conditions, consumers protesting shoddy or overpriced merchandise, and minority groups seeking nondiscriminatory hiring policies that a contrary decision here would have. Business enterprises located in downtown areas would be subject to on-the-spot public criticism for their practices, but businesses situated in the suburbs could largely immunize themselves from similar criticism by creating a cordon sanitaire of parking lots around their stores. Neither precedent nor policy compels a result so at variance with the goal of free expression and communication that is the heart of the First Amendment.

. . . Logan Valley Mall is the functional equivalent of a "business block" and for First Amendment purposes must be treated in substantially the same manner.

Justice Black dissented. *Marsh* required that "private property be treated as though it were public" only "when that property has taken on *all* the attributes of a town, i.e. , 'residential buildings, streets, a system of sewers, a sewage disposal plant and a "business block" on which businesses are situated' " (quoting *Marsh*). Otherwise, for the Court "to confiscate a part of an owner's property and give its use to people who want to picket on it" is a "taking" within the meaning of the Fifth Amendment, for which just compensation must be awarded. Justice White also dissented, elaborating on the difference between the company town in *Marsh* and the Logan Valley shopping center:

Logan Valley Plaza is not a town but only a collection of stores. In no sense are any parts of the shopping center dedicated to the public for general purposes or the occupants of the Plaza exercising official powers. The public is invited to the premises but only in order to do business with those who maintain establishments there. The invitation is to shop for the products which are sold. There is no general invitation to use the parking lot, the pickup zone, or the sidewalk except as an adjunct to shopping. No one is invited to use the parking lot as a place to park his car while he goes elsewhere to work. The driveways and lanes for auto traffic are not offered for use as general thoroughfares leading from one public street to another. Those driveways and parking spaces are not public streets and thus available for parades, public meetings, or other activities for which public streets are used. It may be more convenient for cars and trucks to cut through the shopping center to get from one place to another, but surely the Court does not mean to say that the public may use the shopping center property for this purpose. Even if the Plaza has some aspects of "public" property, it is nevertheless true that some public property is available for some uses and not for others; some public property is neither designed nor dedicated for use by pickets or for other communicative activities. The point is whether Logan Valley Plaza is public or private property, it is a place for shopping and not a place for picketing.[20]

20. Justice White did not reiterate Justice Black's suggestion that the Court's decision amounted to an unlawful taking of respondents' property. Indeed, he concluded the opinion by noting that "[i]f it were shown that Congress has thought it necessary to permit picketing on private property, either to further the national labor policy under the Commerce Clause or to implement and enforce the First Amendment, we would have quite a different case." (Justice Harlan dissented, believing that federal labor legislation arguably was applicable, but that since petitioners had failed to raise this nonconstitutional question, the Court should dismiss the writ of certiorari as improvidently granted.)

Logan Valley was severely limited four years later by Lloyd Corp. v. Tanner, 407 U.S. 551 (1972), which held that respondent leafleteers were not entitled to an injunction against petitioner's interference with their distribution of antiwar tracts in the interior mall of petitioner's large enclosed shopping center. Writing for the Court, Justice Powell distinguished *Logan Valley* on two grounds. First, unlike the picketing in the earlier case, the distribution of leaflets here "had no relation to any purpose for which the center was . . . being used"; "the message sought to be conveyed by respondents was directed to all members of the public, not solely to patrons of Lloyd Center. . . ."[21] Second, in *Logan Valley,* the picketers "would have been deprived of all reasonable opportunity to convey their message to the patrons of the [supermarket] had they been denied access to the shopping center." Here, by contrast, the shopping mall was surrounded by public sidewalks, and "[i]t would be an unwarranted infringement of property rights to require them to yield to the exercise of First Amendment rights under circumstances where adequate alternative avenues of communication exist." Justice Powell also emphasized, though not by way of distinction, that Lloyd Center had a nondiscriminatory policy "enforced against *all* handbilling." The opinion concludes by reiterating the suggestion, voiced by Justice Black in *Logan Valley,* that the petitioner's right to control its private property is rooted in the Fifth Amendment:

> [Property does not] lose its private character merely because the public is generally invited to use it for designated purposes. Few would argue that a freestanding store, with abutting parking space for customers, assumes significant public attributes merely because the public is invited to shop there. Nor is size alone the controlling factor. The essentially private character of a store and its privately owned abutting property does not change by virtue of being large or clustered with other stores in a modern shopping center. This is not to say that no differences may exist with respect to government regulation or rights of citizens arising by virtue of the size and diversity of activities carried on within a privately owned facility serving the public. There will be, for example, problems with respect to public health and safety which vary in degree and in the appropriate government response, depending upon the size and character of a shopping center, an office building, a sports arena, or other large facility serving the public for commercial purposes. We do say that the Fifth and Fourteenth Amendment rights of private property owners, as well as the First Amendment rights of all citizens, must be respected and protected. The Framers of the Constitution certainly did not think these fundamental rights of a free society are incompatible with each other. There may be situations where accommodations between them, and the drawing of lines to assure due protection of both, are not easy. But on the facts presented in this case, the answer is clear.[22]

Justice Marshall joined by Justices Douglas, Brennan, and Stewart, dissented. Pointing out that petitioner allowed schools, presidential candidates, and service

21. In *Logan Valley* the Court had stated that it did not decide "whether respondents' property rights could, consistently with the First Amendment, justify a bar on picketing which was not . . . directly related in its purpose to the use to which the shopping center property was being put."

22. Although Justice Powell purports to distinguish and limit, rather than overrule, *Logan Valley,* the opinion incorporates much language from the dissents in the earlier case. Justice Marshall suggests in dissent that "one may suspect from reading the opinion of the Court that it is *Logan Valley* itself that the Court finds bothersome" and that the major difference is that "the composition of this Court has radically changed in [the] four years" since *Logan Valley.*

and veterans' organizations to speak, hold ceremonies and rallies, and solicit funds in the mall, he contended that "respondents' activities were directly related in purpose to the use to which the shopping center was being put." But, in any event, there was no "logical reason to treat differently speech that is related to subjects other than the Center and its member stores." In each case, rather, a balance must be struck between the "preferred freedom" to speak and the property owner's interest. Justice Marshall argued that "the only way [respondents] can express themselves to a broad range of citizens on issues of general public concern is to picket, or to handbill, or . . . to speak in those areas in which most of their fellow citizens can be found. One such area is the business district of a city or town or its functional equivalent." He dismissed petitioner's argument that the respondents' leafletting would disturb the Center's customers, noting that their message was less likely to deter potential customers from patronizing the stores than leafletting directed against the stores themselves (as in *Logan Valley*); and he found "patently frivolous petitioner's argument that . . . [it] would face inordinate difficulties in removing litter from its premises." Justice Marshall concluded:

> It would not be surprising in the future to see cities rely more and more on private businesses to perform functions once performed by governmental agencies. The advantage of reduced expenses and an increased tax base cannot be overstated. As governments rely on private enterprise, public property decreases in favor of privately owned property. It becomes harder and harder for citizens to find means to communicate with other citizens. Only the wealthy may find effective communication possible unless we adhere to Marsh v. Alabama and continue to hold that "[t]he more an owner, for his advantage, opens up his property for use by the public in general, the more do his rights become circumscribed by the statutory and constitutional rights of those who use it."

Hudgens v. NLRB, 424 U.S. 507 (1975), held that, in the absence of congressional legislation, the Constitution did not protect a union's right to picket a store located in a shopping center to protest the employer's practices at a different location. A majority agreed that *Logan Valley* had overruled *Lloyd* or that, in any case, *Lloyd* should now be overruled.

Note: Does the Finding of No State Action Entail a Right Protected Against State Regulation?

In the aftermath of *Hudgens* and the formal overruling of *Logan Valley,* some analysts suggested that the cases stood for the proposition that the property owners had in effect been found to possess a strong property right protected against state regulation. And in PruneYard Shopping Center v. Robins, 447 U.S. 74 (1980), a shopping-center owner invoked Justice Powell's language in *Lloyd* to argue that the California Supreme Court violated the Fourteenth Amendment when it interpreted the California state constitution to grant political petitioners a right of access to the center.[23] The owner argued, among other things, that this

23. See also p.375 supra.

constituted a taking. The Supreme Court, through Justice Rehnquist, unanimously rejected the claim:

> Our reasoning in *Lloyd* . . . does not ex proprio vigore limit the authority of the State to exercise its police power or its sovereign right to adopt in its own Constitution individual liberties more expansive than those conferred by the Federal Constitution. . . . [I]t is, of course, well established that a State in the exercise of its police power may adopt reasonable restrictions on private property so long as the restrictions do not amount to a taking without just compensation or contravene any other federal constitutional provision.

Does this suggest that the "state action" limitation is best understood in terms of concerns about federalism or separation of powers rather than of an affirmative desire to safeguard individual autonomy as such?

2. *The Park Case*

In 1911, Senator Bacon devised Baconsfield to the city of Macon, Georgia, for use as a park for whites only. The city adhered to the terms of the will until some time after *Brown,* when it opened the park to Negroes. In Evans v. Newton (the *Park* case), the park's managers sued to remove the city as trustee and replace it with private trustees who would enforce the racial limitation, Negro citizens intervened in opposition, and heirs of the senator requested that the property revert to them unless the conditions of the will were met. The state court accepted the resignation of the city as trustee and appointed individual trustees to avoid failure of the trust.

The Court held that the private trustees could not exclude Negroes from the park. The central holding of Evans v. Newton is premised on the government's involvement of many years in maintaining and caring for the park.

EVANS v. NEWTON, 382 U.S. 296 (1966): DOUGLAS, J. . . . For years it was an integral part of the City of Macon's activities. From the pleadings we assume it was swept, manicured, watered, patrolled, and maintained by the city as a public facility for whites only, as well as granted tax exemption under Ga. Code Ann. §92-201. The momentum it acquired as a public facility is certainly not dissipated ipso facto by the appointment of "private" trustees. So far as this record shows, there has been no change in municipal maintenance and concern over this facility. Whether these public characteristics will in time be dissipated is wholly conjectural. If the municipality remains entwined in the management or control of the park, it remains subject to the restraints of the Fourteenth Amendment just as the private utility in Public Utilities Commn. v. Pollak, 343 U.S. 451, 462, remained subject to the Fifth Amendment because of the surveillance which federal agencies had over its affairs. We only hold that where the tradition of municipal control had become firmly established, we cannot take judicial notice that the mere substitution of trustees instantly transferred this park from the public to the private sector.

This conclusion is buttressed by the nature of the service rendered the community by a park. The service rendered even by a private park of this character is municipal in nature. It is open to every white person, there being no selective element other than race. Golf clubs, social centers, luncheon clubs, schools such as Tuskegee was at least in origin, and other like organizations in the private sector are often racially oriented. A park, on the other hand, is more like a fire department or police department that traditionally serves the community. Mass recreation through the use of parks is plainly in the public domain; and state courts that aid private parties to perform that public function on a segregated basis implicate the State in conduct proscribed by the Fourteenth Amendment. Like the streets of the company town in Marsh v. Alabama, the elective process of Terry v. Adams, and the transit system of Public Utilities Commn. v. Pollak, the predominant character and purpose of this park are municipal.[24]

HARLAN, J., joined by Stewart, J., dissenting [criticized the first of the Court's grounds as based on unsupportable assumptions and conjecture, and then attacked the "public function" theory:] . . . More serious than the absence of any firm doctrinal support for this theory of state action are its potentialities for the future. Its failing as a principle of decision in the realm of Fourteenth Amendment concerns can be shown by comparing — among other examples that might be drawn from the still unfolding sweep of governmental functions — the "public function" of privately established schools with that of privately owned parks. Like parks, the purpose schools serve is important to the public. Like parks private control exists, but there is also a very strong tradition of public control in this field. Like parks, schools may be available to almost anyone of one race or religion but to no others. Like parks, there are normally alternatives for those shut out but there may also be inconveniences and disadvantages caused by the restriction. Like parks, the extent of school intimacy varies greatly depending on the size and character of the institution.

For all the resemblance, the majority assumes that its decision leaves unaffected the traditional view that the Fourteenth Amendment does not compel private schools to adapt their admission policies to its requirements, but that such matters are left to the States acting within constitutional bounds. I find it difficult, however, to avoid the conclusion that this decision opens the door to reversal of these basic constitutional concepts, and, at least in logic, jeopardizes the existence of denominationally restricted schools while making of every college entrance rejection letter a potential Fourteenth Amendment question.

While this process of analogy might be spun out to reach privately owned orphanages, libraries, garbage collection companies, detective agencies, and a host of other functions commonly regarded as nongovernmental though paralleling

24. See also Justice Douglas' introductory passage:

> There are two complementary principles to be reconciled in this case. One is the right of the individual to pick his own associates so as to express his preferences and dislikes, and to fashion his private life by joining such clubs and groups as he chooses. The other is the constitutional ban in the Equal Protection Clause of the Fourteenth Amendment against state-sponsored racial inequality.

fields of governmental activity, the example of schools is, I think, sufficient to indicate the pervasive potentialities of this "public function" theory of state action. It substitutes for the comparatively clear and concrete tests of state action a catch-phrase approach as vague and amorphous as it is far-reaching. It dispenses with the sound and careful principles of past decisions in this realm. And it carries the seeds of transferring to federal authority vast areas of concern whose regulation has wisely been left by the Constitution to the States.

3. *The White Primary Cases*

In Nixon v. Herndon, 273 U.S. 536 (1927), the Court struck down under the equal protection clause a Texas statute providing that "in no event shall a negro be eligible to participate in a Democratic party primary election." Texas responded by enacting a measure delegating to the state executive committee of the Democratic Party the authority to prescribe qualifications for voters in the primary. The committee then disqualified Negroes from voting. But in Nixon v. Condon, 286 U.S. 73 (1932), the Court found that the statute effectively made the committee an agent of the state and held that the committee's action violated the equal protection clause. Texas enacted no new statute, but the state Democratic convention then voted to exclude Negroes from the primary. In Grovey v. Townsend, 295 U.S. 45 (1935), the Court unanimously refused to invalidate the convention's rule, holding that the state was no longer unconstitutionally involved.

Grovey survived for only nine years. In Smith v. Allwright, 321 U.S. 649 (1944), the Court held that the all-white primary mandated by the state convention violated the Fifteenth Amendment: Where the primary is an "integral part" of a state's election machinery, the state may not "[cast] its electoral process in a form which permits a private organization to practice racial discrimination in the election."

The final decision of the series was Terry v. Adams, 345 U.S. 461 (1953). The Jaybird Democratic Association was a county political club in Texas that held a preprimary election, not recognized or assisted by the state or by the state Democratic Party, in which all white voters in the county were eligible to participate. Winning the Jaybird election carried no legal consequences, but Jaybird candidates almost invariably won the Democratic primary and the general election. In three opinions, none of which commanded a majority, the Court held that the Fifteenth Amendment prohibited the exclusion of Negro voters from the preprimary.

Justice Black, joined by Justices Burton and Douglas, noted that the Fifteenth Amendment reached "any election in which public issues are decided or public officials selected" and that the state could not constitutionally permit the Jaybird's discriminatory "duplication of its election processes," which had the effect of denying Negroes "an effective voice in governmental affairs."[25] Justice

25. See also Rice v. Elmore, 165 F.2d 387 (4th Cir. 1947), cited with approval by Justice Black: "Having undertaken to perform an important function relating to the exercise of sovereignty by the people, [a political party] may not violate the fundamental principles laid down by the Constitution for its exercise."

Clark, joined by Chief Justice Vinson and Justices Reed and Jackson, took a similar approach, noting that the Jaybird Democratic Association is the "decisive power in the county's recognized electoral process":

> Accordingly, when a state structures its electoral apparatus in a form which devolves upon a political organization the uncontested choice of public officials, that organization itself, in whatever disguise, takes on those attributes of government which draw the Constitution's safeguards into play.[26]

4. *The Public Utility Case*

JACKSON v. METROPOLITAN EDISON CO., 419 U.S. 345 (1974): [The facts of the case are presented above on page 1310.] REHNQUIST, J. . . . Petitioner next urges that state action is present because respondent provides an essential public service required to be supplied on a reasonably continuous basis by [state law] and hence performs a "public function." We have of course found state action present in the exercise by private entity of powers traditionally exclusively reserved to the State. If we were dealing with the exercise by Metropolitan of some power delegated to it by the State which is traditionally associated with sovereignty, such as eminent domain, our case would be quite a different one. But while the Pennsylvania statute imposes an obligation to furnish service on regulated utilities, it imposes no such obligation on the State. The Pennsylvania courts have rejected the contention that the furnishing of utility services are either state functions or municipal duties.

Perhaps in recognition of the fact that the supplying of utility service is not traditionally the exclusive prerogative of the State, petitioner invites the expansion of the doctrine of this limited line of cases into a broad principle that all businesses "affected with the public interest" are state actors in all their actions.

We decline the invitation for reasons stated long ago in Nebbia v. New York, 291 U.S. 502 (1934), in the course of rejecting a substantive due process attack on state legislation: "It is clear that there is no closed class or category of businesses affected with a public interest. . . . The phrase 'affected with a public interest' can, in the nature of things, mean no more than that an industry, for adequate reason, is subject to control for the public good. . . ."

Doctors, optometrists, lawyers, Metropolitan, and *Nebbia's* upstate New York grocery selling a quart of milk are all in regulated businesses, providing arguably essential goods and services, "affected with a public interest." We do not believe that such a status converts their every action, absent more, into that of the State. . . .

MARSHALL, J., dissenting. . . . The fact that the Metropolitan Edison Company supplies an essential public service that is in many communities supplied by the

26. Justice Frankfurter also wrote a concurring opinion that is somewhat obscure. He found state action in the fact that "those charged by State law with the duty of assuring all eligible voters an opportunity to participate in the selection of candidates at the primary — the county election officials who are normally leaders in their communities — participate by voting in the Jaybird primary" and thus "condone" its subversion of the laws regulating the state primary. Only Justice Minton dissented, finding that no state action had been shown.

government weighs more heavily for me than for the majority. The Court concedes that state action might be present if the activity in question were "traditionally associated with sovereignty," but it then undercuts that point by suggesting that a particular service is not a public function if the State in question has not required that it be governmentally operated. This reads the "public function" argument too narrowly. The whole point of the "public function" cases is to look behind the State's decision to provide public services through private parties. In my view, utility service is traditionally identified with the State through universal public regulation or ownership to a degree sufficient to render it a "public function."

I agree with the majority that it requires more than a finding that a particular business is "affected with the public interest" before constitutional burdens can be imposed on that business. But when the activity in question is of such public importance that the State invariably either provides the service itself or permits private companies to act as state surrogates in providing it, much more is involved than just a matter of public interest. In those cases, the State has determined that if private companies wish to enter the field, they will have to surrender many of the prerogatives normally associated with private enterprise and behave in many ways like a governmental body. And when the State's regulatory scheme has gone that far, it seems entirely consistent to impose on the public utility the constitutional burdens normally reserved for the State. . . .

5. The Olympic Committee Case

The complainants in the *United States Olympic Committee* case, p.1314 supra, also argued that state action was present there because of the "public function" served by the Committee. Justice Powell responded that while the Court has "found action to be governmental action when the challenged entity performs functions that have been 'traditionally the *exclusive* prerogative of the Federal Government,' . . . [t]he Act merely authorizes the USOC to coordinate activities that have always been performed by private entities. Neither the conduct nor the coordination of amateur sports has been a traditional governmental function."

Justice Brennan, joined by Justice Marshall, dissented on this point as well:

> The USOC performs a distinctive, traditional governmental function: it represents this Nation to the world community. The USOC is by virtue of [the statute] our country's exclusive representative to the International Olympic Committee (IOC), a highly visible and influentatial international body. The Court overlooks the extraordinary representational responsibilities that Congress has placed on the USOC.

Justice Brennan goes on to review some of the recent history of the Olympic Games in order to establish their great national and international importance. He notes that one source of the statute was concern about American performance in the Games, which led President Ford in 1975 to appoint a Commission on Olympic Sports to consider the situation. In its report it advised "the institution of a central sports organization for the United States." Thus, he concludes, "[t]he better analogy . . . is to the company town in *Marsh* or to the private political party in *Terry* [rather than to the private nursing home in *Blum* or to the private school in *Rendell-Baker*.]"

6. The Warehouseman's Lien Case

In Sniadach v. Family Finance Corp., 395 U.S. 337 (1972), the Court struck down a Wisconsin statute under which, when a creditor filed the appropriate papers, the clerk of court issued a garnishment order to an allegedly defaulting debtor's employer. The clerk's task was purely ministerial, and the order issued without notice to the debtor. The Supreme Court held that prejudgment garnishment without notice and a prior hearing deprived the debtor of her property without due process. *Sniadach* involved a contract between a finance company and a consumer. In North Georgia Finishing, Inc. v. Di-Chem, Inc., 419 U.S. 601 (1975), the Court extended the holding to prohibit the prejudgment garnishment of a commercial debtor's bank account under similar circumstances. Fuentes v. Shevin, 407 U.S. 67 (1972), relied on *Sniadach* to invalidate state statutes that authorized the sheriff to seize household goods sold under conditional sales contracts on the basis of a writ issued by the clerk of court upon the seller-creditor's ex parte application.

The only contested issue in these cases was whether the due process clause required a hearing before the debtor's property was garnished or seized. Both the majority and the dissenting Justices assumed, without discussion, the existence of state action — that is, they assumed that the challenged procedures or transactions were constrained by the requirements of the due process clause of the Fourteenth Amendment.

In the years following *Sniadach,* other creditors' remedies were challenged on due process grounds. These included various "self-help" remedies, whereby creditors having security interests in goods repossessed them from defaulting debtors simply by taking them — without even the ministerial intervention of a state official. Such self-help repossession by secured creditors has long been permitted in many jurisdictions, and the practice is codified by section 9-503 of the Uniform Commercial Code: "Unless otherwise agreed a secured party has on default the right to take possession of the collateral. In taking possession a secured party may proceed without judicial process if this can be done without breach of the peace." Most courts dismissed constitutional challenges to section 9-503 on the ground that, in the absence of any participation by a state official, self-help repossession was private rather than state action and therefore not within the purview of the Fourteenth Amendment. In Flagg Brothers, Inc. v. Brooks, the Supreme Court addressed a variant of the self-help procedure and held that the debtors' complaint was properly dismissed on these grounds.

FLAGG BROS., INC. v. BROOKS

436 U.S. 149 (1978)

Certiorari to the United States Court of Appeals for the Second Circuit

REHNQUIST, J.

The question presented by this litigation is whether a warehouseman's proposed sale of goods entrusted to him for storage, as permitted by New York Uniform Commercial Code §7-210 (McKinney 1964), is an action properly attributable to the state of New York. . . .

I

According to her complaint, the allegations of which we must accept as true, respondent Shirley Brooks and her family were evicted from their apartment in Mount Vernon, N.Y., on June 13, 1973. The city marshal arranged for Brooks' possessions to be stored by petitioner Flagg Brothers, Inc., in its warehouse. Brooks was informed of the cost of moving and storage, and she instructed the workmen to proceed, although she found the price too high. On August 25, 1973, after a series of disputes over the validity of the charges being claimed by petitioner Flagg Brothers, Brooks received a letter demanding that her account be brought up to date within 10 days "or your furniture will be sold." A series of subsequent letters from respondent and her attorneys produced no satisfaction.

Brooks thereupon initiated this class action in the District Court under 42 U.S.C. §1983, seeking damages, an injunction against the threatened sale of her belongings, and the declaration that such a sale pursuant to §7-210 would violate the Due Process and Equal Protection Clauses of the Fourteenth Amendment. . . . [T]he District Court, relying primarily on our decision in Jackson v. Metropolitan Edison Co., 419 U.S. 345 (1974), dismissed the complaint for failure to state a claim for relief under §1983.

A divided panel of the Court of Appeals reversed. . . .

II

. . . [R]espondents allege that Flagg Brothers has deprived them of their right, secured by the Fourteenth Amendment, to be free from state deprivations of property without due process of law. Thus, they must establish not only that Flagg Brothers acted under color of the challenged statute, but also that its actions are properly attributable to the State of New York.

It must be noted that respondents have named no public officials as defendants in this action. The city marshal, who supervised their evictions, was dismissed from the case by the consent of all the parties. This total absence of overt official involvement plainly distinguishes this case from earlier decisions imposing procedural restrictions on creditors' remedies such as North Georgia Finishing, Inc. v. Di-Chem, Inc., 419 U.S. 601 (1975); Fuentes v. Shevin, 407 U.S. 67 (1972); Sniadach v. Family Finance Corp., 395 U.S. 337 (1969). . . . While as a factual matter any person with sufficient physical power may deprive a person of his property, only a State or a private person whose action "may be fairly treated as that of the State itself," *Jackson*, may deprive him of "an interest encompassed within the Fourteenth Amendment's protection." Thus, the only issue presented by this case is whether Flagg Brothers' action may fairly be attributed to the State of New York. We conclude that it may not.

III

Respondents' primary contention is that New York has delegated to Flagg Brothers a power "traditionally exclusively reserved to the State." *Jackson.* They argue that the resolution of private disputes is a traditional function of civil government, and that the State in §7-210 has delegated this function to Flagg Brothers. Respondents, however, have read too much into the language of our previous cases. While many functions have been traditionally performed by governments, very few have been "exclusively reserved to the State."

One such area has been elections. While the Constitution protects private rights of association and advocacy with regard to the election of public officials, our cases make it clear that the conduct of the elections themselves is an exclusively public function. This principle was established by a series of cases challenging the exclusion of blacks from participation in primary elections in Texas. Terry v. Adams, 345 U.S. 461 (1953); Smith v. Allwright, 321 U.S. 649 (1944); Nixon v. Condon, 286 U.S. 73 (1932). Although the rationale of these cases may be subject to some dispute, their scope is carefully defined. The doctrine does not reach to all forms of private political activity, but encompasses only state-regulated elections or elections conducted by organizations which in practice produce "the uncontested choice of public officials." *Terry,* supra, at 484 (Clark, J., concurring). . . .

A second line of cases under the public-function doctrine originated with Marsh v. Alabama, 326 U.S. 501 (1946). Just as the Texas Democratic Party in *Smith* and the Jaybird Democratic Association in *Terry* effectively performed the entire public function of selecting public officials, so too the Gulf Shipbuilding Corp. performed all the necessary municipal functions in the town of Chickasaw, Ala., which it owned. Under those circumstances, the Court concluded it was bound to recognize the right of a group of Jehovah's Witnesses to distribute religious literature on its streets. The Court expanded this municipal-function theory in Food Employees v. Logan Valley Plaza, Inc., 391 U.S. 308 (1968), to encompass the activities of a private shopping center. It did so over the vigorous dissent of Mr. Justice Black, the author of *Marsh*. . . . This Court ultimately adopted Mr. Justice Black's interpretation of the limited reach of *Marsh* in Hudgens v. NLRB, 424 U.S. 507 (1976), in which it announced the overruling of *Logan Valley*.

These two branches of the public-function doctrine have in common the feature of exclusivity.[a] Although the elections held by the Democratic Party and its affiliates were the only meaningful elections in Texas, and the streets owned by the Gulf Shipbuilding Corp. were the only streets in Chickasaw, the proposed sale by Flagg Brothers under §7-210 is not the only means of resolving this purely private dispute. Respondent Brooks has never alleged that state law barred her from seeking a waiver of Flagg Brothers' right to sell her goods at the time she

a. Respondents also contend that Evans v. Newton, 382 U.S. 296 (1966), establishes that the operation of a park for recreational purposes is an exclusively public function. We doubt that *Newton* intended to establish any such broad doctrine in the teeth of the experience of several American entrepreneurs who amassed great fortunes by operating parks for recreational purposes. We think *Newton* rests on a finding of ordinary state action under extraordinary circumstances. The Court's opinion emphasizes that the record showed "no change in the municipal maintenance and concern over this facility" after the transfer of title to private trustees. That transfer had not been shown to have eliminated the actual involvement of the city in the daily maintenance and care of the park.

authorized their storage. Presumably, respondent Jones, who alleges that she never authorized the storage of her goods, could have sought to replevy her goods at any time under state law. See N.Y. Civ. Prac. Law §7101 et seq. (McKinney 1963). The challenged statute itself provides a damages remedy against the warehouseman for violations of its provisions. N.Y.U.C.C. §7-210(9) (McKinney 1964). This system of rights and remedies, recognizing the traditional place of private arrangements in ordering relationships in the commercial world,[b] can hardly be said to have delegated to Flagg Brothers an exclusive prerogative of the sovereign.[c]

Whatever the particular remedies available under New York law, we do not consider a more detailed description of them necessary to our conclusion that the settlement of disputes between debtors and creditors is not traditionally an exclusive public function. Cf. United States v. Kras, 409 U.S. 434, 445-446 (1973). Creditors and debtors have had available to them historically a far wider number of choices than has one who would be an elected public official, or a member of Jehovah's Witnesses who wished to distribute literature in Chickasaw, Ala., at the time *Marsh* was decided. Our analysis requires no parsing of the difference between various commercial liens and other remedies to support the conclusion that this entire field of activity is outside the scope of *Terry* and *Marsh*.[d] This is true whether these commercial rights and remedies are created by statute or decisional law. To rely upon the historical antecedents of a particular practice

b. Unlike the parade of horribles suggested by our Brother Stevens in dissent, this case does not involve state authorization of private breach of the peace.

c. It is undoubtedly true, as our Brother Stevens says in dissent, that "respondents have a property interest in the possessions that the warehouseman proposes to sell." But that property interest is not a monolithic, abstract concept hovering in the legal stratosphere. It is a bundle of rights in personalty, the metes and bounds of which are determined by the decisional and statutory law of the State of New York. The validity of the property interest in these possessions which respondents previously acquired from some other private person depends on New York law, and the manner in which that same property interest in these same possessions may be lost or transferred to still another private person likewise depends on New York law. It would intolerably broaden, beyond the scope of any of our previous cases, the notion of state action under the Fourteenth Amendment to hold that the mere existence of a body of property law in a State, whether decisional or statutory, itself amounted to "state action" even though no state process or state officials were ever involved in enforcing that body of law.

The situation is clearly distinguishable from cases such as North Georgia Finishing, Inc. v. DiChem, Inc., 419 U.S. 601 (1975); Fuentes v. Shevin, 407 U.S. 67 (1972); and Sniadach v. Family Finance Corp., 395 U.S. 337 (1969). In each of those cases a government official participated in the physical deprivation of what had concededly been the constitutional plaintiff's property under state law before the deprivation occurred. The constitutional protection attaches not because, as in *North Georgia Finishing*, a clerk issued a ministerial writ out of the court, but because as a result of that writ the property of the debtor was seized and impounded by the affirmative command of the law of Georgia. The creditor in *North Georgia Finishing* had not simply sought to pursue the collection of his debt by private means permissible under Georgia law; he had invoked the authority of the Georgia court, which in turn had ordered the garnishee not to pay over money which previously had been property of the debtor.

d. This is not to say that dispute resolution between creditors and debtors involves a category of human affairs that is never subject to constitutional constraints. We merely address the public-function doctrine as respondents would apply it to this case.

Self-help of the type involved in this case is not significantly different from creditor remedies generally, whether created by common law or enacted by legislatures. New York's statute has done nothing more than authorize (and indeed limit) — without participation by any public official — what Flagg Brothers would tend to do, even in the absence of such authorization, i.e., dispose of respondents' property in order to free up its valuable storage space. The proposed sale pursuant to the lien in this case is not a significant departure from traditional private arrangements.

would result in the constitutional condemnation in one State of a remedy found perfectly permissible in another.

Thus, even if we were inclined to extend the sovereign-function doctrine outside of its present carefully confined bounds, the field of private commercial transactions would be a particularly inappropriate area into which to expand it. We conclude that our sovereign-function cases do not support a finding of state action here. . . .

[W]e would be remiss if we did not note that there are a number of state and municipal functions not covered by our election cases or governed by the reasoning of *Marsh* which have been administered with a greater degree of exclusivity by States and municipalities than has the function of so-called "dispute resolution." Among these are such functions as education, fire and police protection, and tax collection. We express no view as to the extent, if any, to which a city or State might be free to delegate to private parties the performance of such functions and thereby avoid the strictures of the Fourteenth Amendment. . . .

IV

Respondents further urge that Flagg Brothers' proposed action is properly attributable to the State because the State has authorized and encouraged it in enacting §7-210. Our cases state "that a State is responsible for the . . . act of a private party when the State, by its law, has compelled the act." *Adickes.* This Court, however, has never held that a State's mere acquiescence in a private action converts that action into that of the State. The Court rejected a similar argument in *Jackson*. . . .

It is quite immaterial that the State has embodied its decision not to act in statutory form. If New York had no commercial statutes at all, its courts would still be faced with the decision whether to prohibit or to permit the sort of sale threatened here the first time an aggrieved bailor came before them for relief. A judicial decision to deny relief would be no less an "authorization" or "encouragement" of that sale than the legislature's decision embodied in this statute. It was recognized in the earliest interpretations of the Fourteenth Amendment "that a State may act through different agencies, — either by its legislative, its executive, or its judicial authorities; and the prohibitions of the amendment extend to all action of the State" infringing rights protected thereby. Virginia v. Rives, 100 U.S. 313, 318 (1880). If the mere denial of judicial relief is considered sufficient encouragement to make the State responsible for those private acts, all private deprivations of property would be converted into public acts whenever the State, for whatever reason, denies relief sought by the putative property owner. . . .

Here, the State of New York has not compelled the sale of a bailor's goods, but has merely announced the circumstances under which its courts will not interfere with a private sale. Indeed, the crux of respondents' complaint is not that the State *has* acted, but that it has *refused* to act. This statutory refusal to act is no different in principle from an ordinary statute of limitations whereby the State declines to provide a remedy for private deprivations of property after the passage of a given period of time. . . .

STEVENS, J., joined by White and Marshall, JJ., dissenting. . . .

In my judgment the Court's holding is fundamentally inconsistent with, if not foreclosed by, our prior decisions which have imposed procedural restrictions on the State's authorization of certain creditors' remedies. See North Georgia Finishing, Inc. v. Di-Chem, Inc., 419 U.S. 601; Fuentes v. Shevin, 407 U.S. 67; Sniadach v. Family Finance Corp., 395 U.S. 337.

There is no question in this case but that respondents have a property interest in the possessions that the warehouseman proposes to sell. It is also clear that, whatever power of sale the warehouseman has, it does not derive from the consent of the respondents. The claimed power derives solely from the State, and specifically from §7-210 of the New York Uniform Commercial Code. The question is whether a state statute which authorizes a private party to deprive a person of his property without his consent must meet the requirements of the Due Process Clause of the Fourteenth Amendment. This question must be answered in the affirmative unless the State has virtually unlimited power to transfer interests in private property without any procedural protections.[a]

In determining that New York's statute cannot be scrutinized under the Due Process Clause, the Court reasons that the warehouseman's proposed sale is solely private action because the state statute "*permits* but does not compel" the sale (emphasis added), and because the warehouseman has not been delegated a power "*exclusively* reserved to the State," (emphasis added). Under this approach a State could enact laws authorizing private citizens to use self-help in countless situations without any possibility of federal challenge. A state statute could authorize the warehouseman to retain all proceeds of the lien sale, even if they far exceeded the amount of the alleged debt; it could authorize finance companies to enter private homes to repossess merchandise; or indeed, it could authorize "any person with sufficient physical power" to acquire and sell the property of his weaker neighbor. An attempt to challenge the validity of any such outrageous statute would be defeated by the reasoning the Court uses today: The Court's rationale would characterize action pursuant to such a statute as purely private action, which the State permits but does not compel, in an area not exclusively reserved to the State.

As these examples suggest, the distinctions between "permission" and "compulsion" on the one hand, and "exclusive" and "nonexclusive," on the other, cannot be determinative factors in state-action analysis. There is no great chasm between "permission" and "compulsion" requiring particular state action to fall within one or the other definitional camp. . . . In this case, the State of New York, by enacting §7-210 of the Uniform Commercial Code, has acted in the most effective and unambiguous way a State can act. This section specifically authorizes petitioner Flagg Brothers to sell respondents' possessions; it details the procedures that petitioner must follow; and it grants petitioner the power to convey good title to goods that are now owned by respondents to a third party.

. . . New York has authorized the warehouseman to perform what is clearly a state function. The test of what is a state function for purposes of the Due Process

a. It could be argued that since the State has the power to create property interests, it should also have the power to determine what procedures should attend the deprivation of those interests. See Arnett v. Kennedy, 416 U.S. 134, 153-154 (Rehnquist, J.). Although a majority of this Court has never adopted that position, today's opinion revives the theory in a somewhat different setting by holding that the State can shield its legislation affecting property interests from due process scrutiny by delegating authority to private parties.

Clause has been variously phrased. Most frequently the issue is presented in terms of whether the State has delegated a function traditionally and historically associated with sovereignty. See, e.g., Jackson v. Metropolitan Edison Co., 419 U.S. 345, 353; Evans v. Newton, 382 U.S. 296, 299. In this Court, petitioners have attempted to argue that the nonconsensual transfer of property rights is not a traditional function of the sovereign. The overwhelming historical evidence is to the contrary, however,[b] and the Court wisely does not adopt this position. Instead, the Court reasons that state action cannot be found because the State has not delegated to the warehouseman an *exclusive* sovereign function.[c] This distinction, however, is not consistent with our prior decisions on state action; is not even adhered to by the Court in this case[d] and, most importantly, is inconsistent with the line of cases beginning with Sniadach v. Family Finance Corp., 395 U.S. 337.

Since *Sniadach* this Court has scrutinized various state statutes regulating the debtor-creditor relationship for compliance with the Due Process Clause. See also North Georgia Finishing, Inc. v. Di-Chem, Inc., 419 U.S. 601; Mitchell v. W.T. Grant Co., 416 U.S. 600; Fuentes v. Shevin, 407 U.S. 67. . . .

[These cases] must be viewed as reflecting this Court's recognition of the significance of the State's role in defining *and controlling* the debtor-creditor relationship. The Court's language to this effect in the various debtor-creditor cases has been unequivocal. In Fuentes v. Shevin the Court stressed that the statutes in question "abdicate[d] effective state control over state power." And it is clear that what was of concern in *Shevin* was the *private* use of state power to achieve a nonconsensual resolution of a commercial dispute. The state statutes placed the state power to repossess property in the hands of an interested private party, just as the state statute in this case places the state power to conduct judicially binding sales in satisfaction of a lien in the hands of the warehouseman.

. . . Yet the very defect that made the statutes in *Shevin* and *North Georgia Finishing* unconstitutional — lack of state control — is, under today's decision, the

b. . . . I fully agree with the Court that the decision of whether or not a statute is subject to due process scrutiny should not depend on " 'whether a particular class of creditor did or did not enjoy the same freedom to act in Elizabethan or Georgian England.' " Nonetheless some reference to history and well-settled practice is necessary to determine whether a particular action is a "traditional state function." See Jackson v. Metropolitan Edison Co., 419 U.S. 345. Indeed, in *Jackson* the Court specifically referred to Pennsylvania decisions, rendered in 1879 and 1898, which had rejected the contention that the furnishing of utility services was a state function.

c. As I understand the Court's notion of "exclusivity," the sovereign function here is not exclusive because there may be other state remedies, under different statutes or common-law theories, available to respondents. Even if I were to accept the notion that sovereign functions must be "exclusive," the Court's description of exclusivity is incomprehensible. The question is whether a particular action is a uniquely sovereign function, not whether state law forecloses any possibility of recovering for damages for such activity. For instance, it is clear that the maintenance of a police force is a unique sovereign function, and the delegation of police power to a private party will entail state action. See Griffin v. Maryland, 378 U.S. 130. Under the Court's analysis, however, there would be no state action if the State provided a remedy, such as an action for wrongful imprisonment, for the individual injured by the "private" policeman. This analysis is not based on "exclusivity," but on some vague, and highly inappropriate, notion that respondents should not complain about this state statute if the State offers them a glimmer of hope of redeeming their possessions, or at least the value of the goods, through some other state action. Of course, the availability of other state remedies may be relevant in determining whether the statute provides sufficient procedural protections under the Due Process Clause, but it is not relevant to the state-action issue.

d. As the Court is forced to recognize, its notion of exclusivity simply cannot be squared with the wide range of functions that are typically considered sovereign functions, such as "education, fire and police protection, and tax collection."

factor that precludes constitutional review of the state statute. The Due Process Clause cannot command such incongruous results. If it is unconstitutional for a State to allow a private party to exercise a traditional state power because the state supervision of that power is purely mechanical, the State surely cannot immunize its actions from constitutional *scrutiny* by removing even the mechanical supervision. . . .

Whether termed "traditional," "exclusive," or "significant," the state power to order binding, nonconsensual resolution of a conflict between debtor and creditor is exactly the sort of power with which the Due Process Clause is concerned. And the State's delegation of that power to a private party is accordingly, subject to due process scrutiny. . . .

It is important to emphasize that, contrary to the Court's apparent fears, this conclusion does not even remotely suggest that "all private deprivations of property [will] be converted into public acts whenever the State, for whatever reason, denies relief sought by the putative property owner." The focus is not on the private deprivation but on the state authorization. "[W]hat is always vital to remember is that it is the *state's* conduct, whether action or inaction, not the *private* conduct, that gives rise to constitutional attack." Friendly, The Dartmouth College Case and The Public-Private Penumbra, 12 Texas Quarterly, No. 2, p.17 (1969) (Supp.) (emphasis in original). The State's conduct in this case takes the concrete form of a statutory enactment, and it is that statute that may be challenged.

My analysis in this case thus assumes that petitioner Flagg Brothers' proposed sale will conform to the procedure specified by the state legislature and that respondents' challenge therefore will be to the constitutionality of that process. It is only what the State itself has enacted that they may ask the federal court to review in a §1983 case. If there should be a deviation from the state statute — such as a failure to give the notice required by the state law — the defect could be remedied by a state court and there would be no occasion for §1983 relief. . . .

On the other hand, if there is compliance with the New York statute, the state legislative action which enabled the deprivation to take place must be subject to constitutional challenge in a federal court. . . .

Finally, it is obviously true that the overwhelming majority of disputes in our society are resolved in the private sphere. But it is no longer possible, if it ever was, to believe that a sharp line can be drawn between private and public actions.[e] The Court today holds that our examination of state delegations of power should be limited to those rare instances where the State has ceded one of its "exclusive" powers. As indicated, I believe that this limitation is neither logical nor practical. More troubling, this description of what is state action does not even attempt to reflect the concerns of the Due Process Clause, for the State-action doctrine is, after all, merely one aspect of this broad constitutional protection.

In the broadest sense, we expect government "to provide a reasonable and fair framework of rules which facilitate commercial transactions. . . ." Mitchell v.

e. See, e.g., Thompson, Piercing the Veil of State Action: The Revisionist Theory and A Mythical Application To Self-Help Repossession, 1977 Wis. L. Rev. 1; Glennon & Nowak, A Functional Analysis of the Fourteenth Amendment "State Action" Requirement, 1976 S. Ct. Rev. 221; Black, Foreword: "State Action," Equal Protection, and California's Proposition 14, 81 Harv. L. Rev. 69 (1967); Williams, The Twilight of State Action, 41 Texas L. Rev. 347 (1963); Van Alstyne & Karst, State Action, 14 Stan. L. Rev. 3 (1961).

W.T. Grant Co., 416 U.S., at 624 (Powell, J., concurring). This "framework of rules" is premised on the assumption that the State will control nonconsensual deprivations of property and that the State's control will, in turn, be subject to the restrictions of the Due Process Clause.[f] The power to order legally binding surrenders of property and the constitutional restrictions on that power are necessary correlatives in our system. In effect, today's decision allows the State to divorce these two elements by the simple expedient of transferring the implementation of its policy to private parties. Because the Fourteenth Amendment does not countenance such a division of power and responsibility, I respectfully dissent.[27]

Discussion

1. Is Justice Rehnquist correct that it is irrelevant whether the state has indicated its decision not to act in a statute, in a judicial decision, or simply by not acting?

2. On what theory, if any, could the Court have required a hearing in *Flagg Bros.* without holding that every government decision not to intervene in a private dispute implicated the state in the dispute?

EDMONSON v. LEESVILLE CONCRETE CO.

111 S. Ct. 2077 (1991)
On certiorari from the Fifth Circuit Court of Appeals

[In an African-American's civil suit for negligent injury, the defendant exercised peremptory challenges to strike prospective African-American jurors. The plaintiff argued that Batson v. Kentucky, page 664 supra, required defendant to articulate a race-neutral explanation for the peremptory strikes. Defendant argued, and the district court agreed, that *Batson* applied only to criminal trials. The Court of Appeals for the Fifth Circuit, en banc, affirmed the district court, holding, *inter alia,* that, in contrast to a prosecutor, a private litigant's use of peremptory challenges did not involve state action. Writing for a six-justice majority, Justice Kennedy reversed, holding both that *Batson* applied to civil trials and that

f. Mr. Justice Harlan explained this principle as follows:

> American society, of course, bottoms its systematic definition of individual rights and duties, as well as its machinery for dispute settlement, not on custom or the will of strategically placed individuals, but on the common-law model. It is to courts, or other quasi-judicial official bodies, that we ultimately look for the implementation of a regularized, orderly process of dispute settlement. Within this framework, those who wrote our original Constitution, in the Fifth Amendment, and later those who drafted the Fourteenth Amendment, recognized the centrality of the concept of due process in the operation of this system. Without this guarantee that one may not be deprived of his rights, neither liberty nor property, without due process of law, the State's monopoly over techniques for binding conflict resolution could hardly be said to be acceptable under our scheme of things. Only by providing that the social enforcement mechanism must function strictly within these bounds can we hope to maintain an ordered society that is also just. It is upon this premise that this Court has through years of adjudication put flesh upon the due process principle.

Boddie v. Connecticut, 401 U.S. 371, 375.

27. Justice Brennan did not participate.

requisite state action was present. The excerpts below focus only on the state action issue.]

KENNEDY, J.

We begin our discussion within the framework for state action analysis set forth in Lugar v. Edmonson Oil Co., 457 U.S. 922, at 937 (1982). There we considered the state action question in the context of a due process challenge to a State's procedure allowing private parties to obtain pre-judgment attachments. We asked first whether the claimed constitutional deprivation resulted from the exercise of a right or privilege having its source in state authority and second, whether the private party charged with the deprivation could be described in all fairness as a state actor.

There can be no question that the first part of the *Lugar* inquiry is satisfied here. By their very nature, peremptory challenges have no significance outside a court of law. . . . Peremptory challenges are permitted only when the government, by statute or decisional law, deems it appropriate to allow parties to exclude a given number of persons who otherwise would satisfy the requirements for service on the petit jury. . . .

Without [the] authorization, granted by an Act of Congress itself, Leesville would not have been able to engage in the alleged discriminatory acts.

. . . [T]he remainder of our state action analysis centers around the second part of the *Lugar* test, whether a private litigant in all fairness must be deemed a government actor in the use of peremptory challenges. . . . Our precedents establish that . . . it is relevant to examine the following: the extent to which the actor relies on governmental assistance and benefits; whether the actor is performing a traditional governmental function; and whether the injury caused is aggravated in a unique way by the incidents of governmental authority. Based on our application of these three principles to the circumstances here, we hold that the exercise of peremptory challenges . . . was pursuant to a course of state action.

. . . [A] private party could not exercise its peremptory challenges absent the overt, significant assistance of the court. The government summons jurors, constrains their freedom of movement, and subjects them to public scrutiny and examination. The party who exercises a challenge invokes the formal authority of the court, which must discharge the prospective juror, thus effecting the "final and practical denial" of the excluded individual's opportunity to serve on the petit jury. Without the direct and indispensable participation of the judge, who beyond all question is a state actor, the peremptory challenge system would serve no purpose. By enforcing a discriminatory peremptory challenge, the court "has not only made itself a party to the [biased act], but has elected to place its power, property and prestige behind the [alleged] discrimination." Burton v. Wilmington Parking Authority, 365 U.S., at 725. . . .

[W]e next consider whether the action in question involves the performance of a traditional function of the government. A traditional function of government is evident here. The peremptory challenge is used in selecting an entity that is a quintessential governmental body, having no attributes of a private actor. The jury exercises the power of the court and of the government that confers the court's jurisdiction. . . . [The jury performs] traditional functions of government, not of a select, private group beyond the reach of the Constitution.

If a government confers on a private body the power to choose the government's employees or officials, the private body will be bound by the constitutional mandate of race-neutrality. [Justice Kennedy goes on to discuss, among other cases, the Texas "white primary" decisions and quotes from Justice Clark's concurring opinion in Terry v. Adams the principle that "any 'part of the machinery for choosing officials' becomes subject to the Constitution's constraints."]

. . . Though the motive for a peremptory challenge may be to protect a private interest, the objective of jury selection proceedings is to determine representation on a governmental body. . . . The fact that the government delegates some portion of this power to private litigants does not change the governmental character of the power exercised. The delegation of authority that in *Terry* occurred without the aid of legislation occurs here through explicit statutory authorization.

We find respondent's reliance on Polk County v. Dodson, 454 U.S. 312 (1981), unavailing. In that case, we held that a public defender is not a state actor in his general representation of a criminal defendant, even though he may be in his performance of other official duties. While recognizing the employment relation between the public defender and the government, we noted that the relation is otherwise adversarial in nature. . . .

In the ordinary context of civil litigation, in which the government is not a party, an adversarial relation does not exist between the government and a private litigant. In the jury-selection process, the government and private litigants work for the same end. Just as a government employee was deemed a private actor because of his purpose and functions in *Dodson,* so here a private entity becomes a government actor for the limited purpose of using peremptories during jury selection. The selection of jurors represents a unique governmental function delegated to private litigants by the government and attributable to the government for purposes of invoking constitutional protections against discrimination by reason of race. . . .

If peremptory challenges based on race were permitted, persons could be required by summons to be put at risk of open and public discrimination as a condition of their participation in the justice system. The injury to excluded jurors would be the direct result of governmental delegation and participation.

Finally, we note that the injury caused by the discrimination is made more severe because the government permits it to occur within the courthouse itself. Few places are a more real expression of the constitutional authority of the government than a courtroom, where the law itself unfolds. . . .

Race discrimination within the courtroom raises serious questions as to the fairness of the proceedings conducted there. Racial bias mars the integrity of the judicial system and prevents the idea of democratic government from becoming a reality. . . . To permit racial exclusion in this official forum compounds the racial insult inherent in judging a citizen by the color of his or her skin.

Justice O'CONNOR, with whom the Chief Justice and Justice Scalia join, dissenting:

. . . [The Court's conclusion rests] primarily on two empirical assertions. First, that private parties use peremptory challenges with the "overt, significant participation of the government." Second, that the use of a peremptory challenge by a private party "involves the performance of a traditional function of the government." Neither of these assertions is correct.

A

. . . The peremptory challenge "allow[s] parties," in this case *private* parties, to exclude potential jurors. It is the nature of a peremptory that its exercise is left wholly within the discretion of the litigant. . . . In both criminal and civil trials, the peremptory challenge is a mechanism for the exercise of *private* choice in the pursuit of fairness. The peremptory is, by design, an enclave of private action in a government-managed proceeding.

The Court amasses much ostensible evidence of the Federal Government's "overt, significant participation" in the peremptory process. Most of this evidence is irrelevant to the issue at hand. . . . All of this activity, as well as the trial judge's control over *voir dire,* are merely prerequisites to the use of a peremptory challenge; they do not constitute participation *in* the challenge. That these actions may be necessary to a peremptory challenge — in the sense that there could be no such challenge without a venire from which to select — no more makes the challenge state action than the building of roads and provision of public transportation makes state action of riding on a bus.

The entirety of the Government's actual participation in the peremptory challenge process boils down to a single fact: "When a lawyer exercises a peremptory challenge, the judge advises the juror he or she has been excused." This is not significant participation. . . .

As an initial matter, the judge does not "encourage" the use of a peremptory challenge at all. The decision to strike a juror is entirely up to the litigant, and the reasons for doing so are of no consequence to the judge. It is the attorney who strikes. The judge does little more than acquiesce in this decision by excusing the juror. . . .

The alleged state action here is a far cry from that the Court found, for example, in Shelley v. Kraemer. In that case, state courts were called upon to enforce racially restrictive covenants against sellers of real property who did not wish to discriminate. The coercive power of the State was necessary in order to enforce the private choice of those who had created the covenants. . . . Moreover, the courts in *Shelley* were asked to enforce a facially discriminatory contract. In contrast, peremptory challenges are "exercised without a reason stated [and] without inquiry." A judge does not "significantly encourage" discrimination by the mere act of excusing a juror in response to an unexplained request.

There is another important distinction between *Shelley* and this case. The state court in *Shelley* used coercive force to impose conformance on parties who did not wish to discriminate. "Enforcement" of peremptory challenges, on the other hand, does not compel anyone to discriminate; the discrimination is wholly a matter of private choice. Judicial acquiescence does not convert private choice into that of the state. See Blum v. Yaretsky, 457 U.S., at 1004-1005.

Nor is this the kind of significant involvement found in Tulsa Professional Collection Services, Inc. v. Pope, 485 U.S. 478 (1988). There, we concluded that the actions of the executrix of an estate in providing notice to creditors that they might file claims could fairly be attributed to the State. The State's involvement in the notice process, we said, was "pervasive and substantial." In particular, a state statute directed the executrix to publish notice. In addition, the District Court in that case had "reinforced the statutory command with an order expressly requiring [the executrix] to 'immediately give notice to creditors.' " Notice was not only encouraged by the State, but positively required. There is no comparable state involvement here. No one is compelled by government action to use a peremptory challenge, let alone to use it in a racially discriminatory way.

The Court relies also on Burton v. Wilmington Parking Authority. But the decision in that case depended on the perceived symbiotic relationship between a restaurant and the state parking authority from whom it leased space in a public building. . . . Among the "peculiar facts [and] circumstances" leading to that conclusion was that the State stood to profit from the restaurant's discrimination. . . . [T]he government's involvement in the use of peremptory challenges falls far short of "interdependence" or "joint participation." . . .

Jackson v. Metropolitan Edison Co. is a more appropriate analogy to this case. Metropolitan Edison terminated Jackson's electrical service under authority granted it by the State, pursuant to a procedure approved by the state utility commission. Nonetheless, we held that Jackson could not challenge the termination procedure on due process grounds. The termination was not state action because the State had done nothing to encourage the particular termination practice. . . .

To the same effect is Flagg Bros., Inc. v. Brooks. . . . [I]n the absence of compulsion, or at least encouragement, from the government in the use of peremptory challenges, the government is not responsible. . . .

B

The Court errs also when it concludes that the exercise of a peremptory challenge is a traditional government function. . . . Whatever reason a private litigant may have for using a peremptory challenge, it is not the government's reason. The government otherwise establishes its requirements for jury service, leaving to the private litigant the unfettered discretion to use the strike for any reason. This is not part of the government's function in establishing the requirements for jury service. . . .

The peremptory challenge is a practice of ancient origin, part of our common law heritage in criminal trials. Congress imported this tradition into federal civil trials. The practice of unrestrained private choice in the selection of civil juries is even older than that, however. . . . Peremptory challenges are not a traditional government function; the "tradition" is one of unguided private choice. . . .

[In regard to the various "white primary" cases,] we explained that the government functions in those cases had one thing in common: exclusivity. The public-function doctrine requires that the private actor exercise "a power traditionally exclusively reserved to the State." In order to constitute state action under this doctrine, private conduct must not only comprise something that the government traditionally does, but something that *only* the government traditionally does. Even if one could fairly characterize the use of a peremptory strike as the performance of the traditional government function of jury selection, it has never been exclusively the function of the government to select juries; peremptory strikes are older than the Republic. . . .

C

None of this should be news, as this case is fairly well controlled by Polk County v. Dodson. We there held that a public defender, employed by the State, does not act under color of state law [— the statutory equivalent of the "state action" requirement under the Fourteenth Amendment —] when representing a defendant in a criminal proceeding. In such a circumstance, government employment is not sufficient to create state action. More important for present purposes, neither is the performance of a lawyer's duties in a courtroom. This is because a lawyer, when representing a private client, cannot at the same time represent the government.

Trials in this country are adversarial proceedings. Attorneys for private litigants do not act on behalf of the government, or even the public as a whole; attorneys represent their clients. . . .

It cannot be gainsaid that a peremptory strike is a traditional adversarial act. . . . The Court does not challenge the rule of *Dodson,* yet concludes that private attorneys performing this adversarial function are state actors. Where is the distinction?

The Court wishes to limit the scope of *Dodson* to the actions of public defenders in an adversarial relationship with the government. At a minimum, then, the Court must concede that *Dodson* stands for the proposition that a criminal defense attorney is not a state actor when using peremptory strikes on behalf of a client, nor is an attorney representing a private litigant in a civil suit against the government. Both of these propositions are true, but the Court's distinction between this case and *Dodson* turns state action doctrine on its head. Attorneys in an adversarial relation to the state are not state actors, but that does not mean that attorneys who are not in such a relation *are* state actors.

The Court is plainly wrong when it asserts that "[i]n the jury-selection process, the government and private litigants work for the same end." In a civil trial, the attorneys for each side are in "an adversarial relation"; they use their peremptory strikes in direct opposition to one another, and for precisely contrary ends. The government cannot "work for the same end" as both parties. In fact, the government is neutral as to private litigants' use of peremptory strikes. That's the point. . . .

II

Beyond "significant participation" and "traditional function," the Court's final argument is that the exercise of a peremptory challenge by a private litigant is state action because it takes place in a courtroom. In the end, this is all the Court is left with. . . . The Court is also wrong in its ultimate claim. If *Dodson* stands for anything, it is that the actions of a lawyer in a courtroom do not become those of the government by virtue of their location. This is true even if those actions are based on race.

Racism is a terrible thing. . . . But not every opprobrious and inequitable act is a constitutional violation. . . .

[A dissenting opinion by Justice Scalia is omitted.]

Discussion

1. Return to *Flagg Brothers* and assume that the warehouse had followed a policy of selling the goods of African-Americans 30 days following the purported nonpayment of service charges while retaining the goods of whites for 90 days. Should *Edmundson* change the result?

2. Do any of these cases bring us closer to solving the riddle of state action? If not, is it because the riddle is insoluble or because you think that the Supreme Court is simply giving the wrong answer(s)?

Note: Congressional Regulation of "Private Action" under the Thirteenth and Fourteenth Amendments

This chapter has focused on cases brought under the Fourteenth Amendment by claimants asserting direct rights under the Fourteenth Amendment or under federal statutes prohibiting the deprivation of civil rights "under color of" state laws or customs. The state action issue has also arisen, however, in suits brought under certain federal antidiscrimination statutes that are not limited to conduct under "color of law." Congress might enact such provisions pursuant to its power to enforce the Thirteenth and Fourteenth Amendments, and the question is whether either of these provisions (or both) authorizes Congress to forbid discrimination by private persons. In Griffin v. Breckenridge, 403 U.S. 88 (1971), the Court considered a prosecution for a conspiracy brought against Mississippi whites who assaulted African-American civil rights workers as part of an effort to prevent them and others "from seeking the equal protection of the laws and from enjoying the equal rights, privileges, and immunities of citizens . . ." protected by 42 U.S.C. §1985(3). Holding that the statute indeed reached private conspiracies, the Court did not offer a general approach to Congress' Fourteenth Amendment power. (Recall that the Court had invalidated the Civil Rights Act of 1875 in the Civil Rights Cases precisely because Congress did not have the power to regulate merely private action.) Instead, it observed that "Congress was wholly within its powers under §2 of the Thirteenth Amendment in creating a statutory cause of action for Negro citizens who have been the victims of conspiratorial, racially discriminatory private action aimed at depriving them of the basic rights that the law secures to all free men."

The issue of state action under the Thirteenth Amendment has arisen almost exclusively in the application of federal statutes derived from the Civil Rights Act of 1866. This Act, of course, preceded the addition of the Fourteenth Amendment, and it was therefore based on the Thirteenth Amendment, which became part of the Constitution in December 1865.

Jones v. Alfred H. Mayer Co., 392 U.S. 409 (1968), is the leading case. There the Court construed 42 U.S.C. §1982, which provides that "[a]ll citizens of the United States shall have the same right . . . as is enjoyed by white citizens thereof to inherit, purchase, lease, sell, hold, and convey real and personal property," to apply to a realtor who had allegedly refused to sell a home to an African-American on racial grounds. Although the central debate in the case involved the intent of the 1866 Congress in passing the Civil Rights Act, a collateral issue concerned the constitutional propriety of congressional regulation of the private housing market through the Thirteenth Amendment. Justice Stewart, writing for the majority, wrote:

> As its text reveals, the Thirteenth Amendment "is not a mere prohibition of State laws establishing or upholding slavery, but an absolute declaration that slavery or involuntary servitude shall not exist in any part of the United States." Civil Rights

> Cases, 109 U.S. 3, 20. It has never been doubted, therefore, "that the power vested in Congress to enforce the article by appropriate legislation" includes the power to enact laws "direct and primary, operating upon the acts of individuals, whether sanctioned by State legislation or not." Id. at 23.
>
> Thus, the fact that §1982 operates upon the unofficial acts of private individuals, whether or not sanctioned by state law, presents no constitutional problem. If Congress has power under the Thirteenth Amendment to eradicate conditions that prevent Negroes from buying and renting property because of their race or color, then no federal statute calculated to achieve that objective can be thought to exceed the constitutional power of Congress simply because it reaches beyond state action to regulate the conduct of private individuals. The constitutional question in this case, therefore, comes to this: Does the authority of Congress to enforce the Thirteenth Amendment "by appropriate legislation" include the power to eliminate all racial barriers to the acquisition of real and personal property? We think the answer to that question is plainly yes.

Justice Harlan, joined by Justice White, dissented, primarily on statutory grounds. He noted, though, that "[i]n holding that the Thirteenth Amendment is sufficient constitutional authority for §1982 as interpreted, the Court also decides a question of great importance. Even contemporary supporters of the aims of the 1866 Civil Rights Act doubted that those goals could constitutionally be achieved under the Thirteenth Amendment, and this Court has twice expressed similar doubts." Justice Harlan did not go on to consider the constitutional question. He noted the recent enactment of the Civil Rights Act of 1968, which covered much housing discrimination, and suggested that under the circumstances the Court should dismiss the writ of certiorari as improvidently granted.

Jones was followed in Runyon v. McCrary, 427 U.S. 160 (1976), which was in turn specifically reaffirmed by a unanimous Court in Patterson v. McLean Credit Union, 491 U.S. 164 (1989). In both of the later cases, some Justices suggested that *Jones* had been wrongly decided as a matter of statutory construction, but indicated that they would adhere to it because of the importance of following precedent. (The Court in *Patterson* held that the protection against discrimination in the making of contracts did not extend to protection against racial harassment on the job. This holding was overruled by the Civil Rights Act of 1991.)

Chapter 13
Constituting an American Community

The United States is unusual among the major countries of the world because, from the start, its population consisted largely of immigrants.[1] "For most peoples national identity is the product of a long process of historical evolution involving common ancestors, common experiences, common ethnic background, common language, and usually common religion."[2] By contrast, in the United States, people of different national backgrounds, races, and religions contended with one another over the constitution of an "American" identity.

We have seen some of the dimensions of this contention, particularly with respect to Native Americans and African Americans. This chapter focuses on the tension between the desire to create an "American people" with a shared self-understanding and the reality of diverse and sometimes antagonistic self-understandings of subgroups within the overall American social order. Although this tension is often expressed in terms of individual conscience versus the state, that way of putting it may be misleading: The individual complainant in the cases presented in this chapter typically is a member of a *group* claiming that the majority culture is not sufficiently sensitive to the group's legitimate desire to abide by different norms.

We begin the chapter by examining the idea of citizenship as a formal marker of membership in the American political community. We then examine a variety of problems that might be subsumed under the general heading of the constitutional protections of cultural pluralism within the American social order.

I. The Predicates of United States Citizenship

A. Becoming a Citizen: "Constitutional Attachment" as a Precondition to Naturalization

Most citizens of the United States achieve that status by being born within the territory of the United States, as provided by section 1 of the Fourteenth Amendment.[3]

1. This obviously begs the question of the status of the Native Americans who were already here at the beginnings of the European settlement. The Native Americans were scarcely interested in constituting a new political community and, indeed, fought vigorously to preserve their own independence. See, e.g., the discussion of the *Cherokee Nation* case, Chapter 2 supra. It is also clear that not all of the immigration was voluntary; black slaves scarcely chose to leave Africa.

2. Samuel P. Huntington, American Politics; The Promise of Disharmony 23 (1981).

3. Birthright citizenship was not extended to American Indians born on reservations until 1924 by an act of Congress. Professors Schuck and Smith have suggested that the Fourteenth Amendment

The alternative to citizenship by birth is citizenship by naturalization, i.e., by complying with the procedures established by Congress pursuant to Article I, §8, cl. 4. (See Chapter 2, supra, for a discussion of the early history of naturalization.) Among other things, applicants for citizenship must show that they are "attached to the principles of the Constitution of the United States and well disposed to the good order and happiness of the United States."[4] As David Weissbrodt writes, "The purpose behind this requirement is the admission to citizenship of only those persons who are in general accord with the basic principles of the community."[5] This assumes, of course, that the *pluribus* of American society is sufficiently enclosed within a *unum* that allows us to identify "basic principles" either of the Constitution or of the general community — what Huntington in his book terms "the American creed."[6]

SCHNEIDERMAN v. UNITED STATES

320 U.S. 118 (1943)

Certiorari to the Circuit Court of Appeals for the Ninth Circuit

[William Schneiderman became a naturalized citizen of the United States in 1927, while he was a high official in the American Communist Party. Under then-existing naturalization law, a candidate for citizenship had to behave as a person "attached to the principles of the Constitution." In 1939, the Department of Justice moved to cancel his citizenship on the ground that it had been procured illegally because, as an active member of the Communist Party, Schneiderman could not be attached to the principles of the Constitution. The district court below and the Ninth Circuit Court of Appeals accepted the Department's argument. The Supreme Court reversed.]

MURPHY, J., delivered the opinion of the Court.

We brought this case here on certiorari because of its importance and its possible relation to freedom of thought. . . .

[Section 15 of the Naturalization Act of 1906] gives the United States the right and the duty to set aside and cancel certificates of citizenship on the ground of "fraud" or on the ground that they were "illegally procured." The complaint charged that the certificate had been illegally procured in that petitioner, at the time of his naturalization, and during the five years proceding his naturalization "had not behaved as, a person attached to the principles of the Constitution of the United States and well disposed to the good order and happiness of the United States, but in truth and in fact during all of said times, [Schneiderman] was a member of and affiliated with and believed in and supported the principles

---

need not be read as an automatic grant of citizenship to children born to parents who are in the United States without the government's consent, i.e., "illegal aliens." They argue that no plausible political theory supports an absolute right to citizenship by birth, and they cite the legal history of Indian citizenship to rebut a contrary textualist claim based on the Fourteenth Amendment. Peter Schuck and Rogers Smith, Citizenship without Consent (1984). Their book has proved extremely controversial. See, e.g., David Martin, Membership and Consent: Abstract or Organic, 11 Yale J. Intl. L. 278 (1985).

4. 8 U.S.C. §1427(a) (1983). The general topic of this section is examined in Sanford Levinson, Constitutional Faith, chapters 3 and 4 (1988).

5. David Weissbrodt, Immigration Law and Procedure in a Nutshell (1984), excerpted in T. Alexander Aleinikoff and David Martin, Immigration: Process and Policy 863 (1985).

6. Huntington, supra note 2, at 13-30.

of certain organizations then known as the Workers (Communist) Party of America and the Young Workers (Communist) League of America, whose principles were opposed to the principles of the Constitution of the United States and advised, advocated and taught the overthrow of the Government, Constitution and laws of the United States by force and violence." . . .

This is not a naturalization proceeding in which the Government is being asked to confer the privilege of citizenship upon an applicant. Instead the Government seeks to turn the clock back twelve years after full citizenship was conferred upon petitioner by a judicial decree, and to deprive him of the priceless benefits that derive from that status. In its consequences it is more serious than a taking of one's property, or the imposition of a fine or other penalty. For it is safe to assert that nowhere in the world today is the right of citizenship of greater worth to an individual than it is in this country. It would be difficult to exaggerate its value and importance. By many it is regarded as the highest hope of civilized men. This does not mean that once granted to an alien, citizenship cannot be revoked or cancelled on legal grounds under appropriate proof. But such a right once conferred should not be taken away without the clearest sort of justification and proof. So, whatever may be the rule in a naturalization proceeding, in an action instituted under §15 for the purpose of depriving one of the precious right of citizenship previously conferred we believe the facts and the law should be construed as far as is reasonably possible in favor of the citizen. Especially is this so when the attack is made long after the time when the certificate of citizenship was granted and the citizen has meanwhile met his obligations and has committed no act of lawlessness. It is not denied that the burden of proof is on the Government in this case. For reasons presently to be stated this burden must be met with evidence of a clear and convincing character that when citizenship was conferred upon petitioner in 1927 it was not done in accordance with strict legal requirements.

. . . [Although] we assume, without deciding, that in the absence of fraud a certificate of naturalization can be set aside under §15 as "illegally procured" because the finding as to attachment would later seem to be erroneous, we are of the opinion that this judgment should be reversed. . . . The Government's evidence in this case does not measure up to this [required standard that the proof be "clear, unequivocal, and convincing"].

Certain facts are undisputed. Petitioner came to this country from Russia in 1907 or 1908 when he was approximately three. In 1922, at the age of sixteen, he became a charter member of the Young Workers (now Communist) League in Los Angeles and remained a member until 1929 or 1930. In 1924, at the age of eighteen, he filed his declaration of intention to become a citizen. Later in the same year or early in 1925 he became a member of the Workers Party, the predecessor of the Communist Party of the United States. That membership has continued to the present. His petition for naturalization was filed on January 18, 1927, and his certificate of citizenship was issued on June 10, 1927, by the United States District Court for the Southern District of California. He had not been arrested or subjected to censure prior to 1927 and there is nothing in the record indicating that he was ever connected with any overt illegal or violent action or with any disturbance of any sort. . . .

[Schneiderman] testified . . . that during all the time he has belonged to the League and the Party he has subscribed to the principles of those organizations.

He stated that he "believed in the essential correctness of the Marxist theory as applied by the Communist Party of the United States," that he subscribed "to the philosophy and principles of Socialism as manifested in the writings of Lenin," and that his understanding and interpretation of the program, principles and practice of the Party since he joined "were and are essentially the same as those enunciated" in the Party's 1938 Constitution. He . . . specifically denied that he or the Party advocated the overthrow of the Government of the United States by force and violence, and that he was not attached to the principles of the Constitution. He considered membership in the Party compatible with the obligations of American citizenship. . . .

I

The Constitution authorizes Congress "to establish an uniform Rule of Naturalization" (Art. I, §8, cl. 4), and we may assume that naturalization is a privilege, to be given or withheld on such conditions as Congress sees fit.

But because of our firmly rooted tradition of freedom of belief, we certainly will not presume in construing the naturalization and denaturalization acts that Congress meant to circumscribe liberty of political thought by general phrases in those statutes. As Chief Justice Hughes said in dissent in the *Macintosh* case, such general phrases "should be construed, not in opposition to, but in accord with, the theory and practice of our Government in relation to freedom of conscience."

When petitioner was naturalized in 1927, the applicable statutes did not proscribe Communist beliefs or affiliation as such. They did forbid the naturalization of disbelievers in organized government or members of organizations teaching such disbelief. Polygamists and advocates of political assassination were also barred. Applicants for citizenship were required to take an oath to support the Constitution, to bear true faith and allegiance to the same and the laws of the United States, and to renounce all allegiance to any foreign prince, potentate, state or sovereignty. And, it was to "be made to appear to the satisfaction of the court" of naturalization that immediately preceding the application, the applicant "has resided continuously within the United States five years at least, . . . and that during that time he has behaved as a man of good moral character, attached to the principles of the Constitution of the United States, and well disposed to the good order and happiness of the same." Whether petitioner satisfied this last requirement is the crucial issue in this case.

To apply the statutory requirement of attachment correctly to the proof adduced, it is necessary to ascertain its meaning. On its face the statutory criterion is not attachment to the Constitution, but behavior for a period of five years as a man attached to its principles and well disposed to the good order and happiness of the United States. Since the normal connotation of behavior is conduct, there is something to be said for the proposition that the 1906 Act created a purely objective qualification, limiting inquiry to an applicant's previous conduct. If this objective standard is the requirement, petitioner satisfied the statute. His conduct has been law abiding in all respects. According to the record he has never been arrested, or connected with any disorder, and not a single written or spoken statement of his, during the relevant period from 1922 to 1927 or thereafter, advocating violent overthrow of the Government, or indeed even a statement, apart from his testimony in this proceeding, that he desired any change in the Constitution has been produced. The sole possible criticism is petitioner's membership and acitivity in the League and the Party, but those memberships *qua* memberships, were immaterial under the 1906 Act.

In United States v. Schwimmer, 279 U.S. 644, and United States v. Macintosh, 283 U.S. 605, however, it was held that the statute created a test of belief — that an applicant under the 1906 Act must not only behave as a man attached to the principles of the Constitution, but must be so attached in fact at the time of naturalization. We do not stop to reexamine this construction for even if it is accepted the result is not changed. . . .

The claim that petitioner was not in fact attached to the Constitution and well disposed to the good order and happiness of the United States at the time of his naturalization and for the previous five year period is twofold: First, that he believed in such sweeping changes in the Constitution that he simply could not be attached to it; second, that he believed in and advocated the overthrow by force and violence of the Government, Constitution and laws of the United States.

In support of its position that petitioner was not in fact attached to the principles of the Constitution because of his membership in the League and the Party, the Government has directed our attention first to petitioner's testimony that he subscribed to the principles of those organizations, and then to certain alleged Party principles and statements by Party Leaders which are said to be fundamentally at variance with the principles of the Constitution. At this point it is appropriate to mention what will be more fully developed later — that under our traditions beliefs are personal and not a matter of mere association, and that men in adhering to a political party or other organization notoriously do not subscribe unqualifiedly to all of its platforms or asserted principles. Said to be among those Communist principles in 1927 are: the abolition of private property without compensation; the erection of a new proletarian state upon the ruins of the old bourgeois state; the creation of a dictatorship of the proletariat; denial of political rights to others than members of the Party or of the proletariat; and the creation of a world union of soviet republics. Statements that American democracy "is a fraud" and that the purposes of the Party are "utterly antagonistic to the purposes for which the American democracy, so called, was formed," are stressed.

Those principles and views are not generally accepted — in fact they are distasteful to most of us — and they call for considerable change in our present form of government and society. But we do not think the government has carried its burden of proving by evidence which does not leave the issue in doubt that petitioner was not in fact attached to the principles of the Constitution and well disposed to the good order and happiness of the United States when he was naturalized in 1927.

The constitutional fathers, fresh from a revolution, did not forge a political strait-jacket for the generations to come. Instead they wrote Article V and the First Amendment, guaranteeing freedom of thought, soon followed. Article V contains procedural provisions for constitutional change by amendment without any present limitation whatsoever except that no State may be deprived of equal representation in the Senate without its consent. This provision and the many important and far-reaching changes made in the Constitution since 1787 refute the idea that attachment to any particular provision or provisions is essential, or that one who advocates radical changes is necessarily not attached to the Constitution. . . . Criticism of, and the sincerity of desires to improve the Constitution should not be judged by conformity to prevailing thought because, "if there is any principle of the Constitution that more imperatively calls for attachment than any other it is the principle of free thought — not free thought for those who agree with us but freedom for the thought that we hate." United States v. Schwimmer, 279 U.S. 644 (Holmes, J., dissenting). Whatever attitude we may individually hold toward persons and organizations that believe in or advocate extensive changes in our existing order, it should be our desire and concern at all times to uphold the right of free discussion and free thinking to which we as a people claim primary attachment. To neglect this duty in a proceeding in which we are called upon to judge whether a particular individual has failed to manifest attachment to the Constitution would be ironical indeed.

Our concern is with what Congress meant to be the extent of the area of allowable thought under the statute. By the very generality of the terms employed it is evident that Congress intended an elastic test, one which should not be circumscribed by attempts at precise definition. In view of our tradition of freedom of thought, it is not to be presumed that Congress in the Act of 1906, or its predecessors of 1795 and 1802, intended to offer naturalization only to those whose political views coincide with those considered best by the founders in 1787 or by the majority in this country today. . . . The Government agrees that an alien "may think that the laws and the Constitution should be amended in some or many respects" and still be attached to the principles of the Constitution within the meaning of the statute. Without discussing the nature and extent of those permissible changes, the Government insists that an alien must believe in and sincerely adhere to the "general political philosophy" of the Constitution. Petitioner is said to be opposed to that "political philosophy." . . . It was argued at the bar that since Article V contains no limitations, a person can be attached to the Constitution no matter how extensive the changes are that he desires, so long as he seeks to achieve his ends within the framework of Article V. But we need not consider the validity of this extreme position for if the Government's construction is accepted, it has not carried its burden of proof even under its own test.

. . . With regard to the constitutional changes he desired petitioner testified that he believed in the nationalization of the means of production and exchange with compensation, and the preservation and utilization of our "democratic structure . . . as far as possible for the advantage of the working classes." He stated that the "dictatorship of the proletariat" to him meant "not a government, but a state of things" in which "the majority of the people shall really direct their own destinies and use the instrument of the state for these truly democratic ends." None of this is necessarily incompatible with the "general political philosophy" of the Constitution as outlined above by the Government. It is true that the Fifth Amendment protects private property, even against taking for public use without compensation. But throughout our history many sincere people whose attachment to the general constitutional scheme cannot be doubted have, for various and even divergent reasons, urged differing degrees of governmental ownership and control of natural resources, basic means of production, and banks and the media of exchange, either with or without compensation. And something once regarded as a species of private property was abolished without compensating the owners when the institution of slavery was forbidden. Can it be said that the author of the Emancipation Proclamation and the supporters of the Thirteenth Amendment were not attached to the Constitution? We conclude that lack of attachment to the Constitution is not shown on the basis of the changes which petitioner testified he desired in the Constitution.

Turning now to a seriatim consideration of what the Government asserts are principles of the Communist Party, which petitioner believed and which are opposed to our Constitution, our conclusion remains the same — the Government has not proved by "clear, unequivocal and convincing" evidence that the naturalization court could not have been satisfied that petitioner was attached to the principles of the Constitution when he was naturalized.

We have already disposed of the principle of nationalization of the agents of production and exchange with or without compensation. The erection of a new proletarian state upon the ruins of the old bourgeois state, and the creation of a dictatorship of the proletariat may be considered together. The concept of the dictatorship of the proletariat is one loosely used, upon which more words than light have been shed. Much argument has been directed as to how it is to be achieved, but we have been offered no precise definition here. In the general sense the term may be taken to describe a state in which the workers or the masses, rather than the bourgeoisie or capitalists are the dominant class. Theoretically it is control by a class, not a dictatorship in the sense of absolute and total rule by one individual. So far as the record before us indicates, the concept is a fluid one, capable of adjustment to different conditions in different countries. There are only meager indications of the form the "dictatorship" would take in this country. It does not appear that it would necessarily mean the end of representative government or the federal system. The Program and Constitution of the Workers Party (1921-24) criticized the constitutional system of checks and balances, the Senate's power to pass on legislation, and the involved procedure for amending the Constitution, characterizing them as devices designed to frustrate the will of the majority. The 1928 platform of the Communist Party of the United States, adopted after petitioner's naturalization and hence not strictly relevant, advocated the abolition of the Senate, of the Supreme Court, and of the veto power of the President, and replacement of congressional districts with "councils of workers" in which legislative and executive power would be united. These would indeed be significant changes in our present government structure — changes which it is safe to say are not desired by the majority of the people in this country — but whatever our personal views, as judges we cannot say that a person who advocates their adoption through peaceful and constitutional means is not in fact attached to the Constitution — those institutions are not enumerated as necessary in the Government's test of "general political philosophy," and it is conceivable that "ordered liberty" could be maintained without them. The Senate has not gone free of criticism and one object of the Seventeenth Amendment was to make it more responsive to the public will. The unicameral legislature is not unknown in the country. It is true that this Court has played a large part in the unfolding of the constitutional plan (sometimes too much so in the opinion of some observers), but we would be arrogant indeed if we presumed that a government of laws, with protection for minority groups, would be impossible without it. Like other agencies of government, this Court at various times in its existence has not escaped the shafts of critics whose sincerity and attachment to the Constitution is beyond question — critics who have accused it of assuming functions of judicial review not intended to be conferred upon it, or of abusing those functions to thwart the popular will, and who have advocated various remedies taking a wide range. And it is hardly conceivable that the consequence of freeing the legislative branch from the restraint of the executive veto would be the end of constitutional government. By this discussion we certainly do not mean to indicate that we would favor such changes. Our preference and aversions have no bearing here. Our concern is with the extent of the allowable area of thought under the statute. We decide only that it is possible to advocate such changes and still be attached to the Constitution within the meaning of the Government's minimum test.

If any provisions of the Constitution can be singled out as requiring unqualified attachment, they are the guaranties of the Bill of Rights and especially that of freedom of thought contained in the First Amendment. We do not reach, however, the question whether petitioner was attached to the principles of the Constitution if he believed in denying political and civil rights to persons not members of the Party or of the so-called proletariat, for on the basis of the record before us it has not been clearly shown that such denial was a principle of the organizations to which petitioner belonged. Since it is doubtful that this was a principle of those organizations, it is certainly much more speculative whether this was part of petitioner's philosophy. Some of the documents in the record indicate that "class enemies" of the proletariat should be deprived of their political rights. Lenin, however, wrote that this was not necessary to realize the dictatorship of the proletariat. The party's 1928 platform demanded the unrestricted right to organize, to strike and to picket and the unrestricted right of free speech, free press and free assemblage for the working class. The 1928 Program of the Communist International states that the proletarian State will grant religious freedom, while at the same time it will carry on anti-religious propaganda.

We should not hold that petitioner is not attached to the Constitution by reason of his possible belief in the creation of some form of world union of soviet republics unless we are willing so to hold with regard to those who believe in Pan-Americanism, the League of Nations, Union Now, or some other form of international collaboration or collective security which may grow out of the present holocaust. A distinction here would be an invidious one based on the fact that we might agree with or tolerate the latter but dislike or disagree with the former.

If room is allowed, as we think Congress intended, for the free play of ideas, none of the foregoing principles which might be held to stand forth with sufficient clarity to be imputed to petitioner on the basis of his membership and activity in the League and the Party and his testimony that he subscribed to the principles of those organizations, is enough, whatever our opinion as to their merits, to prove that he was necessarily not attached to the Constitution when he was naturalized. The cumulative effect is no greater.

Apart from the question whether the alleged principles of the Party which petitioner assertedly believed were so fundamentally opposed to the Constitution that he was not attached to its principles in 1927, the Government contends that petitioner was not attached because he believed in the use of force and violence instead of peaceful democratic methods to achieve his desires. In support of this phase of its argument the Government asserts that the organizations with which petitioner was actively affiliated advised, advocated and taught the overthrow of the Government, Constitution and laws of the United States by force and violence, and that petitioner therefore believed in that method of governmental change.

Apart from his membership in the League and the Party, the record is barren of any conduct or statement on petitioner's part which indicates in the slightest that he believed in and advocated the employment of force and violence, instead of peaceful persuasion, as a means of attaining political ends. To find that he so believed and advocated it is necessary, therefore, to find that such was a principle of the organizations to which he belonged and then impute that principle to him on the basis of his activity in those organizations and his statement that he subscribed to their principles. The Government frankly concedes that "it is normally true . . . that it is unsound to impute to an organization the views expressed in the writings of all its members, or to impute such writings to each member. . . ." But the Government contends, however, that it is proper to impute to petitioner certain excerpts from the documents in evidence upon which it particularly relies to show that advocacy of force and violence was a principle of the Communist Party of the United States in 1927, because those documents were official publications carefully supervised by the Party, because of the Party's notorious discipline over its members, and because petitioner was not a mere "rank and file or accidental member of the Party," but "an intelligent and educated individual" who "became a leader of these organizations as an intellectual revolutionary." Since the immediate problem is the determination with certainty of petitioner's beliefs from 1922 to 1927, events and writings since that time have little relevance, and both parties have attempted to confine themselves within the limits of that critical period.

For some time the question whether advocacy of governmental overthrow by force and violence is a principle of the Communist Party of the United States has perplexed courts, administrators, legislators, and students. . . . This Court has never passed upon the question whether the Party does so advocate, and it is unnecessary for us to do so now.

With commendable candor the Government admits the presence of sharply conflicting views on the issue of force and violence as a Party principle, and it also concedes that "some communist literature in respect of force and violence is susceptible of an interpretation more rhetorical than literal." It insists, however, that excerpts from the documents on which it particularly relies, are enough to show that the trial court's finding that the Communist Party advocated violent overthrow of the Government was not "clearly erroneous," and hence can not be set aside. . . . [T]he documents published prior to 1927 stressed by the Government . . . are The Communist Manifesto of Marx and Engels; The State and Revolution by Lenin; The Statutes, Theses and Conditions of Admission to Communist International; and The Theory and Practice of Leninism written by Stalin. The Government also sets forth exerpts from other documents which are entitled to little weight because they were published after the critical period. The bombastic exerpts set forth in Notes 35 to 38, inclusive, upon which the Government particularly relies, lend considerable support to the charge. We do not say that a reasonable man could not possible have found, as the district court did, that the communist party in 1927 actively urged the overthrow of the government by force and violence. But that is not the issue here. We are not concerned with the question whether a reasonable man might so conclude, nor with the narrow issue whether administrative findings to that effect are so lacking in evidentiary support as to amount to a denial of due process. As pointed out before, this is a denaturalization proceeding in which, if the Government is entitled to attack a finding of attachment as we have assumed, the burden rests upon it to prove the alleged lack of attachment by "clear, unequivocal and convincing" evidence. That burden has not been carried. The Government has not proved that petitioner's beliefs on the subject of force and violence were such that he was not attached to the Constitution in 1927.

In the first place this phase of the Government's case is subject to the admitted infirmities of proof by imputation. The difficulties of this method of proof are here increased by the fact that there is, unfortunately, no absolutely accurate test of what a political party's principles are. Political writings are often over-exaggerated polemics bearing the imprint of the period and the place in which written. Philosophies cannot generally be studied in vacuo. Meaning may be wholly distorted by lifting sentences out of context, instead of construing them as part of an organic whole. Every utterance of party leaders is not taken as party gospel. And we would deny our experience as men if we did not recognize that official party programs are unfortunately often opportunistic devices as much honored in the breach as in the observance. On the basis of the present record we cannot say that the Communist Party is so different in this respect that its principles stand forth with perfect clarity, and especially is this so with relation to the crucial issue of advocacy of force and violence, upon which the Government admits the evidence is sharply conflicting. The presence of this conflict is the second weakness in the Government's chain of proof. It is not eliminated by assiduously adding further excerpts from the documents in evidence to those culled out by the Government. . . .

A tenable conclusion . . . is that the Party in 1927 desired to achieve its purpose by peaceful and democratic means, and as a theoretical matter justified the use of force and violence only as a method of preventing an attempted forcible counter-overthrow once the Party had obtained control in a peaceful manner, or as a method of last resort to enforce the majority will if at some indefinite future time because of peculiar circumstances constitutional or peaceful channels were no longer open.

There is a material difference between agitation and exhortation calling for present violent action which creates a clear and present danger of public disorder or other substantive evil, and mere doctrinal justification or prediction of the use of force under hypothetical conditions at some indefinite future time — prediction that is not calculated or intended to be presently acted upon, thus leaving opportunity for general discussion and the calm processes of thought and reason. Because of this difference we may assume that Congress intended, by the general test of "attachment" in the 1906 Act, to deny naturalization to persons falling into the first category but not to those in the second. Such a construction of the statute is to be favored because it preserves for novitiates as well as citizens the full benefit of that freedom of thought which is a fundamental feature of our political institutions. Under the conflicting evidence in this case we cannot say that the Government has proved by such a preponderance of the evidence that the issue is not in doubt, that the attitude of the Communist Party of the United States in 1927 towards force and violence was not susceptible of classification in the second category.

. . . We conclude that the Government has not carried its burden of proving by "clear, unequivocal, and convincing" evidence which does not leave "the issue in doubt," that petitioner obtained his citizenship illegally. In so holding we do not decide what interpretation of the Party's attitude toward force and violence is the most probable on the basis of the present record, or that petitioner's testimony is acceptable at face value. We hold only that where two interpretations of an organization's program are possible, the one reprehensible and a bar to naturalization and the other permissible, a court in a denaturalization proceeding, assuming that it can re-examine a finding of attachment upon a charge of illegal procurement, is not justified in canceling a certificate of citizenship by imputing the reprehensible interpretation to a member of the organization in the absence of overt acts indicating that such was his interpretation. . . .

[Concurring opinions by Justices Douglas and Rutledge are omitted.]

STONE C.J., joined by Justices Frankfurter and Roberts, dissenting.

The two courts below have found that petitioner, at the time he was naturalized, belonged to Communist Party organizations which were opposed to the principles of the Constitution, and which advised, advocated and taught the overthrow of the Government by force and violence. . . .

I think these findings are abundantly supported by the evidence, and hence that it is not within our judicial competence to set them aside — even though, sitting as trial judges, we might have made some other finding. The judgment below, cancelling petitioner's citizenship on the ground that it was illegally obtained, should therefore be affirmed. . . .

It is important to emphasize that the question for decision is much simpler than it has been made to appear. It is whether petitioner, in securing his citizenship by naturalization, has fulfilled a condition which Congress has imposed on every applicant for naturalization — that during the five years preceding his application "he has behaved as a man . . . attached to the principles of the Constitution of the United States, and well disposed to the good order and happiness of the same." . . . We must decide not whether the district court was compelled to find want of attachment, but whether the record warrants such a finding.

. . . The United States has the same interest as other nations in demanding of those who seek its citizenship some measure of attachment to its institutions. Our concern is only that the declared will of Congress shall prevail — that no man shall become a citizen or retain his citizenship whose behavior for five years before his application does not show attachment to the principles of the Constitution.

. . . Under the laws and Constitution of the United States, no person is given any right to demand citizenship, save upon compliance with those conditions. . . .

Hence the issue before us is whether petitioner, when naturalized, satisfied the statutory requirements. It is the same issue as would be presented by an appeal from a judgment granting or denying naturalization upon the evidence here presented, although it may be assumed that in this proceeding the burden of proof rests on the Government which has brought the suit, to establish petitioner's want of qualifications.

. . . As we are not here considering whether petitioner's certificate of naturalization was procured by fraud, there is no occasion, and indeed no justification, for importing into this case the rule, derived from land fraud cases, that fraud, which involves personal moral obliquity, must be proved by clear and convincing evidence. The issue is not whether petitioner committed a crime but whether he should be permitted to enjoy citizenship when he has never satisfied the basic conditions which Congress required for the grant of that privilege. We are concerned only with the question whether petitioner's qualifications were so lacking that he was not lawfully entitled to the privilege of citizenship which he has procured. . . .

The statute does not, as seems to be suggested, require as a condition of citizenship that a man merely be capable of attachment to the principles of the Constitution — a requirement which presumably all mankind could satisfy. It requires instead that the applicant be in fact attached to those principles when he seeks naturalization. . . .

The prescribed conditions for the award of citizenship by naturalization are few and readily understood, and we must accept them as the expression of the Congressional judgment that aliens not satisfying those requirements are not worthy to be admitted to the privilege of citizenship. Congress has declared that before one is entitled to that privilege he must take the oath of allegiance "that he will support and defend the Constitution and laws of the United States against all enemies, foreign and domestic, and bear true faith and allegiance to the same." And as I have said, the applicant must make it appear to the court admitting him to citizenship that for the five years preceding the date of his application he has resided continuously within the United States and "that during that time he has behaved as a man of good moral character, attached to the principles of the Constitution of the United States, and well disposed to the good order and happiness of the same."

Moreover, at the time of petitioner's naturalization, the statutes of the United States excluded from admission into this country "aliens who believe in, advise, advocate, or teach, or who are members of or affiliated with any organization, association, society, or group, that believes in, advises, advocates, or teaches: (1) the overthrow by force or violence of the Government of the United States. . . ." The statutes also barred admission to the United States of "aliens who . . . knowingly circulate, distribute, print, or display, or knowingly cause to be circulated, distributed, printed, published, or displayed . . . any written or printed matter . . . advising, advocating, or teaching: (1) the overthrow by force or violence of the Government of the United States. . . ." And by §2 of the Act of October 16, 1918, it was provided that any alien who, after entering the United States, "is found . . . to have become thereafter, a member of any one of the classes of aliens" just enumerated, shall be taken into custody and deported. Quite apart from the want of attachment to the Constitution and the consequent disqualification of such aliens for citizenship, their belonging to any of these classes would disqualify them for citizenship since their presence in the United States, without which they cannot apply for citizenship, would be unlawful. . . . [E]ven the Court's opinion concedes "We do not say that a reasonable man could not possibly have found, as the district court did, that the Communist Party in 1927 actively urged the overthrow of the Government by force and violence." In addition, the evidence makes it clear beyond all reasonable doubt that petitioner, up to the time of his naturalization, was an alien who knowingly circulated or distributed, or caused to be circulated or distributed, printed matter adovcating the overthrow of the Government by force or violence.

Wholly apart from the deportation statute, the judgment should be affirmed because the trial court was justified in finding that petitioner, in 1927, was not and had not been attached to the principles of the Constitution. My brethren of the majority do not deny that there are principles of the Constitution. The Congress of 1795, which passed the statute requiring an applicant for naturalization to establish that he has "behaved as a man . . . attached to the principles of the constitution," evidently did not doubt that there were. . . . In the absence of any disclaimer I shall assume that there are such principles and that among them are at least the principle of constitutional protection of civil rights and of life, liberty and property, the principle of representative government, and the principle that constitutional laws are not to be broken down by planned disobedience. I assume also that all the principles of the Constitution are hostile to dictatorship and minority rule; and that it is a principle of our Constitution that change in the organization of our government is to be effected by the orderly procedures ordained by the Constitution and not by force or fraud. With these in mind, we may examine petitioner's behavior as disclosed by the record, during the five years which preceded his naturalization, in order to ascertain whether there was basis in the evidence for the trial judge's findings. . . .

Petitioner, who is an educated and intelligent man, took out his first papers June 10, 1927, when nearly twenty-two. Since his sixteenth year he has been continuously and actively engaged in promoting in one way or another the interests of various Communist Party organizations affiliated with and controlled as to their policy and action by the Third International, the parent Communist organization, which had its headquarters and its Executive Committee in Moscow. The evidence shows petitioner's loyalty to the Communist Party organizations; that as a member of the Party he was subject to and accepted its political control, and that as a Party member his adherence to its political principles and tactics was required by its constitution. . . .

At the end of 1924, petitioner joined the Workers Party (which later changed its name to the Workers Communist Party and still later to the Communist Party of the United States of America). . . . The Party constitution, at the time petitioner became a member, provided that "every person who accepts the principles and tactics of the Workers Party of America and agrees to submit to its discipline and engage actively in its work shall be eligible to membership." Applicants for membership were required to sign an application card reading as follows: "The undersigned declares his adherence to the principles and tactics of the Workers Party of America as expressed in its program and constitution and agrees to submit to the discipline of the party and to engage actively in its work." It was likewise provided that "all decisions of the governing bodies of the Party shall be binding upon the membership and subordinate units of the organization," and that "any member or organization violating the decisions of the Party shall be subject to suspension or expulsion." . . .

After his naturalization, petitioner attended the Sixth World Congress of the Communist International, at Moscow, in 1928; and from 1929 to 1930 he was district organizational secretary of the Party for a district which included Arizona, Nevada and California. At various subsequent times he was district organizer in Connecticut, in Minnesota, and in California. He ran twice as the Party's candidate for governor of Minnesota. He held other official positions in the Party, and at the time of the hearing in the district court was California State Secretary of the Party and a member of the State Central Committee. These facts, while not directly probative of his behavior during the five-year period 1922-1927, at least establish that his early devotion to the Party organizations was not transitory, nor inconsistent with his genuine and settled convictions.

The evidence shows and it is not denied that the Communist Party organization at the time in question was a revolutionary party having as its ultimate aim generally, and particularly in England and the United States, the overthrow of capitalistic government, and the substitution for it of the dictatorship of the proletariat. It sought to accomplish this through persistent indoctrination of the people in capitalistic countries with Party principles, by the organization in those countries of sections of the Third International, by systematic teaching of Party principles at meetings and classes held under Party auspices, and by the publication and distribution of Communist literature which constituted one of the basic principles of Party action. . . .

Perusal of the record can leave no doubt of petitioner's unqualified loyalty to the Communist Party. His continuous services to the Party for twenty years in a great variety of capacities, and his familiarity with Party programs and literature, are convincing proof of his complete devotion to Communist Party principles, and his desire to advance them. . . .

There is abundant documentary evidence . . . to support the court's finding that the Communist Party organizations, of which petitioner was a member, diligently circulated printed matter which advocated the overthrow of the Government of the United States by force and violence, and that petitioner aided in that circulation and advocacy. From the beginning, and during all times relevant to this inquiry, there is evidence that the Communist Party organizations advocated the overthrow of capitalistic governments by revolution to be accomplished, if need be, by force of arms. We need not stop to consider the much discussed question whether this meant more than that force was to be used if established governments should be so misguided as to refuse to make themselves over into proletarian dictatorships by amendment of their governmental structures, or should have the effrontery to defend themselves from lawless or subversive attacks. For in any case the end contemplated was the overthrow of government, and the measures advocated were force and violence. . . .

In order to determine whether petitioner's behavior established his attachment to the principles of the Constitution, we are entitled to consider the political system which his Party proposed to establish and toward which his own efforts in promoting the Communist cause were directed. About this there is and can be no serious dispute. Under the new system existing constitutional principles were to be abandoned. In the new government to be established by the Communists, the freedoms guaranteed by the Bill of Rights were to be ended. . . .

The aims of the Communists could be achieved only by "the annihilation of the entire bourgeois governmental apparatus, parliamentary, judicial, military, bureaucratic, administrative, municipal," and it was necessary for the Communists "to break and destroy" the "apparatus." The annihilation of the existing political structure was deemed as necessary in the United States as elsewhere. If elected to public office the Communist was directed to "facilitate this task of destruction" of the existing "apparatus," since the "bourgeois State organizations" were to be utilized only "with the object of destroying them."

. . . The evidence . . . show[s] a basis for finding in the Party teachings, during the period in question, an unqualified hostility to the most fundamental and universally recognized principles of the Constitution. On the argument we were admonished that petitioner favored change in our form of government, which is itself a principle of the Constitution, since the Constitution provides for its own amendment, and that in any case the Communist Party had greatly modified its aims in more recent years. It is true that the Constitution provides for its own amendment by an orderly procedure but not through the breakdown of our governmental system by lawless conduct and by force. It can hardly satisfy the requirement of "attachment to the principles of the Constitution" that one is attached to the means for its destruction.

. . . It would be little short of preposterous to assert that vigorous aid knowingly given by a pledged Party member in disseminating the Party teachings, to which reference has been made, is compatible with attachment to the principles of the Constitution. . . .

Yet the Court's opinion seems to tell us that the trier of fact must not examine petitioner's gospel to find out what kind of man he was, or even what his gospel was; that the trier of fact could not "impute" to petitioner any genuine attachment to the doctrines of these organizations whose teachings he so assiduously spread. It might as well be said that it is impossible to infer that a man is attached to the principles of a religious movement from the fact that he conducts its prayer meetings, or, to take a more sinister example, that it could not be inferred that a man is a Nazi and consequently not attached to constitutional principles who, for more than five years, had diligently circulated the doctrines of Mein Kampf.

In neither case of course is the inference inevitable. It is possible, though not probable or normal, for one to be attached to principles diametrically opposed to those, to the dissemination of which he has given his life's best effort. But it is a normal and sensible inference which the trier of fact is free to make that his attachment is to those principles rather than to constitutional principles with which they are at war. A man can be known by the ideas he spreads as well as by the company he keeps. And when one does not challenge the proof that he has given his life to spreading a particular class of well-defined ideas, it is convincing evidence that his attachment is to them rather than their opposites. In this case it is convincing evidence that petitioner, at the time of his naturalization, was not entitled to the citizenship he procured because he was not attached to the principles of the Constitution of the United States and because he was not well disposed to the good order and happiness of the same.

[Justice Jackson did not participate. He noted that the initial case was instituted by the Justice Department in 1939 "and tried in December of that year. In January 1940, I became Attorney General of the United States and succeeded to official responsibility for it. This I have considered a cause for disqualification, and I desire the reason to be a matter of record." What Justice Jackson did not indicate was that his predecessor as Attorney General — and thus the individual with formal responsibility for initiating the case — was Frank Murphy, the author of the majority opinion.]

Discussion

1. Is Congress as unconstrained by the Constitution as Justice Murphy implies when he says "that naturalization is a privilege, to be given or withheld on such conditions as Congress sees fit"? In *Dred Scott,* Chief Justice Taney mentioned that the first Congress limited naturalization to white immigrants. Would the

Constitution in the 1990s permit such a limitation? Well into the the twentieth century, the United States explicitly took race and national origin into account in deciding who was eligible (and ineligible) for American citizenship, though the races singled out were other than Negro. Natives of both China and Japan were ineligible for citizenship. Moreover, the 1924 immigration act established quotas on immigration based on the percentage of ethnic groups within existing American society. Thus, for example, many more immigrants from the British Isles were entitled to entry than were persons from Southern or Eastern Europe, let alone Asia. This criterion for immigration was not changed until the 1960s. Congress may also use political criteria for naturalization that would raise significant First Amendment problems if applied to birth-right citizens. For example, Congress in 1952 amended the naturalization law to provide, in 8 U.S.C. §1424, that "no person shall hereafter be naturalized as a citizen of the United States . . . who is a member of or affiliated with . . . the Communist Party of the United States" or a variety of other "Communist-front" organizations.

2. How do the majority and dissenting opinions differ in terms of their willingness to ascribe the views of the Communist Party to Schneiderman himself? A variant of this issue arises in Scales v. United States, 367 U.S. 203 (1961), one of the Smith Act cases testing Congress' power to punish knowing membership in an organization advocating violent overthrow of the government. The Court upheld Scales' conviction for membership in the Communist Party in the face of a First Amendment challenge, though Justice Harlan's majority opinion construed the statute in a way that significantly restricted its reach: The government must prove that a defendant had "knowledge of the proscribed advocacy before he may be convicted." And if the organization has legal as well as illegal aims, the government must show by "clear proof that a defendant specifically intend[s] to accomplish [the aims of the organization] by resort to violence."

Note: Loyalty Oaths

To become a naturalized citizen, one must take an oath of loyalty to the Constitution. Article VI of the Constitution requires senators, representatives, and state officials to take a similar oath. And such an oath is often required as a condition for engaging in licensed occupations, including the practice of law. What limits does the Constitution place on such ascertainments of loyalty?

COLE v. RICHARDSON

405 U.S. 676 (1972)

Appeal from the United States District Court for the District of Massachusetts

[The appellee was dismissed shortly after her employment as a research sociologist by Boston State Hospital because she refused to take an oath required of all public employees in Massachusetts: "I do solemnly swear (or affirm) that I will uphold and defend the Constitution of the United States of America and the Constitution of the Commonwealth of Massachusetts and that I will oppose the overthrow of the government of the United States or of this Commonwealth by force, violence or by any illegal or unconstitutional method."

A three-judge district court held the oath unconstitutional. The Supreme Court reversed.]

BURGER, C.J. . . .

A review of the oath cases in this Court will put the instant oath into context. We have made clear that neither federal nor state government may condition employment on taking oaths that impinge on rights guaranteed by the First and Fourteenth Amendments respectively, as for example those relating to political beliefs. Nor may employment be conditioned on an oath that one has not engaged, or will not engage, in protected speech activities such as the following: criticizing institutions of government; discussing political doctrine that approves the overthrow of certain forms of government; and supporting candidates for political office. Employment may not be conditioned on an oath denying past, or abjuring future, associational activities within constitutional protection; such protected activities include membership in organizations having illegal purposes unless one knows of the purpose and shares a specific intent to promote the illegal purpose. . . . And finally an oath may not be so vague that "men of common intelligence must necessarily guess at its meaning and differ as to its application, [because such an oath] violates the first essential of due process of law." Concern for vagueness in the oath cases has been especially great because uncertainty as to an oath's meaning may deter individuals from engaging in constitutionally protected activity conceivably within the scope of the oath.

An underlying, seldom articulated concern running throughout these cases is that the oaths under consideration often required individuals to reach back into their past to recall minor, sometimes innocent, activities. They put the government into "the censorial business of investigating, scrutinizing, interpreting, and then penalizing or approving the political viewpoints" and past activities of individuals.

Several cases recently decided by the Court stand out among our oath cases because they have upheld the constitutionality of oaths, addressed to the future, promising constitutional support in broad terms. These cases have begun with a recognition that the Constitution itself prescribes comparable oaths in two articles. Article II, §1, cl. 8, provides that the President shall swear that he will "faithfully execute the Office . . . and will to the best of [his] Ability, preserve, protect and defend the Constitution of the United States." Article VI, cl. 3, provides that all state and federal officers shall be bound by an oath "to support this Constitution." . . .

Bond v. Floyd, 385 U.S. 116 (1966), involved Georgia's statutory requirement that state legislators swear to "support the Constitution of this State and of the United States," a paraphrase of the constitutionally required oath. The Court there implicitly concluded that the First Amendment did not undercut the validity of the constitutional oath provisions. . . . The Court read the Georgia oath as calling simply for an acknowledgment of a willingness to abide by "constitutional process of government." . . .

The District Court in the instant case properly recognized that the first clause of the Massachusetts oath, in which the individual swears to "uphold and defend" the Constitutions of the United States and the Commonwealth, is indistinguishable from the oaths this Court has recently approved. Yet the District Court applied a highly literalistic approach to the second clause to strike it down. We view the second clause of the oath as essentially the same as the first.

The second clause of the oath contains a promise to "oppose the overthrow of the government of the United States of America or of this Commonwealth by force, violence or by any illegal or unconstitutional method." The District Court sought to give a dictionary meaning to this language and found "oppose" to raise the specter of vague, undefinable responsibilities actively to combat a potential overthrow of the government. That reading of the oath understandably troubled the court because of what it saw as vagueness in terms of what threats would constitute sufficient danger of overthrow to require the oath giver to actively oppose overthrow, and exactly what actions he would have to take in that respect.

But such a literal approach to the second clause is inconsistent with the Court's approach to the "support" oaths. One could make a literal argument that "support" involves nebulous, undefined responsibilities for action in some hypothetical situations. . . .

We have rejected such rigidly literal notions and recognized that the purpose leading legislatures to enact such oaths, just as the purpose leading the Framers of our Constitution to include the two explicit constitutional oaths, was not to create specific responsibilities but to assure that those in positions of public trust were willing to commit themselves to live by the constitutional processes of our system. . . . Just as the connotatively active word "support" has been interpreted to mean simply a commitment to abide by our constitutional system, the second clause of this oath is merely oriented to the negative implication of this notion; it is a commitment not to use illegal and constitutionally unprotected force to change the constitutional system. The second clause does not expand the obligation of the first; it simply makes clear the application of the first clause to a particular issue. Such repetition, whether for emphasis or cadence, seems to be the wont of authors of oaths. That the second clause may be redundant is no ground to strike it down; we are not charged with correcting grammar but with enforcing a constitution.

The purpose of the oath is clear on its face. We cannot presume that the Massachusetts Legislature intended by its use of such general terms as "uphold," "defend," and "oppose" to impose obligations of specific, positive action on oath takers. Any such construction would raise serious questions whether the oath was so vague as to amount to a denial of due process.

Nor is the oath as interpreted void for vagueness. As Mr. Justice Harlan pointed out in his opinion on our earlier consideration of this case, the oath is "no more than an amenity." It is punishable only by a prosecution for perjury and, since perjury is a knowing and willful falsehood, the constitutional vice of punishment without fair warning cannot occur here. Nor here is there any problem of the punishment inflicted by mere prosecution. There has been no prosecution under this statute since its 1948 enactment, and there is no indication that prosecutions have been planned or begun. The oath "triggered no serious possibility of prosecution" by the Commonwealth. Were we confronted with a record of actual prosecutions or harassment through threatened prosecutions, we might be faced with a different question.

DOUGLAS, J., dissenting.

The part of the oath that says "I will oppose the overthrow of the government of the United States of America or of this Commonwealth by force, violence or by any illegal or unconstitutional method" is plainly unconstitutional by our decisions.

Advocacy of basic fundamental changes in government, which might popularly be described as "overthrow," is within the protection of the First Amendment even when it is restrictively construed. In Brandenburg v. Ohio, a case involving criminal syndicalism, this Court ruled that a State may not "forbid or proscribe advocacy of the use of force or of law violation except where such advocacy is directed to inciting or producing imminent lawless action and is likely to incite or produce such action." . . .

The present oath makes such advocacy a possible offense under a restrictive reading of the First Amendment.

The views expressed by Mr. Justice Black and me give the First Amendment a more expansive reading. We have condemned loyalty oaths as "manifestation[s] of a national network of laws aimed at coercing and controlling the minds of men. Test oaths are notorious tools of tyranny. When used to shackle the mind they are, or at least they should be, unspeakably odious to a free people." . . . The line between the permissible control by a State and the impermissible control is "the line between ideas and overt acts." . . . This oath, however, requires that appellee "oppose" that which she has an indisputable right to advocate. . . .

MARSHALL, J., joined by Brennan, J., dissenting. . . .

The first half of the oath, requiring an employee to indicate a willingness to "uphold and defend" the state and federal Constitutions, is clearly constitutional. It is nothing more than the traditional oath of support that we have unanimously upheld as a condition of public employment. . . .

I would . . . strike down the second half of this oath as an overbroad infringement of protected expression and conduct. The Court's prior decisions represent a judgment that simple affirmative oaths of support are less suspect and less evil than negative oaths requiring a disaffirmance of political ties, group affiliations, or beliefs. Yet, I think that it is plain that affirmative oaths of loyalty, no less than negative ones, have odious connotations and that they present dangers. We have tolerated support oaths as applied to all government employees only because we view these affirmations as an expression of "minimal loyalty to the Government." Such oaths are merely indications by the employee "in entirely familiar and traditional language, that he will endeavor to perform his public duties lawfully."

It is precisely because these oaths are minimal, requiring only that nominal expression of allegiance "which, by the common law, every citizen was understood to owe his sovereign," that they have been sustained. That they are minimal intrusions into the freedom of government officials and employees to think, speak, and act makes them constitutional; it does not mean that greater intrusions will be tolerated. On the contrary, each time this Court has been faced with an attempt by government to make the traditional support oath more comprehensive or demanding, it has struck the oath down.

When faced with an "imminent clear and present danger," governments may be able to compel citizens to do things that would ordinarily be beyond their authority to mandate. But, such emergency governmental power is a far cry from compelling every state employee in advance of any such danger to promise in any and all circumstances to conform speech and conduct to opposing an "overthrow" of the government.

Discussion

1. Chief Justice Burger indicates that the Massachusetts oath did not "create specific responsibilities," but was intended instead "to assure that those in positions of public trust were willing to commit themselves to live by the constitutional processes of our system." To what "constitutional processes" do persons taking the oath commit themselves? Consider, for example, the status of the civil disobedient, who disobeys what she considers an immoral law in order to bear witness to a "higher reality" than the Constitution. Is such activity — by, say, someone harboring a fugitive slave — an indication of lack of "attachment" to the Constitution and its "principles," one of which prior to 1863 was the sanctity of that particular form of private property known as chattel slavery? If we have sometimes honored law-breakers because of their contributions to constitutional change, does this mean that our constitutional tradition includes such disobedience as an accepted "constitutional process"? Is it clear, for example, that Abraham Lincoln can so easily be portrayed as "attached" to the "constitutional process" of the 1861 Constitution as Justice Murphy assumes in *Schneiderman*?

B. The Problem of Involuntary Denaturalization: Is Citizenship a Permanent Status (Unless One Chooses to Resign)?

The right of voluntary "expatriation" — i.e., voluntary relinquishment of citizenship — has been recognized since early in American history. By contrast, the question whether Congress has the power to expel a person from the political community through "denationalization" has been controversial. Ironically, as Alexander Aleinikoff notes,[7]

> the recognition of a right of expatriation proved to be a double-edged sword for U.S. citizens. Once it was firmly established that Americans could cast off their allegiance [to the United States], it left room for the government to argue that certain objective conduct evidenced expatriation — such as naturalization elsewhere or residence of a naturalized citizen in his or her country of origin. . . .
>
> The 1907 Expatriation Act was primarily aimed at problems occasioned by dual nationality. It provided that a U.S. citizen "shall be deemed to have expatriated himself" when he has been naturalized in, or taken an oath of allegiance to, a foreign state. The Act also created a rebuttable presumption that a naturalized alien who resided for two years in his native country "has ceased to be an American citizen." Finally, it provided that any American woman who married a foreigner "shall take the nationality of her husband" (for so long as the marriage lasted).

The earliest Supreme Court case examining the issue was Mackenzie v. Hare, 239 U.S. 299 (1915), in which the Court upheld the denaturalization of a native-born California woman for marrying an Englishman. It was irrelevant that Mackenzie had no desire to give up her American citizenship; it was enough that she had voluntarily entered into the marriage "with notice of the consequences." The Court referred to the "ancient principle" of the "identity of husband and wife,"

7. T. Alexander Aleinikoff, Theories of Loss of Citizenship. 84 Mich. L. Rev. 1471, 1476 (1986).

and wrote that the "marriage of an American woman with a foreigner" may "bring the Government into embarrassments and, it may be, into controversies."[8]

Perez v. Brownell, 356 U.S. 44 (1958), upheld a congressional statute that stripped citizenship of a person voting in a foreign election. Justice Frankfurter wrote for the majority: "Congress has interpreted [voting in a foreign election], not irrationally, as importing not only something less than complete and unswerving allegiance to the United States but also elements of an allegiance to another country in some measure, at least, inconsistent with American citizenship." Moreover, as in *Mackenzie*, the withdrawal of citizenship could be viewed by Congress as a means of avoiding embarrassing situations that might "jeopardiz[e] the successful conduct of international relations." Chief Justice Warren, joined by Justices Black and Douglas, dissented. He labeled citizenship "man's basic right, for it is nothing less than the right to have rights." Moreover, the United States "was born of its citizens" and he stated that "it is without power to sever the relationship that gave rise to its existence."

On the same day that *Perez* was decided, the Court took the first step toward limiting the power to denaturalize.

TROP v. DULLES
356 U.S. 86 (1958)
Certiorari to the United States Court of Appeals for the Second Circuit

WARREN, C.J., joined by Justices Black, Douglas, and Whittaker.

. . . The facts are not in dispute. In 1944 petitioner was a private in the United States Army, serving in French Morocco. On May 22, he escaped from a stockade at Casablanca, where he had been confined following a previous breach of discipline. The next day petitioner and a companion were walking along a road towards Rabat, in the general direction back to Casablanca, when an Army truck approached and stopped. A witness testified that petitioner boarded the truck willingly and that no words were spoken. In Rabat petitioner was turned over to military police. Thus ended petitioner's "desertion." He had been gone less than a day and had willingly surrendered to an officer on an Army vehicle while he was walking back towards his base. . . . A general courtmartial convicted petitioner of desertion and sentenced him to three years at hard labor, forfeiture of all pay and allowances and a dishonorable discharge.

In 1952 petitioner applied for a passport. His application was denied on the ground that under the provisions of Section 401(g) of the Nationality Act of 1940, as amended, he had lost his citizenship by reason of his conviction and dishonorable discharge for wartime desertion. In 1955 petitioner commenced this action . . . , seeking a declaratory judgment that he is a citizen.

Section 401(g), the statute that decrees the forfeiture of this petitioner's citizenship [was amended in 1944] to provide that a convicted deserter would lose his citizenship only if he was dismissed from the service or dishonorably discharged. At the same time it was provided that citizenship could be regained if the deserter was restored to active duty in wartime with the permission of the military authorities.

8. Marriage to a foreigner was eliminated as a denaturalizing act by Congress in the Acts of September 22, 1922, 42 Stat. 1022, and March 3, 1931, 46 Stat. 1511.

Though these amendments were added to ameliorate the harshness of the statute, their combined effect produces a result that poses far graver problems than the ones that were sought to be solved. Section 401(g) as amended now gives the military authorities complete discretion to decide who among convicted deserters shall continue to be Americans and who shall be stateless. By deciding whether to issue and execute a dishonorable discharge and whether to allow a deserter to re-enter the armed forces, the military becomes the arbiter of citizenship. And the domain given to it by Congress is not as narrow as might be supposed. Though the crime of desertion is one of the most serious in military law, it is by no means a rare event for a soldier to be convicted of this crime. The elements of desertion are simply absence from duty plus the intention not to return. Into this category falls a great range of conduct, which may be prompted by a variety of motives — fear, laziness, hysteria or any emotional imbalance. The offense may occur not only in combat but also in training camps for draftees in this country. The Solicitor General informed the Court that during World War II, according to Army estimates, approximately 21,000 soldiers and airmen were convicted of desertion and given dishonorable discharges by the sentencing courts-martial and that about 7,000 of these were actually separated from the service and thus rendered stateless when the reviewing authorities refused to remit their dishonorable discharges. Over this group of men, enlarged by whatever the corresponding figures may be for the Navy and Marines, the military has been given the power to grant or withhold citizenship. . . .

I

. . . It is my conviction that citizenship is not subject to the general powers of the National Government and therefore cannot be divested in the exercise of those powers. The right may be voluntarily relinquished or abandoned either by express language or by language and conduct that show a renunciation of citizenship.

Under these principles, this petitioner has not lost his citizenship. Desertion in wartime, though it may merit the ultimate penalty, does not necessarily signify allegiance to a foreign state. . . . This soldier committed a crime for which he should be and was punished, but he did not involve himself in any way with a foreign state. . . .

Citizenship is not a license that expires upon misbehavior. The duties of citizenship are numerous, and the discharge of many of these obligations is essential to the security and well-being of the Nation. The citizen who fails to pay his taxes or to abide by the laws safeguarding the integrity of elections deals a dangerous blow to his country. But could a citizen be deprived of his nationality for evading these basic responsibilities of citizenship? In time of war the citizen's duties include not only the military defense of the Nation but also a full participation in the manifold activities of the civilian ranks. Failure to perform any of these obligations may cause the Nation serious injury, and, in appropriate circumstances, the punishing power is available to deal with derelictions of duty. But citizenship is not lost every time a duty of citizenship is shirked. And the deprivation of citizenship is not a weapon that the Government may use to express its displeasure at a citizen's conduct, however reprehensible that conduct may be. As long as a person does not voluntarily renounce or abandon his citizenship, and this petitioner has done neither, I believe his fundamental right of citizenship is secure. On this ground alone the judgment in this case should be reversed.

II

. . . [T]he action taken in this case exceeds constitutional limits, even under the majority's decision in *Perez.* The Court concluded in *Perez* that citizenship could be divested in the exercise of the foreign affairs power. In this case, it is urged that the war power is adequate to support the divestment of citizenship. But there is a vital difference between the two statutes that purport to implement these powers by decreeing loss of citizenship. The statute in *Perez* decreed loss of citizenship — so the majority concluded — to eliminate those international problems that were thought to arise by reason of a citizen's having voted in a foreign election. The statute in this case, however, is entirely different. . . . The constitutional question posed by Section 401(g) would appear to be whether or not denationalization may be inflicted as a punishment, even assuming that citizenship may be divested pursuant to some governmental power.

But the Government contends that this statute does not impose a penalty and that constitutional limitations on the power of Congress to punish are therefore inapplicable. We are told this is so because a committee of Cabinet members, in recommending this legislation to the Congress, said it "technically is not a penal law." How simple would be the tasks of constitutional adjudication and of law generally if specific problems could be solved by inspection of the labels pasted on them! Manifestly the issue of whether Section 401(g) is a penal law cannot be thus determined. . . .

In form Section 401(g) appears to be a regulation of nationality. The statute deals initially with the status of nationality and then specifies the conduct that will result in loss of that status. But surely form cannot provide the answer to this inquiry. A statute providing that "a person shall lose his liberty by committing bank robbery," though in form a regulation of liberty, would nonetheless be penal. Nor would its penal effect be altered by labeling it a regulation of banks or by arguing that there is a rational connection between safeguarding banks and imprisoning bank robbers. The inquiry must be directed to substance.

. . . In deciding whether or not a law is penal, this Court has generally based its determination upon the purpose of the statute. If the statute imposes a disability for the purposes of punishment — that is, to reprimand the wrongdoer, to deter others, etc., it has been considered penal. But a statute has been considered nonpenal if it imposes a disability, not to punish, but to accomplish some other legitimate governmental purpose. The Court has recognized that any statute decreeing some adversity as a consequence of certain conduct may have both a penal and a nonpenal effect. The controlling nature of such statutes normally depends on the evident purpose of the legislature. The point may be illustrated by the situation of an ordinary felon. A person who commits a bank robbery, for instance, loses his right to liberty and often his right to vote. If, in the exercise of the power to protect banks, both sanctions were imposed for the purpose of punishing bank robbers, the statutes authorizing both disabilities would be penal. But because the purpose of the latter statute is to designate a reasonable ground of eligibility for voting, this law is sustained as a nonpenal exercise of the power to regulate the franchise.

The same reasoning applies to Section 401(g). The purpose of taking away citizenship from a convicted deserter is simply to punish him. There is no other legitimate purpose that the statute could serve. Denationalization in this case is not even claimed to be a means of solving international problems, as was argued in *Perez.* Here the purpose is punishment, and therefore the statute is a penal law.

It is urged that this statute is not a penal law but a regulatory provision authorized by the war power. It cannot be denied that Congress has power to prescribe rules governing the proper performance of military obligations, of which perhaps the most significant is the performance of one's duty when hazardous or important service is required. . . . If this statute taking away citizenship is a congressional exercise of the war power, then it cannot rationally be treated other than as a penal law, because it imposes the sanction of denationalization for the purpose of punishing transgression of a standard of conduct prescribed in the exercise of that power.

The Government argues that the sanction of denationalization imposed by Section 401(g) is not a penalty because deportation has not been so considered by this Court. While deportation is undoubtedly a harsh sanction that has a severe penal effect, this Court has in the past sustained deportation as an exercise of the sovereign's power to determine the conditions upon which an alien may reside in this country. . . . This view of deportation may be highly fictional, but even if its validity is conceded, it is wholly inapplicable to this case. No one contends that the Government has, in addition to the power to exclude all aliens, a sweeping power to denationalize all citizens. . . .

Section 401(g) is a penal law, and we must face the question whether the Constitution permits the Congress to take away citizenship as a punishment for crime. If it is assumed that the power of Congress extends to divestment of citizenship, the problem still remains as to this statute whether denationalization is a cruel and unusual punishment within the meaning of the Eighth Amendment. Since wartime desertion is punishable by death, there can be no argument that the penalty of denationalization is excessive in relation to the gravity of the crime. The question is whether this penalty subjects the individual to a fate forbidden by the principle of civilized treatment guaranteed by the Eighth Amendment.

At the outset, let us put to one side the death penalty as an index of the constitutional limit on punishment. Whatever the arguments may be against capital punishment, . . . the death penalty has been employed throughout our history, and, in a day when it is still widely accepted, it cannot be said to violate the constitutional concept of cruelty. But it is equally plain that the existence of the death penalty is not a license to the Government to devise any punishment short of death within the limit of its imagination.

The exact scope of the constitutional phrase "cruel and unusual" has not been detailed by this Court. But the basic policy reflected in these words is firmly established in the Anglo-American tradition of criminal justice. . . . The basic concept underlying the Eighth Amendment is nothing less than the dignity of man. While the State has the power to punish, the Amendment stands to assure that this power be exercised within the limits of civilized standards. . . . This Court has had little occasion to give precise content to the Eighth Amendment, and, in an enlightened democracy such as ours, this is not surprising. But when the Court was confronted with a punishment of 12 years in irons at hard and painful labor imposed for the crime of falsifying public records, it did not hesitate to declare that the penalty was cruel in its excessiveness and unusual in its character. Weems v. United States, 217 U.S. 349. The Court recognized in that case that the words of the Amendment are not precise, and that their scope is not static. The Amendment must draw its meaning from the evolving standards of decency that mark the progress of a maturing society.

We believe . . . that use of denationalization as a punishment is barred by the Eighth Amendment. There may be involved no physical mistreatment, no primitive torture. There is instead the total destruction of the individual's status in organized society. It is a form of punishment more primitive than torture, for it destroys for the individual the political existence that was centuries in the development. The punishment strips the citizen of his status in the national and international political community. His very existence is at the sufferance of the country in which he happens to find himself. While any one country may accord him some rights, and presumably as long as he remained in this country he would enjoy the limited rights of an alien, no country need do so because he is stateless. Furthermore, his enjoyment of even the limited rights of an alien might be subject to termination at any time by reason of deportation. In short, the expatriate has lost the right to have rights.

This punishment is offensive to cardinal principles for which the Constitution stands. It subjects the individual to a fate of ever-increasing fear and distress. He knows not what discriminations may be established against him, what proscriptions may be directed against him, and when and for what cause his existence in his native land may be terminated. He may be subject to banishment, a fate universally decried by civilized people. He is stateless, a condition deplored in the international community of democracies. It is no answer to suggest that all the disastrous consequences of this fate may not be brought to bear on a stateless person. The threat makes the punishment obnoxious.

The civilized nations of the world are in virtual unanimity that statelessness is not to be imposed as punishment for crime. It is true that several countries prescribe expatriation in the event that their nationals engage in conduct in derogation of native allegiance. Even statutes of this sort are generally applicable primarily to naturalized citizens. But use of denationalization as punishment for crime is an entirely different matter. The United Nations' survey of the nationality laws of 84 nations of the world reveals that only two countries, the Philippines and Turkey, impose denationalization as a penalty for desertion. In this country the Eighth Amendment forbids that to be done. . . .

[A concurring opinion by Justice Black, joined by Justice Douglas, is omitted.]

BRENNAN, J., concurring.

. . . I reach a different conclusion in this case [than in *Perez*] because I believe that §401(g) . . . lies beyond Congress' power to enact. It is, concededly, paradoxical to justify as constitutional the expatriation of the citizen who has committed no crime by voting in a Mexican political election, yet find unconstitutional a statute which provides for the expatriation of a soldier guilty of the very serious crime of desertion in time of war. The loss of citizenship may have as ominous significance for the individual in the one case as in the other. Why then does not the Constitution prevent the expatriation of the voter as well as the deserter?

Here, as in Perez v. Brownell, we must inquire whether there exists a relevant connection between the particular legislative enactment and the power granted to Congress by the Constitution. . . . Harsh as the consequences may be to the individual concerned, Congress has ordained the loss of citizenship simultaneously with the act of voting because Congress might reasonably believe that in these circumstances there is no acceptable alternative to expatriation as a means of avoiding possible embarrassments to our relations with foreign nations. And where Congress has determined that considerations of the highest national importance indicate a course of action for which an adequate substitute might rationally appear lacking, I cannot say that this means lies beyond Congress' power to choose. Cf. Korematsu v. United States, 323 U.S. 214.

In contrast to §401(e), the section with which we are now concerned, §401(g), draws upon the power of Congress to raise and maintain military forces to wage war. No pretense can here be made that expatriation of the deserter in any way relates to the conduct of foreign affairs, for this statute is not limited in its effects to those who desert in a foreign country or who flee to another land. Nor is this statute limited in its application to the deserter whose conduct imports "elements of an allegiance to another country in some measure, at least, inconsistent with American citizenship." Perez v. Brownell, 356 U.S. 61. The history of this provision, indeed, shows that the essential congressional purpose was a response to the needs of the military in maintaining discipline in the armed forces, especially during wartime. There can be no serious question that included in Congress' power to maintain armies is the power to deal with the problem of desertion, an act plainly destructive, not only of the military establishment as such, but, more importantly, of the Nation's ability to wage war effectively. But granting that Congress is authorized to deal with the evil of desertion, we must yet inquire whether expatriation is a means reasonably calculated to achieve this legitimate end and thereby designed to further the ultimate congressional objective — the successful waging of war.

. . . It is difficult, indeed, to see how expatriation of the deserter helps wage war except as it performs that function when imposed as punishment. It is obvious that expatriation cannot in any wise avoid the harm apprehended by Congress. After the act of desertion, only punishment can follow, for the harm has been done. The deserter, moreover, does not cease to be an American citizen at the moment he deserts. Indeed, even conviction does not necessarily effect his expatriation, for dishonorable discharge is the condition precedent to loss of citizenship. Therefore, if expatriation is made a consequence of desertion, it must stand together with death and imprisonment — as a form of punishment.

To characterize expatriation as punishment is, of course, but the beginning of critical inquiry. As punishment it may be extremely harsh, but the crime of desertion may be grave indeed. However, the harshness of the punishment may be an important consideration where the asserted power to expatriate has only a slight or tenuous relation to the granted power. In its material forms no one can today judge the precise consequences of expatriation, for happily American law has had little experience with this status, and it cannot be said hypothetically to what extent the severity of the status may be increased consistently with the demands of due process. But it can be supposed that the consequences of greatest weight, in terms of ultimate impact on the petitioner, are unknown and unknowable. Indeed, in truth, he may live out his life with but minor inconvenience. He may perhaps live, work, marry, raise a family, and generally experience a satisfactorily happy life. Nevertheless it cannot be denied that the impact of expatriation — especially where statelessness is the upshot — may be severe. Expatriation, in this respect, constitutes an especially demoralizing sanction. The uncertainty, and the consequent psychological hurt, which must accompany one who becomes an outcast in his own land must be reckoned a substantial factor in the ultimate judgment.

In view of the manifest severity of this sanction, I feel that we should look closely at its probable effect to determine whether Congress' imposition of expatriation as a penal device is justified in reason. Clearly the severity of the penalty, in the case of a serious offense, is not enough to invalidate it where the nature of the penalty is rationally directed to achieve the legitimate ends of punishment.

The novelty of expatriation as punishment does not alone demonstrate its inefficiency. . . . [R]ehabilitation is but one of the several purposes of the penal law. Among other purposes are deterrents of the wrongful act by the threat of punishment and insulation of society from dangerous individuals by imprisonment or execution. What then is the relationship of the punishment of expatriation to these ends of the penal law? It is perfectly obvious that it constitutes the very antithesis of rehabilitation, for instead of guiding the offender back into the useful paths of society it excommunicates him and makes him, literally, an outcast. I can think of no more certain way in which to make a man in whom, perhaps, rest the seeds of serious antisocial behavior more likely to pursue further a career of unlawful activity than to place on him the stigma of the derelict, uncertain of many of his basic rights. Similarly, it must be questioned whether expatriation can really achieve the other effects sought by society in punitive devices. Certainly it will not insulate society from the deserter, for unless coupled with banishment the sanction leaves the offender at large. And as a deterrent device this sanction would appear of little effect, for the offender, if not deterred by thought of the specific penalties of long imprisonment or even death, is not very likely to be swayed from his course by the prospect of expatriation. However insidious and demoralizing may be the actual experience of statelessness, its contemplation in advance seems unlikely to invoke serious misgiving, for none of us yet knows it ramifications.

. . . [T]he Government argues that the necessary nexus to the granted power is to be found in the idea that legislative withdrawal of citizenship is justified in this case because Trop's desertion constituted a refusal to perform one of the highest duties of American citizenship — the bearing of arms in a time of desperate national peril. . . . I cannot see that this is anything other than forcing retribution from the offender — naked vengeance. . . .

It seems to me that nothing is solved by the uncritical reference to service in the armed forces as the "ultimate duty of American citizenship." Indeed, it is very difficult to imagine, on this theory of power, why Congress cannot impose expatriation as punishment for any crime at all — for tax evasion, for bank robbery, for narcotics offenses. As citizens we are also called upon to pay our taxes and to obey the laws, and these duties appear to me to be fully as related to the nature of our citizenship as our military obligations. But Congress' asserted power to expatriate the deserter bears to the war powers precisely the same relation as its power to expatriate the tax evader would bear to the taxing power.

. . . [T]he requisite rational relation between this statute and the war power does not appear — for in this relation the statute is not "really calculated to effect any of the objects entrusted to the government . . . ," M'Culloch v. Maryland, 4

Wheat. 316, 423 — and therefore that §401(g) falls beyond the domain of Congress.

FRANKFURTER, J., dissented, joined by Justices Burton, Clark, and Harlan:

. . . One of the principal purposes in establishing the Constitution was to "provide for the common defence." To that end the States granted to Congress the several powers of Article I, Section 8, clauses 11 to 14 and 18, compendiously described as the "war power." Although these specific grants of power do not specifically enumerate every factor relevant to the power to conduct war, there is no limitation upon it (other than what the Due Process Clause commands). . . .

Probably the most important governmental action contemplated by the war power is the building up and maintenance of an armed force for the common defense. . . . Congress may justifiably be of the view that stern measures — what to some may seem overly stern — are needed in order that control may be had over evasions of military duty when the armed forces are committed to the Nation's defense, and that the deleterious effects of those evasions may be kept to the minimum. Clearly Congress may deal severely with the problem of desertion from the armed forces in wartime; it is equally clear — from the face of the legislation and from the circumstances in which it was passed — that Congress was calling upon its war powers when it made such desertion an act of expatriation.

Possession by an American citizen of the rights and privileges that constitute citizenship imposes correlative obligations, of which the most indispensable may well be "to take his place in the ranks of the army of his country and risk the chance of being shot down in its defense." Harsh as this may sound, it is no more so than the actualities to which it responds. Can it be said that there is no rational nexus between refusal to perform this ultimate duty of American citizenship and legislative withdrawal of that citizenship? Congress may well have thought that making loss of citizenship a consequence of wartime desertion would affect the ability of the military authorities to control the forces with which they were expected to fight and win a major world conflict. It is not for us to deny that Congress might reasonably have believed the morale and fighting efficiency of our troops would be impaired if our soldiers knew that their fellows who had abandoned them in their time of greatest need were to remain in the communion of our citizens.

. . . Petitioner contends that loss of citizenship is an unconstitutionally disproportionate "punishment" for desertion and that it constitutes "cruel and unusual punishments" within the scope of the Eighth Amendment. Loss of citizenship entails undoubtedly severe — and in particular situations even tragic — consequences. . . . However, like denaturalization, expatriation under the Nationality Act of 1940 is not "punishment" in any valid constitutional sense. Simply because denationalization was attached by Congress as a consequence of conduct that it had elsewhere made unlawful, it does not follow that denationalization is a "punishment," any more than it can be said that loss of civil rights as a result of conviction for a felony is a "punishment" for any legally significant purposes. . . . Since there are legislative ends within the scope of Congress' war power that are wholly consistent with a "non-penal" purpose to regulate the military forces, and since there is nothing on the face of this legislation or in its history to indicate that Congress had a contrary purpose, there is no warrant for this Court's labeling the disability imposed by §401(g) as a "punishment."

Even assuming, arguendo, that §401(g) can be said to impose "punishment," to insist that denationalization is "cruel and unusual" punishment is to stretch that concept beyond the breaking point. It seems scarcely arguable that loss of citizenship is within the Eighth Amendment's prohibition because disproportionate to an offense that is capital and has been so from the first year of Independence. Is constitutional dialectic so empty of reason that it can be seriously urged that loss of citizenship is a fate worse than death? The seriousness of abandoning one's country when it is in the grip of mortal conflict precludes denial to Congress of the power to terminate citizenship here, unless that power is to be denied to Congress under any circumstance.

Many civilized nations impose loss of citizenship for indulgence in designated prohibited activities. Although these provisions are often, but not always, applicable only to naturalized citizens, they are more nearly comparable to our expatriation law than to our denaturalization law. Some countries have made wartime desertion result in loss of citizenship — native- born or naturalized. In this country, desertion has been punishable by loss of at least the "rights of citizenship" since 1865. The Court today reaffirms [earlier decisions] sustaining the power of Congress to denationalize citizens who had no desire or intention to give up their citizenship. If loss of citizenship may constitutionally be made the consequence of such conduct as marrying a foreigner, and thus certainly not "cruel and unusual," it seems more than incongruous that such loss should be thought "cruel and unusual" when it is the consequence of conduct that is also a crime. In short, denationalization, when attached to the offense of wartime desertion, cannot justifiably be deemed so at variance with enlightened concepts of "humane justice," see Weems v. United States, 217 U.S. 349, 378, as to be beyond the power of Congress. . . .

Nor has Congress fallen afoul of [the Eighth Amendment] because a person's post-denationalization status has elements of unpredictability. Presumably a denationalized person becomes an alien vis-à-vis the United States. The very substantial rights and privileges that the alien in this country enjoys under the federal and state constitutions puts him in a very different condition from that of an outlaw in fifteenth-century England. He need not be in constant fear lest some dire and unforeseen fate be imposed on him by arbitrary governmental action — certainly not "while this Court sits." . . . [T]he assumption that brutal treatment is the inevitable lot of denationalized persons found in other countries is a slender basis on which to strike down an Act of Congress otherwise amply sustainable.

Note: Subsequent Cases

1. Statutory denaturalization was considered again in Kennedy v. Mendoza-Martinez, 372 U.S. 144 (1963), and Schneider v. Rusk, 377 U.S. 163 (1964), by a Court that now included Arthur Goldberg in place of Felix Frankfurter. The first case involved a person who had left the United States in order to avoid military service. The second concerned a *naturalized* American citizen who had returned to her native country and resided there for three years. In neither case did the Court adopt Chief Justice Warren's suggestion that involuntary denaturalization *per se* violated the Constitution. Mendoza-Martinez's citizenship was

saved because of procedural deficiencies in the statute; Schneider's, because the majority considered her a victim of illegitimate discrimination as between native-born and naturalized citizens.

2. Two years later, in Afroyim v. Rusk, 387 U.S. 253 (1967), the Court expressly overruled *Perez.* Justice Black wrote: "Our holding does no more than to give to this citizen that which is his own, a constitutional right to remain a citizen in a free country unless he voluntarily relinquishes that citizenship." Rogers v. Bellei, 401 U.S. 815 (1971), upheld a statute requiring a United States citizen born abroad, in order to maintain that citizenship, to come to the United States before the age of 23 and to live there for five years between the ages of 14 and 28. Nonetheless, the Court reaffirmed the central thrust of *Afroyim* in Vance v. Terrazas, 444 U.S. 252 (1980), where it stated that loss of citizenship required proof by the government that an "expatriating act was accompanied by an intent to terminate United States citizenship."

3. *The case of Meir Kahane.* The United States conditions naturalization on renunciation of any previous political loyalties. However, American nationals do not lose their citizenship by becoming citizens of other nations so long as they do not renounce allegiance to the United States. Meir Kahane, a native-born American citizen, became a citizen of Israel, which does not require the renunciation of prior allegiance. In 1984, Kahane, an extreme right-wing religious Zionist, was elected to the Israeli parliament, the Knesset. In 1985, the United States Department of State declared that Kahane had lost his citizenship by virtue of a section of the Immigration and Nationality Act providing for the denaturalization of any citizen "accepting, serving in, or performing the duties of any office, post, or employment under the government of a foreign state . . . if he has or acquires the nationality of such foreign state." Kahane, who traveled frequently to the United States in order to raise funds for his political party,[9] specifically denied any intent to relinquish his American citizenship. Still, he admitted having a "primary loyalty . . . to Israel" and stated that he "would have long since given . . . up [U.S. citizenship] if I did not fear — and with justification — that if I gave it up, the American Government would place great obstacles . . . to enter America for lecture tours."

Does the sequence of cases from *Trop* through *Terrazas* indicate that citizenship can be retained so long as the citizen does not utter certain canonical words, e.g., "I hereby state my intention to renounce American citizenship"? Even if that is the correct interpretation of the cases, is it a correct interpretation of the Constitution? Consider the following discussion:

ALEXANDER ALEINIKOFF, THEORIES OF LOSS OF CITIZENSHIP

84 Mich. L. Rev. 1471 (1986)

. . . The underlying issue that I address in this essay is whether the Constitution ought to be read to prohibit denationalization of U.S. citizens. (I will use the term "denationalization" to refer to the government's act of terminating citizenship. "Expatriation" will be used to refer to the individual's voluntary relinquishment of citizenship.) In examining this question, I will explore citizenship from four different perspectives — rights, consent, contract, and community. . . .

9. Kahane was assassinated in November 1990 while on a visit to the United States.

I. Reasons for Denationalization

One can imagine a number of reasons why a nation might want to terminate citizenship of individuals. I will put denationalization grounds into three categories: allegiance, punishment, and public order.

Citizenship is often thought of in terms of allegiance. From the earliest American naturalization laws, aliens seeking to become U.S. citizens have been required to "renounce and abjure absolutely and entirely all allegiance" to any sovereign and "to bear true faith and allegiance" to "the Constitution of the United States." A person's breach or denial of allegiance may be viewed by some as severing the link between citizen and nation, thereby entitling the state to denationalize. . . .

[However, a]llegiance is not necessarily indivisible. Just as people may feel loyalty to different family members, different groups, or different institutions of higher learning, so might a person have allegiance to more than one nation. Here the problem for the state is not a transfer of allegiance [from the United States to some other state], but *divided allegiance*. . . .

A citizen may also demonstrate a *lack of allegiance* without having allegiance elsewhere. This is the situation of either active disloyalty (for example, treason) or simply no loyalty at all (apathy or unconcern about the fate of the nation). To the extent a nation seeks a citizenry dedicated to the support and defense of the country, it may want to rid itself of enemies or deadbeats.

. . . Denationalization . . . may [also] be justified as *punishment.* Congress has enacted several denationalization grounds that fall within this category, such as violation of laws against subversion, draft evasion, and desertion from the armed forces in time of war. Interestingly, these grounds have an "allegiance" ring to them. But nothing under the punishment theory would prevent denationalization for any anti-social conduct — for example, murder, child abuse, or failure to pay taxes.

A final set of denationalization grounds would include loss of citizenship for individuals or groups that the state deems threats to *public order* . . . [or who otherwise pose] a substantial problem for the maintenance of the status quo or the pursuit of other national objectives. . . . The most horrific recent example is the "homelands" policy of South Africa: blacks living in South Africa were stripped of South African citizenship and given citizenship in "independent" homelands based on tribal background. . . .

[After discussing the history of the relevant statutes and the judicial response to them, Aleinikoff goes on to discuss "Perspectives on Loss of Citizenship":]

Is there a theory — an understanding of citizenship implicit in our constitutional system — that supports the current doctrine? . . .

A. The Rights Perspective

In *Perez,* Warren describes citizenship as "the right to have rights." Black's majority opinion in *Afroyim* finds "a constitutional right to remain a citizen" of the United States. Understanding citizenship in "rights" terms, at first glance, appears quite reasonable. . . . Unfortunately, major difficulties beset a "rights" understanding of citizenship.

From where might such a "right to citizenship" derive? The Court in *Afroyim* points to the fourteenth amendment. But the message from the fourteenth amendment is hardly clear. . . . The citizenship clause was primarily intended to disavow Justice Taney's conclusion in *Dred Scott* that black Americans were not citizens. . . . To be sure, certain rights may flow from holding the status of "citizen." But that does not make citizenship itself a "right." . . .

If the fourteenth amendment does not do much to establish an irrevocable right to citizenship, perhaps the importance of the interest argues for such a result. The claim would be that citizenship is a "fundamental right" protected by a substantive reading of the fifth amendment's due process clause or, perhaps, implicit in the structure of the American constitutional system.

The denationalization cases may be exercises in substantive due process, but they do not read that way. Typically, in a substantive due process case, the Court will define the individual interest at stake and then examine the nature and strength of competing government interests. But in the denationalization cases there is no careful balancing, no discussion of less burdensome alternatives. It is as if the Court viewed citizenship as some kind of "super-right" — one that cannot be balanced away. This seems to be what Chief Justice Warren was driving at when he described citizenship as "the right to have rights."

But Warren's characterization is a dramatic overstatement of the importance of citizenship in the United States today. Aliens residing in the United States — even illegal aliens — are protected by the Constitution. They are entitled to nearly all the public and private opportunities and benefits afforded citizens. The deportation of aliens is significantly constrained by the fifth amendment's due process clause. A central benefit of citizens in other countries — the ability to transmit citizenship to one's children — is far less important in the United States because, by virtue of the fourteenth amendment, children born to aliens in this country are automatically American citizens. Citizenship, of course, does carry with it certain benefits, including the ability to travel on a U.S. passport, to claim protection by the U.S. government overseas, and the right to vote and hold office. But it is far more accurate to adopt the characterization of citizenship in recent equal protection cases — as membership in the political community entitling a person to exercise part of the sovereign power of the nation — that to describe it as the "right to have rights." It is primarily residence in the United States, not citizenship, that affords rights to individuals.

One may properly respond that denationalization threatens residence in the United States as well [because of the possibility of deportation]. But I would urge caution in reaching this conclusion for several reasons. First, the Court's fear that denationalization can create "rightless" people is in large part due to its own unwillingness to impose any substantive limits on Congress' power to deport aliens. There is something quite peculiar about our constitutional doctrine here. Although permanent resident aliens are entitled to nearly all the rights and privileges that citizens enjoy, Congress has *no* power to remove citizenship and virtually *plenary* power to deport aliens. If restrictions on loss of citizenship are based on the deprivations denationalization entails, then some limits ought to be placed on deportation, because it is the removal of the person from the United States that occasions the severest injuries.

Second, aliens are not (yet) deported to outer space or Devil's Island. The United States must find some other country to accept them. Deported aliens are at least entitled to the rights the receiving country extends to aliens. These may not be many, but they are likely to be a far cry from Warren's description of denationalization as "the total destruction of the individual's status in organized society."

Finally, and most important, denationalization can hardly be said to entail loss of the "rights to have rights" when it does not bring about statelessness. Many of the denationalization grounds contemplate the acquisition or existence of citizenship elsewhere. Dual nationals (Rabbi Kahane, for example) certainly have the right to have rights in another polity. . . .

In sum, Chief Justice Warren may have been correct that denationalization sometimes imposes serious, even devastating, harms on individuals. But . . . it seems particularly inappropriate to conceive of citizenship in rights terms at all. Citizenship is not a *right* held *against* the state; it is a *relationship with* the state or, perhaps, a *relationship among* persons in the state. It is membership in a common venture. The notion that membership decisions can turn simply on the will of an individual — and allow no role for other members or the group as a whole — ought to strike us as odd. . . .

B. THE CONSENT PERSPECTIVE

Citizenship is sometimes conceived of as membership in a state generated by mutual consent of a person and the state. . . .

Whatever the merits of seeing citizenship in consent terms, it cannot explain the current constitutional doctrine regarding denationalization. As [Peter Schuck and Rogers Smith, who, in Citizenship Without Consent, defended consent-based citizenship] concede, "a thoroughgoing commitment to pure consensual membership might seem to imply a national power to denationalize citizens at will." . . . If a citizen's right to expatriate himself rests upon the significance of mutual consent to the relationship, it is hard to see how the state can be denied the same right to withdraw consent through denationalization. Thus the consent perspective seems dramatically inconsistent with the asymmetry of the right to "de-consent" produced by *Afroyim*. . . .

C. THE CONTRACTARIAN PERSPECTIVE

Dissenting in *Perez,* Chief Justice Warren examined denationalization from the perspective of the underlying political philosophy of those who founded the nation:

> What is this Government, whose power is here being asserted? And what is the source of that power? The answers are the foundation of our Republic. To secure the inalienable rights of the individual, "Governments are instituted among Men, deriving their just powers from the consent of the governed." I do not believe the passage of time has lessened the truth of this proposition. It is basic to our form of government. This Government was born of its citizens, it maintains itself in a continuing relationship with them, and, in my judgment, it is without power to sever the relationship that gives rise to its existence. I cannot believe that a government conceived in the spirit of ours was established with power to take from the people their most basic right.

One interpretation of Warren's argument is that it is an application of contract theory — that is, a perspective that focuses on agreements among individuals made in the process of creating a state. (Contract theory, as I am using it, looks to agreement among individuals; consent theory looks to agreements between an individual and the state.)

Contract theory may be a sensible perspective for thinking about citizenship and denationalization because membership is a question that precedes, or at least accompanies, the formation of a state. Some group of human beings must come together to form a government, and that group must have some understanding of what constitutes them as a group. . . .

We can take contract theory in two directions. Either we could ask what agreement we believe the framers of our social contract — the Constitution — reached regarding citizenship; or we could investigate the agreement that a hypothetical group of founders, similar to us and sharing our basic political philosophy, would reach were they asked to address the question. . . .

I will not pursue the first line of inquiry here, as it is a well-traveled ground. It is sufficient to note that the prevailing view at the time of the drafting of the Constitution was that citizenship was acquired by birth or naturalization and could be lost only with the consent of the sovereign. As to denationalization, we have little evidence either way.

The second version of contract theory is the more interesting. . . . The project here is to ask: How might a hypothetical group of people interested in creating a political community construct rules regarding attainment and loss of membership? . . .

First, it seems reasonable that those creating a nation would seek to ensure that they will be counted as members once the state comes into being. It is further likely that they will want their children to be members as well. Thus, I will assume that there will be agreement that the children of citizens will be citizens. No doubt the state will want some mechanism for making new members — that is, some kind of naturalization law. . . .

The notion of citizenship by birth and naturalization does not entail perpetual allegiance. It seems sensible that the founders would not want to force a person to remain within the state against his will. . . . Recognition of some kind of right of expatriation is therefore likely.

The denationalization question, however, is not easily resolved in this thought experiment. One can imagine arguments against a broad power to denationalize that might be persuasive to the founders. If denationalization were viewed merely as an exercise of ordinary politics, majorities could tyrannize minorities by threatening them with loss of citizenship. Or, less perniciously, denationalization could be seen as a convenient means of achieving domestic or foreign policy objectives. . . .

Perhaps these considerations would produce agreement that denationalization on "public order grounds" should be prohibited — or, at least, not permitted without a very strong justification by the state. But is there any reason to believe that the hypothetical contractors would not allow denationalization for at least some of the allegiance categories? They might well conclude that, if a person shows himself to be fundamentally opposed to the core principles of the society, he has surrendered any right he has to remain within it. Excommunication, of course, is an old tradition. Furthermore, the founders could well wish that members be willing to undertake obligations necessary for the survival (or smooth functioning?) of the state. Anyone who does not undertake such obligations, they may believe, ought not to be able to claim the benefits of living in their state. These arguments might support a denationalization power for citizens demonstrating a lack of allegiance — as evidenced, perhaps, by treason, armed insurrection, espionage on behalf of a foreign power, draft evasion, and desertion. Similarly, it is not clear why the contractors would protect the continued membership of citizens who have transferred or divided their allegiance. Abandonment and adultery are traditional grounds for terminating marriages. . . .

[T]he notion of citizenship absolutely unrevokable by the state does not appear to follow from contract theory.

D. THE COMMUNITARIAN PERSPECTIVE

"Citizenship in this Nation is a part of a cooperative affair," wrote Justice Black in *Afroyim*. "Its citizenry is the country and the country is its citizenry." This may appear to be a vacuous tautology, or even a frightening appeal to some notion of a "fatherland." But it may also be read as an appeal to a communitarian perspective on citizenship.

. . . Communitarian theory begins with individuals situated in a real society, not in a hypothetical state of nature or on the brink of contract. The individual is seen as an "encumbered" self. He is defined — or constituted — in part by his relationships, roles, and allegiances. His relationship with the state is based on his identification with and immersion in the society's history, traditions, and core asumptions and purposes. If the bywords of liberal theory are freedom, choice, and consent, the bywords of communitarian theory are solidarity, responsibility, and civil virtue. The operative metaphors for the state are "family," "community," or "a people." From the communitarian perspective, citizenship is seen as an organic relationship between the citizen and the state.

The claim here is *not* that either the Constitution or American society is communitarian. . . . Rather, I am suggesting that thinking about membership from a communitarian perspective may shed some light on our current understandings of citizenship. . . .

The communitarian perspective is grounded in the fourteenth amendment's citizenship clause. The vast majority of American citizens attain citizenship by birth, not by choice or consent. By the time most Americans are old enough to understand the concepts of loyalty or allegiance, they have already developed a conception of self that incorporates American citizenship. Of course nationality may be cast off, just as one's family or religion may be abandoned. But for the most part, we live our lives within the identifications into which we are born. Change of nationality, like conversion, is a noteworthy experience. . . .

Viewing citizenship in communitarian terms brings to light two considerations that support limits on denationalization. The first derives from the description of the harm that denationalization may impose on individuals. . . . Denationalization may grossly intrude upon a person's conception of self. It is akin to forced conversion. . . .

This may sound like an overstatement, but test the proposition in your mind. Imagine that you awake one morning to find that your American citizenship has been taken away. What springs to mind? That travel to Europe may be difficult without an American passport? That no country will seek your release if you become a hostage overseas? That it will be impossible to vote in the next presidential election? I doubt that any of these issues are on the top of your concern list. More likely, you feel violated, naked. You ask, how can I not be an American? What am I, then? A part of oneself is gone.

A second argument against denationalization from the communitarian perspective flows from the state's responsibility for the individuals it has helped to constitute. An analogy to the family may help here. Leaving legal obligations aside, it seems common moral ground that parents are responsible for the care, security, and education of their children. Children, after all, do not choose to be brought into the world; they exist because of the choices (or at least the acts) of others. A child's moral, political, and religious beliefs, notions of responsibility and the good — at least until the child reaches maturity — are primarily based on the lessons, either intended or unintended, of the family. I believe that these considerations create a strong basis for a moral principle that parents may not throw a child out or turn him away (even though the child may be free to walk away). . . .

While the leap from family to state is not unproblematic, I think the analogy is permissible here. The state has helped to endow the citizen with a set of values and relationships that precede any conscious choice by the citizen (at least a citizen at birth). In much the same way that the parent is responsible for the child, so the state is responsible for the citizen. Under this reasoning the state — like the family — could punish, but it could not banish.

Understanding citizenship from a communitarian perspective thus lends support to the Court's results in the loss-of-citizenship cases. . . . But it is doubtful that communitarian analysis takes us as far as the intent-to-relinquish test of *Afroyim* and *Terrazas.*

Why, from a communitarian perspective, must a state tolerate the continued membership of a disloyal citizen — a person who has made clear that he has no commitment to (or outright disdain for) the society's core principles? The analogy of family responsibility takes us only so far. At some point, a child grows up and assumes responsibility for his actions. . . . [I]f, as a mature adult, he condemns the family's mores and announces that he feels no responsibility toward family members or goals, it hardly seems immoral for the family to state that the ties that bound have been severed. Disinheritance may be harsh, but it isn't always unjust.

Furthermore, where the citizen has, in effect, declared war on society, the claim that denationalization destroys one's concept of self is much less persuasive. The citizen's actions must be the best signal that the individual's conception of self does not include attachment to the core principles of society. In such a case, denationalization may simply ratify an unfortunate social fact; it would not sever the self. Thus, denationalization could be a justifiable response to treason, or subversion, and perhaps even to desertion in wartime.

This reasoning would also tolerate denationalization in the case of transferred loyalty. The denationalized individual may lose the benefits of United States citizenship, but there should be little or no harm to the person's conception of self. . . .

Divided loyalty presents a more difficult case. On the one hand, we live in a world of overlapping and multiple allegiances — to ethnic group, home town, occupation, and baseball team. To stretch the family analogy perhaps to the breaking point, divided allegiance may be no more troubling than holding allegiance to one's own family and one's "in-laws." At some point, however, the demands of conflicting loyalties may necessitate the choice. (A person can fight for only one of two opposing armies.) It is not clear why a community, under the communitarian perspective, may not put a citizen to a choice when there exists an inescapable conflict in allegiances. In such a situation, the individual will suffer harm no matter what; conditions demand that some part of self be sacrificed. The best that can be done is that the citizen be given a choice.

The arguments from harm and responsibility would not seem to permit denationalization as a routine form of punishment — say, for failure to pay taxes, or for burglary. A communitarian perspective ought to recognize, to some extent, social causes of crime; and forgiveness for even serious misconduct is a central feature of family relationships. Under the rights perspective, Chief Justice Warren's conclusion that denationalization is cruel and unusual punishment seemed vulnerable. But the communitarian perspective exposes both the cruel (destruction of self) and unusual (families forgive, they don't banish) aspects of punishment. . . . Yet, at some point, I can imagine the communitarian argument running out. Some conduct may be so egregious, so outside the bounds of tolerable behavior, that the perpetrator may be seen as having disassociated himself from the community. . . .

In sum, the communitarian perspective may do a good job of describing our intuitions about citizenship and the dramatic harm that denationalization entails. But it cannot serve as a foundation for constitutional principles that leave loss of citizenship solely to the individual.

V. Beyond Intent-to-Relinquish

. . . The problem . . . is to turn the insights of the contractarian and communitarian approaches into consitutional doctrine. The thrust of both analyses is reorientation of doctrine away from intent-to-relinquish and toward notions of allegiance. But there are very serious risks in making this move without careful thought.

Shifting to an allegiance-based understanding of denationalization will naturally lead to government investigations of the loyalty of citizens. The State Department's brief in the *Kahane* case is an ugly example of what can happen when constitutional standards turn on proof of allegiance. The Department combed Kahane's speeches and writings in an attempt to prove that his true allegiance lay with Israel. The chilling effect that such an approach may have on speech and conduct ought to be apparent. . . .

One answer — and I think the correct one — is to insist that denationalization be based on conduct, not belief. That is, Congress ought to be restricted to identifying specific acts that demonstrate lapsed, transferred, or divided allegiance. But even here we must be careful. Past experience indicates that Congress might either make too-easy assumptions that particular conduct evidences lost allegiance (e.g., desertion), or disguise public order grounds as allegiance grounds (e.g., voting in a foreign election). The history of the denationalization statutes, combined with the harms imposed by loss of nationality, suggests that the Court ought not to defer to congressional judgments as to what conduct constitutes a loss of allegiance. . . .

Under this analysis, it may be possible to craft narrow denationalization grounds for transferred allegiance. . . . But naturalization in another country, by itself, can hardly be deemed to indicate a transfer of allegiance. People may seek citizenship in other countries in order to remain with family members or obtain employment. Such conduct in many (if not most) cases says little about continued allegiance to the United States. Other conduct, such as service in a foreign military or voting abroad, is equally unreliable evidence of transferred allegiance.

It may be difficult to define categories of conduct evidencing loss of allegiance. Perhaps joining the army of an invading enemy or working for the violent overthrow of the state may properly be seen as indicating no further attachment to the community. But even here . . . , such assumptions are problematic. If allegiance is understood not as loyalty to the government but rather as attachment to the core principles of a community, then aiding in the overthrow of a government that had demonstrated a "lack of allegiance" to the Constitution would indicate no loss of allegiance. . . .

We ought to be suspicious of governmental assertions about the degree of allegiance a citizen holds. However, some objective indicia may disclose cases where the maintenance of two allegiances becomes untenable. The State Department's Board of Appellate Review has adopted this kind of test in ruling on denationalization cases following *Terrazas*. According to a study of more than one hundred Board decisions, "the Board . . . analyzes each case [where no renunciatory oath is present] to ascertain whether the expatriatory act 'would render it impossible for [the citizen] to perform the obligations of U.S. citizenship.' " . . . [T]he test does three things properly: it captures a set of cases beyond the set of the intent-to-relinquish test that, under my analysis, ought to be permissible grounds for denationalization; it puts the burden on the government to establish the conflict; and it makes irrelevant the state-of-mind evidence used by the State Department in the *Kahane* case.

How does all this play out in the case of Meir Kahane? The mere assumption of a seat in a foreign government ought not to be one of the per se categories of transferred or lapsed allegiance. Indeed, the Board of Appellate Review has already so concluded in the case of another [American citizen elected as a] Knesset member. . . . [T]he case ought to be decided by comparing the duties of a Knesset member with the obligations of U.S. citizenship.

. . . I would . . . require the State Department to be quite specific in detailing the obligations of U.S. citizenship that a member of the Israeli Knesset cannot fulfill. Until the Department meets that burden, under my analysis, Meir Kahane ought to remain a citizen of the United States.

C. Resident Aliens as Members of the American Community

Assume that *Trop* had been decided the other way, and that the petitioner had been consigned to a status of "statelessness." This would not have resulted in his deportation from the United States; indeed, ironically enough, Trop initiated his lawsuit because the United States would not give him a passport and thus allow him to leave the country. His status, according to the United States, was basically that of a resident alien (although, unlike most other resident aliens, he was not a citizen of some foreign nation). As of the 1980 census, approximately 7 million of the 226.5 million residents of the United States (3.1 percent) were noncitizens.[10]

We turn now to some issues raised by the fact that an alien — by definition a noncitizen and thus without the formal status of a full-fledged member of the political community — nonetheless enjoys considerable constitutional protection. Both the division of the polity into citizen and noncitizen and constitutional limitations on the use of this division as the basis for allocating benefits or burdens raise profound questions about the nature of the American political community.

1. *Resident Aliens and the Distribution of Welfare Benefits*

GRAHAM v. RICHARDSON[11]

403 U.S. 365 (1971)

Appeal from the United States District Court for the District of Arizona

BLACKMUN, J., delivered the opinion of the Court.

. . . The issue here is whether the Equal Protection Clause of the Fourteenth Amendment prevents a State from conditioning welfare benefits either (a) upon the beneficiary's possession of United States citizenship, or (b) if the beneficiary is an alien, upon his having resided in this country for a specified number of years.

I

[Arizona required citizenship or 15 years of residence in the United States in order to receive welfare benefits. Appellee Richardson had emigrated from Mexico in 1956 and resided in Arizona from that time. At the time of the litigation she was "permanently and totally disabled," but was ineligible for benefits because she had retained Mexican citizenship and had not lived in Arizona the requisite length of time. A Pennsylvania statute limited welfare only to citizens.]

II

. . . It has long been settled . . . that the term "person" [in the Fourteenth Amendment] encompasses lawfully admitted resident aliens as well as citizens of the United States and entitles both citizens and aliens to the equal protection of the laws of the State in which they reside. . . .

Under traditional equal protection principles, a State retains broad discretion to classify as long as its classification has a reasonable basis. . . . But the Court's decisions have established that classifications based on alienage, like those based on nationality or race, are inherently suspect and subject to close judicial scrutiny. Aliens as a class are a prime example of a "discrete and insular" minority (see U.S. v. Carolene Products Co., 304 U.S. 144, 152-153, n.4 (1938)) for whom such heightened judicial solicitude is appropriate. . . .

10. See 1980 Census of Population, Vol. 1 — Characteristics of the Population at 1-10f. Of the approximately 220 million citizens, 212.5 million were native-born and 7.1 million had received their citizenship through naturalization.

11. Together with Sailer v. Leger, on Appeal from the United States District Court for the Eastern District of Pennsylvania.

Arizona and Pennsylvania seek to justify their restrictions on the eligibility of aliens for public assistance solely on the basis of a State's "special public interest" in favoring its own citizens over aliens in the distribution of limited resources such as welfare benefits. It is true that this Court on occasion has upheld state statutes that treat citizens and noncitizens differently, the ground for distinction having been that such laws were necessary to protect special interests of the State or its citizens. Thus, in Truax v. Raich, the Court, in striking down an Arizona statute restricting the employment of aliens, emphasized that "[t]he discrimination defined by the act does not pertain to the regulation or distribution of the public domain, or of the common property or resources of the people of the State, the enjoyment of which may be limited to its citizens as against both aliens and the citizens of other States." And in Crane v. New York, 239 U.S. 195 (1915), the Court [upheld] a New York statute prohibiting the employment of aliens on public works projects. The New York court's opinion contained [then Justice of the New York Court of Appeals Cardozo's] well known observation:

> To disqualify aliens is discrimination indeed, but not arbitrary discrimination, for the principle of exclusion is the restriction of the resources of the state to the advancement and profit of the members of the state. Ungenerous and unwise such discrimination may be. It is not for that reason unlawful. . . . The state in determining what use shall be made of its own moneys, may legitimately consult the welfare of its own citizens rather than that of aliens. Whatever is a privilege rather than a right, may be made dependent on citizenship. In its war against poverty, the state is not required to dedicate its own resources to citizens and aliens alike.

Whatever may be the contemporary vitality of the special public-interest doctrine . . . , we conclude that a State's desire to preserve limited welfare benefits for its own citizens is inadequate to justify Pennsylvania's making noncitizens ineligible for public assistance, and Arizona's restricting benefits to citizens and long-time resident aliens. First, the special public interest doctrine was heavily grounded on the notion that "[w]hatever is a privilege, rather than a right, may be made dependent upon citizenship." But this Court now has rejected the concept that constitutional rights turn upon whether a governmental benefit is characterized as a "right" or as a "privilege."[12] Second, as the Court recognized in Shapiro v. Thompson,

> [A] State has a valid interest in preserving the fiscal integrity of its programs. It may legitimately attempt to limit its expenditures, whether for public assistance, public education, or any other program. But a State may not accomplish such a purpose by invidious distinctions between classes of its citizens. . . . The saving of welfare costs cannot justify an otherwise invidious classification.

Since an alien as well as a citizen is a "person" for equal protection purposes, a concern for fiscal integrity is no more compelling a justification for the questioned classification in these cases than it was in *Shapiro*.

Appellants, however, would narrow the application of *Shapiro* to citizens by arguing that the right to travel, relied upon in that decision, extends only to citizens and not to aliens. . . . The Court has never decided whether the right applies spe-

12. See the discussion of the so-called unconstitutional conditions doctrine in Chapter 9, supra.

cifically to aliens, and it is unnecessary to reach that question here. It is enough to say that the classification involved in *Shapiro* was subjected to strict scrutiny under the compelling state interest test, not because it was based on any suspect criterion such as race, nationality, or alienage, but because it impinged upon the fundamental right of interstate movement. . . . The classifications involved in the instant cases, on the other hand, are inherently suspect and are therefore subject to strict judicial scrutiny whether or not a fundamental right is impaired. . . .

We agree with the three-judge court in the Pennsylvania case that the

> justification of limiting expenses is particularly inappropriate and unreasonable when the discriminated class consists of aliens. Aliens like citizens pay taxes and may be called into the armed forces. Unlike the short-term residents in *Shapiro*, aliens may live within a state for many years, work in the state and contribute to the economic growth of the state.

There can be no "special public interest" in tax revenues to which aliens have contributed on an equal basis with the residents of the State.

Accordingly, we hold that a state statute that denies welfare benefits to resident aliens and one that denies them to aliens who have not resided in the United States for a specified number of years violate the Equal Protection Clause.

III

An additional reason why the state statutes at issue in these cases do not withstand constitutional scrutiny emerges from the area of federal-state relations. The National Government has "broad constitutional powers in determining what aliens shall be admitted to the United States, the period they may remain, regulation of their conduct before naturalization, and the terms and conditions of their naturalization." Pursuant to that power, Congress has provided . . . that "[a]liens who are paupers, professional beggars, or vagrants" or aliens who "are likely at any time to become public charges" shall be excluded from admission into the United States and that any alien lawfully admitted shall be deported who "has within five years after entry become a public charge from causes not affirmatively shown to have arisen after entry." . . . But Congress has not seen fit to impose any burden or restriction on aliens who become indigent after their entry into the United States. . . .

State laws that restrict the eligibility of aliens for welfare benefits merely because of their alienage conflict with these overriding national policies in an area constitutionally entrusted to the Federal Government. . . .

Congress has broadly declared as federal policy that lawfully admitted resident aliens who become public charges for causes arising after their entry are not subject to deportation, and that as long as they are here they are entitled to the full and equal benefit of all state laws for the security of persons and property. The state statutes at issue in the instant cases impose auxiliary burdens upon the entrance of residence of aliens who suffer the distress, after entry, of economic dependency on public assistance. . . .

[Justice Blackmun goes on to quote from a passage of *Truax* considering the consequence of allowing states to limit the opportunities of aliens for employment:]

> [I]f such a policy were permissible, the practical result would be that those lawfully admitted to the country under the authority of the acts of Congress, instead of enjoying in a substantial sense and in their full scope the privileges conferred by the admission, would be segregated in such of the States as chose to offer hospitality.

The same is true here, for in the ordinary case, an alien, becoming indigent and unable to work, will be unable to live where, because of discriminatory denial of public assistance, he cannot "secure the necessities of life, including food, clothing and shelter." State alien residency requirements that either deny welfare benefits to noncitizens or condition them on longtime residency, equate with the assertion of a right, inconsistent with federal policy, to deny entrance and abode. Since such laws encroach upon exclusive federal power, they are constitutionally impermissible.[13]

2. *Access of Resident Aliens to Occupations*

BERNAL v. FAINTER
467 U.S. 216 (1984)
On Certiorari to the United States Court of Appeals for the Fifth Circuit

MARSHALL, J., delivered the opinion of the Court.

The question posed by this case is whether a statute of the State of Texas violates the Equal Protection Clause of the Fourteenth Amendment . . . by denying aliens the opportunity to become notaries public. . . .

I

[Bernal], a native of Mexico, is a resident alien who has lived in the United States since 1961. He works as a paralegal for Texas Rural Legal Aid, Inc., helping migrant farmworkers on employment and civil rights matters. In order to administer oaths to these workers and to notarize their statements for use in civil litigation, [he] applied in 1978 to become a notary public. . . . The Texas Secretary of State denied [Bernal's] application because he failed to satisfy the statutory requirement that a notary public be a citizen of the United States. . . .

II

As a general matter, a state law that discriminates on the basis of alienage can be sustained only if it can withstand strict judicial scrutiny. In order to withstand strict scrutiny, the law must advance a compelling state interest by the least restrictive means available. Applying this principle, we have invalidated an array of state statutes that denied aliens the right to pursue various occupations. In Sugarman v. Dougall, 413 U.S. 634 (1973), we struck down a state statute barring aliens from employment in permanent positions in the competitive class of the state civil service. In In re Griffith, 413 U.S. 717 (1973), we nullified a state law excluding aliens from eligibility for membership in the State Bar. And in Exam-

13. Justice Harlan, who joined in the judgment, concurred only in part III of the above opinion.

ining Board v. Flores de Otero, 426 U.S. 572 (1976), we voided a state law that excluded aliens from the practice of civil engineering.

We have, however, developed a narrow exception to the rule that discrimination based on alienage trigger strict scrutiny. This exception has been labeled the "political function" exception and applies to laws that exclude aliens from positions intimately related to the process of democratic self-governance. The contours of the "political function" exception are outlined by our prior decisions. In Foley v. Connelie, 435 U.S. 291 (1978), we held that a State may require police to be citizens because, in performing a fundamental obligation of government, police "are clothed with authority to exercise an almost infinite variety of discretionary powers" often involving the most sensitive areas of daily life. In Ambach v. Norwick, 441 U.S. 68 (1979), we held that a State may bar aliens who have not declared their intent to become citizens from teaching in the public schools because teachers, like police, possess a high degree of responsibility and discretion in the fulfillment of a basic governmental obligation. They have direct, day-to-day contact with students, exercise unsupervised discretion over them, act as role models, and influence their students about the government and the political process. Finally, in Cabell v. Chavey-Salido, 454 U.S. 432 (1982), we held that a State may bar aliens from positions as probation officers because they, like police and teachers, routinely exercise discretionary power, involving a basic governmental function, that places them in a position of direct authority over other individuals.

The rationale behind the political-function exception is that within broad boundaries a State may establish its own form of government and limit the right to govern to those who are full-fledged members of the political community. Some public positions are so closely bound with the formulation and implementation of self-government that the State is permitted to exclude from those positions persons outside the political community, hence, persons who have not become part of the process of democratic self-determination.

> The exclusion of aliens from basic governmental processes is not a deficiency in the democratic system but a necessary consequence of the community's process of political self-definition. Self-government, whether direct or through representatives, begins by defining the scope of the community of the governed and thus of the governors as well: Aliens are by definition those outside of this community.

We have therefore lowered our standard of review when evaluating the validity of exclusions that entrust only to citizens important elective and nonelective positions whose operations "go to the heart of representative government." . . .

To determine whether a restriction based on alienage fits within the narrow political-function exception, we devised in *Cabell* a two-part test.

> First, the specificity of the classification will be examined: a classification that is substantially overinclusive or underinclusive tends to undercut the governmental claim that the classification serves legitimate political ends. . . . Second, even if the classification is sufficiently tailored, it may be applied in the particular case only to "persons holding state elective or important nonelective executive, legislative, and judicial positions," those officials who "participate directly in the formulation, execution, or review of broad public policy" and hence "perform functions that go to the heart of representative government."

III

[Does the Texas statute satisfy the *Cabell* test? It applies only to appointment as a Notary Public and therefore] does not indiscriminately sweep within its ambit a wide range of offices and occupations but specifies only one particular post with respect to which the State asserts a right to exclude aliens. Clearly, then, the statute is not overinclusive. . . . Less clear is whether [it] is fatally underinclusive. Texas does not require court reporters to be United States citizens even though they perform some of the same services as notaries. Nor does Texas require that its Secretary of State be a citizen, even though he holds the highest appointive position in the State and performs many important functions, including the supervision of the licensing of all notaries public. We need not decide this issue, however, because of our decision with respect to the second prong of the *Cabell* test.

. . . [T]he State emphasizes that notaries are designated as public officers by the Texas Constitution. . . . This Court, however, has never deemed the *source* of a position — whether it derives from a State's statute or its Constitution — as the dispositive factor in determining whether a State may entrust the position only to citizens. Rather, this Court has always looked to the actual *function* of the position as the dispositive factor. The focus of our inquiry has been whether a position was such that the officeholder would necessarily exercise broad discretionary power over the formulation or execution of public policies importantly affecting the citizen population — power of the sort that a self-governing community could properly entrust only to full-fledged members of that community. . . .

The State maintains that even if the actual function of a post is the touchstone of a proper analysis, Texas notaries public should still be classified among those positions from which aliens can properly be excluded because the duties of Texas notaries entail the performance of functions sufficiently consequential to be deemed "political." The Court of Appeals ably articulated this argument:

> With the power to acknowledge instruments such as wills and deeds and leases and mortgages; to take out-of-court depositions; to administer oaths; and the discretion to refuse to perform any of the foregoing acts, notaries public in Texas are involved in countless matters of importance to the day-to-day functioning of state government. The Texas political community depends upon the notary public to insure that those persons executing documents are accurately identified, to refuse to certify any identification that is false or uncertain, and to insist that oaths are properly and accurately administered. Land titles and property succession depend upon the care and integrity of the notary public, as well as the familiarity of the notary with the community, to verify the authenticity of the execution of the documents.

We recognize the critical need for a notary's duties to be carried out correctly and with integrity. But a notary's duties, important as they are, hardly implicate responsibilities that go to the heart of representative government. Rather, these duties are essentially clerical and ministerial. In contrast to state troopers, notaries do not routinely exercise the State's monopoly of legitimate coercive force. Nor do notaries routinely exercise the wide discretion typically enjoyed by public school teachers when they present materials that educate youth respecting the information and values necessary for the maintenance of a democratic political system. To be sure, considerable damage could result from the negligent or dishonest performance of a notary's duties. But the same could be said for the duties performed by cashiers, building inspectors, the janitors who clean up the offices of public officials, and numerous other categories of personnel upon whom we depend for careful, honest service. What distinguishes such personnel from those to whom the political-function exception is properly applied is that the latter are invested either with policymaking responsibility or broad discretion in the execution of public policy that requires the routine exercise of authority over individuals. Neither of these characteristics pertains to the functions performed by Texas notaries.

The inappropriateness of applying the political-function exception to Texas notaries is further underlined by our decision in In re Griffiths, in which we subjected to strict scrutiny a Connecticut statute that prohibited noncitizens from becoming members of the State Bar. Along with the usual power and privileges accorded to members of the bar, Connecticut gave to members of its Bar additional authority that encompasses the very duties performed by Texas notaries — authority to "sign writs and subpoenas, take recognizances, administer oaths and take depositions and acknowledgements of deeds." In striking down Connecticut's citizenship requirement, we concluded that "[i]t in no way denigrates a lawyer's high responsibilities to observe that [these duties] hardly involve matters of state policy or acts of such unique responsibility as to entrust them only to citizens." If it is improper to apply the political-function exception to a citizenship requirement in a state bar, it would be anomalous to apply the exception to the citizenship requirement that governs eligibility to become a Texas notary. We conclude, then, that the "political function" exception is inapplicable . . . and that the statute is therefore subject to strict judicial scrutiny.

IV

To satisfy strict scrutiny, the State must show that [the statute] furthers a compelling state interest by the least restrictive means available. Respondents maintain that [the statute] serves "its legitimate concern that notaries be reasonably familiar with state law and institutions" and "that notaries may be called upon years later to testify to acts they have performed." However, both of these asserted justifications utterly fail to meet the stringent requirements of strict scrutiny. There is nothing in the record that indicates that resident aliens, as a class, are so incapable of familiarizing themselves with Texas law as to justify the State's absolute and classwide exclusion. . . . Furthermore, if the State's concern with ensuring a notary's familiarity with state law were truly "compelling," one would expect the State to give some sort of test actually measuring a person's familiarity with the law. The State, however, administers no such test. . . . Similarly inadequate is the State's purported interest in ensuring the later availability of notaries' testimony. This justification fails because the State fails to advance a factual showing that the unavailability of notaries' testimony presents a real, as opposed to a merely speculative, problem to the State. Without a factual underpinning, the State's asserted interest lacks the weight we have required of interests properly denominated as compelling.

REHNQUIST, J., dissenting.

I dissent for the reasons stated in my dissenting opinion in Sugarman v. Dougall, 413 U.S. 634, 649 (1973). [In *Sugarman* and its companion case, In re Griffiths, Justice Rehnquist wrote:]

The Court . . . holds that an alien is not really different from a citizen, and that any legislative classification on the basis of alienage is "inherently suspect."[14] The Fourteenth Amendment, the Equal Protection Clause of which the Court interprets as invalidating the state legislation here involved, contains no language concerning "inherently suspect classifications," or, for that matter, merely "suspect classifications." The principal purpose of those who drafted and adopted the Amendment was to prohibit the States from invidiously discriminating by reason of race, Slaughter-House Cases, and, because of this plainly manifested intent, classifications based on race have rightly been held "suspect" under the Amendment. But there is no language used in the Amendment, or any historical evidence as to the intent of the Framers, which would suggest to the slightest degree that it was intended to render alienage a "suspect" classification, that it was designed in any way to protect "discrete and insular minorities" other than racial minorities, or that it would in any way justify the result reached by the Court. . . .

I

The Court, by holding . . . that a citizen-alien classification is "suspect" in the eyes of our Constitution, fails to mention, let alone rationalize, the fact that the Constitution itself recognizes a basic difference between citizens and aliens. That distinction is constitutionally important in no less than 11 instances in a political document noted for its brevity. . . .

Not only do the numerous classifications on the basis of citizenship that are set forth in the Constitution cut against both the analysis used and the results reached by the Court in these cases; the very Amendment which the Court reads to prohibit classifications based on citizenship establishes the very distinction which the Court now condemns as "suspect." . . . In constitutionally defining who is a citizen of the United States, Congress [in proposing the Fourteenth Amendment] obviously thought it was doing something, and something important. Citizenship meant something, a status in and relationship with a society which is continuing and more basic than mere presence or residence. . . .

Decisions of this Court holding that an alien is a "person" within the meaning of the Fourteenth Amendment are simply irrelevant to the question of whether that Amendment prohibits legislative classifications based upon this particular status. . . .

[T]he Court now relies in part on the decisions in Truax v. Raich, 239 U.S. 33 (1915), and Takahashi v. Fish Comm's, 334 U.S. 410 (1948). In *Truax*, the Court invalidated a state statute which prohibited employers of more than five persons from employing more than 20% noncitizens. The law was applicable to all citizens. In holding that the law was invalid . . . , the Court . . . noted that "it should be added that the act is not limited to persons who are engaged in public work or receive the benefit of public moneys." . . .

14. Elsewhere in the opinion, Rehnquist wrote that what "would most disturb native-born citizens and especially naturalized citizens who have worked diligently to learn about our history, mores, and political institutions and who have successfully completed the rigorous process of naturalization, is the intimation, if not statement, that they are really not any different from aliens."

Takahashi involved a statute which prohibited aliens "ineligible for citizenship" under federal law from receiving commercial fishing licenses. . . . Two features of that law should be noted. First, the statutory classification was not one involving citizens and aliens; it classified citizens and those resident aliens eligible for citizenship into one group, and resident aliens ineligible for citizenship into another. No reason for discriminating among resident aliens is apparent. Second, and most important, is the fact that, although the Court properly refused to inquire into the legislative motive, the overwhelming *effect* of the law was to bar resident aliens of Japanese ancestry from procuring fishing licenses. [United States law at the time prohibited persons of Japanese ancestry from becoming naturalized citizens.] The Court was not blind to this fact, or to history. The state statute that classifies aliens on the basis of country of origin is much more likely to classify on the basis of race, and thus conflict with the core purpose of the Equal Protection Clause, than a statute that, as here, merely distinguishes between alienage as such and citizenship as such. . . .

[Justice Rehnquist then turns to Graham v. Richardson, supra. He focuses on the Court's reliance on footnote 4 of United States v. Carolene Products Co.].

The mere recitation of the words "insular and discrete minority" is hardly a *constitutional* reason for prohibiting state legislative classifications such as are involved here. . . .

Our society, consisting of over 200 million individuals of multitudinous origins, customs, tongues, beliefs, and cultures is, to say the least, diverse. It would hardly take extraordinary ingenuity for a lawyer to find "insular and discrete" minorities at every turn in the road. Yet, unless the Court can precisely define and constitutionally justify both the terms and analysis it uses, these decisions today stand for the proposition that the Court can choose a "minority" it "feels" deserves "solicitude" and thereafter prohibit the States from classifying that "minority" differently from the "majority." I cannot find, and the Court does not cite, any constitutional authority for such a "ward of the Court" approach to equal protection.

The only other apparent rationale for the invocation of the "suspect classification" approach in these cases is that alienage is a "status," and the Court does not feel it "appropriate" to classify on that basis. This rationale would appear to be similar to that utilized in Weber v. Aetna Casualty & Surety Co., 406 U.S. 164 (1972)[, in which the Court, with Justice Rehnquist dissenting, indicated that classifications based on the "illegitimacy" of a child would be subject to special scrutiny]. . . . But there is a marked difference between a status or condition such as illegitimacy, national origin, or race, which cannot be altered by an individual and the "status" of the appellant. There is nothing in the record indicating that their status as aliens cannot be changed by their affirmative acts.

II

These statutes do not classify on the basis of country of origin; the distinctions are not between native Americans and "foreigners," but between citizens and aliens. The process of naturalization was specifically designed by Congress to require a foreign national to demonstrate that he or she is familiar with the history, traditions, and institutions of our society in a way that a native-born citizen would learn from formal education and basic social contact. Congress specifically provided that an alien seeking citizenship status must demonstrate "an understanding of the English language" and "a knowledge and understanding of the fundamentals of the history, and of the principles and form of government, of the United States." The purpose was to make the alien establish that he or she understood, and could be integrated into, our social system. . . .

I do not believe that it is irrational for [states to require civil servants] to be citizens, either natural born or naturalized. The proliferation of public administration that our society has witnessed in recent years, as a result of the regulation of conduct and the dispensation of services and funds, has vested a great deal of *de facto* decisionmaking or policymaking authority in the hands of employees who would not be considered the textbook equivalent of policymakers of the legislative or "top" administrative variety. Nevertheless, as far as the private individual who must seek approval or services is concerned, many of these "low level" civil servants are in fact policymakers. Goldberg v. Kelly, 397 U.S. 254 (1970), implicitly recognized that those who apply facts to individual cases are as much "governors" as those who write the laws or regulations the "low-level" administrator must "apply." Since policymaking for a political community is not necessarily the exclusive preserve of the legislators, judges, and "top" administrators, it is not irrational for New York to provide that only citizens should be admitted to the competitive civil service.

But the justification of efficient government is an even more convincing rationale. Native-born citizens can be expected to be familiar with the social and political institutions of our society; with the society and political mores that affect how we react and interact with other citizens. Naturalized citizens have also demonstrated their willingness to adjust to our patterns of living and attitudes, and have demonstrated a basic understanding of our institutions, system of government, history, and traditions. It is not irrational to assume that aliens as a class are not familiar with how we as individuals treat others and how we expect "government" to treat us. An alien who grew up in a country in which political mores do not reject bribery or self-dealing to the same extent that our culture does; in which an imperious bureaucracy historically adopted a complacent or contemptuous attitude toward those it was supposed to serve; in which fewer if any checks existed on administrative abuses; in which "low-level" civil servants serve at the will of their superiors — could rationally be thought not to be able to deal with the public and with citizen civil servants with the same rapport that one familiar with our political and social mores would, or to approach his duties with the attitude that such positions exist for service, not personal sinecures of either the civil servant or his or her superior. . . .

Connecticut's requirement of citizenship [for lawyers] reflects its judgment that something more than technical skills are needed to be a lawyer under our system. I do not believe it is irrational for a State that makes that judgment to require that lawyers have an understanding of the American political and social experience, whether gained from growing up in this country, as in the case of a native-born citizen, or from the naturalization process, as in the case of a foreign-born citizen. I suppose the Connecticut Bar Examining Committee could itself administer tests in American history, government, and sociology, but the State did not choose to go this route. Instead, it chose to operate on the assumption that citizens as a class might reasonably be thought to have a significantly greater degree of understanding of our experience than would aliens. . .

Discussion

1. Community and alienage. It seems clear that a state can deny the right to vote to resident aliens. But why? One assumes that what justifies the denial of the most "fundamental" of all interests in a democratic polity is that an alien is not a member of the political community and is, therefore, not entitled to help shape the community's decisions. See Chapter 10 supra. But what constitutes citizens as a political "community" (rather than simply a collection of persons who happen to share the common legal category of citizenship)? What is it that joins in political fellowship a group of citizens of the United States composed of a Jehovah's Witness from Maine, a Vietnamese refugee living in Houston, and a member of the Ku Klux Klan?

In this context, examine Justice Rehnquist's assumptions about the consequences of growing up in the United States or preparing for naturalization. How plausible are they, and how would you prove or disprove their validity? (Who ought to have the burden of coming forth with relevant evidence?) Does the persuasiveness of Justice Rehnquist's dissent ultimately turn on these assumptions?

2. Equal protection or preemption. Note the difference between parts II and III of the Court's opinion in Graham v. Richardson. Does it matter which theory one chooses to explain the state's inability to discriminate against aliens? Which of these parts proves determinative in *Bernal*, and does it matter?

In Toll v. Moreno, 458 U.S. 1 (1982), the Court, through Justice Brennan, emphasized "the preeminent role of the Federal Government with respect to the regulation of aliens within our borders" while striking down a Maryland statute imposing special costs on aliens attending the state university. The Court quoted a passage from *Takahashi* stating that "[u]nder the Constitution the states . . . can neither add to nor take from the conditions lawfully imposed by Congress upon admission, naturalization and residence of aliens in the United States or the several states." And Justice Brennan went on to acknowledge in a footnote that several "commentators have noted . . . that many of the Court's decisions concerning alienage classifications . . . are better explained in preemption than equal protection terms."[15]

If one were to adopt such a focus, the operative rule might be something like this: When Congress adopts legislation resulting in the permanent residence of an alien, a state cannot interfere with the national policy by setting up barriers to the resident alien's ability to flourish in the United States unless those barriers can survive strict scrutiny.

The Court considered Congress' power over lawfully admitted aliens in Mathews v. Diaz, 426 U.S. 67 (1976), and Hampton v. Mow Sun Wong, 426 U.S. 88 (1976). In *Diaz*, a unanimous Court upheld a congressional limitation on the participation of aliens in federal Medicare programs to aliens who had both been admitted as permanent residents and had been continuously resident in the United States for five years. Writing for the Court, Justice Stevens noted that "[i]n the exercise of its broad power over naturalization and immigration, Congress regularly makes rules that would be unacceptable if applied to citizens."

15. See Note, The Equal Treatment of Aliens: Preemption or Equal Protection, 31 Stan. L. Rev. 1069 (1979); Note, State Burdens on Resident Aliens: A New Preemption Analysis, 89 Yale L.J. 940 (1980).

Justice Stevens wrote: "It is obvious that Congress has no constitutional duty to provide *all aliens* with the welfare benefits provided to citizens." The only question was whether the classifications were reasonable; the Court held that they were. Distinguishing *Graham*, the Court emphasized the difference between states and Congress:

> Insofar as state welfare policy is concerned, there is little, if any, basis for treating persons who are citizens of another State differently from persons who are citizens of another country. Both groups are noncitizens as far as the State's interests in administering its welfare programs are concerned. Thus, a division by a State of the category of persons who are not citizens of that State into subcategories of United States citizens and aliens has no apparent justification, whereas, a comparable classification by the Federal Government is a routine and normally legitimate part of its business. Furthermore, whereas the Constitution inhibits every State's power to restrict travel across its own borders, Congress is explicitly empowered to exercise that type of control across the borders of the United States.
>
> . . . [I]t is not "political hypocrisy" to recognize that the Fourteenth Amendment's limits on state powers are substantially different from the constitutional provisions applicable to the federal power over immigration and naturalization.

In *Hampton*, Justice Stevens wrote for a five-Justice majority to invalidate a United States Civil Service Commission regulation that barred resident aliens from competing for positions in the federal civil service. The Court rested the decision on pure due process grounds, explicitly declining to hold that the regulation violated the equal protection component of the Fifth Amendment that had been applied against the national government since Bolling v. Sharpe. Justice Stevens emphasized the far-reaching consequences of the prohibition and the facts that it had not been directly ordered by either Congress or the President nor had its merits been fully considered by the Commission. The Court acknowledged "that overriding national interests may provide a justification for a citizenship requirement in the federal service even though an identical requirement may not be enforced by a State," but denied that "the federal power over aliens is so plenary that *any agent* of the National Government may arbitrarily subject all resident aliens to different substantive rules from those applied to citizens." (Emphasis added.)

> The rule enforced by the Commission has its impact on an identifiable class of persons who, entirely apart from the rule itself, are already subject to disadvantages not shared by the remainder of the community. Aliens are not entitled to vote and . . . are often handicapped by a lack of familiarity with our language and customs. The added disadvantage resulting from the enforcement of the rule—ineligibility for employment in a major sector of the economy, is of sufficient significance to be characterized as a deprivation of an interest in liberty. Indeed, we deal with a rule which deprives a discrete class of persons of an interest in liberty on a wholesale basis. By reason of the Fifth Amendment, such a deprivation must be accompanied by due process.

Following the decision in *Hampton*, President Ford issued an Executive Order making citizenship a condition for federal employment. The order has not subsequently been reviewed by the Supreme Court. Consider, though, Professor

Tribe's suggestion that the Fifth Amendment's equal protection component "would invalidate even congressional or presidential discrimination against resident aliens as such where no substantial justification could be shown."[16]

May Congress *authorize* states to discriminate against aliens? In Graham v. Richardson, the Court considered Arizona's suggestion that its 15-year durational residency requirement for aliens was authorized by federal law. The Court rejected Arizona's construction of the relevant federal statutes and then went on to say:

> But if [the statutes] were to be read so as to authorize discriminatory treatment of aliens at the option of the States, [that would present] serious constitutional questions. Although the Federal Government admittedly has broad constitutional power to determine what aliens shall be admitted to the United States, the period they may remain, and the terms and conditions of their naturalization, Congress does not have the power to authorize the individual States to violate the Equal Protection Clause. Under Art. I, §8, cl. 4, of the Constitution, Congress' power is to "establish an uniform Rule of Naturalization." A congressional enactment construed so as to permit state legislatures to adopt divergent laws on the subject of citizenship requirements for federally supported welfare programs would appear to contravene this explicit constitutional requirement of uniformity.[a]

Is the Court's advisory construction of the "uniformity" provision persuasive? So long as all immigrants are equally liable to the decisions of the states wherein they happen to reside, wouldn't the "uniformity" provision be satisfied?

II. The United States as a Culturally Pluralist Community: Recognizing the Pluribus *Within the* Unum

A. Creating Communities Through Patriotic Exercise: The Case of Compulsory Flag Salutes

This chapter began by considering the ideas of constitutional attachment and loyalty to the United States. We continue exploring this theme in the context of compulsory flag salutes — a device for symbolizing and inculcating in children a sense of membership in the national polity.

The day after the United States declared war on Spain in 1898, the New York legislature passed the nation's first law requiring public-school students to begin the day with a salute to the American flag.[17] Five other states enacted flag-salute laws in the next two decades, and in the aftermath of World War I, the American Legion and other groups began a national campaign to foster "one hundred per-

16. See Laurence Tribe, American Constitutional Law 1546 n.12 (1988).

a. We have no occasion to decide whether Congress, in the exercise of the immigration and naturalization power, could itself enact a statute imposing on aliens a uniform nationwide residency requirement as a condition of federally funded welfare benefits.

17. See Peter Irons, Courage of Their Convictions 16 (1988). The following discussion of the *Gobitis* case is taken from chapter 1 of Irons' book.

cent Americanism" through patriotic activities of this sort. By 1935, eighteen states and many school boards required flag salutes.

The most persistent challenges to flag salute requirements came from Jehovah's Witnesses, a largely American religious sect teaching the supremacy of the laws of God to those enacted by temporal government. The Witnesses interpret the commandment in Exodus 20:4-5 — "Thou shalt not make unto thee any graven image, or any likeness of any thing that is in heaven above, or that is in the earth beneath, or that is in the water under the earth; Thou shalt not bow down thyself to them, nor serve them" — as a prohibition of saluting the "image" of the flag. (Germany banned the Jehovah's Witnesses in 1933 for, among other reasons, their refusal to give the Nazi salute in schools and public events, and 10,000 Witnesses were subsequently imprisoned in German concentration camps.)

The first constitutional challenge arose in Minersville, Pennsylvania, when William and Lillian Gobitas were expelled from school for refusing to comply with the school board's requirement to salute the flag. During the trial in the district court, the Minersville school superintendent, after describing the children as "indoctrinated," stated that tolerating their noncompliance would be "demoralizing" and would spread "a disregard for our flag and country," especially among the "foreigners of every variety" who needed training in the precepts of Americanism. The district judge found it "clear from the evidence that the refusal of these two earnest Christian children to salute the flag cannot even remotely prejudice or imperil the safety, health, morals, property or personal rights of their fellows" and ordered their readmission to school. His opinion was affirmed by the Third Circuit Court of Appeals. The school board appealed to the United States Supreme Court, which, in an opinion by Justice Frankfurter, reversed and upheld the constitutionality of the compulsory flag salute. Minersville School District v. Gobitis [sic], 310 U.S. 586 (1940).[18]

At the judicial conference discussing the case, Justice Frankfurter, himself a naturalized citizen who had immigrated from Austria in 1894, had made what Chief Justice Hughes described as a "moving statement . . . on the role of the public school in instilling love of country." Frankfurter's opinion described the flag as a symbol fostering "the binding tie of cohesive sentiment" among the citizenry. Frankfurter, much concerned about the war that was already consuming Europe and that threatened to involve the United States, noted that "[n]ational unity is the basis of national security." Only Justice Stone dissented.

"In the two years following the decision," wrote officials of the United States Department of Justice, "the files of the Department of the Justice reflect an uninterrupted record of violence and persecution of the Witnesses. Almost without exception, the flag and the flag salute can be found as the percussion cap that sets off these acts." Acts included the burning down of a Kingdom Hall in Kennebunk, Maine, and, in Nebraska, the beating and castration of a Witness by vigilantes. In some communities, police officials joined in mob violence against Witnesses.

Gobitis triggered the adoption of more flag-salute laws. In addition to expulsion, some of these laws also threatened to send the children to reformatories and to punish the parents for causing delinquency. In Jones v. Opelika, 316 U.S. 584

18. Richard Danzig, Justice Frankfurter's Opinions in the Flag Salute Cases: Blending Logic and Psychologic in Constitutional Decisionmaking, 36 Stan. L. Rev. 675 (1984).

(1942), Justices Black, Douglas, and Murphy indicated that they had significant doubts about the correctness of *Gobitis*. On June 14, 1943 — Flag Day — the Court overruled the precedent.

WEST VIRGINIA STATE BOARD OF EDUCATION v. BARNETTE

Appeal from the United States District Court for the Southern District of West Virginia
319 U.S. 624 (1943)

JACKSON, J., delivered the opinion of the Court. . . .

[In West Virginia the Witnesses offered a substitute for the required pledge: "I have pledged my unqualified allegiance and devotion to Jehovah, the Almighty God, and to His Kingdom, for which Jesus commands all Christians to pray. I respect the flag of the United States and acknowledge it as a symbol of freedom and justice to all. I pledge allegiance and obedience to all the laws of the United States that are consistent with God's law, as set forth in the Bible." The state rejected the offer and Walter Barnette was expelled for "insubordination" for failing to comply with the West Virginia statute.]

. . . Children of this faith have been expelled from school and are threatened with exclusion for no other cause [than failure to salute the flag].

. . . This case calls upon us to reconsider a precedent decision, as the Court throughout its history often has been required to do. Before turning to the *Gobitis* case, however, it is desirable to notice certain characteristics by which this controversy is distinguished.

The freedom asserted by these appellees does not bring them into collision with rights asserted by any other individual. . . . [T]he refusal of these persons to participate in the ceremony does not interfere with or deny rights of others to do so. Nor is there any question in this case that their behavior is peaceable and orderly. The sole conflict is between authority and rights of the individual. The State asserts power to condition access to public education on making a prescribed sign and profession and at the same time to coerce attendance by punishing both parent and child. The latter stand on a right of self-determination in matters that touch individual opinion and personal attitude.

. . . [T]he State may "require teaching by instruction and study of all in our history and in the structure and organization of our government, including the guaranties of civil liberty which tend to inspire patriotism and love of country." Here, however, we are dealing with a compulsion of students to declare a belief.

They are not merely made acquainted with the flag salute so that they may be informed as to what it is or even what it means. The issue here is whether this slow and easily neglected route to aroused loyalties constitutionally may be short-cut by substituting a compulsory salute and slogan. This issue is not prejudiced by the Court's previous holding that where a State, without compelling attendance, extends college facilities to pupils who voluntarily enroll, it may prescribe military training as part of the course without offense to the Constitution. It was held that those who take advantage of its opportunities may not on ground of conscience refuse compliance with such conditions. Hamilton v. Regents, 293 U.S. 245 (1935). In the present case attendance is not optional. That case is also to be distinguished from the present one because, independently of college privileges or requirements, the State has power to raise militia and impose the duties of service therein upon its citizens.

There is no doubt that, in connection with the pledges, the flag salute is a form of utterance. Symbolism is a primitive but effective way of communicating ideas. The use of an emblem or flag to symbolize some system, idea, institution, or personality, is a short cut from mind to mind. Causes and nations, political parties, lodges and ecclesiastical groups seek to knit the loyalty of their followings to a flag or banner, a color or design. . . .

Over a decade ago Chief Justice Hughes led this Court in holding that the display of a red flag as a symbol of opposition by peaceful and legal means to organized government was protected by the free speech guaranties of the Constitution. Stromberg v. California, 283 U.S. 359 (1931). Here it is the State that employs a flag as a symbol of adherence to government as presently organized. It requires the individual to communicate by word and sign his acceptance of the political ideas it thus bespeaks. Objection to this form of communication when coerced is an old one, well known to the framers of the Bill of Rights.

It is also to be noted that the compulsory flag salute and pledge requires affirmation of a belief and an attitude of mind. . . .

It is now a commonplace that censorship or suppression of expression of opinion is tolerated by our Constitution only when the expression presents a clear and present danger of action of a kind the State is empowered to prevent and punish. It would seem that involuntary affirmation could be commanded only on even more immediate and urgent grounds than silence. But here the power of compulsion is invoked without any allegation that remaining passive during a flag salute ritual creates a clear and present danger that would justify an effort even to muffle expression. To sustain the compulsory flag salute we are required to say that a Bill of Rights which guards the individual's right to speak his own mind, left it open to public authorities to compel him to utter what is not in his mind.

Whether the First Amendment to the Constitution will permit officials to order observance of ritual of this nature does not depend upon whether as a voluntary exercise we would think it to be good, bad or merely innocuous. Any credo of nationalism is likely to include what some disapprove or to omit what others think essential, and to give off different overtones as it takes on different accents or interpretations. If official power exists to coerce acceptance of any patriotic creed, what it shall contain cannot be decided by courts, but must be largely discretionary with the ordaining authority, whose power to prescribe would no doubt include power to amend. Hence validity of the asserted power to force an American citizen publicly to profess any statement of belief or to engage in any ceremony of assent to one presents questions of power that must be considered independently of any idea we may have as to the utility of the ceremony in question.

Nor does the issue as we see it turn on one's possession of particular religious views or the sincerity with which they are held. While religion supplies appellees' motive for enduring the discomforts of making the issue in this case, many citizens who do not share these religious views hold such a compulsory rite to infringe constitutional liberty of the individual.

It is not necessary to inquire whether non-conformist beliefs will exempt from the duty to salute unless we first find power to make the salute a legal duty.

The *Gobitis* decision, however, assumed, as did the argument in that case and in this, that power exists in the state to impose the flag salute discipline upon school children in general. The Court only examined and rejected a claim based on religious beliefs of immunity from an unquestioned general rule. The question which underlies the flag salute controversy is whether such a ceremony so touching matters of opinion and political attitude may be imposed upon the individual by official authority under powers connected to any political organization under our Constitution. We examine rather than assume existence of this power and, against this broader definition of issues in this case, reexamine specific grounds for the *Gobitis* decision.

It was said that the flag salute controversy confronted the court with "the problem which Lincoln cast in memorable dilemma: 'Must a government of necessity be too *strong* for the liberties of its people, or too *weak* to maintain its own existence?' The answer must be in favor of strength." Minersville School District v. Gobitis, 310 U.S. 586. We think these issues may be examined free of pressure or restraint growing out of such considerations.

It may be doubted whether Mr. Lincoln would have thought that the strength of government to maintain itself would be impressively vindicated by our confirming power of the state to expel a handful of children from school. Such oversimplification, so handy in political debate, often lacks the precision necessary to postulates of judicial reasoning. If validly applied to this problem, the utterance cited would resolve every issue of power in favor of those in authority and would require us to override every liberty thought to weaken or delay execution of their policies.

. . . Free public education, if faithful to the ideal of secular instruction and political neutrality, will not be partisan or enemy of any class, creed, party, or faction. If it is to impose any ideological discipline, however, each party or denomination must seek to control, or failing that, to weaken the influence of the educational system. Observance of the limitations of the Constitution will not weaken government in the field appropriate for its exercise.

2. It was also considered in the *Gobitis* case that functions of educational officers in states, counties and school districts were such that to interfere with their authority "would in effect make us the school board for the country."

The Fourteenth Amendment, as now applied to the States, protects the citizen against the State itself and all of its creatures — Boards of Education not excepted. These have, of course, important, delicate, and highly discretionary functions, but none that they may not perform within the limits of the Bill of Rights. That they are educating the young for citizenship is reason for scrupulous protection of Constitutional freedoms of the individual, if we are not to strangle the free mind at its source and teach youth to discount important principles of our government as mere platitudes.

Such Boards are numerous and their territorial jurisdiction often small. But small and local authority may feel less sense of responsibility to the Constitution, and agencies of publicity may be less vigilant in calling it to account. The action of Congress in making flag observance voluntary and respecting the conscience of the objector in a matter so vital as raising the Army contrasts sharply with these local regulations in matters relatively trivial to the welfare of the nation. There are village tyrants as well as village Hampdens, but none who acts under color of law is beyond reach of the Constitution.

3. The *Gobitis* opinion reasoned that this is a field "where courts possess no marked and certainly no controlling competence," that it is committed to the legislatures as well as the courts to guard cherished liberties and that it is constitutionally appropriate to "fight out the wise use of legislative authority in the forum of public opinion and before legislative assemblies rather than to transfer such a contest to the judicial arena," since all the "effective means of inducing political changes are left free."

The very purpose of a Bill of Rights was to withdraw certain subjects from the vicissitudes of political controversy, to place them beyond the reach of majorities and officials and to establish them as legal principles to be applied by the courts. One's right to life, liberty, and property, to free speech, a free press, freedom of worship and assembly, and other fundamental rights may not be submitted to vote; they depend on the outcome of no elections.

. . . It is important to note that while it is the Fourteenth Amendment which bears directly upon the State it is the more specific limiting principles of the First Amendment that finally govern this case. . . . These principles grew in soil which also produced a philosophy that the individual was the center of society, that his liberty was attainable through mere absence of governmental restraints, and that government should be entrusted with few controls and only the mildest supervision over men's affairs. We must transplant these rights to a soil in which the laissez-faire concept or principle of non-interference has withered at least as to economic affairs, and social advancements are increasingly sought through closer integration of society and through expanded and strengthened governmental controls. These changed conditions often deprive precedents of reliability and cast us more than we would choose upon our own judgment. But we act in these matters not by authority of our competence but by force of our commissions. We cannot, because of modest estimates of our competence in such specialties as public education, withhold the judgment that history authenticates as the function of this Court when liberty is infringed.

4. Lastly, and this is the very heart of the *Gobitis* opinion, it reasons that "National unity is the basis of national security," that the authorities have "the right to select appropriate means for its attainment," and hence reaches the conclusion that such compulsory measures toward "national unity" are constitutional. Upon the verity of this assumption depends our answer in this case.

National unity as an end which officials may foster by persuasion and example is not in question. The problem is whether under our Constitution compulsion as here employed is a permissible means for its achievement.

Struggles to coerce uniformity of sentiment in support of some end thought essential to their time and country have been waged by many good as well as by evil men. Nationalism is a relatively recent phenomenon but at other times and places the ends have been racial or territorial security, support of a dynasty or regime, and particular plans for saving souls. As first and moderate methods to attain unity have failed, those bent on its accomplishment must resort to an ever-increasing severity. As governmental pressure toward unity becomes greater, so strife becomes more bitter as to whose unity it shall be. Probably no deeper division of our people could proceed from any provocation than from finding it necessary to choose what doctrine and whose program public educational officials shall compel youth to unite in embracing.

Ultimate futility of such attempts to compel coherence is the lesson of every such effort from the Roman drive to stamp out Christianity as a disturber of its pagan unity, the Inquisition, as a means to religious and dynastic unity, the Siberian exiles as a means to Russian unity, down to the fast failing efforts of our present totalitarian enemies. Those who begin coercive elimination of dissent soon find themselves exterminating dissenters. Compulsory unification of opinion achieves only the unanimity of the graveyard.

It seems trite but necessary to say that the First Amendment to our Constitution was designed to avoid these ends by avoiding these beginnings. There is no mysticism in the American concept of the State or of the nature or origin of its authority. We set up government by consent of the governed, and the Bill of Rights denies those in power any legal opportunity to coerce that consent. Authority here is to be controlled by public opinion, not public opinion by authority.

The case is made difficult not because the principles of its decision are obscure but because the flag involved is our own. Nevertheless, we apply the limitations of the Constitution with no fear that freedom to be intellectually and spiritually diverse or even contrary will disintegrate the social organization. To believe that patriotism will not flourish if patriotic ceremonies are voluntary and spontaneous instead of a compulsory routine is to make an unflattering estimate of the appeal of our institutions to free minds.

We can have intellectual individualism and the rich cultural diversities that we owe to exceptional minds only at the price of occasional eccentricity and abnormal attitudes. When they are so harmless to others or to the State as those we deal with here, the price is not too great. But freedom to differ is not limited to things that do not matter much. That would be a mere shadow of freedom. The test of its substance is the right to differ as to things that touch the heart of the existing order.

If there is any fixed star in our constitutional constellation, it is that no official, high or petty, can prescribe what shall be orthodox in politics, nationalism, religion, or other matters of opinion or force citizens to confess by word or act their faith therein. If there are any circumstances which permit an exception, they do not now occur to us.

The decision of this Court in Minersville School District v. Gobitis . . . [is] overruled.

BLACK, J., and Justice Douglas, concurring.

. . . Religious faiths, honestly held, do not free individuals from responsibility to conduct themselves obediently to laws which are either imperatively necessary to protect society as a whole from grave and pressingly imminent dangers or which, without any general prohibition, merely regulate time, place or manner of religious activity. Decision as to the constitutionality of particular laws which strike at the substance of religious tenets and practices must be made by this Court. The duty is a solemn one, and in meeting it we cannot say that a failure, because of religious scruples, to assume a particular physical position and to repeat the words of a patriotic formula creates a grave danger to the nation.

[A concurring opinion by Justice Murphy is omitted. Justices Roberts and Reed "adhere to the views expressed by the Court in Minersville School District v. Gobitis and are of the opinion that the judgment below should be reversed."]

FRANKFURTER, J., dissenting.

One who belongs to the most vilified and persecuted minority in history is not likely to be insensible to the freedoms guaranteed by our Constitution. Were my purely personal attitude relevant I should whole-heartedly associate myself with the general libertarian views in the Court's opinion, representing as they do the thought and action of a lifetime. But as judges we are neither Jew nor Gentile, neither Catholic nor agnostic. We owe equal attachment to the Constitution and are equally bound by our judicial obligations whether we derive our citizenship from the earliest or the latest immigrants to these shores. As a member of this Court I am not justified in writing my private notions of policy into the Constitution, no matter how deeply I may cherish them or how mischievous I may deem their disregard. The duty of a judge who must decide which of two claims before the Court shall prevail, that of a State to enact and enforce laws within its general competence or that of an individual to refuse obedience because of the demands of his conscience, is not that of the ordinary person. It can never be emphasized too much that one's own opinion about the wisdom or evil of a law should be excluded altogether when one is doing one's duty on the bench. The only opinion of our own even looking in that direction that is material is our opinion whether legislators could in reason have enacted such a law. . . . I cannot bring my mind to believe that the "liberty" secured by the Due Process Clause gives this Court authority to deny to the State of West Virginia the attainment of that which we all recognize as a legitimate legislative end, namely, the promotion of good citizenship, by employment of the means here chosen. . . .

The precise scope of the question before us defines the limits of the constitutional power that is in issue. The State of West Virginia requires all pupils to share in the salute to the flag as part of school training in citizenship. . . . All that is in question is the right of the state to compel participation in this exercise by those who choose to attend the public schools. . . .

Under our constitutional system the legislature is charged solely with civil concerns of society. If the avowed or intrinsic legislative purpose is either to promote or to discourage some religious community or creed, it is clearly within the constitutional restrictions imposed on legislatures and cannot stand. But it by no means follows that legislative power is wanting whenever a general non-discriminatory civil regulation in fact touches conscientious scruples or religious beliefs of an individual or a group. Regard for such scruples or beliefs undoubtedly presents one of the most reasonable claims for the exertion of legislative accommodation. . . . That wisdom might suggest the making of such accommodations and that school administration would not find it too difficult to make them and yet maintain the ceremony for those not refusing to conform, is outside our province to suggest. . . .

Conscientious scruples, all would admit, cannot stand against every legislative compulsion to do positive acts in conflict with such scruples. We have been told that such compulsions override religious scruples only as to major concerns of the state. But the determination of what is major and what is minor itself raises questions of policy. For the way in which men equally guided by reason appraise importance goes to the very heart of policy. Judges should be very diffident in setting their judgment against that of a state in determining what is and what is not a major concern, what means are appropriate to proper ends, and what is the total social cost in striking the balance of imponderables.

What one can say with assurance is that the history out of which grew constitutional provisions for religious equality and the writings of the great exponents of religious freedom — Jefferson, Madison, John Adams, Benjamin Franklin — are totally wanting in justification for a claim by dissidents of exceptional immunity from civic measures of general applicability, measures not in fact disguised assaults upon such dissident views. . . . Jefferson and the others . . . knew that minorities may disrupt society. It never would have occurred to them to write into the Constitution the subordination of the general civil authority of the state to sectarian scruples.

. . . Any person may . . . believe or disbelieve what he pleases. He may practice what he will in his own house of worship or publicly within the limits of public order. But the lawmaking authority is not circumscribed by the variety of religious beliefs, otherwise the constitutional guaranty would be not a protection of the free exercise of religion but a denial of the exercise of legislation.

. . . The validity of secular laws cannot be measured by their conformity to religious doctrines. It is only in a theocratic state that ecclesiastical doctrines measure legal right or wrong.

. . . [A]n act promoting good citizenship and national allegiance is within the domain of governmental authority. . . .

The subjection of dissidents to the general requirement of saluting the flag, as a measure conducive to the training of children in good citizenship, is very far from being the first instance of exacting obedience to general laws that have offended deep religious scruples. Compulsory vaccination, see Jacobson v. Massachusetts, 197 U.S. 11, food inspection regulations, see Shapiro v. Lyle, 30 F.2d 971, the obligation to bear arms, see Hamilton v. Regents, 293 U.S. 245, 267, testimonial duties, see Stansbury v. Marks, 2 Dall. 213, compulsory medical treatment, see People v. Vogelgesang, 221 N.Y. 290, 116 N.E. 977 — these are but illustrations of conduct that has often been compelled in the enforcement of legislation of general applicability even though the religious consciences of particular individuals rebelled at the exaction.

Law is concerned with external behavior and not with the inner life of man. It rests in large measure upon compulsion. . . . The consent upon which free government rests is the consent that comes from sharing in the process of making and unmaking laws. . . . One may have the right to practice one's religion and at the same time owe the duty of formal obedience to laws that run counter to one's beliefs. Compelling belief implies denial of opportunity to combat it and to assert dissident views. Such compulsion is one thing. Quite another matter is submission to conformity of action while denying its wisdom or virtue and with ample opportunity for seeking its change or abrogation.

In Hamilton v. Regents, 293 U.S. 245, this Court unanimously held that one attending a state-maintained university cannot refuse attendance on courses that offend his religious scruples. That decision is not overruled today, but is distinguished on the ground that attendance at the institution for higher education was voluntary and therefore a student could not refuse compliance with its conditions and yet take advantage of its opportunities. But West Virginia does not compel the attendance at its public schools of the children here concerned. West Virginia does not so compel, for it cannot. This Court denied the right of a state to require its children to attend public schools. Pierce v. Society of Sisters, 268 U.S. 510. As to its public schools, West Virginia imposes conditions which it deems necessary in the development of future citizens precisely as California deemed necessary the requirements that offended the student's conscience in the *Hamilton* case. The need for higher education and the duty of the state to provide it as part of a public educational system, are part of the democratic faith of most of our states.

The right to secure such education in institutions not maintained by public funds is unquestioned. But the practical opportunities for obtaining what is becoming in increasing measure the conventional equipment of American youth may be no less burdensome than that which parents are increasingly called upon to bear in sending their children to parochial schools because the education provided by public schools, though supported by their taxes, does not satisfy their ethical and educational necessities. I find it impossible, so far as constitutional power is concerned, to differentiate what was sanctioned in the *Hamilton* case from what is nullified in this case. . . .

Parents have the privilege of choosing which schools they wish their children to attend. And the question here is whether the state may make certain requirements that seem to it desirable or important for the proper education of those future citizens who go to schools maintained by the states, or whether the pupils in those schools may be relieved from those requirements if they run counter to the consciences of their parents. Not only have parents the right to send children to schools of their own choosing but the state has no right to bring such schools "under a strict governmental control" or give "affirmative direction concerning the intimate and essential details of such schools, intrust their control to public officers, and deny both owners and patrons reasonable choice and discretion in respect of teachers, curriculum and textbooks." Farrington v. Tokushige, 273 U.S. 284, 298. Why should not the state likewise have constitutional power to make reasonable provisions for the proper instruction of children in schools maintained by it?

When dealing with religious scruples we are dealing with an almost numberless variety of doctrines and beliefs entertained with equal sincerity by the particular groups for which they satisfy man's needs in his relation to the mysteries of the universe. There are in the United States more than 250 distinctive established religious denominations. In the state of Pennsylvania there are 120 of these, and in West Virginia as many as 65. But if religious scruples afford immunity from civic obedience to laws, they may be invoked by the religious beliefs of any individual even though he holds no membership in any sect or organized denomination. Certainly this Court cannot be called upon to determine what claims of conscience should be recognized and what should be rejected as satisfying the "religion" which the Constitution protects. That would indeed resurrect the very discriminatory treatment of religion which the Constitution sought forever to forbid. . . .

We are told that a flag salute is a doubtful substitute for adequate understanding of our institutions. The states that require such a school exercise do not have to justify it as the only means for promoting good citizenship in children, but merely as one of diverse means for accomplishing a worthy end. We may deem it a foolish measure, but the point is that this Court is not the organ of government to resolve doubts as to whether it will fulfill its purpose. Only if there be no doubt that any reasonable mind could entertain can we deny to the states the right to resolve doubts their way and not ours.

We are told that symbolism is a dramatic but primitive way of communicating ideas. Symbolism is inescapable. Even the most sophisticated live by symbols. But it is not for this Court to make psychological judgments as to the effectiveness of a particular symbol in inculcating concededly indispensable feelings, particularly if the state happens to see fit to utilize the symbol that represents our heritage and our hopes. . . . To deny the power to employ educational symbols is to say that the state's educational system may not stimulate the imagination because this may lead to unwise stimulation.

The right of West Virginia to utilize the flag salute as part of its educational process is denied because, so it is argued, it cannot be justified as a means of meeting a "clear and present danger" to national unity. In passing it deserves to be noted that the four cases which unanimously sustained the power of states to utilize such an educational measure arose and were all decided before the present World War. But to measure the state's power to make such regulations as are here resisted by the imminence of national danger is wholly to misconceive the origin and purpose of the concept of "clear and present danger." To apply such a test is for the Court to assume, however unwittingly, a legislative responsibility that does not belong to it. To talk about "clear and present danger" as the touchstone of allowable educational policy by the states whenever school curricula may impinge upon the boundaries of individual conscience, is to take a felicitous phrase out of the context of the particular situation where it arose and for which it was adapted. . . . [Justice Holmes] was not enunciating a formal rule that there can be no restriction upon speech and, still less, no compulsion where conscience balks, unless imminent danger would thereby be wrought "to our institutions or our government."

The flag salute exercise has no kinship whatever to the oath tests so odious in history. For the oath test was one of the instruments for suppressing heretical beliefs. Saluting the flag suppresses no belief nor curbs it. Children and their parents may believe what they please, avow their belief and practice it. It is not even remotely suggested that the requirement for saluting the flag involves the slightest restriction against the fullest opportunity on the part both of the children and of their parents to disavow as publicly as they choose to do so the meaning that others attach to the gesture of salute. All channels of affirmative free expression are open to both children and parents. Had we before us any act of the state putting the slightest curbs upon such free expression, I should not lag behind any member of this Court in striking down such an invasion of the right to freedom of thought and freedom of speech protected by the Constitution.

. . . [J]udicial opinions, even as to questions of constitutionality, are not immutable. As has been true in the past, the Court will from time to time reverse its position. But I believe that never before these Jehovah's Witnesses cases (except for minor deviations subsequently retraced) has this Court overruled decisions so as to restrict the powers of democratic government. Always heretofore, it has withdrawn narrow views of legislative authority so as to authorize what formerly it had denied.

In view of this history it must be plain that what thirteen Justices [in previous cases, including *Gobitis*] found to be within the constitutional authority of a state, legislators can not be deemed unreasonable in enacting. Therefore, in denying to the states what heretofore has received such impressive judicial sanction, some other tests of unconstitutionality must surely be guiding the Court than the absence of a rational justification for the legislation. But I know of no other test which this Court is authorized to apply in nullifying legislation.

. . . Of course patriotism cannot be enforced by the flag salute. But neither can the liberal spirit be enforced by judicial invalidation of illiberal legislation. Our constant preoccupation with the constitutionality of legislation rather than with its wisdom tends to preoccupation of the American mind with a false value. The tendency of focusing attention on constitutionality is to make constitutionality synonymous with wisdom, to regard a law as all right if it is constitutional. Such an attitude is a great enemy of liberalism. Particularly in legislation affecting freedom of thought and freedom of speech much which should offend a free-spirited society is constitutional. Reliance for the most precious interests of civilization, therefore, must be found outside of their vindication in courts of law. Only a persistent positive translation of the faith of a free society into the convictions and habits and actions of a community is the ultimate reliance against unabated temptations to fetter the human spirit.

Discussion

1. Recall the earlier discussion of loyalty oaths. Note that Cole v. Richardson was decided well after *Barnette*. Does this at all call into question the magnitude of Justice Jackson's "fixed star" of the Constitution? What accounts for the difference beween the Court's reaction to loyalty oaths in *Cole* and its response to flag salutes in *Barnette*? Does the distinction lie more in the differences between the actions elicited — support of the Constitution as against "allegiance" to the flag — or in the differences between those from whom the action is sought — public officials (or at least public employees) as against youngsters attending public schools? Could a state require school teachers to begin each day with the pledge of allegiance (thereby setting a model for their students) and to invite any students who so wished to participate in the pledge?

2. Recall also the earlier discussion, Chapter 11 supra, of the issue of "unconstitutional conditions." To what extent does Justice Frankfurter's argument rest on the assumption that public education is a "privilege" rather than a "right," so that the State can condition access to publicly funded education on the requirement of pledging allegiance to the flag? What would his "rationality standard" *not* allow the state to require as a condition for accepting the offer of public education?

3. *The limits of Witness exemption from ordinary law: Prince v. Massachusetts.* The doctrinal significance of Justice Jackson's focusing on an expression-based right to be free from coerced statements of belief, rather than a free-exercise-based right to be exempt from a law that could have applied to the secular dissident, is underscored in a case decided the following year. Prince v. Massachusetts, 321 U.S. 158 (1944), upheld a Jehovah's Witness' conviction for violating the state child labor statute by having her nine-year-old niece distribute pamphlets on a public street. The petitioner argued both that members of the sect are under a religious duty to spread the Witness doctrine by distributing religious tracts and that the particular labor involved presented none of the evils ordinarily associated with "child labor." The child testified that she believed that she would receive everlasting destruction at the apocalyptic battle, Armageddon, if she did not sell the pamphlets.

Justice Rutledge (generally viewed as one of the most liberal members of a predominantly liberal Court) emphasized the general dangers of child labor. "It is too late now to doubt that legislation appropriately designed to reach such evils is within the state's police power, whether against the parent's claim to control of the child or one that religious scruples dictate contrary action." Only Justice Murphy dissented on the merits: "Religious freedom is too sacred a right to be restricted or prohibited in any degree without convincing proof that a legitimate interest of the state is in grave danger."[19] We return to this issue toward the end of the chapter.

4. *The American flag as a sacred communal object.* See section III of Chapter 8, which addresses the constitutionality of laws prohibiting desecration of the American flag.

B. Religious Diversity: The Problem of Mormonism

America has always been notable for its religious diversity, and the Jehovah's Witnesses who challenged the compulsory flag salute are only one of a number of sects whose tenets appeared unacceptably "deviant" from the perspective of their fellow American citizens. The social conditions of the United States have given rise to a variety of religious groups, whose interactions have presented fundamental questions about the limits of cultural pluralism.

The particular history of one church — the Church of Jesus Christ of Latter-Day Saints, more popularly known as the Mormons — provides an interesting example of the constitutional dimensions of these questions. The Mormon Church was founded by Joseph Smith, a New York farmer, who in 1827 proclaimed the discovery of a cache of golden plates to which he was directed by a vision of the angel Moroni. The plates (which were later swept away by another angel) were transcribed and became the Book of Mormon, which detailed "the wanderings, vicissitudes, and battles of America's pre-Columbian inhabitants."[20] These inhabitants included the sons of Nephi, extinguished in recurrent battle with the evil sons of Laman. Two Nephites, Mormon and his son Moroni, buried their chronicles in 384 A.D., to be discovered 1,450 years later by Smith. As Fawn Brodie points out, Mormonism was "no mere dissenting sect" within Christianity, which featured a multiplicity of sects by the early nineteenth century, especially in America. "It was a real religious creation, one intended to be to Christianity what Christianity was to Judaism: that is, a reform and a consummation."[21]

Following the 1830 publication of the Book of Mormon, Smith gathered adherents to the new faith. These members attempted to construct new communities, first in Ohio, then later in Missouri and Illinois. The hostility and violence that greeted these efforts is exemplified by Smith's lynching in Illinois in 1844, after which his successors, including Brigham Young, led his followers to new

19. Justice Jackson, joined by Justices Roberts and Frankfurter, also dissented on technical doctrinal grounds, but there is no doubt that they would otherwise have voted to uphold the law.

20. Sydney E. Ahlstrom, A Religious History of the American People 502-503 (1972). Except where indicated, the information about the Mormon Church in this and the next two paragraphs comes from Ahlstrom at 501-507.

21. Id. at 502, quoting Fawn Brodie, No Man Knows My History: The Life of Joseph Smith, the Mormon Prophet viii (1945).

settlements in the Great Salt Lake basin of Utah. The first wagon train arrived there in July 1847. A constitutional convention in 1849 established the autonomous state of Deseret as a church-regulated community.

Upon the conclusion of the war with Mexico, the United States extended its jurisdiction to Utah in 1850, and tensions between the new government and the state of Deseret immediately developed. These tensions were exacerbated by the 1852 publication of Smith's revelations concerning the duty of plural marriage. President Buchannan's replacement of Young by a non-Mormon as territorial governor in 1857 led to the Mormon War, which included the massacre by Mormons of a group of non-Mormon settlers bound for California.

In 1862, Congress specifically outlawed bigamy "in a Territory, or other place over which the United States have exclusive jurisdiction." A second statute in 1882 denied polygamists the right to vote. Five years later Congress annulled the corporate charter of the Mormon Church and declared most of its property forfeit. In 1890, the Mormon Church formally abandoned the teaching and practice of polygamy, though it is still practiced by some small dissenting sects.

A series of cases involving the Mormons provided the first formal tests of the meaning of the free exercise clause of the First Amendment and the protections that would be given to groups within American society whose behavior diverged in fundamental ways from that of the larger society.[22]

REYNOLDS v. UNITED STATES

Error to the Supreme Court of the Territory of Utah
98 U.S. 145 (1878)

[George Reynolds was convicted of violating the federal antibigamy statute and sentenced to two years in prison and a $500 fine. He appealed his conviction, invoking the Free Exercise Clause of the First Amendment. The Supreme Court unanimously rejected his claim.]

WAITE, C.J. . . .

[Reynolds] proved that at the time of his alleged second marriage he was, and for many years before had been, a member of the Church of Jesus Christ of Latter-Day Saints, commonly called the Mormon Church, and a believer in its doctrines; that it was an accepted doctrine of that church

> that it was the duty of male members of said church, circumstances permitting, to practice polygamy; . . . that this duty was enjoined by different books which the members of said church believed to be of divine origin, and among others the Holy Bible, and also that the members of the church believed that the practice of polygamy was directly enjoined upon the male members thereof by the Almighty God, in a revelation to Joseph Smith, the founder and prophet of said church; that the failing or refusing to practise polygamy . . . , when circumstances would admit, would be punished, and that the penalty for such failure and refusal would be damnation in the life to come.

22. See generally Linford, The Mormons and the Law: The Polygamy Cases, Part I, 9 Utah L. Rev. 308 (1964). See also Edwin Brown Firmage & Richard Collin Mangrum, Zion in the Courts: A Legal History of the Church of Jesus Christ of Latter-Day Saints, 1830-1900, 129-209 (1988).

[T]he question is raised, whether religious belief can be accepted as a justification of an overt act made criminal by the law of the land. . . .

Congress cannot pass a law . . . which shall prohibit the free exercise of religion. . . . The question to be determined is, whether the law now under consideration comes within this prohibition. . . . [W]hat is the religious freedom which has been guaranteed[?]

[The Court reviews some of the history of the First Amendment, ascribing particular significance to the views of Thomas Jefferson. Waite quotes from Jefferson's letter to the Danbury Baptist Association, where he used the metaphor of "a wall of separation between church and state." Jefferson wrote that "religion is a matter which lies solely between man and his God; that he owes account to none other for his faith or his worship; that the legislative powers of the government reach actions only, and not opinions. . . ."] Coming as this does from an acknowledged leader of the advocates of the measure, it may be accepted almost as an authoritative declaration of the scope and effect of the amendment thus secured. Congress was deprived of all legislative power over mere opinion, but was left free to reach actions which were in violation of social duties or subversive of good order.

Polygamy has always been odious among the northern and western nations of Europe, and, until the establishment of the Mormon Church, was almost exclusively a feature of the life of Asiatic and of African people. . . . [F]rom the earliest history of England polygamy has been treated as an offence against society. It is a significant fact that on [December 8,] 1788, after the passage of the [Virginia Act guaranteeing religious freedom] and after the convention of Virginia had recommended as an amendment to the Constitution of the United States the declaration in a bill of rights that "all men have an equal, natural, and unalienable right to the free exercise of religion, according to the dictates of conscience," the legislature of that State substantially enacted the statute of James I, death penalty included, because, as recited in the preamble, "it hath been doubted whether bigamy or poligamy be punishable by the laws of this Commonwealth." From that day to this we think it may safely be said there never has been a time in any State of the Union when polygamy has not been an offence against society, cognizable by the civil courts and punishable with more or less severity. In the face of all this evidence, it is impossible to believe that the constitutional guaranty of religious freedom was intended to prohibit legislation in respect to this most important feature of social life. Marriage, while from its very nature a sacred obligation, is nevertheless, in most civilized nations, a civil contract, and usually regulated by law. Upon it society may be said to be built, and out of its fruits spring social relations and social obligations and duties, with which government is necessarily required to deal. In fact, according as monogamous or polygamous marriages are allowed, do we find the principles on which the government of the people, to a greater or less extent, rests. Professor Lieber says, polygamy leads to the patriachal principle, and which, when applied to large communities, fetters the people in stationary despotism, while that principle cannot long exist in connection with monogamy. Chancellor Kent observes that this remark is equally striking and profound. An exceptional colony of polygamists under an exceptional leadership may sometimes exist for a time without appearing to disturb the social condition of the people who surround it; but there cannot be a doubt that, unless restricted by some form of constitution, it is within the legitimate scope of the power of every civil government to determine whether polygamy or monogamy shall be the law of social life under its dominion.

In our opinion, the statute immediately under consideration is within the legislative power of Congress. . . . This being so, the only question which remains is, whether those who make polygamy a part of their religion are excepted from the operation of the statute. If they are, then those who do not make polygamy a part of their religious belief may be found guilty and punished, while those who do, must be acquitted and go free. This would be introducing a new element into criminal law. Laws are made for the government of actions, and while they cannot interfere with mere religious belief and opinions, they may with practices. Suppose one believed that human sacrifices were a necessary part of religious worship, would it be seriously contended that the civil government under which he lived could not interfere to prevent a sacrifice? Or if a wife religiously believed it was her duty to burn herself upon the funeral pile of her dead husband, would it be beyond the power of the civil government to prevent her carrying her belief into practice?

. . . To permit [exemption of Reynolds on grounds of his religious belief] would be to make the professed doctrines of religious belief superior to the law of the land, and in effect to permit every citizen to become a law unto himself. Government could exist only in name under such circumstances.

Subsequently, Murphy v. Ramsey, 114 U.S. 15 (1885), upheld an act of Congress excluding polygamists and bigamists from voting or holding office. Praising monogamy as "the sure foundation of all that is stable and noble in our civilization; the best guaranty of that reverent morality which is the source of all beneficent progress in social and political improvement," the Court readily supported Congress' "endeavor to withdraw all political influence from those who are practically hostile to its attainment." Similarly, Davis v. Beason, 133 U.S. 333 (1890), upheld a law of the Territory of Idaho that limited the right to vote to those persons otherwise eligible who would swear not only that they were not practicing polygamists but also that they did not support the practice or even belong to any that "teaches, advises, counsels or encourages its members, devotees or any other person to commit the crime of bigamy or polygamy. . . ." After denouncing polygamy, Justice Field defined religion "as having reference to one's views of his relations to his Creator." He went on to explain that "it was never intended or supposed that the [First Amendment] could be invoked as a protection against legislation for the punishment of acts inimical to the peace, good order and morals of society":

> Probably never before in the history of this country has it been seriously contended that the whole punitive power of the government for acts, recognized by the general consent of the Christian world in modern times as proper matters for prohibitory legislation, must be suspended in order that the tenets of a religious sect encouraging crime may be carried out without hindrance. . . . Crime is not the less odious because sanctioned by what any particular sect may designate as religion.

Justice Field appended a short "Note" to the end of his opinion:

> The constitutions of several states, in providing for religious freedom, have declared expressly that such freedom shall not be construed to excuse acts of licentiousness, or to justify practices inconsistent with the peace and safety of the State. Thus the constitution of New York of 1777 provided as follows: "The free exercise and enjoyment of religious profession and worship, without discrimination or preference, shall forever be allowed, within this State, to all mankind: *Provided*, That the liberty of conscience, hereby granted, shall not be so construed as to excuse acts of licentiousness, or justify practices inconsistent with the peace or safety of this State." The same declaration is repeated in the constitution of 1821 and in that of 1846, except that for the words "hereby granted," the words "hereby secured" are substituted. The constitutions of California, Colorado, Connecticut, Florida, Georgia, Illinois, Maryland, Minnesota, Mississippi, Missouri, Nevada and South Carolina contain a similar declaration.

The final Mormon case of this period was The Late Corporation of the Church of Jesus Christ of Latter-day Saints v. United States, 136 U.S. 1 (1890). Congress in 1887 passed an act repealing the corporate charter of the Mormon Church, which had initially been granted in 1851 by an assembly of the State of Deseret and thereafter confirmed by the territorial legislature of Utah. The purpose of the Church was defined as promoting charity and religion. Congress repealed the incorporation on the grounds that a major purpose of the Church was the promotion of polygamy. The act mandating disincorporation directed the court to distribute all of the Church property in accordance with the original purpose. The court below ordered the property sold and the proceeds used to operate public schools within Utah. The Act was upheld in an opinion written by Justice Bradley. He condemned as "a return to barbarism" the practice of polygamy and pronounced it "contrary to the spirit of Christianity and of the civilization which Christianity has produced in the Western world." Chief Justice Fuller, joined by Justices Field and Lamar, dissented solely on the ground that Congress had exceeded its enumerated power over the Territories.

As late as 1946, in Cleveland v. United States, 329 U.S. 14, the Court interpreted the Mann Act (which prohibited the transportation across state lines of "any woman or girl for the purpose of prostitution or debauchery, or for any other immoral purpose") to extend to members of a Mormon sect who continued to practice polygamy long after it had been formally disavowed by the general Mormon Church. Several of those convicted had transported their plural wives across state lines. Quoting *Reynolds* and *Church of Jesus Christ of L.D.S.* Justice Douglas commented: "The establishment or maintenance of polygamous households is a notorious example of promiscuity. . . . [P]olygamous practices have long been branded immoral in the law." As to the suggestion that marriage and divorce was a matter to be regulated by the states alone, Douglas noted simply that "[t]he power of Congress over the instrumentalities of interstate commerce is plenary; it may be used to defeat what are deemed to be immoral practices."

Discussion

Professor Stephen Pepper suggests that the term "free exercise" contains a "clear connotation of at least some degree of freedom of *action*."[23] going beyond

23. Stephen Pepper, *Reynolds, Yoder,* and Beyond: Alternatives for the Free Exercise Clause, 1981 Utah L. Rev. 309 (1981).

the simple right to hold abstract views of theology. Consider a revised First Amendment that guaranteed only "freedom of belief concerning religion." We shall return later in this chapter to problems posed by the claimed duty of the state to take special (and beneficial) cognizance of certain religious "exercises" that are otherwise prohibited by the general law.

C. Americans as "a Religious People"

Recall Justice Bradley's reference to Christianity to support the immorality of polygamy. Was he suggesting that the United States is in some sense a "Christian nation" or that behavior not in accord with Christian doctrine is somehow "un-American"? Though one will not often find such language in modern judicial opinions, Justice Douglas in 1953 wrote that Americans are "a religious people."[24]

The First Amendment provides: "Congress shall make no law respecting an establishment of religion." In 1947, the Court extended this prohibition to the States through the Fourteenth Amendment. One of the most controversial subsequent interpretations of the Establishment Clause has involved the propriety of school prayers and Bible readings. In Engel v. Vitale, 370 U.S. 421 (1962), the Court struck down a prayer composed by the state of New York: "Almighty God, we acknowledge our dependence upon Thee, and we beg Thy blessings upon us, our parents, our teachers and our Country." Justice Black wrote for the 8-to-1 majority: "It is no part of the business of government to compose official prayers for any group of the American people to recite as a part of a religious program carried on by government."

The next year, School District v. Schempp, 374 U.S. 203 (1963), struck down a Pennsylvania requirement that "[a]t least ten verses from the Holy Bible shall be read, without comment, at the opening of each public school on each school day. Any child shall be excused from such Bible reading, or attending such Bible reading, upon the written request of his parent or guardian." Each morning Abingdon Township broadcast ten verses, chosen and read by students, over its internal communications system. This was followed by the recitation of the Lord's Prayer, with the students in the various classrooms being asked to stand and join in repeating the prayer in unison. The exercise closed with the flag salute. The Schempp children, members of the Unitarian Church, objected to the ceremony. Their parents did not ask that they be excused from the classroom because they believed "that the children's relationships with their teachers and classmates would be adversely affected." Instead, they argued that the reading constituted an illegal establishment of religion. The Supreme Court, through Justice Clark, agreed:

> The fact that the Founding Fathers believed devotedly that there was a God and that the unalienable rights of man were rooted in Him is clearly evidenced in their writings, from the Mayflower Compact to the Constitution itself. This background is evidenced today in our public life through the continuance in our oaths of office from the Presidency to the Alderman of the final supplication, "So help me God." Likewise each House of the Congress provides through its Chaplain an opening

24. See Zorach v. Clausen, 343 U.S. 306 (1952).

prayer, and the sessions of this Court are declared open by the crier in a short ceremony, the final phrase of which invokes the grace of God. Again, there are such manifestations in our military forces, where those of our citizens who are under the restrictions of military service wish to engage in voluntary worship. Indeed, only last year an official survey of the country indicated that 64% of our people have church membership, while less than 3% profess no religion whatever. It can be truly said, therefore, that today, as in the beginning, our national life reflects a religious people who, in the words of Madison, are "earnestly praying, as . . . in duty bound, that the Supreme Lawgiver of the Universe . . . guide them into every measure which may be worthy of his [blessing. . . .]"

This is not to say, however, that religion has been so identified with our history and government that religious freedom is not likewise as strongly imbedded in our public and private life. . . .

[T]his Court has rejected unequivocally the contention that the Establishment Clause forbids only governmental preference of one religion over another. Almost 20 years ago, in Everson v. Board of Education, 330 U.S. 1 (1947), the Court said that "[n]either a state nor the Federal Government can set up a church. Neither can pass laws which aid one religion, aid all religions, or prefer one religion over another." . . .

The wholesome "neutrality" of which this Court's cases speak thus stems from a recognition of the teachings of history that powerful sects or groups might bring about a fusion of governmental and religious functions or a concert or dependency of one upon the other to the end that official support of the State or Federal Government would be placed behind the tenets of one or of all orthodoxies. This the Establishment Clause prohibits. . . .

We agree with the trial court's finding as to the religious character of the exercises. Given that finding, the exercises and the law requiring them are in violation of the Establishment Clause. . . . [E]ven if its purpose is not strictly religious, it is sought to be accomplished through readings, without comment, from the Bible. Surely the place of the Bible as an instrument of religion cannot be gainsaid, and the State's recognition of the pervading religious character of the ceremony is evident from the rule's specific permission of the alternative use of the Catholic Douay version [of the Bible] as well as the recent amendment permitting nonattendance at the exercises. None of these factors is consistent with the contention that the Bible is here used either as an instrument for nonreligious moral inspiration or as a reference for the teaching of secular subjects. . . . Nor are these required exercises mitigated by the fact that individual students may absent themselves upon parental request. . . .

It is insisted that unless these religious exercises are permitted a "religion of secularism" is established in the schools. We agree of course that the State may not establish a "religion of secularism" in the sense of affirmatively opposing or showing hostility to religion, thus "preferring those who believe in no religion over those who do believe." We do not agree, however, that this decision in any sense has that effect. In addition, it might well be said that one's education is not complete without a study of comparative religion or the history of religion and its relationship to the advancement of civilization. It certainly may be said that the Bible is worthy of study for its literary and historic qualities. Nothing we have said here indicates that such study of the Bible or of religion, when presented objectively as part of a secular program of education, may not be effected consistently with the First Amendment. But the exercises here do not fall into those categories. They are religious exercises, required by the States in violation of the command of the First Amendment that the Government maintain strict neutrality, neither aiding nor opposing religion. . . .

The place of religion in our society is an exalted one, achieved through a long tradition of reliance on the home, the church and the inviolable citadel of the indi-

> vidual heart and mind. We have come to recognize through bitter experience that it is not within the power of government to invade that citadel, whether its purpose or effect be to aid or oppose, to advance or retard. In the relationship between man and religion, the State is firmly committed to a position of neutrality.

In a concurring opinion, Justice Goldberg, joined by Justice Harlan, cautioned against an "untutored devotion to the concept of neutrality [that] can lead to invocation or approval of results which partake not simply of that noninterference and noninvolvement with the religious which the Constitution commands, but of a brooding and pervasive devotion to the secular and a passive, or even active, hostility to the religious."

Justice Stewart dissented, as he had in *Engel*:

> For me there is involved in these cases a substantial free exercise claim on the part of those who affirmatively desire to have their children's school day open with the reading of passages from the Bible. . . .
>
> [A] compulsory state educational system so structures a child's life that if religious exercises are held to be an impermissible activity in schools, religion is placed at an artificial and state-created disadvantage. Viewed in this light, permission of such exercises [as Bible reading] for those who want them is necessary if the schools are truly to be neutral in the matter of religion. And a refusal to permit religious exercises thus is seen, not as the realization of state neutrality, but rather as the establishment of a religion of secularism, or at the least, as government support of the beliefs of those who think that religious exercises should be conducted only in private. . . .
>
> The dangers both to government and to religion inherent in official support of instruction in the tenets of various religious sects are absent in the present cases, which involve only a reading from the Bible unaccompanied by comments which might otherwise constitute instruction. . . .
>
> In the absence of coercion upon those who do not wish to participate — because they hold less strong beliefs, other beliefs, or no beliefs at all — such provisions cannot, in my view, be held to represent the type of support of religion barred by the Establishment Clause. For the only support which such rules provide for religion is the withholding of state hostility — a simple acknowledgment on the part of secular authorities that the Constitution does not require extirpation of all expression of religious belief. . . .
>
> [I]t seems to me clear that certain types of exercises would present situations in which no possibility of coercion on the part of secular officials could be claimed to exist. Thus, if such exercises were held either before or after the official school day, or if the school schedule were such that participation were merely one among a number of desirable alternatives, it could hardly be contended that the exercises did anything more than to provide an opportunity for the voluntary expression of religious belief. On the other hand, a law which provided for religious exercises during the school day and which contained no excusal provision would obviously be unconstitutionally coercive upon those who did not wish to participate. And even under a law containing an excusal provision, if the exercises were held during the school day, and no equally desirable alternative were provided by the school authorities, the likelihood that children might be under at least some psychological compulsion to participate would be great. In a case such as the latter, however, I think we would err if we *assumed* such coercion in the absence of any evidence.

The Court returned to the issue of religion within the school in Wallace v. Jaffree, 472 U.S. 38 (1985), which involved an Alabama statute authorizing one-minute periods of silence in public schools "for meditation or voluntary prayer." Justice Stevens held it unconstitutional, noting that the statute was passed "for the sole purpose of expressing the State's endorsement of prayer activities. . . . Such an endorsement is not consistent with the established principle that the Government must pursue a course of complete neutrality toward religion."

Separate dissents were written by Chief Justice Burger, Justice White, and Justice Rehnquist. The Chief Justice noted "that on the very day we heard arguments in this case, the Court's session opened with an invocation for Divine protection" and went on to state that the majority indeed manifested "hostility toward religion." "As I read the filed opinions," said Justice White, "a majority of the Court would approve statutes that provided for a moment of silence but did not mention prayer. But if a student asked whether he could pray during that moment, it is difficult to believe that the teacher could not answer in the affirmative. If that is the case, I would not invalidate a statute that at the outset provided the legislative answer to the question 'May I pray?' " Justice Rehnquist disputed the majority's historical analysis of the meaning of the Establishment Clause of the First Amendment.

Note: Religious Expression in Public Places

Douglas Laycock writes:[25]

> The Supreme Court has adhered to its decisions in the school prayer cases despite continued political attack. But it has not enforced the principle of those cases in other contexts. . . . [It] has permitted state sponsored prayer or religious observance in contexts other than schools. Thus it allowed states to hire legislative chaplains to open each legislative session with a prayer. Marsh v. Chambers, 463 U.S. 783 (1983). And it permitted a municipal Nativity display that was part of a larger display that included Santa Claus, reindeer, and other nonreligious symbols. Lynch v. Donnelly, 465 U.S. 668 (1984).
>
> The Court made no serious attempt to reconcile its decisions in these cases with those in the school prayer cases. In the legislative prayer case it noted that the First Congress had both proposed the establishment clause and appointed a chaplain; long historical usage suggested that legislative prayer was permissible. In the Nativity display case the Court invoked a variety of rationales, not all of them entirely consistent. It said that the history of legislative chaplains and of Thanksgiving proclamations showed that some government support for religion was permissible. Then it said that there could be no single test for deciding what support of religion was permitted and what was forbidden. Then it said that the creche display was not an attempt to express a religious message, but that it "principally" depicted "the historical origins of this traditional event" and that to do so was a "secular purpose." The Court also seemed to assume that Christmas carols in the public schools were permissible.[26]

25. Douglas Laycock, A Survey of Religious Liberty in the United States, 47 Ohio St. L.J. 409, 442-444 (1986).

26. The Supreme Court continued this pattern of confusion in County of Allegheny v. American Civil Liberties Union, decided together with City of Pittsburgh v. ACLU, 492 U.S. 573 (1989), where a highly divided Court held that (1) a display of a Christmas crèche on the Grand Staircase of the Allegheny County Courthouse violated the Establishment Clause, but (2) the display by the City of Pittsburgh by the entrance to its city offices of a menorah signifying the Jewish holiday of Chanukah did

Discussion

Neutrality revisited. The basic notion underlying *Schempp* is that the state must stay "neutral" when resolving issues between the religious and the secular.

During the Jacksonian period of American history, a significant controversy was sparked by the practice of keeping post offices open on Sunday, which was bitterly criticized by people who saw this as state-sponsored desecration of the Sabbath.[27] The general problem has not been resolved 150 years later. In McGowan v. Maryland, 366 U.S. 420 (1961), which upheld a Maryland law that required businesses to be closed on Sundays, Chief Justice Warren noted that, whatever the initial motivation for the Sunday closing law, it was now justified by the secular purpose of assuring of a common day of rest or recreation. In many states, Jewish state employees must expend vacation days to take time off to observe the High Holy Days of Rosh Hashanah and Yom Kippur, while a Christian employee need never expend a vacation day to observe Christmas or to attend religious services on Sunday. Does the Court's rationale in *McGowan* extend to making Christmas a holiday? Should the state prevail by observing that it is not promoting Christianity so much as recognizing the social fact that most of the citizenry is in fact Christian and regards Christmas as a holiday?

D. Reproducing the Minority Community: America as a Community of Communities

WISCONSIN v. YODER
Certiorari to the Supreme Court of Wisconsin
406 U.S. 205 (1972)

[Several members of the Old Order Amish and Conservative Amish Mennonite Church were convicted for violating Wisconsin's compulsory school-attendance law by failing to send their children to school. The children in question — Vernon Yutzy, 14 years old, and Frieder Yoder and Barbara Miller, both 15 — had completed the eighth grade but were then withdrawn from further schooling. The parents defended their action on the grounds that application of the law to them violated the Free Exercise Clause of the First Amendment. The Wisconsin Supreme Court overturned the convictions, and the United States Supreme Court affirmed.][28]

BURGER, C.J., delivered the opinion of the Court. . . .

The trial testimony showed that respondents believed, in accordance with the tenets of Old Order Amish communities generally, that their children's attendance at high school, public or private, was contrary to the Amish religion and way of life. They believed that by sending their children to high school, they would not only expose themselves to the danger of the censure of the church community, but, as found by the county court, also endanger their own salvation and that

---

not violate the Clause. The Court split 5-4 on the first holding and 6-3 on the second. Nothing would be gained by attempting to summarize the tortuous distinctions drawn between the crèche and the menorah.

27. See, e.g., Arthur M. Schlesinger, Jr., The Age of Jackson 138-139 (1945).

28. Justices Powell and Rehnquist did not participate in the case.

of their children. The State stipulated that respondents' religious beliefs were sincere.

[The history of the Amish goes back to the struggles of the sixteenth-century Reformation, when Swiss Anabaptists] rejected institutionalized churches and sought to return to the early, simple, Christian life de-emphasizing material success, rejecting the competitive spirit, and seeking to insulate themselves from the modern world. As a result of their common heritage, Old Order Amish communities today are characterized by a fundamental belief that salvation requires life in a church community separate and apart from the world and worldly influence. This concept of life aloof from the world and its values is central to their faith.

. . . Amish beliefs require members of the community to make their living by farming or closely related activities. Broadly speaking, the Old Order Amish religion pervades and determines the entire mode of life of its adherents. Their conduct is regulated in great detail by the Ordnung, or rules, of the church community. Adult baptism, which occurs in late adolescence, is the time at which Amish young people voluntarily undertake heavy obligations, not unlike the Bar Mitzvah of the Jews, to abide by the rules of the church community.

Amish objection to formal education beyond the eighth grade is firmly grounded in these central religious concepts. They object to the high school, and higher education generally, because the values they teach are in marked variance with Amish values and the Amish way of life; they view secondary school education as an impermissible exposure of their children to a "wordly" influence in conflict with their beliefs. The high school tends to emphasize intellectual and scientific accomplishments, self-distinction, competitiveness, worldly success, and social life with other students. Amish society emphasizes informal learning-through-doing; a life of "goodness," rather than a life of intellect; wisdom, rather than technical knowledge; community welfare, rather than competition; and separation from, rather than integration with, contemporary worldly society.

Formal high school education [is also] contrary to Amish beliefs . . . because it takes them away from their community, physically and emotionally, during the crucial and formative adolescent period of life. . . . [A]t this time in life, the Amish child must also grow in his faith and his relationship to the Amish community if he is to be prepared to accept the heavy obligations imposed by adult baptism. In short, high school attendance with teachers who are not of the Amish faith — and may even be hostile to it — interposes a serious barrier to the integration of the Amish child into the Amish religious community. . . .

The Amish do not object to elementary education through the first eight grades as a general proposition because they agree that their children must have basic skills in the "three R's" in order to read the Bible, to be good farmers and citizens, and to be able to deal with non-Amish people when necessary in the course of daily affairs. They view such a basic education as acceptable because it does not significantly expose their children to wordly values or interfere with their development in the Amish community during the crucial adolescent period. While Amish accept compulsory elementary education generally, wherever possible they have established their own elementary schools in many respects like the small local schools of the past. . . .

On the basis of such considerations, [an expert witness] testified that compulsory high school attendance could not only result in great psychological harm to Amish children, because of the conflicts it would produce, but would also, in his opinion, ultimately result in the destruction of the Old Order Amish church community as it exists in the United States today. . . .

I

There is no doubt as to the power of a State, having a high responsibility for education of its citizens, to impose reasonable regulations for the control and duration of basic education. See, e.g., Pierce v. Society of Sisters, 268 U.S. 510, 534 (1925). Providing public schools ranks at the very apex of the function of a State. Yet even this paramount responsibility was, in *Pierce,* made to yield to the right of parents to provide an equivalent education in a privately operated system. . . . As that case suggests, the values of parental direction of the religious upbringing and education of their children in their early and formative years have a high place in our society. Thus, a State's interest in universal education, however highly we rank it, is not totally free from a balancing process when it impinges on fundamental rights and interests, such as those specifically protected by the Free Exercise Clause of the First Amendment, and the traditional interest of parents with respect to the religious upbringing of their children so long as they, in the words of *Pierce,* "prepare (them) for additional obligations."

It follows that in order for Wisconsin to compel school attendance beyond the eighth grade against a claim that such attendance interferes with the practice of a legitimate religious belief, it must appear either that the State does not deny the free exercise of religious belief by its requirement, or that there is a state interest of sufficient magnitude to override the interest claiming protection under the Free Exercise Clause. . . .

II

A way of life, however virtuous and admirable, may not be interposed as a barrier to reasonable state regulation of education if it is based on purely secular considerations; to have the protection of the Religion Clauses, the claims must be rooted in religious belief. Although a determination of what is a "religious" belief or practice entitled to constitutional protection may present a most delicate question, the very concept of ordered liberty precludes allowing every person to make his own standards on matters of conduct in which society as a whole has important interests. Thus, if the Amish asserted their claims because of their subjective evaluation and rejection of the contemporary secular values accepted by the majority, much as Thoreau rejected the social values of his time and isolated himself at Walden Pond, their claims would not rest on a religious basis. Thoreau's choice was philosophical and personal rather than religious, and such belief does not rise to the demands of the Religion Clauses.

. . . [T]he record in this case abundantly supports the claim that the traditional way of life of the Amish is not merely a matter of personal preference, but one of deep religious conviction, shared by an organized group, and intimately related to daily living. . . . The respondents freely concede, and indeed assert as an article of faith, that their religious beliefs and what we would today call "life style" have not altered in fundamentals for centuries. Their way of life in a church-oriented community, separated from the outside world and "worldly" influences, their attachment to nature and the soil, is a way inherently simple and uncomplicated, albeit difficult to preserve against the pressure to conform. Their rejection of telephones, automobiles, radios, and television, their mode of dress, of speech, their habits of manual work do indeed set them apart from much of contemporary society; these customs are both symbolic and practical.

. . . The Amish mode of life has thus come into conflict increasingly with requirements of contemporary society exerting a hydraulic insistence on conformity to majoritarian standards. . . . [T]he values and programs of the modern secondary school are in sharp conflict with the fundamental mode of life mandated by the Amish religion; modern laws requiring compulsory secondary education have accordingly engendered great concern and conflict.

The conclusion is inescapable that secondary schooling, by exposing Amish children to worldly influences in terms of attitudes, goals, and values contrary to beliefs, and by substantially interfering with the religious development of the Amish child and his integration into the way of life of the Amish faith community at the crucial adolescent stage of development, contravenes the basic religious tenets and practice of the Amish faith, both as to the parent and the child.

The impact of the compulsory-attendance law on respondents' practice of the Amish religion is not only severe, but inescapable, for the Wisconsin law affirmatively compels them, under threat of criminal sanction, to perform acts undeniably at odds with fundamental tenets of their religious beliefs. Nor is the impact of the compulsory-attendance law confined to grave interference with important Amish religious tenets from a subjective point of view. It carries with it precisely the kind of objective danger to the free exercise of religion that the First Amendment was designed to prevent. As the record shows, compulsory school attendance to age 16 for Amish children carries with it a very real threat of undermining the Amish community and religious practice as they exist today; they must either abandon belief and be assimilated into society at large, or be forced to migrate to some other and more tolerant region.[a]

In sum, the unchallenged testimony of acknowledged experts in education and religious history, almost 300 years of consistent practice, and strong evidence of a sustained faith pervading and regulating respondents' entire mode of life support the claim that enforcement of the State's requirement of compulsory formal education after the eighth grade would gravely endanger if not destroy the free exercise of respondents' religious beliefs.

III

[Wisconsin's] position is that the State's interest in universal compulsory formal secondary education to age 16 is so great that it is paramount to the undisputed claims of respondents that their mode of preparing their youth for Amish life, after the traditional elementary education, is an essential part of their religious belief and practice. . . .

a. Some States have developed working arrangements with the Amish regarding high school attendance. However, the danger to the continued existence of an ancient religious faith cannot be ignored simply because of the assumption that its adherents will continue to be able, at considerable sacrifice, to relocate in some more tolerant State or country or work out accommodations under threat of criminal prosecution. Forced migration of religious minorities was an evil that lay at the heart of the Religion Clauses.

Wisconsin . . . argues that "actions," even though religiously grounded, are outside the protection of the First Amendment. . . . But to agree that religiously grounded conduct must often be subject to the broad police power of the State is not to deny that there are areas of conduct protected by the Free Exercise Clause of the First Amendment and thus beyond the power of the State to control, even under regulations of general applicability. This case, therefore, does not become easier because respondents were convicted for their "actions" in refusing to send their children to the public high school; in this context belief and action cannot be neatly confined in logic-tight compartments.

. . . The State advances two primary arguments in support of its system of compulsory education. It notes, as Thomas Jefferson pointed out early in our history, that some degree of education is necessary to prepare citizens to participate effectively and intelligently in our open political system if we are to preserve freedom and independence. Further, education prepares individuals to be self-reliant and self-sufficient participants in society. We accept these propositions.

However, the evidence adduced by the Amish in this case is persuasively to the effect that an additional one or two years of formal high school for Amish children in place of their long-established program of informal vocational education would do little to serve those interests. . . . It is one thing to say that compulsory education for a year or two beyond the eighth grade may be necessary when its goal is the preparation of the child for life in modern society as the majority live, but it is quite another if the goal of education be viewed as the preparation of the child for life in the separated agrarian community that is the keystone of the Amish faith.

The State attacks respondents' position as one fostering "ignorance" from which the child must be protected by the State. No one can question the State's duty to protect children from ignorance but this argument does not square with the facts disclosed in the record. Whatever their idiosyncrasies as seen by the majority, this record strongly shows that the Amish community has been a highly successful social unit within our society, even if apart from the conventional "mainstream." Its members are productive and very law-abiding members of society; they reject public welfare in any of its usual modern forms. . . .

It is neither fair nor correct to suggest that the Amish are opposed to education beyond the eighth grade level. What this record shows is that they are opposed to conventional formal education of the type provided by a certified high school because it comes at the child's crucial adolescent period of religious development. Dr. Donald Erickson, for example, testified that their system of learning-by-doing was an "ideal system" of education in terms of preparing Amish children for life as adults in the Amish community. . . .

There can be no assumption that today's majority is "right" and the Amish and others like them are "wrong." A way of life that is odd or even erratic but interferes with no rights or interests of others is not to be condemned because it is different.

The State, however, supports its interest in providing an additional one or two years of compulsory high school education to Amish children because of the possibility that some such children will choose to leave the Amish community, and that if this occurs they will be ill-equipped for life. . . . However, on this record, that argument is highly speculative. There is no specific evidence of the loss of Amish adherents by attrition, nor is there any showing that upon leaving the

Amish community Amish children, with their practical agricultural training and habits of industry and self-reliance, would become burdens on society because of educational shortcomings. Indeed, this argument of the State appears to rest primarily on the State's mistaken assumption, already noted, that the Amish do not provide any education for their children beyond the eighth grade, but allow them to grow in "ignorance." To the contrary, not only do the Amish accept the necessity for formal schooling through the eighth grade level, but continue to provide what has been characterized by the undisputed testimony of expert educators as an "ideal" vocational education for their children in the adolescent years. There is nothing in this record to suggest that the Amish qualities of reliability, self-reliance, and dedication to work would fail to find ready markets in today's society. Absent some contrary evidence supporting the State's position, we are unwilling to assume that persons possessing such valuable vocational skills and habits are doomed to become burdens on society should they determine to leave the Amish faith, nor is there any basis in the record to warrant a finding that an additional one or two years of formal school education beyond the eighth grade would serve to eliminate any such problem that might exist.

Insofar as the State's claim rests on the view that a brief additional period of formal education is imperative to enable the Amish to participate effectively and intelligently in our democratic process, it must fall. The Amish alternative to formal secondary school education has enabled them to function effectively in their day-to-day life under self-imposed limitations on relations with the world, and to survive and prosper in contemporary society as a separate, sharply identifiable and highly self-sufficient community for more than 200 years in this country. In itself this is strong evidence that they are capable of fulfilling the social and political responsibilities of citizenship without compelled attendance beyond the eighth grade at the price of jeopardizing their free exercise of religious belief. . . .

The requirement for compulsory education beyond the eighth grade is a relatively recent development in our history. Less than 60 years ago, the educational requirements of almost all of the States were satisfied by completion of the elementary grades, at least where the child was regularly and lawfully employed. The independence and successful social functioning of the Amish community for a period approaching almost three centuries and more than 200 years in this country are strong evidence that there is at best a speculative gain, in terms of meeting the duties of citizenship, from an additional one or two years of compulsory formal education. Against this background it would require a more particularized showing from the State on this point to justify the severe interference with religious freedom such additional compulsory attendance would entail.

IV

. . . The dissent argues that a child who expresses a desire to attend public high school in conflict with the wishes of his parents should not be prevented from doing so. There is no reason for the Court to consider that point since it is not an issue in the case. The children are not parties to this litigation. The State has at no point tried this case on the theory that respondents were preventing their children from attending school against their expressed desires, and indeed the record is to the contrary. . . .

Our holding in no way determines the proper resolution of possible competing interests of parents, children, and the State in an appropriate state court proceeding in which the power of the State is asserted on the theory that Amish parents are preventing their minor children from attending high school despite their expressed desires to the contrary. Recognition of the claim of the State in such a proceeding would, of course, call into question traditional concepts of parental control over the religious upbringing and education of their minor children recognized in this Court's past decisions. It is clear that such an intrusion by a State into family decisions in the area of religious training would give rise to grave questions of religious freedom comparable to those raised here and those presented in *Pierce*. On this record we neither reach nor decide those issues.

. . . The history and culture of Western civilization reflect a strong tradition of parental concern for the nurture and upbringing of their children. This primary role of the parents in the upbringing of their children is now established beyond debate as an enduring American tradition. . . .

[T]he Court's holding in *Pierce* stands as a charter of the rights of parents to direct the religious upbringing of their children. And, when the interests of parenthood are combined with a free exercise claim of the nature revealed by this record, more than merely a "reasonable relation to some purpose within the competency of the State" is required to sustain the validity of the State's requirement under the First Amendment. To be sure, the power of the parent, even when linked to a free exercise claim, may be subject to limitation . . . if it appears that parental decisions will jeopardize the health or safety of the child, or have a potential for significant social burdens. But in this case, the Amish have introduced persuasive evidence undermining the arguments the State has advanced to support its claims in terms of the welfare of the child and society as a whole. The record strongly indicates that accommodating the religious objections of the Amish by forgoing one, or at most two, additional years of compulsory education will not impair the physical or mental health of the child, or result in an inability to be self-supporting or to discharge the duties and responsibilities of citizenship, or in any other way materially detract from the welfare of society.

In the fact of our consistent emphasis on the central values underlying the Religion Clauses in our constitutional scheme of government, we cannot accept a parens patriae claim of such all-encompassing scope and with such sweeping potential for broad and unforeseeable application as that urged by the State.

V

. . . It cannot be overemphasized that we are not dealing with a way of life and mode of education by a group claiming to have recently discovered some "progressive" or more enlightened process for rearing children for modern life.

Aided by a history of three centuries as an identifiable religious sect and a long history as a successful and self-sufficient segment of American society, the Amish in this case have convincingly demonstrated the sincerity of their religious beliefs, the interrelationship of belief with their mode of life, the vital role that belief and daily conduct play in the continued survival of Old Order Amish communities and their religious organization, and the hazards presented by the State's enforcement of a statute generally valid as to others. Beyond this, they have carried the even more difficult burden of demonstrating the adequacy of their alternative mode of continuing informal vocational education in terms of precisely those overall interests that the State advances in support of its program of compulsory high school education. In light of this convincing showing, one that probably few other religious groups or sects could make, and weighing the minimal difference between what the State would require and what the Amish already accept, it was incumbent on the State to show with more particularity how its admittedly strong interest in compulsory education would be adversely affected by granting an exemption to the Amish. . . .

[In concurring, Justice Stewart, joined by Justice Brennan, emphasized that "[t]his case in no way involves any questions regarding the right of the children of Amish parents to attend public high schools, or any other institutions of learning, if they wish to do so."]

WHITE, J., with whom Justices Brennan and Stewart join, concurring.

This would be a very different case for me if respondents' claim were that their religion forbade their children from attending any school at any time and from complying in any way with the educational standards set by the State. . . .

It is possible that most Amish children will wish to continue living the rural life of their parents, in which case their training at home will adequately equip them for their future role. Others, however, may wish to become nuclear physicists, ballet dancers, computer programmers, or historians, and for these occupations, formal training will be necessary. There is evidence in the record that many children desert the Amish faith when they come of age. A State has a legitimate interest not only in seeking to develop the latent talents of its children but also in seeking to prepare them for the life style that they may later choose, or at least to provide them with an option other than the life they have led in the past. In the circumstances of this case, although the question is close, I am unable to say that the State has demonstrated that Amish children who leave school in the eighth grade will be intellectually stultified or unable to acquire new academic skills later. The statutory minimum school attendance age set by the State is, after all, only 16. . . . I join the Court because the sincerity of the Amish religious policy here is uncontested, because the potentially adverse impact of the state requirement is great, and because the State's valid interest in education has already been largely satisfied by the eight years the children have already spent in school.

DOUGLAS, J., dissenting in part.

I

[N]o analysis of religious-liberty claims can take place in a vacuum. If the parents in this case are allowed a religious exemption, the inevitable effect is to impose the parents' notions of religious duty upon their children. Where the child is mature enough to express potentially conflicting desires, it would be an invasion of the child's rights to permit such an imposition without canvassing his views. . . . [I]f an Amish child desires to attend high school, and is mature enough to have that desire respected, the State may well be able to override the parents' religiously motivated objections.

Religion is an individual experience. It is not necessary, nor even appropriate, for every Amish child to express his views on the subject in a prosecution of a single adult. Crucial, however, are the views of the child whose parent is the subject of the suit. Frieda Yoder has in fact testified that her own religious views are opposed to high-school education. I therefore join the judgment of the Court as to respondent Jonas Yoder. But Frieda Yoder's views may not be those of Vernon Yutzy or Barbara Miller. I must dissent, therefore, as to respondents Adin Yutzy and Wallace Miller as their motion to dismiss also raised the question of their children's religious liberty.

II

This issue has never been squarely presented before today. Our opinions are full of talk about the power of the parents over the child's education. See *Pierce*; Meyer v. Nebraska, 262 U.S. 390. And we have in the past analyzed similar conflicts between parent and State with little regard for the views of the child. Recent cases, however, have clearly held that the children themselves have constitutionally protectible interests. . . .

[T]he education of the child is a matter on which the child will often have decided views. He may want to be a pianist or an astronaut or an oceanographer. To do so he will have to break from the Amish tradition.

It is the future of the student, not the future of the parents, that is imperiled by today's decision. If a parent keeps his child out of school beyond the grade school, then the child will be forever barred from entry into the new and amazing world of diversity that we have today. . . . It is the student's judgment, not his parents', that is essential if we are to give full meaning to what we have said about the Bill of Rights and of the right of students to be masters of their own destiny. If he is harnessed to the Amish way of life by those in authority over him and if his education is truncated, his entire life may be stunted and deformed. The child, therefore, should be given an opportunity to be heard before the State gives the exemption which we honor today.

III

. . . The Court rightly rejects the notion that actions, even though religiously grounded, are always outside the protection of the Free Exercise Clause of the First Amendment. In so ruling, the Court departs from the teaching of Reynolds v. United States, 98 U.S. 145, 164. . . . What we do today, at least in this respect, opens the way to give organized religion a broader base than it has ever enjoyed; and it even promises that in time *Reynolds* will be overruled.

In another way, however, the Court retreats when in reference to Henry Thoreau it says his "choice was philosophical and personal rather than religious, and such belief does not rise to the demands of the Religion Clauses." That is contrary to what we held in United States v. Seeger, 380 U.S. 163, where we were concerned with the meaning of the words "religious training and belief" in the Selective Service Act, which were the basis of many conscientious objector claims. We said:

> Within that phrase would come all sincere religious beliefs which are based upon a power or being, or upon a faith, to which all else is subordinate or upon which all else is ultimately dependent. The test might be stated in these words: A sincere and meaningful belief which occupies in the life of its possessor a place parallel to that filled by the God of those admittedly qualifying for the exemption comes within the statutory definition. This construction avoids imputing to Congress an intent to classify different religious beliefs, exempting some and excluding others, and is in accord with the well-established congressional policy of equal treatment for those whose opposition to service is grounded in their religious tenets.

Discussion

1. *Individual and community.* Justice Jackson described *Barnette* as a case concerning the conflict "between authority and rights of the individual." Justice Douglas in *Yoder* refers to religion as an "individual experience." With respect to the subjects of litigation in these cases, the Barnettes and Yoders probably would have described themselves, not as individuals, but as members of a religious community sworn to accept the authority of a sovereign other than the State. Is this sociological fact relevant to their constitutional claim? Should the First Amendment treat a member of a small (even one-person) idiosyncratic sect differently from the members of a larger, traditional one?

2. *The child as contested territory between parent and state.* Justice Douglas thought that the teen-age Amish children's own educational preferences should have been honored if they had conflicted with those of their parents and, thus, of the Amish community in general. To the extent that you are sympathetic with this argument, does it derive from general support of the rights of children to make their own decisions or from something more specific to the issues surrounding education? Consider in this context, for example, the debate, noted briefly in Chapter 9 above, concerning the duty of teen-age women to notify their parent(s) if they wish to get an abortion.

In any event, it is unlikely that Justice Douglas or most other judges or theorists would accord the same degree of autonomy to seven-year-olds. Rather, the debate most often concerns who, as between the parents and the state, will exercise control over the child and shape her future.

Professor Amy Gutmann writes that education concerns "what might be called 'conscious social reproduction,' " i.e., the recreation of the central values and behaviors of the group in question — family, religious sect, political community — in the next generation. Debates about the control of such reproduction go back at least as far as Plato's Republic and extend up to the present day. Gutmann contrasts a model of the "family state" with the "state of families."[29]

> The defining feature of the family state is that it claims exclusive educational authority as a means of establishing a harmony — one might say, a constitutive relation — between individual and social good based on knowledge [of the good]. Defenders of the family state expect to create a level of like-mindedness and camaraderie among citizens that most of us expect to find only within families (and now perhaps not even there). . . . Citizens of a well-ordered family state learn that they cannot re-

29. Amy Gutmann, Democratic Education 14 (1987).

alize their own good except by contributing to the social good, and they are also educated to desire only what is good for themselves and their society.[30]

By contrast, "[t]he state of families places educational authority exclusively in the hands of parents, thereby permitting parents to predispose their children, through education, to choose a way of life consistent with their familial heritage."

There are problems with each conception. The first is radically antipluralistic, while the second seems to negate the meaningfulness of a shared social life that goes beyond the enclosure of the family or sect. Does it really raise the specter of totalitarianism, for example, for the state to require that the education of the young lead to their self-perception as members of an American political community sharing some common heritage and reponsibility for the future? Can one develop any helpful generalizations about how these tensions are to be resolved? Can one do any better than say that the Constitution requires some balancing between the two conceptions and recognition of both their positive and negative aspects?

Consider the claim of Vicki Frost, who objected that her children be required to read certain books as part of their Tennessee public education. Mozert v. Hawkins County Board of Education, 827 F.2d 1058 (6th Cir. 1987). A born-again Christian, Frost did not object to Tennessee's right to assign books *per se*, but argued that her children should be given alternative assignments when assigned books that offended their religious values. She specifically objected, for example, to any stories that suggested tolerating "all religions [as] merely different roads to God." The Court of Appeals for the Sixth Circuit rejected Ms. Frost's constitutional claim: Pupils are not exempt from confrontation with offensive ideas so long as they are not compelled "to affirm or deny a religious belief or to engage or refrain from engaging in a practice forbidden or required in the exercise of a plaintiff's religion." The court rejected the claim that "[i]t is a violation of the religious beliefs and convictions of the plaintiff students to be required to read the books and a violation of the religious beliefs of the plaintiff parents to permit their children to read the books."

3. *Substantiality of state interests.* To "balance" obviously requires an assessment of interests. Both Justice Jackson in *Barnette* and Chief Justice Burger in *Yoder* seem to denigrate the substantiality of the asserted state interest. It seems clear that Justice Jackson views the flag salute as in fact a trivial activity with no ascertainable importance in instilling a sense of community membership. Similarly, both Chief Justice Burger and Justice White, in his concurrence, emphasize the relative insignificance of the two additional years of required schooling beyond what the Amish were willing to provide their children.

The Court of Appeals in *Mozert* noted that Tennessee law specifically prohibits "regulating the selection or faculty or textbooks or the establishment of a curriculum in church-related schools." Ms. Frost could thus have escaped state regulation entirely by sending her children to a church school. Does the exemption of private church schools undercut Tennessee's argument that it has a "compelling interest" in requiring students to read all assigned materials in the public schools?

30. Id. at 22-33.

E. Pluralism and Private Education

Justice Frankfurter in *Barnette* and, the Court of Appeals in *Mozert* emphasized the availability of private or sectarian schools as an alternative to public education. Is the state constitutionally required to permit such schools, however, and what limits, if any, does the Constitution impose on the state's power to prescribe their curricula and other practices?

The Supreme Court confronted the first question in Pierce v. Society of Sisters, 268 U.S. 510 (1925), page 944 supra, which arose out of a popular initiative, passed in Oregon in 1922, requiring that children be educated only in public schools. David Tyack describes the initiative's background:[31]

> [In 1922, the King Kleagle of the Ku Klux Klan] and his hooded colleagues helped persuade the citizens of Oregon to pass an initiative requiring all children between eight and 16 to attend public schools and essentially outlawing private elementary schools. . . .
>
> Grotesque though it may be to imagine the KKK as defender of the common school and liberty, the Oregon experiment with compulsion was not a lonely aberration but a cresting of social attitudes and political currents that had flowed and ebbed in the past. . . . [T]he Oregon events present in bold outline a widespread American fear of diversity and an impulse to coerce uniformity through public schooling. . . .
>
> Anti-Catholic, anti-immigrant, anti-elite, and anti-intellectual attitudes were hardly new. But in the early 1920s in Oregon the KKK and their allies in the school fight found that many citizens were responsive to their peculiar mixture of fear, paranoia, nostalgia, and hope. This hope was in some ways the most traditional and yet puzzling part of the story. The Klan taught the inherent superiority of [white Anglo-Saxon Protestants] and the inferiority of aliens, blacks, Catholics, and Jews, and yet it somehow persuaded itself that to force all children to attend public schools together would avert the ruin of the republic. . . . [T]he common school could produce social solidarity by mixing all ethnic groups. . . .
>
> The provisions of the Oregon initiative were Draconian: if a parent did not send children to public schools between the ages of eight and 16, they were subject to fines for each day of delinquency and to jail terms of not less than two days.
>
> . . . A defender of the initiative . . . declare[d] that "young children in private schools have no defense against any private ideas antagonistic to our free institutions. We cannot afford to run this risk any longer, and we positively know that traitors are now at this deadly task." . . .
>
> In 1920 the state had only 13 percent foreign-born inhabitants (one-half of them naturalized), only 0.3 percent blacks, only about 8 percent Catholics. . . . Only 7 percent of elementary pupils attended private schools and the ratio was dropping fast. . . .
>
> Why, then, Oregon? Perhaps it was because Oregon did approximate the ideal WASP society that partisans like the Klansmen chose it as a test case for compulsory public education: there were so many of US and so few of THEM. A similar plan had failed in Michigan, but if the Oregon campaign proved successful, a dozen other states were next in line.

31. Compulsory Public Schooling and the Perils of Pluralism: The Case of Oregon, 1922, in David Tyack, Thomas James, and Aaron Benavot, Law and the Shaping of Public Education, 1785-1954, 177-192 (1987). See also Clement E. Vose, Constitutional Change: Amendment Politics and Supreme Court Litigation Since 1900, 139-160 (1972) (chapter on The Catholic School Issue).

In *Pierce*, the Society of the Sisters of the Holy Names of Jesus and Mary and the Hill Military Academy each sued, challenging the initiative on constititutional grounds. The State's brief defended the law on the ground that "the great danger overshadowing all others which confront the American people is the danger of class hatred. . . . [We] don't know any better way to fortify the next generation against that insidious poison than to require that the poor and the rich, the people of all classes and distinction, and of all different religious beliefs, shall meet in the common schools, which are the great American melting pot, there to become . . . the typical American of the future." The Supreme Court unanimously struck down the law.

The Court had first addressed the question of government control over the curriculum of private schools shortly before *Pierce* in Meyer v. Nebraska, 262 U.S. 390 (1923), page 944 supra. Sparked by World War I and the desire to distance "true Americans" from the hated German culture, Nebraska had passed a law prohibiting teaching a foreign language to any child not yet in the eighth grade. With Justices Holmes and Sutherland dissenting, the Supreme Court held the law unconstitutional.

In a 1925 article, Can the Supreme Court Guarantee Toleration?,[32] Professor Felix Frankfurter criticized *Meyers* and *Pierce* as exemplifying the Court's willingness to stifle "social experiments" that it disliked. Although he described these two particular cases as "just cause for rejoicing," they nonetheless followed from the spirit of *Lochner*, and the country would be better served, overall, by rejecting that spirit.

Although the two cases are often cited today in a jurisprudential culture that has rejected their "freedom of contract" overtones, their meaning and justification remain controversial. In his *Yoder* concurrence, for example, Justice White took issue with Chief Justice Burger's seeming reliance on *Pierce* to support plenary parental authority over the education of their children:

> *Pierce* lends no support to the contention that parents may replace state educational requirements with their own idiosyncratic views of what knowledge a child needs to be a productive and happy member of society; in *Pierce*, both the parochial and military schools were in compliance with all the educational standards that the State had set, and the Court held simply that while a State may posit such standards, it may not pre-empt the educational process by requiring children to attend public schools. . . .

In fact, state regulation of private education is pervasive.

> Most states prescribe a core curriculum for private schools that seeks to satisfy the compulsory education requirements. These begin with the usual litany of reading, writing, spelling, arithmetic, and American history, but in some states the core includes instruction in patriotism or good citizenship. . . . About a dozen states require that teachers in private schools be certified.[33]

32. Felix Frankfurter, Can the Supreme Court Guarantee Toleration?, The New Republic, June 17, 1925, reprinted in Philip Kurland, ed., Felix Frankfurter on the Supreme Court: Extrajudicial Essays on the Court and the Constitution 174-178 (1970).

33. Mark Yudof et al., Kirp & Yudof's Educational Policy and the Law 45-46 (2d ed. 1982).

The recent growth of schools organized by members of fundamentalist Christian groups has resulted in contemporary litigation about the scope of state regulation of private schools. In Ohio v. Whisner, 47 Ohio St. 2d 181, 351 N.E.2d 750 (1976), for example, organizers of the Christian Tabernacle School objected to the imposition of Ohio's "minimum standards" on their school, arguing that various aspects of these standards violated their religious rights. The Ohio Supreme Court held for the complainants, observing that

> the state retains the power to regulate the . . . content of the curriculum that is taught, the manner in which it is taught, the person or persons who teach it, the physical layout of the building in which the students are taught, the hours of instruction, and the educational policies intended to be achieved through the instruction offered. . . . [T]he effect . . . is to obliterate the 'philosophy' of the school and impose that of the state. . . .

Over a decade later in New York the question arose whether the state could require nonpublic school education to be "substantially equivalent" to public school education. In Blackwelder v. Safnauer, 689 F. Supp. 106 (N.D.N.Y. 1988), religious parents educating their children at home objected to officials' on-site visits to verify that the home education met state standards. The district judge held against the parents, distinguishing *Yoder* by emphasizing the Supreme Court's assumption

> that the Amish children were to be provided training designed to prepare them for life in an agrarian community separated from the outside world. In contrast, the children here will be required to live and work in modern society upon reaching the age of maturity. . . . *Yoder* must be limited to its unique facts. . . . Unless the child is a member of an identifiable religious sect with a long history of maintaining a successful community separate and apart from American society in general, it must be assumed that the child must be intellectually, socially, and psychologically prepared to interact with others who may not share the views of the parents.

May the state require that all schools, private or public, teach an American history course designed to make students aware of their membership in specifically American social, political, and cultural communities? Michigan requires that private educators select "textbooks that recognize the accomplishments of ethnic and racial groups."[34] May this requirement be imposed on a parochial schools whose religious tenets include the inferiority of particular racial groups?

F. Religious Pluralism, Education, Unemployment, and Peyote

The decisions in *Meyer* and *Pierce* did not turn on the *religious* claims of the private schools involved. Indeed, the complainant in the former case and one of those in the latter were not religious schools. Do some of the subsequent cases suggest a departure from *Reynolds*, establishing a religiously based constitutional exemption from the operation of at least some laws? Compare Justice Douglas in *Yoder*

34. Id.

with Justice Douglas in *Cleveland*, which blandly followed *Reynolds* and its progeny.[35]

In several cases, beginning with Sherbert v. Verner, 374 U.S. 203 (1963), the Court considered the states' authority to deny unemployment compensation to people whose religious beliefs forbade them to comply with conditions imposed on claimants generally. Sherbert, a member of the Seventh Day Adventist Church, had been discharged from her job in a South Carolina textile plant because of her unwillingness to work on Saturday, her Sabbath day. South Carolina required persons claiming unemployment compensation to be "available for work," though the law provided that "no employee shall be required to work on Sunday . . . who is conscientiously opposed to Sunday work." Upon South Carolina's refusal to pay Sherbert unemployment compensation, she sued, claiming denial of her constitutional rights. Although the Court might well have treated this as a distinctly non-neutral preference for Christians who celebrate Sunday as the Sabbath, the majority, per Justice Brennan, took a more substantive position, emphasizing that only state interests "of the highest order" could justify the state's refusing to honor a claimant's religious duty not to work on her Sabbath.

Later, in Thomas v. Review Board of the Indiana Employment Security Division, 450 U.S. 707 (1981), Indiana was ordered to pay unemployment compensation to a Jehovah's Witness who had voluntarily left his job in a defense plant because the military nature of the work violated his conscience. The Court deemed it irrelevant that other Witnesses chose to continue working at the plant. Individual conscience, rather than denominational requirements, seemed to triumph in this particular case. The Court followed *Thomas* in Hobbie v. Unemployment Appeals Court of Florida, 480 U.S. 136 (1987), where the Adventist complainant was discharged from her job in a jewelry store because she would not work on Saturday. Justice Brennan wrote that the claimants in these three cases could not be "forced to choose between fidelity to religious belief and continued employment; the forfeiture of unemployment benefits for choosing the former over the latter brings unlawful coercion to bear on the employee's choice."

The Court was not sympathetic to religious-based claims for exemptions in other contexts, however. Gillette v. United States, 401 U.S. 437 (1971), refused to grant conscientious objector status to a Catholic who believed the Vietnam War "unjust" for religious reasons but who was not a complete pacifist, as required by federal law. United States v. Lee, 455 U.S. 252 (1982), rejected the plea by Amish employers to be exempt from paying social security taxes on their Amish employees. "The Court found the Social Security tax indistinguishable from any other tax and found the government interest in collecting its revenues to be compelling. The Court used the example of war tax resisters to illustrate how unworkable it would be to let people refuse to pay taxes for programs to which they had religiously motivated objection."[36]

Religious claimants also lost in Bob Jones University v. United States, 461 U.S. 574 (1983), and Goldman v. Weinberger, 475 U.S. 503 (1986). The first case upheld the Internal Revenue Service's denial of a tax exemption on the ground that

35. See Lucas A. Powe, Evolution to Absolutism, 74 Colum. L. Rev. 371 (1974).

36. See Laycock, A Survey of Religious Liberty in the United States, 47 Ohio St. L.J. 427-431 (1986), from which the comments below are taken.

the University's religiously based commitment to racial separation was contrary to public policy. Chief Justice Burger wrote: "Denial of tax benefits will inevitably have a substantial impact on the operation of private religious schools, but will not prevent those schools from observing their religious tenets." Moreover, the government had a compelling interest, in "eradicating racial discrimination in education."[37] In *Goldman,* a sharply divided Court refused to invalidate military rules that prevented an Orthodox Jewish officer from wearing his yarmulke along with his regular uniform. The Court emphasized the need to defer to the military's asserted need for uniformity of dress.

Douglas Laycock argues that the decisions in this area are inconsistent. He acknowledges that some of them can be reconciled by saying that the state's interest "in raising armies in *Gillette,* in collecting taxes in *Lee,* and in racial integration in *Bob Jones,* are more compelling than its interest in preserving unemployment compensation funds or forcing Amish children to get two more years of formal education."

> But that formulation conceals a deeper difference in the cases. The Court has defined the government interests at inconsistent levels of generality.
>
> The state interest in educating children is surely compelling, but that is not how the Court posed the question in *Yoder.* Rather, it assessed the state's interest in requiring ninth and tenth grade for Amish children who would reside in an agricultural community that eschewed modern technology and trained its own youth in skills important to that community. The comparable formulation in *Bob Jones* would not be the interest in eliminating racial discrimination in education, but rather the interest in protecting interracial dating among students at a small, private, and pervasively religious school that restricted student conduct in many other ways. The comparable formulation in *Lee* would not be the interest in collecting taxes, but the interest in collecting taxes for Amish employees of Amish employers, all of whom lived in a tight-knit community that, as a matter of religious belief, took care of its own needy members. A broad or narrow formulation of the governmental interest virtually determines the result.

Professors Mayer Freed and Daniel Polsby[38] argue that recognizing rights of religious conscience in *Gillette, Lee,* and *Bob Jones* would invite significant numbers of questionable claims from persons fearing combat, wishing to minimize their taxes, or detesting racial minorities. Unless a court accepted all claims of religious conscience without examination, one would have to devise ways, themselves raising profound constitutional questions, of distinguishing genuinely religiously motivated persons from opportunistic frauds. The scholars argue that cases upholding religious claims are distinguishable: In the unemployment compensation cases, the claimants, after all, had given up their jobs, and *Yoder* rejected a free public education for his children. Few besides the sincerely religious would be likely to test the state's generosity, at least in the absence of a lavish unemployment compensation scheme.

37. For a suggestion that the decision in *Bob Jones* was mistaken, see Douglas Laycock, Tax Exemptions for Racially Discriminatory Schools, 60 Tex. L. Rev. 259 (1982). See also Robert Cover, The Supreme Court 1982 Term, Foreword, *Nomos* and Narrative, 97 Harv. L. Rev. 4, 62-67 (1983).

38. Mayer Freed and Daniel Polsby, Race, Religion, and Public Policy: Bob Jones University v. United States, 1983 Sup. Ct. Rev. 1.

Consider the results, and rationales, of all of these decisions in light of the following 1990 decision by the Supreme Court.

EMPLOYMENT DIVISION, DEPARTMENT OF HUMAN RESOURCES OF OREGON v. SMITH

110 S. Ct. 1595 (1990)

Certiorari to the Oregon Supreme Court

[Alfred Smith and Galen Black, both members of the Native American Church, were employed by a private drug rehabilitation organization, which fired them because they had ingested peyote, an hallucinogenic drug, during religious services off the premises. When they applied to the Employment Division of the Department of Human Resources of Oregon for unemployment compensation, they were held ineligible for benefits because they had been discharged for work-related misconduct. In the ensuing litigation, the Oregon Supreme Court held that state criminal law prohibited the possession or ingestion of peyote, with no exception for the sacramental use of the drug. (Prescription for medical use is exempted.) The court went on, however, to hold that the failure to exempt sacramental use violated the free exercise clause; thus, denying unemployment compensation in these circumstances unconstitutionally burdened Smith's and Black's religious practices. The Supreme Court reversed.]

SCALIA, J., delivered the opinion of the Court.

This case requires us to decide whether the Free Exercise Clause of the First Amendment permits the State of Oregon to include religiously inspired peyote use within the reach of its general prohibition on use of that drug, and thus permits the State to deny unemployment benefits to persons dismissed from their jobs because of such religiously inspired use. . . .

II

Respondents' claim for relief rests on our decisions in Sherbert v. Verner, Thomas v. Review Board, and Hobbie v. Unemployment Appeals Commission of Florida, in which we held that a State could not condition the availability of unemployment insurance on an individual's willingness to forgo conduct required by his religion. . . . [H]owever, the conduct at issue in those cases was not prohibited by law. . . . [T]he Oregon Supreme Court has confirmed that Oregon does prohibit the religious use of peyote, [and] we proceed to consider whether that prohibition is permissible under the Free Exercise Clause.

A

. . . The free exercise of religion means, first and foremost, the right to believe and profess whatever religious doctrine one desires. . . .

But the "exercise of religion" often involves not only belief and profession but the performance of (or abstention from) physical acts. . . . It would be true, we think (though no case of ours has involved the point) that a state would be "prohibiting the free exercise [of religion]" if it sought to ban such acts or abstentions only when they are engaged in for religious reasons, or only because of the religious belief that they display. It would doubtless be unconstitutional, for example, to ban the casting of "statues that are to be used for worship purposes," or to prohibit bowing down before a golden calf.

Respondents in the present case, however, seek to carry the meaning of "prohibiting the free exercise [of religion]" one large step further. They contend that their religious motivation for using peyote places them beyond the reach of a criminal law that is not specifically directed at their religious practice, and that is concededly constitutional as applied to those who use the drug for other reasons. They assert, in other words, that "prohibiting the free exercise [of religion]" includes requiring any individual to observe a generally applicable law that requires (or forbids) the performance of an act that his religious belief forbids (or requires). As a textual matter, we do not think the words must be given that meaning. It is no more necessary to regard the collection of a general tax, for example, as "prohibiting the free exercise [of religion]" by those citizens who believe support of organized government to be sinful, than it is to regard the same tax as "abridging the freedom . . . of the press" of those publishing companies that must pay the tax as a condition of staying in business. It is a permissible reading of the text, in the one case as in the other, to say that if prohibiting the exercise of religion (or burdening the activity of printing) is not the object of the tax but merely the incidental effect of a generally applicable and otherwise valid provision, the First Amendment has not been offended. . . .

Our decisions reveal that the latter reading is the correct one. We have never held that an individual's religious beliefs excuse him from compliance with an otherwise valid law prohibiting conduct that the State is free to regulate. [Quotations from *Gobitis, Reynolds,* and *Prince* are omitted.] . . .

The only decisions in which we have held that the First Amendment bars application of a neutral, generally applicable law to religiously motivated action have involved not the Free Exercise Clause alone, but the Free Exercise Clause in conjunction with other constitutional protections, such as freedom of speech and of the press, see Cantwell v. Connecticut, 310 U.S. 296 (1940) (invalidating a licensing system for religious and charitable solicitations under which the administrator had discretion to deny a license to any cause he deemed nonreligious); Murdock v. Pennsylvania, 319 U.S. 105 (1943) (invalidating a flat tax on solicitation as applied to the dissemination of religious ideas); Follett v. McCormick, 321 U.S. 573 (1944)(same); or the right of parents, acknowledged in Pierce v. Society of Sisters, 268 U.S. 510 (1925), to direct the education of their children, see Wisconsin v. Yoder, 406 U.S. 205 (1972). . . .

The present case does not present such a hybrid situation, but a free exercise claim unconnected with any communicative activity or parental right. Respondents urge us to hold, quite simply, that when otherwise prohibitable conduct is accompanied by religious convictions, not only the convictions but the conduct itself must be free from governmental regulation. We have never held that, and decline to do so now. There being no contention that Oregon's drug law represents an attempt to regulate religious beliefs, the communication of religious beliefs, or the raising of one's children in those beliefs, the rule to which we have adhered ever since *Reynolds* plainly controls. . . .

B

Respondents argue that even though exemption from generally applicable criminal laws need not automatically be extended to religiously motivated actors, at least the claim for a religious exemption must be evaluated under the balancing test set forth in Sherbert v. Verner, 374 U.S. 398 (1963). Under the *Sherbert* test, governmental actions that substantially burden a religious practice must be justified by a compelling governmental interest.

Applying that test we have, on three occasions, invalidated state unemployment compensation rules that conditioned the availability of benefits upon an applicant's willingness to work under conditions forbidden by his religion. We have never invalidated any governmental action on the basis of the *Sherbert* test except the denial of unemployment compensation. . . . In recent years we have abstained from applying the *Sherbert* test (outside the unemployment compensation field) at all. In Bowen v. Roy, 476 U.S. 693 (1986), we declined to apply *Sherbert* analysis to a federal statutory scheme that required benefit recipients to provide their Social Security numbers. The plaintiffs in that case asserted that it would violate their religious beliefs to obtain and provide a Social Security number for their daughter. We held the statute's application to the plaintiffs valid regardless of whether it was necessary to effectuate a compelling interest. In Lyng v. Northwest Indian Cemetery Protective Association, 485 U.S. 439 (1988), we declined to apply *Sherbert* analysis to the Government's logging and road construction activities on lands used for religious purposes by several Native American Tribes, even though it was undisputed that the activities "could have devastating effects on traditional Indian religious practices." In Goldman v. Weinberger, 475 U.S. 503 (1986), we rejected application of the *Sherbert* test to military dress regulations that forbade the wearing of yarmulkes. In O'Lone v. Estate of Shabazz, 482 U.S. 342 (1987), we sustained, without mentioning the *Sherbert* test, a prison's refusal to excuse inmates from work requirements to attend worship services.

Even if we were inclined to breathe into *Sherbert* some life beyond the unemployment compensation field, we would not apply it to require exemptions from a generally applicable criminal law. The *Sherbert* test, it must be recalled, was developed in a context that lent itself to individualized governmental assessment of the reasons for the relevant conduct. . . . As the plurality pointed out in *Roy*, our decisions in the unemployment cases stand for the proposition that where the State has in place a system of individual exemptions, it may not refuse to extend that system to cases of "religious hardship" without compelling reason.

Whether or not the decisions are that limited, they at least have nothing to do with an across-the-board criminal prohibition on a particular form of conduct. . . . We conclude today that . . . the approach in accord with the vast majority of our precedents, is to hold the test inapplicable to such challenges. The government's ability to enforce generally applicable prohibitions of socially harmful conduct, like its ability to carry out other aspects of public policy, "cannot depend on measuring the effects of a governmental action on a religious objector's spiritual development." *Lyng*. To make an individual's obligation to obey such a law contingent upon the law's coincidence with his religious beliefs, except where the State's interest is "compelling" — permitting him, by virtue of his beliefs, "to become a law unto himself," *Reynolds* — contradicts both constitutional tradition and common sense.

The "compelling government interest" requirement seems benign, because it is familiar from other fields. But using it as the standard that must be met before the government may accord different treatment on the basis of race or before the government may regulate the content of speech is not remotely comparable to using it for the purpose asserted here. What it produces in those other fields — equality of treatment, and an unrestricted flow of contending speech — are constitutional norms; what it would produce here — a private right to ignore generally applicable laws — is a constitutional anomaly.

Nor is it possible to limit the impact of respondents' proposal by requiring a "compelling state interest" only when the conduct prohibited is "central" to the individual's religion. It is no more appropriate for judges to determine the "centrality" of religious beliefs before applying a "compelling interest" test in the free exercise field, than it would be for them to determine the "importance" of ideas before applying the "compelling interest" test in the free speech field. What principle of law or logic can be brought to bear to contradict a believer's assurance that a particular act is "central" to his personal faith? . . . Repeatedly and in many different contexts, we have warned that courts must not presume to determine the place of a particular belief in a religion or the plausibility of a religious claim.

If the "compelling interest" test is to be applied at all, then, it must be applied across the board, to all actions thought to be religiously commanded. . . . Any society adopting such a system would be courting anarchy, but that danger increases in direct proportion to the society's diversity of religious beliefs, and its determination to coerce or suppress none of them. . . . [W]e cannot afford the luxury of deeming *presumptively invalid*, as applied to the religious objector, every regulation of conduct that does not protect an interest of the highest order. The rule respondents favor would open the prospect of constitutionally required religious exemptions from civic obligations of almost every conceivable kind — ranging from compulsory military service, see, e.g., Gillette v. U.S., 401 U.S. 437 (1971), to the payment of taxes, see, e.g., U.S. v. Lee, 455 U.S. 252 (1982); to health and safety regulation such as manslaughter and child neglect laws, see, e.g., Funkhouse v. State, 763 P.2d 695 (Okla. Crim. App. 1988), compulsory vaccination laws, see, e.g., Cude v. State, 237 Ark. 927, 377 S.W.2d 816 (1964), drug laws, see, e.g., Olsen v. Drug Enforcement Administration, 878 F.2d 1458 (1989), and traffic laws, see Cox v. New Hampshire, 312 U.S. 569 (1941); to social welfare legislation such as minimum wage laws, see Susan and Tony Alamo Foundation v. Secretary of Labor, 471 U.S. 290 (1985), child labor laws, see Prince v. Mass., 321 U.S. 158 (1944), animal cruelty laws, see, e.g., Church of the Lukumi Babalu Aye Inc. v. City of Hialeah, 723 F. Supp. 1467 (S.D. Fla. 1989), environmental protection laws, see U.S. v. Little, 638 F. Supp. 337 (Mont. 1986), and laws providing for equality of opportunity for the races, see, e.g., Bob Jones University v. U.S., 461 U.S. 574 (1983). The First Amendment's protection of religious liberty does not require this

Values that are protected against government interference through enshrinement in the Bill of Rights are not thereby banished from the political process. Just as a society that believes in the negative protection accorded to the press by the First Amendment is likely to enact laws that affirmatively foster the dissemination of the printed word, so also a society that believes in the negative protection accorded to religious belief can be expected to be solicitous of that value in its legislation as well. It is therefore not surprising that a number of States have made an exception to their drug laws for sacramental peyote use. [Justice Scalia cites statutes from Arizona, Colorado, and New Mexico. In her concurring opinion, Justice O'Connor indicates that at least eleven states have such statutes; and Justice Blackmun, in his dissent, suggests that a dozen other states have achieved the same outcome through judicial construction of statutes.] But to say that a nondiscriminatory religious-practice exemption is permitted, or even that it is desirable, is not to say that it is constructively required, and that the appropriate occasions for its creation can be licensed by the courts. It may fairly be said that leaving accommodation to the political process will place at a relative disadvantage those religious practices that are not widely engaged in, but that unavoidable consequence of democratic government must be preferred to a system in which each conscience is a law unto itself or in which judges weight the social importance of all laws against the centrality of religious beliefs.

Because respondents' ingestion of peyote was prohibited under Oregon law, and because that prohibition is constitutional, Oregon may, consistent with the Free Exercise Clause, deny respondents unemployment compensation when their dismissal results from use of the drug. . . .

O'CONNOR, J., concurring in the judgment (joined, in part II by Justices Brennan, Marshall, and Blackmun). . . .

II

The Court today extracts from our long history of free exercise precedents the single categorical rule that "if prohibiting the exercise of religion . . . is . . . merely the incidental effect of a generally applicable and otherwise valid provision, the First Amendment has not been offended." Indeed, the Court holds that where the law is a generally applicable criminal prohibition, our usual free exercise jurisprudence does not even apply. To reach this sweeping result, however, the Court must not only give a strained reading of the First Amendment but must also disregard our consistent application of free exercise doctrine to cases involving generally applicable regulations that burden religious conduct.

A

. . . [T]he "free *exercise*" of religion often, if not invariably, requires the performance of (or abstention from) certain acts. . . . "[B]elief and action cannot be neatly confined in logic-tight compartments." *Yoder*. Because the First Amendment does not distinguish between religious belief and religious conduct, conduct motivated by sincere religious belief, like the belief itself, must therefore be at least presumptively protected by the Free Exercise Clause. . . . A person who is barred from engaging in religious motivated conduct is barred from freely exercising his religion. . . .

The Court responds that generally applicable laws are "one large step" removed from laws aimed at specific religious practices. The First Amendment, however, does not distinguish between laws that are generally applicable and laws that target particular religious practices. Indeed, few States would be so naive as to enact a law directly prohibiting or burdening a religious practice as such. Our free exercise cases have all concerned generally applicable laws that had the effect of significantly burdening a religious practice. If the First Amendment is to have any vitality, it ought not be construed to cover only the extreme and hypothetical situation in which a State directly targets a religious practice. . . .

To say that a person's right to free exercise has been burdened, of course, does not mean that he has an absolute right to engage in the conduct. . . . Instead, we have respected both the First Amendment's express textual mandate and the governmental interest in regulation of conduct by requiring the Government to justify any substantial burden on religiously motivated conduct by a compelling state interest and by means narrowly tailored to achieve that interest. . . .

The Court endeavors to escape from our decisions in *Cantwell* and *Yoder* by labeling them "hybrid" decisions, but there is no denying that both cases expressly relied on the Free Exercise Clause and that we have consistently regarded these cases as part of the mainstream of our free exercise jurisprudence. Moreover, in each of the other cases cited by the Court to support its categorical rule, we rejected the particular constitutional claims before us only after carefully weighing the competing interests. . . . That we rejected the free exercise claims in those cases hardly calls into question the applicability of the First Amendment doctrine in the first place. . . .

B

Respondents, of course, do not contend that their conduct is automatically immune from all governmental regulation simply because it is motivated by their sincere religious beliefs. . . . Rather, respondents invoke our traditional compelling interest test to argue that the Free Exercise Clause requires the State to grant them a limited exemption from its general criminal prohibition against the possession of peyote. The Court today, however, denies them even the opportunity to make that argument. . . .

In my view, however, the essence of a free exercise claim is relief from a burden imposed by government on religious practices or beliefs, whether the burden is imposed directly through laws that prohibit or compel religious practices, or indirectly through laws that, in effect, make abandonment of one's own religion or conformity to the religious beliefs of others the price of an equal place in the civil community. . . .

Indeed, we have never distinguished between cases in which a State conditions receipt of a benefit on conduct prohibited by religious beliefs and cases in which a State affirmatively prohibits such conduct. . . . [A] neutral criminal law prohibiting conduct that a State may legitimately regulate is, if anything, *more* burdensome than a neutral civil statute placing legitimate conditions on the award of a state benefit.

. . . Once it has been shown that a government regulation or criminal prohibition burdens the free exercise of religions, we have consistently asked the Government to demonstrate that unbending application of its regulation to the religious objector "is essential to accomplish an overriding governmental interest," or represents "the least restrictive means of achieving some compelling state interest." To me, the sounder approach — the approach more consistent with our role as judges to decide each case on its individual merits — is to apply this test in each case to determine whether the burden on the specific plaintiffs before us is constitutionally significant and whether the particular criminal interest asserted by the State before us is compelling. Even if, as an empirical matter, a government's criminal laws might usually serve a compelling interest in health, safety, or public order, the First Amendment at least requires a case-by-case determination of the question, sensitive to the facts of each particular claim. Given the range of conduct that a State might legitimately make criminal, we cannot assume, merely because a law carries criminal sanctions and is generally applicable, that the First Amendment *never* requires the State to grant a limited exemption for religiously motivated conduct.

. . . The Court today gives no convincing reason to depart from settled First Amendment jurisprudence. . . . As the language of the [Free Exercise] Clause itself makes clear, an individual's free exercise of religion is a preferred constitutional activity. A law that makes criminal such an activity therefore triggers constitutional concern — and heightened judicial scrutiny — even if it does not target the particular religious conduct at issue. . . .

[T]he Court today suggests that the disfavoring of minority religions is an "unavoidable consequence" under our system of government and that accommodation of such religions must be left to the political process. In my view, however, the First Amendment was enacted precisely to protect the rights of those whose religious practices are not shared by the majority and may be viewed with hostility. The history of our free exercise doctrine amply demonstrates the harsh impact majoritarian rule has had on unpopular or emerging religious groups. . . . The compelling interest test reflects the First Amendment's mandate of preserving religious liberty to the fullest extent possible in a pluralistic society. For the Court to deem this command a "luxury," is to denigrate "[t]he very purpose of a Bill of Rights."

III

The Court's holding today not only misreads settled First Amendment precedent; it appears to be unnecessary to this case. I would reach the same result applying our established free exercise jurisprudence.

A

There is no dispute that Oregon's criminal prohibition of peyote places a severe burden on the ability of respondents to freely exercise their religion. Peyote is a sacrament of the Native American Church and is regarded as vital to respondents' ability to practice their religion. . . . Under Oregon law, as construed by that State's highest court, members of the Native American Church must choose between carrying out the ritual embodying their religious beliefs and avoidance of criminal prosecution. That choice is, in my view, more than sufficient to trigger First Amendment scrutiny.

There is also no dispute that Oregon has a significant interest in enforcing laws that control the possession and use of controlled substances by its citizens. . . . Indeed, under federal law (incorporated by Oregon law in relevant part), peyote is specifically regulated as a Schedule I controlled substance, which means that Congress has found it has a high potential for abuse, that there is no currently accepted medical use, and that there is a lack of accepted safety for use of the drug under medical supervision. . . . [R]espondents do not seriously dispute that Oregon has a compelling interest in prohibiting the possession of peyote by its citizens.

B

Thus, the critical question in this case is whether exempting respondents from the State's general criminal prohibition "will unduly interfere with fulfillment of the governmental interest." Although the question is close, I would conclude that uniform application of Oregon's criminal prohibition is "essential to accomplish" its overriding interest in preventing the physical harm caused by the use of a Schedule I controlled substance. Oregon's criminal prohibition represents that State's judgment that the possession and use of controlled substances, even by only one person, is inherently harmful and dangerous. Because the health effects caused by the use of controlled substances exist regardless of the motivation of the user, the use of such substances, even for religious purposes, violates the very purpose of the laws that prohibit them. Cf. State v. Massey, 229 N.C. 734, 51 S.E.2d 179 (denying religious exemption to municipal ordinance prohibiting the handling of poisonous reptiles), appeal dism'd sub. nom. Bunn v. N.C., 366 U.S. 942 (1949). Moreover, in view of the societal interest in preventing trafficking in controlled substances, uniform application of the criminal prohibition at issue is essential to the effectiveness of Oregon's stated interest in preventing any possession of peyote. Cf. Jacobson v. Mass., 197 U.S. 11 (1905) (denying exemption from small pox vaccination requirement).

For these reasons, I believe that granting a selective exemption in this case would seriously impair Oregon's compelling interest in prohibiting possession of peyote by its citizens. Under such circumstances, the Free Exercise Clause does not require the State to accommodate respondents' religiously motivated conduct. Unlike in *Yoder,* where we noted that "[t]he record strongly indicates that accommodating the religious objections of the Amish by forgoing one, or at most two, additional years of compulsory education will not impair the physical or mental health of the child, or result in an inability to be self supporting or to discharge the duties and responsibilities of citizenship, or in any other way materially detract from the welfare of society," a religious exemption in this case would be incompatible with the State's interest in controlling use and possession of illegal drugs.

Respondents contend that any incompatibility is belied by the factor that the Federal Government and several States provide exemptions for the religious use of peyote. But other governments may surely choose to grant an exemption without Oregon, with its specific asserted interest in uniform application of its drug laws, being *required* to do so by the First Amendment. Respondents also note that the sacramental use of peyote is central to the tenets of the Native American Church, but I agree with the Court that because "[i]t is not within the judicial ken to question the centrality of particular beliefs or practices to a faith," our determination of the constitutionality of Oregon's general criminal prohibition cannot, and should not, turn on the centrality of the particular religious practice at issue. . . .

BLACKMUN, J., with whom Justices Brennan and Marshall join, dissenting. . . .

I

In weighing respondents' clear interest in the free exercise of their religion against Oregon's asserted interest in enforcing its drug laws, it is important to articulate in precise terms the state interest involved. It is not the State's broad interest in fighting the critical "war on drugs" that must be weighed against respondents' claim, but the State's narrow interest in refusing to make an exception for the religious, ceremonial use of peyote. . . . Failure to reduce the competing interests to the same plane of generality tends to distort the weighing process in the State's favor. . . .

The State's interest in enforcing its prohibition, in order to be sufficiently compelling to outweigh a free exercise claim, cannot be merely abstract or symbolic. . . . In this case, the State actually has not evinced any concrete interest in enforcing its drug laws against religious users of peyote. . . .

Similarly, this Court's prior decisions have not allowed a government to rely on mere speculation about potential harms, but have demanded evidentiary support for a refusal to allow a religious exemption. . . .

The State proclaims an interest in protecting the health and safety of its citizens from the danger of unlawful drugs. It offers, however, no evidence that the religious use of peyote has ever harmed anyone. The factual findings of other courts cast doubt on the State's assumption that religious use of peyote is harmful.

The fact that peyote is classified as a Schedule I controlled substance does not, by itself, show that any and all uses of peyote, in any circumstance, are inherently harmful and dangerous. The Federal Government, which created the classification of unlawful drugs from which Oregon's drug laws are derived, apparently does not find peyote so dangerous as to preclude an exemption for religious use. . . .

The carefully circumscribed ritual context in which respondents used peyote is far removed from the irresponsible and unrestricted recreational use of unlawful drugs. . . .

Moreover, just as in *Yoder,* the values and interests of those seeking a religious exemption in this case are congruent, to a great degree, with those the State seeks to promote through its drug laws. Not only does the Church's doctrine forbid nonreligious use of peyote; it also generally advocates self-reliance, familial responsibility, and abstinence from alcohol. There is considerable evidence that the spiritual and social support provided by the Church has been effective in combatting the tragic effects of alcoholism on the Native American population. . . . Far from promoting the lawless and irresponsible use of drugs, Native American Church members' spiritual code exemplifies values that Oregon's drug laws are presumably intended to foster.

The State also seeks to support its refusal to make an exception for religious use of peyote by invoking its interest in abolishing drug trafficking. There is, however, practically no illegal traffic in peyote. . . . Peyote simply is not a popular drug; its distribution for use in religious rituals has nothing to do with the vast and violent traffic in illegal narcotics that plagues this country.

Finally, the State argues that granting an exception for religious peyote use would erode its interest in the uniform, fair, and certain enforcement of its drug laws. The State fears that, if it grants an exemption for religious peyote use, a flood of other claims to religious exemptions will follow. It would then be placed in a dilemma, it says, between allowing a patchwork of exemptions that would hinder its law enforcement efforts, and risking a violation of the Establishment Clause by arbitrarily limiting its religious exemptions. This argument, however, could be made in almost any free exercise case. This Court . . . consistently has rejected similar arguments in past free exercise cases, and it should do so here as well.

The State's apprehension of a flood of other religious claims is purely speculative. Almost half the States, and the Federal Government, have maintained an exemption for religious peyote use for many years, and apparently have not found themselves overwhelmed by claims to other religious exemptions. Allowing an exemption for religious peyote use would not necessarily oblige the State to grant a similar exemption to other religious groups. The unusual circumstances that make the religious use of peyote compatible with the State's interests in health and safety and in preventing drug trafficking would not apply to other religious claims. Some religions, for example, might not restrict drug use to a limited ceremonial context, as does the Native American Church. See, e.g., Olsen v. Drug Enforcement Administration, 878 F.2d 1458, 1464 (1989) ("the Ethiopian Zion Coptic Church . . . teaches that marijuana is properly smoked 'continually all day' "). Some religious claims involve drugs such as marijuana and heroin, in which there is significant illegal traffic, with its attendant greed and violence, so that it would be difficult to grant a religious exemption without seriously compromising law enforcement efforts.

That the State might grant an exemption for religious peyote use, but deny other religious claims arising in different circumstances, would not violate the Establishment Clause. Though the State must treat all religions equally, and not favor one over another, this obligation is fulfilled by the uniform application of the "compelling interest" *test* to all free exercise claims, not by reaching uniform *results* as to all claims. . . .

III

Finally, although I agree with Justice O'Connor that courts should refrain from delving into questions of whether, as a matter of religious doctrine, a particular practice is "central" to the religion, I do not think this means that the courts must turn a blind eye to the severe impact of a State's restrictions on the adherents of a minority religion. . . .

Respondents believe, and their sincerity has *never* been at issue, that the peyote plant embodies their deity, and eating it is an act of worship and communion. Without peyote, they could not enact the essential ritual of their church. . . .

If Oregon can constitutionally prosecute them for this act of worship, they, like the Amish, may be "forced to migrate to some other and more tolerant region." *Yoder*. This potentially devastating impact must be viewed in light of the federal policy — reached in reaction to many years of religious persecution and intolerance — of protecting the religious freedom of Native Americans. . . .

IV

For these reasons, I conclude that Oregon's interest in enforcing its drug laws against religious use of peyote is not sufficiently compelling to outweigh respondents' right to the free exercise of their religion. Since the State could not constitutionally enforce its criminal prohibition against respondents, the interests underlying the State's drug laws cannot justify its denial of unemployment benefits. Absent such justification, the State's regulatory interest in denying benefits for religiously motivated "misconduct," is indistinguishable from the state interests this Court has rejected in [the unemployment compensation cases]. The State of Oregon cannot, consistently with the Free Exercise Clause, deny respondents unemployment benefits.

Discussion

1. Is Justice Scalia saying — to quote Marshall's comment in *McCulloch* — that it is a "perplexing inquiry, so unfit for the judicial department, what degree" of imposition on the free exercise of religion is "legitimate" and "what degree may amount to an abuse of that power"?[39] Justice Scalia has elsewhere denounced approaches to constitutional interpretation that require judicial "balancing" of competing values. (See, e.g., Washington Can Corp. v. Washington State Department of Revenue, 483 U.S. 232 (1987) (dormant commerce clause).) Indeed, he counters Justice O'Connor's frank acceptance of a judicial duty to balance by stating that "it is horrible to contemplate that federal judges will regularly balance against the importance of general laws the significance of religious practice." Can judges avoid balancing and at the same time protect vulnerable minorities against majoritarian oppression?

2. In a footnote to his dissenting opinion, Justice Blackmun suggests that the Native American Church's

> use of peyote seems closely analogous to the sacramental use of wine by the Roman Catholic Church. During Prohibition, the Federal Government exempted such use of wine from its general ban on possession and use of alcohol. However compelling the Government's then general interest in prohibiting the use of alcohol may have been, it could not plausibly have asserted an interest sufficiently compelling to outweigh Catholics' right to take communion.

Under Justice Scalia's approach, could a "dry" state or county refuse to exempt the sacramental use of wine?

3. How would someone Justice Blackmun's analysis decide a modern *Reynolds* or *Cleveland* case involving bigamous marriage by fundamentalist Mormons or, indeed, by Moslem immigrants to the United States who wish to practice polygamy as allowed by at least some branches of Islam?

39. See George Kannar, The Constitutional Catechism of Antonin Scalia, 99 Yale L.J. 1297, 1307 (1990), where Scalia is described as "not only positivist and textualist" in his constitutional methodology, "but also formalistic, in many respects a throwback to more 'mechanical' days."

G. A Concluding Problem: The Cultural Autonomy of Native Americans

As we saw in Chapter 2, the status of Native American tribes and their members within the structure of American constitutionalism has been problematic from the beginning.[40] We conclude this chapter by considering a case that presents the conflict between the customs of some Native Americans and those of the surrounding majority.

The background of the Indian Civil Rights Act of 1968 (ICRA) is set out by Professors Getches and Wilkinson:[41]

> Recognizing that Indian tribes are not subject to the Bill of Rights and other constitutional guaranties limiting the federal and state governments, Talton v. Mayes, 163 U.S. 376 (1896), [Senator Sam Ervin, the primary sponsor of the legislation] believed that Indians and non-Indians should be protected from potential abuses by tribal governments.
>
> Indian response was mixed during the legislative process. Some tribes had no objection in principle but believed that the legislation was unnecessary. Others argued that the legislation would unduly formalize tribal court systems. Still others, including the traditional pueblos of the Southwest, opposed any incursions whatsoever on their tribal sovereignty. The resulting legislation imposed on tribes, as a matter of statutory law, requirements tracking many of the constitutional restraints on states and the federal government. Notably absent are limitations similar to the establishment of religion clause, the guarantee of a republican form of government, the privileges and immunities clauses, the provisions involving the right to vote, the requirement of free counsel for an indigent accused, and the right to a jury trial in civil cases.

The ICRA does provide, however, that "[n]o Indian tribe in exercising powers of self-government shall . . . deny to any person within its jurisdiction the equal protection of the laws." This provision was at the heart of Santa Clara Pueblo v. Martinez, 436 U.S. 49 (1978), where the Court was faced with a 1939 tribal ordinance of the 600-year-old New Mexico tribe that specified tribal membership on the basis of patrilineal descent: Children whose fathers were not members of the tribe were not themselves entitled to membership.

The ordinance was challenged by Julia Martinez, a tribal member, and her daughter Audrey, who had been denied membership because her father (i.e., Julia's husband) was not a member of the tribe. (He was a Navaho Indian, who had married Julia in 1941, two years after the passage of the ordinance in question.) As described by the Supreme Court, "[a]lthough the children were raised on the reservation and continue to reside there now that they are adults, as a result of their exclusion from membership they may not vote in tribal elections or hold secular office in the tribe; moreover, they have no right to remain on the reserva-

40. See Jane Smith, Republicanism, Imperialism, and Sovereignty: A History of the Doctrine of Tribal Sovereignty, 39 Buffalo L. Rev. 927 (1988/89); Milner Ball, Constitution, Court, Indian Tribes, Am. Bar Found. Research J. 1.

41. David H. Getches and Charles F. Wilkinson, eds., Cases and Materials on Federal Indian Law 367-368 (2d ed. 1986). See also Burnett, An Historical Analysis of the 1968 "Indian Civil Rights" Act, 9 Harv. J. Legis. 557 (1972); Comment, The Indian Bill of Rights and the Constitutional Status of Tribal Governments, 82 Harv. L. Rev. 1343 (1969).

tion in the event of their mother's death, or to inherit their mother's home or her possessory interests in the communal lands."[42]

The district court, though recognizing the comparative recency of the tribal rule, found that it reflected (in the words of the Supreme Court) "traditional values of patriarchy still significant in tribal life. The court recognized the vital importance of respondents' interests, but also determined that membership rules were 'no more or less than a mechanism of social . . . self-definition,' and as such were basic to the tribe's survival as a cultural and economic entity." The Court of Appeals for the Tenth Circuit reversed, finding the tribe's sex-based classification "invidious" and unsupported by any compelling interest.

Writing for seven Justices,[43] Justice Marshall reversed. "As separate sovereigns pre-existing the Constitution, tribes have historically been regarded as unconstrained by those constitutional provisions framed specifically as limitations on federal or state authority." However, Congress does possess "plenary authority to limit, modify or eliminate the powers of local self-government which the tribes otherwise possess," as exemplified by the ICRA itself.

At this point, the opinion took a procedural turn. After deciding that the tribe had sovereign immunity that protected it from being sued directly, the Court went on to hold that the ICRA had not granted federal courts jurisdiction over the dispute even in an action against tribal officials who lacked sovereign immunity. Federal courts had jurisdiction only to grant habeas corpus, where a person claimed to be confined in violation of the Constitution. Otherwise, enforcement of the ICRA was left up to the tribal courts. "[W]e must bear in mind that providing a federal forum for issues arising under [the equal protection section of the ICRA] constitutes an interference with tribal autonomy and self-government beyond that created by the change in substantive law itself."

Justice White, dissenting, "agree[d] with the majority that . . . Congress was . . . concerned with furthering Indian self-government. I do not agree, however, that this concern on the part of Congress precludes our recognition of a federal cause of action to enforce the terms of the Act. The major intrusion upon the tribe's right to govern itself occurred when Congress enacted the ICRA. . . . The extension of constitutional rights to individual citizens is *intended* to intrude on the authority of government."

Discussion

1. Why doesn't the Fourteenth Amendment apply directly to the Santa Clara Pueblo? Is it because an Indian tribe's activity is "private" rather than "state action"? (Does the tribe exercise a "traditional governmental function" of determining who is legally entitled to live within the community?) Should we view the tribe as a (conquered) semi-sovereign entity — as a special kind of "state" that retains a measure of political independence from the norms of the conquerors?

2. Just as the polygamy involved in *Reynolds* offended the dominant society, we suspect that the gender discrimination practiced by the Santa Clara Pueblo offends many readers of this book. But by what criteria should one assess govern-

42. Getches and Wilkinson state, at page 376, that "[t]he dispute . . . arose in part because the Martinez children were denied the services of the Indian Health Service on the ground that they were not enrolled tribal members."

43. Justice Blackmun did not participate, and Justice White wrote a dissent.

ment interference in so fundamental an issue as the tribe's definition of membership in its own community?

3. Catherine MacKinnon writes of *Martinez:*[44]

> Missing from the Supreme Court's account of the case is the history of the tribal rule. I am told that the rule was made in 1939 after the General Allotment Act divided up communal lands into individually held parcels, in something like an attempt to make Indians into proper agrarians. Although this law did not apply to the Pueblos, they recognized that Congress could apply it to them at any time. In the experience of tribes it did apply to, lands were being taken away by white men marrying Native women. The Santa Clara rule was passed to prevent women who married out from passing land out, in an attempt to secure the survival of a culture for which land is life. Without knowing this, which I have by word of mouth, it is hard to understand what the Supreme Court meant when it said that this rule was " 'no more or less than a mechanism of social . . . self-definition,' and as such [was] basic to the tribes' survival as a cultural and economic entity." The rule was seen as basic to survival because it discouraged Native women from marrying white men — or white men from marrying Native women, depending on how you see who does what — because that was taking away Native land. When Native men married white women, the experience apparently had been that white women more often integrated with the tribe.
>
> Given this history, which the tribe did not choose or make, I imagine the tribe saying, we need this rule. I imagine Julia Martinez replying: I understand that history, it is also my history, but this is a male supremacist solution to a problem male supremacy created. The rule keeps Indian women for Indian men at the price of loss of tribal rights, from a time when Native women did not have formal power in rule-making. What would be wrong with preventing *any* child from inheriting land from parents who were not both tribal members? Whose system is it that ties ownership of land to ownership of women? Is that *our* tradition? Why it is seen as a matter of cultural survival when men guarantee exclusive access to Indian women as a requirement of tribal membership, but when an Indian woman attempts to claim that her family is an Indian family, to choose who to make a family with, it's called a *threat* to cultural survival? Whose culture is this culture? Is male supremacy sacred because it has become a tribal tradition? Under what conditions? . . .
>
> I want to suggest that cultural survival is as contingent upon equality between women and men as it is upon equality among peoples. The sex division in this case undermined the ability of Native Americans to survive as autonomous cultures. It was certainly not a means of promoting that survival. This is not the case because Julia Martinez fought over it, and because she fought it in the white man's court, but because the tribe was willing to sacrifice *her tribal connection,* her full membership in the tribal community, in the face of a white male supremacist threat. Their rule did nothing to address or counteract the reasons why Native women were vulnerable to white male land imperialism through marriage — it gave in to them, by punishing the *woman,* the Native person. Sex inequality, looked at close up, may threaten the cultural survival of Native peoples just as going outside the culture to resolve it threatens tribal sovereignty. But this only appears if one recognizes that the systematic vulnerability of Native women marriages that can destroy the tribe indicates the *tribe* has a problem — and not a problem to be solved by punishing Native women through their children to provide a disincentive. Why is excluding women always an

44. Catherine MacKinnon, Whose Culture? A Case Note on Martinez v. Santa Clara Pueblo (1983), in Feminism Unmodified: Discourses on Life and Law 65-69 (1987).

option for solving problems men create between men? Maybe women's loyalty would be more reliable if their communities were more equitable.

. . . [T]he aspiration of women to be no less than men — not to be punished where a man is glorified, not to be considered damaged or disloyal where a man is rewarded or left in peace, not to lead a derivative life, but to do everything and be anybody at all — is an aspiration indigenous to women across place and across time. I think the tribal rule in the *Martinez* case is male supremacist, not just sex differentiated.

4. Does the Constitution accord non-Indian organizations a degree of autonomy from government-imposed norms that interfere with the organizations' self-definition? Consider the trio of cases, Roberts v. United States Jaycees, 468 U.S. 609 (1984); Board of Directors of Rotary International v. Rotary Club of Duarte, California, 481 U.S. 537 (1987); and New York Club Association v. City of New York, 487 U.S. 1 (1988), where the Court upheld, against First Amendment and equal protection challenges, the application of state public accommodations law to prohibit discrimination by ostensibly private clubs. Although the Court ackowledged the constitutional status of freedom of association, Justice Powell wrote in *Rotary International* that "the relationship among Rotary Club members is not the kind of intimate or private relation that warrants constitutional protection." Moreover, even if the California law there at issue "does work some slight infringement on Rotary members' right of expressive association, that infringement is justified because it serves the State's compelling interest in eliminating discrimination against women." That "compelling interest in assuring equal access to women extends to the acquisition of leadership skills and business contacts as well as tangible goods and services." In *New York Club Association*, while upholding the law against a challenge on its face, Justice White wrote that "an association might be able to show that it is organized for specific expressive purposes and that it will not be able to advocate its desired viewpoints nearly as effectively if it cannot confine its membership to those who share the same sex, for example, or the same religion."

5. Can you imagine any circumstances under which a government could require a religious group to adapt its rules of membership to the ostensible requirements of the Constitution? For example, membership by birth in traditional Judaism is by matrilineal descent.[45] This means, among other things, that children of Jewish fathers (but not of Jewish mothers) who have been raised as Jews must undergo formal conversion ceremonies before being accepted as members in Jewish congregations; children of Jewish mothers and non-Jewish fathers need not convert. Could the state constitutionally forbid congregations from applying such clearly discriminatory rules? Or imagine that a legislature attempts to promote the "leadership skills" of female Catholics by making illegal the Roman Catholic Church's refusal to allow women into the priesthood?[46]

If you read the Constitution to prohibit "direct" governmental regulation of such practices, are you similarly skeptical of the ability of government to regulate

45. The Reformed wing of American Judaism, however, recognizes patrilineal descent as well.

46. See Comment, Title VII and the Appointment of Women Clergy: A Statutory and Constitutional Quagmire, 13 Colum. J.L. & Soc. Probs. 257, 260-67 (1977), which discusses the implications of the fact that Title VII of the Civil Rights Act of 1964, the basic federal statute prohibiting discrimination in employment, allows religious institutions to take religion, but not race, sex, or national origin into its hiring decisions.

them "indirectly" by imposing them as conditions for the receipt of benefits, such as continued exemption from having to pay property taxes. (See the discussion of "unconstitutional conditions" in Chapter 11 and of *Bob Jones University*, page 1440 supra.) Consider, for example, a restriction on tax exemptions to only those religious organizations that grant men and women equal access to positions of religious leadership. If you resist upholding such laws what permits Congress to impose the norms of the United States Constitution on Indian tribes? Are churches more "sovereign" than the tribes?

Chapter 14
The Allocation of Decisionmaking Authority

Chapter 11 examined a number of arguments for and against judicial review, on the tacit assumptions that all constitutional questions were subject to adjudication and that the decisions of the judges were final. This chapter questions these assumptions. We begin by returning to the subject of "nonjusticiable" or "political" questions, touched upon in connection with the *Reapportionment* cases, Chapter 7 supra. Then we turn to two provisions of the Constitution — section 5 of the Fourteenth Amendment and Article III — that arguably empower Congress to countermand or limit the effectiveness of judicial decisions.

I. The Commitment of Constitutional Questions to Nonjudicial Agencies

Article III grants federal courts the power to decide cases or controversies "arising under this Constitution." Are there cases arising under the Constitution that are nonetheless not suitable for adjudication?

At various times in its history, the Supreme Court has refused to adjudicate cases or controversies on the ground that they were "political questions." This term has not had a consistent meaning or application. In Baker v. Carr, 369 U.S. 186 (1962), p.1048 supra, one of the Court's more recent discussions of the "political question" doctrine, Justice Brennan wrote:

> It is the relationship between the judiciary and the coordinate branches of the Federal Government . . . which gives rise to the political question. . . . The nonjusticiability of a political question is primarily a function of the separation of powers. . . .
>
> Prominent on the surface of any case held to involve a political question is found a textually demonstrable constitutional commitment of the issue to a coordinate political department.

This section focuses on two arguably "political," or "nonjusticiable," questions — the House of Representatives' decision to exclude a member-elect, and the Senate's judgment of conviction in an impeachment proceeding.

POWELL v. McCORMACK

395 U.S. 486 (1969)

Certiorari to the United States Court of Appeals
for the District of Columbia

WARREN, C.J.

[Adam Clayton Powell, a long-time African-American member of the House of Representatives from New York City, was not permitted to take his seat in the 90th Congress, which convened in January 1967. The basis of this denial was a finding by a Special Subcommittee of the House that Powell had abused his office as chair of the House Committee on Education and Labor, including deceiving the House authorities about travel expenses and, apparently, making certain illegal salary payments to his wife. Upon Powell's being asked to "step aside while the oath [of office] was administered to the other members-elect," the House passed a resolution calling for the appointment of a Select Committee to determine Powell's eligibility to take his seat. The Committee, composed of nine lawyer-members of the House, found both that Powell met the qualifications set out by the Constitution in Article 1, §2, and that he had engaged in a variety of wrongful acts. The Committee therefore recommended that he be seated but that he also be censured by the House, fined $40,000, and be deprived as well of his considerable seniority (and therefore of his office as Chair of the Education and Labor Committee).

Upon the House debate on the Select Committee's recommendation, an amendment was offered calling for the "exclusion" of Powell from the House and a declaration that his seat was vacant. The Speaker of the House ruled that a majority vote was sufficient to pass such an amended resolution. The amendment was adopted by a vote of 248-176. The House then adopted by a vote of 307-116 the resolution as amended, "thereby excluding Powell and directing that the Speaker notify the Governor of New York that the seat was vacant."

Powell, joined by several voters from his district, filed suit; among the defendants were John W. McCormack, the Speaker of the House, the Doorkeeper and Clerk of the House, who were refusing to perform certain services available to members of Congress, and the Sergeant of Arms, who refused to pay Powell his salary. Although Powell was elected to and seated by the 91st Congress, the Court held that the case was not moot because of the presence of the back-salary claim for the term for which he was excluded. The Court also held that the suit could proceed against the House employees, even though the speech and debate clause of the Constitution prevented suit against Speaker McCormack.

Finally, the Court emphasized that House Resolution No. 278, as voted upon, was avowedly an "exclusion" proceeding rather than one "expelling" Powell. Although the final resolution drew the two-thirds majority that would have been necessary for "expulsion," the Speaker had specifically ruled that a majority vote was sufficient for "exclusion." Some members of the House had stated that members could not be "expelled" for preelection conduct, and the Court refused "to speculate" whether the House would have voted to "expel" Powell had the issue been squarely presented. The Court therefore treated it as "exclusion."]

V. SUBJECT MATTER JURISDICTION

As we pointed out in Baker v. Carr, 369 U.S. 186, 198 (1962), there is a significant difference between determining whether a federal court has "jurisdiction of the subject matter" and determining whether a cause over which a court has subject matter jurisdiction is "justiciable." The District Court determined that "to decide this case on the merits . . . would constitute a clear violation of the doctrine of separation of powers" and then dismissed the complaint "for want of jurisdiction of the subject matter." Powell v. McCormack, 266 F. Supp. 354, 359, 360 (D.C.D.C. 1967). However, as the Court of Appeals correctly recognized, the doctrine of separation of powers is more properly considered in determining whether the case is "justiciable." We agree with the unanimous conclusion of the Court of Appeals that the District Court had jurisdiction over the subject matter of this case. Hoever, for reasons set forth in Part VI, infra, we disagree with the Court of Appeals' conclusion that this case is not justiciable.

In Baker v. Carr, supra, we noted that a federal district court lacks jurisdiction over the subject matter (1) if the cause does not "arise under" the Federal Constitution, laws, or treaties (or fall within one of the other enumerated categories of Art. III); or (2) if it is not a "case or controversy" within the meaning of that phrase in Art. III; or (3) if the cause is not one described by any jurisdictional statute. . . .

Respondents . . . contend that this is not a case "arising under" the Constitution within the meaning of Art. III. They emphasize that Art. I, §5, assigns to each House of Congress the power to judge the elections and qualifications of its own members and to punish its members for disorderly behavior. Respondents also note that under Art. I, §3, the Senate has the "sole power" to try all impeachments. Respondents argue that these delegations (to "judge," to "punish," and to "try") to the Legislative Branch are explicit grants of "judicial power" to the Congress and constitute specific exceptions to the general mandate of Art. III that the "judicial power" shall be vested in the federal courts. Thus, respondents maintain, the "power conferred on the courts by Article III does not authorize this Court to do anything more than declare its lack of jurisdiction to proceed."

We reject this contention. Article III, §1, provides that the "judicial Power . . . shall be vested in one supreme Court, and in such inferior Courts as the Congress may . . . establish." Further, §2 mandates that the "judicial Power shall extend to all Cases . . . arising under this Constitution. . . ." It has long been held that a suit "arises under" the Constitution if a petitioner's claim "will be sustained if the Constitution . . . [is] given one construction and will be defeated if [it is] given another." Bell v. Hood, 327 U.S. 678, 685 (1946). . . . Thus, this case clearly is one "arising under" the Constitution as the Court has interpreted that phrase. Any bar to federal courts reviewing the judgments made by the House or Senate in excluding a member arises from the allocation of powers between the two branches of the Federal Government (a question of justiciability), and not from the petitioners' failure to state a claim based on federal law.

Respondents next content that the Court of Appeals erred in ruling that petitioners' suit is authorized by a jurisdictional statute, i.e., 28 U.S.C. §1331(a). Section 1331(a) provides that district courts shall have jurisdiction in "all civil actions wherein the matter in controversy . . . arises under the Constitution. . . ." Respondents urge that even though a case may "arise under the Constitution" for purposes of Art. III, it does not necessarily "arise under the Constitution" for purposes of §1331(a). . . .

We have noted that the grant of jurisdiction in §1331(a), while made in the language used in Art. III, is not in all respects co-extensive with the potential for federal jurisdiction found in Art. III. Nevertheless, it has generally been recognized that the intent of the drafters was to provide a broad jurisdictional grant to the federal courts. And, as noted above, the resolution of this case depends directly on construction of the Constitution. The Court has consistently held such suits are authorized by the statute. . . .

VI. Justiciability

Having concluded that the Court of Appeals correctly ruled that the District Court had jurisdiction over the subject matter, we turn to the question whether the case is justiciable. Two determinations must be made in this regard. First, we must decide whether the claim presented and the relief sought are of the type which admit of judicial resolution. Second, we must determine whether the structure of the Federal Government renders the issue presented a "political question" — that is, a question which is not justiciable in federal court because of the separation of powers provided by the Constitution.

A. General Considerations

In deciding generally whether a claim is justiciable, a court must determine whether "the duty asserted can be judicially identified and its breach judicially determined, and whether protection for the right asserted can be judicially molded." Baker v. Carr. . . . Respondents do not seriously contend that the duty asserted and its alleged breach cannot be judicially determined. If petitioners are correct, the House had a duty to seat Powell once it determined he met the standing requirements set forth in the Constitution. It is undisputed that he met those requirements and that he was nevertheless excluded.

Respondents do maintain, however, that this case is not justiciable because, they assert, it is impossible for a federal court to "mold effective relief for resolving this case." Respondents emphasize that petitioners asked for coercive relief against the officers of the House, and, they contend, federal courts cannot issue mandamus or injunctions compelling officers or employees of the House to perform specific official acts. Respondents rely primarily on the Speech or Debate Clause to support this contention.

We need express no opinion about the appropriateness of coercive relief in this case, for petitioners sought a declaratory judgment, a form of relief the District Court could have issued. The Declaratory Judgment Act, 28 U.S.C. §2201, provides that a district court may "declare the rights . . . of any interested party, . . . whether or not further relief is or could be sought." The availability of declaratory relief depends on whether there is a live dispute between the parties, . . . and a request for declaratory relief may be considered independently of whether other forms of relief are appropriate. We thus conclude that in terms of the general criteria of justiciability, this case is justiciable.

B. POLITICAL QUESTION DOCTRINE

1. *Textually Demonstrable Constitutional Commitment.* Respondents maintain that even if this case is otherwise justiciable, it presents only a political question. It is well established that the federal courts will not adjudicate political questions. In Baker v. Carr we noted that political questions are not justiciable primarily because of the separation of powers within the Federal Government . . . [for example, because there is] "a textually demonstrable constitutional commitment of the issue to a coordinate political department. . . ."

Respondents' first contention is that this case presents a political question because under Art. I, §5, there has been a "textually demonstrable constitutional commitment" to the House of the "adjudicatory power" to determine Powell's qualifications. Thus it is argued that the House, and the House alone, has power to determine who is qualified to be a member.

In order to determine whether there has been a textual commitment to a coordinate department of the Government, we must interpret the Constitution. In other words, we must first determine what power the Constitution confers upon the House through Art. I, §5, before we can determine to what extent, if any, the exercise of that power is subject to judicial review. Respondents maintain that the House has broad power under §5, and, they argue, the House may determine which are the qualifications necessary for membership. On the other hand, petitioners allege that the Constitution provides that an elected representative may be denied his seat only if the House finds he does not meet one of the standing qualifications expressly prescribed by the Constitution.

If examination of §5 disclosed that the Constitution gives the House judicially unreviewable power to set qualifications for membership and to judge whether prospective members meet those qualifications, further review of the House determination might well be barred by the political question doctrine. On the other hand, if the Constitution gives the House power to judge only whether elected members possess the three standing qualifications set forth in the Constitution,[a] further consideration would be necessary to determine whether any of the other formulations of the political question doctrine are "inextricable from the case at bar."[b] Baker v. Carr.

In other words, whether there is a "textually demonstrable constitutional commitment of the issue to a co-ordinate political department" of government and what is the scope of such commitment are questions we must resolve for the first

a. In addition to the three qualifications set forth in Art. I, §2, Art. I, §3, cl. 7, authorizes the disqualification of any person convicted in an impeachment proceeding from "any Office of honor, Trust or Profit under the United States"; Art. I, §6, cl. 2, provides that "no Person holding any Office under the United States, shall be a Member of either House during his Continuance in Office": and §3 of the 14th Amendment disqualifies any person "who, having previously taken an oath . . . to support the Constitution of the United States, shall have engaged in insurrection or rebellion against the same, or given aid or comfort to the enemies thereof." It has been argued that each of these provisions, as well as the Guarantee Clause of Article IV and the oath requirement of Art. VI, cl. 3, is no less a "qualification" within the meaning of Art. I, §5, than those set forth in Art I, §2. Dionisopoulos, A Commentary on the Constitutional Issues in the Powell and Related Cases, 17 J. Pub. L. 103, 111-115 (1968). We need not reach this question, however, since both sides agree that Powell was not ineligible under any of these provisions.

b. Consistent with this interpretation, federal courts might still be barred by the political question doctrine from reviewing the House's factual determination that a member did not meet one of the standing qualifications. This is an issue not presented in this case and we express no view as to its resolution.

time in this case. For, as we pointed out in Baker v. Carr, "[d]eciding whether a matter has in any measure been committed by the Constitution to another branch of government, or whether the action of that branch exceeds whatever authority has been committed, is itself a delicate exercise in constitutional interpretation, and is a responsibility of this Court as ultimate interpreter of the Constitution."

In order to determine the scope of any "textual commitment" under Art. I, §5, we necessarily must determine the meaning of the phrase to "be the Judge of the Qualifications of its own Members." Petitioners argue that the records of the debates during the Constitutional Convention; available commentary from the post-Convention, pre-ratification period; and early congressional applications of Art. I, §5, support their construction of the section. Respondents insist, however, that a careful examination of the pre-Convention practices of the English Parliament and American colonial assemblies demonstrates that by 1787, a legislature's power to judge the qualifications of its members was generally understood to encompass exclusion or expulsion on the ground that an individual's character or past conduct rendered him unfit to serve. When the Constitution and the debates over its adoption are thus viewed in historical perspective, argue respondents, it becomes clear that the "qualifications" expressly set forth in the Constitution were not meant to limit the long-recognized legislative power to exclude or expel at will, but merely to establish "standing incapacities," which could be altered only by a constitutional amendment. Our examination of the relevant historical materials leads us to the conclusion that petitioners are correct and that the Constitution leaves the House without authority to *exclude* any person, duly elected by his constituents, who meets all the requirements for membership expressly prescribed in the Constitution. . . . [The Court's lengthy historical survey is omitted.]

Had the intent of the Framers emerged from these materials with less clarity, we would nevertheless have been compelled to resolve any ambiguity in favor of a narrow construction of the scope of Congress' power to exclude members-elect. A fundamental principle of our representative democracy is, in Hamilton's words, "that the people should choose whom they please to govern them." 2 Elliot's Debates 257. As Madison pointed out at the Convention, this principle is undermined as much by limiting whom the people can select as by limiting the franchise itself. In apparent agreement with this basic philosophy, the Convention adopted his suggestion limiting the power to expel. To allow essentially that same power to be exercised under the guise of judging qualifications, would be to ignore Madison's warning, borne out in the *Wilkes* case and some of Congress' own post-Civil War exclusion cases, against "vesting an improper & dangerous power in the Legislature." 2 Farrand 249. Moreover, it would effectively nullify the Convention's decision to require a two-thirds vote for expulsion. Unquestionably, Congress has an interest in preserving its institutional integrity, but in most cases that interest can be sufficiently safeguarded by the exercise of its power to punish its members for disorderly behavior and, in extreme cases, to expel a member with the concurrence of two-thirds. In short, both the intention of the Framers, to the extent it can be determined, and an examination of the basic principles of our democratic system persuade us that the Constitution does not vest in the Congress a discretionary power to deny membership by a majority vote.

For these reasons, we have concluded that Art. I, §5, is at most a "textually demonstrable commitment" to Congress to judge only the qualifications expressly set forth in the Constitution. Therefore, the "textual commitment" formulation of the political question doctrine does not bar federal courts from adjudicating petitioners' claims.

2. *Other Considerations.* Respondents' alternate contention is that the case presents a political question because judicial resolution of petitioners' claim would produce a "potentially embarrassing confrontation between coordinate branches" of the Federal Government. But, as our interpretation of Art. I, §5, discloses, a determination of petitioner Powell's right to sit would require no more than an interpretation of the Constitution. Such a determination falls within the traditional role accorded courts to interpret the law, and does not involve a "lack of the respect due [a] coordinate [branch] of government," nor does it involve an "initial policy determination of a kind clearly for nonjudicial discretion." Baker v. Carr, 369 U.S. 186, at 217. Our system of government requires that federal courts on occasion interpret the Constitution in a manner at variance with the construction given the document by another branch. The alleged conflict that such an adjudication may cause cannot justify the courts' avoiding their constitutional responsibility.[c] . . .

Nor are any of the other formulations of a political question "inextricable from the case at bar." Baker v. Carr. Petitioners seek a determination that the House was without power to exclude Powell from the 90th Congress, which, we have seen, requires an interpretation of the Constitution — a determination for which clearly there are "judicially . . . manageable standards." Finally, a judicial resolution of petitioners' claim will not result in "multifarious pronouncements by various departments on one question." For, as we noted in Baker v. Carr, it is the responsibility of this Court to act as the ultimate interpreter of the Constitution. Marbury v. Madison, 1 Cranch 137 (1903). Thus, we conclude that petitioners' claim is not barred by the political question doctrine, and, having determined that the claim is otherwise generally justiciable, we hold that the case is justiciable.

VII. Conclusion

To summarize, we have determined the following: (1) This case has not been mooted by Powell's seating in the 91st Congress. (2) Although this action should be dismissed against respondent Congressmen, it may be sustained against their agents. (3) The 90th Congress' denial of membership to Powell cannot be treated as an expulsion. (4) We have jurisdiction over the subject matter of this controversy. (5) The case is justiciable.

Further, analysis of the "textual commitment" under Art. I, §5 . . . has demonstrated that in judging the qualifications of its members Congress is limited to the standing qualifications prescribed in the Constitution. Respondents concede that Powell met these. Thus, there is no need to remand this case to determine whether he was entitled to be seated in the 90th Congress. Therefore, we hold that, since Adam Clayton Powell, Jr., was duly elected by the voters of the 18th Congressional District of New York and was not ineligible to serve under any provision of the Constitution, the House was without power to exclude him from its membership.

c. In fact, the Court has noted that it is an "inadmissible suggestion" that action might be taken in disregard of a judicial determination. McPherson v. Blacker, 146 U.S. 1, 24 (1892).

Petitioners seek additional forms of equitable relief, including mandamus for the release of petitioner Powell's back pay. The propriety of such remedies, however, is more appropriately considered in the first instance by the courts below. . . . [Reversed and remanded.[1]]

A. Types of Nonjusticiable Questions: Some Conceptual Issues

1. Questions "Arising Under This Constitution"

Many issues of government policy do not present questions "arising under" the Constitution or any laws or treaties and are, for that reason alone, committed to decision by nonjudicial agencies. For example, whether the United States should recognize the People's Republic of China, whether Congress should appropriate $10 million or $100 million for a weapons defense system, and whether the Federal Reserve Board should raise its discount rate 0.25 percent, do not present (nonfrivolous) constitutional questions. Assuming that no relevant statutes or treaties were involved, a federal complaint challenging these actions would be dismissed under Rule 12(b)(6) of the Federal Rules of Civil Procedure for "failure to state a claim upon which relief can be granted."[2]

The interesting kind of nonjusticiable question for purposes of this chapter is one that arguably *does* arise under the Constitution, but which the courts may nonetheless not adjudicate. A court could not properly dismiss such a claim under Rule 12(b)(6) because, by hypothesis, the court has no business deciding the merits. Rather, the court should invoke Rule 12(b)(1) — lack of jurisdiction over the subject matter.

Assuming that the decision to exclude a member of Congress is nonjusticiable, is it nonjusticiable in the first sense (i.e., because it does not present a question "arising under this Constitution"), or in the second?

2. Discretion and Finality

Please review the summary of Ronald Dworkin's distinction between the concept of "finality" and various concepts of "discretion" in the notes to *Marbury* in Chapter 2 supra.

In *Marbury* itself, Chief Justice Marshall discussed the respondent's contention that delivery of the commission was within the executive's discretion:

> [W]hatever opinion may be entertained of the manner in which executive discretion may be used, still there exists, and can exist, no power to control that discretion. The subjects are political. They respect the nation, not individual rights, and being intrusted to the executive, the decision of the executive is conclusive. . . .

1. A concurring opinion by Justice Douglas and an opinion by Justice Stewart, dissenting on the ground that the controversy is moot, are omitted.

2. A totally frivolous complaint might also be dismissed for want of jurisdiction, but the lack of jurisdiction would be grounded in the lack of merits. See Bell v. Hood, 327 U.S. 678 (1946).

> [W]here the heads of departments are the political or confidential agents of the executive, merely to execute the will of the President, or rather to act in cases in which the executive possesses a constitutional or legal discretion, nothing can be more perfectly clear than that their acts are only politically examinable. . . .
>
> The power of nominating to the senate, and the power of appointing the person nominated, are political powers to be exercised by the President according to his own discretion. When he has made an appointment, he has exercised his whole power, and his discretion has been completely applied to the case. . . . [I]f the officer is by law not removable at the will of the President; the rights he has acquired [by appointment] are protected by the law, and are not resumable by the President. . . .
>
> The question whether a right has vested or not, is, in its nature, judicial, and must be tried by the judicial authority.

What kind of discretion does Marshall indicate the president has with respect to the nomination and appointment of cabinet officers? Would a person who was passed over for nomination or whose nomination was withdrawn, whatever the reason, have a cause of action "arising under" the Constitution of the United States?[3]

What is the relationship between *discretion* and *finality* and the two kinds of nonjusticiable questions described in the preceding subsection? If the House of Representatives' decision to exclude Mr. Powell is unreviewable, does this imply that the House has (a) plenary discretion, (b) standard-application discretion, and/or (c) the power of finality?

3. *Finality in the Definition of Standards versus Finality in Their Application*

Standards often are defined through the process of applying them to particular fact situations. There are important instances, however, in which definition and application are separated: The judge instructs the jury based on her interpretation of the governing standards, and the jury applies her charge to the facts of the case at bar.

Is this the distinction that the Court makes in footnote b of *Powell* where it leaves open the question of whether "federal courts might still be barred by the political question doctrine from reviewing the House's factual determinations that a member did not meet one of the standing qualifications"? If the Court adhered to the footnote, and the House excluded Powell on the ground that he was under 25 years old, would Powell have a claim arising under the Constitution? If so, would he therefore have a judicial "case" arising under the Constitution?

3. Cf. Alexander Bickel, The Least Dangerous Branch 186 (1962):

> [T]here are discretionary functions of the political institutions which are unprincipled on principle, because we think "that the job is better done without rules." . . . Such questions call for no avoidance: they call for principled adjudication. . . . [S]hould a cabinet officer sue for back pay on the ground that the President had dismissed him arbitrarily, because of his race, and without a hearing . . . , it is not difficult to articulate the reasons that the President should have such arbitrary power. His whim should rule, because it is desirable to enlarge as much as possible his personal political responsibility, and this demands a special kind of loyalty and responsiveness of his immediate subordinates.

B. The Relevance of *Marbury*

In United States v. Nixon, 418 U.S. 683 (1974), President Nixon refused to comply with a subpoena to produce tape recordings and documents relating to his conversations with aides and advisors. He argued that the Executive possessed an absolute privilege and that the judicial branch lacked authority to review his assertion of the privilege. The Court rejected the claim of absolute privilege, on the ground that it conflicted with legitimate judicial functions, and held that need for evidence in pending prosecutions outweighed the Executive's inherent but nonabsolute privilege. In rejecting the President's claim that "the separation of powers doctrine precludes judicial review of a President's claim of privilege," Chief Justice Burger elaborated on the Court's assertion in *Powell* and Baker v. Carr that "it is the responsibility of this Court to act as the ultimate interpreter of the Constitution":

> In the performance of assigned constitutional duties each branch of the Government must initially interpret the Constitution, and the interpretation of its powers by any branch is due great respect from the others. The President's counsel, as we have noted, reads the Constitution as providing an absolute privilege of confidentiality for all presidential communications. Many decisions of this Court, however, have unequivocally reaffirmed the holding of Marbury v. Madison, 1 Cranch 137 (1803), that "it is emphatically the province and duty of the judicial department to say what the law is."
>
> No holding of the Court has defined the scope of judicial power specifically relating to the enforcement of a subpoena for confidential presidential communications for use in a criminal prosecution, but other exercises of powers by the Executive Branch and the Legislative Branch have been found invalid as in conflict with the Constitution. In a series of cases, the Court interpreted the explicit immunity conferred by express provisions of the Constitution on Members of the House and Senate by the Speech or Debate Clause, U.S. Const. Art. I, §6. Doe v. McMillan, 412 U.S. 306 (1973); Gravel v. United States, 408 U.S. 606 (1973); United States v. Brewster, 408 U.S. 501 (1972); United States v. Johnson, 383 U.S. 169 (1966). Since this Court has consistently exercised the power to construe and delineate claims arising under express powers, it must follow that the Court has authority to interpret claims with respect to powers alleged to derive from enumerated powers.
>
> Our system of government "requires that federal courts on occasion interpret the Constitution in a manner at variance with the construction given the document by another branch." . . . Notwithstanding the deference each branch must accord the others, the "judicial power of the United States" vested in the federal courts by Art. III, §1 of the Constitution can no more be shared with the Executive Branch than the Chief Executive, for example, can share with the Judiciary the veto power, or the Congress share with the Judiciary the power to override a presidential veto. Any other conclusion would be contrary to the basic concept of separation of powers and the checks and balances that flow from the scheme of a tripartite government. We therefore reaffirm that it is "emphatically the province and the duty" of this Court "to say what the law is" with respect to the claim of privilege presented in this case. Marbury v. Madison.

Does *Marbury* entail the results in *Powell* and *Nixon?* Recall the ambiguity in Marshall's assertion that it is "the province and duty of the judicial department to say what the law is" (¶52 of *Marbury,* page 86 supra). This might imply that the judiciary performs a special role in constitutional interpretation, which, in turn, might imply that the Court should have the final word in all constitutional disputes. The traditional understanding, however, is the more modest one articulated by Professor Herbert Wechsler — that federal courts pass on constitutional issues only because "they must decide a litigated issue that is *otherwise within their jurisdiction* and in doing so must give effect to the supreme law of the land."[4] On this reading, *Marbury* goes no further than to indicate that the Court has jurisdiction to decide whether it has jurisdiction to decide the merits.

C. Justiciability and the Merits

Consider Professor Terrance Sandalow's criticism of *Powell:*[5]

> Having begun by asking the right question, whether there was a "constitutional commitment of the issue" to the House, the Court proceeded to answer a quite different one, whether the "qualifications" which Article I, Section 5 authorized the House to "judge" were only those specified in Article I, Section 2 (and perhaps elsewhere in the Constitution). The opinion reflects, in short, a classic instance of confusion between "jurisdiction" — the power to decide — and "the merits" — the correctness of decisions.
>
> The source of this confusion, it seems fairly clear, is the Court's assumption that it bears "responsibility . . . to act as the ultimate interpreter of the Constitution." On that premise, it is but a short step to the conclusion that the Court is obligated to intervene when another branch of government acts in a manner prohibited by the Constitution. If the Constitution permits the House to judge only the "standing" qualifications of those who have been elected to membership, i.e., those specified in the Constitution, the Court, as the body ultimately responsible for the Constitution, must have the authority to review the decisions of the House to assure that constitutional limitations have been observed. . . .
>
> Stated in general terms, the analysis seems to lead to a conclusion that the Court may review decisions committed by the Constitution to other branches of government at least to the extent necessary to permit a determination that any standards of decision imposed by the Constitution have been respected. If the Court may review a determination by the House that its power to judge qualifications is not limited by the standing qualification of the Constitution, it is difficult to see, for example, why it may not similarly review expulsions from the Congress or the removal of judges or other officers upon conviction after impeachment. Both of the latter powers are in terms conferred upon the Congress but as to each there is a substantial basis for arguing that the Constitution limits the grounds upon which the Congress may act. Thus, as the Court notes, both houses have doubted their power to expel a member for conduct prior to his election. It would, moreover, do no violence to the language of the Constitution to construe it as authorizing expulsion only in situations in which a member was guilty of "disorderly behavior." Article II, Section 4, similarly, suggests that the "President, Vice-President, and other civil officers of the United States" may be removed from office only "on impeachment for, and conviction of,

4. Wechsler, The Courts and the Constitution, 1965 Colum. L. Rev. 1001, 1005-1006 (emphasis added).

5. Terrance Sandalow, Comments on Powell v. McCormack, 17 U.C.L.A.L. Rev. 1, 172-174 (1969).

treason, bribery, and other high crimes and misdemeanors." And under Article III, judges are entitled to hold their offices "during good behavior."

A conclusion that it is the Court, not Congress, which has the ultimate authority to determine the governing law in exclusion, impeachment, and expulsion proceedings is so contrary to historical practice and to the understanding of students of constitutional law that a re-examination by the Court of the steps leading to that conclusion is plainly in order. The point at which it might profitably begin that re-examination is with its unexamined assumption that it has the responsibility to act as the ultimate interpreter of the Constitution. The basis for that assumption is far from clear. Yet unless the assumption can be justified, *Powell* rests on an inadequate foundation.

Is Professor Sandalow correct that the Court confused the issue of justiciability with the merits? Without considering the "merits" to the extent that it did, could the Court have determined *what* was committed to a coordinate branch? Does Sandalow imply that the Court should have interpreted Article I, section 5, to provide, "Each House shall have sole power to determine whether or not to seat its own Members"? Does his criticism also apply to the Court's decision on the merits in *Marbury* that the right to the commission had vested?

D. Absence of Judicially Manageable Standards and of Information Necessary for Decision

This section introduces two related reasons for nonjusticiability — lack of standards and lack of relevant information.

In Coleman v. Miller, 307 U.S. 433 (1939), members of the Kansas legislature who had voted against ratification of the child labor amendment (proposed by Congress in 1924 to overturn the *Child Labor* cases) (see Chapter 4 supra) sued to restrain state officials from certifying the legislature's adoption of a ratifying resolution in 1937, on the ground, among others, that "by reason of . . . the failure of ratification within a reasonable time the proposed amendment had lost its vitality." The Court affirmed the state court's denial of relief. Chief Justice Hughes explained why the issue of "reasonable time" for ratification was not justiciable:[6]

> Where are to be found the criteria for such a judicial determination? None are to be found in Constitution or statute. In their endeavor to answer this question petitioners' counsel have suggested that at least two years should be allowed; that six years would not seem to be unreasonably long; that seven years had been used by the Congress as a reasonable period; that one year, six months and thirteen days was the average time used in passing upon amendments which have been ratified since the first ten amendments; that three years, six months and twenty-five days has been the longest time used in ratifying. To this list of variables, counsel add that "the nature and extent of publicity and the activity of the public and of the legislatures of the several States in relation to any particular proposal should be taken into consid-

6. Though entitled "opinion of the Court," his opinion reflected the views of only three of the seven Justices in the majority. Justice Frankfurter, joined by Justices Roberts, Black, and Douglas, argued that the legislators lacked standing. Justice Black, joined by Justices Roberts, Frankfurter, and Douglas, argued that the Constitution commits all aspects of the amendment process exclusively to Congress.

eration." That statement is pertinent, but there are additional matters to be examined and weighed. When a proposed amendment springs from a conception of economic needs, it would be necessary, in determining whether a reasonable time had elapsed since its submission, to consider the economic conditions prevailing in the country, whether these had so far changed since the submission as to make the proposal no longer responsive to the conception which inspired it or whether conditions were such as to intensify the feeling of need and the appropriateness of the proposed remedial action. In short, the question of a reasonable time in many cases would involve, as in this case it does involve, an appraisal of a great variety of relevant conditions, political, social and economic, which can hardly be said to be within the appropriate range of evidence receivable in a court of justice and as to which it would be an extravagant extension of judicial authority to assert judicial notice as the basis of deciding a controversy with respect to the validity of an amendment actually ratified. On the other hand, these conditions are appropriate for the consideration of the political departments of the Government. The questions they involve are essentially political and not justiciable. They can be decided by the Congress with the full knowledge and appreciation ascribed to the national legislature of the political, social and economic conditions which have prevailed during the period since the submission of the amendment.

Coleman involves interrelated problems of defining standards and assessing relevant data. Could the Court have adopted a standard that avoided the difficulties alluded to by the Chief Justice and that was also responsive to the policies underlying Article V? Was part of the difficulty that any definite standard — e.g., seven years — would necessarily be somewhat arbitrary?[7]

Consider the problem of standards and information in Chicago & Southern Air Lines v. Waterman Steamship Corp., 333 U.S. 103 (1948), in which the Court noted:

> The President, both as Commander-in-Chief and as the Nation's organ for foreign affairs, has available intelligence services whose reports are not and ought not to be published to the world. It would be intolerable that courts, without the relevant information, should review and perhaps nullify actions of the Executive taken on information properly held secret. Nor can courts sit in camera in order to be taken into executive confidences.

In United States v. Nixon, 418 U.S. 683 (1974), the Court cited this passage after noting that the President "does not place his claim of privilege on the ground [that the confidential communications] are military or diplomatic secrets. As to these areas of Art. II duties the courts have traditionally shown the utmost deference to presidential responsibilities."

7. But cf. the rule against perpetuities developed by common law courts. Cf. also Dunn v. Blumstein, 405 U.S. 330 (1972), implying that Tennessee could not require more than 30 days residency to vote in state elections. Concurring in the result, Justice Blackmun wrote: "It is, of course, a matter of line drawing. . . . But if 30 days pass constitutional muster, what of 35 or 45 or 75?" In Burns v. Fortson, 410 U.S. 686 (1973), the Court held that Georgia could close its registration books 50 days before the election but noted that "the 50-day registration period approaches the outer constitutional limits in this area."

E. Prudential Considerations

In The Least Dangerous Branch 184 (1962), Professor Alexander Bickel thus describes "the foundation . . . of the political question doctrine":

> the Court's sense of lack of capacity, compounded in unequal parts of (a) the strangeness of the issue and its intractability to principled resolution; (b) the sheer momentousness of it, which tends to unbalance judicial judgment; (c) the anxiety, not so much that the judicial judgment will be ignored, as that perhaps it should but will not be; (d) finally ("in a mature democracy"), the inner vulnerability, the self-doubt of an institution which is electorally irresponsible and has no earth to draw strength from.

Professor Bickel provides three illustrations: Luther v. Borden, 48 U.S. (7 How.) 1 (1849); Dred Scott v. Sandford, 60 U.S. (19 How.) 393 (1857); and the 1877 election dispute between Hayes and Tilden, which was decided by a margin of one vote by a special electoral commission that included five Justices of the Supreme Court sitting extrajudicially. In a later case,[8] the Court described Luther v. Borden thus:

> Luther v. Borden, though in form simply an action for damages for trespass was, as Daniel Webster said in opening the argument for the defense, "an unusual case." The defendants, admitting an otherwise tortious breaking and entering, sought to justify their action on the ground that they were agents of the established lawful government of Rhode Island, which State was then under martial law to defend itself from active insurrection; that the plaintiff was engaged in that insurrection; and that they entered under orders to arrest the plaintiff. The case arose "out of the unfortunate political differences which agitated the people of Rhode Island in 1841 and 1842," and which had resulted in a situation wherein two groups laid competing claims to recognition as the lawful government. The plaintiff's right to recover depended upon which of the two groups was entitled to such recognition; but the lower court's refusal to receive evidence or hear argument on that issue, its charge to the jury that the earlier established or "charter" government was lawful, and the verdict for the defendants, were affirmed upon appeal to this Court. . . . [*Luther* might properly be deemed nonjusticiable because of] the commitment to other branches of the decision as to which is the lawful state government; the unambiguous action by the President, in recognizing the charter government as the lawful authority; the need for finality in the executive's decision; and the lack of criteria by which a court could determine what form of government was republican.[9]

But Chief Justice Taney, who wrote the opinion of the Court, also suggested a different reason:

> [T]he question presented is certainly a very serious one. For, if this court is authorized to enter upon this inquiry . . . , and it should be decided that the charter government had no legal existence during the period of time above mentioned — if it had been annulled by the adoption of the opposing government — then the laws passed by its Legislature during that time were nullities; its taxes wrongfully collected; its salaries and compensation to its officers illegally paid; its public accounts improperly

8. Baker v. Carr, 369 U.S. 186, 218-219 (1962).
9. Id. at 222.

settled; and the judgments of the courts in civil and criminal cases null and void, and the officers who carried their decisions into operation answerable as trespassers, if not in some cases as criminals.

In *Dred Scott,* the legal issues of the citizenship of a slave and the validity of the Missouri Compromise were not intrinsically different from many justiciable questions. Rather, Bickel argues, "a question which involved a Civil War can hardly be proper material for the wrangling of lawyers."[10] And the point of his reference to the Hayes-Tilden dispute was that it "brought the country as close as it has ever come to a Latin American sort of a crisis."[11]

The Court has seldom avowed Professor Bickel's notion of political questions. It did not, of course, decline to adjudicate *Dred Scott,* and it has addressed the merits of a variety of "momentous" issues, including the federal income tax, New Deal legislative programs, the steel mill seizure, the relocation program for Japanese-Americans, school desegregation, legislative apportionment, and executive privilege. Moreover, in Powell v. McCormack, the Court implied what the Court of Appeals made explicit in Nixon v. Sirica, 487 F.2d 700 (D.C. Cir. 1973), that "the want of physical power to enforce its judgments does not prevent a court from deciding an otherwise justiciable issue."

On the other hand, one can question whether the Court's refusal to decide challenges to United States military involvement in Southeast Asia[12] and to intervene in the dispute over the seating of delegates to the 1972 Democratic National Convention[13] may not have reflected prudential considerations of the sort espoused by Professor Bickel. Consider also Professor Fritz Scharpf's comments on Coleman v. Miller, supra:[14]

10. Bickel, supra note 3, at 185 (quoting Maurice Finkelstein).

11. Id. The election dispute might have been deemed nonjusticable for other reasons, e.g., a commitment to Congress. In any event, Justice Bradley viewed the matter as presenting "a pure judicial question":

> whether the members of the two houses, when assembled to hear the count of votes for President and Vice President, could go behind the returns, (not of the electors), but of the elections of the electors, and institute a scrutiny into the original elections: or, whether the action of the state authorities on that subject was final.

Letter of October 28, 1882, quoted in Charles Fairman, Mr. Justice Bradley, in Mr. Justice 79 (Kurland & Dunham eds. 1956).

12. See, e.g., Mora v. McNamara, 389 U.S. 934 (1967); Massachusetts v. Laird, 400 U.S. 886 (1970).

13. O'Brien v. Brown, 409 U.S. 1 (1972). California and Illinois delegates sued to prevent the Democratic National Convention from implementing the Credentials Committee's recommendations not to seat them. The California plaintiffs, all committed to George McGovern, challenged the committee's rejection of the state's winner-take-all primary election law. The Illinois plaintiffs (Mayor Daley's delegation) challenged their exclusion for nonrepresentativeness. The plaintiffs argued that they were denied due process and that their constituents the candidates of their choice; the Illinois delegates also argued that the committee had established racial, ethnic, and sexual quotas in violation of the equal protection clause. The suits were filed on July 3, 1972. On July 5, the court of appeals reversed the district court's dismissal of the actions as nonjusticiable and proceeded to determine the merits in favor of the California delegates and the Illinois delegates. On July 7, with the convention only three days off, the Supreme Court stayed the court of appeals' judgments. The short per curiam opinion emphasized the lack of time to consider the issues adequately, the "availability of the convention as a forum to review the recommendations of the Credentials Committee," and "the absence of authority supporting the action of the Court of Appeals in intervening in the internal determinations of a national political party, on the eve of its convention, regarding the seating of delegates." Justices Douglas, White, and Marshall dissented.

14. Fritz Scharpf, Judicial Review and the Political Question, 75 Yale L.J. 517, 586 (1966).

It is one thing for the Court to strike down the Child Labor Law as incompatible with its choice of constitutional values, and it is difficult enough to square this with democratic principle, but it would seem to be quite a different matter if the Court could, by a narrow interpretation of the amendment procedures, prevent the ratification of the amendment which was intended to overrule Hammer v. Dagenhart. Of course, the amendment process is itself governed by the Constitution, and it is by no means inconceivable that an amendment might be unconstitutional. But this seems to be one instance in which the Court cannot assume responsibility for saying "what the law is" without, at the same time, undermining the legitimacy of its power to say so.

F. The Authority to Decline the Exercise of Jurisdiction

May a federal court properly decline, for prudential reasons, to decide a case that is within its mandatory statutory jurisdiction, that is not committed by the Constitution to another agency, and that is susceptible to judicial resolution? A negative answer follows from Chief Justice Marshall's assertion in Cohens v. Virginia, 19 U.S. (6 Wheat.) 264 (1821):

> It is most true that this Court will not take jurisdiction if it should not: but it is equally true, that it must take jurisdiction if it should. The judiciary cannot, as the legislature may, avoid a measure because it approaches the confines of the constitution. We cannot pass it by because it is doubtful. With whatever doubts, with whatever difficulties, a case may be attended, we must decide it, if it be brought before us. We have no more right to decline the exercise of jurisdiction what is given, than to usurp that which is not given. The one or the other would be treason to the constitution.

Marshall may have been referring only to the Court's obligation to obey the law, including section 25 of the Judiciary Act of 1789, which vested the Court with mandatory jurisdiction over certain state appeals. Some scholarly commentators have implied, however, that an assertion of discretion to refuse to decide a properly presented case undermines the very foundations of judicial review as established in *Marbury*. For example, Professor Herbert Wechsler writes:[15]

> For me, as for anyone who finds the judicial power anchored in the Constitution, there is no . . . escape from the judicial obligation . . . to decide the litigated case and to decide it in accordance with the law. . . .
>
> It is true . . . that the courts themselves regard some questions as "political," meaning thereby that they are not to be resolved judicially, although they involve constitutional interpretation and arise in the course of litigation. . . . [But] all the doctrine can defensibly imply is that the courts are called upon to judge whether the Constitution has committed to another agency of government the autonomous determination of the issue raised, a finding that itself requires an interpretation. . . . Difficult as it may be to make that judgment wisely, whatever factors may be rightly weighed in situations where the answer is not clear, what is involved is in itself an act of constitutional interpretation, to be made and judged by standards that should

15. Herbert Wechsler, Toward Neutral Principles of Constitutional Law, 73 Harv. L. Rev. 1, 6-9 (1959) (emphasis added). Cf. Bickel, supra note 3, at 117-119, 124-127; Gerald Gunther, The Subtle Vices of the "Passive Virtues," 1964 Colum. L. Rev. 1.

> govern the interpretive process generally. That, I submit, is toto caelo different from a broad discretion to abstain or intervene.

Is this position persuasive? To be sure, *Marbury's* justification for judicial review entails that if a court decides a case at all, it cannot avoid deciding a constitutional question (other, perhaps, than a true political question) that might affect the judgment. But by what logic does *Marbury* prevent a court's dismissing the case without deciding anything?

The argument made above applies most strongly to trial and intermediate appellate courts, which are obligated to decide *all* cases brought before them. By contrast, the Supreme Court is almost never duty bound to decide any particular case. This was not always so. Until 1925 the Court had almost no formal control over its docket. The Court's discretionary jurisdiction grew during the following half century, and with the elimination of most mandatory appeals in 1988, the Court has had almost complete discretion whether to hear any given case.[16] Bennett Boskey and Eugene Gressman describe this as completing "an historic transformation" based on the principle that the Supreme Court is "the best judge of what cases, out of the thousands put forward each year, are from the national standpoint the most deserving of a hearing on the merits."[17] Given this discretion, what remains of Marshall's claim of duty when the Court assesses the constitutionality of legislation? Should we expect the Justices to use "principled" criteria when determining which cases are to be granted review, or is the decision to review itself (properly) an exercise of political judgment?

G. Concluding Problem: Judicial Review of Matters Pertaining to Impeachment

Article I, sections 2 and 3, of the Constitution provide:

> The House of Representatives . . . shall have the sole power of impeachment. . . .
>
> The Senate shall have the sole power to try all impeachments. When sitting for that purpose, they shall be on oath or affirmation. When the President of the United States is tried, the Chief Justice shall preside: And no person shall be convicted without the concurrence of two thirds of the members present.

Article I, section 3, provides:

16. Since the establishment of the discretionary writ of certiorari in 1925, most of the Court's decisions have resulted from its issuance of this writ rather than from "mandatory" appellate jurisdiction. Still, an important portion of the Court's docket came from its "appellate" docket, though the Court was often criticized for treating this mandatory docket as if it were discretionary. See generally Note, The Discretionary Power of the Supreme Court to Dismiss Appeals from State Courts, 1963 Colum. L. Rev. 688. A dramatic example is Naim v. Naim, 350 U.S. 985 (1956), an appeal from a Virginia judgment upholding the state's antimiscegenation law. The Court dismissed the appeal on spurious jurisdictional grounds, presumably because of its disinclination to confront the constitutionality of "mixed" marriages just two years after Brown v. Board of Education, at a time when Virginia in particular was practicing "massive resistance" against that decision. The Virginia law enforced in *Naim* was unanimously struck down 15 years later in Loving v. Virginia, 388 U.S. 1 (1971), by which time the decision was uncontroversial.

17. See Bennett Boskey and Eugene Gressman, The Supreme Court Bids Farewell to Mandatory Appeals, 109 S. Ct. 412, 430 (1988 interim ed.). Mandatory appellate jurisdiction does continue in a small category of cases, set out in 28 U.S.C. §1253.

Judgment in cases of impeachment shall not extend further than to removal from office and disqualification to hold and enjoy any office of honor, trust, or profit under the United States: but the party convicted shall nevertheless be liable and subject to indictment, trial, judgment, and punishment according to law.

A major issue during the inquiry into the impeachment of President Richard M. Nixon was whether the president could be impeached for misconduct that was neither a crime at common law nor under the United States criminal code. Mr. Nixon's lawyer, James St. Clair, argued that the President could only be impeached for criminal conduct.[18] The staff of the Impeachment Inquiry of the House Judiciary Committee concluded that impeachment could be based "upon conduct seriously incompatible with either the constitutional form and principles of our government or the proper performance of constitutional duties of the presidential office."[19] This issue was debated within the Judiciary Committee, which drafted Articles of Impeachment premised in part on noncriminal misconduct along the lines of the Inquiry staff's standard. The first two Articles charged:

Article I

In his conduct of the office of President of the United States, Richard M. Nixon, in violation of his constitutional oath faithfully to execute the office of President of the United States and, to the best of his ability, preserve, protect, and defend the Constitution of the United States, and in violation of his constitutional duty to take care that the laws be faithfully executed, has prevented, obstructed, and impeded the administration of justice, in that:

On June 17, 1972, and prior thereto, agents of the Committee for the Re-election of the President committed unlawful entry of the headquarters of the Democratic National Committee in Washington, District of Columbia, for the purpose of securing political intelligence. Subsequent thereto, Richard M. Nixon, using the powers of his high office, engaged personally and through his subordinates and agents, in a course of conduct or plan designed to delay, impede, and obstruct the investigation of such unlawful entry; to cover up, conceal and protect those responsible; and to conceal the existence and scope of other unlawful covert activities.

The means used to implement this course of conduct or plan included one or more of the following: . . .

(6) endeavoring to misuse the Central Intelligence Agency, an agency of the United States; . . .

(8) making false or misleading public statements for the purpose of deceiving the people of the United States into believing that a thorough and complete investigation had been conducted with respect to allegations of misconduct on the part of personnel of the executive branch of the United States and personnel of the Committee for the Re-election of the President, and that there was no involvement of such personnel in such misconduct. . . .

Article II

Using the powers of the office of President of the United States, Richard M. Nixon, in violation of his constitutional oath faithfully to execute the office of Presi-

18. St. Clair et al., Summary of an Analysis of the Constitutional Standard for Presidential Impeachment (1974).

19. Report by the Staff of the Impeachment Inquiry, House Committee on the Judiciary, 93d Cong., 2d Sess., Constitutional Grounds for Presidential Impeachment (Comm. Print 1974).

dent of the United States, and to the best of his ability, preserve, protect, and defend the Constitution of the United States, and in disregard of his consitutional duty to take care that the laws be faithfully executed, has repeatedly engaged in conduct violating the constitutional rights of citizens, impairing the due and proper administration of justice and the conduct of lawful inquiries, or contravening the laws governing agencies of the executive branch and the purposes of these agencies.

This conduct has included one or more of the following:

(1) He has, acting personally and through his subordinates and agents, endeavored to obtain from the Internal Revenue Service, in violation of the constitutional rights of citizens, confidential information contained in income tax returns for purposes not authorized by law, and to cause, in violation of the constitutional rights of citizens, income tax audits or other income tax investigations to be initiated or conducted in a discriminatory manner.

(2) He misused the Federal Bureau of Investigation, the Secret Service, and other executive personnel, in violation or disregard of the constitutional rights of citizens, by directing or authorizing such agencies or personnel to conduct or continue electronic surveillance or other investigations for purposes unrelated to national security, the enforcement of laws, or any other lawful function of his office; he did direct, authorize, or permit the use of information obtained thereby for purposes unrelated to national security, the enforcement of laws, or any other lawful function of his office; and he did direct the concealment of certain records made by the Federal Bureau of Investigation of electronic surveillance.

(3) He has, acting personally and through his subordinates and agents, in violation or disregard of the constitutional rights of citizens, authorized and permitted to be maintained a secret investigative unit within the office of the President, financed in part with money derived from campaign contributions, which unlawfully utilized the resources of the Central Intelligence Agency, engaged in covert and unlawful activities, and attempted to prejudice the constitutional right of an accused to a fair trial.

(4) He has failed to take care that the laws were faithfully executed by failing to act when he knew or had reason to know that his close subordinates endeavored to impede and frustrate lawful inquiries by duly constituted executive, judicial, and legislative entities concerning the unlawful entry into the headquarters of the Democratic National Committee, and the coverup thereof, and concerning other unlawful activities, including those relating to the confirmation of Richard Kleindienst as Attorney General of the United States, the electronic surveillance of private citizens, the break-in into the offices of Dr. Lewis Fielding, and the campaign financing practices of the Committee to Re-elect the President.

Suppose that Richard M. Nixon had not resigned the presidency in 1974, that the House of Representatives had adopted the Articles of Impeachment, and that the Senate had tried and convicted him. Suppose that he sought judicial review on the ground that the conduct for which he was convicted was not criminal and that a President can only be impeached for committing criminal offenses.

In what court might Mr. Nixon have sued whom for what relief? On what constitutional provision(s) would the claim have been premised? What constitutional and statutory provisions would support federal subject matter jurisdiction? Would his claim "arise under" the Constitution? If so, would it be justiciable?

Especially on the last question, consider the meaning of the impeachment provisions of Article I, section 3, the implications of The Federalist No. 65, and the contrasting views of Irving Brant and Charles Black.

In The Federalist No. 65, Hamilton explained why the power to try impeachments was reposed in the Senate rather than the Supreme Court:

> Where else than in the Senate could have been found a tribunal sufficiently dignified, or sufficiently independent? What other body would be likely to feel *confidence enough in its own situation* to preserve, unawed and uninfluenced, the necessary impartiality between an *individual* accused and the *representatives of the people, his accusers?*
>
> Could the Supreme Court have been relied upon as answering this description? It is much to be doubted whether the members of that tribunal would at all times be endowed with so eminent a portion of fortitude as would be called for in the execution of so difficult a task; and it is still more to be doubted whether they would possess the degree of credit and authority which might, on certain occasions, be indispensable towards reconciling the people to a decision that should happen to clash with an accusation brought by their immediate representatives. A deficiency in the first would be fatal to the accused; in the last, dangerous to the public tranquillity. The hazard, in both these respects, could only be avoided, if at all, by rendering that tribunal more numerous than would consist with a reasonable attention to economy. The necessity of a numerous court for the trial of impeachments is equally dictated by the nature of the proceeding. This can never be tied down by such strict rules, either in the delineation of the offense by the prosecutors or in the construction of it by the judges, as in common cases serve to limit the discretion of courts in favor of personal security. There will be no jury to stand between the judges who are to pronounce the sentence of the law and the party who is to receive or suffer it. The awful discretion which a court of impeachments must necessarily have to doom to honor or to infamy the most confidential and the most distinguished characters of the community forbids the commitment of the trust to a small number of persons.

IRVING BRANT, IMPEACHMENT: TRIALS AND ERRORS
181-186 (1972)

[I]mpeachment without constitutional warrant is a bill of attainder. Such impeachment is also an ex post facto law.[20] The Constitution says: "No bill of attainder or ex post facto law shall be passed." Once these constitutional realities are recognized in relation to impeachment, the entire situation falls into focus and the remedy is at hand.

Bills of attainder under any guise are subject to judicial review, and so are ex post facto laws. Thus judicial review constitutes the only protection against these prohibited actions by Congress. That is the basic provision of the Constitution for protection against legislative tyranny. Judicial review of bills of attainder was affirmed by way of illustration in Marbury v. Madison in 1803. It has been universally recognized by Congress. It was tacitly recognized but not acknowledged by the impeachers of Andrew Johnson. . . .

Following the injection of that issue into the Johnson trial by former Supreme Court Justice Curtis, Manager John Bingham, without saying a word about at-

20. A bill of attainder is a legislative enactment punishing specified individuals without a judicial proceeding. An ex post facto law is a criminal statute enacted applied retroactively to conduct occurring before its enactment. Art. I, §9, cl. 3, provides: "No Bill of Attainder or ex post facto Law shall be passed."

tainder, launched a violent attack against the idea of review of impeachment by the Supreme Court. . . . He said:

> . . . What has this question to do with the final decision of the case before the Senate? I say if your Supreme Court sat today in judgment upon this question it has no power and can have none over the Senate. The question belongs to the Senate, in the language of the Constitution, exclusively. The words are that "the Senate shall have the sole power to try all impeachments"!

This, Bingham declared, covered every aspect of the case:

> The sole or only power to try impeachments includes the power to try and determine every question of law and fact arising in a case of impeachment. It is in vain that the decision of the Supreme Court or of the circuit court or of the district court or of any court outside of this [the Senate] is invoked for the decision of any question arising in this trial, between the people and their guilty President.

Had the clause relating to the Senate's "sole power" stood alone, there would be some slight plausibility to Bingham's interpretation. But the true meaning is found in its relation to a preceding clause. Putting the two together:

"The House of Representatives . . . shall have the sole power of impeachment.

"The Senate shall have the sole power to try all impeachments."

In combination, what are these but a mere division of functions between House and Senate? They say that the Senate shall have no part of the power to impeach, and that the House shall have no part of the power to try impeachments. . . .

[Bingham also said:]

> The Senate, having the sole power to try impeachments, must of necessity be vested by every intendment of the Constitution with the sole and exclusive power to decide every question of law and of fact involved in the issue . . . and the Supreme Court of the United States has no more power to intervene either before or after judgment in the premises than does the Court of St. Petersburg. . . .

He backed this with another impediment to judicial review. Quoting the provision of Article III that "The judicial power shall extend to all cases in law and equity arising under this Constitution, the laws of the United States, and treaties made, or which shall be made," he protested: "Impeachment is not a case 'in law or equity,' within the meaning of the terms as employed in the third section of the Constitution, which I have just read. It is in no sense a case within the general judicial power of the United States."

This expanded Bingham's original fallacy that the Senate's "sole power to try all impeachments" (a mere denial to the House of any share in the trial) gives the Senate power to override constitutional limitations without judicial review. If impeachment, by its very nature, cannot produce a "case in law or equity" when conducted in violation of the Constitution, that rule must apply to state as well as federal impeachments. It would follow, then, that states could set up racial qualifications and remove Negro officers by impeachment (there have been times when this could have happened), with no possibility of appeal to the Supreme Court under the Fourteenth Amendment. . . . Or House and Senate, acting together, could extend liability to include the impeachment of private citizens and their perpetual disqualification to hold office. Under Bingham's construction, such violations of the Constitution would not produce a case in law or equity for the victims of them.

Every unconstitutional action of Congress that works definite and substantial injury to a specific individual gives that person standing to present a "case in law or equity" to the courts of the United States. The only question, therefore, is whether removal by impeachment in violation of the Constitution produces substantial injury. Financially it may be no injury at all, but in social standing and human dignity the penalty is fearful. Suppose, however, that we treat it as only a passing episode of little stigma. What about the provision that the party convicted may be disqualified "to hold any office of honor, trust or profit under the United States"? Nobody, surely, would contend that this lifelong punishment, if imposed in violation of the Constitution, is too trivial to give rise to a case in law or equity. But no distinction based on differing penalties can be drawn. If a case in law or equity exists in relation to perpetual disqualification, it must exist in relation to every violation of constitutional provisions on impeachment.

Above all, this right of judicial review is implicit in the prohibition of bills of attainder and ex post facto laws — the only processes of criminal law that are singled out by the original Constitution (there are others in the amendments) for complete and unqualified prohibition of action by Congress. Thus they stand out above all others within the mandate that the judicial power shall extend "to all cases in law or equity" arising under the Constitution. . . .

Contrast Professor Brant's impassioned plea for judicial review of impeachments with Professor Charles Black's opposing view:[21]

> . . . The most powerful maxim of constitutional law is that its rules ought to make sense. Let us try to imagine the situation which could be produced by providing judicial review of a senatorial judgment of removal.
>
> Picture, if you will, a president whose conduct has attracted such unfavorable notice as to be thoroughly investigated by the Judiciary Committee of the House of Representatives. The result of this investigation has been a formal recommendation to the whole House that Articles of Impeachment be voted. After the fullest debate, with the attention of the country focused on the issue, the House concludes that the president ought indeed to be impeached. . . . The Senate, after plenary trial and fullest arguments of counsel, and after debate among senators on fact and law, votes by a two-thirds majority to convict and remove the president.
>
> The president now appeals to the Supreme Court. The jurisdiction of that Court over the appeal is to say the least quite unclear, but it takes jurisdiction anyway. On the merits, the Court disagrees with the House and with the Senate on some point, let us say, as to the meaning of "high Crimes and Misdemeanors," or on some procedural question of weight (perhaps dividing 5 to 4, perhaps filing nine opinions no five of which espouse the same reasoning). So *it puts the impeached and convicted president back in for the rest of his term. . . .*
>
> I don't think I possess the resources of rhetoric adequate to characterize the absurdity of that position.

21. Charles Black, Impeachment: A Handbook 53 (1974).

Discussion

1. Does the language of the Constitution imply anything one way or the other about the justiciability of impeachments?

2. Do Hamilton's explanations for the Senate's jurisdiction to try impeachments imply that the judiciary may not review the Senate's judgment of conviction?

3. Assuming that Professor Brant is correct that impeachment without constitutional warrant is a bill of attainder and an ex post facto law, does this imply that convictions of impeachment are justiciable?

4. How would you characterize Professor Black's argument against judicial review of impeachments? That is, what *kind* of an argument is it? Is it persuasive as applied to impeachments of *all* officers, or just certain ones such as presidents? (If just certain ones, are other impeachments justiciable?) What consequences does Professor Black's argument have for the justiciability of school segregation, legislative apportionment, and the issue presented in *Powell*?

5. Might one consistently hold that the "legal" question of what constitutes an impeachable offense is justiciable but that the Senate's application of the law to facts is not justiciable? Does the answer to this depend on one's opinion on the merits of what constitutes an impeachable offense?

6. Representative Gerald Ford once asserted that "an impeachable offense is whatever a majority of the House of Representatives considers [it] to be at a given moment of history."[22] Recurring to the concepts of finality and discretion raised in this section, what might this remark mean? What does it suggest about judicial review of convictions of impeachment?

II. Congressional Implementation of the Civil War Amendments: The Allocation of Constitutional Decisionmaking Authority Between Congress and the Judiciary

In 1981, Senator Helms and Representative Hyde introduced a bill into the Congress "to provide that human life shall be deemed to exist from conception." As amended by a subcommittee of the Senate Judiciary Committee, sections 1-3 of S. 158 provided:

> Section 1. (a) The Congress finds that the life of each human being begins at conception.
>
> (b) The Congress further finds that the fourteenth amendment to the Constitution of the United States protects all human beings.
>
> Sec. 2. Upon the basis of these findings, and in the exercise of the powers of Congress, including its power under section 5 of the fourteenth amendment to the Constitution of the United States, the Congress hereby recognizes that for the purpose of enforcing the obligation of the States under the fourteenth amendment not to deprive persons of life without due process of law, each human life exists from conception, without regard to race, sex, age, health, defect, or condition of dependency, and for this purpose "person" includes all human beings.

22. 116 Cong. Rec. 1913 (April 15, 1970).

Sec. 3. Congress further recognizes that each State has a compelling interest, independent of the status of unborn children under the fourteenth amendment, in protecting the lives of those within the State's jurisdiction whom the State rationally regards as human beings.

The Civil War Amendments are self-executing: The first section of each amendment prohibits certain practices even in the absence of implementing legislation. But each of the amendments also provides (with minor stylistic variation) that "Congress shall have the power to enforce this article by appropriate legislation."[23] Roe v. Wade, 410 U.S. 113 (1973), p.982 supra, was decided under the due process clause of section 1 of the Fourteenth Amendment. The first two sections of S. 158 tacitly assume that Congress has the power, under section 5 of the Amendment, to overrule Roe v. Wade.

We have already seen one instance in which Congress could overrule a judicial decision. Since the *Wheeling Bridge* decision (1852), p.169 supra, Congress has had the final say about whether a state regulation of interstate commerce is impermissibly burdensome. The commerce clause is in terms *solely* a grant of legislative power to Congress; its self-executing aspect had to be inferred and was, indeed, disputed well into the nineteenth century. Moreover, the nature of congressional judgments implementing the commerce power is essentially different from judgments under the Fourteenth Amendment. When Congress legislates under the commerce clause, it need not concern itself with the constitutionality of any state statutes that the proposed law will affect or preempt; Congress must only determine that the proposed law is within its delegated powers and does not contravene any constitutional limitations.[24] By contrast, implicit in congressional legislation pursuant to the implementing clauses of the Civil War Amendments is a finding that the legislation is both an appropriate remedy for *unconstitutional* state laws or practices and, as in the case of S. 158, a corrective for an erroneous constitutional determination by the judiciary.[25]

The scope of congressional power to revise the constitutional judgments of courts is a crucial and unresolved issue in the allocation of constitutional decisionmaking authority in the American polity. It is the central issue of this section. We approach it by surveying the (brief) history of congressional implementation of the Civil War Amendments.

A. Congressional Implementation of Judicially Declared Constitutional Rights

Until the mid-1960s, most congressional legislation under the Civil War Amendments was essentially procedural, designed narrowly to implement and enforce

23. This is also true of the Nineteenth, Twenty-fourth, and Twenty-sixth Amendments.

24. A typical example is the Federal Surface Mining Control and Reclamation Act of 1977, upheld in Hodel v. Virginia Surface Mining and Reclamation Assn., Inc., 452 U.S. 264 (1981), as a valid exercise of Congress' power under the commerce clause. The Act displaced a number of state regulations of strip mining, but Congress had no need to find, or even to inquire into the possibility, that these laws were "unconstitutional." It was enough that Congress found them hindrances to an effective national policy regarding strip mining.

25. As a related point, there also may be a significant difference between the legislative and congressional roles in making decisions affecting the national economy and protecting individual rights.

judicially declared rights. For example, 42 U.S.C. §1983, which is invoked in virtually all civil rights litigation, does not purport to invalidate any state practices that a court has not independently held unconstitutional.

By contrast, the Voting Rights Act of 1965 invalidated state practices that no court had, or has to this day, declared unconstitutional. In South Carolina v. Katzenbach, 383 U.S. 301 (1966), the Court sustained the provision of the act that suspended literacy tests throughout the South, although only a few years earlier, in Lassiter v. Northampton Board of Elections, 360 U.S. 45 (1959), it had unanimously upheld identical tests against constitutional attack.

SOUTH CAROLINA v. KATZENBACH
383 U.S. 301 (1966)
On Bill of Complaint

WARREN, C.J.

By leave of the Court South Carolina has filed a bill of complaint, seeking a declaration that selected provisions of the Voting Rights Act of 1965 violate the Federal Constitution, and asking for an injunction against enforcement of these provisions by the Attorney General. . . .

The Voting Rights Act was designed by Congress to banish the blight of racial discrimination in voting, which has infected the electoral process in part of our country for nearly a century. The Act creates stringent new remedies for voting discrimination where it persists on a pervasive scale, and in addition the statute strengthens existing remedies for pockets of voting discrimination elsewhere in the country. Congress assumed the power to prescribe these remedies from §2 of the Fifteenth Amendment, which authorizes the National Legislature to effectuate by "appropriate" measures the constitutional prohibition against racial discrimination in voting. We hold that the sections of the Act which are properly before us are an appropriate means for carrying out Congress' constitutional responsibilities and are consonant with all other provisions of the Constitution. We therefore deny South Carolina's request that enforcement of these sections of the Act be enjoined.

I

The constitutional propriety of the Voting Rights Act of 1965 must be judged with reference to the historical experience which it reflects. Before enacting the measure, Congress explored with great care the problem of racial discrimination in voting. . . .

Two points emerge vividly from the voluminous legislative history of the Act contained in the committee hearings and floor debates. First: Congress felt itself confronted by an insidious and pervasive evil which had been perpetuated in certain parts of our country through unremitting and ingenious defiance of the Constitution. Second: Congress concluded that the unsuccessful remedies which it had prescribed in the past would have to be replaced by sterner and more elaborate measures in order to satisfy the clear commands of the Fifteenth Amendment. We pause here to summarize the majority reports of the House and Senate

Committees, which document in considerable detail the factual basis for these reactions by Congress.

The Fifteenth Amendment to the Constitution was ratified in 1870. Promptly thereafter Congress passed the Enforcement Act of 1870, which made it a crime for public officers and private persons to obstruct exercise of the right to vote. The statute was amended in the following year to provide for detailed federal supervision of the electoral process, from registration to the certification of returns. As the years passed and fervor for racial equality waned, enforcement of the laws became spotty and ineffective, and most of their provisions were repealed in 1894. The remnants have had little significance in the recently renewed battle against voting discrimination.

Meanwhile, beginning in 1890, the States of Alabama, Georgia, Louisiana, Mississippi, North Carolina, South Carolina, and Virginia enacted tests still in use which were specifically designed to prevent Negroes from voting. Typically, they made the ability to read and write a registration qualification and also required completion of a registration form. These laws were based on the fact that as of 1890 in each of the named States, more than two-thirds of the adult Negroes were illiterate while less than one-quarter of the adult whites were unable to read or write. At the same time, alternate tests were prescribed in all of the named States to assure that white illiterates would not be deprived of the franchise. These included grandfather clauses, property qualifications, "good character" tests, and the requirement that registrants "understand" or "interpret" certain matter.

The course of subsequent Fifteenth Amendment litigation in this Court demonstrates the variety and persistence of these and similar institutions designed to deprive Negroes of the right to vote. Grandfather clauses were invalidated in Guinn v. United States, 238 U.S. 347, and Myers v. Anderson, 238 U.S. 368. Procedural hurdles were struck down in Lane v. Wilson, 307 U.S. 268. The white primary was outlawed in Smith v. Allwright, 321 U.S. 649, and Terry v. Adams, 345 U.S. 461. Improper challenges were nullified in United States v. Thomas, 362 U.S. 58. Racial gerrymandering was forbidden by Gomillion v. Lightfoot, 364 U.S. 339. Finally, discriminatory application of voting tests was condemned in Schnell v. Davis, 336 U.S. 933; Alabama v. United States, 371 U.S. 37; and Louisiana v. United States, 380 U.S. 145.

According to the evidence in recent Justice Department voting suits, the latter stratagem is now the principal method used to bar Negroes from the polls. Discriminatory administration of voting qualifications has been found in all eight Alabama cases, in all nine Louisiana cases, and in all nine Mississippi cases which have gone to final judgment. Moreover, in almost all of these cases, the courts have held that the discrimination was pursuant to a widespread "pattern or practice." White applicants for registration have often been excused altogether from the literacy and understanding tests or have been given easy versions, have received extensive help from voting officials, and have been registered despite serious errors in their answers. Negroes, on the other hand, have typically been required to pass difficult versions of all the tests, without any outside assistance and without the slightest error. The good-morals requirement is so vague and subjective that it has constituted an open invitation to abuse at the hands of voting officials. Negroes obliged to obtain vouchers from registered voters have found it virtually impossible to comply in areas where almost no Negroes are on the rolls.

In recent years, Congress has repeatedly tried to cope with the problem by facilitating case-by-case litigation against voting discrimination. The Civil Rights Act of 1957 authorized the Attorney General to seek injunctions against public and private interference with the right to vote on racial grounds. Perfecting amendments in the Civil Rights Act of 1960 permitted the joinder of States as parties defendant, gave the Attorney General access to local voting records, and authorized courts to register voters in areas of systematic discrimination. Title I of the Civil Rights Act of 1964 expedited the hearing of voting cases before three-judge courts and outlawed some of the tactics used to disqualify Negroes from voting in federal elections.

Despite the earnest efforts of the Justice Department and of many federal judges, these new laws have done little to cure the problem of voting discrimination. . . .

The previous legislation has proved ineffective for a number of reasons. Voting suits are unusually onerous to prepare, sometimes requiring as many as 6,000 manhours spent combing through registration records in preparation for trial. Litigation has been exceedingly slow, in part because of the ample opportunities for delay afforded voting officials and others involved in the proceedings. Even when favorable decisions have finally been obtained, some of the States affected have merely switched to discriminatory devices not covered by the federal decrees or have enacted difficult new tests designed to prolong the existing disparity between white and Negro registration. Alternatively, certain local officials have defied and evaded court orders or have simply closed their registration offices to freeze the voting rolls. The provision of the 1960 law authorizing registration by federal officers has had little impact on local maladministration because of its procedural complexities. . . .

II

The Voting Rights Act of 1965 reflects Congress' firm intention to rid the country of racial discrimination in voting. The heart of the Act is a complex scheme of stringent remedies aimed at areas where voting discrimination has been most flagrant. Section 4(a)-(d) lays down a formula defining the States and political subdivisions to which these new remedies apply. The first of the remedies, contained in §4(a), is the suspension of literacy tests and similar voting qualifications for a period of five years from the last occurrence of substantial voting discrimination. Section 5 prescribes a second remedy, the suspension of all new voting regulations pending review by federal authorities to determine whether their use would perpetuate voting discrimination. The third remedy, covered in §§6(b), 7, 9, and 13(a), is the assignment of federal examiners on certification by the Attorney General to list qualified applicants who are thereafter entitled to vote in all elections. . . .

COVERAGE FORMULA

The remedial sections of the Act assailed by South Carolina automatically apply to any State, or to any separate political subdivision such as a county or parish, for which two findings have been made: (1) the Attorney General has determined that on November 1, 1964, it maintained a "test or device," and (2) the

Director of the Census has determined that less than 50% of its voting age residents were registered on November 1, 1964, or voted in the presidential election of November 1964. These findings are not reviewable in any court and are final upon publication in the Federal Register. §4(b). As used throughout the Act, the phrase "test or device" means any requirement that a registrant or voter must "(1) demonstrate the ability to read, write, understand, or interpret any matter, (2) demonstrate any educational achievement or his knowledge of any particular subject, (3) possess good moral character, or (4) prove his qualifications by the voucher of registered voters or members of any other class." §4(c).

Statutory coverage of a State or political subdivision under §4(b) is terminated if the area obtains a declaratory judgment from the District Court for the District of Columbia, determining that tests and devices have not been used during the preceding five years to abridge the franchise on racial grounds. . . .

South Carolina was brought within the coverage formula of the Act on August 7, 1965, pursuant to appropriate administrative determinations which have not been challenged in this proceeding. On the same day, coverage was also extended to Alabama, Alaska, Georgia, Louisiana, Mississippi, Virginia, 26 counties in North Carolina, and one county in Arizona. Two more counties in Arizona, one county in Hawaii, and one county in Idaho were added to the list on November 19, 1965. Thus far Alaska, the three Arizona counties, and the single county in Idaho have asked the District Court for the District of Columbia to grant a declaratory judgment terminating statutory coverage.

SUSPENSION OF TESTS

In a State or political subdivision covered by §4(b) of the Act, no person may be denied the right to vote in any election because of his failure to comply with a "test or device." §4(a).

On account of this provision, South Carolina is temporarily barred from enforcing [its literacy test]. . . .

REVIEW OF NEW RULES

In a State or political subdivision covered by §4(b) of the Act, no person may be denied the right to vote in any election because of his failure to comply with a voting qualification or procedure different from those in force on November 1, 1964. This suspension of new rules is terminated, however, under either of the following circumstances: (1) if the area has submitted the rules to the Attorney General, and he has not interposed an objection within 60 days, or (2) if the area has obtained a declaratory judgment from the District Court for the District of Columbia, determining that the rules will not abridge the franchise on racial grounds. These declaratory judgment actions are to be heard by a three-judge panel, with direct appeal to this Court. §5.

South Carolina altered its voting laws in 1965 to extend the closing hour at polling places from 6 P.M. to 7 P.M. The State has not sought judicial review of this change in the District Court for the District of Columbia, nor has it submitted the new rule to the Attorney General for his scrutiny, although at our hearing the Attorney General announced that he does not challenge the amendment. There are indications in the record that other sections of the country listed above have also altered their voting laws since November 1, 1964.

FEDERAL EXAMINERS

In any political subdivision covered by §4(b) of the Act, the Civil Service Commission shall appoint voting examiners whenever the Attorney General certifies either of the following facts: (1) that he has received meritorious written complaints from at least 20 residents alleging that they have been disenfranchised under color of law because of their race, or (2) that the appointment of examiners is otherwise necessary to effectuate the guarantees of the Fifteenth Amendment.... These certificates are not reviewable in any court and are effective upon publication in the Federal Register. §4(b).

The examiners who have been appointed are to test the voting qualifications of applicants according to regulations of the Civil Service Commission prescribing times, places, procedures, and forms. §§7(a) and 9(b). Any person who meets the voting requirements of state law, insofar as these have not been suspended by the Act, must promptly be placed on a list of eligible voters.... A person shall be removed from the voting list by an examiner if he has lost his eligibility under valid state law, or if he has been successfully challenged....

On October 30, 1965, the Attorney General certified the need for federal examiners in two South Carolina counties, and examiners appointed by the Civil Service Commission have been serving there since November 8, 1965. Examiners have also been assigned to 11 counties in Alabama, five parishes in Louisiana, and 19 counties in Mississippi....

III

... [T]he basic question presented by the case [is]: Has Congress exercised its powers under the Fifteenth Amendment in an appropriate manner with relation to the States?

The ground rules for resolving this question are clear. The language and purpose of the Fifteenth Amendment, the prior decisions construing its several provisions, and the general doctrines of constitutional interpretation, all point to one fundamental principle. As against the reserved powers of the States, Congress may use any rational means to effectuate the constitutional prohibition of racial discrimination in voting. Cf. our rulings last Term, sustaining Title II of the Civil Rights Act of 1964, in Heart of Atlanta Motel v. United States, 379 U.S. 241, and Katzenbach v. McClung, 379 U.S. 294. We turn now to a more detailed description of the standards which govern our review of the Act.

Section 1 of the Fifteenth Amendment ... has always been treated as self-executing and has repeatedly been construed, without further legislative specification, to invalidate state voting qualifications or procedures which are discriminatory on their face or in practice.

South Carolina contends that the cases cited above are precedents only for the authority of the judiciary to strike down state statutes and procedures — that to allow an exercise of this authority by Congress would be to rob the courts of their rightful constitutional role. On the contrary, §2 of the Fifteenth Amendment expressly declares that "Congress shall have power to enforce this article by appropriate legislation." By adding this authorization, the Framers indicated that Congress was to be chiefly responsible for implementing the rights created in §1. "It is the power of Congress which has been enlarged. Congress is authorized to *enforce* the prohibitions by appropriate legislation. Some legislation is contemplated to make the [Civil War] amendments fully effective." Ex parte Virginia, 100 U.S. 339, 345. Accordingly, in addition to the courts, Congress has full remedial powers to effectuate the constitutional prohibition against racial discrimination in voting.

Congress has repeatedly exercised these powers in the past, and its enactments have repeatedly been upheld. . . . The basic test to be applied in a case involving §2 of the Fifteenth Amendment is the same as in all cases concerning the express powers of Congress with relation to the reserved powers of the States. Chief Justice Marshall laid down the classic formulation, 50 years before the Fifteenth Amendment was ratified: "Let the end be legitimate, let it be within the scope of the constitution, and all means which are appropriate, which are plainly adapted to that end, which are not prohibited, but consist with the letter and spirit of the constitution, are constitutional." McCulloch v. Maryland, 4 Wheat. 316, 421. The Court has subsequently echoed his language in describing each of the Civil War Amendments:

> Whatever legislation is appropriate, that is, adapted to carry out the objects the amendments have in view, whatever tends to enforce submission to the prohibitions they contain, and to secure to all persons the enjoyment of perfect equality of civil rights and the equal protection of the laws against State denial or invasion, if not prohibited, is brought within the domain of congressional power. Ex parte Virginia. . . .

We therefore reject South Carolina's argument that Congress may appropriately do no more than to forbid violations of the Fifteenth Amendment in general terms — that the task of fashioning specific remedies or of applying them to particular localities must necessarily be left entirely to the courts. Congress is not circumscribed by any such artificial rules under §2 of the Fifteenth Amendment. In the oft-repeated words of Chief Justice Marshall, referring to another specific legislative authorization in the Constitution, "This power, like all others vested in Congress, is complete in itself, may be exercised to its utmost extent, and acknowledges no limitations, other than are prescribed in the constitution." Gibbons v. Ogden, 9 Wheat. 1, 196.

IV

Congress exercised its authority under the Fifteenth Amendment in an inventive manner when it enacted the Voting Rights Act of 1965. First: The measure prescribes remedies for voting discrimination which go into effect without any need for prior adjudication. This was clearly a legitimate response to the problem, for which there is ample precedent under other constitutional provisions. See Katzenbach v. McClung, 379 U.S. 294, 302-304; United States v. Darby, 312 U.S. 100, 120-121. Congress had found that case-by-case litigation was inadequate to combat widespread and persistent discrimination in voting, because of the inordinate amount of time and energy required to overcome the obstructionist tactics invariably encountered in these lawsuits. After enduring nearly a century of systematic resistance of the Fifteenth Amendment, Congress might well decide to shift the advantage of time and inertia from the perpetrators of the evil to its victims. The question remains, of course, whether the specific remedies prescribed in the Act were an appropriate means of combatting the evil, and to this question we shall presently address ourselves.

Second: The Act intentionally confines these remedies to a small number of States and political subdivisions which in most instances were familiar to Congress by name. This, too, was a permissible method of dealing with the problem. Congress had learned that substantial voting discrimination presently occurs in certain sections of the country, and it knew no way of accurately forecasting whether the evil might spread elsewhere in the future. In acceptable legislative fashion, Congress chose to limit its attention to the geographic areas where immediate action seemed necessary. . . .

SUSPENSION OF TESTS

We now arrive at consideration of the specific remedies prescribed by the Act for areas included within the coverage formula. South Carolina assails the temporary suspension of existing voting qualifications, reciting the rule laid down by Lassiter v. Northampton County Bd. of Elections, 360 U.S. 45 (1959), that literacy tests and related devices are not in themselves contrary to the Fifteenth Amendment. In that very case, however, the Court went on to say, "Of course a literacy test, fair on its face, may be employed to perpetuate that discrimination which the Fifteenth Amendment was designed to uproot." The record shows that in most of the States covered by the Act, including South Carolina, various tests and devices have been instituted with the purpose of disenfranchising Negroes, have been framed in such a way as to facilitate this aim, and have been administered in a discriminatory fashion for many years. Under these circumstances, the Fifteenth Amendment has clearly been violated.

The Act suspends literacy tests and similar devices for a period of five years from the last occurrence of substantial voting discrimination. This was a legitimate response to the problem, for which there is ample precedent in Fifteenth Amendment cases. Underlying the response was the feeling that States and political subdivisions which had been allowing white illiterates to vote for years could not sincerely complain about "dilution" of their electorates through the registration of Negro illiterates. Congress knew that continuance of the tests and devices in use at the present time, no matter how fairly administered in the future, would freeze the effect of past discrimination in favor of unqualified white registrants. Congress permissibly rejected the alternative of requiring a complete re-registration of all voters, believing that this would be too harsh on many whites who had enjoyed the franchise for their entire adult lives.

REVIEW OF NEW RULES

The Act suspends new voting regulations pending scrutiny by federal authorities to determine whether their use would violate the Fifteenth Amendment. This may have been an uncommnon exercise of congressional power, as South Carolina contends, but the Court has recognized that exceptional conditions can justify legisiative measures not otherwise appropriate. See Home Bldg. & Loan Assn. v. Blaisdell, 290 U.S. 398. . . . Congress knew that some of the States covered by §4(b) of the Act had resorted to the extraordinary stratagem of contriving new rules of various kinds for the sole purpose of perpetuating voting discrimination in the face of adverse federal court decrees. Congress had reason to suppose that these States might try similar maneuvers in the future in order to evade the remedies for voting discrimination contained in the Act itself. Under the compulsion of these unique circumstances, Congress responded in a permissibly decisive manner.[26] . . .

The bill of complaint is dismissed.

BLACK, J., concurring and dissenting.

I agree with substantially all of the Court's opinion sustaining the power of Congress under §2 of the Fifteenth Amendment to suspend state literacy tests and similar voting qualifications and to authorize the Attorney General to secure the appointment of federal examiners to register qualified voters in various sections of the country. . . .

I dissent from its holding that every part of §5 of the Act is constitutional. . . . Section 5 [provides] that a State covered by §4(b) can in no way amend its constitution or laws relating to voting without first trying to persuade the Attorney General of the United States or the Federal District Court for the District of Columbia that the new proposed laws do not have the purpose and will not have the effect of denying the right to vote to citizens on account of their race or color.

My . . . basic objection to §5, is that Congress has here exercised its power under §2 of the Fifteenth Amendment through the adoption of means that conflict with the most basic principles of the Constitution. As the Court says, the limitations of the power granted under §2 are the same as the limitations imposed on the exercise of any of the powers expressly granted Congress by the Constitution. The classic formulation of these constitutional limitations was stated by Chief Justice Marshall when he said in McCulloch v. Maryland, 4 Wheat. 316, 421, "Let the end be legitimate, let it be within the scope of the constitution, and all means which are appropriate, which are plainly adapted to that end, *which are not prohibited, but consist with the letter and spirit of the constitution,* are constitutional." (Emphasis added.) Section 5, by providing that some of the States cannot pass state laws or adopt state constitutional amendments without first being compelled to beg federal authorities to approve their policies, so distorts our constitutional structure of government as to render any distinction drawn in the Constitution between state and federal power almost meaningless. One of the most basic premises upon which our structure of government was founded was that the Federal Government was to

26. *Developments under §5*. Allen v. State Bd. of Elections, 393 U.S. 544 (1969), held that the following changes in state election laws were subject to the approved requirements of §5: election of county supervisors at large rather than by district; appointment, rather than county option of appointment or election, of school superintendents; more onerous requirements for the qualification of independent candidates; barring of voters from voting for write-in candidates by affixing labels rather than writing their names on the ballots. Chief Justice Warren concluded that §5 covered "any state enactment which altered the election law of a covered State in even a minor way." Justice Harlan, dissenting on this issue, argued that §5 applied only to changes in voting qualifications and the manner in which elections are conducted. Justice Black dissented for the same reasons he dissented in South Carolina v. Katzenbach. In Georgia v. United States, 411 U.S. 526 (1973), the Court held that §5 applied to changes in legislative apportionment.

have certain specific and limited powers and no others, and all other power was to be reserved either "to the States respectively, or to the people." Certainly if all the provisions of our Constitution which limit the power of the Federal Government and reserve other power to the States are to mean anything, they mean at least that the States have power to pass laws and amend their constitutions without first sending their officials hundreds of miles away to beg federal authorities to approve them. . . . A federal law which assumes the power to compel the States to submit in advance any proposed legislation they have for approval by federal agents approaches dangerously near to wiping the States out as useful and effective units in the government of our country. I cannot agree to any constitutional interpretation that leads inevitably to such a result. . . .

In this and other prior Acts Congress has quite properly vested the Attorney General with extremely broad power to protect young rights of citizens against discrimination on account of race or color. Section 5 viewed in this context is of very minor importance and in my judgment is likely to serve more as an irritant to the States than as an aid to the enforcement of the Act. I would hold §5 invalid for the reasons stated above with full confidence that the Attorney General has ample power to give vigorous, expeditious and effective protection to the voting rights of all citizens.

Discussion

1. How do the provisions of the Voting Rights Act of 1965 upheld in *South Carolina* differ from the pre-1960s civil rights legislation described near the beginning of this section?

2. In Lassiter v. Northampton County [North Carolina] Board of Elections, 360 U.S. 45 (1959), the Court held that, although the Fifteenth Amendment prohibited the discriminatory administration of literacy tests, the tests were not unconstitutional as such. What is the status of *Lassiter* after enactment of the Voting Rights Act and the decision in *South Carolina?* What is the constitutional status of South Carolina's literacy test?

3. If the Fifteenth Amendment had not contained section 2, would Congress nonetheless have been empowered to enact the Voting Rights Act? In determining the scope of Congress' power to implement the Fifteenth Amendment, the Court quotes Justice Marshall's expansive language in *McCulloch,* which concerned the exercise of Congress' Article I powers. Is *McCulloch* applicable?

4. The Voting Rights Act amendments of 1970 suspended for a period of five years the use of literacy tests in any federal, state, or local election anywhere in the United States. In Oregon v. Mitchell, 400 U.S. 112 (1970), although the Court divided on all other aspects of the 1970 act, it unanimously sustained this provision. There was no majority opinion. In one opinion, Justices Brennan, White, and Marshall wrote:

> The legislative history of the 1970 Amendments contains substantial information upon which Congress could have based a finding that the use of literacy tests in Arizona and in other States where their use was not proscribed by the 1965 Act has the effect of denying the vote to racial minorities whose illiteracy is the consequence of a previous, governmentally sponsored denial of equal educational opportunity. The Attorney General of Arizona told the Senate Subcommittee on Constitutional Rights that many older Indians in the State were "never privileged to attend a formal

school." Extensive testimony before both Houses indicated that racial minorities have long received inferior educational opportunities throughout the United States. And interstate migration of such persons, particularly of Negroes from the Southern States, has long been a matter of common knowledge.

Justices Black and Douglas, in separate opinions, made essentially the same point. Justice Stewart, joined by Chief Justice Burger and Justice Blackmun, wrote:

> Because the justification for extending the ban on literacy tests to the entire Nation need not turn on whether literacy tests unfairly discriminate against Negroes in every State in the Union, Congress was not required to make state-by-state findings concerning either the equality of educational opportunity or actual impact of literacy requirements on the Negro citizen's access to the ballot box. In the interests of uniformity, Congress may paint with a much broader brush than may this Court, which must confine itself to the judicial function of deciding individual cases and controversies upon individual records. The findings that Congress made when it enacted the Voting Rights Act of 1965 would have supported a nationwide ban on literacy tests. . . . Experience gained under the 1965 Act has now led Congress to conclude that it should go the whole distance. This approach to the problem is a rational one: consequently it is within the constitutional power of Congress under §2 of the Fifteenth Amendment.

Although Justice Harlan found the issue "not free from difficulty," he concluded:

> Despite the lack of evidence of specific instances of discriminatory application or effect, Congress could have determined that racial prejudice is prevalent thoughout the Nation, and that literacy tests unduly lend themselves to discriminatory application, either conscious or unconscious. This danger of violation of §1 of the Fifteenth Amendment was sufficient to authorize the exercise of congressional power under §2.

5. The Voting Rights Act was extended and supplemented in 1975. 42 U.S.C. §1973aa(a) now provides: "No citizen shall be denied, because of his failure to comply with any test or device, the right to vote in any Federal, State, or local election conducted in any State or political subdivision of a State," thus making permanent the earlier five-year nationwide prohibition of literacy and similar tests. In a new series of provisions, Congress finds that voting discrimination against citizens of language minorities is "pervasive and national in scope," and prohibits such discrimination as violative of the Fourteenth and Fifteenth Amendments. "Language minorities" are defined as "persons who are American Indian, Asian American, Alaskan Natives, or of Spanish heritage." Among other remedies, 42 U.S.C. §1973aa-la(b) provides:

> Prior to August 6, 1985, no State or political subdivision shall provide registration or voting notices, forms, instructions, assistance, or other materials or information relating to the electoral process, including ballots, only in the English language if the Director of the Census determines (i) that more than 5 percent of the citizens of voting age of such State or political subdivision are members of a single language minority and (ii) that the illiteracy rate of such persons as a group is higher than the national illiteracy rate.

6. Contrast City of Mobile v. Bolden, 446 U.S. 55 (1980), with City of Rome v. United States, 446 U.S. 156 (1980), decided on the same day. In *Mobile,* an action challenging the city's "commission" form of government directly under the Fourteenth and Fifteenth Amendments, the Court held that section 1 of those amendments prohibited only *intentional* discrimination.[27] Cf. Keyes v. Denver School District, page 628 supra. *Rome* involved the Voting Rights Act of 1965. Because the State of Georgia is a jurisdiction covered by section 4(b) of the Act, a change in voting practices by a Georgia municipality must be approved in advance by the attorney general or the United States District Court for the District of Columbia, on a finding that the practice "does not have the purpose and *will not have the effect* of denying or abridging the right to vote on account of race or color" (emphasis added).

In *Rome,* the attorney general and district court had not approved of some annexations and changes in the city's electoral system. The district court found that the city had no discriminatory purpose, but that the changes would have a discriminatory effect on the city's black residents. The Supreme Court affirmed in an opinion by Justice Marshall. It held that only the state, and not a subdivision, may invoke section 4(a) of the Act, which permits a covered jurisdiction to bail out by proving that it has not used a voting test or device discriminatorily for the preceding 17 years. "[South Carolina v. Katzenbach] makes clear that Congress may, under the authority of §2 of the Fifteenth Amendment, prohibit state action that, though in itself not violative of §1, perpetuates the effects of past discrimination." These prohibitions are valid so long as they are

> "appropriate," as that term is defined in McCulloch v. Maryland . . . , [to attack racial discrimination]. In the present case, we hold that the Act's ban on electoral changes that are discriminatory in effect is an appropriate method of promoting the purposes of the Fifteenth Amendment, even if it is assumed that §1 of the Amendment prohibits only intentional discrimination in voting. Congress could rationally have concluded that, because electoral changes by jurisdictions with a demonstrable history of intentional racial discrimination in voting create the risk of purposeful discrimination, it was proper to prohibit changes that have a discriminatory impact.[28]

Justice Powell dissented, arguing that if "section 4(a) imposes the burden of preclearance on Rome, the same section must also relieve that burden when the city can demonstrate its compliance with the Act's quite strict requirements for bailout," and that a contrary interpretation could not be sustained under the Fifteenth Amendment. Justice Rehnquist, joined by Justice Stewart, also dissented:

> Neither reason nor precedent supports the conclusion that here it is "appropriate" for Congress to attempt to prevent purposeful discrimination by prohibiting conduct which a locality proves is *not* purposeful discrimination. . . .

27. Justice Stewart wrote for a plurality including Chief Justice Burger and Justices Powell and Rehnquist. Justice Stevens concurred in the judgment. Justices White, Brennan, and Marshall wrote dissenting opinions. *Mobile* calls into question White v. Regester, 412 U.S. 755 (1973), which was thought to have held that, at least in some circumstances, the Constitution prohibited discriminatory impact in electoral matters.

28. The city invoked National League of Cities v. Usery, Ch. 5 supra, to argue that Congress could not interfere with the structure of state institutions. Marshall responded that "principles of federalism that might otherwise be an obstacle to congressional authority are necessarily overridden by the power to enforce the Civil War Amendments 'by appropriate legislation.' "

Congress had before it evidence that the various governments were enacting electoral changes and annexing territory to prevent the participation of blacks in local government by measures other than outright denial of the franchise. Congress could of course remedy and prevent such purposeful discrimination on the part of local governments. See Gomillion v. Lightfoot. And given the difficulties of proving that an electoral change or annexation has been undertaken for the purpose of discriminating against blacks, Congress could properly conclude that as a remedial matter it was necessary to place the burden of proving lack of discriminatory purpose on the localities. South Carolina v. Katzenbach. But all of this does not support the conclusion that Congress is acting remedially when it continues the presumption of purposeful discrimination even after the locality has disproved that presumption. Absent other circumstances, it would be a topsy-turvey judicial system which held that electoral changes which have been affirmatively proved to be permissible under the Constitution nonetheless violate the Constitution. . . .

Thus, the result of the Court's holding is that Congress effectively has the power to determine for itself that this conduct violates the Constitution. This result violates previously well-established distinctions between the Judicial Branch and the Legislative or Executive branches of the Federal Government. See United States v. Nixon; Marbury v. Madison.

B. From Implementation to Interpretation: Congressional Expansion and Contraction of Judicially Declared Constitutional Rights

KATZENBACH v. MORGAN

384 U.S. 641 (1966)

Appeal from the United States District Court for the District of Columbia

BRENNAN, J.

These cases concern the constitutionality of §4(e) of the Voting Rights Act of 1965. That law, in the respects pertinent in these cases, provides that no person who has successfully completed the sixth primary grade in a public school in, or a private school accredited by, the Commonwealth of Puerto Rico in which the language of instruction was other than English shall be denied the right to vote in any election because of his inability to read or write English. Appellees, registered voters in New York City, brought this suit to challenge the constitutionality of §4(e) insofar as it pro tanto prohibits the enforcement of the election laws of New York requiring an ability to read and write English as a condition of voting. . . . A three-judge district court was designated. Upon cross motions for summary judgment, that court, one judge dissenting, granted the declaratory and injunctive relief appellees sought. The court held that in enacting §4(e) Congress exceeded the powers granted to it by the Constitution and therefore usurped powers reserved to the States by the Tenth Amendment. . . . We reverse. . . .

Under the distribution of powers effected by the Constitution, the States establish qualifications for voting for state officers, and the qualifications established by the States for voting for members of the most numerous branch of the state legislature also determine who may vote for United States Representatives and Senators, Art. I, §2; Seventeenth Amendment. But, of course, the States have no power to grant or withhold the franchise on conditions that are forbidden by the Fourteenth Amendment, or any other provision of the Constitution. . . .

The Attorney General of the State of New York argues that an exercise of congressional power under §5 of the Fourteenth Amendment that prohibits the enforcement of a state law can only be sustained if the judicial branch determines that the state law is prohibited by the provisions of the Amendment that Congress sought to enforce. More specifically, he urges that §4(e) cannot be sustained as appropriate legislation to enforce the Equal Protection Clause unless the judiciary decides — even with the guidance of a congressional judgment — that the application of the English literacy requirement prohibited by §4(e) is forbidden by the Equal Protection Clause itself. We disagree. Neither the language nor history of §5 supports such a construction. As was said with regard to §5 in Ex parte Virginia, 100 U.S. 339, 345, "It is the power of Congress which has been enlarged. Congress is authorized to *enforce* the prohibitions by appropriate legislation. Some legislation is contemplated to make the amendments fully effective." A construction of §5 that would require a judicial determination that the enforcement of the state law precluded by Congress violated the Amendment, as a condition of sustaining the congressional enactment, would depreciate both congressional resourcefulness and congressional responsibility for implementing the Amendment. It would confine the legislative power in this context to the insignificant role of abrogating only those state laws that the judicial branch was prepared to adjudge unconstitutional. . . .

Thus our task in this case is not to determine whether the New York English literacy requirement as applied to deny the right to vote to a person who successfully completed the sixth grade in a Puerto Rican school violates the Equal Protection Clause. Accordingly, our decision in Lassiter v. Northampton Election Bd., 360 U.S. 45 (1959), sustaining the North Carolina English literacy requirement as not in all circumstances prohibited by the first sections of the Fourteenth and Fifteenth Amendments, is inapposite. *Lassiter* did not present the question before us here: Without regard to whether the judiciary would find that the Equal Protection Clause itself nullifies New York's English literacy requirement as so applied, could Congress prohibit the enforcement of the state law by legislating under §5 of the Fourteenth Amendment? In answering this question, our task is limited to determining whether such legislation is, as required by §5, appropriate legislation to enforce the Equal Protection Clause.

By including §5 the draftsmen sought to grant to Congress, by a specific provision applicable to the Fourteenth Amendment, the same broad powers expressed in the Necessary and Proper Clause, Art. I, §8, cl. 18. . . . Correctly viewed, §5 is a positive grant of legislative power authorizing Congress to exercise its discretion in determining whether and what legislation is needed to secure the guarantees of the Fourteenth Amendment.

We therefore proceed to the consideration whether §4(e) is "appropriate legislation" to enforce the Equal Protection Clause, that is, under the McCulloch v. Maryland standard, whether §4(e) may be regarded as an enactment to enforce the Equal Protection Clause, whether it is "plainly adapted to that end" and whether it is not prohibited by but is consistent with "the letter and spirit of the constitution."[a]

a. Contrary to the suggestion of the dissent, §5 does not grant Congress power to exercise discretion in the other direction and to enact "statutes so as in effect to dilute equal protection and due

There can be no doubt that §4(e) may be regarded as an enactment to enforce the Equal Protection Clause. Congress explicitly declared that it enacted §4(e) "to secure the rights under the fourteenth amendment of persons educated in American-flag schools in which the predominant classroom language was other than English." The persons referred to include those who have migrated from the Commonwealth of Puerto Rico to New York and who have been denied the right to vote because of their inability to read and write English, and the Fourteenth Amendment rights referred to include those emanating from the Equal Protection Clause. More specifically, §4(e) may be viewed as a measure to secure for the Puerto Rican community residing in New York nondiscriminatory treatment by government — both in the imposition of voting qualifications and the provision or administration of governmental services, such as public schools, public housing and law enforcement.

Section 4(e) may be readily seen as "plainly adapted" to furthering these aims of the Equal Protection Clause. The practical effect of §4(e) is to prohibit New York from denying the right to vote to large segments of its Puerto Rican community. Congress has thus prohibited the State from denying to that community the right that is "preservative of all rights." Yick Wo v. Hopkins, 118 U.S. 356, 370. This enhanced political power will be helpful in gaining nondiscriminatory treatment in public services for the entire Puerto Rican community.[b] Section 4(e) thereby enables the Puerto Rican minority better to obtain "perfect equality of civil rights and the equal protection of the laws." It was well within congressional authority to say that this need of the Puerto Rican minority for the vote warranted federal intrusion upon any state interests served by the English literacy requirement. It was for Congress, as the branch that made this judgment, to assess and weigh the various conflicting considerations — the risk or pervasiveness of the discrimination in governmental services, the effectiveness of eliminating the state restriction on the right to vote as a means of dealing with the evil, the adequacy or availability of alternative remedies, and the nature and significance of the state interests that would be affected by the nullification of the English literacy requirement as applied to residents who have successfully completed the sixth grade in a Puerto Rican school. It is not for us to review the congressional resolution of these factors. It is enough that we be able to perceive a basis upon which the Congress might resolve the conflict as it did. There plainly was such a basis to support §4(e) in the application in question in this case. Any contrary conclusion would require us to be blind to the realities familiar to the legislators.

The result is no different if we confine our inquiry to the question whether §4(e) was merely legislation aimed at the elimination of an invidious discrimina-

---

process decisions of this Court." We emphasize that Congress' power under §5 is limited to adopting measures to enforce the guarantees of the Amendment: §5 grants Congress no power to restrict, abrogate, or dilute these guarantees. Thus, for example, an enactment authorizing the States to establish racially segregated systems of education would not be — as required by §5 — a measure "to enforce" the Equal Protection Clause since that clause of its own force prohibits such state laws.

b. Cf. James Everard's Breweries v. Day, 265 U.S. 545 (1924), which held that, under the enforcement clause of the Eighteenth Amendment, Congress could prohibit the prescription of intoxicating malt liquor for medicinal purposes even though the Amendment itself only prohibited the manufacture and sale of intoxicating liquors for beverage purposes. Cf. also the settled principle applied in the *Shreveport* Case . . . and expressed in United States v. Darby, 312 U.S. 100, 118, that the power of Congress to regulate interstate commerce "extends to those activities intrastate which so affect interstate commerce or the exercise of the power of Congress over it as to make regulation of them appropriate means to the attainment of a legitimate end. . . ."

tion in establishing voter qualifications. We are told that New York's English literacy requirement originated in the desire to provide an incentive for non-English speaking immigrants to learn the English language and in order to assure the intelligent exercise of the franchise. Yet Congress might well have questioned, in light of the many exemptions provided,[c] and some evidence suggesting that prejudice played a prominent role,[d] whether these were actually the interests being served. Congress might have also questioned whether denial of a right deemed so precious and fundamental in our society was a necessary or appropriate means of encouraging persons to learn English, or of furthering the goal of an intelligent exercise of the franchise. Finally, Congress might well have concluded that as a means of furthering the intelligent exercise of the franchise, an ability to read or understand Spanish is as effective as ability to read English for those to whom Spanish-language newspapers and Spanish-language radio and television programs are available to inform them of election issues and governmental affairs. Since Congress undertook to legislate so as to preclude the enforcement of the state law, and did so in the context of a general appraisal of literacy requirements for voting, see South Carolina v. Katzenbach, supra, to which it brought a specially informed legislative competence,[e] it was Congress' prerogative to weigh these competing considerations. Here again, it is enough that we perceive a basis upon which Congress might predicate a judgment that the application of New York's English literacy requirement to deny the right to vote to a person with a sixth grade education in Puerto Rican schools in which the language of instruction was other than English constituted an invidious discrimination in violation of the Equal Protection Clause.

There remains the question whether the congressional remedies adopted in §4(e) constitute means which are not prohibited by, but are consistent "with the letter and spirit of the constitution." The only respect in which appellees contend that §4(e) fails in this regard is that the section itself works an invidious discrimination in violation of the Fifth Amendment by prohibiting the enforcement of the English literacy requirement only for those educated in American-flag schools (schools located within United States jurisdiction) in which the language of instruction was other than English, and not for those educated in schools beyond the territorial limits of the United States in which the language of instruction was also other than English. This is not a complaint that Congress, in enacting §4(e), has unconstitutionally denied or diluted anyone's right to vote but rather that Congress violated the Constitution by not extending the relief effected in §4(e) to those educated in non-American-flag schools. . . .

c. The principal exemption complained of is that for persons who had been eligible to vote before January 1, 1922.

d. This evidence consists in part of statements made in the Constitutional Convention first considering the English literacy requirement, such as the following made by the sponsor of the measure: "More precious even than the forms of government are the mental qualities of our race. While those stand unimpaired, all is safe. They are exposed to a single danger, and that is that by constantly changing our voting citizenship through the wholesale, but valuable and necessary infusion of Southern and Eastern European races. . . . The danger has begun. . . . . We should check it." . . .

e. See, e.g., 111 Cong. Rec. 11061 (Senator Long of Louisiana and Senator Young), 11064 (Senator Holland), drawing on their experience with voters literate in a language other than English. See also an affidavit from Representative Willis of Louisiana expressing the view that on the basis of his thirty years' personal experience in politics he has "formed a definite opinion that French-speaking voters who are illiterate in English generally have as clear a grasp of the issues and an understanding of the candidates, as do people who read and write the English language."

Section 4(e) does not restrict or deny the franchise but in effect extends the franchise to persons who otherwise would be denied it by state law. . . . We need only decide whether the challenged limitation on the relief effected in §4(e) was permissible. In deciding that question, that principle that calls for the closest scrutiny of distinctions in laws *denying* fundamental rights is inapplicable; for the distinction challenged by appellees is presented only as a limitation on a reform measure aimed at eliminating an existing barrier to the exercise of the franchise. Rather, in deciding the constitutional propriety of the limitations in such a reform measure we are guided by the familiar principles that . . . "reform may take one step at a time, addressing itself to the phase of the problem which seems most acute to the legislative mind," Williamson v. Lee Optical Co., 348 U.S. 483, 489. . . . In the context of the case before us, the congressional choice to limit the relief effected in §4(e) may, for example, reflect Congress' greater familiarity with the quality of instruction in American-flag schools, a recognition of the unique historic relationship between the Congress and the Commonwealth of Puerto Rico, an awareness of the Federal Government's acceptance of the desirability of the use of Spanish as the language of instruction in Commonwealth schools, and the fact that Congress has fostered policies encouraging migration from the Commonwealth to the States. . . . We hold . . . that the limitation on relief effected in §4(e) does not constitute a forbidden discrimination since these factors might well have been the basis for the decision of Congress to go "no farther than it did."

We therefore conclude that §4(e), in the application challenged in this case, is appropriate legislation to enforce the Equal Protection Clause and that the judgment of the District Court must be and hereby is [r]eversed.

DOUGLAS, J., joins the Court's opinion except for the discussion of the question whether the congressional remedies adopted in §4(e) constitute means which are not prohibited by, but are consistent with "the letter and spirit of the constitution." On that question, he reserves judgment until such time as it is presented by a member of the class against which that particular discrimination is directed.

[In Cardona v. Power, 384 U.S. 672 (1966), decided on the same day as *Morgan,* the New York Court of Appeals had sustained the English literacy requirement against the challenge of appellant; a resident of New York, educated in Puerto Rico, but whose complaint did not allege that she had completed sixth grade (as required by §4(e) of the Voting Rights Act). The Supreme Court vacated the judgment and remanded the case to allow the state court to determine whether appellant was covered by §4(e), and, alternatively, whether "in light of this federal enactment, those applications of the New York English literacy requirement not in terms prohibited by §4(e) have continuing validity." Justice Douglas, joined by Justice Fortas, dissented, arguing that aside from §4(e), the requirement could not survive the strict scrutiny to which Harper v. Virginia Board of Elections, 383 U.S. 663 (1966), page 1054 supra, subjected abridgments of the franchise. Justice Harlan's dissent from *Cardona* and *Morgan* follows.]

HARLAN, J., joined by Stewart, J., dissenting.

Worthy as its purposes may be thought by many, I do not see how §4(e) of the Voting Rights Act of 1965, can be sustained except at the sacrifice of fundamentals in the American constitutional system — the separation between the legislative and judicial function and the boundaries between federal and state political authority. By the same token I think that the validity of New York's literacy test, a question which the Court considers *only* in the context of the federal statute, must be upheld. It will conduce to analytical clarity if I discuss the second issue first.

I. The *Cardona* Case

This case presents a straightforward Equal Protection problem. . . . The Equal Protection Clause of the Fourteenth Amendment . . . forbids a State from arbitrarily discriminating among different classes of persons. . . . It is suggested that a different and broader equal protection standard applies in cases where "fundamental liberties and rights are threatened," which would require a State to show a need greater than mere rational policy to justify classifications in this area. . . . I do not believe that any such approach is consistent with the purposes of the Equal Protection Clause, with the overwhelming weight of authority, or with well-established principles of federalism which underlie the Equal Protection Clause. . . .

I believe the same interests recounted in *Lassiter* indubitably point toward upholding the rationality of the New York voting test. It is true that the issue here is not so simply drawn between literacy per se and illiteracy. Appellant alleges that she is literate in Spanish, and that she studied American history and government in United States Spanish-speaking schools in Puerto Rico. . . .

Although to be sure there is a difference between a totally illiterate person and one who is literate in a foreign tongue, I do not believe that this added factor vitiates the constitutionality of the New York statute. Accepting appellant's allegations as true, it is nevertheless also true that the range of material available to a resident of New York literate only in Spanish is much more limited than what is available to an English-speaking resident, that the business of national, state, and local government is conducted in English, and that propositions, amendments, and offices for which candidates are running listed on the ballot are likewise in English. It is also true that most candidates, certainly those campaigning on a national or statewide level, make their speeches in English. New York may justifiably want its voters to be able to understand candidates directly, rather than through possibly imprecise translations or summaries reported in a limited number of Spanish news media. . . . Given the State's legitimate concern with promoting and safeguarding the intelligent use of the ballot, and given also New York's long experience with the process of integrating non-English-speaking residents into the mainstream of American life, I do not see how it can be said that this qualification for suffrage is unconstitutional. I would uphold the validity of the New York statute, unless the federal statute prevents that result, the question to which I now turn.

II. The *Morgan* Cases . . .

The pivotal question in [these cases] is what effect the added factor of a congressional enactment has on the straight equal protection argument dealt with above. The Court declares that since §5 of the Fourteenth Amendment gives to the Congress power to "enforce" the prohibitions of the Amendment by "appropriate" legislation, the test for judicial review of any congressional determination in this area is simply one of rationality; that is, in effect, was Congress acting rationally in declaring that the New York statute is irrational? . . . I believe the Court has confused the issue of how much enforcement power Congress possesses under §5 with the distinct issue of what questions are appropriate for congressional determination and what questions are essentially judicial in nature.

When recognized state violations of federal constitutional standards have occurred, Congress is of course empowered by §5 to take appropriate remedial measures to redress and prevent the wrongs. But it is a judicial question whether the condition with which Congress has thus sought to deal is in truth an infringement of the Constitution, something that is the necessary prerequisite to bringing the §5 power into play at all. Thus, in Ex parte Virginia, 100 U.S. 339 (1879), involving a federal statute making it a federal crime to disqualify anyone from jury service because of race, the Court first held as a matter of constitutional law that "the Fourteenth Amendment secures, among other civil rights, to colored men, when charged with criminal offences against a State, an impartial jury trial, by jurors indifferently selected or chosen without discrimination against such jurors because of their color." Only then did the Court hold that to enforce this prohibition upon state discrimination, Congress could enact a criminal statute of the type under consideration. See also . . . South Carolina v. Katzenbach. . . .

Section 4(e), however, presents a significantly different type of congressional enactment. The question here is not whether the statute is appropriate remedial legislation to cure an established violation of a constitutional command, but whether there has in fact been an infringement of that constitutional command, that is, whether a particular state practice or, as here, a statute is so arbitrary or irrational as to offend the command of the Equal Protection Clause of the Fourteenth Amendment. That question is one for the judicial branch ultimately to determine. Were the rule otherwise, Congress would be able to qualify this Court's constitutional decisions under the Fourteenth and Fifteenth Amendments, let alone those under other provisions of the Constitution, by resorting to congressional power under the Necessary and Proper Clause. In view of this Court's holding in *Lassiter,* that an English literacy test is a permissible exercise of state supervision over its franchise, I do not think it is open to Congress to limit the effect of that decision as it has undertaken to do by §4(e). In effect the Court reads §5 of the Fourteenth Amendment as giving Congress the power to define the *substantive* scope of the Amendment. If that indeed be the true reach of §5, then I do not see why Congress should not be able as well to exercise its §5 "discretion" by enacting statutes so as in effect to dilute equal protection and due process decisions of this Court. In all such cases there is room for reasonable men to differ as to whether or not a denial of equal protection or due process has occurred, and the final decision is one of judgment. Until today this judgment has always been one for the judiciary to resolve.

I do not mean to suggest in what has been said that a legislative judgment of the type incorporated in §4(e) is without any force whatsoever. Decisions on questions of equal protection and due process are based not on abstract logic, but on empirical foundations. To the extent "legislative facts" are relevant to a judicial determination, Congress is well equipped to investigate them, and such determinations are of course entitled to due respect. In South Carolina v. Katzenbach such legislative findings were made to show that racial discrimination in voting was actually occurring. Similarly, in Heart of Atlanta Motel, Inc. v. United States, 379 U.S. 241, and Katzenbach v. McClung, 379 U.S. 294, this Court upheld Title

II of the Civil Rights Act of 1964 under the Commerce Clause. There again the congressional determination that racial discrimination in a clearly defined group of public accommodations did effectively impede interstate commerce was based on "voluminous testimony," which had been put before the Congress and in the context of which it passed remedial legislation.

But no such factual data provide a legislative record supporting §4(e)[a] by way of showing that Spanish-speaking citizens are fully as capable of making informed decisions in a New York election as are English-speaking citizens. Nor was there any showing whatever to support the Court's alternative argument that §4(e) should be viewed as but a remedial measure designed to cure or assure against unconstitutional discrimination of other varieties, e.g., in "public schools, public housing and law enforcement," to which Puerto Rican minorities might be subject in such communities as New York. There is simply no legislative record supporting such hypothesized discrimination of the sort we have hitherto insisted upon when congressional power is brought to bear on constitutionally reserved state concerns.

Thus, we have here not a matter of giving deference to a congressional estimate, based on its determination of legislative facts, bearing upon the validity vel non of a statute, but rather what can at most be called a legislative announcement that Congress believes a state law to entail an unconstitutional deprivation of equal protection. Although this kind of declaration is of course entitled to the most respectful consideration, coming as it does from a concurrent branch and one that is knowledgeable in matters of popular political participation, I do not believe it lessens our responsibility to decide the fundamental issue of whether in fact the state enactment violates federal constitutional rights.

In assessing the deference we should give to this kind of congressional expression of policy, it is relevant that the judiciary has always given to congressional enactments a presumption of validity. However, it is also a canon of judicial review that state statutes are given a similar presumption. Whichever way this case is decided, one statute will be rendered inoperative in whole or in part, and although it has been suggested that this Court should give somewhat more deference to Congress than to a state legislature,[b] such a simple weighing of presumptions is hardly a satisfying way of resolving a matter that touches the distribution of state and federal power in an area so sensitive as that of the regulation of the franchise. Rather it should be recognized that while the Fourteenth Amendment is a "brooding omnipresence" over all state legislation, the substantive matters which it touches are all within the primary legislative competence of the States. Federal authority, legislative no less than judicial, does not intrude unless there has been a denial by state action of Fourteenth Amendment limitations, in this instance a denial of equal protection. At least in the area of primary state concern a state statute that passes constitutional muster under the judicial standard of rationality should not be permitted to be set at naught by a mere contrary congressional pronouncement unsupported by a legislative record justifying that conclusion. . . .

a. There were no committee hearings or reports referring to this section, which was introduced from the floor during debate on the full Voting Rights Act. . . .

b. See Thayer, The Origin and Scope of the American Doctrine of Constitutional Law, 7 Harv. L. Rev. 129, 154-155 (1893).

Note: Remedial Protection of Judicially Declared Constitutional Rights versus Substantive Constitutional Decisionmaking

Justice Brennan supports section 4(e) of the Voting Rights Act of 1965 under two alternative theories: (1) as a provision to secure nondiscriminatory treatment of Puerto Ricans in the provision of public services; and (2) as the embodiment of a congressional judgment that disfranchising the persons covered by §(e) is itself an unconstitutional discrimination.

Under the first theory, Congress does not engage in independent constitutional interpretation but only implements a judicial interpretation of the equal protection clause. Established judicial doctrine holds that discrimination in the provision of public services based on the recipients' ethnic origin violates the Fourteenth Amendment. Congress has merely made the factual determinations (a) that New York is discriminating in this fashion and (b) that enfranchising Puerto Ricans will tend to ameliorate such discrimination.

Under the alternative theory, Congress makes a generic substantive constitutional decision not previously or subsequently made by the Court. Although the Court has held that classifications affecting access to the franchise deny equal protection unless they serve compelling interests, it has never adjudicated the constitutionality of a requirement of English literacy.[29] Such a determination is not simply one of fact; it encompasses a choice of values of the sort involved in most adjudication under the Fourteenth Amendment.

Even under Justice Brennan's alternative theory, Congress is engaging in constitutional decisionmaking well within a doctrinal framework created by the judiciary. Read expansively, however, the second theory authorizes Congress to create novel Fourteenth Amendment doctrine, not only in the Court's silence, but even in the face of judicial doctrine. For example, notwithstanding San Antonio Independent School District v. Rodriguez, 411 U.S. 1 (1973), page 1249 supra, Congress might determine that unequal school expenditures deny equal protection and might enact legislation requiring states to equalize the resources available to school districts throughout the jurisdiction. Which theory is relevant to a congressional finding that New York's literacy test was discriminatorily motivated?

We shall return after Oregon v. Mitchell to evaluate the *Morgan* theories and their implications. In reading that case, note which theories the various opinions invoke in assessing the legislation at issue.

OREGON v. MITCHELL[30]

400 U.S. 112 (1970)
On Bill of Complaint

[These original actions challenged the national suspension of literacy tests and two other provisions of the Voting Rights Act Amendments of 1970. Title II, section 202 of the Act abolished state durational residency requirements for voting in presidential elections and established uniform standards for registration and

29. But cf. Lassiter v. Northampton County Bd. of Elections, 360 U.S. 45 (1959).
30. Together with Texas v. Mitchell; United States v. Arizona; and United States v. Idaho.

absentee balloting, under which persons could register within 30 days of a presidential election. The provisions were prefaced by congressional findings that existing practice

> (1) denies or abridges the inherent constitutional right of citizens to vote for their President and Vice President; (2) denies or abridges the inherent constitutional right of citizens to enjoy their free movement across State lines; (3) denies or abridges the privileges and immunities guaranteed to the citizens of each State under Article IV, section 2, clause 1, of the Constitution; (4) in some instances has the impermissible purpose or effect of denying citizens the right to vote for such officers because of the way they may vote; (5) has the effect of denying to citizens the equality of civil rights and due process and equal protection of the laws that are guaranteed to them under the fourteenth amendment; and (6) does not bear a reasonable relationship to any compelling State interest in the conduct of presidential elections.

Title III, section 302, prohibited the denial of suffrage in any election for citizens 18 years of age or older on account of their age, and was accompanied by congressional findings that the imposition of an age requirement of 21 years

> (1) denies and abridges the inherent constitutional rights of citizens eighteen years of age . . . to vote — a particularly unfair treatment of such citizens in view of the national defense responsibilities imposed upon such citizens; (2) has the effect of denying to citizens eighteen years of age . . . the due process and equal protection of the laws . . . and (3) does not bear a reasonable relationship to any compelling State interest.

The Court upheld the durational residence and absentee voting provisions of Title II, with only Justice Harlan dissenting. By a 5-to-4 vote, the Court upheld the 18-year-old vote provision of Title III as applied to federal elections and invalidated it as applied to state elections. Justices Douglas, Brennan, White, and Marshall voted to uphold all of Title III; Chief Justice Burger and Justices Harlan, Stewart, and Blackmun voted to invalidate all of Title III; Justice Black believed that Title III was constitutional as applied to federal, but not to state, elections.]

BLACK, J. . . .

I

The Framers of our Constitution provided in Art. I, §2, that members of the House of Representatives should be elected by the people and that the voters for Representatives should have "the Qualifications requisite for Electors of the most numerous Branch of the State Legislature." Senators were originally to be elected by the state legislatures, but under the Seventeenth Amendment Senators are also elected by the people, and voters for Senators have the same qualifications as voters for Representatives. In the very beginning the responsibility of the States for setting the qualifications of voters in congressional elections was made subject to the power of Congress to make or alter such regulations if it deemed it advisable to do so. This was done in Art. I, §4. . . . Moreover, the power of Congress to make election regulations in national elections is augmented by the Necessary and Proper Clause. See McCulloch v. Maryland, 4 Wheat. 316 (1819). . . .

The breadth of power granted to Congress to make or alter election regulations in national elections, including the qualifications of voters, is demonstrated by the fact that the Framers of the Constitution and the state legislatures which ratified it intended to grant to Congress the power to lay out or alter the boundaries of the congressional districts, . . . Surely no voter *qualification* was more important to the Framers than the *geographical qualification* embodied in the concept of congressional districts. . . . There can be no doubt that the power to alter congressional district lines is vastly more significant in its effect than the power to permit 18-year-old citizens to go to the polls and vote in all federal elections.

. . . I would hold, as have a long line of decisions in this Court, that Congress has ultimate supervisory power over congressional elections. Similarly, it is the prerogative of Congress to oversee the conduct of presidential and vice-presidential elections and to set the qualifications for voters for electors for those offices. It cannot be seriously contended that Congress has less power over the conduct of presidential elections than it has over congressional elections.[a]

On the other hand, the Constitution was also intended to preserve to the States the power that even the Colonies had to establish and maintain their own separate and independent governments, except insofar as the Constitution itself commands otherwise. . . . No function is more essential to the separate and independent existence of the States and their governments than the power to determine within the limits of the Constitution the qualifications of their own voters for state, county, and municipal offices and the nature of their own machinery for filling local public offices. Moreover, Art. I, §2,[b] is a clear indication that the Framers intended the States to determine the qualifications of their own voters for state offices, because those qualifications were adopted for federal offices unless Congress directs otherwise under Art. I, §4. It is a plain fact of history that the Framers never imagined that the national Congress would set the qualifications for voters in every election from President to local constable or village alderman. It is obvious that the whole Constitution reserves to the States the power to set voter qualifications in state and local elections, except to the limited extent that the people through constitutional amendments have specifically narrowed the powers of the States. Amendments Fourteen, Fifteen, Nineteen, and Twenty-four, each of which has assumed that the States had general supervisory power over state elections, are examples of express limitations on the power of the States to govern themselves. . . .

a. With reference to the selection of the President and Vice President, Art. II, §1, provides: "Each State shall appoint, in such Manner as the Legislature thereof may direct, a Number of Electors, equal to the whole Number of Senators and Representatives to which the State may be entitled in the Congress. . . ." But this Court in Burroughs v. United States, 290 U.S. 534 (1934), upheld the power of Congress to regulate certain aspects of elections for presidential and vice-presidential electors, specifically rejecting a construction of Art. II, §1, that would have curtailed the power of Congress to regulate such elections. Finally, and most important, inherent in the very concept of a supreme national government with national officers is a residual power in Congress to insure that those officers represent their national constituency as responsively as possible. This power arises from the nature of our constitutional system of government and from the Necessary and Proper Clause.

b. "The House of Representatives shall be composed of Members chosen every second Year by the People of the several States, and the Electors in each State shall have the Qualifications requisite for Electors of the most numerous Branch of the State Legislature."

Of course, the original design of the Founding Fathers was altered by the Civil War Amendments and various other amendments to the Constitution. . . . Above all else, the framers of the Civil War Amendments intended to deny to the States the power to discriminate against persons on account of their race. While this Court has recognized that the Equal Protection Clause of the Fourteenth Amendment in some instances protects against discriminations other than those on account of race, . . . [t]he Fourteenth Amendment was surely not intended to make every discrimination between groups of people a constitutional denial of equal protection. Nor was the Enforcement Clause of the Fourteenth Amendment intended to permit Congress to prohibit every discrimination between groups of people. . . .

As broad as the congressional enforcement power is, it is not unlimited. Specifically, there are at least three limitations upon Congress' power to enforce the guarantees of the Civil War Amendments. First, Congress may not by legislation repeal other provisions of the Constitution. Second, the power granted to Congress was not intended to strip the States of their power to govern themselves or to convert our national government of enumerated powers into a central government of unrestrained authority over every inch of the whole Nation. Third, Congress may only "enforce" the provisions of the amendments and may do so only by "appropriate legislation." Congress has no power under the enforcement sections to undercut the amendments' guarantees of personal equality and freedom from discrimination, see Katzenbach v. Morgan, 384 U.S. 641, 651 n.10 (1966), or to undermine those protections of the Bill of Rights which we have held the Fourteenth Amendment made applicable to the States.

Of course, we have upheld congressional legislation under the Enforcement Clauses in some cases where Congress has interfered with state regulation of the local electoral process. . . . Katzenbach v. Morgan, . . . South Carolina v. Katzenbach. . . . Where Congress attempts to remedy racial discrimination under its enforcement powers, its authority is enhanced by the avowed intention of the framers of the Thirteenth, Fourteenth, and Fifteenth Amendments.

In enacting the 18-year-old vote provisions of the Act now before the Court, Congress made no legislative findings that the 21-year-old vote requirement was used by the States to disenfranchise voters on account of race. I seriously doubt that such a finding, if made, could be supported by substantial evidence. Since Congress has attempted to invade an area preserved to the States by the Constitution without a foundation for enforcing the Civil War Amendments' ban on racial discrimination, I would hold that Congress has exceeded its powers in attempting to lower the voting age in state and local elections.[31] On the other hand, where Congress legislates in a domain not exclusively reserved by the Constitution to the States, its enforcement power need not be tied so closely to the goal of eliminating discrimination on account of race. . . .

31. Is Justice Black persuasive that Article I, §2, delegates to the states the power to set voter qualifications so as to insulate all state voting qualifications from the prohibitions of the Fourteenth Amendment? Judging from the context in which the provision appears, what was the purpose of Article I, §2? Does Justice Black's position entail that a state could impose religious voting qualifications? In view of this position that congressional districting involves voter "qualifications," is Justice Black's view of Article I, §2, consistent with his joining the majority in the *Reapportionment* cases, e.g., Reynolds v. Sims, 377 U.S. 533 (1964)?

III

In Title II of the Voting Rights Act Amendments Congress also provided that in presidential and vice-presidential elections, no voter could be denied his right to cast a ballot because he had not lived in the jurisdiction long enough to meet its residency requirements. Furthermore, Congress provided uniform national rules for absentee voting in presidential and vice-presidential elections. In enacting these regulations Congress was attempting to insure a fully effective voice to all citizens in national elections. What I said in Part I of this opinion applies with equal force here. Acting under its broad authority to create and maintain a national government, Congress unquestionably has power under the Constitution to regulate federal elections. . . .

DOUGLAS, J.

I dissent from the judgments of the Court insofar as they declare §302 unconstitutional as applied to state elections and concur in the judgments as they affect federal elections, but for different reasons. I rely on the Equal Protection Clause and on the Privileges and Immunities Clause of the Fourteenth Amendment.

The grant of the franchise to 18-year-olds by Congress is in my view valid across the board. . . . Congress might well conclude that a reduction in the voting age from 21 to 18 was needed in the interest of equal protection. The Act itself brands the denial of the franchise to 18-year-olds as "a particularly unfair treatment of such citizens in view of the national defense responsibilities imposed" on them. The fact that only males are drafted while the vote extends to females as well is not relevant, for the female component of these families or prospective families is also caught up in war and hit hard by it. Congress might well believe that men and women alike should share the fateful decision.

. . . The right to "enforce" granted by §5 of that Amendment is, as noted, parallel with the Necessary and Proper Clause whose reach Chief Justice Marshall described in McCulloch v. Maryland. . . .

Equality of voting by all who are deemed mature enough to vote is certainly consistent "with the letter and spirit of the constitution.". . . [E]lection inequalities created by state laws and based on factors other than race may violate the Equal Protection Clause, as we have held over and over again. The reach of §5 to "enforce" equal protection by eliminating election inequalities would seem quite broad. Certainly there is not a word of limitation in §5 which would restrict its applicability to matters of race alone. . . .

BRENNAN, WHITE, and MARSHALL, JJ., dissent from the judgments insofar as they declare §302 unconstitutional as applied to state and local elections, and concur in the judgments in all other respects, for the following reasons. . . .

II

Section 202 of the 1970 Amendments abolishes all durational state residence requirements restricting the right to vote in presidential elections. . . .

[W]e believe there is an adequate constitutional basis for §202 in §5 of the Fourteenth Amendment. For more than a century, this Court has recognized the constitutional right of all citizens to unhindered interstate travel and settlement.

Passenger Cases, 7 How. 283, 492 (1849) (Taney, C.J.); Crandall v. Nevada, 6 Wall. 35, 43-44 (1868); Paul v. Virginia, 8 Wall. 168, 180 (1869); Edwards v. California, 314 U.S. 160 (1941); United States v. Guest, 383 U.S. 745, 757-758 (1966); Shapiro v. Thompson, 394 U.S. 618, 629-631, 634 (1969). From whatever constitutional provision this right may be said to flow, both its existence and its fundamental importance to our Federal Union have long been established beyond question.

By definition, the imposition of a durational residence requirement operates to penalize those persons, and only those persons, who have exercised their constitutional right of interstate migration. Of course, governmental action that has the incidental effect of burdening the exercise of a constitutional right is not ipso facto unconstitutional. But in such a case, governmental action may withstand constitutional scrutiny only upon a clear showing that the burden imposed is necessary to protect a compelling and substantial governmental interest. Shapiro v. Thompson. And once it be determined that a burden has been placed upon a constitutional right, the onus of demonstrating that no less intrusive means will adequately protect compelling state interests is upon the party seeking to justify the burden.

In the present case, Congress has explicitly found both that the imposition of durational residence requirements abridges the right of free interstate migration and that such requirements are not reasonably related to any compelling state interests. 1970 Amendments, §§202(a)(2), (6). The latter finding was made with full cognizance of the possibility of fraud and administrative difficulty. . . . Accordingly, we find ample justification for the congressional conclusion that §202 is a reasonable means for eliminating an unnecessary burden on the right of interstate migration.

III

The final question presented by these cases is the propriety of Title III of the 1970 Amendments, which forbids the States from disenfranchising persons over the age of 18 because of their age. Congress was of the view that this prohibition, embodied in §302 of the Amendments, was necessary among other reasons in order to enforce the Equal Protection Clause of the Fourteenth Amendment. See §§301(a)(2), (b). . . .

We believe there is serious question whether a statute granting the franchise to citizens 21 and over while denying it to those between the ages of 18 and 21 could, in any event, withstand present scrutiny under the Equal Protection Clause. Regardless of the answer to this question, however, it is clear to us that proper regard for the special function of Congress in making determinations of legislative fact compels this Court to respect those determinations unless they are contradicted by evidence far stronger than anything that has been adduced in these cases. We would uphold §302 as a valid exercise of congressional power under §5 of the Fourteenth Amendment.

A

All parties to these cases are agreed that the States are given power, under the Constitution, to determine the qualifications for voting in state elections. But it is now settled that exercise of this power, like all other exercise of state power, is subject to the Equal Protection Clause of the Fourteenth Amendment. . . . The right to vote has long been recognized as a "fundamental political right, because preservative of all rights.". . . Consequently, when exclusions from the franchise are challenged as violating the Equal Protection Clause, . . . "the Court must determine whether the exclusions are necessary to promote a compelling state interest."

In the present cases, the States justify exclusion of 18- to 21-year-olds from the voting rolls solely on the basis of the States' interests in promoting intelligent and responsible exercise of the franchise. There is no reason to question the legitimacy and importance of these interests. . . . Every State in the Union has concluded for itself that citizens 21 years of age and over are capable of responsible and intelligent voting. Accepting this judgment, there remains the question whether citizens 18 to 21 years of age may fairly be said to be less able.

State practice itself in other areas casts doubt upon any such proposition. Each of the 50 States has provided special mechanisms for dealing with persons who are deemed insufficiently mature and intelligent to understand, and to conform their behavior to, the criminal laws of the State. Forty-nine of the States have concluded that, in this regard, 18-year-olds are invariably to be dealt with according to precisely the same standards prescribed for their elders. This at the very least is evidence of a nearly unanimous legislative judgment on the part of the States themselves that differences in maturity and intelligence between 18-year-olds and persons 21 years of age and over are too trivial to warrant specialized treatment for *any* of the former class in the critically important matter of criminal responsibility. Similarly, every State permits 18-year-olds to marry, and 39 States do not require parental consent for such persons of one or both sexes. . . . No State in the Union requires attendance at school beyond the age of 18. . . . Whether or not a State could in any circumstances condition exercise of the franchise upon educational achievements beyond the level reached by 18-year-olds today, there is no question but that no State purports to do so. Accordingly, that 18-year-olds as a class may be less educated than some of their elders cannot justify restriction of the franchise, for the States themselves have determined that this incremental education is irrelevant to voting qualifications. And finally, we have been cited to no material whatsoever that would support the proposition that intelligence, as opposed to educational attainment, increases between the ages of 18 and 21.

One final point remains. No State seeking to uphold its denial of the franchise to 18-year-olds has adduced anything beyond the mere difference in age. We have already indicated that the relevance of this difference is contradicted by nearly uniform state practice in other areas. But perhaps more important is the uniform experience of those States — Georgia since 1943, and Kentucky since 1955 — that have permitted 18-year-olds to vote. We have not been directed to a word of testimony or other evidence that would indicate . . . that 18-year-olds in those States have voted any less intelligently and responsibly than their elders. . . . On the other hand, every person who spoke to the issue in either the House or Senate was agreed that 18-year-olds in both States were at least as interested, able, and responsible in voting as were their elders.

In short, we are faced with an admitted restriction upon the franchise, supported only by bare assertions and long practice, in the face of strong indications that the States themselves do not credit the factual propositions upon which the restriction is asserted to rest. But there is no reason for us to decide whether, in a proper case, we would be compelled to hold this restriction a violation of the Equal Protection Clause. For as our decisions have long made clear, the question we face today is not one of judicial power under the Equal Protection Clause. The question is the scope of congressional power under §5 of the Fourteenth Amendment. To that question we now turn.

B

As we have often indicated, questions of constitutional power frequently turn in the last analysis on questions of fact. This is particularly the case when an assertion of state power is challenged under the Equal Protection Clause of the Fourteenth Amendment. For although equal protection requires that all persons "under like circumstances and conditions" be treated alike, such a formulation merely raises, but does not answer the question whether a legislative classification has resulted in different treatment of persons who are in fact "under like circumstances and conditions."

Legislatures, as well as courts, are bound by the provisions of the Fourteenth Amendment, Cooper v. Aaron, 358 U.S. 1, 18-20 (1958). When a state legislative classification is subjected to judicial challenge as violating the Equal Protection Clause, it comes before the courts cloaked by the presumption that the legislature has, as it should, acted within constitutional limitations. . . .

But, as we have consistently held, this limitation on judicial review of state legislative classifications is a limitation stemming, not from the Fourteenth Amendment itself, but from the nature of judicial review. It is simply a "salutary principle of judicial decision," one of the "self-imposed restraints intended to protect [the Court] and the state against irresponsible exercise of [the Court's] unappealable power." The nature of the judicial process makes it an inappropriate forum for the determination of complex factual questions of the kind so often involved in constitutional adjudication. Courts, therefore, will overturn a legislative determination of a factual question only if the legislature's finding is so clearly wrong that it may be characterized as "arbitrary," "irrational," or "unreasonable."

Limitations stemming from the nature of the judicial process, however, have no application to Congress. Section 5 of the Fourteenth Amendment provides that "[t]he Congress shall have power to enforce, by appropriate legislation, the provisions of this article." Should Congress, pursuant to that power, undertake an investigation in order to determine whether the factual basis necessary to support a state legislative discrimination actually exists, it need not stop once it determines that some reasonable men could believe the factual basis exists. Section 5 empowers Congress to make its own determination on the matter. See Katzenbach v. Morgan, 384 U.S. 641, 654-656 (1966). It should hardly be necessary to add that if the asserted factual basis necessary to support a given state discrimination does not exist, §5 of the Fourteenth Amendment vests Congress with power to remove the discrimination by appropriate means.

The scope of our review in such matters has been established by a long line of consistent decisions. "It is not for the courts to re-examine the validity of these legislative findings and reject them." "[W]here we find that the legislators, in light of the facts and testimony before them, have a rational basis for finding a chosen regulatory scheme necessary . . . our investigation is at an end." Katzenbach v. McClung, 379 U.S. 294, 303-304 (1964); Katzenbach v. Morgan.[c]

This scheme is consistent with our prior decisions in related areas. The core of dispute over the constitutionality of Title III of the 1970 Amendments is a conflict between state and federal legislative determinations of the factual issues upon which depends decision of a federal constitutional question — the legitimacy, under the Equal Protection Clause, of state discrimination against persons between the ages of 18 and 21. Our cases have repeatedly emphasized that, when state and federal claims come into conflict, the primacy of federal power requires that the federal finding of fact control. The Supremacy Clause requires an identical result when the conflict is one of legislative, not judicial, findings.

Finally, it is no answer to say that Title III intrudes upon a domain reserved to the States — the power to set qualifications for voting. It is no longer open to question that the Fourteenth Amendment applies to this, as to any other, exercise of State power. . . .

C

[Justices Brennan, White, and Marshall respond at length to Justice Harlan's detailed historical argument "that the Fourteenth Amendment was never intended to restrict the authority of the States to allocate their political power as they see fit." They conclude:]

The historical record left by the framers of the Fourteenth Amendment, because it is a product of differing and conflicting political pressures and conceptions of federalism, is thus too vague and imprecise to provide us with sure guidance in deciding the pending cases. We must therefore conclude that its framers understood their Amendment to be a broadly worded injunction capable of being interpreted by future generations in accordance with the vision and needs of those generations. We would be remiss in our duty if, in an attempt to find certainty amidst uncertainty, we were to misread the historical record and cease to interpret the Amendment as this Court has always interpreted it.

D

There remains only the question whether Congress could rationally have concluded that denial of the franchise to citizens between the ages of 18 and 21 was unnecessary to promote any legitimate interests of the States in assuring intelligent and responsible voting. . . . Proposals to lower the voting age to 18 had been before Congress at several times since 1942. The Senate Subcommittee on Constitutional Amendments conducted extensive hearings on the matter in 1968 and

c. As we emphasized in Katzenbach v. Morgan, supra, "§5 does not grant Congress power to . . . enact 'statutes so as in effect to dilute equal protection and due process decisions of this Court,' " 384 U.S., at 651 n.10. As indicated above, a decision of this Court striking down a state statute expresses, among other things, our conclusion that the legislative findings upon which the statute is based are so far wrong as to be unreasonable. Unless Congress were to unearth new evidence in its investigation, its identical findings on the identical issue would be no more reasonable than those of the state legislature.

again in 1970, and the question was discussed at some length on the floor of both the House and the Senate.

Congress was aware, of course, of the facts and state practices already discussed. It was aware of the opinion of many historians that choice of the age of 21 as the age of maturity was an outgrowth of medieval requirements of time for military training and development of a physique adequate to bear heavy armor. It knew that whereas only six percent of 18-year-olds in 1900 had completed high school, 81 percent have done so today. Congress was aware that 18-year-olds today make up a not insubstantial proportion of the adult work force; and it was entitled to draw upon its experience in supervising the federal establishment to determine the competence and responsibility with which 18-year-olds perform their assigned tasks. As Congress recognized, its judgment that 18-year-olds are capable of voting is consistent with its practice of entrusting them with the heavy responsibilities of military service. See §301(a)(1) of the Amendments. Finally, Congress was presented with evidence that the age of social and biological maturity in modern society has been consistently decreasing. Dr. Margaret Mead, an anthropologist, testified that in the past century, the "age of physical maturity has been dropping and has dropped over 3 years." Many Senators and Representatives, including several involved in national campaigns, testified from personal experience that 18-year-olds of today appeared at least as mature and intelligent as 21-year-olds in the Congressmen's youth.

Finally, and perhaps most important, Congress had before it information on the experience of two States, Georgia and Kentucky, which have allowed 18-year-olds to vote since 1943 and 1955, respectively. . . .

In sum, Congress had ample evidence upon which it could have based the conclusion that exclusion of citizens 18 to 21 years of age from the franchise is wholly unnecessary to promote any legitimate interest the States may have in assuring intelligent and responsible voting. If discrimination is unnecessary to promote any legitimate state interest, it is plainly unconstitutional under the Equal Protection Clause, and Congress has ample power to forbid it under §5 of the Fourteenth Amendment. We would uphold §302 of the 1970 Amendments as a legitimate exercise of congressional power.

STEWART, J., joined by Burger, C.J., and Blackmun, J., concurring in part and dissenting in part. . . .

II

A

Congress, in my view, has the power under the Constitution to eradicate political and civil disabilities that arise by operation of state law following a change in residence from one State to another. Freedom to travel from State to State — freedom to enter and abide in any State in the Union — is a privilege of United States citizenship. . . . Congress brings to the protection and facilitation of the exercise of privileges of United States citizenship all of its power under the Necessary and Proper Clause. Consequently, as against the reserved power of the States, it is enough that the end to which Congress has acted be one legitimately within its power and that there be a rational basis for the measures chosen to achieve that end. McCulloch v. Maryland, 4 Wheat. 316, 421.

. . . Congress could rationally conclude that the imposition of durational residency requirements unreasonably burdens and sanctions the privilege of taking up residence in another State. The objective of §202 is clearly a legitimate one. Federal action is required if the privilege to change residence is not to be undercut by parochial local sanctions. No State could undertake to guarantee this privilege to its citizens. At most a single State could take steps to resolve that its own laws would not unreasonably discriminate against the newly arrived resident. Even this resolve might not remain firm in the face of discriminations perceived as unfair against those of its own citizens who moved to other States. Thus, the problem could not be wholly solved by a single State, or even by several States, since every State of new residence and every State of prior residence would have a necessary role to play. In the absence of a unanimous interstate compact, the problem could only be solved by Congress. Quite clearly, then, Congress has acted to protect a constitutional privilege that finds its protection in the Federal Government and is national in character.

B

But even though general constitutional power clearly exists, Congress may not overstep the letter or spirit of any constitutional restriction in the exercise of that power. . . . I have concluded that, while §202 applies only to presidential elections, nothing in the Constitution prevents Congress from protecting those who have moved from one State to another from disenfranchisement in any federal election, whether congressional or presidential.

The Constitution withholds from Congress any general authority to change by legislation the qualifications for voters in federal elections. . . .

Contrary to the submission of my Brother Black, Art. I, §4, does not create in the Federal Legislature the power to alter the constitutionally established qualifications to vote in congressional elections. That section provides that the legislatures in each State shall prescribe the "Times, Places and Manner of holding Elections for Senators and Representatives," but reserves in Congress the power to "make or alter such Regulations, except as to the Places of chusing Senators." The "manner" of holding elections can hardly be read to mean the *qualifications* for voters, when it is remembered that §2 of the same Art. I explicitly speaks of the "qualifications" for voters in elections to choose Representatives. It is plain, in short, that when the Framers meant qualifications they said "qualifications." That word does not appear in Art. I, §4. Moreover, §4 does not give Congress the power to do anything that a State might not have done, and [under Art. I, §2 and the Seventeenth Amendment] no State may establish distinct qualifications for congressional elections. . . .

Different provisions of the Constitution govern the selection of the President and the Vice President. Article II and the Twelfth Amendment provide for election by electors. Article II specifies that each State shall appoint electors "in such Manner as the Legislature thereof may direct." Because the Constitution does not require the popular election of members of the electoral college, it does not specify the qualifications that voters must have when the selection of electors is by popular election. This is left to the States in the exercise of their power to "direct" the manner of choosing presidential electors. . . .

The issue, then, is whether, despite the intentional withholding from the Federal Government of a general authority to establish qualifications to vote in either congressional or presidential elections, there exists congressional power to do so when Congress acts with the objective of protecting a citizen's privilege to move his residence from one State to another. Although the matter is not entirely free from doubt, I am persuaded that the constitutional provisions discussed above are not sufficient to prevent Congress from protecting a person who exercises his constitutional right to enter and abide in any State in the Union from losing his opportunity to vote, when Congress may protect the right of interstate travel from other less fundamental disabilities. . . . As I have sought to show above, federal action is required if this privilege is to be effectively maintained. We should strive to avoid an interpretation of the Constitution that would withhold from Congress the power to legislate for the protection of those constitutional rights that the States are unable effectively to secure. For all these reasons, I conclude that it was within the power of Congress to enact §202.

III

Section 302 added by the Voting Rights Act Amendments of 1970 undertakes to enfranchise in all federal, state, and local elections those citizens 18 years of age or older who are now denied the right to vote by state law because they have not reached the age of 21. Although it was found necessary to amend the Constitution in order to confer a federal right to vote upon Negroes and upon females, the Government asserts that a federal right to vote can be conferred upon people between 18 and 21 years of age simply by this Act of Congress. Our decision in Katzenbach v. Morgan, 384 U.S. 641, it is said, established the power of Congress, under §5 of the Fourteenth Amendment, to nullify state laws requiring voters to be 21 years of age or older if Congress could rationally have concluded that such laws are not supported by a "compelling state interest."

In my view, neither the *Morgan* case, nor any other case upon which the Government relies, establishes such congressional power, even assuming that all those cases were rightly decided. . . . For the reasons that I have set out in Part II of this opinion, it is . . . plain to me that the Constitution . . . withholds from Congress the power to alter by legislation qualifications for voters in federal [as well as state] elections, in view of the explicit provisions of Article I, Article II and the Seventeenth Amendment.

To be sure, recent decisions have established that state action regulating suffrage is not immune from the impact of the Equal Protection Clause. But we have been careful in those decisions to note the undoubted power of a State to establish a qualification for voting based on age. Indeed, none of the opinions filed today suggest that the States have anything but a constitutionally unimpeachable interest in establishing some age qualification as such. Yet to test the power to establish an age qualification by the "compelling interest" standard is really to deny a State any choice at all, because no State could demonstrate a "compelling interest" in drawing the line with respect to age at one point rather than another. Obviously, the power to establish an age qualification must carry with it the power to choose 21 as a reasonable voting age, as the vast majority of the States have done.[a]

Katzenbach v. Morgan does not hold that Congress has the power to determine what are and what are not "compelling state interests" for equal protection purposes. . . . The Court upheld [§4(e)] on two grounds: that Congress could conclude that enhancing the political power of the Puerto Rican community by conferring the right to vote was an appropriate means of remedying discriminatory treatment in public services; and that Congress could conclude that the New York statute was tainted by the impermissible purpose of denying the right to vote to Puerto Ricans, an undoubted invidious discrimination under the Equal Protection Clause.[32] Both of these decisional grounds were farreaching. The Court's opinion made clear that Congress could impose on the States a remedy for the denial of equal protection that elaborated upon the direct command of the Constitution, and that it could override state laws on the ground that they were in fact used as instruments of invidious discrimination even though a court in an individual lawsuit might not have reached that factual conclusion.

But it is necessary to go much further to sustain §302. The state laws that it invalidates do not invidiously discriminate against any discrete and insular minority. Unlike the statute considered in *Morgan,* §302 is valid only if Congress has the power not only to provide the means of eradicating situations that amount to a violation of the Equal Protection Clause, but also to determine as a matter of substantive constitutional law that situations fall within the ambit of the clause, and what state interests are "compelling.". . . I cannot but conclude that §302 was beyond the constitutional power of Congress to enact.

HARLAN, J., concurring in part and dissenting in part. . . .

[Justice Harlan undertakes an extensive survey of the history surrounding the adoption of the Fourteenth Amendment. His conclusion is stated in the following paragraph.]

II

The history of the Fourteenth Amendment with respect to suffrage qualifications is remarkably free of the problems which bedevil most attempts to find a reliable guide to present decision in the pages of the past. Instead, there is virtually unanimous agreement, clearly and repeatedly expressed, that §1 of the Amendment did not reach discriminatory voter qualifications. . . .

a. If the Government is correct in its submission that a particular age requirement must meet the "compelling interest" standard, then, of course, a substantial question would exist whether a 21-year-old voter qualification is constitutional even in the absence of congressional action, as my Brothers point out. Yet it is inconceivable to me that this Court would ever hold that the denial of the vote to those between the ages of 18 and 21 constitutes such an invidious discrimination as to be a denial of the equal protection of the laws. The establishment of an age qualification is not state action aimed at any discrete and insular minority. Cf. United States v. Carolene Products Co., 304 U.S. 144, 152 n.4. Moreover, so long as a State does not set the voting age higher than 21, the reasonableness of its choice is confirmed by the very Fourteenth Amendment upon which the Government relies. Section 2 of that Amendment provides for sanctions when the right to vote "is denied to any of the male inhabitants of such State, *being twenty-one years of age*, and citizens of the United States. . . ." (Emphasis added.)

32. Is this a complete or accurate statement of the alternative holding of *Morgan*?

[T]he very fact that constitutional amendments were deemed necessary to bring about federal abolition of state restrictions on voting by reason of race (Amdt. XV), sex (Amdt. XIX), and, even with respect to federal elections, the failure to pay state poll taxes (Amdt. XXIV), is itself forceful evidence of the common understanding in 1869, 1919, and 1962, respectively, that the Fourteenth Amendment did not empower Congress to legislate in these respects.

It must be recognized, of course, that the amending process is not the only way in which constitutional understanding alters with time. The judiciary has long been entrusted with the task of applying the Constitution in changing circumstances, and as conditions change the Constitution in a sense changes as well. But when the Court gives the language of the Constitution an unforeseen application, it does so, whether explicitly or implicitly, in the name of some underlying purpose of the Framers. This is necessarily so; the federal judiciary, which by express constitutional provision is appointed for life, and therefore cannot be held responsible by the electorate, has no inherent general authority to establish the norms for the rest of society. It is limited to elaboration and application of the precepts ordained in the Constitution by the political representatives of the people. When the Court disregards the express intent and understanding of the Framers, it has invaded the realm of the political process to which the amending power was committed, and it has violated the constitutional structure which it is its highest duty to protect.

As the Court is not justified in substituting its own views of wise policy for the commands of the Constitution, still less is it justified in allowing Congress to disregard those commands as the Court understands them. Although Congress' expression of the view that it does have power to alter state suffrage qualifications is entitled to the most respectful consideration by the judiciary, coming as it does from a coordinate branch of government, this cannot displace the duty of this Court to make an independent determination whether Congress has exceeded its powers. The reason for this goes beyond Marshall's assertion that: "It is emphatically the province and duty of the judicial department to say what the law is." Marbury v. Madison, 1 Cranch 137, 177 (1803).[a] It inheres in the structure of the constitutional system itself. Congress is subject to none of the institutional restraints imposed on judicial decisionmaking; it is controlled only by the political process. In Article V, the Framers expressed the view that the political restraints on Congress alone were an insufficient control over the process of constitution making. The concurrence of two-thirds of each House and of three-fourths of the States was needed for the political check to be adequate. To allow a simple majority of Congress to have final say on matters of constitutional interpretation is therefore fundamentally out of keeping with the constitutional structure. Nor is that structure adequately protected by a requirement that the judiciary be able to perceive a basis for the congressional interpretation, the only restriction laid down in Katzenbach v. Morgan, 384 U.S. 641 (1966).

a. In fact, however, I do not understand how the doctrine of deference to rational constitutional interpretation by Congress, espoused by the majority in Katzenbach v. Morgan, 384 U.S. 641 (1966), is consistent with this statement of Chief Justice Marshall or with our reaffirmation of it in Cooper v. Aaron, 358 U.S. 1, 18 (1958): "[*Marbury*] declared the basic principle that the federal judiciary is supreme in the exposition of the law of the Constitution, and that principle has ever since been respected by this Court and the Country as a permanent and indispensable feature of our constitutional system."

It is suggested that the proper basis for the doctrine enunciated in *Morgan* lies in the relative factfinding competence of Court, Congress, and state legislatures. In this view, as I understand it, since Congress is at least as well qualified as a state legislature to determine factual issues, and far better qualified than this Court, where a dispute is basically factual in nature the congressional finding of fact should control, subject only to review by this Court for reasonableness.

In the first place, this argument has little or no force as applied to the issue whether the Fourteenth Amendment covers voter qualifications. Indeed, I do not understand the adherents of *Morgan* to maintain the contrary. But even on the assumption that the Fourteenth Amendment does place a limit on the sorts of voter qualifications which a State may adopt, I still do not see any real force in the reasoning.

When my Brothers refer to "complex factual questions," they call to mind disputes about primary, objective facts dealing with such issues as the number of persons between the ages of 18 and 21, the extent of their education, and so forth. . . . [However, the] disagreement in these cases revolves around the evaluation of . . . largely uncontested factual material. On the assumption that maturity and experience are relevant to intelligent and responsible exercise of the elective franchise, are the immaturity and inexperience of the average 18-, 19-, or 20-year-old sufficiently serious to justify denying such a person a direct voice in decisions affecting his or her life? Whether or not this judgment is characterized as "factual," it calls for striking a balance between incommensurate interests. Where the balance is to be struck depends ultimately on the values and the perspective of the decisionmaker. It is a matter as to which men of good will can and do reasonably differ.

I fully agree that judgments of the sort involved here are beyond the institutional competence and constitutional authority of the judiciary. See, e.g., Baker v. Carr, 369 U.S. 186, 266-330 (1962) (Frankfurter, J., dissenting); Kramer v. Union School District, 395 U.S. 621, 634-641 (1969) (Stewart, J., dissenting). They are pre-eminently matters for legislative discretion, with judicial review, if it exists at all, narrowly limited. But the same reasons which in my view would require the judiciary to sustain a reasonable state resolution of the issue also require Congress to abstain from entering the picture.

Judicial deference is based, not on relative factfinding competence, but on due regard for the decision of the body constitutionally appointed to decide. Establishment of voting qualifications is a matter for state legislatures. Assuming any authority at all, only when the Court can say with some confidence that the legislature has demonstrably erred in adjusting the competing interests is it justified in striking down the legislative judgment. This order of things is more efficient and more congenial to our system and, in my judgment, much more likely to achieve satisfactory results than one in which the Court has a free hand to replace state legislative judgments with its own.

The same considerations apply, and with almost equal force, to Congress' displacement of state decisions with its own ideas of wise policy. The sole distinction between Congress and the Court in this regard is that Congress, being an elective body, presumptively has popular authority for the value judgment it makes. But since the state legislature has a like authority, this distinction between Congress and the judiciary falls short of justifying a congressional veto on the state judgment. The perspectives and values of national legislators on the issue of voting qualifications are likely to differ from those of state legislators, but I see no reason a priori to prefer those of the national figures, whose collective decision, applying nationwide, is necessarily less able to take account of peculiar local conditions. Whether one agrees with this judgment or not, it is the one expressed by the Framers in leaving voter qualifications to the States. The Supremacy Clause does not, as my colleagues seem to argue, represent a judgment that federal decisions are superior to those of the States whenever the two may differ. . . . In this area, to rely on Congress would make that body a judge in its own cause. The role of final arbiter belongs to this Court.

III

Since I cannot agree that the Fourteenth Amendment empowered Congress, or the federal judiciary, to control voter qualifications, I turn to other asserted sources of congressional power. My Brother Black would find that such power exists with respect to *federal* elections by virtue of Art. I, §4, and seemingly other considerations that he finds implicit in federal authority.

The constitutional provisions controlling the regulation of congressional elections are [Art. I, §§2 and 4, and Amdt. XVII]. . . . Surely nothing in these provisions lends itself to the view that voting qualifications in federal elections are to be set by Congress. . . .

As to presidential elections, the Constitution provides: "Each State shall appoint, in such Manner as the Legislature thereof may direct, a Number of Electors. . . ." Art. II, §l, cl. 2. "The Congress may determine the Time of chusing the Electors, and the Day on which they shall give their Votes; which Day shall be the same throughout the United States." Art. II, §1, cl. 4. Even the power to control the "Manner" of holding elections, given with respect to congressional elections by Art. I, §4, is absent with respect to the selection of presidential electors. And, of course, the fact that it was deemed necessary to provide separately for congressional power to regulate the time of choosing presidential electors and the President himself demonstrates that the power over "Times, Places and Manner" given by Art. I, §4, does not refer to presidential elections, but only to the elections for Congressmen. Any shadow of a justification for congressional power with respect to congressional elections therefore disappears utterly in presidential elections.

IV

With these major contentions resolved, it is convenient to consider the . . . sections of the Act individually to determine whether they can be supported by any other basis of congressional power.

A. VOTING AGE

The only constitutional basis advanced in support of the lowering of the voting age is the power to enforce the Equal Protection Clause, a power found in §5 of the Fourteenth Amendment. For the reasons already given, it cannot be said that the statutory provision is valid as declaratory of the meaning of that clause. Its validity therefore must rest on congressional power to lower the voting age as a means of preventing invidious discrimination that is within the purview of that clause.

The history of the Fourteenth Amendment may well foreclose the possibility that §5 empowers Congress to enfranchise a class of citizens so that they may protect themselves against discrimination forbidden by the first section, but it is unnecessary for me to explore that question. For I think it fair to say that the suggestion that members of the age group between 18 and 21 are threatened with unconstitutional discrimination, or that any hypothetical discrimination is likely to be affected by lowering the voting age, is little short of fanciful. I see no justification for stretching to find any such possibility when all the evidence indicates that Congress — led on by recent decisions of this Court — thought simply that 18-year-olds were fairly entitled to the vote and that Congress could give it to them by legislation. . . .

B. RESIDENCY

For reasons already stated, neither the power to regulate voting qualifications in presidential elections, asserted by my Brother Black, nor the power to declare the meaning of §1 of the Fourteenth Amendment, relied on by my Brother Douglas, can support §202 of the Act. . . . The remaining grounds relied on are the Privileges and Immunities Clause of Art. IV, §2, and the right to travel across state lines.

While the right of qualified electors to cast their ballots and to have their votes counted was held to be a privilege of citizenship in Ex parte Yarbrough, 110 U.S. 651 (1884), and United States v. Classic, 313 U.S. 299 (1941), these decisions were careful to observe that it remained with the States to determine the class of qualified voters. It was federal law, acting on this state-defined class, which turned the right to vote into a privilege of national citizenship. As the Court has consistently held, the Privileges and Immunities Clauses do not react on the mere status of citizenship to enfranchise any citizen whom an otherwise valid state law does not allow to vote. Minors, felons, insane persons, and persons who have not satisfied residency requirements are among those citizens who are not allowed to vote in most States. . . .

The right to travel across state lines, see United States v. Guest, 383 U.S. 745, 757-758 (1966), and Shapiro v. Thompson, 394 U.S. 618, 630 (1969), is likewise insufficient to require Idaho to conform its laws to the requirements of §202. Mr. Justice Stewart justifies §202 solely on the power under §5 of the Fourteenth Amendment to enforce the Privileges and Immunities Clause of §1 which he deems the basis for the right to travel. I find it impossible to square the position that §5 authorizes Congress to abolish state voting qualifications based on residency with the position that it does not authorize Congress to abolish such qualifications based on race. Since the historical record compels me to accept the latter position, I must reject the former.

Mr. Justice Brennan, Mr. Justice White, and Mr. Justice Marshall do not anchor the right of interstate travel to any specific constitutional provision. Past decisions to which they refer have relied on the two Privileges and Immunities Clauses, just discussed, the Due Process Clause of the Fifth Amendment, and the Commerce Clause. The Fifth Amendment is wholly inapplicable to state laws; and surely the Commerce Clause cannot be seriously relied on to sustain the Act here challenged. With no specific clause of the Constitution empowering Congress to enact §202, I fail to see how that nebulous judicial construct, the right to travel, can do so. . . .

1. *Section 5 from Congress' Viewpoint*

Reread the Note at page 1502 supra and consider the grounds on which Congress might have determined that the provisions examined in *Morgan* and *Oregon* were "appropriate legislation" under section 5 of the Fourteenth Amendment to implement the equal protection clause.

a. Remedial Protection of Judicially Declared Rights

On what, if any, factual assumptions might Congress have concluded that the durational residency and voting age provisions of the Voting Rights Amendments of 1970 were appropriate measures to protect judicially declared constitutional rights?

b. Substantive Constitutional Decisionmaking

Justice Brennan suggested in *Morgan* that Congress might have concluded that disfranchisement of Puerto Ricans under the circumstances described in section 4(e) amounted to an intrinsically unconstitutional discrimination under the equal protection clause, without regard to its effect on access to public services. Similarly, Congress might have determined that depriving 18-year-olds of the franchise in itself denied them equal protection. Leaving aside the merits of the decisions, does section 5 empower Congress to make generic constitutional determinations of this sort, or is that exclusively a judicial function?

If Congress is authorized to determine that a state practice is intrinsically unconstitutional, what criteria should it employ? Is *McCulloch*'s description of the scope of congressional powers — "let the end be legitimate," etc. — relevant to this question? What, if any, deference should Congress accord the supposed judgment of a state legislature that its practice promotes desirable or important objectives?

If section 4(e) or the voting age provision is premised on the intrinsic unconstitutionality of the invalidated state practices, should Congress be as free to repeal these as any other laws, or do they have a precedential force akin to the Court's constitutional decisions?

2. *Judicial Review of Congressional Legislation under Section 5*

Throughout this book, we have considered factors that weigh for and against deference in the exercise of judicial review. Which of these seem relevant when a court reviews legislation pursuant to section 5 of the Fourteenth Amendment (1) designed to protect judicially declared rights and (2) based on an independent congressional determination that a state practice violates section 1?

Judicial deference in the first case presents few, if any, novel problems. However, judicial deference to Congress' judgment that the state practice is intrinsically unconstitutional — especially the extreme deference implied by *Morgan's* "some basis" standard — seems to compete with *Marbury*'s assertion that "[i]t is emphatically the province and duty of the judicial department to say what the law is," and, a fortiori, with the Court's assertion of judicial supremacy in Cooper v. Aaron, 358 U.S. 1 (1958). Consider three arguments favoring judicial deference to a congressional determination of this sort.

a. Line Drawing

Professor Robert Burt argues:[33]

> Congress is less burdened by the principled constraints under which courts labor. . . . Congress can make distinctions among classes that the Court would itself be hard put to explain on principled grounds both because Congress is more sensitively tuned to the competing social interests that demand accommodation and because the institutional legitimacy of a legislative act depends not so much on the rational persuasiveness of its decisions as on the simple fact that a majority of "responsible" elected officials were willing to vote for the proposition. . . . Thus the *Morgan* Court could argue that it does not authorize Congress to impose its value preferences on the states, but rather that Congress "enforces" the Court's value preferences, under the Fourteenth Amendment, on the states in circumstances where the Court does not feel able to do so itself.

Professor Burt suggests, as an example, that the Court was institutionally ill suited to extend the Fourteenth Amendment to private discrimination, because it "could not independently proscribe some private discrimination without its proclaimed principle expanding to proscribe all discrimination. [And] . . . embracing such a principle would wholly sacrifice the competing values" in privacy and property. On the other hand,

> Congress, using no principle but fiat by majority vote, could act, for example, to permit Mrs. Murphy to turn away black lodgers [from her boarding house] so long as she lived with her other lodgers in a house that could accommodate no more than four families. Congress could easily conclude that in Mrs. Murphy's case, but not in others closely analogous, the values involved in free choice of companions should predominate. The Court would have much greater difficulty independently constructing an exemption for Mrs. Murphy, no matter how important some such exemption might be, in order to mediate the clashing principles and political pressures at stake. . . . In this context — devising appropriate adjustment of directly conflicting principles — the legislative mechanism is greatly superior to the courts.

In the context of *Morgan* and *Oregon,* Congress was similarly able to draw "arbitrary" lines — sixth-grade education in an accredited Puerto Rican school; 30

33. Robert Burt, *Miranda* and Title II: A Morganatic Marriage, 1969 S. Ct. Rev. 81, 112, 113-114.

days registration period; 18 years old — where no "principled" justification could be given for drawing the line at any particular place.[34]

Discussion

Under Professor Burt's theory, the Court would inquire whether congressional legislation enforces its "value preferences." How would *Morgan* and *Oregon* be decided on this theory? How would the Court respond to congressional legislation that (a) enforced the due process clause by prohibiting states from punishing consensual sexual conduct or the sale and possession of marijuana; (b) enforced the equal protection clause by prohibiting classifications based on intelligence or homosexuality or by requiring that all school districts spend the same amount on each child's education; (c) enforced both clauses by making any interracial assault a federal crime?[35]

In Branzburg v. Hayes, 408 U.S. 665 (1973), a closely divided Court held that the First Amendment did not afford newsmen a privilege against appearing and testifying before state and federal grand juries. Justice White wrote that "we perceive no basis for holding that the public interest in law enforcement and in ensuring effective grand jury proceedings is insufficient to override the consequential, but uncertain, burden on news gathering that is said to result from insisting that reporters, like other citizens, respond to relevant questions put to them in the course of a valid grand jury investigation or criminal trial." He emphasized the difficult problems of definition and line-drawing that would face a court trying to formulate a rule that accommodated these competing interests. He went on to note:

> At the federal level, Congress has freedom to determine whether a statutory newsman's privilege is necessary and desirable and to fashion standards and rules as narrow or broad as deemed necessary to deal with the evil discerned and, equally important, to refashion those rules as experience from time to time may dictate. There is also merit in leaving state legislatures free, within First Amendment limits, to fashion their own standards in light of the conditions and problems with respect to the relations between law enforcement officials and press in their own areas.

Under Professor Burt's theory, could Congress enact a newsman's privilege that applied to state as well as federal proceedings?

b. Fact Finding

Professor Archibald Cox argues:[36]

34. Although, as Professor Burt indicates, courts typically do not draw arbitrary lines of the sorts embodied in the Voting Rights Act, occasionally they do. For example, Duncan v. Louisiana, 391 U.S. 145 (1968), held that defendants subject to imprisonment for more than six months are entitled to trial by jury.

35. Cf. Jones v. Alfred H. Mayer Co., 392 U.S. 409 (1968) (power under Thirteenth Amendment to define "badges and incidents of slavery"), p.1352 supra; United States v. Guest, 383 U.S. 745 (1966) (concurring opinions: power to punish private action that interferes with Fourteenth Amendment rights).

36. Archibald Cox, The Role of Congress in Constitutional Determinations, 40 U. Cin. L. Rev. 199, 228-229 (1971).

[T]he *Morgan* decision follows logically from the basic principles determining the respective functions of the legislative and judicial branches outside the field of preferred constitutional rights. Whether a State law denies equal protection depends to a large extent upon the finding and appraisal of the practical importance of relevant facts. In the case of the English literacy requirement, it turned upon such considerations as the extent to which the requirement served as an incentive to learn English and ease the process of assimilation, the availability of Spanish-language newspapers and their sufficiency to enable non-English-speaking voters to exercise the franchise intelligently, the importance of the franchise, and the relative effectiveness of other inducements to learn English. The conventional formula, unless qualified by notions of preferred rights, would call for the Court to presume the existence of facts giving validity to State legislation. But section 5 of the fourteenth amendment gives Congress a concurrent power to enforce the fourteenth amendment even though that means invalidating State legislation.

There is also a presumption that facts exist which sustain federal legislation and a principle of deference to congressional judgment upon questions of proportion and degree, as illustrated by the due process and commerce clause cases. . . . In *Morgan* the federal and State statutes appeared to rest upon inconsistent findings and legislative evaluations of the conditions determining whether the discrimination against citizens literate only in Spanish was permissible or invidious. The Court, forced to choose between conflicting presumptions, applied the rule of deference to Congress and required the State to yield to the federal enactment thus found valid.

Some commentators have suggested that there is no reason to suppose that the congressional findings reflect the truth more accurately than the findings of a State legislature. The observation seems accurate but irrelevant. When Congress and a State legislature reach different conclusions, the supremacy clause makes the federal determination paramount regardless of its intrinsic merit.

Discussion

Does Professor Cox explain persuasively why the Court should defer to the (supposed) factual findings of Congress that would invalidate the state legislation rather than to those of the state legislature that would sustain it?

Does Professor Cox's theory imply that a court should pay equal deference to all congressional determinations of the constitutionality of state practices, or should judicial scrutiny vary with the extent to which the determination depends on facts and the court's ability independently to determine them? How can a court separate Congress' findings of fact from its judgments on questions of values? Under Professor Cox's theory, how should the Court have decided *Morgan, Oregon,* and the hypothetical cases described at p.1521 supra?

Recall Justice Harlan's criticism of the first rationale of *Morgan* — that New York's supposed discrimination in providing public services was not supported by a legislative record. Should a court be as free to hypothesize legislative facts to sustain a law under Professor Cox's theory as when it sustains a law under a purely remedial rationale (as in South Carolina v. Katzenbach)? Should Congress' formal "findings" incorporated in the Voting Rights Act Amendments of 1970 be conclusive of whatever facts they purport to find? Was there an adequate "record" to support the findings?

c. The Political Safeguards of Federalism

Professor William Cohen argues that "Congress has no institutional competence superior to that of the state legislatures in second-guessing the courts as to the minimal content of liberty reflected in the due process and equal protection clauses."[37] Citing Herbert Wechsler's essay on The Political Safeguards of Federalism,[38] however, Cohen goes on to assert:[39]

> [A] congressional judgment resolving at the national level an issue that could — without constitutional objection — be decided in the same way at the state level, ought normally to be binding on the courts, since Congress presumably reflects a balance between both national and state interests and hence is better able to adjust such conflicts.

Discussion

To what extent is the Court's post-1937 treatment of Congress' Article I powers premised (a) on these "safeguards," or (b) on the judiciary's institutional incompetence to determine the "appropriateness" of legislation, or (c) on the Court's (re)adoption of *McCulloch's* substantive understanding of the breadth of Congress' powers? To what extent do these rationales apply when the Court reviews congressional determinations that state practices are unconstitutional? Under Professor Cohen's theory, how should the Court have decided *Morgan, Oregon*, and the hypothetical cases described at p.1521 supra?

C. Modification of Judicially Declared Rights: Roe v. Wade versus S. 158

The Subcommittee on the Separation of Powers of the Senate Judiciary Committee heard 57 witnesses regarding S. 158 (the Helms-Hyde Bill). Some of the testimony involved the question of when "human life" begins; various doctors and geneticists expressed differing points of view.

Many of the witnesses addressed the issue of the bill's constitutionality, and the testimony revealed divisions within both the practicing and academic bar. For example, of the 13 law professors who testified, seven thought the bill constitutional, while six viewed it as unconstitutional either in part or in whole. Among the latter was Robert Bork, who described *Roe* as "an unconstitutional decision, a serious and wholly unjustifiable judicial usurpation of state legislative authority," but who also argued that to enact S. 158 would be "to adopt unconstitutional countermeasures to redress unconstitutional action by the Court." (Hearings on S. 158 Before the Subcomm. on the Separation of Powers of the Senate Comm. on the Judiciary, 97th Cong., 1st Sess. (Serial No. J-97-16) 315-316 (1981).)

We present below excerpts from the testimony of Judge Noonan, who at the time was a professor at Boalt Hall (University of California Law School) and Professor Cox, who teaches at Harvard Law School.

37. William Cohen, Congressional Power to Interpret Due Process and Equal Protection, 27 Stan. L. Rev. 603, 614 (1975).

38. In Wechsler, Principles, Politics, and Fundamental Law (1961), at p.422 supra.

39. Cohen, supra note 37, at 614.

TESTIMONY OF JOHN T. NOONAN, JR.

Hearings on S. 158 Before the Subcomm. on the Separation of Powers of the Senate Comm. on the Judiciary, 97th Cong., 1st Sess. 263-270 (1981)

1. The Source of Congressional Power. The Fourteenth Amendment, section 5 declares, "The Congress shall have power to enforce, by appropriate legislation, the provisions of this article." The key terms of this constitutional grant of power are "appropriate legislation" and "enforce." In general, there must be said of this part of the Constitution what Chief Justice Marshall said in McCulloch v. Maryland of congressional power under the "Necessary and Proper" Clause of Article I: "1st. The clause is placed among the powers of Congress, not among the limitations on those powers. 2nd. Its terms purport to enlarge, not to diminish the powers vested in the government. It purports to be an additional power, not a restriction on those already granted."

It should be added that the enforcement of the Fourteenth Amendment by *congressional* action has solid historical roots. As the Supreme Court said unanimously in 1879 in Ex parte Virginia, the Thirteenth, Fourteenth, and Fifteenth Amendments "derive much of their force" from the sections conferring power on Congress. "It is not said that the *judicial power* of the government shall extend to enforcing the prohibitions and to protecting the rights and immunities guaranteed. . . . It is the power of Congress which has been enlarged." Even if today the judicial branch has taken to itself a more active part in enforcing the Amendments, surely its more assertive role cannot deprive Congress of the power which the framers of the Amendment intended to confer.

2. The Power of Congress Where the Supreme Court Is in Doubt. In Roe v. Wade the Supreme Court declared, "We need not resolve the difficult question of where life begins. When those trained in the respective disciplines of medicine, philosophy, and theology are unable to arrive at any consensus, the judiciary at this point in the development of man's knowledge, is not in a position to speculate as to the answer." The Court went on to note the varying treatment of the unborn in the law of torts and property and concluded, "In view of all this, we do not agree that by adopting one theory of life, Texas may override the rights of the pregnant woman that are at stake." In short, the judiciary was in no position to answer, common and statutory law gave various answers, and a state did not have power to define life.

Congress is acting with better sources of information than the Court — for the Court took no biological evidence and no historical evidence. It is acting with a better ability than the Court to balance competing value considerations that go to the assessment of the facts. Further, Congress is performing an essential function in the enforcement of the Fourteenth Amendment; for if the judiciary is not "in a position to speculate" when life begins, the Fourteenth Amendment must fail, in a significant way, to be implemented, unless Congress draws on its power to supply an answer.

3. The Power of Congress When the Supreme Court Has Made a Contrary Determination. The objection will be raised, however, that the Supreme Court has done more than acknowledge its incompetence to decide when life begins. The Court in Roe v. Wade has formally held that "the word 'person' as used in the Fourteenth Amendment, does not include the unborn." Does not the proposed statute squarely conflict with this holding of the Court and, if it does so, is not the statute void?

It is clear that Congress will reach, if the proposed statute is enacted, a conclusion different from the Court's in Roe v. Wade on the meaning of person in the Fourteenth Amendment. It does not follow that the statute is void. It follows, rather, that the Court may, and should, change its mind, give deference to the congressional findings and declarations, and overrule Roe v. Wade.

In the area of the Fourteenth Amendment the Court has already provided just such an example of retreating from its own announced understanding of the Constitution in deference to congressional action taken after, and contrary to, the Court's announcement of what it found the Constitution to mean. In Lassiter v. Northampton Election Board, 360 U.S. 45 (1959), the plaintiff complained that a literacy test for voting was unconstitutional. The Supreme Court, unanimously, held that Article I, section 2 of the Constitution expressly reserves to the States the power to determine the qualifications of electors. Seven years later in Katzenbach v. Morgan, 384 U.S. 641 (1966), the Court considered an Act of Congress eliminating literacy in English as a condition for voting. If the Court followed *Lassiter,* this Act of Congress was a clear infringement on a power constitutionally reserved to the States; and the Act was clearly contrary to the holding of the Court in *Lassiter.*

The Court, however, found *Lassiter* "inapposite." Speaking through Justice Brennan and quoting Ex parte Virginia of 1879, the Court held the congressional action a proper exercise of congressional power under section 5 of the Fourteenth Amendment. The act was "plainly adapted" to furthering the aims of the Equal Protection Clause by securing for Puerto Ricans in New York not only the right to vote but, indirectly, nondiscriminatory treatment in public schools, public housing, and law enforcement. The action of Congress, directly contrary to the interpretation of the Constitution by a unanimous Supreme Court, was upheld by the Court. In Oregon v. Mitchell, 400 U.S. 112 (1970), while splitting on other issues, the Court unanimously upheld Congress' total elimination of literacy tests. Justice Black's opinion specifically deferred to the "substantial, if not overwhelming, evidence" on which Congress acted and to the exercise of Congressional power under section 5.

4. Congressional Action Affecting Personal Liberties. In Shapiro v. Thompson, a case involving the welfare residency requirement of California, it was said by way of dictum that even if Congress had consented to the residency requirement — which the Court held it had not — the requirement was invalid, because "Congress may not authorize the States to violate the Equal Protection Clause." Similarly, in a footnote to Katzenbach v. Morgan, Justice Brennan declared that section 5 "grants Congress no power to restrict, abrogate or dilute" the guarantees of the Fourteenth Amendment. In a footnote to his dissent in Oregon v. Mitchell, Justice Brennan repeated this view, and added apropos of state statutes found to be based on unreasonable legislative findings, "Unless Congress were to unearth new evidence in its investigation, its identical findings on the same issue would be no more reasonable than those of the state legislature." The question is thus presented whether the proposed Act authorizes states to violate the Equal Protection Clause, dilutes or abrogates Fourteenth Amendment guarantees, or is based on the same evidence on which state legislatures acted unreasonably.

In recognizing the unborn as persons, so far as protection of their lives is concerned, the proposed Act treats no one unequally but gives equal protection to one class of humanity now unequally treated. It does not dilute a Fourteenth Amendment guarantee, but expands the rights of a whole class. It is based not on evidence before the state legislatures — what that evidence was we do not know — but on evidence freshly taken from leading geneticists and physicians.

Yet the question will be pressed, "Does not the Act dilute or abrogate the right to an abortion?" Necessarily, the expression of the rights of one class of human beings has an impact on the rights of others. The elimination of literacy tests in this way "diluted" the voting rights of the literate. It is inescapable that congressional expression of the right to life will have an impact on the abortion right; but in the eyes of Congress, if it enacts this law, there will be a net gain for Fourteenth Amendment rights by the expansion and the attendant diminution.

Further, it must be noted that the correctness of Justice Brennan's footnotes has been questioned by a careful scholar of Constitutional law, Professor Archibald Cox. Professor Cox suggests that Congress is free to act where "the Court has formulated some corollary to a constitutional command upon a different view of contemporaneous conditions than the legislatures" and where "the problems of application quite genuinely involved investigation and evaluation of facts." There are, Cox adds, "areas in which Congress has at least some claims to superior competence while the Court has none." In these areas, Justice Brennan's footnotes "run against the demands of logical consistency." They run also, Cox observes, against evenhandedness. If Congress has been given power under the Constitution, that power is to be exercised as Congress finds "appropriate" to the furtherance of the guarantees of the Fourteenth Amendment.

A number of Justices have, indeed, signalled their disagreement with Justice Brennan's "dilution" test.

5. Section 5 and Marbury v. Madison. The cornerstone of the judicial power, Chief Justice Marshall's opinion in Marbury v. Madison, announces that the Constitution "controls any legislative act repugnant to it" and imposes on the judges the duty to determine this repugnancy. Does the proposed Act defy or subvert these fundamental principles?

Not in the least. Congress is not ousting the Court of jurisdiction, "overruling" the Court, or declaring its will superior to Constitution or Court. On the basis of hearings and fresh evidence, Congress is taking a position which in one important particular disagrees with the Court's interpretation of the Constitution in Roe v. Wade. Under the principles of Marbury v. Madison, it will be for the Court to decide whether, following such precedents as Katzenbach v. Morgan, it should now defer to Congress' interpretation.

To suppose that the statute proposed is a challenge to judicial review assumes a radical — I am inclined to say willful — misunderstanding of the functions of Court and Congress. A decision of the Supreme Court interpreting the Constitution is neither infallible nor eternal nor unchangeable. The Court has often been wrong. The Court has often corrected itself. There is nothing in our constitutional theory that says the Court must remain forever in a mistaken position, and much contrary example to its so doing. The proposed Act is an invitation to the Court to correct its error itself.

It was once settled constitutional doctrine that if the States could not regulate interstate commerce, Congress could not give them power to do so. The classic case on this point, Cooley v. Wardens of Philadelphia, 12 How. 299 (1851), was one of the great unshakable landmarks of constitutional interpretation by the Supreme Court. It declared in ringing terms, "If the Constitution excluded the States from making any law regulating commerce, certainly Congress cannot regrant or in any way reconvey to the States that power." But in 1945, in the teeth of the *Cooley* doctrine, Congress enacted the McCarran Act, conferring on the States the power to regulate insurance. The Court in Prudential Insurance Co. v. Benjamin, 328 U.S. 408 (1946), unanimously sustained the delegation, the opinion for the Court recognizing in Congress a "plenary and supreme authority" over interstate commerce. What had once been the Court's interpretation of the Constitution had yielded to the congressional teaching.

The story is an old one, frequently retold. The Supreme Court is not immune to reason and to instruction. It reverses itself. It listens to Congress. Those who want an institution immoveable and beyond the reach of popular instruction must look elsewhere.

STATEMENT OF ARCHIBALD COX

Hearings on S. 158 Before the Subcomm. on the Separation of Powers of the Senate Comm. on the Judiciary, 97th Cong., 1st Sess., 334-344 (1981)

The two decisions putting the broadest interpretation upon the "power to enforce . . . by appropriate legislation" are South Carolina v. Katzenbach, 383 U.S. 301 (1964), and Katzenbach v. Morgan, 384 U.S. 641 (1966). But those decisions . . . do not sustain the constitutionality of S. 158. . . .

South Carolina v. Katzenbach upheld the power of Congress to prohibit conduct which is not unconstitutional — the use of a literacy test — under circumstances in which the conduct is likely to lead to racial discrimination violating an established constitutional right — there, the right of citizens to vote regardless of race or color.

The decision in South Carolina v. Katzenbach gives no support to S. 158 because S. 158 does not seek to protect any established constitutional right. On the contrary, S. 158 seeks by legislative definition of "life" and "person" to create new constitutional rights. Thus, although S. 158 apparently would prohibit conduct which is not otherwise unconstitutional — State aid to any interference with the natural development of a fetus — the analogy to South Carolina v. Katzenbach breaks down because S. 158 does not and cannot impose the prohibition in aid of an established Fourteenth Amendment right. A fetus is not a "person" under the established constitutional meaning of the word. Roe v. Wade, 410 U.S. 113, 158, and cases cited. Only persons within the meaning of the Constitution have Fourteenth Amendment rights.

Katzenbach v. Morgan, 384 U.S. 641 (1966), grew out of a constitutional challenge to Section 4(e)(2) of the Voting Rights Act of 1965 which provided that no person who had successfully completed the sixth grade in a Puerto Rican school where instruction was in Spanish should be denied the right to vote because of inability to read or write English. The Court, by a vote of seven to two, upheld the statute. One branch of opinion sustains congressional removal of the State's requirement of English literacy on the ground that Congress might have viewed the removal as a measure adapted to securing the Puerto Ricans residing in New

York against unconstitutional discrimination in the provision of government services, such as public schools, public housing and law enforcement. 384 U.S. at 652-653.

The first branch of Katzenbach v. Morgan gives no support to S. 158, Section 1, for the same reason that South Carolina v. Katzenbach is distinguishable. Section 4(e)(2) was upheld as a means of securing a separate and established constitutional right — the right to equal treatment in public services without regard to race or color. Enactment of S. 158 would not protect any established constitutional right. S. 158 simply attempts to create a constitutional right for the unborn, even though it is established constitutional law that the unborn are not "persons" within the meaning of the Fourteenth Amendment.

South Carolina v. Katzenbach and the first branch of Katzenbach v. Morgan are plainly inappropriate for a further reason. In creating a new constitutional right for the unborn, S. 158 — if effective — would cut back upon the established constitutional right of a woman to decide during the first two trimesters of pregnancy whether she wishes to bear a child. Neither of the cited precedents involved an act of Congress attempting to cut back or dilute existing constitutional rights. On the contrary, the opinion in Katzenbach v. Morgan specifically notes the difference between adding and taking away protection, and goes on to state that the rationale of the opinion does not extend to legislation curtailing individual rights.

The second branch of the opinion in Katzenbach v. Morgan is somewhat closer to the mark, but it too gives no significant support to proponents of the constitutionality of S. 158, Section 1. The New York law that Congress was seeking to supersede denied citizens literate in Spanish the same voting rights as citizens literate in English. The discrimination was under attack as a violation of the equal protection clause in another judicial proceeding, but the Court assumed that it would not be judged unconstitutional without the aid of legislation. Nevertheless, the Court went on to say in the *Morgan* case, "We perceive a basis upon which Congress might predicate a judgment that the application of New York's English literacy requirement . . . constituted an invidious discrimination in violation of the Equal Protection Clause." 384 U.S. at 670-671. For this reason, the Court held that the New York statute must yield even though Congress' decision might differ from that which the Court would have rendered.

The essential point to be observed is that the second branch of Katzenbach v. Morgan involved only *deference to congressional determinations upon what are truly questions of fact.* There was general agreement that the legislative classification resulting from the English-speaking literacy test was unconstitutional only if the classification bore no rational relationship to some permissible public purpose. That was the applicable legal standard. Section 4 of the Voting Rights Act made no effort to change that standard. Whether a State law violates that standard often depends to a large extent upon the finding and appraisal of the practical importance of relevant facts. In the case of the English literacy requirement, it turned upon such considerations as the extent to which the requirement served as an incentive to learn English and ease the process of assimilation, the availability of Spanish-language newspapers and their sufficiency to enable non-English-speaking voters to exercise the franchise intelligently, the importance of the franchise, and the relative effectiveness of other inducements to learn English.

The conventional constitutional formula called for the Court to presume the existence of facts giving validity to State legislation and to defer to any State legislative findings of fact unless the findings were irrational. There is also a presumption that facts exist which sustain federal legislation and a principle of deference to congressional judgment upon questions of fact. In *Morgan* the federal and State statutes appeared to rest upon inconsistent findings and legislative evaluations of the practical conditions determining whether the discrimination against citizens literate only in Spanish was permissible or invidious. The Court, forced to choose between conflicting presumptions, applied the rule of deference to the congressional findings of fact.

S. 158, Section 1 does not rest upon any "findings of fact" in the sense in which those words were used in Katzenbach v. Morgan and the ensuing professional commentary. The bill does not ask Congress to make or declare new knowledge of actual facts or to appraise the practical operation of facts. Even the proposed finding that there is "a significant likelihood that actual human life exists from conception" rests entirely upon giving a particular meaning to the word "life." What is "life" is not simply a question of fact. Over the years many sincere people have believed that life begins at the moment of conception. Everything depends upon what one means by "life." The meaning may be established by agreement upon a dictionary definition. The meaning may represent a theological, philosophical, moral, legal or other normative declaration of when a particular collection of phenomena should be given the same theological, philosophical, moral, legal or other normative consequences as the "life" we recognize in human beings after birth and before anything that might be determined to be "death." Because the meaning of "life" must first be fixed, the existence of life is not simply a question of fact.

The rest of Section 1 of S. 158 does not even purport to deal with the facts: it says that "life" shall "be deemed" to commence at the moment of conception; it defines "person" to include any unborn person from the moment of conception.

For these reasons even the second branch of Katzenbach v. Morgan gives no support to S. 158.

For similar reasons S. 158, Section 1 presents very different constitutional questions from the 1971 amendment to the Voting Rights Act reducing the voting age in all state and federal elections from 21 years old to 18 years old. The constitutional question was whether classifying 18- to 21-year-old citizens as ineligible to vote while citizens over 21 years old are permitted to vote violated the Equal Protection Clause. The classification was not invidious in the sense that it rests upon hostility or prejudice; age is relevant to the permissible State objective of securing an informed, intelligent and responsible electorate. Thus, using the twenty-first birthday to draw the line was permissible if, but only if, the knowledge, experience, maturity, and appreciation of one's stake in the community necessary for an intelligent and responsible vote of those over 21 is sufficiently greater than that of those between 18 and 21 to justify excluding the younger group from participation in self-government. These are questions of fact in the first instance, of characterization or degree after the raw data is assembled, and ultimately, of balance or relative importance.

Section 302 of the Voting Rights Act in nowise sought to change the constitutional principle. Among other supporters of the reduction I urged that Congress honestly could and should find *purely as matters of fact* that the spread and improvement of education, the age at which young people take jobs, pay taxes, marry and have children, the tremendous interest of young people in government and public affairs, and their increased knowledge and sophistication everywhere as a result of new forms of mass communications had made 18- to 21-year-old citizens as able to cast informed, intelligent and responsible votes as those over 21 years old.

S. 158 is altogether different because, as I have repeatedly pointed out, it does not find facts but simply and directly seeks to change the applicable constitutional standards. The second branch of Katzenbach v. Morgan, even when read most broadly, gives no support whatever to an attempt to change the meaning of the Constitution, to redefine the words used in the Constitution, by simple legislative majorities. As I wrote ten years ago, "Nothing in *Morgan* suggested that the Court should defer to Congress in the process of deriving the applicable legal standard from the document and other sources of law; the opinion seemed to require Congress to *apply the same standard* as the Court, merely leaving it free to apply the standard differently where the application turned upon 'questions of fact.' "

S. 158 does not apply the same legal standard as the Court established in Roe v. Wade. S. 158 rejects the Court's standard. In Roe v. Wade the Court held that "the word 'person,' as used in the Fourteenth Amendment, does *not* include the unborn." S. 158 would reject this standard by enacting that " 'person' shall include all human life as defined herein (i.e. from the moment of conception)," thereby including the unborn. In Roe v. Wade the Court held that the woman's freedom to choose during the first two trimesters of pregnancy whether to carry an unborn child until birth is constitutionally superior to any interest in or of the fetus up to the time of viability, regardless of when "life" may begin. S. 158 rejects that legal standard also; it adopts one view of when life begins and then declares, contrary to the existing rule of law, that its view of when life begins shall be controlling under the Fourteenth Amendment.

Thus, my present view that S. 158, Section 1, is patently unconstitutional is completely consistent with that I wrote of the power of Congress under Section 5 of the Fourteenth Amendment in 1971.

> [The argument] affects only the latitude available to Congress in applying general rules of law to what it finds to be actual social conditions, always within the legal framework supplied by the Constitution and the principles developed by the Court. No one suggests that the Congress can read into the Constitution new general rules of law that have been rejected by the Court, regardless of whether they expand or dilute constitutional rights.

Discussion

1. What are the issues in dispute between Professors Noonan and Cox? Do they join issue over the true meaning of Katzenbach v. Morgan and Oregon v. Mitchell or over the true meaning of section 5 of the Fourteenth Amendment? Might Congress properly enact S. 158 based on its conclusion that, whatever the Court may have said or held in these cases, section 5 authorizes the congressional action?

2. What deference should the Court give to the judgments that may underlie the act? Congress heard extensive testimony concerning medical, moral, and legal issues bearing on S. 158, but what does it mean to say that *"Congress* heard"?

Even if "it" did hear, should — and could — a reviewing court be concerned with how well it listened?

3. Could the Court consistently apply different standards in reviewing laws that "expand" and those that "contract" constitutional rights? Recall Professor Cohen's distinction between judicial review of decisions concerning individual rights and states' rights, and consider Professor Cox's similar argument:

> There is no a priori reason for linking power to expand constitutional safeguards with power to dilute them. One can assert without logical fallacy that, since the chief function of the Supreme Court is to protect human rights, it should never defer to any legislative determination which restricts those rights without making its own investigation and characterization of the interests affected, even though it welcomes any legislative determination that extends human rights and is subject to challenge only as an unconstitutional extension of federal power at the expense of the states.[40]

Does S. 158 expand or contract constitutional rights?

THE HUMAN LIFE BILL (S. 158): REPORT TO THE COMMITTEE ON THE JUDICIARY OF THE UNITED STATES SENATE

Made by its Subcommittee on Separation of Powers

III. Need for This Legislation

To protect the lives of human beings is the highest duty of government. . . . Today there is a strong concern among many citizens that government is not fulfilling its duty to protect the lives of all human beings. Since 1973 abortion has been available on demand nationwide, resulting in more than one and one-half million abortions per year. Yet this abrupt and fundamental shift in policy occurred without any prior inquiry by any branch of the federal government to determine whether the unborn children being aborted are living human beings. Nor has any branch of the federal government forthrightly faced the question whether our law should continue to affirm the sanctity of human life — the intrinsic worth and equal value of all human life — or whether our law should now reject the sanctity of life in favor of some competing ethic. Only by determining whether unborn children are human beings, and deciding whether our law should and does accord intrinsic worth and equal value to their lives, can our government rationally address the issue of abortion. . . .

Since the fourteenth amendment expressly confers on Congress the power to enforce the protections of that amendment, including the protection of life, it is appropriate for Congress as well as the Supreme Court to ask whether a particular class of individuals are human beings. . . .

In its hearings on S. 158, the Subcommittee has exhaustively addressed all questions relevant to the protection of lives of unborn children under the fourteenth amendment. Through these hearings we have also come to recognize that the fundamental question concerning the life and humanity of the unborn is two-

40. Cox, supra note 36, at 253.

fold. Not only must government answer the biological, factual question of when the life of each human being begins; it must also address the question whether to accord intrinsic worth and equal value to all human life, whether before or after birth.

These two questions are separate and distinct. The question of when the life of a human being begins — when an individual member of the human species comes into existence — is answered by scientific, factual evidence. Science, however, is not relevant to the second question; science cannot tell us what value to give to each human life. This second question can be answered only in light of the ethical and legal values held by our citizens and expressed by the framers of our Constitution.

The two congressional findings contained in section 1 of S. 158 correspond to these two distinct questions. The congressional finding in section 1(a) of the bill addresses the first question and rests on a factual, scientific determination. The congressional finding in section 1(b) of the bill reflects the conclusion of the Subcommittee that the fourteenth amendment answers the second question by affirming the intrinsic worth and equal value of all human lives. . . .

IV. The Scientific Question: When Does a Human Life Begin?

During the course of eight days of hearings, fifty-seven witnesses testified on S. 158 before the Subcommittee. Of these witnesses, twenty-two, including world-renowned geneticists, biologists, and practicing physicians, addressed the medical and biological questions raised by the bill. Eleven testified in support of the bill and eleven in opposition.

The testimony of these witnesses and the voluminous submissions received by the Subcommittee demonstrate that contemporary scientific evidence points to a clear conclusion: the life of a human being begins at conception, the time when the process of fertilization is complete. Until the early nineteenth century science had not advanced sufficiently to be able to know that conception is the beginning of a human life; but today the facts are beyond dispute.

Physicians, biologists, and other scientists agree that conception marks the beginning of the life of a human being — of a being that is alive and is a member of the human species. There is overwhelming agreement on this point in countless medical, biological, and scientific writings. . . .

V. The Value Question: Should We Value All Human Lives Equally?

The answer to the scientific question casts the value question in clear relief. Unborn children are human beings. But should our nation value all human lives equally? Scientific evidence is not relevant to this question. The answer is a matter of ethical judgment.

Deeply engrained in American society and American constitutional history is the ethic of the sanctity of innocent human life. The sanctity-of-life ethic recognizes each human life as having intrinsic worth simply by virtue of its being human. If, as a society, we reject this ethic, we must inevitably adopt some other standard for deciding which human lives are of value and are worthy of protection. Because the standards some use to make such decisions turn on various qualities by which they define which lives are worthy of protection, the alternative to the sanctity-of-life ethic is often termed the "quality-of-life ethic." A sharp division exists today between those who affirm the sanctity-of-life ethic and those who reject it in favor of the quality-of-life ethic. The Supreme Court has never purported to decide which ethic our Constitution mandates for valuing the lives of human beings before birth. Nevertheless, deciding which ethic should apply is fundamental to resolving the abortion issue under the Constitution. . . .

Our constitutional history leaves no doubt which ethic is written into our fundamental law. The Declaration of Independence expressly affirms the sanctity of human life: "We hold these truths to be self-evident, that all men are created equal, that they are endowed by their Creator with certain unalienable rights, that among these are life, liberty, and the pursuit of happiness."

The proponents of the fourteenth amendment argued for the amendment on the basis of these principles. Congressman John A. Bingham of Ohio, who drafted the first section of the fourteenth amendment, stated after the adoption of the Joint Resolution of Congress proposing this amendment:

> Before that great law [of the United States,] the only question to be asked of the creature claiming its protection is this: Is he a man? Every man is entitled to the protection of American law, because its divine spirit of equality declares that all men are created equal.

Cong. Globe, 40th Cong., 1st Sess. 542 (1867).

Similarly, Abraham Lincoln emphasized the importance of holding to the concept of the sanctity of human life and of never denying the inalienable value of every human being.

> I should like to know if taking this old Declaration of Independence, which declares that all men are equal upon principle and making exceptions to it where will it stop. If one man says it does not mean a negro, why not another say it does not mean some other man? If that declaration is not the truth, let us get the Statute book, in which we find it and tear it out! . . . let us stick to it then . . . let us stand firmly by it then.

Speech during the Lincoln-Douglas senatorial campaign (July 10, 1858), reprinted in 2 The Collected Works of Abraham Lincoln 484, 500-01 (R. Basler ed. 1953) (footnote omitted).

As the framers planned it, all human beings were to fall within the ambit of the amendment's protection. Congressman Bingham spoke of the rights guaranteed by the amendment as applying to "any human being." Cong. Globe, 39th Cong., 1st Sess. 1089 (1866). Bingham also said the amendment would protect the rights of "common humanity." Cong. Globe, 40th Cong., 2d Sess. 514 (1868). . . .

Because it affirms the Constitution, the Subcommittee cannot accept any legal rule that would allow judges, scientists, or medical professors to decide that some human lives are not worth living. We must instead affirm the intrinsic worth of *all* human life. We find that the fourteenth amendment embodies the sanctity of human life and that today the government must affirm this ethic by recognizing the "personhood" of all human beings. Earlier we found, based upon scientific examination, that the life of each human being begins at conception. Now, basing our decision not upon science but upon the values embodied in our Constitution, we affirm the sanctity of all human life. Science can tell us whether a being is alive and a member of the human species. It cannot tell us whether to accord value to that being. The government of any society that accords intrinsic worth to all human life must make *both* a factual determination recognizing the existence of all human beings *and* a value decision affirming the worth of human life.

VI. Legal Effect of S. 158

. . . The first effect of S. 158 is to require the Supreme Court to reconsider its holding in Roe v. Wade that unborn children are not persons entitled to protection of their lives under the fourteenth amendment. With the findings of S. 158, the Court faces a fundamentally different issue than it faced in Roe v. Wade. In that case it addressed the personhood issue without purporting to know whether unborn children are human beings and without considering whether all human lives are to be accorded intrinsic worth and equal value under our Constitution. . . .

The second legal effect of S. 158 will be to require the Supreme Court to reconsider its 1973 holding that found the right of privacy to include abortion and that permitted abortion on demand throughout the term of pregnancy. . . .

The third legal effect of S. 158 is that no state will be able to deprive an unborn child of life without due process of law. Under Supreme Court precedent, states could thus perform or fund abortions only when necessary to protect compelling state interests. Protection of the life of the mother would surely be interpreted as one such compelling state interest. See Roe v. Wade, 410 U.S. at 173 (Rehnquist, J., dissenting). . . .

What S. 158 will not do is also important to recognize. First, S. 158 establishes no criminal penalties; the passage of S. 158 will not make abortion a crime.

. . . [W]hile S. 158 will prevent states from funding or performing abortions on demand, it will not automatically prevent the performance of abortions by private means. The fourteenth amendment only provides that no *state* shall deprive any person of life without due process of law. See Martinez v. California, 444 U.S. 277, 284 (1980). The amendment does not directly affect private action; therefore S. 158 will not directly affect the performance of abortions by private clinics. A state's failure to act to protect unborn children against privately performed abortions, moreover, would not likely be deemed state action. See Jackson v. Metropolitan Edison Co., 419 U.S. 345 (1974); Reitman v. Mulkey, 387 U.S. 369, 381 (1967). . . .

Consequently, abortions will become illegal in the wake of S. 158 only if state legislatures choose to make them illegal. It is incorrect to state that S. 158 will make abortion "murder." S. 158 will not make abortion murder because it does not even make abortion a crime. . . .

S. 158 will not allow states to outlaw any forms of contraception. S. 158 allows states to protect unborn children only after they have come into existence at conception. Contraceptives, by definition, prevent conception. They do not terminate the life of any living human being. Furthermore, drugs and devices that do act to perform abortions after conception will not be prohibited following enactment of S. 158 unless states so legislate.

Fourth, S. 158 will not require state legislatures to categorize abortion as murder. State legislatures will have discretion, within limits of reason, to set penalties for abortion as for any other crime. They may consider mitigating circumstances for the crime of abortion, just as for any other degree of homicide or any other crime. States, furthermore, may make exceptions from an abortion statute where there is a compelling state interest for doing so. Such an interest would certainly exist in a case where an abortion was necessary to save the life of the mother, assuming that in such cases all practicable means are taken to preserve the life of the child. Here, as before, other difficult cases will have to be resolved by the courts on a case-by-case basis.

VII. CONSTITUTIONALITY OF S. 158

Congress has constitutional power to enact S. 158 despite the holding of Roe v. Wade that unborn children are not persons and there is a right to abort them. The findings of S. 158 that unborn children are human beings as a matter of biological fact and that the sanctity-of-life ethic is central to our Constitution create a fundamentally different question of constitutional law than the Supreme Court faced in Roe v. Wade. The factual question whether unborn children are human beings is central to deciding whether their lives are protected by a constitutional amendment that is intended to protect all human beings. The value decision of whether to accord intrinsic worth and equal value to all human life is also central to the enforcement of the fourteenth amendment's protection of life. The Supreme Court's Roe v. Wade opinion found the judiciary unable to address the first question, whether unborn children are human beings. It did not therefore address the question whether the lives of unborn human beings are to be accorded intrinsic worth and equal value along with other human lives. When the Supreme Court faces these two congressional determinations in the course of reviewing the constitutionality of S. 158, it will therefore face a constitutional question far different from that decided in Roe v. Wade.

Congress has the authority and, indeed, the duty to address questions of fact and value that are central to the interpretation and enforcement of constitutional provisions. The task of interpreting the Constitution in the context of specific cases is ultimately for the Supreme Court. But when the Supreme Court has professed an inability to address underlying questions that are fundamental to the interpretation of a constitutional provision, Congress is entirely justified in expressing its view on such questions, subject to Supreme Court review. . . .

The purpose of this legislation is not to impair the Supreme Court's power to review the constitutionality of legislation, but to exercise the authority of Congress to disagree with the result of an earlier Supreme Court decision based on an investigation of facts and on a decision concerning values that the Supreme Court has declined to address. The Supreme Court retains full power to review the constitutionality of S. 158, and the Subcommittee believes that the bill *should* be reviewed by the Supreme Court. A primary purpose of S. 158 is precisely to produce a new consideration by the Supreme Court of its abortion decision in light of both the biological facts concerning unborn human life and the principle that all human life is of intrinsic worth and equal value. If the Supreme Court finds the determinations of Congress to be persuasive, it will change its constitutional decision as to the availability of abortion on demand. If the Supreme Court finds Congress's determinations unsubstantiated and unpersuasive, it can refuse to follow them. In either case, the Supreme Court will have an opportunity to interpret S. 158 in light of the Constitution.

Some critics of S. 158 argue that even if Roe v. Wade was wrongly decided and ought to be overruled, S. 158 is unconstitutional because Congress must act in conformity with Supreme Court decisions until the Court itself chooses to overrule them. This criticism rests on a profound misapprehension of the doctrine of judicial review espoused in Marbury v. Madison, 5 U.S. (1 Cranch) 137 (1803). Under *Marbury,* the Supreme Court, presented with a proper case, must rule in accordance with its own interpretation of the Constitution rather than with a contrary congressional interpretation, because the Justices have taken an oath to uphold the Constitution. As Chief Justice Marshall stated in *Marbury,* automatic judicial deference to a legislative interpretation of the Constitution would constitute an implicit violation of the Justices' oath of office; the Justices would thereby "close their eyes on the constitution, and see only the law." 5 U.S. (Cranch) at 178. It does not follow, however, that once the Court has interpreted a provision of the Constitution members of Congress must automatically defer to the judicial interpretation. Indeed, members of Congress take the same oath that the Justices take to uphold the Constitution. Confronted with a proposed law that is consistent with his own honest construction of the Constitution and with his view of sound policy, but that conflicts with what he regards as an erroneous Supreme Court decision, a member of Congress has at least the right and perhaps the duty to vote for the bill. To do otherwise would be to close his eyes on the Constitution and see only the case. Through its power to issue judgments that are binding on the parties to litigation, the Supreme Court will as a practical matter generally have the final word in any dispute over constitutional interpretation. But this does not preclude the possibility of a responsible dialogue between Congress and the Court. . . .

Assessing various attempts by Congress to counter judicial doctrine by offering its own reflections on constitutional meaning, Paul Brest argues, in Congress as a Constitutional Decisionmaker and Its Power to Counter Judicial Doctrine, 21 Ga. L. Rev. 57 (1986), that "Congress has neither a strong tradition nor trustworthy procedures for addressing constitutional questions." He goes on to note that several scholars "have suggested that Congress' ability to contradict the Court's constitutional interpretations . . . may serve to maintain 'a desirable tension between Congress and the Court' or encourage 'a dialectical process of constitutional growth.'" Whatever the merits of this as a normative notion, Brest views

> Congress' traditions and practices of considering constitutional questions [as] so weak and untrustworthy that it is not ready to enter into a dialogue. It needs a tutorial first. . . .
>
> Until and unless Congress develops systematic and trustworthy procedures of constitutional decisionmaking, Congress may not counter the Court's decisions either by direct legislation or by jurisdiction-limiting measures under Article III [which shall be considered in the next section], but must rely on the amendment process. By "may not," I mean that Congress *currently lacks the authority* to counter judicial doctrine — although Congress might in the future develop procedures that would give it the authority.

This is an unusual sort of argument: We conventionally think of the allocation of authority among institutions as being determined by the Constitution itself and hence immutable except by amendment. Or at least we usually talk of "institutional competence" in theoretical terms rather than consider how well an institution actually does its job. But the written Constitution does not determine the central issue at stake here. In any event, the notion of immutable constitutional doctrine does not comport with the reality of American legal history. Issues involving the allocation of authority tend more than many others to be resolved by the course of the institutions' practices. While our history is not unequivocal, it is largely one of congressional acquiescence in judicially-declared constitutional doctrine. Not only would it be inappropriate to alter the tradition at present, it would be constitutional error.

This does not mean that Congress must be forever barred from attempting to counter judicial doctrine. Congress has ample opportunity to develop trustworthy practices of constitutional decisionmaking in the course of enacting *ordinary legislation*, where the issues involve Congress' powers under Article I and the limitations imposed by the Bill of Rights and the separation of powers. Only after it has succeeded in the realm of ordinary legislation can Congress assess how its constitutional decisionmaking procedures compare with the Court's and consider whether it has the authority to contradict the Court.

The distinction between ordinary legislation and legislation that has the purpose or effect of contradicting or subverting judicial doctrine is usually evident. However, it is worth mentioning two situations where the issue may not be clear. One involves the expansion of judicially-declared rights under the fourteenth or fifteenth amendment. . . . If the Court's refusal to hold a state practice unconstitutional is based on its interpretation of the text or original history of the Constitution, legislation based on a different congressional interpretation would certainly count as a contradiction. But the Court's failure to hold a state practice unconstitutional may reflect real or supposed institutional limitations on judicial inquiry into legislative motivation, the determination of legislative facts, or the drawing of arbitrary lines. To the extent that the legislative process is free from these constraints, a different congressional decision does not necessarily contradict judicial doctrine. On the other hand, as Justice Harlan suggested in Oregon v. Mitchell, such legislative determinations are typically intertwined with value judgments having a constitutional dimension. The general principle suggested by the argument of this article is that Congress should not contradict judicial value judgments of this sort.

The second situation is one where Congress' disagreement with the Court results in a decision *not* to enact legislation that Congress could well decide not to enact on other grounds as well. Imagine, for example, Congress returning to the pre-1937 view of its article I powers while the Court retains its expansive interpretation. Such a state of affairs does little if any injury to the principles in this article.

In conclusion, let me reiterate that this article is addressed primarily to Congress, not the Court. The argument that Congress may not contradict or subvert the enforcement of judicial doctrine does not entail that the Court may strike down or ignore a statute that purports to do so. That depends on issues of institutional competence and authority beyond those canvassed here — for example, the Court's capacity to assess the quality of Congress' decisionmaking processes.

Discussion

1. Please assess the quality of Congress' inquiry into the constitutionality of the Helms-Hyde Bill as presented earlier in this chapter. If you think you need more information to answer the question, what is it, precisely, that you would like to know and for what reason?

2. If you *do* find Congress' inquiry inadequate, for whatever reason, does this automatically translate into a view that the Court should invalidate the Bill (had it ever passed)?

III. Congress' Use of its Article III Powers to Respond to Judicial Constitutional Interpretation[41]

Sections 4 and 5 of S. 158 provide:

> Sec. 4. Notwithstanding any other provision of law, no inferior Federal court ordained and established by Congress under article III of the Constitution of the United States shall have jurisdiction to issue any restraining order, temporary or permanent injunction, or declaratory judgment in any case involving or arising from any State law or municipal ordinance that (1) protects the rights of human persons between conception and birth, or (2) prohibits, limits, or regulates (a) the performance of abortions or (b) the provision at public expense of funds, facilities, personnel, or other assistance for the performance of abortions: Provided, That nothing in this section shall deprive the Supreme Court of the United States of the authority to render appropriate relief in any case.
>
> Sec. 5. Any party may appeal to the Supreme Court of the United States from an interlocutory or final judgment, decree, or order of any court of the United States regarding the enforcement of this Act, or of any State law or municipal ordinance that protects the rights of human beings between conception and birth, or which adjudicates the constitutionality of this Act, or of any such law or ordinance. The Supreme Court shall advance on its docket and expedite the disposition of any such appeal.

A. Background

These sections present another unresolved issue in the allocation of constitutional decisionmaking authority — the extent to which Congress can use the powers conferred by Article III (to create and regulate the jurisdiction of federal courts) in order to express disagreement with and thwart the enforcement of judicially declared constitutional doctrines it deems erroneous. The language of Article III is sparse:

> The judicial Power of the United States shall be vested in one supreme Court, and in such inferior Courts as the Congress may from time to time ordain and establish. . . .
>
> In all Cases affecting Ambassadors, other public Ministers and Consuls, and those in which a State shall be a Party, the supreme Court shall have original Jurisdiction. In all the other Cases before mentioned, the supreme Court shall have ap-

41. The issues considered here constitute one part of an arcane area taken up in courses in federal courts and considered by aficionados of the subject to lie at its very core.

> pellate Jurisdiction, both as to Law and Fact, with such Exceptions, and under such Regulations as the Congress shall make.[42]

Few areas of constitutional law have been the subject of such sweeping and inconsistent judicial statement as the authority of Congress to regulate the jurisdiction of the federal courts — and hence to control the circumstances in which they can exercise judicial review. At the one extreme, in dictum in Martin v. Hunter's Lessee, 14 U.S. (1 Wheat.) 304 (1816), page 72 supra, Justice Story wrote:

> The language of [Article III] throughout is manifestly designed to be mandatory upon the legislature. Its obligatory force is so imperative, that congress could not, without a violation of its duty, have refused to carry it into operation. The judicial power of the United States *shall* be vested (not *may* be vested) in one supreme court, and in such inferior courts as congress may, from time to time, ordain and establish. . . .
>
> If, then, it is a duty of congress to vest the judicial power of the United States, it is a duty to vest the whole judicial power. The language, if imperative as to one part, is imperative as to all. If it were otherwise, this anomaly would exist, that congress might successively refuse to vest the jurisdiction in any one class of cases enumerated in the constitution, and thereby defeat the jurisdiction as to all; for the constitution has not singled out any class on which congress are bound to act in preference to others.
>
> The next consideration is, as to the courts in which the judicial power shall be vested. It is manifest, that a supreme court must be established; but whether it be equally obligatory to establish inferior courts, is a question of some difficulty. If congress may lawfully omit to establish inferior courts, it might follow, that in some of the enumerated cases, the judicial power could nowhere exist. The supreme court can have original jurisdiction in two classes of cases, only, viz., in cases affecting ambassadors, other public ministers and consuls, and in cases in which a state is a party. Congress cannot vest any portion of the judicial power of the United States, except in courts ordained and established by itself; and if in any of the cases enumerated in the constitution, the state courts did not then possess jurisdiction, the appellate jurisdiction of the supreme court (admitting that it could act on state courts) could not reach those cases, and consequently, the injunction of the constitution, that the judicial power "shall be vested," would be disobeyed. It would seem, therefore, to follow, that congress are bound to create some inferior courts, in which to vest all that jurisdiction which, under the constitution, is exclusively vested in the United States, and of which the supreme court cannot take original cognisance. They might establish one or more inferior courts; they might parcel out the jurisdiction among such courts, from time to time, at their own pleasure. But the whole judicial power of the United States should be, at all times, vested, either in an original or appellate form, in some courts created under its authority.

Is Justice Story's deduction from the text persuasive? Professors Hart and Wechsler argue that his view is inconsistent with a deliberate compromise between those who advocated a constitutionally mandated inferior federal judiciary and those who wanted no lower federal courts at all: The matter was to be left to

42. Article III, §§1 and 2. See also Article I, §8, cl. 18: "The Congress shall have Power . . . [t]o make all Laws which shall be necessary and proper for carrying into Execution . . . all . . . Powers vested by this Constitution in the Government of the United States, or in any Department . . . thereof."

Congress' discretion.[43] Moreover, the Judiciary Act of 1789 implicitly rejected Story's position by vesting the federal judiciary with less than the full jurisdiction authorized by Article III. For example, the act (a) created no general "federal question" jurisdiction, (b) limited diversity jurisdiction to suits involving more than $500, and (c) refused to authorize Supreme Court review of all state cases arising under the Constitution, laws, and treaties of the United States.

At the other extreme, the Court has often characterized Congress' control over the jurisdiction of the federal judiciary (except the Supreme Court's original jurisdiction) as plenary. For example, in Sheldon v. Sill, 49 U.S. (8 How.) 440 (1850), in holding that a circuit court had no jurisdiction over a case that met the constitutional, but not the statutory, requirements for diversity jurisdiction, Justice Grier wrote:

> [C]ongress may withhold from any court of its creation jurisdiction of any of the enumerated controversies. Courts created by statute can have no jurisdiction but such as the statute confers. . . . The Constitution has defined the limits of the judicial power of the United States, but has not prescribed how much of it shall be exercised by the Circuit Court; consequently, the statute which does prescribe the limits of their jurisdiction, cannot be in conflict with the Constitution, unless it confers powers not enumerated therein.

And in The Francis Wright, 105 U.S. 381 (1881), Chief Justice Waite observed:

> [W]hile the appellate power of this court under the Constitution extends to all cases within the judicial power of the United States, actual jurisdiction under the power is confined within such limits as Congress sees fit to prescribe. . . . What those [appellate] powers shall be, and to what extent they shall be exercised, are, and always have been, proper subjects of legislative control. Authority to limit the jurisdiction necessarily carries with it authority to limit the use of the jurisdiction. Not only may whole classes of cases be kept out of the jurisdiction altogether, but particular classes of questions may be subjected to re-examination and review, while others are not.

Ever since the Judiciary Act of 1789, Congress has regulated the original and appellate jurisdiction of federal courts, in response to federalistic and procedural considerations, to allocate business between the federal and state systems and to channel federal litigation efficiently. Over the past several decades some jurisdictional measures of a quite different sort have been introduced in the Congress. Generated by disagreement with the substance of particular Supreme Court decisions, these bills typically have sought to eliminate both the Supreme Court's appellate jurisdiction and the original jurisdiction of inferior federal courts over particular subjects.[44] For example, the Jenner bill (1958) provided that "the Supreme Court shall have no jurisdiction to review . . . any case where there is drawn into question the validity" of citations for contempt of congressional committees, the discharge of federal employees "whose retention may impair the security of the United States Government," state regulations designed "to control

43. Hart & Wechsler, The Federal Courts and the Federal System 11-12 (Bator et al. eds., 2d ed. 1973) (hereinafter Hart & Wechsler). For a weak argument supporting Story, see Julius Goebel, Antecedents and Beginnings to 1801 at 246-247 (1971) (I History of the Supreme Court of the United States).

44. See Hart & Wechsler, supra note 43, at 360; Walter Murphy, Congress and the Court (1962).

subversive activities," and decisions "pertaining to the admission of persons to the practice of law."[45] In a similar vein, the Tuck bill (1964) provided:[46]

> The Supreme Court shall not have the right to review the action of a Federal court or a State court of last resort concerning any action taken upon a petition or complaint seeking to apportion or reapportion the legislature of any State of the Union or any branch thereof.
>
> The district courts shall not have jurisdiction to entertain any petition or complaint seeking to apportion or reapportion the legislature of any State of the Union or any branch thereof. . . .

A section of the Omnibus Crime Control and Safe Streets bill (1968) provided:[47]

> Neither the Supreme Court nor any inferior court ordained and established by Congress under article III . . . shall have jurisdiction to review or to reverse, vacate, modify, or disturb in any way, a ruling of any trial court of any State in any criminal prosecution admitting in evidence as voluntarily made an admission or confession of an accused if such ruling has been affirmed or otherwise upheld by the highest court of the State having appellate jurisdiction of the cause.

Read without qualification, the dicta of Sheldon v. Sill and The Francis Wright imply that these measures pose no constitutional problems whatsoever. Although those dicta have their modern supporters,[48] they have also been criticized as incautiously broad. It has been argued that Congress' power over the jurisdiction of federal courts is not plenary but is subject to both explicit and implicit constitutional limitations.

B. Limitations on the Jurisdiction of Lower Federal Courts

Professors Noonan and Cox, who testified regarding the constitutionality of sections 1 and 2 of S. 158, also testified about sections 4 and 5. Professor Noonan said:

> As Justice White wrote in Palmore v. United States, 411 U.S. 389, at 400-401 (1973), in an opinion joined by Chief Justice Burger and Justices Brennan, Stewart, Marshall, Blackmun, Powell, and Rehnquist, "The decision with respect to inferior federal courts, as well as the task of defining their jurisdiction, was left to the discretion of Congress." Congress, he went on to say, was not constitutionally required to create Article III courts nor, if they were created, "required to invest them with all the jurisdiction it was authorized to bestow." Until 1875 "the state courts provided the only forum for vindicating many important federal claims." It needs no further argument to show that the restriction on the jurisdiction of the inferior federal courts — leaving unaffected the jurisdiction of the United States Supreme Court and the state courts — is constitutional.
>
> The only question that can appropriately be raised is whether the restriction is wise. Here the experience of the last eight years must be referred to. The judges of

45. S. 2646, 85th Cong., 2d Sess. (1958).
46. H.R. 11926, 88th Cong., 2d Sess. (1964).
47. S. 17, 90th Cong., 2d Sess. (1968).
48. See Herbert Wechsler, The Courts and the Constitution, 1965 Colum. L. Rev. 1001.

the inferior federal courts have shown themselves in many instances to be zealous, partisan, and prejudiced champions of those seeking and those providing abortions. They have shown a marked insensitivity to values at stake besides the abortion liberty and a marked disregard for the constitutional restraints on judicial action in this area.[49]

Professor Cox testified:

It is well known that the Constitution gives to the Congress the power to establish such inferior federal courts as it deems appropriate. This broad power to establish lower federal courts has been interpreted to include the power for Congress to limit the kinds of cases that can be brought in those courts. Thus, there are numerous precedents that allow Congress to limit the jurisdiction of the inferior federal courts so long as the right of an aggrieved party to ultimately bring his constitutional claim to the Supreme Court is preserved.

The power of Congress to limit lower federal court jurisdiction is not, however, without bounds. This congressional power, like all others, is constrained by the other provisions of the Constitution, and must be exercised in conformance with other constitutional protections. Thus, Congress may limit federal court jurisdiction only if it does so consistent with, for instance, Fifth Amendment Due Process guarantees.

The jurisdictional limitation is S. 158 raises grave questions on this basis. The bill proposes that Congress deny to the lower federal courts the power to hear cases asserting particular federal constitutional rights. In singling out one set of constitutional rights for disfavored treatment, the bill burdens the exercise of those rights. The Supreme Court has often held that Congress may not discriminate against particular constitutional rights by burdening their exercise. See Shapiro v. Thompson, 394 U.S. 618 (1969); Sherbert v. Verner, 374 U.S. 395 (1963). To do so violates both the equal protection and due process guarantees of the Fifth Amendment. I thus believe that the jurisdictional limitation in S. 158 is of dubious constitutionality, even though I cannot categorically say it would be held unconstitutional.

The most extensive testimony arguing against constitutionality of section 4 of S. 158 was offered by Professor Theodore Eisenberg of the University of California at Los Angeles Law School.[50]

TESTIMONY OF THEODORE EISENBERG

Hearings on S. 158 Before the Subcomm. on the Separation of Powers of the Senate Comm. on the Judiciary, 97th Cong., 1st Sess. 586-605 (1981)

. . . One of Section [4]'s principal difficulties is that it undermines an essential role of the federal judiciary. Perhaps above all else the framers intended the national judiciary to be able to hear and to do justice in all cases involving federal constitutional rights. At the time of the Constitutional Convention and the Judiciary Act of 1789, this function could be performed solely by the Supreme Court.

49. Hearings on S. 158 Before the Subcomm. on the Separation of Powers of the Senate Comm. on the Judiciary, 97th Cong., 1st Sess. 261 (1981). Professor Cox's statement (which follows) is from id. at 344-346.

50. See also Theodore Eisenberg, Congressional Authority to Restrict Lower Federal Court Jurisdiction, 83 Yale L.J. 498 (1974).

But this function no longer can be performed solely by the Court. Therefore, to maintain an essential function of the national judiciary, litigants need access to lower federal courts. . . .

A compelling indication that the framers intended the federal judiciary to afford a forum at some level for all cases within its jurisdiction comes from an omission from Article III. Neither the final arrangement nor any of the five judiciary plans submitted to the Convention authorized federal courts to decline to hear a case. Discretionary review by the Supreme Court did not originate until 1925. The framers' failure to confer, or even consider conferring, discretionary review powers upon courts suggests that federal tribunals, including the Supreme Court, were thought capable of providing a forum in all cases within their jurisdiction. . . .

Accepting the national judiciary's role as a protector of federal rights, how was the new judiciary to fulfill that role? The right to appellate review by the Supreme Court would provide litigants with an opportunity to have their cases heard by a national tribunal.

The expectation that there would be few federal cases supports the view that Supreme Court review was believed adequate to implement the role of the national judiciary. If there were to be few cases, the Supreme Court, by appellate review, would be capable of vindicating each litigant's federal rights.

Willingness to implement the federal judiciary's role through Supreme Court review was perfectly understandable at the time. Without question, the Supreme Court was then capable of providing a forum for all federal cases. Between 1789 and 1801 the Supreme Court disposed of fewer than 90 cases. During the first four terms of the Court, not a single case was argued. Since the Court's jurisdiction was not discretionary, any litigant whose case fell within the federal judicial power and who desired to have a federal forum hear his case could obtain such a forum.

However content one might have been in 1789 to have the Supreme Court by itself fulfill the national judiciary's role, such an approach clearly will not work in today's world. Contrast the above figures for the Supreme Court's early terms with the status of a modern Court term. During the 1979 Term, the Supreme Court was asked to hear 4,781 cases but disposed of only 278 on the merits, including 149 by full opinion. This increase in case load has had significant consequences for both the Supreme Court and the lower federal courts. The Supreme Court is no longer capable of providing a federal forum to hear the merits of every case involving a federal constitutional question.

As the federal caseload has grown the role of lower federal courts has undergone change. Today the lower federal courts are more than mere federal trial forums for cases falling within the Article III jurisdictional grant. First, in those instances where the Supreme Court makes a pronouncement of nation-wide impact regarding federal rights or interests, access to the lower courts is needed to enforce and apply it. Moreover, as Supreme Court review becomes more selective, the lower courts have become the primary vindicators of federal rights. . . .

To a significant extent the contemporary guarantors of federal rights are not the nine Supreme Court Justices but the judges of the district courts and courts of appeals. The lower judges are not authorized to decline to hear a federal matter within their jurisdiction. Hundreds of important issues are determined with practical finality by lower federal judges.

B. THE CONSTITUTIONALITY OF SECTION [4]

In passing on the validity of any federal statute one must determine its natural or probable effect and measure that effect against constitutional requirements. For example, a jurisdictional statute prohibiting black plaintiffs from bringing actions in the lower federal courts would fall as a violation of equal protection. Although I suggest below theories under which Section [4] could be deemed unconstitutional, each theory is in some sense speculative. The modern Court never has faced this precise problem.

1. Section [4]'s Abridgment of the Right of Access to a Federal Forum. A statute depriving both federal and state courts of jurisdiction to hear a claim has an obvious, drastic impact. Statutes that foreclose only lower federal court jurisdiction have more subtle but nevertheless serious substantive effects. Consider a statute like S. 158 that deprives lower federal courts, but not state courts, of jurisdiction to hear a class of cases. The provision cannot be justified, as some might claim, on the ground that inferior federal jurisdiction is not necessary to vindicate federal rights because of the availability of Supreme Court review of state court decisions. No litigant has any assurance that the Court even will agree to hear his case. And, in the aggregate, litigants with federal claims, even constitutional claims, have absolute assurance that the Court will not hear each of their cases.

It is not enough to say that state courts might perform well in abortion cases or that the Supreme Court might grant certiorari or that the lower federal courts might not be up to the task of protecting federal rights. These results may all occur with some frequency. The crux of the argument is independent of state court performance. The framers undoubtedly realized that state courts often would suffice, but they chose to rely on independent and life-tenured federal judges for the vindication of federal rights. They knew that in some places, at some times, pressures are brought to bear on state courts that cannot be brought to bear on federal courts.

History has not proven them wrong. One is reminded of recent efforts in California to recall or to prevent reelection of state Supreme Court justices because of disagreement with their decisions. The state trial judge in the Los Angeles school desegregation case was the subject of a recall movement. The efforts failed but they display the continuing pressures state judges must face. Some might argue that such popular pressure on courts is desirable. But with respect to federal constitutional rights, at least, our system was meant to offer litigants life-tenured, independent judges. . . .

2. Section [4] as Abridging Abortion Rights. The Supreme Court's inability to review each case suggests a second potentially unconstitutional effect of S. 158, an effect going beyond the availability of a federal forum. To an individual whose federal claim is rejected by state courts and who fails to obtain Supreme Court review, the effect of a federal jurisdictional withdrawal may be indistinguishable from that of a substantive statute foreclosing his claim. . . . [W]here state courts do not vindicate constitutional rights, the effect of a federal jurisdictional limitation on an individual denied Supreme Court review is strikingly close to a substantive law limitation. Any substantive statute with such effects on the vindication of federal constitutional rights would be struck down. Jurisdictional statutes should receive similar scrutiny. If they have unconstitutional substantive effects, they are themselves unconstitutional.

3. Discrimination Against Abortion Rights. Section [4] singles out one class of constitutional rights, abortion rights, for less protection than Congress affords all other constitutional rights. This discriminatory treatment suggests two overlapping bases for arguing that Section [4] is unconstitutional.

First, it is possible to argue that Section [4] should fall because it is motivated by hostility to an established constitutional right. . . . S. 158 may be subjected to motive scrutiny because there can be little doubt about the motives behind it. It is a frank effort to eliminate the rights found to exist in Roe v. Wade. And the motive underlying the effort, hostility to abortion rights, may well be viewed as unconstitutional.

Second, regardless of the motives underlying Section [4] it discriminates on its face against one class of litigants, those seeking to vindicate abortion rights. This raises the question whether Section [4] violates the principles of equal protection made applicable to federal legislation by the fifth amendment.

Under existing equal protection doctrine, Section [4] possesses neither of the characteristics that lead to virtually automatic invalidation of a challenged provision. That is, it neither affects a known fundamental right nor contains a suspect classification. Abortion rights have yet to be declared fundamental and discrimination among constitutional rights has yet to be declared a suspect classification. Nevertheless, abortion rights are closely related to rights of procreation and familial relations that are viewed as fundamental. The status of abortion rights for purposes of equal protection analysis must therefore be regarded as unsettled. It also is possible that Section [4] will be found to fall into a category of statutes for which a substantial though not necessarily compelling governmental interest must be found. In that event as well, it is difficult to predict the results of the Court's analysis.

There is one other common mode of analysis under equal protection doctrine. All statutory classifications must be rationally related to a permissible purpose. If Section [4]'s evident purpose, the contraction of abortion rights, is viewed as impermissible, Section [4] may be one of those extremely rare laws that falls for want of a rational relation to a permissible purpose. It is possible, however, to state Section [4]'s purposes more sympathetically than the evil-sounding purpose "to contract a constitutional right." One could characterize Section [4] not as an effort to contract abortion rights, but rather as an effort to protect fetuses. Such a purpose hardly sounds like a basis for upsetting a statute and its acceptance as S. 158's purpose would undermine the motive-based argument against S. 158 as well as the straightforward equal protection argument. If, however, one accepts the natural, inexorable linkage between an increase in fetal rights and a decrease in those of women, a desire to protect fetuses may have to be viewed as the functional equivalent of a desire to contract the rights of pregnant women.

The conclusion that Section [4] may violate constitutional principles does not necessarily lead to the conclusion that courts would grant any particular relief from its operation. Serious problems of enforcement and interbranch relations attend any judicial decree in this area. That a constitutional right may not be readily amenable to judicial enforcement, however, does not deprive the right of its status. It becomes all the more important in such cases for Congress to be sensitive to constitutional values.

C. ARTICLE III DOES NOT CONFER UNLIMITED DISCRETION UPON CONGRESS TO ENACT JURISDICTIONAL PROVISIONS

. . . One reading of Article III is that Congress has discretion to ordain and establish lower federal courts. Given that power, Congress at least generally must be able to choose the cases in which lower federal courts have jurisdiction. Do these statements translate into a constitutional argument supporting Section [4]?

There are two reasons for believing that they do not. First, in light of what has been shown to be the central role of the lower federal courts in fulfilling the role of the national judiciary, the previous paragraph's argument is seriously incomplete. . . .

Second, whatever guidance one derives from the text of Article III with respect to Congress' power to create lower federal courts, . . . Article III provides no express guidance with respect to Congress' control over their jurisdiction. In light of the fact that the framers expected Congress to create lower federal courts, that Congress did so, and that their existence spans the nation's existence, it seems particularly unrealistic to derive any additional control over the courts from some theoretical power to abolish them. In addition, constitutional infirmities that stem from the discriminatory aspects of Section [4] do not depend on whether Congress has plenary control of lower court jurisdiction. They depend only on finding the Constitution applicable to jurisdictional statutes.

Nevertheless, it seems clear that *in general* Congress must have the power to control lower federal court jurisdiction. There simply is no rational alternative. Can one articulate principles under which Congress has general control over jurisdiction without having authority to withdraw constitutional cases in general or the cases embraced by Section [4] in particular? The answer is yes.

III. CONGRESS' POWER TO CONTROL JURISDICTION AND REMEDIES

The conclusion that lower federal courts are essential to fulfilling the role of the national judiciary, and that S. 158 may therefore be unconstitutional, does not mean that *any* effort by Congress to control jurisdiction is unconstitutional. For even though federal courts were intended to vindicate federal rights, Congress has a substantial role to play in creating, refining or restricting federal rights.

In particular, Congress may enact jurisdictional laws that accomplish what it could have accomplished by means of a substantive rule. That is, it may enact any jurisdictional statute that does not prevent vindication of a constitutional right. In cases in which Congress may constitutionally prescribe a rule of decision, no federal right that could be vindicated under a constitutional claim is excluded from the federal courts by the withdrawal of jurisdiction. Thus, if no abortion rights survive enactment of Section 1 of S. 158, Section [4]'s curtailment of jurisdiction is constitutional.

In addition, because Section [4] does not completely remove lower federal court jurisdiction to hear abortion cases, the question remains whether the federal jurisdiction available under Section [4] is sufficient to vindicate abortion rights. Unless one of the remedies provided by Section [4] sufficiently protects abortion rights, Section [4] remains unconstitutional despite some residual federal jurisdiction to hear abortion cases. Section [4] does not foreclose inferior federal court jurisdiction (1) to hear damage actions against officials who enforce unconstitutional antiabortion laws, or (2) to grant federal habeas corpus relief to those prosecuted under such laws. It is therefore necessary to decide whether either form of relief adequately protects abortion rights.

Neither remedy seems a sufficient mechanism through which to vindicate abortion rights. An antiabortion law has two effects. In some cases, it discourages a woman from seeking (or a physician from performing) an abortion. In other cases it imposes criminal penalties on women who obtain (or physicians who perform) abortions. As to those discouraged from seeking abortions by an unconstitutional antiabortion law, neither habeas corpus nor damages is an effective remedy. Relief from criminal liability is no consolation for those who obey an unconstitutional law, with a resulting unwanted birth. Damages at best are a crude form of compensation for an unwanted child. This truly is an area in which there is no adequate remedy at law.

The basic problem with both remedies is that they are retrospective in nature. They only function after the fact. Because of the irreversible nature of the birth process, abortion may be an area in which prospective relief, such as the declaratory and injunctive relief banned by Section [4], is the only effective relief. The remedial rule here simply cannot require, as it does in the case of most taxes, initial obedience to the law followed by litigation. The later litigation too often will be too late. S. 158 seems to attempt to remove the only effective relief.

There is one other important class of jurisdictional statutes that may be within Congress' power. One should not jump to the conclusion that Congress just vest lower federal courts to hear all constitutional cases. An overabundance of federal forums with unrestricted jurisdiction to hear all federal cases could in fact undermine the judiciary. A number of factors suggest the necessity for line-drawing. First, the expense of such a system might make it impracticable. Second, a large increase in the caseload would inevitably mean an increase in the number of judges and a decrease in the prestige attached to being a federal judge. Many commentators have stated that such prestige is needed if the federal bench is to continue to attract qualified lawyers, especially in areas where private practice is more lucrative. "Any deterioration in the quality of the district judges individually or of their performance collectively would destroy the very values the federal court system is meant to attain."

Thus Congress needs some authority to limit federal jurisdiction. The authority to curtail, however, is limited by its origins. It should not be used to restrict jurisdiction over narrowly defined classes of cases, such as those covered by Section [4] that pose little threat to efficiency; such selective curtailments would bear no rational relationship to the end sought, namely preservation of the quality of federal justice. The power to curtail is limited to prudent steps which help avoid case overloads. In fact, Congress' control of lower federal court jurisdiction has tracked the principles here enumerated. Any Congress enacting legislation not within these guidelines is not only risking a constitutional confrontation but also is breaking with the mainstream of its own traditions.

Note: State Courts as Enforcers of Federal Constitutional Rights

The testimony concerning S. 158 makes partly explicit an assumption shared by lawyers and politicians on both sides of the issue — that federal judges tend to be more solicitous of individual rights than state court judges. Professor Paul Bator has argued that this belief has unfortunate consequences.[51]

> Let us remind ourselves, briefly, of the arguments put forward to justify the conclusion that the federal courts are the preferred forum. The federal bench constitutes a relatively small elite. Its judges are better paid and have more prestige than state judges; more competent lawyers are, therefore, attracted to the federal bench. That competence is reinforced by the expertise derived from specialization in questions of federal law. Protected by life tenure, federal judges are insulated from majoritarian pressures and will therefore be more receptive to controversial and unpopular constitutional principles. Further, the institutional bias of federal judges will be in favor of federal rights; state judges are more likely to be grudging when local authority is attacked on federal grounds. . . .
>
> Assume that we are, more or less, persuaded that the federal forum is, on these grounds, preferable. What should we make of this? . . .
>
> [I]t is virtually inevitable that the state courts will in fact continue to be asked to play a substantial role in the formulation and application of federal constitutional principles; the arguments in favor of the federal forum will not lead to a monopoly. If this is so, a new problem of fundamental significance emerges: we must try to create conditions to assure optimal performance by the state courts. . . .
>
> Ideally, we hope that state judges will conceive of the supreme federal law to be part of their own law, not an alien intrusion. We want state judges to think of themselves as really being charged, "*equally* with the courts of the Union," with an obligation to "guard, enforce, and protect every right granted or secured by the Constitution." How can such an attitude be fostered? . . .
>
> Competence and sensitivity are themselves not static phenomena. Conscientiousness, dedication, idealism, openness, enthusiasm, willingness to listen and to learn — all the mysterious components of the subtle art of judging well — are at least to some extent best evoked by a sense of responsibility, by the realization that one has been entrusted with a great and important task. I can think of nothing more subversive to the judge's inner sense of responsibility than the notion that, to the greatest possible extent, all the important shots will be called by someone else because we don't believe in his or her competence and sensitivity. If we want the state judges to internalize the sense that they, too, speak for the Constitution — that it is *their* Constitution — we must not too easily construct our jurisdictional and remedial rules on the premise that they can't and won't speak for the Constitution. If we want state judges to feel institutional responsibility for vindicating federal rights, it is counterproductive to be grudging in giving them the opportunity to do so. . . .
>
> Moreover, . . . [t]he hidden assumption of the argument [in favor of federal courts] is that the Constitution contains only one or two *sorts* of values: typically, those which protect the individual from the power of the state, and those which assure the superiority of federal to state law.
>
> But the Constitution contains other sorts of values as well. It gives the federal government powers, but also enacts limitations on those powers. *The limitations, too, count as setting forth constitutional values.* Will the federal judge be more sensitive than the state judge . . . [e.g.] to the values underlying the tenth amendment? . . .

51. Paul Bator, The State Courts and Federal Constitutional Litigation, 22 Wm. & Mary L. Rev. 605, 623-625, 631-632, 633, 634 (1981).

> [T]he claim that cases should be channeled to the federal court because of the special receptivity of federal judges to constitutional values may embody a narrow and partisan vision of what constitutional values are. . . .
>
> One more speculation remains. The argument that cases should, as much as possible, be directed toward the federal courts seems to me to embody, at a deep level, what might be called the positivist reflex, one which conceives of lawmaking in hierarchical terms and sees fidelity to law primarily as a matter of complying with pronouncements coming from a higher authority. The moral task is, fundamentally, the duty to obey. On this view, it is easy to fall into the habit of assuming that the task of the state judge, too, is to obey; the elaboration of federal constitutional law is a hierarchical task, in which commands come from the federal bench and, eventually, from the United States Supreme Court.
>
> But there is a different, richer, and more coherent account of lawmaking which asserts that it is a cooperative enterprise in which each participant, including the citizen, shares in the privilege and duty of principled elaboration. And this competing account is not inapplicable to federal constitutional law. In respect to federal constitutional principles, too, there is a moral and legal community which is mutually, and reciprocally charged with the mutual and reciprocal elaboration of these principles. We are not entitled to deny to state court judges the competence to participate in this process; to do so would deny them pro tanto membership in this cooperative moral and legal community.

Note: The Independent Importance of State Constitutions

Professor Bator was addressing, in his own words, "the role of the state courts in the elaboration of *federal* constitutional law and the enforcement of *federal* constitutional principles" (emphasis added). You should be aware, however, of the importance, especially in recent years, of *state* constitutions and the enforcement of *state* constitutional protections. To be sure, states have no right to diminish the scope of individual rights protected under the federal Constitution. However, in a number of important areas state supreme courts have construed their own constitutions to grant rights considerably broader than those currently found in the United States Constitution by the current Supreme Court.[52] Examples of such state enhancement include the rights of criminal defendants; the prohibition of capital punishment; the requirement of egalitarian financing of public schools; and the striking down of state prohibitions of certain sexual behavior, including fornication and sodomy.

As retired Judge Hans Linde of the Oregon Supreme Court has pointed out,[53] it is professionally derelict for lawyers to be unaware of the implications of their respective state constitutions. Moreover, Judge Linde argued that lawyers should always present state constitutional claims first in their arguments, using federal constitutional claims only as default arguments should the state constitution be determined not to protect their clients. It should be obvious that almost all of the

52. See, e.g., William Brennan, State Constitutions and the Protection of Individual Rights, 90 Harv. L. Rev. 489 (1977); Developments in the Law — The Interpretation of State Constitutional Rights, 95 Harv. L. Rev. 1324 (1982); Bradley McGraw, ed., Developments in State Constitutional Law (1985).

53. Hans Linde, First Things First: Rediscovering the States' Bills of Rights, 9 U. Balt. L. Rev. 379 (1980).

interpretive dilemmas presented by the United States Constitution will also face the analyst trying to construe a state constitution.

IV. The Last Word

"It is always a doubtful course, to argue against the use or existence of a power, from the possibility of its abuse. . . . From the very nature of things, the absolute right of decision, in the last resort, must rest somewhere — wherever it is vested it is susceptible of abuse." Martin v. Hunter's Lessee, 14 U.S. (1 Wheat.) 304 (1816) (Story, J.).

Granting Story's main point, in what sense is it true that "the absolute right of decision, in the last resort, must rest somewhere"?

1. In Cooper v. Aaron, 358 U.S. 1 (1958), the Governor and legislature of Arkansas had attempted to prevent the Little Rock school board from complying with a federal court's desegregation order, claiming that the board was not bound by the Supreme Court's holding in Brown v. Board of Education, 347 U.S. 483 (1954).

In an opinion signed by each of the nine Justices, the Court responded in sweeping terms:

> It is necessary only to recall some basic constitutional propositions which are settled doctrine. Article VI of the Constitution makes the Constitution the "supreme Law of the Land." In 1803, Chief Justice Marshall, speaking for a unanimous Court, referring to the Constitution as "the fundamental and paramount law of the nation," declared in the notable case of Marbury v. Madison, 1 Cranch 137, 177, that "It is emphatically the province and duty of the judicial department to say what the law is." This decision declared the basic principle that the federal judiciary is supreme in the exposition of the law of the Constitution, and that principle has ever since been respected by this Court and the Country as a permanent and indispensable feature of our constitutional system. It follows that the interpretation of the Fourteenth Amendment enunciated by this Court in the *Brown* case is the supreme law of the land, and Art. VI of the Constitution makes it of binding effect on the States "any Thing in the Constitution or Laws of any State to the Contrary notwithstanding." Every state legislator and executive and judicial officer is solemnly committed by oath taken pursuant to Art. VI, cl. 3, "to support this Constitution."

2. Thomas Jefferson wrote to Abigail Adams:

> You seem to think it devolved on the judges to decide on the validity of the sedition law. But nothing in the Constitution has given them a right to decide for the Executive, more than to the Executive to decide for them. Both magistracies are equally independent in the sphere of action assigned to them. The judges, believing the law constitutional, had a right to pass a sentence of fine and imprisonment; because that power was placed in their hands by the Constitution. But the Executive, believing the law to be unconstitutional, was bound to remit the execution of it; because that power has been confided to him by the Constitution. That instrument meant that its co-ordinate branches should be checks on each other. But the opinion which gives to

the judges the right to decide what laws are constitutional, and what not, not only for themselves in their own sphere of action, but for the Legislature & Executive also, in their spheres, would make the judiciary a despotic branch.[54]

3. Recall President Andrew Johnson's message of July 10, 1832, vetoing the bill to recharter the Bank of the United States, p.49 supra. On the floor of the Senate, Daniel Webster responded to Jackson's veto:

The President is as much bound by the law as any private citizen, and can no more contest its validity than any private citizen. He may refuse to obey the law, and so may a private citizen; but both do it at their own peril, and neither of them can settle the question of its validity. The President may say a law is unconstitutional, but he is not the judge. Who is to decide that question? The judiciary alone possesses this unquestionable and hitherto unquestioned right. The judiciary is the constitutional tribunal of appeal for the citizens against both Congress and the executive, in regard to the constitutionality of laws. It has this jurisdiction expressly conferred upon it, and when it has decided the question, its judgment must, from the very nature of all judgments that are final, and from which there is no appeal, be conclusive. Hitherto, this opinion, and a correspondent practice, have prevailed, in America, with all wise and considerate men. If it were otherwise, there would be no government of laws; but we should all live under the government, the rule, the caprices of individuals. If we depart from the observance of these salutary principles, the executive power becomes at once purely despotic; for the President, if the principle and the reasoning of the message be sound, may either execute or not execute the laws of the land, according to his sovereign pleasure. He may refuse to put into execution one law, pronounced valid by all branches of the government, and yet execute another, which may have been by constitutional authority pronounced void.[55]

4. Recall Lincoln's and Douglas' comments on the binding nature of *Dred Scott*, pp. 211-213 supra.

5. In a speech in Elmira, New York, in 1907, Charles Evans Hughes, who later became Chief Justice of the United States, said: "We are under a Constitution, but the Constitution is what the judges say it is."[56]

6. In a period of constitutional crisis, then-Professor Felix Frankfurter wrote to his friend, President Franklin Roosevelt:

It is a creditable aspect of human nature that it wants some object of veneration, and veneration to no small degree thrives on mystery and mysticism. . . . People have been taught to believe that when the Supreme Court speaks it is not they who speak but the Constitution, whereas, of course, in so many vital cases, it is *they* who speak and *not* the Constitution. And I verily believe that that is what the country needs most to understand.[57]

7. Ronald Dworkin has argued that American constitutionalism "does not make the decision of any court conclusive":

54. 8 Writings of Thomas Jefferson 310-311 (Ford ed. 1897).
55. The Age of Jackson 92 (Remini ed. 1972).
56. Charles Evans Hughes, Addresses and Papers 133, 139 (1908).
57. Roosevelt and Frankfurter: Their Correspondence 1928-1945, at 383 (Freedman ed. 1967) (letter of February 18, 1937).

Sometimes, even after a contrary Supreme Court decision, an individual may still reasonably believe that the law is on his side. . . . [A] citizen's allegiance is to the law, not to any person's view of what the law is, and he does not behave unfairly so long as he proceeds on his own considered and reasonable view of what the law requires. . . . [I]f the issue is one touching fundamental personal and political rights, and it is arguable that the Supreme Court has made a mistake, a man is within his social rights in refusing to accept that decision as conclusive.[58]

10. On remand from the Supreme Court's decision in United Steelworkers v. Weber, 443 U.S. 193 (1979), p.734 supra, Judge Gee wrote (611 F.2d 133 (5th Cir. 1980)):

Obedient to the mandate of the Supreme Court, we vacate the trial court's judgment, as well as ours affirming it, 563 F.2d 216, and remand the cause to that court for further proceedings in conformity with the opinion above.

For myself only, and with all respect and deference, I here note my personal conviction that the decision of the Supreme Court in this case is profoundly wrong.

That it is wrong as a matter of statutory construction seems to me sufficiently demonstrated by the dissenting opinions of the Chief Justice and of Mr. Justice Rehnquist. To these I can add nothing. They make plain beyond peradventure that the Civil Rights Act of 1964 passed the Congress on the express representation of its sponsors that it would not and could not be construed as the Court has now construed it. What could be plainer than the words of the late Senator Humphrey — defending the bill against the charge that it adumbrated quotas and preferential treatment — that "the title would *prohibit* preferential treatment for any particular group . . ."? The Court now tells us that this is not so. That it feels it may properly do so seems to me a grievous thing.

But sadder still — tragic, in my own view — is the Court's departure from the long road that we have travelled from Plessy v. Ferguson, 163 U.S. 537 (1896), toward making good Mr. Justice Harlan's anguished cry in dissent that "[o]ur Constitution is color-blind, and neither knows nor tolerates classes among citizens." Id. at 559. I voice my profound belief that this present action, like *Plessy,* is a wrong and dangerous turning, and my confident hope that we will soon return to the high, bright road on which we disdain to classify a citizen, *any* citizen, to any degree or for any purpose by the color of his skin.

Though for the above reasons I think it gravely mistaken, I do not say that the Court's decision is immoral or unjust — indeed, in some basic sense it may well represent true justice. But there are many actions roughly just that our laws do not authorize and our Constitution forbids, actions such as preventing a Nazi Party march through a town where reside former inmates of concentration camps or inflicting summary punishment on one caught red-handed in a crime.

Subordinate magistrates such as I must either obey the orders of higher authority or yield up their posts to those who will. I obey, since in my view the action required of me by the Court's mandate is only to follow a mistaken course and not an evil one.

58. Ronald Dworkin, Taking Rights Seriously 211, 214-215 (1978).

Appendix
Table of Justices of the Supreme Court

	Administration	Chief Justice	2	3	4	5	6	7	8	9	Major Cases
1789	Washington	John Jay	John Rutledge	William Cushing	James Wilson	John Blair					
1790							James Iredell				
—			Thomas Johnson								
—											
—			William Paterson								
—											
1795		John Rutledge									
—		Oliver Ellsworth				Samuel Chase					
—	J. Adams				Bushrod Washington						
—											Calder v. Bull (1798)
—							Alfred Moore				
1800		John Marshall (Adams)									
—	Jefferson										
—											Marbury v. Madison (1803)
—											
—							William Johnson				
1805											
—			H. Brockholst Livingston								
—								Thomas Todd			
—											
—	Madison										
1810											Fletcher v. Peck (1810)
—				Joseph Story		Gabriel Duvall					
—											
—											
—											
1815											
—											
—	Monroe										
—											McCulloch v. Maryland (1819)
—											
1820											
—											
—											
—			Smith Thompson								Gibbons v. Ogden (1824)
—											
1825	J. Q. Adams										
—								Robert Trimble			
—											
—											
—	Jackson							John McLean			

1830					Henry Baldwin						
—											Barron v. Baltimore (1833)
1835							James M. Wayne				
—		Roger B. Taney				Philip P. Barbour					
—	Van Buren								John Catron	John McKinley	Mayor v. Miln (1837)
1840						Peter V. Daniel (Van Buren)					
—	W. Harrison Tyler										
—											Prigg v. Pennsylvania (1842)
1845	Polk		Samuel Nelson (Tyler)	Levi Woodbury							
—					Robert C. Grier						
1850	Taylor Fillmore										
—				Benjamin R. Curtis							
—	Pierce									John A. Campbell	
1855											
—											Dred Scott v. Sandford (1857)
—	Buchanan			Nathan Clifford							
1860											
—	Lincoln										
—						Samuel F. Miller		Noah H. Swayne		David Davis	
—									10* Stephen J. Field		Prize Cases (1863)
—		Salmon P. Chase									
1865	A. Johnson										
—†											
—	Grant										

*In 1863 Congress established a tenth seat, to which Stephen J. Field was appointed.

†In 1866 Congress reduced the size of the Court to six justices. Consequently, the seats of Justices Catron and Wayne remained unfilled after their deaths in 1865 and 1867. Congress restored the Court to nine seats in 1869.

	Administration	Chief Justice	2	3	4	5	6	7	8	9	Major Cases
1870					William Strong		Joseph P. Bradley				
—											
—			Ward Hunt								Slaughter-House Cases (1873)
—		Morrison R. Waite									
—											
1875											
—											
—	Hayes									John M. Harlan	
—											Reynolds v. U.S. (1879)
—					William B. Woods						
1880				Horace Gray (Arthur)							
—	Garfield Arthur							Stanley Matthews (Garfield)			
—			Samuel Blatchford								
—											Civil Rights Cases (1883)
—											
1885	Cleveland										
—											
—		Melville W. Fuller			Lucius Q. C. Lamar						
—											
—	B. Harrison							David J. Brewer			
1890						Henry B. Brown					
—											
—					Howell E. Jackson (Harrison) Rufus W. Peckham		George Shiras				
—	Cleveland										
—			Edward D. White								
1895											
—											Plessy v. Ferguson (1896)
—	McKinley										
—									Joseph McKenna		
—											
1900											
—	T. Roosevelt										
—				Oliver W. Holmes							
—							William R. Day				
—											
1905											Lochner v. N.Y. (1905)
—						William H. Moody					
—											
—											
—	Taft				Horace H. Lurton						

1910		Edward D. White	Willis Van Devanter			Joseph R. Lamar		Charles E. Hughes			
										Mahlon Pitney	
	Wilson				James C. McReynolds						
1915											
						Louis D. Brandeis		John H. Clarke			
											Debs v. U.S. (1919)
1920											
	Harding	William H. Taft									
							Pierce Butler	George Sutherland		Edward T. Sanford (Harding)	
	Coolidge										
1925									Harlan F. Stone		
	Hoover										
1930		Charles E. Hughes								Owen J. Roberts	
				Benjamin N. Cardozo							Minnesota Mortgage Moratorium Case (1934)
	F. D. Roosevelt										
1935											
			Hugo L. Black								West Coast Hotel v. Parrish (1937) U.S. v. Carolene Prods. (1938)
						William O. Douglas		Stanley F. Reed			
				Felix Frankfurter							
1940							Frank Murphy				
		Harlan F. Stone			James F. Byrnes				Robert H. Jackson		
					Wiley B. Rutledge						Korematsu v. U.S. (1944)
1945	Truman									Harold H. Burton	
		Fred M. Vinson									
					Sherman Minton		Tom C. Clark				
1950											
	Eisenhower	Earl Warren									Steel Seizure Case (1952) Brown v. Bd. of Ed. (1954)

	Administration	Chief Justice	2	3	4	5	6	7	8	9	Major Cases
1955									John M. Harlan		
—					William J. Brennan						
—								Charles E. Whittaker		Potter Stewart	
—											
—											
1960											
—	Kennedy							Byron R. White			
—				Arthur J. Goldberg							
—	L. B. Johnson										Katzenbach v. McClung (1964)
—											
1965				Abe Fortas							Griswold v. Conn. (1965)
—							Thurgood Marshall				
—											
—		Warren E. Burger									N.Y. Times v. U.S. (1971)
—	Nixon										
1970				Harry A. Blackmun					William H. Rehnquist		Roe v. Wade (1973)
—			Lewis F. Powell								San Antonio v. Rodriguez (1973)
—											
—											
—	Ford										
1975						John Paul Stevens					Washington v. Davis (1976)
—											
—	Carter										U. Cal. v. Bakke (1978)
—											
—											
1980											
—	Reagan									Sandra Day O'Connor	MUW v. Hogan (1982)
—											
—											
—											
1985											Bowers v. Hardwick (1986)
—		William H. Rehnquist						Ginsberg	Antonin Scalia		Richmond v. J.A. Croson Co. (1989)
—			Anthony M. Kennedy	Breyer							
—											
—	Bush										
1990					David H. Souter		Clarence Thomas				Oregon v. Smith (1990)
—											
—											

Table of Cases

Index